Contemporary Literary Criticism

Volume 12
Young Adult Literature

Contemporary Literary Criticism

Excerpts from Criticism
of the Works of Today's
Novelists, Poets, Playwrights,
and Other Creative Writers

Dedria Bryfonski
Editor

Gerard J. Senick
Project Editor

Gale Research Company
Book Tower
Detroit, Michigan 48226

STAFF

Dedria Bryfonski, *Editor*

Gerard J. Senick, *Project Editor*

Sharon R. Gunton, *Associate Editor and Production Editor*
Dennis Poupard, Jean C. Stine, David J. Szymanski,
Carolyn Voldrich, *Assistant Editors*

Phyllis Carmel Mendelson, *Contributing Editor*

Linda M. Pugliese, *Manuscript Coordinator*
Thomas E. Gunton, *Research Coordinator*
Emily W. Barrett, Anna H. Crabtree, Catherine E. Daligga,
Jeanne A. Gough, Tom Ligotti, Marsha R. Mackenzie,
Nancy C. Mazzara, James E. Person, Jr., *Editorial Assistants*

L. Elizabeth Hardin, *Permissions Coordinator*
Dawn L. McGinty, *Permissions Assistant*

Library of Congress Catalog Card Number 76-38938
ISBN 0-8103-0122-9

Contents

Preface

The last thirty years have brought about a type of literature which is directed specifically to a young adult audience. These works have recognized the uniqueness of young adult readers while preparing them for the subjects, styles, and emotional levels of adult literature. Much of this writing has also had a definite appeal for adult readers and a discernible influence on their literature. Because of the importance of this subject matter and its audience, *Contemporary Literary Criticism* is planning to devote periodic volumes to writers whose work is directed to or appreciated by young adults. Until now, a collection of opinion has not existed which has centered on writers for the junior high to junior college age group. These special volumes of *CLC*, therefore, are meant to acknowledge this genre and its criticism as an important and serious part of recent literature.

The Plan of the Work

In this special volume we have broadened the definition of young adult literature to include not only writers who fit into the classic young adult mode, such as M. E. Kerr and Robert Cormier, but also authors and poets such as Frank Herbert, Harper Lee, and E. E. Cummings, whose works are received enthusiastically by the young even though they were not originally the intended audience. In the latter category are writers whose works have such relevance for the YA sensibility that they have achieved mass appeal, such as J. D. Salinger, Richard Brautigan, and J. R. R. Tolkien. A distinctive feature of these special volumes will be the inclusion of criticism on writers whose work is not restricted to book form. Many songwriters, for instance, are recognized by young people as today's poets. Their lyrics have been critically analyzed and accepted as serious literary creations. Since young people look to film, television, and the theater to expand their knowledge and reflect their world view, there will be criticism on screenwriters, scriptwriters, and playwrights who appeal to the young, including Mel Brooks, Norman Lear, and Elizabeth Swados in the present volume. Humorists and cartoonists such as Garry Trudeau and Charles M. Schulz, whom young people look to for both social comment and entertainment, will also be included.

The annual special volume on young adult literature is designed to complement other volumes of *CLC* and will follow the same format with some slight variations. The list of authors will continue to be international in scope and will fall into the same time period as the other authors in the *CLC* series; that is, they must be living now or have died after January 1, 1960. However, since each special volume is intended to provide a definitive overview of the authors included, the author list will be limited to approximately 65 writers, as compared to 150 writers in each standard volume.

Criticism has been selected with the levels and interests of the young adult in mind. The essays represent the criticism to date of the work of each writer; thus, in the case of a writer with the longevity of Agatha Christie, the criticism spans six decades. Many young adult authors have also written for younger children. Criticism of these works has been included when it is felt that their interest and level of competence extends to the young adult.

Each excerpt is fully identified for the convenience of readers who may wish to consult the entire chapter, article, or review excerpted. Beginning with *CLC*, Volume 5, the method for referring to pages in the original sources was standardized. Page numbers appear after each fragment (unless the entire essay was contained on one page). Page numbers appear in citations as well only when the editors wish to indicate, with an essay or chapter title and its *inclusive* page numbers, the scope of the original treatment.

A table of contents, cumulative indexes to authors and critics, and an appendix will continue to be standard features of these special volumes. The appendix lists the sources from which material is reprinted in each volume. It does not, however, list books or periodicals merely consulted during the preparation of the volume.

A Note on Bio-Bibliographical References

Parenthetical material following several of the identification paragraphs includes references to biographical and critical reference books published by the Gale Research Company. These include past volumes of *CLC*, *Contemporary Authors*, *Something about the Author*, *Children's Literature Review*, and *Yesterday's Authors of Books for Children*.

Acknowledgments

The editors wish to thank the copyright holders of the excerpts included in this volume for their permission to use the material, and the staffs of the Detroit Public Library, Wayne State University Library, and the libraries of the University of Michigan for making their resources available to us. The editors also wish to thank Russel Nye, R. Serge Denisoff, and Peter Knobler for the information they provided.

Suggestions Are Welcome

If readers wish to suggest authors they are particularly anxious to have covered in coming volumes, or if they have other suggestions, they are cordially invited to write the editors.

Authors Forthcoming in *CLC*

With the publication of *Contemporary Literary Criticism,* Volume 12, the series has expanded its scope to encompass songwriters, screenwriters, cartoonists, and other creative writers whose work is often evaluated from a literary perspective. These writers take their place with the novelists, poets, dramatists, and short story writers who will continue to be the primary focus of *CLC*. Volume 13 will include criticism on a number of authors not previously listed, and will also feature criticism of newer works of authors included in earlier volumes.

To be Included in Volume 13

Alice Adams (American short story writer and novelist) Will feature criticism on new collection of short stories, *Beautiful Girl*

A. Alvarez (British essayist, poet, and novelist) Will feature criticism on new novel, *Hunt*

Kingsley Amis (British novelist, short story writer, poet, and essayist) Will feature criticism on new novel, *Jake's Thing*

Donald Barthelme (American short story writer and novelist) Will feature criticism on new collection of short stories, *Great Days*

Ann Beattie (American short story writer and novelist) Will feature criticism on new collection of short stories, *Secrets and Surprises*

Marie-Claire Blais (French-Canadian novelist and poet)

Jorge Luis Borges (Argentine short story writer, poet, and essayist)

Anthony Burgess (British novelist and essayist) Will feature criticism on new novel, *Abba Abba*

Arthur C. Clarke (British science fiction writer) Will feature criticism on new novel, *The Fountains of Paradise*

Lawrence Durrell (British novelist and essayist) Will feature criticism on new novel, *Livia; or Buried Alive*

T. S. Eliot (Anglo-American Nobel-Prize-winning poet and critic)

Carlos Fuentes (Mexican novelist, poet, and short story writer) Will feature criticism on new novel, *The Hydra Head*

Doris Grumbach (American novelist and critic) Will feature criticism on new novel, *Chamber Music*

Elizabeth Hardwick (American critic and novelist) Will feature criticism on new novel, *Sleepless Nights*

John Irving (American novelist and short story writer) Will feature criticism on new novel, *The World According to Garp*

André Malraux (French novelist and essayist)

Edna O'Brien (Irish novelist and short story writer) Will feature criticism on new collection of short stories, *A Rose in the Heart*

Flannery O'Connor (American short story writer, essayist, and novelist) Will feature criticism on her collected letters, *The Habit of Being*

Bernard Pomerance (American dramatist) Will feature criticism on Tony Award-winning play, *The Elephant Man*

Katherine Anne Porter (American Pulitzer-Prize-winning short story writer, essayist, and novelist)

Ishmael Reed (Black American novelist and poet) Will feature criticism on new collection, *Shrovetide in Old New Orleans*

Susan Sontag (American novelist, essayist, and short story writer) Will feature criticism on new collection of short stories, *I, etcetera*

Muriel Spark (Scottish novelist, poet, and dramatist) Will feature criticism on new novel, *Territorial Rights*

John Updike (American novelist, short story writer, and essayist) Will feature criticism on new novel, *The Coup*

Yevgeny Yevtushenko (Russian poet)

E. M. Almedingen

1898-1971

(Born Martha Edith von Almedingen) Almedingen was a Russian-born British novelist, translator, lecturer, poet, playwright, and short story writer. She is best known for her biographical and autobiographical novels for young adults, many of which draw upon her Russian heritage and family history. Born in St. Petersburg (now Leningrad), a city fondly remembered in many of her works, she was a distinguished student and later teacher of medieval history and literature at the University of Petrograd. The years 1917-22 were pivotal for her as well as for Russia; she survived the revolution and later wrote about her experiences in *My Saint Petersburg: A Reminiscence of Childhood* and *Tomorrow Will Come*. Almedingen, who emigrated to England in 1923, wrote for almost twenty years before she achieved critical recognition with the publication of *Tomorrow Will Come*, which was awarded the 1941 Atlantic Monthly prize for best nonfiction book of the year. One of her most popular books, *Katia*, is based on her great-aunt Catherine Almedingen's best-selling autobiography, *The Story of a Little Girl*. Although she was a prolific writer who wrote for adults, teenagers, and children, most critics agree that Almedingen's most successful works are her translated ancestral diaries and accounts, interwoven with Russian history and her personal reminiscences. (See also *Contemporary Authors*, Vols. 1-4, rev. ed., and *Something about the Author*, Vol. 3.)

Grimness and splendour, personal and dynastic, are the keynotes of *The Nibelunglied*, the German heroic epic, on which *The Treasure of Siegfried* is based. [Miss Almedingen] has achieved an exceptionally clean story line, yet enveloped it in a panoply and fairy-tale atmosphere that is positively Wagnerian. Indeed young music enthusiasts who read this may find it a great help towards understanding the monumental framework and Teutonic intensity of Wagner's work on the same theme. (p. 371)

The Junior Bookshelf, *December, 1964.*

PRISCILLA L. MOULTON

Similar in many ways to the Arthurian legends, Kiev Cycle stories were collected and written down about one century ago, although their aural age is closer to ten centuries. Twelve of the more noteworthy tales are translated and retold [in *The Knights of the Golden Table*,] a collection for older children. . . . The contemporary rendition of these full-blooded legends makes them simpler to tell than some other hero tales. Colorful and dramatic, their surprisingly democratic spirit is a zestful antidote to the gloom sometimes associated with Russian life. (pp. 55-6)

Priscilla L. Moulton, in The Horn Book Magazine (*copyright © 1965, by The Horn Book, Inc., Boston*), *February, 1965.*

SR. M. DENNIS, R.S.M.

Almedingen writes in the fierce, bold style characteristic of the original epic [in *The Treasure of Siegfried*], portraying the legendary figures with cold sharp realism, particularly Kriemhild, who changes from a paragon of virtue to a veritable demon avenging her every offender. (p. 310)

Sr. M. Dennis, R.S.M., in Best Sellers (*copyright 1965, by the University of Scranton*), *November 1, 1965.*

[*The Ladies of St. Hedwig's*], moving with dignity to its tragic conclusion, shows Miss Almedingen's considerable talents to good advantage. A convent of nuns, most of them Polish, has been long settled in St. Petersburg. But it is rocked and wrecked by the Polish Mutiny of 1863 and by the savage outbreaks of anti-Polish violence in Russia which follow it. The prioress, half-Polish and half-American, is a well-realized character. She possesses the strength and serenity which sustain the community through mounting tribulations, re-establish it in Siberian exile, and inspire it to face ultimate martyrdom without flinching. This is a sombre, quiet book with no false emphases. (p. 1007)

The Times Literary Supplement (*© Times Newspapers Ltd. (London) 1965; reproduced from* The Times Literary Supplement *by permission*), *November 11, 1965.*

ETHNA SHEEHAN

E. M. Almedingen has adapted "The Treasure of Siegfried" from the German verse epic "The Nibelungenlied." To make the narrative suitable for children, some episodes have been softened and others omitted. While the story makes swift and entertaining reading, the language is flat, peppered with clichés and often with inept phrasing. The dialogue is at times quaintly Victorian, at others jarringly modern and the metamorphosis of Kremhild from a gentle, lovable, generous young woman to a vengeful fury is too drastic for credibility. (p. 66)

Ethna Sheehan, in The New York Times Book Review (© 1965 by The New York Times Company; reprinted by permission), November 14, 1965.

Turgenev and Chekhov are writers for the mature reader, [and] even the most precocious adolescent is hardly likely to make anything of them. . . . E. M. Almedingen's *Little Katia* [published in the United States as *Katia*], therefore, plunges into strange territory, a land where servants kneel to take off the shoes and stockings of the children of the house, where a journey to your grandmother's house may take three weeks and you run the risk of your throat being slit on the way, where a serf who displeases his master can be sent for twenty-five years' servitude in the army and well-born girls finish their schooldays in institutes for the nobility where there are no holidays, no release until their education is complete. These details are authentic, for the author has adapted her great-aunt's memoirs for modern readers.

Catherine Almedingen was born in 1829 and died in 1893. She was editor of a successful children's magazine, but it was *The Story of a Little Girl* which brought her her greatest fame. . . . The earlier version was far too long for modern taste, but on the other hand must have contained allusions which required lengthy explanation. All this has been done with great skill, it is impossible to detect which is the great-aunt, which the niece, and the whole forms the most readable and delightful portrait, both of a little girl growing up, and of a vanished regime. It can be compared to Laura Ingalls Wilder's autobiographical accounts for children of pioneering days in America. It has the same simplicity of style, vigorous dialogue, acute observation of child and adult characters, and the same fundamental goodness.

"A Russian Childhood," in The Times Literary Supplement (©Times Newspapers Ltd. (London) 1966; reproduced from The Times Literary Supplement by permission), May 19, 1966, p. 433.

LEWIS BATES

Miss Almedingen's *The Romanovs* is an enjoyable sketch by a supporter of the dynasty who is shocked by the frequency with which its members were bloody and incompetent. She keeps a reasonble balance between vivid gossip about loves and rages and more far-reaching questions about access to the Baltic and Black Sea, the condition of the people and Russia's ramshackle administrative institutions. Her introduction pleads firmly for personal history to supplement the history of the group or mass and she gives the mystical rapport between Little Father and peasants its due as a historical fact. When she reaches the final Tsardom, personal feeling tugs hard at judicial impartiality. This is certainly not a rose-tinted picture of the *ancien régime* but it is a sadly affectionate one. . . . Very quietly, Miss Almedingen expresses regret that the chances of swift, systematic reform in the early years of the century were lost when blood-thirsty confusion became endemic on the Left as it had been on the Right. (p. 893)

Lewis Bates, in Punch (© 1966 Punch Publications Ltd.; all rights reserved), June 15, 1966.

[Miss Almedingen's *The Romanovs*] follows the pattern she has earlier established in her biographies of individual

Romanovs—that is to say, it is mainly concerned with the dynasty in its personal and intimate aspect and shows little grasp of the historical context. On the other hand, the sheer juxtaposition of such differing personalities as Peter the Great and Nicholas II or of Catherine and Nicholas I makes for great entertainment value.

Curiously enough, however, for all the personal emphasis inherent in Miss Almedingen's work, it is precisely in this respect that her portrayal of Nicholas II is at its weakest. Here surely, was the most ill-fated of the dynasty. It was nothing unusual for a Romanov to die by assassination—the deaths of Paul and Alexander II were precedents—but actually to be instrumental in bringing the dynasty to a close was the most ignominious fate of all.

Is this to exaggerate the role of Nicholas II? Possibly. But given the autocratic structure of government the person and character of the autocrat could not but be of overwhelming importance. It would not, perhaps, be too fanciful to portray the background of the revolution of 1917 in terms of Nicholas's personality. . . .

Perhaps the most noteworthy feature of the Tsar's character was his determination to maintain intact his autocratic prerogatives. . . .

Miss Almedingen's failure to bring out this dominating feature in the outlook of the last of the Romanovs is clearly detrimental to her portrayal. But all in all, here is a book that within its modest compass brings to life a line of the most vivid personalities.

"Tsars in Their Courses," in The Times Literary Supplement (© Times Newspapers Ltd. (London) 1966; reproduced from The Times Literary Supplement by permission), August 18, 1966, p. 739.

HANS KOHN

The Emperor Alexander I [is] a movingly written portrait. . . . Mrs. Almedingen wrote her book not for the historian but for the general public, to which it can be warmly recommended. Not a "romantic" or fictional biography, but based on letters and memoirs of the period, the book frankly acknowledges the disastrous weakness in Alexander's character and political judgment. Nevertheless the work profits by its warm sympathy with the elusive personality of its hero. (p. 38)

Hans Kohn, in Saturday Review (© 1966 by Saturday Review, Inc.; reprinted with permission), September 17, 1966.

RUTH HILL VIGUERS

Katia's relationships with her many relatives of all ages, her adjustment to her beautiful young stepmother, whom she came to love, and all the details of luxurious living, including parties and holiday festivities, of a well-to-do family in Czarist Russia make [*Katia*] a story with the romantic appeal of an almost fairy-tale world. The children are completely real in their reactions and behavior. Quite apart from its significance as a picture of a vanished era, the book is important because it is such irresistibly good reading. (p. 210)

Ruth Hill Viguers, in The Horn Book Magazine (copyright © 1967, by The Horn Book, Inc., Boston), April, 1967.

Miss Almedingen's [*St. Francis of Assisi*] makes no pretense of being a definitive biography. Indeed, her approach is too romantic and simplistic, and the book therefore too dependent on the author's attempts to surmise what was in Francis' mind (e.g., " . . . even if he had known it, the knowledge would not have influenced his resolve," etc., etc.), for it to be taken very seriously as biography. Nonetheless, the work is very readable and will undoubtedly be useful to those who are more concerned with being inspired than instructed. (p. 911)

> *Kirkus Service (copyright © 1967 Virginia Kirkus' Service, Inc.), August 1, 1967.*

There might at first seem little reason to add yet another to the numerous biographies of St. Francis, especially since Miss Almedingen is at pains to disclaim any new approach or to have had access to any new sources. But the attractiveness of the saint of Assisi is such that he continues to find fresh admirers who, even though they have nothing to say that will attract the scholar's interest, yet succeed in commending Francis to every generation.

Miss Almedingen has sensibly based [*St. Francis of Assisi*] on the primary biographies that were written by men who had personal knowledge of Francis. Sensibly, because . . . [these biographies] transmit an authentic flavour that matters more than a merely factual accuracy—even if that were possible to attain. She tells the familiar story with an engaging lyricism, that is not without its occasional rhetoric (with words and thoughts ascribed to Francis that have no basis in recorded history). But, unlike many other biographies in English, this life maintains a reasonably cool attitude on Francis the animal lover and on Francis the simple man confronted with the horrors of ecclesiastical power. And the historical and geographical background is adequately indicated.

> *"Not So Simple," in The Times Literary Supplement (© Times Newspapers Ltd. (London) 1967; reproduced from The Times Literary Supplement by permission), September 14, 1967, p. 823.*

SHIRLEY L. HOPKINSON

[*The Ladies of St. Hedwig's* is a] well-written historical novel . . . based on facts told to the author in 1919 by an elderly, secular priest. . . . Miss Almedingen has skillfully woven a tale from the meager facts, a story of fallible and very human people who, nevertheless, knew what they must do in an environment of endless contradictions, bewilderment, and despair of the future. Miss Almedingen portrays these believable characters sympathetically but never mawkishly, and her excellent descriptive prose helps to establish the mood. (p. 4025)

> *Shirley L. Hopkinson, in Library Journal (reprinted from Library Journal, November 1, 1967; published by R. R. Bowker Co. (a Xerox company); copyright © 1967 by Xerox Corporation), November 1, 1967.*

ELLEN LEWIS BUELL

[*The Story of Gudrun*, as retold] from a 12th- or 13th-century German epic . . . , has the quality of a folk tale within the framework of a brief novel. Gudrun, daughter of one king and betrothed to another, is a romantic and heroic figure. . . . [She] deserves to be better known than she is and I am grateful to Miss Almedingen for this vigorous portrait, set against a richly detailed background. (p. 167)

> *Ellen Lewis Buell, in Book World—Chicago Tribune, Part II (© 1967 Postrib Corp.), November 5, 1967.*

Miss Almedingen's picaro's-eye-view of Russia in the eighteenth century [in *Young Mark—the Story of a Venture*] is authentic and she has obviously done her reading assiduously. Particularly impressive is her description of Mark's arrival in St. Petersburg, which must certainly have appeared icily unwelcoming and alien to a young Ukrainian vagrant just forty years after its foundation. . . . [Mark's] story is arresting and unusual enough to speak for itself. It is a pity therefore that Miss Almedingen has laid on the ending quite so thickly. (p. 1139)

> *The Times Literary Supplement (© Times Newspapers Ltd. (London) 1967; reproduced from The Times Literary Supplement by permission), November 30, 1967.*

Young Mark is based on a true incident in the life of one of the author's ancestors. . . . [Mark's] placid personality, however, and the lack of climax in his telling of his story, makes it seem much less exciting than it must have been. The historical background is not very clearly drawn and may confuse anyone not already familiar with the Russia of the Empress Elizabeth's time. (p. 383)

> *The Junior Bookshelf, December, 1967.*

JESSIE B. KITCHING

["Tomorrow Will Come" is a] reading experience not soon forgotten. This autobiographical account of a childhood and girlhood in St. Petersburg (now Leningrad) up to 1922 (when Miss Almedingen escaped to Italy) is extraordinarily moving and beautifully written. The book was first published in 1941. It is being republished on the strong advice of librarians, because it is a classic which should never have gone out of print. . . .

Though this is the story of how one young life was affected by the Russian Revolution, it is not a political book but a very personal saga, taut with emotion and drama. (p. 88)

> *Jessie B. Kitching, in Publishers Weekly (reprinted from the February 19, 1968, issue of Publishers Weekly by permission of the critic, published by R. R. Bowker Company, a Xerox company; copyright © 1968 by Xerox Corporation), February 19, 1968.*

ZENA SUTHERLAND

Based on the third part of an anonymous German epic of the twelfth or thirteenth centuries, [*The Story of Gudrun*] is a romantic tale of stoicism and valor, good overcoming evil, and of the court intrigue of feudal life. . . . The story is retold in a most fitting style, dignified yet graceful, with that larger-than-life portentousness that distinguishes the epic from folk literature. (p. 154)

> *Zena Sutherland, in Bulletin of the Center for Children's Books (copyright 1968 by The University of Chicago; all rights reserved), June, 1968.*

ROGER SALE

[E. M. Almedingen's preface to the 1967 edition of *Tomorrow Will Come*] is sour, clear and simple about her loathing of the revolution and Soviet Russia, but the narrative is different, written with loving care of the blinding pain and loneliness that was her childhood and with little regard to what the adult writer "makes" of it all. (p. 549)

The first third of the book is simply magnificent, sharp and poignantly seen vignettes in which the girl's way of seeing is everything—her older brother is drowned in an act of childish bravery, but we get the faces at the door, the hushed conversations, the worry for mother that precedes worry for self because the girl cannot fathom what has happened, then her first meeting with her father, and a move to a shabbier home.... Miss Almedingen takes each event for itself and assumes that if each experience is accepted fully the patterns must necessarily appear by themselves. In each scene the people are "there" so completely that they can barely be seen as personalities.

There is a slight falling off when the revolution comes and life becomes so crushing and grim and aimless that the narrative method itself is partially victimized by the staggering events. Hunger, marginal jobs, a rescue into the cloister of the University and even into a teaching position, typhus, relief work, Moscow and finally escape to Italy—there is no sense of history here because the girl could not have one, and the form is thus forced to imitate the effortful and empty quality of the events. The buildings become communal and people are moved endlessly and nothing is repaired; shops are closed, bread lines are long, clothes are made from curtains, the winters bring bitter cold and the summers epidemic. But none of this is seen politically because Miss Almedingen could not afford the luxury of a self, could not see the need for one beyond simple, pathetic efforts for people to be helpful to each other.... [The] line between respect and contempt in the rendering of one's youth [is delicate]. Miss Almedingen is [often] unembarrassedly serious about what [happens to her characters].... [The experiences in the book] her mind cannot naturally grasp, but that is her work's strength, and rare beauty. (pp. 549-50)

> *Roger Sale, in* The Hudson Review *(copyright © 1968 by The Hudson Review, Inc.; reprinted by permission), Vol. XXI, No. 3, Autumn, 1968.*

GUY DAVENPORT

[*Tomorrow Will Come*] is a book about a woman who remained sane in a time of madness. It was written in 1936, written lucidly, truthfully, and with a firm exactitude that seems at times understatement, until we realize that only a few have been gifted with the mastery of words necessary to present such turbulence in its proper fire. Here we have instead cold truth exactly put. (p. 1072)

The first impact of this strange and heroic book is its realistic account of a revolution from the underside, wholly from the point of view of a young lady who knew nothing of it until it happened, and who had to survive it as a victim. The second is that it pictures the collapse of a civilization. The story has been told over and over, in history books and in fiction. By now the Russian Revolution has taken on the dimensions of legend. Madame Lenin spoke of its "slow grandeur"; the moving-picture *Doctor Zhivago* made it look as sweet as the Salvation Army marching against sin.

Miss Almedingen offers no political opinions, makes no passionate statements about civilization, extracts no conclusions; she is not writing that kind of book. Brilliant historian that she is, she chose rather to write a book in which one can feel page by page the anguish of the revolution and the loss of the civilization it destroyed. But it is the kind of book every wise reader prefers to the cold diagrams of the history book. Facts hide the knowledge they pretend to convey; real history is knowing that there was a time in one of the most civilized of cities when a broken shoelace was the last shoelace in the world. (p. 1073)

> *Guy Davenport, "They Call It a Revolution," in* National Review *(© National Review, Inc., 1968; 150 East 35th St., New York, N.Y. 10016), October 22, 1968, pp. 1072-73.*

ROSEMARY NEISWENDER

Miss Almedingen is especially adept at translating history into terms dramatic enough to capture the imagination of younger readers without sacrificing accuracy. Readers of an older generation will remember her *Tomorrow Will Come* ..., a vivid evocation of the author's early life in pre-Revolutionary Russia and of her later emigration to England.... [In *The Retreat from Moscow*] the author presents the story of Napoleon's ill-fated 1812 march across Russia to Moscow.... This is told from a pro-Russian viewpoint, and while it is scarcely a postage-stamp *War and Peace*, it contains many lively, colorful vignettes and can be considered good fictionalized history. (p. 1)

> *Rosemary Neiswender, in* School Library Journal *(reprinted from the April, 1969 issue of* School Library Journal, *published by R. R. Bowker Co. A Xerox Corporation; copyright © 1969), April, 1969.*

ZENA SUTHERLAND

The story line [of *A Candle at Dusk*] is of minor importance, although it reflects historical events; the major interest in the book is the recreation of a period, and this is effected with notable success. The pattern of life on a Frankish freehold, the struggle for power within the church, and the pressing fear of Saracen invasion are vividly evoked. (pp. 59-60)

> *Zena Sutherland, in* Saturday Review *(© 1969 by Saturday Review, Inc.; reprinted with permission), May 10, 1969.*

Many of Miss Almedingen's previous books combine historical data with fictionalization but [*Stephen's Light*] may well be her least successful. Set in a "composite" late fifteenth century town, it focuses on lackluster Sabina, a merchant's daughter, and the social convolutions of being jilted when her Richard runs off with Dame Adela of the local cloister. The story would be dull enough with just the woebegone thoughts of and slights to the girl ...; written as it is, tiresomely, the detail-studded social fabric unravels endlessly. Besides the convent life ..., there are shaky flirtations with grand historical movements ..., seen from both the kitchen and the main hall. Also, the frequent inclusion of parts of medieval Christian ceremonies will just bug most readers. *Te deum* tedium. (p. 1154)

> *Kirkus Reviews (copyright © 1969 The Kirkus Service, Inc.), November 1, 1969.*

MARGARET N. COUGHLAN

[*Stephen's Light*] fails as a compelling, engaging narrative. The late 15th Century, with its decadent church and rise of the burghers, provides the background for the story of Sabina, only child of a wealthy burgher.... Though the story is well written and the setting authentic, neither characters nor incidents are fully realized. There's no fire in the telling, and the book is, at best, a supplementary item for libraries needing more period fiction for girls. (p. 56)

> *Margaret N. Coughlan, in* School Library Journal *(reprinted from the December, 1969 issue of* School Library Journal, *published by R. R. Bowker Co. A Xerox Corporation; copyright ©* 1969), *December, 1969.*

[Miss Almedingen was born in St. Petersburg] and spent her childhood and youth there. Her parents were separated and though they both came from good families she and her mother were very poor. The child seems to have been allowed a great deal of freedom to wander round the city and these wanderings she describes as if they were yesterday.... [*I Remember St. Petersburg* (published in the United States as *My St. Petersburg*)] is a really honest book ... conveying the history and atmosphere of one of the most beautiful cities in Europe which no amount of hardship and seige can change. One hopes that by reading it children will come to a deeper understanding of Russia. (p. 91)

> The Junior Bookshelf, *April, 1970.*

[*The Scarlet Goose* is so] very recondite a novel as to seem deliberately evasive—evasive of its own story line which is itself obscure, set in a 1492 Germany that mirrors little Renaissance glow. As plotted, the action is potentially dramatic, but as structured it becomes linear and fragmented, diffuse; the drifting of focus from one character or situation to another suggests perhaps a cinematic realization where palpables would convey what antique diction and strained syntax cannot.... Money, oaths, and prayers fly round the market gossip as the badly executed mosaic of social, religious, and mercantile machinations comments on a people imprisoned according to station in a medieval world. Starker, darker still than *Stephen's Light* (1969), the story is stripped of identifying clues or guideposts and whittled into a massive patter-nostrum. (p. 463)

> Kirkus Reviews *(copyright © 1970 The Kirkus Service, Inc.), April 15, 1970.*

Fanny ... grew up to be a writer herself, and the story of her first fourteen years, on the family's estates in Kaluga province or in the restricting Moscow town house, is told in her own words [in *Fanny*], translated and skilfully expanded from other family sources, by her niece E. M. Almedingen. Such memoirs suit this writer's slow, detailed style exactly. Reminiscences of childhood in any time or place told with such understanding would have been worth reading, but here there is also historical interest, in the vivid picture of pre-Revolutionary Russia at the end of the nineteenth century.... A new world is made real with the descriptions of the Russian countryside and daily life at Fanny's beloved Avchourino.... (pp. 157-58)

> The Junior Bookshelf, *June, 1970.*

VIRGINIA HAVILAND

[*Ellen* is another chapter in the story of E. M. Almedingen's] extraordinary English-Russian forebears. Fictional in form, but with no fictional characters or events, it is a lively biography of her Kentish grandmother, Ellen, the mother of Frances whose life is told in *Fanny*.... The book is closely related to the author's previous writing about old Russia.... [It] is rich in ample details of rural life in a large home near Canterbury and in the full-bodied characterizations of children, servants, relatives, and visitors. It is unusually effective for its portrait of the English family surrounding a lovable, spirited child and young woman. (p. 53)

> *Virginia Haviland, in* The Horn Book Magazine *(copyright © 1971 by The Horn Book, Inc., Boston), February, 1971.*

JOHN W. CONNER

Adolescent girls who love to read stories about nineteenth-century, middle-class English country maidens who marry wealthy European noblemen have an inviting ... novel in store for them. *Ellen* is a book for these young readers to cherish. E. M. Almedingen relates the true story of her grandmother, Ellen Southee, with great affection and excellent taste.

Ellen is a beautifully developed character. Miss Almedingen sees her as a temperamental, sometimes lazy young lady who must mature when her mother dies leaving Ellen's family under the haphazard guidance of her fun-loving, free spending father....

There are a great many characters in *Ellen*. Yet, somehow Miss Almedingen makes them all real people as they aid or resist Ellen Southee. Ellen's prodigal father comes off rather too well, considering his inability to manage his own family responsibilities, and Ellen's mother will be remembered as an ever-ailing saint who keeps her family solvent and respectable for as long as she lives. Every reader will regret the moment when the Southeee's English home is abandoned and the faithful servants are sent away to spend their remaining years in somewhat less hospitable households. And every reader will share Ellen's excitement as she takes possession of her enormous Russian household.

It is easy to become involved in the lives presented in *Ellen*. An adolescent reader may sigh with regret as Ellen's adventures end. This is a book for quiet, personal enjoyment with an intrinsic timeless quality. *Ellen* should be a popular reader's choice for many years to come! (p. 405)

> *John W. Conner, in* English Journal *(copyright © 1971 by the National Council of Teachers of English), March, 1971.*

ANN THWAITE

There seems to be no end to the extraordinary family papers this lucky author has to draw on. She has already told the stories of other relations in *Little Katia, Young Mark* and *Fanny*. In the preface to *Ellen* she tells us she has not included a single 'invented happening or imagined person'. She writes in the first person and it is difficult to believe she is not remembering it herself. It has its inconsistencies and longueurs, as the autobiography of any elderly lady would have, but it is also carefully packed with plenty of good stories and meaningful detail. The last quarter of the book, from the arrival in Russia, is by far the most interesting. (p. 312)

> *Ann Thwaite, in* New Statesman *(© 1971 The Statesman & Nation Publishing Co. Ltd.), March 5, 1971.*

E. M. Almedingen's devotees are familiar with the great

sweeping serf-run estates of the Poltoratzkys at Avchourino, snowbound through the long winter months, a fairyland in spring and summer. They understand the deep fissures, social and cultural, which divide the serfs from the aristocratic French-speaking Russian family in the big house; and they are aware of the dilemma of the head of the family who deplores serfdom yet knows it is the basis of the Russian economy, who would like to free his own serfs but is sufficiently practical to realize that Russia will not be defeudalized through the humanitarian thinking of a mere handful of aristocrats.

So that when Kentish Ellen, heroine of E. M. Almedingen's [*Ellen*], arrives at Avchourino in the middle of the nineteenth century, having married Serge Poltoratzky whom she met while travelling Europe with her debt-laden but delightful father, the seasoned Almedingen reader comes ''home''—while the heroine and the new reader (who could do worse than begin here and follow on with *Fanny, Little Katia* and *Young Mark* in that order) are on fresh and strange territory.

Ellen is an absorbing book, better tailored than its immediate predecessor *Fanny* and therefore, though long, easier to read. . . .

Ellen, like so many of the Poltoratzky family she was to marry into, was a born writer. She saw stories everywhere and filled notebook after notebook with her fantasies. Through her diaries and jottings—over which Miss Almedingen has waved her magic wand—the atmosphere of a big family . . . springs from the page. Especially vivid is the description of Ellen's old grandfather who lived near Canterbury in a house full of objects which stirred little Ellen's imagination. . . .

Another chapter in the Poltoratzky family history—one of the best—has been written. What a chronicle it is! (p. 381)

The Times Literary Supplement (© Times Newspapers Ltd. (London) 1971; reproduced from The Times Literary Supplement by permission), April 2, 1971.

One must admit that, though the best of [*Ellen*] has the enchanting quality of Miss Almedingen's other recreations of her family's past, the style here is uneven, and at times relationships are tediously analysed in adult fashion, or the daily routine whipped up to appear, for instance, ''the black year'' 1828: it seems all the milder for the humdrum waiting for events which never happen in Ellen's part of Kent. The centuries' old home of the Kentish yeoman family is lovingly drawn, and there are delightful characters. . . . The ruin of their fortunes after their mother's death, when their father relapsed into gambling and betting, and their breathless progress across Europe, living alternately in luxury and dire poverty, is as lively as any of the earlier Russian tales, and Ellen's romance with Count Poltoratsky, their marriage, early tragedies and joys, are delightfully told. It is a fascinating record of an unfamiliar period. . . . (pp. 173-74)

The Junior Bookshelf, *June, 1971.*

VALERIE ALDERSON

Among contemporary writers of English children's books, E. M. Almedingen probably had one of the most colourful family backgrounds, and this was reflected in much of her writing, particularly in the later years when she turned to children's books. (p. 149)

[Characters] in her adult novels such as *The Scarlet Goose* or *Stand Fast Beloved City* or even *Frossia*, seem dead—indeed they do have '. . . wood in their breast and water in their veins', as she herself said, although potentially, the stories could have lent themselves to much livelier treatment. (p. 151)

[It] is in her last two books for children, *Fanny* and *Ellen* that one can most clearly make the comparison between her writing for adults and for children. The first of these stories is based on the surviving notes of her aunt Frances-Hermione, who used to visit them in St. Petersburg, and is an account of the life of her mother's family at Avchourino, their country estate in Russia, and the early years of their exile to France. The second volume, *Ellen,* tells the story of the childhood and early married life of grandmother Ellen, up to the birth of Frances, with a brief epilogue covering the remainder of her life. This is a straight re-working for children of the biography first published in 1958. It is possible to compare details, seeing where an incident has been adapted, a sentence changed to suit the younger readership, and it is fascinating to observe the way in which characters who were merely flat descriptions on the pages of the first book come alive under their new treatment. E. M. Almedingen never wrote down to children; one never feels in the reading that she made *conscious* concessions to vocabulary or understandings, but clearly she was more at ease in the less complex, freer world of childhood than in the emotional entanglements of the adult novel. (pp. 151-52)

I suspect that it will be for her children's books, written during the last few years, that she will be best remembered. It would seem that her family were quite right in their belief that 'literature was a realm to be won only after a mature and solemn dedication'. In children's books she had found her true *metier* and it is a great pity that she did not live long enough to exploit it fully. Had she lived, I am sure that sooner or later she would have returned to her own story, begun in the reminiscences of *I Remember St. Petersburg*, bringing early twentieth-century Russia to life as no textbook could do, and providing a magnificent foil to those less personally involved who have already made the attempt. (p. 152)

Valerie Alderson, ''E. M. Almedingen 1898-1971: An Appreciation,'' in Children's Book Review (© 1971 by Five Owls Press Ltd.; all rights reserved), October, 1971, pp. 149-52.

Children fascinated by the legendary figures of Russia's early history will be grateful [for the publication of] *Rus into Muscovy* by . . . E. M. Almedingen; twenty-three short chapters sketch in the major upheavals from 862, when the Slav tribes became one nation, to 1613, when Michael Romanov was proclaimed Tsar. One cannot pretend that the prose is limpid, and those sufficiently interested to persevere will surely be scholarly enough to regret that there is no index. (p. 1518)

The Times Literary Supplement (© Times Newspapers Ltd. (London) 1971; reproduced from The Times Literary Supplement by permission), December 3, 1971.

MARGERY FISHER

[*The Retreat from Moscow* is a] brief, brisk account of Napoleon's campaign in Russia, in essence a paean of praise to Alexander I. The author has used a good deal of invented dialogue to diversify her facts; this is very much a novelist's book, for as always she sees history mainly in terms of individuals. (p. 1884)

Margery Fisher, in her Growing Point, *January, 1972.*

[*Rus into Muscovy: The History of Early Russia* (published in the United States as *Land of Muscovy*) is a] posthumous work by an author who always loved Russia and knew it well. It is a history of the early days of the country from A.D. 862 to the 17th Century, that is from the Slav invasion and settlement to the beginning of unity for this vast country under the first of the Romanov dynasty. The story is a dramatic and tragic one, full of bloodshed and cruelty....

A book of this kind with its many stories of fantastic and colourful personalities could be read by a wide age range. It does much to explain the events of our own century in the Soviet Union and is valuable background material. (p. 103)

The Junior Bookshelf, *April, 1972.*

The stories of this sensitive and gifted writer, all based on the chronicles of her family in the eighteenth and nineteenth centuries, are infused with devotion and nostalgia. . . . [*Anna*] marks the end of an era. Although she does not shirk the social implications of a feudal society which persisted into our century, the author empathizes so completely with the heroine, Anna, that the reader sees the book as autobiographical fiction in the best tradition of "the good old days". Anna is nearly drowned crossing a river in an overloaded ferry boat and later set upon by wandering ruffians who are subsequently hanged, but it is difficult to feel that the calm of the house of the scholarly eighteenth-century seed-merchant is ever really threatened.... [*Anna*] is all that a remarkable matriarch should be in childhood, a gifted linguist, her father's helper, a little princess in the mercantile world of her Moscow suburb. The virtues of the intense identification of the author with her subject are seen in the details of occupations, food, the rituals of the Orthodox year, the benevolent paternalism. The shadows of coming events are short. Anna's life is a scholarly idyll, beautifully written. It is unlikely there will be any more of this kind. (p. 476)

The Times Literary Supplement (© *Times Newspapers Ltd. (London) 1972; reproduced from* The Times Literary Supplement *by permission), April 28, 1972.*

In her last book [*Anna*] E. M. Almedingen recaptures once more a past age and brings it vividly to life. She dips for the last time into her family papers and brings out this time her great-grandmother, who grew up in the changing world of the late eighteenth century, acutely aware of the atmosphere of revolution and playing her very small part in the transformation of society. It is an enchanting portrait, not less for being lightly drawn. No writer of our day has used understatement with more subtle effect. A beautifully written story, tender, affectionate, but—like the heroine—utterly without fuss. (p. 235)

The Junior Bookshelf, *August, 1972.*

ZENA SUTHERLAND

Familiar to young readers as the author of many stories set in Russia and based on the history of her own aristocratic family, E. M. Almedingen has written, in *Land of Muscovy*, a book as dramatic and colorful as any of her novels. The text traces Russian history from the times of the first scattered, nomadic tribes to the beginning of the Romanov dynasty; it has enough action, intrigue, tragedy, and triumph to fashion a handful of opera libretti. (p. 70)

Zena Sutherland, in Bulletin of the Center for Children's Books (© *1973 by the University of Chicago; all rights reserved), January, 1973.*

SHEILA G. RAY

Although the stories which she has written for young people do not have a contemporary setting, E. M. Almedingen does manage to convey the sense of spaciousness, the richness of tradition and the mixed character of the Russian people which are still as true of the country as they were before 1917. Even though the political system was very different in the days of which she writes in most of her books, they may nevertheless help to understand the way of life in Eastern Europe....

[She] was an expert on Russian history and many of her books reflect this fact. (p. 301)

The Poltoratzkys represent E. M. Almedingen's maternal relations. Catherine von Almedingen, the heroine of *Little Katia*, was a great aunt on her father's side; this book is a rewriting of Catherine's own story published in Russia in 1874 as *The Story of a Little Girl*, which established Catherine's reputation as a leading children's author. This, like all the stories previously mentioned, is written in the first person.

Frossia is the only one of these stories written in the third person and this alone does not purport to be fiction based on fact. Frossia, however, is of the same age and generation as E. M. Almedingen herself, and lives through the days immediately after the 1917 Revolution, determined to survive and inspired by love of her country despite the changed political situation.... She describes how she grew up, devoted to her native city, and how, in spite of the poverty in which she and her mother lived . . . , she considered herself 'rich because I had St Petersburg'. Reading *Frossia* immediately after this autobiographical account of life before 1917, it is impossible to disassociate the two central characters—they have so much in common.

E. M. Almedingen allows her own love of St Petersburg to be reflected in *Frossia.* . . . Her dealings with bureaucracy are a good introduction to the way things still operate in the USSR.

In many ways *Frossia* . . . is the best. The fact that it is written in the third person means that the author can range widely—we are not restricted to scenes and incidents where Frossia herself is present.... Frossia, with her gift for learning languages, is very much a heroine in the tradition of the author's ancestresses. (pp. 302-03)

Anna, Ellen and *Fanny;* the last three to be published, are longer and more demanding; they are most likely to appeal to girls in their teens, since, although the heroines all describe incidents of early childhood . . . , they dwell much more on the problems of growing up and adapting to the adult world. Older girls will also enjoy fitting the stories together and will gain some sense of historical perspective from doing so. Anna is the kind of heroine with whom many girls will like to identify; she is extremely learned, capable and energetic; before she marries (at sixteen!) she has learnt six languages, but there are plenty of reminders that she is living in an earlier age. . . .

Ellen and Fanny, as well as Catherine Almedingen, had the urge to write. Their descendant has made good use of the rich material they left in their memoirs, and the panorama which she has woven out of their jottings and out of her own experience gives to the reader some understanding of why the USSR is the country which it is today. (p. 303)

> *Sheila G. Ray, in* The School Librarian, *December, 1973.*

ETHEL L. CHAMBERLAIN

[E. M. Almedingen] is a crafter of the first order, she plays with words and images, and, early on, her story casts its spell. . . . (p. 553)

[*Too Early Lilac*] is the story of Lena Stelling, of her growing up in a pampered, aristocratic household, of her maturing and of her coming to grips with that question. Indeed it is strange that in turn-of-the-century St. Petersburg nothing constructive is happening around her. True, she studies French and literature with a governess from Limoges, and Russian History with a tutor from the university, but all is stagnant, as much idle chatter as the talk of the kitchen help. . . . It is as if events outside the door do not affect these people, and Miss Almedingen fails to bring any touch of reality, of social milieu, of political condition to her story. Indeed it is entertaining, a fairy tale. (pp. 553-54)

> *Ethel L. Chamberlain, in* Best Sellers *(copyright 1975, by the University of Scranton), March 15, 1975.*

Maya Angelou

1928-

(Pseudonym of Marguerita Johnson) American autobiographical novelist, poet, dramatist, composer, actress, and dancer. Angelou's life has become a source of great interest since the publication of her first autobiographical novel, *I Know Why the Caged Bird Sings*. Her story is noteworthy for its candid descriptions of the adjustments and struggles of Angelou's early life. Despite the pain involved in writing about her past, she feels her story is beneficial to young people, whom she warns, "You may encounter many defeats, but you must not be defeated." Angelou has done editorial work on the *Arab Observer* of Cairo and administrative work for the School of Music and Drama at the University of Ghana. She speaks six languages and has taught and lectured at several universities. In 1976, she was named Woman of the Year in Communications by *Ladies' Home Journal*. She has also been nominated for various awards, including the Pulitzer Prize and the Tony Award. A member of a number of prominent associations, such as the Directors Guild of America, she has also served on the advisory board of the Women's Prison Association, and on the National Commission on the Observance of International Women's Year and the American Revolution Bicentennial Council. (See also *Contemporary Authors*, Vols. 65-68.)

ERNECE B. KELLY

[*I Know Why the Caged Bird Sings*] is a poetic counterpart for the more scholarly [*Growing Up in the Black Belt: Negro Youth in the Rural South* by Charles S. Johnson]. For it is an autobiographical novel about a "too big Negro girl, with nappy black hair, broad feet and a space between her teeth that would hold a number-two pencil" ... scratching out the early outlines of self in a small Arkansas town.

Miss Angelou confidently reaches back in memory to pull out the painful childhood times: when children fail to break the adult code, disastrously breaching faith and laws they know nothing of; when the very young swing easy from hysterical laughter to awful loneliness; from a hunger for heroes to the voluntary Pleasure-Pain game of wondering who their *real* parents are and how long before they take them to their authentic home.

Introducing herself as Marguerite, a "tender-hearted" child, the author allows her story to range in an extraordinary fashion along the field of human emotion. With a child's fatalism, a deep cut ushers in visions of an ignoble death. With a child's addiction to romance and melodrama, she imagines ending her life in the dirt-yard of a Mexican family—among strangers! It is as if Miss Angelou has a Time Machine, so unerringly does she record the private world of the young where sin is the Original Sin and embarrassment, penultimate.

While she expertly reminds us of the pain of children trapped by time in the unsympathetic world of adults, she stretches out to the human environment too. Although the elements that go to make up the Black southern and rural experience—customs, values, superstitions—most interest Miss Angelou, she carries us "across the tracks" occasionally to the white world in experiences which corroborate the observation Marguerite's uncle makes: "They don't know us. They mostly scared." ... (p. 681)

[Marguerite's] view of the truth about interracial encounters in this land is often expressed in phrasing that seems dated in its naturalistic grounding. Speaking of a white receptionist who gives her the run-around about a job, for instance, she says, "I accepted her as a fellow victim of the same puppeteer." ... Such a fatalistic point-of-view would be quickly smothered in the current climate of social/political activism. Activists see the possibility and necessity for change—moderate to revolutionary—in the racial roles this society assigns us. Interestingly, the author moves out from under her fatalism by the end of the novel when she successfully demands a job as a streetcar conductor in San Francisco, a position traditionally denied women who are Black.

Miss Angelou accommodates her literary style to the various settings her story moves through. She describes a rural vignette which is "sweet-milk fresh in her memory." ... Her metaphors are strong and right; her similes less often so. But these lapses in poetic style are undeniably balanced by the insight she offers into the effects of social conditioning on the life-style and self-concept of a Black child growing up in the rural South of the 1930's.

This is a novel about Blackness, youth, and white American society, usually in conflict. The miracle is that out of the War emerges a whole person capable of believing in her worth and capabilities. On balance, it is a gentle indictment of white American womanhood. It is a timely book. (p. 682)

Ernece B. Kelly, in Harvard Educational Review

(copyright © 1970 by President and Fellows of Harvard College), November, 1970.

The natural feeling that made *I Know Why the Caged Bird Sings* such a special reminiscence gives [the verses of *Just Give Me a Cool Drink of Water 'Fore I Diiie*] their claim to poetry. They're mostly short and rhymed, in simple forms or freeform, not sophisticated but sensitive all the same to the aural possibilities of rhythm and diction. Of the two sections, one of lyrics on love as the black woman knows it and the other, longer pieces on angrier universal themes of blackness, the first seems the truer. Poems like "They went Home" and "No Loser, No Weeper," slight as they are, carry the weight of experience. "Times-Square-Shoe-Shine-Composition" (in a "Dozens" cadence) and "The Calling of Names" flash among the serious but less well realized pieces of the second group but nothing in either is a match for Miss Angelou's prose, where her real poetry flows without restraint. (p. 775)

Kirkus Reviews *(copyright © 1971 The Kirkus Service, Inc.), July 15, 1971.*

SIDONIE ANN SMITH

Maya Angelou's autobiography, like [Richard] Wright's, opens with a primal childhood scene that brings into focus the nature of the imprisoning environment from which the self will seek escape. The black girl child is trapped within the cage of her own diminished self-image around which interlock the bars of natural and social forces. The oppression of natural forces, of physical appearance and processes, foists a self-consciousness on all young girls who must grow from children into women. Hair is too thin or stringy or mousy or nappy. Legs are too fat, too thin, too bony, the knees too bowed. Hips are too wide or not wide enough. Breasts grow too fast or not at all. The self-critical process is incessant, a driving demon. But in the black girl child's experience these natural bars are reinforced with the rusted iron social bars of racial subordination and impotence. Being born black is itself a liability in a world ruled by white standards of beauty which imprison the child *a priori* in a cage of ugliness: "What you looking at me for?" This really isn't me. I'm white with long blond hair and blue eyes, with pretty pink skin and straight hair, with a delicate mouth. I'm my own mistake. I haven't dreamed myself hard enough. I'll try again. The black and blue bruises of the soul multiply and compound as the caged bird flings herself against these bars.... If the black man is denied his potency and his masculinity, if his autobiography narrates the quest of the black male after a "place" of full manhood, the black woman is denied her beauty and her quest is one after self-accepted black womanhood. Thus the discovered pattern of significant moments Maya Angelou superimposes on the experience of her life is a pattern of moments that trace the quest of the black female after a "place," a place where a child no longer need ask self-consciously, "What you looking at me for?" but where a woman can declare confidently, "I am a beautiful, Black woman." (pp. 367-68)

[This] autobiography of Black America is haunted by [Maya and her brother Bailey], children beginning life or early finding themselves without parents, sometimes with no one but themselves. They travel through life desperately in search of a home, some place where they can escape the shadow of loneliness, of solitude, of outsider-ness. Al-

though Maya and Bailey are travelling toward the home of their grandmother, more important, they are travelling away from the "home" of their parents. Such rejection a child internalizes and translates as a rejection of self: ultimately the loss of home occasions the loss of self-worth. "I'm being sent away because I'm not lovable." The quest for a home therefore is the quest for acceptance, for love, and for the resultant feeling of self-worth. Because Maya Angelou became conscious of her displacement early in life, she began her quest earlier than most of us. Like that of any orphan, that quest is intensely lonely, intensely solitary, making it all the more desperate, immediate, demanding, and making it, above all, an even more estranging process. For the "place" always recedes into the distance, moving with the horizon, and the searcher goes through life merely "passing through" to some place beyond, always beyond....

The aura of personal displacement is counterpointed by the ambience of displacement within the larger black community. The black community of Stamps [, Arkansas, where the two children are sent by their estranged parents] is itself caged in the social reality of racial subordination and impotence. The cotton pickers must face an empty bag every morning, an empty will every night, knowing all along that the season would end as it had begun—money-less, credit-less. (p. 369)

Nevertheless, there is a containedness in this environment called Stamps, a containedness which controls the girl child's sense of displacement, the containedness of a safe way of life, a hard way of life, but a known way of life. The child doesn't want to fit here, but it shapes her to it. And although she is lonely, although she suffers from her feelings of ugliness and abandonment, the strength of Momma's arms contains some of that loneliness.

Suddenly Stamps is left behind. Moving on, the promise of a place. Her mother, aunts, uncles, grandparents—St. Louis, a big city, an even bigger reality, a totally new reality. But even here displacement: St. Louis, with its strange sounds, its packaged food, its modern conveniences, remains, a foreign country to the child who after only a few weeks understands that it is not to be her "home." (p. 370)

Back to Stamps, back to the place of grayness and barrenness, the place where nothing happened to people who, in spite of it all, felt contentment "based on the belief that nothing more was coming to them although a great deal more was due."... Her psychological and emotional devastation find a mirror in Stamps' social devastation. (p. 371)

One gesture, however, foreshadows Maya's eventual inability to "sit quietly" and is very much an expression of her growing acceptance of her own self-worth. For a short time she works in the house of Mrs. Viola Cullinan, but a short time only, for Mrs. Cullinan, with an easiness that comes from long tradition, assaults her ego by calling her Mary rather than Maya. Such an oversight offered so casually is a most devastating sign of the girl's invisibility. In failing to call her by her name, a symbol of identity and individuality, of uniqueness, Mrs. Cullinan fails to respect her humanity. Maya understands this perfectly and rebels by breaking Mrs. Cullinan's most cherished dish. The girl child is assuming the consciousness of rebellion as the stance necessary for preserving her individuality and affirming her self-worth. Such a stance insures displacement in Stamps, Arkansas.

But now there is yet another move. Once again the train, travelling westward to San Francisco in wartime. Here in this big city everything seems out of place. . . . In Stamps the way of life remained rigid, in San Francisco it ran fluid. Maya had been on the move when she entered Stamps and thus could not settle into its rigid way of life. She chose to remain an outsider, and in so doing, chose not to allow her personality to become rigid. The fluidity of the new environment matched the fluidity of her emotional, physical, and psychological life. She could feel in place in an environment where everyone and everything seemed out-of-place.

Even more significant than the total displacement of San Francisco is Maya's trip to Mexico with her father. The older autobiographer, in giving form to her past experience, discovers that this "moment" was central to her process of growth. Maya accompanies her father to a small Mexican town where he proceeds to get obliviously drunk, leaving her with the responsibility of getting them back to Los Angeles. But she has never before driven a car. For the first time, Maya finds herself totally in control of her fate. Such total control contrasts vividly to her earlier recognition in Stamps that she as a Negro had no control over her fate. Here she is alone with that fate. And although the drive culminates in an accident, she triumphs.

This "moment" is succeeded by a month spent in a wrecked car lot scavenging with others like herself. Together these experiences provide her with a knowledge of self-determination and a confirmation of her self-worth. With the assumption of this affirmative knowledge and power, Maya is ready to challenge the unwritten, restrictive social codes of San Francisco. Mrs. Cullinan's broken dish prefigures the job on the streetcar. Stamps' acquiescence is left far behind in Arkansas as Maya assumes control over her own social destiny and engages in the struggle with life's forces. She has broken out of the rusted bars of her social cage.

But Maya must still break open the bars of her female sexuality: although she now feels power over her social identity, she feels insecurity about her sexual identity. (pp. 372-73)

Only [her] pregnancy provides a climactic reassurance: if she can become pregnant, she certainly cannot be a lesbian (certainly a specious argument in terms of logic but a compelling one in terms of emotions and psychology). The birth of the baby brings Maya something totally her own, but, more important, brings her to a recognition of and acceptance of her full, instinctual womanhood. The child, father to the woman, opens the caged door and allows the fully-developed woman to fly out. Now she feels the control of her sexual identity as well as of her social identity. (pp. 373-74)

Maya Angelou's autobiography comes to a sense of an ending: the black American girl child has succeeded in freeing herself from the natural and social bars imprisoning her in the cage of her own diminished self-image by assuming control of her life and fully accepting her black womanhood. The displaced child has found a "place." With the birth of her child Maya is herself born into a mature engagement with the forces of life. In welcoming that struggle she refuses to live a death of quiet acquiescence. . . .

One final comment: one way of dying to life's struggle is to suppress its inevitable pain by forgetting the past. . . . Once [Maya Angelou] accepted the challenge of recovering the lost years, she accepted the challenge of the process of self-discovery and reconfirmed her commitment to life's struggle. By the time she, as autobiographer, finished remembering the past and shaping it into a pattern of significant moments, she had imposed some sense of an ending upon it. And in imposing that ending upon it she gave the experience distance and a context and thereby came to understand the past and ultimately to understand herself. (p. 374)

Her genius as a writer is her ability to recapture the texture of the way of life in the texture of its idioms, its idiosyncratic vocabulary and especially in its process of image-making. The imagery holds the reality, giving it immediacy. That she chooses to recreate the past in its own sounds suggests to the reader that she accepts the past and recognizes its beauty and its ugliness, its assets and its liabilities, its strength and its weakness. Here we witness a return to and final acceptance of the past in the return to and full acceptance of its language, the language a symbolic construct of a way of life. Ultimately Maya Angelou's style testifies to her reaffirmation of self-acceptance, the self-acceptance she achieves within the pattern of the autobiography. (p. 375)

Sidonie Ann Smith, "The Song of a Caged Bird: Maya Angelou's Quest after Self-Acceptance," in The Southern Humanities Review *(copyright 1973 by Auburn University), Fall, 1973, pp. 365-75.*

ANNIE GOTTLIEB

Maya Angelou writes like a song, and like the truth. The wisdom, rue and humor of her storytelling are borne on a lilting rhythm completely her own, the product of a born writer's senses nourished on black church singing and preaching, soft mother talk and salty street talk, and on literature: James Weldon Johnson, Langston Hughes, Richard Wright, Shakespeare and Gorki. Her honesty is also very much her own, even when she faces bitter facts or her own youthful foolishness. In this second installment of her autobiography, as in her much praised first book, "I Know Why the Caged Bird Sings," Maya Angelou accomplishes the rare feat of laying her own life open to a reader's scrutiny without the reflex-covering gesture of melodrama or shame. And as she reveals herself so does she reveal the black community, with a quiet pride, a painful candor and a clean anger.

"Gather Together in My Name" is a little shorter and thinner than its predecessor; telling of an episodic, searching and wandering period in Maya Angelou's life, it lacks the density of childhood. In full compensation, her style has both ripened and simplified. It is more telegraphic and more condensed, transmitting a world of sensation or emotion or understanding in one image—in short, it is more like poetry. . . .

"The South I returned to . . . was flesh-real and swollen-belly poor." "I clenched my reason and forced their faces into focus." Even in these short bits snipped out of context, you can sense the palpability, the precision and the rhythm of this writing. The reader is rocked into pleasure, stung into awareness. And the migrant, irresolute quality of the story—a faithful reflection of her late adolescence in the forties—resolves into a revelation. The restless, frustrated trying-on of roles turns out to have been an instinctive self-education, and the book ends with Maya Angelou finally gaining her adulthood by regaining her innocence. (p. 16)

In "Gather Together in My Name," the ridiculous and touching posturing of a young girl in the throes of growing up are superimposed on the serious business of survival and responsibility for a child. Maya Angelou's insistence on taking full responsibility for her own life, her frank and humorous examination of her self, will challenge many a reader to be as honest under easier circumstances. Reading her book, you may learn, too, the embrace and ritual, the dignity and solace and humor of the black community. You will meet strong, distinctive people, drawn with deftness and compassion; their blackness is not used to hide their familiar but vulnerable humanity any more than their accessible humanity can for a moment be used to obscure their blackness—or their oppression. Maya Angelou's second book about her life as a young black woman in America is engrossing and vital, rich and funny and wise. (p. 20)

> *Annie Gottlieb, in* The New York Times Book Review *(© 1974 by The New York Times Company; reprinted by permission), June 16, 1974.*

LYNN SUKENICK

Maya Angelou's rendering of three years of her innocent, awkward, and admirably nervy late adolescence in ["Gather Together in My Name"], the second volume of her autobiography, resembles the performance of a professional dancer trying to imitate someone who can't dance. The grace and competence show through and it's hard to believe in the high incidence of failure she describes in her youth. Thus we are entertained but kept safe from the roughness and painful uncertainty of real ineptitudes.

Angelou's prose is sculpted, concise, rich with flavor and surprise, exuding a natural confidence and command. The fault—since I have found one—lies more in the tone of the book. It is healthy, warm, and tough, winning our affection partly through its refusal to gloss over stupidities, mistakes, and cruelties. Yet this refusal to let her earlier self get off easy, and the self-mockery which is her means to honesty, finally becomes in itself a glossing over; although her laughter at herself is witty, intelligent, and a good preventative against maudlin confession (she shrugs off deprivations of family feeling that would make our ordinary psychoanalyzed citizen curl up in self-pity), it eventually becomes a tic and a substitute for a deeper look.

The book is a comedy of self-deception. I don't mean to say that it should be something sober and earnest—indeed, Angelou's style and flair come from her ability to move rather than brood. Yet a revelation of youthful foolishness usually implies that something will take its place, build slowly to edge it out, and the book does not build; it is a chain of anecdotes, and Maya's innocence must re-establish itself at the start of each in order to her mistakes to function as the punch lines they tend to be. Comedy is liberating precisely because there is in it an absence of long-range consequences, and it is not consequences but transitions that I miss—whether of motivation, or musing, or adjustments of emotion. Transitions are a graph of how people cope, and wanting to know how people cope is one of our most urgent reasons for reading autobiography. That Angelou is within the space of three years a mother, a

Creole cook, a madam, a tap dancer, a prostitute, a chauffeurette, and so on, is amazing, but I'm not content to be amazed, and I'm annoyed when flippancy runs interference; she gets me to like her and I want to know what it is inside her that makes those choices, however little they may have seemed like Choices at the time. . . .

The realest thing about autobiography is the teller, not the tale. Temperament tends to linger and infuse us long after the anecdotes are forgotten. On the strength of "I Know Why the Caged Bird Sings" I will continue to read whatever autobiographical prose Maya Angelou produces, but I hope that next time she will let simmer a little longer and make it a little less Entertaining, however much a publisher, or even her readers, urge her on. (p. 31)

> *Lynn Sukenick, in* The Village Voice *(reprinted by permission of* The Village Voice; *copyright © The Village Voice, Inc., 1974), July 11, 1974.*

DORIS GRUMBACH

[*Gather Together in My Name*] is the second volume in the story of [Maya Angelou's] life, a series that she intended to continue "every three years until she is recognized as the contemporary Black Proust." It may be that she will fall short of that avowed ambition but, if one recalls her first successful book *I Know Why The Caged Bird Sings* . . . , and reads this second one, it is apparent that Angelou is keen, sharp, earthy, imaginative, lyrical, spiritually bold, and seems destined for distinction.

The book concerns her travails in California between the ages of 17 and 19 at the end of World War II. . . . Rita [the name Maya calls herself in this book] scrapes, in these two frantic years, from the bottom to the level at the end of the book when, like Voltaire's Candide, she asserts: "I had given a promise and found my innocence. I swore I'd never lose it again."

Angelou has kept that promise. . . . A truly remarkable person, she is able to re-create events of her own life and make them seem part of the reader's imaginative experience. (p. 32)

> *Doris Grumbach, in* The New Republic *(reprinted by permission of* The New Republic; *© 1974 by The New Republic, Inc.), July 6 & 13, 1974.*

FRANK LAMONT PHILLIPS

[Maya Angelou begins *Gather Together In My Name*] with a brief history of Black American thought and culture after the second World War; it is not a precise history, certainly not history as viewed coolly and through statistics. It is not even "accurate," but viewed from the vantage of almost 30 years, as one might hear it on the streets: biased, authoritative, hip, almost wildly funny, like certain urban myths. It seems right, and if this is not history as it was, it is history as it should have been.

In many ways, autobiography is the most demanding fiction, and few can, *à la* Chester Himes' *The Quality of Hurt*, whip the form into anything more appreciable than the cotton candy of a life that might have been anyone's. Richard Wright succeeded with *Black Boy* because he approached it as fiction. (p. 52)

Maya Angelou is not the stylist that Himes is, nor a Richard Wright. She manages, however, a whirry poetic flow (intensely more successful than in her book of poems,

Just Give Me A Cool Drink of Water 'fore I Die) that is sometimes cute, sometimes lax, often apt. The events of her life making interesting if somewhat lurid reading: an unwed mother, she is unlucky in love; she becomes a prostitute, enduring every nadir of fortune, her motherly instincts intact, her ability to adapt to adversity functioning.

Miss Angelou has the right instincts, that mythomania which one who is given to prattling about his life seems always to possess. She applies it cannily, preserving the fiction that one can recall and, from a distance, whole conversations and surrounding trivia—as if she were a reel of recording tape, consuming for later regurgitation a problematic life. Further, she is schooled in situation ethics, licensing them retroactively to cover her having been a prostitute, making it seem almost enviable that she pulled it off so well.

It can also be said that Miss Angelou possesses an ear for folkways; they spawn abundantly in the warm stream of narration, adding enough mother wit and humor to give the events a "rightness." To some extent she is coy, never allowing us a really good, voyeur's glimpse into the conjugal bed that several male characters enjoy with her; rather, she teases. And though the author is never mawkiskly sentimental, she shows herself to have been, like most of us, silly, only more so than many of us will admit. Yet she is proud. She stumbles, falls, but like the phoenix, rises renewed and wholly myth. (p. 61)

> *Frank Lamont Phillips, in* Black World *(copyright © July, 1975, by* Black World; *reprinted by permission of Johnson Publishing Company and Frank Lamont Phillips), July, 1975.*

MARY SILVA COSGRAVE

[*Oh Pray My Wings Are Gonna Fit Me Well* is an] eloquent collection of poems that sing out like spirituals from the heart of the poet. She writes of love and loneliness, childhood and womanhood, communication, rejection, fairness, and justice; of Africa waking up and America still sleeping. The verses in "Pickin Em Up and Layin Em Down" catch the stomping rhythm of a fickle lover dancing his way to the next town. In "Song for the Old Ones," the Uncle Toms and Aunt Jemimas used their wits, cunning, and smiles to insure the survival of their race. In "Take Time Out," the contemporary world is urged to pause and reflect: "If you know that youth / is dying on the run / and my daughter trades / dope stories with your son / we'd better see / what all our / fearing and our / jeering and our / crying and / our lying / brought about." (p. 78)

> *Mary Silva Cosgrave, in* The Horn Book Magazine *(copyright © 1976 by the Horn Book, Inc., Boston), February, 1976.*

The 36 poems in [*Oh Pray My Wings Are Gonna Fit Me Well*] are grouped, arbitrarily it seems, into five parts, the first four of which contain pieces that are all surface. The themes, chiefly lost or wronged love or frustrated desire, and their treatments are akin to country-western music. It is in the treatment that the superficiality is most obvious: Motives not explored, little depth or interpretation of feelings, no sense of time or change, no allusion or any rich ambiguity, little melody. Some are merely cute. Most could be as effectively stated in declarative sentences. A few poems capture some sense of loneliness, but without con-

veying any insight or universal values. The twelve poems in part five are generally better, containing some developed images, a degree of music, while also finding deeper meanings in man's actions or inactions. (p. 82)

> *Virginia Quarterly Review (copyright, 1976, by the* Virginia Quarterly Review, The University of Virginia), *Vol. 52, No. 3 (Summer, 1976).*

SANDRA M. GILBERT

I can't help feeling that Maya Angelou's career has suffered from the interest her publishers have in mythologizing *her*. *Oh Pray My Wings Are Gonna Fit Me Well* is such a painfully untalented collection of poems that I can't think of any reason, other than the Maya Myth, for it to be in print.... All this is especially depressing because Angelou ... is a stunningly talented prose writer, whose marvelous *I Know Why The Caged Bird Sings* has quite properly become a contemporary classic. Why should it be necessary, then, for her to represent herself publicly as the author of such an embarrassing tangle as

> I'd touched your features inchly
>   heard love and dared the cost.
> The scented spiel reeled me unreal
>   and found my senses lost.

And why, instead of encouraging Angelou, didn't some friendly editor Block (as *The New Yorker* would say) the following Metaphor:

> A day
> drunk with the nectar of
> nowness
> weaves its way between
> the years
> to find itself at the flophouse
> of night. . . .

To be fair, not all the verse in *Oh Pray* . . . is quite as bad as these two examples. A few of the colloquial pieces— *Pickin Em Up and Layin Em Down* or *Come. And Be My Baby*—have the slangy, unpretentious vitality of good ballads. *The Pusher* ("He bad / O he bad"), with its echoes of Brooks's "We real cool", achieves genuine scariness. And *John J.* might be a portrait in verse of Bailey, the handsome brother Angelou renders so beautifully in *I Know Why*. . . . But these are only four or five poems out of the thirty-six in this collection. And most of the others, when they're not awkward or stilted, are simply corny.... Angelou can hardly be accused of self-parody: for one thing, most of the poetry here is too unself-conscious, too thoughtless, to be in any sense parodic. But, for whatever reason, the wings of song certainly don't seem to fit her very well right now. (pp. 296-97)

> *Sandra M. Gilbert, in* Poetry *(© 1976 by The Modern Poetry Association; reprinted by permission of the Editor of* Poetry), *August, 1976.*

JUNE JORDAN

[The heroine of *Singin' and Swingin' and Gettin' Merry Like Christmas,* a] real-life memoir (that frequently borders on the light and fantastical style of comic opera) paces you through the extraordinarily eventful days and nights of her life as a single young woman who is amply gifted and clearly on the bigger-and-better-make scene. (p. 40)

We accompany Angelou from city to city, from triumph to

triumph, you might say, until her worries about her son (left with her mother, who is somebody I'd sure like to know more about) catapult her back to the States, her son, and, presumably, more merry adventures, to be disclosed, if not concluded, in the next book-long chapter of her life.

Well, this is sometimes delightful reading, and sometimes not. The unabashed, positive energies and the happy resourcefulness of this woman compel your respect, and certainly you wish her well as she hurtles from week to week, place to place, trial to victory.

When she tries to prepare her mother for her impending interracial marriage, her mother asks her why she'll marry the man since Angelou evidently does not love him, or doesn't say she does. Angelou replies: "Because he asked me." The starved sorrow of that response strongly suggests that there are dimensions to Angelou's life that she is not ready to share, yet. I wish she would; that would make it real for me. In the meantime, reading this account, you will not be able to guess about the year, or know about anything remotely political and, in that sense, general. Perhaps Angelou wrote her story that way, *in vacuo,* so that she could righteously declare, to paraphrase Langston Hughes if I may, "Life for me ain't been no big despair." (pp. 40-1)

June Jordan, in Ms. *(© 1977 Ms. Magazine Corp.), January, 1977.*

ALLEEN PACE NILSEN

Besides the always present Angelou zest and style, a value of [*Singin' and Swingin' and Gettin' Merry Like Christmas*] is that it covers the period of her life when she made the transition from being a part-time clerk in a record store to being "somebody." The part of the book that fascinated me the most was the recounting of her tour as a featured dancer in "Porgy and Bess" when it played in Italy, France, Greece, Yugoslavia, and Egypt. Because of the cast of characters, Angelou's keen sense of observation, and her lively writing, this is no ordinary travelogue. For readers who have a harder time getting into poetry than into prose, this book might make an exciting introduction to Angelou's poetry. (pp. 87-8)

Alleen Pace Nilsen, in English Journal *(copyright © 1977 by the National Council of Teachers of English), September, 1977.*

JANET BOYARIN BLUNDELL

Angelou's [*And Still I Rise*] enlarges on themes from her autobiographical writings and earlier poetry, although the quality of individual poems varies.... The poems that work have language close to speech or more nearly to song, while the others get mired in hackneyed metaphor and forced rhyme. Despite its unevenness, the book succeeds as a statement of one black woman's experience, and of her determination not only to survive but to grow. (p. 1640)

Janet Boyarin Blundell, in Library Journal *(reprinted from* Library Journal, *September 1, 1978; published by R. R. Bowker Co. (a Xerox company); copyright © 1978 by Xerox Corporation), September 1, 1978.*

[In *And Still I Rise*], Maya Angelou proves once again that audacity can pay off. Seemingly unafraid to approach anything, she includes comments on aging, the disappointments of love, anger at the abuse of black people, and the everyday aspects of womanhood. The moving spirit is summed up in the poem "Still I Rise" when she says "Does my sassiness upset you? / Why are you beset with gloom? / 'Cause I walk like I've got oil wells / Pumping in my living room...." The music of these lines is continued throughout the book: indeed Angelou's use of the refrain often serves to break up a poem when the tension grows overwhelming.... Angelou's most glaring weakness is a tendency towards obvious and rhetorical statement, as in "Ain't that Bad," which lists items commonly associated with blacks (Stevie Wonder, rice and beans, etc.) in a way that fails to dramatize any point. However, through her use of music and direct, uninhibited statement, she has written a distinctive and energetic volume. (p. 1127)

Kirkus Reviews *(copyright © 1978 The Kirkus Service, Inc.), October 1, 1978.*

Jules Archer
1915-

American young adult nonfiction writer, biographer, and screenwriter. Archer is noted for writing histories and biographies for young adults that do not gloss over the unpleasant aspects of history and that present famous figures realistically, with human failings and weaknesses. He began writing for young adults when he saw the material available to his three sons in junior high and high school, textbooks and supplementary reading that he felt fed "American youngsters . . . pap and Pollyanna tales instead of the honest truth; the good and the bad alike." Archer served in the Air Force and became a war correspondent during World War II. From these experiences he gained background for some of his popular biographies of World War II figures, including *Front-Line General: Douglas MacArthur* and *Battlefield President: Dwight D. Eisenhower*. Archer actively researches each of his books, examining unpublished as well as published sources and traveling extensively, and often comes up with unusual or little-known facts that contribute to the interest of his works. He has a reputation for being somewhat of a George Plimpton, and in his search for material swam in the Seine at midnight, shot the rapids, climbed a live volcano by camel, and snorkeled among barracuda, among other activities. He is especially well respected for his studies of Eastern culture and history. (See also *Contemporary Authors*, Vols. 9-12, rev. ed., and *Something about the Author*, Vol. 4.)

HELENE CANTARELLA

In selecting Benito Mussolini as the subject of [*Twentieth Century Caesar: Benito Mussolini*], Jules Archer deliberately accents the negative to achieve the positive. To prove that the ruler who teaches his people to hate blindly ultimately falls victim to that violence, he has chosen to focus on the meteoric rise and fall of the son of a small-town blacksmith and an overworked schoolmistress, who was to become Il Duce of Fascism and founder of the now vanished Italian Empire.

Nothing in the life of this ruthless, strutting demagogue inspires, either admiration or compassion. He made his way from the start through betrayal of every cause he ever espoused and every friend who ever held out to him a helping hand. . . .

All this Mr. Archer makes unmistakably clear despite minor orthographic and factual inaccuracies. His swift-moving account recaptures in substance the complex historical events that made possible the rise of the preposterous characters who played a major role in shaping them. (p. 24)

> Helene Cantarella, in The New York Times Book Review (© 1964 by The New York Times Company; reprinted by permission), November 1, 1964.

[*Man of Steel: Joseph Stalin*] is worth having. It's readable, it's cautious in its judgments and its facts are traceable without the heavy presence of footnotes. . . . What Jules Archer has attempted with some success is the sort of unemotional analysis history's great villains seldom get. His major thesis is that Stalin personally reflected all the barbarism of a semi-primitive country and also mirrored all its crude strength when forcing it, (without any commitment to the ethical principles of Western civilization) to join the 20th century in military power and technological skills. He minimizes none of the despotic characteristics, nor does he fail to point up the always disturbing questions of ends and means. Well-done—it makes you stop and think, and perhaps discuss. (p. 988)

> Virginia Kirkus' Service (copyright © 1965 Virginia Kirkus' Service, Inc.), September 15, 1965.

Two-thirds of [*Laws that Changed America*] is cursory information forced into a predetermined format, but the balance may be worth your attention. To claim that the first Federal Bank Act, the Sixteenth Amendment (permitting the levying of an income tax), the Federal Reserve Act (creating a flexible currency) and the Glass-Steagall Act (insuring deposits) "made us prosper" is ipso facto ridiculous and obscures what it intends to reveal—the interdependence of economics and the political process; further, the chapter as a whole is too condensed, the information too abstracted from the context of history, to be useful. Likewise the sections bearing on American expansion, guarantee of rights, foreign policy, conservation, and civil rights—and much of this material is widely available elsewhere. The balance is both fuller and less frequently assembled: laws pertaining to labor, to health, education and welfare, and to the farmer. There's a candid, comprehensive discussion of temperance and prohibition and (under "red-white-and-blue laws") an extensive summary of the loyalty syndrome from the first repressive acts (and the limitation of immigration) to the McCarthy era. (pp. 568-69)

Kirkus Service *(copyright © 1967 Virginia Kirkus' Service, Inc.), May 1, 1967.*

EDWARD J. BANDER

[*Laws That Changed America*] was well conceived but poorly executed. The author gives chapters on the settlement of this country, economic measures, the Bill of Rights, laws that shaped our foreign policy, conservation laws, labor laws, anti-trust laws, health-education-welfare laws, laws for the farmer, conscription, civil rights, etc. Well over 100 laws are raced through helter-skelter, with the impression that liberalism was the guiding force behind all beneficial enactments. No attempt is made to explain how laws are passed or to distinguish between bills, acts, vetoes, joint resolutions, constitutional amendments or court cases. Citations to the acts are not given, nor is there any indication as to where they can be found. If all the reader wants is a list of memorable laws, classified as indicated above, he has it here. (p. 3192)

Edward J. Bander, in Library Journal *(reprinted from Library Journal, September 15, 1967; published by R. R. Bowker Co. (a Xerox company); copyright © 1967 by Xerox Corporation), September 15, 1967.*

The provocative title [of *The Dictators*] covers a multitude, and they're not all sinners—some (Lenin, Castro, Tito) improved the life of their people, others started well but became demagogues (Ataturk, Mao, Peron, Nasser). Among the out-and-out villains are not only Hitler, Mussolini and Stalin but also such American embarrassments as Chiang, Trujillo and Batista—and it is the presence of the latter that gives the book its greatest interest. The life and career of each is sketched in eight or nine pages of highly colored prose—not enough space (or detachment) for the complex political, economic and social background of the more prominent, appropriate rather to a petty tyrant (and this includes Duvalier, possibly the very different Salazar). An introductory chapter attempts, via a hypothetical chronology of events, to trace the rise of a representative dictator; it's an effective device even if the example doesn't apply universally. Of less value is the last chapter, an editorializing comparison of dictatorship and democracy. What's left are the lives, too personal and particular to provide a framework for understanding dictatorship generally, too cursory and controversially selective to be good history, but useful perhaps for the minor figures. (p. 1221)

Kirkus Service *(copyright © 1967 Virginia Kirkus' Service, Inc.), October 1, 1967.*

[*World Citizen: Woodrow Wilson*] is significant for its realistic portrayal of Wilson's character and its lively coverage of the negotiations and controversies engendered by the Mexican War and the Versailles Treaty. Focusing mainly on the Presidential years, Archer's account of Wilson's childhood and youth underlines those influences which had a lasting effect on his personality and thought. It concludes with a summary of pro and con opinions by Wilson's critics and defenders. (p. 920)

The Booklist and Subscription Books Bulletin *(reprinted by permission of the American Library Association; copyright 1968 by the American Library Association), April 1, 1968.*

DAVID CORT

As a crash course in fundamentals, ["*The Dictators*"] has its distinct virtues, and it gives a net impression of the absolute hell this century has been through. The author has a wonderfully simple point of view: dictators who died poor are better than dictators who died rich. The Communist examples, even Stalin, are given a better image than is the general custom. Mao and Lenin are pretty fine here; Chiang is awful. And so is Ataturk, who was only the salvation of the modern Turkish nation. On the other hand, Franco and Salazar come off better than one would expect. (p. 26)

David Cort, in The New York Times Book Review *(© 1968 by The New York Times Company; reprinted by permission), May 5, 1968.*

[*The Unpopular Ones* is] a book you may agree with and yet not approve of because of its implicit polemic, its explicit parallels with the present. Most of the profiles begin with a dramatic incident—a prosecution which is also a persecution—then recap the subject's life briefly, dwelling in detail only on his divergent ideas and the consequences thereof—for the individual, for his time, for posterity. The last aspect is overstated to the point of insulting the reader: Joseph Palmer went to jail rather than remove his beard, hippies have been harassed for wearing beards, etc. The first three—Roger Williams, Zenger, Paine—are expected choices whose contributions are made quite clear; the next, Anne Royall, who skewered many sacred cows, is little known and worth knowing; Horace Greeley and Thoreau are utilized primarily to advance the author's purposes though he does include much of Greeley's history, much of Thoreau's writing; Jonathan Walker, another obscure figure, is here because his branded hand (punishment for helping slaves to escape) made him an instrument of the Abolitionists; Bethenia Owens, "the first lady doctor in the West," would qualify for an inspirational biopsy. Which brings us to the controversial core of the book: a tribute to Debs that lacks background and balance; a treatment of Wilson that attributes the Fourteen Points to Bolshevik disclosures of secret treaties, forcing him to dispel the taint of imperialism; strong chapters on Margaret Sanger and Robert Oppenheimer, both of which are quite judicious (though the former unfortunately refers to *impending* Papal reconsideration). And then there's Fulbright, who gets twice as much space as most of the others for what is, in effect, a long critique of, first, the McCarthy period, then, more particularly, of American foreign policy of the past twenty-five years. Uneven as collective biography, both interesting and irritating as a nay-sayer's slant on history. (p. 989)

Kirkus Service *(copyright © 1968 The Kirkus Service, Inc.), September 1, 1968.*

DALLAS Y. SHAFFER

This competent fictionalized biography [*Red Rebel: Tito of Yugoslavia*] emphasizes Tito's early years and resistance fighting during World War II and clearly explains the historical background and intricacies of Yugoslavian politics. The postwar developments in the country are handled vaguely, but the confrontation between Stalin and Tito is well described, as is the importance of Yugoslavia in contemporary world politics. The style is generally good, except for some corny chapter titles such as "Have Gun, Will Travel." (p. 92)

Dallas Y. Shaffer, in School Library Journal *(reprinted from the November 1968 issue of* School Library Journal, *published by R. R. Bowker Co. A Xerox Corporation; copyright © 1968), November, 1968.*

Kenyatta's passage from Kikuyu village to the Prime Ministery of an independent Kenya—via London, Moscow and long imprisonment—is equal to Mr. Archer's penchant for grandiloquence: it is an extraordinary story. And it's to the author's credit that he notes the nuances [in *African Firebrand: Jomo Kenyatta*]: the protracted conflict between the British Colonial Office and the local settlers over the rights of Africans; the latter's misunderstanding of African tribal customs, especially with regard to land ownership; the Africans' (and Kenyatta's) disillusionment with Christianity, adherence to Christ; Kenyatta's disapproval of Mau Mau, refusal to disavow it. This most inflammatory episode is placed in perspective: caused by white denial of concessions, aggravated by the arrest of Kenyatta, it led to brutal excesses on both sides and a massive loss of African lives.... The book balances excitement with assessment and provides a welcome introduction to a salient figure. (p. 318)

Kirkus Reviews (copyright © 1969 The Kirkus Service, Inc.), March 15, 1969.

CLAUDE URY

[*The Extremists: Gadflies of American Society* is a] unique, very stimulating analysis of the extremist views and their proponents—whether right, left or center—that have influenced the American scene, from Colonial days to the present.... [Particularly] excellent is the last chapter on extremism in the '60's. The author's thesis is that extremism is an element necessary to an open-minded democracy.... His factual, unbiased presentation will serve to help develop readers' potential for critical thinking. (pp. 124-25)

Claude Ury, in School Library Journal *(reprinted from the November, 1969 issue of* School Library Journal, *published by R. R. Bowker Co. A Xerox Corporation; copyright © 1969), November, 1969.*

DOROTHY S. LATIAK

Today's young people should dig William Lloyd Garrison! He wanted "freedom now" and his battle cry was "I will be heard." Beginning as a moderate on the issue of slavery, his soon became the strongest voice against the evil which was tearing our country apart. Jules Archer presents Garrison [in *Angry Abolitionist: William Lloyd Garrison*] as a human being as well as the tireless abolitionist who edited the *Liberator* throughout its existence.... This book will be useful to supplement material on African-American history. (p. 127)

Dorothy S. Latiak, in School Library Journal *(reprinted from the March, 1970 issue of* School Library Journal, *published by R. R. Bowker Co. A Xerox Corporation; copyright © 1970), March, 1970.*

Mr. Archer sees the course of military and foreign affairs from colonial days to the present in terms of a contest between "hawks" and "doves" [in *Hawks, Doves and the Eagle*]. And while he disclaims "hard-and-fast classifications," individuals and groups are so categorized on vir-

tually every page as per the doctrinaire lines drawn at the beginning ("Hawks favor military alliances, but doves frown on obligations to supply troops to fight beyond our borders," etc., etc.). Consequently issues of civil liberties, of profiteering, of proper conduct and economic policy are obscured.... As history the book is both insufficiently explicative (the Versailles Treaty is an undefined "disaster") and frequently erroneous (T. R. was Leonard Wood's second-in-command rather than vice versa . . .). Meanwhile individual "hawks" are vilified . . . or ridiculed.... The good that this might have done—as a record of anti-war sentiment and pacifist protest—is negated by unreasonableness and untrustworthiness. (p. 391)

Kirkus Reviews (copyright © 1970 The Kirkus Service, Inc.), April 1, 1970.

In a backhanded backpat, Mr. Archer introduces Lieutenant General William Harney . . . [in *Indian Foe, Indian Friend*] as "an ideal choice as a camera of his times" a propos of U.S. treatment of the Indians. To the extent that Harney, a foremost Indian fighter, was sufficiently enlightened to see U.S. intransigence as self-defeating, sufficiently humane to bridle at slaughtering women and children, he may be said to have been the Indians' friend; but considering that government perfidy didn't deter him from pursuing the Seminoles nor the justice of the Sioux cause (in resisting invasion of treaty-lands) affect his willingness to take command against them, one wonders if he is quite the 'remarkable unsung hero' he's made out to be.... Harney's sentiments, acknowledged by other authorities and supported by documents, are inflated here by ascribing to him thoughts that cannot be verified: did he indeed 'reflect bitterly' on "the government's attempt to use laws to rob the Indians for the benefit of a powerful clique of unscrupulous businessmen?" Evidence points rather to his respect for the Indians and regard for fair play, no mean qualities at the time. Incidental ennobling occurs also: Harney had long been separated from his family when he becomes "numb with grief and guilt" at his wife's death (no mention is made of his remarriage) & his role in the Oregon boundary dispute is viewed much less leniently elsewhere. Had Harney been seen as a soldier with a conscience (and a man like any other), he would be a more convincing historical presence. (p. 467)

Kirkus Reviews (copyright © 1970 The Kirkus Service, Inc.), April 15, 1970.

HARVEY DUST

[*Thorn in Our Flesh: Castro's Cuba*] is uneven in quality and [weak] on pre-revolutionary history. [Archer] is often negligent with his facts, sometimes so marshalling them as to draw unintended, meaningless, or misleading conclusions. For example, though Castro was not Communist until 1961, Archer gives the impression . . . that the conversion was earlier. Also, he overstates the influence of Raul and Che without offering proof of the same. He tends to conveniently overlook certain facts: e.g., Batista traded with the U.S.S.R. but no one ever accused him of being a part of the Soviet economic bloc. Archer's strengths lie mainly in his account of the Bay of Pigs . . . , and in his last two chapters, "Reporters Look at Cuba" and "Fidelism Tomorrow"; these exhibit a depth and objectivity lacking in the main body of his book. (p. 167)

Harvey Dust, in School Library Journal *(reprinted*

[In *The Philippines' Fight for Freedom*] Mr. Archer fixes upon the quest for self-determination and equalization and slights internal politics except as they pertain . . . ; but he is assiduous in reporting relevant developments (the recurring guerrilla movements are portrayed with particular acumen) and pinning opinions down in contemporary quotes. Not only is his evidence irrefutable, his tone is, given the material, quite equable: the subject is well worth airing, and well aired. (pp. 1254-55)

> *Kirkus Reviews (copyright © 1970 The Kirkus Service, Inc.), November 15, 1970.*

WILLIAM D. EDWARDS

[*The Philippines' Fight for Freedom* is an] in-depth examination of the almost 400-year struggle of the Philippines for independence. The misery and suffering of the native people and the injustice by Spain, Church, and the U.S. dominate the account. A revealing picture of the barbarity of the times and of the situation is depicted in the chapters dealing with the U.S. take-over after the Spanish-American War. Archer forcefully introduces the Philippine leaders, their hopes for the country . . . and the broken promises of the U.S. Learning of the war fought by the natives against us is much like reading a story of the war in Vietnam today. (p. 57)

> *William D. Edwards, in* School Library Journal *(reprinted from the December, 1970 issue of* School Library Journal, *published by R. R. Bowker Co. A Xerox Corporation; copyright © 1970), December, 1970.*

JAMES NELSON GOODSELL

In what is nothing short of dispassionate treatment, Jules Archer's *Thorn in Our Flesh* looks at Cuba and the appeal that it has to American youth—and suggests some of the reasons why. It will not please the ardently pro-Castro reader, nor will it receive plaudits from the staunchly anti-Castro reader. But that in itself lends merit to the book.

Archer's theme is that "if we understand why the Cuban revolution happened, we may be able in the future to avoid repeating the tragic mistakes that have proved so costly to us in Cuba and Vietnam." His book does not give all the answers, but it is written for the teenager whose awareness of the vast economic and social forces at work in Latin America is not as broad as it will become in the years ahead.

One point stands out in Archer's description of U.S.-Cuban relations. "Castro himself finds it ironic," he writes, "that a country born in rebellion against injustice should have been so insensitive to Cuban suffering and rebellion." (p. 48)

> *James Nelson Goodsell, in* The Progressive *(reprinted by permission from* The Progressive, *408 West Gorham Street, Madison, Wisconsin 53703; copyright © 1971 by The Progressive, Inc.), January, 1971.*

JACK FORMAN

1968 *was* an incredibly eventful year and in some ways, as

[*1968: Year of Crisis*] points out, a year of many crises for this country. Archer . . . succeeds here in catching some of the excitement of the year through his fastpaced, colorfully written narrative. However, because the book is not a history . . . , but instead a kind of retrospective, interpretative journalism, Archer does not succeed in proving that the year was a "turning point" in American history. The treatment is generally superficial; transitions between the various events described tend to be forced. Archer's bias is openly anti-war, anti-Nixon, but he does attempt throughout to be fair to all sides. On balance, while the reference value is minimal because most of the information offered can be found elsewhere, the book will be useful where students read this kind of popular history. (p. 71)

> *Jack Forman, in* School Library Journal *(reprinted from the May, 1971 issue of* School Library Journal, *published by R. R. Bowker Co. A Xerox Corporation; copyright © 1971), May, 1971.*

JANET G. POLACHECK

[*Revolution in our Time* is a] confusing account of world revolutions in the past century. There is little continuity between chapters which move from the New Left to black power to whether a new American revolution can succeed and whether revolutionists should be tolerated. While many interesting anecdotes are offered, the abrupt jumps in time . . . and from place to place . . . make this book almost impossible to read and follow coherently. (p. 287)

> *Janet G. Polacheck, in* School Library Journal *(reprinted from the January, 1972 issue of* School Library Journal, *published by R. R. Bowker Co. A Xerox Corporation; copyright © 1972), January, 1972.*

[*Mao Tse-Tung* is a] responsible, undemanding biography of Chairman Mao which personalizes and updates the story of *The Rise of Red China* told by [Robert] Goldston in 1967. As demonstrated by a wealth of anecdotes—about Mao's readiness to volunteer for hazardous duty, his fatherly concern for his young orderly on the Long March, etc.—Archer clearly admires the self-sacrifice and political acumen which characterized the Chairman's youth. But he is far from uncritical—attributing Mao's parochialism partly to his long retreat in Yenan, tracing the growth of Maoist cult of personality and outlining the failures of the Great Leap Forward and the Hundred Flowers campaign. Of necessity this is a portrait of the public man, except for the few private conversations passed on by Malraux, Robert Payne and Jules Roy, but Archer's value lies in his ability to assess Mao's strengths and weaknesses unemotionally. (p. 268)

> *Kirkus Reviews (copyright © 1972 The Kirkus Service, Inc.), March 1, 1972.*

["Mao Tse-Tung: Red Emperor" is a] good book on Mao for the high school library and young adult readers. Archer is a competent writer who has produced some smoothly written but undistinguished biographies for the popular market. His gift is not meticulous research or political sophistication; but here he manages his narrative of Mao's career with simplicity and clarity—overdramatizing and "novelizing" to sustain interest, but on the whole offering younger readers a good headstart in their education on modern China. (p. 79)

MERLE GOLDMAN

There is an advantage in having a professional writer for young people, like Archer, write on historical events because he has the knack to entice his reader on almost every page. ["Mao Tse-Tung"] is a thriller. Perhaps there has been no more exciting account of Mao. The problem is that it is too exciting.

Because he is not an expert in this field, certain aspects of Mao's life, important in understanding him, are missing. As Mao achieves power, Archer gives him the appearance of a superman. His feats of strength, ingenuity and wisdom overwhelm insurmountable obstacles. Yet Mao did falter, made mistakes and was brutal toward his internal enemies in the early stages of his movement. Though he was flexible and tolerant in Yenan, for example, he treated some left-wing intellectuals harshly. Despite its deficiencies, Mr. Archer's book is bound to whet the student's appetite and lead him to other interpretations. (pp. 8, 10)

ELIZABETH H. WELCH

This detailed biography [*Ho Chi Minh: Legend of Hanoi*] reads like the most exciting adventure story. Archer, though always favorable to Ho, is plausible, and he bases his writings on historical events and documents. In this book, Ho, to most Americans a mysterious and formidable leader, is shown more warmly, with "human" qualities, as he matured and as he developed his political philosophy. The emphasis is that Ho was *not* a servant of China nor of Russia. He was first a nationalist with a fierce love for his country. (p. 912)

[In *Strikes, Bombs & Bullets: Big Bill Haywood and the IWW*] Archer pulls no punches with regard to Big Bill's tolerance of/involvement with violence in the mineworker and IWW ranks ("No socialist can be a law-abiding citizen," was a Haywood credo), but the exhaustively described tyranny of the mine owners stands as an implicit defense. The Wobblies' differences with Gompers and the AFL are crystallized in matters of style . . . and principle . . . , and background characters are humanized in a few, quick strokes. . . . A fair and non-simplistic rendering of the factual background is combined here with a dramatic, high-interest journalistic style, and, like the contemporary newspaperman he quotes, Archer successfully communicates his qualified admiration for fiery, headstrong Big Bill. . . . (pp. 808-09)

TARIQ ALI

[*Ho Chi Minh, Legend of Hanoi*] is insipid, dull even by the standards of bourgeois journalism and totally superfluous. Since Lacouture's biography is available in English, one wonders why . . . [the publishers] decided to publish this book at all. Certainly it does provide some information, but on the level of a bad colour supplement article which is what it should have been restricted to. (p. 86)

HUBERT HUMPHREYS

According to Major General Smedley Butler a faction of the anti-Roosevelt Liberty League conspired to use him to overthrow the U.S. government and establish an American fascist dictatorship. Archer . . . uses some unpublished records of a short-lived congressional investigation and some limited interviews in an attempt to prove the validity of this assertion [in *The Plot to Seize the White House*]. Unfortunately his evidence, like that presented to the 1934 McCormack-Dickstein Committee, is very limited and doesn't prove anything. Archer, by repetitiously reciting hearsay evidence and using a long biographical sketch of Butler (to verify Butler's integrity and veracity), expands a fascinating footnote of history into an intriguing book that attempts to convince the reader there was a conspiracy. However, unless more hard evidence is ferreted out of the camp of the supposed conspirators and their Establishment protectors, the story will remain an intriguing footnote. (pp. 1480-81)

The most notorious examples of American intervention in Mexico . . . have been amply covered in last year's spate of Mexican histories. However, Archer alone has been willing to tackle the more complex dynamics of the post-Wilsonian era, and he acknowledges that in spite of the friendlier diplomatic climate there was still political pressure on Mexico to align with us in the Cold War and economic pressure to slow down the revolution in the interest of American investors. The compressed, fast moving account [in *Mexico & the United States*] incorporates observations by American journalists Lincoln Steffens, John Reed and Walter Lippmann and sheds some light on political divisions in the U.S. as well as in Mexico. . . . Lucid, well organized, and more outspoken than most. (p. 694)

[In *Trotsky: World Revolutionary*] Archer has conscientiously marshaled his facts to outline the substance of Trotsky's views and accomplishments, but he fails to explain (much less prove) his initial claim that Trotsky's appeal "has never been more compelling than it is today." Indeed one feels that the author is bending over backwards to be fair to a subject who, because of his vanity and incompetence in practical politics, has little appeal to him. This carefully objective portrait lacks the kind of human interest glimpses found in [Bertram David] Wolfe's *Three Who Made a Revolution* which add to Trotsky's stature as a radical folk hero. The result is a solid, if disappointingly colorless, supplement to such basic histories as [Robert] Goldston's *Russian Revolution*. (pp. 889-90)

> Kirkus Reviews *(copyright © 1973 The Kirkus Service, Inc.), August 15, 1973.*

MRS. JOHN G. GRAY

In [*Famous Young Rebels,* an] excellent collection of short biographical sketches of famous people, and some not so commonly included in collective works, the author has chosen as common denominator the fact that all twelve subjects were regarded as radicals of their day. . . . Offbeat life styles and goals, and intimate touches from the private lives of such well-known men and women, present attractive social study material. (p. 332)

> *Mrs. John G. Gray, in* Best Sellers *(copyright 1973, by the University of Scranton), October 15, 1973.*

JACK FORMAN

According to Archer, the Number Two man in Red China, Chou, is the man who has made Maoism work. In describing his life and up-and-down relationships with Chiang-Kai-Shek and Mao-Tse-Tung, the straightforward, chronological narrative [of *Chou En-Lai*] brings out Chou's personal qualities of charm, compromise, and patience. Archer also shows how Chou's western education contributed to his political successes in China. What comes through as clearly as Chou's character is the ability of the Chinese people to pull together in defense against foreign invasion. Some fictional dialogue is included, but the well-written account is factual overall. Together with Archer's equally well-done biography, *Mao-Tse-Tung,* . . . a fascinating history of Communist China emerges. (p. 3460)

> *Jack Forman, in* Library Journal *(reprinted from* Library Journal, *November 15, 1973; published by R. R. Bowker Co. (a Xerox company); copyright © 1973 by Xerox Corporation), November 15, 1973.*

HENRY J. STECK

[*Resistance*] is a disappointing book. Having started with a good idea and having collected a goodly body of information, the author fails to follow through. He seeks to answer a series of questions that have become compelling in recent years: Why do people resist? How far should resistance to legitimate and illegitimate authority go? What are the consequences of resistance? How can we learn from earlier examples? His historical examples range from Christ and Thoreau through resistance to Hitler and Stalin to various resistance movements today. But his assertions lack coherence, analytical depth, and persuasiveness. All forms of resistance appear to be thrown together, thus obscuring necessary historical and other distinctions. (p. 59)

> *Henry J. Steck, in* Library Journal *(reprinted from* Library Journal, *January 1, 1974; published by R. R. Bowker Co. (a Xerox company); copyright © 1974 by Xerox Corporation), January 1, 1974.*

JACK FORMAN

In [*Trotsky: World Revolutionary,* a] sympathetic and fair portrait of Trotsky, Archer clarifies without oversimplifying the muddled political situation of the Russian Revolution in 1917. He describes Trotsky's growth and development as an important Communist leader within the context of 19th- and early 20th-Century Russian history. An idealistic and sometimes fanatical believer in world revolution, Trotsky is seen as a charismatic speaker and a Communist theoretician. Archer believes his contributions to the Revolution are often overlooked because his political ambitions were not as great as either Lenin's or Stalin's. This well-written biography of Trotsky . . . captures the excitement and tragedy of the era when Czarist rule was overthrown by the Marxist revolution. (p. 68)

> *Jack Forman, in* School Library Journal *(reprinted from the February, 1974 issue of* School Library Journal, *published by R. R. Bowker Co. A Xerox Corporation; copyright © 1974), February, 1974.*

In a brief, analytical foreword [to *Riot: A History of Mob Action in the United States*] Archer makes the now well-recognized point that American history has had its share of civil violence and singles out several causative factors. . . . The remaining descriptive chapters are fairly comprehensive, beginning with Bacon's Rebellion and covering the broad spectrum of populist revolts, "vigilantism," race riots, labor unrest, even the Kent State shooting and the Days of Rage. . . . This is a solid treatment by an experienced commentator who, as usual, manages to take the broad, unhysterical view of a loaded topic. Nevertheless, anyone seriously interested in gaining a historical perspective ought to consider beginning at the adult level with [Richard] Hofstadter and [Michael] Wallace's *American Violence: A Documentary History.* (p. 1163)

> Kirkus Reviews *(copyright © 1974 The Kirkus Service, Inc.), November 1, 1974.*

RICHARD J. WALTON

[*The Plot to Seize the White House*] is great fun. It reads like a "best-selling novel soon to be made into a major motion picture." . . . The trouble is that this book is hard to take seriously. There is certainly a place for popular history and there is a foundation of fact for the belief that there was a plot to seize the White House paid for by right-wing Wall Streeters. But the alleged plotters were so inept—it makes the Kissinger kidnap caper seem sensible—and Jules Archer provides so little documentation for his assertions that one wishes he had written it consciously as a comedy instead of as the unconscious comedy his terrible earnestness sometimes makes it.

There's another problem. It takes so few pages to record all the facts known about the plot that the only way to eke it out to book length is by padding. Some of the padding is accomplished by simple repetition but most of it is achieved by means of a vastly entertaining mini-biography of the book's principal figure, Maj. Gen. Smedley Darlington Butler, who was quite an extraordinary man. . . .

Since Butler was the focal point of the strange plot, it was only appropriate that Archer give the reader some idea of what kind of man he was, but chapter after chapter is simply too much. . . . (p. 603)

Archer does little more than retell an old story, using material printed a generation ago by writers like George Seldes and John L. Spivak. He uncovered nothing new, and so we still do not know whether a serious, dangerous plot was in the works or whether it was merely a case of boardroom daydreaming exploited by a hustler who fattened his wallet at the expense of those whose hatred for "that man in the White House" allowed them to be conned. But his book certainly does whet my appetite for more on that cantankerous Smedley Darlington Butler. (p. 604)

> *Richard J. Walton, "Wrong Man on Horseback," in* The Nation *(copyright 1974 by the Nation Associates, Inc.), December 7, 1974, pp. 603-04.*

A shade less emotional than Archer's lives of *Trotsky* and *Mao Tse-Tung*, [*China in the 20th Century*] is still a fast-paced, vivid narration of 20th century Chinese history and is especially outspoken about the KMT and its place in United States foreign policy, the Sino Soviet split and Chinese foreign relations in general. Archer also details Mao's periodic struggles to retain his leadership of the Party and the "Yenan complex" that has sometimes led him to misjudge the temper of the people. Many lively quotes—from Mao himself, General Stilwell, western journalists and observers—are woven into the history, and though enthusiasm for Chinese accomplishments runs high, this paints a less idealistic, more hard-headed picture than, say, [Gil and Ann D.] Loeschers' *Chinese Way*. . . . The prolific Mr. Archer is always in top form when the subject is China, and this well-balanced introduction is less demanding than most at this level, yet without a trace of condescension. (p. 1312)

> Kirkus Reviews *(copyright © 1974 The Kirkus Service, Inc.), December 15, 1974.*

ERNEST DUNBAR

In an analysis that simplifies issues without being simplistic, [*Washington vs. Main Street: The Struggle between Federal and Local Power*] traces the shifts of power that occurred as the U.S. evolved from a colonial society in which localities had considerable autonomy to its contemporary character wherein most disputes have ramifications beyond the communities in which they may arise. To its credit, the book goes beyond the formal decision-making machinery of Congress or city hall to deal with the vast influence wielded by lobbyists, pressure groups and other special interests who actually determine many of the laws under which we live. It is particularly praiseworthy for its candid assessment of the treatment of minority people by both federal and local governments. Archer does not allow the shorthand symbols of "Washington" and "Main Street" to obscure the fact that at times a president or Congress may reflect popular sentiment more than do locally-elected bodies.

The book would have been improved by the inclusion of footnotes for its specific references. But that is a small flaw in a work that does much to clarify for young people the complex interplay of federal and local power which has formed the backdrop for the development of the American system. This is a valuable study. (p. 3)

> *Ernest Dunbar, in* Interracial Books for Children Bulletin *(reprinted by permission of* Interracial Books for Children Bulletin, *1841 Broadway, New York, N.Y. 10023), Vol. 6, No. 2, 1975.*

CYNTHIA SEYBOLT

[In *China in the Twentieth Century*] Archer presents a balanced view of developments in China since 1900 emphasizing political history and the men who made it. The au-

thor traces the rise of the Communist Party and outlines the policies and programs it has implemented to change Chinese society. Problems, failures, and struggles within the Party, as well as its triumphs, are described accurately and thoroughly. An excellent final chapter deals with aspects of life in China today. . . . [This book] emphasizes the role of the people rather than the leaders in recent Chinese history. (p. 61)

> *Cynthia Seybolt, in* School Library Journal *(reprinted from the April, 1975 issue of* School Library Journal, *published by R. R. Bowker Co. A Xerox Corporation; copyright © 1975), April, 1975.*

Although the author's anti-Nixon administration bias is in evidence and his use of the present tense throughout the narrative is sometimes disconcerting, his treatment of Watergate [in *Watergate: America in Crisis*] is thorough and well organized. Archer unfolds the whole story from the June 1972 break-in to the president's resignation and pardon and also fills in details of Nixon's earlier political career, the Ellsberg affair, the gamut of campaign "dirty tricks," and various financial scandals. Archer concludes, like many others, that flaws in Richard Nixon's character led to his downfall; he ends his account, however, with discussion of constructive changes that have and may yet come out of Watergate. (pp. 1122)

> The Booklist *(reprinted by permission of the American Library Association; copyright 1975 by the American Library Association), July 1, 1975.*

Archer sees Soviet-American relations as essentially a conflict between grass roots friendship and official suspicion. As he shows [in *The Russians and the Americans*], Russian admiration for American society goes back a long way. . . . Aside from being noticeably unanalytical, Archer tends to underplay the negative aspects of Soviet society, including the purges, and their impact on American opinion. This is, however, a provocative though somewhat simplistic critique of America's postwar policies. And Archer shows why the Soviets have had good reason to fear U.S. aggression—a viewpoint which should be an eye-opener for youngsters who've only heard it the other way around. (p. 784)

> Kirkus Reviews *(copyright © 1975 The Kirkus Service, Inc.), July 15, 1975.*

VICTOR S. NAVASKY

The case for Jules Archer's "Watergate: America in Crisis" is quite simply that it is the first attempt at a comprehensive account of Watergate for young citizens. . . .

Here is a tough-minded, skillful distillation of the Watergate events. The literary strategy is to tell the story not as it unfolded (as Woodward and Bernstein did in "All the President's Men") but as it happened. The style is clear but unpatronizing. The political premise and perspective are that Mr. Nixon was indeed "a crook."

Rather than pretending to present anything new, Mr. Archer recollects. Remember the "third-rate burglary attempt"? Where were you when John Mitchell said, "When the going gets tough the tough get going"? . . .

Nevertheless, the Archer genre raises a number of troublesome questions. First, there is the whole matter of transforming jury-findings of guilt into historical narratives. Louis Nizer did much the same thing for adults in his re-creation of the story of Julius and Ethel Rosenberg, "The Implosion Conspiracy." Such enterprises run fact-risks inadequately signaled in the text.

Then there are the author's dubious and sometimes facile judgments, such as his assertion that "On January 1, 1975, President Ford signs into law the most sweeping political campaign reform bill in the nation's history, preventing repetition of the abuses that had been at the heart of the Watergate scandal." For one thing, Watergate involved the breaking of laws, not the absence of them. For another, the bill is under severe constitutional attack and new loopholes are being discovered on what seems to be a daily basis.

More important, perhaps, is the fact that those old enough to understand this book (teens and pre-teens, I would say) are also old enough to understand such books as Theodore White's incomparably more valuable account of Mr. Nixon's fall or to await J. Anthony Lukas's forthcoming in-depth history. For those too young to have followed Watergate, the book doesn't do enough by way of context-re-creating; the cast of characters is too large, the pace of events too swift.

Does that mean there is no room for a Watergate book for the young citizen? Not at all. Especially since Watergate contains so many issues which speak to the next generation. What, for example, is the obligation of a junior staff member confronted with an order or action which appears unwise, immoral or illegal? When is he obliged to speak up, violate the chain of command, walk out, go to the authorities? One is curious to hear more about the dilemma faced by the President's daughters, and why and how Julie chose to fight while Tricia stayed silent. What about young Gordon Strachan's advice, not mentioned here, that the moral of the story for young people interested in a career in politics and government is to "stay away"?

Having said all of that, I am glad Mr. Archer has given us this readable guide to the players and actions in the Watergate drama. At a minimum, it should be useful to anyone, young or old, who wants a quick explanation of how a "third rate burglary" resulted in the fall from power of an "unindicted co-conspirator."

Victor S. Navasky, "Watergate," in The New York Times Book Review (© 1975 by The New York Times Company; reprinted by permission), August 3, 1975, p. 8.

DAVID A. LINDSEY

[*Watergate: America in Crisis* is a] chronological recapitulation—almost minute-by-minute—of the Watergate Affair from the break-in, through Richard Nixon's pardon to the signing of a major political campaign reform bill by President Ford. The present tense gives a sense of immediacy and urgency to the narrative, and the account is liberally laced with pertinent and cogent quotations. Informative background chapters summarize Nixon's character and political career and sketch in his closest henchman. The highlight of the book, however, is the final chapter where Archer concludes that Nixon's insatiable desire for power and sense of opportunism foreshadowed the happenings of Watergate, and that the affair itself dramatically unveiled to the nation how the system of checks and balances had been subverted. (p. 116)

David A. Lindsey, in School Library Journal (reprinted from the September, 1975 issue of School Library Journal, published by R. R. Bowker Co. A Xerox Corporation; copyright © 1975), September, 1975.

PATRICIA McCUE MARWELL

[*The Russians and the Americans*] study of 230 years of official and unofficial relations between the two countries is disjointed and boring. In content, simplistic statements occur too frequently, and stylistically Archer tries to be both analytical and anecdotal, changing gears abruptly and awkwardly. Vocabulary and concepts are beyond the ken of most junior high students, and older readers will do better with George Kennan's or John Gunther's adult works. (p. 50)

Patricia McCue Marwell, in School Library Journal (reprinted from the February, 1976 issue of School Library Journal, published by R. R. Bowker Co. A Xerox Corporation; copyright © 1976), February, 1976.

CYNTHIA T. SEYBOLT

[*The Chinese and the Americans*] is an extensive yet detailed history of U.S.-China relations from their beginnings to the present.... Using a great variety of sources, from official documents to onlookers' observations, Archer conveys the enormous complexity of events and attitudes and helps to dispel many stereotyped American views by emphasizing the Chinese perspective. The writing is clear, and the factual narrative is frequently interspersed with quotations, interesting incidents, and amusing anecdotes. Readers with no background might find some of the detail and digression confusing, and the vast amount of material presented has necessitated some oversimplification. On the whole, however, this is a sound and interesting presentation. (p. 66)

Cynthia T. Seybolt, in School Library Journal (reprinted from the May, 1976 issue of School Library Journal, published by R. R. Bowker Co. A Xerox Corporation; copyright © 1976), May, 1976.

Assuming that his readers know little or nothing of the Arab viewpoint, Archer proposes to plead their case [in *Legacy of the Desert: Understanding the Arabs*], beginning with the history of the Rise of Islam, the humiliation of Turkish takeover during the Ottoman Empire ..., and the "streak of emotionalism" and rich linguistic heritage which he sees as dominant strains of the Arab culture. Surprisingly, it is on the touchstone issues of Palestinian refugees and Israeli confiscation of Palestinian property that the defense is strongest: Archer argues largely through the naive statements of Zionists, such as David Ben Gurion's 1917 declaration that Palestine was "in a historical and moral sense ... a country without inhabitants." For readers who have little idea of, say, the influence of Nasser on Arab nationalism, or of social and political differences within the Arab bloc, Archer's outline should be required reading. And though Archer doesn't claim to present both sides of Arab-Israeli differences, his essay is one of the more objective and nonrhetorical introductions available.... (pp. 1146-47)

Kirkus Reviews (copyright © The Kirkus Service, Inc.), October 15, 1976.

From the first strange symptoms to the epidemiologists' investigations and countermeasures, Archer describes the course of a number of variously spectacular recent epidemics and potential outbreaks [in *Epidemic! The Story of the Disease Detectives*].... Collective heros are WHO, which has effectively wiped out smallpox worldwide, and, more centrally, Atlanta's Center for Disease Control; Archer ignores recent criticism of the CDC, and though he's as up-to-date as the identification of the Legionnaires' microbe he never mentions swine flu or the innoculation fiasco. In closing, environmental poison is mentioned as a major problem for the future, but the same final chapter cites the successful use of aerosol insecticide in airplanes without even an ironic aside. But, in lieu of issues, there is plenty of detection and arresting detail.... And, if Archer's choppier treatment is less involving than the closeup focus on individual cases perfected by Bertrand Roueche (whose adult books cover many of the same diseases), in itself this is a readable and unsensationalized roster. (p. 437)

> Kirkus Reviews *(copyright © 1977 The Kirkus Service, Inc.), April 15, 1977.*

DENISE M. WILMS

There's an overenthusiastic tone to this account of naturalist-explorer Roy Chapman Andrews [*From Whales to Dinosaurs: The Story of Roy Chapman Andrews*] that rings hollow after a while. The dynamic scientist takes on the dimensions of a heroic cardboard figure despite mention of his disregard for cultural values and, later, of the single-mindedness that led to the breakup of his marriage. Yet the nature of Chapman's full-steam-ahead personality and his remarkable museum work show how such a stylistic problem could occur. The outlines of his scientific expeditions into the Gobi Desert do point to his luck-blessed genius and make interesting reading in themselves; his adventures there carry the book more than anything else. (p. 1343)

> Denise M. Wilms, in Booklist *(reprinted by permission of the American Library Association; copyright 1977 by the American Library Association), May 1, 1977.*

Prefaced with a reminder of Nixon administration violations and a working definition of "police state," [*Police State: Could It Happen Here?*] is mainly a series of predigested, broad-stroke profiles of other totalitarian regimes—most of which have been the subject of previous Archer books. Thus historical highlights and selective impressions of Hitler's Germany, Soviet Russia, and modern China are followed by more rapid tours of "variations" on the left (Cuba, Yugoslavia, Eastern Europe) and right (Spain, Chile). By no means is all the material relevant to an examination of how a police state operates or comes into being, though Archer does point out in a simplistic way how

"you" as a citizen of each of these countries might have been taken in. He doesn't dig very far for cogent commentary, at times seeming content with just about any quotation that represents a balancing viewpoint.... Archer ends with a review of anti-libertarian measures in this country ..., concluding that "a police state could happen here. But not if enough informed Americans are aware of dictatorial threats and developments early enough and unite to prevent (them)." This has only sketchy application toward that end—though it's certainly a convenient shortcut for the impatient student. (p. 1105)

> Kirkus Reviews *(copyright © 1977 The Kirkus Service, Inc.), October 15, 1977.*

[*Superspies: The Secret Side of Government*] is chiefly a chronicle of agency abuses, from the CIA's secret tapping of King Farouk's urinal to the Cleveland police taps on their own mayor's phones. Young people previously unaware of such violations might well be shocked, which is all to the good, and there is much to be said for simply extending the exposure to a wider, younger audience. But those disinclined to believe the horror stories will find no citations to check and no clues as to how and when the facts came to light; and more disappointing is the absence of analysis that might make readers not only informed about past abuses but wise to their patterns and rationalizations. (Archer's complacent acceptance of Carter's promise to "strip away secrecy in government" is hardly the example we'd expect him to set.) Archer does muster a damning abundance of specific, dramatic examples—very handy for packing term papers, but only where one source is considered as good as the next and evaluation of evidence is not considered at all. Overall, more fuel for righteous outrage than food for thought. (p. 1105)

> Kirkus Reviews *(copyright © 1977 The Kirkus Service, Inc.), October 15, 1977.*

R. C. VICKERY

Beginning with an account of the recent legionnaires disease epidemic, Archer has produced an entertaining and informative story of world-wide epidemiological investigations [in his *Epidemic! The Story of the Disease Detectives*]. The subject is treated in a nonalarmist manner, informing the reader of possible health hazards to the community as well as some of the procedures used to investigate and correct them. Technical terms are either avoided entirely or clarified when necessary. The work of epidemiologists at the Center for Disease Control and at other such organizations received long overdue recognition. This book is recommended reading for any budding young student considering a career in epidemiology. (p. 212)

> R. C. Vickery, in Science Books & Films *(copyright 1978 by the American Association for the Advancement of Science), Vol. XIII, No. 4 (March, 1978).*

Ruth M(abel) Arthur
1905-

British novelist, poet, and short story writer. Arthur, who blends a romantic approach with contemporary topics and problems, is a leading writer of Gothic novels for young adults aimed at a predominately female audience. Born in Glasgow, Scotland, she began writing as a child and had her first short stories published when she was eighteen. Also during this period Arthur told stories for children on radio broadcasts. She was a kindergarten teacher before her marriage and wrote primarily for younger children until her own children became teenagers, when she started writing for the older reader. Most of her young adult novels follow a similar structural pattern: her protagonist, who is usually a teenage girl, comes to a greater sense of self-awareness and understanding through her handling of the difficulties thrust upon her. These difficulties usually revolve around relationships, especially family relationships. Setting plays an important role in Arthur's fiction. She generally chooses places she has lived as backgrounds but imbues them with mysteriousness through the introduction of supernatural events, travels in time, and local superstitions. Although Arthur on occasion has been criticized for formulaic plotting and an overwrought prose style, her novels are recognized as a creditable contribution to the popular genre of Gothic romance. (See also *Contemporary Authors*, Vols. 9-12, rev. ed., and *Something about the Author*, Vol. 7.)

[*Dragon Summer*] rings true to life—its moral tone is good and its simplicity and acceptance of life will endear it to many young girls. The fantasy is normalised and kept in proportion yet there are points here to stretch a girl's imagination and help her to overcome some of the common obstacles of life. (p. 124)

The Junior Bookshelf, *July, 1962.*

ETHEL L. HEINS

Told in the first person as a sensitive reminiscence, [*My Daughter, Nicola*] is the story of a girl in a mountain village of Switzerland early in the twentieth century. . . . Local legend, skillfully woven into an original plot, adds to the vivid sense of place in a story that is rich in wisdom and memorable characterizations. (p. 501)

Ethel L. Heins, in The Horn Book Magazine *(copyright © 1965 by The Horn Book, Inc., Boston), October, 1965.*

The candle lights up a flickering sense of evil [in *A Candle in Her Room*], an indefinable but distinct presence. As in *Dragon Summer* (1963) the author has managed to convey a sense of black magic although other elements of the story are not achieved with the same finesse. . . . The most compelling moments occur when the characters become aware of the malignant spread of evil. Judith is rarely more than objectified as an evil force and Melissa is disappointingly bland. Often the minor characters are lost in the story but many girls will be pleased with the gothic change of pace and will find it hard to shrug off the mood. (p. 111)

Virginia Kirkus' Service *(copyright © 1966 Virginia Kirkus' Service, Inc.), February 1, 1966.*

RUTH HILL VIGUERS

[*A Candle in Her Room*, an absorbing story], is laid in Wales in a beautiful old house by the sea where the lives of three generations of girls are changed by a strange antique doll, Dido. . . . That Dido can be responsible for what seems to be an evil spell on the house is not wholly convincing, but the quality of mystery pervading the story is real enough to create strong suspense. Dilys' mother, Judith, is like a beautiful, wicked character from a Daphne du Maurier novel, but the story has symbolism and more dimensions than the usual suspense tale; and though the mystery of Dido is never solved, her eventual destruction brings a sweep of fresh air through the haunted rooms. (pp. 195-96)

Ruth Hill Viguers, in The Horn Book Magazine *(copyright © 1966, by The Horn Book, Inc., Boston), April, 1966.*

JEAN FRITZ

The old wooden doll found by the three Mansell sisters living in turn-of-the-century England was obviously something that attracted evil [in "A Candle in her Room"]. . . . [Three] generations is a long time to cover in 200-odd pages. The reader just warms up to one heroine when, whoosh, he has to be whisked off to the next generation and a new heroine. Then whoosh again. This isn't magic, either; it's only a rather charming author in too much of a hurry. (p. 24)

Jean Fritz, in The New York Times Book Review *(© 1966 by The New York Times Company; reprinted by permission), August 7, 1966.*

Is *A Candle in her Room* a book about witchcraft or about the enduring power of love? A bit of both, perhaps, as well as a touching story of family conflict and affection. The raw material of this book belongs almost to women's magazine fiction, but the author has lifted her story on to an altogether higher plane. . . .

[The subtlety with which Ruth Arthur unfolds her remarkable story] takes hold of the reader with something of the uncanny power which Dido exercised over her victims; one does not readily put it out of mind. In a very quiet way, and with no stylistic tricks, Miss Arthur adapts her theme to its three narrators, but gives the whole a unity of mood. This is fundamentally a very sad story, but it is relieved by much tenderness and understanding. Girls suffering the bewildering growing pains of adolescence, for whom so few good books exist, may find here some of the answers to their problems and a strength with which they can identify themselves.

A Candle in her Room is a book which is much bigger than its parts. . . . (p. 1070)

> The Times Literary Supplement (© *Times Newspapers Ltd. (London) 1966; reproduced from* The Times Literary Supplement *by permission), November 24, 1966.*

LAVINIA RUSS

If we dare to hope that in the present torrent of curriculum-oriented, multi-cultured, *molto*-boring books, we can find the golden books that John Rowe Townsend promises will make today "the second golden age," surely Ruth Arthur's name will be on one of them. As anyone knows who remembers her "Candle in Her Room," she is a seasoned traveler in both the real and the dream world. *She* remembers that when you are young, you can cross their borders with imagination as your passport. In ["Requiem for a Princess"] . . . , there is the same haunting quality that made [Daphne du Maurier's] "Rebecca" a memorable novel. (p. 61)

> *Lavinia Russ, in* Publishers Weekly *(reprinted from the March 20, 1967, issue of* Publishers Weekly *by permission of the critic, published by R. R. Bowker Company, a Xerox company; copyright © 1967 by Xerox Corporation), March 20, 1967.*

VIRGINIA HAVILAND

Willow Forrester, who hopes someday to become a concert pianist . . . , suffers a "nervous breakdown" when she learns she has been adopted; and she has to be absent from boarding school for a term. In the quiet atmosphere and beauty of a Cornish guesthouse by the sea, Willow shakes off her depression. . . . [*Requiem for a Princess*] is remarkable not only for its vivid expression but also for its unusual structure—the paralleling of Willow's situation with that of another orphan through Willow's dreams of a sixteenth-century girl. . . . (p. 211)

> *Virginia Haviland, in* The Horn Book Magazine *(copyright © 1967, by The Horn Book, Inc., Boston), April, 1967.*

Requiem for a Princess is a much less subtle performance than [Ruth Arthur's] earlier book of youth and hauntings [*A Candle in Her Room*]. . . . [Willow, the narrator,] is a schoolgirl with unusual gifts as a pianist. Though happy enough with her parents, she is appalled to learn, from a tactless friend, that she is their *adopted* daughter. . . . Ill and dispirited, she goes with her mother to Cornwall, where they stay at a private hotel, once an Elizabethan manor, home of the Tresilian family. . . .

[Something] does catch Willow's interest—a portrait of a young girl in Elizabethan clothes "with huge dark eyes and elaborate hair style" [who turns out to be an ancestor of the family, also an adopted daughter.] . . .

Obsessed by the Spanish girl, Willow has a series of dreams which take her through Isabel's story; she emerges with thoughts of her own, of reconciliation, gratitude, and the wish to give, not take. A good enough conclusion but far too heavily achieved. Isabel, who takes so much of the tale with her Spanish ambience, is a pasteboard figure throughout. Her problems are those of circumstance, not of personality, and Willow's lose their edge along with hers. (p. 1141)

> The Times Literary Supplement (© *Times Newspapers Ltd. (London) 1967; reproduced from* The Times Literary Supplement *by permission), November 30, 1967.*

[*Requiem for a Princess*] is less impressive than *A Candle in Her Room*, but a deft weaving together of interesting strands; recommended to both pre- and present du Maurier fans. (p. 384)

> The Junior Bookshelf, *December, 1967.*

To her usual preoccupation with evil incarnate, preceded by uneasiness and omens, Miss Arthur adds a shadow of miscegenation and anxiety over an autistic child, and it would be easy to dismiss [*Portrait of Margarita*] as pretentious melodrama if Margarita weren't the quintessentially empathetic mousey adolescent growing into glowing womanhood; if guardian Cousin Francis weren't the archetypical rich British bachelor, handsome and accomplished; if the settings, a mellow Oxfordshire mill and a dramatic Italian lakeside villa, weren't so cinematically alluring. None of this cancels out the phoniness of Francis' old nurse Miss Laura's malevolent threat to Margarita and to his sister before (jealousy, jealousy), nor the objectionable and untimely nature of Margarita's color-consciousness. . . . You *suspect*—it's all very hush-hush—but you don't *know* until the next-to-last page that Margarita's grandmother was black. . . . The trouble with this sort of thing is that it's insidious and girls will wallow in it, maybe even swallow it. (p. 121)

> Kirkus Service *(copyright © 1968 Virginia Kirkus' Service, Inc.), February 1, 1968.*

A strong element of mystery akin to horror underlines the plot [in *Portrait of Margarita*], when a former governess to Margarita's guardian issues sinister threats to her, and finally attempts to have her drowned. The whole story moves swiftly, and makes very compelling reading. . . . Teen-age girls will like this story very much, and if it has some of the ingredients of escapist literature, then the author's skill creates a haunting story from them. (pp. 232-33)

> The Junior Bookshelf, *August, 1968.*

MARGERY FISHER

The characters in *The whistling boy* are absorbed in the

past for one reason or another, often to the exclusion of the present. In an East Anglian setting, we follow the parallel journeys of a boy and a girl—his into a past which has confused him, hers towards a better understanding of her young stepmother. The idea of possession of one person's mind by the projection of another—doll, person, idea—has persisted through many of Ruth Arthur's books and each time she deepens the feeling of mystery by her close attention to the temperament and the perplexities of young people in the present. In this story, also, her skill in bringing a particular landscape before our eyes and making it important in the story is particularly to be admired.... The author's gift for suggesting personality through description and talk is seen especially in the way she brings working-class Sammie to life; this boy of trenchant speech and determination lends colour to a crowded but somehow, light-weight story. (pp. 1397-98)

> *Margery Fisher, in her* Growing Point, *October, 1969.*

The Whistling Boy offers a dream-like first person narration by a brooding, self-centred adolescent girl passing through a ''difficult'' phase. The sea-washed setting, too, is intentionally part of the drama; and again, as in earlier books, the girl's restlessness catches something super-natural in the air, a link, perhaps with the place's bygone history. To make such a narrator likeable—to avoid the commonplaces and even vulgarities of the private thoughts of a heroine of this kind—is far from easy, as earlier books have shown, but in the present novel one senses a caution about these pitfalls. (p. 1199)

> The Times Literary Supplement (© *Times Newspapers Ltd. (London) 1969; reproduced from* The Times Literary Supplement *by permission), October 16, 1969.*

[*The Saracen Lamp* is decidedly] queer like its predecessors, though not quite as sinister, perhaps; and hauntedly reminiscent of one in particular—the *Requiem for a Princess* (1967).... Something's awry with three grotesquely pathological heroines—not to mention, materially, how much the long-suffering plot is wounded by the leaps and bounds. (p. 248)

> Kirkus Reviews (copyright © *1970 The Kirkus Service, Inc.), March 1, 1970.*

Ruth Arthur usually speaks through an adolescent girl, and the girl (if sympathetic) is always the same: full of sensibility and idealism, often handicapped, but brave withal. If the girl is unsympathetic, she tends to become monstrously melodramatic, like Alys in this story, *The Saracen Lamp.* Romantic magazine fiction geared to the young girl, it is compounded of the author's richest, sweetest ingredients: the enchanting old house exerting its spell, the ancient feature uncovered in the garden, the ''talisman'' ... which brings blessing, the ''possession'' of a healthy person by a malicious ghost. Three girls of the family tell their tales, in 1300, in the sixteenth century, and now. The first, Mélisande's, is the most appealing: her wedding procession is like a picture in a French Book of Hours. Romantic girls, from Catherine Morland to the present ones, adore family seats and secrets, ghosts and talismans, and will doubtless revel in this story. Life, soon enough, can be trusted forcibly to inject some realism. (p. 711)

> The Times Literary Supplement (© *Times Newspapers Ltd. (London) 1970; reproduced from* The Times Literary Supplement *by permission), July 2, 1970.*

ELINOR S. CULLEN

[Ruth Arthur] is adept at giving vitality to characters and incidents of the past. Unfortunately, there is a surfeit of plot and people in [*The Saracen Lamp*], and no one character becomes absorbing. The multi-character/century technique has been used before by this author and more successfully; in *A Candle in Her Room* ..., the evil influence of the doll held the story together and maintained reader attention much more effectively than the amorphous device of the Saracen Lamp does here. (p. 136)

> *Elinor S. Cullen, in* School Library Journal *(reprinted from the October, 1970 issue of* School Library Journal, *published by R. R. Bowker Co. A Xerox Corporation; copyright © 1970), October, 1970.*

NINA DANISCHEWSKY

Ruth Arthur's books have a soothing air of unreality about them; they deal with familiar, entirely human emotions and behaviour, but always from a safe distance.... [In] *The Little Dark Thorn* the heroine's problems have already been resolved before the reader hears of them, for Merrie tells her own story, from the tranquil vantage point of someone who has begun to rationalise her feelings and to see her past behaviour in perspective.... There are homely details of everyday life that recreate different backgrounds of very distinctive identities, the story Merrie tells is an interesting one. Like all Ruth Arthur's books its appeal is specifically feminine. It is a well-written, quiet, 'comfortable' book over which the soft-hearted may shed a tear or two without being greatly moved. (p. 193)

> *Nina Danischewsky, in* Children's Book Review *(© 1971 by Five Owls Press Ltd.; all rights reserved), December, 1971.*

MARGERY FISHER

It is the really personal note that I miss in *The little dark thorn.* Merrie is taken from her Malayan mother when she is six and is brought up by a great-aunt; some years later she has to adjust again, to her father's young Norwegian wife, and to bear some of the responsibility for the tragic death of her young stepsister. The story covers the whole childhood and much of the adolescence of the heroine, who tells her own story. Her narrative is sober and monotonous and does not really give an individual impression; Merrie's feelings are not realised strongly enough to sustain so long a life-span or such a succession of difficult adjustments. (p. 1864)

> *Margery Fisher, in her* Growing Point, *January, 1972.*

[*The Little Dark Thorn*] is quite an unusual story and is concerned very largely with personal relationships. The central figure in it is Merrie, daughter of a British father and a Malayan mother.... It is told in the first person and such an adult mental approach is given to the child's thoughts, reactions and attitudes in the first year or two that much of the part ''Aunt Emma's house'' suffers as a result.... The story otherwise moves well, maintains the interest and many episodes are related with realism. (p. 103)

The Junior Bookshelf, April, 1972.

JUDITH ALDRIDGE

Ruth Arthur is reputed to have written well in previous books of teenage emotions, intrigue and the supernatural. [*The Autumn People*] fails to convince in any of these areas. . . .

Throughout the story emotional attachments are portrayed at the level of a girls' magazine, characters are static and Rodger's occult powers in particular very stagey. The writer fails to convey any sense of period or to make the autumn people credible. After a quite promising opening the book tails away sadly. (p. 80)

> Judith Aldridge, in Children's Book Review (© 1973 Five Owls Press Ltd.; all rights reserved), June, 1973.

Ruth Arthur is an adept at creating an eerie atmosphere and in building her stories for older girls round a mystery of the past. [*The Autumn People*] suffers, for when the reader reaches the third part he already knows what has happened in the past, and Romilly's discoveries are an anti-climax. Romilly's contact with the "Autumn people" lacks atmosphere and a feeling of the supernatural. The ending of the story seems unnecessarily fortuitous. (p. 324)

The Junior Bookshelf, October, 1973.

JEAN F. MERCIER

Even for young readers, [*After Candlemas*] will lack interest. Though suspense and romance are hinted at and the essentials of entertainment are here, they are never developed past simplicity. (p. 56)

> Jean F. Mercier, in Publishers Weekly (reprinted from the March 25, 1974, issue of Publishers Weekly by permission of the critic, published by R. R. Bowker Company, a Xerox company; copyright © 1974 by Xerox Corporation), March 25, 1974.

Harriet [the main character in *After Candlemas*] holds the story firmly together; her personality emerges mainly from her contacts with Gramma Cobbley, the old lady who eases her into village life and its secrets, and Birney, the runaway. Harriet finds some excitement in her unconventional behaviour: helping to hide and protect a young criminal has its frightening moments but caring has its compensations. All ends happily, of course . . . but without any irritating twists of fortune or probability.

Punctuation, especially of conversation, seems to have gone awry. (p. 161)

The Junior Bookshelf, June, 1974.

GABRIELLE MAUNDER

[*After Candlemas* is a] book whose style and language entirely diminish the basic intent of the plot which concerns the black arts, an essence of re-incarnation and a flavour of the Old Religion in bleakest Dorset. Such ominous themes should command a style which reinforces the atmospheric tension so the chatty, negative approach of the girl narrator seems quite inadequate. There is a distinct flavour of the

schoolgirl's annual and one constantly finds the characters not *saying* things but 'laughing' or 'grumbling' them, a common characteristic of thirdformers in the dorm. The book is a suitable soporific for the undemanding. (p. 61)

> Gabrielle Maunder, in Children's Book Review (© 1974 Five Owls Press Ltd.; all rights reserved), Summer, 1974.

Betony tells her story [in *On the Wasteland*] with a languid sophistication that seems inappropriate to a thirteen-year-old nicknamed "Gipsy" by her more conformist fellow orphans. And the lassitude carries over into the plot which alternates between Betony's first tenuous friendships . . . and her wanderings out on the salt marsh where she sights a Viking ship and, now and then, finds herself transformed into Estrith, sister of Thorkell and betrothed to a Saxon prince. The mixture seems half-hearted rather than dreamlike, and considering the number of heroines who have similar experiences nowadays there isn't much reason for anyone to get overexcited. . . . [This] is pleasantly literate. Still, the props—a moor, a handful of picturesque types, a soupcon of time travel—have never been more gratuitous. (p. 710)

> Kirkus Reviews (copyright © 1975 The Kirkus Service, Inc.), July 1, 1975.

CECILIA GORDON

[Ruth M. Arthur writes with] insight; but *On the Wasteland* reads like two separate stories uneasily linked. . . . Betony's "real" life is a convincing narrative of her growing understanding and developing relationships. The frequent shifts into her fantasy life are doubtless meant to illuminate this main theme, but instead they so interrupt its flow that their cumulative effect is to disrupt the story. (p. 1455)

> Cecilia Gordon, in The Times Literary Supplement (© Times Newspapers Ltd. (London) 1975; reproduced from The Times Literary Supplement by permission), December 5, 1975.

GORDON PARSONS

There is a delicate lyricism about [*On the Wasteland*]. Betony's first-person narrative is one of moving self-discovery, as she seeks survival in her orphaned, children's home existence, by clinging desperately to a sense of place. . . .

Ruth Arthur's novel modulates between the fantasy and the reality of the maturing girl's experience with consummate ease. We know, for all its dream-like seductiveness, the former can offer only temporary solace, while involvement in the lives of those, themselves in need of affection and understanding, who surround Betony in real life points the way through.

[It is a] superb piece of low-keyed but effectively engaging writing. (p. 140)

> Gordon Parsons, in School Library Journal (reprinted from the June, 1976 issue of School Library Journal, published by R. R. Bowker Co. A Xerox Corporation; copyright © 1976), June, 1976.

The characters [in *An Old Magic*] are no more than quick studies, and this sort of mild romance-laced story is as old as the hills—or the moors in this case. But Arthur is on intimate terms with the terrain and this is made to order for the future fans of R. F. Delderfield. (p. 1102)

Kirkus Reviews (copyright © 1977 The Kirkus Service, Inc.), October 15, 1977.

The old magic indeed, as only Ruth Arthur can distil it. Few writers have a stronger sense of *lacrimae rerum,* or a finer gift for conveying the brooding menace of places. . . .

As usual any attempt to summarize briefly a Ruth Arthur novel runs into serious trouble. Suffice it to say that, in the context, [*An Old Magic*] is a strongly logical story into the main stream of which each episode flows most satisfactorily. There is tragedy, tenderness, an aching love of life and of the land, everything, in fact, but humour. It is tempting to categorize it as a novel for teenage girls, but that is far too limiting. What Miss Arthur does supremely well is show the interrelationship and the interdependence of the generations. It is a story for all ages and for all those readers who desire total involvement with the characters and who can give generously of their sympathy and love. (p. 147)

The Junior Bookshelf, June, 1978.

JOYCE BANKS

To say that [*An Old Magic*] is a typical Ruth Arthur story, is to predicate wholesome characters of the present day who have contact with a world outside of present time and space. Here, the mysterious element is provided by gypsies on a mountain overlooking a Welsh farmhouse and their influence on the farm family through four generations. The strangeness of being a twin is another theme explored. Just occasionally the characters seem to be symbols rather than real people and one or two incidents seem slightly contrived, but such is the author's gift of storytelling that it is impossible not to read on. (p. 256)

Joyce Banks, in The School Librarian, *September, 1978.*

MARCUS CROUCH

Ruth Arthur, in . . . *An Old Magic,* returns to one of her persistent themes, the genius of place. Places—mountains, pools, houses, rocks—are not passive recipients of experience; they absorb, store up and give out the experiences gained in and around them. (p. 239)

Miss Arthur is not in the strict sense a regional writer. She ranges wide for her settings between Italy and the Scottish Isles—and even, indirectly, Malaya—and she writes always from personal knowledge. She seems to return most fondly to West Wales . . . , East Anglia and Cumberland. . . . Only one has a completely foreign setting and that the least characteristic of all her work—*My Daughter Nicola.* Her treatment of settings is a model for aspiring writers in this field. Direct description is rare. She builds up a picture in the reader's mind by a host of small touches incorporated in the narrative. This, I fancy, is not just because of the remembered tedium of Sir Walter Scott or because she is consciously gearing her style to the needs and the capabilities of young readers, but because this is her own method, a very personal technique developed by trial and error. The rare set pieces of description, when they come, are the more impressive. Witness, for example, the magnificent vision of an undermountain hall of quartz in *My Daughter Nicola* and half a page distilling the essence of a Cumbrian

winter in *The Little Dark Thorn:* "the stillness brought by the snow, the hooting of an owl in the darkness or the light bark of a fox took on a new sound, a quality of magic".

"Magic" is a recurring word, not as an easy refuge from reality but as the key to a deeper reality.

The first of Miss Arthur's stories of girls growing up contains many of the elements which have become part of her professional equipment. *Dragon Summer* . . . appeared in 1962. (pp. 239-40)

[Contained in *Dragon Summer*], in embryo or fully developed, are many of the Arthur characteristics. The heroine, as always, is the narrator. A leading character—not in this case the heroine—has difficult family circumstances. There is a benevolent retainer. The house and its surroundings play an active part in the action. The house is haunted, not by a spirit from the remote past but by an owner only recently dead.

These are features which recur again and again. Miss Arthur could be accused, by those who look only on the surface, of making plots by formula. Willow in *Requiem for a Princess,* who is troubled by the discovery that she is adopted, is not unlike Kirsty in *The Whistling Boy,* who cannot get on with her stepmother. Both girls solve their problems by going to stay with strangers and becoming involved in mysteries from the past. Willow [in *Requiem for a Princess*] and Betony in *On the Wasteland* both discover the past in dreams. The special communion of spirit between twins is a theme in *Portrait of Margarita, The Whistling Boy* and *An Old Magic.* Perdita in *The Saracen Lamp,* like Willow, becomes obsessed with someone from the past, almost to the exclusion of the present.

It is not the similarity of material that matters but the variety of treatment. The formula writer uses the same sequence of events, the same set of types, merely changing the names and the superficial features from story to story. Each of Miss Arthur's novels is an individual work, presenting and solving its own problems.

A more serious criticism might be made on stylistic grounds. At one stage in her writing, not, curiously enough, the first, Miss Arthur seemed prodigal to the point of self-indulgence in the use of adjectives and adverbs. Every noun, however unimportant, became associated, qualified and adorned by its accompanying epithet, so that the prose became—what it must never be—predictable. Well, Homer had the same weakness and so had most of the world's great writers. Miss Arthur has purged herself of the habit now. It is strongly in evidence in some of the middle novels, and one accepts it, readily enough, as part of the small price to pay for the enjoyment of some superb story-telling and much acute observation.

The books do not fall easily into the categories devised by tidy-minded adults for the classification of children's fiction. Although more often than not the characters are on holiday, the books are not holiday novels as written by Arthur Ransome. They are not even stories about children. Adults play very important parts in them, and in some—I would say the best—the narrative spans several generations. No, they are not school stories or holiday stories or historical stories, although the interpretation of the past is an important theme in several; they are novels, studies of the interaction of human beings and of the reaction of people to their environment and their times.

If one must classify, these are novels for adolescent girls. (How is it that they have such a strong and personal message for me, an aged male?) Miss Arthur knows well, through her own training and experience as a teacher and a parent, what problems trouble a child. In three books she looks at the effects upon children of a parent's remarriage. Stepmothers are a byword in traditional children's stories. (pp. 240-41)

So too Miss Arthur deals, quietly and with complete integrity, with the problem of the adopted child—in *Requiem for a Princess,* of the orphan—in *On the Wasteland,* and of the coloured child—in *Portrait of Margarita.* She wins the respect of her readers by finding no easy solutions. On the young the burden of growing up weighs heavily and it is the writer's role to share the load, not to pretend that it is not there. A quiet unobtrusive wisdom illuminates all she says.

Miss Arthur owes this uncompromising honesty, and a toughness of spirit, to her Scottish origins and ancestry. It is the Celt in her, I suppose, which is responsible for a persistent concern with the supernatural. Only one of her books—*My Daughter Nicola*—is completely without a ghost, witch or some other supranormal feature. In itself this is not unusual. Plenty of writers are obsessed with the inexplicable. Miss Arthur's ghosts however are highly individual. . . . In *An Old Magic* a living gypsy's music plays on in the house where she had been happy and unhappy, sending a message to the child who is to carry on her genius.

The message of the tales is always one of continuity. "I had always known that patterns had to be complete", as Romilly says in the moving conclusion of *The Autumn People,* a story in which past and present are but different sides of the same coin. Romilly steps easily into the century of her own great-grandmother and indeed becomes her in the company of the Autumn People. She, like other heroines in these stories, derives her strength from "roots in the past, a recurring pattern of family life".

All Miss Arthur's wisdom and understanding would stand for naught were she not also an incomparable story-teller. She knows exactly how to squeeze the heart with suspense and to permit the relief of tears. These are not tales for escape. They are tales for involvement. Unless the reader is at one with the heroine the message is lost. But one readily surrenders to these narrators, so varied, so tough, so vulnerable. Readers will have their favourites . . . but they have one characteristic in common; they are all portraits from the life, not types taken from stock.

The first book to show Miss Arthur's powers in full maturity was *A Candle in Her Room,* her third; and it still seems to me to be in many important ways her best. Its compass is wide, covering three generations, and the construction is tight. (pp. 241-42)

This story, told by narrators of the three generations, is marvellously sustained, deeply moving, uncompromisingly true to itself. The blending of story and setting, the conflict of characters, are masterly. For me one of the dozen books of the last two decades which stands above criticism.

It is hard for a writer who peaks too soon. Succeeding books were not of this quality. They were however of their kind extremely good. . . . Then in 1977 Miss Arthur did it again, producing in *An Old Magic* the same kind of triumph she had achieved eleven years earlier in *A Candle in Her Room*. . . . Again the story is beautifully tailored, filled with absorbing and relevant detail, and action, character and setting are dovetailed in masterly fashion. (p. 243)

The theme of all the books is, in essence, self-discovery. These heroines, finding their way through the bewildering complexities of adolescence, are, each in her way, learning to distinguish between fancy and reality. At first "unsure of reality" like Harriet in *After Candlemass,* they in time learn to turn their attention "to real people and the worthwhile things in my *real* life". As Betony says, percipiently: "I think it was then that I really began to grow up". (pp. 243-44)

Marcus Crouch, "The Painful Art of Growing Up: The Novels of Ruth M. Arthur," in The Junior Bookshelf, *October, 1978, pp. 239-44.*

Margot Benary-Isbert

1889-1979

German-born American novelist, short story writer, and poet. Benary-Isbert was most noted for her humane presentation of the postwar German experience. She began writing at an early age, publishing her first story when she was nineteen. The Nazi regime put an end to her publications from 1933-45 because she would not join the Nazi writers' organization. The U.S. Army liberated her section of Germany in 1945, only to hand it over to the Russians ten weeks later. Not wanting to live under another totalitarian government, Benary-Isbert and her family fled to West Germany. Life during World War II and the postwar German experience are the primary concerns of her novels. Her portraits of the German people are life-like, presenting the mixture of good and evil that exists in most people. Her books deal with vital problems of the twentieth century, such as government-sanctioned hatred and violence. But she also depicts the eternal qualities of life that survive under even the harshest of conditions, such as a young girl's first love and the warmth of family life. She does not peddle a ready-made morality about the German experience. Her readers are allowed to draw their own conclusions. As she says about the young reader, "He does not like to feel that the author wants to hand him out a moral, to educate him. He wants nothing more or less than a good story. . . . But don't we all remember our own childhood and what we felt when we had been given one of those books about wonderfully good children, living patterns of virtue, diligence and good behaviour, books which we detested because they bored us to death! We smelled the moral —and turned away." Benary-Isbert wrote in German but collaborated closely with her English translators. She has been widely praised for bringing the German experience of this century to young people of other cultures. (See also *Contemporary Authors*, Vols. 5-8, rev. ed., and *Something about the Author*, Vol. 2.)

[*The Ark* is a] heart felt story of a post-war German refugee family of five, but one that falls short of significance by way of sentimentality and an appeal to a too-sunny attitude towards life. From Pomerania, the Lechows . . . come to the town of Hesse in West Germany and are allotted two rooms in the house of Mrs. Verduz. With spirit—and it is here that there are the overdoses of gaiety—they settle down and find the friends who will keep them company. . . . Superficial treatment of more vital elements in pinioned country however, makes the book a disappointment. (p. 41)

Virginia Kirkus' Bookshop Service, *January 15, 1953.*

MARJORIE FISCHER

In ["The Ark,"] one of the first books for young people to come out of post-war Germany, we meet the Lechow family, refugees from the East Zone. . . .

The setting is unusual and interesting. But the best part of the book deals with the birth, death and care of the animals on the farm, described with knowledge and affection. The story is handled rather amateurishly, with too many characters seen from too many points of view, so that the reader is sometimes confused, and the effect is scattered. Moreover there is constant self-pity and a feeling of a world too small and isolated. Apparently all these people have been living in a political vacuum, where no one of them has ever felt sympathy for the Nazis (who are never mentioned); there is something—to this adult reader, at least—disingenuous about the picture.

Marjorie Fischer, "The Refugees," in The New York Times Book Review *(© 1953 by The New York Times Company; reprinted by permission), March 1, 1953, p. 32.*

ANNE CARROLL MOORE

Mrs. Benary-Isbert is a born storyteller who [in *The Ark*] has been able to create living characters in the midst of the aftermath of war in a defeated country. Whether drawn from life or from the imagination of the author, every one of them takes a natural place in the story. While it is a true picture of life and death among a homeless people, it is lighted by a courage and a warm human sympathy and understanding that leave a glow in the heart of the reader. (p. 102)

Anne Carroll Moore, in The Horn Book Magazine *(copyrighted, 1953, by The Horn Book, Inc., Boston), April, 1953.*

VIRGINIA HAVILAND

[*The Ark,* a] rare and perceptive book, reflecting something of the author's own experience, contains much of importance to reach the hearts and minds of young Americans. With an acute awareness of the effect of war on children and adolescents; with a consciousness of homely details that interest them; and with a wonderful depth of feeling for country things, she pictures a year's experiences of a close-knit German refugee family whose father, a doctor, is missing in Russia. Following bravely optimistic Mummy Lechow and her four children to assigned rooms in a German town and later to the Ark (a railroad car converted into a more cheerful home on a farm) is like accompanying real people. Lonely Margret, with her intimate attachment to the animals and her rapt learning of animal husbandry when at fourteen she becomes a kennel maid, will especially appeal to young readers. Although happiness comes to this family with the father's final return, there is no minimizing of their sufferings and sacrifices. (p. 124)

> *Virginia Haviland, in* The Horn Book Magazine *(copyrighted, 1953, by The Horn Book, Inc., Boston), April, 1953.*

LAVINIA R. DAVIS

["The Shooting Star" tells of when Annagret and her mother were getting over pneumonia and] were sent from their German home to the mountain village of Arosa in Switzerland for three months convalescence.... [Annagret's discovery of Alpine pleasures and] her new friendships constitute a deceptively simple story with ... warmth and unself-conscious goodness.... The effect upon Annagret of the beautiful mountain country is conveyed with rare skill.

> *Lavinia R. Davis, "The Happy Exile," in* The New York Times Book Review *(© 1954 by The New York Times Company; reprinted by permission), February 28, 1954, p. 24.*

FRANCIS LANDER SPAIN

"Rowan Farm" carries on the story of the Lechow family begun by Mrs. Benary-Isbert last year in "The Ark." The latter volume, it will be recalled, transmitted a sense of excitement and tension in its account of a family experiencing displacement and rehabilitation. This is lacking in "Rowan Farm"; but the new book does portray the maturing of the children, the satisfactions of accomplishment, and the feeling of security that comes from problems faced and at least partially solved. (p. 35)

> *Francis Lander Spain, in* The Saturday Review *(Entire issue copyright 1954 by Saturday Review Associates, Inc.; reprinted with permission), August 21, 1954.*

LOUISE S. BECHTEL

[The Margret of "Rowan Farm"] is a teen-age girl in postwar Germany. She is working hard on a farm, ... and involved in various hopes and dreams of rebuilding her part of her war-torn country. She also is experiencing the difficulties of first love and making decisions that will shape her adult life. Her story, however, is the basic thread of a family story that gives many aspects of reconstruction in Germany. It includes interesting adults who have felt the war in different ways. It pierces the problems of war guilt as a teen-ager would feel it. So the book is truly a junior "novel," giving us a rich, full slice of life and the emotions and development of an admirable girl, whose inner life will be recognized as true by girls in any country....

The young twin brothers bravely solving a black market mystery, the stuffy mayor, and the red tape of German bureaucracy, provide incidents showing traditional unlovable sides of the German character.

It is a leisurely book, which through its length builds up a deep impression of the hard work of the farm, the beauty of country life, the variety of family problems and the different thinking of varied young people, from serious Margret to the siren from Frankfurt.... [A sequel to "The Ark," there] are sufficient throwbacks so that it could be read without reading "The Ark" first. Reading both will be a rewarding experience for any girl over twelve; more than any other postwar books for this age, they strike to the heart of problems of our time. Their final effect is one of hope and of beauty, for this writer is deeply imbued with the cycles of nature. (p. 7)

> *Louise S. Bechtel, in* New York Herald Tribune Book Review *(© I.H.T. Corporation; reprinted by permission), August 22, 1954.*

ELLEN LEWIS BUELL

[Margret's] experience as kennel-maid with the farm animals, the temptation to take a job in America, her inevitable romance with the landowner's son give continuity to ["Rowan Farm,"] a many-faceted, rather complicated narrative of family activities.

Like "The Ark" this is an uneven performance. It is frequently sentimental and even a little banal, yet it has little of the Teutonic self-pity which seeped through the earlier book. Its horizons are wider and there are times when the author makes the reader sharply aware of the emotional as well as the physical devastation which follows war. (p. 38)

> *Ellen Lewis Buell, in* The New York Times Book Review *© 1954 by The New York Times Company; reprinted by permission), October 10, 1954.*

How many readers of *Little Women* remember that it was set in a grim post-war period? The poverty of the March family is ... evident, but it is the richness of character, incident, and above all, of spirit, which makes their story memorable. The same kind of feeling is left by [*The Ark,* a] German story of a refugee family whose happy life in Pomerania has been overlaid by successive war and post-war calamities, who begin the book making a brave new start in two attic rooms in a bomb-scarred town, and close it, with even higher hopes for the future, in a converted railway carriage on someone else's farm.

Mrs. Lechow, like Mrs. March, is a woman of parts, and her four children are lively and intelligent, eager to learn, and able to make a great deal out of next to nothing. Fourteen-year-old Margret is the central figure, but the others are made equally real, and their problems and friends provide a surprisingly comprehensive picture of post-war German life.... [Throughout the book Margot Benary-Isbert] communicates her pleasure in family life and in the strength and promise of young people, developing and maturing. The people are made vivid, almost visible.... There are several very moving Christmas chapters, and as an added delight, rather than a climax, the safe return of first Mrs. Almut's son and then Dr. Lechow from Russian camps, a return made probable simply because it hasn't been made a necessary pivot of the story. These people can stand on their own feet whatever happens, or wherever they might live—even the hint of coming romance between young Almut and Margret could be ignored by such well-established characters. Altogether, then, a book to grow on, with much wisdom and compassion to offer re-readers in particular. (p. 295)

The Junior Bookshelf, *December, 1954.*

In a different vein from *The Ark* and *Rowan Farm* which were two stories of postwar German refugees, [*The Wicked Enchantment*] takes life under more "normal" conditions in the enchanting little town of Vogelsang. . . . Real story telling, this has clever satire and the ringing clarity of German forest land. (p. 538)

Virginia Kirkus' Service, *August 1, 1955.*

As is the way of sequels, [*Rowan Farm*] is less perfect than its predecessor, *The Ark,* being more loosely constructed, more concerned with the immediate present, and probably attempting too much. It still has much to recommend it and the Lechows' projects and personalities are still worth recording. The story contains much that will please those in search of light entertainment and also contrives to deal with personal and public matters of interest to thoughtful adolescents—and it is the air of contrivance which keeps the book below the level established by *The Ark.* However, there are many good scenes and real, vigorous people. . . . Mrs. Benary respects her readers' right to the truth; she is not afraid to mention death and the existence of difficult problems, and by neither over-emphasizing nor under-stating, gives a balanced picture of post-war German life. . . . [The reforming zeal of her young characters] is necessary if the more permanent values of sympathy, hope and faith are to be kept alive, and Mrs. Benary is very much on the side of life. Her positive approach, her sanity and understanding, keep this book from floundering in the multiplicity of incident. (pp. 218-19)

The Junior Bookshelf, *October, 1955.*

LOUISE S. BECHTEL

[In *The Wicked Enchantment,* Mrs. Benary-Isbert] offers a modern fairy-tale full of suspense, fun, excitement, answering children's love of animals, the circus and magic. She uses an Old World setting and plays with an old German legend, weaving in her memories of old arts of Europe; the book is both gay and serious, ending in the cathedral on Easter Eve, where, listening to the ancient bells, we know that love and courage can overcome superstition and tyranny. . . .

With all its wealth of detail the story is clearly told and its very real human relations balance its magic. The pages glow with . . . colorful imagery. . . . It is a rare book to stimulate the wits of bright children besides stirring their hearts. (p. 7)

Louise S. Bechtel, in New York Herald Tribune Book Review *(© I.H.T. Corporation; reprinted by permission), October 2, 1955.*

MARY LOUISE HECTOR

Leni Winkelberg is 16 in 1948, a lean year in post-war Germany [as depicted in "Castle on the Border"]. Determined upon theatrical stardom, Leni arranges her life with calculation and detachment, habits wherewith she had survived as an orphaned refugee from bombed Berlin. . . . Slowly she develops into a young woman of maturity, able finally to talk about her parents; to participate in Advent and Christmas traditions for their meaning, beyond the sorrow of memory; to attend her gentle uncle at the hour of his death.

Leni's finely drawn problem works itself out amid events that move constantly, and among people widely representative of the courageous national effort to rebuild a life and a land. "Castle on the Border" is a splendid book for teenage readers of advanced ability. (p. 34)

Mary Louise Hector, "Rebuilding a Life," in The New York Times Book Review *(© 1956 by The New York Times Company; reprinted by permission), May 6, 1956, p. 34.*

JENNIE D. LINDQUIST

[*Castle on the Border*] is an unusually rich book for young people, for the author gets so much of life into it. There are Leni and her brother and their friends determined to conquer all obstacles in order to make the Castle Theater Company a success. There are Aunt Friderike and Uncle Hubertus and their courage in beginning life again after escaping from the East Zone, he working on his scientific study of spiders, she making a home of the castle and trying to bring beauty back to its gardens. There are children and animals to lighten the story; and to give it added depth there are the refugees coming over the border and hiding away a night or two in the castle. And there is the effect all this has on Leni and her growth not only as an actress but, more important, as a person. It is a serious book but it has gaiety in it, too; I think it will live a long time. (p. 273)

Jennie D. Lindquist, in The Horn Book Magazine *(copyrighted, 1956, by The Horn Book Inc., Boston), August, 1956.*

NORMA RATHBURN

There is much to recommend this superior teen-age novel ["Castle on the Border"]. Romance, humor and gaiety, the satisfaction in unselfish living, the understanding which can exist between the aged and the young, the joys of a creative life, and a sensitive response to nature are all skilfully interwoven.

Mrs. Benary-Isbert is an author who knows that one faces life with courage and she transfers this truth to young people with the conviction that they will understand. (p. 37)

Norma Rathburn, in The Saturday Review *(Entire issue copyright 1956 by Saturday Review Associates, Inc.; reprinted with permission), August 18, 1956.*

[In *The Wicked Enchantment*] Anemone lives happily with her widowed father and pet dog in Vogelsang, a German town of medieval fairy-tale quality, until the mysterious disappearance of a statue and gargoyle from the Cathedral casts troubled shadows of eerie foreboding upon most of its inhabitants. . . . [Her] aunt, together with her pets, a little magic, and Anemone, solve the mystery and bring happiness and stability to the town once more. This fantasy is sharp and bold with a down to earth quality that gives it the appearance of a clear cut black and white etching. The narrative is sometimes a little too rough and coarse, as though it had been ground down, losing in the process its depth and mirrored movements of light and shade. But for much of the time the ingredients of true fantasy are there and while the story resembles many of its kind it is worth individual recommendation. The author gives evidence of a living faith and that faith sheds a light on the story, and a light that reveals a vital truth. (p. 202)

The Junior Bookshelf, *October, 1956.*

MARY LEE KRUPKA

Just as Kay Boyle's short stories painted vivid portraits of post-war Germany for adult readers, so have Margot Benary-Isbert's novels traced a similar pattern for teenagers. ["The Long Way Home"] covers somewhat wider ground, detailing the journey of a 13-year-old orphan boy from an impoverished East Germany to a longed-for permanent home in California.

There is a basic honesty in Mrs. Benary-Isbert's writing, refreshing to find in young people's literature. Characterization is fully dimensioned, each personality being clearly defined without glossing or patly resolving weaknesses. And through the travels of a wide-eyed yet mature Christoph Wegener, American youngsters will discover the coast-to-coast wonders of their own land. It's a well-rounded picture. Certainly the most poignant section is the Chicago episode, when the young boy is placed with a kind but busily distracted family in a dingy Loop apartment—quite alone among strangers.

Gracefully the author has also threaded in characters from her other books.

> Mary Lee Krupka, "West from Germany," in The New York Times Book Review (© 1959 by The New York Times Company; reprinted by permission), May 10, 1959, p. 10.

HELEN E. KINSEY

Too long-winded, over-crowded with people, places, and events, and less deeply felt than [Margot Benary-Isbert's] first books, the story of Chris Wegener's experiences [in The Long Way Home] is nonetheless a perceptive and often moving one. Readers will be interested not only in Chris's plight but also in a view of themselves and their country as seen through the eyes of a stranger. (p. 575)

> Helen E. Kinsey, in The Booklist and Subscription Books Bulletin (reprinted by permission of the American Library Association; copyright 1959 by the American Library Association), June 1, 1959.

It is easy to be sentimental about refugees without being practical and without really thinking about them as human beings, but [in The Long Way Home] Margot Benary concentrates all her craft on the theme of "home" and while refugees of one sort or another besides Christoph become woven into the plot, the basis of the story is always the personal need to belong which affects others than displaced persons but is concentrated in Christoph's eventual arrival and his consciousness of "fitting in." (p. 222)

> The Junior Bookshelf, October, 1960.

MARGARET SHERWOOD LIBBY

[Dangerous Spring is the story of a spring] in Karin Lorenz' life, sixteen, almost seventeen, and in love with Helmut Lobelius, almost twelve years her senior, a young idealistic pastor with an imperturbable passion for truth and indifference to worldly things. It was a desperately dangerous spring. The Third Reich was tottering. The American army would be in Erfurt, Karin's city, any day, and word had gone forth that the city was to be defended. . . .

Karin accompanies Lobelius on his parish calls and watches his sympathy for the heterogeneous group of refugees who crowd his home and bicker constantly, nerves snapping under the long strain. She wonders if she can be the tower of strength this dedicated man needs as a wife, but as danger grows she does her part. There is a superb climax when, just as Karin offers to interpret for the mayor a capitulation of the town to the Americans so it will escape annihilation, he receives orders by telephone from the military commander to offer opposition. . . .

With quiet competence the author, who knows this situation from personal experience, shows the changing mood of the people, a phrase here, a quiet action there . . . , as well as all points of view and all kinds of people. The minor characters ring true while the main ones are completely realized. Even the full implications of Buchenwald are conveyed to the reader, as they reach Karin and Lobelius, with a force that is all the more effective because it is restrained.

Because this is a love story, though a bitter-sweet one, it will appeal to girls especially, yet we hope boys will read it too, not only to appreciate the character of Lobelius, but for Till, . . . educated as a Hitler youth, who had to see a boy almost murdered by the SS before he could quite believe that he had been trained by evil. An outstanding book, not only the best this very fine author has done but superb by any standard. It is deeply moving and wise. It offers insights into the complexities of the human heart, its confusions especially, its evil passions and its holiest. . . . (p. 8)

> Margaret Sherwood Libby, in New York Herald Tribune Book Review (© I.H.T. Corporation; reprinted by permission), May 14, 1961.

MARY LOUISE HECTOR

Based on diaries kept by the author and her husband, "Dangerous Spring" is an extraordinary success on two-interdependent levels, fiction and document. The story is well-constructed and minutely controlled. . . . [The] documentation strikingly reveals that, behind the solid mass of German national guilt, there were conscientious and distressed individuals. (p. 18)

> Mary Louise Hector, "The Americans Came," in The New York Times Book Review (© 1961 by The New York Times Company; reprinted by permission), May 14, 1961, pp. 16, 18.

RUTH HILL VIGUERS

The varied cast of characters [of Dangerous Spring], many of whom are refugees sheltering in Helmut's home, have surely been drawn from life. Especially appealing are Karin, deeply in love but unaware of the necessary practical qualifications of a minister's wife, and her young brother Till, fanatically devoted to the Hitler Youth Movement to whom the desperate last-ditch activities of the Storm Troopers bring complete disillusionment. A fine book which can do more than a library of factual accounts to make young people see the senselessness of war, and the idealism that can survive in great hearts even through the most devastating experiences. (p. 272)

> Ruth Hill Viguers, in The Horn Book Magazine (copyright, 1961, by the Horn Book, Inc., Boston), June, 1961.

[Dangerous Spring] is a remarkable book; the most cynical of teenagers, if persuaded to read beyond the first chapters, is likely to recognise its truth and its contemporary relevance. (pp. 293-94)

It is a tough story and Mrs. Benary, although she never dwells on horror, spares not her heroine nor her readers. She blends her tones most brilliantly; here are neither heroes nor villains, blacks nor whites, but here too the reader is in no doubt as to where goodness lies. The portrayal of character, not only that of the charming perplexed heroine, is most skilful, and so is the unobtrusively lovely painting of landscape. The author shows the last spring of war in all its incongruous beauty.

Mrs. Benary has . . . [a] pervading sense of goodness; her values are . . . complex. . . . Mrs. Benary has written another book of high distinction, one which treats of life-size problems with dignity and without condescension. She respects her readers. . . . (p. 294)

The Junior Bookshelf, November, 1961.

MARY LEE KRUPKA

To American teen-agers viewing the Germany of the nineteen-thirties from film clips and history books, the decade emerges as a kaleidoscope of goose-stepping Nazis and Hitler's frenetic gestures. In ["Time to Love"], Margot Benary-Isbert proposes that within certain upper-class German families who detested the political pattern of the times, it was possible to enjoy a productive life in relative seclusion from the horrendous events taking form in their land—at least for a time. (p. 14)

The author subtly injects politics into the story, but merely in relation to the Benninger family, to whom Hitler's ambitions are at first a remote annoyance. By book's end, however, the war erupts about them, and their gentle life seems doomed. (p. 18)

> *Mary Lee Krupka, in The New York Times Book Review (© 1962 by The New York Times Company; reprinted by permission), November 11, 1962.*

There are things in [*A Time to Love*] that are easily dislikable, because it has that German mixture of sentimentality, smugness and earnestness which can grate upon an English mind. But Mrs. Benary's people are people; they are solid, real characters, their lives and their hopes and their sorrows matter to the reader, and the setting of their lives . . . all is clear and concrete. This is what children and young people like, nor do they despise a certain moral preoccupation. And the setting is really German, not just a scene yanked abroad for a change. . . . It is a well-written book and one cannot but be absorbed by it. (p. 974)

> *The Times Literary Supplement (© Times Newspapers Ltd. (London), 1963; reproduced from The Times Literary Supplement by permission), November 28, 1963.*

KEITH HARRISON

[*Under a Changing Moon* is] the story of a bourgeois family in the Rhineland in 1865. The family is large and respectable—ruled over by a benign father who is the local magistrate, and a busy wife who, with the help of her daughter Paula, just out of convent, manages to keep her many sons in order. The whole novel is the record of a year's domestic minutiae, quite elegantly written, but with an attitude so coy that I can only assume it was intended for a certain kind of child. Most kids wouldn't be convinced. People like this may have lived a hundred years

ago, but that's not the point. Maybe I have misread the book—indeed, I hope I have. (p. 214)

> *Keith Harrison, in The Spectator (© 1965 by The Spectator; reprinted by permission of The Spectator), August 13, 1965.*

[In *Under a Changing Moon*] Mrs. Benary proves that it is still possible to write movingly and to a certain extent sentimentally about a young girl's emergence from adolescence into womanhood without suggesting the word "sex" anywhere along the line. Her heroine, Paula, returns to the bosom of her very large family in the provincial town of Limburg, from her convent schooling, in the year 1886. She falls in love, and is fallen in love with, but all does not come right at once, as is proper in a story and usually in life also. But her own story is given a background and an emphasis by the actions of her mother, father, brothers, uncles, aunts and family servants. . . . Though Mrs. Benary does not labour the facts, all her young characters have problems of one sort or another to solve, crises of character which must be faced alone, and which must be overcome for the sake of future development and personal integrity. The whole is tempered with the kind of humour which comes of a mind at peace if not at rest. This is just the right kind of book for the adolescent and the pre-adolescent who needs some reassurance about moral values and integrated behaviour. (p. 303)

The Junior Bookshelf, October, 1965.

The older girl who enjoys a quiet, slow-moving narrative will return to [*Under a Changing Moon*] time and again, and still find it richly rewarding. Its accounts of the progression of the seasons and the Church's year, of family relationships, and life in a provincial German town are evocative and moving. But the author is also to be commended for the way she handles moral issues soberly and without embarrassment; few children's writers nowadays can do this. (p. 1145)

> *The Times Literary Supplement (© Times Newspapers Ltd. (London), 1965; reproduced from The Times Literary Supplement by permission), December 9, 1965.*

MARCUS CROUCH

Vogelsang [of *The Wicked Enchantment*] is a German city. It is not obviously detached from the rest of the world, but through many centuries it has gone its own way, living for the most part contentedly beneath the shadow of the great Gothic cathedral. People from other towns say 'We are all a little touched', but the Vogelsanger madness is of an agreeable kind and the ghosts who haunt the town are mostly 'nice and respectable'. But evil comes to Vogelsang; to be precise, it comes from within the town, from the forgotten vault beneath the cathedral where Earl Owl of Owlhall rests uneasily. (The parallel with Nazi Germany is implicit.) (p. 133)

Margot Benary adopted an appropriately Gothic frame for her story, with an extravagance of style and numerous side-chapels and pinnacles of episode and sub-plot. The book has its share of Teutonic sentimentality too, but the general impression is, like the cathedral, of a unified and harmonious structure. The little world of Vogelsang, in turmoil or at peace, is the true hero of the story. (p. 134)

[The characters of *The Ark*] belong to the defeated race who have to rebuild their lives in the shadow of occupation. (p. 180)

The charm of *The Ark* springs from its concern with the realities of love and hunger. Food was a constant preoccupation of the families who clung to life in the harsh years of recovery, and the book is full of the bitterness of hunger and the glorious smell of food.... Children's literature is full of feasts, but few are described with such loving concern over each mouthful than the Lechows' Advent party with its four miraculous cakes.

The wonder of *The Ark* is not that it is a good book, for in many ways it falls short of excellence, but that it should have been written at all. It came out of war and defeat and out of the chaos that preceded reconstruction. Of the war there is little in the book; the author and the characters avoid direct reference to it when they can. Dieter, the young musician, recalls briefly his work on the West Wall and remembers: 'At home we never cared much for all the heiling and hurrahing'. After the war there is extreme hardship, humiliation as well as hunger, and the boredom of queueing. Mrs. Benary and the Lechows rise above it, largely through a strong sense of family which extends to their motley collection of friends, partly because deprivation and suffering help them to comprehend fundamental truths. (pp. 180, 182)

In its warmth and tenderness *The Ark* comes often to the brink of sentimentality. It never quite topples over. Mrs. Benary always harnesses sentiment to reality. Her finest achievement is the character of Margret, who more than the others carries into peacetime the scars of war. There is a remarkable episode in which she fights for the life of the puppies in her charge at Rowan Farm. Somehow the animals become associated in her mind with the dead children she had seen on the refugees' marches. It might be an incongruous and embarrassing moment were the writer's touch less sure. But the reader accepts that 'all the world's suffering had come down at once upon her.' (p. 182)

Benary approaches [the theme of growing up in wartime in] *Dangerous Spring*.... Karin, the adolescent daughter of a German liberal doctor, falls in love with a saintly pastor.... Karin is perhaps in love with him, or with life, or with the spring; in the last weeks of war she is wide open to influences, from art and nature and religion, and the lame and half-blind pastor provides the catalyst for her teeming emotions. It is a tender, pathetic, very slightly comic, picture of young love. But growth is accelerated in wartime, and during the terrors of bombing and greater perils from the liberating Russians, Karin grows up and gains the strength to lose her pastor.

This is a wise story, authentic in its details, which are based on the author's own experiences, yet surprisingly detached; the reader remains an observer instead of becoming . . . a partisan. (p. 203)

> *Marcus Crouch, in his* The Nesbit Tradition: The Children's Novel in England 1945-1970 (© *Marcus Crouch 1972*), *Ernest Benn, 1972.*

CAROLYN T. KINGSTON

The Ark is a story of how one family managed to survive when their home, possessions, father, and one son were swept away during World War II. As all those chosen by Noah to come into the ark survived, so this story shows that life can be ongoing despite floods and wars, or holocaustal conditions. (p. 108)

The tragic moments of the story are the times when Margret faces the loss of something or someone she loves. The first tragedy is conveyed in retrospect, a device that helps to cushion the sorrow the reader must feel in learning of the loss of Margret's happy home and the death of her twin brother.... One day she meets an old woman who has lost an only son in the war. Mari has found a way to cope with her sorrow and shares her illumination with the refugee girl. "When what you love best departs, there's a long time afterward when you're never at home anywhere. But wait, the dead come back. They come to life again within us; we have only to have patience and let it happen." . . . (pp. 108-09)

The old woman tells Margret that some people learn to remember differently, whereas others must forget. But she says that remembering is the best medicine. And so Mari states the story's theme, which the girl finds to be the means of coping with the problems war has brought into her experience, and her former happiness does have an inner rebirth.

The second tragic moment happens on the farm where Margret is taking care of the livestock.... One dog with tortured, pleading eyes drags herself to the girl and dies with her head on Margret's lap. The helplessness of having done all one can without avail wells up in Margret, and in her sorrow she remembers the refugee mothers and fathers who carry their dead children on their backs for many miles, clinging to this last presence of a dear one for whom no more can be done. Thus the girl understands and gains compassion for others through her own tragic experience. Going later into the barn, however, she finds that the mare has given birth to a beautiful colt, and deeply stirred, Margret whispers, "life!" In her moment of sorrow she has tasted the bitterness of death and now experiences the joy of new birth, feeling something of the reciprocal quality of the two emotions, the latter made richer by the former.

A third moment of tragedy comes with the news of the death of Mrs. Verduz, the woman with whom the family first found refuge.... As in the second tragic instance, however, the death of the kind landlady is more than balanced by the homecoming of their father. (p. 109)

At the conclusion of the story, the family has found a new way of life that approximates the old. It is bittersweet because it is touched with the remembrance of people and objects no longer present, but it is a life enriched by suffering, resulting in a more comprehensive compassion for the troubles of humanity. The catharsis conveyed by the story is this clarification the family receives concerning life's ongoingness despite devastating conditions.

But the story is always tragedy, although it contains an affirmative outlook. There is no substitute for Margret's twin brother. What she finds is that a void created by death can be filled, but that part of the new is made more beautiful by remembrance of the old.

The story's message is emotionally touching and satisfying as well as realistic. There is no need for the construction of a fairy-tale approach to life. Comfort comes from looking deep, rather than turning aside, and, as the old woman told Margret, this kind of remembrance is the best medicine.

The author is able to create moods and atmospheres successfully. The wind-blown icy night with its desolate streets symbolizes cold despair at the outset of the story. The warmth and peace of life on the farm with father, war-scarred but present among them in The Ark, seems symbolic of the peace Margret and her family have found after the suffering of the war years. (pp. 109-10)

Carolyn T. Kingston, in her The Tragic Mode in Children's Literature *(copyright © 1974 by Teachers College, Columbia University; reprinted by permission of the publisher), New York: Teachers College Press, 1974.*

Melvin Berger

1927-

American young adult nonfiction writer, biographer, and lecturer. Berger is a popular and prolific author of nonfiction works which explain aspects of science and music to a young adult audience. He is perhaps best known for his *Scientists at Work* series, which deals with pollution, cancer, crime detection, oceanography, weather, and medical research. A related concern is with the environment, and in *The New Air Book, Jobs That Save Our Environment,* and *The New Water Book* Berger demonstrates the impact that technological advances have had on nature. A graduate of the Eastman School of Music and a professional violist, he has written several introductions to instruments, noted musicians, and types of music. Believing that "all music is related to the world in which it was created or is being performed," he writes books that "relate the art of music to the social, political, and scientific ideas of the time." Although most critics praise his ability to simplify complicated theories, there are dissenters who maintain that his explanations lack precision. The majority of his books describe related jobs and their qualifications, a useful feature for the young adult planning a career. Recently Berger has begun collaborating with his wife, Gilda, herself an author of nonfiction for young people. (See also *Contemporary Authors,* Vols. 5-8, rev. ed., and *Something about the Author,* Vol. 5.)

EVELYN SHAW

In *Triumphs of Modern Science,* by Melvin Berger . . . , there is emphasis on the individual's participation in scientific discoveries. (Actually, I would like to know what prompted some of the inclusions as part of modern science, unless by "modern" the author means anything between 1900 and 1960.)

Each chapter is a biography of the scientist identified with a particular discovery, and includes the histories of penicillin, viruses, antibiotics, X-rays, DNA, radioactivity, and relativity. I like the human element in this type of reporting, because I think that young readers can relate to it and see the possibilities that exist for their own achievements in science studies. However, I wish the author had emphasized somewhere that many discoveries are not made suddenly, but usually have, as a foundation, years of work carried out by many people and leading to one individual's spectacular "breakthrough." (p. 17)

Evelyn Shaw, in Natural History *(copyright © the American Museum of Natural History, 1965; re-printed with permission from* Natural History*), November, 1965.*

A science book with the humanities reader in mind, [*Famous Men of Modern Biology*] investigates the work of fourteen biologists from Pasteur to the *Double Helix* duo. . . . [Each chapter develops] some personality through anecdotes, such as the preoccupied Salk assuring his neglected wife, "My dear, I'm giving you my *undevoted* attention." Mr. Berger does for biology what Bernard Jaffe did for chemistry in *Crucibles;* the two are similar in style of presentation, selection of known names . . . , and the ability to relate the technical in relevant, stimulating terms. . . . (p. 468)

Kirkus Service (copyright © 1968 The Kirkus Service, Inc.), April 15, 1968.

In [*Famous Men of Modern Biology*] the author presents the story of the remarkable accomplishments and discoveries of 14 researchers in the biological sciences. . . . The biographies tend to be superficial, as would be expected in a collection of this sort. The book might be useful for introducing younger readers to more detailed biographies of the scientists. For this reason, it is especially unfortunate that the author included no bibliographies. (pp. 118-19)

Science Books (copyright 1968 by the American Association for the Advancement of Science), Vol. 4, No. 2 (September, 1968).

[*For Good Measure*] more clearly belongs on the science bookshelf than do most which deal with measurement, a reflection not of its relative quality—although it is a fine book—but of the fact that others get so involved with numbers and scales and the rationale for standardized measures that little time is left to explore the scientific uses of measurement. Here the organization is around areas such as sound, electricity and magnetism, light and radiation, though there are chapters on such standard topics as mass, length and time. Each unit is treated historically. . . . Thus a great deal of scientific development in the fields is covered in exploring the changing nature of measuring. In contrast, a more common approach such as [Philip B.] Carona's (in *Things That Measure*) offers simply a historical outline of devices. (p. 318)

Kirkus Reviews (copyright © 1969 The Kirkus Service, Inc.), March 15, 1969.

[Few] laymen know the history of the development of standardized weights and measures, and for them Mr. Berger has supplied a complete, readable and not-too-technical little book [*For Good Measure: The Story of Modern Measurement*]. The introductory portion traces the genesis of measurement as a long historical process, first by describing the concepts of magnitude or dimension conveyed by man's natural senses.... The book goes on step by step beyond the internationally accepted and adopted basic standards of length, weight and mass, to discuss some of the modern concepts and methods in metrology.... An appreciation is developed for the fact that absolute accuracy in measurement has not been and may never be achieved.... Here and there interesting experiments are suggested which should interest many young people—would that there were more. Additional illustrations would have enriched a factually correct but occasionally dry text.... It is good collateral study material as well as for general reading. (p. 104)

> *Science Books (copyright 1969 by the American Association for the Advancement of Science), Vol. 5, No. 2 (September, 1969).*

HAROLD F. DESMOND, JR.

A strong point of [*For Good Measure: The Story of Modern Measurement*] is its inclusion of many experiments, but there is no glossary for the numerous technical terms.... On the whole, however, this is a very solid treatment, both for students and teacher reference and review. (p. 3826)

> *Harold F. Desmond, Jr., in* Library Journal *(reprinted from* Library Journal, *October 15, 1969; published by R. R. Bowker Co. (a Xerox company); copyright © 1969 by Xerox Corporation), October 15, 1969.*

HARRY C. STUBBS

[*Tools of Modern Biology*] is good and describes a lot of apparatus well, but I fear we are not yet at the point where the electron microscope and pH meter can show very clearly why Beethoven could write a symphony and I cannot. I do hope, though, that scientific *measuring*, which forms the entire foundation for Mr. Berger's book, may someday make a big difference to the *science* of psychology. (p. 408)

> *Harry C. Stubbs, in* The Horn Book Magazine *(copyright © 1970 by The Horn Book, Inc., Boston), August, 1970.*

WILLIAM J. MURRAY

[*Tools of Modern Biology*] is principally a history of the development of the methods (Intellectual Tools) and instruments that have contributed to the growth and development of the Modern Biological Body of Knowledge. It is made more interesting by the fact that the works of some of the major researchers in the field are cited throughout.

Perhaps the most important contribution that this book offers to the reader is that it gives him meaningful insights into scientific process and method and a better understanding of the men who are engaged in scientific endeavors....

The scientific "Truth" is only as good as the methods and instruments employed and the data which support them.

This point is so well made by the author's development of his subject that this alone is enough to recommend the book....

His treatment of the scientific method is one of the best yet for real insight and understanding. His treatment of Biometrics demonstrates his skill at taking a fairly complicated topic and making it simple and quite understandable for the average reader.

The author's chapters on the use of various scientific instruments such as light and electron microscopes, radioactive tracers and others are excellent. (p. 296)

> *William J. Murray, in* Best Sellers *(copyright 1970, by the University of Scranton), October 15, 1970.*

Everyday tasks of the weather observer, radar operator, forecaster, "hurricane hunter," and other meteorological technicians are surveyed [in *The National Weather Service*] to convey an appreciation of "what goes into preparing those simple sounding weather reports." Covered in the process are the functions and handling of such tools as the weather balloon, satellite, barometer, even ... the inter-station teletype machine. The attention to office routine is sometimes excessive.... Procedures in making weather maps are closely followed ..., but those wavy lines (isobars) that appear on the pictured maps are never mentioned.... In short, this easy once-over provides a clear picture of what the various weathermen do (at a younger level than Bixby's *Skywatchers*), but only a foggy notion of what it's all about. (p. 590)

> *Kirkus Reviews (copyright © 1971 The Kirkus Service, Inc.), June 1, 1971.*

Mr. Berger has presented almost a travelog of a trip to the South Pole Station [in *South Pole Station*].... His style is pleasant and rather low key, however he manages to inject an amazingly large amount of factual material without bogging down in detail. He presents the day-to-day life of the South Polar scientist at work and play.... The major emphasis is on the scientific program and how the various individuals and their investigations contribute to an overall study of the South Pole. This book is generally restricted to the pole station and its inhabitants rather than a broader view of the South Pole. In this context, as an introduction to a particular scientific environment, rather than as one of the many already available books about Antarctica, the book is well worth reading. (p. 131)

> *Science Books (copyright 1971 by the American Association for the Advancement of Science), Vol. VII, No. 2 (September, 1971).*

HENRY LELAND CLARKE

Melvin Berger has presented his readers with the story of fourteen leading composers of the century [in *Masters of Modern Music*]. He has selected Stravinsky, Schoenberg, and Bartók to represent "Musical Explorers"; Richard Strauss, Sibelius, Hindemith, Prokofiev, Copland, and Britten, "Music in the Main Stream"; Gershwin, Richard Rodgers, and Menotti, "Music for the Many"; and John Cage and Vladimir Ussachevsky, "The New Music." All fourteen were born before the outbreak of World War I, and there is not a French, Yankee, or black composer among them. Within these limitations his list has been well chosen, despite a few possible objections. Surely, for instance, Webern should be added to the first three men, as one of the "composers who have pointed out the new directions of modern music." . . . [The author] has followed the present trend of placing Hindemith only among those "composers who have carried forward the musical traditions of the past." In addition, certain statements in the text raise the question of whether Richard Strauss and Sibelius are modern enough to be included at all. (p. 70)

In any case, the composers chosen are attractively presented. Each is introduced by a striking incident or characterization, which brings him close to the reader at the outset. The style is readable and especially appealing to the young person looking for a guide. One result of this format is that it makes the work suitable as a novel but not as a source book for specific data. Although the text is accurate in giving the general sense of things, the very cursive style that makes it move sometimes blurs particular points and allows years to slip into each other. . . .

The last paragraph of the book raises a dated question: "Will the growth of electronic music mean the end of concerts and live performers?" When young Stockhausen swept the country with his tapes back in 1958, it was already apparent that the days of pure electronic music were numbered. Today, it is generally recognized that no matter how avant-garde a composition is, there has to be at least one live body on the stage along with the appliances.

The text contains no musical examples. Berger has provided a very short bibliography and discography, which are to be praised for their selectivity. The portraits of The Fourteen are fine if formal. The recommendation for *Masters of Modern Music* is read it, but don't lean on it. (p. 71)

> *Henry Leland Clarke, in* Music Educators Journal *(copyright © 1971 by Music Educators National Conference; reprinted with permission), December, 1971.*

ZENA SUTHERLAND

In a fascinating survey of research and findings, [Melvin Berger] makes a complicated subject clear [in *Enzymes in Action*], explaining the nature of enzymes, the ways in which they act, and the isolation . . . of a pure enzyme that led, in addition to other experimental work, to the production . . . of a synthetic enzyme. . . . Lively, informal, and informative, this is not only good science for the layman, but also a good picture of scientific method. (pp. 117-18)

> *Zena Sutherland, in* Bulletin of the Center for Children's Books *(© 1972 by the University of Chicago; all rights reserved), April, 1972.*

[*The Violin Book* is variously] entertaining and inspiring background material for young performers. . . . Berger also gives some hints about repertoire and advice on career possibilities, but since he still believes in the efficacy of the self-organized New York debut ("You hope that the newspaper critics who usually attend these concerts will write rave reviews") it's hard to place much faith in the practicality of his recommendations. (p. 411)

> *Kirkus Reviews (copyright © 1972 The Kirkus Service, Inc.), April 1, 1972.*

[*Enzymes in Action*] is a short up-to-date review of enzymology and its practical application in industry. Berger

covers adequately such topics as the role of enzymes in digestion, food production, and preparation of beverages; enzymes as drugs; enzymes and diseases; and enzymes at work. He describes historic and salient discoveries including the latest achievements in enzymology. The book is written in a highly simplified style. Because the vocabulary is simple, the book can be read easily by a layman. The text can be used with great profit as a collateral reading by a freshman student of biochemistry, biology, agronomy, agriculture, or medicine. Although the author uses no chemical formulas, such classical effects on enzyme activity as those of pH, temperature, and concentrations of enzyme and substrate should have been mentioned. (p. 46)

> Science Books *(copyright 1972 by the American Association for the Advancement of Science), Vol. VIII, No. 1 (May, 1972).*

Though none of it is essential to their music making, young flutists [reading *The Flute Book*] will enjoy meeting their famous predecessors from Frederick the Great to Jean-Pierre Rampal, tracing the innovations that led to the standard flute designed by Theobald Boehm in 1847, seeing how modern instruments are made, and learning a little about the physics of the flute's sound and a little more about the highlights of the concert repertoire. And, given the instrument's resurgent 20th century popularity, those with a sense of humor will appreciate the 19th century image of the flutist: "He always has a pointed nose, marries a near-sighted woman and dies run over by a bus." Grace notes all, but pleasantly orchestrated. (p. 561)

> *Kirkus Reviews (copyright © 1973 The Kirkus Service, Inc.), May 15, 1973.*

LEONE R. HEMENWAY

Such books as [Erik] Bergaust's *Oceanographers in Action* . . . and [Charles] Coombs's *Deep-Sea World: the Story of Oceanography* . . . cover the techniques, tools, and projects of ocean scientists, but [*Oceanography Lab*] is unique in describing the Woods Hole Oceanographic Institution (WHOI). . . . [This is a] generally well-conceived and well-executed presentation. (p. 2190)

> *Leone R. Hemenway, in* Library Journal *(reprinted from* Library Journal, *July, 1973; published by R. R. Bowker Co. (a Xerox company); copyright © 1973 by Xerox Corporation), July, 1973.*

[*Pollution Lab*] . . . or how "today's pollution scientists strive to make the world a cleaner and more healthful place for us to live." Dedicated to "the men and women of the Environmental Protection Agency," this is an establishment-oriented guided tour through field stations and laboratories involved in monitoring air and water quality, researching solid waste control and recovery of resources, operating a sewage disposal plant, gathering evidence for an EPA sewage pollution suit, or trying out the many "promising methods" for dealing with oil and other spills. . . . [As] in his other *Scientists at Work* books [Berger's] sentences are often blandly unsubstantial (the obvious introductory pronouncement that as world population multiplied and technology developed, "scientists were called in to lead the fight against pollution" doesn't even pose the questions of who called them in, where the barricades are, or how scientists "lead") and in the same indifferent manner the photos of technicians at work show us what their machines and devices look like from the outside but don't reveal what they are for or how they work. (p. 537)

Kirkus Reviews *(copyright © 1974 The Kirkus Service, Inc.), May 15, 1974.*

PHYLLIS G. MORDAS

[*Jobs in Fine Arts and Humanities* is a] satisfactory introduction to career opportunities in art, dance, drama, music, and the humanities. Berger emphasizes the skills and training needed and the opportunities for advancement. Of the many jobs described only five are in the field of the humanities. Job coverage in the fine arts, however, is well done with helpful examples and photographs. (p. 116)

Phyllis G. Mordas, in Library Journal *(reprinted from* Library Journal, *October 15, 1974; published by R. R. Bowker Co. (a Xerox company); copyright © 1974 by Xerox Corporation), October 15, 1974.*

ZENA SUTHERLAND

Although [*Jobs in Fine Arts and Humanities*] gives some information about careers, it covers far too broad an area to be anything but superficial in treatment.... Adequately written, but not very useful. (p. 38)

Zena Sutherland, in Bulletin of the Center for Children's Books *(© 1974 by the University of Chicago; all rights reserved), November, 1974.*

[*The New Air Book* is a companion to *The New Water Book*. With] simple experiments worked into the text wherever possible, Berger introduces just about everything he can think of that has to do with air—breathing, atmosphere, wind, weather, flying, and pollution (this last, mostly assurances about the EPA's effectiveness and instructions for measuring different kinds of pollution). The writing is clear, [and] the experiments relevant to the matter at hand ...; what is missing is a sense of overall direction. (p. 1254)

Kirkus Reviews *(copyright © 1974 The Kirkus Service, Inc.), December 1, 1974.*

DAVID G. HOAG

Much of this book about air, the atmosphere, and weather, is excellent. The text [of *The New Air Book*] for the most part is clear and well organized.... The many experiments described should be instructive and fun. But here and there are factual flaws and incomplete or misleading statements. Ignoring buoyancy in the balloon air-weighing experiment or saying nothing about the chemical and pressure changes in the candle, glass and water experiment are unfortunate. This potentially excellent book could have made the mark if it had been more carefully checked before being published! I recommend it in spite of the problems for its generally good quality science and the many experiments included. The last few chapters on air pollution are carefully done without overstatement. (p. 7)

David G. Hoag, in Appraisal *(copyright © 1975 by the Children's Science Book Review Committee), Winter, 1975.*

H. C. WOHLERS

The New Air Book provides an excellent description of one of man's natural resources. The author takes a detailed look at the technical aspects of air, describing what it is physically and chemically in an easy-to-understand text. In addition, Berger discusses the importance of air, weather, flying and air pollution, and what the public can do to learn more about the problems of air quality.... A number of pedantic scientific questions could be raised concerning the complete correctness of some explanations used in the book. In an attempt to simplify complex problems, Berger has sometimes oversimplified. One hopes that the book will provide the reader with an incentive to delve further into the science of air to obtain more fundamental knowledge. (p. 34)

H. C. Wohlers, in Science Books & Films *(copyright 1975 by the American Association for the Advancement of Science), Vol. XI, No. 1 (May, 1975).*

As in his *Flute* and *Violin* books Berger gives beginning musicians a modest boost [in *The Clarinet & Saxophone Book*] by introducing the history, manufacture and repertoire of their chosen instrument. His look at how reeds are made and evaluated and a rundown of the various members of the clarinet and saxophone families will be most useful here. There are several pages of discography, listing jazz as well as classical performances, but the omission of Charlie Parker from a chapter on famous players is a good indication of Berger's lack of interest in jazz. (p. 1231)

Kirkus Reviews *(copyright © 1975 The Kirkus Service, Inc.), November 1, 1975.*

ESTHER H. READ

Preceded by a foreword of deep feeling, this rather comprehensive book on cancer for young people [*Cancer Lab*] proceeds to discuss, in turn, all types of cancer therapists and researchers involved in treatment and study.... In a book such as this for older children, it seems unnecessary to confine the writing to very short sentences—they become tedious. Nevertheless, the boy or girl already interested in science or in the medical field will find this up-to-date work rewarding. (pp. 9-10)

Esther H. Read, in Appraisal *(copyright © 1976 by the Children's Science Book Review Committee), Winter, 1976.*

JOHN DAWSON BONIOL, JR.

The increasingly important role of the police laboratory in law enforcement work is skillfully presented in this well-written and profusely illustrated book [*Police Lab*]. Berger covers the entire range of the criminologists' work and explains very lucidly the scientific processes in such areas as serology, toxicology, spectrography, chromatography, and pathology. Although the text points out that laboratory tests can be used to corroborate innocence, the examples presented show mainly how these tests can be used to prove guilt. With an increasing general interest in police work, this is a very good and up-to-date addition.... (p. 43)

John Dawson Boniol, Jr., in School Library Journal *(reprinted from the February, 1976 issue of* School Library Journal, *published by R. R. Bowker Co. A Xerox Corporation; copyright © 1976), February, 1976.*

"It is not really terribly important to put a label on every single song," says Berger, in a sensible attempt to define his subject—which he goes on to illustrate with representative ballads, work songs, protest music [in *The Story of Folk Music*]. The many examples, reinforced by repeated suggestions that the way to know folk music is to listen, sing and, if possible, play it for yourself, bolster a quick overview of the origins of ethno-musicology, the most popular folk instruments, the use of folk melodies by "art" composers, the careers of the Lomaxes, Leadbelly, and Woody Guthrie, and modern hybrids such as folk-rock. But the ten record discography that lists Judy Collins, Tim Hardin, and Bob Dylan, and then suggests sending away for a Folkways catalog, is indicative of Berger's overall slackness. A glancing introduction at best, but one that has no competition at this level. (p. 1096)

> Kirkus Reviews *(copyright © 1976, The Kirkus Service, Inc.), October 1, 1976.*

BEVERLY B. YOUREE

This well-written survey of the evolution of American folk music includes brief explanations of how folk music is created as well as descriptions of folk instruments and biographies of folk singers and instrumentalists. An unusual feature [of *The Story of Folk Music*] is the inclusion of instructions on how to make some simple musical instruments at home and compose one's own songs. . . . [It is an] extremely interesting book on a very popular subject. (p. 54)

> Beverly B. Youree, in School Library Journal *(reprinted from the November, 1976 issue of* School Library Journal, *published by R. R. Bowker Co. A Xerox Corporation; copyright © 1976), November, 1976.*

[Considering the scope and beauty of the work, *The Story of Folk Music*] is only necessarily superficial. [Berger's] information on the pathways of folk music, on its relationship to formally composed music, on popular instruments, and on twentieth-century American musicians is all reputable and easy to absorb. . . . One may quibble with Berger's statement that "more people than ever before are listening to, singing, and composing folk songs," especially since the appended bibliography-discography argues the reverse quite well. (p. 603)

> Booklist *(reprinted by permission of the American Library Association; copyright 1976 by the American Library Association), December 15, 1976.*

JOHN D. BONIOL

Covering the training and work of Special Agents, the operations of the Laboratory and the Identification Division but not the activities of the director and other high-level administrators, [*FBI*] is a glorification of the bureau. There is no mention of past illegal FBI maneuvers nor of the controversies that have surrounded the agency, and the inclusion of current "Ten Most-Wanted Criminals" posters is useless since these will quickly become out of date. (p. 46)

> John D. Boniol, in School Library Journal *(reprinted from the December, 1977 issue of* School Library Journal, *published by R. R. Bowker Co. A Xerox Corporation; copyright © 1977), December, 1977.*

DOROTHY BICKERTON

Medical Center Lab belongs on the vocational guidance shelf in school libraries. The book covers both clinical labs . . . , which assist the medical staff in diagnosis, and research labs . . . , which seek new knowledge and new techniques of treatment. . . . Because of the diversity of jobs in medical center labs and the brevity of the text, no particular aspect is discussed in depth; what is presented is an overall view of the many and varied careers which come together in medical center laboratories. This is done in the context of the treatment of actual patients, which is really what work in these labs is all about. (p. 151)

> Dorothy Bickerton, in Science Books & Films *(copyright 1977 by the American Association for the Advancement of Science), Vol. XIII, No. 3 (December, 1977).*

DAPHNE ANN HAMILTON

The title [*Medical Center Lab*] is a slight misnomer, as the author describes the work of nine different labs which might be found in a large modern medical center. . . . While continually stressing the value of . . . research, Berger's one method of citing typical work done in the labs is much less applicable to research than to clinical labs, with the consequence that this section of the book is much less interesting and the work appears less vital—a distinct disservice to the subject. A few other problems occur: ECG is used for electrocardiograph, with no mention made of the less correct but more familiar term EKG; and in one account of a heart function experiment, the results are so exactly reflective of the reasons for choosing the experimental groups in the first place that one wonders why the experiment was conducted—or at least why it was recounted here. The book as a whole . . . is uneven. . . . (p. 10)

> Daphne Ann Hamilton, in Appraisal *(copyright © 1978 by the Children's Science Book Review Committee), Winter, 1978.*

[Melvin and Gilda Berger's] coverage of proteins, carbohydrates, and fats is admirably clear [in *The New Food Book*], and more extensive than that in Hettie Jones' *How to Eat Your ABC's* . . . which concentrates on vitamins; but on the whole the level and direction of nutritional advice is comparable. . . . The Bergers then go on to other food-related matters, but their treatment of world hunger is characteristically bland, and their discussion of the Green Revolution, food shopping, additives, and food production is naive and complacent compared to Sara Gilbert's report on the industry in *You Are What You Eat*. . . . In place of Gilbert's genuine independent investigation, the Bergers riddle their text with simple "experiments"—e.g., check for the presence of starch in different foods or observe its breakdown in cooked potato slices—which function more as a nuisance than anything else. (p. 498)

> Kirkus Reviews *(copyright © 1978 The Kirkus Service, Inc.), May 1, 1978.*

ZENA SUTHERLAND

In a fairly objective assessment of the occult sciences, Berger covers a wide range of topics adequately if not comprehensively [in *The Supernatural: From ESP to UFOs*]. Separate chapters are devoted to such subjects as astrology, faith healing, parapsychology, witchcraft, and UFOs. Case histories and anecdotes add variety to the text, which includes some exposes and some unexplained, but documented phenomena. Not unlike other books on the supernatural, this does a workmanlike job of introduction. (p. 154)

> *Zena Sutherland, in* Bulletin of the Center for Children's Books *(© 1978 by the University of Chicago; all rights reserved), June, 1978.*

SARAH GAGNÉ

[*The Supernatural: From ESP to UFOs* is a] searching, unbiased study of supernatural reports. The first chapter sets the tone: The author describes a disquieting encounter he once had with a stranger in an art gallery, who spoke of actual events in Berger's life. Was the stranger receiving mental messages? The author purposely does not give an answer. The remaining eight chapters of the book examine several categories of supernatural phenomena. . . . (p. 308)

> *Sarah Gagné, "Supernatural Phenomena," in* The Horn Book Magazine *(copyright © 1978 by the Horn Book, Inc., Boston), June, 1978, pp. 308-09.*

MONTAGUE ULLMAN

[*The Supernatural; From ESP to UFOs*] is a book that will be of little use to the serious reader of any age. Loose and inaccurate, it lumps together a smattering of scientific research in parapsychology (most of which is behind the times) with astrology, witchcraft, spiritualism and UFOs. Even the effort at being impartial comes off poorly. In hit-and-run fashion, the author selects dramatic, rather than evidential, material and then cites critics and skeptics in a way that whitewashes the initial impact. Nowhere is there a valid sifting out of the real from the spurious. (p. 142)

> *Montague Ullman, in* Science Books & Films *(copyright 1978 by the American Association for the Advancement of Science), Vol. XIV, No. 3 (December, 1978).*

SHARON HENDRICKS

On the blurb Mr. Berger is described as a "meticulous researcher," and [*The Supernatural from ESP to UFO's*] does have a bibliography and a list of organizations that deal in supernatural phenomena. It is not a book that presents both sides of an issue. The author clearly believes in all the mysterious things about which he writes. Any librarian who . . . has been trying to keep the shelves stocked with this type of drivel will at once recognize that this book offers nothing new. It is a rehash with a new cover. (p. 17)

> *Sharon Hendricks, in* Young Adult Cooperative Book Review Group of Massachusetts, *December, 1978.*

JEAN F. MERCIER

A true craftsman, Berger is a favorite with readers whose interests he covers in nonfiction. [In "The World of Dance"] he discusses the numerous ramifications of the dance, its history from ancient times to the present. . . . Berger doesn't fail to include information about great names in the dance in an absorbing book. One finds but one quotation to question. Scholar Curt Sachs says, ". . . dancing . . . is simply life on a higher level." (Make that "a different level" or add "sometimes.") (p. 69)

> *Jean F. Mercier, in* Publishers Weekly *(reprinted from the December 11, 1978, issue of* Publishers Weekly *by permission of the critic, published by R. R. Bowker Company, a Xerox company; copyright © 1979 by Xerox Corporation), December 11, 1978.*

DAPHNE ANN HAMILTON

[Melvin and Gilda Berger] have produced a low-key but highly informational book which should fill in a blank spot in most children's collections. . . . [*The New Food Book: Nutrition Diet, Consumer Tips, and Foods of the Future*] strikes a good balance between the traditional and health food viewpoints, avoiding both textbook dullness and over-enthusiastic proselytising. The authors don't hesitate to give the claims on both sides of an argument and leave the conclusion to further investigation by scientists, and . . . the reader. Very simple experiments illustrating a number of "food facts" are scattered throughout the book, smoothly merging into the text; they might provide some different science fair projects. Broader based than most books on this subject, this readable, well-organized, and informative introduction deserves a larger readership than it will probably get. (p. 5)

> *Daphne Ann Hamilton, in* Appraisal *(copyright © 1979 by the Children's Science Book Review Committee), Winter, 1979.*

BARBARA ELLEMAN

[The Legionnaires' disease] provides the basis for Berger's discussion of the Center for Disease Control [*Disease Detectives*]. He follows the painstaking research of each department—bacteriology, virology, and toxicology—in the race to locate the epidemic's cause, describing the broader scope of their work along the way. Explanations of technical terms are integrated into the text; and though [Jules] Archer's *Epidemic!* . . . is wider in scope, the concise writing style and detective story approach make this more accessible for slightly younger readers. (p. 748)

> *Barbara Elleman, in* Booklist *(reprinted by permission of the American Library Association; copyright 1979 by the American Library Association), January 1, 1979.*

BARBARA ELLEMAN

In a broad overview beginning with evidence of its primitive use in Paleolithic times, Berger traces the history of dance in a straightforward, perfunctory manner [in *The World of Dance*]. The discussion touches on the styles that developed in ancient Egypt, Greece, the Orient, and Medieval Europe and comments on reasons for these developments. Ballet receives far more attention as Berger describes its evolution, explaining terms, summarizing story plots, and mentioning dancers and choreographers responsible for its present form. Also included is the influence of Isadora Duncan, Martha Graham, and Twyla Tharp on the formation of modern dance techniques. . . . A useful history for music and social studies reports. (p. 748)

> *Barbara Elleman, in* Booklist *(reprinted by permission of the American Library Association; copyright 1979 by the American Library Association), January 1, 1979.*

Unlike Berger's other entries in the *Scientists at Work* series, [*Disease Detectives*] sticks to one story—the Legionnaires' Disease mystery—to demonstrate the workings of the federal Center for Disease Control in Atlanta. . . . [As usual for the series,] Berger's text also tends to overemphasize routines and devices—but the Legionnaire's Disease case gives the book focus and continuity. (pp. 67-8)

Kirkus Reviews *(copyright © 1979 The Kirkus Service, Inc.), January 15, 1979.*

Judy Blume

1938-

American young adult and adult novelist. Blume is one of the most controversial authors today writing for young adults for her frank consideration of such topics as menstruation, masturbation, and teenage sexuality. Although her books are popular with young adults, having sold more than six million copies, many school libraries consider them inappropriate for adolescent readers. With the publication in 1970 of *Are You There God? It's Me, Margaret*, Blume became a leading writer of teenage fiction. This novel has two themes: Margaret's preoccupation with the physical signs of puberty, and her search for a religious identity. Blume was praised for her accurate rendering of teenage dialogue and her warmly humorous treatment of a universal female concern, although several critics considered her descriptions of Margaret's bodily changes overly graphic. *Forever . . .*, with its detailed description of a first sexual encounter, is even more controversial. Blume does not moralize, although her books do emphasize the importance of social responsibility. Her books are set in suburbia, reflecting her own East Coast, middle-class background. While adults may criticize her work, citing her lack of depth and stylistic limitations, her popularity with young adults indicates that she has an accurate sense of their concerns. (See also *Children's Literature Review*, Vol. 2, *Contemporary Authors*, Vols. 29-32, rev. ed., and *Something about the Author*, Vol. 2.)

LAVINIA RUSS

With sensitivity and humor, Judy Blume has captured the joys, fears and uncertainty that surround a young girl approaching adolescence [in "Are You There, God? It's Me, Margaret"]. Margaret Simon, almost 12, frequently chats with God, relaying all her problems concerning puberty and religion (she is the only child of non-religious, mixed-marriage parents). Margaret's story is any young girl's story, but when Judy Blume writes it there is an exception—it is directed toward each reader individually. (pp. 62-3)

> *Lavinia Russ, in* Publishers Weekly (*reprinted from the January 11, 1971, issue of* Publishers Weekly *by permission of the critic, published by R. R. Bowker Company, a Xerox company; copyright © 1971 by Xerox Corporation), January 11, 1971.*

JOHN W. CONNER

Karen Newman in *It's not the end of the world* suspects the worst when her father is absent from home for two days without explanation, but Karen's mother does not tell Karen and her brother and sister that a divorce is pending until they are having Sunday lunch in a restaurant with Mrs. Newman's sister and her husband. Stunned by the announcement, Karen resents her mother's failure to explain her father's absence earlier and the public place her mother chose to make the announcement. Karen's world disintegrates. . . .

Karen resists the divorce, hoping she can bring her parents together again preserving the family unit Karen loves. Karen's brother Jeff seemingly accepts the pending divorce but it is he who forestalls it by running away from home just before Karen's father is expected to go to Las Vegas to gain his freedom. *It's not the end of the world* explores the deep anxieties adolescents feel when their home structure is uprooted. . . .

[Judy Blume] does not try to solve Karen's problem, only present the aching uncertainty which Karen, and girls like her, suffer when their parents part. (p. 936)

> *John W. Conner, in* English Journal (*copyright © 1972 by the National Council of Teachers of English), September, 1972.*

ZENA SUTHERLAND

Katherine had liked Michael when they met at a party, she was delighted when he asked for a date, and she knew it was only a question of time until they became lovers. . . . They are deeply in love, wholly committed. Forever. And then, due to parental insistence, Kath goes to work in a summer camp and finds she is attracted to another man. And that's it—the end of forever. No preaching (Blume never does) but the message [of *Forever . . .*] is clear; no hedging (Blume never does) but a candid account by Kath gives intimate details of a first sexual relationship. The characters and dialogue are equally natural and vigorous, the language uncensored, the depiction of family relationships outstanding. (p. 106)

> *Zena Sutherland, in* Bulletin of the Center for Children's Books (© *1976 by the University of Chicago; all rights reserved), March, 1976.*

ALLEEN PACE NILSEN

[*Forever . . .*] may be just the book to replace the now

dated *Seventeenth Summer* even though it is officially coming out as an "adult" book. . . . Once the thousands of girls who grew to love Judy Blume when she led them through their first menstrual periods with *Are You There God? It's Me, Margaret* find that she is now offering to lead them through their first experiences with sexual intercourse, they will seek out the book regardless of whether or not we have it at school—which in this day of book banning and censorship struggles is unlikely.

One of the reasons that as an adult book about young love, *Forever* stands out in vivid contrast to the adult movies about young love is that if adults do read it, it will be adult women—not men. Instead of erring (or perhaps *leaning* is a better word) on the side of pornography, it errs on the side of romance. The boy and the whole affair is almost too perfect.

For three semesters I've used Blume's *Are You There God?* . . . in my "Children's Literature for Parents" class. The mothers love the book and nostalgically chuckle over Margaret's consternation about her first period. Then inevitably they begin to wish their own first period had been as one woman put it, so "satisfying." I suspect female readers will have a similar response to *Forever.* Those who have already experienced their first love will inevitably compare. In my generation nice girls clung doggedly to their virginity and our reactions are apt to be tinged with regret, i.e. we missed out on something truly beautiful. Girls still looking forward to their first love will revel in anticipation, though in real life it is highly unlikely that many of them will have a similar experience. (p. 90)

Alleen Pace Nilsen, in English Journal *(copyright © 1976 by the National Council of Teachers of English), March, 1976.*

PELORUS

How the world turns. Twenty years exactly after Beverly Cleary's *Fifteen* . . . was first published, in which it took Our Hero 174 out of 175 pages to kiss Our Heroine, appears *Forever* . . . by Judy Blume . . . in which the first kiss is accomplished on page 3. By page 20 they're discussing virginity ("No boy had ever come right out and asked me . . ."), and by page 25 the groping has begun.

In fact, this story is about first-time intercourse, explicitly described, just as *Fifteen* was about a first, explicitly described, date. That's the change. Otherwise things haven't altered too much. Judy Blume's style has colloquial ease, humour and just enough romantic patina to give the everyday . . . a semblance of the desirable.

Certainly it is good to have sex written about without the embarrassment and pertness we've been used to in books for young people. But until there have been a number of *Forever*s I doubt that it will be possible to have a story in which the sex act is just one element in something more complex. I rather think we're still at the stage where the relevant pages will get thumb-marked from overly specific reading. (p. 149)

Pelorus, in Signal *(copyright © 1976 Pelorus; reprinted by permission of the author and The Thimble Press, Lockwood Station Road, South Woodchester, Glos. GL5 5EQ, England), September, 1976.*

NICHOLAS TUCKER

[*Forever* . . .] is a story as told by the adolescent heroine,

about an affair with another seventeen-year-old that germinates, burgeons and finally goes to seed. As a narrative technique, talking straight from the adolescent's mouth can also act as camouflage for slack writing, not entirely avoided here. Although it may be in character for the narrator to rhapsodize about eyes that are "very dark, with just a rim of green and other times they sparkle and are greenish-gray all over", it is still no less tedious to read. So if the author does manage to catch the almost inexorable egotism of some adolescents at this age, it is at the cost of producing a dull novel about two very dull young people, told in prose of the same soggy consistency as the used tissues that play such an important part in the couple's post-amatory techniques.

But it is just in this area, perhaps, that the book either justifies itself or not; if it is sex that is wanted, there is plenty of it here. . . . Yet even as a fictionalized sex manual, *Forever* is nowhere near as explicit as other material available for everyone today, nor is it as erotic as, for example, that "jolly little story" *Fanny Hill.* In fact, it is not erotic at all: its protagonists couple and separate like two well-lubricated automata, and if this novel is remarkable for anything, it is in its ability to trivialize sex, something that so far no puritan has ever managed to, perhaps even intended to do. There is an absence of poetry or passion about this couple; an emotional impotence in the midst of perfect physical health. (p. 1238)

Nicholas Tucker, in The Times Literary Supplement *(© Times Newspapers Ltd. (London) 1976; reproduced from* The Times Literary Supplement *by permission), October 1, 1976.*

ANNE REDMON

Sex, for all its sometimes gruesome oughts and shouldn'ts, never deserved *Forever* . . . . Judy Blume takes more than just a peek at Kath and Michael making it in Summit, NJ. From first base all the way to home, we get the blow by blow. Kath loses her virginity with one qualm—she doesn't have an orgasm. 'Maybe it was the rubber,' Michael says. Maybe it was. Anyhow, they work it out (they love each other, don't they?): but satisfaction leaves tristesse and Mom and Dad think marriage is appalling at 18. Wasn't she lucky she was careful? Isn't it great they were both so well adjusted? Their friend Artie, a closet queer, tries suicide when vamped beyond endurance by raunchy Erica. That's good too: 'Now at least, Artie will get the kind of professional help he's needed all along.' Kath bops off with another guy, a better candidate for the deep relationship than sniffling Mike, who's taught her two positions —and love. (p. 644)

Anne Redmon, in New Statesman *(© 1976 The Statesman & Nation Publishing Co. Ltd.), November 5, 1976.*

DOROTHY NIMMO

[*Forever* . . .] is a very explicit account of a teenage love-affair written in the style of a magazine story, peppered with the three dots that used to be left for the imagination to fill in although in this case nothing whatever is left to the imagination. . . . All the right messages are put over, about responsibility and birth-control and not having abortions and illegitimate babies, but all the same I think it is pornography and so a limiting rather than a widening of experience. It suggests patterns, it imposes expectations. (p. 335)

> Dorothy Nimmo, in The School Librarian, December, 1976.

Maintaining a strictly neutral moral tone, unless acceptance is synonymous with approval, this story of young love [*Forever* . . .] is surely the frankest exposition we have yet had from America. True, it is "a novel for young adults" and the protagonists are in their later teens, but it will without doubt be pored over (or pawed over) by younger readers. . . .

Judy Blume's aim is serious and responsible enough and her revelation of young love is probably typical of many relationships today. . . . But, however sympathetic towards adolescent problems Judy Blume is, I am left wondering how *Forever* . . . will really help its readers. The young tend to follow the life-style of their peers: will Katherine and Michael's affair help to impose yet another imprimatur on casual sex? It may well minimise a sense of guilt but will it encourage the need for firm and satisfying relationships? Perhaps the final irony is in the title of the book itself. . . . (p. 49)

> The Junior Bookshelf, *February, 1977.*

DIANE HAAS

There is little plot and even less point to [*Starring Sally J. Freedman as Herself*]; the writing lacks the wit and insight of her earlier books, and the rare moments of humor are aimed at adults. Sally's obsession with Hitler, while certainly plausible and understandable, does not fit smoothly into the context of the book, and is often unnecessarily violent in its expression. For example, one of Sally's daydreams goes as follows, "Hitler . . . gets his knife and slowly slashes each of her fingers . . . her blood drips onto his rug . . . 'Look what you've done, you Jew bastard,' Hitler cries hysterically. 'You've ruined my rug!'" It seems almost painfully obvious that this is autobiographical, but in exorcising the demons of her youth, Blume is ignoring her eager audience and forgetting what she does best. (p. 59)

> Diane Haas, in School Library Journal (reprinted from the May, 1977 issue of School Library Journal, published by R. R. Bowker Co., A Xerox Corporation; copyright © 1977), May, 1977.

JULIA WHEDON

[Witnessing the awkward, then tender, reunions of her parents in "Starring Sally J. Freedman as Herself," Sally] feels the impact of their need for one another without fully understanding what it means. It's a reminder to all of us that there's a time when children know the facts of life without understanding them. Beyond that, the book is largely a chronicle of Sally's adjustment to a new life, of wishes and nervousness and fun, and the author's memories of the 1940's.

Interestingly, Mrs. Blume herself has become a much discussed subject of the sub-teen culture she writes about. Kids read her books with a blushing curiosity once reserved for certain words in the dictionary, parts of the Bible and naughty passages in Hemingway. They know they will find some frank discussion of prurient matters like breasts and menstruation. Some of her readers may also have read

[Erica Jong's] "Fear of Flying," yet they reread "Are You There God? It's Me, Margaret." It's evident her appeal goes beyond sexual frankness: She must be conveying a certain emotional reality that children recognize as true. Portnoy may complain all he wants, but kids will go right on needing reassurance that there is a time of slow awakening, of normal curiosity and confusion about what they are learning and feeling. And this is soft at the core, not hard.

While Mrs. Blume's book is teeming with social value, its redeeming literary qualities are less conspicuous. Her characters are so recognizable they don't matter. She describes the 40's in a banal shorthand that misses a good chance to describe what it was really like growing up then. Just as my generation thinks of the 20's as bathtub gin and Clara Bow, I worry that the next generation can be bought off with Margaret O'Brien and Murphy beds.

> Julia Whedon, "The Forties Revisited," in The New York Times Book Review (© 1977 by The New York Times Company; reprinted by permission), May 1, 1977, p. 40.

BRIGITTE WEEKS

A huge, unquestioning audience awaits any book by the author of *Are You There God? It's Me, Margaret*. But even Judy Blume's young teenage fans may find [*Starring Sally J. Freedman as Herself*] hard going in places. Blume still captures the anxieties and dreams of her heroines, but an uneventful winter in Florida for a 10-year-old from New Jersey fails to bring Sally close to the reader. The year is 1947, and Sally's preoccupation with Hitler's atrocities among the Jews (including some of her own relations) is a potentially important theme, but it is trivialized by poor taste and unnecessarily ghoulish fantasies. To further weaken the novel, Sally's own Jewish family is surprisingly stereotyped. *Sally Freedman* is described as autobiographical, which may account for its rambling attention to trivia and its inconsequential plot. The resulting novel is too long and too slow-moving for the age group and certainly lacks the sympathetic spark of *Margaret*. (p. F4)

> Brigitte Weeks, in Book World—The Washington Post (© 1977, The Washington Post), August 14, 1977.

ANN EVANS

Are You There, God? It's Me, Margaret . . . is about menstruation and religion, in that order. Margaret Simon, aged twelve, has two crushing anxieties on her young shoulders: when will she begin to menstruate? and in which church will she, born of Jewish father and Christian mother, find the official seat of the God she chats to so cosily in moments of stress? The story is inconsequential. The book consists largely of the endless body-obsessed prattle of Margaret and her friends, and as such will prove irresistible to readers of her age. Alas, the generation gap yawns wide. The adult reader quickly becomes satiated, to the point of nausea, and is left with the sad conviction that here is a book of scant worth. Its candour overreaches itself and Margaret's private talks with God are insufferably selfconscious and arch. Much of this could be forgiven if it were funny, but the odd incident apart, it is not. (p. 383)

> Ann Evans, in The Times Literary Supplement (© Times Newspapers Ltd. (London) 1978; reproduced from The Times Literary Supplement by permission), April 7, 1978.

MARGERY FISHER

Are American children exceptionally articulate about their problems, I wonder? I find it hard to imagine a group of small girls here anxiously discussing a longed-for puberty in the way the heroine of *Are you there, God? It's me, Margaret* does, though the author assures us that she is recalling her own pre-'teen emotions. At all events, this comedy depends on the discussion which Margaret, who is rising twelve, holds with the rest of her gang about menstruation and chest measurement and (in the same breath) about religious faith.... One or two scenes provoke at least a smile—notably, the scene at Norman Fishbein's party where a handsome schoolmate, idol of the little girls, forgets his manners; but for many tastes the book may seem cute and sentimental. (p. 3325)

> *Margery Fisher, in her* Growing Point, *May, 1978.*

GEORGE W. ARTHUR

Margaret is 12 years old and has just moved with her parents from New York to Farbrook, New Jersey. She soon makes friends with three other girls and they call themselves 'the four PTS's' (Pre-Teen Sensations). They share secrets, gossip on the phone for ages, and worry about acquiring busts, boyfriends, bras and their periods.... Basically, [*Are You There, God? It's Me, Margaret*] is a very funny book with plenty of incidents to keep a girl, and only a girl, reader of 11 or 12 amused—such as how you actually kiss a boy once you have him alone.... However, there are features of the book which are over-stressed and detract from the author's easy handling of most of the topics she covers. I refer to the excessive, almost obsessive, concern with a girl's period. Perhaps the physical details given could have fitted into the structure of the novel naturally, but when the author rhapsodises about the wearing of a sanitary napkin, the effect is banal in the extreme, and disbelief is total. Suddenly a sensitive, amusing novel has been reduced to the level of some of the advertising blurb in the 'confidential' section of a teenage magazine. You can carry didacticism much too far. This is the only novel by Judy Blume I have read so far, but I certainly want to read more, if only to find out whether she gets the balance right in them. (p. 22)

> *George W. Arthur, in* Book Window (© *1978 S.C.B.A. and contributors), Summer 1978.*

R. A. SIEGAL

One hesitates to speculate on what the theme of the next book for the pre-adolescent market will be for a writer whose muse seems to be Haim Ginott rather than Calliope. One can be assured, however, that it will mirror what people have been talking about lately in Darien and Short Hills and San Fernando, that it will be rendered with a cheerful, reassuring suburban sameness, and that it will have the same relationship to a truly significant exploration of social problems that a Stanley Kramer film does.

It's no secret that kids like Blume books ... but it's doubtful that the novelty of her themes alone is responsible for her popularity. After all, this kind of "realism" has become the cliched substance of Norman Lear situation comedies, and Judy Blume's books are really old-fashioned by comparision with, say, Norma Klein. In spite of the many, tiresome allusions to Bloomingdale's, these are not really trendy books and the values they promote are very much those of mainstream, Middle America.

Nor does it seem that Blume's books, or any other "problem" novels, ought to be discussed and evaluated on the basis of what they teach children about handling specific social or personal problems.... Their success depends on the author's handling of narrative techniques and their meaning and educative value is embedded in those same techniques. To discover the key to Blume's popularity, one has to look beyond the realistic trappings and didactic intentions of the "problem" book to a closer study of why her narrative techniques work especially well with children. To understand what her books really teach children, one has to understand the way in which these techniques are used to communicate a style of experiencing and perceiving the self and the world and a definition of what it means to be a pre-adolescent child in suburban America.

As is often the case with popular fiction, Blume's books are successful for what they *are not* as much as for what *they are*. That is, her books are not very demanding and they make for the kind of easy, rapid reading that children like to relax with. Since all her books are told through the voice of a child narrator, the vocabulary is necessarily limited and the sentence construction basic and repetitive.

Her plots are loose and episodic: they accumulate rather than develop. They are not complicated or demanding and the pace is sometimes sloppy, as in *Blubber*, where Jill's change of heart seems too sudden and contrived. She has a repertoire of stock minor characters—the annoying older or younger sibling, the steadfast friend—who can be counted on as plot machinery or for comic effects. In the tradition of children's books, parents are kept harmlessly out of the way. And in the vein of recent American children's books, these parents are usually well-meaning but ineffectual characters whose efforts at communication are often comic failures.

On the other hand, Judy Blume is a careful observer of the everyday details of children's lives and she has a feel for the little power struggles and shifting alliances of their social relationships. She knows that children can be cruel to one another and that they are deeply concerned with peer group judgments. She can be funny in a broad, slapstick way, as in *Tales of a Fourth Grade Nothing*, but her humor is more often based on regarding her characters with cloying adult irony. (pp. 72-3)

Blume's most characteristic technique and the key to her success is the first-person narrative: through this technique she succeeds in establishing intimacy and identification between character and audience. All her books read like diaries or journals and the reader is drawn in by the narrator's self-revelations. Creating the illusion that one is having an intimate conversation with a close friend, the first-person narrative succeeds especially in children's books because children enter so readily into a partnership with fictional narrators and because they tend to experience books as extensions of other types of personal relationships. (p. 74)

What strikes one immediately about Blume's narrators is the sameness of voice.... Essentially the same voice speaks to the reader in *Deenie* and *Margaret*, in all of Blume's books, in fact, and the effect of this sameness on the child reader is probably reassuring, like discovering an old friend in a new neighborhood.

Blume's choice of first person narrative and her didactic intentions make it imperative that her characters be perceptive and self-conscious and that they continually draw conclusions from their experience. . . . Blume's narrators are always cogitating, earnestly trying to be honest to their own feelings and to discover meaning and truth in the world: one has the sense that they will grow up to be characters in a John Fowles novel.

None of this can be taken very seriously as an accurate description of the mental processes of pre-adolescent children: kids of this age are beginning to become self-aware but this is too formulated, too pat, and thought crystallizes too readily into truism to be convincing. What seems important to note here, however, is that self-consciousness is offered as a model for children to identify with and that self-awareness and the awareness of other people's feelings are presented as goals in themselves.

Self-consciousness and self-awareness, however, can turn rapidly into self-absorption. Blume's books are remarkable in the number of narcissistic incidents they portray: Margaret examining herself in a mirror, Tony's masturbation, and so on. The pattern of such incidents suggests that they are fundamental to Blume's conception of the pre-adolescent child's nature.

One of the disturbing results of this preoccupation with the self is the loss of tangible intimacy with any concrete thing or object: the texture of lives lived in a specific, particular place is missing. Although the geography of the world of Blume's books is rather limited—Jersey City, Radnor, the urban or suburban Northeast—these places exist only as proper nouns, generalized abstractions. For all the reader knows about the sights and sounds and smells of these places, they might as well be Omaha or Anaheim. To put it another way, Blume makes Any Place into No Place, a talent which should not be confused with that of, say, E. B. White, who can turn Any Place into Every Place, an idealized but vividly realized setting. (pp. 74-6)

In the end . . . Judy Blume's books are impoverished because she fails to establish a vital relationship between place and character. She creates no place for her characters to inhabit except the self, and more importantly, no world for her readers to live in. Things are not encountered by her characters; they are understood through intellection and rationalization.

In traditional children's literature, characters went out into the world, encountered it on non-subjective terms, and came to self-awareness in situations and through social actions which were meaningful in themselves. In Blume's novels, the quest turns inward, self-awareness becomes a goal and not a product, and actions are valuable only in so far as they authenticate the feelings of the narrators. This may be good training for life in narcissistic, self-absorbed, suburban America but, in the long run, it is poor nourishment for the imagination of children. (p. 76)

R. A. Siegal, "Are You There, God? It's Me, Me, Me!: Judy Blume's Self-Absorbed Narrators," in The Lion and the Unicorn *(copyright © 1978 The Lion and the Unicorn),* Fall, 1978, pp. 72-7.

Frank Bonham

1914-

American novelist, short story writer, nonfiction writer, and screenwriter. Most of Bonham's young adult novels are concerned with minority youths and the problems they face. His books, which examine the lives of young blacks, Chicanos, Indians, and Japanese-Americans, are realistic accounts of modern life based on first-hand observation and his experiences in volunteer social work. In Dogtown, the prototypical West Coast ghetto that recurs in his work, Bonham has mapped out an area that is as well defined and intimately known as Faulkner's Yoknapatawpha County. Bonham's work is insightful and compassionate, but he doesn't mouth platitudes or depict the harsh lives of his characters simply to elicit sympathy. Rather, he writes directly for underprivileged young adults, trying to involve them in literature by depicting life as they know it. As he says, "*Durango Street* was probably welcomed, not because it was an exceptional book, but because it filled a need. It is a book in which many Negro teenagers can see themselves." This concern for his reader is evident in all of his work, from the tough realism of *Durango Street* to his later, more fanciful books such as *The Missing Persons League*. (See also *Contemporary Authors*, Vols. 9-12, rev. ed., and *Something about the Author*, Vol. 1.)

When Rufus Henry was released on parole from the reformatory, his social case worker found him a job and told him that he must not join a gang. Within two days Negro Rufus left his job and became a member of the Moors. . . . As the Moors, who shortly came under Rufus' leadership, slug it out with the [rival gang, the] Gassers, the author tastefully but honestly makes it clear just how dangerous these battles are [in *Durango Street*]. While the organization of gangs is undoubtedly more complex than the all-important matter of life or death, the frank recognition of this factor and of how serious life is for the teenager make this book welcome. Although it is with Rufus and his associates that readers will sympathize, the book is actually supposed to be about Special Service for Groups, an organization which sends group leaders to try to reorient gangs and eventually break them up. The S.S.G. representative who managed to attach himself to the Moors is a shadowy sort of person, and it is never quite clear why Rufus respects him more than the other social workers. His success is somewhat ephemeral (as presumably is often the case in reality), and the book ends with one problem cooperatively and successfully surmounted but with the future still unknown. This is a forth-right presentation of a social problem which teenagers want and deserve to know more about. (p. 689)

Virginia Kirkus' Service, *July 15, 1965.*

JAMES McBRIDE

Projected in a style far closer to screen documentary than conventional narrative, "Durango Street" describes a summer in the life of Rufus Henry. . . .

Mr. Bonham's opening chapters are by far his best. . . . [The] author creates a macabre montage that compels belief. Durango Street could be any sink of misery in any American city. The fact that Mr. Bonham has done his research in Los Angeles gives his book an added relevance.

Unfortunately, when this documentary runs out of camera angles, the author—as an honest reporter—has nowhere else to go. A youth counselor takes over, with highly doubtful results. A Negro pro football star appears as a totally unconvincing peacemaker. Rufus's halfhearted decision to go back to school is only a device to ring down the curtain. One closes this disturbing book with all the sensations of a tourist who has just been down nightmare alley in a prowl car—only to be whisked out again, at the moment when Rufus, like his doomed supporting cast, was about to assume a third dimension. Since Mr. Bonham was on the outside looking in, it is perhaps unrealistic to ask for more. (p. 20)

James McBride, in The New York Times Book Review (© *1965 by The New York Times Company; reprinted by permission), September 5, 1965.*

ZENA SUTHERLAND

[*Durango Street* is a] candid and powerful novel about teen-age gangs and the tortuous protocol of intramural gang fights. . . . The boys are neither overdrawn nor sugarcoated; the attitudes of parents, neighbors, and police are utterly convincing. Although most of the characters are Negro, this is not a story about Negroes, but a story about the breeding grounds of delinquency. (p. 27)

Zena Sutherland, in Bulletin of the Center for Children's Books (*copyright 1965 by the University of Chicago; all rights reserved), October, 1965.*

ZENA SUTHERLAND

[*Mystery in Little Tokyo* is a] rather good middle-grades mystery story despite the somewhat contrived plot. The story is set in the Japanese section of Los Angeles, where Dan and Carol are visiting their grandparents. Danny . . . helps solve the mystery of the [disappearance of his grandfather's samurai sword] . . . and also helps end the feud between his grandfather and an elderly neighbor who had once been a good friend. The writing style is adequate, the characters are well-drawn, and the setting is very nicely developed; the author draws Little Tokyo as a solid neighborhood community with a rich tradition. (p. 70)

> *Zena Sutherland, in* Bulletin of the Center for Children's Books *(copyright 1967 by the University of Chicago; all rights reserved), January, 1967.*

Twins Tom and Andy Croft, who volunteered together, are separated by a snafu in England; [*The Ghost Front*] follows them through Germany and Belgium during the Battle of the Bulge. Each comes to despise the military realities as, fresh from training . . . , they face the enemy . . . and look into themselves. The nitty-gritty of army life is bared while the movement of each boy is related . . . , and the modified realism (e.g. the language goes beyond "heck," but not often) makes sense: the soldiers sweat and retch, bleed and desert, but not in excessive detail. Battalions have varied compositions without the usual one-man/one-creed constituencies, but the problems of cultural clash do not arise; neither is there any questioning of war itself. Finally, there's the personal adjustment to separation from the other self: Andy must learn to think for himself, Tom to move without pushing another, even gently. The dual vision works effectively. . . . (p. 12)

> Kirkus Service *(copyright © 1968 Virginia Kirkus' Service, Inc.), January 1, 1968.*

LEORA OGLESBY

[*The Ghost Front* is a] realistic novel, which might well appeal to reluctant readers all the way up to senior high, about the 106th Infantry Division. . . . The grim brutality of war is amply demonstrated as Mr. Bonham shows its effects on the 18-year-old twins Andy and Tom Croft. . . . As they change from innocent youths to gaunt, bearded, mud-soaked men, the chaos and senselessness of much that happens in war is vividly conveyed. (p. 88)

> *Leora Oglesby, in* School Library Journal *(reprinted from the February, 1968 issue of* School Library Journal, *published by R. R. Bowker Co. A Xerox Corporation; copyright © 1968), February, 1968.*

NANCY W. FABER

["The Ghost Front"] is furnished with the ritual trappings of the [war story] genre, from the tough-talking Sarge to the melting-pot platoon roster. Times have changed to the point where it is implied that soldiers have occasion to swear. Many characters are introduced only to die unpleasant deaths, without heroics. There are even some bum officers. More important, the enemy is given his due; usually faceless, he is nonetheless competent and not the sauerkraut-stuffed clown so humorously depicted on TV these days. (p. 20)

> *Nancy W. Faber, in* The New York Times Book Review *(© 1968 by The New York Times Company; reprinted by permission), April 14, 1968.*

PAUL HEINS

It is not often that mystery and urban social problems are brought together [as they are in *Mystery of the Fat Cat*]. . . . Surprisingly, the mystery is solved by Buddy's mentally retarded brother Ralphie. [Bonham] has blended characters and plot so well that the reader thinks only incidentally of the boys as Negroes, although a powerful contrast is developed in the persons of Mr. Hannibal, the Boys Club director, who looks like an African delegate to the U.N.; and Shriker, the scheming Negro chauffeur. . . . A simple but uncondescending style and a judicious use of colloquialisms give immediacy to the problems of the underprivileged without undermining the basic plot. (pp. 426-27)

> *Paul Heins, in* The Horn Book Magazine *(copyright © 1968 by The Horn Book, Inc., Boston), August, 1968.*

JANE MANTHORNE

Only gradually does [Bonham in "Mystery of the Fat Cat" paint his] characters brown or the color of dark rosewood, revealing them as blacks or "beans" (Mexican-Americans). They emerge as realistic guys of the ghetto, ready in their boredom to shoot out street lights or roll winos. Their humor, a jaunty cynicism born of poverty, rings true: the cockroaches, they claim, stand in line at the snack bar; the rats are so fierce that they storm the gym wearing green berets. Particularly in his handling of encounters between citizens and cops and of alert boys with a mentally retarded youngster, Bonham shows slum people the way they are, with honest pragmatism and tough vitality. (p. 24)

> *Jane Manthorne, in* The New York Times Book Review *(© 1968 by The New York Times Company; reprinted by permission), August 25, 1968.*

ZENA SUTHERLAND

[The characters'] unraveling of the mystery [in *Mystery of the Fat Cat*] is believable and exciting. The characters are lively, the dialogue natural, and the inclusion of a backward child as a sympathetic—and contributing—character adds to the book's appeal. (p. 23)

> *Zena Sutherland, in* Bulletin of the Center for Children's Books *(copyright 1968 by The University of Chicago; all rights reserved), October, 1968.*

ED MARCINIAK

[Bonham] has again mapped an adventurous trail through the nitty-gritty world of a Negro teenager living in "Dogtown," a poor, big-city neighborhood.

Following that trail is Charlie Matthews, a near-dropout from high school, seeking directions to his future vocation. . . .

The Nitty Gritty follows his career struggle through a series of offbeat adventures which includes a boxing match in an oil-slicked ring, a raid into a rocky ravine for sackfuls of ladybugs, and an illegally sponsored cock fight. Breathing Man, a sedentary wizard who exchanges advice for hot dogs; Cowboy, leader of a rat pack, and the other characters who plop into Charlie's life are as real and tough as those whose names land on a police blotter.

Youngsters will not be the only ones charmed by Charlie

and his Dogtown friends. Oldsters, especially those who deal with young boys, will appreciate Bonham's professional insight into juvenile psychology. While Charlie is burdened by some special hang-ups as a Negro, readers will also recognize that his are the growing pains of every high school youth. (p. 20)

> *Ed Marciniak, in* Book World—Chicago Tribune, *Part I (© 1968 Postrib Corp.), November 3, 1968.*

JOHN GILLESPIE

In [*The Nitty Gritty,* Bonham] returns to Dogtown, a Negro ghetto that was [also] the locale of . . . *Mystery of the Fat Cat.* In a more serious vein than [that] book, Bonham tells of 17-year-old Charlie Matthews, who decides to escape his life of poverty by running away with itinerant, fast-talking Uncle Baron, whom Charlie hero-worships. . . . The plot is suspenseful, and the characters are well drawn. There are many amusing incidents, though the generally somber tone and serious confrontation with adult failure make this a novel of more limited appeal . . . than *Mystery of the Fat Cat.* . . . (pp. 64-5)

> *John Gillespie, in* School Library Journal *(reprinted from the January, 1969 issue of* School Library Journal, *published by R. R. Bowker Co. A Xerox Corporation; copyright © 1969), January, 1969.*

JANE MANTHORNE

For Charlie Matthews of "The Nitty Gritty" the only way to be somebody is to get out of Dogtown. He decides to "buy in" with flashy, fast-talking Uncle Baron and take to the road, following the racing season from track to track. Charlie has really "gotta hustle" to get enough cash. His get-rich-quick schemes include dump picking, ladybug hunting, boxing and a final violent, blood-spattered scene unique in children's literature. . . .

Faithful to the argot and atmosphere of the city, ["The Nitty Gritty" is a hard-hitting story] of ghetto people, some still striving for something better, some surrendering to poverty. . . . "The Nitty Gritty" is played out in a . . . casual, light-hearted mood. Parents drink their beer and send their truant kids off to make a few pennies at the shoeshine parlor. (p. 28)

> *Jane Manthorne, in* The New York Times Book Review *(© 1969 by The New York Times Company; reprinted by permission), January 19, 1969.*

ZENA SUTHERLAND

[When] his father disappeared [in *The Vagabundos*], Eric Hansen was deeply disturbed and determined to follow the slim lead he had. . . . For a thousand miles he trails his father by wheel, boat, and foot; living the simple life of the Baja fishermen, the *vagabundos,* Eric finds a satisfaction and maturity he was never able to achieve in the luxurious atmosphere of a wealthy home. By the time he locates his father, he understands why Mr. Hansen has decided to stay on the peninsula and run a business. The contrast between the rigidity of the home setting and the freedom of the *vagabundos'* life is sharply effective, and, brightened by the striking people Eric meets, the book has the urgent mood of a perilous voyage. (p. 59)

> *Zena Sutherland, in* Saturday Review *(© 1969 by Saturday Review, Inc.; reprinted with permission), August 16, 1969.*

JAMES FORMAN

Mr. Bonham lavishes too much attention on [the] psychiatric first chapters [of "The Vagabundos"]. Once over them, the reader can almost hear the author sigh with relief as he enters a land he knows and loves—Mexico. Adventures involving the natives, pirate gold, dug-out canoes, sharks and a lovely blonde enliven the tour south. When the pursuit ends, both Erics have found themselves. . . .

The characters are adequate to carry a busy, offbeat story. What matters is Baja California, its flora, fauna and its people. The author makes one want to go there, splash about and become a *vagabundo del mar.* (p. 34)

> *James Forman, in* The New York Times Book Review *(© 1969 by The New York Times Company; reprinted by permission), September 7, 1969.*

ZENA SUTHERLAND

Keeny was on parole, wanting to make it this time but driven by the ceaseless nagging at home, the latest stepfather (an Anglo!), the ugly squalor of the housing project, the pressure from other Chicanos. . . . [*Viva Chicano*] is powerful and almost depressing, its only weakness the long-sustained situation in which Keeny (and a girl) reverently cling to a cardboard display dummy, stolen from a theater, of the Mexican hero Zapata—which talks to them. It is not explained fully: the voice of conscience? (but the gang of boys hear it) drug-induced hallucination? schizophrenia? The parole officer offers the theory that it is "the dark side of your mind," that the many facts that the voice knows are facts that Keeny's father had told him years ago. (p. 55)

> *Zena Sutherland, in* Bulletin of the Center for Children's Books *(© 1970 by the University of Chicago; all rights reserved), December, 1970.*

DIANE GERSONI STAVN

[Frank Bonham is guilty of] misleading use of words and minimal objectivity [in his treatment of women]. In Bonham's 1956 title, *The Loud, Resounding Sea,* the most admirable female character is Delphine the Dolphin, with whom the young hero, Skip Turner, enjoys a marvelous rapport based on mutual trust, affection and respect. Skip's attitude toward pretty, blonde Leslie, with whom he works in a lab during the summer, is a lot less flattering: "Like most girls, she was about as practical as a chicken-wire fishbowl." Bonham does a fair enough job with Skip's mother; she's a hard-working schoolteacher, and the mainstay of her family because her husband, a skilled cook and restaurateur, has advanced wanderlust and is rarely at home. Mr. Turner himself is a basically amiable character, yet Skip does express resentment at the burden he puts on Mrs. Turner. In the end, it's stated that the itinerant chef will undertake a steady business right near home. He tells Skip: "'I need a woman to tell my plans and troubles to. What man doesn't? An understanding wife to help him into his cardboard armor in the morning, and put back together at night.'" Very true. How about a woman's right to the same kind of support? Bonham doesn't negate it here, but silence is *not* always affirmative.

In the didactic *The Vagabundos,* his sympathy for roving dads becomes an adulatory obsession, and mom becomes a drag, on both husband and son. Eric Hansen pursues his father to Baja when the retired, wealthy, middle-aged—and bored—Southern Californian, who is believed to have a heart condition, leaves his family behind and sets out to do his thing—whatever that may be. . . . [Later] "Eric . . . suddenly perceived that the whole Ranch Sereno game—parties, clubs, feuds, hobbies—was a sort of complex machine designed and manufactured by women—but very inexpertly—so that it took all the time of every man on the Ranch to keep it from flying apart . . . He fantasied the reunion with his father on the beach . . . No drying stockings, hair curlers, and other woman-stuff for a while. Just camping, skindiving, living in the sun." It is never acknowledged that a major part of the Ranch Sereno game was invented by men; that since success in business leads to power, men seeking such power will organize parties, clubs, etc. to make business contacts. As for the beach-side activities, women have been known to indulge happily in camping and such.

Dr. Nestor, [a] "wise" character whom Eric encounters while tracking down Dad, says: "'Just because a man's always been a house-cat type doesn't mean there isn't a little wildcat blood left in him. And if that kind of blood is kept bottled up forever, it curdles in the brain . . . Do you want to know what's the matter? Women in the States, especially in areas like yours, have forgotten how to be women; but they haven't yet learned how to be men. They've turned into harpies, and their men into zombies. God, it's pitiful!'" It's pitiful indeed that all women be held responsible for the lack of integrity and purpose in some men. Eric himself really doesn't need much encouragement in male chauvinist ideas: "He knew that in Mexico a husband was a king; his behavior was not to be questioned by his family. In the abstract, the idea had appeal."

For a short time, Eric takes Dr. Nestor's daughter Polly, a big, beautiful blonde, along on his quest. Her father comments about her: "'Remember—she's a female, and full of tricks.'" Thinks Eric: "Men . . . liked to talk about women as though they had some sort of special malignant power, a witchlike ability to control men. But Polly was honest and open, a real sweet kid. Joanie [a girlfriend of sorts back home] had some of the witch in her, and would do mean things just to make you burn." However, though Polly is supposedly an unusually fine specimen of female, she later pulls all kinds of teasing tricks and says "'I'm a witch . . . I *was* being nasty . . . Girls just do those things, I guess. We're really not aware of doing them . . .'" Using girls to damn girls to boys is a remarkably low trick, and Mr. Bonham is at subterranean level here. He has Eric agree with Polly: "'Even old girls like my mother. If she hadn't torpedoed my father's idea to buy a garage, he might not have taken off.'"

Later, a "wise" Mexican contributes his version of what the score is: "'The women should run some things. But not all . . . American women . . . They wear pants and shout like boys. Are they men or women? They don't seem to know, and the men don't know enough to tell them to shut up.'" Eric: "'That's it right there. [Polly] . . . began to think she should run the show. That's where I had to straighten her out. And after I got her straightened out she seemed happier.'"

Given all this, it is not unreasonable to wonder at Mr. Bonham's problems with American women. But it is certainly most reasonable to doubt the fairness of propagandizing young boys in this way. The jacket copy says about this book: ". . . it has some wise things to say about the role of men and women in each other's lives . . ." I think it has some revealing things to say about the antediluvian concepts and personal conflicts reeling around in Mr. Bonham's head. . . . (pp. 68-9)

Diane Gersoni Stavn, in School Library Journal *(reprinted from the January, 1971 issue of* School Library Journal, *published by R. R. Bowker Co. A Xerox Corporation; copyright © 1971), January, 1971.*

Dogtown has been Bonham's regular beat for a while now but [in *Cool Cat*] he strikes out: the story is shapeless, an agglomerate just like the West Coast ghetto, and it zigzags from one to another touchstone. . . . A self-conscious scenario wrought with a paucity of inspiration and a barrage of theatrical incidents . . . not to mention the toplofty verbiage whereby "Buddy saw everything through an opalescent haze of hope." (p. 179)

Kirkus Reviews *(copyright © 1971 The Kirkus Service, Inc.), February 15, 1971.*

PAMELA BRAGG

Frank Bonham's newest Dogtown story ["*Cool Cat*"] is a disappointment. Some familiar faces are back, along with some rather exaggerated new ones. Although the ghetto scene, with dope and pill-popping, is contemporary, the disjointed, shifting scenes are cumbersome and difficult to follow. (p. 53)

Pamela Bragg, in Publishers Weekly *(reprinted from the March 22, 1971, issue of* Publishers Weekly *by permission of the critic, published by R. R. Bowker Company, a Xerox company; copyright © 1971 by Xerox Corporation), March 22, 1971.*

ZENA SUTHERLAND

Some of the characters of *Mystery of the Fat Cat* appear again in [*Cool Cat,*] another story of ghetto youth: again, the acceptance by adolescents of a retarded child is one of the assets of the book, although a minor aspect. Several boys pool their money to buy an old truck so that they can do some hauling; they are persecuted by the Machete gang and reprisals follow. In and out of the action is the cool cat, Cal Brown, whose behavior has made the others suspicious. A pusher? But Cal turns out to be a narcotics agent, and he gets his man. There is no hint of this until the very end of the book, which—although it is well-written and grimly mirrors the ghetto scene—lacks direction or focus. (p. 152)

Zena Sutherland, in Bulletin of the Center for Children's Books *(© 1971 by the University of Chicago; all rights reserved), June, 1971.*

[The character] Chief has what it takes to keep [*Chief*] on its feet even when Bonham is not on his toes and starts to run away with it. . . . [Hereditary leader of a band of Santa Rosa Indians, he wants his lawyer to] make a case for Indian land rights in Harbor City. Barton Shackleford is as willing as he seems unable, being somewhat the worse for drink and the schizo-fantasy that he's Clarence Darrow defending Leopold and Loeb, but he claims that there is a loophole and offers to serve on a contingency basis so Chief figures they have nothing to lose. There's no reason why Chief couldn't have read the [legal] papers for himself and there's no call for a lot of the extravagances that follow: length-wise especially, Bonham stretches his basic design to the breaking point. But Chief is a sturdy rallying point and the fabric is intrinsically resilient enough to withstand the weight of all the embroidery; the dialogue is sharp —easygoing but resonant—and the problems and patterns of acculturation do emerge. (pp. 813-14)

> *Kirkus Reviews (copyright © 1971 The Kirkus Service, Inc.), August 1, 1971.*

FEENIE ZINER

To avoid [the dangers and pitfalls of ghetto life], Buddy needs exactly the right combination of suspicion and compassion, ambition and discretion. . . .

For the reader unfamiliar with the everyday problems of black urban youth, ["Cool Cat"] can be an eye-opener. Although it relies rather heavily on turns of plot for excitement, "Cool Cat" offers a guided tour through a section of the Other America most young readers know too little about. (p. 8)

> *Feenie Ziner, in* The New York Times Book Review *(© 1971 by The New York Times Company; reprinted by permission), August 8, 1971.*

DALLAS SHAFFER

The plot [of *Chief*], which includes a few improbable twists, essentially revolves around what happens when old treaties reveal that [an Indian] band owns a portion of the city where Chief lives. Despite the slangy language, lower-class milieu and rough characters, the lack of in-depth characterization makes this novel not much closer to reality than more conventional middle-class fare. But, like most of Bonham's other books . . . it's a fast-paced, smoothly written, lively read. (p. 120)

> *Dallas Shaffer, in* School Library Journal *(reprinted from the November, 1971 issue of* School Library Journal, *published by R. R. Bowker Co. A Xerox Corporation; copyright © 1971), November, 1971.*

[In *Hey, Big Spender* seventeen year old] Cool Hankins finds himself fronting for an old vagrant named Breathing Man who's inherited over half a million dollars and philanthropically assigned it all to what Cool dubiously calls a hard luck lottery. Cool is to be paid $100 a week to interview applicants at the Hope office, report each evening to the underground storm drain that is Breathing Man's summer home . . . and deliver . . . a suitable sum to the day's winner. But Cool becomes increasingly upset by the cases and the need to reject all but one each day; he's further discouraged when the hustlers and the nuts come to outnumber the "real heartbreakers." . . . Then Cool's aunt steps in and talks Breathing Man into setting up a chain of foster homes on the order of the one in which she herself has raised Cool and dozens of other abandoned waifs. In a way Aunt Josie's intervention is a relief for all, but it does make the whole enterprise even more of an essay, and the excitement that often turns Bonham's social service into fiction is not abundant here. Not a Dogtown event, then, but the characteristic light touch, nice people, and easy dialogue (which seems true without seeming to try) redeem. (p. 201)

> *Kirkus Reviews (copyright © 1972 The Kirkus Service, Inc.), February 15, 1972.*

JOHN W. CONNER

The same volatile active narrative which holds an adolescent reader's interest in *Durango Street* is apparent in *Chief*. Again the story concerns an adolescent who is oppressed by an adult society but who does not have direct recourse because his problem is not considered important by a strong segment of adult society.

Sixteen-year-old Henry Crowfoot [or Chief, as he is called by his friends,] is the hereditary chief of a small band of eighty-seven Indians, most of whom reside on a reservation high in the hills above Harbor City. . . . *Chief* is the story of the fight to regain [Indian property rights and the court-appointed] derelict lawyer's successful fight to regain confidence in himself.

The action is so swift and the narrative so fascinating that this reader was totally absorbed in *Chief*. Many of the minor characters are stereotypes, but they appear as such because Chief sees them as stereotypes. (p. 435)

Money and what lengths people will go to get it is a major theme in *Chief*. (p. 436)

> *John W. Conner, in* English Journal *(copyright 1972 by the National Council of Teachers of English), March, 1972.*

MAY HILL ARBUTHNOT and ZENA SUTHERLAND

Although *Durango Street* . . . has a black youth as its protagonist, it is less about black delinquents than it is about the slum neighborhood that breeds delinquency. Rufus is a paroled adolescent more suspicious of the social worker assigned to his case than he would be if Alex Robbins were white. While the patient, firm Robbins does have a realistically small effect on Rufus and his gang, the book is more interesting as a fictional study of gang behavior and protocol than as a story.

In *The Nitty Gritty* . . . , another black adolescent is torn between the indolent life of his favorite uncle and the benefits of continuing his education. Again, the story lacks impetus but in perceptive in interpretation of character and motivation, its candor lightened by moments of humor. (p. 466)

> *May Hill Arbuthnot and Zena Sutherland, in their* Children and Books *(copyright © 1947, 1957, 1964, 1972 by Scott, Foresman and Company; reprinted by permission), fourth edition, Scott, Foresman, 1972.*

ZENA SUTHERLAND

[In *The Friends of the Loony Lake Monster* the] fanciful and the realistic are nicely blended in a tale with good characterization and a briskly-paced plot; it's a deft story with an active heroine who should receive the Fem. Lib. seal of approval, and it is also a plea for conservation. (p. 71)

> *Zena Sutherland, in* Bulletin of the Center for Children's Books *(© 1973 by the University of Chicago; all rights reserved), January, 1973.*

HARRIET MORRISON

Bonham combines fantasy, mystery, and adventure in [*Hey, Big Spender,* which is] set in a present-day West coast ghetto. Black, teenaged Cool is aware of the drug abuse, racial prejudice, poverty, and crime which surround him, but he is above it. Living with Aunt Jo, he helps her maintain a ramshackle foster home where love is more abundant than food. Cool is also employed by enfeebled, seemingly penniless "Breathing Man" to help him give $650,000 to the needy. . . . Despite [a slow start, the story] picks up and concludes strongly. Unfortunately, the realities of present-day ghettoes makes it hard to swallow Bonham's romantic picture of life in them. (p. 74)

> *Harriet Morrison, in* School Library Journal *(reprinted from the January, 1973 issue of* School Library Journal, *published by R. R. Bowker Co. A Xerox Corporation; copyright © 1973), January, 1973.*

ZENA SUTHERLAND

[In *Hey, Big Spender* the] writing is casually smooth, dialogue excellent, and characterization vivid if not profound; unlike Bonham's other stories about the black citizens of Dogtown, this is less a biting study than an excursion into escape fiction despite the plight of some of Cool's cases. (p. 120)

> *Zena Sutherland, in* Bulletin of the Center for Children's Books *(© 1973 by the University of Chicago; all rights reserved), April, 1973.*

MARILYN R. SINGER

Bonham is not at his best in [*A Dream of Ghosts,* a] contrived ghost story. An American family moves to France and into a 15th-Century castle inhabited by the ghosts of its original owners. Eleven-year-old Gwen, a computerized Nancy Drew, sets out to solve all the mysteries, with the questionable aid of her obnoxious younger brother. The characters are outdated stock figures adorned with a few contemporary props, and they often seem more unreal than the ghosts. . . . But none of that is important. What is supposed to matter is Gwen's realization that "you can't measure everything or put it under a microscope. You just have to keep trying . . . " Bonham introduces some fascinating supernatural material, but, unfortunately, it's the book's punch line rather than its premise, and the story ends just where it seems to begin. (p. 46)

> *Marilyn R. Singer, in* School Library Journal *(reprinted from the November 1973 issue of* School Library Journal, *published by R. R. Bowker Co. A Xerox Corporation; copyright © 1973), November, 1973.*

[In *The Golden Bees of Tulami*] a mysterious African stranger comes to [Dogtown], bringing with him a hive of bees and a supply of honey candy that is an instant turn-on to peace and humankindness. Gang tensions melt away after the African, Mr. Kinsman, arranges a "brotherhood ceremony" with tastes of Tulami honey for all, and Kinsman hopes to persuade the White House to exchange his queen bees—and their potential as a social panacea for the developmental dollars the tiny kingdom of Tulami needs. Despite many straight-faced assertions that the honey, which has no negative effects whatsoever, is "not a drug," readers can't be prevented from coming to their own conclusions. So it's not at all surprising that our government tries to destroy Kinsman and co-opt his product because peace would be economically disastrous. But what-

ever satire may (and it may not) be intended doesn't cut very deep; no one questions the rightness of the police using the honey to control crime, and no character ever objects to the gift of artificial bliss. In fact, Bonham is never quite specific enough about the nature of the honey high; he at least ought to have convinced us that it induced creativity, not just passivity. (p. 1159)

> Kirkus Reviews *(copyright © 1974 The Kirkus Service, Inc.), November 1, 1974.*

GLORIA LEVITAS

["The Golden Bees of Tulami"] teeters—sometimes precariously—between imagination and reality. Bonham's didacticism seems more obvious in this book than in his previous stories of the Dogtown ghetto, and his ironic humor here serves less as commentary than background. . . . Bonham hopefully suggests that myths can help to nourish, even if they cannot ensure, a happy and more human future. (p. 10)

> *Gloria Levitas, in* The New York Times Book Review *(© 1974 by The New York Times Company; reprinted by permission), November 10, 1974.*

The shallow plot of *Mystery in Little Tokyo* traces the disappearance and recovery of a trunkful of old samurai swords by Danny and Carol Nomura, who are staying with their grandparents in Los Angeles' "Little Tokyo" community.

Visions of inscrutable, strange and mysterious "Orientals" haunt the story, taking such forms as the unscrupulous, "shifty eyed" Mr. Kaji. . . . In one scene, Mr. Kaji threatens to kill himself rather than lose face, in keeping with the romanticized stereotype of Japanese as superproud people.

Central to the plot is a foolish and longstanding feud between the dogmatic and spiteful Grandpa Nomura and his neighbor, the "stubborn" Mr. Shinoda, over a prized samurai sword which they both covet. Both characters are merchants. . . . An offensively negative image of the Japanese American community as a tourist trap for shoppers is presented through the character of a Japanese American policeman, one of whose main jobs is to keep order in "Little Tokyo" so that the merchants won't "be ruined" by people who "would be afraid to shop here."

Grandma Nomura is a clucking, apologetic woman who cooks her way through the story (in one scene she is criticized for not getting the breakfast waffles to the table fast enough). . . .

Despite some effort on the author's part to examine life in a Japanese American community, the book remains essentially a superficial and exploitative venture. (p. 18)

> Interracial Books for Children Bulletin *(reprinted by permission of* Interracial Books for Children Bulletin, *1841 Broadway, New York, N.Y. 10023), Vol. 7, Nos. 2 & 3, 1976.*

[*Burma Rifles: A Story of Merrill's Marauders*] describes the heroic service of Nisei men as combat interpreters for "Merrill's Marauders" in Burma during World War II. Based on fact, the story is a readable and interesting "war adventure." . . . However, its adventurous tone detracts from the author's attempt to show that the Nisei were expected to be 200 per cent Americans despite the racist violence committed against them.

The fault is not only one of omission, but of emphasis. The author's description of white American attitudes toward the Nisei during the months following Pearl Harbor, and prior to the internment of West Coast Japanese Americans, is good but does not reveal the depth of white hostility. Mr. Bonham leads readers to believe that abuse of Japanese American property was the fullest extent of that hostility when, in fact, the Nisei feared for their lives. The cruel herding of the Nisei into wartime assembly centers is not cited except to say that they were limited to "one suitcase each" and were picked up by trucks (in reality, they were often transported like cattle). No mention is made of the machine gun-toting guards or of the barbed wire that surrounded the camps. In the absence of such references, readers may not grasp the irony of a situation in which young Nisei had to demonstrate loyalty and heroism in service to a country which had confined them and their families in concentration camps as "traitors." . . .

Mr. Bonham admires the Nisei but, like many white "friends" of Japanese Americans, he seems to believe that his good will allows him latitude. One seriously questions how well the author understands the real reason the Nisei soldiers fought to prove their loyalty to this country—that despite being considered "Japs," they struggled against prejudice and suspicion to be regarded as "Americans." . . . (p. 20)

> Interracial Books for Children Bulletin (reprinted by permission of Interracial Books for Children Bulletin, 1841 Broadway, New York, N.Y. 10023), Vol. 7, Nos. 2 & 3, 1976.

The oxygen-and vitamin-starved environment of San Diego some years in the future [in *The Missing Persons League*] makes [twentieth-century] Dogtown look like paradise. . . . [Brian Foster's] trouble begins when he determines to track down his mother and sister, who disappeared a year before in an apparently patternless epidemic of missing persons. The response to his ad in the Personals column of the local newspaper includes visits from the Environmental Police, who leave a bugging device in the kitchen; a letter, apparently from Charles Dickens, which directs him to an anti-matter planet called Arret; and the friendly interest of Heather Morse. Heather herself is brainwashed by someone who calls every night with instructions cued in by strains of a Brahms lullaby, and she puts Brian in touch with his own "conductor", the yellow-coveralled Gumball King. . . . Oddly, only the utopian dream held out by the ending seems like science fiction; Brian's stainless steel wrapped, quick frozen reality is chillingly convincing, and this time round the hypnotically slick gimmicks that turn Bonham's plot into a minefield are part and parcel of the message. (p. 909)

> Kirkus Reviews (copyright © 1976 The Kirkus Service, Inc.), August 15, 1976.

ZENA SUTHERLAND

[In *The Missing Persons League*] Bonham depicts a society that has adjusted to pollution and its ignoring of conservation, to the policing of individual lives, and to the constant need for pills and palliatives. In this, the story is most con-vincing. It is rather less so in plot, for the ending is an intricate chase-and-evade sequence between the good guys and the bad guys. (p. 39)

> Zena Sutherland, in Bulletin of the Center for Children's Books (© 1976 by the University of Chicago; all rights reserved), November, 1976.

STEPHEN KRENSKY

Bonham squeezes considerable tension and suspense from the proceedings [in "The Missing Persons League"], but little else of note. His characters are never in focus except when occupying center stage; their background machinations—which contribute significantly to the plot—are left blurred, unresolved by the ending.

Most important, perhaps, the book is a muddled example of science-fiction. Notwithstanding a willing suspension of disbelief, I could not reconcile the indiscriminate hash Bonham has made of things to come. Pontiac Firebirds and "nailhead transmitters" simply do not mix. Too many of the touchstones in speech, clothing and technology are contemporary; they don't blend into the evolved setting the plot requires. If the future is really as confused as Bonham depicts it, whatever happens will serve us right. (p. 10)

> Stephen Krensky, in The New York Times Book Review (© 1977 by The New York Times Company; reprinted by permission), January 9, 1977.

ZENA SUTHERLAND

[*The Rascals from Haskell's Gym* is a] story about girl gymnasts [which] seems constructed to emphasize the increasingly popular sport, since the plot is contrived and the sub-plot tangential. Adequately written, save for technical terms that are unexplained, the book focuses on the enmity between two gymnastic schools; the protagonist, Sissy, is worried about her own performance . . . and about beating the "Haskell's Raskell's" in a team competition. She's also worried about whether or not her father will be able to hold a piece of property that the hostile Mr. Haskell wants. There's a nice father-daughter relationship, but the rest of the story is labored. (p. 42)

> Zena Sutherland, in Bulletin of the Center for Children's Books (© 1977 by the University of Chicago; all rights reserved), November, 1977.

JOHN T. GILLESPIE

Through Chief's eyes [in the novel *Chief*], the reader is able to experience the struggle of the exploited modern-day Indian in finding a rightful and just place in society. The Indians' plight is realistically portrayed without sermonizing or condescending, although many of the characters express a natural bitterness and disillusionment with the values of present-day America. Many of the characters, particularly boozy Uncle Horse and the enterprising hero, are very well drawn. (p. 53)

> John T. Gillespie, in his More Juniorplots: A Guide for Teachers and Librarians (copyright © 1977 by John Gillespie; reprinted by permission of the R. R. Bowker Company), Bowker, 1977.

DENISE M. WILMS

It's clear from the outset [of *Devilhorn*] that Tom Fox is a resourceful, determined sort. The split from his shallow, temperamental father and brassy new stepmother is painless. The 93 goats he has in tow in the forested Oregon countryside promise to insure a hand-to-mouth existence to start with, maybe something better if plans for herding and cheesemaking work out. . . . The story, set in 1939, is absorbing despite several instances of contrived plotting. Details of goat-tending and cheesemaking so thoroughly woven through prove unexpectedly interesting, and Tom's levelheaded, independent nature is appealing. A flawed but worthwhile, enjoyable read. (p. 1676)

> *Denise M. Wilms, in* Booklist *(reprinted by permission of the American Library Association; copyright 1978 by the American Library Association), July 1, 1978.*

Richard Brautigan

1935-

American novelist, short story writer, and poet. Brautigan is often seen as one of the major practitioners of the New Fiction and as the literary representative of the sixties' counterculture. His works resist categorization, combining imagination, comedy, and unconventional plots and language to present a melancholy vision of American life. Brautigan's books show a recognition of and a dissatisfaction with current absurdity at the same time that they long nostalgically for the past. He mourns the betrayal of the American dream, and the theme of much of his early work has been the search for an American Eden. *Trout Fishing in America* is considered the best representation of this theme. His overall philosophy is a stoic acceptance of our declining culture, and a belief that the use of good humor and the power of imagination gives zest and humanity to life. Brautigan's literary view has been compared to that of novelist Kurt Vonnegut, Jr., and it was Vonnegut who successfully introduced Brautigan's work, published originally by California small presses, to a national publishing company. The popularity of Brautigan's books spread across the country, finding many readers among college students who identified with his philosophy and were excited by the unorthodox use of language and structure of his poetry and fiction. Brautigan's gentleness and whimsicality appealed to the youth of the late sixties, as did his references to popular music, sexual freedom, and drug experiences. Often writing from the point of view of an adolescent, Brautigan presented himself as a writer who related to youth. However, he has been criticized for being too hip, clever, and bizarre, and his works have been called insubstantial and facile. Recently Brautigan has been writing parodies of Gothics, science fiction, and mysteries. These works are generally considered less successful than his earlier efforts. Although critics occasionally wonder if Brautigan has passed his time of relevance, it is generally agreed that his best work transcends temporal limitations and holds a unique place in American literature. (See also *CLC*, Vols. 1, 3, 5, 9, and *Contemporary Authors*, Vols. 53-56.)

PHILIP RAHV

Richard Brautigan's beat-story *A Confederate General from Big Sur*—strikes me as very crude indeed. In it the beatnik tendency to disorganization of form and inconsequence of content reaches a new low. (p. 8)

There is little to say of Richard Brautigan's *A Confederate General from Big Sur* except that it is no story at all but only a series of improvised scenes in the manner of Jack Kerouac. It is pop-writing of the worst kind, full of vapid jokes and equally vapid sex-scenes which are also a joke, though scarcely in the sense intended by the author. Its two protagonists, inevitably, are a couple of young men who have made scrounging for food, liquor, and women their life-career. The only connection with the Confederacy is that one of the young men fraudulently claims descent from a general in the Civil War. And what is so terribly funny about that remains the author's secret. (p. 10)

Philip Rahv, in The New York Review of Books *(reprinted with permission from* The New York Review of Books; *copyright © 1965 Nyrev, Inc.),* April 8, 1965.

GILBERT SORRENTINO

[*The Galilee Hitch-Hiker*] has nine short poems which take their shape from quotations from Baudelaire, and from the kind of residue in the reader's mind concerning his recollection of Baudelaire's life—or what we take his life to have been, relying on his poems. Sometimes they work and sometimes they don't. The perfect poem is the second one, *The American Hotel* . . .—which is really a kind of comic genius. It might be useful to note that these poems have a sense of "camp" about them, clearly manifested, and much more intriguing than what is now going down as wit. . . . But they are very subtle and literary, and function dryly. (p. 59)

Gilbert Sorrentino, in Poetry (© *1968 by The Modern Poetry Association; reprinted by permission of the Editor of* Poetry), *April, 1968.*

PAMELA RITTERMAN

[*Trout Fishing in America*] has been around for a while, enjoying some underground success. It's really about trout fishing in America. There's something of Hemingway, but also of Izaak Walton in this small compendium of anecdotes, observations, a few recipes. Brautigan can write whimsy that, miraculously, is neither cute nor embrassing. *Trout Fishing* is a funny, delightful book that draws freely on American mythic attitudes, the tones and rhythms of drifting, searching out trout streams, thinking slow thoughts in wide country. (p. 601)

Pamela Ritterman, in Commonweal (*copyright © 1969 Commonweal Publishing Co., Inc.; reprinted by permission of Commonweal Publishing Co., Inc.), September 26, 1969.*

ALBERT H. NORMAN

Richard Brautigan's novels are as informal as an open house—everyone and everything is welcome. (p. 54)

"Trout Fishing in America" is not a book for the sportsman to get hooked on. Brautigan is an outdoorsman, but far out. His work abounds with wildlife, but not of the Field and Stream variety. A compleat angler, Brautigan drops his lines into a clear pool of consciousness, and reels in some very strange fish.

Brautigan lures the reader with eclectic bait. He combines the surface finality of Hemingway, the straightforwardness of Sherwood Anderson and the synesthetic guile of Baudelaire. Blunt and sparing with his words, Brautigan packs his creel with evocative symbols. His stories are at once as open as the Pacific Northwest, and as meticulous as a water-bug on Salt Creek. Wandering from stream to stream, Brautigan small-talks, writes letters, concocts recipes, makes love and even catches trout. His stories collapse like an accordion, bending everything out of shape. It all takes place so fast that his books must be called subliminal suites. . . . (pp. 54-5)

Brautigan wants to befriend the earth, not shake it. His style and wit transmit so much energy that energy itself becomes the message. . . . Brautigan strains to live, he explodes every simile ("His eyes were like the shoelaces of a harpsichord"), makes all the senses breathe. Only a hedonist could cram so much life onto a single page.

Brautigan's collected poems, "The Pill Versus the Springhill Mine Disaster," are too uneven to be truly satisfying. He lacks the abstract depth of Wallace Stevens and the focus of William Carlos Williams. The poems are too casual, like an untucked shirt. . . .

"In Watermelon Sugar," a novel in three parts, is Brautigan at his best. Every page is gracefully complex. The characters in this naïve allegory are as sweet as sugar. The writing melts in your mouth. He creates a backwater civilization reminiscent of Tolkien, a fragile world of polite chit-chat, talking tigers and multicolored suns. . . .

"Our lives we have carefully constructed from watermelon sugar," says the hero, "and then traveled to the length of our dreams, along roads lined with pines and stones." Brautigan . . .—is carrying his craft down those same roads. . . . Traveling on sheer whimsy, the Brautigan novel speeds by like a dream, encompassing everything. . . . (p. 55)

Albert H. Norman, "Energy and Whimsy," in Newsweek *(copyright 1969 by Newsweek, Inc.; all rights reserved; reprinted by permission), December 29, 1969, pp. 54-5.*

GUY DAVENPORT

Mr. Richard Brautigan's *Trout Fishing in America, The Pill versus the Springhill Mine Disaster* and *In Watermelon Sugar* are experimental pieces of quite spirited conception. (p. 158)

Mr. Brautigan's solicitude for the world he lives in and his impatient grasp of essences continue from their clear emergence in this opening passage all the way through an in-spired book. Trout Fishing in America is a person, a place, a quality; anything, in fact, the author surrealistically wants it to be. It functions as a nonsense phrase of great power, and the author's spirited faith that he need never explain it is the happy—and only—ground on which we may approach the book.

Most of what's printed in our time is either spiel or bilge. Mr. Brautigan locates his writing on the barricade which the sane mind maintains against spiel and bilge, and here he cavorts with a divine idiocy, thumbing his nose. But he makes it clear that at his immediate disposal is a fund of common sense he does not hesitate to bring into play. He is a kind of Thoreau who cannot keep a straight face.

His prose is handy with apt similes. "Like astigmatism, I made myself at home." His imagination is magnificently nimble. His sense of the ridiculous is delirious, a gift from the gods. "The Lysol sits like another guest on the stuffed furniture, reading a copy of the *Chronicle,* the Sports Section. It is the only furniture I have ever seen in my life that looks like baby food."

Mr. Brautigan is not a Surrealist, nor yet a fantasist. I would place him among the philosophers, for his central perception is that the world makes very little sense to a man with a plain mind. He has made his will stubborn against the tinsel and whorish fabric of society. He might even claim that he has described the world with a strong measure of accuracy; Lord knows novelists who sound a lot less peculiar than Mr. Brautigan have tampered with their subjects more than he to achieve such astounding fairy tales as the mysteries of Erle Stanley Gardner.

In Watermelon Sugar is a more sober and mysterious work than *Trout Fishing in America.* Mr. Brautigan calls it a novel, and it satisfies that designation in a very strange and new way. *Trout Fishing* is a festival, and invites a musical analogy; *In Watermelon Sugar* is myth, and is closer to the poem than the novel. Both these works show Mr. Brautigan to be one of the most gifted innovators in our literature. (pp. 159-60)

Guy Davenport, in The Hudson Review *(copyright © 1970 by the Hudson Review, Inc.; reprinted by permission), Vol. XXIII, No. 1, Spring, 1970.*

J. D. O'HARA

[Richard Brautigan, in *Trout Fishing in America, The Pill versus the Springhill Mine Disaster,* and *In Watermelon Sugar*] is funny but seldom satiric, sometimes bored but hardly ever angry, frequently happier than you but never holier than thou. One of his verses imagines "a cybernetic meadow / where mammals and computers / live together," a world of people "returned to our mammal / brothers and sisters, / and all watched over / by machines of loving grace"; and this gently witty reconciliation of disparate worlds is one of his repeated achievements. Another is acceptance. His existence is like ours, full of aggravations and failures, but without being at all Pollyanna-ish he manages to make the best—however mediocre it might be—of a seedy world. . . .

Brautigan's heroes are generally himself, more or less costumed; but unlike the modern author-hero he doesn't come on as a ramrod, a love machine, a superstar; in sex as in other areas he's mild, unassuming, and given to self-deprecation. In one of his verses, in fact, he laments: "If I were dead / I couldn't attract / a female fly." Such Twainian exaggeration and understatement locate Brautigan in an old tradition of West Coast humor, while the many fishing scenes recall the pastoral side of Hemingway. It's not a close resemblance, however. Hemingway's heroes go to nature (and women) to prove themselves and to escape civilization; Brautigan's couldn't care less about proving themselves, and they connect nature and civilization effortlessly.

Connection, in fact, is what Brautigan is best at; it characterizes his style. Here's his title poem:

> When you take your pill
> it's like a mine disaster.
> I think of all the people
> lost inside of you.

His prose is even better, and is loaded with pleasing connections: "a few stubborn rainbow trout, seldom heard from, but there all the same, like certified public accountants"; "when the sun went behind a cloud, the smell of the sheep decreased, like standing on some old guy's hearing aid." Sometimes connection achieves larger ideas, for instance Shorty, in *Trout Fishing*, "a legless, screaming middle-aged wino . . . descended upon North Beach like a chapter from the Old Testament," but before Brautigan's through with him he's a Western Ratso Rizzo, foully lovable. And what a fine connection of disparates lies behind one of *Trout Fishing*'s best chapters, "The Cleveland Wrecking Yard," in which the Yard has a used trout stream for sale (by the foot).

Alas for the hazards of being reviewed: Brautigan at secondhand is all too likely to sound merely whimsical and cute. He is not; what underlies these games is a modern fatalism, not maudlin fatheadedness. . . .

Like his *Confederate General from Big Sur* . . . , *Trout Fishing* is about life in reality. In *Watermelon*, the scene is sweetly fantastic and the narrator is not a Brautigan but a simple-minded fellow chuckleheadedly pursuing happiness with, or at the expense of, two women. In the earlier novels the prosaic workaday surface of reality was repeatedly illuminated by the charm of the narrator's happy imaginings. In this one the spun-sugar simplifications of organized happiness the naive placidity of the narrator are repeatedly darkened by our perception of real misery, jealousy, frustration and unrequited love. It is more complicated technically and more disturbing emotionally than the earlier works, and it suggests that you should, while reading all the Brautigan now available, look forward to the Brautigan yet to come.

> *J. D. O'Hara, "Happier (But Not Holier) Than Thou," in* Book World—Chicago Tribune *(© 1970 Postrib Corp.), January 11, 1970, p. 3.*

RON LOEWINSOHN

One difficulty in reviewing Brautigan's books is that you're tempted to try to do in your own prose what he does in his. He makes it look so easy. . . . Many reviewers have tried to do that, & of course they can't. But I don't even want to review *Trout Fishing in America*. I just want you to read it because it is one of the funniest books you will ever read, a book you may not want to read on the bus to work because it will keep you laughing out loud & everyone else on the bus will turn to see what's the matter with you, but you

won't be able to stop reading, or laughing. It is also a very moving book. Sometimes you will finish a chapter & you will just put the book down in your lap & look out the window for a while, trying to keep the fleeting savor of what Brautigan has made you feel, a feeling you will not have any words to describe. I don't.

Brautigan's language is magical, & absolutely accurate, a kind of lens which allows you to see his vision of America, an America you never suspected was there, but of course it has been there all along, & you have lived in it, & now you recognize it. His prose is a poet's prose, in which each word, each image, has been chosen with intelligent & sensitive care. Yet it is not "poetic," but usually flat, modulating at times into an intensely understated lyricism. (p. 288)

So it's a fun book, & a moving one. It's also an important book: it may be the *Great Gatsby* of our time. & I would ask those people who think it's not a novel at all, but merely a collection of amusing vignettes—What's Benjamin Franklin's function in the novel? How does economics function there? How does nature? How does the past—both of America's history & its literature—figure in it? Why are trout described in the second chapter as "a precious & intelligent metal," but not silver, rather steel? & having answered that, what is John Dillinger doing in there? Finally, how is the last chapter, together with its prologue, a final summation of a noble yet un-'Romantic' statement of the human condition?

In Watermelon Sugar is another story. Its atmosphere is at once concrete & evanescent. . . . The surface of the novel is gentle, even banal, but under that surface lurk predictability and repression—self-repression. The irony is all the more cutting for its subtlety. (pp. 228-29)

The Pill versus The Springhill Mine Disaster collects most of the poems Brautigan has written & published over the past ten years. Most of them are short, & many of them are funny. There are some real gems here, poems that stand up to repeated readings: "A Postcard from Chinatown," "The Sidney Greenstreet Blues," "The Fever Monument," or "1942." . . . But mostly his poems are either very clever or very sentimental. Further, he seems not to have much sense of the possibilities the line proposes, so that the poems often seem like one-liner jokes chopped up into verse. But if you read these poems in the light of Brautigan's own "Private Eye Lettuce" . . . , you will see that he is concerned more deeply with naming things, or re-naming them, finding their true, secret name, than with any of the sentiments or jokes which form these poems' surfaces. That yields mixed results: while it's an admirable concern, it gets in the way of his perceiving the *process* involved in the things he names or defines. Definition is just that, a closing off, & what Brautigan leaves outside the door of classification is any acknowledgment of the on-going-ness of things, & of himself. That's why the poems are so easy to take. You finish one & go immediately on to the next, because the poems don't resonate beyond their final (usually very final-sounding) line. In his prose he gives himself more room & more time, & there he is more enduringly satisfying. (pp. 229-30)

> *Ron Loewinsohn, in* TriQuarterly 18 *(© 1970 by TriQuarterly), Spring, 1970.*

KATE ROSE

Reading Mr. Brautigan's [*Rommel Drives on Deep Into*

Egypt], I'm struck by the fact that [he] cannot be aspiring to poetdom as it is commonly conceived these days.

Brautigan's poems suggest his presence as an imaginative, sensitive, and unexceptional observer. However, they neither explore his personality nor offer a reader anything else on a very deep or elaborate scale. The poetry is not tense, not particularly noble, not, seemingly, aspiring to anything other than the presentation of somebody's reactions, clarified and reduced into tasteful bites. A simpler way of saying this is that *Rommel Drives on Deep Into Egypt* should be gulped, like a session of *Laugh In*, that Mr. Brautigan is attempting to be an entertainer rather than a Great Figure in Literature, and that from anybody's point of view the attempt is worth having around. After all, his emphasis on entertainment is his distinction; attempts at presenting the thoughts of a plain man have been around since Catullus.

How, then, are we to be entertained? As entertainer Brautigan downplays himself and needs good jokes, which, short and strung together through the book, hit a response say, seven times out of ten. The material has a fresh touch, is clearly presented, and is delivered as a series of one-time tries. The effect he seems to be after is sensibility-tweaking. He presents a world which is comfortable, if pleasingly strange, and which will carry a reader along with very little effort. This makes him a good guest-room poet, if you like, but he does manage to tweak enough to make the show come off, one way or another. (And how much can be said of other poetry?) (p. 115)

Ideas, tough, involving ideas, are not Brautigan's speciality. He tends toward gestures and insights and words, but anyone who's been afraid of poetry because of its formality, glumness, bookish references, obscure, private visions, long words or politics can read this book. The man is not writing to poets or his educated peers; he may be writing instant culture, but he will be read. (p. 116)

> *Kate Rose, "The Grand Penny Tour: Brautigan's 'Rommel Drives on Deep into Egypt'," in* The Minnesota Review *(copyright 1970 by The Minnesota Review), Vol. X, Nos. 3 & 4, 1970, pp. 115-16.*

HUGO WILLIAMS

Though much has been made of [Brautigan's] years in the wilderness, it has fallen to him, as far as his poetry is concerned, to be the popularizer of other men's work. Somewhere in [*The Pill Versus the Springhill Mine Disaster*] you will find hidden the sweetened and simplified faces of Frank O'Hara, James Wright, Robert Creeley, Dudley Fitts, not to mention Buddy Holly, Walt Whitman and all. He is the author of two original and poetic prose works called *In Watermelon Sugar* and *Trout Fishing in America* which have become something of a cult on the West Coast. Short, visionary inscapes on the American nightmare, they might indeed have required some kind of exile to complete. . . . Sugary, predigested and schoolgirlish, his naiveté is actually cynical it is so accurately researched to touch the dewy and vulgar adolescent heart. With his own heart safely given over to justified lines he has been able without a qualm to write down as low as needs be to reach that smiling majority who are always waiting. . . . He deserves a sucky medal with a picture of himself on it for his own personal sweetness. (pp. 83-4)

Hugo Williams, in London Magazine *(© London Magazine 1971), February, 1971.*

MASON SMITH

Of an order apart from most books, "Trout Fishing in America" was a totally original novel plotted in the changing shapes of a heart-breaking symbol for what is happening to America. "Trout Fishing in America" was a legless wino, a cheap hotel, a revolutionary slogan chalked on the backs of schoolchildren; it was the political disguise of the murderous "Mayor of the Twentieth Century"; it was a brooding spirit that remembered "people with three-cornered hats fishing in the dawn" and Lewis and Clark discovering the Great Falls of the Missouri. It was dead, extinct as the dinosaur (trout had become steel, streams had become stores), but seemed to live, transformed again, in the life and prose and person of Brautigan himself. Every chapter had a secret hook to set, a steel meaning in a sparely tied fly of anecdote and metaphor, a valuable and accurate surprise. Just another book like that is what you pray for every time you crack a new one.

The fact is we are still getting Brautigan writings from a time before "Trout Fishing" made the world his oyster. ["The Abortion"] has been around a while and owes more to "In Watermelon Sugar," which itself was written a couple of years or more before "Trout Fishing" was published. The commonplace short dialogues of greeting, eating and bedding—"Conversations and things that happen every day. (Work, baths, breakfast and dinner)"—that gave "In Watermelon Sugar" so many relaxed, seemingly vacuous pages illustrated the novel's point about peaceful coexistence with mortality. They also suggested analogously that with regard to literary mortality the way to sanity was "watermelon ink"—which one imagines to be vaguely pink and fading while one reads. The new book is written almost entirely with the sugar-water *sprezzatura* of an artist who hands it in to a dead-end library and never expects to see it again.

The story is simple and straightforward. Two people help each other out of temporary blockages; an abortion, ironically, the agency of their delivery. . . .

[The book] addresses, in an oddly frontal way, the Women's Lib themes of abortion and sex-objectification. It will be read in part as a rather uncomradely attack on Brautigan's fellow girl-watchers, and perhaps as some sort of statement about the nastiness and dishonesty of our social and legal pressures around the subject of abortion. But it's doubtful if the author of "Trout Fishing"—who did his damning there in the permanent and hard, artistic war—has his heart in such a lazy undertaking. There is something spooky and funny here, pale pink and fading. (p. 4)

"The Abortion" is short, swift and formally neat, and though it contains some very offhand writing, this experiment along the limits of the watermelon thinness of Brautigan's ink is cheeky enough, and there are enough indelible stretches where the watermelon ink rinses out some India, to be just a little more than just another book. (p. 26)

> *Mason Smith, in* The New York Times Book Review *(© 1971 by The New York Times Company; reprinted by permission), March 18, 1971.*

THOMAS LASK

"The Abortion," Richard Brautigan's new novel, is split

almost evenly down the middle. Half of it is amiable fantasy, half realistic documentary so factual you can draw a map from its pages. It is possible to tie the two halves together symbolically or rather hang one half on the other. But that possibility depends more on the ingenuity of the commentator than on the merit of the work. . . . In spite of the fact that people come and go in this book and that part of it involves a journey by auto van, plane and bus from San Francisco to Tijuana and back, the work is essentially static. It never moves off center, never gets off the ground. One reason for this malaise is the author's catch-as-catch-can approach to the black page. He grabs at a chapter and throws it to the mat. But his victories are easy ones.

The author's flip attitude is like watered whiskey. Only a whiff of the original comes through. The off-beat, the surreal, the neat observations of "Trout Fishing in America" have been changed into self-indulgent literary ticks. And the manner shows, I won't go so far as to say that Mr. Brautigan is contemptuous of those who put down hard coin of the realm for his books, but the substance of "The Abortion" is thin to the point of insensibility.

In "The Abortion," the "I" who tells the story is in charge of a fabulous library, open 24 hours a day, seven days a week. It's a great place; books are never deposited and they are books that have only just been written. Anybody with a finished manuscript can bring it into the library and leave it there. . . .

[Before] the reader knows it, or has a chance to back away, he is in the middle of a novel in which a guy takes a girl in out of the rain, they decide to share his bed, she becomes pregnant, they decide not to have the child. Sounds original, doesn't it? The last half of the book is a step-by-step account of how the two travel to Tijuana, how Vida has her abortion and how they return. Anyone interested in having such an operation in Tijuana or in the details of securing such surgery will find "The Abortion" tense with excitement. The rest of us (some 200 million maybe) will find it a paralyzing bore.

If one is determined enough, a moral can be drawn from this fiction. Maybe the library is the same way station for the unborn spirit as the abortion mill is for the unborn child. Maybe the author is condemning the waste in both instances. Maybe he is trying to draw attention to those inarticulate and dumb spirits who are unable to give form to their yearnings, who die unmarked and unnoticed in the man-swarm of humanity. Maybe—but I doubt it. For the book is so morally neutral, so entirely without nuance or reflection that it could easily be a chapter in a West Coast travel guide. No theorizing can prop up this jerrybuilt substitute for entertainment.

Brautigan has wandered a long way from "Trout Fishing in America." There was an irreverent, unstructured, slightly wacky quality to those sketches that revealed an off-beat mind, a flexible, informal and tangy prose style and an original way of looking at the commonplace. . . .

And the life that wanders in and out of that book, defying the Establishment, normal economic laws and bourgeois morality, has a raffish and wry charm. But it's not a style that works with everything. "In Watermelon Sugar" was a feeble and amateurish exercise. It took 30 minutes to read and seemed interminable. There were things in it that could only be excused on the grounds that the author was being

paid so much a word. "The Abortion" is not so great a failure, but it is a greater disappointment. Mr. Brautigan has let a good idea wither for lack of nourishment.

> *Thomas Lask, "Move Over, Mr. Tolstoy," in The New York Times (© 1971 by The New York Times Company; reprinted by permission), March 30, 1971, p. 33.*

ROBERT ADAMS

The Brautigan phenomenon, California filtered through Brautigan, has been working itself out, in prose and verse, for several years now. How far has it got, and where is it going? Like the hitchhikers who stand beside Route 1 thumbing rides simultaneously in *both* directions, it is a distinctive phenomenon which is hard to assess. . . .

We begin by distinguishing: on the one hand there is Brautigan's poetry, on the other Brautigan's prose. About the poetry, I can't pretend to offer a very assured judgment. There is a great deal of it, and I haven't seen it all. What I have seen is in a minor key: it comes on rather like the more playful poems of e. e. cummings. There are lots of lively small poems on small, occasional topics; considerable charm, a nicely understated wit—it is deft writing, and that, for a poet, is not much of a compliment.

One of the best things about this poetry is that it doesn't try very hard. Its metaphors drop neatly into place without any agony of thought or torment of feeling. The largest statements I have seen the poet undertake verge on sentimentality ("The Galilee Hitch-Hiker") or nostalgia ("1942"); a good deal of what he turns out is what used to be called *jeux d'esprit, vers de circonstance*, or some other French name implying more sauce than substance. . . .

The prose pieces (one can't call them novels or even fictions—they may well go down in literary history as Brautigans) now number four, and, to this reader's taste, they are much more impressive than the poetry. But they are not easy to describe. . . .

[*In Watermelon Sugar*] is a good place to jump off on one's Brautigan readings, precisely because it's so apparent that there is a great deal . . . to it. It seems to me a fable, but also a nightmare, of innocence. (p. 24)

Like Agnes Varda's lovely movie *Le Bonheur*, which it resembles in many ways, this fable of Brautigan's seems to me deeply ambiguous; you can read it forward (with Pauline and the iDEATH people as the civilized element) or backward (with inBOIL and pals as the outcast-pariah heroes) or neutrally, with a shrug of the shoulders for poor Margaret. Our narrator, with his aspirations toward a "gentle life," can't conceivably come off very well, and the simple fact that nobody in the book blames him for Margaret's death may be read as an invitation to the reader to do so. . . .

Trout Fishing in America is the earlier . . . and, in this reader's judgment, the next best Brautigan; but one must note respectfully that it seems to have had a better press than *In Watermelon Sugar*. Probably this is because it feels like a bigger book. I found it more diffuse and episodic, a little more forced in some of its fun, a little more disposed to rely on obscenity for easy effects. Without any of the structure of *In Watermelon Sugar*, it is wilder and more fantastic in its use of language, more eloquent and various in its accounts of some very quirky people—a kind of visionary comic-book apocalypse about fresh-water Americans and their nature. If it gets less than top marks with this accountant, that's probably due to a basic preference for more controlled books which I couldn't begin to justify logically. *Trout Fishing* and *In Watermelon Sugar*, whichever one happens to prefer, are a pair of vigorous and original books, and the crown of Brautigan's achievement so far.

By contrast, I couldn't get very excited over *A Confederate General from Big Sur*, the first of the lot. . . . The problem here is simply that, being unsure of itself, it tries too hard. In essence the book amounts to an extended version of those stories that begin, "I met this guy in North Beach last summer, you'll never believe it, was he wacky, just let me tell you." Self-consciousness is the curse of the Brautigan characters; when they start assuring us how quaint they are and performing quaint capers to prove the point, the cause is as plainly lost as it was when Longstreet called on Pickett to charge.

So it's clear, when one looks back over the line of Brautigans from last published to first, that the author has been growing in assurance, in control, in ambition. But the books are still very different from one another, especially in organization; and it wouldn't have been at all easy to predict, from the three previous ones, what the fourth book, just published, would be like. As a matter of fact, there is some reason to feel that, despite publication dates, *The Abortion: An Historical Romance 1966*, may have been planned if not written before *Trout Fishing* and *In Watermelon Sugar*. It is a good deal less grotesque and fantastic than its forerunners, a good deal less ambitious as well. It doesn't play as many tricks with the prose or with the surface of things; it is a milder, blander book than either of its immediate predecessors. (p. 25)

What makes the situation [in *The Abortion*] go is its radical instability. Our hero is presented as such a helpless innocent, Vida is so frantically desirable to all passing males, and the situation is so plainly fraught with the possibilities of hideous misfortune that one is spooked on every page by phantoms of multiple catastrophe. But, like all other Brautigan innocents, this pair seems to enjoy a special immunity. Evil quietly evaporates around them, and none of the hideous destinies to which Candide heroes are traditionally prone actually befalls them. . . .

[By] the end of the book, our hero has built himself a certain status as practically everyone's favorite puppy-dog; and unless Mr. Brautigan is a much clumsier artist than I think him to be, he wants that fact to trouble the reader at least some.

The surfaces of the new book are a good deal less skewed than those of the previous two; it has none of those fey watermelons, trouts, and verbal knots in the grain of the narrative. What is queer about the world of *The Abortion* is mostly the librarian's exaggerated, artless simplicity of mind; it makes for a series of small jokes. . . .

There is a touch of the cunning and tricksy about these jokes; one feels a deliberate element in their simplicity, so that the narrator seems already to have settled into his destined role as campus character. The worst things that can happen to him aren't very bad, and best aren't very good. He's evidently a victim of that creeping California disease which amounts to saying, to yourself or to others, "What the hell, I'm pretty much okay the way I am, right?" There

are a lot of places in the world where it depends; there is a real chance you may be—oh well, like stupid or maybe infantile, and sometimes it even matters, to the point of doing something about it. Not here. It would be too much to ask of Mr. Brautigan that he commit himself to a point of view on his characters: it really would, that's not just sarcasm.

He leaves us the possibility of irony; nailing it down explicitly would narrow, not widen, his effect. His art lies in making things out of a scene, and the things he chooses to make aren't moral judgments, they're not even compatible with moral judgments. But the things he makes can and must involve large or trifling attitudes, maybe not toward people (I think Brautigan is too modern to care a damn about people), but toward the language and vision that are his special gift.

The Abortion, I feel, doesn't make generous use of the qualities manifested in the previous two novels. It isn't a bad book, it just isn't much of a book. . . . Brautigan has done too much in the genuinely imaginative, powerfully controlled way of vision to be accepted readily as an artificer of the country cute. (p. 26)

Robert Adams, "Brautigan Was Here," in The New York Review of Books *(reprinted with permission from* The New York Review of Books; *copyright © 1971 Nyrev, Inc.), April 22, 1971, pp. 24-6.*

JOSEPH BUTWIN

Richard Brautigan's novels have taken their place among the standard extra-curricular reading of college students. Their special appeal to the young may lie in Brautigan's capacity to make a myth that satisfies the demands of recent American experience, for he writes refreshing comedy that happens to accommodate a growing sense of disaster. A young man in his latest novel says, "I think we have the power to transform our lives into brand-new instantaneous rituals that we calmly act out when something hard comes up that we must do. We become like theatres." Hard times are with us, and Richard Brautigan provides readers with the ritualistic and theatrical equipment appropriate for survival.

In *The Abortion* the question of survival is raised by a girl cursed with beauty. (p. 52)

The trails of Vida form an implicit critique of our culture: The physical beauty, bombs, industrial proliferation, and commercial techniques we cherish have gotten us into trouble. And the price we are paying for them reverberates through our movie theaters and paperback bookshops—the temples of youth. A pile of money, an American flag, and a beautiful machine leave Peter Fonda's "easy rider" burning in a ditch, and his prophetic words, "We blew it," reach beyond the roadside into all aspects of our national experience. In *The Abortion* Brautigan tells that sad story in a new way. His Captain America is a woman, and the possibility of love and a fresh start survives the premature termination of life in America.

If Brautigan himself is a hero among students it is precisely because his writing is not academic, in the sense that an "academic" question produces no repercussions in the world. He creates a myth and convinces readers that he actually lives it. A new life can be reconstructed, he seems to say, out of the rubble of American failure, along the model of a renaissance that strangely follows abortion. Take a few steps back to the point where things began to go wrong and then start over again. . . .

That a cult should grow around Brautigan is no accident: he plans it that way. . . . Everything he writes reinforces the modern sense that a literary style might also be a life-style. His writing is as brief and immediate as a telegram or a message left on a door for a friend. The dedication of *The Abortion*—"Frank: come on in—read novel—it's on table in front room. I'll be back in about 2 hours. Richard."— sets the simple style of writing and of living, and Brautigan offers himself as an exemplar of simplicity in a complex age. Literature transforms itself immediately into cult.

A cult of this kind meets resistance. Can the simple persona survive in the aura of theatricality that surrounds Brautigan and his friends and disciples? Is it possible to make a myth about oneself and still remain sufficiently humble and human not to offend the audience? It may be that myths cannot be manufactured but must evolve slowly and accidentally to answer the unspoken demands of a society. Brautigan himself begins to confront these contradictions in his understanding that "we become like theaters" even as we perform our "brand-new instantaneous rituals." He recognizes that a mythology adequate to the task of reconstruction will need models and *The Abortion* is an attempt to supply one. (p. 67)

Joseph Butwin, in Saturday Review (© *1971 by Saturday Review, Inc.; reprinted with permission), June 12, 1971.*

MICHAEL FELD

[Psychiatrists] doing a roaring trade in rich young ladies who've lost the will to live tip Richard as therapy in an each way double with Christina Rossetti. . . . [He's] currently heavily backed by pushers of brown sugar and watercress and nut omelettes—people so determined to achieve a more beautiful and profound vision of things they reconcile the implacable eating of 'natural' food with the swallowing, inhaling and injecting of various chemical concoctions? Indeed, he's namedropped in most places where there's lots of sensitivity and modernity and drugs and no commonsense going on, where cool languid personalities slump about passing joints like sweaty kisses, speaking of power to the people and freedom and the plight of the gipsies. Such figures are fully paid-up members of the ever expanding market for Richard and his california prose pertry, an eminently greasy brand of verbal psychedelicatessen. (p. 150)

I suffer an oleagineous tasting aftermath from Richard's recipes. I burp and adjudge the flavour is similar to (*a*) wet and spurious Winifred God. Or (*b*) Papa Hemingway— when the emphasis was on the pap and his heart was in the wrong place, i.e. in his mouth. . . . Or (*c*) the kind of honest injun copywriting favoured by cartels and monopolies in 'prestige' flashyglib ads appearing in the 'quality' press with the message, though we're vast we're no Sheriff of Nottingham, we're Robin Hood, do you realise half our turnover goes in developing new products for the benefit of humanity? (p. 152)

Michael Feld, "A Double with Christina," in London Magazine (© *London Magazine 1971), August-September, 1971, pp. 150-52.*

JOHN CLAYTON

I want to talk out my feelings about Richard Brautigan's *Trout Fishing in America*—about Brautigan's sense of life and about his politics. Because his politics are those of lots of my own people, maybe sometimes of my own life—and they disturb me.

Brautigan is talking . . . to the WE of a subculture—a subculture I'm a part of. He is creating for us a mental space called Trout Fishing in America where we can all live in freedom. He's not preaching about it to us: he assumes we're already there, or just about there. But I'm also in an unfree America, not by mental choice but by condition. And the politics of imagination is finally not enough for me. It's not enough for *us*. (p. 56)

[The critic proceeds to quote from the chapter "The Cleveland Wrecking Yard."] The view I'm offered at the Cleveland Wrecking Yard's window is of bitterness and deadening brick. But Brautigan lets me out of dealing directly with that desperate reality (and I want to be let out); he snatches me up inside his *process of imagination*—the magazines eroding like the Grand Canyon, the magical perception of the patients' complaints. I am given imaginative magic as a liberation from decay.

Later in the same episode, the narrator goes himself to the Cleveland Wrecking Yard "to have a look at a used trout stream." He sees the sign:

> USED TROUT STREAM FOR SALE.
> MUST BE SEEN TO BE APPRECIATED.

Another writer might have produced an obvious satire on destruction and commercialization of the pastoral—a trout stream sold by the foot length. Of course the American trout stream has been sawed into pieces, animals extra. But this satire Brautigan soft-pedals: if the pastoral stream is no longer available, the pastoral of the imagination *is* available. I am seduced by his stoned imagination, which can *conceive of* a trout stream sold by the board foot; which can make a pastoral in a junkyard. What I am finally hooked by is the sensibility which can create a lyrical space in our heads by play, by metaphor.

Brautigan's sensibility is personally liberating. It makes me happy by letting me feel my freedom. To the weight of this world he does not counterpose the *concept* of the imagination; he allows us to join him in his *process* of imaginative re-creation. *Imaginative re-creation* is not a fanciful critical term in talking about Brautigan; it is precise. . . . (pp. 57-8)

It is always a trout stream of the imagination that Brautigan fishes in. Like the stream the narrator as a boy creates out of a flight of stairs: "I ended up by being my own trout and eating the slice of bread myself." And even though Trout Fishing in America replies, "There was nothing I could do. I couldn't change a flight of stairs into a creek," we have already been part of exactly that magic transformation— and we are now presented with another: the transformation of a *topic* into a *character*, Trout Fishing in America, a character who signs a letter to the narrator with a wobbly signature; and into a book cover; and into the nickname of another character, Trout Fishing in America Shorty; and into a hotel; and into a gourmet. . . . (p. 58)

Finally, it's a place: "I've come home from Trout Fishing in America, the highway bent its long smooth anchor about my neck and then stopped." It's a place of rambling, of freedom, of closeness with a peaceful, natural world. . . .

And if it's disappearing in a reality of institutionalized campgrounds with flush toilets, it remains alive in Brautigan's way of seeing. Salvation through perception: the politics of inner freedom.

The mental space we enter with Brautigan's narrator is shaped by an attitude toward language, by tone, and by narrative structure as well as by metaphor. It is a political space in that it reinforces "our" values—the values of a subculture that sees itself as flipped outside of goal-oriented, psychically and socially repressive, exploitative, aggrandizing American technological society. It is political in that to go into that space is to decide *not* to confront that other society. (p. 59)

Part of the magic [of Brautigan's writing] is in the discontinuity itself. If *Trout Fishing in America* is in part a life-style of freedom and rambling, these qualities are present not only in the metaphorical transformations and illogical connections but in the apparent looseness, casualness, easy rambling of the narrator's talk. It isn't true that the parts of *Trout Fishing in America* could be shuffled at random— some, for instance, are necessary preconditions for others to make sense; but we are intended to *feel* that there is absolutely no ordering. And within a chapter Brautigan creates the stance of careless rambler just as Arlo Guthrie does in the record of *Alice's Restaurant*. In "The Cleveland Wrecking Yard," for example, Brautigan begins with the experience of his friends, talks about the mansion of a dead actor, then about two Negro boys discussing a champion twister—all before he gets to the story of his adventure with the trout stream in the wrecking yard. (p. 60)

["Sea Sea Rider"] does wonderful things to my head. I feel the freedom, the openness, of the narrator's trip. He becomes a Sea Rider. I remember the song—sometimes called "See, See, Rider" or "Easy Rider"—from which the chapter title comes. It's a blues about rejection after love-making. But the problem of that blues is gone; getting laid is easy; the narrator becomes a Sea Rider, spinning his fantasies like wheels in the sea. . . .

What the bookstore-owner-teacher does for the narrator [in this chapter], Brautigan's style does for me: his simple narratives, his synapses of logic, his assumption that we will of course accept what he says without asking for explanations, his rambling structure, his metaphorical shifts, his gentle pastoral imagery. We are become as little children, just as the listeners to Jesus' parables must have been as much transformed by the simple diction and syntax and childlike transitions as by the stories themselves. Sometimes Brautigan actually *describes* a way of life. . . . But it's not the description—it's my sharing, our sharing, in Brautigan's imaginative process that really does such beautiful things to us. (p. 63)

Brautigan's style says I can discard categorized living, since *his* perceptions are free to bounce in and out of categories at will. It says I can discard consciousness of causality and rational connections. . . . The style says I can ignore moral dicta, says this by its acceptance of people and events without even asking whether they should be accepted. Things simply *are*. And underlying this sense of life are gentleness and mental freedom.

Brautigan's style undercuts the long tradition of realistic fiction. *Trout Fishing in America* is not an anti-novel; it is an un-novel. Brautigan has no interest in character—in in-

trospection or psychological insight, in interpersonal dynamics; no interest in materiality; no interest in time or causality. The book runs profoundly counter to the bourgeois instincts of the novel. It runs counter to the bourgeois world view of practicality, functionality, rationality. But it isn't a rebellious, individualistic book. Not at all. There is *no* rebellion in it. It accepts everything, even the world that is destroying the pastoral possibilities it asserts. And even though the chapters are often solitary adventures, it is still the book of a subculture, of a WE who are so different from bourgeois expectations as not to need explanations about our way of life.

I am not arguing—not at all—that Brautigan *denies* death and suffering. They are very necessary parts of the book. The bookstore owner floated on the Atlantic till "death did not want him." Again and again death and suffering are connected with beauty. That is the point—that Brautigan *transmutes* ugliness and sadness. (p. 64)

[The] episode "Worsewick" [is] a playful pastoral which contains elements of death as matters of simple fact. Brautigan doesn't solemnize or moralize death; it is just *there*. (p. 65)

The [narrator's] voice [in "Worsewick"] says that everything is cool. When a writer like Hemingway connects love and death it is to counter love with death and death with love. For Brautigan they are both *okay*.

The style of *Trout Fishing in America* sucks us into the politics of no politics—the politics of a subculture alive in *another place*. For Brautigan, America itself is "often only a place in the mind." Unfortunately, however, America is real. . . . Brautigan can get away with his freedom by living mentally in the interstices of the manipulative social structure and by ignoring both imperialism and racism. He is not alone there. Brautigan has been taken up as a tribal hero, along with the plain-folks Mister Dylan of "Country Pie" and the pastoral evocations of the uncomplicated South (The Band, Creedence Clearwater Revival). He is part of what's been called the Woodstock Nation, living . . . as if "our" revolution had already happened. (pp. 65-6)

I, and many of my friends and students, having been very excited by Richard Brautigan, have begun to see *why* he's been so much a cult hero: like the Beatles, he gives people the assurance that they can be free and part of a community of free people, *now*. (p. 66)

I want to live in the liberated mental space that Brautigan creates. I am aware, however, of the institutions that make it difficult for me to live there and that make it impossible for most people in the world. Brautigan's value is in giving us a pastoral vision which can water our spirits as we struggle—the happy knowledge that there is another place to breathe in; his danger, and the danger of the style of youth culture generally, is that we will forget the struggle. (pp. 67-8)

John Clayton, "Richard Brautigan: The Politics of Woodstock," in New American Review *(copyright © 1971 by The New American Library, Inc.), No. 11, 1971, pp. 56-68.*

GURNEY NORMAN and ED McCLANAHAN

Gurney: The other day when the review copy of Richard Brautigan's new volume of stories [*Revenge of the Lawn: Stories: 1962-70*] came in the mail, Ed and I got into a discussion about whether or not Brautigan's stories belong to the literary genre formally known as "the short story." I said I thought they probably didn't, that they seemed to me too short to be short stories. . . .

Ed's reply to that was something like: bullshit, Brautigan's stories are prime short stories, absolutely within the tradition of the modern epiphany as perfected in this century by writers like Joyce and Hemingway. . . .

Ed: [The] thematic similarities between "Forgiven" and [Ernest Hemingway's] "Big Two-Hearted River" are as real as they are apparent: both are about solitary young men trout-fishing in streams in which they recognize some dark, mysterious power that fills them with a nameless dread when they feel it tugging at them. (Not uncharacteristically, Brautigan's sensitive, finely-tuned hero flees the ominous place in panic, whereas Hemingway's Nick Adams permits himself only the merest hint of a mental shudder before he manfully turns his back on his forebodings and stalks away.) But the point is that, in terms of both visual expansiveness and psychological complexity, "Forgiven" really *does* compare favorably to "Big Two-Hearted River." . . .

I think the density of the language throughout [*Revenge of the Lawn*] provides the best defense to date against the argument that Brautigan's work is too often slight, fey, even cute. He is still Richard Brautigan, of course, and there are still moments when his natural impulse to be playful gets the upper hand and trivializes an idea. ("The Gathering of a Californian," for instance, is rendered almost indecipherable by such overly cunning similes as "like a metal-eating flower" and "like the Taj Mahal in the shape of a parking meter.") But by and large the language in this book has a density and power unequaled anywhere in his work, not even in *Trout Fishing in America;* and there is scarcely a page without at least one image—such as the "large unmade bed that looked as if it had been a partner to some of the saddest love-making this side of the Cross," or the Point Reyes Peninsula landscape "which of course unfolded like layers of abstraction and intimacy constantly being circled by hawks," or the senile old lap-dog that "had been dying for so long that it lost the way to death"—which, if you yield to it, will break your heart.

Gurney: I think your phrase "yield to it" is important, because Brautigan is not a hard-sell kind of writer. It's not his style to overload the senses. He very softly invites you into his fictional world. But once inside, indeed, your heart may well be broken, because within these apparently delicate pieces are people up against the ultimate issues of love, loneliness, and death.

"Coffee" is a story about loneliness. A man goes to visit a former girl friend. She is not glad to see him. When he asks for a cup of coffee, she sets out a cup and a jar of instant coffee, puts water on to boil, then disappears into another room until he leaves. Then that night the man visits another ex-girl friend. "What do you want?" she asks. "I want a cup of coffee." The second girl tells him where the instant is, then she too goes into the bedroom and closes the door behind her. (p. 66)

The story is only four pages long, but this lonesome guy's world is so fully rendered that the reader is inevitably sucked into it, and made to feel pretty damn lonely himself. The story is powerful because it's about experience that

everyone can claim as his own. Everybody gets lonely from time to time. And practically everybody drinks coffee. Readers can't help but be effected subliminally by its repetition throughout the story (21 times in four pages). After about the tenth time, the reader is damn near salivating, longing for the warmth of the cup in his hands, the hot liquid on his tongue, the vitalizing influence of coffee in his system. He wants coffee the way the protagonist wants coffee, which is to say, he wants love and warmth like the protagonist wants it, from *some* body on such a cold and lonely night as this.

Ed: Exactly; it's the old shock-of-recognition trick, it's what pathos is all about, actually—epiphany, too, for that matter—those painful, joyous moments when, in the artist's experience, we recognize our own.

And that sense of recognition is just as vital to good comic writing—of which there's an abundance in this book—as it is to pathos. (pp. 66, 68)

Then, too, of course, there is the other kind of comic writing, the rollicking, imaginative variety which depends on surprise and exaggeration, the sort of crazy, downhome burlesque that Faulkner and Flannery O'Connor [are] wonderfully good at. . . .

Gurney: I'm glad you cited Faulkner and Flannery O'Connor. I think you can go farther into Brautigan off of them than you can off of someone like Hemingway, who is a little too one-tracked in his attitudes and concerns to delight me forever. Hemingway doesn't laugh much. Maybe that's why he committed suicide. Suicide may have been inevitable for Hemingway, but you'd never think such a thing about Faulkner, Flannery O'Connor, or Brautigan. Not that they are "happy" writers by any means. Their fiction can be as heavy and as grotesque as life itself, but what's refreshing, as you say, is that they have a supreme comic sense as well as a tragic vision. They're double-edged, sharp on both sides.

The fascinating thing about Brautigan is that he's more than double-edged. He's got more edges, more places to grab hold, than anyone else I can think of now writing. He's a poet and a novelist and a short story writer. And then he's something else besides. He's a curious kind of inventor, which takes me back to what I said earlier: that, to me, the short pieces like "Lint" and "The Scarlatti Tilt" do not fit the genre of the "short story" as I understand it, while "Coffee" and, say, "The World War I Los Angeles Airplane" (which encompasses an entire lifetime in five pages) and several others most certainly do. Brautigan is one of those rare writers who can operate within traditional form, and outside it. Most writers place themselves in one camp or another, seeking either to master an inherited set of rules or else to discover new ones. A story like "Coffee" is a story out of settled literary places. But when he writes that curious "Lint," I think Brautigan is out on the frontier of something. He goes out, and then he comes back in again. He plays in the interface, at that special meeting-place of underground and overground, of the familiar and the avant-garde. The tension between those opposing directions is one of the main sources of the energy behind the stories in this volume, stories about common things, told in very uncommon ways.

I think it's in there somewhere that Brautigan's enormous popular success is explained. He's popular because he is a man peculiarly of his time, and place. He's a very contemporary guy. He's a California writer, and his perception is "stoned." He gets *behind* the little episodes of these stories, gets into the emotion behind the action, in a way that more intellectual writers seem incapable of, or at least not very interested in. Feelings flow freely in Brautigan's fiction, sweet feelings as well as bitter ones, and that makes it a rare commodity in a country as violent and repressed as the United States. As a California writer, he stands as a kind of gift from the West Coast to the rest of the nation which, judging from the enormous circulation of his books, is a gift the country willingly accepts.

And *Revenge of the Lawn* is the latest of Brautigan's lovely gifts to us all. (p. 68)

> *Gurney Norman and Ed McClanahan, in* Rolling Stone *(by Straight Arrow Publishers, Inc.* © *1971; all rights reserved; reprinted by permission), Issue 97, December 9, 1971.*

TONY TANNER

[Brautigan's writing seems to float easily away from the *dreck* of the contemporary environment] like clouds over the Pacific. . . . Although his work is indeed extremely funny, there is a pervasive sense of loss, desolation and death in it which amounts to an implicit formulation of an attitude towards contemporary America. The first word of his first novel, *A Confederate General from Big Sur* . . . , is 'attrition', and the book manages to combine fleeting reminiscences of the obvious attritions of the Civil War with the less obvious attritions of life on the Californian coast today. The book is the reverse of didactic, and one would be missing the whole point to look for a specific moral to it. In appearance indeed it is very carefree. (p. 406)

And yet one feels that the engaging humour, naive and fantastic, is being maintained on the edge of a great emptiness. . . . The narrator offers multiple endings for his novel, but the dominant sense is of things thinning away into air, drawn back into the sea, fading away to the silent stillness of an old photograph. . . . This most insubstantial of worlds is being rapidly reabsorbed into an immense vacancy.

What the narrator has to sustain him is a gentle gaiety among words and a habit of instant fantasy. (p. 407)

One could call Brautigan's book an idyll, a satire, a quest, an exercise in nostalgia, a lament for America, or a joke—but it is a book which floats effortlessly free of all categories, and it is just this experience of floating free which is communicated while one is reading the book. There is certainly a feeling for a pastoral America which has vanished or been despoiled by mechanization, crime, accumulating garbage, and various kinds of poison and violence. In addition there is a sense that the original reality of America has been replaced by fabricated dreams of which the movies are the clearest example. (p. 410)

But the book is nothing like a polemic: Brautigan, it is clear, would not engage in anything so formulaic and recognizable as an established genre. That, after all, is someone else's movie. He has found himself a place beyond society and has exempted himself from all the usual modes and conventions. His novel is like no other novel and is one only because he says so, since it flouts all the usual prescriptions for the writing of fiction. The list of contents, the chapter divisions, the 'characters', the narrative episodes,

all mock the forms of conventional fiction by pretending to add up to a recognizable structure which is not there when you come to look for it. He retains the illusion of orthodox syntax and grammar, but the sentences are continually turning off into unexpectedness in ways which pleasantly dissolve our habitual semantic expectations. At the same time Brautigan is constantly, cunningly, deviating into sense; there is enough linguistic coherence left for us to experience the book as communication, and enough linguistic sport for Brautigan to demonstrate his own freedom from control.

Among other things the book is a typographical playfield. On the title-page, the words of the title are arranged to simulate a trout jumping. In the course of the text we find blocks of words from signs and monuments, signatures, recipes, a square from a map, addresses, labels, quotations, notes, words from headstones, underlinings, and—'4/17 OF A HAIKU'. With such good-humoured caprices Brautigan shows how free he feels to make his own patterns, and how uncircumscribed he is by the traditional ones. Each chapter is a separate fragment, unpredictable because unrelated in any of the usual ways. Each one engages us for a moment with its humour, or strangeness, or unusual evocation, and then fades away. The writing is like skywriting; even while articulating it is receding back into silence, dissolving its own patternings before it gets fixed in them. . . . It is one of Brautigan's distinctive achievements that his magically delicate verbal ephemera seem to accomplish their own vanishings.

Clearly this might all add up to a recipe for whimsy, and a style with such a light touch cannot always hope to avoid coyness, false naivety and sentimentality. These are certainly to be found in Brautigan's work, but hardly at all in this novel. The evanescent quality of the writing, the elusive metamorphoses of sense and form (like clouds) nevertheless leave one in possession of something extremely haunting, evocative, and capable of making subtle solicitations to a whole range of authentic feelings. Unhysterical, unegotistical, often magical, Brautigan's work contains some of the most original and refreshing prose to appear in the 'sixties. (pp. 410-12)

[*In Watermelon Sugar*] is a charming and original work with touches of magic, but is perhaps too obvious in its parabolic form. It suggests a commitment to a rather *too* simple-minded version of things which the previous novels avoid. It is a pastoral dream in which the dominance of fantasy and imagination over the Forgotten Works and the wrecking yard is perhaps too effortlessly achieved.

To return to the last two chapters of *Trout Fishing in America* is almost to return to where we started, for they are about language. Brautigan first quotes passages from three books concerning the origin of culture and more particularly the mystery of the origin and evolution of language. He then adds that he himself, 'expressing a human need', has always wanted to write a book that ended with the word mayonnaise. The final chapter he calls 'The Mayonnaise Chapter'. It turns out to be a letter of condolences sent to some people on the passing away of Mr Good. The letter has a P.S. which reads, 'Sorry I forgot to give you the mayonnaise.' Master of his own verbal terrain, Brautigan has satisfied his need, indulged his whim, exercised his freedom—there are any number of ways of expressing the possibilities open to a writer in the City of Words. But this final gesture is not merely frivolous. In an earlier chapter while walking through one of the many graveyards in the book, the narrator takes note of the pathetic improvised markers on the graves of the poor. On one of them is a mayonnaise jar containing wilted flowers commemorating, so he gathers from the inscription, an eighteen-year-old boy who was murdered in a bar; it was left there by his sister who is now in 'the Crazy Place'. The mayonnaise jar rests on one of the graves of the American dream; similarly Brautigan's lexical games rest lightly, but distinctly, on the panorama of violence, decay and death which is recognized as the real world. A gift for play and a sense of annihilation come together in the placing of the last word of his book, just as they do in his work as a whole. Borrowing a phrase from Gary Snyder, we may say that Brautigan's writing offers 'Flowers for the Void'. In it we can feel his disengagement from a malign reality—not by ignoring it (for it haunts him), but by moving to that realm where all is Great Play and Transformation, the liberations of fantasy once again triumphing over the constrictions of environment. (pp. 413-15)

> *Tony Tanner, in his* City of Words: American Fiction 1950-1970 *(copyright © 1971 by Tony Tanner; reprinted by permission of Harper & Row, Publishers, Inc.; in Canada by Jonathan Cape Ltd), Harper, 1971.*

GERALD LOCKLIN and CHARLES STETLER

What intrigues us most about Richard Brautigan's novel, *A Confederate General from Big Sur*, is its strong resemblance to [Ernest Hemingway's] *The Sun Also Rises* and [F. Scott Fitzgerald's] *The Great Gatsby*, little as the comparison might be appreciated by the authors of those classic works. In narrative technique the novel most closely resembles *Gatsby*. Jesse, like Nick Carroway, is a first person peripheral narrator. The subject of his narration is a flamboyant, "romantic" character who, like Gatsby, reflects the materialistic values of the country. Gatsby and Lee Mellon decline in glamor in the course of the novels, but the former transcends his context and the latter does not. At the end of each novel the most prominent character is the narrator and both have witnessed the end of a dream.

This is the novel of a generation, The Sixties, which many would consider equally as "lost" or even more so than that of The Twenties. It details the sort of good and bad times of a social clique that one finds in the Hemingway book. Both groups are expatriates, although in the more recent novel the locale and expatriation is the "Confederate State" of Big Sur. Still, like the Hemingway group and unlike the protagonists of *Easy Rider*, the Brautigan characters are instinctively trying to escape from America.

There is the striking parallel of the physical impotence of Jake Barnes with the concluding psychological impotence of Jesse.

In both works the "fiesta" ends in an existential hangover. The drugs and whiskey of the Brautigan novel correspond to the obsessive wine-drinking of the Hemingway novel.

The Twenties were faced with the search for a new morality in the light of the Dead Gods. The Sixties were similarly aware of that *Gotterdammerung*. Jesse, like Jake, is trying to evolve an ethic. Lee Mellon isn't even bothering.

Like *The Sun Also Rises*, *A Confederate General* is a war novel, or, more properly, a post-war novel. Hemingway, Mailer, Jones selected wars from their experience. Brautigan, like Stephen Crane, selects the Civil War. Brautigan, like Faulkner, feels that America has been in decline since that war. He calls it "the last good time this country ever had." (pp. 72-3)

For Brautigan the morally and spiritually crippling effects of the war have spread with Manifest Destiny across the continent, reaching at last the Coast. . . . (p. 73)

By mentioning him in the same breath with John Stuart Mill, Brautigan encourages us to think of Lee Mellon as a man of stature. He has like Mill a "truly gifted faculty." Whereas, however, Mill learned to translate Greek at the age of three, Lee Mellon's gift is for "getting his teeth knocked out."

The above is to some extent facetious, for Lee Mellon *is* a genius of sorts, a Mill without humanism. His ambition is to become "one of the dominant creatures on this shit pile." He is the master of the put-on, the con. He is ruthless and without a shred of altruism. He might, a century before, have been a robber baron. Hence, his surname.

In what sense is Lee Mellon a Confederate General? In that sense in which "confederate" equates with "counterfeit"? Probably. He is gradually reduced in stature throughout the novel, just as is his ancestor, August Mellon, in a series of flashbacks very reminiscent of the interchapters of [Hemingway's] *In Our Time*. Augustus Mellon turns out to have been no general at all, but merely a goof-off soldier, a sort of character out of *Catch-22*. . . . (p. 74)

But for about a hundred pages [Augustus'] exploits seem generally funny. Then we find ourselves in the same position in which Calder Willingham places us in *Eternal Fire*: we are rooting for the wrong side, or for both sides. (pp. 74-5)

Lee Mellon is man reduced to animal, man stripped of his ideals, and those who come in contact with him suffer a like fate. . . .

We first notice Jesse's increasing mental instability about two-thirds of the way through the novel when he half-heartedly jokes about the damage to the soul of a steady diet of Lee Mellon's cooking. Up to this point, Jesse has remained in the background, portraying Lee Mellon for us, sometimes dazzling us with his imagery, but making no value judgments and telling us little of his own feelings. Soon, though, we find him irritated with Roy Earle's offer to buy Elaine for the night and, shortly thereafter, he states, "I wanted reality to be there. What we had wasn't worth it. Reality would be better." This is a crucial remark, for the progress of the book to this point (and the spiritual thrust of the Sixties as well) has been in the direction of a *sur*-reality, mind-expansion, a psychedelic rejection of the ordinary, the established, the banal. They have been playing at insanity, but confronted with Roy Earle they can see that real mental illness is no laughing matter. Worse, they have played insane to the point where they have actually gone a little mad, the lot of them. (p. 76)

Significantly it is in the midst of their highest moments on dope that Roy Earle, a nightmare image, appears "at the edge of the firelight. He was chained to a log he had dragged from God knows where. It was just horrible." Furthermore, it is during the the dope chapter that Brautigan switches from Civil War metaphors to images drawn from modern warfare. (pp. 76-7)

Walking, Jesse [later] says, "I would not fight it this time." Does he mean he won't fight reality or won't fight sanity? We're not sure, but on the next page he refuses to accept one of Roy Earle's fantasies—the first time in the book that any character has insisted on literal reality. (One recalls Jesse's fiction with Susan of not having seen Lee Mellon—even with Lee Mellon standing next to him.) (p. 77)

[We] come to a conclusion distinctly reminiscent of the catastrophe of [Nathanael West's] *The Day of the Locust*—the simultaneous disintegration of society and of the self. Insanity reigns, as the characters search for a lost pomegranate, but only Jesse is aware that there is anything crazy about the whole thing. And both books conclude near the Pacific limits of America, the nation of the Dream.

Jesse's final comment: "There was nothing else to do, for all this was the destiny of our lives. A long time ago this was our future, looking now for a lost pomegranate at Big Sur." There are strong echoes of Faulkner in the rhetoric and also in the theme of historical determinism. (pp. 77-8)

In the novel, Brautigan writes, "A seagull flew over us, its voice running with the light, its voice passing historically through songs of gentle color. We closed our eyes and the bird's shadow was in our ears." This is not prose logic. This is closer to the poetic logic of associations espoused by the Symbolists and Surrealists and condemned by such critics of obscurantism as Yvor Winters. (p. 78)

Brautigan's style is touched by the spirit of Dada. In the early chapters in particular there is an irreverence, a sansouciance, a willingness to trust to the random association, which places it in the tradition of Tzara, Arp, [West's] *Balso Snell*, S. J. Perelman, and the Marx Brothers. There is a sense of fun, a relaxed quality to the prose. Brautigan makes reference to [Kenneth] Patchen's *Journal of Albion Moonlight*, and that work certainly is a predecessor of the present novel, but we are spared the earlier work's heavy symbolism, its self importance, its verbosity—all the plagues of the off-beat novel. *In Watermelon Sugar* reminds one more of the Patchen novel.

The mention of Dada reminds us of two points that must not be obscured by our analyses: (1) although this is a serious work and definitely not an anti-novel, it is nonetheless a very funny book as well, especially the early chapters . . . and (2) one runs the risk of over-interpreting any work that rings of Dadaism—Brautigan is surely not one to bind himself too rigidly to consistency, symmetry, the unities. He rules by fiat.

The novel might also be approached as a series of character studies of the young women of the Sixties, reminiscent again of *The Great Gatsby* with its incomparable cameos of Daisy, Jordan Baker, Mrs. Wilson. . . . (pp. 79-80)

[Elaine] is the most complicated and profound of Brautigan's portrayals. (p. 80)

Jesse provides symbolic keys to her personality by linking her with Alice and Ophelia. For Alice was, after all, the prototypal woman of the Sixties (cf. the Jefferson Airplane's hit, "White Rabbit."). Alice is the queen of psychedelia, she who dispenses the pills that make you larger and the pills that make you smaller. Elaine is perfectly at

home in the "wonderland" of Lee Mellon's Confederate State of Big Sur. Ophelia, like Alice, left one insane world for another.

Brautigan concludes the novel with 186,000 alternative endings per second, of which several are sketched for us. The endings represent stylistic variations. Jesse's breakdown and the search for the pomegranate are not contested. . . .

The endings produce a deliquescent effect, a *Tempest*-like dissolution but without the harmony of Shakespeare's play. (p. 81)

The world of the novel is one devoid of moral and psychological constants. Elizabeth and Elaine have learned to cope with such a world. Lee Mellon rises to military dictator. It is more a commentary on the world itself than on Jesse that he simply can't handle it. It is the mark of tragic heroes, Hamlet for instance, that they are incompatible with the world. (pp. 81-2)

Lee Mellon's great-grandfather, Augustus Mellon, died in 1910. Brautigan reminds it was that ominous year in which Mark Twain also died, and the year of Halley's Comet. Is this an effort to reinforce the whole theme of America in decline? . . .

There is a schoolteacher from Jesse's boarding house who journeys to Europe. He dies on the gangplank while returning home: "He didn't quite make it. His hat did though. It rolled off his head and down the gangplank and landed, plop, on America." Is this a parody on America as the promised land? Cf. Elia Kazan's *America, America*. . . .

To come full circle: like *A Sun Also Rises, A Confederate General from Big Sur* is a very funny, very sad, and very important novel. (p. 82)

Gerald Locklin and Charles Stetler, "Some Observations on 'A Confederate General from Big Sur'," in Critique: Studies in Modern Fiction *(copyright © by* Critique *1972), Vol. XIII, No. 2, 1972, pp. 72-82.*

CHERYL WALKER

Richard Brautigan is an epiphenomenon in American literature. He seems to represent some sort of insubstantial alternative. While the academy of letters reads Beckett, Borges, and Nabokov, the kids read Brautigan. . . . His appeal consists primarily in an irrepressible optimism (probably the brand of a woodsy Pacific Northwest background), a style flashing with artifice, and a total disregard for effete university culture. Mr. Brautigan is not himself the product of American higher education or of much formal training of any kind. Furthermore, his fund of simplicity and optimism is a relief for some from the profound despair of writers like Beckett. To complete the picture, I need only add that his flashy technique, in reality concealing a great deal of carelessness, on first reading must strike some readers as more exciting than the whittled style and carefully constructed works of Borges.

Thus he has risen almost by accident to a prominence far beyond his expectations or desserts. He emerged conveniently at a time when surface display is applauded by many readers, weary with education and its sacred fund of difficult literary exercises. The convenience extends to his natural bent toward living close to the earth which coincided happily with a burgeoning interest in ecology and the retreat from the cities to a more rural existence. There is no doubt that Mr. Brautigan has become a kind of cult figure. (pp. 308-09)

However, it is not fair to limit the appeal of Mr. Brautigan to the young. An enormous number of reviews have appeared in a wide range of journals which indicate that many members of the older generation have fallen under his spell as well. . . . (p. 309)

[*Trout Fishing in America*] is a collage of scraps about life in California, about the Pacific Northwest, about various experiences trout fishing, all of which the author seems to want to coalesce into some kind of statement about America itself, often as he says "only a place in the mind." Unfortunately, Mr. Brautigan's mind does not seem to be able to concentrate on anything long enough or hard enough to discover its meaning, to unlock its mystery, to do much more than make a few stray notes about the logistics of experience.

The logistics of experience are precisely what Mr. Brautigan seems to be interested in. His characters are hardly characters at all but they do interact. Thus gesture replaces psychology, travel replaces self-exploration, and accidental disappointments replace existential despair. Mr. Brautigan's characters are not alienated and the America he describes in *Trout Fishing* is sometimes unjust but never hostile. Unanalyzably present and mutely assertive, America becomes a mere extension of his ego like the various women who appear and disappear throughout his work.

The source of interest in this world comes from Brautigan's liberal use of tricks, puns, wild images, and surprising juxtapositions. (p. 310)

Mr. Brautigan is sincere, or would at least like to convince the reader of his sincerity. Unfortunately, one is hardly repaid for the sentimental flaccidness of his prose by the experience of feeling that he might after all be serious. Hovering behind many of his stories, behind "The Surgeon" in *Trout Fishing* for example, is a desire to flaunt the author's moral sensitivity. In *The Abortion* it is Vida who decides to get rid of her baby but it is Mr. Brautigan who looks for the credit of her decision. This leads to a kind of sententiousness on the part of the character which hardly seems necessary in her situation.

> Vida: Maybe another time, perhaps for certain another time, but not now. I love children, but this isn't the time. If you can't give them the maximum of yourself, then it's best to wait. There are too many children in the world and not enough love. . . .

The sentiments are respectable enough and yet they sound maudlin because they are expressed in prose with so little originality, so little bite to it. They are the well-chewed maxims of sociology texts. The sentimental Mr. Brautigan peeps from his pages so often in moments like this that one is tempted to cultivate an acerbic irony just to freshen the air.

Interestingly enough, Mr. Brautigan for all his attempts to be part of the avant-garde often falls into the very old pit of the moral fable. (pp. 311-12)

What Brautigan does well—the single insight about fleeting human experience—is more suited to poetry than it is to prose. In *The Pill Versus the Springhill Mine Disaster* he occasionally hits it. "Widow's Lament" which follows in full is nice in its minor way.

> It's not quite cold enough
> to go borrow firewood
> from the neighbors.

However, such understatement is rare, and more often than not Mr. Brautigan's poetry simply illustrates his lack of understanding of the medium. His lineation is based on grammatical units rather than on any principle inherent in the poem itself. Furthermore, he does not know how to build: development of character or statement or scene is as alien to his poetry as to his prose.

Some readers have mistaken this weakness for a statement about the meaninglessness of existence, the fragmentary quality of experience, the mute surfaces of modern life. Unfortunately, Mr. Brautigan himself brings events into moral relations which his readers are so kind as to forget. In "1692 Cotton Mather Newsreel" a child's prank becomes emblematic of the New England witch hunts and the genocide of Nazi Germany. The story itself does not in the least warrant such extensions of meaning. It sounds like an incident from *To Kill a Mockingbird*, though Harper Lee never made such grand claims as these. A couple of boys dare each other to sneak into the house of a helpless lady whom they think of as a witch. One boy completes the dare and then, frightened at himself, runs screaming away, joined by his pal outside who also begins to scream. The story ends: "We ran screaming through the streets of Tacoma, pursued by our own voices like a 1692 Cotton Mather Newsreel.

This was a month before the German Army marched into Poland."

There are, of course, other writers in America today who use the fragmented series to form a collage. William Gass' "In the Heart of the Heart of the Country" and Donald Barthelme's "Robert Kennedy Saved from Drowning" are two works of fiction which succeed brilliantly at Brautigan's game. Gass gives a more complicated picture of America in his Indiana collage than Brautigan does in the whole of *Trout Fishing in America*. Furthermore, Gass like Barthelme says a great deal that is interesting about the creative process as well. Both men keep one guessing, keep one's mind awake and working even when they are relating a seemingly meaningless list of facts. Brautigan, on the other hand, is all somersault, all splash and glitter. One grows weary of this and stops paying much attention to the pages as they turn. There is no organizing consciousness behind the phenomena he presents to our view. It's only some kind of shell game with Brautigan hoping he can keep your interest distracted from the fact that there is nothing under his shiny cups after all. (pp. 312-13)

> *Cheryl Walker, "Richard Brautigan: Youth Fishing in America," in* Modern Occasions (*copyright © Modern Occasions 1972), Spring, 1972, pp. 308-13.*

JOHN DITSKY

Richard Brautigan's fiction shares many of the qualities of his poetry—charm, brevity, whimsy, and in many cases a total inability to leave a residue in the consciousness. His narrative voice, in its matter-of-factness, resembles that of that other Californian, [John] Steinbeck, but lacks the older writer's coherent philosophy and sense of apparent purpose. Yet even in these respects Brautigan's writing seems consistent with that of the more intellectual practitioners of experiment fiction, such as Coover, Gass, Barthelme, and Barth. Moreover, Brautigan writes stories and chapter units of minimal length, like those of W. S. Merwin and Leonard Michaels. In addition, he is accessible on a level just a cut above sentimentality and mass-art: obviously beyond Rod McKuen, but perhaps on a par with Kurt Vonnegut.

Brautigan's *Revenge of the Lawn* . . . is similar in tone to *Confederate General from Big Sur, In Watermelon Sugar,* and his best known work, *Trout Fishing in America.* If it lacks the slackness of *The Abortion,* its predecessor in publication, it shares with it an only temporarily disarming casualness about the motivation for the creative act. . . . Autobiographical fragments, often achieving easy effects, even flirt with the maudlin, as in "One Afternoon in 1939," where Brautigan repeats a daughter's favorite story about her father as a child. A little charm goes a long way, and Brautigan has the good sense to keep his pieces short, as much out of prudence as out of art. Wit is the soul of his brevity, time-killing his morality, and the experience of others a kind of clay: "I put it in my pocket. I took it home with me and shaped it into this, having nothing better to do with my time." Even in the more successful stories, like the tightly-constructed "The World War I Los Angeles Airplane," where the experience of recounting a failed man's life collides with the facts of his death and the necessity of informing his daughter, we are given a clue to Brautigan's suspicions of conventional fiction: "Always at the end of the words somebody is dead." (pp. 304-05)

John Ditsky, in The Georgia Review *(copyright, 1972, by the University of Georgia), Fall, 1972.*

ROGER SALE

Richard Brautigan . . . the only writer of the sixties recommended to me by students whom I enjoyed, [is] author of the charming *Trout Fishing in America,* and author, alas, of *The Hawkline Monster,* which is decidedly uncharming and literary, obvious, empty, Butch Cassidy and the Sundance Kid stuff. . . . There are maybe a hundred [edgeless and pointless] chapters in *The Hawkline Monster.* . . . When Brautigan tires of gunmen he writes about identical women named Miss Hawkline whose father made a monster, and when he tires of that he has the Miss Hawklines see the dead butler in the hall and say "I'd like to get fucked." It's a terrible book, deeply unfunny, in no need of having been written. (pp. 624-25)

Roger Sale, in The Hudson Review *(copyright © 1974 by The Hudson Review, Inc.; reprinted by permission), Vol. XXVII, No. 4, Winter, 1974-75.*

VALENTINE CUNNINGHAM

When you take on the surreal you must clearly watch out for its near and merely embarrassing neighbours, triteness and banality. Richard Brautigan is not, on the whole, half watchful enough. . . .

[The plot of *The Hawkline Monster* is one] that leaves one decidedly out of thrall much of the time. And as for Gothicism: as oddities, this lot scarcely packs much of a *frisson.* "What does supernatural mean?" Cameron asks. "It

means out of the ordinary", one of the Misses Hawkline informs. But, though events in *The Hawkline Monster* can certainly range far out of the ordinary, the more bizarre they come the flatter tends to be their impact. The dull, accepting tone is largely to blame, and there is little to be said for it as a narrative means except perhaps that it can welcome the ordinary quite unhectically. It is extremely liberating to find everyday things like four-letter words, the sexual act, and the desire of women for men, making for once an unstrident appearance in fiction. "'Fuck me', Magic Child said. . . . Greer blew the lantern out and she fucked Greer first."

But even—perhaps *especially*—in regard to sexual events narrative inertness speedily numbs. In fiction where nothing is allowed to perturb, the reader quickly feels nothing matters all that much. "An Early Twentieth Century Picnic" is the chapter heading when Hawkline Manor blazes, the Monster dies, and "a scientific dream" ends. But the novel is much too enervated to make the implied case about our times actually stick on anyone or anything.

Valentine Cunningham, "Whisky in the Works," in The Times Literary Supplement *(© Times Newspapers Ltd. (London) 1975; reproduced from* The Times Literary Supplement *by permission), April 11, 1975, p. 389.*

MICHAEL ROGERS

[The guileless and unprepossessing Brautigan style] has finally, after a few tentative passes, collided firmly with the harsh and nasty seventies.

Brautigan's sixth novel, "Willard and His Bowling Trophies," is essentially about sex and violence. Willard, in standard Brautigan fashion, really has very little to do with any of it. He is, in fact, a mysterious papier-mâché bird, housed off the lower floor of a two-unit apartment building, and surrounded by a collection of stolen bowling trophies. Precisely who stole the trophies is not clear, but the original owners are a trio of brothers who lose their jobs, self-respect, and ultimately commit senseless murder in a misguided attempt at revenge. It is, in all, a fairly slim story for 167 pages, but then the art of loose unraveling is a Brautigan cornerstone. This time, however, the unraveling is not a very happy process. . . .

While the rest of the book never gets much more intentionally unpleasant than the first few pages, it doesn't get much lighter, either, and the Brautigan humor that used to pop up in even the grimmest places is here little in evidence. . . .

Brautigan's most durable work, in fact, has been his short fiction and verse—shorter pieces containing wit, innovative imagery and unexpected turns of phrase that will almost certainly retain a lasting audience. "Willard," unfortunately, shows few of those virtues.

Perhaps Brautigan should make a brief retreat from the novel form. Or perhaps that flat, almost banal, ingenuous style, that worked so well for wistful depictions of loves lost and gained, of good luck and bad luck and loneliness, just isn't right for a long bleak gaze at unhappy sex and senseless murder. (p. 4)

Michael Rogers, in The New York Times Book Review *(© 1975 by The New York Times Company; reprinted by permission), September 14, 1975.*

L. J. DAVIS

It strikes me that the secret of Richard Brautigan's fiction and poetry is that, like the symbolism of D. H. Lawrence, it means exactly what it seems to mean. Trying to delve deeply into it is like trying to delve deeply into a cigar box; what's in it may be good, bad or indifferent, but there really isn't very much of it and its pleasures are soon exhausted. It may be a sign of the times (or something) and it is certainly a symptom of the current state of American fiction that some critics doggedly persist in treating Brautigan as if he were a Joseph Conrad instead of an Art Buchwald: it is such a blessed relief to find someone who writes so *nicely*. There is no denying that he turns a pretty phrase and does so often; it is his greatest gift, and not one to be stinted. But it should also not be overlooked that turning a pretty phrase is just about all that he does. There is a streak of sadness in him that is refreshingly without self-pity and a streak of kindness that is almost magically free of condescension, but the fact remains that he is a constructor of sentences, not a fabricator of situations. When he looks out on the world, he sees shapely prose and not the dark and vagrant mysteries of the human condition. The reader will find no sense of majesty here, or of its loss, no irritating complications such as madness and thwarted hope, no terror but a good deal of pity. Richard Brautigan will give no one bad dreams. He is sorry for us, and he is fun to read. When one has said that about him, one has said about all there is to say.

Willard and His Bowling Trophies finds the mixture much the same as before. . . .

I think the bowling trophies and the Logans' search for them are meant to represent the sleaziness and degrading pointlessness of American life. I think Brautigan thinks so too. (What Willard means is anyone's guess; I think Brautigan wants it that way.) The novel tells the story of the end of the brothers' three-year quest. It is not a happy ending but, like everything Brautigan attempts, it is nicely done.

Richard Brautigan has a sort of modified Midas touch: instead of gold, everything turns into feathers. They are handsome feathers and they have been arranged with the skill of a Japanese floral designer; I am going to place the book in my extensive collection of Brautiganiana, with my thanks to the author for having provided me with a relaxing 90 minutes, my face sometimes touched with the ghost of a smile, sometimes with the ghost of a frown. (p. 30)

> L. J. Davis, in The New Republic *(reprinted by permission of* The New Republic; © *1975 by The New Republic, Inc.), September 20, 1975.*

ROBERT KERN

Brautigan's work in both poetry and prose . . . provides a post-modernist instance of primitivist poetics in as pure a form as one could wish and also helps to clarify some of the differences between modernism and post-modernism in general. (p. 52)

As a poet and maker of fiction, Brautigan seems to come as close to a painter like Grandma Moses as it is possible for a writer to do; though sometimes his allegorical intentions and utopian or pastoral politics suggest a greater affinity with the early nineteenth-century Quaker and primitivist painter of a long series of variations on the theme of the Peaceable Kingdom, Edward Hicks. Insofar as his prose books can be considered novels, they are a re-invention of the novel, a project carried out in seeming ignorance of the history of literature and representing a kind of childhood of fiction, personal to the point of self-indulgence, open-ended, radically picaresque. This is probably most true of *Trout Fishing in America,* which often gives the impression of being invented or created *ex nihilo,* in a kind of isolation from the entire world, past and present, of literary method and discourse. But on another level Brautigan's ahistorical naiveté is deliberate, a calculated assertion of freedom from convention or the willful and sometimes arbitrary satisfaction of a whim. "Expressing a human need," he says near the end of *Trout Fishing,* "I always wanted to write a book that ended with the word Mayonnaise." And he then proceeds to fulfill the wish by giving us . . . "The Mayonnaise Chapter." . . . Thus Brautigan ends his book by introducing into its imaginative confines an artifact (whether invented or authentic makes no difference) that could never be mistaken for "literature" but that is a fully serviceable if highly oblique metaphor for his vision of pathos and continuity in American life. Brautigan's willingness to use such texts, the fact that he grants them entry into "literature," is indicative of his primitivist impulse not only to clear the ground but to widen it as well, to make it hospitable to utterances and verbal shapes and even inarticulate desires whose literary value and viability are essentially unrecognized. To this extent he goes even further than [William Carlos] Williams in the democratization of literature, in the offer of recognition and "a say," so to speak, not only to the ordinary and the familiar but to motives and impulses that just barely make their way into written form. (pp. 53-4)

It is tempting, though probably misleading, to regard Brautigan's work as a revolutionary act of sabotage directed against the institution that American literature becomes in [the final image of his short story "⅓, ⅓, ⅓"]. He wants, after all, not to destroy the institution but to throw open its gates and allow for a greater intermingling between what goes on inside them and the rest of the verbal world. In the larger field of his fiction, at any rate, the distinction between his own sophisticated writing and the primitivism of his sources and subject-matter remains clear despite the intermingling. But in his poetry we come into contact with a voice and a strategy that can usually be categorized as belonging pretty definitely to the primitivist side of the distinction. Its minimalist tendencies, along with the gentle, almost unconscious wit and innocence of its speakers, suggest that in his poetry Brautigan is viewing the world from *inside* a primitivist perspective as opposed to the juxtaposition and manipulation of several perspectives that take place in his fiction. Nor do his poems carry the same sorts of social and political implications to be found in his stories and novels. For the most part turned in upon themselves, they are almost narcissistic in their self-involvement and self-regard. (p. 55)

More than anything else, it is probably the flatness and the apparent artlessness of his poetry that are boring and even offensive to some of Brautigan's readers. But it is precisely these elements that constitute what is meant by a primitivist poetics (though Brautigan, admittedly, takes them to a blatant extreme). His disregard for the conventionally "poetic" is grounded in the assumption that anything more than a direct, immediate and simple response to things would be dishonest, while on another level it implies that he *does not know how* to write in highflown, literary language, which he distrusts anyway as a distraction, an intrusion between him and unmediated experience. But the most fundamental assumption behind this resistance to the "poetic" in Brautigan is that "poetry" does not reside in language or even in the text of the poem; it is, instead, a latent possibility in reality and can "happen" at any moment. In this sense his poems are opposed to the romanticism of the confessional mode, in which it is assumed that the poet is a special person whose perception is privileged and whose work gives voice to experience that is unique and intensely charged. For a poet like Brautigan . . . , poetry is whatever happens to him, a continuing, everpresent possibility, and he is, almost helplessly, its servant, rather than the other way around. In one poem he records how he has to get out of bed and put his glasses on in order to write it down, so that a good deal of his poetry amounts to a commentary on itself. Accordingly, Brautigan's poems are often reproductions of the circumstances which brought them into being. . . . [For] example, "April 7, 1969":

> I feel so bad today
> that I want to write a poem.
> I don't care: any poem, this
> poem.

Poetry of this sort works like a self-fulfilling prophecy and involves a kind of magic. It delights and surprises because it is so outrageously self-conscious. Before our eyes a desire to write transforms itself into something written. A desire to produce a poem, by virtue of a sheer act of self-recognition, becomes a poem. There can be no better dramatization of the notion that poetry is an act of recognition as well as one of craft, and in Brautigan the craft is pared down to the recognition itself. The result may be disturbingly quiescent in the sense that, given the attitudes behind such work, the writer is left helpless before experience, neither exercising control over it nor attempting to interpret it. It may be artless in fact and even trivial, but the undeniable insistence in such writing is that poetry is ultimately located in experience itself, an insistence that demotes the text to an occasion of recognition. And what is recognized is that the true ground of poetry lies beyond all texts, in the world outside the institution of literature. (pp. 56-7)

> *Robert Kern, in* Chicago Review *(reprinted by permission of* Chicago Review; *copyright © 1975 by* Chicago Review), *Vol. 27, No. 1, 1975.*

DUNCAN FALLOWELL

Willard and his Bowling Trophies is a humorous downtown fantasy and might strike someone not *au fait* with post-colonic literature as unusual, disgusting even. This is not so. Brautigan couldn't split an infinitive to save his life. In the manner in which he handles his God-given culture he could be the nearest America comes to producing an updated P. G. Wodehouse. But his originality, let alone longevity, has suffered from an overdose of small beer exacerbated by a material lack of concentration. The most concentrated sentence is 'After he came his penis would slowly soften inside of her and their bodies would be very quiet together like two haunted houses staring across a weedy vacant lot at each other.' A minor planetary system spirals inside that sentence. He used to be throwing them up all the time.

Stretched beyond endurance, with these big gaps all over the show, the book is finally embarrassed by the exaggerated attention brought to bear upon its whimsy. 'They

would tear a nice hole in you and provide you with enough death to last forever'—ugh, coy, and it is often like that. Even the basic idea is forced, a Caesarean attempt at lunacy. The Logan Brothers are nice boys until one day their bowling trophies are stolen; they hit the road to recover them in an anti-social frame of mind, and end up committing murder on a peculiar couple called Bob and Constance who are trainee sado-masochists innocent of theft.

The funniest episodes observe this couple's entanglement with venereal warts. (p. 30)

> *Duncan Fallowell, in* The Spectator *(© 1976 by* The Spectator; *reprinted by permission of* The Spectator), *May 29, 1976.*

BRAD HAYDEN

In [*Trout Fishing in America*] the trout stream is a central metaphor for the shrinking American wilderness and the social values which are associated with it. The narrator of Brautigan's novel seeks a pastoral life in nature but does not succeed; his search ends in frustration and disillusionment. Enroute he comments upon social and personal values in America with an equal sense of despair.

Brautigan's method, looking at society through nature, is not new. A number of literary artists and philosophers in various ages have done the same—the most notable of whom is probably Henry David Thoreau. Indeed, similarities between Thoreau's *Walden* and Brautigan's novel are very striking both in the form their arguments take, as well as in the arguments themselves.

Both works are written as first person narratives. Each reflects upon experiences in nature which conveniently span one year's time, and consequently, both have (in Charles B. Anderson's words on *Walden*) "sought an asymmetrical pattern that would satisfy the esthetic sense of form and still remain true to the nature of experience, art without the appearance of artifice." . . . (p. 21)

On a surface level, Brautigan's work appears to be a series of disjunctured ramblings (interestingly enough, the same criticism was made of Thoreau by his early critics) with no apparent form. Yet like *Walden* various levels of structure do appear to serious readers. The most obvious is that structure of a year's quest. It begins with the narrator's search for an amiable trout stream and terminates with the last chapters commenting upon the disappearance of nature in America. The work ends with the narrator and his family having decided to live in a friend's cabin in California.

A similar structure is also found in Brautigan's treatment of the narrator's maturation into manhood and the loss of innocence through knowledge. The narrator's personal growth parallels the picture of nature he presents. The wilderness, which represents a kind of innocence, is fouled by society, while the narrator's boyhood idealism turns into disillusionment. By using flashbacks of past life in the one-year narrative, the two levels of experience complement one another. Thoreau, of course, does much the same in his "digressions" in *Walden*. He uses his discussions of his more metaphysical concerns to color his commentary on nature. Brautigan's method in handling nature is also similar to Hemingway's. Like Jake Barnes fishing the mountains of Spain in *The Sun Also Rises*, Brautigan's narrator seeks through nature a means of communing with the surrounding world. Neither of the characters is highly successful. (pp. 21-2)

Trout Fishing in America conveys its thematic message through a series of short episodes concerned with the materialistic wasting away of the American wilderness and the decay of personal morality. Like Thoreau among the ponds surrounding Concord, Brautigan's narrator sojourns through the wilderness of Idaho hoping to find idyllic meaning in a primitive natural order, to be [in the words of Ralph Waldo Emerson] "part and particle" of the organic harmony between fish and stream, animal and forest. This then is related through episodes describing direct natural experience of nature: And within this naturalist order is intertwined, in a *Walden*-like manner seemingly at random, episodes which deal with society and the narrator's personal level of awareness of the world surrounding him. For example, in one of the beginning chapters, "Another Method for Making Walnut Catsup," the concept of trout fishing in America is personified as a rich gourmet. In this chapter this character "trout fishing in America" and his girlfriend, Maria Callas, prepare exotic, yet homemade, dishes together in the moonlight, "on a marble table with beautiful candles". . . . At first a reader might be taken back. What does this chapter have to do with the book's structural order, why is it there? One reason is found in the chapter's ritualistic use of language—the language of recipes and of cause and effect. The primary connotations of such language concerns order: follow the prescribed steps and the desired result will always be attained. And, by introducing Maria Callas, a glamorous and famous woman, the scene takes on the added connotations of the American Dream: follow the prescribed steps and success will naturally follow. The concept of formula is stressed and a kind of ordering is presented; Maria Callas then smiles and the moonlight comes out. Thoreau does the same in *Walden* through his early presentation of the ordered life. He certainly does not have a character comparable to Maria Callas but from the recipe for financial living which is presented in *Walden*'s opening chapter "Economy" to the final rebirth of spring in the work's latter stages, Thoreau too definitely stresses order and harmony. (p. 22)

The basic structure of *Walden* leads to transcendence, from the climactic reflection of the heavens in the waters of Walden pond to nature's, and Henry David's, renewal and rebirth with the coming of spring. The structure of Brautigan's novel, however, leads to frustration. Instead of achieving his desired unity with nature, Brautigan's narrator finds disjunction. The major significant difference between *Trout Fishing in America* and *Walden* is that in Brautigan's story there is no personal transcendence. Yet, this brings out the logical question, if the methods are similar, why is the end result not the same?

The answer lies in the physical reality of *Walden*'s nature in contrast to its theory of nature. That is, such critics as Anderson have noted the importance of the proximity of Concord to Walden pond. Thoreau in theory was able to merge himself in the wilderness despite the society which enveloped it. But the fact does remain that in his southwesterly walks Thoreau did face an essentially unexploited continent in America. A virgin wilderness may not have existed around Concord, but it did hypothetically exist for Thoreau in America's western regions.

For Brautigan's narrator no such conceptual nature exists. Indeed, the most significant aspect of the work is that for the narrator such nature does not in reality have substance.

Even though the primary level of description concerns the narrator's direct experience with nature, time after time he journeys into the wilderness and is frustrated. (p. 23)

Society itself occupies a greater role in Brautigan's narrative than in Thoreau's and is used as an essential manifestation of Brautigan's novel failing to achieve satisfaction in nature. The mentality and values of the society Brautigan describes accounts for the narrator's failure to find the pastoral life. Of course, the interpretations of experience which Thoreau and Brautigan employ are different. To Thoreau experience is seen on a cosmic and metaphysical level: man achieving a synthesis between himself and the natural world which in turn unifies him with what Ralph Waldo Emerson identified as the "over-soul." Brautigan is less concerned with man's position with the cosmos than he is with man's position in society itself. *Trout Fishing in America* is basically social criticism of our contemporary American society. And while Thoreau certainly criticizes society in *Walden*, his emphasis is upon the individual ascension of man into universality. (p. 24)

Brautigan's final commentary on life in contemporary America is pessimistic to say the least; it's certainly not like Thoreau's commentary in the final stages of *Walden*, which ends optimistically. Thoreau is successful in achieving his dream, whereas Brautigan's narrator is not. Yet all is not hopeless in Brautigan's world. Mention is made periodically thoughout the book of "Trout Fishing in America Terrorists"; persons who oppose the society and, like Thoreau, live according to the dictates of conscience rather than those of social law. Brautigan's narrator too is not crushed by the world he views. Like Thoreau, he moves on looking forward to live new lives in the future. (p. 25)

Brad Hayden, "Echoes of 'Walden' in 'Trout Fishing in America'," in Thoreau Journal Quarterly, *July, 1976, pp. 21-6.*

THOMAS R. EDWARDS

As a Barthelme-like exercise in discontinuous modes, lyrical, topical, and confessional, [*Sombrero Fallout: A Japanese Novel*] is amusing but somehow self-cancelling. The parable about mindless public violence is too harmlessly droll, the love story too sentimental, the portrait of the artist too routinely self-loathing. Remembering Brautigan's *Trout Fishing in America*, I would be glad to like *Sombrero Fallout* better, but his charm seems to be increasingly calculated. (p. 100)

Thomas R. Edwards, in Harper's *(copyright © 1976 by* Harper's *Magazine; all rights reserved; reprinted from the October, 1976 issue by special permission), October, 1976.*

DENNIS PETTICOFFER

Brautigan insists that [*June 30th, June 30th*] is a "different" collection of poetry. Written in diary form, it contains impressions of his seven-week tour of Japan in 1976. . . . Taken individually, many of these poems do not hold up well. Brautigan himself concedes that the collection is "uneven." Taken together, it portrays a mood of alienation and loneliness, as might be expected when a poet finds himself immersed in an alien culture, unable to communicate with, or be understood by, the world around him. But "Japan" is not necessarily on the other side of the world—it can be just across the street. The book's prime appeal will be to college audiences, but it may prove less enticing than Brautigan's earlier works. (p. 465)

Dennis Petticoffer, in Library Journal *(reprinted from* Library Journal, *February 15, 1978; published by R. R. Bowker Co. (a Xerox company); copyright © 1978 by Xerox Corporation), February 15, 1978.*

MARY HOPE

As a newcomer to the Brautigan cult, I can only think that [*Dreaming of Babylon*] must be a bit of a spare-time exercise: an after-dinner conversational joke which got out of hand. . . .

Much of the action takes place in the morgue, the cemetery, or the hero's head; either way, the effect is fairly deadly. Brautigan's style depends on the premise that one bad joke deserves another: he sets up what starts off as a respectable one-liner and then kills it stone dead by trying to make it into two. If he'd honed down the cracks, the book would be even shorter than it is, but much funnier. There is not much point in parodying a style unless there is a valid alternative statement to make: this is just a thin idea, made thinner by the disparity between the master's theme and the pupil's variations. (p. 24)

Mary Hope, in The Spectator *(© 1978 by The Spectator; reprinted by permission of* The Spectator*),* April 22, 1978.*

ARIAN SCHUSTER

[*June 30th, June 30th* is a] collection of eighty brief poems, several just fragments—written from May 13 to June 30th on a visit Brautigan made to Japan, somewhat in the spirit of a memorial journey for the Japanese and American war dead. . . . Like so many literary journeys, it becomes a point of departure for an exploration of the self in relation to the world of the nonself. The Brautigan wit is fleetingly present, but there is a haunting feeling of loneliness in the poetry—a sense of a stranger in a strange land—that ultimately makes Japan seem like a metaphor for alienation. Brautigan fans may like this; but he has moved away from the concerns of the young adult, and if one already has Brautigan books, skip this one. (p. 18)

Arian Schuster, in Young Adult Cooperative Book Review Group of Massachusetts, *December, 1978.*

Mel Brooks

1926-

(Pseudonym of Melvin Kaminsky) American scriptwriter, director, actor, and comedian. Involved for many years in comedy writing for television, Brooks is now best known for directing zany films in which he often acts. His humor is frequently concerned with Jewish subjects and characters. He explains his position in this way: "Unrelieved lamenting would be intolerable. So, for every ten Jews beating their breasts, God designated one to be crazy and amuse the breast-beaters. By the time I was five I knew I was that one." Brooks's career took off when he began writing for Sid Caesar's television series "Broadway Revue" and "Your Show of Shows." His first filmscript won him an Academy Award in 1963. It was an animated short, "The Critic," inspired by an old immigrant who sat behind Brooks in the theater, mumbling his negative opinions of an abstract animated film. Brooks asked his friend, Ernie Pintoff, to draw a similar piece and as he viewed it for the first time, he improvised a prejudiced reaction to it, using the comments as the final sound track. Brooks began directing because he considered it his only defense against rewrite experts. Although his first film, *The Producers*, won the 1968 Academy Award for best original screenplay, it was not a great success, financially or critically. In subsequent years, however, his reputation has soared. He is, at this time, lauded by many critics as one of the best comedy directors in America. His work in films is characterized by his broad humor, which many times borders on slapstick. However, Brooks has noted that the loss of his father when he was two years old gave him an awe and fear of death. This recurs in his work in a variety of ways, such as the desperation to create life *(Young Frankenstein)* or the denial of mortality (the character of the 2000 Year Old Man). Although not always apparent, such serious comments are an important aspect of his humor, an undercurrent of its surface absurdity. (See also *Contemporary Authors*, Vols. 65-68.)

RENATA ADLER

["The Producers"] is a violently mixed bag. Some of it is shoddy and gross and cruel; the rest is funny in an entirely unexpected way. It has the episodic, revue quality of so much contemporary comedy—not building, laughter, but stringing it together skit after skit, some vile, some boffo. . . .

Strangely enough, the first act of "Springtime for Hitler: A Gay Romp with Adolf and Eva in Berchtesgaden" is the funniest part of this fantastically uneven movie. The Ge-

stapo chorines, the opening number, "Look Out, Here Comes the Master Race"—well, it loses absolutely everything in transcription. But there is just enough talent and energy to keep this blackest of collegiate humors comic. Barely.

Then, the movie makes a terrible and irreversible mistake. It allows the audience onscreen to find the play funny. This turned the real audience in the theater off as though a fuse had blown. Hardly anyone laughed again. Partly, it must be admitted, because "Springtime for Hitler" itself gets less funny at this point. . . . But mainly, because there is nothing like having your make-believe audience catch on to a joke—and a joke that absolutely capsizes the plans of your leading characters—to make your real audience really hostile to you.

The ending, when all the comic props are supposed to be in motion . . . goes better than one might think. On the whole, though, "The Producers," leaves one alternately picking up one's coat to leave and sitting back to laugh. (p. 38)

Renata Adler, in The New York Times (© *1968 by The New York Times Company; reprinted by permission), March 19, 1968.*

ANDREW SARRIS

[Mel Brooks' "The Producers"] did not make me laugh as much as I had anticipated, and perhaps anticipation is part of the problem. Let us suppose that an acquaintance stops us in the street with the announcement that he is going to tell us the funniest joke ever told. But first, he tells us, he is going to synopsize the joke, describe its high and low points, analyze the style of its telling, compare it with other jokes in the same genre from other eras, and psychoanalyze those listeners who will laugh at it and those who will not. Then and only then does he tell us the joke. Do we laugh? Not likely. The element of surprise is gone because we listen with too many preconceptions. In short, we listen more to the how of style than to the what of content. . . .

The idea that two Jewish producers would engage in a project called "Springtime for Hitler" even as part of a swindle is more a cabaret idea than a movie idea. Even on the Borscht Circuit, a Jewish comedian can assume a Nazi role as a temporarily shocking point of departure to arouse black laughter in his audience. . . . Cabaret characterizations are entirely hypothetical. If you accept such and such a premise, such and such will occur. Screen characterizations are historical. The characters played by Zero Mostel and Gene Wilder are obviously if not blatantly Jewish, and they carry their pasts around with them while they humor a psychotic Nazi author to the point of singing "Deutschland Uber Alles" and wearing swastika armbands. . . .

However, even if we assume that there were two Jewish producers greedy enough to do something so distasteful, it is difficult to laugh, however blackly, at a plot device that has received so much advance publicity. As it turns out, the whole movie is based on this one plot premise that is supposed to attest to the New Audacity in movies. Instead everything in "The Producers" attests to the New Vulgarity.

Except for two or three expert sequences, the direction of Mel Brooks is thoroughly vile and inept. Everyone in the film down to the least extra mugs with an extravagance not seen since the most florid silent days. When "Springtime for Hitler" is finally staged, the audience looks with collectively wide-eyed, wide-mouthed shock and amazement at a hilariously professional mixed chorus of boys and girls in black jackets and swastikas tapping, kicking, and prancing away. But why should an audience be so shocked at a show called "Springtime for Hitler?" What did they expect? the realistic conscience of the medium keeps whispering in my ear. To make matters worse, the audience within the film begins roaring with laughter at precisely that instant when the spectacle on the stage within the film ceases to be amusing. . . .

At a time when film aestheticians are solemnly debating the merits of looking directly at the camera to talk to the audience, Mel Brooks indulges in asides too stagey even for the stage. . . .

"The Producers" resembles "Enter Laughing" both in its conceptual and directorial crudity and in its isolated moments of hilarity with stage struck mediocrities. "The Producers" is in a class by itself as a movie that completely ignores the existence of women except as props, toys, or old bags. I hope this isn't a trend in the bright new world of sophisticated cinema. (p. 47)

> *Andrew Sarris, in* The Village Voice *(reprinted by permission of* The Village Voice; *copyright © The Village Voice, Inc., 1968), March 28, 1968.*

PAULINE KAEL

Brooks not only isn't a director—he isn't really a writer, either. He's the cutup in the audience whose manic laughter and unrestrained comments stop the show. Essentially, he *is* the audience; he's the most cynical and the most appreciative of audiences—nobody laughs harder, nobody gets more derisive. He was perfectly cast in the short "The Critic." His humor is a show-business comment on show business. Mel Brooks is in a special position: his criticism has become a branch of show business—he's a critic from the inside. He isn't expected to be orderly or disciplined; he's the irrepressible critic as clown. His comments aren't censored by the usual caution and sentimentality, but his crazy-man irrepressibility makes him lovable; he can be vicious and get away with it because he's Mel Brooks, who isn't expected to be in control. His unique charm is the surreal freedom of his kibitzer's imagination.

The other side of the coin is that he isn't self-critical. And, as his new picture, "Blazing Saddles," once again demonstrates, he doesn't have the controlling vision that a director needs. It's easy to imagine him on the set, doubled up laughing at the performers and not paying any attention to what he's supposed to be there for . Mel Brooks doesn't think like a director; he's not a planner. He doesn't even do any formal, disciplined routines; he's a genius at spontaneous repartee—which the movies have never yet been able to handle, though television can, and that's where Brooks is peerless. Out of nowhere, he says things that people talk about for decades. . . . [In "Blazing Saddles," the] story is about a modern black hipster (Cleavon Little) who becomes sheriff in a Western town in the eighteen-sixties—a core idea without much energy in it to start with, a variant of the plot of such movies as "The Paleface," with Bob Hope. (pp. 378-80)

Brooks's humor is intentionally graceless; he seems to fear subtlety as if it were the enemy of all he holds dear—as if it were gentility itself. Brooks *has* to love the comedy of chaos. He wants to offend, and he also wants to be loved for being offensive. We can share his affection for low-comedy crudeness and the comedy of chaos, but not when he pounds us over the head with strident dumb jokes, and not when we begin to feel uncomfortable for the performers —mugging and smirking and working too hard. Brooks's sense of what's funny has sunk to sour, stale faggot jokes, and insults, and to dirtying up mildewed jokes, as if that would make them fresh. I never imagine I'd think back longingly on Brooks's first film, "The Producers"—but it never sank to this. His second film, "The Twelve Chairs," was bland and pokey, but Brooks himself was funny in it. (p. 380)

Mel Brooks is always looking for laughs—and he's beginning to laugh much more easily than we do. The movie is a rehash of "Hell-zapoppin" and other slapstick burlesques, and it may appeal to those who enjoyed the rehashed humor of "What's Up, Doc?," but it doesn't have the wit that made Mel Brooks a hero. He's become like a gag writer with a joke-book memory who cracks up at every terrible joke he recalls. Most of the gags in "Blazing Saddles" never were very funny, and probably Brooks knows that and thinks that what's funny about those rotten old jokes is how unfunny they are. But as a director he doesn't have enough style to make the unfunny funny. In "Blazing Saddles" he makes the unfunny desperate. (p. 381)

> *Pauline Kael, "O Consuella" (originally published in* The New Yorker, *February 18, 1974), in her* Reeling *(copyright © 1974 by Pauline Kael; reprinted by permission of Little, Brown and Co. in Association with the Atlantic Monthly Press), Atlantic-Little, Brown, 1974, pp. 374-81.*

COLIN L. WESTERBECK, JR.

Mel Brooks has a truly baroque sense of humor, as his new film, *Blazing Saddles,* demonstrates. Such an eccentric wealth of material comes out of his imagination that this film is usually working full tilt on three different levels at once: social satire, straight, old-fashioned slapstick comedy, and parody of various other Hollywood genres, most notably, of course, the Western. . . . It is, as the saying goes, a sketch.

Unhappily, that's often all it is: a sketch. It's not enough to make up a whole movie. Despite generating some material that works on all three levels, Brooks doesn't always have what he needs to keep the film going. . . . Moreover, the multiple levels on which the film is attempting to work don't always enhance each other. At times, in fact, they cancel each other out, especially where Bart is concerned. This is because the social satire and the slapstick comedy make contrary demands on his role.

In Brooks' view the former requires that, as a black man, Bart see through the bigotries, hypocrisies and illusions of the whites. He must be capable of a knowing, almost indulgent reaction to them. For instance, when he first arrives in Rocky Ridge, the town where he's to be sheriff, the entire population draws on him. To escape Bart pulls out his own gun as if he too were getting the drop on himself. Having thus taken himself hostage, he edges himself through the crowd toward the refuge of the jail.

This is a funny bit too, until Bart makes it to safety and at once shrugs off these gullible yokels with an unconcerned air. Before the comedy has successfully run its course, such a gesture of bemusement, repeated at the conclusion of skit after skit, kills the laugh every time. Whatever the gesture might do for the social satire, it is a wet blanket on the slapstick. The *mise en scène* of slapstick is destroyed when the protagonist suddenly switches from being the hapless victim of society to being a wry, ironic observer of it—when he unexpectedly turns out to be not so much the butt of the joke as the practical joker himself.

It might seem that Brooks has just decided he must ultimately sacrifice the slapstick to the satire. But in truth I think it is a weakness in the social satire, not its strength, that interferes with the total effect of the film at these moments. The fact is that Brooks is letting us off easily, and by *us* I mean the audience for whom the film was made, the white middle-class audience with whom the film will have to make its nut. Out of consideration for our touchy sensibilities, Brooks shies away from any really acerbic visions of race relations. Bart takes whitey's abuse in stride as if the problem were for him to be tolerant of white society rather than vice versa. He can even manipulate the white man and avoid the consequences of his malice so handily, that malice need not be thought of as a legitimate problem anyway. *Blazing Saddles* is thus careful—too careful—not to offend us. Like *All in the Family*, Brooks' film makes our prejudices seem so apparent and inept that we might conclude they must be harmless as well. The trouble with *Blazing Saddles* is that it's a comedy not black enough.

In the end, however, it's the Hollywood parody that comes to the top and dominates both the social satire and the slapstick. . . . Brooks' zaniness, his instinct for incongruities, doesn't fail him here. These closing scenes all go in a dozen different directions at once. But somehow they are still not as funny as they ought to be considering all the energy they are expending.

Maybe Brooks himself has tried to go in too many different directions at once. He has not only tried to work on too many levels of consciousness at the same time, but has taken on too many jobs: actor, director, writer, producer, lyricist, etc. There are two separate roles in which Brooks appears as an actor. . . . And even when these characters are not on the screen, Brooks still seems to be there in the

person of Bart. Bart's ambiguity, this too agile dexterity of his which allows him first to participate in a scene, then to stand aside and admire his handiwork, seems to reflect Brooks' own dilemma as director. Like Bart, Brooks has to juggle too many points of view for his own good. (pp. 61-2)

> *Colin L. Westerbeck, Jr., in* Commonweal *(copyright © 1974 Commonweal Publishing Co., Inc.; reprinted by permission of Commonweal Publishing Co., Inc.),* March 22, 1974.

JAY COCKS

Of course [*Young Frankenstein*'s] funny. And of course it's grating, flatulent, desperate—all in the best and the worst manner of Mel Brooks. As comic and as film maker, Brooks wants to knock you cockeyed. For a laugh, he will do anything, try anything. He rains gags. After a Brooks bit, audiences can be exhausted; after a Brooks film, there is the lingering feeling of having been pummeled. Brooks is like a young, slightly skittish fighter whose energy compensates for lack of finesse. He hits out wildly, continuously, hoping that a few punches will land. . . . The bedrock of all Brooks films is frenzy; the nominal subject of *Young Frankenstein*—the skyhook for all the madness—is a satirical exhumation of Mary Shelley's classic. The Shelley story ought to have turned wormy by this time from virtually constant exposure. It is, however, still a powerful myth. One good measure of its resiliency is that even when Brooks is lampooning it, the story remains compelling, nearly inviolate. When Gene Wilder's Dr. Frankenstein tries to zap life into a grotesque, inanimate form, the movie goes serious despite itself. The myth is better, more involving than the jokes being made about it. . . .

Brooks is always at his best making fun of the delicious stupidities of popular entertainment (recall *Springtime for Hitler* in *The Producers*), and this scene, with scientist and subject in top hat and tails performing *Puttin' On the Ritz*, is some sort of deranged high point in contemporary film comedy.

For moments like that, Brooks can be forgiven almost anything. He always furnishes plenty that needs forgiving, but his best scenes are madder, funnier, more inspired than anything being done in movies today, including the rather coddled comedy of Woody Allen. Brooks must also have got tired of people telling him what a maladroit technician he has been, and he has taken some pains to correct that failing here. *Young Frankenstein* is his best-crafted film so far.

> *Jay Cocks, "Monster Mash," in* Time *(reprinted by permission from* Time, The Weekly Newsmagazine; *copyright Time Inc. 1974),* December 30, 1974, p. 2.

COLIN L. WESTERBECK, JR.

The Frankenstein story, as we all know, is about a creature made up entirely of misappropriate and mismatched parts. That's pretty much the way Mel Brooks has made his new film, *Young Frankenstein*, too. Since all comedy has to be based on some sort of incongruity, this approach works out pretty well for Brooks. Most of the parts he has misappropriated come out of other people's movies. Besides having stolen the whole idea for this movie from James Whale's *Frankenstein* (1931), Brooks has, for instance, stolen the hairdo for one of his stars, Madeline Kahn, from Elsa

Lanchester in *The Bride of Frankenstein* (1935). At times, as when Miss Lanchester's streak job is set atop Miss Kahn's head, the stolen parts hardly look out of place at all. At other times, as when Brooks' monster (Peter Boyle) clomps his way through a Fred Astaire number of about the same vintage as the hairdo, Brooks is purposely letting all the sutures show. (p. 421)

A good deal of Brooks' energies in *Young Frankenstein* have been devoted to keeping up our awareness of his movie as a movie. He realizes that the culture on which his insanity really feeds is not Mary Shelley's England nor Transylvania nor even America at large, but just Hollywood. For this reason *Young Frankenstein* is, from its overall composition to its isolated details, a comedy of production errors. The whole movie has been thrown together from spare parts of other movies as if it were a bin full of out-takes, a face off the cutting-room floors where Hollywood's campiest films were made. The migration of Igor's hump and the switch-hitting the chief does with his prosthesis look like the mental lapses of some script girl who should be maintaining continuity in such details, but isn't quite up to her job. In vowel shifts that occur in a single one-liner, as in the execution of entire sequences, movie conventions fly through the air in this film in a mad jugglery that never lets us get down to earth for a moment. (p. 422)

> *Colin L. Westerbeck, Jr., in* Commonweal *(copyright © 1975 Commonweal Publishing Co., Inc.; reprinted by permission of Commonweal Publishing Co., Inc.), February 28, 1975.*

HERBERT GOLD

[Brooks] is the little boy, the youngest son, so beloved by his family and continually tossed in the air that his feet didn't touch the ground till he was 6 years old. He has been resting securely on the wind ever since. He knows he can always get home. He also gives an audience this dreamy assurance: They can wander in fantasy and nightmare, but with Kafka or Lenny Bruce, other Jewish masters of controlled psychosis, they were not sure of getting home from the dream. With Mel Brooks, they are merely up in the air, dandled, comfortable, blowing homeward to familiar hatreds (Germans, creeps, squares) and comfortable nostalgias (food, neighborhood, kids, old folks, Jews, Italians). The 1,000-watt kid is finally shedding his light for Southern drive-ins, Western small towns, the suburbs and exurbs and nonurbs filled with chuckling customers who never saw the originals which spawned him. In stagflation time, something that allows laughter is worth any price, especially since the price will probably go up.

Benevolent rivals for kingship in this domain of comfortable and consoling comedy are Woody Allen and Mel Brooks. They share several qualities—unthreatening physical presence, a bewildered yet focused eye, a language which slips out of the loose grasp of immigrant speech into desperate precision. Survival is never certain for them, and yet their perturbation is somehow comfortable. The audience is implicated, but not bound. Both Allen and Brooks violate rules, but not law: or perhaps it is law but not rules—they go far, but not too far. Fred Allen and Jack Benny filled some of these needs in another time. Isolation, anomie, frustration, love-lost and lovelorn fate, the common comic themes are stroked. Woody Allen and Mel Brooks are good at it. They do not threaten total revolution, but they play with nihilism. They are wanters—of love and comfort—like

the audience. They also want distraction, and they give it, and they get good rewards from an audience in need. There is room for both Woody Allen and Mel Brooks at the top. (pp. 28, 30)

Mel Brooks has learned the philosopher's truth: The mystery of life is not a problem to be solved, but a reality to be experienced—or, in his case, to be worked over in yoks. Like Lenny Bruce and Mort Sahl, he is playful with ideas and sounds, and introduces a bound-for-college tentative intellectuality; like the Borscht Belt comics, the Jackies and Sheckies and Jerries, he knows his job is to keep the customers awake and agape and, if you don't like this joke, wait seven seconds for the next one. His special qualities—boyish hope, a few obsessions (Jews and Italians good, Germans bad), the image of the 2,000-year-old man, a loving attention to the street fantasy of the kids of his generation (the western, the horror film, the verbal pratfall)—are not really unique, either, but he has finally mobilized the Mel Brooks Cult into a Mel Brooks Championship. (p. 30)

The audience achieved by Brooks's careful attention to his own insanity now seems to include everybody—critics, the young, the old, the nostalgic and the backers of movies. People want an excuse to laugh, any excuse, and Brooks is willing to give them good value for their money. They sense his yearning beyond the wisecracks, his appeal to love, his small-boy dirty-face cuteness, no matter how outrageous he might seem—flatulence, a dirty word here and there, a touch of bemused sadism. Where Lenny Bruce shocked, Mel Brooks consoles. He is funny because he wants to be funny. He is attractive about his funniness, corrosive in a healing manner, because he likes his actors, he likes his audience, he likes himself. As an amateur doctor, he wants to make people well—also himself. He is one unusual comic. . . . He is no revolutionary. He is a consoler in a time of too many instant revolutions. (p. 31)

> *Herbert Gold, "Funny Is Money," in* The New York Times Magazine *(© 1975 by The New York Times Company; reprinted by permission), March 30, 1975, pp. 16-17, 19, 21-2, 26, 28, 30-1.*

JACOBA ATLAS

[Brooks'] films abound in lovingly precise dialect humor, a near-balletic control of physical comedy, and whirlwind pacing that begins in chaos and ends in sweet lunacy.

Superficially, Brooks' movies . . . seem less careful than carefree. But Brooks says he does not believe in chance: his films are the result of meticulous construction, especially in the scriptwriting stage. . . .

At their core, his films come surprisingly close to being "male" love stories. You can see it in the sadomasochistic friendship in *The Producers* (with Zero Mostel as the S., and Gene Wilder as the M.), the love-hate relationship of Frank Langella and Ron Moody in *The Twelve Chairs*, the easy warmth between Wilder and Cleavon Little in *Blazing Saddles*, even the sympathetic if hysterical bond established between Wilder as Dr. Frankenstein and Peter Boyle as the Creature.

> *Jacoba Atlas, in her introduction to her "Mel Brooks Interview," in* Film Comment *(copyright © 1975 by The Film Society of Lincoln Center; all rights reserved), March-April, 1975, p. 54.*

JOHN RUSSELL TAYLOR

[*Young Frankenstein*] is remarkably restrained considering

that Brooks made it with the triumphant commercial success of *Blazing Saddles* under his belt; and that, it seems to me, gets across mainly by taking easy targets and bludgeoning them mercilessly until the last, dullest member of the audience must have seen the joke. The classic horror movie would seem to offer targets just as obvious. But evidently Brooks has more sympathy for it than he does for the Western, and a lot of the sympathy and enjoyment comes through. This time we are dealing with the story of *the* Baron Frankenstein's grandson, a humble, sane anatomy teacher who just wants to forget his family's reputation—until, that is, he arrives at the castle and falls under the spell of his grandfather's books and machines (the originals from [director] James Whale's day).

The gags are nearly all of the very slowburn variety rather than the straight belly-laugh. . . . No good to describe, but perfect examples of the 'it was funny when he did it' syndrome. And the film itself, shot in black and white which has deliberately been given the grainy, faded quality of the average print of a horror classic as we now see them, has often an uncanny look of James Whale at his best. To appreciate *Young Frankenstein* fully, you have to be pretty well acquainted with his legitimate grandfather. (pp. 125-26)

> *John Russell Taylor, in* Sight and Sound *(copyright © 1975 by The British Film Institute), Spring, 1975.*

TOM MILNE

Young Frankenstein begins on a dark and stormy night, with the camera panning lovingly over a torchlit courtyard, zooming slowly in to a dusty window, and dissolving as the clock strikes midnight into a caressing inspection of the Gothic inscription on a coffin reposing within a dank and doomladen crypt. A brilliant pastiche of the horror film's studied quest for atmospherics, the sequence suggests not only that Mel Brooks has added some sort of cinematic style to his bag of tricks, but that he knows his genre and intends to stick to it. An illusion that is dashed all too soon . . . as one discovers that anything goes even more frantically than it did in *Blazing Saddles*. . . . [All] too often Brooks resorts to the most clichéd sort of *Carry On* smut ("What knockers!" says Frederick, looking at Inga's décolletage but referring to the brasswork on Castle Frankenstein's portals), he repeats himself endlessly (the witless joke about Frau Blücher's name is done five times), he does the film a serious injury by allowing Marty Feldman to indulge some grotesquely unfunny mugging, and he even sinks to the perpetration of an Abbott and Costello routine. He also commits the unpardonable error of trying to milk laughs from something—Lionel Atwill's wooden arm in *Son of Frankenstein*—which was treated with much surer wit in the original. The real pity of all this is that two sequences not only come very close to brilliance, but also show the path a really good parody might have followed. One is the Monster's game of throwing flowers into the water with the little girl, staged with the same tender, fragile charm as in Whale's original but in which, as the little girl wails "Oh dear, nothing left, what shall we throw in now?", the monster turns to stare knowingly but doubtfully at the camera: he, too, has seen the movie. The other is the Monster's encounter with the blind hermit who, in trying to be hospitable to his new friend, accidentally pours soup over him, showers him with wine and splinters of glass in drinking his

health, and finally drives him out gibbering with terror and rage after setting fire to him in error for a cigar. In both these sequences, Brooks extends the spirit of the originals, confounds expectations, and creates a sort of poetry of his own very much in keeping with, in particular, *The Bride of Frankenstein*. But after *The Producers* and *Blazing Saddles*, no doubt one has to accept that a Mel Brooks film is a ragbag containing both best and worst. (pp. 90-1)

> *Tom Milne, in* Monthly Film Bulletin *(copyright © The British Film Institute, 1975), April, 1975.*

JOHN COLEMAN

Mel Brooks uses bad taste rather as you and I would pass the salt. *The Twelve Chairs* is basically an unjustifiable nonsense, done in Yugoslavia on the cheap side . . . , presumably after *The Producers* and before *Blazing Saddles*. Set in a Brooksian notion of post-revolutionary Russia, it agitates itself about fellows chasing up a dozen gilt chairs in the hope of disembowelling the one that contains a tsar's ransom in jewels. . . . Mr Brooks, who almost wrecks the outing by turning up too successfully in it himself, as a masochistic ex-valet and all-purpose serf . . . , has thoughtfully written a flabby role which comes over as improvised as silly putty left to its own devices. (pp. 418-19)

> *John Coleman, in* New Statesman *(© 1975 The Statesman & Nation Publishing Co. Ltd.), October 3, 1975.*

DEREK ELLEY

There are frequently sound reasons, both commercial and artistic, why many films remain on the shelf, but [*The Twelve Chairs*] thankfully falls prey to none of them. It is a genuine discovery in every way, and provides an opportunity to see Brooks working within stricter limitations than his other forays have provided. These take the form of Ilf and Petrov's famous satire on greed and cupidity in post-Revolutionary Russia—well-known within the USSR, perhaps less so elsewhere. . . . Despite the limitations of working from a literary source, Brooks has nonetheless produced a thoroughly personal version, as much impregnated with his brand of Jewish-American humour as anything from *The Producers* or *Blazing Saddles*. If the complete lunacy of his other films is generally missing in *The Twelve Chairs*, then that is no bad thing, although it no doubt accounts for the film's obscurity. Character is more to the fore and there is no small amount of sadness in much of the playing. (p. 38)

[Though] Brooks pays lipservice to the original in his main title sequence (showing the title first in Russian), he cannot resist the opportunites offered by having signs in English throughout: Marx, Engel, Lenin and Trotsky Street (with the Trotsky crossed out), or a placard advertising *Hamlet and the October Revolution* by William Shakespeare and Ivan Poppov. Because the overall temperature of the film is less high than in Brooks's other works, there are fewer damp squibs and a greater feeling of the film being equal to the sum of its parts. That sum is never very much, and it certainly will not make your ribs ache, but there is an unaccustomed warmth to the picture which is very winning indeed. (p. 39)

> *Derek Elley, in* Films and Filming *(© copyright Derek Elley 1976; reprinted with permission), March, 1976.*

JACK KROLL

Mel Brooks's "Silent Movie" is a take-off on silent movies, but it also uses the silent movie as a way of getting a fresh angle on today's world. In many ways it's Brooks's best film, less pushy than "Blazing Saddles," less shticky than "Young Frankenstein." . . . Brooks is one of our few authentic mad comic poets, and his daring to make a movie without spoken dialogue is an audaciously creative act in this bet-hedging time. . . .

The gags as usual vary in quality from gold to zinc, but what makes "Silent Movie" more than a string of gags is the comic sensibility of Brooks. Believe it or not, the master of bad taste becomes almost endearing in this film—as when he pays homage to the good old bump and grind with a pelvic paroxysm by the pneumatic Bernadette Peters. The film's foremost quality is a genuine sweetness of tone as the three maniacs ricochet around contemporary Los Angeles in search of stars and success. Brooks knows that the quality common to the old silent comedies was this rippling rhythm of sweet, silly humanity, and he captures it to a remarkable degree without any camp or condescension.

> *Jack Kroll, "Funny Business," in* Newsweek *(copyright 1976 by Newsweek, Inc.; all rights reserved; reprinted by permission), July 12, 1976, p. 69.*

JOHN SIMON

Mel Brooks's comic gift, such as it is, is largely verbal and stands to lose too much in a silent movie; and . . . what was once done so well was done out of necessity, the need to overcome the limitations of a mute medium. Remove the necessity, which is the mother of invention, and you come up with test-tube babies of scant viability.

In the event, *Silent Movie* has some quite funny sight gags, though the invention wears progressively thinner; it also has exaggerated sound effects that have good and bad moments. . . .

The scenario is basically no sillier than those of the old silent comedies, but the innocence is gone. Some gags are too elucubrated and esoteric; other are takeoffs on the old ones, and seem to kid something that depended on its deadpan dedication. (p. 84)

Yet it would be less than honest to say that there are no laughs; it must, however, be stressed that laughter, like other forms of sustenance, varies in taste. There are sweet or spicy laughs that leave a vivifying aftertaste in the mouth; there are sharp or sour ones that a good chef can likewise put to stimulating use. But there are also those laughs that are so stupidly bland, so bitter, or so tasteless as to leave behind an acrid taste or none at all. Such queasy laughs one is soon ashamed of having laughed, and *Silent Movie* (sigh! sob!) has far too many of them. (pp. 84, 87)

> *John Simon, in* New York Magazine *(copyright © 1976 by News Group Publications, Inc.; reprinted with the permission of* New York Magazine*), July 19, 1976.*

STANLEY KAUFFMANN

[*Silent Movie* is Brooks's] best picture to date. That's limited praise, surely, still this is his most organic film, the least desperately outrageous. No one sequence stands out like the punching of the horse in *Saddles* or the monster-doctor vaudeville routine in *Frankenstein,* but those were highlights amidst messy frenzy. *Silent Movie* takes a comic line and hews to it fairly consistently, fairly inventively.

Some viewers have assumed that, by making a silent film, Brooks is automatically challenging Chaplin and Keaton, particularly since he also plays the leading role. . . . [But he] is simply pursuing his parodic way—last time monster pictures, this time silent slapstick, next time maybe Ingmar Bergman. Like all parody, it's a form of homage, but that's not the same thing as competition. The only question is whether the parody amuses. . . .

I didn't laugh at the picture as much as I just *liked* it. Even when gags go on too long, like Brooks and friends in armor in a studio commissary, *Silent Movie* has the feeling of goodhearted spoof. And most of this comes from Brooks himself. Up to now his screen performing has been blasted by life-of-the-party mania. But here the absence of language seems to have forced him back, not on technical excellence, which he doesn't have, but on his personality. What holds this picture together is that Brooks comes across as—yes, I was surprised, too—rather sweet. (p. 20)

> *Stanley Kauffmann, "Laff Time" (copyright © 1976 by Stanley Kauffmann; reprinted by permission of Brandt & Brandt Literary Agents, Inc.), in* The New Republic, *July 31, 1976, pp. 20, 33.*

ROBERT ASAHINA

I have never been an admirer of Mel Brooks, although I enjoyed *Young Frankenstein* when it came out a little over a year ago. To be sure, his *oeuvre* has included some hilarious moments—the "Springtime for Hitler" sequence in *The Producers,* for example—but these were practically buried beneath an indiscriminate flurry of flat jokes. As Pauline Kael has aptly noted, his films embody the spirit of gagwriting, not screenwriting. They do not work as cinematic comedies because they are essentially extended strings of raucous and vulgar one-liners, better suited to the nightclub floor than to the moviehouse. . . .

Still, since my quarrel is with his style of verbal bombardment, I was prepared to be open-minded about *Silent Movie,* Brooks' attempt to write and direct a comedy without dialogue. Unfortunately, the production fails on much the same grounds as his talking pictures.

Silent Movie simply isn't very funny. . . .

It is never clear why this comedy about the making of [a silent] movie should itself be silent. Brooks seems to think the humor of this conceit is self-evident, and that it provides a sufficient mainspring for everything he is going to show us. But nothing follows from this empty joke—except a catalogue of the various blunders that can be committed in the name of comedy, silent or otherwise. We are left confused and puzzled throughout about his intentions.

Like all of Brooks' works (with the possible exception of *Young Frankenstein*), this one is guilty of obviousness. That is not to say that the humor is excessively broad—though it happens to be—but rather that it is at the level of a dull five-year old. . . .

[A] blatant gag can only succeed when contrasted to more subtle humor. But Brooks provides no shadings; he never misses a chance to stick his finger in your eye—twice in a row, if possible. Funn, Egg and Bell drive past a Szechwan restaurant, and through a picture window they see steam rising from the mouths of customers. We are then immediately shown the same scene through a *second* window, so the joke is hammered home with elephantine skill. (p. 23)

The relentless pounding of *Silent Movie* is further heightened by the mechanical setups Brooks ineptly employs. Funn, Egg and Bell try to recruit several Hollywood stars (who play themselves in cameo roles) for their film. (pp. 23-4)

When the three go after Liza Minnelli, they corner her at lunch in the studio commissary. Since they have taken the time to dress in heavy suits of armor, we are, again not surprisingly, exposed to awkward attempts at sitting down, considerable clanking about, broken dishes, and smashed tables and chairs. Yet there is no apparent reason for the sequence: We never learn why they put on the armor in the first place.

Justifying such unnatural contrivances by appealing to a sense of the ridiculous simply won't do. Humor can indeed be founded on a non sequitur; it can be illogical and even artificial. But it cannot be utterly arbitrary. Moreover, when it is as mechanically contrived as it is in this instance, it is completely predictable. The setups here are so patently engineered, they telegraph rather than lead into the sequences that follow.

What all this suggests is a complete inability to appreciate the cinematic constraints on comedy. For a funnyman, Brooks has a lamentably poor sense of timing, a handicap that hampers his verbal comedy, and is almost fatal to the visual gags. In *The Producers,* for instance, the "Springtime for Hitler" episode combined outrageous sight gags with a hilarious musical number. It succeeded in spite of, not because of the editing, which almost destroyed the sequence by awkwardly cutting back and forth between the stage and the audience.

In *Silent Movie* there is even greater need for careful editing. In one potentially funny sequence involving a car chase, Funn, Egg and Bell are rushing to the theater with the unfinished film, while Vilma is trying to distract the impatient audience waiting for the movie premiere. Intercutting in the best Keystone Cops tradition would have been effective. Instead, Vilma's ever more explicit displays convey no sense of her increasing desperation; the car chase is literally stalled at several points and fails to build any feeling of comic frustration and urgency.

It would be easy to blame the editors of *Silent Movie* for this, however I suspect the fault lies with Brooks; totally insensitive to the rhythm of movie comedy, he botched what should have been an effective sequence. . . .

Brooks' anarchic, machine-gun spray of gags reduces everything to its lowest common denominator and then ridicules it. This is the reason toilet humor figures so prominently in his comic scheme—we are all equally vulnerable on the seat. But that is precisely why we choose to preserve some privacy, some dignity; if we are all in the same position, no one can mock others without demeaning himself.

This apparently has not occurred to Brooks. And I suspect audiences do not recognize his misanthropy for what it is because he is so unremittingly cheerful. . . .

Comedy, of course, is not something that occurs only in a socially or politically neutral context. More often, in fact, it is aimed at deflating empty pretension, attacking class differences, exposing hypocrisy—in other words, it is culturally motivated. Brooks' purpose is to communicate sheer anarchy. Thus only audiences equally anarchic could find his films funny: His comic nihilism feeds the nihilism of his audiences. That is what troubles me about hearing otherwise sensitive people laugh at his *Silent Movie.* (p. 24)

> *Robert Asahina, "Suffering in Silence," in* The New Leader *(© 1976 by the American Labor Conference on International Affairs, Inc.), August 2, 1976, pp. 23-4.*

JUDITH CRIST

[In *Silent Movie*] Brooks has concocted a talkie with a gimmick. The gimmickry here involves parodies of silent-movie jokes and simplistic plotting. The absence of realistic sound and speech is complete with the exception of one word—spoken, of course, by the mime Marcel Marceau. Above all, it's an oral comedy, with its verbal humor obvious in signs, names, and title cards. Like *Blazing Saddles,* the Brooks film this most closely parallels, *Silent Movie* is clearly the work of gag writers. . . . It's even more clearly the work of Mel Brooks, not merely as the co-author, director, and leading man, but also as the overall comic persona, replete with his satiric eye, sophisticated social perception, gut approach, and unfortunate tendency toward the scatological, not to mention his gift for the outrageous and—though I have sworn off the word as blurbily destructive—the hilarious. . . .

[There] are sight gags galore: slapstick and pratfalls and rib tickles and rib pokes; shticks and bits and skits and lunacy —and lapses of taste and timing. (p. 44)

And there are falters: Marceau in a Bip bit serves only to jolt us into the realization that we are watching speechless rather than silent comedy; the villainies of Harold Gould and his E & D associates are basically uninspired. . . . As a tour de force, it's amusing on a superficial level. As a Mel Brooks movie, it's more of the same—and while we do indeed ask for more we keep hoping for the "something different" he's come up with before. (pp. 44-5)

> *Judith Crist, "Mel Brooks Tackles the 'Pickford Paradox'," in* Saturday Review *(© 1976 by Saturday Review/World, Inc.; reprinted with permission), August 7, 1976, pp. 44-5.*

TOM ALLEN, S.C.

Mel Brooks, along with Woody Allen, has progressed as a prolific, one-man source of American screen comedy. Both comedians have picked up where Jerry Lewis died off and have actively participated in the writing, acting, producing and directing of their films. Neither has settled for a personal, distinctive style yet, but they are giving the previous, well-defined comic personae, such as W. C. Fields and the Marx Brothers, stiff competition. They work in safe ranges well below the level of the great silent comedians; but their comic, sometimes cosmic, daring is far superior to the steady diet of Bob Hope, Red Skelton and other postwar schlemiels.

Mel Brooks's *Silent Movie,* a consistently funny grab bag of routines, is perched in style somewhere between the boorish excesses of *Blazing Saddles* and the disciplined mimicry of *Young Frankenstein.* It has the feel of a throw-away lark, which, in its way, is a healthy symptom of survival under the pressure of the rarefied field of creative comedy. . . .

He has not made a movie for theoreticians who are still puzzling over why the giants of American screen comedy died out in the talkie era. He has, it appears, handicapped himself with a silent film only to turn on the creative juices for other outlets: to write more puns in the title frames, to tinker with the type of sound effects that no truly silent movie ever had and to sharpen his sense of timing in the visual gags of slapstick. (p. 100)

Tom Allen, S.C., in America *(© America Press, 1976; all rights reserved), September 4, 1976.*

LAWRENCE WESCHLER

You need only be informed that in [*High Anxiety*] . . . , Brooks is sending up Alfred Hitchcock, and you will instantly surmise that here, on the last day of the 54-day shoot, he is trying to bury *The Birds* once and for all. Hitchcock's protagonists suddenly found themselves prey to a swarm of man-pecking birds. In Brooks's version, the psychiatrist-protagonist—''a reincarnation of the classic Hitchcockian hero, the tall, handsome innocent who gradually becomes ensnared in a nefarious plot breaking out all about him,'' played by Himself—is relaxing on a park bench one afternoon as gradually, one by one, a flock of pigeons convenes on a nearby jungle gym. Gradually, one by one, the birds take off, swoop in low, and strafe. Slowly, calmly, Brooks assesses the situation, rises, begins to walk away, nonchalantly quickens his pace—the birds, in droves now, continue the pursuit—and, finally, breaks into headlong flight, seeking refuge at last in the ill-fated gardener's shed. *High Anxiety* may not be the first time Brooks has stooled to conquer, but in this scene, he offers one of the most outrageous samples of his *mise en merde* directorial style.

In the general public imagination, Mel Brooks is perceived as something of a madcap maniac, an image Brooks resents but at the same time helps to foster. In reality, however, his filmmaking persona is anything but out of control. From screenwriting through directing and then editing, Brooks is in complete command of his medium, utterly considered in his deployment of its resources. And the central preoccupation at every stage is vigilant attention to pacing and nuance. In this context, it is not surprising to learn that he first forged into show business as a drummer, snaring out summers in the Catskills. For Brooks, the process of creating a film is entirely one of orchestration, He has an uncanny sense of what will make an audience laugh, and how long and in what manner it will make them laugh. His directing metaphors are often musical: He inserts rests, changes key, quickens tempo, measures out the beat. He directs with an eye to editing, acutely aware of the jokes on either side of the one he is at that moment positing. And the entire process, for all its lunatic jangles, is intensely cerebral. (pp. 35, 37)

Yet *High Anxiety* displays more than mere technical virtuosity on Brooks's part, As an homage to Alfred Hitchcock, he has had to fashion a film that works simultaneously as a comedy and a suspense thriller, the two elements playing against each other. The stratification of jokes is much more complex than in his earlier efforts, ranging from straight

shtick to subtle allusion and on out to blatant parody. The plot and the characters are more boldly drawn and clearly articulated: He is eliciting a wider range of performances from his repertory company of actors. . . .

There is the usual Brooksian mixture of slapstick, snidery, double entendre, and character blitz. But what makes *High Anxiety* special is its homage to the cinematic style of the master. We know we are in Hitchcock's universe, or why else would our point of view be scrunched below a glass table, looking up at the huge knees and dwarfed faces of the two archvillains as they conspire to yet commit another murder? Hitchcock fans will probably be most titillated by the sidelong tributes to specific films, for the plot, while contained in itself, is continually surfacing, like some stray submarine, in the middle of some other classic Hitchcock movie. The comic impact derives from the shudder of recognition as the Brooks film momentarily tumbles into the Hitchcock, and just as quickly, picks itself up, scrapes off the birdshit, and moves on.

In many ways, *High Anxiety* may stand, as Brooks insists it does, as his greatest film to date. Nevertheless, . . . I find myself harboring a grudging reluctance to throw myself wholeheartedly into the chorus of praise. This is partly because *High Anxiety* continues the string of Brooks parodies of other films. *The Producers* and, to a lesser extent, *The Twelve Chairs,* his first two films, seemed somehow extensions of a personal self. . . . But, starting with *Blazing Saddles,* and continuing with *Young Frankenstein, Silent Movie,* and now *High Anxiety,* Brooks has developed an almost formulaic approach: Unlike *The Producers,* which he wrote alone, these scripts are the products of television-style brainstorming sessions between shifting collections of comic writers. And they all work primarily as take-offs on earlier, cliché-ridden genres. (p. 37)

The core attribute of Mel Brooks is a sort of hypersensitivity to the outside world. On the one hand, this is reflected in an almost naive celebration, an unmediated delight in the sheer richness of the everyday lifeworld, the human provenance. Here is the source of his richest comedic material, in his extraordinary attention to nuance and detail. . . . And that anxiety, in turn, skews the artistic production: Trying to please the largest possible audience, he confects another genre parody rather than hazarding a more personal statement. Or within any given film, some small, delicate insight is blasted home, rendered utterly blatant, so that there's no doubt that everyone will get it.

My thoughts drifted to Brooks's extraordinary propensity for metaphors of combat whenever he's discussing his cinematic intentions. The dovetailing between the languages of comedy and violence is by now proverbial: Jokes die; monologues bomb; when successful, comics kill their audiences. But his language is especially charged, and the confrontation seems somehow more personally intense. In a curious sort of way, the audience is forever the potential enemy: At any moment, it could break out in apathy. This danger has to be smashed. The point is not merely to survive but to gain the victory. The explosion he plots is the audience's uncontainable laughter. He triumphs when, momentarily, he utterly disarms his would-be adversaries. His expansive generosity arises simultaneously with his tenacious defensiveness. Perhaps a similar process is at work in the self-exposure of other comedians, but with Brooks its operations are more transparent, and, one imagines, more intense. His comedies only hint at the drama of their creation. (p. 38)

Lawrence Weschler, "Is Mel Brooks Going Crazy?" in The Village Voice *(reprinted by permission of* The Village Voice; *copyright © The Village Voice, Inc., 1977), December 26, 1977, pp. 35, 37-8.*

CHARLES M. YOUNG

High Anxiety could well be Brooks' funniest movie yet. The plot is disarmingly rhythmic, sucking you into suspense-movie clichés and then exploding them with a joke.... The camera and the music are also important characters, contributing to several wonderfully surreal gags. Not every joke works: one dissident doctor dies of a brain hemorrhage from listening to rock & roll (now *that's* offensive, it's been done before, and the music should have been by Sick Dick and the Volkswagens). The key, I think, is that *High Anxiety* transcends schtick enough that you are glad when Brooks wins the fight, gets married to Madeline Kahn and lives happily ever after in the suburbs. That's a Brooks trademark that may reflect his own marriage to actress Anne Bancroft and their living happily ever after in the suburbs. Where the satirist Jonathan Swift (also obsessed with bodily orifices) argued for people to live logically, the comedian Mel Brooks only wants them to live happily. (p. 34)

Charles M. Young, "Seven Revelations about Mel Brooks: A Study in Low Anxiety," in Rolling Stone *(by Straight Arrow Publishers, Inc. © 1978; all rights reserved; reprinted by permission), Issue 258, February 9, 1978, pp. 33-6.*

Carlos Castaneda

1935?-

American writer of autobiographical anthropology field studies. While attempting to write a thesis on medicinal plants, Castaneda met a Yaqui Indian *brujo* (a sorcerer or medicine man) named don Juan Matus. He has written of his experiences with don Juan in several books that relate his search for a nonrational reality and his attempts to become a Yaqui warrior, "to balance the terror of being a man with the wonder of being a man." Although Castaneda calls these books anthropological field studies, there are critics and scholars who consider them fiction. Castaneda's life is shrouded in mystery. His birth date has been given as ranging from 1925 to the late 1930s. Most sources agree that he was born in Brazil, but accounts of his childhood differ greatly. He moved to Los Angeles either with his family or on his own to study at UCLA. He claims to have served in the United States Army but his service record cannot be found by the Defense Department. The ambiguity of his past can be attributed to Castaneda's habit of either avoiding the subject or supplying conflicting information. He adheres to don Juan's belief that a warrior must divorce himself from his past and is not much more candid about his present, stating that "to weasel in and out of different worlds you have to remain inconspicuous." *The Teachings of Don Juan* was the first product of Castaneda's lengthy apprenticeship with don Juan. This chronicle of Castaneda's bizarre experiences, many of which are drug-related, enjoyed wide popular success. Castaneda contends, however, that his work is often misunderstood. He denies the charge that he is merely relating the experiences of drug trips, and claims that he was less convinced of the validity of his experiences when they resulted from drug use. In his later books, in fact, drugs and medicinal plants play a much smaller part in his learning processes. He wrote *Journey to Ixtlan* as his doctoral thesis, and in 1973 received his Ph.D. from UCLA's department of anthropology. Despite the controversy over his hallucinogenic experiences, Castaneda's books are praised as unique anthropological studies of the Yaqui culture and philosophical treatises on the existence of alternate ways of viewing reality. (See also *Contemporary Authors*, Vols. 25-28, rev. ed.)

DUDLEY YOUNG

The fundamental issue which ["The Teachings of Don Juan"] confronts is as old as civilization, and of the utmost importance. Throughout his history man has tried to rationalize his suffering by attributing it to the existence of demonic spirits, which he has then attempted to propitiate.

Our highly technological society clearly does not encourage belief in demonic forces. Science is our answer to the primitive's propitiation rituals. . . .

The contemporary argument against our scientific rationalism is, broadly, that by ignoring the nether world we are only half-alive, truncated individuals cut off from the rich sources of both good and evil. . . . [We] should still go out to meet the devil, not perhaps in search of power over others but in search of power over ourselves, and a fuller humanity.

Such then is the debate that this volume seeks to illuminate. Mr. Castaneda's descriptions of his experiences with peyote are both interesting and moving. It made him violently ill, and disclosed to him both terror and ecstasy. Towards the end of his fourth year he began to have what the layman might describe as a nervous breakdown, and after a particularly shattering evening with the Don, he abruptly broke off relations. It was only several months later that he decided to write about his experiences in book form.

Don Juan emerges as an enigmatic, ultimately sinister *guru* figure; ascetic and authoritarian, he confidently imposes complex interpretations on the hallucinated visions of his bewildered and highly suggestible student. The spirits of his underworld, contacted through drugs, can protect and ennoble those they fancy, but destroy those who lack discipline of reverence. The Don was convinced that his disciple was well-favored by the gods, but if this is so, one shudders to think what happens to the ill-favored ones.

Since we are given virtually no information about the Don's credentials as a sorcerer (or indeed about his family or friends) it is very difficult to decide whether his symbology has genuine ethnic roots in Yaqui culture, whether he is just a more or less harmless crank, or whether he was seeking a corrupting kind of power over his disciple (have we not all heard the threat latent in the phrase, "I want to turn you on"?). Certainly the author's final hallucination, during which he threw a rock at his master who seemed bent on destroying him, would support such a suggestion. But Mr. Castaneda nowhere considers this possibility.

The second half of the book is called "A Structural Analysis," in which the author attempts to analyze his experiences in the language of the social sciences. His ponderous discussion of suggestibility is vitiated by his failure to consider either the Don's motivation or the possibility that his demonology was arbitrarily composed on an ad hoc basis. His attempt to establish criteria for testing the coherence and objectivity of the Don's system are surprisingly simpleminded: a sophomoric essay on the phenomenology of perception, about which the author clearly knows very little.

This book is unsatisfying because it falls uneasily between ethnography, spiritual autobiography, and travel literature. As ethnography it is both too ambitious and not ambitious enough. . . .

As confessional literature it is tantalizingly incomplete. One feels that the author's "scientific" scruples led him to withhold several chapters of the story. One would like to know for example, what kind of religious desire made him turn to peyote, how he found the courage to trust the Don, if and when that trust was lost, how his experiences with peyote affected his daily life, and whether it left him a stronger or a weaker man. One admires his daring but one regrets his reticence.

> *Dudley Young, "The Magic of Peyote," in* The New York Times Book Review (© *1968 by The New York Times Company; reprinted by permission), September 29, 1968, p. 30.*

EDWARD H. SPICER

[*The Teachings of Don Juan*] achieves three things: (1) it presents a description of personal experience with peyote, datura, and hallucinogenic mushrooms; (2) it describes the relationship between a student anthropologist and an elderly North Mexican Indian; and (3) it offers an analysis of a set of concepts and a pattern of thought concerning a realm of knowledge important in the Indian's world view. (pp. 30-1)

The description of the young anthropologist's hallucinogenic experiences, under the tutelage of the Indian, is remarkably vivid and compelling. Certainly what Castaneda has put on paper, recording the highlights of his several experiences with each of the three drugs, ranks with the best accounts by experimental psychologists, such as those by Havelock Ellis and Weir Mitchell with peyote and the Wassons with hallucinogenic mushrooms. They seem to me superior to the various literary accounts, such as those of Aldous Huxley. While the evocative descriptions are at least on a par with Huxley's, Castaneda's accounts seem based on more systematic use of notes and less after-the-experience reworking. Castaneda's literary skill led me to complete absorption in what seemed almost the direct experience itself. I think that this comes about in part through the skillful delineation of the immediate setting, namely, the personal relationship between the author and his teacher, which provided the motivation and the meaning of the activities.

It is in the presentation of this relationship that Castaneda is at his very best. With the skill of an accomplished novelist, utilizing suspense in character unfoldment and compelling suggestion rather than full exposition of place and situation, the intense relationship developed between the young and groping anthropologist and the richly experienced old teacher engrosses the reader. To me this is the chief value of the book and represents a remarkable achievement. It seems to me, further, that anthropologists concerned with preparing students for significant field relationships will find Castaneda's presentation of his experience immensely useful. The many facets of participant observation are available here for illuminating analysis and discussion of what this kind of fieldwork involves. (pp. 31-2)

It seems wholly gratuitous to emphasize, as the subtitle does, any connection between the subject matter of the book and the cultural traditions of the Yaquis. One suspects that the publisher went beyond Castaneda's intention, for the text itself provides no data for such a connection. . . . I am forced to the conclusion that Don Juan is one of those many persons to be encountered in Mexico and Arizona who, although Yaqui in family origin perhaps, have never participated in Yaqui group life or at best have done so only sporadically. (pp. 32-3)

Insofar as the reader is informed by this book, the teachings of Don Juan exist in a cultural limbo. Within the bounds of this serious limitation, it is nevertheless an excellent piece of work. One hopes that Castaneda will cultivate his exceptional gift for writing expressive prose and continue to employ it in his further contributions to anthropology. (p. 33)

> *Edward H. Spicer, in* American Anthropologist (*copyright 1969 by the American Anthropological Association; reproduced by permission of the American Anthropological Association), Vol. 71, No. 2, 1969 (and reprinted in* Seeing Castaneda: Reactions to the "Don Juan" Writings of Carlos Castaneda, *edited by Daniel C. Noel, G. P. Putnam's Sons, 1976, pp. 30-3).*

EDMUND LEACH

[The reader of *The Teachings of Don Juan*] can ignore the fact that at all relevant times the author was a graduate student in the Department of Anthropology at the University of California, Los Angeles. Despite the last fifty pages of jargon-loaded "structural analysis," this is a work of art rather than of scholarship, and it is as a diary of unusual personal experience that the book deserves attention. Assessed on this basis the book is not of superlative quality perhaps, but very good indeed.

The don Juan of the title is an old man, a Yaqui Indian from Sonora in Mexico, who now lives at an unspecified locality in Arizona. This is all we are told about him. The book contains no bibliography and no further clues about the Yaqui and their way of life. Indeed if don Juan had been described as a man from Mars it would have made little difference. The text is narrowly confined to the personal interactions between don Juan and the author between the summer of 1960 and the autumn of 1965. It is a relationship which is at once intimate yet tense, as between Moby Dick and Ahab, God and Job, or any psychoanalyst and his patient. (p. 12)

The book is a step by step record of how, in seeking to learn about don Juan's secrets, Castaneda gradually became his apprentice. Don Juan taught his craft by initiation. The pupil was first induced to take a drug; then, while under its influence or subsequently, he was persuaded, by means of hypnotic commands or less direct modes of suggestion, to accept the teacher's interpretation of the drug-induced experience. From the teacher's point of view, this was a road to true knowledge. Just how far Castaneda himself came to believe in don Juan's fantasies is left carefully obscure. And the undoubted fascination of the book lies precisely in this: the uncertainty of the author's own attitude. It is don Juan, not Castaneda, who has the dominant voice.

So this is not just another account of the joys and terrors of mescalin-induced visions, for it has the novelty that we are led to apprehend the contours of the other world according to don Juan's categories rather than as figments of a bemused American's imagination. (pp. 12-13)

In between descriptions of the techniques of drug preparation and vivid accounts of Castaneda's personal hallucinations, don Juan is presented as a mystic spouting the universal jargon of the apocalypse. . . . But just how much of this "philosophy" is really that of don Juan and how much is Castaneda (or even don Juan himself) regurgitating the Book of Revelations is hard to say. The Yaqui Indians incidentally have been Catholic Christians of a sort for several hundred years. What I find worrying is that although the reader is likely to end up with a strong impression of what don Juan must be like, we are, in fact, told practically nothing about him. All that we know concerns his attitudes toward the sources of his magic, and although these seem coherent enough in the setting of this book, they have no obvious connection with Yaqui culture as it has been described for us by other authors. . . .

The patients of psychoanalysts are unreliable witnesses of either the personality or the doctrine of their mentors, and Castaneda is no exception. It seems to me that he has just fitted don Juan into a mold that is ready-made.

Potentially his theme is very big. He is trying to describe a non-logical cosmos in terms which we can accept as constituting a "reality." But somehow, despite the author's sensitivity to the poetic symbolism which is implicit in his often terrifying experiences, the whole business gets reduced to triviality. Perhaps it is simply that the size of the canvas is too small for what it is meant to portray. (p. 13)

> *Edmund Leach, in* The New York Review of Books *(reprinted with permission from* The New York Review of Books; *copyright © 1969 Nyrev, Inc.), June 5, 1969.*

JOSEPH GRANGE

The full significance of drugs as an alternative metaphysics of existence awaits something more than the pseudo-apocalyptic prose of Leary or its neo-Zen endorsement by Alan Watts. In [*A Separate Reality,* an] intensely personal account of his apprenticeship to a Yaqui Indian shaman, Carlos Castaneda draws a terrifying yet compelling portrait of the concrete demands and rewards of a life lived in and through the use of the hallucinogens. As a result, the outline of the significance of drugs for the Western mind is sketched and the full seriousness of such an alternative way of life made apparent. . . .

There are thrills galore in this book, but a recounting of the bizarre and mysterious experiences undergone by Castaneda—he travels through water, is pursued by irreal objects, and witnesses a number of states of non-ordinary reality—would not do justice to the importance of this work. *A Separate Reality* is not a Disneyland outing; it is a remarkable probe of the consequences of seriously exploring worlds not recognized by Western Consciousness. As such, it contains an ontology, an epistemology and an ethics.

The theory of reality that undergirds Don Juan's cosmos is similar to that of contemporary process thought. There is a fleeting "really real" world behind the stolid facade of things; to catch it, one must rely on the speed provided by the hallucinogens. But the mere ingestion of these drugs is not sufficient, for one is required to follow a strict regimen of analysis in order to become "a man of knowledge" (Don Juan's term for the profession of shaman). The rigors of this epistemology are as exacting as that of any contemporary scientific methodology, requiring close attention to detail and the precise performance of sophisticated techniques for successful experimentation.

The major consequence of this exploration of an alien culture, however, lies in the tacit ethic practiced by Don Juan. As a mode of concrete existence, this way of life demands a supreme and unbending effort of the will. Drugs, in other words, are not spiritual vitamins gulped down to ward off the evils of capitalism. Rather only a magnanimous stoicism exhibiting severe indifference to pain and loss but tempered by a sense of the comic can allow one to live in this world of mystery and magic. The courage of the warrior who has put aside fear and exercises a constant and unbending intent to fathom the inexhaustible worlds of creative wonder is the required code of conduct. . . .

In the *Politics of Experience* R. D. Laing suggests that a new breed of priest-psychiatrist is called for: men of knowledge capable of helping others to endure and understand the voyage through the depths of time to the sources of existence. Don Juan's tutelage of Castaneda bears a striking resemblance to such a feat. Kind but emphatic, serious yet at times hilarious in his humor, he is the model of the good teacher evoking self-understanding rather than dispensing barren factual explanations after the manner of present-day scientism.

In an age that upholds discursive analysis as the paradigm of intelligence, the significance of the irrational vanishes. . . . *A Separate Reality* restores the irrational to its proper place: the reality of the unexpected together with its accompanying terror are part of the birthright of man. (p. 482)

Post-industrial modes of awareness have shrunk to the level of predictability and efficient performance, and the element of creative surprise has all but withered. While not everyone can follow the paths of Don Juan, his message should stir our sleeping depths: "We are men and our lot is to learn and to be hurled into inconceivable worlds. . . . *Seeing* is for an impeccable man. Temper your spirit now, become a warrior, learn to *see,* and then you'll know that there is no end to the new worlds for our vision." Castaneda's courageous effort to do so warrants our thanks and his work our careful attention. (pp. 482-83)

> *Joseph Grange, in* Commonweal *(copyright © 1971 Commonweal Publishing Co., Inc.; reprinted by permission of Commonweal Publishing Co., Inc.), September 17, 1971.*

RICHARD GOTT

[*The Teachings of Don Juan* dealt with Castaneda's] own reaction to the experiences he submitted himself to, but it was also an attempt to see into a non-Western system of thought, to go further into the culture of the Yaqui Indians than anyone had penetrated before. The book has become something of a cult book in the United States where it is obviously grist to the mills of the expanding population of opters-out. For the first time, if I'm not mistaken, Castaneda's investigation of a Yaqui 'way of knowledge' has given some degree of cultural and historical authenticity to the use of what have become known as psychedelic drugs.

Whether in the spirit of true inquiry, or whether impelled by his bank manager . . . , Castaneda returned to Mexico in 1968 and took up the conversations with Don Juan that he had abandoned three years earlier.

A Separate Reality is an account of his latest 'experiences' with Don Juan, together with a few from the earlier period that had got buried in his voluminous notes. It is a more commercial book than the first one, written more for his cult addicts than for the academics. He is now concerned with the mechanics of story-telling, not with explanation or analysis.

Not surprisingly he was sent away with a flea in his ear when he told Don Juan how he had tried to explain in the first book just what social pressures were at work to make a mitote—a meeting where peyote is ingested—a success. The techniques of the contemporary social scientist are ill-adapted to cope with other 'realities', and Don Juan merely laughed. Learning his lesson, Castaneda in this book simply tries to tell what happened to him as he drove about Mexico with Don Juan, ate a variety of mushrooms, and met an extraordinary collection of people capable of doing things like crossing cataracts by using their tentacles. (pp. 51-2)

A belief in other realities is of course a dangerous creed, subversive of both capitalism and socialism. Where it seems to me extremely attractive is that it allows pre-industrial non-Europeans to have a commendable reality of their own. American opters-out, who turn to Zen or the ways of the Yaqui, are, I suspect, playing an important role in educating their own society to accept that it does not have a monopoly over reality. (p. 52)

> Richard Gott, *"Mushrooms," in* New Statesman *(© 1972 The Statesman & Nation Publishing Co. Ltd.), January 14, 1972, pp. 51-2.*

PAUL RIESMAN

Taken together—and they should be read in the order they were written—[Carlos Castaneda's books] form a work which is among the best that the science of anthropology has produced. Three aspects of the work have profoundly influenced my response to it: first, the interest and value of the teachings of Don Juan are extraordinary in themselves; second, Carlos Castaneda has conveyed these teachings with great artistry so that they affect us at many levels; third, he shows us the conditions under which the teachings were transmitted to him, and not only makes us feel the relation he had with his teacher, but also reveals something of his personal struggle with standard Western reality whose thrall kept preventing him from accepting Don Juan's lessons on their own terms. (p. 7)

The story [these books] tell is so good, and the descriptions so vivid, that I was utterly fascinated as I read. What makes these books great is that Castaneda has not been afraid to commit things to paper that he himself does not understand. . . . Luckily, something in Castaneda's guts told him that there was more to his experiences than what he could understand, so rather than give us the pabulum of

analyzed data, he has done a wonderful job of conveying his experiences while under the tutelage of Don Juan. (pp. 7, 10)

Mescalito, the "spirit" of the Peyote plant, indicated to Don Juan that Carlos was the "chosen" one, the person to whom Don Juan should pass on his knowledge.

The result of this has been, for us, a very happy collaboration, and it is because of the collaborative nature of the work that it is appropriate, I think, to call it science. Castaneda modestly says that he is letting Don Juan's words speak for themselves, but this is true only in that Castaneda does not burden them with qualifications or alter them while trying to explain them. The fact is that the words would not be there at all if Castaneda had not been there "with unbending intent," and if he had not put his very being on the line so that Don Juan would also give him his utmost. . . .

Although I feel he should do even more of this, Castaneda does reveal enough of himself for us to see some of the ways in which we are like him (or unlike him, as the case may be). In fact, his courage lies not only in the fact that he persists in his effort to become a "man of knowledge"—a path that involves continuing openness to the unknown—but also in the fact that he is willing to speak of things concerning himself that most people would prefer to hide from themselves as well as others. Yet it is these things, the truths that hit you in the pit of the stomach, that enable us to see that our image of man is just that—an image—and that suggest entirely other ways of perceiving man and the world. I am not thinking here of Castaneda's strange, beautiful and disconcerting experiences in what he calls "non-ordinary reality," but rather of some simpler, more everyday ones which I am sure nearly every reader of these books can recognize as his own. (p. 10)

Castaneda, like nearly every member of Western civilization, feels himself to be superior to members of other cultures and in fact to all other entities in the world. But since such feelings conflict with our democratic ideology, he claims that Don Juan is his equal [in a scene described in "Journey to Ixtlan"]. Don Juan not only sees through this, but also sees that Castaneda is pimping in the sense that Castaneda's reason for being there in the first place is not to learn something but to collect information for someone else: to add to the corpus of anthropological knowledge, for instance, by writing a Ph.D. thesis that will add to what is already known so that others can then add even more and it will appear that our knowledge is actually increasing.

But knowledge of what? This is the crux of the matter. . . . In their studies of the cultures of other people, even those anthropologists who sincerely love the people they study almost never think that they are learning something about the way the world really is. Rather, they conceive of themselves as finding out what other people's *conceptions* of the world are. For the longest time Castaneda, too, thought this way about what Don Juan was telling him.

It is stupid and wasteful, however, to think of Don Juan's knowledge—and that of other non-Western peoples—as no more than conceptions of some fixed reality. Castaneda makes it clear that the teachings of Don Juan do tell us something of how the world really is, and I feel that this is knowledge of great value. I don't have the space to put down my own reading of what Don Juan is saying, and I can't even begin to point out all the delights to be found in these books. In any case, the excellence of Castaneda's writing ensures, I believe, that readers will discover these things for themselves. (p. 14)

> Paul Riesman, in The New York Times Book Review (© 1972 by The New York Times Company; reprinted by permission), October 22, 1972.

JOSEPH KANON

Castaneda's third, and presumably final, account [A Separate Reality] does not deal at all with hallucinogenic drugs . . . , but it is no less interesting—if anything, it is more strangely beautiful and provocative for being less dramatic.

Don Juan's point all along has been that drugs were merely alternative, if not incidental, routes to becoming a "man of knowledge," but Castaneda had been almost exclusively concerned with their role in the process. Now, in what is more an amplification than a revision of the earlier books, Castaneda has sifted through ten years of notes to study Don Juan's nondrug techniques for "stopping the world" (i.e., shifting to the perception of another reality) and arranged this material into seventeen chapter "lessons," most of which are designed to splinter the ego and erase self-consciousness. The master/student relationship—Don Juan, arch and playfully enigmatic; Castaneda, earnest and desperately trying to "see" rather than "look"—has by now become so engaging a part of Castaneda's running saga that, as with Holmes and Watson, the interplay of the characters alone can buoy up even those chapters that don't prompt one to fill the margins with question marks of wonder. (p. 67)

The extraordinary thing about Castaneda's books has been their experiential authority, their ability to make us believe the unbelievable because it is presented as having really happened. His very academic skepticism so draws the reader to his side (a man of reason, after all) that, when he "sees," beyond doubt, we have no choice but to stay with him and follow the course. And if all this begs the question of solipsism, it does so in the most fascinating and basic way. "Why should the world be only as you think it is?" Don Juan asks. "Who gave you the authority to say so?"

It was evidently a point well taken; to his credit, Castaneda refuses to present this newly perceived reality as anything more than "one of many descriptions." Even his own spiritual experience, which provides the dramatic climax of the book, is not used as a pitch for recruitment. He does not proselytize; he merely gives information. And insofar as the Indian culture he describes is alien to most readers, this information alone makes fascinating reading. The nature whose "flow" the brujo must perceive is not the cozy green most Americans now say they want to get back to, but the primitive brutality of the Sonora Desert, a world where nature is an interlocking series of "powers," few of them benign, and where life itself under the shifting desert light shimmers with impenetrable mystery. This sense of landscape, and the awe it inspires, so fills the book that at times it takes on the magical air of legend telling over a campfire, when anything seems possible. It is truly another world, foreign enough to make us suspend judgment, and Castaneda's achievement is that he makes it tangible for us. (p. 68)

> Joseph Kanon, in Saturday Review (© 1972 Saturday Review Inc.; reprinted with permission), November 11, 1972.

JOYCE CAROL OATES

Paul Riesman's review of Carlos Castaneda's three books ("The Teachings of Don Juan," "A Separate Reality," and "Journey to Ixtlan") [see excerpt above], while a respectful and illuminating commentary, left me more bewildered than ever.

Since I am by no means familiar with anthropology, and have not yet read Castaneda's most recent book, "Journey," I should make it clear that my reaction is certainly an amateur's and no doubt very private . . . but is it possible that these books are non-fiction?

I realize that everyone accepts them as anthropological studies, yet they seem to me remarkable works of art, on the Hesse-like theme of a young man's initiation into "another way" of reality. They are beautifully constructed. The dialogue is faultless. The character of Don Juan is unforgettable. There is a novelistic momentum—rising suspenseful action, a gradual revelation of character . . . the moment when Don Juan sees in the narrator a certain secret he clung to as a child, which must be overcome if he is to become a "man of knowledge."

It is quite possible that Don Juan represents a "non-ordinary reality" so strange to me that I cannot accept it, and must try to reason my way out of believing. But I don't think so. The voice of Don Juan has always been with us. . . . (p. 68)

> Joyce Carol Oates, "Anthropology—or Fiction?" in The New York Times Book Review (© 1972 by the New York Times Company; reprinted by permission), November 26, 1972 (and reprinted in Seeing Castaneda: Reactions to the "Don Juan" Writings of Carlos Castaneda, edited by Daniel C. Noel, G. P. Putnam's Sons, 1976, pp. 68-9).

WESTON LaBARRE

Having made out with a good thing in "The Teachings of Don Juan: A Yaqui Way of Knowledge," Carlos Castaneda now writes a kind of "Don Juan Revisited" [with "A Separate Reality: Further Conversations with Don Juan"]. There is a certain poignancy in the picture of a raw young anthropologist in his encounter with a wise old man of another culture, and in both books Castaneda has played this for all it is worth, even to his own indignity. But no professional anthropologist who read the first book was ever able to suppose it made any contribution to Yaqui ethnography, and it is even unclear to what degree Don Juan was Yaqui in culture. The Appendix purporting to be "A Structural Analysis" shows an abrupt change of style and was evidently tacked on at the behest of a thesis committee, in order to retrieve otherwise woefully inadequate ethnography. But this tedious attempt to play dutiful Lévi-Straussian games can have satisfied neither committee nor the general reader.

The long disquisition of Don Juan and the detailing of each confused emotional reaction of the author, in the present volume, imply either total recall, novelistic talent, or a tape recorder. No banality goes unrecorded, nothing is summarized, nothing is spared us, and yet the nourishment of it all hardly matches that in Jello. The total effect is self-dramatizing and vague, and Castaneda curiously manages to be at once disingenuous and naïve. Even as belles lettres the book is wanting, for the writing is pretentious (twice we read of "insidious hair," as though the writer were enamoured of his concoction). The *smoking* of the "psilocybe" (mushroom) raises some wonder too.

There seems to exist a sizeable public with a taste for the plastic flowers of science-writing in Ardrey, Heyerdahl, and Desmond Morris, and that public will no doubt be pleased with this new production. One longs for sheer information on datura and narcotic mushrooms beyond the oblique words of Don Juan and the empty feelings of the acolyte, and both books together advance our knowledge of peyotism not a whit. But perhaps it is unfair to expect this of an ego trip. Everything is smarmy with self-important and really quite trivial feelings and narcissistic self-preoccupation.

One's impatience is aroused by the most obvious questions being left unasked. For example, is "a separate reality" the same for every society, or even for two individuals? And is a toxic state of the brain any earnest for the existence of another "reality"? The book is pseudo-profound, sophomoric and deeply vulgar. To one reader at least, for decades interested in Amerindian hallucinogens, the book is frustratingly and tiresomely dull, posturing pseudoethnography and, intellectually, kitsch. (pp. 41-2)

> *Weston LaBarre, "Stinging Criticism from the Author of 'The Peyote Cult'," (1972) (© 1972 by The New York Times Company; reprinted by permission), in Seeing Castenada: Reactions to the "Don Juan" Writings of Carlos Castenada, edited by Daniel C. Noel, G. P. Putnam's Sons, 1976, pp. 40-2.*

RONALD SUKENICK

One of the first things I talked about with Castaneda when we met was the novelistic quality of his books. I told him frankly that as a novelist the first thing that occurred to me when I noticed the similarities between our books [Castaneda's "A Separate Reality" and Sukenick's "Out"] was that he too must be writing a novel. Since Joyce Carol Oates's letter to the Sunday Times Book Review raising the same possibility [see excerpt above], I understand this must be a natural speculation for novelists and perhaps for others.

Castaneda, when I first met him two years ago, was rather different from the way he is now, and the change in him reflects the course the books have taken. That evening he struck me as a kind of Candide parrying with a schizophrenic episode, and in fact a kind of cultural schizophrenia —parallel to what one might call the controlled pathology induced by Don Juan—has been the key to his books since the first one, with its experiential reportage in the body of the book, and its attempt at an abstract objective analysis added on at the end. (p. 111)

[Being] overly concerned with the factuality of Castaneda's account seems in itself literal-minded. Castaneda is a visionary and in what sense does one ask whether a vision is "true"? A vision is beyond the category of fact, other than the fact of its having happened at all. Like a story, it is neither true nor false, only persuasive or unreal, and I think there are few people who would argue that Castaneda's accounts of his experience are not persuasive, as persuasive in fact as the most accomplished novels. (p. 112)

Part of the enormous impact of Castaneda's books is due to the fact that they come at a time when [our commitment to statistics] is beginning to crumble in many quarters, when the empirical tradition has come to appear obviously inadequate, and the fact that Don Juan's teachings have so many similarities with Zen, with "The Book of the Dead," with witchlore, with Sufism, with various Eastern disciplines, with the Western mystical tradition, with Jungian speculations, and perhaps most interestingly with Wilhelm Reich and his followers, only indicates that it is part of an important subplot in the story of the culture, and in stories, . . . everything comes together. A major peripeteia is about to come off: what seemed true begins to lose credibility, and the incredible looks more and more likely.

Part of this cultural turnabout is the discovery that all accounts of our experience, all versions of "reality," are of the nature of fiction. There's your story and my story, there's the journalist's story and the historian's story, there's the philosopher's story and the scientist's story about what happens in the atomic microcosm and the cosmic macrocosm (scientists have a corner on the stories of creation and genesis these days). . . .

This is the key statement in all of Don Juan's teachings, and is also crucial, I believe, for our particular cultural moment. The secret of the sorcerer's power, it follows, is to know that reality is imagined and, as if it were a work of art, to apply the full force of the imagination to it. The alternating descriptions of reality that Don Juan works with are possible only by working through, and on, the imagination. (p. 113)

Don Juan is Prospero. The world of the sorcerer is a stage and in Castaneda's books Don Juan is the skillful stage manager. What is he trying to teach Castaneda is not the primacy of one description over another, but the possibility of different descriptions. He is teaching Castaneda the art of description. And in so doing he breaks down, for the alert reader, that false separation of art from life, of imagination from reality that in our culture tends to vitiate both. (p. 114)

The next time I saw Castaneda, to return to our story, was many months later when he came to lecture at the university where I was teaching at the time, and I went to talk to him for a while afterward. (p. 115)

On that occasion I tried to draw him out on the resemblances between what he was involved with and the processes of the imagination in art, but his conception of art seemed a rather crude one, amounting to something like an idea of decoration. But if Castaneda's works aren't novels they're still stories, Castaneda's story about Don Juan's story, and I keep thinking of them in connection with other stories that explore similar areas for our culture.

In "Journey to Ixtlan," for example, Castaneda, wandering through the Mexican mountains amid a landscape animated by spirits and powers, reminds me exactly of the early Wordsworth wandering in the English hills that are alive with immanent spirit. Or how about another Hispanic sorcerer, Cervantes, Castaneda's Sancho Panza to Don Juan's Quijote. Except that in this version of the story all the power is on the Don's side, which leads us to the thought that maybe Quijote was right all along, that maybe the culture, not to mention the novel itself, has conceded too much to the pragmatic Sancho.

Here it is Sancho Castaneda who undergoes the conversion, who finally has to admit that the windmills are giants, and that he has to struggle with them. Here it turns out that the Don is sane after all and the rest of us are mad, or if not mad at least gross dullards. These are works of art . . . , but works of art don't have to be novels. They are works of art compared, say, with Tom Wolfe's account of Kesey in "The Electric Kool-Aid Acid Test," not because one is factual and the other is not, but simply because Castaneda's books attain a high level of imaginative power and coherence, of precision in language, of inventive selection, and Wolfe's book does not, though it may be an exemplar of the new journalism.

Must we really wait on the testimony of anthropologists about the value of these books? If the anthropological establishment were to rise up and cry fraud—and since it hasn't by now one can be certain it's not going to—wouldn't that, in a way, be even more exciting in imaginative terms. (pp. 115-16)

> *Ronald Sukenick, "Upward and Juanward: The Possible Dream," in* The Village Voice *(reprinted by permission of* The Village Voice; *copyright © The Village Voice, Inc., 1973), January 25, 1973 (and reprinted in* Seeing Castaneda: Reactions to the "Don Juan" Writings of Carlos Castaneda, *edited by Daniel C. Noel, G. P. Putnam's Sons, 1976, pp. 110-20).*

Indeed, though [Don Juan] is an enigma wrapped in mystery wrapped in a tortilla, [Castaneda's books are] beautifully lucid. [His] story unfolds with a narrative power unmatched in other anthropological studies. Its terrain—studded with organ-pipe cacti, from the glittering lava massifs of the Mexican desert to the ramshackle interior of Don Juan's shack—becomes perfectly real. In detail, it is as thoroughly articulated a world as, say, Faulkner's Yoknapatawpha County. In all the books, but especially in *Journey to Ixtlan,* Castaneda makes the reader experience the pressure of mysterious winds and the shiver of leaves at twilight, the hunter's peculiar alertness to sound and smell, the rock-bottom scrubbiness of Indian life, the raw fragrance of tequila and the vile, fibrous taste of peyote, the dust in the car and the loft of a crow's flight. It is a superbly concrete setting, dense with animistic meaning. This is just as well, in view of the utter weirdness of the events that happen in it. . . .

Why, . . . in an age full of descriptions of good and bad trips, should Castaneda's sensations be of any more interest than anyone else's? First, because they were apparently conducted within a system—albeit one he did not understand at the time—imposed with priestly and rigorous discipline by his Indian guide. Secondly, because Castaneda kept voluminous and extraordinarily vivid notes. . . . Perhaps most important, Castaneda remained throughout a rationalist Everyman. His one resource was questions: a persistent, often fumbling effort to keep a Socratic dialogue going with Don Juan. . . . (p. 37)

[In] some quarters Castaneda's works are extravagantly admired as a revival of a mode of cognition that has been largely neglected in the West, buried by materialism and Pascal's despair, since the Renaissance. . . .

But such endorsements and parallels do not in any way validate the more worldly claim to importance of Castaneda's books: to wit, that they are anthropology, a specific and truthful account of an aspect of Mexican Indian culture as shown by the speech and actions of one person, a shaman named Juan Matus. That proof hinges on the credibility of Don Juan as a being and Carlos Castaneda as a witness. Yet there is no corroboration—beyond Castaneda's writings—that Don Juan did what he is said to have done, and very little that he exists at all. (p. 38)

Like the various versions of Castaneda's life, the books are an invitation to consider contradictory kinds of truth. At the core of his books and Don Juan's method is, of course, the assumption that reality is not an absolute. It comes to each of us culturally determined, packaged in advance. "The world has been rendered coherent by our description of it." Castaneda argues, echoing Don Juan. "From the moment of birth, this world has been described for us. What we see is just a description." (p. 44)

It is not [the] years of study but the nature of the revelation he offers that has run Castaneda afoul of rationalists. To join another man's consensus of reality, one's own must go, and since nobody can easily abandon his own accustomed description it must be forcibly broken up. The historical precedents, even in the West, are abundant. Ever since the ecstatic mystery religions of Greece, our culture has been continually challenged by the wish to escape its own dominant properties: the linear, the categorical, the fixed.

Whether Carlos Castaneda is, as some leading scholars think, a major figure in an evolution of anthropology or only a brilliant novelist with unique knowledge of the desert and Indian lore, his work is to be reckoned with. (p. 45)

> *"Don Juan and the Sorcerer's Apprentice," in* Time *(reprinted by permission from* Time, The Weekly Newsmagazine; *copyright Time Inc. 1973), March 5, 1973, pp. 36-45.*

Of Carlos Castaneda it might be said that he is a social-anthropological drop-out in much the same way that many psychoanalysts might consider R. D. Laing to be a psychoanalytical one. From the point of view of their respective orthodoxies both have gone over to the enemy. They have rejected the objective and scientific approach to their subject-matter in favour of an extravagant empathy with the human object of their studies. In their view you cannot understand the "primitive" without becoming "primitive" any more than you can understand the mad without tasting madness yourself. Though such anti-scientific frivolity may have estranged both from their respective orthodoxies, it has catapulted them both from academic obscurity into the full glare of publicity. . . .

In *A Separate Reality* [Castaneda] described how, in the interests of science, he had put himself into the hands of [a] strange backwoodsman, and how he emerged from his peyote-induced trance experiences an altered and badly shaken man. Like William James and Aldous Huxley before him, the drug had revealed to him a "separate reality" quite as real as that of everyday consciousness—more real indeed in that what he saw and experienced far exceeded anything he had ever imagined possible both in beauty and, even more, in sheer terror.

In *Journey to Ixtlan* the author resumes his story and seems to bring it to its conclusions. Much of the ground has already been covered in his earlier books—but from a different angle. The drug experiences here are put in their proper setting: they are no more than aids to help one understand that there *is* a "separate reality" of which they may provide a glimpse, though little more. This "reality" cannot be explained in words, and many of Mr Castaneda's readers will have been infuriated by Don Juan's refusal even to try to explain the properties of his magical world, and even more so by his habit of lapsing into giggles at the very moments when his investigator-apprentice is reduced to a state of terror.

Why is he so obstinately uninformative? Since he cannot express what the sometime anthropologist is so anxious to learn, he must, then, be either very simple or a mystic (since, as everyone knows, the mystics can never describe their transports but can only hint at what they have undergone). He is certainly not simple, but his terminology and general demeanor would indeed appear to rank him among the mystics, if by "mystic" we mean the Taoists and Zen Buddhists of every degree of enlightenment. He talks a great deal of "power" and "knowledge" and above all of "*seeing*" (always italicized to distinguish it from what we normally understand of "seeing"), but these verbalizations have hitherto not got us very much further. . . .

In this book Don Juan is no less exasperating but he does become more explicit—on his own terms which are, however, not terms familiar to the average social anthropologist or the average anyone, come to that. But it is not the words that matter but a whole series of monstrous happenings which constitute the ordeal of the social anthropologist turned sorcerer's apprentice. That these horrors had to be endured is patiently explained because, if one is ever to learn to *see,* one must first become a "warrior" who has learnt to store his magic power. Only then will he be able to "stop the world". "Stopping the world" is perhaps the keyword of this book, and it is precisely what the Buddhists understand by *Nirodha* ("putting a stop to" the phenomenal world) which is a synonym for Nirvana. . . .

Whether the reader takes this book seriously or whether he prefers to regard it as an "entertainment" *à la* Graham Greene, he is unlikely to be bored. Perhaps its greatest merit is that Carlos Castaneda emerges as a firm believer in his "separate reality" and yet manages to combine this with the healthy scepticism with which he started.

> *"Stopping the World,"* in The Times Literary Supplement (© *Times Newspapers Ltd.* (London) 1973; reproduced from The Times Literary Supplement *by permission*), June 15, 1973, p. 663.

ELSA FIRST

Carlos Castaneda has [placed us inside the shaman's consciousness] and this is why his work is original and important. . . .

In order to show us a world in which "non-ordinary" states of reality are given an equal valence with waking consciousness, Castaneda has devised a powerful literary strategy. He describes "non-ordinary" experiences as they occurred subjectively, often taking him overwhelmingly by surprise. Only afterwards does he give his attempts to understand them rationally—and always in the form of dialogues with his teacher, so that the terms of the discussion are those of Don Juan's world, not ours. Castaneda's narrative surface thus modulates from one state of consciousness to another without transition.

This has caused considerable bewilderment among the group of naive skeptics who say that such things don't occur. Castaneda deliberately leaves out the helpful signposts that might read "hallucinatory state" or "trance." . . .

There is a more knowledgeable form of skepticism which holds that Castaneda's experiences are almost too good to be true: Don Juan's teachings are strikingly similar to those of all of the world's great esoteric traditions (such as Sufism, the higher yogas or Tantric Buddhism) and the figure of Don Jaun himself has increasingly assumed the outline of paradigmatic spiritual teacher or guru. Why, for example, do Castaneda's shamans seem to possess a close analogue to the Hindu Chakra system when this has not been reported by others? At this point all we can say is that Castaneda's reported experiences closely resemble much cross-cultural data—and this could well be explained by the fact that the "natural mind" everywhere perceives similarly. (p. 35)

"Tales of Power" starts out only a few months after "Journey to Ixtlan" left off (it is based on Castaneda's experiences in 1971 and '72) but we soon see that the pace is accelerated and the scale is grander. . . .

This is a splendid book, for all that it may seem ungainly, at times ponderous, at others overwrought. . . . "Tales of Power" could well be read as a farcical picaresque epic of altered states of consciousness. Carlos adventures through many strange modes of perception and suffers many enchantments as well. . . .

In all the great examples of the picaresque genre we meander through tales within tales until we feel we are in danger of getting lost. The central section of "Tales of Power" takes place largely in Mexico City where Don Juan shatters Carlos's romanticism and ours by appearing in a well-tailored suit, and there we do seem to get definitely lost: Suddenly, Carlos finds himself whirled away from an acquaintance who has been tailing him in the hopes of being led to the real Don Juan. Carlos lands a mile and a half away near some familiar market stalls which, as he discovers when he tries to confirm the event later, were not in fact open that day. . . . (p. 38)

Carlos has come a long way. Just as Casteneda's style has changed from the factual precision of the first book to the lunatic extravagance of this last, so too his *persona* Carlos's understanding of the states of "non-ordinary reality" has grown from book to book. His relationship with Don Juan has developed too, since that moment in "A Separate Reality" when Don Juan uncovered Carlos's forgotten childhood vow that he would fail—a striking example of how the shaman-guru may act as a psychotherapist as he deals with the interferences to his apprentice's "seeing." One of the finest things in "Tales of Power," however, stylized or fictional it may be, is the convincing portrait of a spiritual teacher working away at his student's tendency to "indulge" in self-dramatization and self-pity. . . .

Over the last six years the figures of Carlos and Don Juan have assumed a peculiar status in the imagination of an entire generation. They loom as do the great characters of fiction, Sancho Panza and Don Quixote, say, who marked Western civilization's fall into materialism as Carlos and Don Juan signify the attempt to emerge from it. But we also remain aware that somewhere there is a real Carlos who apparently has painstakingly learned how to ''stop the internal dialogue'' which continually reconstitutes the ego-bound world. (p. 40)

Elsa First, in The New York Times Book Review
(© 1974 by The New York Times Company; reprinted by permission), October 27, 1974.

WILLIAM KENNEDY

[Castaneda], who once thought he was a student and wrote his first book as a doctoral thesis, is unquestionably a teacher. His books are as didactic as Plato's and just as fat with instructional dialogue. His Don Juan, who constantly tells Carlitos to end his own internal dialogue, is as garrulous as Jonathan Winters and just as fractured by his own jokes. And yet if Castaneda is not about to inseminate Western culture with a vision of how it really is, he is at least on the cusp of twisting its head a few millimeters. He is a cult figure now, especially with the young but not exclusively so, approaching Hesse, Vonnegut, Golding and Salinger. (p. 29)

[According to Castaneda, we achieve the totality of ourselves] by seeing in a special way what few others see, by dreaming, by will, by stopping our internal dialogue. We get there by learning to end our self-pity and by taking responsibility for what we have done. We get there by eliminating our past as a source of anxiety and by living in the present, by being in touch with all the fine detail of life that those who wallow in their own grief or exhausted past histories never can appreciate.

The message [in *Tales of Power*] is at times very like Thornton Wilder's in *Our Town*. It is also like Salinger invoking Zen to urge us not to seek rewards for our work. The direction is blessedly free from moral stricture (we are admittedly dealing in the black magic of the spirit), free also from sex (there are no significant women in this book), and free from any worldly temptation except that of slipping back into the muck and dreck of reason. Reason alone . . . is slow death. Of course death, if we only knew it, is the way to life. (pp. 29-30)

Being so full of such bromidic salvation, it would seem the book is useless. But Castaneda has the skills of a superb but flawed novelist. He has structured his philosophy novelistically and structured it with great care. For instance, before he fully advises us how to split ourselves, and how to dream ourselves into the nagual, he conjures up a ''magical'' event for Carlitos to experience—seeing himself sleeping in two different places, witnessing two separate sets of events. He is thus able to transcend space and time, which his teachers, Don Juan and especially Don Genaro, are so adept at doing. Don Genaro leaps up and down canyons, walks upside down on trees.

By book's end it is clear that Carlitos is not really talking about magic at all; that the whole work is, like that dual sleeping scene, an elaborate and admirably detailed metaphor with the aim of guiding the reader out of the humdrum and into self-awareness. The magical events are no further out of our reach than our next wilfully weird daydream.

It has been said that Castaneda has dressed out his Mexican spirit world as thoroughly as Faulkner detailed Yoknapatawpha County, a ridiculous thing to say. Castaneda's strength is in pictorializing his philosophy with surreal metaphors. But when he begins to detail a man, or a real cabin,

or a city park, he is as ill at ease as a brick mason trying to point up gold leaf on the Taj Mahal. His dialogue is fluid but often gawky, acceptable finally because you don't believe he's even trying to simulate reality. The behavior of Don Juan and Carlitos is so thinly and repetitiously imagined when they are not involved in dialogue or dream, that it would earn the author a revoked passport to any decent creative writing class. . . .

[However, his] plot, wherever it began in his personal life, whether on some mushroom orgy in a Los Angeles apartment or a spooky walk along some dusky chaparral in Mexico, has turned into something nifty for a great many people. Who can object to wising up the human race? . . .

The way to his secrets is not easy. You have to wade through a lot of silly prose. But when you get there you like Castaneda for all his effort. He is as welcome as any other novelist who gives his whole being to his books. He really doesn't know any more than any of the other would-be wise men among us, but he thinks he does. And that determines what winds up on our bookshelves. (p. 30)

William Kennedy, ''Fact or Fiction,'' in The New Republic (reprinted by permission of The New Republic; © 1974 by The New Republic, Inc.), November 16, 1974, pp. 28-30.

H. S. McALLISTER

The fourth and final book of the don Juan series, *Tales of Power*, answers some of the questions the books have raised, leaves many other questions unanswered, and ends on a tentative note quite different from the open-ended, serial conclusion of the first books. *Tales of Power* is inconclusive, but as the book draws to its close the reader feels a strong sense of completion, a sense that Castaneda has said all he will say.

Like the previous books, *Tales of Power* repudiates much that has gone before. Drugs, we learned in *Journey to Ixtlan*, are not essential to the apprenticeship in sorcery. In the closing book, don Juan reveals that sorcery is not an end in itself, that it is not to be sought as the alternative to our commonplace sense of ''reality.'' The sorcerer's way is not alternative but complementary to the average person's way. The normative sensibility which don Juan seems now to mean with his term, the tonal, is, he asserts, necessary to our existence: we need the describing, assessing, ordering principle to exist as personalities, but if that principle is allowed total control of our experience, we lose our sense of the nagual (all that is not tonal), the creative principle. The sorcerer's way is an extension of the tonal, and a way of regaining the experience of the nagual. The experience of the nagual, the culminating moment of the book, is the peak and purpose of Carlos' training.

Don Juan seems, as usual, to be most interested in disorienting his pupil, forcing him to constantly question the validity of both old and new assumptions he makes about reality. . . . Clearly one of don Juan's primary purposes is to force Carlos to avoid complacency about any detail of experience; recognition of this purpose explains some of the confusing contradictions in the earlier books. Don Juan is not concerned about honesty or facts in the sense we might use those terms. As he tells Carlos in *Journey to Ixtlan*, everything he does is sincere and the behavior of an actor.

The question of these books' authenticity remains unanswered and, I believe, irrelevant. Don Juan, after all, is an outcast Yaqui, a "diablero" or witch, so he does not speak for Yaqui culture or religion. The way of the sorcerer is not a version of an established, organized religion, whether Castaneda made it up or not. It is, however, a cogent description of an "Indian" perspective, particularly in these last two books. The sense of one's relationship to the natural world, the evocation of a non-Europeanized perspective on reality, both are valuable to anyone who wishes to step out of his White education, however briefly, and walk in the shoes of any other culture. One of Castaneda's powers as a writer is his ability to describe such perspectives, to reify the "unreal": the descriptions of drug experience in the first two books, of disoriented sensory experience in the whole tetralogy, of the magical transformations which are at once fantastic, believable and even commonplace by the time we reach *Tales of Power*.

The magic in don Juan's teaching is intended to bring Carlos to his encounter with the nagual, an encounter which we can only share vicariously. Thus, it would be simplistic to assume that the series of books is intended to teach us to perform magic tricks. The philosophy of the Yaqui's teachings, however, summed up in a recapitulation or "disintoxication" at the center of *Tales of Power*, is accessible to the reader as well as to the apprentice. This philosophy has a precisely Indian center, the recognition that the life of a "warrior" is joyful "because it is based on his affection, his devotion, his dedication to his beloved, "the earth," "this lovely being, which is alive to its last recesses and understands every feeling." (pp. 75-6)

This consuming love for the natural is the ruling principle of the warriors' lives, and the expression of that Indian sensitivity is masterful here in Castaneda's final volume.... [However] the problem of authenticity makes it impossible to legitimately present these books ... as unequivocal "Indian" books. If used with an acknowledgement of this problem ..., *Journey to Ixtlan* and *Tales of Power* are valuable additions to the bibliography of literature of the Indian and the American West. (p. 76)

> *H. S. McAllister, in* Western American Literature *(copyright, 1975, by the Western Literature Association), Spring, 1975.*

DOUGLAS McFERRAN

In my college course in the philosophy of the occult it would be impossible to ignore Castaneda, and I would hardly want to. His books are dramatic presentations of an ideal of magical involvement that are among the most powerful and compelling to be found in any literature. To ignore them because don Juan may be solely a creature of Castaneda's imagination would be to sidestep a major challenge to conventional religious and social ideals. After all, if the image of the sorcerer as "the man of knowledge" is an attractive one, it may not really matter that it has been embodied in a curious type of fiction rather than in the records of a factual encounter.

Carlos Castaneda has definitely touched a nerve in modern consciousness. In an industrialized society, it is difficult to feel respected as a true individual: "the games people play" include the totality of life. The one who, like Nietzsche's Zarathustra or Kazantzakis' Zorba the Greek or Castaneda's don Juan, is completely his own master, unfettered by

dogmas or by the expectations of others, appears to have won a victory the rest of us can only admire. The vindication of his power is not only supreme self-confidence, but a preternatural control of his environment. (pp. 162-63)

The Mexican sorcerers, as portrayed by Castaneda, were one up on their urban neighbors because they knew that if one's experiences depended on his definitions, totally revising these definitions could lead to the experience of a "separate reality" in which literally anything was possible.

Has Castaneda ever experienced this "anything is possible" world for himself? According to his books, he has, and I am inclined to think this the case regardless of whether the incidents he describes ever occurred. Castaneda has clearly wanted to see the world as a sorcerer; the intensity of his descriptions suggests that, in some manner at least, he has succeeded. The real question, however, would be whether he succeeded before or after he began writing the pages that he presents as the field notes of his tutelage under don Juan. If it was before, as a result of his own experiences in transforming consciousness (with or without drugs), that would explain certain odd biases he displays. (p. 163)

What finally remains of Castaneda's challenge if, on the one hand, he is entirely discounted by fellow anthropologists and, on the other, the ideal of the sorcerer proves less lasting than the ideal of the one awaiting the kingdom? My guess is that his books will pass into the body of occultist literature read only by a handful of true believers, and Castaneda, who ironically has made it difficult for himself to be read as anything but the disciple of don Juan, will either have to keep adding to his series or disappear into literary oblivion. . . .

The don Juan series has been popular because its readers want to believe it possible to become a "man of knowledge"—in short, a Gnostic. That itself is saying something about the times we live in. We may now have moved to a next stage in which magic has surrendered to talk of the millennium, but this would be only a substitution of heresies. There is still the sense of alienation, the frustration with established values—and there is also the danger of self-destructive action. Understanding Castaneda is part of what it takes to understand the entire religious scene of the present. (p. 164)

> *Douglas McFerran, "The Castaneda Plot," in* America (© *America Press, 1977; all rights reserved), February 26, 1977, pp. 162-64.*

SAM KEEN

Does Don Juan exist? Yes or no? The skeptical mind insists on the facts. Strip the legendary hero of the adornment of miracle and find the core of historical truth. Placed under the microscope, Don Juan shrinks. My guess is that he is Carlos Castaneda's imaginary playmate. . . .

The most important question we can ask is not: "Can Juan Matus be located in 1977 in Sonora, Mexico?" It is rather: "What does Don Juan tell us about ourselves, about the millions in this country and abroad, who have read his words in 11 languages?" As an archetypical hero, Don Juan may reveal to us something, about the contours of the collective unconscious and the longings of our time. (p. 40)

With Don Juan, the classical hero (with a thousand faces) returns to the scene. The wise old man has finally arrived to share the knowledge of the fathers. There is somebody over 30 we can trust. The fathers of the last generation were too busy making it to initiate the sons and daughters. And because they gave their hearts to IBM, they lacked the charisma and authority of elders. We have grown up with the image of a world governed by adolescent or, worse, infantile adults. It is good to have an image of an old man, lean and bursting with spirit, and with power enough to go fiercely into that good night.

There is also more than a sprinkling of folly in the appeal of Don Juan. He plays upon romantic hopes as well as profound needs (which is not to deny that we may have a profound need for romantic hopes). The old sorcerer rides in on the wave of the Indian mystique. We are experiencing a cultural return of the repressed. Indians can do no wrong. The nostalgia for feathers and turquoise among urban cliff-dwellers reflects a fatigue with urban life. We want our salvation to come from the wilds beyond the suburbs, from a desert that is devoid of the marks of technology or bureaucracy. In fact, the innocent longing for a pure life in the heart of nature is traditionally American.

Don Juan finds a natural point of entrance into the modern American psyche because he addresses our deepest obsession—the quest for power. The sorcerer game, like that of the Pentagon, is the accumulation of power. Granted, Don Juan is concerned with personal power, and the military-industrial complex with military power. But the logic of power leads them to a similar view of the world. Power breeds paranoia. For generals and sorcerers, the world is very dangerous. Enemies are lurking everywhere. Don Juan and the CIA create a fantastic cast of enemies and an esoteric armamentarium to combat them.

Don Juan is so charming that it is easy to overlook the obvious—the organizing metaphors for his world are martial. The man of knowledge is a warrior who accumulates power. (pp. 42, 124)

We might see Don Juan as a walking parable of the world of the primal particle that is being opened up by the new physics. Mysticism and science are joining hands. Black holes in space suggest that matter may disappear into a void where there is no space and time. So why shouldn't Don Juan slip into the nagual and reappear at an unexpected place? Both the sorcerer and the blackhole physicist agree that there may be "worm holes in space" that might allow us to cut through the universe faster than the speed of light. Both suggest that any event in the universe has some effect on every other part of the universe (Bell's theorem). And everyone knows by now that we can no longer model the universe solely on evidence based on common sense or the five senses. (p. 124)

The technology of transcendence of Don Juan could be paralleled in most mystical traditions. Zen and Christian mysticism and Gestalt therapy emphasize stopping the inner dialogue and entering the silence. The notion of ego-death, going beyond the persona, or "shrinking the tonal," is standard in religion and psychotherapy. And there are few traditions that have not advocated the use of some drugs as an aid.

Unfortunately, both the symbolism and the spiritual disciplines of Christianity and Judaism are currently suffering from a bad case of the blahs. Our native Western religious forms have ossified into institutionalized dogma, ritual, and moralism. Religion has become solemn business. Don Juan has brought back some of the delight, humor, and playfulness into the quest for the underlying or overarching reality.

But often Don Juan slips over the line that divides mystery and mystification. He does a few too many cheap miracles. We don't need Don Juan to produce a squirrel out of mid-air. The black magic and esoteric rites of the sorcerers often seem a parody and substitute for rituals and manners that bind those who live and struggle together. It seems that when a people can no longer look to any real bonding, no mutual trust, no purpose beyond survival, to hold them together in one body politic, then the esoteric and the occult become important. Don Juan raises the question of how to quiet the inner dialogue that haunts the lonely and obsessed self, so that the silence of nature can be heard. He does not help us to discover how to be gentle again, to trust and nurture.

Whatever his excesses or deficiencies, whether he is actual or fictional, Don Juan has found a firm place in the contemporary spirit. He inhabits the nagual of our time. It is good to have him around, reminding us to stop the world and wonder. (p. 140)

> *Sam Keen, "Don Juan's Power Trip," in* Psychology Today *(copyright © 1977 Ziff-Davis Publishing Company), December, 1977, pp. 40-2, 124, 140.*

ROBERT BLY

Whether there is a don Juan or not, Castaneda's five books embody a myth. The myth, broken into statements, says: You can gain power by picking the brains of men in cultures more primitive than ours. To gain power Western people have to reject all the perceptions of reason. No work on your shadow, or dependent side, is necessary. The male does not have to develop his feminine side, and relations with women are not important. But, as Blake would say, the contraries of these four statements are true, namely: 1. Only by reaching to the work of a more highly articulated culture can your own interior energy come forth. 2. The rational structure of our culture is a form of energy. The student goes through it, not around it. 3. No dependent person can make progress. 4. Spiritual instruction without the presence of women is worthless.

Don Juan's teaching of a Californian (Castaneda) couldn't possibly work anyway because the whole experience of grounding is missing. No one can ground on someone else's land. Inside, the Westerner has to ground through Western culture, either present or past. By his second book, it was clear that Castaneda was making up the conversations. It's a hoax. Joyce Carol Oates noticed it in 1972, and Weston LaBarre, the most distinguished researcher in the peyote field, called Castaneda a charlatan without mincing around [see excerpts above]. Castaneda as a novelist has the right to try a long novel in parts with an imaginary Mexican shaman as a hero, why not? Anthropologists are the ones embarrassed. . . .

There is something charming and good-natured about Castaneda's mass-paperback instruction. He doesn't insist on himself, as some Asian gurus do, but cancels himself, even going so far as to present himself as stupid. He has an interest in ideas, though he doesn't live them. In between books, he ransacks the work of genuine researchers . . .

and dishes out a sample goulash with new vegetables, standing behind the counter of what Turngpa Rinpoche accurately calls the spiritual supermarket. . . .

Castaneda good-naturedly gives the capitalist college students what they want—fantasies of gaining power without becoming more compassionate or more honest. (p. 7)

Castaneda's little essay in the first book on the four enemies of power was lovely and still is. Good little lectures are scattered around all his books. His not-doing is a harmless rephrasing of Taoist ideas. His "tonal-nagual" concept, which describes the gap between the ordinary world and a mysterious nonverbal world, owes a lot to the work of split-brain researchers in rational laboratories and to sophisticates like Robert Ornstein. He then attributed these ideas to an American slang-speaking Mexican native. But his finding of these ideas shows good taste. What I don't like so well is the air of regression that surrounds the language.

The attitude that surrounds all of Castaneda's teaching is the attitude of the pre-genital stage, the stage Freud identified as the anal. The absence of women in the first four books is striking. There is not a single thinking woman, and not one woman at all lovable in the way the frolicsome men are. Genital energy is not felt anywhere. . . .

[What] is curious in Castaneda is that teaching created by men and women climbing a powerful spiritual stair, or by men and women living in a joyful genital stage, are presented in the language of the anal stage. Naturally this shows in content, where no one ever goes off behind the bushes without being noticed. But the regression shows most clearly in the poor vocabulary, the thin texture of language, the poverty of metaphor, the monotonous way people talk, the tawdriness of image. The use of clichés deadens all of Castaneda's teaching. . . .

As his books go on, Castaneda learns more and more interesting ideas, but the regression deepens. I had the oddest sense in reading "The Second Ring of Power" that I was not in a house in Mexico at all, but in a kindergarten. . . .

In "The Second Ring of Power," all the women are frightful, empty and power-mad: Doña Soledad wants to kill Castaneda and steal his "luminosity." All are greedy. Sexual scenes, usually involving a woman lying heavily on top of Carlos, or he on her, contain horror always. People who offer to present occult information cheaply, in fantasy form, probably have this anti-female material in their psyche also, and as you read Castaneda's books you are absorbing the anti-female stuff, even though St. Paul is not present. (p. 22)

> Rober Bly, "Carlos Castaneda Meets Madame
> Solitude," in The New York Times Book Review
> (© 1978 by The New York Times Company; re-
> printed by permission), January 22, 1978, pp. 7,
> 22.

THOMAS LeCLAIR

Reading [The Second Ring of Power] I felt like the man going to St. Ives. Don Juan has gone by, leaving a band of apprentice sorceresses and their magical cats and kits to multiply his teachings. The dusty magus, now only remembered, gave earlier Castaneda books a personality and an interest absent here. In The Second Ring of Power we have only the residue of myth, odds and ends of folklore that suggest Castaneda has finally run out of material. . . .

As journalism, The Second Ring of Power is mind-mush. It is anecdotal anthropology and monochromatic drug vision. As religious teaching, it is repetitive and banal. As fiction—which is how I've come to read Castaneda—it is mute. (p. 38)

> Thomas LeClair, in Saturday Review (© 1978 by
> Saturday Review Magazine Corp.; reprinted with
> permission), February 4, 1978.

RICHARD de MILLE

[Castaneda's first] three volumes of field reports sold millions of copies coast to coast and around the world. That's unusual.

Don Juan, the mystical old Mexican Indian, was an imaginary person. That's extraordinary.

"Is it possible that these books are nonfiction?" exclaimed Joyce Carol Oates [see excerpt above]. Novelists Oates and William Kennedy and science fiction writer Theodore Sturgeon were quick to recognize Castaneda as a fellow story teller.

Carlos (as I call the young anthropologist in the story told by Castaneda) goes to Arizona to learn how the Indians use peyote but to his utter amazement is chosen by the imperious don Juan . . . to become "a man of knowledge," which means he will after long and arduous training enter "a separate reality" and *see* the essence of the world as mystics do. Published during the psychedelic years, *The Teachings of Don Juan* and *A Separate Reality* recount twenty-two wondrous drug trips through which don Juan guides Carlos, but as new-age consciousness gained favor in the media, *Journey to Ixtlan* suddenly discovered a wealth of neglected drugless techniques in some piles of old field notes Carlos had stupidly set aside. *Tales of Power* and *The Second Ring of Power* reflected later popular trends toward occultism and feminism.

If the trendy Castaneda could write at least five best sellers in a row, why did he bother with the anthropology hoax? An obvious economic reason is that the competition was too steep in the fiction market. Defective style, weak dramatic structure, poverty of detail, cardboard characters that do not develop (but are suitable for allegory), stereotyped emotions, and absence of ordinary human relationships make his books unsalable except as fact. Readers love a true adventure, even if badly told.

A more important, psychological reason is that anyone who would keep up such a difficult and complicated hoax for eight years before getting any reward is a person who habitually refuses to follow the rules of society and insists on winning the game of life by playing tricks. As with Castaneda, this lifelong pattern often includes personal charm, high intelligence, and some genuine accomplishments along with the con job. . . .

First, the so-called field reports contradict each other. Carlos meets a certain witch named La Catalina for the first time in 1962 and *again* for the first time in 1965. Though he learns a lot about *seeing* in 1962, unaccountably he has never heard of it in 1968. . . .

A second kind of proof arises from absence of convincing detail and presence of implausible detail. During nine years of collecting plants and hunting animals with don Juan, Carlos learns not one Indian name for any plant or animal and precious few Spanish or English names. No specimen of don Juan's hallucinogenic mushroom was brought back for verification, though Gordon Wasson had challenged its identification in 1968. Don Juan's desert is vaguely described, his habitations are all but featureless. Incessantly sauntering across the sands in seasons when . . . harsh conditions keep prudent people away, Carlos and don Juan go quite unmolested by pests that normally torment desert hikers. Carlos climbs unclimbable trees and stalks unstalkable animals. With prodigious speed and skill he writes down "everything" don Juan says to him under the most unlikely conditions. No one but Carlos has seen don Juan. . . .

A third kind of proof is found in don Juan's teachings, which combine American Indian folklore, oriental mysticism, and European philosophy. Indignantly dismissing such a proof, don Juan's followers declare that enlightened minds think alike in all times and places, but there is more to the proof than similar ideas; there are similar words. When don Juan opens his mouth, the words of particular writers come out. An example will show what I mean. Though I have condensed lines and added italics, I have not changed any words:

> The Human Aura is seen by the psychic observer as a *luminous* cloud, *egg*-shaped, streaked by fine lines like stiff *bristles* standing *out in all directions*.

> A man looks like an *egg* out of circulating fibers. And his arms and legs are like *luminous bristles* bursting *out in all directions*.

Of these two passages, the first comes from a book published in 1903, the second from *A Separate Reality*, a direct quote from don Juan. What I find piquant about this seventy-year echo is the contention that don Juan spoke only Spanish to Carlos. Somehow, in the course of translating don Juan's Spanish, Castaneda managed to resurrect the English phrases of Yogi Ramacharaka, a pseudonymous American hack writer of fake mysticism whose works are still available in occult bookstores.

Could such correspondence be accidental? Despite the close matching of words and ideas, one would have to allow the possibility if this were the only example, but it is not. . . .

Proofs like those I have just offered do not impress the loyal clients of Castaneda-Shaman. Contradictions, they say, don't matter, because Castaneda was not trying to write a factual account; he was trying to convey a subjective experience. If, then, his reports are nowhere tied to ordinary fact, how shall we distinguish them from ordinary fiction? . . .

Science requires facts; story-telling can take them or leave them. Scientific reports in which "specific details can often be justifiably questioned" are likely to be discredited, because specific details are often crucial in science; the fabric of observation and reporting can display only so many holes before being tossed into the trashcan. As science, the don Juan books are a farce. As fiction, they form an ingenious allegory in which experts . . . can recognize much anthropological truth.

Richard de Mille, "The Shaman of Academe: Carlos Castaneda" (copyright © 1979 by Richard de Mille), in Horizon, *April, 1979, pp. 64-8, 70 (the full text of this essay appears in* The Don Juan Papers: Further Castaneda Controversies, *edited by Richard de Mille, Ross-Erikson Publishers, 1980).*

Betty Cavanna

1909-

(Has also written under the names Betsy Allen and Elizabeth Headley) American young adult novelist, journalist, and author of fiction and nonfiction for younger children. Cavanna has been writing for and about the adolescent girl since 1943. Her books are distinguished by their insight into teenage living and their accurate descriptions of background and setting, and show a keen awareness of the uniqueness of the teen years. Her earlier novels center mainly on all-American girls from small towns as they deal with anxiety, jealousy, and most importantly, love. These books have been criticized for being too simplistic and predictable, and for presenting weak heroines who often have to rely on men. However, several of her books are recognized as classics, especially *Going on Sixteen*. The changing lifestyle of the American teenager is reflected in Cavanna's novels of the late sixties and early seventies. These novels incorporate more controversial themes, such as mother/daughter rivalry and conflicts between races and cultures, and feature plots built around such contemporary events as kidnapping and drug smuggling. With the exception of *Jenny Kimura*, these novels were not well received by critics. Most recently Cavanna has been rewriting earlier books into contemporary times and writing original novels set in the past. Cavanna's books have been accused of attracting an undemanding, unsophisticated audience. She has, however, developed a large, loyal following who appreciate her unpretentiousness and can identify with her characters as they face the numerous upheavals involved in growing up. (See also *Contemporary Authors*, Vols. 9-12, rev. ed., and *Something about the Author*, Vol. 1.)

MAY LAMBERTON BECKER

["The Black Spaniel Mystery" is an] excellent mystery for young folks beginning to grow up: . . .

Both "long" and "involved" are words of praise: a good mystery for young folks should go on a good while and have plenty in it, and should not be so easily unraveled that you see the end of the thread before you reach it. . . .

This is a mystery that can and will be read more than once. (p. 5)

> *May Lamberton Becker, in* New York Herald Tribune Book Review *(© I.H.T. Corporation; reprinted by permission), June 10, 1945.*

MAY LAMBERTON BECKER

[Seldom] one finds a story so well within [the world of the teenage girl as "Going on Sixteen."] . . .

The feature of "Going on Sixteen" is that it keeps level with the time [but in the mode of the moment deals with matters with which every girl has to deal]. . . .

Miss Cavanna's "Black Spaniel Mystery" stood out in its class because it had real young people and real dogs; ["Going on Sixteen"] is another proof of such understanding. (p. 8)

> *May Lamberton Becker, in* New York Herald Tribune Book Review *(© I.H.T. Corporation; reprinted by permission), May 5, 1946.*

JANE COBB and HELEN DORE BOYLSTON

[*A Date for Diane*] is written with skill, sympathy, and an abundant humor which laughs with, but never at, the fourteen-year-olds. And it's all there—the anxiety about the first date, the frenzies about clothes, the interminable telephone conversations, the picnics that go haywire, the inexplicable reaction of parents to lipstick and low-cut evening dresses, and the desperately important school activities, all presented from the serious point of view of fourteen. There is no caricaturing of the young in this book, no visible preaching, no patronage. These wholesome, normal kids feel as fourteen has always felt, and always will feel. (p. 166)

> *Jane Cobb and Helen Dore Boylston, in* The Atlantic Monthly *(copyright © 1946 by The Atlantic Monthly Company, Boston, Mass.; reprinted with permission), December, 1946.*

ELLEN LEWIS BUELL

Diane's sophomore year in high school [in "A Date for Diane"] begins as all small-towners will understand, just before school opens, with her first date. Into that one evening are crammed all the misgivings and embarrassments of 14-going on-15. . . .

We cannot conscientiously recommend as a pattern of behavior her tactics with the visiting cousin, whose aggressive femininity almost disrupts the gang, though we thoroughly enjoyed her ingenuity. We can, however, recommend this story for the light-hearted perception with which it treats those first suspenseful days of dates and dances. (p. 18)

Ellen Lewis Buell, in The New York Times Book Review *(© 1947 by The New York Times Company; reprinted by permission), January 5, 1947.*

ELLEN LEWIS BUELL

Betty Cavanna who has written several light-hearted but perceptive novels for the 'teen-aged, turns to the uncertain days of 1859 in this story of the Underground Railway ["Secret Passage"]. . . .

Almost any bright youngster will guess the outcome of its very simple plot, but they will like warm-hearted, curious Sally, and Miss Cavanna has a nice sense of period and place which gives flavor to the thin narrative. (p. 35)

Ellen Lewis Buell, in The New York Times Book Review *(© 1947 by The New York Times Company; reprinted by permission), February 23, 1947.*

MAY LAMBERTON BECKER

["Secret Passage"] is the sort of story for which libraries are always looking, one that, while keeping the taboos of the "mystery for girls," is sound in substance, well written, and likely to be remembered for something other than the solution of a problem. The action is permeated with atmosphere of the time, the year of Harper's Ferry, and though the Brintons' stand against slavery is firm and the Padbury type of slave-owner is shown in action, the Carringtons are treated as sufferers rather than oppressors. (p. 11)

May Lamberton Becker, in New York Herald Tribune Book Review, *(© I.H.T. Corporation; reprinted by permission), May 11, 1947.*

ELLEN LEWIS BUELL

Balletomanes are going to find that they have a lot in common with Topsy. . . .

More serious in theme than "A Date for Diane," ["Take a Call, Topsy"] lacks something of that book's quick spontaneity and finish, but like it, this one too portrays the 'teenager's world—the parties, the dates, the first pangs of hero-worship—with understanding of their importance, even to one who is dedicated to her art. (p. 25)

Ellen Lewis Buell, in The New York Times Book Review *(© 1947 by The New York Times Company; reprinted by permission), July 20, 1947.*

MAY LAMBERTON BECKER

An aviation story for girls must have something besides aviation to hold their attention, or it will be read only by the comparatively few who really want to fly and are willing to work for it. Betty Cavanna, whose books for growing girls are exactly suiting a great many of them, has put much more than flying into this sound, reasonable flying story ["A Girl Can Dream"]; her heroine is a girl who doesn't quite fit into everyday social life in a small city, and while envying the ease with which other girls do, makes no effort to imitate them. . . . Miss Cavanna herself knows what it is to learn to fly, but so do several other writers: she has the added grace of understanding the average girl. (p. 10)

May Lamberton Becker, in New York Herald Tribune Book Review *(© I.H.T. Corporation; reprinted by permission), April 11, 1948.*

VIRGINIA H. MATTHEWS

[Betty Cavanna] knows how to make her characters express the true, live intensity of being 17 and how to state in simple terms the experiences that bring maturity and wisdom. Kate's bright infatuation for a handsome young fisherman [in "Paintbox Summer"] is beautifully handled, as is the growth of her deeper and more lasting feeling for another boy at the summer's end. Finally when all the emotional and mental energies fuse into happy sense of direction and she decides to go to art school in the fall, each teen-age reader will be delighted, but sorry, that a wonderful story has come to an end. (p. 22)

Virginia H. Matthews, in The New York Times Book Review *(© 1949 by The New York Times Company; reprinted by permission), May 15, 1949.*

MARY GOULD DAVIS

It is rare to find a story for girls that tells so honestly and so sensitively the thoughts and emotions of first love [as "Paintbox Summer"]. . . . Against the background of Cape Cod in summer with the Peter Hunt school as its focal point, the story develops naturally and with unflagging interest. It has a touch of humor and it is completely honest in its human relationships. It is a good choice for any girl who is beginning to think of the years ahead. (p. 34)

Mary Gould Davis, in The Saturday Review of Literature *(copyright, 1949, by The Saturday Review Co., Inc.; reprinted with permission), August 13, 1949.*

ALICE BROOKS McGUIRE

There is a "Cinderella" theme in Betty Cavanna's ["Spring Comes Riding"]. . . .

Miss Cavanna is second only to Maureen Daly in her ability to see into the hearts of teen-age girls and present convincingly the problems and emotional unrest that plague them. Her characters are natural and even family relations do not always reflect sweetness and light. . . .

Adolescent girls will associate themselves completely with this story and rightly so, for the whole narrative is quite convincing even to the adult reader. (p. 10)

Alice Brooks McGuire, in Chicago Sunday Tribune, *Part 4, November 12, 1950.*

GLADYS CROFOOT CASTOR

[In "Spring Comes Riding"] Meg learns what kind of girl she herself is, and what she can mean to those who are important to her.

To a lively story of family fun, of horses, dates, parties and romance in the persons of two attractive young college men, Betty Cavanna has added her special ability to see into the heart of a teen-age girl.

Gladys Crofoot Castor, "Teenage Hurdle," in The New York Times Book Review *(© 1950 by The New York Times Company; reprinted by permission), November 12, 1950, p. 16.*

MAY LAMBERTON BECKER

In Camden in 1917 there were just two possible careers for a "nice" girl—normal school or marriage—and Ellen [in "Catchpenny Street"] had no bent for teaching. There was one handsome, steady youth who had intentions and lived in a more distinguished neighborhood: an unpredictable medical student complicated her choice. To this the situation can be reduced.

But that gives little idea of how good the book is, or of how contemporary it is in spite of taking place as the first world war was coming to a boil. The problem of individual choice keeps coming up with each individual girl—provided she remains an individual and not a mass production—and a story in which it is successfully and recognizably worked out is always timely. Girls of 1951 who want to marry for security and are not quite sure what kind of security they want will be friends with Ellen, who did find out, though it took a fire, a war, a dachshund and a polio epidemic to enlighten her. (p. 12)

> *May Lamberton Becker, in* New York Herald Tribune Book Review *(© I.H.T. Corporation; reprinted by permission), June 17, 1951.*

DWIGHT L. BURTON

Books by Betty Cavanna have been among the most popular with young high school readers. Her principal characters are adolescent girls, her setting is the environs of Philadelphia, and her theme usually is the struggle of an adolescent girl to gain self-confidence. Of her five or six novels, one, *Going on Sixteen,* is noteworthy. The others are neither better nor worse than the dozens of innocuous girls' stories which have flowed from the press in recent years.

Going on Sixteen is compounded of the humdrum in adolescent life. It rests upon its genuineness and sincerity rather than upon melodrama. Julie, the heroine, is a somewhat shy, nondescript girl who lives on a farm with her father and commutes to the town high school by bus. The story carries her through three years of high school to a point where she has apparently "found herself." The theme of the novel, although familiar, is handled well. The author avoids the easy assumptions present in many books with a similar theme, including others by herself. Boys, though they have a place in Julie's life, are not the magic medium through which she suddenly blossoms. Julie does not go to the prom with the football captain or with any "dreamy" new boy who moves to town; nor does any aunt come to visit who teaches Julie how to dress and change her personality. Julie does not blossom at all; there is no metamorphosis, but there is realistic evolution of character brought about by Julie's own efforts and recognition of her faults and by the sympathetic guidance of a teacher.

Miss Cavanna's principal general strength lies in the perception with which she presents adolescents together. Her best scenes, notably in *Spring Comes Riding* and *Going on Sixteen,* are those in which groups of adolescents are at dances, movies, or in drugstores, situations in which the unique social mores and conventions of adolescence are in operation. In *Going on Sixteen* the freshman dance scene is a bit of rare artistry.

Miss Cavanna is weakest perhaps in her treatment of family relations and in characterization. Her fathers and mothers, except in *Going on Sixteen,* where the father is a well-drawn individual, run to stereotypes. The mothers are young, attractive, and laden with patient wisdom; the fathers are intelligent, somewhat indulgent, and in a state of mild frustration with their daughters, who wheedle them. Real family problems do not exist. Miss Cavanna is in-

clined to categorize her characters and then proceed to the business of the story.... It is difficult to create a really believable adolescent in fiction, because in personality the adolescent, even more than the adult, is now one thing and now another. (pp. 164-65)

> *Dwight L. Burton, in* English Journal *(copyright © 1951 by the National Council of Teachers of English), September, 1951 (and reprinted in* Readings about Adolescent Literature, *edited by Dennis Thomison, The Scarecrow Press, Inc., 1970).*

MARGARET A. EDWARDS

The nearest contemporary rival in popularity [to Maureen Daly is probably Betty Cavanna]. *Going on Sixteen* and *A Date for Diane* have much to say to shy girls who must learn that the road to self-assurance and popularity is paved with thoughts and deeds that center around other people rather than one's self. And in her stories this author says these things in a style that is entertaining and persuasive. (p. 70)

> *Margaret A. Edwards, in* English Journal *(copyright © 1952 by the National Council of Teachers of English), September, 1952 (and reprinted in* Readings about Adolescent Literature, *edited by Dennis Thomison, The Scarecrow Press, Inc., 1970).*

NORA KRAMER

[The] lightly romantic story [of *Love, Laurie*] will lift the heart of the quiet girl whose natural reserve seems an added hurdle in growing up. It will comfort those who inwardly despair as other girls with ready tongues make flip rejoinders to the easy banter of the boys they know. . . .

To help her recover from the shock of her mother's recent death, [her father] leaves to Laurie decisions involved with the building [of a new house]. This seems a drastic "cure," but Laurie's understanding of her father's rationalizing is part of her growing up, as is her honest self-appraisal in her friendship with each of three young men.

The plot is thin, yet Laurie is real and will be remembered for her strength and dignity.

> *Nora Kramer, "Laurie Grows Up," in* The New York Times Book Review *(© 1953 by The New York Times Company; reprinted with permission), November 15, 1953, p. 8.*

RICHARD S. ALM

[Betty Cavanna] is a writer of some importance. In Rette Larkin, the heroine of *A Girl Can Dream,* she creates a tomboy whose unconventional behavior and ambitions make her a conspicuous member of the senior class. Unfortunately, the characterization is not carefully sustained, and the story ends too neatly with all *i*'s dotted and all *t*'s crossed. In *Going on Sixteen,* an earlier story, the shy, withdrawn Julie Ferguson develops into a more self-confident, poised adolescent. This heroine is a convincing figure throughout the story. Changes in Julie are carefully prepared for and are neither abrupt nor exaggerated. The one opportunity for giving the story a fairy-tale twist—Julie's attempting to sell her sketches of puppies to an art editor to earn enough money to buy Sonny, the thoroughbred Collie —Cavanna turns instead into an experience that helps Julie to grow up. Betty Cavanna is sensitive to the happiness as well as the pain of adolescence, and her stories of teen-agers reflect both. (p. 318)

Richard S. Alm, in English Journal *(copyright © 1955 by the National Council of Teachers of English), September, 1955 (and reprinted in* Readings about Children's Literature, *edited by Evelyn Rose Robinson, David McKay Company, Inc., 1966).*

ALBERTA EISEMAN

Angela Dodge, the "Angel on Skis," . . . is 14 when we first meet her. Angry and resentful at having to help run the guest house, she dreams only of the day when she'll be able to afford a pair of skis. When we leave her, two years later, she's on the threshold of becoming a top-notch skier. We follow her through her first sitzmarks, the thrill of discovering that she's truly talented, the disappointment of losing a race, the slow, painful learning to be a good sport. Miss Cavanna captures fully the excitement of skiing and the breathtaking beauty of the landscape. The characters are believable, the story line uncluttered. This one's a gem. (p. 18)

Alberta Eiseman, in The New York Times Book Review *(© 1957 by The New York Times Company; reprinted by permission), December 15, 1957.*

ALBERTA EISEMAN

Betty Cavanna is a fine storyteller, and as such she can always carry you along from page to page, asking no questions as to consistency or motivation until after you have finished the book. Many of her very popular novels for young people are satisfactory on all counts. But after the last page of "Stars in Her Eyes" is turned, many questions remain unanswered. . . .

[Magda Page, pudgy 14-year-old daughter of a famous television personality,] takes her first steps toward independence by working as a waitress during her vacation, then persuades her parents to let her spend ten months in Paris, studying singing and ballet as well as attending a French school. When she returns home, slim and poised, she is truly ready to embark upon her new career, and mature enough to be grateful for her father's help.

Why does Maggie decide to go to Paris? On page 163 the idea is mentioned for the first time, "dredged out of her subconscious." On page 167, without further discussion, her parents have agreed, and she's off. And why does Scoop, the knowledgeable young TV script writer, exclaim "aha! The independent type!" twice during the space of a few pages, both times to Maggie? There is much of validity in the book, but it seems to have been written hurriedly, without much regard for details. (p. 50)

Alberta Eiseman, in The New York Times Book Review *(© 1958 by The New York Times Company; reprinted by permission), October 26, 1958.*

ALBERTA EISEMAN

[Betty Cavanna] has nicely captured the thrill of learning to sail, and the conflict between native Cape Codders and summer residents is amusingly sketched [in *The Scarlet Sail*]. The minor characters are sharply drawn, especially Mike, Andrea's young sailing instructor, and his wise little

sister Hannah. But it is the warm, sympathetic handling of the heroine herself which will make this book a favorite with young readers. (p. 58)

Alberta Eiseman, in The New York Times Book Review *(© 1959 by The New York Times Company; reprinted by permission), November 15, 1959.*

VIRGINIA HAVILAND

There is sufficient reality in this summer romance [*The Scarlet Sail*] to make the reviewer wish it went a few steps beyond. The author has a believable heroine, who wrestles with normal enough problems in getting used to life with a new, and most understanding, stepfather; in adjusting to a new Cape Cod environment with a new set of teen-agers; and in learning to sail her new birthday boat—but the characterizations, tensions, and incidents fail to grip the reader with a strong enough pull. It's all too facile, although of course it is sure to be one of the author's most popular books. (p. 39)

Virginia Haviland, in The Horn Book Magazine *(copyright, 1960, by The Horn Book, Inc., Boston), February, 1960.*

RUTH HILL VIGUERS

The understanding and skillful interpretation of present-day teen-age girls that so characterizes this author's work marks also her entrance into the field of historical fiction. . . . [*A Touch of Magic* is a] moral tale certainly, and there is a tendency to allow details of setting to slow up the story, but there are interesting contrasts in the historical background and evidence that Miss Cavanna can write with depth and compassion. (p. 273)

Ruth Hill Viguers, in The Horn Book Magazine *(copyright, 1961, by the Horn Book, Inc., Boston), June, 1961.*

[Betty Cavanna] uses the pleasant background of Nantucket Sound, and holidaying and sailing there against which to set [*The Scarlet Sail*, a] story of a girl's growth and development. The story is a useful one for older girls, dealing as it does with the difficulties common to many but the author is perhaps a little too self-consciously preoccupied with the problem [of adjusting to a new stepparent]. The treatment of the theme becomes almost clinical, while the moral is perhaps too pointedly made to be readily acceptable. The red sails and the seashore assume the too thin semblance of an attractive veneer which fails to fit the heavy solidarity beneath. (pp. 126-27)

The Junior Bookshelf, *July, 1962.*

MARGARET SHERWOOD LIBBY

Betty Cavanna has set the stage for [the visit of Japanese-raised Jenny to America in *Jenny Kimura*] and depicted the characters, both Japanese and American, extremely well. We found three-quarters of the book absorbing reading, with Jenny's problems very real and complex. Then the mechanics of a light teen-age romance took over, and the characters became unconvincing puppets acting out a contrived and sentimental happy ending. (p. 28)

Margaret Sherwood Libby, in Book Week *(© I.H.T. Corporation; reprinted by permission), November 29, 1964.*

BECKY WELZ

I think "Mystery at Love's Creek" is too young for teen-agers. . . .

The thief was obvious to me in the second chapter. From then on the author tries to make a mystery by presenting other suspects.

Carlie is supposed to be sixteen, but by the way she talks it is hard to believe she is a teen-ager. For example, the word "dandy" would never come out of a teenager's mouth today. (p. 11)

> Becky Welz, in The Christian Science Monitor (reprinted by permission from The Christian Science Monitor; © 1965 The Christian Science Publishing Society; all rights reserved), November 4, 1965.

[In *Jenny Kimura*] Jenny Kimura Smith (it had to be Smith) lives in Tokyo with her Japanese mother and her American father. At sixteen she is going on a visit to her paternal grandmother in Kansas City. One can almost see those good intentions skimming through the author's mind. What an ideal backcloth against which to show that Japanese and American customs may differ but a little forbearance on both sides will bridge the gap! But what do we learn? That Japanese girls envy the freedom of their American counter-parts? That the kimono is not fancy dress but what you wear when you want to show respect? That Kansas City matrons are all for fraternization but all against inter-marriage? That the child of a mixed marriage looks strangely fair to one set of grandparents but noticeably dark to the other? These obvious pointers would be acceptable if they were integrated into a worthwhile story, but Jenny's infatu-ations with the boring Alan and George Yamadu, second-generation American, are tedious and trivial. It is a pity that Betty Cavanna, who writes well, could not think of more original adventures for her heroine. (p. 442)

> The Times Literary Supplement (© Times News-papers Ltd. (London) 1966; reproduced from The Times Literary Supplement by permission), May 19, 1966.

[*A Breath of Fresh Air*] is disappointingly stale from this extremely popular author. Miss Cavanna is usually quite precise in her understanding of teenagers' reactions and feelings, but here the viewpoint often seems too old to suit her heroine. The situation is affecting—Brooke Lawrence, a senior in high school, has to reconcile herself to her par-ents' inevitable divorce. At the same time she starts to re-alize that in spite of her suspicions of romance and mar-riage, she is really falling in love with her long time friend, David Hale. The incompatibility of the Lawrences, both very likeable people, is very well handled, but Brooke's compassion towards them sometimes seems beyond her age and experience, and this is heightened by the author's ten-dency to refer to the parents by their first names. . . . The subject [Brooke picks for her English term paper] is Louisa May Alcott, and even though she lives near the Alcott home, she seems too old to empathize with Louisa, too young to be taking the studious interest she does. The ro-mance is bound to please girls, and the split home is de-scribed satisfyingly; however the discrepancies in Brooke's personality, and the tendency of the writing to become cliched, detract from the book's potential. (p. 914)

> Virginia Kirkus' Service (copyright © 1966 Vir-ginia Kirkus' Service, Inc.), September 1, 1966.

"Christmas in a castle—an Irish castle!" So begins [*The Ghost of Ballyhooly*] which proceeds directly to an ap-parent murder on Ballyhooly grounds, teases with legends and glimpses of a castle ghost who roams the tower, and links the mystery's culprits to pollution in a half-hearted play for up-to-date relevance. . . . The story reveals a quaintly off-target notion of an intellectual family's conver-sations and an even remoter sense of a bright 16-year-old's preoccupations; there's just enough tepid romance, pallid local color and puzzling occurrences to sustain those com-mitted Cavanna fans who grow younger every year. (p. 881)

> Kirkus Reviews (copyright © 1971 The Kirkus Service, Inc.), August 15, 1971.

Instead of trying to keep up with today's manners and out-look, Betty Cavanna wisely sets [*Joyride*] in the '20's, where concern about decorating the school gym for a dance seems in keeping with *The Sheik* under the mattress and "I'll See You In My Dreams" on the gramophone. . . . Cavanna's non-judgmental handling of Susan's mother is commendable in a YA novel; Mrs. Cucci's vitality, grace-less discontent and sometimes insensitive devotion to her daughter elicit both sympathy and impatience. Less well realized is Susan's artist friend Mary, who is good for the plot and for Susan's development but whose comments on contemporary artists are too anonymously correct to convey her claimed personal enthusiasm. In the same way Susan's own reactions to Dreiser, Hemingway, etc., read like capsule evaluations hacked out for some commercial outline series and the author's attempts to integrate con-temporary events and issues are just as much ruled by con-ventional retrospective wisdom. Serious Cavanna, this is a bit too slow and uneventful for her mystery fans yet lacking in interest for teenagers like Susan who read real literature. However, the outsider's problems of adjustment in a time when joyriding seems *de rigueur* will be readily accessible to correspondingly tentative members of the Pepsi genera-tion. (p. 1012)

> Kirkus Reviews (copyright © 1974 The Kirkus Service, Inc.), September 15, 1974.

LILLIAN N. GERHARDT

The roar of the 1920's is reduced to a squeak in this misfit-makes-good-in-high school novel [*Joyride*]. . . . It's all purest escape, never real: Susan's purity never falters as she faces up to school life, her conservative parents, her problems making friends, getting dates, fending off joy-riding boys, and bathtub gin; the "fast girl" in her class gets pregnant, of course; the guzzling college boy who got her that way goes blind on wood alcohol. Nobody over the age of nine would doubt that Susan could come through unscathed and nobody over the age of ten with all her mar-bles is likely to read this. (p. 40)

> Lillian N. Gerhardt, in School Library Journal (reprinted from the December, 1974 issue of School Library Journal, published by R. R. Bowker Co. A Xerox Corporation; copyright © 1974), December, 1974.

Cavanna starts out [*Ruffles and Drums*] with a highly top-ical combination—feminist sentiments in a Bicentennial setting. And at first it seems she has taken a more realistic tack, for though Sarah Devotion Kent longs to join the fighting men of Concord she is soon reduced to winding cartridge papers and nursing a wounded British officer. As it turns out, Sarah's main preoccupation is the parceling out of her affections between her betrothed sweetheart, Tom Fletcher, and the Englishman, James Butler. . . . But the only interest here—a lagging one—lies in how long it will take Sarah to rationalize the switch from Tom to James. A tired formula . . . almost an instant artifact. (p. 716)

Kirkus Reviews (copyright © 1975 The Kirkus Service, Inc.), July 1, 1975.

CYRISSE JAFFEE

Betty Cavanna has produced a wholly unremarkable novel [*Ruffles and Drums*] to add to the already glutted Bicentennial market. Set in Concord in 1775, this relates the story of Sarah Devotion Kent, her family and neighbors, beginning with the fight at the North Bridge. The descriptions of colonial Concord life and the historical details are well-drawn. But Cavanna sticks rigidly to her tired old formula. Sarah must choose between Thomas, literally the "boy-next-door," and James Butler, a handsome and charming enemy soldier wounded at the North Bridge and nursed back to health by Sarah and her mother. The stereotypical, predictable characterizations fail to make the important events come alive. (p. 96)

Cyrisse Jaffee, in School Library Journal (reprinted from the October, 1975 issue of School Library Journal, published by R. R. Bowker Co. A Xerox Corporation; copyright © 1975), October, 1975.

[*Jenny Kimura*] is a perfect textbook for versing teenagers in the attitudes towards class, race, sex and success held and promoted by the establishment. To her credit, the author has done her homework regarding Japanese culture and lifestyles, writes interestingly and tells a good tale.

Jenny is the sixteen-year-old daughter of an American father and Japanese mother on a first visit to the U.S. . . . Jenny enthusiastically embraces the carefree ways and goals of American girls (boys, clothes, boys, sports, boys, boys, boys) and deals with the racism she encounters with quiet and calm. The only non-whites in this environment are a "black-skinned, plump, and kindly" maid and a woman who writes book reviews.

Racism is overcome at the end through individual, not group or societal, solutions. Jenny ends up believing in the "essential goodness of America" and is left to decide whether to go to Radcliffe or Wellesley, depending upon which boy she wants to be near. . . . A clear value judgment is placed on the desirability of success, materialism, and other American ways of life. (p. 17)

Interracial Books for Children Bulletin (reprinted by permission of Interracial Books for Children Bulletin, 1841 Broadway, New York, N.Y. 10023), Vol. 7, Nos. 2 & 3, 1976.

KAY HAUGAARD

Sarah Devotion Kent. What a wonderfully upright, colonial name. A farm girl of Concord during the Revolutionary War, Sarah has spunk and spirit so that you keep expecting her to have some goal in mind—something to worry about,

feel about. No such luck. We learn more about James, the wounded British officer taken in by Sarah's family, than we do Sarah.

[*Ruffles and Drums* is a] loosely plotted tale about the Revolution in which everyone is amazingly reasonable, sweet and understanding, and nothing of significance hangs in the balance. (p. 80)

Kay Haugaard, in Journal of Reading (copyright 1976 by the International Reading Association, Inc.; reprinted by permission of Kay Haugaard and the International Reading Association), October, 1976.

A trip to Thailand with her glamorous photographer father, the attentions of a young hippie . . . , and the chance to solve a mystery at the behest of the king of Thailand himself, by discovering the missing emerald buddha hidden in a vat of whitewash. . . . Lisette's summer is chock full of excitement. But as Cavanna's notion of characterization is transparent [in the *The Mystery of the Buddha*] . . . , as her idea of romance is having a woman ostentatiously called Professor Goodfellow throughout relinquish her title for marriage and joint credit on Father's book; and as her villains can be spotted a mile away, the appointments evoke plastic and naugahyde instead of emerald and jade. Strictly a low budget package tour. (p. 1100)

Kirkus Reviews (copyright © 1976 The Kirkus Service, Inc.), October 1, 1976.

ZENA SUTHERLAND

[In *You Can't Take Twenty Dogs on a Date*, Jo Redmond] decides to use the kennels and runs back of her home, purchased from a dog breeder, for a summer boarding kennel. While the story has a slight plot thread (two strands: will the project succeed; will attractive Steve Chance remain interested in her) it is primarily an account of Jo's problems and plans. The writing style is adequate, but no more; the characterization is adequate but without depth. The positive aspects of the story are the believable and warm family relationships, Jo's dedication and her sense of responsibility, and the sensible way in which she copes with practical and emotional obstacles. For some readers, the affection for, and descriptions of dogs will be an added appeal. (p. 30)

Zena Sutherland, in Bulletin of the Center for Children's Books (© 1977 by the University of Chicago; all rights reserved), October, 1977.

PHYLLIS INGRAM

Using as historical background the 1866 voyage of a troopship of young women from New York through the Straits of Magellan to Seattle, Cavanna has fashioned a routine romance [in *Runaway Voyage*]. . . . The story is thickly larded with descriptive passages of the travel-folder type. The dialogue is embarrassingly clichéd, and so are the characters—the hard-working, resourceful orphan, the spoiled rich girl, the wise sea captain, and the rascally promoter—not to forget the good-hearted prostitute. (p. 153)

Phyllis Ingram, in School Library Journal (reprinted from the October, 1978 issue of School Library Journal, published by R. R. Bowker Co. A Xerox Corporation; copyright © 1978), October, 1978.

JEAN F. MERCIER

Of approximately 40 popular novels that Cavanna has created, few can compete in liveliness, romance and genuine appeal with her new story ["Runaway Voyage"]. She bases it on "Mercer's Belles," *New York Times* reporter Roger Conant's diary. He sailed on the *Continental* in 1866 from New York to Seattle with shifty Asa Mercer, who escorted a bevy of maidens eager to find new lives and husbands in the raw territory. Cavanna invented Eliza, an orphan, who steals money for a train trip to board the vessel and is a stowaway, hidden by a friendly sailor, Harry.

She is most endearing and her adventures—sad, scary, funny and victorious—keep the reader glued to the pages. (p. 61)

> *Jean F. Mercier, in* Publishers Weekly *(reprinted from the October 23, 1978, issue of* Publishers Weekly *by permission of the critic, published by R. R. Bowker Company, a Xerox company; copyright © 1978 by Xerox Corporation), October 23, 1978.*

DENISE M. WILMS

Cavanna's practiced hand moves [*Runaway Voyage*] along nicely via the particulars of Eliza's lengthy sea voyage. Shipboard characters run to type . . . but create color as they shape action. In the end Eliza's circumstances are definitely bettered (as you knew they would be). . . . [The] story constitutes an interesting sidelight on history and does well as untaxing, satisfying recreational reading. (pp. 476-77)

> *Denise M. Wilms, in* Booklist *(reprinted by permission of the American Library Association; copyright 1978 by the American Library Association), November 1, 1978.*

HELEN GREGORY

[*Ballet Fever*, the rewriting of Cavanna's 1947 *Take a Call, Topsy*] does no major revision to the plot—the story of a girl who must give up a posh finishing school and her football hero boyfriend for a career in dance, and overcome her schoolgirl crush on an instructor; with a subplot showing the growth of her little sister during a crisis following an auto accident in which her mother breaks her leg. The revision, renamed perhaps to cash in on "Saturday Night Fever," simply removes out-of-date references (Vera Zorina, snoods, "bids" to dances, etc.), streamlines the prose, cuts back on detailed descriptions of clothing, and changes the heroine's name from "Topsy" to an innocuous "Teddi." While the plot is centered on her ballet career choice and the dance references are generally accurate and interesting background, there isn't a lot of real dancing, and the image of Teddi as "a pretty picture in the frothy ballet skirt . . . small and well made, with blonde hair that fell heavy and shining to her shoulders" leaves something to be desired. . . . It's not bad reading, the work of a craftsman, if not an artist. (p. 60)

> *Helen Gregory, in* School Library Journal *(reprinted from the January, 1979 issue of* School Library Journal, *published by R. R. Bowker Co. A Xerox Corporation; copyright © 1979), January, 1979.*

Alice Childress

1920-

Black American playwright, novelist, nonfiction writer, and editor. Childress's works examine the complexity of relationships between blacks and whites and the various ways blacks survive in contemporary society. She is sharply observant and unsentimental, and uses a strong theatrical sense in both her drama and her fiction. While Childress is considered a talented playwright, her works have been infrequently produced. An early play, *Trouble in Mind*, deals with a group of black actors rehearsing a white play about blacks. Although it was critically acclaimed as an off-Broadway production and won the 1956 Obie Award, it was never performed on Broadway due to disputes over theme and interpretation which caused Childress to withdraw it. However, it was her first work to be seen outside Harlem, and was a precursor of the black naturalistic plays of the late 1960s. Childress feels she got her dramatic bent from her grandmother, a theatrical storyteller, and from the influences of the Bible, Shakespeare, and black poet Paul Laurence Dunbar. As an actress, she was one of the original members of The American Negro Theatre, and later served as a director there for twelve years. Childress turned to writing plays in the late 1940s when a one-act play, *Florence*, was favorably reviewed for its realistic dialogue and strong characterization. Her first novel, *A Hero Ain't Nothin' But a Sandwich*, was praised for similar reasons, and has become recognized as a classic portrayal of a young urban heroin addict and his world. Despite a small output, Childress has developed a reputation as a writer of realistic works of quality. (See also *Contemporary Authors*, Vols, 45-48, and *Something about the Author*, Vol. 7.)

ARTHUR GELB

The author of "Trouble in Mind" is Alice Childress, a writer with a quick eye for the foibles and crotches, the humor and pathos of backstage life in the type of Broadway production that utilizes a predominantly Negro cast.

Miss Childress . . . has some witty and penetrating things to say about the dearth of roles for Negro actors in the contemporary theatre, the cut-throat competition for these parts and the fact that Negro actors often find themselves playing stereotyped roles in which they cannot bring themselves to believe.

She also has some sharp comments to make about the jumpy state of nerves in the much-investigated entertainment media. But it is all done with good humor and, except

for the last [sections of dialogue], manages to avoid any impassioned sermonizing. (p. 23)

> Arthur Gelb, in The New York Times (© 1955 by The New York Times Company; reprinted by permission), November 5, 1955.

LOFTEN MITCHELL

Miss Childress writes with a sharp, satiric touch. Character seems to interest her more than plot. Her characterizations are piercing, her observations devastating. Apparently, she feels the American race problem is a family fight but not in the sense that a Dixiecrat would claim the problem in the South is the South's alone. Miss Childress seems to believe there is a direct relationship between black and white, that these are grandchildren and cousins who are being denied human decency. She, therefore, calls on the nation to reexamine itself morally.

[Her] play, *Wedding Band*, suggests this in bold terms. Here she deals with an interracial couple that cannot marry because of southern laws. The play reaches a rousing climax when the Negro woman defines for a white woman exactly what the Negro has meant in terms of southern lives. (p. 221)

Wedding Band is, to all who have heard it, an exceptionally well-written, humorous, dramatic piece, positive in its approach and fully deserving a first-rate production. (p. 222)

> Loften Mitchell, in The Crisis (copyright 1965 by The Crisis Publishing Company, Inc.), April, 1965.

CLIVE BARNES

[Childress's one-act play "String"] was suggested by the Guy de Maupassant story of the Norman peasant Hauchecorne, called "The Piece of String." The short story is concerned with the ironically narrow balance between guilt and innocence, and Maupassant, with that crisply impersonal cynicism that is almost the crest of Romanticism, treats it with a brief wit and a long compassion. The play does not.

The play in fairness is completely different. Only the memory remains. Miss Childress has set her play at a black block party picnic. The characters are nicely judged. The Cadillac-bar-owning bully, the happily socially weaving bourgeois matrons, and the cryptomiser, accused of theft; these people are part of an incandescently recognizable scene. It was the recognition of that scene that was itself interesting.

The fault of the piece was simply that it was too prolonged for its subject. The Maupassant short story makes its obliquely satiric point in a matter of minutes. The play drags out. It is worth noting, in passing, that short stories very rarely serve well as plays if only because the time span is so different. (p. 37)

> *Clive Barnes, in* The New York Times *(© 1969 by The New York Times Company; reprinted by permission), April 2, 1969.*

DORIS E. ABRAMSON

Alice Childress has been, from the beginning, a crusader and a writer who resists compromise. She tries to write about Negro problems as honestly as she can, and she refuses production of her plays if the producer wants to change them in a way which distorts her intentions. (p. 190)

The title [of] *Trouble in Mind* comes from a blues song of the same name. Alice Childress chose to tell about trouble in a milieu that she knows well—the theatre. The three acts of *Trouble in Mind* take place during rehearsals in a Broadway theatre.... The play being rehearsed is one about Negroes and whites....

Trouble in Mind has interesting characters and dialogue, though both tend to ring false whenever they are saturated with sermonizing. The setting, the stage of a theatre during rehearsals, invites an audience to participate in a ritual usually forbidden them and therefore tantalizing. The plot amounts to very little—a group of actors rehearse a play, quarrel about interpretation, get the director to agree to ask the playwright to make changes in the script. What lends the play significance is that the cast is predominantly Negro. As attitudes in the company are modified, people's lives are affected, and this play about a rehearsal makes a comment on life itself.

And yet, too much of *Trouble in Mind* is willed—what the French call *voulu.* A reader of the script is very much aware of the author pulling strings, putting her own words into a number of mouths. This is not, however, to deny the theatrical effectiveness of the play in production. (p. 203)

To read the play is to be much more aware than [seeing it in production] of the extent to which Miss Childress loaded the play with Negro problems....

It would be better if she did not assault race prejudice at every turn, for she sometimes sacrifices depth of character in the process....

The characters need a humanizing complexity to keep them from ever becoming the stereotypes featured in "Chaos in Belleville" [the play being rehearsed within Childress' play]. (p. 204)

> *Doris E. Abramson, in her* Negro Playwrights in the American Theatre: 1925-1959 *(copyright © 1967, 1969 Columbia University Press; reprinted by permission of the publisher), Columbia University Press, 1969.*

DONALD T. EVANS

Black people have recognized the need for their own the-

ater. To give voice to our esthetic meant that we had to be free of the white man's evaluation, his standards of quality. It goes without saying that this need for our own encompasses much more than just theater, but *Trouble in Mind* by Alice Childress begins with the hassle of the Black artist. She shows the difficulty of working in *the man's* theater and maintaining one's integrity and identity. She shows why the Black Arts Movement had to come about. White America doesn't want to know about Black people, she says. They are much more comfortable with the half-human creatures they created and maintained in asinine comedy after comedy. (p. 44)

> *Donald T. Evans, in* Black World *(copyright © February, 1971, by* Black World; *reprinted by permission of Johnson Publishing Company and Donald T. Evans), February, 1971.*

CLIVE BARNES

["Wedding Band"] is a romantic play, and does not entirely escape the charge of sentimentality.

The writing is rather old-fashioned in its attempt at Ibsenite realism, and neither the situation nor the characters really change from the beginning of the play to the end. But perhaps that was par for the course in South Carolina in 1918, and the play has a cosy efficiency that always holds the attention. It is a sweet old love story about hard, dusty times in a hard, dusty place.

What did black people think and talk about in 1918? We are so used to the black stereotypes thrust on us by the white literature of the time or to the films of a period just a little later that it is difficult to judge the credibility of a black play deliberately set more than half a century ago, almost midway between Abolition and now.

Miss Childress very carefully suggests the stirrings of black consciousness, as well as the strength of white bigotry. Interestingly, the stirrings are most strongly felt in the young black soldier about to go to France, for it was during this world war and the one that followed it that the seeds of social change were most abundantly implanted. The play also has a great deal of compassion.

Indeed its strength lies very much in the poignancy of its star-cross'd lovers, but whereas Shakespeare's lovers always had a fighting chance, there is no way that Julia and Herman are going to be able to beat the system. Niggers and crackers are more irreconcilable than any Montagues and Capulets.

The background to the lovers—the black neighbors and his white mother and sister—is conventionally drawn. The blacks are more comic than bitter, and the white family is rigidly racist. You just know that the mother would think there was a better use for white sheets than putting them on a bed. But in the two lovers themselves, Miss Childress strikes the note of the genuine playwright....

[The play] does also offer a modest gloss on a period of black history that often goes unremarked. There after all was quite an interregnum between slavery and militancy, and this play is right in there explaining. (p. 30)

> *Clive Barnes, in* The New York Times *(© 1972 by The New York Times Company; reprinted by permission), October 27, 1972.*

EDITH OLIVER

["Wedding Band" is a play about] a pair of lovers no longer

young. She is black, he is white; she is a seamstress, he is a baker named Herman. The time is 1918, while the United States is still at war, and the place is a city in South Carolina. . . .

Much of the wealth of ''Wedding Band'' is in the small scenes of byplay among the neighbors. For the most part, Miss Childress . . . [succeeds] in creating a whole style of life at that time and in that place. . . . All through the action, things are on the move: two little girls run around and scream and play, a nasty white peddler wanders in and out, and everyone minds everyone else's business, sometimes in a very kind and supportive way. The first act is splendid, but after that we hit a few jarring notes, when the characters seem to be speaking as much for the benefit of us eavesdroppers out front in 1972 as for the benefit of one another. At one point, . . . [the seamstress], in a farewell toast, talks of her hopes for the future, when blacks will be free to go to ''parks and museums.'' It is a dreadful speech, made straight to the audience, that sounds like something out of a bad Russian movie. Whether these spurts of spuriousness are the fault of the writing . . . I cannot say, but . . . they do not spoil the evening. (p. 105)

Edith Oliver, in The New Yorker *(© 1972 by The New Yorker Magazine, Inc.), November 4, 1972.*

WALTER KERR

[''Wedding Band'' is an] honest and provocative look into black life in America just as World War I was giving way to the Twenties, though it has its vitamin deficiencies as drama. . . . Using a kind of South Carolina backyard chorus as counterpoint to a private tug-of-war between [a seamstress and her white lover of long standing] . . . , Miss Childress is at her best with the peripheral figures who lead prayer, read letters for one another, and spy upon the forbidden liaison with generous candor. . . .

The play, as it stands, does little more than illustrate what we have already known: that intermarriage, especially in redneck districts, is apt to be opposed. . . .

[The] play moves only at its edges; the center feels, and is, impotent, a joint surrender rather than a joined battle. (p. 323)

Walter Kerr, in The New York Times, *Section 2 (© 1972 by The New York Times Company; reprinted by permission), November 5, 1972.*

HAROLD CLURMAN

[*Wedding Band*] has an authenticity which, whatever its faults, makes it compelling. . . .

The play's basic theme emerges from the portrayal not only of the bigoted opposition of Herman's family, with its vile Klan spirit, but just as saliently in the suspicion and fear with which the blacks confront the two lovers. Herman, on the verge of death during the influenza epidemic which raged at the time, proves his deep attachment to Julia by buying her a ticket to New York even as he lies helpless, still in the grip of his wretched family. She on the other hand, though convinced of his love and freedom from racial bias, despairs of overcoming the barriers between them.

There is an honest pathos in the telling of this simple story, and some humorous and touching thumbnail sketches re-

veal knowledge and understanding of the people dealt with. The fact that black and white interrelationships have somewhat changed since 1918 does not make the play less relevant to the present. Constitutional amendments and laws do not immediately alter people's emotions; the divisions and tensions which *Wedding Band* dramatizes still exist to a far more painful extent than most of us are willing to admit. (p. 475)

Harold Clurman, in The Nation *(copyright 1972 by the Nation Associates, Inc.), November 13, 1972.*

ED BULLINS

There are too few books that convince us that reading is one of the supreme gifts of being human. Alice Childress, in her short, brilliant study of a 13-year-old black heroin user, ''A Hero Ain't Nothin' But a Sandwhich,'' achieves this feat in a masterly way by telling a real story of the victims of today's worst urban plague, heroin addiction, and it reaffirms the belief that excellent writing is alive and thriving in some black corners of America. (pp. 36, 38)

This surprisingly exciting, entertaining book demystifies the pusher and the problem he sells by centering on the unwitting victim, Benjie, and the disintegration of a black family. With their own voices the people in this story tell the truths of their lives. The writer uses her considerable dramatic talents to expose a segment of society seldom spoken of above a whisper; she exposes the urban disease that hides behind the headlines of drug abuse, the child junkies, drug rehabilitation programs and the problem of sheer survival in the black urban community.

There is a suggestion of hope in this book, but there is also the unconcealed truth. . . . You don't even have to be heroic to discover it. Just read. (p. 40)

Ed Bullins, in The New York Times Book Review *(© 1973 by The New York Times Company; reprinted by permission), November 4, 1973.*

NORMA ROGERS

In *A Hero Ain't Nothin' But a Sandwich*, Alice Childress intimately portrays the oppression of the working class people living in Afro-American communities. With fine perception, she tells about thirteen year old Benjie Johnson, a victim of drug addiction, his family, friends and neighbors living in the Harlem ghetto. (pp. 72-3)

Alice Childress has written a moving story that vividly describes life in the ghettos of Black America. It is a grim picture that holds little or no promise for the children's future. (p. 74)

The author has presented an examination of society on the decline in the United States. The salient question regarding the survival of Afro-American children as total human beings can only be answered with positive social changes.

The book has been written with pathos and humor. I highly recommend this fine piece of literature for young adults and older readers. (p. 75)

Norma Rogers, ''To Destroy Life,'' in Freedomways *(copyright 1974 by Freedomways Associates, Inc.; reprinted by permission of Freedomways, 799 Broadway, New York, New York, 10003), Vol. 14, No. 1, 1974, pp. 72-5.*

JAMES V. HATCH

Bill Jameson [in *Wine in the Wilderness*] is the product of the old black bourgeois values. Sonny-Man and Cynthia are also victims of this old social order. They are educated; They consciously and unconsciously label themselves "better" than Tommy and Oldtimer. They are empty, artificial people, preaching blackness, brotherhood, and love simply because it is in vogue. Innately they are cold, cruel, and self-centered individuals. They are reflections of the old slave masters, imitators of white middle-class, who accept Oldtimer (they don't even know his name) because they find him amusing, and Tommy only because they feel she can be used. . . . [Bill's] orientation is white; no matter how hard he tries to assert his blackness, it remains surface and insignificant. . . . The only "real" people in the play are Tommy and Oldtimer. They are both honest, not living under the illusion of false reality. True, Tommy "hopes" that Bill will seriously fall for her, but if he doesn't, she is prepared to move on: ". . . don't nothin' happen that's not suppose to." She is a sensible woman without pretense. The beauty of *Wine in the Wilderness* is in part due to the author's sensitive treatment of Tommy, "a poor, dumb chick that's had her behind kicked until it's numb," but whose warmth, compassion, inner dignity, and pride make her more of a woman than Cynthia will ever be. She is indeed the "wine in the wilderness" that Bill has conceived; when she undergoes a metamorphosis before his eyes, he suddenly becomes aware that she is the source of inspiration that he and the others so desperately need to find themselves, and their blackness. Alice Childress has created a powerful, *new* black heroine who emerges from the depths of the black community, offering a sharp contrast to the typically strong "Mama" figure that dominates such plays as *Raisin in the Sun*. (p. 737)

> *James V. Hatch, in his* Black Theater, U.S.A: Forty-five Plays by Black Americans *(reprinted with permission of Macmillan Publishing Co., Inc.; copyright © 1974 by The Free Press, a Division of Macmillan Publishing Co. Inc.),* The Free Press, *1974.*

RAY ANTHONY SHEPARD

The young adult novel seems to be here to stay, and with books like Alice Childress's *A Hero Ain't Nothin' But a Sandwich* . . . one can see why.

Young and Black Benjie Johnson is a junkie. Through a series of brillliant vignettes, we see Benjie through his own eyes and through the eyes of those around him as he nods his way through his thirteenth year.

Benjie wants someone to believe in him, but since heroes are only sandwiches, the question for Benjie is who can be his hero? . . .

In short, there is no one so Benjie tries to become his own hero.

Finally, [it is] Butler Craig, the common man—not the sports hero or movie star or street corner preacher or Black intellectual who are usually paraded out for Negro History Week in local schools—who reaches out and pulls Benjie over the edge. Butler is willing to believe in Benjie and be his father a hundred times. With that kind of pulling maybe Benjie, and all of us, can make it. (p. 4)

> *Ray Anthony Shepard, in* Interracial Books for Children Bulletin *(reprinted by permission of In-*

terracial Books for Children Bulletin, *1841 Broadway, New York, N.Y. 10023), Vol. 6, No. 1, 1975.*

ZENA SUTHERLAND

There is little movement in this one-act drama [*When the Rattlesnake Sounds*], but a wealth of poignant dialogue. . . .

The title refers to [Harriet Tubman's] consoling Celia about her fear by saying, "Child, you lookin at a woman who's been plenty afraid. When the rattlesnake sounds a warnin . . . it's time to be scared." Despite the lack of action, the play is moving because of its subject and impressive because of the deftness with which Childress develops characters and background in so brief and static a setting. (p. 140)

> *Zena Sutherland, in* Bulletin of the Center for Children's Books *(© 1976 by the University of Chicago; all rights reserved), May, 1976.*

MARY M. BURNS

Generally, plays written especially for young people are reviewed as useful rather than as literary works. [*When the Rattlesnake Sounds*], however, is a poignant celebration of courage, a beautifully crafted work drawn from the life of Harriet Tubman. Rather than attempting the usual chronological panoramic pageant, replete with trite dialogue and a cast of thousands, the author has wisely chosen to confine her drama to one act, focusing on the summer during which Harriet worked as a hotel laundress in Cape May, New Jersey, in order to raise money for the abolitionist cause. Skillful use of introductory notes, stage directions, and the scene-within-a-scene device gives insight not only into the life of the heroine who led hundreds of her people to freedom but also into the universality of human emotions. . . . [The] book offers the young reader a rare opportunity for an aesthetic experience while becoming aware of the techniques used by the dramatist to develop situation and characters. (p. 301)

> *Mary M. Burns, in* The Horn Book Magazine *(copyright © 1976 by the Horn Book, Inc., Boston), June, 1976.*

JOHN T. GILLESPIE

Alice Childress' experience as playwright and actress is revealed in the brilliant characterization and dialogue in *Hero*, essentially the story of a 13-year-old black boy, Benjie Johnson, and his near-fatal brush with permanent heroin addiction. It is told honestly in the vital, but strong, street idiom of Harlem by several people close to Benjie, and by Benjie himself. While each monologue is part of the story, it also presents a different point of view and helps to develop a gallery of memorable characters. (p. 54)

Hero is not just a family of blacks and their problems: it deals with themes and experiences that are universal, such as rejection, love, the importance of family ties, poverty, and the problems of growing old. It also depicts the frustration and despair of lives warped by discrimination and want; at the same time showing that people must believe in themselves. Lastly, it is a horrifying picture of the effects of dope that make a fine boy become an enemy in his own home. (pp. 56-7)

> *John T. Gillespie, in his* More Juniorplots: A Guide for Teachers and Librarians *(copyright ©*

1977 by John Gillespie; reprinted by permission of the R. R. Bowker Company), Bowker, 1977.

MIGUEL ORTIZ

Each chapter [in *A Hero Ain't Nothin but a Sandwich*] is essentially a monologue delivered by each of the different participants in the story. This allows for utmost flexibility in portraying the conflicting interest of the several characters. It is difficult, though not impossible, to show a situation in all its complexity and yet convince a reader that it is a child's perception. Alice Childress avoids this predicament with a most felicitous result. No doubt the fact that she is a playwright has a great deal to do with her ability to let each character speak for him or herself.

The monologue technique not only has the advantage of describing the action from several vantage points, but it also enables the author to clearly show the discrepancy between what one character thinks he or she is doing and what is perceived by the others, without violating the integrity of any of them. This discrepancy between intention and result is most obvious in the case of Nigeria Greene, a black teacher in Benjie's school. He is, to hear him speak, a gung-ho black nationalist. He tries instilling in his pupils a sense of black pride. That, he feels, comes first, over and above any academic skill he might be able to impart to them. His room is decorated with portraits of Marcus Garvey, W.E.B. Du Bois, and Malcom X. He constantly runs at the mouth about those blacks who cow-tow to whitey's ways. But he is unable to escape the fact that being a teacher puts him in an economic bracket that pulls him toward the style of life more consistent with the white middle class than with most of his fellow blacks in Harlem. Nigeria Greene seems confused by this phenomenon, and the only thing he can do to protect himself from this inner conflict is to spout more rhetoric.

The portrait of whites is more realistic in this book, more compassionate, and at the same time, because it is believable, more scathing. Bernard Cohen, Benjie's other teacher, is the typical middle class liberal. He wants to do a good job, but he is confused as to what that means. He doesn't want to rock the boat. When he notices Benjie's nodding off, he assumes the boy stays up late watching television. He doesn't want to have to deal with turning a kid in. He only takes action after Nigeria forces the issue. Bernard Cohn is no less confused than Nigeria. Cohn fears that blacks will drive him out of his job, and that keeps a muffled racism alive in him. The principal, the only other white in the book, is counting the days to his retirement. He has three years to go. He wants as few headaches as possible in that remaining time. He is not a stupid man, nor an evil one. He is only an ordinary man trying to do a job too big for him.

The book conveys very strongly the message that we are all human, even when we are acting in ways that we are somewhat ashamed of. The structure of the book grows out of the personalities of the characters, and the author makes us aware of how much the economic and social circumstances dictate a character's actions. We see how people are forced to deviate from their moral standards by the exigencies of their economic self-interest. This is achieved without neglecting to observe the psychological complexity of each human being. Every character is presented as unique. There are no evil characters in the book, though there are

evil consequences; a perfect example of hating the sin, but not the sinner.

A Hero has a strong but simple dramatic structure. The story builds to a climax which is resolved in an optimistic denouement. Benjie, as a potential junkie, is the ultimate repository of all the evil that racism and capitalism can inflict upon human beings. The main drama is played out between him and his step-father, Butler Craig. Butler is the strongest person in the book, the only one who is able to come to a clear resolution of his inner conflict, and the only one who is able to reach Benjie. It is interesting to note that Butler is a working class black, in contrast with [Benjie's teacher] Nigeria Greene, who despite his rhetoric is unable to see and accept Butler for what he is. Butler, on the other hand, has Nigeria pegged from the beginning: Butler says: ". . . seems like I'm knowing him, but he can't know me; however I don't hold that against him. . . . The cat is strainin' so hard to get to me, till I just have to encourage him." Butler comes across as a heroic character, worthy of admiration . . . , yet the reader is able to identify with his struggle in trying to deal with Benjie. Benjie too is sensitively drawn. The author, without condoning or relieving him of the responsibility which is rightfully his, shows him becoming a junkie, but does not lose sight of the fact that he is a child who is hurting, in trouble, and worthy of our sympathy.

A Hero Ain't Nothin but a Sandwich works, both on an aesthetic and political level, because it is true to its characters. . . . Alice Childress, in successfully portraying the complexity of character, has been able to show the effect of economic class and historical antecedent on the people she writes about. (pp. 13-15)

Miguel Ortiz, in The Lion and the Unicorn *(copyright © 1978 The Lion and the Unicorn), Fall, 1978.*

SALLY R. SOMMER

Trouble in Mind is a play about black actors rehearsing a pretentious, liberal, anti-lynching play written by whites, produced by whites, and directed by whites—it is a comedy and its humor is black. Writing in 1955 (three years before Genet's *The Blacks*), Alice Childress used the concentric circles of the play-within-the-play to examine the multiple roles blacks enact in order to survive. Twenty-three years later we can look at the play and see its double cutting edge: It predicts not only the course of social history but the course of black playwrighting. The plot is about an emerging rebellion begun as the heroine, Wiletta, refuses to enact a namby-Mammy, either in the play or for her director. The best parts of the play, its multi-leveled language and seething, funny role-enactments, prefigure the tough black style of '60s plays—naturalistic dramas that hit hard, inset with sermon-like arias for solo performers.

Hundreds of years of stereotyping are condensed in a few lines. . . .

The most powerful scene occurs when Wiletta begins to "mind" about the stereotypes she has succumbed to, and Sheldon, a sly, canny, skilled role-player, tells her: "Yeah, we all *mind*, but you gotta swallow what you mind. 'Mind' don't buy beans." While Wiletta is the awakening protagonist, Sheldon's self-awareness gives him heroic stature, even as it forces him into yet another role, another survival tactic. He describes in a moving soliloquy how he really saw a lynching when he was a boy—which completely devastates the liberal pretentions of the "anti-lynching" play being rehearsed. . . .

The drama is not without its weaknesses, which lie in the genre of play-rehearsal-within-a-play. For me, at least, that conceit has only worked on the page. In print and theory, it appears to offer the perfect structure for examining role-enactment, reality vs. fiction. But the *playing* of it I have always found cumbersome and unwieldy. . . .

Sally R. Sommer, "Black Figures, White Shadows," in The Village Voice *(reprinted by permission of* The Village Voice; *copyright © The Village Voice, Inc., 1979), January 15, 1979, p. 91.*

Agatha Christie

1890-1976

(Has also written under the names Mary Westmacott and Agatha Christie Mallowan) English novelist, playwright, short story writer, and poet. Christie is best known for her detective stories, which are characterized by their ingenious plots and psychological clues. Many of them are considered classics of their genre. Christie has been called the "Queen of Crime," having written nearly 100 books during a fifty-year span. She created one of literature's most popular detectives in Hercule Poirot, a retired Belgian who uses his "little grey cells" to solve crimes in partnership with the bumbling Hastings. Her other popular characters are sleuths Miss Jane Marple, a spinster, and husband-and-wife team Tommy and Tuppence Beresford. Christie's first detective novel, written to meet a challenge by her sister, was *The Mysterious Affair at Styles*. Published in 1920, it has never been out of print. *The Murder of Roger Ackroyd*, with its surprising dénouement, is credited by Howard Haycraft as exemplifying "The Golden Age of Detective Story Writing." *The Mousetrap*, which Christie adapted from her novella "The Three Blind Mice," is the longest running play in modern theater history. Her works have been translated into over 100 languages and have been outsold only by the Bible and Shakespeare. A true mystery still surrounds Christie's ten-day disappearance during the break-up of her first marriage. Nor does *An Autobiography* shed light upon this event, which gave her valuable publicity and which she claimed at the time was due to amnesia. Her second marriage to archaeologist Max Mallowan and her subsequent travels with him throughout the Middle East provided material for several of her novels. *Come, Tell Me How You Live* is a personal account of these expeditions. Christie also wrote several romantic novels under the pseudonym Mary Westmacott. Many of her works were adapted for the screen with *Murder on the Orient Express* being perhaps the most successful. *Witness for the Prosecution* won the New York Drama Critics Circle Award in 1955 as the best foreign play of the year. Before she herself died, Christie wrote *Curtain* and *Sleeping Murder* in which Poirot and Miss Marple die. Adverse criticism of her work focuses on her undistinguished style and on the lack of depth in her rather stereotyped characters, on the absence of any sociological analysis of the crimes, and on her repeated use of the "least-likely-person" device. In spite of, or perhaps because of these characteristics, Christie's varied and imaginative plot puzzles have consistently entertained her many fans for almost sixty years. (See also *CLC*, Vols. 1, 6, 8, and *Contemporary Authors*, Vols. 17-20, rev. ed.; obituary, Vols. 61-64.)

["The Murder on the Links"] is a remarkably good detective story which can be warmly commended to those who like that kind of fiction. . . .

The plot has peculiar complications and the reader will have to be very astute indeed if he guesses who the criminal is until the last complexity has been unraveled. The author is notably ingenious in the construction and unraveling of the mystery, which develops fresh interests and new entanglements at every turn. She deserves commendation also for the care with which the story is worked out and the good craftsmanship with which it is written. Although there is not much endeavor to portray character, except in the case of M. Poirot, several of the personages are depicted with swiftly made, expressive and distinctive lines. M. Poirot is an ingenious and interesting addition to the gallery of fictional detectives. He stands out from the author's pages with a real vitality. (p. 14)

The New York Times Book Review (© 1923 by The New York Times Company; reprinted by permission), March 25, 1923.

When in the first of M. Poirot's adventures [*Poirot Investigates*] we find a famous diamond that has once been the eye of a god and a cryptic message that it will be taken from its possessor "at the full of the moon," we are inclined to grow indignant on behalf of our dear old friend the moonstone [in Wilkie Collins's *The Moonstone*]. But we have no right to do so, for the story is quite original. Moreover, if Captain Hastings, who tells the story, is a little like Watson always anxious to display his cleverness and always getting snubbed, every detective has had a foil since the days of Lecoq. In fact M. Poirot is a thoroughly pleasant and entertaining person, an admirable companion for a railway journey. (pp. 209-10)

The Times Literary Supplement (© Times Newspapers Ltd. (London) 1924; reproduced from The Times Literary Supplement *by permission), April 3, 1924.*

Hercule Poirot of "Poirot Investigates" is the latest of a long line of successors to the immortal [Sherlock] Holmes who carry on the industry of criminal investigation during intervals that elapse between the resurrections of the wizard of Baker Street. There seems no reason why the dynasty should ever come to an end. Any character with strongly marked national eccentricities [can be made to serve]. . . .

[Agatha Christie's hero] is traditional almost to caricature, but his adventures are amusing and the problems which he unravels skillfully tangled in advance. Poirot does not have recourse to morphia or improvise on the violin. He arrives at his deductions, sometimes incredibly swift, by means of a process which he himself terms "the little gray cells," but it is to be feared that some of the evidence he collects would fare badly in criminal courts. . . .

Mrs. Christie's new book, in a word, is for the lightest of reading. But its appeal is disarmingly modest and it will please the large public which relishes stories of crime, but likes its crime served decorously. (p. 5)

> The New York Times Book Review (© 1924 by The New York Times Company; reprinted by permission), April 20, 1924.

[*The Murder of Roger Ackroyd*] is a well-written detective story of which the only criticism might perhaps be that there are too many curious incidents not really connected with the crime which have to be elucidated before the true criminal can be discovered. . . . It is all very puzzling but the great Hercule Poirot, a retired Belgian detective, solves the mystery. It may safely be asserted that very few readers will do so. (p. 397)

> The Times Literary Supplement (© Times Newspapers Ltd. (London) 1926; reproduced from The Times Literary Supplement by permission), June 10, 1926.

There are doubtless many detective stories more exciting and bloodcurdling than "The Murder of Roger Ackroyd," but this reviewer has recently read very few which provide greater analytical stimulation. This story, though it is inferior to them at their best, is in the tradition of [Edgar Allan] Poe's analytical tales and the Sherlock Holmes stories. The author does not devote her talents to the creation of thrills and shocks, but to the orderly solution of a single murder, conventional at that, instead. . . .

Roger Ackroyd is murdered one night under particularly perplexing circumstances. . . . In conventional detective-story style, seemingly trivial and extraneous details become clarifying evidence to [Poirot] while they baffle the reader only the more. It is really Poirot's method which holds the reader's interest. Matters become more and more complicated, till one surprising fact after another begins to reveal itself. . . . Miss Christie is not only an expert technician and a remarkably good story-teller, but she knows, as well, just the right number of hints to offer as to the real murderer.

In the present case his identity is made all the more baffling through the author's technical cleverness in selecting the part he is to play in the story; and yet her non-commital characterization of him makes it a perfectly fair procedure. The experienced reader will probably spot him, but it is safe to say that he will often have his doubts as the story unfolds itself.

"The Murder of Roger Ackroyd" cannot be too highly praised for its clean-cut construction, its unusually plausible explanation at the end, and its ability to stimulate the analytical faculties of the reader. It soars far above the crude, standardized mystery stories which have become such customary merchandise. (p. 18)

> The New York Times (© 1926 by The New York Times Company; reprinted by permission), July 18, 1926.

WILLIAM ROSE BENÉT

"The Murder of Roger Ackroyd" really turns a new trick in detective fiction, surely a difficult enough achievement "with the competition so strong." Most writers of detective stories develop their own special detectives, following the lead of the famous. Agatha Christie's pet detective is Hercule Poirot. . . .

Poirot is merely one factor in a tale so ingeniously constructed, so dextrously plotted as to warrant our complete admiration. It is unfortunate for us that we may not indicate here the most original element in Miss Christie's planning of the story. But that would be treachery to the author, and the reader has no right to be too well informed in advance. . . .

Suffice it to say that Miss Christie's dedication of the book is to one "who likes an orthodox detective story, murder, inquest, and suspicion falling on every one in turn!" So she set herself to write such an orthodox story, with the strange result that she has succeeded in producing one of the few notable for originality.

For those who prefer certain backgrounds to others for their mystery tales we may say that Miss Christie's are always English in setting. To those who hate "loose ends" we may remark that this author ties all her knots neatly and bites off the thread. Her characterization is sharp in outline, her motivation is sound, complications of the plot never "get away from her." Everything in the puzzle falls neatly into place, and the complete picture leaves upon us an ineradicable impression. There are no inexplicable and glozed-over details. It is all an almost mathematical demonstration so far as the fundamental brainwork goes. Yet that it is no mere clever intellectual exercise, witness the fact that the reader is left with the strongest emotions of pity and wonder over the disastrous coil the weak and erring weave. There are indications, in fact, of an even deeper psychological insight than can be actively exercised in a book of this kind. For a detective story must move. The author cannot pause to philosophize. But one is rather closer in touch, in this tale, with the mad logic of actual criminality, with the criminal as a mainly average human being with one tragic twist, than is at all usual.

We do not overpraise this story, we believe, when we say that it should go on the shelf with the books of first rank in its field. The detective story pure and simple has as definite limitations of form as the sonnet in poetry. Within these limitations, with admirable structural art, Miss Christie has genuinely achieved.

> William Rose Benét, "Out of the Usual," in The Saturday Review of Literature (copyright, 1926, by The Saturday Review Co., Inc.; reprinted with permission), July 24, 1926, p. 951.

[*The Mysterious Affair at Styles*] is a well-knit tale, which advances steadily to plausible conclusion without attempting the mystification of the reader by the introduction of unnecessary detail and false clues. Yet at one time or another suspicion is thrown on all the leading characters, and thrown on them with sufficient naturalness to be justified even after the story has reached its conclusion. Miss Christie writes with economy of incident, and the stereotyped properties of the usual detective of fiction. (p. 600)

The Saturday Review of Literature (copyright, 1927, by The Saturday Review Co., Inc.; reprinted with permission), February 19, 1927.

To describe adequately such a book as ["Partners in Crime"] is no easy matter. It is a group of short detective stories within a detective novel, for there is a rather sketchy, but nonetheless absorbing, plot which holds the separate tales together. The entire book and the separate stories may be taken as hilarious burlesque or parodies of current detective fiction, or they may be taken as serious attempts on the part of the author to write stories in the manner of some of the masters of the art. Taken either way, they are distinctly worth while.... Thomas Beresford and his wife, known to their friends as Tommy and Tuppence, are requested by Tommy's chief in the Foreign Office to take charge of a private detective agency whose owner has been arrested for certain activities without the law.... Both are omnivorous readers of detective fiction, and they decide to try out, one after the other, the methods of Sherlock Holmes, Father Brown, Inspector French and other fiction heroes, including Agatha Christie's own Hercule Poirot. The result is the merriest collection of detective stories it has been our good fortune to encounter. (p. 38)

The New York Times Book Review (© 1929 by The New York Times Company; reprinted by permission), September 22, 1929.

PROTEUS

It is a pity that publishers and too friendly critics write in an extravagance of praise, especially when writing about fiction, for surely works of genius do not appear at the rate of half a dozen a month? Take Miss Westmacott's book [*Giant's Bread*], for example, which is one of the most loudly heralded. One advertisement states that its fluency and facility are so great that it is incredible that it can be a first novel. This is true enough, but it is cause for apprehension rather than hope. The fluency and facility which Miss Westmacott shows, particularly in the opening third of her novel, suggest not so much the born novelist as the born novel-reader with a gift for easy imitation; the childhood of Vernon Deyre and the various friends and relatives who surround him are described with rapid competence, but no better than in fifty other novels which concern themselves with the trials of young genius growing up. There is nothing particularly real about Vernon or any part of his career ..., and the easy flow of the narrative makes one fear that Miss Westmacott could turn out, two a year, a dozen more novels of the kind.

This, however, is not all the truth, and our hopes for the author are roused by finding that in her own book she has provided the contrast. Even in the first part there are some touches, such as the gentleman who uttered the magic word "Brummagem," which are fresh and charming; and when Miss Westmacott reaches the world of music, which she really knows, her book suddenly comes alive and vivifies her characters with it. Jane, the singer, is a live and withal a charming personality, and in her presence the rather pallid

and inadequate figure of Vernon's wife takes on for a while a real existence. The chapters in which Jane appears are worth the rest of the book put together, and make one wish to encourage Miss Westmacott to go on writing—but to prune her gift for imitating what half a hundred other authors can do. (p. 151)

Proteus, in New Statesman (© 1930 The Statesman Publishing Co. Ltd.), May 10, 1930.

I. M. PARSONS

Giant's Bread is yet another of those stories which begin at the end and then go back to the beginning. In this case it is the life of a musician, a composer of genius.... [Miss Westmacott] traces the life of the composer from early childhood upwards, carefully emphasizing the influences of heredity, sex, and environment. As a first novel the book has obvious merits, though at the same time it is crowded with faults. Pre-eminently Miss Westmacott is not yet sufficiently certain of herself to know what to put in and what to leave out. Her sense of selection is still undetermined. She has, also, a tendency to be always on the side of the angels (though, of course, of the modern angel) and some of her characters are a little grotesque. Mrs. Deyre, for example, mother of the future genius, is a little too good (or bad) to be true. Granted that mothers of this type exist, and sometimes may even produce a genius, it is seldom that they contain *all* the attributes of maternal impossibility—hysteria, selfishness, stupidity and an overweening affection for their offspring—in the manner of Mrs. Deyre. However, when Miss Westmacott has learnt to tighten up her dialogue, and to *imply* more than she states, she will be able to give fuller effect to her capacity for telling a story, and her very saving sense of humour. They are qualities not to be rated low in a first novel. (p. 913)

I. M. Parsons, in The Spectator (© 1930 by The Spectator; reprinted by permission of The Spectator), May 31, 1930.

WILL CUPPY

["Murder in the Calais Coach" is] your best mystery bet of the moment by quite some distance—a thoroughly up-to-snuff Christie that ought to go down in history as one of the author's slickest. Or should we say one of Hercule Poirot's slickest since that famous sleuth is again on the trail, his egg-shaped head and amusing locutions working overtime? Before we forget it, "Murder in the Calais Coach" seems to us just as good as "The Murder of Roger Ackroyd." ...

One of Mrs. Christie's charms is, of course, that she writes in the civilized manner, and that always helps. Then, her mystery technique is nothing short of swell. She's probably the best suspicion scatterer and diverter in the business. If you find your old friend, credibility, seeming to slip in the later stages of this exciting tale, don't worry—for Mrs. Christie is working up to something most unusual by this very means. There's an alibi for everything that appears a leetle stretched. Indeed, we'll go so far as to say that "Murder in the Calais Coach" is a tour de force in the way of an artificial and no less gripping riddle. But you'll have to read it to find out just what is meant by this profound judgement. (p. 12)

Will Cuppy, in New York Herald Tribune Book Review (© I.H.T. Corporation; reprinted by permission), March 4, 1934.

NICHOLAS BLAKE

The Garden-of-Live-Flowers incident in the Alice-mythos anticipates the method of the modern detection-fan. To find the Red Queen he has learnt to go in the most unlikely direction. So now the hard-pressed writer is inclined to try a double bluff and make his criminal the obvious suspect throughout. It would give away her whole plot to tell which of these bluffs Mrs. Christie employs in [*The A.B.C. Murders*]: one can only chalk up yet another defeat at her hands and admit sadly that she has led one up the garden path with her usual blend of duplicity and fairness. This is all the more riling, as she conveys throughout the book a subtle suggestion that she is not playing fair.... Moreover she deceives us, not by irrelevant red herrings, but by the identical trick the A.B.C. murderer uses to deceive the police.... The characters, particularly that of the murderer, are rather too perfunctorily sketched. Apart from this, one can have nothing but praise for *The A.B.C. Murders,* which is really a little masterpiece of construction. (pp. 271-72)

> *Nicholas Blake, in* The Spectator (© *1936 by* The Spectator; *reprinted by permission of* The Spectator), *February 14, 1936.*

RALPH PARTRIDGE

Mrs. Christie has designed her latest masterpiece [*Death on the Nile*] as if she intended it to illustrate a text-book on detective writing. In Part I the characters are collected from different parts of the world and assembled in Egypt ready for anything; in Part II the individuals are moulded by social intercourse into a tragic group ready for murder; in Part III the predestined victim is killed and the reader should be ready with his solution. But is he? You can take your choice of motive: revenge, robbery, to escape exposure, jealousy, a political assassination or an act of social retribution. Each motive has an appropriate representative on board that Nile steamer. Those who imagine they have an inkling of Mrs. Christie's psychology will take a sly look at some of the faces.... As Poirot put it, and you can always believe Poirot: "It is more than odd—it is impossible! The sequence of events is impossible." But as Colonel Race replied (the Colonel from *Cards on the Table,* and you ought to be able to believe that Colonel, surely): "Not impossible since it happened." That is Mrs. Christie's magic—her crime is unbelievable, but her solution will not only be believed, but rapturously believed. (p. 1067)

> *Ralph Partridge, in* The New Statesman & Nation (© *1937 The Statesman & Nation Publishing Co. Ltd.), December 18, 1937.*

WILL CUPPY

Trust Agatha Christie to turn out the brightest and generally slickest mystery currently at hand. Once more [in "Death on the Nile"] she makes most of her rivals look a bit silly with her skill in every department of the puzzler's art—or is it a science? Her main achievement this time—for she always performs some outstanding feat—probably lies in covering up the killer who ran amuck on the S.S. Karnak while some highly polished friends and enemies were returning from the Second Cataract; among them, fortunately, was Hercule Poirot, the little Belgian with the egg-shaped head who saw death coming well in advance....

Mrs. Christie gives you a bird's-eye view of the whole situation and its ramifications before she starts the fatal Egyptian holiday, introducing her characters in their natural habitats in a brief first part, with everybody converging toward the land of the Nile.... The trip has not a dull moment, and if things may not often happen like that in real life, few fans will object to that. The amount of pertinent material our author gets into her tale without breaking the melodic line, as it were, is quite amazing, and should be a lesson to the thinner bafflers. (p. 9)

> *Will Cuppy, in* New York Herald Tribune Book Review (© *I.H.T. Corporation; reprinted by permission), February 6, 1938.*

GILBERT NORWOOD

Mrs. Christie is known to all connoisseurs of detective stories as beyond comparison the finest practitioner of this delightful craft. She should long ago have received the Order of Merit, as having given more and richer pleasure to the English-speaking race than all other living persons, except perhaps Mr. [Charlie] Chaplin, Mr. [George Bernard] Shaw and Mr. [P. G.] Wodehouse. It is marvellous that anyone should invent a new method of putting experienced readers off the scent, but almost beyond belief that this should be done repeatedly by one writer: in *The Man in the Brown Suit, Peril at End House, Lord Edgware Dies, Death on the Orient Express,* as in no other stories, she has invented an entirely new device, and the new device has been different each time. The point of course is that, readers being so sophisticated and alert, it is not enough to (deceptively) clear the real criminal in their eyes: the frightfully difficult task is somehow to prevent them even from considering the real criminal at all. (p. 458)

Death on the Nile is excellent, but by no means at the level of her best. I realized who committed the murder—and even before it was committed: this I have never before achieved in a Christie book. And there are too many red herrings—exceedingly rufous and big as salmon. In a word, the story is far more mechanical than is usual. But the characterization, dialogue, the descriptions of Egyptian sights, sounds and life are all charmingly done. (pp. 458-59)

> *Gilbert Norwood, "Another Christie," in* The Canadian Forum, *April, 1938, pp. 458-59.*

RALPH PARTRIDGE

[It is no use trying to compare Mrs. Christie] with other writers of detection. She stands *hors concours,* in a class of her own. No one else in the world would have attempted seriously to manipulate a plot like that of *Ten Little Niggers* without a hopeless presentiment of failure.... Mrs. Christie disdains contraptions. She faces her readers with her bare hands and her sleeves rolled up; and she sells them ten dummies beautifully, one after the other, with the exquisite timing of a Rugby International three-quarter going through a pack of clumsy yokels to score a try under the posts.... There are ten people cooped up on Nigger Island who put on a gramophone record and hear their death-sentence. After sentence has been executed Scotland Yard asks "Who did it?" But only Mrs. Christie survives to tell. Apart from one little dubious proceeding there is no cheating; the reader is just bamboozled in a straightforward way from first to last. To show her utter superiority over our deductive faculty, from time to time Mrs. Christie even allows us to know what every character present is thinking —and still we can't guess! If it were not for that iota of hanky-panky *Ten Little Niggers* would be the most colossal achievement of a colossal career. As it is the book must rank with Mrs. Christie's previous best, alongside *Roger Ackroyd, Lord Edgware, Styles, The Man in the Brown Suit,* and *Death on the Nile,* on the top notch of detection. (pp. 726, 728)

Ralph Partridge, in The New Statesman & Nation *(© 1939 The Statesman & Nation Publishing Co. Ltd.), November 18, 1939.*

RUPERT HART-DAVIS

For thirteen years Mrs. Christie's admirers have been waiting for her to reproduce the superlative form of *The Murder of Roger Ackroyd.* Once or twice their hopes have been raised: *The A.B.C. Murders* very nearly came up to scratch, but the common run of Poirot's adventures has produced little more than a half-light from the little grey cells. Now at last the expected *chef-d'oeuvre* has appeared. *Ten Little Niggers* is as near a perfect crime puzzle as we are likely to see. It is short, *sans* Poirot, exciting, baffling, and scrupulously fair. To divulge any of the plot would be to take the edge off the reader's enjoyment. It should be enough to say that the book is Agatha Christie's masterpiece. (p. 878)

Rupert Hart-Davis, in The Spectator *(© 1939 by* The Spectator; *reprinted by permission of* The Spectator*), December 15, 1939.*

ISAAC ANDERSON

Eight guests, two servants, but no host or hostess—that is the situation [of "And Then There Were None", published in Great Britain as "Ten Little Niggers"] in the luxurious mansion on Indian Island off the coast of Devon. The servants say that they have been hired from an employment agency and have never seen their employers. The guests have been brought to the place on various pretexts, and each of them professes to know nothing about the missing Mr. and Mrs. Owen, who are supposed to be their hosts. If one may believe the Voice, which makes a startling announcement after dinner, all of these persons are doomed to die for crimes which they are alleged to have committed. Hanging in each bedroom is a framed copy of doggerel verse about "Ten Little Indian Boys," and this, too, predicts the fate of the ten. When you read what happens after that you will not believe it, but you will keep on reading, and as one incredible event is followed by another even more incredible you will still keep on reading. The whole thing is utterly impossible and utterly fascinating. It is the most baffling mystery that Agatha Christie has ever written, and if any other writer has ever surpassed it for sheer puzzlement the name escapes our memory. We are referring, of course, to mysteries that have logical explanations, as this one has. It is a tall story, to be sure, but it could have happened. (p. 15)

Isaac Anderson, in The New York Times Book Review *(© 1940 by The New York Times Company; reprinted by permission), February 25, 1940.*

RALPH PARTRIDGE

Is any bowler more dreaded by the batsmen of detection than Mrs. Christie? *Towards Zero* will get a great many wickets, or I'm heavily mistaken in the acumen of my friends. Halfway through the book I've asked them "Who

did it?" Three-quarters way through I ask them again—and the names they reluctantly murmur are never the same both times. It is not a trick of Mrs. Christie's: it's her devilish art. There are about six subjects in *Towards Zero,* and she focuses our attention on each in turn. Some look too guilty; some look too innocent. Some have an opportunity, but where's the motive? Some have a motive, but where's the opportunity? So it goes on. The reader wobbles and wavers, and *shrinks from a decision:* and Mrs. Christie quietly bowls you out. . . . [The] struggle to coach victims against Mrs. Christie is utterly hopeless.

The scene of the murder in *Towards Zero* is a country house by an estuary on the South Coast. I can devise no way of outlining the plot without forestalling some of the excitement and bewilderment. But the solution is by Superintendent Battle, not by Poirot. That indicates that Mrs. Christie does not regard this work as flawless by her own supreme standard. The flaw is that the solution is only completed by the criminal's confession; and there should be no need for confession in a perfect specimen of detection. (p. 94)

Ralph Partridge, in The New Statesman and Nation *(© 1944 The Statesman and Nation Publishing Co. Ltd.), August 5, 1944.*

ROSE FELD

"If you'd nothing to think about but yourself for days on end I wonder what you'd find out about yourself." This is the keynote of Mary Westmacott's fine novel, "Absent in the Spring." . . .

Joan Scudamore, on her way back to England from Baghdad, had the opportunity to do a thorough job of soul-searching and self-evaluation. With admirable skill, sensitive and subtle, Miss Westmacott portrays the woman, first, as model wife and mother, second, in the more penetrating role of a woman who had, in one way or another, warped and distorted the lives of the members of her family. . . .

With mounting effect, Miss Westmacott builds up her portrait of an insensitive, calculating woman who never in her life entered the hearts of the people whose lives she shaped. Outwardly the structure seemed strong and admirable; inwardly it was crumbling with rebellion and frustration. . . .

The book closes on a note honest as the sun in its concept and characterization. Miss Westmacott's novel is a gem of a psychological portrait, the writing sensitive and probing, the outlines intense and arresting.

Rose Feld, "She Saw a Stranger in Herself," in New York Herald Tribune Book Review *(© I.H.T. Corporation; reprinted by permission), September 10, 1944, p. 2.*

EDMUND WILSON

[The puzzle mystery has] been brought to a high pitch of ingenuity in the stories of Agatha Christie. So I have read also the new Agatha Christie, *Death Comes as the End,* and I confess that I have been had by Mrs. Christie. I did not guess who the murderer was, I was incited to keep on and find out, and when I did finally find out, I was surprised. Yet I did not care for Agatha Christie and I hope never to read another of her books. I ought, perhaps, to discount the fact that "Death Comes as the End" is supposed to take place in Egypt two thousand years before Christ, so that the book has a flavor of Lloyd C. Douglas not, I understand, quite typical of the author . . . ; but her writing is of a mawkishness and banality which seem to me literally impossible to read. You cannot *read* such a book, you run through it to see the problem worked out; and you cannot become interested in the characters because they never can be allowed an existence of their own even in a flat two dimensions but have always to be contrived so that they can seem either reliable or sinister, depending on which quarter, at the moment, is to be baited for the reader's suspicion. . . . Mrs. Christie, in proportion as she is more expert and concentrates more narrowly on the puzzle, has to eliminate human interest completely, or rather fill in the picture with what seems to me a distasteful parody of it. In this new novel she has to provide herself with puppets who will be good for three stages of suspense: you must first wonder who is going to be murdered, you must then wonder who is committing the murders, and you must finally be unable to foresee which of two men the heroine will marry. It is all like a sleight-of-hand trick, in which the magician diverts your attention from the awkward or irrelevant movements that conceal the manipulation of the cards, and it may mildly amuse and amaze you, as such a sleight-of-hand performance may. But in a performance like *Death Comes as the End*, the patter is a constant bore and the properties lack the elegance of playing cards. (pp. 234-35)

Edmund Wilson, "*Why Do People Read Detective Stories*" (originally published in a slightly different version in The New Yorker, *October 14, 1944*), *in his* Classics and Commercials: A Literary Chronicle of the Forties (*reprinted with the permission of Farrar, Straus & Giroux, Inc.; copyright © 1950 by Edmund Wilson; copyright renewed © 1978 by Elena Wilson*), *The Noonday Press, 1950, pp. 231-37.*

[Miss Mary Westmacott] studies men in their singularity [in *The Rose and the Yew Tree*]; she is concerned with the diversity of their lives. Her point is that the diversity is radical; the rose and the yew tree have different patterns but, in Mr. T. S. Eliot's words, their moments are of equal duration, because the patterns are complete. One cannot be measured against the other. Success and failure are relative terms, and the nature of each individual person to whom we apply them is unique. Thus stated, the argument recalls M. [Jean-Paul] Sartre, but the tale which supports is suggests, in its technical aspect, the influence of Mr. Somerset Maugham. Miss Westmacott writes crisply and is always lucid. (p. 621)

The Times Literary Supplement (© *Times Newspapers Ltd. (London) 1968; reproduced from* The Times Literary Supplement *by permission*), *November 6, 1948.*

ROBERT KEE

The Rose and The Yew Tree is an intense inexperienced story about a mysterious unscrupulous scoundrel. . . . He has won the V.C. in the war, and after it sets out to win a seat in the election in the Conservative interest, not because he believes in Conservatism but because it suits his ambition at the moment. He abandons politics immediately after winning the seat in order to ruin the life of an innocent, aristocratic but extremely tough young girl. [His story] takes a very long time to tell, and it is told (via a

first-person medium) with the self-confidence of someone who is perhaps not quite sure of himself. Twists are added to the story in desperation; but no satisfactory whole merges—only a collection of twists. Isabella is an interesting character, and Miss Westmacott may well write a much better book than this one day. (p. 28)

Robert Kee, in The Spectator (© *1949 by* The Spectator; *reprinted by permission of* The Spectator), *January 7, 1949.*

[*They Came to Baghdad*] is more of a thriller than a detective story, though there are plenty of mysteries and two surprises reserved for the closing chapters: one of these is perhaps [Miss Christie's] best since the unmasking of the criminal in *The Seven Dials Mystery*. . . . [The] easy expertise of the writing is once more a matter for admiration. There are several satisfactory suspects; an excellent intelligence chief, done in the modern manner; a delightful *hôtelier*, and a very human heroine, whose powers of invention, like those of her creator, never fail her. (p. 241)

The Times Literary Supplement (© *Times Newspapers Ltd. (London) 1951; reproduced from* The Times Literary Supplement *by permission*), *April 20, 1951.*

ANTHONY BOUCHER

Since Agatha Christie is so pre-eminently the mistress of the straight detective story, we're apt to forget how good she can be on her occasional ventures into the spy-suspense-intrigue novel. And so well has she exploited the English countryside that we may also forget how intimately she knows the Middle East. These two neglected facets of Miss Christie glisten brilliantly in ["They Came to Baghdad"]. This is a story of little detection or mystery, but much intricacy and surprise, revolving around the preparations for a top level East-West conference in Baghdad and the machinations of a new kind of international intrigant who makes the Fascists and Communists of the average thriller seem almost innocuous. All of this is embellished by authentic first-hand details on Iraq archaeology and the fine, easy sketching of a large cast. All in all, the most satisfactory novel in some years from one of the most satisfying of novelists. (p. 19)

Anthony Boucher, in The New York Times Book Review (© *1951 by* The New York Times Company; *reprinted by permission*), *June 3, 1951.*

Miss Christie's [*A Pocket Full of Rye*] belongs to the comfortable branch of detective fiction; it never harrows its readers by realistic presentation of violence or emotion or by making exorbitant demands on their interest in the characters. Crime is a convention, pursuit an intellectual exercise, and it is as if the murderer of the odious financier did but poison in jest. The characters are lightly and deftly sketched and an antiseptic breeze of humour prevails. It is a pleasure to read an author so nicely conscious of the limitations of what she is attempting.

Three murders (generally regarded, since Edgar Wallace's time, as the maximum permissible) take place, apparently with nothing but the nursery rhyme about four-and-twenty blackbirds to connect them. Inspector Neele, an intelligent C.I.D. officer but no genius, has the good fortune, however, to be assisted by Miss Marple, and the assassin is duly unmasked. Miss Christie has a reputation for playing fair with the reader who likes to assume detective responsibility, and also for being one too many for him. In the present case it may be felt that the hidden mechanism of the plot is ingenious at the expense of probability, but the tale is told with such confidence that (like murder itself, in this pastoral atmosphere) it does not matter very much. (p. 773)

The Times Literary Supplement (© *Times Newspapers Ltd. (London) 1953; reproduced from* The Times Literary Supplement *by permission*), December 4, 1953.

ANTHONY BOUCHER

Any of you who long, as I often do, for nostalgic time-travel back to those days in the Thirties when the detective story *was* a detective story, and not ''a novel of suspense,'' can at least rejoice annually upon the appearance of a new Agatha Christie; and you'll be delighted to learn that ''A Pocket Full of Rye'' [represents Christie in top form]. . . .

[This] is the best of the novels starring Christie's spinster-detective, Miss Marple (who has usually been more effective in short stories). Christie's unanalyzable gift for thumbnail characterization is also at its best and . . . you aren't apt to find a better job of professional craftsmanship this year. (p. 23)

Anthony Boucher, in The New York Times Book Review (© 1954 by The New York Times Company; reprinted by permission), April 18, 1954.

The solution of *Ordeal by Innocence* is certainly not below the level of Mrs. Christie's customary ingenuity, but the book lacks other qualities which her readers have come to expect. What has become of the blitheness, the invigorating good spirits with which the game of detection is played in so many of her stories? *Ordeal by Innocence* slips out of that cheerful arena into something much too like an attempt at psychological fiction. It is too much of a conversation-piece and too many people are talking—people in whom it is hard to take the necessary amount of interest because there is not space enough to establish them. The kind of workmanship which has been lavished on this tale is not a kind in which the author excels and the reader feels that Miss Marple and Poirot would thoroughly disapprove of the whole business. (p. 726)

The Times Literary Supplement (© *Times Newspapers Ltd. (London) 1958; reproduced from* The Times Literary Supplement *by permission*), December 12, 1958.

ANTHONY BOUCHER

Agatha Christie wisely refrains from overworking her star detective, Hercule Poirot, knowing that it's better for us to yearn for more Poirot stories than to complain of a surfeit. . . . [''Ordeal by Innocence''] introduces Dr. Arthur Calgary, Antarctic explorer. Once more Mrs. Christie's skill in puzzle-making and storytelling is so consummate that we never think of missing the little Belgian octogenarian. . . .

The book is unusually long for Christie and may sag a bit in the middle; but family tensions and suspicions are adroitly handled, and the solution is characteristically surprising, trickily constructed and yet firmly based in character. (p. 18)

Anthony Boucher, in The New York Times Book

Review (© 1959 by The New York Times Company; reprinted by permission), March 15, 1959.

'Owing to the influential connections at Meadowbank the murder of Miss Springer had been played down very tactfully in the press.' 'Meadowbank' is the smartest girls' school in Europe, with princesses among its pupils, and 'Miss Springer' its games mistress, and if Miss Christie believes that the press would play *that* murder down, she will believe anything. But it is nothing to what she asks *us* to believe [in *Cat among the Pigeons*]. Her girls and mistresses are as true to boring old type as the boys and masters of Greyfriars and St. Jim's, and the plot calls for mysterious strangers in shrubberies; forgery, kidnapping, and a couple more killings; 'a small wicked-looking automatic'; a secret-service operator disguised as a gardener; and, at last, on page 183, M. Hercule Poirot *luimême*, ejaculating '''*Nom d'un nom d'un nom!*'' in an awe-inspired whisper.' How did we ever come to take Miss Christie seriously? (p. 641)

The Spectator (© 1959 by The Spectator; reprinted by permission of The Spectator), November 6, 1959.

Miss Agatha Christie, like many writers before her, is often praised for the wrong virtues. It is not for feats of detection that we turn to her, nor even, since her early *tours de force*, for the criminological ingenuity of her plots, workmanlike though they are. Her cardinal virtue is simpler and more subtle. It is sheer readability; her books can be gulped down like cream or invalid jelly. This is not a matter of good writing. Miss Christie can write abominably (''nobody will mind whether he's been killed or not, and doesn't care in the least who's done it'' says a character in her new book), but she has a gift almost as rare and intangible as the poet's gift of poetry.

This gift is there, clear enough, in *The Pale Horse,* which is not a Poirot story nor a Miss Marple but just a Christie extravaganza. . . .

Miss Christie has a surprise or two in hand, of course, and a relatively convincing solution to her rather implausible mystery: but the point is that the story holds unflaggingly, and holds with a grip which is gentle as well as firm. There are never any midnight horrors about Miss Christie's murders; she transmutes them into a cosy tea-time game. She is a peculiarly English writer producing a uniquely English type of book. (p. 851)

The Times Literary Supplement (© *Times Newspapers Ltd. (London) 1961; reproduced from* The Times Literary Supplement *by permission*), November 24, 1961.

Agatha Christie is really astonishing. She is an old lady now, and her gentlewoman detective, Miss Marple, an older one; but, unlike too many of her contemporaries, she capitalizes instead of concealing the facts. So *At Bertram's Hotel* is an old-lady book, about old Miss Marple's receiving the present of a holiday in an exquisitely old-fashioned London hotel, and discovering (this is what one might call the Moral) that nostalgia is dangerous and to cash in on it a safe cover for depravity.

Miss Christie has lost none of her toughness. Almost alone among nice English detective writers she has never excluded any characters from possible revelation as murderers, not the sweet young girl, the charming youth, the wise old man, not even the dear old lady. And neither does she here. (p. 1112)

> *The Times Literary Supplement (© Times Newspapers Ltd. (London) 1965; reproduced from* The Times Literary Supplement *by permission), December 2, 1965.*

ANTHONY BOUCHER

I strongly suspect that future scholars of the simon-pure detective novel will hold that its greatest practitioner, outranking even Ellery Queen and John Dickson Carr in their best periods, has been Agatha Christie—not only for her incomparable plot construction, but for her extraordinary ability to limn character and era with so few (and such skilled) strokes. And while Queen and Carr have offered recent books well below their highest standards, Christie . . . is virtually as good as ever—as she roundly demonstrates in ''At Bertram's Hotel.'' . . .

Miss Jane Marple revisits a quietly superlative London hotel which she had known as a girl, and finds it still a marvel of Edwardian elegance and conservatism—with a disturbing off-color touch of something new, and definitely of the sixties. The puzzle of the tone of Bertram's Hotel is the primary puzzle of the novel (which runs most of its length without overt violence). Miss Marple has a worthy investigative colleague in the unconventional Chief Inspector Davy; and the book is a joy to read from beginning to end, especially in its acute sensitivity to the contrasts between this era and that of Miss Marple's youth. (p. 61)

> *Anthony Boucher, in* The New York Times Book Review *(© 1966 The New York Times Company; reprinted by permission), September 25, 1966.*

SUMI YAMASHITA

Despite the author's many mysteries successfully recommended for [young adults, *Third Girl*] is too tame to hand over to anybody. Norma, an English flower-child type, shares an apartment with two other girls after her long-lost father returns from Africa with a new wife. Norma is always on the scene clutching incriminating implements but with no recollection of events when poisoning, knifing, and murder take place. Hercule Poirot repetitively mulls over the clues, arriving at last at the incredible solution: transformed by a wig, the villainous stepmother is also the third roommate and has been harrassing and drugging the dim-witted Norma. The *Third Girl* is a bore. (p. 4272)

> *Sumi Yamashita, in* Library Journal *(reprinted from* Library Journal, *November 15, 1967; published by R. R. Bowker Co. (a Xerox company); copyright © 1967 by Xerox Corporation), November 15, 1967.*

Miss Christie makes the most of it [in *By the Pricking of My Thumbs*] of being a woman, of being a country woman, an archaeologist's wife, and now, of being old. Her hero and heroine Miss Christie has resuscitated from the 1920s, her even then tiresome Tommy and Tuppence, now sprightly oldsters. The general theme is senility. (p. 1414)

> *The Times Literary Supplement (© Times Newspapers Ltd. (London) 1968; reproduced from* The Times Literary Supplement *by permission), December 12, 1968.*

MARCIA KELLER

[*By the Pricking of My Thumbs* is a] mystery centered on senior citizens which will nevertheless appeal to younger girls. Tommy and Tuppence Beresford visit an aging aunt in a rest home, and a few stray remarks by a supposedly senile companion lead to revelations concerning crimes of infanticide which had long been thought solved. The clues occasionally come too fast and heavy, and at times there are too many characters, but all is neatly tidied up in the end. Particularly good is the way the confused, befuddled, genteel and elderly Beresfords, the woman working from womanly intuition and the man from reason and logic, plow through the morass of hints and suspicions to finally half-deduce, half-stumble on the answer to the mystery. Competent Christie, in its own way bridging the generation gap. (p. 1346)

> *Marcia Keller, in* Library Journal *(reprinted from* Library Journal, *March 15, 1969; published by R. R. Bowker Co. (a Xerox company); copyright © 1969 by Xerox Corporation), March 15, 1969.*

ANTHONY LEJEUNE

Compared, not only with Sherlock Holmes and Father Brown, but with Nero Wolfe or Dr Fell or Lord Peter Wimsey, Poirot is a distinctly cardboard character, an obvious artefact. Agatha Christie herself prefers Miss Marple, and her new book, *Passenger to Frankfurt*, contains neither of them.

The fact remains, however, that Poirot, like a survivor from an almost extinct race of giants, is one of the last of the Great Detectives: and the mention of his name should be enough to remind us how much pleasure Agatha Christie has given millions of people over the past fifty years. . . .

So what is it, this quality which Agatha Christie possesses and so many imitators have lacked?

The secret does lie partly in her plots. *The Murder of Roger Ackroyd, Murder on the Orient Express, The ABC Murders* and her other classic *tours de force* deserve their fame. If they seem hackneyed or contrived now or even too easily guessable, that is precisely because they left so permanent an impression on the detective story genre. These books are famous because each of them turns on a piece of misdirection and a solution which, in their day, were startlingly innovatory: but there are many others—*Crooked House, Cards on the Table, Death on the Nile, Mrs McGinty's Dead, 4.30 from Paddington*—which, in their overall construction, the ingenuity of their clues and the satisfactory smoothness with which their unexpected solutions fall into place, are just as good and perhaps better. It would be silly to pretend that Mrs Christie has never written a bad book. She has—several: but, compared with the size of her output, amazingly few. Almost always, skilled professional that she is, she can out-plot her readers, tripping them up with an extra twist in the tail of the story.

But this isn't all. The real secret of Agatha Christie is subtler. It lies not in the carpentering of her plots, excellent though that is, but in the texture of her writing; a texture smooth and homely as cream. Her books are the easiest of reading. They 'go down a treat', as the saying is.

In a literary sense she doesn't write particularly well. But there is another sense, which for a writer of fiction is perhaps even more important. The ability to buttonhole a reader, to make (as Raymond Chandler put it) 'each page throw the hook for the next', is a separate and by no means common art. . . .

She has one other key quality—the quality of cosiness. There are no nightmares in her books, nothing nasty, nothing horrid, as Jane Austen would say. . . . This is an important attribute of the true detective story. Its secure and restful formality is part of the pleasure; we don't really have to weep for the victim or for the villain; we ought not to be harrowed, any more than we are by the loss of pieces in a game of chess.

This type of book—and therefore this type of pleasure—has become rare. One reason, the main one probably, is that every new detective story, unlike other kinds of fiction, needs an at least marginally new idea—a new way of committing a murder, or of concealing a murderer's identity, or of solving a murder: and, in the nature of things, finding such new devices gets harder all the time. . . .

Mrs. Christie herself has sometimes ventured a little outside the classic field; *Passenger to Frankfurt,* as it happens, is an example. But she belongs fairly and squarely in the old tradition. . . .

The Great Detectives were—and, in Mrs. Christie's hands, thank goodness, still are—engaged on a great business. They move, untouched, incorruptible, undefeated, among the mysteries of life and death, teaching us in a parable that there is a reason for everything, that puzzles were made to be solved, that what seems like chaos may be only the observed effects of unknown causes; in short, that the world, instead of being as meaningless as a modern novel, may be like a good detective story, in which the truth and a happy ending are kept for the final chapter.

> Anthony Lejeune, "The Secret of Agatha Christie," in The Spectator (ⓒ 1970 by The Spectator; reprinted by permission of The Spectator), September 19, 1970, p. 294.

HOWARD HAYCRAFT

Of the impressive list of [Mrs. Christie's] volumes, mostly about Poirot, . . . the best known and most widely discussed is the brilliant *The Murder of Roger Ackroyd.* . . . At the present late date it is betraying no secret to say that this remarkable story, a tour de force in every sense of the word and one of the true classics of the literature, turns on the ultimate revelation of the narrator as the criminal. This device (or trick, as the reader may prefer) provoked the most violent debate in detective story history. Scarcely had the ink dried on the pages before representatives of one school of thought were crying, "Foul play!" Other readers and critics rallied as ardently to Mrs. Christie's defense, chanting the dictum: "It is the reader's business to suspect *every one.*" The question remains unsettled to-day, and the inconclusive argument will probably continue as long as detective stories are read and discussed. (p. 130)

Happily, Poirot richly merited the attention he [has] received. For when he is at the top of his form few fictional sleuths can surpass the amazing little Belgian—with his waxed mustaches and egg-shaped head, his inflated confidence in the infallibility of his "little grey cells," his murderous attacks on the English language—either for individuality or ingenuity. His methods, as the mention of the seldom-forgotten "cells" implies, are imaginative rather

than routine. Not for Poirot the fingerprint or the cigar ash. His picturesque refusal to go to Holmes-like on all fours in pursuit of clues is classic in the literature. (But his inventor does not scorn to employ one of the tritest of the Conanical devices almost ad nauseam, in the person of Captain Hastings, easily the stupidest of all modern Watsons.) Not quite an arm-chair detective, Poirot nevertheless spurns the aid of science. He is the champion of theory over matter. What this postulate may lack in verisimilitude it gains in dramatic possibilities, which the author knows well how to exploit to advantage.

The only really serious grounds for criticism of the stories, in fact, is Mrs. Christie's too great reliance on, and not always scrupulous use of, the least-likely-person motif. (pp. 131-32)

Mrs. Christie occasionally turns her hand, for diversion, presumably, to stories in which other detectives appear; but none of these secondary creations has ever seriously rivaled the mustachioed Belgian. His own investigations, one regrets to report, have begun to reveal now and then symptoms of ennui, so that the publication of "a new Christie" . . . is not always now the item of interest to the discriminating reader that it once was.

Nevertheless, few sleuths have been more rewarding than Poirot at the height of his powers. He still comes closer to symbolizing his profession in the popular mind than any story-book detective since the Holmes whose methods he professes to deplore—but with whose essential histrionism he has so much in common. The hypercritical may feel that Mrs. Christie sometimes allows her hero to lean too heavily on intuition, and that her own art could be improved by a little greater variety in method and closer attention to the probabilities and the canons of fair play. But none can gainsay that at her frequent best Agatha Christie is easily one of the half-dozen most accomplished and entertaining writers in the modern field. (pp. 132-33)

> Howard Haycraft, in his Murder for Pleasure: The Life and Times of the Detective Story (copyright, 1969, by Howard Haycraft; reprinted by permission of the author), revised edition, Biblo and Tannen, 1972.

ERIC SHORTER

Once upon a time (and a very good time it was) the Abbey's Lady Gregory said: 'We went on giving what we thought good until it became popular'. No better motto could be found for theatrical managers, but how many heed it? The motto now is to give what the manager thinks will be popular until it is generally thought good. Hence *The Mousetrap.* It must be good because it has run for so long.

Agatha Christie's thriller has now been on for 21 years. It has broken every conceivable theatrical record. (p. 51)

What indeed does anybody know to explain the tenacity of this routine, country house whodunnit? (pp. 51-2)

[Whether seeds of immortality] are to be found in the text or the performance, the theatre or its position, its management or its publicity, is a question which nobody can answer for sure. (p. 52)

And it all began because the BBC wanted something by Agatha Christie, at Queen Mary's request, to celebrate Queen Mary's 80th birthday. So Mrs. Christie ran up a short story called *Three Blind Mice* which she subsequently stretched into a play. . . .

And the idea of the thriller? Timelessly conventional. Into the lounge hall of a snowed-up panelled, home counties hotel just opened by a diffident young couple drift a careful assortment of independent types (grave, comical, foreign, peculiar, chatty, silent and so forth), one of whom is in due course bumped off. Thereafter suspicion falls, with the help of red herrings, on the survivors variously in turn; and before the final unmasking a mild degree of curiosity, even excitement, certainly tension is aroused. The suspense, if not intense, is agreeable; and the plotting is unquestionably neat. (p. 53)

> Eric Shorter, "*Quite a Nice Run*," in Drama, *Spring, 1974.*

MARGOT PETERS and AGATE NESAULE KROUSE

Critics of the British detective novel have generally agreed that it is a conservative genre. The detective functions as the guardian of the status quo: he brings to justice criminals who have threatened middle-class stability by threatening the foundation of that stability—money. Not surprisingly, the genre itself is a product of the nineteenth century, for only this century saw the triumph of a class into which an outsider could buy his way—as he could not into the aristocracy—if only he could get his hands on capital. The getting of capital, therefore, motivates most criminals to murder in detective fiction, and the detective is worshiped by the middle classes who understand that their wealth and position will eventually be safe in his hands.

Given the conservatism of the genre, one can further predict that stereotypes of character will seldom be violated. Thus, upon opening an [Margery] Allingham, a [Dorothy] Sayers, or a Christie, one finds many of the familiar sexist attitudes toward women that one might otherwise expect these women writers to avoid. Christie offends the least, but still offends. (p. 144)

Christie is the mistress of plot rather than character. Her young men are tall, dark, and tense; her clergymen delightfully fuddled; her old solicitors discreet; her retired colonels bluff. How does she characterize women? Looking over the vastness of seventy—or is it eighty?—mysteries, we find a few inevitable types occurring again and again. Her women are garrulous, talking inconsequentially and at length about irrelevancies. If young, they are often stupid, blonde, red-fingernailed gold diggers without a thought in their heads except men and money. Her servant girls are even more stupid, with slack mouths, "boiled gooseberry eyes," and a vocabulary limited to "Yes'm" and "No'm" unless, of course, they're being garrulous. Dark-haired women are apt to be ruthless or clever, redheads naïve and bouncy. Competent women, like Poirot's secretary Miss Lemon, are single, skinny, and sexless. A depressing cast of thousands.

Christie often prefaces her novels with thumbnail sketches [of the characters]. (pp. 149-50)

Granted that some of the sketches are meant to be misleading, this brief juxtaposing of Christie's male and female characters reveals her prejudice against women. The men are by and large presented as professional, active, and rational. The women are portrayed, on the other hand as social aberrants—exotics, witches, sea nymphs, woodsprites;

as unattractive—snoopy, whining, foreign; or as mentally confused—"an imaginative if untidy mind."

In defense of Christie, one can argue that her novels are filled with students, secretaries, widows, headmistresses, actresses—independent women making it in society on their own brains, skills, and energies. Unfortunately, too many of Christie's competent women are portrayed as either deadly or destructive. . . . [Independent] and ambitious women are hostile and criminal, whereas the dizzy females are at least harmless. One hopes there is no significance to the fact that Christie's only murderous child is a girl.

Christie also exhibits sexism in depicting her detectives. Her most popular sleuth is Hercule Poirot. His fame rests on his "little grey cells": he is a purely cerebral armchair detective who solves his crimes by rationality and method. His geometrical apartment reflects his worship of regularity, precision, and order; his happiness is complete at the invention of square scones for his tea. While Christie smiles at Poirot's overweening pride in his luxurious moustaches and his patent leather shoes, his egotism is founded on a secure sense of self and male superiority. He praises rationality—a male attribute—and deplores intuition: in *The ABC Murders* . . . he reproves Hastings, his Watson, for suggesting that the great Poirot has employed instinct: "'Not instinct, Hastings. Instinct is a bad word. It is my *knowledge,* my *experience*—that tells me that something about that letter is wrong—'"

Not surprisingly, Miss Marple, Christie's spinster detective, owes her success chiefly to intuition and nosiness. Operating on the theory that human nature is universal, she ferrets out the criminal by his resemblance to someone she has known in her native village of St. Mary Mead, since her knowledge of life extends little farther. Her method does, of course, involve analogy, a ratiocinative process (although her reliance on physical types has a disturbing similarity to the "science" of phrenology), but Christie presents Miss Marple as chiefly intuitive, operating with a sixth sense rather than the "little grey cells." Concomitantly, while Poirot looks upon crime rationally as a sociological ill, Miss Marple takes the reactionary medieval view that a tangible spirit of wickedness or evil walks abroad in the world: murderers can be detected by "the pricking of the thumbs." Again, unlike Poirot, Miss Marple lacks self-confidence; she apologizes, demurs, and patiently waits her turn to speak, a forbearance impossible to imagine in Poirot.

Mrs. Ariadne Oliver, a writer of detective fiction, also appears in Christie's novels as an amateur sleuth. Christie portrays her as a muddled, untidy woman whose trail is strewn with hairpins and apple cores. Mrs. Oliver's mind is as untidy as her appearance. And when she does come up with a right answer it's a lucky guess—in other words, her "feminine intuition." She almost always functions as a foil for Poirot's logical brilliance, and as the butt of his chauvinistic jokes. . . . (pp. 150-52)

Yet Christie is not as sexist as Sayers and Allingham in one respect. Both spinster and widow are self-sufficient, possessing a zest for life depending in no way on a man's support and approval. Neither manifests insecurity at being a single woman; both have interests that absorb them creatively. Neither succumbs to romance or marriage: Christie takes it for granted that without youth, beauty, or a husband a woman can still be fulfilled. (p. 152)

Margot Peters and Agate Nesaule Krouse, in Southwest Review (© *1974 by Southern Methodist University Press), Spring, 1974.*

DICK DATCHERY

There's life in the old girl yet—but I do wish she could be persuaded to stop writing. This one [*Postern of Fate*] is a disaster. It is confused (Mutton Chop did *not* send Tommy to Mr. Robinson), rambling, garrulous, and just plain silly. There are not one but two dogs whose innermost thoughts are revealed to the reader and the dialogue by members of the lower-classes is unbelievable. Mostly this latest by Dame Christie suggests that through her years she has probably been overrated and that her detecting heroes and heroines (Miss Marple, Tommy and Tuppence and Hercule Poirot) are just too damn cute. If there is an audience, it's the geriatric set, there'll-always-be-an-England division. (p. 75)

Dick Datchery, in The Critic (© *The Critic 1974; reprinted with the permission of the Thomas More Association, Chicago, Illinois), March-April, 1974.*

FRANCIS WYNDHAM

Of course nobody is expected to care in any humanist sense: it is, quite simply, that one has to know. Agatha Christie at her best writes animated algebra. She dares us to solve a basic equation buried beneath a proliferation of irrelevancies. By the last page, everything should have been eliminated except for the motive and identity of the murderer; the elaborate working-out, apparently too complicated to grasp, is suddenly reduced to satisfactory simplicity. The effect is one of comfortable catharsis.

During the Second World War, just after finishing *The Body in the Library*, Agatha Christie wrote two novels which she intended to reserve for publication after her death. They described the last cases of her two most famous detectives, Poirot and Miss Marple. Now she has generously decided to release at least one of them while she is still alive. *Curtain*, therefore, belongs to the period when her power to puzzle was at its formidable height. . . .

[Its] solution, when it is finally sprung, turns out to be as outrageously satisfying as those of *The Murder of Roger Ackroyd, Ten Little Indians, Murder on the Orient Express* and *Crooked House*. As she presumably intended, in this one Agatha Christie has brought off the bluff to end them all.

Francis Wyndham, "Animated Algebra," in The Times Literary Supplement (© *Times Newspapers Ltd. (London) 1975; reproduced from* The Times Literary Supplement *by permission), September 26, 1975, p. 1078.*

PETER PRESCOTT

Probably no detective story in history has met with such instantaneous success as ["Curtain"]. . . . Poirot dead? It seems incredible. The little Belgian detective had been most active between 1900 and 1904; by 1920, when he appeared in Christie's first novel, "The Mysterious Affair at Styles," he was officially retired. And yet he went on to star in 40 of his author's 86 books—which is about as firm a grip on immortality as a literary man can get. For this reason, his death comes as an unexpected jolt. (p. 91)

"Curtain" is one of Christie's most ingenious stories, a tour de force in which the lady who had bent all the rules of the genre before bends them yet again. Like all her stories, it is scrupulously honest. In a detective story, as in an allegory, much that happens—the concrete details that provide an illusion of reality—actually points to something else, and in "Curtain" so many events are not quite what they seem that the reader may at the end feel as foolish as Hastings. To believe in the killer's motivation requires belief in some truly hokey psychology, but never mind: the credibility of the design, not the people, is what distinguishes the best of Christie's stories. (p. 92)

Peter Prescott, "The Last Act," in Newsweek (*copyright 1975 by Newsweek, Inc.; all rights reserved; reprinted by permission), October 6, 1975, pp. 90-2.*

[*Curtain* is much] ado about very little. As almost everyone knows by now, this is Hercule Poirot's *schwanenlied*. His death turns out to be as silly as his life. This is better than recent Christies—which isn't saying a hell of a lot. Ms. Christie is one of the most over-rated writers of our time and her present phenomenal popularity simply proves that most readers cannot distinguish between mediocre and good suspense novels. Her one talent is intricate plotting but plot alone does not a novel make. (pp. 91-2)

The Critic (© *The Critic 1975; reprinted with the permission of the Thomas More Association, Chicago, Illinois), Winter, 1975.*

ADAM ULAM

It must have been the heady atmosphere of those World War II days that made Edmund Wilson mount a frontal assault at one of the mainstays of Western civilization. "Who cares who killed Roger Ackroyd," he thundered in the title of his essay denigrating detective fiction. But having discharged this salvo the eminent critic must have been seized by some inner doubts. Obviously hundreds of thousands have cared, the vast legion of readers who for 300 pages have struggled with the plethora of clues, only to be left dazzled and emotionally drained by the astounding conclusion of Agatha Christie's masterpiece. Wilson thus beat a retreat to a higher, supposedly safer, ground: "Friends," he wrote, "we represent a minority but Literature is on our side. . . . There is no need to bore ourselves with this rubbish." But this maneuver left him even more vulnerable. The masses don't buy and certainly don't read boring books, that is unless they have been certified as Literature by eminent critics. Wilson's last desperate move was a traditional one for those who run out of rasoned arguments: call for repression. He would have detective fiction proscribed. . . . (p. 21)

Fortunately his impious suggestion remained unheeded. Where would we be now, how could we have survived the alarms and anxieties of the Cold War, the Great Society, and the Greening of America without the distraction and solace of the mystery novel? As against senseless violence that surrounds us on all sides, this novel is an oasis of *sensible* violence: fictional, orderly and intellectually stimulating.

Some indeed would still make us feel guilty for spending a few hours with a mystery. . . . Our reading matter should be chosen so as to enhance our anxieties. . . . But how does it help us to read just for pleasure?

Yet quite apart from being tiresome, our moralists miss the point. In addition to being fun, the mystery novel has a lot to teach us about the modern world. This novel has always been a force for progress.... Few who have immersed themselves in Agatha Christie's immortal work can miss her close affinity to many of the advanced causes of our own day. Take her militantly democratic spirit. To a superficial reader, this statement might appear absurd. Isn't a classical Christie story woven around a country house tittle-tattle interrupted only by servants bringing in brandy and soda, and the thud of falling corpses? Precisely! Only a writer with a profound sympathy for the underprivileged would make her typical murderer an upper-or upper-middle-class person. (pp. 21-2)

True, most of the writer's lower-class characters are portrayed, with the exception of a few of the proverbial old faithful retainers, as rather imbecilic, and, well, common, prone to dishonesty, and, especially if maid-servants, to vulgar promiscuity. Yet the attentive and perceptive reader will see immediately that such stereotypes add up to a burning indictment of the class society that was the England of the author's time....

It must have given Dame Agatha great pleasure to live to see the dawn of social justice in her country. There have been many scholarly accounts celebrating this salutary evolution of England from a decadent class-ridden society to a dynamic one inspired by the ideals of equality and democracy. None of them, it is fair to say, can match the fictional evocation contained in our author's *Curtain*. Its scene is set in the very same locality where some 40 years before Hercule Poirot tackled his first case. Then the rich played and murdered in their luxurious manor house, while the sole function of the denizens of the village was to serve them and provide a picturesquely primitive backdrop for their betters' amusements. But now on arriving Poirot's friend notices immediately signs of change: "Styles St. Mary was altered out of all recognition. Petrol stations, a cinema, two more inns and rows of council houses." As against this fuller, richer life for the masses, how poignant the retribution visited upon the erstwhile idle rich! The once stately home is now dilapidated, the drive leading to it "badly kept and much overgrown with weeds," the edifice itself "badly needed a coat of paint." And, the supreme irony of all, Styles is now a *boarding* house, its proprietors and most of the boarders the last remnants of the parasitic class, justly reduced to this inelegant style of living. (p. 22)

Need one stress the obvious: the close link between our genre of novel and the cause of Women's Liberation? ... On the issue of women's rights, we must consider Agatha Christie to have been a pioneer.... With Christie, women cease to be a mere plaything or a misleading clue. Occasionally she picks up a gun herself and knows how to use it on a male chauvinist. Over and above such advances in character development, Dame Agatha in an affirmative action of her own broke the male exclusiveness of the circle of great detectives. In her quiet way Miss Marple certainly belongs there, even though few would rank her as equal to Hercule Poirot. But then who is? (pp. 22-3)

[Let] us not neglect the ingenuity of her plots and the high literary merit of her writing. To be sure she has had detractors on both counts.... It has been said that solutions of crimes in her stories are unfairly devious, her style tends to be flat, her characters one-dimensional. Yet such criticisms

do an injustice to the meticulous honesty of Christie's clues and the robust concise quality of her prose. What can be more precise, insightful and straightforward than the following characterization: "He had the resolute, competent manner of a man accustomed to meeting with emergencies." Is there anything more that we need to know to visualize the individual in question, and yet to feel shaken, though not entirely surprised, when some 200 pages later he turns out to have been the murderer?

Were Edmund Wilson alive today he would, one hopes, reconsider his hasty verdict of 30 years ago. Certainly the great critic would not hold crime fiction at a disadvantage when compared with the pretentious rubbish that passes so often for a serious discussion of current affairs, or with that amalgam of pornography and dime store psychology that is the typical contemporary "serious" novel. The mystery story and Literature, far from being enemies, are natural allies. There are few ways of wiling away our time that can be as delightful, profitable and innocent as in trying to find out who killed Roger Ackroyd. (p. 23)

Adam Ulam, "The Issue Is Murder," in The New Republic *(reprinted by permission of* The New Republic; © *1976 The New Republic, Inc.), July 31, 1976, pp. 21-3.*

JULIAN BARNES

Ingenious to the last, Agatha Christie kept back one Poirot and one Miss Marple story, each written some 30 years ago, for publication after her death. The date of its vintage, of course, doesn't matter in the least, since Christieland is as socially frozen and lacking in specifically dating detail as the world of [P. G.] Wodehouse or [Ivy] Compton-Burnett. It's all as ordered, stiff and unlikely as an everlasting flower: from gay, happy young couples and solid professional oldsters to servants who can't spell and gardeners who can't even pronounce the names of plants properly. Here, murders are by definition a trifle insane; good men tend to attract bad women; psychiatrists have just been heard of, though Miss Marple prefers to call them ironically 'mental specialists'; and the phrase for a girl who enjoys a bit of a fling (gosh, the idiom is catching) is 'man mad'.

Sleeping Murder has nice newlyweds Gwenda and Giles settling in the West Country in a house which gives Gwenda a strange sense of familiarity.... It all seems excruciatingly slow at first—by halfway there's only a situation, not a sniff of a suspect; but the second half is full of intricate Christie crochet-work. I fingered the villain pretty easily, on the grounds that a) he was extremely unlikely, b) he was a respectable solicitor, and c) he stayed at home every evening and played piquet with his mother. Ah well, wrong again. (p. 522)

Julian Barnes, in New Statesman (© *1976 The Statesman & Nation Publishing Co. Ltd.), October 15, 1976.*

JULIAN SYMONS

It was the plotting of crime that fascinated [Agatha Christie], not its often unpleasant end, and it is as a constructor of plots that she stands supreme among modern crime writers. Raymond Chandler once said that plotting was a bore, a necessary piece of journeywork that had to be done, and that the actual writing was the thing that gave the author pleasure. Agatha Christie's feelings were almost the opposite of these....

Her most stunningly original plots are those in *The Murder of Roger Ackroyd, The A.B.C. Murders* and *Ten Little Niggers* (also evasively called *And Then There Were None* and *Ten Little Indians*), but although these are her major achievements, she showed from the beginning an extraordinary assurance in handling the devices in a detective story plot.

Her first book, *The Mysterious Affair at Styles,* was published in 1920 but written some years earlier. . . . In general it is true that nothing becomes out-of-date more quickly than an old detective story but *Styles,* which was turned down by several publishers, remains wonderfully readable today. In part this is because of Poirot, but it is chiefly a tribute to the plot.

Most Christie plots are based upon a single and fairly simple circumstance, which is then elaborated and concealed. In *Styles* the plot springs from the fact that in England somebody acquitted of a crime may not be tried for it again. (pp. 27-8)

There are other felicities in *Styles,* in particular several of those deductions that trick us by their very simplicity. . . .

Styles was a splendid beginning. Not all of the books that succeeded it were on the same level, and the semi-thrillers that used what has been called a 'master criminal' theme seem to me inferior in almost every way to the orthodox detective stories. But as Agatha Christie's skills developed, a pattern emerged which might be called the typical Christie plot form. It was used by other people too, but by none so well or so variously as in her books. The form consisted of gathering a number of people together in a particular place preliminary to one of them being murdered, and of showing the reasons for their presence. It is a way of creating a totally closed society, and one can see it happening in very different books: *Death in the Clouds* (1935) (*Death in the Air* in America), *Cards on the Table* (1936), *Death on the Nile* (1937), and *Ten Little Niggers* (1939). To look at the way in which these plots are devised and carried through is to see the high skill that was, with almost deceptive casualness, employed in them. (p. 29)

[*The reader should be aware of the*] kind of trap she sets— there are people who claim to be able always to tell the villain in any Christie story by such an awareness. I couldn't make this claim myself, and indeed I doubt whether it is possible to be specific about the 'kind of trap'. Even the pattern I have called the typical Christie plot form does not apply to the majority of her books, although it is used in a high percentage of the best ones. But her work is astonishingly varied. There is a whole slew of books that take their settings from the fact that her second husband Sir Max Mallowan is an archaeologist, concerned chiefly with Assyrian culture, and that she often accompanied him and to some extent shared his interests. But although archaeology has a place in several stories her readers are never oppressed by a feeling of ignorance. She had an instinctive awareness of just how far her audience would wish her to go in showing expert knowledge, and no Agatha Christie mystery depends for its solution on a knowledge of ancient artefacts. (pp. 32-3)

One sees certain things more clearly in looking back at her work than was apparent when reading the books as they were published. One is the supremacy of the best Poirot stories over the rest of what she wrote. She became tired of

Poirot herself and preferred Miss Marple, who did not appear in a novel until 1930, with the feeble *Murder at the Vicarage.* Miss Marple, she said, was more fun, and like many aunts and grandmothers was 'a splendid natural detective when it comes to observing human nature'. Only a minority of readers agreed with her. If one prefers Poirot it is not only because he is an altogether livelier character, but also because his insights are more rational and less inspirational than Miss Marple's. A second thing that becomes apparent is her frequent carelessness in leaving deplorably loose ends, and a third is the highly verbal nature of her plotting. It is not just that you don't need to know about ancient artefacts to solve a Christie puzzle, but that you need no specialized knowledge at all. . . . The basic difference in plotting between her and most detective story writers is that the central clue in almost all of her best books is either verbal or visual. We are induced to give a meaning to something that has been said, or something that has been seen, which is not the true meaning or not the only possible meaning. (pp. 33-4)

Such visual and verbal clues, when they are used with subtlety and fairness, seem to me the very best things in the classical detective story. At her best Dame Agatha Christie was an incomparable deceiver.

That the level of her work varied greatly has to be acknowledged. Most of her finest performances belong to the 1920s and 1930s. The following decade more or less maintained this high level, but after that the decline was steady and near the end it was steep. The books of her last few years were, with only one or two exceptions, no more than faint echoes of her best work. A book like *The Clocks* (1963) opens very promisingly with a body found in a room full of clocks, most of which have no right to be there. The explanation of this anomaly, which would have been the heart of an earlier novel, is both casual and disappointing. And the people have become shadowy too, as inevitably she lost touch with contemporary life and feeling.

A survey of her whole output shows that she was often slapdash from the beginning in dealing with the technical details from which she flinched. *Murder on the Links* (1923), for instance, has been justly praised for its complicated and brilliant plotting, and for the way in which details of a twenty-year-old murder are interwoven with a current one. It contains one of her most characteristically clever touches of deception, and what must be called an almost equally characteristic carelessness in handling an important plot detail. (pp. 34-5)

In the end Agatha Christie's claim to supremacy among the classical detective story writers of her time rests on her originality in constructing puzzles. This was her supreme skill, and it is [displayed best] in three books, *The Murder of Roger Ackroyd, The A.B.C. Murders* and *Ten Little Niggers.* Some would add to these, which I regard as her most dazzling performances, *Murder on the Orient Express* (1934) (in the US *Murder in the Calais Coach*) or *Peril at End House* (1932) or even the last Poirot story *Curtain* (1975). But the crime writer who relies on a puzzle is like a tight-rope walker. A perfect achievement is a perfect marvel, but anything less, any slight swaying on the line, leaves us sharply critical. Both *Murder on the Orient Express* and *Curtain* are for me too obviously and purely tricks, and although I rate *Peril at End House* much more highly than do most critics, it cannot quite be ranked with Christie's best. (p. 35)

The trouble with plot devices is that they often obtrude, so that we have all plot and no story. Part of *Roger Ackroyd*'s triumphant success rests in the fact that the rest of the story is so perfectly typical of the period. (p. 36)

One might feel that ingenuity in plot construction could hardly be taken further than *Roger Ackroyd*. Rather more than a decade after its publication, Dorothy L. Sayers suggested that the detective story as a pure puzzle was in gentle and painless decline, partly because those devices that had seemed so ingenious in the form's early days—the poisoned toothbrush, the evaporating ice dart, the pistol timed to fire when the grandfather clock in the library struck twelve—were worn out from too much use, and partly because readers' tastes had changed, so that they were increasingly asking for crime stories in which the characters were as important as the plot. She has proved a truthful prophet, although some of the crime story's developments would have surprised and displeased her. Agatha Christie's ingenuity, however, had always been verbal and visual rather than mechanical and scientific, and she responded to the idea that the detective puzzle was worn out by inventing new and still more dazzling conjuring tricks.

Are *The A.B.C. Murders* (1935) and *Ten Little Niggers* (1939) as good as *Roger Ackroyd*? Not quite, because the trick played on the reader is deliberately artificial rather than fitting naturally into the story. In the later books the Christie cleverness again leaves us gasping, but second and third readings show that the plot has been built around the device used, with total disregard for our belief in the story itself. Who can believe that those ten guilty people would in fact have accepted that mysterious invitation to stay on the small island in *Ten Little Niggers*? Who can believe in a murderer so reckless, and in a gull so stupid, as the characters in *The A.B.C. Murders*? Yet the books remain triumphs of ingenuity, and it is worth trying to see just how the tricks are done. (pp. 36-7)

What are Agatha Christie's chances of survival as a writer who will be read a century from now? . . .

To answer yes, as I would do, is not to say that she was a great or even a good writer, but rather to say that although the detective story is ephemeral literature, the puzzle which it embodies has a permanent appeal. . . . If her work survives it will be because she was the supreme mistress of a magical skill that is a permanent, although often secret, concern of humanity: the construction and the solution of puzzles. (p. 38)

> Julian Symons, "*The Mistress of Complication*," in Agatha Christie: First Lady of Crime, *edited by H.R.F. Keating (copyright © 1977 by Weidenfeld & Nicolson; reprinted by permission of Holt, Rinehart and Winston, Publishers; in Canada by Weidenfeld & Nicholson Ltd.), Holt, Rinehart and Winston, 1977, pp. 25-38.*

EMMA LATHEN

Why do Americans gulp down Agatha Christie in such quantity? Our most eminent literary critics have asked the question with genuine and growing bewilderment. Their pardonable zeal to espy a new [Leo] Tolstoy or [Fyodor] Dostoyevsky blinds them to the essence of Gutenberg's invention. They fail to recognize that, ever since the availability of the printing press, mankind has been evincing a dogged determination to read. And Americans, as usual, have taken a simple human desire and run away with it. . . .

Now genius is just as rare in literature as it is every place else. The world has long accepted the fact that the lack of a [Christopher] Wren or a [Charles] Bulfinch has never prevented people from erecting buildings. Instead they have settled for the nearest reliable craftsman. . . . (p. 85)

In the same sense, Agatha Christie has become a vernacular art form in her own right. And there is no doubt at all about the nature of her functionalism. She writes a readable book, a book that remains readable come hell or high water. This in itself is enough to explain her sales in the US, in the world.

American enthusiasts of James Joyce or Virginia Woolf do not see it this way. An embattled crew—as they have to be—they fight every inch of the way. Very well, they concede grudgingly, Agatha Christie is an honest, reliable craftsman. What's so wonderful about that? Surely there are plenty of them around. What makes this one so attractive to the American reading public?

In some circles it is tactless to reply that readable writers are not really thick on the ground. Provocative, insightful, gritty . . . yes. Readable . . . no. Narrative thrust, as we must all admit, is hopelessly old-fashioned. But then, so are most book readers, at least in this country. Coteries may be interested in the psyche; people still like stories. Agatha Christie is, *par excellence,* a story-teller.

Fortunately the second reason is less invidious. By making her works so quintessentially English, by becoming a chronicler of British small beer, Christie creates a special dimension of interest for her foreign audience, including Americans. Her intricate embroidery of domestic trivia obscures some of her consistent defects, such as shallow characterization and hackneyed situations. At the same time it leaves untouched her great strengths—the absolute mastery of puzzle, the glinting edge of humour, the accurate social eye. There are millions of us ready to attest that this is a more than satisfactory trade-off.

A chorus of unanimity rises on at least one of these points. Friend and foe alike bow to the queen of the puzzle. Every Christie plot resolution has been hailed as a masterpiece of sleight-of-hand; she herself as a virtuoso of subterfuge. Tributes like these are heartwarming and deserved. They are not, however, altogether accurate. Agatha Christie's brilliance lies in her rare appreciation of the Laocoon complexities inherent in any standard situation. She herself rarely condescends to misdirect; she lets the cliché do it for her. When a sexually carnivorous young woman appears on the Christie scene, the reader, recognizing the stock figure of the home wrecker, needs no further inducement to trip down the garden path of self-deception. Wilfully misinterpreting every wrinkle, he will have strayed so far into the brambles by the time of the inevitable murder that nothing can get him back on course. Then the solution, the keystone of which is simply the durability of the original marriage or attachment, comes as a startling *bouleversement* for him—not to mention the carnivore. The contrapuntal variations on this theme are explored in *Evil Under the Sun, Murder in Retrospect* (in Britain *Five Little Pigs*), and *Death on the Nile.*

The same deadly common sense informs the Christie approach to impersonation and collusion. After all, any mystery aficionado worth his salt knows how to react when a large fortune and several dubious claimants are trailed enticingly before him. Like Pavlov's dog, he's been there before. Then comes the grand finale, the bland Christie assumption that, if an inheritance is worth shenanigans now, it was worth even more one death back. Therefore—good heavens!—the impostor is not any of those obvious suspects but is the man, or woman, who is already enjoying full possession of the money bags. So runs the logic of *A Murder Is Announced, There Is A Tide* (*Taken at the Flood* in Britain), and *Dead Man's Folly.* The twist is then reversed for *Funerals Are Fatal* (*After the Funeral*), where the skulduggery begins one death later, instead of one death sooner, than expected.

This Christie penchant for exhaustive combinations and permutations really blossoms whenever two people conspire to commit a crime. Outlandish yokings of every description abound. But, by and large, it is safe to say that whenever an obvious male ne'er-do-well exists, no woman is ineligible to be his accomplice. In this respect Dame Agatha showed her colours as early as *The Mysterious Affair at Styles,* where the gruff, middle-aged companion, complete with tweeds and walking shoes, emerges as a passionate partner in murder. From these promising beginnings she has made a clean sweep of the field, including the devoted secretary (*Sparkling Cyanide*), the protective Swedish child lover (*Ordeal by Innocence*), the subnormal housemaid (*A Pocket Full of Rye*), and the crisply independent poor relation (*The Patriotic Murders,* in Britain *One, Two, Buckle My Shoe*). Yet for a ruthless exploiter of every conceivable possibility, these achievements were not enough. The apotheosis of Christie conspiracy is reserved for *Murder in the Calais Coach,* otherwise the *Orient Express,* where everybody is guilty.

All of this lies well within the canon of the classic detective story and is deeply satisfying to those of us who like to see a rigid form explored to its outermost limits. But inevitably the further Agatha Christie wanders off the beaten track, the closer she comes to overshooting the bounds of credulity. Here is where her export market enjoys a clear-cut advantage. An English reader may boggle at palpable absurdities. Not so an American. By the time we have absorbed the larger realities of English life, together with the special aspects illustrated by St Mary Mead [Miss Marple's village] we are not going to strain at gnats. For example, there is the geography of England. To American eyes, this involves an incredible number of people in a very constricted space. What's more, instead of trying to spread out, they all seem to be going to London constantly. (pp. 85-7)

And there is the eternal question of age. Who counts as young, who counts as old? Above all, when do people retire? Every American, assiduously working his way through the Christie *oeuvre,* can grasp the broad outlines of employment in the colonial civil services. But what is he to make of all those fifty-year-old men, coming home to marry and start families as country gentlemen of leisure? . . .

Which raises the ultimate mystification. What in the world do these people do, day in, day out? . . .

Even before he stumbles over a body in the library, the American reader realizes that he lacks the proper yardstick to measure normal English behaviour. (p. 88)

The list could continue indefinitely, but the moral is self-evident. To read Agatha Christie, an American is required to abandon all his own social experience and surrender himself to a never-never world where voices are rarely raised, where breeding is more important than money, and where a really good herbaceous border matters more than anything else. . . .

If the lulling background is English, the humour is universal —at least in the vintage Christie, which can be defined roughly as running from the mid thirties through the end of the fifties. At the beginning of her career she strayed into broad set pieces, with Bundle Brent rocketing adorably around the countryside and Hastings functioning as all-purpose stooge. But with success came relaxation and the introduction of fleeting vignettes and brief asides reflecting the author's point of view. Taken as a whole, they constitute an irresistible interpretation of the human condition. (p. 89)

For extra measure, the Christie assemblage includes a gallery of bystanders who transcend minor considerations of reality, creatures of inspired fantasy. These amiable *jeux d'esprit,* who can well be incorporated under the title of The Crazy Ladies, rarely figure as prominent members of the cast. But they are forever memorable. (p. 90)

No, Agatha Christie is not a comic writer. Black humour, mordant wit, condescending irony are—thank God—alien to her native genius. She is the author of straightforward light fiction who uses humour as leavening so that, throughout her great period, everything she wrote breathes a spirit of sanity, kindliness and detachment. It is quite enough to endear her to millions of readers.

And then, while their guard is down, she tells them more about what has happened to England since the First World War than *The Times*—either of London or New York. That quick and unerring eye for the homely detail is worth volumes of social history. In *Styles* we start out with servants, with open fires, with bedroom candles. Little by little, the servants fade away, electric lights reach the bedroom, and central heating warms good and bad alike. No one, including *The Economist,* has tracked the shift of English household practice from labour-intensive to capital-intensive with such unobtrusive persistency.

Outside the home her characters, even if they are derived from a golden world that never existed, move competently through one social upheaval after another. Wartime rationing, austerity, National Health—all formed part of Agatha Christie's accurately observed England. So too did educational grants and youth hostels in London, West Indian hospital nurses and bus conductors, the very rich staying rich in a welfare state. Dame Agatha mentioned these things to us long before anybody else did because she had a noticing eye. Capital punishment disappeared for Christie malefactors, and young people left those bed-sitters with the ubiquitous gas ring in order to share apartments—and Agatha Christie registers the fact, then casually passes it on. The Empire dies, employment goes up and down, the youth movement is spawned and it is all there, as seen from the Aga stove. There is no pretension, no didacticism. But it is the record of an era, drawn dispassionately and effectively.

Even on the delicate ground of American characters, Christie rarely sets a foot wrong. Here her victory consists less in attracting a devoted American audience than in avoiding its alienation. Refined creative instinct, or a lot of horse sense, saved Christie from the fatal error of sending Hercule Poirot to New York, or Miss Marple to Washington, DC. (English readers must often yearn for a little reciprocity along these lines.) Indeed, Christie was generally sparing in her use of Americans. (pp. 90-1)

So much for the content of Christie's work. There is one final point to be made concerning her record in the United States. All those impressive sales figures stress the insatiable demand for her books. But there is another side to the coin. In addition to mass consumption, Agatha Christie represents mass production. Her long, hard-working life has filled the shelves with title after title. Now mystery reading often presents some of the symptoms of addiction, with the hardened fanatic devouring larger and larger dosages until a book a night is required to satisfy the craving. Everyone who has ever been bitten by the bug knows the joy of unearthing a new, appealing author, followed by the bitter discovery that his entire output consists of two volumes. With Christie, there is no such brief encounter; she is with you for life. And by the time there are over forty works to a writer's credit, re-reading becomes more than a possibility, it becomes an insurance policy. Nothing makes us feel safer than an Agatha Christie we read twenty years ago. (pp. 92-3)

> *Emma Lathen, "Cornwallis's Revenge," in* Agatha Christie: First Lady of Crime, *edited by H.R.F. Keating (copyright © 1977 by Weidenfeld & Nicolson; reprinted by permission of Holt, Rinehart and Winston, Publishers; in Canada by Weidenfeld & Nicholson Ltd.), Holt, Rinehart and Winston, 1977, pp. 79-94.*

J. C. TREWIN

Through the years playgoers and critics joined in keeping any secret Mrs Christie confided to them, and her trust was honoured; it astonishes us now that after a quarter of a century in London *The Mousetrap* can still be acted before audiences with no idea of its development or climax.

Agatha Christie, by herself, wrote twelve full-scale plays (one published, not performed) and three in a single act. She collaborated in another full-length play; four more, from her novels or short stories, were adapted by other hands. . . . Whatever else was wrong, nobody sustained a problem as she did, or solved it so quickly without a tedious explanatory huddle. This was her Midas gift to the theatre. 'Upon my soul,' exclaimed [Charles] Dickens's Barnacle Junior, 'you mustn't come into the place saying you want to know, you know.' Agatha Christie's fans did want to know. In the later plays they may have found it a lagging wait. Never mind: having been in at the death they insisted on a post-mortem verdict. (p. 133)

Agatha Christie put action before character. Too often, in early plays or late, her people were stereotyped. Like [Oscar] Wilde's minor epigrams, they could have been transferred, as needed, from plot to plot, hall to manor, court to vicarage: a doctor there, a spinster here. Attendants on a body, they rarely had life of their own. Naturally, we remember Poirot—even he could be something of a stereotype—and Mrs Boynton in *Appointment with Death*, Romaine in *Witness for the Prosecution*, Clarissa in *Spider's Web*, and Lady Angkatell in *The Hollow* do linger. Others can coil out in a greyish procession of names. (p. 140)

Dame Agatha's strength in the theatre was her power of plotting. She could do most things with a body, but it became increasingly hard to animate the gap between death and revelation. Usually people and dialogue were functional, though at times, as in the whole of *Witness for the Prosecution*, in much of *The Mousetrap*, in the second acts of *The Hollow* and *Ten Little Niggers*, in the incidental comedy of *Spider's Web*, and in *The Unexpected Guest*, the stage could flash swiftly to life. Very few detachable lines keep a play in memory; humour often stiffened to mannerism. (pp. 152-53)

That admitted, Agatha Christie had more narrative impulse than anyone of her day. Frequently her end would justify the means. She was a technician when, among critics, the word had mildewed. Our pleasure in her major puzzles was the pleasure of a testing anagram, of an exact mortise-and-tenon, of filling the space at 27 down and closing an awkward corner. In fine, the pleasure of solution, the answer to a precisely stated challenge. In the matter of life and death within her world of artifice, she could be past-mistress of the artificial: no leopardess, no organ at midnight, not even a vault. She failed when her heart was not with the problem (*Towards Zero, Go Back for Murder, Verdict*). When she had persuaded herself she could soon persuade others: in the period's most rubbed jargon, there might not be many 'insights', but the machine did 'work'.

Agatha Christie fortified the theatre of entertainment; she knew about plays of menace before the tag was modish. At least three of her plays should live beyond the century. . . . (pp. 153-54)

> *J. C. Trewin, "A Midas Gift to the Theatre," in* Agatha Christie: First Lady of Crime, *edited by H.R.F. Keating (copyright © 1977 by Weidenfeld & Nicolson; reprinted by permission of Holt, Rinehart and Winston, Publishers; in Canada by Weidenfeld & Nicholson Ltd.), Holt, Rinehart and Winston, 1977, pp. 131-54.*

NAOMI BLIVEN

"An Autobiography," by Agatha Christie . . . is the work of a writer who depended upon a skeleton—the formal structure of the detective story—in order to allow herself to imagine in public. These memoirs are like nothing else she wrote: they are vivid, stylish, subtle, relaxed, and wholly uncarpentered. . . . [Mrs. Christie's] tone provides a sense of freshness, of discovery, as if she were inviting us along as she finds out how she came to be who she was. She also demonstrates, by the way, how intense and complex emotions take shape in narrow little societies. Sometimes she justifies the past in ways we cannot accept. For instance, she thinks that late-Victorian parents, like her own, were "realistic" in labelling their children early, and tells us, with no apparent resentment, "I myself was always recognized, though quite kindly, as 'the slow one' of the family." This judgment was nonsense, and I think it harmed her, deepening her shyness, her sense of inadequacy, and her self-distrust, to which she repeatedly refers. Humiliating stagefright ended her aspiration for a career as a concert pianist, and throughout her life she seems to have feared attention, or even admiration. I see a parallel to her published work, which is always tearing along to divert us, as if she feared she might be a bore.

In her memoirs, by contrast, she is candid and ample. She

does not conceal trouble (loss of money) or sorrow (loss of love), and she writes freely of her idiosyncrasies, her joys, her pleasures, her sources of pride. Her publishers note that she does not describe what they call her "celebrated disappearance"—an amnesiac flight during the breakup of her first marriage—but she is remarkably precise about the onset of her nervous breakdown, and evokes its peculiar frightfulness: her feelings of loneliness and confusion, of knowing she was somehow "off" but not knowing exactly how or why. And, for once allowing herself the freedom of space, she has room to let character develop. Though she seems to have gone on believing that she was partly to blame for the failure of that marriage, the reader will see, I think, what Mrs. Christie was too self-belittling to recognize: that she was a superior woman married to a mediocre man. The happiness of her second marriage, to a distinguished archeologist, shows her success with a husband who was her equal in brains, character, and taste.

Mrs. Christie's amplitude also offers a fascinating mass of detail about the past—about the shapes of Victorian trunks, say, and the way Edwardian women wore hairpieces. She has a sense of humor, a sense of fun, and a sense of the point of things. No matter how much she appears to digress, she is such a gifted narrator that her story never slackens. It unfolds with an effect of absolute naturalness, which, of course, is never achieved by nature but only by art. During her life, Agatha Christie was recognized as a first-rate entertainer; in this work she reveals the artist she did not believe she was, and was too shy to let herself be. (pp. 105-6)

Naomi Bliven, in The New Yorker *(© 1978 by The New Yorker Magazine, Inc.), January 30, 1978.*

E. F. BARGAINNIER

Hercule Poirot and Jane Marple are the detectives of Agatha Christie known to millions; somewhat less well known are Tuppence and Tommy Beresford and Inspector Battle. In all four cases, Christie wrote novels, as well as short stories, using these characters. However, there are two other Christie "detectives" who never appear in a novel, only in short stories. The quotation marks are necessary, for neither of these men fulfill the usual image of the British detective. They are Mr. C. Parker Pyne and Mr. Harley Quin. With the latter must be included his friend Mr. Satterthwaite. . . . The stories of Pyne and Quin illustrate two different elements of Christie's mystery fiction—elements that are not part of her works about the other detectives. In the Pyne stories she combines detection, or at least deduction, and the manipulation of human lives to achieve their happiness, while in the Quin stories she combines detection and fantasy.

There are fourteen Parker Pyne stories. Of these seven can hardly be called detective stories; rather they are cases in which Pyne manipulates people to give them the happiness they desire—the mystery element is how he accomplishes the task. The other seven involve detection by Pyne when he is asked to help an unhappy person. (p. 110)

As a result of Pyne's omnipotence, Christie's stories about him can be considered improbable. His ingenious schemes to provide people happiness by manipulating their views of their world, his astounding ability at classification, and his insight into human character based upon that classification

are far beyond the powers of most people. The improbability is lessened, however, by the nature of most of his cases. They are human interest stories, dealing with problems that face most people: problems of love, boredom, and money. Also, Pyne has none of the usual eccentricities of so many English detectives of the period in which he was created; rather, he is presented as an "ordinary," elderly English middle-class man in his tastes and personal life. It is in the blending of improbable action and ordinary characters that these stories are distinctive.

If Parker Pyne is omnipotent in his cases, Harley Quin is omniscient in the thirteen stories in which he appears, though he denies it. . . .

Quin is based upon the harlequin of the English pantomime, which is a descendant of the sixteenth-century *commedia dell'arte*. . . . Harlequin was not originally a supernatural character, but by the nineteenth century, he and Columbine, as presented on the English stage, had become fairy-like creatures not bound by time and space. (p. 112)

The resemblance to motley and the eerie effect of light on his appearance conjoin the elements of the stage harlequin and the supernatural being within Quin.

However, other characteristics of the supernatural are included in his presentation. The most obvious are his sudden appearances and disappearances. . . . (p. 113)

[One] cannot discuss Quin without including his mortal partner, Mr. Satterthwaite. (p. 114)

Quin and Satterthwaite are a team, a matching of the supernatural and the human—surely one of the most unusual detective teams in fiction. . . .

Neither Quin nor Pyne will ever have the popularity of Poirot, Marple, or the Beresfords. The short story form does not allow for the development of character which the novel does. Apparently, Christie did not see her way to extending Pyne's manipulation of people or the supernatural characteristics of Quin to the length of a novel. . . . Though Pyle is a basically colorless figure, the disquieting Quin and the little dried-up Satterthwaite are difficult to forget, and one can only regret her abandonment of them. But whatever one may think of the characters and the stories in which they appear, the fact remains that the twenty-seven stories are significant examples of Christie's experimentation in adding narrative interest to the detective genre by employing elements not generally considered compatible with it. (p. 115)

E. F. Bargainnier, "Agatha Christie's Other Detectives," in The Armchair Detective *(copyright © 1978 by The Armchair Detective), April, 1978, pp. 110-15.*

JULIAN SYMONS

Agatha Christie's success has not been checked by death. . . . What is it that has made the books live?

Certainly not the quality of the writing, which is at best no more than lively. . . .

Yet if Agatha Christie was an indifferent writer, she was a most intelligent craftsman, who had considerable sensibility about the form in which she worked. . . .

Other bad writers have been skillful craftsmen without lasting like Agatha Christie. Perhaps the nearest one can get to explaining the puzzle of her enduring popularity is to suggest that although the detective story is ephemeral, the riddle's attraction is lasting. There are those who find the detective story's origins in the Apocrypha, the story of Oedipus, or Voltaire's Zadig, but these are scholastic arguments. What is certainly true is that human beings have a passion equally for concealment and revelation. Agatha Christie's stories appeal strongly to very many people because they fulfill this passion in the world of the fairy tale, a world only nominally linked to reality. (p. 39)

> *Julian Symons, "The Christie Mystery," in* The New York Review of Books *(reprinted with permission from* The New York Review of Books; *copyright © 1978 Nyrev, Inc.),* December 21, 1978, pp. 37-9.

DAVID I. GROSSVOGEL

Agatha Christie wrote her first detective story, *The Mysterious Affair at Styles*, in 1920. Thereafter, and for over half a century, she was the most popular purveyor of the genre. During that time she wrote works that would not fit quite as well within the narrowest definition of the genre. But detective fiction is a form that loses definition in proportion as it extends beyond its intentional narrowness—a truism confirmed by the lasting appeal of even as rudimentary a work as *The Mysterious Affair at Styles.* . . . The detective story requires characters only in sufficient numbers, and sufficiently fleshed out, to give its puzzle an anthropomorphic semblance and to preserve the reader from boredom for as long as the veil of its "mystery" is drawn. When it restricts itself to this kind of functional stylization, it exposes little to the dangers of age: how many novels written at the end of the First World War could find such a ready, face-value acceptance today?

To say that the detective story proposes a puzzle is not quite accurate either: one must assume that only an infinitesimally small number of Agatha Christie's half billion readers ever undertook or expected to solve her stories in advance of Jane Marple or Hercule Poirot. What the detective story proposes instead is the *expectation* of a solution. The detective story offers confirmation and continuity at the price of a minor and spurious disruption. The continuity that it insures includes, ultimately, that of the genre itself: nearly every part of the world within which *The Mysterious Affair at Styles* is set must surely be dead and gone by now (if it ever actually existed), and yet thousands of readers who have never known that world still accept it as real, with little or no suggestion of "camp."

The world was the one possibly enjoyed for yet awhile by the English upper class after 1918. . . . Styles Court exists only in our expectation of what it might be if it were a part of our imaginings. It comes into being through a process of diluted logic that assumes, since mystery is given as an unfortunate condition that can, and should be, eliminated, that life without such unpleasantness must perforce be agreeable and desirable. In a place like Styles, the plumbing is never erratic (unless for the limited purpose of serving the plot), personal sorrow is as evanescent and inconsequential as a summer shower, age and decay cannot inform the exemplary and unyielding mien of its people: the young know that they will be young forever, the professionals are admirably suited to their faces. . . . In such a garden of delightfully fulfilled expectations, there rarely occurs anything worse than murder.

Where the corpse of Laius was a scandal that affronted even the gods, the poisoning of Emily Inglethorp at Styles is an event that is just barely sufficient to disrupt the tea and tennis routine. (pp. 40-2)

It is not the act of murder that casts a pall over this idyllic landscape. The pity of murder is that, as slugs ruin lettuce beds (something that would be unheard of at Styles, of course), murder spoils what was otherwise good. Styles St. Mary (or Jane Marple's identical St. Mary Mead) is not the world of high romance: it is the bucolic dream of England. . . .

The people in that landscape are as tautological as the landscape itself: an adjective or two are sufficient to call their identity to mind. There is "Miss Howard. She is an excellent specimen of well-balanced English beef and brawn. She is sanity itself." . . . The reader's store of familiar images conjures her out of seven words when he first encounters her: "A lady in a stout tweed skirt," . . . the moral qualities of stoutness combining with the British virtue of tweed to convey the instant vision of a hearty, hardy, and honest soul. Thereafter, Evelyn Howard turns into the manifest emblem of her inner nature: "She was a pleasant-looking woman of about forty, with a deep voice, almost manly in its stentorian tones, and had a large sensible square body, with feet to match—these encased in good thick boots." . . . Agelessness, together with an utter lack of gender or esthetic qualities, confer on her the quintessential merit visually attributed to John Bull. . . .

But once murder has been committed, the tautological evidence can no longer be trusted. . . . (p. 44)

[The] characters lay no claim to being people: they are dyspeptic evidence of a déjà vu. Out of such reminders of minor unpleasantness within the world, the detective story creates the temporary annoyance to which it reduces an otherwise all-enclosing mystery. (p. 46)

[In] 1920 Agatha Christie could still rely on her world and the responses of her people. The canniest person in *The Mysterious Affair at Styles* is neither the criminal (doomed to defeat within the expectations of the genre) nor, obviously, the singularly inept narrator, Hastings. But it is not Hercule Poirot either: it is Agatha Christie herself. She moves in a world she knows so well she can pretend not to be a part of it, counting on the reader's prejudice that associates him with her characters, while she herself avoids contamination. Her mode allows her to show the guilty and the innocent in what appears to be the same light by dissociating herself ostensibly from the convention on which she relies, while in reality she knows that she is casting suspicion on those who should not be suspect. (pp. 47-8)

The assurance of the detective's infallibility results in structural difficulties that are further evidence of the skillful dosing required by the genre. Too manifest an expectation of the detective's success will weaken fatally the delicate tension that must be maintained during the time of subtle unpleasantness that extends between the crime and its resolution. However infallible the detective (and, in the traditional genre, all are equally infallible), he cannot be so percipient as to reveal instantly the sham for what it is. In proportion as Poirot's foes were relatively easy to dispose of at the time of his first introduction to the world, Poirot himself was proportionally the more flawed. . . . Poirot has little to recommend him to us or to denizens of Styles

Court. From the first he is marred by the same imperfection as the other aliens—his conspicuous foreignness: nowhere is it more evident than in the fact that he is *short*. Even before he appears, he has been patronizingly dismissed by most of the Britishers in the cast.... Of course, this is meant to be a joke on [the doubters] ..., but it is a double-edged joke nevertheless; though it confirms Poirot in the end, it helps to blend him a little better with the "alien" quality of murder until the final and brief moment of his triumph. (p. 49)

The author was aware of the faintly ridiculous figure cut by Poirot when she baptized him. She named him after a vegetable—the leek (*poireau,* which also means a wart, in French)—to which she apposed the (barely) Christian name Hercule, in such a way that each name would cast ridicule on the other. Virtues that might have been British in someone of normal stature were undercut by Poirot's height—five feet four inches. (p. 50)

Such indignities were visited on Poirot by virtue of his birth; but in the parts of his personality over which he might have been expected to exercise some self-control, he showed a deplorable tendency to indulge his foreignness. His English was unaccountably Gallicized ..., with altogether too many exclamation marks, too much boastfulness ..., and an excess of continental posturing.... Even Poirot's single greatest asset—his brain—is ostentatiously displayed in a head exactly like an egg. But perhaps the most serious injury inflicted by Poirot's shameless exuberance is the extent of the overstatement into which he forces those who must describe him, starting with the hapless Hastings.

However, these imperfections notwithstanding, Poirot is not entirely dismissible, either. Part of the artificial surprise of the detective story is contained within the detective who triumphs, as he brings the action to a close, over even his own shortcomings.... Agatha Christie is faithful to her method in distancing herself from the aspersions cast at her detective. Not only is his intelligence the brighter for having to shine through his mannerisms, but he has been endowed by his maker with a saving grace of no mean consequence: Gallicized as he might be, Poirot is still not quite French. Rather, he is as Nordic as can possibly be someone using the French language—he is Belgian. (pp. 50-1)

Lastly, Poirot is conferred a kind of honorary citizenship in being awarded a sacrificial, native goat—Hastings—used for purposes of contrast and to ask Poirot questions, the withholding of whose answers is necessary for suspense within the story (very properly, the predetermined time during which disclosure of what was known all along is *suspended,* held up). Hastings is wholly functional: until the arrival of Poirot, that is to say, before the story can devolve from a dialectical process, Hastings is the sole reliance of the reader.... But once Poirot enters the scene, Hastings becomes no more than a bumbling foil.... Just as the unsatisfactory Watson is positioned between the reader and Sherlock Holmes, Hastings acts as the reader's intercessor to the intercessor—though he is manifestly the most obtuse of the characters. Presumed to be the spyglass through which the reader is able to "follow" Poirot, he in fact prevents the reader from seeing much. (pp. 51-2)

And so, the trivial unpleasantness that was contrived for the pleasure of ending it is brought to a close. A spoilsport old lady has been eliminated, foreigners (or those who act like them) have either been justly punished or made to disappear. Those who were only half-foreigners, but actually good, emerge as their better halves. The lovers are reunited, the upper-middle-class ritual is once again resumed. Law, order, and property are secure, and, in a universe that is forever threatening to escape from our rational grasp, a single little man with a maniacal penchant for neatness leaves us the gift of a tidy world, a closed book in which all questions have been answered.

The detective story treats the reader's expectations and prejudices with gentle solicitude. Alongside its disposable annoyances, the planetary triumphs of James Bond are unsettling: the evil he overcomes is of such magnitude that, even when undone, it leaves a menacing trace. We are left wondering whether the secret agent with license to kill is not, in his apotheosis, a reincarnation of what he has eliminated. In a novel by Ian Fleming, an anxiety caused by the awareness that such a tale could be told seeps through the closed covers within which that anxiety was meant to be contained. The anxiety we feel is, of course, more than its fiction intended, and its seepage is an accident. But that seepage makes the world that writes Bond into being much like ours: both are one. Agatha Christie's world, on the other hand, was never more than nostalgia and illusion. Her continued success suggests only that the illusion has not yet receded completely beyond our ken. (pp. 52)

David I. Grossvogel, "Agatha Christie: Containment of the Unknown," in his Mystery and Its Fictions: From Oedipus to Agatha Christie *(copyright © 1979 by The Johns Hopkins University Press), The Johns Hopkins University Press, 1979, pp. 39-52.*

Mavis Thorpe Clark

1912?-

(Has also written under pseudonym of Mavis Latham) Australian young adult novelist, adult biographer and short story writer, and scriptwriter for children's radio programs. Either the outback, the virgin forests of Victoria, the opal mines, the islands off Tasmania, or some other well-researched Australian setting is the background for each of Clark's teenage novels. Her gift for atmosphere combined with strong plot development makes her books extremely popular in her native Australia, where she has won several awards, most notably the 1967 Children's Book of the Year award for *The Min-Min*. This novel, which most critics consider to be her best, brought Clark to the attention of British and American young adult readership. Most of her subsequent books have been published in Great Britain and America as well as Australia. Her novels tend to be concerned with social issues, to the detriment of her characters and plot, some critics contend. (See also *Contemporary Authors*, Vols. 57-60, and *Something about the Author*, Vol. 8.)

Reg in *The Min-min* is a young tough whom neither father nor schoolmaster can control. His sister Sylvie is beginning to look beyond the cramped, uneasy life her family leads in the settlers' camp on the Australian railroad, and when Reg is finally threatened with "an institution" they leave home to cross the desert to the home of the Tucker family. The descriptive matter has all the attractive menace of the Australian landscape, yet the actual flight of the children is less gripping than one expects. The min-min, the will o' the wisp light in the desert, is an inconstant symbol in every way. . . . The inevitable resolution is not shirked, however. Sylvie returns to look after the family, Reg faces the institution with increased self-control. (p. 454)

> The Times Literary Supplement (© *Times Newspapers Ltd. (London) 1967; reproduced from* The Times Literary Supplement *by permission), May 25, 1967.*

In Britain it is hard to imagine a land where it hardly ever rains, where the sun blazes down day after day, and where it is possible to go for miles without seeing any sign of life or habitation. Mavis Thorpe Clark has chosen this setting for [*The Min-Min*] and made it possible to realise that such conditions do exist. Her characters are real people, so that along with them one can feel the heat and the thirst and wonder if one will die a lingering death out in the Australian desert. . . . Children of all ages will appreciate this story because it will mirror their own lives, to a certain extent, and yet give them a glimpse into a completely different way of life at the same time. (p. 179)

> The Junior Bookshelf, *June, 1967.*

Blue Above the Trees is a brilliantly fresh example [of pioneer literature]. In the 1870s the Whitburns have come from Devon to cultivate 600 acres of infinitely ancient forest in Victoria, Australia. . . .

[There are family tensions enough] to keep any story going, and the author makes the most of them: very subtly, too, for the way of life of the family of lyrebirds that Simon observes year after year is ironically but unobtrusively contrasted with the dissatisfactions and strains within the human family. All is well in the end, but not until after real excitements—of achievement or setback. The story gives one a haunting familiarity with the forest, the paths through it, the growing areas of cultivation. (p. 583)

> The Times Literary Supplement (© *Times Newspapers Ltd. (London) 1968; reproduced from* The Times Literary Supplement *by permission), June 6, 1968.*

The plot [of *Blue Above the Trees*] is gripping, the characterization strong and the background authentic. The Whitburn family come out from England in the middle of the nineteenth century to retrieve their fortunes in the great virgin forest of Victoria. . . . The blue above the trees of the title is symbolic of the clearing of the vast forest and also one feels of the clearing of their way of life. In the raw, problems are stripped to their basic conceptions. The period is a part of the development of the Commonwealth that we in Britain know very little about and this book will be a good introduction for teenage readers, both boys and girls. The descriptions of life in early cabins, both domestic and social, are interesting and those of the primitive jungle are magnificent, one can almost smell it. Thirteen to fifteen year olds will be fascinated by it and in a strange way will possibly identify themselves, subconsciously, with their Whitburn contemporaries in their struggle for freedom, parental and otherwise. (pp. 235-36)

> The Junior Bookshelf, *August, 1968.*

JANE MANTHORNE

With powerfully simple understatement Mavis Clark paints [in "*The Min-Min*"] the harsh land down under and the people and wild things which survive there. Her strong, terse prose is reminiscent of Mary Patchett's "Cry of the Heart" and evokes tears. Her images are pragmatic and original: the rising moon looks like the "round full yoke of a yellow egg," and an approaching train sounds like "wind in the earth's stomach." (p. 26)

> Jane Manthorne, in The New York Times Book Review (© 1970 by The New York Times Company; reprinted by permission), January 25, 1970.

MARGERY FISHER

The interplay of action and character in *Spark of opal* marks this as a book which has something to say to the 'teens; boys and girls may recognise problems of their own in its pages, even if it is unlikely that many of them will find themselves in exactly comparable situations. . . . With the thrills of opal-mining to dominate the plot, the growing pains of the young people and their friends provide a second theme of absorbing interest. . . . The author makes her points forcibly in the context of a community with its own customs and prejudices, and the background of the story is as fascinating as its events. (p. 1709)

> Margery Fisher, in her Growing Point, April, 1971.

Mavis Clark explores [in *Spark of Opal*] several sets of relationships skilfully—within the Watson family, between the aborigines and the settlers, between the various groups of opal-mad miners. The conflicts, friendships and enmities are deftly traced and interwoven, and the unusual, lonely setting gives a lively impression of pioneer days and ways with modern trimmings. (p. 240)

> The Junior Bookshelf, August, 1971.

[*Iron Mountain* is a] successor to *The Min-Min* (1969) which doesn't sag under the virtues of the first book and again surfaces with a firmly realistic contemporary story of the land down under where, in the far West, there are new worlds as well as selves to conquer. . . . The story is authoritatively framed and in itself has lots of grit and go-ahead momentum. (p. 1020)

> Kirkus Reviews (copyright © 1971 The Kirkus Service, Inc.), September 15, 1971.

VIRGINIA HAVILAND

Joey, a troubled boy on probation for reckless driving in Melbourne, leaves his cheerless home and is fortunate in hitching a two-thousand-mile ride to a mining community in western Australia [in *Iron Mountain*]. . . . Joey's unsuccessful attempt to hide his past, and the problems of the individuals in Leah's family fill an engrossing, well-told story. The exaggerated geographical conditions heighten tensions; and the hot, dust-filled iron-mining country, where workers receive hardship bonuses and air-conditioned company houses, even becomes a protagonist. One can easily envision the mining operations, the dangers of the trackless mountain terrain and the cyclones, and Joey's and Woodie's follies. Joey, who could become excited because of the impressiveness and the beauty of the mountain colors, makes a strong central figure; and his decisions from first to last are convincing. (p. 561)

> Virginia Haviland, in The Horn Book Magazine (copyright © 1972 by The Horn Book, Inc., Boston), February, 1972.

[*Iron Mountain*, an Australian novel,] has a sense of purpose, of didacticism even, which belongs to a developing art; this country's freedom from it is perhaps a sign of incipient decadence. *Iron Mountain*, for all its contemporary technology, is a moral tale and a remarkably good one. The action becomes suspended from time to time while the actors listen to a lecture on geology or metallurgy. None of the information is gratuitous, for everyone in the story is caught up in some way with the adventure of Tom Price Mine and the terrible, beautiful deserts of Western Australia.

The mine and the mountain help Joey to discover himself. . . . The mountains, too, strengthen his resolve to abandon new-found security and friendship to face his past. The awkward, confused product of the slums has something in common with Leah, eldest and most beautiful of the Rose family, with whom he throws in his lot. . . . The reader scents romance, but there are no easy solutions to the dilemmas of this tough, honest, rather slow-moving tale. (p. 803)

> The Times Literary Supplement (© Times Newspapers Ltd. (London) 1972; reproduced from The Times Literary Supplement by permission), July 14, 1972.

[*Iron Mountain*] is aptly named, for the iron ore mountain in Western Australia plays the leading role; to it come a family from the east, together with a lad from a city slum whom they have picked up on the way. On this new western frontier everything is biggest and best, and [Mavis Thorpe Clark] is full of enthusiasm for the whole set-up notwithstanding dust and flies, and in her eagerness to involve the reader she is far too prone to slip in lumps of undigested information about mines and mining with its brash new towns springing up in what was hitherto desert. The reader from an older civilisation is likely, however, to have doubts for the future of the miners when he reads of company stores, company houses and other symptoms of an out-of-date paternalism. This sort of thing will not worry the young reader as long as the book is readable, which it undoubtedly is, and it seems to give a very fair likeness of life in such a town at the present day. But the older reader may also question the advisability of making the chief human character a boy on the run from the police who seems likely to get away with breaking his parole and even to benefit from it. (p. 241)

> The Junior Bookshelf, August, 1972.

C.E.J. SMITH

Mavis Thorpe Clark evokes her locale and creates her characters [in *Iron Mountain*] with the same expertise she showed in *Spark of Opal* and *Blue Above the Trees*. While one is concerned about Woodie Rose's escapade on the loading wharf at Dampier, or with Amanda Rose's getting lost in the bush, one does not realise how much technical and topographical detail the author is using to sustain her narrative. (p. 113)

> C.E.J. Smith, in Children's Book Review (© 1972 by Five Owls Press Ltd.; all rights reserved), September, 1972.

The rough, desolate ambience of an isolated Australian mining town is [*Spark of Opal's*] only distinguishing feature, though Liz' attitudes toward the aborigine children she befriends . . . are sometimes as paternalistic as they are altruistic. The opposition between the visionary, adventurous menfolk and the cautious, guilty women . . . is infuriatingly banal typecasting, but the unusual locale and background on opal mining methods should hold most readers' attention. (p. 1432)

> *Kirkus Reviews (copyright © 1972 The Kirkus Service, Inc.), December 15, 1972.*

KARIN K. BRICKER

Opal mining provides an interesting and well-integrated background [for *Spark of Opal*]: however, most of the characters show only minimal development and the plot unfolds through exposition rather than action. (p. 73)

> *Karin K. Bricker, in* School Library Journal *(reprinted from the April, 1973 issue of* School Library Journal, *published by R. R. Bowker Co. A Xerox Corporation; copyright © 1973), April, 1973.*

The wildfire that periodically ravages Victoria, Australia is the villain and chief protagonist [in *Wildfire*], and ranged against it are the Mob, a predictably varied lot of local children who find themselves trapped together in an old wooden cabin behind the fire lines. . . . [Events] are vivid enough to rivet the attention of the most blase bystanders. In contrast, the children's reactions are pretty much straight out of their leader Bill's volunteer Book of Operations and the final discovery that the fire was started—not by gentle, absent-minded Steven—but by churlish farmer Brown cuts the fragile threads of human guilt and irony that held the Mob to the fire as more than casual victims. Plenty of large-scale danger and excitement, but not the equal of [Ivan] Southall's very similar *Ash Road*. (pp. 633-34)

> *Kirkus Reviews (copyright © 1974 The Kirkus Service, Inc.), June 15, 1974.*

MARGERY FISHER

In *Wildfire* there is a deliberate, vital contrast between two boys of fourteen. . . . [Their] hostility to one another becomes serious when a runaway bushfire threatens the district. The subject of bushfires may be common enough in stories from Australia, but this one commands attention for the vivacity and force of the author's descriptions and narrative technique, and above all for her manipulation of her characters. (p. 2428)

> *Margery Fisher, in her* Growing Point, *July, 1974.*

VIRGINIA HAVILAND

The first third of [*Wildfire*], in which many characters are introduced, moves with a relatively slow pace; but the narrative turns suddenly to descriptions of the frenzied onrush of wind, smoke, and flame as wildfire erupts. As brilliantly graphic as the succession of fire scenes is the quiet aftermath, when, with rain falling, the forest is seen "burned into stillness." Central to the story are four individualized teenagers and an eight-year-old. . . . When the holocaust is over, each of them is a different person. . . . (p. 140)

> *Virginia Haviland, in* The Horn Book Magazine *(copyright © 1974 by The Horn Book, Inc., Boston), October, 1974.*

[Mavis Thorpe Clark's account in *Wildfire*] of the ravages of forest fire in Victoria . . . would have been exciting enough as a documentary. The fact that she has moulded it into a shapely piece of fiction with controlled inter-connections of plot and personality has naturally intensified the elements of suspense and disaster which must be present year after year in this part of the world, and on which she bases the urgency of action and survival techniques. . . . [The author] adds a confident handling of events and dialogue, the result of long practice and first-hand experience of her native environment and of more remote areas where man is so much at the mercy of nature and his own carelessness or indifference to the safety of others. In "the Mob", consisting of Bill, Jan, Pete, Steve and Shane, not always co-existing in perfect harmony, we have a band of convincing characters sufficiently varied to strike the necessary sparks from human relationships as well as to carry out the exploits which are illustrative of the theme. (p. 291)

> The Junior Bookshelf, *October, 1974.*

Even if the structure and plot of *The Sky is Free* were less effective, Mavis Clark's picture of an opal mining town and its Australian environment almost deserves the epithet "devastating". Her gift for atmosphere is enough to make one feel breathing is difficult and it is dangerous to touch any sheet metal, and food does not get a chance to melt in your mouth. She plants within this climatic maelstrom the runaways, Sam and Tony, and sets them to work while a charge of burglary hangs over their uncertain heads. There is a harmless element of girl-interest which both helps to soften the work-obsessive atmosphere and establishes contact with a more normal world. Both boys achieve regeneration of a kind. Above all, they decide to give home another try. *The Sky is Free* is altogether well composed. (p. 262)

> The Junior Bookshelf, *August, 1975.*

ROBERT UNSWORTH

Although the evocation of the dreariness of the strip-mined land is well done, the lore of the Chinese immigrants who worked the mines interesting, and the description of the near disaster in the tunnel excellent, there are problems [in *If the Earth Falls In*]. The opening chapters, abounding with characters and characterization, are slow going; Louise [the 15-year-old protagonist] is unusually introspective for her young years; and many readers will be stumped by the Australian jargon . . . for which there is no glossary. This is an intelligent novel; however, there are too few tenacious readers who will see it through to its exciting finish. (p. 50)

> *Robert Unsworth, in* School Library Journal *(reprinted from the February, 1976 issue of* School Library Journal, *published by R. R. Bowker Co. A Xerox Corporation; copyright © 1976), February, 1976.*

VIRGINIA HAVILAND

[The tactics used by three young people to escape from a caved-in mine shaft], described in graphic detail, advance [*If the Earth Falls In*] with increasing pace and make the three characters intensely alive for the reader. Subsidiary to this action, but important to Louise's resolution, is the disposition of a valuable painting on glass. . . . The combination of smoothly interwoven elements makes for engrossing reading. (p. 161)

Virginia Haviland, in The Horn Book Magazine (copyright © 1976 by the Horn Book, Inc., Boston), April, 1976.

REBECCA J. LUKENS

Although complexity and variety in themes may be one of the strongest proofs of [a] work's excellence, most literature for children seems to center upon a *primary theme*. When a story contains a variety of themes, they are often linked. The central idea, for example, of young people trying to find the best direction for their lives is explored in Mavis Thorpe Clark's *Spark of Opal*, a story set in the opal mines of Australia. The young people work the opal mine with inadequate equipment: Youth proves itself by daring to do adult jobs. Liz Watson nearly decides to fail so the family need not move to a school town: One can be torn between love of family and need to develop one's self. Liz and her mother are weary of waiting for a lucky opal strike: Yearning for an ordered life can disrupt the lives of others. Four dissimilar young people chart different courses for themselves: Each of us has different skills with which to serve. These multiple themes are related and support the central or main theme. (p. 84)

Rebecca J. Lukens, in her A Critical Handbook of Children's Literature (copyright © 1976 by Scott, Foresman and Company), Scott, Foresman, 1976.

ZENA SUTHERLAND

[There is an unexpectedly touching ending to *The Sky Is Free*,] a story that reflects the flinty, harsh life of the opal mining country. Characterization, dialogue, and setting are of equally high quality. (p. 73)

Zena Sutherland, in Bulletin of the Center for Children's Books (© 1977 by the University of Chicago; all rights reserved), January, 1977.

[*The Hundred Islands*] takes place on an island off Australia where Greg, Jenny, and Darryl have grown up together and where Greg, dead serious about the island's ecology, now confronts his hard-working sheep farmer father, who thinks feeding people is more important than saving wildlife. Greg is willing to help Dad on the farm if it's run his way (no poison, a vermin-proof fence), but when Dad sticks to *his* terms Greg leaves home. . . . The problem though is not that Greg, like many his age, thinks in self-righteous black and white, but that Clark's presentation of the issues and actors is just as heavyhanded. (p. 672)

Kirkus Reviews (copyright © 1977 The Kirkus Service, Inc.), July 1, 1977.

Set among the hundred islands in the Bass Strait off Tasmania, this story is centred on two teenagers, Greg and Jenny, and their deeply-felt concern for the islands' wildlife. *The Hundred Islands* is a sensitive and poignant novel, with an important message about conservation and the future. Mavis Thorpe Clark creates a vivid atmosphere and a sense of isolation and beauty in her descriptions of the islands and the birds and animals. The relationship between Greg and Jenny is developed carefully and convincingly, although it never dominates the story completely it is the means by which we are given hope for the future. (p. 232)

The Junior Bookshelf, August, 1977.

SUSAN SPRAGUE

The author's concern about endangered Australian wildlife certainly comes across [in *The Hundred Islands*]: however, the pages and pages describing birds' migrating, mating, and behavior patterns swamp this story of a young man's struggle to go to college. . . . Some of the characters are overdone and don't ring true—Jenny's too dedicated to her cause, Greg's mother is so timid she feigns a toothache to get out of the house—and the plot with its plethora of puzzling words (not defined in context) is forced and melodramatic. (p. 123)

Susan Sprague, in School Library Journal (reprinted from the September, 1977 issue of School Library Journal, published by R. R. Bowker Co. A Xerox Corporation; copyright © 1977), September, 1977.

MARGERY FISHER

The fairy-tale rags-to-riches plot [of *Pony from Tarella*] will be redeemed for some readers, though not for all, by the precise topography and agreeable open-air atmosphere of this Australian story. (p. 3190)

Margery Fisher, in her Growing Point, October, 1977.

Robert Cormier

1925-

American novelist, short story writer, editor, and journalist. Rather than the explorations of interpersonal relationships favored by many young adult novelists, Cormier deals with the outside forces that test the individual and often maliciously oppose him. His themes are powerful and not often considered in young adult fiction: betrayal, vulnerability, guilt, paranoia, fear, and psychosis. His protagonists enter or are forced into situations which place them in direct opposition to powerful adversaries, both identified and faceless. Without any help or support, these characters all come to the realization, as does Adam in *I Am the Cheese*, that in order to survive they must learn to stand alone. Many of Cormier's topics and subjects stem from personal experience, much of it gained during his career as a newspaper reporter and human interest columnist. For instance, the models for Gracie of *A Little Raw on Monday Mornings* and Tommy Battin of *Take Me Where the Good Times Are* were interviewed by Cormier while on assignment. His father's death from cancer was the stimulus for *Now and at the Hour,* and his son's refusal to sell candy for his high school served as the background for *The Chocolate War,* Cormier's first book for young adults. Since *The Chocolate War,* Cormier has written exclusively for young adults. His novels are written with an emphasis on dialogue, which he uses rather than narrative description to develop his characters. The novels are extremely fast-moving and establish personality and situation in short, quick strokes. Cormier has been criticized for the bleak, depressing endings of his books and has been accused of pessimism by some critics. Although the vision in his novels acknowledges the darker side of life, Cormier's attitude seems to be one of awareness of evil rather than agreement with it. Without moralizing, Cormier's novels stress the importance of self-reliance and self-respect. His combination of realism, sensitivity, and originality has made him popular with both readers and critics, and has moved him to the forefront of recent young adult novelists. (See also *Contemporary Authors,* Vols. 1-4, rev. ed., and *Something about the Author,* Vol. 10.)

PHOEBE ADAMS

[*Now and at the Hour*] has the ring of personal experience, which the setting, a New England factory town, and the social level, that of skilled labor just below the promotable-to-management level, unobtrusively reinforce. It is not likely that a writer who did not know this particular kind of world at first hand could present it so casually or with such conviction. Mr. Cormier does not give much attention to his background, for his interest runs in another direction, but every detail that he provides is right. . . .

It is quite a task to make an interesting hero of a man who has done no great deeds, committed no crimes, suffered no psychological upheavals, never been painfully poor or even mildly rich, and who has in the course of the book nothing to do but think, an activity which he carries on at a quite uncomplicated level and without a trace of imagination. Mr. Cormier not only succeeds in making Alph interesting, he creates considerable suspense with the question of how long the man can keep up his pretense of ignorance. There are moments when Alph seems in danger of becoming too good to be true, but the author always manages to avoid the saccharine and the sentimental, and ends by creating a touching picture of a man who is not nearly as ordinary as he himself thinks.

Phoebe Adams, "Heroism Unsung," in The Atlantic Monthly *(copyright © 1960 by The Atlantic Monthly Company, Boston, Mass.; reprinted with permission), September, 1960, p. 118.*

RILEY HUGHES

[In *Now and at the Hour*] Alph Le Blanc, an ordinary, family man who is a factory worker, lies in bed during (what he fears and cannot at first accept) the last weeks of his life. . . . In the narrowing circumference of his days he comes to know pain, the glimpse of forsythia and visits from falsely cheerful friends and family.

He has the force of his faith behind him as he comes quietly to realize the power of an uneventful but good life. . . .

Now and at the Hour is, surprisingly (considering the author's control and incisiveness), a first novel. In spite of its subject, it is anything but repellant, for Alph's humanity and his courage—and not his illness—are its center. This is writing and perceiving of a rare fineness and distinction. I recommend this poignant book with the greatest earnestness and pleasure. Reading it has been an exciting and rewarding experience. (p. 182)

Riley Hughes, in Catholic World *(copyright 1960 by The Missionary Society of St. Paul the Apostle in the State of New York), December, 1960.*

WILLIAM B. HILL, S.J.

The most engaging feature of [*A Little Raw on Monday*

Mornings] is its wonderfully honest realism. It is so plain at times that it is tiring; the reality is obvious, familiar, and occasionally a bit flat. At its best, however, the story is bright and appealing; and at its very infrequent worst, it still has the merit of a rare sort of artistic integrity. . . .

There may be a touch of unreal coincidence in the circumstances leading to Gracie's pregnancy; and there is too much of the type, too little of the individual in the character of Terry, Gracie's fellow worker and confidante. Otherwise there is an abundance of real artistry in this clear, sometimes inevitably depressing account of a poor, stumbling woman caught in a sorry situation. The stuff of tragedy is not here—Gracie is much too pathetic to be tragic; but there is plenty of human sympathy expressed in and demanded by this living story about one of the sorry little faceless people who inhabit the ugly and nameless buildings in our drab streets. There is no tremendous relief at the book's end, no purging of pity and fear, but there does arise some wonder at heroism's many unsuspected dwelling places.

The author is a trifle awkward in a few very brief passages dealing with the actualities of sex; the interludes are embarrassing because Mr. Cormier seems to be trying to prove that he and his markedly Catholic publishers are as sophisticated as the next person. (p. 222)

William B. Hill, S.J., in Best Sellers *(copyright 1963, by the University of Scranton), October 1, 1963.*

MARTIN LEVIN

[In "Take Me Where the Good Times Are"] an oldster named Tommy Bartin has a brief but violent furlough from the Monument City Infirmary, so called because "nobody is supposed to say 'poorhouse' anymore." . . . Mr. Cormier depicts his inevitably disastrous odyssey with an admirable lack of hokum, bypassing the easy sentimentality that this drab El Dorado invites. . . . It is a pleasure to add that the sum total of [Bartin's] failures to recapture his identity in Mr. Cormier's refreshing little history inspires respect rather than pity. (p. 43)

Martin Levin, in The New York Times Book Review *(© 1965 by The New York Times Company; reprinted by permission), April 25, 1965.*

HAROLD C. GARDINER

To chronicle the small pleasures, the larger troubles and the rare triumphs of the somewhat seedy poor in such a way as to make the characters interesting and even strangely attractive is no small achievement. Mr. Cormier is apparently fully launched on a career of detailing the annals of the poor, and his special cachet is that he manages this intractable material without sentimentality, without crying out at the culpability of society (that convenient scapegoat of the sociologically-minded novelist), and even with a deep respect for the human dignity of his people. He did this quite impressively in his earlier *A Little Raw on Monday Mornings,* and if [*Take Me Where the Good Times Are*] is not quite as impressive, it still deserves a thoughtful reading. . . .

This is a good, sound, if unspectacular book. It is deceptively simple. And it rings true. Mr. Cormier has staked out a field that he plows very well indeed, and with each succeeding book he has plowed deeper into some of the fundamental realities of life. (p. 717)

Harold C. Gardiner, in America *(© America Press, 1965; all rights reserved), May 15, 1965.*

MICHELE MURRAY

Few literary tricks can be more annoying to a reader—to this reader, at least—than to find the author pleading for sympathy for a character when that character is clearly dreadful, hopeless, impossible to cherish. Think of the legions of virginal young damsels who bloom in the lush gardens of 19th-century English fiction. How our feelings are played upon! How we are hectored to love them! . . .

Whatever else has happened to fiction these past fifty years, we can be grateful for the passing of the Sweet Young Thing. But the same kind of novelistic sleight-of-hand is still going on, with the same unhappy effect: witness [Saul Bellow's] *Herzog* and, much lower down the same ladder, *Take Me Where the Good Times Are.*

In Robert Cormier's book, it is an old man, poor and alone —the 20th-century equivalent of the Young Girl apparently will be the Senior Citizen. . . .

Alas, alas, Mr. Cormier has chosen to tell this story in the first person, thus making the unpleasant character of Tommy Bartin even more unpleasant, for the reader loses any reliable guide as to whether he is to take Tommy straight (as Tommy takes himself) or to read between the lines for the author's subtle indicators that Tommy is not to be trusted. Given the love for irony of so much modern fiction, the inclination would be to jazz up the book by picking the second alternative, but judging by this book itself, I'd say that we are meant to take Tommy straight, and that is too bad.

For Tommy in action is a selfish old man, innocent of intelligence or experience for all his seventy years, weak on judgment and long on talk. He spends most of his big day in bars, drinking and getting drunk, behaving foolishly; at the end, when he gets involved with some young motorcycle toughs who have given the retarded girl a ride to a motorcycle rally (but done nothing more), misjudges them completely, is rolled, then smuggled beneath the tarpaulin of the statue which is to be dedicated the next day in the town square, so that he is revealed as the statue is unveiled, one is neither sorry for Tommy nor amused, merely disgusted.

The book has a little of everything, with the search for Annie and the motorcycle boys providing the thread of plot: a bit of nostalgia, some mild humor, characters, suicide, very pure and distant sex, some gentle grotesques. Nevertheless, the book is not pleasant, the character of Tommy Bartin is not pleasant, and the author is playing a con game with our sympathies. The book jacket calls Tommy Bartin a good man but one must disagree. He is not good, only innocent, which is not at all the same thing. (p. 477)

Michele Murray, in Commonweal *(copyright © 1965 Commonweal Publishing Co., Inc.; reprinted by permission of Commonweal Publishing Co., Inc.), July 2, 1965.*

THEODORE WEESNER

["The Chocolate War"], written for teen-agers but a strong read for adults, is a story with a highly serious message not only about the usurpation and misuse of power but about power's inevitable staying. "The Chocolate War" is masterfully structured and rich in theme; the action is well crafted, well timed, suspenseful; complex ideas develop and unfold with clarity. The novel may be faulted only for its general short-changing of character. The characters are quick studies, recognizable at a glance, two-dimensional.

The stuff of this novel is serious . . . and although a mushy, carameled battle is expected, and although humorous scenes do precede the novel's denouement, an easy out does not occur. Rather, like most rebellions, the action here is turned rather quickly, and there with a disturbing impact is the point, the message of the story and the conclusion of the novel.

''The Chocolate War,'' presenting as it does a philosophical plateau between childhood and adulthood, seems an ideal study for the high school classroom. The characters, although not deeply drawn, are accurate and touch close enough to raise questions of identification, questions of one's location within an arena of power, and also provide some hard recognition of the functions of power within a society. A scene, frightening in its overtones, shows Brother Leon persuading a classroom that its star pupil is in fact a cheat and a liar. Of course the boy is neither—the character assassination is merely one of Brother Leon's odd teaching devices—but the class is swayed and a message in extention of the larger theme is delivered. When the story ends, one wishes only that one had known the characters better, to better understand their responses to the importance of the message. (p. 15)

> Theodore Weesner, in The New York Times Book Review (© 1974 by the New York Times Company; reprinted by permission), May 5, 1974.

RICHARD PECK

The big book of this YA autumn is clearly—and justifiably —Robert Cormier's *The Chocolate War*. . . . Too many young adult novels only promise an outspoken revelation of the relevant. *The Chocolate War* delivers the goods.

The goods in the story are 20,000 boxes of chocolates that a depraved teaching brother means for the students of a tottering parochial school to sell. Sweet charity is the mask for Brother Leon's sharp and shady fund-raising. Since nothing is petty to the institutionalized, the chocolate sale consumes the school.

The plot paces to a cataclysmic conclusion. The young will understand the outcome. They won't like it, but they'll understand.

The Chocolate War is surely the most uncompromising novel ever directed to the ''12 and up reader''—and very likely the most necessary. It depicts the mass psychology behind the looming menace of the gangs that have never been more omnipotent than now. In his moneymaking venture, Brother Leon enlists the aid of Trinity School's invisible empire, a club of middle-class thugs who deal in mental —and ultimately physical—torture.

Significantly, we never learn the family backgrounds of the gang leaders. The author, who is free of the fatal susceptibilities of a guidance counselor, judges them unforgivingly on the evidence of their corruption. The measure of Brother Leon's own depravity is plumbed when he explains away the gang's excesses: ''Oh, once in a while they get carried away but it's good to see all that energy and zeal and enthusiasm.'' . . .

[The gangs'] victim—and the reader's surrogate—is Jerry Renault. He is a boy who says no to the gang's demands repeatedly, and finally once too often. The values of our time being what they are, we are probably only at the beginning of a Literature of the Victim. Jerry is a notable example, for he is no quiet recipient of his fate. He resists to his limits. And anyone looking for a pat triumph of the individual had better avert his eyes.

In his *New York Times* review [see excerpt above], Theodore Weesner recommends *The Chocolate War* as ''an ideal study for the high school classroom.'' It's ideal too for a teacher-training program. And anyone banning this book for its locker-room-realistic language is committing a crime against the young. (p. 492)

> Richard Peck, in American Libraries (reprinted by permission of the American Library Association; copyright 1974 by the American Library Association), October, 1974.

[The Chocolate War] is a thoroughly nasty book about a thoroughly nasty American private school. The characters have that dedication to corruption which seems to flourish in small closed societies presided over by an evil mind. . . . Watergate is the next step.

This may be a brilliantly written tour de force but despite the publisher's claim it is no more a children's book than is *The Exorcist*. The forces of good and evil are better balanced in *The Lord of the Flies* and the cruelty of *Portrait of an Artist as a Young Man* is compensated by the presence of a lyricism of awakening adolescence. *The Chocolate War* depicts a life without hope in which boys prey upon each other like prohibition gangsters, masturbate in the lavatory and drool over girlie magazines. It presents in one neat package all the most repellent aspects of the American way of life. Here in embryo are the forces of commercialism, of corruption, of sadism and the triumph of the beast. If you are an adult and an American it may shock you out of your complacency but English children will at the best be confused and at the worst enjoy it as a sadistic spectacle.

There is no place on the shelves of a children's library for such a delight in the destruction of innocence. (pp. 194-95)

> The Junior Bookshelf, *June, 1975.*

MARGERY FISHER

The Chocolate War, a brutal, forthright study in violence, ends in doubt—one might say, in an inglorious draw. Presumably the author was not evading an ending but honestly intended to suggest that no decision between Good and Evil was really possible. Extreme as his picture is, it can only too readily be believed. . . . Brother Leon's actions, seem entirely from the point of view of his pupils, are never truly motivated; he is, ultimately, a Bogyman, an embodiment of Evil who is, perhaps, only temporarily halted in his course. This is not a book for the squeamish and it contains a note of cynicism which might perhaps have been less obvious if the character of Brother Leon had been developed in depth, as the story seems to demand that it should be. (pp. 2657-58)

> Margery Fisher, in her Growing Point, *July, 1975.*

PELORUS

[The Chocolate War] will surely be one of those books that

sweep through teenage readers with the fervent interest that *Catcher in the Rye* roused in its day. . . .

I've . . . spoken to adult readers whom it worries. . . . Their charge against it has nothing to do with the book's compulsion. On the contrary. They say it is *too* attractive, too compelling, too persuasive. They say that such a hopeless ending—hopeless, not (colloquially) unsuccessful—should not be presented to young people.

But to say that is to argue that books form ideas and behaviour according to the conclusions of their stories. In other words a novel's happy ending helps towards happy endings for people. Christian novelists make Christian readers. And I doubt that anyone actually holds such a literary philosophy to be true.

Robert Cormier obviously doesn't believe it. He dedicates the book to his son: which indicates that he's understood entirely what literature is about. It presents an image for us to contemplate. It says—in the case of his book—let's follow to their logical conclusion certain facets of society as you and I see them (remembering that *The Chocolate War* was written during the Watergate/Nixon debacle) and let's take that image to *its* logical conclusion and see what happens.

The idea is to ask the question, Do you want a world like this? The answer has to be, No. In which case I would argue, and I fancy Cormier would too, that the real point of his book is to cause young readers to see the result of certain kinds of human behaviour and to opt not for the hopeless end that the logically worked-out image presents, but for just the opposite.

It seems to me that too many children's book "professionals"—commentators, teachers, librarians, even writers—still work on the assumption that literature makes people better only so long as the books themselves show a life, however unreal, which is the "better" they want children and young people to be.

However, whether they like it or not—and I like it—*The Chocolate War* is well on its way to becoming one of those books every young person will have to read. (p. 146)

Pelorus, in Signal *(copyright © 1975 Pelorus; reprinted by permission of the author and The Thimble Press, Lockwood Station Road, South Woodchester, Glos. GL5 5EQ, England), September, 1975.*

NEWGATE CALLENDAR

Cormier has written a novel of psychological suspense [in "I Am the Cheese"]. He is a fine technician and this is an absorbing, even a brilliant job. The book is assembled in mosaic fashion: a tiny chip here, a chip there, and suddenly the outline of a face dimly begins to take shape. Everything is related to something else; everything builds and builds to a fearsome climax. At the end the boy discovers that he is indeed the cheese—the bait around which the rats gather. Little can he do about it, except react the way God and Freud have provided. The ending is grim indeed.

It is not that "I Am the Cheese" is in any way sensational, sadistic or anything like that. Cormier merely has the knack of making horror out of the ordinary, as the masters of suspense writing know how to do. The story moves along quietly enough. The bicycling adventures of the boy are the

kind of adventures anybody today could experience. Where the tension enters is in the mind of the boy, who (as it turns out) is faced with a situation with which no child should have to cope.

The book is written in a highly sophisticated style, and the plotting and literary workmanship will delight the connoisseur. But, one wonders, will the style and, indeed, some of the actual content be above the heads of most teen-agers? It may be, however, that kids are more sophisticated today and that nothing much comes as a surprise to them.

Newgate Callendar, "Boy on the Couch," in The New York Times Book Review *(© 1977 by The New York Times Company; reprinted by permission), May 1, 1977, p. 15.*

PAUL HEINS

[*I Am the Cheese*], a magnificent accomplishment, begins innocuously with a first-person narrative: "I am riding the bicycle and I am on Route 31 in Monument, Massachusetts, on my way to Ruttersburg, Vermont, and I'm pedaling furiously because this is an old-fashioned bike. . . ." The reader, however, is suddenly jolted by a shift in point of view: the appearance of the official-looking transcript of a taped dialogue between the protagonist of the story and Brint, a mysterious interlocutor. The dialogue, in turn, is interspersed with an account of the events as related by an omniscient third-person narrator. Skillfully, an intertwining pattern for the whole book is created, rhythmically alternating the three devices; but much more than a brilliant technical tour de force is achieved. These devices, as expertly as they are used, build the necessary dynamic structure to encompass the onward-pacing story full of tension, mysteries, and secrets—the disclosure of the fate of a young protagonist whose life is inextricably entangled in a series of thorny predicaments. (p. 427)

As in *The Chocolate War*, Mr. Cormier is actually writing about human integrity; and in the course of doing so, he cogently uncovers the lacerations that evil often inflicts upon the innocent. . . . Truly a novel in the tragic mode, cunningly wrought, shattering in its emotional implications. (p. 428)

Paul Heins, in The Horn Book Magazine *(copyright © 1977 by the Horn Book, Inc., Boston), August, 1977.*

LANCE SALWAY

For [*I am the Cheese*] Robert Cormier has returned to the theme which dominated his outstanding earlier book, *The Chocolate War*: that of innocence and morality destroyed by the ruthless ambition of the masters of a corrupt society. In *The Chocolate War*, this society was a private school, and the victim a boy who alone stood out against corruption. Now, in *I am the Cheese,* Robert Cormier has extended this dark theme. The hero is an unwilling, uncomprehending and truly innocent victim of a greater, more hideous conspiracy; the corrupt society is our own, and the innocent victim must be completely destroyed in order to sustain it.

At first sight, the narrative construction of the novel seems difficult and pretentious. . . . As the novel nears its end, the point and meaning of the book's construction become plain, and the narrative strands combine in a climax of depressing violence and a conclusion of almost intolerable despair. . . .

I am the Cheese is, first and foremost, a novel of suspense through which the reader is lured by the excitement and tension of the story. But the book is more than just a good thriller: Robert Cormier has written a chilling study of a mind on the verge of disintegration, and presented us with a view of our society that is too dire to contemplate. Robert Cormier does not hesitate to challenge and disturb his readers and although *I am the Cheese* is no book for the emotionally squeamish, it deserves to be widely read. Beside it, most books for the young seem as insubstantial as candyfloss. (p. 1415)

> *Lance Salway, in* The Times Literary Supplement *(© Times Newspapers Ltd. (London) 1977; reproduced from* The Times Literary Supplement *by permission), December 2, 1977.*

MARGERY FISHER

The technique in *I am the Cheese* . . . is an exacting one, and to follow the tripartite narrative readers will have to be alert as well as concerned if they are to realise its full value. There is no mitigation of the terror or the peril of Adam Farmer, a boy of fourteen whose privacy is invaded and whose mind is almost destroyed by the secret, unassailable agencies of government. . . . Through hints, half-truths, the brutal insistence of Brint the questioner and the pathetic delusion of the boy, the author presents his case for the liberty of the individual, his case against the menace of institutional power. As the title suggests, Adam has lost his family (the "Farmer in the Dell" and the farmer's wife) and, like the cheese, he stands alone. He does still stand—so much we guess from the enigmatic end of the book; but his prospects are bleak, unspoken and undefined, and the tone of the book is tragic. Literary technique can sometimes destroy the candour of a book or mask its structure. In [*I am the Cheese*], more consistently balanced for young readers than *The Chocolate War*, technique has added something positive and integral to the whole. (p. 3286)

> *Margery Fisher, in her* Growing Point, *April, 1978.*

Powerful but puzzling, [*I Am the Cheese*] has a message hidden in its tantalising relevations. Young Adam Farmer is cycling from Monument in Massachusetts to Rutterburg in Vermont where his father is in hospital. Apart from the hazards of the journey, Adam is facing a psychological investigation which keeps intruding painfully into his narrative. What secrets are buried in the boy's mind? . . .

Tension mounts with inexorable and terrifying certainty as Adam nears the end of his journey—and not until the final line of the book is his own fate disclosed. Destruction, manipulation, ice-cold ruthlessness swamp Adam; it is not an easy book to read but a disturbing comment on current society, not another cosy tale for tired teenagers but a serious and challenging thriller of considerable merit. (pp. 150-51)

> The Junior Bookshelf, *June, 1978.*

WALTER M. HUMES

Set against the background of a prestige American school, [*The Chocolate War*] explores the theme of corruption on various levels—the corruption of the adolescent through fear and group pressure, the corruption of those in authority who betray their ideals, ultimately the corruption of

all institutions because of human weakness. The narrative is powerful and compelling, and Robert Cormier's portrayal of the psychology of a wide range of characters . . . is very impressive. Both language and events are frank and realistic, features which serve as an antidote to sentimental accounts of adolescence. (p. 26)

> *Walter M. Humes, in* Book Window *(© 1978 S.C.B.A. and contributors), Summer 1978.*

ROBERT BELL

Young Adam's bicycle journey . . . begins ordinarily enough [in *I am the Cheese*], and his recollections of the events leading up to the accident seem at first coherent and believable, but when the narrative begins to be interspersed with transcripts of recorded interrogations of the boy by a patient but cold and remorseless interviewer, the picture gradually takes on a nightmare quality. The nightmare becomes wilder and wilder, the suspense tauter and tauter, and the climax, when Adam's true situation is revealed, is searing and horrifying. It affords the reader naught for his comfort when it is realised that, for his own sake, Adam must not let his interrogator make him remember the past completely. 1984 looms alarmingly close. Sixteen is young enough, I feel, for the harrowing experience of encountering this remarkably powerful book. Very strongly recommended, for any age beyond that. (p. 281)

> *Robert Bell, in* The School Librarian, *September, 1978.*

BRUCE CLEMENTS

There is a striking similarity between the end of Robert Cormier's *The Chocolate War* and the end of William Shakespeare's *Hamlet*. In both works the hero gives a final message to his closest friend, one whose suffering has been chiefly that of a spectator. (p. 217)

Like Shakespeare's play, *The Chocolate War* is concerned with putting things right in a world gone rotten. Jerry's story of standing out for conscience is carefully, convincingly built, and if its obsessive concern with the evil of Brother Leon and Archie needed justification—which it does not—Shakespeare again provides a model. He, too, was fascinated by the creative springs which can be tapped, in some men and women and children, only by the impulse to control and destroy. Even in *Othello*, where the destructive will works itself out in a particularly perverse way, Shakespeare finally asserts the grandeur of life; and in *Romeo and Juliet*, where youth and energy and beauty all die, hope does not.

Juliet and Romeo and Jerry and [his friend] Goober are the same age.

In 1848 the Danish philosopher Søren Kierkegaard published an essay about Juliet ["Crisis in the Life of an Actress"]. . . . In the essay Kierkegaard describes the "astonishing" power of youth in art, its possibilities and limitations. The young heroine has, first, an overwhelming confidence in the present moment and in her ability to control it forever. . . . In her absolute confidence the audience finds rest and assurance, a deeply grounded cheer.

From the beginning the audience knows that Juliet will fall victim to the hatred and posturing and false reassurances of the adult world. It must be so. The child heroine can triumph, says Kierkegaard, only on a dark and heavy stage.

A heavy object can weigh something down. But conversely, it can also conceal the fact that it is heavy, and express its heaviness in the opposite way, by lifting something up in the air. . . . One becomes light by means of —heaviness. One swings up high and free by means of—a pressure.

(pp. 217-18)

In *The Chocolate War* Kierkegaard's "heavy object" overwhelms. That would matter less if the novel were not so skillfully written. Robert Cormier's prose is clear and consistent and tight; the pace is steady; the individual scenes are well tuned and ordered. We care about Jerry and Goober. The novel, in short, engages the reader's heart and mind and carries him along. But in the end, life and art are both overwhelmed. The stage has gone black, the hero has been broken, his friend reduced to silence, and the final word seems to be Iago's. (p. 218)

> *Bruce Clements, "A Second Look: 'The Chocolate War'," in* The Horn Book Magazine *(copyright © 1979, by the Horn Book, Inc., Boston), April, 1979, pp. 217-18.*

STANLEY ELLIN

In two justly admired novels, "The Chocolate War" and "I Am the Cheese," Robert Cormier has dealt with the betrayal of youth, creating landscapes familiar but unnervingly strange—as in a di Chirico painting—in which one sees a boy in mid-adolescence, exceptionally decent and sensitive, standing alone as invisible forces gather against him.

The betrayals themselves, perpetrated by the elders who were by nature designed to be the boy's strength and support, are breaches of trust that lead to the extinction of trust and the spirit it fires. Parents, teachers, mentors, Mr. Cormier makes plain, can each have their own self-serving need to manipulate the young people in their charge, and when they act on that need the consequences can be deadly.

Presented in narrow focus, never moralizing, written in a lean and graphic prose that creates great tension, the novels provided an experience that this reader cannot shake off. The images and ethical questions they raised are still fresh and troubling, and provided an emotional background for the reading of Mr. Cormier's new book, "After the First Death."

Here, fixing on the same theme of betrayal, the author widens his focus. A busload of small children on their way to a New England day camp is hijacked by a gang of what we may surmise from the few clues offered is one of the more bloodthirsty adjuncts of the Palestine Liberation Organization. From different points of view we watch the events, minute by minute, until the climax; the pressure mounts steadily until it seems enough to blow the eardrums. (pp. 30-1)

In this small epic of terrorism and counter-terrorism and their consequences, Mr. Cormier pulls no punches. The brutality is all there, the intimations of sexuality in the young, the sour judgments of values by their elders, whose values have been rotted by political cant—all are presented without sermonizing in a marvelously told story. "After the First Death" more than sustains the reputation its author

has won with "The Chocolate War" and "I Am the Cheese"; it adds luster to it.

Putting all three books together, one disturbing aspect becomes clear: Their basic theme, no matter how brilliant the variations on it, suggests unrelieved despair. The world of Mr. Cormier's people is a Dantean Inferno without any hint of Purgatorio or Paradiso. This is, of course, an antidote to the mindless Happy Ending school of literature but, like most such medicine, it does leave a bitter taste in the mouth. (p. 31)

> *Stanley Ellin, in* The New York Times Book Review *(© 1979 by The New York Times Company; reprinted by permission), April 29, 1979.*

E(dward) E(stlin) Cummings

1894-1962

American poet, novelist, and playwright. One of the most controversial and innovative poets of the twentieth century, Cummings wrote verse which was revolutionary in typography and style but traditional in theme. His work is characterized by its humor, its unusual configurations on the page, and its themes of love, loss of innocence, the dignity of the individual, and nature. It also shows the thematic influence of writers like Ralph Waldo Emerson, bearing witness to the significance of Cummings's New England upbringing. An Emersonian emphasis on individualism remained an important theme throughout Cummings's career, and in particular figured in his novel, _The Enormous Room_. Based on his experiences in a French detention camp during World War I, it is an account of the preservation of dignity in a degrading and dehumanizing situation. After the war Cummings went to Paris to study art; there he became acquainted with the poet Louis Aragon and the painter Pablo Picasso. In addition to his writing, Cummings also gained recognition as a painter. His background in the visual arts was a significant influence on the radical typography of his poetry. Although his work was accepted by critics with a variety of reactions from acclaim to derision, he was given several distinctions and awards during his lifetime. Notably, Cummings was selected to present the Charles Eliot Norton lectures at Harvard. These were later published as _i: six nonlectures_. Written in Cummings's characteristically rambling prose style, they reveal a great deal about his life and influences. It has been argued that Cummings never grew artistically and that his poetry never evolved into a mature style. However, his influence on modern poetry is irrefutable and his humor refreshingly atypical of his time. (See also _CLC_, Vols. 1, 3, 8, and _Contemporary Authors_, Vols. 73-76.)

JOHN DOS PASSOS

[Here's] a book that exists because the author was so moved, excited, amused by a certain slice of his existence that things happened freely and cantankerously on paper. And he had the nerve to let things happen. . . . _The Enormous Room_ seems to me to be the book that has nearest approached the mood of reckless adventure in which men will reach the white heat of imagination needed to fuse the soggy disjointed complexity of the industrial life about us into seething fluid of creation. There can be no more playing safe. (p. 98)

Along with Sandburg and Sherwood Anderson, E. E.

Cummings takes the rhythms of our American speech as the material of his prose as of his verse. It is writing created in the ear and lips and jotted down. For accuracy in noting the halting cadences of talk and making music of it, I don't know anything that comes up to these . . . passages. . . .

> Sunday: green murmurs in coldness. Surplice fiercely fearful, praying on his bony both knees, crossing himself. . . . The Fake French Soldier, alias Garibaldi, beside him, a little face filled with terror . . . the Bell cranks the sharp-nosed priest on his knees . . . titter from bench of whores—
>
> And that reminds me of a Sunday afternoon on our backs spent with the wholeness of a hill in Chevancourt, discovering a great apple pie, B. and Jean Stahl and Maurice le Menusier and myself; and the sun falling roundly before us.
>
> (p. 99)

This sort of thing knocks literature into a cocked hat. It has the raucous directness of a song and dance act in cheap vaudeville, the willingness to go the limit in expression and emotion of a negro dancing. And in this mode, nearer the conventions of speech than those of books, in a style infinitely swift and crisply flexible, an individual not ashamed of his loves and hates, great or trivial, has expressed a bit of the underside of History with indelible vividness. (p. 100)

John Dos Passos, in The Dial _(copyright, 1922, by The Dial Publishing Company, Inc.), July, 1922._

MARK VAN DOREN

["X LI Poems"] continues in almost every phase the tradition which Mr. Cummings established for himself two years ago with "Tulips and Chimneys." No long poems are here, but there are Songs, Portraits, Chansons Innocentes, Sonnets, and, war-pieces; and always the same man is writing, with the same unquestionable power and the same unnecessary tricks. The tricks are unnecessary because without them the power would be quite as apparent as it is now, if not a little more so. . . .

Essentially Mr. Cummings is an educated poet. For all his surface radicalism, for all his insistence that his mind is "a big hunk of irrevocable nothing'' which performs ''squirms of chrome'' and executes ''strides of cobalt,'' for all his warning to the timid reader that he will ''utter lilac shrieks and scarlet bellowings,'' he is saturated with Chaucer, Spenser, and Shakespeare—to name only three of the great poets to whom he obviously has gone to school. Why should he not disregard the timid reader, as they did in their different ways, and fill his pages still fuller of the interesting and beautiful work of which he is capable? He has a richly sensuous mind; his verse is distinguished by fluidity and weight; he is equipped to range lustily and long among the major passions. May not his future lie in the direction of his second sonnet, which is a hymn in the grand style—but his grand style—to love?

> Mark Van Doren, ''First Glance,'' in *The Nation* (copyright 1925 by The Nation Associates, Inc.), July 8, 1925, p. 72.

RICHARD P. BLACKMUR

Mr. Cummings is a school of writing in himself; so that it is necessary to state the underlying assumptions of his mind, and of the school which he teaches, before dealing with the specific results in poetry of those assumptions.

It is possible to say that Mr. Cummings belongs to the anti-culture group; what has been called at various times vorticism, futurism, dadaism, surrealism, and so on. Part of the general dogma of this group is a sentimental denial of the intelligence and the deliberate assertion that the unintelligible is the only object of significant experience.... It is argued that only by denying to the intelligence its function of discerning quality and order, can the failures of the intelligence be overcome; that if we take things as they come without remembering what has gone before or guessing what may come next, and if we accept these things at their face value, we shall know life, at least in the arts, as it really is. Nothing could be more arrogant, and more deceptively persuasive to the childish spirit, than such an attitude when held as fundamental. It appeals to the intellect which wishes to work swiftly and is in love with immediate certainty. (pp. 1-2)

The central attitude of this group has developed, in its sectaries, a logical and thoroughgoing set of principles and habits.... Jazz effects, tough dialects, tough guys, slim hot queens, barkers, fairies, and so on, are made into the media and symbols of poetry. Which is proper enough in Shakespeare where such effects are used ornamentally or for pure play. But in Cummings such effects are employed as substance, as the very mainstay of the poetry. There is a continuous effort to escape the realism of the intelligence in favour of the realism of the obvious. What might be stodgy or dull because not properly worked up into poetry is replaced by the tawdry and by the fiction of the immediate. (pp. 2-3)

By denying the dead intelligence and putting on the heresy of unintelligence, the poet only succeeds in substituting one set of unnourished conventions for another. What survives, with a deceptive air of reality, is a surface. That the deception is often intentional hardly excuses it. The surface is meant to clothe and illuminate a real substance, but in fact is is impenetrable. We are left, after experiencing this sort of art, with the certainty that there was nothing to penetrate. The surface was perfect; the deceit was childish; and the conception was incorrigibly sentimental: all because of the dogma which made them possible.

If Mr. Cummings' tough-guy poems are excellent examples of this sentimentality, it is only natural that his other poems —those clothed in the more familiar language of the lyric— should betray even more obviously, even more perfectly, the same fault. There, in the lyric, there is no pretence at hardness of surface. We are admitted at once to the bare emotion. What is most striking, in every instance, about this emotion is the fact that, in so far as it exists at all, it is Mr. Cummings' emotion, so that our best knowledge of it must be, finally, our best guess. It is not an emotion resulting from the poem; it existed before the poem began and is a result of the poet's private life.... This is the extreme form, in poetry, of romantic egoism: whatever I experience is real and final, and whatever I say represents what I experience. Such a dogma is the natural counterpart of the denial of the intelligence. (pp. 3-4)

Assuming that a poem should in some sense be understood, should have a meaning apart from the poet's private life, either one of two things will be true about any poem written from such an attitude as we have ascribed to Mr. Cummings. Either the poem will appear in terms so conventional that everybody will understand it—when it will be flat and no poem at all; or it will appear in language so far distorted from convention as to be inapprehensible except by lucky guess. In neither instance will the poem be genuinely complete. It will be the notes for a poem, from which might flow an infinite number of possible poems, but from which no particular poem can be certainly deduced. (p. 4)

The question central to [this] discussion will be what kind of meaning does Mr. Cummings' poetry have; what is the kind of equivalence between the language and its object. The pursuit of such a question involves us immediately in the relations between words and feelings, and the relations between the intelligence and its field in experience—all relations which are precise only in terms themselves essentially poetic—in the feeling for an image, the sense of an idiom.... In the examination of Mr. Cummings' writings the grounds will be the facts about the words he uses, and the end will be apprehended in the quality of the meaning his use of these words permits. (pp. 4-5)

If a reader, sufficiently familiar with these poems not to be caught on the snag of novelty, inspects carefully any score of them, no matter how widely scattered, he will especially be struck by a sameness among them. This sameness will be in two sorts—a vagueness of image and a constant recurrence of words.... In *Tulips and Chimneys* words such as these occur frequently—thrilling, flowers, serious, absolute, sweet, unspeaking, utter, gradual, ultimate, final, serene, frail, grave, tremendous.... [None] of them, taken alone, are very *concrete* words; and ... many of them are the rather *abstract,* which is to say typical, *names* for precise qualities, but are not, and cannot be, as *originally important* words in a poem, very precise or very concrete or very abstract: they are middling words, not in themselves very much one thing or the other, and should be useful only with respect to something concrete in itself. (pp. 6-7)

[One example, the word ''flower,'' is used repeatedly and in a variety of usages, such as flower-terrible, flowers of kiss, and world flower.] The question is, whether or not the reader can possibly have shared the experience which Mr. Cummings has had of the word; whether or not it is possible to discern, after any amount of effort, the precise impact which Mr. Cummings undoubtedly feels upon his whole experience when he uses the word. (p. 8)

[In] his use of the word "flower" as a maid of all work [Mr. Cummings has let his ideas run away with him]. The word has become an idea, and in the process has been deprived of its history, its qualities, and its meaning. . . . In Mr. Cummings' poetry we find [that] the word "flower," because of the originality with which he conceives it, becomes an idea and is used to represent the most interesting and most important aspect of his poem. Hence the centre of the poem is permanently abstract and unknowable for the reader, and remains altogether without qualifications and concreteness. It is not the mere frequency of use that deadens the word flower into an idea; it is the kind of thought which each use illustrates in common. By seldom saying *what* flower, by seldom relating immitigably the abstract word to a specific experience, the content of the word vanishes; it has no inner mystery, only an impenetrable surface.

This is the defect, the essential deceit, we were trying to define. Without questioning Mr. Cummings, or any poet, as to sincerity . . . it is possible to say that when in any poem the important words are forced by their use to remain impenetrable, when they can be made to surrender nothing actually to the senses—then the poem is defective and the poet's words have so far deceived him as to become ideas merely. (pp. 9-10)

Mr. Cummings has a fine talent for using familiar, even almost dead words, in such a context as to make them suddenly impervious to every ordinary sense; they become unable to speak, but with a great air of being bursting with something very important and precise to say. "The bigness of cannon is *skilful* . . . enormous rhythm of *absurdity* . . . *slimness* of *evenslicing* eyes are chisels . . . electric Distinct face haughtily vital *clinched* in a swoon of *synopsis* . . . my friends's being continually whittles *keen* careful futile *flowers*," etc. With the possible exception of the compound *evenslicing* the italicized words are all ordinary words; all in normal contexts have a variety of meanings both connotative and denotative; the particular context of being such as to indicate a particular meaning, to establish precisely a feeling, a sensation or a relation.

Mr. Cummings' contexts are employed to an opposite purpose in so far as they wipe out altogether the history of the word, its past associations and general character. To seize Mr. Cummings' meaning there is only the free and *uninstructed* intuition. (p. 16)

The general movement of Mr. Cummings' language is away from communicative precision. If it be argued that the particular use of one of the italicized words above merely makes that word unique, the retort is that such uniqueness is too perfect, is sterile. If by removing the general sense of a word the special sense is apotheosized, it is only so at the expense of the general sense itself. The destruction of the general sense of a word results in the loss of that word's individuality. . . . (pp. 16-17)

When Mr. Cummings resorts to language for the *thrill* that words may be made to give, when he allows his thrill to appear as an equivalent for concrete meaning, he is often more successful than when he is engaged more ambitiously. . . . Thrill, by itself, or in its proper place, is an exceedingly important element in any poem: it is the circulation of its blood, the *quickness* of life, by which we know it, when there is anything in it to know, most intimately. To

use a word for its thrill, is to resurrect it from the dead; it is the incarnation of life in consciousness; it is movement.

But what Mr. Cummings does, when he is using language as thrill, is not to resurrect a word from the dead: he more often produces an apparition, in itself startling and even ominous, but still only a ghost: it is all a thrill, and what it is that thrilled us cannot be determined. (pp. 22-3)

[There] is an exquisite example of the proper use of this strangeness, this thrill, in [a] poem of Mr. Cummings: where he speaks of a cathedral before whose face "the streets turn *young* with rain." While there might be some question as to whether the use of *young* presents the only adequate image, there is certainly no question at all that the phrase is entirely successful: that is, the suggestive feeling in *young* makes the juncture, the emotional conjugation, of streets and rain transparent and perfect. . . . Just because reference is not commonly made either to young streets or young rain, the combination here effected is the more appropriate. The surprise, the contrast, which lend force to the phrase, do not exist in the poem; but exist, if at all, rather in the mind of the reader who did not forsee the slight stretch of his sensibility that the phrase requires—which the phrase not only requires, but necessitates. This, then, is a *strangeness* understood by its own viableness. No preliminary agreement of taste, or contract of symbols, was necessary.

The point is that Mr. Cummings did not here attempt the impossible, he merely stretched the probable. The business of the poet who deals largely with tactual and visual images, as Mr. Cummings does, for the meat of his work, is to escape the prison of his private mind; to use in his poem as little as possible of the experience that happened to him personally, and on the other hand to employ as much as possible of that experience as it is data. (pp. 25-6)

The proper process of poetry designs exactly what the reader will perceive; that is what is meant when a word is said to be inevitable or *juste*. But this exactness of perception can only come about when there is an extreme fidelity on the part of the poet to his words as living things; which he can discover and control—which he must learn, and nourish, and stretch; but which he cannot invent. This unanimity in our possible experience of words implies that the only unanimity which the reader can feel in what the poet represents must be likewise exterior to the poet; must be somehow both anterior and posterior to the poet's own experience. The poet's mind, perhaps, is what he is outside himself with; is what he has learned; is what he knows: it is also what the reader knows. So long as he is content to remain in his private mind, he in unknowable, impenetrable, and sentimental. All his words perhaps must thrill us, because we cannot know them in the very degree that we sympathise with them. But the best thrills are those we have without knowing it. (p. 27)

Richard P. Blackmur, "Notes on E. E. Cummings' Language" (originally published in Hound & Horn, *January-March, 1931), in his* The Double Agent: Essays in Craft and Elucidation *(copyright, 1935, by Richard P. Blackmur), Arrow Editions, 1935 (and reprinted by Peter Smith, 1962), pp. 1-29.*

MARIANNE MOORE

Style is for Mr. Cummings "translating;" it is a self-demonstrating aptitude for technique, as a seal that has been swimming right-side-up turns over and swims on its back for a time—"killing nears in droves slaying almost massacring myriads of notquites": "the worm knocks loud", "sit/ the bum said"—with numerous finds in the realm of unconscious bourgeois obnoxiousness: "eye buleev money rules thith woyl"— . . . "wen uh man's gut thad bright gole thing in his fist, he's strong." This pluck-the-duck, scale-the-fish 15th century appetite for aliveness equivalent to a million trillion musical light years, results in some effects [in *Eimi*] which are as much better than those in *The Enormous Room* (the germ for these) as *Viva* is an improved vagueness and judicious anonymity over most of what preceded. And the typography, one should add, is not something superimposed on the meaning but the author's mental handwriting. There courteous innocently penguin-eyed comrade capitalist Cummings gets the best of strong publisher and boorish public. (p. 278)

One does not like to praise, then take away the praise—and will not; but there are a few queries. (a) Not to be confused with Virgil's necessary artificial argot of politeness, the sharkskin papillae pebble-pattern of the Italian garden-walk, undesirably changes now and then to polished white mosaic: "Not only has Turk been up; he's been doing"; (b) a Saint Sebastian—as our Dante probably knows—may be hid by too many arrows of awareness; (c) a tag is perhaps too much a certain kind of tag for a' that it is used by a poet; (d) one is never going to be able to score words as one scores sounds, "condesfusionpair" being not hard on the brain but awkward for it; (e) the book should have an index though it may be like suggesting that the kangaroo pouch accommodate a grown kangaroo; (f) Which freedom wears best? that of a leprechaun a leopard a leper a hyperholiest priest of Benares, or of the mystic for whom leprosy becomes negligible? Mr. Cummings' obscenities are dear to him, somewhat as Esau's hairiness is associated with good hunting, but one thing is certain: if an otherwise divine burlesque is a bouquet that has a stench, a chair that was a garbage-pail—then a grin, a smirk, a smile, are synonymous; B is not for Beatrice but for bunk, and i am not Dante. (pp. 279-80)

"Birdlike and boy," "defunct," "dwarfish," "chipmunk lion," "mr/ cricket" and mr crab (the 5-year vermin), Comrade Can't, and "So do I" recall Mr. Civility, Pick-thank, and Cutpurse, and this to some extent children's story, by an author whose kindness to comrade stunned, equals America, has traits in common with Hashimura Togo, Ezra Pound, Gertrude Stein, T. S. Eliot, and the Guls Horn-book; the consanguinity with James Joyce being the nostalgic note, quite as much as a similarity in harmonics. . . . (p. 280)

Marianne Moore, "A Penguin in Moscow," in Poetry (© *1933 by The Modern Poetry Association; reprinted by permission of the Editor of* Poetry; *excerpted by permission of The Estate of Marianne C. Moore), August, 1933, pp. 277-81.*

JOHN PEALE BISHOP

[Cummings] appeared as a young and romantic poet. But he was one unmistakably of his time. That he derived from Keats and had been instructed by the poets of the last century was obvious; but even in the earliest poems, where their trace is most strong, the movement of Cummings' verse is already his own. His charm, at once, is his ra-

pidity. The influence of the romantic tradition was soon left behind; but not the romantic attitude. That was authentic and not taught—at least, not by the English poets. It stood no more in critical favor than it does now, however the cry against it in some quarters has changed. This poetry was aware, as only poetry can be, of what was going on. The sensibility of the poet was singularly uncontaminated. He defied, indeed, every principle which Ezra Pound had taught us was right for poetry; and there was none of us then who had not listened with attention to Pound. Here was no effort for the one precise word; instead adjectives, which were Pound's abhorrence, were piled one on another in a sort of luminous accumulation. If Cummings, in writing, had kept his eye on the object, it was of no avail, for the objects had their outlines distorted, or else they dissolved, leaving behind only an impression of their qualities. Here was a poetry as shining and as elusive as quicksilver. If there was anything precise about it, it was, as Cummings was to note later, that precision which aims at creating movement. Yet none but a poet could have been so preoccupied with words; nor could anyone not a poet have so enlivened them with his presence.

Here was no Prince Hamlet, nor was meant to be; here was quite another figure, fine, impertinent, full of shocks and capers, in the midst of some absurd mockery suddenly turning surpassingly lyrical. Here was Mercutio. (p. 174)

At the time when Cummings' manner was formed, it seemed not only possible, but imperative, that every element of technique should be recreated. He was aware of Joyce's experiments in prose in *Ulysses;* some of them he has repeated, concentrating them, as he might well do in the smaller space of a poem; in his own prose he has carried them still further, especially in *Eimi,* by accelerating their performance. He had before him the example of Picasso, who had already passed through three or four periods, each representing a progress in emotion and a prodigious renewal of technique. What could be more natural than that Cummings, who is painter as well as poet, should attempt to emulate in literature the innovations of his contemporaries in painting? In Picasso, as in some others who were renewing the painter's art, he saw what intensity might follow distortion of line and immensity of form. And Cummings has taught himself to see somewhat as they see, but without losing his personal vision. He juxtaposes words as they do pigments. The effect is not altogether a happy one, for what is gained in intensity may be lost in meaning. When a painter distorts a line, he may increase its functional value; but a sentence can easily be so dislocated that it will no longer work. The impressionist method, so apt to seize the aspect of a momentary world, permits Cummings to rely on the vaguest associations. It has led him as a poet, not to weight, but merely to touch his words with meaning. In fact, the significance of his words is often in their position. Then, too, it is probably the example of the Post-Impressionists and the Picasso of the *papier collé* period that has persuaded him to admit to his poetry much that was tawdry, trivial, and lewd—material whose advantage to him is certainly in part that it has hitherto been considered inadmissible. (pp. 177-78)

His art is personal. It could not well be anything else; for it reposes upon a conviction that each man's world is his own and that no other can be known. . . . Other poets have professed some such philosophy, but, so far as I know, Cummings is the first actually to carry it into his writing. He does not write as a common sense dualist. He was born and brought up in Cambridge, Massachusetts; and though he has constantly cried his repudiation of his birthplace and all its academic works, including the late Josiah Royce, it is only as a child of Cambridge that he can be so passionately private and peculiar. (p. 178)

[Cummings] is constantly trying to affect us by other than purely literary means. He attempts to seduce us without departing from his solitude. Cummings' faults are those of the sensitive writer, and the interest of his poetry is that it is a product of his sensibility. No one poem is unintelligible. On the contrary, it is much more likely that if we try to take it as complete, its meaning will be too soon exhausted. For its concern is with the immediate and with the moment. It may charm or amuse; but it is only by Cummings' poetry as a whole that we are profoundly impressed. It is not unattached to his personality; but the interest of that personality is in its singular capacity to report the age.

The problem is not one of escaping personality (for that way impotence lies) but of transcending it. And that a poet may do in one of two ways: he may dramatize his personal desires directly, or he may find in the outer world some drama, into whose actors he can fuse his own desires and in whose catastrophe he can, though only on an imaginative plane, resolve his personal conflict. . . . Cummings has almost no imagination. He is said to be confined in his own world; but it is a world which has too much in common with ours to make communication impossible. He is subject there to a conflict of contrary desires: he would be like others and yet utterly unlike; he would be like the man who suffers, but not like the man who dies. He has taken the only known way to immortality. Out of this conflict he has made his poems, both lyrical and satirical. But nothing has made him a dramatic poet.

Cummings' prose has never had anything like the attention it deserves. *The Enormous Room* came out . . . when a reaction had set in against almost all that had then been written about the War. It did not exploit that reaction and failed, as so many later books did not, to profit from it. *Eimi*, which is an account of a journey made through the U.S.S.R. in 1931, appeared . . . in the midst of the depression communism. It was derided or ignored. And yet, *The Enormous Room* has the effect of making all but a very few comparable books that came out of the War look shoddy and worn. It has been possible to read it, as I have done, at intervals over the seventeen years since its publication, and always to find it undiminished. So it has slowly found readers. But those who were attracted to *The Enormous Room*, because of the compassion Cummings showed there for the lowly and despised, were repulsed by *Eimi*, which makes it clear that he will have nothing to do with the communist effort to improve the condition of mankind. The one book is, nevertheless, the complement of the other, and the only change in Cummings to be marked between them is the change from youth to maturity. And in *Eimi*, he makes every other writer on Russia appear dishonest or credulous.

These books have behind them what must be regarded as the two most important events of our time. And the backgrounds, in so far as they affect his narratives, are set before us with great vividness. The incidental characters are presented with an admirable skill and they remain convinc-

ing, even though in the parts they play there is almost always some exaggeration, comic or pathetic. For again and again, as Cummings produces a character, we are reminded of Dickens. But the center of *The Enormous Room* is not the War, nor that of *Eimi* the Russian Revolution. At the core of each is a spiritual crisis. (pp. 179-81)

[In *The Enormous Room*, the] narrator met a problem much older than the War. In his own soul he met it: the significance of human suffering. He met it with the intensity of youth and knowing that upon some solution of it depended his sanity. It is a problem much greater than that of injustice, for it includes it. And it is worth noting that it is not with its injustice that Cummings reproaches the French government, but with its stupidity, in confining to the Enormous Room specimens of humanity as small as these.

The mind provides no answer to the problem of suffering. The answer must come from elsewhere. (p. 181)

Here, at the very start, we have in Cummings what has been called his cult of unintelligence. He was one who could not but seek a wholesome being. He emerged from imprisonment profoundly shaken. Where else was he to look for what he sought in a world dead at the top if not below? And in Cummings there is from now on, in all he writes, an exaltation of the lowly and the lively. He is himself, and he accepts his common lot. With the others, he suffers; he exults alone, and in a world of his own. But something happens to alter this attitude shortly after he crosses the Polish border into the Soviet Union and in the customs house encounters upon one wall, framed in bunting, the colored photograph of Nicolai Lenin.

The style which Cummings began in poetry reaches its most complete development in the prose of *Eimi*. Indeed, one might almost say that, without knowing it, Cummings had been acquiring a certain skill over years, in order that, when occasion arose, he might set down in words the full horror of Lenin's tomb. It is brought to us through every sense: the solid stench of numberless multitudes endlessly waiting, endlessly treading downward into the darkness to look on the maker of their world, the corpse of the man with the small, not intense, face and the reddish beard, secret, being dead, as when alive, intransigeant even in mortality. For in Russia, Cummings was not only in a new country; he was in a new world. Impressions pressed, one on another, in such confusing rapidity that no one with less than his skill could possibly have caught and recorded them. (pp. 182-83)

Throughout *Eimi*, Cummings maintains an analogy, never too hard pressed, between his own progress from circle to circle of soviet society and Dante's passage through Hell. The moment at which he emerges to see the stars is when he returns to Europe, where it is once more possible for him to assume the full responsibility of being a man. In prison he had learned a passive acceptance of his lot. It was on his return to freedom . . . that he experiences that sense of the wholeness of life—that complete vision which includes both divinity and depravity—that allows him, as he approaches the borders of Italy, without presumption, to call upon the name of Dante. For now he knows there is but one freedom, a freedom active and acquiescent in the vision, the freedom of the will, responsive and responsible, and that from it all other freedoms take their course. (p. 186)

John Peale Bishop, "The Poems and Prose of E. E. Cummings," in The Southern Review *(copyright, 1938, by John Peale Bishop), Vol. IV, No. 3, Summer, 1938, pp. 173-86.*

S. I. HAYAKAWA

No modern poet to my knowledge has such a clear, child-like perception as E. E. Cummings—a way of coming smack against things with unaffected delight and wonder. This candor . . . results in breath-takingly clean vision. . . . No modern poet, furthermore, is less self-important than Cummings—none so delicately shy about asserting his will upon others. These are not, so far as I am aware, the customary opinions of his work, but if one keeps his attention for a time strictly upon the lyrical verses in the *Collected Poems,* without permitting himself to be startled or shocked (and therefore sidetracked) by the typographical fireworks or the satire, he will find qualities in Cummings' poetry that are reminiscent of nothing so much as a sensitive and well-mannered child. . . . Leave him alone, and he will play in a corner for hours, with his fragilities, his colors, and his delight in the bright shapes of all the things he see. . . . (pp. 284-85)

The important point about E. E. Cummings is, however, that he was not left alone. He was dumped out into the un-innocent and unlyrical world—the world of chippies, broads, and burlesque shows such as are discovered by Harvard undergraduates "seeing life"—and after that into the infinitely more shocking world of the blood, vermin, murder, commercialized idealism, and patriotic hysteria of the Great War. Cummings wrote about these two worlds (which frequently merge into each other) his fiercest satirical verse. His lyricism, shy enough at best, ran completely for cover, and he turned upon the nightmare worlds of reality partly with the assumed callousness and defensive self-mockery of the very sensitive, and partly with the white and terrible anger of the excessively shy.

The self-mockery that served to conceal his innocence and lyricism (principally from himself, one suspects) begins to find expression toward the end of *Tulips and Chimneys,* and recurs in his poetry throughout the rest of his work. Poems of this kind, dealing principally with prostitutes, yeggs, and perverts, are, like his play *Him,* powerful, phantasmagoric—as if the poet, having left his fragilities behind him, were exploring with unfeeling but lively curiosity a nether world peopled by hideous automatons. There is in these poems none of the sentimentality in reverse that made the "scarlet woman" and disreputable hang-outs the subjects for delicious shudders among the fin-de-siècle poets. (pp. 285-86)

Now and then, however, the world offers a situation which overcomes his indifference—and when this happens Cummings condenses such pity and terror into a sudden stanza or turn of phrase (all the more terrible because unexpected) that the reader is taken with a quick, sharp thud, right in the pit of his consciousness. These (perhaps involuntary) revelations of his carefully concealed ethical passion—not frequent, but frequent enough so that we know they are not accidental—constitute an unobtrusive claim by which we are compelled to grant that he has written some poetry that we cannot call anything but great. (p. 287)

Anger is the central passion of his war-poetry—the white anger, as I have said, of the excessively shy. Although

many have already conceded his *Enormous Room* to be one of the greatest war-books, only few have as yet realized that Cummings has written what are certainly our greatest war-poems. (pp. 287-88)

E. E. Cummings' descent into Hell is a trip from which he has not come up. He is still there (or here). Perhaps there is no coming up if, as Eliot has said, in prose one may be concerned with ideals, but in poetry one deals with reality. The brilliant mind that early took refuge in sophistication is now profoundly sophisticated. . . . More frequently in his recent poetry he seems to be returning, although with elaborate precautions lest he be caught acting like a softie, to his naturally tender delicacy of sentiment—his almost sentimentality. (pp. 288-89)

Perhaps this fact explains the eccentricities of his technique. Partly they are a disguise—a man so sick of the "poetry" and rotten idealism of his time, a man so acutely aware of the ludicrous figure presented by people with beautiful souls in a world of brutes and slobberers, is forced if he is most indubitably a poet to present an exterior that will make it impossible for anyone to think of him as a "poet" as commonly understood. (p. 289)

Another reason for his technique is his attempt, perhaps illegitimate, to represent by words and typography experiences *just the way they happened,* without regard to the formalities or the "laws" of thought. This results in the most daring of his technical innovations. . . . These are probably "not poetry", but I am not sure that this matters greatly, since they succeed eminently in doing what they set out to do. Mr. Cummings is not interested in the "legitimacy" of his experiments.

Can one say, following current critical fashions, that Cummings is up a blind alley, and so saying dismiss him as a left-over from the futilitarian twenties? This is not to ask whether he has said all he is capable of saying. The question is whether the exercise and discipline of our sensibilities to which his poetry submits us are still useful. If we find that they are, it is merely churlish to complain that he is no "fructifying force". His profound scepticism is regarded now, of course, as "dating" him. I am not at all sure that this is a fault in him—for his scepticism is of a kind that ought not to be lightly abandoned. His is not the easier way. (pp. 290-91)

S. I. Hayakawa, "Is Indeed 5," in Poetry *(© 1938 by The Modern Poetry Association; reprinted by permission of the Editor of* Poetry*), August, 1938, pp. 284-92.*

JOHN FINCH

The career of E. E. Cummings, from his first appearance at Harvard to his last, has been the consistent statement of an attitude toward authority. His entire work raises the question whether this attitude can much longer continue to be a creative one, or even a possible one for the artist. The question remains unanswered, but merely to have raised it so sharply as he has done is a peculiar achievement.

It involved first the definition of a world in which poems, Cummings's kind of poems, might be written. . . . And this meant a rigid, wilful ordering of experience according to a moral standard, a reduction of all things into the two categories of the lyric affirmatives (flowers, kisses, children, birds, love) and the sterile negatives (machines, money, advertisements, respectability, death). In a world thus ordered, it then became the poet's task to find means of asserting with finality the truth and beauty and goodness of the former category and the falseness, ugliness, and evil of the latter. For Cummings there are two ways of doing this. His perceptions are lyrical, almost mystical. If he can restate them in wholly lyrical terms, they become valid truths in so far as they succeed as poetry. But the lyric impulse lags: its strength is fitful and capricious. And the poet's chosen world is an infinite dualism containing the denial of poetry as well as its affirmation. When lyricism fails him, he has the other method left, the assertion of himself, a conscious, willing self, as the supreme authority, and the appeal simply to that.

These, of course, are the methods of romanticism, and no one will deny that Cummings is a romantic poet. He shares much with the romantic poets of the past. (pp. 643-44)

[It] is to American romanticism in particular that he is most closely related, that type which is above all didactic.... His confident and continual preaching is truly Emersonian.... But not all the native attitudes in Cummings are out of Emerson. The exclusiveness of his individualism suggests Thoreau. His metaphysical impertinence recalls, again and again, Emily Dickinson. And in celebrating "my body when it is with your body" or "the poetic carcass of a girl," he becomes remotely Whitmanesque. To suggest any of these names as literary influences is beside the point. Cummings, in a different century, is preaching and practising the way of life for which they stood. His career presents, in peculiarly sharpened terms, a test case for romantic individualism long after romanticism's day.

This underlying attitude, which can best be characterized, perhaps, as a denial of external authority, determines every aspect of his writing. It is there in his technique as a consistent rejection of the authority of form, or rather an assertion of the authority of self over material and convention. By such a process he worked out his highly personal typography, distractive to a perennial crowd of readers and critics. It is surely not of central importance to his poetry. He neither stands nor falls thereby. Yet one can say that, using it, Cummings, at least part of the time, *controls* his poems to a greater extent than other writers. He has orchestrated them, choreographed them upon the page to such a degree that our reading, when we have recovered from the first shock of visual strangeness, must approximate his. (pp. 644-45)

More pertinent, certainly, is the question of his vocabulary. Over words, the real material of verse, Cummings again asserts the individual authority.... [If] Cummings's poetry at its worst is a destructive violation of language, at its best this same poetry is a new affirmation of the vitality of our speech. And here too he is allied with an American tradition. The history of our poetry, that part of it which has enduring life, could be told almost entirely in terms of its continuous experimentation with the fluid, native vocabulary. And it is with this vocabulary wholly that Cummings works. By virtue of his delicate bullying of words and grammar, punctuation and typography, he achieves a remarkable poetic freshness—catches, at times, the most elusive shadings of sensation. He can impart to language, which in his hands is forever, to be sure, in danger of its life, a rare, pervasive excitement.

But it is in his implacably individualistic approach to experience that Cummings's final predicament is uncovered. The hundred years since Emerson's *Self-Reliance* have altered the validity, or at least the practicability, of this romantic way of life.... [Cummings] is put on the defensive from the start. His whole career has been a long process of digging in. From *Tulips and Chimneys*, whose very title suggests the dualism, to *No Thanks*, labeled with a rejection, the poetry has grown steadily sharper, more dogmatic, more bitter. Affirmations are necessarily less frequent, and belligerence becomes the poet's customary manner. (pp. 646-47)

A platform of moral isolation like this does offer certain advantages to the artist. From it, for one thing, he can speak with a private intensity; he can muster a heady indignation. Also, a quiet room, with all the doors shut and windows barred, is a good place to tell the heart's secrets, to celebrate the lone things which happen only to the man alone. This is the proper business of the lyricist, and surely no contemporary poetry is more thoroughly lyric than Cummings's. But in such a place the danger is that one may forget what is going on outside, how men speak to each other and what happens to men together. When a poet's attitude distorts his perception of the outer world, it begins to deny the possibilities of poetry. Here, one supposes, is the likeliest source for all the obscurity in Cummings's work. (pp. 647-48)

[However] sensitive he may be, obvious values escape him when they are outward values. Affirming only the authority within himself, he has been forced, by the logic of his position, into a rejection of social authority. His two prose works show, no less than his poetry, what has happened. *The Enormous Room* remains one of the best books of the last war, largely because of its magnificent human sympathy. The author's consciousness is open to embrace his fellow prisoners, Zoo-loo, Surplice, Jean Le Nègre, and all the rest. But between that and *Eimi*, the closing which Cummings hates has taken place. Lenin's tomb reminds him only of Coney Island, and Russia is viewed entirely from a far cold point of isolation. The attempted affirmation of "I Am" with which the book is labeled sounds like an old-fashioned tune grimly whistled in the dark. There is not enough humanity left. Rejection has become the poet's habit until he has rejected the one food that might nourish him. Here is perhaps the last irony of individualism: that it must in the end be loveless.

Cummings has worked desperately and long to escape a natural heritage. He was born into it, a New England clergyman's son, and it proved at the last inescapable.... To him, as to so many of the young literati of the 1920's, this force was stultifying and restrictive. It was a death force. Taking his cue from a prevailing drift of the '20's, Cummings tried to abuse this threatening conservatism out of his path. He became the *enfant terrible* of a generation of terrible children. (pp. 650-51)

Since 1933 he has acquired another antipathy. That was the year of the Russian travel diary, *Eimi*. Whereas in 1926 he had noticed that "the communists have fine Eyes," he now burst out bitterly against the "Kumrads."... As satire or invective the poems of this later political bias are greatly inferior to the scornful sting of the earlier attacks on native conservatism. Their accents are shrill, almost fanatical. And the mere assertion of a romantic abstraction, "life" or "love," is inadequate as a positive platform from which to utter these sweeping denouncements. But the most striking consideration of all is that in these poems Cummings, on slightly different grounds, is fighting the very battle of conservatism. He is joining the New England merchants and politicos in the angry assertion of their free, individual rights against the remotest threat. Like them, he is a champion of moral *laissez faire*. (pp. 651-52)

I have tried to suggest the remarkable unity of Cummings's work. In spite of a surface versatility, in itself consistent, and in spite of abrupt shifts of direction such as that just noted, the poems, the prose, and for that matter, the pictures of *CIOPW*, the play *him*, and the ballet scenario *Tom* are all strongly of a piece. Their unity derives from the basic romantic premises on which he has worked out his particular creative experiment. If this experiment is a failure, it is largely these premises which are at fault. Cummings brought to it an extraordinary talent and conducted it with uncompromising honesty. A possible conclusion is that, in poetry as elsewhere individualism of the nineteenth-century kind, no matter how we may translate it into twentieth-century words or disguise it with contemporary gestures, remains tragically out of date. The lonely gospel of isolated manhood can no longer nourish man. (pp. 652-53)

Put against the background of contemporary verse in America, his work takes on one other elusive quality. It is a quality so important to the well-being of poetry that merely to mention it seems hardly adequate. It is the thing which is central to such of his poems as those about Buffalo Bill, death's poker game with love, niggers, or Jimmie's goil. It informs most of his conceits and it peoples his volumes with mice and elephants, grasshoppers, tough guys, and busted statues. Cummings's poetry has—what today's poetry sorely needs—the rare quality of fun. (p. 653)

> John Finch, "New England Prodigal," in The New England Quarterly *(copyright 1939 by* The New England Quarterly*), December, 1939, 643-53.*

JOHN ARTHOS

E. E. Cummings is one of the few modern poets who write about beautiful things simply. Much contemporary poetry is concerned with the analysis of states of mind for the sake of philosophic or social comment. . . . There are exceptions, of course, but most modern poets are not concerned very much with declaring that the beauty of their experience is proof of the power of beauty. . . . Cummings is surely the modern poet who has most consistently aimed at lyric expression in the direct manner. . . . He has remained a lyric poet because he has not been interested in questioning and doubting; he has been constantly searching but he has always known what he is searching for. (p. 372)

Cummings's career in print began with a novel, *The Enormous Room*. . . . After graduating from Harvard he had served with an ambulance corps in France before the United States entered the war, and there through one of the blunders of the French he and a friend were confined to a concentration camp near the Pyrenees for some months, confined with people who by the record might appear to have been the scum of the earth. But Cummings found some of them to be characters of overpowering excellence. . . . Here Cummings discovered and re-created such

virtue and beauty as are hardly to be found in any other contemporary writer. And here he seems to have taken a direction he was never to give up, a strict and rich attention to the particular beauty that belongs to the humble.

But in the strange world of New York and Paris after the war such simple service was very often undertaken as part of the revolt against a society that for many people no longer seemed to deserve much loyalty. As after any great collective effort when individuals are closely confined in their personal aims, there was the reaction to extreme individualism and much disillusionment. Cummings was one of those swept by this anarchic surge. . . . Still believing in virtue, he seemed to assert it was to be found only among the downtrodden, which is a rather comfortable way of escaping from Brattle Street. Insofar as he was rebelling against complacency and dullness and arrogance he was being true to himself, but in exaggerating the virtues of the underworld he submitted himself to an unnecessary strain and artificiality. (pp. 373-74)

He has spent his feeling, then, with some confusion, and it is useful for any consideration of his poetry to examine how he has done this. It is significant that many of the chapter headings of *The Enormous Room* are taken from *The Pilgrim's Progress*. Several of the late poems are explicitly religious, but without these we may see many indications that he has consistently striven to be pious. In spite of himself he has remained a Puritan, though for him despair, his Valley of Despond, has been the hatred of the senses Puritanism approved and fostered. . . . As fortune would have it, some of his intensity of feeling is guarded by the singleness of mind that provides one of the great strengths of Puritanism, so much so that he is led by the same virtue to become a missionary, to make beauty a cause. He is sometimes obliged, praising whatever is Spring-like, to worship defiantly. . . . To do justice to the claims of the senses he turned to the world Brattle Street considered most debased, and he did this in a conscientious and Puritan way. (p. 374)

His love poems, which show both his loyal intentness and his unhappy confusion, describe countless affairs, crude as well as fine. Sometimes they are very beautiful, and at other times they are detached and hard. Sometimes they are merely obscene jokes. He told Puritanism off even while shocking himself, and this became a habit. It was right and necessary to tell his Puritan ancestors that the life of the senses is good, but it does the senses no favor to consider their restlessness their essential virtue. Their value consists really in their aptitude for constancy, in service that is rewarding to the whole individual, whereby the attachment of the senses is deeply and lastingly fixed.

His paganism, then, is corrupted with an idea, that the casual experience of the senses provides a sufficient truth for living. Falling in love, he is really serving this idea, and his experience of what is more deeply human is restricted. (p. 375)

In the very earliest poems, "Puella Mea" and "Epithalamion," Cummings began with the praise of love, with sensuous and fragrant language and a kind of delicacy that is like Catullus. Later he was to make epigrams in the manner of the Latin poet, but here the stronger reminiscences are of Spenser and Keats, with here and there, curiously enough, a tone that seems to come from Milton. . . . [There] is much that is clumsy, and sometimes the language is pitifully insecure. But they are left as a remainder of a genuine striving. The surer grace came in certain sonnets, where there is a kind of fragile charm. . . . (pp. 376-77)

What is immediately striking here is the language of the images, more perhaps than the images themselves: the *threaded moment,* the *shadowy sheep,* eyes *frailer* than dreams. Something of this same love of language is in Spenser and Milton, where abstract words are treated like material ones, *the very skillful strangeness of your smile.* The method seems to be to use the abstraction to express the essential quality of a thing, and a sensuous or material epithet is attached in order to clinch the image referred to in such a way that all the associations implied in the abstraction are drawn on. When unsuccessful, such phrasing points to a kind of vagueness of language and perhaps feeling. But the failures only indicate the nature of the successes, which seem to prove that any beautiful particular depends upon something ineffable, something not exclusively comprehended in the image alone—*eyes frailer than most dreams are frail.* (p. 378)

I think one of Cummings's first inclinations must have been to write in a convention, even while he was intent on forming an individual style. He must have taken forms from the past that were roughly adapted to the things he had to write about. He found these forms of course in the poets he admired, Spenser and Keats, the Spenserian stanza, the sonnet, the iambic rhythm. And in the beginning he found a language there he wanted, and a way of phrasing. However fresh the feelings he had to express seemed to him, he knew that it was impossible merely to take over the language of daily speech with no wider knowledge of its capacity than is to be gained in conversation. He has had an extraordinary gift of his own with which to extend our language, and it is understandable that at times he should have distorted language beyond recognition. (pp. 378-79)

A Protestant rebelling against Protestantism, he has a particular stake in asserting the value of his feeling, and he has the conjunct necessity to establish a language worthy of his rebellion. (p. 379)

His failures come most often when he relies on a strident exaggeration of language to express feelings that are unripe for expression, when he is confusedly intent. I think it can be said that his obscure poems are bad, and they are bad because he is in them affirming the values of his sensibility at the expense of his conviction. This is like the hope of most adolescent writers that personal feelings may be communicated with images whose connotations are not supported by the logic of the syntax. . . . There is still something else to be said, I think, about the insecurity of Cummings's language, and about his persistent crudeness next door to excellence. (pp. 380-82)

The punctuation Cummings employs often distracts and antagonizes readers, but at times it can be shown to serve a useful purpose. (p. 383)

At times his scheme certainly causes the reader to pay special attention to the sound of the words. But at other times it seems to provide a puzzle of such complexity that interest in the poem is lost for the sake of the puzzle. At times Cummings is merely thumbing his nose at convention and at the reader. Occasionally I think Cummings is making jokes, and I for one am amused, but then, some of these are threadbare jokes.

When this unorthodox punctuation is good, it is excellent. When it is less than that it is of doubtful value, for I think that ambiguity in these matters indicates a lack of interest in the poem by the poet himself. The punctuation is worked out in terms of a word or phrase, or two or three phrases, and almost never is there a logic to it which supports the meaning of the whole poem. (The Buffalo Bill poem, as an exception, is a very short poem.) Very often those poems in which the punctuation is most complicated are poems which fall apart, which are without unity of meaning. And conversely, those poems which are sustained and unified are most simply punctuated. In general, I think, his unorthodox punctuation is most successful when it leaves out signs. It is most often unsuccessful when it elaborates on the conventional scheme by amplification.

However obscure Cummings's language may become at times and however absurd his typography, it is clear that he is an intelligent poet. He is not interested in intellectual subtleties as Eliot and MacLeish are, and on the other hand he does not belong to the cult of unintelligibility. Actually his intellectual position is respectable and rather coherently maintained. He is a Platonist, absorbed in the discipline of contemplation and devoted to the perception of being. Existence means more to him than action. The highest praise he can give to people is to say they are; the Zulu Is. That which is alive in the truth, and is capable of growth and fulfillment, Is. (pp. 387-88)

In [his latest] poems I find a firmness and strength which is new to Cummings. All along he has maintained his knowledge of the invaluable worth of the individual . . . , and some of his limitations of belief have hindered him from social comment. But now I think he more clearly understands the nature of the rebellion he has been waging; it is clearer to him, and his experience can be put to wiser use. . . . His imagery and his thought are more frequently informed with Christian doctrine. I do not believe Cummings yet has a fully reasoned philosophy, but it is evident that he is now able to express more serious convictions by virtue of greater sympathy with Christianity. The judgments in the recent poems are not perhaps profound, but they are never foolish. They are responsible judgments. He is now more sure that he belongs to the world of all of us. This, I think, is growth, and provides a means whereby Cummings may now avoid errors he once made, and develop more fully what was originally sound in his perceptions. As from the beginning he has given us things of immeasurable worth, so I think he will continue to increasingly.

He should not be allowed to fall from sight, or to be remembered only as one of the wild experimenters who came along after the last war. For he represents even now, in a more terrible war, something that is valid and sweet in the human spirit, and something profound and strong—in short, beauty. (pp. 389-90)

John Arthos, "The Poetry of E. E. Cummings," in American Literature *(reprinted by permission of the Publisher; copyright 1943 by Duke University Press, Durham, North Carolina), Vol. 14, January, 1943, pp. 372-90.*

PHILIP GREEN

This unessay is also about communication which is like flowers and moons only not really whom flowers and

moons are only for feel (ing o isn't that nice), but communication is more like razor-blades and electric eggbeaters; it is
made for use It is utilitarianand so at least partially rational
and so unfortunately is any

po (iloveyou) em. . . .

what you and i and cummings have in common even more
than roses is . . . language but also the Same Language ie
english; a frenchman would have a hell of a time reading
cummings' poetry unless he happened to speak english
which unfortunately most frenchmen do not [and that
would not help more than littlemuch even if he did for many
of cummings' poems] (and the really go

　　　　　　　　　　　　　　　　go
　　　　　　　　　　　　　　　　　　　good ones like
somewhere I have never travelled or my love thy head

　　or the great advantage of being alive are not really very
unsame from any other uninpoems)

because most of them are not very anything but tricks and
games saying unthings nearly or things that leave you with
a vague feeling of feeling (my red red rose) goodness which
is often not nearly poetry but unorganized sound or emotion like if i wrote I love you i Love you i lOve you i loVe
you i lovE you i love You six times.)

What eecummings is doing withah-POETRY!? in his own
syntactical way is really allthetime the same things which I
shall describe to wit . . . he is recreating his emotional experiences of looking at treesmoonsrainsnowlovemo-
therskythighetc or maybe even his dreams and he wants
you to too and see how undead and thingish they are . . .
what gets in his way is paper and Language which is why:
once feeling is described it is not feeling any more but it is
anaboutfeeling which is a farfar differentthing and you do
not feel it but the telling about it in words which have logical relations hips topreposition eachadjective othersub-
stantive and that must therefore be intelligent in some way
or one might say (or might not) rational (lyordered) and
which are as i said not pure feeling which is immediate and
emotional and unconventionally ordered.

eecummings is trying to get away from unliveness which
destroys his feelings so he if i may quote someone else
frEEEs language, that is he destroys ITS order until he
thinks it looks (and this is where the problem) the same as
HIS feeling and/or (comes in) he uses words which are
things with both denotations and connotations purely for
their connotative which is usually emotional effect. ! Thus
he combines images which are so unrelated to each other as
to be almost unimages merely because of their associational
quality which gives you the feeling he wants. . . . He does
this very well and it is why many of his poems are extremely unbad. . . .

and similarly is what else he does to us with his syntactics,
in two ways: first with normalwordorder and pun, ctu!
ation? which is most ordinary when he merely reverses it or
leaves it out; he does often much more fiendish, things?
Second with the parts of speech which he mixes up like the
muchness of summer rain until all, being being, are one
with each other. this is not nocuous when he simply forgets
capitaL letters and periods and other unbeautiful whatnots
that aren't the snow soaking into the belly of the Earth or
what have you;? after the first shock which was in the
1920's anyway you don't notice because these things are
not either logical or illogical in themselfish's being only
conveniences like a woman in a bar

And he is *often* (SUCCESS)

　　　　　　full, mixing up which's and whom's and all the
King's words. . . .

However, in most of his poetry if you use the criterion of
merely　counting　noses　like　any　anaesthetized-
impersonalunbeing mathematician which don't get down
and sssss

　　　　　　UCK the good earth, or mud when it rains, it
fails. (p. 24)

What eec is doing is to take words ordinarily denotative and
make them connotative like fragile which he uses to qualify
almost everything under the sun not to mention the sun, or
also to invent new connotations for words ordinarily used
in a connotative sense. What happens too often is that the
burden of meaning he puts on a denotative or convention-
　　　　　　　　　　　　　　　　　　　　eak
ally connotative and therefore w　　is too heavy: the word
　　　　　　　　　　　　　　　　ord
snapS and we are left with no meaning at all or an incoherent meaning as if he were stroking your back, it feels so
nice but can you tell me about it? The weight referred to is
that of mr cummings' private experience and perceptions
which of necessity mustin their original state be unshared
by the reader who has had his own experience and has
found the triangular why of a dream is not to quote mr
cummings blue and is furthermore not triangular and is indeed not why. Of course i am not saying that eec must only
use words which a particular reader understands in context
—the, line, we draw for permissibly avoiding unlive-
massman convention is a pragmatic one at best but unfortunately eec is prone to overstep it. even at its most tolerant,
as in the foregoing quotation which may sound very
pleasant but poetry is unhappily not music it is impossible
to elucidate the meaning or even the feeling of the phrase.
The poet must grant the reader some rapport even if he
doesn't like us because we're not undead or else his poetry
becomes purely subjectivistic which is fine for writing on
your tablecloth but not necessarily so good for printing in a
public place unless you happen to be an anarchist, which I
am not and you are probably not.

Second, we must refer to the similar but much more destructive problem of cummings' punc (tuation)? and typography which is to say that he　　ow
　　　　　　　　　　　　　all
　　　　　　　　　　　　　　　　s
some
　　　　his poem　　　　　　　of
　　　　　s
　　　　　　　　　　　　v
to sprawl all　　　　　o　　　e
　　　　　　　(r)
the printed to use the word loosely page, with little marks
that used to be commas and similar unthings stuck in un-
Godly places,

Mr cummings is in this regard working on the theory of direct communication i assume that i referred to earlier,
which is that he is desir-ous of avoiding the stultification of
prescribed form which will hinder the direct expression of
　　　　　　　　　　　　　　　　　　　　　　　　i
his experiences. So that if he wants . . . to describe a k e he
　　　　　　　　　　　　　　　　　　　　　　　　t
makes some kind of arrangement which is supposed to sug-

gest a kite but is not a kite and cannot even really suggest a kite because a kite is a thing is unwords and exists in space not in time which is what words exist in; and because words are not things but are things ABOUT things or symbols and are experienced not directly but at one remove from experience. They are descriptions and a poem too in a description and since comprehension of descriptions occurs through the use of the intelligence the description itself must be intelligent even if this is unwhich and notmost. The trouble with cummings' poems which are really unpoems may be stated also psychologically; cummings breaks up w/o(r)-ds and chops them into pieces and mis: punctuate, s and extraCAPITALIZES and half-parenthesizes and (all to emphasize what he thinks are the feelings inherent in ordinary boring words like anonymous which has an US in it which is i suppose you and i making love. But this unphotographicminded reader reads one word at a time and must therefore rearrange as he goes along because words will be words and demand that they be perceived in the same oldreary way that they have been for the last few hundred years, i. e. one at a time and oneafteranother and in one (1) piece and even spelled bourgeoiscorrectly.

                If i scrawl   f,
                        o*
                l   a   tin,
                        g! ( )

in little pieces from here to eternity you are still going to read it as floating eventually if you die in the attempt and your effort to do this creates a battle between the reader and the poem which has nothing to do with the usual tension of unprose. It is just a damnuisance.

on the whole of course cummings has written a lot of doublemuchunugly poems which are very nice to read because he knows lots of not beautiful words which are unthings but words about beautiful things. . . . But most of these poems are ones in which the images have at least something to do with anyone or anything and the words are written one after another. As a matter of fact which is a subtle way of saying that my next sentence will probably be incorrect, those unconventional oddities of eec's which are good, such as what if a much of a which of a wind, are good precisely because they combine the best features of innovation with convention being in the most respected ladyyourlipsaredivineandiloveyou tradition: they are in a given context logical (he'd never forgive me for saying this) changes, structured intelligently and (your pardon ee) rationally; in short they make (o world o death) sens

                                                            E.

                                                    (pp. 25-6)

Philip Green, "an unessay on ee cuMming S," in The New Republic *(reprinted by permission of* The New Republic; © 1958 by The New Republic, Inc.), *May 19, 1958, pp. 24-6.*

NORMAN FRIEDMAN

[The] relationship between Cummings and his speaker is of the [kind which Friedman defines earlier as an author who "may deliberately create a poetic persona and then transform himself in its image, organizing his personal life and concerns to conform to that pattern"], and it has been made possible by endurance—or better still, integrity—rather than by a private income. His speaker is never involved in the world of work and routine which takes up the largest part of the lives of most men. . . . He is a detached observer and commentator rather than a participant; he is always either alone or with his lady; he never has a time clock to punch, a train to catch, a bill to pay, or a baby to feed. (p. 9)

[The incredible thing about Cummings' poetry is] how completely the man has been transformed into the artist, for his mode of life has involved absolutely no compromise between the character of the speaker he has created and the demands of everyday existence. It is just possible, indeed, that Cummings himself fully believes and acts exactly as his speaker believes and acts.

The speaker of Cummings' poems, then, is always a poet and a painter, and this has been a matter of endurance almost ritualistic in its disciplined and consistently sustained self-abnegation: the man has in effect died that the artist might live. For if the artist enjoys a certain amount of freedom from drudgery and nagging routine of which we of the "really unreal" world might feel somewhat envious, he also in exchange denies himself the solace of family and physical security which most of us would be reluctant indeed to surrender. And even more "dangerously" (a favorite word of his) he has taken, by a deliberate effort of will, his destiny altogether into his own hands, so that whatever becomes of him, he is entirely responsible. It has been, for him, an exchange of one kind of responsibility for another, and this voluntary assumption of freedom is a conclusive sign, if a sign is needed, of his absolute moral seriousness. (pp. 9-10)

[Cummings'] speaker sees this world as cleanly divided between good and evil, right and wrong, and, in so doing, simply rises above the whole struggle into a transcendent world which is one, and full of love. (p. 13)

Perhaps the key to the thought of Cummings' persona is to be found in the fact that, in his universe, there is evil but no sin. It is as if we were all still living in an Eden in which no command has yet been given, and all, except the speaker and a few others like him, are afraid of eating of its fruits. (pp. 13-14)

His reaction to suffering and evil is, since they are wholly manmade, hate unalloyed with pity; he has no sense at all of man's helplessness due to historical or metaphysical causes. And his reaction to courage and love is, since they are wholly divine, admiration unspoiled by second thoughts; he has no idea whatever of man's fundamental ambivalences due to environmental and psychological causes. (pp. 14-15)

This sense of detachment also partially explains the unusual virulence of his satire, for if we are ourselves wholly responsible for whatever foolishness we are guilty of and whatever betrayals we commit, then it follows that the satirist can bite and snarl, laugh and rage, fume and storm in his effort to get us to change our ways, and be without pity for those who refuse to listen. It helps to explain the rare tenderness of his love poetry as well, for the lover is not affrighted by the skull beneath the skin when he kisses his lady, nor is he dismayed by the tug of guilt as he embraces her. (p. 15)

There are three or four areas of human thought and experience about which Cummings' speaker has any ideas: love, death, and time; the natural and the artificial; society and the individual; and dream and reality. Transcendence means freedom from limitations and has its source in a sinless universe. Each of these topics, therefore, involves an opposition that illustrates this general freedom in a particular way: love transcends death and time; the individual transcends the group; the natural transcends the artificial; and the dream is the true reality. (p. 16)

If the character and thought of this speaker represent select aspects of the character and thought of its creator, so also do the subjects he dwells upon and the circumstances that give rise to his dramatic responses represent select aspects of the poet's actual environment. As the speaker, in other words, is a created persona, so his subjects and situations form a created world of images. And here also, taking them up in the order of their importance, we will learn as much from the omissions as from the inclusions.

Love always was and still is Cummings' chief subject of interest. The traditional lyric situation, representing the lover speaking of love to his lady, has been given in our time a special flavor and emphasis by Cummings. Not only the lover and his lady, but love itself—its quality, its value, its feel, its meaning—is a subject of continuing concern to our speaker.

Cummings is furthermore in the habit of associating love, as a subject, with the landscape, the seasons, the times of day, and with time and death—as poets have always done in the past. Love and lovers, not only traditionally but also as a logical consequence of the speaker's thought, are seen against the background of, and in harmony with, nature and natural process. . . . (pp. 27-8)

Ideas constitute his next most significant subject. It is frequently said that Cummings, happy primitive and sensuous anti-intellectual that he is, is undistinguished as a thinker. Whatever we may think of such a lack in a lyric poet, it is simply not true that he shares this quality with, say, Campion or Lovelace. The more one reads the complete poems, the more one is impressed by the relatively high proportion of nondramatic and satirical poems, the subjects of which are exclusively values and concepts, to say nothing of the many dramatic poems that express or imply abstract ideas in connection with the thought and character of the speaker as he responds to a variety of circumstances. (p. 29)

We have already discussed the detachment from the normal world of work and routine of Cummings' persona, and we may note here, in relation to his third most important poetic subject matter, the conspicuous absence of interest in marriage, children in relation to parents, working, groceries, bills, illness, diapers, dishes, laundry, worry, mundane responsibility, and social life. (p. 30)

The truth of the matter is that, for Cummings as well as for his speaker, what most of us call the "real" world simply does not exist, not necessarily and just because it is evil but rather because it is external and abstract. No one can feel History, or see a Government; they are made up, they are fake. The artist's country is himself, and treason or loyalty have meaning only in relationship to that citizenship; people who live in the unworld, since they exist in terms of that world, change when that world changes, succeed when that world succeeds, and collapse when that world collapses (witness the mass suicide of businessmen after the Crash). They are dead because they are not true to themselves. (p. 34)

The poet, then, creates the character, thought, and world of his persona out of internal necessity, and the critic need only ask if out of this necessity are created serious and beautiful peoms. A sensual mystic, Cummings is not of this world. If he is immature, it is the immaturity of a visionary; his persona represents no mere aesthetic pose. (p. 35)

We inquire now into the kinds of responses that Cummings portrays his speaker as acting out in consequence of endowing him with a certain character, set of beliefs, and subject matter. And the kinds of responses that a speaker may experience in a lyric are, commonly, to praise, to blame, to persuade, to react emotionally, to describe, to meditate, to reflect, and to set forth or argue a proposition. (p. 36)

Description, praise and eulogy, satire, reflection, and persuasion . . . are the kinds of responses that Cummings' persona is most frequently portrayed as enacting, and in that order. And these poems account for almost 90 per cent of the total, the rest being a numerically, if not a relatively, substantial scattering of poems of proposition and emotion. (p. 40)

These, then, are the kinds of responses around which Cummings most characteristically organizes his poems. His five major forms are: the description, that locates its speaker in the presence of some sensory stimulus and represents him as perceiving; praise and eulogy, that place him in relation to some person, type, or idea, and represent him as admiring; the satire, that places him in relation to society and that represents him as its critic; reflection, that places him before scenes and people and represents him as interpreting and commenting; and persuasion, that places him in the presence of someone else and represents him as speaking to him or her. . . . [There] are several additional minor ones which we have not been able to examine in any detail.

A speaker who has over five roles to play simply cannot be characterized as lacking in dramatic and rhetorical range, and thus the usual song-satire distinction will not serve to describe it. Furthermore, a thorough inquiry into Cummings' use of these situations has not supported the contention that he is a static poet, for each of them has an individual history in his work, an origin in time, a rise, and perhaps a fall. There is a decrease in description as he gets older and less absorbed in the immediacy of sensation; a rise, a dip, and a rise in his use of praise and eulogy as he gets a firmer grip on his moral values; a strong current of satire, more and more clearly defining his social values; and a gradual decline in reflection and persuasion as he turns more and more outward toward approbation rather than interpretation, instruction, and consolation. If his growth reveals no crises, it does show a steady development. (pp. 59-60)

If the poet's vision determines in general the kinds of poems he writes, then it is the kinds of poems he writes that determine the styles he uses. (p. 61)

[Nothing is more characteristic of Cummings'] style than its range and variety. He makes fun of what he praises, and mocks what he reveres; he is seriously funny, comically serious, and classically romantic. He can use obscenities in a love poem and archaisms in a topical satire; he can mix concrete adjectives with abstract nouns and see colors in terms of sounds. Thus I shall call his general stylistic quality "mixed." Although the mixed style is characteristic of much modern poetry, what is impressive is the particular nature of Cummings' mixture and the special way he handles it.

The components of this mixture—whether appearing alone or in combination—range, reading from right to left on the linguistic spectrum, from "formal" or "archaic," to "neutral," to "mock" or "burlesque." These three modes and their various mixtures constitute an instrument of great dramatic and rhetorical precision which Cummings has forged to characterize the subtlety and variety of his speaker's attitudes and responses. Since there appears to be almost no limit to what his speaker can say in a given situation—he may talk out of the side of his mouth, or sing, or speak grandiloquently, or combine various voices—this verbal freedom is his chief pitfall. But here, as elsewhere, Cummings' freedom transcends danger—or rather lives on danger—and comes out finally as discipline. (pp. 62-3)

There are at least two reasons why Cummings' growth has been called into question: first, because many of his critics, being of his generation, have apparently never been able to forget the startling impression that his early work made in their younger days, and therefore have been unable to read his middle and later work without being impressed most by the echoes they find there of the early work; and second, because they cherish a special and limited notion of what constitutes poetic development. (pp. 159-60)

A chronological reading of his complete poetry reveals very real developments in thought, form, expression, and technique, and therefore the facts simply will not support the charge that he has remained static. (p. 160)

Their view, secondly, of what constitutes development seems to be limited to the kind that involves a reversal of some sort: from profane to sacred verse, as in Donne; from lushness to restraint, as in Yeats; from despair to faith, as in Eliot; or from Marxism to Freudianism to Protestantism, as in Auden. What they require, apparently, is that the poet grow through a series of discarded hopes and repudiated enthusiasms, and this they value as a sign of maturity. This is related also to their doctrine of the tragic vision, of giving the devil his due, on the assumption, it seems, that one can only know in terms of opposites, that Good can be understood only after one has embraced Evil, that the repentant sinner is more to be valued than the consistently virtuous man. Also involved is the rather faddish doctrine that a poet must mirror his times; if the age is complex, then poetry must be complex; if the age is ambivalent, the poet must be ambivalent.

The fact is, however, that many of our best poets have not developed in this way. . . . Cummings has grown . . . by remaining faithful to himself; if he has not changed his vision of life, he has nevertheless deepened it and given it a more serious turn; if he has not evolved from one sort of poetic form to another, he has nevertheless developed a variety of forms and revealed a less purely sensuous emphasis in many of them; if he has shown a consistent preference for certain words, he has nevertheless rejected some and added others in the interest of greater efficiency of style; and if he has not entirely abandoned his more eccentric typographical techniques, he has nevertheless come to use them with less frequency in favor of and in combination with other and stricter disciplines. (pp. 160-61)

For he has grown, as all artists must, by remaining faithful

to himself in his own way and by being dedicated as few others are. This is called, all things considered, integrity—which we are prepared by now not to confuse with immaturity—a quality the possession of which by any poet, nay, by any man, qualifies him as a citizen of immortality. (p. 167)

Norman Friedman, in his E. E. Cummings: The Art of His Poetry *(© 1960 by The Johns Hopkins Press), The Johns Hopkins University Press, 1960.*

DAVID RAY

Cummings is one of our society's best haters; functioning as a Juvenalian satirist, he has long attacked our society's worst indulgences in materialism, hypocrisy, "hypercivic zeal," scientific unwisdom and the following of false heroes and tawdry ideals. He most bitterly, in poems like "plato told him . . . " reproaches us for not taking the words of our philosophers seriously, but rather insisting on mouthing (vulgarizing and debasing) the poetry of their utterances. (p. 287)

["Buffalo Bill's Defunct,"] based on the poet's intense anger, is part of Cummings's broadside assault on several traditions, particularly that of our national sentimentality toward figures like Buffalo Bill. Cummings seems to be saying, with an appearance of flippancy that has often been regarded by critics as rather adolescent, that we as a nation are adolescent in our infatuation for such fraudulent "heroes." Even the subjects of our grief are unworthy. (p. 288)

To understand the poem's irony it is necessary to make the chronological perspective within the poem very clear. The persona is that of a mature man who, as a child, was awed by Bill . . . and who, hearing of Bill's death, first grieves for him, and then (and these functions are simultaneous) adds additional fuel to his hatred of "Mister Death," the destroyer of everything, by reflecting that he was defrauded and deprived by Bill as well as by "Mister Death." In this sense the poet both laments and curses the fraudulence of his childhood hero-worship. These shifts are clearly signalled by the change of tense from present to past (to the boy's view) and back again to the angry persona of the present tense. There is, of course, a very obvious shift of tone that goes along with the shift of tense; the mellifluous "watersmooth silver stallion" image, almost caressed, is a sharp contrast to such a nasty word as *defunct* or to such a sneering phrase as "how do you like your blueeyed boy."

It is important to note, in making a case for the redirection of the poet's fury to Bill, that Bill, in the poem, functions as a destroyer, an agent of death. What has been destroyed, of course, is rather all-embracing. Bill has been destroyed; the poet's childhood, and the kind of innocent faith and wonder that went along with it has been destroyed by his subsequent disillusionment with Bill; the clay pigeons have been destroyed. The poet is in many ways blaming Bill for disappointing both his expectations of childhood and of America. . . . (pp. 288-89)

Cummings's poem is, then, an assault on everything held dear by a sentimentalist or a hero-worshipper. Following his usual practice, his first offense is directed at the grammarians; he then turns to attack the tradition of a respectful stance toward the subject of death . . . , the heroism of Buffalo Bill, and—most importantly—the entire convention of the elegy. Cummings assaults everything, in short, in this finest of his "hate" poems except what he manages to assert by this anger—a sense of fundamental decency outraged with everything that corrupts life or makes it fraudulent. (pp. 289-90)

David Ray, "The Irony of E. E. Cummings," in College English (copyright © 1962 by the National Council of Teachers of English), January, 1962, pp. 282-90.

GEORGE WESOLEK

Cummings' depth and poetic vision is intense enough to excite and revivify. He confronts himself with cosmic dichotomies that take him to the core of man's reality. He questions, probes, ridicules. The undercurrent of a Cummings' joy is most often cynicism, betraying to us the lonely man, the man of "helpless pain" beleaguered by a "piercing sense of dislocation." . . . (p. 3)

Cummings runs away in his cynicism. He flees the hellbent, tortuous world that offers the evil of man as his own God. He flees the oppressing, lackluster world of scientifically organized man. . . . He lifts himself above this banality searching for the God of his poetic joy. . . . He is like Byron following the venturesome Don Juan to a fairy island or Whitman losing himself in the surging rivers and pliant grass. (pp. 3-4)

Cummings breaks the chains that bind him to conventional matters and casts off the "common motives of humanity." Because of this, he deserves the respect, admiration, and envy due all poets by the more unfortunate who must cast their lot with banality. He is above other men because he places himself there and his success depends upon his supraview of nature, of the heaven in his back alley or the public park. He expresses his joy and it remains with him. Most people cannot partake in it for his acts of poetry are naked and obscene exposures of an inner daimonia. They are of "infinite loneliness." In a sense, they communicate only the loneliness, the longing that emptiness brings to a super-sensitive prophet of beauty. The great mass of men, the "mostpeople" of Cummings, cannot fathom this unreal search for reality. . . . Mostpeople is rather the "Cultured aristocrat yanked out of his hyperexclusively ultravoluptuous superpallazzo, and dumped into an incredibly vulgar detentioncamp swarming with every conceivable species of undesireable organism." But not "You and I," says Cummings. "You and I are human beings; mostpeople are snobs." You and I are the visionaries, the oracles of a hellishly mysterious world. . . .

The fantastic tension created between mostpeople and you and I is the medium of Cummings' poetry. (p. 4)

Cummings, the poet, exemplifies the alienation of the searcher for beauty and truth from the world. Monklike, he follows a discipline which liberates his vision. He turns his head with pride to the heavens and seeks out the stars that shine brilliantly through dirty windows, or over the towering mountain of a steel city, or in the mud of a garden path. He proclaims the star in man, the mystery that will never be solved by the furious machinations of a mind:

> when skies are hanged and oceans drowned,
> the single secret will still be man.

Reason stifles the gropings of man's real need. Cummings emphasizes this point over and over again. It is at the basis of his flight from what mostpeople call reality. It is at the crux of his alienation. He would rather see a dirt-encrusted garbage can and partake of its beauty than to scientifically evaluate its dimensions. . . .

This transcendency over the mind brings Cummings to damn all abstractions. He wants to accept the world and reality as it is, to become a part of it, to enter into it with all the verve and passion of a lover. We are unable to communicate with such an irregular view of reality for any length of time. We are not "existential" enough. When all is said and done, and our momentary fit of poetic romanticism has passed, we have to return to a world of "reality." Cummings' "real" and our "real" cannot breathe the same air. (p. 5)

In himself and by himself . . . the artist may travel where he pleases. There are no restrictions on creativity in his private domain. If two plus two equals four in the "real world," the poet can make it five. The "nonmakers" are content with four, Cummings cannot be. This ingredient of freedom may be called license by some, but it is definitely not by Cummings. It is, rather, the *meontic* freedom of Berdyaev and the *willful* freedom of Nietzsche. Man is Godlike. He can create and destroy as he wills. The pity of the situation is that there is no absolute quality to creativity. It is extremely difficult to transcend with blazing visions when all things are restricted by man's myopia. On the poetic level, there is the problem of fitting the vastly beautiful three dimensional reality into two dimensional forms. In an effort to escape this, Cummings uses form, words, spacing and punctuation as he wills. He tries to create reality that surpasses limitations. In reading his more unorthodox work, one feels his soul struggling upwards while not understanding totally. (pp. 5-6)

A great amount of pain can arise in a sensitive soul which is constantly at the core of such tension. The battleground is not soaked in blood but in the sweat of loneliness. The poet stands at the pinnacle of a paradox. He can see his stars and feel their heat but he cannot communicate this adequately to others. . . .

No vision in its completeness can pass between Cummings and mostpeople. "Worms are the words," they convey "a dawn of a doom of a dream." The breach is unsurpassable and heightens Cummings' sense of isolation. It forces him to turn in on himself and encounter whatever good or evil he may find there. The isolation also directs him to an Other, but an Other that is worthy of him—a Being that transcends even his visions. This Other is a most fundamental part of his search. It is the end toward which all his dreams are focused. It is the essence of his complete transcendency and pursuit of this "object" becomes the central theme of all Cummings' work.

Is it God? Is it Love? In a sense, it is both of these, but really and basically it is something beyond them. (p. 6)

The truth is that neither God nor Love can fill the void in Cummings. The emptiness remains as a symbol of man's condition—the plight of uncertainty and existence in a befouled world. For Cummings, the feeling is much more acute. By his talent and vision, the infinite gap between heaven and earth takes on gigantic proportions. The pain travels paradoxically through his poetry in the form of joy —a joy which is an enigmatic consolation now. (p. 7)

Words can be deceiving, and they are very apt to be deceiving in the case of Cummings. He is definitely not a children's poet although he does exude a warmth and charm that is childlike in quality. He is not a poet of rebellion and pessimism although he does allow himself cynical, rebellious overtures. More pointedly, it can be said that he embodies both of these things to a certain extent while still pursuing more elusive and profound realities. He is a poet in the tradition of Homer, Shakespeare, and Whitman. Cummings searches for a vision which will satisfy and complete him. He struggles forward in a special way, in a decidedly modern way, in a way that has been conditioned by nuclear turmoil and despair. He expresses a boundless Faith in Man and his courage to overcome these difficulties and keep on searching in the face of opposition and even annihilation. He is a lonely man, a man isolated from most-people, estranged from the herd, alienated from the common trivia of earthly life. In short, he is a poet and a mystic, and because of this, he is doomed to a position of grandeur—grandeur that is so lofty and so immersed in captured destiny that the horizon of humanity becomes a very distant line never again to be seen by human eyes. (p. 8)

> *George Wesolek, "E. E. Cummings: A Reconsideration," in* Renascence *(© copyright, 1965, Marquette University Press), Autumn, 1965, pp. 3-8.*

ROBERT E. WEGNER

For Cummings, self-discovery was supremely important and the only valid motive for writing a poem; it separated his awareness from stereotyped awarenesses, separated his identity as an artist from his conventional identity as a member of society. If the truth of human existence is to be uncovered and recognized, it will be accomplished through the perspective of the artist. (pp. 12-13)

In the process of writing a poem, the poet discovers his identity, which paradoxically is one of fusion and harmony with the eternal forces of change. The artist discovers his identity in the eternal by resisting the current of temporal affairs; at the same time, it is in the temporal world that the artist discovers the eternal and spiritual. This unfolding of identity is never-ending: it depends upon an honest appraisal of felt experience. (p. 13)

The happiness of Cummings' early life, his sense of being loved, and his devotion to his parents have found expression in many poems. Two of the most obvious and best known are the famous elegies: "my father moved through dooms of love" . . . and "if there are any heavens my mother will (all by herself) have." . . . (p. 14)

The concept of love as a positive force to be equated with joy and growth had its source in Cummings' experience as a child; he grew up in an aura of love. From the same source, from his study of Greek literature, and no doubt from other sources, came his conviction of the essential dignity of the individual. Both are central to his writing. Love is the propelling force behind a great body of his poetry. In time he came to see love and the dignity of the human being as inseparable. (pp. 15-16)

Cummings' satiric thrusts at his conventional New England background with its decorum, propriety, and respectability spring from the same source as his poems of eulogy and joy —namely his convictions about love and human dignity. Cummings defends these values against any force or idea that would threaten them. Rules and regulations about what is correct and proper stifle spontaneity, thwart joy, stunt spiritual growth; they may prevent love, may prevent the realization of one's dignity. You cannot know who you are if you are concerned only with what society demands that you should be. Hence Cummings ridicules the stuffy elements of his own New England, Puritan heritage. (p. 17)

Throughout his career Cummings insisted that the artist must maintain fidelity to himself. (p. 25)

The most extended analysis of the problem of maintaining individuality as a man and fidelity to self as an artist occurs in the play *Him.* . . . The dramatic tension of the play rises from the struggle of the character Him to determine what is genuine and what is false, what truly exists and what he is deceived into thinking exists. (pp. 26-7)

Two key words in Cummings' mystique are *failure* and *nothing*. These two words help clarify each other. *Nothing* represents the spirit or essence of existence; it is no thing. For Cummings the apparent confusion and chaos of the visible and tangible world dissolves when one becomes aware of the spiritual world inherent in it. The task of the poet is to attempt to come to grips with this world of spirit, to show that behind the tumultuous and disparate impressions lies a world of harmony, order, and unity of spirit. This world is more real than the superficial world of unrelated sense impressions: it is the world of *nothing*, wherein lies the truth of our existence. (pp. 30-1)

But the poet, by being nothing in society, by cultivating himself, is alone with such basic phenomena as stars, twilight, the moon, and (in this particular poem) flowers, which all serve as symbols of a cycle of growth and love. Moreover, these phenomena renew themselves, and to this extent they are in accord with the universal will of creation. Ironically, they are so taken for granted, so constantly before us, that they are perceived as nothing in the usual sense of the word—devoid of significance. But to the poet they speak completeness, fulfillment, and rebirth—the ultimate of *nothing*.

For Cummings, then, the word *nothing* implies the "awful responsibility" the artist assumes, knowing he will fail. Finally, *nothing* is the ultimate goal of the Artist-Man-Failure, who in order to attain it must of necessity maintain fidelity to himself. (pp. 35-6)

Cummings is concerned with the whole man, and in writing a poem he attempts to make the poem become the man. That is, he attempts to portray for his readers that image of man which is splendid rather than sordid, magnanimous rather than petty. (p. 38)

In reading Cummings' poetry . . . it is helpful to know that he differs from most of his contemporaries in two basic ways: in his general attitude toward life, and in his method of employing subjects and images. His attitude toward existence largely informs and controls his poetic methods. . . . Cummings finds illimitable joy in everything truly alive. He turns an oftentimes brilliant and vitriolic satire upon those people who do not respond to life and upon the conventions, institutions, and beliefs with which they surround themselves to avoid or disguise reality.

Because of this basic attitude his poems often take on a radical appearance on the page. Subjects are presented for the simple purpose of calling attention to the properties of their vitality or for the purpose of dispelling set notions or beliefs about them. Hence [his poems] . . . either intrigue readers with the ingenuity of their technique or cause them to decide that Cummings is writing in a private language to please only himself and perhaps the esoteric few. (pp. 40-1)

Where other poets begin with an idea (or perhaps a general conviction or awareness) which they exemplify with subjects and images—a process which T. S. Eliot has termed the discovery of an "objective correlative"—Cummings often begins with and goes no further than the subject or incident itself, assuming that the subject, seen for itself, will reveal its inherent significance. Here we have two polarities of method which, when effectively employed, converge upon very similar results. With Cummings, however, it is important to recognize how his method differs from conventional practice, as an aid to understanding his poetry.

Cummings does not present a system of thought; instead he presents a response to life. His statements express this response; his subjects and images embody it. They do not stand for something outside the poem (they are not symbols in the true sense of the word), but represent only themselves, as possessing life and vitality or not possessing it. They may be thought of as symbols only in relation to Cummings' statement that life is a mystery, an unknown quantity, and that in order to be alive one must constantly be aware of this fact.

Cummings' major subjects are love, birth, growth, dying, and their antitheses. . . . Given his convictions about what constitutes value in life, these subjects are most appropriate; for they remain largely unknown (mysterious). It may even be that the poet alone (or a person of poetic temperament) has anything to say about them that is interesting or exciting. (pp. 47-8)

Although he occasionally called himself a "nonhero," the meaning Cummings attaches to two key terms in his lexicon —*freedom* and *individual*—is much more apropos to his stance as a member of society and his vision as a poet. (p. 66)

Cummings believed that a man is free when he is allowed to *be* himself. He believed that a man can be himself only when he is not shackled to creed, beliefs, dogma, ideologies. . . . A man can be himself by reflecting on his responses and feeling awarenesses. If he accepts the truth he senses, he is free. If, however, he lives by the creeds and slogans he has been taught to believe, he is not free. One of the foremost attributes of the individual is that he resists the tyranny of thinking and practices the freedom of feeling alive.

In his freedom the individual retains the right, always, to decline making a choice between mental alternatives or hypothetical distinctions. (pp. 67-8)

Cummings' concept of the individual did not emerge fully developed at the beginning of his career to be reaffirmed through successive volumes of poetry without any perceptible change or increase in significance, as has too often been stated. Rather, the early volumes primarily celebrate the simply joy of living through the senses, though they also contain some of Cummings' best satiric pieces.

The middle volumes, beginning approximately with *is 5* . . . , reaching a culmination with *no thanks* . . . , and showing evidence of a changing emphasis with *50 Poems* . . . , reveal a heightened and defensively sensitive aware-

ness of the individual in relation to his social environment. A noticeably larger number of poems are satiric in tone; they expose specific incidents, occupations, and conventions in thought and behavior that in Cummings' view threaten the individual perception. Poems of objective detail without overt statement now appear on occasion in the form of a pictogram or ideogram. Primarily, however, sensory perception during this middle period is used as a test or a contrast to reveal disparity between what the individual perceives as truth and what the intellect has inculcated. (pp. 80-1)

With the publication of *50 Poems* another important dimension becomes evident in Cummings' poetry. Beginning approximately with this volume and extending through *95 Poems* . . . and *73 Poems* . . . , we find Cummings examining the positive impact that the individual exerts upon his fellow men. As we have seen, what the individual has to offer, what the pattern of his life illustrates, is love. . . . This role of the individual adds a new dimension to Cummings' themes; but nothing of major emphasis in the earlier poetry has been discarded. It is this integrated thematic unity that has misled certain critics into assuming that Cummings' poetry has shown neither growth nor change. The charge is not just. Although Cummings' basic position has never wavered, his poetry does reveal growth in perception and a steady increase in depth and significance. (pp. 81-2)

These are the basic themes of all of Cummings' writing. They are interdependent. Taken in the order Cummings has emphasized them in his poetry, they may be listed as follows:

1. The primacy of sensory awareness (of feeling).
2. The integrity of the individual.
3. The realization of love.

In the order listed these themes point up Cummings' growth as a poet.

The earliest poetry not only affirms that the senses are the means by which life is revealed, but the poetry itself is sensuous, replete with archaic terms suggesting romantic distance and exotic images around which cluster vague emotions suggested through the connotative value of abstract adjectives. . . . However, Cummings soon came to recognize that the simple presentation of sensual exuberance was not enough, that the value of a phenomenon resided in its inherent essence as revelation about the meaning of life. As a consequence a number of things occurred: the romantic imagery and setting were dropped along with archaic terms and the many allusions to myths and mythological figures. In their stead we find poems dealing with the immediate scene although suitable to any historic time, past, present, or future—the wonder evoked by spring, by the beauty of flowers, by twilight and other natural phenomena, and by the emotion of love. In addition, the poet's language becomes far less extravagant; the rich and vaguely sensuous gives way to the more precise and definite, yet manages to convey impressions that are sensuous and emotionally charged. Word spacing, syntactical distortion, and all the typographical oddities for which Cummings is known are motivated by the same desire to capture, by heightening the impression, the essence of the phenomenon perceived. However, through all this experimentation in the early poetry, his fundamental belief in the importance of sensual perception remained steadfast. (pp. 82-3)

The majority of Cummings' early poems neither state nor indicate by contrast that sensory perception is the only valid test of reality; rather they proceed on this assumption. As poems they deal with experiences or impressions that in themselves may seem slight. Their intention seems to be merely that of reproducing the emotional sensation of physical love, of response to the natural manifestations of life, of response to vivid childhood memories, or of the felt reaction towards sterility. Behind these poems there resides no implicit body of ideology or philosophic idea. Rather the attempt seems to be that of recording an impression or experience in such a way that the reader is compelled to share it with the poet. (pp. 89-90)

From an early poetry of exuberance and sensory detail in which values were seldom pointedly stated, Cummings moved during the mid-twenties to a position from which he more pronouncedly rejects the sham values and superficial by-products of social convention. However, the charge that in his middle and later poetry he became so obsessed with his own integrity as an individual that he could neither accept nor find place for the opinions of others is without warrant in the light of the many poems he has written for the express purpose of giving credit and extending praise to those he admired. Equally unwarranted is the assertion that the characters of his poems are so shallowly depicted as to emerge almost entirely as caricatures, intensely presented in objective detail but lacking in substance of thought or feeling. Numerous poems and prose comments indicate the opposite, among them those lauding Hart Crane, Ezra Pound, Froissart, Ford Madox Ford, Picasso, Sally Rand, Jimmy Savo, Sam (whose ''heart was big/ as the world aint square),'' his father, and Olaf, ''a conscientious object-or,'' to name those that come most readily to mind. (p. 99)

The individual in Cummings' poetry emerges because of the recognition of two basic precepts: that the codes of behavior and accepted belief of society are stultifying, and that the values residing in nature are not perceived or understood by those who subscribe to the dictates of propriety. The result is that the individual is one set apart not because he wants to be, because he prizes a discipline of some kind for the sake of the discipline, but because his integrity warns him that he must constantly beware of doctrine that is false by the test of the unstereotyped response. (p. 101)

With the publication of *50 Poems* . . . it became evident that the individual of the earlier poems was becoming aware of himself as one who not only exults in love but also practices that love which is the only real ingredient of life. In a sense the individual becomes in the later poems both the embodiment of and the spokesman for the love that reveals the basic kinship of men. The earlier poems reflect an exuberance about the physical aspect of love. Poems published during the 1930's indicate an awareness of love as the force that perpetuates life and existence beyond death through a kind of transcendental communion with the forces of the universe. But not until the later poems do we find the individual as a disciple of and commentator on love, one who brings an awareness of the force and beauty of love into the lives of others through the simple procedure of being his uninhibited self in action and words. To be sure, these later poems dealing with love are more didactic than the earlier ones; where the earlier poems deal largely with the physical sensations of love and as a result are to a certain degree

dramatic, with a recognized speaker or actor involved, the later poems proceed much of the time from an uninvolved voice commenting upon those mystic qualities of love that induce growth, renewal, and harmony. In short, the development has been from poems dealing with the sensations of love to those in praise of a realization of love.

The best known of these later love poems are those that metaphorically figure the wonder and strength of love in the form of a recognizable person, verging on a type. Examples would be his father, anyone of ''anyone lived in a pretty how town,'' Sam of the poem ''rain or hail,'' and the knife-sharpener of ''who sharpens every dull.'' The characters in each of these poems are superb examples of the Cummings hero, the individual who lives and practices love, who is an ambassador of love without consciously striving to be, without the slightest trace of altruism, living his life according to the only valid principle he knows, fidelity to self. However, the majority of the later love poems are not so strikingly dramatized; rather they exist as disembodied statements about love, identifiable with the human situation only as we can hear and accept the voice of the poet. (pp. 109-10)

What growth or depth has Cummings' poetry revealed over the years? From my observations I would say that the poet has steadily approached an ideal which can be summarily stated as follows: the purpose of life is the realization of love. Love, however, to be realized, depends upon an individual who applies to himself for the truth as it is perceived and felt. (p. 114)

Cummings wrote poetry for the purpose of discovering himself; the purpose of his satire was to preserve himself, his identity as an individual. In contrast to what he celebrated (birth, growth, love, joy), there is what he impugned (hypocrisy of any kind, cruelty, unfeeling disregard for human dignity, and death regarded as complete cessation). At its best, Cummings' satire reveals the joy of knowing and discovering ourselves in an amazing if not fantastic world versus the ever-present danger of losing ourselves in a human mass, of succumbing to concocted stimuli presented on a massive scale. On this level his satire is brilliant revelation: trenchant, penetrating, sometimes explosive in its humorous ribaldry. At times, however, the reason for the poet's scorn seems to be lost in a barrage of abuse and name-calling. When this happens two things are apparent: precision of statement is lacking, and the attack seems to be launched from a position in itself conventional and stereotyped. These two failings are, of course, related; when the poet is not himself, he cannot write like himself. Good satire depends upon more than a personal bias: it is based upon the assumption that human dignity is more to be cherished than all or any forms or manners of living.

The basis of Cummings' satire is the unfulfilled ideal of human dignity he cherished. For Cummings human dignity could not exist without love. (pp. 116-17)

Without an awareness of what Cummings considers the motive of satire, a reader is likely to come to the unjustifiable conclusion that the poet is only bitter, that he is something of a cynic, that he is inhabiting the ghost-town of solipsism, or that he is skating along the brink of nihilism. These charges have been made; and they have probably been made out of shock or amazement at the vituperation Cummings unleashes against the forces of negation which he loathes. But there is always the other side of the coin: Cummings never stops expressing his admiration, respect, and love for the vital. As he pointed out, love expresses itself through both affirmation and denial. (p. 122)

Cummings' name is associated with unconventional punctuation and capitalization, word displacements, and unusual arrangements of stanzas, lines, words, and even individual letters to produce visual typographical forms. His poems range in prosodic shape from the terse, cryptic ideogram (or pictogram), which in appearance may resemble a column of Chinese script, to conventional stanzaic forms with regular line lengths, meter, and rhyme. Most of his poems fall between these two extremes; nevertheless, an unwary reader may mistake a Cummings sonnet for a poem in free verse. (p. 142)

The ideogram is probably Cummings' most difficult form. These most terse of peoms combine visual and auditory elements, and must be viewed in much the same way as an intaglio. Sounds are suggested, but they may be onomatopoeic rather than linguistic—that is, heard, associated with a visual image, but not pronounced. (p. 143)

The ideogram compresses perception, feeling, and realization until they are no longer distinguishable, until, as Keats observed, beauty is truth and truth is beauty. Cummings responded to the beauty of twilight, a first star, the new moon. His purpose in striving for compression in these poems was to realize more fully the truth about love and being alive that he felt resided in something as simple as seeing a flake of snow—or a whole snowstorm. He has written numerous poems on these subjects. But the progress he made in realizing their significance can best be seen by comparing an early poem with a later one—for instance, "in the rain-" from *XLI Poems* with "a-/float on some" from the volume *I X I*. They are very much alike in subject matter and in the tone of voice. However, they show a great difference in technical accomplishment, and they illustrate the poet's development, a matter which has concerned many critics. (p. 148)

Cummings wrote poems that even Mrs. Grundy would recognize as such. Established stanzaic patterns, strict metrical lines, and rhyme have always been part of his technical repertoire, and poems with these characteristics can be found in every volume of poetry he published. They show a precision, particularly in his later volumes, as meticulous as that found in the ideogram. In addition, traditional forms seemed to allow him more freedom: he indulged in wit, humor, narrative, satire as well as fleeting impressions and brief incidents. The ideogram is a moment of coalesced awarenesses. The poem written in traditional prosody may be, for Cummings, a philosophical reflection, a complete episode, a character sketch, or a narrative summary of an entire life. He put established forms to more uses than he did the very terse poem of impression. The broader confines allowed him to investigate more than one perspective. . . . (pp. 157-58)

Cummings is a versatile poet, a skilled craftsman. But regardless of what form he employs, from the highly elliptical ideogram to the flawlessly metrical and rhymed stanza, his purpose remains the same: through technique to achieve that precision which conclusively demonstrates the spiritual harmony of the physical universe. At their best, his techniques are the embodiment of his themes. (p. 162)

Robert E. Wegner, in his The Poetry and Prose of E. E. Cummings *(copyright © 1965 by Robert E. Wegner; reprinted by permission of Harcourt Brace Jovanovich, Inc.), Harcourt, 1965.*

MARILYN GAULL

E. E. Cummings, particularly in *The Enormous Room*, assumed the multiple task of demonstrating not only the discrepancy between language and experience but also the corrosive effects of this discrepancy on the human psyche, and, perhaps his most significant achievement, offered a means for overcoming it in the creation of new relationships between language and experience. (p. 646)

[Principles] for restoring value to a benumbed and misleading language were displayed by Cummings throughout his work. His characteristic device was the manipulation of contexts, associating symbols with their functional referents rather than traditional ones. Such a device, however, in the spare and unelaborated idiom of his poetry was actually a source of confusion. . . . In the poetry . . . Cummings' assault on the traditional values of words appears to be little more than evocative eccentricity. Within the more flexible bounds of prose, however, Cummings was able to build up new contexts, to provide the precise associations upon which a creative and functional use of language depends.

In *The Enormous Room,* Cummings' creative use of language is most successful because it is most integral to the form and theme of the novel. His attack on the traditional symbols, his portrayal of the distorted values and behavior arising from the tyranny of these symbols over reality and his ultimate creation of a language which accurately describes and thereby recreates his world serve as a paradigm for the experience of the narrator. For the novel traces the narrator's disenchantment and betrayal by a world that contradicts its own cultural tradition; it follows the slow erosion of his personality, and his gradual awakening as a creative consciousness.

The major technical problem of a narrative which involves such complex objectives is point of view. Primarily, Cummings' point of view is retrospective. The narrator serves as the persona of Cummings-past, so to speak, through whom the author re-enacts his self-development. The ironic detachment of much of the novel is accounted for by Cummings' having used the innovations in perception and language which were the product of his entire experience. (pp. 647-48)

The Introduction, written in 1932, focuses on the opposition around which the book is structured. In a dialogue between an anonymous interviewer and Cummings, the author opposes a member of what he calls the "everyday humdrum world" and the artist. . . . (pp. 648-49)

Cummings establishes through this dialogue that the artist, by which he means anyone who creates symbols in wood, music, paint or words, achieves identity or selfhood. . . . It is, if you like, the hypothesis of *The Enormous Room*, evolved during his writing of the novel ten years earlier. (p. 649)

The central problem of the book . . . was a subjective one, the solution to which allowed the book to be written. Before Cummings could perceive and create a viable correspondence between language and experience, he had to rescue himself, a perceiver or identity, from the dehumanizing pressures of his environment. During most of his stay in the Enormous Room, the problem of selfhood was latent. He resided in a limbo between the loss of the official or external and the discovery of the essential self. Deprived of the possibility, indeed, the necessity for motivated action, Cummings functioned simply as an intensely aware and receptive but frozen intelligence. Since it was, as Cummings discovered, through his art that he was able to become himself . . . , his search for an authentic self was a search within for a nucleus of creativity, the artist's Archimedean point.

Basic to this self-discovery was a condition which characterized his entire imprisonment: a suspension of time. The temporal order is another external structure which, by tying the individual to his own past, introduces the confusion between the self and what is merely an accumulation of experience or events. Consequently, after a detailed description of one day's schedule in prison, Cummings discards the temporal as even an organizational device. . . . Having established his truancy from time, he confines himself to an empirical present. . . . (pp. 658-59)

Cummings remains in this state of suspended animation until the departure of his companion "B," the last link with his own past and culture. With this event, the dissolution of external bases of identity rapidly increases and intensifies. . . . In his indifference to a set of Shakespeare which he receives in the mail, Cummings recognizes the failure of intellectual or cultural affinities as possible bases for self-definition, for they, like one's past or friends, are only external points of reference. . . . Finally, his physical appearance deteriorates, and with it the most superficial but conventional basis for a definition of self in the objective world, the last external symbol of a social being. . . . Gradually, the "Machine of decomposition" . . . destroys the surface layers of Cummings' identity until he is reduced to an almost prenatal passiveness: "I felt myself to be, at last, a doll—taken out occasionally and played with and put back into its house and told to go to sleep." . . . What appears here as a total defeat by the official structure is in fact the most crucial point in Cummings' self-realization. In this total apathy he no longer depends upon his environment or his accumulated experience for either a vision of self or an interpretation of events.

Cummings makes the first positive gesture toward self-realization when he responds to a natural phenomenon directly rather than through a perception cluttered with inherited, non-functional symbols. The instrument of this response is the imagination, and its awakening marks the emergence of the artist, the basis of his authentic self. . . . (pp. 659-60)

In establishing the imagination as the inviolable point of reference for understanding his world, Cummings defines his identity as an artist. Whenever he articulates his personal vision of the world, whenever, in other words, he assigns symbols to experience, he both re-creates that world and affirms his identity. The whole process has something of the magical self-generation of the phoenix in it. In order to create, one must have a sense of selfhood; selfhood is affirmed through the act of creation. The ultimate significance, however, of the creative act is contained in the final self-surpassing goal: words, symbols, language. (p. 661)

Like the creative writers of the war generation, he was preoccupied with the failure of traditional symbols in representing the critical experience of his time. But Cummings did not seem to respond in either of the two fashions which characterized these writers. He neither denied the world, excluding it from his proper artistic concerns; nor did he defy it, assuming the self-defeating posture of protest. Rather, he incorporated the world within himself, interpreted it in personal terms, and arrived at a separate, private but communicable peace. Like the semanticists, Cummings' approach to language was functional or empirical. But the goal of the semanticists was social: a community of understanding based upon universally verifiable experience. However admirable this goal may have been, it could not be attained. The semanticists were either caught in debate over the universality of their definitions or imposed new orthodoxies to escape from the morass of whether X should equal Y, Z or buttercups. Cummings escaped both these dilemmas by resisting the claims of society on his art and himself. Experience had shown him that the only possible and authentic gesture was in the preservation of self through a creative act, the making of symbols, which could be as minimal and only as social as conversation. (pp. 661-62)

With the imagination as his source of value, Cummings' ultimate allegiance is to an aesthetic norm which is not restricted to art, one with social, political and ethical implications. Like an earlier devotee of the imagination, Cummings found a liberating and enlarging ideal in the Beauty that is Truth, and Truth that is Beauty. While the truth which he pursued may be more mundane than Keats', it is also more concrete and therefore more available. The beauty, however, that is its measure is encompassing, including the entire range of the living sensate world and everything which animates it. *The Enormous Room* then, on almost every level—language, form, theme, character—may be considered as a metaphor for the Edenic experience of the creating imagination. (p. 662)

> *Marilyn Gaull, "Language and Identity: A Study of E. E. Cummings' 'The Enormous Room'," in* American Quarterly *(copyright © 1967 Trustees of the University of Pennsylvania), Winter, 1967, pp. 645-62.*

PATRICK B. MULLEN

It is generally overlooked that E. E. Cummings had an avid interest in various forms of American popular culture, especially burlesque, circuses, amusement parks, comic strips, animated cartoons, and movies. . . . To Cummings, burlesque and the other popular arts were alive with a spontaneous, unrehearsed quality. He wanted to capture the same quality of spontaneity in his poetry, both in content and technique. In a limited way, Cummings wrote about popular culture of the 1920's-1930's much the same as Tom Wolfe was writing about it in the 1960's. Cummings was one of the few writers of his day to deal with mass entertainment, and his fondness for it shows through in his poetry.

Burlesque had a more direct influence on Cummings' poetry than the other popular forms. (pp. 503-04)

In analyzing the art of burlesque Cummings emphasizes its incongruous and paradoxical qualities: "'opposites' occur *together*. For that reason, burlesk enables us to (so to speak) *know around* a thing, character, or situation.'' In ordinary painting, on the other hand, we can only know one side of a thing. As an example of "knowing around" Cummings cites his favorite burlesque comic Jack Shargel. . . . Opposites occur together when Shargel delicately and lightly tosses a red rose to the floor. It floats downward and when it lands, a terrific ear-splitting crash is heard.

> Nothing in 'the arts' . . . has moved me more, or has proved to be a more completely inextinguishable source of 'aesthetic emotion,' than this *knowing around* the Shargel rose; this releasing of all the unroselike and non-flowerish elements which—where 'rose' and 'flower' are ordinarily concerned—*secretly or unconsciously* modify and enhance those rose—and flower—qualities to which (in terms of consciousness only) they are 'opposed.'
>
> (p. 504)

The verbal comedy of the burlesque comic also appealed to Cummings' sense of the ridiculous. In the foreword to *Is 5*, Cummings uses burlesque in explaining his theory of technique.

> I can express it in fifteen words, by quoting The Eternal Question And Immortal Answer of burlesk, viz. 'Would you hit a woman with a child?—No, I'd hit her with a brick.' Like the burlesk comedian, I am abnormally fond of that precision which creates movement.

The joke expresses some of Cummings' favorite poetic techniques: movement, incongruity, and surprise. These same elements are inherent in his juxtaposition of opposites, but surprise can arise from other incongruities. For instance, in one of his poems on the effect of science on mankind, Cummings juxtaposes incongruous elements for humorous and satiric purposes. In "pity this busy monster, manunkind" the line occurs, "Progress is a comfortable disease." A new understanding of progress is gained by modifying "disease" with a word which is associated with an opposite feeling. . . . The incongruity between man's scientific illusions and the reality of his insignificance leads to Cummings' famous advice in the last two lines, "listen: there's a hell/of a good universe next door; let's go." Part of the surprise humor in the ending arises out of the contrast between the colloquial tone of these words and the pseudo-technical tone of the rest of the poem, "hypermagical ultraomnipotence."

Science and technology represent the dead world of nonfeeling and nonloving, and Cummings satirizes them mercilessly. But burlesque was a part of the alive world which he celebrated in many of his poems and articles. . . . [When] John Dos Passos took Cummings to Irving Place one day,. . .Cummings witnessed the strip tease for the first time. The comedian was no longer the center of attention.

> Humor, filth, slapstick, and satire were all present, but they functioned primarily to enhance the Eternal Feminine. And when you saw that Feminine you understood why. It was no static concept, that pulchritude. It moved, and in moving it revealed itself, and in revealing itself it performed such prodi-

gies of innuendo as made the best belly dancer of the *Folies Bergere* entr'acte look like a statue of liberty.

(pp. 506-07)

Cummings transfers his love of movement to the printed page in his poetry. Cummings' poems never sit still; they move across the page in unusual typography, and the words themselves often suggest movement. . . . In one poem Cummings attempts to emulate the bumps and grinds of a stripper performing her act. . . . [In the poem that begins "sh estiffl," the] letters and words are so arranged as to suggest the mystery and "peek-a-boo," tantalizing, teasing quality of the stripper. We never see it all, but we see enough to keep us interested. . . . The halting and provocative unbuttoning of her gown is suggested by the repetition of parts of the word until they all fall together, and by the question marks at the end of each line. When the stripper grinds, the words grinds ("gRiNdS"). The vicarious participation of the men in the audience almost becomes an orgasm at the end of the poem. Besides the type swooping all over the page, the words also imply movement, "struts," "slips," "twitching," "steps," "flipchucking," "grinds," "loop," "mime," "hurl," "swoop," "swirl," "whirling," and "climb." The words and typography suggest the spontaneity of the burlesque art which the poem describes.

Another popular form of entertainment which delighted Cummings was the circus, and like burlesque it too was noted for movement. . . . The circus as an art form has something which even burlesque lacks, a sense of reality. "Within 'the big top,' as nowhere else on earth, is to be found Actuality." There is nothing phoney when the lion tamer faces the lion and when the trapeze artist defies death. Again, there are opposites occurring together as the terror of death is juxtaposed with the antics of the clowns. (pp. 508-10)

"Aliveness" and "beauty" seem to be the qualities which Cummings seeks in art, and if painting, fiction and drama ever lack them, then they are not art in those instances; but if mass forms of entertainment, the burlesque and circus, have them, then they are appreciated as true art. (p. 510)

Cummings also saw beauty and aliveness in amusement parks, especially his favorite, Coney Island. . . . Besides displaying beauty and aliveness, Coney Island performs a unique function of fusing humanity. . . . The performance at this "circus-theatre" is joined with the audience, a fact which is significant for art. The audience participates by doing circus tricks themselves, by riding the death-defying roller coasters and loop-the-loops. . . . Cummings seems to have anticipated the current interest in participatory arts, widely expressed in the "living theatre" and in art which requires the viewer to enter its structure or manipulate it in some way. Having actors embrace members of the audience and using electronic media are not the only ways to involve the audience; the printed page has long been used to make the reader participate in an experience. This is what Cummings attempts to do in his poetry, to fuse the reader with the poem, to make the poem become the reader. He wants the poem to be an emotional experience for the reader. Most of Cummings' poems could be offered as examples of this, especially his love poems and nature poems. (p. 511)

Another form of mass entertainment which Cummings analyzed was the comic strip. . . . [He has described George Herriman's comic strip character Krazy Kat in an article for the 1946 spring issue of *Sewanee Review.*]

"Krazy is herself. Krazy is illimitable—she loves. She loves in the only way anyone can love: illimitably.". . . . Krazy Kat's love reminds us of the "spiritual force" which is missing from our lives. Cummings' poetry was not directly affected by his appreciation of comic strips, but there is a parallel between his interest in Krazy and one of the main themes of his poetry, love. Like George Herriman, Cummings uses the symbolism of a comic situation to awaken our dead sensibilities to a spiritual awareness of love.

Cummings often used the comic exuberance of youth to evoke an awareness of love in his readers. . . . He was often accused of being an "adolescent songster," and this remark probably gave him great delight because he tried to maintain the aliveness of youth in his adult life. This may partially explain his fondness for entertainments associated with childhood and adolescence: circuses, amusement parks, comic strips, and animated cartoons.

Cummings' love for comic strips was intensified when they took on the motion of animated cartoons. . . . His fascination with film animation lies in the fact that this is a world where nothing is impossible: animals talk, rabbits save other rabbits from being tied to railroad tracks, trains split in half, people walk on air. Miracles take place when we are in this dream world. . . . Here again are the opposites occurring together, and a new awareness and understanding arising from it. The awareness comes about through laughter at the contradictions. (pp. 513, 515)

Cummings often created a dream world, a world where the impossible is possible, in his poems, and laughter was often the vehicle for entering this realm. One of these creations is the world of candy figurines [in Cummings' poem which begins "this little bride & groom are."]. . . . The whimsical humor comes from the building intensity throughout the poem. The reader is swept along by rhythms and sounds, much as a viewer is moved by the rapid action in an animated cartoon, until he is almost breathless and limp by the time the climax occurs in the last line. Cummings builds the reader up tier by tier through the unreality of the cake and then hits him with a startling metaphysical statement. Our world is separated from reality just as the cake is cut off from the outside by cellophane. We are no more real than figurines on top of a cake. The poem is a statement of Cummings' transcendent vision: the physical world is not the ultimate reality, and we can only reach reality through the imagination and emotions. The laughter evoked by the surprise statement at the end is a vehicle for seeing beyond the physical and into the spiritual.

Laughter is also the central element in another of Cummings' movie favorites, Charlie Chaplin. Cummings was a life-long fan of Chaplin's cinematic creations. . . . Chaplin's creation "The Tramp" is closely akin to many of the personages in Cummings' poetry, the hoboes, balloonmen, organ grinders, and other social misfits who bring joy into the lives of others. Cummings' technique of combining pathos with humor is parallel to the feeling evoked by "The Tramp." He is probably the only modern American poet who can achieve to the same degree this fusion of pity and joy. . . . [Some] Cummings' poems which reflect Chaplin-

esque technique and subject matter are "in Just-spring," "my uncle Daniel," and all of the poems about Joe Gould, the Greenwich Village beggar.

Cummings' poetry was only indirectly influenced by popular culture, but he definitely absorbed the rhythms and styles of America from 1920 through 1960 as they were expressed in mass entertainment. He considered burlesque, circuses, amusement parks, comic strips, animated cartoons, and movies as true art forms, because, at their best, they demonstrate qualities of aliveness, spontaneity, and beauty. Cummings' interest in mass culture shows his own anti-intellectualism. He wanted no part of an art that was just for a small elite; functioning art had to appeal to the masses. Several of these popular arts exhibit techniques found in Cummings' poetry: the juxtaposition of opposites, incongruity, movement, and surprise. The themes of many of Cummings' poems have similarities with mass entertainment: love, women, youth, and comedy. Cummings saw the popular arts as a means of transcending reality, and his poetry often functions in the same way. . . . Laughter is often a means to this end. Humor runs through all the forms of popular culture which appealed to Cummings, and his own work is made up of many humorous poems. No matter how great or how small the actual influence of popular arts was on Cummings' poetry, there is no doubt that he was in harmony with American mass culture. (pp. 516-17, 519)

> *Patrick B. Mullen, "E. E. Cummings and Popular Culture," in* Journal of Popular Culture *(copyright © 1971 by Ray B. Browne), Winter, 1971, pp. 503-20.*

BETHANY K. DUMAS

Cummings is not significantly a "free verse" poet in the popular sense of that term. From first to last, he was a poet thoroughly in the tradition of English prosody; he experimented freely with given forms, but it will be seen that he molded traditional forms to new uses more often than he simply invented new ones. In this he resembles Swinburne as much as any other predecessor, and it is possible that he was heavily influenced by Swinburne's metrics. Second, though there are no important "periods" in Cummings' life, as there are in the lives of poets like Eliot and Yeats, it is not true that there is no development in his poetry. He has been accused of such a lack of development, partly because he did not move from one clearly-defined "position" to another—politically or otherwise—during his lifetime. This has been somewhat unusual in twentieth-century America, though there are also the examples of Stevens and Frost. However, Cummings certainly matured and developed: the fact that his development cannot be charted in terms of "periods" does not belie that fact.

Further, Cummings was writing squarely in a tradition that began in America in the first half of the nineteenth century. Like Henry David Thoreau and Ralph Waldo Emerson, and later Walt Whitman, Cummings identified himself as an individual and poet similar to the model transcendentalist described in Emerson's essay, "The Transcendentalist." Like him, Cummings believed in the ultimate value of the egocentric individual and of love. He valued childhood. He scorned materialism and found society and institutions dangerous. Emerson's "spiritual principle" can be equated with Cummings' "love." Cummings was different from the early transcendentalists in one important way, though. He denied the flesh no more than did Whitman. Indeed, he sometimes appeared to have a naïve faith that if "spring omnipotent goddess" returns often enough and if people learn to "live suddenly without thinking," all will be well. That is, of course, a gross oversimplification of Cummings' philosophy, particularly as set forth in his mature poems, though it is true that when there is a choice to make, he is more likely than not to opt for the heart, not the head. It is important to keep in mind that Cummings was not often a victim of the "either/or" fallacy, that notion which says that things are good or bad, right or wrong, black or white. In many ways, in fact, his whole life was a protest against that fallacy.

In *Tulips and Chimneys* he set forth his basic concerns as a young poet. In later volumes, he was to refine his techniques of expression, modify his metaphysics, and move away from an early romanticism that threatened to dominate his poems, but he did not alter his basic concerns, which remained love and the individual. (pp. 58-9)

Since the unconventional aspects of Cummings' poetry are sometimes concentrated on to the exclusion of other features, it might be well to begin with a brief examination of some misunderstandings of these elements. Observations about them are often inaccurate and lead to serious misreadings of the poems. Though it should, for instance, go without saying that the poems of Cummings, like those of all true poets, are written primarily for the ear, not the eye, the fact of the matter is that many are disposed to take Cummings at his most atypical and single out the exceptions for the rule. His "eye-poems" constitute a negligible percentage of his total body of poems. . . . (p. 70)

Just as Cummings' poems are directed primarily to the ear, so are the various devices by means of which he gets his poems arranged on the page largely directed to the oral readings of the poems. It is important to look at these devices closely, both because they have annoyed and puzzled some readers, and because they are important and interesting in their own right. The easiest way to approach them is to hear them in action; that can be done by listening to recordings of Cummings reading his poems. It is highly instructive to follow the text of a given poem while listening to the poet's reading of it. Parentheses, commas, spaced-outwards, bunched-up words—all these devices emerge as stage directions of a sort. The simplest devices are those of disjunction and displacement. These devices are sometimes combined; an element of a word may appear parenthetically within another word. This is one way of suggesting a simultaneity of action or experience which cannot be expressed by ordinary syntax. Inherent in the English language is a false chronology which announces that one thing always follows another thing. A language built on a subject-verb-object rendering of experience must be wrenched a bit if one is to portray experience more nearly as it is. (p. 73)

Cummings' use of words is such that he gets greater mileage from even such simple words as "a" and "and" and "the" than the writer of an ordinary English sentence is likely to. Word coinages are another trademark of Cummings. . . . Cummings most often created new words by the use of inflectional or derivational affixes. In this respect, he was typical of his period, for other writers—Dos Passos and Faulkner certainly come to mind—used affixes to create new words. What is unusual is that Cummings did this in poetry, while others used the technique mostly in prose writings.

More important than the specific devices used by Cummings is the use to which he puts the devices. That is a complex matter; irregular spacing, either of whole words or parts of words, for instance, allows both amplification and retardation. Further, spacing of key words allows puns which would otherwise be impossible. Some devices, such as the use of lowercase letters at the beginnings of lines and for the first person personal pronoun, allow a kind of distortion that often re-enforces that of the syntax. Friedman has suggested that both seem to spring from a conviction that it is necessary to transform the word in order to transform the world. All these devices have the effect of jarring the reader, of forcing him to examine experience with fresh eyes.

Not all the devices are used with the same frequency throughout Cummings' career as a poet. The earliest poetry is characterized by a great deal of synaesthesia, personification, metaphor, and simile. It is much more conventional than the later poetry, which relies increasingly on symbol, allegory, paradox, word-coinage, typographical spacing, and oxymoron. (p. 74)

The subject matter of Cummings' poems may be approached in terms of the stylistic breakdown [previously set forth]. Some initial generalizations will be useful. The romantic poems, predictably, have for their subjects such things as love, nature, Spring, birds, flowers, kisses, sunsets, youth, rain, stars—mostly the little and potentially intimate natural occurrences. The satiric poems deal with quite different kinds of subjects; love may appear, but it will do so only in terms of its physical manifestation, and most often on city streets where the actors will be whores and pimps and their customers or potential customers. This is not to suggest that Cummings was opposed to sex—quite the contrary!—but rather to suggest that once sex becomes exclusively a commercial venture, it is subject to the same ridicule and contempt as any form of commercial exploitation. . . . (pp. 74-5)

The subjects of the portrait poems are, of course, individuals. . . . For many of them Cummings the poet has appreciation, his tone implying neither approval nor indignation. The portrait poems . . . include conventionally acceptable subjects [as well as unsavory characters]; in fact, characters from the demimonde diminish in later volumes. Finally, the subjects of the typographs, the "tricky" poems, sometimes with epigrammatic and sometimes with haiku effect, tend to be similar to those of the romantic poems. They often involve the celebration of sensation; since they are organic structures which often show process, Becoming as opposed to Being, they tend to depict, rather than delimit. Thus, they are seldom characterized by attitudinal strictures. . . .

The "devices" discussed above are elements of Cummings' order in his poems, and, as such, they play an important role in the shaping of the poems. Of greater importance, though, is poetic meter strictly defined: a more or less regular linguistic rhythm, resulting from the heightened, organized, and regulated natural rhythmical movements of colloquial speech—so that pattern emerges from the relative phonetic haphazardness of ordinary utterance—which is the most fundamental technique of order available to the poet. Some other poetic techniques of order—rhyme, line division, stanzaic form, and over-all structure—are in a sense projections and magnifications of the kind of formal repetition which is meter. (p. 77)

Those who think of Cummings as the poet of lowercase letters, scrambled words, and largely unpronounceable poems are always surprised to learn how many and what excellent poems he wrote using traditional metrical features. Really, the most interesting—and often the most successful—of his poems are those which are nonce forms using traditional metrical patterns. They become most important after *is 5,* which begins a turning point in Cummings' poetic development. As Norman Friedman has pointed out, it is by that volume becoming apparent that in general Cummings reserves metrical stanzas for his more "serious" poems, while he uses experiments for various kinds of free verse embodiments of satire, comedy, and description. The "serious" poems are not all solemn. They are serious in that they embody a more complex view of the universe—and man's place in it—than is possible in the other poems. It is in these that Cummings' transcendent vision is more thoroughly revealed and in which love is described in terms of a transcendental metaphor. Satire is also included. . . . (p. 84)

The more serious of the satiric poems always contain a sense of moral indignation, sometimes moral outrage. Like other satirists, Cummings sometimes makes use of scatalogy and the so-called four-letter Anglo-Saxon words to communicate his outrage. (p. 85)

Cummings felt very strongly that "noone who hopes to write poetry should attempt what used to be called free verse until he or she has mastered the conventional forms" . . .; he himself mastered the traditional forms early, though the only ones he continued to write with any degree of regularity after the *Tulips and Chimneys* manuscript were sonnets, various kinds of satirical poems, and rhymed and metrical quatrains. The sonnets are an extremely important category of Cummings' poems, both because of the number he wrote and because of their quality. Further, they are of interest because they show the extent to which Cummings was able to experiment with and vary a traditional form. His accomplishment in the sonnet ranges from fairly regular and highly metrical Shakesperian sonnets to such typographically eccentric sonnets that they are often identified as irregular free verse poems. (p. 91)

The truth is that it is impossible to classify Cummings' poems on the basis of any single classification scheme. He was a lyric poet whose range was extraordinary. He greatly enlarged the boundaries of the possible where the lyric was concerned. His accomplishments in the lyric ranged from the highly melodic—a number of his poems have been set to music, some of them more than once—to the literally unpronounceable. Many of his individual volumes of poems give, in miniature, a picture of the range of his interests and visions and talents. Frequently, the poems are set within a kind of framework in which the first poem is a typograph of some sort, while the final poem of the volume is a love poem in some traditional form, often a sonnet. Since Cummings was painstaking in his attention to the arrangement of his poems, it is surely noteworthy that this framework is used, and that it is within such a framework that the various poems occur. There is a move from a celebration of the moment, with its accompanying metaphysical implications, to an ordered and orderly picture of the universe. Form implies meaning, and the progression is significant: "love is the whole and more than all." . . . (pp. 105-06)

Readers who have found in Cummings' work an apparent preponderance of romantic love or indignation should re-

member that the turn of a page may bring with it the reverse of the coin. Great love for individuals often goes hand in hand with a large capacity for moral outrage at their ill-treatment. Cummings was not a man for all seasons, nor are his poems a storehouse of "something for everyone." He was, however, a man who genuinely loved men and the craft of poetry and hated those things which make men less than men and poetry mere words. That is sufficient to recommend him to the ages. (p. 106)

E. E. Cummings' prose works are as original and as exciting as the best of his poems. In fact, Cummings felt that his identity as a writer lay in prose as much as in poetry. (p. 107)

The style of *The Enormous Room* is on the whole fairly conventional; . . . it is a great deal more conventional than one realizes until it is compared with later prose works, notably *Eimi.* There do occur here and there in the book bits and pieces of prose which more nearly resemble poems than ordinary prose. They are characterized by a wrenching of syntax that renders them in effect asyntactical. The wrenching is deliberate; Cummings was striving to develop not only the notion that conventional use of language is a habit that has to be broken if one is to deal honestly with experience, but also a style—or set of styles—by which that notion could be demonstrated. He does not develop that style—or set of styles—in this book, but he begins the development. (p. 119)

[*Eimi*], his second full-length work of prose, bears similarities to *The Enormous Room;* both are records of personal experience, recorded in more-or-less chronological order; both result from a strong conviction, based on personal experience, that there are things desperately wrong in the world; and both are modelled loosely on other literary works, this time *The Divine Comedy.* They are, however, rather different sorts of books. Cummings valued the later book more; his stated conviction that *Eimi* helped explain his stance as a writer is re-enforced by the fact that he devoted a significant part of his sixth lecture at Harvard to comments about and a reading from the book. It is, as he says, "written in a style of its own," and it is admittedly difficult reading.

The very title of the book (Greek for "I am") makes it sound more typically Cummings; increasingly important in his developing awareness of the transcendent nature of reality was his insistence on what he sometimes calls "isness," the notion that only in the verb could one express the kinetic quality of life. In his lecture about *Eimi,* Cummings' announced topic for the evening was "i & am & santa claus." And if, as Cummings thought, *The Enormous Room* was not the "war book" he felt people expected it to be, it is certainly true that *Eimi* was even less what people expected it to be: another *Enormous Room.* However, he suggests that there were in both instances close relationships between what was expected and what was actually presented. *The Enormous Room* used war, to explore the nature of the individual; *Eimi* explores the individual again, "a more complex individual in a more enormous room." (pp. 124-25)

Some of the specific techniques used by Cummings to share his vision of the universe have been discussed. What has not been discussed is the broad implication of his use of specific poetic techniques. While his techniques of typography, capitalization, punctuation, etc., are all very interesting in and of themselves, they are even more interesting when considered together as a pattern of linguistic signalling. Their major significance seems to be as what we might call code-labels; they signal a level of usage and therefore have a function other than that of carrying a message—though they also do that, of course, and on several levels. Of great significance where Cummings' writings are concerned is the fact that he makes greater use of intimate and casual styles than other poets writing at the same time . . . so much so that he may be said to have deliberately used the characteristic features of intimate and casual styles, where other poets might have used casual and consultative styles. He did so, I think, because he felt that conventional language usage—consultative style for consultation, casual style for casual discourse, etc.—was bankrupt. He made an attempt to break down certain barriers between himself and his reader. He did this by treating his reader with a greater degree of intimacy than his reader was always prepared for. Many of his poems have the external features of highly intimate letters. Some readers have been put off by some of the poems, I think, because they have felt unable to respond to such intimacy. These people are in the position of having opened letters that appear not to be directed to them. They are, I think, somewhat embarrassed and perhaps a little resentful. Theirs is an unfortunate, if natural reaction.

In addition to using the intimate style so often, Cummings also deviated from general usage by mixing styles, using more than two in alternation, occasionally jumping steps. In ordinary discourse, a speaker—or writer—confines himself to two neighboring styles alternately, it being considered anti-social for a speaker to shift two or more steps in a single jump, for instance from casual to formal. Cummings' disregard for this convention is, I think, partly responsible for the critical reception of some of his early poetry, where he most blatantly mixed styles. The early poems in which style-mixing is most obvious are those in which there is a mixture of archaisms and colloquialisms. (pp. 144-45)

Cummings' deviation from convention is certainly not the result of carelessness or ignorance. It amounts to a deliberate and highly informed departure from the rules of conventional discourse. The rules are those of his early life, and they are important as much when they are being challenged as when they are being followed blindly. We must not forget that Cummings was as thoroughly a product of his milieu as any American poet, and even his radical poetry is a constant reminder that he was formed by the area bounded by Boston's State House, Harvard University, the Charles River, the Field of Lexington, and Concord's bridge. It is not possible to deviate from rules which are not thoroughly established; there is, therefore, a certain amount of implied respect for the conventions of his early environment in all of Cummings' writings.

I have used the word "radical" in connection with Cummings' poetry; he was radical in his metaphysics and in his

anti-societal stance, certainly. He was linguistically radical in the sense that his wit is concerned with the roots of syntax and grammar. He shows throughout his poetry great consciousness of the close relationship between life and grammar. (p. 146)

There is, thus, no reason to think of Cummings as a simple-minded idealist. Nor is he a romantic in the nineteenth-century sense of that term. He has been called a "neo-romantic" and perhaps he is. . . . Clearly of the twentieth-century, Cummings does not fit neatly into twentieth-century categories. If he is a "neo-romantic," it is important to distinguish between his quest and those of such people as Novalis, looking for his little blue flower, and Dostoevsky's Underground Man, determined that two plus two shall be five, out of spite. Cummings certainly reveals himself to be a transcendentalist, but he is as far from being a romantic, in any "pure" sense of that word, as his volume title *is 5* is from that illogical statement that two plus two is five.

Cummings' major accomplishments were two: first of all, he revived the lyric as a viable poetic form and transformed it greatly, enlarging its horizons and multiplying its poetic possibilities; second, he created a poetic language by means of which he forced his reader to consider action, motivation, and character from viewpoints new to him. At his best, he forced the reader into the kind of re-reading that results in the finest kind of education available to most of us, that in which we continue to educate ourselves.

I do not think that poets can be ranked or graded. I would not know where to put Cummings on a numerical scale, nor would I know whether he should be judged an A+ or B− poet. He clearly has a place among the leading poets writing in English in the twentieth century. He was in some interesting ways a poet ahead of his time, particularly with respect to his achievement in bending language to his will. In that respect, he was different from some other important poets of the century. While others are now *behind* us, he is, I think, often still *ahead* of us. For that reason, it is still too early to define his place in twentieth-century literature, though we can say that in some respects it will be found to be to one side of the poets who constitute the various "main-streams" of twentieth-century English and American poetry. Twin streams merge in Cummings, those of traditionalism and innovation, and they do so in ways that they do not in other poets of the century. Ideologically, Cummings was an American transcendentalist; he sought to express his vision of the transcendent universe by stretching the shape of the lyric poem. His description of himself as "an author of pictures, less a draughtsman of words" re-enforces our own conviction that as a poet he was the most traditional of innovators and the most innovative of traditionalists. (pp. 147-48)

Bethany K. Dumas, in her E. E. Cummings: A Remembrance of Miracles *(© 1974 Vision Press; by permission of Harper & Row, Publishers, Inc.; Barnes & Noble Books; in Canada by Vision Press), Vision Press, 1974, Barnes & Noble, 1974.*

Julia W(oolfolk) Cunningham

1916-

American young adult and children's novelist and editor. Cunningham, whose controversial *Dorp Dead!* is considered the first existential novel aimed specifically at a young adult audience, writes fiction that is complex, sophisticated, and rich in symbolism and psychological meaning. While *Dorp Dead!*, which deals uncompromisingly with evil, is generally conceded to be a beautifully written novel, it is considered by many critics too grim to be suitable for the age group for which it was written. Strong elements of fantasy, allegory, and gothic romanticism flavor Cunningham's fiction, with the medieval French background of some of her stories attributable to her stay in France in the 1950s. Cunningham is a unique figure in young adult literature, writing both realistic and symbolic stories that emphasize the absolute importance of individualism and self-realization. (See also *Contemporary Authors*, Vols. 9-12, rev. ed., and *Something about the Author*, Vol. 1.)

AILEEN PIPPETT

[*Dorp Dead*'s] Gilly Ground was a lonely orphan boy who decided to stay that way. He felt tough enough to stand many more blows from fate. He obeyed the orphanage rules but would make no friends, muff at games and pretend to be stupid. At last the orphanage gave up on him and sent him to work for Kobalt the ladder-maker, a surly giant, who lived by the clock and who kept a mud-colored dog too dejected to wag its tail. Through the dog Gilly learned that Kobalt was cruel, not just hard-hearted. . . .

This is a grim tale with an exciting climax told in Gilly's own words after he escaped from Kobalt. Now broken out from the cage he had built about himself, he has given up the idea that people can live without love. In the future he will have friends and fun; he will even learn to spell—which is the only clue to the odd title, a hidden joke that explodes into a laugh at the end of this enthralling book. (p. 26)

Aileen Pippett, in The New York Times Book Review *(© 1965 by The New York Times Company; reprinted by permission), April 25, 1965.*

JUDITH CRIST

[*Dorp Dead*] is the story of a boy who discovers himself, who basically comes to grips with that most contemporary of problems, the isolation of the individual. It is told within the near-classic framework of the story of the orphan who survives and escapes maltreatment to find love, but it is told in frank, literate terms in the lingo of today's youngsters. And it has, as an additional dimension, a touch of the Gothic tale, a tinge of terror and a shade of romanticism, as it evolves as a fast-moving, first-person, present-tense adventure story that never descends to the sensational. . . .

"Dorp Dead" is Gilly's final message to those who would build cages for the young—Gilly is a bad speller, with his non-conformity extending to the sequence of letters. . . . But however Gilly spells, he speaks for his contemporaries in their terms.

And this is the distinction that Miss Cunningham brings to a field that this season brims with excitement in the area of non-fiction but brings little in the way of either imagination or even simple literary, let alone literate, adventure to a particular age group of children who, having learned to cope with books, should proceed to revel in them. Here is one author who has recognized the sophistication of young readers geared to an age of television and films—and shows that a book can be as hip and as exciting and far more memorable. (p. 5)

Judith Crist, in Book Week—The Sunday Herald Tribune *(© I.H.T. Corporation; reprinted by permission), May 9, 1965.*

Because of the controversy over *Dorp Dead*, [*Viollet*] will be of considerable interest to librarians, but it is not likely to carry much conviction for children. The flaw is fundamental, in the form: this story of animals who talk and act as humans is neither fable nor fantasy nor allegory. (Not fantasy because fantasy requires either an imaginary world or a bridge from the real to the imaginary; not allegory because the chief conflict is individual and personal.) Viollet is a thrush, a natural musician who is afraid to sing except when she is alone. . . . [She and some other] animals plot together to protect [their] beloved Count. . . . The beauty of the book is in the character of each of the animals and their relationships to one another; the weakness is in their intervention in the affairs of men. The old count is a credible character until his final transformation, but Tressac is a villain without dimension, a loathsome, petty person. Viollet La Grive is believable, but her story is not. (pp. 1054-55)

Virginia Kirkus' Service *(copyright © 1966 Virginia Kirkus' Service, Inc.), October 1, 1966.*

BARBARA WERSBA

["Viollet"] is a Gothic tale, in the true sense of the word, set amid the ruins of a French castle, and as ominous as a thundery sky. Presiding over the castle and its famous vineyards is the Count de la Tour, an aging and unworldly nobleman. As harvest time approaches, three animals learn of a foreman's plans to murder the Count and usurp his dynasty.... The empathy that unites these creatures is superb—the author having been wise enough to keep their world separate from the human. Because of this, the animals' rescue of their beloved Count is credible; and when the four finally spend an evening together, graced by Viollet's first public (and sober) performance, the reader is genuinely touched.

If the best children's books speak to the adult in the child, and the child in the adult, then Julia Cunningham's work is of this genre. Her prose is sensitive yet uncompromising.... (p. 40)

> *Barbara Wersba, in* The New York Times Book Review, *Part II (© 1966 by The New York Times Company; reprinted by permission), November 6, 1966.*

Short, tense, piercing, remarkable, [*Dorp Dead*] is a book that stands alone. It uses no magic-machinery, but possibly something of symbolism; yet this may after all be no more than the grotesqueries of the child's eye-view....

[After] peaks of nightmare (good stuff of climb and hunt at ordinary schoolboy reader's level), brightness ends the scene, and starts a new beginning for [Gilly].... The writing of all this ... gives the book an intense completeness—something, too, of the sustained compulsion of a dream. (p. 1141)

> The Times Literary Supplement *(© Times Newspapers Ltd. (London) 1967; reproduced from* The Times Literary Supplement *by permission), November 30, 1967.*

MARGERY FISHER

Dorp Dead is a fable, sensational in plot and severely concrete in detail. The reader must give substance to the hero (an orphan boy bent on freedom but incapable of recognising it); he must make his own mental picture, from hints, of the house where the boy enters into apprenticeship with Master Kolbert the carpenter, and imagine the utensils and clocks and walls of this house where he meets danger to mind and body. The approach through deliberate anonymity is just what is needed to drive the story onward emotionally. (p. 1070)

> *Margery Fisher, in her* Growing Point, *March, 1968.*

CHARLOTTE S. HUCK and DORIS YOUNG KUHN

[*Dorp Dead*] tells of a boy's growing toward maturity as he changes his concepts of security and freedom.... Told in the first person, the style of the narrative is unrealistic, for most children would not use such beautiful language. This is one clue that indicates the book goes beyond mere "reality of presentation." (p. 261)

Dear Rat ... is a tremendous spoof on a hard-boiled detective story....

[*Macaroon*] is a more subtle and gentle animal fantasy....

Viollet is a rather sinister animal fantasy.... It combines some elements of both *Dear Rat* and *Macaroon*, but does not have the humor of the first or the loving compassion of the second.... Fantasy and realism become too mixed in this story for believability. While the characters are clearly drawn, they lack focus. It is Viollet's story, yet the reader only meets her at the beginning and the end. One's sympathies are directed more towards Oxford, the hound, and Warwick, the old fox. (p. 348)

The controversial *Dorp Dead* ... [is] allegorical in nature. Gilly Ground represents all youth caught between its need to be non-conforming and its need for security; Kobalt, the laddermaker, *is* evil, the epitome of all evil that would control and damage basic personalities. The Hunter whose gun has no bullets may represent love or the meaning of life.... The plot of this story is sinister, but evil is overcome, and the integrity of Gilly Ground's personality preserved. Viewed as realistic fiction, this story seems too evil and unbelievable. Seen as allegory, *Dorp Dead* becomes an exceptional book indeed. (p. 361)

> *Charlotte S. Huck and Doris Young Kuhn, in their* Children's Literature in the Elementary School *(copyright © 1961, 1968, by Holt, Rinehart and Winston, Inc.; reprinted by permission of Holt, Rinehart and Winston, Publishers), second edition, Holt, 1968.*

PAUL HEINS

It is certainly important and necessary at times to consider children's literature purely as literature. Questions of style, structure, and technical subtlety are as applicable to children's literature as to any of the other branches of literature. Julia Cunningham's *Dorp Dead* ... may be considered as an exemplar of the Gothic novel; and one could learn much by comparing the structure of her story with that of *Jane Eyre*. (p. 77)

> *Paul Heins, in a speech delivered at the University of Utah, Salt Lake City, Utah, on June 18, 1969, in his* Crosscurrents of Criticism: Horn Book Essays 1968-1977, *edited by Paul Heins (copyright © 1977 by The Horn Book, Inc.), Horn Book, 1977.*

MAY HILL ARBUTHNOT

Dorp Dead has the quality of a bad dream.... The realism of the beginning of the story occasionally fades into fantasy, but the plight of the boy, helpless for a time in the hands of a psychotic man, is startlingly real. This haunting story suggests that children in the grasp of cruel older people must put up stiff resistance if they are to survive. It is a memorable scare story that will give children chills up their backbones. (pp. 175-76)

> *May Hill Arbuthnot, in her* Children's Reading in the Home *(copyright © 1969 by Scott, Foresman and Company; reprinted by permission), Scott, Foresman, 1969.*

ELEANOR CAMERON

Dorp Dead, besides being taut and original, has guts and danger, a danger that possibly many a tender-hearted eleven-and twelve-year-old could not endure.... Certainly there is no niceness here. The treatment of brutality has nothing of the objectivity found in fairy tales.... The brutality in *Dorp Dead* is subjective, very slow, psychotic.

Throughout most of the book, the villain, Kobalt, thoroughly enjoys his sadistic treatment of both boy and dog—poor Mash, who he says must "learn to die"—but, of course, Kobalt is surely insane, and in the name of insanity one can go to any lengths one pleases entirely without motivation. Many of the teen-agers who are enthusiastic about the book are possibly in rebellion against the contrived, shallow rubbish of the average teenage fiction and feel a sense of identity with Gilly, who broke out of an emotional cage as well as a physical one when he escaped from the house in which he was imprisoned. (pp. 210-11)

> *Eleanor Cameron, in her* The Green and Burning Tree: On the Writing and Enjoyment of Children's Books *(copyright © 1962, 1964, 1966, 1969 by Eleanor Cameron; reprinted by permission of Little, Brown and Co. in association with The Atlantic Monthly Press), Atlantic-Little, Brown, 1969.*

SHEILA EGOFF

In *Dorp Dead* Julia Cunningham . . . portrays life as she sees it, believing that, in the total experience, the unhealthy lip-licking kind of brutality that she has been accused of exploiting is actually inseparable from the realization of love and personal fulfilment of the young protagonist, Gilly: had he not been the victim of a sadistic adult, he would have become entrapped in a cage of self-alienation.

The disapproving critical reception of [this unusual novel] . . . suggests that while mediocrity is acceptable or at least tolerated, distortion for artistic reasons and anything pathological are not, even when they are used to widen the reader's vision of life and society. It is sadly apparent that the majority of adult critics of children's books prefer a message imposed from without rather than one that grows out of the novel itself. (pp. 440-41)

> *Sheila Egoff, in* Only Connect: Readings on Children's Literature, *edited by Sheila Egoff, G. T. Stubbs, and L. F. Ashley, (© Oxford University Press (Canadian Branch) 1969), Oxford University Press, Canadian Branch, 1969.*

BARBARA WERSBA

Comparisons may be odious, but compared to recent children's books, "Burnish Me Bright" stands out like a torch. There are all kinds of things wrong with it—illogic, melodrama, sentimentality—but from first page to last, the story glows. . . .

It is unnecessary to reveal the chilling climax to this book, and equally unnecessary to state that its theme is the destruction of the innocent, those who are brave—or simple—enough to be "different." Suffice it to say that Julia Cunningham is no ordinary writer. Like her characters, she understands the substance of magic. (p. 26)

> *Barbara Wersba, in* The New York Times Book Review *(© 1970 by The New York Times Company; reprinted by permission), May 24, 1970.*

SADA FRETZ

The author's previously evident talent for creating a scene or a mood is evident [in *Burnish Me Bright*], but the story has neither the psychological depth nor the compelling plot of her previous *Dorp Dead!* . . . The style of *Burnish Me Bright*, like the title, verges on the sentimental and the self-consciously "beautiful"; the plot, though well constructed, lacks wide appeal, and its miracles are unconvincing. Also, the familiar characters (the ailing-because-overprotected little girl, the heartless guardian, the witch-hunting villagers) live neither as individuals nor as archetypes. (pp. 158-59)

> *Sada Fretz, in* School Library Journal *(reprinted from the September, 1970 issue of* School Library Journal, *published by R. R. Bowker Co. A Xerox Corporation; copyright © 1970), September, 1970.*

VIRGINIA HAVILAND

Praise for the originality and the skillful, sensitive writing of the author for earlier work is due in complete measure again [for *Burnish Me Bright*]. . . . Poetry fills the writing—spare, evocative, intense—leaving a haunting blend of scenes brilliantly conceived and character relationships delicately limned. (pp. 386-87)

> *Virginia Haviland, in* The Horn Book Magazine *(copyright © 1970 by The Horn Book, Inc., Boston), August, 1970.*

Adumbrated in words that are not childlike [*Wings of the Morning* tells of] an experience unlike that of most children—who, finding an inert bird by the roadside, assume it to be hurt or dead and react fearfully or protectively according to their nature. But this bare-footed, blue-jeaned, otherwise otherworldly youngster, feeling her aloneness on the wide road, thinks that it is sleeping, "waiting there for me all morning." It "needs someone to fly beside it"—and so she spreads its wings and tosses it into the air. Immediately it falls and she is devastated, to recover only in the security of her father's arms. Manifestly metaphorical, this is nonetheless problematic: was the bird dead at the outset? if wounded, would she not unwittingly have killed it? These are the questions that would occur to a child, and the fact that the photographer's daughter is the girl to whom this happened does not answer them. Indeed, the simulation—i.e. photographic recreation—of such intense reality is itself suspect. And coupled with the poeticizing, [it is ineffectual by comparison with the creative simplicity of the Margaret Wise Brown-Remy Charlip *Dead Bird*]. (p. 229)

> Kirkus Reviews *(copyright © 1971 The Kirkus Service, Inc.), March 1, 1971.*

MARGERY FISHER

Burnish me bright does not move on fashionable tram-lines but has the almost inconsequent unpatterned feel of reality in it. The author is wholly committed to her principal characters, a dumb boy grudgingly reared by a mean-minded widow in a small French village, and old Hilaire, once a famous artiste in mime, now living in an isolated, decaying mansion. The old man devotes the last of his strength to teaching the boy his craft and so gives him a new freedom to express himself and to help the chemist's frail little daughter to conquer her listlessness. . . . The indirect plea for charity shines through a text cut with economy out of a unique living language. Simple words carry a wealth of meaning, of landscape detail and of human feeling. This is a special book for thoughtful readers, who must accept it as an organic whole. (p. 1759)

> *Margery Fisher, in her* Growing Point, *July, 1971.*

SHEILA R. COLE

A child finds a bird in Julia Cunningham's "Wings of the Morning." . . . She thinks it is sleeping.

The story raises more questions than it answers. It does not provide much that might help a child cope with his first encounter with death. In fact it does not face up to the issue at all. The prose is self-consciously poetic. . . . (p. 10)

> Sheila R. Cole, in The New York Times Book Review (© 1971 by The New York Times Company; reprinted by permission), September 26, 1971.

In a crumbling 11th century castle hedged with roses, the power of a young widow's gentleness tames a trio of thugs and repels a haughty baron [in *The Treasure Is the Rose*]. . . . Cunningham's heavy romanticism is a little easier to take than the drippy sentimentality of her recent Tallow stories, but as usual her talent for simulating a trance exceeds her sensibility, so that from the opening disclaimer that "To tell about Ariane is to try to grow a rose on paper without the touch of sun and moon, rain and snow that make it real and growing," she comes as close to parody as she does to sharing a vision. (p. 1095)

> Kirkus Reviews (copyright © 1971 The Kirkus Service, Inc.), October 1, 1971.

PAUL HEINS

[*Far in the Day,* the sequel to *Burnish Me Bright,* finds] the mute French boy who had been trained by the famous mime Hilaire, . . . part of Michael Duffy's Circus traveling the roads of Ireland. Although he endears himself to most of the members of the depleted troupe (the circus had seen better days), the mute boy, now dubbed Tallow, arouses the undying hatred of crass, brutal, corpulent Mme. Althea Creel—fortune teller and cook for the company. . . . Mme. Creel dominates the action of the story until she is outwitted by Tallow in a final scene fraught with suspense. Despite occasional lapses into melodrama and emotionalism, the narrative sensitively conveys the power of the human spirit to transcend successfully a disintegrating environment; Tallow, who seems to bear a charmed life, silently triumphs over a powerfully portrayed antagonist, the very incarnation of vulgarity and evil. (p. 268)

> Paul Heins, in The Horn Book Magazine (copyright © 1972 by The Horn Book, Inc., Boston), June, 1972.

BARBARA WERSBA

"The Treasure Is the Rose" is surely [Julia Cunningham's] finest accomplishment. (p. 40)

There is great beauty in the writing—an aura of color and light, words shimmering on the page as if sunshine illumined them. But the author's consummate achievement has been to probe her characters to the point where we see the secret self that hides within all of them, waiting for someone to bring it forth. Yarrow, the youth who Ariane finally comes to love, is probably the most interesting character Miss Cunningham has ever created—and, upon several readings, her book becomes a pool into which the reader throws tiny pebbles. The rings continue outward. (p. 42)

> Barbara Wersba, in The New York Times Book Review (© 1973 by The New York Times Com-

pany; reprinted by permission), November 4, 1973.

PAUL HEINS

Although the events of the narrative [in *The Treasure Is the Rose*] are skillfully articulated and suggest a medieval tale, the mood and style are redolent of a Pre-Raphaelite kind of romanticism. . . . The characters are exaggerated conventions; and the final effect of the story is one of emotional preciosity. (pp. 49-50)

> Paul Heins, in The Horn Book Magazine (copyright © 1974 by The Horn Book, Inc., Boston), February, 1974.

The gray vacuum that is Gravel Winter's soul will remind you of the aloof presence of Gilly in *Dorp Dead,* but [in *Come to the Edge*] it is kindness more than cruelty which threatens the integrity of a boy's alienation. . . . [At times] Gravel is so full of his own message that you want to shake him and indeed, in the twelve years since *Dorp Dead,* Cunningham has acquired such baggage as symbolic roses. Yet the dichotomy between possessiveness and the bonds of trust, as acted out by the sniveling miser Gant and Paynter. . . . seems to inspire this author's best efforts; even her constricted solipsistic manner is oddly complementary to the theme. (p. 4)

> Kirkus Reviews (copyright © 1977 The Kirkus Service, Inc.), January 1, 1977.

BARBARA WERSBA

[In the world of children's literature Miss Cunningham is] an original. She [writes] with unabashed romanticism and her prose [has] an edge of steel. She [has] a charming sense of humor beneath which [lurks] despair. Most of all, she [is] able to write about childhood as though she had never left it.

["Come to the Edge"] deals with fear—and will therefore be meaningful to many children. . . .

What Miss Cunningham has created—despite a few Gothic twists—is a parable about love and man's inability to accept it in the face of his own unworthiness. The fact that Gravel [the protagonist] does eventually learn to love and be loved, makes a moving ending; but even if the resolution had been different, I would have been shaken by this story. Miss Cunningham tells the truth about life and tells it in ways that are completely her own. In other words, she is an artist. (p. 21)

> Barbara Wersba, in The New York Times Book Review (© 1977 by The New York Times Company; reprinted by permission), July 10, 1977.

ETHEL L. HEINS

Never a trendy writer, [Julia Cunningham] has chosen, probably by pure coincidence, a currently fashionable subject—an abandoned, abused boy. But her essential theme is far more profound, and it subtly pervades the brief, pointed story [of *Come to the Edge*]. . . .

Disciplined, metaphorical writing adds its own rewards to a tense, mature, and thought-provoking story. (p. 449)

> Ethel L. Heins, in The Horn Book Magazine (copyright © 1977 by the Horn Book, Inc., Boston), August, 1977.

Peter Dickinson

1927-

British novelist, poet, and editor. Dickinson is an eclectic and original writer equally respected for his young adult fantasies and adult mysteries. He expands the limits of both genres, blending his flights of imagination with a strong historical and cultural sensibility and using multiple interests and themes. He often writes from the viewpoint of an anthropologist, emphasizing the importance of custom and ritual. In *The Poison Oracle*, for example, he creates an imaginary Arabian kingdom which he culturally analyzes in great detail. Dickinson is considered a creator of sophisticated, ingenious mysteries which are full of atmosphere and reflect much research. His first novel, *Skin Deep*, describes a tribal murder in the heart of London, and sets up several social questions and themes that are detailed in his later novels. It also introduces Inspector Jimmy Pibble, an observant sleuth who idealizes the days of Edwardian rule. Dickinson received the Crime Writer's Association Golden Dagger Award in 1968 for this title, which was published in the United States as *The Glass-Sided Ants' Nest*, and in 1969 for *A Pride of Heroes*, published in the United States as *The Old English Peep-Show*. As a writer for young people, Dickinson achieved immediate success. He published the volumes of his Changes trilogy within months of each other and received much critical affirmation. This fantasy series, considered his most popular work, deals with an imaginary England which has turned against machinery and has regressed to a dark age of superstition. The novels are concerned with human nature under stress and emphasize the necessity of love, understanding, and brotherhood in a world set askew. Dickinson is often praised for his storytelling ability, and for the economy and liveliness of his prose style, due perhaps to his seventeen years as an editor of *Punch* magazine. He is occasionally criticized for contriving plots for the sake of suspense and for ignoring characterization in favor of extensive background. Some critics feel that Dickinson's books for young people far outshine his adult titles, since he seems to operate best when he takes the child's point of view. Dickinson writes for this audience since "it seems such an obvious thing to do, almost like breathing." For many of his readers, appreciating his varied titles amounts to much the same thing. (See also *Contemporary Authors*, Vols. 41-44, and *Something about the Author*, Vol. 5.)

The Weathermonger [is] a remarkable story which seems at first like an anti-science-fiction novel but which by degrees becomes a fantasy of the Celtic fringe. It all began when Mr. Furbelow, a little chemist from Abergavenny, found Merlin sleeping beneath a rock in the Black Mountains and . . . woke him up. The mighty spirit of Merlin spreads out over England, turning everything to the likeness of the fifth century.

But all this is at the climax of a masterly story. The country is rescued from the past by an assault force composed of one boy, aged sixteen, and his sister, aged eleven. They escape from ceremonial drowning to a France firmly established in mid-twentieth century. Here a French general, drawn with just the finest touch of irony, briefs them for their forlorn expedition. This, when it comes, is an admirable piece of narrative. . . .

What gives [this story] an individual quality is that, like all the best and only the best fantasies, it is firmly grounded in reality. The reader accepts the huge improbabilities because they are placed in a setting which is consistent and convincing. The author does not attempt to cheat. There are no easy solutions. The children achieve their task not just by luck—although there is an acceptable amount of this —but by courage and resolution, and by Sally's skill in oral Latin.

Above all, this is very good storytelling. The reader—and not only the child reader—is on the edge of his chair with the excitement of the drive across England, and the earthquake in which the nigromancer's dark tower falls, in a night of chaos and terror, is finely described. In face of such convincing writing disbelief is readily suspended.

In the end England returns to rainy skies and the reek of petrol. Was it all worth it? It is an adult's question. Children will be content with a fine tale and a modern world in which to read it.

> *"The Sleeper Wakes," in* The Times Literary Supplement (© *Times Newspapers Ltd. (London) 1968; reproduced from* The Times Literary Supplement *by permission), March 14, 1968, p. 257.*

N. DANISCHEWSKY

[The] first chapter [of *The Weathermonger* jolts the reader] out of present time and space into a marvellously unpredictable, incredible story; and since he knows no more than the boy Geoffrey knows, he shares Geoffrey's frightening bewilderment at finding himself, without memory of the past five years, on a rock with an unknown girl in Weymouth Harbour. . . . (p. 143)

The children's escape to France, their superbly funny interview with General Turville, their return to England to find the cause of disruption—"not for France or the world or anything, but just to know", makes a fast-moving, very original story. I imagine it will be most enjoyed by the imaginative child, able to read anything and interested in everything. (pp. 143, 145)

> *N. Danischewsky, in* Children's Book News *(copyright © 1968 By Children's Book Centre Ltd.), March-April, 1968.*

Whatever the faults of our age there is something very encouraging about the emergence of authors of . . . quality; surely the children who respond to the intense awareness of life manifested by [Alan] Garner, [William] Mayne, [Philippa] Pearce and now Peter Dickinson will continue to respond more intelligently to both life and literature and will take a livelier interest in the world as a whole? The "better" authors have always appealed primarily to the "better" readers and this situation is unlikely to alter, but for many decades better reading tended to lead the reader to an ivory tower; these new authors are able to blend traditional and topical themes in a way which promises to lead to a keener appreciation of both modern problems and universal concepts. Thus [*The Weathermonger*], written sheerly for entertainment and extremely entertaining and readable, includes both some very shrewd comments on war and the military mentality, and a brief but memorable appearance by Merlin which opens up a whole world of possibilities under the reader's feet. The description of the 1909 Rolls Royce Silver Ghost can impress even those usually left cold by cars of any vintage, and the horse Maddox is a considerable creation. Amongst its other achievements, such as originality of plot, ease of writing, feeling for place and credibility of action, the book is one of that most civilized group which prove it is possible to have suspense and drama without making anyone play the villain; even the con-man schoolmaster, even the General, is likable. The plot is too good to give away. . . . Invigorating stuff, stylistically experimental in a way which should intrigue more than the literary, with a climax which should intrigue *anybody*. (p. 176)

> The Junior Bookshelf, *June, 1968.*

ALLEN J. HUBIN

The mystery novel without an integrated background is missing a useful dimension; there's the disturbing sense that the action could have taken place anywhere, or at any time. Few mystery writers in recent years have settled their tales in more ingenious environments than Peter Dickinson—who created an entire New Guinean society for his first novel last year ("The Glass-Sided Ant's Nest"). Any minor reservations I had about that book do not apply to his second, "The Old English Peep Show" . . . , which marks the reappearance of Scotland Yard Superintendent Jimmy Pibble.

Here, Mr. Dickinson turns an irreverent eye toward a pair of doddering British war heroes. . . . Read this tale carefully. It's a jewel. (p. 34)

> *Allen J. Hubin, in* The New York Times Book Review *(© 1969 by The New York Times Company; reprinted by permission), April 13, 1969.*

[In *Heartsease*] Mr. Dickinson proposes a thought-provoking situation in his story of children living on a Cotswold farm at a time when an extraordinary social revolution has outlawed all machines and the traditions associated with them. While there might be some sense in this, there is less in the extension of the feeling that machines are immoral to the resurrection of suspicions of witchcraft among the less fortunate members of the community who behave oddly or ineffectually. The irrationality of the witch-hunting is as galling as the incidents at Salem to the practical mind. . . . [This is] an exciting story in which thoughtful young readers may read a significance which is at once frightening and maturing. *Heartsease* should prove to be an outstanding achievement. (p. 177)

> The Junior Bookshelf, *June, 1969.*

Peter Dickinson made a startling debut last year with *The Weathermonger*, surely one of the most original of first novels. Mr. Dickinson showed an England which, not far in the future, had turned against the machine. The situation was highly intriguing; the explanation just a little hard to swallow. *Heartsease* describes an episode in the same period, this time without a solution, and the story is the better for the omission. . . .

Mr. Dickinson's imaginative control is absolute. He makes the reader feel the weight of the spirit of this strange age, so that the children's success in resisting it is the more impressive. . . .

Heartsease scores very high marks for sheer story-telling, narrative which is packed full of suspense and pace and in which the action springs from the clash of personalities and the stress of circumstance. It is more than a very good yarn. The scene-painting is masterly, discreet and economical and always consistent. Some of the characters are types or ciphers, but Margaret, the central figure, is finely conceived. . . .

[There] is a satisfying, unpredictable ending to [this] remarkable and moving story. In Mr. Dickinson we have another of those writers, in whom this age is so rich, who push back the boundaries of the children's novel.

> *"After the Machine Age," in* The Times Literary Supplement *(© Times Newspapers Ltd. (London) 1969; reproduced from* The Times Literary Supplement *by permission), June 26, 1969, p. 687.*

L. E. SALWAY

In ["Heartsease"], Mr. Dickinson has returned to the situation which he used so effectively in ["The Weathermonger"]: England in the grip of the ideas and superstitions of the Middle Ages. But although the setting is the same the mood is not and the humour and originality which characterised "The Weathermonger" have been replaced in "Heartsease" by a more serious and straightforward attempt to examine life in a society dominated by fear of machines and adherence to ancient superstition.

The story concerns a group of children who rescue an American spy from death by stoning and smuggle him out of the country. It is an exciting story and Mr. Dickinson tells it well but the plot is less interesting than the background and the characterisation of the children themselves is less effective than that of the adults who are their enemies.

There is no weathermongering and no Merlin in "Hearts-ease" and the book is less a fantasy than a realistic adventure in an alien setting. Children of ten to twelve will enjoy it as such but admirers of "The Weathermonger" will, I think, be disappointed. (p. 201)

> *L. E. Salway, in* Children's Book News *(copyright © 1969 by Children's Book Centre Ltd.), July-August, 1969.*

Peter Dickinson has written the best thriller likely to be published this year [with *The Sinful Stones*]. Is that a rash statement to make in June? Not very. *Both* his previous books won best-thriller awards and the new one is better still. This Scottish yarn is like a lightweight, well-woven, expertly tailored Harris tweed. To scramble metaphors, the cunning mechanism of the plot purrs like a Rolls, and the writing style is luscious thick Devon cream There's been nothing like it in British mystery fiction since Michael Innes and Edmund Crispin. . . . [This is a] racing adventure story, spiced with genuine detection and told with rare wit. (p. 25)

> The New Republic *(reprinted by permission of* The New Republic; © 1970 The New Republic, Inc.), *June 13, 1970.*

MARGERY FISHER

The Devil's children is the third book in which the Changes in a near-future Britain are described through their effect on certain individuals and places. In this book we are at a point not long after the mysterious antipathy towards machines has exposed Britain to a new ideological tyranny. In Shepherds Bush a girl of twelve has been separated from her parents in a panic evacuation of the disease-ridden city. Nicola is adopted by a band of Sikhs looking for somewhere to settle; because of their race they are immune to the Changes and regard Nicola in the light of a "canary" able to warn them of danger. . . . The progress of the story is a dual one. The journey through Surrey is meticulously plotted and the hillside farm where the Sikhs settle is described so well that you feel you are present at every conference, at the meeting with the giant Barnard, ex-farm worker, who keeps the village under his thumb, and through the terrible days when thugs wearing armour fashioned from beaten tins occupy the place and persecute the inhabitants. Through this action, logically developed and utterly absorbing, runs the parallel journey of Nicky's heart —for this, sentimental though it may sound, is just what it is. Quite rightly the story does not end with the victory over the invaders nor with the village festival (described with sly humour) in which brown people and white celebrate their better understanding; it ends with Nicola's departure to France to look for her parents and to try to become human once more. Using the Changes to illustrate the growing-up of a girl, the author has given them an emotional dimension deeper than that of the earlier books. (pp. 1559-60)

> *Margery Fisher, in her* Growing Point, *July, 1970.*

ALLEN J. HUBIN

If Peter Dickinson's "The Sinful Stones" . . . had been a first novel, I would have praised it as a rewarding debut of unusual character; but inasmuch as Mr. Dickinson's previous two crime novels (especially the second, "The Old English Peep Show") have disclosed the awesome range of his creativity, my enthusiasm for "Stones" is somewhat muted. It is uncommon of milieu and well peopled, but less than compelling of plot. (p. 41)

> *Allen J. Hubin, in* The New York Times Book Review *(© 1970 by The New York Times Company; reprinted by permission), July 12, 1970.*

SARA BLACKBURN

In which one of the perils of series novels is illustrated: James Pibble, the British detective hero of Peter Dickinson's [*The Lizard in the Cup*], is apparently beloved for his past adventures in previous novels, but the author has forgotten to re-create his character in this current episode, set on a Greek island. We find Pibble reluctantly hard at work there among the highly exotic entourage of Thanassi Thanatos, an Onassis-type zillionaire who is, perhaps, about to be murdered. . . . Dickinson . . . weaves all [his] plots and counterplots with skill, and with an obvious passion for his setting, which is lovingly conveyed here. Yet my own response was to sit idly by, enjoying the scene but indifferent as to whether or not Thanatos was safe because I was never sure just who Pibble was: He is clearly in the low-key, even depressed tradition of [Per Wahlöö's and Maj Sjöwall's] lovable Martin Beck, but Dickinson has been unforgivably presumptuous about his renown for previous adventures, and it's hard to root for Pibble's client with no allegiance to the shadowy hero himself. I harp on this major flaw at such length only because this is a novel one wants to become absorbed in and to admire for its obvious virtues, which include a respect for the details of both exterior landscape and interior human emotion that is preciously rare in its genre.

One final complaint: In a closing act, Pibble demonstrates that he's on the side of right by turning over to the authorities one of the major members of the cast, a woman whose crimes have been unrelated to the mystery at hand. He does so, Dickinson would have us believe, because he's against the violence she represents. This seems a weird act of gratuitous goody-goodiness on the murky Pibble's part, for Dickinson has had ample opportunity throughout to deplore the far more lethal violence of the regime that rules over the idyllic Greek setting of his novel. (p. 13)

> *Sara Blackburn, in* Book World—Chicago Tribune *(© 1970 Postrib Corp.), July 19, 1970.*

A. L. ROSENZWEIG

[*The Sinful Stones*] has the great virtue of being different, just like Peter Dickinson's two earlier stories featuring Inspector Pibble of New Scotland Yard. And that's rare with a character in a series. In each adventure Pibble's persona grows in the round so that by the opening scenes of his current case the middle-aged cop is engaged in retracing time lost. . . . The story is laced with mystery and a kind of nostalgia for the Edwardian days which Pibble must re-live to make the present bearable. (p. 15)

> *A. L. Rosenzweig, in* Book World—Chicago Tribune *(© 1970 Postrib Corp.), July 19, 1970.*

MARGERY FISHER

[The] cunning narrative scheme and the peculiarly subtle divulging of the central surprise bring [*Emma Tupper's diary*] closer to Peter Dickinson's detective stories than to the "Changes" books. Here, it is true, is the same concern for the state of Britain, the same obsession about machines, that have informed all his children's books; man's effect on his environment provides a firm, if implied, moral for an exceptionally exciting story. . . . Tension and surprise are beautifully managed, in regard to human and extra-human affairs. One can only be thankful for an author who conceives his books for the young on the same grand scale as his adult novels and puts into them ebullient humour and stylishness of expression. (pp. 1749-50)

Margery Fisher, in her Growing Point, *May, 1971.*

NEWGATE CALLENDAR

In recent years, Peter Dickinson has been attracting attention for a series of low-keyed mysteries written with extraordinary concentration. It is not so much that the man is an unusually fine prose stylist. Even more, he has the ability to suggest, to leave things unsaid, and over his books hangs a suspended cloud that can scare the reader.

Dickinson maintains his high standard in "Sleep and His Brother." . . .

[Elements in the book include] a Greek billionaire, a pair of doctors with problems of their own, a denouement in which matters are none too satisfactorily settled. The author strings together these various elements like the virtuoso he is, and "Sleep and His Brother" should be high on the list when annual awards are considered. (p. 40)

Newgate Callendar, in The New York Times Book Review *(© 1971 by The New York Times Company; reprinted by permission), May 9, 1971.*

Comedy of manners? ecological allegory? adventure? farce? the disparities don't reconcile. Dickinson starts [*Emma Tupper's Diary*] with a houseful of savvy Scots and sets them to launching a juvenile hoax—disguising the family submarine (Grandfather McAndrews was an inventor) as a Loch monster. . . . It's hard to believe that Fiona and Andy who are 18 and 22 have nothing better to do, and the motives Dickinson supplies are unbecomingly flimsy. . . . Clever in spots but in no wise the equal of the first or third volumes in Dickinson's recent trilogy, partly because it's paunchy (or flabby round the middle), but mostly because the signals cross incompatibly. (pp. 953-54)

Kirkus Reviews (copyright © 1971 The Kirkus Service, Inc.), September 1, 1971.

FRANK EYRE

Peter Dickinson [is] a comparatively new writer whose stories about 'The Changes', a time when men in England had learned to fear and dread machines, and so destroy them, have been one of the most refreshing discoveries of the last few years. (p. 124)

The first of these three books, *The Weathermonger*, is a straightforward and vividly exciting adventure story. The Changes have only affected Britain; Europe is still as she was, but she cannot mount a rescue expedition because, for reasons which are described with convincing ingenuity, all forms of power fail as the English coast is approached. Two children are found who have been unaffected by the Changes. They are taken to France, given careful instructions and then taken across the Channel in a sailing yacht back to England. . . .

Their object is to drive across England to Wales, and get as near as they can to a spot which has been located as the source of the trouble. They succeed in doing this, discover the cause of the Changes and are able to reverse them. This is a wonderfully imaginative adventure story, of a kind that seemed almost to have ceased to exist, and no one who has read it will be surprised that its author should also have written a series of detective stories (or something like detective stories) which are as unique in their own way as *The Weathermonger* is among children's adventure stories of today. The second book about The Changes, *Heartsease*, is even better, because the story is just as exciting but there are also strongly drawn characters. The girl who is the centre of the story is clearly drawn and the villagers and other adults are only too true to life. This is a story of prejudice and oppression, that paints an all-too-recognisable picture of what English villages could become in a time of such Change. Peter Dickinson's third book, *The Devil's Children*, takes the reader back to the beginning of the Changes. . . . This is a book which, once the basic situation is accepted, is completely real. There are no gratuitous sensations, no thrills for the sake of thrills, and no easy solutions, but the author leaves us a believable hope. (pp. 124-25)

Frank Eyre, in his British Children's Books in the Twentieth Century *(copyright © 1971 by Frank Eyre; reprinted by permission of the publishers, E. P. Dutton & Co., Inc., in Canada by Penguin Books Ltd.), Longman Books, 1971, Dutton, 1973.*

Peter Dickinson, who has already proved his mastery in two very different types of story, now tries his strength in another. *The Dancing Bear* is a magnificent tale of adventure, a penetrating study of history, and a close examination of human and animal relationships. In each it is an outstanding achievement. . . .

Bubba's is a fine portrait, for she, although never more than animal, is full of personality. From her first appearance, playing cat-and-mouse with the live crabs which are her supper and weeping because the honey jar she has filched has fallen just out of reach, till at Silvester's betrothal feast she gets drunk and has a "hideous hangover", Bubba gains the reader's unconditional devotion. There are more convenient companions for an odyssey than a slow, moody, thick-headed dancing bear, but none more endearing.

Mr. Dickinson is firmly established as one of the most original, versatile and uncommitted of contemporary writers for the young. He confirms and extends this reputation in a novel which tells a great story with restrained eloquence, with deep human understanding, and above all with tolerance. There are no villains in *The Dancing Bear*, not even the Empire, only people following their destinies towards happiness or disaster. (p. 485)

The Times Literary Supplement *(© Times Newspapers Ltd. (London) 1972; reproduced from* The Times Literary Supplement *by permission), April 28, 1972.*

NEWGATE CALLENDAR

Any book in which James Pibble appears is, *ipso facto*, going to be a good book, and so it is in Peter Dickinson's "The Lizard in the Cup." . . .

The book is not only a travelogue about one of the Greek islands, and a basic introduction to drug traffic. It is about people. Dickinson is one of the most natural and literate of mystery writers. His people talk as people really talk; they have understandable motivations; and each person emerges as a believable character in his own right. But Dickinson never forgets that he is writing a mystery story. There is plenty of action, and the plotting is impeccable. "The Lizard in the Cup" is Dickinson at his best. If it does not have the macabre terror of last year's "Sleep and His Brother," it has a different but equally intriguing buildup. (p. 35)

> *Newgate Callendar, in* The New York Times Book Review *(© 1972 by The New York Times Company; reprinted by permission), May 14, 1972.*

In some ways, Mr. Dickinson's [*The Dancing Bear*] suggests that he is a worthy successor to the late Henry Treece, in bringing alive little-documented historical periods. Based on actual events, his reconstruction of decadent sixth-century Byzantium, beseiged by barbarians, has a vivid reality and truth.... The plot is fast-moving and quite strong meat.... [Dickinson brings unique qualities to the plot], particularly the humour of his earlier children's books, here applied to the absurd trivialities of Byzantine life, to Bubba's endearing antics, and Holy John, perched on his pillar in the palace courtyard, arguing theological niceties alike with servants or the Count's guests (and carried in on a special portable pillar). A more serious thread in the narration, a mystical sense of the City as a living being, and an awareness of unspoken human ties and responsibilities, will make due impact on thoughtful readers. (pp. 176-77)

> The Junior Bookshelf, *June, 1972.*

BILL MESSER

[With *The Dancing Bear*, the] author shows how individuals adjust in alien surroundings. He also points to the need of adolescents to establish their own identities: the daughter seems happy to adopt Hun society while the slave, trying to decide whether he is merely a thing, or an individual in his own right, accepts the Roman model for its civilized standards. These are important matters. That he uses them as the backbone in an absorbing tale is a measure of the quality of this writer. (pp. 252-53)

> *Bill Messer, in* The School Librarian, *September, 1972.*

PAUL HEINS

A boy, a bear, and a holy man are the three chief characters in [*The Dancing Bear*], a historical novel set in sixth-century Byzantium.... The author has successfully made use of historical details to further the plot of the story, since a knowledge of the sophisticated civilization of the Byzantines and an insight into the customs and habits of the ancient Slavs and Huns are essential to an understanding of Silvester's experiences. The story itself consists of a series of lively and amusing roadside adventures, but in a larger sense, it is a comedy—the high comedy of Silvester's learning how to value and to accept freedom. Actually, several comedies are enacted at once; for Bubba's antics smack of slapstick and Holy John's preachments are delightfully preposterous. Background, character, and

comedy are skillfully blended in a combination that is—at once—witty, rich, and evocative. (pp. 470, 472)

> *Paul Heins, in* The Horn Book Magazine *(copyright © 1973 by The Horn Book, Inc., Boston), October, 1973.*

[*Sleep and His Brother* is brilliantly] original as always in setting, a charitable home for children suffering from sleepiness leading to early death: engaging as always in characters, with Pibble now retired, doctors real and false, a devoted spinster, a Greek millionaire: ingenious as always in situational gimmickry—but this time the story is sadly diffuse and constructionally poor, the promising telepathy left hanging unexplored, and likewise the bait of the horror-murderer from the past: a disappointing book to come from one of our best new crime writers. (p. 253)

> The Times Literary Supplement *(© Times Newspapers Ltd. (London) 1974; reproduced from* The Times Literary Supplement *by permission), April 12, 1974.*

If we were asked which modern writer could pull off a detective story based on anthropology and psycholinguistics, the answer could only be Peter Dickinson. Anthropology Mr Dickinson has already brought brilliantly to book in his first detective novel, *Skin Deep*. Thereafter we have had some quirky, original, always enjoyable stories, but all well below that standard. Now he is on it again and even above it, with a story that is both a good novel and excellent detection....

It is hard to praise [*The Poison Oracle*] too highly. The interweaving of strands, all intrinsic, each of its own story-telling value, is brilliant. Characterization is more than adequate, and not least of Morris himself, a kindly man of low sexual drive but intense devotions. He is no commonplace thriller hero, simply an intelligent scholarly man, acting throughout within limited capacities which turn out to be those exactly meeting the situations. There is no intention of asking us to accept this as a serious novel of art and insight. Instead, it is a model of the highest weight of novel a detective story can bear.

> *"Chomsky among the Chimps," in* The Times Literary Supplement *(© Times Newspapers Ltd. (London) 1974; reproduced from* The Times Literary Supplement *by permission), April 12, 1974, p. 385.*

NEWGATE CALLENDAR

What puts "The Poison Oracle" considerably above most books of its kind is its thoroughness of detail. Dickinson, as might be expected from the author of so scary and offbeat a novel as "Sleep and His Brother" ... has an unusual kind of mind. He also is a first-rate researcher who seems to know a great deal about Arabic languages, linguistic theory and Arabic customs. Thus "The Poison Oracle" transcends the pure mystery. But between the covers is a classic mystery with a more or less standard denouement except for the chief witness—the most unlikely witness any writer is going to introduce for a long time. (p. 31)

> *Newgate Callendar, in* The New York Times Book Review *© 1974 by The New York Times Company; reprinted by permission), June 16, 1974.*

MARY M. BURNS

Davy Price [of *The Gift*] had the unique ability to see other

171

people's thoughts in his own mind. . . . Past and present, legend and fact are woven into an intricate web of suspense and climax in the psychologically charged confrontation of the boy with a crazed killer whose violent thoughts have been forced into Davy's consciousness. Adult emotions and experiences . . . are handled subtly and honestly. The author has avoided sensationalism by consistently retaining the perspective of his adolescent protagonist both in dialogue and in narration. Superb touches of humor, contrasting sharply with the gravity of the situations, give depth to the characterizations and balance to the structure without destroying the feeling of thrill and suspense. A novel which can be classified according to many of the currently fashionable categories—social realism, psychological analysis, interest in occult phenomena—but which remains in the memory first and foremost as a masterful example of storytelling. (pp. 141-42)

> *Mary M. Burns, in* The Horn Book Magazine *(copyright © 1974 by The Horn Book, Inc., Boston), October, 1974.*

JANE ABRAMSON

In Dickinson's first-rate novel about second sight, Davy Price has inherited *The Gift* of clairvoyance from a legendary Welsh ancestor. . . . [The] gift becomes a terrifying burden when Davy's mind is flooded with the mad imaginings of a half-wit out to destroy the Prices. From Wolf's distorted visions which are masterfully described as Van Gogh-esque nightmares of swirling shapes and overly bright colors, Davy discovers and helps foil a robbery scheme involving his father. Ironically, through his special relation with Wolf, Davy's numbed emotions are awakened and he comes to a fuller understanding of his own family—the tangled relationships between his self-sufficient brother and sister; his parents (a pair of middle-aged adolescents who are Dickinson's weakest characters); and his Welsh grandparents who are accorded a passion and depth rarely seen in children's books. A consummate craftsman, Dickinson skillfully mixes folklore and modern suspense to create an affecting story about perception—both the extrasensory and everyday kinds. (p. 118)

> *Jane Abramson, in* School Library Journal *(reprinted from the October, 1974 issue of* School Library Journal, *published by R. R. Bowker Co. A Xerox Corporation; copyright © 1974), October, 1974.*

RICHARD E. GEIS

[*The Poison Oracle* is] a bit of Strange, rather bizarre. Set in Now, in the real world, in which an English psycholinguist is working with a "genius" chimp in animal/human communication while in the employ of an oil-rich Arab ruler at the unique "castle" of the ruler. . . .

The plot—the "suspense"—is more the psycholinguist's survival in the swamp in the clutches of the sacrificial-minded natives than solving the puzzle of who killed the Sulton and how it was done. . . .

What is superb in this book is Dickinson's creation of the marsh people, their complicated society, culture and customs, and their meticulously worked-out language and its effect/link on/with the marsh people. Dickinson's skill in this area should turn many sf writers green with envy and

admiration. He makes the natives and their culture so real . . . I'm still not totally sure they don't really exist.

> *Richard E. Geis, "A Chimp in Time," in* The Alien Critic *(copyright © 1974 by Richard Geis for the contributors; reprinted by permission of Richard E. Geis), November, 1974, p. 30.*

JOHN ROWE TOWNSEND

Peter Dickinson's three books about the 'Changes', which cause the people of England to turn against machinery and withdraw into a dark age of malicious ignorance, appeared at almost the same time as [John Christopher's 'White Mountains' trilogy]. . . . Peter Dickinson is even farther from the SF mainstream than John Christopher. In the first book to appear, [*The Weathermonger*, Geoffrey] and his sister Sally set off through hostile countryside in a splendid antique Rolls-Royce from the Beaulieu motor museum to find the cause of the Changes. This part of the book is a vivid adventure story, and the passages in which the hero practises his mysterious art of conjuring up a different weather are fine and poetic, but the book comes a sorry tumble in the end with its incongruous attribution of the Changes to a revived but drug-sick Merlin. (p. 216)

The second book, *Heartsease* . . . , moves back in time from *The Weathermonger*. Two children, using horses and an old tugboat, contrive the escape of a young man who has been stoned as a witch and left for death. This is the most unified, most consistently gripping, and for my money the best book of the trio. Finally, *The Devil's Children* . . . goes back to the beginning of the Changes. . . . The fact that the three books were written in reverse order to the events they describe emphasizes that they are three linked stories and not, like the 'White Mountains' three, a true trilogy. This does not in itself detract from their merits, but it was possible to feel after *The Devil's Children* appeared that the author's obvious inventive and storytelling abilities had not quite produced the achievement they might have done. (p. 217)

> *John Rowe Townsend, in his* Written for Children: An Outline of English-Language Children's Literature *(copyright © 1965, 1974 by John Rowe Townsend; reprinted by permission of J. B. Lippincott Company; in Canada by Kestrel Books), revised edition, Lippincott, 1974.*

JOANNA HUTCHISON

Peter Dickinson's first three children's books, *The Weathermonger*, *Heartsease* and *The Devil's Children*, form a trilogy. They are all set in a Britain chronologically of the near future yet also of the past, for the 'Changes' have taken place, causing the country to become an island

> . . . fragmented into a series of rural communities, united by a common hostility to machines of any sort and by a tendency to try to return to the modes of living and thought that characterized the Dark Ages. . . .

This basic hypothesis, that Britain has changed in this way, provides the mainspring of the trilogy.

The other two books simply ask one to accept the Changes without explanation, and are more successful because of it. *Heartsease* takes place about five years after the Changes, and *The Devil's Children* is set at the very beginning of the

Changes, when people are leaving in their thousands for other countries. I think I was fortunate in reading *The Devil's Children* first, for it seems to me that the weakness of the trilogy lies in the cause of the Changes, and in *The Devil's Children* this seems irrelevant, or certainly obtrudes least. Any fantasy asks one to accept a certain hypothesis, to exercise a 'willing suspension of disbelief', and this one agrees to do if the book has an inner consistency and if our credulity is not expected to stretch beyond what we feel to be the probable or likely outcome of the original hypothesis. I feel that this is what *The Weathermonger* does expect of us. (pp. 88-9)

When I told my class the explanation for the Changes given in *The Weathermonger*, they were both puzzled and derisive to find that it is Merlin, discovered and then held in the drugged sway of Mr Furbelow, who is causing Britain to revert to a more familiar time. It was as if the book had stepped outside its own borders of probability.

I was often niggled by other inconsistencies in *The Weathermonger* and *Heartsease*—inconsistencies which perhaps only strike one when one is reading in a more critical fashion and not when one is being swept along by the excitement of the story. Why is Geoffrey, who is so strongly affected by the Changes that he acquires the powers to become a weathermonger, not affected by the antimachine feeling so that all through the Changes he regularly services his motor boat? Why isn't Mr Furbelow returned to the Dark Ages in the same way as the other people in the book? Why are some people only partially affected by the Changes? Jonathan in *Heartsease* wonders if the immunity is, '. . . something to do with children's minds. . . . Not being so set in their ways of thinking.' But one would in fact expect memories of machines and their usefulness to be much weaker in their minds, and that those minds should be equally susceptible to an exterior force driving them in a particular direction.

The fact that it is an exterior force is the cause of another weakness of the books—their attitude to machines. I'm not suggesting that the books should have come out wholeheartedly for or against machines. But they do invite one to consider the good and bad effects of machines, although this is done rather vaguely and weakly. Mr Gordon, the evil old sexton in *Heartsease,* and the rabble that he is able to arouse, are against machines not because they see them as something with a power to harm because of what they can *do;* they loathe machines for what they think they *are*— the Devil's work, evil for reasons they cannot clearly justify. Their hatred of machines becomes simply another superstition of the Dark Ages. And yet one seems to be asked to give serious consideration to this superstition. . . . (pp. 89-90)

[What Jonathan calls 'Mr Gordon and his lot' have] turned against machines not because they are *machines* but because they are at variance with the forces that are causing them to revert to the Dark Ages. I sense an uneasiness in the books over this question. In *The Weathermonger* there is obvious admiration for the beauty of the Rolls Royce Silver Ghost but not for 'those little French beetles whining about'. Part of the trouble is that in *The Weathermonger* and *Heartsease* the antimachine feeling is so negative. The world without machines that we are presented with has little in its favour. People are withdrawn, ignorant, superstitious, suspicious of each other: 'Nobody liking or trusting

anybody—it couldn't have been like that before the Changes. Or in the Dark Ages?' Given this, it is difficult to feel more than token regret when Britain is removed from the crazed grip of a morphine addict, even when one reads in the last line of *The Weathermonger*, 'And the English air would soon be reeking with petrol.'

It is in this regard that I feel that *The Devil's Children* is better than the other two books in the trilogy. Machines don't figure so largely, though the attitude towards them comes across very vividly when Nicky is overcome by a sort of madness as one of the Sikhs starts up an abandoned bus. More important, the community life of the Sikhs . . . presents a kind of positive side to life without machines. I admit much of this comes through the Sikhs themselves. They have a generosity and dignity that the rather mean and ignorant villagers lack. (Partly, it must be owned, because they are not affected mentally by the Changes, not having been a part of Britain in the Dark Ages.) But even the villagers in this book are not so unpleasant as the ordinary people one meets in *The Weathermonger* and *Heartsease*. They are more recognizable as human beings, and when the two communities come together at the end of the book, one can see a value in their way of life that forms a definite counterbalance to a noisy, industrialized Britain, whose rotting relics are left behind at the beginning of the book.

I have rather ungenerously started by saying what I don't like about the trilogy, but there are many positive elements in the books. Peter Dickinson knows that familiar and concrete objects lend an air of reality to a story that in other ways is fantastic. (pp. 90-1)

Peter Dickinson seems concerned that places in the stories be real places. . . . The author describes mechanical processes in such detail that one feels quite sure they would work in reality—processes such as the mending of the motor boat's cooling system in *The Weathermonger* or the ways in which the various bridges in *Heartsease* operate. . . . (pp. 91-2)

Another of Peter Dickinson's strengths is his ability to pack a story full of exciting incident. A journey often figures in the books, giving opportunity for a wide-ranging and swiftly changing sequence of events. As one might expect from an author who also writes detective fiction, he is a skilful manager of plot and knows how to grip the reader's interest. Despite my criticisms of it, I would acknowledge *The Weathermonger* to be an exciting tale. . . . Feeling as I do that it is not the best of Peter Dickinson's books, I don't particularly encourage [my pupils] to read it, nor would I choose to read it to a class. I have noticed that *Heartsease* is popular with girls in my classes, who are interested in horses, for they can identify with its heroine and the sympathy she has with her pony. It is a book which I recommend. Apart from the exciting story, there is greater reflection in it, greater self-realization. Margaret, the principal character, has to come to acknowledge the particular strengths of Lucy, whom she has before now dismissed as a lazy and inefficient servant. And there is an interesting contrast between the peculiar virtues and weaknesses of the very different characters of Margaret and her cousin Jonathan. (p. 92)

[The] link between ancient superstition and current prejudice is strong in *The Devil's Children*, whose title indicates the way in which the native Englishmen see the Sikhs, whom we discover to be a warm, friendly, courageous and dignified people. Our sympathies are with them throughout the book.

The element of self-realization that we find in *Heartsease* is developed further in this book. Nicky Gore is a more tangible heroine than Margaret in *Heartsease,* and alongside the story of the Sikhs' journey to Felpham and their coming to terms with the village is Nicky's coming to terms with herself. (pp. 94-5)

This greater complexity of characterization makes *The Devil's Children* the most satisfying of the trilogy for me, though I would have to agree with Peter Dickinson that:

> A children's book which concentrates much
> on the development of character and much
> of whose plot hinges on character, is not of
> as great interest to children as it would be to
> an adult.

The Devil's Children has its highly exciting moments but the story's beginning does not have such an impact as in the other two books. . . .

Emma Tupper's Diary breaks away from Britain under the Changes and turns to Scotland of the present day. Here again Peter Dickinson brings in his carpet tacks of reality to anchor the fantasy. The submarine in which the children discover animals surviving from prehistoric times is described in loving detail, and its working operations are carefully explained. (There is also a diagram at the front of the book which makes things quite clear!) And like the submarine, the arguments for the existence and survival of the Plesiosaurs are carefully and convincingly worked out. In fact I found the submarine and Plesiosaurs rather easier to accept than the people. Peter Dickinson seems to have a liking for somewhat bizarre and eccentric characters. It is from them that he derives much of his humour both in his children's books and in his adult novels, where I feel they are more successful. When plot depends on character it is important that character can sustain this. Several incidents in the story spring from the constant quarrels of the Mc-Andrew brothers, Andy and Roddy, which I found unconvincing and tedious. Poop Newcombe, a luscious, dumb, blonde kleptomaniac, who keeps an eye on the children while they keep an eye on her, is perhaps typical of the kind of unusual character that Peter Dickinson seems to enjoy creating. She adds to Emma's sense of displacement from her ordinary and stolid surroundings, but like the other McAndrews, her credibility tends to suffer when compared with tangible objects like the submarine. (p. 95)

The journeys in the submarine are exciting, though the story moves rather slowly to the point where the machine is got into working order, and the scene where Emma and Roddy surface in the reeking, nightmarish cave where the creatures live is superbly described and, I think, the highlight of the book. (pp. 95-6)

The Dancing Bear is quite different again. Its setting is the Byzantium of 558 A D, whose atmosphere is colourfully and vividly evoked in all its complexity, vitality, beauty and squalor. . . . As well as its complexity and wealth of incident, *The Dancing Bear* has excitement and charm. The journey which forms the central line of the book allows a great variety of setting and never allows one's interest to flag.

[Bubba] is a superb bear and very real. She never takes on anthropomorphic features. It is often her very stupidity and lack of understanding, her desire for a wrestling match at a most inopportune moment and her dismay when she slides down a bank and then turns it into a new game that make her so engaging and so credible. (p. 96)

[*The Gift*] contains an element of fantasy, but here it is even more securely anchored to the familiar and recognizable. The fantasy concerns the 'Gift', now possessed by fourteen-year-old Davy Price, of being able to receive images from other people's minds, to see the pictures that they are conjuring up in the mind's eye. The history of the Gift is contained in Welsh legend. . . .

This legend, contained in a skilfully wrought piece of verse, is delicately and characteristically handled by the author. It isn't made a focal part of the story as in Alan Garner's *Owl Service,* but introduced subtly as an explanation for those who choose to believe it. Or one can think like Davy's grandfather that the poem could have been written at some later time to account for the existence of a power which is not so far from known forms of extrasensory perception as to stretch our credulity.

The story is chiefly anchored to the familiar through its setting, a world of comparative ordinariness; a housing estate, a small Welsh farm, school and a building site. (p. 97)

It is a story of suspense, mystery and excitement and also one in which character is drawn with great sympathy and understanding, not only in the case of Wolf, who becomes a figure more pathetic than frightening, but also in the cases of Davy's father, irritating and unstable yet likeable, and his grandmother, with her unforgiving and wounded pride. People are portrayed convincingly with all their weaknesses yet without being judged. Much of this insight into other people is shown through Penny, whose sensitivity to others is a gift too, a gift which the book suggests is of greater value and more reliable than Davy's. (pp. 97-8)

Joanna Hutchison, "Peter Dickinson Considered, in and out of the Classroom," in Children's literature in education (© 1975, Agathon Press, Inc.; reprinted by permission of the publisher), No. 17 (Summer), 1975, pp. 88-98.*

MARGERY FISHER

The distinction between the three concepts in the title of this fascinating compendium [*Chance, Luck and Destiny*] is enforced by the story of Oedipus, told in sections and, at first, without identification, with the finding of the exposed infant standing for Chance, his adoption by the childless rulers of Corinth for Luck and the final tragedy for Destiny. Between the several parts of the story of Oedipus lie anecdotes, reflections, examples, statistics. . . . A curious mixture of guesswork, reason and offhand belief characterises this unusual book, which should by no means be confined to young readers. (pp. 2751-52)

Margery Fisher, in her Growing Point, *November, 1975.*

MARGERY FISHER

Stage properties, the line-drawings at the head of each chapter, scenery, plot and theme of *The Blue Hawk,* all suggest a very early period of Egyptian culture, but this is not an historical novel. Peter Dickinson leaps still further from any actual historical starting-point than he did from Byzantium in *The Dancing Bear*. As in that book, he produces an illusion of authenticity while taking freedom to arrange events and choose characters as it suits him. At the same time, the associations with an exotic past that flock into the mind as we read cannot but add to our enjoyment of this complex, circling narrative. (p. 2811)

This is not the first story of the clash between tyranny and freedom of thought and it will not be the last, but it is certainly one of the most specific and compelling. Quotations from the texts prescribed by the priests for any and every contingency, religious or domestic, texts committed to memory by acolytes like Tron, are inserted naturally in the story and provide evidence of the power of the priesthood beyond what is obvious from their actions, whether honest or conspiratorial; these snatches of chanted words seem to go right to the heart of the matter. The tight quasi-verse structures, as well as the elaborate, concentrated descriptions of ritual, create a strong atmosphere of ancient mystery; the tyranny of O and AA, or rather, of those who purport to interpret Sun and Moon to the people, is in this book a great deal more than a mere matter of statement. Again, Peter Dickinson stresses through their speech the contrast between the inexorably formal priests and the human, freedom-loving King whom they must destroy if they are not to lose their unique status in the kingdom.

The patterns of action and feeling in this book are as various as its style. Harsh, vivid descriptions of conflict; evocations of riverside, mountain gorge, the secret tunnels of the Palace; soldiers' banter, the uncouth mumblings of outland folk, the innocent exchanges between Tron and the shepherd girl Taleel; continual changes of colour, sound and scene contribute to the creation of a world as absolute as if it had really existed. (pp. 2811-12)

> *Margery Fisher, in her* Growing Point, *March 1976.*

DAVID CHURCHILL

Virtually unreviewable is Peter Dickinson's unusual and absorbing book [*Chance, Luck and Destiny*]. Its four sections, 'Magic and Witchcraft' being added to the three of the title, are anthologies of facts and fictions, unquestionably enhanced by the author's commentary, which never seeks to make mystery where there is none and frequently dismisses fallacy, yet reveals the strangeness of the workings of chance and coincidence in people's lives. . . . Difficult to evaluate as such a cauldronful of intriguing entertainment may be, it is certainly unlikely to be left unread if placed on the library shelves of any secondary school. (p. 57)

> *David Churchill, in* The School Librarian, *March, 1976.*

MARCUS CROUCH

Peter Dickinson is the critic's joy, as well as the child's. Other writers, including the best, settle into a uniform excellence which is wholly to be admired but which scarcely lends itself to individual appreciation.

Mr Dickinson keeps us guessing. Will the next be about a society without machines, or a school of Loch Ness monsters, or the second sight, or the Byzantine Empire? Probably not, for he has had his say on these matters. *The Blue*

Hawk seems to be about Pharaonic Egypt. . . . A little reflection suggests that this is too facile a view. The sacred river Tan whose waters keep the land fertile may seem like the Nile, but she flows south. Other details are equally disconcerting, and they give rise to more fundamental doubts. Are we in the past? The kingdom operates according to rituals whose rigidity suggests a civilization moving towards decay. It is not just that the revolution which is the main theme of the story is overdue. There are hints of a greater, more sophisticated civilization in the remote past. Can it be that we are, in fact, not in the past but the future, and that —flattering thought—the Wise whose memory and relics remain are ourselves?

It is to be hoped that such considerations will not distract readers from the pure and wholehearted enjoyment of this magnificent tale. It is acknowledged that in the children's book the fine art of story-telling has its last manifestation, and—setting aside his political, sociological and psychological concerns—Mr Dickinson is the past-master story-teller of our day.

> *Marcus Crouch, "Ritual or Revolution," in* The Times Literary Supplement (© *Times Newspapers Ltd. (London) 1976; reproduced from* The Times Literary Supplement *by permission), April 12, 1976, p. 375.*

T. J. BINYON

One of the main differences between the thriller and the detective story proper is that the former demands an open, the latter a closed environment. The classic example of the second is the country-house murder. Peter Dickinson, in a series of highly intelligent novels, has taken this formula and stood it on its head by creating a succession of strange closed societies that are not simply neutral arenas for the conflict between murderer and detective but are fascinating in their own right. In them the crime and its detection are defined by the bizarre environment, and it is probably this which has forced his detective, Jimmy Pibble, most sympathetic of fictional policemen, into premature retirement; the normal procedures of investigation are unavailing in the outré worlds conceived by Mr Dickinson. . . .

Peter Dickinson tends to look at things from the standpoint of an anthropologist: custom and ritual bulk larger than individual character or emotion. In *King and Joker* he has chosen as his subject the English royal family. . . .

King and Joker is witty and extremely ingenious. There seems to be a slight shift from the anthropologist's to the novelist's point of view: the characters are more memorable (the Dowager Princess of Wales, for instance), and Peter Dickinson has adopted from his children's books— which are considered by some people to be even better than his books for adults—the technique of looking at the action (or some of it) through a child's eyes: here those of the thirteen-year-old Louise, for whom the events are interwoven with the difficulties of growing up and of coming to terms with her role as a princess.

> *T. J. Binyon, "Murder at the Palace," in* The Times Literary Supplement (© *Times Newspapers Ltd. (London) 1976; reproduced from* The Times Literary Supplement *by permission), April 30, 1976, p. 507.*

MARGARET MEEK

The great reward of writers for the young is that they are

expected to tell stories. The readers look for secondary worlds to find themselves in and the critics examine 'How does the author do it?' The virtues of narrative, response and criticism meet in this remarkable novel [*The blue hawk*], the story of Tron, the young priest in an Egyptian (?) land where the Gods hold sway and the priests make the rules. Rarely have I read such vividly imagined scenes as that of the dead king's barge floating down the great river and the lifting of an age-old curse. It is a spiritual autobiography, the kind of book written with power and commitment for which no adult outlet exists. I will promote this story with fervour, but only experienced readers could read it, and they usually want something else. (p. 146)

> *Margaret Meek, in* The School Librarian, *June, 1976.*

ANATOLE BROYARD

In "King and Joker," Peter Dickinson paints an oxzymoronic picture . . . of an imaginary British royal family. . . .

On a social level, the members of the royal family are rather like high-wire performers in a circus. If they fall, they have so far to go; there is suspense in the spectacle of their keeping their balance.

Disturbing that balance is the purpose of the Joker. . . . He is bent on proving that the jewels in the crown are false, that nobility is an anachronism, that it would be better if the British public were disillusioned once and for all, disabused of its favorite fairy tale, that old anti-Freudian dream of an ideal father and mother. . . .

"King and Joker" is full of Mr. Dickinson's usual flourishes: When the King inspects a guard of honor, he looks at the constables not with a military but with a medical eye and delivers silent diagnoses: "Asthma, poor sod . . . Whisky . . . can that moonface be the start of Addison's disease?" Because the author loves a plot convolution in much the same way that a lecher loves a voluptuous curve, the King has a double, a "look-alike," whom he keeps around for amusement. It becomes crucial to the plot to know whether it is the double or the King himself who is discovered in the under-nurse's bed.

While the Joker's pranks grow increasingly vicious and violent, they are not the center of the action. They simply provoke a series of revelations into the life and intimate history of the royal family, a succession of agonizing re-appraisals. . . . The Joker's real crime—and here we see the moral of Mr. Dickinson's novel—is the invasion of privacy. Instead of assassinating the King in classical style, the Joker wants to assassinate his reputation in what one might call the modern style. . . .

Mr. Dickinson's antic touches seem to grow with each book, as he settles into his idiosyncratic style. Old Nanny Durdy still greets the Prince and Princess with, "Have you done your business?" . . . The King's mother disparages British royalty: "This country has no history," she scoffs. "How many Kings have you assassinated? One! And you did that by committee."

In "King and Joker," Mr. Dickinson continues to move away from the conventional suspense novel and his characters are becoming more convincing with each book. King Victor is especially good. We know him so well that we can

feel with him even when he is infuriated by government figures who say "refute" when they mean "repudiate." . . .

Who killed the concept of nobility?—not who killed Roger Ackroyd?—is the theme of "King and Joker." If we take nobility in its wildest sense, we might say that Mr. Dickinson's subject is the crime of the century.

> *Anatole Broyard, "The Crime of the Century," in* The New York Times *(© 1976 by The New York Times Company; reprinted by permission), June 1, 1976, p. 33.*

PETER HUNT

[*Annerton Pit*] is Peter Dickinson rather below par, with a trendy plot showing the terrible brittleness of the ultra-contemporary. The theme may be eternal—do ends justify means?—but the militant conservationists who blow up motorways and plan to take over an oil rig are a dismally catchpenny collection. . . . [These] conspirators are a weak pastiche of newspaper realities. . . . Peter Dickinson has at hand a [rich] and . . . subtle substructure. The book is masterly in its presentation of the thirteen-year-old Jake, whose consciousness carries the narrative. Jake is blind, and the modulation of experience through heightened senses other than sight, the acceptance of blindness as normality, and the deep rapport with and respect for Jake which are built up, are very impressive indeed. Interpersonal relationships really mean something—especially between Jake and his impetuous but very caring elder brother. Equally, the ghostly terrors of the abandoned coal-mine, Annerton pit itself, and Jake's final encounter with the terrors in his own mind, all evolve, are all integral with the pervasive sightlessness. It is only the slackness of the central incidents, and the unnecessary striving for "excitement" and "significance" which undercut the real potential of the book. (p. 358)

> *Peter Hunt, in* The Times Literary Supplement *(© Times Newspapers Ltd. (London) 1977; reproduced from* The Times Literary Supplement *by permission), March 25, 1977.*

Peter Dickinson's stories have a way of settling around you, so that when [in *Annerton Pit*] thirteen-year-old Jake is disclosed to be blind, the news seems simply to confirm his extraordinary powers of observation. And it is these powers—aptly, the ability to "see" in the dark—that will safeguard Jake and older brother Martin when their ghost-hunting grandfather disappears. . . . [When] the three are trapped in Annerton Pit, . . . it's the devil's own cave to escape from, with *something* present even rational, home-in-the-dark Jake can't shake. Until, within him, the dark lifts. . . . The exorcism of Jake's ghost entails prolonged groping about, literally and figuratively, and the analogy between the pit's terror and political terrorism—both extinguished by a mine detonation—is forced upon the reader. But this intelligent, literate, thoughtful thriller—so intrinsically a blind child's experience—is worth having on any terms. (pp. 788-89)

> Kirkus Reviews *(copyright © 1977 The Kirkus Service, Inc.), August 1, 1977.*

T. J. BINYON

As his other books show, Peter Dickinson has a liking for outré societies; the one portrayed in *Walking Dead* seems a less artificial construction than has sometimes been the case and its characters are more human—which compensates for a rather thin plot. But this is a minor criticism of a highly intelligent, witty and elegant book. (p. 1483)

T. J. Binyon, in The Times Literary Supplement *(© Times Newspapers Ltd, (London) 1977; reproduced from* The Times Literary Supplement *by permission), December 16, 1977.*

NEWGATE CALLENDAR

Leave it to Peter Dickinson to dream up something unusual. This British writer creates mysteries that can have all kinds of threatening undertones, and that have an unusual milieu. . . . Dickinson has imagination, and he also is a sensitive writer. Every new book of his can be approached with anticipation.

His latest is "Walking Dead." . . . In it he poses an ethical problem. A scientist who is an expert on rat and monkey behavioral patterns finds himself framed for murder on a Caribbean island. The dictator orders him to investigate the potentialities of a new drug. But this time he is not to experiment on animals. He is given a group of blacks who are enemies of the state. Go to work—or else.

This ethical dilemma is the main thrust of the book. But there is another one almost as important. Dickinson skillfully works into the plot the confrontation between old magic and new science. . . . Things are never black and white in Dickinson's books. The ending, incidentally, rather unexpectedly follows the rules of a standard murder mystery. The scientist, as it turns out, is also a detective. Don't miss this one. (p. 27)

Newgate Callendar, in The New York Times Book Review *(© 1978 by The New York Times Company; reprinted by permission), January 29, 1978.*

ETHEL L. HEINS

A powerful, wholly original novel is constructed with enormous skill and written with rare perception and intuition [in *Annerton Pit*]. [In the story of the characters'] incarceration and of their attempts to escape from the chill, slimy, terrifying underground labyrinth, the horror of the deliberate, detailed writing approaches that of Poe. But there are also intimations of Dostoevsky, for the greatest impact of the novel is psychological. Martin, who has secretly been an idealistic young supporter of the revolutionists, is placed in an agonizing situation; after the rescue by the police he must, ironically, become "the tool of the very system that scarred the green hills, poisoned river and sea, murdered plant and creatures and spun mankind faster and faster towards destruction." Moreover, he realizes miserably, "It's not much of a problem *being* right. It's *doing* right where the trouble begins—doing it and going on doing it while life comes up and hits you with situations where there aren't any rights to do." And left alone in the mine, sightless Jake undergoes a devastating mental experience and suffers the worst trauma of all; physically agile, intellectually keen, and uncannily sensitive, he is the real hero of the book. (p. 150)

Ethel L. Heins, in The Horn Book Magazine *(copyright © 1978 by the Horn Book, Inc., Boston), April, 1978.*

MARGERY FISHER

The classic journey-adventures of the past, from [Frederick] Marryat and [Walter] Scott downwards, have most of them been journeys of body and spirit together: the most stringent and compelling accidents have their full effect when we can see how they have changed the protagonist other than by merely breaking his head. The divagating and dangerous journey taken [in *Tulku*] by Theodore Tewker into Tibet is, to outward appearance, a flight; surviving a Boxer raid on his father's mission in China, the boy attaches himself to chance-met travellers without any particular plan or hope. It is not for many months that he is able to admit that there was a pattern, mysterious and inexplicable, in his journeying. . . . [Safely] back in England, he admitted to himself that if "the foundations which Father had given him had been shaken", he had "discovered other foundations beneath, broader and more enduring", not by denying the value of the old Lama's teaching or reacting against his father, but by growing into himself.

It is difficult, for reviewer as for writer, to indicate this kind of growth without smudging the total effect of adventure-narrative, a genre which at its best should achieve the reader's belief in emotional change not through sermonising but through a passionate reality of character, action and place fused together, a veracity of detail so strong that he cannot fail to be drawn into the secondary world. *Tulku* is a most impressive and artfully wrought book. It has the outward trappings of a great adventure—an exotic setting of mountain, plateau and river, expert variations of pace and tension and strong character-drawing. (p. 3462)

The small but brilliantly conceived group of monastic dwellers and incoming strangers is presented to the reader in dialogue, description and action with precisely chosen detail and with an illusion of reality supported by the setting, the vividly imagined foothills and mountain fastnesses of Tibet as they might have been seventy years ago. Descriptions are at times extremely simple and direct. . . . At other times statement gives place to images as surprising as they are appropriate. . . . The effect of a piece of action is often enhanced in an image that works like a mentally visual shock in the reader. At the beginning of the journey Mrs. Jones, holding bandits at bay with a shot-gun, orders Lung to cut their trouser-belts, as she says, "from . . . belt to arse":

> "He darted forward, grabbed up a knife and bent behind the right-hand man, then moved down the line like a gardener performing some rapid piece of pruning on a row of fruit-trees. As he left each man a dramatic change took place, the shabby but serviceable pantaloons tumbling down to ankle-level, leaving some with bare buttocks and some with a twist of loin-cloth."

The humour and the sharpness of activity clash together with musical force. The image is important too for its place in the theme of the book, the idea of the growing points of personality. Plants and gardens run fugally through the narrative. Daisy Jones is a plant-hunter, working alone as she once worked with the lover she generously renounced for his social good: the undescribed yellow lily she finds on the hillside seems to symbolise the love she enjoys with Lung: the book ends on a note of mingled humour and philosophy as the lily bulb she has sent by Theodore to her erstwhile lover is unpacked and pronounced to be dried out but still living. It will grow in the greenhouse just as Theodore, by the owner's help, is to be planted again to grow more sturdily than before. Action, image and feeling come together in a few sentecnes to demonstrate the incalculable power of the right word in the right place to embody a strong imaginative vision. (pp. 3462-63)

> *Margery Fisher, in her* Growing Point, *March,* 1979.

Bob Dylan

1941-

(Born Robert Zimmerman) Songwriter, singer, poet, musician, novelist, and screenwriter. Dylan was the voice of the sixties, writing songs which defied middle-class mores and expressed feelings of isolation, anxiety, and the quest for self-identity. Starting as a composer of ballads and protest songs of an unmistakable literary bent, his works eventually transformed the genre of popular music with their combination of the lyrical, the obscure, and the daring. Dylan was born in Duluth, Minnesota and grew up in Hibbing, a tiny iron-ore mining town. Dissatisfied with what he considered a staid, middle-class life, he ran away from home repeatedly. While wandering and working a variety of jobs he also cultivated an interest in music, teaching himself to play piano, guitar, harmonica, and autoharp. By the time he was twenty, he was living in New York City, singing in coffeehouses, and recording with Columbia. His first album, *Bob Dylan*, included little of his own material and was not immediately popular. There were two deciding factors which catapulted him to success: a favorable review of his performance by Robert Shelton for the *New York Times* and the release of "Blowin' in the Wind" performed by Peter, Paul, and Mary. Critics have cited scores of songwriters and musicians as being influential in Dylan's stylistic evolution. His music is said to contain elements reminiscent of Chuck Berry, Leadbelly, Hank Williams, Woody Guthrie, Little Richard, and others. But Dylan's work is very much his own. Rooted in the tradition of folk music with its local color and diction, his songs are also characteristically modern. In fact, this hybrid effect has been called "folk-rock" and Dylan is considered by many the creator and high priest of this genre. Idolized as much more than a musician/composer, Dylan rose to his greatest popularity during the sixties as a result of highly imaginative, symbolic lyrics on timely subjects and emotions. Equally important as his lyrics, his singing voice—raspy with the intonations of the southern folk singers he emulated—made Dylan's appeal incredibly widespread. Some of his recent projects have not achieved universal popularity. The film *Renaldo and Clara* and several of his recent albums have been criticized for their lack of clarity and cohesion. However, the power, variety, influence, and literary quality of Dylan's works have assured his position as one of his generation's most gifted contemporary musicians. (See also *CLC*, Vols. 3, 4, 6, and *Contemporary Authors*, Vols. 41-44, rev. ed.)

ROBERT SHELTON

A bright new face in folk music is appearing at Gerde's Folk City. Although only 20 years old, Bob Dylan is one of the most distinctive stylists to play in a Manhattan cabaret in months. . . . Mr. Dylan is both comedian and tragedian. Like a vaudeville actor on the rural circuit, he offers a variety of droll musical monologues: "Talking Bear Mountain" lampoons the overcrowding of an excursion boat, "Talking New York" satirizes his troubles in gaining recognition and "Talking Havah Nagilah" burlesques the folk-music craze and the singer himself. (p. 17)

Mr. Dylan's highly personalized approach toward folk song is still evolving. He has been sopping up influences like a sponge. At times, the drama he aims at is off-target melodrama and his stylization threatens to topple over as a mannered excess.

But if not for every taste, his music-making has the mark of originality and inspiration, all the more noteworthy for his youth. Mr. Dylan is vague about his antecedents and birthplace, but it matters less where he has been than where he is going, and that would seem to be straight up. (p. 18)

Robert Shelton, "Boy Dylan: A Distinctive Folk-Song Stylist," in The New York Times (© 1961 *by The New York Times Company; reprinted by permission), September 29, 1961 (and reprinted in* Bob Dylan: A Retrospective, *edited by Craig McGregor, William Morrow and Company, 1972, pp. 17-18).*

GIL TURNER

[Dylan's] vocal style is rough and unpolished, reflecting a conscious effort to recapture the earthy realism of the rural country blues. It is a distinctive, highly personalized style combining many musical influences and innovations. . . .

Bob Dylan, while capturing some really superb performances, does not show the breadth of his talent. It contains only one humorous selection—a talking blues about some of his own composition, "Song to Woody." With this relatively minor reservation, the record can be wholeheartedly endorsed as an excellent first album. . . . (p. 24)

While Bob is a noteworthy folk performer with a bright future, I believe his most significant and lasting contribution will be in the songs he writes. . . . Dylan avoids the terms "write" or "compose" in connection with his songs. "The songs are there. They exist all by themselves just waiting for someone to write them down. I just put them down on paper. If I didn't do it, somebody else would." His method of writing places the emphasis on the words, the tune almost always being borrowed or adapted from one he has heard somewhere, usually a traditional one. (p. 25)

> *Gil Turner, "Bob Dylan—A New Voice Singing New Songs," in* Sing Out! *(reprinted with permission from* Sing Out!*), October-November, 1962 (and reprinted in* Bob Dylan: A Retrospective, *edited by Craig McGregor, William Morrow & Company, Inc., 1972, pp. 22-7).*

JOSEPH HAAS

There are few healthier signs of our times than that many of our young people heed and respect the grim pessimism of Bob Dylan. This drawn and weary balladeer writes songs as timely and as real as the gunshot that murdered Medgar Evers or the poverty that drove Hollis Brown to destroy his wife, his five children and himself.

Dylan is becoming a one-young-man Grecian chorus chanting of our sins of pride and prejudice and warning that the gods have struck down men for less—if there are any gods, of course. Dylan seems, in his gloomy cynicism, even to question the validity of such a comforting notion. . . .

Dylan's style, admittedly, isn't easy to take for someone who is accustomed to pop singing, especially of the folkum variety. His voice is flat, nasal and limited in range, and he has confined his guitar and harmonica accompaniment to skeletal chording or a raw country blues framework. But he has style, unmistakably his own and ideally suited to his raw, outspoken material.

Some may question his right to set himself up as a conscience of society. After all, he's only 21 or so, with not much more than a high school education, and he dresses like a beatnik. But really, what other credentials does he need than talent, sensitivity, the gift of poetry, and the validity of his judgments—by these criteria, he more than justifies his right to be heard.

His ballad, *The Lonesome Death of Hattie Carroll*, is hardly more than simple reporting of a Maryland killing. . . . It would be difficult to achieve greater impact in reporting this story than Dylan has done with his plain ballad.

The tragedy of *The Ballad of Hollis Brown* is in the meaninglessness of it and the seeming indifference of god and man to Brown's insurmountable poverty. After the poor South Dakota farmer has slaughtered his family and himself, Dylan finds the ideal line to emphasize the awful absurdity of the deaths: "Somewhere in the distance, there's seven new people born. . . ." (p. xx)

> *Joseph Haas, in* Chicago Daily News *(reprinted with permission of* Field Enterprises, Inc.*), March 7, 1964.*

NAT HENTOFF

It is Dylan's work as a composer . . . that has won him a wider audience than his singing alone might have. Whether concerned with cosmic spectres or personal conundrums, Dylan's lyrics are pungently idiomatic. He has a superb ear for speech rhythms, a generally astute sense of selective detail, and a natural storyteller's command of narrative pacing. His songs sound as if they were being created out of oral street history rather than carefully written in tranquillity. (p. 78)

> *Nat Hentoff, "The Crackin', Shakin', Breakin' Sounds," in* The New Yorker *(© 1964 by The New Yorker Magazine, Inc.), October 24, 1964, pp. 64-90.*

ISRAEL G. YOUNG

Bob Dylan has become a pawn in his own game. He has ceased his Quest for a Universal Sound and has settled for a liaison with the music trade's Top Forty Hit Parade. He has worked his way through dozens of singers and poets on both sides of the Atlantic, and he has left them all behind. Because he is a Genius, he need not, and does not, give credit to anyone—all the way from Jack Elliott to Allen Ginsberg. He has given up his companions for the companionship of the Charts. Currently, the Charts require him to write rock-and-roll; and he does. And he is no mere imitator. Where there is life, vivacity, statement, and protest in the original, Dylan has added a bitterness and loneliness that can't be helped. He adds a sense of violence that is cloaked by a brilliant obscurity. It leaves you depressed and alone instead of wanting to join with others in life and song.

As Dylan gets further and further away from his original leanings, there is no question that his singing voice has improved. But he doesn't always use his "better" voice. It depends on the market he is singing for. So as not to miss out on any markets, he sings with two voices, clear and unclear, and, I might add, with two sets of costumes. If necessary, he'll sing songs he repudiated. For example, he sang many songs in England he no longer sings here because the English audience is two years behind his American image. Next year, he'll be writing rhythm-and-blues songs when they get high on the charts. The following year, the Polish polka will make it, and then he'll write them, too. By then, he'll be so mired in the popularity charts that he'll be safe enough for the State Department to have them send him to entertain troops at whatever battlefront we're on at the time. As much as he's popular, the American Public would love to see him fall, just like Andy Griffith in *A Face in the Crowd* or Marilyn Monroe in real life. I don't think it's worth it, Bob. If you don't watch out, you'll become commerical. (pp. 93-4)

> *Israel G. Young, "Frets and Flails," in* Sing Out! *(reprinted with permission from* Sing Out!*), November, 1965 (and reprinted in* Bob Dylan: A Retrospective, *edited by Craig McGregor, William Morrow & Company, Inc., 1972, pp. 93-4).*

THOMAS MEEHAN

Most of Dylan's reputation rests on his talents as a performer and a writer of lyrics rather than as a composer, for his melodies are fairly ordinary and decidedly derivative—although perhaps unique in that they mix for the first time the sounds of Negro blues with the twang of Nashville country music. . . .

As a literary stylist, he seems something of an anachronism, for many of his songs are written in a manner reminiscent of the protest "Waiting for Lefty" pseudo poetry of the thirties. (p. 132)

On the other hand, future Ph.D. candidates in English, writing their theses on Dylan, will not find him that easy to pigeonhole, for he tends to write in a number of styles, among them an extraordinarily lyrical and traditional folk-song style. (p. 133)

At the same time, oddly enough, mixing a traditional folk-song style with the techniques of modern poetry, Dylan can at times be extremely obscure. . . . Those conditioned by the likes of "Red River Valley" to think of folk songs as simple and uncomplicated are inevitably confused by Dylan's songs. Dylan, however, claims that folk songs have always been difficult to comprehend.

[At] times his verses sound like those of a hillbilly W. H. Auden—specifically the earlier Auden of such poems as "September 1, 1939," as these lines from Dylan's "It's Alright Ma (I'm Only Bleeding)" might suggest:

> Disillusioned words like bullets bark
> As human Gods aim for their mark
> Made everything from toy guns that spark
> To flesh colored Christs that glow in the dark

Perhaps Dylan's principal appeal to the young (and to an increasing number of the not-so-young) is his rude defiance of all authority and scorn for the Establishment, which he puts down with unrelenting and unforgiving bitterness. . . . (pp. 133-34)

Those students who claim that Dylan is the best writer in America today point not only to his lyrics but also, curiously enough, to the copy Dylan writes for his record liners. This is usually a hundred lines or so of free verse, like [the] characteristic, somewhat Brechtian (with punctuation by Cummings) excerpts from the liner of the recent album "Bringing It All Back Home." . . . (p. 135)

Dylan's fellow poets tend . . . to be somewhat divided in their assessment of him, as in the opinions of:

Stanley Kunitz— "I listen with pleasure to Bob Dylan but I would term him a popular artist, a writer of verse rather than of poetry. All in all, though, I think the interest taken in him is a healthy sign, for there is no reason why popular art and a more selective, esoteric art can't cheerfully co-exist. And popular art is the foundation on which fine art rests. Thus, the higher the level of taste there is in the popular arts, the more promising is the hope for the evolution of great fine art."

Louis Simpson—"I don't think Bob Dylan is a poet at all; he is an entertainer—the word poet is used these days to describe practically anybody. I am not surprised though, that American college students consider him their favorite poet—they don't know anything about poetry."

W. H. Auden—"I am afraid I don't know his work at all. But that doesn't mean much—one has so frightfully much to read anyway." (p. 136)

Thomas Meehan, "Public Writer No. 1?" in The New York Times Magazine *(© 1965 by The New York Times Company; reprinted by permission), December 12, 1965, pp. 129-30, 132-36.*

IRWIN SILBER

[*Highway 61 Revisited*] is the logical extension of [Bob Dylan's] last three LPs. Somehow, I feel that most critics (and admirers) of the "new" Dylan have missed the main point. They have made Dylan's electrification the point of demarcation between the old and the new. The fact is that "Desolation Row" is not less (or more) "folk music" than "The Death of Hattie Carroll." Whether what Dylan does should or shouldn't be called "folk" is about the most unimportant question one can ask. (p. 102)

No, it is not by amplification or vocal technique that audiences have ever responded to (or rejected) Bob Dylan. It has always been by the substance of what he had to say— sometimes clearly articulated, sometimes couched in incredibly involved and frequently challenging symbolism.

Like it or not, by choice or necessity, Bob Dylan's thing is his message. Listening to *Highway 61 Revisited*, one realizes more clearly than ever before the essentially existentialist philosophy that Dylan represents, filtered, of course, through his own set of eye and brain images. Song after song adds up to the same basic statement: Life is an absurd conglomeration of meaningless events capsuled into the unnatural vacuum created by birth and completed by death; we are all living under a perpetual sentence of death and to seek meaning or purpose in life is as unrewarding as it is pointless; all your modern civilization does is further alienate man from his fellow man and from nature. (pp. 102-03)

Irwin Silber, "Topical Song: Polarization Sets In," in Sing Out! *(reprinted with permission from Sing Out!), February-March, 1966 (and reprinted in Bob Dylan: A Retrospective, edited by Craig McGregor, William Morrow & Company, Inc., 1972, pp. 102-03).*

RALPH J. GLEASON

With hit recordings blaring forth from every radio, with his songs being sung by individual vocalists and played by rock 'n' roll groups everywhere, Dylan is telling the American audience (and through that audience telling the world) that it is better to make love than to make war, that the only loyalty is to oneself ("it is not he or she or them or it that you belong to") that politics are irrelevant ("you say nothin's perfect and i tell you again there are no politics") that the leadership cult of the Great Society is a fraud ("don't follow leaders, watch the parkin' meters") that the old fashioned virtues of hard work and thrift and a clean tongue are obsolete ("money doesn't talk it swears; obscenity who really cares").

He is saying, in short, that the entire system of Western society, built upon Aristotelian logic, and upon a series of economic systems from Hobbes to Marx, does not work.

And mirable dictu *what* he is saying, is getting an unbelievably intense reaction from a generation thirsting for answers other than those in the college text books. (p. 174)

[Dylan] is the first poet of that all-American artifact, the juke box, the first American poet to touch everyone, to hit all walks of life in this great sprawling society. The first poet of mass media, if you will. . . .

Is Dylan a poet? The only dissent comes from those who are not moved by him. But even his advocates do not think of him as the poet sublime, at least not completely. Allen Ginsberg says Dylan is still hung up having to rhyme words and Ferlinghetti wonders if Dylan would be effective as a poet without the guitar. (p. 176)

Dylan thinks of songs—all songs, his own included—as pictures. He's said that numerous times in one way or another and this, coupled with his remark about writing in "chains of flashing images" is a clue to the technique he uses.

Dylan's world is a nightmare world—except for his songs of wry romance and even some of them have touches of it.

The world is like a dream. . . . Recurring figures in the Dylan poetry include the monk, the hunchback, the side-show geek and clown and Napoleon. It's a gaudy, depressing, grotesquerie rivalled only by the inmates of "The Circus of Dr. Lao" or the images of Rimbaud's "Season in Hell."

For Dylan sees the world around him—and this is I suspect the core of his attraction for the young—as a world run by a vast machine and by men who are heartless men and part of that machine. He looks at this scene surrealistically, linking together his mosaics of images like a ceiling by El Greco. He sings of alienation, of the emptiness of the adult society; he is the clown, the Napoleon in rags, a Don Quixote of today riding across a neon-lighted jungle, across the moon country, past lines of empty drive-in movies showing vista-vision pictures of what's happening. The vision is apocalyptical, the images glowing, and he is articulating the re-alignment of priorities first heralded by the wordless revolt of the jazzmen's horns. There's something in Dylan for everybody. "You who philosophize disgrace" he screams at the law-makers in "The Lonesome Death of Hattie Carroll" (a song about the fatal beating given a Negro servant by a Maryland farmer). He sneers at the groves of academe, "the old folks' home in the college," at religion, "utopian hermit monks," Madison avenue, "grey flannel dwarfs" and "propaganda all is phony"; the war machine "With God on Our Side" and hard work "I ain't gonna work on Maggie's farm no more . . . 'sing while you slave' and I just get bored."

The new generation is a lonely one ("it's always silent where I am," Dylan said at a press conference and at another time wrote "there is no love except in silence and silence doesn't say a word") born in the shadow of the Bomb and straining to make sense out of a life governed, stratified and resting upon assumptions of another age. Dylan dramatizes this—the growing realization of the surrealism of our real world has produced the novelist-turned-reporter like Ken Kesey and Joseph Heller and James Baldwin and the reporter-turned-poet like I. F. Stone. It has also produced Dylan. (pp. 177-78)

The magnetism that Dylan possesses for those under thirty (and remember the remark by Jack Weinberg of the Free Speech Movement—"they have a saying, in the movement, 'you can't trust anyone over thirty'") may very well be the fact that they, too, see the world as he sees it.

"Bob Dylan says the things I feel but don't know how to say" one college student wrote me. And when these young people find someone else describing the world around them as Dylan describes it (mystically, poetically, surrealistically) they say "Yes!" and "Amen!" and "Yes!" again. (p. 180)

One fundamental result of the acceleration of life in this technological society is to have begot a generation that is a lot smarter than its predecessors and a lot smarter than we give it credit for. And lines like Dylan's hit home immediately to the New Youth who sees all around him, everywhere from high to low position, pretense, dishonesty, absurdity, contradiction, cupidity, in fact, all the biblical sins of sloth, arrogance and greed. Dylan describes a world in which naturalness is forbidden, creativity is the enemy and beauty is assassinated. Youth, struggling to keep from growing up absurd in a land of TV commercials and high-

rise rapacity, sees this world and sees, too, that we adult members accept it and then they hear Dylan describe it. And when he describes it, it is either in a voice reminiscent of the juke box or in words on paper in a language they understand. Youth knows intuitively, if not empirically, that this is a true state of the nation message. (p. 181)

Ralph J. Gleason, "The Children's Crusade," in Ramparts *(copyright 1966 by Ramparts Magazine Inc.; reprinted by permission), March, 1966 (and reprinted in* Bob Dylan: A Retrospective, *edited by Craig McGregor, William Morrow & Company, Inc., 1972, pp. 173-91).*

RICHARD GOLDSTEIN

[The sound of "Blonde On Blonde"] is neither mysterious nor forbidding. "Blonde On Blonde" is Dylan's least esoteric work. At the same time, it signifies a major step in his development as an entertainer and folk-poet. It belongs with "The Times They Are A-Changin'" and "Bringing It All Back Home," as key albums in the Dylan momentum.

With "Blonde On Blonde," Dylan buries the put-down song, a genre he perfected in "Like a Rolling Stone" and "Positively Fourth Street," and then lost in unsuccessful songs like "Please Crawl Out of Your Window." There was an increasing sense of futility in listening to this Dylan because, even when he destroyed with acid skill, the question lingered stubbornly—would too many Newports of the soul become Dylan's trademark?

The songs on this new LP are all about women (possibly many, possibly one) but they take us far beyond the J. D. Salinger phony-circuit. This work is in appreciation and—more important—in celebration. There is a softness of imagery, a mellowing of tone; even the voice is huskier. It is as though someone somewhere has sandpapered Dylan's sensibilities. But softness does not imply limpness. The message, and the impact, are as sharp as ever.

The most moving song on the LP is "Just Like a Woman." Like any good poem, it captures essences—almost scents—in a series of images that build until, by its conclusion, there is a sense of intimate knowledge. Like any good song, its refrain stings: "She takes just like a woman / She makes love just like a woman / She aches just like a woman / But she breaks just like a little girl."

"I Want You" should especially appeal to the teens in Dylan's growing audience because, while it remains complex in imagery, it expresses its theme in simple phrases like "I need you so bad." "Memphis Blues Again" and "Leopard Skin Pillbox Hat" come close to being put-downs, but even in these songs, we laugh rather than snicker.

A personal favorite is "Sad-Eyed Lady of the Lowlands" because all that is necessary to appreciate the willowy beauty of its lyrics is to think closely of a personal sad-eyed lady and let the images do the rest. Critics who claim that Dylan's songs are a hodge-podge of his own associations, meaningless beyond the perimeter of Gramercy Park, should listen to the "Sad-Eyed Lady . . ." side. . . .

It's good to see motion again, and it's good to see—in this LP—not a rehash but a reshaping. It's especially good because there can be no such thing as a poet of the put-down.

Richard Goldstein, "The Pop Bag," in The Village Voice *(reprinted by permission of* The Village

Voice; *copyright* © *The Village Voice, Inc., 1966), September 22, 1966, p. 18.*

O. B. BRUMMELL

Bob Dylan and his peers exist on the fringes of music, on the fringes of entertainment and, above all, on the fringes of political potency. And somehow they all participate in the delusion that they ride the eye of the hurricane. Dylan's poetry is ridiculously inept; his voice is as bad as his guitar playing, which is abysmal. Only his ballads, and very few of these, have any value. And his total impact on the course of America and the world measures nil—even though he and his coterie, perhaps mercifully, believe otherwise. Some of his early songs, notably *Blowin' in the Wind* and *With God on Our Side,* wrenched the heart. But his own incredibly mannered interpretations—the consciously antimusical, harsh voice coupled with an asinine woolhat dialect—cheapened even these.

In "Blonde on Blonde" you won't find any songs of conscience.... Yet, there is one pure gem—a piece called *Sad-Eyed Lady of the Lowlands,* harking back in its imagery to the stylized metaphors of the Child Ballads. One entire side is devoted to this single song, etched against a calm instrumental backdrop, and I, for one, respond to it both emotionally and aesthetically. It is Dylan's finest achievement.

On balance, the album is a banal production. It spotlights all of Dylan's horrendous shortcomings. But, through one luminous selection, it reminds us that somewhere in the dross there may gleam a fugitive vein of gold.

O. B. Brummell, "Bob Dylan—A Far Cry from Aristotle," in High Fidelity (*copyright* © *by ABC Leisure Magazines, Inc.), October, 1966, p. 125.*

JACK NEWFIELD

Dylan, the Brecht of the juke box, has already won this generation of rebels, just as Kerouac and Camus have won earlier generations. Dylan's words, values, imagery, even his eccentric life-style, are grooved into more under-30 brains than any other writer's. And the miracle of it is that almost nobody over 30 in the literary and intellectual establishments even pays attention to his electronic guitar-coated nightmare visions of America.... (p. 1)

Two cultural traditions have grown up in America, one enshrined in respectability and the other quarantined by its illegitimacy. One is the university and the fashionable periodicals and it runs from T. S. Eliot to Edmund Wilson to Saul Bellow. But for a century now there has been an angry subterranean brook cutting away the bedrock beneath the arid soil of the New Yorker. This bastard tradition goes back to Whitman and Poe, and includes Charlie Parker, Lenny Bruce, William Burroughs, and now Bob Dylan. Its energy comes from slums, alleys, and jails, instead of libraries, classrooms, and editorial offices.

At the most obvious level of his impact, Dylan has "exploded" popular music the way critic Leslie Fiedler says William Burroughs has "exploded" the traditional form of the novel with his cut-outs and syntactical innovations.... [His] exploding of both form and content opened up folk and pop music to new plateaus for poetic, content-conscious songwriters. Dylan, as seminal innovator, has made Lennon and McCartney, Phil Ochs, and the Byrds possible, just as Lenny Bruce made Woody Allen possible. In so

mass a media as juke boxes and records, Dylan's effect is already deeper and more durable than Sinatra's, Rodgers and Hammerstein's, and Presley's. Dylan Thomas put song back into poetry, and Bob Dylan has put poetry into song.

Some artists develop vertically, digging even deeper into the fiber of their own obsession. Hemingway, James Baldwin, and John Osborne fit this category. Other artists, more restless, mature horizontally, changing passions and styles like seasons; Picasso, Norman Mailer, and Dylan among them. (pp. 1, 12)

Dylan's transcendent vision [is] that life is absurd and the only way to endure in this mad and routinized society is to see everything as a meaningless game juggling reality and illusion constantly....

[Dylan's] writing is very uneven and undisciplined. He is capable of such silly lines as "walk a rugged mile" and "I'm weary as hell." Too often his compulsion to rhyme diminishes his imagery and music. He is hardly yet the equal of Lowell, Ginsberg, or John Ashbery.

But he has single-handedly revolutionized pop music and folk music. To a whole generation he has become the nation's number one public writer.

And he is a poet. If Whitman were alive today, he too would be playing an electric guitar. (p. 12)

Jack Newfield, "Bob Dylan: Brecht of the Jukebox, Poet of Electric Guitar," in The Village Voice (*reprinted by permission of* The Village Voice; *copyright* © *The Village Voice, Inc., 1967), January 26, 1967, pp. 1, 12.*

ELLEN WILLIS

Dylan's refusal to be known is not simply a celebrity's ploy, but a passion that has shaped his work. As his songs have become more introspective, the introspections have become more impersonal, the confidences of a no-man without past or future. Bob Dylan as identifiable *persona* has been disappearing into his songs, which is what he wants. This terrifies his audiences. They could accept a consistent image—roving minstrel, poet of alienation, spokesman for youth—in lieu of the "real" Bob Dylan. But his progressive self-annihilation cannot be contained in a game of let's pretend, and it conjures up nightmares of madness, mutilation, death. (pp. 219-20)

Many people hate Bob Dylan because they hate being fooled. Illusion is fine, if quarantined and diagnosed as mild; otherwise it is potentially humiliating (is he laughing at me? conning me out of my money?). Some still discount Dylan as merely a popular culture hero (how can a teen-age idol be a serious artist—at most, perhaps, a serious demagogue). But the most tempting answer—forget his public presence, listen to his songs—won't do. For Dylan has exploited his image as a vehicle for artistic statement. The same is true of Andy Warhol and, to a lesser degree, of the Beatles and Allen Ginsberg.... Dylan has self-consciously explored the possibilities of mass communication just as the pop artists explored the possibilities of mass production. In the same sense that pop art is about commodities, Dylan's art is about celebrity.

This is not to deny the intrinsic value of Dylan's songs. Everyone interested in folk and popular music agrees on their importance, if not their merit. As composer, interpreter, most of all as lyricist, Dylan has made a revolution. He expanded folk idiom into a rich, figurative language, grafted literary and philosophical subtleties onto the protest song, revitalized folk vision by rejecting proletarian and ethnic sentimentality, then all but destroyed pure folk as a contemporary form by merging it with pop. (pp. 220-21)

Yet many of Dylan's fans—especially ex-fans—miss the point. Dylan is no apostle of the electronic age. Rather, he is a fifth-columnist from the past, shaped by personal and political nonconformity, by blues and modern poetry. He has imposed his commitment to individual freedom (and its obverse, isolation) on the hip passivity of pop culture, his literacy on an illiterate music. He has used the publicity machine to demonstrate his belief in privacy. His songs and public role are guides to survival in the world of the image, the cool, and the high. And in coming to terms with that world, he has forced it to come to terms with him. (p. 221)

"Rolling Stone" opened Dylan's first all-rock album, *Highway 61 Revisited.* More polished but less daring than *Bringing It All Back Home,* the album reworked familiar motifs. The title song, which depicted the highway as junkyard, temple, and arena for war, was Dylan's best face-of-America commentary since "Talking World War III Blues." . . . "Desolation Row" was Dylan's final tribute to the götterdämmerung strain in modern literature—an eleven-minute freak show whose cast of losers, goons and ghosts wandered around in a miasma of sexual repression and latent violence underscored by the electronic beat: "Einstein disguised as Robin Hood . . . / passed this way an hour ago with his friend, a jealous monk / now he looked so immaculately frightful as he bummed a cigarette / then he went off sniffing drainpipes and reciting the alphabet."

The violent hostility of traditionalists to Dylan's rock-and-roll made the uproar over "My Back Pages" seem mild. Not only orthodox leftists but bohemian radicals called him a sellout and a phony. . . . Actually, Dylan's work still bristled with messages; his "opportunism" had absorbed three years of his life and produced the finest extensions of traditional music since Guthrie. But the purists believed in it because they wanted to. Their passion told less about Dylan than about their own peculiar compound of aristocratic and proletarian sensitivities. (pp. 229-30)

It is a truism among Dylan's admirers that he is a poet using rock-and-roll to spread his art: as Jack Newfield put it in the *Village Voice,* "If Whitman were alive today, he too would be playing an electric guitar." This misrepresentation has only served to discredit Dylan among intellectuals and draw predictable sniping from conscientious B-student poets like Louis Simpson and John Ciardi. Dylan has a lavish verbal imagination and a brilliant sense of irony, and many of his images—especially on the two *Blonde on Blonde* records—are memorable. But poetry also requires economy, coherence and discrimination, and Dylan has perpetrated prolix verses, horrendous grammar, tangled phrases, silly metaphors, embarrassing clichés, muddled thought; at times he seems to believe one good image deserves five others, and he relies too much on rhyme. His chief literary vitue—sensitivity to psychological nuance—belongs to fiction more than poetry. His skill at creating character has made good lyrics out of terrible poetry, as in the pre-rock "Ballad in Plain D," whose portraits of the singer, his girl and her family redeem lines like: "With unseen consciousness I possessed in my grip / a magnificent mantelpiece though its heart being chipped."

Dylan is not always undisciplined. As early as *Freewheelin',* it was clear that he could control his material when he cared to. But his disciplines are song-writing and acting, not poetry; his words fit the needs of music and performance, not an intrinsic pattern. Words or rhymes that seem gratuitous in print often make good musical sense, and Dylan's voice, an extraordinary interpreter of emotion though (or more likely because) it is almost devoid of melody, makes vague lines clear. Dylan's music is not inspired. His melodies and arrangements are derivative, and his one technical accomplishment, a vivacious, evocative harmonica, does not approach the virtuosity of a Sonny Terry. His strength as a musician is his formidable eclecticism combined with a talent for choosing the right music to go with a given lyric. The result is a unity of sound and word that eludes most of his imitators.

Dylan is effective only when exploiting this unity, which is why his free verse album notes are interesting mainly as autobiography (or mythology) and why *Tarantula* is unlikely to be a masterpiece. When critics call Dylan a poet, they really mean visionary. . . . With the rock songs on *Bringing It All Back Home,* Dylan began trying to create an alternative to poetry. (pp. 233-34)

Formally, [*Blonde on Blonde*] was his finest achievement since *Freewheelin',* but while the appeal of the *Freewheelin'* songs was the illusion of spontaneous folk expression, the songs from *Blonde on Blonde* were clearly artifacts, lovingly and carefully made. The music was rock and Nashville country, with a sprinkling of blues runs and English-ballad arpeggios. Thematically, the album was a unity. It explored the sub-world pop was creating, an exotic milieu of velvet doors and scorpions, cool sex ("I saw you makin love with him, / you forgot to close the garage door"), zany fashions ("it balances on your head just like a mattress balances on a bottle of wine, / your brand-new leopard-skin pill-box hat"), strange potions ("it strangled up my mind, / now people just get uglier and I have no sense of time"), neurotic women ("she's like all the rest / with her fog, her amphetamine, and her pearls").

The songs did not preach: Dylan was no longer rebel but seismograph, registering his emotions—fascination, confusion, pity, annoyance, exuberance, anguish—with sardonic lucidity. (p. 235)

The fashionable, sybaritic denizens of *Blonde on Blonde* are the sort of people despised by radicals as apologists for the system. Yet in accepting the surface that system has produced, they subvert its assumptions. . . . *Blonde on Blonde* is about this love of surface.

Dylan's sensitivity to pop comes straight out of his folk background. Both folk and pop mentalities are leery of abstractions, and Dylan's appreciation of surface detail represents Guthriesque common sense—to Dylan, a television commercial was always a television commercial as well as a symbol of alienation. From the first, a basic pragmatism tempered his commitment to the passionate excesses of the revolutionist and the *poète-maudit* and set him apart from hipster heroes like James Dean. Like the beats, who admired the total revolt of the hipster from a safe distance, Dylan is essentially non-violent. Any vengefulness in his songs is either impersonal or funny, like the threats of a little boy to beat up the bad guys; more often, he is the bemused butt of slapstick cruelty. (pp. 235-36)

Dylan's basic rapport with reality has also saved him from the excesses of pop, kept him from merging, Warhol-like, into his public surface. *John Wesley Harding*, released after twenty months of silence, shows that Dylan is still intact in spirit as well as body. The songs are more impersonal—and in a way more inscrutable—than ever, yet the human being behind them has never seemed less mysterious. For they reveal Dylan not as the protean embodiment of some collective nerve, but as an alert artist responding to challenge from his peers. Dylan's first rock-and-roll songs were his reaction to the changes in life-style the new rock represented; *John Wesley Harding* is a reaction to the music itself as it has evolved since his accident. The album is comprehensible only in this context. (pp. 236-37)

The new melodies are absurdly simple, even for Dylan; the only instruments backing his guitar, piano and harmonica are a bass, a drum, and in two songs an extra guitar; the rock beat has faded out and the country and English ballad strains now dominate. The titles are all as straight as "John Wesley Harding": most are taken from the first lines of the songs. The lyrics are not only simple but understated in a way that shows Dylan has learned a trick or two from Lennon-McCartney, and they are folk lyrics. Or more precisely, affectionate comments on folk lyrics—the album is not a reversion to his early work but a kind of hymn to it. (pp. 237-38)

Several of the songs are folk-style fantasies. "Frankie Lee and Judas Priest" is both a folk-ballad (based on another stock situation, the gambler on the road) and one of Dylan's surrealist dream songs; "As I Walked Out One Morning" describes a run-in with an Arthurian enchantress as if she were a revenue agent or the farmer's daughter. This juxtaposition of the conventional and the fantastic produces an unsettling gnomic effect, enhanced in some cases by truncated endings—in "The Drifter's Escape," the drifter's trial for some unknown offense ends abruptly when lightning strikes the courthouse, and he gets away in the confusion; "All Along the Watchtower" ends with a beginning, "Two riders are approaching, the wind began to howl." The aura of the uncanny that these songs create is probably what Dylan meant when he remarked, years ago, that folk songs grew out of mysteries.

But some of the album is sheer fun, especially "Down Along the Cove," a jaunty blues banged out on the piano, and "I'll Be Your Baby Tonight." . . .

John Wesley Harding does not measure up to *Blonde on Blonde*. It is basically a tour de force. But it serves its purpose, which is to liberate Dylan—and the rest of us—from the *Sgt. Pepper* straitjacket. Dylan is free now to work on his own terms. It would be foolish to predict what he will do next. But hopefully he will remain a mediator, using the language of pop to transcend it. If the gap between past and present continues to widen, such mediation may be crucial. In a communications crisis, the true prophets are the translators. (p. 239)

> Ellen Willis, "Dylan," in Cheetah (copyright © 1967 by Ellen Willis; reprinted by permission of Ellen Willis), March, 1967 (and reprinted in Bob Dylan: A Retrospective, edited by Craig McGregor, Morrow, 1972, pp. 218-39).

CHARLES E. FAGER

John Wesley Harding is, on the surface at least, utterly different from *Blonde on Blonde*. Gone is electricity, except for a discreet, subdued steel guitar in one or two cuts. Gone is the sense of opaque interior monologue; most of the songs are so apparently uncomplicated that they almost defy interpretation. And, most surprising, gone are the striking verbal images that were practically the hallmark of his style.

Small wonder, then, that Dylan fans haven't been able to make sense of their hero's new effort. Only one of the *Harding* songs, "I Pity the Poor Immigrant," sounds much like anything that went before, and it is reminiscent of Dylan's second and third albums, not of the three later ones. Two other songs, "Down Along the Cove" and "I'll Be Your Baby Tonight," are plainly exercises in simple musicianship, with straight lyrics and fetching, uncomplicated tunes that carry echoes of country and western—a new departure for Dylan. Five of the songs are third-person expositions of strange scenes and events. Of these, only "Drifter's Escape" moved me at all. If the rest have inner meaning, I missed it. The remaining songs are first-person pieces. Two of them—"I Dreamed I Saw St. Augustine" and "Dear Landlord"—are impressive. The "I" of a third, "I am a Lonesome Hobo," cannot be Dylan: lonesome the young millionaire may be, but a hobo, no. In several songs there is what could be called a rudimentary religious element—something new for Dylan.

In general, I found too many of the songs to be far below the standards of powerful image and hunting sound that distinguished the better cuts on even the very personal *Blonde on Blonde*. Either that, or the new songs' meaning went completely over my head. Dylan has put out bad records before; notably his fourth, *Another Side of Bob Dylan;* so the conclusion that *John Wesley Harding* just doesn't make the grade is not disconcerting. I can wait until next time. (p. 821)

> *Charles E. Fager, in* Criticism *(copyright © 1965 by the Christian Century Foundation), June 19, 1968.*

JEAN STROUSE

Bob Dylan's new album, *John Wesley Harding,* is like the feeling left long after seeing "Bonnie and Clyde": gently anarchic. It is the anarchy of everyone doing his own thing, assuming that freedom can exist only outside the laws and layers of society. The outsiders—outlaw, hobo, immigrant, joker, thief, girl in chains, drifter, saint—form an existential community simply in reaction to them". But Dylan is hardly simplistic: the album is a collection of narratives in precise moods and voices, and its affirmation lies in the community between artist and audience, in the poet's certainty that his vision is shared by those capable of understanding it. (p. 406)

The lyrics combine various formal conventions—ballad structures, allegorical characterizations, the epic distance of moral tales—with enigmatic Dylanisms. He is the master of the put-on as he sings narratives with no dramatic action, eluding meaning-seekers while drawing attention to the tone, imagery and assumptions of the voice he adopts. For example, "John Wesley Harding" is about an American Robin Hood, friend to the poor, who "never hurt an honest man." Dylan sings of the "time they talk about"—but skips the expected climax and we learn only that "he took a stand'' and soon the situation was ''all but straightened out.'' The only quality making Harding the hero of the song (and, as it is the title song, of the album) is his lawless goodness: he carries a gun in ''every'' hand but his virtues are gentle, even Christian.... Dylan's playful use of syntax here (''a gun in every hand'') and of rhyme and pronunciation elsewhere (in ''The Ballad of Frankie Lee and Judas Priest'' *fright* is pronounces ''freight'' to rhyme with *sight* pronounced ''sate,'') contrasts with clichés like ''always lend a helping hand,'' trite rhymes like ''moon . . . spoon'' and tortured word orders for the sake of rhyme. Is Dylan mocking the rules and limitations of language, using them to move beyond convention—or is he simply hung up trying to find rhymes and meters for his thoughts so they will somehow become songs? There is no reason why he would have to use rhymes if felt they were only hanging him up. The rest of his verbal games are so sophisticated that this ineptitude seems to be part of a colossal and maybe defensive put-on. The attractive thing about put-ons is that you can wait for others' reactions before deciding how straight you want to play.

Dylan plays high on a tightrope strung out between richly religious, allusive moralizing and an arch tone of complete put-on. The Christian metaphors in ''I Dreamed I Saw St. Augustine'' are used straight, without undercutting.... [The] final image of the speaker (''I put my fingers against the glass / And bowed my head and cried'') leaves a very real but mysterious sense of fear, guilt and aloneness: the old symbols work in vague emotional evocation, but any precise ''interpretation'' must follow the jaunty mockery of the harmonica's coda to a different end.

The sense of vague secular apocalypse is strongest in ''All Along the Watchtower,'' a song that gets better all the time.... [It] condences and reflects much of the rest of the album.... Roughly paraphrased [the lyrics say]: society is a total assault on jokers and thieves (Shakespeare's fools, biblical outcasts, the outsiders-as-social critic;) but rather than bitter invective, the reaction here is a casual certainty of revolution. ''We'' out here just have to get ourselves together and it will happen; ''they'' (princes, their women and barefoot servants) in there are doomed. The magnificent vagueness of ''the wind began to howl,'' which could be the beginning of the song, is totally unlike the lack of climax in ''John Wesley Harding.'' The title song is in the past tense, and we are assured by the narrative voice that everything came out all right, and that the specific action is irrelevant where the *style* of the hero becomes morality and affirmation. But here the issue is a kind of religious *belief*— hippie faith in the drug revolution, political faith in the third world and guerrilla warfare—a hope for radical change in the future-present that becomes apocalyptic as one becomes increasingly committed to it. Still, the belief that ''it'' will happen is tempered here by the frozen imminence of apocalypse, and it remains as accessible to doubts and hopes as the present. (p. 407)

> *Jean Strouse, "Bob Dylan's Gentle Anarchy," in* Commonweal *(copyright © 1968 Commonweal Publishing Co., Inc.; reprinted by permission of Commonweal Publishing Co, Inc.), June 21, 1968, pp. 406-07.*

ELLEN WILLIS

[''Nashville Skyline'' is Dylan's tribute to the game of country music.] The usual relationship between Dylan's words and his melodies is reversed. ''Nashville Skyline'' is primarily *sound*—country sound of several varieties. Most of the lyrics are pastiches of country-western and pop clichés (''I was cruel. / I treated her like a fool. / I threw it all away'') whose function is to provide the proper setting for the music. In the past, Dylan has used country music as a vehicle for self-expression; in this album he subordinates self to genre. (pp. 157-58)

Dylan's mood of acceptance, his use of clichés in the attempt to fashion ''generic'' songs, his revived interest in his past were all evident on ''John Wesley Harding,'' though here these concerns are treated more casually and playfully. (p. 161)

Dylan has always combined frankness about the power struggle between men and women with reticence about sex —an unusual combination. The conventional approach in pop music is to combine realism with a display of sexual power—indeed, to identify the two—or else to soften the whole male-female relationship with fantasy. The first tendency comes out of blues and is bound up with the myth of black sexuality; the second is the product of white music and puritanism. Before Dylan (and the Beatles), American bohemians and radicals who rebelled against the hypocrisies of white middle-class culture almost invariably used blackness as a central metaphor. Dylan never did. Like all the other folkies, he learned blues riffs and sang about Mississippi, but his radicalism was modelled on Woody Guthrie's and his bohemianism on Allen Ginsberg's, and blues sensibility contributed little to his melodies (diatonic and crude), his rhythms (English-*cum*-hillbilly), his lyrics, or his sexual attitude. Now he is discovering that romantic fantasy, staple of the white pop tradition, has its place. His attitude toward women, like his attitude toward everything else, has softened considerably. ''Nashville Skyline'' is an album of tender, humor-filled love songs—not a putdown in the lot. (pp. 161-62)

> *Ellen Willis, in* The New Yorker *(© 1969 by the New Yorker Magazine, Inc.), April 26, 1969.*

ALBERT GOLDMAN

Nashville Skyline is Bob Dylan through rose-tinted shades....

What is most remarkable about this metempsychotic album is not simply the change it has wrought in Dylan's image but the revolution it has made in his art. Dylan of yore was possessed of glossolalia, afflicted with logorrhea: he used more words per song than any man since W. S. Gilbert. His music and his singing were just a rough-skinned conveyer belt on which he heaped the riches of his verbal imagination. Snarling and hollering, fleering and jeering, he cranked out more symbols and myths, more allegories and apothegms than a whole Bowery of Beat poets. Now he's lost the gift of gab. Rock's greatest rhetorician has become a mouther of romantic cliches.... Has Dylan ''matured,'' as a good many of the early reviewers happily report—or has he just gone soft as apple butter?

The test is clearly the tunes themselves, which in this album carry the weight once borne by Dylan's poetry. The songs range from the maudlin *Girl from the North Country* . . . through the lime-tart, gittar-twanging *Country Pie* to the deftly campy *Peggy Day,* all straw-hat throwaway lines and goony goony stee-el guitar glissandos. Every one of these songs is attractive, distinctive and skillfully sung (perhaps the word is "put over"), but the materials from which they have been made are paper thin and plainly derivative. Dylan's ditty bag is patched together from Country & Western clichés and his delivery is not quite good enough to be believed. He comes on either as a semipro entertainer lightheartedly recollecting *Grand Ole Opry* or he's a sandlot lover self-consciously revealing a newly won masculinity that somehow seems to sit on Bob Dylan like the first growth of beard on a teen-age boy. . . .

Significance is precisely what *Nashville Skyline* is packed with for people who are apprehensive about the drooping state of America pop music. If a performer of the shrewdness of Bob Dylan can delude himself into thinking his former style—tough, complex and wholly original—was merely the product of "big city" influences operating on a basically simple and bucolic temperament, then there is every reason to believe that the whole pop music scene may soon slide inexorably back into the slough of sentimentality from which it was lifted a number of years ago when the first hard rockers began their program of rural electrification.

> Albert Goldman, "That Angry Kid Has Gone All Over Romantic," in Life (copyright © 1969 by Albert Goldman; reprinted by permission of The Sterling Lord Agency, Inc.), May 23, 1969, p. 18.

MICHAEL ROGERS

Once in a while, you can cross a street, walking down the backward abysm of time, and hear the sounds of early Byrds, *Meet the Beatles, Bringing It All Back Home.* Today, after having seen the succession of Dylan's new faces on *Nashville Skyline, Self Portrait,* and *New Morning,* you might again feel the mystery of time's reversing warp as the beautiful and androgynous, light-dark 1966 Dylan face stares in bookstores out through the cover of his five-year-old *Tarantula.* . . .

It's difficult to know how *Tarantula* would have read five years ago. The relationship between cultural disintegration and its literary exemplification in *Tarantula* might have been considered very far out at the time. Today, *Tarantula*'s close to 50 schismatic and disjointed "fables," "poems," "scenes," "hallucinations," whatever, suggest only an imitative fallacy, for they are literally about too much of nothing. . . .

Suppose, as one anti-formalist critic does, that "art is simply what occurs in a setting and a situation appropriate to a certain kind of attention." Then, by that measure, what is there to attend to in *Tarantula?* It mirrors, of course, the Dylan world. . . .

Tarantula often seems like the hallucination of a method-up poker player, rapidly dealing the cards, all of which reveal only parts of himself in a cosmically tricked deck.

The book suffers from hypertrophied images: "a bearded leprechaun . . . wearing a topless mafia cape" freak and goon show humor: Cunk selling "fake blisters at the world's fair," "a sauerkraut hits him in the face"; punched-out allegorical names: Plague the Kid, Weep the Greed, Tom the Wretched; and a wiseacre wit: "ed Sullivan and Fresh kid, a relative of Prince Rainier and visiting this country as a guest of Cong Long, a grandson of Huey Long —seen escaping with catcher's mitts."

There are, of course, stunning episodes, like the story of Simply That, or the section beginning "back betty, black bready" with its "blam de lam!" chorus. . . .

Whereas writers like Lautreamont, Rimbaud, and William Burroughs insist on combining a careful delineation of the minute particulars of their demonic visions with a tone of insouciant, often lyrical cruelty, Dylan's Season in Hell reveals too often merely the fragments of an exploding conscience drifting away from any moral or esthetic center. His assaults against the "wall of dollar" and "the intoxicating ghosts of dogma" are rebuffed as his "hipster's dictionary" suffocates him with too many words.

Dylan, who in his songs has captured and distilled as true a representation of the American idiom as Mark Twain, William Carlos Williams, or Chuck Berry, suffers in *Tarantula* from a case of self-inflicted tarantism a jittery, uncontrolled language dance. In a way, the book's manifest self-indulgence can be seen as a painful consequence of what must have been for Dylan a period of near self-abolition. (p. 52)

> Michael Rogers, in Rolling Stone (by Straight Arrow Publishers, Inc. © 1971; all rights reserved; reprinted by permission), June 24, 1971.

WILFRID MELLERS

While Dylan's originality is his strength, his art *has* roots, and these are a strength also. Primarily, one looks to the words, since the significance of early Dylan is inseparable from his articulateness. The basic source is the traditional folk ballad, both in its British origins and in its American permutations. Closely allied to the ballad are children's rhymes, British and American; Negro blues poetry; the Bible, the mythology of which permeates the American mid-west; and runic verses of all kinds, reminding us of, and possibly even including, the lyrical poems of Blake.

Dylan's musical sources are both white and black. Most fundamental is the American transmutation of British ballad style. In the world of the "poor white," the grand modal themes survive, but the line becomes harder, tighter, the rhythm more cabined and confined in the metres of hymnody. . . . The happiness is eupeptic, even if also a bit euphoric: for the shutting out of pain involves a wilful hardening of sensibility.

The contrast with black folk music is pointed; and although Dylan is white, it is significant that in his art black and white sources are inextricably linked. Most basic among his black roots is the Negro holler—the unaccompanied, usually pentatonic, ululation which the black man chants to the empty fields. Scarcely less primitive is the talking blues which cannot aspire to song: the Negro mumbles to himself whilst vamping an accompaniment on guitar or piano. (pp. 398-99)

Bob Dylan, like Beethoven and the Beatles, has three periods: which correspond to an evolution towards music and a maturing of sensibility. In the first period the young mind and senses are preoccupied with the world OUTSIDE, which is regarded as at once separate and hostile: so that most of the songs are in some sense protest. In many songs of this phase music is minimal. Thus "Talking World War III Blues" has NO tune, no lyricism; the words are spoken against a rudimentary blues sequence on guitar, and the piece differs from a Negro talking blues mainly in that the words are sophisticated, acid in their comment on the plight of modern man, yet with a touch of fantasticality that distances the experience. The songs proper in the early period fall roughly into three types. The first is narrative, based on the American mutation of British balladry. A fine example is the "Ballad of Hollis Brown." ... The music could hardly be more primitive, more deprived, counteracting the flashes of poetic metaphor in the verse: for it consists of an almost pre-pentatonic reiterated incantation, supported by an unchanging ostinato of tonic and dominant chords on guitar. (pp. 399-400)

In the second type of song protest hits back by way of satire and (sometimes) lyricism. "With God On Our Side" recounts American military history with savage humour; and unlike "Hollis Brown" it *has* a tune (related to the hillbilly waltz) which is memorable if not affecting. Despite the bitterness of the words, their wit and the tune's memorability make the song affirmative, even comic.

Because such songs are positive in total effect, they tie up with the third type of song from the early period, wherein satire is transcended into the apocalyptic. In these songs both words and tune are often a permutation of real folk sources. "A Hard Rain's A-Gonna Fall" is a recreation of the ballad of Lord Rendal. The poetic imagery has a genuine affinity with runic folk verse and there are lines of visionary splendour that recall Bunyan and Blake. The incremental treatment of the original tune is preserved, but the modality of the melody is translated into a diatonic hillbilly waltz.

Interestingly enough, these apocalyptic songs often spring from topical and local events: "Who killed Davey Moore?" for instance, deals with a real and specific human situation, but makes out of it an experience as universal as the Cockrobin rhyme it transmutes. Not surprisingly, it was these visionary songs that provided the transition from Dylan's first to his second period, wherein the drama turns within the mind. Wheareas his first phase had been a kind of antiliturgy, exorcising the devil in an unlyrical, even at times unmusical, rasping, cawing and talking style, raucous and rancid: the evolution from protest to acceptance is also a move towards lyricism and music. (pp. 400-01)

As Dylan explores within the mind, the key-songs of his second period contain the complementary poles of DREAM and NIGHTMARE. "Mr. Tambourine Man" is the first great Dylan tune, no longer definable in term of sources, though it has something in common with celtic folksong and American hillbilly, if little in common with the Negro blues. Far from being socially committed, it looks as though it might be an escape song, and is so, in that a tambourine man is a peddler of pot. Yet Dylan says he's "not sleepy," even though there ain't no place he's going to; and his pied piper myth encourages us to follow the unconscious where spontaneously it may lead us. This is subtly suggested by the wavery refrain and by the irregularity of both verbal and musical clauses, which pile or float up like smoke rings. As the rings unfurl, we are liberated: so the song turns out to be about recharging our spiritual batteries today in order to find life again tomorrow. The song is unexpectedly disturbing because its mythology plumbs unexpectedly deep.

But going back to the world of instinct means accepting everything that the mind contains; the Edenic dream of "Mr. Tambourine Man" couldn't be valid if Dylan hadn't

also faced up to the mind's darker depths. So the great dream-songs are complemented by the songs of nightmare; and significantly, whereas "Mr. Tambourine Man" is folky, countrified, with natural guitar, "Ballad of a Thin Man" is in city-blues style, late Chicago vintage, with driving rhythm and electrophonic amplification. ... Dylan is no longer outside his victim; the nightmare is both without and within: and the dark thread inherent in melody, harmony and the driving pulse is poles removed from the self righteous arrogance of the early protest songs.

So in his second phase Bob Dylan has turned from the world without to the world within; and has expressed this by complementary songs of dream and of nightmare. In the double album *Blonde on Blonde*—which provides a transition to his third period—dream and nightmare have become almost indistinguishable. All the songs would seem to be concerned with the drug experience and the rediscovery of identity; and the verses contain a fair proportion of what looks like "automatic" writing by free association. This release of "consciousness" leads to further musical enrichment; and "Sad Eyed Lady of the Lowlands" stands with "Mr. Tambourine Man" as perhaps the most insidiously haunting pop song of our time. (pp. 401-02)

Dylan's third period is initiated with *John Wesley Harding,* for me his finest disc thus far. The songs' maturity comes from their fusion of the social commitment of the early phase with the commitment to the inner life manifest in the second period; the public and private manners become one, in a style that is all song. While the words have gained undertones and overtones from Dylan's submission to dream and nightmare, they're now always meaningful, if not unambiguously so. Complementarily, the tunes are more complex in organization; and the inter-relationship of line, rhythm and harmony powerfully "incarnates" the words. A relatively simple example is "Dear Landlord" in which the music directly expresses the equivocation of the title. Though we all know that landlords must be wicked and the adjective "dear" ironic, we end up feeling a wry compassion: the reason being partly melodic (the tune, lingering almost caressingly on the "dear," combines an upward aspiring tenderness with strength)—and partly harmonic (the sudden change, at the top of the phrase, from the triad of C to that of E is a revelation—our ears open in a tragi-comic wonder, if not dismay, at the realisation that Dylan and landlord might learn to accept one another). (p. 403)

John Wesley Harding ... ends with "I'll Be Your Baby Tonight," a simple song of heterosexual love: which is a two-way relationship between individuals. The point, if obvious, is important: for Dylan is no longer concerned with himself in opposition to the external world, nor with the mazes of his dream or nightmare; he's concerned with himself in relationship to another human being. Superficially, the music seems corny, ragtimely, almost cosy, whilst the quietly comic words forestall emotional indulgence. Yet the time, lyrically extended in the silence of the night, is so beautiful that in total effect the song, far from being comfortable, almost stills the breath. The music tells us that it's *true* that there's "no need to be afraid": that all the bleeding and dying and all minatory Thin Men are banished from this silent room and warm bed. ... The song leaves us warm and at peace—yet also vulnerable; we live through the experience of love in a way it would hardly be extravagant to call magical. So the song, though it seems homelier, is really no less mysterious than Dylan's other great lyrical songs, "Mr. Tambourine Man" and "Sad Eyed Lady."

This song could have been written only by a young man; none the less its balance of stresses—between tenderness and irony, joy and pain—is remarkably mature. Perhaps Dylan has never equalled it since, though it's the springboard from which most of his later songs derive. The disc *Nashville Skyline* effects a rebirth of country and western music, in which eroticism and heterosexual lovingness are experienced, not commercially manipulated. (pp. 404-05)

Dylan, unlike most pop artists, has grown up and offers potential for future development. His significance lies in the fact that he cannot be categorized. At bottom he's a traditional folk artist, a white drifter and outsider; yet he's seen this experience as directly relevant in an urban metropolis and in so doing has called upon industrial techniques and even "commercial" values. In this respect there are parallels between Dylan and the two pop composers of indubitable genius from an earlier generation, Gershwin and Ellington. Gershwin as Jewish Outsider, Ellington as Negro Outsider, "incarnated" values that denied Tin Pan Alley; yet they made it possible for their public to accept a range of experience which it didn't know it could apprehend, let alone believe in. Dylan began as the Adolescent Outsider, with Nashville substituting for Tin Pan Alley. He has an advantage over his predecessors in that he has a public that identifies with him and is (even intellectually) aware of what he stands for. It remains to be seen, however, whether Dylan's young public can grow older with him, or whether the superficially articulate militants will carry the day in maintaining that Dylan has been a Judas in moving from callow denunciation of other people's values to a recognition of mutual responsibility. (p. 406)

> *Wilfrid Mellers, "Bob Dylan: Freedom and Responsibility," in* Bob Dylan: A Retrospective, *edited by Craig McGregor (copyright © 1972 by Craig McGregor), William Morrow & Company, Inc., 1972, pp. 398-407.*

GENE BLUESTEIN

Dylan became a major innovator by immersing himself in Whitman's "swimmy waters." That is, he initiated the movement toward an Emersonian esthetic, adapting the most sophisticated verse techniques to a basically folk style, thus reproducing on the level of popular song what had been a major literary approach since Whitman. The resulting style is sometimes called folk-rock and is exemplified in the work of Dylan, Simon and Garfunkel, and a great many imitators. Folk-rock relies heavily on a *Waste Land* imagery that attempts to expose the alienation and absurdity of modern civilization.... Dylan's song, "A Hard Rain's A Gonna Fall," begins with lines that recall the old ballad, "Lord Randall"; but in place of the dramatic narrative one expects in ballad tradition, Dylan provides a catalogue of apocalyptic images.... This is the mode Dylan has continued to develop, and although many of his efforts are what pop musicians call "message songs," the elements of protest are clearly subordinated to the exercise of a complex imagery which is notably different from the straightforward affirmations of Guthrie's songs. (pp. 146-47)

> *Gene Bluestein, in his* The Voice of the Folk: Folklore and American Literary Theory *(copyright © 1972 by the University of Massachusetts Press), University of Massachusetts Press, 1972.*

PETER KNOBLER

Writings and Drawings by Bob Dylan . . . contains all of the works, except *Tarantula*, which individually have comprised the whole of the public Dylan, and through it one can trace the development of a public figure and a private sensibility. . . .

But why now? This is an important step; one doesn't collect his life's work on a whim. . . . Is Dylan closing an era, in effect saying, "This is what it was when it was"? . . .

Possible, but not very likely. Writing, singing and playing music has been what he's done best. It would be hard to shelve your strength, no matter how interesting your weakness, and Dylan still hasn't painted his "masterpiece."

It could be a looking back to find how he arrived at the present before pressing forward. Dylan is no doubt at a crossroads now. He must have come close to accomplishing what drove him to his limits; he has been a known man, a celebrity, a Superstar, an international influence, a mover of men. There seems little doubt that on some level that's what he was after, and he got it. Long ago. At the same time he is young enough to remember individual insights, yet old enough to have the details blurred. The fact of retrieving all his work may have served to refreshen his memory, and either reinforce or temper his decisions. (p. 43)

If the book serves no other purpose than to bring Dylan records back into extensive currency, it has served well. But there is so much more here. One can see the development of a writer, from the bald yet insistent pounding of the "Ballad of Emmett Till" to the slightly more sophisticated "Only A Pawn In Their Game" and then (and this is the marvel of the book, the availability of comparison) in an incredible yet fully evident quantum leap to the brilliance of "Mr. Tambourine Man." The meter tightens and the words fall instead of being placed, but you *can* "hear vague traces of skippin' reels of rhyme," and there is something to tracing a man's creative history which puts you in closer touch with his present and one's own hopes for the future.

The Dylan wit is very apparent throughout the book, strongest when Dylan is at his ambiguous best and fading when he tries too hard. *Don't Look Back* showed how he used it as a defense and a weapon, but on paper one can trace its growth from puppy dog snip to teething protest yowl to snarling amphetamine put-down to a final joke on himself. He had the presence of mind, for instance (and I missed this when the record came out), to follow "Chimes of Freedom," his densest, most complex and wondrous work to that date, with "I Shall Be Free No. 10," which starts, "I'm just average common too . . ." It was the pixie behind the prescience and it was part of Dylan's charm. Much of his appeal, in fact, was to join him (if you could) in his joke.... Right about then, around *Another Side* . . . when Dylan started putting young adult universals into enchanted language, was when people started tossing his phrases into their word-salad conversations like precious avocados. (pp. 44-5)

Dylan's intuition ran deep. He became in touch (on many levels, often below the conscious) with a gut consistency that if you had to define it you couldn't feel. He began it as a wise-ass kid when his songs refused to come unstuck in their rambling detail. He was linear, a story-teller ("Hattie Carroll," "North Country Blues," "Boots of Spanish Leather" and many others are detailed narratives with a *tone* at the core), but he could turn a phrase like a bandit and was topical on exactly the right topics. When he grew less linear, when the tone came forth and the narrative became oblique, it was this consistency which unified even the most frenetic images. He could throw words around like spangles in a wind and they'd *have* to mean something. They couldn't miss. He was *in touch*. (pp. 45-6)

Blonde on Blonde was the apex of that fragmented vision. His songs were regularly shattered like mirrors into jagged sections, each with its own unique yet truly reflective viewpoint. But interpretations did get out of hand, and the gut magic reached people with twisted guts and distorted like never before.

It was getting pretty crazy. With every step somehow accepted, there were no standards. Dylan could have been sloppy or tight and largely have gotten away with either. He was the biggest individual superstar since Elvis and had none of the seered guidelines rock idols can follow today. Even in coping with epic lunacy, Dylan led the way. (p. 46)

When he reemerged [after his motorcycle accident], there seemed a conscious denial of the past madness. Gone was the sardonic wit, replaced by an austere diction and entirely new symbol system which left many of his former devotees with no immediate grasp on exactly what he was saying. There were few concrete—no more honky-tonk lagoons or escapades out on the D train to latch on to. About the time you started wondering what all this *meant*, you realized your gut wasn't telling you. Dylan's magic gut consistency was gone.

John Wesley Harding was austere and deep like a quarry pool. It was a head album, Dylan's first. *Nashville Skyline* again steered clear of intuitive connections, Dylan preferring to sing about such universals as love and love's constancy without using concrete examples from anyone's life, including his own. As if to maintain the purity of his privacy, he offered no glimpse into his concrete world. *Nashville Skyline* could take place anywhere, or nowhere. *Self Portrait* was the same.

But there was a strange stirring, some forgotten shifting of stomach juices, when *New Morning* appeared unannounced one autumn afternoon. Dylan's voice seemed to rasp again, and there were some vaguely recognizable scenes set in language that brought sly grins to all my friends' faces. "Day of the Locusts" had a concrete base—you could feel Dylan's presence, his old ambivalence up-dated by the twin behemoths, security and maturity. The overtones were ominous—locusts buzzed alluringly throughout the song—but Dylan both braved them and escaped. Once again he was talking about a recognizable self and a personalized yet still universal fear. Once again a head was exploding, but this time it wasn't his.

"One More Weekend" was a married man's "Pledging My Time" in which Dylan introduced his kids, if only to leave them for a while. That was a first. He seemed remarkably forthcoming with his details, relaxed as he let them fall. The gem of the album, the song which spoke for the entire year, was "Went to See the Gypsy," in which Dylan vis-

ited a figure I assume to be Presley. The song has all the banter, the vague yet potentially decipherable phrasing of classic Dylan without the manic frightrush. In the song Dylan is again tempted, ambivalent. He admits implicitly to fear (of exposure? of a lunatic relapse?) and to the desire to break away from watching himself, to go "through the mirror." Ultimately he lets it ride, but he has to go all the way home to "that little Minnesota town" to do it. It seems he was feeling the stirrings too. (pp. 46-7)

The final two pages of writing faces "Watching the River Flow" with ["When I Paint My Masterpiece"]. . . . This wide-ranging book which includes Dylan at his most publicly profound is almost made to end with "I don't have much to say . . ." It's an irony not wasted on a man who has been criticized in his lifetime for saying both too little and too much, simultaneously.

But that tempting absurdity is flush against Dylan's statement that he's not finished. The masterpiece is not painted but not out of mind. Dylan wants it; he must or he wouldn't have called such final attention to it. But both of his latest works (each copyright 1971) are near parodies of that desire; they talk *about* tranquility and high art without ever achieving either. And no amount of joking will bring them closer. Dylan approached the peak of his powers during the madness of the amphetamine express. He can't be expected to return to those lunatic days, they almost did him in. But the thread which ran through *Another Side . . .*, *Bringing It All Back Home*, *Highway 61 Revisited* and *Blonde on Blonde*, and which resurfaced for a continuing, fascinating moment in *New Morning*, is still potentially reachable. The urgency has been dulled but the core of the man remains. His concretes vary, and some could well inspire him. (pp. 47-8)

Peter Knobler, "Bob Dylan: A Gut Reaction," in Crawdaddy *(copyright © 1973 by Crawdaddy Publishing Co., Inc.; reprinted by permission of Peter Knobler), September, 1973, pp. 42-8.*

JON LANDAU

Bob Dylan may be the Charlie Chaplin of rock & roll. Both men are regarded as geniuses by their entire audience. Both were proclaimed revolutionaries for their early work and subjected to exhaustive attack when later works were thought to be inferior. Both developed their art without so much as a nodding glance toward their peers. Both are multitalented: Chaplin as a director, actor, writer and musician; Dylan as a recording artist, singer, songwriter, prose writer and poet. Both superimpose their personalities over the techniques of their art forms. They rejected the peculiarly 20th century notion that confuses the advancement of the techniques and mechanics of an art form with the growth of art itself. They have stood alone. . . .

When I criticize Dylan now, it's not for his abilities as a singer or songwriter, which are extraordinary, but for his shortcomings as a record maker. Part of me believes that the completed record is the final measure of the pop musician's accomplishments. (p. 43)

If Dylan isn't a great rock artist per se, he is a great artist, period. He has transcended his limitations more successfully than anyone else in rock. He succeeded in making himself indispensable. The records may be indispensable in only the first moments in which they are perceived, but they can transmit as much force in those moments as others do in hours, days and years.

Dylan considered in total—as a man, myth, singer, writer and, yes, maker of records—hasn't been merely immediate and urgent: He's given rock its drama. He creates tensions within his audience beyond anyone else's reach. If he isn't as good a record maker as Chuck Berry, he's a much better actor. As an actor and as a personality, Dylan hasn't handled every role with equal skill. . . .

Like James Dean and Marlon Brando, he was better at playing the rebel than the citizen, the outsider than the insider and the outlaw than the sheriff.

Much of the critical enthusiasm for *Blood on the Tracks* is really a sigh of relief that he's shaken off the role of contentment that Jonathan Cott also has found never rang true. But in returning to his role as disturber of the peace, Dylan hasn't revived any specific phase from the past, only a style that lets his emotions speak more freely and the state of mind in which he no longer denies the fires that are still raging within him and us. He is using elements of his past to make an album about his past. . . .

The writing is the source of the record's power. It's been a long time since Dylan has composed a melody line as perfectly suited to his voice as "Tangled Up in Blue," and though the lyrics are both confessional and narrative, Dylan makes it all sound like direct address. There are times when he sounds closer, more intimate and more real than anyone else. . . .

I like everything about it; the good, the bad and the ugly. It all matters: the title "Tangled Up in Blue"; and the way that song propels itself relentlessly forward (even though it is about the past) and always winds up leaving Dylan and us standing in the same place; the lines, "I helped her out of a jam, I guess / But I used a little too much force"; the way that the song sounds so right for the Byrds of 1965; the compassion, not rage, of "You're a Big Girl Now"; the lines "I can make it through / You can make it too"; the innocence and unqualified beauty of Dylan's reprise of his folk music roots on "Buckets of Rain"; the awkwardness of the music for "If You See Her, Say Hello"; the childishness (without any redeeming child-like wonder) of so much of "Idiot Wind"; the holiness of the last verse of "Shelter from the Storm"; the extension of the apocalyptic mood of his earlier work into something still forceful, but mellower, more understanding, more tolerant and more self-critical; the indifference to the subject of women as a generality and his involvement with women and love as something specific, and above all, the arrogance—that defiant indifference to whatever it is others think he ought to be doing. He still stands alone.

Blood on the Tracks will only sound like a great album for a while. Like most of Dylan, it is impermanent. But like the man who made it, the album answers to no one and was made for everyone. It is the work of someone who is not just seeing through himself, but looking through us—and still making us see things that we haven't seen before. (p. 51)

> Jon Landau, "After the Flood," in Rolling Stone (by Straight Arrow Publishers, Inc. © 1975; all rights reserved; reprinted by permission), Issue 182, March 13, 1975, pp. 43, 49, 51.

STEPHEN HOLDEN

Blood on the Tracks is easily Bob Dylan's strongest, most moving album since *Blonde on Blonde*. Like no other singer/poet, Dylan at his best transmutes personal frustration, anger, self-pity and moral intolerance into an inspired litany of rage and remorse, and *Blood* contains not one less than excellent song. My favorite is "Idiot Wind," whose overlapping metaphors and jumbled images work because of, not in spite of, their crudity; its intensity scares me. The same holds for Dylan's singing, which integrates the shouting self-parody of *Before the Flood* with the gruff sensitivity of his preelectric albums. . . . *Blood on the Tracks*, though suffused with pain, also bursts alive with the triumphant exhilaration of having survived. It is outrageously great. (p. 53)

> Stephen Holden, in Rolling Stone (by Straight Arrow Publishers, Inc. © 1975; all rights reserved; reprinted by permission), Issue 182, March 13, 1975.

NAOMI LINDSTROM

Certainly it is not possible that a mutation in the human brain caused people to be able to take in poetry just as fast as it could be sung. Yet by the sixties it was accepted, at least by those who were willing to listen to Bob Dylan, that a Dylan song might contain such a welter of images, discontinuous narrative, curious metaphors, and phrases so hermetic as to exclude every listener except Dylan, that, even after hearing it through more than once, a listener might have only a vague notion of what it was about. Lines such as "My penthouse has your Arabian drum / shall I leave it now beside your gate / or, sad-eyed lady, shall I wait?" left listeners with nothing more definite than that the poetic *I* was addressing himself, in tones of hesitation and only tentative approach, to a mysterious woman. From other lyrics one could eventually figure out that while the sad-eyed lady had had a great many men figure in her life, none of them was capable of offering her the sort of total commitment and support she demanded, an attitude on her part which might explain the singer's hesitancy to approach her. Describing the sad-eyed lady's hangers-on, an unsavory lot, the singer concluded brutally, "Who among them do you think would ever carry you?" After giving out only this much information, the song retreats into obscurity, effectively excluding the listener from deciphering it in its totality. It would be hard to think of a more effective refutation of the idea that song lyrics must render up their meanings on the spot in order to satisfy.

The reaction to, for instance, the Dylan songs on *Blonde on Blonde* was an almost overwhelming concern with thematics. One group of listeners seemed most intent on determining whether the narrative voice or any of the characters in a given song were under the influence of drugs or using drug-induced experiences as referents. Such a concern was not only somewhat reductive, but hopeless, since the lyrics were so ambiguous that various sets of referents could be plugged in. Other special-interest groups sifted through Dylan lyrics seeking statements on generational conflict, attitudes toward women, possible calls to revolution, deification of new heroes, and so forth. Naturally, there were those concerned that listening too often to Dylan might cause the listener to abandon his moral standards. (p. 133)

The major arguments against giving Dylan the status of poet seemed to be that he reelaborated the same to-hell-with-you material too often and that many of his Rimbaud-evoking songs used mere obscurity to give an impression of something profound going on, while the images in the poems were really thrown together quite arbitrarily, without regard for the total rhetoric of the song.

Certainly a tiny stock of themes has never prevented non-singing poets from being classified as such. The charge of incoherence and randomness makes more sense, for some Dylan texts are remarkably loose and fragmented, failing to satisfy because they give the listener no clue as to how he is to fit the barrage of images into some coherent system. However, most of Dylan's songs make an approximate sort of sense. The poetic *I* usually takes such a markedly emotional stance toward his subject, whether one of contempt, despair, or longing, as to provide evidence of what is supposed to be going on.

The arguments against Dylan-as-poet seem to be trying to disqualify him by applying to his work standards not used in cases where the poet refrains from singing his texts. This double standard suggests that what really bothers these objectors to Dylan-as-poet is that he violates the distinction between poetry and song. Many poets fail to make their signs sufficiently clear or to impart to their works a unified feel, but Dylan was a poet of modern times spreading his unsimplified work with a song. (p. 134)

> Naomi Lindstrom, *"Dylan: Song Returns to Poetry,"* in The Texas Quarterly (© 1976 by The University of Texas at Austin), Winter, 1976, pp. 131-36.

W. T. LHAMON, JR.

Desire has about it the feel of a State of the Disunion message, sung, chanted and talked by a man with great power, if indirect, and greater integrity, certainly, than most of the people addressing us this year. When he hears from his partner in "Isis" that they will return from their odyssey to the North "by the fourth," and replies, that's the "best news I've ever heard"—then that suggests one attitude toward America. But when he sings, in "Black Diamond Bay," that "there's really nothing anyone can say" about the land's hard luck stories—that tells something different. Would-be patriotism and resigned cynicism are the oil and water of this record. (p. 23)

Desire grows more interesting exactly because of the way the parts have a will of their own, a recalcitrance to Dylan's will. If in his affectionate liner notes Allen Ginsberg calls "One More Cup of Coffee" a "Hebraic cantillation never heard before in US song," there are few who can call him on the judgment. But perhaps I can add as a Tallahassee Texan that there's a whole heap of Country and Western hunkered down in the midst of that Jewish mysticism. And the point is that whoever this Jewish-poet-cowboy cantilating country music is, and whatever his song's stubborn parts, they all differ vastly from Hurricane Carter and *his* song, from Sara and *hers;* and these have only Dylan's compulsion, sense of national absurdity and consistent instrumentation tying them to the dying dreamer of "Romance in Durango," or to the sister of "Oh, Sister."

Preferring honest anarchy to pretended order, Dylan's new work senses without making, without constructing, without building a concrete structure, without giving audiences easy handles to hold. . . . [Many] people are going to claim that an album like *Desire* doesn't make sense. It doesn't. If there is any sense in the grooves, it will be private sense,

drawn in on a gasp and breathed out in a sigh; it will be sensual. It will not be consensual. For at the heart of Dylan's work these days is the assumption that consensus values are really gone.

Nor shall they be replaced. This is an album of maturity, not of resignation but of acknowledgment—where desire is an everyday affliction, where dream-songs are written on rising before going back to sleep for 40 more winks, where apocalypses happen in nearly every tune only to be passed over casually. (pp. 23-4)

> W. T. Lhamon, Jr., "Bicentennial Dylan," in The New Republic (reprinted by permission of The New Republic; © 1976 by The New Republic, Inc.), February 14, 1976, pp. 23-4.

DAVE MARSH

Desire is a very special album, although Bob Dylan's adamantly antimusical approach keeps it from greatness. Somehow, though, Dylan's antimusic winds up being very seductive. . . .

[It's hard] to determine who is responsible for the most meaningful change in Dylan's writing, which is expressed in the songs concerning women. Previously, Dylan has recognized only two kinds of women: "angels," whose function was to save man (from the women themselves as often as not), and "bitches," whose function was to let him down, if not by overt attempts to ruin and confuse, at least by their failure to save. The bitches enjoyed their heyday during the "Just like a Woman" period, of course, and their prominent return on *Blood on the Tracks* was one of the principle reasons why that album was believed to be a return to the golden age. The angels dominated from *Nashville Skyline* to *Planet Waves,* and there is reason to believe that Dylan still holds onto something of that vision: "Sara," one of two songs on *Desire* which he wrote alone, again speaks of his wife as a "sweet virgin angel." (p. 55)

But love songs aren't the focus of *Desire,* which is one of the things that differentiates it from Dylan's other post-rock work. On the best songs, Dylan returns to the fantastic images, weird characters and absurdist landscapes of the Sixties. The metaphors work on so many levels they're impossible to sift, and just when you think you have one firmly defined, it slips off into something else again. The crucial ideas are cinematic; in fact, one song, "Romance in Durango," seems to be an explicit parable about making *Pat Garrett and Billy the Kid* in 1973. There are the usual romances, the stories of hard-luck kids from rough slums, a couple of other westerns, even a bit of travelogue ("Mozambique"). Some of the songs, like "One More Cup of Coffee" (which is apparently based on a story Ramblin' Jack Elliott used to tell), seem ancient, as though Dylan were once more using the resources of traditional folk music for his melodies and themes.

But the bulk of the songs are nightmares, visions of a man on the run from something he can't define, or else stories about the fear of having nowhere to turn (as in "Oh, Sister" and "One More Cup of Coffee"). . . . In "Black Diamond Bay" this is carried to its extreme. In a madhouse hotel where suicidal Greeks are mistaken for Soviet diplomats, the terrified protagonist, running again from something unnamed, loses her identity—she can't even remember the face on her passport. Open a door, and like a Rube Goldberg contraption, the Greek is hung, a volcano explodes, the island falls into the sea. And the desk clerk, meanwhile, simply sits and smiles: he's seen it all before. . . .

The record only falters, in fact, when it attempts to write or rewrite real history. I believe Dylan's confession about "Sad-Eyed Lady of the Lowlands" in "Sara" but I don't trust it. "Hurricane" is a setup. The whole thing is too improbable for real life, though . . . it did happen. Dylan even sings with a measure of disbelief and, in the end, his rage is rather impotent. . . .

This problem presents itself most explicitly and awkwardly in "Joey," a hymm to Joey Gallo. . . . Dylan would obviously like to write an outlaw ballad, making a sort of Billy the Kid or Pretty Boy Floyd from a modern-day thug. . . .

[Dylan rationalizes his lionizing of Joey] because he spent his time in prison "readin' Nietzsche and Wilhelm Reich," because he came out of prison dressed like Jimmy Cagney. For this sense of style, Dylan is willing to forgive him his numbers and gambling rackets—even slyly attempting to deny that he ever was involved with such things. But his neatest ellipsis is to avoid all mention of the public execution of Joseph Colombo, which the evidence suggests the Gallo mob ordered. (p. 57)

Gallo was an outlaw, in fact, only in the sense that he refused to live by the rules of the mob—it's as hard to be sympathetic to him as it is to be comfortable with Robert De Niro's crazy Johnny in *Mean Streets*. Is an intellectual Mafioso really that much more heroic than an unlettered hood? This is elitist sophistry of the worst sort, contemptible even when it comes from an outlaw radlib like Bob Dylan.

Specious as it is, "Joey" is musically seductive. Its chorus is perhaps the most memorable on the album, and there's a passion in the singing and playing that is uplifting. This doesn't excuse the sophomoric idea that animates that passion but it does provide some kind of measure of Dylan's continued power as a songwriter and mythmonger. Liking *Desire* is hardly the point—there are those of us who will always believe that Dylan is copping out until he returns to the fiery rock & roll that drove his middle Sixties work, just as there are those who will never truly love his music again until he writes an album full of "Hurricanes." The test of Bob Dylan's talent is really that all of us continue to listen and hope. (p. 59)

> *Dave Marsh, "Desire under Fire: Mythic Images of Women and Outlaws," in* Rolling Stone *(by Straight Arrow Publishers, Inc. © 1976; all rights reserved; reprinted by permission), Issue 208, March 11, 1976, pp. 55-9.*

TIMOTHY LEARY

The post-Hiroshima generation was the first completely *electroid* generation. At exactly the time when this enormous genetic wave opened to receive a post-Einsteinian reality, SHAZAM! . . . 4,000 years of Old Testament pessimism popped up in the person of the Electronic Pad-Trip Evangelist.

The one song "It's All Over Now, Baby Blue" probably caused more biological and philosophical suicides than any poem in Western history. This is a tribute, not to the dismal poet, but to electronic amplification.

Give a close reading, if you can, to the Zimmerman lyrics of the 1960s—snarling, whining, scorning, mocking. "Just like a Woman." "No, No, No, It Ain't Me, Babe." "Subterranean Homesick Blues." "It's All Right, Ma, I'm Only Bleeding."

The classic techniques of brainwashing are unconsciously employed in these albums. First, the dogmatic command, "Everybody Must Get Stoned," encourages a chemically induced state of neural receptivity. Note the semantics: *stoned*. Don't get high; don't space out; don't trip (with its multireality flexible implication); don't get blissed out. You "must get stoned," sung to a heavy, slow, plodding beat. And accompanied by the other nihilist hits that systematically converted a generation to neurotic complaint.

Read, if you dare, the lyrics to "Like a Rolling Stone" and cringe at the deliberate trampling on hope and self-confidence. Barbiturate Barbarism. "How Does It Feel?" It feels like that Old Testament Masochism Bob.

The evil of the Zimmerman Effect is not just that it imprints destructive, nasty realities on young brains, but that it produces a fake alienation from direct experience. The Zimmerman Effect alienates because the media manipulator broadcasts about other people's experience, *not his own*. To an anonymous audience. Did Dylan stand on picket lines? Get his head busted by company police? March at Selma in the hard rain? Get tear-gassed at Chicago? Sleep in the mud at Woodstock (just down the road from his comfy retreat)? Lie on a roach-ridden mattress in a state prison? Put his body on the line in any real action? Live the fugitive Life? Go into exile? Or put his nervous system on the line in neuronaut exploration? Yes, we know what he was against. But what was he for? (Besides fake nostalgia.) When an entire generation was on the move, swirling into uncharted neurogenetic territory, where was the young millionaire waif? Protected, dear boy, in the arms of producer Al Grossman, promoter Bill Graham, Golda Meir, Allen Ginsberg, Joan Baez, and a supporting brigade of mother figures.

Looking back at that wretched reality we see that Dylan truly never understood that it ain't no good to let other people get your kicks for you. . . .

[There] are two factors that make the Zimmerman Effect a perversion of the ancient and honorable bardic role:

1. Zimmerman portrays not the glory and the heroic pride of an evolving species, but the dark, craven themes of the loser cult.

2. The true minstrel sings in person; wanders around in face-to-face contact with those he is influencing. He is forced into eyeball confrontations with Mr. Jones and Maggie's Father and everyone watches to see if he's for real or if he's all talk. It just ain't no good to let the agents, record producers, and tax lawyers take your kicks for you. You gotta get down and look into the eyes of the Squeaky Frommes you are urging into rebellion. (p. 390)

We can now speak frankly about the Zimmerman Effect because it is waning. We can now view with compassion, not only the passive, but the active casualties of Electroid Brainwash. Zimmerman, like Manson, was the original victim of the Effect, which occurs when electronic and chemical neural-vulnerabilities are ripped off by commercial exploiters. Dylan whined endlessly for himself and his own Lost Innocence. In recent statements and actions, however, it is clear that Dylan is beginning to sense that it was no accident that he was propelled into premature pop-star status by forces he himself detests. He is beginning to discover that you can't look back. He now seems to be listening, learning. He seems able, at last, to sidestep the literary Mafia that sought to freeze him as a beatnik poet. (pp. 390, 410)

Timothy Leary, in National Review (© *National Review, Inc., 1976; 150 East 35th St., New York, N.Y. 10016), April 16, 1976.*

THOMAS S. JOHNSON

What was Bob Dylan doing when he moved into rock music in mid-career? His first albums were in a folk-protest idiom. His later albums tended to return to a folk-country idiom close to his first albums. But the latter were markedly different because of three central albums that intervened: *Bringing It All Back Home; Highway 61, Revisited;* and *Blonde on Blonde.* Perhaps now, knowing where his music went, we can begin to look back and try to understand what were the underlying motives for that excursion. There are certain songs on these three albums that stand out from the rest as highly individualistic even within Dylan's own canon. They establish a continuity and developing attitude that seems to underlie Dylan's work in this period, an attitude which proved untenable and which finally forced him out of rock altogether.

The common interpretation of "Mr. Tambourine Man" is that it describes a drug high, the Tambourine Man being the dealer, his song being a hint of the visions he will give the poet through drugs. The imagery of the song would tend to back this up. In the first verse the poet states his readiness to begin to trip out. In the second verse the actual high begins to take effect: the singer's hands and feet grow numb and "lose their grip," and he loses his hold on reality. In the third verse he is "laughing, spinning, swinging madly across the sun," and in the fourth verse he travels down through his mind, seeing the various things buried deep beneath the "waves" of his subconscious. Such specific imagery can be compounded and the song becomes simply the description of a drug high, but this does not explain everything in the lyric. . . . Throughout the song there is imagery referring to music and dancing and singing. In both verse one and three another obvious mood is that of wandering, searching. The entire song is operating in the imperative form of the verb: the poet asks the Tambourine Man to play his song, he demands "take me on a trip"—he is ready to go, and in the second verse he promises to go. In the last verse he says "take me disappearing," and "let me forget about today." The song ends with the repetition of the chorus, which is quite clearly calling on the Tambourine Man to play him a song, which he will follow, the spell of which he will go under. . . . This point of view of the singer in relation to the Tambourine Man is the key to the song. The imagery points to the feelings evoked by the singer's realization of his place and its implications and consequences for him.

Dylan begins the song, and presents his basic attitude, in the chorus. He is awake, waiting for somewhere to go. The first verse specifies his position—"evening's empire" has turned to sand that has slipped through his fingers, and he is blind, weary, stranded, alone on an empty street "too

dead for dreaming." Evening's empire is the realm of dreams. (pp. 135-36)

In the second verse he points out his readiness to begin his trip, to fade "into my own parade." On the one hand this implies fading into his own mind, his own world. He also recognizes that what he needs is an idiom of his own, a "parade" moving down his own road, to replace the dead form he has worked in. Again the chorus, and he calls on the Tambourine Man for inspiration, to help him find his way.

The narrative point of view then shifts from the first person to an ironic second person. The point of view becomes that of the Tambourine Man as the poet conceives of him, and the third verse considers what the Tambourine Man must think of this poet and his songs. (pp. 136-37)

The singer then looks into himself to find what he will see, given the inspiration of the Tambourine Man. He wishes to delve into his mind to escape his consciousness and his subconscious fears, the "haunted frightened trees," the "foggy ruins of time," and the world he lives in, to realize a fresh elemental vision, represented by the setting of sea, sand, and sky. On the beach, confronting the sea, the primordial element of nature, he would drown memory, time, fate and its consequences, and experience a pure poetic vision. . . .

The poet is on a street "too dead for dreaming." But with no dreaming there can be no new vision. There is no one on the street to lead him, and so he called on the Tambourine Man to help him. But the Tambourine Man exists in another world and either cannot or will not help him, and the poet on his own cannot make the leap into that world. Thus the cry at the end of the song is a cry of futility. (p. 137)

And so what is he to do now? He chooses to take a closer look around, both at the street and at the world just off of the street. The results are not edifying, for the remainder of this album and much of the next detail a catalog of grotesquery and nightmares almost unparalleled in contemporary poetry. A good example of this, and perhaps Dylan's most powerful single lyric, is "Desolation Row" on the *Highway 61, Revisited* album. (pp. 137-38)

In "Desolation Row" Dylan turns his back on drug visions and visionary hopes to face reality as he sees it, and he sees the world in the aspect of a carnival, specifically a freak show, with all the grotesques on prominent display. The lyric tells of the parade of grotesques that pass before the poet, a stream of images generated by a letter full of gossip he has just received from an old acquaintance.

The opening is primarily an impressionistic panoramic overview of the world around his street, setting the scene for the specific and deeper probings to follow. The first three phrases present three spot images, one of them grotesque postcards of a hanged man, reminiscent of the hanged god of *The Waste Land,* another failed symbol of fertility and redemption. The fourth phrase gives us the setting of the lyric: "The circus is in town." (p. 138)

There are two important women on the Row, Cinderella and Ophelia. Cinderella is a prostitute, confronting Romeo, the idealistic lover, who is told to leave. On this street there is no place for such a ridiculous adolescent. An ambulance carries away the dead Romeo, leaving Cinderella to her perennial task of sweeping up. There will be no Prince

Charming here. Ophelia is just the opposite of Cinerella, a professional virgin. Although only twenty-two, she is already an old maid because she has sacrificed love and affection for her career, armored herself, and become one of the iron maidens of modern business. The iron vest she wears is a likely metaphor for the way she has armored her mind and body against love and sexuality.

Science and medicine fare about as well as sentimental love and affection here. Albert Einstein, the symbol of modern science and technology, is presented in the guise of Robin Hood, perhaps representing his symbolic position today as the bringer of the riches (and horrors) of modern living to the everyday man. For Dylan, all he can ultimately do is bum cigarettes, sniff drainpipes, recite the alphabet—absurd activities. Science and technology and all they involve, represented in this man, have become a meaningless and occasionally grotesque parody of humanity. (p. 139)

There is no hope even in the stars. The third verse, the first "Eliotesque" verse, so called because of allusions to *The Waste Land* in the figure of the fortune-teller, the mechanical lovemaking, and the motif of waiting for rain, begins with the blacking out of the stars and moon, standard symbols of romance and the aspirations of men. The fortune-teller has given up the ghost and gone inside—there is no fortune to tell without the stars. The only ones left who aren't waiting for release from their lives are Cain and Abel and the Hunchback of Notre Dame, the first an image of death and hate where there should be love, the second an image of ignorant and deformed love. The Good Samaritan is also dressing for the show—he too is now a freak, to go on display in the modern carnival freak show.

And so the stage is set for the presentation in verse seven of the main show of the carnival. The central figure is Casanova, standard representative of sexual energy, and the occasion is his punishment. His crime? Not his dissolute life, which in its essential sterility is in keeping with modern life, but rather his trip to Desolation Row. Casanova has been to the Row and as a result has lost his assurance, his potency. On Desolation Row he has experienced the nothingness of his life—the end of the road, the absolute nihilism, the knowledge of his irrelevance, which comes when he must face the fact of his own ultimate impotence. The result of this experience is that he must be spoon-fed if his illusions are to be revived and he is to become again one of the carnival's proper functionaries. He is not being killed and poisoned literally; rather his experience on Desolation Row, where he lost his self-confidence, must be purged by means of false self-confidence and the superficiality of words. This, to Dylan, is as good as death, because the loss of assurance is implicitly the beginning of true insight. (pp. 139-40)

The larger world is not pleasant looking. Verse eight is a Kafkaesque verse, with its dominating image of the castles. It is midnight, but instead of witches and werewolves, it is the agents, crew, and insurance men from the castles who sweep down to scour the land.... Their prey is anyone who rises above the common lot, anyone who has greater knowledge than they.

Carnival imagery is now of less importance. The song has expanded in its significance by positing a dark and mysterious power at the center of the world, the castles. What these castles are is not explicit, as was also true in the

Kafka novel. The important thing is that they exist out there and threaten all aspects of contemporary life.

One escape route is posited by Dylan, however—the Titanic. In verse nine, the Titanic is to sail at dawn. In "Tambourine Man" dawn and the ship were to bring a new vision. Here they bring death and destruction to one of man's great creations. From this point on this can be seen as the second "Eliotesque" verse, with specific references to Eliot and Pound and to the calling mermaids of "Prufrock." The central image again refers to the dissolution of the poet's idiom or inspiration. One of Dylan's major influences is the poetry of these two men, but they are doomed without even realizing it, so caught up are they in their own petty arguments. With the sinking of the Titanic comes the death of the meaningfulness of Eliot's and Pound's poetic idiom. Fishermen and calypso singers laugh at the two men for their irrelevance to real life.... All of these people have ignored, in fact never really recognize, Desolation Row, and therefore are destined to irrelevance forever. (p. 141)

Since he was forced to give up the dream of the Tambourine Man, Dylan has forced himself to see the place where he stands for what it is, has moved toward the nadir point of his existence where old values, institutions, and aspirations are obliterated or distorted in an absolute negativity. He is surviving. The experience of all this is recounted in "Desolation Row," and this experience he has resolved into a tremendously powerful lyric. But he is not yet free. The experience has not been weighed, balanced, judged. Indeed it seems as though, given the poet's detached place in the song, it has not even been fully absorbed yet. It remains to be seen at this point whether he will find any resolution. He takes up this problem in "Visions of Johanna."

"Visions of Johanna" is probably Dylan's most difficult lyric, made up of a series of highly personal and shifting images and references. It is also filled with sexual and drug imagery, important vehicles in establishing the theme and motif of the song, the only song on the *Blonde on Blonde* album that uses this imagery in such concentration and profusion.

The motif of the song is the unstructured stream-of-consciousness thoughts of a young man (the poet) sitting in a room with a girl named Louie and her lover. The basic theme of the lyric would seem to be the poet's feelings of being abandoned, left alone to face the Visions of Johanna. The definition of these Visions is developed slowly through the poem. They are not the inspiration Dylan has been seeking since "Tambourine Man," for the world of this song is a bizarre one derived directly from "Desolation Row," even to the position of the poet in a room above a street of grotesques. They are visions of love prostituted, and of the negation of life and vitality this prostitution implies, all of which contrasts violently with an idealized love the poet recognizes he cannot have. The conflict throughout the lyric between visions of negation and of an idealized love lost and prostituted sets up a tension that leads to the final dissolution of the song. The ideal and the real are irreconcilable, and end by destroying each other.

This duality in "Visions of Johanna" is the result of the combination of two image patterns that have developed in previous songs. The idealized vision of the Tambourine

Man, the poet's vision of an energizing relationship, is now conceived of in terms of a lost love relationship. The visions of the nihilism of life in "Just Like Tom Thumb's Blues" and "Desolation Row," also included here, imply the complete breakdown of the poet's world and by implication of his own mind. (pp. 142-43)

With this song, it would seem that Dylan was unable to pull out of the situation he found himself in on Desolation Row and in "Tambourine Man." He found no saving grace to reinject hope and vitality into his poetry. Negativity (as he saw in "Just Like Tom Thumb's Blues") has resulted in a superabundance of grotesqueries, pornography, deviation. There has been no vision, and negativity did not see him through.

Dylan has sung his rock-song, and there is no Madonna waiting for him. And so he picks up his folk guitar and begins to sing again. The *John Wesley Harding* album is a reversion to a country-folk idiom, changed significantly because of his experiences through three albums, but still basically a return to a previous idiom. Yet before he steps back into folk music he has a few final remarks to make on it all.

In "All Along the Watchtower," the I-persona is abandoned for a third person narrative, but the concerns and theme follow directly from the songs I have been considering. It is constructed in three verses that continue one story straight through. The third verse suddenly cuts off the narrative, and the song is left unfinished. I believe this is so because Dylan was reviewing the same conflict he couldn't resolve previously, and dropped it in favor of his new-old idiom.

The setting and characters have an almost mythic quality. The place is a medieval castle, so distant from our time that it can take on an otherworldly aspect. The two main characters are a joker and a thief, both the disinherited of their society. The joker as a character in, for example, Shakespearean drama, always knew what was going on around him, in fact was frequently the only one who knew this, but was unable to act on his knowledge. (p. 145)

"'There must be some way out of there,' said the joker to the thief. / 'There's too much confusion, I can't get no relief.'" The fragmented world and chaotic life his previous poetry dealt with is too much for him; he can't support it. None of the common people (plowmen or businessmen) can understand his problem. Wine is a conventional symbol of blood, and the businessmen drinking his wine are sucking his life, his creativity, out of him. Thus these common people actually become oppressors. And of course, as in previous lyrics, none of them know the real value of any of his work. At the end of the first verse Dylan's whole situation, running through all his rock lyrics, has been defined. He has been pushed around, drained, and wasted, turned into some kind of freak in his own freak show, and no one realizes what has been happening.

The thief replies to the joker. He understands the joker's position, and also sees life as a cruel joke (reminiscent of verse four of "Visions of Johanna"). But as he points out, the two of them are through all that confusion now, and there is another destiny awaiting them. Perhaps this is the thief that hung beside Christ, as some like to speculate. The joker then becomes a version of the hanged god (as in verse one of "Desolation Row") who brings fertility to the land

through his death, and salvation to those who drink his blood. The late hour would be the hour of their death. Thus a hint of possible redemption enters the poem. (pp. 145-46)

What did it all mean? Dylan seems to have overthrown the question, and in the bedlam escaped the trials of it all with his drifter and headed for the tall timber ("The Drifter's Escape"). In *John Wesley Harding,* the rock medium was highly modified for the same reason the rock lyrics were modified—he found the less structured nature of his idiom insupportable just as he found the "real" world grotesque and unacceptable. The results of this clash in both music and lyrics was a return to a simpler, clearer, "cleaner" world, a return to a "primitivist" idiom, accompanied by a self-imposed exile. Dylan seems to have come to the conclusion that the ultimate truths were to be found in those things that "whisper a few simple things eternally." . . . Dylan's songs at this point seem to imply that the ultimate way a man should be is to have a simple humane concern for his fellow men, and that such basic human emotions are the sources of peace and order. (pp. 146-47)

Thomas S. Johnson, "Desolation Row Revisited: Bob Dylan's Rock Poetry," in Southwest Review *(© 1977 by Southern Methodist University Press), Spring, 1977, pp. 135-47.*

TONY PALMER

Without question, the most important figure in the protest renaissance of the 1960s was Bob Dylan. Like his idol Woody Guthrie, Dylan believed he was "trying to be a singer without a dictionary, and a poet not bound with shelves of books." He had a voice caught in barbed wire, he looked like a cross between Harpo Marx and the younger Beethoven. "What I do," he said, "is write songs and sing them and perform them. Anything else trying to get on top of it, making something out of it which it isn't first, brings me down." Yet his song "A Hard Rain's A-Gonna Fall" was about, or at least inspired by, the 1962 Cuban Missile confrontation; the "Ballad of Hollis Brown" commemorated a particularly bloody killing of a Dakota dirt farmer; "Oxford Town" concerned the ordeal of James Meredith; his recent return to activist singing, "Hurricane," is about a black prize fighter wrongly jailed (so it is claimed) for murder.

Dylan's protest songs are full of savage melancholy, flinty and drawling. Their subject matter is intolerance and the loss of liberty. (p. 208)

[His] lyrics have brought eloquence to an age that has little, dignity to a generation that tends to forget its meaning, and a terrible honesty to a society which prefers deceit. A prophet of reasoned defiance, he works in a medium where such an attitude had been virtually unknown among whites, though it is now seen as a cornerstone of future musical development. Like other folk artists, he steals from the past to revitalize the present. His debt to black music and to the blues in particular is often unacknowledged and damaging to both. But as a lyricist, his example stands as a warning to those who "go mistaking Paradise for that home across the road." (pp. 208-09)

Tony Palmer, in his All You Need Is Love: The Story of Popular Music *(copyright © Theatre Projects Film Productions Limited, EMI Television Productions Limited and Phonogram Limited, 1976; all rights reserved; reprinted by permis-*

sion of Viking Penguin Inc.), Viking Penguin, 1977.

ANDREW WARD

It is a shame . . . that so few are going to forgive Bob Dylan for *Renaldo & Clara*. I am afraid it is only going to alienate further those whose irritation with Dylan's incarnations has kept them from turning out the lights and trying to understand his music. Perhaps the uninitiated do not concern Dylan particularly, and perhaps they shouldn't, but even for his most fanatic fans, *Renaldo & Clara* is a long and bumpy ride.

The sudden transformations of self that have sparked Dylan's songs over the years do not seem to work in film, or at least not in this film. Throughout *Renaldo & Clara* identities shift, overlap, and collide.

Since no one is positively identified within the movie itself, you need to commit the credits to memory before the houselights dim. Bob Dylan plays Renaldo, a character in whiteface who seems to represent Dylan's poetic self. Ronnie Hawkins plays Bob Dylan as a celebrity. Mrs. Dylan plays Clara, a character I never quite got a handle on, unless she was Renaldo's wife and thus a female counterpart to Dylan's poetic self. Ronee Blakley plays Mrs. Dylan in her public manifestation, although she looks (as do most of the ladies in Dylan's entourage) like Joan Baez, who in turn appears as herself, as a whore, and as a mysterious Woman in White. During the course of the film various characters are mistaken for Bob Dylan, including Bob Neuwirth, who plays the Masked Tortilla. . . .

During the course of the movie, Allen Ginsberg gets a shave and a woman carries a rope to a car. A bunch of morons in a greasy spoon talk about the decline of the Movement, and Joan Baez is traded for a pony. Dylan drives a van to a cathouse, and the Tuscarora nation has everyone over for lunch. Lourdes, Toronto, and Kerouac's grave are visited. A lot of brunettes wander around delivering roses and experiencing anxiety. Palms are read. An elderly woman accompanies herself on a ukelele.

But just when I found myself thinking that Dylan and his friends were listless, self-indulgent fools, Dylan would suddenly appear as the white-faced Renaldo in performances filmed during his brilliant Rolling Thunder Review concert tour, singing his greatest songs at the peak of his powers as if to ask, "If we're such fools, how do you account for all this amazing music?" In some of the most beautifully photographed concert footage I've ever seen, he performs his mad waltzes of retribution and redemption with the wild-eyed urgency of Jeremiah. (p. 125)

But not even the magnificent music could rescue the muddled bulk of *Renaldo & Clara*. Dylan has shown courage in making this film, and in championing it so fervently in interview after interview, but the film itself is tentative and parsimonious. His sense of privacy, which has served him so well as a songwriter, works against him as a director, for it prohibits him from manipulating his cast. Instead of exercising his poetic gifts, he too often allows his cast, as wooden offstage as it is electric onstage, to provide the dialogue. Dylan might have been better served by professional actors who would have demanded more from him as a director than knowing nods and smiles of reassurance, but improvised dialogue, with its hesitancies, is rarely convinc-

ing, even in the best of hands, and in *Renaldo & Clara* it is often downright silly. He seems to have made all his assertions in the editing room with coy flashbacks and jarring juxtapositions.

Dylan's movie is an ego trip, but that isn't its problem. Art consists of ego trips. The problem is that it obscures rather than illuminates his obsession. The best that can be said for it is that it records, however fitfully, some of his greatest performances, and has reportedly spurred him on to write a new album's worth of songs. What worries me is that Dylan actually believes he denuded himself in *Renaldo & Clara*, when all he wound up doing was disrobing in a fog. (pp. 125-26)

Andrew Ward, "Bob Dylan's Amateur Night," in The Atlantic Monthly (copyright © 1978 by The Atlantic Monthly Company, Boston, Mass.; reprinted with permission), April, 1978, pp. 122, 125-26.

GREIL MARCUS

Most of the stuff here [on *Street-Legal*] is dead air, or close to it. (p. 51)

The most interesting—if that's the word—aspect of *Street-Legal* is its lyrics, which often pretend to the supposed impenetrability of Dylan's mid-Sixties albums, the albums on which his reputation still rests. But the return is false; you may not have known why Dylan was singing about a "Panamanian moon" in "Memphis Blues Again" (or, for that matter, have had any idea why the blues were Memphian rather than Bostonian), but you knew what "Your debutante just knows what you need / But I know what you want" meant, and it meant a lot. In *Street-Legal*'s "Señor (Tales of Yankee Power)"—the parenthetical part of the title is the most inspired thing on the record—the lines, "Well, the last thing I remember before I stripped and kneeled / Was that trainload of fools bogged down in a magnetic field," are just a gesture, just a wave at the fans. Not that the effect of the lines can't hurt: it's hard not to hear the older songs now in terms of the new numbers that appear to resemble them, and then conclude that at bottom "Absolutely Sweet Marie" and "Highway 61 Revisited" are as empty as "Where are You Tonight? (Journey through Dark Heat)," even though that isn't remotely true. (p. 53)

Greil Marcus, " 'Street-Legal': A Misdemeanor," in Rolling Stone (by Straight Arrow Publishers, Inc. © 1978; all rights reserved; reprinted by permission), August 24, 1978, pp. 51-3.

JON PARELES

When Bob Dylan writes from his wounded heart, he can be eloquent. When he writes from the head, he can be clairvoyant. And when Dylan the man teams with Dylan the yarn-spinner, lines are written that could serve as epigraphs to whole lives: "If you don't believe there's a price for this sweet paradise / Just remind me to show you the scars." Regardless of Dylan's musical trappings, people still search his albums for lines that strong; I know I do. *Street-Legal* has quite a few. . . .

The Dylan I respect . . . is the free associator, the crazed doggerel genius whose songs make sense a hundred different ways. A lot of fools write love songs, but there's only one "Highway 61 Revisited." The best thing about

Street-Legal is that Dylan's letting his mind ramble again, going further afield than he did on *Blood on the Tracks*, making *Desire* sound like setting-up exercises. It might be a conscious new direction: The opener, "Changing of the Guards," is about a revolution, and the closer, "Where Are You Tonight?," announces "There's a new day at dawn and I've finally arrived." . . .

Nothing is explained; foreboding is all. "Changing of the Guards," moving along at a forthright clip, is a montage with no discernible narrative, just mysterious scenes. . . .

The final step is the transcendent merger of autobiography and imaginary epic; most recently consummated in "Tangled Up in Blue." "No Time to Think" makes the attempt; its allusive verses read like a spiritual diary:

> You've murdered your vanity,
> burned your sanity
>
> For pleasure you must now resist
> Lovers obey you but they cannot sway you
> They're not even sure you exist

But the lyrics bog down with lists of abstract nouns ("Socialism, hypnotism / Patriotism, materialism"), and the music is a tiresome 18-verse sea chanty. . . .

Dylan still needs a producer, still has his turgid moments, still shouts when he could be quiet and plays it cool when he could open up. Yet *Street-Legal*, for all its lapses, has kept the spark that makes Dylan irreplaceable.

> Jon Pareles, *"Untangling from the Blues,"* in Crawdaddy *(copyright © 1978 by Crawdaddy Publishing Co., Inc.; reprinted by permission of Peter Knobler), September, 1978, p. 65.*

MARK KIDEL

Renaldo and Clara is not a straight movie. It is a tortuous and uncompromising film, unlikely to appeal to anyone but those already captured by Bob Dylan's magic and susceptible to the many mythological references scattered throughout the 3 hours 52 minutes of its length. The portrait of the artist as a rock musician on the road . . . might at first appear self-indulgent and narcissistic, given that the epic was written and directed by Dylan himself. No other rock musician, after all, has ever dared present his audience with a similar self-portrait.

Dylan succeeds however, because he has refused, in characteristic style, to define himself: it is this mutability, the absence of a recognisable image, which makes the film and its ridiculously self-effacing hero (he hardly speaks at all) so absorbing. Dylan has always preferred expressing himself in song rather than press interviews, preferring ambiguity to interrogation. The structure of the film—or perhaps more accurately its lack of structure, relying on echo and unsettling juxtaposition rather than simple and coherent narrative —reflects the same love of the oblique, an unwillingness to be trapped by easily digested clarity. . . .

The deliberate confusion between drama and *vérité* scenes helps create an atmosphere which is free of illusion and pretence. Nothing is absolutely real or true—including the conventional fly-on-the-wall documentary material; there are only different levels of fantasy: masks, roles and games, myths which are played out, consciously or unconsciously.

The entire film has a dreamlike quality, flowing unpredicta-

bly, advancing and returning through time and space with no apparent logic. There are recurrent images of madness, magic and wild eccentricity. . . .

Dylan is almost overshadowed by the beautiful women that surround him. . . . They haunt the film like a team of competing enchantresses. It is through his relationship with women 'who hold the keys', as the voice-over in the film declaims, that he will progress on his 'quest'. For *Renaldo and Clara*, like most of the road movies before it, is not just a simple travelogue. Kerouac, the first to chronicle his own drift towards self-discovery, is clearly acknowledged in a graveside pilgrimage made by Dylan and Ginsberg. The road is a very American search for freedom, but it is also symbolic of the spiritual path, the solitary suspension that Dylan has so clearly chosen in preference to the cosiness of conventional stardom.

In most of the concert sequences, Dylan sings with unnerving force. . . . There is also a deeply stirring and quite un-self-pitying openness and vulnerability: Dylan (and Renaldo) may not talk too much, but in his songs, and by extension this film, he has revealed far more of his personal feelings than most other rock musicians. (p. 308)

> Mark Kidel, *"On the Road,"* in New Statesman *(© 1978 The Statesman & Nation Publishing Co. Ltd.), September 8, 1978.*

ALAN RINZLER

After the more deferential, less personal politesse of his first album [*Bob Dylan*], . . . *Freewheelin'* Bob Dylan throws open all the windows and tears the sheets off the furniture. . . . [There is] an immortal spiritual anthem which made him famous everywhere and opens up this album: "Blowin' in the Wind."

"Blowin' in the Wind" has withstood the test of time. It stands as a song not just for a special period or generation but for all time and every generation. (p. 15)

The range of *Freewheelin'* is tremendous: humor, anger, bombast, wit; loveliness, loneliness, irony, and spit. . . . His ability to reflect not only his own feelings but some simpler, more general emotions he felt around him, was uncanny. And however mythic, two-dimensional, or adolescent these feelings were, he was usually able to rescue them with the brilliance of his music and his performance. (p. 19)

Most of the songs on [*The Times They Are A-Changin'*] are devastating in their power of political persuasion. The title song is a solemn, dead-serious sermon delivered in a flat, righteous voice with a heavy drone-like beat. And that name, the repeated litany of that declaration: *The Times They Are A-Changin'*. It sounds like an expression we've known all our lives or heard a lot somewhere, before. But we haven't. Dylan just made it up, the perfect expression of our sentiment, our innate desire. If ever a song crystallized the passions of a generation, it's this one. (p. 23)

[*Another Side of Bob Dylan*] is a conscious effort . . . to break free of any constricting stereotypes, get off the soapbox and turn inward. Consequently this album has an emphasis on love rather than rhetoric, on relationships rather than revolution. A full eight of the eleven songs are about women. Nevertheless there's still an undertone of anger and apocalypse to many of the songs and not only in those which are still overtly political. . . . (p. 31)

This album has attempted to back off from the near-caricature image of the "protest" singer deliberately constructed in *The Times They Are A-Changin'*, and to a degree, it has succeeded. We are convinced Dylan isn't as simple as anything we've thought of him so far, that he's still searching, and that there's no telling where his quest will lead. (p. 36)

The title [of] *Bringing It All Back Home* accurately describes Dylan's intention: to escape the folk and protest music and return to his first love: rock 'n' roll. To bring back or withdraw his creativity and psychic energy from the public posture of folk purist or political dissident and return to his center, his home, his heart, the music he grew up with: rock 'n' roll. In fact the break is not so clean cut or simple. This is not completely a rock album but rather a transitional collection with some big electric sound as well as some acoustic compositions on Side Two. But the album is a departure, and it's amazing to consider how it shocked and outraged fans and critics at the time. (p. 39)

There's a lot of energy on [*Highway 61 Revisited*]: driving, burning, speeding, it's focused in feelings of bitterness and revenge. Actually, the underlying theme of this album is defiance and *revenge*. Dylan seems so angry, so tired of having to explain, so mad at lots of people . . . or is it that he is just plain *mad*. . . .

People who'd never have listened during the blue-jeans and work-shirt days were now enormously turned on by his electric, hard-driving, violent songs of rebellion. In fact, Dylan was doing more to revolutionize and influence American society now, singing rock 'n' roll, than he had ever been able to accomplish as a folk-music protest singer. More individual, more personal, Dylan's songs nonetheless have stimulated self-understanding, change and revolution in each of us. . . . (p. 47)

The first cut [on *Blonde on Blonde*] sets the tone for many of the thirteen to follow: "Rainy Day Women # 12 & 35" is a gas: a stoned-out shouter, a fine song for marching down the street. The music and the high-stepping beat and the vigorous performance are so full of camaraderie, humor, and fun, they contrast sharply with the words which, if read alone, sound like a paranoid fantasy—just the sort of ironic vision one might very well experience when stoned. (p. 51)

Blonde on Blonde marks the apex of Dylan's career as a rock 'n' roll star. At this point in his life he really was as big as Elvis Presley. Moreover, the content of Dylan's songs convinces many idolatrous fans that he *knows,* that he has some cosmic *answer,* that he can tell them the truth about their lives—an assumption which he himself both encourages and disdains. "Listen to me," he says; but "Don't listen to me. . . ." The responsibility is too great, the pressure becomes immense. (p. 55)

John Wesley Harding is a sermon disguised as a series of narrative ballads. The songs on this album are like gentle admonitions, sung in a mellow and persuasive voice. Like all of Dylan's music, there's a lot between the lines. There *is* a message. But instead of beating us over the head, Dylan herein assumes the mantle of a teacher, a rabbi, and a patriarch who shows the way through example, through moral allegory, and through parable. Each of the songs is short and to the point. Dylan takes a position. He has reappeared, liberated from the madness that had surrounded him. Apparently he is also free of those personal devils that had plagued him: anger, jealousy, bitterness. He reincar-

nates himself before our very eyes, regroups his energy, which had been faint, and carefully applies it to a new position. For all his protestation to the contrary, Dylan tells us once again: this is it!

And what is it? The *Bible*. Mostly Old Testament. . . . Dylan's previous moralizing had been so adolescent and simplistic, so good-versus-bad, us-versus-them. Now he's saying something much subtler: he's older and matured; he's learned something from all those years in the crucible; now he's saying in these cunningly plain, simple songs— with no electricity, with understatement rather than hyperbole—now he's advising us to love each other and take responsibility for our lives. (pp. 57, 59)

Nashville Skyline is a *hoot,* a joyous celebration, a happy revelation. This has to be the happiest album Dylan has made till now: gentle, playful, calm, and serene. Everything about it conveys Dylan's new role of the family man, unperturbed, peaceful, patient, loving, and loved. What a difference between this country gentleman and the surly, angry, strung-out-looking guy on the front of his precrash albums *Highway 61* and *Blonde on Blonde*.

Dylan wants to tell us what's making him so happy, something he started to do on the last two cuts of *John Wesley Harding*. Let's count our blessings, he says, chief among which are our love and our loving families, the basic, mundane things in life—all the old eternal verities which country music has always been about. (p. 63)

There's a loose sort of foolin' around feeling on *Self-Portrait*, with some odd little fillips thrown in, as if to say: I'm all these things; *this* is me and *this* is me and, wait a second, *this* is me, too. Dylan feels good. He's asking for a little self-indulgence, a chance to relax after all these years, just for himself. He wants to be outrageous. And outrage *was* the general reaction to this album at the time. *It drove people right up the wall.* (p. 68)

As the dust settled and years passed, *Self-Portrait* has become more appreciated for what it is: experimental, self-indulgent, foolin' around, with peculiar lapses but odd flashes of brilliance and innovation. (p. 69)

The doubting Thomases crucified him for *Self-Portrait*— seen in historical perspective as a kind of busman's holiday. But Dylan quickly returns to deliver a new album full of light and love, tight energetic songs and some terrific piano playing. Not just romantic songs idealizing this love, but rather showing us how he's working out the snags and doubts and anxieties. Complexity, variety, clear-thinking, direct-saying, virtuoso musicality—the new, improved, renewed, risen again *New Morning*. (p. 77)

Planet Waves marks the beginning of a new cycle. It's a powerful, ambitious album, by far his best since *New Morning*. The entire project radiates high energy, tremendous intensity, and deliberate intent. Dylan wants to tell us something, and he's back to doing everything himself, just to make sure we get the message. These songs are *Planet Waves;* they're emanations from far within the earth, from the center: great washes and tides, powerful forces from deep inside of us and our world. As it says on the front of the album, these songs are cast-iron songs, sturdy, solid, permanent, tough, and well-built. And they're torch ballads of love—love with a fire, flaming passions, hot and sultry and burning. (p. 89)

Nine out of ten songs on *Planet Waves* are love songs, and a great deal of what they convey is gratitude coupled with desperation. This valedictory "Wedding Song" is the most confessional and explicit of them all, exposing most profoundly the singer's hunger, his continuing yearning *and* his anxiety. . . .

Dylan has come a long way from the confidence and serenity of *Nashville Skyline* and *New Morning*. Those rosy-colored love songs were much simpler and happier. There's been a change now, four years later: malaise, hunger, jealousy, and sadness burn throughout these torch ballads. . . .

After a relatively long silence, he's given us a progress report, a state of the artist, a consolidated self-portrait of his mind and feelings and his intentions—his ambitions to renew, to continue his quest, to reiterate his moral and spiritual positions even more adamantly. Sober, determined, still hopeful in loving, he rides out again to do battle in his own life and to share, teach, exhort, and inspire us to do the same. (p. 95)

Blood on the Tracks could have been subtitled *Love's Labor Lost*. For whereas *Planet Waves*, released earlier the same year, was about hanging on to love, *Blood on the Tracks* takes place after the fall. The overwhelming theme of nearly every song on the record is lost love, breaking up, the dissolution of a very important relationship. What distinguishes this album from both other work on the same subject and from Dylan's previous love songs is that this group of ballads all approach the same subject from a variety of disparate angles. Dylan reacts to a cataclysmic event with all the complexity it deserves: he's mad, he's resigned, he's vindictive, he's forgiving, he's hurt and bitter, he's playful and ironic, he's understanding—he doesn't understand, he's filled with rage and frustration, he's philosophical, he's content, he's discontent. This album is a *tour de force* on the subject of breaking up with someone, someone with whom you've shared a whole lot of your life, someone who's always going to be very important, forever in your consciousness. (pp. 99-100)

[*Planet Waves, Blood on the Tracks,* and *Desire*] represent the most fully realized expressions of a great artist in his maturity. Because *Desire*, more than anything that has come before, explodes with Dylan's openhearted power in a rich variety of virtuoso styles over a broad spectrum of deeply felt emotions, flights of illumination, universal fantasy, and personal, gut-issue messages—from his heart to ours.

Dylan's greatness has always been his ability to express what we are experiencing; adolescent rebellion, sociopolitical apocalypticism and rampant naiveté, hot fucks, perhaps children, love paranoia, crazy speed, consciousness catapulting, hurt, rejection, the breakup of an important relationship or two, death nearby and coming closer, self-realization leading to doubt, ambivalence, vulnerability, compassion, empathy, diversity, flexibility, alternatives. *Desire* expresses all this; the album, the songs, the metaphor—the great East Indian holy men say we are all living now in the Desire World, that everything we do and feel is motivated by DESIRE. Freud said something like that, too, and certainly all the passions and issues on this album come from desire: for freedom and justice, for love, salvation, and fulfillment. But there's a subtitle to this album: *Songs of Redemption*. An interesting choice of

words for a man who chooses his words very carefully. Redemption means to buy back, to liberate by payment, or on a more spiritual level, to free from the bondage of sin, to change for the better or REFORM; or, heavier yet, to atone for or expiate. Once again, as in "My Back Pages" and "I Am a Lonesome Hobo," Dylan seems to be in a mood for self-criticism, for paying some dues, for reevaluating his prior positions, and exposing his own process of change. (pp. 107-08)

Desire is an album by a mature artist at the height of his powers. Undiminished. Stronger than ever. Everything about this album is polished to a new level of perfection. . . . (p. 113)

[The] mood of *Street-Legal*—hard, strained, deliberate, depressing—may be as ephemeral as many others he has passed through. We hope for something more uplifting, more optimistic, more loving . . . and in the meantime we remain fascinated and attentive. (p. 120)

> *Alan Rinzler, in his* Bob Dylan: The Illustrated Record *(copyright © 1978 by Alan Rinzler; used by permission of Harmony Books), Harmony Books, 1978.*

JOHN WELLS

Dylan is an important artist whose writings portray unique societal themes, symbolic representations and structures of consciousness found in contemporary society. Furthermore, these topics are deeply rooted within a socio-historical context and provide linkages to similar themes throughout other historical settings.

This essay does not attempt a total evaluation of Dylan's lyrics from this standpoint, but more specifically it concentrates on a re-occurring theme in his work: the notion of the grotesque through his dramatic representation of a fictional cosmos. . . .

[The period between 1965 and 1966] can be considered the "surrealistic chains of rhyming images" phase of his career and particularly lends itself to the present discussion. (p. 39)

[Two] components of the term grotesque . . . are formed most frequently in Dylan's lyrics. These include elements of disharmony and alienation of the individual within a social milieu. In creating a fictional cosmos composed of many people who seem "bent out of shape from society's pliers," Dylan represents a picture of reality separated from its ordinary psychic underpinnings. His characters are often fantastic or distorted persons caught in a terrible moral drama. For Dylan in his surrealistic phase, the ordinary world and a nightmare madhouse are virtually undistinguishable.

In *Bringing It All Back Home* Dylan's songs reflect a man trapped in an insane world not quite of his own making. For example, in the song "Maggie's Farm" (which could easily be interpreted as modern society) the continuing refrain, "I ain't gonna work on Maggie's farm no more" echoes Dylan's resentment against a woman whose brother "hands you a nickel, hands you a dime, asks you with a grin, if you're having a good time." Here Dylan is wrestling under disturbing conditions superimposed upon his own sensibilities to the point where he just can not manage to function anymore. Maggie's farm is a grotesque place not only because it represents an overtly authoritarian locality, but offers a contradictory view of his existence. The normal routine patterns of life are juxtaposed against jumbled confusion. His attitude toward his "job" at Maggie's farm contradicts the excessive bureaucratic operations which rule our so-called familiar world. Disharmony and alienation arise through a desparate attempt to maintain his personal identity in the face of a world gone mad with the routinization of specialized, boring tasks. Dylan proclaims at the end of the song that he trys to be as he is, but everybody wants you to be like they are and while other people sing while they slave, Dylan just gets bored. A similar reaction, one even more grotesque, is displayed in "On the Road Again".... Dylan's use of incongruent scenes and stark images are reminiscent of the French symbolist poets, particularly Rimbaud and Baudelaire. One of the key functions of these poets was to provoke their audience into a different kind of perception by presenting to the ordinary eye an object or person so dazzling that it would destroy the dominant temporal-spatial order and rational mode of consciousness. Indeed, Dylan's creations of grotesque disharmonies reveal a farcical universe not founded upon any systematic and logical representations. . . .

Highway 61 Revisited contains some of the best poetic imagery Dylan has ever written. His blurring of reality and irreality in such songs as "Desolation Row," "Tombstone Blues," "Ballad of a Thin Man," and "Highway 61 Revisited" further challenges the familiar world to which we are accustomed. (p. 41)

In "Desolation Row" Dylan descends completely into the abyss of modern society. Here is a place inhabited by extremely grotesque figures in a cold cunning and mechanical environment. As he descends into this Dantesque netherworld he meets a riot squad who needs some place to go, sexless patients trying to blow-up a leather cup, Ophelia who is an old maid on her twenty-second birthday, Einstein disguised as Robin Hood, the Titanic sailing at dawn, and Ezra Pound and T. S. Eliot fighting in a captain's tower. In one of the more chilling choruses Dylan declares:

> Now at midnight all the agents and the
>   superhuman crew
> Come out and round up everyone that knows more
>   than they do

Obviously Dylan is experiencing a radically different kind of existence and the surrealistic images he projects cause one to shudder because they reflect a totally estranged world. It is his own season in hell and here especially the similarities between Dylan and Rimbaud are quite apparent. Rimbaud, almost a century earlier, experimented with all sorts of drugs, underwent hunger, exhaustion and other extreme physical deprivations to produce a "com-

plete deregularization of the senses." Through this method Rimbaud hoped to achieve poetic visions which would loosen the moorings of ordinary consciousness through the dissolution of ordinary reality.... [Dylan makes] numerous references to drugs in his songs and one may safely say that he used some method similar to Rimbaud's to gain visionary insights and surrealistic chains of rhyming images devoid of any conscious control by a rationalistic state of mind. (pp. 41-2)

Blonde on Blonde has one song which somehow perfectly captures the grotesque disharmony and alienation themes with which we are dealing: . . . the superbly written "Stuck Inside of Mobile with the Memphis Blues Again." . . . Dylan sings as if this is his last day on earth. When he delivers the repeated refrain of every chorus, "Oh Mama can this really be the end—to be struck inside of Mobile with the Memphis blues again", there is no doubt that this is a man crying from the utter depths of experience. It has been said that with the Beatles you thought you had a chance; with the Rolling Stones you knew you didn't want one. In this song Dylan confirms that you will never have a chance. This, as he says, is *really* the end.

After repeated listening one realizes that Mobile no longer just means being stuck in an Alabama city, but more symbolically, Mobile represents the grotesque turbulent world we all inhabit. In this song Dylan drinks some Texas medicine which strangles up his mind and experiences people getting uglier, loses his sense of time and wonders what price he has to pay for going through all these things twice.... Dylan may be stuck in an insane world, but he somehow maintains his sanity by not taking the world or himself too seriously. This may be a terrible place to live, but it is also something of a joke and if a person reaches the point where something has strangled up his mind, he has no sense of time, people just get uglier, and he wonders why he has to go through all these things twice then it is obvious that "normal reality" has no meaning whatsover. The world has become transformed and transformed into a grotesque madhouse. As Benjamin Nelson has noted [in an article he wrote in *The Psycho-analytic Review*], "Images of the grotesque . . . regularly seem to multiply when large numbers of people find it impossible to function, much less thrive, in their everyday worlds." This is why Dylan's work remains important from a sociological point of view. (p. 43)

John Wells, "Bent Out of Shape from Society's Pliers: A Sociological Study of the Grotesque in the Songs of Bob Dylan," in Popular Music and Society *(copyright © 1978 by R. Serge Denisoff), Vol. VI, No. 1, 1978, pp. 39-43.*

Esther Forbes

1891-1967

American historian, biographer, and fiction writer. Born and raised in New England, Forbes had an early interest in the life styles and folklore of that region. This blossomed into serious historical research, prompted by the many varied and intriguing stories she heard concerning her own ancestors, including the tale of a woman who died in jail, accused of witchcraft. Forbes won the Pulitzer Prize in History in 1943 for her biography, *Paul Revere and the World He Lived In*. It was while working on this book that she uncovered information about the apprentices of the Revolutionary period and contemplated writing a book which dealt with this subject. At this time, the impending World War II was thrusting young men into positions and responsibilities of adulthood not unlike the situation prior to the Revolutionary War. The combination of these two stimuli brought about the creation of one of Forbes's most remarkable novels. On the day after the bombing of Pearl Harbor, she began work on *Johnny Tremain: A Novel for Old and Young*, which told the story of a silversmith's apprentice and his maturation in pre-Revolution Boston. She was awarded the Newbery Medal in 1944 for this book and it was almost universally acclaimed for its historical accuracy as well as its depth of insight and emotion. Throughout the years, it has maintained a high status as a source of information on colonial New England while remaining a favorite for pure reading enjoyment. (See also *Contemporary Authors*, Vols. 13-14; obituary, Vols. 25-28, rev. ed.; *Contemporary Authors Permanent Series*, Vol. 1, and *Something about the Author*, Vol. 2.)

ANNE PARRISH

["O Genteel Lady!"] is the strange story of Lanice Bardeen, beautiful bluestocking of the Boston of Holmes, Emerson and the Alcotts. No one else in the book matters much, although there are many characters. But Lanice lives, and her life is shown us with honesty and rather bitter laughter.

Esther Forbes is able to keep her characters in costume without letting the costumes smother the characters. The book is brilliant with color. You really see picture after picture—the ladies of fashion in their autumn-tinted dresses, "burnt orange, dull crimson, russet, and a bright, light green, the shade of the winter rye," and their Paisley shawls, sweeping up the fallen leaves with their full skirts. . . .

The book remains true to its period in its costumes and settings. These are perfect. But although Lanice is a contemporary of Louisa Alcott, she is, in the flaming passion of her untrammeled love for Anthony Jones, her independent career as illustrator and author, and her lonely wanderings in Italy and England, more modern than the moderns. . . . The speech of the characters, on the other hand, is far too old-fashioned. It needs brocade and powdered hair, and even then is unconvincing. The characters, with the exception of the burlesqued Augustus, really live until they begin to talk, then the same voice speaks through each mouth in rounded literary periods. We see and feel them, and believe. We hear them, and say "This is not true." . . .

Anthony Jones is convincing only through his effect on Lanice. Roger Cuncliffe, the dying young lover of her dead mother, gives the feeling of the sorrow of spring, the death in birth that one finds in Botticelli's paintings, and then opens his mouth and talks like an elegant guidebook to Italy. Literary celebrities, English and American, are scattered as thickly through the pages as currants through a cake, and remain as important as currants, except the Tennysons, amusingly sketched.

The book is original and uninfluenced, although some, on reading of crinolines and "Mamma," may murmur, "May Sinclair." But in spite of the general impression Laurence Stallings did not invent the war, A. A. Milne did not invent children and May Sinclair did not invent mammas and crinoline.

Anne Parrish, "Always Genteel?" in New York Herald Tribune Book Review (© I.H.T. Corporation, reprinted by permission), May 9, 1926, p. 7.

Timed though it is by crinoline and attitude towards ankle, "O Genteel Lady!" is timeless in its presentation of a romantic woman's demands upon life. Lanice Bardeen is an alluring young creature who quits the college town from which her mother has eloped with a student, and goes to Boston to find freedom, love, and a career. The career develops in a publishing house, love comes with the assistance of a colorful English adventurer who finds the lecture platforms of the New World excellent financial backing for explorations in the Old. Freedom is more elusive and comes late and in disguise.

Although the novel derives much of its charm from its period and setting—the classical era of American life, when Emerson and Dr. Holmes were familiar figures on Boston streets, it is wholly modern in its interpretation of the moods and desires of its young heroine. . . .

"O Genteel Lady!" has as much literary distinction as any of this year's crop of novels. It might easily, in less skillful hands, have become a pretty, sentimental story relying on its picturesque background and the author's grace of style for a perfectly legitimate interest and popularity. Instead of this it has a robustness of theme and of characterization which would give it importance quite apart from Miss Forbes's ingratiating presentation.

> *"A Romantic Woman," in* The Saturday Review of Literature *(copyright, 1926, by The Saturday Review Co., Inc.; reprinted with permission), May 29, 1926, p. 823.*

EDITH OLIVIER

[In "A Mirror for Witches" is found] that deep, tragic irony which culminates in St. John's Gospel, in the creations of the Greek dramatists, in Thomas Hardy. [Esther Forbes's] story has that human poignancy which tears the heart in the account of those witches who really were done to death at Salem, and as one reads "A Mirror for Witches" one feels stream over one the force of that same evil, reasonless torrent.

The scene is set "upon the skirts of Cowan Corners, and but six miles removed from Salem," and the action takes place some twenty or thirty years before the Salem witch-findings. As far as I know (though I may be mistaken), it is not founded on historical fact, but is a rarer thing,—a creation compact of imagination and of sure historic instinct. It is indeed a *tour de force*.

[The] story is the commonplace, almost sordid, one, of a panic-stricken child, pursued by spite and jealousy in a world where frightful beliefs can clothe the happenings of every day with a fiendlike supernatural character. It is there that lies the amazing technique of the writing. There is its unique ironic quality. As one reads the story, one sees that all its events are entirely normal. But in the poisoned light of fear and superstition they cast huge shadows, which swallow them up and engulf them, till they are no longer the doings of human people, but the awe-inspiring movements of some spectre of the Brocken. And so completely does Miss Forbes identify herself with the mental attitude of the period, that one realizes how the fantastic beliefs generated in a soil of ignorance and fanaticism, can permeate every-where, so that even the little victim herself believes at last that she is possessed and loved by a demon lover. The atmosphere of the book is entirely true to the seventeenth century.

And the characters which move in this atmosphere are clearly and delicately drawn. They come very near, in spite of their remote setting. The tiny, stunted figure of Doll is full of pathos and beauty; and Jared, with all the characteristics of the conventional sea captain, yet succeeds in being individual and charming. Hannah is a detestable woman, but she is not a fiend, and it must have been very hard not to make her one. She is a disappointed, jealous, credulous creature, with that belief in her own infallibility which attacks the weak mind nurtured on an infallible Book. Mr. Zelley (evidently drawn from the Rev. George Burroughs, and of all the characters in the book, the nearest to history)

succeeds in being lovable in spite of the fact that he is described from the point of view of an antagonist. But that is where the originality of the treatment lies all through. Miss Forbes writes in the spirit of the seventeenth century, but her vision is the vision of to-day, and she conveys to her readers this double standpoint.

The "historical novel" is, as a rule, but a hybrid artistic form, and is commonly neither historical nor a novel; but Miss Forbes could, without misgiving, have dedicated this book, with its rare subtlety and insight, to Calliope and Clio for their joint acceptance.

> *Edith Olivier, "Witchcraft at Work," in* The Saturday Review of Literature *(copyright, 1928, by The Saturday Review Co., Inc.; reprinted with permission), June 2, 1928, p. 930.*

KENNETH B. MURDOCK

[*Paradise*] cracks the moulds in which too many historical novels of early New England have been cast. [Miss Forbes] has written the story of a seventeenth-century Massachusetts Bay family with the emphasis on flesh and blood, not on an artificially contrived system; on drinking, eating, breeding, not on pious meditation; and on the dramatic struggle of white man and Indian, ending bitterly in war, not on the tamer operations of religious zealots. . . .

To be sure there are ghosts of the old lay figures in the minister whose soul wars with his body, in the little girl tormented ostensibly by conviction of sin, and there is certainly in Bathsheba a strong hint of the familiar "exotic" woman so useful in Puritan romances. But even these do not degenerate into the puppets of convention. Each of them has some color of individuality, and they share in a God's plenty of action, against a vivid setting. (p. 6)

Perhaps it is inevitable that where action is to the fore, characters lose in depth, but no one of the actors in "Paradise" is quite completely drawn. Bathsheba, for example, physically lovely and frankly seductive, never able to give herself wholly, married to one brother and the mistress of another without ever being really a lover for either, seems at any moment likely to become a rounded and defined character, but cheats the reader by going mad. . . . But the characters are fully enough drawn to make the action realizable, and far more fully drawn than the early New Englanders of most novels.

Possibly a severely scholarly historian might find details in which Miss Forbes errs, but apparently she has taken pains to build her action and setting on a careful study of Puritan life and the events of colonial history. Here and there she falls into the trap that yawns for the historical novelist and makes her characters talk a bastard tongue, neither of the seventeenth century nor of the twentieth. . . . What really matters, however, is that for the most part she writes of New England three centuries ago as though its men and women had passions as well as fears, positive impulses as well as repressions, as though they delighted in color, sound, sunshine, space, and the verities of flesh and the soil. Only the credulous can believe that the Massachusetts pioneers common in fiction and the more conventional histories ever existed, but there were pioneers and they were men and women. By realizing this simple truth Miss Forbes has managed to write a good story, and has breathed something of the life of reality into the bare facts of colonial adventurings. (pp. 6-7)

Kenneth B. Murdock, "Flesh and Blood Puritans," in The Saturday Review of Literature (copyright, 1937, by The Saturday Review Co., Inc.; reprinted with permission), February 27, 1937, pp. 6-7.

EDITH H. WALTON

Unlike so many historical novelists, who either overstress background or are content to use it as a pretty costume device, Miss Forbes has achieved a balance, an integration between character and environment which is responsible for the living quality of ["Paradise"]. Period color is not permitted to dwarf individuals, and the family of Jude Parre loom larger than their setting. What is more important, and certainly more rare, they act, feel, think like children of their age. As with Hawthorne, upon whose territory she is trespassing, Miss Forbes seems to feel in her bones the spiritual climate of Puritan New England. Her characters are less mystical and less austere, but on their own, more worldly plane they mirror as faithfully the temper of the times. . . .

Quoting the words of Miss Forbes . . . , I have called this novel a historical romance. Actually—and this is perhaps the highest tribute one can pay it—"Paradise" impresses one as realism rather than romance. Dramatic and glamorous as its story is, one has the most vivid convictions throughout that it is true to essential fact. These people, the Parres and their servants and their friends, are somehow believable and right. They act as such people must have acted; they are subject to the superstitions and compulsions of Puritanism and their times, yet one feels that those compulsions have not been duly exaggerated. Taking a vast deal of knowledge in her stride, Miss Forbes has written a book which seems to be entirely compelling. "Paradise," I think, is as fine a historical novel as any one could reasonably ask.

Edith H. Walton, "A Major Novel by Esther Forbes," in The New York Times Book Review (© 1937 by The New York Times Company; reprinted by permission), February 28, 1937, p. 2.

WILLIAM SOSKIN

New England is traditionally the home place of the American humanists, the American conscience troubled by its appetites, heckled by its morality, crucified by its intelligence. Its stern Puritan fathers have never successfully concealed the essential physical yearnings and the lusts which made begetting patriarchs of them and scandalous males, even as they erected their picket fences of respectable morality and visited Old Testament wrath upon unconventional sinners, witches and adulterers. . . .

[Rarely] has the conflict been so dramatically presented in terms of historical fiction as it is in Esther Forbes's novel of the early days of the Massachusetts Bay Colony, "Paradise." An accomplished artist in psychological fiction dealing with the eccentrics, witches, fanatics, romancers and other types characteristic of New England communities, Miss Forbes is an excellent historian as well, a student of detail of the type which has made Margaret Mitchell's "Gone With the Wind" historically unassailable and dramatically powerful. . . .

Fenton's sister, Jazan, is the most appealing woman in the story, a symbol of the sturdy, passionate, fine-grained

woman who had the patience to bear and the understanding to love [the] men of New England. With infinite pains and good imagination Miss Forbes reveals the drama of frustration in Jazan's marriage to the young preacher, Forethought Fearing, a man whose intense religious vision destroys natural passions. In Fearing, the brave idealist who stands up on the Common to defend Bathsheba and Christopher as Jesus defended an adulteress, but who cannot apply tolerance and understanding to the emotional needs of his own and Jazan's life, we have an excellent if not startlingly original portrayal of the New England dualist.

Miss Forbes has woven many romances, many strange tales of the Indians and their friendship and hatred for the white settlers, many glowing pictures of the farming community, many histories of marriages, births and deaths into this large tapestry. She has not been timid. She has taken her people into Boston and given us fresh, rich and pungent pictures of that town's early history. She has carried her story into the forests and the communities of the Indians, and she has capped it all with an amazingly real account of an Indian uprising which hurls all her characters into a maelstrom of death and savage blood-letting.

The book has none of the flavor of artificially synthesized historical fiction. It is deeply felt and built in terms of character magnificently realized. If at times the style seems jerky and erratic, at other times it is brilliant narrative that journeys inward to the secret recesses of the hearts of these New England pioneers, and outward to the astonishing courage of their physical exploits.

William Soskin, "Pagans among the Puritans," in New York Herald Tribune Book Review (© I.H.T. Corporation; reprinted by permission), March 7, 1937, p. 4.

WALTER D. EDMONDS

[Once in a great while] a book appears that so fuses history and the life of its protagonists that it makes a class of its own. In recent years I think of James Boyd's "Long Hunt" in this class, and now there is another one: Esther Forbes's new book, "The General's Lady."

To my way of thinking books like these express the essence of what historical writing should be. It is easy enough to snatch episodes out of history and string them on a heroic line, but it is hard for the reader to forget that he is reading history. That is what every reader should forget. His imagination should not be allowed to dwell in the past while he reads; the book should have its own inner present and future. Every one must have come across some author's sad attempt to create this "futurity" by putting copy prophecy into the mouth of a character, the stunned ox feels no happier.

"The General's Lady" ceases to be history within a very few pages of the start, and as it progresses with emotional inevitability to its conclusion, there is not a person involved that does not emerge in his own right as a living, breathing, feeling human being. History with its capital H makes no more difference to them than it does to the average person today as far as his emotional life is concerned; yet it is history that makes the pattern of actual events that produces their story, and it is their reaction to the pattern that makes the tragedy inevitable. . . .

The story is neither sordid nor heroic; [Morganna] cannot

rise to such heights any more than the rank and file of other human beings, and yet within her own limits her end has courage and pathos. Like other such endings it resolves the lives of the minor characters in tragedy and hope.

It is really these minor people (minor as they are related to her life) that make the book to me, at least, unusual. The girl Lavandar is excellently done; the loud, strong and sincere husband whom she does not understand until he dies, and her end is near, is a man of flesh and blood; his son, by his first marriage, is a really extraordinary character, the essence of New England strength and weakness. The minister, who is her friend and proves the instrument of her doom; the attorney general who brings her to justice; the Negro servant, are all drawn with a sure hand and an unfailing ability to get at their human inwardness.

I do not think a reader who once starts this book can lay it down. And I do not think that he, any more than I, will realize as he reads that he is living for the moment, in America at the end of the Revolution. That is the way history should be written.

> *Walter D. Edmonds, "A Noble Historical Novel," in* New York Herald Tribune Book Review *(© I.H.T. Corporation; reprinted by permission), October 2, 1938, p. 5.*

CARL VAN DOREN

Not every historical novelist can write a good biography, but the right kind of historical novelist has some of the qualities most needed in a good biographer. Esther Forbes is that kind of novelist, and her biography of Paul Revere ["Paul Revere and the World He Lived In"] takes at once a high and lasting place in American literature. Miss Forbes credits her mother, Harriette M. Forbes, with doing "most of the work on the original papers, court records, deeds, etc., newspapers, manuscript diaries, and letters": this is absolutely first-rate work. To Miss Forbes must go the credit for knowing how to make the richest use of so valuable a collaborator and how to turn these original documents into a fresh, creative record of men and times and actions that can never again seem remote or dim. . . .

The story of Revere's most memorable day has never been told so truly and so well as in this book. Though in certain necessary details Miss Forbes has to correct the legend as presented by Longfellow, her chief concern is to visualize the day's happenings, hour by hour, till the reader can feel he is also a spectator. (p. 1)

The Lexington episode, though so important in Revere's general reputation, makes up only about a tenth of his whole story as Miss Forbes tells it, reconstructing every chapter out of endless precise facts put together with affectionate and vivid art. Here is the finest account yet written of the career of any early American craftsman, expert in regard to the craft, sympathetic in regard to the man. . . .

Miss Forbes is no less informed and skillful in her account of political affairs during the last years of Thomas Hutchinson's governorship and the subsequent months leading up to armed conflict and revolution. Fair to both the conservative Hutchinson and the radical Samuel Adams, she is amused by John Hancock, the rich young man who chose the rebel side. She is fond of the gallant Joseph Warren, ironic about the treacherous Benjamin Church. But Revere, unspeculative, tireless, a man of action without malice or

resentments, is her hero, as he deserves to be. For this is a history of Boston during certain classic years, told fully for the first time from the point of view of plain men like Revere, who was chief among Boston's plain men, not a Harvard graduate or a clergyman or a lawyer or merchant or a landowner but an artisan—a mechanic, as Revere would have said. Told from this point of view, it gains not only in freshness but also in substance and reality.

In turning from fiction to biography, Miss Forbes has kept her novelist's eye for the visual image, the revealing trait, the outward evidences of customary life like food and clothing and furniture and houses and tools and vehicles and amusements. These, too, are history. But she has not failed to look behind them to the movements of opinion and crises of action which are history's more usual topics. Her special merit is her ability to combine the two arts without awkwardness or confusion. Her "Paul Revere" is a story told so absorbingly that many readers will stop to think, and few will care if they do stop and think whether this is a biography or a novel. What does it matter?

This is the exciting, convincing life of a human being. (p. 2)

> *Carl Van Doren, "Paul Revere, Mechanic, and His Moonlit Ride," in* New York Herald Tribune Book Review *(© I.H.T. Corporation; reprinted by permission), June 28, 1942, pp. 1-2.*

God did not make Paul Revere a very exciting person, and for all her skill and devotion Biographer Esther Forbes has not managed to do much better. But . . . [*Paul Revere & the World He Lived In*] is absorbing reading. Reason: Paul Revere lived so close to the center of the historical storm of Boston (colonial population about 15,000) which influenced world history ever since that the context makes him impressive.

Biographer Forbes . . . is a persistent rummager in regional attics. She sometimes dotes a little too much on research (even noting a change in the size of the armholes of the Governor of Massachusetts' coat). But her life of Paul Revere is: 1) a levelheaded account of Boston's part in the American Revolution; 2) an engaging slide lecture on colonial and early republican life in New England; 3) a lengthy portrait gallery of revolutionists like Samuel Adams and Joseph Warren, Tory Governor Thomas Hutchinson. (pp. 76, 78)

> *"Early American," in* Time *(reprinted by permission from* Time, The Weekly Newsmagazine; *copyright Time Inc. 1942), June 29, 1942, pp. 76, 78-9.*

BURKE BOYCE

Paul Revere has not left us many words. He was an artisan, not a philosopher; a creator, not a talker. But the words he has left are enough, in sympathetic hands, to bring him to life as he was, and he is solid, human, and refreshing.

Esther Forbes has done well by Paul Revere [in *Paul Revere and the World He Lived In*]—the actual Revere, a Boston workman of French descent, cool, canny, successful, the husband of two wives and the father of sixteen children, loving his home and the skill he wrought with his hands, a maker of silver, bells, ships' bottoms, and artificial teeth. The legendary Revere, he of the upraised arm and the rearing horse at the farmhouse door, succumbs with surprising ease. Miss Forbes does no debunking. She simply tells the truth, and the truth is more real in her retelling of it than any legend could be. Perhaps it is not suited so well to oratory and high-school declamations, but Paul Revere shrewdly picking out his route on the Sunday before his ride, Paul Revere forgetting his spurs, Billy Dawes falling off his horse at Lexington, and the forty-ish, family Paul Revere carrying his half of John Hancock's trunk around the corner of a house as the first shot snaps across the Lexington Green give the picture a nearness to us—and an understanding which the legend with its heroics never had.

The real Revere is more of a problem for Miss Forbes. "He seems," she says, "to have been a man of no spite, envy, or vindictiveness." And when she adds that there is something about this quality which is hard to dramatize, those of us who write can detect the wistfulness in her tone. If the real Revere does not at first glitter for us, or strike imaginative sparks, if some parts of his biography even verge toward the dull, that is his fault, not Miss Forbes's—and ours, who come at him with the legendary vision.

> *Burke Boyce, "A Messenger of Freedom," in The Atlantic Monthly (copyright © 1942 by The Atlantic Monthly Company, Boston Mass.; reprinted with permission), July, 1942, p. 98.*

JAMES TRUSLOW ADAMS

Revere has been one of the best known legendary heroes of our country, embedded in the customary errors of [Longfellow's poem]. As Esther Forbes . . . says, the legend was to swallow the actual man. It has been her task [in *Paul Revere and the World He Lived In*] to bring the real man to life, and to paint his portrait against the background of his times.

The original material for the purpose has apparently not been excessive, but it has been sufficient, and the author has evidently gone through it with care and discrimination. This is her first non-fiction book, but shows, like the five novels dealing with New England conditions which preceded this historio-biography, an extremely competent knowledge of the history of her section. . . . Esther Forbes wears her learning lightly, and in her easy style transmits to her readers some of the pleasure, and even fun, she has had in her work. . . .

There are two themes in this book. One is the life of Revere himself, and the other the daily life of New Englanders in the stormy pre-Revolutionary, Revolutionary, and post-Revolutionary periods which his life spanned. . . .

Miss Forbes tells us much about the real Revere, without, however, the slightest "debunking," for none is necessary. . . . Altogether, we get a very satisfactory picture of the man, his character, career, and his family and social relations, with no overdone hero worship.

In her other theme, the life of his times, Miss Forbes has been equally successful. In the broader political and military aspects there is little that is new. A good deal of it is rather antiquarian than historical, but it is so well done that one does get a new sense of what those days were like and what their problems were for our ancestors. There are many interesting glimpses down historical side-alleys, such as the pages on dentistry and bad teeth as compared with such matters among then contemporary Europeans. . . .

The only serious criticism I would have of the author's treatment of her background is her account of Shays's Rebellion, which I think, in view of the general scale on which topics are treated, is far too short and gives a somewhat false impression. During most of the Rebellion, which in itself, in spite of scant treatment here, was an important factor in creating the American Constitution, Bowdoin and not Hancock was governor of Massachusetts, Hancock having stepped aside until he could safely reap the glory of ending it.

However, I can heartily recommend the book as a whole as both enjoyable reading and sound history.

> *James Truslow Adams, "A New Paul Revere," in The Saturday Review of Literature (copyright, 1942, by The Saturday Review Co., Inc.; reprinted with permission), July 11, 1942, p. 7.*

MARGARET LEECH

Because [Miss Forbes] is a novelist, she is interested in character. British redcoats and Boston tories, James Otis and Sam Adams and John Hancock, are delineated sharply and judicially [in "Paul Revere and the World He Lived In"], with the novelist's eye for idiosyncrasy. The daily habit of life—business, political, domestic, and social—is admirably recreated. Miss Forbes occasionally permits herself the luxury of too much detail. It appears to be a fault of the novelist turned historian. Sometimes, when the available facts limit her scope, she overindulges in speculation on the probabilities. It does not, for example, increase our understanding of the Revere household in 1770 to have Miss Forbes muse that the eldest child, Deborah, aged twelve, was "a great help to her mother and grandmother, unless she was unusually backward." It merely raises a disagreeable and apparently unwarranted suspicion about Deborah.

But these are minor flaws in a book which, in the fidelity of its research and the wisdom of its presentation, makes an important contribution to American history. Miss Forbes has ably and graciously performed the task of setting hard facts against the fabric of a well-loved story. (p. 163)

> *Margaret Leech, "Legend and Hard Fact," in The Yale Review (© 1942 by Yale University; reprinted by permission of the editors), Autumn, 1942, pp. 161-63.*

ALLEN FRENCH

[*Paul Revere and the World He Lived In*] is a novelist's biography, but it is (thank Heaven!) not fictionized, nor yet (more thanks!) dramatized. But the historian's weighing of evidence, the giving of reasons for decisions, the noting of sources, are mostly lacking. (p. 521)

Even so, the facts were thoroughly assimilated, and the skill of the practised novelist makes for brisk movement and color. The double title of the book represents the two tasks which the author set herself. She has carried them out well. Under her hand old Boston becomes a personality. No one else has so mastered and shown the intricacies of relationship and neighborhood in the town of that day. Perhaps she over-emphasizes the mobbishness of Boston, particularly in the Andros case. After all, the leading men usually led. But the author brings to light many a forgotten person or neglected fact. The houses, crowded together and themselves crowded within, the narrow and crooked streets, the inquisitive people, instantly responding to any excitement or alarm—these have never been better pictured. . . . This is a perfect background for Revere himself, whom Miss Forbes rescues from the too poetic garb by which he is generally known. . . . Nor does Revere lose in the process: rather he gains. From a dimly seen legendary hero he becomes a man of solid worth, artist in his own right, responsible public man, inventive manufacturer, speaking to New England still from the tongues of his bells, and on his domestic side a considerate husband, father, and neighbor. Revere emerges as a hero of the sort needed today, a Yankee citizen whom we are lucky to have as a model. (p. 522)

> *Allen French, in* The New England Quarterly *(copyright 1942 by The New England Quarterly), September, 1942.*

ALICE M. JORDAN

The publication of *Johnny Tremain* gives young people an outstanding novel of Revolutionary days in Boston, and may well be counted a red-letter event in children's books. Esther Forbes has now preserved for young people's reading some of the very background of her *Paul Revere*, with its details of domestic life, its penetrating knowledge of colonial Boston, its perception of character, its artistry. . . . Johnny's personal story, however, holds absorbed attention throughout the book. Following an accident to his hand, which barred him from his loved trade, he rode for the patriotic newspaper, *Observer,* and as messenger for the Sons of Liberty. So he came in touch with the Whig leaders, with many of the Tories and the British Army officers. Sam Adams, James Otis, Dr. Warren, General Gage —they are alive and real as they have never been in a children's book. Quick-tongued Johnny is no prodigy, he plays no important rôle in memorable deeds, but he is a true, likable boy, growing up to manhood at sixteen, to understand, as many boys are understanding today, the meaning to all men of the Liberty for which they fight. (p. 413)

> *Alice M. Jordan, in* The Horn Book Magazine *(copyrighted, 1943, by The Horn Book, Inc., Boston), November, 1943.*

MARY GOULD DAVIS

If Jonathan Lyte Tremain never lived in the flesh, he lives vividly with the men of his time in [*Johnny Tremain*]. So we dare to put him among the people of importance. . . .

This story of Johnny Tremain is almost uncanny in its "aliveness." Esther Forbes's power to create, and to recreate, a face, a voice, a scene takes us as living spectators to the Boston Tea Party, to the Battles of Lexington and of North Creek. It takes us, with Johnny, to the secret meetings of the Sons of Liberty, to the secret training of the Minute Men. We hear and see Samuel Adams and John Hancock and Paul Revere. Over and over again, we share some little incident that makes those days in Boston as exciting and as vital as Washington and London and Moscow are today. . . . Always the people *live* as people do live under the pressure of great events. Johnny suffers and doubts, grouches and *grows*. (p. 44)

> *Mary Gould Davis, in* The Saturday Review of Literature *(copyright, 1943, by The Saturday Review Co., Inc.; reprinted with permission), November 13, 1943.*

ELLEN LEWIS BUELL

Only a master craftsman, and one who has worked so much

in the period that it has become a kind of second home in time, would dare to undertake that most familiar of themes —Boston at the outbreak of the war. Such a novelist is Esther Forbes and to ["Johnny Tremain"] she brings such freshness and vitality that one reads it with the avidity with which one follows today's news, with the extra dividend of pleasurable recognition of half forgotten episodes thrown in.

The reason, of course, is that Miss Forbes not only knows the wharves, the inns, the very cobblestones of eighteenth-century Boston about as intimately as her own back yard, but because she creates three dimensional people. Historical figures are clothed in flesh as well as good broadcloth, even casual street figures are endowed for the moment of their appearance with reality, and thus we see the temper of a city and a period. . . .

The proportion between [Johnny's] personal fortunes and the larger theme of the Revolution is so delicately balanced that never for a moment does one forget either. The one is part and parcel of the other, true test of the novelist's skill. Miss Forbes calls this a novel for young and old, and adults will read it for its richness of color, its wit and humor, its illumination of a noble period, but it would be unfair to compare it to her major novels, for basically, in scope and concept, it is a novel for the teen age, and as such the most distinguished one we have had in years.

> *Ellen Lewis Buell, "A Story of Boston and the Revolution," in* The New York Times Book Review *(© 1943 by The New York Times Company; reprinted by permission), November 14, 1943, p. 5.*

MAY LAMBERTON BECKER

The sub-title [of "Johnny Tremain"], "a novel for old or young," will serve if you bear in mind that the young will read for Johnny's sake and the old for the sake of Esther Forbes. Here is history treated with a realism that may be an eye-opener to boys' books. The Revolution goes through the story with a rush and scramble and in its surge men and boys alike are caught up. The inside of people's minds often has as much to do with the story as the outside layer of their actions. This is adult treatment but the establishment of Johnny's relationship to the Lytes has the curve of a juvenile plot. The book's chief value is that it brings back Boston and the road to Lexington in a year when boys of sixteen had to be adult. (p. 8)

> *May Lamberton Becker, in* New York Herald Tribune Book Review *(© I.H.T. Corporation; reprinted by permission), November 21, 1943.*

ALICE M. JORDAN

Johnny Tremain may well be counted the first classic story of Boston for young people. This is not alone because of the accurate picture of the pre-Revolutionary town, with its wandering streets and busy wharves, its crafts and trades, markets and merchants, nor because of the rich abundance of details about the manners of the period, its ways of living and customs of trade, nor even because it is an arresting portrayal of the stubborn resistance of the Patriots and townspeople against arbitrary acts of the British Parliament. It is a distinguished book, primarily, because the people in it are vigorously endowed with the human quality which binds one generation to another. (p. 270)

Alice M. Jordan, "Esther Forbes, Newbery Winner," in The Horn Book Magazine (copyrighted, 1944, by The Horn Book, Inc., Boston), July-August, 1944, pp. 268-70.

ELLERY SEDGWICK

["The Boston Book"] is a rarely delightful picture book. Here is the Boston Bostonians dream they live in, the Hurleyless, Curleyless, Tobinless Boston, where the Common is not littered with last night's newspapers, where the street cleaners do not wait for spring rains and the native Yankee has not fled to the suburbs. It is the Boston of hills and crooked streets, of Peter Faneuil and the Adamses. Boston down to Dr. Holmes, with only touches on the age of Koussevitzky, baseball and the atom. . . .

For a picture book Esther Forbes' text is informing and adequate, but stirs few recollections of the excellence of her "Paul Revere." With all her talent, she is—unfortunately—a peripheral Bostonian. But her outsider's feeling for us is sympathetic and friendly.

Ellery Sedgwick, "Dream of the Boston Brahmin," in New York Herald Tribune Book Review (© I.H.T. Corporation; reprinted by permission), September 7, 1947, p. 6.

EDWARD WEEKS

To her books Miss Forbes brings a deep and delving delight in the past, a feeling for the New England character by turns shrewd and romantic, and the pepper and salt of everyday living which she translates so accurately into another century.

The Running of the Tide is the story of Salem in the early 1800's when the ships bound out of the skimpy, silted harbor (no vessel larger than four hundred tons could get into it), in their trade with Russia, the West Indies, China, and India, were making it the wealthiest port in the world. (p. 98)

The Salem which Miss Forbes has painted for us is the Salem ashore, not afloat. . . . The feminine, the distaff side of the town is revealed in a hundred deft touches, and when the ships return and the men walk in we see them highlighted as it were against the emotion of homecoming or the passionate omen of departure. The color and essential masculinity of the town when the fleet is making ready have the touch of authenticity, but the chapters at sea and the snatches of seafaring talk as they come back to us from the parlors do not carry an equal force. . . . It is of men ashore and of women who wait that Miss Forbes writes—and that, after all, was essentially the Salem which was at last left high and dry. (p. 100)

Edward Weeks, "Salem and Her Ships," in The Atlantic Monthly (copyright © 1948 by The Atlantic Monthly Company, Boston, Mass.; reprinted with permission), October, 1948, pp. 98, 100.

CARL VAN DOREN

Most historical novels are nothing if they are not historical—and they are not historical. In particular, they have a way of finding in the past what the present assumes must have been there. In the ordinary historical novel a character visiting the Salem custom house about 1845 or thereabouts, and finding the surveyor of the port a youngish, shy man,

"handsome with his mane of heavy hair and the dark eyes, half-melancholy and half amused," would be certain to recognize Nathaniel Hawthorne and likely to have a premonition that the surveyor was even then writing a novel on some such theme as, say, adultery in early Massachusetts.

Esther Forbes is not an ordinary historical novelist. In "The Running of the Tide," the surveyor makes his momentary appearance in the final chapter without any mention of his actual name or future renown. This is true history. For Hawthorne was not regarded by Salem in 1845 or so as one of its most famous figures, which he not yet was, and the visitor would not have known him by sight or by such reputation as his short stories then had brought him. These are the facts of the case. To misrepresent them would be false history.

"The Running of the Tide" is remarkably free of such false history. Not that the book is slavish in its adherence to bare facts, Mrs. Forbes admits that the Inman with which her story is chiefly concerned has points in common with the Crowninshield family of the real Salem. . . . Such likenesses have no importance except as the actual brothers furnish various solid details of reality to the brothers Mrs. Forbes has imagined. She takes what she finds and needs, and uses it for her own purpose, which is to create a Salem family of ship captains and merchants in Salem's great days and afterwards. . . .

With what mastery Mrs. Forbes presents small things: the houses people live in, the clothes they wear, the food they eat, the swarming variety of men, women and children! There is the superb Mr. Africanus, a blind Negro in high hat and Hessian boots who is a pauper in the Charity House but who earned money by remembering things that people with eyes forgot. There is Linda, who dances in back alleys with a lighted candle on her head. There are the rowdy, bawdy characters of the docks, and the elegant young ladies of the fine houses that shipping built. It is a full bodied story, and full blooded. Life in this Salem does not run smooth, and it does not run cool. . . .

This is Salem, convincingly set forth, in a living panorama of fifty years: good history presented in good fiction. I know no chronicle of a New England town that is better than "The Running of the Tide," nor any Salem novel to be compared with it since Hawthorne.

Carl Van Doren, "The Life and Death of a New England Town," in New York Herald Tribune Book Review (© I.H.T. Corporation; reprinted by permission), October 3, 1948, p. 5.

ALEXANDER LAING

The historical novel, latterly, has come to depend more and more upon the old picaresque formula which had, in its origins, nothing in particular to do with history. As if plotted upon a sine wave, the story must soar to a lush bit of four-poster ecstasy every fifteen pages, and plummet in the interstices into violence and cruelty. It is therefore something of a relief to come upon a tale [such as The Running of the Tide] which does not rely upon such gaudy devices at all. Miss Forbes approaches her task and material respectfully. The faults of her novel, in so far as it is faulty, are those of too laborious an attention to details. (p. 15)

The publishers, . . . to quote the dust wrapper, call it "a titanic struggle of conscience rarely equaled in American fiction.'' Given the circumstances, it could be such a conflict, but it is not. On the level of plot, the people and circumstances are rather more exasperating than piteous and terrible. The background is vivid, true, and convincing—if we allow for the historical novelist's almost inevitable quota of minor slips. The ethical problem is well stated, and inevitably worked out. The trouble is with the people. They are not unlike the personalities that lurk behind the letters printed in such old journals as Miss Forbes has drawn upon for much of her material. We think: ''This is a real statement, from a real person, deeply concerned over a real problem.'' And yet it requires a separate act of the imagination to cut back through time and space into this real person's consciousness. It is because, in nearly every such case, the writer was not a creative artist.

A multitude of *things,* however true and orderly, may stand between us and the fact of character. In this story, they do. Miss Forbes uses a hundred pages to get the *Victrix* off to sea on her first voyage. All of these pages are good reading, but it is only at this late point that the nature of the moral conflict even begins to be revealed. The dramatic crises, thereafter, are almost muted. Frequently the action slides the circumstance. The stuff of a first-rate scene is foreshadowed. Then it is handled in reminiscence. So far as characters in immediate activity are concerned, it has never occurred at all. . . .

No, this is Salem's book, from first to last. The fact remains that most of it is good reading, even if there is much too much of it at all points except the dramatic climaxes. Many of the minor characters are excellently conceived and drawn. The smell, the mood, the color of the town are always convincing. . . .

Miss Forbes writes much more understandably of women than of men, and rather better about dogs than about human beings of either persuasion. But the true heroine of her book is a town and its personality. Some of the most loving writers about Salem have been the least endearing. It has become something of a tradition for hardshell reactionaries to hold up this particular accident of time, place, and circumstance as an example of what the whole country might still be, if no central government had ever meddled with it. Miss Forbes skirts this temptation with good humor and grace, admitting that her Inmans are not Jeffersonians, and letting the picture, as she has drawn it, point its own morals. It is too bad, I think, that she did not content herself with the task of writing the biography of Salem, rather than the insufficiently realized tragedy of the Inmans and the two women, aristocrat and peasant, whose lives they complicated into a tragedy that dwindles away in the telling. (p. 16)

> *Alexander Laing, ''Salem's Aristotles and Magpies,'' in* The Saturday Review of Literature *(copyright, 1948, by The Saturday Review Co., Inc.; reprinted with permission), October 9, 1948, pp. 15-16.*

DIANA TRILLING

''The Running of the Tide'' is so clearly a pot-boiler—and this despite Miss Forbes's reputation as a historian—that it really should not be reviewed at all in a serious magazine. In fact, I had already set it aside, when I saw it written about on the front page of the New York *Times Book Review* as if it were a major artistic achievement. While it may

not be entirely fair to submit an author to harsh judgment in one periodical just because she was unduly praised in another, I think it would be even less fair to allow the readers of this magazine to discover the disappointment of Miss Forbes's novel for themselves. Actually Miss Forbes's story of the seafarers of Salem has but a single thing to recommend it—its presumable historical accuracy. For the rest it is a tedious romance aimed at the movies, as remote as it could be from the important experience it was called by the newspaper which is the chief molder of literary opinion in this country. (p. 500)

> *Diana Trilling, in* The Nation *(copyright 1948 by the Nation Associates, Inc.), October 30, 1948.*

JAMES THOMAS FLEXNER

The mood of Esther Forbes's charming novel ''Rainbow on the Road'' is that of a sunlit summer day, variegated with thunderstorms which pass quickly, leaving behind them an even brighter landscape. . . .

Mrs. Forbes uses not sex—there never was a purer book—or dagger to lure the reader from page to page, but relies on a skill which most modern historical novelists seem to regard as secondary, on literary style, on the ability to evoke the wonders of everyday living. In brilliant passages, so simple that their artistry is never obvious, she reveals a clear morning, the strange personality of a ballad-singer walking the highways, all the luxuriant human life that pours out upon a traveler who knocks on many doors.

In other novels Mrs. Forbes has most effectively dipped her brush in somber hues, but this novel is so lyrical, so gay that when she uses darker notes for more than contrast they seem slightly out of key. The book does have a plot in the conventional sense—Jude Rebaugh is mistaken for a Robin-Hoodlike bandit who turns into a murderer—but all this seems an afterthought; the plot does not make a real appearance until we are halfway through her delightful pages. Although in themselves extremely well done, the scenes of violence necessitated by the plot—they are few—break the mood.

Mrs. Forbes . . . never forgets the difference between historical fiction and history. She pulls no actual characters in by the hair; she gives us no classroom lectures, but uses her vast erudition as food for her imagination. She treats the past no differently from the way other skilful novelists treat the times in which they themselves lived. . . .

''Rainbow on the Road'' will long be read and cherished not because of the facts it contains, but because of its imaginative power.

> *James Thomas Flexner, ''New England Traveler,'' in* The Saturday Review *(Entire issue copyright 1954 by Saturday Review Associates, Inc.; reprinted with permission), January 30, 1954, p. 19.*

HENRY COMMAGER

Miss Forbes is in love with New England, and [''Rainbow on the Road''] is her confession and her declaration. It is, to be sure, about New England of a century ago, but much of it is familiar, both the appearance and the character. This view of New England is a welcome change from current fashion—early autumns or desire under the elms or last puritans or George Apleys—and it is a long time since we have had a book that delighted in the granite ledges and the noisy brooks and the little white villages and the flavor of the villages. . . .

"Rainbow on the Road" is a picaresque novel. As with most picaresque novels, the story itself is not very important. . . .

Ruby Lambkin comes to dominate the book, though not wholly. If Miss Forbes owes little to Freud, she owes much to Hawthorne, and this is a sort of picaresque Marble Farm situation. Everywhere Jude goes he hears tell of Ruby Lambkin:

> Ruby Lambkin is my name
> In breaking jails I've won my fame
> I give to poor and steal from rich
> No law of man's can hold me.

There were many other verses, as many as there were adventures, real or imagined. He was (so at least Jude thought), a sort of Robin Hood; he represented much that Jude himself wished to be and to have—freedom and adventure and love and sense of power. Jude looked like the famed Ruby, and soon he was identifying himself with Ruby. At first it was something of a joke. . . . In time it came to be an obsession. . . .

This sounds like a bit of heavy weather, but it is not. What is memorable about "Rainbow on the Road" is the humor and the good humor, the high spirits, the sense of the richness of life and the beauty of the land. There are stories that are inevitably destined for a hundred anthologies. . . . There is a whole gallery of characters, Jude's wife Mitty, so firm and angular and righteous; the relatives who would never invite Jude in until they were sure he had brought along a ham; the assorted squires and tavern keepers and peddlers and Shakers and sheriffs and teachers—many of whom can be met in New Hampshire or Vermont today. And there is, on every page, that almost sensuous feeling for the countryside, for the birch trees and the willow trees and the willows and the elms, for the changing skies and the changing seasons.

> *Henry Commager, "A Picaresque Tale Laid Among New England's Hills and Streams," in* New York Herald Tribune Book Review (© *I.H.T. Corporation; reprinted by permission), January 31, 1954, p. 3.*

FRANCES GAITHER

["Rainbow on the Road"] concerns an itinerant painter who found his craft so little humdrum, so zestful in daily practice, that, although he could and did earn his every casual supper, he was never in the least averse to singing for it, too. He does so in a taproom largesse of tales, true and fabricated, rendered in a manner to enliven anybody but some old tract-reading deacon or surly band of pig drovers. For he was by disposition a kind of traveling harlequin—and is as easy and entertaining company as a novel reader could hope to encounter. (p. 5)

The narrative style [of the book] is artless, intensely objective, focusing one's attention as immediately as those small household wonders that used to be handed to children to play with: a prism fallen from a chandelier, perhaps, with a whole spectrum in its insides, or a domed glass paperweight, wherein the lightest touch could set a "real" snowstorm flying about a needle-sharp church spire and red village roofs.

Actually, the story gets off to a slow start. But the grownup reader, like the boy observer, cherishes the smallest item in the winter's preparations. . . . (pp. 5, 18)

The country [the boy and the painter] traveled through resounded with the exploits, real and imputed, of a footloose bandit then operating along the Connecticut River. . . .

Now, as any reader acquainted with this author's earlier work knows, Miss Forbes needs no more than a slight weakness in a protagonist and a strand or so of innuendo afloat in an atmosphere of provincial alarm to stitch together a plot as dainty—and as treacherous—as a spider web. She knows the occult implications of the simplest fact. For she, like this Jude and the shifting, irresponsible crowds his personality drew about him at every stop, stems, too, from a folk who, ordinarily acting, and even thinking of themselves, as plain God-fearing people could believe in witches and warlocks enough to hang them.

Although Phineas Sharp, by virtue of his calling and his mischievous imagination, is as necessary to the dramatic action of this novel as the blind man who brought the black spot to that of "Treasure Island," he often seems—to one reader at least—out of character in his self-assumed role of wayside philosopher. One's attention, accommodated so comfortably to Eddy's double-lensed boy-and-man viewpoint, is annoyingly distracted by Mr. Sharp's between-act warblings of such a song as "How Far Is Far Away?"—with sententious asides thrown in for good measure. And when he dares to take "Illusion" as his text for preachment, poking his platitudes right through the gossamer veil itself, he seems as much out of place as people who talk aloud at a concert.

Every other participant in this light fantasy, however, acts as if "from nature". . . . (p. 18)

> *Frances Gaither, "The Itinerant Painter," in* The New York Times Book Review (© *1954 by The New York Times Company; reprinted by permission), January 31, 1954, pp. 5, 18.*

CAROLYN HOROVITZ

It should be no surprise, if *Johnny Tremain*, by Esther Forbes, finds its way into the upper "rare" stratosphere of literary excellence. Lauded ever since it first appeared, it continues to be read and regarded as a fine historical novel. It is a book much praised, but it has not, as far as I know, been critically examined. (p. 139)

Basically, the story is one of character development, of a boy's struggle with his feelings of inferiority and worth, his attempts to find a place for himself, his problems about establishing relationships with people. It is almost as if he were a symbol of his time: a boy with promise and great natural ability but shackled by a sense of shame and inferiority. Aside from these symbolic values, this boy has the character and attitude of his own time, when men and boys were expected to make their own way. . . . He is not described as showing these traits and qualities of the times; he actively displays them. Although he is a boy of all ages in his teasing and carefully guarded tender feelings, he is a boy of *his* time. In our day and age, such a boy would be sent to juvenile hall.

But in those days, Johnny was needed and soon came to be valued for his courage, just as he came to find values for which to fight and by which to live. In a time of growing, the boy grew in answer to needs greater than his own. The answer to the question, ''why *time?*'', is apparent in this novel. This boy is of the time, bred, illuminated, and developed. Although presented in far greater precision than a symbol, he does have symbolic value.

Place comes alive sensuously with the first sentence, the first paragraph. . . . Miss Forbes brings Boston awake at the same time that the reader plunges into a sense of place —smelling, breathing, hearing, seeing. The novel has base in this way, from start to finish; never is skillful use of place merely a garnish or a layer in a sandwich. Speech and clothes and manner of behavior are all of a piece, but not an undifferentiated piece. (pp. 139-40)

This book does not merely deal with another time and place; it is impregnated with these elements. And the hero, in working out his destiny, is under the same inevitable compulsion that people in the past have always appeared to feel. There was no other way. Yet, during the telling, as during the actual happening, nothing seemed certain, nothing seemed inevitable. . . . There is a sense of the meaning of life, of creed and ethics, of human behavior. . . . Paul Revere's heroism was accepted casually with believability, credibility, coming through the illumination of small detail. One instance is the description of Revere's ride to Portsmouth, before his famous ride. The weather was bad that night:

> From the lowering December sky handfuls of snowflakes were falling, but as soon as they came to earth they turned to ice. It was a bleak, bad, dangerous day for the long ride north.

Revere's wife was in bed, recovering from having borne another child. She rapped on a windowpane at Johnny to come and get a note her husband had almost forgotten, a note about his sick grandmother with which to allay the suspicions of the British soldiers.

In this way, Esther Forbes brings about what Hilaire Belloc [in *One Thing and Another*] calls ''the resurrection of the past'' by the use of sudden illumination, proportion, and imagination:

> . . . upon the discovery of the essential movements and the essential moments in the action; and upon imagination, the power of seeing the thing as it was; landscape, the weather, the gestures and the faces of the men; yes, and their thoughts within.

Wonderful as Miss Forbes' work is, it is not a work which can be neatly pigeonholed as ''suitable for children.'' It is ''suitable'' for anyone who wishes to read a good story of this period. The excitement of the times is used to its fullest extent in building plot interest; the boy's involvement in the Revolution is so intrinsic a part of the plot that reading about Johnny Tremain becomes reading about the American Revolution. If any book can be called a prototype of all that historical fiction should be, this book merits that appellation. (pp. 140-42)

> *Carolyn Horovitz, ''Dimensions in Time: A Critical View of Historical Fiction for Children'' (originally published in* The Horn Book Magazine, *June, 1962), in* Horn Book Reflections: On Children's Books and Reading, *edited by Elinor Whitney Field (copyright © 1969 by The Horn Book, Inc., Boston),* Horn Book, *1969, pp. 137-50.*

MARGERY FISHER

[*Johnny Tremain*] was first published in the United States in 1943 and is now accepted as a classic in both our countries. [Fisher is a British critic.] It deserves the title because the author has so skilfully related personal and national issues, but far more because in Johnny she has created a very real person, a boy whose faults are first his undoing and then his salvation. To see a self-satisfied boy become a man, under stress, is just as exciting as it is to read of how the ideal of freedom was fought for and died for. Beyond the fascination of technical and period detail, and the easy narration, there is in this historical novel a depth of compassion and a lively intelligence that makes it essential and acceptable reading for all young people.

> *Margery Fisher, ''An Old Favourite,'' in her* Growing Point, *May, 1965, p. 516.*

JOHN ROWE TOWNSEND

[*Johnny Tremain* has an] inspirational note: 'We fight, we die, for a simple thing. Only that a man can stand up.' . . . [It] is a true historical novel, concerned with actual historical events; and it seems to me (though not for this reason) that it has true classic quality. I have the impression that the author may even have known she was writing a classic; for *Johnny Tremain* has an air of absolute sureness and solidity; like one of its redoubtable New Englanders it knows where it is going and knows it will be treated with respect. (pp. 181-82)

A feature of the book is its strong pictorial quality. The best set pieces not merely are colourful but have a powerful sense of historical occasion, as in the description of the 'great scarlet dragon' of the British brigade, seen first with its head resting on Boston Common, and later marching off on its thousands of feet. The book's main fault is a slight lack of cohesion between its two components: the personal story of Johnny, the smart apprentice whose expectations are dashed by injury, and the broad general subject of the rebellion. The first few chapters might be the start of quite a different kind of book. But the strengths far outweigh this weakness. And there is a fine sense of fair play in the recognition that men of all persuasions are good, bad and indifferent; in the willing acknowledgement that the crowds who sullenly watch the scarlet dragon are all Englishmen, fighting for English liberty. (p. 182)

> *John Rowe Townsend, in his* Written for Children: An Outline of English-Language Children's Literature *(copyright © 1965, 1974 by John Rowe Townsend; reprinted by permission of J. B. Lippincott Company; in Canada by Kestrel Books), revised edition, Lippincott, 1974.*

DOROTHY H. NELSON

[*Johnny Tremain*] is a natural for the Bicentennial year.

Students can identify with Johnny, for his was the arrogance of today. He plunged heart and soul into the rebellious spirit of his time. His quick temper and his cocksure air (for he *was* a clever boy) make him so human and alive that Johnny carries with him whole classrooms of youngsters who learn to feel and to experience that Spirit of '76. No other book about early America can cast the spell that *Johnny Tremain* does. . . . The thrill, the justice of the Revolutionary War, as felt by those early New Englanders, exudes from these absorbing pages. A sense of pride in the

American cause shines through, as Johnny and his brave, inspiring friend, Rab, prepare to meet the enemy.

Probably it is the drama of James Otis which strikes the ultimate chord, as he talks with and to the Sons of Liberty. . . .

In this day of sagging patriotism, America's two-hundredth anniversary offers a chance to rekindle the spirits of our young Americans. An indepth study of *Johnny Tremain* will reveal that it's not all speeches and flag waving. The romance of childhood sweethearts, the pathos of a crippling injury, the violence of a tar and feathering, the shock of the firing squad, the humor of a feather-bed disguise, the delight of the silversmith's perfection—they're all there in this Colonial epic to be lived through vicariously by the reader. Esther Forbes' masterpiece contains all the inspiration of the early American patriots. It's a Bicentennial MUST.

> *Dorothy H. Nelson, "'Johnny Tremain'—A Bicentennial Natural!" in* Language Arts *(copyright © 1976 by the National Council of Teachers of English), January, 1976, p. 45.*

CHRISTOPHER COLLIER

Johnny Tremain, with its message of ideologically moti-

vated war, is so much the product of World War II that one who grew up in the 1940's must honor its clear one-sidedness. Younger historians, products of the 1960's who are currently busy reviving the Progressive interpretation of a generation ago, would be less tolerant. But without denying its outstanding literary merit, Miss Forbes' presentation of the American Revolution does not pass muster as serious, professional history. Not so much because it is so sharply biased, but because it is so simplistic. Life is not like that—and we may be sure it was not like that two hundred years ago. Such an event as a war involving the three major European nations, with implications for the western power structure for centuries to come, is bound to be a complex matter. To present history in simple, one-sided—almost moralistic—terms, is to teach nothing worth learning and to falsify the past in a way that provides worse than no help in understanding the present or in meeting the future. (p. 240)

> *Christopher Collier, "Johnny and Sam: Old and New Approaches to the American Revolution" originally published in* The Horn Book Magazine, *April, 1976), in* Crosscurrents of Criticism: Horn Book Essays 1968-1977, *edited by Paul Heins (copyright © 1977 by The Horn Book, Inc., Boston), Horn Book, 1977, pp. 234-40.*

Babbis Friis-Baastad

1921-1970

(Has also written under the names Eleanor Babbis and Babbis Friis) Norwegian young adult novelist. Like many young adult and children's authors, Friis-Baastad began her literary career by telling and writing stories for her own children. Her audience gradually widened and she eventually found herself contributing on a regular basis to children's radio broadcasts in the 1950s. Her best known books, *Kristy's Courage* and *Don't Take Teddy*, are unsentimental treatments of young adults coping with mental and physical handicaps. Friis-Baastad became interested in this topic through her acquaintance with a handicapped child. Her interest in this field grew as she began an intensive study to gain background for her fiction and culminated in the publication of *Du ma vakne Tor*, which translates as "Wake up, Tor," and was written for an audience of mentally handicapped young adults. This book was quite controversial in Scandinavia, with some critics feeling that the text was too complex for its audience. (See also *Contemporary Authors*, Vols. 17-20, rev. ed., and *Something about the Author*, Vol. 7.)

When seven year old Kristy wakes up in the hospital after having been hit by a car, she does not realize how deformed she will seem to the outside world. It is only after she goes, in typical excitement, to her first day at a new school that Kristy, taunted and stared at by the other children, begins to think of her facial scar as ugly. . . . The author [of *Kristy's Courage*] has a rare gift for conveying a child's sensitivity in a way other children will be able to understand. There are moments of real humor and tenderness and (most unusual) snatches of very real sounding adult conversation, the sort every child overhears. . . . [This] is a realistic treatment of a situation some children experience and it is movingly told. (p. 678)

Virginia Kirkus' Service, *July 15, 1965*.

ANNE IZARD

[*Kristy's Courage*] is a realistic story of the thoughtless cruelty that can make tragedy for children. Kristy learns not to run away but to face life. Her story will hold all children and make them think. (p. 5076)

Anne Izard, in Library Journal (*reprinted from* Library Journal, *November 15, 1965; published by R. R. Bowker Co. (a Xerox company); copyright © 1965 by Xerox Corporation*), November 15, 1965.

MARGARET BERKVIST

Probing the subject [of youngsters adjusting to physical disabilities] with complete honesty and a lack of sentimentality, the Norwegian author Babbis Friis begins ["Kristy's Courage"] as Kristy is recovering consciousness following an automobile accident. Though time will mend the child's injuries, for the present she must live with a scarred face and distorted speech. . . . Miss Friis's readers will appreciate her understanding of how cruel the world can be to children on occasion. (p. 26)

Margaret Berkvist, in The New York Times Book Review (© *by The New York Times Company; reprinted by permission*), December 12, 1965.

Kersti is a young girl who is involved in a car accident. As a result she is left with a horrible scar on her cheek which turns up one side of her mouth into a permanent smile. This story tells of the troubles she has in coming to terms with her scar and the way her friends and school-fellows react. [*Kersti*, published in the United States as *Kristy's Courage*,] is quoted as being "a study in child psychology for girls interested in teaching and nursing." This is rather a narrow field but it is a fairly accurate description of the type of readership who will enjoy it. The book is too adult in its approach for the younger reader, and the main character is too young for the older reader. It is a well-written, deep-thinking book but can hardly be called intriguing fiction, or even a fascinating story. (pp. 179-80)

The Junior Bookshelf, *April, 1966*.

"What we'd always dreaded at home . . . had happened at last. Teddy had done something really wrong. He'd harmed someone." And afraid that his mentally defective older brother will be taken away by the police, thirteen-year-old Mikkel takes Teddy himself and runs away. . . . [The story of their traumatic flight is told by Mikkel in *Don't Take Teddy*] in an interior monologue of such affectiveness and mounting intensity that the reader is left limp. The denouement is a sensible solution but an emotional manipulation: to the horror of Mikkel who thinks his brother is being abandoned, Teddy is entered in a school for mental defectives—but it is revealed suddenly that he will be a day student living at home, and talk turns to ways of helping mental defectives generally. As she demonstrated in *Kristy's Courage* . . . , Mrs. Friis-Baastad has unusual skill in depicting subtle appreciation of the qualities of a mental defective and his importance to his family. This needs introduction but it will be remembered. (p. 137)

> Kirkus Service *(copyright © 1967 Virginia Kirkus' Service, Inc.), February 1, 1967.*

ZENA SUTHERLAND

[*Don't Take Teddy*] is quite a remarkable book, because the author teaches a lesson without preaching. In Mikkel's love for his brother there is a realistic embarrassment but no shame; there is a realistic range of reactions from people he meets, and a realistic acceptance of the limits of the educability of the retarded. The book is a plea for understanding, but the plea is not made directly by the author; by having the story told by Mikkel, the communication is more direct and most touching. (p. 100)

> *Zena Sutherland, in* Saturday Review *(© 1967 by Saturday Review Inc.; reprinted with permission), April 22, 1967.*

MARGARET A. DORSEY

Mikkel's first-person account [in *Don't Take Teddy*] communicates the tension and the strain of a very real boy over-reacting to a responsibility he's too young to cope with or fully understand. Although his series of problems tend toward repetitive similarity, the book is an active adventure novel, not at all obscured by its message, one that can reach any reader who may ever undertake the care of a more helpless being. (p. 56)

> *Margaret A. Dorsey, in* School Library Journal *(reprinted from the May, 1967 issue of* School Library Journal, *published by R. R. Bowker Co. A Xerox Corporation; copyright © 1967), May, 1967.*

GRETA WALKER

Mrs. Friis-Baastad presents [in "Don't Take Teddy"], with commendable directness, the wrenching problems of the family with a retarded child. Teddy, with a mental age of 2½, has been lovingly protected by his parents and younger brother from the hostility and ridicule of outsiders. In the end a nurse specializing in retardation, whom the runaways meet on their journey, convinces the family that Teddy can be helped to find his own strengths—not by being shielded and kept at home, but by going to special schools that will develop, as much as possible, his mind and muscles. Although the plot is forced, the author does contribute to understanding in a neglected area. (p. 30)

> *Greta Walker, in* The New York Times Book Review *(© 1967 by The New York Times Company; reprinted by permission), May 21, 1967.*

Svein's burning but abstract desire for a "super horse" [in *Wanted! A Horse!*] involves him in a series of down to earth challenges. . . . Svein's impressionistically internalized emotions and the warmly diffused imagery of a Nor-

wegian Christmas nurture a fragile atmosphere of growth, though sometimes threatened by uncertainties of tone and awkward syntax. It's more of a reverie about the changes people go through than a vicariously satisfying daydream about horses—likely to frustrate those searching for equine adventure, but to please readers who can follow the gently meandering prose through Svein's successive hopes and disappointments. (pp. 1256-57)

> Kirkus Reviews *(copyright © 1971 The Kirkus Service, Inc.), December 1, 1971.*

ZENA SUTHERLAND

While [*Wanted! A Horse!*] doesn't have the strong story line or the dramatic impact of the author's *Don't Take Teddy!* it has the same sympathetic, no-nonsense understanding of children and a smooth writing style, and it is particularly sensitive to the relationships with a family and the effect that home situations and external relationships have upon each other. (p. 122)

> *Zena Sutherland, in* Bulletin of the Center for Children's Books *(© 1972 by the University of Chicago; all rights reserved), April, 1972.*

ZENA SUTHERLAND

Twelve-year-old Svein is disappointed at not getting the horse he'd hoped to receive as a birthday present. But he cheers up when he hears he can take riding lessons at a reduced rate in return for working in the stables. Save for the malicious behavior of another boy and Svein's friendship with two sisters, [*Wanted! A Horse!*] has little plot. It is, however, filled with incidents that have action and appeal. Svein's family relationships, and the problems the two sisters face in adjusting to their parents' recent divorce and to a new home are described with considerable realism and commendable restraint. (p. 84)

> *Zena Sutherland, in* Saturday Review *(© 1972 Saturday Review Inc.; reprinted with permission), April 22, 1972.*

ROSE S. BENDER

Despite the title [*Wanted! A Horse!*], horse enthusiasts will not find much to satisfy them in this muddled story. Friis has woven together the standard strands: silly, non-understanding parents; two young girls whose family has been broken by divorce and whose relationship to the hero, Svein, is both nebulous and contrived; and some sophisticated and unmotivated teenagers, including one whose behavior is meant to be an example of modern destructiveness. . . . Even the addition of a touch of mystery fails to produce the desired suspense, and the denouement is slow, unclear and boring. (p. 2960)

> *Rose S. Bender, in* Library Journal *(reprinted from* Library Journal, *September 15, 1972; published by R. R. Bowker Co. (a Xerox company); copyright © 1972 by Xerox Corporation), September 15, 1972.*

Leon Garfield

1921-

British novelist, short story writer, and nonfiction writer. Garfield has used the content and background of English history in his works to create an interpretation both modern and unique. Operating out of the tradition of writers such as Henry Fielding, Jane Austen, Charles Dickens, and Robert Louis Stevenson, he has brought an original viewpoint and style to such established literary forms as the adventure novel and picaresque romance. Many of his works are novels of experience which employ a journey motif, often describing the involvement of a young homeless or rootless hero with characters and situations that lead him to an understanding of his true identity. He will often provide twists in narrative and characterization to show both hero and reader the deceptiveness of appearances, especially as they relate to good and evil. Garfield's heroes uniformly search for values that are solid and permanent, and his fiction has been said to reflect his own similar concerns and desires. He had an unsettled childhood, with a neurotic mother and an irresponsible father whom he has compared to the character of Mr. Treet in *Devil-in-the-Fog*. Garfield originally wanted to become an artist, but World War II interrupted his studies. Following the war, he worked for twenty years as a biochemical technician in a London hospital, and wrote in his spare time. Both art and chemistry have influenced Garfield's style, since he has a painter's eye for composition and detail, and a scientist's predilection for research, detail, and fact. Although the times and events he describes are only occasionally particularized, such as the French Revolution in *The Prisoners of September,* he makes them appear believable and authentic, and presents attitudes to such subjects as mental illness without overemphasis or sentimentality. Garfield has been criticized for concentrating on atmosphere over plot and for being too wordy, melodramatic, and hard to read. Some critics also feel that he tries too hard to be allusive and symbolic. The modern reinterpretations of Greek myths which Garfield wrote with Edward Blishen have especially been criticized for their loftiness, and for losing the significance of the myths in the psychological theorizing of the authors. However, he is often considered among those contemporary writers who are headed towards classic status, and whose works are closing the gap between literature for adults and the young. *Devil-in-the-Fog* was the winner of the first Guardian Award for children's fiction in 1967, and *The God Beneath the Sea* was awarded the 1971 Carnegie Medal. (See also *Contemporary Authors*, Vols. 17-20, rev. ed., and *Something about the Author*, Vol. 1.)

[*Jack Holborn*] is not easy reading, for the plot is involved, and there are slight lacunae in its unfolding, as if the book had been cut and certain connecting links lost. Yet the brilliantly written episodes, of which the appearances of mad Taplow's "ghost" are among the most graphic, remain in one's mind, alight with promise for Mr. Garfield's future. . . .

A book for rather older children, it requires some patience, even rereading in places, for the author does not always treat his plot expertly. He seems unable to control his main themes through the tortuous paths of shipwreck, slavery and mistaken identity. A firmer editorial hand might have clarified the issues. Nonetheless, a vividly painted rogue's gallery and a robust style that owes something to [Tobias] Smollett—a statement intended as a compliment—make Mr. Garfield an author worth watching. (p. 1072)

The Times Literary Supplement (© *Times Newspapers Ltd. (London) 1964; reproduced from* The Times Literary Supplement *by permission), November 26, 1964.*

There is more action to the square page in [*Jack Holborn*] than can be adequately condensed. . . . [Leon Garfield] writes well and uses a myriad of absorbing detail to make you see, hear and smell the disparate sections of 18th century London and the world. The cast of characters is enormous of course, but the dialogue is so well done that each of the many voices emerges as a distinct personality, partly through the descriptions of Jack Holborn, the young narrator, and partly through their own choices of revealing words and identifying phrases. (Jack has the master gossip's great ear for reporting whole conversations.) The book is proof positive that all good stories deserve re-telling, because in lesser hands, each of the amazing dramatic turns Jack's story takes would be just a series of thundering cliches. . . . It's done with such terrific good nature and flair that you begin by liking Jack, whose instincts are good, and wind up enjoying the whole teeming book. (p. 1082)

Virginia Kirkus' Service (*copyright © 1965 Virginia Kirkus' Service, Inc.), October 15, 1965.*

MARGARET SHERWOOD LIBBY

Jack Holborn [is] a taut, tough and exciting story, complicated but so well-told that it held me to the last page. The old cliches [about pirate tales] are given fresh turns, and the spectacular additions to the formula include a desperate trek through an African wilderness, a tense slave-market auction and a London trial in which the prisoner claims a place on the judge's bench. . . .

[Jack Holborn] plays a more effective part in the story than most young pirate victims, and the ups and downs of his fortunes provide as good an incursion into the world of derring-do as any older boy would wish while many a younger one . . . will find this his dish. (p. 42)

> *Margaret Sherwood Libby, in* Book Week—The Sunday Herald Tribune *(© I.H.T. Corporation; reprinted by permission), October 31, 1965.*

GEOFFREY TREASE

Devil-in-the-Fog is 18th-century—not history, but luscious melodrama, complete with wicked baronet, missing heir, convenient recognition scar, the lot. And much more than the usual lot, because Mr Garfield has humour too and ingenuity in mixing old ingredients to produce something fresh. This is first-person narrative, with showers of exclamation-marks, a proliferation of parentheses, and enough lines of dots to demarcate the parish boundaries on an ordnance map. But the warmth and gusto are genuine enough, the characters swagger, the drama is riveting. (p. 708)

> *Geoffrey Trease, in* New Statesman *(© 1966 The Statesman & Nation Publishing Co. Ltd.), November 11, 1966.*

JEAN C. THOMSON

If readers of Stevenson delighted in "Jack Holborn," Garfield's first book, "Devil-in-the-Fog" will suit devotees of Dickens. Such comparisons are only approximate, for this author's inventions are original, and his tempo is modern. He writes with such dazzling ease that all else falls effortlessly into place, and his artistry is more satisfying than any conjurer's—begging Mr. Treet's pardon. (p. 55)

> *Jean C. Thomson, in* The New York Times Book Review *(© 1966 by The New York Times Company; reprinted by permission), November 20, 1966.*

Devil-in-the-Fog [is] doubly disappointing after the author's *Jack Holborn*. Mr. Garfield's earthy, fantastic style, so at home in an exotic pirate setting, here seems altogether too clever. It was a mistake to make the young travelling actor George recount his own adventures. He speaks in character ("Oh God, I whsipered, Why? Why?") and his eighteenth-century grammar, even if accurate, is difficult to read. When the mysterious stranger who overshadows the lives of the Treets pays his last visit and George takes up his apparently rightful position as son and heir to Sir John Dexter, strange characters crowd confusingly in. . . . The identity of the wicked Principal remains a fairly good secret until the end. There are humorous moments, like the seven little Treets perched on the stocks where their father sits, but that gentleman, reminiscent of both Vincent Crummles and Wilkins Micawber, scarcely merits George's extravagant adulation. The characters of eighteenth-century high life are unreal, and we feel little involvement until the end, when George finds himself back among those who love him for his own sake. (p. 1078)

> The Times Literary Supplement *(© Times News-*

papers Ltd. (London) 1966; reproduced from The Times Literary Supplement *by permission), November 24, 1966.*

MARGERY FISHER

The dead little gentleman—what a title that would have been for [*Devil-in-the-fog*, a] strange compound of mystery, violence and Dickensian humour. Did the infant George Dexter die in truth or was he really farmed out among the numerous progeny of Mr. Treet the itinerant actor? There is a search for identity in this book, as there was in *Jack Holborn*, worked out in just such a way, with dropped hints, evasive half-answers, events acquiring meaning bit by bit as the story winds on. The theme is implicit in the first lines ('My father is put in the stocks again! Oh, the injustice of it! My father is a genius—as are all of we Treets') as it is in the last ('For the dead little gentleman sleeps in the churchyard close by his father . . .). Father and son, character inherited or acquired—the theme is carried like a refrain through the story. . . .

Artistry is a matter of painstaking work relaxed, finally, in personal ease. One of Leon Garfield's devices, implied in his title, is to sustain the image of fog all through the book. In the abstract, for everyone is in a fog about the meaning of events. In the everyday life of the Treets, since their claim to respect rests on the Lucifer's Smoke and Devil's Fire they are so adept at producing. And in event after event—the November fog that heralds the arrival of the Stranger; the mists of Sussex 'like clumps of wool from a giant's sheep' through which the Treet's waggon rolls towards the Hall; the mist-hung thicket where George ventures to meet his disreputable and perhaps murderous uncle. To notice this is a pleasure for the reader, but not an effort; every part of the book is natural and inevitable. Yet what a strange, almost tormented prose it is, really—a mass of asterisks and dots and exclamation marks, of whimsical detail and Joycean phrase (the footman has 'conspiracy-shaped eyes,' and the fumes of Mr. Treet's smoke jostle 'like a crowd at a wedding or a hanging'). It is all . . . closely suited to the late eighteenth century period. . . . A strange book, more than life-size and yet life-like for the feelings and attitudes of the characters: a book to leave firmly out of categories and accept thankfully for what it is —a masterpiece. (p. 809)

> *Margery Fisher, in her* Growing Point, *December, 1966.*

Mr. Garfield is a difficult writer to praise highly—yet. His gift for language is remarkable and he can evoke a scene so vividly that you see, feel, hear and smell it, but his first novel, *Jack Holborn*, was a broken-backed story, and *Smith*, his third, suffers equally from Mr. Garfield's episodic treatment and the unlikeliness of his plot. The author's knowledge of the underworld of eighteenth-century London enables him to paint a splendidly convincing backcloth. He invents a set of characters to people his stage. They must, of course, talk and act, and so they do, in a series of episodes. Moreover, Mr. Garfield likes to give his characters typical catch-phrases, so that they are recognizable by what they say rather than by what they are. . . .

Mr. Garfield is fascinated by the mixture of romantic bravado and unutterable squalor that characterized eighteenth-century low life, but is he moved by those who lived in it? The alleys, taverns and rat-ridden dens that lay under the shadow of Newgate and the hangman's noose are brilliantly evoked, but the misfortunes of Smith . . . hardly ever stir the feelings. Characters are drawn in bold, Dickensian strokes, and a wry humour pervades the writing. Indeed, there is so much to admire that one is impatient with the weakness of the plot, especially its sentimental ending.

Mr. Garfield can take his readers with him into the stench and filth of footpad London, across the snowbound heath where the pistols of the high toby, Lord Tom, flashed "blue daylight", into the sunless swarming warren of Newgate prison, and the cellar of the rickety old Red Lion tavern, but he cannot make them believe in the convoluted plot or involve them in the fortunes of those who partake in it. This is, perhaps, a basic weakness of many picaresque novels. (p. 446)

The Times Literary Supplement (© Times Newspapers Ltd. (London) 1967; reproduced from The Times Literary Supplement *by permission), May 25, 1967.*

NAOMI LEWIS

Smith crosses the line into brilliance.

Smith himself [is] a pickpocket by trade. . . . After he has taken—something—from a troubled-looking old gentleman, he sees his victim murdered and searched by two men in brown. His find is a document: but Smith cannot read. . . . The tale leaps on in a series of dazzling scenes—a session in Newgate where Smith is held for the old man's murder; an eerie flight through a kind of ventilator; the reading at last of the script; the tomb with the black stone angel to which it leads; the extraordinary climax. Leon Garfield speeds with shrewd or crackling or poignant wit through the London of dark thieves' kitchen and gentleman's mansion, in and out of St Paul's, St Andrew's and the Old Bailey. To follow is an electrifying experience. (pp. 732-33)

Naomi Lewis, in New Statesman *(© 1967 The Statesman & Nation Publishing Co. Ltd), May 26, 1967.*

MARGERY FISHER

Smith is an outstanding book on many counts. Set in the author's favoured period, the mid-eighteenth century, the story owes its unerring sense of period partly to the characters. But though they are, you might say, period types . . . they transcend costumes, idiom, manners, because the author uses them to communicate more than just a sense of the past. This intricate mystery of ancient wrongs and present revenge has the kind of tempo and vitality we expect from Leon Garfield. Adventure is here, initiated when Smith . . . witnesses a murder seconds after he has snatched a document from the pocket of the victim. What the document holds, how Smith worries at its secret and what danger his curiosity brings—explanations follow logically on event in scenes in Newgate, in the streets of Holborn, on Highgate Heath—and for these scenes the author has first worked at background facts and then felt himself into the past. The prose in this book is noticeably less staccato than that of *Devil-in-the-fog* and there is more time allowed for reflection and for the proper emerging of character. For the reader is not *told* but *shown* how to understand that two paths converge—the path of the vagrant boy, independent, shunning affection, unwilling to trust or to like, and that of the magistrate who has to come to compas-

sion a different way, by seeing the limitations of the legal form which has comforted his physical blindness. I doubt if anyone in 1967 will write a book so rich in the furnishings of historical fiction which offers also such a fascinating and such a valid study of human beings. (p. 935)

Margery Fisher, in her Growing Point, *July, 1967.*

Leon Garfield's first book, *Jack Holborn*, marked him out at once as an historical novelist with an individual style. Mr. Garfield really knows the eighteenth-century scene and his background is impressively authentic. What gives this knowledge wings and makes him so readable is his command of a vivid, fast-moving prose. But there is something more than style and pace to [*Black Jack*]. The progress from *Jack Holborn* to *Black Jack* shows that as Mr. Garfield's appetite for his chosen century grows, especially for the macabre elements in it, so does his skill in telling his tale, while his interest has shifted beyond the picaresque rogues' gallery of his previous books. Now he gives us a compassionate treatment of the emotions of his chief characters that brings real depth to his new novel. . . .

Mr. Garfield's prose style has always had distinction, but in this novel it is employed in service to a far better story than he has yet written. There is no disparagement intended in pointing out that it owes much of its vividness to a certain verbal device employed by Dickens, a constant cross-reference from material objects to human life. . . .

[There] is a richness about this book, both in physical detail and in human feeling, that makes it a notable contribution to the genre of the historical novel. (p. 1369)

The Times Literary Supplement (© Times Newspapers Ltd. (London) 1968; reproduced from The Times Literary Supplement *by permission), December 5, 1968.*

GEOFFREY TREASE

Leon Garfield has quickly established himself by general acclamation as one of the most gifted and individual writers for the older child. He has staked out a special corner for himself; one is tempted to say 'a graveyard plot', so macabre is his fancy, but that description would belie the vitality, the exuberant gusto, with which he claps his skeletal grip upon the bristling nape and sends his delicious frissons down the spine.

Those who seek absorption, and dislike short-story collections, need not be put off by the title of his new book, *Mister Corbett's Ghost and other stories* . . . , for there are only three stories, and two are of novella length. Both [novellas] have Mr Garfield's favourite period and setting, the seamier side of the 18th century. . . . Both, and the short story between them . . . are related in Mr Garfield's characteristic style, by turns humorous and horrific, earthy and fantastical, scintillant with new-minted phrases.

The style is superb. Of the content I am not so sure. It poses the question that always crops up at parents' meetings on children's reading tastes. Is horror undesirable, or does it provide a healthy release? . . . [I wish] that Mr Garfield, having given us four books of this genre, would emerge from the shadow of the gallows and exercise his splendid powers in a wider historical field. (p. 700)

Geoffrey Trease, in New Statesman *(© 1969 The Statesman & Nation Publishing Co. Ltd), May 16, 1969.*

VIRGINIA HAVILAND

[*Black Jack* is another] graphic eighteenth-century story from this master of prose [which] suggests his earlier macabre situations and characters, but also possesses an overriding warmth of human kindness. . . . [Leon Garfield] has reached his highest level in the fresh, rich period story so dramatically told. His full realization of scenes, incidents, and problems indicates the vast research which must lie behind the vivid detail. (pp. 310-11)

> *Virginia Haviland, in* The Horn Book Magazine *(copyright © 1969 by The Horn Book, Inc., Boston), June, 1969.*

The successful Mr. Garfield is best taken in small doses, and so [*Mr. Corbett's Ghost and other stories*] is my book. His stylistic bravura and professional technique in fact conceal a remarkably narrow range, so that in time the long atmospheric stories begin to pall. In this book he offers two novellas with, as meat for this sandwich, a brilliant miniature in the Dutch manner. The first ghost story is nearly all atmosphere, ghostly and not far short of ghastly. Devilish clever but not endearing. 'The Simpleton' is . . . less dependent on stylistic tricks and the better for this. The tale has a neat twist. The centrepiece is 'Vaarlem and Tripp', a marvellous thumbnail portrait of a great Dutch painter drawn by his reluctant apprentice. In fifteen pages Mr. Garfield establishes himself as the master he has often been claimed to be. (p. 180)

> The Junior Bookshelf, *June, 1969.*

MARGERY FISHER

The separation of mind and feeling is the theme of *Mr. Corbett's ghost*, the first of three stories which confirm the pattern of Leon Garfield's language and thought. He has never rendered atmosphere with as much power as he does in the scenes of his first story, making Hampstead Heath an expanding place of terror and possession. The bitter struggle of a young apprentice to free himself from a cruel master is shown, literally, on the frontiers of the human spirit. . . . To his chill and mysterious detail Leon Garfield adds a wry and mature understanding of the indignities of human nature. So finely is his story worked out that we are hardly aware that strong form and verbal dexterity have done their part in carrying the force of its theme. In a lighter vein but still with a sombre irony, *Vaarlem and Tripp* shows a glimpse of cowardice and genius in the setting of a seventeenth century sea battle. At sea again, in *The simpleton*, a boy transported through the trickery of evil associates finds himself in the company of jailbirds and unexpectedly protected by the worst of them. A pretty passenger further complicates his situation until the wheel of fortune brings him fortune and revenge in a way that provokes laughter and thought alike in the reader. The paradoxes and quips of this tale alone would be enough to make Leon Garfield as a craftsman of the first rank; his serious comment on human beings is never allowed to extrude from a literary form which is part and parcel of it. (p. 1374)

> *Margery Fisher, in her* Growing Point, *September, 1969.*

RUTH HILL VIGUERS

An outstanding English writer of the sixties is Leon Garfield, whose books have pace, humor, and unusually good characterizations. In each of his books mystery is focused on a strange, dominating figure. . . . *Smith* . . . , the tale of a small pickpocket of the eighteenth century, is a triumph of story telling, characterization, and suspense. Few present-day writers combine the attributes that seem so effortless in Mr. Garfield's work: well-built plots, suspense, a writing style suited to the mood of each book, and characters that come to life. (pp. 491-92)

> *Ruth Hill Viguers, in* A Critical History of Children's Literature, *by Cornelia Meigs, Anne Thaxter Eaton, Elizabeth Nesbitt, and Ruth Hill Viguers, edited by Cornelia Meigs (copyright © 1953, 1969 by Macmillan Publishing Co., Inc.), revised edition, Macmillan, 1969.*

SHEILA EGOFF

The rising star in [the field of the British historical novel] is Leon Garfield, who has called forth comparions with Fielding, Hogarth, and Dickens. Not merely concerned with creating a strict historical setting, he conveys the very atmosphere of time past. Using the ingredients of melodrama —pickpockets, highwaymen, smiling villains, cut-throat sailors, stolen documents and diamonds, escapes and hurried journeys—he welds them into tales of high adventure that have their own inner purpose. The only direct problem Mr Garfield poses to readers is how to put a book of his down. (pp. 442-43)

> *Sheila Egoff, in* Only Connect: Readings on Children's Literature, *edited by Sheila Egoff, G. T. Stubbs, and L. F. Ashley (© Oxford University Press (Canadian Branch) 1969), Oxford University Press, Canadian Branch, 1969.*

MARGERY FISHER

Leon Garfield's imagination is disciplined so that the surprises and bizarre events in his stories are properly related to the whole. He makes it seem natural, and yet astonishing [in *The Drummer boy*], that Charlie Samson the drummer boy, the "golden lad" of the regiment, should be the link between the General who gave orders (or said he did) in anticipation of ambush, his son-in-law who disastrously failed to carry them out and the young soldier whose remarkably unheroic death will deprive the General's daughter of life and love—unless Charlie is prepared to stand substitute. . . . What is heroism? What is love? How can a mere boy, trained to lead with the sound of his drum, learn to work out his own orders for life? Perhaps none of Leon Garfield's parables of innocence tarnished has been quite as moving or as sharply considered as this one. In his quick, pointed sentences he uses visual images to establish a mood or a scene or to make a point about character; the whole book is imbued with the red and gold of destruction. . . . It is most particularly an artistic whole, this book, an enormously stimulating and touching one. It will not teach children historical fact but will open the past for them. (pp. 1534-35)

> *Margery Fisher, in her* Growing Point, *May, 1970.*

[*The Drummer Boy*] may dismay many a reader whose experience and ability have been limited by circumstance or natural imagination, but the persistence shown by Mr. Garfield in creating his atmosphere is justified in his final effect. . . . It is difficult at times to be sure where the nightmare begins and where reality ends, and even some of the real people have a nightmare quality which makes them forbidding as well as amusing.... [The] sense of period and of what might perhaps be called human unpredictability are combined to create a moving story in which humour and optimism always underlie the misery and misfortune which in the end are transmuted into a modest happiness while unhappy memories are softened into a sadness left far behind. (p. 164)

The Junior Bookshelf, June, 1970.

TED HUGHES

There have been many retellings of Greek myths for children but this interweaving of about twenty of them [in *The God Beneath the Sea*] must be among the best. It is difficult to add authentic language and atmosphere to such old and familiar stories. [Leon Garfield and Edward Blishen] have succeeded.

Victorian moralizing dullness was more concentrated on the ancient Greeks, and on what children should be taught from them, than on almost anything else. This dullness is monumentalized in masses of poetry and literature for children. Very few writers have been able to touch, let alone release, the real life sealed up in those old shapes. The joint authors of this book deliberately set out to crack the Victorian plaster, and the result may be a surprise to some people. These stories are, after all, primitive revelations, the life they dramatize is not a little demonic. (p. 66)

Beginning with the birth of Hephaestus, [the authors] follow a developing series of about twenty stories through the war with the Titans, the creation of the main gods and of men, down to Hera's unsuccessful attempt to dethrone Zeus. These goings on—usually so cloudy and familiar and abstract—are made vividly new, interesting, often exciting. The authors obviously enjoyed the job greatly. Their zest sweeps you along. It is a real feat, to make everything sound so first hand. These are in fact genuine imaginative retellings—the dramatic urgency, the casual invention of many beautiful details, the characterization, the striking flashes of language, the hectic impressionistic scenes, are just what you get in very good retellings of folktales by practised traditional narrators. Everything jumps to life in front of your eyes. Some moments are really wonderfully visualized. The authors have stripped away the pseudo-classical draperies and produced an intense, highly coloured, primitive atmosphere. We are reading about the elemental gods of tribes just awakening—with their dreams fresh—from barbarism and animal unconsciousness. Frequently, they read like Norse myths, or like some African myths—with richer, more suggestive vistas. (pp. 66-7)

It will be a good thing if the authors can be persuaded to make another collection as shapely and vivid as this one. (p. 67)

Ted Hughes, in Children's literature in education *(© 1970, Agathon Press, Inc.; reprinted by permission of the publisher), No. 3 (November), 1970.*

ALAN GARNER

With so many books published annually, and so little space available to a critic, it seems extravagant to pay attention to rubbish, but in this case there may be a lesson to be won from the experience. *The God Beneath the Sea* . . . is very bad. It is almost impossible to read, let alone assess.

The editor is to blame as much as anybody. Personal taste is one thing, but *The God Beneath the Sea* is quite another; and whoever accepted the manuscript in its published form has rendered a disservice to the authors. Leon Garfield and Edward Blishen have fallen into the trap they tried to avoid. The prose is overblown Victoriana, 'fine' writing at its worst, cliché-ridden to the point of satire, falsely poetic, groaning with imagery and, among such a grandiloquent mess, intrusively colloquial at times.

Worst of all, the authors are so coy in their efforts to be 'frank' about sexuality that only the cumulative absurdity saves them from prurience: '. . . and in a white passion of wings, [he] quenched his restless heat' . . . , 'The Titan's daughter was already quick with child' . . . , 'Her time was at hand' . . . , 'Her gown was torn, her hair awry and everything about her proclaimed her ruin.... All that is missing is, 'Afterwards, they slept.'

It's necessary to quote, because destructive criticism is cheap and easy, and the authors must speak for themselves—which they do at length in an Afterword that is embarrassing in its hubris:

> . . . those re-tellings that now have most currency among the young form a haphazard sequence of tall tales often related in a manner which arises from certain conventions of translation from Greek poetry, and have little in them of the literary voice of our own time. We wondered if it might be possible to discover some new style of telling these stories—a language freed in some important respects from those conventions.

A statement such as that makes the book the more deplorable: to have been aware of what was wrong, and to have written a pastiche of all that was worst. (p. 606)

The text of *The God Beneath the Sea* demonstrates what is dead in our feeling for Classical myth. But if that were all, there would be no justification for wasting energy on the book, except to warn readers from being conned into buying it on the strength of the authors' prestigious names. (p. 607)

Alan Garner, "The Death of Myth," in New Statesman *(© 1970 The Statesman & Nation Publishing Co. Ltd.), November 6, 1970, pp. 606-07.*

CLIVE PEMBERTON

There is a type of book which operates both on an adult and a juvenile level. I am not thinking of books like *Robinson Crusoe* or *Gulliver's Travels*, which probe deeply into the human condition and to which the child may bring his own uncluttered and innocent responses, taking from the surface of the work an enjoyable fiction comprehensible within the limits of his own world. Nor do I have in mind those books (Alan Garner's *The Owl Service* may be one) which have been written with professional competence for a specific market, but which hold within them a range of interpretation that may seriously activate and perhaps even tax the critical and intellectual faculties of an intelligent adult. I am thinking of a third and rarer type of book, one which may well have been written in ignorance of the readership it will eventually find, and which operates successfully on the adult and the juvenile level simultaneously.

I suggest as examples of this an acknowledged classic,

Robert Louis Stevenson's *Treasure Island* . . . and a modern story of adventure on the sea set in a similar historical period, Leon Garfield's *Jack Holborn.* . . . The former was produced when a writer of genius descended into the realm of juvenile fiction. Stevenson's integrity and devotion to his craft would not allow him to produce anything that was not the best he could write. The latter was written when an author whose talent in the field of juvenile fiction was shortly to be recognized set out to write an adult novel. Converging upon the dual level from opposite directions they appeal powerfully to the boy in man as well as the man in boy.

Superficially the two books appear to have a good deal in common. They both set out to tell a story crisply, clearly and with excitement. Involvement begins on the first page and our function as readers 'is to lay by our judgment', as Stevenson himself reminded Henry James, 'to be submerged by the tale as by a billow'. It is the familiar appeal of the romance, a willing suspension of all that may impede our enjoyment of the adventure and the journey. Thus the story is set in both cases in a world far removed from the one with which we are familiar, but a world, nonetheless, with whose outlines and general shape we feel a kind of distant blood-relationship. The pirates, the sea and the island in both cases spring at us from a dimmed past; they are something we half recognize and cannot fully forget. (pp. 113-14)

And as with setting, so with character. The people who are our companions on the voyage will be clearly enough delineated in their outlines for us to know who they are and what they stand for, but not so densely probed or explored that they will obscure the free flow of the story. 'Character', wrote Stevenson, in *A Humble Remonstrance,* 'to the boy is a closed book. For him a pirate is a beard, a pair of wide trousers, and a liberal complement of pistols.' . . . The narrator, in both cases, is adequate for the role he has to play but is seldom in danger of developing his own personality beyond the orthodox limits of the genre. And the assorted collection of squires, doctors, Trumpets and Morrises slide like greased counters around the set, every now and again erupting into a spasm of activity which rivets our interest, but never holding it at the expense of the progress of the story.

In the progress of the story, skilfully and effectively managed in both cases, one can observe an interesting variant of technique. In *Treasure Island,* as Mr. G. S. Fraser has pointed out . . . , the heightened moments often occur, paradoxically, at moments when the action is arrested. . . . [The] situation is lingered over, the tension deliberately drawn out, and both are resolved violently and suddenly as breaking point is reached. With Garfield, by contrast, there seems a definite effort to keep things continuously on the boil, to move as quickly as possible through the many hazards of the plot to the dramatic climax of the story. The impression is of a series of scenes in pictures, almost like a succession of colour slides, and with the same heightened colour that one often associates with such slides. Noises are added, the picture is set moving, and at the resolution of the scene the next slide is already in place. (p. 114)

[*Jack Holborn*] was conceived as an adult book and the intention was to deal with problems of good and evil through the medium of an exciting and well told tale. The 'doppelganger' theme, treated here through the good and evil captains of the Charming Molly, is at the centre of the complicated plot and everything else in the story revolves around it. Indeed, the fact that there are two captains, though the reader may have guessed it earlier, is not explicitly revealed until the contrived and vivid courtroom scene which is the climax of the book. There is a strong element of the detective story in the tale and a marked difference of voice in the manner of telling it.

The basic register of Jack in narrating the tale is that of the unaffected raconteur, eager to give a straightforward account of the extraordinary adventure that has befallen him, relaxed in the knowledge that the events themselves are sufficient to enthral all who are willing to be held. But nothing less than the melodramatic mode will do as the story gets under way and climaxes succeed one another with bewildering rapidity. The professional storyteller takes over, and the rhetorical devices of the raconteur, the measured delivery of key sentences, the pause for effect, the writer's equivalent of the distended eyeball and the stabbing forefinger, make themselves felt through the prose.

Sometimes the lyrical is attempted, as in the description of Jack's diamond in the bartering sequences. Sometimes the horrible is vividly represented; one remembers, perhaps, the extended treatment of Mr. Trumpet's unfortunate experience in the swamp. And sometimes the lyrical and the horrible are fused in a single description, suggesting again how good and evil may be aspects of the same thing. The river, for instance, which leads the weary party through the weird experiences of the middle section of the book, runs 'directly out of the sun to wind its uncanny way through the dark of the world'. At one point 'it had sparkled like a necklace', while later it is revealed as 'a creeping hearse of dead branches, and rotted vegetation, endlessly slit by the sinful smile of crocodiles'. That last image, straight out of the nursery, is an excellent example of the way in which a child's range of reference is used throughout this section to create a deep sense of adult evil. In this way, and sometimes in the simple but effective juxtaposition of opposites, as in the river's 'silver treachery', the prose reflects the main intention. The voice is not, perhaps, as personal, as controlled, or as consistent as Stevenson's, but it knows clearly enough what it is trying to say, and it is trying to say something very similar.

Similar to what? Not, surprisingly enough, the child's adventure story, *Treasure Island,* which fashioned the literary tradition in which it can now clearly be seen to lie and which its author had not previously read. But *The Master of Ballantrae,* that adult novel of the struggle between a powerful, evil man and a weak, good man, which Garfield admired and which provided him with the idea of a book in which the weak rather than the evil go to the wall. To this he added another major theme taken from the nineteenth century romances—Melville in *Moby Dick* particularly, and Victor Hugo in a number of his novels—the idea of nature as an active, evil force.

The attempt to bring this out permeates the book. In addition to the river there is the extraordinary prominence given to the dark storm, which follows the ship throughout its voyage and is invariably described as a tiger. When the party lands on the African coast the image is again there to meet them as the trees crouch like an enormous animal. And the courtroom scene itself, the climax of the book, is carefully and quite deliberately presented as a kind of storm. Not all of this is, I think successful, nor is it as obvious in the present version as its author might like to think. But in the original draft, twice as long and written as an adult book, the intention was clear enough. It is hardly surprising that the work carries with it to its different market at least some of the qualities which characterized the intention of the original. (pp. 115-17)

Clive Pemberton, in The Use of English *(© Granada Publishing Limited 1971), Winter, 1971.*

CATHERINE STORR

[A] writer who ridicules villainy, though the tone of most of his books is not comic but deeply serious and moving, is Leon Garfield. He involves his readers in a situation where, identified with the hero, they see the forces of evil moving to engulf them and then, suddenly, by a delicate twist of phrase, he shows not the wickedness of the villain but his weakness and, above all, his vanity. As Thackeray pointed out, once you understand a man's vanity, he is in your power; for this reason the Garfield villians evoke almost as much sympathy as terror. (p. 125)

Catherine Storr, "Things That Go Bump in the Night" (reprinted by permission of the author), in The Sunday Times Magazine, *March 7, 1971 (and reprinted in* The Cool Web, *edited by Margaret Meek, Aidan Warlow, and Griselda Barton, The Bodley Head, 1977, pp. 120-27).*

RICHARD CAMP

Karl Kraus said: "There are two kinds of writers, those who are and those who aren't. With the first, content and form belong together like soul and body; with the second, they match each other like body and clothes." Leon Garfield in *The Drummer Boy* has become one of "those who are". It is no more a children's book than *Gulliver's Travels* is a travel book; but the fact that it had to be prepared for the children's market may be the reason why it is so perfect a work of art: enforcing compression of complex ideas within the accepted length of a children's novel, and enforcing exclusion of all that may not have been central to them. (p. 47)

[The] landscape of the book is, as in [D. H.] Lawrence, a real landscape, and a landscape of the inner world. (pp. 47-8)

Much of the last part of the book is set in the New Forest, with its royal associations stressed. Charlie's father, we are told, was "a great forest lover—in every sense of the word". When Charlie arrives in the Forest he feels at home there: to the other, inglorious, survivors it is nefarious shelter; for Charlie "all about him there lingered memories of the love that must have brought him into the world". . . . Charlie . . . was conceived at King's Hat. After his birth, Mrs. Samson preferred to keep to the safety of her husband's inn, pregnantly called The Doe's Rest. At the very end of the book Charlie and Charity, his down-to-earth (in every sense of the word) future wife, are walking through the forest. "Suddenly her smile seems to fill the forest and the night . . . so Charlie Samson shuts his eyes, and kisses it . . . Bushes turn into patient, watchful does, and the upper air is full of the proud, branching antlers of leaping stags." Their love, so described, takes place in Knightwood Oak. . . . Charlie is now a great forest lover like his father, and he appropriately delivers Charity home to the safety of The Doe's Rest. This is no glossing over the act of physical love for the protection of child readers; in the book's context it has poetical force which no strictly realistic description could have. The book is full of real objects that are the indirect, universalized expression of feelings which have analogous resemblance to them.

Each character is welded to one such object, objects often emotionally reinforced by their colour. With Charlie this object is, of course, his white-faced drum, the symbol of all his ideals. As he leads his regiment into battle, the prose mimes splendidly the forward movement of the zealous soldiers and the drum-beats: "The drúmmer bóy is théir gólden lád, and he's cáught the rhýthm óf their héarts." All too soon afterwards, the prose again mimes in heavy stresses the miserable aftermath: "slów and héavy, he was thúndering óut the Fúneral Retŕeat for the glóry of the fállen in the gráss." Charlie's military illusions are shattered, but he, like his drum, emerges from battle with a whole skin, and he gratefully recovers his drum. The next time Charlie nearly faces death, this time from water, the drum recovers him; the sailors throw it into the sea after him; it floats; he catches it "in full embrace" and it "sustains him". . . . At the end, in the Forest, when the ignominious survivors of the French battle finally part and say their farewells, Charlie beats a last defiant Advance into life. He beats so hard he splits the drumskin. "He wept for his broken drum; he wept for his dream of Sophia Lawrence, and for the drums of all such as he; he wept for the ten thousand scarlet men who slept on the hillside and would dream no more." This is as Ralph weeps at the end of *Lord of the Flies* "for the end of innocence, the darkness of man's heart, and the fall through the air of his true, wise friend, called Piggy". But Charlie still has his true, wise friend, called Charity. She was never impressed by the drum which so thrilled Sophia; her first suggestion was that Charlie should sell it to a tinker for a shilling. When Charlie drums through his long vigil outside Sophia's house, Charity the maid tells him roundly "to give over that grisly row". Finally, she agrees to give the drum houseroom as a vegetable basket; so Charlie himself retains only the fading shell of his own ideals. The drum was empty before anyway.

Charity, of course, is charity; the name of this kind of love is mentioned several times in the book before she is. She is characterized simply by the often-mentioned white petticoat which keeps "dancing out of her gown as if it was putting its tongue out at the world". Sophia, the General's daughter, is characterized by her blood-red gown, which, as she stands at a window of the house, gives the impression "of a drop of blood clinging to the house's face". . . . She is a vampire figure, living on other blood. When she is dying, Charlie observes a spot of bright red on her bosom; but it moves, and flies away, for it is only a *ladybird* "mocking blood". This image goes back to the book's opening, where in the battle that so thrills Sophia "grown men crash . . . bearing crimson medals on their scarlet chests" and sombrely lie wearing their scarlet "with a difference", like the soldiers of Wilfred Owen's *The Send-Off*. . . . (pp. 48-50)

Sophia is, as her name suggests, sophisticated; a town version of Hardy's Eustacia Vye, pining for emotion. . . . By the time Eustacia had consumed Clym Yeobright, the native, who returned with so many fine ideals, he is stripped of them and reduced to the belief that "instead of men aiming to advance in life with glory they should calculate how to retreat out of it without shame". That other returned native, Charlie Samson, is similarly diminished by his service to Sophia; Charlie's only ambition at the end is "to undo what he has done, and leave the world without the stain of having lived in it".

Mister Shaw accurately diagnoses Sophia's complaint: "she sits in her little room at the top of the house quite shut away, feeding . . . feeding. . . . The father feeds her—and she feeds him. She feeds him on vanity; and he feeds her on death, endless, endless, death." Charlie's battle story, and the lie that her lover, James Digby, died bravely, nourishes her; on the third day of his lovelorn vigil outside her house, Charlie is said to be "fading". When he finally enters the house again, Sophia reproaches him for growing so pale, especially as she herself seems to be gaining in strength. "You fade while I bloom. It should not be so, drummer boy." This is exactly the situation of the male innocent in Blake's *Mental Traveller*. . . . And, as in Blake, the Male revives as the Female loses her strength, and the action is reversed. . . . (pp. 50-1)

Owing to Mister Shaw's frenzied, caring determination to make him see the truth of things, Sophia's spell is broken, and Charlie sees fear and hatred in Sophia's serpent eyes. Sophia says on her grimy deathbed: "Remember how we talked of my blossoming while you faded? Now it's changed about." (pp. 51-2)

All the imagery in the book is functional, never merely decorative. We are told, for example, that "the gathering clouds of the General's fall" will destroy Sophia; but nearly thirty pages before that, the author says: "it was the presence of Sophia Lawrence that brooded over the house like an ominous cloud." She is the cloud, the cause of her father's ruin and of her own; we are only permitted to see this through the linking metaphors, which are much more dark and powerful than finite statements.

Much of the imagery is "black", but set against this there is assertion of love in the sense of charity. The most eloquent assertion of charity is not made by Charity, but by Mister Shaw: "Oh God, Charlie—do you know what love is? It ain't just the spitting flicker of green wood catching. It's a mighty weapon, Charlie! It's the defender of the faith —it's the only thing we still have on our side! Even my talent, Charlie, only exists because of love!" (p. 54)

The human conflicts in the book are of great intensity, reminiscent even of Blake and Hardy. The recurrent images compress and universalize the human drama: birds, clouds, drum, flowers, teeth, wind and woods; these are reinforced by colour motifs: gold, silver, black, white and red. Never are the metaphors forced, and there is no moment when objects become awkwardly something inward and subjective; for their outward form and their inward meaning coexist with no conflict, fusing into a perfect work of art. The body and the soul of the book are one. (p. 55)

Richard Camp, "Garfield's Golden Net," in *Signal* (copyright © 1971 Richard Camp; reprinted by permission of the author and The Thimble Press, Lockwood Station Road, South Woodchester, Glos. GL5 5EQ, England), May, 1971, pp. 47-55.

BARBARA WERSBA

A re-creation of myriad Greek legends, this long and detailed book ["The God Beneath the Sea"] quivers with excitement. Its language is like a mosaic of fiery, precious jewels; and its interwoven plots are brilliantly handled. Beginning with the creation of the world, the book advances swiftly to the creation of the gods and then to the creation of man. The cast of characters is enormous, yet each god takes on a distinct personality. Nothing is omitted here, whether it be the agony of the bound Prometheus or the tragic fate of crippled Hephaestus or the wild lusts of Zeus. The making of mankind from a few handfuls of clay is perhaps the most moving part of the story. . . . The death of the first pitiful man, the unleashing upon the world of evil and sickness by Pandora—all these episodes touch the heart quite strangely. They are only myths, yet they seem to be a total dream-history of the world. Authors Garfield and Blishen have written a strong, sensual and complicated book for adolescents, who are of course the very people that will appreciate it most. (p. 46)

Barbara Wersba, in The New York Times Book Review (© 1971 by the New York Times Company; reprinted by permission), May 2, 1971.

PETER GEOFFREY TOWNSEND

In an Afterword the co-authors [of *The God Beneath the Sea*] explain that their aim in re-telling the Greek myths to the young is to avoid 'A haphazard sequence of tall tales' often related in a manner arising from certain conventions of translation from Greek poetry, but rather, to relate, 'as a continuous narrative' using a 'literary voice of our own time'. The manner in which many of the better known myths are put within a dramatic framework and given a coherence, both chronological and psychological, is indeed probably the greatest achievement of the book.

The narrative is strung between the two falls of the god, Hephaestus, hurled from Olympus first by Hera, his mother, and later by Zeus. After his first fall, 'the god beneath the sea' is told by his guardians, Thetis and Eurynome, of the great Creation myth. . . . Hephaestus' birth and fall is also recounted and then by a clever narrative twist, typical of the book, the maker of a marvellous brooch is summoned to Olympus, and found, of course, to be the formerly rejected, misshapen artist—God. The making of men, and finally some of the Greek myths concerning the inter-relations of the two, are retold in the latter half of the book. There is, perhaps inevitably, after so fine a reworking of the earlier myths, a slight loss in narrative cohesiveness in the last section of the book. Nevertheless, this detracts little from the effectiveness of thematic and narrative motifs, such as the coral brooch, which help tie together the disparate myths so well.

The authors felt it was the intention of the myths, 'if not to explain life then to provide a pattern that would act as a vast imaginative alternative to an explanation'. In attempting to convey this significance they have been especially successful in dealing with Prometheus's creatures; in the cause for the frail hold on life, the blind hand of fate, and the warring human passions where 'all aspirations would be lamed, all achievement warped as man eternally fought within himself a battle that could neither be lost nor won'. The characterisation in broad, sweeping strokes and incisive details of the high passions of the gods adds to the essentially dramatic presentation of the myths. . . . Two things only mar this admirable book. The first of these is somewhat similar to Milton's mistake in *Paradise Lost*, where God is made to speak. Although dealing with pagan gods who are human on a vast scale, the dialogue cannot always match the action. Secondly, in a number of places the elevated prose tends to overreach itself, 'His head was bent, his eyes were deep, and his fathomless mind reached regions even out of Hermes scope'. These flaws notwithstanding, I can thoroughly recommend this book for older child and adult alike. (pp. 332-33)

> *Peter Geoffrey Townsend, "Greek Myths Retold," in* Contemporary Review *(© 1971 Contemporary Review Co. Ltd.), June, 1971, pp. 332-33.*

MARGERY FISHER

What is a children's book? What is a young adult? What pigeon-hole is big enough for Garfield? The answers to these questions must depend finally on each reader's discretion. Certainly [*The strange affair of Adelaide Harris*] is a book for all to read—all, that is, from a reasonably sophisticated eleven years upwards, for an intricate plot, a devastating mock-heroic tone demand some such starting point of age. As for the top limit, this is a comedy, a superb comedy whose slapstick, irony and farce may be readily accepted by adults on its own terms. All the same, there is one respect at least in which this book is within the particular reach of young people; to use [Edward] Blishen's phrase, there really is 'a child's eye in the centre'.

Imbroglio is the only word for the swift, bewilderingly intricate plot. (p. 1817)

What I want to stress is that though this is a mature and extremely cultivated book, with a humour as sharp as a scalpel and as entertaining as the Marx Brothers, it is all the time subtly keyed to the boys [Bostock and Harris]. The animal passions evinced by Ralph Bunnion and the egregious Sir Walter, the monstrous drunkenness of Mrs. Bonney, are hilarious rather than sordid partly because we see them through the eyes of the two boys, naturally coarse and self-centered, who find the grown-ups splendid if inexplicable fun to watch. Even when the boys are not present their attitude still colours the story. When you have into the bargain a mock-heroic style worthy of *Tom Jones* that mitigates near-seduction and greed and stupidity just through ribaldry, you have a book which can be called 'for the young' or 'for the general reader' with equal truth.

Certainly Leon Garfield's talent in word-spinning and word-choosing are here exercised to the full. The book must be read slowly and often for the full richness of its flavour to be appreciated, and for the last ramification of the cunning plot to be properly noted. I doubt whether we shall see such a shrewd comedy for many years. (pp. 1817-18)

> *Margery Fisher, in her* Growing Point, *November 1971.*

Intrigued delight takes hold of one with the very first sentence of Leon Garfield's *The Strange Affair of Adelaide Harris* and never lets go till the hapless plottings of those old friends Bostock and Harris, having tangled themselves into a positive cat's cradle of complication, pull finally clear. It is a fourfold delight, deriving as much from the invention which can place at all the string-pulling vantage points such a variety of entertaining characters as from the author's dry comments on their thoughts and motives; as

much from the ingenuity that twitches them round Brighton and its countryside in a dance of such fascinating intricacy as from the never-failing brilliance of Mr. Garfield's style. Lighter and more pointed than ever, now deliciously witty too, it is a constant joy, and . . . this new story gives the impression of being a contemporary engraving, first exquisitely drawn and then coloured vividly by hand. . . .

For good measure there is a host of lesser characters, resting somewhere between Dickens and Jane Austen. . . . The whole book sparkles with richness and to try and quote from it would be useless, for in searching for one felicity another yet more delightful would appear and so one would never stop.

Yet—and in spite of all these superlatives there is still a reservation, faint as a breath of wind across the downs, but persistent nevertheless—in the very way that one praises is implicit a faint regret. One talks of period prints rather than actuality, of characters that are skilfully manipulated rather than moving with their own life; one seems to see the whole story through a bioscope, or as though it were a picture in a frame and the characters at one remove. This new story of Leon Garfield's touches most delectably the fancy but not, as his earlier stories so notably have done, the heart. Perhaps it isn't meant to; after the white-hot intensity of *The Drummer Boy* he may well have needed the relief of a change, but one hopes that the change may be only temporary.

One final, very small carp, a skirmish in a private war. Do the page or two of Sir William's bawdry, of Harris's crude assessment of Bosty's awakening dreams, add anything to the story; are they really necessary to art or literature? (p. 1509)

> The Times Literary Supplement *(© Times Newspapers Ltd. (London) 1971; reproduced from* The Times Literary Supplement *by permission), December 3, 1971.*

FRANK EYRE

Leon Garfield is one author who has invented what is almost a new category of his own. . . . His books are not historical novels—though they are set in the past—nor are they simply adventure stories—it is even possible to see them, in some lights, as fantasies. But they are more likely to be read and enjoyed by those who like stories with plenty of action and excitement, than by lovers of historical stories or fantasy. . . . (p. 98)

Although Leon Garfield's work has strengthened with each book, his manner and method has remained unchanged and it is impossible to mistake any book by Garfield for one by any other writer. They are all set in a not too precisely defined part of the eighteenth century; a period which seems to have been chosen more for the opportunities it presents than for any special reason of historical interest or research. It is not an imaginary period, in the sense that Joan Aiken's settings are imaginary, . . . but no serious attempt is made at historical accuracy. No doubt some reading must have been done to get the general picture of the period into the author's mind, but would not be the kind of research that a Rosemary Sutcliff or a Stephanie Plowman undertakes before writing a historical novel and there are, as a result, occasional anachronisms and inaccuracies. But these are minor blemishes and it is clearly not Leon Garfield's intention to aim at an accurate historical picture. (pp. 98-9)

Leon Garfield's second book, *Devil-in-the-Fog,* is not his best book, but it is an excellent example of the author's manner and serves as a good introduction to his work. If the reader likes this he will like all the author's work, if he dislikes it he will probably dislike them all. It is the story of George Treet, the eldest son of a family of strolling players, who learns suddenly that he may be the son of a nobleman and the heir to great wealth.... *Devil-in-the-Fog* is as stagey, theatrical and melodramatic as Treet's own performances no doubt were. The style of writing is high-pitched, inflated, with all the marks of the kind of historical writing which earlier had brought historical novels into disrepute. One almost expects a character to burst out with 'Gadzooks!' at any moment, and there are as many exclamation marks, leaders, and dashes as there ever were in Herbert Strang.... (pp. 100-01)

Yet despite all this the book succeeds with most readers, who are carried along by the impetuosity and verve of the author's writing and attracted by the very theatricality and staginess of the period atmosphere which other readers find overdone. (p. 101)

The book in which Leon Garfield comes nearest to making a complete success of the unique mixture of sinister characters, complex, sometimes obscure plots and macabre set-pieces that he has made peculiarly his own, is *Black Jack.* (pp. 101-02)

It would be difficult to imagine a more unlikely story. Yet Leon Garfield makes it not only readable, but compulsively so by the pace and tension of his writing and the almost frenzied 'come along quickly, let's get on with action and not bother too much about what is really supposed to be going on' that is the special mark of his manner. (p. 102)

His third book, *Smith,* is probably his best known, and is the one that has attracted most critical attention. It is a closely woven pastiche of the darker side of eighteenth-century London.... It is in many ways more like a miniature, and of course infinitely lesser, novel by Dickens than a children's book but there is no doubt at all that many children do read this, and all his books, with zest and find them both exciting and stimulating. His most recent book, *The Drummer Boy,* carries his strange tales even farther along the road to confusion. It is full of things that no other living author for children could achieve, but it would be an intelligent child indeed who could follow the author's tortuous threads to the true centre of his maze. Much as one has to admire his set pieces, and some excellent humorous writing, there is too much in this book that strikes false notes and too much that will mystify, confuse and unnecessarily distress young readers for it to be completely satisfying. Whatever may be true of *Jack Holborn, Devil-in-the-Fog* or *Black Jack,* or *Smith,* this book, one feels, should be in the adult section, because adults will be better equipped to get most value from it.

Leon Garfield's books, in fact, like those of some other writers, raise the question whether, in an age when the telling of straight narrative stories is no longer acceptable in adult novels, some writers may not be driven into children's books as the only way to make use of the gift that has been given them. I remember hearing an Australian writer, Ivan Southall, tell a seminar audience that this was why he wrote children's books, and one wonders whether Leon Garfield . . . may not be [a novelist manqué].

Leon Garfield's work has been highly praised, and many good critics admire it, but it seems to me too early for a reliable judgement to be formed on it.... It is always difficult for an adult critic to be completely objective about children's books—so many of them are so much beneath notice to an informed mind that anything at all unusual stands out sometimes undeservedly—and this is particularly so with a writer like Leon Garfield who is, as he himself so shrewdly analysed, doing something that is neither quite for adults nor quite for children. But it seems unlikely that he can continue to produce at regular intervals a succession of the same kind of pseudo-historical firework displays. If he does, he will become type-styled and of less interest, but he has such obvious talent, as a born novelist of the true story-telling kind, that he may well develop his work along other lines that are of more interest to critics and readers like myself, to whom his present work does not greatly appeal because of its basic unreality. (pp. 103-05)

> *Frank Eyre, in his* British Children's Books in the Twentieth Century *(copyright © 1971 by Frank Eyre; reprinted by permission of the publishers, E. P. Dutton & Co., Inc.; in Canada by Penguin Books Ltd.),* Longman Books, 1971, Dutton, 1973.

JOHN ROWE TOWNSEND

Of all the talents that emerged in the field of British writing for children in the 1960s, that of Leon Garfield seems to me to be the richest and strangest. I am tempted to go on and say that his stories are the tallest, the deepest, the wildest, the most spine-chilling, the most humorous, the most energetic, the most extravagant, the most searching, the most everything. Superlatives sit as naturally on them as a silk hat on T. S. Eliot's Bradford millionaire. They are vastly larger, livelier and more vivid than life. They are intensely individual: it would be impossible to mistake a page of Garfield for a page written by anybody else. They are full of outward and visible action, but they are not just chains of events, for everything that happens on the surface has its powerful motivation beneath. And they create their own probabilities. Wildly unlikely it may be that the waif Smith should be rewarded with ten thousand guineas by the not-conspicuously-generous heirs to a fortune, but like many farther-fetched events this is entirely acceptable because nothing less would have matched the size of the story.

Although Garfield is endlessly versatile within his range, the range itself is narrow. His novels so far are all set in the eighteenth century, mostly in London and southern England. His themes are few and recurrent: mysteries of origin and identity; the deceptive appearances of good and evil; contrasts of true and false feeling; the precarious survival of compassion and charity in a tempestuous world. His characters, though never cardboard, are seldom of great psychological complexity as we understand the phrase these days, and often themselves appear to represent underlying forces or passions or even humours.

The choice of the eighteenth century is an unexplained mystery of the Garfield writing personality. It could be that it allows release from the realistic inhibitions that increasingly gathered round the novel from mid-Victorian times onwards. Garfield's is a lawless world; or, more precisely, a world in which the rule of law is itself a contender, is trying to assert itself but is not to be relied on for protection. Men are greatly dependent on their own quickness of hand, of foot, of eye, of wit. The world is one in which great and small rogues are forever busy and the Devil is there to take the hindmost. The author seems steeped in his period; even when writing in the third person he commonly puts 'mistook' or 'forsook' or 'forgot' for 'mistaken' or 'forsaken' or 'forgotten', and he will write 'twenty pound' rather than 'twenty pounds'. But this is not the eighteenth century that might be reconstructed by an historical novelist. It is original, organic, springing straight from the Garfield imagination; though I believe that the work of other writers, and artists, has provided an essential compost. You may well discern something of Stevenson in Garfield's first book, *Jack Holborn* (1964), and something of Dickens everywhere. You may be sure that Garfield knows the work of Fielding and Hogarth, among much else from the eighteenth century itself. There are less obvious writers whose work can fruitfully be considered in relation to his: the great Russian novelists, especially Dostoievsky; even Jane Austen; even Emily Brontë. A rich literary soil is not simply constituted.

The first novel, *Jack Holborn*, showed many of its author's qualities already strongly developed, and immediately appeared remarkable when it first came out. In comparison with later books it has several weaknesses. On the surface it is a tale of piracy, murder, treasure, treachery, shipwreck and ultimate fortune, all in the best tradition of the sea adventure story. And so it will be read by children and by most other readers. There are also two separate questions of identity. One is simple: just who *is* the hero-narrator, the foundling Jack Holborn, so named from the parish in which he was abandoned? The other is disconcerting: how can it be that identical faces cover such different personalities as those of the distinguished Judge and the wicked pirate captain? Confusion between real and apparent good and evil is a recurrent Garfield theme; but the device used in *Jack Holborn*—the introduction of identical twins of opposite character—is crude in comparison with, for instance, the moral complexity of *The Drummer Boy* five years later. And *Jack Holborn* has other flaws. The story, of which the first three quarters are gripping, falls away in the final quarter; the narrator is brave, generous and well-meaning, but he is not interesting. Yet the Garfield style and vision are already unmistakable, and although the writing is not yet fully ablaze with metaphor in the later Garfield manner it rises at times to a staccato poetry.

Devil-in-the-Fog (1966), the second novel, again revolves at length around questions of identity. The narrator George Treet, from being a member of a family of travelling players, is translated suddenly to the position of heir apparent to Sir John Dexter, baronet. In the misty grounds of the great house lurks Sir John's unloving brother, newly cut out of the succession. But who is the true villain, and is George really gentleman or player? The book shows one clear advance on *Jack Holborn*: the difficulty of making the narrator into an effective character in his own right is overcome. The artless George, in telling his story, allows us to see more of him than he can see of himself; we perceive, for instance, the honest vulgarity that makes him unacceptable to Sir John as an heir. And here enters another Garfield theme, that of true and false feeling; for we can contrast and appraise at their proper values the simple vanity of the Treets and the chilly pride of Sir John. But the story, although straightforward in theme and feeling, is complicated in terms of actual incident; and not even the Garfield

energy is quite enough to drive it successfully through its own convolutions and lengthy denouement. . . . *Devil-in-the-Fog* still seems to me to display outstanding promise rather than outstanding achievement.

Smith (1967), the first of Leon Garfield's third-person narrations, was a stronger and more straightforward story than either of its predecessors. (pp. 97-100)

In *Smith,* it seems to me that the forward progress of the story is no longer hindered by entanglement in complications; it knows where it is going and drives steadily towards its powerful climax. It is more unified, more of a novel than its two predecessors or its successor; it is not Garfield's richest book but it is the most obviously successful of his first four.

Black Jack (1968) is a more complex book than *Smith,* and, in its beginning and end, more powerful. It is however less satisfactory in structure. (pp. 100-01)

[The] structure is perhaps more like that of a symphony—one with powerful opening and closing movements and quieter ones in between—than that of a novel, in which one might wish for a more continuous progress, a build-up of tension towards the climax.

Garfield's latest novel so far, *The Drummer Boy* (1970), is the most ambitious of all and the most complex in ideas and feeling although not in plot. Its hero Charlie Samson is everyone's golden lad, the embodiment of all unfulfilled dreams and lost ideals. With Charlie the story moves from the field of battle, in which ten thousand scarlet soldiers have been mown down, to London, where the responsible General is trying to save his skin. In thrall to the General's beautiful and apparently dying daughter Sophia, Charlie is ready to perjure himself and shift the General's guilt to a haunted wretch of a scapegoat. He is brought to his senses by the cowardly, fat, pansy surgeon Mister Shaw and the common servant-girl Charity.

Clearly the book is concerned with the evils of false romanticism. The brief and doubtful glory of the battlefield is a poor exchange for the slow ripening of a lifetime which we see awaiting Charlie in the story's happy ending. The brief and doubtful glory of serving belle-dame-sans-merci Sophia and her exalted, hollow father is nothing in comparison with the warmth of an honest wench with twenty pounds in the bank and a loving nature. Again there is the bewildering interchange of good and evil; for the apparently natural love of Charlie for Sophia turns out to be a deadly menace, while the seemingly unnatural love of Mister Shaw for Charlie, though it is hopeless, pathetic, incapable of fruition, is beneficent. It would be possible to see Mister Shaw as the ambiguous hero of this story: himself the battlefield, with his healing gift at war with half a dozen ignoble purposes. Charlie as hero is so much a receptacle for the hopes and dreams of others that in himself he is an empty vessel. But at last he loses his drum, the symbol of his virginity of mind and body, and returns with Charity on his arm to the New Forest where he began. The real story of Charlie Samson starts where the book leaves off.

I do not think *The Drummer Boy* is quite the major triumph that Garfield has been promising ever since *Jack Holborn*, but I am sure it will come. In the meantime, he has one small but perfect work to his credit in *Mister Corbett's Ghost*, which was published in England in 1969 as part of a triptych with two other stories. It is the tale of an apothecary's apprentice, Benjamin, who wishes his harsh master dead, and on New Year's Eve finds an old man who can grant the wish, at a price. But the ghost of Mister Corbett lingers with Benjamin and is more pitiable, more human even, than Mister Corbett was in life; and the boy is happy, in the end, to undo his bargain. Whether this is a story of the supernatural or an externalizing of inner processes is a matter of interpretation, or perhaps of the reader's own development. The themes are those of responsibility for one's actions and of the dreadful destructiveness of revenge; and in his dealings with Mister Corbett as corpse and then as ghost Benjamin goes through the stages of guilt: fear, shame, remorse, compassion. This is a tale told with total command; its temperature goes down, down, far below zero before returning all the more effectively to the warmth of living flesh. I would say, and not lightly, that it can be compared to [Dickens's] *A Christmas Carol.*

The most obvious characteristic of Leon Garfield I have left until the end. He treats the English language with a mastery that sometimes verges on outrage. Effortlessly, page after page and line after line, he creates his individual and vivid images. 'He jerked the candle down, thereby causing banisters and certain pieces of respectable mahogany furniture to take fright and crouch in their own shadows.'.... Garfield's metaphors tend to be strongly visual. But he does not only see; he touches, tastes and smells. (An analysis of the smells in his novels might be curiously illuminating.) As a man with medical knowledge he is well aware of the perishable human body, the too too solid, or sullied, flesh. In treating of life as it comes, more rough than smooth, he is not unduly fastidious. Yet he can be gentle, as in the love of Belle and Tolly in *Black Jack.*... Leon Garfield can do anything with words and his touch is very sure.... I do not believe in singling out a writer as 'the best'; books and their authors are only to a limited extent comparable, and should not be seen as competing against each other. But I have livelier expectations from Leon Garfield than from anyone else whose work is being published on a children's list in England today. (pp. 101-04)

> *John Rowe Townsend, "Leon Garfield," in his* A Sense of Story: Essays on Contemporary Writers for Children *(copyright © 1971 by John Rowe Townsend; reprinted by permission of J. B. Lippincott Company), Lippincott, 1971, pp. 97-106.*

GLADYS WILLIAMS

Leon Garfield's latest, *The Strange Affair of Adelaide Harris,* is a glorious, non-sensible frolic, with carefully erudite period roots, that will charm and refresh adults as well as the teenagers for whom it is primarily intended. Garfield has always seemed to have power to summon the ghosts of both [Robert Louis Stevenson] and Dickens to his elbow when he starts to write, interweaving the sinister blood-chill of Blind Pew and Long John Silver with the stench and slime of Simon Tappertit and cronies' underground cellar. But this time he's taken an unexpected turn into the sunlight, and added Saki to his established familiars. A lovely outburst of joyful, impudent satire has resulted, with horror and violence in full retreat. What's more, Mr Garfield has dared to come all out on the side of age against youth, and it is the plans of the over-cocky young that go astray, while their poor, browbeaten, bullied classics master wins his heart's desire. (p. 96)

> *Gladys Williams, in* Books and Bookmen (© *copyright Gladys Williams 1972; reprinted with permission), February, 1972.*

BRIAN W. ALDERSON

It is Bostock and Harris who are responsible for 'the affair' [in *The Strange Affair of Adelaide Harris*], they (or at least Harris) having decided to expose Harris's sister Adelaide on the down above Brighton in the hopes that she will be adopted by a wolf. This decision sets in train a sequence of events of extraordinary complexity, their relationship to real life being a fragile one, but their existence for the sake of Mr. Garfield's art being amply justified. Casting aside the elements of romantic drama which characterised such books as *Jack Holborn* and *Black Jack,* and turning his back on the pretensions of *The Drummer Boy,* he has allowed full play to the ingenuity and wit that are also present in those books.

It is impossible to chart the convolutions of the story—and indeed, an inquiry-agent brought in to do just this succeeds only in confounding matters even more.... What can be singled out is the sureness of the comedy: the descriptions (Mrs. Bunnion asleep 'like a stately ship rising and falling at anchor'), the characterisation, even of the walk-on parts (poor Adam, the apostate monk from Basingstoke, who was too wet to burn) and a farcical cross-talk that is at times reminiscent of Christopher Fry. The book has its flaws—some of the jokes are repetitious, and there is superfluous hat tipping towards our newly-acquired freedom of expression in 'children's literature'—but it is a fresh and original addition to that rather rare species: the comic novel. (p. 14)

> *Brian W. Alderson, in* Children's Book Review (© *1972 by Five Owls Press Ltd.; all rights reserved), February, 1972.*

ELEANOR CAMERON

Devotees of Leon Garfield's distinctive way of expressing himself will take pleasure in [*The Ghost Downstairs*].... A tale whose meaning dances full circle, it is for any child, teenager, or adult who delights in fantasy. Despite its verve, however, it may grow too fantastical for those not sufficiently enchanted by its style to enter into a willing suspension of disbelief. (p. 13)

> *Eleanor Cameron, in* Book World—Chicago Tribune (© *1972 Postrib Corp.), May 7, 1972.*

J. ALLAN MORRISON

[Sir John Theophilus Lee is portrayed in *Child O' War*] as an ingratiating nonentity.... His one substantial claim on the regard of posterity, apart from the memoir around which *Child O' War* is built, issues from a judiciously negotiated contract for the supply of lemon-juice to the navy.

A pretty slender target, you may think, for Mr. Garfield's bubble-pricking broadsides. But Lee's is by no means the only character to be raked, for little good is said of any of the actors in the revolutionary drama. Callous heads are hacked broadcast from fat, bemedalled bodies on both sides of the Channel; all politicians are pompous fools, or worse; only the First Consul himself is allowed—true to the multiple standards of our own time—to escape his due share of invective. Well, of course we all know that war is a rude game played by less elevated minds—but what would Mr.

Garfield and his able annotator, David Proctor, have done about Napoleon? Batter him into submission with adjectives, perhaps? (p. 86)

J. Allan Morrison, in Children's Book Review *(© 1972 by Five Owls Press Ltd.; all rights reserved), June, 1972.*

GILLIAN TINDALL

Splendidly logical is Leon Garfield's *The Ghost Downstairs* . . . , with the spooky originality one expects from this writer. I'm not sure how old a child would have to be to appreciate the true meaning of its Faustian theme, let alone the chilling concept of selling one's own childhood: I suspect that this is really a tale for adults. But then so were some of the most enduring children's books ever written. (p. 760)

Gillian Tindall, in New Statesman *(© 1972 The Statesman & Nation Publishing Co. Ltd.), June 2, 1972.*

MARGERY FISHER

The ghost downstairs tantalises with fleeting likenesses—among them Bosch and Breughel, Coleridge and M. R. James; the last not only because "a ghost in the sunshine is a fearful thing" but also because of Leon Garfield's urbane, polished style. . . .

The Pathetic Fallacy is used brilliantly in this book; fog and sunshine, the gloom of a basement and the fiery flickering of a steam train, by turns reflect and represent the alternating moods of greedy hope and sharp despair as the clerk, who has sold not his soul but seven years of his childhood to the old man downstairs, realises his mistake and tries in vain to think of a way out of the ingenious legal contract he has devised so cunningly. The book takes the form of a novella in two parts, with an elaborate system of loud and soft passages leading to a colossal crescendo and then to a coda of piercing sweetness. This is a fine piece of writing. . . . This is not a book for all children, or exclusively for children. Certainly it is not for anyone who reads for the story alone and has no feeling for words. Ultimately its value lies in its whole and not in its parts, as a piece of original, stimulating literature in an inevitable form. (p. 1973)

Margery Fisher, in her Growing Point, *July, 1972.*

[In] Leon Garfield's *Child O' War* . . . the author presents both the hero and the sea battles he takes part in stereoscopically. Sir John Theophilus Lee, the youngest boy—at the age of five and a half—ever to join His Majesty's Navy, and on whose actual memoirs the story is based, is shown to us not only as a snobbish old man reminiscing but through the eyes of his own children watching him; the stark facts of a British sailor's life and the peerless actions they fought in are shown in a fuzz of extemporization, through receding archways of fretwork, as it were.

Though Leon Garfield's inventive re-creation of the Victorian scene is as ingenious as ever, though, even at several removes and through the pen of Sir T. Lee, the clear facts of the sea battles compel their own lucid prose, the two do not mix; it is as though someone had spun a cocoon of candy floss round a piece of steel. There are two stories here, one of fanciful family life and the other of straight, unwhimsical action, and though both may be in the memoirs each would seem to be for an entirely different taste. It is difficult to believe that a young reader following Alexander and Swiftsure into action would want to be switched to Euphemia's predilection for jelly, or that anyone sharing Henrietta's romantic dreams would care much about the line of battle at Cape St Vincent. Between them the interest flickers hither and thither, like a compass needle gone mad. (p. 807)

The Times Literary Supplement *(© Times Newspapers Ltd. (London) 1972; reproduced from* The Times Literary Supplement *by permission), July 14, 1972.*

RHODRI JONES

Leon Garfield dislikes being described as a writer for children. He regards this as a publisher's convenience—a slot into which his books can be easily put. What interests him is the novel as narrative, and since the modern novel for adults tends to be concerned with psychological states and sexual exploration rather than with the telling of an intricate and neatly dove-tailing story, Garfield's novels are regarded as being more suitable for children. Certainly they appeal very strongly to young readers and a very important element of this appeal is the strong story-line.

Each of his novels is built on a complicated but firm plot, following the adventures of the main character through a series of clues and discoveries until the complications are resolved and the mysteries revealed as the novel comes to a close. The plots are usually based on a search of some kind —in *Jack Holborn* and *Devil-in-the-Fog* for the truth about the hero's origin, in *The Drummer Boy* for what is real and what is false. Always there is the search for knowledge.

Another factor which gives the novels an appeal for young people is the type of hero that Garfield depicts. Garfield's heroes are on their own. They have to make their own way in the bewildering adult world, finding out for themselves what is reality and what is illusion, learning by trial and error whom to trust and who is merely making use of them. There is Smith, for instance, the twelve-year-old pickpocket stealing a living in fog-swirled eighteenth-century London, who learns that mere survival is not enough and that compassion is more important than wounded pride or self-interest. Or Charlie Samson, the golden drummer boy, whose goodness is taken advantage of and who learns that the adult world of pride and privilege is not all that it seems. It is through heroes like these that children can explore the strange adult world into which they are moving and against whom they can weigh their own experience.

The style Garfield uses also appeals to children. His language is highly coloured, full of imagery and humour, shot through with irony and ambiguity (which last may not always be grasped by children). Sometimes the imagery is used decoratively . . . ; often, it is used more organically as part of the meaning of the novel. In *Smith,* the dead eyes of the magistrate are a symbol of his inward blindness. In *The Drummer Boy,* the golden lad is in danger of having his innocence tarnished by the world.

Even in the most grim situation—for Garfield shuns little from murder to madness—humour keeps breaking through. (pp. 34-5)

The opening of *Smith* illustrates . . . the assurance with which Garfield establishes a style and a tone for his novels, a skill he may have learned from Jane Austen who has certainly influenced his use of irony. . . . (p. 35)

The other main influence on Garfield's writing seems to be Dickens, although he did not read Dickens until after he had written his first novel *Jack Holborn*. This can be seen partly in the characterisation of the minor figures with their one easily recognisable catch-phrase or trait (Meg in *Smith* with her 'Learning? Give you a farthing for it!' or Pobjoy in *Jack Holborn* with his thirst for gin). It can be seen partly in the gusto and skill of the narrative. The whirling end of *Black Jack* is like a speeded-up version of the crescendo of crisis upon crisis at the end of *A Tale of Two Cities* or *Oliver Twist*. It can be seen partly in the use of symbolism. The travelling actors of *Devil-in-the-Fog* and the fair people of *Black Jack* with their casual, free-and-easy emotional world bear the same significance as the circus people in *Hard Times*. It can be seen in the way in which, once he gets going, Garfield's prose takes on a lyrical lilt and rhythm reminiscent of Dickens in full flight.... It is ... exuberant exaggeration and vitality in the use of words that Garfield shares with Dickens. He also shares a warmth of heart and feeling. Virtue is triumphant. Goodness is seen to be good, without in any way descending to Dickens' sentimental excesses. This is not to say that Garfield is a greater artist than Dickens—merely that he has a better sense of proportion.

Garfield's novels are set in the eighteenth century. He has said (in an interview in *The Guardian*, 9 June 1971): 'It's like science fiction in reverse: you take a moral problem out of context to observe it better; you have the reality of the past to latch on to.' Through the vividness of his writing, his choice of detail and the generosity of his characterisation, Garfield does bring a past age to life. *Smith* has the exuberance, the violence, the high spirits, and the squalor of *The Beggar's Opera*. But his novels are more than costume charades. Moral questions and their reverberations loom very large. The search for identity is made concrete by having his hero literally search to find out who his father is in *Jack Holborn* and *Devil-in-the-Fog*. Moral choice is a very important element in *Smith*. Learning to distinguish between outward beauty, respectability or rank and inward corruption, self-seeking, and wickedness is the basis of *Black Jack* and *The Drummer Boy*. (pp. 35-6)

And this is, perhaps, one of the most important aspects of Garfield's novels. They deal with the same kind of themes as adult literature, but in terms that children can understand. By identifying with the heroes, children can appreciate the moral choices that arise, and can see that the world is not entirely black and white but varying shades of grey. When they go on to read Shakespeare, Dickens, George Eliot or Jane Austen, they are prepared for similar complexities of feelings and responses to character and situation. If they do not go on to read these classics, they have had a valuable and easily approachable substitute. (p. 36)

Rhodri Jones, "Leon Garfield" (1972), in Good Writers for Young Readers, *edited by Dennis Butts (copyright selection and arrangement © 1977 Hart-Davis Educational), Hart-Davis Educational, 1977, pp. 34-40.*

MARCUS CROUCH

Leon Garfield seems to have had no 'prentice period. His first book, *Jack Holborn* ..., has all his characteristic qualities; indeed if one were to be unkind one might venture to say that he has gone on telling the same story ever since.... [The book includes] mutiny, shipwreck, jungle trekking, a slave-market and a great trial scene. The ingredients are all conventional enough. It is the author's expert chemistry—appropriately he is a biochemist by calling—which makes the unpromising materials react to produce tension and atmosphere.

Jack Holborn is sustained through great physical ordeals by the hope that he will discover his identity.... When the truth is made known ... it is unspectacular. Jack's mother is not a duchess but a treasure of a housekeeper to a foolish Sussex knight. In *Devil-in-the-Fog* ... the situation is reversed. George Treet, one of a travelling showman's brood, discovers early on that he is in fact the long-lost son and heir to a wealthy Sussex knight.... At last it appears that he is not the heir, but that he has been called upon to play a part with innate professionalism.

What makes these absurd plots not merely acceptable but absorbingly fascinating is Garfield's craftsmanship. He has a gift for creating sharp larger-than-life characters, like Mister Solomon Trumpet in *Jack Holborn* and Mr Thomas Treet, genius and loving father who allowed his infant son to be scarred for life in return for payments down and to come, in *Devil-in-the-Fog*. He excels in equivocal characters, leaving the reader to puzzle through the course of a long story whether they are good or evil. More important than characterization is style. Written in conventional modern English, these stories would scarcely find a reader, let alone a publisher. But Leon Garfield tells his stories in an extraordinary evocative language all his own (it is no more the language of the Eighteenth Century than Jeffery Farnol's equally artificial stylistic mannerisms were). Garfield hypnotizes the reader, wooing him with strange sounds and haunting circumlocutions into a willing co-operation. The words are like an incantation. Archaisms abound, and common words are disguised as unfamiliar contractions—'to've' and 'so's'. The pressure never eases. Garfield has remarkable skill in focusing attention on a situation or a character by a telling description. When Jack Holborn sees for the first time the agent of Nemesis—characteristically in the fog—'he never spoke nor nodded nor waved to any living soul, but stared and stared across the dirty sea as if he was looking for a particular wave.' Here the device is effective and functional, but at times it seems a form of self-indulgence or exhibitionism. (pp. 34-6)

Leon Garfield's craft is at its most brilliant, and is most at the command of his theme, in *Smith*.... In this story of a 'sooty spirit of the violent and ramshackle town' and of the London underworld the stylistic mannerisms are comparatively subdued, and the story moves almost as swiftly as Smith, beside whom 'a rat was like a snail'. Smith is a fine creation, a most complex blending of apparent contradictions.... In this book there are qualities lacking in most of Garfield's work, compassion and involvement. It is not just a masterly exercise in story-telling, but a book through which the reader shares in the triumphs and disasters of Smith and his admirable sisters, Miss Bridget and Miss Fanny.... (pp. 36, 38)

Marcus Crouch, in his The Nesbit Tradition: The Children's Novel in England 1945-1970 *(© Marcus Crouch 1972), Ernest Benn, 1972.*

MYLES McDOWELL

What is one to say ... of the view of life expressed in, for example, *Smith,* by Leon Garfield: is that simplistic? The word hardly seems an apt description for a kaleidoscopic view of fortune and deservings such as Garfield presents. Schematic, I suggest, is the more appropriate word. And in this word, I think, is contained one of the essential differences between an adult's and a child's view of life. By and large adults have effected a bifurcation between the moral and the physical imperatives. But this understanding is itself of fairly recent growth, having its springs in the development of scientific rationality during the last three centuries; and in popular terms perhaps is restricted to presently living generations of 'advanced' countries. A common nineteenth-century European view, in all strata of society, would have been that a moral power could, and frequently did, overrule the physical laws. A personal accident that befell one was not explicable in terms of a chain of physical cause and effect, but as a 'judgement' for some earlier moral failing. This schematic moral view of life is essentially childlike; and what is more, it is inconceivable that one should reach the more sophisticated state of discriminatory thinking about the varieties of cause and effect without going through the more primitive stage of belief that an omnipotent, omnipresent, omniactive power controlled all manifestations. From a child's point of view not only is such a view safe and reassuring, it is also optimistic. Good *will* triumph, and not because it has public support and sympathy (that being almost one of the characteristics of what we call good), but because it *must*. Evil *will* be punished, again a benign power reigns. (p. 54)

> Myles McDowell, in Children's literature in education (© 1973, Agathon Press, Inc.; reprinted by permission of the publisher), No. 10 (March), 1973.

GERARD BENSON

In *The Golden Shadow* [Garfield and Blishen] have combined a number of stories from disparate sources into a literary whole. Gods, demi-gods and god-like humans strive, love, lust, inhabiting a landscape whose very rocks and stones, whose tides are alive with menace and promise. The stories are linked through the figure of an aged storyteller who wanders from place to place, always, like the hero of Ted Hughes's *Bedtime Story,* inattentive at the crucial moment; so that he is there when the events happen, but never sees them happen.... It is an interesting device, and a successful one, as if the authors had imaginatively become this archetypal figure, and tried to eavesdrop on the scenes they described.

Since so many stories are packed within 150 pages, some, inevitably, suffer. At times the authors try too hard to work up to a climax in too short a time.... The result at such moments is a sub-Keatsian, orgasmic kind of writing, overladen with imagery. Here for instance is Atalanta running her final race:

> The rushing wind painted her tunic against
> her breasts and flying thighs ... she laughed
> aloud; she and the inquisitive air were one.
> She was a spirit—a dream in men's minds to
> be possessed only in sleep and death.

Good. Yes very. But you can have too much of a good thing.

However, when the authors settle down to the central episode, the story of Heracles, his childhood, his madness, his crime, punishment and expiation, his heroic act of mercy towards the chained Prometheus, and his eternal reward, the book becomes very good indeed, moving with remarkable narrative power. Here the myth is transmuted into something new: utterly modern in its writing and still Greek in feeling. (p. 782)

> Gerard Benson, in New Statesman (© 1973 The Statesman & Nation Publishing Co. Ltd.), May 25, 1973.

In *The God Beneath the Sea* [Leon Garfield and Edward Blishen] dealt mainly with the birth and conflicts of the gods and only incidentally with man. This new book, *The Golden Shadow,* is less lofty in its theme and all the better for it. The Olympian framework is still there, ... but this time it is man who holds the centre of the stage.

As in the earlier book, a number of different stories have been woven together to make a more or less coherent whole. The threads of continuity are provided by the adventures of Heracles and by the tale of Peleus and Thetis. The connecting link is a shortsighted storyteller, wandering from place to place, always arriving just too soon or too late, before or after the event, missing the gods or not knowing them and forever fated to inspire belief in others while unable to experience it himself for longer than the space of his song.

Oddly enough it is in this character of the compulsive artist, yearning after the ineffable but unable to resist pulling it to pieces to pluck out the heart while ordinary mortals simply marvel and accept, that the authors have come closest to the real quality of myth. Aging, tired, cynical, endlessly inquisitive, trudging the blinding roads, turning his head from side to side "with an eager, desperate smile—as if at any moment his short-sighted eyes would at last see a god": this is a creature that we recognize. Elsewhere, too often, it is still Charles Keeping's staggering illustrations which carry the burden of imagination, soaring onto a plane of pity and terror never reached by the laboured, adjectival prose.

Often, but not always. The writing has its moments. And as there is more humanity in this book, so there is less need for the inflated phrase. The descriptions of Heracles's madness, falling like warm rain out of a clear sky ... have their own staccato horror.... There is humour, too, in Heracles's relations with Iolaus (not here his nephew), and in the cleansing of the Augeian stables. Certainly, there is a depth and texture often missing from the run of retellings.

So far, so good. Allowing for a somewhat Procrustean attitude to the time scale, Messrs Blishen and Garfield have succeeded in weaving their chosen myths into the likeness of a continuous narrative. What they have also done, in clothing these bones with flesh of their own, is to impose a specific character on them. There is nothing against it. It is what writers have been doing ever since Homer. It is even what they must do. Whether, supposing one had never heard of the Greek myths, one would wish for this or that version as an introduction to them, remains a matter of individual choice. Where the authors may be held to fail is where the flesh is inadequate to the bones it has to cover, and in this case that happens at some point between the human and divine worlds. Prometheus glimpses as a tormented cliff shape through the wreathing mists of the Caucasus is fine, but in action he lacks the stature of the Aeschylean Titan. The creatures of myth are scaled down, Chiron the Centaur is reduced to running a kind of public school for heroes, and in the end, what we are left with is no more than crude couplings in caves, a poor exchange for the triumphant mating of a goddess with a man. (p. 675)

The Times Literary Supplement (© *Times Newspapers Ltd.* (London) 1973; reproduced from The Times Literary Supplement *by permission*), June 15, 1973.

[*The Golden Shadow*] is a companion to *The God Beneath the Sea* which was the subject of one of the most controversial of all Carnegie Medal Awards. It is likely to arouse equally violent passions of love and hate.

Let us waste no time in discussing whether it is for children. Neither [Garfield nor Blishen] is likely to believe in the existence of a separate category of "children's books"; both have been concerned to make a book as eloquent, true and passionate as human limitations permit.

Like the Greek tragedies—and it is a measure of the book's importance that one makes a comparison with no sense of incongruity—*The Golden Shadow* presupposes in the reader a knowledge of the subject-matter. . . . One must start with the ground-plan of Greek legend clearly in mind. Then one may relish the subtlety and the profound logic of the Garfield-Blishen interpretation which reconciles inconsistencies in the familiar versions and squeezes universal truths out of the irrational and often immoral behaviour of gods and mortals.

This is a book in which one cannot isolate for critical examination theme and style, for every element . . . depends on all the others. The flexible, highly artificial language is entirely at the service of the subject, and the writers, each a master of his craft, at no time indulge their virtuosity. The book is long and complex but tightly interwoven and constructed with strict economy. The principal themes, of Prometheus, Thetis, Hercules and the story-teller, interact and mirror one another in the most complex and satisfying counterpoint.

An important book? Unquestionably. A great book? Maybe; time must be allowed to work on both book and reader to determine this. An enjoyable book? Yes; the kind of enjoyment which grows as the book progresses and continues long after it is finally closed. (p. 330)

The Junior Bookshelf, *October, 1973.*

JUDITH VIDAL-HALL

[*The Golden Shadow*] is in no way a conventional retelling of the deeds of a strong-arm bully whose heroism is measured in monsters slain and enemies lying dead in heaps. It is every bit as idiosyncratic an interpretation as [*The God Beneath the Sea*], concerned more with the hero as a man than a superman, and questioning the nature of heroism itself. If there are two ways into myths as has been suggested, it is true to say that this book takes the inward route, looking beneath the outer religious and moral purpose of the stories to their inner preoccupations. We feel Heracles primarily as a man, still larger than life, but in weakness as well as in strength; the archetype not of the hero as species, but of everyman's heroic suffering in his quest through life. It is this dimension—the massive humanity of Heracles—that the authors have added to the

traditional story. It may be an interpretation nearer to our ways of thinking than to the original conception of the Greeks, and perhaps we lose here something of the old heiratic grandeur of the Myth, but we gain far-reaching insights, investing the story with a new and valid relevance. (pp. 182-83)

The Golden Shadow is for all who will read and are of an age to understand. It is not an easy book; its narrative devices are as complex as the ideas it contains. Despite the moments of humour, of broad comedy even, it is a sombre story told as a tragedy with all the violence and blood-letting that implied for the Greeks as well as Shakespeare. The language of its telling, only, is simpler than in the earlier book, more nearly reaching the poetic than the often tortured prose of that other. (p. 183)

Judith Vidal-Hall, in Children's Book Review (© 1973 Five Owls Press Ltd.; all rights reserved), December, 1973.

SHULAMITH OPPENHEIM

"There is no doubt about it," wrote Thomas Mann in 1936, "the moment when the story-teller acquires the mythical way of looking at things . . . that moment marks a beginning in his life." And with this gem of a book ["The Golden Shadow"] to back me up, I would add: the moment the listener, in this case the young adult reader, is confronted with such a story-teller, this moment must mark a beginning of a deeper insight into the dark recesses of man's fantasy life.

Is this saying a great deal? I mean to. One should not underestimate the literary gift of a thoroughly successful work, one that is sure to influence the inner life of every child *and* adult who reads it.

The original story-tellers here already worked with myth. But the book would not be what it is, a re-creation of the Heracles legend that makes us feel witness to its birth, were Leon Garfield and Edward Blishen themselves not endowed with the mythical perspective. In the hands of those less skilled and less sensitive, such a re-creation would be hubris.

Here time flows. The tales are stunningly interwoven. And like a true poem, time flows in the round. (p. 8)

Shulamith Oppenheim, in The New York Times Book Review (© 1974 by The New York Times Company; reprinted by permission), February 3, 1974.

C. S. HANNABUSS

The richly styled atmospherics of Leon Garfield form one of the salient literary features in the landscape of the last decade and a half of children's books. . . . [His] tales of misty derring-do, replete with coincidental encounters and nightmare villainies that work an insidious chemistry on the imagination of the reader, will remain on booklists for a long while. Nevertheless the strength of stories like *Devil-in-the-Fog* and *Black Jack* and *Smith* should be seen side by side with the pastiche heaviness of *Child O' War*, the manneristic parody of *The Strange Affair of Adelaide Harris*, and now the sense of self-imitation that arises in *The Sound of Coaches*. . . .

The play's the same but the company are tired after a long season. Episodes trickle along, description doing the work of action. The characters are not able to support this amplitude, for they thrive in the pell-mell that continually entertains and delightfully confuses the reader. The greater scope to show the hero's feelings is impaired by a hang-dog prolixity with none of the wry self-knowledge that exonerates, say, Tom Jones from being tiresome. *The Sound of Coaches* has few of the haunting harmonics one yearns to hear again: in fact it is rather a weary sound, going on a bit too long. (p. 110)

> *C. S. Hannabuss, in* Children's Book Review *(© 1974 Five Owls Press Ltd.; all rights reserved), Autumn, 1974.*

ETHEL L. HEINS

A favorite Garfield theme—the mystery of the hero's identity—forms the backbone of [*The Sound of Coaches*]; and a few lines quoted from *The Beggar's Opera* sets a theatrical atmosphere for the picaresque tale.... The threads of the skillfully-woven plot are almost too neatly tucked in at the end of the story; and after all the expended energy, the final chapter seems to go a bit limp. But the book bears many of the author's hallmarks—his melodrama; his discerning character development; and his humor: "two ... professional ladies in the company ... both not so much past their prime as having missed it altogether." And Garfield is still an alchemist with language, whipping it into a fine froth, extravagant images spilling out, one after the other. (p. 142)

> *Ethel L. Heins, in* The Horn Book Magazine *(copyright © 1974 by The Horn Book, Inc., Boston), October, 1974.*

C. E. J. SMITH

[*The Prisoners of September* is a] real reader's book. The plot is as nicely convoluted and ironically involved as one has come to expect; the characters have a touch of the eccentric excess that so delights: but the great fascination to the committed reader is that Mr. Garfield uses words so well, so prodigally, so precisely, so colourfully, powerfully, brilliantly. (p. 66)

Here are mystery and madness, violence and virtue, terror, conspiracy, coincidence, character, humour and surprise....

Mr. Garfield has been accused of self-indulgence—there seems little here. And it is asked: For whom does Mr. Garfield now write? Surely he writes for those who love fine words and a strong story. However, it will be a well-schooled adolescent that copes easily with this. (p. 67)

> *C.E.J. Smith, in* Children's Book Review *(© 1975 Five Owls Press Ltd.; all rights reserved), Summer, 1975.*

[*The Prisoners of September*] marks a turning-point in Leon Garfield's career. It is not only that he has chosen to leave the strange never-never land of *Smith* and *Jack Holborn* in favour of the authentic historical past. He has abandoned too his standpoint of ironic detachment; if he does not identify with his characters now he certainly takes them very seriously indeed.

If this should seem too sober a view, it must be added that Mr. Garfield has a great sense of fun, and exercises all his old virtuosity in description and happy turns of phrase. (p. 263)

The story is of Sussex and of France under the Revolution. Mr. Garfield for once introduces historical figures, notably the Comtesse de la Motte-Valois, victim or villain of the Queen's Necklace affair, whose introduction to bourgeois Sussex society ends disastrously. The first scenes, freshly evoking the atmosphere of the Downs and introducing affectionately the naive and accident-prone hero, are delightful. The story is richly humorous, but seriousness breaks in very soon. The Revolution is no joke....

This seems to me to be Mr. Garfield's best book to date. He writes as well as ever, and captures atmosphere with all his old mastery. It has sometimes seemed in the past that he exercised these crafts almost for their own sakes. Here his skills are at the service of a strong theme, a subtle and complex plot, and a gallery of very individual, entertaining and, for the most part, entirely credible characters. In writing *The Prisoners of September* he demonstrates once again, and this time most tellingly, the meaninglessness of classification into 'children's' or 'adult' books. This is a Book. (p. 264)

> The Junior Bookshelf, *August, 1975.*

MARGERY FISHER

This splendidly unclassifiable novel [*The Prisoners of September*] opens in a mood of exuberant mock-Gothic comedy, with a hero as gullible, though hardly as winning, as Catherine Morland: it ends in tragedy, in the victory of violence and compromise over idealism and innocence. Events of great moment in the past—the French Revolution in general and the Septembrist massacres in particular—are treated with the opportunism of a Dickens or a Dumas, used to give a positive turn to the lives of two heroes who prove, in the end, to be anti-heroes. (p. 2679)

I have no doubt that *The Prisoners of September* will be read with an eye to its relevance to the present day, for the very direct look at the self-perpetuating nature of violence, the implied comment on political ignorance and uninstructed idealism, the negation of conventional heroics. I hope it will also be read as an excellent story. The twists of the plot are contrived through the two main characters but also through a great many minor characters delineated strongly and with an almost genial humour. Dialogue and description are managed with a skill and firmness which I do not think Leon Garfield has ever equalled. In particular, his predilection for the off-beat or unexpected verbal image is, in this book, kept in bounds and used only when it really contributes to the story in one way or another.... [Though] I may have seemed to suggest otherwise, this is a pleasing book to read—pleasing because it does so well what it sets out to do, pleasing because of the conclusion on which the story rests, so unexpected and yet so right; pleasing, above all, because in it, Leon Garfield expresses once more, in the indirect way proper to a novel, his respect for humanity. (p. 2680)

> *Margery Fisher, in her* Growing Point, *September, 1975.*

GORDON PARSONS

Leon Garfield has said that we are all the ghosts of what we were. Unfortunately, if we are to afford Garfield the level of critical response his remarkable achievements demand, it must be acknowledge that [*The Prisoners of September*] echoes uncomfortably the stylistic brilliance of earlier works without developing into significant, fresh areas.

It is as if he is drawn spectre-like to the scene of previous triumphs. The characters are disconcertingly recognisable, patchwork creations from the dramatis personæ of earlier novels, while the relationships too explore familiar ground —the love-lorn boy drawn irresistibly to the blood-sucking woman for instance.

I hasten to add, however, that second-class Garfield is far in advance of the generality of writing for children. Perhaps the core weakness of *The Prisoners of September* lies in its construction, unlike his other books, around a specific historical event, the French revolutionary September massacres. This has forced upon the author a particular 'political' position. So, what had in *Smith* and *Black Jack* seemed a rich recognition of the complexity of human nature and the interdependence of human beings, here appears a slightly cynical, distanced observation of human motivation.

Adelaide Harris shared this tone but being much more broadly comic, it succeeded. Now we have a somewhat tired repetition of the unique style, presenting a disillusioned liberal-humanist world view. (pp. 244, 247)

> *Gordon Parsons, in* The School Librarian, *September, 1975.*

RUSSELL HOBAN

Leon Garfield is an example of what talent can do to a children's book writer: it can drive him out of children's books as he follows the development of his material wherever it takes him, and that is precisely what's happened. *The Strange Affair of Adelaide Harris,* for instance, has to be considered as an adult book. Comedy is a serious business in that it relies on dead accuracy of insight—the laughs don't happen unless we recognize ourselves and others in each situation. And the depth of recognition for *Adelaide Harris* requires adult experience.

Garfield's outstanding characteristic has always been energy and exuberance, his gusto in using words; and this has sometimes led him into overwriting. In *The Ghost Downstairs,* however, after a characteristically twinkling opening, he settles into what I think is his best and tightest writing to date. His variation of the Faust legend is a conception of frightening power, and wholly a book for grownups.

The measure of his invention is the shocking vitality of his 'What if?': What if it isn't necessarily the Devil who wants to buy the soul of Mr Fast? What if the canny seller offers the mysterious Mr Fishbane seven years of his life in return for wealth, but seven years from the *beginning* of it? What if, having signed away with his childhood all that was bright and wondrous in him, he finds existence a perdition of betrayal through which he haplessly pursues the self that he has sold?

In this book the theme has dominated the writer and freed him from mannerism and self-consciousness. His sensitivities are heightened, his sense of detail is remarkable: the sound of an iron hoop rolled by the ghost of childhood; a marvellous model of St Paul's made by a cabinetmaker 'long since retired from life size', with the craftsman's giant spectacles lying on miniature Ludgate Hill; the 'gently outstretched hands' of a young man sleeping in a train compartment—darks and lights evolved within the reader build a shifting chiaroscuro through which moments flash occulting one by one until the end:

> 'Where shall we go now?' whispered the little phantom, its pale face smiling up into the old man's.
>
> 'God knows', answered Mr Fishbane, and his beard streamed out to catch the stars.

The echo of Marlowe's 'See, see where Christ's blood streams in the firmament!' is not out of place; it closes a book that is eerily insightful, demonically vital, and not quite definable, a story in which the unhappy present destroys itself by betraying the innocent past. (pp. 74-5)

> *Russell Hoban, "Thoughts on Being and Writing" (© 1975 by Russell Hoban), in* The Thorny Paradise: Writers on Writing for Children, *edited by Edward Blishen, Kestrel Books, 1975, pp. 65-76.*

ANNE WOOD

All [Garfield's] books deal in some way with an atmosphere of concentrated evil shot through with possibilities for good. Perhaps his wartime experiences have had something to do with the springs of his writing inspirations. On the other hand, the press handouts all tell us that he "has a passion for secrets and mystery". However they are sparked off, Leon Garfield's books are unique in children's literature.

He is as aware as any other author for children of the need for frequent action. Never a page is turned but something happens, and yet the overwhelming contribution of his books is that they deal in that old-fashioned quality, morality. At the centre of each story is a young person, a boy usually, whose life is impinged upon by mysterious forces for good and evil, their rightness or wrongness obscured by different shows and pretences or seemingly accidental occurrences. Is everything as it seems? Part of the fascination of reading Leon Garfield is penetrating the camouflage of his precision-made plots. These are not historical novels in the accepted sense. An interpretation of history is certainly not what they are about. An interpretation of life perhaps.

The young men in *Prisoners of September* involved in the bloodier side of the French Revolution could just as easily be young men caught up in the violence of the I.R.A. Pickpocket Smith has his modern counterpart and Leon Garfield's latest long novel, *The Pleasure Garden,* "a garden of dreams where the old and ugly imagine themselves to be beautiful, the poor rich, and the damned saved—where all fantasies are played out" is as much a reflection of contemporary Britain as any part of eighteenth century London.

I therefore approached Leon Garfield's contribution to Andre Deutsch's Mirror of Britain series with heightened anticipation. I just didn't believe he could write a conventional general introduction to the Georgian Period. *The House of Hanover* proved my theory. Taking the brilliant device of viewing the period through the portraits of its leading figures, he proceeds to follow this through literally by making the entire book an account of a visit to the National Portrait Gallery. It is brilliantly done, never flagging for a second in breathless interest and amusement. It is entirely personal. Hogarth is featured on the front cover, Handel is lingered over, while Alexander Pope is gone over as quickly as is decent and Gainsborough comes a very poor second to Capability Brown. (pp. 2-3)

The House of Hanover must surely be one of the most entertaining introductions, not just to the artistic life of a particular period but to the relationship between art and life in any age, ever written. And if we seem to have moved away from the realms of childhood, consider for a moment the central question that a child on the point of growing up is concerned with, or for that matter, that the child that remains in all of us is concerned with. Who am I? Am I good or bad? The question does confront us and it needs audacity and a sense of humour to even contemplate it.

The line between good and evil is very thin and not always easily seen—it is a mystery to be probed. In his preoccupation on the grand scale with the devil's interference in the affairs of mankind, Leon Garfield does write the same book again and again. He has fabricated a totally convincing world dressed up in eighteenth century costume, endlessly fascinating to himself. Inside it he worries at dramatic situations presenting them to the rest of us with a flourish of style and wit. But more important than all of this, is that he presents them in terms that children, too, can enjoy and understand. (p. 3)

> Anne Wood, "Portrait of an Author: Leon Garfield," in Books for Your Children (© Books for Your Children 1976), Summer, 1976, pp. 2-3.

MARGERY FISHER

"Garfield's Apprentices" opens with two stories—*Mirror, Mirror* and *The Lamplighter's Funeral*—which offer examples of cruelty and compassion, defeat and victory. . . . Though the tales are short and structurally simple, they will appeal mainly to children experienced enough to catch the tone of a writer's voice and listen to his unspoken message. Both tales are full of imagery—the brilliance of jewellery and glass in the first, the revelations of torch light in the second. . . .

These are stories intended not to teach children history but to surprise them into realising that time does not change humanity very much. Leon Garfield's particular version of the London of Fielding and Hogarth offers its own private, searching history lesson. (p. 2913)

> *Margery Fisher, in her* Growing Point, *July, 1976.*

PETER HUNT

[With *The Pleasure Garden*] Leon Garfield has produced another rich meal from his sub-Smollett/Hogarth/Dickens recipe, and as a heavily decorated thriller it is very impressive. The cameos and grotesques are all alive—the staymakers, beggars, blackmailers, half-innocent urchins, the whores. But this time, his packed world is paralleled by an equally packed symbolism, centred on the microcosm of Mrs Bray's Mulberry Pleasure Garden with its masks, confessions, and dubious redemptions. Thus the Reverend Justice Young's search for a murderer is also a search for his own salvation; the trouble is that he often seems to be wading knee deep in symbols as well as red herrings.

Perhaps it is all too much of a good thing, for Mr Garfield's cleverness is also his Achilles' heel. His verbal dexterity does as much to create his atmosphere as do his scenes, and for most of the time it works well. Thus the noise of children on cellar steps "suggested that a small-sized hailstorm had got inside the house and panicked". But to say that "the revellers go out of the pleasure garden, out into the black garden of pain" is to go out into pretentiousness. It is not that the allegory is inappropriate, or that the ambi-

valence of everything (including, centrally, sex) is not well conveyed. It is more that Garfield is too insistent; his overstressing of the cosmic leads to overwriting, almost to self-parody, so that episodes such as Martin Young's struggle with the flesh . . . collapse under the weight of biblical significance.

But at least Mr Garfield's clichés are his own, and on this showing he remains someone to set standards by. (p. 880)

> *Peter Hunt, in* The Times Literary Supplement *(© Times Newspapers Ltd. (London) 1976; reproduced from* The Times Literary Supplement *by permission), July 16, 1976.*

PAUL LANGFORD

[*The House of Hanover*] takes the form of a stroll through the Hanoverian portions of the National Portrait Gallery, with a running commentary on the principal personalities of the age as they appear. It is a short book, but the approach is self-indulgent, with lengthy accounts of conversations between the author and a garrulous attendant, and a good deal of jovial jocularity. It is page forty before we actually reach the age of Hanover, though the result hardly justifies the effort of getting there. Each character is treated in a few superficial words, which convey Leon Garfield's prejudices, such as they are, but little of interest or consequence. There is no attempt to relate the artists and writers discussed to the major cultural, let alone social developments of the period, no attempt to transmit the essential flavour and character of Hanoverian England, no attempt to impose any kind of framework.

> *Paul Langford, "Georgian Stroller," in* The Times Literary Supplement *(© Times Newspapers Ltd. (London) 1976; reproduced from* The Times Literary Supplement *by permission), July 16, 1976, p. 886.*

[*The Pleasure Garden*] includes transvestism, prostitution, blackmail and murder. Meat for the kiddies? On the one hand Mr. Garfield has always maintained his contention that there are no books for children, only books; on the other his view of Georgian London is so enriched by imagination, persuasive detail, humour and dazzling wit that children and adults alike have no option but to surrender to his appeal. (p. 226)

The complex and flawlessly constructed plot unfolds with adequately sustained suspense.

There are too many good things here for full enumeration. One may mention briefly the brilliant character-drawing which is never very deep but always colourful, and the writing, which offers, literally, never a dull moment. Just one example: here the well-built Mrs. Bray stands beside her assistant who seems "really no more than a mere slice of a man who might have come off Mrs. Bray in a carelessly slammed door". In this, as in his mastery of colour and his control of a crowded canvas, Mr. Garfield is the Dickensian writer of our times. (p. 227)

> The Junior Bookshelf, *August, 1976.*

MARGERY FISHER

I would hesitate to offer *The House of Hanover* to anyone who did not already possess a reasonably good idea of the sequence of events in the eighteenth century and their own views on some at least of the century's writers. On the other hand, those who do already relish the period are likely to find Leon Garfield's dish somewhat over-spiced. This is, by intention, a very personal view of the period and one which is almost disavowed by the author when, having made a rapid and dogmatic tour of the National Portrait Gallery, he is adjured by the attendant to ''Go through the gallery again—and come out with a different answer''. So, we must accept, even if we do not like, echo or agree with, the attitudes he takes up in this book. He is lengthy and serious about Handel, coyly respectful of Johnson, disagreeably superficial about Pope (surely the fashion for describing the poet as a cold projector of strategems went out generations ago), sentimental about Swift, inadequate about George III. The idea of seeing the eighteenth century by way of a sequence of portraits was a good one and the book's epigraph, Pope's line ''The proper study of mankind is man'', says something valid about a period when individuals still steered historical event. Still, there is dangerously little of history here to anchor the throw-away literary comment, and a chronological scheme somewhat resembling Dunne's theory of Time is likely to confuse rather than enlighten a young reader not equipped with the essential skeleton of dates. The book may send some to the literary figures who are its chief subject and that (Leon Garfield implies) is his chief aim: it is a logical if unusual interpretation of the brief of the ''Mirror of Britain'' series, which is by definition a many-faceted cultural history. But history the series is, and history is both orderly and layered. I do not feel that Leon Garfield's contribution to the series is either. The many stimulating and pointed comments are lost in imagery that at times seems like self-parody and in chats with the gallery attendant which remind me uncomfortably of the father-son chats in [A. A. Milne's] Pooh books. And this could have been such a good book! (pp. 2944-45)

> *Margery Fisher, in her* Growing Point, *September, 1976.*

C. S. HANNABUSS

The Lamplighter's Funeral and *Mirror, Mirror* [are] . . . very much in the style of books like *The Ghost Downstairs* and *Black Jack*. The misanthropic lamplighter Pallcat in *The Lamplighter's Funeral* has a strange nocturnal meeting with Possul, a street urchin with disconcertingly innocent eyes and, when he becomes Pallcat's apprentice, with an uncanny and disturbing way of lighting up scenes of human misery in the murky Victorian streets. Travellers learn to avoid him, but Pallcat's thoughts are changed by this boy and by the bizarre way the boy views his job. *Mirror, Mirror,* too, develops a story both sinister and symbolic: apprentice Daniel Nightingale, working for a master-carver of mirror-frames, has to learn to cope with a house full of mirrors and full of the unreasonable sadism of his master's daughter. The mirrors seem to multiply his fears until he finds a way of using them to show her what she really looks like. Leon Garfield's distinctive melodrama allows him to write a compelling adventure and at the same time to explore the sinister side of life in ways children understand. . . . This is clear from books like *Smith* and *Devil-in-the-Fog,* and it is clear in [these stories], even if symbolism of a high Gothic kind sometimes makes some of the imagery a private adult literary experience. (p. 24)

> *C. S. Hannabuss, in* Children's Book Review (© 1976 Five Owls Press Ltd.; all rights reserved), *October, 1976.*

J. ALLAN MORRISON

[There] is too much of Garfield [in *The House of Hanover: England in the Eighteenth Century*] and he is showing-off like mad. The first person singular may have appeared in the earlier books, but I recall no instance; Garfield however talks as much about himself as about his characters and in that exuberance of verbiage which is a delight in his novels but which is quite out of keeping here. The smooth continuity of the [*Mirror of Britain*] series is rudely jarred. He is always readable, but I am not sure that he is believable. (p. 29)

> *J. Allan Morrison, in* Children's Book Review (© 1976 Five Owls Press Ltd.; all rights reserved), *October, 1976.*

JULIA BRIGGS

Leon Garfield [presents] his simple people simply as they are [in *Moss and Blister*], in a comic view that surprisingly avoids being patronizing while delighting in absurdity at every social level. His laughter is quite without contempt, despite the fact that his methods are akin to caricature. . . . *Moss and Blister* is the latest in Garfield's series of ''apprentices'', odd little books whose length suggests a slightness that their energy contradicts. Moss the midwife and her scrawny apprentice are a splendidly comic duo, plying their trade of delivering babies—itself seen as essentially comic, perhaps for the first time since Dr. Slop—on Christmas Eve. (p. 1545)

> *Julia Briggs, in* The Times Literary Supplement (© *Time Newspapers Ltd. (London) 1976; reproduced from* The Times Literary Supplement *by permission), December 10, 1976.*

A preliminary glance at [*The Book Lovers*] raises suspicions that it is nothing but an attempt to entice reluctant readers. A young man worships a librarian from afar and follows her from ''Lending'' to ''Reference'', where he presses his suit by means of love scenes in the books he reads, ostensibly to prepare an anthology on love. One should have more faith in Leon Garfield! In the first place, the framework story is deliciously funny. . . . Secondly, the extracts are all from nineteenth-century authors, and though some are inevitable, the choice from Dickens, Trollope, Jane Austen and Charlotte Brontë is by no means obvious. Other authors are less well-known to modern readers. . . . Most readers will have their horizons broadened—one extract is quite startlingly uncensored!—and the disparate elements fuse well into an entertaining whole. (p. 50)

> The Junior Bookshelf, *February, 1977.*

MARGERY FISHER

Leon Garfield's ''Apprentice'' stories are not for a young reading age, despite the somewhat misleading format and plentiful illustration. In these terse, ironic tales there is a concentration of imagery, an elusive technique of characterisation and a breadth of social comment which demand an alert reader (I suggest, ten and over) ready to accept an idiosyncratic but authentic view of the past. Like their predecessors in the series, the present books, numbered 5 to 8, contain several linking devices. The London scene shifts from one street to another within the City, from St. Martin's Churchyard in *The Valentine* to a dingy yard off Old 'Change in *Labour in Vain*, from a Jewish clockmaker's in Carter Lane in *The Fool* to Drury Lane and its alleyways in *Rosy Starling*. Each tale is marked by a festival. . . . Beyond the links of place and circumstance there are deeper links in theme, for each of these caustic, sharply documented tales turns on imposture, self-deception, change and—in a sense—growing up. When the sequence is complete I am sure it will stand out as one of the most notable individual commentaries of our time on the vanity of human wishes, a lesson anyone could learn willingly through this unique combination of historical detail and universal feeling. (pp. 3199-200)

Margery Fisher, in her Growing Point, *November, 1977.*

That Leon Garfield is a fine writer is unquestionable, but even so, many of his books have been beyond the range of many children. This is not a criticism of the writer, more one of the level at which many children are able to read and interpret what they read. His books have been a delight to those with the ability to appreciate them but above the limits of many. This makes the Apprentice series so much more welcome; the style, the skill of a superb story teller, the imaginative tale are all here in miniature and this has made the best in modern children's literature possible for a much wider readership. *The Valentine* tells of a young girl, daughter of an undertaker who pines after one of her father's previous "clients". A rival firm employs an apprentice, Hawkins, whom she loathes as being instrumental in taking business away from her family's business. The two young people are isolated in their macabre trade, their romance starts among the graves. There is a wry humour and great sympathy in this story which is beautifully written. (p. 351)

The Junior Bookshelf, December, 1977.

RHODRI JONES

Leon Garfield's five early novels—*Jack Holborn, Devil-in-the-Fog, Smith, Black Jack,* and *The Drummer Boy*—established very clearly the kind of world we associate with Garfield's writing. Since then, he has continued to produce prolifically, but the sense of unity, the sense of direction, seems to have become dissipated. It is not just a question of wanting or expecting him to go on writing as he has done or to write about the same things as before. After all, one doesn't expect each of William Mayne's books, for example, to be the same—in fact, one is surprised and gratified that each new novel is different and unpredictable. Nor does Garfield's later work lack quality—*The God Beneath the Sea, The Strange Affair of Adelaide Harris,* and *The Ghost Downstairs* are as fine as anything he has written. But nevertheless, looking back at the work he has produced since *The Drummer Boy*, there is a slight nagging sense of disappointment as though Garfield has missed his footing or somehow stumbled from the path and only intermittently found it again. He seems to be turning round seeking new directions, not all of which lead to successful destinations.

The quintessential Garfield world of the early novels is most instantly recognisable in his subsequent short novels. Stories like *The Boy and the Monkey, The Captain's Watch,* and *Lucifer Wilkins* show the characteristic delight of playing with words and images and the creation of chirpy characters. The more recent *Mirror, Mirror* and *The Lamplighter's Funeral*, two of a projected twelve under the general heading of 'Garfield's Apprentices', mark a very definite return to the London of narrow streets and evocative names, of master craftsmen and beggared children—though perhaps the squalor is more readily revealed. . . .

Another element which has previously been evident in Garfield's writing—though not, strangely, in the major novels—is an interest in the supernatural, but none of his ghost stories has been as extended and successful as *The Ghost Downstairs*. It is innovatory in that it is set outside the eighteenth century, in the time of children's sailor suits, of cabs and trains. . . . The story is told with grim power though not without the touches of irony and humour that are characteristic. (p. 41)

Comedy is always bursting out in Garfield's work, but with *The Strange Affair of Adelaide Harris* comedy has taken over completely. The story has the riotous to-ing and fro-ing of a farce by Feydeau. The characters are all swept along in a fantastic dance as complication upon complication is piled up to a masterly dénouement. Every detail is right; every incident builds up our knowledge of the characters and tangles or untangles the skein of the plot more. No word is wasted. It is a virtuoso performance, whose virtuosity can be gauged by comparing it with the short story *The Restless Ghost,* where the two schoolboy heroes, Bostock and Harris, who set the dance going by exposing the infant Adelaide on the hillside in emulation of Ancient Sparta, made an earlier appearance. In the short story, Bostock and Harris are merely rather mischievous schoolboys involved in a prank that becomes too big for them. In *The Strange Affair of Adelaide Harris* they have been purified and refined; they have come into focus. Harris is the one with the cunning brain and the deep thought, Bostock his more sensitive but rather dense friend (except that it is Bostock who shows the real intelligence) with an undying admiration for and devotion to his supposed genius of a hero. They are not just schoolboys, they are quintessential schoolboys. (p. 42)

Another direction Garfield was moving in was towards collaboration. *The Ghost Downstairs,* for instance, could almost be described as a joint work with the illustrator, Antony Maitland. But the most important collaboration has been with Edward Blishen in their retelling of the Greek myths in *The God Beneath the Sea* and *The Golden Shadow,* where the myths are given a fresh power and a new and strong narrative unity. The strength of these two books lies in the sweep of the story-telling and in the austere nobility of the tone, which except in occasional ironic asides is strangely unlike the Garfield of the earlier novels and shows a greater restraint. The characters come alive without losing dignity. The stories are filled in with details that convince—the hawkers selling purses of sand stained with the blood of the Nemean Lion in the market place of Mycenae, for example—so that a sense of bustling life is given to this strange mixture of heroic endeavour, godly power and human frailty without in any way diminishing the grandeur and awesomeness of the events. Both volumes (*The Golden Shadow* marginally less so) are splendid achievements, and rescue the myths from past flat and fustian versions—even if one may sometimes have to go back to those versions to find out what the myths actually and factually were.

It is with the three major novels that Garfield has written since *The Drummer Boy* that doubts really begin to press. *The Sound of Coaches* has a theme reminiscent of the earlier *Jack Holborn* and *Devil-in-the-Fog* with its hero Sam searching for his real father and finding disillusionment along the way. The world of the coaching trade and the travelling actors that Sam joins are vividly portrayed, but somehow Sam is too pale a character for us to care very much about him. *The Prisoners of September* deals with the involvement of two young Englishmen in the massacres of September 1793 in Paris. They are like two halves of the same character, one glorying in the brutality while believing himself to be fighting for freedom, the other repelled by the horror of it. Unthinking idealism takes a hard knock. *The Pleasure Garden* is set in a kind of open-air brothel, based presumably on Vauxhall Gardens, where children hide all night in the trees and report on the goings-on for the purpose of blackmail.

It is not simply that these novels display an increasing though only occasional coarseness of language and violence. There is the cellarman Joe in *The Sound of Coaches*, for instance, talking about the sun 'shining out of the tiddler's arse'; there is Richard Mortimer in *The Prisoners of September* inciting the crowd to tear a young woman's body to pieces and the vision of packs of wild dogs rushing through the streets of Paris with the private parts of princesses in their jaws; there is the whole idea of children being involved in voyeurism and blackmail in *The Pleasure Garden*. These were crude and violent times, and foul language can be justified in terms of character, but are such things suitable reading for children? (pp. 42-3)

[There] have been violent and unpleasant episodes in [Garfield's] earlier novels, but the subject-matter of his recent novels seems more suitable for adults than for children. They raise the question of what is a children's writer, which is a large topic but a part of whose answer is to do with tone, the way the author addresses his imagined audience. And while Garfield is writing about things which more suitably concern adults than children, his tone is still that which one would use when talking to children alone, with the result that the end-product is satisfactory neither to one nor to the other. . . . He wants to communicate, and he wants to communicate to children and adults, but this is only possible in exceptional circumstances—and usually long after the author is dead. It seems appropriate that the figure of Prometheus should loom so large in *The God Beneath the Sea.* (p. 43)

> *Rhodri Jones, in her postscript to "Leon Garfield," in* Good Writers for Young Readers, *edited by Dennis Butts (copyright selection and arrangement © 1977 Hart-Davis Educational), Hart-Davis Educational, 1977, pp. 41-4.*

PHILIP HOLLAND

Garfield's novels appeal to young readers for reasons which should become clear in looking at them individually. All his work has a strong narrative line and his books are worlds of violent adventure. Theatricality and melodrama are part of their fabric. The hero's search is not only for his identity but also for moral certainties in the shifting sands of good and evil. The hero is usually an adolescent boy, bewildered by the duplicity of the adult world. He is a valuable point of identification for the young reader. The moral choices he has to make are presented not in terms of psychological analysis (until we come to *The Pleasure Garden*) but in terms of action and discussion which offer a high level of vicarious experience. Garfield's style also has a

wide appeal; its level of complexity varies, and while it is never easy for any other than the literate child the vocabulary is not particularly unusual or difficult. The imagery is strongly visual and colourful and he appreciates children's curiosity for detail. He will thread an idea or an image through a story so that it becomes a signpost of the plot, providing a thrill of recognition or anticipation. Such detail contributes to the vividness of his writing and often to its humour, for even in the grimmest situation—and ''the stench of Newgate gaol'' pervades almost all the novels—an ironic humour breaks through.

Most of Garfield's fiction is set in the eighteenth century, the better to observe the moral issues he wishes to examine. . . . He homes in on a small area—mostly London and the South of England—and, within this area, certain institutions—the prisons, the courts, the inns, the households—and in a controllable and documented time and space he is able to examine more clearly the motives and actions of his characters. . . . Period and setting are certainly central to the unities he wishes to observe.

The grip that Garfield now has on his plots is something that has come with time. In his first two novels, he told the stories as first person narrations and therefore placed on himself constraints which do not suit his style. In both, the hero is seeking his identity—Jack Holborn, the foundling, completely on his own, and George Treet from a position of unexpected elevation as heir to Sir John Dexter. For both, the theme of identity goes beyond the simple discovery of origin. There is a confusion in *Jack Holborn* between two brothers, one a judge, the other a pirate captain—but which is good and which is evil? Likewise, in *Devil-in-the-Fog,* Sir John's brother lurks in the shadows, possibly seeking revenge. Which of the brothers is telling the truth? Exciting though these stories are, the devices are crude compared with later novels. Identical twins and coincidences are cornerstones of the plots. In *Jack Holborn* particularly, Garfield nudges us along relentlessly; three times Jack must save the Captain's life. There are similar nudgings in *Devil-in-the-Fog*—the picture missing from the frame for example. They are clumsy devices, and neither of the two novels is fully satisfying. In *Jack Holborn* the interest level of the story diminishes towards the end apart from the two set pieces—the slave auction and the courtroom climax. The narrator is dull and too vaguely drawn to maintain our interest. And although George Treet in *Devil-in-the-Fog* is more lively, his theatrical ways fitting uneasily into the home of the reserved Dexters, the story is too crowded with incident and false trails, all rushed to an end in an ungainly final chapter of explanation upon explanation. The book has power . . . , but seen in the perspective of later Garfield achievements, it is unpolished and unsure.

The next two novels show a considerable advance. *Smith* is more firmly plotted and unified around the hero's search for understanding of the document he steals from a man he sees murdered shortly afterwards. There is a tension and suspense in the book created at the outset in the dimly lit streets where Smith carries errands for the prisoners of Newgate. From early in the story Smith is watched and followed—as are so many of Garfield's characters—but now those awkward plot warning signals turn into anticipatory chapter ends which are used so well in later novels. The search for identity is still present in a minor way—who is the mysterious Mr Black, the one-legged prime-mover of villainy? More important now, though, is the confusion between good and evil, the difficulty of the blind magistrate to whom "devils and angels are all one." This is a key issue in the Garfield world. . . . The environment's shaping of our nature is explored in some depth in *Smith*. Billing tells Smith "Life's a race for rats. . . . We're all rats, Smith —and it's eat or be eaten." But through Lord Tom's death Smith learns of the redeeming power of love, a theme of increasing importance for Garfield. There is a great deal of emotional knowledge to be learned in the book. . . . Smith's literal journey through the snow with the blind magistrate is one of the most vivid scenes in the book and more closely integrated with theme and subject than are the set pieces of the earlier novels. There is also the humour—varied from the pantomime undressing of Smith . . . and the slapstick quality of Miss Mansfield trying to get Smith out of bed . . . , to the more subtle use of irony in description. *Smith* is the first of the important novels.

Tolly Dorking, the hero of *Black Jack* doesn't have the resilience of Smith, but goes through more alarming experiences before finding joy in love for himself and salvation for Belle Carter. The horrors of this story are terrific, as the characters are aware—"if you was to know a part of all the wickedness done in a single day, you'd not sleep of nights." Tolly, however, manages to influence for the good almost all those around him, including the ruffianly Black Jack. . . . Hatch, Dr Carmody's apprentice, who turns to blackmail and becomes a keeper at the madhouse is a really evil youth, Garfield's most vicious creation. The novel becomes really frightening towards the end as the Northern Lights "spread their sombre finery across the sky," an earthquake shakes London and the end of the world is prophesied—when Hatch releases the lunatics and arms one of them with a chopper to go after Tolly and Belle. Hatch is as evil as Dr Dormann in *The Pleasure Garden*, but the latter is not so vicious and more subtle. Both come to a murky end in the waters of the Thames. As Hatch dies Garfield writes of "the ending of Hatch's world" and this is important with young readers in mind. Garfield never destroys hope; he never suggests his heroes won't pull through. Tolly and Belle triumph over the corruption and wickedness that seem set to destroy them. They find each other and in doing so discover themselves.

Black Jack was followed in 1968 by *Mr Corbett's Ghost*, published with two other stories in 1969. In these stories, *The Ghost Downstairs*, and the latest series of *Garfield's Apprentices*, the writer explores in some depth the relationship of the young to the adult world. The master-apprentice relationship runs through the novels also—the youthful apprentice always potentially good, energetic and full of hope; the master figure ranging from the world-weary Mr Mansfield, through the cynical Black Jack, the jaded, harsh Mr Corbett, to the vicious Bartlemann in *The Simpleton* and the evil Dr Dormann. The young may influence the old for the good: in *The Lamplighter's Funeral* the bitter Pallcat is devastated when he thinks his young apprentice might leave him, even though he treats him with great suspicion. . . . Both [the ghost] stories can be read as supernatural tales. They can also be read as wish-fulfilment stories, in which case they seem more powerful. It all depends on the maturity of the reader.

The Drummer Boy is a deeper-probing novel. Charlie Samson, the hero, is an innocent who is used by spiritually bankrupt adults. The plot is more subtly built, and Charlie's search is not only the literal one for Maddox, the adult failure, but for his own adulthood, free from the corruptions around him. . . . The material world is seen as hollow and the glories of the battlefield are sham and destructive. In the end Charlie destroys his drum, the symbol of a false manhood and finds the real one in the genuine love of Charity, Sophia's maid, and returns with her to the home of his father, which he had earlier left in defiance. Once again the hero is redeemed by love.

Garfield's surer touch is seen in a more subtle use of humour, from the depiction of the grotesque "teeth-fitter," Gamaliel Voice . . . to the more subtle jokes about Charlie's father—"a forest lover, in every sense of the word" whose children had been conceived in various outdoor places of historical significance. . . . (pp. 159-64)

That Garfield was trying his hand at creating humour became apparent in *The Strange Affair of Adelaide Harris*, a novel with a farcical structure. The raison d'être is superb. . . . We are in a different world from other Garfield stories. Even the young are selfish and stupid, but once again love conquers all for Mr Brett (supposedly a self-portrait) and Tizzy Alexander. Garfield concentrates his energies on the intricate plotting, but ultimately, I think, it is disappointing. He is forced into absurdity to keep the plot going. The characters have no imagination at all; the inquiry agent, Selwyn Raven, is presented as peculiarly blind to the obvious. His extreme patience and obtuseness are an irritation. The point at which Adelaide is discovered at the poorhouse, about halfway through the book, is really a point of conclusion, but Garfield has created so many ramifications of the plot that it continues on and on. The investigation of Adelaide's disappearance and the duel are really nonevents. I think the novel shows that Garfield needs the suspense and tension of a mystery, the puzzle of identity as material for a plot. (pp. 164-65)

With *The Sound of Coaches* Garfield returned to the subject matter and manner of approach which he handles so well and this novel is outstanding. Sam Chichester's life is traced from birth to manhood. One of the main themes of the book is the happiness we are able to bring to each other, and part of its richness lies in the fact that this is seen as a two-way process. Garfield builds up suspense and anticipation through a plot developed at considerable length (it is longer than *Adelaide Harris*) which never flags for a moment. In the early pages he weaves the motifs of the ring and the pistol through climactic chapter ends . . . until the pistol leads to the discovery of Sam's father, the old ham, Daniel Coventry. Suspense is created in little matters as well as large ones and the plot is built on revelations. (p. 165)

Among the many themes we can recognise in this novel— the search after truth, appearance and reality, fate and destiny, there are two that are of major interest. One is the passage of time, made concrete in the ever turning wheels of the coach that Sam's adoptive father drives. Time brings change, but change and knowledge do not necessarily bring happiness, and Sam must make his own decisions about the life he wishes to lead. The young must supplant the old and Daniel Coventry is a vain and ridiculous figure as he tries to prevent his natural son's talents from outshining his own. The weakness of character and moral turpitude of Coventry is finely presented for a young reader's understanding. And this indicates the second major theme—the relationship between environment and heredity. Until this novel all Garfield's heroes have got from their parents has been a name. Sam, however, is a fuller character with an inheritance in his nature. (pp. 165-66)

Given the strength of the plot and characterisation and the opportunity to explore a range of themes, Garfield constructs a splendid novel and his humour finds its element within the larger framework. The book is less sombre than many of its predecessors, for the characters are seen less as victims of environment and more capable of hammering out their own lives, even if fate does occasionally take a cruel hand. (p. 166)

In the two novels published since *The Sound of Coaches* Garfield has shown a widening of interest and range. He has begun to explore territory perhaps outside the appreciation of the younger reader but not of the older adolescent, and he still offers a strong narrative. Both *The Prisoners of September* and *The Pleasure Garden* are exciting novels and the latter is compulsive reading. The central characters are no longer innocents but young adults who know the world is no Garden of Eden, but who are unprepared for the depravity of their fellow creatures. (p. 167)

[*The Pleasure Garden*] is almost an allegory of the evil man has wrought in the world. The Pleasure Garden is at once the world where man takes his pleasures, but where no man is safe, and a Garden of Eden whose serpent hides in the trees in the form of the urchins who spy upon the couples and report back to the devilish Dr Dormann. The evil that Garfield conjures up in this novel is far more terrifying than the petty wickednesses he has chronicled in others. Although the book has the framework of a murder mystery, this is not the aspect that Garfield is interested in. The identity of the murderer is not significant. He uses the elements of the plot as a catalyst for his story of the struggle between good and evil, to enable him to study, more than ever before, the mind of his central character, who, with his "great gift" of gentleness and compassion, tries to lead people to goodness. Garfield is particularly good in this novel at letting the reader see the difference between a character as perceived and a character in reality. . . . As in *The Prisoners of September* the tone at the end is optimistic, but the struggle to come through is harder for an adult than for a child.

Garfield's style is his unique characteristic. His highly coloured imagery and extravagant descriptions appeal to children even though not everything may be immediately accessible. His books are worth rereading to explore further the pictures he paints, or the thematic use of imagery such as that of the sea in *Black Jack*. (p. 168)

Very occasionally the imagery is merely decorative but usually it is an organic part of the writing. I think, to use Eliot's idea, Garfield possesses "a mechanism of sensibility" which can devour experience and turn it into effortless imaginative expression. I have heard him say that his style is not the result of endless reworkings, but the natural mode of expression of his subject matter. His war service, his seafaring experiences, his scientific training, his medical knowledge are all part of his imaginative reservoir. Of his character Bostock in *Adelaide Harris* he writes: "He did not have the creative imagination that seizes on matters,

apparently of little use and far apart, and instantly divines the link between them." Garfield does have this quality and his creative imagination is fertile. (p. 169)

[Garfield] is a master of mystery and a master of style. The latter is probably seen to best effect in the short stories, where he polishes words like diamonds. (p. 170)

Different writers have different aims, but Garfield's attempt to produce books for the family is a notable one. It is commonplace to find him compared in reviews to Dickens. His literary antecedents include Stevenson and Fielding, but certainly he brings Dickens to mind. He creates a similar sort of London, he enjoys the theatrical and melodramatic nature of events, he constructs a stong narrative, he attacks materialism, he hates the law—"red in tooth and clause" he writes in one story—he loves eccentric characters. In *The Prisoners of September* he has given us his *Tale of Two Cities* and in *Mr Corbett's Ghost* a story that stands comparison with *A Christmas Carol*. As Dickens did, he seems to be moving from reliance on narrative strength to a compassionate observation of the meaning of life for an individual. Like Dickens, I think he is capable of creating his own audience, for a taste for the early novels can lead any reader to explore the latest works. We already have a rich set of novels and stories and his work with Edward Blishen on the retelling of the Greek myths as continuous narrative or his "fictional history" in *Child O' War* suggests that he is a writer of whom we can entertain great expectations. (pp. 170-71)

Philip Holland, "Shades of the Prison House: The Fiction of Leon Garfield," in Children's literature in education *(© 1978, Agathon Press, Inc.; reprinted by permission of the publisher), Vol. 9, No. 4, 1978, pp. 159-72.*

No writer can convey the spirit and sheer liveliness of the eighteenth century as can Leon Garfield. . . . [*The Fool* is a] lively account of the rough and tumble of city life before the days of social services and modern sanitation. Garfield has traced back his apprentices in eighteenth century books and manuscripts and no detail is omitted, no subtlety of plot missed. A rare masterpiece. . . . (pp. 25-6)

The Junior Bookshelf, *February, 1978.*

Trust Leon Garfield, always literate in 18th-century London, to transform off-beat material into an engrossing read. Here [in *The Apprentices*] he introduces a string of apprentices in separate chapters, assigns them authentic occupations and identities, and just perceptibly interlocks their stories through several months of fictional time. Thus Possul, the lamplighter's linkboy, walks by most of the characters after his opening chapter; the midwife and the mirror-frame carver both stop in the mirror-maker's house; and virtually all have some contact, passing or more lasting, with the Noades funeral. And the stories themselves have integrity. . . . Subtle class distinctions and the daily grime emerge as well as religious and political items: as the Jewish clockmaker's family celebrates Passover, an uninvited guest appears at the door opened for Elijah, and the printer's apprentice has the wrong stock burned to please an author's appealing daughter. Clever—an assemblage of Dickensian names . . . and distinct faces. (p. 252)

Kirkus Reviews *(copyright © 1978 The Kirkus Service, Inc.), March 1, 1978.*

The kind of story currently being given a place in publisher's lists of books for young people differs very much from those deemed suitable for [the teenage] group even a very few years ago. Now there is virtually no subject considered unsuitable, and characters are permitted to use any sort of language. One wonders indeed for what readership the authors and the publishers intend such stories, and whether it would not be better to publish them on an adult list.

These two latest additions to the ''Garfield's Apprentices'' series [*Tom Titmarsh's Devil* and *The Dumb Cake*] concern scenes from life behind the counter in an eighteenth century bookshop, and the superstitions and customs associated with Midsummer's Eve some two hundred years ago.

Few authors have painted the seamier side of eighteenth century life with such minute attention to detail as Leon Garfield has and the result is a certain compelling style of writing, but whether these two books are entirely suitable for teenage readers remains highly questionable. (p. 153)

The Junior Bookshelf, June, 1978.

ANN A. FLOWERS

[Leon Garfield], noted for his Dickensian novels about London, has written [with *The Apprentices*] an ingeniously linked series of twelve tales about apprentices set in successive months, so that the book covers one year; each tale has a relationship to at least one of the others and each deals with a different craft. Many of the stories tell of some unlikely and unexpected good deed. For instance, ''The Lamplighter'' is the tale of Pallcat, a dirty, stingy old man, who reluctantly takes a pathetic waif as his apprentice and, to his own surprise, becomes attached to him. . . . Characters appear and reappear, sometimes as major figures, sometimes as passersby. A lamplighter or a linkboy crops up in almost every story, demonstrating the themes of light and dark, good and evil that dominate the book. The sights, the sounds, and especially the smells of eighteenth-century London are vividly presented, making a brilliantly impressionistic and amusing book. (p. 402)

Ann A. Flowers, in The Horn Book Magazine *(copyright © 1978 by the Horn Book, Inc., Boston), August, 1978.*

RONI NATOV

Leon Garfield has been hailed as one of the best contemporary writers for adolescents for his lively and unmistakable style, his ability to weave a series of endlessly fascinating plots, and for his quirky and unforgettable characters. He draws richly and with originality from our great masters of fiction: Fielding, Smollett, and Dickens. His debt to Fielding and Smollett is most obvious in terms of the settings of his novels, all of which take place in the 18th century. Many of them make use of the picaresque episodic structure and the complex combination of comedy and violence found in those early works. Encounters with all kinds of rogues, kidnappings, attempted and actual murders are not unusual in a Garfield novel. In fact, his own particular use of the adventure story, varied and expansive as it is, involves exploring and indulging in melodrama, which allows, of course, for suspenseful plots and characters that undergo extreme states of feeling.

But while any Garfield novel uses all the conventional

melodramatic devices, his sense of humor tempers, refines, and adds complexity, so his novels don't feel corny or staged. Like Fielding, Garfield seems to embrace humanity in all its pettiness and smugness, and is appreciative of man's ingenuity. He is interested in exploring what we do to survive—and how, in the direst of circumstances, we are often deprived of the luxury of being moral, upright, and clean. While Garfield takes us through slums, onto pirate ships, into prisons, his touch is always lightened by humor, and therein lies his chief debt to Dickens. It is obvious that at least two of his novels draw their style and format from Dickens' work. *Smith* is as much like *Oliver Twist* and *Prisoners of September* like *A Tale of Two Cities* as they could be without being actual copies or parodies of those earlier works. But chiefly Dickens' pervasive comic sense of character is what Garfield borrows and makes his own. His characters explode with idiosyncratic verbal tics and gestures, which become their signatures, though the characters rarely lose their complexity.

So Garfield comes to adolescents as a particularly rich writer, and one who defies categories. . . . Garfield's adventure stories stand apart. . . . They are romances—sea stories, picaresque adventures, historical novels—which confront the same problems that all the ''relevant'' adolescent novels hinge on: the quest for identity, coming to terms with one's roots and heritage, learning to distinguish between authenticity and artifice, and finding a place for oneself in the world. Yet the use of the 18th century, which for Garfield is ''more of a locality than a time,'' allows a fresh look at these essential themes. The reader is glued to his seat, much in the way 18th and 19th century novelists held their readers in suspense, while Garfield plunges into these issues. He feels compelled to write about the quest for identity because, as he says, ''I have a passion for secrets and mystery. And the secret and mystery of another individual seems to me the only mystery one can unravel endlessly. . . .''

So while his readers can revel in the sheer joy of good storytelling, Garfield is one of the few writers of adolescent novels who doesn't cheat them by ending his responsibility with suspenseful narration. Nor does he simplify the world in an attempt to satisfy the adolescent impulse toward closure. In other words, he does not make the world sweeter, or the obstacles in his stories darker, uglier, more or less threatening than they are. In his warmth and humor he urges an acceptance of humanity and a tolerance of ambivalence which is unique to the world of adolescent fiction. And it is this tolerance that allows for an honest, substantial, and mature point of view.

Garfield's first novel, *Jack Holborn* . . . , is a sea adventure, and the plot is constructed out of the traditional motifs of the genre: sailing to strange and faraway places, shipwreck, treasure hunting, mutiny and piracy. It is often cumbersome, melodramatic, and unconvincing, but it is exciting. We are drawn into the story immediately as Jack, the young hero, stows away in the hold of the ship, the ''Charming Molly,'' while it is taken over by pirates and the original crew murdered. This dramatic and violent opening is described through the eyes of the child, Jack, who is about the same age Stevenson's Jim Hawkins was when he set sail for Treasure Island. But Garfield's hero, though he remains relatively undeveloped at the end of the novel, is a far more interesting character. Unlike Jim, he is a waif and has the cynical viewpoint of an abandoned child. (pp. 44-6)

[Jack's quest] involves learning who to trust, how to distinguish between good and evil, and how to detect deception. And the adults in this novel are certainly difficult to decipher.

In Stevenson's *Treasure Island,* on which this novel draws heavily, Jim's maturity can be plotted by noting his responses to Long John Silver. Tossed between trusting and fearing him, Jim must sift out what Long John appears to be from what he really is. And just as Jim confronts a series of father figures after the death of his own father, culminating in the confrontation with Long John, Jack goes through a similar process in which he comes to terms with a gallery of strange and ambiguous male figures. (p. 46)

However, the man who figures most centrally in Jack's quest is the Captain, and it is his identity which is most mysterious. . . . We learn that the Captain is really two men, identical twins: the distinguished judge, Lord Sheringham, and the vicious, deceptive Captain Rogers. Explaining away the Captain's paradoxical behavior with a case of mistaken identity is, as John Townsend points out [in his *A Sense of Story,* see excerpt above], a crude device, but the portraits of most of the characters are vivid and complex. Through them, Jack comes to understand how two seemingly opposing traits can and do coexist. The sinister pirate captain has a real sense of integrity and dignity, and Trumpet becomes a kind and loving friend. (p. 49)

[The question of Jack's] identity is solved with a surprising little twist. Instead of discovering, in typical fairy tale fashion, or in the tradition of *Tom Jones,* that the foundling was really of noble birth after all, we discover, as the name Holborn suggests, that we needn't look to be what we aren't and that we need only to be ourselves to develop whatever is already within us. . . .

Trumpet's message to Jack—"'So d'you see, Jack, right from the beginning you've been yourself without knowing it!'" . . .—could also be said to be the underlying theme of Garfield's next novel, *Devil-in-the-Fog.* . . . The democratic impulse that characterizes much of Garfield's work is more fully and concisely developed in this Dickensian adventure story. (p. 50)

Devil-in-the-Fog takes a real leap from *Jack Holborn.* Garfield's humor is more developed here than in the earlier novel, and his use of the first person narrative more sophisticated. But the resolution to the question of identity is similar. In the end George reclaims Treet as his father and rejects the aristocrats' offers to adopt him as their son and heir. Though the aristocrats are presented as generous and affable, it is another victory for the lower-middle classes and for ordinary people.

This is also true of Garfield's next novel, *Smith* . . . , which is reminiscent of the Newgate or crime novels of [William Harrison] Ainsworth and [Edward] Bulwer Lytton, popular in Dickens' time. Actually, it is most like Dickens' own attempt at this genre, *Oliver Twist,* particularly in its plot. It is the story of the adventures of a young street urchin who is taken in by a rich old gentleman and his devoted daughter. Like *Oliver Twist,* it contrasts the criminal life of the slums of London with the comfortable safety of the old gentleman's world. . . . This hero has none of the choir boy

markings of Oliver. The portrait of Smith is less sentimental and more realistic. (pp. 54, 57)

[Although] the novel is always suspenseful, it is often unconvincing in its machinery and detail. What *is* convincing, however, is the child-terror of Smith's many narrow escapes and betrayals. The world is depicted, as it was in both *Jack Holborn* and *Devil-in-the-Fog,* as a dangerous place, where children must develop extra sharp senses to ward off violence. This vision never gets too threatening, however; it is offset by a series of comic incidents and satiric jokes. (p. 57)

There seem to be two visions of life that control the novel. One is cynical and is presented by the criminals. . . . (p. 58)

However, a more optimistic, romantic feeling presides, particularly in the relationship between the blind magistrate and Smith, whose growing bond and affection is able to work great changes in them. . . . And Smith stays with the blind magistrate, risking his own life, and is rewarded with the protection of a good home for himself and his sisters. All this, of course, suggests a sentimental happy ending. (pp. 58-9)

In *Black Jack* . . . , Garfield's next adventure story, the predominant Garfield themes prevail. The young hero straddles the two opposite worlds of the lower and upper classes. As he matures, he is reconciled with his humble origins, though he gains security and comfort from exposure to the aristocracy. But in this novel, these themes are transformed: they seem to have been sunk beneath the surface. The settings are dream landscapes and the themes are surrealistically played out. There are two main story lines and two important relationships, with Tolly, the young hero, at the center of the opposing poles. The first, Tolly's relationship with the criminal, Black Jack, seems to dominate; however, the developing love between Tolly and Belle, the young daughter of the wealthy Carter family, absorbs our interest and, at times, threatens to take over the novel. This is the first Garfield novel in which romantic love plays a part. As in the previous novels, the hero goes through an identity crisis which involves coming to terms with parental figures. But here it is the love relationship that helps the hero to mature. (p. 59)

This novel is the most satisfying of Garfield's work thus far. It is a suspenseful picaresque adventure, a rich tapestry into which Garfield weaves a variety of fascinating characters. His satirical portraits of the many hypocritical doctors are reminiscent of Dickens' lawyers, and the scenes of the inmates and their keepers at the madhouse are hilarious and piercing. Out of this gallery of quacks and eccentrics, Belle, the mad child, emerges, dazzles us, and captures our hearts. And even though this view of madness (fitting as it may be for an 18th century historical novel) is erroneous and romantic, Garfield's depiction of Belle's erratic behavior convinces and fascinates us. (p. 61)

Belle grows stronger and more coherent through persistent love and understanding; by loving her, Tolly comes to accept the forces of the irrational in himself; and the union of Belle and Tolly suggests a harmonious balance. As always, Garfield ends his novels with a bonding. In the earlier novels, it is between parent and child. Here, as in the later novels, two lovers are united. In this sense *Black Jack* is a turning point. But, as in the earlier novels, the message is the same: order is restored but characters maintain their ambiguous qualities and human frailty is accepted. (pp. 61-2)

With *The Sound of Coaches* ..., Garfield expands his picaresque adventure novel to include the kind of psychological probing found in the modern domestic novel. The hero here is a fuller, more complex young man and we watch him grow from infancy to manhood. We observe his adopted parents closely, and establish the motivation behind the characters' actions. While *The Sound of Coaches* is another story of a young man in search of his identity, the problems of growing up are here more accurately described. Garfield exposes the underlying competition and jealousy between father and son, the impulsiveness of adolescent sexuality, and the illusions of youth and inevitable disillusionment with parents and lovers. (p. 62)

Throughout, ... Garfield never loses the hard edge of honesty. He remains true to his characters. He understands that noble acts are done for less than noble motives. (p. 64)

Garfield's last adolescent novel and his most complex is *The Prisoners of September*.... It is his first full-blown historical novel, a fictionalized and personalized account of the French Revolution and its effect on the lives of two young men. And it is about the illusions and the inevitable disillusionments of adolescence.

In many ways this work is a departure from Garfield's other adventure stories. For one thing, it has two heroes. They function dialectically, each providing a context for the other. And they are older than the typical Garfield hero; rather than searching to reclaim a mysterious heritage, they define themselves within their larger society and actively participate in the outside world, in this case, in a specific event in history. Garfield explores the psychological motivation behind individual choices and their larger political context. The movement is from the personal to the political and back to the personal. For one of the heroes, the results are tragic; for the other, they are conventionally comic. At the end, one of the heroes is killed and the other is about to marry. If the marriage does not suggest an overwhelming sense of society's regeneration, there is at least for the couple a personal sense of acceptance.

The story is in many ways reminiscent of Dickens' historical novel about the French Revolution, *A Tale of Two Cities*. In *The Prisoners of September*, however, there are no simple solutions, no wholly moral characters. (pp. 64-6)

The characters collide with each other demonstrating Garfield's golden principle—that no one is pure. (p. 66)

The two young women in this novel, Henrietta and Gilberte, are counterparts in the same way that the heroes are. Their experiences of the world have been diametrically opposed and they assume opposing viewpoints. But both are courageous and both are flawed. In order to survive, Gilberte has had to calculate and deceive. Henrietta resents Gilberte's ability to manipulate her brother with her aristocratic manners.... Each character's pretensions are revealed and each is in some way justified.

This balance between characters is one example of the order that pervades this novel. It is a carefully structured work, divided into three sections, each prefaced with a slogan from the French Revolution. The first subtitle, "*Liberté*," ironically describes the two young men's visions of their own liberation.... The middle section, "*E-galité*," follows suit. The kind of equality hinted at here is doubly ironic. The aristocrats are imprisoned and beheaded so that death and degradation seem to be the true equalizers. In that sense Garfield's view of the Revolution is close to Dickens'. (pp. 67-8)

In the final section, though "*Fraternité*" is not achieved, a softer note is struck. The Revolutionary government survives, though we are not encouraged towards great optimism. (p. 69)

That everything is not resolved and all ends tied is a testament to Garfield's loyalty to the truth. Ideals do go astray and we live most of our moments filled with ambivalence. (p. 70)

> Roni Natov, "'Not the Blackest of Villains ... Not the Brightest of Saints': Humanism in Leon Garfield's Adventure Novels," in *The Lion and the Unicorn* (copyright © 1978 The Lion and the Unicorn), Fall, 1978, pp. 44-71.

GORDON PARSONS

The final two stories in Leon Garfield's 'Apprentices' series [*The enemy and the filthy beast*] introduce respectively the love-lorn Hobby, apprenticed to a modeller of plaster statuettes, and Shag, the trainee house painter who spends most of his life venting his earthy humour from his precarious scaffolding perch on those who pass below. These apprentices like their predecessors are, however, first and foremost apprentices to the business of life. (pp. 349-50)

I have not yet read all twelve 'Apprentices' but I suspect that the characteristic Garfield style, with its distinctive imagery and knowing, gentle irony, while weighing a little too heavily in the context of a single short volume, may well work effectively to bind together the separate tales into a coherent pattern, offering something different but as satisfying as the full-length novels.

It is the unique colouring of Garfield's style that tends to obscure that he is above all a moralist—and none the worse for that! Like all his fiction, the 'Apprentices' communicate the need for human beings, despite all their individual quirks and eccentricities, to recognise their shared vulnerability and homogeneity of feeling. (p. 350)

> Gordon Parsons, in *The School Librarian*, December, 1978.

Even at this late stage in his career Leon Garfield still has a surprise or two left. [*The Confidence Man*] is one of them. It is, too, perhaps his most mature and consistent novel to date.

The scene, for half the story, and the theme are new to him. He has found—in history or in his head?—the record of an emigrant community from Southern Germany who pulled up their roots and went to America in the eighteenth century. They are Protestants in a Catholic town—unnamed—and subject to the intermittent and mindless persecution of the majority.... The Captain is one of Mr. Garfield's finest creations, a wonderfully enigmatic character. Is he just a professional 'con' man, or is he moved by more complicated motives? Even at the end of the story we cannot quite be sure. Moving among his host, encouraging, cheering the despondent, he is a moving and magnificent figure who inspires confidence as well as fear....

Admirable as Mr. Garfield is as storyteller, he is even better at evoking atmosphere. His picture of life in a Protestant ghetto is beautifully done; that of London with its pharisees passing the abandoned refugees by on the other side is even better. And for a portrait to match that of the Captain for complexity, he produces Geneva Brown, the cockney kid whose ambition is to be 'advertised' at Billingsgate and so find a worthy mate. There are memorable smaller sketches, of which that of Zipfel the pot-boy is outstanding. Altogether a most exciting book, written with all this master's exuberance and gift for the vivid image.... There is material here for a dozen books, spilled out with the utmost prodigality. Let us once again salute one of the contemporary masters of this fine art. (p. 115)

The Junior Bookshelf, *April, 1979.*

Alex Haley

1921-

Black American journalist, essayist, and historical novelist. Haley is best known for *Roots: The Saga of an American Family*, a "literary-television" sociological phenomenon which vaulted him into celebrity status during the late 1970s. It is a fictionalized account of seven generations of his own family based on twelve years of research in Africa, Europe, and America. The story of slave Kunta Kinte and his descendants has become almost legendary, and has spawned an intense interest in genealogy and a pride in black ancestry. By personalizing the Afro-American experience, Haley has universalized it. He first became known for his thoughtful collaboration on *The Autobiography of Malcolm X*, a powerful portrait of this controversial leader and his espousal of and final disenchantment with the Black Muslim movement. Haley has been given the credit for gaining the confidence of Malcolm X and for giving the book its final shape. He first decided to research his own story after retiring from the Coast Guard as chief journalist and spending several years as interviewer and magazine writer. The book *Roots* was well-received by critics and was awarded special citations from the National Book Awards Committee and the Pulitzer Prize Committee, but it was not until its adaptation was televised that its full influence was realized. Haley did not have the final approval of the script for *Roots* and he feels that it did not accurately represent his viewpoint. However, he served as consultant for the second television series, *Roots: The Next Generations*. This is a continuation of the saga of his family as they became caught up in the black struggle for equality following the Civil War and deals particularly with his own efforts to retrace his lineage. Haley has been criticized for his idealization of history, for his stilted and artificial dialogue, for reverse racism, and for factual errors. He was recently charged with plagiarism but settled out of court. Haley calls his story "faction," neither fact nor fiction, and it is this dual nature which saves it from being a romantic melodrama or a scholarly treatise and seems to give it its power. (See also *CLC*, Vol. 8, and *Contemporary Authors*, Vols. 77-80.)

ROBERT PENN WARREN

[Malcolm X was a latter-day example of] the man who "makes it," the man who, from humble origins and with meager education, converts, by will, intelligence, and sterling character, his liabilities into assets. (p. 161)

Malcolm X fulfills, it would seem, all the requirements—success against odds, the role of prophet, and martyrdom—for inclusion in the American pantheon. (p. 162)

[*The Autobiography of Malcolm X*] is "told" to Alex Haley. . . . From 1963 up to the assassination, Haley saw Malcolm for almost daily sessions when Malcolm was in New York, and sometimes accompanied him on his trips. Haley's account of this period, of how he slowly gained Malcolm's confidence and how Malcolm himself discovered the need to tell his story, is extremely interesting and, though presented as an Epilogue, is an integral part of the book; but the main narrative has the advantage of Malcolm's tone, his characteristic movement of mind, and his wit for Haley has succeeded admirably in capturing these qualities. . . . (pp. 163-64)

[The story of Malcolm X] shows the reader the world in which that truth can operate; that is, it shows the kind of alienation to which this truth is applicable. It shows, also, the human quality of the operation, a man in the process of trying to understand his plight, and to find salvation, by that truth. (p. 167)

[Malcolm X] was the black man who looked the white man in the eye and forgave nothing. . . . To put it another way, Malcolm X let the white man see what, from a certain perspective, he, his history, and his culture looked like. It was possible to say that that perspective was not the only one, that it did not give the whole truth about the white man, his history, and his culture, but it was not possible to say that the perspective did not carry *a* truth, a truth that was not less, but more, true for being seen from [his] angle. . . . (p. 169)

As one reads the *Autobiography*, one feels that, whatever the historical importance of Malcolm Little, his story has permanence, that it has something of tragic intensity and meaning. One feels that it is an American story bound to be remembered, to lurk in the background of popular consciousness. . . . (p. 171)

Robert Penn Warren, "Malcolm X: Mission and Meaning," in The Yale Review *(© 1965 by Yale University; reprinted by permission of the editors), Winter, 1966, pp. 161-71.*

NAT HENTOFF

Clearly [Malcolm X] had charisma, but powering that charisma was his capacity to understand and articulate his own American experience and so link it with that of other blacks that he was indeed a spokesman. . . . The nature of his own experience and its series of "conversions" . . . is distilled with candor and cutting clarity in [*The Autobiography of Malcom X*] (with writer Alex Haley serving as an admirably unobtrusive and astute organizer of the material). . . .

The autobiography is revelatory not only of Malcolm but also of diverse black members of this "pluralistic" society whom hardly any whites have yet begun to know—their values, their affirmations, their evasions, their ways of wit, rage and sorrow. Malcolm himself, as was clear to those who knew him, emerges as a man of warmth as well as fury, of wry perception, and most importantly, as a man with the ability to change and grow. He was, as the book demonstrates, at the beginning of a new stage of understanding himself and the society when he was killed. (p. 511)

> *Nat Hentoff, "The Odyssey of a Black Man," in* Commonweal *(copyright © 1966 Commonweal Publishing Co., Inc.; reprinted by permission of Commonweal Publishing Co., Inc.), January 28, 1966, pp. 511-12.*

COLIN MacINNES

The modest hero of [*The Autobiography of Malcom X*] is really Alex Haley, who provides, in his introduction, a frank and just appreciation of Malcolm X, and whose task it was, at snatched moments over two hectic years, first to win Malcolm's confidence and then persuade him to tell his story fully. The result is beyond praise, for one must instantly feel that though this is, technically, a 'ghosted' book, it is Malcolm's thought and voice we are hearing all the time. . . .

Malcolm foresaw his martyrdom and he knew his heroic mould. And it is impossible to read this book without becoming convinced that Malcolm was a hero. . . .

The cause of the break with the Muslims isn't satisfactorily explained even in this frank book, and one suspects that Malcolm, in talking to Haley, still had reticences. . . .

I suspect many English readers will dismiss Malcolm as a fanatic who preached the sword and perished by it. But any such reader can have no comprehension whatever of the virulent despair and aggression of the American Negro. . . .

What Malcolm achieved was to give coherence to the feelings of millions. Until and unless absolute economic and social equality are won by Negroes, these feelings will remain and grow. Internationally, they are allied to all those of non-white peoples throughout the world. If anyone doubts this, and doubts the anger of it, Malcolm's biography will be a corrective. (p. 668)

> *Colin MacInnes, in* The Spectator *(© 1966 by* The Spectator; *reprinted by permission of* The Spectator), *May 27, 1966.*

CAROL OHMANN

The Autobiography of Malcolm X testifies to the black experience in America. More precisely, it testifies to the personal cost of the black experience in America. The first chapter records the death of Malcolm's father, the victim apparently of whites who resented his propagandizing for Marcus Garvey's back-to-Africa movement; in the "Epi-

logue," Alex Haley describes the assassination of Malcolm X. . . . The lives of father and son alike were fundamentally shaped to their violent ends by the fact that they were born black in America and tried to combat the inferiority to which their color condemned them.

And yet, at the same time that the *Autobiography* unforgettably tells those of us who do not know it about the black experience, and helps to explain it to those who know it and have yet to understand it—at the same time, the *Autobiography* is in many ways a traditionally American work. The evidence of the book itself insists on both its differences from and its similarities to the general American experience. At a time when one hears so often simply that Black is Different . . . , it seems to me useful to note some of the ways in which Malcolm X's story . . . reflects American culture. Despite the fact that Benjamin Franklin could not have bought a bottle of Red Devil lye, and would have had no need or wish to, his *Autobiography* and *The Autobiography of Malcolm X* resemble each other in the conceptions of the self they convey, in the categories by which they apprehend men and events, in the standards by which they judge them, and in the ways, looking backward as autobiographers do, they pattern or structure the raw materials of their own lives. Roughly, what Benjamin Franklin wanted and got for himself and his fellow citizens, Malcolm X also wanted for himself and his people—until in the last year of his life he changed his mind. To put this in a practical academic way, *The Autobiography of Malcolm X* belongs not only in an Afro-American course but in a course in American literature or American autobiography. Both Benjamin Franklin and Malcolm X testify to certain strengths and certain weaknesses in our national ethos, strengths and weaknesses that have characterized us very nearly from, if not from, the beginning. (pp. 131-32)

Both books tell, despite the episodic unfolding to which their genre and the particularly versatile achievements of their respective authors dispose them, stories of men who move from inexperience to sophistication, from ignorance to enlightenment, from obscurity to worldly prominence. Both books offer spectacular contrasts between then and now. . . . (p. 133)

In the pages of *The Autobiography of Malcolm X* . . . two sets of values compete, and two conceptions of the self; side by side with the would-be lawyer, hustler and black nationalist, another self, or another dimension of the self, struggles toward expression. (p. 142)

While *The Autobiography of Malcolm X* is in many striking ways analogous to Franklin's *Autobiography,* our prototypical American story of secular success, it may also be compared to our, still earlier, Puritan examinations into the nature of the inner life, examinations which include, indeed stress, the life of the heart. Hustler, Trapped, Caught, Satan, Saved, Savior, Minister Malcolm X. The paradigmatic curve suggested here is that of the sinner repentant, touched by grace, submissive to God, and saved, like Thomas Shepard, like Cotton Mather, like Jonathan Edwards and like John Bunyan before them, and Saint Augustine before him. (p. 145)

Recording the experiences of Muzdalifa and Mecca, *The Autobiography of Malcolm X* does separate itself from Franklin's *Autobiography;* here the late account finds no equivalent, whether straight or ironic, in the earlier one. At

Muzdalifa and Mecca, an impulse sent from heart to mind from private self to public, effected a personal integration. The power to feel intensely, the power to feel connection with other human beings, the power to express that feeling, all were freed from the limits previously set on them by black/white divisions and hostilities. The emotional dimension of the self joined the rational dimension and gave it cause to reconceive the nature of the individual and of his relationship to the world. In the reconception, every man is subject rather than object, to be cherished rather than managed or manipulated, and true brotherhood excludes no one. (pp. 147-48)

The similarity between the autobiographies of Franklin and Malcolm X points finally, ... to common areas of experience and suggests that, black and white, we share a common problem: to render human or humane the ideas by which we have traditionally shaped ourselves and our programs or institutions. (p. 148)

> Carol Ohmann, "'The Autobiography of Malcolm X': A Revolutionary Use of the Franklin Tradition," in American Quarterly (copyright © 1970 Trustees of the University of Pennsylvania), Spring, 1970, pp. 130-49.

WARNER BERTHOFF

[No one can listen to the voice transcribed in *The Autobiography of Malcolm X*] or the printed versions of his public speeches, without forming the sense of an extraordinary human being: fiercely intelligent, shrewdly and humanely responsive to the life around him despite every reason in the world to have gone blind with suspicion and hate, a rarely gifted leader and inspirer of other men. The form of autobiographical narration adds something further; he comes through to us as the forceful agent of a life-history that was heroic in the event and has the shape of the heroic in the telling, a protagonist who (in Francis R. Hart's fine description) has himself created and now recreates "human value and vitality in each new world or underworld he has entered."

The power of Malcolm's book is that it speaks directly out of the totality of that life-history *and* the ingratiating openness of his own mind and recollection to it. It seems to me a book that ... does not require any softening or suspension of critical judgment. In the first place it is written, or spoken, in a quick, pungent, concrete style, again the plain style of popular idiom, improved and made efficient by the same sort of natural sharpness and concentration of attention that gives life and color to the best of Mark Twain's recollective writing, or Franklin's, or [John] Bunyan's. In the run of the narrative the liveliness of observation and recollection, the "histrionic exuberance" (Professor Hart again), are continuously persuasive—and incidentally confirm as elements of a true style Alex Haley's assurance that the book is indeed Malcolm's own and not a clever piece of mimicry or pastiche. The casually vivid rendering of other persons is worth remarking, a test some quite competent novelists would have trouble passing. . . . [All] these figures are precisely defined, according to their place in the story. The grasp of the narrative extends in fact to whole sociologies of behavior. The Harlem chapters in general, with their explanation of hustling in all its major forms—numbers, drugs, prostitution, protection, petty in-ghetto thievery—offer one of the best accounts in our literature of the cultural underside of the American business system,

and of the bitter psychology that binds its victims to it. . . . Most generally it is [the] blending of his own life-story with the full collective history of his milieu and the laws of behavior controlling it that gives Malcolm's testimony its strength and large authority—and sets it apart, I think, from the many more or less skillfully designed essays in autobiography we have had recently from writers like Frank Conroy, Claude Brown, Norman Podhoretz, Willie Morris, Paul Cowan, David McReynolds, to mention only a few; sets it apart also from the great run of novels about contemporary city life.

But it is Malcolm himself, and his own active consciousness of the myth of his life's progress, that most fills and quickens the book, making it something more than simply a valuable document. His past life is vividly present to him as he speaks; he gives it the form, in recollection, of a dramatic adventure in which he himself is felt as the precipitating agent and moving force. It is not unreasonable that he should see himself as someone who has a special power to make things happen, to work changes on the world around him (and to change within himself); and thus finally as one whose rise to authority is in some sense in the natural order of things, the working out of some deep structure of fortune. (pp. 317-18)

The force of this continuously active process of self-conception and self-projection is fundamental to the book's power of truth. It gives vitality and momentum to the early parts of the story. . . . Most decisively, this force of self-conception is what brings alive the drama of his conversion, and his re-emergence within the Nation of Islam as a leader and teacher of his people. For Malcolm's autobiography is consciously shaped as the story of an "education," and in so describing it I am not merely making the appropriate allusion to Henry Adams or the *Bildungsroman* tradition; "education" is Malcolm's own word for what is taking place.

Above all, the book is the story of a conversion and its consequences. (p. 318)

And always there is Malcolm's own fascination with what has happened to him, and what objectively it means. As if establishing a leitmotif, the climaxes of his story repeatedly focus on this extraordinary power to change and be changed that he has grown conscious of within himself and that presents itself to him as the distinctive rule of his life. . . . He has a driving need to understand everything that happens to him or around him and to gain a measure of intelligent control over it; it is a passion with him to get his own purchase on reality.

It thus makes *narrative* sense, of a kind only the best of novelists are in command of, that he should discover his calling in life as a teacher and converter. (pp. 318-19)

[The] last academic point I want to make about the literary character of Malcolm's book is that ... as a political statement, its form is recognizably "classic." The model it quite naturally conforms to is that of the Political Testament, the work in which some ruler or statesman sets down for the particular benefit of his people a summary of his own experience and wisdom and indicates the principles which are to guide those who succeed him. . . . My argument is not that Malcolm was in any way guided by this grand precedent, merely that in serving all his book's purposes he substantially recreated it—which is of course what the work of literature we call "classic" does within the occasion it answers to. (p. 321)

Warner Berthoff, in New Literary History *(copyright © 1971 by* New Literary History, *The University of Virginia, Charlottesville, Virginia), Winter, 1971.*

MICHAEL G. COOKE

[The] distinctive feature of the *Autobiography* is its naturalistic use of time, the willingness to let the past stand as it was, in its own season, even when later developments, of intellect or intuition or event, give it a different quality.... The atmosphere in which the *Autobiography* operates is remarkably practical and quick-moving; its genius springs from being so and at the same time remarkably responsive to crystallizations of meaning.... (pp. 274-75)

Michael G. Cooke, in Romanticism: Vistas, Instances, Continuities, *edited by David Thorburn and Geoffrey Hartman (copyright © 1973 by Cornell University; used by permission of the publisher, Cornell University Press), Cornell University Press, 1973.*

DAVID HERBERT DONALD

As the reconstruction of a genealogy, Haley's [*Roots*] is a *tour de force*.... [It] reminds us how even in appallingly adverse circumstances blacks often maintained, through oral traditions, a full account of their lineage and a proper sense of their individual identities. Skillfully, Haley checked his oral history against surviving written documents, and the family tree that he has outlined seems not just plausible but authentic. It is easy to accept Haley's statement: "To the best of my knowledge and of my effort, every lineage statement within *Roots* is from either my African or American families' carefully preserved oral history, much of which I have been able conventionally to corroborate with documents." (p. 70)

Readers should not expect to find in these pages an accurate history of Haley's family, any more than they would look for a factually complete account of the Civil War in Stephen Vincent Benet's *John Brown's Body*. In a work of this sort it is enough to have a high level of historical plausibility coupled with enough literary skill to make the characters credible.

By this standard, parts of *Roots* come off very well. Since I am not an Africanist, I cannot judge the historical accuracy of Haley's reconstruction of Kunta Kinte's boyhood in an 18th-century Mandinka village. Perhaps for this reason I found this section of *Roots* both imaginative and persuasive. My colleagues who do know African history warn that Haley tends to romanticize the beauties and comforts of primitive society.... Haley's account of the Middle Passage—the dreaded voyage from Africa to America—is ... a convincing recreation of that horror....

Once Haley gets Kunta to America, however, the historical plausibility of his story begins to deteriorate. On page after page there are factual errors as well as distortions. No one of these in itself is weighty, but cumulatively they create disbelief. (p. 72)

The most serious historical blunder in *Roots* concerns Kunta's grandson George—called "Chicken George" because of his skill in training gamecocks. In the 1850's when George's master loses a disastrous wager on his birds, he

pays his debt by giving his slave to a visiting Englishman, who takes him to Britain for five years to train fighting cocks there. Despite Lord Mansfield's 1772 ruling in the Sommersett case, announcing that once a slave set foot on British soil he became free, Haley has George remain a slave to the British lord. Sent back to America in 1860, George continues a slave, even though he stops off in New York, where the personal liberty laws would certainly have guaranteed his freedom, and he returns docilely to the South to entreat his master for liberty.

The point should be obvious: whatever Mr. Haley may know about Africa, he simply has not done enough reading about the South, about slavery, about American agriculture—to say nothing about general American history—to give his novel a convincing background.

Nor has Haley mastered the literary technique of historical fiction. Perhaps it does not make much difference that his characters are one-dimensional and wooden, for psychological subtlety can be as distracting in a historical novel as in a detective story. But it is awkward that the only way Haley can devise to introduce chronology is to have house slaves rush down to the quarters announcing the latest big-house gossip.... It is awkward, too, that Haley has written most of *Roots* in heavy dialect....

Indeed, Haley's fictional technique closely resembles that of [Joel Chandler] Harris and other ... late 19th-century Southern historical romancers ... and *Roots* should be read as a continuation of this hoary tradition—but with the racial signs reversed....

Just as traditional Southern white historical novelists wrote of "darkeys" instead of Negroes, so Haley can hardly bring himself to speak of whites but refers to them throughout as "toubob"—presumably a word of African origin. And finally, just as in the conventional Southern historical romance of the 1880's, Haley's family emerges from its trials unscathed, or rather ennobled, and at the end its members live happily and prosperously ever afterward.

Since we are all used to making allowances for the white racism that permeates so many 19th-century historical novels, there is no special reason why we should not be equally resigned to the black racism in Haley's story. The problem, however, is that Haley's racism leads to an unfortunate distortion of his family's history. Admitting embarrassment that he himself is of mixed blood and feeling humiliated in the presence of truly black Africans, Haley is uncomfortable in dealing with the history of his family during the past hundred years, because that history is one of people with mixed blood who accepted, emulated, and excelled in the white American world.... Only in the sketchiest outline does he tell us of the migration of that family as a unit to Tennessee, of their creation of a vigorous and prosperous new black community, of their economic success.... This is the real story of Haley's family, a typically American success story. That story of triumph over adversity would have been far more inspiring, as well as far more historically accurate, than any romanticized account of African ancestors. (pp. 73-4)

David Herbert Donald (reprinted from Commentary *by permission; copyright © 1976 by the American Jewish Committee), in* Commentary, *December, 1976.*

ARNOLD RAMPERSAD

A narrative history of the family from the birth of Kunta Kinte to the maturity of Haley himself, *Roots* is a hybrid work. It links the detective skills of a superior investigative reporter to the powers of a would-be fiction writer, and the product is a work of extremely uneven texture but unquestionable final success. (p. 23)

Haley's search for his ancestors is not conducted to discover unvarnished truth but rather, from one perspective, to justify the history of blacks in America—as if that history needed justification. There is a dominant angle of vision in *Roots;* almost the entire story is seen from the vantage point of a belief in the necessity of social and political justice, which is the principal romantic illusion to inform the text. From an artistic and intellectual point of view there is what may be for some readers a fateful shift of emphasis from the pathos and ingenuity of the author's search for his family toward the elevation of its members to mythical level as accurate representatives of the black race in America, with Kunta Kinte as the archetypal African warrior prince. Side by side in the book, then, exist these twin desires for the illumination of truth and the cultural propaganda. What furthur complicates this odd combination is the absence of radical political belief on the author's part; Haley's values, except concerning the worth of black people, are those of the masses of Americans, to whom the book is in fact dedicated.

In one sense Haley's ancestral family bears its mythic burden well; with the exception of Kunta Kinte, after all, the members are really ordinary. But it is on Kinte that the book is based. Though Haley's account of his hero's African childhood sometimes reads like a dramatization of a master's thesis on childhood and youth among the Mandinko people in the mid-18th century, more often it is suffused in the light of Haley's reverence for the Africa of his ancestors and his loving account of their society. His re-creation of Kinte's middle-passage journey in the hold of a slave ship is harrowing, the major place in the book where facts are incontrovertibly alchemized into vivid narrative; and his presentation of Kinte's unfolding consciousness of the strange new white world of America is brilliant, yielding startling insights into the psychological process of American slavery, and into aspects of American culture then and now. Kunta Kinte's rage for freedom—one foot is cut off after his fourth attempt to escape—impressed on succeeding generations a respect, however muted, for the integrity of their origins and their dignity as well.

On the other hand, the middle of the book is dominated by the flamboyant figure of Kinte's grandson, Chicken George, reared by his white father—and owner—to be an expert trainer of gamecocks. Haley's accounts of cockfighting in the South in the 19th century are lively (though there are too many of them), but Chicken George himself is about as interesting as a plucked bird. Survival and endurance replace defiance as the central concern of Kunta Kinte's clan, and it is at this point that its members become History. Haley's integration of personages and events from the American past into his narrative is the stuff of pageants or some other moribund medium, such as television, and fails to conceal the fact that uncovering the truth about the past does not necessarily make it interesting.

The solemnity of the basic theme of *Roots* also cannot obscure the fact that the Afro-American novel is too accomplished in its basic skills for *Roots* to pass as a well wrought novel or romance. Technically, the work is so innocent of fictive ingenuity that it seldom surpasses the standards of the most popular of historical romances. Haley's ability to write dialogue and dialect is competent at best, and stilted and artificial far too often. Nor is the work helped much by the strange and fitful dramatic strokes its author casts into the void (Kinte, for example, does not sleep with a woman until he marries at the age of 39 . . .). Similarly, sociological and historical scholarship on both West Africa and the American slave centuries is too developed for Haley's uncoverings to be met as revelations. Undoubtedly the book will make history and sociology more familiar to its readers, but that role in itself can hardly be the reason for the possibly long-lasting consequence of this narrative.

One pushes through *Roots,* sometimes swiftly, sometimes laboriously, as often captivated as irritated by the limitations of its concern with form. But there is no denying the extraordinary force of individual passages and episodes or —more importantly—the exhilaration with which one bursts forth, as from the underbrush of dried fact and tangled genealogical vines, into the present time and the living presence of the author. For one dazzling moment, from which it seems impossible to recover, the past becomes the present, and the present becomes the past, and there is a sense of circularity, of completeness, of integration of sensibility within the black American experience that is unparalleled, to my knowledge, in either fiction or scholarship concerning Afro-America.

The primary effect of *Roots* is not, however, partisan, if only because the implied relationship between the sense of political identity imposed by racism on the American black and the sense of genetic identity with Africa is minimal in its intellectual dignity. *Roots* is the record of the voluntary location of an individual in the context of the past. Haley may have intended to make the justification of Afro-America the locus of his effort; he has succeeded, in spite of his intentions and his personal reticence, in making himself, as an individual, vital to the book's meanings. The peculiar essence of *Roots* is that the author, prostrating himself before the past, is himself called upon to justify his existence before the power of history and the court of the past. . . . And it is this test of the individual life before the sacrifices and disasters of a common ancestry that Haley passes most movingly. In the display of intelligence, industry and humanity out of which the substance of the book evolves—its limitations as fiction are really insignificant in comparison—one finds preserved not pride of family or race or a smattering of heirloomed words but those qualities of spirit that, as Kunta Kinte knew in preferring mutilation to servility, make freedom not a privilege but a necessity. When Haley stands at the end of *Roots* before his African country-cousins and feels himself "impure" because of their richly black skin, there is behind the tedious racial romanticism the felt truth of a confrontation between the individual and his—and in this case—personified past. Haley has nothing to be ashamed of, at least not in this book; Kunta Kinte would have respected him. (pp. 24-5)

Arnold Rampersad, in The New Republic *(reprinted by permission of* The New Republic; © *1976 The New Republic, Inc.), December 4, 1976.*

RUSSELL WARREN HOWE

After a decade of research in Africa, Europe and the United States [Alex Haley] was able to piece together his family tree. [*Roots*], although represented as nonfiction, is a monumental novel, a *Forsyte Saga* of a part-African, part-Irish, part-Cherokee family. . . .

Written mostly in slave dialect, it is crammed with raw violence and makes valid demands on the tearducts of the dourest reader. (p. 23)

The American passages—by far the best and most convincing—are on a par with Victor Hugo's *Les Miserables,* fully worthy of the praise lavished by reviewers. Yet for all Haley's undeniable achievement and painstaking research, implying a claim to authenticity, the key historical portions are marred by serious factual errors.

A major one occurs in the book's main episode—the story of Kinte's capture. Like characters from *Tarzan,* white seamen armed with slaves stalk through the long grass, ready to pounce on isolated tribesmen. Allowing outsiders to participate in slavehunting was as unthinkable in 18th-century West Africa as permitting them to harvest their own peppers or shoot ivory. Slaves were the region's most lucrative export, and the middlemen—the African beach traders who reaped the greatest profit in this commerce—bought from African captors and sold to the ships.

Haley's fictionalized ancestor angrily also thinks of his captors as "traitors." Such an idea never could have occurred to Kinte. The people of his village, Juffure, did not see all "Africans" as brothers. Indeed, they had no concept of "Africa" (Haley's characters use the term). Nor did the question of treason arise, since slaveraiders only captured foreigners, not members of their own clans. (pp. 23-4)

Haley's people speak of "The Gambia," the name given to the Kamby River colony created more than a century later, and "Senegal," the French name for the Sunuga River that first became the title of an imperial claim at the Berlin Conference of 1884.

There is talk, too, of "Senegalese" and of "Northern Guinea." Elders mention Benin (1,200 miles away), pygmies and Batutsi (who live as far from Juffure as New York is from San Francisco), and Zimbabwe (a vanished kingdom still further south).

The Juffure of the 1750s is portrayed almost as it appears today. For instance, the village's main crop is rice, which was not introduced until this century and only became Gambia's staple diet after World War II. Kinte is weaned at 13 months—conceivable now, when every Mauritanian storekeeper in Gambia sells powdered milk and formula, but unthinkable in traditional West Africa before the age of three or later. Adults in the village know their ages—an unlikely situation even today.

Kinte's mother, Binta, fears her husband, Omoro, will take a second wife. Today, when large families are often uneconomical, Binta might well protest. She might even object for feminist reasons. In 1760—and as recently as 1960—the new mate would mean Binta's promotion to senior wife, to less work and more respect. In *Roots,* the women of Juffure kiss children; in traditional Africa it would be revolting to use the mouth for anything but eating, drinking and talking.

There are other minor incongruities. . . .

Historians will not quarrel with Haley's graphic description of the foul conditions aboard a slave ship. But much of the gratuitous cruelty in *Roots,* directed against a cargo whose value depended on its condition, belies the logic of commerce and the ample memoirs of the trade.

The book's central flaw is that while it portrays in almost anthropological detail Kinte's Mandinko . . . childhood, and the cultural clash of his initiation into the life of a slave, the wholly American author's persona rather than that of the fictionalized character emerges from the printed page. Only when Juffure has become a distant childhood memory, and Kinte is acculturated into slave America, does the character become arrestingly true.

Kinte's immediate, hysterically sustained reaction to the tragedy of capture is the hindsight rage of today's American. Most slaves went to their fates with resignation, and not surprisingly: Fear, not anger, is the first reaction.

Although resentment at the human instruments of his bondage would be natural enough for Kinte, an illiterate Muslim steeped in animism, the predominant concern would be Why? What Islamic taboo had been broken, what ancestor left unappeased, for his unavoidable sanction to have been imposed? When Kinte cries out on the slave ship that he will never again fail to face Mecca five times a day, Haley comes closest to letting his creation be Mandingo, not American.

The writer admirably describes the gruff discipline and reassuring certainties of life in a traditional West African village. He conveys the local color well and with intelligent sympathy. But despite three or four extended visits to Juffure and other parts of Africa, Haley is necessarily still an outsider. . . .

An African analysis of an American novel, particularly one as good as *Roots,* is perhaps in some ways superfluous. Certainly it should not detract from the author's amazing work in tracing his family tree to a remote hamlet thousands of miles away. But what Haley shows is that—although less has changed in Juffure over 200 years than in Tennessee, where Allah ordained Kinte's tree should sprout—the roots alone can be uncovered; the seed cannot be recaptured. (p. 24)

Russell Warren Howe, "An Elusive Past," in The New Leader *(© 1977 by the American Labor Conference on International Affairs, Inc.), January 3, 1977, pp. 23-4.*

DALE NORTON

[*Roots*] symbolizes the connection of black Americans—and, by association, all Americans—to Africa itself. *Roots* is part of the growing body of literature helping to rediscover the heritage of black Americans which has been outlawed, ignored, or forgotten over the generations. (p. xliii)

As literature the work has faults, but none which overshadow the rightness of its general conception or the triumph of Haley's imagination.

The first half of the book focuses on the life of the African Kunta Kinte and is clearly its most successful part. The dignity of Kunta's family and the soundness of the village culture are thoroughly convincing. . . . Statistics and drawings of slave ships in no way prepare one for the overpowering vividness of the voyage episodes. Equally moving are Kunta's struggles to escape and to salvage his manhood during the first agonizing years of slavery when he cannot communicate even with his fellow slaves. The book's largest virtues are the genuine and convincing heroism of Kunta and the sustained empathy through which Haley is able to convey the curse of slavery.

His portrayal of whites demonstrates equal control in the middle portions of the book. . . . Haley gives us believable representative masters without descending to stereotype. There are moments in the lives of later generations, Chicken George and Tom Murray principally, when Haley is equally successful; but melodrama and other flaws begin to strain at the narrative. . . .

Haley's inspiration also seems to wane for the female generations. . . . Kizzy is surprisingly underplayed compared to the thorough treatment we have become accustomed to with Kunta himself. . . . [She] figures significantly only as a vessel—first for Kunta's determination to perpetuate his African heritage and later for Tom Lea's sexual attacks. (p. xliv)

Tom Murray's daughter Cynthia is also too quickly eclipsed by her husband, Will Palmer. Palmer is unquestionably an inspiring figure, but, having pursued the descent of one family for over five hundred pages, the reader feels gulled to find the operative grandparent overshadowed. Indeed, by the time we reach Haley's own mother, Bertha, the quality of family saga is dissipated to mundane family chronicle. Perhaps Haley's imagination is cramped toward the end of the book, ironically, by too much familiarity with his subject to allow a conclusion consistent with the bulk of the book.

Whatever the cause, the turn to personal history and the account of his investigation is a jarring disappointment at the end of the book. The method is apparent throughout, and the significance of the story for Haley and the reader lies in its basis in fact, but the distance in time and the purity of touch in the earlier portions of the book are ultimately more satisfying. One supposes that even Haley senses this as he accelerates the passage of time through the last three generations. Perhaps it is too much to attempt to breathe life into more than two or three generations in a single volume.

Whatever its flaws in symmetry and consistency of tone, they do not outweigh the power of the early narrative or the significance of the project as a whole. Haley has made an important contribution to our mutual history through an informed imagination. (pp. xliv, xlvi)

> *Dale Norton, "A Usable Past," in* Sewanee Review *(reprinted by permission of the editor;* © *1977 by The University of the South), Spring, 1977, pp. xliii-xlvi.*

ADAM DAVID MILLER

For long we have been fighting the fiction that we maintained nothing of what we brought over from Africa, that we created nothing of cultural value in the South; fighting the belief that because we were not accorded life by the image-makers, that we, in fact, did not exist. We have been fighting to establish that the lives of our fore-parents stood for something other than what was portrayed in the U.S. media.

Roots, because it is based on the result of painstaking scholarship and is therefore accurate in most of its details, will give Afro-Americans, especially the young, a second starting point from which to look at their past. (p. 50)

Haley wants the story of the Kinte family to be seen as "The Saga of an American Family." Will Afro-Americans reading the book think of themselves as more American or less? . . .

Tom the Blacksmith, a Kinte descendant, and his family are shown in 1860 to exemplify the virtues of family loyalty, thrift, hard work, ingenuity, perseverance, and spirituality. . . . My fear is that what Haley may have unwittingly done is to lay the Kinte family open to that other charge against us: Oh, but *you*'re different! Did he write too well? . . .

Haley has brought together an incredibly large body of information, has woven it into story, incident and detail, the result of which is overwhelming. Haley's skill as a writer of adventure stories shows in the live way incidents are portrayed, from cockfighting to the Middle Passage. . . .

Roots will not only help translate Afro-American experience, it will also make possible a more intelligent viewing and reading about Afro-American experience. (p. 51)

> *Adam David Miller, in* The Black Scholar *(copyright 1977 by* The Black Scholar*), April, 1977.*

ALI A. MAZRUI

In terms of political impact, the three most important literary milestones may well turn out to be, first, the publication of Harriet Beecher Stowe's novel *Uncle Tom's Cabin* in 1852; second, the collective Black creative eruption of the Harlem Renaissance in the 1920s; and now, thirdly, Alex Haley's work of "fact-ion," *Roots.* . . .

[Whether] this particular work itself continues to be read or not, its impact at the point of its birth has been sufficiently extensive to make it a major sociological event in modern American history. (p. 6)

Part of the impact of *Roots* is due to the fact that very few Black Americans can trace their origins back to Africa in any personalized or family sense. Because of the nature of the slave-system which prevailed in the United States, Blacks were forced to forget their past. Collective amnesia was imposed on the Black population. Both the book and the television series bring out sharply this strategy of enforced amnesia. Kunta Kinte's vain struggle to retain his African name, and the brutal way in which he was compelled to accept a new identity, dramatized this process. (p. 7)

Following the showing of the television series of *Roots,* many White Americans wondered if it was wise to resurrect the past. . . .

[Collective] amnesia was not only imposed on Blacks; it was also imposed on White Americans by their own guilt complexes. . . . White America longed for at least fitful forgetfulness to drown the cries of anguish of a man in the process of having his foot cut off.

That is why Kunta Kinte's amputated foot had such powerful symbolic meaning—in some ways more powerful than the alternative fate of castration as punishment for attempting to escape. . . . Had Kunta lost his testicles he would have had no procreational *future*; but by losing his foot he was now brutally cut off from his historical *past*. [He could not return physically to Africa.] (p. 8)

The symbolism is heightened by the circumcision episode

earlier in the saga. . . . The comparative symbolism of bloodletting in the two events captured a range of emotive responses: from the promise of puberty to the despair of immobility, from the valor of initiation to the anguish of final submission.

The theme of escape acquired two contradictory meanings in *Roots*. One is psychological escapism—a retreat from harsh realities through make-believe. The lives of Chicken George and his father were particularly illustrative of this trend. (pp. 8-9)

[They indulged in the cheap escapism of cockfighting]—making weaker beings fight unto death without any risk to the cheering human sadists.

And between Chicken George and his father, the father was the greater escapist. . . . [Like] so many other American slave owners, he sought to escape the reality of his own child by maintaining George's status as a saleable commodity. Ultimately George's father was a moral coward—he was himself *chicken*.

The other sense of "escape" in *Roots* is the ambition to escape bondage. Kunta Kinte's attempts to run away were the most explicit aspects of this motif. But there was also the related theme of silent protest through the oral tradition; a constant reminder from generation to generation of a prior existence before slavery. . . .

These twin themes of escape in *Roots* are quite fundamental both to American history as a whole and to America as a human dream. (p. 9)

> *Ali A. Mazrui, "The End of America's Amnesia," in* Africa Report *(published by permission of Transaction, Inc.; copyright © 1977 by The African-American Institute, Inc.), Vol. 22, No. 3, May-June, 1977, pp. 6-11.*

CAROLE MERITT

In presenting [the story of *Roots*] as a novel, Haley has maximized its popular appeal and captured the spirit of its oral tradition. In fact *Roots* may be regarded as the first serious challenge to existing popular mythology on the black man's past—that blacks are without a past, without a culture of their own and therefore, an inferior and unworthy people. If Haley had chosen to provide a factual report of his family's history, it might have had no greater impact than as a quaint and incidental reference in the historiography of American slavery. Instead, with characters drawn from real people, woven into a drama of major events and day-to-day activities, conversations and interrelationships, *Roots* lays hold of our imagination and begins to restructure popular belief about the black experience. (p. 211)

Haley is at his best when recreating Kunta's boyhood in the Gambia. . . . This part of the story is a disciplined account that engages us in the rhythm of Africa. . . . But Haley's narrative becomes difficult in recounting the African-American experience. The development of a distinctive African-American culture is a complex chapter in our history. It does not lend itself to the clarity and simplicity which characterize Haley's portrayal of boyhood in eighteenth century West Africa. How, for example, should the slave's accommodation and resistance to the slave master, his culture and his oppression be treated?

Haley acknowledges African survivals among the slaves:

gestures, facial expressions, cries of exclamation and "these blacks' great love of singing and dancing." These traits, however, are interpreted as incidental and unconscious. What the author apparently considers as weightier matters of culture seem to survive only among the Kintes. For example, the slave community which Haley describes appears not to be composed of families. In sharp contrast to the Kinte family unit, the other slaves in *Roots* appear as a collection of unattached individuals. The implication is that most slaves lived outside the bonds of kinship and marriage. At issue is not literary style or emphasis, but rather the interpretation of the African-American experience. While the Kinte family is among an elite in its oral tradition, it is not unique in its family structure and function.

Recent scholarship on the slave family would have informed Haley's work.

[Nevertheless, our] debt is to Haley for introducing this story to the public and for engaging the nation in pursuit of its past. (p. 212)

> *Carole Meritt, "Looking at Afro-American Roots," in* PHYLON: The Atlanta University Review of Race and Culture *(copyright, 1977, by Atlanta University; reprinted by permission of* PHYLON*), Vol. XXXVIII, Second Quarter (June, 1977), pp. 211-12.*

NANCY L. ARNEZ

Roots, meaning the beginning, captures the essence of an African people. It is the cultural history laid bare upon the canvas of time devoid of the misconceptions and misinterpretations of a people rationalizing their sins against humanity. It sutures the wounds that European and American historical scalpers presented to Blacks as the truth about their heritage in an effort to enslave their minds as well as their bodies. . . . [This] psychological warfare was the most grievous of all crimes wrought upon a people. Haley, with his seminal work, *Roots*, has helped mightily to destroy the chilling terror of ignorance of who we are as a people. He has given our proud heritage back to us. He has given us back our ancestors and our land. He has made us less fearful of white reprisals for we have seen them displayed in all of their ugliness, both in the book and on the screen, reaching the masses of Black people as well as the scholars. He has done this not once but twice—first with *The Autobiography of Malcolm X* . . . , and now with *Roots*, an epic work of classical dimensions. (p. 367)

[The cultural history of African people] is vividly told. It is electrifying in its imagery. The descriptions are rooted in historical truth culled from meticulous research. . . . (p. 368)

Significantly, the story is viewed primarily through the eyes of Kunta Kinte, one of Haley's ancestors. In this way, Haley enables the reader to experience what the rains, hunger, depopulation, love, learning and responsibility meant to the Mandinkas. . . . Each of us becomes Kunta Kinte as he pursues a lifetime in the pages of this work. (pp. 368-69)

[*Roots*] is full of drama, neither all fact nor all fiction. With a little bit of both, Haley has woven together a tale which will be long remembered and which this reviewer believes will have a serious, sustained impact on Civil Rights in this century and the next. (p. 369)

The book *Roots* is a gift of grace to the American people. The television version, despite its flaws, is a milestone in race relations. It provided 130 million out of 200 million Americans a more-or-less realistic view of the most heinious cultural institution in American life—slavery, which was evil crystallized; evil encapsulated. The airing of ''Roots'' spelled out in concrete ways a spirit of black pride and black identity for Black Americans; and for white Americans, a clearer understanding of what slavery did to this country and a whole nation of people. (p. 371)

> *Nancy L. Arnez, "From His Story to Our Story:*
> *A Review of 'Roots',"* in The Journal of Negro
> Education, 46 *(Summer, 1977,) pp. 367-71.*

HOWARD F. STEIN

For all its moving, tender, and grisly historic vividness, *Roots* remains what psychologists call an ''ambiguous stimulus,'' one which is selectively restructured by the observer who is participant. This is not to despair in solipsism, but to emphasize the omnipresence of subjectivity in the never-detached observer; and to stress equally that that subjectivity can be a tool either for un-self-conscious *indulgence,* or for *disciplined* engagement. (p. 12)

For me, what is refreshing about Haley's *Roots* is that reality is not . . . cavalierly held in contempt. While there is much absolutistic either-or in the tale, Haley's world of human bondage does more than outrageously simplify into good guys and bad guys. I would go further: his is an *American* epic that Black and White men and women of good will might read and watch and discuss *together.* For while Haley does lamentably indulge in stereotyping, which I shall consider later, the over-all effect of *Roots* is, for me, a transcendent one, not a one-sided victory. In a sense, *Roots* taps the core of the American experience with its focus on the journey from whence we come, where we are now, where we aspire to, and the ever-new and constantly renewing pioneer settling of a new-found-land in freedom. ''We'' becomes everyone, not a single race. Haley is not fixated on the past: the past is simply, and starkly, and dramatically, the Proud Beginning. Haley does not rest complacently with an origin myth: for roots is *process,* not place. Roots lie not only in the past—but in the present and future as well.

Those who view Haley's message as exclusively a look backward have missed the dramatic unfolding toward the *future.* A sinking and spreading of roots takes place throughout the odyssey. (pp. 11-12)

The American dream became a new image of rootedness. The American cultural value on ''Don't give up hope,'' that ''If I can't attain it, I will help my children to get it,'' these values, in Haley's script, become transformed into *Afro-*American values, making for convergence, congruence, synthesis in cultural aspirations. (p. 13)

The new rootedness is not without anguish and sacrifice and risk. Kunta Kinte must choose among divided loyalties: his choice reveals what sort of man he is, his values, his priorities. He must decide between acting upon his vow to be a free man at any cost, and remaining with his new family. . . . Ultimately, it required greater courage for Kunta Kinte to choose to remain behind, to establish new roots, than it would have been to make a daring escape. To the maturing Kunta Kinte, the freedom of dogged ideological adherence to the individualism of the past became less

attractive than commitment to those who were by love and promise of the future committed to him. He found new reward in meeting the new demands and opportunities of family life. There were other ways of fighting slavery than fleeing it.

Kunta Kinte chooses the limits and different freedoms of responsibility, mutuality, and devotion. Like his future descendant Alex Haley, he is more self-disciplined than self-indulgent. Selfhood is deepened, not suffocated, in relation and commitment—all the more dramatically poignant when the imminence of the master's whim renders impermanent any human relationship. (pp. 13-14)

Haley does frequently indulge himself oversimplifying and overdrawing racial differences to the point of caricature. This results in a reversal of White stereotypes, popular and sociological, and obscures much of the interpersonal complexity and internal anguish in those both Black and White caught *together* in the ''American Dilemma.'' Thus Africans and Afro-Americans are portrayed as strong, courageous, loving, alive, patient, compassionate, determined, proud, moral, having integrity, knowing who they are, resorting to deception and obsequious cunning only out of the necessity of survival. Whites, excepting Old George, are cruel, inhuman, immoral, pretentiously mannered, inured to human suffering, calloused in their emotions, obsessed with property and propriety and order. Freedom in Africa is contrasted with Slavery in America, as though African slavery not only did not antedate White slavers but did not exist. Neither Kunta Kinte, nor Chicken George, nor others in the later succession of Black males, were weak, passive, docile, fatalistic, resigned. For survival they may have feigned what submission the credulous master and mistress needed for their own dehumanizing entertainment. But everything was a finely rehearsed outward act. . . . Defiance was the underlying flame that made brokenness and despair impossible. Rootedness endured. . . .

If in some ways, Haley simplifies history, in other ways, his dramatic autobiographic odyssey of personal lineage is congruent with the findings of current historians of the antebellum South. (p. 14)

With insight and grace, Haley is able to articulate contradictions and ambivalences that less self-aware writers would make a matter of either-or. With empathic historical relativism, he successfully (for me) tries to imagine himself and his audience back in the eras he depicts. . . . There is no denying the human holocaust of American slavery. Yet even in the constraints of such degradation, there was some mutuality, some warmth, some caring, some commitment, some sense of reciprocal obligation. All was not feigned. Haley conveys much of this, even as he exaggerates the virtues and frailties and failings of his characters.

I find and identify with in *Roots* a struggle and process that is incomplete, one which I suspect cannot be finalized without foreclosing or violating the life-long development of identity. Here is where *Roots* parts company with most personal histories, self-disclosures, and autobiographic-ethnic confessionals of the contemporary genre. For if I hear Haley correctly, *Roots* does not denote exclusively African origins. Kunta Kinte is not his protagonist, but a vehicle for the *dramatic unfolding* which is the true protagonist, one of a search for wholeness. I do not find in Haley's agonized itinerary a tale of primeval innocence, despite frequent lapse in characterization. I do not hear an apologia for ethno-racial separatism, since Haley's and *Roots'* odyssey is inextricably Black and White. I do not find Black pride purchased exclusively at the expense of White shame and guilt. Haley is not altogether clear here, but the direction of his resolution is what compels my identification. He is, after all, the biographer of Malcolm X who just before his assassination, transcended the hate-ridden phase of "White Devils" hortatory rhetoric in his pilgrimage to Mecca, discovering that all men could be brothers irrespective of race. *Roots* serves as a reminder that not only is Black history bound up with White, but that White history is inseparable from Black. In a word, Haley's integrity and authenticity outweigh his sins of omission and commission. He has held a mirror before us, one in which we have chosen to peer attentively. Haley has chosen not the deceptive luxury of cozening himself and us into a fixation on the past, but has with sensitivity and self-discipline documented and embellished a continuum of culture and history that is common to the *American* experience.

Roots concludes with homage to the past and hope for the future, a future founded on a fresh start—something peculiarly American. (pp. 15-16)

[This] fairy tale in historical form is designed to make a point. And the degree to which it has touched us, made us more whole, is the extent to which Haley's odyssey is ours also, his hope, ours. In the end, there remains the unanswered question: Quo vadimus? Is it still possible to overcome together? (p. 16)

> *Howard F. Stein, "In Search of 'Roots': An Epic of Origins and Destiny (copyright © 1978 by Ray B. Browne), in* Journal of Popular Culture, *Summer, 1977, pp. 11-17.*

MICHAEL G. COOKE

Perhaps it is time . . . to take a close, steady look at the phenomenon that is *Roots:* what lies at the bottom of its pandemic appeal, what magic does it proffer, and to whom? Three sorts of magic, subtly blended to serve as all things to most people, can be directly identified.

To begin with, the magic of the placebo. *Roots* purports to deal with diseases in the American body politic and the harsh medicine necessary for a cure. But it proves unspeakably mild and conciliatory in fact. . . . Haley has the accent of an adolescent catechist, and the imagination of an adolescent materialist. The vividness of physical slavery virtually exhausts his powers of response. . . . One thinks of André Schwarz-Bart and *A Woman Named Solitude* and wishes that Haley had half so well perceived the *physique* of slavery as a perverse sacrament, an outward sign of inward disgrace, imposed degradation.

The essence of the placebo approach is expressed in the shift from cultural-moral issues to esthetic effects as the novel wears on. The marriage of Tom and Irene . . . is "a lovely, moving occasion" with a "lavish reception dinner" replete with "beaming white families"; and suddenly slavery has evolved into a source of charming occasions and charming sentiments. . . . *Roots* combines a sense that grave problems are under discussion with a basically picturesque and comforting spirit. It is a sort of movie-setting mountain, large and weighty to the credulous eye, and perfect for a time that wants to take up serious cultural-moral questions without difficulty and without discipline.

Then there is the magic of approximation. Haley continually fails to come to grips with a number of thorny issues. . . . But he seems to raise the issues: of time and the power of chance; of memory and the difference between a communal-African and an institutional-American organization of society; of cultural cross-comparison, and the nostalgic cachet of racial recall; of the paradoxicality of black American experience, which produces both dross and gold out of one pot, one personality; and so on. In raising such issues, *Roots* promises a far broader, more candid and more complex engagement than it sustains. It touches rather than taking on its issues. (pp. 145-46)

Finally one may recognize the magic of sentimentality, of emotion released from the demands of its object and expressed in the loose idiom of incredulity. Sentimentality largely prevents *Roots* from breaking into the revolutionary dimension toward which it gestures, and further prevents it from getting into the complex psycho-ecology of a family tree in an alien, indeed hostile soil. . . . It is odd that in his personal life Haley should make such claims for the transformative-redemptive value of the [oral] tradition, and yet in his fiction do so little to substantiate those claims.

In fact, there is a fourth, covert magic about *Roots,* the magic of what may best be called the misplaced genre. The work only just fails to find itself as sado-masochistic pornography . . . ; or as a metaphysical detective story . . . ; or as a victim's history of the United States; or again as a variant of the tale of the self-made man. *Roots* ends up as a smorgasbord when it might have been a mosaic. It is a feast for the transient rather than the sedulous reader. Its very form, marked by short chapters and short paragraphs, is calculated for ease. When it strives to be authentic it manages to be inadvertently comic, as in calling male genitals "foto" or the slave-minded white man "toubob." Because it does not dig in or rear up when serious matters are afoot, it seems easy to get through. But one wonders whether it will not prove also unduly easy to put down. (p. 146)

> *Michael G. Cooke, "'Roots' as Placebo," in* The Yale Review *(© 1977 by Yale University; reprinted by permission of the editors), Autumn, 1977, pp. 144-46.*

DILLIBE ONYEAMA

This saga of one man's twelve-year search for his ancestral origin [*Roots*] owes its success chiefly to white American guilt and Afro-American consciousness. . . . The *Newsweek* critique that *Roots* 'will reach millions of people and alter the way we see ourselves' is one certainly not to be applied to black Africans, who will question the sanity of any man who feels that his ancestral origins are of such significance as to warrant a twelve-year and half-a-million mile search. The inevitable reaction of any such African (I am one) to the resulting book would be . . . *so what?* . . .

This book is sad in a way—from the view that it meant so much to Mr. Haley to embark on this search to find an identity for himself. For this reason only am I happy that he was rewarded with the acclaim and commercial success that the book fetched him. Apart from that, his book is a great disappointment. Through six generations of slaves and freedmen, farmers and blacksmiths, architects and lawyers, lumber mill workers and Pullman porters—and one author, this is a tiresomely long and tediously detailed saga of one Kunta Kinte. . . . As a dramatic novel describing the anguish and sheer hell of slavery, *Roots* must rank as the worst slave-novel I have read (my bookshelves boast scores of them). It is written in a patronising manner that makes the reader feel like a nursery-school child being told a fairy-tale by a sweet-smiling female teacher. During the sixteen years of Kunta Kinte's rosy upbringing in the Gambia (made exaggeratedly rosy to emphasise the enormity of his kidnapping into slavery, no doubt), we see happy Kunta indulge in all the rigorous activities to shape him into manhood, except sexual communication. This essential aspect of nature seems to be totally absent from this lad's life, and the only hint that he is ever aware that such a natural phenomenon exists at all is when he has his first baby as a slave.

The book is rendered tedious after the second chapter by Haley's obsession with antiquated expressions and the weather . . . 'The names, which were great and many, went back more than two hundred rains'. . . .

Haley, we are told, taught himself to write, becoming a magazine writer and interviewer, and ghosting Malcolm X's autobiography. He should now endeavour to teach himself sentence-control. To say that most of his sentences are mouthfuls would be an understatement. . . .

The question that remains is, of course, how valid are the findings of his search? How reliable was the 'griot' in Juffure who supplied Haley with the information that left him in no doubt that he had at long last found his family tree? . . . Haley expresses deep gratitude to the griots of Africa. . . .

However, anyone who read [Mark Ottaway's brilliant] expose in the *Sunday Times* regarding the integrity of the late griot who gave Haley the meat-centre of his various informations, would have been tempted to conclude, as I concluded, that Haley had been taken for a shameful ride. That particular griot, Ottaway alleged, was something of a villain, a master of exaggeration and concoction, who knew in advance what Haley wanted to hear. . . .

On the basis of this, I am inclined to think that *Roots* is a work of pure fiction, albeit unintentional on Haley's part. Nevertheless Haley must be admired for his great efforts and originality. His sincerity is unquestionable.

> *Dillibe Onyeama, "Wrong Roots," in* Books and Bookmen *(© copyright Dillibe Onyeama 1978; reprinted with permission), June, 1978, p. 23.*

ARTHUR UNGER

"Roots," which, on television at least, started out as an entertainment and evolved into a sociological phenomenon, has finally turned into a self-contained environment. . . . "Roots" emerged from the TV screen like a massive tapestry, every square inch imprinted with artifacts of slavery and the period which it ominously dominated. The show's impact on whites as well as blacks is still being studied, but there is almost total agreement that, despite its obvious flaws, "Roots" was proof of the positive impact which a TV series can have on our society. . . .

While ["Roots: The Next Generations"] may lack some of the emotional impact of discovery and recognition of the original mini-series, [it] is superior to "Roots" in just about every other way. It is a tribute to taste, talent, creativity, and commitment. . . .

Deprived of the emotional issue of slavery by the Emancipation Proclamation, the new series touches on just about every black-white, black-black, people-people issue of the past 125 years. And it manages to handle most of them with restraint and subtlety, seldom downgrading the complexities, usually upgrading the emotionalism only as much as necessary for dramatic impact. . . .

The emphasis is not so much on the fight for freedom as it is on the struggle for equality. There is no sign of any queasiness as Kunta Kinte's descendants struggle toward their ultimate goal—assimilation into the American middle class.

Although many whites as well as blacks have been involved in the production of "Roots: The Next Generations," the mini-series looks at the world through the eyes of moderate black America. The perspective is black. And to those eyes, black is not only beautiful—it is upwardly mobile. . . .

Throughout all seven episodes, whenever a baby is born, he is held up to the sky and the moon as was Kunta Kinte. The elders retell a few simple facts about the African origins of the family, deeply rooted in nourishing black African soil. It is an inspiring family chronicle—the family of man, that is.

Certainly there are lapses—every now and then one can spot a kind of yearning for mass-media oversimplification and garishness—which will have you wincing. . . . (p. 23)

"Roots," "Holocaust," and now "Roots: The Next Generations" have all been stupendous projects, conceived with monumental objectives—that is, to illuminate important human events of our time. And as in the case of the mammoth heads of Mt. Rushmore, any close inspection of such a gargantuan creative project reveals flaws, distortion, cracks. But one doesn't examine Mt. Rushmore with a magnifying glass—one looks, one experiences, one marvels.

"Roots I" and now "Roots II" have managed to reflect accurately a long-neglected segment of our humanity, place it once and for all in rational perspective, allow it to take its rightful place in our consciousness. And most important— they have done what only television can do: Make it an integral part of the environment.

> *Arthur Unger, "'Roots' Is Back, in Many Ways a Better Series," in* The Christian Science Monitor *(reprinted by permission from* The Christian Science Monitor; *© 1979 The Christian Publishing Society; all rights reserved), February 16, 1979, p. 19.*

JAMES WOLCOTT

Will Alex Haley's ancestors reconquer American television? After seeing three of [the 14 hours of *Roots: The Next Generations*], I'd have to give a provisional no. With all its whippings and thrashings and swoony palpitations, [*Roots I*] had a pulpy-moralistic excitement reminiscent of that other world-shaking race melodrama, *Uncle Tom's Cabin*. . . . [*Roots II*] is an expensive show-and-tell lecture about Black History and Black Pride, forlornly parading forth good intentions. . . .

[As] drama, it's pulverisingly dull. Unlike the first series, the white characters here aren't all foaming-at-the-mouth racists, but you find yourself wishing that *somebody* would work up a frothy high. . . .

[The later] episodes of *Roots: The Next Generations* . . . celebrate Alex Haley as the great soul-embattled moral explorer of our time. . . . [Despite] dents in Haley's scholarly reputation, he's still a heroic figure for millions of Americans—millions who will loyally handcuff themselves to the TV for all 14 ponderous hours of *Roots II*.

> *James Wolcott, "'Roots II': Provocative (Zzzzzzzzzz)," in* The Village Voice *(reprinted by permission of* The Village Voice; *copyright © The Village Voice, Inc., 1979), February 19, 1979, p. 54.*

JANET MASLIN

In its seventh and final installment, "Roots: The Next Generations" changes shape. Set in the 1960's, it presents an Alex Haley who is a more complex and sharp-edged character than many of his now-famous forebears. And it places him in highly charged situations in which the battle lines aren't clearly drawn. If the earlier episodes, however sweeping, had a tendency to be black and white in outlook as well as subject matter, the conclusion of the series is something else again. This last part of "Roots" is easily strong enough to be watched without reference to the rest of the series. . . .

[The confrontation between American Nazi Party leader George Lincoln Rockwell and Haley] shows each man masking bitterness and rage with an air of exaggerated calm —Mr. Rockwell pretends to unflappable reasonableness, and Mr. Haley counters by being businesslike. The program is at its best when it sets up such intense, furious parallels and then refuses to resolve the situation. The interview scene ends with Mr. Rockwell's becoming so amused by his memories of absurdly childish Nazi anthems that he simply trails off in the middle of the encounter.

Right to the end, "Roots" persists in caricaturing whites who are either too unctuous or too evil. A cocktail party scene, which says as much about the younger Mr. Haley and his ambitions as it does about the era, is slightly marred by its exaggeration of the white hostess's gaucherie.

Later in the program, though, the nature of relations between blacks and whites in the 60's is illustrated with much more delicacy, as Mr. Haley tracks down people from widely varying backgrounds in the course of his hunt for his African relatives, an undertaking that takes an obvious toll on his private affairs before it culminates in a wonderful, stirring moment of triumph.

> *Janet Maslin, "TV: End of 'Roots II' Delineates 60's," in* The New York Times *(© 1979 by The New York Times Company; reprinted by permission), February 25, 1979, p. 46.*

MICHAEL J. ARLEN

Ever since Alex Haley's best-selling documentary novel (or "faction," as he described it) "Roots" first appeared, in 1974, and then reappeared, on television, in 1977, still as "Roots" (or "Roots I"), . . . and then reappeared again a few weeks ago, as "Roots: The Next Generations" (or "Roots II") . . . the story of Mr. Haley's efforts to retrace his lineage to its African beginnings has been talked about in terms of power. To "Roots" in its various forms, though perhaps especially to its television dramatizations, have been attributed the power to uplift the pride of American blacks, the power to raise the racial consciousness of American whites, the power to affect the emotions of all races through its powerful narrative, and the power to teach.

There is obviously no denying the power of a popular story that persistently attracts such huge audiences, although, considering the several weaknesses, dramatic and otherwise, of "Roots II," it is worth speculating about where the real power of the over-all drama resides. For example, it surely does not lie in an enormous respect for historical accuracy, since, despite Haley's much-touted labors of research, the dimensions of the several plagiarism lawsuits brought against him, and of one settlement, indicate that there was at times some more than modest confusion in his mind as to his sources; also, a 1977 challenge by a reporter of the London *Sunday Times* to the plausibility of Haley's *griot*-obtained information about his remote African ancestor Kunta Kinte has cast at least a little doubt on the factual, or detective-story, basis of his adventure. Nor has "Roots II" treated its parent, the original "Roots," with all-embracing fidelity, being content, perhaps, to subject the sacred text to the same poetic process that the author sometimes employed upon his earlier research. (p. 115)

[Chief among the problems concerning "Roots II"], I suppose, is the extraordinarily lopsided nature of Haley's story —a lopsidedness that existed in Haley's book and has only been magnified in both television versions—wherein the black characters are almost uniformly depicted in terms of dignity and moral courage, while the white characters, with but few exceptions, are generally portrayed as loutish and mean-spirited when poor, or weak and corrupt, though superficially genteel, when rich. Thus, in the town of Henning, Tennessee, where most of the first half of "Roots II" takes place . . . one gets not so much a sense of real drama or interplay between the blacks and the whites—of the two peoples' being really involved with one another—as a sort of old-fashioned, static morality play, reminiscent in part of "Uncle Tom's Cabin" and also, in some ways, of those movies about life in the trenches in the First World War, where Allied soldiers are shown in one set of trenches and the Germans are shown in another set of trenches, and the point of the drama seems to be to wait for some captain's whistle to periodically signal an offensive. In "Roots I," the propaganda element was rarely absent, although, perhaps because of the more substantial texture of the story, the racial messages seemed less obtrusive. In "Roots II," there are extended periods when propaganda seems to have been substituted for story—as in the Henning episodes, in which the drama seems to come to life only at those carefully structured intervals when the coarse and violent whites are sent off to brutalize the stoic and philosophic blacks.

The men in "Roots II" are for the most part close to racial caricature; the women are not much better. Black women in "Roots II" tend to be wise, sexual, philosophic, and invariably in touch with basic human emotions; white women are usually superficial and unsexual—or, if sexual, slightly whorish. But there are a couple of exceptions to the general rule of caricature—or, at least, there are attempts at exceptions. . . . Jim [son of the town aristocrat] is clearly intended as a sort of bridge between the races, or trenches, for he marries a black girl (naturally, a college-educated black girl of great sensitivity and good looks) and goes to live on the black side of town. But there is something off-key about the role. On the surface, Jim . . . seems to be a decent sort of white American boy, at least by ''Roots II'' standards, being relatively non-alcoholic, non-corrupt, and non-loutish, but he is also a kind of freak: poetic, sensitive, literary—almost, to use an archaic word, something of a sissy. Thus, while striking a blow for brotherhood in the ''plot,'' the underlying quality of Jim's role suggests, first, that the only way for a white man to escape the inherent wickedness of his nature is by surrendering a large part of his masculinity, and, second, that the surest way to achieve goodness is for him to marry a black girl. ''Roots II'' also suggests a couple of other options open to a white man wishing to achieve some measure of salvation—or, at least, dignity—in Henning, Tennessee, in the late nineteenth century. One of these is to be a sound, progressive, forward-thinking, liberal-minded small businessman. Not just an ordinary businessman, mind you, for, although business is clearly an occupation that attracts a better sort of person than the white trash who commonly engage in rural activities in the South, it nonetheless often brings out the devil in the white soul by driving such a person to drink on the job and become shiftless; as in the case of poor, weak Mr. Campbell. . . . Another option for a white man aspiring to decency is to be Jewish. According to ''Roots II'' there has rarely been as deep and affecting a fondness between two peoples as that which existed in Henning, Tennessee, in the eighteen-eighties and eighteen-nineties between black Americans and Jewish Americans. In fact, except for the forward-looking banker who sets Mr. Palmer up in the lumber business, just about the only decent adult white man anywhere near Henning is a cultivated gentleman called Mr. Goldstein, who runs a small drygoods store in town. (pp. 115-17)

Even when one wants to like ''Roots II,'' it seems to require some effort to peer through the curious racial propaganda, and something of a further effort to care very deeply —beyond the purely reflexive response of not wanting to see helpless people beaten up onscreen—about characters, white or black, whose personalities contain so few ambiguities and no surprises and who are mainly sent off, like freight cars, on their tracks of nobility (for the blacks) and meanness (for the whites) while we wait for them to collide.

There is also another fairly important weakness in the story. For, though the two ''Roots'' dramatizations have been described or appraised in epic terms, in ''Roots II'' (which is supposedly based on the last section of Haley's book together with ''one thousand pages of notes'' that he provided for the project) the television writers seem to have reduced the potentially epic dimensions of the story of Haley's ancestors in this country since the Civil War to a generation-by-generation series of boy-meets-girl encounters. Obviously, there's a place for romance and sexual relationships in a long family narrative, but in much of ''Roots II'' the problems of young love seem to be the real focus of the drama—and in some cases the only focus. At the center of the stage, girl flirts with boy, or boy flirts with girl; girl runs after boy, or boy runs after girl. Around these perpetually romancing kinfolk stand, on one side, the older generation of black men and women, persistently displaying wisdom and dignity, and, on another side, the hostile white people, brandishing clubs and displaying a general air of menace. And behind them, hazily sketched on a backdrop, or sometimes only hinted at, are the larger events of the times that Haley and his ancestors lived through. It seems a

strangely condescending view of black history, or of the part played in it by Haley's ancestors—as if the major moments worth rendering were youthfully romantic ones. (pp. 117-18)

[On] the surface, the power of the ''Roots'' stories remains something of a mystery or a paradox. Their audience-drawing power is evident. . . . But the nature of this power is not so clear. For example, the dramas are alleged to be uplifting to blacks, and so they are, but they are also in many instances subtly and not so subtly condescending toward them. Or they are supposed to be instructive to whites, but in fact the instruction is often inept, implausible, and inaccurate. More important for a popular melodrama, the ''Roots'' episodes, while they are described as a richly dramatic narrative releasing powerful emotions, are for the most part strangely static, with characters not so much acting out tragic patterns as merely being set in their ways, often imprisoned in stereotype, and with the supposed dramatic focus being directed unusually often to the relatively soft and formulaic problems of young love. So where does this power of ''Roots'' come from?

It comes, I suspect, from a most familiar source: from fantasy—or, to be a bit more specific, from family fantasies, those ''remembrances'' of a golden past or golden youth that most of us have dreamed for ourselves at some point or other, and that we apparently still dream at moments when we feel too naked or alone in the world to deal with cold reality. In ''Roots I,'' this element of fantasy was less noticeable, for the first television series was based fairly specifically on events in Haley's book . . . ; yet, even beneath Haley's stolid, journalist's prose and his gruesome scenes of slave whippings, the softer, golden colors of his dreaming could be glimpsed. (pp. 118-19)

If Haley's private fantasies were subterranean in ''Roots I,'' glowing from underneath the dark tales of slavery, in ''Roots II'' they seem to be much closer to the surface. There is one scene in particular, it seems to me, that expresses the underlying fantasy of the whole narrative. . . . What one saw in the scene was this: Haley has recently arrived in Gambia, on the coast of western Africa, in order to seek out traces of his ancestors. Earlier, he has met with some Gambians, who have directed him inland and upriver. Now Haley, holding notebook and pencil, has reached his apparent destination. The sun is shining. There are sand and palm trees. (Arcadia returning!) And a crowd of friendly, smiling Africans approaches across the sand. Haley stands watching them, and then, with mounting excitement, begins to cry, ''I've *found* you! I've *found* you! Kunta Kinte, *I've found you!*'' On the television screen, it is a triumphant moment. . . .

Certainly it is not a fantasy unique to Haley; probably most people have indulged in it at one time or another, and that, I suspect, accounts for its power. Call it the fantasy or dream of Going Home. (p. 120)

[In] print and on television, and especially in the more recent television version, ''Roots II,'' Haley's work seems to be only incidentally a drama of the progress and the tribulations of black people in America. This is the overlay of the story: the plot; the journalistic message that people tell themselves they are responding to. The deeper energy of the story, and its real strength in terms of audience appeal, proceeds from Haley's own fantasies about Going Home, and above all from his apparent willingness to leave the fantasies intact and unchallenged in much the same way that his audience does. One could almost say that the power of "Roots" lies in its weakness, albeit a most human weakness, for nearly all of us seem prey to fears that our ancestors were *not*—at least, at some point in the remote and golden past—mighty warriors, noble, sexual, and brave; and, worse, that if one of our kinfolk should now come before us, having travelled from a distant century or a far-off county, he would only let us down and make us look bad. "Kunta Kinte, at last I've found you, and I sure hope you make me *look good*!" Of course, if Haley had bitten the bullet and broken through the dream he was so movingly trapped in, he would have had to write a different, braver, and almost certainly much less popular book; but then he might have given his people, and also other peoples, a truer Kunta Kinte, clothed, however dangerously, in his real humanity, and who knows but that in the long run this might have turned out to be the greater gift? (pp. 124-25)

Michael J. Arlen, "The Prisoner of the Golden Dream," in The New Yorker (© *1979 by The New Yorker Magazine, Inc.), March 26, 1979, pp. 115-20, 123-25.*

Earl Hamner, Jr.

1923-

American novelist and writer for radio and television. Hamner is perhaps best known for *The Waltons,* a successful television series which is based on his autobiographical novels *Spencer's Mountain* and *The Homecoming* and on which he serves as executive story consultant. This series presents an idealized look at a large Depression-era family in Virginia's Blue Ridge Mountains. The early episodes revolved around the eldest son, John-Boy, an aspiring writer based on Hamner himself. After a slow start in 1972, it steadily gained popularity with both viewers and critics, who found its essential gentleness and quiet messages both touching and inspiring. Hamner's series has been criticized for its sentimentality, unreality, and excessive wholesomeness, but his characters have become as familiar as friends to many viewers, whom critics seem to feel have found stability and security in the family's solid structure and who can appreciate the program's nostalgic simplicity. (See also *Contemporary Authors,* Vols. 73-76.)

CHARLES LEE

If a novel may be described as an education in people, problems and places, Mr. Hamner has a claim to being a good teacher [with ''Fifty Roads to Town'']. Not everyone will want to sit in on a demonstration of life among the Holy Rollers in a small Virginia mountain town, of course, but those who do will find their sympathies as well as their interest engaged. The book is picturesque in its psychological oddities and setting. But it does not so lose itself in hillbilly comedy and terror as to alienate the reader's sense of compassion. Indeed, it goes to the sorrowful core of the human condition.

> *Charles Lee, ''Mountain Preacher,'' in* The New York Times Book Review *(© 1953 by The New York Times Company; reprinted by permission), October 11, 1953, p. 28.*

JOHN COOK WYLIE

In the apt phrase of the publisher, this Southern novel [''Spencer's Mountain''] is a ''happy'' one. Advance-reader Harper Lee colloquially called it ''splendid,'' and Jesse Stuart spoke of the sheer beauty of its simple writing.... In short, the book shows every promise of realizing at least a brief sojourn on the cenotablets of best-sellerdom. Or, to put it another way, with his second novel Mr. Hamner has become unmistakably the full-fledged William Makepeace Thackeray of Nelson County, Virginia.... [Mr. Hamner] remembers the sights, sounds and smells of his childhood with clarity. He reports them sometimes with brilliance and always with affection. His plot is simplicity itself: Country boy grows up, meets city girl, runs up against Latin syntax, sinks same.

Two things about the work (besides its obviously wide appeal to the vast public of happy-novel readers) call for comment. One is the messing around with symbols. There is an early intrusion of a white deer as a non-symbol, and there is a delicately unjelled use of the myth of Sisyphus in a father image. Neither of these, of course, will bother anyone except reviewers.

The other thing is more important, because it unobtrusively makes the work something of a social document in the history of the passing of the Old South. The author has his philosopher's stone resting at the sectarian University of Richmond, and he makes the object of his youth the breaking free from rural chains. Nothing of this sort could possibly have been written by members of an older generation. They wanted only to keep their children down on a farm, which in most cases was no longer a farm.

That Mr. Hamner belongs to a vibrant, new guiltless generation striving for the metropolis and the liberal arts, is clear everywhere in his book....

Apparently the Civil War at long last is over and the old shibboleths no longer work. The past is suddenly dead, even if it is still lovely. The young, in their freedom, can now remember the days of their youth with happiness and tranquillity.

> *John Cook Wylie, ''A Boy Grows Up in Nelson County, Virginia,'' in* The New York Times Book Review *(© 1962 by The New York Times Company; reprinted by permission), January 14, 1962, p. 48.*

ORVILLE PRESCOTT

[The] one thing we don't expect to find on the sidewalks of New York is fantasy, sentimentality and simple goodness. Yet these are the elements to be found in Earl Hamner's novel, ''You Can't Get There From Here,'' a modern tale about the search of a sixteen-year-old boy for his wandering father through the symbolical dream world of an improbable city called New York. Is this a good novel? It's hard to be certain, but I don't think so. It is a little too sweet and its gossamer thread of story is too frail and artificially contrived. On the other hand, this is an appealing novel, one that makes one feel young and innocent and good just for the few hours it takes to read it. If there is nothing in these whispy pages that can be taken seriously, neither is there anything that isn't pleasant, gently humorous and likable.

It would be as difficult to dislike "You Can't Get There From Here" as to dislike a basket of spaniel puppies. In the cold, hard, raucous world of modern fiction there ought to be room for a sensitive plant like this. (p. 29)

> *Orville Prescott, in* The New York Times *(© 1965 by The New York Times Company; reprinted by permission), June 11, 1965.*

MARTIN LEVIN

"You Can't Get There From Here" . . . is Joe's punchline. "It's too late." Joe is a radio comedy writer whose profession has become obsolete, which is just one of the reasons he has gone A.W.O.L. from his home in Brooklyn Heights with a bad case of "the dooms" and with his 16-year-old son Wes in close pursuit.

You can't get to New York from Mr. Hamner's directions either. The Manhattan through which young Wes hunts for his father is a far cry from the Blue Ridge Virginia the author described so well in "Spencer's Mountain." For the most part, it's real Oz country, inhabited by charming characters. . . . This is the New York that Robert Nathan invented, and if you can take your mind off the smog and the uproar of the city long enough to believe in Wes's innocence and his father's saintliness, it's not a bad place to visit. (p. 32)

> *Martin Levin, in* The New York Times Book Review *(© 1965 by The New York Times Company; reprinted by permission), June 20, 1965.*

JOHN J. O'CONNOR

The plot [of "The Homecoming"] seems to be the problem. Just as one story line gets under way, another appears to sidetrack it.

At the center is the Walton family, seven attractive children overseen by mother . . . grandpa . . . and grandma. . . . The family is awaiting the weekly return of father, who is forced to work fifty miles away during the Depression years. . . .

Traditional family routines keep stumbling into dramatic crises that are oddly resolved. At one point, the oldest son is sent in the middle of the night to look for his father, who may have been hurt in a bus accident. His trip includes a stop for Christmas services at the local Negro church with Cleavon Little doing the preacher-man shtick from "Purlie." Then he winds up with two genteel spinsters who are part-time boot-leggers.

That is about the extent of the son's search for his father, who finally shows up anyway and turns out to be a fount of love and understanding. "The Homecoming," unfortunately, turns out to be a string of incidents, varying widely in quality, that are never pulled quite firmly enough into a cohesive whole. (p. 75)

> *John J. O'Connor, in* The New York Times *(© 1971 by The New York Times Company; reprinted by permission), December 21, 1971.*

JOHN J. O'CONNOR

The mode [of "The Waltons"] is almost brazenly sentimental.

The narrator is John-Boy, the oldest son, reminiscing from the present. As he puts it, though, the Depression years were harsh, the family was "sustained with gingerbread, laughter and sharing, but, most of all with a wonderful mother and father."

As a special, "The Homecoming" disintegrated into a series of episodes that finally lacked cohesion. The episodic form, however, is precisely what is needed for a weekly series, and "The Waltons" should prove a more satisfactory vehicle for the stories of Mr. Hamner. . . .

The key operating device is a disarming simplicity that carefully avoids becoming simple-minded. John-Boy recalls his father and says, "I remember one morning when his hospitality was put to a challenging test," and the viewer is eased into a story about a deaf girl being left on the Walton family's door-step.

The context is a world of large, closely knit families, friendly sheriffs and doctors who occasionally refuse to accept a fee. John-Boy writes poetry in his spare time. Everyone gathers around the radio to listen to Charlie and Edgar. And violence is something that happens in far-away places. . . .

"The Waltons" deserve an audience. . . . If nothing else, it will be interesting to see if the public has any appetite for good family entertainment. (p. 94)

> *John J. O'Connor, in* The New York Times *(© 1972 by The New York Times Company; reprinted by permission), September 14, 1972.*

ROBERT BERKVIST

"The Waltons," CBS's gift to viewers who were hoping for one, just one, different show this season, seems strangely out of place until you realize what makes it different: you're being asked to care. . . . The wonderful and unusual thing about the Waltons is that they come across as real people.

Add to that a bit. The really unusual thing about the Waltons is that they're poor. All right, let's concede that these aren't the ghettoized victims of today's prosperous poverty. . . . [The] show can't boast the relevance of . . . well, what's your favorite relevant TV show? "Bridget Loves Bernie"? No, the Waltons relate to something else, something important. . . .

The Waltons' adventures, if they can be called that, are pretty mild stuff next to some of TV's improbable happenings. . . .

What does this story of yesterday's people say to us, here, now? What indeed? Most of us will never know what it's like to live in a sprawling old house with a screen door that slams and cocks that crow in the barnyard. Most of our children won't have run through grassy fields alight with wildflowers. Few of us would give a stranger the time of day, let alone shelter. Family life, for many, is a temporary prison en route to . . . what?

The Waltons, I think, remind us where we have been and suggest there was value there. This is a picture of a family in which people, real people, *talk* to one another as people, not as a gaggle of gagwriters for the "Tonight" show.

There's respect here, and affection openly displayed, and both young and old have their own dignity.

Robert Berkvist, "Some People We Can Care About," in The New York Times, Section 2 (© 1972 by The New York Times Company; reprinted by permission), October 8, 1972, p. 23.

JOHN W. DONOHUE

[The] famous opening sentence of *Anna Karenina* suggests that happy families aren't particularly interesting. Why, then, has *The Waltons* done quite well.... The reason usually given is that its characters are *real!* But to tell the truth, they are not all that real. Of course, they are immeasurably more human than the flat cutouts in most TV shows. (p. 549)

Nevertheless, no actual families are this uniformly good-looking and sweet-tempered.... And even in happy families, as Willa Cather once said, there's an unavoidable tension, for each one "is clinging passionately to his individual soul, is in terror of losing it in the general family flavor." *The Waltons* doesn't peer into depths of that sort, though it hints at them when John-Boy, the oldest of the children, feels himself divided between his hope of becoming a writer and his family affections and responsibilities.

But lack of realism is beside the point because what is being evoked here is not so much a real as an ideal world. Although it is a sophisticated, corporate work, *The Waltons* has something of the charm and purity of the Peaceable Kingdom, that world painted by such highly individual American primitives as Edward Hicks and Grandma Moses.... [The Waltons has the] power of suggesting what life ideally ought to be and of awakening a nostalgia for it.

In fact, it's a kind of morality play made unusually concrete and poignant by expert craftsmanship and the naturalness that films can achieve. Although in *The Waltons*, as Earl Hamner admits, even the "heavies" are not very villainous, many of its episodes are built around the morality's favorite theme: the conflict between light and darkness. Some outsider whose values are false or ambiguous comes across the Waltons and gets straightened out: a youthful preacher too preoccupied with sin and judgment; a German Jewish refugee who wants to forget his religious heritage; John Walton's World War I buddy who has never grown up. Sometimes the stranger, despite his own weakness, clarifies values for a Walton.... In each encounter the values the Waltons embody—family love, kindness, honesty, hard work—are not only highlighted but reassuringly prevail. (pp. 549-50)

John W. Donohue, "Arcadia Recalled: 'The Waltons'," in America (© America Press, 1972; all rights reserved), December 23, 1972, pp. 549-50.

PEGGY HUDSON

When I say that *The Waltons* perpetuates a myth, I am saying that the show is based on a certain concept of what life was like in the 1930's—and that there is probably little resemblance between this view and the way things really were.

I agree that the trappings of the story are enormously appealing—the big family, the simple life, the strong father figure, the household at rest and peace as darkness falls.

Whatever happens, safety and security close around the family at the end of each show. What a welcome relief from the problems of so many other TV shows, and the strains of our own lives.

Of course, things go wrong on *The Waltons*, but somehow a miraculous recovery is always made. (pp. 22-3)

Certainly there is nothing wrong with happy endings. Most of us watch TV to be entertained. We have problems of our own, which we want to forget for a few minutes. We want people on TV to solve their problems and be happy. But we shouldn't kid ourselves that what we're watching is necessarily a slice of reality....

[*The Waltons*] is not a "new" form of TV entertainment, as some have said, nor is it "history" in action. But it is wholesome, family-oriented entertainment, and that's achievement enough. (p. 23)

Peggy Hudson, in Senior Scholastic (copyright © 1973 by Scholastic Magazines, Inc. reprinted by permission), May 7, 1973.

ANNE ROIPHE

A bobwhite cry breaks the quiet of night among the firs and pines of the Blue Ridge Mountains of Virginia.... "Good night, Ma." "Good night, John-Boy." "Good night, Pa." "Good night, John-Boy...." and the lights of the Walton house on Walton's Mountain sometime in the early nineteen-thirties dim and a million viewers turn away from their television sets, eyes wet, souls heavy with false memory and hopeless longing. C.B.S. has filled another Thursday night with nostalgia, bathos, soap opera, formula plot, tear-jerking junk, and I and all those other viewers share a moment of tender shame at having been so painfully touched by such obvious commercial exploitation....

What myth or memory has caught so many of us? Why are we watching Mary Ellen go to a dance with her first boyfriend; Grandpa and Grandma relive a youthful jealousy; John-Boy befriend a midget, an actress or a big-city delinquent; Ma give up her career as a singer, overcome polio and gentle a wild, dying raccoon? What keeps us watching this obviously corny, totally unreal family?

Since every Thursday night I am reduced to ridiculous tears, I had to ask these questions and explore the program's skill at piercing tough hides, revealing sentimental ooze that can no more be controlled than the shift of dreams that still wake us screaming every now and then....

Man has always invented stories, gods and heroes to give him a sense of understanding and control of the lightning, the thunder, accident and death. I think we use our television set in many of the same ways. We huddle about its blue light looking for relief, control and understanding, magic to be worked on all those confusing forces that push us about. "The Waltons" may be romantic nonsense, may bear only superficial and misleading resemblance to real life, but it is very good magic. It is a good, workable dance to scare away the evil spirits of loneliness, isolation, divorce, alcoholism, troubled children, abandoned elders—the real companions of American family life, the real demons of the living room. (p. 40)

[The] Walton family is the ideal family as we all wish ours was: the one we would choose to come from; the one we would hope to create. Three loving generations live in one large house in the beautiful mountains where nature has not yet been destroyed by strip miners or other industrial nightmares. . . . (p. 41)

Is John Walton, who carries his sick child in his arms to the hospital, who teaches an arrogant young Baptist preacher humility and grace, who protects a troubled juvenile delinquent, who teaches trust and honor, love for all God's creatures to his children—is that John Walton too good to be true? Of course he is. Why do so many of us believe him, then—work-stained but proud, his seven children and two parents depending on him week after week? It can only be real to us, not a cartoon or a mockery of truth, because we want to believe it, we need to believe it. John Walton's down-home goodness (American as apple pie, turkey and cranberries, Mom) isn't a lie—or so our magic circles tell us on Thursday nights, weaving designs of make-believe we willingly admire. (pp. 41, 130)

[Olivia Walton] is the mother we all wish we had. She is the mother we all would like to be. She is the image that gives us guilt on days when we are irritable or tired, when we are selfish, when we wander away from home, when we fail to stay married; when we produce children who drop out of school, turn to drugs; when we can't find what's wrong or remember how to talk to our parents or how to explain to ourselves the disappointments that line the edges of our life. Olivia Walton has confidence in herself. Her strength seems infinite and we mere mortal mothers and wives shrink to nothing, contorted twisted versions of what was once good and pure. Not for one mad second do I think Olivia Walton is a real person, but watching her serving an enormous breakfast to 10 people, scouring pots and saving money in the kitchen cabinet, I ache with wanting the television to be presenting a documentary—not a soap opera but a genuine model of what it might all be. (pp. 130-31)

In our days of middle-class affluence we tend to associate poverty with an elevated moral sense as if it were our refrigerators, cars and swimming pools that were the source of the corruption of moral values, as if in the good old days without such material excesses people were better. A romantic myth if ever there's been one, and yet I suppose we need to feel that in the past, in the rougher, harder moments of our history, we were a fine people because surely we don't feel that way about ourselves now, and just as surely a John Walton character set in modern suburbia would be so unbelievable that the show would be howled right out of the Burbank studio, where it originated, into oblivion.

From a feminist viewpoint Olivia's decision to abandon her career as a singer is dreadful—one hopes she is not an inspiration to the next generation of women whom we are counting on to lead productive, intellectual, active lives outside of the home. However, Mrs. Walton's refusal to follow the now-popular path reminds us that, after all, happiness is the point and some women may indeed still find—even with fewer children and modern appliances—deep happiness in the roles of wife and mother.

The Waltons are equal partners in their family just as truly as if they were a team of neurosurgeons. This, I suppose, is part of the unreality of the program, and it is an important factor in the ideal image of family life it presents. (pp. 131-32)

[The] program, like fake electric fires in the fireplace, creates an illusion of warmth. As with the myth of Achilles or Hercules, no real man should measure his success by the activities of the gods and yet humanly enough we all do.

The Walton show, which must produce a full-hour-length story every week, has found a very successful formula for easily capturing our attention. To Walton's Mountain come all kinds of strangers, all of them troubled outcasts, fragmented or harmed by the value systems, the dizziness of the world beyond this sweet rural community. . . . [All] these characters create some kind of tension in the Walton household, tensions which are resolved through understanding, love and growth of the family. The single characters themselves are somewhat healed by their contact with the Waltons and the simple values the Waltons exude. We, the audience, are suckers for these stories because we all know we are that outsider, that troubled person whose life, like an X-ray with dark spots, holds threat of bad things. We identify with the outcasts, the loners, the poorly valued, isolated people who don't have the security of the Walton family, and we also identify with the Walton family itself, not so much from recognition as imagination or mythical cultural memories of the way it ought to be. Since we think of ourselves as outsiders and we wish we were part of the cohesive, good, happy family, we eagerly sink into the story, two sides of ourselves playing against each other, and in the end we feel pleasurably sad—even though, of course, everything has turned out all right. We are sad because we know things aren't that way at all and yet we're not angry or provoked because we've enjoyed playing around with the images of family life as they might be (we determine, not consciously, to bring our own families closer together), and as with New Year's resolutions the lack of accomplishment is nothing compared to the sincerity of the attempt.

What really are the factors that make the Waltons' life so ideal? It is obvious that nothing disastrous ever does really happen. . . . (pp. 132-33)

The disasters, physical and economic and psychological, that would actually befall a real family only threaten here for purposes of dramatic tension. (p. 133)

God is always watching over the Walton family—that seems still to be a part of our happiness myth, if only a small part of our reality. (p. 134)

The Walton family drama takes place in our recent past, but all those experimenting with new forms of marital-family relationships, all those parents planning the birth of a first child, all those of us midway in family life are constantly trying to achieve in our private ways the protective, humane, decent loving family that seems to come so easily to the Waltons. Never mind that we all fail; it's a journey worth taking. (p. 146)

Anne Roiphe, "Ma and Pa and John-Boy in Mythic America: The Waltons," in The New York Times Magazine *(© 1973 by The New York Times Company; reprinted by permission), November 18, 1973, pp. 40-1, 130-34, 146.*

Christie Harris

1907-

Canadian novelist, short story writer, essayist, playwright, and editor. Harris has written historical fiction, novels about contemporary young adults, and several volumes of Indian legends retold for the modern reader. As a child, she lived with her homesteader parents in a log cabin in western Canada and credits this with her affinity for tales of that area. The West she depicts is a peaceful one, in contrast to the violence of the American West. Her interpretations of Indian myths are sensitive and stress universal concerns against the unfamiliar background of Indian life. She says, "I've found it a real challenge to take their tragic history, their magnificent culture, and their fascinating legends; and then make it all real and understandable to today's young people." Her research has not been confined to historic accounts and anthropological archives: she has also spent much time with the Indians themselves. Harris's historical fiction also deals with the Canadian West but is often criticized for lacking life-like dimensions: her facts are accurate and her research is painstaking but the characters often seem wooden and their actions implausible. In addition, she has written several works of fiction dealing with the lives of her children; however, these novels seem to lack the artistic distance necessary to develop convincing characterization. Harris seems to be at her weakest when attempting to present a moral. The Indian legends, which confine this didacticism best, are her most successful works. (See also *Contemporary Authors*, Vols. 5-8, rev. ed., and *Something about the Author*, Vol. 6.)

RUTH HILL VIGUERS

[The stories in *Once Upon a Totem*] have the complexity, variety of human beings and supernatural creatures, and conflicts between good and evil that characterize all great hero stories and reflect mythology, history, and intricate social systems. . . . The brief introductions, one for each story, throw light on unusual customs or traditions and give the book additional value. (p. 173)

Ruth Hill Viguers, in The Horn Book Magazine *(copyright, 1963, by the Horn Book, Inc., Boston), April, 1963.*

ETHNA SHEEHAN

Tribal law and its abuse is [a significant theme] in Christie Harris's legends of the New World [collected in "Once upon a Totem"]. Ancient custom was the basis of the legal, moral and social code of the North Pacific Indians; disobe-

dience brought punishment, always certain if sometimes delayed. The totems were the heraldic symbols of the clans, and behind each crest was a story of heroic achievement or sacrifice. . . . These tales memorialized on clan totems are not bloodcurdling tales of savagery; they are the records, here evocatively and sensitively retold, of a disciplined and artistic people. (p. 28)

Ethna Sheehan, in New York Times Book Review (© *1963 by The New York Times Company; reprinted by permission), May 12, 1963.*

HELEN M. KOVAR

[*You Have to Draw the Line Somewhere*] is the story of a young Canadian girl who aspires to become a *Vogue* fashion artist. The British Columbia setting is refreshing, and the style humorous. Although the emphasis is on the heroine's pursuit of her career, there is enough of family life and boy-dates-girl to interest a wide variety of readers. It is a frank picture of the non-glamorous side of fashion art and modeling and the amount of work necessary to become first-rate in either profession. With a light touch the story offers depth and mature values. . . . This has much more to offer than most girls' fiction. (p. 72)

Helen M. Kovar, in School Library Journal *(reprinted from the April, 1964 issue of* School Library Journal, *published by R. R. Bowker Co. A Xerox Corporation; copyright* © *1964), April, 1964.*

MARGARET SHERWOOD LIBBY

Christie Harris has achieved a minor miracle [in *You Have to Draw the Line Somewhere*], a romance-career story that is sparkling and well written, filled with humor that springs naturally from character and situation. . . .

More detailed than *Cheaper by the Dozen*, it is just as funny. The scenes of family life are wonderful—everyone quipping at the parents' expense, never-failing brotherly wisecracks, and the two young sisters—ardent young conformists—trying to hide their ambitions, their originality and their parents' delightful eccentricities from their young friends. . . . [This book is a genuine slice of life giving equal attention to] frustrations, successes, and dull stretches. . . . (p. 19)

Margaret Sherwood Libby, in Book Week—The

Washington Post (© *I.H.T. Corporation; reprinted by permission*), *May 17, 1964.*

RUTH HILL VIGUERS

Linsey Ross-Allen [the protagonist of *You Have to Draw the Line Somewhere*] tells the story of the long road—from her dreams at the age of nine—to her successful career as a fashion artist. The book is episodic, without real plot, reading like lively autobiography, which it comes close to being. . . . Because this is first of all the story of a career, no great effort is made to develop the characters; but, even so, the parents particularly emerge very clearly. . . . The book gives a special bonus by continuing after Linsey's marriage to show how she meets the challenge of being simultaneously successful in home and career. Written with verve and humor, it is often very funny and should find a wide audience among teen-age girls and their mothers. (pp. 290-91)

Ruth Hill Viguers, in The Horn Book Magazine *(copyright © 1964, by The Horn Book, Inc., Boston), June, 1964.*

BENJAMIN CAPPS

The journal of two Englishmen . . . who crossed western Canada in 1863 is the basis for this fictionalized account ["West with the White Chiefs"] of a perilous trip through little-known, difficult land. . . .

Comic relief is supplied by a roguish Irishman, a ridiculous, helpless freeloader who intrudes into the party and makes the journey with the explorers. He quotes Latin aphorisms, is generally unavailable for any work, always makes outrageous demands on the others. He is a wonderful creation, a delightful contrast to the hard-working, serious Indians and Englishmen, but he loses some of his appeal as the author overworks his helplessness and, in the end, makes a completely unsympathetic character of him. (p. 22)

Benjamin Capps, in The New York Times Book Review *(© 1965 by The New York Times Company; reprinted by permission), April 4, 1965.*

PRISCILLA L. MOULTON

Characters are overdrawn and not always convincing [in *West with the White Chief*], but an abundance of humor—a rare quality in exploration accounts—Louis' faith in his father, the nature of the expedition, and the now-Canadian setting distinguish the story from others of its type. Once past a confusing first chapter, boys will find entertainment and adventure with a satisfying conclusion. (p. 280)

Priscilla L. Moulton, in The Horn Book Magazine *(copyright © 1965, by The Horn Book, Inc., Boston), June, 1965.*

PRISCILLA L. MOULTON

[Christie Harris has] rediscovered and reproduced a dignified and inspiring picture of [Haida] culture in a work of epic proportions [*Raven's Cry*]. Painstaking research and intense absorption in anthropological details have enabled the author to write with rare commitment and involvement from the Haida point of view. She sings the saga of the three chieftains, of their larger-than-life deeds, of the people they led, of the gods they honored. Her account is richly adorned with details of custom, ceremony, and costume. Dealing as it does in a highly artistic and complicated

manner with the whole range of human emotion and character, it makes demands of the reader but rewards him with new understanding of the forces that shape civilizations. . . . This distinguished work, probably classified as fiction, will occupy a respected position in historical, anthropological, and story collections. (pp. 574-75)

Priscilla L. Moulton, in The Horn Book Magazine *(copyright © 1966, by The Horn Book, Inc., Boston), October, 1966.*

PHILIP and PHYLIS MORRISON

[*Raven's Cry*] is so thoroughly immersed in the life of the Haida, the remarkable industrial Indians of British Columbia . . . that the book is first-rate ethnography. . . . The story is poignant: firearms, Bible, gold, whiskey and smallpox play their traditional roles. But the Haida are so like us in their determination to excel—in skill, in trade, in wealth, in status—that the story is much richer than the pastoral tragedy of so many tribes. (p. 144)

Philip and Phylis Morrison, in Scientific American *(copyright © 1966 by Scientific American, Inc.; all rights reserved), December, 1966.*

HELEN M. LOTHIAN

[*Confessions of a Toe-Hanger* is a companion book to *You Have to Draw the Line Somewhere* and] tells of the struggle of Linsey's younger sister Feeny to find herself. It is too episodic for children looking for a story and although older girls would enjoy the romance it is doubtful if they would be interested in the early chapters of the young Feeny or her later struggles as a young wife and mother.

Although the book is told in the first person it left one with the feeling that the insights into the central character were those of a loving and understanding mother rather than Feeny's own. Mrs. Harris is not only loving and understanding but a good writer, and I would look forward to more books such as *Raven's Cry* rather than another about her family. (p. 14)

Helen M. Lothian, in In Review: Canadian Books for Children, *Summer, 1967.*

COLIN M. TURNBULL

Raven's Cry . . . does not pretend to be any more than a novel.

As such it catches the interest and holds it, while at the same time introducing, almost by sleight of hand, many very real and pertinent anthropological observations. Social institutions such as the potlatch, totems, family structure, and trade are brought into the picture like the sweetest sugar-coated pills, and anyone reading this book is, whether he likes it or not, going to emerge not only interested but informed. Yet the book is utterly without pretense. (p. 28)

Colin M. Turnbull, in Natural History *(copyright © the American Museum of Natural History, 1967; reprinted with permission from* Natural History*), November, 1967.*

RUTH HILL VIGUERS

The author's ability to create convincingly alive characters is as evident [in *Forbidden Frontier*] as in her other books, but Mrs. Harris has such a lot to say about the times, the people, and the problems that she has crammed too much into one story. Events move fast enough to hold readers, however, and girls who read the book for the story of Alison and Megan will learn a great deal about the settlement of the Far West. (pp. 182-83)

> *Ruth Hill Viguers, in* The Horn Book Magazine *(copyright © 1968 by The Horn Book, Inc., Boston), April, 1968.*

KATHRYN C. JAMES

The arrival of farmers and gold seekers to the Canadian West brought change and upheaval. To the Indian it meant adjustment to a new way of life often with disastrous results. To the fur trader it meant the loss of livelihood. To Alison Stewart, daughter of a chief trader and an Indian princess it brought grief and bitterness. To Ross MacNeil, the son of a chief trader and a Shuswap Indian it brought ignominy and revolt. To Megan Scully, newly come to the West and with the memory of an Indian massacre fresh in her mind, it meant fear and a chance for wealth. Through their eyes, the conflict of Indian and white settlers is portrayed with honesty and fairness [in *Forbidden Frontier*]. . . .

In spite of real and vivid characters, the story often lacks cohesion and often becomes a mere recital of case histories. (p. 15)

> *Kathryn C. James, in* In Review: Canadian Books for Children, *Summer, 1968.*

JULIE LOSINSKI

[In *Let X Be Excitement*, which is based on the life of her son, Harris] has created a new, commendable addition to her collection of family portraits. For Ralph, discovering his life's occupation meant finding a job that offered intellectual challenge and satisfied his love of excitement and the outdoors. . . . Ralph's satisfaction in doing what comes naturally, combined with a sense of humor, results in an appealing zest for living. Readers (boys particularly) facing career decisions will empathize with Ralph, and enjoy, even though they may not be able to equal, his adventures. (p. 124)

> *Julie Losinski, in* School Library Journal *(reprinted from the September, 1969 issue of* School Library Journal, *published by R. R. Bowker Co. A Xerox Corporation; copyright © 1969), September, 1969.*

PENELOPE M. MITCHELL

More than a who-wore-what version of the history of dress, [*Figleafing Through History: the Dynamics of Dress*] attempts to show that clothing has never been merely utilitarian, that it is a reflection of mores, rank, and philosophies. As a result, what is had here is a brief history of civilization—Eastern and Western—as seen through man's bodily adornment. Simplification has not distorted the overview, and the necessary postulation of changes in attitude during pre- and early history does not seem out of line. The author's personal bias does occasionally emerge. especially in the final (approving) chapter on current Western trends in dress. (p. 127)

> *Penelope M. Mitchell, in* School Library Journal *(reprinted from the September, 1971 issue of* School Library Journal, *published by R. R. Bowker Co. A Xerox Corporation; copyright © 1971), September, 1971.*

"Anything uncanny is stlalakum," and practically everything uncanny [that happens in *Secret in the Stlalakum Wild*]—sasquatches, sprites, lie detector evidence of plants' emotions, and a very unlikely British Columbian faery named Siem—plays a role in convincing hard-headed Morann that the real treasure of the Stlalakum Wild is not gold but natural beauty. It's a little disappointing that more isn't made of these fantasy elements after they've been introduced: the sasquatch is dismissed as "a pitiful buffoon. . . . Big as a grizzly, yet timid as a rabbit"; the wonderful Ogress Squirrel plays only a minor role; and the encounter with the two-headed Seexqui is inconclusive—it's supposed to be a test of courage, but Morann *would* have run away if she could have gotten her sleeping bag unzipped. Perhaps if we knew earlier that the Wild was being threatened by miners, Morann's quest would seem more purposeful. As it is, the mix of Indian legends, scientific speculation and traditional make-believe is powerfully suggestive, even though it never really coalesces. . . . (p. 478)

> *Kirkus Reviews (copyright © 1972 The Kirkus Service, Inc.), April 15, 1972.*

FRANCES POSTELL

[*Secret in the Stlalakum Wild* is an] interesting although not entirely successful attempt to use the lore of the Northwest Coast Indians in a message fantasy. The Stlalakums (spirits of the Old Coast Salish Indians in British Columbia) begin to speak to Morann, a normal little girl with a very active imagination, and urge her to find what she understands to be a great treasure. She joins in the quest reluctantly at first, but later gains enthusiasm when she comes to believe that finding treasure will make her important in her family. Morann eventually discovers that the treasure is the wilderness itself which the Stlalakums want people to love and save. After this initial build-up, the ending may disappoint some children. . . . (p. 77)

> *Frances Postell, in* School Library Journal *(reprinted from the May, 1972 issue of* School Library Journal, *published by R. R. Bowker Co. A Xerox Corporation; copyright © 1972), May, 1972.*

[*Once More Upon a Totem* contains three] more lengthy stories compiled from folk material of the Indians of the Northwest coast, with an introductory evocation of the potlatch atmosphere in which they were originally told. The first tells rather incoherently of a prince's dealings with the hypnotic, ritualistically recycled salmon people; the second is essentially a string of anecdotes about the supernatural trickster Raven, a former prince who is a slave to his voracious belly; and the last and most concise is a "ghost story" about a proud shaman prince who goes too far in his ostentatious meddling with the dead. . . . [Background] notes are woven into the narratives, and Harris' authoritative and intimate knowledge of the cultures (Tlingit, Haida, Tsimshian and Kwakiutl) is evident. As stories however these are unevenly successful. (p. 257)

> *Kirkus Reviews (copyright © 1973 The Kirkus Service, Inc.), March 1, 1973.*

[*Sky Man on the Totem Pole?* is] the history of a people—or, rather, two peoples: a tribe of Northwest Coast Indians whose growing arrogance, stemming from their belief in the divinity of a skyman ancestor, brings disaster; and the mechanized, technologically advanced population of a distant planet whose greenery is dying because, heretics whisper, the people do not talk to plants or recognize their spirits. The novel (?) is based on an Indian legend about a Man-from-the-Sky who carried off an Indian princess and returned her to earth years later with six grown children; Harris, who suggests that the skyman could have been a real man from space, retells the tribe's story in terms of Velikovsky's *Worlds in Collision,* Von Daniken's *Chariots of the Gods?* and Tompkins and Bird's *The Secret Life of Plants.* . . . The problem is that Harris takes these pseudo-scientific sources as literally and as grimly as her inevitable muttering elders take the endless portents of delayed disaster—omens which become, here, less effective in sustaining tension the more frequently they are evoked. (p. 317)

Kirkus Reviews (copyright © 1975 The Kirkus Service, Inc.), March 15, 1975.

VIRGINIA HAVILAND

[*Sky Man on the Totem Pole?*] combines mythological beliefs with the possibility of men coming from outer space and with modern theories about bioplasmic energy in an attempt to explain what might have happened in Temlaham, the Indian's Promised Land. The story's structure is confusingly episodic, weaving back and forth with changes of scene and points of view. An Indian community sees a falling star or comet; it turns out to be the spaceship *Colonizer,* directed to the planet Tlu's colony on Earth. After the Indians migrate to Temlaham, the narrative returns to the spaceship. It is aiming to save its doomed planet when data banks show the extermination of growing things to be imminent and Doomsday only 102 years away. Finally, after the spaceship's landing, the men from Tlu lead the Indians to regard scientific phenomena as manifestations of the spirit world. The conglomeration of ideas could provide material for fresh and interesting science fiction, but the story lacks suspense and clarity, and the sum of its parts does not make a successful whole. (pp. 380-81)

Virginia Haviland, in The Horn Book Magazine (copyright © 1975, by the Horn Book, Inc., Boston), April, 1975.

KENNETH RADU

The general competency of *Secret in the Stlalakum Wild* is surely the result of years of tending to the craft of writing for young readers. The hallmark of [Harris's] style is a good-humored briskness which carries the story along in an uncomplicated, well-paced narrative. . . .

Indian folk-lore and mythology have quite clearly made their imprint upon Mrs. Harris's imagination. Her finest work is directly concerned with the Indian life and legends of the Northwest. *Raven's Cry* . . . remains a singularly moving paean to the now extinct Haida civilization of the Queen Charlotte Islands. Fully and accurately researched, *Raven's Cry* portrays the complexities and uniqueness of the Haida culture with insight, wonder, and compassion. Mrs. Harris's view is neither sentimental, romantic, nor patronizing. She reports Haida life as it was lived on the islands with the clear eye and honesty of the sympathetic chronicler. Mrs. Harris returns to the Haida again in her later novel, *Forbidden Frontier* (1968). In the character of Djaada, the Haida wife of a Hudson's Bay Company offi-

cial, Mrs. Harris created a figure of dignity and pride, a woman who could ignore the white man's insults and stupidity but who could not ignore the loss of Haida self-respect. Again, one trusts the historical accuracy of the writing. (p. 75)

The morality of *Secret in the Stlalakum Wild* . . . shows signs of [a] tendency in Canadian fantasy literature [to fail to integrate fully the moral lesson]. Morann, the heroine of the story, is introduced as a somewhat dissatisfied young girl who feels particularly ignored by her family. . . . Morann's feelings of neglect are very real and stem from her own sense of worthlessness. Unable to believe in herself and her special qualities, she is prone to saying and doing tiresome and foolish things, in a vain attempt to be noticed.

The ultimate point of Mrs. Harris's fantasy, it would seem, is to teach Morann that she has unique value and individual worth. To this end, Morann's self-education process becomes involved with her quest for treasure which, an Indian spirit informs her, has been built up over millions of years, a fact that provides some indication of its fabulous value. (p. 76)

There is marvellous opportunity here for the creation of a convincing, secondary world, even if the world is represented by a single agent. More importantly, such a meeting is a chance for the suggestive qualities of an evocative, subtle prose to play upon the reader's imagination. The author disappoints us.

> A shimmer of pearl flashed up onto a hummock of grass. It was a little person. Yet it wasn't a little person.
> A UFO has landed, Morann thought. A flying saucer. It's a little being from Outer Space.
> It was a little person. Yet it wasn't a little person . . .

Morann's response, as Mrs. Harris portrays it, is anticlimactic. The odour of cliché hovers about such terms as "flying saucer," and "UFO." The description of the spirit immediately after this is not without its fine touches; but unfortunately the book stylistically remains one of occasional effects. The writing is more consistently functional than inspired.

The limited quality of the prose seems to be the natural consequence of Mrs. Harris's uncertain grasp of the nature of fantasy. She is not primarily a writer of fantasy literature, and the prose of *Raven's Cry,* significantly enough, is considerably more interesting than that of *Stlalakum.* Because of her inexperience in the genre, the author persistently undercuts the fantasy elements of the novel. Instead of creating a logic which arises from and supports the fantasy, Mrs. Harris relies upon the empirical data of the real world to give scientific respectability to the central fantastical conception, the Indian view that all nature is richly endowed with communicating spirits or stlalakums who are sensitive to the presence of humanity. This is unfortunate because it wastes so much time at the beginning of the book where Mrs. Harris, for example, quotes directly from an article in an issue of *Wildlife* magazine concerning experiments about the psychogalvanic reflex of plant cells to prove that they do indeed "react emotionally to every threat to their well being." . . .

The point of this information has its thematic relevance later when Morann discovers what constitutes the real treasure she takes such great pains to seek. Hence, one is aware of the basic contrivance of the fantasy; but, to her credit, Mrs. Harris does show the creative good sense to translate the jargon of the article into comic terms. (pp. 76-7)

Siem is the most important fantastical character in the novel; but the difficulty with his characterization is that one cannot really believe in him as either an Indian or a spirit. He sounds too much like Henry Higgins. In response to Morann's exclamation, "Leaping leppercorns!" Siem says: "Do not conjure up those grasping immortals" . . . ! Later he adds: "I distinctly heard you summoning leprechauns, though your pronunciation leaves something to be desired." . . . Too often as well, he is a mouthpiece for castigating the white man's stupidity about the wilds. (p. 77)

As a character, Siem illustrates what is wrong with *Secret in the Stlalakum Wild* . . . : the absence of memorable characters who are unmistakably a part of a richly imagined fantasy and who never sound a false note therein. When an author concentrates upon getting the story told and making the moral point clear, however, character is evidently sacrificed. . . .

[The] chapters describing Morann's ordeal of being alone, stuck in her sleeping bag, in forbidding surroundings are among the best in the book. Mrs. Harris is quite capable of creating a very tense mood, of depicting an environment which could, seemingly, come alive to destroy an intruder. . . .

Morann's moral education whereby she becomes an individual of real worth now depends upon her recognition that the fabulous treasure of the Stlalakum wild is really the awesome beauty and mystery of nature herself. (p. 78)

Secret in the Stlalakum Wild works hard to be a "relevant" book for young readers. Hence, the moral vision, if one can call it that, sounds a bit thin, a kind of truism which it is now fashionable to introduce into a book of this kind. Because Mrs. Harris's fantasy is not provided with its own controlling logic and is by and large undeveloped as a fantasy, because it is not conveyed in a prose of "poetic overtones," because no single character emerges strongly and memorably, *Secret in the Stlalakum Wild* is not a success as an example of significant fantasy fiction.

That should not, however, blind us to the novel's real merits. It is a book that asks us to respect the natural world. It is a book that describes some of the beauty of that world with love and precision. It is a book of good humour and good companionship. (p. 79)

Kenneth Radu, "Canadian Fantasy," in Canadian Children's Literature: A Journal of Criticism and Review (Box 335, Guelph, Ontario, Canada N1H 6K5), No. 2, 1975, pp. 73-9.

PAT MITTON

Christie Harris combines her considerable talents for writing richly evocative legends and imaginative novels in [*Sky Man on the Totem Pole?,* a] fascinating Man-from-the-Sky legend. . . .

The author has not zipped off a trendy tale to cash in on books like *Chariots of the Gods* by von Daniken, but has provided her readers with a thoughtful piece of writing recognizing the values of both modern and primitive thought on how to best work with nature to preserve both the natural and human elements. (p. 34)

Pat Mitton, in In Review: Canadian Books for Children, *Autumn, 1975.*

SHEILA EGOFF

The potential for children's literature inherent in the Indian legends is most fully realized by Christie Harris on *Once Upon a Totem.* . . . Other collections may have more charm, or a more fluid style, but the legends chosen by Harris and her interpretation of them are outstanding in that they seek quietly to illuminate universal values. The stories are very much a part of early Indian life and very much a part of today.

The book contains five legends relating to the Indians of the North Pacific Coast, a people unusually rich in myth and legend. (pp. 24-5)

Harris does not interpret the intricate character of the trickster-hero Raven but is concerned to present a group of separate stories, each of which has its own shape and development. Her task is therefore somewhat easier than that of those writers who have endeavoured to put some order into the cyclic Indian tales.

The first story in the collection, 'The One-Horned Mountain Goat', [reveals] dramatically the Indian concept of respect for animals. (p. 25)

Although the legend loses nothing in a simple retelling—such is its innate power—Christie Harris has enhanced it with detail and in so doing has added a new dimension, much as Walter de la Mare re-clothed the old folktales in his *Tales Told Again.* . . .

The author's style is simple and vivid, as when she is describing the vengeance of the goats, and one feels the rhythm of the archetypal legend. . . . (p. 26)

Many Indian legends have a quality of anonymity. In their original form, characters may not even be identified, or their traits may be so little individualized as to make them types rather than people. But Harris, in her first sentence, brings her hero close to the reader: 'Long, long ago there lived an Indian boy, Du'as, who found one northern summer almost endless. It seemed to him that the golden tints of autumn would never brighten the aspen trees along the lower slopes of Stek-yaw-den.'

At the same time Harris does not sacrifice authenticity to literary values. The five stories retold in this collection are based on ethnological reports and on the author's direct experience of mingling with the Indians as much as possible in their homes and in their villages listening to the stories being told. Three stories have overtones of European folktales but stand sturdily on their own feet as indigenous products. The author tells us that the last tale—'Fly Again Proud Eagle'—is a historical adventure, based firmly on actual happenings. Be that as it may, it is also a portrayal of the longing, as old and as new as human experience, to recapture a lost homeland.

Most stories from the oral tradition are improved by pruning, honing, polishing, and refining until not a word seems out of place and the basic concept emerges with clarity, but with enough depth and mystery to allow readers to make their own interpretation. In Harris's . . . *Once More Upon a Totem* . . . , the considerable risk inherent in the embellishment of myth and legend is all too apparent. The first story, 'The Prince Who was Taken Away by the Salmon', is a famous Tsimshian tale, which . . . has a definite mythological shape. In transferring it to the short-story or novelette form, Harris has destroyed its legend quality and, indeed, its basic pattern. Length becomes even more of a hazard in the second story, 'Raven Travelling', which is long and repetitious to the point of boredom; while the third one, 'Ghost Story', is so long and involved that it cheats the reader of the shivers promised by the title.

Alongside Harris's rather sophisticated talents, the older retellings seem now to be somewhat naïve. . . . (pp. 26-7)

[The young heroine of *Secret in the Stlalakum Wild,*] Morann, rather pettishly unhappy with her family role, is sidetracked from her search for recognition into an understanding of nature and conservation. . . . [She] comes to learn that healthy green and golden nature is more valuable than the green or gold in man's pockets. Thus Harris gives us a substantial ecology theme in the tradition of Ruskin, Kingsley, and Tolkien. (pp. 73-4)

Harris's brief entries into the realm of fantasy in the 'Stlalakum Wild' are jerky and stagey and finally almost spoil her overt purpose, which is to teach her youthful readers the importance of conservation. Morann is probably the most bouncy and outgoing heroine since L. M. Montgomery's Anne—a strong contrast to children in most fantasies, who tend to be somewhat lonesome and alienated from their everyday surroundings. Morann is healthy, open, and modern, a very ordinary girl who is almost dragged into an adventure for the common good. The opening paragraph sets the tone of practicality:

> Life seemed only too predictable to Morann on the blistering hot day her father's sister Sarah was due to arrive. So much so that she took steps to start things off in a new direction. Determined to be somebody's favourite for a change, she went at the day head on. She brushed her hair hard, and she reeked of perfume when she finally emerged from the bathroom.

The rather hearty manner of the opening is not entirely typical of the style. It ranges from some fine descriptive passages to 'modern' conversations riddled with schoolgirl and schoolboy colloquialisms. If a break in high style is considered a fault in fantasy, it should be remembered that the same criticism has been levelled against C. S. Lewis in his Narnia Chronicles—but with far less justification.

Harris has a deep and demonstrable knowledge of West Coast Indian myth. Her books of Indian legends have been justly acknowledged as important contributions to the literature. She also has a deep feeling for the landscape of British Columbia; but [her concern is self-consciousness]. . . . (pp. 74-5)

[*You Have to Draw the Line Somewhere*] is based on episodes in the family life of the author and tells about a Canadian girl in British Columbia from her elementary school days to her success (but not outstanding success) as a fashion artist in New York. It has style, characterization,

fun, and gaiety. Writing such as this, with its sense of reality, its sanity and humour, its roots grounded in real family life, makes *You Have to Draw the Line* an unusual example of light writing and of what can happen when even a writer with a stereotyped idea begins a book with a creative spark. . . . (pp. 190-91)

Sheila Egoff, in her The Republic of Childhood: A Critical Guide to Canadian Children's Literature in English (© *Oxford University Press, Canadian Branch, 1975), Second edition, Oxford University Press, Canadian Branch, 1975.*

RICHARD B. DAVIDSON

Christie Harris *Sky Man on the Totem Pole?* . . . concerns, among other things, the relation between the Indian and White cultures. In the vein of von Daniken, the question is this: did visitors from other planets furnish the images for the mythology of Earth's denizens? In this novel, might spacemen have provided the Indians of the Northwest with the basic imagery and narrative core of their central legend of Temiaham? . . .

I am sorry to say that while I am aware of Harris' reputation and respectful of her impulse to do something fresh and new, I do not find this a good book. It is contrived, made up of elements that work against each other. For example, if you write a novel and introduce character in the psychological sense, as Harris does at the outset with the brothers Adinak and Say-ok, you raise expectations which are shortchanged if the characters are suddenly transposed into the mythic mode wherein psychology is irrelevant and the "character's" *emblematic* function is the important thing. (p. 511)

Legend and myth are not amenable to certain narrative devices and points of view. Harris goes inside the characters' heads, but will come right out when myth requires their demise. And while myth depends on the calm reiteration of incident, the author tries to dramatize cyclic incident with a breathless style that, for me, soon ceases to be generative of any emotion at all. I think this novel is not controlled: there is too much aimed for, not enough hit. Sad, because there are possibilities here. (pp. 511, 513)

Richard B. Davidson, in Journal of Reading (*copyright 1976 by the International Reading Association, Inc.; reprinted by permission of Richard B. Davidson and the International Reading Association), March, 1976, pp. 511-12.*

All six stories in Harris' third collection of Northwest Coast Indian tales [*Mouse Woman and the Vanished Princesses*] deal with princesses who are kidnapped or captured by animals or spirits. . . . Reading all six together makes the unifying themes seem only repetitive, and Harris sometimes plays Mouse Woman for her marginally cloying cuteness while playing the rest of it straight. . . . [But separately the stories] stir up enough atmospheric mischief, and reveal enough of Haida and Tsimshian culture, to put this on the level of the author's *Once More Upon a Totem*. . . . (p. 476)

Kirkus Reviews (*copyright © 1976 The Kirkus Service, Inc.), April 15, 1976.*

S. YVONNE MacDONALD

[*Mouse Woman and the Vanished Princesses,* a] collection

of legends from the mythology of the Northwest Coast Indians of Canada is uniquely linked through the character of Mousewoman, a Narnauk or Supernatural Being. . . . The stories are clearly and lyrically told, with perhaps the most distinctive quality being the characterizations of the Narnauks. Harris manages to evoke the magical and essentially alien World of the Supernaturals and also its familiarity to the Indians, for these spirits were a daily part of their lives. . . .

There is a surprising amount of variety in this collection, given the confines of the theme, vanishing princesses. Some of the tales are poignant, others almost grisly in their outcome. All of the retellings reveal the author's detailed knowledge of Northwest Indian culture and customs, in addition to the actual legends. (p. 41)

Mousewoman and the Vanished Princesses follows other books of Indian mythology by Christie Harris such as *Once Upon a Totem* and *Once more Upon a Totem*. By comparison, they have a more scholarly approach to Indian mythology, because of the introductory essay preceding each tale, perhaps. In these essays, Harris formally discusses Northwest Coast Indian life. . . . They could easily be used by an adult studying cultural anthropology. . . .

[*Raven's Cry* and *Forbidden Frontier*] combine the author's knowledge of Indian folklore and custom with historical fact to describe the collision between European white man's civilization and Indian culture. Harris writes with sympathy for the Indians, apparently determined to tell their side of the story. Her characterizations of Indian children and adults are as human, if not more so, than those of the white people in the novels, stressing the pride and dignity of the Indian people before their degradation by the fur traders and other whites. *Forbidden Frontier* . . . seemed more sketchily written than *Raven's Cry*, which drew more upon the author's specialised knowledge of Indian mythology. This knowledge of legend and folklore seems to me to be the author's main strength, whether in her collections of myths or in her novels. She is at her best when she is recreating the stateliness and traditional tone of the Northwest Indian culture, the main theme in all her writings. (p. 42)

> *S. Yvonne MacDonald, in* In Review: Canadian Books for Children, *Autumn, 1976.*

GWYNETH F. EVANS

Sky Man on the Totem Pole? has some fine moments in it [but] . . . Christie Harris attempts too many disparate tasks. Ultimately *Sky Man* falls apart from lack of internal unity or sense of development. The heart of the book, and its real strength, is its retelling of the legends of [the] people of Temlaham; the adaptation of such legends into exciting and appealing stories for children is Mrs. Harris's forte. (pp. 117-18)

The chief weakness of *Sky Man* is the didacticism which imposes a kind of superficial unity on the disparate elements of the book, but which is obtrusive, often shrill, and remains stated rather than felt. Didacticism is certainly not alien to fantasy—George MacDonald and C. S. Lewis are two notable practitioners of both—but to avoid stifling the fantasy it must remain implicit, must be at the heart of the author's vision, rather than a message baldly stated by the author, as it tends to be in *Sky Man*. Christie Harris takes

up in this book the idea which she elaborated, again not altogether successfully, in *Secret in the Stlalakum Wild:* plants have a sensitivity and consciousness which the Indians expressed through the idea of their individual spirits and which modern technological society must come to realize and respect. (p. 118)

Mrs. Harris has a good feeling for her readership, and she is not wrong in assuming that modern children will be interested in an interpretation of Indian legends which accounts for their supernatural elements by reference to visitors from outer space. But such an interpretation does not of itself create a good fantasy, nor does it ultimately do justice to the mythology which it interprets. The basic assumption of *Sky Man* is that the legends gain in significance and validity if they can be seen as in some sense scientifically "true", if they refer to events which once literally happened. The dedication of the book is "To everyone who suspects that legends are fanciful records of history—recountings of actual events that were often misunderstood at the time." That a legend-teller of Christie Harris's reputation should espouse such a simplistic view of myth, apparently ignoring its symbolic, psychological and spiritual basis, is surprising. Ironically, this assumption that legends are justified by receiving a rational, historical explanation places her in the camp of her own Tlu-men, who do not think that a belief has any value unless it can be scientifically demonstrated to be true.

The story of Tlu might have been developed into a good science fiction novel on its own; science fiction is traditionally hospitable to speculation and messages of warning about human behaviour. But juxtaposed to the Temlaham legends and offered as an explanation of them, it is thin and tawdry. The process by which the Tlu-men project images on the rocks in order to lure the wasteful goat-hunters to the mountains is confusing, unconvincing, and adds nothing at all to the original legend. If one must have a rational explanation for the story, it is not difficult to think of a more plausible one than this. One might question, too, in a book directed at children, the emphasis placed on the theories of *Chariots of the Gods* and *The Secret Life of Plants:* these theories have not, on the whole, been accepted by reputable scientists, but the manner in which they are presented in *Sky Man on the Totem Pole?* belies the question mark at the end of its title. (pp. 118-19)

In structure and style, as well, *Sky Man* is seriously flawed. The book closes with the Indian boy, Billy Charlie, discovering that modern science is confirming many of his tribe's old beliefs. . . . Whatever one may think of the concept, this is not a felicitous way of expressing it and concluding the novel. Similarly, a potentially beautiful vision of the legendary Temlaham is spoilt by theorizing about the Findhorn gardeners and an odd reference to everyone making the desert bloom with forty-pound cabbages.

The figure of Billy Charlie, a modern Indian boy who comes to appreciate the traditions of his people, might have been used more effectively to integrate the book: why not begin with Billy as well, instead of with the thoughts and feelings of a boy who shortly drowns and is forgotten? Mrs. Harris attempts to impose continuity on her material by the reiteration of her message, but the constant changes of protagonist, both among the Indians and among the Tlu-men, are distracting. The book needs a character, and not just an idea, at its centre. Skawah, although she reappears several times in the course of the book, is never sufficiently developed as a character to serve the purpose, and remains a *dea ex machina*.

Sky Man contains several potentially good books within it, but fails to integrate this material into a convincing whole.... If the story itself had made its hypotheses more subtly and delicately, and found some means to blend its components into an artistic whole, it would be both more charming in its fantasy and more convincing in its theories. (pp. 119-20)

Gwyneth F. Evans, "On the Gitskan Indians of B.C.," in Canadian Children's Literature: A Journal of Criticism and Review *(Box 335, Guelph, Ontario, Canada N1H 6K5), Nos. 5 & 6, 1976, pp. 116-20.*

JANE ABRAMSON

[The] seven cautionary folk legends [in *Mouse Woman and the Mischief-Makers*], told with spare strength and humor, are exceptional for revealing the bedrock upon which the Northwest Indian culture stood. Harris recreates a world where balance and harmony among living creatures are valued above all and where even supernatural narnauks (including proper little Mouse Woman herself) can occasionally become "mischief-makers." (p. 67)

Jane Abramson, in School Library Journal *(reprinted from the April, 1977 issue of* School Library Journal, *published by R. R. Bowker Co. A Xerox Corporation; copyright © 1977), April, 1977.*

FRANCES M. FRAZER

The young heroines of [*Mouse Woman and the Vanished Princesses*] are not sweet and simple variations on Pretty Redwing, but accomplished, haughty young ladies who guard their dignity even more strenuously than they do their personal safety. And although the narnauks of these stories, like the supernatural beings of other Indian cultures, can change their physical forms, they confine themselves to two guises, one animal, the other human. Consequently, the ground-rules of the fantasy are kept reasonably clear, and the stories seem less arbitrary than most others of the *genre*....

Beyond her ability to shift her own shape, and on one occasion in this book to lend mouse guise to a human being, Mouse Woman is not a miracle-worker. But she is benevolent and wise, within the confines of her Grundy-like concern for proprieties. Her only moral weakness is a lust for wool to ravel with her 'ravelly little fingers', a lust that makes her demanding and sometimes pushes her to the brink of larceny. Otherwise she is a stauch defender of good sense and good etiquette among narnauks as well as people. She is also a champion of justice, although she occasionally exhibits alarming powers of rationalization, discovering ingenious reasons for believing that things have been 'made equal' even when her well-meant interferences are not entirely successful. Her quirks, her civilized intelligence, and her very limitations, which accommodate suspense, make her an interesting and effective intermediary between the real and the supernatural worlds.

Of the six stories in the book, the first, "The Princess and the Feathers", is by far the strongest. It has a clean-lined, exciting plot, and, apart from one lapse (of princesses who

vanish permanently, we are told, "Again and again they vanished."), it is lucidly as well as briskly written. Wy-en-eeks the Eagle Princess is a spirited, resourceful heroine who keeps her head in horrifying circumstances, and Mouse Woman, appearing briefly as a white mouse to help the princess save herself, does only what any mouse might do by happenstance. Magic is present, but it does not detract from the achievement of the human heroine. The story also, unemphatically but clearly, introduces the remorseless justice that the Indians of old evidently approved, as Wy-en-eeks calls down terrible but just retribution upon her murderous enemy....

In contrast, "The Princess and the Bears" is a strange mixture of pathos and mordant humour about a bizarre case of miscegenation which seems likely to evoke awkward questions from young readers despite the narration's careful avoidance of suggestive details. (p. 29)

The short emphatic sentences and half-sentences and the relatively undemanding diction are well suited to child readers; the tale itself is not, though it has a ruefully whimsical appeal.

The remaining four stories fall between these two stools; they are somewhat less interesting and satisfying than the first, but free from the sadness and perversity of the second. Supernatural wonders tend to accumulate in them, with proportional losses to human endeavour and hence in human interest. (p. 30)

But when the fault-finding comparisons have been made, it must be stressed that all of these stories are entertaining— and fascinatingly different from the myths of eastern tribes that have dominated the field, numerically at least, to date.

And for the most part, Mrs. Harris does them justice with her pleasant tone and economical style. She does have some irritating habits. In or out of season, whether the subject matter is tense or active or neither, she habitually uses short snappy sentences (all too many beginning with "for") and sentence fragments that carry a story forward at a rapid clip but also produce a staccato, hiccoughing effect. Her typographical emphases are obtrusively frequent. Ritualistic repetitions that probably echo the verbal formulas of oral storytellers become monotonous and suggestive of laziness, at least to adult eyes and ears. A penchant for word-play and verbal whimsy sometimes misleads her into near-coyness or even downright obscurity, as in "At the other end of awesomeness, there was Mouse Woman...." Nevertheless, her descriptions are concisely evocative, and she places her bits of information and her provocative hints with a sure hand. (pp. 30-1)

Frances M. Frazer, "Indian Folklore and Fantasy," in Canadian Children's Literature: A Journal of Criticism and Review *(Box 335, Guelph, Ontario, Canada N1H 6K5), No. 7, 1977, pp. 28-31.*

JESSICA LATSHAW

The primary source for the tales [of *Mouse Woman and the Mischief-Makers*] is not given so it was impossible to check the authenticity of her version. The tales, however, are not as carefully written as the author's earlier collections and are needlessly interrupted by a restatement of the underlying moral principle involved. (p. 47)

Jessica Latshaw, in In Review: Canadian Books for Children, *Spring, 1978.*

JANICE BICK

[*Mystery at the Edge of Two Worlds* is an] imaginative, well-told story of two teenagers, Lark and brother Joe who take a trip to visit their Gran and learn the art of sailing from Gran's neighbour Skipper Peery. Lark had been told by her mother that it was time she got out and did things, not just sit and think and read. . . . However, the unravelling of the mystery of Lucy Island and the meeting with red-haired Andy Fergus did much to change Lark's summer. . . .

With all the magic potions needed to make a successful mystery, Christie Harris draws undivided attention from her reader. Characters are well-drawn, the plot moves at a swift pace and enough chills and excitement complete the story. Although carefully researched, facts do not overburden the novel's impact, yet add to the quality of the tale. (p. 49)

> *Janice Bick, in* In Review: Canadian Books for Children, *February, 1979.*

Frank Herbert

1920-

American novelist, short story writer, and journalist. Herbert is a science fiction writer who questions the limits of the physical and spiritual qualities of mankind and comments on the future effects of ecological abuse. His novels combine the technological and the psychological, and have as their theme the problems inherent in man's manipulation of his environment. Herbert's *Dune* trilogy contains many of his literary characteristics. It is an epic description of the quest and destiny of a superior human, Paul Muad'Dib, who seeks enough water to save his planet. Herbert created a complete civilization in these works, including full descriptions of its history, philosophies, and physical makeup. Although the novels have been criticized for their complexity, they are popular and well respected among science fiction readers, and are often cited by those who maintain that science fiction should be considered serious literature. *Dune* was the winner of the 1965 Nebula Award and cowinner of the 1966 Hugo Award. Herbert's interest in social and ecological concerns is reflected in his background. He served as a consultant in these areas in Pakistan and Vietnam, as well as in the United States. He has had many varied occupations, such as oyster diving, and has taught both creative writing and jungle survival. Herbert has edited several newspapers, and has contributed short stories to magazines such as *Astounding Science Fiction*, which printed the first versions of the *Dune* mythology. His first novel, *Dragon in the Sea*, was the cowinner of the 1956 International Fantasy Award. Although Herbert has been consistently popular, he has become something of a cult figure during the present decade. Despite the esoteric and extremely detailed nature of some of his works, young adults have found that they can relate his subjects and concerns of the future, especially the ecological situations, to their own questions about themselves and their world. (See also *Contemporary Authors*, Vols. 53-56, and *Something about the Author*, Vol. 9.)

J. FRANCES McCOMAS

["The Dragon in the Sea"] is a sea story of an imaginary war that comes very close to matching—in suspense, action and psychic strain—any chronicle of real war by C. S. Forester or Herman Wouk. Frank Herbert writes of the next war, a conflict wherein the "curtains" are so impenetrable that the only theatre of action is under the sea. In marvelously convincing fashion, he tells the grim saga of a "subtug," venturing across the Atlantic to raid the enemy's subterranean oil reserves. . . . In this fine blend of speculation and action, Mr. Herbert has created a novel that ranks with the best of modern science fiction.

J. Frances McComas, "Water War," in The New York Times Book Review (© 1956 by The New York Times Company; reprinted by permission), March 11, 1956, p. 33.

R. Z. SHEPPARD

[Professional] science-fiction writers have rarely been encouraged to be good stylists. . . . This is partly because SF publishing and marketing methods make little distinction between the kind of star-schlock in which intergalactic cops battle hypothyroid blobs, and a well-wrought literary work in which far-reaching concepts and social problems are dramatized with intelligence, wit and verbal skill. . . .

More important, critics and reviewers who confer literary status rarely know much about science or technology. . . . Even journeymen practitioners of SF are likely to know more about literature than most novelists and critics know about science. And in the 20th century, ignorance of the fundamentals—and social implications—of physics, chemistry, biology and mathematics constitutes an embarrassing form of illiteracy.

Despite much misunderstanding over the past half-dozen years, SF has undergone an explosive growth. . . . In perspective, the interest in SF can be seen as part of the natural anxiety about the future of the planet. . . .

Unlike many bestselling popular novelists who squint at headlines for topical book ideas, SF writers often prove to be commercially farsighted. [One] of the most spectacularly successful SF novels of recent years, Frank Herbert's *Dune* . . . [is a good example] of how public concerns and infatuations catch up with the science-fiction imagination. [It has] been extremely popular with youth, which is greatly involved with the power of mysticism and the impieties of earthly industrial civilization. (p. 86)

Paul Atreides, the hero of *Dune*, is . . . well equipped [with psychic abilities and Christlike symbolism]. A superior thought-hypnotist, swordsman (of the old school) and ecologist, he is descended from an ancient line of space migrants whose antitechnology religion is summed up in the commandment, "Thou shalt not disfigure the soul." Set on the nearly waterless planet of Arrakis thousands of years in the future, *Dune* is a swashbuckling account of how human civilization, as it is now known, is reborn in a desert.

Like most science fiction, . . . [*Dune* is] conceptually rich. [It] . . . has 541 pages crammed with the canned fruits of Herbert's researches into ecology, desert cultures and history. There are even extensive appendices outlining the soil growth and planting schedules that Atreides projected for his centuries-long ecological project to make Arrakis bloom. (pp. 86-7)

> *R. Z. Sheppard, in* Time *(reprinted by permission from* Time, The Weekly Newsmagazine; *copyright Time Inc. 1971), March 29, 1971.*

ROBERT C. PARKINSON

Dune Messiah should be considered not as a sequel to the massive *Dune* novel, but as the penultimate section of an as-yet-incomplete work—whether trilogy, tetralogy or five-act epic matters not.

The objection to criticizing *Dune Messiah* as a simple sequel to the earlier novel is that almost invariably it has been seen as some sort of "repeat performance," and as such judged in terms of what the critic thought were the important themes of its predecessor. Considering it merely as a further installment, on the other hand, allows the critic the possibility that the important themes may only now be becoming apparent. (p. 16)

I suspect that in a large part the admiration *Dune* has commanded has come from the scope and the detail of its author's creation. . . . But the true scope of science fiction is not as an exhibition of the author's fertile and untrammeled imagination, but as a place to examine important human themes under radically altered circumstances.

Now in depth of background-detail, *Dune Messiah* does not significantly advance the reader's knowledge of the planet Arrakis, nor (as might have been expected of a sequel) does it tell of the wider universe in which this planet exists. There are one or two new wonders . . . but these were not entirely absent in the earlier novel, and they are not integrated into a vast interlocking ecology in the way that the parts of Arrakis were in *Dune*. This, however, seems of minor importance. If we are to judge *Dune* on its wealth of physical and social creation, then we should look at its flaws also—in its politics, to give one example, which far from being the sophisticated creation of a distant future are an almost straight "lift" from the later Turkish Empire.

But Arrakis is, after all, only a planet. What *Dune Messiah* does do is to continue the unfolding story and the philosophical problems begun in *Dune*. Among other things it converts a straight adventure "success story" into high tragedy.

What is *Dune* about, anyway?

Let me ask another question, which may give us a clue to the first. Why does Paul Atreides fear so much the consequences of following his vision? And if he does fear it so much, why does he never step aside from it?

This is the first obvious continuing theme of both books. . . . By looking at this theme, it becomes possible to see that most of the ecological interactions of the first book are simply characteristics of that part of the work, and not what the total work is about. Not as they stand.

Ecology does have a large part to play in the Dune novels. . . . And Kynes, the ecologist of the book, commends the young Paul for having understood a fundamental law of ecology: that ". . . the struggle between life elements is the struggle for the free energy of a system."

But it is a simplistic view of ecology. In particular it is a simplistic view when applied to human political systems as ecology. If an ecology is seen as a closed and dynamically balanced system, then one of the implicit lessons of the Dune novels . . . is that ultimately a political system which sees itself in these terms cannot achieve this balance. (pp. 16-17)

It is possible that Herbert's axiom only really holds for closed and collapsing societies, and even then a "superhuman" figure like Paul Atreides may disturb the system sufficiently to destroy its balance.

Just as, by his political actions, he probably destroys the delicately evolving artificial ecology of Arrakis. (pp. 17-18)

The struggle in *Dune* is obvious enough. Paul Atreides (and there is more than a trace of symbolism in that name; indeed, one could put a deal of orthodox Freudian interpretation into the book) comes from the wet world of Caladan to the desert world of Arrakis (and the parallel with human birth is explicitly underwritten . . .), and is immediately threatened by his hereditary enemies, the Harkonnens. He is therefore pitchforked into a situation where he must learn to survive both in the hostile environment of Arrakis and under the attack of the Harkonnens. As might be expected, Herbert is a good enough storyteller to make sure that the solution to the one problem—how to survive on Arrakis—is the solution to the other. . . .

Indeed, even the ecological themes parallel one another. The secret of Arrakis is that it has water, and that its ecology is being deliberately disturbed to the point at which a wet-cycle ecology can be self-sustaining. And in the wider universe, Paul Atreides has found that the political ecology which would squeeze him out must be altered to the point at which it is self-sustaining *for* him. It is no longer sufficient that he should no longer be hunted; at the end he must be emperor.

Dune Messiah apparently repeats the cycle, showing how Paul—now Muad'dib, emperor and prophet—having achieved success, is threatened again, this time by elements of the ecology that he has displaced—the Bene Gesserit, the Guild, the Tleilaxu. But this time the solution to the problem ends in his own death. . . .

Dying and life are what the Dune novels are about. Consider the opening. Right at the beginning Paul learns about *melange*—the geriatric spice. . . . (p. 18)

[Possibly] *melange* is no more than a senility-inhibitor. But it is obviously addictive, and it appears to be addictive in the manner of Herbert's "residual poisons" in that it offers life up to the point at which it is withdrawn. . . .

[It] seems to me that [the] emphasis on the value of and greed for *melange* serves only to keep the action of the story going; it is subsidiary to the theme.

In particular, *melange* is addictive to Paul in its capacity to induce prescient visions. Significantly this prescient role is always referred to as a secondary characteristic. But for Paul *melange* is not important as a rejuvenator, but as a religion-substitute. (p. 19)

[Religious] mysticism permeates the pages of the Dune novels. Herbert has contained within his novel the cynical view ("religion is the opium of the masses" . . .) and the miraculous view . . . ; but he also has managed to show that he understands the essence that lies much closer to the heart of the religious impulse—that which gives the individual's life significance.

This is why Paul becomes the Fremen prophet—because he gives their existence significance. But it is something that Paul himself cannot share. Paul must seek his own significance in becoming immortal. His instrument to achieving that end is his oracular vision. (pp. 19-20)

It is in that addiction to the oracular vision that the clue lies as to why Paul never once steps aside from the path of his vision.

His whole course is set towards minimizing the risk that he suffers. (p. 20)

So the chaos of the jihad rages through the universe and he does not step aside—because to do so would increase his own personal area of risk. In the first books, in *Dune,* Paul Atreides appears as a sympathetic character—a youngster having to defend himself against hopeless odds. In *Dune Messiah* Paul Muad'dib is more distant, but the reader still tends to identify him as a "good" character. This is the author's art winning out over the reader's objectivity. That the essential sympathy is retained at least to the end of *Dune Messiah* is essential if the story is to have its full impact, although it will be necessary to see Paul in the perspective of the final part before the full extent of his tragedy becomes apparent. The essential fact is that at the end of *Dune Messiah* Paul Muad'dib, corrupted by his own power, has become evil without wishing to be. (p. 21)

The need for a knowledge of the future drives right through Herbert's books, right from the first page of *Dune.* But by the beginning of *Dune Messiah,* he is prepared to state flatly—prophecy is lethal.

I began by saying that the Dune novels were a tetralogy. It is now possible to interpret them as a growth series.

It begins with birth, the threat that thrusts Paul Atreides out of the warm damp of Caladan into the hostile "real world." It continues through his growth, in the rest of *Dune,* to his maturity in *Dune Messiah.* Ultimately in that mature phase his death is a consequence of the fact that he has stopped growing. At the end of *Dune Messiah* the growth cycle has achieved its ultimate objective—death. But because it is a human growth cycle, and because religion is a major theme of the composite novel, that death proves not unexpectedly a doorway to immortality. To continue living at the end of *Dune Messiah,* Paul would have to make an adaption so radical that he would no longer be Paul—even though it is an adaptation that he has toyed with ever since his destiny became apparent:

> 'A creature who has spent his life creating one particular representation of his selfdom will die rather than become the antithesis of that representation,' Scytale said.

The novels are about the temptation of life. Notice that the temptation offered by the Tleilaxu, the temptation which Paul comes closest to succumbing to, is—life! He resists it through the knowledge of a greater prize—his own immortality.

It is this fear that he will not achieve his immortality that gives him his real concern, not the casualties of the jihad with which he deceives himself and others. Even at the last possible moment, when his enemies are destroyed and he cannot avoid his own death any longer, he can turn destiny aside by stepping down, by showing his mortality. Physically at this moment he has nothing to lose or gain. The right action would be to step down. "Greater love hath no man than this, that a man lay down his life for his friends." But Paul lays down his for his own immortality.

Let us look for a moment at the nature of this immortality. It is a state in which he still exercises control over the galaxy at large: over the thoughts, actions and loyalties of his people. . . . But at the same time it is an unchanging state. He seeks to maintain what he has. He imagines that he can fix it through his own death. In many ways this immortality is that offered by the traditional religions—heaven, nirvana, paradise. The whole concept of eternity is something "out of time," and failing to hold onto life with its change, Paul opts for this.

Now we can hazard a guess at the nature of the final book. (pp. 21-2)

If Herbert can bring it off, can marry together all the left-over elements of the first books—Muad'dib's immortality, Alia, the children—to complete the sequence and revise the reader's opinions of all that has gone before with the insight and skill shown in the first works, then the final tetralogy, five-act-epic, or what you will, will surely be a *tour de force* of science fiction. By putting the appropriate anchor points into *Dune Messiah,* Herbert has made a small announcement that he is prepared to gamble his skill (and probably the very best of his skill, for while he is technically competent, other of his novels are not up to the standard of the Dune novels) on producing that *tour de force,* with the alternative that he may spoil what was, after all, a rather good work of science fiction. (pp. 23-4)

> *Robert C. Parkinson, "'Dune'—an Unfinished Tetralogy," in* Extrapolation *(copyright 1971 by Thomas D. and Alice S. Clareson), December, 1971, pp. 16-24.*

JONI BODART

[The author of *The Gods Makers*] creates a new world peopled by a cast of unusual characters. . . . The characters are believable and interesting, the plot moves quickly, and suspense is maintained. The most enjoyable part of the book is the writings of various characters which begin each chapter, giving their personal philosophies. The result is an insightful novel which should be popular with fans of *Dune.* (p. 126)

> *Joni Bodart, in* School Library Journal *(reprinted from the March, 1973 issue of* School Library Journal, *published by R. R. Bowker Co. A Xerox Corporation; copyright © 1973), March, 1973.*

BRIAN W. ALDISS

If you can't be great, be big! Frank Herbert's *Dune* (1965) is certainly big, and many people have found it great.

Dune is enjoying something like the same success as [Robert Heinlein's] *Stranger in a Strange Land,* and probably for the same reason, because its readers can indulge in a fantasy life of power and savour a strange religion. But there is more than that to *Dune* and its successor, *Dune Messiah* (1969). Although Campbellian science fiction is still present, so, too, is an attention to sensuous detail which is the antithesis of Campbell; the bleak, dry world of Arrakis is as intensely realised as any in science fiction. The obvious shortage of water, for instance, is presented not just diagrammatically, but as living fact which permeates all facets of existence. (pp. 274-75)

[*Dune* and *Dune Messiah*] are dense and complex books, repaying careful reading. While they contain many ideas, the main informing idea is an ecological one; which makes them—together with all the other things they are!—very trendy books.

Herbert has long been known as an impressive writer. His great . . . *Under Pressure*—reprinted . . . [as] *Dragon in the Sea*, and *21st Century Sub*—also has strong religious elements, and is well worth seeking out for its study of obsessed men engaged in undersea warfare some time in the future. (p. 276)

> *Brian W. Aldiss, in his* Billion Year Spree: The True History of Science Fiction *(copyright © 1973 by Brian W. Aldiss; reprinted by permission of Doubleday & Co., Inc.), Doubleday, 1973.*

G. ROBERT CARLSEN

A book that builds with spellbinding intensity is [*Soul Catchers,* the] story of a young Indian graduate student in anthropology who works summers as a counselor in a boys camp. Slowly he becomes convinced that his mission is to expiate the sins of the white man toward his people by taking the life of an "innocent." . . . The values of the old Indian culture are highlighted in this moving story which can lead to an exciting exchange of ideas among students. (p. 91)

> *G. Robert Carlsen, in* English Journal *(copyright © 1974 by the National Council of Teachers of English), February, 1974.*

JOHN OWER

The very rawness and naivete of popular culture are signs of a vitality which can, without a breach with its origins, transcend itself in the inspiration of fine art. This fertile paradox is illustrated by Frank Herbert's *Dune*. It is the unstultified vigor of Herbert's imagination which is responsible for the complexity, the depth, and the symbolic virtuosity of his novel. At the same time, his art is rooted in the naive elements of good storytelling. The setting of *Dune* is an adventure—a wonder-land elaborately spun from the author's imagination. However, it coheres perfectly in its solidity of specification, never abandoning the concreteness and verisimilitude which are primal sources of pleasure. *Dune* at once captures our interest with the immediacy of its dense and vivid detail, and it intrigues us because it is strange and labyrinthine. Through his appeal to our curiosity and wonder, Herbert leads us beyond a childlike fascination with his fictional surface to the intellectual and visionary depths behind it. Every aspect of *Dune* is meaningful in relation both to a cultural environment and to an inner spiritual realm linking man with the transcendent.

Dune thus has associations with both realistic fiction and romance—the narrative of psychological and metaphysical symbolism in which the protagonist has supernatural powers, and in which character, event, and setting can be more

clear-cut and highly colored than is considered proper to the "mimetic" modes. This "romantic" quality is largely responsible for Herbert's success in combining popular appeal with genuine profundity. *Dune* makes liberal use of the exoticism, the adventure, and the melodrama of "space opera," but these express spiritual forces of good and evil —of death and renewal—at work in a civilization. In addition, much of the power of *Dune* arises from Herbert's exploitation of a tension implicit at the heart of romance: a union-in-opposition of earthly and supernal realities, of the humanity of the hero and his preternatural stature. Hence, despite its conventionally happy ending, *Dune* incorporates the complexities and conflicts of a genuinely tragic vision.

As a romance, *Dune* is related to the contemporary vein of "fantasy." However, it displays three concerns which, taken together, distinguish science fiction as an essentially "realistic" form. These are the historical, the socio-economic, and the technological. Like Asimov's *Foundation* trilogy, *Dune* explores these areas both through a highly developed and galaxy-wide civilization and through an enormous time-span which sees sweeping cultural changes. The "epic" scope of *Dune* allows Herbert to pursue the conjectural bent of science fiction with a boldness and complexity worthy of his predecessor. (pp. 129-30)

Herbert pours all of his wide knowledge into the fictional "models" through which he investigates civilization. However, his perspective reaches beyond scientific rationalism to a religious awareness of the universe as a spiritually vitalized and unified organism, in which everything entails everything else; it is a cornucopia of endless possibility.

The time-dimension of *Dune* is given a fullness commensurate with its speculative and visionary compass through a network of historical echoes and allusions. (p. 130)

Herbert's conception of history grows from his vision of the organic unity of the universe. Although this oneness is dynamic, it can be approached in simplified "cross-section" through Paul's static "spatial" awareness of time:

> He held himself poised in the awareness, seeing time . . . spread like a net gathering countless worlds and forces.

This net can be seen as a cosmic "field" analogous to those of gravitation and electricity. . . . The universe . . . parallels the ecology of Arrakis in being a developing energy-system. Power is funneled into it through revolutionary irruptions. These take place at "nexuses," involved knots of possibility occurring at points where the lines of force radiated by the various elements of the field are concentrated and cross. It is the movement of supernal energy into the universe which produces the flow of time. Thus, a major religious and cultural upheaval is released through the nexus created when Paul Muad'Dib, who himself embodies a complex of forces, becomes the conductor of the spiritual "electricity" latent in the tribes of the desert-planet Arrakis.

The spiritual therefore stands in approximately the same relationship to the temporal as does energy to matter in the physical world. Energy drives matter through an endless succession of changes, but these are governed by immutable laws. This combination of variation and repetition also characterizes historical time. The spiritual is at once a dynamic current which "dissolves, diffuses, dissipates" established patterns of culture and a set of paradigms which ensures that the new will bear some resemblance to the old. . . . [Thus] although Fremen culture resembles that of the Arabs while Paul is reminiscent of both Mohammed and T. E. Lawrence, Herbert deliberately does not make the correspondences too close. Rather, he sees history as a kaleidoscope of similar but endlessly shifting patterns.

The interaction of the spiritual and the physical, of eternity and time, is expressed in *Dune* through the symbols of desert and water. These images root Herbert's metaphysic in the natural and human life of Arrakis. Water carries its traditional connotations of the flow of time and of material flux. The image of the river—with its wave-patterns, currents, and eddies—deftly renders Herbert's conception of history as a movement combining variation and change with order and design. The cognate symbol of the swimmer suggests the tension in Paul's career between the necessity of submitting to the onrush of destiny, and his power to modify its course through his own initiative. The sand desert of Arrakis implies not only the "sea" of time in which man is immersed, but also the forbidding "otherness" of eternity. As Herbert indicates through his romantically "sublime" images of the desert windstorm, the explosive "spice-blow" and the gigantic sand-worm, eternity is the maker of time through the discharge of its limitless energy. These irruptions are awesome both in their unpredictability and their power. The death of the ecologist Liet-Kynes in a spice-blow is a sudden and violent avatar of the truth that the material order is finally determined by the spiritual and that science is therefore inferior to religion as a means of comprehending and controlling history.

The dialectic which creates history is rendered in rich symbolic detail by the biology of Arrakis. Because the organic is the incarnation and avatar of the spiritual, it relates at once to the transcendent and to the human world. The huge size of the Arrakeen sand-worm, along with its honorific "Old Father Eternity," indicates that it is an image of immanent divine energy. Its epithet of "maker" suggests eternity as the creator of time. Like swimming, the riding of the worm renders the paradox that the hero-prophet must move with destiny, and yet can guide its direction. (pp. 130-32)

The spice-drug which matures Paul's prophetic awareness is a by-product of the life-cycle of the sandworm, and it conveys a similar complex of meaning. . . . The spice-blow suggests how history is gestated at nexuses in the cosmic field, which lie in and behind the physical. It also implies the double paradox that the birth of history in an outrush of vital energy is the "death" of a portion of the eternal, which is, however, necessary to mature its transcendent purposes. The connection of the spice with irruptions of the spirit is also indicated by its geriatric properties and by its stimulation of the prophetic power. Its addictive nature once again suggests the paradoxical lot of the prophet, who is not only the mediator and guide of the eternal but also the slave of its "terrible purpose."

The setting of *Dune* thus provides a coherent structure of symbols. This implies the oneness of reality in a spiritual field through its correspondence between the natural, the human, and the supernal. The central term in this cosmic equation is the ecology of Arrakis which, in linking Paul and the Fremen with the eternal, indicates how they "conduct" its energy into universal human history. *Dune* is,

accordingly, a paradigm of the connection of the sacred with the manifold aspects of the secular. The revolution born on the planet has ramifications for every aspect of man's life from the genetic to the religious. (p. 132)

Herbert's consideration of the complex reality with which Paul must deal is focused upon four interrelated aspects of human existence. These are the physical, the psychological, the socioeconomic, and the religious. The most basic is man's bodily life, which involves his instinctual drives. Herbert's stress upon the need to accept suffering and privation expresses his belief that the senses and the passions must be controlled and channelled in the service of the social, the moral, and the religious. This, and not an ascetic denial of the flesh, is the meaning both of the stoic endurance of the Fremen and of the torture which the Reverend Mother Gaius Helen inflicts upon Paul to test his "humanity." The same idea is embodied in the riding of the sandworm as a Fremen initiation rite, for it implies that the harnessing of the sexual drive is fundamental to the attainment of personal and social maturity. The absolute necessity of such discipline is highlighted by the Harkonnens, whose unrestrained self-indulgence has perverted both their bodily appetites and their higher faculties. (pp. 132-33)

Such arrested development is opposed to Herbert's ideal of a maturity achieved through suffering and love. This is exemplified by Paul, who eventually attains a Jungian psychic wholeness. When the novel opens, Paul is in the critical period of adolescence. In order to realize his great potential, he must become independent of his parents, and yet internalize their exceptional powers and presence. It is only through such an "atonement" that he can encompass both masculine force and clarity and the dark wisdom of the female. (p. 133)

In attaining the feminine endowments, Paul's relationship with his mother is a delicate balance of alienation and communion, in which his liberation from her political schemes permits his more elevated use of her gifts.

Other essentials of Paul's commanding stature come from his father, from the Atreides retainers, and from the Fremen warriors. Through the discipline and the example which these men provide in the skills and the values involved in statecraft and war, Paul gains much that is necessary to the great leader. . . . Paul's growth to a maturity, which embraces both masculine and feminine capacities, takes place mainly through the prolonged and painful "initiation" entailed by the tragic breakup of his father's household and by his difficult entry into the Fremen fold. (pp. 133-34)

Paul's maturation takes place within two closely-knit communities: the feudal and the tribal. This illustrates Herbert's social ideal of a symbiosis between the individual and the group. Both the feudal retinue and the tribe suggest that the purpose of society is to foster each of its members who, in turn, finds his fulfillment in giving himself to his fellows. . . . The strict discipline of the feudal court and of the tribe is also balanced by their family atmosphere. Because true social life is rooted in the emotions and in interpersonal relationships, the basic and paradigmatic unit of the community is the family. Both the Atreides retinue and the sietch are extended families, in which the leader acts as a father to his followers. It is only through this intimacy that the group can function symbiotically and act as a unit.

The decadent society of the Imperium parodies Herbert's symbiotic ideal. Thus, a radical self-centeredness and the breakdown of moral restraint have reduced the Harkonnens to the law of the jungle. (p. 134)

The secular struggles within the Imperium suggest its reversal of a higher goal implicit in the symbiotic society: a spiritual and cultural integration of man with the divine, with nature, and with other men. . . . The dissociation and conflict which characterize imperial culture are reflected in its technology. The defensive shield is both a practical and a symbolic manifestation of social scission, as is the ultrasophisticated use of science in various other weapons of war and assassination. The spice "crawler" suggests the economic ravishment of nature, while the use of drugs such as semuta and melange involves a sort of mechanized parody of visionary experience. Such a "rape" and death technology implies that the only interactions within the Imperium are those involving conflict, exploitation, and subjection. This is suggested particularly by the technologization of human beings. . . .

Unlike the Imperium, Fremen culture is marked by a creative unity of men with one another, with nature, and with the divine. This organic community is conveyed by the image of water. The practice of rendering down a dead man's body for its moisture implies not only the economic co-operation which centers in the public cistern, but also the emotional readiness of the individual to sacrifice his life for his fellows. . . . At the same time, water paradoxically becomes through its scarcity on Arrakis an image indicative of the close association of the Fremen with nature. . . .

The movement of historical time is governed by the three "paradigms" of "ecology," "nexus," and "kaleidoscope." Ecology is based upon an interaction which involves both conflict and interdependence. (p. 135)

The most obvious example of the ecological principle in *Dune* is provided by Arrakis. The physical geography, the flora and fauna, and the Fremen tribes of the planet together form an intricate system, in which a bitter struggle for survival creates a self-perpetuating and mutually beneficial biological matrix. . . .

The concept of ecology is applied metaphorically in *Dune* to human life, and thus emerges as one of the principles of analogy which indicates the organic unity of reality. Paul's complex personality, in which disparate and sometimes conflicting forces are integrated in a *discordia concors,* can be described as a psycho-ecology. This steadily evolves during his lifetime, begin progressively enriched by experience and by infusions of supernal vision. Similarly, Fremen society not only exists within, but is itself, an eco-system. Just as Paul's character subsumes opposites within a higher unity, so individual self-assertion is harmonized and channelled by the Fremen community for the benefit of the greater whole. . . .

The Imperium is a parodic eco-system, which can be described by the biological metaphors of parasitism and predation. In the Empire, conflict leads not to mutual co-operation and stability, but rather to a precarious balance of power. (p. 136)

Like the eco-system, the nexus involves the interplay of many diverse elements in time and thus suggests how the universe acts as a unified whole. In particular, the nexus involves a concept of organic causation. This differs radically from the simple, mechanistic notion of a chain of events that is derived from "classical" physics. As the junction of a number of lines of spiritual force or historical development, the nexus suggests that each result is produced not by a single cause, but rather by a complex of apparently disparate factors acting simultaneously. Similarly, any one thread or event at the nexus radiates out into a multiplicity of possible and actual consequences. The notion of nexus also suggests the organic unity of past, present, and future. (p. 137)

A further indication of the organic coherence of the universe is that time is to some degree teleological. For example, the Bene Gesserit genetic plan is both a sign and an instrument of the "terrible purpose" which is moving humanity toward an order encompassing all antinomies. However, as Herbert suggests through the labyrinth of choices confronting Paul, the unfolding of history toward its goal is conditioned by its entanglement in brute particulars. These include the free choice of the individual. . . . History thus involves both a union and a tension of the universal and the particular, of the changing and the eternal. This means that kaleidoscope, which balances an overall design against the passing and the specific, is a fundamental pattern in the movement of time.

Kaleidoscope and the duality from which it arises are manifested especially in religious history. Although the hero and the prophet apply unchanging myths and principles, the particular circumstances through which they must work are always different. Similarly, a new religion will be periodically required to readapt the transcendent to altered conditions. . . . [Paul] resembles all valid prophets in at once giving the spiritual a "local habitation and a name," and in universalizing the parochial. This "kaleidoscopic" balance weds his new religion to history. Although it will inevitably pass away, in its very dissolution it will flow into the future, permeating all subsequent culture and contributing to all new religions.

Although *Dune* possesses a broad popular appeal which is often denied to the "highbrow" novel, it reveals itself to formal literary analysis as a subtle, complex, and carefully crafted work of art. It thus constitutes an eloquent comment on the increasing maturity of science fiction as a form. Certainly *Dune* does not suffer from disparity between ambitious conception and literary execution which characterizes such earlier "epics" as Delany's *Fall of the Towers* and Asimov's *Foundation* trilogy. . . . In view of the central importance of popular inspiration to English literary tradition, the recognition accorded to *Dune* may be a bright prognosis for the future of science fiction as a form. (pp. 137-38)

> *John Ower, "Idea and Imagery in Herbert's 'Dune'," in* Extrapolation *(copyright 1974 by Thomas D. and Alice S. Clareson), May, 1974, pp. 129-39.*

ELIZABETH HALL

Using the movie *The Hellstrom Chronicle* as a springboard, Frank Herbert has written a compelling novel. But *Hellstrom's Hive* . . . is straightforward science fiction, no nature story in disguise. Herbert has concentrated on what he does best, the creation of a balanced civilization. This time the aliens are among us, except that they are mutants. . . . The time is now. Hellstrom's Hive, founded secretly 300 years ago beneath an Oregon farm, is beginning to feel swarming pressure. And its 50,000 inhabitants are the object of a Government investigation. This book doesn't reach the heights of *Dune*, but *Hellstrom's Hive* does provide the ultimate group experience. (p. 20)

Elizabeth Hall, in Psychology Today *(copyright © 1974 Ziff-Davis Publishing Company), August, 1974.*

THEODORE STURGEON

Expectedly from a writer of Frank Herbert's great competence, [*Hellstrom's Hive*] is fascinating reading, but one has the feeling that he got tired of it five-sixths of the way through, and let his drama get melo. (p. 39)

Theodore Sturgeon, in The New York Times Book Review *(© 1974 by The New York Times Company; reprinted by permission), September 8, 1974.*

ROBERT SCHOLES

Few would deny that *Dune* is a "great read," as Tolkien's *Lord of the Rings* is a "great read." It gives us strongly defined heroes and villains, engages us in an action which is simple in essence but full of events, twists, complications. *Dune* and its sequel, *Dune Messiah*, first appeared as serial fiction, and they exhibit the frequent climaxes and moments of great suspense which the serial format requires. *Dune* is a romance of adventure, and it is not my intention here to suggest that this romance hides great speculative profundities. What makes it exceptional is the systematic way in which the narrational events are imbedded in a particular ecological setting, and the thoughtfulness and delicacy that have gone into the major characterizations. By choosing as his main location a planet that is naturally a desert, Herbert has alloted the ecosystem a major role in structuring his narrative. And he has developed this role with a wonderful rigor and attention to detail.

This is one great strength of *Dune*. Another is in Herbert's attention to the mechanisms by which religious and political "greatness" are achieved. The imaginary sands of Dune owe a good deal to the real sands of Arabia, and somewhere behind this novel stands T. E. Lawrence's *Seven Pillars of Wisdom*, in which Lawrence speculated on the curious propensity of the semitic geography for producing prophets and mystics. Paul Atreides, who becomes the religious leader Muad'Dib, finds himself cast for the role of prophet in a holy war. . . . Herbert is saved from operating at the adventure story level—saved by a greater ability to transfer something of actual political maneuvering into narrative form, and to an even greater extent saved by his ability to characterize Paul as a young man who *knows* that he has been cast for a role, that he is enacting a myth with which he is not entirely in sympathy. Like the comic-mythic heroes of John Barth's *Chimera*, Paul Atreides has a powerful sense of the artificiality in his own situation. But where Barth's bumbling heroes struggle to enact their mythic roles fittingly, forcing us to laugh at their comic ineptitude, Paul simply takes a sardonic attitude toward "greatness" and tries to ride the mythic whirlwind and tame it for the sake of the people on his adopted planet.

Herbert wisely avoids loading the story with a greater conceptual weight then the romance of adventure can comfortably handle, nor does he often try to philosophize beyond his own intellectual range. He works within the traditional formula, achieving his effects through care and consistency, and through considerable tact in the use of extraordinary mental and physical events. Paul's prophetic powers, for instance, reveal not one future to him, but many possible futures, projections of present history which he may try to actualize or avoid. The other extraordinary mental feats performed by various characters are logical, almost reasonable extensions of the practices of yoga or the possibilities of bio-feedback. Tact, consistency, and restraint are what make this adventure story an exceptionally mature and interesting one. And nowhere do these qualities emerge more clearly than in Herbert's presentation of the ecology of Dune and the various human responses to that ecology. Here he is most structural, most aware of system and necessity, and this awareness is the backbone of the book. (pp. 67-70)

Robert Scholes, in his Structural Fabulation: An Essay on Fiction of the Future *(copyright ©1975 by University of Notre Dame Press; Notre Dame, IN 46556), University of Notre Dame Press, 1975.*

LEON E. STOVER

That we are in for a portentous rendering of great issues in philosophy is signaled at the outset [of *Santaroga Barrier*] by the name of the hero, Dr. Gilbert Dasein. *Dasein* in German means "being there" and is the key concept of existential thinking in the philosophy of Karl Jaspers, whose own name figures in the drug with which the townsmen of Santaroga infuse their beer, cheese, and other foods.

Karl Jaspers . . . is associated with a number of critics of modern society who together have built what is probably the most influential social theory of our day: the theory of mass society. . . . [They] are concerned less with the general conditions of freedom in society than with the freedom of those persons who possess the intelligence to cultivate a sense of the individual self over and above the dim self-awareness of mass man. The criticism of mass society brought to bear by Karl Jaspers is above all an aristocratic critique. Therein lies the source of his appeal: the defense of creative individuality. (p. 160)

The decline of cultural standards in order to meet the consensus needs of the classless multitudes of average people has brought about a crisis of individual consciousness. . . . In the absence of a cultured elite born or educated to command, true leadership is replaced by organization men who strive for position and power with an opportunistic cunning that stands in the way of responsibility for one's actions, with the result that true selfhood is denied to others as well; for where power depends on the mobilization of popular appetites in politics and business, leadership cannot tolerate individuality, reason or self-expression in the target population. It is a world of mass mediocrity, from top to bottom. Given this cultural decline, is the realization of the self still a possibility?

To that question the inhabitants of Santaroga, a small town in California, answer *yes*. They have erected a barrier against mass society behind which the personal values of their counter-culture may flourish. But their unanimity of purpose is mediated by a drug, Jaspers, whose pernicious effects result in the heightening of empathy and the awareness of others at the expense of self-awareness. . . . But ironically, in their reliance on the drug Jaspers to restore a traditional sense of community which the individual may imbue with his selfhood, they too are reduced to a mindless mass of functional parts. . . .

In the course of finding an answer to [the question of why Santarogans won't trade with outsiders], Dr. Dasein himself [an outside investigator] becomes a Santarogan. (p. 161)

In tracing the hero's philosophical progress, Frank Herbert is faithful to the essential pessimism of Karl Jaspers' message: that people in general lack the capacity to resist deception; that both the manipulators and the manipulated in mass society lack the will to see reality as it is actually constituted. And the reality is human mendacity; people are not, in fact, honest or kind. The discovery that life among dishonest men is not worth living is the discovery made by the Santarogans, and Dr. Dasein joins with them in creating a community of like minds. The stress in the philosophy of Karl Jaspers is the dependence of the self upon social and linguistic interaction. The Santarogans are living examples of Jaspers' belief that we humans are what we are only through a community of mutually conscious understandings, that truth is communicability.

The fallacy that makes Santaroga a black utopia is that it is a community of vital sympathies merely, minus the freedom to reject the communications of one's fellows in favor of the promptings from an inner source. This enforced awareness of others, mediated by the drug Jaspers, makes for a caricature of everything Karl Jaspers the philosopher ever stood for. . . . It is all group awareness and no individual freedom. In fact, the Santarogans are not aware individually that their collective will communicates hostility to outsiders. They murdered a number of outside investigators but actually believe these deaths resulted from unfortunate accidents. . . .

The first thing that Dasein notes about Santaroga, when it is his turn to investigate it, is its conservatism; it resists change.

[Far] from pioneering an exportable counter-culture against mass society, as it believes it is doing, the rest of the world is moving away from it. (p. 162)

In the end, Dasein understands the Santarogans so well that he becomes one of them. But not before he is addicted to Jaspers for life when he ingests a massive dose of the drug abstracted from a wheel of Jaspers cheese. . . . Up until this time he had escaped unharmed from all attempts to murder him. . . . The collective will to kill him finally almost succeeds in the person of Jenny, but like the others she lacks any individual knowledge of this; Dasein understands and forgives her. After his conversion, he himself murders Dr. Selador, a psychiatrist colleague, in the same unconscious manner. (p. 164)

[The] unconscious communication of hatred for outsiders is Santaroga's version of raw, ungoverned power; the Santarogans take Jaspers as their "Consciousness Fuel," . . . but it fuels a sense of communal awareness at the total expense of individual awareness. . . . [With] his engagement to Jenny, Dasein leaves behind all such attempts to intellectualize his experience:

> He settled his mind firmly then onto

thoughts of the home Jenny had described, pictured himself carrying her across the threshold—his wife. There'd be presents: Jaspers from 'the gang,' furniture . . . Santaroga took care of its own.

> *It'll be a beautiful life,* he thought. *Beautiful . . . beautiful . . . beautiful. . . .*

These concluding words are meant to be ironic; the Santarogan utopia turns out to be a totalitarian utopia, in which men are domesticated for community life at the sacrifice of their souls. Like all utopian goals, those of Santaroga are beyond human reach—they intended nothing less than to overcome the sum of human alienation caused by the rise of modern civilization. But the result was a replication of the worst feature of mass society—"all people . . . everywhere alike." In addition, there were a number of individuals who did not respond well to the drug; it turned them into nullities, moronic rejects who were chained to the production lines of Santaroga's cheese industry. For the others, all that remains in place of a spiritually informed existence is a collectivity of primal selves. (p. 165)

In conclusion, I believe that Frank Herbert's presentation of Santaroga as a black utopia is the means by which he criticizes the theory of mass society itself and its romantic hostility to the modern world. Everyone is against atomism and for organic living, but if we substitute "totalitarian" for "organic" and "individualistic" for "atomistic," the argument is turned around. The picture of mass society as debauched by concessions to popular taste is overdrawn. And if it be granted that mass society is superficial in personal relations, utilitarian, competitive, acquisitive and mobile, the good side must also be shown—the right to privacy, the free choice of occupation and friends, social status on the basis of merit not pedigree, a plurality of norms and standards rather than monopolistic control by a single dominant group.

For mass society, Dr. counter-culture prescribes Jaspers beer and cheese. Once again, the cure is worse than the disease. (pp. 166-67)

> *Leon E. Stover, "Is Jaspers Beer Good for You?: Mass Society and Counter Culture in Herbert's 'Santaroga Barrier'," in* Extrapolation *(copyright 1976 by Thomas D. and Alice S. Clareson), May, 1976, pp. 160-67.*

WILLIS E. McNELLY

Frank Herbert's long-awaited finale of his *Dune* trilogy, *Children of Dune,* cannot be dismissed casually as just another space opera. To be sure, there is plenty of traditional science-fiction action for the true believer, but, as with the earlier novels, *Dune* and *Dune Messiah,* there's much to satisfy ecologists, anthropologists and speculative theologians, as well.

Arrakis, the desert planet, sole source in the universe of a genuine life-prolonging drug, is the real hero. . . . *Children of Dune* opens as the changes begun decades before are taking place. . . . The vast spectrum of characters, many of whom illustrate some Jungian mythic archetype, are either unaware of, or unconcerned with, these changes. . . . The consequences make up the plot of *Children of Dune.*

In the hands of skilled writers like Herbert, science fiction becomes a tool or a device to say something meaningful about our contemporary world. In this sense, science fiction verges on allegory, but without the burden usually associated with that word. We need to understand what we are doing to our own environment, Herbert seems to be saying, because some of the things we've done, e.g., disruption of the ozone layer, may already be beyond redemption, with disastrous consequences for the earth and for human life. But Herbert is too good a writer to draw such obvious conclusions in his novel. Rather, he stimulates the reader to think about these problems, while he goes on telling a rattling good story. . . .

Moreover, some of the questions it asks are ones not normally associated with science fiction: Given a genuine avatar, what will be the psychological (and ecological) effects on him and his planet if, because of the violent nature of the planet, he must choose as his method of redemption, not the traditional means of mercy and love, but violence? What are the effects of a ritualistic religion on a planet undergoing a change from static to dynamic?

Dune was deservedly a popular success, and it has become something of a cult object among its readers. *Children of Dune* will be no disappointment to them, and its quality may finally convince those who haven't yet accepted the fact that science fiction can be good. (p. 570)

Willis E. McNelly, in America (© *America Press, 1976; all rights reserved), June 26, 1976.*

GERALD JONAS

To appreciate Frank Herbert's achievement in the Dune trilogy, which concludes with "Children of Dune" . . . , you have to be a devotee of obsession. On the surface, the Dune books offer an unlikely combination of old-fashioned space opera, up-to-date ecological concern and breathtakingly ecumenical religiosity. The space opera elements include a decaying galactic empire, heroes and villains of nearly superhuman power, and truly formidable monsters. The ecology centers around the planet Dune, which is one vast desert, yet which supports a population of remarkably disciplined human beings known as Fremen. . . .

Herbert's vision of a people forced by circumstance into total ecological awareness is worked out in convincing detail; and since the first book in the trilogy, "Dune," was published in 1965, he can hardly be accused of mere faddishness. . . .

What sets these books apart from their competitors is the obsessive quality of Herbert's imagination. . . . To read the Dune trilogy is to plunge into someone else's obsession. As in Tolkien's "The Lord of the Rings," nothing in these books is real, yet everything has a life-or-death importance.

Whatever else the characters in Herbert's books have to worry about, none suffers from that common malady of our day: a sense of meaninglessness. Virtually every page in the trilogy contains a sentence that hints at the momentousness of the events being described. This is where the religiosity comes in. Herbert keeps interrupting the action with quotes from made-up sources that reinforce the atmosphere of millennial conflict and resolution. . . .

But the whole point of an obsession is that it cannot be criticized from the outside; what distinguishes a successful obsessional tale from a failure is that the reader is held, like Coleridge's Wedding Guest, so that "he cannot choose but

hear," no matter what his other faculties tell him. On this criterion, I would personally rate the Dune trilogy an unqualified success. (p. 18)

Gerald Jonas, in The New York Times Book Review (© *1976 by The New York Times Company Company; reprinted by permission), August 1, 1976.*

HAROLD L. BERGER

[What makes *The Heaven Makers*] unique among mind-invasion science fiction stories is [its] historical orientation. [It attributes] the madness and misery of past and present to mind-warping incubi—vampires feeding on man's creative energy or string-holders of the Punch-and-Judy show called history, whose scenario human beings imagine they have written. (pp.111-12)

The Heaven Makers stirs recollections of Samuel Johnson's satiric criticism, "A Review of Soame Jenyns' *A Free Inquiry into the Nature and Origin of Evil.*" "He [Jenyns] imagines," Johnson writes, "that as we have not only animals for food, but choose some for our diversion, the same privilege may be allowed to some beings above us, *who may deceive, torment, or destroy us for the ends only of their own pleasure or utility.*" Johnson proceeds to demolish Jenyns' speculations, pricking him with exquisite ridicule, and concludes, "The only end of writing is to enable the readers better to enjoy life, or better to endure it: and how will either of those be put more in our power by him who tells us, that we are puppets, of which some creature not much wiser than ourselves manages the wires." Yet that is the thesis of Herbert's story.

The Chem, immortal, invisible, goblin creatures, imprisoned in eternity, find relief from oppressive timelessness by molding "voices and faces and entire races" for their amusement. Having little else to relieve their boredom but voyeurism, the Chem have made earth (and other worlds too) one vast theatrical stage. From his storyship beneath the ocean, director-scenarist Fraffin had sent shooting crews "filming" the pageants of history to entertain the Chem on universal "pantovive" (a kind of television). "I touch a nerve," says Fraffin, explaining his art to a Chem visitor. "Greed here, a desire there, a whim in the other place—and fear. Yes, fear. When the creature's fully prepared, I arouse its fears. The whole mechanism performs for me then. They make themselves ill! They love! They hate! They cheat! They kill! They die! . . . And the most amusing part . . . the most *humorous* element is that they think they do it of and by themselves." (pp. 113-14)

It is curious that the mind-invasion stories of . . . Herbert . . . should lean toward an interpretation of history. Does this approach signal the beginning of a trend? Shakespeare's metaphor, "All the world's a stage, And all the men and women merely players," has been held literally, as theology and superstition reveal. If man continues to move inexorably toward yawning, calculable hells, will fiction—will man—look to demonism for answers?

There is an ironic moment in *The Heaven Makers*, which touches [its] philosophic core. . . . Fraffin, looking through his scanners for some activity among "his creatures," focuses upon a pitchman's flea show, the fleas dancing and leaping, wrestling and racing. The Chem wonders, "Do those fleas know they're someone else's property?" The mind-invasion story asks, Whose property is man? (pp. 115-16)

Harold L. Berger, in his Science Fiction and the New Dark Age *(copyright © 1976 by The Popular Press), Popular Press, 1976.*

ROBIN ADAMS

[*Santaroga Barrier*] is exciting and suspenseful; but there is a good message here as well. Santaroga seems utopian: perfectly adjusted, with no crime or reported mental illness. But there are failures—mental cripples who could not handle the Jaspers. Even the psychologist's own professional experience fails to help him under the drug's high. The message is not judgemental: Herbert likes to explore the possibilities of altered states of consciousness. . . . When Dasein overdoses on the drug, we are left wondering whether what is left is an omniscient superman, or a euphoric idiot. (p. 6)

Robin Adams, in Young Adult Cooperative Book Review Group of Massachusetts, *October, 1977.*

MICHAEL S. CROSS

[*The Dosadi Experiment*] is full of the characteristics that irritate the [non-science-fiction fan]: the combination of "hard" sf with a fantasy style; the plethora of names, institutions, and civilizations dropped in with little or no identification; the swashbuckling plot. Fans, however, will delight in all of these. And, as usual with Herbert, some of the conceits are intriguing. Here the plot rotates about the peculiar legal philosophy and institutions of a people called the Gowachin, a quite fascinating portrayal of alien minds. (p. 2084)

Michael S. Cross, in Library Journal *(reprinted from* Library Journal, *October 1, 1977; published by R. R. Bowker Co. (a Xerox company); copyright © 1977 by Xerox Corporation), October 1, 1977.*

GERALD JONAS

The first thing that must be said about ["The Dosadi Experiment"] is that it takes place in an entirely different universe from his justly celebrated and popular "Dune" trilogy. The "Dune" novels are superb space opera—persuasively detailed fiction set against the broadest backdrop imaginable. By contrast, everything about "The Dosadi Experiment" is claustrophobic—the basic premise, the setting, even the writing. Sometime in the past, an illicit experiment was established on the barely habitable planet of Dosadi. . . .

The result of this cold-blooded venture in Social Darwinism is, as expected, a planet full of cunning survivors. But the experiment has been *too* successful—the survival skills of the Dosadis are so awesome that the experimenters are afraid their guinea pigs will eventually escape from the planet and conquer the galaxy. To guard against this possibility, they decide to destroy Dosadi. (p. 42)

[A] number of important elements in this novel were first introduced to Herbert's readers in an earlier novel, "Whipping Star." This may account for the insubstantiality of "The Dosadi Experiment." The motives of the leading characters are never quite clear; everyone seems to know something the reader doesn't know.

All this would be bearable if the behavior of the super-survivors of Dosadi were as satisfying to watch as the behavior of the Fremen, or the Bene Gesserit, or the Mentats

in the "Dune" trilogy. Alas, the feats of the Dosadis—both human and Gowachin—are no more remarkable that those of many other s.f. heroes. The Dosadis approach life as a cutthroat chess game, and they are always one or two moves ahead of their opponents. But somehow, from Herbert's big buildup, I expected more. (pp. 42-3)

Gerald Jonas, in The New York Times Book Review *(© 1977 by The New York Times Company; reprinted by permission), November 27, 1977.*

TIMOTHY O'REILLY

Dune is a novel rich in ideas as well as imagination. . . . (p. 41)

Recalling the origins of *Dune,* Herbert says:

> It began with a concept: to do a long novel about the messianic convulsions which periodically inflict themselves on human societies. I had this theory that superheroes were disastrous for humans, that even if you postulated an infallible hero, the things this hero set in motion fell eventually into the hands of fallible mortals. What better way to destroy a civilization, a society or a race than to set people into the wild oscillations which follow their turning over their judgment and decision-making faculties to a superhero?
>
> (p. 42)

[Detail] by painstaking detail, Herbert constructed a world, in an exercise of ecological imagination as gradual, as delicate, and as complex as such a planetary transformation itself might be. (p. 43)

[Paul Atreides, the hero of *Dune,*] is not merely a prophet, but a here-and-now messiah with more than a visionary dream with which to inspire a following. . . . In Paul, Herbert has a vehicle to explore the many factors that go into the creation of a messianic "superhero." Herbert lays out in detail the structure of aristocratic leadership, the use of psychological manipulation, the birth of an irresistible legend from individually insignificant events, and an unusual psychogenetic theory of history. (p. 45)

The feudal and paramilitary structure of the Empire and House Atreides reveals an important aspect of what Herbert describes as the superhero mystique. Feudalism is a natural condition into which men fall, he contends, a situation in which some men lead and others, surrendering the responsibility to make their own decisions, follow orders. (p. 46)

This then is the first layer of the superhero mystique: the hierarchical structure of leadership. Paul is trained to lead and his followers are trained to follow.

At the same time as Herbert was delineating the social structure of the Empire, he was introducing another layer. . . . Through the Bene Gesserit, Herbert psychoanalyzes the role of the unconscious in human affairs and the potential for its manipulation by the knowledgeable and unscrupulous. Most people are only half-awake—they react to external stimuli without really knowing why they respond the way they do. By contrast, the Bene Gesserit have schooled themselves to understand and master their own unconscious reflexes. This is graphically demonstrated in the test of the *gom jabbar*, as well as in other almost fantastic feats of psychological and physiological control. In addition, the Bene Gesserit have refined the ability to perceive and to play on the unconscious weaknesses of others. Their power to influence the course of politics depends almost entirely on this ability, applied both to individuals and to groups. (p. 47)

The significance of this power is easy to miss if we get caught up in the question of whether or not such a thing is possible. Herbert is extrapolating powers of suggestion and psychological manipulation far in advance of anything available today, but the power itself is not the main point. He is saying something about who we are as human animals. In Western civilization, we have placed so much emphasis on conscious thought and rationality that we have forgotten how much of our behavior is unintentional and uncontrolled by consciousness. We make choices for reasons of the flesh and feelings, as well as of the mind. The attraction of the superhero, as Herbert sees it, is a case in point. The Fremen do not follow Paul for logical reasons, but precisely because logic is not enough for comfort in a hostile world. Unconscious needs for security, belonging, and surety play a much larger role in a messianic upheaval than the conscious content which masquerades as the "cause." (p. 48)

Paul does in fact have remarkable powers, but far more important in the end is how the Fremen respond to them. There is a strong, unconscious projection that makes him even more special than he is. Part of this projection depends on the legends planted by the Bene Gesserit and the way they crystallize around Paul, but even more depends on the faculty of his followers for wishful thinking, the unconscious will to believe there is someone out there with answers they lack. Unable to find adequate strength of purpose in themselves, they look for a truth, a cause, and a leader to supply it. It is the same mutually supportive relationship of leaders and followers which was explored in the feudal setup of House Atreides.

Thus far, Herbert's portrayal of the "superhero syndrome" follows recognizable paths of social and psychological analysis. He drew first of all on the traditional messianic pattern, the longing for a better future exhibited by oppressed peoples. He then showed the structure of leadership—how a society functions with built-in expectations of who will lead and who follow—and explored the nature of charismatic myths and the possibility for manipulation of the unconsciousness in all of us. Each of these was to an extent an extrapolation from accepted understanding. But there is one other concept Herbert built his story on that is unique. This is what we might call his genetic theory of history.

Once again, Herbert uses the Bene Gesserit and the inner powers Paul has gained from them as his vehicle. The source of the almost supernatural abilities of the Bene Gesserit is a substance they call the Truthsayer drug, which allows their Reverend Mothers to draw on profound inner knowledge and the accumulated wisdom of the past. But it is only women who can master the inner changes brought on by the drug. It has always been death for a man. The Bene Gesserit have embarked accordingly on a centuries-long program of selective breeding to produce a man who can take the drug and live. . . . It is hoped that Paul may be this figure, but he has been born a generation too soon in the plan and is consequently not completely under their control. He has his own destiny to follow. (pp. 49-50)

[What] Paul's heightened inner powers give him is the same ability to perceive unconscious motivation with regard to masses of people as the Bene Gesserit Reverend Mothers have with individuals. And aided by a process of "Mentat" computation, he is in effect able to see the future as the Reverend Mothers see the past. (pp. 50-1)

In his visions, Paul comes face to face with the universe as it really is, a vastness beyond any hope of human control. . . . Paul confronts the vision of infinity, and learns to yield to it, to ride the currents of infinite time and not to restrain them. And then, symbolically, he leads his troops to victory on the backs of the giant sandworms, the untamable predators of the desert who may yet be ridden by those bold enough to take the risk.

These are difficult concepts—far more serious than are found in the average science fiction novel—and Herbert went to a great deal of trouble to see that they became more than concepts in the reader's mind. In the novel, the ideas are not presented in a linear manner, as they have been here, but are woven into the texture of plot and imagery and character. When the same idea is shown again and again in many different forms—as with the "superhero" concept—it begins to take on a life independent of any of them.

Herbert is also a master of the use of obscurity and shadow in lending depth to a novel. *Dune* has been so often praised for its fullness of detail that it is easy to overlook the fascination of what has been left out. Certain ideas or scenes that were crucial at one point in the development of the story later dropped out, leaving mysterious signs in the way others are handled. Other significant pieces of background were left deliberately unfinished, to draw the reader's attention deeper into the story and to keep him involved long after it was over. . . . Herbert is endlessly willing to hint, but not to explain. If, as a result, there are ideas that seem to hang unsupported, this only lends fire to the reader's conviction that it is a real world he is exploring, with mysteries that have defied even the author. (pp. 52-3)

Herbert is convinced that the sound of a passage is subconsciously reconstructed by the reader even though he reads silently, and furthermore, that it has a powerful unconscious effect. As a result, he wrote a great many crucial passages in the book as poetry—sonnets, haiku, and many other different forms depending on the mood—and then concealed them in the prose. On a larger scale, he very carefully controlled the pacing of the book to underscore the sexual nature of the jihad. The ending of *Dune* is a tour-de-force, in which action, character, and themes are brought to an explosive climax. Literally. Herbert admits:

> It's a coital rhythm. Very slow pace, increasing all the way through. And when you get to the ending, I chopped it at a nonbreaking point, so that the person reading skids out of the story, trailing bits of it with him.

The end result of all this art is a novel packed with ideas that cannot easily be shaken from the mind. This is more than good entertainment. Herbert has said that the function of science fiction is not always to predict the future but sometimes to prevent it. Many of the features of the superhero mystique that he unveils in *Dune* haunt our own culture. By increasing our awareness of a problem, science fiction can be a powerful tool for change. When it reaches the subconscious levels where the old, inappropriate response patterns are rooted, as *Dune* so clearly does, it goes beyond being even a cautionary fable and becomes, in Herbert's own words, a "training manual for consciousness." (p. 54-5)

Timothy O'Reilly, "From Concept to Fable: The Evolution of Frank Herbert's 'Dune'," in Critical Encounters: Writers and Themes in Science Fiction, *edited by Dick Riley (copyright © 1978 by Frederick Ungar Publishing Co., Inc.), Ungar, 1978, pp. 41-55.*

James Herriot
1916-

(Pseudonym of James Alfred Wight) British nonfiction writer and autobiographer. Herriot is best known for his autobiographical accounts revolving around his simple life as a country veterinarian in the Yorkshire farmlands. He began writing about the personal rewards of his practice and lifestyle when he was in his fifties. The popularity of his books is widespread, but some critics question how well future works will be received if he continues along the same vein. Critics generally agree that his writing style is as simple and free as the life he lives, and often use words like "earthy" to describe it. Herriot confirms this, saying his aim is to write his stories as if they were being told at a country pub. In an age that celebrates country living, his love of life and nature is an appealing factor in his best selling books, such as *All Creatures Great and Small*, which was recently adapted into a film and a television series. (See also *Contemporary Authors*, Vols. 77-80.)

NELSON BRYANT

["All Creatures Great and Small"] shines with love of life. It is not surprising that James Herriot still ministers to his charges in the same location, for the reader soon feels that the man and his work should never be separated from Yorkshire and its people. . . .

Herriot's portrayal of his mercurial and charming boss [Siegfried Farnon] and his boss's fey brother Tristan is delightful. Indeed, every character in the book emerges with force and clarity. There is humor everywhere, including the often futile attempts of a domineering woman to bring some order to Siegfried's slapdash bookkeeping. . . .

However, Herriot's book is more than a collection of well-told anecdotes and sharply drawn personalities. Laced through it is the author's growing awareness that he is in the right place doing the right thing. . . .

Herriot charms because he delights in life, embraces it with sensitivity and gusto and writes with grace. Reading him, one is reminded that there are still, nearly 40 years after the time of his story, country places where the wind blows clean, places where men and women find pleasure in hard work and simple living.

Nelson Bryant, "A Place Where the Wind Blows Clean," in The New York Times Book Review *(© 1973 by The New York Times Company; reprinted by permission), February 18, 1973, p. 10.*

WILLIAM R. DOERNER

What the world needs now, and does every so often, is a warm, G-rated, down-home, unadrenalized prize of a book that sneaks onto the bestseller lists for no apparent reason other than a certain floppy-eared puppy appeal.

However, it is only partly because warm puppies—along with cows, horses, pigs, cats and the rest of the animal kingdom—figure as his main characters that James Herriot's [*All Creatures Great and Small*] qualify admirably. . . .

Young Dr. Herriot is forever stripping to the waist in some drafty Darrowby barn and soaping up his arm to plunge it into one troubled animal orifice or another. For Herriot, and the reader, the rewards of such expeditions range from delivery of little nibbling creatures who sometimes get stuck in the process of being born, to the periodic relief administered to Tricki Woo, a pampered little Pekingese constantly overfed by her mistress. . . .

The author naturally dwells longer on his successes than his missteps, but even the latter provide moments of fine humor. Having refused to accept Herriot's expert diagnosis that his cow had a broken pelvis, one stubborn dalesman proceeded to apply an ancient cure used by his father. . . . The cow turned out to be suffering only from loose pelvic ligaments, which happened to cure themselves almost at the moment the useless home remedy was applied. For years thereafter—which the author would be well advised to cover in a sequel—the animal was triumphantly introduced far and wide by its owner as "the cow Mr. Herriot said would never get up n'more."

William R. Doerner, "How Now, Brown Cow?" in Time *(reprinted by permission from* Time, The Weekly Newsmagazine; *copyright* Time Inc., *1973), February 19, 1973, p. 88.*

PHOEBE ADAMS

[*All Creatures Great and Small*] is full of recalcitrant cows, sinister pigs, neurotic dogs, Yorkshire weather, and pleasantly demented colleagues. It continues to be one of the funniest and most likable books around. (p. 91)

Phoebe Adams, in The Atlantic Monthly *(copyright © 1974 by The Atlantic Monthly Company, Boston, Mass.; reprinted with permission), August, 1974.*

EDWARD WEEKS

All Things Bright and Beautiful continues the story of [James Herriot's] youthful practice in an earthy profession: with growing confidence and strong arms he learns to cope with calves that are strangling in birth and with complications like husk, grass staggers, calcium deficiency, or "wool ball on t'stomach." His courtship of Helen Alderson prevails despite her testy father and Herriot's undiplomatic judging of the Pet Show. The warmth which she brings into his life is as truly told as the admiration he feels for his gifted senior partner. His prose gives us the sound of sheep, the sight of lambs, the smell of spring in the Dales; perhaps the least successful chapters are those about the scamp Tristan, whose escapades border on the fictitious. But the laughter and fidelity in the writing arise from the fact that Dr. Herriot loves his work—and is still at it in Yorkshire. (pp. 114-15)

> *Edward Weeks, in* The Atlantic Monthly *(copyright © 1974 by The Atlantic Monthly Company, Boston, Mass.; reprinted with permission), October, 1974.*

EUGENE J. LINEHAN, S.J.

Was it not W. C. Fields who claimed that a man could not be all bad if he disliked animals and young children? Allow me a suggestion: even if the reader dislikes animals and pets and children, he will like [*All Things Bright and Beautiful*]. It brings the world of animals and people into a ring of beauty, precisely because it touches the human often and with skill. The title is a first line from a hymn of Mrs. Cecil Alexander whose second line is the title of James Herriot's first book: All Creatures Great and Small. As that work was received with enthusiasm, so should this be. It's a joy. (pp. 304-05)

> *Eugene J. Linehan, S.J., in* Best Sellers *(copyright 1974, by the University of Scranton), October 1, 1974.*

PAUL SHOWERS

James Herriot is at it again with that easy, ingratiating way of telling a story. Readers of his best-selling "All Creatures Great and Small" are undoubtedly ready to devour its sequel in one gulp. Which may not be the best way to approach this supplementary collection of reminiscences of the Yorkshire country vet before World War II. It deserves more leisurely treatment, a few chapters at a time.

Again Mr. Herriot is evoking those faraway days when even veterinarians made house calls in the middle of the night.... And there is something about a succession of ewes' *accouchements*, horse castrations and teat stitching that, taken without a break, tends to neutralize narrative suspense.

Such technical items, of course, are not the point of the book. It does not confine itself to a specialist's account of his specialty. This, in today's fashionable cliché, is James Herriot's enthusiastic endorsement of a simple, unpretentious lifestyle. No wonder the earlier book was so popular. Here is a man who actually enjoys his work without worrying about the Protestant Ethic; he finds satisfaction in testing his skill against challenges of different kinds. Beyond that, he delights in the day-to-day process of living even when things aren't going too well.... It's reassuring to come across an affirmation of this sort every now and

then, even though it seems to be inspired more readily by the remote past than the immediate present.

> *Paul Showers, "A Country Vet Remembers," in* The New York Times Book Review *(© 1974 by The New York Times Company; reprinted by permission), November 3, 1974, p. 61.*

RICHARD R. LINGEMAN

[*All Things Wise and Wonderful*] is the third of James Herriot's remembrances of the quiet rural joys of practicing veterinary medicine in Yorkshire. It is cut from the same bolt of nubbly cloth as his previous books....

In "All Things Wise and Wonderful," we find the good animal doctor coping with R.A.F. training at the outset of World War II. Don't worry, Herriot-lovers, this is not a book about the service. Although Herriot is in the R.A.F., his heart is in the lovely Yorkshire moors and glens and fells. He is homesick for his new wife, Helen, and for his memories of the 1930's when, as a young man fresh out of vet's school, he worked for the fearsome older vet, Siegfried, and strove to prove himself to the crusty, laconic Yorkshire farmers....

The quiet sense of accomplishment Herriot takes in his homely labors and the honest descriptions of the veterinarian's life ... give the books a reasonably sturdy keel. The sense of the beauties of the rural countryside is there, too, as well as rural humanity in colorful diversity—my favorite being the lord who works alongside his hired hands in the muck and manure.

What allays one's pleasure, though, is a sense of formula creeping into the stories, of mechanical plot-shifts, as though Herriot were straining to heighten and point up a diminishing store of materials; he also skirts close to Disneyization, i.e. rule by lovable animals. On the whole, "All Things Wise and Wonderful" is as ingratiating as the previous ones; niceness still triumphs, but this time around, it's a near thing.

> *Richard R. Lingeman, "Animal Doctor," in* The New York Times Book Review *(© 1977 by The New York Times Company; reprinted by permission), September 18, 1977, p. 13.*

JANE MANTHORNE

Each chapter [of *All Things Wise and Wonderful*] is a separate vignette which is filled with drama and emotion, particularly the case of a beautiful collie—"mouth gaping, tongue lolling, eyes staring lifelessly"—which Herriot revives. All in all, this is another remarkable and engrossing view of humans and beasts, and YA's will look forward to the next which will surely be titled *The Lord God Made Them All*. (p. 131)

> *Jane Manthorne, in* School Library Journal *(reprinted from the October, 1977 issue of* School Library Journal, *published by R. R. Bowker Co. A Xerox Corporation; copyright © 1977), October, 1977.*

[*All Things Wise and Wonderful* is the] third of the delightful, autobiographical series by the Yorkshire veterinarian. [It] starts with his induction into the Royal Air Force in World War II and wisely interweaves flashbacks to his family and the country practice, now famous from the first two accounts. Compassion and humor prevail in his dealing with all creatures such as a tough drill sergeant, a home-loving cow sold to the market, a juvenile delinquent, and Oscar, the cat who attends local meetings. This installment ends as the young doctor, mustered out by a medical discharge, walks through the gentle hills of home toward his new son, his dear wife, and surely more adventures. (p. 30)

Virginia Quarterly Review *(copyright, 1978 by the Virginia Quarterly Review, The University of Virginia), Vol. 54, No. 1 (Winter, 1978).*

JOY K. ROY

James Herriot's account of his veterinary experience in Yorkshire . . . can give a higher boost to morale than alcohol, drugs, or a visit to the doctor. These books start in World War I and take place in Yorkshire, England, a harsh region of the country which produces hardy folk who endure. Herriot's understated and uncomplaining lot is ameliorated by his sense of humor and steered by his sensitivity.

The author's matter-of-fact recounting of hardship, study, and practice displays courageous fortitude. He shows a sympathy and love for the animals he treats. This unusual vicarious experience helps the reader climb out of his or her own private Slough of Despond. The reader will be stunned by the amount of hardship encountered as a matter of course; one's own lot is bound to be better by comparison. Herriot's writings epitomize the process of bibliotherapy: they are written in love; they can be used to inspire, to nurture, to brighten and to help the reader endure. Nature, being neither kind nor unkind in this objective view, can be a balancer of thought. "Coping behavior" may generally be increased; this reading can patch up the human spirit. (p. 57)

Joy K. Roy, in English Journal *(copyright © 1979 by the National Council of Teachers of English), March, 1979.*

Jamake Highwater

1942-

(Also writes under pseudonym J Marks) American novelist, biographer, playwright, journalist, and nonfiction writer. Highwater, the son of a Blackfoot and a Cherokee Indian, is noted for his authentic presentations of Amerindian culture to a young adult audience. Highwater holds degrees in music and anthropology, and both areas have served as subjects for his books. *Anpao: An American Indian Odyssey* is generally considered his most successful work. It has been compared to Homer's *Odyssey* for the way in which it blends oral tradition with the exciting adventures of a young man. In *Song from the Earth* Highwater explores the Indian conception of great art as art which contains "good spirit" as opposed to "beauty." In a like manner, he presents the Indian view of dance in *Dance: Ritual of Experience*. (See also *Contemporary Authors*, Vols. 65-68.)

A picture-text book *à la* the fantastically popular "The Medium Is the Massage," [*Rock and Other Four Letter Words*] seems to us to be a far more successful and appropriate use of the wayout layout. At any rate, we think it's groovy; it rocks along with surprises on every page . . . and reveals the world of rock music with more excitement than one expects to see in a book. The author claims that the format is based on the standard 32-bar rock melody (melody!?!); that the book builds to crescendos and that it is a circle, with no beginning and no end. Yes, well. There are murder mysteries based on chess problems, too, and we don't dig chess. But we dig the Jefferson Airplane, the Who, Cream, the Jimi Hendrix Experience, and others, and they are all in this book. (p. 51)

Publishers Weekly (*reprinted from the November 11, 1968, issue of* Publishers Weekly *by permission of the critic, published by R. R. Bowker Company, a Xerox company; copyright © 1968 by Xerox Corporation), November 11, 1968.*

ALICE K. TURNER

["Mick Jagger"] is a book less about Jagger than about Jagger's vibes. Man, you're supposed to *know* something about Jagger before you read this book because if you don't, you're *lost*. *Pasticheur* Marks has put together bits of Stones' history, running narratives of the Altamont victim approaching his fate and a Holly Woodlawn type waiting for tickets to the big birthday concert, snippet sketches of the '72 tour, long conversations with one David Dalton about the emerging book to hand. . . . The result is a Marks creation, not a Jagger revelation. Not a bad creation, but Jagger remains the enigmatic figure he has determinedly molded himself to be and this is not *his* book. (p. 75)

Alice K. Turner, in Publishers Weekly (*reprinted from the June 25, 1973, issue of* Publishers Weekly *by permission of the critic, published by R. R. Bowker Company, a Xerox company; copyright © 1973 by Xerox Corporation), June 25, 1973.*

["Fodor's Indian America" is an] admirably written, rich history of each major Amerindian group. . . . Himself an Indian, [Highwater] quickly journeys down the millennia to the white man's takeover after Columbus. Without bidding for sympathy, he describes the death-ridden Trail of Tears and the crowding on today's reservations. Rather than harp on Manifest Destiny as it seemed to justify the Anglos' land-grab and genocide, he tactfully produces a travel guide . . . —everything needed for a better appreciation of Indian culture and customs. A guide that follows a different drummer, invaluable for travelers seriously interested in Indian life and lore. (p. 46)

Publishers Weekly (*reprinted from the November 11, 1974, issue of* Publishers Weekly *by permission of the critic, published by R. R. Bowker Company, a Xerox company; copyright © 1974 by Xerox Corporation), November 11, 1974.*

PHOEBE-LOU ADAMS

After a quick summary of things before Columbus, Mr. Highwater makes an extensive survey of recent Indian painting [in *Song from the Earth*]. . . . Aesthetic rows liven up the test, which includes interviews with current artists of varied training and principles. The most interesting talker is Blackbear Bosin, who explains, "In my paintings there is *absolutely* no recognition—*none* of our defeat. I am describing America as if 1492 simply had never happened." Bosin states plainly an attitude detectable in the work of many of his colleagues; it probably accounts for the strain of prettified romanticism which the Anglo eye perceives. . . . (p. 117)

Phoebe-Lou Adams, in The Atlantic Monthly (*copyright © 1977 by The Atlantic Monthly Company, Boston, Mass.; reprinted with permission), March, 1977.*

JOHN C. EWERS

[*Song from the Earth: American Indian Painting's*] greatest weakness lies in its provincial assumption that no Indian painting was important unless it was created by an Indian who was a resident of, or was schooled or taught in the Southwest. No mention is made of Angel De Cora, the most influential Indian artist, teacher, and spokesman for Indian art at the beginning of the century. She was a Winnebago Indian from Nebraska. Forgotten also are the Indian artists who actively contributed to WPA art programs during the depression years. (p. 58)

> *John C. Ewers, in* The American West *(copyright © 1977 by the American West Publishing Company, Cupertino, California), March/April, 1977.*

One must add [*Song from the Earth: American Indian Painting*] to Dorothy Dunn's *American Indian painting of the Southwest and Plains area* . . . as an antidote to the latter's parochial taste and outlook regarding the uniqueness of "modern" Indian art. . . . Highwater's terse descriptions and analytic comments on the artworks are close to the actual visual material; his artistic evaluations seem balanced and comparisons made with artists in the Euro-American tradition are thought-provoking. Equally important are his comments on the appearance and revitalization role of native American art as a reaction to white society's destructiveness, acculturation pressures, and socio-economic influences. . . . Highwater also takes up contemporary-style painters and the mutual reactions of advocates of the old and new styles. . . . Highwater is a native American free-lance writer with an excellent grasp, familiarity, and sensitivity to the subject matter. . . . One warning; Chap. 2 ("The Indian in history") is full of nonsense. The book is an invaluable step toward a better grounded and more detailed study. It can, however, be read with pleasure and scholarly profit. . . . (pp. 358-59)

> Choice *(copyright © 1977 by American Library Association), May, 1977.*

LOIS SONKISS

[Perhaps] the most valuable portion of [*Song from the Earth: American Indian Painting*] is the section containing interviews and comments from artists themselves. (p. 66)

For the most part, Highwater's presentation of the artists' comments and works, and the events and attitudes that shaped them, is very sensitive. But the first three chapters of the book are biased, so biased that it takes the reader another three chapters to recognize the depth and validity of the material that follows those introductory chapters. The book is aimed at a non-Indian, awed audience, and the author overemphasizes the "otherness" of Indians, placing Native American and their art on a pedestal, beyond the comprehension of an Anglo critic. In his efforts to ennoble modern Indian artists through a discussion of the attempts of many to preserve or recall their ethnic identity, Highwater refuses to recognize prehistoric American Indian art as a conscious endeavor. Making Indian artists, prehistoric or modern, too different from other artists deprives them of their right to enjoy visual and perceptual games and be creative in the manner recognized in Western society. It is only in his concluding chapter that Highwater loosens up and considers the many different social aspects involved in the production of historic and modern Indian art and the implication these factors have in the works themselves.

Highwater's concise history of prehistoric Indian art contains some misconceptions as well as misinformation. . . . Forewarned of Highwater's over-ethnic approach to his subject, this history of contemporary American Indian art is as capable as the next. It is the bonus of interviews with many of the artists themselves that sets this book apart. (pp. 66-7)

> *Lois Sonkiss, in* Museum News *(copyright 1977 American Assoc. of Museums), May-June, 1977.*

ELLEN SISCO

[*Anpao*] takes many of the native American Indian tales and weaves them together into one story—a kind of Odyssey—which relates creation, the beginnings of Death, and even the coming of the White Men.

This book would be a delight to read, especially in the context which the author in his afterword explains; for while [the hero] Anpao journeys through many of the customs and tribal rites of many native Americans, he also journies through their histories. This book would be a good introduction to the evolution of oral history—the manner in which the stories are told has captured that oral tradition, even down to sounds and calls of animals. (p. 7)

> *Ellen Sisco, in* Young Adult Cooperative Book Review Group of Massachusetts, *October, 1977.*

[In *Anpao: An American Odyssey*] Highwater's subtitle, no idle choice, is a measure of his ambition in this ordering of traditional tales and elements around the wanderings of the invented hero Anpao ("the Dawn"). His story parallels Indian history from creation to white domination. . . . Highwater was warned by fellow Indians, he reports, that whites might not understand such business—but one suspects that it is not the pre-literate world-view with its vision of transformations, etc., but the author's artificial sequencing of separate motifs and tales that makes such serious matters as dying seem totally lacking in consequence. In the end, the character Anpao, through a handy device, lends neither depth nor drama to the material. Nevertheless, Highwater has a firm command of his sources, and this is a serious, craftsmanlike work. (pp. 1053-54)

> Kirkus Reviews *(copyright © 1977 The Kirkus Service, Inc.), October 1, 1977.*

Highwater's spare but evocative prose is a perfect vehicle for the Amerind tribal legends he interweaves in his story of the adventures of the Indian boy Anpao. . . . Anpao's arduous journey brings him into contact with a myriad of characters who reveal to him the mysteries of his birth and of life and the foibles and frailties of humankind. A vivid, sensitive rendering of the unique Indian concept of all things, certain to conjure up images long after its last page has been completed. (p. 542)

> Booklist *(reprinted by permission of the American Library Association; copyright 1977 by the American Library Association), November 15, 1977.*

JAMES A. NORSWORTHY

Highwater has created an exceptional book of rare beauty and insight [in *Anpao*]. To say that Highwater did for American Indian culture what Homer did for the people of Ancient Greece may seem astonishing or perhaps overstated, but it is true. . . . Two of the stories, "The Farting

Boy'' and ''Deer Woman'' have elements that may be objectionable to some readers: however, they are presented with such good taste that they are likely to offend no one except those who can't wait to be offended. The moral tone of the stories is by nature Indian and will provide an interesting comparison and contrast to those of the Judeo-Christian tradition. (p. 235)

> *James A. Norsworthy, in* Catholic Library World, *December, 1977.*

JUDITH McPHERON

Like many current books about native Americans, there is a contradiction inherent in [*Ritual of the Wind: North American Indian Ceremonies, Music, and Dances*]. The photographs, gorgeous and exotic, beckon us, while the text, clumsy and overwritten, warns us constantly that we are invaders and besmirchers of the sacred. Of course, historically, this has been true, but if the sense of violation is so great, one wonders why a book about Indian ceremonialism, aimed primarily at a non-Indian audience, is attempted at all. The book is an eclectic mix, with bits and pieces from many cultures, and that is its strongest point. (p. 102)

> *Judith McPheron, in* Library Journal *(reprinted from* Library Journal, *January 1, 1978; published by R. R. Bowker Co. (a Xerox company); copyright © 1978 by Xerox Corporation), January 1, 1978.*

MARY M. BURNS

With a storyteller's rhythmic cadences, [*Anpao: An American Indian Odyssey*] chronicles the adventures of Anpao as he persists in his arduous quest for the love of the beautiful Ko-ko-mik-e-is.... Because the oral tradition upon which Anpao's adventures are based includes many diverse elements, the book may be perceived as a unique blending of history and mysticism. These elements range from cosmological stories originating in the multilayered consciousness of a world predating contemporary notions of time and space to tales inspired by relatively recent events, such as the coming of the white man. As noted in the final explanatory chapter, ''there is no pan-Indian history, for Indian cultures are far too diversified to accommodate a uniform view of history or to embrace a single cultural hero . . . the tales of *Anpao* are selected from a large body of oral history, in much the way that Homer's tales in the *Odyssey* represent only a fragment of the tales of all the tribes of the Aegean.'' The author has developed a prose saga which skillfully interweaves various tales into a coherent entity reflective of the Indian's earthy humor as well as of his transcendent view of the universe. A magnificent, long-needed achievement.... (pp. 55-6)

> *Mary M. Burns, in* The Horn Book Magazine *(copyright © 1978 by the Horn Book, Inc., Boston), February, 1978.*

RUTH M. STEIN

[In *Anpao*] Highwater spins ancient and more recent tales of Indian tribes, focused around one fictional character, and set as stories-within-a story. A unified structure reflects the unity Native Americans feel with the earth, sky, water and people.... Art, songs, stories, poems, and sayings do justice to a rich and relatively unknown heritage full of adventure, mysticism, and even ribald humor. Though complex in concept, the style of writing brings this within the range of most youngsters. (pp. 213-14)

> *Ruth M. Stein, in* Language Arts *(copyright © 1978 by the National Council of Teachers of English), February, 1978.*

JANE YOLEN

Jamake Highwater, of Blackfeet/Cherokee heritage, calls himself the Indian Homer who has written in ''Anpao'' an American Indian Odyssey. He almost pulls it off.

Anpao, the main character in Highwater's novel, is, in his words, ''a fabrication,'' but the adventures the boy completes on his way to becoming a man are borrowed from the folklore of many American Indian tribes. Indeed, Highwater annotates the novel so that each adventure is set in its originating culture as well as being part of the continuing narrative....

The novel is well written, smooth, pleasing to the eye and ear. But as a novel it is no more than the linking of old tales. The character of Anpao is never developed. His more interesting brother Oapna dies in the first section. Ko-ko-mik-e-is is simply a beautiful and faithful woman, a little like Penelope perhaps, but with none of Penelope's inventive dedication. Folk characters in any culture tend to be types, prototypes who serve the theme of the tale. Highwater has written an extended folktale, not a novel, for his characters never breathe....

I applaud Highwater's effort. His retelling of the tales is fluid and in many instances compelling. The book cries to be read aloud. But it is not a novel. And it is nowhere near as great a narrative as the ''Odyssey.'' (p. 26)

> *Jane Yolen, in* The New York Times Book Review *(© 1978 by The New York Times Company; reprinted by permission), February 5, 1978.*

VIRGINIA HAVILAND

Occasionally, not often enough, in the world of young people's books—or anyone's—there appears a timeless work which defies delimiting of audience. Such a book is *Anpao*, a synthesis of native American folklore....

[Highwater] has woven across the main threads of his legendary hero's quest a significant weft of American Indian mythology, just as Homer in his famous epic of a Greek's journey homeward from Troy introduced tales of supernatural encounters which extended the dangers of that voyage.

None of these tales, says Highwater, is of his own invention, although the words are new, his own. Most exist in many versions, but in his meticulous bibliography of sources he cites at least one book in which each tale can be read in its oral form. Some of these are ancient; some emerged out of experiences after the invasion by white men....

[Not] only the uniqueness and significance of the content make this an enduring book, but also the author's gift for using the poetic, dignified language required of tellers of great epics.

> *Virginia Haviland, ''Tales of the Tribes,'' in* Book World—The Washington Post *(© 1978, The Washington Post), February 12, 1978, p. G4.*

[''Dance: The Ritual of Experience''] is a most interesting attempt to analyze dance from a fresh viewpoint, to tear away the superstructure built by years of Western dance conventions and get down to basics. Some may find the idea controversial, but clearly Highwater has important things to say and says them well. (p. 63)

Publishers Weekly *(reprinted from the* March 20, 1978, *issue of Publishers Weekly by permission of the critic, published by R. R. Bowker Company, a Xerox company; copyright © 1978 by Xerox Corporation),* March 20, 1978.

N. SCOTT MOMADAY

["Many Smokes, Many Moons" is a general survey which] treats the Americas as a whole. Mr. Highwater writes in his preface: "This book is an effort to make bridges across the vast spaces between Indians and non-Indians and to explore the America of native Americans as it is made visible through Indian art." Actually, the book is not nearly so ambitious as that sentence suggests. The "bridges" are simply brief chronological entries in a calendar of events that mark the experience of American Indians from prehistoric to contemporary times. The book, then, is a kind of clock, the bare outline of an enormous record yet to be set down in writing. As such it is more nearly a reference book than anything else.

Yet the principle of selection seems highly arbitrary; indeed, it seems at times curiously rhetorical, even contentious. Under 1528-36, for example, the single entry refers to the incredible odyssey of Cabeza de Vaca and his three companions, who walked across the American Southwest and were the first white men to encounter the Indians of that region. Theirs is surely one of the great stories of survival in human history; they must have suffered unimaginable hardships. But Mr. Highwater ends the entry with this sentence: "Though Spanish history books made these men out to be heroes, Indians have accused the party of exploitation and aggression, and Esteban, in particular, is looked upon by Pueblo Indians as a thief and a rapist." This may be true, so far as it goes, but it certainly isn't the whole truth, nor is it the point that ought to be made here.

Again, under the crucial year 1776, we have this entry only, which I quote in its entirety:

> The rebels of the American Revolution cited as one of the offenses committed by England's King George III the arousing of antagonism between Indians and colonists. The American Declaration of Independence, adopted on July 4, stated, 'He has excited domestic insurrections amongst us, and has endeavoured to bring on the inhabitants of our frontiers, the merciless Indian Savages, whose known rule of warfare, is an undistinguished destruction, of all ages, sexes and conditions.' The United States of America was born.

It is, of course, deplorable that such a prejudicial sentence should contaminate the language of so great a document as the Declaration of Independence, but why deplore it here, I wonder. Surely there are more significant points to make, better bridges to build between Indians and non-Indians. (p. 52)

N. Scott Momaday, in The New Times Book Review *(© 1978 by The New York Times Company; reprinted by permission), April 30, 1978.*

BARBARA NEWMAN

[*Dance: The Ritual of Experience*] examines the shifting role of ritual, "a tribal, expressive form of man's relationship to the power of nature," in the development of dance through the ages, with specific attention to its manifestations in ten contemporary dance works. . . . Despite sometimes haphazard organization, several factual errors, and a distinct bias for the ritual practices of the American Indian, Highwater has made an interesting, if cursory, exploration of an important subject. However, this book seems more an introductory investigation than the fully developed study the topic could easily sustain. (p. 1193)

Barbara Newman, in Library Journal *(reprinted from* Library Journal, *June 1, 1978; published by R. R. Bowker Co. (a Xerox company); copyright © 1978 by Xerox Corporation), June 1, 1978.*

JEAN F. MERCIER

In a preface to his engrossing and eloquent work [in *Many Smokes, Many Moons,* Highwater] gives an example of fundamental differences in understanding between native Americans and whites. Subsequent chapters pinpoint historic and cultural events to express the seldom-heard Indian view. . . . Sad to say, it includes an almost unbroken account of whites' betrayals of a conquered people. (p. 65)

Jean F. Mercier, in Publishers Weekly *(reprinted from the July 3, 1978, issue of* Publishers Weekly *by permission of the critic, published by R. R. Bowker Company, a Xerox company; copyright 1978 by Xerox Corporation), July 3, 1978.*

The subtitle [of *Many Smokes, Many Moons: A Chronology of American Indian History Through Indian Art*] is misleading. Handsomely designed, this really consists [more] of archaeological, [than of] historical snippets. . . . A typical early sequence notes that the Pinto Basin culture, based on an economy of fish and shellfish, dominated the Far West around 7000 B.C. . . . After 1492 the coming of Europeans and the subsequent great changes and disasters are seen (sometimes) from the Indians' viewpoint—but not as eloquently or informatively as in Nabakov's *Native American Testimony.* . . . As for American Indian art as a subject for comment, Highwater makes passing mention of several developments but with no apparent system or sense of proportion; political observations are similarly sketchy and unconnected. The pictures as a group do not make this a notable art book; neither is it a coherent history or a particularly pointed reminder of the human diversity Highwater emphasizes in his introduction. (p. 813)

Kirkus Reviews *(copyright © 1978 The Kirkus Service, Inc.), August 1, 1978.*

Jesse Jackson

1908-

Black American young adult novelist and biographer. Jackson utilizes his own cultural heritage in his novels about black teenagers growing up in America. *Call Me Charley*, published in 1945, was one of the first young adult books to deal openly with racial prejudice. Although Jackson's treatment of the black-white confrontation in this novel seems dated today, he was a pioneer in treating this subject matter realistically and his work retains historical significance. In this work and in his subsequent fiction, Jackson writes simply and eloquently of the universal problems and joys of adolescence while also considering the more specialized problems of the black ghetto teenager. (See also *Contemporary Authors*, Vols. 25-28, rev. ed., and *Something about the Author*, Vol. 2.)

MAY LAMBERTON BECKER

[The story of Charles Moss, the first colored boy in Arlington Heights,] can be matched under like circumstances all over the United States, except that in some parts it would not work out so well as [in "Call Me Charley"]. (p. 18)

Even Tom—whose solid, unemotional friendship was quickened by constant proof that whenever they both got into trouble the colored boy would get the blame—was often impatient with the patience of Charley and thought him scared. Perhaps he was but of something larger than what happened. (pp. 18, 20)

A straight story of American boy-life, it is told largely in dialogue; the young author, whose ear is uncommonly sensitive, reproduces the staccato touch and distinctive turn of Negro speech without attributing dialect to educated Northern Negroes. His book is a contribution to understanding. (p. 20)

> *May Lamberton Becker, in* New York Herald Tribune Book Review *(© I.H.T. Corporation; reprinted by permission), November 11, 1945.*

JANE H. CLARKE

In *Tessie*, a young girl from Harlem encounters an entirely different city and an entirely different world when she wins a scholarship to Hobbe and becomes the first Negro student to attend the private school. . . .

Although it is unlikely that Tessie's first day at Hobbe could have happened as it did, [Jesse Jackson] writes compassionately of a girl's struggle to face a strange world and be true to herself. (p. 34)

> *Jane H. Clarke, in* Book World—Chicago Tribune, *Part II (© 1968 Postrib Corp.), May 5, 1968.*

MARY LOUISE BIRMINGHAM

[In "Tessie" a] ninth-grader from Harlem wins an ivy-clad scholarship and runs the gantlet of her first year in a mythical private school named Hobbe. . . . [Tessie's] conflict is so dense with implications for all of us, so absorbing in itself, that pages turn willy-nilly. All the same, the book is a barely passable effort to bridge communication gaps between the races, the generations, or the sexes.

One embarrassemnt is the author's . . . assumption that black ritual and idiom never leak from the inner city. . . .

This is bloodless drawing-room tragicomedy, even narrower in scope than "Guess Who's Coming to Dinner." Miscegenation is dismissed at the outset as a potentiality, although Hobbe is coeducational and almost lily-white. Tessie scoffs at the thought of any love other than her soul-buddy, Jimmy, and thinks that "the question only showed how little her parents understood."

The author seems to agree with Tessie. To the pure all things are very pure indeed, and few problems so knotty that they cannot be straightened out with patience and a heated comb. (p. 30)

> *Mary Louise Birmingham, in* The New York Times Book Review *(© 1968 by The New York Times Company; reprinted by permission), May 26, 1968.*

DORIS INNIS

Juvenile books about Harlem and its residents fall into three main categories (or traps); those that romanticize life in Harlem, those that oversimplify it, and those that portray Harlem as a place from which the lucky ones escape. *Tessie* falls partly into the second category, but mostly into the third. These attitudes are obvious from the beginning. Bright 14-year old Tessie returns from a summer camp stay which has apparently dimmed her memories of unpleasant aspects of Harlem life and reacts as if she's returned to a minor nightmare. Tessie's escape route opens up when she wins a scholarship to Hobbe, an exclusive private school. . . . Tessie takes her scholarship, and the story chiefly concerns her resulting cross pressures; to win acceptance by Hobbe students without having her Harlem friends feel she has changed. The author handles this basic conflict in such confused and unconvincing ways that the end product is almost a hymn to the rather prevalent notion, more challenged now than ever before: to be white and middle class. Tessie's addiction to white social and aesthetic values is exemplified in the entire chapter devoted to what the author calls Tessie's hair problem, which, since it is kinky, she straightens, to conform to white standards of what hair should look like. Readers will inevitably be left with the unfortunate impression that Tessie, her verbal protestations to the contrary, has chosen the world of Hobbe and that it is the best of all possible worlds. (p. 169)

> *Doris Innis, in* School Library Journal *(reprinted from the October, 1968 issue of* School Library Journal, *published by R. R. Bowker Co. A Xerox Corporation; copyright © 1968), October, 1968.*

BETTY ZOSS

Twelve-years old and living in Columbus, Ohio, Stonewall Jackson [protagonist of "The Sickest Don't Always Die The Quickest"] suspects being black is a sin. . . . With Stoney, who has a spot on one lung, the reader lives and learns. It is better (literally) to swim than sink: the sickest do not always die the quickest.

Stoney's world will be news to many of all ages, black and white. . . .

While our busy hero survives more sad-funny, boy-growing up scrapes than one week (in July, 1920) and a book this size, can quite afford, TSDADTQ is fresh, warm, honest Americana about a real American boy. Stoney should make a lot of friends. (p. 20)

> *Betty Zoss, in* The New York Times Book Review *(© 1971 by The New York Times Company; reprinted by permission), February 14, 1971.*

JOHN W. CONNER

Jesse Jackson is a very funny writer. In *The Sickest Don't Always Die the Quickest* he has created a black Tom Sawyer (Steeplehead) and a black Huckleberry Finn (Stonewall) who cavort irreverently through two weeks of hot July afternoons in 1920. . . .

To support Steeplehead and Stonewall, the author recreates the black society which attends Calvary Baptist Church in Columbus, Ohio. These people and the white folks who control jobs held by blacks are a microcosm reflecting the foibles of a world with which the innocent but ornery Steeplehead and Stonewall constantly collide. (p. 665)

Stonewall and Steeplehead are twelve and thirteen respectively. Neither is willing to shed the superstitions which adults around them practice; both boys want to be true to their own beliefs but find this difficult when threatened by adults. Jesse Jackson's adult characters often behave more like children than Stonewall and Steeplehead do. The author implies that children's honesty is warped to fit adult misconceptions. Not that a reader will believe that Stonewall and Steeplehead will be warped! These two adolescent free thinkers will survive adult misconceptions despite adult pressures! (pp. 665-66)

Jesse Jackson's frank language and the chapter in which

Stonewall makes his weekly paper route collections may make *The Sickest Don't Always Die the Quickest* unacceptable for some readers. Read this book before recommending it to adolescents. You will enjoy it. Jesse Jackson's humor will leave a thought-provoking tingle at the end of your funny bone. (p. 666)

> *John W. Conner, in* English Journal *(copyright 1971 by the National Council of Teachers of English), May, 1971.*

[*The Fourteenth Cadillac* is less] a finished novel than impressionistic sketches of Calvary—or black Columbus, Ohio, in 1925, as experienced by teen-aged Stonewall Jackson. . . . Jackson doesn't attempt to construct a plot out of Stonewall's problems in landing a suitable job (and avoiding one as the undertaker's apprentice) or appeasing his girl Talitha who resents his refusal to join the church. Instead, this is to be read—by youngsters who don't require narrative tension, psychological depth or even polished writing—for Stonewall's passing observations on Calvary funeral protocol and pretension . . . and the distinctly evoked social surfaces of this church-centered community where the altar is equipped—are you ready?—with a white telephone hooked up with heaven. (p. 1152)

> *Kirkus Reviews (copyright © 1972 The Kirkus Service, Inc.), October 1, 1972.*

MAY HILL ARBUTHNOT and ZENA SUTHERLAND

Jesse Jackson has given a full and moving account of the kind of discriminations a black child may encounter. In *Call Me Charley* . . . the young black, the only one in the neighborhood, is not welcome in the school but is tolerated. He has some bitter disappointments but gradually wins the respect and friendship of some of the boys. It is a touching story made more poignant by Charley's quiet, patient acceptance of his lot. . . . The author has too realistic an approach to suggest a complete solution, but he tells a good story of a brave, likable boy in a difficult world.

Charley Starts from Scratch . . . , a sequel, finds Charley graduated from high school and trying to find a job in a strange city. Many doors are closed to him, but coming in first in Olympic trials gives Charley fresh courage and convinces several employers of the boy's worth and perseverance. Like the first book, this story is sensitively told.

Tessie . . . is the story of a fourteen-year-old girl in Harlem who wins a scholarship to an all-white private school. Her parents are apprehensive, but Tessie is determined to use her educational opportunity even if it means social rebuffs —as it does, both from her new schoolmates and from her old friends. The development is believable, with actions that proceed logically from attitudes and motivations, so that Tessie's firm insistence on making the best of both her worlds is natural. (p. 457)

> *May Hill Arbuthnot and Zena Sutherland, in their* Children and Books *(copyright © 1947, 1957, 1964, 1972 by Scott, Foresman and Company; reprinted by permission), fourth edition, Scott, Foresman, 1972.*

JOHN W. CONNER

Adolescent readers who enjoyed meeting Stonewall Jackson and his pal Steeplehead in one of Jesse Jackson's previous books, *The Sickest Don't Always Die the Quick-*

est, will welcome the continued adventures of these two black adolescents who try to find jobs in a Southern city in 1925. But, before Stonewall starts job-hunting in earnest, Jesse Jackson treats his readers to the laying out, the funeral, and the survivor's feast in honor of Aunt Hettie, Stonewall's favorite aunt.

Jesse Jackson has a talent for combining description and fast-paced narrative. . . .

The Fourteenth Cadillac is great fun to read. It will touch many adolescents where their weaknesses in familial relationships occur. Stonewall's younger brother is a hypocrite and a tattletale, his mother has enormous ambitions for Stonewall which are far beyond his capacities to fulfill, only Stonewall's father feels that a seventeen-year-old boy has a right to honest failure.

Adolescent readers will laugh with Stonewall and occasionally fear for him as he faces a situation for which he seems ill-prepared. But, readers know that Stonewall and Steeple will come through any situation relatively unscathed and confident of a brighter future. *The Fourteenth Cadillac* suggests that the human foibles of 1925 are much like those of 1973. Jesse Jackson, I think you are right! (p. 307)

> *John W. Conner, in* English Journal *(copyright 1973 by the National Council of Teachers of English), February, 1973.*

DOROTHY M. BRODERICK

Call Me Charley was the first book to present anything resembling a genuine black-white confrontation. (p. 166)

The verbal exchange and the threatening gestures do not lead to physical combat . . . at any time in the book. . . .

[The bigot who gives Charley the most trouble is George.] He is pampered, a victim of his parents' prejudices, and the parents are shown as not really class people: a little too loud, a little too pushy.

This idea that "class" people do not behave badly is a direct descendant of the slave attitude that masters were "quality" folk and the nonslave-owning population was "poor white trash." It is also related to the idea that "happy slaves" had good masters, while on occasion there was a bad master whose lack of good behavior caused the slaves to be unhappy. (p. 167)

> *Dorothy M. Broderick, in her* Image of the Black in Children's Fiction *(copyright © 1973 by Dorothy M. Broderick; reprinted by permission of the R. R. Bowker Company), Bowker, 1973.*

ZENA SUTHERLAND

[*Black in America* is a] survey of black history in this country. . . . Emphasis is on the long struggle for freedom and equality. The text is adequately written and the photographs well chosen, but the book seems somewhat random in choice of material. . . . Although most of the black history books are written for slightly older readers, they are so much better written and so much more informative that a history as sketchy as this one pales in contrast. (pp. 130-31)

> *Zena Sutherland, in* Bulletin of the Center for Children's Books *(© 1974 by the University of Chicago; all rights reserved), April, 1974.*

LORAINE ALTERMAN

[Jesse Jackson's biography, *The Life of Mahalia Jackson, Queen of the Gospel Singers*] details the course of her life from her early years in New Orleans, where she first impressed people with her singing at age 5, through her triumphs all over the world and her brave participation in the civil rights movement. . . .

Jesse Jackson makes it clear that she lived and breathed to spread the word of peace and love through gospel music.

Jesse Jackson tells the story well—explaining vividly why Miss Jackson stuck with gospel rather than singing the blues and how she was willing to do the toughest kind of housework for white people so that she could sing. There are times when the author tries to convey in the narrative what Miss Jackson was thinking. I'm a little suspicious of this, and it makes no sense in view of the disclaimer which appears in the acknowledgments: "The author regrets not having space for more of the wonderful things Mahalia said about her life, her music, the black experience, religion, and God." I would have preferred more of Mahalia Jackson, less of Jesse Jackson. . . .

But on the whole it will induce young readers to listen to some of Mahalia Jackson's recordings and to discover for themselves what made her gift so special.

> *Loraine Alterman, "Make a Joyful Noise unto the Lord," in* The New York Times Book Review *(© 1974 by The New York Times Company; reprinted by permission), June 16, 1974, p. 8.*

JOHN ROWE TOWNSEND

[Among stories which were "contemporary" at the time but which now look dated is *Call Me Charley*, concerning] the acceptance of a black boy in a suburban community generally.

[In this book] the black characters bear injustice with a patience which now appears Uncle Tommish. . . . Charley Moss's mother in *Call Me Charley* advises him on the last page, 'As long as you work hard and try to do right, you will always find good [white] people like Doc Cunningham or Tom and his folks marching along with you in the right path.' Actually Charley is not without spirit; when someone addresses him as Sambo he says, 'My name is Charles. Sometimes I'm called Charley. Nobody calls me Sambo and gets away with it.' Hence the book's title. Nevertheless, there is some resemblance to the treatment of the poor in books by well-meaning Victorians. Just as the poor were expected to rely on and be grateful for the beneficence of the rich, so the black must rely on and be grateful for the beneficence of the white. Of course we have no right to sneer from our vantage-point in the 1970s at advice which was sensible when it was given. But well might poor or black have retorted, 'Damn your charity, give us justice.' (p. 272)

> *John Rowe Townsend, in his* Written for Children: An Outline of English-Language Children's Literature *(copyright © 1965, 1974 by John Rowe Townsend; reprinted by permission of J. B. Lippincott Company; in Canada by Kestrel Books), revised edition, Lippincott, 1974.*

Jim Jacobs

1942-

Warren Casey

1942(?)-

American playwrights and composers. Jacobs and Casey are the creators of *Grease*, the rock'n'roll musical which parodies the fifties while rendering it timeless. One of Broadway's most popular plays, its success stems primarily from its authentic depiction of high school kids interacting naturally without adult interference. It is based on the standard boy-meets-girl theme, such as in the clichéd teen romance movies of Troy Donahue and Sandra Dee, but the several original twists it applies to this theme give it a lively and unhackneyed approach. The emphasis of *Grease* is on the camaraderie of young people, and it subtly comments on group acceptance and psychology. However, it avoids any direct references to the era's serious events and resolves any problems that its characters have by the end of the play. *Grease* presents the fifties as a decade of fun and good times, and it is considered responsible, along with George Lucas's film *American Graffiti*, for spawning the nostalgia trend of the early 1970s. Both of its authors grew up during the fifties, and recall and recapture it without sentimentality. Jacobs is an actor, writer, and musician who used his own experiences as a high school greaser as the basis for much of the play's plot and dialogue. Casey is a songwriter and actor whose theatre company, The Kingston Mines, staged the original production of *Grease* in Chicago. Their lyrics and dialogue are clever and full of double entendres, sexual raunchiness, and many fifties' allusions. Their songs reflect both teenage trauma and celebration, and are done tongue-in-cheek in the styles of performers such as Elvis Presley, the Everly Brothers, and the Teen Queens. *Grease* has been criticized for an overall lack of seriousness, unmemorable musical material, and for what some critics feel is a thin storyline. It is generally considered, however, to have successfully merged rock and musical theater much in the manner of *Hair* and *Godspell*. Designed purely for entertainment, its youthful high spirits and universal good humor keep it fresh and enjoyable for contemporary young people.

WALTER KERR

"Grease" is a mostly agreeable musical about the very last moment in time when boys submitted to haircuts (though they were training them to duck-tails), when cigarettes and wine were the makings of girls' pajama parties, when hubcaps were highly thought of as objects worth snatching, and when at least one of the kids around Rydell High ('59) could be heard cursing himself for having forgotten it was Friday and having eaten a hamburger. . . .

The show's state of mind is disarming, its sociology would seem to be accurate (I wasn't in high school at the time), its tunes by Jim Jacobs and Warren Casey are often attractive in themselves as well as wryly nostalgic, and its two principals are so personable and so skilled that I wish the composer-librettists had had the plain good sense to concentrate on them more. . . .

If "Grease" becomes attenuated and rather wearing in the second half, it's because it keeps replaying its atmospheric effects instead of getting on with what probably ought to be the love story. It dawdles over jargon too much, as though just hearing the lunchroom, street-corner, school-gym inflections of the period would be enough to keep us content between numbers. It wastes time on a rumble that's going nowhere and doesn't quite seem to belong to begin with. And it starts up paths—one of the girls gets pregnant—it isn't going to bother to pursue. The book rambles, and has to keep picking up after itself, which is a chore.

But some of the numbers . . . are worth the waiting even if you didn't graduate from Rydell in '59. Those who did are probably going to be entirely happy. (p. 3)

Walter Kerr, in The New York Times (© *1972 by The New York Times Company; reprinted by permission), February 2, 1972.*

EDITH OLIVER

["Grease"] is—if such a thing is conceivable—an exercise in dry-eyed nostalgia for the nineteen-fifties, the era of Elvis Presley and radio disc jockeys. Jim Jacobs and Warren Casey, who wrote the book, score, and lyrics, have apparently steeped themselves in a period when any nuisance or personal misfortune, however transitory, was good for a lament. Three of the best and funniest numbers are "It's Raining on Prom Night," "Alone at a Drive-In Movie," and "Beauty School Dropout." The tone of the show is tongue-in-(and-out-of-) cheek, and perhaps it is true that the best way to parody the fifties is simply to imitate them, for the songs here are just fifties songs, and pretty good ones. The book, such as it is, is entirely concerned with the activities of a high school class—lunchroom gossip and lunchroom plotting, a pajama party, and abortive gang rumble, a school dance, a pregnancy scare, and holdout virginity. There are some amusing lines, and everything certainly looks and sounds authentic. . . .

And yet, as I sat watching it, I kept feeling that I should be having a better time. . . . [The characters] are neither interesting nor especially attractive, and Mr. Jacobs and Mr. Casey certainly haven't bothered to give them anything interesting to do, relying instead, perhaps, on that nostalgia to be generated in the audience. A mistake. Who wants to be bothered remembering the fifties? The thirties and forties, yes, and the sixties, yes indeed, but the nineteen-fifties made one of the dullest decades on record and are better forgotten. (p. 68)

Edith Oliver, in The New Yorker *(© 1972 by The New Yorker Magazine, Inc.), February 26, 1972.*

HARRIS GREEN

["Grease" is the] kind of musical that Broadway has needed for some time. . . .

Somehow, it has managed to combine the two commodities everyone agrees our theater most requires: younger audiences and what I can best describe—not too ponderously, I trust—as "older virtues." That is, "Grease" deserves the adjectives we once awarded shows like "Pal Joey," "Kiss Me Kate," "Guys and Dolls" and "The Pajama Game" but haven't had much call for recently. (p. 1)

For several seasons we haven't had many musicals that deserve to be hailed as: "brash . . . charming . . . unsentimental . . . light-hearted . . . spunky . . . high-spirited . . . unpretentious." Good word, that "unpretentious"! Thanks to "Grease," all are applicable once more. The musical comedy is both musical and comic once more. . . .

Jacobs and Casey view [the fifties] with that rare blend of affection and consternation that Sandy Wilson brought to "The Boy Friend."

They are so unsentimental about the brutishness of Elvis and the inanities of Annette that it wouldn't surprise me to learn they'd dashed the whole show off one weekend—possibly after watching an old beach-party flick on TV—when the pluperfect mindlessness of what they'd once taken seriously struck them with such force that each sprang to his typewriter or guitar, writhing with inspiration. Nowhere in "Grease" is there that mad delight in the insipid past that has permitted nostalgia to rage like a plague on Broadway. . . .

Jacobs and Casey have no other cause but entertainment in mind in "Grease." I confess that I had my doubts about their being true to it, at least as far as I was concerned, for they have created a very unappetizing student body for Rydell High, their archetypal school of the fifties where much of "Grease" is set. Many of the boys of Rydell's Class of '59 look as if they've slouched out of "The Blackboard Jungle" while the girls look like camp followers of "The Wild One," and everyone uses the kind of language that will drive most benefit-matinee ladies right up the wall. . . .

The awesome purity of our heroine, Sandy Dumbrowski . . . , should be restorative enough for anyone overwhelmed by the lack of morality of the other girls. So ominous is Sandy's fresh-scrubbed goodness that the creep of her dreams, Danny Zuko . . . , twitches like a puppet at the mercy of a spastic puppeteer at her very approach. To mend his worldly ways, he virtually runs for his life: he goes out for the track team. Can he reform before both of

them exhaust their supply of idiotic songs about the hammer-strokes of fate visited upon us in adolescence . . . ?

Jacobs and Casey resolve their dilemma amid a welter of wrenched clichés, in a manner that now seems as unimprovably right—for this show—as its title.

Not content with knocking about such familar cult figures of a decade and a half ago as Pat Boone or smarmy disk jockeys, "Grease" has a great deal of fun with one of today's more deserving targets: O'Horgan's "Jesus Christ Superstar," with its desperate, unimaginative use of hand mikes. This simultaneous debasement of the musical and Christianity must surely be the inspiration for the way everyone in "Grease" plucks microphones out of the very air, it would seem, at every opportunity. . . .

How jolting, then, to find a show this high-spirited and irreverent, which apparently had no pretensions about rock and its capability of bearing messages of great seriousness, suddenly grinding to a halt for a dreary salute to unwed motherhood ("There Are Worse Things—I Could Do" . . .). I do believe Jacobs and Casey have succumbed to that tradition Rodgers and Hammerstein set: pausing for a moment of Higher Seriousness. I wish they hadn't. . . .

"Grease," [however,] for the most part, is [high spirited and unpretentious]. (p. 13)

Harris Green, "'Grease'? Groovy," in The New York Times *(© 1972 by The New York Times Company; reprinted by permission), June 4, 1972, pp. 1, 13.*

HENRY HEWES

Dispensing with the conventional charm and nostalgia one might expect, *Grease* takes a tough midwestern city high school named Rydell and describes its coarseness with unsentimental accuracy. The opening scene is an anniversary to which graduates of the class of '59 return. They sing a typical alma mater, which, of course, is utter hypocrisy. Suddenly the boring decorum is shattered. The alma mater uproariously changes to a mocking cataloging of their real and mostly scatological memories of Rydell. The banquet table disappears, and the graduates re-enact scenes from their last year at school.

This makes *Grease* different from the *Best Foot Forward* kind of musical that uses the youthfulness of its performers to enchant us. In *Grease* we are always aware that the performers are more mature than the teen-agers they are depicting, and therefore they can be harsher and more unflinching in their parody of their former selves.

The plot follows a dozen kids through typical high school incidents, with its main thread being a "romance" between Danny Zuko and Sandy Dumbrowski. . . .

Ultimately, of course, there is a "happy" ending, with Sandy deciding to run with the pack and enjoy the same kind of sexual liaison with Danny that some of the other girls have with their uncommitted boy friends. Does this bring her true love and happiness? Probably not. But she does find her new personality more comfortable in the high school milieu. One suspects that *Grease* is celebrating the courage these kids must have for living according to cool-generation mores. This courage is best expressed, not by Sandy, but by another girl who bravely pretends to her boy friend that some other guy was responsible for her pregnancy. In a song, "There Are Worse Things I Could Do," she movingly describes and defends her new morality.

However, the success of *Grease* owes less to its fulfillment of Danny-gets-Sandy expectations than it does to its vivid creation of the whole scene around them. A pajama party at which the girls trade catty remarks and notes about boys features a ballad sung Supremes-style by the girls. A beat-up, secondhand wreck of a car is vigorously serenaded as "Greased Lightning," a vehicle guaranteed to thrill the chicks into sexual surrender. And one boy rhapsodizes about his success at "Mooning," a boyish trick of sticking one's bare behind out the window at passing girls. All these things are essentially ugly and debasing. Yet *Grease* treats them unevasively and with good comic effect. . . .

[Although] *Grease* has no magical story to tell and although its music is an imitation of rock hits of the past, it does what it sets out to do with admirable thoroughness and entertains from start to finish.

> *Henry Hewes, "Kid Stuff Retrospective," in Sat-urday Review (© 1972 Saturday Review, Inc.; reprinted with permission), July 15, 1972, p. 64.*

MICHAEL FEINGOLD

Grease does not discourse about our presence in Saigon. Nor does it contain in-depth study of such other 50's developments as the growth of mega-corporations and conglomerates, the suburban building boom that broke the backs of our cities, the separation of labor's political power from the workers by union leaders and organization men. Although set in and around an urban high school, it does not even discuss one of the decade's dominant news stories, the massive expansion of the university system, and the directing of a whole generation of war babies toward the pursuit of college degrees. *Grease* is an escape, a musical designed to entertain, not to concern itself with serious political and social matters. But because it is truthful, because it spares neither the details nor the larger shapes of the narrow experience on which it focuses so tightly, *Grease* implies the topics I have raised, and many others. So I think it is a work of art, a firm image that projects, by means of what it does contain, everything it has chosen to leave out. And between the throbs of its ebullience, charm, and comedy, it conveys a feeling, about where we have been and how we got to where we are, that is quite near despair, if one wants to dwell on it.

Nostalgia is a pretty unhealthy emotion. In the theater it evades, more often than not, the reality of both past and present. . . . *Grease,* however, does not evade; in that sense it is not a nostalgia show. One has to have some affectionate memory of a period one has outlived, and the musical does not scruple to show its affection for every person and thing involved; it is, I believe, utterly without hate. Yet it is objective about the triviality and emptiness of the lives it portrays, about the sweeping changes that have now rendered those lives obsolete, about the sweet manu-factured insipidity of the music and lyrics that were a con-stant background to a 1950's adolescence.

The people of *Grease* are a special class of aliens, self-apppointed cynics in a work-oriented, upwardly mobile world. We know from the prologue that history has played its dirty trick on them before they even appear: They are not at the reunion; they will not be found among the pros-perous Mrs. Honeywells and the go-getting vice-presidents of Straight-Shooters, Unlimited. Nor, on the other hand, did they actively drop out: that was left to their younger siblings and cousins. . . . They were the group who thought they had, or chose to have, nowhere to go. They stayed in the monotonous work routine of the lower middle class, acquiring, if they were lucky, enough status to move to one of the more nondescript suburbs, and losing their strongest virtue—the group solidarity that had made them, in high school, a force to be reckoned with. It is appropriate that the finale of *Grease* celebrates that solidarity, with the saving of its heroine, and the reclamation of its hero, from the clutches of respectability. . . . (pp. 1-2)

Grease is in possession of a truth, one of its strongest, about the media and how they worked on us. This is of course best seen in its superb, sharp-eared songs. The mus-ical basis of 50's rock is fractured by comedy quite early in the enumeration of "Those Magic Changes." After that it is a matter of astonishment how many delicate subforms there were to the songs of the period, and how many dif-ferent comic approaches Jim Jacobs and Warren Casey use to pin them down: Imitative *hommage* ("Rock 'n Roll Party Queen"), outright burlesque ("Sandra Dee"), ironic, look-the-other-way dirty joke ("Mooning"), character satire ("Freddy, My Love"), improbable-situation parody ("Beauty School Dropout"), and, best of all to my taste, the quiet revelation of fact as an antidote to the sentimen-tality of the originals. Take "It's Raining on Prom Night":

> I don't even have my corsage, oh gee,
> It fell down a sewer with my sister's I.D.

Truthful, admittedly, but pretty squalid. Small. Petty. Not the deep sentimental tragedy you will find in a prototypical "serious" song like "Tell Tommy I Miss Him" or "Teen Angel." This song is easier to laugh at than some of the others because it is more firmly distanced—not a report of something that actually happens to our heroine, just a con-venient index to her momentary emotions.

"There Are Worse Things I Could Do" seems a harder case, momentarily: What is this ostensibly serious, "dra-matic" song doing in the middle of this rumbustious, frivo-lous show? But after all, it, too, is a parody. The serious-ness of the situation is equalled only by its smallness: "Even though the neighborhood / Thinks I'm trashy and no good . . ." Here again the point is not sympathy, or dra-matic urgency, but history: This feeling, now obsolete, was recorded during the 1950's. Make of it what you will. The greatest achievement of *Grease* . . . is its perfect deadpan objectivity about everything in it: A d.a. haircut, a new gui-tar, a missed period, a falsetto backup group, a preposter-ously accurate hand-jive. It is a loving, funny, museum of where we were, perhaps even, when we scream and stomp our feet at it, a gentle attempt to exorcize the parts of our-selves we left back there, a tribute to the many small, stupid things that happened to us during "the decade when nothing happened." If, after we see it, after we have our hearty laugh and our tender glow at the memory of where we were, we scream silently, "How did we end up here?", or shudder at the memory of the greasers we left back there —if we do that, it is entirely up to us. The authors have left the case open, and the depths are there only if you want to dig for them—it's equally easy to have a good time and look no further. But we might as well face the fact that sooner or later we all have to say "goodbye to Sandra Dee," and to her cohorts in the field of illusion. *Grease* is a warm, laugh-loaded, relaxing way to get disillusioned, as honest in its comedy as any great musical of the 20's or 30's. So don't let anybody tell you they don't make shows like that anymore. (pp. 2-4)

Michael Feingold, "Goodbye to Sandra Dee" (copyright © 1972 by Winter House Ltd.), in Grease *by Jim Jacobs and Warren Casey, Winter House Ltd., 1972, pp. 1-4.*

ROY HOLLINGWORTH

Grease offers a good stench of cheeseburgers, soda, flick-knives and floosies, stocking tops and schools hops, and rrrrrrockanroll. And hey, that can't be bad!

I always approach rock musicals with a vast amount of suspicion. . . .

But let me tell you this maybe is the first valid rock 'n' roll musical. The reason is very simple. It's all about rock 'n' roll. It's authentic, it's brilliantly written, and the cast is just NEAT. Take all that and add hilarious humour and I reckons you've got entertainment.

It's a pretty wet storyline, but that couldn't have been better for something that's supposed to mirror the wild scenes that went on behind teachers' back at High School Circa 1957. . . .

The teen-talk is just superb, fast and slick, and bitchy as you like. The girls look like sisters of sin. Hate to think what would melt in their mouths.

And the guys—just incredible. There's Danny Zuko, . . . Sonny La Teirra, and Kenickie. Cuban heeled winkles, tight jeans, slicked back hair, and slicked-back conversation. They're not caricature roles—guys like this did exist.

The book, music and lyrics were written by Jim Jacobs and Warren Casey, and you've got to hand it to them—they pinned it all right down to the last onion on the last burger.

Roy Hollingworth, "The Roar of the Grease," in Melody Maker *(© IPC Business Press Ltd.), July 7, 1973, p. 16.*

M. E. Kerr
1928(?)-

(Pseudonym of Marijane Meaker) American novelist. Although she has only been writing young adult fiction since 1972, Kerr has firmly established herself as one of that genre's most popular authors. Her novels explore such contemporary topics as breaking free from parental guidance and misguidance and the recognition and acceptance of human fallibility. These concerns are presented with poignancy and humor, in novels that have been praised for their credibility and relevance. Some critics, however, look with disfavor on Kerr's contemporaneity, accusing her of superficiality with trendy plots and flippant dialogue. Kerr began her literary career as a mystery writer for adults, publishing her first mystery novel, *Whisper His Sin*, under the name Vin Packer, the first of several pseudonyms she has used. While writing steadily, Kerr began to teach creative writing on a volunteer basis at Manhattan's Central High. The background and characters in her first young adult novel, *Dinky Hocker Shoots Smack!*, were based on this experience. She discovered the stimulus for her latest novel, *Gentlehands*, in her brother, a former World War II Navy pilot and Vietnam veteran who had difficulty in readjusting to peacetime. In an area where authors often stereotype teenagers' concerns, Kerr is noteworthy for her presentation of realistic situations and responses.

Don't be put off by the title [*Dinky Hocker Shoots Smack!*]; this is not another anti-drug sermon and in fact Dinky does not shoot smack nor is she about to; she only makes the announcement, in Day-Glo graffiti throughout her Brooklyn Heights "community," so that her do-gooding mother who's into rehabilitating addicts will give her some attention. Refreshingly the only junkie in the cast is not a straw heavy constructed to bear the cautionary burden of pity or scorn, but a credible, humorously immature minor character—and an even greater relief from recent YA typecasting is the brilliant, fiercely reactionary P. John Knight, maligned by all the liberal Heights parents who should be pondering his favorite quotation, "don't understand me too quickly." Mrs. Hocker, who sabotages P. John's relationship with the overweight Dinky and his attempts to help her get thin, is in fact the only heavy here, but if mother's smug insensitivity is a little thick she's real enough to rouse your fury all the same. Dinky herself is a troubled girl who is never at a loss for flip and brittle words ("the meek inherit the shaft," she tells a black child she's working with at her mother's neighborhood center), and her

friend Tucker who tells the story has some wry lines and risibly recognizable problems of his own. Unlike the tiresome bulk of Now novels, this view of the contemporary scene . . . is neither hostile nor hortatory nor exploitative. Instead Kerr's honesty, evident respect and consistently on-target wit will keep Dinky's and Tucker's contemporaries laughing and nodding agreement. (pp. 1152-53)

Kirkus Reviews (copyright © 1972 The Kirkus Service, Inc.), October 1, 1972.

JEAN STAFFORD

["Dinky Hocker Shoots Smack!"] is not only a revolting and cryptic title . . . ; it is, as well, a put-on. Dinky, whose perfectly reasonable real name is Susan, is not a hophead but a lunchhead, and hers is the story of the ups and downs of weight-watching with her obese and mossback boyfriend, P. John Knight, whose admiration for the late Senator Joe McCarthy is not less credible than this gobbet of dialogue:

> "Does heroin give you pimples?" Tucker asked.
>
> 'All junk does. Junkies love sweets," Dinky said authoritatively. "I never met a junkie who didn't verge on bulbous acne."

The publicity people at Harper & Row are so struck with the verve and know-how of their heroine that they begin their flap copy with this come-on. I hope the original Harper Brothers have long ago become insentient mycelium. (p. 190)

Jean Stafford, in The New Yorker *(© 1972 by The New Yorker Magazine, Inc.; reprinted by permission of Russell & Volkening, Inc., as agents for the author), December 2, 1972.*

DALE CARLSON

The pages rush by in ["Dinkey Hocker Shoots Smack!"] by M. E. Kerr, who has an ear for catching the sound of real people talking and a heart for finding the center of real people's problems. . . .

The problems to be coped with are real, contemporary in a contemporary world. The writer is sensitive not only to the dialogue, but to the themes of today's preoccupations. You get the feeling it could all be happening next door.

This is a brilliantly funny book that will make you cry. It is full of wit and wisdom and an astonishing immediacy that comes from spare, honest writing. Many writers try to characterize the peculiar poignancy and the terrible hilarity of adolescence. Few succeed as well as M. E. Kerr in this timely, compelling and entertaining novel.

Dale Carlson, "Smack," in The New York Times Book Review (© 1973 by The New York Times Company; reprinted by permission), February 11, 1973, p. 8.

DIANE GERSONI-STAVN

Despite its pretentious title, self-conscious, first-person style, and some caricatures, [If I Love You, Am I Trapped Forever?] is an interesting, entertaining novel. Alan Bennett—a handsome, popular, Protestant jock going steady with a beautiful cheerleader—anticipates a glorious senior year in high school. Then ugly, Jewish, unathletic Duncan Stein transfers in and unexpectedly *becomes* in, as do his passion for poetry and belief in unrequited love. Going steady—and Alan—are suddenly out.... [Alan] can't decide if love is the warmth of going steady or the excitement of a brief encounter, a comfortable feeling for a contemporary or admiration for someone older. Can love be distinguished from human weakness or need? Is a strong person one who pulls out of an unsatisfying marriage or who works to make it better? When is parental love selfish? At the end of the story, Duncan falls in love with Alan's former steady; having now experienced rather than intellectualized love, Duncan decides he wants to go steady too. Ephemeral love as a school fad dies, but Alan retains his new-found awareness of its power and appeal. The turnabout's a bit too pat but still acceptable and, fortunately for readers, there are more questions than answers. (p. 75)

Diane Gersoni-Stavn, in School Library Journal (reprinted from the April, 1973 issue of School Library Journal, published by R. R. Bowker Co. A Xerox Corporation; copyright © 1973), April, 1973.

CAROLYN BALDUCCI

Had M. E. Kerr restrained her literary and academic impulses, "If I Love You, Am I Trapped Forever?" would have been a first-rate young adult novel. Her book is like a Möbius strip onto which are stapled bits of World Lit, Pop-Psych, letters, classified ads, writing style tips and news items. It poses the eternal rhetorical question: "What Is Love?" yet supplies only the basis for a one-dimensional reply....

Alan spends [a weekend] with his father who had run off with a woman he despises as he despises himself. This is a shattering encounter for Alan that forces him to probe deeper into the meaning of "Love." However, judging from what kids fantasize about parents from an early age onward, the effect of this meeting on a 16-year-old boy (presumably aware of similar genetic matter existing in his own chromosomes) should have been more profound than making him become impossibly vague with his girlfriend. Thus, the boy's involvement with an older woman upon his return home is not as unconnected as the book would like us to believe. Alan—unlike Sonny in "The Last Picture Show" or Ben in "The Graduate"—does not attempt to have a physical relationship with Mrs. Stein. He has no opportunity, therefore, of resolving his emotional turmoil:

indeed, putting emotions into action is something Alan seems no longer capable of accomplishing.

At the very end, Alan's breaking down and weeping when he hears that his "ideal" has run off with a man he deems unworthy does not portend a happy heterosexual future. Alan's decision to become a writer suggest that while love may come in as many varieties as there are people, those who are emotionally castrated are those who understand Romance the best. (p. 8)

Carolyn Balducci, in The New York Times Book Review (© 1973 by The New York Times Company; reprinted by permission), September 16, 1973.

The idiom [of "Dinky Hocker Shoots Smack!"], and probably the situation too, is wholly American; we could do with a British Dinky, but numerous attempts at realistic writing about adolescents have lacked Miss Kerr's sureness of touch.

[In her "On Children's Literature," Isabelle] Jan reckons that three-quarters of the novels written for boys and girls since 1850 tell the story of a lost or orphaned child in search of a family, and this novel too is about rejection. But the theme has become subtler, and not only because children are less easily orphaned these days: Mrs Hocker never says, like the mother in Victor Hugo's "Les Miserables", that she is sick of her child, but, in late-twentieth-century style, she fails to communicate.

But the real joy of "Dinky Hocker" is that Miss Kerr is knocking this jargon-cum-way-of-life: the parents' efforts to "adjust", to "communicate", to "participate", are seen through quite clearly by their teenage children, who are yet never repellent, misunderstood martyrs. The narrative never fails to be funny. Miss Kerr is also taking a swipe at parental preoccupation with drugs. "People," says young Tucker of Dinky, "who don't shoot smack have problems too". But best of all, Miss Kerr is not of the all-too-large school of authors who believe you achieve realism in children's novels by injecting sex and then lose their nerve and superimpose a moral fable. Tucker is cooler about sex than his parents, who are constantly telling him he is too young to go steady and longing to be contradicted. At the end of a cross-examination about his girl friend, he gives the perfectly adolescent answer: "I'm waiting for the fall". Time, Miss Kerr so brilliantly understands, looks different when it is on your side. (pp. 59-60)

The Economist (© The Economist Newspaper Limited, 1973), December 29, 1973.

MARY M. BURNS

Small-town Vermont is the backdrop against which two bright, brittle teenagers, both misfits in their disparate social orders, gain insight into themselves and their families.... A blending of sophistication and innocence develops the characters [of The Son of Someone Famous] as credible teenagers, despite the soap-opera banalities of the plot. Unfortunately, the whole is less than the sum of its parts, for characters and situations are not as fully integrated as in Dinky Hocker Shoots Smack!; although the dialogue and description are superb, the incidents seem patched together from speculation about a life style sensed but not experienced. (pp. 384-85)

Mary M. Burns, in The Horn Book Magazine *(copyright © 1974 by The Horn Book, Inc., Boston), August, 1974.*

JEAN STAFFORD

Heretofore, although I have recognized the ability of M. E. Kerr, I have not liked her novels. But her new one, "The Son of Someone Famous" . . . , entertained me greatly. . . . Miss Kerr's pace is brisk, the characters are distinct and are faithful to their individual charms and quirks, the wisecracks are uncontrived and they range from good to first-rate, the agonies of loneliness and self-doubt, of jealousy and of resentment are recognizable and are not pummelled with exposition, and the virtues of compassion, forgiveness, and loyalty are straightforward and have no frills and furbelows attached. (pp. 187-88)

Jean Stafford, in The New Yorker *(© 1974 by The New Yorker Magazine, Inc.; reprinted by permission of Russell & Volkening, Inc., as agents for the author), December 2, 1974.*

MRS. JOHN G. GRAY

Gauze, voile, organdy, net, chiffon, silk—somewhere there's a word that will give the reader the precise feel, one that says it all about [*Is That You, Miss Blue?*].

The everyday happenings of a typical "climber's" girl's school and the hodgepodge of characters enrolled are misted over by the "mist-ical" Miss Blue, a teacher who truly waits for the Lord's knock on her bedroom door. . . . Miss Kerr can dig deep and scurry around in the loneliest, saddest corners of a reader's soul and always come up with a perceptive thought for teenagers to mull over. (p. 49)

Mrs. John G. Gray, in Best Sellers *(copyright © 1975 Helen Dwight Reid Educational Foundation), May, 1975.*

LAVINIA RUSS

In time, M. E. Kerr may write something that's not real, touching, poignant, funny and marvelous. And, in time, Gibraltar may crumble. . . . Her books get better; ["Love Is a Missing Person"] is the finest yet. . . . The ultimate lesson here is that we are never so brave or right as we think and that we hurt others more than we can bear to admit. (p. 58)

Lavinia Russ, in Publishers Weekly *(reprinted from the June 30, 1975, issue of* Publishers Weekly *by permission of the critic, published by R. R. Bowker Company, a Xerox company; copyright © 1975 by Xerox Corporation), June 30, 1975.*

MARY M. BURNS

Much of [*Is That You Miss Blue?*'s] power is derived from its delineation of character while consistently maintaining the young narrator's perspective. As seen through Flanders' eyes, the conflicting personalities are Dickensian types, skillfully limned but exaggerated. And the author achieves a balance between pathos and humor in documenting Miss Blue's disintegration. In a spare, wryly funny, genuinely moving book, M. E. Kerr surpasses all of her previous achievements. (p. 365)

Mary M. Burns, in The Horn Book Magazine *(copyright © 1975 by The Horn Book, Inc., Boston), August, 1975.*

ZENA SUTHERLAND

While Suzy Slade, the fifteen-year-old who tells the story [of *Love is a Missing Person*], is a strongly delineated character, she functions primarily as the commentator on the problems of the other people with whom she is involved. . . . This is one of Kerr's best, honest and poignant and perceptive. She gives no easy answers to the intricate problems in the lives of her characters, offers no lulling conclusions. The characterization and the dialogue are convincing and trenchant; while the ending is (as it was in *Is That You, Miss Blue?*) left open. . . . it is the right ending, but what is left is not bitterness, it is an aching compassion. (p. 48)

Zena Sutherland, in Bulletin of the Center for Children's Books *(© 1975 by the University of Chicago; all rights reserved), November, 1975.*

MARY KINGSBURY

I'm not going to describe in detail the very personal things that take place. . . . I'm not writing this book for a bunch of voyeurs. . . . It's a story about people and how their minds work. . . . What's fascinating about people is, no one thinks or acts the same way. I am writing about the why of people.

Alan Bennett's Apologia in *If I Love You, Am I Trapped Forever?* . . . describes M. E. Kerr's purpose in each of her five novels. If, as Irene Hunt suggests, the strain of excellence to be looked for in an outstanding book is the author's ability to clarify "some problem of the human family, some aspect of human behavior, some quality of the human heart or mind or conscience" and the author's "sensitivity to the problem he has perceived, the credibility and grace with which he has recorded what he has perceived," the novels of M. E. Kerr can be judged as among the most outstanding being published today. For in each of them and with varying degrees of "credibility and grace," she attempts to clarify the why of people. Her willingness to confront serious issues coupled with her artistic abilities lifts her novels above the myriad problem-novels that have little to recommend them but their topicality. Not that Kerr's novels fail to reflect the age in which they are written. They do reflect the 1970s, but they also offer the reader much more than a commentary on contemporary problems. They introduce themes that will continue to puzzle mankind in the future just as they have troubled him in the past. (pp. 288-89)

Reading all [Kerr's] novels brings the realization that a common theme appears in each of them, a theme that makes one of the strongest comments on the human condition in literature for young people today. The author is concerned with love, its presence and, more commonly, its absence in the lives of her characters. Virginia Woolf noted in *The Common Reader* . . . that writers are disappointing if they are concerned with the body but not with the spirit. Kerr gave early assurance that she was not going to fall into that trap. The why of people can, in most instances, be explained in terms of who or what they love and whether they receive the love they need from others. The spiritual element that Virginia Woolf found wanting in much of modern fiction is not lacking in the novels of M. E. Kerr.

A theme in all her novels becomes the title of her latest— *Love Is A Missing Person*. . . . In her first book, *Dinky*

Hocker Shoots Smack! . . . , Dinky fails to get the love and attention she needs from her parents until she makes an extraordinary effort to communicate her feelings. . . .

The theme of love is less well defined in Kerr's third and least successful novel, *The Son of Someone Famous.* . . . Adam, called "A. J." by his father, has allowed his identity to be defined by his father's. The book raises the problem all adolescents must solve to achieve maturity. An individual can never become a person in his own right if he is always living up to the expectations of those who love him. (p. 289)

Is That You, Miss Blue? . . . is a tightly constructed novel that makes a harsh but truthful statement about man's inhumanity to his fellows. The book strips away the veneer of righteousness that adorns many who are, in fact, inwardly honeycombed with hypocrisy. Miss Blue's open display of love for Christ leads to her dismissal from the ostensibly Christian boarding school. The ultimate irony is that in a school dedicated to religious principles and practices, a teacher is dismissed for being too fervent in her convictions. Miss Blue loves too much, and her ways of expressing love are unacceptable to those in authority. By saying that the school is a microcosm of the world, Kerr implies that the injustices perpetrated there are only smaller versions of the injustices in the larger world.

Suzy Slade, the narrator of M. E. Kerr's latest book, feels alienated from her mother and unwanted by her father. For her, love is a missing person. Gwen Spring's former sweetheart has been missing from her life for twenty-five years, yet she continues to love him. Suzy's sister, Chicago, falls in love and literally becomes a missing person. The author, as in all her books, is preoccupied with love, the varied relationships it engenders, and man's inability to give and to receive the love that might be expected in such relationships. For most of her characters, in fact, love is a missing person.

In addition to this common theme, the novels share a pattern of elements and literary devices. Each introduces at least one contemporary issue such as mental illness, drug addiction, anti-Semitism, alcoholism, and racism. Each portrays the development of adolescent sexuality, and several offer insight into adult sexuality as well. Adolescents in all the books begin to view their parents more realistically and with greater understanding. Sharply drawn minor characters abound in all the books; frequent use is made of irony, humor, and quotations from literary sources.

The world Kerr creates is more than an adolescent world, for it includes adult characters who are far different from the unsympathetic ones usually portrayed in much realistic fiction. Moreover, she displays great skill in conveying the complexities of the parent-child relationship. (p. 290)

In *Love Is A Missing Person*, Suzy Slade . . . begins to see her father in a different perspective. "I'd never questioned his behavior in my whole life. . . . Now I just wondered about him, not as Daddy, and not as the man in *Who's Who.* . . . But Barry Slade, the individual. Did I even like him anymore?"

Suzy's ponderings point up an obvious strength in the Kerr novels, one that sets them apart from the many contemporary novels nearly devoid of well-developed adult characters. A reader of the majority of books written for young adults learns what motivates the adolescent characters but seldom learns what makes the adult characters act as they do. The adult characters are so fully realized, however, that readers acquire some idea of the pressures on adults in American society. The books offer a series of "possible futures" for their readers, a veritable gallery of "there but for the grace of God" vignettes. Flan Brown speculates, for example, about what changed the popular "Nesty" into the shunned Miss Blue. "Could it happen to anyone? To me? And what would it take to make it happen?" (pp. 291-92)

The only flaw in Kerr's depiction of her characters is that they never elicit from the reader a complete sense of identification. The adolescent narrators, for example, are not as memorable as several of the adult characters, possibly because the young people act as observers of the actions of more colorful characters. This is not to say that the reader cannot identify with Kerr's adolescent characters. Tucker's fears about his social acceptability, Flan's feeling of guilt about Miss Blue, and Suzy Slade's disillusionment with her father and ambiguous feelings about her mother can be shared. But rarely, if ever, does a character totally capture both the interest and emotions of the reader. Her characterizations appeal more to the head than to the heart, but they are, nevertheless, fascinating.

Consider Evelyn Slade in *Love Is A Missing Person*. To dismiss her as "the alcoholic mother" is to miss one of the most complex characters in recent fiction. She relies on her bottle of I. W. Harper whenever she is under pressure: "That was Mother's courage." In the solarium, decorated with yellow and white wicker furniture, she wears a dress from her yellow and white solarium collection. This is a woman who refuses to join an exclusive club because it does not admit Jews and who says that "bravery isn't tested during big moments but in little, everyday ones, in the way one faces people and faces up to problems with them." In the furor over the stolen painting, she tells Suzy to go to her job at the library. "'In a crisis . . . you do the same as you do every day, as far as possible. That's what holds things together. Routine is fiber, and in a crisis, fiber binds.'" Yet this wise woman later makes a fool of herself trying to get back a husband she doesn't really want; she is an adult who combines a high degree of perceptiveness with a goodly share of human foibles.

Contrast the elegant Evelyn Slade with Suzy's friend, Gwen Spring, a throwback to the 1940s in her saddle shoes and white socks, a memorial to unrequited love. When Susie says she wishes she could write something as beautiful as "Wild Nights," Miss Spring tells her to "'[w]ish instead that you could *feel* anything so beautiful as that poem.'" Another time she tells Suzy that life isn't answers, but questions. She admits that she has wasted herself in a "'futile fantasy. I grew wrinkles from dreaming. Wrinkles should come from living, not imagining that you are.'"

Evelyn Slade and Gwen Spring are examples of a literary device evident in all of M. E. Kerr's novels, a device used in other books, such as Ruth Sawyer's *Roller Skates* . . . and Louise Fitzhugh's *Harriet the Spy.* . . . [These characters] present a range of views on life and the human dilemma through their own statements or quotations from others. . . . Quotations from a variety of sources ranging from the Bible, Shakespeare, and Dostoevsky to Tennessee Williams, Norman Mailer, and the Beatles are integrated into Kerr's books in a number of ways—as part of an English class activity, in a letter, or in notes on bulletin boards. No other contemporary writer exposes young readers to so much material for reflection.

Another discernible pattern is formed by the balancing of two opposing sets of values—P. John's conservative views offset by the liberal views of his father and the Hockers, the views on atheism of Cardmaker and Flan's father countered by Flan's own ponderings, the two views of life represented by Brenda Belle's mother and her aunt, the contrasting life styles of Tucker's father and his Uncle Jingle. M. E. Kerr offers her readers a choice. One takes from these books a genuine sense of the ambiguity of life and the difficulty, if not the impossibility, of pinning down definite answers. "'Life isn't answers.... It's questions.'" Nor is there an answer that fits all people. "'The right way is what you grow to learn is right for you.'" Young people, in reading these novels, have the opportunity to think about their responsibility for defining the old people they will become. Always there is the sense, however, that we cannot control our lives entirely—that, as Alan's mother cautioned, our lives are influenced by other people and by circumstances over which we have little or no control. Can fiction become more realistic than that? (pp. 292-94)

Matthew Arnold's definition of literature as a "'criticism of life'" points up the seriousness of the literary endeavor. For Arnold it was not enough that a work of literature provide diversion. Nor, seemingly, is it enough for Irene Hunt with her criterion that an outstanding book must provide a perceptive commentary on the human condition. Judged by these standards, the novels of M. E. Kerr stand out from the general run of contemporary books. With style, wit, and compassion she describes adolescents coming to the realization that those they love will, more often than not, fail to live up to their expectations. Her concern with themes that have universal significance, her ability to create a variety of characters, her sensitivity to the sufferings of others, her humor and, finally, her use of irony all contribute to the power of her books. She has a clever style that never offends by being too clever. Moreover, she is subtle; where others are heavy-handed, she is light, sharp, and deft—using a rapier but never a sledge hammer.

Having published five books in four years, Kerr demonstrates the capability for sustained effort that is necessary to achieve a lasting place in literature. Time alone will determine the longevity of these novels, but it is worth noting that the last two are the best of the five. Short of writing a masterpiece, an author can establish a claim to fame by producing a number of superior books. M. E. Kerr is well on her way to that goal. (p. 295)

> *Mary Kingsbury, "The Why of People: The Novels of M. E. Kerr," in* The Horn Book Magazine *(copyright © 1977 by the Horn Book, Inc., Boston), June, 1977, pp. 288-95.*

JANET P. BENESTAD

From the title [of *I'll Love You When You're More Like Me*], this novel ... sounds like just another "story with a message." Well, it is. The message, simply stated, is that "you have to step out of line to give the world something special." Unfortunately, the story used to portray this sound moral is trite, not unlike a half-dozen recent movies, and it is hardly inspiring....

Ms. Kerr is obviously trying sympathetically to depict a very disconcerting event in many a teenager's life—the realization that he is ashamed of his parents and wants to be anything but like them. I think, however, that such a subtle problem warrants more than the glib, avant-garde dialogue and facile solutions offered in *I'll Love You*. And I believe that the young adult audience to whom this book is addressed deserves better heroes than Sabra and Wally. (p. 294)

> *Janet P. Benestad, in* Best Sellers *(copyright © 1977 Helen Dwight Reid Educational Foundation), December, 1977.*

JEAN F. MERCIER

Kerr's earlier novels, splendid as they are, seem like a prelude to ["Gentlehands"]. It's a marvel of understatement, diamond insights, irony and compassion. (p. 81)

> *Jean F. Mercier, in* Publisher's Weekly *(reprinted from the January 9, 1978, issue of* Publishers Weekly, *by permission of the critic, published by R. R. Bowker Company, a Xerox company; copyright © 1978 by Xerox Corporation), January 9, 1978.*

ALLEEN PACE NILSEN

In thinking about Kerr's writing, I am reminded of what Richard Peck said in a speech for the Adolescent Literature Assembly a couple of years ago. He observed that what many teenagers like in their light reading is *unreality* masked as *realism*. Kerr is a genius at providing this combination.

The unreality in *I'll Love You When You're More Like Me* centers around an unlikely combination of characters and events....

Kerr uses several techniques to make [the unlikely] seem believable. The book is written in first person with chapters from Wally alternating with chapters from Sabra. It is the clever dialogues and the flip comments that give readers the feeling that Kerr is one of them. But even this isn't really the way teenagers talk. Instead it is the way teenagers fondly imagine themselves to talk. There is probably one kid in every crowd who occasionally comes close. But as for the rest of them it is only in their I-wish-I-would-have-said daydreams that they sound like the characters in Kerr's books.

Nevertheless Kerr's exaggerations all fit together, and her books are undeniably fun to read. Her affable style gets readers involved so that they feel like cheering the absurdities. (p. 99)

> *Alleen Pace Nilsen, in* English Journal *(copyright © 1978 by the National Council of Teachers of English), February, 1978.*

RICHARD BRADFORD

The 16-year-old hero of ["Gentlehands"]—and he is a hero, in the only ways he can be—is William Raymond "Buddy" Boyle.... [His] parents are not just lower-middle class but resentfully snobbish about it; and he is in love with Skye Pennington, who summers with her parents near Montauk and possesses wealth and beauty in amounts F. Scott Fitzgerald might have hesitated to describe.

Buddy is tall and handsome, which explains Skye's interest

in him, but he's diffident and hopeless in the presence of her sophistication. . . .

Overcoming this social and financial gulf is the lesser of Buddy's problems. The larger one concerns his grandfather, and it is insuperable.

His grandfather, the mysterious and wealthy Frank Trenker, alienated from Buddy's mother, welcomes visits from his gauche grandson, and impresses even Skye with his charm, his wisdom, his kindness, his easy and tasteful use of wealth and his nice sense of civilization. Buddy, not entirely free of snobbery himself, is delighted to have at least one presentable relative to show off to Skye. Frank Trenker—multilingual, an opera buff, a man who cooks for and feeds the wild animals near his large house—is certainly presentable. Without making an issue of it, Trenker begins to steer and shape Buddy's mind and his future.

A summer guest of the Penningtons is Nick De Lucca, an investigative reporter whose young cousin was among the Roman Jews murdered at Auschwitz in 1943 by an SS officer known as Gentlehands. (The ironic nickname arose from his custom of taunting Italian prisoners with a recording of Mario's aria from "Tosca," "O dolci mani," before sending them to their deaths.) De Lucca's anti-Nazi research has led him to Frank Trenker, whom he accuses in a detailed newspaper article of being the infamous Gentlehands.

Buddy refuses to believe it. Skye refuses to believe it. The reader—this reader, anyway—refuses to believe it. . . .

De Lucca's documentation is flawless, however. Trenker is —was—Gentlehands. Before he can be questioned by the Immigration and Naturalization Service he disappears, leaving a note for Buddy: "I live in the present between two unfathomable clouds, what was and what will be."

Buddy is the last person to accept the incomprehensible fact of his grandfather's identity, but at the end, on a final visit to Trenker's empty, vandalized house, he accepts the truth, as he must.

The incriminating newspaper article is filled with horrible detail—strong stuff for young people; strong stuff for anyone. But Nazism, that ghastly pit of the human soul, was real, and a young generation of Americans knows of it only vaguely, if at all. There are muted connections in the book between the airy, thoughtless anti-Semitism of Skye and her crowd and the bloody nightmare of Auschwitz that haunts this pocket of the modern world.

Miss Kerr's book is important and useful as an introduction to the grotesque character of the Nazi period, as well as to the paradoxes that exist in the heart of man. Her ear for youthful American speech is superb; her understanding of youthful feelings, and youth's occasional lack of them, is sure. If she fails to explain thoroughly the alarming enigma of Frank Trenker's double life, it is only because there is, finally, no explanation possible.

> *Richard Bradford, "The Nazi Legacy: Undoing History," in* The New York Times Book Review *(© 1978 by the New York Times Company; reprinted by permission), April 30, 1978, p. 30.*

VIRGINIA WILDER

High-school student Wallace Witherspoon, Jr., heir-apparent to directorship of funerals in Seaville, Long Island,

and Sabra St. Amour, teenage goddess of daytime television soap opera, spend a star-crossed summer getting to know themselves through each other and through the other wildly overdrawn characters in [*I'll Love You When You're More Like Me*]. Nasty Harriet Hren has used "female" tactics to get herself engaged to Wally. Wally's gay friend, Charlie, has just come out of the closet. Sabra's mother, Madame St. Amour, is vicariously living out her own aborted stage career through Sabra. . . .

The theme, "I'll love you when you are more like me," is . . . borne out by all relationships except the one existing between Wally and Sabra. . . .

Wally and Sabra share happy endings, each taking active steps towards the particular future they yearn for. Charlie, in the meantime (although not hit by a car or otherwise killed off as gay men tend to be in adolescent fiction), chooses to bury himself forever in a small town where no gay life-style is possible. So while we finally have a book with a nice straight-boy, gay-boy friendship, the future promises a sex life only to straight Wally. (p. 14)

> *Virginia Wilder, in* Interracial Books for Children Bulletin *(reprinted by permission of* Interracial Books for Children Bulletin, *1841 Broadway, New York, N.Y. 10023), Vol. 9, No. 3, 1978.*

BRIGITTE WEEKS

As always M. E. Kerr writes sensitively and catches precisely the agonies of growing up, but she lapses dangerously into stereotypes [in *Gentlehands*]: the policeman's son is *too* naive and the rich girl a little too monogrammed. The plot then thickens to involve an escaped Nazi turned from monster into animal lover, invoking a further host of moral issues. The story is overburdened and slightly unlikely, which is a pity, because despite it all Buddy Boyle is an interesting and not unsubtle character. (p. E4)

> *Brigitte Weeks, in* Book World—The Washington Post *(© 1978, The Washington Post), July 9, 1978.*

PATRICIA RUNK SWEENEY

The imprisonment of one's true self in a shell of one's own making is a pervasive theme in [*Dinky Hocker Shoots Smack!*] and its five successors. Though each of [Kerr's] novels tell a different story, the same concern for self-realization—a concern shared, we may assume, by every adolescent who reads these books—dominates both plot and subplot. And overall the message is an optimistic one: many of her characters do succeed in releasing the person shut up inside them, as Susan is shut up inside "Dinky," or Priscilla inside "Chicago" (in *Love is a Missing Person*). And even for some of the apparent failures, there is hope. At least they have become aware of the possibility of change and they have gained insight into their own identity.

Of course, not all change is for the better. Kerr's characters have free will, and they must ultimately decide whether they are really "grabbing the reins" . . . and "stretching" toward the ideal . . . or simply toward something different. But often they can only find out by trial and error. Revolt for its own sake may not seem much better than passivity, but some of Kerr's characters must "act out" before they understand what they are really disturbed about. When Carolyn Cardmaker, for example, starts an atheists' club in *Is That You, Miss Blue?* she is rebelling not against religion but against a world that hypocritically exalts religion while allowing most of its clergymen (including her father) to live on the edge of indigence. Since her quarrel is really with society, she returns, in the last pages to the novel, to her church and her family. But she is more aware, at the end, of the "system" that has beaten her down. . . . Progress, Kerr shows us, cannot always be measured in a straight line. (pp. 37-8)

Like all Kerr's work, [*Dinky Hocker Shoots Smack!*] deals with the many different forms of escapism to which we are all subject at one time or another—obesity, alcoholism, psychosomatic disorders—and with the prejudices and hypocrisies we often adopt. Drug addiction is just a particularly dramatic example, a metaphor used to bring Kerr's readers face to face with their own dependencies. And in every instance, in her work, the recourse is the same: one must take charge of one's own life.

All the novels follow the same basic structure: two plots centering around two characters, one ordinary and afraid to diverge from the norm . . . , the other in some way extraordinary and trying to reach a truce with the rest of the world. . . . The two plots often split off into one involving a romantic relationship and the other involving relationships between parents and children. With the exception of *Dinky Hocker,* all are written in the first person, and two, *The Son of Someone Famous* and *I'll Love You When You're More Like Me,* employ a variation of that technique, the double first person. The two alternating voices produce a more complex point of view and help to create dramatic irony.

Certain motifs are repeatedly used in Kerr's work to express the state of mind of her characters. Food is one; clothing is another. A third and particularly interesting one is her use of names. Many of Kerr's characters have strange names or nicknames, and explanations about their genesis appear frequently. The characters' names express the way they feel about themselves, illuminate their relationships with their parents, and allow them to adopt and reject various *personae.* Like P. John, children drop names to rebel against their parents, and re-assume them when they've reconciled. Mrs. Hocker attempts to wield power over her daughter by calling her "Dinky." Mothers' maiden names keep coming up, perhaps to remind children how unfair it is for women to lose a part of their identity by the simple act of marrying. It is one symbolic example of how, "if I love you, I am trapped forever." Characters also use their mothers' maiden names as alternative identities for themselves; having other available names gives them some psychic room to grow. The name changing expresses Kerr's overall theme: the struggle to define and articulate who one is, and it also makes the point that identities are always shifting. What is important is that characters feel the freedom to fiddle with what may seem unchangeable, to recognize that they are never really "stuck" unless they choose to be.

But one cannot change unless the alternatives are more appealing than what one has, and unless the action is really getting at the heart of the problem. (pp. 38-9)

[Ideologies] are generally suspect in Kerr's books. Emotion is a much more effective motivator. In *Dinky Hocker* especially, Kerr shows that ideological allegiances often create smokescreens which, under the right circumstances, can easily be put aside. What can't be put aside and what must guide change are the strong feelings characters have for one another. Chicago Slade [in *Love Is a Missing Person*] tells her sister Suzy that love can make a "missing person" of you, a "shed skin" of your old, false self. . . .

Love also helps Kerr's characters to understand the needs and choices of those around them. Thus Chicago's love for a brilliant but poor black student, Roger Coe, makes her tolerant of her Father's infatuation with a nineteen year old former cocktail waitress. And the romances in Kerr's books often demand this kind of tolerance, for they are frequently unconventional. She encourages the notion of "chemistry," of following one's instincts. (pp. 39-40)

Perhaps the notion of chemistry and the celebration of the unconventional are important to Kerr because they involve a surrendering of the staid and sensible—the ostensibly easy but often stifling way—and an embracing by each character of something fresh and different, not only in their loved ones but ultimately in themselves. Such risk-taking relationships also make characters feel special, loved not for their *persona,* their conventional role, but for the real person inside themselves. At the risk of oversimplifying, I can say that all Kerr's protagonists are looking for this kind of love—love for the hidden, needy person inside of them. And what they also seek is a love that lets them be. The ideal relationship in a Kerr novel involves each character recognizing the other's strengths and weaknesses, feeling committed because of, or in spite of, those qualities, and being willing to let the other fly free. (p. 40)

While this ideal is most dramatically demonstrated in the romantic aspects of the novels, relationships between parents and children also demand acceptance and a letting go. The problems between parents and children in Kerr's works often stem exactly from the unwillingness of parents to recognize this. The parents find it difficult either to let their children make their own mistakes or to let them solve their own problems. For Kerr makes the subtle point that parents often take solace in their children's problems and the resulting dependencies, so that they frequently create "double binds" for them, urging them to change at the same time that they are covertly pressuring them to maintain old, destructive habits. . . . While both [Dinky's mother and P. John's father in *Dinky Hocker*] claim to be concerned about their children's obesity, they are ambivalent about letting them do something about it. If a rebirth is to occur, the parents want to assist at it themselves. At least then, if they lose their fat children, they can take credit for the metamorphoses. What the children are asking for, though, is something more difficult. They are asking to be loved for what they are. *That* will help them to change.

In her later novels, Kerr's characters deal with situations of increasing complexity and gravity. She shifts focus a bit, moving from the need for change to the point at which her characters must accept who they are and then direct themselves back to the community. . . . While the concerns are not far from those of the earlier works—what does one owe to one's loved ones and what does one owe to oneself—in these later works Kerr is going one step further, stating not only that one has to help oneself, but also that one ultimately has responsibilities toward others. (pp. 41-2)

Progressively, the novels . . . tell us to see and embrace our differences, to take responsibility for ourselves, and then, recognizing our common humanity, to move back toward those around us.

In showing her readers so many patterns of discovery, revolt, and return, M. E. Kerr is providing them with hope and a wonderful relish for the variety in human nature. Wondering why, with her impressive gifts, she did not choose to write for adults, the answer I came up with is that she likes young people better. She is sympathetic to adults, depicting their struggles throughout her books, revealing them not only as bumblers and seekers, but as occasional finders as well. But her strongest sympathies and her greatest hope seem to be with young people. . . . [However] squelched and trampled by life, they have the potential to grow up and out—into something not only bigger but better. (p. 42)

Patricia Runk Sweeney, "Self-discovery and Rediscovery in the Novels of M. E. Kerr," in The Lion and the Unicorn *(copyright © 1978 The Lion and the Unicorn), Fall, 1978, pp. 37-42.*

RUTH CHARNES

[*Gentlehands* is a] slick little tale in which the Holocaust and Nazi exterminators become cheap devices to move the plot forward. Whatever the author's intention, I was infuriated by this book, which seems to give equal weight to the questions of morality raised by the Holocaust and to an unrealistic teen-age romance. It's also hard to tell what the author intends with her anti-Semitic jokes and anti-gay remarks and her stereotypic portrayal of Nick De Lucca who—to further complicate the plot—is apparently gay. The book's glorification of conspicuous consumption and of a very spoiled and bratty young woman were the last straws! The author's "amusing" and witty style and her trendy subject matter no doubt are responsible for her popularity with young readers; it's a great pity that her writings are so devoid of a moral heart. (p. 18)

Ruth Charnes, in Interracial Books for Children Bulletin *(reprinted by permission of* Interracial Books for Children Bulletin, *1841 Broadway, New York, N.Y. 10023), Vol. 9, No. 8, 1978.*

Larry Kettelkamp

1933-

American nonfiction writer and illustrator. Kettelkamp's nonfiction works for young adults spring primarily from his own varied interests and hobbies. A versatile musician, he has written several introductory books to the families of instruments, such as *Flutes, Whistles, and Reeds*. Magic and his fascination with hobby crafts have resulted in books such as *Magic Made Easy* and *Kites*. His most extensive work, however, has been done in the realm of the paranormal, covering subjects as diverse as haunted houses and hypnosis. Kettelkamp is a firm believer in reincarnation and ESP, beliefs that have led to studies like *Sixth Sense* and *Investigating Psychics*. He approaches his topics scientifically, presenting evidence from research studies and experiments as he explains the history of mankind's views of such phenomena. He has often been criticized, however, for promoting his own beliefs instead of giving objective, even-handed studies of as yet unprovable hypotheses. Kettelkamp was formerly a teacher and an art director, and he has illustrated all of his own books as well as the works of authors such as Herbert S. Zim. (See also *Contemporary Authors*, Vols. 29-32, rev. ed., and *Something about the Author*, Vol. 2.)

MARJORIE HALDERMAN

[*Spooky Magic* is] an excellent beginning for the would-be magician. The tricks are simple to perform, and after careful rehearsals to make the stunts smooth and believable any youngster can amaze and entertain his bewildered audience.

Mr. Kettelkamp understands his magic and knows how to explain it to youngsters so that they can follow his instructions, and no expensive or hard-to-obtain props are needed to handle these tricks. (p. 74)

> Marjorie Halderman, in The Saturday Review *(Entire issue copyright 1955 by Saturday Review Associates, Inc.; reprinted with permission), November 5, 1955.*

OLIVE MUMFORD

[In *Singing Strings*, Kettelkamp] has attempted three things: to give a brief history of stringed instruments, to explain the scientific basis for such sound production, and to show how easily simple versions of these instruments can be made. These overlapping purposes result in confusion, as there is little continuity. Fifth and sixth-grade chil-

dren capable of understanding the text would find the glossary of musical terms inadequate. (p. 3009)

> Olive Mumford, in Library Journal *(reprinted from* Library Journal, October 15, 1958; published by R. R. Bowker Co. (a Xerox company); copyright © 1958 by Xerox Corporation), October 15, 1958.*

VIRGINIA HAVILAND

For music appreciation, or hobby and craft fun, [*Drums, Rattles, and Bells*] is an attractive and useful brief book. It gives something of the history and international use of percussion instruments and, also, directions for making noisemakers or rattles, drums of many kinds . . . , keyboard percussion instruments, and bells. Children should readily be intrigued. (p. 172)

> Virginia Haviland, in The Horn Book Magazine *(copyright, 1961, by the Horn Book, Inc., Boston), April, 1961.*

Librarians who have searched in vain for a simple text on how the voice functions—the mechanics of voice production—and the functions of the voice—speech and song, will welcome [*Song, Speech, and Ventriloquism*, a] careful, clearly illustrated explanation. It should be especially helpful to the parent coping with a speech problem, the voice teacher training the young. The section on ventriloquism . . . provides a technical explanation of the phenomenon and additional bait in the form of a sample routine with a dummy. A much-needed book by a well-qualified author. (p. 135)

> Kirkus Service *(copyright © 1967 Virginia Kirkus' Service, Inc.), February 1, 1967.*

PHILIP and PHYLIS MORRISON

The mechanisms of speech and voice are taken apart for readers in the upper grades [in *Song, Speech, and Ventriloquism*], with sensible model experiments and the tricky tests you can make with the black box of your own speech. Then the whole sense of understanding is put to real use, by building up a rationale from which anyone who will try hard, and practice, can become a genuine ventriloquist. There are even a few lines of properly old jokes. Original and intriguing, and possibly a low-key means of improving one's speech. (p. 151)

[*Dreams* is a] refined distillation of modern theories proceeding from simple to complex in a meaningful idiom. [This] demands from any reader the ability to make logical progressions from once-presented information, which restricts the potential audience. (p. 277)

Dreams, a topic important to all of us, is treated somewhat superficially [in "Dreams"]. This account explains their historical, psychological and social significance and gives brief mention to the symbolism used in their interpretation. It is in this last area that the book misses (probably on purpose) the major factor, sex. Because sex—at least to Freudians—is the dominant theme in dream symbolism, the subject (symbolism) might better have been ignored than covered inadequately in deference to the young age group. (p. 52)

ZENA SUTHERLAND

A topic that is of universal interest is explored in a simple, lucid book [*Dreams*] which describes early theories about dreaming and goes on to discuss the more scientific approach of Freud, Jung, and later research workers. This isn't comprehensive, but it is a good summary of the experiments that have been made and the facts that have been established. (p. 40)

[*Dreams* is a] popular monograph [that] ostensibly deals with the history and current research in the study of dreams.... Additional description of [current dream research using drugs and the electro-encephalograph] might have rendered the book more scientific and less speculative, though possibly less "popular." The latter part of the book concentrates on considerations from parapsychology, culminating in a do-it-yourself six-point program for recording one's own dreams. Interesting, but of questionable scientific worth. (p. 81)

JEROME BEATTY, JR.

There are two approaches to ghost stories. The emotional one is to sit around a campfire at night, or lie abed in the dark, and exchange eerie tales till you're covered with goose pimples. ["Haunted Houses"] takes the second, journalistic, scientific way. It is about as spooky as a Mickey Mouse cartoon.... As a matter-of-fact look at spectral phenomena, the book serves its purpose. The final chapter is an "explanation," offering some theories to chew on.... It's all bound to be interesting to a young reader on the phantom trail, but don't look for goose pimples. (p. 26)

[In *Dreams*] Mr. Kettelkamp begins by summing up the work of Freud and Jung shortly and simply: this is well done. His somewhat idiosyncratic interpretations of the meaning of certain objects or events observed in dreams may not command universal approval and are of doubtful value for the young. His account or recent work on eye movements during sleep, which is now being carried out in the United States, is of interest, but seems to give undue importance to theories which have not yet been proved. (p. 702)

MARGARET A. DORSEY

[*Sixth Sense* is a]lucid overview of various types of psychic phenomena. The author clearly explains the nature of telepathy, clairvoyance, and precognition, and also discusses psychometry, retrocognition, astral projections, mediums, possession, psychokinesis, psychic photography and healing, and the tricks of phony mediums and mentalists. Suggestions for testing and developing one's own ESP are given at the end. The author cites various case histories, the experiences of such people as Edgar Cayce, Jean Dixon and Ted Serios, and the results of laboratory experiments whenever possible, to give a generally accurate and balanced picture of present knowledge about parapsychology; however, when discussing more nebulous, untestable areas such as retrocognition (intuitive knowledge of the past), Mr. Kettelkamp does not suggest that such knowledge may be due to a form of clairvoyance, but appears to lean toward the belief that such manifestations support theories of reincarnation. The same criticism applies to the discussion of mediumistic experiences as indicative of survival after death and, partially, to that of astral projection. Nevertheless, this is a clearly written, well-organized book on a fascinating subject, and it will be popular. (p. 49)

RANDOLPH HOGAN

Who among us has not experienced the physical re-enactment of a dream. This feeling, sometimes called déjà vu, is one of the many fascinating and often chilling subjects discussed in ["Sixth Sense," an] excellent book about psychic phenomena....

Beginning with a few documented cases of telepathy and clairvoyance, the author then deals with prediction of the future and its opposite number, the recollection of past events.... From here he goes to traveling consciousness, or the mind's (and sometimes the body's) ability to be in two places at the same time.

Mr. Kettelkamp also discusses mediums . . . ; psychic photography . . . ; mind over matter . . . ; and concludes with some good advice about quacks and frauds and some suggestions about conducting simple psychic experiments.

This is a serious and worthwhile book which adults as well as younger readers will enjoy. (p. 22)

> *Randolph Hogan, in* The New York Times Book Review (© 1971 by The New York Times Company; reprinted by permission), February 21, 1971.

An eight-page chapter, late in [*Sixth Sense*] on magicians and frauds mentions that much so-called magic is illusion, prestidigitation, or outright fraud, which is true also of some ESP experiences. All phases of the book might well have been subjected to the same type of questioning, and therefore the material in this chapter should have been introduced as the second chapter.... The statement by the publisher on the jacket blurb that the book has been "thoroughly researched" cannot be accepted because the author is not a professional psychologist capable of evaluating human behavior objectively, and because there are no references or literature citations (titles of books and authors strewn in the text without other identifying information is not proper documentation). If the substance of the final chapter, "Understanding Psi," had been used, together with other basic introductory material from psychology, as an initial or orientation chapter, then the author might have been able to embark on a successful book for young readers. The "suggested experiments" in the final chapter should have been worked in at appropriate points in the text to assist the reader in attempting his own evaluations of some of the theories or phenomena presented. As they stand, the youngster will flounder about with no real orientation for conducting a valid test or experiment. (pp. 276-77)

> *Science Books (copyright 1971 by the American Association for the Advancement of Science), Vol. 6, No. 4 (March, 1971).*

ZENA SUTHERLAND

[*Sixth Sense* is a] discussion of psychic phenomena and some of the supportive research, of which a small amount is anecdotal, most of the evidence being documented.

All of [the] topics are treated seriously and briefly, and the final pages define levels of consciousness and suggest ways in which the reader can increase the possibility of having psychic experiences. Simply written, a good introduction to a fascinating topic. (p. 138)

> *Zena Sutherland, in* Bulletin of the Center for Children's Books (© 1971 by the University of Chicago; all rights reserved), May, 1971.

[*Investigating UFO's* takes us once] more around the UFO controversy, with essentially the same stopovers as those visited in numerous previous saucer books.... Kettelkamp's review of official studies has the usual implication of a conspiracy of silence, and his catalog of incidents invites belief, though a chapter on "illusions, pranks and hoaxes" acknowledges that some have faked saucer sightings and that various visual conditions can simulate the phenomenon.... Overall, it's a concise if somewhat weighted summary of saucer lore, well organized and attractively laid out, by a master of far-out subjects; but the need for still another rehash is debatable. (pp. 878-79)

> *The Kirkus Reviews (copyright © 1971 The Kirkus Service, Inc.), August 15, 1971.*

[*Investigating UFO's*] primarily presents the case for UFO's, with only a brief look at the case against them. Although it is full of interesting anecdotal material on the sightings of flying saucers (and sometimes their inhabitants) and contains a number of photographs and sketches, the book leaves, this reviewer with the feeling that it would have been better if a more balanced treatment of the subject had been presented. There is certainly a case that can be made for investigating UFO's, but some of the incidents reported here with little or no critique are of very doubtful authenticity.... Nevertheless, the author does present a concise survey of the kinds of sightings that have been reported. (pp. 328-29)

> *Science Books (copyright 1972 by the American Association for the Advancement of Science), Vol. VII, No. 4 (March, 1972).*

Dreams, Haunted Houses, Investigating UFO'S, Sixth Sense—the titles of Larry Kettelkamp's previous books—give some indication of the slant he takes in [*Religions East and West,* an] ever so brief survey of the origins of world religions. The work of Edgar Cayce and James Churchward's theories about the continent of Lemuria (Mu), reviewed in a chapter on "New Trends in Faith," receive as much space as Christianity. And the chapter on Christianity is itself a curious mixture of basic facts, esoterica ... and fuzzy thinking.... Similarly, the discussion of Egyptian religion centers on the legendary travels of Osiris ..., and continues with a disproportionately long tribute to Ikhnaton's short-lived monotheism. This ill-informed introduction to comparative religion is useless except in so far as it serves as a cautionary example of the encroachment of occult mumbo jumbo into apparently serious juvenile books. (p. 1157)

> *Kirkus Reviews (copyright © 1972 The Kirkus Service, Inc.), October 1, 1972.*

SISTER MARY ETHELDREDA SMELTZER

[*Religions East and West*] comes at a time when the study of comparative religions is of the essence. The unusually clear treatment of Eastern Religions will prove interesting and informative to our youth in search of truth. (p. 448)

> *Sister Mary Etheldreda Smeltzer, in* Catholic Library World, February, 1973.

DENISE MURKO WILMS

Kettelkamp's journalistic three-part survey of astrology [*Astrology: Wisdom of the Stars*] offers a broad view of the historical development and present-day status of "the first science."... Part two contains the standard fare of traditional astrology.... Not a how-to manual for would-be forecasters, but rather a nice effort at defining the scope and content of astrology today. (p. 340)

> *Denise Murko Wilms, in* The Booklist (reprinted by permission of the American Library Association; copyright 1973 by the American Library Association), November 15, 1973.

It should be possible to talk about hypnosis without getting into ESP, but Kettelkamp's historical survey [*Hypnosis: The Wakeful Sleep*] emphasizes apparent telepathic feats by hypnotic subjects, later chapters wax credulous about clairvoyance and "artificial reincarnation" in which subjects remember past lives, and this ends with the claim that "researchers today," unlike mechanistic scientists of the past, view consciousness as creating the physical universe. . . . [It's] unlikely that Kettelkamp's simple instructions will live up to his claims for self suggestion, which can drain off tension, change pulse rate and body temperature, or turn the shy into public speakers. (No doubt it can, but not without some practice and direction unavailable here.) To be sure, his Mickey Mouse exercises are probably harmless in terms of the experimentation they will prompt, but as a model of disinterested investigating this ranks with TV commercials. (p. 1291)

> *Kirkus Reviews (copyright © 1975 The Kirkus Service, Inc.), November 15, 1975.*

You might well question the need for a book on biofeedback at this level, but otherwise you won't fault Kettelkamp's reasonable, realistic report on laboratory experiments and training sessions [in *A Partnership of Mind and Body: Biofeedback*]. In a chapter on each of five areas of investigation, he describes instances of autocontrol of body temperature . . . , heart and blood pressure . . . , involuntary muscles . . . , skin resistance . . . and brain waves. . . . Though kids may not need it, "the potential for bringing mind and body together" can probably intrigue at any level. (p. 846)

> *Kirkus Reviews (copyright © 1976 The Kirkus Service, Inc.), August 1, 1976.*

Apparently [*Hypnosis: The Wakeful Sleep*] was written as an introduction to hypnosis for the general public. Much of it is well written and reasonably accurate, but there are several serious flaws. The idea that hypnosis can be used to foster creativity and serve as an aid to ESP is uncritically presented. No bibliography is given to help those who would check such claims, and the extensive modern research which renders these claims doubtful at best is inadequately represented. Enough nonsense is abroad in the area of hypnosis without adding to the burden—as this book will unfortunately do. (p. 66)

> *Science Books & Films (copyright 1976 by the American Association for the Advancement of Science), Vol. XII, No. 2 (September, 1976).*

HERBERT J. STOLZ

[*Hypnosis: The Wakeful Sleep*,] Kettelkamp's discussion of the history and techniques of hypnosis and its present use in such fields as medicine, psychotherapy, and psychic phenomena research, is scientifically accurate. The text is written in clear, simple language and is a good introduction to a fascinating topic. Included are a few simple, safe experiments for self-hypnosis. Larry Kettelkamp knows how to write good juvenile books. (p. 26)

> *Herbert J. Stolz, in Appraisal (copyright © 1976 by the Children's Science Book Review Committee), Fall, 1976.*

ZENA SUTHERLAND

Kettelkamp's books are always authoritative and objective, and in [*A Partnership of Mind and Body: Biofeedback*, a] lucid examination of a provocative and still controversial subject, he carefully restricts discussion to recorded scientific research. Each chapter describes research experiments in a different area: the brain, the smooth muscles, the skin, etc. In each case, the text includes theory, testing equip-

ment, experiments, and results; some of the results are merely informative, while others have already been put to practical use by the medical profession. . . . A stimulating subject; a fine survey. (pp. 76-7)

> *Zena Sutherland, in Bulletin of the Center for Children's Books (© 1977 by the University of Chicago; all rights reserved), January, 1977.*

SARAH GAGNÉ

Exciting new developments in biofeedback are starting to receive widespread attention, and with advertisements appearing for brain wave machines, children are in need of a book [such as *A Partnership of Body and Mind: Biofeedback* which explains] the subject. . . . The chapter on brain waves is the most interesting because of their influence on the state of creativity and "quiet awareness" and because of the resultant implications for mind control. As with other books by Kettelkamp, striking events are presented within the context of the subject rather than for mere sensation. (pp. 78-9)

> *Sarah Gagné, in The Horn Book Magazine (copyright © 1977 by the Horn Book, Inc., Boston), February, 1977.*

ANNE C. RAYME

[*Investigating Psychics: Five Life Histories*] provides an overview of current developments and future directions in the new science of psi or parapsychology plus profiles of five gifted psychics. Results of controlled laboratory experiments are outlined to document the claims of [the five subjects]. The coverage is objective and responsible and includes cautions against laymen attempting dangerous feats in order to explore their psi potential. While not an exhaustive nor conclusive investigation, this easily digestible introduction to psi research won't be a shelf sitter. (p. 130)

> *Anne C. Rayme, in School Library Journal (reprinted from the March, 1978 issue of School Library Journal, published by R. R. Bowker Co. A Xerox Corporation; copyright © 1978), March, 1978.*

E. VIRGINIA DEMOS

Investigating Psychics—Five Life Histories is clearly written by a believer in parapsychology, whose treatment of the subject cannot be accurately described as an "investigation". The author, Mr. Larry Kettelkamp, starts with a brief introduction to parapsychology and psychic or "psi" effects that is entirely one-sided. He then proceeds to describe the life stories of five self-declared psychics, using only secondary source materials, which he accepts without question. Since he has chosen to write about people who are alive today, and have been to the United States, or live here, it is odd and distressing that Mr. Kettelkamp has made no effort to interview these people personally, or to obtain first hand information about their psychic abilities, life histories, etc. Finally, the book ends with an almost evangelical chapter on how to increase one's own psychic powers. Throughout the book the author exaggerates the degree of acceptance of psychic events by the scientific community, and fails to mention the considerable contrary evidence. The book represents a distorted and misleading view of the topic. Kettelkamp's purpose seems to have been not to educate, but to convert the young reader. (pp. 19-20)

E. Virginia Demos, in Appraisal *(copyright © 1978 by the Children's Science Book Review Committee), Spring, 1978.*

MONTAGUE ULLMAN

It is apparently the intent [of Kettelkamp in *Investigating Psychics*] to introduce the younger reader to the field of parapsychology by presenting its stellar performers, the men and women who have become newsworthy in recent years.... Biographical sketches of the psychics are given along with a summary of their most striking achievements. A dramatic picture emerges, based partly on fact but more often on uncritical assessment of claims. The style is largely anecdotal. No sources are given. The accomplishments of these five psychics, regardless of their interest and importance, cannot convey an accurate or balanced picture of the field of parapsychological research. Kettelkamp is more apt to give a somewhat distorted picture to the uninformed reader. (p. 142)

Montague Ullman, in Science Books & Films *(copyright 1978 by the American Association for the Advancement of Science), Vol. XIV, No. 3 (December, 1978).*

Kettelkamp's conception of holistic medicine leads him to treat every manner of healing [in *The Healing Arts*], from natural herbs to acupuncture to cryosurgery to laying on of hands, as complementary methods that "share certain important [but unspecified] basic principles." Besides giving ... a broad perspective on the subject, this ecumenical approach gives Kettelkamp the opportunity to bring up ... a variety of intriguing current topics ... but it doesn't lend itself to rigorous assessment of ideas and evidence. Many interesting but tentative findings are simplistically presented as established fact, and [the] final chapter on spiritual healing is especially irresponsible in its implication that various claims for psychic healing, the relationship between intuition and electromagnetic fields, etc., represent serious scientific conclusions. (pp. 129-30)

Kirkus Reviews (copyright © 1979 The Kirkus Service, Inc.), February 1, 1979.

KATHRYN WEISMAN

[*The Healings Arts* is a] survey of the various approaches to healing the body [and] includes discussions of herbal and nutritional medicine, body rhythms, osteopathy, chiropractic, acupuncture, mental and spiritual healing techniques, as well as discussions of traditional Western medical and surgical techniques. Kettelkamp does not try to promote one method of healing over another; rather he strives to give an unbiased explanation of each and then attempts to show its scientific basis.... [Few of the other survey books available] cover the range of topics that Kettelkamp does here. (pp. 140-41)

Kathryn Weisman, in School Library Journal *(reprinted from the March, 1979 issue of* School Library Journal, *published by R. R. Bowker Co. A Xerox Corporation; copyright © 1973), March, 1979.*

Stephen King
1947-

American novelist, short story writer, and screenwriter. King is primarily known for his modern Gothic novels in which supernatural disturbances reflect psychological or moral problems, as in *Carrie* and *The Shining*. Critics praise King as a stylist whose characterizations are much better than those that are generally found in Gothic suspense novels. He is criticized, however, for lack of originality in plot and for being derivative in a field that too easily lends itself to imitation and cliché. King treats horror fiction as a serious outgrowth of mainstream fiction. As he says, "Fear and death are two of the human constants. But only the writer of horror and the supernatural gives the reader such an opportunity for total identification and catharsis. . . ." King's work is a hybrid, utilizing the styles of both the traditional horror tale, as practiced by Edgar Allen Poe and Bram Stoker, and the modern commercial thriller which utilizes phenomena such as parapsychology and ESP. (See also *Contemporary Authors*, Vols. 61-64, and *Something about the Author*, Vol. 9.)

[*Salem's Lot* is a] super-exorcism that leaves the taste of somebody else's blood in your mouth and what a bad taste it is. King presents us with the riddle of a small Maine town that has been deserted overnight. . . . Vampirism, necrophilia, *et* dreadful *alia* rather overplayed by the author of *Carrie*. . . . (p. 935)

> Kirkus Reviews *(copyright © 1975 The Kirkus Service, Inc.), August 15, 1975.*

ELIZABETH HALL

Poltergeists, psychokinesis (called telekinesis or TK in this book), and religious fundamentalism mix to produce *Carrie* . . . , Stephen King's novel that probably holds the record for the number of deaths perpetrated within its covers by a single adolescent. Sin, sex, and the unpopularity of an adolescent girl endowed with TK begin to come together when the naive Carrie is shocked by the sudden onset of her first menstrual period. The fatal results indicate the value of sex education. (p. 76)

> *Elizabeth Hall, in* Psychology Today *(copyright © 1975 Ziff-Davis Publishing Company), September, 1975.*

WALTER BOBBIE

Stephen King's *'salem's Lot* (Jerusalem's Lot) is a novel of such chilling beginnings that we look forward to losing sleep over it. . . . It is the kind of goose bump fiction that makes grown men afraid of the dark.

It is to Stephen King's credit as a stylist that he has charmed us into such familiar territory. Sparing the endless atmospheric creaks and cobwebs and cupolas of this New England landscape, he thrusts us into the private terror of his characters. A wise choice. An equally familiar assortment of types achieves a personal dimension and life's blood that grounds us. King gives this stock company a contemporary resonance and wit. Instead of stalking among their dusty antiques, he lets us peek into their souls.

It is here that the writer proves a master of this genre. He juggles character vignettes into a structural crossfire that is hypnotic. A thousand detailed portraits become the broad canvas of *'salem's Lot*.

Unfortunately, we mystery fans are an odd lot, opting for a good story over a well-written one any night of the week. . . . And it is here, ultimately, that *'salem's Lot* disappoints. No one minds a good retelling of an old legend when there is a new finale. But the final confrontation is labored, obvious, and familiar. King has added nothing new to this legend. . . . (p. 304)

> *Walter Bobbie, in* Best Sellers *(copyright © 1976 Helen Dwight Reid Educational Foundation), January, 1976.*

JACK SULLIVAN

To say that Stephen King is not an elegant writer . . . is putting it mildly. But inelegance is not precisely the problem in "The Shining." . . . [In] "The Shining," memories and fantasies often find themselves pretentiously enclosed in parentheses. Sometimes non-punctuation or italics are used—quite arbitrarily—for gimmicky stream of consciousness effect. Occasionally we are subjected to all capitals in parentheses with triple exclamation points (!!! ON BOTH MARGINS !!!)! This is Mr. King's way of being climactic. . . .

Mr. King lifts images and plot fragments from books (Poe, Blackwood, Lovecraft) and films ("Diabolique," "Psycho," "Village of the Damned") as if his characters and readers are indeed noticing them "for the first time."

Occasionally Mr. King seems aware of his triteness, but instead of playing the awareness for laughs, he offers apologies. In one scene, a character has an epiphany over a wasps' nest: "He felt that he had unwittingly stuck his hand into The Great Wasps' Nest of Life. As an image it stank. As a cameo of reality, he felt it was serviceable." Like an admission of guilt, the apology only makes things worse. . . .

To be sure, "The Shining" does have its chilling moments. There is a bathtub apparition that, though derivative, is wonderfully frightening. And there are others, though the hyperbole and stylistic fumblings make an equal number unintentionally funny.

H. P. Lovecraft once remarked that "atmosphere is the all-important thing" in this genre. A compelling atmosphere can make us forget the clichés. But since atmosphere is so much a function of style—which Mr. King hasn't developed yet—the clichés in "The Shining" stand out in ghoulish, jeering relief. (p. 8)

> Jack Sullivan, in The New York Times Book Review (© 1977 by The New York Times Company; reprinted by permission), February 20, 1977.

FREDERICK PATTEN

[*The Shining*] has flaws, some minor and some serious. . . .

But when all's said, the novel *works*! It makes one tremble in anticipation of the day when King gets it all together and writes a 'perfect' book. . . . King's style . . . is his most obvious fault. It's all *good* writing, it's all pertinent, but it goes on and on. . . . Setting a realistic scene and creating believably complex characters are laudable traits, but King seriously overdoes it.

King builds his mood slowly, at first establishing the idyllic setting of the peaceful old Overlook. . . . Minor ominous incidents occur at intervals between lengthy flashbacks to Jack's and Wendy's youth, showing the childhoods that molded their personalities. Gradually the story stabilizes in the present as the hallucinations become more vicious, and the Torrances are increasingly hard-pressed to rationalize them as imaginary. . . .

King continues to add . . . detail, building upon minor incidents, filling in a mosaic of horror which has unsuspected depths. . . .

There's [another] annoyance that's obvious . . . , King does not portray Danny as a five-year-old child. He's too mature; he seems nine or ten at least. Even granting that a telepathic boy might be emotionally older than his peers, it's important for plot reasons that Danny be no more than five. Whenever King switched to a lengthy scene with the boy, the story suddenly became less convincing. There are also some subplots that don't really fit the story; they're too obviously just to give the reader some extra chills.

Most of the flaws are in the nature of loose ends that the reader is bothered at finding unresolved. Some may be setups that King decided to drop, such as an old canvas firehose that has a 'disturbingly coiled' aspect, we are told several times, but which never does do anything. Some may be due to deliberate vagueness; King doesn't seem to want us to be sure at what point the hotel's manifestations pass from the illusory plane to the actual one. . . . A list of other loose ends would be tedious to those who haven't read the book yet, so I'll just say that the totality leaves the

reader with a distinct wish that King had spent less time on the Torrances' past and on their emotional complexes, and more on finishing the story in a complete manner.

But it's still the goddamnedest best horror novel I've read in over two decades. (p. 6)

> Frederick Patten, in Delap's Fantasy and Science Fiction Review (copyright © 1977 by Richard Delap), April, 1977.

[King demonstrates in *Night Shift* that he] is as effective in the horror vignette as in the novel. His big opening tale, "Jerusalem's Lot"—about a deserted village—is obviously his first shot at '*Salem's Lot* and, in its dependence on a gigantic worm out of Poe and Lovecraft, it misses the novel's gorged frenzy of Vampireville. But most of the other tales go straight through you like rats' fangs. . . . Bizarre dripperies, straight out of *Tales from the Crypt* comics. . . . (p. 1285)

> Kirkus Reviews (copyright © 1977 The Kirkus Service, Inc.), December 1, 1977.

W. H. LYLES

Most [of the stories of *Night Shift*] could be classified as "horror stories," yet they lack the true horror of Henry Kuttner . . . , the obsessiveness of H. P. Lovecraft, the variety of Richard Matheson, the humor of John Collier, the richness of Ray Bradbury. But all the stories are competently done, some ("The Mangler," "Quitters, Inc.") much above that. (p. 385)

> W. H. Lyles, in Library Journal (reprinted from Library Journal, February 1, 1978; published by R. R. Bowker Co. (a Xerox company); copyright © 1978 by Xerox Corporation), February 1, 1978.

MICHAEL MEWSHAW

Some of [Stephen King's plots in his short story collection "*Night Shift*"] are . . . imaginative, even ingenious. (p. 13)

But it seems not to have occurred to Mr. King that style is crucial to story, as are characterization and theme. His own characters seldom serve any purpose save as ballast for his bizarre plots. . . . His worst stories strain mightily to generate one last *frisson*, using twist endings that should have died with O. Henry, the hoariest clichés of the horror-tale subgenre ("I was shaking in my shoes") and lines that provoke smiles rather than terror. . . . It's baffling to think that anybody might find these stories fascinating or frightening. . . . (pp. 13, 23)

> Michael Mewshaw, in The New York Times Book Review (© 1978 by The New York Times Company; reprinted by permission), March 26, 1978.

BILL CRIDER

[The stories of *Night Shift*] all begin in our normal world, where everything is safe and warm. But in almost every instance, something slips, and we find ourselves in the nightmare world of the not-quite-real. (p. 6)

Such stories require a willing suspension of disbelief, of course, but they also require an author who is an expert manipulator, one who can make horror seem not only plausible but almost logical. King is an expert, and many of these stories will not be easily forgotten. . . . Perhaps

["The Mangler"] is the best example of King's skill at what he does. The idea of a steam ironer possessed by a demon seems laughable, but no one who reads "The Mangler" is going to laugh for very long. (pp. 6-7)

> Bill Crider, in Best Sellers (copyright © 1978 Helen Dwight Reid Educational Foundation), April, 1978.

Striking a far less hysterical tone than in *The Shining*, King has written his most sweeping horror novel in *The Stand*, though it may lack the spinal jingles of *'Salem's Lot*. In part this is because *The Stand*, with its flow of hundreds of brand-name products, is a kind of inventory of American culture. "Superflu" has hit the U.S. and the world. . . . Immunity seems to be a gift from God—or the Devil. . . . Good and Evil come to an atomic clash at the climax, the Book of Revelations working itself out rather too explicitly. But more importantly, there are memorable scenes of the superflu spreading hideously. . . . Some King fans will be put off by the pretensions here; most will embrace them along with the earthier chills. (pp. 965-66)

> Kirkus Reviews (copyright © 1978 The Kirkus Service, Inc.), September 1, 1978.

MARC LAIDLAW

The haunted hotel [of *The Shining*] is a stock sort of device, left over from the days when people were still writing straight ghost stories. The struggling family offers the pathos that no doubt is in part responsible for the book's popularity—real characters, beautifully handled for the most part, though some of the development toward the end is a bit too hasty. Even the child with the "gift" is a common theme of Stephen King's. . . . But herein they are combined, redeveloped, slowly woven into a dark, unfamiliar tapestry—something dreadful and inevitable and ultimately terrifying. . . .

King's creation of atmosphere is masterful—the first irrational hint I had that anything unusual might happen terrified me as fully as the later, more logically-constructed episodes. In fact, where the novel falls short is in the fact that the conclusion is not nearly as frightening as the mood that has been predicting it. King takes the stance that he should give the reader a hint of the ultimate horror early in the game, and then—when they're sure to be afraid that it's actually going to happen—give them exactly what they've been nervously waiting for. It's a technique that works rather well, though in this case the intimations of doom are more frightening than the doom itself. (p. 34)

> Marc Laidlaw, in Nyctalops (copyright © 1978 by Harry O. Morris, Jr. and Edward P. Berglund; reprinted by permission of Marc Laidlaw), Vol. 2, No. 7, 1978.

Deadly disease running rampant over the countryside is a natural subject for horror stories; King is a natural teller of such tales. . . . [*The Stand*] elicits fear and dread as completely as he has in previous works . . . , [and] the suspense is underlaid with questions concerning good and evil in human nature. (p. 601)

> Booklist (reprinted by permission of the American Library Association; copyright 1978 by the American Library Association), December 1, 1978.

ANNE COLLINS

In 1980, America dies for its sins (pollution of both landscape and spirit) in a shifting antigen plague leaked from some cavern of government-sponsored biological warfare. But the purge leaves certain issues of good and evil unresolved. In *The Stand*, Stephen King divides the survivors up like tiddledywinks into two camps, one devoted to good . . . , the other to the devil. Will it be Walden III or the Fourth Reich? In the panorama of mass disaster—and with such moral freight to consider—King loses his characterizations . . . in a clutter of place-names and products. . . .

[The] devil (otherwise known as Randall Flagg, an agent provocateur out of the Rolling Stones' *Sympathy for the Devil*) successfully raises hairs on the arms. The prose flows well, describing multiple plague deaths, swollen corpses, and the rantings of idiot savants. . . . But *The Stand* is not a horror story like King's *Carrie* or *The Shining*, and that's why it ultimately bores. Horror lies in that area where known becomes unknown, where ordinary turns menacing.

Too much of King's new book deals with a little leaguer's vision of American democracy somehow smiling through apocalypse; good and evil are set up like so many kindergarten blocks. Bad is Las Vegas where those survivors who sell their souls gather; good is Boulder, Colorado, and the American constitution. Similar equations act like dry rot on the plot.

> Anne Collins, "No Sympathy for the Devil," in Maclean's Magazine (© 1978 by Maclean's Magazine; reprinted by permission), December 18, 1978, p. 51.

J. JUSTIN GUSTAINIS

Stephen King has been writing very good and very scary novels and short stories for a number of years now. *The Stand* is something of a departure for him. This is not to suggest that it is not good, or, in its own way, scary. But the word which best describes it is one not heard much today outside of English classrooms: epic. Another word should also be resurrected too, this one out of the dusty tomes of Biblical scholarship: apocalyptic. . . .

[He sets the stage] for a conflict, and in reference to that struggle one could dig up one more of those rarely used old words: Armageddon.

Stephen King is a masterful writer. . . . (p. 378)

> J. Justin Gustainis, in Best Sellers (copyright © 1979 Helen Dwight Reid Educational Foundation), March, 1979.

Maxine Hong Kingston

1940-

Chinese-American autobiographer, journalist, and short story writer. Kingston is best known for her 1976 autobiography, *The Woman Warrior: Memoirs of a Girlhood among Ghosts*, which won the general nonfiction award from the National Book Critics Circle. Born to parents who were Chinese immigrants, she grew up experiencing the often painful results of the radical clashes between American and Chinese cultures. Her mother, who was a strong influence on Kingston, wanted her to remain essentially Chinese and instilled in her the superstitions, traditions, and customs of her native country. Many of her stories revolved around the legendary figure of Fa Mu Lan, the woman warrior, whose exploits were in sharp contrast to the traditionally subservient role of the Chinese woman. Fa Mu Lan captured Kingston's imagination, figuring prominently in her childhood fantasies and later in her autobiography. *The Woman Warrior* is the chronicle of Kingston's confrontation with her dual heritage. She is presently writing further stories of Chinese legend and heroes.

[Rarely does East meet West with such charming results as occur in "The Woman Warrior", a] reminiscence of growing up in a Chinese-American culture where Oriental myth and Occidental reality somehow blended. American-born Maxine Kingston begins by exploring her girlhood dream—nourished by the folklore brought to this country by her mother, Brave Orchid—of becoming Fa Mu Lan, the Woman Warrior of Chinese myth. At the same time, she lives among Americans whom her mother terms "ghosts." . . . Along with the quirky humor are . . . myths as rich and varied as Chinese brocade; these are described in prose that often achieves the delicacy and precision of porcelain. An unusual and rewarding book for a specially attuned readership. (p. 72)

Publishers Weekly (reprinted from the August 9, 1976, issue of Publishers Weekly *by permission, published by R. R. Bowker Company, a Xerox company; copyright © 1976 by Xerox Corporation), August 9, 1976.*

WILLIAM McPHERSON

The Woman Warrior is a strange, sometimes savagely terrifying and, in the literal sense, wonderful story of growing up caught between two highly sophisticated and utterly alien cultures, both vivid, often menacing and equally mysterious. Reality in its bewildering complexity is at the heart of it: what appears to our senses, the mind transforms, into a whole set of myths and phantoms (language, number, emotion, relation, abstraction) to become what we perceive as real. Ghosts from the Chinese past may thus be as real—and as unreal—as persons from the California present; and vice versa. Is a parent any the less real to us, less true, because he is dead? It is not the same as not existing. Mrs. Kingston mulls over these mysteries, these paradoxes in this extraordinary book.

William McPherson, "Ghosts from the Middle Kingdom," in Book World—The Washington Post *(© 1976, The Washington Post), October 10, 1976, p. E1.*

JANE KRAMER

["The Woman Warrior"] is a brilliant memoir. It shocks us out of our facile rhetoric, past the clichés of our obtuseness, back to the mystery of a stubbornly, utterly foreign sensibility, and I cannot think of another book since Andre Malraux's melancholy artifice, "La Tentation de l'Occident," that even starts to do this. "The Woman Warrior" is about being Chinese, in the way the "Portrait of the Artist" is about being Irish. It is an investigation of soul, not landscape. Its sources are dream and memory, myth and desire. Its crises are the crises of a heart in exile from roots that bind and terrorize it. (p. 1)

Maxine Kingston writes with bitter and relentless love. Her voice . . . is as clear as the voice of Ts'ai Yen, who sang her sad, angry songs of China to the barbarians. It is as fierce as a warrior's voice, and as eloquent as any artist's. (p. 20)

Jane Kramer, in The New York Times Book Review *(© 1976 by The New York Times Company; reprinted by permission), November 7, 1976.*

PAUL GRAY

Exiles and refugees tell sad stories of the life they left behind. Even sadder, sometimes, is the muteness of their children. They are likely to find the old ways and old language excess baggage, especially if their adopted homeland is the U.S., where the race is to the swift and the adaptable. Thus a heritage of centuries can die in a generation of embarrassed silence. *The Woman Warrior* gives that silence a voice.

312

Subtitled *Memoirs of a Girlhood Among Ghosts,* this astonishingly accomplished first book . . . haunts a region somewhere between autobiography and fiction. Yet it hardly matters whether the woman who tells (or muses) the book's five stories is literally Maxine Hong Kingston. Art has intervened here. The stories may or may not be transcripts of actual experience. They are, unquestionably, triumphant journeys of the imagination through a desolation of spirit. . . .

Though it is drenched in alienation, *The Woman Warrior* never whines. Author Kingston avoids rhetoric for a wealth of detail—old customs and legends, the feel of Chinese enclaves transported to the California of her childhood. Even at their most poignant, her stories sing. Thousands of books have bubbled up out of the American melting pot. This should be one of those that will be remembered.

> Paul Gray, "Book of Changes," in Time (reprinted by permission from Time, The Weekly Newsmagazine; copyright Time Inc. 1976), December 6, 1976, p. 91.

SARA BLACKBURN

Maxine Hong Kingston illuminates the experience of everyone who has ever felt the terror of being an emotional outsider. It seems to me that the best records of the immigrant experience and the bittersweet legacy it bestows upon the next generation fascinate us because of the insights they provide into the life of the family, that mystified arena where we first learn, truly or falsely, our own identities. It should therefore not be very startling—as it was to me—that this dazzling mixture of pre-revolutionary Chinese village life and myth, set against its almost unbearable contradictions in contemporary American life, could unfold as almost a psychic transcript of every woman I know—class, age, race, or ethnicity be damned. Here is the real meaning of America as melting pot.

Kingston alternates the experiences of her parents and their generation, in China and the Chinatowns of California, with her own. In a starving society where girl children were a despised and useless commodity, her mother had become a physician, then joined her long-ago immigrated husband in America, where she was hence to labor in the laundry which was their survival in the terrifying new land. Their children, raised in the aura of the old myths and their parents' fears for their children and themselves, alternated between revering and despising them. . . .

In the book's finest scene, which somehow manages to be both hilarious and devastatingly painful, Kingston's elderly aunt is brought over from China and forced to try to reclaim the now-Americanized husband she had married years before at home. In the traditional style, he had been supporting her from California though he had long ago married another woman. The confrontation is a microcosm of the book's impact: he is a svelte, classy brain surgeon, surrounded by all the American trappings of wealth and prestige; she is a provincial old village woman, and falls back, dumbfounded, at his eerie power. . . . (p. 39)

A tragic dynamic gets played out here. Taught that our own needs are illegitimate, too many of us repress them and spend our lives serving what we perceive to be the more legitimate needs of others. It is in this way that Kingston's ambivalent responses to growing up in this family and culture evoke the history of women around the world. The

author's own early fantasies dwelt on how she is miraculously trained to be a fierce, proud warrior, who liberates the suffering people of the Chinese past from the terrible oppression of the landowners. Only her lover knows that she is, in reality, a woman!

In the book's climax, Kingston, now in high school, lashes out at her mother in an extraordinary, liberating tirade in which she claims at last her own shaky identity. And her mother, who once struggled so valiantly for her own, first denies her feelings and then tries to convey the dangers, real and imagined, which have molded her own attitude toward this beloved, maddening stranger. The gap is too wide, for the teenage Maxine has perceived more of her mother's fear than her love, more of her culture's confines than its richness and beauty. The possibilities of love and forgiveness will have to be postponed for the more immediate necessities: the struggles for autonomy, on the one hand, and assimilation on the other. The depiction of these twin struggles is this memoir's great strength.

The Woman Warrior is not without flaws: much of the exquisite fantasy material comes too early in the book, before we're properly grounded in the author's own "reality," and we can appreciate its full impact only in retrospect. There's often a staccato, jarring quality in transition from one scene to another, and we have to work hard placing ourselves in time and event. Prospective readers should not be discouraged by these minor problems. What is in store for those who read on is not only the essence of the immigrant experience—here Chinese, and uniquely fascinating for that—but a marvelous glimpse into the real life of women in the family, a perception-expanding report for the archives of human experience. Praise to Maxine Hong Kingston for distilling it and writing it all down for us. (pp. 39-40)

> Sara Blackburn, "Notes of a Chinese Daughter," in Ms. (© 1977 Ms. Magazine Corp.), January, 1977, pp. 39-40.

MIRIAM GREENSPAN

Kingston reveals to readers the very different world inhabited by her immigrant parents—the world of legends, folklore, customs, and manners of China. She writes, simply and movingly, of the pain of an American-born child who inevitably rejects the expectations and authority of her family in favor of the values of the new land and of her own bond to her mother—a survivor, a woman of enormous strength and vitality. In a rich, poetic, original style, Kingston captures the struggle, the conflict, the bewilderment, and the love that imbue a complex mother-daughter relationship. (p. 108)

> Miriam Greenspan, in School Library Journal (reprinted from the January, 1977 issue of School Library Journal, published by R. R. Bowker Co. A Xerox Corporation; copyright © 1977), January, 1977.

DIANE JOHNSON

Maxine Hong Kingston's memoir of a Chinese-American girlhood presents . . . the female side of growing up in a tradition, perhaps any tradition. Women perform for any society the service of maladjustment that Kingston here brilliantly performs for the society of Chinese immigrants in California. She . . . (unlike most Chinese-Americans) fulfills an American pattern by moving away from an ethnic tradition the distance required to memorialize and cherish it. . . . (p. 19)

Like many other women, Kingston does not wish to reject female nature so much as the female condition, and at that she would reserve the female biological destiny. . . . But of course [there] are the bindings on every woman's feet. In the vivid particularity of her experience, and with the resources of a considerable art, Kingston reaches to the universal qualities of female condition and female anger that the bland generalities of social science and the merely factual history cannot describe.

Women may reject the culture that rejects them, but such brave and rare disassociations are not without serious cost. Kingston is dealing here with the fears and rebellions that recur in much women's writing, often displaced in other ways, and dramatized or actually experienced as suicide, catatonia, hysteria, anorexia—maladies common to many female protagonists, both fictional and alive, from Brontë heroines to Sylvia Plath. Kingston recounts such a gesture of protest in her own life, a period of refusal to play culture's game. (pp. 19-20)

> *Diane Johnson, in* The New York Review of Books *(reprinted with permission from* The New York Review of Books; *copyright © 1977 Nyrev, Inc.), February 3, 1977.*

ELIZABETH FIFER

In autobiography, the told story often is accompanied by the untold one. In Maxine Hong Kingston's *The Woman Warrior,* the idea of autobiography is accompanied by the vision of the stuttering girl, the woman of whom nothing is known, the girl who refuses to speak, the girl with the cut tongue, the one whose throat hurts, the one who quacks like a duck, and the one who talks so much that she is considered mad. Even as Kingston gives a voice to her own life, she is also offering us their suppressed collective biographies, a record of their lives that she has intuited from her own participation in their defeated silences. To do this, Kingston, an American of Chinese descent, must absorb and synthesize the experience of her two cultures, and come to understand her alienation from American life and the particular cruelty towards women in Chinese culture as two central metaphors for the general human experience. *The Woman Warrior* thus enlarges on the autobiographical genre, making it include not only the actual events of her own life, but also the reconstructed stories of the past that she can only approach through the powers of a sympathetic imagination.

Starting with the image of the abandoned and suicidal aunt, who gave birth to her illegitimate baby in a pigsty and drowned herself in a well, the book moves to the images of superwomen: the mythic woman warrior herself, Fa Mu Lan, about whom the narrator learns in her mother's chant, and the mother herself, Brave Orchid, a seer who has led two complete lives: a doctor in China and a mother in the United States. These chapters, devoted to strong women, are interspersed with chapters about women who could not cope: her aunt, Moon Orchid, who goes mad after coming to America, and the author herself, a prototypical silent Chinese girl, for whom the act of writing itself constitutes a convincing heroism.

The narrator is a traveler in a world of ghosts—the white

Americans, the Chinese Americans who have forgotten their origins, the actual supernatural beings who inhabit the dead and the inanimate—all of whom must be combatted with a special conjuring.

The author's quest, as a half-ghost herself, is both to be accepted by her large and diverse family, and to make sense of the social norms of the Chinese culture, and still to be able to assert her own worth and identity. To do this, Kingston superimposes the heritage of the past on her own historical present with her unique blend of history, myth, Americana, childhood memories, movies, scenes from pre-Revolutionary China (as her mother experienced it), and even a few glimpses of post-Revolutionary China. . . . (pp. 68-9)

[Her] mother, Brave Orchid, a real shaman, is Kingston's best subject. Brave Orchid haunts her children like a ghost, and like ghosts, they rarely visit, though she longs to know more of their lives, just as they long to understand hers. She "talks-story" so well that her daughter often has trouble sorting out her own reality from her mother's acts of the imagination. . . .

The sections keep retelling the same "talk-story," trying to wind it ever-tighter, to compress it more fully inside a replica of itself, as in a series of Chinese boxes. The last section, "Song for a Barbarian Reed Pipe," is still concerned with not being able to talk—another version of Moon Orchid's story, or the narrator's childhood, the little Chinese girl trying to make herself speak. Linear progression is sacrificed to the continued repetition of the old stories. Yet the lips of the half-ghost not only flesh the old traditions and memories, but give new utterance to them.

This memoir is a poetic, thoughtful, wonderfully subtle reclamation of self, an important book, setting a high standard for autobiography. More than personal history, it is a personal mythology. (p. 69)

> *Elizabeth Fifer [Lehigh University], in* The International Fiction Review *(© copyright International Fiction Association), January, 1978.*

LINDA B. HALL

In this exquisitely written book [*The Woman Warrior*], Maxine Hong Kingston has given us a picture of the American life of a Chinese-American woman, mediated through the stories and myths that her mother has told her about China. The interweaving of experience, legend, and history, played against the background of two totally different cultures, gives an extraordinary sense of both worlds. Yet the most important contribution of the book is the entrance into the mind and emotions of this complex and fascinating woman.

The book is never didactic. The insights are conveyed not explicitly, but rather implicitly in the web of the stories and incidents she relates. . . .

It is the author's mother who has conveyed to her her sense of her own restricted place as a woman and at the same time told her the legends which feed her ambitions for a full, accomplishing, and contributing life of her own. This paradox forms the center of the book. The woman who relates to her daughter the story of the legendary woman warrior who saves China is the same woman who drives her child to hysteria by repeating Chinese aphorisms. . . . (p. 190)

This book is remarkable in its insights into the plight of individuals pulled between two cultures, and the position of women in both the United States and China. The reader can only be grateful that Maxine Hong Kingston has found her voice. (p. 191)

> *Linda B. Hall, "Internal Wars of a Chinese-American Woman," in* Southwest Review *(© 1978 by Southern Methodist University Press), Spring, 1978, pp. 190-91.*

Joseph Krumgold

1908-

American novelist, filmmaker, screenwriter, director, and producer. Krumgold's young adult novels . . . *And Now Miguel*, *Onion John*, and *Henry 3* form a trilogy built around the theme of the awakening of awareness in youth of self, of human nature, and of how to fit into society. These works describe the processes, both internal and external, that turn boys into men, pinpointing in minute detail this time of change. They are set in very different cultures: a tradition-laden rural Mexican community, an American small town, and an American suburb, but show the universality of the maturation experience. Krumgold's works are notable for their strong sense of place, which is developed through the observations of a first-person narrator. These characters are used as reflectors for the world outside themselves. Krumgold's background in film has had a direct influence on his fiction. He uses a cinematic style in his novels, incorporating a stark visual sense and a flair for drama. At the age of twelve, Krumgold decided to devote himself to making movies. He began working for MGM studios in New York, and went to Hollywood as a Chinese dialogue writer for an ill-fated Lon Chaney film. After working on feature films for twelve years, he began concentrating solely on his own documentaries, for which he has won several international awards, including an Academy Award nomination. While in New Mexico, he worked on a film about the world of a shepherd boy, "Miguel Chavez," which served as the model for his first novel for young readers, . . . *And Now Miguel*. This book received the 1954 Newbery Award. His second novel, *Onion John*, was also based on a real character, an East European hobo living in Hope, New Jersey, where Krumgold also lives. This book was given the 1960 Newbery Award, giving Krumgold the distinction of being the first two-time winner of this prize. Krumgold has been criticized for the solidly male concerns of his novels, and for the lack of inclusion of women in his stories except in derogatory terms or in superficial ways. However, his perceptive understanding and realistic depiction of contemporary young people as they grow into adulthood have affected the emotions of many readers. (See also *Contemporary Authors*, Vols. 9-12, rev. ed., and *Something about the Author*, Vol. 1.)

ISAAC ANDERSON

If you are fed up with those supermen, the brilliant amateur detectives who are always compelling the reluctant admiration of their rivals on the regular police force, then you should by all means meet Michael Vestry [in "Thanks to Murder"]. Mike is an earnest young man who is convinced, as who is not, that there is something wrong with the world. He believes that the remedy lies in the strict application of scientific principles. What is more, he intends to do something about it. He selects for his first point of attack the crime problem. . . .

As a detective Vestry is a complete flop, but that may be because the cases he chooses to investigate do not come up to the standards of the best detective fiction. Consequently, all his elaborate deduction goes to waste, except in so far as it provides him and others with some extremely exciting moments, to say nothing of bringing about his meeting with a girl who is not a bit like the other girls he has met. The story of Vestry's investigation into the death of the man called Phillips is a most hilarious chronicle of cockeyed sleuthing by an amateur whose chief qualification for the job is a pull with The District Attorney. One begins the story with the impression that Vestry is a mere fool, but one soon learns to like him in spite of his blundering. Unfortunately, the author has so thoroughly put an end to his pretensions as a detective that we are not likely to meet him again in that role. However, Mr. Krumgold may have other tricks up his sleeve, and in the meantime he is to be congratulated upon having produced one of the funniest detective novels in years. (p. 14)

Isaac Anderson, in The New York Times Book Review (© 1935 by The New York Times Company; reprinted by permission), May 26, 1935.

CLAIRE HUCHET BISHOP

Miguel Chavez lives in New Mexico. From time immemorial the Chavez have raised sheep. Every year the men take the sheep to graze on the Sangre de Cristo Mountains. Miguel, who is twelve, has a secret wish: to go with the men and the sheep to the Sangre de Cristo Mountains.

Such is the theme of ". . . And Now Miguel" which develops into a beautiful symphony where everything enters: factual and detailed information on sheep raising, on the family life of those of Spanish descent, on the heart yearnings of a boy, and some simple dialogues which tackle the problem of human destiny. Miguel himself tells the story and he does not use any word that a boy of his age could not use. What comes out is a tale of grandeur, tenderness, and sheer beauty. . . .

This is a distinguished, unforgettable book. . . . (p. 62)

Claire Huchet Bishop, in The Saturday Review
(Entire issue copyright 1953 by Saturday Review
Associates, Inc.; reprinted with permission),
November 14, 1953.

MARJORIE FISHER

The style [of "... And Now Miguel"] is sometimes genuinely simple and primitive, though at times with the sentences flattening to pools, there is a suggestion that Miguel
has been reading Ernest Hemingway instead of minding
sheep.

Marjorie Fisher, "Shepherd," in The New York
Times Book Review, Part II (© 1953 by The New
York Times Company; reprinted by permission),
November 15, 1953, p. 28.

VIRGINIA HAVILAND

There is a rare closeness to life in [*... and Now Miguel,*]
this poetic telling by the boy Miguel of his yearning to grow
up, to join the men of his family taking sheep for summer
pasturing into the Sangre de Cristo Mountains. Beauty,
simple dignity, and humor are in the boyish words that
share his innermost plans and secrets and describe the progression of life in the flock. Miguel is twelve and he understands sheep with unique insight.... A young reader will
not forget Miguel's searching spirit and the challenge, the
fun and the fervor of his twelfth year, concluded by his realization of a great moment on the mountain. The Taos
country, the members of his large family, and the way of
the sheep-raisers are well shown.... (p. 456)

Virginia Haviland, in The Horn Book Magazine
(copyrighted, 1953, by The Horn Book, Inc., Boston), December, 1953.

PAMELA MARSH

"Onion John" is as different from most children's books as
Onion John is different from the man next door. Instead of
cardboard-thin characters cut to fit the plot, the story grows
out of the actions and reactions of people too real to be forgotten when the book is closed. Packed with humor, odd
information (why witches ride broomsticks), descriptions
that never burden the action, and warmth, it will appeal to
the more sensitive 10-14's. And to most adults. (p. 5B)

Pamela Marsh, in The Christian Science Monitor,
(reprinted by permission from The Christian Science Monitor; © 1959 The Christian Science Publishing Society; all rights reserved), November 5,
1959.

VIRGINIA HAVILAND

Mr. Krumgold has created another penetrating picture of a
boy growing up. The interrelationships of his new
characters—the boy Andy and his adult friend Onion John
and Andy's father—become as important as those in ...
And Now Miguel. The story [of *Onion John*] emerges from
the point of view of the twelve-year-old boy and centers on
him and Onion John, who is a squatter of sorts on two
garden acres allowed him in a New Jersey town....
Written with extraordinary perception, humor, and vivid
turn of speech, in the language of Andy who tells the story,
the book has a lingering effect on the reader. It has depths
that mean interest on more than one level and is particularly recommended for adults and children to share in
family reading aloud. (pp. 482-83)

Virginia Haviland, in The Horn Book Magazine
(copyright, 1959, by the Horn Book, Inc., Boston), December, 1959.

ELLEN LEWIS BUELL

Ever since Huck Finn and Jim rafted down the Mississippi
a popular theme among writers has been the friendship of a
boy with a philosophic man, who may be an eccentric, an
outcast or a recluse. It is a rare relationship—not many
boys today have the time or the opportunity for one, but in
fiction it can still be ... a prospective theme....

The title character in Joseph Krumgold's "Onion John" is
a robustly individual soul, a small-town handyman who
uses the town dump as his supermarket, has four bathtubs
in his one-room shack and has, also, a fund of esoteric
knowledge irresistible to young boys.... Once 12-year-old
Andy ... understands Onion John's complicated English
the two become best friends, and this irritates Andy's
father, who has his own plans for his son—he is to be a scientist and away with all these superstitions. Andy is caught
between his father's love, his insistence upon a rational
way of life and the wonderful come-day, go-day self-reliance of John, who is simple but no simpleton, good and
wise. When Andy's father tries to remodel John along
twentieth-century lines, the situation gets really complicated and suddenly, almost ruefully, Andy finds he has
grown up.

Mr. Krumgold ... tells all this with wit and comedy, some
wry, good-natured satire on conventional do-gooders and a
great deal of sympathy for all concerned. Never mind if the
stage manager's hand sometimes shows; he has given the
serious reader a lot to think about. (p. 16)

Ellen Lewis Buell, in The New York Times Book
Review (© 1960 by The New York Times Company; reprinted by permission), January 3, 1960.

[*Onion John*] is certainly one of the distinguished books of
our time with all the literary finesse and perceptiveness of
"Miguel" and stronger story appeal. The problems it deals
with are basic: how understanding can we be of the bits of
alien culture and superstition an immigrant clings to? Can
we realize that "what we think is proper and what John
thinks is proper, they're two different things. What are we
trying to prove to him, that he's wrong?" How far may a
father influence his son in passing on career dreams of his
own? How does a 12-year-old boy meet his father on a
man-to-man basis after a conscientious struggle inside? ...
[The] writing has dignity and strength. There is conflict,
drama, and excellent character portrayal. There should be
more of this kind of realism in children's books. (p. 147)

Junior Libraries (reprinted from the March, 1960
issue of Junior Libraries, published by R. R.
Bowker Co. A Xerox Corporation; copyright ©
1960), March, 1960.

In *Onion John* Mr. Krumgold has established a character
worth cherishing in a materially-minded world for he cares
nothing for the trimmings of civilisation, and though he may
be a trifle cracked on the subject of spells and magic formula he is on the other hand completely self-sufficient....
Local Rotary builds him a new house with all mod. con.
which John's unfamiliarity with modern living promptly
reduces to ashes. Whose fault was it? Was it really right to
transfer John into an environment for which he was temper-

amentally unsuited? Was he best left to his life of comparative squalor and drifting activity? Within his portrait of an American small town and character-studies of John and Andy, the author poses these questions without imposing on the reader any sociological clap-trap. . . . One feels the author has something to say which here and there a sensitive reader will absorb. (p. 169)

The Junior Bookshelf, *July, 1964.*

CAROLYN HOROVITZ

Onion John does not appear to me to be a work for children but instead, a "teaching" story, a parable, aimed at parents. Onion John, in spite of minute description, is a personification of an abstraction. Except for what he does in an accidental way, the boy who narrates the story is really not involved as an active participant; it is his father's struggle that is central and resolved at the moment of climax. (pp. 160-61)

> *Carolyn Horovitz, in* Newbery and Caldecott Medal Books: 1956-1965, *edited by Lee Kingman (copyright © 1965 by The Horn Book, Inc., Boston), Horn Book, 1965 (and reprinted by Horn Book, 1966).*

Mr. Krumgold catches the quintessence of suburbia [in *Henry 3*]: the lawns and shrubs like stage sets, the subtleties of social climbing from the crib on, the insecurity that insists too much. His kids come across loud and clear and so, sadly, do their elders. . . . Because it is fast and funny and refreshing reading, because it probes—deep—the problems which bug kids, it should have an enormous impact. (p. 886)

> Kirkus Service *(copyright © 1967 Virginia Kirkus' Service, Inc.), August 1, 1967.*

ZENA SUTHERLAND

[*Henry 3*] is a thoughtful and perceptive book, well written but just a bit slow of pace. Although the characterization is excellent, the story doesn't quite achieve the impact of Mr. Krumgold's two Newbery Award books. (p. 49)

> *Zena Sutherland, in* Saturday Review *(© 1967 by Saturday Review, Inc.; reprinted with permission), September 16, 1967.*

JEAN FRITZ

Crestview [in "Henry 3"] is the Establishment; it is Suburbia, the perfect backdrop for a man like Henry Lovering's father, ripe for a vice-presidency. Crestview is a place where survival itself depends on cultivating the right people. This, as it turns out, does not include Fletcher Larkin and his father. . . .

Although Henry has a great time as a member of the most in-group, eventually he comes to see the phoniness. . . . And what can a young man do at the end of such a book? There is no place to go since Crestview is not an isolated community; it is every community. About all Henry can do is to leave the future open.

Unfortunately the story and characterization are not wholly convincing, sometimes verging on caricature, sometimes naiveté. One remembers the satisfying stories and subtle, many-sided characters Mr. Krumgold has created in the past in two Newbery Award books and regrets that, al-

though the theme of the present book is provocative, the story is presented in such black and white terms. (p. 40)

> *Jean Fritz, in* The New York Times Book Review *(© 1967 by The New York Times Company; reprinted by permission), October 8, 1967.*

HOUSTON L. MAPLES

In *Henry 3* Joseph Krumgold continues the dialogue between the generations which he has explored with such sensitivity and insight in his previous works. Once again he presents us with a boy on the verge of the adult world, torn between affection for his parents and the need to establish his own values. . . . Mr. Krumgold's style is beautiful in its suppleness, economy and nuance, his story rich in variety of character and incident; yet one will look in vain for that undercurrent of poetic identification with rural or village scene which illuminated *And Now Miguel* or *Onion John*. Crestview, by contrast, is a dismal and disturbing manifestation of spiritual poverty and cold-blooded opportunism, the symptoms described with uncanny accuracy and, underneath, a humorous disdain. (p. 8)

Has Mr. Krumgold written a sociological treatise or a story for children? Despite the underlying concern with social issues and moral values, this is a warm and engaging story about a special boy, his friends and, most of all, his parents. Crestview with its neon-lit shopping center and fourteen different style houses is dreadful to the eye of the sophisticated reader, but, within the framework of the child's world, it is merely where Henry lives, and better than where he lived before. Mr. Krumgold's primary concern is with the beauty and humor and sadness of human aspirations and the human condition; consequently his characters, who speak in a spontaneous and wonderfully revealing manner, engross us in a personal and individual way simply as people working out their destinies, rather than as symbols manipulated to demonstrate a theory.

It is often said that children's literature is the literature of optimism. *Henry 3* belongs firmly to that tradition. If there are no easy answers in Henry's world, neither is there cause for cynicism or despair. An affirmative belief in human goodness is real and palpable throughout the story. The relationship between the boy and his parents is remarkable in its directness and wealth of affection. Even when Henry is obliged to reject their values and to make his disappointment known, he does so thoughtfully and with a candor which testifies to the depth of their mutual love. It is this capacity for love, so beautifully understated, which enables the parents to recognize the need of their son and their own limitations. How they provide for that need gives the story a surprising and moving conclusion. (p. 34)

> *Houston L. Maples, in* Book World—Chicago Tribune, *Part II (© 1967 Postrib Corp.), November 5, 1967.*

ETHEL L. HEINS

With his keen intelligence and a boy's clear, uncluttered vision, Henry began to penetrate the apparent hypocrisy of the world of adults [in *Henry 3*]. Only in a time of crisis when a hurricane brought tragedy and destruction to the town, did Henry glimpse the nobility and truth in people. His encounter with life—his first realization of human strengths and weaknesses—was the beginning of maturity. Henry's story makes a long, thoughtful book which speaks directly to young people with far more vitality, immediacy, and compassion than either of the author's two Newbery Medal books. (p. 71)

Ethel L. Heins, in The Horn Book Magazine *(copyright © 1968 by The Horn Book, Inc., Boston), February, 1968.*

JOSEPH KRUMGOLD

[Running] into fairy tales is a familiar professional predicament of mine. It happened with each of the three books that make up the trilogy I've written on how we grow up. In each case, I started out to write a thoroughly realistic story of how a child turns adult in one of three different areas of our society. In each case, I found I was writing, by the time I got halfway through the book, simply a new variation of a well-known fairy tale. . . .

[In . . . *and now Miguel*] the fairy tale was the story of the Three Wishes, totally appropriate to a boy who grows up in a tradition-bound religious society. He must learn that the rewards of maturity come through believing in a wisdom far more universal than his own. . . .

In *Onion John* the fairy tale proved to be the one about the Hero Who Learns the Language of the Animals. We're told that this story may preserve the dim memory of a prehistoric knack we had of communicating with our fellow beasts at a time when we domesticated some of them. It sets up the problem of identity—whether one is indeed a man or an animal—and ends with the hero trying to exploit, and being repudiated by, the creature whose language he's come to know. The boy in *Onion John* follows this pattern. Confused as he is by the changing values of an American small town, his search is for his identity. The magic and adventure of speaking an unknown language doesn't help in the end. He finds out who he is and turns adult only when he forces a new acknowledgement of kinship with his own kind, with his own father. . . .

Henry's suburb turns out to be a community far more antique, in one respect, than either the small town of Onion John or the church town of Miguel. This suburb is a woman's town. . . .

By happy coincidence, it happened that while working on *Henry 3* I found myself in the exact place where recorded history did dawn—in the Mediterranean. . . .

[One] of the common ties binding these seaboard people together is the heritage of the Goddess, and her worship. . . .

[This heritage] goes back to the garden civilization that immediately preceded the writing of history, the culture of crop and cattle in which the woman had taken the place of the hunter as chief provider. The history of these unrecorded times, this matriarchy, comes to us as myth. . . . [Most] students of folklore agree that the widespread myth is a dramatization of a common religious festival, the fertility rite that petitioned the powers on high to keep things growing. (p. 113)

One fixed episode of the fertility rite is the testing of the hero who will marry the Princess and live happily ever after, until he is in turn sacrificed. In the folk tales these tests have to do with the Seven Heroic Labors, or the Dragon and Glass Mountain . . . , or, as turns out to be the case with *Henry 3*, the story we all know of the Hero Who Is Given Three Puzzles To Solve. . . .

I was more than halfway through *Henry 3* when I discovered that this was the story I was actually trying to write. And again, for a boy growing up in the new matriarchy of our big-city suburb, this fairy tale, when it did appear, seemed to be wonderfully apt. For Henry 3 did have puzzles to solve and indeed they're impressive enough. . . . But even more significant for me is the very pattern of the fairy tale I was now faced with. It described the world that Henry and most of us live in. . . .

We're puzzle solvers. This is our basic faith. We live with the conviction that given enough information, enough data, enough facts—and enough computers into which we can program this flow—we can solve any puzzle. The operative word here, for our society, is *enough*. Whatever problems we face remain problems, we're sure, only because we don't have *enough* facts to bring them to decision. All we have to do is dig into ourselves a little deeper, such is our optimism, to measure ourselves a little more minutely, and all the questions of race and class and the individual and his purposes will be answered.

We seem to have no fear that the better we do this job the more we fade into an abstraction. . . .

That's Henry's problem. He lives in this abstract world. He's as sure about himself, within his statistically bound community, as Miguel is in his religious one. With this difference. Miguel can begin to tell us his story with the simple affirmation "I am Miguel." Henry's affirmation is simple enough, but it's a decimal. "I am," he tells us, "154 percent normal." Henry's surest description of himself is an abstraction. And his struggle to grow up is a search for reality. . . .

There's nothing real here for Henry to find. But it's the way he goes about his search that makes it even tougher. He simply adopts current procedure and goes ahead confident that if he can solve his own puzzles he'll reach fulfillment. And solve them he does, even to finding a way to go around the world in a parked automobile. Henry even finds a way to stop wars. But with all this, he fails. It doesn't work.

What Henry bumps up against, of course, is the end of that old fairy tale. The hero always does manage to solve his three puzzles, you remember. But always he's denied his reward—by the wicked King or the jealous Queen or the calculating wizard. Always something more, something different is needed. No matter how bright we are, how intellectual, what kind of an I.Q. we have or how magic a computer, it's not enough, says the old fairy tale. It takes courage. We have to stand up for ourselves, we need to prove our moral and physical courage, as well, to reach our goal. It's a switch, as we used to say in story conferences. The fairy tale turns us from a story about a brain to one about the heart that's in us.

It's this switch that makes me an optimist. It seems to point to a cultural switch that we as a people are going through today, right now. One that may be the very start of the pendulum swing that will save our own species from the brink of success. (p. 114)

With his three puzzles behind him, all neatly solved, Henry 3 does manage to summon up the courage required by the old fairy tale. He looks beyond his father and mother to reach for what's real with the help of a kid his own age. . . .

And with this reassurance the last sentence of the book was written. Henry 3 says, "I am Miguel." It's the opening line of the first book. This was my way of telling myself that the circle of the trilogy was turned, that more of us increasingly come to where we can undertake the spiritual adventure of a shepherd boy who climbs a mountain. (p. 115)

> *Joseph Krumgold, "Archetypes of the Twentieth Century," in* School Library Journal *(reprinted from the October, 1968 issue of* School Library Journal, *published by R. R. Bowker Co. A Xerox Corporation; copyright © 1968), October, 1968, pp. 112-15.*

CHARLOTTE S. HUCK and DORIS YOUNG KUHN

When Andy discovers he has an ability to communicate with an immigrant town bum, *Onion John*, he transfers his loyalty and resents his father's interference with the superstitions and rituals of Onion John. He is hurt by the way his father and the townspeople try to change Onion John into a "proper citizen" by building an acceptable home for him. Finally, Andy is freed from his father's dominance and the superstition of Onion John. Each of these men contributes to Andy's growing independence. The closing scene is a beautifully written description of the communication of a father and son through gesture and smiles. (p. 223)

> *Charlotte S. Huck and Doris Young Kuhn, in their* Children's Literature in the Elementary School *(copyright © 1961, 1968, by Holt, Rinehart and Winston, Inc., reprinted by permission of Holt, Rinehart and Winston, Publishers), second edition, Holt, 1968.*

MAY HILL ARBUTHNOT

[. . . *And Now Miguel*], set in the sheepherding country of New Mexico, is one of the great books for children. . . . Miguel's goal is special—to become an expert sheepherder like the rest of the men in his family. But his problem is a universal one for twelve-year-olds. . . . The boy struggles to fulfill competently all the tasks of sheepherding that come his way, but he feels that he fails more frequently than he succeeds. He always measures himself by adult standards, and there is no part of the four-hundred-year-old skills in sheep care and breeding that Miguel does not love and strive to learn. This is a remarkable story on many counts—deep family love, pride in the family skills and work, passionate desire for independent achievement and competence, and a boy's love for his grown-up brother. The discussion of prayer between the two boys, Gabriel and Miguel, is unique in children's literature as is the rather subtle style in which this book is written. (p. 117)

> *May Hill Arbuthnot, in her* Children's Reading in the Home *(copyright © 1969 by Scott, Foresman and Company; reprinted by permission), Scott, Foresman, 1969.*

RUTH HILL VIGUERS

Joseph Krumgold's three books, different in settings, characters, mood, and style are, nevertheless, related. They make up, in a sense, a trilogy having for its basic theme the problems of adolescence: of understanding the loved and imperfect people around one and being respected by them as a mature person, of accepting the world of people with widely divergent views and attitudes, and of recognizing the values fundamental to the wholeness of one's personality and life. . . .

Mr. Krumgold received the Newbery Medal for each of his first two books. *Henry 3* is even stronger in the development of the theme and characterizations, and more absorbing and exciting in plot. (p. 594)

> *Ruth Hill Viguers, in* A Critical History of Children's Literature, *by Cornelia Meigs, Anne Thaxter Eaton, Elizabeth Nesbitt, and Ruth Hill Viguers, edited by Cornelia Meigs (copyright © 1953, 1969 by Macmillan Publishing Co., Inc.), revised edition, Macmillan, 1969.*

ELEANOR CAMERON

In extended imagery, Krumgold gives us in *Henry 3* the following inscape about losing, about the sensation of knowing you're losing, and here . . . the rhythm of these lines, their very flow, is an inherent part of Krumgold's meaning. (These lines, too, are a fine example of how a novel can be written in the first person, the person here being a thirteen-year-old boy, can reflect the disciplined and sensitive style of the author himself, and yet sound perfectly natural and unliterary, in the pejorative sense of the word "literary.")

> . . . losing became a part of whatever went on. There's even a color to losing. It's brown, like the one dead leaf on a full green tree is brown, twisting slow and waiting to drop. And the smell of losing is sour as a dirty T-shirt the morning after a ball game. There's a taste to it, too, that's dry and salty. You could be running a temperature, the way losing tastes. And the sound of it is far off. Losing is an echo of all the noises you pass through while you think only of what's wrong. It's brittle, losing, like the feel of toothpicks you snap between your fingers in Pirelli's Pharmacy, trying to answer questions.
>
> (p. 150)

> *Eleanor Cameron, in her* The Green and Burning Tree: On the Writing and Enjoyment of Children's Books *(copyright © 1962, 1964, 1966, 1969 by Eleanor Cameron; reprinted by permission of Little, Brown and Co. in association with The Atlantic Monthly Press), Atlantic-Little, Brown, 1969.*

DIANE GERSONI STAVN

[Joseph Krumgold] uses . . . state-of-the-sexes observations to "explain" the sad state of modern society. His . . . *And Now Miguel*, a capably written book, concerns a farm-dwelling family and particularly the next to the youngest son. Miguel's mother and sisters seem to exist only because the author assumed the men of the family would have to come into contact with women sometimes. They're alluded to primarily in terms of their familial roles: e.g., Miguel wonders "'. . . what there could be for supper.'" . . . Given the farm setting, such role delineation is realistic enough. Krumgold begins to slide with *Onion John*, a dull book that touts the glories of rugged individualism by focusing on the antics of a superstitious old man who is befriended by 12-year-old Andy. Andy's housewife mother is an innocuous, really irrelevant character, visible a little more often than Miguel's mother but just barely. . . .

In *Henry 3*, a book set in wealthy suburbia, Krumgold through his characters laments the fact of commuting fathers and tortuously and speciously indicts the presumably eviscerating "matriarchal" suburban values. Henry Lovering is a kid with an embarrassingly high I. Q. His dad during the day is a fawning corporate climber; his mom *likes* life in suburban Crestview. When the Loverings are ostracized because of the bomb shelter they have installed in their home (Mr. Lovering's in the shelter biz), it seems likely that the family will have to leave Crestview. Henry's upset about this, but the old sage of the book, his friend Fletcher's ruggedly individualistic grandfather, tells him to shed no tears; that Crestview's no place for a boy to grow to manhood in because it's "'. . . a woman's world around here. Crestview is her idea . . . these women have to be safe. They have their children to protect. Their first big idea is to get enough security to bring up a family. And the second, they have to be in fashion. Because in a place like this a woman can't grow old . . . the ideas it (Crestview) lives by. They're about thirty-five hundred years old. That's how far back you'd have to go to find a world anything like Crestview, a matriarchy. . . . A society that's ruled by women. And there you have it, why Crestview's wrong . . . Fashion's fine and so is security, but they're not enough to control a lot of machinery. If we can't find anything better to live by than those two things, we might as well give this particular planet back to the ants.'"

Now, even so general a source as the *Encyclopaedia Britannica* states: "No peoples on earth are known to be organized matriarchically, nor are there reliable historical records of such societies. If there ever were matriarchates in the very earliest times, there is no trustworthy evidence for their existence . . . the society as a whole has never been found in which women in general have authority over men in general." Given that any intelligent discussion of matriarchy must involve uncertainty, it is revealing that Mr.

Krumgold has a sympathetic character impart a rigid theory —the basis of which is emphatically in disfavor—in ringing, pontifical tones to young readers. Even if one were to accept his patently absurd generalizations regarding all women in suburbia, it's difficult to follow Krumgold's logic. Is Crestview the woman's idea? Isn't it just as valid to postulate that suburbia is the status symbol of the rising young executive? *If* women can't grow old in Crestview, is that a situation of their own choosing? Do they enjoy the fashion treadmill? Or must they maintain their youthful, fashionable looks in order to be acceptable assets to their husbands? (p. 284)

MAY HILL ARBUTHNOT and ZENA SUTHERLAND

[. . . *And Now Miguel*] written in the first person, may have to be introduced to children, but it is well worth the time and effort. Here are strong family love and loyalty with a profound respect for the family tradition of work, and here is pride in the expert performance of that work. Here too is the hero worship of a younger for an older brother. There is a feeling for the cycle of the seasons, each one bringing its special work and special satisfactions. And finally there is a closeness to God that makes prayer a natural part of life. (p. 458)

Jean Lee Latham

1902-

(Also has written under pseudonym Julian Lee) American young adult biographer, novelist, poet, playwright, and editor, and adult playwright and essayist. Latham is considered a leading writer of fictionalized biography. She chooses doctors, inventors, scientists, naturalists, and mathematicians as her subjects, people ahead of their time in pioneering technical advancement. Latham reduces massive data into a form that is understandable to her young adult audience, and she has consistently detailed the important aspects of her subjects and their achievements without disturbing the flow of her narratives. She is also an extremely thorough researcher who uses the letters and samples of the work of her subjects to enhance and verify her narratives. Formerly a dramatist, Latham claims that it is the suspense in a person's life and his ability to achieve despite setbacks that makes him appealing as a subject. She began writing plays in high school, and eventually became both an actress and a drama teacher. She was editor-in-chief of the Dramatic Publishing Company in Chicago for six years, and wrote her first book about acting and directing. She has also written many plays for both stage and radio. During World War II, Latham was appointed civilian in charge of the National Training Program for Signal Corps inspectors. After the war she concentrated solely on narrative writing. Latham discovered Nathaniel Bowditch, the American astronomer and authority on navigation, when she read the introduction to *The American Practical Navigator*, which he wrote in 1799 at the age of twenty-six and which is still considered the standard work among sailors. *Carry On, Mr. Bowditch* renewed interest in its subject and won the 1956 Newbery Medal. She aimed this work at a specific reader, the adolescent boy. Most of her works have male heroes and have their greatest appeal to those with an interest in technical subjects. She has been criticized for these aspects, and for a writing style that is sometimes stilted and choppy. However, Latham's works have introduced young people to real characters from whose accomplishments they can learn and with whose dreams they can identify. (See also *Contemporary Authors*, Vols. 5-8, rev. ed., and *Something about the Author*, Vol. 2.)

T. MORRIS LONGSTRETH

Thanks to Miss Latham's investigation of seamanship in 1800 and of the Bowditch household [in "Carry On, Mr. Bowditch"], the reader is kept at Nat's elbow, from the age of six, sharing the poignant and difficult events as they come along. . . .

Miss Latham's courage in attempting the life of a calculator has paid off in several directions. She has added a lovable genius to our roster of great Americans. She has put in a plug for education, subtly but surely, through her skill in picturing Nat. She has made us understand character better, for none can read this book without benefitting by Nat's example. Her keen feeling for human relationships and her economical style round out her achievement. As my sextant figures it, "Carry On, Mr. Bowditch" is a book not only for the pre-teens, but for everybody. (p. 13)

> *T. Morris Longstreth, in* The Christian Science Monitor *(reprinted by permission from* The Christian Science Monitor; © *1955 The Christian Science Publishing Society; all rights reserved), September 22, 1955.*

ALICE BROOKS McGUIRE

The author of ["Carry On, Mr. Bowditch"] merits special commendation for her writing ability. She has created out of a mass of involved, technical material a living, dramatic story which will hold the interest of most young people. It reads like a lively sea yarn, yet does not skimp on the mathematical and navigation data. In fact, Bowditch's own simple explanation to his unlettered crew could not have been any more lucid than Miss Latham's account of the discoveries of this "human calculating machine." (p. 8)

> *Alice Brooks McGuire, in* New York Herald Tribune Book Review, Part 2 *(© I.H.T. Corporation; reprinted by permission), November 13, 1955.*

Matthew Fontaine Maury was a fighter. . . . He was destined to fight all his life against odds for his ideas. . . . [In "Trail Blazer of the Seas"] Jean Latham dramatizes his struggle to get his wind and current charts made and their conclusions accepted. The reader rushes ahead as full of interest in these achievements as in a battle at sea. It is the technique used successfully in the Newbery Prize-winning "Carry On, Mr. Bowditch." In her Newbery acceptance speech Mrs. Latham said it was being "back yard familiar" with the world of her story before she proceeded to "flesh the bones with reality." It is no small achievement to do this with a fairly uneventful life. . . . (p. 12)

> New York Herald Tribune Book Review, Part 2 *(© I.H.T. Corporation; reprinted by permission), November 18, 1956.*

ELLEN LEWIS BUELL

[Miss Latham] has a knack of making the people of the past seem very much alive. In this robust, full-bodied story ["This Dear-Bought Land"] she not only does that but also gives the reader an understanding of the immensity of [the undertaking of establishing the colony of Jamestown]. (p. 34)

> *Ellen Lewis Buell*, in The New York Times Book Review (© 1957 by The New York Times Company; reprinted by permission), March 31, 1957.

IRVING T. MARSH

["This Dear-Bought Land"] is written with the zest one gives a favorite subject, is dramatic and paints a vivid picture of [a] desperate venture.

[Jean Lee Latham] also offers very ingenious suggestions in explanation of the early silence of Captain John Smith about many incidents which he reported in his later years. David Warren, hurt and insulted by Captain John Smith the first time he meets him, reluctantly grows to admire him. Thus the readers gain an understanding picture of the thorny and indomitable character. David's story begins dramatically with a hold-up and murder. There is a deft use of Christmas carols, first in his English home before the tragedy and again when he and Captain John Smith are in Powhatan's power, threatened with death. (p. 29)

> *Irving T. Marsh*, in New York Herald Tribune Book Review (© I.H.T. Corporation; reprinted by permission), May 12, 1957.

MARGARET WARREN BROWN

[*Young Man in a Hurry: The Story of Cyrus W. Field*] is powerfully written, and intensely exciting. The solving of the numerous apparently unsolvable problems involved in the manufacture and laying of thousands of miles of cable becomes spellbinding. Drama and suspense reach a great climax on the deck of the *Great Eastern* . . . when with Field we finally see the cable successfully laid. A magnificent book. (pp. 390-91)

> *Margaret Warren Brown*, in The Horn Book Magazine (copyright, 1958, by the Horn Book, Inc., Boston), October, 1958.

HOWARD BOSTON

In most history textbooks only passing reference is made to Cyrus W. Field. No reader of Jean Lee Latham's latest fictionalized biography will ever be disposed to dismiss the enterprising Field so briefly. This lively and convincing book brings the man most responsible for the Atlantic Cable unforgettably to life. . . . The account really takes off . . . when Field throws himself into the project of tying the Old and New Worlds with a submarine cable. The staggering problems he tackles—and the heartbreaking setbacks he receives—make absorbing reading.

Laying underseas cable and sending messages through it are highly technical operations, but Miss Latham makes them not only crystal clear but exciting. A cable splicing in mid-Atlantic becomes as dramatic an achievement as a delicate surgical operation. Readers of this fast-moving, conversation-packed biography will be genuinely impressed with Field's integrity and perseverance. (p. 28)

> *Howard Boston*, in The New York Times Book

Review (© 1959 by The New York Times Company; reprinted by permission), January 18, 1959.

Hero or pirate? This is the question not only history but his contemporaries asked of Francis Drake. According to [*Drake: The Man They Called A Pirate*], the bold Englishman, servant to Queen Elizabeth, was every inch the patriot. . . . In his capacity of self-elected protector of England's rights against Spain often the tactics that he used were unorthodox. Alone, he and the men of his ship raided Spanish vessels and harried the Spanish fleet in the Caribbean. But this he did in order to cut off supplies from Philip. The author . . . stresses the fact that he refused to kill women, children or unarmed men. Sir Francis Drake's life . . . was one of colorful achievement and this biography does much to convey the richness of event and atmosphere which was the portion of one of Elizabeth's most celebrated knights. (p. 96)

> *Virginia Kirkus' Service, February 1, 1960.*

VIRGINIA HAVILAND

[*Drake, The Man They Called a Pirate* is a] full biography which reads like historical fiction. . . . Heavily conversational but without earlier speech and salty language, the book lacks period flavor, yet gives a clear account of Drake's genius as a mariner and the historical background of his adventuring. (p. 301)

> *Virginia Haviland*, in The Horn Book Magazine (copyright, 1960, by the Horn Book, Inc., Boston), August, 1960.

LEARNED T. BULMAN

As she did with Nathaniel Bowditch and Matthew Maury, Jean Lee Latham has made an impressive figure of a nearly forgotten man [John Ericsson, in "Man of the Monitor"]. Again she stops at a focal point—the battle of the Monitor and the Merrimac; Ericsson died twenty-seven years later. Again one misses a chronology. But, like all of her fictionized biographies, this is fast-paced, informative reading. (p. 30)

> *Learned T. Bulman*, in The New York Times Book Review (© 1962 by The New York Times Company; reprinted by permission), May 20, 1962.

MARGARET SHERWOOD LIBBY

["Man of the Monitor" is] more alluring to the average 12-year-old than the more sober narrative of Constance Buell Burnett, "Captain John Ericsson." Having attracted the young readers Miss Latham, like a competent craftsman, tries to hold their interest by squeezing as much excitement as possible out of the many frustrations of her hero's life. She is less successful in this than in her ["Carry On, Mr. Bowditch" or even "This Dear-Bought Land"]. Perhaps this is because all her characters talk alike, in a pleasantly ordinary modern speech. Whatever the reason, a less vivid picture of the ever-optimistic inventor of the "Monitor" is given here than in Mrs. Burnett's book. . . . (p. 9)

> *Margaret Sherwood Libby*, in New York Herald Tribune Books (© I.H.T. Corporation; reprinted by permission), July 1, 1962.

[*Retreat to Glory: The Story of Sam Houston*] is probably intended as a biography cum fictionalized dialogue of

Houston. However, since the dramatization is heavy, and the historical details have been played up according to their effectiveness with respect to the total narrative, the book's value is as an exciting adventure based on actual events. The most vivid part of the book occurs during Houston's leadership of the rebel armies against Mexico. The vastness of Texas and the complexity of varying events throughout the state is made quite clear. This is an outstandingly realistic portrayal of a war. Houston's oft repeated battlecry, when it comes, is strong and fresh in its impact. The opening of the book, which deals with young Sam as a mischievous little boy, seems rather foolish, but once it reaches the time in his adolescence when he joined an Indian tribe it becomes a compelling drama of a hero who seems more than human. The book continues through Houston's career as Governor and U.S. Senator. . . . It is an exciting pageant dealing with a great man, born to be a legend. (p. 318)

> *Virginia Kirkus' Service (copyright © 1965 Virginia Kirkus' Service, Inc.), March 15, 1965.*

LON TINKLE

Jean Lee Latham makes Sam Houston a believable and very human hero [in "Retreat to Glory: The Story of Sam Houston"]. . . .

The private personality behind this flamboyant public figure is as interesting as the career. With impressively swift pace, Miss Latham, who knows what to omit or merely suggest, does not skimp Sam's character at all. It is clear why as a boy, bored with country school and storekeeping in Tennessee, he ran off to live with the neighboring Cherokees. It is clear why he later became Andy Jackson's protégé, clear how his courage and personal sense of honor dominated the major events in his life. . . . This superior account makes both man and history clear and absorbing. (p. 24)

> *Lon Tinkle, in The New York Times Book Review (© 1965 by The New York Times Company; reprinted by permission), June 13, 1965.*

PETER C. LAWRENCE

The ambitious attempt of Miss Latham to portray Sam Houston as a human being as well as a patriot [in *Retreat to Glory, the Story of Sam Houston*] in no way detracts from her explanation of the life and times in which he lived. Throughout the narrative Houston's many faceted personality is merged with the tumultuous events of American History from the War of 1812 through the secession of Texas in the Civil War, and from the merger of man with events comes a picture of a citizen with the courage of his convictions.

The story, written in a simple, straightforward style, serves several purposes. The issues that faced our growing nation —war and our military system, Indian problems, expansion, political maneuvering, and the many problems associated with sectionalism—are explained in terms of their social, political and economic impact using the episodes of Houston's life as a focal point. The problems are removed from text book sterility and made real through the author's skillful use of dialogue. The explanation of events involving the settling of Texas and its struggle for independence and statehood is particularly effective.

Perhaps more important than the relating of history is the character study of Houston. The adolescent of today can readily identify with the young man who appeared to be the typical square peg in a round hole. There are also opportunities for the young reader to be inspired by Houston's courage to find a suitable life, work hard for what he wanted, and fight bravely in defense of his beliefs. In light of the sometimes cynical questioning of motives and men today, this narrative becomes a welcome partial explanation of American greatness. (pp. 80-1)

> *Peter C. Lawrence, in The Social Studies (copyright © 1967 Helen Dwight Reid Educational Foundation), February, 1967.*

RAYMOND W. BARBER

[*Anchors Aweigh: the Story of David Glasgow Farragut* is a] vivid picture of the U.S. Navy from 1810 through 1869 and a less skillful, fictionized depiction of David Farragut who gained fame in the Civil War naval battles of New Orleans and Mobile Bay. . . . Despite the addition of much fictionized dialogue, Farragut is seen solely as a Navy man and never comes across as a believable human being. The historical background is interesting but as a biography, this falls flat. (p. 4420)

> *Raymond W. Barber, in Library Journal (reprinted from Library Journal, November 15, 1968; published by R. R. Bowker Co. (a Xerox company); copyright © 1968 by Xerox Corporation), November 15, 1968.*

IVAN SANDROF

["Anchors Aweigh" is] told in the form of a novel by Jean Lee Latham. . . . She is a bright writer, always in command, despite a tendency to furl too much sail. (She dismisses the death of young Farragut's beloved mother in seven bald lines.) But her narrative flows, her pace is swift, her knowledge of matters nautical considerable. (p. 12)

> *Ivan Sandrof, in The New York Times Book Review (© 1968 by The New York Times Company; reprinted by permission), December 22, 1968.*

NANCY BYERS

In a very much to-the-point fashion [*The Columbia, Power House of North America*] tells the river's history, its discovery, the building of Astoria to promote fur trade, the gradual settlement of the territory by the Americans, the river's development and finally the building of the huge dams to produce hydro-electric power. In more recent years [Canadian] interest, and much controversy, has been aroused by the Columbia River Treaty of 1964 which has been summarily dealt with in 10 lines near the end of the book. . . . [The] text, written in an easy-to-read style, is reasonably successful, making this a good "project" book. However, as the book concentrates on the American end of the river and the American end of things it would seem it would be of more use to American students. (p. 29)

> *Nancy Byers, in In Review: Canadian Books for Children, Spring, 1970.*

"You're going to go far." Shoulders squared and mind alert . . . , the young James Cook follows his star . . . right out of biography into the heady gambits of historical fiction [in *Far Voyager: The Story of James Cook*]. . . . [This] whole venture [is] composed of dramatic scenes, vigorous dialogue, colorful personalities—it's eminently readable,

not unreliable, just somewhat flushed (and in the case of his wife, affected: "There are some things [like danger] a man doesn't tell a woman"). (p. 507)

Kirkus Reviews *(copyright © 1970 The Kirkus Service, Inc.), May 1, 1970.*

MARY M. BURNS

Thoroughly conversant with the equipment, traditions, and living conditions aboard eighteenth-century sailing ships, the author has written Cook's story [in *Far Voyager: The Story of James Cook*] with the flair and pace of a first-rate adventure yarn set against the background of the Seven Years' War and the American Revolution.... His metamorphosis from seaman to commissioned officer in His Majesty's Navy is substantial material in itself for an engrossing narrative. His exploits as one of history's greatest navigators and explorers add dramatic tension as well. Today's young reader for whom the world has already become too small should find it illuminating to consider an era —merely two centuries ago—when much of the Pacific Ocean was unknown. By demonstrating the magnitude of Cook's accomplishments during his Pacific explorations, the biography presents him as no casual thrill seeker but rather as a meticulous and dedicated scientist. Respected for his knowledge and humanitarianism, Cook nevertheless was separated by his visionary genius from ordinary friend-

ships and the full companionship of his wife and family—a subtheme to which the author gives sympathetic attention. His death in 1779, due in part to the Hawaiians mistaking him for the man-god "Lono," is the stuff of tragedy, and the author makes of it a dramatic yet dignified conclusion to her narrative. (pp. 400-01)

Mary M. Burns, in The Horn Book Magazine *(copyright © 1970 by The Horn Book, Inc., Boston), August, 1970.*

LEARNED T. BULMAN

[*Carry on, Mr. Bowditch*] is a really accomplished piece of writing. Miss Latham has succeeded in making a comparatively unknown person come alive on every page of her book. Unlike a number of the Newbery winners, which seem to be chosen by librarians more because they have a beauty of writing (usually lost on the child) than because they tell a good story and do it well, *Carry on, Mr. Bowditch* has been well received by the youngsters and may be just the book to give to the not-so-good reader who needs a book with bounce. (pp. 85-6)

Learned T. Bulman, in English Journal *(copyright © 1958 by the National Council of Teachers of English), November, 1958 (and reprinted in* Readings about Adolescent Literature, *edited by Dennis Thomison, Scarecrow Press, 1970).*

Norman Lear

1922-

American writer of screenplays and television scripts, movie and television producer, and film director. Lear has been credited with expanding the boundaries of television with the situation comedies he created, which brought current social concerns and formerly taboo subjects to viewing audiences. Before *All in the Family* appeared in 1971, television comedy series were often considered mindless, unrealistic entertainments with no relevance to real life. This program was the first to present issues such as rape, breast cancer, homosexuality, and, especially, prejudice on the home screen. Revolving around Archie Bunker, a bigoted white working man in Queens, it was immediately controversial, although not immediately successful. It gradually became accepted and popular through its appealing combination of comedy and reality, a premise which Lear has used as the basis for all his other series. Lear took the ideas for several of his early shows from programs already established on British television. *Till Death Do Us Part* became *All in the Family* and *Steptoe and Son* was turned into *Sanford and Son,* a program which openly ventilated ethnic humor from the black viewpoint. Fred Sanford was the black equivalent of Archie Bunker, just as the character of Maude, an ultra-liberal feminist, was his antithesis. *Maude,* a spinoff series from *All in the Family,* continued its tradition by introducing controversial topics such as abortion, mental illness, and suicide. Along with his partner, Bud Yorkin, Lear created a group of successful spinoff series, and at one time had eight situation comedies running concurrently. One of Lear's biggest successes was *Mary Hartman, Mary Hartman,* an offbeat, often outrageous parody of soap operas which dealt with the travails of a befuddled housewife. As well as spawning series like *Fernwood 2-Night,* a satire of talk and variety shows, *Mary Hartman* was the first program to be marketed independently to individual stations. Lear has won many Emmy awards for his programs, and has been recognized several times with awards from his professional colleagues. Not all of Lear's ideas have been successful. *All That Glitters,* which dealt with male/female role reversal, lasted for only a few episodes. His programs have been criticized for their increased trendiness and a tendency towards shock effect and excessive cuteness. However, many of them have been commended for their accurate portrayal of the family unit. Lear has based many of his ideas and dialogue on his own life; the character of Archie Bunker, for instance, was based on his father. Much of the success of his programs has been attributed to good timing, but Lear feels that the American people "have always been ready" for the depiction of adult themes on television. Whatever the reasons for Lear's success, most critics feel that he has had an undeniable influence on the forward movement of the television industry. (See also *Contemporary Authors,* Vols. 73-76.)

BOSLEY CROWTHER

[The satire, "Divorce American Style," screenplay by Norman Lear] is not as funny or trenchant as it tries very hard to be. Indeed, it is rather depressing, saddening and annoying, largely because it does labor to turn a solemn subject into a great big American-boob joke.

[A key reason for its weakness] is that [director] Mr. Yorkin and Mr. Lear do not establish any viable reason for their quarreling couple to become divorced. They simply ask us to accept the premise that [two people] . . . could be conned into separating, after 17 years of marriage, by a caricature of a marriage counselor and a couple of catty friends.

Sure, they may be a little rattled by too suddenly achieving affluence and too desperately trying to keep up with the other Joneses in a split-level section of Los Angeles. But the feeling one gets is that the authors simply wanted to pull these people apart so they could show the comical convulsions of a fellow trying to make out on what he has left after paying alimony to his divorced wife. . . .

But the main trouble with this picture . . . is that it makes glib fun of something that doesn't fit the frisky mood of farce. (p. 30)

Bosley Crowther, in The New York Times Film Review (© 1967 by The New York Times Company; reprinted by permission), July 20, 1967.

FRED FERRETTI

Tonight the Columbia Broadcasting System Television Network will find out if Americans think bigotry and racism, as the prime elements of a situation comedy, are funny.

It is funny, for example, to have the pot-bellied, churchgoing, cigar-smoking son of Middle America, Archie Bunker, the hero of "All in the Family," fill the screen with such epithets as "spic" and "spade" and "hebe" and "yid" and "polack"? Is it funny for him to refer to his son-in-law as "the laziest white man I ever seen?" Or to look at a televised football game and yell, "Look at that spook run . . . It's in his blood"?

The answer, I say, is no. None of these is funny. They shock because one is not used to hearing them shouted from the television tube during prime-time family programs. They don't make one laugh so much as they force self-conscious, semi-amused gasps.

They are not funny because they are there for their shock value, despite C.B.S.'s protestations that what are being presented are "familiar stereotypes" with "a humorous spotlight on their prejudices . . . making them a source of laughter," so "we can show how absurd they are." What is lacking is taste.

> *Fred Ferretti, "TV: Are Racism and Bigotry Funny?" in* The New York Times *(© 1971 by The New York Times Company; reprinted by permission), January 12, 1971, p. 70.*

STEPHANIE HARRINGTON

"All in the Family," is kind of like wishing for a little more frankness in political dialogue and getting your wish in the form of Spiro Agnew. A working-class family situation series with a message, "All in the Family" is vulgar and silly. And after the disgust-at-first-shock wears off, the vaudeville clinkers passed off as humor are totally predictable, both in themselves and as means of conveying the show's moral: All prejudice—racial, class, sophisticated against unsophisticated and vice versa—is bad.

It cannot even claim the shock value of being courageously, uncompromisingly, true to life. In an attempt to discredit stereotyping, it resorts to stereotypes. In its sledgehammer determination to tell it like it is, it over-tells, and, instead of being the breakthrough in courage it was meant to be, it over-kills itself.

> *Stephanie Harrington, "The Message Sounds Like 'Hate Thy Neighbor'," in* The New York Times, *Section 2 (© 1971 by The New York Times Company; reprinted by permission), January 24, 1971, p. 17.*

LAURA Z. HOBSON

I have a most peculiar complaint about the bigotry in the hit TV comedy, "All in the Family." There's not enough of it.

Here, spade, spic, coon, Polack—these are the words that its central character, Archie Bunker is forever using, plus endless variations, like jungle bunnies, black beauties, the chosen people, yenta, gook, chink, spook and so on. Quite a splashing display of bigotry, but I repeat, nowhere near enough of it.

Let me back up a little. Years ago, after "Gentleman's Agreement," I decided I'd never again write about bigotry or prejudice, at least not about the racial or religious kinds. I've stuck to it. No lectures, no articles, no books about discrimination against Jews, against blacks, against whites, against Puerto Ricans. Perhaps I did not want to keep harping on one theme, perhaps I had nothing to say.

But after 24 years something happened. A television show that treated bigotry for laughs appeared on the screens of the nation. . . . (p. 1)

[I felt the show to be irresponsible] but beyond that I began to be haunted by the notion that there was something else I had to get hold of, for myself if for nothing else. Something the critics weren't saying, something nobody seemed to be saying, not even the people I sought out as experts in the field of race relations. As I kept on ploughing through all the reviews, the feeling intensified. I was pulled up often by the phrases "honest show" and "honest laughter" and "a lovable bigot." . . .

A lovable bigot. Your friendly neighborhood bigot. This is an honest show. This is the way it really is. (p. 12)

[The night I really tangled with "All in the Family" was during the Emmy Awards.]

Johnny Carson wisecracked, "Norman Lear—a nice guy for a Hebe." The audience roared with laughter.

I suppose Norman Lear laughed too. Would he have laughed, I suddenly wondered, if Johnny Carson had said, "Norman Lear, a nice guy for a kike"?

Unthinkable, Johnny Carson would never never—

I know he wouldn't. Besides, it was never never used in the show. Hebe, yes; chosen people, yes, yenta, yes, yid, yes. But kike? Never.

I began to listen for it as I began my little study of the re-runs. Never. And sheeny? Never.

Had Norman Lear never realized that what bigots really called Jews was kike or sheeny? That they didn't really go around talking about the chosen people or one of that tribe or yenta? That their own words, the words they actually used, were kike and sheeny? Then why did Norman Lear, in this honest portrayal of the bigot next door, never say either? . . .

And that other word. Where was that one, among the spades and coons and jungle bunnies and black beauties? I was listening to the shows regularly by then, pad and pencil at the ready, jotting down the actual words Archie was so free with, and I never once heard it. . . .

You know the word they use. The one word, the hideous word.

Unthinkable too, Don't even print it. Nigger.

You know and I know and Mr. Lear knows and the anonymous vice president of the Press Relations Department at CBS knows that Archie Bunker in the flesh would be holding forth about niggers moving in next door, and not breaking bread with no niggers, and getting up a petition for keeping niggers from wrecking real estate values on the street.

Everybody knows it. Then why doesn't this honest show use the real words that real bigots always use?

Is there a little list of Forbidden Words floating around CBS? Is it a little list self-imposed by Mr. Lear himself? Or is it a little list imposed by the Program Practices Department, and the CBS executives in charge of that department?

That was my one big question. Instinctively I knew the answer, but tied into it was that other point: what was that list for? Were the honest producer and the responsible network trying to make bigotry more acceptable? Were they trying to clean it up, deodorize it, make millions of people more comfy about hearing it, indulging in it?

It strikes me that, unconsciously or not, that's just what they were doing. And of course it was the essential trick, to make this show laughable not only to the bigots among that 100 million out there, but also to the "bigotees," the very Hebes and coons and spades and spics and Polacks themselves.

Do you think that any of the nation's blacks would laugh if Archie Bunker constantly said nigger? Do you think many Jews would laugh if he said kike? . . .

Don't risk it. Don't tell it like it is. Clean it up, deterge it, bleach it, enzyme it, and you'll have a show about a lovable bigot that everybody except a few pinko atheistic bleedin' hearts will love.

Well, I differ, I don't think you can be a bigot and be lovable, nor an anti-Semite and lovable. And I don't think the millions who watch this show should be conned into thinking that you can be.

And there you have the basis for my peculiar complaint [that] there's nowhere near enough bigotry in "All in the Family," not by a long sight. How about showing the real thing for a while, before accepting any more praise for honest shows and honest laughter? What about laying it on the line about bigots and then seeing whether CBS switchboards light up with nothing but cheers?

But this is supposed to be a comedy! I know, but a network is supposed to care about the public interest. And one thing that's nearly as nasty as exposing those millions, and their children, week after week to bigotry, is to expose them constantly to hypocrisy. (p. 27)

> Laura Z. Hobson, "As I Listened to Archie Say 'Hebe' . . . ," in The New York Times Book Review, *Part II* (© 1971 by The New York Times Company; reprinted by permission), September 12, 1971, pp. 1, 12, 27.

NORMAN LEAR

I have a most peculiar complaint about Mrs. Hobson's complaint [see excerpt above]. Nigger, kike, and sheeny were the words she found missing from in "All in the Family," which, according to her, made the show dishonest. But there is another word some bigots use—some liberal bigots. You know the word they use. The one word, the hideous word. Don't even print it.

No, Mrs. Hobson, not nigger. Schwartze.

Mrs. Hobson didn't mind our not using that word. Not, I expect because she knows Archie Bunker isn't Jewish: she did acknowledge his use of the word "yenta." I'll offer another reason later. . . .

What . . . is Mrs. Hobson's motive in taking out pad and pencil? Does she feel a sense of proprietorship, of having been the first, and therefore the authority, on the brave new ground of striking-out-at-bigotry? Have we poached on her unconsciously owned territory and must we be driven off by fair means or specious ones?

Mrs. Hobson asks: "Had Norman Lear never realized that what bigots really call Jews was kike and sheeny? . . . Then why did Norman Lear, in his honest portrayal of the bigot next door, never say either?"

Because, Mrs. Hobson, Norman Lear was presenting what to him, out of his knowledge and his life experience, was his honest portrayal of the bigot next door. . . .

If kike and sheeny were the words that bigots really called Jews, as Mrs. Hobson insists, I wasted a lot of tears, and some blood in my lifetime on such pleasantries as yid, hebe, and dirty Jew.

The important thing about bigots and their choice of expressions, however, is that unless they are conversing with other known bigots, they will always tread very carefully, testing before coming out directly. . . .

Archie Bunker does that. A bigot motivated not by hate, but by fear—fear of change, fear of anything he doesn't understand—he knows that Mike and Gloria will jump his every bigoted remark, which indeed they do, so he tries forever to sneak them by.

Mrs. Hobson, however, feels that Mike and Gloria provide no real rebuttal to Archie. I disagree. Mike is always the one who is making sense. Archie at best will work out some kind of convoluted logic to make a point. But it's always foolish. Totally foolish. The biggest point, however, is that we mustn't expect Mike to convince Archie of anything. A liberal will not change the mind of a bigot that way, not on television and not in real life, so week after week, Mike the liberal doesn't defeat Archie. (p. 17)

Speaking of the honest use of words, some bigots say—about as often as they draw a breath. I think an Archie Bunker would use that word down at Kelsey's saloon. As a matter of fact, if my only goal was total honesty, I could not do without that word. But here I fess up. I would not use that word on TV for fear of offending too many people. Not so with nigger, kike, and sheeny. You don't hear them on "All in the Family"—(a) because I feel they are words from another decade, and (b) they are words that connote real hatred, and Archie, as I mentioned earlier, is not motivated by hatred but by fear. (pp. 17, 30)

"All in the Family" can never satisfy Mrs. Hobson. It can't because I believe I know how Mrs. Hobson likes to see her bigots portrayed in the mass media. I know because her generation has provided dozens of stereotypes for my generation—in movies, books, magazines, radio, etc. I grew up with them. . . .

How many of us have ever known a man who has raped a black woman in a squad car? Then how do we relate to him? How do we see a little of ourselves in him? On the other hand, most of us have known people who drop words like spade; and people who with a sly smile have tossed a yenta into the conversational waters to see if it would float. And I have also known people to use that word. The hideous one. Don't print it again.

Schwartze.

More about that in a minute. There is something deeper lurking here. Why do Mrs. Hobson's bigots have to be such outrageous haters to qualify as bigots? . . .

My hope is that the public won't discount Archie Bunker at all. My hope is that they won't feel so superior to him that he becomes as much a stereotype as the white man raping the black woman. . . .

And now about that word. The hideous one. In the publishing world, at a literary dinner, at a cocktail party, sometime in your lifetime, dear lady, have you ever heard the word schwartze pass through the lips of an otherwise respectable, outstanding, humane and even lovable person? . . .

I believe there is a good chance Mrs. Hobson has heard that word, which brings me to my biggest complaint about Mrs. Hobson's complaint. Why didn't she object to our not using schwartze on "All in the Family" along with nigger, kike, and sheeny? She didn't object because she doesn't associate the highly educated, very sophisticated, upperclass individual who uses the word schwartze with a common, lower-class bigot like Archie Bunker. Well, I do. The lower class bigot may hurt the feelings of a hundred people in a lifetime with his racial epithets and perhaps keep one black family out of a white neighborhood. The upperclass gentleman who says schwartze may never hurt the feelings of a black man with his racial epithets; but he just may run a business that employs hundreds of people, none of them black. The thing about bigots, and this includes Archie Bunker, is that they do not know they are prejudiced.

If prejudice were to disappear at noon tomorrow from the hearts of all the good people in the world, there would be no real problem at all.

I am 22 years your junior, Madam, and meaning you no disrespect, if you have not known lovable bigots of different stripes and attitudes, and in varying degrees, we are obviously aging in different wine cellars.

Towards the end of her piece, Mrs. Hobson threw an extra zinger our way concerning the effect she feared "All in the Family" might have on children. I don't wish to get into this at length, except to say I disagree with her in every particular. Life teaches children that "they aren't wanted in certain neighborhoods," and that "there's something that makes people call them names." "All in the Family" simply airs it, brings it out in the open, has people talking about it. And there, in my opinion, is the big effect "All in the Family" can have on children. They will ask questions about the bigotry they see on "All in the Family" and parents will have to answer. Conversations in the home; how bad can that be? (p. 30)

Norman Lear, "As I Read How Laura Saw Archie . . . ," in The New York Times, Section 2 (© 1971 by The New York Times Company; reprinted by permission), October 10, 1971, pp. 17, 30.

ROBERT LEWIS SHAYON

Sanford and Son. . . . is the second BBC comedy series to be transplanted from British to American television. . . . *All in the Family* was the first. . . . *Sanford and Son* will succeed, I hope, although its virtues are not as spectacular as those of its predecessor. . . . I have seen only the first two programs of *Sanford and Son*, but already it is clear that there is a common pattern in the transplant experiences of both series.

The key to that pattern is in the program's lead characters. The prototype of Archie Bunker was a thoroughly unsympathetic bigot in the original British series, *Till Death Do Us Part*, which was designed for a short run. Presumably the allegedly tough-minded British telly viewers could tolerate such a sour character briefly. But for softer-brained American audiences, who must live with their television saints and sinners indefinitely, our Archie had to be made into a "lovable" bigot.

Sanford and Son was based upon the British *Steptoe and Son*. In his pre-transplant incarnation, the main character

was the bitter, irascible, lower-class proprietor of a second-hand shop. In the American version, he has been changed into an essentially sympathetic sixty-five-year-old black named Fred Sanford. . . . Although the changes made in both Archie and Fred solved some problems, they also resulted in new ones. In the case of *All in the Family*, some critics and viewers charged that presenting Archie Bunker as a warm and funny bigot served only to celebrate intolerance of racial and ethnic minorities and to make sick hatreds into laughing matters. Social responsibility demanded muting Archie's prejudices; yet the dramatic fate of the series rested on the unreconcilable tension between Archie's frailties and society's desired behavioral norms. In recent episodes, [there have been] . . . moments of self-awareness as the bigot suffers the arrows of bigotry himself and teeters momentarily on the brink of crucial changes in his belief-system. Given the exigencies of commercial television, this is about the best that can be done in the circumstances. But ultimately this deepening of character makes Archie more interesting, for we are always tantalized by the possibility of his transformation.

In *Sanford and Son*, draining the bitterness and cynicism out of Fred Sanford and casting the role with an actor [Redd Foxx] who has empathic, comic gifts have also brought a transplant difficulty that requires adjustment. Sanford, as presented in the first two episodes, was simply a rather querulous, grouchy old man, incapable of receiving with any measure of appreciation the care, consideration, and gifts of Lamont . . . , his adult son and partner in their junkyard business. Both father and son are caught in an understandable symbiotic-love-hate relationship. The father is a cultural isolate, apparently unaware of any world beyond his cluttered premises combining home and shop. The son is ambitious and eager for upward social mobility. He loves his father and is tolerant of his frailties and needs.

Although he is forever threatening to leave, Lamont doesn't go. The problem for the series is that Fred appears to be a one-dimensional character. While we can understand his abrasive insistence on maintaining his own identity, we could probably not endure indefinitely his inability to acknowledge love offered. As in *All in the Family*, there is a tension that cannot utterly be reconciled—in this case, the tension between Lamont's desire to strike off on his own and his deep affection for his father. Nevertheless, Lamont's patience would become incredible if Fred refused ever to suggest that he had some wells of gratitude, however shallow, within him. Fred himself would ultimately be rejected by the viewers if he persisted in his extremity of perversity.

Sanford and Son is America's first TV comedy series featuring a warm, sympathetic relationship between black males. As such, it is very welcome, but its long-run chances might be enhanced by minor surgery. Endowing father and son with strong social and political attitudes . . . would offer an even better solution; but, regrettably, American TV is still not ready for full-dimensional black males in its entertainment programs.

Robert Lewis Shayon, "The Trouble with Transplants," in Saturday Review (© 1972 Saturday Review Inc.; reprinted with permission), February 19, 1972, p. 14.

PEGGY HUDSON

The situation itself has great potential for comedy—the generation gap, an offbeat way of life, a kind of "anti-establishment" way of thinking. Best of all, perhaps, is the fact that *Sanford and Son* is a network show that treats black people with respect and affection. It isn't "true to life." What situation comedy is? But it's a lot less phoney than *Julia* was.

That's why I hate to see it fail in what I consider some important areas. It is basically a two-character comedy. For this kind of comedy to work, on a weekly basis, it seems to me there should be some kind of balance. I don't *want* to laugh at Fred Sanford every week. If I'm to laugh at him because he's old and out of touch, shouldn't I *sometimes* be able to laugh with him and say, "Hurray for you, Fred Sanford, you really showed them"? Shouldn't he sometimes show traces of intelligence, compassion, humor —and maybe even spunk?

One of the strengths of *All in the Family* is that no matter how much Archie rants and raves, you know the rest of the family can take care of themselves. . . . There is a *balance* in the characterizations—each one has its particular strong points. The cards haven't been stacked against any one of the various characters.

They *have* been stacked pretty heavily against Fred Sanford and I hope he'll break loose. *Sanford and Son* has great potential, but it's going to need more than funny one-liners to keep it going. (pp. 22-3)

> *Peggy Hudson, in* Senior Scholastic *(copyright ©
> 1972 by Scholastic Magazines, Inc.; reprinted by
> permission), May 8, 1972.*

CHARLES L. SANDERS

Suddenly we have a new American hero. He's not an Audie Murphy or a Charles Lindbergh or an Ike or a Huck Finn or anybody like that. He's a wholly ignorant, lower middle-class, white Anglo-Saxon Protestant, beer-bellied bigot. This hero, this St. Archie [of *All in the Family*], must be dealt with seriously for he has become much more than a mere television character; he has become a social force engaging the minds and hearts of vast millions of Americans—many of them the people who still significantly control black lives. . . .

[There] is the probability that, week after week, Archie Bunker is saying things and projecting attitudes that stir up anti-black passions and trigger all kinds of racial wickedness. . . .

One hesitates to consider what psychological damage is done to the black children who not only absorb Archie's racial assaults on Saturday evenings but who must also deal with racial superiority complexes developing among white children in their schools and neighborhoods. How great the damage if even one black child begins turning inward toward self-hatred while striving for acceptance by his white schoolmates through a process of "whitenizing" and being anything other than "jig" or "coon"? As has been said, Archie Bunker—who he is and what he represents—must be dealt with quite seriously.

The contention—on the part of *AITF*'s producer and the apologists for the CBS network—is that, by bringing bigotry out into the open, and by holding up the Archie Bunkers to all kinds of put-downs and ridicule, the "boil of racism" will somehow miraculously ripen and burst and the pus will run out, thus permitting the healing process. Certain reality in the nation opens up that contention to serious questioning, of course. Can anyone claim, with any degree of seriousness, that white racism has become any less pervasive . . . [since] St. Archie has been canonized? (p. 188)

What does it all mean—this Archie cult, this affection for, and identification by millions of white Americans with, The Nation's Number One Bigot? Perhaps it can be explained as conditioned reflex: an appreciation for, a taking to the bosom of, anyone who celebrates in even the smallest and crudest ways the White Superiority Syndrome. Or perhaps it is that, finally, right out in the open, on network television, the white "little man" has a spokesman, a quite appealing one who, like most white people, doesn't actually lynch niggers or even use cattle prods on 'em (why, he even lets one come over to his house now and then); who is, actually, in white minds, a really quite lovable guy.

But also, what does it mean that all the people who worship St. Archie are not white? Thousands upon thousands of blacks are among his fans. . . .

Black people must be reminded that they ought always hold in contempt Archie Bunker and his kind. They, above all others, ought to do so not because of "paranoid touchiness" but because of their special intimacy with a history they have bought with such a high price in suffering and struggle and murdered black heroes. Black people know the Archie Bunkers—well. Thus they must know that he, no matter how "lovable," symbolizes the very real flesh and blood white man who, for centuries, has crushed black hope and stifled every black dream. . . . (p. 190)

> *Charles L. Sanders, "Nation's New Hero is a
> Beer-Bellied Bigot with 60 Million Fans," in*
> Ebony *(© copyright, 1972, by Johnson Publishing
> Co., Inc.), June, 1972, pp. 186-88, 190, 192.*

FRANK LEVY

To assert, as the program's apologists do, that "All in the Family" is satire like "Till Death Do Us Part" is plainly to misunderstand what satire is. The kind of laughter which Bergson once described as "froth with a saline base" can hardly rivet 60 million people to the television set Saturday nights.

This is not to criticize the escape that situation comedy provides. Laughter for its own sake is an important part of television. Great comedians like Abbot and Costello, Jack Benny, Burns and Allen, all steadfastly avoided politics or social reality of any kind. Where "All in the Family" differs from the tradition of television comedy or situation comedy is that it *purports* to deal with reality satirically. And what is reprehensible is that by taking real issues and extirpating all evidence of cruelty or consequence "All in the Family" essentially indoctrinates its 60 million viewers to believe they don't exist. Archie, unlike his precursor on the BBC, Alf Garnett, is no grotesque exaggeration, but a rather effective apologist for bigotry and reaction. Rather than allowing the American public to hold a mirror up to itself, "All in the Family" does just the opposite. Its pleasure comes primarily from producing forgetfulness, encouraging the hope that racism, welfare or discimination don't really exist and that the major problems of contemporary American society are the fantastical conjurings of "malcontents," "hopheads," "libs," "pinkos" and "eggheads." (p. 26)

Frank Levy, "In Defense of Prejudice . . . ," in The New Republic (reprinted by permission of The New Republic; © 1972 by The New Republic, Inc.), August 5 & 12, 1972, pp. 25-6.

RICHARD A. BLAKE

How the tears flowed for CBS and its stellar producer Norman Lear when all the sponsors and 36 of 189 affiliates dropped the reruns of "Maude's Dilemma," . . . as though they were tainted with plague bacilli. . . .

What about "Maude's Dilemma"? The problem is not controversial content, but the mode of treatment; there are distinctions among the different genres. *Maude* is a comedy; it does not present a discussion of abortion by experts, offer the editorial position of a station, which by law must be identified as editorial and which may be answered by an opposing view under the equal time provision of the Fairness Doctrine, nor, finally, does it present a serious dramatic conflict in which a woman faces a tragic decision. Unless I am very much mistaken, any of these formats would meet only marginal objection.

In "Maude's Dilemma," abortion is not a matter of life and death; it is a joke with a deadly message: the divorced daughter tells Maude to outgrow her childhood hang-ups, since repugnance for abortion is a silly old-fashioned idea.

In comedy, taste is the all important criterion for acceptability. Some topics are agreed to be completely unacceptable for comedy: belief in God, homosexuality, drug addiction, genocide. . . .

Situation comedy presents its own special problems of taste since it presents approximations of real people as the basis of humor. Maude is such a character, and her joke involves contemplating, for laughs, what many people consider the murder of a human being. Her hesitations, and consequently the moral beliefs of many in her audience, are held up to ridicule. Her decision to go ahead with the abortion is more than black humor; it is grotesque.

Mr. Lear, whose success with *All in The Family* was built largely on his willingness to break the taboos of ethnic humor to arrive at a larger truth, is an effective social critic. But, in "Maude's Dilemma," he passed beyond social satire and became merely offensive to those of many faiths who oppose abortion.

Richard A. Blake, "O Maude, Poor Maude," in America (© America Press, 1973; all rights reserved), September 1, 1973, p. 120.

Coming off its great abortion brouhaha, CBS's "Maude" launched a two-part treatment of alcoholism. Like abortion, of course, alcoholism is no laughing matter—but then Maude is just the right sort to tackle something sobering without sacrificing her sass. (p. 65)

Predictably, the two-parter tries to leave 'em laughing: the reformed Walter substitutes his craving for the sauce with a craze for sex. But for a few wrenching moments, "Maude" stands tall in the new family of sitcoms. Bunkerisms about "spades" and "fags" may shock, but they remain oneliners. By at least trying to reach for an issue's bottom line, "Maude" defines its own—and the medium's—potential. (p. 66)

"The Tube and the Bottle," in Newsweek (copyright 1973 by Newsweek, Inc.; all rights reserved; reprinted by permission), September 24, 1973, pp. 65-6.

JOHN J. O'CONNOR

Despite some fascinating touches, the [situation of "The Jeffersons"] is somewhat shaky. The character of Mr. Jefferson, snobbish, and given to frequent temper tantrums, verges on the unattractive. Even Archie Bunker is an "appealing" bigot. And much of the humor is based on insult, what used to be called "playing the dozens," when content can become secondary to delivery. On "The Jeffersons," too much of the content is very secondary. . . .

And then there is the Willis couple, new neighbors of the Jeffersons. Mr. Lear has carefully cultivated a reputation for dealing with the unusual and controversial: breast cancer, menopause, abortion, economic inflation. This time, however, in terms of network television and wherever the collective psyche of the nation may be at the moment, he is teetering on the verge of the explosive.

Mrs. Willis . . . is black, Mr. Willis . . . is white. Weekly TV entertainment has produced its first interracial marriage, and Mr. Lear is not about to be coy about it. Not for him the liberal tentativeness of a film like "Guess Who's Coming to Dinner?"

John J. O'Connor, "TV: Lear's 'Jeffersons'," in The New York Times (© 1975 by The New York Times Company; reprinted by permission), January 17, 1975, p. 67.

CHILTON WILLIAMSON, JR.

I was . . . taken instantly with [the] clever show [*All in the Family*], and count myself today as one of its many yet unjaded enthusiasts. Part of my delight in Lear's scripts is traceable, I suspect, to my longstanding admiration of Sinclair Lewis' work: surely Archie Bunker is the McLuhanesque counterpart of the Gutenbergian George Babbitt of half a century ago. The American appetite for social satire is, it seems, nearly as voracious as the English: indeed, every American social class with the exception of course of the noble subproletariat has by now been depicted as a set of clowns. After watching Archie thrash about recently in the tatters of his precarious and blusterous self-complacency, I summarily canceled *The Jeffersons* and reached for my copy of the Lewis novel. (pp. 401-02)

The working class in America has come of age, and since 1970 it has had its own George Babbitt as the badge of its maturity.

Lear's brilliantly witty scripts . . . suggest that the liberal middle class, as the mastermind of the sluggishly evolving Great Society, has formulated its own ideas of class responsibility. . . . Its members are too polite to refer, even among themselves, to "wops" or "kikes" or "culluds" or "broads"; they have signed too many full-page primal screams in the *New York Times* and fed too much Piper-Heidsieck to too many Panthers to flay themselves into the rehabilitation of their liberal psyches. In their hearts they know they're right: now they have only to activate their high principles, roll up their sleeves, get off their rumps. They are not gauche, for heaven's sake, and they are full of Concern. But there are others who yell "Polack" and "Dingbat," sleep in their underwear, and don't give a damn. . . . The blue collar boys aren't terribly bright and they're not very talented, so they can't write sociological guidelines for affirmative action or whip the law round Southerners' ankles. But at least they can be expected to learn the right *attitude*.

Which is to say, they can be flogged with all the proper middle class mores of the sort that for a couple of hundred years have been saving the world for democracy. *All in the Family* is not preaching a new consciousness for a greening America: the virtues it pushes are as established as the concept of debt repayment. . . . Most of what the Archie show is saying is that middle class decencies, the Ten Commandments, and a number of the civil statutes make sense, though they have been imperfectly taken to heart by people who were but recently working for 25 cents a day, drinking too much, pilfering bakeries, and going on strike at every possible opportunity. The much praised "frankness" and "courage" of the show in handling such touchy subjects as breast cancer, menopause, and homosexuality are not its lodestone. At bottom, *All in the Family* is a sort of media hornbook, stuffed with the Sunday School pieties of Grosse Pointe, Michigan. . . .

America is . . . still separated into clearly defined social strata that are perceived even—or perhaps especially—by those who are most vocal about the need for homogenizing them. During the first decade and a half of the present century, the genteel Progressives set about reforming and uplifting everybody below the social rank of librarian. Today they discover that, at least partly as a result of their past labors, the old proletariat is now rubbing neighborhoods and bank accounts with the middle classes, and this at a time when the new sub-proletariat has become the subject of a new romantic movement. We must have new victims of society to agonize with and suffer for. As for the victims of old, they are now part of the problem. Materially speaking, they need no uplifting. But they do require refinement in the ways of responsible respectability. (p. 402)

Chilton Williamson, Jr., "All in 'Your' Family," in National Review (© *National Review, Inc., 1975; 150 East 35th St., New York, N.Y. 10016), April 11, 1975, pp. 401-02.*

ROGER ROSENBLATT

Comedy and death are old companions . . . , not merely in graveyard and funeral jokes, but in substance. . . . Both are forms of criticism and reality, shattering pretense, showing people for what they are. To make a joke of something is to kill it. The terms of comedy are the terms of death: you're a riot, a scream; you break me up; you're killing me.

These terms have a special companionship in "All in the Family" because "All in the Family" was dead on arrival. We knew from the outset that the four main characters always would be impervious to change. . . . On the surface Archie's humor seems more variable. At times he appears as Hate, Stubbornness, Selfishness or Cowardice, but all of these group under the presiding humor of Death itself, which governs every form of immovability, in Archie and his kin.

Despite the formal stagnation of their lives, the Bunkers reappear every week as if reborn for the week's occasions. They do not learn from past mistakes. They repeat old jokes and epithets. None seems to have much of a memory for former events which might guide their present decisions. . . .

By blocking out the past, of course, they block out the future. . . .

But the Bunkers do not live in the present, either. Instead of a state of time, they live in a state of mind, specifically Archie's. When the week's problem is announced, the humors gather 'round to offer different perspectives on, for example: What is the meaning of individual honesty in a mechanized world where machines can cheat and be cheated? What are the meanings of death and truth in such a world? These questions appear to be up for grabs, but they are in Archie's control from the start, control that is manifested by childishness and panic. Because Archie always represents the worst response to problems, he bears the focus for possible solutions. Because no solutions are ever offered or desired on "All in the Family" Archie also always wins the day.

This is the death that the program promotes: the death of motion and enlargement of spirit. . . .

Is "All in the Family" funny? Sometimes. . . . But the fun is piecemeal, not connected to a fluid life. It is meant to interfere between surprise and understanding, and then to boing like an overwound watchspring so that once laughing we must start at zero again, and rebuild the situation. . . .

Comedy, like death, must embrace the whole life, if it works. It may deny change, but must also acknowledge the possibility of change, of past and future, thereby in its denials suggesting a moral base. The comedy of the Bunkers, which is not of the whole life, which is the blurtings of topical and toilet jokes, rapid fire, scattergun, automatic, depending on our habitual courtesy to laugh at familiar things —this comedy is of a different death, a death where life never was. There is nothing intense and nothing to care for. The family are bunkers against our caring. (p. 31)

Roger Rosenblatt, in The New Republic *(reprinted by permission of* The New Republic; © *1975 by The New Republic, Inc.), May 24, 1975.*

LOUIE ROBINSON

Bombastic, frenetic, boastful, ill-mannered, prejudiced and scheming, George Jefferson, his wife Louise, and a cast of other interesting characters have become a success in *The Jeffersons*. . . . (p. 112)

Spun off from the front-running *All In The Family, The Jeffersons* appear to some as the flip side of the Archie Bunkers. Unlike Archie, however, who has never risen above his blue-collar status, George has, in the words of the show's theme music, moved on up to that big East Side apartment in the sky. . . . (pp. 112, 114)

For those who may still be looking for a deep and satisfying social significance in black shows on television, the wait goes on. Although *The Jeffersons* portrays blacks on a different socio-economic level than other black TV shows, it is nevertheless, like the others, broad comedy and has to be accepted as such. But this is true, in one form or another, for most white shows, and thus TV must be realized, if not accepted, for what it is. (p. 115)

Louie Robinson, "The Jeffersons: A Look at Life on Black America's New 'Striver's Row'," in Ebony (© *copyright, 1976, by Johnson Publishing Co., Inc.), January, 1976, pp. 112, 114-15.*

JOHN J. O'CONNOR

[With ''Mary Hartman, Mary Hartman,'' Lear and his company] are taking the venerable broadcasting form of soap opera and are attempting to work simultaneously on two levels: one straight, to be taken seriously; the other slightly bent, to be sampled with a sense of humor that is ''satirical, humanistic, and realistic.'' . . .

A press kit explains that ''far from being a broad parody of soaps, the series would subtly satirize people as they behave in day-to-day situations—never straying from reality.'' The problem is that the soap-opera form itself tends to resist satire, except perhaps in brief spurts of broad parody. In its pure form, soap opera already can work on straight or slightly bent levels, depending on the inclinations of the viewer. Tinkering with the original may degenerate rather easily into unneccesary underlining.

''Mary Hartman, Mary Hartman'' wanders amiably down a path of wide-eyed wonder, or dumbness, in which every object or event is precisely equal to any other object or event, in which the murder of a family down the street elicits the same emotional concern as the buildup of yellowing wax on the kitchen floor. . . .

And there is much that is very funny. Mary's neighbors—a 22-year-old aspirant to country music fame and her older, baldish and adoring husband—strike a nice balance between appalling and appealing. And Mary's 80-plus grandfather is properly irascible as the town ''flasher,'' picked up for indecent exposure in a public school playground.

Many of the bits and pieces do work very well indeed, but the overall concept may contain its own seeds of self-destruction. After grandpa has been arrested for indecent exposure, what can he do for an encore? Well, later this week, he is arrested again on the same charge, this time for doing his performance at the Fernwood Hospital's luau party for graduating nurses. The end is still funny, but the means are escalated noticeably. . . .

According to the Lear organization, the networks, in rejecting the series, maintained that the public ''was not sophisticated enough to understand its many facets.'' But the opposite is very possibly true. The public is too sophisticated to take ''Mary Hartman, Mary Hartman'' on a straight, serious level. That leaves the bent, humorous approach, and the inevitable demands for novelty will perhaps transform an interesting experiment into standard situation comedy.

> *John J. O'Connor, ''TV: Lear's 'Mary Hartman,' Interesting Innovation,'' in* The New York Times *(© 1976 by The New York Times Company; reprinted by permission), January 6, 1976, p. 63.*

RICHARD SCHICKEL

It must have seemed a good idea doing a parody soap opera. For the opening minutes of its first episode last week, *Mary Hartman, Mary Hartman* . . . still seemed like a good idea. . . .

But the art of parody lies in brevity. The trick is to catch and tickle to death a form's conventions and hastily flee the scene. In a very few minutes any reasonably clever group of comic writers and players can exhaust the rather limited parodistic possibilities inherent in the soaps. Then the problem is what to do next. The only answer, of course, is to do exactly what the soaps do—give the characters some

issues to turn over and over in their tiny minds. There is a mass murder down the block, the grandpa who is discovered to be a flasher, the husband suffering from impotence.

These matters do not turn out to be the height of hilarity. In fact, they are depressing. Drawing the characters in the series not from the middle-class world where most soap opera people live but from the blue-collar class where most of their viewers reside seems, like so many Norman Lear notions, condescending rather than clever. *Mary Hartman, Mary Hartman* is silly stupid, silly stupid.

> *Richard Schickel, ''Tickled to Death,'' in* Time *(reprinted by permission from* Time, The Weekly Newsmagazine; *copyright Time Inc. 1976), January 19, 1976, p. 64.*

JAMES WOLCOTT

Confession: ''Mary Hartman, Mary Hartman'' caught me almost completely by surprise. It doesn't broadly parody soap operas, and it isn't the sort of flamboyantly ''controversial'' sit-com that one has come to expect from Norman Lear; which is to say that ''Mary Hartman'' doesn't signal its comedy in any of the usual ways. . . . ''Mary Hartman'' has its awful jokey spasms, as when a character is called a ''prevert'' . . . but when the residents of Fernwood are so involved in themselves that the laughter comes leaking out of their self-absorption, it's the most subtly, disconcertingly funny show ever to appear on television. . . .

The loopiness of the characters is treated with genial matter-of-factness . . . and *that* is what makes the show so liberating, not the ''frank'' subject matter. For nothing would have been more tiresomely predictable than a nightly farrago of abuse and hurled dirt. Lear has gone as far as he can go (at least I hope he has) with the almost Homeric sarcasm of ''Maude'' and ''All in the Family,'' and the gentle, laconic absurdity of ''Mary Hartman'' shows. . . . What ''Mary Hartman'' takes from the soaps is the sense that the camera is another character in the room, indeed that the camera is the most observant character of all.

And what is that camera attentive to? Not sin, really, but the discovery of sin: embarrassment. Embarrassment is the experience of being trapped in one's own lies or, even worse, discovering that one is inadequate in dealing with society's demands. . . .

The nihilistic edge to ''Mary Hartman'' is that though the characters are trapped in those soap-opera rooms, the viewer is always aware of the chaotic world outside. Mary's knocked-out quizzicality seems almost a response to, and a comment on, all the pounding action that is on prime time before 11; she's been so battered by the violence on ''Hawaii 5-0'' that a mass-murder in her neighborhood just doesn't connect with her feelings.

What *does* connect with her feelings is sex, or rather, the lack of it. Mary feels sorrowful embarrassment not for something she's done, but for something she can't bring herself to do: masturbate. The bedroom scene in which she confessed to her husband that she doesn't masturbate, that she's never been able to masturbate, wasn't shocking; it was sad, achingly sad. When her husband nervously changes the subject, Louise Lasser's Mary sighs, ''I can't do it and you can't talk about it,'' and the line was charged with the pain of disconnectedness, and it was like watching a spacey American ''Scenes From a Marriage.'' It was a piercingly tender moment and one didn't have to endure hours of schematic plotting, studied drabness, and deadening Bergmanian sobriety in order to reach it.

As in "Scenes From a Marriage," the center of the narrative is a perplexed woman who finds the scaffoldings of her life giving way. . . .

So far, "Mary Hartman, Mary Hartman" is loose and fitful, ham-handed at times, and often too close to the edge of Carol Burnett burlesquerie, but it has verve, affection, and a loving attentiveness to the nuanced banalities of everyday talk, and in its best moments the comedy reveals the raw nerves of love's loneliness. It's not only more entertaining than "Scenes From a Marriage," it's better art.

> James Wolcott, "'Hartman' Is the Best Thing about Lear," in The Village Voice (reprinted by permission of The Village Voice; copyright © The Village Voice, Inc., 1976), January 19, 1976, p. 117.

JOHN J. O'CONNOR

The time may have arrived for the Norman Lear factory to close down and take serious stock of its product. The machine may be overworked. No matter how well "One Day at a Time" may be doing . . . in the ratings, the character of the older daughter is an abrasive drag. No matter how many sophisticated excuses are proffered for deadpan monotony of "Mary Hartman, Mary Hartman," the syndicated series is tedious in extended doses. And now . . . the hastily concocted product is "The Dumplings."

Joe and Angela Dumpling operate a lunch counter in a New York office building. [They] are a fat couple very much in love with each other. At work or at home, they are surrounded by oddball characters, from hostile customers to Angela's neurotic sister. . . .

No doubt, Mr. Lear will argue that he is saying something positive about love, about ordinary people. In fact, he is being insultingly patronizing. It's not that his lovers are fat, but that they are forced to verge on the grotesque, constantly mooning or pawing or waxing stupidly sentimental. They are allowed Mr. Lear's conception of love. The first of the world is condemned to neuroses and hysteria. People don't speak; they shout. People don't communicate; they bombard. Thrown together with the loving Dumplings, the mixture did not work. . . .

> John J. O'Connor, "'Dumplings,' the Story of Fat, Loving Couple," in The New York Times © 1976 by the New York Times Company; reprinted by permission), January 29, 1976, p. 67.

JOHN J. O'CONNOR

Although perhaps only temporarily, the Lear product has become noticeably strained. A good deal of the humor has settled into a monotonous groove of hostility. The situations, particularly those dealing with sex, are getting predictable enough to trigger charges of easy exploitation. . . .

Despite a good cast and a promising premise—a divorced woman attempting to raise two teenage daughters—["One Day at a Time"] has been generally mediocre. The character of the older daughter, something of a hysterical brat, is positively repulsive. Mr. Lear counters that my strong reaction to a TV character may be worthwhile. Probably, but not when the reaction is strong enough to get the TV set turned off.

"The Dumplings" . . . is not getting good ratings. It doesn't deserve good ratings. Interestingly, Mr. and Mrs. Dumpling, characters taken from a Canadian comic strip, are just about the only couple in a Lear production who do not use hostile humor on each other. They are "uncomplicated and so much in love," according to Mr. Lear, "in the face of all odds," . . . "they've managed somehow to keep their innocence and optimism."

But evidently a price must be paid for innocence and optimism. For the Dumplings . . . it is fat. Both he and she are militantly overweight, swooning at the mention of just about any cholesterol-laden food dish. They adore each other's girth, of course, but the message still is that fat is funny. Even the fortunate few who can be described as "so much in love" or "too pure" for the world cannot escape a touch of the grotesque.

"Mary Hartman, Mary Hartman" does indeed represent a fascinating departure for the Lear organization. Brilliantly cast, the ultimate exploration of soap opera techniques is almost recklessly uneven. Many elements, including Louise Lasser's overuse of Mary's blank stare, are tiresome. But some, a quite respectable portion, are insanely funny. A recent funeral service held in Mary's kitchen for a sports coach who drowned in a bowl of chicken soup offered ten minutes of the most hilarious TV that is likely to be seen this year.

Yet, the use of misuse of soap-opera gimmicks for TV comedy would seem to be rather limited. At this stage, Mr. Lear is still forced to confront the problem of new future directions. Will he expand, or will he settle for merely additional products from the same cookie cutter? His record has been astonishingly inventive. He has transformed TV comedy into a form that can deal with serious personal and social problems. In his warm and lovable persons, he denies that he has been influential. "Bull----!" he declares with typical modesty. But his shrewdness and cold calculation will undoubtedly keep him fighting for a while.

> John J. O'Connor, "Is Norman Lear in a Rut?" in The New York Times (© 1976 by The New York Times Company; reprinted by permission), March 21, 1976, p. 23.

STEPHANIE HARRINGTON

[On] "Mary Hartman"—the material is there, just as life is there; the writers respond to the absurdities they perceive around them; the actors either identify with the writers' impulses or substitute their own. . . .

And this is appropriate since, if "Mary Hartman" is about anything, it is about reactions. Specifically, it is about the way working-class people in a factory town of tract homes, who are intellectually, morally, and emotionally outfitted by soap operas, television commercials, and the Reader's Digest, respond to insecurity, disappointment, rejection, frustration, infirmity, and death. . . . But the success of "Mary Hartman"—it has achieved the status of a media event—indicates that the show has also hooked subscribers of Psychology Today, who don't worry about waxy yellow buildup because they have installed terra-cotta tile floors in their kitchens. Moreover, it has attracted equal numbers of men and women. (p. 53)

To watch—more important, to listen to—the folks in Fernwood respond to [their] calamities is to be plugged into a slapstick of free association orchestrated by Terry Southern and the *Ladies' Home Journal*.

For them, there are no priorities. All levels of experience are equal. . . .

[Worrying] about the yellow on your floor doesn't mean you aren't upset about five people being murdered. And baking a cake doesn't mean you aren't worried about your daughter. And wanting to be a superstar doesn't mean that you don't care about your best friend. It's just that all of this coexists in unlikely juxtaposition inside our heads. It is a mix on our psychic tapes. But in real life we edit our responses so people won't misunderstand. We all worry about what to wear to a funeral and whether to try to do the laundry before we go. But we don't *tell* anybody. On "Mary Hartman," the tapes are not edited. (p. 54)

But [the heaviest insights about Mary Hartman come from her portrayer, actress Louise Lasser], who is strangely hard on Mary. Leading up to her perception of Mary, she asks, "Do you like existential novels? Have you read *The Stranger*?" And connecting Mary Hartman with, of all things, what is probably Camus's bleakest statement of life's meaninglessness, Lasser condemns Mary as a person who "is not aware of herself in space and time." And, as if Camus were not enough, she judges Mary lacking by Aristotelian standards, as a "survivor who misses being a tragic heroine because she is not aware of her plight." (But Mary's complexities are limitless; she seems to have something for everyone.) . . .

Existentialism, tragic heroine, "wise fool"—has the carbon monoxide blowing north from the Santa Monica Freeway propelled all the brains here in Learville into a self-deluding literary high? (p. 55)

Or are we really ready for graduate courses on "Existentialism in the Media: The Presentiment of 'Mary Hartman' in the Work of Albert Camus"? Well, why not? The written word is passé, and the novel of experience, when last glimpsed, was embalmed and lying in state at the British Museum waiting for Stanley Kubrick to make another movie. And "Mary Hartman" may be as engaging a replacement for the socially conscious literary potboiler as this culture will come up with. The melodramatic pileup of calamities is outrageous, but the writers and actors maintain an impressive balance, never going over the edge of satire into camp. They are hilariously ruthless about impaling our public and private evasions and delusions for microscopic inspection without ever failing to make us care about the characters and what happens to them. . . .

As for Mary, as Lasser points out, she is still a little girl trying to grow up. There is a woman in there trying to get out, but the braids, the tight, puffy-sleeved little-girl dresses are holding her in. Lasser has said that Mary is trying to live properly. And to her, living properly is living by rules laid out by *Family Circle* and Dr. Joyce Brothers and the johnsonswaxtidybowllemonfreshjoy commercials. She tries to be a good mother, a loving wife, an interesting sex partner, and a thorough housewife. She waxes her floors relentlessly, sanitizes the toilet every Friday, borrows library books to solve her sexual problems, takes Geritol twice a day, and waits for happiness and fulfillment to find her.

And is this antiwoman—this concept of the passive little girl determined by an environment she seems unable to act

on? I think not. The men in the show—particularly her husband Tom—are as trapped on the assembly line as Mary is in the kitchen, bound by rules and regulations that reduce them to the powerlessness of little boys. And they are, if anything, even more out of touch with themselves. Tom does not even try to find out why he isn't happy. He doesn't even admit his unhappiness to himself. Mary, at least, risks asking the questions.

But she is striving, says Lasser, "for something that can't work out." Lasser has said, in an interview with John Wilson in the New York *Times*, that Mary is a survivor in a world that may not be worth surviving in. . . .

I would doubt that Mary will develop in opposition to Lasser's sense of human limitations. For one thing, she is Lasser's character. Moreover, although she certainly has moments when she seems strong enough to rebel, if she does, in fact, do so—if she develops attitudes of her own and chooses an alternative role for herself, she will be in danger of becoming a caricature of a point of view—perhaps even a feminist one.

As it is, we are confident that no matter what life does to her, Mary will survive. This may not be tragically heroic, but it is as heroic as most of us can get. And her successes and failures as a survivor give us insights, at least, into our own.

If Mary's character becomes too assertive and she ceases to let life wash over her and, Candide-like, confront calamity with a cup of coffee and a non sequitur, if she ceases to expose the myths we live by by religiously observing their rituals, we may have to invent Mary Hartman all over again. (p. 98)

> Stephanie Harrington, "Mary Hartman: the Unedited, All-American Unconscious," in Ms. (© 1976 Ms. Magazine Corp.), May, 1976, pp. 53-5, 98.

HARRY F. WATERS with MARTIN KASINDORF

Love it or loathe it, "Mary Hartman, Mary Hartman" is the nation's latest pop-culture craze—a sort of video Rorschach test for the mass audience. Norman Lear's comedy soap opera is the most talked-about new TV series since America was assaulted by his Archie Bunker. (p. 54)

Thematically, the serial is something of a mishmash, and even the show's creators seem at a loss to define exactly what they are trying to do. . . . Lear originally envisioned "MH2" as a kind of split-level soap. On one level, it would be a *reductio ad absurdum* of every soap-opera convention, including the inane commercials. But the show would also be human enough to make viewers care for its characters—just as they feel for the folks on "As the World Turns."

It was an audacious game plan, but one probably destined to miss as often as hit. At its best, "Mary Hartman" is a biting satire on our mass-consumer society and a wacky, surrealistic evocation of contemporary life. Unsure where the commercials on her TV leave off and her own life begins, with her psyche constantly flashing overload, Mary can never manage to get her priorities in order. (pp. 54-5)

Nonetheless, "MH2" does have its serious undercurrents. At times, the show's impact is as wrenchingly poignant as [John] Cassavetes's "A Woman Under the Influence." Mary is no deep thinker; her favorite gurus are Abigail Van

Buren, Joyce Brothers and the Reader's Digest. Yet she is perceptive enough to sense that her life *en famille* is out of synch with her glossy expectations—the product of a lifetime's diet of junk food for thought. . . .

The mirror that "Mary Hartman" holds up to our neuroses may come from a funhouse, but its reflections can be unnervingly sharp.

At its worst, however, the new hybrid inhabits a deadly dull vacuum between comedy and melodrama. Half the characters play out their gothic disasters fully in earnest while the rest of the cast clowns and mugs its way through the factory-town soap like high-school amateurs. As the show's satirical shots misfire—and they frequently do—perplexed viewers are returning Mary's perpetually blank stare. (p. 55)

> *Harry F. Waters with Martin Kasindorf, "The Mary Hartman Craze," in* Newsweek *(copyright 1976 by Newsweek, Inc.; all rights reserved; reprinted by permission), May 3, 1976, pp. 54-63.*

PETER SOURIAN

I accuse Lear of being a closet scholar. Like most creators with the broad touch necessary for quality-*cum*-success, he seems sure enough of his own originality not to hesitate to steal from past masters. His earlier shows, still running, reflect this. *The Jeffersons*'s black bourgeois dry cleaner . . . is "movin' on up" so nearly in the footsteps of Molière's Monsieur Jourdain, that it is hard to believe that Lear has not been rereading the *Bourgeois Gentilhomme*. Furthermore, both Jefferson and his white counterpart, Archie Bunker, of Lear's *All in the Family*, are typically Molièresque central figures: authoritarian male family heads, narrow-minded and covertly decentish in their willful ignorance. (p. 157)

[Each] of these shows is classical in that the laughter results from discrepant human engagements with an implicit moral norm, which norm is (usually too blandly) re-established by the end of each episode after a (usually too even-handed) degree of social criticism and topical commentary along the way.

But *Mary Hartman, Mary Hartman* is different. It is not classical. It is dark and it is grim, even though millions of people watch and laugh. There is no norm, and Lear avoids restorative climaxes simply by seeing to it that there are no climaxes at all. Instead of a discrete half-hour unit per week of continuing characters but new episodes, he's running a relentless narrative that is always promising resolutions and conclusions that absolutely never arrive. As a compound of the situation comedy and soap-opera genres, with their respective modes of sensibility, *Mary Hartman* becomes a genre unto itself, which—like the novel at its beginnings—permits fresh art to exercise itself where it could not do so within an older rigidified convention. Thus, good as some of the other sitcoms are, they are becoming as formal as the sonnet, with only fine ensemble acting to permit them life.

To illustrate what I mean about there being no norm, only a dreadful abyss: the recent season's concluding episode left Mary on the edge of her daily nervous breakdown, this time in New York where, selected as America's Typical Consumer Housewife, she is about to go on the *David Susskind Show*. ("But I'm separated from my husband and my daughter hates me." "That's great. According to our statis-

tics that puts you right in line for the title.") Mary wanders into F.A.O. Schwarz and asks the price of a big doll's house there on display. When told it's not for sale she insists hysterically that she must have it, with each little doll, every chair, table, plate, knife, fork perfectly in its proper place. She desperately craves a norm. But it is not a norm, this doll's house interior; it cannot be had. The point is that Mary is insane to keep on insisting it can be had, when it's only a display item in the greatest toy store in the world.

Mary Hartman, Mary Hartman is recognizable as a Norman Lear production in that it too displays plenty of creative "stealing." I repeat my closet scholar accusation, with further specifications: Lear has read Flaubert on received ideas, heard Chekhov's characters talk self-absorbedly past one another in comic-tragic scenes depicting the fatal erosion of a society too removed from the most ordinary truths, applied and even developed Marx's concept of alienation. He's had the nerve to exploit these systematically in a tough mass market not only because he has sensed that this may be where we are at but also because he believes that *we* have sensed that this may be where we are at: in no-norm's-land. (pp. 157-58)

He gets to say his fine things but he never insists; delighted if audiences are simply laughing and/or crying, he won't complain ungratefully, like Shaw, that he's not being taken seriously. . . .

TV people have begun to realize that there is a blue-collar class out there, 65 million strong, with frustrations, hidden injuries. . . . But *Mary Hartman, Mary Hartman* is the first and only working-class soap opera to come to grips with blue-collar frustrations and despairs. . . .

Incidentally, there is no show which so insightfully and deliberately depicts TV itself as an important part of the lives of people. During a mass murder right down the block, showing live on TV, Mary frets over the "waxy yellow build-up" on her kitchen floor, unable to distinguish between the news and the commercials. Such off-the-point reactions are a staple feature of the show, akin to Lear's Chekhovian dialogue, and Marxist in their underlying sense of the anatomy of alienation possible in a large-scale capitalist society. . . .

[Extraneous] ideas have a more compelling place in Mary's brutally one-dimensional existence than either desire or fidelity, kindness or venality. Yet—and this is the sweet and terrible pathos of Lear—we know that, steam-rollered as she is, Mary has plenty of frantic desire, fidelity, kindness, venality.

Lear's Marxism has to do with the notion of man's alienation through certain kinds of work. Tom, screwing in the dome lights for which he can have no feeling, is unable to touch his wife, for whom he has a kind of drowned but real feeling. Lear sees virtually everything in our culture—even and especially that which is most intrinsically valuable—being ground up into a commodity to be packaged and sold, regardless of need or real appetite, and he is busy depicting the manifold extensions of this fact. The goods must be moved off the shelf, and no matter whether or how they are absorbed. The cups of instant coffee are gobbled up by people who may at bottom legitimately desire to sleep, not stay awake. The people who do not love nor wish to love buy paperbacks on how to love and study them hard. The chicken soup is slurped up by men who have been told it is good for them; the fact that they may be drowning in the stuff is incidental to the system, since they are incidental.

These monster manufacturers are constantly rising up in Lear's show. But his best general insight is that, more damaging than the possibly useful and quite efficient household appliances, waxes, polishes and foodstuffs, are the ideas, originally of value, but now ground up, packaged, purveyed, swallowed and scarcely digested. We are the most sophisticated people in the world, even those of us who live in Fernwood, yet we know nothing; we are intolerably burdened with ideas, a most heavy baggage, without even a rudimentary sense of their use. . . .

For the genial Lear it's no joke. He likes his characters. He hates what has happened to them and in an ironic way this forces him to end up with distaste for the characters he likes. It is a bitter, bitter business—so much so that I will no longer watch *Mary Hartman, Mary Hartman.* (p. 158)

> *Peter Sourian, in* The Nation *(copyright 1976 by the Nation Associates, Inc.), August 28, 1976.*

JAMES WOLCOTT

Blazing with large intentions, Norman Lear's new series *All That Glitters* . . . is a firebird that never takes flight: It flutters, sputters, then falls. Like Eve Merriam's entertainment *The Club* and Lina Wertmuller's *Swept Away, All That Glitters* is a dramatic exercise in role-and-gender reversal. The women here are queen bees in a corporation known as Globatron and have no need of subscriptions to *Savvy*—they've already mastered the martial arts of careermanship. The men are little more than stingerless drones, but unlike drones they are forced into labor as secretaries, toga-clad waiters, househusbands. . . .

Fifteen years ago, it might have been subversive to mock sexual stereotypes, for those sterotypes were firm in the public mind. . . . Since then such stereotypes have largely melted. . . . What *is* a shock is that the women of *Glitters* are so rapaciously Nixonian. Is this intended to mirror the male corporate world, or is it meant to suggest that once women possess power they'll be every inch as ruthless and vulpine as men? When they ogle their boy secretaries, is it a parody of male lust or an illustration of how sexually exploitative women can be? Actually, it fizzles either way since the Boy Fridays are so mincingly fey that it's easier to imagine them making it with other boys than with their bosses. . . .

What links *The Club* and *Swept Away* and *All That Glitters* is that all are fundamentally incoherent. . . . *All That Glitters* displays women in caricatures of maleness, men in caricatures of femaleness, and the sexiest woman turns out to be a transsexual. . . . *The Club* at least has some liveliness as a lesbian jamboree, but *Glitters* doesn't provide any kicks with its confusions—it makes one long for Milton Berle in Southern-bell drag. *All That Glitters* is a Myra Breckenridge whirlpool and everyone gets sucked under.

> *James Wolcott, "The Bitter Tears of Petra Von Lear," in* The Village Voice *(reprinted by permission of* The Village Voice; *copyright ©* The Village Voice, Inc., 1977*), May 9, 1977, p. 87.*

ROBERT MacKENZIE

"What would life be like in a world where women have always held the key positions in business, in politics, in the home and in society?" asks the publicity for this syndicated Norman Lear serial [*All That Glitters*].

Apparently it would be like this: the women would be unscrupulous maneuverers, frauds, lechers and jerks of all description. The men would be dreary, simple-headed drudges or simpering sexpots. Nothing much would happen, conversation would reach unprecedented abysses of dullness, and relations between men and women would be conducted at a level of callousness that would stun Germaine Greer.

Does Lear really think this cumbersome collection of reversed stereotypes represents the way we live now? He is coy about it. "Is it a reflection of life? It is whatever the audience thinks it is," he says. Well, this part of the audience thinks it is pretty obvious stuff, mostly out of date, not nearly funny enough and altogether doggone wearying. Nothing's perfect, of course.

There were moments during the first few episodes when we thought *Glitters* might be funny and even insightful. . . .

There is still enough sexual polarization around to make some of [its] gags trenchant and amusing. But the series took the easy way from the start, creating grotesques that don't correspond to men and women, role-reversed or otherwise, but to cliches we've already outgrown. . . .

There's nobody to like in this series. We just ache for Mary Hartman to drop in and give us a sad little grin.

There is something faintly medicinal about all Lear's shows, but usually he gives us the dose with a syrup of compassion and wit. *Glitters* leaves us with the uncomfortable feeling that the writers hate men, aren't crazy about women and have been hibernating somewhere for the past 10 years. (p. 2)

> *Robert MacKenzie, in* TV Guide® Magazine, *(copyright © 1977 by Triangle Publications, Inc. Radnor, Pennsylvania; reprinted by permission), June 25, 1977.*

JOHN J. O'CONNOR

There is hardly anything new about satirizing talk shows. In some cases, the form almost satirizes itself, and it has long been the butt of comedy routines, from "Laugh In" to "Monty Python's Flying Circus." But "Fernwood 2-Night" goes beyond the talk-show form to ridicule contemporary convictions and foibles in a wide range of aspects. Anti-Semitism and religious deprogramming have little or nothing to do with talk shows, but they have been put to extremely clever use on "Fernwood 2-Night."

The concept of a fictional talk show may contain its own self-destruct mechanism. The form itself is limited, and the pressures to be outrageous can only escalate. Where do you go after you've given them a pianist in an iron lung? . . .

There is a little something to offend just about everybody. There may also be a bit too much cruelty, too much smug adolescent superiority to sustain the humor for very long. But in this opening week of "Fernwood 2-Night," only the certifiably enbalmed will fail to laugh out loud several times along the outrageous way.

> *John J. O'Connor, "TV: 'Fernwood 2-Night' a Little 2 Much," in* The New York Times *(© 1977 by The New York Times Company; reprinted by permission), July 6, 1977, p. 19.*

JAMES WOLCOTT

After the first season, *Mary Hartman, Mary Hartman* deteriorated into an off-off-Broadway nightmare—a druggy *No Exit*, where hell was other suburbanites—but *2-Night*'s new characters, plus *MH* regulars who will pop in from time to time, should lift the Fernwood saga out of its surreal doldrums. . . . Unless my instincts have gone glitchy, *Fernwood 2-Night*, with its *Gong Show* gooniness, can't fail to be a hit. Which will fill Norman Lear's bulletin board with happy returns. . . .

I laughed at much of *Fernwood 2-Night*, but I didn't really like it, and I don't think it should bring silver to Lear's reputation. *2-Night* is shrewdly, confidently coarse—was Norman Lear born with one nostril? taste is hardly his talisman—and the coarseness is used for a self-consciously stupid put-on effect. Except for a satirical bit about "deprogramming" a Catholic priest, the jokes here—about iron lungs, senior citizens, Vietnamese refugees—aren't vulgarly liberating but pricky and mean; it's insensitivity masquerading as a parody of "insensitivity."

But what's wrong with *2-Night* goes deeper than show-biz bumminess. . . . Lear's depiction of the working class *is* shaped by snobbery and ignorance. . . . *Fernwood 2-Night*, like *Mary Hartman*, is a televisionized fantasy of life in the heartland, and the Middle America of Norman Lear is every bit as phony and crass as the haystack-and-moonshine South of *Hee Haw*. . . .

If *Fernwood 2-Night* were merely midsummer madness . . . , then it could be shrugged off, but like *Mary Hartman* . . . , it will probably become ridiculously influential. Norman Lear has, in *2-Night*, brought together two fashionable post-McLuhan notions—the world as soap opera, the world as talk-show—and given us a meta-world in which everyone is linked not by blood or class or affection but by a flow of put-on banter. . . . Norman Lear probably believes he is being entertainingly uplifting, but the Yahoo mockery of *Fernwood 2-Night* serves only to dislocate people from the real sources of rage, oppression, and attrition. Is Vietnam so faraway in our memories that we can cheerfully make jokes about "gooks"?

> *James Wolcott, "The Other Side of Fernwood,"*
> *in* The Village Voice *(reprinted by permission of*
> The Village Voice; *copyright © The Village*
> Voice, Inc., 1977), July 11, 1977, p. 71.

HARRY F. WATERS

Alas, "Forever Fernwood" reads funnier than it plays. Norman Lear's syndicated sequel to "Mary Hartman, Mary Hartman" arrived on TV last week, not only without Louise Lasser's Mary but largely devoid of its predecessor's angst-ridden subtlety. The charm of the original flowed from its skill at meshing soap-opera satire with poignantly vulnerable characters. The second time around, the denizens of Fernwood have sold out their humanity for all-out parody. Lear's split-level soap now reflects not recognizable neuroses but lunatic posturings.

> *Harry F. Waters, "Forever—or a Day?" in* News-
> week *(copyright 1977 by Newsweek, Inc.; all*
> *rights reserved; reprinted by permission), October*
> 17, 1977, p. 106.

M. J. SOBRAN, JR.

All in the Family we have always with us. It is now reduced to buttocks humor—at the expense, of course, of Archie's arse. The latest episode showed him sitting on a knitting needle and later getting pinched on the backside. The poor guy can never do anything right, at least not until his immaculately liberal Gloria and her husband the Meathead have conspired with humiliating Experience to show him the light. It's an old TV joke—sit-comdaddies are always feckless . . . —but it's a durable one. . . .

Consider: every time Archie defames some minority, he is instantly confuted by the materialization of an urbane Representative thereof, who invariably speaks in epigrams so polished as to make one wonder why affirmative action (let along police action) was ever thought needful. His bigotries are not only ethnic: one show exposed his shameful prejudice against transvestites. The aforementioned episode also showed him seething with irrational hostility toward an Old Person, merely because she, an uninvited guest in his house, relentlessly insulted him, corrected his grammar, and complained of his cigars. Whereupon the Meathead gave him a lecture on the necessity of respecting one's elders. Season after season, Michael tirelessly explains a) that They are no different from Us, and b) that to the extent They *are* different, They're just that much more adorable.

Needless to say, the show is fueled by sneaking sympathy for Archie, and the Meathead—that sniveling social conscience—is there just to keep the pressure groups from growling. (p. 230)

> *M. J. Sobran, Jr., in* National Review *(© Na-*
> *tional Review, Inc., 1978; 150 East 35th St., New*
> *York, N.Y. 10016), February 17, 1978.*

MICHAEL NOVAK

[The] fact that Norman Lear's "All That Glitters" didn't strike gold doesn't mean that it didn't have importance for our culture. It did. . . .

The first hour shown to the press had all the marks of high ideology. "All That Glitters" coruscated like a tract. Women in power, men subservient—the script seemed catechetical. Lines and scenes reached out to nudge the audience: "Get it? Get it?" In real life, any man who dared to behave like the women-imitating-men in this show would be treated with scorn. . . . American society today is far more complex than the reverse-stereotypical images of males and females in "Glitters." The show seemed for a moment to be carrying the nation backward. It seemed to be a consciousness-lowering exercise.

In addition, Lear's new experiment failed to solve an important narrative problem. Too many couples and too many subplots burdened each episode. Watching night by night, one couldn't get a clear narrative line, and the individual segments were too short. . . .

Lear needed two hours or so every night in order to get all eight major characters through each turn in the plot. With the story segmented, unity fell apart.

Seeing the episodes in larger blocks, moreover, I discovered a theme exactly the opposite of the one I had expected. "All That Glitters" is one of the most effective refutations of errant feminism yet encountered. There is an obvious point to the show's title—the glittering role of men in the man's world, it turns out when women take it up, isn't gold. The deeper (and perhaps unintended) theme, however, is that, try as they might, women are not men and men are not women. . . .

The fundamental idea of "Glitters" was to show female executives in a multimillion-dollar public relations firm, Globatron, assisted by male secretaries and supported by male househusbands (and male waiters, etc.), engaged in a major business conflict. . . .

In the past, Norman Lear's acute sense for the concrete realities of daily life gave his shows a distinctive realism. From "The Brady Bunch" to "All in the Family" was a long step indeed. In this show, however, the gap between the Lear team's sharp eye for real detail and the fantasy of a world of inverted sex roles constantly disrupts the story, the texture and the point. (p. 246)

In part, the texture of the show confounds sex with class. All the women . . . speak with the elegant, precise, grainy diction of the upper class. In the accents of nearly all the men one hears the echoes of working-class voices from the south, New England, California and the middle west. . . . The class struggle in "Glitters" somehow turns out to be more significant than the sexual one.

Indeed, even the definition of the sexual struggle in this show doubles back upon itself. The premise of the show supposes that the stereotypes generated by the women's movement—machismo versus helplessness—are true, and need only to be reversed. . . . The show reeks of contempt for the stereotypical woman, played by men. It glorifies the macho man, played by women.

In this respect, the show is like a trip backward in time. In fact, everywhere today one meets exceedingly gentle, almost "feminine" men, and decisive women lawyers and managers. Instead of fantasizing what the world "might" look like if roles were suddenly reversed, Lear and company might simply have looked around at today's multiplicity of roles.

More than this, the basic gimmick in the show—the transformation of Leonard Murkland to Linda Murkland (the Wilmington girl) through a trans-sexual operation—supposes that there *is* a definitive female personality, sometimes trapped in a male body, and the reverse. This premise supposes some inseparable chasm between being female and being male. (pp. 246-47)

The real differences between men and women in the real world also keep breaking though the script. Only by leaving pregnancy, breast-feeding and childbirth out of the picture can the show's premise proceed at all. One can believe a "househusband" caring for a grown child—the only child in the show—but can one avoid the questions of infancy? That

is to request the greatest suspension of disbelief in history. Other suspensions follow. It is plausible to imagine (who has not encountered?) sexually avaricious and aggressive females. But when one recalls that the sexually unassertive, distracted males of "Glitters" *also* have to become hard, and have to do the impregnating, the dynamics of the sexual petting in "Glitters" become absurd. . . .

Women can, of course, imitate the decisiveness, crispness, air of authority, and strength of men rather easily. . . . But when the males on the show imitate females, they look for all the world like limp-wristed gays. . . .

Lear and company fail to teach the male actors the secrets of female strength, competency and power. They are not playing females; they are playing *failed* females. Perhaps the most unrealized image in our generation is that of the strong, decisive female. . . . The strength of the female eludes the imagination of our creative artists and our journalists. In real life, we recognize strengths in women which men lack; but we seem to have no words or images to give names to these forms of power. The show suffers for this lack. It puts women down, through the reverse symbolism of men playing weak and dumb.

"Glitters" solves this problem very nicely so long as men are not on camera. When the women deal with one another, their strength is apparent and the screen comes alive with genuine drama. . . .

The nation owes Norman Lear a work of thanks, nonetheless, for this flawed experiment. Against it, one can see that the realities of contemporary life are far more complex than stereotypes suggest. . . . Our society is already further along in the reversal of roles than the wooden stereotypes of "Glitters" suppose. Indeed, meeting scores of women lawyers, activists, actresses, managers and executives, one has already met the male female of "Glitters." (p. 248)

On the other hand, when men become emasculated or too far feminized, women begin to despise them, and they despise themselves as well. Failing legitimate praise for specifically masculine aggressions, many will seek bogus forms of masculinity. In such cultural despair, the Nazi man arose. . . .

Is women's liberation, essentially, a cry of despair about the feminization of the male? "Glitters" experiments with female males. It doesn't work. Not much that glitters in contemporary theories of sexual differentiation comes up gold. (p. 249)

Michael Novak, "Norman Lear's Failed Experiment," in The Christian Century *(copyright 1978 Christian Century Foundation; reprinted by permission from the March 8, 1978 issue of* The Christian Century), *March 8, 1978, pp. 246-49.*

(Nelle) Harper Lee

1926-

American novelist. Lee's only work to date is her 1960 Pulitzer Prize-winning novel, *To Kill a Mockingbird*. A descendent of Robert E. Lee, she was born and raised in a small town in Alabama. Her decision to attend law school is attributed to the strong influence of her lawyer-father, who later served as a model for the main character in her novel, Atticus Finch. Her study of law and its principles helped her develop a lucid prose style; her southern upbringing gave her the raw material which she incorporated into the novel. In a time of the burgeoning civil rights movement, her book was met with popular acclaim and was later adapted for film. Critics agree that it is a literary success, comparing her easy flowing prose style to that of Mark Twain. Her promise of a second novel has yet to be fulfilled. (See also *Contemporary Authors*, Vols. 13-16, rev. ed., and *Something about the Author*, Vol. 11.)

The shadows of a beginning for black-white understanding, the persistent fight that Scout carries on against school, Jem's emergence into adulthood, Calpurnia's quiet power, and all the incidents touching on the children's "growing, outward" have an attractive starchiness that keeps this southern picture pert and provocative [in *To Kill a Mockingbird*]. (p. 360)

Virginia Kirkus' Service, *May 1, 1960.*

FRANK H. LYELL

Harper Lee writes with gentle affection, rich humor and deep understanding of small-town family life in [Maycomb,] Alabama [in "To Kill a Mockingbird"]. (p. 5)

Maycomb has its share of eccentrics and evil-doers, but Miss Lee has not tried to satisfy the current lust for morbid, grotesque tales of Southern depravity. . . . [She] illustrates the importance of developing an open, unprejudiced, well-furnished mind of one's own. . . . (pp. 5, 18)

The dialogue of Miss Lee's refreshingly varied characters is a constant delight in its authenticity and swift revelation of personality. The events connecting the Finches with the Ewell-Robinson lawsuit develop quietly and logically, unifying the plot and dramatizing the author's level-headed plea for interracial understanding. . . .

The praise Miss Lee deserved must be qualified somewhat by noting that oftentimes the narrator's expository style has a processed, homogenized, impersonal flatness quite out of keeping with the narrator's gay, impulsive approach to life

in youth. Also, some of the scenes suggest that Miss Lee is cocking at least one eye toward Hollywood. Moviegoing readers will be able to cast most of the roles very quickly, but it is no disparagement of Miss Lee's winning book to say that it could be the basis of an excellent film. (p. 18)

Frank H. Lyell, "One-Taxi Town," in The New York Times Book Review (© 1960 by The New York Times Company; reprinted by permission), July 10, 1960, pp. 5, 18.

RICHARD SULLIVAN

"To Kill a Mockingbird" is a first novel of such rare excellence that it will no doubt make a great many readers slow down to relish the more fully its simple distinction. . . .

The style is bright and straightforward; the unaffected young narrator uses adult language to render the matter she deals with, but the point of view is cunningly restricted to that of a perceptive, independent child, who doesn't always understand fully what's happening, but who conveys completely, by implication, the weight and burden of the story.

There is wit, grace, and skill in the telling. From the narrator on, every person in the book is every moment alive in time and place. Maycomb, Ala., itself comes alive, as a town abundantly inhabited by individual human beings, each one possessed of his or her own thoroughly convincing nature and personality. And each one contributes to the quiet, sustained humor, the occasionally intense drama, the often taut suspense which all rise out of this rich and variegated complex of human relationships.

Gradually, the novel unfolds and reveals not only a sharp look at a number of people but a view of the American south, and its attitudes, feelings, and traditions.

This is in no way a sociological novel. It underlines no cause. It answers no questions. It offers no solutions. It proposes no programs. It is simply an excellent piece of story telling, which on the way along suggests that there are in Maycomb, Ala., persons of good will in whom love and generous loyalty supersede law, and others in whom meanness—along with envy and fear—breeds lying persecution, under law. . . .

"To Kill a Mockingbird" is a novel of strong contemporary national significance. And it deserves serious consideration. But first of all it is a story so admirably done that it must be called both honorable and engrossing.

Richard Sullivan, "Engrossing First Novel of Rare Excellence," in Chicago Sunday Tribune, July 17, 1960, p. 1.

PHOEBE ADAMS

To Kill a Mockingbird is a . . . successful piece of work. It is frankly and completely impossible, being told in the first person by a six-year-old girl with the prose style of a well-educated adult. Miss Lee has to be sure, made an attempt to confine the information in the text to what Scout would actually know, but it is no more than a casual gesture toward plausibility. . . . What happens [in the story] is . . . never seen directly by the narrator. The surface of the story is an Alcottish filigree of games, mischief, squabbles with an older brother, troubles at school, and the like. (p. 98)

A variety of adults, mostly eccentric in Scout's judgment, and a continual bubble of incident make *To Kill a Mockingbird* pleasant, undemanding reading. (pp. 98-9)

Phoebe Adams, in The Atlantic Monthly *(copyright © 1960 by The Atlantic Monthly Company, Boston, Mass.; reprinted with permission), August, 1960.*

KEITH WATERHOUSE

The innocent childhood game that tumbles into something adult and serious is a fairly common theme in fiction, but I have not for some time seen the idea used so forcefully as in *To Kill a Mockingbird*. . . . The game is 'Making Boo come out' which the children of a Southern lawyer play outside the old home of a family of foot-washing Baptists where, according to one among many legends, Boo Radley has been kept chained up for years and years for stabbing his father with the scissors. Pretty soon we are in the adult game, based on the same fear and fascination of the dark: the ugliness and violence of a Negro's trial for rape and the town's opposition to the children's father for defending him. Miss Lee does well what so many American writers do appallingly: she paints a true and lively picture of life in an American small town. And she gives freshness to a stock situation. (p. 580)

Keith Waterhouse, in New Statesman *(© 1960 The Statesman and Nation Publishing Co. Ltd.), October 15, 1960.*

To Kill a Mockingbird . . . [is] laden with well-deserved praise. In situation and tone it has something in common with [Carson McCullers'] *The Member of the Wedding*, though its development and its atmosphere are more commonplace. . . . The early parts of the book are pure delight. Miss Lee excels in recapturing her childhood, and the children she writes about are worth knowing. . . .

[When a negro is accused of raping a white girl,] Scout's father undertakes the defence, and the novel thereafter runs the way of its many predecessors. But the plot is well constructed, the tone of the opening preserved to the end, and the message one that can stand repetition. (p. 697)

The Times Literary Supplement (© Times Newspapers Ltd. (London) 1960; reproduced from The Times Literary Supplement *by permission), October 28, 1960.*

LEO WARD

Both the style and the story [of *To Kill a Mockingbird*]

seem simple, but no doubt it is quite an achievement to bring them to that happy condition. What a greenhorn from the North may enjoy most is how quietly and completely he is introduced to ways of seeing and feeling and acting in the Deep South. . . . [Harper Lee, unknown until this book appeared,] will not soon be forgotten. (p. 289)

Leo Ward, in Commonweal *(copyright © 1960 Commonweal Publishing Co., Inc.; reprinted by permission of Commonweal Publishing Co., Inc.), December 9, 1960.*

NICK AARON FORD

To Kill a Mockingbird . . . is the complete antithesis of [Leon Odell Griffiths's] *Seed in the Wind*. Instead of stereotyped Negroes, this novel presents living, convincing characters—neither saints nor devils, neither completely ignorant or craven or foolish, nor completely wise or wholly courageous. Instead of blatant propaganda from beginning to end, the socially significant overtones do not begin to appear until the story has progressed a third of the way and then they creep in unobtrusively, as natural as breathing. . . .

The story is told by Jean Louise Finch . . . , aged six at the beginning and eight at the end. It is dominated by [her] complete love and devotion for her father and older brother, her admiration for a boy her own age, her acceptance of Negroes as fellow human beings with the same rights and privileges as those of white people, and her hatred of all hypocrisy and cant. Her dramatic recital of the joys, fears, dreams, misdemeanors, and problems of her little circle of friends and enemies gives the most vivid, realistic, and delightful experiences of a child's world ever presented by an American novelist, with the possible exception of Mark Twain's *Tom Sawyer* and *Huckleberry Finn*. (p. 122)

Nick Aaron Ford, in PHYLON: The Atlanta University Review of Race and Culture *(copyright, 1961, by Atlanta University; reprinted by permission of* PHYLON*), Vol. XXII, Second Quarter (June), 1961.*

EDGAR H. SCHUSTER

Students enjoy reading *To Kill A Mockingbird*, but my experience has been that their appreciation is meager. Over and over again their interpretations stress the race prejudice issue to the exclusion of virtually everything else. . . .

In the pages that follow I shall set forth both a practical classroom approach to the novel and an interpretation of *To Kill a Mockingbird* based on that approach. The reader should bear in mind that I am dealing here primarily with the elements of theme and structure. . . .

It is not difficult to teach students the distinction between full and summary rendering. Furthermore, through their work in composition they are already familiar with the principle that the more space one gives an incident or idea, the more emphasis it receives. In fiction, it follows that those incidents that are fully rendered and those that are relatively long will be keys to the author's intention. (p. 506)

If *Mockingbird* is primarily a race relations novel, why is it that the author gives such a full treatment to episodes that seem totally unrelated to this theme? . . .

Another process of examination has to do with the discovery and tracing of thematic motifs. . . .

My students and I have identified five thematic motifs in *To Kill a Mockingbird*. (p. 507)

One of the motifs—largely understated due to the novel's point of view—concerns Jem's physiological and psychological growth. Although this growth motif may have more to do with character than with theme, the two elements are ultimately bound; moreover it seems clear that the growth of Jem (and of his sister as well) is intimately related to the theme and structure of the novel.

A second thematic motif is centered around what Miss Lee calls the "caste system" in Maycomb. This motif—brought up in many places throughout the book—is obviously related to other motifs, such as growth, superstition, and education. Furthermore, it is within the context of the "caste system" motif that Aunt Alexandria's "missionary circle" and all their talk about the Mrunas and J. Grimes Everett is to be understood.

Thirdly, the title of a novel, students should know, often points to one of its key themes, and this is obviously the case in *To Kill a Mockingbird*. Mockingbirds are mentioned in several places throughout the book, often in key scenes. Best of all, the tracing of this motif will reveal clearly to the students that Tom Robinson is not the only "mockingbird" in the novel.

Finally, the thematic motifs that I would like to discuss in fuller detail are those dealing with *education* and *superstition*. The education motif comes up early in the novel and persists until very near the end. . . . Reflection will reveal . . . that the education motif—far from being incidental—is a center for the ironic contrast between what is "taught" and what is "learned," a contrast that lies at the very heart of the novel.

In the course of their growing up the children do a great deal of learning, but little of that learning takes place in school. . . . Their most effective "teacher," . . . is life itself, their experience. (pp. 507-08)

Superstition is another key motif running through the novel. Superstitions are, of course, the product of fear and ignorance. We expect them to disappear as fear and ignorance are replaced by security and knowledge, and this is clearly what happens, at least to the children, as the novel progresses.

The most memorable superstition in the book is the one concerning the "hot places." Because of its uniqueness, it stands as a kind of symbol of superstition in general. (p. 508)

The novel opens with the reference to Jem's bad arm and the argument between the children over who started it all. Scout blames it on the Ewells, but Jem claims that it began when Dill first came and gave them the idea of making Boo Radley come out. Although Atticus says that both children are right, the author tacitly confirms Jem's view by devoting her first fully rendered scene to the meeting with Dill and Jem's "foray" on the Radley Place.

It is also in this chapter that Dill wagers his copy of *The Gray Ghost* against two Tom Swifts that Jem won't touch Radley's house. Here, too, we learn of the "summertime boundaries" of the children—the Dubose house two doors to the north and the Radley Place three doors to the south. Mrs. Dubose is "gray" in age; Radley lives in a "gray

house." Both characters are "ghosts" in the sense that the children do not know them; fear and prejudice and superstition surround both homes. All these facts should be kept in mind as the novel moves toward fulfillment. (p. 509)

A discovery of the structure of *To Kill a Mockingbird* must begin by focusing on the first chapter: the summertime boundaries, the "gray ghosts," the tension centered in the question of what Boo Radley is really like. How do these phenomena fit into the over-all design?

If that design is to be truly "over-all," it is obvious that the final chapter, too, must play a key role. It is in this chapter —just after having escorted the real Boo Radley home— that Scout makes the point about growing up and algebra; it is here that she says that one never knows a man unless he stands in his shoes and walks around in them; here that she realizes that "nothin's real scary except in books"; and here, finally, that Atticus reads to her from *The Gray Ghost*. The novel concludes with Scout revealing some of the content of that book:

> "An' they chased him 'n' never could catch him 'cause they didn't know what he looked like, an' Atticus, when they finally saw him, why he hadn't done any of those things . . . Atticus, he was real nice. . . ."
>
> His hands were under my chin, pulling up the cover, tucking it around me.
>
> "Most people are, Scout, when you finally see them."

And so the gray ghosts—Dubose and Radley in particular —and superstitions and prejudices of *all* kinds are gone, banished by security and knowledge—the security stemming from the love and example of Atticus, the knowledge coming from real contact with real people.

The achievement of Harper Lee is not that she has written another novel about race prejudice, but rather that she has placed race prejudice in a perspective which allows us to see it as an aspect of a larger thing; as something that arises from phantom contacts, from fear and lack of knowledge; and finally as something that disappears with the kind of knowledge or "education" that one gains through learning what people are really like when you "finally see them." (p. 511)

> *Edgar H. Schuster, "Discovering Theme and Structure in the Novel," in* English Journal *(copyright © 1963 by the National Council of Teachers of English), October, 1963, pp. 506-11.*

EDWIN BRUELL

Miss Lee does write like a woman. She paints Scout in warm tones, and we like the child. (p. 659)

Miss Lee uses high and telling humor when she depicts the myopic do-gooders of the local missionary circle who alternately squealed and sighed over the remote plight of the Mrunas who were safely distant in the dark continent, the while they stirred up a falsely labeled "Christian" hell for the racially different in their home town. Yes, and there was cutting irony and blanched white sarcasm too when the authoress seemingly reaches the outer limits of her fine sense of tolerance even for the bigoted. (p. 660)

> *Edwin Bruell, in* English Journal *(copyright ©
> 1964 by The National Council of Teachers of
> English), December, 1964.*

Madeleine L'Engle

1918-

American novelist, poet, playwright, and essayist. L'Engle's works are characterized by their spirit, optimism, and subtle religious undertones. Her novels for young adults couple traditional action and adventure with modern philosophical and scientific problems and discoveries. A central concern is the importance of a secure and caring family life; this theme is fundamental to *A Wrinkle in Time*, L'Engle's best known novel. Nurtured in a loving atmosphere, the Murry children find inner strength as they conquer the paralyzing forces of evil and mass conformity in order to save their father. It is in part the thematic universality of *A Wrinkle in Time* that brought it the distinction of several awards, including the 1963 Newbery Medal. It is also the first science fiction novel for young people to be considered a part of the mainstream of children's literature, and it spawned several sequels. The solidarity of the Murrys was anticipated by L'Engle's popular books about the Austin family. Although more conventional and less intricate than her other series, *Meet the Austins* and its sequels presented a close-knit family who solved their problems together. L'Engle was criticized for creating a too-perfect family with the Austins, for cluttering her other novels with an overabundance of character and incident, and for overemphasizing her themes. She does not consider herself a didactic writer, and claims to be only a storyteller. Although her abilities as such are unquestionable, her books give her readers deep thought provocation, which attests to her statement that she writes for young people when the subject is "too difficult for grownups." (See also *Contemporary Authors*, Vols. 1-4, rev. ed., and *Something about the Author*, Vol. 1.)

MARY ROSS

[The charm of "The Small Rain"] is its naturalness as a record of childhood and youth. . . .

Miss L'Engle tells the story straightforwardly, without sentimentality, but with quick insight into the keen and contradictory emotions of the years when a girl is struggling to find out what she is and what she wants. In this her picture of the girls at boarding school is notable. . . .

"The Small Rain" is in no way the too common story of unhappy and misunderstood childhood which many novelists seem impelled to write. Miss L'Engle gives you Katherine and her family and friends with an objectivity that makes you respect and like them as individuals. The setting and the events of the story are in themselves interesting. Its distinction, however, arises from the clarity and naturalness with which it recaptures the protean course of youth, reminding you that what has happened by age twenty is neither simple nor important. (p. 2)

> *Mary Ross, in* New York Herald Tribune Book Review *(© I.H.T. Corporation; reprinted by permission), March 11, 1945.*

NINA BROWN BAKER

Katherine [of "The Small Rain"], despite her quite special environment, seems typical rather than unique. Her heartaches and raptures, her yearning for "someone you can really talk to," her high resolves and black despairs, are nothing but the old achingly familiar process of growing up. And yet, the young (and those who have not forgotten how it feels to be young) should find this a moving story. . . . "The Small Rain" gives evidence of a fresh new talent.

> *Nina Brown Baker, "Storm-Tossed Adolescence," in* The New York Times Book Review *(© 1945 by The New York Times Company; reprinted by permission), March 11, 1945, p. 8.*

EDWARD WEEKS

Madeleine L'Engle is a newcomer and I mention her first novel, *The Small Rain*, because in it she succeeds in creating the character of a young artist, one of the most difficult assignments in the whole range of writing. This is the young and refreshing story of a musician growing surely with self-dedication in the midst of Bohemian New York, a realm which can so easily be cheapened, sentimentalized, or exaggerated. Her novel is written with good taste and clear understanding, and while she has much to learn in the pointing up of conversation and in the natural cutback of introspection, the undeniable vitality of her writing is good to discover. (p. 125)

> *Edward Weeks, in* The Atlantic Monthly *(copyright © 1945 by The Atlantic Monthly Company, Boston, Mass.; reprinted with permission), June, 1945.*

EUNICE HOLSAERT

Miss L'Engle's second novel ["Ilsa"] does not warrant the enthusiasm with which her first offering, "The Small Rain," was received. The novel is told in the first person by Ilsa's perennial admirer, a sapless youth of the old

South, whose sensitivity and humility do little to relieve the tedium of his perpetual, unspoken devotion. . . .

[L'Engle's characters] would probably not survive on a soap opera.

> Eunice Holsaert, "Hollow Lives," in The New York Times Book Review (© 1946 by The New York Times Company; reprinted by permission), April 28, 1946, p. 14.

ELLEN LEWIS BUELL

There are poignant overtones in ["And Both Were Young"], for the time is today, and the shadows cast by the war give depth and veracity to Philippa's enlarging perspective. The ending seems a little anticlimactic, following as it does a dramatic and significant episode. But teen-aged girls will find this a satisfying story, sensitive, understanding and stimulating.

> Ellen Lewis Buell, "Boarding School Days," in The New York Times Book Review (© 1949 by The New York Times Company; reprinted by permission), May 22, 1949, p. 28.

ROSE FELD

When does a child cease to be a child and stand in the isolation of an individual? When do parents cease being parents and become unknown human beings? These are the questions, fraught with deeply rooted emotional complications, that Madeleine L'Engle explores in her new novel, "Camilla Dickinson."

Camilla, herself, fifteen years old, is the narrator of the story. It is through her eyes, her feelings, her fears and her bewilderment that the sensitive, fragile texture of a girl's coming of age takes form and pattern. . . .

Perceptively, with a tender understanding of the vulnerability of a growing girl lost in the confusion of intuitive but formless knowledge, Miss L'Engle portrays the shock with which Camilla discovers that Jacques Nissen, a frequent caller at the Dickinson home, is her mother's lover. . . .

Telling her story through Camilla, Miss L'Engle succeeds admirably in portraying the painful awakening of a finely wrought adolescent. She is less successful in portraying some of the adults in the story. But in the realm of troubled, questing youth, Miss L'Engle has the sensitive touch of one whose emotional remembrance has the clarity of the living moment.

> Rose Feld, "A Child Grows Up," in New York Herald Tribune Book Review, (© I.H.T. Corporation; reprinted by permission), August 26, 1951, p. 4.

TRUDIE OSBORNE

Like many a gossip who, in talking about others, chiefly reveals herself, this novel about adolescence ["Camilla Dickinson"] throws its strongest light on adulthood—a state which, if this book is correct, can only be described as a mess. (p. 14)

Most of the cast bespeaks hopelessness and futility and generally leaves a bad taste in the mouth. All the characters intrigue, but not all are clearly realized. In two cases the author has resorted to annoying tricks of speech to supplant inadequate characterization. They are Camilla's mother, who never ends a sentence, and David, a young veteran, who never properly begins one.

Camilla herself passes the fictional test of growth. In the opening pages she combines a precocious adult perception with the childish innocence of another age. It is a combination that might have stepped, if not from a book by one of the Brontës, certainly from the pages of a manuscript written with a quill. By the end of the story the innocence has vanished, and Camilla's awareness, if not her understanding, has caught up with her perception.

Miss L'Engle has chosen New York as a backdrop. Her present-day New York is recognizable but, as often happens, it remains a fictional vacuum. No author to ignore challenges, she has further elected to write in the first person, from the point of view and in the thought idiom of 15-year-old Camilla. It is a narrative path thick with pitfalls. On the whole, she has traversed it well. (pp. 14-15)

> Trudie Osborne, in The New York Times Book Review (© 1951 by The New York Times Company; reprinted by permission), August 26, 1951.

HARRISON SMITH

A month ago J. D. Salinger told the story of what happened to a sixteen-year-old boy in the three days' interval between his dismissal from a private school and his return to his parents' home in New York's Park Avenue, ill and in a state of mental and physical shock. "Catcher in the Rye" is rapidly climbing toward the top of the best seller lists, and now it seems likely that Madeleine L'Engle's latest novel, which is concerned with two weeks in the life of a fifteen-year-old Park Avenue girl, may follow in its steps. There is a remarkable similarity in these two diverse books. Both are told in the first person, and both are concerned with the problems of a sensitive adolescent faced suddenly with the necessity of crossing the dividing line between childhood and maturity.

Miss L'Engle's "Camilla Dickinson" has more innate strength and stability than Salinger's Holden Caulfield. (p. 18)

The success of Miss L'Engle's appealing novel depends on the sensitivity and the understanding with which she reveals the mind of a charming young girl. There is nothing wrong with Camilla, who has courage and imagination, and who, unlike Mr. Salinger's Holden Caulfield, could not be made to endure what was ugly, cruel, or false among his fellows or the adult world. But there is a deeper division between "Camilla Dickinson" and "Catcher in the Rye." Mr. Salinger's magic depends for the most part on the authenticity of Holden's language which gives the illusion of being taken from life itself. Camilla's words and thoughts have the appearance of being interpreted at times though the novelist's words. Sometimes it is Camilla speaking directly to the reader but more often it is Miss L'Engle. It is unlikely, for example, that a fifteen-year-old girl could recall accurately every sentence of a long dialogue she listened to when she was five years old. This is perhaps a distinction without a difference, and it does not destroy the charm, the pathos, and the meaning of her book. (pp. 18-19)

> Harrison Smith, in The Saturday Review of Literature (Entire issue copyright 1951 by Saturday Review Associates, Inc.; reprinted with permission), September 1, 1951.

RUTH HILL VIGUERS

Anyone who has traveled with four children, or even less,

over thousands of miles, camping nearly every night in a different spot, knows how much can happen. "Adventures" become almost commonplace. Perhaps no one family could have had all the variety of experiences that the Austins had on their journey [in *The Moon by Night*], but not one of the events is impossible or even unbelievable. From time to time I found myself thinking, "Oh, why didn't they stop there long enough to see . . ." and then remembered I was reading a *story*. If a veteran reviewer could be so convinced of the reality of a book, it will surely be alive for young readers.

Vicky matures to the point of feeling life is still worth living after having her young belief in the inevitability of justice shattered. Her efforts to find herself, to help the boy who needs her friendship, to put in perspective all she has been taught of life and death, human relationships, and religious faith, involve much thoughtful analysis and bring this story very close to young people. Woven through are passages that some might consider sermonizing, but they are so in character and so spiced with reality and humor that I think young people looking for answers to their many questions will appreciate them.

Idealistic and wise, this is also absorbing reading and very much a story of today, contemporary in feeling, incident, and characterizations. Elizabeth George Speare, in her Newbery Acceptance last June quoted Joseph Wood Krutch, "If Love, and Honor, and Duty can be salvaged, then someone must write about them in a fashion which carries conviction." In this book Madeleine L'Engle has done just that. (pp. 165-66)

> *Ruth Hill Viguers, in* The Horn Book Magazine *(copyright © 1963, by The Horn Book, Inc., Boston), April, 1963.*

ALICE DALGLIESH

[*The Moon by Night*] is another, and independent, book about Vicky and her family, who first appeared in *Meet the Austins*. [The Austins are] as real a family as you find in a book. . . .

Vicky, the narrator, meets a boy who interests her because he is so different—but he is disturbing to her family. His effect on Vicky's slightly uncertain but really firm faith in God—and in life—makes a good story, one that may, in so far as it is possible, give reassurance to girls who need it. But occasionally they may wish that Vicky and Zachary did not take themselves quite so seriously. (p. 77)

> *Alice Dalgliesh, in* The Saturday Review *(Entire issue copyright 1963 by Saturday Review Associates, reprinted with permission), May 11, 1963.*

Judging by the frequency of their appearance books with some sort of gimmick involving the fourth dimension have substantial appeal for younger readers. [*A Wrinkle in Time*] adds a fifth, though it is not quite clear what it is, which enables persons with the right "equipment" to translate themselves (if that is the right word) to other planets, or, indeed, other points in time. It would not be fair to the author to disclose even a hint of the development, in the second half of the book, of this technique, but one thing can be said at once: Meg, little Charles Wallace, and the older Calvin are far more interesting and appealing as children before that development than at any time after and they do not as creations deserve the strain and fear that is part of

their treatment as the story moves on. It is rather terrifying to reflect on the realities of modern life which make Madeleine L'Engle's science fantasy possible and I am not at all certain that the book ought to fall into the hands of highly imaginative children who may still be afraid of the dark. Still, as there is now a swing of opinion away from the theory of horror in fairy stories and the corrupting influence of adult cinema, it may in this case be all right. There is no doubt that she writes well—devilish well—though her beneficent replacements for the Three Witches, Mrs. Whatsit, Mrs. Who and Mrs. Which are not altogether convincing, one might think. (pp. 154-55)

> The Junior Bookshelf, *July, 1963.*

RUTH HILL VIGUERS

I have often wished it were not necessary to review a book immediately upon publication. Children's reactions and acceptances are always important and there should be time to be aware of them. The critic's own perspective on a book is often clearer months after it is read. I felt that way about Madeleine L'Engle's *A Wrinkle in Time*. I reviewed it favorably upon publication. Months later the book's extraordinary power began to show itself in the way incidents kept coming to mind, in the hold it had taken on my imagination.

I cannot forget the personalities of the children: precocious little Charles Wallace; Meg, whose faults alone—anger, impatience, stubbornness—could save her; the three strange beings who emerge at times as eccentric but very kind old ladies. (p. 25)

Miss L'Engle has referred to her book as a parable; but it is first of all an exciting adventure story, with something important added—the overtones that will make it worth reading many times and will give new meanings with each new reading.

Here is a book which the analytical reviewer might characterize in this way:

> A mingling of realism and science fantasy which incorporates the concepts of time travel, extrasensory perception, and inhabited planets in outer space. Excellent writing style, involved plot. Vocabulary and literary references too difficult for the average fairy-tale audience.

An imaginative analyst might compare the three spirits with the witches of Macbeth, point out analogies to modern life, and cite the value (or confusion to the unread child) of the literary quotations. Both reviewers would be doing what C. S. Lewis calls judging "the instrument by anything rather than its power to do the work it was made for," criticizing "the lens after looking *at* it instead of *through* it."

> We are so busy doing things with the work that we give it too little chance to work on us. Thus increasingly we meet only ourselves.

Here certainly is a book which should not be used but should be received, full of words which are "exquisitely detailed compulsions on a mind willing and able to be so compelled." Here is a book requiring an approach which allows margin for surprise. (pp. 26-7)

> *Ruth Hill Viguers, in her* Margin for Surprise: About Books, Children, and Librarians *(copyright © 1964 by Ruth Hill Viguers; reprinted by permission of Little, Brown and Co.), Little, Brown, 1964.*

CAROLYN M. LIGHT

Following the theme which characterizes her last two books, that of young protagonists who make travel and an interest in science the roads of maturity, Madeleine L'Engle has created a . . . novel [*The Arm of the Starfish*] demanding a place on all young adult bookshelves. . . .

[It presents] that type of smooth running plot which immerses one to its end in story alone, and only then delivers in brilliant flashes a shower of meaning and application. Some handlings of situation are overdrawn, being perhaps too intense pockets of the author's perceptive sensitivity. Usually the tone is even and natural, suspense building up through the clash of events upon the perplexed and wary minds of both boy and reader. It is a book about love and loyalty, about the difficulty but necessity of committing oneself to a cause the implications of which extend to "Heaven and the future's sakes." Could anything be more relevant to the challenges facing Adam's generation today? Could any problem be for them more pressing than his—to find selfhood and vocation "Where love and need are one." (pp. 36-7)

> *Carolyn M. Light, in* Best Sellers *(copyright 1965, by the University of Scranton), April 15, 1965.*

ALICE DALGLIESH

The qualities that made *A Wrinkle in Time* popular are all [in *The Arm of the Starfish*], though the plot and characters are kept under better control. At first the story seems a cloak-and-dagger affair; it teeters on the edge of melodrama, becomes mystical in tone, and, if you read the note in the front matter, appears also to be science fiction. There is a "message," which is more skilfully presented than that of the former book. The characters are alive and possible—including the Jesus-like Joshua, who proclaims his non-belief in a personal God, yet cares about humanity even to the fall of a sparrow. (p. 45)

> *Alice Dalgliesh, in* Saturday Review *(© 1965 by Saturday Review, Inc.; reprinted with permission), April 24, 1965.*

CAROLYN HOROVITZ

A most popular and original book is *A Wrinkle in Time*. The book sparkles with the author's vitality and imagination and proceeds at a fast pace with recognizable character types. Her contributions are ingenious but not deep. The climactic scene in which Meg stands crying before Charles Wallace bothers me for two reasons. First of all, I find it hard to understand why she could not have done this before; secondly, if Mrs. Whatsit could tesser her and Charles Wallace away from IT, why couldn't she have been with them before and saved them from their father's inept tessering? Here, it seems to me, the ground rules of the plot have been violated. In the previous visit to IT, the children had to go alone; now Mrs. Whatsit is there to tesser them off. This may seem minor, but it is of a piece with the main criticism I have to make of this book; there is a facility about it, a slickness in characterization and dialogue which makes me feel that I have been dealt with less than directly.

There is no question but that the book is good entertainment and that the writer carries the story along with a great deal of verve; there is some question about the depth of its quality. (p. 159)

> *Carolyn Horovitz, in* Newbery and Caldecott Medal Books: 1956-1965, *edited by Lee Kingman (copyright © 1965 by The Horn Book, Inc., Boston), Horn Book, 1965 (and reprinted by Horn Book, 1966).*

ELAINE MOSS

Madeleine L'Engle's *Meet the Austins* . . . deserves notice because it takes one small step towards filling the yawning spiritual gap in novels for the young. As unfashionable as covered knees, it explores, from the secure anchorage of a happy American family, the meaning of life and death. (p. 702)

> *Elaine Moss, in* The Spectator *(© 1966 by The Spectator; reprinted by permission of The Spectator), June 3, 1966.*

[*Meet the Austins*] might perhaps be sub-titled "The Family That Never Was." Nevertheless, there is a refreshingly wholesome feeling about this New England doctor's family who weather a report of sudden death, a bicycle accident, and the disruption caused by a spoilt orphan, determined by any means to be the centre of attention. The four children and the outsider, ranging in age from about six to thirteen, are delightfully true to life, excellently observed, and the parents, so understanding and sane, are as parents should be, finding time to share with the whole family the beauty of a night sky or frost in the moonlight. (p. 253)

> The Junior Bookshelf, *August, 1966.*

JEAN C. THOMSON

[The bizarre story of *The Young Unicorns*] turns on a power-mad brain surgeon's discovery of the stunning potential in a micro-laser to control men's minds. What's most fun here is the author's outrageous imagination coupled with her ability to characterize so many people adequately; the sheer number, however, will occasionally leave readers bewildered. Dave, a troubled youth, begins and ends the book, but in between the action sways away from him, and nearly all the characters receive equal time. Surprisingly, the supernumeraries and suspense-gorged plot are so integrated as to add up to a carnival show for young readers in a giddy, mind-stretching book. (pp. 149-50)

> *Jean C. Thomson, in* School Library Journal *(reprinted from the March, 1968 issue of* School Library Journal, *published by R. R. Bowker Co. A Xerox Corporation; copyright © 1968), March, 1968.*

PAUL HEINS

[*The Journey with Jonah*, a dramatization of the story found in the Old Testament Book of Jonah,] amplifies the humor of the original and retains its basic meaning. Jonah, the somewhat pompous prophet, may be at odds with God and man, but he is not left alone. On every step of his way he is confronted by animal creation. His motives are probed by a pedantic Owl, a silly Goose, and a pert Jay—among others; the Rat family witness his ejection from the ship; and he engages in a conversation with the Whale. Through the prose and the verse, the rhymes and the puns, is witnessed the animal world's revelation of the incomprehensibility of God's mercy, which Jonah finally acknowledges. (p. 184)

> Paul Heins, in The Horn Book Magazine (copyright © 1968 by The Horn Book, Inc., Boston), April, 1968.

GERALDINE E. LaROCQUE

The Journey with Jonah abounds with delightful puns and saucy animals that reflect their common characteristics such as the wise old owl and the foolish goose. I am inclined to say that *everyone* will love *The Journey with Jonah* because I am so taken with it and because I find it impossible not to pile orchid after orchid upon Newbery Prize winner L'Engle; but experience impels me to moderate that "everyone" in spite of myself.

So compelling is the play that students reading it may want to read the story of Jonah in the Bible. Because the subject matter is open to treatment in depth or to understanding on a literal level, I believe the play can be read anywhere from Grades 7 to 12. The animals may appeal to younger students, and their symbolic attributes will appeal to the more mature. The same is true of the style; its refinements can be appreciated by the better reader but its intent can be grasped by the less proficient. (p. 753)

> Geraldine E. LaRocque, in English Journal (copyright © 1968 by the National Council of Teachers of English), May, 1968.

GERALDINE E. LaROCQUE

A very unusual novel, both frighteningly realistic and highly imaginative, *The Young Unicorns* ... maintains Madeleine L'Engle's reputation as one of the finest of the present day authors writing for young people. (p. 296)

Because the manner of the telling and the sense of confusion and mystery created by the unknowns are integral to the enjoyment of the book, recounting the plot here would be a real disservice; but it is important to say that the book deals with profound questions of philosophy and psychology. A special novel, which can be read by some junior high school boys and girls but which, because of the intricacies of plot and philosophy, might be recommended more successfully to older readers.

Barbara M. Castellano ... sees the book as the story of the development of one of the main characters, Dave, as he learns to love and trust people, as he breaks down the barriers of his disillusion with others. In speaking of Canon Tallis who solves the mystery of the sinister events, Barbara Castellano says:

> He is a profound thinker, deeply concerned with moral-theological issues. It is he who provides the masked theme of the book: the immorality of establishing a Utopia at the expense of human freedom. His point of view corresponds to the Miltonian concepts of liberty and license. Man can only have dignity if he can *choose* good. The villain of the piece proposes to eliminate that choice, and L'Engle's argument against such control of the human spirit is as good as any in contemporary adult fiction.

(pp. 296-97)

> Geraldine E. LaRocque, in English Journal (copyright © 1969 by the National Council of Teachers of English), February, 1969.

"The dragons and the owls honor him because he gives waters in the wilderness, and rivers in the desert, and drink to his people." The words of the child's mother articulate what has become apparent during the procession of real and fabled creatures to the desert caravan's overnight camp. Each in his own way does obeisance to the joyful little boy; it is the "extraordinary night ... when nobody was afraid and everybody danced." As designed, [*Dance in the Desert*] as a whole is a desert night on the journey into Egypt, the text appearing against the glowing sands, the flickering fire, the shadowy dunes; fittingly, the last picture is an almost traditional Madonna and Child. What may seem florid (in the illustrations) and sticky (in the story) to some is, if taken in the spirit in which it was meant, a fervent testimonial (p. 372)

> Kirkus Reviews (copyright © 1969 The Kirkus Service, Inc.), April 1, 1969.

These poems [in *Lines Scribbled on an Envelope and Other Poems*] are less traditional, both in style and substance, than much of the poetry written for children (no chirpy birds or sticky eccentricities) but they have a familiar large optimism and heavy social consciousness.... Several flirt with Biblical lines—both "Shout Joy" and "The Baby in the Bath" use echoes from the psalms—while others concern light exotica—the unicorn, the phoenix, the roc ("But the only meal of suitable elegance / For a flock of young roc is a handful of elephants. / Rockabye, rocklings, roc, roc, roc a bye"). The verse forms vary considerably—simple rhyme, sonnets, free verse—but only a few are strong and forceful and the very personal projections of uplift and enthusiasm are limited in appeal. (p. 681)

> Kirkus Reviews (copyright © 1969 The Kirkus Service, Inc.), July 1, 1969.

The Young Unicorns seems a more resolved and complete work than *A Wrinkle in Time*, the book by which the author is so far known here. That, too, was about the battle of good and evil, in a world of modern science and ancient forces, and it had some unforgettable passages of fairy-tale magic and witchery; but it had its weaknesses too, not the least of them something over-local and over-sentimental in the politics of the message. *The Young Unicorns* (where, in spite of the prevailing strangeness, nothing of the seeming-supernatural is left without a rational explanation) is a good deal more subtle in its complexities. And even those young readers who contrive to bypass the thought and the allegory, cannot but be impressed by the sheer melodramatic thrills of the plot. A triumph of the possible rather than the probable, one might think, but it is logically credible and certainly imaginatively so.

> "Of Good and Evil," in The Times Literary Supplement (© Times Newspapers Ltd. (London) 1969; reproduced from The Times Literary Supplement by permission), October 16, 1969, p. 1190.

JOHN CONNER

Young readers who remember Madeleine L'Engle for her exciting *A Wrinkle in Time* may enjoy "The Sea Monster,"

"Summer City," "The Monkey," "The Dragon," "Song of Simeon," and "The Parrot" in [*Lines Scribbled on an Envelope*]. These poems present a segment of life in a quasi-humorous way sustained by a youthful point of view. They also represent Madeleine L'Engle's marvelous gift for combining dissimilar elements from opposing historical periods.

But most of the poems in this collection will appeal to older adolescent and adult readers because the poet views her subject matter in retrospect. She is a concrete adult wondering about present day values in terms of birth, death, passion, and religious experience. I believe it must be these poems which made Madeleine L'Engle hesitate about publishing this book. In her preface to the volume she writes of being afraid "of making myself vulnerable to people I don't know." She is aware that the distilled language of verse magnifies her thoughts.

A marvelous image of an unhappily thrashing sea monster in the poem of the same name who waits forever for ships to fall off the horizon because people no longer believe the world is flat contrasts with the symbolic hole in the world in "Lines After M. B.'s Funeral" through which the poet hopes to see where the wind comes from and where the light begins. These examples suggest the range of images in this brief volume of verse. Individual poems may appeal to widely different audiences.

Reading *Lines Scribbled on an Envelope* is a deeply moving experience. I'm glad Madeleine L'Engle had the courage to reveal herself to her readers. (p. 302)

> *John Conner, in* English Journal *(copyright 1970 by the National Council of Teachers of English), February, 1970.*

In [*Dance in the Desert,* a] fairy tale about the Flight into Egypt, the desert animals and birds come by night to the caravan with which the Holy Family is travelling and dance to Jesus by the light of the campfire. . . . The story is rather hard to accept: not so much the inclusion with real animals of the dragon and unicorn (vindicating the Virgin's purity by placing his head in her lap), as the unconcern of the rest of the caravan at these unusual happenings. (p. 88)

> The Junior Bookshelf, *April, 1970.*

JOHN W. CONNER

A generation of adolescent readers has been charmed by the many writing moods of Madeleine L'Engle; perhaps the sense of togetherness in *Meet the Austins,* the mystery and suspense of *A Wrinkle in Time,* or the romantic adventure of *And Both Were Young.* Miss L'Engle's new novel, *The Other Side of the Sun,* is an adult one, but older adolescent L'Engle fans will welcome a new facet of this fine author's talent.

Madeleine L'Engle has a very special way with words. She shapes sentences so that the syntax suggests movement and feeling beyond the descriptive power of the words themselves. Never has this been more apparent than in *The Other Side of the Sun.* (p. 1154)

The Other Side of the Sun moves sedately, revealing little by little the complex familial intrigue which threatens various members of the Illyria family. Slowly Miss L'Engle builds the tension. Finally it is released in an eruption of witchcraft, conflagration, and vigilante slayings. Early in the novel the words of the first white co-mistress of Illyria set the theme: "Only on love's terrible other side is found the place where lion and lamb abide." It is the search for that other side of love which motivates a reader to unravel the mysteries of Illyria. And it is a fruitful search. . . .

Adolescent readers will be intrigued by the value systems employed by various characters in *The Other Side of the Sun.* I think they will be shaken, as I was, by the pervading sense of evil in the practices of witchcraft. *The Other Side of the Sun* is excellent reading fare for the older adolescent who is prepared to consider the ultimate price a human being must pay for the values he upholds. Miss L'Engle is to be congratulated for adding an important new dimension to her varied writings. (p. 1155)

> *John W. Conner, in* English Journal *(copyright © 1971 by the National Council of Teachers of English), November, 1971.*

POLLY LONGSWORTH

Anyone who has read many of Madeleine L'Engle's excellent novels for young people must hanker to know something about *her,* to find out why beautiful mothers and radiantly warm family life recur in her books, and why her female characters achieve fuller dimension than her male, and how she dares champion the forces of good in these dark times.

The chance to know her comes on like a Newfoundland puppy in "A Circle of Quiet," a long, loosely-structured, personal statement of her convictions, experiences, ponderings, self-analyses and philosophizings in which the reader discovers her discovering herself.

At age 51 Madeleine L'Engle is experiencing what [Carl] Jung called individuation, and she calls ontology—a coming to the real self. She employs the image of the burning bush —with everything non-essential burned away and only the real remaining—to describe the process she is undergoing and to justify culling her journals and her recent experiences to explain who and where she is. The result is an amorphous grouping of short essays focusing on the intrinsic values of her life as mother, wife, writer and friend. It is a fusion of autobiographical detail, practical advice to writers, demonstration of her craft, short intellectual excursions in search of truth and definition, passionate defense of the need for love, charity, compassion, laughter, community and commitment in our lives, and, most important to the author, a confirmation of her evolving belief in a loving Creator.

Any human confession presents the opportunity to play God, and the responsibility for doing so with justice. "A Circle of Quiet" reveals a loyal, wise and passionate individual, whose response to life has influenced others through friendship and through her writing. She has made a highly vulnerable declaration, sprawling, flawed, and full of material redolent of women's magazines. That she is cognizant of her faults doesn't entirely justify them. For instance, she makes a lot of perfectly obvious, ordinary observations which rob the book of a penetrating quality. This is disappointing.

Miss L'Engle does not pretend to be an intellectual; she buffers her good intelligence with faith and feeling. Nor is she writing a work of fiction. But there is an unnecessary Oz effect here. The all-too-human individual revealed behind the apparent magician has failed to make full use of her very real powers, for she can and has made magic. In this instance her talent for imaginatively transfiguring experience has been sacrificed at the altar of ontology. *Isness,* getting to the core of herself, has required admirable honesty, but she has let her artistic self down in the process. Perhaps the book suffers from the author's being both writer and chief character. . . .

The question hanging over "A Circle of Quiet" is, who is it for? . . .

I doubt that many young adults will read this book. Not because they disagree with what she says, but because they reject odyssey as a route to *Isness,* and because they won't agree with Madeleine L'Engle that there are answers.

The author emphasizes her inability to distinguish in her own writing between books for children and books for adults, but she demonstrates that there is a difference through her search for answers. She has a penchant for locating paradoxes, for tidying ambivalences, for catching up life's many loose, meaningless ends—in short, for moralizing. Books for children (including lots of adult books) come to conclusions. We don't put them down feeling hopeless and lost. "A Circle of Quiet" is an effort at conclusion for the author.

Not that the author is drawing her life to a close, but its chronology is now plain to her, and in seeking to become ontological she is searching for the denouement of her own life's story. For her, both the real and imaginary worlds fuse in "affirmation of a universe which is created by a power of good." That moral of affirmation sings through this personal narrative. It explains why Madeleine L'Engle is a wonderful writer of books for children. But morals now seem inadequate to many of the troubled adults who earlier drew nourishment from those books. (p. 28)

> *Polly Longsworth, in* The New York Times Book Review *(© 1972 by The New York Times Company; reprinted by permission), February 13, 1972.*

JOHN W. CONNER

Madeleine L'Engle is an avid spectator of life. Her word portraits of personalities she includes in *A Circle of Quiet* reveal a respectable ability to get into the character of another, feeling about until she hits a responsive nerve. (p. 767)

Snatches of *A Circle of Quiet* keep reoccurring in my memory as I go about the business of daily living. For example, chapters sprinkled throughout the book contain excellent advice for fledgling writers. I find myself explaining how the author uses her journals, or the importance of *showing* a reader rather than *reporting* to a reader when writing fiction, or the reality in characterization which comes only from allowing an imaginary character to develop naturally. A thread of irrepressible humor runs through *A Circle of Quiet.* Madeleine L'Engle has reached a stage in her maturity where she can easily smile at her own foibles. It is wonderfully refreshing to read her thoughtful reactions to today's tensions—what a contrast to the up-tight concerned prose of the daily press!

Is *A Circle of Quiet* for adolescents or adults? My initial reaction favored adults. . . . But I have had second thoughts. Many adolescents have enjoyed a number of

Madeleine L'Engle's books. They might be as curious as I to meet the real Madeleine L'Engle.

And so, *A Circle of Quiet* has found its way into this column, and I predict it will find its way into the hearts of Madeleine L'Engle's fans, adolescent and adult. (pp. 767-68)

> *John W. Conner, in* English Journal *(copyright © 1972 by the National Council of Teachers of English), May, 1972.*

MAY HILL ARBUTHNOT and ZENA SUTHERLAND

[*Meet the Austins* is one of the first family-centered books] since *Little Women* to handle the death of a loved one so well (p. 462)

The children's ups and downs, a serious brother-sister conflict, some funny and some grave situations—all develop against a background of family love. This is a fine family story, as unusual and provocative throughout the whole book as is its first chapter. (p. 463)

> *May Hill Arbuthnot and Zena Sutherland, in their* Children and Books *(copyright © 1947, 1957, 1964, 1972, by Scott, Foresman and Company, reprinted by permission), fourth edition, Scott Foresman, 1972.*

JOHN ROWE TOWNSEND

The most ambitious of American SF stories for young people is Madeleine L'Engle's *A Wrinkle in Time.* . . . Heroine Meg Murry, who wears spectacles and has braces on her teeth, sets off with precocious small brother Charles and friend Calvin O'Keefe to rescue her scientist father from the grip of IT; a great brain that controls the lives of the zombie population of a planet called Camazotz. The power of love and the help of three witches who appear also to be angels enable Meg to triumph over evil (evil being the extermination of individuality). There is a luminous confusion about *A Wrinkle in Time*; it seems to be trying to do too many things at once. But it is an attractive book, splendidly unafraid of being clever or out-of-the-ordinary, and not concerned to reinforce the image of the regular guy or girl. (p. 215)

> *John Rowe Townsend, in his* Written for Children: An Outline of English-Language Children's Literature *(copyright © 1965, 1974, by John Rowe Townsend; reprinted by permission of J. B. Lippincott Company; in Canada by Kestrel Books), revised edition, Lippincott, 1974.*

ROBERT BELL

Adult admirers of Miss L'Engle will appreciate [*A Wind in the Door*], her most virtuoso performance in fantasy to date, but I have a lingering doubt if any but the more virtuoso young readers will be able to escape a good deal of bewilderment. The plot is enormously exciting, though I have the same kind of reservations about the solution as some reviewers had about that in Alan Garner's *The Owl Service.* The book will not be for every child; a good many will find it puzzling, but for the discerning readers who are able to appreciate the symbolism it will make a lasting impression. (pp. 247-48)

> *Robert Bell, in* The School Librarian, *September, 1975.*

WAYNE DODD

[Madeleine L'Engle's *A Wind in the Door*] attempts to get

to the spiritual by way of fantasy/science fiction. But she also takes other routes as well: namely both the ''dragon'' road and that familiar street that runs through the unnoticed gap in the everyday and into the beyond. The result is that, in terms of wonder, we get nowhere. Mrs. L'Engle really can't make up her mind whether she wants the reader to be involved in the realistic dimension of her story (which is rendered with superfluous and unselective detail) or to be caught up in the discovery of the ''other'' in our lives. The idea for this story is a promising one: the discovery (by the children) of the presence, in the strange illness of one little boy, of a whole universe of struggle between good and evil, order and chaos, integration and disintegration. This is the same territory C. S. Lewis worked, both in the chronicles of Narnia and in the Perelandra series for adults. The difference is that genuine wonder is never present in *A Wind in the Door*. The problem appears to be one of writing, primarily. For not only is there a confusion of routes (lack of commitment?) but also the spiritual (galactic) dimension, once moved into, is simply too confusingly vague and obscure to win acceptance. In addition, the treatment of the realistic point of departure is too charmingly eccentric, even, finally, clichéd—that is, cliché ideas of charmingly eccentric people. Moreover, *A Wind in the Door* shares what appears to be the burden of all fantasy/science fiction: only the idea really interests the writer. (p. 174)

> *Wayne Dodd, in* Children's Literature: Annual of The Modern Language Association Seminar on Children's Literature and The Children's Literature Association, *Vol. 4, edited by Francelia Butler (© 1975 by Francelia Butler; all rights reserved), Temple University Press, 1975.*

[The O'Keefe family from *The Arm of the Starfish* are on hand in *Dragons in the Waters*] to join Simon Bolivar Renier and his spooky Cousin Phair on a freighter voyage from Savannah to Venezuela which looks at the outset a bit like L'Engle's version of [Katherine Anne Porter's] *Ship of Fools*. The O'Keefe kids haven't outgrown their arrogance —Poly is given to bragging about her family's doctorates real and potential, and excuses Simon's eavesdropping because this is the end of the century when ''Things are falling apart. The center doesn't hold.'' But there's little time for metaphysical wrangles as we are introduced to the Orion's passengers and crew, while Simon survives several attempts on his life and Cousin Phair is murdered.... [In the rush of new developments] one can be immune to the lure of the Quiztanos or even unimpressed by the murder mystery's solution and still be well entertained. Of all L'Engle's novels, we find this the most satisfying, perhaps because it doesn't demand to be taken with such deadly seriousness. Deduct ten points at the beginning for self-importance and enjoy the rest for a lark. (pp. 470-71)

> Kirkus Reviews *(copyright © 1976 The Kirkus Service, Inc.), April 15, 1976.*

BARBARA ELLEMAN

[In *Dragons in the Waters*] L'Engle writes a taut, intricately layered novel, charged with suspenseful twists and faceted into a thoughtful yet climactic conclusion. As in her other books, the power of love and cohesive force of caring are underlying themes, and the perceptively drawn characters, some of whom appeared in *The Arm of the Starfish*,

are realistic in their conception, credible in their actions, and extremely human. (p. 1266)

> *Barbara Elleman, in* The Booklist *(reprinted by permission of the American Library Association; copyright 1976 by The American Library Association), May 1, 1976.*

CYNTHIA BENJAMIN

There is enough adventure in ''Dragons in the Waters'' to make Nancy Drew and her chums squirm: a shipboard murder that could have been committed by any one of the passengers or crew; a kidnapping; an attack by a wild boar; a young boy lost in the Venezuelan jungle.... And much more....

The plot of ''Dragons in the Waters'' is complex and might be confusing to less able readers. The narrative is an intriguing mixture of contemporary allusions and gothic mystery. But does it work? Will readers find Simon's decision to remain in the primitive Quiztano village believable? It is a credit to the author's skill at characterization that they will. (p. 22)

> *Cynthia Benjamin, in* The New York Times Book Review *(© 1976 by The New York Times Company; reprinted by permission), June 20, 1976.*

CRAIG WALLACE BARROW

Madeleine L'Engle's *A Wrinkle in Time* is a splendid fantasy; ... it seldom violates reality. The Murry family relationships, Calvin's relationship to his parents, and Meg's relation to school authorities and the community, as well as the character portraits, are probable and realistic. Envy of the Murrys, gossip about the supposedly runaway father-husband, malice, selfishness, and even Charles Wallace's arrogance, are unflinchingly presented. Tesseracting, a seemingly instantaneous movement in time and/or place, is given a metamorphic fifth-dimension explanation. The witches who were formerly stars dying in the struggle against the evil shadow fight a symbolic battle steeped in classical and Gospel-of-John traditions, a battle that is psychically realistic even though symbolic. One can even relate Mrs. Whatsit's, Mrs. Who's, and Mrs. Which's actions to current theories of black holes in space and neutron stars; even the life style on Camazotz has an affinity to entropy. The only weakness in the novel is the confrontation with the It-brain by Mr. Murry and the children; the shift from the symbolic to the actual confrontation is a dramatic collapse of an antagonist from the infinite to the finite much like the cannon battle in [John Milton's] *Paradise Lost*. (pp. 295-96)

> *Craig Wallace Barrow, in* Children's Literature: Annual of The Modern Language Association Seminar on Children's Literature and The Children's Literature Association, *Vol. 5, edited by Francelia Butler (© 1976 by Francelia Butler; all rights reserved), Temple University Press, 1976.*

REBECCA J. LUKENS

A Wrinkle in Time [is] a fantasy which uses many of the devices of science fiction, but which does not rely on its machinery to produce story. Space and time fantasy can have fully developed character, and yet retain the ingenuity we find in science fiction. Even though the characters of *A Wrinkle in Time* have special mental powers, they do not lose their humanness. Father, the brilliant scientist, through sheer human weariness has lost his fight with IT, the huge, disembodied brain. Meg struggles to hold back Charles Wallace, who—arrogantly believing in the superiority of mind—is drawn into IT's control. Meg's human stubbornness helps her rescue her father, but in the process she leaves Charles Wallace. Sustained by the strength of an indomitable human force, love, Meg returns to rescue her brother and reunite the family. These are round, three-dimensional characters; they can be found in science fiction. We can be made to care about the action, the ideas, the characters, and their relationships—when the characters are believable. (p. 27)

> *Rebecca J. Lukens, in her* A Critical Handbook of Children's Literature *(copyright © 1976 by Scott, Foresman and Company; reprinted by permission), Scott, Foresman, 1976.*

JEAN F. MERCIER

The cast from the Newbery-award novel, "A Wrinkle in Time" and "A Wind in the Door" returns [in "A Swiftly Tilting Planet"] with the Murry children now grown.... Shivery and elegant twists of plot ensue as Meg and Charles Wallace employ time travel, telepathy, a Welsh rune and other means to prevent annihilation of the universe by a mad dictator. L'Engle's gifts are at their most impressive here. Her ability to draw attention to familiar details of settings and characters is such that she slips searingly abstract scientific and moral principles into the reader's consciousness, smoothly but surely. (p. 65)

> *Jean F. Mercier, in* Publishers Weekly *(reprinted from the July 3, 1978, issue of* Publishers Weekly *by permission of the critic, published by R. R. Bowker Company, a Xerox company; copyright © 1978 by Xerox Corporation), July 3, 1978.*

L'Engle's irksomely superior Murry family reassembles [in *A Swiftly Tilting Planet*] for Thanksgiving dinner, about ten years after Meg and Charles Wallace braved the *Wrinkle in Time*.... [Precocious] Charles Wallace, now 15, leaves his tesseract model and goes off to his star-watching rock to see what he can do to avert disaster. There, with the wind

making the decisions and the evil *echthroi* trying to catch him en route, Charles rides a unicorn back in time and goes "Within" a series of individual consciousnesses.... The idea, according to the unicorn, is for Charles to influence a Might-Have-Been which determines whether Branzillo is descended from the good or the bad line, and thus (?!) whether he will or will not start a nuclear war—a shaky if not asinine premise on which to build an earth-tilting adventure. The Madoc-Maddok-Maddox-Mad Dog family saga grows in interest as Charles gradually figures out all the connections, but—though his mission succeeds somewhere in the 19th century—we never see him as anything but a passive, if uniquely present, onlooker. Meg's role is even more passive and less engaging, as she alternates between wringing her hands in the family kitchen and stroking a strange dog on her attic bed while fretfully following Charles Wallace's adventures in her "kything" mind. (p. 754)

> Kirkus Reviews *(copyright © 1978 The Kirkus Service, Inc.), July 15, 1978.*

KAREN M. KLOCKNER

[In *A Swiftly Tilting Planet*, the] author picks up themes from earlier books—time as a relative phenomenon, the interdependency of people and events, the importance of the individual—and presents them in an unusual framework. She considers the possibility of one person's altering the course of history by traveling back in time and entering the consciousness of other individuals: "What happens in one time can make a difference in what happens in another time, far more than we realize.... Nothing, no one, is too small to matter." ... On one level the book takes place in the course of an evening; on another it spans centuries. Unfortunately, the different episodes are not well integrated, and the author's tendency to philosophize interrupts the smooth flow of the narrative. Characterization, though, is carefully handled, and if the book is flawed on a structural level, it is impeccable on an emotional one. (pp. 525-26)

> *Karen M. Klockner, in* The Horn Book Magazine *(copyright © 1978 by the Horn Book, Inc., Boston), October, 1978.*

John Lennon

1940-

Paul McCartney

1942-

British songwriters, musicians, producers, arrangers, actors, and filmmakers. Lennon and McCartney were the chief writers for the Beatles, the rock quartet by whose success all other groups are now measured. Without formal musical training, they created music that had universal appeal, yet was sophisticated enough to be appreciated by musical scholars. They expanded the boundaries of popular music, gave it respectability, and helped to bring it, both artistically and commercially, to its present state. The Beatles played a major role in defining the cultural climate of the sixties. From their hair and clothing to their interests in drugs and meditation, young people emulated them and their lifestyles. The Beatles achieved an uncanny balance of personality and talent, with each member of the group (which also included George Harrison and Ringo Starr) strongly individual as well as complementary to the others. Their music reflected this diversity: Lennon wrote songs that were often rebellious, aggressive, and satirical; McCartney's were lyrical, sweeter, and more sentimental. As songwriters, the difference in their natures seemed to aid in the success of their collaborations as each complemented the other's writing style. Later Harrison also became a composer, and his works most often reflected his interest in Eastern music and mystical thought. The Beatles, along with Bob Dylan, are considered responsible for renewing an interest in the power of words to the listening audience of the sixties. From the beginning, their lyrics were fresh and devoid of cliché. As they matured, their songs increased in complexity, and they moved from boy/girl romantic themes to subjects infrequently used in popular songs. Lennon's "Norwegian Wood," for instance, dealt with a clandestine affair, and McCartney's "Eleanor Rigby" painted a touching picture of the life and death of a lonely woman. Lennon also published two inventive books, *In His Own Write* and *A Spaniard in the Works*, which have been recognized as serious contributions to the genre of comic literature in the vein of James Joyce and Edward Lear. The zenith for the band was *Sgt Pepper's Lonely Heart's Club Band*, an ambitious album which was not only unified thematically, but which was also the last representation of the Beatles working together as a unit. It treats illusion, escape, and reality within its structure of an English music hall show, and includes the song "A Day in the Life," which many critics have called the finest synthesis of the talents of Lennon and McCartney. The release of *Sgt Pepper* in 1967 was a landmark in the history of popular music. Its success and influence solidified the Beatles's reputation as major musical innovators, and provided the first example of a popular work worthy of analysis as art, with criterion similar to that of more classical forms. On their successive albums, the Beatles began to work independently of each other, and created works that went into more unconventional musical directions but were less cohesive. The Lennon and McCartney songwriting partnership disbanded due to personal and musical differences, and some critics complained that without the balancing effect that the composers had on each other, their compositions were marred by the excesses of their individual writing styles. These complaints were intensified after the breakup of the group in 1970, when both Lennon and McCartney began releasing solo albums. Many critics felt that each artist operated from either side of an extreme: Lennon was accused of making musical editorials of his songs, while McCartney became considered an intellectual lightweight with songs that, although melodic, had no more meaning than nursery rhymes. Despite McCartney's recent commercial success and Lennon's deified position as a reclusive genius, the most consistent opinion has been that Lennon and McCartney are less successful individually than they were with the rest of the Beatles. However, as the creative forces behind the most potently influential musicians of the last twenty years, very few of us have been left untouched by the magic of their words and music.

FRANCIS NEWTON

The Beatles are an agreeable bunch of kids, quite unsinister (unlike some of the American teenage comets), with that charming combination of flamboyance and a certain hip self-mickey-taking, which is the ideal of their age group. They are in fact the 'new Elizabethans' for whom the bishops called 10 years ago. Much of their appeal has nothing to do with music at all, but with clothes, haircuts and stance. What they sell is not music, but 'the sound', a slightly modified version of the heavily accented, electronically amplified noise which has long been familiar to rock-and-rollers and could at a pinch be described as the *musique concrète* of the masses. Anyone can produce that sound, and practically everyone with the money for the rather expensive gear has done so. . . . Mersey-side—and the Beatles—emerged as the recognised Nashville of Britain about a year ago, when entrepreneurs first became aware of the size of the market for the beat groups which had grown up spontaneously in provincial cellars and halls. . . . There is generally only one idol and it happens that this sympathetic group of lads has been cast for the part. They are probably just about to begin their slow descent: the moment when someone thinks of making a film with a pop idol normally marks the peak of his curve. In 20 years' time nothing of them will survive. (p. 673)

> Francis Newton, *"Beatles and Before," in* New Statesman (© *1963 The Statesman & Nation Publishing Co. Ltd.), November 8, 1963, pp. 673-74.*

This has been the Year of the BEATLES. Whatever triumphs or disasters 1963 has held for the rest of us, for countless thousands of young Britons it has been a time when the world has revolved around these four energetically nonchalant young men. The phenomenon is not, of course, new. Plenty of people in their day have caught a generation's fancy. Some of us can remember a PRINCE OF WALES who had only to sport a boater to set an instantaneous fashion. . . .

Educationists should be thinking about them. But is that not a trite suggestion? What have educationists been doing already? Some indeed have had no option but to think about the BEATLES. . . .

Only connect! These Liverpool boys have achieved a degree of communication overnight that all the educational pundits in being could never aspire to in a month of Sundays. We tire the years debating how we can get across to the young. They open their mouths and in a second half the youngsters in Christendom are sharing their world. . . .

But what do we really know about them? If the BEATLES were nothing else they would still be a sobering reminder to us of what tiros we are in this business of knowing the child.

They are, in fact, much more than that. When the techniques of promotion and advertisement that surround them are stripped away they still epitomize by their very demeanour a striking quality of present-day youth. It is their complete freedom from adult hypocrisies. The young today have a candour about them, born perhaps of the Bomb, that accepts no assumptions just because they are accepted and takes over no values untried. For all their ignorance they set us an example of intellectual honesty that should make us feel ashamed. If we cannot match their integrity we shall never get on terms with them. We shall be squaring the hypotenuse or expounding the ablative absolute. They will be humming to themselves "All My Loving", "I Wanna Be Your Man" or "Hold Me Tight".

> *"Heroes of the Year," in* The Times Educational Supplement (© *Times Newspapers Ltd. (London) 1963; reproduced from* The Times Educational Supplement *by permission), December 27, 1963, p. 939.*

JACK GOULD

The Beatles of Britain were seen in their first complete song on American television last night as Jack Paar presented a film of the mop-headed quartet on his variety show. . . .

The young men from Liverpool, whose Merseyside version of rock 'n' roll has bestirred English teen-agers and sociologists to a communion of interest, aurally suggested a Presley multiplied by four. Visually, their calisthenics were

wider and, upon somewhat fuller examination, might prove infinitely more amusing. . . .

While trade papers of the United States entertainment world indicate that recordings made by the Beatles should find favor among indigenous teen-agers, it would not seem quite so likely that the accompanying fever known as Beatlemania will also be successfully exported. On this side of the Atlantic it is dated stuff.

Hysterical squeals emanating from developing femininity really went out coincidental with the payola scandal and Presley's military service. . . .

On last night's very limited evidence it would appear that the main joy of Beatlemania for the English is its British manufacture; it is no time for neighbors of the Paramount Theatre to point out that hereabouts it happens once a generation—e.g., Frank Sinatra and Alan Freed.

From a nation where the best-selling record is now The Singing Nun's delicate and charming "Dominique" there can be extended to the British the comforting assurance that an occasional cultural purgative can have a beneficial effect.

> *Jack Gould, "TV: It's the Beatles (Yeah, Yeah, Yeah)," in* The New York Times (© *1964 by The New York Times Company; reprinted by permission), January 4, 1964, p. L47.*

Of all the odd by-products of the great Beatle craze (wigs, boots, sweaters, jelly-babies) none is more unexpected or more promising than [*John Lennon in His Own Write*. It consists] of brief sketches and poems which hover in a linguistic never-never land somewhere between Joyce, Lewis Carroll and [Daisy Ashford's] *The Young Visiters*, with decorations in a line that seems part Milligan, part Thurber.

As a phenomenon they are remarkable; they are a world away from the trite sentiments and underdeveloped language of the Lennon-McCartney songs (heaven knows what the fans are going to make of them), and the fact that such a real and lively talent can spring up as part of a spontaneous, popular and extremely youthful movement is most encouraging. They are also very funny—Mrs. Weatherby who accuses her neighbour of desecrating the church by "drawing bad Christians on the graves"; the ballad of Deaf Ted, Danoota, and me; the story of No Flies on Frank (starting "There were no flies on Frank that morning—after all why not?"); or the opening character Partly Dave, who would disconcert his wife by muttering "I am partly Dave" over his breakfast. . . . And so the nonsense runs on, words and images prompting one another in a chain of pure fantasy, where only the occasional forced bathos or neo-conventional sick joke (spastics, sudden slaughter, amputations) intrudes.

Slight as [the book] is, it is worth the attention of anyone who fears for the impoverishment of the English language and the British imagination. From Beachcomber and Myles na Gopaleen to the Goons and *Itma* the humorists have done much more to preserve and enrich these assets than most serious critics allow. Theirs is arguably our liveliest stream of "experimental writing" and Mr. Lennon shows himself well equipped to take it farther.

> *"A Comedy of Letters," in* The Times Literary Supplement (© *Times Newspapers Ltd. (London) 1964; reproduced from* The Times Literary Supplement *by permission), March 26, 1964, p. 250.*

TOM WOLFE

Literary London, from parlor to arty mews, has been one great wide open door for noble primitives, even though London literati still live in the mental atmosphere of the 19th-century aristocracy, in the world of the universities, nutty sherry, curly Shelley hair, parlor floor libraries with trestle ladders, and mandarin wit. The enthusiasm for genius-savages has been in part a guilty sympathy for the proles and primitives and in part a romantic awe of raw vitality. Nevertheless, the case of John Lennon is exceptional. He is one of the few Englishmen whom English literati have hailed as a genius of the lower crust. He comes out of the very vortex of something intellectuals all over the West have begun to turn to as a new fashion in artistic taste: namely, mass culture, which has been the material, in painting, for the genre known as "pop art." The pop artists sit on the floor wearing levis and Zorrie sandals in the same old calcimined lofts painting pictures of comic strips, tail fins, motel archways, tuxedo ads, housing development floor plans. But Lennon steps right out of mass culture, the "Beatlemania," without benefit of a middle man, we are assured, and becomes the artist himself. . . .

[The stories and poems in *In His Own Write* are] nonsense writing, but one has only to review the literature of nonsense to see how well Lennon has brought it off. While some of his homonyms are gratuitous word play, many others have not only double meanings but a double edge.

His inspiration in verse seems to be Lewis Carroll. . . . (p. 4)

But Lennon adds an anarchic cynicism that, for better or worse, goes beyond Carroll's kind of jabberwocky:

> With faithful frog beside us,
> Big mighty club are we
> The battle scab and frisky dyke
> Deaf Ted, Danoota, and me.

He seems to take the general format for his stories, fables, playlets, poems and drawings from a British humorist named Spike Milligan. But the underlying bitterness of much of what Lennon writes about marriage and family life, for example, as well as his Joycean excursions into language fantasies, are something else altogether. (pp. 4, 10)

The time to watch will be next time around. Nonsense humor is a bit of an easy crutch, even for James Joyce. John Lennon's real test will come when he turns loose his wild inventiveness and bitter slant upon a heavier literary form. (p. 10)

> *Tom Wolfe, "A Highbrow under All That Hair?" in* Book Week—The Washington Post (© *I.H.T. Corporation; reprinted by permission), May 3, 1964, pp. 4, 10.*

PETER SCHICKELE

[*In His Own Write*] not only has a style of its own, but at its best it has a very sure and delightful style. Moreover, it is not about the author or the group which made him famous; it is a collection of brief whimsies and simple drawings—pure fancy and nonsense concocted by someone who loves jumbling words and images.

In reviews of the book, all sorts of literary wheels have been mentioned as influences—Edward Lear, Lewis Carroll, James Thurber (I keep thinking of Kenneth Patchen, too—and it's easy to see why . . .). . . . Even James Joyce has been mentioned, and certainly [some] passages . . . have a wild and heavy quality which goes beyond word play. . . . (p. 588)

But Lennon is Lennon; he has his own brand of jumbleword, particularly in the prose pieces (it often sounds like someone with a cold speaking cockney-rhyming slang), and his own satiric way of looking at things. Sometimes his satire is extremely cutting, although several stories are marred to my taste, by a sort of surface viciousness that comes out like the cute snicker of sick jokes.

These places, however, are more than balanced by pages of inspired madness in the form of small poems, tiny stories, minute plays, a letter, a television survey, speech instructions, and a few even less classifiable items. The pieces range from quietly clever to outrageous, and occasionally there is even a touching moment. The drawings are very uneven; some are just right, while others look amateurish, as if they'd been drawn by a professional rock 'n' roll singer rather than by someone who attended the Liverpool Art College. But before rounding off my applause for John Lennon I must, as a fan of the Beatles and much R 'n' R in general, register one complaint: why hasn't any of this fine wordplay penetrated the lyrics of Beatles' songs? I've heard many (though not all) of their numbers, and the only trace of literary wit I can find is the name of the group itself (after all, they could have called themselves the Rolls-Royces or the Gyrations). Admittedly, the commercial R 'n' R field is probably not very congenial to flights of literary fancy, but nowhere in the Beatles' songs have I heard even the elementary wit of one of the Coaster's old numbers [*Poison Ivy* or] . . . the poignancy of Elvis Presley's early hit *Heartbreak Hotel*. . . . (pp. 588-89)

Elvis has become such a picture of clean living in his middle age that it's easy to forget the days when he aroused wrath right and left, and supposedly answered a question about marriage with, "Why buy a cow when you can get milk through the fence?" The Beatles have the same perspective and seem to enjoy themselves more than Elvis ever did. (p. 589)

> *Peter Schickele, "About the Awful," in* The Nation (*copyright 1964 by the Nation Associates, Inc.), June 8, 1964, pp. 588-89.*

["*A Spaniard in the Works*"] is as fresh and alive as "In His Own Write." Lennon still rocks and rolls with the English language. Indeed, his style has become surer and richer, his subjects more literary, and his manner more spicy, without loss of his already established zest and buoyant playfulness. Apparently his earlier success has encouraged him to think of his audience as more sophisticated than screaming teenage girls, for in this volume his political attacks and his take-offs on literary standards assume an adult awareness and proffer mature fun. Ringo may have a future as a comic, but there can be no question that John Lennon has proven himself a writer of talent and bountiful imagination. No one is writing satire today with the flair that he has demonstrated in his first two books. (p. cxlvii)

> Virginia Quarterly Review (*copyright, 1965, by the* Virginia Quarterly Review, The University of Virginia), *Vol. 41, No. 4 (Autumn, 1965).*

JONATHAN COTT

The question is: why do we need *A Hard Day's Night* so much that we keep showing it as often as we do? (p. 84)

Childhood is our goal. Concomitant with being a child exists the pleasure one gets from playing and the intolerable displeasure one gets from realizing one's dependency on others. Thus the Beatles play on the rugby field in that most pleasurable scene which you want to see again and again. Four boys mock space and time—the sequence lasts under three minutes—as they play to "Can't Buy Me Love." Every moment seems spontaneous and joyful. Actions and movements are speeded up and slowed down. What we see is how we once wanted to feel. "Genital organization is a tyranny in man because his peculiar infancy has left him with a lifelong allegiance (i.e., fixation) to the pattern of infantile sexuality" (Norman O. Brown). If this is correct, why does the playing terminate? After that beautiful scene of exhaustion when the Beatles—lying on the grass, hands under their heads—count or talk silently to themselves? The answer is that 1) Mr. Genital Reality orders them off his field; and that 2) the Beatles have a TV rehearsal waiting for them. They have escaped from their duties: no job, no "Money"—which song comments obversely on that working-day world situation which "Can't Buy Me Love" attempts to fantasize away. The balding TV director ("It's a young man's business") depends on the manager who depends on the Beatles who depend on both, even when they do not wish to admit it. When Ringo gets led astray by the clean old id man, he assumes independence, and, in the tramp sequence, appears comic to us —the Bergsonian object-butt—but we have lost our goal, we laugh at the child in us now. The jokes are on Ringo, but he does not enjoy them. For the Beatles are boys, not bums, and they try their best not to "grow up." (p. 85)

A Hard Day's Night does not, in Keats' words, unperplex bliss from pain; still, it strives honorifically towards our longed-for goal of childhood by focusing on the four boys in action. The great Sung neo-Confucianist philosopher Chu Hsi wrote: "Nature is the state before activity begins, the feelings are the state when activity has started. . . ." The verb "to act," in fact—which, in a general sense, means "to begin," "to lead," and eventually "to rule" (from the Greek *archein*) and also "to put in motion" (from the Latin *agere*)—suggests the Beatles' style of life. Their actions and their songs are impelled not from what they know but from what they are—from feelings rather than from states of mind. Boys and girls are naturally active, and it takes a bit of acculturation before they become bored, depressed, and hung-up. Talking at press conferences, taking a bath, dancing, singing, playing cards, running in and out of jail (even the car thief and the cops become game-playing boys again—society's standards are demolished)—all these actions are invested with pleasurable feeling. The Beatles need only themselves for their own resources. Most important is the fact that each Beatle makes an ideal of himself; and that is why we suddenly realize in amazement that the Beatles sing love songs like "If I Fell" and "I'm Happy Just to Dance with You" only to themselves. "You" means "me" in these songs. There is no "other," but they can say "we" to themselves and to each other. The Beatles' state of nature—to refuse Chu Hsi for a moment—is just this state of self-idealized and self-absorbed activity. (pp. 85-6)

It has been observed that *A Hard Day's Night* is not strong on plot. This is of course true. But it is not jokes—"campy," anti-Nazi, anti-cops—as good as they are that hold your interest. Rather it is the director's total dependence on showing the physical immediacy of the events and persons observed that generates the film's excitement and pleasure. I can think of no major feature film other than Dreyer's *Passion of St. Joan* that emphasizes the physical fact in such an unmitigated fashion. In Dreyer's film, the fly on Joan's eye, the warts on the interrogator's face, the cripples hanging around, the child sucking the mother's breast just when Joan, about to die, says: "Where will I be tonight?" —all these observed events heighten Dreyer's outraged sense of the flesh, all the more heightened as they contrast with Joan's saintliness. And yet her face, revealing all the confusion and suffering, is the most excruciating of physical facts.

The Beatles' faces and the parts of their faces, however, are the exultantly observed images—if not the heroes—of *A Hard Day's Night*: eyes, noses, hair, teeth. The image of a hand caressing a guitar, first seen on the studio's TV screen, is as close to suggesting a sense of sexual love as the film allows and so eerily reverberates with more force than had it been employed in a different context—say in an Italian comedy, where everyone is touching. (pp. 87-8)

Then, too, there are the faces of the girls and women. Their faces reveal as much about them as the humors reveal the characters in [Ben] Jonson's plays. Just a second's sight of them unimaginably expresses the essence of girlhood. As the Beatles sing on TV, you see the girls in the audience, eyes dilating, each one unique from any other in her ecstasy and the force of her early but veritable sexuality. And if the girls seem womanly, the women seem girlish: the wonderfully shy creature talking to Ringo at the press conference, the women dancing at the party, the sexy secretary putting on her shoes who leads George into the shirt designer's office. The Beatles enable the women to become girls; the girls, women—even if only for a moment or the length of a song. (p. 88)

Rock and roll is the new mysticism for those too experienced and cynical to believe much in anything anymore—a mysticism which you can accept for three minutes, a veritable even if noninterpersonal giving of oneself, because there is no fear of losing out. (There is here, too, also a return to the undifferentiated world of early childhood experiences.)

The hard day's night, the race to the train, the playing and singing—this is the passion of the world. But in the end, the Beatles in their helicopter fly up to Heaven. Is this not the Easter revelation we all have need of re-experiencing? *A Hard Day's Night* combines radical innocence and religious revelation, inviting ecstasy and salvation to that soul Yeats wrote about: "self-delighting, self-appeasing, self-affrighting"; whose "own sweet will is Heaven's will." (p. 90)

Jonathan Cott, "A Hard Day's Knights" (copyright © 1965 by Jonathan Cott; reprinted by permission of the author), in Ramparts, October, 1965 (and reprinted in The Young American Writers, edited by Richard Kostelanetz, Funk & Wagnalls, 1970, pp. 83-90).

RICHARD GOLDSTEIN

If being a critic were the same as being a listener I could just enjoy "Sergeant Pepper's Lonely Hearts Club Band." Other than one cut which I detest ("Good Morning, Good Morning"), I find the album better than 80 per cent of the music around today; it is the other 20 per cent (including the best of the Beatles' past performances) which worries me as a critic. . . .

When the Beatles' work as a whole is viewed in retrospect, it will be "Rubber Soul" and "Revolver" which stand as their major contributions. When the slicks and tricks of production on this album no longer seem unusual, and the compositions are stripped to their musical and lyrical essentials, "Sergeant Pepper" will be Beatles baroque—an elaboration without improvement.

I find it easier to explain that statement by comparing a song like "She's Leaving Home" with "Eleanor Rigby" because while the musical motifs are similar, a profound sense of tragedy is conveyed in the earlier song through a series of poignantly ironic vignettes. This "tactile" agony within detail has exercised a profound influence on the poetry of rock; you can see it in Donovan's brooding "Young Girl Blues" and in the Bee Gees' stark "New York Mine Disaster."

"She's Leaving Home" is unlikely to influence anyone except the Monkees. Its lyrical technique is uninspired narrative, with a dearth of poetic irony. All the despair is surface, and so, while "Eleanor Rigby" seethed with implication, "She's Leaving Home" glistens with a flourish of tragedy. . . . "She's Leaving Home" is too apparent to be worth the trouble. . . .

I feel the same about most of the music on this album. It is dazzling because it is the most spectacularly produced record in pop, but fraudulent because, beyond the razzmatazz, the songs just aren't as good as they were on "Revolver." . . .

In "Revolver" I found a complexity that was staggering in its poignancy, its innovation, and its empathy. I called it a complicated masterpiece. But in "Sergeant Pepper" I sense a new distance, a sarcasm masquerading as hip, a dangerously dominant sense of what is stylish.

Much of the radicalism on Sergeant Pepper has appeared elsewhere, in a less sophisticated form. There was musical posturing in a song like "Something Happened to Me" (on the Rolling Stones' "Between the Buttons") which resembles "Sergeant Pepper." (p. 14)

"Sergeant Pepper" is not a work of plagiarism, but neither does it represent a breakthrough. It is an in-between experience, a chic.

The Beatles, I am informed, are "head composers." To turn on, goes the reasoning, will admit the enlightened to a whole range of associations and subtleties unfathomable to the straight mind. My experience till now has been that what I like straight, I like all the time. The idea that certain progressions, tonal nuances, or lyrical flights, are comprehensible only to the turned-on smacks of critical fascism. I think of the psychedelic experience as an elaboration of a given reality—not a substitute.

Since Lennon-McCartney reflect almost all of pop in 1967 (this should be, since they define it), it would be difficult to avoid a thorough awareness of their interests and influence. The Beatles are the creators of the rock ethic. Without them there could be no such discipline as "rock criticism." The new music is their thing. (p. 25)

The physical continuity on this album invites a structure, just as the printed lyrics cry for textual analysis, but in unadorned fact, the Beatles had composed a healthy chunk of this new work before they wrote the "Sergeant Pepper" theme and thought of centralizing it. The "banding" innovation came later too. Only in mid-production then did the thought of producing an album which would resemble a concert take hold, and the finished product shows this late commitment to the idea of unity. George Harrison's piece has no place in a band concert, and neither do "A Day in the Life" or "Lucy in the Sky with Diamonds." . . .

The only conceivable way to treat "Sergeant Pepper" would seem to be as caprice. "Sit back and let the evening go." But you and I know the best Beatle music is only deceptively casual. . . .

Part of the trouble with "Sergeant Pepper" is its determination to be a game, and the shallowest cop-out is to excuse this work by reporting jubilantly that it has no meaning. It does. "A Day in the Life" is no caprice, and it knocks me out to hear it. "When I'm Sixty Four" is delicately melancholy; they are not just funning.

All the cuts on this album have something to say. The difficulty comes in interpreting the work as a whole. It is much more sensible to talk of mood than actual structure on "Sergeant Pepper." The Beatles have always avoided producing "theme" albums, and despite its quasicontinuity, "Sergeant Pepper" represents no significant break with this tradition. There are no recurrent themes (outside of the reprise), and only hints (in the background vocalising) of what should have been repeating motif. Nevertheless, the album has a mood, even if it is only defined by its aims. "Rubber Soul" strove for tonal beauty and it is super-melodic. "Revolver" attempted to be eclectic; its compositions stand as utterly distinct and self-contained. "Sergeant Pepper" is a circus of sour.

"The Beatles" are dead; we are all watchers at their wake, where "a splendid time is guaranteed for all." They are no longer screaming "yeah yeah yeah," or crooning "Meeechelle." The new thing is pop destruction; the new technique is inundation; the new mood is merry nihilism. It shows everywhere in current English music.

Lennon and McCartney are destroying the popsong and with it, the old melodic Beatles. . . .

"Sergeant Pepper" is an interim, and that is why, in retrospect, it is an "engaging curio" and not more. Nothing is real herein, and nothing to get hung about. Too bad. I have a sweet tooth for reality. I like my art drenched in it, and even from fantasy I expect authenticity. What I worship about the Beatles is their forging of rock into what is real. It made them artists; it made all of us fans. . . . (p. 26)

Richard Goldstein, "I Blew My Cool through 'The New York Times'," in The Village Voice *(reprinted by permission of* The Village Voice; *copyright © The Village Voice, Inc., 1967), July 20, 1967, pp. 14, 25-6.*

GENE LEES

No album in recent years has been issued in the midst of so much 'fuss and foofaraw as "Sgt. Pepper's Lonely Hearts Club Band." . . .

The title tune, *Sgt. Pepper's Lonely Hearts Club Band,* is the latter: redundant without making a point by the redundancy. Its lyric is vague and cluttered. The rock intellectuals will claim it is full of meaning, of course. If it becomes desperately important for you to find meaning in it, a little grass will help: pot makes *everything* seem significant.

The second song of the album, *A Little Help from My Friends,* features more of the meandering, unstructured, free-association do-it-yourself-Rorschachism that Lennon and McCartney too often pass off as lyric writing, "I get by with a little help from my friends, I get high with a little help from my friends . . ." What are the friends? Roaches? Who knows whether they mean drugs, or actual real-live friends. This lyric isn't profound; it's just indefinite.

But suddenly, in the third track, the album comes to life. *Lucy in the Sky with Diamonds,* almost certainly a deliberate evocation of the visual effect of an LSD high, opens in three-four. A melotron—an electronic keyboard instrument that here sounds like a reverberated harpsichord—provides an eerily beautiful accompaniment. The song begins, "Picture yourself in a boat on a river, with tangerine trees and marmalade skies. Somebody calls you, you answer quite slowly, a girl with kaleidoscope eyes." In the refrain line, "Lucy in the sky with diamonds," the song switches to four-four time and a flavor of mild hysteria. The song's effect is of genuine beauty and startling shimmering interflowing images.

Yet the next song, *Getting Better,* slides off the rail again: it tosses in a little protest against the rigidities of conventional education—something no one in his right mind has tried to defend for the last thirty years. . . .

Good Morning, Good Morning is [a] case of the Beatles spraying contempt at the audience. Sound effects are dubbed fore and aft: chickens, dogs, a hunting horn, a chirping bird. This will be seen as profound by the convinced. Actually, it is Lennon and McCartney saying, "We can throw in any kind of garbage, and the kids will buy it." . . . [The album's best song is] the startling *A Day in the Life.* By indirection and imagery, this melancholy, disturbing little piece suggests the spiritual deadness of today's world, the dreary and corrupt quality of the life—and it tends to suggest too why the kids (the intelligent ones, anyway) don't trust our political and academic and business leaders. Using a large orchestra, the song sets a dark mood. Then there is tape acceleration—the orchestra speeds up, and its rising pitch evokes the mounting horror of contemporary life.

At first hearing, *A Day in the Life* is just another of the wearisome dope songs. ("He blew his mind out in a car . . ." and "I'd love to turn you on.") But, perhaps in spite of itself, it is much more.

There are, then, three, maybe four important songs in this album, a few that are so-so, and a couple that can be considered authentically insignificant. But the Beatles are growing, growing quickly. The level of literacy in their writing has been raised to a startling degree: gone are the

frothy pitches to teen-aged libidos. They are trying hard to say important things. At times they are succeeding.

Gene Lees, "Beatles, Op. 15," in High Fidelity (copyright © by ABC Leisure Magazines, Inc.), August, 1967, p. 94.

DON HECKMAN

That "Sgt. Pepper" is different from [the Beatles'] previous albums should surprise no one. Every edition of their work has revealed change, sometimes intensive, sometimes casual. A large measure of the Beatles' attractiveness is centered around this basic—and probably intuitive—need to extend the limits of their art. Lennon is a natural lyricist in much the way, I would say, that Larry Hart was. Lennon makes banal rhymes and gets away with it. He can rhyme "I was mean" with "I'm changing my scene"; he can match "Nothing to say" with "but what a day" and couple successive phrases like "I get by," "I get high" and "going to try," and make them all work. Why? Because he is a masterful storyteller, even with abstract material; that is, he can string together seemingly unrelated fragments with just enough connective material to make things appear sequential (see his published books for more specific examples). In addition, the simple classical song forms used by McCartney for his melodies give a sense of continuity to Lennon's lyrics that they might otherwise lack. Insofar as the symbolism of Lennon's lyrics is concerned, I do not really feel that it is that important to be aware of all the allusions to LSD, pot, and the other purely topical matters he frequently examines. A song that describes the fixing of a ". . . hole where the rain gets in, And stops my mind from wandering . . ." is pertinent to *any* sensitive listener, whether it be a teenybopper who understands Lennon's specific reference or a 45-year-old square who sees something quite different, but equally meaningful.

Perhaps the most noticeable change in "Sgt. Pepper" is in the music. McCartney never has been a particularly complex melodist, but he has written a number of tunes—*Michelle* is the obvious example—that go beyond the repeated line patterns of most contemporary popular music. In this collection he adopts even less complex means, structuring most of the songs in simple verse/chorus fashion. (p. 168)

All in all, "Sgt. Pepper" is a major achievement of popular entertainment art. I cannot view it—as many listeners do—as a totality, but I can appreciate the glowing creativity that has made many of the individual tunes into new classics. It will be a long time indeed before this group, or anyone else, comes up with a piece that combines music, lyrics, orchestration and performance as effectively as *A Day in the Life.* (p. 169)

Don Heckman, in The American Record Guide *(© by The American Record Guide, Inc., 1967), October, 1967.*

ROBERT CHRISTGAU

The Beatles really started the whole long-haired hippie business four years ago, and who knows whether they developed with it or it developed with them? All those hours of analysis are a gauge of how important the Beatles have become to . . . *us.*

One song on Sgt. Pepper, "Being for the Benefit of Mr. Kite", seems to me deliberately one-dimensional, nothing more than a description of a traveling circus. It fits beautifully into the album, which is kind of a long vaudeville show, but I feel almost certain it has no "meaning". Yet one girl, age fifteen, writes that it presents "life as an eerie, perverted circus." Is this sad? silly? horrifying? contemptible? From an adult it might be all four, but from a fifteen-year-old it is simply moving. A good Lennon-McCartney song is sufficiently cryptic to speak to the needs of whomever listens. (p. 45)

One of the nice things The Beatles do for those of us who love them is charge commonplace English with meaning. I want to hold your hand. It's getting better all the time. Yeah, yeah, yeah. "Fixing a Hole" ... is full of such suggestive phrases. I'll resist temptation and quote only five lines: "And it really doesn't matter if I'm wrong or right / Where I belong I'm right / Where I belong. / See the people standing there who disagree and never win / And wonder why they don't get in my door." This passage not only indicates the intricate things The Beatles are doing with rhyme, skewing their stanzas and dispensing almost completely with traditional song form. It also serves as a gnomic reminder of the limitations of criticism. Allow me to fall into its trap by providing my own paraphrase, viz: "in matters of interpretation, the important thing is not whether you're 'wrong' or 'right' but whether you are faithful to your own peculiar stance in the world. Those who insist on the absolute rectitude of their puny opinions will never attain my state of enlightenment."

Well, there it is; I've finally done it. Pompous, right? Sorry, I'm just not John Lennon. But like everyone else, I feel compelled to make Our Boys My Boys. . . . Now, after several false starts that had me convinced for a while I think I've got it. It is not surprising that their ideas are so much like my own. That's what they're saying, isn't it?

For, just like [their fans], I have my own Beatles. As far as I'm concerned, "Fixing a Hole" is not like other songs by stupid groups that say I am alienated and junk like that. And I have other prejudices. I can't believe The Beatles indulge in the simplistic kind of symbolism that turns a yellow submarine into a Nembutal, or a banana—it is just a yellow submarine, damn it, an obvious elaboration of John's submarine fixation, first revealed in *A Hard Day's Night*. I think they want their meanings to be absorbed on an instinctual level, just as their new, complex music can be absorbed on a sensual level. I don't think they much care whether *Sgt. Pepper* is that classic moldy fig, Great Art. I think they are inordinately fond (in a rather recondite way) of what I call the real world. They want to turn us on, all right—to everything in that world and in ourselves. (pp. 45-7)

Robert Christgau, "Secular Music" (originally published in a slightly different version in Esquire *Magazine, December, 1967), in his* Any Old Way You Choose It: Rock and Other Pop Music, 1967-1973 *(copyright © Robert Christgau, 1967, 1968, 1969, 1973; reprinted by permission of Penguin Books and the author), Penguin, 1973, pp. 12-85.*

ALEJANDRO ENRIQUE PLANCHART

The Beatles' music, up to the time of their first movie, still belongs in the earlier tradition of rock 'n' roll. Each new album had one or two really remarkable songs that today seem to anticipate the later pieces. But I have the feeling that there was a real change at about the time of *A Hard Day's Night,* and that the seeds of that change were literary rather than musical. They came essentially from Lennon's acute sensitivity to the spiritual world and to the hang-ups of the British middle class. While most critics were surprised by how good *A Hard Day's Night* was (where had they been?), Lennon's *In His Own Write* and the later *A Spaniard in the Works* brought about mixed reactions. Many reviewers who had apparently enjoyed reading the books appeared embarrassed to say so. The Joycean surface of the writing, thin though it is, put people off. Critics found it a transparent and perhaps pretentious game, and teeny-boppers did not find much fun in Lennon's wit. The surface of the writing is, in fact, playful, but I find it delightful. Behind it, there is a remarkably acute perception of the petit-bourgeois, his narrow world, his mechanically repetitive life, and his dreams, often as feeble and prosaic as his reality, to escape it.

If this vision is hidden behind a clever surface in the books, it comes out fully in the lyrics of the songs. Some, such as *She Is Leaving Home,* have an obvious moral to them, but many are only observation and description, with the music itself serving as social commentary: *Paperback Writer, Eleanor Rigby, Lovely Rita,* and *A Day in the Life* are among them. . . .

The poetic and musical categories intertwine in the different songs to create new variations that are the delight of the oversubtle Beatle fan. Contrary to *Time* magazine's opinion, Baroque rock, whatever it may be, begins with the chromatic bass line and invention-like texture of *Michelle,* takes a more romantic turn with *Yesterday,* and goes on to the marvelously ugly string playing in the *concerto-grosso* parody that accompanies *Eleanor Rigby.* Poetically, however, *Yesterday*'s ancestor is *I Don't Want to Spoil the Party;* both songs are vivid pictures of dazed, uncomprehending dejection, when no explanations are sought because none would make adequate sense. In *Yesterday* this is achieved in great part by the performance itself. The strings have a reserved, dry sound, not the *molto espressivo* with lots of vibrato that one usually associates with this type of song. There is also McCartney's straight, absolutely dead-pan delivery, straining at the high notes and giving the feeling that, if the top note of the piece (on Yester-*day*) lasted a split-second longer, his voice would crack. This is a perfect example of what I have called "dry lyricism": its plainness and lack of "schmaltz" leave the tune alone, giving it a feeling of sincerity that reinforces the lyrics and produces a staggering effect. . . .

The change in the Beatles' style took the form of real explosion in the sense that they moved in many directions at once, taking in influences as they went, and transforming their discoveries into an integral part of their style. Folksong, Indian, Baroque and electronic music, all became grist for their mill. These were not necessarily innovations: Dylan was doing folk-rock before them and the Byrds were using the sitar and experimenting with Indian music before Harrison. It is the quality and the inventiveness of what the Beatles did with these influences that makes them remarkable. (p. 37)

The first fruits of the change in the Beatles' style originally expressed themselves in a few singles and in the album collection of songs from their movies. *A Hard Day's Night* was the least satisfactory among them because the album included material other than the Beatles' own songs; but there is no song in it with quite the elegance and appeal of the title song of the movie *Help!* Then came two magnificent collections: *Rubber Soul* and *Yesterday and Today.* Every piece in them is beautiful: they represent the first crystalization of the Beatles' own style. *Rubber Soul* is probably the ''softest,'' most melodically graceful, and thus melody dominated album which the Beatles have produced. This may be perhaps an illusion created by the beauty of three tunes: *I've Just Seen a Face, Norwegian Wood,* and *Michelle.* The first two approach folk-songs although not quite as openly as *Rain. Michelle* is often paired with *Yesterday* but it is really a unique piece in the Beatles' output: it is their most traditionally lyrical and intimate song, and, up to that time, the one with the most elaborate harmonic surface. (pp. 37-8)

Yesterday and Today is an even better collection—it is one of those extreme rarities: a perfect album. Not only are all the songs beautiful; they are, despite the different styles, remarkably consistent. *Yesterday* stands out, but almost all of the other songs in the album are equally good. In *Rubber Soul* there are one or two pieces that, in spite of their excellence, do not have a very clear profile; each is just another ''lovely song'' (although that is certainly enough). But every piece in *Yesterday and Today* is also quite distinctive and memorable. The album as a whole is an example of the old cliche of ''unity in variety,'' and, as usual, when that trick is turned, it is very hard to say why or how. . . .

After *Yesterday and Today* another element begins to appear in both the text and music of the Beatle songs: a certain whimsy which at times borders on surrealism. Some of it can be explained as a result of their experience with drugs, but it also appears as a delayed reaction from *A Hard Day's Night* and even more from *Help.* the musical counterparts of the visual trickery and the improbable situations in both movies are *Yellow Submarine, Mr. Kite, Sgt. Pepper,* and *I Am the Walrus.* The *Yellow Submarine* may be also some sort of psychedelic Mother Goose song, since yellow submarine is the Britsh slang name for drug capsules. In this case, the piece would be a variation of *Strawberry Fields.* It is more likely, however, that the song is more nursery rhyme than psychedelic, spawned by the literal meaning of the title irrespective of the context in which the Beatles came across it. This impression is strengthened by the silly and catchy tune of the song. It is the archetype of the kind of tune that kids sing around summer campfires. The electronic trickery and sound effects build up progressively a gleeful nuttiness, filled with the same kind of clutter that one finds in *Mad* magazine cartoons. A charming detail which actually reinforces this impression appears in the last stanza, when the caller's words follow, rather than precede, the sung ones, and end with a mad cackle which for no good reason always brings back to my mind the remarks about ''the very *clean* old man'' in *A Hard Day's Night.* (p. 38)

Sgt. Pepper is, like *Yesterday and Today,* another perfect album. Artistically and technically, songs like *Paperback Writer, Eleanor Rigby, Strawberry Fields* or even *Penny Lane,* already point the way to *Sgt. Pepper.* But none of these is as complex as some of the pieces in this album. Because of its strangely reserved sound, few of the songs reach out and grab you; in fact, it takes two or three hearings to catch on, always a danger in pop music, but one

which the Beatles have succeeded in overcoming. This, indeed, is the innovation of most consequence in the record, rather than the conception of the entire album as a ''show.'' Nevertheless, it is the sense of continuity which carries the listener through many of the rough spots at first hearing. The balance of reserve and communicativeness in *Sgt. Pepper* gradually draws the listener in instead of hitting him over the head.

The vision of the petit-bourgeois, which seeps through earlier collections, pervades *Sgt. Pepper* from the very beginning. It is there in the surrealist title piece, in *Lovely Rita,* and in *When I'm Sixty-four.* The vision takes a more disquieting turn in *A Little Help from My Friends* and in *She's Leaving Home,* and becomes hideously oppressive in *A Day in the Life.*

A Day in the Life, which borders on expressionism, is one of the Beatles' masterpieces, comparable only to *Eleanor Rigby.* Sound effects as such are used very sparingly (the alarm clock, the panting) but with a deadly accuracy. The dream section here is more effective in its articulateness than *Lucy in the Sky,* which suffers a bit from the fact that the lyrics are better than the tune. Finally, there are the inner musings, sung in that feeble falsetto, trailing off in an aimless slow trill on ''I'd love to turn you on,'' and followed by the huge orchestral *glissando.* This passage is all the more chilling because it appears as a direct reference to one of the few genuinely frightening pieces of music ever written—Alban Berg's *Wozzeck.*

The symbolic appropriateness of the allusion at this point makes it either a master-stroke or a fantastic case of blind luck, depending on whether the Beatles know Berg's masterpiece or not. The contrast between the narrator's life, on the one hand, and his dreams and musings, on the other, is further heightened by the mechanically driving music that accompanies the narration, and by the sound effects in the middle section of the piece. The panting after ''I noticed I was late'' turns the whole section, and hence the narrator's conscious life, into a caricature. (pp. 38-9)

The songs which follow *Sgt. Pepper* are, if anything, more diverse. In addition, the Beatles seem to be using some of their earlier tunes as points of departure. *Baby, You're a Rich Man* combines some of the procedures of *A Little Help from My Friends* and *Lucy in the Sky* in a marvelous vignette-song that contains some acid commentaries on the vacuity of jet-set life. The instrumentation adds an incongruous ''exoticism'' to the piece with literary implications that go beyond their mere use as musical color. . . .

I Am the Walrus is one of the weirdest pieces ever to pass as a pop song. Here the Joycean aspect of Lennon's writing shows itself in full force not only in the lyrics but also in the music. (p. 39)

Much has been made of the Beatles' influence on rock. It is difficult to say how much of today's immense activity is really derived from them rather than from the folk-rock tradition. The direct imitations of the Beatles by other groups are often feeble and inept. The one song by another group which does sound like a Beatle song, and still remains a really beautiful piece, is the Rolling Stones' *Ruby Tuesday.* But the connection between what the *Jefferson Airplane, The Byrds, The Grateful Dead, The Lovin' Spoonful, The Association,* or *The Mothers of Invention* are doing and what the Beatles have done remains a tenuous one. Quite apart from their music, it has been the Beatles' example to break consistently from the restrictions and cliches of rock and still achieve immense popularity. Their example, rather than their influence, has been liberating, but what other groups do with this freedom is their own. Few have shown the Beatles' remarkable combination of inventiveness and consistency. (p. 40)

> *Alejandro Enrique Planchart, "The Musical Landscape of the Beatles," in* The Yale Literary Magazine *(copyright by the Yale Literary Society 1966), March, 1968, pp. 36-40.*

FREDERIC V. GRUNFELD

[The] Beatles are now in a position to do anything at all and have it listened to. Their recent *oeuvre,* notably *Sgt. Pepper's Lonely Hearts Club Band* and the *Magical Mystery Tour,* is a great eclectic circus of Indian raga, Salvation Army, Benjamin British, tailgate, gutbucket, and aleatoric chance-music, all handled without hang-ups or uptightness. There is a lovely lawlessness about it that reminds one of the "indeterminacy" experiments of John Cage, the father of random music-making. Cage did this sort of thing for years, but he had to explain himself. The Beatles do it without explaining: "You don't say love, you do it" is an old psychedelic proverb. (p. 56)

Rhythmically [the] early Beatle numbers were lineal descendants of "race records," Mississippi blues, Alabama field hollers, and such. But while the thumb was playing with blues tension, the windpipe was enunciating British sentiments closer to Bea Lillie than Lead Belly. The words were surprisingly bland, coming from a generation whose mod/rocker antics were just then making headlines and whose taste for unabated high volume was blowing the roof off the discotheques.

Apparently the Beatles had got to the root of some secret sorrow and made it articulate: the first groping love efforts of a generation that had undergone the trauma of permissive parenthood and demand feeding. Beneath the tough-sounding surface of this music one could detect a vaguely oedipal predicament: Don't be bad to me; Hold me love me; I call your name but you're not there; I'm a loser; Did you have to treat me oh so bad? These are clearly songs of innocence rather than experience, and when Lennon and McCartney ask, "Don't go 'way I'm afraid that I might miss you," they touch on the same anguish that an earlier British poet [A. A. Milne] summed up so poignantly in the line: "You must *never* go down to the end of the town without consulting me."

What had begun as an *art brut,* all capitals and no lower case, gradually acquired more subtle shades of pop impressionism. (pp. 56-7)

In "We Can Work It Out" echoes of a French musette band broke like a thunderclap across a pop scene that had heard nothing but four-four time for fifty years; the Beatles had independently invented waltz time, here disguised as triplets, and even this simple rhythmic innovation shook the pop world to its foundations.

These were the Beatles' *Wanderjahre,* and though their

efforts to shore up the British pound took them as far west as Texas and California, their whole style was moving further and further toward the East. George Harrison (afterward to spend a semester in India with Ravi Shankar) took up the uncertain sitar that is to be heard twanging for the first time in "Norwegian Wood." It was a decisive addition to the arsenal of Beatle sounds. In time, after some other experiments with Indian ragas and gurus, the Beatles found their real depth as the mind-expanding dragomans of the love generation, translating Yoga into pop and interpreting the new Vedanta for the Western scene.

Their poetry loses its shrill note of sexual urgency and goes softly out of focus: "We all live in a yellow submarine, yellow submarine . . . " The *Revolver* album . . . stakes out the boundaries of the Beatles' expanded domain, now no longer circumscribed by the Mersey beat. "Taxman," the opening song in the album, offers a first attempt at social protest for people in the upper income brackets: "If you get too cold I'll tax the heat, If you take a walk I'll tax your feet." "Good Day Sunshine" revives the spirit of barrelhouse and barbershop; "For No One" borrows a romantic French horn obbligato from Schubert's *Hirt auf dem Felsen.* Though love appeals are more casual than ever— "I'll make love to you if you want me to"—the group is not above reverting to an old-fashioned crooner ballad, intoned so beatifically that butter wouldn't melt in their guitars. Harrison's sitar, improving with practice, appears in "Love You To" and "Tomorrow Never Knows," proclaiming a new-found doctrine of flower power: "Turn off your mind, relax and float downstream," at which point the sound does become very relaxed and unpremeditated, close to the edge of indeterminacy. But the album's real *pièce de résistance,* "Eleanor Rigby," is actually a kind of Lennon-McCartney passion chorale. . . .

In the outline and texture of its string accompaniment "Eleanor Rigby" bears a more than fleeting resemblance to the *Bachianas Brasileiras* of Villa-Lobos. (p. 57)

Intentionally or not, the Beatles had already breached the wall between classical music—passé, insuperable—and whatever it was they had been doing. With their next single they arrived at virtually the same intersection between the square and the amoebic that Kurt Weill had reached, for some brief but glorious moments, in his Berlin theatre songs of the 1920's. "Penny Lane" opens up neobaroque vistas, with Bach trumpets blowing hallelujahs for the fireman who "likes to keep his fire engine clean, it's a clean machine." And "Strawberry Fields Forever," on the other side, completes the job of utterly demolishing the form and formula of the erstwhile "pop single." (pp. 57-8)

The Beatles have come to the point where the message has outgrown the medium. *Sgt. Pepper* contrives to be a sort of play within a play, à la Brecht, with the Beatles already at one remove from their former cherubic selves. . . . Musically it is all done with mirrors—the happiest orgy of free association since Wagner invented his ninety leitmotifs: jangling harps and harpsichords, wheezing accordions, the gatling-gun rhythms of the Tamla-Motown Detroit Negro style, Caliban thumping a high-hat, electric guitars going off like wobbly oboes, a choral *fugato* on "We shall scrimp and save," dogs barking, cocks crowing, paeans to a "Mr. K" who could be [Franz] Kafka or [Paul] Klee, memories of Fred and Adele Astaire, a charge of light brigades and an instant-gamaka Hindu chant about saving the world through love. As usual the libretto is illumined by flashes of brilliant psychological insight. . . .

The music is basically neobaroque, but as full of miscellanea as a *basura* joint bought in a Tangier café: trumpets, saxophones, random noises of the Zen-Cage school, and footnotes from "yeah, yeah, yeah" and "Greensleeves." Several further wrinkles and refinements are added in "I Am the Walrus," which is really the more interesting side of their next single though it is "Hello, Goodbye" that gets all the plays. "Hello" is a palpable hit on account of its neatly posited dialectics: "I don't know why you say goodbye, I say hello." But "Walrus" takes a much bigger and more significant step toward the abolition of determinacy. It finds grist for its mill in retreaded 1947 Hollywood movie chords, choruses inspired by early laughing-gas dentistry, and "Elementry penguin singing Hare Krishna." Amid the inchoate prenatal or postprandial noises of this "Walrus," the universe resounds with the mighty cry of "I am the eggman" and intimations of the great ooohm, muttered through mink teeth. The record also marks their first tentative exploration of forbidden territory: "boy you been a naughty girl, you let your knickers down." (p. 58)

"Walrus" also turns up in the filmic *Mystery Tour* package, where the idea of carelessness is carried beyond iconoclasm and raised to the status of an organizing principle. The title song and "The Fool on the Hill" represent the Beatles' two current brands of hot and cold running expressionism: on the one hand, "They've got everything you need / Satisfaction guaranteed," and on the other, "The Fool on the Hill / Sees the sun going down and the eyes in his head / See the world spinning round."

Elsewhere in the album, particularly in "Your Mother Should Know," the Beatles reaffirm their ties to the great western tradition of J. Brahms and the close-knit family. "Your mother should know" is the motto, repeated and repeated. (pp. 58-9)

The sheer irrelevance of much of this music suggests that possibility of another put-on, but McCartney has made it quite plain that "Elementry penguin singing Hare Krishna" and "Love is all you need" constitute an authoritative pronunciamento from Beatle headquarters. "I believe that love is the one thing that can supersede everything else," he explains. "Love is a groove . . . Love is the only natural thing . . . God is in everything. . . . It just happens that I've realized all of this through acid, but it could have been through anything. It really doesn't matter how I made it . . . The final result is all that counts."

Already the Beatles have nearly succeeded in bringing the two mainstreams of music, serious and pop, Bach and barrelhouse, flowing back in the same broad channel—something that hasn't happened since the days when they were dancing *bourrées* in the streets. What a relief it is to turn on a radio and hear the blare of poetry instead of drivel: "Lovely Rita meter maid" or "Expert texpert choking smokers don't you think the joker laughs at you? Ha ha ha!"

When their revolution is complete and the Beatle millennium arrives, the art of music will once more be a continuum instead of a series of soundproof compartments. For a generation bent on enlarging the spectrum of its sensations, the Beatles—like Beethoven before them—have permanently expanded the limits of the world we live in, the world of vibrations. (p. 59)

Frederic V. Grunfeld, "On Polyphony and a New Vocal Quartet" (copyright © 1968 by Frederic V. Grunfeld; reprinted by permission of Wallace & Sheil Agency, Inc.), in Horizon, *Spring, 1968, pp. 56-9.*

SUSAN LYDON

Time was when the Beatles could be viewed as the vanguard of a cultural revolution without so much as bothering their heads about politics. Just what was implicit in their music was enough: an assumption of generational revolt and the existence of sub-cultures with alternative life styles. (p. 65)

In the beginning, the Beatles never had to attack the system overtly; their very success implied the criticism. Being isolationist and apolitical was in itself a departure from the values of the older generation; in English terms it meant not giving a damn about the Queen and her crumbling empire. . . .

The Beatles were more than a rock band. They offered up their whole lives as a kind of entertainment, with an invitation to kids to imitate them: live free, fuck off, you don't have to play the game by society's rules to make it. Taking on the Beatles' life style was an implicitly political act that may have been valid, at that particular time, for English kids.

But the revolt that seemed so promising for England proved, in time, to be merely one-dimensional: the bank clerks and office juniors who donned Mod clothes and danced to the Beatles remained bank clerks and office juniors; the class structure that the Beatles were supposed to be breaking down never quite broke down enough to include their fans. And the attempt to import it to America, where intellectuals were increasingly political, was doomed to disaster from the beginning.

To Americans, the defiant spirit of post-Beatles rock and roll seemed so vital, so in tune with what they were feeling, that they wanted desperately to believe it could offer a total world view. There was an aspect of the new rock that appealed particularly to some political activists: that it seemed finally, irrevocably unrespectable, and un-cooptable by society. (pp. 65-6)

They saw things in Beatles songs that were never there; they sang "Yellow Submarine" as though John and Paul had personally sat down to chart a new direction for the radical movement and provide it with an anthem.

To be fair, the Beatles had protested all along that they were apolitical. (p. 66)

By Christmas of 1965, when "Rubber Soul" was released, most of the world's youth population was pretty firmly under the thumb of the Beatles. Knowing there were millions who would approve anything they did gave the Beatles virtually unlimited freedom to experiment. They began to withdraw into palaces of the imagination, taking a lot of people along on the trip.

Popularity is one thing; unlimited influence another. Soon even the culture heroes began to take themselves seriously as arbiters of the youth revolution. They began to prescribe: take drugs, don't take drugs, turn on to transcendental meditation and find yourself. It was their downfall. The Beatles, smooth, musical virtuosi, astute on matters of the heart, have done nothing but make fools of themselves since they got into philosophizing: Flower Power, the Maharishi, All You Need Is Love. And their choice of a phony and rather reactionary philosophy made fools of radicals who idealized them as well.

"Revolution" is the final blow to the radicals' illusions. With their latest record, the Beatles have plunged directly into the politics of youth. It is an explicit political statement, and must be judged in that context.

"Revolution" is a put-down. "You say you want a revolution / We-ell you know / We all want to change the world." Maybe on the basis of that last line you can argue that the song only puts down *violent* revolution. But the sarcasm seems too apparent. "If you go around carrying pictures of Chairman Mao / You ain't gonna make it with anyone anyhow," they sing; and they moralize: "You say that it's the institution / We-ell you know / You better free your mind instead."

Can the Beatles ultimately resolve the question of what to think about Chairman Mao? I doubt it. If you free your mind, can you free the world? There was a time when American radicals thought so. . . . But the dropouts' style of life was co-opted, and the "blow their minds" politics that had evolved, while more fun than picketing or marching, didn't change the repressive institutions either. Obviously more forceful tactics were necessary. Street fighting became the order of the day.

The really disturbing thing about "Revolution" is that it confirms the Beatles' process of intellectual ossification. Times have changed but the Beatles remain the same, singing a narcissistic little song called "Revolution" that, in these troubled times, preaches counter-revolution.

And what's the thing that really bugs them? "You say you want a contribution." They're not giving "money to people with minds that hate." They've gotten so far away from thinking of "contribution" to a political cause as meaning what they can do as artists that they conceive of their role essentially as that of millionaires. The chorus of the song is, "And you know it's gonna be all right." Well, it isn't. You *know* it's *not* gonna be all right; the song, in fact, is one of the few Beatles songs that, even artistically, lacks conviction.

In view of recent events, it's no longer possible to believe that it's enough just to imitate the buoyant optimism of the Beatles or to live as they do. It is no longer a matter of music but rather one of betrayal. They come off with a whining affirmation of their own values—all you need is love—while the kids build barricades in the streets and the cops bash heads.

> Susan Lydon, *"Would you want your sister to marry a Beatle?"* in Ramparts *(copyright 1968 by Ramparts Magazine, Inc.; reprinted by permission), November 30, 1968, pp. 65-6, 68.*

TOM WOLFE

September. . . . The Merry Pranksters are getting ready to head bombed out into the mightiest crazed throng in San Francisco history, come to see the Beatles at the Cow Palace. (p. 178)

Inside the Cow Palace it is very roaring hell. Somehow [Ken Kesey, the leader of the Merry Pranksters] and Babbs lead the Day-Glo crazies up to their seats. The pranksters

are sitting in a great clump, a wacky perch up high in precipitous pitch high up pitching down to the stage and millions of the screaming teeny freaks. The teeny freaks, tens of thousands of little girls, have gone raving mad already, even though the Beatles have not come on. Other groups, preliminaries, keep trooping on. . . . (p. 181)

Each group of musicians that goes off the stage—the horde thinks *now* the Beatles, but the Beatles don't come, some other group appears, and the sea of girls gets more and more intense and impatient and the screaming gets higher, and the thought slips into Norman's flailing flash-frayed brain stem ::: the human lung cannot go beyond this ::::: and yet when the voice says *And now—the Beatles*—what else could he say?—and out they come on stage—*them*—John and George and Ringo and uh the other one—it might as well have been four imported vinyl dolls for all it was going to matter—that sound he thinks cannot get higher, it doubles, his eardrums ring like stamped metal with it and suddenly *Ghhhhhhwoooooooooowwwwww*, it is like the whole thing has snapped, and the whole front section of the arena becomes a writhing, seething mass of little girls waving their arms in the air, this mass of pink arms, it is all you can see, it is like a single colonial animal with a thousand waving pink tentacles—it *is* a single colonial animal with a thousand waving pink tentacles,

—vibrating poison madness and filling the universe with the teeny agony torn out of them. It dawns on Kesey: it is *one being*. They have all been transformed into one being.

—Mountain Girl grins and urges them on—its scream does not subside for a moment, during after or between numbers, the Beatles could be miming it for all it matters. But something else . . . does . . . matter . . . and Kesey sees it. One of the Beatles, John, George, Paul, dips his long electric guitar handle in one direction and the whole teeny horde ripples precisely along the line of energy he set off— and then in the other direction, precisely along that line. It causes them to grin, John and Paul and George and Ringo, rippling the poor huge freaked teeny beast this way and that

—

Control—it is perfectly obvious—they have brought this whole mass of human beings to the point where they are one, out of their skulls, one psyche, and they have utter control over them—but they don't know what in the hell to do with it, they haven't the first idea, and they will lose it. (p. 182)

Ghhhhhhwoooooooooowwwww, thousands of teeny bodies hurtling toward the stage and a fence there and a solid line of cops, fighting to hurl the assault back, while the Beatles keep moving their chops and switching their hips around sunk like a dumb show under the universal scream. In that surge, just when you would have thought not another sound in the universe could break through, it starts—*thwaaaack— thwaaaack*—the sound of the folding chairs on the arena floor collapsing and smashing down on the floor, and the remains are down there amid the pink tentacles, crushed to a pulp, little bits and splinters that used to be folding chairs, debris being passed out from hand to hand traveling over the pink tentacles from one to the other like some hideously diseased lurching monster cockroaches. And then the girls start fainting, like suffocation, and getting tromped on, and they start handing out their bodies, cockroach chair debris and the bodies of little teeny freaks being shuttled out over the pitched sea like squashed lice picked off the beast, screaming and fainting and *Ghhhhhwoooooowwwwww* again up against the cop fence while the Beatles cheese and mince at them in the dumb show, utterly helpless to ripple them or anything else now, with no control left—

CANCER—Kesey has only to look and it is perfectly obvious—all of them, the teeny freaks and the Beatles, are one creature, caught in a state of sheer poison mad cancer. The Beatles are the creature's head. The teeny freaks are the body. But the head has lost control of the body and the body rebels and goes amok and that is what cancer is. (p. 183)

> *Tom Wolfe, in his* The Electric Kool-Aid Acid Test *(copyright © 1968 by Tom Wolfe; copyright © 1967 by the World Journal Tribune Corporation; reprinted with the permission of Farrar, Straus and Giroux, Inc.), Bantam Books, Inc., 1968.*

ALFRED G. ARONOWITZ

By the weight of the crate, *The Beatles* is the most ambitious album of their career. It took five months to produce through a session of doubt as Paul was changing friends, John was changing wives and the four of them were trying to build a corporate Garden of Eden where they could walk naked, have their Apple and eat it, too. They were off the Maharishi but still whistling tunes they had written on the road to Rishikesh. *I'd give you everything I've got for a little peace of mind!* shouts John. His suffering in this album becomes as heavy as the cement that holds the Beatles together. Poor John. With his songs so patently autobiographical, how must one react to lines like, *I feel so suicidal, just like Dylan's Mr. Jones?* How must Paul, George and Ringo have reacted to it? With pleasure? I doubt it.

It wasn't until after they met Dylan that the Beatles realized there's more to a song than the pretty cinemascopic colors they give to its sound. They still come tumbling out of your hi-fi speakers and into your living room like old friends bringing gifts but ever since they learned they'd have to live out their lives in public their lyrics have become more like snapshots from a family album. . . .

Many of the songs in this album were written of, by and for children. The Beatles are still trying to lead the fight against an older generation that acts as if youth has been purse-snatched from it by the kids. John's tenderest moments are when he sings to Mia Farrow's younger sister, Prudence, who kept herself locked in her room when the Beatles were meditating in Rishikesh: *Dear Prudence, won't you come out to play?* Or to his mother, Julia, who was killed by a car when he was 17: *Half of what I say is meaningless/But I say it just to reach you, Julia.*

George is right. The more songs you write, the wiser you become. The Beatles are only in their late 20s and already they're world savants. In spite of themselves, they've reached a new peak of popularity and God knows what songs they're going to write next.

> *Alfred G. Aronowitz, "Wisdom of Their Years,"* in Life *(courtesy of* Life *Magazine; © 1969 Time Inc.; reprinted by permission of the author), January 31, 1969, p. 12.*

JOHN GABREE

The Beatles, ninety minutes of music on two records, is massively boring, a collection of mediocre compositions given some of the most flaccid performances of recent months. The only tension on the album is between the quartet's snottiness and their indifference to the audience.

A good deal of the new album is taken up with a variety of homages and parodies (and, by and large, parody is a lazy man's art form): mock country-and-western, mock West Indian, mock Beach Boys, mock teeny rock, mock electronic music, mock '30s pop, and especially mock Beatles. Most of it doesn't work and some of it is even offensive: for example, the parody of the Beach Boys is sloppy and unconvincing (although the song itself, *Back in the U.S.S.R.,* is quite funny), and I imagine the blues and c & w copies are insulting to people for whom these are meaningful forms. Even the very best cuts are disappointments. *The Continuing Story of Bungalow Bill* finally can't sustain Lennon's cuteness. *Happiness Is a Warm Gun* is, despite its title, a song about sexual aggression, not peace. The cut I like best is Ringo's *Don't Pass Me By,* but that may be because his singing is simple and straightforward and the group is playing plain old rock. (p. 84)

> *John Gabree, "The Beatles' Ninety-Minute Bore, and the Rolling Stones' Beggars Banquet,"* in High Fidelity *(copyright © by ABC Leisure Magazines, Inc.), March, 1969, pp. 84-5.*

ELLEN SANDER

There are no nagging inconsistencies in *Abbey Road,* no finger-pointing or exasperating enigmas, just a whole mess of sublimely executed, elegantly composed Beatles music.

Yea, team.

Shimmering brilliance and unbounded creative energy grace every moment of *Abbey Road.* It is alternately bright, silly, warm, funny, childlike, funky, and glib, seamlessly bound into a perfectly molded entity born fresh into the day. All the insecure raggedness of the plain white album is gone and *Abbey Road* emerges a glowing tour de force.

It opens with a fresh, salty rock 'n' roll stompalong, "Come Together," peppered with spicy Lennon one-liners, underpinned with a jolly boogie beat. It's a midnight mover, good old rock 'n' roll.

"Maxwell's Silver Hammer," in the best McCartney-music-hall, rinky-tink tradition . . . , [is] a jolly ditty of mischief and manslaughter, full of musical imagination and lyrical buffoonery. You can hear his losing battle to keep a straight face while singing.

"Oh! Darling" is a blistering rock 'n' roll wailing wall, a grand old [Paul McCartney] screamer. It's constructed simply around a conventional rock 'n' roll chord pattern, reaches its height with steamroller guitar assaults, the vocal roaring, gasping, and gagging until its relieved last, dying breath. . . .

The first side is the spectacular, programed for abrupt contrast and crisp definition of the material. Songs of completely different character are placed next to one another with a conscious sense of pace. The result is that each song is set off to the ultimate advantage of its contents and is surrounded by material that complements it, leaving its identity intact.

If Side 1 is the study in contrasts, Side 2 is the ultimate in tonal blending and rhythmic balance. It is the sun side, suffused with mellowed warmth, woven together with motifs, bridging, reprises, surprises, with all the songs set within one another. It opens with "Here Comes the Sun," an awakening, an exaltation of the dawn, "sun, sun, here we come." "You Never Give Me Your Money," a song of estrangement, business, and art, follows, leading through with the same sonic quality. "Sun King," picking up the tonality and theme of the first cut, is next; then come five mini-songs interwoven in a casual suite, exerting the identity of each section gently but firmly in a careful but easy structure. . . .

The album is completely cycled, ready to be played from the start again and again. The balance and feeling for the material on this album is a brilliant example of the Beatles' perspective on their own work, the variety and ultimately the synthesis of the sounds they make.

> Ellen Sander, "The Beatles: 'Abbey Road'," in Saturday Review (© 1969 by Saturday Review, Inc.; reprinted with permission), October 25, 1969, p. 69.

MICHAEL WOOD

Lennon and McCartney's early lyrics were thin and conventional. There was rain in the heart, there were stars in the sky, birds were always threatening not to sing. The tunes were good, some of them as good as those of Rodgers or Leonard Bernstein. But the gap between words and music in pieces like "If I Fell," "And I Love Her," "Ask Me Why," "Not a Second Time," was embarrassing for anyone who wanted to take the songs seriously. The best lyrics, which went with up-tempo numbers like "I Feel Fine," "All My Lovin'," "Can't Buy Me Love," were the ones which said the least. They said yeh, approximately. I'm not suggesting that Lennon and McCartney didn't know how conventional they were being, or that they couldn't have done better. But they didn't do better, presumably because they weren't interested.

Now they are interested. We get the sharpness of "Your day breaks/Your mind aches," where the rhyme really does something. People, characters, begin to take the place of the anonymous lover of the early songs. . . .

But still, the music has developed more than the language, and the language is not a main attraction in these songs. Lennon and McCartney's words are still less important than those of Bob Dylan, or Lorenz Hart, or Cole Porter, or Ira Gershwin. (p. 124)

Think of the titles: "Yesterday," "The Night Before." Think of the nostalgia in songs like "Things We Said Today," or "In My Life": "There are places I'll remember all my life." Think of the echoes of melodrama and music hall in the *Sergeant Pepper* album, the jaunty George Formby tone of "When I'm Sixty-four." In "Good Morning, Good Morning" we take a walk past the old school— "Nothing has changed, it's still the same"—and "She Said She Said" flings a bewildered boy out of the classroom on to a hard life. The girl tells him that she knows what it's like to be dead, and he can only reply, "No no you're wrong when I was a boy everything was right . . ." Lennon and McCartney in their songs do indeed "live the past in the present," as Richard Poirier wrote about them. . . . But it is a personal and sentimental past, not a historical one—it is the specific past of good school days, when the world was simpler and adults looked like fools.

Lennon and McCartney are not naïvely nostalgic, but they are nostalgic. Their songs and Lennon's stories express the good child's hostility to grown-ups. That is what we mean by the youth of the Beatles, an attitude, not an age—after all, they were in their twenties when they began to make it around 1962. The attitude is not dangerous, at worst it deserves a detention, and this is why adults have been so keen to endorse the Beatles. This is safe play for children, mild naughtiness, and much better than breaking up Margate or digging up Paris.

The Beatles are a middle generation between the old conformers and the new rebels, between those who find it hard to believe that the world will change and those who know it's got to. Lennon and McCartney protest against the world adults have made, of course. They hate its pain and loneliness. But their protests are quiet. . . . (pp. 124-25)

> Michael Wood, "Arts in Society: John Lennon's School Days" (reprinted by permission of Peter Matson, Agent), in The Age of Rock: Sounds of the American Cultural Revolution, edited by Jonathan Eisen, Random House, 1969, pp. 121-25.

SPENCER C. BENNETT

[The Beatles'] format is that of anonymity and role playing. Although this group is comprised of multitalented individuals, nobody thinks of them as anything less than a unity. Their anonymity is purposeful and deliberate. They cultivate their ability to assume many roles but they never do so at the expense of fragmentizing that strong outline of the four of them in any one song or film. It's Sergeant Pepper's Lonely Hearts Club Band but Sergeant Pepper is a corporate entity.

They also deal with time and space in terms of their universal implications. Time is important as a medium through which transtemporality can be expressed. The same is true of space. . . . The Beatles are concerned with age, human improvement and death. Although they are not above a thrust at human foibles such as greed ("Piggies") and immature idealism ("Revolution I") they are for the most part optimists about the possibilities of human nature. (pp. 97-8)

[All] of their songs are relevant to the aura of our cultural patterns but none of them can be pinned down to specific event. They depend on electronic media but they do not manipulate them without allowing them first to suggest aural possibilities. Thematically they deal in mythology and parable rather than allegory. Rolewise, they assume the position of the exorciser more than any other. They attempt to speak to alienation and move the listener or the subject from the position of self-containment into community. For all of their eccentricities, the Beatles have a social view of man. The symphonic form of *Sergeant Pepper's Lonely Heart's Club Band* centers on the movement into and out of common communion.

> You're such a lovely audience,
> We'd like to take you home with us,
> We'd love to take you home.

The magical side of the Beatles and their view of themselves as exorcisers of evil spirits in the community [is] especially clear in the film *The Yellow Submarine*. Besides creating a revolution in the format of the cartoon, the film dwells upon some very real forms of human alienation. The lonely sterility of Eleanor Rigby, the hollow shell of intellectual activity which comprises the life of the Nowhere Man, and the threat of the Meanies who attain metaphorical status by draining the color and sound out of life—all of these comprise a Beatle-like statement about human isolation and its consequences. In the film the Beatles represent a rejuvenating force. They are the Four Horsemen of the Apocalypse in a submarine. Sergeant Pepper's music has restorative powers in a world that has lost its zest for life. The band explores the sense of celebration through fantasy without attempting to paraphrase the soap opera atmosphere of Walt Disney. And because the Beatles depend as much on the innovative use of the cartoon as a medium as they do upon their music to convey the need for communical celebration, they emerge as magicians who use illusion to tell us something very true about ourselves. (p. 99)

> *Spencer C. Bennett, "Christ, Icons, and Mass Media," in* Icons of Popular Culture, *edited by Marshall Fishwick and Ray B. Browne (copyright © 1970 by the Bowling Green University Popular Press), Bowling Green University Press, 1970, pp. 91-102.*

RUSSEL NYE

While the Beatles' audience might be preponderantly pubescent, at the same time their musical ideas attracted and influenced serious, sophisticated, professional musicians. A substantial part of their popularity among the young was perhaps more sociological than musical, and it seems safe to assume that a large number of teen-age Beatle enthusiasts had little or no concept of the musical content of their recordings. Their exuberant vitality, their delicate handling of sentimentality, and their real lyrical gifts offered something new and fresh to popular music. At the same time, their topical, carefully-coded lyrics, with concealed references to sex, drugs, and rebellion, captivated restless and uncertain youth everywhere. (Although their rebelliousness has proved to be partly ironic, and not half so destructive as their critics have assumed.) Their extravagantly eccentric dress, wild hair styles, and public antics implied a lifestyle which proved instantly attractive to the adolescent. . . .

The Beatles' importance to popular music, however, had little to do with screaming adolescents, for they brought to it a fund of ideas and a musical style that have since exerted enormous influence on the field. Whatever their eccentricities of dress and behavior, they were, as a musical organization, highly skilled, imaginative, daring, and thoroughly competent professionals. (p. 352)

> *Russel Nye, in his* The Unembarrassed Muse: The Popular Arts in America *(copyright © 1970 by Russel Nye; reprinted by permission of The Dial Press), Dial, 1970.*

BUD SCOPPA

When I first heard *Ram* in bits and pieces on the radio several weeks ago, I hated it. I didn't care much for the single, either. But then, feeling myself getting swept up in the anti-McCartney backlash that seems to be building daily, I promised myself to listen to the album with open ears. I did, and now I have to admit that I like most of it very much. Musically, it's easily the most successful post-Beatle album yet.

McCartney excels at composing riffs; he doesn't write concertos. His genius is most evident in the sheer simplicity of his creations. Side two of *Abbey Road* is McCartney at his best: first conceiving, then executing, finally juxtaposing a rainbow pattern of simple melodic and lyrical ideas. *Ram* works in a similar way, although the juxtapositions occur for the most part within single songs. "Uncle Albert// Admiral Halsey," for example, pits several ideas, all of which could easily stand up by themselves, against each other, and the product resembles "A Day in the Life" structurally if not dramatically. . . . I haven't the slightest idea what it's all about, but I find the song affecting nonetheless.

"Long Haired Lady" is the other side of the coin. Each of the pieces of the song is attractive by itself, but the pattern the pieces form when strung together has none of the charm or movement of the individual segments themselves. In this case, the juxtaposition of parts negates their value. Perhaps the song fails because Paul's manipulations here are visible to the point of obviousness, or perhaps the listener can sense that he's straining to be clever.

Paul *is* clever, of course, while John is powerful and George is earnest. To be clever, powerful, and earnest all at the same time, can produce spectacular results, as we've all learned; but each of these stances alone is somewhat limited, as we've lately discovered. Still, clever is a very good thing to be, and Paul can be clever better than anyone else in popular music. That's why you should take those pronouncements that *Ram* is a lousy album with a full shaker of salt. Between the typically inspired melodies, cryptic lyrics, great singing, sharply etched musical parody, and generally brilliant execution, McCartney's album contains as much meat as a gross of average pop albums. If even that much is less than the listener expects of him, that's quite a tribute to Paul, I'd say.

Speaking of those aspects of the album, Paul seems to have something to say on *Ram*, and I didn't get the impression on his first solo venture. I'll leave the interpretation to someone else, but there's a great deal more than punning here. It's interesting and perhaps significant to note that while Lennon does his best to speak clearly and literally in his work, McCartney often seems to deliberately *obscure* his meaning in riddles and metaphors; while John sincerely seems to be living each image he adopts, I always get the feeling that Paul is *hiding behind* the faces he reveals. The literal mind and the metaphorical mind can compliment each other perfectly when the match is right, but too much of either can be irritating. Still, clever is as clever does, and you have to accept Paul's posing in order to come to terms with his work. . . .

After *McCartney*, I yearned to hear the Beatles perfect all those half-finished ideas that Paul had come up with. On *Ram*, he's proved that he can do most of it himself. Not quite, of course—too much of one thing is always, well, too much—but he's come close enough to make him look awfully good. (p. 27)

> *Bud Scoppa, in* Rock, *(reprinted by permission of Countrywide Publications, Inc. and* Rock *Magazine), July 29, 1971.*

BEN GERSON

Imagine raises the question how much further John can progress with the vocabulary of concepts and feelings laid down on *John Lennon / Plastic Ono Band.*

POB's importance lay not in the fact that it is the culmination of certain tensions which can be seen in John's work since the beginning (the lyrical directness and vocal intensity, for example), but that it was also their solution. As an early adolescent, John chose rock as both his artistic and therapeutic medium. Rock and roll's way of solving problems is simply stating and restating them (''I Can't Get No Satisfaction'' is the classic example) and through the resulting emotional and physical exhaustion, the pressure is temporarily alleviated. However, the intervention of the primal therapy experience forced John to redefine his approach in a subtle but decisive way. Where he had sung ''Twist and Shout'' with the urgency of someone who had to get something off his chest, he sang the songs on *POB* as a final recreation of his original traumas, and as a document of their cure. *POB* is a profoundly ''ultimate'' album, because it unbends the mainspring of at least one man's rock and roll career. . . .

The problem of following an album as perfect as *POB* is of course more than a stylistic one. *POB* took an individual course. Where the trend of rock over the past few years had been one of increasing complexity and sophistication (certainly John, with songs like ''Strawberry Fields Forever'' and ''I Am the Walrus'' is as responsible for this as anyone). *POB* represented a return to rock's most visceral, and still implicit origins. Of course, it was not done naively, but with a full regala of theoretical justifications. But it is a style which, because it is so bound up with a particular experience at a moment in time, is obsolete once it is expressed.

On the evidence of *Imagine*, I don't think John has resolved the manner in which a masterpiece and an artistic dead-end like *POB* can successfully be followed. In its technical sloppiness and self-absorption, *Imagine* is John's *Self-Portrait*. Most of it centers around issues which have already been dealt with on *POB*, only here handled less passionately and, strangely, less fastidiously as well. . . .

''Imagine,'' for instance, is simply the consolidation of primal awareness into a world movement. It asks that we imagine a world without religions or nations, and that such a world would mean brotherhood and peace. The singing is methodical but not really skilled, the melody undistinguished, except for the bridge, which sounds nice to me.

I first heard ''Crippled Inside'' on my car radio. I didn't know right off who it was . . . , but was convinced that only someone very famous, in this age of banal competence, would dare put out something so haphazard. The song's refrain and theme is ''One thing you can't hide / Is when you're crippled inside,'' and is another pitch for John's personal outlook. It sports an Ed Sanders-type vocal.

It is not clear whether ''It's So Hard'' came before or after John's primal therapy experience. ''It's so hard, it's really hard / Sometimes I feel like going down.'' John sings, and the words can have the most general meaning, or, applied to John's own past, the most specific. . . .

In sheer viciousness, nothing on the album surpasses ''How Do You Sleep.'' It begins with the orchestra tuning up, a la *Sgt. Pepper*, and proceeds to lay waste to Paul's character, family and career. John is still a wicked punster, and lines like ''The only thing you done was yesterday'' hit their mark. But beyond the cruelty of it, it is offensive because it is unjust. Paul's music may be muzak to John's

ears, but songs like ''Oh Yoko'' or ''Crippled Inside'' are no more consequential than anything on *McCartney* or *Ram*. And while a song like ''It's So Hard'' is more ''serious'' than much of what's on those two albums, it is certainly no better.

The motives for ''Sleep'' are baffling. Partly it is the traditional bohemian contempt for the bourgeois; partly it is the souring of John's long-standing competitive relationship with Paul. When they were both Beatles their rivalry was channeled towards the betterment of the Beatles as a totality. Apart, it is only destructive.

Most insidiously, I fear that John sees himself in the role of truth-teller, and, as such, can justify any kind of self-indulgent brutality in the name of truth. In ''Gimme Some Truth,'' John complains, ''I've had enough of watching scenes / Of schizophrenic-egocentric-paranoic-prima donnas''; who is he speaking about now? Personally, I'm interested in John the man, his personal trials and dramas, because he has revealed them to us as John the extraordinary artist. If he does not continue as such, his posturings will soon seem not merely dull but irrelevant. It seems to me that John is facing the most extraordinary challenge of his career, both personally and artistically. But then, great artists, of whom John is one, are nothing if not resourceful. (p. 48)

> *Ben Gerson, in* Rolling Stone *(by Straight Arrow Publishers, Inc.* © *1971; all rights reserved; reprinted by permission), Issue 94, October 28, 1971.*

ALBERT GOLDMAN

The history of the Beatles is pop culture's redaction of the myth of innocence and experience. When the famous four set out on their careers, they knew nothing of art or life. At home only in the rough-and-tumble world of the Liverpool cellar club or the Hamburg *Lokal*, they were a shaggy and ignorant crew. They could not read music, they could barely play their instruments, and their idea of a joke was to come out on the bandstand wearing toilet seats around their necks. Since then their careers and lives have mounted upward and outward in dizzying gyres that have swept them around the whole world of twentieth-century life and culture and set them on terms of respect and familiarity with some of the most sophisticated minds in the contemporary arts. (pp. 18-19)

The appearance in 1966 of their album *Revolver* signaled an important transformation of the Beatles. First, the album soured the milky innocence of ''I Want to Hold Your Hand'' and ''Michelle'' with the sardonic tone of the city citizen, personified in the acrid sounds and sarcastic lyrics of ''Taxman.'' The second change was formal: instead of singing in their one basic style, the Beatles became virtuosos and produced a pastiche of modes. (p. 20)

Revolver points the way to the variety mix, but it furnishes no general context for its excellent songs, and hence they gain nothing from being on one record. *Sgt. Pepper* remedies this deficiency by assembling its tunes inside the framework of an old-time band concert. Offering itself as a record of such an occasion, it harmonizes the stylistic eclecticism of its contents by presenting each song as an individual vaudeville turn. At the same time the opportunity is created to step beyond the artificial glare of the footlights and deliver with chilling effect the final revelation of ''A Day in the Life.''

The effect of this last song is like that of awakening from turbulent but colorful dreams to stare at the patch of gray that signals dawn in the city. What we awake to in the song is the modern oscillation between anomie and anxiety punctuated periodically by the sound of a dynamo that has just been switched on. This sound is itself the ultimate symbol of the Beatles' world. It represents the state of being turned on, of getting high and escaping from our deadened selves; but at the same time, its alarming crescendo of speed and power suggests an acceleration to the point of explosion (an implication underscored by the Beethoven-like chords of a symphony orchestra, portending doom). The end of the song is a single tonic chord struck on the piano and then allowed to float away for half a minute, like a slowly dissolving puff of smoke.

"A Day in the Life" is a skillfully contrived microcosm of the contemporary world. Called by one critic "the Beatles' *Waste Land*," and by another "a little Antonioni movie," its brilliance lies in the exquisite adjustment of its tone, calibrated finely between apathy and terror. Reflecting meaning from every facet, the song not only evokes the chug-chug of a mechanistic society and the numbed sensibilities of its anonymous inhabitants, but also sound with conviction the note of apocalypse.

That a song of such intellectual sophistication and artistic resourcefulness should arise out of the same tradition that only a dozen years ago was spawning ditties like "Rock Around the Clock" seems almost unbelievable. But the very swiftness of the development indicates its real nature. Unlike other popular arts, rock has not been forced to spin its substance out of itself. Instead, it has acted like a magnet, drawing into its field a host of heterogeneous materials that has fallen quickly into patterns. No other cultural force in modern times has possessed its power of synthesis. (pp. 21-2)

> *Albert Goldman, in his* Freakshow *(copyright © 1959, 1962, 1963, 1964, 1965, 1966, 1967, 1968, 1969, 1970, 1971 by Albert Goldman; reprinted by permission of The Sterling Lord Agency, Inc.), Atheneum Publishers, 1971.*

RICHARD POIRIER

Any close listening to musical groups soon establishes the fact that as composers and performers the Beatles repay attention altogether more than does any other group, American or English. They offer something for nearly everyone and respond to almost any kind of interest. (pp. 120-21)

More aloof from politics than the Stones, their topicality is of music, the social predicaments, and especially the sentiments traditional to folk songs and ballads. Maybe the most important service of the Beatles and similar groups is the restoration to good standing of the simplicities that have frightened us into irony and the search for irony; they locate the beauty and pathos of commonplace feelings even while they work havoc with fashionable or tiresome expressions of those feelings. (p. 124)

One of the Beatles' most appealing qualities is . . . their tendency more to self-parody than to parody of others. The two are of course very close for performers who empathize with all the characters in their songs and whose most conspicuous moments of self-parody occur when they're emulating someone whose style they'd like to master. At such moments their boyishness really does shine forth as a musical virtue: giving themselves almost wholly to an imitation

of some performer they admire, their necessary exaggeration of his style makes fun of no one so much as themselves. It's a matter of trying on a style and then—as if embarrassed by their own riches, by a self-confident knowledge that no style, not even one of their own invention, is more than a temporary exercise of strength—of laughing themselves out of imitation. (p. 127)

Parody from the Beatles tends usually, and increasingly, to be directed toward musical tradition and their own musical efforts. This is at least one reason why "All You Need Is Love," recorded on the reverse side of "Baby You're a Rich Man," is one of their most revealing. Along with the *Sgt. Pepper* album, it indicates so sophisticated an awareness of their historical achievements in music as to make it evident that they could not continue much longer without still further changes of direction. . . . "All You Need Is Love" is decisive evidence that when the Beatles think together (or apart) about anything they think musically and that musical thinking dictates their response to other things: to "love," in this instance, to drugs and social manners in "Baby You're a Rich Man" and throughout the *Sgt. Pepper* album. (p. 128)

Lennon and McCartney's musical recognition that the "need" for love [in "All You Need Is Love"] is historical and recurrent is communicated less in the lyrics than by instrumental and vocal allusions to earlier material. The historical allusiveness is at the outset smart-alecky—the song opens with the French National Anthem—passes through the Chaplin echo, if that's what it is, to various echoes of the blues, and boogie-woogie, all of them in the mere shadings of background, until at the end the song itself seems to be swept up and dispersed within the musical history of which it is a part and of the electronics by which that history has been made available. The process begins by a recurrence of the "love, love, love" phrase, here repeated and doubled as on a stalled record. It then proceeds into a medley of sounds, fractured, mingled musical phrases drifting into a blur. . . . We can make out fragments of old love songs condemned to wander through the airways for all time. . . . Far from being in any way satiric, the song gathers into itself the musical expression of the "need" for love as it has accumulated through decades of popular music.

This historical feeling for music, including their own musical creations, explains I think, something centrally important about the Beatles: their fascination with the invented aspects of everything around them. They respond with a participatory tenderness and joy to styles and artifact, and it is what makes them so attractively responsive, for older as well as younger listeners, to the human and social landscape of contemporary England. It's as if they naturally see the world in the form of *son et lumière:* as they say in a beautiful neighborhood song about Liverpool, "Penny Lane is in my ears and in my eyes." Not everyone their age is capable of seeing the odd wonder of a meter maid—after all, a meter maid's a meter maid; fewer still would be moved to a song of praise like "Lovely Rita" ("When it gets dark I tow your heart away"); and only a Beatle could be expected, when seeing her with a bag across her shoulder, to have the historically enlivened vision that "made her look a little like a military man."

Now of course English boys out of Liverpool can be expected, it says here, to be more intimate than American boys from San Francisco with the residual social and cultural evidences from World War II and even from the First World War. In response to these and other traces of the past, however, the Beatles display an absolutely unique kind of involvement. It isn't simply that they have an instinctive nostalgia for period styles, as in "She's Leaving Home" or "When I'm Sixty-four," or that they absorb the past through the media of the popular arts, through music, cinema, theatrical conventions, bands like Sgt. Pepper's or music-hall performers. (pp. 130-31)

No, the Beatles have the distinction in their work both of *knowing* that this is how they see and feel things and of enjoying the knowledge. It could be said that they know what Beckett and Borges know but without any loss of simple enthusism or innocent expectation, and without any patronization of those who do not know. In the loving phrases of "Penny Lane," "A pretty nurse is selling poppies from a tray, / And tho' she feels as if she's in a play, / She is anyway." (pp. 131-32)

Without even willing it, we picture ourselves much of the time anyway, see ourselves and the world in exotic images usually invented by someone else. This is the suggestion throughout the *Sgt. Pepper* album. . . . In "A Day in the Life," the last song and a work of great power and historical grasp, the hapless man whose role is sung by Lennon wants to "turn on" himself and his lover—maybe us too—as a relief from the multiple controls exerted over life and the imagination by various and competing media. (p. 133)

Lennon and McCartney in their songs seem as vulnerable as the man in "A Day in the Life" to the sights and sounds by which different media shape and then reshape reality, but their response isn't in any way as intimidated, and "turning on" isn't their only recourse. They can also tune in, literally to show how one shaped view of reality can be mocked out of existence by crossing it with another. They mix their media the way they mix musical sounds; lyrics in one tone are crossed with music of quite another; and they do so with a vengeance. It's unwise ever to assume that they're doing only one thing musically or expressing themselves in only one style. "She's Leaving Home" does have a persistent cello background to evoke genteel melodrama of an earlier decade, and "When I'm Sixty-four" is intentionally clichèd throughout, both in its ragtime rhythm and in its lyrics. The result is a satiric heightening of the love-nest sentimentality of old popular songs. (p. 136)

The *Sgt. Pepper* album and the singles released . . . just before and after it—"Penny Lane," "Strawberry Fields Forever," "All You Need Is Love" and "Baby You're a Rich Man"—constitute the Beatles' most audacious musical effort up to that point, works of such achieved ambitiousness as to give an entirely new retrospective shape of their whole career. Nothing less is being claimed by these songs than that the Beatles now exist not merely as a phenomenon of entertainment but as a force of historical consequence. They have placed themselves within a musical and historical environment more monumental in its surroundings and more significantly populated than was the environment of any of their early songs. Listening to the *Sgt. Pepper* album one thinks not simply of the history of popular music but of the history of this century. (pp 136-37)

Richard Poirier, "*Learning from the Beatles*" (*originally published in a slightly different version in* Partisan Review, *Fall, 1967*), *in his* The Performing Self (*copyright* © *1971 by Richard Poirier; reprinted by permission of the author*), Oxford University Press, 1971, pp. 112-40.

BARBARA SUCZEK

An interesting example of the social construction of a mystery occurred in the late months of 1969, when a strange surge of excitement spread across the country, fomented, apparently, by persistent rumors relating to the nature and circumstances of the alleged death of Beatle Paul McCartney. (p. 61)

The story, in gist, is as follows: Paul McCartney was allegedly killed in an automobile accident in England in November 1966. The remaining Beatles, fearing that public reaction to the news would adversely affect the fortunes of the group, agreed among themselves to keep the matter a secret. Since it was obvious that Paul could not simply disappear from their midst without rousing a storm of embarrassing questions, they hit upon the idea of hiring a double to play his part in public. . . . (p. 63)

For some unspecified reason, however, and at some unspecified time, the plot seems to have undergone a qualitative change. "What began," according to the *Berkeley Tribe* . . . , "for John Lennon as a scheme of deception conceived during moments of personal shock—and perhaps despair—developed into an all-encompassing religious vision."

Lennon's "all-encompassing religious vision," we are asked to believe, was oddly manifested by inserting cryptic messages relating to McCartney's death into the lyrics of songs and among the decorations on the Beatles' album covers. . . .

It is undoubtedly difficult for anyone not immediately caught up in the collective excitement generated by this macabre story to take seriously the symbols regarded as significant by those who were intensely involved in it. Nevertheless, for a period of several weeks they *were* taken seriously and by a surprisingly diverse body of people. (p. 64)

To account for the initial appearance of the rumor is, perhaps, the most perplexing aspect of the phenomenon. It seemed to emerge from out of nowhere, in response to nothing in particular and, as if at once to explain and justify its presence, the clues seemed similarly to emerge. But to realize the fact of the death depended upon recognizing the existence of the clues, and the clues were only recognizable if one were aware of the death. And so there is no external logic to guide a decision as to where the fundamental ambiguity lies—in the death or in the clues—since it is impossible to establish a priority between them. (p. 66)

Clearly, the rumor's underlying logic is difficult to discern —so difficult, in fact, that—if logic can be said to exist at all —it appears that it must be sought outside the immediate subject of discourse. If this is the case, the rumor should be regarded as essentially symbolic, its characters and events standing for as yet unknown (and perhaps unknowable) social concerns. As such, its function is symptomatic; expressive rather than expository, problem-indicative rather than problem-solving.

The intriguing question inevitably poses itself as to why a group of young English pop singers should become the symbol for the expression of a social malaise. A clear answer is not easy to provide. It does seem reasonable to assume, however, that it is in some way related to the climate of intense excitement the group universally seemed to evoke. (p. 67)

The most striking characteristic of the McCartney phenomenon is probably its preoccupation with the covert. Whether emphasizing *concealment* as in the idea that the rumor was covering a sales promotional gimmick or *revelation* that it stemmed from John Lennon's motivation to communicate "the truth"—the "hidden meaning" motif recurs thematically both in the content of the rumor and in the explanations put forth to account for it.

There are, in all likelihood, many and various reasons for a public fascination with the idea of the concealed. The death rumor may be, for example, an inconsequential but interesting expression of the ethos of the Freudian epoch: an essentially artistic creation indicating public awareness of the concept of the unconscious—a folk equivalent of Surrealism.

Again, the fact that many persons apparently resisted all reasonable explications offered in the mass media, preferring to accept interpretations stressing occultism and deceit, may point to a widespread lack of faith in the reliability of information received through formal channels of communication. It may indicate that the much-discussed "credibility gap" is taking its toll by developing publics increasingly inclined to turn to folk communicational resources.

However, the strange content of the rumor and its obdurate quality—the previously discussed failure of its publics to interest themselves in reaching consensual explanation—both suggest that there is something more than a mistrust of news agencies involved in this instance.

Another possibility is that there is demonstrated here a process of ordering seemingly random and chaotic facts into a system of meaning, the sense of the covert being somehow related to an inherent significance which is assumed to *underlie* the events of the world.

The Beatles had, over the years, moved from the straightforward, comprehensible statements of the "I Want to Hold Your Hand"—"I Saw Her Standing There" period of 1963 to the confusing and seemingly unintegrated verbal streams that are characteristic of many of the 1967 songs: "Lucy in the Sky with Diamonds," for example, and "I Am the Walrus."

The "absurdity" of the songs was reflected in the style of the album cover decorations, those of the later years being typically designed as collages of apparently unrelated and randomly selected items.

Randomness can create a fertile field for subjective interpretation: one man's nonsense is another's apocalypse. To avoid the terror stemming from idiosyncratic isolation, however, it is necessary to establish a social basis of confirmation—some criterial standard—that what one takes to be a meaning is accepted and shared by others. Some such meaning-establishing process seemed to be indicated by the behavior of the younger adolescents as they busily conferred with one another evaluating the orthodoxy of the existence and interpretation of specific "clues."

It may be that the McCartney rumor reflects a search for meaning that runs much deeper than a seemingly frivolous preoccupation with pop song lyrics and album cover art would seem to suggest. In periods of social unrest and upheaval, when traditional sources of authority are being challenged and overthrown, there is always the danger that human institutions will dissolve into primal meaninglessness.... Perhaps there is a search for a new basis of authority and understanding represented here that is as profound as, on the surface, it may appear ridiculous.

That this fascination with the mystic seems particularly prevalent among the young makes sense when explained in the theoretical terms of adolescent identity crisis. Since it is this age group that most typically lacks the integrated convictions that might help to sustain a sense of basic meaning in times of extreme and rapid change, these are logically the ones whose worlds are most vulnerable when established bases of authority are assaulted.

In the past, it has surely been the function of great religions to organize and sustain the meanings and values of a society, but ours is a secular age. Basic religious tenets have been increasingly challenged by science; basic religious values have been subordinated to marketplace competition. It is probably not strange, then, that many aspects of the McCartney death story suggest an abortive attempt to apotheosize Paul McCartney.

There are five specific properties of the McCartney phenomenon that would seem to support a conjecture that a myth- or legend-creating process was at work.

> (1) The content was relatively stable, lacking the ongoing, developmental quality that usually characterizes a news story. Among its believers, the story was taught and learned, deviations from the theme were definitely discouraged, and the fundamental details were memorized like a litany.

> (2) The story shared with the legend a quality of empirical irrelevance. To whom, after all, but a few academicians, does it matter if legendary heroes actually lived and did the deeds attributed to them? The significance of the story transcends the details of individual biography. The fact, or lack of it, of the death of Paul McCartney seemed similarly irrelevant to its publics. The inference, then, is that the Paul McCartney of this story was a symbol, a social construct that no longer required the facts of a personal existence to sustain it.

> (3) An almost Gothic engrossment with death and the occult permeated virtually every aspect of the phenomenon—twin themes that are fundamental to myth.

(The above properties, taken together, seem to fall into a familiar and ancient pattern. One senses in their conjunction a curious mandate that something must be fulfilled, calling for the recapitulation of a legend.)

> (4) The content of the story recalls the pattern that categorically defines a cyclical myth. The untimely death of a beautiful youth who is subsequently transformed into or revealed to be a god is a recurrent mythical theme and is presumed to reflect the

cyclical process in nature. The legends of Osiris, Adonis, Dionysis, and Jesus have all conformed, in some major way to this pattern. It may be that the McCartney rumor represents an aborted attempt to re-create such a myth. Perhaps in the present, as in the past, humans may be trying to make sense out of the apparent senselessness of their own deaths by suggesting, analogously, the possibility of reincarnation. Alternatively, such a myth may be a process whereby socially valued qualities of an exemplary youth can be abstracted into an idealized model and thus preserved from the eroding onslaughts of ongoing reality (a motivation described by Wallace Stevens as "nostalgia for perfection.")

Whatever the reason for the recurring beautiful-dead-youth theme, its resonance in the McCartney story was clearly discernible. An embarrassed but eerie longing for the story to be true—for Paul to be really dead—was repeatedly expressed, such expression being invariably accompanied by protestations of admiration or love for the singer.

> (5) Clearly the rumor had high entertainment value. Not only did it provide a fascinating subject for conversation, but it also invoked —particularly among younger adolescents— a fearful, brooding, supernatural mood which they obviously found rather more enjoyable than otherwise. The entertainment component is an important factor in the promulgation of a myth since the pleasure of its company makes its repetition a likelihood.
>
> (pp. 68-72)

Mystery resulting from ignorance can pose a potential and serious threat to human survival; as such, it urges the pursuit of knowledge to dispel it. Mystery, on the other hand, can provide a basis for human meaning, its sacred (and secret) premises upholding the perception of reality. In its latter function, it can be created and preserved by social volition; it can be institutionalized into a religion. (p. 73)

The public stir attending the "death" of Paul McCartney was obviously an amusing but trivial social phenomenon: short-lived and probably inconsequential. That it should have spread as widely and as rapidly as it did, however, suggests that there are processes of social interaction at work that it might well behoove us to examine more carefully. However foolish its guise, the McCartney rumor clearly indicates that there is a potential for irrational belief and action—be it constructive or be it destructive to what or whose values—that is alive and well in the modern, industrialized, "enlightened" world. (p. 74)

> Barbara Suczek, "The Curious Case of the 'Death' of Paul McCartney," in Urban Life and Culture (copyright © 1972 by Sage Publications, Inc.; reprinted by permission of the Publisher, Sage Publications, Inc.), Vol. 1, No. 1 (April 1972), pp. 61-76.

BRUCE HARRIS

Since the breakup of The Beatles, Paul has had the unhappy role of playing villain, a problem that has been ampli-

fied by things John Lennon has said and sung, statements that Paul has not answered extensively in any interview. Only in his lyrics do we discover any of his attitudes, and even there Paul backs off the subject, being clever but not really incisive: "Too many people sharing party lines, / Too many people never sleeping late. / Too many people paying parking fines, / Too many hungry people losing weight." (*Too Many People* by Paul McCartney.)

That's really not much of an answer to "I've seen religion from Jesus to Paul," or "Those freaks was right when they said you was dead, / The one mistake you made was in your head." According to Paul, in *Too Many People,* John's one mistake is that he missed his "lucky break," but it's all too vague. Paul works through personas even in his most deeply felt personal statements. It is his chosen mode of expression and he is remarkably successful at it. But Lennon is like a journalist: he is specific, he deals in names, dates, places. *Too Many People* is about a lot of things besides John Lennon. *How Do You Sleep At Night,* is about nothing but Paul McCartney.

It is, however, more than irrelevant how Paul fares against John in this verbal shooting match, or which of them is more mature or clever about it. That's not the point. Each of The Beatles should be seen on his own terms. We shouldn't be comparing *Ram* or *Imagine* or *All Things Must Pass* to *Abbey Road*. It just doesn't make sense. On their own, neither Paul McCartney, nor John Lennon, nor George Harrison (though he tries hardest), nor Ringo in any way constitute the group known as The Beatles. We ought to know that by now. (pp. 18-19)

McCartney, Paul's first solo album, is, of course, a homemade recording with Paul playing all the instruments, and it suffers from the kind of rough edges that such an album must inevitably have. Much of the material is not complete. There are fragments, and worse still, fragments of fragments. The instrumentals, *Valentine Day, Momma Miss America,* and such are fluffy bits of melody loosely strung together. It's the kind of music Paul makes in his sleep. If you were Paul's friend, this is probably just the stuff he'd hum to you in the car driving down to get a pack of cigarettes. It gives the album a warm, friendly, homey feeling, and that's nice; but its immense lack of ambition leaves the listener somewhat unsatisfied.

On the other hand, even on a homemade album, a musical genius like Paul can't help but include a few classics, of which *Junk, Teddy Boy,* and *Maybe I'm Amazed* are the most formidable.

Ram presents us with a far greater critical problem, because it is really terribly ambitious all the way through. Even its silliest cuts, *Three Legs* and *Ram On* demand a certain amount of attention. Critics of Paul McCartney, beware! If this is a dumb album, it sure is dumb in the strangest ways.

In fact, *Ram* is anything but dumb. Its only failing is perhaps that in certain ways it asks too much of the listener. So many tunes, so much music, so much going on all the time that it takes a while before you can reach an overview of the whole thing, a point from which you can perceive the ways it functions as a totality.

Side One of *Ram* focuses on Paul's relation with John Lennon, but as suggested before, it's all in terms of personas, and it would be possible to hear it all without once thinking of John Lennon and still have all the songs make sense. But that fact in itself makes it quite a feat. It is the incorporation of personal feelings into universally understood statements. (p. 19)

As the most wholly realized work on the album, *Back Seat of My Car* raises many critical problems. It is not imagistic, but extremely straightforward, and so in discovering what it *means,* we are forced to deal with something that is quite concrete and right to the point. To toss it off as mere fluff would be to toss off *Maxwell's Silver Hammer* or *Blackbird* as mere fluff. The central theme in *Back Seat Of My Car*—the implicit war between young and old—is stated so simply, so obviously, and so naturally that it is easy to miss. Yes, the song is primarily a love song, but it is a love song that acknowledges an unhappy alternative to love. It is a statement of a very basic human problem. If we insist on seeing the couple as Paul and Linda, we are not allowing Paul the artistic freedom of creating fictional characters. After all, Maxwell Edison and Rocky Racoon and JoJo (in *Get Back*) are not Paul McCartney.

Seeing the singer as a fictional creation, *Back Seat Of My Car* is most closely related to another McCartney song *She's Leaving Home,* for in both, children oppose their parents. In *Back Seat,* the objections are highly moral. We choose either the singer's song, which is a song of love, or the girl's father's song, which is a song of hate, in which "making love is wrong." (pp. 19, 22)

The car works on many levels as a means of escape. Don't forget that these lovers flee by riding in the *back* seat of a car. They're not really going to make it to Mexico City, or anywhere for that matter. Not yet, at least. The sexual implications of hiding and riding in the back seat are obvious enough, but coupled with a moral statement like, "We believe that we can't be wrong," they take on new meanings. Love in itself completely vanquishes "her daddy's song," and in the end, what remains is a joyous tribute to that love, "We believe that we can't be wrong!"

Ram is such a complex album musically that it is painfully superficial to attempt this kind of brief analysis of some of the lyrics. Songs like *Long Haired Lady* function so much in terms of the kinds of musical changes they go through that it is really a bit misleading to discuss them in terms of their lyrical wit, no matter how subtle and beautiful they may be.

The past few months have found Paul succeeding only with the public who still apparently find him at least entertaining. *Ram* was attacked viciously for being vacuous and random, a mere pastiche of amiable, but superficial sounds. . . .

Paul's latest album, *Wild Life,* made with his new group Wings, has only made matters worse. A new group featuring Paul McCartney seems rife to be compared with that other group he was once in, and that's pretty much of a losing battle. *Wild Life* is also a very unambitious album. . . .

A lot of the way *Wild Life* is just what the critics said *Ram* was: superficial, shallow, empty-headed. It is a very simple record, and its only excuse is that it was intended to be so. There is no evidence to believe that the best that the writer of *Hey Jude* and several dozen other great songs can do

now is compose lines like "the word 'wild' applies to the words 'you and me.'" It is very layed back. It sounds like everyone had fun making it. Sometimes, it is even fun in itself.

But for the most part, it does lack depth, and that's a problem that must be dealt with. Its self-indulgence is obvious as are its curious pretensions. Like *McCartney,* it has a basement quality to it, but with very few exceptions, it never really rises above that level.

Paul can do better, and Paul knows it. In a recent interview, he implied that he had been greatly disappointed to the critical response to *Ram,* and that *Wild Life* is an example of what happens when a musician stops caring.

But Paul McCartney will return. The next album will be better, because Paul knows that it has to be. *Dear Friend,* the closing song of *Wild Life,* directs us toward the future. Its subtle brilliance is more a sign of things to come than anything else. Paul is closing one door, only to open another. (p. 22)

Bruce Harris, "In Defense of Paul McCartney," in Words & Music *(copyright © 1972 by Hampshire Distributors Ltd.; reprinted by permission of the author), June, 1972, pp. 18-19, 22.*

STEPHEN HOLDEN

[*Some Time in New York City*] represents only another logical step in [John's and Yoko's] artistic devolution. More than on any previous album it shows [them] actively functioning as an interdependent unit. Five songs are collaborations; of the other five, three are by Yoko and two by John. The overall ideology takes the Maoist view that art, life, and politics should be inseparable and, in the ultimate order of things, indistinguishable. *Some Time in New York City* is thus entirely devoted to propaganda. But as proganda it is so embarrassingly puerile as to constitute an advertisement against itself.

The songs on *Some Time in New York City* are a little better than "Power to the People" and "Happy Xmas." But when compared to the songs on *John Lennon/Plastic Ono Band,* or even *Imagine,* they are sad indeed. The first album, a masterpiece that by its very nature could never be repeated, nevertheless seemed to signal the beginning of something important—the formulation of a new kind of populist art song—elegant in its careful simplicity and radically honest to a degree perhaps never before attempted in Western music. If there was a weakness in the album, it was that the melodies were shallow and derivative. But then, one could argue, wasn't the whole point to be as direct and unprettified as possible.

That first album represented a painful and profound self-exorcism and self-renewal, so daring and so successful that one would have expected Lennon's subsequent work to radiate out from that central core, away from the self to express a deepening complexity of awareness and taste. And it did, to some extent, though *Imagine* had the same relation to *John Lennon/Plastic Ono Band* as *Magical Mystery Tour* had to *Sgt. Pepper:* prettier but weaker. I liked many things on *Imagine*—in particular the title cut and "Oh Yoko!" but had to force myself to ignore the ominous "How Do You Sleep?," a song so spiteful and self-indulgent that it sanctified the victim and demeaned the accuser. Such anger, it seemed to me, was far more effective when channeled into the political didacticism of "Gimme Some Truth," itself a cut that barely rose above the level of simplistic ranting.

On *Some Time in New York City* the Lennons attempt to turn chants and slogans into songs. Their strategy seems to be to try to radicalize what they must envision as an ignorant stupid mass of working-class teenagers and ghetto-dwellers by "getting down to their level." Does John's repeated phrase "Que pasa, New York?" in "New York City" say anything meaningful to or about New York's Puerto Rican community? To me it sounds like one more radical-chic allusion in a rush to touch all bases.

Except for "John Sinclair" the songs are awful. The tunes are shallow and derivative and the words little more than sloppy nursery rhymes that patronize the issues and individuals they seek to exalt. Only a monomaniacal smugness could allow the Lennons to think that this witless doggerel insult the intelligence and feelings of *any* audience. . . .

"Woman Is the Nigger of the World" is built around two slogans—the words of the title and the repeated incantation "We make her paint her face and dance." In between, almost every feminist truism is mentioned. There is no narrative development or explication of an idea; the song is simply a list of injustices clumsily set so that herds of syllables packed into each line make the whole thing almost unintelligible. Sure, the sentiments are fine. But they are shouted at us in the tone of a newsboy yelling "Extra/ Extra/ Read all about it!" Well we *have* read all about it and heard all about it from plenty of sources more coherent and persuasive than the Lennons.

Throughout their artistic careers, separately and together, the Lennons have been committed avant-gardists. Such commitment takes guts. It takes even more guts guts when you've made it so big that you don't need to take chances to stay on top: the Lennons should be commended for their daring. What is deplorable, however, is the egotistical laziness (and the sycophantic milieu in which it thrives) that allows artists of such proven stature, who claim to identify with the "working class hero," to think they can patronize all whom they would call sisters and brothers.

> Stephen Holden, "'Que pasa, New York?' Indeed, What Do You Say about Artistic Suicide?" in Rolling Stone (by Straight Arrow Publishers, Inc. © 1972; all rights reserved; reprinted by permission), Issue 113, July 20, 1972, p. 48.

DAVID R. PICHASKE

Some of the lyrics of The Beatles, Bob Dylan, Jefferson Airplane, and Leonard Cohen are the vaguest of all pop songs except, of course, for those that degenerate into utter absurdity. They are not different from much of contemporary poetry, which has also become so subtle and indirect as to admit to a wide variety of possible interpretations. . . . Very little can definitely be said about the theme of "I Am the Walrus," except that it is an exceptionally unpleasant song about death or ugliness or perversion or a combination of the three and even more. "Norwegian Wood" is a hauntingly beautiful lyric on a more pleasant but equally vague theme. . . . More than one individual has suggested that this is a narrative about a drug trip and that "Norwegian Wood" is yet another slang term for marijuana. But apart from the surrealism of the action and perhaps the exotic instrumental accompaniment, a result of the use of the sitar for the first time in rock music, there is little to support such an argument. The girl suggests a sexual relationship and perhaps even love, although it is certainly casual and impermanent. . . . The woman is intriguing, even intoxicating, as many women are, but the poet does not seem to miss her when she leaves. Their relationship is pleasant while it lasts, but not mourned when it is over. Most importantly and most perplexingly, we are not sure whether this is a real woman or whether she represents something else—like marijuana. On the other hand, for all its ambiguities, the song does have a reasonably definite subject and theme: it is about an enjoyable, transient experience, and it suggests that pleasant experiences may all be temporary and should be accepted as such and not mourned excessively when they end. Within these limits, the individual reader is free to set up his own definite interpretation, provided that it is supported by evidence within the poem. (pp. 15-16)

[The] Lennon-McCartney song "All You Need is Love" [contains obvious deliberate ambiguity]. "What kind of love?" we ask ourselves, and scraps of music playing in the back of the song give us all sorts of answers: the modern, unromanticized love of "She Loves You, Yeh, Yeh, Yeh," the romantic love of "Greensleeves," the Christian *agape* of Christmas and the old carol "What Child Is This?" But it is possible, we discover when we think about it, that "love" encompasses all of these meanings, that they encompass each other, and that the love we need is multidimensional. The song exploits the possibilities of an ambiguous love to make an important—if not particularly original—point. (p. 134)

The most clearly ambiguous phrase (to use an oxymoron) [in "Let It Be"] is the title "Let It Be." To what does "it" refer? To an answer? An answer to what question? And just how do we "let it be?" But another and perhaps more important ambiguity may lie in "Mother Mary," who speaks the words of wisdom. In rock lyrics Mary is frequently a personification of marijuana . . . , and she may be just that here. But Mother Mary suggests Mary, Christ's mother, and some religious implications are added to the poem. If the figure is deliberately ambiguous, what would be the point of combining the associations of the Virgin Mary and marijuana? Does the rest of the poem assume added meaning in light of this ambiguous Mary? Does it explain what the answer might be, how "it" might be, what "it" might resolve? (p. 136)

Sergeant Pepper has a kind of unity absent on most rock albums. The individual lyrics are, of course, impressive, and they are the place to begin a discussion of that album; but a discussion of any one lyric must soon give way to a discussion of the meaning of the whole. . . . (p. 290)

[The] two "Sergeant Pepper" songs frame a series of distinct studies of great musical and poetic variety, putting the whole album in the context of a stage performance (the illusion is furthered by "A Little Help From My Friends"). The last cut on the second side is parenthetical, outside the performance context, a new perspective on all that has gone before.

The place to begin a consideration of the album is with the individual lyrics, some of which have already been the subject of considerable discussion. Only after one has grasped the songs individually can one begin drawing patterns of meaning from the whole album. "Lucy In the Sky" is widely interpreted as an acid trip and an acrostic for LSD. Certainly both the tonal distortions of the music and the rich sensual imagery of the poem suggest the popular conception of such a trip. . . . ''Lucy In the Sky'' is a powerful poem even if it is not an acid song: the title image suggests an awareness that the rest of the song develops, an awareness of the most common of things in the most uncommon of contexts, imbueing Lucy with mystical attraction. Perhaps the song is really about the awareness of the extraordinary within the ordinary—but then that is precisely what LSD is reported (perhaps erroneously) to open one's eyes to. (pp. 301-02)

''A Day in the Life'' is, with the possible exception of ''Lucy in the Sky,'' the most haunting and the most ambiguous song on the album. Madison Avenue has managed to make the phrase ''turn on'' virtually meaningless by applying it to everything from shades of cosmetics to chocolate malts, but the expression always did have a certain ambiguity to it. First, of course, it means drugs. . . . But the other images in the song suggest that we are being asked to turn on to an awareness of the bankruptcy of life as we usually live it in the twentieth century, and to an awareness of what life might be. The man blew his mind out just when he finally made the grade, the war was won but nobody really cared. Life goes on, a collage of nearly missed buses and holes to be carefully counted. If ''Lucy in the Sky'' was a trip that turned us on to the magic of what is conventional, all that magic has disappeared in ''A Day in the Life.'' The trip is over, and it was a bummer.

The comparison between these two songs brings us to a more important question: what kind of a statement does the album as a whole make? Everyone . . . agrees that yes, it does have a unity, and it is obvious that the unity is intentional. . . . But what kind of a statement does this unity make?

The context of the whole album is provided by the opening two songs: this is a performance by Sergeant Pepper (Ringo Star, alias Billy Shears—he wears the sergeant's stripes on his uniform) and his lonely hearts club band. Two things are important: the band is lonely, and it is performing. Perhaps the two are interrelated: performers are generally lonely people, lonely people perform when they pretend not to be lonely and in an attempt to escape their loneliness. What is especially significant, however, is that Sergeant Pepper and his band are aware of that fact that they are performing, that they are acting out an illusion—others are not as aware, but then again they are probably not as lonely. Some are off into a drug thing; others tell themselves that things are, after all, getting better all the time, or rationalize their disillusionment by excusing themselves. Some withdraw into self-isolation and others drown any misgivings they might have in the noise and excitement of a circus performance. ''What we were talking about,'' says George Harrison bluntly in ''Within You Without You,'' ''is what is hypocritical and what is honest, and who hides behind what walls of illusion.'' But if the lyrics of this song outline inadequate responses people make when they are vaguely aware that something is wrong with their lives, the next three songs present us with a gallery of incredibly shallow individuals. The first proposes the most mundane of marriages to a mail-order bride; the second falls in love with a meter maid he happens to see writing up tickets; the third drives in self-impressed fashion aimlessly around town

looking for pick-ups. What makes the whole despicable crowd especially disgusting (and The Beatles' comment especially morose) is the irrepressible high spirits of the music, which ironically mocks the words themselves and piles irony on top of irony. And then the band, Sergeant Pepper's Band, Sergeant Pepper's Lonely Hearts Club Band, breaks in with its initial statement, now made depressingly meaningful: ''Sergeant Pepper's lonely.'' The ''l'' is lower case; the phrase ends with a period. The band is making a statement: ''Sergeant Pepper is lonely,'' and that's what we've been talking about for the duration of this performance. By now we as listeners have begun to feel a trifle lonely too, and ''A Day In the Life,'' with the alienated, impassive attitude of the observers and its resounding chord dying-out-to-nothing at the end is almost too much. But it is too much not simply because of the song itself, but because the entire weight of the whole album comes crashing down on that final chord. And the whole weight of *Sergeant Pepper* is a lot of weight. (pp. 302-04)

> David R. Pichaske, *in his* Beowulf to Beatles Approaches to Poetry, *edited by David R. Pichaske (reprinted with permission of Macmillan Publishing Co., Inc.; copyright © 1972 by the Free Press, a Division of The Macmillan Publishing Company), The Free Press, 1972.*

WILFRID MELLERS

[What] kind of world did [the Beatles] evoke in their early years, from [their] interfusion of American black blues and white rock and Country-Western, of Anglo-Irish folk music and song and dance from music-hall and pub? From the start the Beatles were individualities who sought a corporate identity. Though only during the first year or two did Lennon and McCartney actually compose *together,* there's point in the ascription of the songs to their joint authorship. They needed one another for their fulfilment: needed, in a rather different way, the other two Beatles; and the separate ways in which they grew up were affected by the identity they'd sought for in the early years. . . . [Their] 'group' sense—their corporate identity—is complemented by the themes of the early songs; which concern the euphoric happiness of togetherness, though it's significant that this togetherness is identified with the two-way relationship of heterosexual love—which sometimes becomes synonymous with 'home', security, mum.

One of the most famous of early Beatle songs—*She loves you*—is also quintessential. It is simply an affirmation, epitomised in its 'Yeah yeah yeah' refrain; and it exists in the moment, without before or after. . . . The timeless, present-affirming modality is instinctive; and the words, if . . . perfunctorily vacuous, are no longer *merely* magic talismen, abracadabra. They do concern a basic, life-affirming human experience; and the conjunction of the words with the music makes evident that this experience matters because it is true; and is true because—even in the face of the commercial pressures and discords of modern industrial life—the Beatles are, through their music, as though new-born. It's this pristine quality that helps us to understand the potency of their appeal, the relevance of their mythology. (pp. 32-3)

The basic Beatle song is Edenic: as is manifest on the first LP in *I saw her standing there.* . . . (p. 33)

One couldn't claim that [its] words are oral poetry, in the

sense that Dylan's songs—even the earliest ones—are: though in the course of time the Beatles 'grew into' oral poetry, largely by way of Dylan's example. What [the] verses do have is an uncanny instinct for the ways in which people of the Beatles' generation spoke and felt, rather than thought; and they're prepared to accept their inarticulateness rather than substitute for it the 'poetic' insincerities—the moon-June clichés—of the previous generation's pop songs. (p. 34)

There's a place, by John, should be mentioned . . . because it's the first song concerned with *self*-reliance. Despite its melismata and parallel triads, it is curiously austere, resolutely diatonic, virtually without modulation. The 'place' where he thinks of her (again the song, performed by John and Paul, is at once individual and corporate) is his own mind: which is ultimately inviolable, even by her: 'There's a place where I can go When I feel low, When I feel blue, And it's my mind and there's no time When I'm alone.' This is probably the first song wherein we realise that John might be an 'oral' poet, and that in terms of poetic-musical experience he had a long way to travel. (p. 41)

Over and above the sheer physical impact [the Beatles] inherited from commercialised rock, they evoke a young happiness that haunts one because it is true; and is true because it's experience reborn into innocence. The technical manifestations of this are the songs' preoccupation with 'pure' folk-like melody (basically pentatonic and monodic) as against ordered harmony, with its Western, 'cultivated', associations: so that the vocal lines are marvellously fresh, whether with Paul's lyricism or John's toughness. The Beatles' music is more open, whiter, fresher, tenderer than the age-old black blues, for its Anglo-Irish affiliations lead it towards innocence rather than ecstasy, pleasure rather than pain, wholeness rather than blueness. Even the harmony provoked intuitively by modal melody and blue guitar techniques effects a kind of re-Renaissance—in wide-eyed, open-eared wonder at the 'pure' sensuality of thirds and sixths. . . . None the less, the ambivalence of the Negro blues. . . . is not entirely alien to Beatle music, even in their early days. Blue rawness and 'reality' temper their innocence; whilst their innocence transmutes aggression. It's this synthesis of qualities —American black and Anglo-Irish white—that makes the physical beat, which is their music's most *immediately* recognisable quality, a stimulus rather than a narcotic; and this again is what makes the happiness not mindlessly euphoric, but for real. The irony, or comedy, that often springs from this fusion is also pertinent here; the objectivity their songs achieve reconciles individual with corporate identity, and this helps to explain their tremendous impact on a whole generation. They were simply and sensuously affirmative; babes newborn, rejecting the past, yet singing for *dear life.*

None the less, because Beatle happiness was true, it had latent within it the awareness of pain and the negative emotions. (pp. 41-2)

Beatles' initiation . . . is a ceremony of birth. On [their] disc, *A hard day's night,* they're concerned with adolescence and growing up; and the rituals are those of puberty. The title song is another number about Love, identified with Home; but a more 'experienced' quality is evident in the verses, which use less youthfully abstract jargon, more down to earth fact. John has been 'working like a dog' to get money to buy his girl *things.* He should now, after his

hard day, be 'sleeping like a log', but knows he won't be, because the things she'll do when he gets home will make him 'feel alright'. So there's again a division between innocence (the ecstasy of being 'held tight') and experience (things, making money, the tedium of work, suggested by the long repeated notes in the tune's first phrase). Both poetically and musically, however, this is subtler, because more equivocal, than in any previous song. Indeed one might say that the song sees innocence and experience as interdependent; the freedom couldn't be so lovely were it not for the tedium. (p. 43)

The starkness of [*Anytime at All*] provides a transition to Paul's *Things we said today,* for me the Beatles' most beautiful and deep song up to this point. Again it concerns the reality of love, involving responsibility and wonder as well as pleasure.

[This] song makes incarnate the Beatles' truth to experience. The words tell us little by themselves, for the point is precisely that the love-experience is too deep for words: 'Someday when we're dreaming, deep in love, not a lot to say, Then we will remember Things we said today.' The music, with its faintly liturgical flavour, genuinely acts this out, creating an experience no longer just happy, but full of awe. Here the fade-out legitimately carries us outside Time. (pp. 47-8)

The immediate nostalgia of [*Yesterday*] is without suspicion of sentimentality. . . .

Being lost, the song tells us, is part of the painful process of growing up. He believes in yesterday, as we all do, because then love was 'an easy game to play'. Now he needs a 'place to hide away' from the shadow; and with the words 'O yesterday came suddenly', the sense is inverted, for 'yesterday' becomes the recognition of the shadow itself, the moment of truth. Negatively, one can attribute this merely to the slack syntax which the Beatles share with all pop lyricists, the words trickling or spurting out to fit, or help to make, the tune. Positively, one can regard it as a beautiful example of the functioning of an 'oral' poetry which is pre-syntactical, and in which the emotional ambivalence is the kind of accident that may happen to an intuitive artist. As the Beatles grow up, such accidents occur with increasing frequency; and there is probably no precedent for this outside relatively primitive folk cultures. Baby Mozart, or even teenage Schubert, didn't function thus empirically, since they worked within a stable and literate tradition. Mozart seems miraculously to have missed out on puberty; Schubert's teenage songs do not noticeably differ, in the range of their themes or even their technical sophistication, from those of his maturity. (p. 57)

[*Rubber Soul*] may be an inverted positive—a move towards self-reliance, in reaction to the Nowhere Man. Certainly John's *Run for your life,* a totally explicit anti-girl song, generates a joyous exuberance from its mediant alternations, so that its brusqueness is not synonymous with cruelty. Similarly, Paul's *I'm looking through you* pierces through pretences as it answers its upward flowing phrases with a resigned descent from the subdominant's flat seventh. . . . [In] these songs there's a toughness, beneath lyricism or comedy, that is not evident in earlier songs.

The best songs on *Rubber Soul* are not, however, overtly satirical; certainly the anti-girl elements in John's *Girl* are complemented by a lyricism so touching in its simplicity that the ironies take us by surprise. (pp. 60-1)

The word, a joint composition, . . . is a ritual love-spell. . . . [The] Word that is evoked may be Love, with overtly sexual implications in the upward thrusting arpeggio and the lacerating false relations; yet the sacramental connotations of the Word are also latent, since the song's potency is grave, almost austere, in its modality.

This little song is of some importance in the Beatles' development, for the magical and runic qualities which we have seen to be implicit in many of their early songs here become explicit. In their Hard Day's Night they've learned that love isn't the simple boy-meets-girl relationship it had seemed to be; at least the feelings released by such basic heterosexual contacts are both confused and confusing: inseparable from other people and the 'world outside': inseparable, it would seem, from metaphysical as well as physical sanctions, using the term literally and without pretention. Inevitably, there's a tie-up between the widening range of the Beatles' experience and the expansion of their technical resources. In any case, their next disc, *Revolver,* is at once a break-through in technique and a new kind of experience. (pp. 65-6)

Though *Revolver* still contains ritual elements, one can no longer discuss it in terms of adolescent ceremonial, nor is it relatable to the conventions of commercialised pop music. Halfway between ritual and art, it's both verbally and musically an extraordinary break-through. . . . (p. 69)

With remarkable verbal articulateness, though at a poetic level beyond intellectual formulation, . . . *Sgt. Pepper's Lonely Hearts Club Band* . . . explores the perennial as well as current problems of adolescence—loneliness, friendship, sex, the generation gap, alienation, fear, nightmare; and perhaps could do so because the Beatles' early 'corporate identity' was always a synthesis of four separate individualities. Yet if *Pepper* is, in this relatively traditional sense, art, it is also a ritual involving the young—through its electronic extension of musical sounds into the environment of the external world—in a ceremonial togetherness, without the prop of church or state. This two-way function as art and ritual remains valid, even though the Beatles, in common with most pop groups, disclaim both moral responsibility and artistic technique: for that responsibility and technique may be intuitively independent of conscious volition is the heart of the matter.

No longer do the Beatles offer us a miscellany of songs; we rather have a sequence of intricately related numbers, forming a whole and performed without break. The verses, though still composed 'orally', by trial and error, are printed on the record sleeve, so that we may go back and read them again, 'like a book': just as on disc we may repeat bits of the music, as one cannot in a live (especially in part improvised) performance. None of the songs is a love song; and that the main theme of the sequence is loneliness would seem to admit that the Beatles' early attempts at tribal togetherness had failed—not as music, but as a way of life. (pp. 86-7)

Sgt. Pepper makes the climacteric point in the Beatles' career, their definite breach with the pop music industry, however materially successful the disc . . . may have been. Henceforth, the world they've created is *sui generis,* bringing its own criteria. The pattern of their young lives seems clear. In their boyhood they discovered a lost Eden, creating a danced music of which the euphoria was valid because newborn. Their first period ends with their hard day's night's discovery of human relationships and responsibilities; and this 'second period' is consummated in *Sgt. Pepper's Lonely Hearts Club Band.* If Pepper, however, is the apotheosis of the second period, he also initiates the third: much in the same way as *A Hard Day's Night* had one foot in the first period, the other in the second. For whereas many songs in *Pepper* are concerned with the young mind and senses in relationship to the external world, others follow *Tomorrow never knows* (from *Revolver*) in re-entering the world of dream. This preoccupation with the life 'within you' is no longer child-like and innocent, for its absorbs the experience of the Beatles' middle years. (p. 101)

[It's] interesting that the musical development in *Abbey Road* goes along with a partial relinquishment of the verbal, poetic life progressively explored in *Rubber Soul, Revolver* and *Sgt. Pepper.* The verses in *Abbey Road* are certainly more runic, more oral, less concerned with human relationships, though the unconscious springs touched on are now far from being Edenic. (p. 122)

Revolver, Sgt. Pepper and *Abbey Road* are the three great milestones in the Beatles' career: *Revolver* because it was a breakthrough from the world of pop into a world that hasn't yet been categorised; *Pepper* because it's the most comprehensively realised Beatle testament; *Abbey Road* because it's their most dangerous adventure. It may be that the personal-cum-mythical statement they made in *Sgt. Pepper* couldn't, once made, be repeated; nor could they have strayed further down Abbey Road without surrendering their 'corporate identity', becoming a different kind of phenomenon. In effect, this is what happened; after *The end of Abbey Road* the Beatles pursued separate paths. This is true even though *Abbey Road* was not in fact the last 'corporate' disc the Beatles issued: for *Let it Be* is a deliberate reversal to earlier manners and to a considerable extent consists of earlier—sometimes very early—material. . . . It is . . . legitimate to relate the *White Album,* as an aftermath, to *Let it Be,* in that it is retrospective in the same sense, if on a larger scale, as were the companion songs *Baby, you're a rich man now* and *All you need is love.* It looks back, with remarkable richness of invention and variety of mood, on the Beatles' career; and submits almost all their own and other peoples' song-modes to the kind of serious parody at which [they were] adept. Though this doesn't necessarily lessen the commitment of individual songs, the consistency of the parodistic approach implies a rejection of the past: which perhaps was necessary before the *Magical Mystery Tour* could find its consummatory way into *Abbey Road.* (p. 125)

[The] Beatles' initiation was their discovery of their Liverpudlian corporate identity. As they grew up their Rubber Souls, armed with Revolvers, strayed into euphoric Penny Lane and hallucinatory Strawberry Fields; and attained a consummation which owes its power to the fact that their corporate identity allows for such complex nuances of personal stress and distress. Though Sgt. Pepper was pepperily militant in dragooning the circus band, the band itself played to a club of Lonely Hearts. That great record created a solidarity of the youthful whilst being at once pathetically and ironically aware of the solitariness of all hearts, young and old. The songs never proselytise, yet are genuinely a 'criticism of life'.

It was too much to expect that the delicate balance of *Sgt. Pepper* could be sustained. Yet the Beatles' third period, initiated on their *Magical Mystery Tour* and achieving fruition in *Abbey Road*, is a further stage in their evolution in that it accepts, unequivocally and unafraid, whatever darkness, as well as light, rebirth and regression may throw up. That is an astonishing achievement: especially if one thinks of the Beatles against the backcloth of the pop music industry in which they had been nurtured. Nor is it surprising that this precarious honesty was also impermanent. The beginning of disintegration was inherent in it; and although the Beatles threw retrospective glances back at their seemingly distant past . . . they were then obliged, if not content, to Let it be, and to go their separate ways. (p. 143)

[The Beatles'] achievement wouldn't be so heroic had they not suffered as scapegoats and sacrificial victims for us all. The Beatles' lives enacted out the rape of commerce and the electronic media upon us; whilst their music remained as true as truth's simplicity—with the understanding that today's simplicity cannot avoid manifold ironies and ambiguities.

In spite of the commercial stresses, in spite of the lapses into infantile narcissism and into pseudo-mystical twaddle, the Beatles—along with a few other flowers of pop—have occasionally reawakened our ritual sense; and we have to see this phenomenon in relationship to comparable developments in all the arts at all levels, remembering that the public for late Beatles and progressive pop overlaps with that for Stockhausen, Cage, Partch, Berio, even perhaps Tippett's ritual operas and Britten's 'parables for church performance'. That the Beatles, unlike the phenomena listed above, were a cult involving millions of young people is part of their importance: which is not to be diminished by a glib reference to the young's new economic viability. It is rather that such music youthfully demonstrates how man's life, in the words of Octavio Paz, is 'ceasing to be a spatial measurement and changing into a source, a spring, in the absolute present'. Pop has reasserted the spirit of fiesta which, whether secular or religious, allows us, momently released from Time, to 'emerge from our solitude and become one with creation': as were the 'mature' Beatles when they made the affirmation, however ambiguous, of *The end*; as had been the boy Beatles when they wonderingly piped 'I saw her standing there'; as were we ourselves when, as children, chanting 'wallflowers, wallflowers', we mythologised the act and fact of dying, even in the spring of the year. (p. 195)

> *Wilfrid Mellers, in his* Twilight of the Gods: The Music of the Beatles *(copyright © 1973 by Wilfrid Mellers; reprinted by permission of Viking Penguin, Inc.; in Canada by Faber and Faber Ltd),* Schirmer Books, 1973.

JON LANDAU

Band on the Run finds McCartney walking a middle ground between autobiographical songwriting and subtle attempts to mythologize his own experience through the creation of a fantasy world of adventure—perhaps remotely inspired by his having recently written "Live and Let Die." He does it by uniting the myth of the rock star and the outlaw, the original legendary figure on the run.

Up until now, the critical assumption has been that McCartney's lyrics mean little if anything, that he is a mere

stylist, playing games with words and sounds. And it is of course possible that the words to *Band on the Run* don't mean (or weren't intended to mean) as much as I think they do. But I'll take a chance, and say that *Band on the Run* is an album about the search for freedom and the flight from restrictions on his and Linda's personal happiness. It is about the pursuit of freedom from his past as a Beatle, freedom from the consequences of the drug busts that have kept him from the United States and forced him into thinking of himself as an outlaw. . . . It is also about two people becoming what they want to be, trying to decide what they want to do, and asking to be accepted for what they are now rather than what they were then.

If the listener were to ignore the music and the skill with which McCartney has developed his theme, the entire enterprise might seem banal. But he holds the record together through the continual intimation that he enjoys the search for freedom more than he might enjoy freedom itself. In the best tradition of outlaw mythology, he makes being on the run sound so damned exciting. . . .

A lesser talent would have taken the escape concept and perhaps woven a simple story around it. But, consistent with his own past, the songs overlap both in their content and sentiments (some are even reprised), the album forming a unit without ever becoming too schematic, literal, overbearing or overtly accessible.

On *Band on the Run*, there are two separate searches going on: McCartney's for himself and the listener's for McCartney. (p. 48)

The album's abrupt and surprising ending suggests that the McCartneys are afraid they may find what they are looking for only to discover that it, too, fails to satisfy them. Thus they end with only one commitment: to remain a band on the run. That decision has resulted in (with the possible exception of John Lennon's *Plastic Ono Band*) the finest record yet released by any of the four musicians who were once called the Beatles. (p. 50)

> *Jon Landau, "McCartney Takes a Stand," in* Rolling Stone *(by Straight Arrow Publishers, Inc. © 1974; all rights reserved; reprinted by permission), Issue 153, January 31, 1974, pp. 48, 50.*

BEN GERSON

Walls and Bridges shows John Lennon to be as mercurial as ever. I anticipated an unbearable suffering occasioned by the collapse of one of this century's most public love affairs —after all, Yoko Ono was presented as the membrane between agony and peace for Lennon, between illusion and reality. Yet the relative clearheadedness of this album suggests that she may have been only the most recent in a series of causes from which Lennon is extricating himself with customary agility. He seemed more pugnacious, more doctrinaire, more vulnerable when Yoko was supposedly supplying him with bliss than he is today.

For the first time since the formation of .the Beatles, Lennon is on his own and, remarkably, he seems to find that tolerable, though half the numbers on *Walls and Bridges* record his pangs of loss. (pp. 72, 74)

The insights are reformulations of the lessons of *Plastic Ono Band*, with this difference: On *POB* the tearing away of veils only revealed another face to Lennon's utopianism. Then (keeping in mind his crucial inconsistency in idealizing his relationship with Yoko) illusionlessness seemed the ultimate liberation. Today Lennon knows that neither dreams nor their puncturing is the answer. There is no neat answer. When one accepts one's childhood, one's parenthood and the impermanence of what lies between, one can begin to slog along. When John slogs, he makes progress. (pp. 74, 76)

Ben Gerson, "Lennon: Together Again," in Rolling Stone (by Straight Arrow Publishers, Inc. © 1974; all rights reserved; reprinted by permission), Issue 174, November 21, 1974, pp. 72, 74, 76.

JEFF GREENFIELD

When the Beatles broke up in 1970 in a welter of lawsuits and recriminations, the sixties were ending as well—in spirit as well as by the calendar. Bloodshed and bombings on campus, the harsh realities beneath the facile hopes for a "Woodstock nation," the shabby refuse of counterculture communities, all helped kill the dream.

What remains remarkable now, almost 20 years after John Lennon started playing rock 'n' roll music, more than a decade after their first worldwide conquest, is how appealing this dream was; how its vision of the world gripped so much of a generation; how that dream reshaped our recent past and affects us still. . . .

[The] impact of the Beatles cannot be waved away. If the Marx they emulated was Groucho, not Karl, if their world was a playground instead of a battleground, they still changed what we listened to and how we listened to it; they helped make rock music a battering ram for the youth culture's assault on the mainstream, and that assault in turn changed our culture permanently. And if the "dream" the Beatles helped create could not sustain itself in the real world, that speaks more to our false hopes than to their promises. They wrote and sang songs. We turned it into politics and philosophy and a road map to another way of life. (p. 12)

By coming into prominence early in 1964, the Beatles probably saved rock 'n' roll from extinction. Rock in the early nineteen-sixties existed in name only; apart from the soul artists, it was a time of "shlock rock," with talentless media hypes like Fabian and Frankie Avalon riding the crest of the American Bandstand wave. By contrast, the Beatles provided a sense of musical energy that made successful a brilliant public-relations effort. . . .

The Beatles . . . had more than hype; they had talent. Even their first hits, "I Want to Hold Your Hand," "She Loves You," "Please Please Me," "I Saw Her Standing There," had a hint of harmonies and melodies more inventive than standard rock tunes. More important, it became immediately clear that the Beatles were hipper, more complicated, than the bovine rock stars who could not seem to put four coherent words together. . . .

[The] real surprise came at the end of 1965, with the release of the "Rubber Soul" album. Starting with that album, and continuing through "Revolver" and "Sgt. Pepper's Lonely Hearts Club Band," the Beatles began to throw away the rigid conventions of rock 'n' roll music and lyrics. . . . The Beatles were drawing on their memories and feelings, not those cut from Tin Pan Alley cloth. (p. 37)

With the release of "Sgt. Pepper" in the spring of 1967, the era of rock as a strictly adolescent phenomenon was gone. One song, "A Day in the Life," with its recital of an ordinary day combined with a dreamlike sense of dread and anxiety, made it impossible to ignore the skills of Lennon and McCartney. . . .

By using their fame to help break through the boundaries of rock, the Beatles proved that they were not the puppets of backstage manipulation or payola or hysterical 14-year-olds. Instead, they helped make rock music the music of an entire international generation. Perhaps for the first time in history, it was possible to say that tens of millions of people, defined simply by age, were all doing the same thing: they were listening to rock 'n' roll. That fact changed the popular culture of the world. . . .

The teen-agers of the nineteen-fifties had become the young adults of the nineteen-sixties, entering the professions, bringing with them a cultural frame of reference shaped in good measure by rock 'n' roll. The "youth" market was enormous—the flood of babies born during and just after World War II made the under-25 population group abnormally large; their tastes were more influential than ever before. And because the music had won acceptability, rock 'n' roll was not judged indulgently as a "boys will be boys" fad. Rock music was expressing a sensibility about the tangible world—about sensuality, about colors and sensations, about the need to change consciousness. And this sensibility soon spilled over into other arenas. (p. 40)

The real political impact of the Beatles was not in any four-point program or in an attack on injustice or the war in Vietnam. It was instead in the counterculture they had helped to create. Somewhere in the nineteen-sixties, millions of people began to regard themselves as a class separate from mainstream society *by virtue of their youth and the sensibility that youth produced.* (p. 42)

The politicization of youth as a class helped to divide natural political allies and make politics more vulnerable to demagogues. As the Beatles found in their own personal and professional lives, the practical outside world has a merciless habit of intruding into fantasies; somebody has to pay the bills and somebody has to do the dishes in the commune and somebody has to protect us from the worst instincts of other human beings. John Lennon was expressing some very painful lessons when he told "Rolling Stone" shortly after the group's breakup that "nothing happened except we all dressed up . . . the same bastards are in control, the same people are runnin' everything." (p. 43)

For me, the final irony is that the Beatles themselves have unconsciously proven the value of communality. As a group, they seemed to hold each other back from excess: McCartney was lyrical, but not saccharine; Lennon was rebellious but not offensive; Harrison's mysticism was disciplined (Ringo was always Ringo, drummer and friend). Now, the sense of control seems to have loosened. Paul and Linda McCartney seem tempted by the chance to become the Steve and Eydie of rock; Lennon is still struggling to free himself from a Fad of the Month mentality; George Harrison's Gospel According to Krishna succeeded in boring much of his audience. . . . Perhaps the idea they did so much to spread several years ago is not as dead as all that; perhaps we all need a little help from our friends. The enduring power of that idea is as permanent as any impact their music had on us, even if they no longer believe it. (p. 46)

Jeff Greenfield, "They Changed Rock, Which Changed the Culture, Which Changed Us," in The New York Times Magazine *(© 1975 by The New York Times Company; reprinted by permission), February 16, 1975, pp. 12, 37, 42-3, 46.*

PAUL NELSON

As time goes by, John Lennon's importance to the Beatles becomes more and more self-evident. The same old story we've been hearing for years—that Lennon's wit and abrasive probing were needed to balance Paul McCartney's melodic charm and sweetness—is obvious but true. . . .

Lennon probably had nothing whatsoever to do with *Venus and Mars,* the new Wings album, but somehow the ghost of his sincerity not only haunts but also accentuates the cool calculation of the McCartney project, and a jarring primal scream or two might make me feel less enraged by Paul and Linda's chic, unconvincing and blatant bid to be enshrined as pop music's Romeo and Juliet. One can point out that John and Yoko were no better, perhaps even worse, in their similar public insistence—or Bob Dylan on *Planet Waves,* for that matter—but what makes such a comparison appalling is that John and Yoko and Dylan believed what they were saying, or at least desperately tried to, while the McCartneys serve it all up with the offhand air of two uncaring jet-setters presenting us with the very latest in prefabricated TV dinners.

Venus and Mars begins with Paul and Linda's casual and false assumption that the whole world is tremendously interested in the state of their union (whereas John and Yoko and Dylan were driven, I think, more by individual inner needs to say what they did), so they concoct a slick, Broadway/Hollywood exterior romance that is an insult to the very "lovers everywhere" to whom they dedicate the L.P. For all I know, the McCartneys may love each other passionately, but it is self-aggrandizement, not private ardor, that shines through the computerized smoothness of their insubstantial songs; no blood on the tracks here, and no connection with reality either. Perhaps this is too harsh; perhaps Paul and Linda's image of themselves as rock & roll's mythical couple is real in their minds but, as this album proves, an extended trip across that arid area is apt to make even the night thoughts of Johnny Carson appear positively Dostoevskian. (p. 52)

Paul Nelson, "'Venus & Mars': Wings' Nonstellar Flight," in Rolling Stone *(by Straight Arrow Publishers, Inc. © 1975; all rights reserved; reprinted by permission), Issue 192, July 31, 1975, pp. 52, 55.*

ROY CARR and TONY TYLER

[The initial meeting between John and Paul] in the late 'fifties led to events that shook the world.

This is no exaggeration. How many of us can look around and deny that the Beatles at least *seemed* to initiate many of those changes in our social attitudes and tastes that took place in the 'sixties and which still reverberate today? Possibly it was just the group's good luck to be so closely identified with these mass changes in consciousness. Yet many who still view the whole Beatle Phenomenon through wistfully pink-lensed spectacles will *always* secretly be convinced that the Beatles were behind the whole thing from the start. (p. 5)

With the release of [the] superb and historic single ['I Want to Hold Your Hand'], the Beatles proved themselves masters of the difficult art of writing original, memorable and commercial pop singles. The musical structure of 'I Want To Hold Your Hand' is full of subtle tricks and adventurous ploys that reveal a rapidly growing maturity in their work. From the deliberate stumble of the opening time-signature to the calculated dissonances of the chorus, the whole conception of this song was unlike anything attempted before—and owed little or nothing to their well-publicised tap-root American influences.

America, until now a sealed market for British rock acts . . ., sagged to its alpaca knees in awe. Thus is history made. (p. 21)

['With the Beatles' (British title)] is the only LP from the primitive early 'sixties that, well over ten years later, still retains all the freshness and breadth of musical vision that was instantly apparent on the day of issue. It was a simply staggering achievement from every point of view, a landmark *par excellence,* and one of the four best albums the Beatles ever made. (p. 22)

[The] almost flawless album ['Revolver'] can be seen as the peak of the Beatles' creative career. They were later to undertake more ambitious projects which would be crowned with equal critical acclaim, but 'Revolver' is the kind of achievement which any artist would be more than satisfied to regard as some kind of culmination to his career. No less than that. (p. 54)

The overall effect of 'Revolver' is majestic. A subjective opinion: the Beatles were never to surpass the standard of writing and playing which can be found on almost every track. (p. 58)

'Sgt. Pepper' is surely the Beatles' greatest technical achievement and if hindsight reveals many of the contrivances, they weren't in any way apparent in June 1967, high-water-mark of the psychedelic era. (p. 64)

[The] 'White Album'—as it became rapidly known—also indicated the passing of the Beatles *as a group* and the termination of any real desire to feed ideas into a communal pool. On this double LP, *they each act as each others' session men;* didacticism is rampant and it is more of a selection of solo tracks that we hear.

'The White Album' is an odd, patchy collection: informed critics opine that there is enough material here to make one really good single album. Certainly many of the tracks are dispensable, but the best are easily as good as anything they'd done. . . .

McCartney's material reveals the eclecticism which had always dogged him—but this time to creditable effect. From the Beach Boys/Chuck Berry-styled opener 'Back In the USSR' (one of the best Beatle rockers ever written) to the whimsy of 'Martha My Dear' and the curious but extremely beautiful 'Blackbird' (held by many to be a sympathetic gesture towards the then-emergent Black Power movement), he hardly ever falters on this album, except on those tracks which are obvious inclusions for the sake of filling the enormous recording commitment necessitated by any double LP. His rooty-toot persona whisks past in the form of 'Rocky Raccoon' (a Mack Sennett movie set to music) and 'Honey Pie', a speakeasy special with charming flapper overtones. And nobody but McCartney could get away with the closing track, 'Goodnight'. . . .

On the other hand, Lennon's unhappiness and resurgent iconoclasm come through powerfully. Swinging wildly (but sometimes accurately) at almost everything in sight, he scores telling hits on the Hippie Heaven of '67 ('Glass Onion'), a white hunter he'd met in Africa ('Bungalow Bill'), America's National Rifle Association ('Happiness Is a Warm Gun'), the British Blues Boom ('Yer Blues'), the Maharishi ('Sexy Sadie') and activists everywhere ('Revolution 1'). He attacks his own background even more strongly on 'Julia', a wistful blueprint for his later primal-scream recorded histrionics. Lennon's best song on the album is the magnificent 'I'm So Tired', almost a direct continuation of the dream-sequence commenced with 'I'm Only Sleeping' on the 'Revolver' LP. The voice control and dynamics displayed on the later bars of each verse are quite astounding and reveal him as by far the most gifted vocalist in the group. (p. 74)

The brilliance was certainly there but the Beatle Dream was almost over and, try as they might, they couldn't prevent an uncomfortable amount of the sordid world outside from creeping in.

They were no longer invulnerable. (p. 75)

'Abbey Road' is the last real album the Beatles ever made; and it was certainly the last time all four were co-operating together in the studio.

It was actually recorded *after* 'Let It Be'—but continuing problems with the latter delayed editing, then programming, and finally re-mixing; meanwhile, the issue of 'Abbey Road' took place. (p. 80)

Prominent on the first side, McCartney practically carries the second side by himself—and this particular series of tracks still stands as one of the Beatles' supreme recorded achievements. . . .

'Abbey Road' is certainly not unlike 'Pepper'. Both albums have the same glossy finish, noticeably lacking on all subsequent product apart from one or two singles. Both *appear* to follow a concept, though neither do in actuality and, in each case, the high standard of the master tape was arrived at by careful selection and juxtaposition, with effects added afterwards in the studio.

Lennon is strangely subdued once again, surfacing as a prominent vocalist only three times on 'Abbey Road' but with his unmistakable voice prominent on many of the backing layers. 'Come Together', the first song on the album, is his—and is one of the best of the set. Lennon's sardonic voice urges, through a barrage of free association, the exaltation of the simultaneous orgasm. . . .

McCartney himself appears . . . with the rascally 'Maxwell's Silver Hammer', an effortless little tune about a psychotic medical student. McCartney's all-purpose children's TV-style voice makes Maxwell's homicidal progress sound almost banally normal. 'Oh! Darling' (the next track) is McCartney again, aping a Paul Anka two-straws-in-one-malted doo-wop lament. This slight sag in the texture and tension of 'Abbey Road' is given a further weight to contend with in the form of 'Octopus's Garden', a remake of

'Yellow Submarine' with further subnautical noises and little else to commend it.

'I Want You—She's So Heavy' signals Lennon's return; it's a tortuous two-part piece which starts off like an agonised version of Mel Torme's 'Comin' Home Baby' and fades out amid the retreating footsteps of the Grim Reaper, as evoked by several instruments playing the same ominous riff in uncompromising unison. (p. 82)

A slower essay at the same craft, which displays, in parts, some really fine close harmonies, is the Hawaiian-sounding 'Because'. This segues sharply into the piano opening for McCartney's 'You Never Give Me Your Money' '*You only give me your funny paper*', he mourns as the piece builds and further vocal harmonies are layered on top. Graceful and very delicate, it drops abruptly into a boogie centre which leads away from the main theme into 'Sun King', which in turn immediately recalls 'Because' with its rich layers of harmony (and nonsense Spanish).

At this point McCartney leaps to the fore. With one exception, all the remaining tracks on Side Two are his. The sequence in which they are welded produces some of the most accomplished—and surprising—music in Beatle repertoire. 'Mean Mr Mustard'—who, if not a psychopath, is certainly extremely unsavoury—is once again passed off as a whimsical character, a sort of Elder Steptoe. Following very closely is Lennon's final track, 'Polythene Pam', his contribution to that gallery of weirdos who have detailed portraits in 'Abbey Road'. The closing three chords patter along for a while until they usher in McCartney's 'She Came In Through the Bathroom Window'. The 'significance of the symbolism'—'*She came in through the bathroom window / protected by a silver spoon*'—was another nail in McCartney's supposed coffin, but he survived long enough to reprise 'You Never Give Me Your Money' as 'Golden Slumbers'; a beautiful coda. 'The End', acts as a final decorative touch to the album (and particularly to his own final closing suite). Luckily, he had the necessary irreverence to puncture the effect thus created by adding a postscript. 'Her Majesty' lasts precisely twenty seconds.

The overall effect of 'Abbey Road'—especially when seen in its true scheduled context—is one of superb mockery, especially directed at the proliferating numbers of Beatleologists who were busily dissecting all Beatle LPs back to 'Rubber Soul' in a frantic search for Revelation. The music is some of the most polished and most memorable the group ever produced. . . . The album dissatisfies because it is not perhaps their most honest record—but Beatle honesty veered perilously close to masochism on occasion and 'Abbey Roads' slickness is also its salvation. (pp. 82-3)

['Let It Be'] is characteristic for the abandonment of the overdubbing and purely studio effects which had been notable on every LP since 'Rubber Soul'. It is a starkly simple record (as was intended for proper *verité*) except in one or two curious places. Accordingly, the quality suffers, though the authenticity of what comes across is held, in some quarters, to be of greater interest. . . . (p. 90)

[John Lennon / Plastic Ono Band' is a] majestic album and, with Paul McCartney's 'Band On the Run' . . . , one of the two best-ever Beatle solo LPs.

Lennon's solo work had, until now, taken the form of collaborations with wife Yoko which reflected more of her influences than of his. But two years in the wilderness had produced a strong undercurrent of feeling in Lennon which could not be satisfied by lying on art-gallery floors inside large paper bags. His own splintered childhood and his recent discovery of primal scream therapy techniques encouraged him to use the LP medium as confessional, thereby laying some of the ghosts which had haunted him since early adolescence. The result is a remarkable and often moving album, almost brutally honest, and which, though obsessed with personal pain, was a complete artistic statement of great courage and typical candour.

Indeed, so many and so horrendous were the chances taken by Lennon on this LP that, with any lesser talent, the result could have been disastrous. In the word of a review of the time, he placed his balls defiantly on the line; out of sheer respect, the train ground to a halt.

A quick scan of the track titles reveals much of the subject matter: his rejection by the community as an adolescent; his rejection by the world (and his fellow-Beatles) in recent months; his loss of his mother in childhood—nothing is spared the listener, and the fact that such harrowing material succeeds artistically without falling into the trap of sentiment is entirely due to Lennon's natural feeling for economy and sparseness which preclude all forms of conventional musical sentimentality.

Dry-eyed, he sings of his mother, Julia ('Mother', 'My Mummy's Dead'); of painful growing-up and equally painful later rejection ('Working Class Hero'); of sham idolatry as personally experienced ('I Found Out', 'Isolation', 'God')—and, occasionally, of discovery and hope for the future ('Hold On John', 'Love', 'Look At Me'). . . .

This period of Lennon's creativity has recently been harshly parodied—probably because of the excess of agony to be found in the songs. All the same, it was the most worthwhile Beatle LP since 'Abbey Road' and was not to be equalled by any other until late 1973. (p. 93)

'Imagine' . . . still stands as a classic of its kind and the most positive recorded statement Lennon has yet managed to make without the collaboration of Paul McCartney—though certain aspects of its premise have undergone some reassessment.

Pain, the stock-in-trade of the archetypal singer / song writer—and featured in pallid technicolour by Lennon himself on his earlier album—found itself subtly muted in favour of melody, polish, and a surprising sense of optimism. This was his White Period. He wore white, played a white piano, laundered his thoughts to breath-taking freshness (with one curious exception) and breathed white fumes in the white room of his white house at Ascot.

Because of the blanched nature of the publicity surrounding 'Imagine', the album itself seems full of colour. Lennon runs a full gamut of emotions, from 1970 agony to 1971 ecstasy with a sideswipe at arch-litigant Paul McCartney thrown in for good measure and malicious intent. 'How Do You Sleep?' is the most extraordinary song on the entire album. It is a vitriolic open letter, full of nasty insinuations and contemptuous insults. . . .

All the more surprising then, that the majority of the remaining nine tracks display a gentleness and sensitivity far removed from the crude personal level of 'How Do You Sleep'. In fact, Lennon's rediscovery of melody—and it is

nearly *all* melodic music that we encounter on this album—is gratifying in view of his almost total abandonment of this quality, both before and since. But for 'How Do You Sleep?' one would almost declare 'Imagine' a loving album. Perhaps the most lyrical tracks are 'Jealous Guy' and the title track itself. 'Oh My Love' and 'Oh Yoko!' are also tender little tunes. There is some of the 'Plastic Ono Band' period self-flagellation ('Crippled Inside', 'I Don't Want To Be a Soldier' and 'Give Me Some Truth') and, of course, the unique 'How Do You Sleep?'. (p. 97)

If Paul McCartney had been . . . in the wilderness for the previous three years, ['Band On the Run'] certainly re-instated him in the public eye and in the eyes of the numerous critics who had long previously dismissed his talent as 'lightweight' and 'overstylised'. . . .

It reveals McCartney, not unnaturally, producing what McCartney produces best: disciplined arrangements; a strong sense of melody allied to a natural feel for exotic rhythms, the whole thing coupled to a resurgence of self-confidence. He also avoids the use of Beatle stylistic devices: devices are certainly present, but they are McCartney's personal property, and on 'Band On the Run' he uses them in a perfectly satisfactory manner.

Humour is also present: in (long-delayed) answer to Lennon's cruel 'How Do You Sleep' ('Imagine' LP), Paul fights back—gently—with a beautiful and totally sympathetic impersonation of Lennon's own idiosyncratic vocal/production style, 'Let Me Roll It' (complete with Arthur Janov-style primal whimper at the close). The understatement of this track contrasts with Lennon's misplaced viciousness to a marked degree.

Though 'Let Me Roll It' is the track which attracted most attention, many others stand out. 'Jet', which shortly afterwards became a single, is a thundering piece, featuring obscure lyrics and McCartney's own matchless bass; he also plays Moog synthesiser with more taste than most other exponents of this Frankensteinian instrument. His lightweight touch (which has only proved successful when allied to his natural ebullience) works superbly on 'Bluebird' (which recalls 'Blackbird' from 'The White Album') and on 'Mrs Vandebilt'—where Paul asks *'What's the use of worrying?'. 'No use'* he answers himself, and, of course, he's dead right. In fact, it's the self-confidence of this album—especially after his many years in disfavour—which is so refreshing. (p. 110)

> *Roy Carr and Tony Tyler, in their* The Beatles: An Illustrated Record *(copyright © 1975 by Trewin Copplestone Publishing Ltd.), Harmony Books, 1975.*

LESTER BANGS

What has McCartney got that makes people of all ages the world over respond, that makes the media sit up and bark soon as he strolls across the pond, that makes his comeback solo tour a notary-certifiable Event in a day when rock tours are dubbed Events every time you turn around? His albums are, by and large, some of the blandest discs ever piped into a waiting room, and even his hit singles are so eminently forgettable that the titles evade recall without research. The man obviously proved he had a gift for melody in the Beatles, but his lyrics are so dopey they end up making fun of themselves, and on top of all that he insists on trundling his musically illiterate photographer wife with him everywhere, insistently, both on stage and records. (pp. 36-7)

Like the King Family, the McCartneys in their celebration of suburban conjugal joys and hyping of their children are involved in a presentation of nuclear normalcy, a model for the present and future (as *they* see it) based on the conventions of the past. Just like Paul's music, in which *Sgt. Pepper* could draw rock from music hall and be hailed as an avant-garde masterpiece. To be sure, Paul and Linda are marketing themselves, but they are also marketing a *lifestyle*. What lifestyle? *Father Knows Best.* But unlike *Father Knows Best*, which was smug, there is a certain desperation underlying their presentation. They protest too much, and in their very bland rectitude there is a certain wild yearning after their idea of an ordered world. Which is, of course, very British and very middle class. (p. 39)

Much of the result is nursery school music (but there are rules in nursery school, of course, and Paul is a Do-Be), in line with *Ram*'s cover design by Paul which looks like the wall of a child's room. Does he write these ninny-tunes as home cartoons and lullabies for his children? And if so, what does this say about the kind of artist who would devote his public output to such a scheme? From fairy tales with storybook characters ("Band on the Run," jailer man and Sailor Sam) to comic-strips ("Magneto & Titanium Man"), lines like "when I leave my pajamas to Billy Budapest" ("Monkberry Moon Delight") and "Man, I could smell your feet a mile away"—only a child could laugh wholeheartedly at that. Perhaps McCartney has really tapped the vast market available to the musical equivalent of *Benji, The Computer Wore Tennis Shoes, Willy Wonka & the Chocolate Factory;* traditional bubblegum music seems to be a played-out form anyway, and half these songs would be perfect *Sesame Street* fodder. They're cute, with a childish humor that's slightly out of kilter.

Of course, I realize that it is as silly as a McCartney song to analyze his lyrics in any kind of serious detail. The success of any given McCartney song depends not at all upon the lyrics, but on the hook, melody and how much conviction he can infuse into the subverbal core of his sonic truffles. That is, the songs, however fatuous, project an attitude, but that attitude is not to be taken seriously. Because it is irrelevant. As irrelevant as a Slinky. (pp. 39, 71)

McCartney is sterile. Sterility is both the selling point and insurance of ultimate obsolescence for McCartney albums. They're like electronic massages, from which you come away soothed but neither satiated nor fortified. It's this sterility which is fortunately missing from Wings' live presentation. Paul's cleanness and natural sense of showbiz simply makes the energy of his performance breezily expansive. Unfortunately, this amiably mild kick is delivered in Dachau franchises, to bedraggled and benumbed animals. Most don't notice the clash—they've got long hair at the Madison Square—but it renders McCartney's real accomplishment (the translation of his boutique ditties into a rousing party) ultimately meaningless. Kind of like bringing *A Chorus Line* to Folsom Prison. (p. 71)

Paul McCartney, of course, is the antithesis of all the danger that rock 'n' roll used to stand for. People like McCartney because he epitomizes safety—a nice safe boy, safe music, safe marriage, safe kids, safe tours, safe money. Listen to his description of a rock concert in "Venus &

Mars / Rock Show," even the way he sings it, and you know how cutely, albeit affectionately, distanced he is from the tumult and the stoned, stunned ennui.... The man simply seems incapable of a gesture that is not arch. He's a plasticene porter, and for all his coyness lacks the obscene smugness of Elton John. But for all he sings of love, you don't sense much coming out of his music. It's more like a Mattel toy—shiny, synthetic but durable, break-resistant. (p. 73)

Lester Bangs, "Paul and Linda McCartney: Bionic Couple Serves It Your Way," in Creem (© copyright 1976 by Creem Magazine, Inc.) August, 1976, pp. 36-9, 71-3.

R. MELTZER

First and foremost, Paul is still for all intents and purposes a Beatle—which *automatically* makes him *preferable* to Hubert Humphrey or Judy Garland under just about any grid of analysis you'd be likely to name. Second, the great Willie Nelson became the first country singer per se to cut a Beatle song and the one he chose back in '66 or so was of all things "Yesterday," proof that some people besides boobs and assflames actually dig that 4th-rate garbage of his. Third, well I dunno ... y'gotta admit the reviews're still basically mixed ... 30 years from now when he's the Maurice Chevalier of his generation and he's on the Johnny Carson Show talkin' about how swell it's been, *then* is when we'll be able to judge whether close to a lifetime of puke has been justified in any sense of the word. (p. 98)

R. Meltzer, "McCartney Vs. Meltzer: Discography," in McCartney: Beatle on Wings (copyright © 1976 by Countrywide Publications, Inc.), Countrywide Publications, 1976, pp. 80-98.

GREIL MARCUS

[The music on *Meet the Beatles*] was instantly recognizable and like nothing we had ever heard. It was joyous, threatening, absurd, arrogant, determined, innocent and tough....

It was only in the context of the Beatles event that their music was perceived for what it was.

The event was a pop explosion; the second, and thus far the last, that rock and roll has produced. (p. 175)

[At] its heart, a pop explosion attaches the individual to a group—the fan to an audience, the solitary to a generation—in essence, *forms* a group and creates new loyalties—while at the same time it increases one's ability to respond to a particular pop artifact, or a thousand of them, with an intensity that verges on lunacy. Ringo's shout of "All right, George!" just before the guitar in "Boys" becomes a matter of indefinable and indefensible significance; styles on Carnaby Street outdo the pace of the pop charts and change literally by the hour. Yet within it all is some principle of shape, of continuity, of value.

This principle was the Beatles. As was so often pointed out in the mid-Sixties, the sum of the Beatles was greater than the parts, but the parts were so distinctive and attractive that the group itself could be all things to all people, more or less; you did not have to love them all to love the group, but you could not love one without loving the group, and this was why the Beatles became bigger than Elvis; this was what had never happened before. And so it began. The past was felt to dissolve, the future was conceivable only as an expansion of the present, and the present was defined absolutely by its expansive novelty. Towering above Bob Dylan, the Rolling Stones, a score of British groups, American groups, Mary Quant, the Who, whatever and whoever sprung up day by day, the Beatles seemed not only to symbolize but to contain it all—to make history by anticipating it.

The first pop explosion, beginning in 1955 and 1956, began to yield to normalcy by about 1957. The Beatles event, beyond all expectations save perhaps their own, intensified not only in momentum but in magnetism, reaching more and more people with greater and greater mythic and emotional power, for at least four years. The Beatles affected not only the feel but the quality of life—they deepened it, sharpened it, brightened it, not merely as a factor in the cultural scheme, but as a presence. The Beatles affected not only the quality of life—they affected its worth.

Their event reached its height, and in many ways its effective end, with the release of *Sgt. Pepper* on June 2nd, 1967. (pp. 175-76)

Almost immediately, *Sgt. Pepper* was certified as proof that the Beatles' music—or at least this album—was Art. But what mattered was the conscious creation of event—the way in which the summing-up-the-spirit-of-the-times style of the music (which for the most part has not survived its time) was perfectly congruent with the organizing-the-spirit-of-the-times manner in which the album was released and received. Which is to say that *Sgt. Pepper,* as the most brilliantly orchestrated manipulation of a cultural audience in pop history, was nothing less than a small pop explosion in and of itself. The music was not great art; the event, in its intensification of the ability to respond, was. . . .

[It] seemed as if the world really did turn around the Beatles, even if the truth was that this music, as opposed to this event, represented that point at which the Beatles began to be formed more by the times than the other way around. In the next few months Brian Epstein would die, and the Beatles, who had unified the young, would themselves begin to fragment—anticipating, as usual, the fragmentation that in years to come would separate the audience they had created. Still, if *Sgt. Pepper* was an ending, it was an ending that has never been matched. It was perhaps in the nature of the game that it would be all downhill from there. (p. 176)

Since the Beatles disbanded a virtual consensus among rock critics has emerged to argue that the music of the Beatles, enjoyable as it may have been, stands now as distinctly inferior to that of the Stones, Dylan, or even the Byrds or the Beach Boys; the Beatles are conventionally portrayed as imitative, lightweights, yea-sayers, softies, ordinary musicians, vaguely unhip, unimaginative lyrically, and, above all, ''clever''—that is, merely clever. You know—the Beatles just wanted to hold your hand, while the Stones wanted to pillage your town. Etc.

There is some truth to this argument. . . . The Stones wrote from an insistently sexual and aggressive blues tradition; the Beatles worked mostly in the more polite and circumscribed milieu of pop, as defined not only by rock tunesmiths Carole King and Gerry Goffin but by the earlier professional romanticists of Tin Pan Alley. The Beatles' optimism prevailed even when they tried to sound desperate (''Help!''), which sometimes made them sound sappy; the Stones' sullenness prevailed even when they affected optimism (''We Love You''), which usually made them sound all the more attractive.

Which only proves, I think, that comparisons of the Beatles and the Stones (or Dylan or Elvis or any other true titan of rock) are pointless. I cannot make an argument that the Beatles were better at being the Stones than the Stones were (though I can point out that it was the Beatles who opened up the turf the Stones took as their own—there was no possibility of a Left until the Beatles created the Center). The argument that seems to emerge from a close listening to the Beatles' music, on the other hand, is this one: by 1962 the Beatles' mastery of rock and roll was such that it was inevitable they would change the form simply by addressing themselves to it. Unlike the Stones or Dylan, the Beatles came *through* rock; as they went on, extending (if not deepening) their mastery, they defined rock, to the degree that it made sense to speak of ''Yesterday,'' a ballad accompanied only by acoustic guitar and strings, as ''rock and roll,'' simply because the disc was credited to the Beatles. And unlike Dylan, and possibly the Stones, at least until 1966, the Beatles had no fall-back position. They were rock and roll or they were nothing. As such, they were, at their best, the best. (pp. 176, 178)

[The] form of the Beatles contained the forms of rock and roll itself. The Beatles combined the harmonic range and implicit equality of the Fifties vocal group (the Dell-Vikings, say) with the flash of a rockabilly band (the Crickets or Gene Vincent's Blue Caps) with the aggressive and unique personalities of the classic rock stars (Elvis, Little Richard) with the homey this-could-be-you manner of later rock stars (Everly Brothers, Holly, Eddie Cochran) with the endlessly inventive songwriting touch of the Brill Building, and delivered it all with the grace of the Miracles, the physicality of ''Louie Louie,'' and the absurd enthusiasm of Gary ''U.S.'' Bonds. Three of the Beatles wrote, all sang lead, and they played their own music; in sum, they communicated (and generically insisted upon) absolute involvement (it was only after the Beatles that ''rock groups'' had to make their own records and write their own songs). Rock, which in the course of the Fifties had changed from a personal inspiration and affirmation to a process that allowed the most marginal of commitments, became, in the shape of the Beatles, a way of life. . . .

Accompanying the shock of novelty so many experienced on first exposure to the Beatles in 1963 or '64 was a shock of recognition, which bespoke the Beatles' connection to the whole history of rock and roll up to that time: the Beatles had absorbed that history because—year by year, playing and listening and writing, in Liverpool and on the bottoms of British tours and in Hamburg—they had, albeit invisibly, made it.

No one else could touch *this* sort of mastery, and the result was that elusive rock treasure, *a new sound*—and a new sound that could not be exhausted in the course of one brief flurry on the charts. . . .

The beat, first of all, was not big, it was enormous. The entire performance orchestrated it, was built around it (listen to ''There's a Place''). At the same time, there was a lightness to almost every tune, a floating quality, a kind of lyrical attack that shaped but did not lessen the rhythmic power of the numbers. This quality, which can be heard in its most spectacular form in the segues in and out of the middle eight, was perhaps the most important thing John and Paul learned from Goffin-King (and from Ellie Greenwich, Jeff Barry and Phil Spector); it was written right into the compositions, and put across through head arrangements and in the use of rock group dynamics so fluid and intelligent that for years they made nearly everything else on the radio sound faintly stupid (listen to "Every Little Thing," "Anytime at All," "What You're Doing"). (p. 178)

But more than anything else it was the singing that made these records what they were. John and Paul's vocals—and the four Beatles' unpredictable screams, yeah-yeah-yeahs, and head-to-head oooos—communicated urgency first and foremost. Regardless of lyrics, the singers made demands, reached, got, went after more, blew away all that stood before them. They were exhilarated, exuberant, joyous; but all that joy was rooted in determination, as if those nihilistic nights in Hamburg had not just added an edge to the Beatles' music but had lighted a fire in their hearts. In 1964, the freshness of the Beatles' vocal assault was the sound of pure novelty; today, one hears a lovely, naked emotion in those early vocals, a refusal to kid around, to cut the corners of feeling, and a will to say it all, that was not to be heard in rock and roll from any other white performer until Bob Dylan released "Like a Rolling Stone" in the summer of 1965. This spirit surfaced in more obvious form later—consciously and with great craftsmanship, in "Strawberry Fields Forever," "I Am the Walrus," "Yer Blues" and "I'm So Tired"—but it was there from the beginning. In a sense it was the beginning. (pp. 178-79)

Mixing the lyricism of "There's a Place" and the force of "Money," the Beatles' mastery of rock in their first two years of recording was absolute. Without really testing the limits of the form as they had worked it out in the early Sixties, they continued to prove that mastery through 1965, with "Ticket to Ride," the brilliant "Help!," its little-known flip side, "I'm Down" (an astonishing piece of hard rock with a crazed Little Richard vocal from Paul), and "Day Tripper." Still, given Dylan, the Stones, and the Byrds, there was no question that other rockers were testing the Beatles' limits, even if they were not, and so at the end of 1965 the Beatles turned around and dumped *Rubber Soul* on the market.

Though it can be argued that the Beatles' first four LPs, in their British configurations (*Please Please Me, With the Beatles, A Hard Day's Night* and *Beatles for Sale*) were as good as *Rubber Soul*, it may not be worth the trouble. *Rubber Soul* was an album *made* as an album; with the exception of "Michelle" (which, to be fair, paid the bills for years to come), every cut was an inspiration, something new and remarkable in and of itself.

In terms of lyrics, the Beatles were still writing about love, but this was a new kind of love: contingent, scary, and vital in a way that countenanced ambiguities and doubts earlier songs had skimmed right over. "In My Life" was as moving and precise a song about friendship as rock has produced; "Girl," though deceptively straightforward, was a good deal more sophisticated than Dylan's "Just like a Woman."

If the emotional touch was harder, the musical touch was lighter. This music was seduction, not assault; the force was all beneath the surface. . . . (p. 179)

It was the Beatles' most attractive album, perhaps their glossiest, and at the same time their most deeply satisfying. To this listener, it was unquestionably their best.

From this point on the story is not so clear. What was clear, though, what was clear in retrospect even on *Rubber Soul,* was that John and Paul were no longer the songwriting team they had once been. Consistently, John's songs described struggle, while Paul's denied it; Paul wrote and sang the A sides, John the Bs. Mapping out the directions that have governed their careers since the Beatles disbanded, John was already cultivating his rebellion and his anger; Paul was making his Decision for Pop; George was making his Decision for Krishna; and Ringo was having his house painted. All of the Beatles were attaching themselves to the fads and passions of the time, to drugs, transcendence, coats of many colors, the paraphernalia of psychedelia. And as the Beatles became one with the times, merging with them rather than standing above them, they became, musically and in every other way, harder to see truly. The wholeness of the group, the music, and the very idea of the Beatles began to break up, even as "The Beatles," as cultural icons, media personalities, and phenomena, became more exciting than ever. Thus at the time it was obvious that *Revolver,* released in 1966, was better than *Rubber Soul,* just as it was obvious *Sgt. Pepper* was better than both put together. The times carried the imperative of such a choice—though it was not really a choice at all, but rather a sort of faceless necessity. The only road, after all, was onward.

Such a choice does not seem so obvious now, and of course the necessity has faded. *Revolver* retains the flash its title promised, but little of the soul its predecessor delivered. Compared to either, *Sgt. Pepper* appears playful but contrived, less a summing up of its era than a concession to it.

In the final two and a half years of Beatle groupdom, the four remained charming with "All You Need Is Love"; took a fall with *Magical Mystery Tour,* offered a stunning preview of post-Beatles music with the white album; wrapped up their career with the erratic, overly professional *Abbey Road;* and stumbled off the stage they had raised with a botched release of the antiprofessional *Let It Be.*

Out of that sad ending several recordings stand with the best the Beatles ever made. Save Paul's shimmering "Penny Lane," and his bruising "Helter Skelter," all were John's work, and in truth they may have little of the Beatles—the Beatles as something more than four people who sang and played—in them. Still, to this writer, "Strawberry Fields Forever," "I Am the Walrus," "Yer Blues," "I'm So Tired" and "Don't Let Me Down" are each richer than *Sgt. Pepper's* best cut, "A Day in the Life"; in every case, John seemed to be getting closer to the essentials of his soul, which might be identified as a refusal to settle for anything short of perfection combined with a clear understanding that perfection does not exist—a dilemma that, given the history of the Beatles era and the years since, is something more than one man's hangup.

Since 1970, the Beatles have carried on, and it has taken real courage to resist the calls, increasingly intense, to accept a certain defeat and reunite for one last time, or perhaps for longer than that. I think the truth is that the Beatles have accepted that they cannot, in any form, become what they were. John and Paul particularly are engaged in the ultimate pop process of reinventing themselves, and in a manner that defies, or redefines, pop, since pop calls in the moment and their efforts will likely last their whole lives. Today, the Beatles oscillate between genius and self-parody, and only one who does not understand the game that is being played would hope for some final, perfect synthesis. Perhaps what matters is that symbolically or in action, the Beatles, who saved the game close to 15 years ago, have no alternative but to work to keep it going. (pp. 179-80)

Greil Marcus, in The Rolling Stone Illustrated History of Rock and Roll, *edited by Jim Miller (copyright © 1976 by Rolling Stone Press; reprinted by permission of Random House, Inc.), Rolling Stone Press, Random House, 1976.*

NICHOLAS SCHAFFNER

The Beatles will be remembered not only for their considerable contribution as songwriters and recording artists, but also as the most remarkable cultural and sociological phenomenon of their time. During the 1960's they seemed to transform, however unwittingly, the look, sound, and style of at least one generation. They had, of course, a lot of help from a great many friends—but it was more than anyone else, John, Paul, George, and Ringo who set in motion the forces that made a whole era what it was, and, by extension, what it is today.

The impact the Beatles made is incalculable, not only in popular music and in every other fact of the music business —be it album cover design, the quality of recorded sound, or the size of the crowds—but also in innumerable other areas. They were among the first major public figures of our time to break down the barriers dividing the sexes, with their long hair and vivid attire; champion the use of "mind-expanding" drugs and the innovations in sound, design, language, and attitudes these substances inspired; and, in general, show the way to a life style that defied so many of the conventions taken for granted in 1963. There were others in their wake more daring and iconoclastic, but it is unlikely that the Rolling Stones, or David Bowie, or even Bob Dylan, could have accomplished what they did without the Beatles' example.

Imagine what our world might be like today, were it not for the Beatles. Rock 'n' roll as a critically acclaimed and relatively sophisticated popular art form, with words that say something and music that draws from an almost limitless variety of sources: long hair and expressive clothing on men; marijuana and "Eastern mysticism"—all this and more might well still be practically unheard of in the mainstream of society were it not thanks (or no thanks!) to the Beatles.

Of course it might be argued that they merely picked up on trends from less celebrated sources, that they reflected the times rather than made them; one may file that riddle in the chicken-or-the-egg department. But it can safely be said that the Beatles were the medium that first brought many of the present trappings of our culture (a few years back that might have read "counterculture") to the attention of ordinary folks, quite a few of whom emulated what they saw and heard.

The Beatles were great natural talents; that they lacked any formal training yet were so gifted and imaginative enabled them to do things that more conventional entertainers, composers, or musicians simply could never have dreamed of. From the moment that captivated eighty million American T.V. viewers in February 1964 with their catchy ditties and funny haircuts, through the final crescendos of *Abbey Road*, the Beatles never stopped exploring and evolving as songwriters and musicians—and as personalities.

One of their attributes was an ability to live their colorful lives in a virtual fishbowl and yet never for a moment bore or disappoint their millions of riveted voyeurs and eavesdroppers. . . . Despite the formidable pressures of . . . fame, the Beatles (at least until their break-up) never stopped learning and growing with them—as the words and music improved beyond anyone's wildest expectations.

In short, the Beatles were admitted into our consciousness in the guise of a low-brow fad; like the Trojan horse, there proved to be a lot more there than initially met the eye (and ear). Once snared by the cherubic looks and the tasty bubblegum, an unsuspecting world was set off on a magical mystery tour out of which many emerged quite different people from those they might have otherwise been.

Nicholas Schaffner, in his introduction to his The Beatles Forever *(copyright © 1977 by Nicholas Schaffner; with permission of Stackpole Books), McGraw-Hill, 1977, p. 7.*

William Mayne

1928-

(Has also written under pseudonyms of Charles Molin and Martin Cobalt, and, with R. D. Caesar, under joint pseudonym of Dynely James) British young adult novelist and editor and author of picture books for children. Mayne is recognized as a writer whose young adult fiction has broadened the definition of this genre, preparing his audience for the style, content, and complexity of adult fiction. Mayne is not considered an easy writer due to the conciseness of his prose, which sometimes borders on terseness, and the intricacy of his plots. His books often expect readers to answer their own questions and have a particularly British reserve or coolness of emotion, aspects which are sometimes regarded as limiting their popularity with young readers. However, Mayne is an individualistic writer who is not content with recycling standard themes and plots. His books contain sensitive characterizations, skillful use of language, and lyrical evocation of atmosphere, giving them what many critics consider an uncommon depth. As a writer Mayne calls himself an observer, like a camera lens. "All I am doing," he says, "is looking at things now and showing them to myself when I was young." He was born in Yorkshire, the setting reflected in both the atmosphere and dialogue of many of his books. At nine he won a scholarship to Canterbury Cathedral, where he stayed until 1942; he later used his experiences as a choir boy for his cathedral school stories. Mayne began his career writing family stories involving mysteries and treasure hunts, books in which he first explored the nuances in relationships among members of all generations. In 1958 he was awarded the Carnegie Medal for *A Grass Rope*, a book considered the precursor of many of his later works, which investigate the intricacies of time and space, past and present. Perhaps the most successful synthesis of Mayne's literary characteristics is *Earthfasts*. Based on a local Yorkshire legend, it has been recognized as a modern classic of fantasy literature. Mayne has more than fifty books to his credit, including several for younger children, and is the editor of several anthologies dealing with legends and the supernatural. He is also a composer of music, and in 1965 composed the incidental music for *Holly from the Bongs*, by Alan Garner, a British writer to whom Mayne is often compared. As a literary observer, Mayne portrays what he sees in both his imagination and the real world with clarity, making him well respected among those young adults who know his work. (See also *Contemporary Authors*, Vols. 9-12, rev. ed., and *Something about the Author*, Vol. 6.)

Some might quibble at the whimsical humour and allusive conversations in [*The World Upside Down*], but read in the right mood it is delightfully refreshing, with its nice civilized children making quotable (and quotation-filled) remarks, and finding pleasure in being alive as well as a proper treasure of golden crowns and coins. . . . There is style in the writing, warmth and wit in the family relationships, and reality behind each character, even the poacher who sounds almost too much a character to be true. The kind of light reading which will stand up to many re-readings, and pave the way to the best kind of adult light fiction. (p. 247)

The Junior Bookshelf, *November, 1954.*

Without going outside the familiar convention of seek-and-find adventure in an English country setting, William Mayne has quickly established himself as the most original good writer for children in our immediate time. At this stage ([*The Member for the Marsh*] is his fourth) it is possible to see something of the pattern on which his imagination works. He writes on the edge of the past rather than on the edge of the future; he dismisses the age-barrier between friends; he makes his own traditions (among schoolboys, for instance), but they seem to lighten life, not burden it. He also expects his readers to think speedily. If it is a scramble to follow his quick wit at times, the book can always be read again; and the second reading often gives more pleasure than the first.

"The Edge of the Past," in The Times Literary Supplement (© *Times Newspapers Ltd. (London) 1956; reproduced from* The Times Literary Supplement *by permission), May 11, 1956, p. vii.*

William Mayne is certainly the most excitingly original writer for children to emerge in the last five years. This is not to say that he is, even potentially, the most popular. *The Member for the marsh* confirms the impressions of his three earlier novels that he has an insatiable passion for oddities. When many writers are haunted by the shadow of the backward reader, he writes joyously and unashamedly for the top flight of the grammar school, for those who may be expected to enjoy fine style, original and provocative ideas and rich characters. He writes, one suspects, to please himself, as most of the best books are written.

Mr. Mayne is a master of the use of setting. This time his

scene is the fascinating flat country of western Somerset. He knows the country well and communicates his appreciation of its not-very-obvious charms. Into this setting he puts—but no, they live there already—four very odd boys, the Harmonious Mud Stickers. . . . Never were there less typical schoolboys, but each is drawn consistently and convincingly. Their activities, in which schoolboyish fun charmingly breaks through the solemnity, are too good to give away. Mr. Mayne tells a good story, with certainty and without haste. Not a book for children, but definitely a book for the child who can deserve it. (p. 144)

The Junior Bookshelf, July, 1956.

To come to *Choristers' Cake* is to enter a new world, from the flat drabness of monochrome engraving to the colour and movement and depth of real life. The scene is that of *A Swarm in May*, but the viewpoint is changed. The Choir School [of Canterbury] is seen through the eyes, and interpreted by the rather muddled brain, of an older boy, one who does not easily find a place in the cooperative society of school. This is a most skilful study, and there is nothing contrived about Sandy's gradual achievement of self-recognition.

Psychological insight is not the whole of Mr. Mayne's armoury. He is a master—*the* master in contemporary English writing for children—of setting, and the hero of *Choristers' Cake* is not Sandy but the Cathedral. The Cathedral is ever-present. Its traditions provide the story with its main theme. Its services mark the passage of time. The precincts are the boys' home and their playground. The many, and delightful, minor characters are the Cathedral's servants. . . .

Choristers' Cake may be a by-way of children's literature. Its virtuosity and verbal richness, as well as the undoubted oddness of many of its characters, put it beyond the range of the average reader. But for the child who can meet its demands it will be a deep and memorable experience. In insight, in gaiety, in exuberance of idea and language, it is in a class apart. Mr. Mayne is certainly the most interesting, as the most unpredictable, figure in children's books today. He has all the talents, and he has devoted them to the creation of a little world, self-contained and absorbed, in spite of quarrels and rivalries, in its work of praising God. (p. vii)

The Times Literary Supplement (© Times Newspapers Ltd. (London) 1956; reproduced from The Times Literary Supplement *by permission), November 23, 1956.*

Mr. Mayne is not an easy writer, as we know. His love of words, his range of ideas and his interest in psychology, which are the very essence of his art, all act as stumbling-blocks to the young reader. One suspects that Mr. Mayne is not unduly distressed by this. He writes, as he must, to please himself. Will he at the same time please others? Yes, he will delight those who deserve writing of this quality, the children, a minority but not an insignificant one, who can recognise the truth of his observation of boys' behaviour and who can relish the convincing oddity of his adults.

This book is not a sequel to *A Swarm in May*. That inimitable book said the last word on its subject. In *Choristers' Cake* we look at the same school from a different viewpoint. The central character is an older boy than John

Owen, who in this story is a very small and unimportant singing boy. Sandwell is one of those boys who fight a solitary war against school tradition and discipline. He is intensely real. (p. 341)

The Junior Bookshelf, December, 1956.

JENNIE D. LINDQUIST

First published in England in 1955, [*A Swarm in May*] has a most unusual plot. It is based on an old tradition: the youngest Singing Boy is always the Beekeeper; he must "come before the Bishop one Sunday in May, to sing a short solo and recite the ritual assuring the Bishop that the organist will supply good beeswax candles for the Cathedral throughout the coming year." The custom is still carried on though now the candles come from a warehouse and are not made of beeswax. How John Owen the youngest boy refuses at first to be the Beekeeper but comes at last to realize how much the old tradition means forms one thread of the story. Running along with it is the mystery of beehives and a secret missing since the days of Henry VIII. The Cathedral background, the music, the beekeeping and the very real boys combine to make a story that will be loved by those children who are always looking for English books and by others who are lucky enough to have adults share it with them. (pp. 307-08)

Jennie D. Lindquist, in The Horn Book Magazine *(copyrighted, 1957, by The Horn Book, Inc., Boston), August, 1957.*

RUTH WEEDEN STEWART

[*A Swarm in May*] will have limited appeal. The writer presupposes a rather extensive knowledge of music and a knowledge of the slang and colloquialisms of England. The legend of the beekeeper and the ancient custom of presenting the candles to the bishop is charming but does not furnish sufficient spark for a boy's story today. This book is for the special child who has some training and real interest in the life of a chorister. (p. 149)

Ruth Weeden Stewart, in Junior Libraries *(reprinted from the October, 1957 issue of* Junior Libraries, *published by R. R. Bowker Co. A Xerox Corporation; copyright © 1957), October, 1957.*

No one could be more traditional in his material [than is Mayne in *A Grass Rope*]; no one could touch the dead material of the adventure story into vivid life with such sure, individual and wonderful magic.

Mr. Mayne has infinite resources. First, style. He has the gift of describing everyday things as if he were seeing them for the first time, and he shares this freshness of vision with his readers. . . . He has, too, a fine sense of landscape and of atmosphere. The harsh Pennine country to this story is an essential actor in the drama; one sees it all the time, as one feels the hill mists, and hears the distant rush of water and the barking of foxes. He has a deep understanding of children. No one ever acts or speaks out of character. He is, moreover, a fine story-teller, who knows how to set his narrative in motion so that it gains in momentum as it goes. And everything is coloured with his characteristic sober humour.

Is *A Grass Rope* a book for children? It isn't the answer to the C-stream's prayer. It is difficult to read, with the twin obstacles of dialect and uninhibited vocabulary. It depends on subtleties of writing and observation. It is, nevertheless, completely in tune with childhood. It is written from the child's point of view, not from that of an adult thinking about children. . . . *A Grass Rope* is an original and enchanting book. No one else could have written it. (pp. 318-19)

The Junior Bookshelf, *December, 1957.*

No doubt we shall have sober people explaining how in this passage Mr. Mayne has succeeded, in that failed, here written within the child's range, there soared far beyond his grasp. Labour in vain! William Mayne is one of those rare writers—there are seldom more than one or two in each generation—whom one takes on his own terms or not at all. *The Thumbstick* is a very good Mayne; that is, a very good book for intelligent readers of all ages and all environments. Whether it is a children's book depends on one's definition; it recalls C. S. Lewis's dictum: "A children's book which is enjoyed only by children is a bad children's book." It will certainly lift the right child on tiptoe; it is one of those tales in [Charles] Lamb's words "which make the child a man, while all the time he suspected himself to be no bigger than a child."

The Thumbstick is one of Mayne's Yorkshire stories. Like all his books it is a tale of living traditions. It is also about a treasure-hunt. Like every one of Mayne's books, too, it is astonishingly unlike every other one. For all that, it has his characteristic qualities; a style which is a miracle of flexibility and range, a superb sense of atmosphere, brilliant characterisation and subtle observation, above all a poet's interest in the commonplaces of every-day life and an awareness of their cosmic significance. (p. 152)

The Junior Bookshelf, *July, 1959.*

HAMISH FOTHERINGHAM

[Mayne's] first published story was *Follow the Footprints,* the story of a "treasure hunt," a motif which William Mayne has developed with freshness and originality in the majority of his books. Caroline and Andrew Blake come with their parents to live in an old Tollhouse in Cumberland. From local legends the children learn of treasure hidden in the former abbey of Saint Elda and set out to find it. . . . The children are portrayed as being staunchly independent, clever, but never too clever, thank goodness, and neither precocious nor prigs. They are aware that independent action free from adult control can bring with it occasional discomfort and much hard work. (pp. 185-86)

This framework of well described country setting, local legends, excellently drawn pen portraits, sparkling dialogues and a plot rich in incidents is used by the author in his other "treasure hunt" stories. Framework is hardly the correct term. Variations on a theme would perhaps be a better description, for William Mayne has a poet's ear for the music of language—the sound as well as the sense. (p. 186)

The plot [of *The World Upside Down*] is a little complex but utterly logical. The description of the inverted reflection on the wall which provides the main clue—and the title of the story—needs more than one reading to fix the detail, but it fits together perfectly. All the characters have the breath of life. The old poacher Jessop, a likeable old rogue, is particularly well done, although the broad Yorkshire dialect of his speech may offer occasional difficulties.

William Mayne has produced a rich portrait gallery of shrewdly but affectionately observed, well-rounded characters. One thinks of young Mary, the Yorkshire farmer's daughter, in *A Grass Rope* with her unshakeable belief in fairies. Or the brothers in *The Blue Boat,* Hugh, highly imaginative opening up a world of phantasy to the more serious minded Christopher who, thanks to boarding school, feels it is easier to avoid trouble by conforming to the rules imposed by grown ups.

How much of the material in the two books about Canterbury Cathedral Choir School is autobiographical, one wonders? (pp. 186-87)

In *Choristers' Cake* the main figure is Peter Sandwell who tries to shirk being up-graded to the rank of chorister and is, in consequence, sent to Coventry by his school-fellows. His gradual awareness that his behaviour is anti-social is presented with a skill and insight which will be appreciated more by parents than by young readers. The atmosphere of the centuries old cathedral is beautifully fixed. Thanks to Mr. Mayne's art—aided perhaps by having actively shared the milieu—there is nothing "pye" about the choristers. They remain boys throughout, with whom the reader can identify himself, not surpliced and ruffed little angels.

Perhaps William Mayne's chief asset lies in not confining his characters to one particular age group. He always shows complete harmony existing between children of different ages and of both sexes and this same harmony marks the child's relationship with the adult world. Each child possesses a distinct personality with the right—one can almost say the DUTY—of expressing an opinion. They all take an active part in discussing plans and carrying them out. In the "treasure hunt" stories it is quite clear that they are successful in their search only because THEY ARE A GROUP with each child of whatever age making an important contribution to the common aim. (p. 188)

William Mayne is not an easy author. He never writes down and concentration is needed to keep up with his lively imagination. But is this, after all, such a bad thing? There are children prepared to make the effort of meeting an author on his own terms, and to them Mayne's stories are exciting and wholly satisfying. (p. 189)

Hamish Fotheringham, *"The Art of William Mayne," in* The Junior Bookshelf, *October, 1959, pp. 185-89.*

Schoolboy society is in William Mayne's *Cathedral Wednesday*—cathedral choir school society once more. . . .

As always, Mr. Mayne's writing is brilliant—so brilliant that there is a perpetual, restless surface-shimmer that can become tiresomely dazzling. But children learning to appreciate play of language and image will enjoy the wit, even the atrociously ingenious puns. Above all, Mr. Mayne's writing has exactness ("four steamed puddings *robed* in jam") and individuality. (p. xii)

The Times Literary Supplement (© *Times Newspapers Ltd. (London) 1960; reproduced from* The Times Literary Supplement *by permission), November 25, 1960.*

Cathedral Wednesday is, like *A Swarm in May,* a story about responsibility. Owen, in the earlier book, tries to evade the responsibility of his job as Beekeeper; Young, in this, finds it difficult to accept the problems of maintaining discipline when Trevithic goes sick and he find himself Acting Head Boy. The difference between the two books is that *A Swarm in May* works out its social and moral problems through a most original and profoundly interesting treasure-hunt; Andrew Young's dilemma is almost the whole of *Cathedral Wednesday*.

This is not to say that Mr. Mayne's new book is lacking in interest. It shares with the other "Choir School" stories the fascination of the Cathedral setting and of the complex and traditional life of the school; it has too its delightful clutch of odd characters and, because Young is a day boy, glimpses of a typical Mayne domestic interior in which the clarinet is played in the bath and mutton broth is laced with China tea. The writing is as exquisite as ever. Mr. Mayne's dialogue is a miraculous blend of naturalism, wit and individuality. His narrative prose glows. His insight into human behaviour, adult and child, is uncanny. I have no doubt at all that *Cathedral Wednesday* is a very lovely book, with much to delight and amuse and develop the child reader. Many of them however will miss the point and be left wondering if there is a point at all. (p. 370)

The Junior Bookshelf, December, 1960.

ELLEN LEWIS BUELL

William Mayne is a witty, highly individual writer, author of that very British, very special story, "A Swarm in May" and the tricky, imaginative "The Blue Boat." ["Underground Alley"] is possibly the most accessible for the average American reader that we have yet had here.

The setting is a Welsh border town where the townspeople are preparing for the annual Town Day and the visit of a prince. The rather complicated action revolves around the discovery by Patty, a whirlwind of a little girl, of a buried medieval street which explains an ancient mystery and an act of treachery which had long ago cast the town into royal disfavor. . . . There is much coming and going, a good surprise at the end, and general feeling of pre-festival excitement. Patty is so real that one regrets that the author never resolves her half-concealed conflict with her young, well-meaning stepmother—one problem that should never, fictionally, be left hanging.

> *Ellen Lewis Buell, "Festival Towns," in* The New York Times Book Review *(© 1961 by The New York Times Company; reprinted by permission), September 24, 1961, p. 40.*

MARGERY FISHER

Set in the Yorkshire dales, [*A Grass Rope*] is a treasure hunt, like so many of William Mayne's books, but with the difference that one of the characters, young Mary, believes so firmly in magic that her interpretation of events dominates the story rather than her parents' common-sense or Adam Forrest's grammar-school reasoning. (p. 140)

It is certainly not inappropriate to use the word 'magic' of a story where the author makes you aware of the irrational all the time, the poetic below the events of ordinary life, and does this while keeping his characters absolutely real, not eccentric or peculiar, but people with character and drive and personal idiom.

Mayne's particular contribution to the fantastic adventure is the way he makes the vision of certain of his characters

override actual events. In [this book, which has a simple, almost hackneyed plot], the tone is set by Mary's belief in fairyland. . . . (pp. 140-41)

In [Mayne's] three choir-school stories the dialogue is curiously formalized and yet so apposite that it gets nearer to the *real* talk of boys than anything I have read later than *Tom Sawyer*. (p. 174)

From the dialogue and the narrative in Mayne's books you are always aware, too, of the extreme *concreteness* of the junior world (not an easy thing to get into a book). Mary's delight in the 'white stick' in *A Grass Rope*, the absorption of Owen in the ball and key he has found, in *A Swarm in May*, the map on the damp wall in *The World Upside Down*—all these objects are crucial to the stories, but they are also important to the children who handle or observe or find them, for their shape or texture or colour. This is one of the most important qualities of Mayne's work and links him with writers like Walter de la Mare and Elizabeth Coatsworth and Laura Ingalls Wilder, writers who have a particular faculty for reliving the life of the senses which a child cannot communicate directly to an adult. (p. 175)

I know no recent children's stories more *actual* than William Mayne's, whether he is writing about a school or a village or a small town; and perhaps he is a little difficult for children to appreciate just for this reason, because he utterly ignores any compromise, any of the formulas which endear more popular writers to children. But the child who plunges into his stories, forgetting fashion, listening to the dry, crisp dialogue, and seeing in his mind's eye the scenes so minutely and economically visualized, has found a companion for life, no less. (p. 281)

> *Margery Fisher, in her* Intent upon Reading: A Critical Appraisal of Modern Fiction for Children *(copyright © 1961 by Margery Fisher), Hodder & Stoughton Children's Books (formerly Brockhampton Press), 1961 (and reprinted by Franklin Watts, Inc., 1962).*

[William Mayne] is surely the most original and stimulating writer for children of our day. Here [in *A Parcel of Trees*] is the usual bounty of freshly observed scenes, emotions, conversations and characters, each indicated with the minimum of words and contrivance, the maximum of humour and sympathy. The story is one of his most approachable and the problem is less elaborately worked out than some he has evolved. . . . As in real life some of the allusions and explanations are obscure at first but there is plenty to intrigue and please and it is all even better the second time round—and the third and fourth, for the Mayne books make some of the best re-reading ever written and always the wonder grows—how does he do it, all so deftly and astonishingly right without ever forcing the pace or being merely clever? (p. 156)

The Junior Bookshelf, July, 1963.

[*Words and Music*] is splendid stuff. It is not often an author maintains such a vein of uproarious humour which yet keeps the reader quiet, as it were, in case he should miss one of the quips when it comes along. The story does not matter very much, though it has many good moments. What grips the reader's attention is the rapidity and subtlety of Mr. Mayne's picture of life in a choir school where everything is geared to singing and services and every boy is at the mercy of some musical or clerical whim. The author has the details of this "order of service" so thoroughly and intimately taped that one is soon in a fever of excitement and enveloped in the boys' own mild nightmare of assignments and adjustments. As a picture of a school at work it is at once efficient and human and it never slackens off. (p. 351)

The Junior Bookshelf, *December, 1963.*

JOHN ASHLIN

[*Words and Music*] is a sequel to the remarkable trilogy *A Swarm in May, Choristers' Cake,* and *Cathedral Wednesday.* . . . Has the magic been achieved yet again? No one is more conscious than William Mayne of the difficulty of maintaining the level of interest over a number of volumes and in *Cathedral Wednesday* he adopted the unusual and successful device of looking at the school through the eyes of a day-boy. Now we are back again as boarders and with the fabric of the cathedral playing a part in the story as it did in *A Swarm in May.* Readers must judge for themselves but I felt that he has once more met the challenge successfully, but one or two characters such as Trevithic are becoming more remote and vague—time they moved on to their public schools perhaps. The style is just as lucid, clear and clever, and a delight as usual; most of the characters drawn by the author show that he understands the workings of a prep schoolboy's mind as perhaps no one else does. (pp. 206-07)

John Ashlin, in The School Librarian and School Library Review, *July, 1964.*

ROBERT BELL

In both [*A Parcel of Trees* and *Sand*] the author's brilliant story-telling, character drawing, dialogue and perfectly-timed climaxes evoke, as always, the highest admiration.

The 'parcel of trees' is the legal term for a disused orchard, Susan's favourite retreat. When her right to use it is threatened by the railway authorities whose property it apparently is, a friendly lawyer establishes her legal ownership by 'squatter's rights.' The ingenious way in which this is done, and the significance of the intriguing objects in the orchard—a ruined lodge, a horse's skeleton, pieces of aluminum and concrete, and a row of dogs' graves—make a most absorbing story which is outstanding even for this distinguished writer.

Sand is a more hilarious affair, but of comparable excellence. The setting is a coastal town which is being slowly inundated by sand blown from the dunes. The central characters are a group of the most authentic schoolboys imaginable, and their ingenuity in fighting the sand, the uses to which they put the variety of objects they uncover, and the positively sparkling and mirth-provoking dialogue will keep readers absorbed and audibly chuckling from beginning to end.

Both books are 'musts.' (pp. 91-2)

Robert Bell, in The School Librarian and School Library Review, *March, 1965.*

ALBERTA EISEMAN

The background [of "Sand"] is perfect for a suspense story: an old English town by the North Sea where the sand drifts in relentlessly, burying houses and trees beneath

great dunes. . . . Under the constant shifting of scene, each happening tends to become anticlimactic. And it is too bad that against this brooding backdrop, the characters, like footprints in the drifting sand, leave no lasting impression. (p. 46)

Alberta Eiseman, in The New York Times Book Review *(© 1965 by The New York Times Company; reprinted by permission), November 28, 1965.*

[*Pig in the Middle* does not contain] one of Mr. Mayne's complex plots. Indeed it is simple to the point of lacking interest. It is difficult, too, to accept the naivety of the boys and their acceptance of the leadership of John Much, huge, retarded, illiterate. John is a typical Mayne creation, sending out his meaningless summonses in exquisite calligraphy and keeping his "library" of unread books; but one smells here too much of the labour of creation, too little spontaneity.

There remains the accurate painting of the town, its canal and its dark, dirty back streets leading to adventures more exciting and real than those described in this book, and the authentic interior of Michael's house. This, and the cadences of everyday speech, are what Mr. Mayne does supremely well, and they never fail even in, what this is, the least satisfying of his books. (p. 1139)

The Times Literary Supplement *(© Times Newspapers Ltd. (London) 1965; reproduced from* The Times Literary Supplement *by permission), December 9, 1965.*

GEOFFREY TREASE

You either surrender to Mayne's spell or impatiently don't. Myself, I admire so many of his talents singly—his poet's eye and ear, his word-magic, his evocation of atmosphere—but I cannot make the surrender, and feel sure that at no age could I have done so. (p. 708)

Geoffrey Trease, in New Statesman *(© 1966 The Statesman & Nation Publishing Co. Ltd.), November 11, 1966.*

WALLACE HILDICK

The descriptive matter [in *The Battlefield*] is seemingly casual, compressed, beautifully telling. The dialogue is wayward without being rambling, and fascinating in the way the half-formed thoughts jut up like stepping stones. But I couldn't help thinking that too much of this was muted bravura, put on for the benefit of older faithful admirers, especially in the first 30 pages. I'm not one who believes that children's stories should be pared down to their narrative essentials, with everything being used to push forward the plot. Children live in the present. To them any interesting incident *is* the plot. Even so, I feel that nothing need be lost and the whole may be enhanced by establishing the theme of a story as firmly and vividly and early as possible. The blurb announces a 'tale of mystery and strange happenings' in Mayne's native Yorkshire, but the author should have done this job himself, taking care in those first two chapters to hint more strongly at the mystery and strangeness, as well as setting the wintry moorland scene and introducing the delightfully fitful little girls who are the heroines. (pp. 643-44)

Wallace Hildick, in The Listener *(© British*

Broadcasting Corp. 1967; reprinted by permission of Wallace Hildick), November 16, 1967.

MARGARET MEEK

The pace of the plot of William Mayne's latest *tour de force* [*The Battlefield*] is slow and measured, country style. . . . The climax is conceivable only because by the time it comes the girls have woven themselves into the readers' consciousness by the quaint acuteness of their speech, their 'cleverness' in the northern sense. The author exploits the way they experiment with language before reality encroaches on metaphor. The result is an exploration in depth of sense experience, almost Keatsian in its richness, laced with good humour and memorable characters. I smell that shepherd yet. (p. 111)

Margaret Meek, in The School Librarian and School Library Review, *March, 1968.*

The plot of *The Battlefield* is slight: two children with the help of a local tractor-driver unearth an old cannon and spend a night in a tower which is transplanted from the battlefield to the village green. The characteristic touch of Mayne magic is there: how else could a solid stone building move?

A look at the quality of the writing itself, however, confirms once again the reason for Mayne's impressive achievements. Characters are illuminated in a phrase; an adjective brings a noun sharply to life; a verb propels action into conviction—"the saw complained"; "a newly cleaned tooth felt smooth and cool and wideawake"; "Bullocks are great elbow-tasters".

Perhaps the weak jokes of Lesley and Debby will please children more than they will sophisticated adults. But any astute reader, young or old, will recognise the fidelity of Mayne's picture of the Yorkshire village where the story is set and of the local folk who live there: inn-keeper, farmer, stone mason, shepherd.

The subtle, quiet handling of suspense through the story will not be apparent except to the most perceptive young reader and one is left with a feeling that only boys and girls as bright as Debby and Lesley are likely to appreciate the richness of this accomplished book. (p. 117)

The Junior Bookshelf, *April, 1968.*

EDWARD BLISHEN

[What William Mayne's] writing has shown is that stories for children need not drive straight from opening to end; they can shape themselves by a sort of sly oblique process, emerge sideways and even backwards out of dialogue and hints. In fact, all his stories have strong narrative spines; but they are not rigid ones. He has also come so close to the true nature of children's talk and to the way they feel and think that it must be more difficult than it was for a writer of any sensitiveness to reproduce that blunt form of dialogue, always obviously to the purpose, and that falsely consequent rendering of patterns of young thought and feeling, that are conventions of writing for children. In a sense, Mr Mayne has reminded us of the precise nature of children. (p. 79)

William Mayne's stories are full of . . . pure true comedy of talk among children, of talk between children and adults (the adults sometimes exasperated or bemused by it, or

without the leisure that enables the child to give it full attention; though the old, as they are often portrayed in William Mayne's stories, are seen to have re-acquired their sense of the intricate meanings of language). And, apart from his purely comic concern with words, William Mayne understands beautifully that language is itself part of the adventure of being alive and that, by misleading or puzzling or illuminating, it can inspire or direct events.

It is perhaps this feeling he has for the role played in life by language—especially in the lives of children, able to be so attentive—that more than anything makes Mayne a highly original and rare children's writer. He can be arch, and over-playful, and is capable of, as it were, doodling in the style of William Mayne; at times (I detected this especially in a recent story, *The Battlefield*) his children and the way they talk reflect the writer's agility with words, his inability to leave them alone, rather than their credible selves. He is an extraordinarily prolific writer. . . . [Certainly] this large output is responsible for the passages of doodling and of near-self-parody. It is also to be seen as a kind of generosity: he has spread his attention over many audiences, from the youngest to the most sophisticated. And because to each of those audiences, in each of the varied settings of his stories, he addresses himself in the same manner, in the tone of this dancing and devious concern with language (as well as because the structure of his writing is *never* difficult, and he is indeed a master of the short sentence), I cannot believe that those who say he is writing over the heads of children, or only for those with a special taste for words, are analysing the situation correctly. (p. 80)

From the moment you enter one of his stories, all your senses are deeply and very precisely involved. . . . [The] beauty of William Mayne's style is that it is never purple—there is rather [a] constant deft attentiveness to the sensations of being alive, usually expressed with a wholly unstrained wit. (p. 81)

But what is most important is that all this texture, to which I have found it necessary to pay attention before looking at anything else—this perpetual lively alertness to language and to sensations—is wholly at the service of Mr Mayne's stories. It can be enjoyed for its own sake, but it does not exist for its own sake. The little group of books he wrote about life in a choir school—beginning with *A Swarm in May*—stand slightly aside from the rest. They form a loving tribute to a special way of young life. The stories embody characteristic themes—the impact on the present of complex mysteries with their roots in the past, the conflict of attitudes to tradition, the relationships of the young and their elders—but, to my mind, exist as an achievement separate from the rest. They include some of William Mayne's best inventions: for example, the family of Pargales, who have tended the fabric of the cathedral for centuries, and whose notion of time, as of the relation of the generations among themselves, has become tied to the enormously leisurely pace at which stone crumbles, gargoyles weather and fall and must be replaced. In the other stories, two major preoccupations emerge. One is that of the treasure hunt, of the search for clues to some mystery that carries the characters back into the past. This is a common theme in writing for children, but William Mayne handles it in a most uncommon manner. Not only is there his usual teasing obliqueness of narration, at once crystal-clear and devious; but there is also a constant ambiguity that enables a story to be interpreted in the light both of the most sober common sense and of the most extravagant imagination. Fantasy and realism are beautifully enmeshed. This is the manner of stories such as *The Thumbstick, The Rolling Season, The Battlefield:* and is at its best, in my opinion, in *A Grass Rope,* . . . in which the various possible interpretations of the near-magical events have their convincing advocate among the characters: a child who believes in magic, a clever boy who brings scientific reasoning to the quest, the children's parents who are simply sensible about it all. The conclusion is perfectly poised: the reader may believe any of the explanations, and perhaps that reader is most worthy of the author who manages to believe all of them. This is a very serious achievement of William Mayne's, I think: to preserve such an active and enchanting neutrality as between all the levels of our experience. Beside this achievement, much writing for children—wholly embracing fantasy or opting for thorough realism—falls awfully short. (pp. 81-2)

The second large theme often, but not always, stems from this first one. It is the theme of enormous makings and destructions. The boys in *Sand* find what appear to be the remains of a prehistoric creature under the sand; they set out on an elaborate task of secret rescue, trying to retrieve these mysterious bones. The complications of their labour are vast; and so, too, are its consequences. In *Pig in the Middle,* a group of boys set out to transform an old barge into a seagoing vessel; as in *Sand,* they become intricately involved in the task. One of them, when they have achieved part of it, 'suddenly understood the beginnings of the Bible'. It is this business of making things—of planning for a construction, or of actually constructing—that again and again William Mayne celebrates; and again, of course, there could be few things closer to a child's heart. But so often in these stories the making leads to a vast unmaking, a catastrophe. In *The Battlefield,* the children's interest in the old tower in the marshes, the step they take to investigate and make use of it, lead to near-fatal consequences, a huge scene of flood and displacement. The children are in fact warned by an old shepherd that, with so many forces at work—those of nature and of history, for example—those exerted by inquiring man may be too much. The attempt to transform the old barge in *Pig in the Middle* leads to immense disaster again—or at any rate is closely associated with it: the complete collapse of the mill buildings in which the barge is housed. It seems to me that this theme of making and breaking, sometimes separate from the magical theme, sometimes part of it, is again a concern that takes William Mayne close to the young reader, much of whose own life is devoted to bold constructions and to curiosity about the consequences of interfering with nature.

It is easy to say that William Mayne is an uneven writer. That must be true of anyone who writes so much. The comment is sometimes made by critics who appear not to distinguish between the more ambitious stories and those that are less serious in intention. It is also easy, and I think quite wrong, to claim that he is a writer for a highly literate minority; . . . I believe this view is an invention of those who see only the freshness, subtlety and obliquity of the writing, and do not observe that it is always tied to stories of considerable narrative strength or that children everywhere have a delight in verbal ingenuity. These are, in fact, extremely *sensible* stories, and in my experience are recognised as such by a wide range of children. They are sensible

because the heroes are never improbably heroic, and pure villains have no more place in the stories than they have in life itself. They are sensible also because Mr Mayne understands the fluctuating relationships of child with child, the tangle of emotional attitudes which is part of the reality of children's lives, and of which so many children's writers seem inadequately aware. One should add that William Mayne is a brilliant reporter on the nature of family life, on the role of mums and dads. Parents impose a framework, but that is not all that can be said about them; one of the best things about this writer's work is that he understands that, at intervals in their busy round, adults are likely to be as much influenced by their children as their children are by them. The children of the sixties are fortunate to possess a writer who can make such robust and copious literature out of a balance of so many gifts, all of them uncommon. (pp. 82-3)

Edward Blishen, "William Mayne" (1968), in Good Writers for Young Readers, *edited by Dennis Butts (copyright selection and arrangement* © *1977 Hart-Davis Educational), Hart-Davis Educational, 1977, pp. 79-85.*

COLIN FIELD

Once one has accepted the premise that is is possible to see backwards and forwards in time, and to conjure people from the past and the future, the logic of [*Over the Hills and Far Away*] is impeccable, and its unfolding inevitable. Particularly commendable is the portrayal of the children of both periods of history who are faced with situations which they do not understand. It is this portrayal of children exposed to the conflicts in the adult world which spells out Mayne's undeniable qualities as a writer. And, as always, his sense of place and atmosphere is acute and beautifully integrated into the story.

It is often pointed out that William Mayne's stories are not read by many children because of the paucity of action. This criticism cannot be made of *Over the Hills and Far Away,* which is strongly recommended for upper juniors and lower seniors. (pp. 91-2)

Colin Field, in The School Librarian, *March, 1969.*

ELVA HARMON

[*The Hill Road* is adequate] historical adventure cum fantasy. . . . This story is not fully realized as fantasy—perhaps because the picture of life in post-Roman Britain is developed rather casually; perhaps because Dolly and Andrew remain passive, unknowing, almost unthinking participants in their remarkable trip backward through time. Yet it is strengthened by the author's sense of English atmosphere and by his sharply contrasting characterizations of Magra and her stand-in. Fine for readers not yet ready for either the power and poignancy of Rosemary Sutcliff's and Madeleine Polland's realistic stories of the period or Mayne's own evocative, chilling fantasy, *Earthfasts.* . . . (pp. 115-16)

Elva Harmon, in School Library Journal (*reprinted from the April, 1969 issue of* School Library Journal, *published by R. R. Bowker Co. A Xerox Corporation; copyright* © *1969), April, 1969.*

HOUSTON L. MAPLES

Confirming the impression made by *Earthfasts,* William

Mayne shows again the broadening of his talents in [*The Hill Road,* an] artful fantasy of superimposed eras in time. . . .

The atmosphere of moorland and valley is, as we would expect from this writer, exquisitely conveyed, with the underlying sense of slumbering history beautifully heightened by the almost tangible juxtaposition of the two depths of time in the same place. Especially convincing is the author's recreation of the details, customs and mood of primitive life in the Dark Ages—a severe and somber picture made more persuasive by its contrast with the light-hearted puzzlement of the modern children. An engrossing and beautifully polished example of storytelling. (p. 15)

> *Houston L. Maples, in* Book World—Chicago Tribune (© *1969 Postrib Corp.), May 11, 1969.*

RUTH HILL VIGUERS

Mr. Mayne's settings are most often Yorkshire villages, his characters ordinary middle-class people—except that they are never really ordinary. To browse through a number of his books at the same time is to realize how many people he has brought to life in print and how complete an individual each one is. The children disagree, sometimes quarrel and weep, but the atmosphere that one remembers in his many stories is good humor. The relationships are affectionate and amusing, the dialogue full of quips and jokes and amiable insults. *Sand* . . . is an especially good example of the individuality of characters, *The Battlefield* . . . of the quick wit and the lively give and take in the conversations. The Yorkshire dialect sprinkled through the stories is less confusing to American children, I believe, than Mr. Mayne's tendency to make three words do the work of twenty. He has been called a "verbal magician" and his genius in finding the right word and his ability to tell a story almost entirely through dialogue are continually astonishing. The abundance of details packed into a few lines demands the most careful attention or the thread of meaning is lost. There is no racing through Mr. Mayne's books, and herein may lie the reason for the reluctance of some children to read them. (pp. 571-72)

> *Ruth Hill Viguers, in* A Critical History of Children's Literature, *by Cornelia Meigs, Anne Thaxter Eaton, Elizabeth Nesbitt, and Ruth Hill Viguers, edited by Cornelia Meigs (copyright © 1953, 1969 by Macmillan Publishing Co., Inc.), revised edition, Macmillan, 1969.*

ELEANOR CAMERON

William Mayne's *Earthfasts,* which puts him triumphantly among that small group who have shown such an audacious and original grasp of the possibilities of time fantasy, [lures us into a kind of magic]. It is one which, rather miraculously for a fantasy, manages to absorb into itself and to interlace throughout the book, not only legend and folklore, but the kind of dry, witnessing, factual exchanges one would expect to hear at an ESP conference, as well as observations of the author's, through his own words and through the words and thoughts of his boy protagonists, very often phrased in the language of science. At times, indeed, one is almost inclined to say to oneself that this is not fantasy at all but the story of a psychic phenomenon in which the whole countryside has been caught up. And yet, in the end, when Keith enters the cave and beholds, as he

replaces the Candle of Time in its stone socket on the Round Table, King Arthur and his knights change back to stalagmites, what is felt then, purely and simply, is a power brought into play by the supernatural.

Earthfasts is a wild, glimmering, shadowed, elusive kind of book which, like all of William Mayne's best, demands more than one reading. The past, the evocation of legend and folklore, haunt every page and from this evocation wells the magic that grips it. Earthfasts, to begin with, are humps or rises in plowed land, and out of one of these at "half past eight dusk of a day at the end of summer," a "higging" (confusing? cavilling?) time of day, two boys hear a throbbing in the earth which they think may be badgers, or possibly underground water, but which proves to be the drumming of a drummer boy of the time of Napoleon who had gone into a cave under Garebridge Castle to search for King Arthur's treasure. And when he emerges, beating his drum with one hand and in the other holding a candle that burns with a cold, spinning, indestructible flame, he sets loose all the ancient, sleeping forces of this corner of Old England. . . . (pp. 123-24)

The candle is not only a concentrate of time-magic but is as well the moving force of the book, for it compels both boys to action and Keith to a comprehension which brings the story to its climax. Furthermore, its nature serves to reveal, through their reactions to it, the differing characters of the two boys: the essentially reasoning, inquiring, experimental nature of the brilliant David and the usually more subjectively biased, intuitive nature of Keith. (p. 126)

Yet William Mayne is far too much of an artist to see David as purely and simply "the scientific type," devoted only to facts and to logic, for it is David who says that "Science doesn't know everything" and rebukes Keith for thinking it will be interesting to see what the drummer boy will do when he beholds strange and unfamiliar things, saying that it would be cruel to experiment with him. David combines in himself clarity of intellect with compassion; he is, in many ways, more adult than Keith, more spiritually courageous; in the beginning he has qualities which Keith has yet to realize, and it is the candle which brings Keith to a more mature stage of himself. (p. 127)

A mingling of poetic and scientific insights is continual throughout *Earthfasts.* Again and again they are set in juxtaposition, each intensifying the other, setting off the other, as David and Keith by their differences, which are never pure differences, reveal and enhance, bring out aspects of one another. The mood of shadowed, portentous magic, of fatefulness, of inexplicable movements in half darkness (reminding one, in a way, of Ingmar Bergman's film of medieval life, *The Seventh Seal*) is constantly striated by objective observations having to do with cause and effect, while words relating to experiments in physics or chemistry are found in paragraphs of feeling, of intimation, of seventh sense. (p. 129)

The extraordinary uniqueness of William Mayne's conception of simultaneous existences in two different times is nowhere more evident than in his description, through Keith's thoughts, of King Arthur's army waiting outside the boy's window. Keith and that army have not yet arrived at the point where they will stand together in one time, and though the men and their horses seem quite real, he sees them as "set, somehow, against the grain of the world, so that Keith himself felt slightly as if he were leaning.'' It is as though those men in chain mail were obeying the laws of a different field of force; it is what you feel in those incomprehensible fun houses built over magnetic centers where you struggle over a flat floor as up the steepest mountain, or where ''a marble runs up the sloping floor and then up the wall and out of the window.'' He saw the army ''as if they were held, like iron filings, and prickly like them too, against a different force from the one that held Keith to the house and to the floor of the world.'' A moment later, though there is no opening to another time that Keith is aware of—''only the brightening sky and the frosty earth and yonder hill fringed with giants,'' and ''Excalibur with the dull green back and the sharp bronze edge that held light from everywhere, from star and morning and candle'' —Keith and the King are no longer obeying the laws of different force fields, existing at different angles, but are standing on the same plane; they have come to their meeting place. ''And the King had his sword.''

It is the visualization of an idea which the mind and the imagination can play over with the greatest pleasure because of its strangeness and potency; they can go back to it in wonder as they do to Nellie Jack John, the drummer boy, straining toward Keith and David with his hair streaming out behind him and his clothes pressed against his body, but moving at a snail's pace because he is running against the grain of Time instead of with it. (pp. 130-31)

> *Eleanor Cameron, in her* The Green and Burning Tree: On the Writing and Enjoyment of Children's Books *(copyright © 1962, 1964, 1966, 1969 by Eleanor Cameron; reprinted by permission of Little, Brown, and Co. in association with The Atlantic Monthly Press), Atlantic-Little, Brown, 1969.*

EDWARD BLISHEN

We [teachers] might have missed the point about William Mayne.... You have to walk into one of his books sideways—it's an excellent exercise in being a crab, right down to having your eyes on stalks. The books he writes are mysterious, oblique books, the relief of reading which lies in the holiday they give you from the common effort in which we are normally engaged to make a sort of stodgy continuity out of the events and ideas and perceptions in which we are involved. William Mayne I think is one of the few pure wits who have ever written for children. We should be careful about analyzing and using such work until the excitement and delight of it are dispersed. (p. 66)

> *Edward Blishen, in* Children's literature in education *(© 1970, Agathon Press, Inc.; reprinted by permission of the publisher), No. 2 (July), 1970.*

The special features of Mr. William Mayne's enthralling talent sometimes distract attention from those features of it which link him with the most famous and gifted children's authors of the past. There is, for example, the way in which the outline structure of his plots—triumphantly disguised with a daunting ingenuity—is fundamentally uncomplicated and traditional at heart. There is the repeated use of the convention of tireless daring and resourcefulness in children, often used to outwit (though gently) the intentions of their undiscerning elders; the originality of the means and the deep understanding of relationships between generations serve to mask it. And least noticeable of all, perhaps,

is a pervading moral emphasis—worked out through detail and by means of implication rather than proffered by generalization and stark obviousness.

This last feature appears in *Ravensgill* in its usual painstakingly subtle form. Mr. Mayne's greatest gift is his ability to inhabit the moment-to-moment consciousness of the young, remember and understand their confusions, register in an elegantly precise prose narrative and dialogue their partial and yet illuminating sense of the world of objects and people, and enter into their games of perception. It follows, but almost imperceptibly, that the most sensitive are the most virtuous and that the reward of virtue—almost invariably allied, inseparably, with moral strengths like courage and persistence—is triumph. But one notable mark of his originality is that the process of winning is frequently a process also of achieving understanding. The two main child characters in his new novel work away at the mystery which grips and bewilders them, until they solve it in a way which yields a moving comprehension of adult values, rituals and obsessions. . . .

Underneath, but far underneath, the surface, the elements are traditional and familiar. But the skill with which they are re-shuffled and re-interpreted makes *Ravensgill* a solidly original achievement, even if it does not represent Mr. Mayne at his arresting and alarming best.

As always, his sense of setting and his perception of the interrelation of people and places are remarkable. . . . [The] values of old and young are set beautifully and discerningly at odds. No one senses and portrays these shifts and changes more accurately than Mr. Mayne. No one now writes with more knowledge of, and compassion for, people in all their roles. And no one contributes more through sheer sensitivity and virtuosity of style and treatment to our increasing realization of children's fiction as an art in its own right.

> *"Yorkshire Family Quarrel," in* The Times Literary Supplement *(© Times Newspapers Ltd. (London) 1970; reproduced from* The Times Literary Supplement *by permission), July 2, 1970, p. 713.*

MARGARET MEEK

The inner weather of a Mayne novel is as shifting as a spring day and inspires an expressive response rather than a report. As usual [in *Ravensgill*] the plot offers little more than the bare lines of a contrapuntal theme; two farming households, two grandmothers, children and two hired men are linked and separated by a murder mystery and the Yorkshire dales. As the details emerge, so does the pattern of time, place and relationships change, shifting like the elemental landscape features under the influence of the seasons. The language operates at many levels so that the action and the setting are both familiar and strange, as if all ordinary things have new significance. To make this possible Mayne not only invents elderly characters of great singularity but also follows with intensity the line of the growing awareness of the young. . . .

The author may not thank us for comparing this book with [Alan Garner's] *The Owl Service* but it is an achievement of the same order on a similar theme. (p. 333)

> *Margaret Meek, in* The School Librarian, *September, 1970.*

LEON GARFIELD

William Mayne's *Ravensgill* . . . has already been praised highly elsewhere; but that is no reason for not praising it again. It is, I feel, his most considerable book for some time. In addition to the usual brilliance of his writing, there is a chilling depth that lends the story a rare excitement. Little by little a long-forgotten crime is brought to the surface—both literally and metaphorically—and the weird grandmother who stands at the plot's centre becomes a shifting, fascinating character exhibited in the dimension of time. There are many memorable passages in the book, but one in particular stands out. Apparently unrelated to the movement of the plot, yet providing a necessary emotional balance, there is an episode describing a game of French cricket that is pure magic. (p. 608)

> *Leon Garfield, in* New Statesman *(© 1970 The Statesman & Nation Publishing Co. Ltd.), November 6, 1970.*

BRIAN W. ALDERSON

If you were to accuse Mr. Mayne of being 'uncompromising', he would probably stare back at you blankly as one who, despite a formidable vocabulary, has never encountered the word. If, in a given situation, little girls choose to behave petulantly and kick Dad on his bare shins then the narrator must record the sorry fact; . . . [matters like this], however odd, must take their place in the narrative. To compromise by wrapping them up in large dramatic statements would somehow make them incredible; to water them down with explanations would make them look like crude inventions. All Mr. Mayne can do is tell it the way it was.

Royal Harry, therefore, has all the characteristics—impossible to summarise—of a typical Mayne curiosity. Although one may discern a greater obliqueness of manner and even conciser refinements of dialogue and the portrayal of places, it is a book that he might have written at any time since the days of *The Blue Boat* and *Underground Alley*. We are nudged through a sequence of events that hover at one moment on the edge of total naturalism, at the next of inexplicable fantasy. In the end there are just enough explanations to account for so many weird happenings in so obscure a locality; and, as if to confirm that everything is perfectly true, Mr. Mayne, most unusually, steps out of the book's final paragraph and assures us in a passage of grand irony that everyone is living happily ever after.

The real mystification about *Royal Harry*, though, is the source of power that can drive a reader through so much inconsequence and barely perceptible, dry wit. With most authors—especially in a story as eccentric as this one—it would be the pace and strangeness of the plot; but with Mr. Mayne the plot is simply a backdrop for the interplay of character. The flitting family, the winter house, the ship and the paraphernalia of a local kingship-rite are all subordinated to the effects they have on people. Reading *Royal Harry* 'to find out what happens' is almost pointless; but reading it because you discover a quiet sympathy with Harriet Archdale and her unpredictable, unemployed Dad, her sharp, efficient, tolerant Mum, is a different matter. Thereby you enter a world where much is expected of you, where the rewards are very private and barely possible to define. You have come to a demesne of high civilisation. (p. 91)

> *Brian W. Alderson, in* Children's Book Review *(© 1971 by Five Owls Press Ltd.; all rights reserved), June, 1971.*

PAT SMYTH

With [*Royal Harry*], the adult reader finds his attention gripped with the same intensity as that of any child. This is an ideal situation for a genuine sharing of its experience.

What are the qualities of the book that contribute to its peculiarly universal character? The magical appeal of the core of the tale demonstrates ancient fealties and gives us hints of treasure to be discovered and a throne to be regained. The reader is refreshed by his journey deeper into the past and closer into the wild countryside untouched by urban and industrial development; but he is not allowed to make his 'escape'. All the happenings of the story are firmly embedded in the reality of human existence, the same then as now, and the same in childhood as when we are grown up. (p. 262)

Much has been said in praise of William Mayne's dialogue. The conversations in this book have many of the characteristics of the give and take of the best kind of improvised drama. They distil the quality of the relationships, and delight us by their dryness and wit. Much too could be said of the incidental details that enrich the fabric of the story's reality.

'Have you read *Royal Harry*?'. The question from teacher to pupil will indeed be the same question he will ask his friends. They will relish it together. (p. 265)

> *Pat Smyth, in* The School Librarian, *September, 1971.*

NATALIE BABBITT

William Mayne's prose style has a club foot. For the first few pages of [''A Game of Dark''], the phraseology seems awkward, ill-assorted and confusing. . . . And then very subtly Mayne's unique rhythms begin to assert themselves. The reader finds he has fallen into step with them and is no longer parsing sentences to get at their meaning. The gracelessness has become a kind of power instead, a power well suited to such a strange tale as this.

Donald Jackson is a 14-year-old boy who lives, in his English town, a life that is utterly bleak. His mother is humorless and withdrawn, his father an engrossed paralytic, and both, when they speak at all, are given to sermonizing. . . . Donald realizes that he neither loves nor pities his father, and because of this and his own rejection of his family's religious (Methodist) views, he is lost in guilt, shame and confusion. The escape he takes is backward in time into the feudal period and here he acts out a role so laden with symbolism that it must be examined very gently.

In the first place, it seems clear that this is no ''Connecticut Yankee'' fantasy adventure but rather a variety of schizophrenia. Donald slips effortlessly in and out of his imagined world, and embodies there the emotional chaos of his real life in physical forms which he can touch, cope with and understand. He becomes page, then squire, then knight to a feudal lord in a town menaced by a gigantic and voracious worm which eats whatever it can find, including people. In fighting the worm by the rules of honorable combat, the lord is killed and Donald, called only Jackson in this shadow life, becomes lord in his stead. He tries to fight the worm by the rules himself, sees that this means defeat and death, and runs away, returning later to slay it in the only possible way—through guile. By violating the code, he knows he has made himself an outcast, but still his method has been successful and he is still alive. Returning to reality, he discovers that he can now love his father, but his father dies immediately of a fever and Donald "lay and listened to the quiet, and went to sleep, consolate."

What is to be made of this? The worm is unmistakably and grossly phallic, and its killing insistently reminiscent of Zeus's castration of his father, Cronus. On the other hand, the lord whom Jackson serves may be a symbolic Lord of Heaven sacrificed senselessly to the blindness of Christian ethics so that Jackson, in killing the worm dishonorably, is severing his own ties with his parents' loveless piety, thereby setting himself free to love purely outside any prescribed code.

Probably Mayne intends both of these interpretations, though the Zeus-Cronus side is the stronger. I can think of no other reason why Donald, freed, should be "consolate" at his father's death unless the author intends us to understand that the father, castrated, is no longer a threat and can be loved without fear and lost without remorse.

Mayne is relentlessly, gloriously graphic in his descriptions of the horrors of the worm and pitiless in his exposure of the people in Donald's real life. There is no shred of warmth in a single word of the novel—only alienation and the all-pervasive bleakness—but it holds the attention completely nevertheless. However, it will take an extremely unusual young person to pluck from this story anything but the genuine color and suspense of the worm episodes and the surface tensions of Donald's relationship with his father. Like much of modern poetry, the rest is so personal, fragile and involuted that more patience is required to understand it than perhaps it merits. (p. 8)

> *Natalie Babbitt, in* The New York Times Book Review *(© 1971 by The New York Times Company; reprinted by permission), October 10, 1971.*

FRANK EYRE

William Mayne's name must inevitably appear frequently in any discussion of the late twentieth-century children's book. Not only because, despite conflicting views about his work, all critics agree that it is important, but also because he has written so many different kinds of book, for so many different ages. He is the one living writer of real stature who has already established a secure reputation. Whatever else he may write from now on he has written sufficient to demonstrate an instinctive understanding of the real nature of children, an infallibly sure ear for the truth of children's conversation, and a subtly complex way of looking at life, people and things which makes him unique among contemporary writers.

There are still many people who argue about William Mayne's work, who say that children don't like his books; that they sit on the library shelves; above all, that children don't *talk* like that. Anyone who believes this has never listened properly to children talking among themselves. Few children may use the actual words or constructions that Mayne uses, but what he achieves, for those with ears to hear, is the authentic sound and *feel* of children talking.

William Mayne's use of dialogue is, in fact, the distin-

guishing mark of his work. Children (and adults) who do not enjoy the finely strung tension and wit of the kind of dialogue that he writes (and it *is* a sophisticated taste) are not likely to appreciate his books. Because, to a much greater extent than with any other contemporary writer for children, his stories are introduced, developed and concluded with talk. Not to such an extent that, as with Ivy Compton-Burnett's novels, if you do not concentrate on every single word of the dialogue you are likely to miss an essential part of the plot, but at least to the extent that if you have the kind of visual rather than intellectual imagination that demands constant description to keep you 'on scene' you are likely to miss the essential point of his books —and may even lose your way in them. There are few descriptive passages; he rarely sets a scene—and when he does it is not particularly well done—so that the reader sometimes has to work hard to understand what is being described. Instead the reader is made aware of the effect the scene had on the people who were present and becomes vividly aware of what it felt like to be there. His books are about people and feelings rather than things. A 'thing' is often the superficial centre of the plot (an old barge, a disused railway line, a boat, a 'parcel of trees') but it is the people who matter and what they are like is communicated to the reader not by description but by what they say. If he wants his readers to know that a boy who has just come into the room is big and burly and angry he rarely tells you that he is—instead, he makes him *sound* big and burly and angry.

William Mayne is particularly good at conveying by small details of dialogue the inevitable tensions of close family relationships, and there are many fine examples of this in his books. . . . Mayne never makes the mistake of overdrawing these tensions until they become false tragedies. He knows that family life is not like that. But he has a wonderfully sure touch for the complex love-hate, friendship-dislike, need-for-yet-wanting-to-be-away-from that all close families share, and a family, though it is seldom the centre, always plays an important part in his books. He is almost but not quite as good with the relationships between children at school and at play.

The world of William Mayne is an intimate one, restricted to a few people closely observed, and circumscribed always by the normal ranging abilities of children and their inescapable necessity to report home for meals and bed and to school during term-time. It is, in fact, the true world of children. But it is in some ways a *mental* world, the projection of someone whose own deeply-felt love of childhood has never been lost, and who spins his wonderfully fine web of imaginative truth from the truth he knew rather than the truth he sees. It is a world which has something in common with Kenneth Grahame's. Not because there is any similarity between their books, but because both look backwards at childhood with an adult mind. Both are genuinely thinking hard about children, striving to get their essential nature down on paper, to tell us how they think and feel, what life seems like to them, what they think of us, to make it possible for us to share a child's world. But Kenneth Grahame never succeeded, in those of his books which are about children, in making them truly *for* children, whereas William Mayne does. His world is one which children and their parents inhabit equally and this is the second distinguishing mark of his books—that no part of them is ever included cursorily. Everything that is in them is there for a purpose and each part is handled with the same kind of observation and affection. The world of school, the world of home, the world of play are indivisible to him, they are all part of the world of childhood, and that is the world he writes about. (pp. 139-41)

He is unlikely to write a better book [than *A Swarm in May*]. It has all the Mayne qualities, fine dialogue (the way in which the characters of the different masters are brought out in discussion is remarkable) and a lovingly observed *mise-en-scène* superbly served by one of his best plots. . . . The story [of *Sand*] contains some of Mayne's best dialogue, and the talk and behaviour of the girls and boys is not only finely observed and accurately recorded but is also at times very funny. Many of Mayne's stories are set in [a small coastal town or village], where the past is still a living one, the population is small, everyone knows everyone else and relationships are close between a small group of mostly working-class families, shopkeepers, electricians, railwaymen, painters and other tradesmen. *Pig-in-the-Middle* has much the same kind of plot. . . . But, as with *Sand,* it is not the story that matters, it is the people in it, and Michael's family is one of Mayne's best-sustained portraits. (pp. 141-42)

[*Earthfasts*] is an uncanny book, with an extraordinary power of conviction that impresses one again with Mayne's great gifts. The suspension of disbelief while reading is so complete that the sense of chill that the boys experience comes through vividly. Only at the end, when many readers will reject the idea of the drummer-boy being left alive above the ground, to settle down and become an ordinary human boy again, is the reader brought up suddenly by a question. . . . It is interesting to note that he first thought of killing the boy off and only left him alive because others asked him to do so.

I have no wish to belittle William Mayne's work, because I think him the truest and most creative of those few major authors who are genuinely writing *for* children. But it would be a mistake to think that his books will be widely popular, or that all children will enjoy them. So much so that parents, teachers or librarians who try to force children who do not like them to read them are doing the author a real disservice. Those children who do appreciate and enjoy them will come back to them again and again, but they are always likely to be in a minority. (pp. 142-43)

> *Frank Eyre, in his* British Children's Books in the Twentieth Century *(copyright © 1971 by Frank Eyre; reprinted by permission of the publishers, E. P. Dutton & Co., Inc.; in Canada by Penguin Books Ltd.), Longman Books, 1971, Dutton, 1973.*

JOHN ROWE TOWNSEND

William Mayne has never made any concessions to the lazy or inattentive reader; he has never written the fully-automated book. In any case, we cannot all like the same things, and even among books of comparable merit there must always be some that strike a more popular note than others. Nevertheless, the impression of Mayne as a writer of somewhat rarefied excellence—one who operates at a high literary altitude where the air is thin—still persists, and may have some justification. Re-reading many of his novels in a short time—after having previously read and admired them individually at the time of publication—I am inclined

to feel that Mayne as a writer has a characteristic which deprives his work of a substantial and vital element.

This, I think, is a tendency to shy away from the passions. Children feel strong emotion and can be deeply conscious of strong emotion in others, even when it is not understood. Life without it is less than the whole of life. Mayne is aware of the passions, most notably so in *Ravensgill*, but even there he appears to define deep feeling by drawing round its edges rather than plunging in. One senses in *Ravensgill* that the air is full of old guilt and fear, grievance and feud and loss; but one is never there in the middle, experiencing these things. Pity and terror are rare in Mayne's books; the expression of love, in any of its many forms, is to the best of my recollection absent. To say this is not to make an adverse criticism of any book. *Ravensgill* seems to me exceptionally fine, and I do not suggest that the author could or should have written it differently. But there is a limitation here. I suspect that it is a lack of robustness and of red corpuscle in Mayne's work which often causes it to make a less satisfying impact than that of writers who are more crude in their perceptions and far less gifted artistically. (p. 131)

I did not read *Follow the Footprints* when it first came out, so I cannot say how it seemed when Mayne was new and when the number of good current children's books was much smaller. I do, however, recall the first appearance of *A Swarm in May* . . . , which seemed then, and seems now, an outstanding piece of work. In this novel, set in a cathedral choir school based on the one he had attended as a boy, Mayne created or re-created a closed, complete and satisfying world, in which a large cast of characters was clearly distinguished, and in which a story was clearly told and a mystery satisfyingly solved. And behind these individuals, behind the daily life of school and the puzzle from the past, emerging out of the mist to dwarf them all, was the cathedral itself. Indeed, the cathedral seemed in the end to become the frame of the story: a frame filled with cathedral space, a space filled with cathedral music, with the choir's singing and Dr Sunderland's organ-playing. It is hard to fault *A Swarm in May*. Within its limits—and in this case I believe the limits were a source of strength—it is as near to perfection as any children's book of its decade. Even [Philippa Pearce's] *Tom's Midnight Garden* is of no greater formal excellence, although it has a depth which *A Swarm in May* lacks. But then, the latter was a young man's book; indeed, it gives the impression that it might have been written by a marvelously talented schoolboy, a literary Mozart.

In the books which followed, Mayne seemed to be elegantly treading water. Individually his books were of obvious distinction and were duly acclaimed, but, collectively, they began to add up to disappointment. (pp. 132-33)

In 1964 and 1965 a change of direction came with *Sand* and *Pig in the Middle*. These were about the everyday lives of boys and young adolescents, doing quite ordinary things with no elaborate mysteries to be solved. . . . *Sand* comes close to being a very good story, but is marred to my mind by a seemingly-endless account of an attempt by the boys to excavate the tracks of an old narrow-gauge railway. Their persistence in this pointless task is entirely convincing, but the description of it comes to share its own pointlessness. . . . I have heard praise of *Pig in the Middle*, a story about boys in an inner-city district who try to rehabilitate an old barge; but it seems to me that Mayne is not at home in this setting, and its greyness has communicated itself to the book.

At this stage, with the new writers of the 1960s becoming prominent, it seemed that Mayne was almost becoming a back number. But in 1966 he published *Earthfasts:* an extraordinarily fine book in which at last he surpassed his early work. I believe that in *Earthfasts* there is an element of response to the novels of Alan Garner. At last Mayne makes use of the supernatural, which previously he seemed to have avoided, and he uses it superbly. In Garner's manner he brings the fantasy-world into the here-and-now; and to make it more credible he has as his main characters two modern, scientifically-minded schoolboys who look for rational explanations of everything. When *they* are convinced that the impossible has happened, we are all convinced. (pp. 133-34)

The sheer sweep of *Earthfasts,* swift and wide and totally under control, has never been matched by Mayne. It has its flaws at the level of simple surface probability—surely two boys finding themselves in possession of an ever-burning cold candle would have taken it straight to be analysed—but it marks a breakthrough, and it remains, in 1970, its author's best book. It also seems to have begun a new lease of artistic life. In 1968 Mayne took up another time theme, but played it the other way round, with his present-day characters journeying into the past. This was *Over the Hills and Far Away,* in which Dolly and Andrew and Sara, pony-trekking on a visit to their Gran, find themselves switched into post-Roman Britain, into a tale of old unhappy far-off things that they can't understand or even really believe in. And Sara, who has flaming red hair, is looked on by the tribesmen among whom she finds herself as a witch, a saviour, a sacrifice. *Over the Hills and Far Away* is notable for an outstandingly clear, almost transparent, style of writing, and for the effective contrast between the fluid, dreamlike nature of the action and the enduring solidity of the Yorkshire landscape through which it moves. *Ravensgill* . . . is set, yet again, in the Yorkshire dales, and at first sight has a resemblance to Mayne's work of the *Grass Rope* period, a dozen years earlier. Here are families on two farms, estranged by an unsolved crime of half a century ago. Here is an elaborate and ingenious solution to the mystery. But there is a sombre note in *Ravensgill* which is new to Mayne; and the dominant character, Grandma, the impetuous girl who lost her man long years ago and has grown into a foolish, pathetic, but spirited old woman is one that I would once have thought outside his range.

William Mayne is a writer with striking strengths and weaknesses. He has a genuinely distinguished, if sometimes unduly whimsical, mind. He writes superbly. He can evoke a landscape, a time of day or year, a kind of weather, the feeling of the way things are. . . . He has an unfailing gift for the precise and vivid simile. . . . He has a fine imagination, and a gift for story construction and narration when he cares to use it, which is not always. If he feels so disposed he will turn aside from his story to chase images like butterflies, snatching significant and insignificant detail alike from the air. He will allow the action of a story to mount towards climax and then, casually and disappointingly, let it down. His plot structure may sag in the middle, as in *Sand;* and he seems unworried by disconcerting shifts of viewpoint, as in *Over the Hills,* which has a complete change of cast after the first fifty pages.

He is a notable writer of dialogue, and, like many who excel in this field, appears to have a gift of mimicry. In *The Twelve Dancers* almost all the characters are Welsh, and although not a word of Welsh is spoken, their English is Welsh English. His ear is unfailing and one hardly needs to be told that he is a musical man. He knows how things are done, and can tell you; he seems to have an instinctive understanding of all trades, their gear and tackle and trim. But his books are not notable for their characters. Between Dr. Sunderland, the rumbling-voiced choirmaster of *A Swarm in May,* and Grandma in *Ravensgill* fifteen years later, I find that few Mayne characters spring unbidden to mind. On looking through the books, one finds many who are well drawn, and hardly one who fails to ring true, but few who come vigorously off the page with a life of their own.

Mayne has written that 'the best part of a book is the plot . . . I don't bother with the characters until I have begun'. To my mind this is a weakness. There are only a few basic plots, and they have all been used again and again. Character is infinite, and, for my money, characters make novels. But, on the whole, Mayne children mostly resemble other Mayne children. Of the numerous mothers and fathers, the only one who stays firmly in my memory is Marlene's sharp, narrow, down-to-earth mother in *The Twelve Dancers,* who sends three-year-old small brother Porky to school to get him out of the way, but grouses at having to pay dinner-money: 'He can't eat a shilling a day if he tried.'

The reluctance, noted earlier, to become involved with any depth of feeling may have something to do with Mayne's relative failure in the area of characterization. Often one feels that the emotional life of his characters is weak or is simply left blank, and they are correspondingly enfeebled. (pp. 135-37)

[Mayne's] principal work . . . consists of his numerous novels for older children. They are for the most part individual, original, enjoyable, admirable. Their flavour is unlike that of anything else. Some of the recent books have shown the author reaching out towards new achievement: *Earthfasts, Over the Hills and Far Away* and *Ravensgill,* especially, show signs of a maturity as a writer which had been long delayed after early brilliance. In spite of having written forty books, Mayne still has plenty of time on his side, and there is every reason to suppose he will go on filling out as a writer. In 1955 one felt of the author of *A Swarm in May* that he might do anything. In 1970 one feels much the same about the author of *Ravensgill.* (p. 138)

John Rowe Townsend, "William Mayne," in his A Sense of Story: Essays on Contemporary Writers for Children *(copyright © 1971 by John Rowe Townsend; reprinted by permission of J. B. Lippincott Company), Lippincott, 1971, pp. 130-38.*

PAUL HEINS

[In *A Game of Dark* Mayne] again illustrates his technical mastery of plot and his skill in manipulating the elements of time-fantasy. . . . The whole story alternates between the reality of the unhappy events in the life of Donald living in an English town and the fantasy of a world in which he can slay a monster—ultimately a world which he can choose to enter or to reject. The two elements—denoting outer and inner experience, objective and subjective perceptiveness—

are uncannily combined in the dual awareness of Donald Jackson, who by the end of the narrative has solved his problem and can go "to sleep, consolate." Actually, the author has permitted himself to present more genuine human involvement in this story than in some of his earlier ones, but—despite the power of his narrative—his characters remain stand-offish. (p. 59)

> *Paul Heins, in* The Horn Book Magazine *(copyright © 1972 by The Horn Book, Inc., Boston), February, 1972.*

ROBERT BELL

It is almost becoming a *cliché* with reviewers to say that William Mayne's latest book is 'his most powerful to date,' but really one cannot avoid saying it of [*A Game of Dark*]. How he is able to go on giving us books which evoke ever higher and higher praise is nothing short of astounding.... The way the action slips from one world to the other and back again, and the subtle interaction between fantasy and reality, make the story totally absorbing. The dream world, although an escape, is no cosy, fairy-tale place, where everything comes right, but from the grimness and horror, and even his own 'honour rooted in dishonour', Donald derives a strange strength and consolation when his father dies. This is a most profound and moving book which stays long in the mind. (pp. 63-4)

> *Robert Bell, in* The School Librarian, *March, 1972.*

MARGARET MEEK

The day you start work is the initiation ritual. For Mason Ross [in *The Incline*] it means more than 'going to business' at the bank; it includes passing to the men's side and seeing the world of the quarry, where until now his father seemed unchallenged, as a microcosm of human insecurity and his father no stronger than others. (p. 259)

Although we now know how to become enmeshed in Mayne's characters despite the external simplicity of the situation, we can never capture in a short account enough of the complexity of feeling he portrays. This book is more direct than *A Game of Dark*, as if the author were offering us a tale of rural Yorkshire in the early days of this century, but its linear plot is no less subtle than those of the other recent books, and draws the reader into as many contrapuntal moves as any adult novel.... The dialogue is sheerly poetic, yet as tense as steel, a thing of great beauty and wonder.

This is a book to make adolescents pause, if only because it brings boys' matters close to the reader in a way that no adult novel can do so directly any more. For this reason alone Mayne is in a class by himself. (pp. 259-60)

> *Margaret Meek, in* The School Librarian, *September, 1972.*

As usual Mayne has created a solidly organic setting and society [in *The Incline*].... As usual too Mayne's ability to get inside the head of his oddly undemonstrative adolescent hero allows us to share the confusion of Mason's new job, the perplexities of his first love ..., and his dismay in witnessing his father's ostracism as Spitalhouse publicly blames his financial blunders on Ross. There is even one of Mayne's incongruous, mystical scenes when Mason and Moira, who are running away from their fighting fathers,

wake up in a sheep-fold on beds of fleece and view the meaning of existence in a visually disoriented moment. But all of Mayne's skill and effort seems misplaced when we come to the ending.... There is a sort of stodgy humor about [this ending], and Mayne's oddly effective prose and sure narrative sense carry [it off], but it's a disappointingly expedient resolution. The novel on balance is neither as dark and demanding as Mayne's best work nor as insubstantial as *Royal Harry* ... but falls somewhere between in both mood and strength. In the end it's the period setting and the traditional nature of Mason's concerns that one remembers. (pp. 1034-35)

> Kirkus Reviews *(copyright © 1972 The Kirkus Service, Inc.), September 1, 1972.*

MICHELE MURRAY

[William Mayne] is becoming the John Creasey of children's fiction.... [*The Incline* is] his best book in several years. Unfortunately, because it's all very English in its understated, clever dialogue and portrayal of a Yorkshire town at the turn of the century, with all its subtle class antagonisms, I suspect American children are likely to put it down in bewilderment, for all its virtues. In his resolute strangeness and obsession with certain themes, Mayne, like Ivan Southall, is much like a writer of adult fiction who works out of his private vision rather than a purveyor of made-to-order tales. (p. 8)

> *Michele Murray, in* Book World—The Washington Post, Part II *(© 1972—The Washington Post Company), November 5, 1972.*

HELEN STUBBS

In *The Unreluctant Years*, Lillian H. Smith says "that a new book's claim to stand beside a well-loved favorite rests in the degree to which it possesses the magic of a Lewis Carroll or a Stevenson or a Mark Twain."

With what infinite certainty do we realize in Mayne's books that children do things 'with blitheness,' are endlessly searching for lasting truth, and in the process, reveal to us the heart of the matter. "The eager, reaching, elusive spirit of childhood is here. It has its own far horizons and a friendly and familiar acquaintance with miracle." It is because of this quality, which is innate in the books of William Mayne, that we cannot fail to recognize his universality, his disarming truth, his power to re-create for us the essence of the heart of a child, by the strength of his expression and insight into the ways they think and act. This power makes us all renew within ourselves—if for a short time only, the inexpressible things of that rare and fleeting receptive time that was our own childhood. In his studies of children, he is able to express for us their essential thought-workings, projected as they are, from imaginative conception into real adventure. The children think things out before us and act in accordance with intensity and feeling. Everything is real to them and has meaning. Because we can read about ideas as they are being crystallized into action for us through the eagerness of vision that only a child can have, we too are able to draw on inner capacities and can give ourselves, the readers, a rare treat. We are able to feel safe again, in a world which is true, where there are no conventions, and no delusions. They rediscover for us a kind of symbol of the eternal, and the intensity of our pleasure in being able to recapture it, is real indeed.

''The thing that makes a book a good book to a child,'' says Lillian H. Smith, ''is that it is an experience and the spirit of childhood in each generation is attracted to the spirit of writers of those books who collectively have given them a children's literature.'' Surely William Mayne falls into such a category.

If we wonder with C. S. Lewis whether the 'excitement' in a story may not be an element actually hostile to the deeper imagination, we shall wonder again with William Mayne, when we find ourselves accepting with shivers and delight, the range of ideas which are embodied in his tales. We find the secret to our pleasures lies, I think, largely in his style and especially in the style of the dialogue and the undertones and overtones of his settings. It takes the whole story to build up for us the atmosphere that his imagination recreates for us, and it is achieved almost entirely by talking. His appeal is to the whole 'idea' of the things he mentions. If it is 'unicorns' [as it is in *A Grass Rope*], he makes everything which goes into the conception of a unicorn, count. He is able to capture for us the essential truth of the basic idea. (pp. 5-6)

He makes for us, as a story-teller, the kind of 'Secondary World' that Tolkien talks about in his essay on *Fairy-Stories,* which our minds can enter. Inside it, what he relates is true; it accords with the laws of that world. We enter it through the clear, true heart of a child because he makes us aware, with a child's intense feeling, of the immensity and luminous quality of what is for them absolute and eternal. The boundaries of life are for them uncharted, free, innocent, and defy the measurements of time and place. He recreates for us that joyous state of being which was once our own proud, unconscious possession. Whether as a child or as an adult, this intrigues us. We emerge from the experience with our senses quickened.

I think Mayne in all his books is also acutely aware of the fresh, unsullied, direct approach to the world of nature and life in general, that is in the heart of childhood itself. He suggests it to us at every turn of phrase.

''What is the use of a book without conversations,'' says Alice [in *Alice in Wonderland*]. That being so, William Mayne excels here too. Because it is by means of conversations, direct, by implication, at times elliptical and often dialectal, that the motivation and charm of his books unfold. Through his use of conversation we are able to feel the whole process of thought growing in the characters. It is a procession of ideas really, one thing suggesting another. . . . One's appetite is continually being whetted, as the relationship of thought, idea, character, and action, is projected before our eyes.

It is entirely true to the child mind. Based on everyday living, sharpened and attune to legend and tradition, and illuminated by imagination, the 'adventure' of the book is the complete realization of all three. We thus step within that real world of childhood again, when we read the books of this engaging and skilful writer. Children have no such thoughts when they read his stories. They don't have to. They *sense* reality—the reality which is basic in things mortal and immortal.

Tradition or legend to him is unequivocally English, and just as alive today as it was in the Middle Ages. The quality and influence of that tradition penetrates the present and is the motivation behind the writing in his cathedral choir school stories. It absorbs us, the centuries are rolled away and we make our way in and about and around the living cathedral of today.

He shows us the comfortable, easy relationship that can be between boys and masters. His values are sound. His ideas keep us enthralled. They move into other dimensions, particularly the world of the spirit. His motivation—a combination magically mixed—of the real and imaginative stimulation at work in the minds and hearts of the young. Because it is the core of his writings—all adults are swept along with it and move within the radiance of this reality too. We are shown by this creative mind of Mayne that the world of fantasy is really not blurred by the real world, but rather set in motion by it.

Whether it is an English cathedral; whether it is an eerie marsh in Somerset full of untold fears and possible mud monsters that snarl and snap amid close dead stalks; whether it is a mere, an island and a borrowed *Blue Boat;* or Mary wandering in the misty dales of Yorkshire, searching for her unicorn—he gives us a world of heightened reality. The atmosphere he creates lives for us. He has infinite capacity to suggest, rather than describe, and to integrate character, story and a sense of place, with evocative power.

The adults in the books are completely understanding and play their part with an unusual degree of spontaneous lightness of heart, appreciating to the full that the world of a child is very real, both inside and out, and so very rich in a number of inexpressible, unexplainable things.

In all, his style is deceptively simple. His acute perception of boys—their different habits, ways of thinking, their manner of influencing one another and the entirely lovable Mary of *A Grass Rope*—unforgettable. His rich character studies of adults remain extraordinarily vivid in our minds —personalities in the flesh. (pp. 6-7)

[With] subtlety of writing and observation, by being completely in tune with childhood, with provocative ideas, rich characterization, a sense of tradition and landscape, he offers us a unique realization of the power of communication, by which the everyday world in which we live can be transcended. By a subtle blending of all these things and others, yet more intangible, into a whole state of being, and illumined by his imagination, he shows us the mirrors of a mind. The experience to us is an enriching one. It is an art that conceals art. (p. 7)

Mayne's books, with all their tonal variations remain true to the arpeggios of life as he knows them. No false note is ever struck. His style is literary, distinctly original and individualistic in its expression. It can breathe atmosphere in a single phrase, is often incisive in its physical perception, and charms with startling and often unexpected insight into the mind and heart of all his characters, especially children. He writes with a controlled and polished style and is often elliptical, with flashes of humour that tease and delight the imagination with their genuine quality of surprise. Though never of universal popularity in their appeal, his books, in the experience they afford to individuals, cannot be adequately assessed in general terms. A master craftsman in his particular art, he brings together myth, legend, tradition and human nature, and etches in for us their interplay especially in the elusive and thinking minds of children. Because he clothes it all in the cloak of an adventure in imagination he catches for us, with classic art, that particular spark of vitality which feeds its own flame. In a little more than 20 years he has given to the world of children's literature a contribution that vibrates with intimations of immortality. (pp. 13-14)

Helen Stubbs, "William Mayne's Country of the Mind," in In Review: Canadian Books for Children, *Winter, 1972, pp. 5-14.*

PENELOPE FARMER

William Mayne is one of the most considerable, and certainly in some respects the most interesting writer for children now and [*A Game of Dark*] is undoubtedly his best book. Less rich and localized in its fantasy than *Earthfasts;* less rich in human terms than *Ravensgill;* not as affectionately funny as *A Swarm in May,* it is still all those things in a highly concentrated and synthesized form, besides demonstrating Mayne's recurring obsession with mysterious family pasts and relationships. And it goes far deeper than any of the others.

Mayne's sheer brilliance has always been one of his drawbacks as a writer. Some of his books could almost be described as cons—marvellous writing concealing the fact that they are uncontrolled, perverse, peripheral, even one dimensional in human terms (all those patient, understanding mothers . . .). But here he goes straight to the centre, shirking nothing. There are no tricks, no verbal fireworks. It is pared down, precise, plain, using images sparingly, highly economical in form, yet possessing an extraordinary translucence and clarity. It has however drawn upon itself the most surprising and unprecedented abuse culminating in the accusation that Mayne is working out his hangups on adolescents—as if most hangups weren't conceived in childhood and first encountered in adolescence anyway. His, in all events, are beside the point and to say the least it would be impertinent to speculate.

The hangups in the book relate to Donald's family: his cool, priggish, teacher mother who forgets and calls him Jackson at home; his dying minister father and his own ambivalent feelings towards both of them—his horror at his father's illness, his guilt at his lack of felt love. The problems here are intensified maybe, but they seem to me central to adolescence; what we feel—or don't feel—about our families, once we cease to take them for granted, the guilt aroused by our ambivalence. We are a guilt ridden, depressive society, and perhaps, underlying the declared concern for the young in the cries of hate against this book, is a reluctance by many to look at such aspects of themselves. (pp. 37-8)

It is still not an easy or comfortable book. I would not expect it to reach many adolescents (but that does not mean it should not be offered them; to a few it may say a lot). Nor do I think it is flawless. The railcrash is slightly melodramatic. The whole ending is not quite right—you grasp momentarily what it says and feels, and then lose both. But on any reckoning it is important and considerable. (p. 38)

Penelope Farmer, in Children's literature in education *(© 1973, Agathon Press, Inc.; reprinted by permission of the publisher), No. 11 (May), 1973.*

Like another vast and splendid feu d'artifice the poetic prose of William Mayne delights the mind with its subtle glowing lights [in *The Jersey Shore*]. First here, then there,

then somewhere else unexpectedly so that the eye strains to make out the pattern the picture surely comes into being. As it slowly develops and the dark spaces are filled in with brightly coloured patches and luminous lines the full picture appears and lo and behold everything has fallen into place and the old magic has worked once more. We applaud the virtuosity and store away another warm memory. *The Jersey Shore* is just such a book, and when the last chapter has added its final touches we grasp the whole composed of tantalising details, the significance of which all but escaped us at first reading. . . . This is a deeply satisfying book for that rare bird, the sensitive, adolescent reader. . . . (p. 280)

The Junior Bookshelf, *August, 1973.*

BRIAN ALDERSON

It seems to me that *Over the Hills and Far Away* and *A Game of Dark* are as important for their exploration of time and place as ever they are for the stories that they have to tell. In both books we stand like Magra and Korva 'surrounded by a misty edge where one time ran into another' and it is the uncanny skill with which Mayne summons up . . . an utterly convincing past and mingles it with the present in a particular place that gives these two books their peculiarly haunting quality. The effect is fairly obvious in *Over the Hills and Far Away,* but has not been so widely noticed in *A Game of Dark.* Reviewers, with a whiff of Freud in their nostrils, have gone chasing phallic symbols and Zeus/Cronus patterns and have neglected what is emotionally and technically one of the book's triumphs: Donald's ambivalent relationship with his Other World and the absolute reality of that place as a paradigm of his home world.

The skill that has gone into this book and its predecessor can be seen emerging gradually through Mayne's whole writing life—like [*Earthfasts's*] Nelly Jack John from under Richmond Castle—and the success with which it is carried out can perhaps be measured by comparing Mayne's work with that of Alan Garner in the recently published *Red Shift.* For all the force of Garner's historical imagination he does not achieve that fugal intensity with which William Mayne plays off past against present simultaneously so that the reader too feels the chill of 'being in a place before the map knew about it'.

It is through their intricate play with time that *Over the Hills and Far Away* and *A Game of Dark* can be seen as closely related to William Mayne's latest novel *The Jersey Shore.* . . . With considerable daring he has elected to set the scene for what he has to say in the United States in the early 1930's and the small happenings of this part of the story concern a boy, Arthur, and his mother who are spending a longish holiday on 'the Jersey shore' with an oddish aunt. It is quite possible that American readers will find fault with some of Mr. Mayne's characterisations in these scenes and it is for the more knowledgeable to say whether Arthur—who is one quarter escaped Negro slave —speaks, or at least thinks, in a manner altogether too akin to one of Mr. Ardent's young gentlemen.

This part of the book, with the exception of a superb, somewhat enigmatic Negro Preacher, is fairly conventional Mayne family-portrait stuff (however unconventional such may be by most writers' standards of perception). What gives the book its energy are the communings between Arthur and his English grandfather who, incompatible with the aunt, his daughter, ('like two beakers in a bag, we chip off each others' handles') lives farther down towards the shore. In a series of meetings the old man conveys to the boy not just recollections of his own feckless past as a labourer in the Norfolk fen-country, but something which is the essence of that distant locale, its people and the generations of family life. And to say 'conveys' is to be as exact as possible—for communication between the two of them is only partially in words—the brilliantly caught accents of one man from one place—much of it is in transferred images. . . . (pp. 133-34)

With *The Jersey Shore* . . . it seems to me that William Mayne has crossed 'the misty edge' and written a book where the complexity of experience requires more than childish resources for its appreciation. The fulcrum of the story is not Arthur, down there on a visit, but Benj Thatcher and his profound but unco-ordinated recollections. The angle of the obliqueness has shifted decisively against the child, for whom the disparate elements of past and present, place and family will surely not fuse into the compelling unity that they do for an adult. Like so much of William Mayne's writing the tones of the book's voices echo in the mind long after it has been finished, the pictures that it summons up live in the memory, but the truth of its emotion speaks from maturity to maturity. (p. 135)

> *Brian Alderson, "On the Littoral: William Mayne's 'The Jersey Shore'," in* Children's Book Review (© *1973 Five Owls Press Ltd.; all rights reserved), October, 1973, pp. 133-35.*

JANE LANGTON

[No] one merges past and present more seamlessly and masterfully than William Mayne. In some of his settings, the past is embodied in relics and monuments which litter the landscape, it incarnates itself in optical effects of light, it spills out of the cracks in the sky, it moves restively under the soil, it maintains a kind of urgent pressure on the present day. (p. 440)

> *Jane Langton, in* The Horn Book Magazine *(copyright © 1973 by The Horn Book, Inc., Boston), October, 1973.*

PAUL HEINS

Although he lacks the emotional intensity of [Alan] Garner, Mayne does have a sense of story; and despite his willfully oblique manner of style and method, he can convey the significance of events in such books as *Earthfasts, Ravensgill,* and *A Game of Dark.* . . . But although he displays in *The Jersey Shore* his flair for catching colloquial characteristics of speech and idiosyncrasies of character, he suggests a situation without developing it and tells a mere wisp of a story. . . .

Until the epilogue, the narrative is singularly tepid and lacking in the kind of motivation that makes for storytelling. And there is little suspense, though much covert humor, in the detailing of casual events of everyday life. The setting only hazily hints at the New Jersey shore. What is remarkable about the book, however, is its ending—or rather its two endings, that of the original English edition and that of the American edition.

At the end of the English edition, the reader learns that Arthur is black, that his grandmother "had been born a slave"; and for once, the story is given an unexpected

strength—both emotional and romantic—when Arthur is reunited with the English branch of his family. In retrospect, one realizes that Mayne does give fleeting indications of the race of the protagonist. His ancestor was a man who "came from the sea. . . . dragging a chain." One member of grandfather's English family states "'We abide here, and folk bear with us, but we don't belong and look different, so dark we are.'"

The conclusion of the American edition ignores the fact that Arthur is black; but black he must be if Mayne's hints throughout the story are to have any meaning. In the American ending, Arthur's visit to Osney, his grandfather's original home, becomes a mere act of filial piety and destroys whatever emotional impact the book may have. (p. 581)

> *Paul Heins, in* The Horn Book Magazine *(copyright © 1973 by The Horn Book, Inc., Boston), December, 1973.*

CHARLES SARLAND

William Mayne is the great "problem" amongst modern children's writers. Everyone seems agreed that he is a writer of great subtlety and complexity, that he has an uncanny knack of seeing the world through the eyes of children, and that he is the most assured stylist of all modern children's authors. Yet he remains obstinately unread by children, and short of saying that he is a very sophisticated writer, which he is, no one has satisfactorily explained why. I do not intend, in this article, to question his critical standing. . . . I want in particular to look in some detail at the writing style, for it seems to me that valuable clues are to be found in it that go a long way to explaining precisely why many children find it difficult to come to terms with a writer who, on the face of it, would seem to have so much to offer.

On first reading the earliest of the Chorister books, *A Swarm in May,* one is struck by three things: the meticulously detailed descriptions of the physical environment; the uncanny insight into a small boy's concerns; and the wordplay, the witty allusions and puns that inform the book. These three aspects of Mayne's work turn out to be characteristic of his whole output, and all three things relate to his style. First and foremost then, he is concerned to show exactly what it feels like to be a small boy in a choir school. He does this by detailing the physical environment from precisely the point of view of such a small boy, recreating for the adult reader that forgotten time when the immediate physical environment was a continual source of interest and even wonder. (p. 107)

If one examines the wordplay of [this] book one gets some idea of the mental processes that Mayne expects his readers to apply. For instance, one of the teachers, Mr. Sutton, has a nickname, Brass Button. At one point Owen puns on his name "'No fear,' said Owen, 'Brass Button's come quite unsown with me'" and later in the book he develops the metaphor in answer to Dr. Sunderland, "'He won't for me, sir,' said Owen. 'I weaken his threads too much.'" And here is Trevithic, the head chorister, with two musical puns in the same breath, the one obscure and the other more obvious, "'You are burbling out the dullest passages I ever heard,' said Trevithic. 'I think you must have gone slightly decomposed in the afternoon.'" In order to appreciate such jokes—indeed in order to understand them, for their metaphorical applications have specific meaning within the narrative and emotional context of the book—the reader must stand back and make the connecting links that Mayne deliberately leaves out. In other words the wordplay alienates the reader from the drama of the narrative and draws his attention instead to the formal linguistic elements that serve to unite Mayne's delineation of character. In the above example on the two occasions that Owen puns on Mr. Sutton's name the reader is reminded of Owen's apprehension of Mr. Sutton but remains objective in his consideration of that apprehension.

Once again the technique is devoted to dissipating the immediate dramatic impact and replacing it with a contemplative consideration of the situation. The Brechtian term "alienation" would seem to fit the bill very precisely here, for Brecht's alienation devices were conceived with exactly the same purposes in mind. I am not suggesting that Mayne is a Brechtian writer, merely that he has adopted and adapted the technique for his own use. In passages of dialogue the same result is achieved by somewhat different means. Take for example a crucial interchange in *Cathedral Wednesday*. A dayboy, Andrew Young, finds himself acting head chorister because of illness. He has a lot of trouble with the two boys next below him in seniority. Finally he puts them on the prefect's "list", a grave step. There follows this conversation when he meets one of them:

> "Is it . . .?" said Silverman and stopped.
> "Hmm," he said, and shook his head.
>
> "Better line up," said Andrew quietly.
>
> "Yes," said Silverman. He looked fully round at Andrew. "Is it Book Boys?" he said.
>
> "What do you think?" said Andrew.
>
> "But honestly," said Silverman, "we . . ."
>
> "Line up," said Andrew. "Attention, left turn, quick march, left, left, left."

This is, potentially, a highly dramatic exchange in which Andrew, for the first time in the book, asserts his authority. Yet the conversation is interrupted by passages of description . . . so that the passage takes far longer to read than it would have done to say. . . . So clearly Mayne wishes to prevent his readers from becoming emotionally involved either in Silverman's desperation or in Andrew's triumph and they are encouraged instead to take a more objective view.

On other occasions he will deliberately create a situation in which he is forced to break off the narrative in order to explain what is going on. Here is Mr. Lewis, late for breakfast in *Words and Music*: "'. . . go and make the toast for me. It's my breakfast.' He didn't mean that the toast was for him, but that he should have been downstairs seeing that everyone else got it in time." Instead of a clear exposition of the total situation within which the drama can unfold, Mayne gives the reader little snippets of exposition in order to clear up the puzzlement that he himself has created. (pp. 108-10)

In *Choristers' Cake* the central character, Sandwell, is unsympathetic. He is conceited, obstinate and foolish. At various points in the story he makes the wrong decisions. Yet he remains the central character, and it is through his

eyes that we perceive the action. If it were not for his alienation techniques Mayne would never be able to handle such a delicate situation and retain an objective moral viewpoint. But the book requires a degree of sophistication in the reader that would not normally be found in children of the same age as his characters. It is clear from the way that he uses pace, dialogue, causal relationships, puns and wordplay that the last thing that he wants is that the reader should be carried along on the tide of the narrative. Always the requirement is that out of the sense impressions that he supplies the reader should construct his own pace, his own drama, his own causal and verbal links, and it is a measure of Mayne's mastery that they are there to be constructed. He admits no ambivalence of response, but the reader must work hard to pick up all the cues that are laid down for his guidance.

There are a number of conclusions that present themselves. One is that Mayne will quite simply remain a minority taste. Another is that perhaps the publishers could usefully look at the age range for which they are intending his books. There is a case for saying, for instance, that *Choristers' Cake* is suited to a thirteen- or fourteen-year-old audience rather than a ten-year-old audience. Certainly *Ravensgill* would seem out of place in a list of books for eight- and nine-year-olds. One hopes that the fact of his unpopularity will not discourage publishers from ensuring that the best of his books remain in print. (pp. 112-13)

> *Charles Sarland, "Chorister Quartet," in* Signal *(copyright © 1975 Charles Sarland; reprinted by permission of the author and The Thimble Press, Lockwood Station Road, South Woodchester, Glos. GL5 5EQ, England), September, 1975, pp. 107-13.*

RUSSELL HOBAN

William Mayne, in *A Game of Dark,* has taken on not only the Oedipal conflict but the basic existential one of staying or going, holding on or splitting. . . .

Appropriately the story opens with a feeling of sickness and a pervasive stench. The bad smell of Donald's life has carried over into a second life in which he must ultimately fight a stinking worm who leaves a slimy track behind him as he preys on a feudal village. . . .

Mayne is technically unlimited—he can do anything with words—and he handles his psychical shifts suavely. For a time Donald chooses the second life in the feudal village. Eventually he kills the worm, not in the proper knightly fashion but with the ingenuity and tenacity of desperate courage. (p. 73)

Mayne has taken on themes that require considerable force and depth of the writer; how well he has done them is less important to me than that he regards them as being within his province. (p. 74)

> *Russell Hoban, "Thoughts on Being and Writing" (© 1975 by Russell Hoban), in* The Thorny Paradise: Writers on Writing for Children, *edited by Edward Blishen, Kestrel Books, 1975, pp. 65-76.*

NATALIE BABBITT

At first, a William Mayne story always sounds to me as if it had been translated from some other tongue by someone with a rather thin gift for languages. The structures are awkward, and sometimes passages have to be paraphrased to reveal their meaning. But after a few pages, the reader grows accustomed to all this and forgets it, because Mayne's style has a strength all its own and the strength takes over.

This story [of "A Year and a Day"], unlike some others of his, is a gentle, uncomplicated tale. . . .

It has no particular wisdom or message, nor even the traditional—suspense and drama of the folktales it most nearly resembles. The characters do not live on in the imagination after the book is closed. But the sense of something in motion behind this story, and the resonance of its telling, provide a special power, as they do in all of Mayne's work. Perhaps it is simply that he cares very much about what he is doing, that instead of being skimmed from the surface, his stories come from very deep in the well. This is a rare thing in children's fiction and should be celebrated wherever it is found. (p. 40)

Natalie Babbitt, in The New York Times Book Review *(© 1976 by The New York Times Company; reprinted by permission), May 2, 1976.*

SALLY EMERSON

[*A Year and a Day*] is a fairy tale which superbly evokes the potency of words and the wonder of natural things. The language is simple and fresh, reflecting the sisters' sensual and visual appreciation of the beauties around them and their dawning delight in words. . . . The tenderness of the peasant family towards the strange little boy, the essential kindness of the squire and the rector, the humour of small incidents, and the pungency of the Cornish dialogue, provide a warm and realistic backcloth to the resonant tale of the fairy-child who returns to his own. In its simplicity it deviates from William Mayne's usual, more elaborate plots, and should appeal to readers of eight upwards, and upwards. (pp. 80-1)

Sally Emerson, in Books and Bookmen *(© copyright Sally Emerson 1976; reprinted with permission), November, 1976.*

MYLES McDOWELL

In *A Parcel of Trees* Mayne evokes a languid, summery world of long and lazy days and slow quest. He unfolds his story unhurriedly, drowsing and droning, so it seems. But the impression is deceptive—a retrospective impression. In fact, the story seldom stands still, and then only for the shortest passages. (p. 148)

There is with Mayne a sense of a slow, deep, steady current of understanding underlying the lighter surface show. The surface carries the reader buoyantly; the undercurrent it is which is remembered. And this, of course, is Mayne's strength, this hiding of the introspective, reflective quality in dialogue and incident. (p. 149)

Myles McDowell, in Writers, Critics and Children, *edited by Geoff Fox, Graham Hammond, Terry Jones, Frederic Smith, and Kenneth Sterck (© 1976 by Geoff Fox), Agathon Press, Inc., 1976.*

MARY CADOGAN and PATRICIA CRAIG

William Mayne has devised a kind of dialogue in which the character speaks principally to himself, to clarify some facet of his personality for his own benefit. His children are surprisingly articulate but leave much unsaid. The possibilities for ambiguity, for private interpretation, are endless here, but the device is used also to project unequivocal feelings and uncertainties. . . . In *Earthfasts* . . . the author's concern with psychological effect is everywhere apparent: he has got inside the characters who are confronted with a variety of phenomena, in order to express more explicitly their efforts to extend conventional definitions to accommodate their experiences of the supernatural. . . . The author's explanations are entirely convincing; his reordering of "natural" events has in it a matter-of-fact quality and controlled tension which combine authoritatively. Everything is worked into this book; legend, superstition, a "scientific approach", psychological detail, a surface interest, a powerful evocation of scene; and everything *works*, because it is given just the right degree of emphasis. The characters are driven to extremes of feeling and experience (one even "dies") but there is no note of hysteria, no sense even of make-believe. (pp. 356-57)

Mary Cadogan and Patricia Craig, in their You're a Brick, Angela! A New Look at Girls' Fiction from 1839 to 1975 *(© Mary Cadogan and Patricia Craig 1976), Victor Gollancz Ltd., 1976.*

AIDAN CHAMBERS

It does not follow, of course, that a writer who places a child at the narrative centre of his tale necessarily or even intentionally forges an alliance with children. . . .

William Mayne, always published as a children's author but notoriously little read by children and much read by adults, may, for all I know, intend to be a writer for children. But what the tone of his books actually achieves, as Charles Sarland brilliantly uncovered [see excerpt above], is an implied author who is an observer of children and the narrative: a watcher rather than an ally. Even his dramatic technique seems deliberately designed to alienate the reader from the events and from the people described. This attitude to story is so little to be found in children's books that even children who have grown up as frequent and thoughtful readers find Mayne at his densest and best very difficult to negotiate. He wants his reader to stand back and examine what he, Mayne, offers in the same way that, as nearly as I can understand it, [Bertolt] Brecht wanted his audiences to stand back from and contemplate the events enacted on stage. (p. 73)

[There is] an ambivalence about Mayne's work that disturbs his relationship with his child reader. And this is made more unnerving by a fracture between a narrative point of view that seems to want to ally the book with children, while yet containing a use of narrative techniques that require the reader to disassociate from the story—to retreat and examine it dispassionately.

What Mayne may be trying to do—I say "may be" because I am not sure that he *is* trying for it—is not impossible to achieve, though it is very difficult indeed to achieve for children. (pp. 73-4)

Once an author has forged an alliance and a point of view that engages a child, he can then manipulate that alliance as a device to guide the reader towards the meanings he wishes to negotiate. (p. 75)

What such manipulation of the reader's expectations, allegiances, and author-guided desires leads to is the further development of the implied reader into an implicated reader: one so intellectually and emotionally given to the book, not just its plot and characters but its negotiation between author and reader of potential meanings, that the reader is totally involved. The last thing he wants is to stop reading; and what he wants above all is to milk the book dry of all it has to offer, and to do so in the kind of way the author wishes. He finally becomes a participant in the making of the book. He has become aware of the "telltale gaps". (p. 76)

Aidan Chambers, in Signal *(copyright © 1977 Aidan Chambers; reprinted by permission of the author and The Thimble Press, Lockwood Station Road, South Woodchester, Glos. GL5 5EQ, England), May, 1977.*

MARGERY FISHER

In *Max's Dream* William Mayne has returned to the Cornwall of *A Year and a Day*, to the 1890's when, in a small community tightly organised, thirteen-year-old Katie, servant in training to Mrs. Veary, cherishes an unspoken love for Max, the boy who lies in the room above, dominating the household with his precocious speech and his physical helplessness. The story is distanced from the reader not only in date but also in the manner of its telling, for Katie, an old woman waiting for death, is looking back at this critical year in her life, capturing, as the old can, the very ebb and flow of her feelings and the precise detail of cottage kitchen or bedroom, carrier's cart or seaside ferry. The mystery of Max—who he is, what his condition is, when he was orphaned—is unravelled partly as Katie and her peers talk to their elders in the village and partly by their own efforts to break Max's dream of an island, a house full of gold and silver and a silent girl—a girl who, he decides, must be his queen if he is to play the part of king in the midsummer revels on Troy Town. . . . Both [Max's and Katie's] kinds of prose, simple yet resounding and full of ambiguities, further William Mayne's intention in suggesting the magical rightness and sincerity of children's ideas of the world round them—the customs and hierarchies of the village, the relationship of Katie with riotous Trombo and little Hannah, the different approach of the incomer Max to the environment. Like Alan Garner and Lace Kendall, Mayne has worked people and places into a whole by the force of words simple in themselves but meticulously chosen and "in their best order". (p. 3209)

Margery Fisher, in her Growing Point, *November, 1977.*

MARGARET MEEK

To approach *Max's Dream* the reader has to switch into the rhythm of the language of recollection, so that the "then and there" becomes the here and now. Among William Mayne's many gifts is a facility for making memories for those too young to have them, so that his readers go back over experiences they never had. . . .

The reader learns the rhythm of the narrative from William Mayne's delicate pacing. Familiar dialect conversation centres on immediate events, while the before-and-after comes with a slightly breathless tumbling of sentences as events crowd the recollection.

It is impossible to write about William Mayne without sampling the texture of his prose. The tenses of his verbs need a study of their own. "I hanged the kettle over the fire and we had a cup of tea and now it's time for bed." The adult reader looks at the surface structures, the child sees through them, once he is confident, into Max's dream world as it merges with the strenuous efforts Katie makes, her own foot blistered and raw with a burn, to ease his pain. Accidents, fights, and Max near death are swooped over in the long sentence strings, while the ferry with "a sort of gallows and there the bell do hang" and the surgeon with his things "all as black bones and leather" stand out as shaped events. The reader's privilege is to take part in the play of the text and emerge the more literate for his efforts. (p. 1413)

Margaret Meek, in The Times Literary Supplement *(© Times Newspapers Ltd. (London) 1977; reproduced from* The Times Literary Supplement *by permission), December 2, 1977.*

MARGERY FISHER

At first sight Alice Dyson might seem to be in the same position in William Mayne's *It* [as the character of Anne in Robert Westall's *The Watch House*]. But though this girl of nearly twelve might seem to be an obvious medium through which a spirit would reach out to the world of everyday, it is not her state of mild discontent which emotionally directs the release of "It". Instead, the plot of the story—as circular as the position of the four crosses at the city boundary, as circular as the rings Alice cannot help finding—turns on an ancient curse which, subtly and insidiously, affects (or might have affected) many people. . . . (p. 3237)

Certainly William Mayne is not detached about Alice and the state of mind that seizes her after she has unwittingly given the invisible being a chance to escape into the city which had centuries before destroyed its witch creator. Only Alice, haunted and puzzled though she is, realises that this is not a wholly evil spirit, nor the indescribably horrible creature of legend, but a spirit defenceless, lonely and bitterly unhappy in its lack of a way to exist or a place to exist in. All the same, Mayne remains an observer, analysing the total effect of a visitation on a particular place. This place he has described with an intricate simplicity that gives his book the special quality of populousness. If his description of the emergence of "It" reminds one of the similar scene in *Earthfasts* when the two schoolboys open the ground and allow the drummer boy of two centuries before to emerge from the earth, the pattern of social, religious and domestic life in this new book takes one back, rather, to a book like *Underground Alley*, with its picture of a community with all its overlappings and dependencies. Time and again some small detail . . . opens momentarily a new facet of the city into which an ancient wrong has intruded. Mayne's story, like Westall's, ends with an exorcism. In both books there is a compelling movement from near-humour to solemnity, a necessary deepening of tone towards a reconciling of turbulence and distress. In each scene a girl is released from a burden which could have been crippling. But the exorcism performed by Alice's Anglican grandfather and his Catholic counterpart, described with an almost offhand tenderness, releases the whole city, where Westall's scene completes the study of an individual girl. Mayne has completed a circle in his book but he has not drawn a conclusion. "It" remains imperfectly explained and undefined, and in this lies the justification for his choice of subject. Manipulating words and rhythms, hints and half-truths, in his open-ended story, he has stirred in the reader an almost physical sense of something beyond reason. In the deepest sense of the word, his is a true ghost story. (p. 3238)

Margery Fisher, in her Growing Point, *January, 1978.*

William Mayne is full of surprises. There are moments in *It* where one thinks of *Earthfasts* and sometimes of Alan Garner (but always Mayne benefits from the comparison), but the book remains superbly individual and original.

Mayne knows better than anyone how much more convincing the supernatural is when presented in terms of the everyday world. He knows too that places (and he is the supreme living celebrator of the spirit of Place) are made up of past and present and that the two cannot be separated. (p. 45)

[This story] has its share of fun as well as terror. The two elements are always close together. When Alice climbs Eyell Hill and, putting her hand into a hole in the stone at the summit and having it held by another hand "dry and rough", understandably screams and runs away from the Eyell, she says to herself, 'because her throat had to say something, "I yell. . . . Perhaps that's what it means"'.

I will not disclose the plot, because it is as good as it is characteristic of the writer, except to say that it is based firmly in local history and human nature. The terrors are real and logical, and there are no contrived easy solutions to Alice's dilemma. The honours are shared equally between Alice, a child who grows through grappling with her problem, and the city. It is a small place with something of the intimacy of a village. . . . Here is a writer who is incapable of cliché, in character as in phrase. He plays his skilful game with people and with words, a master of style, a master of character, and a master of environment.

It is hardly necessary to add that this book is a book for children only in the sense that children play important parts in the action. It would be absurd, and wickedly wasteful, to limit its readership to the young. Plenty of young people will enjoy the fun and the excitement as they will like being scared stiff, but they must be prepared to share the book with their elders, for this is a book for everyone. (pp. 45-6)

The Junior Bookshelf, February, 1978.

DOMINIC HIBBERD

It is not about IT, a familiar spirit, nor even about Alice, a twelve-year-old who wins a cathedral school scholarship, but about the power of imagination and the reality of free will. Alice, like [J.R.R. Tolkien's] Frodo, inherits a ring of power and can choose whether or not to wield it. The power is represented by the demon, who brings her nine rings by which it could master her; Alice, choosing to retain her freedom, rejects them all and eventually makes a tenth by which she can master the demon. IT manifests itself as a poltergeist and poltergeists, we know, are associated with the emotional conflicts of girls in early adolescence. Fully unleashed, however, this strength which throws eggs about and makes empty chairs kneel in assembly could destroy a cathedral town; or, to put it much more boringly, adolescent feelings that are not controlled can become socially destructive. Laying the demon involves the entire commu-

nity, including the Bishop; Alice cannot become a complete person unaided.

The principal conflict which Alice has to reconcile lies between the values of her parents; her mother, daughter of a scholarly clergyman, insists on "good" English while her father, a local tradesman, speaks broad Yorkshire (it is characteristic of William Mayne that this dilemma is described in terms of language). . . .

I am not sure that William Mayne himself is quite clear about the mechanics of releasing and controlling the familiar but they provide some nice moments of terror and comedy. He expects the reader to work as hard as Alice and he makes the work rewarding. Words are alive in this book and full of possibilities; and they, too, are an expression of Alice, whose mind teems with conceits and images.

She can, for example, imagine, vividly, a flood in the main street, but when the familiar joins her such imaginings can become real. A series of extraordinary events, described with cool precision, involve the family and eventually the whole town, past and present, in making the tenth ring, a great circle round the city. Ghosts walk, choirs sing in a noonday darkness, for the third time Alice sees the Minster already in ruins and—she makes her choice. It is the choice that many children of her age would make, I think; and, as the darkness is rolled back and poor Alice is sick into the gutter, one feels that one has not been convinced by any mere sleight of hand. Yet Mr Mayne, like IT, is undoubtedly a conjurer.

Dominic Hibberd, "Rings of Power," in The Times Literary Supplement *(© Times Newspapers Ltd. (London) 1978; reproduced from* The Times Literary Supplement *by permission), April 7, 1978, p. 376.*

DIANA WAGGONER

The magical blending of times and spells in [*Earthfasts*] is made more effective by Mayne's matter-of-fact attitude. His tight, intricate plotting, skillful prose, and distinctive, individual characters, especially the drummer boy and gentle, passive Keith, combine with the immense profundity of his invention to make this one of the best of all fantasies, a classic of speculative literature. (p. 240)

Diana Waggoner, in her The Hills of Faraway: A Guide to Fantasy *(abridged by permission of Atheneum Publishers; copyright © 1978 by Diana Waggoner), Atheneum, 1978.*

PETER HUNT

Possibly because I am not primarily concerned with children, but rather with books and literary theory, I feel that Mayne is a major writer, who should be recognized as such. That opinion is based on the *oeuvre*, rather than on any single book. . . . In his style, Mayne is an original, one of the few true stylists of the twentieth century; if the language echoes a somewhat idealistic view of a child's perceptive processes, it is nonetheless at its best with the apparently inconsequential, avoiding patronizing either the characters or the implied readers. It sets up, in short, an honest narrative contract.

Consider, for example, the opening of *The Twelve Dancers*. . . . (p. 13)

I feel that the passage offers precisely what literature

should offer; something essentially different; something unique. More prosaically, it is remarkably economical in setting the character and background for the novel, and the irony operates—unlike many other writers'—on both the writer-child and the writer-adult levels. If all that is known is known through the child's eyes, that does not invalidate its acceptance by the adult; and Mayne can extend this technique to virtuoso lengths, as in *Royal Harry*.

It may be true that his characters rarely stand out, being functional parts of enclosed worlds (or, as Mayne himself has said, secondary to the narrative . . .), for some readers rather in the manner of the early Lawrence—and this derives from his total approach. While avoiding direct emotional involvement, his capacity to see over the heads of his characters—as in much of *A Grass Rope*—gives a compensatory dimension, in a tradition running from [Henry] Fielding to Ford Madox Ford and P. G. Wodehouse.

Not to make this a catalogue, I might cite, as others have done, his use of dialogue, which is Pinter-esque, at least in its obliquity and its implication of social infra-structures, if not in its verbal density. This goes hand in hand with his capacity to draw rounded families from suggestions (as in *The Battlefield*) or complete communities from casual details (as in *A Parcel of Trees*). (pp. 14-15)

> *Peter Hunt, "The Mayne Game: An Experiment in Response," in* Signal *(copyright © 1979 Peter Hunt; reprinted by permission of the author and The Thimble Press, Lockwood Station Road, South Woodchester, Glos. GL5 5EQ, England), January, 1979, pp. 9-24.*

(Lula) Carson McCullers

1917-1967

American novelist, short story writer, poet, and playwright. Despite a small literary output, McCullers is considered a leading writer of the American South. She was born and grew up in Georgia, and her novels are deeply rooted in her southern background. Her pervasive themes of spiritual isolation and the loneliness of the individual give unity to her work but have also proved to be a limiting factor. She was often placed in the category of southern Gothic writers who concerned themselves with decay and the grotesque and used horror for its own sake. McCullers, however, used the physical incapacity of her grotesque figures as a symbol of their spiritual incapacity to love or receive love. McCullers originally intended to become a concert pianist but was forced to abandon her plan due to lack of money. Consequently she turned to writing, and often drew on her knowledge of music for the structure of her works. She published her first book, *The Heart Is a Lonely Hunter*, at the age of 23. Her autobiographical portrayals of adolescence as a period of questing, loneliness, fantasy, and rebellion have been called both touching and accurate. In *The Member of the Wedding*, Frankie Addams desperately searches for her identity, which she calls "the we of me." The dramatization of this novel won McCullers the New York Drama Critics Circle Award. Mick Kelly, the teenager in *The Heart Is a Lonely Hunter*, looks for love and meaning as she faces adulthood. McCullers' portrayals of southern blacks have also been praised for their depth and understanding. (See also *CLC*, Vols. 1, 4, 10, and *Contemporary Authors*, Vols. 5-8, rev. ed.; obituary, Vols. 25-28, rev. ed.)

LOUIS B. SALOMON

Around the pivotal character of John Singer, a deaf-mute, and around the theme of man's vital craving for a sympathetic, understanding confidant, Miss McCullers drapes the rather loosely woven texture of [*The Heart Is a Lonely Hunter*], a book flavored with compassion and a gentle melancholy but never with despair. . . .

While Miss McCullers harps perhaps a little too persistently on the one plaintive string of her theme, she leaves several of her people hauntingly engraved in the reader's memory; and she displays a most praiseworthy frankness and lack of affection. The acuteness of character-perception revealed is quite remarkable in an author who . . . is a girl of twenty-two.

Louis B. Salomon, "Someone to Talk To," in

The Nation (copyright 1940 by the Nation Associates, Inc.), July 13, 1940, p. 36.

RICHARD WRIGHT

With the depression as a murky backdrop, ["The Heart Is a Lonely Hunter"] depicts the bleak landscape of the American consciousness below the Mason-Dixon line. Miss McCullers' picture of loneliness, death, accident, insanity, fear, mob violence and terror is perhaps the most desolate that has so far come from the South. Her quality of despair is unique and individual; and it seems to me more natural and authentic than that of Faulkner. Her groping characters live in a world more completely lost than any Sherwood Anderson ever dreamed of. And she recounts incidents of death and attitudes of stoicism in sentences whose neutrality makes Hemingway's terse prose seem warm and partisan by comparison. Hovering mockingly over her story of loneliness in a small town are primitive religion, adolescent hope, the silence of deaf mutes—and all of these give the violent colors of the life she depicts a sheen of weird tenderness. . . .

I don't know what the book is about; the nearest I can come to indicating its theme is to refer to the Catholic confessional or the private office of the psychoanalyst. The characters, Negro and white, are "naturals," and are seen from a point of view that endows them with a mythlike quality. The core of the book is the varied relationships of these characters to Singer, a lonely deaf mute. . . .

The naturalistic incidents of which the book is compounded seem to be of no importance; one has the feeling that any string of typical actions would have served the author's purpose as well, for the value of such writing lies not so much in what is said as in the angle of vision from which life is seen. There are times when Miss McCullers deliberately suppresses the naturally dramatic in order to linger over and accentuate the more obscure, oblique and elusive emotions.

To me the most impressive aspect of "The Heart Is a Lonely Hunter" is the astonishing humanity that enables a white writer, for the first time in Southern fiction, to handle Negro characters with as much ease and justice as those of her own race. This cannot be accounted for stylistically or politically; it seems to stem from an attitude toward life which enables Miss McCullers to rise above the pressures of her environment and embrace white and black humanity in one sweep of apprehension and tenderness.

In the conventional sense, this is not so much a novel as a projected mood, a state of mind poetically objectified in words, an attitude externalized in naturalistic detail.

> *Richard Wright, "Inner Landscape," in* The New Republic *(reprinted by permission of* The New Republic; © *1940 by The New Republic, Inc.),* August 5, 1940, p. 195.

CLIFTON FADIMAN

I have rarely read a work of fiction like "Reflections in a Golden Eye," a novelette in which are held, in unstable equilibrium, a certain not unimpressive intuitive quality (pointedly reminiscent of D. H. Lawrence), a feverish concern with distorted and neurotic types, and a kind of innocence, as if the author had never encountered any of the experiences she describes but were making them up, as a child invents a magical tale. The net effect is completely unconvincing.

Mrs. McCullers' characters make Mr. Faulkner's seem like the folks next door. (p. 78)

Mrs. McCullers was herself in her first novel. In her second effort she seems to be borrowing from her reading of others. This mimicry gives an effect of falseness which is further strengthened by her too obvious desire to create people and situations that are strange and startling. She has undeniable talent. It would grow more harmoniously if she could, right at this point in her development, give herself a humorous once-over. If she did, she might find something to laugh at in the grotesque and forced hallucinations of which "Reflections in a Golden Eye" is composed. (p. 80)

> *Clifton Fadiman, in* The New Yorker *(© 1941 by The New Yorker Magazine, Inc.), February 15, 1941.*

In its sphere, [*Reflections in a Golden Eye*] is a masterpiece. It is as mature and finished as Henry James's *The Turn of the Screw*, though still more specialized. Its story is about life as Carson McCullers sees fit to create it in a Southern Army camp, and is almost desperately psychomedical. Within its 183 pages a child is born (some of whose fingers are grown together), an Army captain suffers from bisexual impotence, a half-witted private rides nude in the woods, a stallion is tortured, a murder is done, a heartbroken wife cuts off her nipples with garden shears.

In almost any hands, such material would yield a rank fruitcake of mere arty melodrama. But Carson McCullers tells her tale with simplicity, insight, and a rare gift of phrase. She makes its tortures seem at least as valid as the dull suburban tragedies from [James T.] Farrell's or [Theodore] Dreiser's Midwest, commonly called lifelike. *Reflections in a Golden Eye* is the Southern school at its most Gothic, but also at its best.

> *"Masterpiece at 24," in* Time *(reprinted by permission from* Time, The Weekly Newsmagazine; *copyright Time Inc. 1941), February 17, 1941, p. 96.*

BASIL DAVENPORT

["Reflections in a Golden Eye"] is a sad disappointment, not only after [Miss McCullers'] remarkable first novel,

"The Heart Is a Lonely Hunter," but after its own opening pages. It is instantly plain that the book is by some one who can *write*, with a haunting power and suggestiveness that can be felt at once; but it all too soon becomes clear that the story is a vipers'-knot of neurasthenic relationships among characters whom the author seems hardly to comprehend, and of whose perversions she can create nothing. On the first page she promises us a murder on an army post, involving "Two officers, a soldier, two women, a Filipino, and a horse"; and it is no joke, but the simple truth, to say of this cast, the horse is the only one for whom one can feel comprehension of his character and pity for his tragedy. . . .

Such a collection of sick and unnatural souls could become the stuff of tragedy only if handled with the greatest comprehension, and woven into a pattern which gave some logical conclusion to the bent of each character. Neither of these conditions is here fulfilled. The murder which we have been promised comes as an anticlimax, not because the preceding emotions are too great, but because so many of the narrative threads do not lead to it, and because it is no resolution even of those which do: the book does not culminate in tragedy, it trails off into futility. And to Miss McCullers her characters' vagaries seem merely something to be cold-bloodedly chosen for their bizarrerie, contemplated, and set down, without pity or comment or any sort of use. (p. 12)

> *Basil Davenport, in* The Saturday Review of Literature *(copyright, 1941, by The Saturday Review Co., Inc.; reprinted with permission), February 22, 1941.*

FRED T. MARSH

[Miss McCullers' concerns in "Reflections in a Golden Eye"], and ours, is what she sees going on within, for her people are masks underneath which pulse strange, distorted psyches.

Miss McCullers is young, but quite of age. . . . "The Heart Is a Lonely Hunter" proved that. It was youthful in its special intensity and in its probing candor, its certain relentless, merciless quality. But it was a remarkable novel, placing a strange, original talent on display. . . . The present much shorter and slighter novel exhibits to some degree the same quality. But it is vastly inferior. Quite unlike the other, it suggests the youthful prodigy; and one suspects it was written first and unwisely pressed into service by the publishers to follow up the success of the first novel. Either that or it has been over-hastily written.

"Look!" cries the Filipino sitting before the fire, staring at the glowing embers, "a peacock of a sort of ghastly green. With one immense golden eye. And in it these reflections of something tiny and"—

"Grotesque," suggests the Major's wife. That gives us title and mood. These people, shifting shadow shapes, are distortions, dancing reflections in a glowing eye shining through an epicene penumbra. And it is, of course, entirely proper for the literary as the pictorial artist to treat of the grotesque and arabesque, of masks and puppets, of distortions and of horror and evil, of things unreal and unknown things, darkly hidden, if such be his way of approach to verity. But the six principals here . . . , moving two by two through a puppet show that appears to be a mere masquerade, seem only costumed. . . .

No one could say, however, that Miss McCullers has not succeeded in making her genuine talent felt, a talent which is less of subtlety than of infant-terrible insight expressed with quite grown-up precision, as yet unmellowed and unhallowed. It should not be forced in order to take advantage of a passing vogue, for it will surely crack up in the hurly-burly of competition. It is a brave talent; but not, I think, a very sturdy plant. It calls for a gentle handling and careful cultivation.

> *Fred T. Marsh, "At an Army Post," in* The New York Times Book Review (© *1941 by The New York Times Company; reprinted by permission), March 2, 1941, p. 6.*

EDMUND WILSON

Carson McCullers is a writer of undoubted sensibility and talent who seems to have difficulty in adjusting her abilities to a dramatically effective subject.... ["The Member of the Wedding"] has no element of drama at all.

The whole book is a formless chronicle of Frankie's musings as she walks about the town, and of her interminable conversations in the kitchen with the maid and the little cousin. These kitchen scenes are very well done in the sense that they create an atmosphere and that the characters are droll and natural: the maid is particularly good; the way she is made to talk is perfect. But they have no internal structure and do not build up to anything. The whole story seems utterly pointless....

I hope that I am not being stupid about this book, which has left me feeling rather cheated. (p. 87)

> *Edmund Wilson, "Two Books that Leave You Blank: Carson McCullers, Siegfried Sassoon" (reprinted with the permission of Farrar, Straus & Giroux, Inc.; copyright 1946 by Edmund Wilson; copyright renewed © 1973 by Elena Wilson), in* The New Yorker, *March 30, 1946.*

GEORGE DANGERFIELD

["The Member of the Wedding"] is Carson McCullers's third book; and we have now, I should think, sufficient evidence for remarking that, while there are quite a few writers who unfortunately resemble her, she fortunately resembles nobody else. She is unique....

["The Member of the Wedding"] is not just a study of adolescence. Frankie Addams, it is true, conforms to a possible pattern of behavior. She does nothing which a twelve-year-old girl might not do. Yet the further you read into "The Member of the Wedding" the more you realize, it seems to me, that Frankie is merely the projection of a problem that has nothing much to do with adolescence.

The three chief characters are Frankie herself, her [cousin] John Henry, and the [cook] Berenice.... Their problem is elementary, unanswerable, and common to all age levels....

In other words, the problem which obsesses them is human loneliness: the basic problem which Virginia Woolf, after years of investigation, could only state in terms of "here is one room, there another." Miss McCullers states it in its most undifferentiated form; places it in this light and in that; looks at it savagely, gleefully, tenderly; seems almost to taste it and to roll it round her tongue; but never attempts to find an answer.

Indeed, what makes this story so unusual is the fact that most of it takes place through the medium of desultory conversations between three really weird people sitting in an even weirder kitchen. Nothing or almost nothing occurs here, and yet every page is filled with a sense of something having happened, happening, and about to happen. This in itself is a considerable technical feat; and, beyond that, there is magic in it....

I would be the last to deny that Miss McCullers has [her limitations]. It must be obvious to everyone who has read her books that her art excludes many important things with which the artist today is rightly preoccupied. It is an exclusive art, not out of choice but out of necessity: not because it does not wish to include but because it cannot.

She is a suggestive rather than an eloquent writer, and often seems to present us less with a meaning than with a hint. And yet the lines of her work are clear and firm. I do not know how this is done; but my ignorance will not deter me from attempting to provide an explanation.

Though she has an acute observation, she does not use it to make rounded people. Her characters invariably remind one of faces one *may have* seen, in a dream perhaps, in a tabloid newspaper possibly, or out of a train window. Their clothes, their gestures, their conversations are selected with an admirable eye and ear to verisimilitude; but the actual inhabitants of these clothes, gestures, and conversations are not themselves quite human. In fact, this book seems more and more to insist that it is, as it were, a monologue furnished with figures.

For Carson McCullers's work has always seemed to me to be a form of self-dramatization. It is true that this can be said of most immature fiction. But Miss McCullers is both a mature and fine writer. She does not dramatize herself in the sense that she is merely autobiographical; but she does dramatize herself in the sense that she seems to invest the various sides of her personality with attributes skilfully collected from the outside world.

From this point of view, "The Member of the Wedding" is a masquerade; but a serious, profound, and poetic masquerade in which the Unconscious (or the Subconscious or whatever you wish to call the subliminal personality) expresses itself, now through the voice of Frankie Addams, now through that of John Henry, now through that of Berenice Sadie Brown. The other characters, who certainly belong to the real world, hover round the edge of this extraordinary monologue, with one foot in it and one out; behaving with none of the awkwardness which you might expect from them in such circumstances; but adding richness to the story and relating it to more normal fiction....

[This] is, to my mind, a marvelous piece of writing. Not merely does it sustain the interest all the way through, but it does so under circumstances which demand the utmost delicacy and balance from the author.

The book avoids what T. E. Lawrence called "the kindergarten of the imagination" on the one hand; on the other hand, it never becomes a mere sequence of neurotic images. It steers a wonderful middle course between these two morasses. It is a work which reveals a strong, courageous, and independent imagination. There are other writers in the contemporary field who are of more importance than Carson McCullers. Of her it should be sufficient to say, once again, that she is unique.

George Dangerfield, "An Adolescent's Four Days," in The Saturday Review of Literature (copyright, 1946, by the Saturday Review Co., Inc.; reprinted with permission), March 30, 1946, p. 15.

MARGUERITE YOUNG

Carson McCullers' *The Member of the Wedding*, astutely and frugally designed, is a deceptive piece of writing, and its candor may betray the unwary reader into accepting it as what it first seems, a study of turbulent adolescence.... [McCullers' portrait of childhood is composed of] a complexus of unreal, real, and surreal events, in a pattern which is itself as delusive as the dream of a total happiness. Merely by thinking in terms of the individual childhood here presented rather than in terms of the many and carefully erected symbols employed by the author in an argument concerned with man in his relation to various kinds of reality, the reader may miss the importance of this curiously spiritual book.... Mrs. McCullers, sometimes depicted as a sensationalist revelling in the grotesque, is more than that because she is first of all the poetic symbolist, a seeker after those luminous meanings which always do transcend the boundaries of the stereotyped, the conventional, and the so-called normal. Here, then, is a fairly clear, explicit writing—explicit even in its use of the anomalous, the paradoxical, the amorphous—the confusions of life. Though its themes are romantic, their working out is classically controlled. There is no wilderness for the reader to get lost in, and if he is lost, it is perhaps because this writing does not weep, gnash, wail, shout, wear its heart on its sleeve. It is rather like a chess game, where every move is a symbol and requires the reader's counter-move. (pp. 151-52)

At first level, it is the story of a boy girl Frankie who, during a torrid summer, plans to join her brother's wedding, to get married to the two who are getting married, to belong, to be a member of something, to break down all barriers of atomic individualism, to be somehow intimately involved with all the intimate concerns of the happy human race. If Frankie can only crash in on this wedding of two other people to each other, being the third member, loving both, loved by both, even though she is excessive, why, then, there will be the kind of perfect happiness which man has always dreamed of, like a union of all the nations.... What Frankie is dreaming of is possible only inside her own creative head, is nowhere else, is very far from possible. The purely imaginary goal is still a goal for Frankie, who cannot easily give up. She and Berenice sit discussing these crucial matters in endless, capacious luxury, capacious for them and for the reader, who can ponder as they ponder, think backward and forward. Then there is an audience, John Henry, aged six, who chimes in every once in a while and provides, in the drama, his own special, peculiar insights. He is beautifully described, once as a little blackbird running against the light. In fact, all three characters, all major, are treated with dignity and revealing tenderness, especially Berenice, whose blue glass eye is like Frankie's dream of the impossible wedding, a dream of almost heavenly harmony on earth. Berenice does not precisely dream of turning white, but her blue glass eye is a terrible commentary on the color line and the arbitrary divisions which shut off people from each other. All this book is a discussion of happiness, done as quietly as *Rasselas* by Dr. [Samuel] Johnson, and the conclusion is faintly similar to

his. There are minor characters moving back and forth like the minor figures on a chessboard, in this case both cosmic and human. Nobody is ever disparaged. The Negro people are always people, thoughtful, mature, at home with Frankie who wants to belong to the human race, at home with John Henry, who is very soon to leave it.... (p. 152)

I see the impossibility of describing the book without describing it in terms of its intricate symbols.... One thing is always described in terms of another. The argument, though veiled by diverse imagery, is never lost. The imagery is functional. In fact, if there is any one statement to define Mrs. McCullers' position as a writer, it is not that she is merely the sensationalist but that she is ... concerned with theories of knowledge—though the by-play of wit does not entice her away from the main themes. There is no lush undergrowth. Control is never absent. The framework is always visible.

People want to be told what they already believe, and Mrs. McCullers, in this case, is not telling most people what they already believe. Rather, she is continually questioning a great many complacent assumptions as to what is what, for she is too closely skeptical and analytical a writer to suppose that in the accepted platitudes lies truth. She weighs, she measures. Wild idealism does not carry her beyond the boundaries of a rigorous common sense world, partly for the reason that she finds the given world itself a sufficient phantasmagoria of lost events. Her attitude toward human nature is patient, behaviorist, clinical. Her writing, brooding and exploratory though it is, remains for these reasons as formal as a problem in geometry, though the perspectives bewilderingly and constantly shift. She sees life as impressionistic, but she herself is not the impressionist. She is a logician in an illogical realm.

Is there a given pattern in the nature of things, a music of the spheres, or was it all, as Mrs. McCullers implies, accident and chaos and fragment to begin with? Mrs. McCullers, speculative like her characters, dreams of an omniscient pattern but finds that such a pattern is rather more man's project than God's and that its realization may comprise another chaos. Then, too, there is the problem of how to make the inner world and the outer world conjoin, the problem immediately faced by Frankie, an anarchist in an old baseball cap. These three people, Frankie, John Henry, and Berenice sit around the kitchen table talking most musically while the green summer heat grows more and more oppressive around them. The focal subject is the impossible wedding, the illusory goal, out of which grow other illusory subjects, all related. John Henry draws crazy pictures on the wall. The piano tuner comes to tune the piano (perhaps next door), and the notes become a visible music climbing to the ceiling. And this is almost all that ever happens in the book but enough to keep the sensitive reader appalled to hear meaning after meaning dissolve, while the old problems continue. Is even green a color that can be said to be green to everybody? The metaphysical grows out of the immediate and returns to it, made no less rich because its origin is known.... Berenice, Frankie, and John Henry, many-dimensioned, talking about what it means to be human, play in an alien system, all the while at a three-handed bridge game, emblematic of their plight. Some of the cards are, though they do not know it, missing from the beginning, maybe like those cards which God threw down at creation—and maybe that is why nothing ever turns out right, why there are expectation and disappointment. John Henry expresses his desire for an angular vision with which to read through and around the cards, a vision that can bend at will, for John Henry is of a philosophic turn of mind besides being a painter of crazy pictures.

At the end of the book, when the strange trilogy is broken up by death and moving away, it seems, in retrospect, a pattern as illusive and perfect as the wedding of three. It can never be recovered. The enchantment is implied in the writing but is not expressed by Frankie, who has come to the banal point of declaring that she just loves Michelangelo. Uncertainty seems to be her future. Either she will grow up, or she will not grow up. (pp. 152-55)

> *Marguerite Young, "Metaphysical Fiction," in*
> The Kenyon Review *(copyright 1947 by Kenyon College), Winter, 1947, pp. 151-55.*

TENNESSEE WILLIAMS

[*Reflections in a Golden Eye*] is a second novel, and although its appreciation has steadily risen during the eight or nine years since its first appearance, it was then regarded as somewhat disappointing in the way that second novels usually are. When the book preceding a second novel has been very highly acclaimed, as was *The Heart Is a Lonely Hunter,* there is an inclination on the part of critics to retrench their favor, so nearly automatic and invariable a tendency that it can almost be set down as a physical law. But the reasons for failure to justly evaluate this second novel go beyond the common, temporal disadvantage that all second novels must suffer, and I feel that an examination of these reasons may be of considerably greater pertinence to our aim of suggesting a fresh evaluation. (p. ix)

I believe that I am safe in assuming that it was [the critics'] identification of the author with a certain school of American writers, mostly of southern origin, that made her subject to a particular and powerful line of attack.

Even in the preceding book some readers must undoubtedly have detected a warning predisposition toward certain elements which are popularly known as 'morbid.' Doubtless there were some critics, as well as readers, who did not understand why Carson McCullers had elected to deal with a matter so unwholesome as the spiritual but passionate attachment that existed between a deaf-mute and a half-wit. But the tenderness of the book disarmed them. The depth and nobility of its compassion were so palpable that at least for the time being the charge of decadence had to be held in check. This forbearance was of short duration. In her second novel the veil of a subjective tenderness, which is the one quality of her talent which she has occasionally used to some excess, was drawn away. And the young writer suddenly flashed in their faces the cabalistic emblems of fellowship with a certain company of writers that the righteous 'Humanists' in the world of letters regarded as most abhorrent and most necessary to expose and attack. (pp. x-xi)

I am not at all sure what title has been conferred upon this group of writers by their disparaging critics, but for my own convenience I will refer to them as the Gothic School. It has a very ancient lineage, this school, but our local inheritance of its tradition was first brought into prominence by the early novels of William Faulkner, who still remains a most notorious and unregenerate member. There is something in the region, something in the blood and culture, of the southern state that has somehow made them the center of this Gothic school of writers. Certainly something more important than the influence of a single artist, Faulkner, is to be credited with its development, just as in France the Existentialist movement is surely attributable to forces more significant than the personal influence of Jean-Paul Sartre. There is actually a common link between the two schools, French and American, but characteristically the motor impulse of the French school is intellectual and philosophic while that of the American is more of an emotional and romantic nature. What is this common link? In my opinion it is most simply definable as a sense, an intuition, of an underlying dreadfulness in modern experience. (pp. xi-xii)

Reflections in a Golden Eye is one of the purest and most powerful of those works which are conceived in that Sense of The Awful which is the desperate black root of nearly all significant modern art, from the *Guernica* of Picasso to the cartoons of Charles Addams. (pp. xvii-xviii)

The first novel had a tendency to overflow in places as if the virtuosity of the young writer had not yet fallen under her entire control. But in the second there is an absolute mastery of design. There is a lapidary precision about the structure of this second book. Furthermore I think it succeeds more perfectly in establishing its own reality, in creating a world of its own, and this is something that primarily distinguishes the work of a great artist from that of a professional writer. In this book there is perhaps no single passage that assaults the heart so mercilessly as that scene in the earlier novel where the deaf-mute Singer stands at night outside the squalid flat that he had formerly occupied with the crazed and now dying Antonopolous. The acute tragic sensibility of scenes like that occurred more frequently in *The Heart Is a Lonely Hunter.* Here the artistic climate is more austere. The tragedy is more distilled: a Grecian purity cools it, the eventually overwhelming impact is of a more reflective order. The key to this deliberate difference is implicit in the very title of the book. Discerning critics should have found it the opposite of a disappointment since it exhibited the one attribute which had yet to be shown in Carson McCullers' stunning array of gifts: the gift of mastery over a youthful lyricism.

I will add, however, that this second novel is still not her greatest; it is surpassed by *The Member of the Wedding,* her third novel, which combined the heart-breaking tenderness of the first with the sculptural quality of the second. But this book is in turn surpassed by a somewhat shorter work. I am speaking of *The Ballad of the Sad Cafe,* which is assuredly among the masterpieces of our language in the form of the novella. (pp. xviii-xix)

I have found in her work, such intensity and nobility of spirit as we have not had in our prose-writing since Herman Melville. . . . [The work she has already accomplished] is not eclipsed by time but further illumined. (p. xxi)

> *Tennessee Williams, in his introduction to* Reflections in a Golden Eye *by Carson McCullers (copyright © 1941 by Carson Smith McCullers; all rights reserved; reprinted by permission of New Directions Publishing Corporation), New Directions, 1950, pp. ix-xxi.*

COLEMAN ROSENBERGER

Here in one omnibus volume ["The Ballad of the Sad

Café''], which includes her three novels, a half dozen short stories, and an unfamiliar longer one which gives the volume its name, is the whole fabulous world of Carson McCullers: the dwarfed and the deformed, the hurt and the lonely, the defeated and the despised, the violent and the homicidal—all the masks and symbols which she has employed over a decade of writing to shock the reader into a shared experience of her own intense sense of human tragedy. When ''The Heart Is a Lonely Hunter'' was published in 1949, it was widely recognized as an original and mature work, and the acclaim for it was mixed with mild astonishment that the book should be the work of a twenty-three-year old writer. Something like that first astonishment is induced by the present collection, which exhibits what an impressive and unified body of work has been produced by Mrs. McCullers at an age when many another writer has hardly started his career. For ''The Ballad of the Sad Café'' makes abundantly clear, which was not generally seen at the time of their separate publication, that ''Reflections in a Golden Eye'' and ''The Member of the Wedding'' extend and broaden the themes of her first book, as do the shorter pieces, so that each takes its place in an expanding structure in which each part augments and strengthens the rest.

A recurring theme throughout Mrs. McCullers' work—perhaps the central theme—is the human tragedy of the failure of communication between man and man, and the sense of loss and separation and loneliness which accompanies that failure. . . .

In Mrs. McCullers' world of symbols the urgent need to communicate is most often presented in the guise of the physically maimed or deformed, who are at once the favored and the damned. (p. 1)

The establishment of communication, the breaking down of the barriers of a torturing separateness, is the ultimate achievement of Mrs. McCullers' characters. . . .

''The Sojourner'' and ''A Domestic Dilemma'' and ''A Tree, A Rock, A Cloud'' are, in their various ways, stories of the separateness which may exist in the ''we'' of man and wife. It is, however, in the title story, ''The Ballad of the Sad Café,'' that Mrs. McCullers' achievement is seen at its most intense. A short novel, or long short story, or novella . . . it is condensed and disciplined and brilliant writing, which carries the reader along so easily on the wave of the story that he may not at first be aware how completely he has been saturated with symbolism. . . . Miss Amelia and the hunchback and Marvin Macy, the instrument of the disaster, are a grotesque crew. . . . Mrs. McCullers' freaks are not to be dismissed: they are Everyman. (p. 13)

> *Coleman Rosenberger, in* The New York Times Book Review *(© 1951 by The New York Times Company; reprinted by permission), June 10, 1951.*

WILLIAM P. CLANCY

The art of Carson McCullers has been called ''Gothic.'' Perhaps it is—superficially. Certainly her day-to-day world, her little Southern towns, are haunted by far more masterful horrors than were ever conjured up in the dreary castles of a Horace Walpole. It seems to me, however, that the ''Gothic'' label misses the essential point. Because Carson McCullers is ultimately the artist functioning at the very loftiest symbolic level, and if one must look for labels I should prefer to call her work ''metaphysical.'' Behind the strange and horrible in her world there are played out the most sombre tragedies of the human spirit; her mutes, her hunchbacks, speak of complexities and frustrations which are so native to man that they can only be recognized, perhaps, in the shock which comes from seeing them dressed in the robes of the grotesque. They pass us on the street every day but we only notice them when they drag a foot as they go by.

At the very opening of the title story [of *The Ballad of the Sad Cafe*], the face of Miss Amelia, the proprietor of the ''Sad Cafe,'' is described as a face ''. . . like the terrible dim faces known in dreams . . . sexless and white, with two gray crossed eyes which are turned inwards so sharply that they seem to be exchanging with each other one long and secret gaze of grief.'' This description, remarkable for its metaphysical fusion of horror and compassion, might serve as a symbol of Carson McCullers' art. And this fusion, I would say, represents an achievement equalled by few other contemporary American writers. (p. 243)

> *William P. Clancy, in* Commonweal *(copyright © 1951 Commonweal Publishing Co., Inc.; reprinted by permission of Commonweal Publishing Co., Inc.), June 15, 1951.*

DAYTON KOHLER

[Few writers] are as consistent and thoroughgoing as Carson McCullers in creating a sustained body of work. This underlying unity is partly the result of her prevailing theme of loneliness and desire, partly the working of the special sensibility which colors her perception of people and events. Her writing has both center and substance. . . . (p. 1)

[Even] though Mrs. McCullers' purpose was frequently misread, there was never any doubt as to the vividness of her writing. She possessed from the first those qualities which distinguish the born writer: the ability to recreate with fidelity and rich complexity a world of sense impressions, an intimation of the mystery surrounding our circle of awareness, and a technique giving form and meaning to the raw lump of experience. (pp. 1-2)

[We] are struck at once by the oddly dreamlike quality pervading her work. Most of her stories reveal some degree of nightmarish intensity because of the indirect lighting on her material. This effect is one of perspective as well as sensibility. Without being archaic, her fiction suggests the faraway and long ago, and with her opening paragraphs she takes us into her own special world. Sometimes it is the lost world of childhood, as in *The Member of the Wedding*. . . . Sometimes Mrs. McCullers' style gives a suggestion of remoteness to the commonplace present. The first sentence of *The Heart Is a Lonely Hunter* could easily begin a medieval legend of piety and grace: ''In the town there were two mutes, and they were always together.'' Instead, we read a story of life in a southern mill town toward the end of the depression. The feeling of distance may come also from her treatment of landscape and setting. The village in *The Ballad of the Sad Café* is ''lonesome, sad, and like a place that is far off and estranged from all the other places in the world.'' This effect of distance is neither sentimental nor quaint; its aesthetic value is to define the point of view from which action and scene are presented in somber aspect. It is a perspective revealing a world of half-lights and shadows. The logic of things in Mrs. McCullers' stories is no longer the daylight logic of everyday life. (p. 2)

At the same time her talent has firm roots in the local scene. The settings of her novels are Georgia mill towns, a dusty crossroads hamlet, an army post in the Deep South. Against this regional background she has created a world of tragic reality, as violent as Dostoevski's, as richly symbolic as Kafka's, though unmistakably her own. It is a limited world, but within it she is capable of precise and evocative effects. She has all the realist's concern for shapes and colors, for the particularities of persons and things. Her books are filled with images drawn, not from the historic tradition of literature, but from the background of particular experience in which her characters are involved. . . .

Her writing develops interesting juxtapositions; the simple and the elusive, realism and imaginative symbolism. To the realist's strict regard for appearances and sense experience she has joined the symbolist's preoccupation with meaning and value. This fusion allows her imagination to operate simultaneously on two levels—one real and dramatic, the other poetic and symbolic. The quality of dualism in her work is best illustrated by her handling of character. The men and women in her novels exist as clearly realized human beings, even while they function as symbols of the human predicament. John Singer, the mute who stands at the center of action and meaning in *The Heart Is a Lonely Hunter,* is such a figure, realistically drawn. . . . His value, however, is symbolic. To the other characters in the novel he is the embodiment of that sense of isolation, of separation from the community, which makes their lives wretched. (p. 3)

Most of the men and women in her world are grotesques in the manner of Sherwood Anderson's people in *Winesburg, Ohio:* social misfits, psychological freaks. Many of them are maimed or deformed. . . . Apparently Mrs. McCullers can realize her own tragic vision of life only through symbols of the misshapen and the hurt, whose physical deformities reveal outwardly the twisted, distorted spirits of their inner lives. (pp. 3-4)

The people in these books feel a desperate need to communicate with their fellows. . . . When they fail to break through the barriers of self, they are driven to moods of violence and despair. The symbolism of the café, that "clean, well-lighted place" for the lonely and the sleepless, is as clearly motivated in Mrs. McCullers' novels as it is in Hemingway's story.

In fact, this is the basic symbol in *The Ballad of the Sad Café*. . . . It is not a perfect story, for there are flaws in its structure and style . . . ; but it brings into perspective and balance the chief elements of her narrative pattern: a plot of double conflict, external and internal, between the individual and a hostile environment; a dramatic structure unfolding the tension of crisis, when the individual realizes that he is separate and lost; a theme of moral isolation presented in terms of social disunity and the wasted human effort to escape the loneliness which life itself imposes; style as technique, to disclose thematic meanings which parallel the dramatic line of action. (p. 4)

This novelette has the casual tone of an old wives' tale, retold with touches of horror and wry humor. . . . It is also a story of compassion and insight, for deeper meanings lie

under the simple narrative pattern. . . . Mrs. McCullers' triumph is that she has made Miss Amelia grotesque without letting her become ridiculous, just as Cousin Lymon is sinister without being melodramatic. In this fable the writer ponders the mystery of love and the hatred which lies close to it, and the ways by which character is shaped for betrayal and ruin. *The Ballad of the Sad Café* is an impressive story because it takes a long, steady look at the moral evil which is also the devouring, obsessive evil of modern society, the isolation of the loving and the lonely.

All of Mrs. McCullers' fiction turns on the single theme of loneliness and longing. . . .

It is this view of moral isolation as the inescapable condition of man which makes *The Heart Is a Lonely Hunter* so impressive as a first novel. (p. 5)

No one, so far as I know, has commented on the thematic structure of this novel—thematic as that term is used to describe form in a musical composition. Mrs. McCullers had her early training in music, and she has drawn upon her knowledge to give the design of her book its structural analogy. Themes and character motifs appear early in the novel, only to be dropped and later resumed, so that the structure becomes one of introduction, repetition, variation, dissonances, unresolved harmonies. The design of the novel alone should have indicated to her first reviewers how far she had progressed beyond realistic reporting.

The Heart Is a Lonely Hunter is the broadest social picture she has attempted. In contrast, the world of *Reflections in a Golden Eye* has grown restricted and intense. Her setting, an unnamed army post, presupposes a particular society and special forms of conduct, so that her novel seems [morally insulated]. . . . The pressure of the narrowed field makes for speed and concentration, and the reader has a feeling of powerlessness before this swift unfolding of physical violence and psychological horrors. (p. 6)

But *Reflections in a Golden Eye* is more than a simple chronicle of violence. For Mrs. McCullers the real thing is not the effect of horror she creates but the enveloping moment which reveals man's capacity for error, cruelty, guilt, self-deception, self-destruction. The book is an example of the planned novel, with every detail and symbol deliberately created and plotted. Story, character, and setting exist as one great metaphor. For the special world of this novel is also the larger world, and its characters—the weak, the impotent, the skeptical, the predatory, the lonely, the unreflecting primitive—are its society. Her method in this novel is that of much modern poetry and fiction, but it is also a method as old as the first myths and fables.

In one sense her stories are never finished, for she has the habit of returning to the same characters and situations and reworking them, as much for her own understanding, apparently, as for that of her readers. There are points of similarity, for instance, between the section of *The Heart Is a Lonely Hunter* dealing with Mick Kelly and *The Member of the Wedding*. . . . In *The Member of the Wedding* she makes us feel that adolescence is the thing she says it is, a haze of loneliness and groping shot through with private fantasy and furious outbreak against a complacent adult society. (p. 7)

It is easy enough to understand why this novel succeeded

as a play. In the story of Frankie Addams Mrs. McCullers has reduced the total idea of moral isolation to a fable of simple outlines and a few eloquently dramatic scenes, set against a background of adolescent mood and experience familiar to us all.

Since all her novels represent some kind of variation on the one theme of human loneliness, a knowledge of her treatment of this theme is necessary to understand the purpose and cast of her writing. We should not take it for granted, however, that her work is in any way systematic or mechanical. Her way is not the course of allegory, tracing an exact correspondency between image and idea, but the way of myth. She is, after all, a novelist haunted by the elusive nature of human truth, and her underlying theme gives coherence to the variety and surprises she has found in the world about her.

By means of theme, symbol, and style she has thrown some light upon a dark corner of human experience. This in itself is no small achievement, especially so in view of the fact that her command of illuminating structure and style has been considerably complicated by the nature of her sensibility. (pp. 7-8)

The general high level of her writing makes all the more apparent . . . the slackening in the tensions of structure and style to be found in *The Ballad of the Sad Café*. In her effort to give this novelette the simple outlines of a ballad story she has let self-conscious archaism creep into her prose at several points. . . . In very much the same way Mrs. McCullers weakens the tightness of her structure by stepping into the foreground of the story to comment on her characters. . . .

[This shows] the writer's capacity for relaxed and wise observation, but [it] may also indicate on her part the feeling of a need to editorialize, as if she thought her story too weak to carry unsupported its burden of theme and sensibility.

These minor flaws in her later work are defects of technique, not of vision, and, since they are not moral, they are curable. . . . Meanwhile she has given us novels of warmth and significance. In doing so, she has exhibited considerable resourcefulness and technical skill. (p. 8)

> Dayton Kohler, *"Carson McCullers: Variations on a Theme,"* in College English *(copyright © 1951 by the National Council of Teachers of English), October, 1951, pp. 1-8.*

V. S. PRITCHETT

Miss Carson McCullers [is] the most remarkable novelist, I think, to come out of America for a generation. Coverage is ignored by her. She is a regional writer from the South, but behind her lies that classical and melancholy authority, that indifference to shock, which seem more European than American. She knows her own original, fearless and compassionate mind. The short novels and two or three stories now published in *The Ballad of the Sad Café*—the sing-song Poe-like title so filled with the dominant American emotion of nostalgia—make an impact which recalls the impression made by such very different writers as Maupassant and D. H. Lawrence. What she has, before anything else, is a courageous imagination; that is to say one that is bold enough to consider the terrible in human nature without loss of nerve, calm, dignity or love. She has the

fearless "golden eye" of the title of one of her stories. She is as circumspect as Defoe was in setting down the plain facts of her decaying Southern scene—a boring military camp, the dying little mill town with its closed café and empty streets, the back-kitchen life of a widower's daughter—and yet the moment she picks out her people, they are changed from the typical to the extraordinary. Like all writers of original genius, she convinces us that we have missed something which was plainly to be seen in the real world. So that if it is a matter of freaks like a gangling, mannish, hard-spitting, hard-hitting old virgin, or the hunchback dwarf she falls in love with, we are made to see that ordinary human love can transform them as it can any other creature: and, reversing the situation, when love gives its twist to a pair of dull officers and their wives at a military station, they become as strange, in their way, as the freaks. Like a chorus the mass of ordinary people crowd round these afflicted hearts. It may be objected that the very strangeness of the characters in a story like *The Ballad of the Sad Café* is that of regional gossip and, in fact, turns these characters into minor figures from some American Powys-land. They become the bywords of a local ballad. But the compassion of the author gives them their Homeric moment in a universal tragedy. There is a point at which they become "great." A more exact definition of the range of her genius would be to say that human destiny is watched by her in the heart alone. She is—but in the highest and most sensitive degree—limited to the subject of personality.

On that subject she is a master of peculiar perception and an incomparable story-teller. The *Ballad,* though it concerns oddities, is a most ingenious and surprising work and, as in her other stories, its invention and surprise are found not in plot but in the contemplation of the characters themselves. She winds her way backwards and forwards into her people in a way that is sometimes too dilatory, but at every digression she cannot fail to come upon some new bearing on their fate. The almost intolerable, magnetised suspense of her stories comes from the leisure of telling and her power to catch the fatal changes in people. (p. 137)

In her power to show the unconscious breaking surface, Miss McCullers is remarkable. She is a wonderful observer—this is rare in Anglo-Saxon writers—of the forms of love. In describing things like a neurotic illness, the seductiveness of a silly woman of slightly feeble mind, a pious soldier suddenly made sinister and exalted by the shock of desire, theory is buried far out of sight; one sees these things as they are in life but one is covertly made to understand the force behind them at the same time. Once again, [in *Reflections in a Golden Eye,*] the atmosphere created from innumerable fine strokes of local detail is momentous, and the winding course of the story adds to its effect. Perhaps, engrossed by her own skill in the devious line of continuity, Miss McCullers digresses or pads too much. There is a portrait of a Filipino servant which is a failure because he too usefully embodies the personal ideal of a moral sensibility that is perfect aesthetically. He is too precious a distillation of insight and humility in a story that is, very properly, a satire on the lethargy of life at a military station.

Although this is the most ambitious story in the book and the most powerful, it did not strike me as having the total originality of *The Member of the Wedding*. . . . Stories of adolescence are apt to be fatally infected by the morbidity, the continued adolescence of their authors. This one is not. Once again, this story goes on too long; it is filled with too many instances; but I have never seen anything on this subject done with a comparable insight. The squalor of dirty-faced, aggressive childhood, its physical awkwardness, its stupidities and jealousies, its ignorance of the world, its gusts of idealism, its lapses into the infantile are rendered in just detail; and when I say "rendered" I do not mean merely stated or analysed but, in the Jamesian sense, dramatised and put into the skin of life. And the terror of life, the fact that, to an intense imagination, life is terrifying from moment to moment because we do not know the fierce shadow inside ourselves or other people, is always conveyed.... A town comes to life in the child's wanderings, a place whose seamy and sinister meanings are half grasped, half ignored. Running wild about this place in her condition, the child is walking a tight-rope between normal human kindness and callous, frightful, casual wickedness and she has no fixed notion of either. So again this is a story of terror, but not of morbid terror. The child is not presented as a little sentimentalised victim of seediness, but as a creature forming itself, becoming a member of life, undergoing a completing experience without knowing she is doing so. For the complete are the scarred. Miss McCullers is a writer of the highest class because of her great literary gifts; but underlying these, and not less important, is her sense of the completeness of human experience at any moment. She is a classic, not a convert. (pp. 137-38)

V. S. Pritchett, in The New Statesman & Nation *(© 1952 The Statesman & Nation Publishing Co. Ltd.), August 2, 1952.*

JANE HART

To all appearances Carson McCullers belongs to a School, the Gothic School of Southern writers unconsciously established by William Faulkner, a school supposedly concerned with the grotesque and the abnormal, with an outlandish love for the morbid, conveniently provided with characters of the decadent aristocracy and depraved poor whites which supposedly make up the population of the South. But whereas other Southern writers, perhaps Eudora Welty and Truman Capote, seem often to have capitalized upon interest created simply by differences and to have delved into strange creatures with artistic and precise surgery, Carson McCullers seems to have been concerned with a larger vision—in which the abnormal figures, it is true, but with a functional purpose, not simply to gain from the instinctive, primitive quickening we have for things strange or perverted. (pp. 53-4)

[It is probably] the tenderness of her seeing, the childlike compassion and interest without any of the more probing adult pity and surgical psychology that gives her writing the air of simple, star-like purity and beauty, the truth and humility of one who has learned to love a rock, a tree, a cloud, and finally all mankind. *The Heart Is a Lonely Hunter* is a novel about the loneliness of all men, abnormal or normal, deformed or whole.... Her vision is a clear, compassionate one of people spiritually isolated each from the other, all as though living in a town that is "lonesome, sad, and like a place that is far off and estranged from all other places in the world." If she has used the grotesque it is because the loneliest of all human souls is found in the abnormal and deformed, the outward and manifest symbol of human separateness....

This pilgrimage through loneliness is symbolized superbly in the relationship of the two mutes, Singer and Antonapoulos, in *The Heart Is a Lonely Hunter*. (p. 54)

But the irony we realize is that only Singer is aware of the tremendous meaning of [their] "togetherness." Antonapoulos is obese, sensual, separate in his own fleshy, far-away world, a complacent Buddha-figure sublimely indifferent to all of Singer's impassioned and spiritual love....

This almost incomprehensible attraction is paralleled again by Miss Amelia and Cousin Lymon in *The Ballad of the Sad Cafe*. (p. 55)

The difference in this relationship is another aspect of the constant theme of human loneliness. It is always the lover who gains, even if the way is sorrow, as indeed it is for Miss Amelia, deserted by the weird little dwarf she has clothed, cared for, and loved, because he too has become a lover and must now follow the object of his love.... This is the love of "A Tree, A Rock, A Cloud," the brilliant and poignant short story of an old man, a tramp, who wanders silent and alone, learning to love through the penance and sorrow of a self-imposed pilgrimage, the *Wanderjahre* of the heart.

Carson McCullers does not limit her stories to the bizarre and the strange (and never for those qualities alone), to the wayfarer, to the traveler who stops in all-night cafes. Mick Kelly and Frankie Addams, who are both really the same girl in different novels, *The Heart Is a Lonely Hunger* and *The Member of the Wedding*, begin seeking in a sudden new world the way to escape the solitude they are discovering with the first brilliant sensitivity of adolescence.... (p. 56)

The theme of loneliness is a constant one, recurring, if not openly to or within a character, symbolically in the imagery or description. The towns are nearly always small and provincial, lonely Southern towns where "in the faces along the streets there was the desperate look of hunger and of loneliness." They are always places where men walk alone, forever strangers and alone but seeking solidarity and kinship with others. (p. 57)

Every detail is selected, every aspect of a description is well chosen; there is nothing which does not contribute either overtly or intrinsically to the theme.

The truth of the theme and of the way Carson McCullers has told her stories is something we recognize instinctively although we may postpone if possible the conscious acceptance of so devastating a knowledge. But she has not left us without a solution to the problem of human loneliness. Sometimes, Carson McCullers shows us, men find for a radiant moment the *Thee* they are seeking and so are lifted above their own loneliness by a sense of togetherness, of being with others in love, sorrow or beauty. They find truth, a moment of pure love, a sudden illumination, and, like Frankie, feel that someone or something is "the we of me." Then, no matter how evanescent the instant, the experience brings a sense of warmth and togetherness that makes the barest solitudes endurable, that gives the heart a brief respite from aloneness. (p. 58)

Jane Hart, "Carson McCullers, Pilgrim of Loneliness," in The Georgia Review *(copyright, 1957, by the University of Georgia), Spring, 1957, pp. 53-8.*

FREDERIC CARPENTER

With greater complexity and greater realism, although perhaps with less art [than J. D. Salinger's *The Catcher in the Rye*], Carson McCullers embodies [the] same problems of adolescence, and its confrontation of the evils of experience, in her novels *The Heart Is a Lonely Hunter* and *The Member of the Wedding*. The latter more resembles *The Catcher in the Rye*, in that it focuses on the failure of the adolescent to adjust to the confusions of the adult world. But *The Heart . . .* is a larger and richer book. (pp. 63-4)

[The disturbed adolescent in *The Member of the Wedding*], Frankie Addams, embodies in exaggeraged form all those traits of immaturity which other novels have described more normally, and thereby rivets our attention on them the more firmly. Frankie's feeling of desperate isolation and alienation drives her to identify herself with her older brother and his fiancée, until she tries to join them even on their honeymoon. But this grotesque situation merely emphasizes the confusion of all adolescents, and of all maladjusted members of human society.

What raises *The Member of the Wedding* above the merely grotesque (as described in the author's other novel *Reflections in a Golden Eye*) is its inclusion of other characters suggesting the parallel tragedies of other alienated people. Berenice Sadie Brown, the Negro mammy whose husband has died leaving her lonely, and her foster-brother "Honey," who runs afoul of the law, suggest the tragedy of Negroes who can never become full "members" of society; the young John Henry is the "gentle boy" who is too good for this world; while over all hangs the cloud of the atom bomb, which everyone discusses casually.

By contrast, *The Heart Is a Lonely Hunter* seems hardly to describe adolescence at all. The youthful Mick Kelly appears a background figure, observing and partly sharing the tragedies of the deaf-mutes, the Negroes, and the labor agitators. . . . [Essentially] it describes the struggle of all these lonely people to come to terms with their world, to become members of their society, to find human love—in short, to become mature. (p. 64)

> *Frederic Carpenter, in* English Journal *(copyright © 1957 by the National Council of Teachers of English), September, 1957 (and reprinted in* Readings about Adolescent Literature, *edited by Dennis Thomison, The Scarecrow Press, Inc., 1970).*

CARSON McCULLERS

Spiritual isolation is the basis of most of my themes. My first book was concerned with this, almost entirely, and all of my books since, in one way or another. Love, and especially love of a person who is incapable of returning or receiving it, is at the heart of my selection of grotesque figures to write about—people whose physical incapacity is a symbol of their spiritual incapacity to love or receive love—their spiritual isolation.

To understand a work, it is important for the artist to be emotionally right on dead center: to see, to know, to experience the things he is writing about. (p. 274)

I understand only particles. I understand the characters, but the novel itself is not in focus. The focus comes at random moments which no one can understand, least of all the author. For me, they usually follow great effort. To me,

these illuminations are the grace of labor. All of my work has happened this way. It is at once the hazard and the beauty that a writer has to depend on such illuminations. After months of confusion and labor, when the idea has flowered, the collusion is Divine. It always comes from the subconscious and cannot be controlled. For a whole year I worked on *The Heart Is a Lonely Hunter* without understanding it at all. Each character was talking to a central character, but why, I didn't know. I'd almost decided that the book was no novel, that I should chop it up into short stories. But I could feel the mutilation in my body when I had that idea, and I was in despair. I had been working for five hours and I went outside. Suddenly, as I walked across a road, it occurred to me that Harry Minovitz, the character all the other characters were talking to, was a different man, a deaf mute, and immediately the name was changed to John Singer. The whole focus of the novel was fixed and I was for the first time committed with my whole soul to *The Heart Is a Lonely Hunter*. (p. 275)

A writer's main asset is intuition; too many facts impede intuition. A writer needs to know so many things, but there are so many things he doesn't need to know—he needs to know human things even if they aren't "wholesome," as they call it. (p. 276)

One cannot explain accusations of morbidity. A writer can only say he writes from the seed which flowers later in the subconscious. Nature is not abnormal, only lifelessness is abnormal. Anything that pulses and moves and walks around the room, no matter what thing it is doing, is natural and human to a writer. The fact that John Singer, in *The Heart Is a Lonely Hunter*, is a deaf-and-dumb man is a symbol, and the fact that Captain Penderton, in *Reflections in a Golden Eye*, is homosexual, is also a symbol, of handicap and impotence. The deaf mute, Singer, is a symbol of infirmity, and he loves a person who is incapable of receiving his love. Symbols suggest the story and theme and incident, and they are so interwoven that one cannot understand consciously where the suggestion begins. I become the characters I write about. I am so immersed in them that their motives are my own. When I write about a thief, I become one; when I write about Captain Penderton, I become a homosexual man; when I write about a deaf mute, I become dumb during the time of the story. I become the characters I write about and I bless the Latin poet Terence who said, "Nothing human is alien to me." (pp. 276-77)

Many authors find it hard to write about new environments that they did not know in childhood. The voices reheard from childhood have a truer pitch. And the foliage—the trees of childhood—are remembered more exactly. When I work from within a different locale from the South, I have to wonder what time the flowers are in bloom—and what flowers? I hardly let characters speak unless they are Southern. [Thomas] Wolfe wrote brilliantly of Brooklyn, but more brilliantly of the Southern cadence and ways of speech. This is particularly true of Southern writers because it is not only their speech and the foliage, but their entire culture—which makes it a homeland within a homeland. No matter what the politics, the degree or non-degree of liberalism in a Southern writer, he is still bound to this peculiar regionalism of language and voices and foliage and memory. (p. 279)

The writer by nature of his profession is a dreamer and a conscious dreamer. How, without love and the intuition that comes from love, can a human being place himself in the situation of another human being? He must imagine, and imagination takes humility, love, and great courage. How can you create a character without love and the struggle that goes with love? (p. 280)

The passionate, individual love—the old Tristan-Isolde love, the Eros love—is inferior to the love of God, to fellowship, to the love of Agape—the Greek god of the feast, the God of brotherly love—and of man. This is what I tried to show in *The Ballad of the Sad Café* in the strange love of Miss Amelia for the little hunchback, Cousin Lymon.

The writer's work is predicated not only on his personality but by the region in which he was born. I wonder sometimes if what they call the "Gothic" school of Southern writing, in which the grotesque is paralleled with the sublime, is not due largely to the cheapness of human life in the South. . . . To many a poor Southerner, the only pride that he has is the fact that he is white, and when one's self-pride is so pitiably debased, how can one learn to love? Above all, love is the main generator of all good writing. Love, passion, compassion are all welded together.

In any communication, a thing says to one person quite a different thing from what it says to another, but writing, in essence, is communication; and communication is the only access to love—to love, to conscience, to nature, to God, and to the dream. For myself, the further I go into my own work and the more I read of those I love, the more aware I am of the dream and the logic of God, which indeed is a Divine collusion. (pp. 281-82)

> Carson McCullers, "The Flowering Dream" (originally published in Esquire Magazine, December, 1959), in her The Mortgaged Heart (copyright © 1963 by Carson McCullers; © 1971 by Floria V. Lasky; reprinted by permission of Houghton Mifflin Company), Houghton, 1971, pp. 274-82.

RUMER GODDEN

[For] me not a word could be added or taken away from this marvel of a novel ["Clock Without Hands"] by Carson McCullers.

Her talent is extraordinary: the name of her first book "The Heart Is a Lonely Hunter" might be a description of it: the steady life-giving beat that is the core of every book: the pursuit of the quarry she sees and would catch and hold for us, often something so fleeting and ephemeral that most authors would quail at trying to catch it in words—and Mrs. McCullers' words are the coin of every day, plain, frank, slangy, unemotional. Above all her gift is apart, aloof, inevitably lonely: it owes nothing to any other writer and is paradoxical, a sure sign of richness: it is powerful yet humble, dignified yet utterly unpretentious. . . .

"Transcendental"; "master of peculiar penetration"; "an incomparable storyteller." These praises of Carson McCullers do not exaggerate, yet I think that she has something more rare: a capacity for telling the unvarnished truth. This sounds simple but it is extraordinarily difficult for a sensitive writer to reach the real truth of what he or she sees; sensitivity glosses with its very depth of feeling; it is the bedevilment of writers, especially women. . . .

Of course truth is not always palatable. There are parts in this book that even now may shock in their matter-of-fact treatment of certain subjects. Truth, too, can give an un-

comfortable bleakness, and one can well understand that, of Mrs. McCullers' novels, only "The Member of the Wedding," a masterpiece, has become universally popular. This book may well be too strange and strong, too frank, for many people. But like J. T. Malone [its main character], it grows richer and quieter as it draws towards its end. . . .

> Rumer Godden, "Death and Life in a Small Southern Town," in New York Herald Tribune Books (© I.H.T. Corporation; reprinted by permission), September 17, 1961, p. 5.

GORE VIDAL

It is hard to believe that twenty-one years have passed since *The Heart Is A Lonely Hunter,* the first novel of Carson McCullers, was published. For those of us who arrived on the scene in the war years, McCullers was *the* young writer. She was an American legend from the beginning, which is to say that her fame was as much the creation of publicity as of talent. The publicity was the work of those fashion magazines where a dish of black-eyed peas can be made to seem the roe of some rare fish, photographed by Avedon; yet McCullers's dreaming, androgynous face in its ikon elegance subtly confounded the chic of the lingerie ads all about her. For unlike other "legends," her talent was as real as her face. Though she was progenitress to much "Southern writing" (one can name a dozen writers who would not exist in the way they do if she had not written in the way she did), she had a manner all her own. Her prose was chaste and severe, and realistic in its working out of narrative. I suspect that of all the Southern writers, she is the most apt to endure, though her vision is by no means as large or encompassing as that, say, of Faulkner, whom she has the grace to resemble not at all. (pp. 208-09)

The first thing to remark in McCullers is her style. From Wolfe to Faulkner, most Southern writing has tended to windy rhetoric of the "lost, lost and by the wind grieved" sort which I find entirely detestable. I can read very little of Wolfe, and much of the admirable Faulkner is ruined for me by that terrible gaseous prose (he went the length of *Requiem for a Nun* obsessively using "euphemistic" for "euphonious"). McCullers writes an exact prose closer to the [Gustave] Flaubert of *Un Coeur Simple* than to *Absalom, Absalom.* But her material is intensely Southern. Although she has had at times a passion for the extreme situation and the gratuitous act (*The Ballad of the Sad Café, Reflections in a Golden Eye*), whose intent I sometimes question, her means have always saved her. She gets entirely within the event told. There is never a false note. Technically, it is breathtaking to watch her set a scene and then dart from character to character, opening up in a line, a phrase, a life. It is marvelous, but . . .

But. Twenty-one years is a long time. *The Member of the Wedding,* her latest novel until now, was published in 1946. During those fifteen years other writers have come and gone. New attitudes, new follies, new perceptions have occurred to us. But most important, the world of the private vision which was her domain has been more and more intruded upon by the public world which threatens to destroy, literally, the actual world. Worse, though it may not do this final thing, the threat of extinction has made many doubt the worth of art. If the planet becomes an empty desert, why make anything, knowing it will soon be no more than a grain or two in the never-to-be-noticed dust? Not every writer of course has this apocalyptic vision, nor does a writer necessarily find the thought of the world's end any reason for not making what he wants to make in the present, which is all. But that ugly final thing *is* there, public and menacing and chilling the day. It is hard not to take it into account. (pp. 211-12)

[With] *Clock without Hands,* Carson McCullers acknowledges the public world for the first time in her work. Though her response is uneasy and uncertain, it is good to note that she writes as well as ever, with all the old clarity and fine tension. But the book is odd, and it is so because what has always been the most private of responses has been rudely startled and bemused by the world outside. The changing South. The Supreme Court Decision. Integration. The aviator as new man. All these things crop up unexpectedly in her narrative. One cannot say she handles these things badly; it is just that they do not quite fit her story. . . . The four characters interact. They are explored. They come alive. Yet one is not convinced by the story told. Symbolically, is it true or merely pat?

At the book's end, the old judge, enraged by the Supreme Court's decision, goes on radio to denounce the Court, but in his dottiness and great age he cannot recall anything to say except, word for word, the Gettysburg Address. Are we to take that as the South's last gasp as a new order begins? If so, I don't believe it. McCullers of course is free to make whatever she wants of a public situation. One quarrels not with her view of things, which is after all intuitive not liberal, but with the effect publicness has had on her art. Everything is thrown slightly out of kilter. She is not the only writer to suffer in this way. More and more of our private artists have fallen silent in the last twenty years, unable to cope with a world which has thrust itself upon the imagination like some clumsy-hooved animal loose in a garden. But even this near failure of McCullers is marvelous to read, and her genius for prose remains one of the few satisfying achievements of our second-rate culture. (pp. 212-13)

Gore Vidal, "Carson McCullers's 'Clock without Hands'" (© 1961 by Gore Vidal), in The Reporter, *September 28, 1961 (and reprinted in his* Rocking the Boat, *Little, Brown, 1963, pp. 208-13).*

CATHARINE HUGHES

[*Clock Without Hands*] probes intensely the human spirit, yet captures indelibly the sights and the sounds, the sorrow and the tensions of the South [Mrs. McCullers] knows so well. Incisively exploring the minds and the motivations, the yearnings and dreams of the young, it at the same time conveys the longing and frustration, the sense of intruding death, of the old. . . .

[Mrs. McCullers'] talent, the dreamlike—almost trancelike —quality of her fiction seemingly precludes her ever being completely uninteresting. Yet, somehow, the reader occasionally finds himself looking for something that is not there. Perhaps it is merely a sense that Mrs. McCullers has seldom permitted her characters to go the whole way, to achieve any final or satisfactory vision of the consequence of their actions. There are, perhaps, too many violent endings; too many questions which are averted by death. And, while it would be wrong to accuse Mrs. McCullers of artificially imposing "shock endings," the result has, on occa-

sion, been very nearly the same as if she had tried to do just that. . . .

The world of Carson McCullers is a world of outcasts; her universe the realm of extraordinary, rather than "normal," happenings. Yet, for all this, she succeeds in establishing a rapport of feeling, an aura of shared experience. (p. 73)

There are few "happy" characters in Carson McCullers' world, yet it is a universe which is somehow not altogether oppressive, for there is transition; there is development and a form of progression even within this lost and lonely humanity. Or at least there had been such a progression and development prior to [*Clock Without Hands*].

"Death is always the same," Mrs. McCullers writes in her opening sentence, "but each man dies in his own way." And, in *its* own way, it is a magnificent beginning; an attempt to explore an almost unbelievably difficult theme. And, by this very fact, because it is so difficult, one must admire any writer undertaking it. But strangely enough, it is not primarily on this level that Mrs. McCullers fails. The faults in *Clock Without Hands* are far more rudimentary and, for all her technical virtuosity, they are almost unavoidably obvious.

J. T. Malone, at the age of forty, thinks he is suffering from a severe case of "spring fever," but finds instead that he has leukemia and will die within a short time. How this affects him, his family, the lives of those around him, would seem a sufficiently fertile area for any novelist. And it is this one expects Mrs. McCullers to do—not so much because it is "logical," but because everything in her opening section points toward it. Instead, she succeeds in introducing another group of characters and another plot which, rather than complementing the original, only manage to provide a diversion. Significantly, the diversion becomes a great deal more intriguing than the original. . . .

While there is a rather tenuous link established between the Judge's story [the sub-plot] and the supposed self-realization undergone by Malone, it is essentially so thin as to seem nearly contrived. On either the physical or metaphysical level, Malone is basically unnecessary to the Clanes; yet he is there. And as the chapters alternate between the two, one looks longingly for the moment at which the fictional gears will mesh. The gears never do manage to mesh —except in a conclusion which, when all else has been said, is as unsatisfactory as the entire attempt to establish their inter-relationship. (p. 74)

Mrs. McCullers has described *Clock Without Hands* as a novel "about response and responsibility—of man toward his own livingness." And, because it is so big a theme, because Mrs. McCullers is so obviously one of a fairly small number of American writers with the potential of successfully realizing it, the reader longs to see her succeed. In the end, however, his hopes are doomed by the conflict which exists within the novel itself and by Mrs. McCullers' inability to focus his attention where she seemingly wished it to be, on J. T. Malone. In saying that *Clock Without Hands* might better have been two novels, one really says relatively little. Perhaps it would be more realistic to admit that, despite its many fine stylistic qualities, it simply doesn't come off *as a novel.* And this, unfortunately, is something even Mrs. McCullers' flashes of genuine brilliance cannot conceal from us.

Brilliance there is, without doubt. For those who have indicted Mrs. McCullers and the whole school of Southern writers for their absorption in what often, for lack of anything better, is termed the "morbid," there can be, of course, no answer. Recognizing what Tennessee Williams has called "an underlying dreadfulness in modern experience," Mrs. McCullers elects to depict it in its own terms —terms sometimes fraught with an almost overpowering feeling of human suffocation in a world beyond control, yet terms ultimately successful through their very irresistible intensity.

In the labyrinth established for the McCullers characters, a world of "no exit," man is caught up in the dizziness of life, is inextricably drawn toward a crisis in which he either recognizes himself or, failing this, is lost forever in frustration and despair. It is a world of either/or, in which there are few half-way measures, where everything is viewed in nightmarish bold relief. Simultaneously unrealistic and yet supra-realistic, it is the unique and unforgettable world of Carson McCullers. (p. 75)

> Catharine Hughes, "A World of Outcasts," in Commonweal (copyright © 1961 Commonweal Publishing Co., Inc.; reprinted by permission of Commonweal Publishing Co., Inc.), October 13, 1961, pp. 73-5.

DONALD EMERSON

All outward experience of the characters of *Clock Without Hands* . . . is conditioned by a sense of moral isolation, a feeling of despair, and baffled search for an identifiable Self. (p. 15)

Mrs. McCullers is most herself as the novelist of inward experience, but in *Clock Without Hands* she attempts to add another dimension by making her characters stand for the whole South. It is a mistake. The private and the symbolic roles are not fused; the individual and the representative do not merge. The result for the reader is confusion arising from what seems to have been Mrs. McCullers' uncertainty about her objective. There is also a looseness of structure which weakens the novel and which apparently came of her attempt to make it a far bigger book than she finally published.

A novelist who begins, "Death is always the same, but each man dies in his own way," must expect to remind her readers of the famous first sentence of *Anna Karenina*. The expectation of a novel of scope is reinforced when it becomes apparent that each of the chief characters has a symbolic role; nothing less than the entire Southern dilemma is to be represented through the tangled private histories of a restricted group in a small city. Mrs. McCullers allows the Supreme Court decision on integration of schools to reach the bedside of a dying man who has sunk beyond any concern with news, in a scene which makes sense only if the large implications are a chief intention. *Clock Without Hands* does not live up to the intention, for the implications of the action undercut the symbolic roles assigned the chief characters.

The title is itself ambiguous. J. T. Malone, the druggist of Milan, Georgia, is under sentence of death from leukemia, a man confusedly watching his time run out on a clock without hands. But when in that last scene Malone's old friend Judge Clane bursts into the sickroom with news of the decision, the reader catches the suggestion that the

Court's "all deliberate speed" is also to be measured by a clock without hands. Behind this scene and the other references to the clock there is the implied warning "It is later than you think." . . . (pp. 15-16)

Besides Malone and Judge Clane, there are two other characters of importance: Jester Clane, the Judge's grandson, and Sherman Pew, a Negro. Both are eighteen. Their connections with Judge Clane provide once more the contrast of youth with age which deepens the pathos of many scenes in *The Heart Is a Lonely Hunter* and *The Member of the Wedding*. They also, in a friendship which holds them in close conflict, repeat the baffling experience which Mrs. McCullers envisions for all friends and all lovers: isolation without hope of communication, within the bonds of an affection that is onerous to the loved one and frustrating to the lover.

The symbolic roles which were to have given *Clock Without Hands* its forceful social reference detract from the effectiveness of the novel on the level of immediate, inward experience where Mrs. McCullers' powers are greatest. Besides, the symbolic action is questionable. J. T. Malone represents the conscience of the South, and at a crucial moment he recoils from violence. His quiet death in bed, however, has doubtful implications for the collective conscience for which he stands. Judge Clane, with all his demagoguery and his delusions, is made the embodiment of the Old South. He is obvious as a type and symbol, but one feels uneasy. Granted that Mrs. McCullers uses him to express contradictions of attitude amounting to bankruptcy of ideas in a class, the Judge as a man is a grotesque. If, on the other hand, he is to be accepted as a pitiable old man whose curse through life has been a combination of sentimentality and invincible stupidity in all human relations, the burden of his symbolic role is too great.

As representatives, the younger characters appear to no better advantage. Jester Clane is forcefully identified as one of the "men of good will" who may redeem their society, but in his symbolic role he is not only ineffectual in aiding his friend (he cannot even persuade Sherman to escape murder), he is incapable of retribution when the wretched human condition of the murderer is brought home to him. Sherman Pew is the rebellious Negro whose accumulated humiliations and frustrations drive him to the senseless cruelty of hanging Jester's dog, and to the open defiance of renting a house in the white section of town. He is isolated by hatred and self-contempt for all men, and his gestures become equally compulsive and self-destructive. More even than the others he is unacceptable as the symbol Mrs. McCullers has tried to make him, for he is an Outsider rather than the representative of a social class.

The crux of the difficulty is most apparent in the portrayals of Sherman Pew and Jester Clane, and it comes of Mrs. McCullers' being sensitively penetrating when she deals with the inner life but fumbling and uncertain when she attempts a social paradigm. (pp. 16-18)

Besides failing to achieve the dimensions which Mrs. McCullers intended, the novel is structurally weak. Mrs. McCullers has customarily restricted the scope of her fictions, and she limits her cast in *Clock Without Hands*. But there is no central character with whom all the others feel the sole relation they all experience, as with the deaf-mute Singer in *The Heart Is a Lonely Hunter*. There is no tight pattern of antipathies such as enmeshed the men, the women, and the horse in *Reflections in a Golden Eye*. No single character such as Frankie Addams of *The Member of the Wedding* exists to give the novel a viewpoint. In her latest novel, Mrs. McCullers begins with Malone and the Judge, neglects this relation to concentrate on the Judge, Jester, and Sherman, and returns to it to put a period to the action. Malone is removed almost from significance in the lives of the others. (pp. 18-19)

Compassionate identification which reveals how Malone, the Judge, Jester and Sherman all grope toward a sense of identity is too far removed from awkward political symbolism for easy reconciliation; the distance explains the defects of the novel, the looseness of plot, and the failure of *Clock Without Hands* to rank with Mrs. McCullers' best work. This same distance, however, justifies praise of Mrs. McCullers' best qualities, which appear even in the disappointing attempt to merge individual and typical roles for a timely social commentary. (p. 19)

Mrs. McCullers' novel contains thematic material which would flesh out a quartet of thin, brainless fictions, but the sum of it is confused, and *Clock Without Hands* is most interesting in the context of all of her work. The same compassionate voice speaks in this novel of the loneliness of mankind, of the frustration of love which makes the lover take refuge in a world of fantasy doomed to violation, and of the inability to communicate either love itself or the despair which follows its defeat. The author finds the search for identity a perennial quest, most touchingly seen in the gropings of the adolescents, the outcasts, and the grotesques of society. The threat of raw physical violence hangs over all of them. (p. 27)

[How] does one regulate a clock without hands? The symbol which Mrs. McCullers has used in her latest novel is emblematic, as is Singer's dream in *The Heart Is a Lonely Hunter,* the changed, flat, prison-like world which Frankie Addams discovers when she tries to flee, or the chained state of the twelve mortal men [in *The Ballad of the Sad Cafe*]. Each symbol reinforces the others, and if *Clock Without Hands* is richest in the context of Mrs. McCullers' other work, it in turn sharpens the contrasts in her picture of man's fate. . . .

[She] discloses a world in which troubles from eternity do not fail and the instrument of their chronology marks no certain hour. (p. 28)

> Donald Emerson, *"The Ambiguities of 'Clock without Hands',"* in Wisconsin Studies in Contemporary Literature (© 1962, Wisconsin Studies in Contemporary Literature), *Fall, 1962, pp. 15-28.*

CHESTER E. EISINGER

[Carson McCullers] is governed by the aesthetics of the primitive. This means that her overview is essentially anti-realistic. She has cut herself off from the world of ordinary experience and ordinary human beings who might entertain ordinary ideas. Her people are bizarre, freakish, lonely, hermaphroditic. This aesthetic dictates an intense concentration on man's most urgent emotional needs: a communion of dialogue and love. For her, further, the truth of the fable is the truth of the heart. It is not concerned with abstractions about the structure of society or with ideological conflicts in the contemporary world. She has banished

these sociological and intellectual matters from her fiction, narrowing its range, perhaps to its detriment, in favor of memory and mood, and above all, feeling. This aesthetic demands a poetic prose and a style which, in Mrs. McCullers' case, often appears childlike. Her prose has a deliberately jerky rhythm and uneven pace, creating a movement which is designed to give the impression of simplicity. Toward that same goal of simplicity, she is occasionally monotonous in tonal qualities and repetitious, again deliberately and to good effect. Her extravagant use of color and sensuous descriptions of food are further evidences of her immersion in the world of the senses.

The purpose of her aesthetic lies in the artist's need to communicate his vision, a need that Mrs. McCullers says she feels intensely. "The function of the artist," she has written, "is to execute his own indigenous vision, and having done that, to keep faith with this vision." If to keep faith is to pursue consistently a single theme, then she has succeeded. For everywhere in her fiction she works at variations on the theme of moral isolation. It is the paradoxes of loneliness and love that impel her characters to a wretched abandonment of hope and leave them to feed on the pain of frustrated communion. She is fascinated by the loneliness of individuals in a world full of individuals. She is possessed by the unceasing failures in the consummation of love, because the lover is always rejected by the beloved, who would himself be a lover, and the lover thus goes on dying, into infinity, his spiritual death. (pp. 243-44)

[Mrs. McCullers] understands the need of the individual to define himself by something outside himself. This is the motive force behind her play on the dialogue of love. The desolation of her characters, and her own pessimism, lie in the failure to achieve the kind of communion that Martin Buber has described, the meeting of *ich und du* [I and Thou], joined in a mystical reciprocity. (p. 244)

Mrs. McCullers' implicit hope is that lovers, all men and women, might flow toward each other as the imperatives of Buber's mystical insight bids them do. But the visible assumptions of her theory of love doom them to inevitable failure and condemn them to eternal loneliness. Their fate is to be at the end what they were at the beginning—half-people.

But it must also be said that the failure of dialogue lies in the carefully selected characters Mrs. McCullers permits to engage in it. She has stacked the deck to guarantee ruptured communion and fruitless love by choosing people whose need, to be sure, is demonstrable but whose capacities are crippled. It is her gothic imagination that dictates this narrowly specialized range of character. It is the gothic principle that drives her to a consideration of the outsider: the adolescent who has no place and no sex, the deaf mute, the beloved hunchback, the bisexual adult, or the maternal male. These bizarre characters, alienated from society and the self, dramatize the problem of their ambiguous sex in a life that is curiously desexualized. . . . It is flight from normative behavior [which is the pattern of her fiction]; it is the frantic flight of the divided soul between the poles of male and female in the prison of the self that interests her. It is her gothic vision that denies a final resting place to this tortured soul, for no resolution of its dilemma is possible.

Although Mrs. McCullers published *The Heart Is a Lonely Hunter* (1940) at an unbelievably early and presumably impressionable age, the novel is indubitably all her own. (p. 245)

[In her statement and treatment of theme] she bares the loneliness of each sentient human being whose need is to create an image of wisdom and receptivity which receives and resolves one's problems, providing release and fulfilment. And here, with magisterial firmness, she condemns her characters to failure. The image they create out of their need has the same need they suffer from. They have wilfully obscured the fallibility of the image. They have stubbornly embarked upon a monologue in the mistaken notion that they have established the reciprocity necessary for dialogue. They are self-deluded in the conversation each holds with himself. And the dimensions of this failure of dialogue are in the collapse of the inner self and the frustration of the social being. Mrs. McCullers does not, in a kind of warmth generated by a barroom milieu, permit her characters to live by the illusions they create. Honesty, not harshness I think, triumphs over warmth when she strips the illusion to reveal its essential nothingness. (p. 246)

It has been claimed that Singer has a God-like function in the novel, but I prefer to see him as the figure of the Virgin Mother and the Son. He has none of the terrible majesty of God, but he does represent for the others [an] all-embracing, comforting, maternal force. . . . [The other characters] do not exist for him, either intellectually or emotionally, in any consequential way. Yet he is at the center of their lives. He is, although they do not yet know it, the false Virgin and the false Son. (p. 247)

The most sensitive treatment of character, and the most successful, is saved for Mick Kelly, the adolescent girl in the novel. She is like all the others in her isolation and in her failure to communicate love, in her case a generalized love for people. Full of dreams and aspirations that will not be realized, she feels herself different from others. She is independent of spirit and rejects God. She yearns for she knows not what. She is forced in upon herself, but she cannot achieve an inner peace. In a word, she is the typical adolescent struggling blindly toward maturity, unaware that the pain of alienation she now endures is the proper preparation for later life. Her refuge in her loneliness is her inner room, where she may create her own world. But the unalterable condition of adolescence is insecurity, and it manifests itself in Mick in the terrible self-consciousness and the trembling uncertainties that overtake her. Stifled like the other characters, she must in addition undergo the painful process of growth. It is growth toward sex awareness, which has its culmination when the boy next door takes her. This event does not altogether end a certain ambiguity about Mick's sex, for she has seemed, in the course of the book, to resist the role of woman toward which she is destined. The adolescent girl, in Mrs. McCullers' fiction, has the problem not only of sex awareness but of sex determination. It is not the responsibility of womanhood that she reluctantly must take up but the decision to be a woman at all that she must make. She is, then, sexless, hovering between the two sexes, this girl with a boy's name. In Brannon and in Singer, the sexes seem to achieve a beneficent union. In Mick they make for a chaotic confusion.

The bedding of Mick is a determination of this sex ambiguity more redolent of surrender than of glory. And this is characteristic of the fate Mrs. McCullers has arranged for her. Afraid and alone as she is during much of the book,

she nevertheless waits with intense excitement upon the infinite possibilities of life. Then she is more or less compelled to take a job at Woolworth's. All her hopes are dashed. She feels trapped and cheated. She can no longer get into her inside room. Her potentiality in music will be dissipated in this numbing descent into the humdrum. Release from the anguish of adolescence, in Mrs. McCullers' view, brings one into nothing better than the stifling world of adulthood. No measured sense of responsibility comes to Mick because she now earns money necessary for the household. She is angry all the time with a bafflement at life's blasted promise. (pp. 250-51)

[*The Heart Is a Lonely Hunter*] elicits a warmth of response from us partly because its psychological problems are placed in a familiar social context. The same cannot be said for *Reflections in a Golden Eye* (1941). Its scene is an army post in the South, but Mrs. McCullers makes no attempt to render it in depth. Neither soldiers nor army life is the subject of this novel. The book is virtually cut off from the external world of recognizable social reality. It creates its own bizarre climate. (p. 251)

It does seem clear, however, that Mrs. McCullers is pursuing a theme that she began to explore in her first novel. Human beings, she seems to say, are not whole. As half-people, their deficiencies prevent them from realizing their humanity; their course in life is errant, unpredictable, painful. (pp. 251-52)

[The] reflections in the immense golden eye of the green peacock are tiny and grotesque. The prevailing tone of the novel derives from this image given back by the bird's eye. The image describes the uneasy and remote relations of the people to each other. It describes the atmosphere through which these people move, so often filled with cold yellow light or blunt splashes of yellow. Mrs. McCullers even makes an attempt to justify the grotesque, insofar as it may be equated with the aberrant. Penderton argues that if human fulfilment is obtained even in an abnormal way, it is good as long as it brings happiness; moral judgments about such means are irrelevant. But the book is not really a defense of the deviant any more than it is an attack upon the heavy-handed, army-shaped moral standards of so essentially conventional a man as Major Langdon. Mrs. McCullers takes a few false steps toward such rhetorical goals out of a sense of rebellion against conventional morality or taboos which could block the natural movement of the personality toward fruition. But her real theme seems to be the impossibility of such fruition, given inherently incomplete human beings.

The Member of the Wedding (1946) takes us from the obsessed and fevered world of *Reflections* to the warmer and more understandable world of the adolescent, where the pursuit of love and human communion is as real as the southern kitchen in which much of the action takes place. The reality of this novel displaces the gothic character of the first two, and in doing so makes it necessary for Mrs. McCullers to skirt carefully around a sentimentalization of her material. She avoids this danger, happily, but she does lay herself open to the charge of repetition. The Frankie Addams of this novel is the Mick Kelly of *The Heart Is a Lonely Hunter*. The themes are those of the first book: that human beings wish to ameliorate their loneliness by joining themselves, one to another, in meaningful relationship, and that the pains of adolescence are succeeded by a growing recognition of the limits of selfhood and the inevitability of aloneness.... The emphasis is on the interior life of her protagonist. The substance of the novel is conveyed in an investigation of feeling—the poignance of adolescence offering so rich an opportunity—offered with an artist's eye to color and a heightened sensitivity to mood. The particular movement in the novel may be charted in this way: Frankie suffers from insecurity and a sense of loss at the beginning; she is then the victim of a self-generated fantasy about belonging; finally, at the end, her effort at joining is frustrated and she resolves her disappointment.

Frankie, who again bears a masculine name as a sign of the not-yet-determined sex of the adolescent girl, is at the beginning a member of nothing at all, the juvenile outsider alienated from her peers and her elders. The world seems separate from herself. Then she determines to join her brother's wedding and become a *we* person instead of remaining an *I* person. She is motivated by the search for love and security that will banish fear. The fear is a compound of the ineffable sadness of growing up, of the melancholy of a summer afternoon, of an undefined sense of guilt, all rendered with a skill that captures the evanescent moment and the inarticulate yearning. The love is the girl's wish to be accepted as a part of the magnetic chain of humanity, and it is the love of man for woman which Frankie does not yet understand. It is her innocence which permits her to think she can join her brother's wedding. It is this innocence the drunken soldier assaults when he tries to seduce her. It is this innocence that Berenice, the Negro cook, quietly dissolves as she instructs Frankie in the meaning of love. Out of all these episodes comes a knowledge of sex, but she has not yet undergone a decisive initiation into sexual love. The limitations of the novel are in its focus on the child's self-centered world in which the macrocosm plays no part. The contribution of the novel is to state once more the universal need for human dialogue. (pp. 254-56)

Out of the still and twisted world in which her imagination dwells, Mrs. McCullers has drawn some truths that come home to all men. She has illuminated the possibilities for loneliness and the capacities for deviant behavior that mark the human lot. But there is a troubling sense of something wanting in what she does. The world of the adolescent child is, after all, only a promise of life to come in adulthood. The crazy, private world of her freakish and tortured adults is on the periphery of our experience, even if a significantly disturbing one. It is a narrow corner of human existence that she has chosen to exploit in her fiction. Her view of man's fate, therefore, adds little, in the largest sense, to the dimensions of our understanding. The gothic view of life has conjured up the terror of life but has not weighed the consequences of that terror. Mrs. McCullers knows something of the conditions under which life must be carried on, but she has gone beyond this to examine how men might endure under these conditions. There is no room in her work for the *consequences* of human action; there is no sense of the continuity of life. She has succeeded perhaps too well in creating an art form that is cut off from life. It is a form cut off from society, from morality, from religion, from ideas, from concern with man's burden or with man's hope. It is a special art form, and its special quality makes it symptomatic of the phenomena we have always with us—a disturbed psyche and a disturbed time. (p. 258)

Chester E. Eisinger, in his Fiction of the Forties

(reprinted by permission of The University of Chicago Press; © *1963 by Chester E. Eisinger), University of Chicago Press, 1963.*

KLAUS LUBBERS

Together with such other writers as Katherine Anne Porter and Eudora Welty, Mrs. McCullers forms a Southern triad that has carried on and modified the basic Faulknerian themes of lust, disease, mutilation, defeat, idiocy and death. All of these notes, with a shift in emphasis, are played in her fiction over and again: disease crops up in the form of permanent distortion in the figures of the cretin, the crippled and the incurable; the theme of death is effectively pitted against that of adolescence; the idea of defeat is narrowed down to personal disillusion resulting from tragic initiation into life or from the failure of a misdirected lifework —it does not carry the historical implications as in Faulkner's concept of the past bearing down heavily upon the present; mutilation is the fate of the social underdog, the Negro, in the fangs of unjust justice; idiocy is used rather in the way Faulkner uses it, as a symbol of futility, of the impossibility of redemption although, again, [Faulkner's] Benjy is given a more comprehensive meaning than is Antonapoulos in *The Heart Is a Lonely Hunter;* finally, lust is transformed into a more complex theme that is central to her prose: it is the constant insistence on the impossibility of mutual love. All of these themes spread a web of sadness, isolation and disenchantment over Carson McCullers' work.

As she follows up the issues of Faulkner's earlier period, most of his later and more significant themes are lacking. She is far more concerned with the present than with the past, and therefore the collective burdens of fathers and forebears have but little weight on the outcome of her novels. In a sense, she entirely forgoes the broad social and historical dimensions that Faulkner and, for that matter, Robert Penn Warren are so keenly aware of. Moreover, she is out of touch with nature or, to put it in Faulkner's phrase, the land, in which he seems to have anchored some of his more recently voiced hope and affirmation. There is but little change of outlook in her development; the same ideas, though intensified and formally varied, are harped on repeatedly. Thirdly, in her attitude toward her themes and characters, she fails to develop Faulkner's passion and obsession; she remains cool and detached, at the most, compassionate. Wherever her heart goes into her pages, it tends to add pathetic touches that, at times, verge on the sentimental. Still, her "ordinary town," the setting of her plots, lies in the middle of the deep South. . . . (pp. 187-88)

The most puzzling novel is undoubtedly *The Heart Is a Lonely Hunter.* . . . What has led to some confusion is the multiplicity of characters, parallel actions and understandings of 'truth' (none of which seems central) without any apparent norm to give the plot perspective. As a consequence, the story gives the impression of being made up of loosely juxtaposed elements which are parts of a barely coherent whole. Unless one can perceive governing patterns, the book leaves in the reader a disjointed, if not chaotic, effect. Almost any of the main figures or 'truths' might then be selected as central, summing up the total experience. (p. 188)

The story is mainly concerned with four figures grappling with life from the different angles of growing childhood, the race problem, socialism and common sense. In addition, there are a couple of deaf-mutes that are closely tied up with the meaning of the whole. (p. 189)

Structurally, Singer as the hub seems to occupy the dominating position in the novel. It is his figure that gives the book its frame in the first section, it is his exit that closes its main portion and causes Copeland, Jake, Mick and Biff to revise their differing experiences with life, now life without the illusive prop. However, there is a neatly elaborated structure running counter to this grouping. It arranges the characters in a different way, namely in proportion to the viability of their ideas. If we exclude Singer, the persons are introduced in the following order at the beginning: Biff dominates the second chapter, the third is mainly about Mick, the fourth is devoted to Jake, the fifth deals with Copeland. . . . They live in their individual divisions as in watertight compartments. This technique of encasing the figures in their separate worlds underscores their isolation in life: each stands by himself. In the epilogue, the third section, the order of presentation is exactly reversed: Copeland is followed by Jake, Mick by Biff. Between the beginning and the end there is thus a chiastic correspondence in the order of presenting the figures. . . . If we accept the different distribution of emphasis . . . we see the figures in a new order of importance ranging from Biff through Mick and Jake down to Copeland. (pp. 190-91)

What does this sequence and this regrouping of the personages that both adds and runs counter to the flight-of-steps image tell us about the meaning of *The Heart Is a Lonely Hunter*? What are the grounds for this double grouping? The main theme of Carson McCullers' first novel is not the social problem nor is it primarily that of human isolation. It is rather the question of truth and illusion (or, disillusionment). Each of the four characters around Singer is in his own way concerned with distinguishing truth from illusion. Biff Brannon . . . looks out for truth behind appearances from behind his restaurant counter. He is a realist, interested in facts and the whys behind them. For the adolescent Mick Kelly, the problem of truth is that of initiation into a drab world. For a long time, she is unable to make her imaginary and her real worlds meet. Her friendly "inside room" is furnished with her dreams and aspirations while the "outside room" of the world leaves her puzzled and perplexed. For Jake Blount . . . the world is similarly split up: there are the "knows" and the "don't knows" according to people's reactions to his socialist good tidings. The fourth person is . . . Benedict Copeland, obsessed with the dissemination of "real truths". He has sacrificed his family life to the pursuit of his "real true purpose" of liberating his race. He is an atheist, suspicious of the heart, living only with his brain. (p. 191)

Reflections in a Golden Eye can best be regarded as a repeated but abortive attempt to deal . . . with a concatenation of bizarre feelings. . . . It lies in the absence of the necessary observer, a Nick Carraway, to give meaning to the last act of the tragedy which the form does not make clear as in *The Heart Is a Lonely Hunter*. The author, obviously aware of this failure, was later to make amends in *The Ballad of the Sad Café*. (p. 196)

There is a rhythm in Carson McCullers' output: full-length treatment alternates with the short novel or *novelette*, a form in which her problems of love and isolation can be stated more cogently. The choice of the intermediary fictional genre seems especially adequate as it allows of con-

densation of atmosphere and detachment of the narrator. *The Ballad of the Sad Café* marks the artistic climax of her writing up to that time. It contains a philosophy of love that has slowly evolved through her earlier works and has now reached a point of completeness where it is not only presented dramatically, but also explicitly in a reflective passage: not only may love not be returned by the beloved, it may also cause the latter to hate the lover. This idea is the result of a consistent development of such relations as between the deaf-mutes, and it accounts for the singular and terrible connection of the characters in her fourth book. (p. 198)

It is a long way from Carson McCullers' first to [*Clock Without Hands*], written with her age in the meantime doubled and with tragic experience behind her. Although the old watermarks still show through the pages—loneliness, freakishness, men in pursuit of separate and clashing dreams, the odd, ironic human chain with the beloved lashing out at the lover—, her writing has apparently entered a new phase. Life has become more wholesome, order and meaning are perceived in it at last, and even mutual love begins to blossom. (p. 201)

Both the latter-day evangelists and the adolescents are important figures in her first and third books and their ideas have to be reduced to proper proportions by means of structural devices and contrasting characters. Thus, order in *The Heart Is a Lonely Hunter* is mainly imposed by the principle of organization . . . , and by the central rôle which Biff Brannon plays. His importance, however, still depends on the place he is given within the *formal* framework of the novel. In *Reflections in a Golden Eye,* the theme of one-sided love is tentatively developed and brought to an unsatisfactory conclusion. The antithesis of the double ethical norm—'square peg' standard versus the feeble judgment passed by Alison as a moral arbiter—is not resolved and leaves the three surviving personages in an unexplained chaos. By a shift in emphasis, reduction of characters and concentration on one major theme, a balanced world emerges at the end of *The Member of the Wedding.* Here, for the last time, the adolescent is allowed a dominating part. This novel as well as the army camp novelette are variations on themes inherent in portions of the first book whereas *The Ballad of the Sad Café* belongs to a new category in matter and manner. The theme of love chasing its tail forms the logical capstone of an evolution through the three previous works. Its morbidity is made bearable and convincing by narrative detachment, remoteness in time and the witnessing town that stays outside the emotional boundary line. With *Clock Without Hands* a new concept of order is announced. Life becomes a state in which, at least at the end, everything is in its right place.

The overall theme of Carson McCullers' books is that of man's problematic and painful existence with various veerings from its proper course. Man's drab life is presented at critical points such as adolescence, loss of friendship, oncoming death, and leads to types of escape, imaginary and real. Escape may be actual as in Frankie's case; but it is of short duration and fails due to lack of direction. In its extreme form, it becomes the negation of meaning in life itself, as in Singer's suicide. Another source of escape is the recourse to the "inner room". Fancy fastens on the distant in time and place; the seashell on Frankie's desk stands for the warm wash of the Gulf of Mexico, her glass snow globe reminds her of cool Alaska, the wedding proves more attractive because it takes place in 'Winter' Hill. Uneventful life is also adorned by lying which provides a form of vicarious life. Yet inevitably, man is brought back from fanciful flights. Without fail his wishful dreams are thwarted by the onslaughts of reality and only his nightmares materialize. His experience is that of being caught, of being left as an alien in a strange land, symbolized in the corresponding images of the prisoner caged in a stone cell with iron bars before the windows and of the chain that both connects and isolates the members of the gang. The song of the "twelve mortal men" mediates between the tragic vision of Biff and the rediscovered little miracles of everyday life that reconcile J. T. Malone with his too early death. His love for his wife has returned just as Martin Meadows in a short story 'A Domestic Dilemma' finds back to "the immense complexity of love." . . . Thus the burden of impersonal love that Biff takes up and that is rationalized in an early story 'A Tree. A Rock. A Cloud' is replaced by mutual personal love for the first time.

The imaginary scope of the author is not wide. Typical figures and ideas, characteristic scenes, forms of behavior recur in all of her books. Nor does her fictional town alter much. It is expanded or contracted as needed, a café or a drugstore forms its significant center: in short, the stage remains, the properties are shifted. On the stage, man's drama is enacted, and it is his attitude toward life that has undergone a change and testifies that, in the second decade of her writing, Mrs. McCullers' themes have changed tending to emphasize the one side of Brannon's vision, putting more stress on 'radiance' and 'faith' than upon 'irony' and 'darkness'. (pp. 203-04)

Klaus Lubbers, "The Necessary Order: A Study of Theme and Structure in Carson McCullers' Fiction, in Jahrbuch Für Amerikastudien *(© 1963 Carl Winter, Universitätsverlag, Gegr. 1822, GmbH., Heidelberg), Band 8, 1963, pp. 187-204.*

JACK B. MOORE

Carson McCullers has frequently employed mythic patterns to explicate the psychological tensions urging her characters. . . . The people in her books, stripped of all irrelevant behavioral flesh, present the heart's core of action that we also see played out for us in legend, fairytale, and folkstory.

Yet her books—such as *Reflections in a Golden Eye, Clock Without Hands, The Heart Is a Lonely Hunter*—are contemporary reports of life in America. . . . As a novelist one of her gifts has been the ability to fuse the demands of verisimilitude and romance, one of her difficulties the occasional splitting of the two—as in *Clock Without Hands*—to the detriment of her work's impact. . . .

[In] *The Heart Is a Lonely Hunter* she successfully employs one of our oldest myths—that of initiation—to solve a delicate problem of verisimilitude, and how at the same time she perfectly retells the myth in convincingly contemporary terms. . . . McCullers' nearly allegoric retelling is amazingly faithful to the heart of the myth's pattern. [Her] reworking handles the complex process of ritual initiation with a natural simplicity and beauty worth noting. In describing young Mick Kelly's poignant loss of virginity, and her more painful loss of childhood, McCullers travels the path of both contemporary novelist and timeless myth-

maker, and shows that, with her at least, the dual roads ultimately converge. (p. 76)

Jack B. Moore, "Carson McCullers: The Heart Is a Timeless Hunter," in Twentieth Century Literature *(copyright 1965, Hofstra University Press), April, 1965, pp. 76-81.*

OLIVER EVANS

[*The Square Root of Wonderful*] is to a large extent autobiographical. When it appeared in book form, the author explained in her preface:

> In *The Square Root of Wonderful* I recognize many of the compulsions that made me write this play. My husband wanted to be a writer and his failure in that was one of the disappointments that led to his death. When I started *The Square Root of Wonderful* my mother was very ill and after a few months she died. I wanted to recreate my mother— to remember her tranquil beauty and sense of joy in life. So, unconsciously, the life-death theme of *The Square Root of Wonderful* emerged.

The play's protagonist is a young woman, Mollie Lovejoy, who has been twice married to and divorced from the same man, a once-famous writer who, after the failure of his latest play, has attempted suicide and is convalescing in a rest home. Mollie has meanwhile fallen in love with an architect, John, and is on the point of marrying him when Phillip, her ex-husband, returns. The two men are opposites: John is dull but strong; Phillip is weak and has learned to use his weakness to advantage with women, but he is charming and perceptive. He does not love Mollie—it is made clear that he is incapable of loving anyone—but he needs her desperately and insists that she love *him*. (pp. 162-63)

From what Mrs McCullers has said in her preface, the reader is obviously expected to identify Phillip with Reeves McCullers, and Mollie Lovejoy with Mrs Smith [Mrs McCullers's mother]. But it is not quite so simple as that; the careful reader will note at once that it is Phillip and not his wife who was successful as a writer, even if he is now a 'has-been'. . . . And the circumstance of Mollie's having married the same man twice reminds us not of Mrs Smith but of Mrs McCullers. What the author has done is to identify herself now with Phillip (in the speeches in which he discusses his writing), now with Mollie (in the dialogue which she exchanges with her ex-husband). This is of course perfectly proper: it is what most authors do when they create characters, so that the result is seldom an authentic portrait of a single individual but a composite or amalgam. But it is useful for us to realize that the author, consciously or unconsciously, has not kept herself out of the play quite as much as her preface might suggest—useful because it explains the lack of aesthetic distance which separates her from her characters. For if this is Mrs McCullers's weakest performance—and I believe it is—the reason for it may well be that she is still too close to her materials. (p. 163)

Though her choice of a life-death theme suggests that Mrs McCullers has consciously chosen a new area of literary interest, the reader will remember that the same theme was present in *Reflections in a Golden Eye*. . . . The polarization of characters in this play also reminds us of *Reflections in a Golden Eye*: John (like Major Langdon) is dull and 'normal' while Phillip (like Penderton) is brilliant and neurotic. The contrast extends also to the women characters: while two men compete for Mollie, Sister is obliged to invent her lovers. . . .

In his inability to love, Phillip personifies the death principle, or, in Freudian terms, the death wish (it is significant that he takes his own life), and Mollie, who is capable of loving more than one man simultaneously, personifies the *élan vital*. Life triumphs over death in the play, and in a sense it is the triumph of the mediocre over the exceptional, for Phillip is certainly the more interesting character. (p. 164)

Subordinate to the primary theme is a variety of minor motifs (too many, possibly, for the play to maintain its unity). . . . Thus, the irrationality of love is again insisted upon. . . . So also is the loneliness that springs from an incapacity for love. . . . (p. 165)

But the most important of the minor themes has to do with time. The relation of time to love is obvious: it is the Great Enemy of love as it is of life, of which love is the surest sign and the happiest manifestation. . . . Its relation to the problem of identity is equally obvious, since one's identity, as Frankie learns in *The Member of the Wedding*, changes with its passage.

In relation to loneliness, however, time takes on yet another significance. . . . Time passes quickly for the lover, and in that sense may be thought of as a traitor and an enemy, but it is an even greater enemy to the loveless. Phillip refers to it as 'that endless idiot that goes screaming round the world'. . . . (pp. 166-67)

Except in the case of Phillip (and, to a less extent, Mollie) the characterization is thin and lacking in complexity. (p. 167)

Technically, *The Square Root of Wonderful* is a well-made play (it makes surprisingly good reading), and the fact that it did not succeed on Broadway may merely mean that a popular audience is less interested in the personal problems of a literary has-been than in those of a fourteen-year-old girl—who might be the one next door—with growing pains. In this play Mrs McCullers is concerned with too specialized an area of human interest and experience—another way, perhaps, of saying that she is too close to her materials. (p. 168)

It is doubtful that any American writer since Hawthorne and Melville has handled the difficult form of allegory quite so well as Carson McCullers. A didactic writer in an age when didacticism, in the United States at any rate, is suspect (unless the message involved be one that flatters the reader at the same time that it does not make very considerable demands upon his intelligence), she may yet live to see the fulfilment of Mr Gore Vidal's prediction [see excerpt above] that 'of all our Southern writers Carson McCullers is the one most likely to endure'. . . . Her writing is almost never peripheral, as that of Faulkner often is: it goes straight to the heart of its subject, and it rarely fumbles. And while it is true that her talent lacks the impressive range of Faulkner's, within its limits she has succeeded in creating certain effects that are inimitable. Had she written nothing except *The Ballad of the Sad Café* her position

among the half dozen or so who comprise the highest echelon of living American authors would still be unassailable. (p. 194)

Oliver Evans, in his The Ballad of Carson Mc-Cullers: A Biography *(copyright © 1965 by Peter Owen Ltd.), Coward-McCann, Inc., 1966.*

ROBERT DRAKE

In the preface to the published version of her play *The Square Root of Wonderful* (1958), the late Carson McCullers posed and answered a question that every writer has come to terms with sooner or later:

> Why does anyone write at all? I suppose a writer writes out of some inward compulsion to transform his own experience (much of it is unconscious) into the universal and symbolical. The themes the artist chooses are always deeply personal. I suppose my central theme is the theme of spiritual isolation. Certainly I have always felt alone. In addition to being lonely, a writer is also amorphous. A writer soon discovers he has no single identity but lives the lives of all the people he creates and his weathers are independent of the actual day around him. I live with the people I create and it has always made my essential loneliness less keen.

Many writers and critics of fiction would agree that Mrs. McCullers' work is an excellent illustration of these views; for her work seems to indicate that she was well aware of the nature of her own talents—and of their concomitant limitations. Further, many of her admirers would say that she always pretty well followed the precepts she set down. I am inclined to think, however, that this was not always the case; that her neglect of her own advice explains many of Mrs. McCullers' artistic failures and will ultimately deny her a place among the most accomplished and compelling practitioners of 20th century American fiction. . . .

I believe that in [*The Heart Is a Lonely Hunter* and *The Member of the Wedding*]—as in hardly any other of her fictions save possibly one or two of her short stories—she came near to finding an inevitable and technically unexceptionable embodiment of the theme she correctly assessed as her principal one. Who could forget the first novel's adolescent Mick Kelly desperately searching for love and meaning? Who could remain untouched by the second's tormented Frankie Addams, trying frantically to be "included" in the wedding—to find what surely all of us are somehow looking for: "the we of me"? These are themes as old as the human heart, and it was Mrs. McCullers' great talent that she was able to discern and present them (especially in her *Hunter*) in a variety of characters and dramatic situations.

And what wisdom there is in these two books! Surely those critics are wrong who argue that it is Mr. Singer, the deaf-mute, who holds the diffuse first novel together, with his constant availability as a listener for all the talkers that work is so full of. More likely it is the colored Portia, herself one of the least and meekest, who constitutes the novel's spiritual center—though probably, and unfortunately, not its structural one. Perhaps Mr. Singer *is* the structural center; but part of the novel's technical weakness may lie just there: its spiritual and structural centers do not coincide. . . .

Another Negro, Berenice, seems to be both the moral and the technical center of *The Member of the Wedding*. Berenice too knows the deep unspoken longings of the human heart. She comes as close as anybody to understanding and helping tomboy Frankie, who passes through the wild romanticism of "F. Jasmine" to the somewhat greater maturity of "Frances" in her lonely search for identity and love. (p. 50)

But love, at its best, does not necessarily seek or hunt for anyone or anything: it simply *is*, and it *gives*. Sometimes Mrs. McCullers implies (as in the story "A Tree—a Rock —a Cloud") that one has to start with smaller things before he can work up to loving whole persons, just as they are. . . . At her best she is never false to this theme, though she is sometimes uncertain and confused in its execution. Even her two finest novels suffer from a considerable degree of incoherence, as though she were trying to tell too many stories at once. And even in these two she occasionally falls into tendentious exploitation of contemporary southern social problems or even of the grand affairs of world politics.

But it is in her lesser works that her defects become fully evident—novels like the kinked-up *Reflections in a Golden Eye* (1941) and the ridiculous *The Ballad of the Sad Cafe* (1951), with its fabricated primitivistic folkishness. Here her keen sense of the grotesque goes wild, and she twists kink into kink until the whole pattern becomes meaningless. . . . Tiresome also is the fictionally meaningless homosexual longing of Jester Clane for the Negro Sherman Pew in *Clock Without Hands*. What does all Mrs. McCullers' *grotesquerie* mean anyhow? Certainly very little where almost everything is grotesque. . . . In this matter Mrs. McCullers is inferior to Flannery O'Connor, with whom she is often compared. Alas, Mrs. McCullers' work is more akin to that of Tennessee Williams or of the young Truman Capote. (pp. 50-1)

I am driven to counter another misleading comparison—the assertion of affinities between Mrs. McCullers and Eudora Welty. Miss Welty's fiction too is very much concerned with the heart's reasons, with the searching love that can bless but, if not carefully regulated, can also destroy. But she always keeps this theme under control; she never uses it as a springboard to launch into topics of the day or plunge into stories irrelevant to the one in hand.

Indeed, I believe that the greatest weakness in Mrs. McCullers' fiction is precisely this lack of *form*. She was truly obsessed by her one story, her principal theme, and at her best she was true to it. But in so many cases she simply did not know what to do with it, how to embody it economically and persuasively in her fictional characters. Why?

It would be provincial, and also perhaps somewhat wide of the mark, to say that she should have stayed at home in Georgia and not gone off to fall among the thieves and vultures of the New York literary salon scene. But there may be some saving truth in this apparently chauvinistic observation. Let me try to put it into critical terminology: Mrs. McCullers wrote best when her head and her heart were working in harmony to produce the fictional music which was uniquely hers. She was at her worst when her head took over, when she forgot or ignored her real story and

started to examine pathological specimens or to write up the news from home—segregation in [*Clock Without Hands*], for example. . . .

I believe that, despite her occasional triumphs—and they *were* valid ones—her talent never came to its full fruition. (p. 51)

Robert Drake, "The Lonely Heart of Carson McCullers," in The Christian Century *(copyright 1968 Christian Century Foundation; reprinted by permission from the January 10, 1968 issue of* The Christian Century*), January 10, 1968, pp. 50-1.*

JEANNE KINNEY

In a sense [*The Mortgaged Heart*] is a writer's dream—to have everything one ever wrote, including a rough outline for a novel, published. What more could an artist hope for? On the other hand, for a perfectionist like Carson McCullers, who rewrote over and over again until the gem was sufficiently polished, it might have been a horror. . . . [As] a specialized collection, it will prove a valuable appendage to devotees of the author's major works. . . .

Her dramatic sense of detail was there from the beginning in character sketches and evolved to maturity in her later stories and essays. The essays are remarkably lucid prose. Worth the price of the book are the seven brief essays on "Writers and Writing." . . .

Carson felt all good prose writing has an element of poetry as well. Her own prose is better poetry than the nine poems included here. It would have honored the author's memory to have left them buried in a bottom drawer somewhere.

Presumably Carson McCullers never meant much of this material for the public and it is with this in mind that the stories and essays provide a sort of autobiographical and literary background that helps to round out the picture of the author as creative person. (p. 371)

Jeanne Kinney, in Best Sellers *(copyright 1971, by the University of Scranton), November 15, 1971.*

JOHN ALFRED AVANT

When a writer dies leaving early work uncollected, it is often uncollected for a very good reason; and readers who come to *The Mortgaged Heart* without previous exposure to Carson McCullers may wonder whether her reputation is justified. This posthumous collection contains 14 stories . . . , an outline for *The Heart Is a Lonely Hunter*, some nonfiction magazine pieces, and five poems. The stories are clearly apprentice works, some of them from the "How I Grew Up Last Summer" school. They use typical McCullers subjects (painful adolescence, loneliness in the big city, youthful exposure to adult sexuality), but what is beautifully fragile in her best writing is too slight in these early exercises to hold one's interest. Most of the nonfiction is undistinguished. A Thanksgiving article from *Mademoiselle* is surprisingly like a blandly pious holiday sermon; and a maudlin recollection of a legless girl with whom McCullers once spent Christmas in a physical therapy hospital is embarrassing, because McCullers uses our knowledge of her own physical pain to achieve pathos in ways that are unworthy of her.

What partially redeems the volume is "The Flowering Dream," a series of fragmented observations on writing and life that don't go very far but are stated with admirable simplicity. (p. 73)

John Alfred Avant, in Library Journal *(reprinted from* Library Journal, *January 1, 1972; published by R. R. Bowker Co. (a Xerox company); copyright © 1972 by Xerox Corporation), January 1, 1972.*

JOSEPH R. MILLICHAP

The use of the bizarre theory of love offered by the narrator of [*Ballad of the Sad Café*] as a formula for interpreting all of McCullers' fiction has hampered analysis not only of the *novella* itself but of her other works as well. The description of her narrative as a ballad, so obviously presented in the title, provides a key to understanding which unlocks the novella's difficulties of literary mode, point-of-view, characterization, and plot structure. (p. 329)

McCullers' ballad concentrates on the strange love triangle formed by a manly giantess, a selfish dwarf, and a demonic bandit. The action unfolds in a few weird events which culminate in an epic battle waged purposely on Groundhog Day to decide the death or rebirth of love. The setting is a romantic wasteland where piney woods and swamps counterpoint the stunning heat of August afternoons. The concrete symbols of the ballad world both explain and motivate the action; buildings lean in precarious decay; trees twist grotesquely in the moonlight; birds and animals provide mysterious analogues to human action.

Clearly this is the traditional world of the ballad, a world of passion and violence, of omens and portents, of the full wild impulsiveness of archetypal human behavior. . . . (pp. 329-30)

Of course, McCullers' ballad is a literary one, wrought by a modern, conscious artistry not by the folk mind or by an artless imagination. . . . The structural and stylistic integrity of the story, especially of narrative voice marks her literary ballad as an unqualified success. McCullers presents a narrator who can spin the fine fabric of romantic fiction from the raw materials of mill-village life without violating either realm. In *Ballad* a ballad-maker evokes from the world of the Georgia back-country a timeless, compelling story of human passion. His voice fixes the style of the novel—a perfect blend of the literate and colloquial, the objective and personal, talky observation. The existence of this filtering personality assures the novella's achievement.

Neither McCullers nor the typical third person omniscient voice, narrates; the ballad-maker tells the tale. (p. 330)

This device also releases McCullers from responsibility for the universalization of the fantastic observations on the mutual exclusiveness of love so often ascribed to her by earlier critics (such as Oliver Evans . . . and Klaus Lubbers) [see excerpts above]. The narrator defines love as "joint experience between two persons," the lover and the beloved. The experience between them is not necessarily the same for each party, for the lover and the beloved "come from two different countries." The lover attaches his love to some person, often without rational purpose. He creates an imaginary world surrounding the beloved and then releases his stored creative energies on this dream vision. "Therefore, the value and quality of any love is determined solely by the lover himself." The narrator continues: "It is for this reason that most of us would rather love than be loved. Almost everyone wants to be the lover. And the curt truth is that, in a deep secret way, the state of being beloved is intolerable to many. The beloved fears and hates the lover, and with the best of reasons. For the lover is forever trying to strip bare his beloved. The lover craves any possible relation with the beloved, even if this experience can cause him only pain.''

The ballad-maker's theory of love is substantiated by the character relationships in the novella, but the limited number of cases prevents immediate acceptance of it as a universal law of human nature; it clearly remains the narrator's hypothesis, not McCullers'. . . . In her later novels and stories love does live for a few people, at least for a time. Yet the earlier novels have partially demonstrated this pattern. (p. 331)

As in both [*The Heart Is a Lonely Hunter* and *Reflections in a Golden Eye*] a geometrically patterned relationship of characters is the basis of symbolism and structure.

After the description of the town, which opens the tale, the narrator introduces Miss Amelia. On the hot, empty afternoons of August, the season when the town seems most desolate and isolated, her strange face peers down crazily from an upper window of the town's largest structure which is now boarded up and fast decaying. The building has "a curious, cracked look that is very puzzling," and Miss Amelia's haunted face with her severely crossed eyes provides the human analogue of the structure. (p. 332)

Plot is developed tightly and economically so as to dramatize the creation of [the love] triangles and to emphasize the role of the balladeer-narrator. . . .

The narrator quickly moves the story through these years of human growth for Miss Amelia, symbolized by the emergence of the café. (p. 336)

The years pass in this fruitful manner until Marvin Macy comes back to the village; bad luck follows him to his home town. . . . Marvin Macy's fearful reputation increases, and in direct proportion so does Cousin Lymon's adoration of him. . . . After the snow Cousin Lymon brings his beloved to stay in the rooms over the café; this final displacement of Amelia precipitates the total collapse on February 2, Groundhog Day. The date proves significant because Cousin Lymon sees the groundhog observe his shadow, an indication of six more weeks of winter ahead and a prefigurement of Marvin Macy's destructive triumph. . . .

The climactic battle begins at seven o'clock, as Miss Amelia sets great store by the mystical number seven. Significantly the fight takes place in the café; the center of companionship and symbol of love has become a place of hatred and combat. (p. 337)

Miss Amelia is severely beaten, and left in disgrace. . . . Cousin Lymon and Marvin Macy leave that night, but, before they go, they completely wreck the café: food, whiskey, decorations, the mechanical piano. The café ends as Miss Amelia's love ends. Slowly she shrivels into an old maid; her muscles shrink and her eyes cross to look inward. After three years of lonesome waiting for Cousin Lymon to return, she has the store-café boarded up. Retreating into the upstairs rooms, she remains there alone and isolated. The town takes on a new loneliness also; a perpetual August drought envelops it in a claustrophobic malaise. Time hangs heavy and dull. (p. 338)

The chain gang [epilogue which takes place in the present] illustrates the prison house aspect of the human condition.

The coda, entitled "Twelve Mortal Men," emphasizes how man can achieve creativity, in this case the beautiful work songs and ballads of the gang, even in the most difficult situations if there is harmony and cooperation. The last sentence of the novella points out that they are only "... twelve mortal men who are together." The picture of the chain gang contrasts with the reader's final vision of Miss Amelia. She could release her creative efforts when she was "together" with Cousin Lymon; alone she can accomplish nothing. Where love and harmony exist much can be created; sadly enough, they exist in few places and for short times—human failings quickly frustrate them, and they are often replaced by hate and isolation. McCullers' other novels demonstrate this condition in the modern social world; the strange ballad of the café that becomes sad traces the roots of these difficulties in the timeless province of the lonely human heart. (pp. 338-39)

> *Joseph R. Millichap, "Carson McCullers' Literary Ballad," in* The Georgia Review *(copyright, 1973, by the University of Georgia), Fall, 1973, pp. 329-39.*

JOHN McNALLY

When one reads the novella [*The Ballad of the Sad Café*] in the understanding that the narrator is a character in the story, he notices a subtle but significant shift in the story's form and subsequent themes. Such a reader finds himself absorbed not so much with the bizarre goings-on in the old café as with the changing perceptions of a person in the process of intense introspection. . . .

The first clue to the actual point of view is the fact that the story begins and ends in the present tense. In itself, the present tense does not a fictive narrator make. Considered in the context of the references to "here" and "now," though, the use of the present suggests a person who is describing the café "on the spot." . . .

To read the story in the light of this perception is to read a very different story indeed—it is to read a story in which, for one thing, the apparent authorial intrusions and digressions are no longer flaws in the narrative but actually key passages in the story's curious network of meanings. . . .

As an actual character, then, the narrator is less to be faulted for digressing than would a simple omniscient narrator—for *real* people do digress when they tell stories.

But there is more to this than mere verisimilitude. As the concern of a character-narrator, the "digression" is more clearly related to the later section in the story in which the narrator describes the effects of the music of the chain gang. For, just as Miss Amelia's liquor had once "warmed his soul," "shown the truth" and the "message hidden there," so now the music causes his "heart to broaden," his soul to "grow cold with ecstasy and fright." The café he had once visited gone, the narrator seeks truth in the music of "the earth itself," of the "twelve mortal men who are together."

Besides the liquor "digression" and the enigmatic chain-gang passage, there are other frequent points in the narrative at which the narrator asserts his personality. . . . (p. 41)

If in these passages the narrator reveals something of himself, what is it? In other words, who is he? What does he mean? (p. 42)

The whole story he remembers—digressions and all—has the effect of changing his perceptions of himself and his present predicament. He realizes, for example, that the characters he has recalled were incapable of sharing love, that each was the other's hell. He recalls a pageant of grotesquery and violence that eventually turns the nostalgia to bitterness and pain. More than anything else, though, he experiences the contrast between the proprietress in her prime and the bent, broken and inward-turned terrible face she now shows at the window.

The recollection done, he is a man who sees himself in the town in which he sits, who sees the town—like the remembered café—as a reflection of his own static image. It is here—after the flashback—that he repeats "Yes, the town *is* dreary. . . ." It is so dreary that "the soul rots with boredom." It is so dreary that he "might as well go down to the Fork Falls highway and listen to the chain-gang." This last paragraph suggests, then, that the narrator is a man who realizes he has refused to obey his impulse to move—to go listen to the chain-gang. It shows him to be a man who has wrestled with the past and who has used the past to reinterpret the present. It shows that he knows that when nothing moves—the spirit dies; "the soul rots with boredom."

The so-called epilogue, "The Twelve Mortal Men," seen in the context of the character-narrator's struggle becomes not a cryptic appendix to a gothic tale but, instead, the positive act of a man of changed perspective. . . . The whole section is seen in direct contrast to the flashback section of the story. Where in the café reminiscences the narrator found free people unwilling or incapable to share love with one another, in the epilogue he finds people in chains who share their suffering and who, in sharing, bring music from the earth and sky. Such music is what keeps the narrator's soul alive.

It has not been my purpose here to insist that the inside story—the flashback about the café that is still remembered—is of minor significance. On the contrary, that story is an intriguing one: it is a grotesque delineation of love's power to destroy. It *has* been my purpose, though, to show that its chief significance lies in what it reveals about the character who, in recalling it, gives it its shape and who, in reaction to it, finds new meaning in his own existence. (pp. 42-3)

What we have in *The Ballad of the Sad Café*, then, is a beautifully sculptured piece of writing. . . . The *Ballad* is a song of the human spirit. (pp. 43-4)

> *John McNally, "The Introspective Narrator in 'The Ballad of the Sad Café'," in* South Atlantic Bulletin *(copyright © 1973 by South Atlantic Modern Language Association), November, 1973, pp. 40-4.*

RICHARD M. COOK

The limits of McCullers's accomplishments are real. One reads through her works with a sharp sense of the highly individual, almost eccentric nature of her achievement, but also with a growing sense of their author's restricted range of interest and abilities. And when one looks closely at the whole course of her career, one is even more struck by its disappointments and unfulfilled promises. For there is something initially inspiring but eventually dispiriting about McCullers's life as a writer. It is almost as if the disappointment felt by the would-be *wunderkind* of her first published story were a prophesy for her own career. (pp. 122-23)

Her fiction does not grow out of a broadening intellectual inquiry into new areas of thought and experience. Rather it is limited to the repeated exploration of one idea or emotional state—the human being in isolation. Though her first and last novels bring up questions of politics, religion, race, and history, her primary concern in these and all her novels remains the same—man alone. For McCullers it was a profound but circumscribed area of concern and one which after *The Heart Is a Lonely Hunter* turned inward on itself, taking her novels into areas increasingly removed from outside contemporary life, areas such as the subjective imagination of a twelve-year-old girl or a remote village in a land of myth and fairy tale "like a place that is far off and estranged from all other places in the world." The failure of *Clock without Hands* to repeat the success of *The Heart Is a Lonely Hunter* only demonstrates further how far removed McCullers's concern with human isolation had grown from contemporary issues. Few Americans have evoked the terrors and the pathos of man alone as well as she has. Loneliness is a feeling pervasive and permanent in the physical world of her novels; it is also a fact in all of her characters' lives, a condition that brings each of them together into fragile communities of mutual isolation. But as if caught within its own terrible meaning, human isolation is a theme that in McCullers's fiction circles further and further inward, leading less and less to concerns beyond itself—a solipsistic pattern that may eventually have strangled her art.

Moreover, restrictions inherent in her theme were further subject to restrictions in time and place. . . . The South as she remembered it as a child was the land of her inspiration. . . . [But after] finishing *The Member of the Wedding,* McCullers turned from the South of her childhood to the urban and suburban North for the material of her short stories and her play, *The Square Root of Wonderful.* She returns to the South in *Clock without Hands,* but to the South of the 1950s of which she had only the most casual understanding. In turning from her childhood memories for her inspiration she lost touch with a world that she knew intimately and exactly, where loneliness, boredom, and frustration merged into an inescapable daily agony. She also lost her capacity to create interesting believable characters. Removed from the wealth of odd and homely details that create in her best works a felt sense of time and place, the people in the short stories and the play never come alive, stand up, and cast real shadows. (pp. 123-25)

But if the muse of isolation was for Carson McCullers inward-turning and at home only in the South of her childhood memories, it inspired her best writing with a rare sympathy for and insight into hidden suffering which, I think, represent the highest accomplishments of her fiction. . . . Running throughout her works is the unstated conviction that no human being can in his inmost, truest self ever be really known, that he is doomed either to eternal loneliness or to compromise with the crass world outside. . . . It is in their vulnerability to the crude, violent, leavening forces in the outside world that McCullers's people are isolated. . . . Grotesque and unfinished in their intense subjectivity, they would risk their ideals and individuality if they joined the outside world of "normal"

public human beings. And yet the loneliness of their incomplete and unjoined state is more than they can bear.

McCullers believed that only through the compassion and empathy of art could such vulnerable inwardness be freed and appreciated for the valuable and rare quality that it was. Her vision of human loneliness is a vision born of love. . . . (pp. 126-27)

McCullers possessed what most of her characters tragically lack, a double vision that enabled her to see the inside and the outside of people: a hopeless love for a departed friend beneath John Singer's deferential politeness, a sincere moral outrage beneath Jake Blount's loud talk and belligerent manner, an uncertainty of identity and terror of the future beneath Frankie's foolishness and irritability, and a desperate, lonely passion beneath Miss Amelia's masculine dress and crafty business practices. In her most successful works McCullers could, as she once claimed, "become" her characters, enter their lonely lives, the places where they lived. And without letting us lose sight of their awkward, sometimes frightening and often amusing outwardness, she let us see into their secret inwardness. (p. 128)

Richard M. Cook, "Carson McCullers's Career: The Achievements, the Disappointments," in his Carson McCullers *(copyright © 1975 by Frederick Ungar Publishing Co., Inc.), Frederick Ungar, 1975, pp. 121-29.*

RICHARD GRAY

There is a peculiar quality of isolation about Carson McCullers's work . . . that owes some of its intensity perhaps to her own status vis-à-vis the South. She does not belong to the great generation of the "renaissance," that is clear enough. . . . But she does not really belong to the new wave of Southern writers either, since apart from *Clock Without Hands*—a book dealing, among other things, with the issue of desegregation, which was not published until 1961—all of her more important fiction had been written by 1946; and was collected into a uniform edition some five years later. Her major period of creativity was very brief, consisting of about five years in all; and the last twenty or so years of her life were so marred by ill health that, in retrospect, it seems remarkable she was able to write the little, during the period, that she did. Certainly, illness offers a sufficient explanation for her gradual lapse into silence. Coming after the great fiction and poetry of the twenties and thirties, but before the more recent examples of Southern Gothic . . . her novels and short stories occupy, consequently, a particular transitional moment of their own in the tradition. Theirs is a special, and especially separate, place in the history of Southern literature, which makes their author seem occasionally like one of her own characters—alone, cut off from all normal channels of communication, and strangely vulnerable.

Other factors, quite apart from her unusual literary situation, probably contributed to McCullers's interest in the dimensions of loneliness. Her childhood, for example, seems to have been a very quiet one. "Almost singularly lacking," as her biographer [Oliver Evans] has put it, "in the excitement of external events." . . . Always afraid of a full commitment to others, searching for the possibility of betrayal and claiming to find it even when it was not there, she seemed to draw a magic circle around herself for much of the time, and live in an inner world that was compounded equally of memory and imagination. . . . [It was] her ghostly, private world, that she tried to reproduce in most of her fiction. She gave it many names, over the years, and placed it consistently in the South. Southern though its geographical location might be, however, it was like no South anybody had ever seen before. It was not the South of newspaper articles and political speeches, nor the South of country humor or magnolia-blossom romance; it was not even the South described so extensively in [William Faulkner's] Yoknapatawpha novels. In effect, it was another country altogether, created out of all that the author had found haunting, soft, and lonely in her childhood surroundings—a new place offering a new perspective on the experience from which it had been drawn. (pp. 265-66)

[The] effect of McCullers's prose is accumulative. She does not work in a series of detached, glittering phrases as, say, Truman Capote does. Nor does she, imitating Faulkner, write sentences that coil up snakelike and then strike, suddenly, before the period. Her language is cool and lucid, almost classical in its precision, her descriptions clipped and occasionally cryptic. A nuance in one place, a repetition or a shading somewhere else: this is all she needs really because . . . she tends to rely on the resonance given to a detail by its total context—and to use concealment almost as a medium of communication. The inertia, the desolation, and the brooding violence of the small-town South are caught in images that are hermetic, despite their apparent candor, and in incidents brimming with undisclosed biography.

The act is performed so quietly that it may tend to go unnoticed: what McCullers has created, . . . is a world where emotion and vision can coalesce—in which, through the agency of her prose, her own particular sense of life can be externalized. The town [in "The Ballad of the Sad Café"] is no dream kingdom, that is clear enough. It is anchored in this world, in a firm if understated way, by such details as . . . references to the bus and train services and by an implicit understanding of its economic function. But it is no ordinary place, either—the kind of town we might easily come across in Georgia, in the South, or anywhere else. Why? Because, quite apart from establishing this anchorage, the writer has used every means at her disposal to reorder, rearrange, and so metamorphose; in a way that must be familiar to us by now, she has created another country out of her own known home. In this respect, the anonymity of the prose ties in with the evasiveness of the narrator, the hermeticism of the imagery with the apparent emptiness of the scene. For together they direct our attention to precisely the same subject; a feeling of "lonesomeness" or loss seems to result from them all. . . . [This feeling is not imposed on the material:] it is there in the Deep South already, waiting to be acknowledged. McCullers has, however, emphasized it almost to the exclusion of everything else and, in doing so, cleverly established a nexus, a point of connection between the geometry of her self and the geography of her childhood surroundings. Gently, she has nudged the regional landscape into the expression of a fresh mood.

McCullers's aims are, of course, not just personal. Quite apart from externalizing her own state she is trying also, through the medium of the South, to anatomize human nature, to chart, in her plan of her region, the coordinates of

all our lives. And in order to make this clear she will occasionally punctuate her narrative with little explanatory passages . . . which suggest that, remembering her own doubts about the possibility of proper contact between man and man—and, perhaps, experiencing some misgivings about her oblique methods elsewhere—the author is afraid the reader will otherwise miss the point. . . . [This] does, naturally, tend to carry its own dangers with it. The "message" may . . . seem a little too pat to be convincing, too limited and limiting even for the purpose of fable. The writer may, in short, end up with didacticism of the crudest possible kind. McCullers is saved from such dangers most of the time, I think, though; and what saves her more than anything else is her constant awareness of the *human* situation —the specifically emotional and imaginative terms into which her ideas have to be translated. Her landscapes, for all their initial sparseness, *are* inhabited. More to the point, the figures inhabiting them possess a special kind of resonance, that sense of roots and a definite history which marks them out as the descendants of recognizable Southern types. They have the substance and immediate credibility of people long brooded over, and so well understood—and to this is added that freshness, the sense of surprise and valuable discovery, which can only come when someone as well known as this is seen from a radically altered standpoint. We may suspect, while we read a McCullers story, that we have seen characters like hers before; in fact, if we have read much earlier Southern fiction we are sure we have. But until now, she makes us feel, we have never been properly acquainted with them: there is something about them, some crucial side of them we have somehow managed to miss. (pp. 267-69)

[The central character of "The Ballad of the Sad Café," Miss Amelia,] is a grotesque, perhaps, but she is a grotesque for the same reason that most of McCullers's subjects are—because, as the author herself once put it, her "physical incapacity" is being used primarily as "a symbol of [her] spiritual incapacity . . . —[her] spiritual isolation." She is not just the comic loser. . . . [She is] "lonesome," and her lonesomeness is intended eventually to figure our own. Like an image seen in a carnival mirror, she is meant to offer us an exaggerated, comically distorted, and yet somehow sadly accurate reflection of ourselves. . . . We are drawn to the woman even while she still seems a little odd to us. The knowledge we have of her by [the end of the story] has, of course, something to do with this development: we understand why she is odd and, understanding, we perhaps suspect that her oddity touches upon ours. . . . [Of immeasurable significance] is something almost indefinable—which, for want of a better phrase, we must call the sheer texture of her prose. . . . [McCullers's style] manages to be lyrical and colloquial, lucid and enigmatic, at one and the same time. . . . [It] is as a direct consequence of this strange combination, really, that we find ourselves held back from Miss Amelia here—and brought close up into a special kind of intimacy with her as well. She is distanced from us by a certain lingering freakishness of expression, a mysterious image, it may be, or a quirky turn of phrase; and yet she is also brought into an immediate contact with us by our sense that this is, after all, a conventional idiom we are listening to—that the language Miss Amelia inhabits, so to speak, belongs to normal, everyday conversation. This is an extraordinarily subtle relationship to set up between character and reader—far subtler than anything we are likely to come across elsewhere, in the work of other writers who have experimented with the Southern comic mode. It has its origins, of course, in McCullers's belief that a paradox lurks at the heart of experience, naturally attaching itself to the idea of a *shared* isolation. As for its issue, that we find in the mood or *ambiance* to which our minds first return when recalling a McCullers novel—our memories of a quiet, but peculiarly inclusive, pathos. (pp. 270-71)

McCullers's fiction, at its best (by which I mean "The Ballad of the Sad Café," *The Member of the Wedding,* and parts of *The Heart Is a Lonely Hunter*) . . . shows, I think, how tough and really critical an emotion pathos can be. Her characters are pathetic, but they are pathetic in the finest sense. . . . [The] pathetic is used as an agent of moral instruction more than anything else, a means of telling us, quietly and sadly, what we are and the most we can do and of advising us, by inference, as to how we should behave.

McCullers's is, then, the definitive use of a specific emotional effect—a pathos that at once lends a strange atmosphere to landscape and character, and helps establish an intimate, unusually searching relationship between tale and reader. This is an impressive achievement—showing the kind of subtlety and even deviousness of intent we are perhaps more inclined to associate with more "difficult" fiction—and its very impressiveness has, I believe, led one or two of McCullers's critics into overestimating her. For there is a tendency, noticeable especially among those with a bias toward the New Criticism, to assume that because her work represents a perfect adaptation of means to ends she is, therefore, more or less unsurpassed among writers of her own region. . . . [However,] the very perfection of McCullers's work depends, after all, upon her own level-headed acceptance of her limitations. She knows that she can describe, quite subtly, one particular dilemma or area of life and she concentrates almost her entire resources on that. There is no place in her fiction, really, for the rich "over-plus" of experience—by which I mean any aspects of behavior that cannot be included under the heading of theme, or any dimensions of feeling that cannot be reconciled with the major effect of pathos. And recognizing this she demonstrates little interest in such matters as the historical and social context, and no commitment either to the idea of a developing consciousness. (p. 272)

As for McCullers's actual achievement, though, setting aside all such exaggeration, that surely is certain and secure. She is not a major writer. . . . But she is a very good minor one—so good, indeed, that she seems to reap a definite advantage from her minor status and turn her limitations into virtues. The absence of the historical dimension is a useful illustration of this. With many other writers, and especially Southern ones, such an absence might prove fatal. . . . With McCullers, however, just the opposite is true; . . . in some strange way she manages to make history function as an *absent presence* in her work. It seems to be not so much omitted from her writing as concealed, made to disappear, and in such a way that the disappearance itself, like the disappearance of the religious perspective from later Victorian fiction, encourages our active comment. McCullers's characters, we infer, have not even this, the mere possibility of a tradition, to sustain them; . . . [they are] so disoriented as to have no point of reference really, no common denominator with which to chart their

disorientation. They may suffer pangs of nostalgia; in fact most of them do, it is a natural consequence of their loneliness. But that nostalgia is for a condition they can hardly define. They may be adrift, homesick; but that homesickness is for a place that has never, personally, been theirs. Just as space seems to recede from them even while it is being described, to try to hide from them in a way, so time in its larger dimension appears somehow to mock them by remaining hidden; the vacuum its departure creates is, we sense, *there* as a positive force in the narrative contributing to their despair. One sometimes wonders if, in all this, McCullers is not trying to add her own idiosyncratic footnote to Nietzsche by suggesting that not only God, that traditional comforter of the lonely and spiritually disfigured, is dead now—history, as a common secular resource and the modern substitute for God, is as well. (p. 273)

Richard Gray, in his *The Literature of Memory: Modern Writers of the American South (copyright © 1977 by Richard Gray), The Johns Hopkins University Press, 1977.*

ROBERT PHILLIPS

[If we take Carson McCullers] at her word, and I believe we should, [the] theme of spiritual isolation is the cornerstone to her house of fiction. One of the smallest rooms of that house is the region of her short stories [published in *The Mortgaged Heart* and *The Ballad of the Sad Cafe*]. . . . Certainly all are typical McCullers, with this exception: they are all less likely to be labeled "Gothic" or "grotesque" when compared to her novels. For whatever reason, there is less physical abnormality in the stories. Instead of mutes and dwarfs, what we generally encounter here are people isolated by circumstance rather than physical appearance or malady. Instead of freaks we find an inner freaking-out. . . .

One of the amazing things in considering McCullers is not only how many variations she played upon this theme [of spiritual isolation] in book after book, story after story, and two plays, but also how early that vision was formulated. It is to be found in her very first story, "Sucker," written when she was a seventeen-year-old school girl. There the title character, Sucker, is an orphan, and therefore unrelated to the family with whom he lives. . . . Sucker desperately wants to be loved, to become a member of the family. . . .

At first "Sucker" seems to be the story of the narrator, Pete, and the pull between *agape* (Pete and Sucker) and *eros* (Pete and Maybelle). But by the time of the story's climax, the awful scene in which Pete tells Sucker he doesn't care for him one bit, we realize the story bears the correct title after all. It *is* Sucker's story, the story of an outsider who tries to fit in. (p. 66)

Being an orphan, then, was McCullers's first projection of a spiritually isolated being. She used the same projection in "The Orphanage." Yet another early story, "Breath from the Sky," depicts a young woman orphaned from her family not by parental death, but by her own invalidism. (p. 67)

Some of Carson McCullers's most successful characterizations of the isolated individual are, of course, her adolescents—characters like Mick Kelly and Frankie Addams, who belong neither to the adult world nor to the world of childhood. One such in-betweener is the thirteen-year-old younger sister in the early story "Like That." Perceiving the pain of growing into womanhood experienced by her older sister, she resists rather than embraces maturation. Like Sucker, she rebels, only her rebellion is against such overwhelming forces as menstruation, sexuality, premature death.

Another adolescent is the heroine of "Correspondence," a slight epistolary story of a one-way correspondence undertaken by a Frankie Addams type, here named Henrietta Evans. . . . That there is no response from the other country is indicative of McCullers's negative world view.

Not all of McCullers's suffering adolescents are female. In the long "Untitled Piece" a boy called Andrew Leander seems a male Frankie, and his father is also a jeweler. The action takes place during one crazy summer, and Berenice Sadie Brown has somehow been transmogrified into a younger black named Vitalis. In his attempt to become joined to something, Andrew commits an act of unpremeditated miscegenation with Vitalis, then flees the town in guilt. His one act of union and love has forced his separation and fear. A later story, "The Haunted Boy," depicts a teenager named Hugh who is also isolated, in his case in the knowledge that his mother is mad and that he may once again discover her in a suicide attempt. The story is marred by a pat ending, but Hugh's fear is made extraordinarily real. (pp. 67-8)

Another category of McCullers's characterizations of young people is that of the adolescent as musician. . . . "Wunderkind" is one of the most famous of all her stories, even though there are several that are better. It concerns the realization of a fifteen-year-old music student that she simply does not possess the emotional capacity to match her facile pianistic technique. Outside she is all glitter; inside, she knows she is empty. . . . In the novels McCullers strove for grand moments; in the stories, for quiet occasions which nevertheless are vital occasions. When the washed-up *wunderkind* flees her piano teacher's studio and hurries "down the street that had become confused with noise and bicycles and the games of other children," the reader comprehends the loss of the girl's childhood, sacrificed to the music she cannot really play well. She is an emotional freak who is outwardly normal.

Another youthful musician appears in "Poldi," an early tale of hopeless love. . . . As in "Sucker," "The Haunted Boy," and the "Untitled Piece," McCullers successfully transforms herself into a young male. (pp. 68-9)

Bridging the generation gap between the author's younger and older short story protagonists is the eighteen-year-old university student in the early tale "Court in the West Eighties." . . . [Here] McCullers injects a potent symbol into the story in the form of a balloon man—that is, a man made of balloons, bearing a silly grin and hanging perpetually from one apartment window. He is an effigy mocking mankind and man's helplessness. In the world of McCullers's imagination we are all dangling, hanged men.

In McCullers's stories portraying adults confronting adult problems—or rather, not confronting them, since most either freak out or flee the situation rather than face it—the characters are occasionally absolutely normal in appearance. Later, however, they are rendered symbolically grotesque, as in "Instant of the Hour After," a mood piece in which a young married couple's love for one another is in-

explicably destroying them. In the story's chief symbol they are seen as two figures in a bottle—small, perfect, yet white and exhausted, like "fleshly specimens in a laboratory." (p. 69)

In "A Domestic Dilemma," the isolated character is a housewife, physically transplanted from Alabama to New York. Unable to adjust to the changes involved in the move or to make friends, she seeks escape through drinking. Without the artifice of alcohol her interior life is insufficient. . . . In this, my personal favorite of her shorter fiction, McCullers explores love/hate relationships in marriage and what she calls "the immense complexity of love."

This inability to adjust to physical change signals a state of spiritual isolation in several of the best stories by McCullers, including "The Sojourner" and "A Tree. A Rock. A Cloud," as well as the more superficial "Art and Mr. Mahoney." (p. 70)

The disintegration of a marriage [creates a] dis-integrated soul in "A Tree. A Rock. A Cloud." The story relates the encounter in a café of a twelve-year-old boy and an old cuckold. . . . Love here is expounded as a condition which must be achieved through small steps. Rather than presuming to begin one's love life with a woman—what the old man (and McCullers) calls "the most dangerous and sacred experience in God's earth"—we should instead begin in very small ways, loving tiny inanimate objects first: a tree, a rock, a cloud. Only when we can relate to the minimal can we hope to possess the maximal. (pp. 70-1)

That McCullers sides with him is made clear by the actions she attributes to Leo, the café owner. Leo not only treats his regular customers stingily, but also does not love himself enough to nourish his body adequately. He grudges himself a bun. But then, in McCullers's love affairs, everyone seems to be grudging their buns. . . .

Mr. Mahoney's inability to adjust, in "Art and Mr. Mahoney," is less dramatic. He is a man of great cultural pretensions and little education to back them up. Inadvertently he reveals his ignorance by clapping at the wrong time in a piano concert. . . . His little embarrassment, however, can in no way be compared to the illuminations experienced by the *wunderkind* and Ferris and the haunted boy, and "Art and Mr. Mahoney" remains a trivial story. (p. 71)

"Who Has Seen the Wind?" is the rather melodramatic tale of Ken, a writer who is blocked after two books. His inability to communicate is driving him mad. . . .

The tale of "Madame Zilensky" is a superb one of a woman so dedicated to music that she is alien to the rest of the world, consequently compensating through lies—living vicariously the experiences she never had time to experience. . . .

In "The Aliens," which is a sketch rather than a story, we are given speculations on the nature of grief from the mouth of a wandering Jew. There once was a time, I hear, when many provincial people thought a Jew was a freak, with horns and a tail. McCullers's Jew has neither horns nor tail, and can in no way qualify as a freak. She uses his Jewishness to emphasize his displacement. He is an alien on the bus of life, as it were—rootless and totally other. (p. 72)

[In "The Jockey"] we do find a freakish fellow. . . . With his diminutive physical stature and his life of mandatory dietary deprivation, he is a man-child in the world of men. A freak.

But more than size and diet separates this jockey from his peers. He is morally outraged by the behavior of the trainer, the bookie, and the rich man who populate the story. . . .

In contrast to the physical and material values of these men, McCullers posits a symbol of the soul—green-white August moths which flutter about the clear candle flames. The soulful jockey and the moths are one. The image is a good one, because in this gallery of wanderers and aliens, failures and outcasts in a world in which all traditional values are, if not reversed, unrecognizable, all are seeking but one thing—the freedom of the moth, the unification of the spirit with the environment, the soul within the body of this earth. In these nineteen short stories, with only one certified freak among them, Carson McCullers depicts this quest with less sensationalism than in the novels, and often with true distinction. (p. 73)

Robert Phillips, ''Freaking Out: The Short Stories of Carson McCullers,'' in Southwest Review *(© 1978 by Southern Methodist University Press), Winter, 1978, pp. 65-73.*

Joni Mitchell
1943-

(Born Roberta Joan Anderson) Canadian songwriter and musician. One of the foremost folk artists of the 1960s, Mitchell has made the transition to the 1970s with music that now incorporates forms of pop, rock, and jazz. Her themes, however, have remained the same—love and the difficulties of maintaining a loving relationship, loneliness, and the pressures of stardom. Mitchell, who taught herself guitar with a Pete Seeger instruction record, performed in coffeehouses in Toronto, Detroit, and, finally, New York in the early 1960s. Her success as a songwriter skyrocketed when "The Circle Game" and "Both Sides Now" were recorded by established folk artists Tom Rush and Judy Collins. It was not until the release of her first album, *Songs to a Seagull*, however, that she became known outside musical circles and achieved recognition as a performer. Her songs are often autobiographical, reflecting not only her intriguing personal life, but the sentiments of women living in times of changing roles. Most critics have noticed a definite maturation in Mitchell's lyrics; she has gone from the simple but pleasant sentiments of "Both Sides Now" to songs like "Coyote," which are replete with ambiguity and exhibit a sense of humor that was not evident in earlier works. Her experimentation with rock and jazz in recent years has destroyed her somewhat stereotyped image as the symbolic "Woodstock generation" folksinger, and has made her work difficult to classify. This has brought varying reactions from both fans and critics, who are unsure of the direction and success of this synthesis. As an innovative musician, she is often considered the female counterpart of Bob Dylan, both in creativity and influence.

KARL DALLAS

["Songs to a Seagull"] is one of the few [albums] I can think of (the others that spring to mind are "Sgt. Pepper" and the [album by the] Mothers of Invention) which successfully hangs together as a complete whole. . . .

Because Joni Mitchell was originally a painter . . . the things that stick in the mind from her songs are all visual. The king she lost, painting the pastel walls of her home brown thinking of ladies in gingham while she is a girl dressed in leather. . . .

And all through this album, the seagull that wheels above you cries, and then is suddenly gone.

I think Joni Mitchell is that seagull.

Karl Dallas, "Joni, The Seagull from Saska-

toon," in Melody Maker (© IPC Business Press Ltd.), September 28, 1968, p. 26.

ELLEN SANDER

Joni Mitchell is an individual who defies conceptualization, and in that defiance comes into her own brilliantly. Her second album, *Clouds* . . . , is one of the most lyrical, skillful, and utterly distinctive presentations of great talent that has ever had to stand on its own. A superlative song writer, Miss Mitchell is fascinated with womanhood. Her songs explore the joys and travails of being loved and unloved, of looking at the world through the eyes of a female.

Clouds shows considerable growth and improvement over her first album; the songs are stronger, the changes braver, her voice more flexible and relaxed. While the first album seemed understated, *Clouds*, which does not have any accompaniment other than that which the artist herself supplies, is a stronger, more personal effort, fuller and richer for what she has put into the songs. (pp. 51, 57)

Ellen Sander, in Saturday Review *(© 1969 by Saturday Review, Inc.; reprinted with permission), July 26, 1969.*

SUSAN DONOGHUE

[*Clouds*] is a whole lot more than an exercise in slickness. Second albums have a tendency to lean heavily on promotion after an unknown "hot" property has shot his load on his debut LP, but this is not the case with Miss Mitchell. If it is possible to become an "old pro" between first and second albums, she has done it. *Clouds* is not *slick,* it is just *smooth,* and it is a joy to hear the composer's touch go into those numbers we've heard as Judy Collins' concert staples *Chelsea Morning* and *The Midway Song.* There is an undeniable power to the sort of "production numbers" these two songs become in a Collins concert, but there is an equally charming quality to Joni Mitchell's delivery of them as sort of tremulous love-confessions. But it would be hard to do anything wrong with the sort of poetry that Miss Mitchell produces. She has a fantastic eye (a "painter's eye", I guess, 'scuse the expression) for combining real, sensual imagery with special, and personal, pleading. . . .

All of Joni Mitchell's songs are gentle, and even the one protest song on the album, *The Fiddle and the Drum,* seems to chide gently, rather than "protest". There's not a single bad apple in the *Clouds* barrel, including her best-known song, *Both Sides Now,* which is new all over again when sung by its mother. (pp. 42-3)

Susan Donoghue, in Jazz & Pop (© 1969 by Jazz Press Inc.; reprinted by permission of the author), September, 1969.

JACOBA ATLAS

Joni Mitchell is a poet whose time has come. Because she uses the vehicle of music, her words and thoughts reach out to countless minds. With Joni, there is no restriction of reading or schooling; she sings her poetry and brings it to the people. . . . Joni has emerged as a major force in music. Her songs, once the exclusive property of a few, have become the catchword of many. . . .

Her songs are reflections of a very feminine way of looking at life. All too seldom in music, and indeed in any art form, is the female view of the world set down. Joni does just that.

One critic suggested that women think in a complicated manner and speak in simple terms. This could certainly be said of Joni's material; but her simplicity reveals a sensitivity and awareness that few composers possess today. With phrases like "know that I will know you" and "while she's so busy being free," we are given an entire picture of a woman's mind and heart at work. . . .

Like many poets, Joni insists that her lyrics be worked over until every word is absolutely necessary and cannot be altered. . . .

Her ability to understand and transform has made her almost a legend. . . . Critics and listeners alike rhapsodise over her songs and her psyche. She is fulfilling something of a "goddess" need in American rock, a woman who is more than a woman; a poet who expresses a full range of emotions without embarrassment.

Her legend is beginning to obscure her work; because she is virtually without competition . . . she is without comparison. Her work for now, goes almost totally without question, without debate.

Jacoba Atlas, "Joni: Let's Make Life More Romantic," in Melody Maker (© IPC Business Press Ltd.), June 20, 1970, p. 24.

SUE DONOGHUE

Ladies of the Canyon, Joni Mitchell's third album, is not aimed at fairly literate ex-folkies who will take anyone's fairly literate word for anything. It is aimed at the world. . . . [Her] voice is narrating twelve stories of different kinds, and consequently needs the top of its range as much as human emotion does, as much as the actress portraying it does. Well and good, so that's what's going on with the unstructured melodies and occasional falsettos for which I couldn't find a corresponding irony in the lyric (ah, me . . .). But what *about* those lyrics? Aren't there fewer of the stunning Mitchell images? Doesn't it seem like only 1966's *The Circle Game,* of all the cuts, is tied as neatly as expected? Well, the images aren't fewer, she just doesn't have to *rely* on them as much, and after all, 1966 was tied more neatly than '67, which was tied more neatly than '68 —and don't imagine that's irrelevant.

In 1966, we still believed in wrapping things neatly—flour-

ish, finish, applause (usually after the downbeat), three or four rhyming stanzas broken as many times by a catchy chorus. And a "statement by the author." Joni Mitchell has gotten so good that she's transcended all the neat little categories and made an invisible film (for brain-viewing). With the best director's eye, she points us in different directions. . . . She's acting (superbly) in the stories, voice recounting her part and the other ones. Big shifts in range and feeling . . . , prosy lines, momentary musical digressions to avoid gilding the lily. A damn fine director . . . as well as composer . . . as well as author . . . as well as performer . . . as well as I've heard anything done. (p. 44)

Sue Donoghue, in Jazz & Pop (© 1970 by Jazz Press Inc.; reprinted by permission of the author), July, 1970.

Yes, it's all here. . . . Everything we need for another volume of vicarious heartache:

Guess that's a pretty sour way to begin a review of what, in many ways, is Joni's most perfect album ["Blue"]. But then her songs have come to mean so much to me over the years that my reactions to this album are hopelessly subjective and ambivalent.

The problem, I suppose, is one of empathy. Her songs are autobiographical and one's reaction to them depends to a large extent on how far one can relate to the experiences she describes. On her previous albums she has dealt with the joys and sorrows of love: the communication has been direct and often . . . sharply poignant.

But now, as they say, the scene changes. The success of those songs has made her a Rock Star. . . . The songs here reflect the hang-ups of such an existence and, for me at least, it's hard to relate to them. There is little pain of passion here: where once she described the nightmare of city life in "Nathan La Freneer" she now muses on the sweet dilemma of being stuck in Paris when she wants to be in California. . . .

None of it is Joni's fault, of course. Her songs continue to reflect her own reality, but where once the truths she distilled were universal, the songs here tend to be inward-looking. . . .

It is, perhaps, as a singer of exquisite, richly-contoured, beautifully singable songs, rather than anything more profound, that she now has her greatest strength. All I know is that despite everything I've said above, this album hasn't been off my turntable in five days. (p. 26)

Melody Maker (© IPC Business Ltd.), July 10, 1971.

PETER REILLY

Joni Mitchell continues to demonstrate that she is not only an actress-singer but a composer of considerable power: her . . . album "Blue" . . . is an unqualified success on both counts. It is a collection of what once were called "torch" songs, but Miss Mitchell adds an extra dimension to her "my man's gone now" theme by introducing a spare, satirical element that is sometimes directed at herself, sometimes at her partners. . . .

And, if her songs are based on personal experience, she certainly does seem to have had a rough time of it in the Game of Love. . . . The subject of *My Old Man* is apparently given to irregular disappearances, thus causing Joni to collide with the blues and to discover that "The bed's too big / The frying pan's too wide." That last phrase (think about it) is a *genuine* image, provocative and palpable. There are others like it running all through her compositions, and they regularly bring the listener to sharp attention with the unmistakable clang of sardonic truth.

Though the subject of all these songs is the blues, Miss Mitchell's extraordinary performances of them quickly remove any possibility that they might all add up to a bad case of the sulks. . . .

I think the finest thing about "Blue" . . . is its message of survival. "Well, there're so many sinking now / You've got to keep thinking / You can make it through these waves / Acid, booze, and ass / Needles, guns and grass / Lots of laughs, lots of laughs. / Well everybody's saying that hell's the hippest way to go / Well, I don't think so." These words sound to me very like a pointed and pertinent warning to that part of a generation that talks a lot about getting it all together but begins to seem less and less capable of really doing so.

> *Peter Reilly, "Joni Mitchell Sings Her Blues," in* Stereo Review *(reprinted by permission of the author), October, 1971, p. 87.*

LESTER BANGS

It took a while for a lot of people to get to Joni Mitchell. Listening to her albums was a frustrating experience if you weren't a convert in front. You could tell that *Blue,* for instance, was an important record and the songs were truly fine, but somehow it seemed almost too personal, too consistently down. Also, her propensity for seemingly cramming every syllable she possibly could into each line became irritating after awhile, at once melodically overcomplex and a conversation style taken to an extreme. . . .

[*For the Roses* is] the best album Joni Mitchell has ever made and, even beyond the songs themselves, it's a *sound* record. . . .

Joni takes the riskiest propositions and somehow pulls them off without a trace of banality. Whoever thought they'd wanna hear another song about groupies and musicians on the road? But "Blonde in the Bleachers" gets it down with some kind of wonder intact: "You're in rock and roll / It's the nature of the race / It's the unknown child / So sweet and wild." (p. 66)

Naturally the album has its share of songs about love gone bad, and nobody is better at this than Joni Mitchell: "Where are you now . . . Are you caught in a crowd / Or holding some honey / Who came on to you? / Why do you have to be so jive?"

Great lines! Old shit but time-tested, and somehow caught in a totally new way. And isn't it the genius of rock'n'roll or any music having anything to do with it to take the most hackneyed forms and situations and breathe some life into them? We need clarification of the same old muddles, and every once in awhile you find it: in Van Morrison, in the Stones, in Dylan and Lou Reed in their prime. I finally found it in Joni Mitchell with this album. She's so fine I don't even miss the backbeat. (p. 67)

> *Lester Bangs, in* Creem *(© copyright 1973 by Creem Magazine, Inc.), February, 1973.*

ARTHUR SCHMIDT

Most female singer-guitarists in folk and pop genres . . . are primarily interpreters of songs others—usually men—write. The Canadian Joni Mitchell, often grouped with them, is exceptional however not so much because she is her own composer and lyricist, but because of the persistence with which she has, at her most characteristic, pursued through five record albums the sexual theme she treats with sophistication surprising in a mass artist. Love songs are nothing new, but the love-hate song is probably Mitchell's invention. . . .

Mitchell celebrates the moral virtue of strength—or, rather the collection of qualities once referred to as "character"; her parallel virtue as composer is tight, economic construction, with chords and words seldom wasted. . . .

Mitchell *sings* fiction, and complex fiction at that. But though she dedicated her first record to "Mr. Kratzman who taught me to love words," it is her musicianship that stretches the pop form to admit qualities that would otherwise be incongruously "literary."

Most stories on that first record, *Songs to a Seagull,* are spare sketches of character revealed in mundane incident or gesture. . . . As in Dylan's best songs, one hears them first as wholes, catching a phrase here and there. Words and phrases fold under chord complexities until, after not one but many listenings, they are heard or suddenly *really* heard.

The best of these sketches is of "Nathan La Franeer," a taxi-driver who "hated everyone who paid to ride / And share his common space." Mitchell's lyrics, melodies, and soprano voice typically possess an old-lace beauty some find off-putting, but here she spares no urban brutality: "an aging cripple selling Superman balloons," police siren careening against guitar as "With gangs and girly shows / The ghostly garden grows." The pain is simply there, but it is her own and not borrowed, and so compassion, in this instance, does not cloy.

Seagull's "The Pirate of Penance" is already full narrative, murder mystery with accusation and defence. Perhaps over-ambitious—since Mitchell sings the two parts, it is unintelligible without recourse to the lyrics printed on the sleeve—it foreshadows the innovative use she later makes of dialogue; as lyricist to tell stories, as composer to introduce conversational rhythms into instrumental as well as vocal phrasings.

Ladies of the Canyon hints at, and her fourth album, *Blue*'s final two songs illustrate by their peripheral placement an attempt at extending the pop-song form. These tunes, one notices, are less "sweet," less accessible, and seem to fragment under the weight of anxious pauses and parentheses. Everyday prose takes over from Mitchell's perhaps self-conscious taste for "beauty". . . . (pp. 340-41)

Her versifying is limited by music, fated to reduction on paper. Her music is limited by the popular form she stubbornly stretches. But she is a "chick singer" (as I have heard her described) in much the same sense that Virginia Woolf is a chick novelist. (p. 345)

> *Arthur Schmidt, in* Popular Music & Society *(copyright © 1973 by R. Serge Denisoff), Vol. II, No. 4, 1973.*

Of all the female writers and singers post-dating Joan Baez in pop music, Joni Mitchell seems to me to have arrived at the most complete definition of herself as an artist. True, she's not witty, like Dory Previn, as sophisticated as Midler or La Streisand, nor as stylistically far-ranging as Carole King, but few other rock musicians, male or female, have so refined personal expression that it succeeds as genuine art.

Of course, this view is to see pop, albeit the best of it, as working self-consciously, and Mitchell, along with James Taylor, has never lacked critics who deplore the egocentric nature of her lyrics, to the extent that the term "singer-songwriter" has tended to fall into disrepute....

But Joni Mitchell isn't like ... Taylor, even though whole albums have been patently devoted to current men in her life and explanations of the relationship.... Even in her most personal revelations, we're involved because she speaks directly to our innermost feelings. This ability to express the most private emotions in a public way, with utmost subtleties and nuances, is the stuff of real poetry, and I have little hesitation in stating that Mitchell is a major poetic force whose stature in the Seventies will have to be evaluated on a very high level indeed.

This is by way of saying that ... "Court And Spark" ... is her most mature piece of work yet, and one in which she deepens the complexities of her art, both in a lyric and musical sense, as well as taking off on her new direction....

If anything, besides being the album's key song, ["Same Situation" is] the most beautifully melodic statement here, with perhaps the most weighted and delicate lyrics she's ever written....

"Court And Spark" strongly underlines a growing belief that Joni Mitchell should be sitting at [Dylan's] right hand. The cards are face up. The King and Queen, they say. (p. 31)

Melody Maker (© *IPC Business Press Ltd.*), *January 26, 1974.*

JON LANDAU

On first listening, Joni Mitchell's *Court And Spark* ... sounds surprisingly light; by the third or fourth listening, it reveals its underlying tensions. The lyrics lead us through concentric circles that define an almost Zen-like dilemma: The freer the writer becomes, the more unhappy she finds herself; the more she surrenders her freedom, the less willing she is to accept the resulting compromise. Joni Mitchell seems destined to remain in a state of permanent dissatisfaction—always knowing what she would like to do, always more depressed when it's done.

Joni Mitchell has composed few songs of unambivalent feeling. Even her most minimal work suggests a need for change and skepticism about its potential results. On *Court And Spark* she has elevated this tendency into a theme: No thought or emotion is expressed without some equally forceful statement of its negation.

The actual opposites of *Court And Spark*—the thrill of courtship modulated by the fear of emotional commitment —suggest a series of choices that Mitchell touches on, passes through, and defines with astounding compression— the alternatives of love and freedom, trust and paranoia, security and rootlessness, concern for herself and for oth-

ers, compromise and pursuit of perfection, and even sanity and insanity.

Her boldest fears come out in her songs about madness, the last two on the album. Her own "Trouble Child" and Lambert-Hendricks-Ross' "Twisted" deal with it in strikingly different ways: The former is tragic, the latter is a piece of comedy with an hilarious punch line that plays on the very notion of schizophrenia. Together they flirt with insanity from a distance safe enough to show she can control even so threatening a concern....

But if Joni Mitchell is capable of subtly edging around the notion of breakdowns, she's unable to keep the same distance when singing about the men who dominate the album. She never seems to know where she wants to draw the line in love, or if a line exists at all. But it is precisely on the songs about love that the new lightness in her music makes so much sense. (p. 54)

["Down To You" is] the album's best love song—sophisticated, subtle and complete in itself. As good as melody, vocal and arrangement are, the lyrics overshadow them, with intimations of the album's opposites....

The special beauty of *Court And Spark* is that it forces us to [laugh and cry], and that it does so with such infinite grace. (p. 55)

Jon Landau, "Joni Mitchell: A Delicate Balance," in Rolling Stone *(by Straight Arrow Publishers, Inc. © 1974; all rights reserved; reprinted by permission), Issue 155, February 28, 1974, pp. 54-5.*

WAYNE ROBINS

Truth is something [Joni Mitchell] sells as well as Ralph Nader, John Wayne, or Guru Maharaj Ji. Unlike Dylan, who sold public truths that inspired social awareness, Joni's truths are private. Most concern The Relationship....

As a result [of her intriguing relationships] her private truths have much to say about the mixed blessings of promiscuity, which may be this era's favorite obsession....

Joni's songs are beachnut California. She sings of canyons rather than fire escapes, of a world that is as attractive as it is repellent to a native New Yorker. How I've learned to tolerate, even appreciate, her "Yin Yang" I don't know, except that maybe what she calls "portrait of a disappointment" is becoming one of my "favorite themes" too. [*Miles of Aisles*] was recorded in California, which may explain the ease and comfort with which she goes through sixteen familiar and two new songs.... Joni thrives ... when she's alone, just the breathless sun sliding into the Pacific vocals and I Ching guitar tuning. "Friends say I have changed," Joni sings in the standard version of "Both Sides Now." Here she adds "And I have." Me too, Joni, me too. I've become a fan as well as an admirer. (p. 69)

Wayne Robins, in Creem *(© copyright 1975 by Creem Magazine, Inc.), March, 1975.*

STEPHEN HOLDEN

With *The Hissing of Summer Lawns*, Joni Mitchell has moved beyond personal confession into the realm of social philosophy. All the characters are American stereotypes who act out socially determined rituals of power and submission in exquisitely described settings. Mitchell's eye for detail is at once so precise and so panoramic that one feels these characters have very little freedom. They belong to the things they own, wear and observe, to the drugs they take and the people they know as much if not more than to themselves. Most are fixed combatants in tableaux, rituals and scenarios that share Mitchell's reflections on feminism.

As might be expected, Mitchell's approach is very cerebral. In "Don't Interrupt the Sorrow," a poem of almost impenetrable mystery, she voices the core of her vision. Among other things, the song parallels modern forms of female subjugation with both Christian and African mythology in imagery that is disjunctive and telegraphic. . . .

Mitchell, never one to disavow the powerful glamour of evil, pulls a brilliant twist [in "The Jungle Line"], uniting images of cannibalism, wild animals, slave ships and industrial squalor with the gorgeously innocent paintings of imaginary jungle scenes by the late-19th-century French Primitive, Henri Rousseau.

Always Mitchell displays enough moral ambiguity in her lyrics to avoid condescension; her latent impulse to anger is consistently redeemed by a compassionate, seemingly genuine sorrow, as well as by a visual artist's impulse to perceive the beauty in all things. The tension between Mitchell's moral and aesthetic principles is resolved with special grace in "Shades of Scarlet Conquering," the full-scale portrait of a southern belle very similar to Tennessee Williams's Blanche DuBois. Here Mitchell's feminist sensibility is implicit in her compassion:

> Beauty and madness to be praised
> It is not easy to be brave
> To walk around in so much need
> To carry the weight of all that greed
>   . . . .

If *The Hissing of Summer Lawns* offers substantial literature, it is set to insubstantial music. There are no tunes to speak of. . . .

The Hissing of Summer Lawns is ultimately a great collection of pop poems with a distracting soundtrack. Read it first. Then play it. (p. 50)

> *Stephen Holden, in* Rolling Stone *(by Straight Arrow Publishers, Inc. © 1976; all rights reserved; reprinted by permission), Issue 204, January 15, 1976.*

NOEL COPPAGE

Joni Mitchell's viewpoint has usually been first-person-singular, with the world seen as an incidental part of the examination of the quandary inside a relationship. In . . . "The Hissing of Summer Lawns," the viewpoint seems more nearly general, less specific, and the stories she tells collectively yield some truths (or maybe they're only suspicions) that are social as well as personal.

There is still the question of how much romanticism balanced against how much "reality" is good for us, but it is complicated this time out by the irony of what has happened to the settings, the environments—the city has paradoxically become the place primeval, while the country (nowadays the suburbs) has become the place where too much civilization is beginning to take its toll. Joni Mitchell shows us people trying to recapture a certain irresponsibility or a spontaneity—the ability to dance, to play—and they come off looking either a bit tawdry or frantic. . . .

It is a difficult album, you see, partly because Mitchell is *not* moralizing, not boiling a situation down so any right-thinking listener can interpret it in only one way. . . . *The Jungle Line,* for example, is about an *asphalt* jungle—but seen as something a beautiful madman such as the "primitive" painter Theodore Rousseau might have created ("Beauty and madness to be praised," she says in another song, about a movie-style greed for the root flavor of life). It is an experiment, a successful one, exquisitely lyrical images enhanced by almost frightening synthesizer whoops and warrior drums, and it doesn't mind being pulled out of the album to be considered as a separate whole. Most of the other pieces don't disengage from the overall context quite so easily. (p. 75)

[The] appeal of Mitchell's metaphors lies in their richness, in how long you can continue to pull new ideas and fresh slants out of them, no matter how many of them came from her head, how many from yours.

I hope I've made it clear that this isn't much of a party record; you'll have to deal with it privately, as you would read a book. But it should keep you occupied for about as long as you want it to—and how often does "popular" music do that? (p. 76)

> *Noel Coppage, "More Than a Sprinkling of Symbolism in Joni Mitchell's 'The Hissing of Summer Lawns',"* in Stereo Review *(reprinted by permission of the author), February, 1976, pp. 75-6.*

NOEL COPPAGE

Sometimes . . . one does sense a degree of California School of Pointless Insight in [Mitchell's] work. Sometimes I feel I've put myself through all manner of tortuous self-analysis with her and am no closer to knowing what to do about it, and the vehicle of escape—whether it be a big yellow taxi, the pick-up pitch of a fast lady trying to compete with the hockey game in the bar of the Empire Hotel, or a street corner where someone is providing free clarinet music—is not always there when I need it. . . . Pretentious, some say [of "The Hissing of Summer Lawns"], meaning (I gather) not artistically but intellectually. Others claim that the less serious parts of it are too full of jive—including too much use of *jive* and words like it—and they don't want her making what she does jibe with this label someone pinned on her, Queen of Rock. . . .

I wonder . . . if "Hissing" may have been a *longer* jump than she could gracefully make. Her liner-note message—"The whole unfolded like a mystery, and it is not my intentions to unravel that mystery for anyone"—reads a little bit nervous, a little bit defensive, to me. This could be merely the eye of the beholder playing its tricks, of course; it does seem that in "Hissing" Mitchell was trying for the kind of ambiguity that the *ear* of the beholder could put to private uses. Spiritually, she may have primed her followers for all this, but stylistically she has not; without giving much warning in previous work, she slips—in ambitious songs like *Don't Interrupt the Sorrow* and *Shadows and Light*—into a sort of Joycean stream-of-consciousness way with words, and a job of making grammatical sense of them must be done before one can start to cogitate upon what they mean. Did she conclude there was no way to be more direct about these things, or did she, consciously or unconsciously, court mystery—was she, consciously or unconsciously, trying to impress those academic types who like to have things as abstract as possible so the rabble can't unscramble them? Too soon to tell, I think, but keep in mind that the simplest answer sometimes *is* the best, and the simplest answer is that she was again flying in the face of, trying to fly away from, a set of rules.

There will be other albums, anyway, that can't help but put this one in better perspective. Mitchell seems to be looking out at sociology more, without leaving the rough stuff of one-to-one relating unattended, and a good observer is a good observer. . . .

[I] see her as a naïve person who knows more than the sophisticates do, a person who may have picked up . . . something from the Indians, Western and Eastern, about truly being able to have something only when you can give it up. For verily, as Eve's chronicler would say, Joni Mitchell has a great stake in innocence—and that's why she has to keep putting it on the line. (p. 67)

> Noel Coppage, *"Innocence on a Spree," in* Stereo Review *(reprinted by permission of the author), April, 1976, pp. 65-7.*

JANET MASLIN

Understanding the singer songwriter's gift involves tracing a pattern of personal evolution . . . rather than isolating the most impressive material. *Court and Spark* (1974) may be Joni Mitchell's finest album, but the continuum that brought her to that point is more exciting than any single effort.

Hindsight helps, of course: when Mitchell made her 1968 recording debut, it would have been difficult to peg her as anything more promising than an obviously gifted but dour and arty poet, more comfortable behind the scenes (supplying material to Judy Collins, Tom Rush, Ian and Sylvia) than she might ever become in the limelight. . . . But that first record [*Songs to a Seagull*] now seems intriguingly disingenuous. Many of the singer/songwriters' early efforts take on this same uneasy feel in retrospect. Mitchell's opening cut, "I Had a King," is a daintily philosophical account of the breakup of her marriage ("There's no one to blame . . .") that is, upon closer scrutiny, surprisingly snide. . . . Yet for all the air of quiet resignation in the lyrics, Mitchell's vocal is baleful, scathing, charged with an anger she cannot bring herself to express directly. Three albums later, in another song about her former spouse ("The Last Time I Saw Richard"), she's still cruel, condemning the man for his drab new wife and his kitchen appliances. But here the resentment is overdrawn, almost caricatured, and tempered by a closing note of loneliness that turns this into a richly dramatic interchange, not a mere sideswipe. (pp. 312, 314)

Over the course of her first six albums, Mitchell had more than mere temper to contend with; it took her almost that long to understand and accept her dependency upon men, to see her giddy romanticism for what it was worth (and take it lightly), to acknowledge the scope of her ambition and yet somehow keep it under control. Her vocal style also has kept fascinatingly close pace with her emotional evolution; where the first album had a glum, thin-lipped sound on most cuts ("Night in the City" is a gloriously high-spirited exception), *Court and Spark* is exquisitely snug, passionate and yet perfectly controlled. "Same Situation," her finest song thus far, enhances a concise, agoniz-

ingly self-aware lyric with a melody that climbs and plummets as dramatically as do the singer's moods, and with the piercingly lovely vocal a work this incisive surely warrants.

If "Same Situation" is Mitchell's most sterling moment (and "For the Roses," the title song from her preceding 1972 album, a close second), it is also an excruciatingly demanding one. "Living on nerves and feelings" as she describes it, may be too much for anyone to bear indefinitely; certainly that seemed true in Mitchell's case when she abruptly changed course after *Court and Spark*, retreating (with 1975's *The Hissing of Summer Lawns*) into coolly detached condemnation of bourgeois and bohemian foibles. This is in many ways (laborious lyrics, experiments with jazz accompaniment) Mitchell's most painstaking album, but it may also have been her easiest, placed at such a comfortable remove from the struggles of the self. (p. 314)

> Janet Maslin, in The Rolling Stone Illustrated History of Rock and Roll, *edited by Jim Miller (copyright © 1976 by Rolling Stone Press; reprinted by permission of Random House, Inc.), Rolling Stone Press, Random House, 1976.*

PERRY MEISEL

Despite Joni Mitchell's reputation as a lyricist, the poetic element in her work has been a growing source of embarrassment to many listeners over the years. Less a measure of ignorance than of optimism, Mitchell's verbal pretensions are a product of her innocence—an innocence that seems unwarranted by the crushed hopes her songs discern in everything from urban blight and stardom to motherhood and love. Usually, Mitchell's melodies have been so compelling that her songs stand up on purely musical grounds, at least until . . . *The Hissing of Summer Lawns*, which sounded so aimless that it put off many of Joni's oldest fans. It is the poetic/lyrical factor, though, that sustains [*Hejira*]. . . .

Hejira presents the Queen of El Lay more explicitly in the guise of a poet than ever before, festooned with cape, beret, slanted pinky, and the backdrop of a resolutely abstract landscape. Well, that's the way poets are supposed to look, I guess, and Mitchell's (self-)portrait here seems to be a little too aware of that. Mitchell, of course, has always tried to pass herself off as a poet by printing out her lyrics on the covers of her recordings. . . . Mixing your metaphors in ignorance is one thing, but flaunting your pretensions in black and white is quite another. Unless . . . unless . . . the vaguely ironic Mitchell that emerged after *For the Roses* is now becoming more overt.

Mitchell's paradoxical history, both personal and artistic, should have prepared us for such a contingency. Here was a lover of words who, by all accounts at least, had spoken for a generation in revolt against language. . . . Mitchell managed to forge an ego-ideal for lots of women, and certainly an ideal for the female vocalizer who was also a versifier, not to mention the lousy poet who could sing. . . .

[*Hejira*] seems to offer a new set of answers to the old questions, beginning with the familiar contrast between the world of "nylons" and the world of "jeans": "You know it was white lace I was chasing / Chasing dreams / Mama's nylons underneath my cowgirl jeans" ("Song for Sharon"). Surprising as it may seem to hear Mitchell opting for the "white lace," self-reliance capitulates to domesticity, the cowgirl to the family. Yes, what is real or natural—what is "underneath"—turns out to be an ego-ideal named "Mama."

Yet the rest of the stanza complicates this moment of self-discovery by scrambling the terms on which it is made: ". . . first you get the kisses / And then you get the tears / But the ceremony of the bells and lace / Still veils this reckless fool here." The "bells and lace," of course, turn out to be just as foolish as the "jeans." Neither is more real or natural than the other. The "veil" of the bride is also the veil of illusion. So the meaning of "underneath," in its Freudian sense of discovery, gets called into question; depth itself becomes a fiction and the self a surface of images, ciphers, or signs. (p. 42)

If Mitchell's language denies the possibility of real discovery, though, what happens to the "nature" that Joni the romantic has always been hellbent on recovering? If there is no ground, how can there be a garden? And if domesticity may be part of humanity's natural rhythms, where is a nature that is separate from society and its attendant constraints?

At this point Mitchell's mythology begins to crumble. Premised on a return to nature, her mini-allegories fairly reek with a nostalgia for the garden and, by implication, for a pre-fallen language as well. Such a paradisiacal language would identify the word with the thing, allowing Mitchell to speak about feelings with all the sincerity for which she yearns. Trouble is, we're all outside the gates of Eden. Language is not an innocent tool of expression; it leads a life of its own, and, more often than not, it helps to manufacture the world in which we live.

Mitchell, though, resists the power inherent in language as such, even the power her own language displays. Despite the fact that her words generate ambiguity and call their own meanings into question, she wants them to stay fixed and believes that they do. A relentless practitioner of figurative speech, Mitchell behaves as though her words are straightforward conduits of expression, "direct from the heart" as it were. I'm more than willing—in fact, I'm eager—to grant Mitchell the title of ironist. Unfortunately, she's not willing to grant it herself.

Indeed, she clutches on to reactionary notions about history and anthropology as eagerly as she clutches her own sincerity. Without a belief, however metaphoric, in the garden beyond or before civilization, there could be no belief in the garden of pure feeling that Mitchell assumes to be growing "underneath" ego and superego in the terrain of the self. For the Mitchell of *Hejira* "history falls / To parking lots and shopping malls" ("Furry Sings the Blues"). Though the trope's manifest meaning is simply that old buildings get torn down by property developers, Mitchell's figurative use of the word "history" also makes a clear (even if unintentional) rhetorical distinction between "history" and "shopping malls" that implies that shopping malls aren't part of human history at all. What's more, this trope is typical of her indulgence in nostalgic fantasies about a simple past she presumes to have existed before technology and industrialization. In this context, the phrase "history falls" turns out to be meaningless: history is a consequence of the fall, not the other way around. In this way the phrase even threatens to invalidate the Christian romance of Mitchell's quest for redemption—of personal and public histories alike.

The question of literary prototypes also raises the question of Mitchell's relation to real Romanticism. The High Romantics themselves were by no means the pantheists our high schools like to teach, nor were they the source of Mitchell's naive assumptions about the status of nature. Shelley, for example, begins his famous poem in awe of Mont Blanc, and ends by asserting that he has imagined it. Not only is there no way back to the garden that Mitchell's "Woodstock" once demanded—nature itself may not even exist. There is no state of innocence down "underneath," where she expects it to be.

So there is finally no paradox involved in Mitchell's having spoken for the nonverbalists of the '60s. Hers is a language on the verge of dissolution, though the dissolution is largely unwitting and unrecognized. Unlike Barthelme or Borges, whose language is intentionally designed to empty out its signifying power in a dissolution that is part of its significance, the dissolution of Mitchell's language falls outside her will and control. Her language is therefore clouded, vague, imprecise, immodest; above all, rampant with figures of speech that break down under scrutiny and that collide in implications they do not intend.

God knows, I've had my heart-throbs for Joni, and I've been moved almost to tears by her stuff. But that's when I've been listening to her sing. Joined with melody and the infinite nuance of her voice, Mitchell's words are something else again. As a batch of syllables no longer bound to the responsibilities of the page and its ironic preconditions, they acquire a new and different kind of life. Puns on "ego" and "eagle" ("Coyote"), for example, are entirely legitimate when they're sung, despite their nonexistence on the page. Even the dangers of imitative form are superseded when Mitchell's voice ascends to meet the heights of "ice cream castles in the air" on "Both Sides Now."

Mitchell's language also creates the kind of phonemic density and variation that only singers like Ella Fitzgerald or Sarah Vaughan can impart to the relatively simple verbal mannerisms of most pop tunes as they are written. Because the phonetic density of Mitchell's lyrics is so high (I'd wager she uses more syllables per song than any songwriter living, Dylan included), her songs are, formally speaking, almost like copied-down scat extensions of a simpler melody line embedded somewhere inside the tune as a whole. From this point of view, Mitchell's style of songwriting seems designed to catch up as best it can with its perception of the essence of jazz singing proper. What it more often resembles, however, is the effort of a patchworker or bricoleur in assembling fragments of inspiration from a bewildering panoply of half-understood sources—blues, folk, opera, music-hall, cabaret, and so on. (pp. 42-3)

Hejira's title . . . is its most enticing trope. The word "hejira" refers to Mohammed's flight from Mecca in 622, a flight for personal survival that preserved the fledgling Islamic religion. Ever since, "hejira" has come to mean such a purposive flight from danger or oppression. Clearly, Mitchell means to take this meaning for her own, to signify her many flights from oppressive relationships, the burdens of stardom, the dirt of the city. In this way, the album's recurrent images of flight—Icarus, jets, crows, and so on—conspire to suggest a Mitchell whose only "refuge" is "the roads." Yet "flight" also signifies the transitory, the ephemeral, the flighty quality of Mitchell's own attempts at meaning. This kind of flight—escape or loss rather than departure for freedom—is far different from the Mohammedan sense of the word, which Mitchell wants to use to grant her own flightiness a weightier sense of purpose than it really possesses. The meanings are at odds, and they fight it out within the word itself.

Ultimately, though, we are left with a question of intentionality: Are all these meanings of "hejira" really "there," or does Mitchell's language comment on itself—indeed, deconstruct itself—outside her control and design? Just how naive is this airy lady of the canyons, whose . . . album seems a witness to the inauthenticity of all sincerity? Mitchell mocks herself on *Hejira,* though just how wittingly it is hard to tell. There seems to be something like bitterness on the album, even if it comes out as a diminished investment in the self and a decline in the earnestness with which the persona is presented. . . .

As an artist, however, Mitchell clearly lacks any real understanding of what her work is and how it behaves. Aware as she may be of the ironies of her pose as a lover and a soothsayer, the finer ironies of what it means to work in language obviously elude her. There are two distinctly different kinds of irony, mind you, and they signify two distinct levels of knowing. The first is dramatic or situational, the way we have of knowing what we don't know, much as Mitchell the self-mocking artiste knows she no longer has the answers. The second, however, is far crueler, since it knows we can never mean what we say. It is this second style of knowing that characterizes all literary language, and that can transform any language into an aesthetic one so long as its syntax displays some delight in the hazards of signification and some deliberation as to how it means to handle them.

These hazards are not only beyond Mitchell's control but also beyond her ken. Her art lacks deliberation because it lacks a knowledge of the instruments it employs. The product of these shortcomings for the artist is the self-consuming artifact that finally consumes its own maker. *Hejira* signifies Mitchell's flight from precisely this fate. The mythology of the garden still has her in its thrall, and until she confronts it within her conscious imagination, her work will be haunted by the prospect of its own annihilation. (p. 43)

Perry Meisel, "An End to Innocence: How Joni Mitchell Fails," in The Village Voice *(reprinted by permission of* The Village Voice; *copyright © The Village Voice, Inc., 1977), January 24, 1977, pp. 42-3.*

ARIEL SWARTLEY

It is the tug of war between the symbolist and the siren that makes Joni Mitchell's albums alternately alluring and forbidding. On the one hand she is the most ruthlessly analytical member of the music-as-therapy songwriting school, and often her songs seem intent only on making private sense of her own experience. On the other hand, as a public performer, Mitchell wants to be heard and even enjoyed. To that end she conducts a cool flirtation with her audience. Like a Victorian gentlewoman, she seems afraid that we won't respect her if she makes obvious advances. Thus, though *Court and Spark* showed Mitchell blossoming into accessibility, . . . *The Hissing of Summer Lawns* brought back the arcane priestess of *For the Roses.* But . . . with *Hejira,* Mitchell has gravely come a-courting once again. (p. 99)

While *Hejira* (the title itself refers to Mohammed's "flight from danger") represents a retreat from the inviting accessibility of *Court and Spark,* it is a retreat with a self-renewing purpose. Mitchell has withdrawn to her roots, to redefine them.

Nearly all the new songs are built from the bare bones of her early work. . . . [*Hejira,* however,] contains no "Raised on Robbery," no "Big Yellow Taxi." The one concession to popular tastes is the dreamy, blowsy "Blue Motel Room," which is too much tongue-in-cheek to sustain the torch-song illusion for long. For the rest, verse after long meditative verse is resolved in a single-line refrain which gains in meaning with repetition. The refrains . . . are the only devices approaching a hook: recurring, memorable tags that sum up the song.

By writing for instruments that she plays well (guitars) and within a genre she understands (folk), Mitchell avoids the self-conscious artiness that marred *The Hissing of Summer Lawns.* Despite its apparent simplicity and spare instrumentation, the sound is as sophisticated and arresting as anything she's done. Mitchell has taken advantage of the music's structural freedom to write some of her most incisive and humorous lyrics. (pp. 99-100)

For *Hejira,* as any glance at the cover or the lyrics will prove, is about the Highway: as a symbol of distance or flight; as a stage for encounters or revelations; as a communal umbilical cord relating separate souls and random experiences. The road runs through every song. The old pastoral conventions have been revived in Mitchell's freeways. Like Shakespeare's Forest of Arden or Mark Twain's Mississippi, the highway is a place where the obligations of power and wealth, or merely the confines of civilization, can be momentarily forgotten.

The road is further represented as Mitchell's only source of anonymity and acceptance. There she can masquerade as one in a gang of vagabonds ("The Refuge of the Roads"), drink and dance with the locals ("Coyote") or find unencumbered solitude ("Hejira," "Amelia"). The desire to escape, to start over, to make things simple again is universal, but in addition the artist often pays for success with a frightening isolation, a woman artist perhaps even more so.

A current of success-induced guilt ran through such earlier Mitchell songs as "For Free" and "People's Parties." Now she openly acknowledges the rewards of achievement along with the penalties, accepting the conflict as inevitable. Her new songs take a long, sometimes painful look at a problem of particular concern to ambitious women: how to reconcile the demands of one's chosen work with the demands of love and family. . . .

The really difficult conflict is between the long-taught myth that a woman should make a total commitment to love and the hard-won discovery that a career may require the same all-consuming passion. . . .

It is to Joni Mitchell's credit that she comes to no glib conclusions. The conflict between freedom for art's sake and the need for love forms the basis of most of her songs, and it is her uncertainty, the alternating warmth and chill, which is most fascinating. But if Mitchell is not always inviting, she is never complacent. With *Hejira* she redefines the elements of her music with as much courage as when she scrutinizes her aims and motivations. And despite the songs of love lost and plans changed, despite the urgent, often stark consciousness of mortality and the absence of comfortable solutions, *Hejira* is a curiously optimistic album. In "Black Crow," Mitchell sings, "In search of love and music / My whole life has been / Illumination / Corruption / And diving, diving, diving, diving . . . ," her voice swooping and spiraling on the repeated word. That is what *Hejira* is about: it is not the answers that are most important but the search itself. (p. 100)

Ariel Swartley, "Mitchell: The Siren and the Symbolist," in Rolling Stone *(by Straight Arrow Publishers, Inc.* © *1977; all rights reserved; reprinted by permission), Issue 232, February 10, 1977, pp. 99-100.*

JON PARELES

Somewhere along the way, Mitchell's reverent audiences convinced her that her every thought is profound. Having concentrated on herself for so long. Mitchell's discrimination has eroded; she can't separate out the trivia anymore. Her intimacy has become exhaustive—she tells all, every flicker of ambivalence, every last rationalization, seemingly anything that pops into her head. You feel like you're drowning in her stream of consciousness. Her perceptions of the outside world are clear and neatly expressed—only between her head and heart do things get muddled. . . .

Where she takes on larger concepts, Mitchell over-writes. "Don Juan's Reckless Daughter," a meditation on the divided self, explains itself endlessly, beating to death a lovely network of images: eagle / airplane / woman / / "clarity" vs. snake / train / man / "blind desire." Lines like "We are all hopelessly oppressed cowards / Of some duplicity / Of restless multiplicity" weigh the song down with literalness. I prefer the verbal fantasias on *The Hissing of Summer Lawns* to this sort of expostulation.

Despite the feverish intellectualizing of its lyrics, *Don Juan's Reckless Daughter* turns out to be soft at the center. Mitchell, all of a sudden, has subscribed to the two most banal '70s panaceas: dancing ("Cotton Avenue," "Paprika Plains") and dreaming ("Paprika Plains," "Otis and Marlena," "Dreamland," "The Silky Veils of Ardor"). She took a hard look at distances, transience and herself on *Hejira;* now it seems she'd rather drift and ruminate. (We are expected, however, to drift with her: Most of the lyrics on "Paprika Plains" are unsung, under the assumption that we'll read the lyric sheet for Mitchell's dream / vision of rebirth while the record plays tasteful movie music. Rather arrogant. . . .) Perhaps Mitchell has become so ingrown that she doesn't notice the clichés she's absorbed. . . .

At this point, dreams are an unfortunate metaphor for Mitchell. In "The Silky Veils of Ardor" . . . , Mitchell gives advice to schoolgirls about men which she herself is unable to follow, sighing "In my dreams we fly." Formless and private, dreams let Mitchell wander anywhere, float into anything, when what she needs most is a sense of proportion.

Jon Pareles, "Four Sides Now," in Crawdaddy *(copyright* © *1978 by Crawdaddy Publishing Co., Inc.; reprinted by permission of Peter Knobler), February, 1978, p. 63.*

RAY STURGEON

Because the songs are stronger [on *Don Juan's Reckless*

Daughter] the lyrics overflow less. [Joni] builds images like they do in movies, a piece at a time. People in her songs sit around, restless, maybe talking, maybe drinking, maybe looking out of the window. Nobody ever gets up to slug the other guy. She has sent us more love letters, on post cards, from long lost bus rides. More rainy memories and blizzard emotions. She circles and pokes that big ol' carcass of life. Everything acts on her, and she records it.

Mitchell fans tell me it's an excellent album. But I wonder if the rest of us have the patience for the serious listening it requires.

I back into Joni Mitchell records. I try not to listen to the words. She knows too much. She knows when you've been sleeping. She knows when you're awake. And when you're trying to get some rest, she wakes you up to tell you what your dreams are, because she knows that, too. Listening to *Don Juan's Reckless Daughter* . . . , one can only be surprised that she has remained so remarkably committed to words, when there are plenty of easier ways to communicate. She loads her songs like a horse and wagon, and takes journal-entry observations for a quick ride through the park. They speed by so fast we can only notice and appreciate. So I listen to the music. (p. 59)

Ray Sturgeon, in Circus Magazine *(copyright* © *1978 by Circus Enterprises Corporation), February 16, 1978.*

JANET MASLIN

[The unpredictable caliber of Joni Mitchell's] work has been as exciting as it is frustrating. Now, for once, she has gambled and lost. The best that can be said for *Don Juan's Reckless Daughter* is that it is an instructive failure.

Since *Blue*, Mitchell has demonstrated an increasing fondness for formats that don't suit her. Not that this awkwardness can't be occasionally successful: on *Hejira*, she clung so resolutely to even the stray flat notes that the impression was an attractive one of stubbornness and strength. But, increasingly, Mitchell's pretensions have shaped her appraisal of her own gifts. At her best, she is a keen observer but not a particularly original one, and she has never been an interesting chronicler of experience other than her own, though [*Don Juan's Reckless Daughter*] finds her trying. . . . Her most resonant lyrics have been simple and concise, spinning out images rather than overburdening them, but lately the endearing modesty of "California" or "Just like This Train" seems far behind her. These days, Mitchell appears bent on repudiating her own flair for popular songwriting, and on staking her claim to the kind of artistry that, when it's real, doesn't need to announce itself so stridently.

Don Juan's Reckless Daughter is a double album that should have been a single album. It's sapped of emotion and full of ideas that should have remained whims, melodies that should have been riffs, songs that should have been fragments. At its worst, it is a painful illustration of how different the standards that govern poetry and song lyrics can be, and an indication that Joni Mitchell's talents, stretched here to the breaking point, lend themselves much more naturally to the latter form. . . .

The painful banality of Mitchell's lyrics—there is nothing said here that she hasn't said better before, except those things she should have kept to herself—is almost the least of her problems. Behind a treacly title like "The Silky Veils of Ardor" lurks an even treaclier notion: that the romantic visions of love put forth by certain folk songs are one thing, that reality is another, and that the singer apparently yearns for both. . . .

"Talk to Me" is the LP's most enduring number: as a terrible, embarrassing song about feeling terribly embarrassed, it has a scary appropriateness. But even though there are no real solutions to the album's mysteries or explanations for its lapses, Joni Mitchell's resilience has been demonstrated often enough to make speculation about such things appear superfluous. She's bound to be back when the time is right and her mood is less drowsy, less disengaged than it seems here. Until then, we're left with *Don Juan's Reckless Daughter,* in all its recklessness.

> *Janet Maslin, "Joni Mitchell's Reckless and Shapeless Daughter," in* Rolling Stone *(by Straight Arrow Publishers, Inc. © 1978; all rights reserved; reprinted by permission), Issue 260, March 9, 1978, p. 54.*

Nicholosa Mohr

1935-

American young adult novelist, short story writer, and illustrator. Mohr's work is noted for its realistic portrayal of life in New York City's Puerto Rican slums. An accomplished painter and printmaker, she received awards both as author and illustrator for her 1973 first novel, *Nilda*. Mohr says of her work: "It incorporates a strong social statement; the plight and constant struggle of the Puerto Ricans on the mainland to receive their basic human rights. Using art, the universal language of humanity, I bring forth the point-of-view of a subculture in America, the Puerto Rican people with all their variety and complexity." She is sometimes criticized for being more concerned with her characters as Puerto Ricans than as human beings, but her concern with the condition of that minority does not obscure her vision. She presents her characters sympathetically, but honestly, revealing their character flaws as well as strengths. Her work often deals with situations that are unconventional in young adult fiction, such as failed marriages, homosexuality, and illegitimacy. (See also *Contemporary Authors*, Vols. 49-52, and *Something about the Author*, Vol. 8.)

Nilda's growing up at first seems to be a chain of just so many unrelated demonstrations of the humiliation that ensues from being poor and Puerto Rican in New York [in 1941], the incidents lack neither sting nor sense of humor.... Quite unexpectedly, the unifying message [of *Nilda*] is delivered by Nilda's mother (previously seen as a hopeless muddle of piety and superstition) who confesses on her deathbed that "I cannot see who I am beyond the lives of the children I bore" and advises Nilda to "hold on to something all yours . . . never give it to nobody . . . not to your lover, not to your kids." The insight might be less of a blockbuster if we knew something of Nilda's own feelings in the matter, but the vigorous portrayal of Nilda's large family and acquaintanceship, the lively Spanglish accent, and the absence of any artificial solutions or epiphanies, gives this autobiographical first novel unusual strength. (p. 1097)

Kirkus Reviews (copyright © 1973 The Kirkus Service, Inc.), October 1, 1973.

MARILYN SACHS

When Nilda Ramirez was nearly 10, a white policeman shouted, "God damn you people," at her and her neighbors. At other times in the course of this sad and beautiful book ["Nilda"], Nilda and her family are called "spics," "animals" and much worse. But they are always "you people" to the teachers, social workers, policemen, nurses and other white Americans who control their world.

What does it feel like being poor and belonging to a despised minority? Over the past 10 years many children's books have been written, exploring these very questions. Few come up to "Nilda" in describing the crushing humiliations of poverty and in peeling off the ethnic wrappings so that we can see the human child underneath.

Nilda is nearly 10 when the book begins in July, 1941, and 13½ when it ends in May, 1945. The Second World War is there in the background, important only in its unimportance to a family whose daily struggles to survive are so overwhelming. This is a very personal book. We see life in the Puerto Rican ghetto of New York City through a child's vision—baffled, resigned, angry and frequently joyful. Nilda is no idealized slum child. She punctuates her speech with four-letter words, and like all children, places her own private griefs ahead of larger, adult sorrows. "Mama, I gotta tell you something, Ma!" Nilda cries, eager to tell her weeping, grieving mother whose husband is dying how Sophie played a mean trick on her.

The main story line concerns Mama's efforts to take care of her large family—five children, sick husband, crazy aunt, and pregnant girl friend of one son. But what makes the book remarkable is the richness of detail and the aching sense of a child's feelings....

[This] book goes far beyond being just another tale from the ghetto. Sad, funny, fascinating and honest, it will appeal to adults as well as children. (pp. 27-8)

Marilyn Sachs, in The New York Times Book Review *(© 1973 by The New York Times Company; reprinted by permission), November 4, 1973.*

MARY M. BURNS

[*Nilda*] succeeds as a sociological documentary but fails to develop the heroine as a unique personality. Nor do the minor characters fare much better—with the exception of the elderly, eccentric Aunt Delia and of the Spanish-born Socialist stepfather, who preserves his anticlerical convictions and profane vocabulary until his final breath. Although somewhat reminiscent of Piri Thomas's autobiographical *Down These Mean Streets* . . . in its frank cataloguing of the sights, sounds, conflicts, and language of Spanish Harlem, the narrative is stilted and, at times, anachronistic: Such expressions as "let's split" and "disc jockey" suggest the fifties and sixties rather than the early forties—an impression supported by the *Dictionary of American Slang*. . . . Effective re-creation of reality in fiction requires more than simple fidelity to fact; the reader must become emotionally involved with the characters and their problems. Thus, Nilda's world is more vividly evoked in the expressionistic black-and-white illustrations—which, as the jacket states, "combine representational art, symbols and words"—than in the text, which attempts to depict times past in terms of present-day emotions and attitudes. (p. 153)

> *Mary M. Burns, in* The Horn Book Magazine *(copyright © 1974 by the Horn Book, Inc., Boston), April, 1974.*

RAY ANTHONY SHEPARD

[*Nilda*] is a sensitive, well written and powerful story of a 10-year-old girl's growth into adolescence. Nilda is on her own because no one else survives. She must not only grow into adolescence, but she must learn what it means to be Puerto Rican and poor in America. . . . [She] must come to grips with a poverty that kills her step-father and eventually her mother. . . .

At times the odds against Nilda, or any child, seem overpowering. At the end of four years her survival is still in doubt; one hopes she survives because as a reader one is so involved in her life, but even as the novel closes one can not be sure.

This is an outstanding first novel. . . . (p. 230)

> *Ray Anthony Shepard, in* Children's Literature: Annual of The Modern Language Association Seminar on Children's Literature and The Children's Literature Association, *Vol. 3, edited by Francelia Butler (© 1974 by Francelia Butler; all rights reserved), Temple University Press, 1974.*

[The] thirteen glimpses of life in El Bronx [in *El Bronx Remembered*] have the ethnic flavor and nostalgia but little of the resilience of *Nilda* (1973). In fact it's the smallest stories that ring true here: Hector faces the embarrassment of wearing his uncle's tacky, pointed-toe shoes (real "matacucarachas") to his high school graduation; a pet hen named Joncrofo (Joan Crawford) defeats Mrs. Fernandez' determination to turn her into a chicken dinner; Hannibal plots to win well-chaperoned Serafina by joining her "aleluya" church. The several longer stories tend to get mired in sentimentality—particularly the memoir of a friendship between feeble, lonely Mr. Mendelsohn and the Suarez family next door, and the drawn-out failure of a marriage between pregnant, teenage Alice and covertly homosexual Hector. Mohr is almost too good at zeroing in on touching incidents; the danger is that her El Bronx can be too easily dismissed as quaint. But given their limited emotional range and narrow focus these will stand as grace notes, augmenting *Nilda*'s more vital theme and spirit. (pp. 1004-05)

> Kirkus Reviews *(copyright © 1975 The Kirkus Service, Inc.), September 1, 1975.*

MARILYN SACHS

Little Ray, in "A New Window Display" [one of the stories in "El Bronx Remembered"], is a newcomer from Puerto Rico who marvels at all the wonders in El Bronx: to every new experience, he says, "*Qué fenomenal!*" His friends have told him about the snow, and he is particularly eager to see it. But he never does. He dies before it comes, and his friends mourn for him in the best possible way—by playing in it themselves, shouting, sliding, turning and crying out for him at its beauty, "*Qué fenomenal!*"

If there is any message at all in these stories, any underlying theme, it is that life goes on. But Nicholasa Mohr is more interested in people than in messages. Essentially, she is an old-fashioned writer, a meat-and-potatoes writer, whose stories stick to your ribs. No complicated symbolism here, no trendy obscurity of meaning, no hopeless despair or militant ethnicity. Her people endure because they are people. Some of them suffer, some of them die, a few of them fail, but most of the time they endure, or others like them endure.

Most brilliant and tender, perhaps, of all these brilliant and tender stories, is "Mr. Mendelsohn," the story of a lonely old Jewish man who is befriended by a Puerto Rican family. Even though Mr. Mendelsohn dies finally, it is no tragedy because his last years have been enriched by kindness and love. Very different for Doña Nereida in the chilling story, "Princess." She is trapped by a narrow love for a dead animal, love she cannot allow to grow into something wider and healthier.

A couple of the stories are tragic, but most of Nicholasa Mohr's characters are too sturdy and resilient for defeat. Yvette and Mildred, the two friends in "The Wrong Lunch Line," are humiliated by teachers when they try to eat their lunch together in school. Friendship, however, is not such a fragile thing, and the two girls, though hurt and confused, can laugh scornfully at the foolishness of adults.

And Hannibal, Joey, Ramona, Maria and Casilda, who grow up in the course of three of the stories, can laugh too —and survive death, betrayal and religious conversion, as they bounce off the pages in the final story on their way to a dance at St. Anselm's and to a future that will always hold for Nicholasa Mohr's characters some promise, some hope.

In her earlier outstanding novel, "Nilda," it was apparent that if any author could make you hear pulses beating from the pages, Nicholasa Mohr was the one. In "El Bronx Remembered," she has done it again. (p. 30)

> *Marilyn Sachs, in* The New York Times Book Review *(© 1975 by The New York Times Company; reprinted by permission), November 16, 1975.*

PAUL HEINS

[*El Bronx Remembered: A Novella and Stories* is a] group of short narratives about Puerto Rican immigrants living in the South Bronx between 1946 and 1956. Despite their poverty and their crowded quarters, the people are generally represented as dwelling in an alien rather than in a hostile environment; and each story is a carefully focused vignette of pathetic and/or comic incidents. . . . Only in the novella, "Herman and Alice," does the author introduce topics of hard-core realism: the homosexual Herman befriends and marries Alice, a teenage pregnant girl. The style is plain and direct, often making use of colloquial Americanisms, and the occasional Spanish expressions are effectively dramatic. At their best, the short Chekov-like narratives reveal universal emotions hovering beneath an urban, ethnic casing. (p. 57)

> Paul Heins, in The Horn Book Magazine (copyright © 1976 by the Horn Book, Inc., Boston), February, 1976.

IRMA GARCIA

[The stories of *El Bronx Remembered* describe] the anxieties, fears, loves, hates, pride, despair, nostalgia and hopes of several Puerto Ricans in the barrio, El Bronx, from 1946 to 1956. The subjects of these well-written and descriptive tales want to escape to suburbia, or into the arms of men, or to be accepted and assimilated into a materialistic society which rejects and exploits them. We have seen their faces. But despite some truths and sharp insights, these are not stories of change, struggle or love. Rather, they are negative stories which reinforce stereotypes.

One incredibly racist story is about Jasmine, a gypsy who wins the acceptance of her classmates by reading palms and telling stories. When Hannibal goes to Jasmine's house to have his fortune read, he gives her all the money he has to be blessed. . . . The ending is obvious: no fortune, no refund, no more Jasmine—she and her family move on "as they all do." The description of Jasmine's appearance reads like a catalogue of prejudices and, as in most of the stories in this book, sexism is prevalent as well.

The novella (a sick soap opera) tells of Alice, a pregnant fifteen-year-old who finds temporary comfort and happiness in the home of a mature, understanding homosexual.

A conversation between Alice and her mother about the pregnancy reeks of puritanism—"I know you are sorry. I am too, Alice, but it's too late now. Because now you see, you can be sorry for the rest of your life."—as does Alice's description of her sexual life. . . . To top it off, Alice forgets all of her labor pain as soon as she looks upon her *son*.

In addition to having internalized myths about females, the novella's characters have also taken to heart certain myths about Puerto Ricans. Herman says of his own people, "Honestly, these people, a bunch of ignorantes, and they just keep making babies and more babies and being miserable." Alice's mother buys her new clothes to go out with the "respectable" homosexual, so that he will not think their family is a bunch of "jíbaros" (peasants).

Although it is unusual to portray a gay person in a book for young people, no new ground is broken here in developing understanding of sexual differences. Those differences are simply presented. Alice marries Herman to escape from her critical mother. For Herman, the marriage serves to pacify his old parents in Puerto Rico who want him to be a husband and father. The characters are neither honest with themselves nor with each other. (p. 16)

> Irma Garcia, in Interracial Books for Children Bulletin (reprinted by permission of Interracial Books for Children Bulletin, 1841 Broadway, New York, N.Y. 10023), Vol. 7, No. 4, 1976.

[*In Nueva York,* a] tighter collection [of stories] than *El Bronx Remembered* (1975) gradually zeros in on a few principals and ends more like an episodic novel. . . . In truth, it

might be negative qualities that make this a juvenile—it's being neither demanding nor really disturbing. But that is not to deny the clarity, wry humor, genuine sympathy, and considerable success with which Mohr brings her neighborhood to life. (p. 360)

> Kirkus Reviews (copyright © 1977 The Kirkus Service, Inc.), April 1, 1977.

[The seven interrelated stories in *In Nueva York*] vividly re-create the struggles inherent in life in a New York City Puerto Rican barrio. . . . While success of the individual stories varies and their direction is occasionally all too obvious, Mohr's sense of place is carefully maintained, her characters are sympathetically and realistically drawn, and teenagers will be easily caught up by the honesty and artless prose that permeates it all. (p. 1415)

> Booklist (reprinted by permission of the American Library Association; copyright 1977 by the American Library Association), May 15, 1977.

GEORGESS McHARGUE

Realism is the order of the day in ["In Nueva York"]—realism with an ethnic garnish. . . . [The book] would provide a profitable unit to a high-school social studies class. . . .

[It] seems, however, too obviously intended as slice-of-life fiction with the result that the characters are busier being Puerto Rican-Americans than being people. Several of the stories present intriguing situations but end inconclusively. An old woman's long lost son turns out to be a dwarf. A gay male marries a gay female. "The English Lesson" embarrassingly recalls H*Y*M*A*N K*A*P*L*A*N without laughs. Happily, [something] better shows itself in the last few stories. In "The Robbery" and "Coming to Terms" a store owner kills a 15-year-old thief during a holdup and is publicly badgered by the dead youth's mother with demands that the storeowner pay for a headstone. In the end the man comes to terms, not with the mother ("This woman is stark raving nuts"), but with the battered alley cat whose life he has been threatening for years. There should have been more of this. All in all, it's Sociologists 8, Readers 4. (p. 29)

> Georgess McHargue, in The New York Times Book Review (© 1977 by The New York Times Company; reprinted by permission), May 22, 1977.

ZENA SUTHERLAND

[In *In Nueva York*] Mohr creates a remarkably vivid tapestry of community life as well as of individual characters. . . . Tough, candid, and perceptive, the book has memorable characters, resilient and responsive, in a sharply-etched milieu. (p. 178)

> Zena Sutherland, in Bulletin of the Center for Children's Books (© 1977 by the University of Chicago; all rights reserved), July-August, 1977.

ALLEEN PACE NILSEN

Like *El Bronx Remembered*, *In Nueva York* is not a novel but instead is a collection of stories tied together by their setting. A number of the characters appear in more than one story and the effect is an intimate look into the most interesting parts of several people's lives without the artificial strain of having them all squeezed into a single plot. For people who like to approach books from the social issues viewpoint, this is an excellent book to help people see beyond the stereotypes. The reader meets several individuals who share a common neighborhood and many common problems, yet each is unique and intriguing. The fact that readers come away with a knowledge of each character's individuality and an empathy for their feelings is due to Mohr's skill as a writer. There is really no way of evaluating a book from the viewpoint of its social effect without also judging its literary effect. On either score *In Nueva York* ranks very high. (p. 100)

Alleen Pace Nilsen, in English Journal *(copyright 1978 by the National Council of Teachers of English), February, 1978.*

MIGUEL A. ORTIZ

Nilda is the story of a Puerto Rican family living in New York. It is narrated from the point of view of a young girl; Nilda is ten years old at the outset of the story which covers a four year period, from 1941 to 1945. I presume the author chose this time period because it coincided with her own childhood and early adolescence. There is no evidence in the novel that there was any other reason. The author was not striving to capture the flavor of the forties. The biggest event of the time, World War II, is incidental to the story. (p. 6)

The accumulation of details without dramatic purpose results in overwhelming boredom. This, I suppose, is more a failure of technique than of intention. The portrait of life in El Barrio is fair enough but the author seems to be depending on the inherent drama of poverty to carry the book. That drama never materializes. The characters have no depth. Though none of their actions strikes a false note, the reader is hard pressed to feel for them. Rarely is the book able to arouse any sympathy, pathos, or humor.

Two incidents in the book are exceptions. One occurs when Nilda goes to camp. The other girls in her bunk persecute a girl who did not have a suitcase—she had brought her clothes in a paper box. To compensate for her poverty she habitually bragged about make-believe luxuries, thus arousing the animosity of the other girls, who retaliate by vandalizing her cardboard box. This incident is handled sensitively and comes across convincingly. The other scene of note involves Jimmy's girlfriend's going back home, after her baby is born. The outraged mother will not open the door to the suppliant daughter. The mother refuses even to acknowledge that it is her daughter on the other side of the locked door. This scene stands out for its dramatic force. Two good scenes however are not enough to make an interesting novel.

Surprisingly, the author creates, then throws away, an opportunity to make incisive political observations. She makes one of the characters, the step-father, a socialist, but proceeds to treat this fact as an aberration in his personality. If one knew nothing at all about socialism one might conclude from this book that all it entails is an irrational hatred of religion. None of the disruption caused by the war is even hinted at. The recent depression, which to this day is on the lips of people who lived through it, is never mentioned by anyone in the book. Spanish Harlem was not so isolated from the rest of New York as to have been so totally unaffected by the larger events of the day. If it had been, that in itself would be something to write about. The dynamics of the Welfare Department go unexplored, though going on public assistance is a traumatic event in the life of the family. Neither is the older brother's experience in prison utilized as social commentary. In fact, we get no hint at all of what personal circumstances and feelings drove him down the path of crime.

Assuming that the author did not digress into any of the above areas in order to concentrate on Nilda's experience, we would have the right to expect a psychological portrait of Nilda. We do not get it; cause and effect are here negated. She seems to be living through events which have no effect on her. (pp. 7-8)

Miguel A. Ortiz, in The Lion and the Unicorn *(copyright © 1978 The Lion and the Unicorn), Fall, 1978.*

Emily Cheney Neville

1919-

American novelist and journalist. Neville was one of the first young adult writers to choose settings other than the affluent suburbs or bucolic countryside and characters other than fair-haired kids with creamy complexions and perfect orthodontia. Her first novel accepted for publication, *It's Like This, Cat*, is a sensitive, low-keyed look at an ordinary teenage boy in New York City. Directed especially to a male readership, it was unusual for its accurate rendering of teenage dialogue and slang and was praised for its perceptive representation of the feelings of an average teenager towards his family and everyday life. Neville wrote the book as a change from the standard boy-and-dog stories of her youth, and as a reaction against her childhood hatred of cats. It was awarded the Newbery Medal in 1964. Neville grew up in a situation quite different from any of her own somewhat urbane characters. She came from a large, closeknit family in a small town, and had only her cousins as companions until the age of eleven. Her bittersweet autobiographical novel, *Traveler from a Small Kingdom*, describes her discovery of the outside world. Neville's understanding of the importance of being accepted in society has come through strongly in her works, due perhaps to her own experience. *The Seventeenth Street Gang* describes a group of urban children dealing with acceptance and rejection, and presents an analysis of some of the internal problems within a group mentality. Neville has brought a strong sense of social justice to her books, and has recently begun a career as a lawyer. Her *Berries Goodman* has as its theme the dawning of the existence of prejudice on a boy in a suburban environment. Neville has consistently refused to sugar-coat the incidents she describes in her works, and has been criticized for her unsubtlety, as well as her creation of stereotyped characters. She claims that "the real world . . . is so much more beautiful than a rigid world of good and bad. It is also more confusing. I think the teenage reader is ready for both." She admits her characters are "somewhat fragmentary," since she lets her dialogue define them. Although some of this dialogue sounds somewhat dated today, the situations she describes for her characters are representative of the universal teenage experience. Her mission as an author, Neville states, "is to show the reader, not how great a hero he could become, because I don't think most people are going to become heroes, but simply how hard it is to be a plain decent human being." (See also *Contemporary Authors*, Vols. 5-8, rev. ed., and *Something about the Author*, Vol. 1.)

ROBERT HOOD

A middle-class, 14-year-old cliff dweller, Dave Mitchell, roams from the Bronx Zoo to the Fulton Fish Market to Coney Island [in "It's Like This, Cat"]. His experiences, although not melodramatic, violent or grim, are the essence of today—shy dates with a girl, friendship with an older boy, affection for a pet, learning to understand Dad. Written in an understated, humorous style, this is superb— the best junior novel I've ever read about big-city life. (p. 2)

> *Robert Hood, in* The New York Times Book Review (© *1963 by The New York Times Company; reprinted by permission), May 12, 1963.*

[In *Berries Goodman*], in a recognizable, believable situation, the difficulty in assigning blame and analyzing motive as well as in tracing the pressures adults exert on children, who are also subject to the pressures of their own codes, is very well done. Unlike the general run of juvenile novels, the issue of anti-Semitism is *not* continuously slugged at, telegraphed or spotlighted. It is through nuance that the social myths go crashing—about being Jewish, looking Jewish and having Jewish names. Berries' first person reporting is sharp. This boy doesn't miss a trick and all the incidental misadventures of transplanting from city sidewalks to suburban folkways are recounted with a direct comic vision which enhances the book's major point without reducing its serious intent. The dialogue is just as natural and relaxed as in *It's Like This, Cat* and indirectly (for instance, Sidney's mother who is in there protecting and pushing and wanting him "to be perfect") some types are well cast. We often recommend adult books for youngsters; you can do the reverse here—anybody can find it both worthwhile and a pleasure to read. (p. 318)

> Virginia Kirkus' Service, *March 15, 1965.*

ELLEN RUDIN

"Berries Goodman" is a children's book which focuses unsmilingly on the Gentile and the Jewish problem. Despite a most readable style, it is a hard, painful book. Berries, whom we meet at age 9, is Gentile. The product of a heterogeneous big-city neighborhood and a laissez-faire family, he has always accepted people for themselves. After his family moves to the suburbs, however, Berries gradually wakes up to the fact of prejudice. It puzzles him and disturbs him. Eventually its ugly complexities cause him to lose his best friend, a Jewish boy named Sidney Fine. . . .

This is a profound subject for a book of children's fiction. Mrs. Neville keeps to the point. She has not tried to explain away the weed of prejudice but only to show its bitter fruit. And that is quite enough. (p. 26)

> *Ellen Rudin, in* The New York Times Book Review *(© 1965 by The New York Times Company; reprinted by permission), April 25, 1965.*

RUTH HILL VIGUERS

Told with understated directness, [*Berries Goodman*] has underlying emotion that makes the reader care greatly about the boys and their friendship. The characters are completely individual, Berries' family is refreshing and real, and events grow naturally from the interplay of personalities. The whole story has the conviction of one that has been a long time maturing in the author's mind. Stronger than the author's *It's Like This, Cat*, and highly recommended. (p. 285)

> *Ruth Hill Viguers, in* The Horn Book Magazine *(copyright © 1965 by the Horn Book, Inc., Boston), June, 1965.*

TALIAFERRO BOATWRIGHT

[*Berries Goodman* is a] completely contemporary tale, as immediate and recognizable as the PTA and advice-to-parents columns. Its central theme—anti-Semitic prejudice in "restricted" communities and how it affects children brought up in ignorance that such things exist—is both important and interesting. Its incidents . . . are the stuff of everyday middle-class life. Its hero, Berries, is as appealing a 9-year-old as you could find. And yet, after the award-winning *It's Like This, Cat*, Mrs. Neville's previous book, this is a disappointment. Probably the trouble is that the material is all too familiar, and there is not enough drama in the story or development in the characters. (p. 16)

> *Taliaferro Boatwright, in* Book Week—The Washington Post *(© I.H.T. Corporation; reprinted by permission), July 11, 1965.*

RUTH HILL VIGUERS

Attitudes and idiom reflect what is considered typical of New York City children [in *The Seventeenth-Street Gang*]. Underneath their defiant independence and their defence against "flots" and adults in general are glimpses of the people they really are—not very different from children of any time and place. The glimpses are brief, however. Instead of the depth of the characterization in the author's *Berries Goodman*, one feels here superficial cleverness, typical of a current genre. Present-day children, recognizing types, may read enough into the story to enjoy it, but the plot is too slim to be remembered long. (p. 570)

> *Ruth Hill Viguers, in* The Horn Book Magazine *(copyright © 1966, by The Horn Book, Inc., Boston), October, 1966.*

THOMAS J. FLEMING

Like all award winners, Emily Cheney Neville will spend the rest of her life competing with herself. Her "It's Like This, Cat" walked (or talked) off with the Newbery Medal several years ago. Is "The Seventeenth-Street Gang" a match for that champion? The answer must be a reluctant no.

Mrs. Neville's eye for the nuances of affection and exasperation between parents and children is still keen, and she creates believable characters, who talk and act like real children and adults. Everyone's favorite in this book is sure to be Minnow, Seventeenth Street's supercharged *femme fatale*. . . . But Minnow's charm is wasted on a very routine plot—the gang's hesitation about taking a new boy named Hollis into the group—and Mrs. Neville must resort to even more routine melodrama to resolve it. (pp. 42, 44)

> *Thomas J. Fleming, in* The New York Times Book Review *(© 1966 by The New York Times Company; reprinted by permission), November 6, 1966.*

ZENA SUTHERLAND

Capricious, mendacious, and notably hostile, Minnow dominates a group of boys and girls of mixed ages and backgrounds living in a heterogeneous New York neighborhood [in *The Seventeenth-Street Gang*]. . . . The resilient Minnow is an *enfant terrible*, but she is more nasty than vicious, and she is utterly believable. The shifting patterns of power plays within the gang are fascinating, as are the stratagems that the children use to maintain their privacy against adults. (p. 50)

> *Zena Sutherland, in* Saturday Review *(© 1966 by Saturday Review, Inc.; reprinted with permission), November 12, 1966.*

MARGERY FISHER

Of [Natalie Savage Carlson's *The Empty Schoolhouse*, Bella Rodman's *Lions in the Way*, and *Berries Goodman*], each pleading for tolerance, *Berries Goodman* seems to me the best balanced. The well-to-do suburb of Olcott does not care for Jews and forces them, by subtle pressure, to live a separate social life. . . . [Racial] antagonism is the cause of action, not the motive for the book. When Berries and Sidney are separated we see family relationships laid bare— the stupid power exercised by Sandra's parents, the appalling powerlessness of children to direct their lives or understand their parents' direction of them. All this emerges as Berries tells the story five years later, a little wiser but still leaving the reader to discover depths in the story for himself. Clever, witty, generous—the book is also, unobtrusively, very wise. (p. 836)

> *Margery Fisher, in her* Growing Point, *January, 1967.*

POLLY GOODWIN

The world Emily Cheney knew as a little girl in the 1920s will seem to today's children as foreign to their experience as a fairytale kingdom, as remote as a planet in outer space. But to Emily, the Place was very real—and secure—inhabited exclusively by Cheneys. . . .

[*Traveler from a Small Kingdom*] is Emily's nostalgic re-creation of that life. It moves at a leisurely pace as it tells of games and pranks with cousins, of holiday celebrations, of exploratory walks with [the governess] Mrs. Goodall, of experiments with their hens and pet goats. Gradually it takes Emily beyond her kingdom. . . .

Children love to know what it was like "when you were a little girl." With the storytelling skill and intuition that won her the Newbery award for *It's Like This, Cat*, Emily Neville makes her childhood and its setting both real and appealing. (p. 4)

Polly Goodwin, in Book World—Chicago Tribune, *Part II (© 1968 Postrib Corp.), May 5, 1968.*

ETHEL L. HEINS

To a generation of children growing up . . . in a world accustomed to war, violence, speed, and technology, [the almost uneventful re-creation of an extinct way of life in *Traveler from a Small Kingdom*] may seem limp and unreal. Perhaps an adult, savoring the reminiscences and the evocative writing, can introduce the book. (p. 335)

Ethel L. Heins, in The Horn Book Magazine *(copyright © 1968 by The Horn Book, Inc., Boston), June, 1968.*

ZENA SUTHERLAND

[*Fogarty*] has the candor and realism of the author's Newbery winner, *It's Like This, Cat* . . . , with a protagonist who is like so many of today's young adults, but no formula situations. The characterizations, not only of Fog but of all the minor characters, is magnificent. (p. 72)

Zena Sutherland, in Saturday Review *(© 1969 by Saturday Review, Inc.; reprinted with permission), November 8, 1969.*

When first met [in *Fogarty*] loafing in front of Malone's garage in Wilbur Flats, Dan Fogarty, twenty-three, college graduate and law school drop-out, is the "town flop"—as he caustically informs a preacher who, like his old schoolteacher, the retired idlers and almost everyone, would have him *be something.* . . . The scenes in and around the garage smack of early Saroyan—the same people stopping by to get gas and bandy Big Ideas, Fog and the preacher peppering each other with Biblical quotations; then we're in the East Village, where Fog sleeps with a self-protective waif, senses the futile drift, sees his play flop. (Oddly, this man who chose to confound Wilbur Flats seems wholly a child in New York.) . . . There's a little obscenity, plus the bedding of Yetta, but this isn't a children's book anyhow, just an adult bind without adult dimension. (p. 1203)

Kirkus Reviews *(copyright © 1969 The Kirkus Service, Inc.), November 15, 1969.*

RUTH HILL VIGUERS

Emily Neville's *It's Like This, Cat* . . . gives a wonderful sense of the sights, sounds, and smells of New York City. Dave Mitchell, fourteen and rebellious—"My father is always talking about how a dog can be very educational for a boy. This is one reason I got a cat"—tells his own story of a year of growing up, especially of going through the tunnel of impatience and irritation with his father and coming at last into the light. Mrs. Neville's second book, *Berries Goodman* . . . , has even more interesting characters and situations. It is the story of a city boy, newly arrived in the suburbs, who has his first brush with antisemitism. Berries Goodman and Sidney Fine, who have found much in common, do their best to keep adult prejudices from interfering with their friendship, but they cannot long maintain their easy, happy relationship in the face of parental pressures. Humor and perspective make it an absorbing story, not a social tract. The emotion underlying the straightforward storytelling makes the reader care greatly about the boys and their friendship. (pp. 595-96)

Ruth Hill Viguers, in A Critical History of Children's Literature, *by Cornelia Meigs, Anne Thaxter Eaton, Elizabeth Nesbitt, and Ruth Hill Viguers, edited by Cornelia Meigs (copyright © 1953, 1969 by Macmillan Publishing Co., Inc.), revised edition, Macmillan, 1969.*

JOSH GREENFELD

Once a domesticated preserve of games and whimsey and fancy, the new children's literature now deals with all the subjects that were once labeled "For Adults Only."

Emily Cheney Neville is certainly one of the better practitioners of the new children's literature. Her "It's Like This, Cat" won the prestigious Newbery Medal in 1964. In "Fogarty" she has an honest ear, a penchant for sharp simile ("He'd forgotten that city water tasted like warm Clorox"), the ability to encapsulate an endearing truth simply (" 'Why,' he thought, 'is it so hard to tell someone you *don't* love them?' ") and, moreover she knows how to underwrite a dramatic scene so that it reverberates with overtones ("He said, 'Don't cry.' Then, a little later, 'Why are you crying?' She broke away from him and said, 'If I knew why, I wouldn't be doing it!' "). Then why does her treatment of Fogarty, a young man caught in the drift of our times, finally seem so disappointingly tame and tepid? . . .

Indeed, there is something second grade and second hand about it all, like most simplistic television drama, tinted with condescension, coming up with stale, pat poses instead of trying to provide some exciting insight into the dynamics of neuroses. Compare Fogarty, with say, Benjamin, of "The Graduate" and one can easily begin to see the difference between old adult literature and so much of the new children's literature. Sex can overwhelm Benjamin, but Fogarty can't even be undermined by it: Charles Webb seems to be following his character, while author Neville seems to be leading hers toward predescribed moral direction with a didactic point of view. The result is that though "The Graduate" like any work of literature may ultimately only serve as a substitute for life, "Fogarty" like so many children's books seems to have as its justification only that it is a substitute for adult literature.

The whole process reeks to me of cultivated cop out. Children's Literature ignores its own potentialities, author Neville denies herself a legitimate literary quest, and kids—or young adults—are short-changed again, asked to settle for less just because they are no more than children. (p. 26)

Josh Greenfeld, in The New York Times Book Review *(© 1970 by The New York Times Company; reprinted by permission), January 11, 1970.*

DIANE G. STAVN

[*Fogarty*], ambitious in aim, is off-target in itself but better than most. . . . Like A. E. Johnson's *A Blues I Can Whistle* . . . , this book depicts the sentimental hold of a small town on even its more rebellious citizens, and features a sensitive young dropout hero who is getting over an unhappy romance, has some measure of artistic talent, and spars mentally with himself about his motivations to action. But *A Blues I Can Whistle* is more sophisticated stylistically, more intrinsically dramatic. Its protagonist, 19-year-old Cody, is recovering from an actual affair; Fog, from a hand-holding relationship. Cody's attempt to prevent his activist friend Barney's philosophically-inspired suicide makes political/social issues immediate and vivid; Fog's emotional shouting (pro ghetto children who have difficulty in school, anti hellfire interpretations of religion) is tedious. The book is obviously intended as a sympathetic record of the gradual maturation of a well-meaning slow bloomer. But, beside Cody, for example, young Fogarty palls. (p. 71)

> *Diane G. Stavn, in* School Library Journal *(reprinted from the January, 1970 issue of* School Library Journal, *published by R. R. Bowker Co. A Xerox Corporation; copyright © 1970), January, 1970.*

[*It's Like This, Cat*] is very American in content and atmosphere. The hero, Dave, acts, talks and thinks in a way which is not readily familiar to the British reader. Coney Island, the subway and the buses are not British in lay-out; and the British child may find it difficult to follow for this reason, but this is a very readable story and brilliantly written. (p. 102)

> The Junior Bookshelf, *April, 1970.*

[*Berries Goodman* is a] perceptive story of relationships for children of ten upwards.... There are two themes—a family moving into the country from New York and the way in which each member adjusts to the different kind of life, and the prejudice of a community towards the Jews in their area....

It is a story of conflict and, to an English reader, there is much that is unfamiliar, especially in the community's attitude towards the Jewish families which is carried to the length of confining them to one quarter and keeping out the children from the local schools. Nevertheless, this is a story which convinces and amuses and, at times, gives food for thoughtful re-assessment of values. (p. 305)

> The Junior Bookshelf, *October, 1970.*

MAY HILL ARBUTHNOT and ZENA SUTHERLAND

There is no startling drama in *It's Like This, Cat* . . . , but it is impressive both for its lightly humorous, easy style and the fidelity with which it portrays a fourteen-year-old boy, Dave, who tells the story. Dave has found the first girl with whom he really feels comfortable (her mother is delightfully sketched as an urban intellectual), and he learns, by seeing the relationship between his father and his friend, that his father really is a pretty good guy. The experience of seeing one's parents through a friend's eyes is a common one, usually revelatory and seldom touched on in books for young people.

Berries Goodman . . . looks back on the two years in which his family lived in a suburb, years in which he had a friend who was Jewish and learned the subtle signs of adult prejudice: the nuances of tone and the light dismissal of subjects with painful implications. He also learns that Sidney's mother is just as biased. The book is an invitation to better understanding, and its serious import is not lessened by a light humor. (p. 464)

> *May Hill Arbuthnot and Zena Sutherland, in their* Children and Books *(copyright © 1947, 1957, 1964, 1972 by Scott, Foresman and Company; reprinted by permission), fourth edition, Scott, Foresman, 1972.*

ELEANOR CAMERON

Chekhov pointed out that the great writer has a sense of absolute freedom within the discipline of his craft, within his moral point of view, his sense of aesthetic distance. He has reached that point where he can be himself to the utmost degree and can say it without descending to the meretricious, the vulgar, or to a cheap voyeurism. And I think that it is this sense of restriction—of not feeling perfectly free to express all he knows to be true of teenage sexual feelings and the teenagers' deepest attitudes toward them—that so often pulls the quality of the writer's work for this age down to the level of the bland and the superficial, to what Josh Greenfeld, in a review of Emily Neville's *Fogarty* [see excerpt above] called "the cultivated cop-out." That cop-out, he said, is what is the matter with most children's books. But what he meant by "the cultivated cop-out" in reference to Emily Neville's novel was her failure to communicate any real understanding of Fogarty as a man desiring a woman. She closed the door on that scene, and on Fogarty's emotions in that moment because she possibly hadn't the knowledge or the power or the courage to face them and delineate them in a way she could handle. And I was sharply resentful at finding a novel about a twenty-three-year-old man reviewed with children's books (and called by Greenfeld a children's book) simply because Emily Neville usually writes for teenagers. But resentful above all because "the cultivated cop-out" in a child's book would have nothing at all to do with lack of frankness about sexual love, but would result in an avoidance of truth regarding some facet of a child's complex emotions before the age of puberty. (pp. 113-14)

> *Eleanor Cameron, in* The Horn Book Magazine *(copyright © 1973 by Eleanor Cameron), February, 1973 (and reprinted in* Crosscurrents of Criticism: Horn Book Essays 1968-1977, *edited by Paul Heins, Horn Book, 1977).*

ERIC A. KIMMEL

The central issue of *Berries Goodman* is that of polite suburban anti-Semitism. . . . (p. 152)

Ms. Neville cannot really be criticized for not presenting a very clear picture of the central issues of Jewish life, for the main action does not involve Jewish characters in any roles other than secondary ones. Still, some points should be noted. Sidney Fine falls victim to a malady common to minority characters in similar situations. Because of the structure of the plot, it is important that he be seen as a sympathetic, regular guy, so nice that any dislike of him is revealed as foolish and unjustified. What really happens in this case and in similar ones is that the character becomes flat. Although Ms. Neville is especially gifted in capturing the speech and thought of children and adolescents, Sidney seems to have nothing to say about what it means to be Jewish in a hostile Gentile environment. A conversation between Berries and Sidney on this subject would have been memorable. However, it never occurs.

Sidney's mother is more interesting, bent on over-protecting her son from what she sees as an overtly hostile environment. But again, we never get a rational statement about her motives. We merely see her reacting, or over-reacting.

A far more serious criticism involves the handling of the issue of anti-Semitism, the book's main theme. We are shown the effects of anti-Semitism, but we never get down to its basic causes. The bigoted characters speak of Jewish ostentation, wealth, and pushiness. These are, obviously, pseudo-reasons. Poor, humble, clannish Jews are not liked any better. Yet, Ms. Neville never really deals with this rationalization directly, other than to try to link it to Hitler's ovens. Her refutation takes the view that since Jews are nice people who behave like everyone else, it is foolish to regard them as different and to dislike them for it. Such a view, adequate for 1952, is out-of-date today. It is as if one tried to explain away racism by stating that Blacks are like everyone else, except for a deeper tan. (pp. 152-53)

Eric A. Kimmel, in The Horn Book Magazine *(copyright © 1973 by The Horn Book, Inc., Boston), April 1973 (and reprinted in* Crosscurrents of Criticism: Horn Book Essays 1968-1977, *edited by Paul Heins, Horn Book, 1977).*

CAROLYN T. KINGSTON

The tragic moments of [*It's Like This, Cat*] ostensibly concern cats, but in a larger sense they are clarifications of two forms of loss.

The first tragic moment occurs after Cat has been seriously hurt in a fight. Cat often returns home wounded from his night rambles, but this time he comes close to death. Kate says that the animal can survive only one or two years in the back alleys, and Dave, loving his pet, realizes that he must decide whether to take Cat to the hospital for an operation. The boy places high value on his pet's masculinity and "catness" and cannot bear that this should be lost, but with tears in his eyes, he decides that the preservation of Cat's life must take precedence. At this moment, Dave becomes a tragic hero. Forced to choose between "two goods," he solves the difficult problem alone, taking the way that seems best, although it involves the loss of something he values. He has found the tragic balance, knowing that it is important to him to keep Cat from further suffering. "I'm sorry," he tells his pet, before they leave for the hospital. "Be tough, Cat, anyway, will you?" (p. 153)

The second tragic moment again involves a cat—this time, one of Kate's kittens. After the spinster inherits her fortune, her quiet apartment is suddenly crowded with reporters and curious persons. A litter of new kittens has recently been born, among them a strong young cat who is of an adventurous spirit and will not stay in his box to avoid the unaccustomed traffic. But his fearlessness becomes his undoing; one of the reporters carelessly steps on him, wounding him horribly. With one swift blow, Kate ends the kitten's agony, and then, without tears, disposes of its corpse in the garbage. To the undiscerning observer it might seem that Kate's action was hardhearted. It is not. She has loved the kitten. But Kate is tough—durable and resilient in spirit. Realizing that the kitten cannot survive, she wastes no time in useless remorse, nor does she permit it to suffer.

These two moments contain the tragic essence. Both present situations in which inevitable tragedy is faced without sentimentality, but with realism and a willingness to go on. The second moment underscores the illumination Dave has received during the first encounter with tragedy. He understands what it means to be tough in the best sense of the word, for it is this resiliency that helps to balance inevitable loss with some gain of the spirit, a clarification that is the cathartic yield of the story. Shakespeare said it more poetically, but his meaning was essentially the same.

Surveying the bloody deeds of a fateful night, Lady MacBeth tells her husband, "What's done, cannot be undone."

The essence of this story could have been washed away with tears if it had been written in a sentimental vein, but Emily Neville, the author, is as tough as her characters. One must look hard to find the deep compassion swelling beneath her unemotional words. This is a story about strays. Cat is called "Cat" because he represents all homeless creatures—loveless and nameless until they find affection and a place to be. The author cares about Tom, about Dave's girlfriend, about Dave and Kate and all the strays, but her emotion has high tensile strength—the kind of strength these characters can understand.

Many stories only seem to be realistic. *It's Like This, Cat* is a realistic story in every sense of the word. Its title states the author's view. "This is the way life is," she says. "What will you do about it?" The incidents she has chosen around which to wrap her tragic atmosphere have an element of shock in them. Their topics do not make polite conversation. But they are of the stuff of life.

The scene of the tale is a none-too-affluent section of a tough city—New York. With its dirt and danger, it is a perfect setting for the two-fisted clarification the story conveys. But despite the realism of unsavory back alleys and inelegant characters, the story rises above the mere presentation of a realistic situation, into the beauty of the tragic realm, because of the author's intense spirit of affirmation. Although loss may occur in life, she seems to say, a balance may be achieved if one can accept the inevitable and go on. Without preachment, she conveys the idea that only spiritual toughness can balance tragedy. (pp. 153-55)

Carolyn T. Kingston, in her The Tragic Mode in Children's Literature *(copyright © 1974 by Teachers College, Columbia University; reprinted by permission of the publisher), Teachers College Press, 1974.*

Almost aimlessly, the narrative [of *Garden of Broken Glass*] skips from one of the four principals' viewpoints to the next, but mostly this is about Brian, who is helped by the others (in the closest thing to a main plot) to face his miserable family situation. It's not that thin—there are minor characters and involving scenes . . . but it is that blandly, painlessly integrated. But even disregarding racial tensions, we wonder at Brian's finding any three such stronger, surer kids who are this indulgent of his dreamy, bumbling ways. (p. 612)

Kirkus Reviews (copyright © 1975 The Kirkus Service, Inc.), June 1, 1975.

DORIS ORGEL

Mrs. Neville makes the slum setting [of " Garden of Broken Glass"] palpably real. Her four main characters have plenty of problems: living on the edge of despair with an abusive drunk for a mother, as Brian, the one white boy, does; being fat, and, as 13-year-old Martha fears, pregnant; knowing, as Dwayne and his girlfriend Melvita do, that "without money, you is nothin!" But problems, as Mrs. Neville knows, are only interesting if the characters move and breathe and think and feel.

Martha is philosophical beyond her years, and perhaps,

beyond belief. The street talk doesn't always ring true. Now and then the author, whose great strength is seeing people from inside, makes extraneous, sociological-sounding comments. Despite such faults, this is an honest, quite powerful book. I hope lots of kids read it. I can even imagine it making a difference in a few of their lives.

> Doris Orgel, "*Garden of Broken Glass*," *in* The New York Times Book Review (© *1975 by The New York Times Company; reprinted by permission), June 15, 1975, p. 8.*

[*Garden of Broken Glass*] is a story of wonderful young people, struggling against heavy odds to avoid being mortally scarred by the sharp edges of a racist and uncaring society. (p. 241)

The oppression of poverty and racism is depicted without evoking sentimental pity for the young characters, who have strengths and are lovable, but who are not idealized. The *Garden of Broken Glass* shows us a spaghetti, Kool-Aid and soda pop world of poverty in which humor, warmth and concern for others are the key to survival and growth. (p. 242)

> Human (and Anti-Human) Values in Children's Books: A Content Rating Instrument for Educators and Concerned Parents, *prepared by CIBC Racism and Sexism Resource Center for Educators (copyright © by the Council on Interracial Books for Children, Inc.; all rights reserved), The Council on Interracial Books for Children, Inc., 1976.*

Andre Norton

1912-

(Pseudonym of Alice Mary Norton; has also written under pseudonym of Andrew North) American novelist, short story writer, and editor. Although she began her literary career by writing historical novels in the 1930s, Norton turned to science fiction in the 1950s and it is in this genre that she has made her most significant contribution. She is generally regarded as one of the foremost writers of "space opera", and is certainly one of the best-selling women authors in the field. As a teenager Norton planned on a career as a history teacher; she eventually became a children's librarian and a professional writer. Both her early interest in history and her library training in research have played significant roles in her writing. Norton extensively researches each of her books, using folklore, legends, history (especially Greek and Roman), archeology, anthropology, and the occult in her fiction. Her careful scholarship is evident in her work, which is frequently praised for its convincing, detailed backgrounds. Norton's first novel, *The Prince Commands*, was accepted for publication before she was 21. She continued to write primarily historical fiction until the 1940s, when she turned to adventure and spy stories. An espionage novel, *The Sword Is Drawn*, was given an award by the Netherlands government in 1946 for its portrayal of that nation at war. Although she had been writing science fiction sporadically for some time, it was only after she had edited several science fiction anthologies that Norton found a publisher for her first science fiction novel, *Star Man's Son*. The success of this book and Norton's subsequent titles helped to open the field for other writers. She aims most of her fiction at a young adult audience; however, her work is also read by a considerable number of adults. Strong elements of fantasy and magic color much of her science fiction, and she has written some pure fantasies. Norton's universe is menacing, with the lines of Good versus Evil clearly drawn. Ambiguity has little place in her vision, and her characters are either heroes or villains. For this reason her works have been likened to Westerns, and her moral certainty has led some critics to consider her pompous or didactic. Although her vision is of a hostile universe, Norton is essentially an optimist, and her protagonists are given the courage and resourcefulness to prevail against tremendous odds. (See also *Contemporary Authors*, Vols. 1-4, rev. ed., and *Something about the Author*, Vol. 1.)

MARGARET ERNST

For those who like a pirate story and a mystery, "Scarface" is a fine one, well written, with plenty of action. . . .

A map of the West Indies would have been a useful addition. And why will authors continue to make their people talk in hard-to-pronounce dialect when no young person likes to read it? As one boy said to me: "I spend so much time figuring out how the words sound that I lose sight of what they mean." Luckily, only a few of . . . Norton's lesser pirates drop "h's" all over the deck. (p. 6)

> *Margaret Ernst, in* New York Herald Tribune Book Review (© *I.H.T. Corporation; reprinted by permission), September 12, 1948.*

MERRITT P. ALLEN

Older readers will compare this well-written and -plotted story ["Scarface"] with Howard Pyle. It has humor and atmosphere and action that never falter. Even the minor characters are sharply drawn. It is "strong meat." There is no softening of the brutality and coarseness of the "men from the sea." To older boys and girls and to adults it will probably emerge as one of the outstanding adventure stories of the year. (p. 37)

> *Merritt P. Allen, in* The Saturday Review of Literature *(copyright, 1948, by The Saturday Review Co., Inc.; reprinted with permission), October 16, 1948.*

RALPH ADAMS BROWN

The story [of "Scarface"] has a complicated and suspense-filled plot. The action is fast and the characterization is excellent. The historical background is accurate. All combine to produce a top-notch story. One of the tests of a good junior novel is the difficulty the youngsters have in getting the book away from their dads. This one should produce a genuine tug-of-war—it is that good. (p. 4)

> *Ralph Adams Brown, in* The New York Times Book Review (© *1948 by The New York Times Company; reprinted by permission), November 14, 1948.*

ALICE M. JORDAN

[*Scarface*] is a vigorous, exciting story dealing with the days when the islands of the West Indies were infested with fearless, bloodthirsty pirates. In particular, it tells about the course of events by which a boy captured in infancy, ill-treated and enslaved by one of the evil and most daring of the "Brothers of the Coast," solved the mystery of his identity. The story has full share of brutality in the tradition of such tales, but it holds to the history of the period and will be eagerly read by young people. (p. 42)

> Alice M. Jordan, in The Horn Book Magazine *(copyrighted, 1949, by The Horn Book, Inc., Boston), January-February 1949.*

ELLEN LEWIS BUELL

Although "Star Man's Son: 2250 A. D." is not science fiction in the strict sense (no space suits or other alluring gadgets) it ought to interest any young reader who has cast a speculative eye upon the future. As a picture of America approximately two centuries after an atomic war it is grim and thought-provoking even if on second thought it isn't wholly convincing. It's a little hard to believe that descendants of a picked group of scientists could have been reduced to quite such a primitive life as is described.

Granting this doubtful premise, however, this is a robust story with a serious theme. . . . Fors' adventures with nightmarish beasts, his encounters with other wandering tribes, his friendship with a dark young hunter, all stress the theme that men cannot afford to be suspicious of each others' differences if they wish to survive.

> Ellen Lewis Buell, "After the Blow-Up," *in* The New York Times Book Review *(© 1952 by The New York Times Company; reprinted by permission), August 31, 1952, p. 12.*

H. H. HOLMES

["Star Rangers" is] an imaginative and moving historical novel. This is a historical novel of the collapse of a decadent Galactic Empire; but it obtains its powerful effect by restricting its action to a small area of the surface of one planet and to the problems of a group of spacemen, abandoned by the empire they had lived only to serve. No cut-and-dried star hopping here, but oddly all the more impact of the awe and wonder of space—as the ocean may have more meaning to a castaway than to a trans-oceanic plane passenger. The plot involves a surprise that should not be mentioned here—an old theme, but one I've never seen so well handled before. In all, an excellent book for the new science fiction reader, and even for the veteran a refreshingly readable one. (p. 9)

> H. H. Holmes, in New York Herald Tribune Book Review *(© I.H.T. Corporation; reprinted by permission), August 23, 1953.*

Superior cloak and dagger, [at *Sword's Points*] follows the trail of quiet, studious 19-year-old Quinn Anders as he is taken on by an independent under-cover outfit, on the Free World's side, and sent to find a valuable set of Belgian statuettes whose large purchase price could be used by the Russians. As carefully and excitingly planned as the operation itself, the book is suspense all the way. . . . Spellbinding and as adept as Andre Norton's more familiar science fiction. (p. 390)

> Virginia Kirkus' Bookshop Service, *July 1, 1954.*

LEARNED T. BULMAN

An excellent fabrication of old and new science-fiction ideas, "The Stars Are Ours!" is based on the theme that man's desire for personal liberty can overcome all adversity. Some readers may feel the ending is incomplete, and

that too much happens in too few chapters, but even they will agree that this is a rip-snorting adventure tale.

> Learned T. Bulman, "Ad Astra," in The New York Times Book Review *(© 1954 by The New York Times Company; reprinted by permission), August 29, 1954, p. 18.*

VIRGINIA HAVILAND

["Yankee Privateer"] is a full-length tale of historical intrigue with more than enough action for one volume as the author invents one hair-raising catastrophe and escape after another, with a tempo that increases rapidly from a moderate beginning. . . .

Among unusual scenes of action Plymouth's Old Mill Prison with its fully described regime stands out particularly.

This is not the best of this author's stories, which are very good indeed, but it is excellent historical adventure, noteworthy for its interpretation of privateering from American, British, and French angles. (p. 14)

> Virginia Haviland, in New York Herald Tribune Book Review *(© I.H.T. Corporation; reprinted by permission), May 15, 1955.*

ROBERT BERKVIST

Two highly diverting offerings from André Norton will not disappoint those who have come to appreciate her flair for the unusual. . . . ["The Time Traders"] combines some fact with much fantasy to produce a believable result. Time travel is not new in science fiction, nor is the anti-social hero a particularly fresh type, but in Miss Norton's skilled hands the story of Ross Murdock's adventures in the past . . . makes fascinating reading.

Time also is an important factor in "Star Gate" . . . , in which Miss Norton again demonstrates her superb talent for creating and sustaining a world of foreign moods. Gorth is such a world . . . torn by a struggle between good and evil. Miss Norton has captured the flavor of a Beowulfian folk epic so thoroughly that some readers may find the going a bit thick at first, but when one has learned how to separate the Styrs from the Wurds and mords the story moves briskly along. (p. 18)

> Robert Berkvist, in The New York Times Book Review *(© 1958 by The New York Times Company; reprinted by permission), December 14, 1958.*

ELAINE SIMPSON

As always, Miss Norton writes an exciting story for SF readers. This reviewer was annoyed by the fact [in *The Beast Master*] that the author has merely rewritten a cowboy-and-Indian story in an alien situation and with the addition of SF terms and trappings: the herds, rustler nesters, trail drive, fights in the frontier saloon, plains natives, etc., etc. are all there. However, perhaps this will not bother teen-agers who have not read westerns. Also, the conclusion is the least convincing of any of this author's books, but even so, this is better than much current SF. (p. 2)

> Elaine Simpson, in Junior Libraries *(reprinted from the September, 1959 issue of* Junior Libraries, *published by R. R. Bowker Co. A Xerox Corporation; copyright © 1959), September, 1959.*

ROBERT BERKVIST

"The Beast Master" might easily have been just another Western played in futuristic terms. Miss Norton, however, endows the story of a homeless, revenge-driven man with her own inimitable touch, blending an acute sense of primitive mystery with still another of her well-conceived foreign worlds. The result is a compelling and compassionate tale. (p. 32)

> *Robert Berkvist, in* The New York Times Book Review *(© 1960 by The New York Times Company; reprinted by permission), January 31, 1960.*

RICHARD M. BUCK

This boys' adventure story of Rebel scouts in the Civil War [*Ride Proud, Rebel!*] is undistinguished, with pedestrian style and prosaic dialogue. . . . Little dramatic conflict, tension, or suspense, and scant character development will not attract many readers. Attempts to set Southern dialect into type are unsuccessful; the "suhs" and "heahs" are distracting. Not recommended. (p. 1996)

> *Richard M. Buck, in* Library Journal *(reprinted from* Library Journal, *May 15, 1961; published by R. R. Bowker Co. (a Xerox company); copyright © 1961 by Xerox Corporation), May 15, 1961.*

[*Judgment on Janus*] is "a science fiction novel," but in spite of its considerable flights of imagination, the flights into space are a less important part of it, and one feels that it scarecely gets into that category. It is an American story of uneven quality which improves in the second half of the book. In the earlier part the conversation belongs much more to the Wild West, and it is indeed a relief when the author drops it later and words and spelling return to normal—albeit American normal. . . . Miss Norton does not quite succeed with this novel, but deserves credit for some very good writing in the second half of it. (p. 317)

The Junior Bookshelf, *November, 1964.*

JANE MANTHORNE

In her latest two S-F concoctions [Andre Norton] shows the varied possibilities of inventiveness within her genre. [*Quest Crosstime*] is a political, villains-and-good-guys adventure, earthbound, with ingenious development of time-travel. . . . Particularly imaginative are the pictures of worlds, like E625, in which crucial alterations of events change the future altogether, so that the United States never comes into being, pre-empted by a part-Mayan, part-English civilization. This intriguing adventure will lure girls into S-F fandom since the lead characters are mind-linked twin girls. . . . (p. 636)

Whereas adventure is paramount in *Quest Crosstime*, atmosphere dominates *The X Factor*. . . . The author goes far beyond good plotting and peopling of fiction to construct a fantastic never-never-land of new color, new sound, new motion. Readers feel truly like off-worlders with off-world eyes suddenly gazing for the first time on obscene creatures of slime, or enchanting red and silver woodlands, or the shadow people of Xcothal. (pp. 636-37)

> *Jane Manthorne, in* The Horn Book Magazine *(copyright © 1965, by The Horn Book, Inc., Boston), December, 1965.*

ALAN MADSEN

Of the two most recent Andre Norton novels, *The X Factor* and *Quest Crosstime, The X Factor* begins with the most promise; but it fails to fulfill that promise. . . .

While this novel might have held "a mirror up to nature," it avoids a most significant issue for the adolescent: how is a man to come to terms with his physical makeup in his *own* culture? Moreover, Norton relies on the cliche that the physically handicapped possess some special affinity for, and sensitivity to, the natural world. Here this cliche is dressed out as "thought projection." Neither the science, which borders on mysticism, nor the slow-moving action will make this novel appeal to younger readers.

Although *Quest Crosstime* is potentially more interesting fare for girls than *The X Factor*, the introductory exposition is so difficult to follow that many readers will never get past the opening chapter. . . . (p. 10)

> *Alan Madsen, in* Chicago Tribune Book Week *(copyright © 1966 by The Chicago Sun-Times; reprinted by permission from The Chicago Sun-Times), February 27, 1966.*

Lord of Thunder takes place on the same planet as an earlier story of Hosteen Storm, the Terran relocated to Arzor, which in these pages was compared with space "western." Although this begins and to a limited extent continues in a similar vein, it diverges fairly soon into complicated scientific ramifications incorporating a system of "translation" of the human body from one location to another by instantaneous means. This is never explained but it accounts for almost half the suspense of the plot. The scientific background to these "translations" is an essential element of the plot also, as it is the overt evidence of a plan to overthrow the political system of Arzor with its duality of social groups and the complications of prejudice among the Terrans against the "natives." It does not give the impression of being so completely successful a book as *The Beast Master* but it is still a good yarn. (p. 315)

The Junior Bookshelf, *October, 1966.*

The problems which may arise if the proliferation of mutants is ever accomplished in a radiation-ridden world are partly explored in [*The X Factor*, a] story of the fate of such a mutant [Diskan Fentress]. . . . The author's main intention appears to be to depict the regeneration of Fentress, enabling him to find a purpose in existence. . . . (p. 135)

The Junior Bookshelf, *April, 1967.*

After the initial shock of finding Arthur and Merlin transported to America, [*Steel Magic*] can be enjoyed thoroughly.

Three children find their way through a deserted garden into the land of Avalon, from whence they cannot return until they free the land from the powers of evil. They are the only ones who can handle iron and steel without harm, and armed with the cutlery from their picnic basket they set out to recover the three magic talismans that have fallen into the hands of the evil powers. Mrs. Norton does not have William Mayne's masterly touch when it comes to transporting her characters to and from present day reality, but she does handle this difficult journey far better than many, and she tells a very good tale. (p. 172)

The Junior Bookshelf, *June, 1967.*

MARGARET A. DORSEY

With Miss Norton's usual skilled writing, solid construction and sympathetic characters, [*Operation Time Search*] is a pleasure to read and to recommend. It begins when a government project's attempt to break through to an alternate world accidentally projects photographer Ray Osborne thousands of years back in time. In this distant era, Atlantis is a powerful but evil nation, now at war with Mu, whose people worship the purity of the Flame. . . . There is little here of the provocative speculation, insight or satire which characterizes the best adult science fiction, just a good moralistic adventure story (with a slightly surprising end) in which the righteous Murians are pitted against the evil rulers of Atlantis. (p. 134)

> *Margaret A. Dorsey, in* School Library Journal *(reprinted from the September, 1967 issue of* School Library Journal, *published by R. R. Bowker Co. A Xerox Corporation; copyright* © *1967), September, 1967.*

Miss Norton's extraordinary imagination is again at work [in *The Zero Stone*] as she reels her hero from a city where they choose sacrificial victims by lottery to a ship where he is condemned as a plague victim through space sans ship where the "Zero stone" acts as a strange propellant to a planet with hidden tombs bearing the bodies of the "Forerunner races," creatures of legend. Good sustaining action in what could be the start of a very nice series. (p. 191)

> *Kirkus Service (copyright* © *1968 Virginia Kirkus' Service, Inc.), February 15, 1968.*

By now it is a truism to say that fantasy must be anchored by a convincing and realistic background. But this can be taken further. Ideally, fantasy and reality should reach the same level of intensity and maturity. Fantasy loses its potential power if the real background, though convincing itself, is also in some senses too lightweight for it.

For this is the chief criticism to be made of Andre Norton's interesting and accomplished *Octagon Magic*. . . . [This is a] very subtle and delicate story; in which little is explained but everything explicable; in which the overtones, the implications are fascinating. The fantasy is marvellously controlled; the careful, loving use of detail reminiscent occasionally of Lucy Boston's work. . . . You are slid imperceptibly from one world to another, never sure how and when the transition will come. Similarly you are given no simple answers. Miss Ashemeade has all the moral severity of her generation; but this is part of her character, not merely the simplistic morality which it didactically expressed in the everyday background of school life. Here the polite introduction of the colour problem in Lorrie's friend Elizabeth is typical. So, too, is the moral for lonely Lorrie: learn to join in dear, be friendly with those with whom you haven't much in common—you will be popular in the end. All the lonely misfits sigh and wish it was as easy as that.

It is as if the fantasy world frees Miss Norton's adult sensibilities—whereas in the real world she is audience conscious and afraid of ambiguity and uncertainty. It seems a pity in this sometimes illuminating and beautiful book, like mouthfuls of porridge in syllabub. (p. 584)

> *The Times Literary Supplement (*© *Times Newspapers Ltd. (London) 1968; reproduced from* The Times Literary Supplement *by permission), June 6, 1968.*

One of the valid remaining distinguishing tests of science fiction is that of thoroughness, distinction in which can raise an exceptional novel above the high level now achieved by most published work in this field. [In *Star Man's Son*] Mrs. Norton wins high regard as the mere length of this work shows. Her situation this time is also fraught with novel possibilities since the period of her story, like that of *Things to Come*, is the one which follows a disastrous nuclear war. . . . To say much more would rob the reader of agreeable reactions of surprise but it must be repeated that Mrs. Norton's treatment is thorough in at least two ways: the implications of the initial situation are fully explored, and the episodes which constitute the plot are developed to the fullest possible extent this side of probability; there is no hint of scrappiness in the writing and this still seems a prerequisite of successful science fiction which aims to emulate the work of the classical masters in this genre. The hero-figure's environment and the characters which oppose or assist him are full of interest in themselves as well as moving the story along very capably. (p. 244)

> *The Junior Bookshelf, August, 1968.*

In the beginning [of *Postmarked the Stars*] Dane Thorson wakes up with the headache the reader will have by the close. This is one of [Andre Norton's] uninhibited efforts where the plot gives up and anything goes. With more "monsters," "oozings" and "blobs" than you can shake a stun gun at. . . . This time Miss Norton's energy is enervating. (p. 1010)

> *Kirkus Reviews (copyright* © *1969 The Kirkus Service, Inc.), September 15, 1969.*

[*Dark Piper* is an] imaginative eventful and fast moving tale but, while one accepts—indeed now expects—an air of unreality in a Science Fiction story, it is unfortunate that this extends so much to the characters, who do not seem to come alive across the ages and through space but retain that air of remoteness. (p. 391)

> *The Junior Bookshelf, December, 1969.*

For at least three-quarters of its duration [*Moon of the Three Rings*] is hard to put down though it appears to lose a little of its fervour as the story closes. Though it could be classed as science fiction, the other-worlds depicted have not the hard, bright patina of much futuristic writing in this genre. Although the ship which takes Krip Vorland to Yiktor is the most advanced imaginable, the society which he visits is at least pre-medieval in its primitive way of life. Thus the same atmosphere which might prevail in a tale of the Great Khan is superimposed on a space-age narrative with the most startling results. Add to this the interest of a kind of sect whose mission is the practice of communication with the animal world and occasionally a metamorphosis into it and you have a sort of grand fairy tale of the interplanetary era. All the normal ingredients of the adventure story proper are here; plot and counter-plot, ambush and escape, rebellion and master-spy contribute to the action, and even the search for the long-lost sister gambit (rather than gimmick) fits dramatically into the pattern of events. It entirely commands the 'willing suspension of disbelief' upon which so many great fictional experiences depend and repays that relaxation with scarcely a pang of scepticism. (pp. 391-92)

The Junior Bookshelf, *December, 1969.*

BARRY McGHAN

It is sometimes unfair to describe an author's writing in a single phrase. However, Andre Norton's stories, more easily classified than many, might be called "romantic adventure"—akin to tales of island castaways, cowboys and indians, and knightly quests. Her heroes are of epic size; her books, filled with action, peril, and mystery, are rich with complex and colourful descriptions of settings, characters, and societies.

Certain themes occur in story after story, There is the "beast master" theme, a quasi-symbiotic relationship between men and animals that involves some kind of direct mind-to-mind communication. There is the "space-opera," often involving a galactic empire (or two). There is the "ancient race" theme, the concept of an old and mysteriously powerful culture that lurks in the background. There is time travel, and the aftermath-of-atomic-war theme. In addition, nearly all books written since 1963 contain the themes of witch powers and parallel universes.

P. Schuyler Miller claims that a prime attraction of this author's writing is that she introduces many intriguing ideas that are never completely wrapped up at the end of the book, thus leaving something to be filled in by the reader's own imagination. He points out that her stories are ageless in the sense that they are set on exotic and far-flung worlds that science cannot make commonplace (at least in the foreseeable future). But despite everything in her favour her work is stigmatised by the appellation "escape literature." (p. 129)

[Why is there an] absence of critical recognition and what can we expect from here on?

During the Fifties and early Sixties literary interest in s.f. shifted to "mental" or subjective events, viewed in themselves or in their relationship to external events in the "real" world—with the adventure story being relegated by critics to the domain of juvenilia. This "demotion" made it easy for critics to dismiss Andre Norton as just another female writer of children's books. (Without trying to settle the question of what is important or acceptable as science fiction, I can observe the snobbery of ignoring work simply because it does not bear the stamp of currently "important" writing.)

Recent years, however, have seen a revival of interest in the fantasy adventures of [Edgar Rice] Burroughs, [Robert] Howard, [Ray] Cummings, and [A.] Merrit . . . , each of whom offers escape to a world more "natural" than our own, where existence is unspoiled by the artificialities of urban civilisation. Of course, Andre Norton returns directly to the primitive mode only in her beast-master and aftermath-of-atomic-war themes, but in each instance the hero's courage and resourcefulness accomplish what city-bred degeneracy could not. Although her writing lacks a single archetypal figure to represent our primitive selves (like Tarzan or Conan), it belongs to the same general *class* as Burroughs' and Howard's and so, I believe, will be given the same critical attention these authors are starting to receive.

Also, with her recent Witch World series, Norton shares the literary primitivism exemplified in the Sword and Sorcery of veteran contemporaries like [Fritz] Leiber and [L.

Sprague] de Camp and newer writers like Ted White, Michael Moorcock, and Lin Carter. Amongst this group, perhaps, Andre Norton will receive the type of recognition she lacked while apart from any other. (pp. 129-30)

Barry McGhan, "Andre Norton: Why Has She Been Neglected?" in Riverside Quarterly *(copyright 1970 by Leland Sapiro), January, 1970, pp. 128-31.*

MARGARET A. DORSEY

After several gripping opening pages in which Dane Thorson, assistant cargo master of a free trader spaceship, awakes from attempted poisoning in unknown surroundings, [*Postmarked the Stars*] lapses into standard cosmic cops and robbers. . . . There's less to the plot than meets the eye, as the last half of the book consists mainly of repetitive captures and escapes; also, the characterizations, dull and two-dimensional, do not live up to the standards of Miss Norton's other books. This book is not likely to win her new readers, and will only disappoint her many fans. (p. 1947)

Margaret A. Dorsey, in School Library Journal *(reprinted from the May, 1970 issue of* School Library Journal, *published by R. R. Bowker Co. A Xerox Corporation; copyright © 1970), May, 1970.*

BAIRD SEARLES

The prolific Andre Norton's science fiction adventures tend to be full of sound and fury, the narrative lines going around in circles rather than forward to a satisfying conclusion. In "Ice Crown" . . . , we are again in the far future with a young female protagonist (a welcome change) who goes with her archeologist uncle to investigate prehuman remains on the planet Clio. They discover the medieval culture thereon to be an artificially conditioned one, set up by long gone, off-world dictators and maintained by planted machine controls. Strictly against orders, the girl gets involved with local dynastic squabbles. Characterization, plot and logic are too often sacrificed to keep the action going. (p. 47)

Baird Searles, in The New York Times Book Review *(© 1970 by The New York Times Company; reprinted by permission), September 20, 1970.*

DIANE FARRELL

A skillful intertwining of unlikely elements—folklore and spacelore, sorcery and science—generates an engrossing adventure [in *Dread Companion*]. . . . Despite its elaborate setting, this science-fiction fantasy boils down to a suspenseful and satisfying teen-age romance. . . . (pp. 483-84)

Diane Farrell, in The Horn Book Magazine *(copyright © 1970 by The Horn Book, Inc.), October, 1970.*

ELIZABETH HAYNES

Miss Norton's contributions have ranged from virtually pure SF to almost equally pure fantasy. [*Dread Companion*] leans heavily toward the latter and is somewhat below her usual high standard. . . . Miss Norton's skill at style and characterization give the book readability and interest, but the plot has a murky vagueness at times. However, female protagonists are rare in juvenile SF, and even a below-average Norton is better than much of the SF//fantasy floating around today. (p. 64)

Elizabeth Haynes, in School Library Journal *(reprinted from the December, 1970 issue of* School Library Journal, *published by R. R. Bowker Co. A Xerox Corporation; copyright © 1970), December, 1970.*

HUGH CRAGO

Andre Norton is a prolific author and like most prolific authors, she has her off-moments. Regrettably, *Ice Crown* appears to have been written in one of them. This story of Roane, the efficient but love-starved girl from an advanced world who becomes embroiled in cloak and dagger work among the aristocracy of the primitive planet Clio, could have been a good one. But after a promising (if extremely compressed and allusive) start, it drags its weary length out . . . without ever really convincing the reader that what is happening matters very much. Except where Roane is facing the antagonism of her own people, and the conflict of loyalties and ways of thinking comes into sharp focus, I was simply bored—no recommendation for a book intended for young readers. The characters are mostly cardboard, the writing tired, the details of life on Clio thin in the extreme—apart from 'duocorns' as horse-equivalents, everything is much the same as in seventeenth century England. Even the plot creaks a bit at times, and Roane's kit of sophisticated tools and weapons is too easy a way of getting her out of trouble, surely? Super-hero stuff like this shouldn't be necessary. . . . ['Potboiler'] is a hard word, but I think it applies here. (p. 91)

Hugh Crago, in Children's Book Review *(© 1971 by Five Owls Press Ltd.; all rights reserved), June, 1971.*

[*Ice Crown*] is another of Andre Norton's off-world stories about a quest on Clio. Clio is a closed planet, closed because its inhabitants have been brain-washed by the Psychocrats (now overthrown) and must not be disturbed by truth. Norton fans will be hooked from the outset, but new readers must be warned that she is an exacting author who demands attentive reading. A whole history and way of life is painted in while the story flows on. The story line is strong. . . . This is a story of real people, of a girl's developing character and the conflicts she must face. The action is set in a fantastic background which is, as always, utterly believable because of Andre Norton's unique imagination and vivid precise writing. (p. 767)

The Times Literary Supplement *(© Times Newspapers Ltd. (London) 1971; reproduced from* The Times Literary Supplement *by permission), July 2, 1971.*

SHERYL B. ANDREWS

In [*Exiles of the Stars,*] the sequel to *Moon of Three Rings,* [Andre Norton] continues with the story of Krip Vorlund, a Free Trader in some future eon, who through shapechanging entered into the body of a wild animal and then, being unable ever again to regain his original form, was forced to claim as his own the body of a Thassa named Maquad. As in the first book, the Thassa Moon Singer Maelen is integrally bound to Krip although she no longer wears the guise of a woman, having been condemned by her people to take the body of her animal-friend Vors when

her own body was broken and dying. . . . The story is told in the first person by Maelen and Krip in alternating though not ordered sequential chapters; and though the final explanations for the motivations of the four ancient crowned beings who seek to control the life force of the [Free Trader ship] *Lydis'* crew remain a bit nebulous, the fast pace of the story and the development of the two major characters carries even the literal-minded reader past the stage of mundane questioning to enjoyment. (pp. 389-90)

Sheryl B. Andrews, in The Horn Book Magazine *(copyright © 1971 by The Horn Book, Inc., Boston), August, 1971.*

[*Shadow Hawk*] will receive a warm welcome, although this is not in [Norton's] popular science-fiction style. Here we have a convincing reconstruction of an aspect of Ancient Egypt in about 2000 B.C. . . . Although the book is not easy reading and has a surfeit of names, it nevertheless presents a very forceful picture of life in Egypt at that time. The military and other actions are handled with great skill and excitement, and the main characters are well drawn. (p. 253)

The Junior Bookshelf, *August, 1971.*

A new departure by an author better known as a writer of science fiction. [In *Bertie and May*] Andre Norton tells of her mother's childhood in Ohio nearly one hundred years ago. The story is founded on her mother's own written account and is supplemented by the many anecdotes she told to her children and grandchildren before her death at 95. The result is a convincing picture of two little sisters and the way of life in the 1870's. It was an unsettled life, for the sisters' father was a miller at a time when his kind of milling was almost outdated, but loyalty and family unity surmounted the hardships.

The adult reader inevitably compares this chronicle with the Laura Wilder books, although the background is not one of pioneer life. Andre Norton's is a much slighter work and the reader's sympathies are not as totally involved with Bertie and May as with Laura. Nevertheless, this is an engaging picture of a real family in a rural township in America and it has humour and warmth. (p. 308)

The Junior Bookshelf, *October, 1971.*

In some ways Mrs. Norton's [*Postmarked the Stars*] is a complicated game of hide-and-seek in outer space, first on board the free-trading spaceship, Solar Queen, eventually on Trewsworld, a planet whose constitutional and industrial status is being undermined by a corrupt scientific organisation. . . . On Trewsworld an exhilarating sequence of discoveries and escapes keeps the reader on tenterhooks for what seems a very long time. Mrs. Norton's detail is, as always, convincing, and her extension of the possibilities of mutation in animal strains carries fascinating but forbidding implications for the human race. (p. 321)

The Junior Bookshelf, *October, 1971.*

JOHN ROWE TOWNSEND

Although [Andre Norton's] fantasies and historical stories have merit, it seems to me that the science fiction is the most interesting part of her work and the basis of her reputation.

Miss Norton's science fiction books are, in the main, 'space opera': stories of galactic and inter-galactic adventure. This is the category of science fiction which is least likely to be found acceptable by the literati. Space opera is associated with pulp magazines, and is apt to be written off on superficial inspection as wild, undisciplined stuff, all about clashing fleets of spaceships, battles with bug-eyed monsters, death and destruction by ray-gun: action of meaningless violence in settings which are spatially enormous but imaginatively minute. Andre Norton has used the standard ingredients of space opera without undue inhibition, but they are not the be-all and end-all of her work. The sheer size of her world, which is infinitely extended in time and space, and in which nothing is outside the bounds of possibility, is matched by the size of the themes she tackles. She has had her artistic failures—quite a number of them—but she has had her successes, too.

She is a highly professional writer, and has always paid full attention to the need to hold the reader, including the young reader who is simply in it for the story. Incident follows incident, sometimes coming so thick and fast as to obscure the main line of the plot. But there is always something beyond the immediate action to be reached for and thought about. Miss Norton's sources of inspiration include Greek and Roman history as well as archaeology and anthropology, myth and folklore. She is not much interested in science-for-science's-sake, and obviously has a strong awareness of the menace of uncontrolled or miscontrolled technological development. One subject which deeply interests her and which occurs again and again is telepathy, often as a means of communication between man and animal. She is also fascinated by mutations and new forms of life, although she does not seem to me to have overcome the problem imposed by the limits of human imagination: we cannot conceive of *really* new forms of life, we tend to think of variations on forms we know, and the result is often ludicrous. (pp. 143-44)

Her first science fiction stories—though they were by no means her first novels—were the four 'Star' books: *Star Man's Son, Star Rangers, Star Guard,* and *Star Gate.* The title of *Star Man's Son* . . . sounds like that of a sequel, but it is not. It is a fairly straightforward story, set in a post-cataclysmic world—our own—where a few small communities survive in a primitive way, and in which the hero sets to look for a lost city which is rumoured to be safe from radiation. The Norton interest in telepathy and mutation is already present; the hero is himself a mutant and has a telepathic relationship with a giant cat; but the book does not have the range and imaginative power of later ones.

The other three 'Star' books, while all set in the future, have classical associations. A foreword to *Star Rangers* (1953) refers to the legend of the Roman Emperor who simultaneously demonstrated his absolute power and the loyalty of his legions by sending one of them to march to the end of the world. . . . This is a big advance on Miss Norton's first science fiction novel; it is probably the best of the early group and certainly the one I would recommend for sampling. Apart from the Roman analogy, her interest in telepathy is developed: there are now 'sensitives' at different levels on the scale of extrasensory perception, and, at one point, a literal battle of wills is described with some success. (pp. 144-45)

The third book, *Star Guard* (1955), is also based on a

Roman Empire situation—in this case a decadent central power-structure trying to hold down vigorous barbarians from Earth—but its main action, the retreat of a legion, has a Greek source, for it is in effect a retelling of the *Anabasis* of Xenophon. The fourth, *Star Gate* (1958), begins with the withdrawal of the wise and great Star Lords from a planet which they have raised from savagery to a feudal civilization. Although this hints at the departure of the legions, the feeling of the story is medieval. And the philosophic interest is something different again. It lies in an exploration of time theory: could there be a parallel world, also existing 'now', in which things have developed differently? The assumption is made that there could; and the 'star gate' is a device for transposing into and out of it. (Incidentally, if time as a single straight line is the fourth dimension, then a time in which parallel developments could take place would require a fifth dimension, that of space-in-time. Miss Norton's field of speculation is wide indeed.) But although Andre Norton is prepared to mix the remote past with the distant future and the might-have-been, her action has to be on a comprehensible human scale, and tends to take place on a reasonably familiar-seeming earth-type planet on which people can move and breathe as we do. The hero of *The Beast Master* (1959) and its sequel *Lord of Thunder* (1962) is, by ancestry, a Navajo Indian, and although he lives at a time when this earth has been reduced to a blue radioactive cinder, the territory he inhabits on another planet is remarkably like the American West.

Of the later Norton science fiction books, which cannot all be discussed in this small amount of space, the most imaginative, though not the most successful, is *Judgment on Janus* (1963), in which the hero finds himself drawn through inward change into membership of an infinitely-remote, green-skinned tree people. There is a sequel, *Victory on Janus.* . . . (pp. 144-46)

[The] blending in these two books of space technology with the myth-infused forest world of the Iftin does not come off. Too often it produces a result which, instead of the intended dramatic clash, is simply a ludicrous inappropriateness.

The value of old ways of life, of the simple and natural against the sophisticated, artificial and ever-changing, is a frequent issue in Miss Norton's work. It may seem odd to compare her with Rosemary Sutcliff, but there are curious correspondences. Miss Norton, as the Roman references may already have suggested, is concerned with civilization under the threat of barbarism; but there is also a part of her which sees that civilization is not all, which is deeply aware of instinctual life, is conscious of the rooting of myth in the cycle of life and death, the turning of the seasons. This is true of Miss Sutcliff, too. It is not a contradiction but a proper ambiguity which perhaps is unavoidable in people who both think and feel. And for all their vast spans of time and distance, the Norton novels can often appear to be bounded in a nutshell as well as free of infinite space, for—as in the Janus books—the conflict of tree people with advance technology may be seen as the externalization of an inner struggle.

Dark Piper (1968) seems to me to be Miss Norton's best book so far, and it draws together most of her enduring themes. In some ways it shows her at her most Roman. (pp. 146-47)

Miss Norton's science fiction books are mainly written in a hard, dry, somewhat impersonal style. Her heroes are young, determined, often afraid but overcoming their fears. They are not characterized in depth, and appear to be blanks for the reader to fill. In the earlier books there are no girls; in the Janus stories there is the forest maiden Illylle, but there is little about her that is flesh and blood. Commonly the heroes are unrooted 'loners' without family or friends, though they make comrades in the course of the action. *Dark Piper* is an exception to nearly all these generalizations. It is a first-person narration, which gives greater immediacy than usual. The children are seen both as distinct individuals and in relationship to the group; and there are real, three-dimensional girl characters in the strong-minded, protective Annet and imaginative Gytha.

Miss Norton handles her gadgetry with great aplomb. She never draws special attention to it; it is simply there. Spaceships are as ordinary as buses. Flitters for moving around in; stunners and blasters and flamers for dealing with your enemies; and 'coms' of all kinds for getting in touch with people are, with countless other devices, casually mentioned in passing without any nudge to the reader. Just occasionally the effects of word-coinage are odd—'he spooned up some lorg sauce and spread it neatly over a horva fritter'—but on the whole this is one of Miss Norton's minor strengths. Few writers are better than she is at inventing things and giving names to them. A more important power, which should not be underrated, is that of telling strong, fast-moving stories.

The Norton universe on the whole is an alarming and hostile one. It is assumed that for thousands of years hence there will be wars and rumours of wars. Peace is there only to be disturbed. Prosperity appears in an unpleasing form on the 'pleasure planet' Korwar, which also houses an intergalactic slum called the Dipple. Corruption and injustice are always around. Nature is red in tooth and claw; man in flamer and blaster. In terms of organized society there seems little to look forward to. It could be of course that strife and confusion are externalized from inner states; divided men who war within themselves will form divided, warring communities; and it is not realistic to expect sudden improvements in human nature.

Miss Norton offers no false comfort in a harsh world. In most of her novels it is quite a triumph even to stay alive. Yet the atmosphere is by no means one of despair. There is always the hope of private happiness, private fulfilment (to be found, as in *Catseye,* in the wild rather than the city), and the development of new faculties, new forms of sympathy and awareness. (pp. 147-49)

> John Rowe Townsend, "Andre Norton," in his A Sense of Story: Essays on Contemporary Writers for Children *(copyright © 1971 by John Rowe Townsend; reprinted by permission of J. B. Lippincott Company), Lippincott, 1971, pp. 143-49.*

Four boys find a magic jigsaw puzzle in a deserted house [in *Dragon Magic*], and as each completes one of the four pictured dragons he is propelled into a mythological fantasy neatly tailored to his cultural background and personal hangups. . . . The legends (particularly the Arthurian material) are cleverly reworked, but the strict parallels of the plot admit little suspense and restrict the fantasies' appeal by making them patly didactic. As always, however, Andre

Norton can be relied upon to convert her magic formulas into adroit entertainment. (p. 485)

> Kirkus Reviews *(copyright © 1972 The Kirkus Service, Inc.), April 15, 1972.*

Dread Companion is as compulsive and relentless as a nightmare—a hideous nightmare to which the reader would not return if the author once allowed him to wake up; but Andre Norton binds her spell tight. . . . [She writes of] a land of monsters and mirages where touch, smell and taste of the indigenous vegetation affect vision and dimension, where age and time take on new and terrifying meanings. (p. 484)

> The Times Literary Supplement *(© Times Newspapers Ltd. (London) 1972; reproduced from* The Times Literary Supplement *by permission), April 28, 1972.*

Set in the distant future on a far planet [*Dread Companion*], though undoubtedly sci-fic., has more in it of magic than of possible scientific developments. A young woman in charge of two children follows them to a frightening and hostile world for which the elder has some barely understood obsession, though she seems to have been bewitched by the Lady of the title, a somewhat shadowy figure reminiscent of Andersen's Snow Queen. The plot could well be taken as an allegory of the seductive yet soul-destroying practice of drug-taking, though readers will make of it what they will and most will enjoy it at face value as the well-written and gripping story that it is. There are enough horrors in it to make the hair stand on end deliciously, yet all through shine the courage and endurance of the heroine and her companion; it is these virtues, bolstered it is true by magic aids, which finally enable these two to bring the children back again to their former world. But the story does not end here, the world has changed and flight once more becomes necessary, pointing the way, the reader hopes, for another adventure of this intrepid girl. This is a book for the adult as well as the junior shelves. (p. 187)

> The Junior Bookshelf, *June, 1972.*

After *Moon of Three Rings* and *Exiles of the Stars* it becomes convincingly evident that Mrs. Norton's work demands a reading at one sitting if possible. It is not that her technical complications are impossibly fanciful—she writes too convincingly for that—but that a substantial proportion of the narrative consists of introspective meditations by two at least of the mutated or transmuted beings who are part of the regular crew of the Free Trader inter-stellar ship, Lydis, especially Krip Vorlund and the semi-creature, Maelen, the one-time moon-singer on the feudal planet of Yiktor in *Moon of Three Rings*. Such passages demand exceptional concentration within the framework of a tale which otherwise deals with rapidly changing situations within a highly-technical environment. For a reader without true leisure this reconciliation of elements proves progressively harder. I am not sure I apprehend fully the projected technicalities of *Exiles of the Stars* but few who essay it will be disappointed. (p. 187)

> The Junior Bookshelf, *June, 1972.*

BERYL ROBINSON

Four boys experience individual adventures in space and time when they explore a deserted old house. Attracted to a jigsaw puzzle lying on a dust-covered table, each boy obeys an irresistible urge to put the puzzle together. As the last piece goes into place and completes one of the four dragons pictured on the cover, each boy is suddenly transported to another time and place, where he bears a different name and identity, and becomes deeply involved in a dangerous adventure. . . . Legend, fantasy, and historical and contemporary situations are interwoven in [Dragon Magic]. Despite the wealth and range of dragon lore and legendry, the story has clarity and immediacy; and the values of courage, loyalty, and strength met in the past help each boy meet problems of the present. Those who read this book may well find themselves seeking eagerly—as did the four adventurers—the hero tales and legends in the library. (p. 373)

> Beryl Robinson, in The Horn Book Magazine (copyright © 1972 by The Horn Book, Inc., Boston), August, 1972.

The plot of [The Crystal Gryphon] adds up to more intrigue and spells and pseudo-medieval dialogue than [its] expressionless protagonists can support. One would like to know more about the past/present world of Ulm, but a little less plot and some evidence that the author possesses a sense of humor would have made Kerovan more fully human. (p. 948)

> Kirkus Reviews (copyright © 1972 The Kirkus Service, Inc.), August 15, 1972.

C. S. HANNABUSS

Readers have rightly come to expect excitement in science fantasy of the 'sword and sorcery' type, and from [Androids at Arms] they will not come away unfed. (p. 150)

Yet readers have come to expect structural efficiency in Andre Norton's science fantasy, and from this book they will come away confused. The plot poses two questions: 'Will Andras win back his throne in the real Inyaga?' and 'Is he android?' In the effort to answer the second, the first is rather forgotten. The first 150 pages, obediently developing the title, continuously revolve around question one. But Andras's journey into the future is one way, so that the climax exists exclusively in the future Inyanga: it is preoccupied with working out question two, leaving the android double untouched upon the throne. Perhaps he/it disintegrates in the general overthrow of evil—if not, much remains to be done. There are two halves of two good books here. (pp. 150-51)

> C. S. Hannabuss, in Children's Book Review (© 1972 by Five Owls Press Ltd.; all rights reserved), October, 1972.

AL JACKSON

Alice Mary Norton is a strange phenomenon in sf. The whole structure and setting of her stories is thirty years out of date. It's as if you took all those raging blood and thunder stories in science fiction of the late thirties and the decade of the forties and combined them into, say, a Sunday edition of The Galactic Times. You would have plenty of headlines and loads of stuff to fill pages and pages of your newspaper. But, what about that little 'human interest' story for the Sunday supplement or the long quiet piece about everyday life you need for a filler on page 96? Well, Miss Norton has striven mightily over the last two decades to fill in all those little byways that must be in the background of Asimov's First Galactic Empire or Heinlein's Future History.

Miss Norton now has over forty sf novels and no one in modern times has stuck more faithfully to their future history. Not that we ever have really found out much about it. We have the Patrol, the Scouts, the Rangers, etc. moving against the background of the same settings that she has used for nearly 20 years now. Yet we have rarely if ever found out what central power (for there must be some organizing agency) plans and knits all these interstellar services together. The hand that rocks the cradle is off there 'somewhere.' It does not matter because Miss Norton has left all that stuff to the front pages.

All this derivative milieu makes Miss Norton a hack of sorts. Yet that is a mean tag to pin on her. For it is easy to see her sincerity and fondness for science fiction. She uses what trappings she needs but does not abuse or pervert them. Ninety percent of her novels have been sold as juveniles and one should keep this in mind. One should tone down his expectations: don't look for characterization, and as Schuyler Miller has pointed out, pay attention to the fine flair of a good story teller. Miss Norton has woven some nice gems like Star Guard, Galactic Derelict, recently the Janus stories and others all straight sf. I am not a fan of her fantasy work, finding the Witch World series somewhat lacking.

Dread Companion falls into a subclass of Norton stories. Namely the mixing of fantasy (of sorts) with straight science fiction. The main character Kilda is led into a parallel universe, with a fantasy superstructure, by the two possessed children for whom she is governess. This adventure fills the middle portion of the book and though most of the action takes place in this parallel world, it only serves to connect two different time slices on the same planet. The major preoccupation of this novel, the action in the fantasy world, seems to serve no recognizable purpose (except to explain in part the possession of the children). It is an aimless adventure and Miss Norton leaves her usual number of loose ends. One gets the impression that she found this parallel world so unappealing that she disposes of it as a plot idea about 3/4 of the way through the book. Just as well, the loose ends left are better off if they drift into oblivion. (p. 53)

> Al Jackson, in Luna Monthly, October-November, 1972.

Andre Norton is among the best and most imaginative present day writers of science fiction. [Android at Arms] is well up to her high standards. It is a mixture of the future in the past. The empire that Andas Kastor claims, could well have been that of the Incas. His problem is, is he the rightful heir or is he an android? He has been imprisoned on an alien planet for an unexplained period and when he returns he brings with him Yolyos, a strange creature from another world who was a fellow prisoner. Together they experience in a haunted palace the future in the past and Andas is so sickened by what he knows will be, he determines at all cost to defeat his rival and enemy. How he does so is powerfully described.

The readership is again hard to define, it is definitely for the older addict of SF, that is the twelve to sixteen-year-old boy or girl—but many adults will also be fascinated by it. (pp. 407-08)

The Junior Bookshelf, *December, 1972.*

VIRGINIA CARPIO

[*Breed To Come* is] above-average science fiction dealing with the effects of evolution on a polluted world deserted by humans and dominated by "the People" (highly intelligent cats), the Barkers (dogs), the Tusked Ones (pigs), and their common enemy, the Rattons (rats). As they become more intelligent, physically refined and acquire the knowledge man left behind, the animal races face the problems of their former masters: greed, hostility, fear and doubt. The dreaded return to earth of four humans triggers a chain of events which makes men and animals search their souls for answers to moral questions shared by all intelligent creatures. The story is well written and absorbing. (p. 82)

Virginia Carpio, in School Library Journal *(reprinted from the December, 1972 issue of* School Library Journal, *published by R. R. Bowker Co. A Xerox Corporation; copyright © 1972), December, 1972.*

MARCUS CROUCH

The two acknowledged masters of mainstream SF for young readers are André Norton and Robert A. Heinlein. Despite their almost parallel careers and their comparable status, their achievements have wide differences in style and manner. André Norton's strength lies in atmosphere. She gives a tangible quality to the most improbable invention by clothing it in vividly imagined detail, and her highly charged style—admittedly a little hard to digest in large quantities—evokes with equal success the terrors of darkness and the blinding glare of light. Hers is an astonishingly complete vision; she describes the topography and the sociology of new worlds as if from the life, giving them a kind of actuality rather like that of Tolkien's *Lord of the Rings*—although in no other way does she approach the breadth and range of his achievement.

André Norton tells a good tale, too, but here she is a shade derivative. For all the wonder of the settings, the action of her stories might almost be that of a Western. The strange worlds are often divided neatly into goodies and baddies, and the latter, after great hazards, bite the dust as convincingly as if they were redskins or rogue cowboys.

Here, however, is a writer who develops with each book; and the naiveties which made a good story like *The Beast Master* . . . difficult to accept with unconditional seriousness, are being gradually purged.

Dark Piper . . . has a concentrated power and, if the word is not unacceptable for an off-world story, humanity which marks a long stride forward. Her books continue to make difficult reading. An imaginative experience so completely realized can only be shared through the reader's total surrender, and not everyone is willing, or able, to follow her along some of her perilous paths. The inability to select which the writer showed in her earlier books, too, is an obstacle which not all young readers can surmount. (pp. 54-5)

Marcus Crouch, in his The Nesbit Tradition: The Children's Novel in England 1945-1970 *(© Marcus Crouch 1972), Ernest Benn, 1972.*

It seems that *Star Born* was first published in 1957 which does not make it easy to relate it to Andre Norton's other science fiction stories. I get the impression she has written tauter, tenser and clearer works since then. Followers of *Star Trek* and *Dr. Who* will have no difficulty in sorting out the differing humanoid life forms who fight each other for survival on a strange planet. The sheer inventiveness of science fiction is half its charm, and yet there is nothing new on the Planet Astra. . . . This is a good story for those for whom suspension of disbelief is easily achieved. Embedded in the space chatter is a philosophic gem which asks the question "What is man?" The science fiction writer's freedom to invent so many life forms may make the question curiously difficult to answer, but it is interesting to note that the question is actually asked and is still relevant. (p. 273)

The Junior Bookshelf, *August, 1973.*

Although Andre Norton writes science fiction stories based on a world of the future, her characters, whether they be the Star men or, as in [*Breed to Come,*] the cats and the rat-like anti-heroes called rattons, are based very much on humanity. Through all the writings shines the quality of deep understanding of peoples. The author weaves into her free imaginative world, human values and human reaction in the handling of their complex affairs. . . .

This deeply moving and sensitive story will be much appreciated by the older teenagers, and it would be a pity if those not addicted to science fiction stories were to miss the depth of meaning, for there is much here about fear, the conflict between good and evil, the creation of society and its structures, and the need to preserve for posterity the best of what we have. . . . (p. 281)

The Junior Bookshelf, *August, 1973.*

S. WILLIAM ALDERSON

Star Born! The title itself is something of a pun on the two groups of the story: those born *on* Astra and those borne *to* Astra.

The events are told from two different viewpoints: on the one hand by a colonist—a descendant of a small group of fugitives from a *1984* life on earth—and on the other, by a member of a party of explorers from the now liberated earth. Andre Norton uses this alternation of narrators to give a broader view of events, but also, more important, to sustain suspense in a way which could not be done by straightforward narrative.

The story tells what happens when the party of explorers lands on Astra during the culmination of a war between the two native races: the Astrans, belligerent, callous and domineering, the former masters of their world, and the Sea People, a gentle, telepathic race of humanoid amphibians. The Sea People have become friends and allies of the Terran colonists and have passed on to them some of their telepathic gifts. . . .

[There is] no major climax, only a series of incidents. Although told from both colonists' and explorers' viewpoints, there is an obvious bias towards the colonists and although the device of alternating viewpoints helps to sustain interest, the book falls short of the standard of the author's *Breed to Come* where she has employed a similar device and plot much more successfully. (p. 113)

S. William Alderson, in Children's Book Review *(© 1973 Five Owls Press Ltd.; all rights reserved), September, 1973.*

The problem for a prolific author, and Andre Norton is surely that, is the increase in critics' nonchalance. So long as the standard seems to be maintained, the products, in this case more than sixty books at the rate of three a year, may go unremarked beyond the nod of acknowledgment. But readers grow and change. Those who know Miss Norton's space fictions may not even be aware of her historical fantasies, or, at the start, may mistake the one for the other.

Those who know Miss Norton's work well appreciate her highly. She belongs to the group of writers whose books appear on the list for the young as the result of shrinkage in the adult novel, although her readers might be of any age over twelve. The background of her stories is a literary one and includes myth and legend and the high tone and seriousness of epic, the dark and brooding matters of tragedy—more Senecan than modern, for in the lives of the heroes much is to be suffered when little can be done to strive against the violence of fate. At first approach, the reader's difficulty is to share the author's context.

The Crystal Gryphon belongs to the category of historical fantasy of the kind that readers may approach through Rosemary Sutcliff or Peter Dickinson. Indeed, Miss Norton and Miss Sutcliff share a common theme in the heroic tale which generates a linguistic and tonal similarity, difficult for the novice, spellbinding for the initiate. For new readers to make the most of her remarkable qualities they should have someone who already appreciates and understands them to discuss them with. *The Crystal Gryphon*, far from being simply the latest in a series, seems an ideal starting place.

The structure is admirably clear, yet subtle. The hero, Kerovan, and the heroine, Joisan . . . , tell, in alternate chapters, of the events which bring them together eight years after their betrothal. . . .

Besides sharing the author's context of legendary tale, the reader has to accept the symbolism of the underlying value structure: simple faith and truth, honour, valour, the cycle of time, the significance of word-bond and kinship, all of which are embodied in the characters and the atmosphere. Power is generated by obedience to the nature of things, by stones that have lain in earth or other talismanic objects whose significance the reader is bound to accept. It is in the nature of Miss Norton's spellbinding that he does so. Set in a time out of time, with a past that looms uncertainly over a present that is still ancient, this heroic tale generates its own linguistic style. Certain word-forms distance it from the reader: "unfriend," "blood-claim," "birthing," the speech of the characters and the forms of greeting and cursing. The convention is well enough established by Rosemary Sutcliff, Ursula Le Guin and others to cause the experienced reader no qualms, but it is to Miss Norton's credit that she maintains the heightened phraseology with no loss of credulity. To those who have been sceptical about the effective continuance of this gifted writer this book offers a chance to begin again; and to the rest of us, a distinctive experience.

> "Sorcery for Initiates," in The Times Literary Supplement (© Times Newspapers Ltd. (London) 1973; reproduced from The Times Literary Supplement by permission), September 28, 1973, p. 1114.

JESSICA KEMBALL-COOK

Andre Norton's [*The Crystal Gryphon*] is an outright tale of sword-and-sorcery. . . .

To tell this story the author has plunged fully into the epic world of Tolkien and [William] Morris, of archaisms and Teutonic phrasing, of birthings, healcraft, wife-right, ensorcelling and signs of the Power. It is a world where chance and coincidence operate on the hero's side, so that miraculous escapes and helpful finds are designed to show that fate rather than luck is at work. . . . This is an outstanding fantasy of the kind which works on symbolic as well as narrative levels, and one of the most carefully and consistently presented works this author has given us in recent years. (p. 179)

> Jessica Kemball-Cook, in Children's Book Review (© 1973 Five Owls Press Ltd.; all rights reserved), December, 1973.

JESSICA KEMBALL-COOK

Ziantha, a highly-trained telepath, makes a 'foray' or mind-search into the times of the Forerunners, an ancient race which predates her own era. While spying for the Thieves' Guild, an interplanetary organisation, she comes across a mysterious stone which magnifies her mental powers and drags her into the personalities of two Forerunner females, each facing a great crisis in their own time. . . .

With its casual references to terms like 'sight distort', 'nightsight', 'psychic energy', 'chewing gratz' and 'veeps', [*Forerunner Foray*] certainly assumes an acquaintance with SF conventions, and takes for granted that we understand what Ziantha is about with her mind-searching. . . . The story has a more general application, however, as it deals with the right of the individual to determine his own future and go his own way apart from those who have trained him. . . .

With its carefully constructed plot and choice of suitable language this book stands above much by inferior writers; yet the pace is slow and sometimes wearying, so that I would only recommend it to Norton fans and SF addicts, who would best appreciate its quality of elegance blended with intellectual argument. (p. 66)

> Jessica Kemball-Cook, in Children's Book Review (© 1974 Five Owls Press Ltd.; all rights reserved), Summer, 1974.

KATHRYN A. LITSINGER

SF fans and animal lovers will relish [*Iron Cage*, a] tale about a new breed of cats that inhabit an outer galactic planet. Initially, the creatures befriend humans who have escaped from the cages of the "Big People," but the plot comes full circle when a space ship brings visitors who intend to cage and study the animals. . . . The only jarring note is a prologue and epilogue which uses a modern day parallel—abandoning a house cat about to deliver kittens in the town dump—to didactically point up the moral. Though not as fast paced as Norton's *Forerunner Foray* . . . nor as involved with scientific data as *Breed to Come* . . . , this is still interesting and complex enough to rate well above most science fiction offerings. (p. 109)

> Kathryn A. Litsinger, in School Library Journal (reprinted from the September, 1974 issue of School Library Journal, published by R. R. Bowker Co. A Xerox Corporation; copyright © 1974), September, 1974.

S. WILLIAM ALDERSON

In *The Zero Stone,* Murdoc Jern . . . inherits a ring, set with the inscrutable 'zero stone', from his murdered father and is himself caught up in the rapids of interstellar intrigue, drawn on—sometimes literally—by the stone and its secrets. . . . Andre Norton constructs a mystery from this dull, pitted, grey stone suggestive of the proverbial mountain out of a molehill, building more and more props into the book as it progresses. Initially, the 'present' is dappled by memories of the 'past' and the events leading up to Murdoc's father's death, but by the end everything is very much in order, firmly steered along the pre-set channels of the story and the close of the book is, itself, a 'break for the ads.' before the theme is taken up again in *Uncharted Stars.*

In *Uncharted Stars,* Murdoc and Eet [an alien mutant] continue their trail of the Zero Stone, and this leads them, after a succession of adventures, to a dead planet where Eet acquires her true shape. The anticlimax of the end does not warrant the lead-up through two books, particularly when the story is as dependent on luck as this one, a feature becoming more and more prominent in Andre Norton's books. She attempts to liven up the story with practically insignificant events, almost immediately cancelled out, and in so doing gives a hint of near desperation. (p. 108)

> *S. William Alderson, in* Children's Book Review *(© 1974 Five Owls Press Ltd.; all rights reserved), Autumn, 1974.*

VIRGINIA HAVILAND

[In *Lavender-Green Magic* a] family of black children is drawn from a here-and-now situation in "Sussex," a community obviously north of Boston, into a mysterious colonial past connected with the Dimsdale estate. . . . Herbs account for many threads in the plot: For the children who take turns sleeping on it, an herbal pillow becomes the means of transport to early Dimsdale; they learn more of the curse put upon the Dimsdales after finding—in the center of an herb-garden maze—the house where two sisters used to mix their herbal brews. The witchlore and herbcraft, superimposed on a family situation, is skillfully worked into the plot, although there is a certain amount of light moralizing. The author succeeds particularly well in creating child personalities. . . . (pp. 137-38)

> *Virginia Haviland, in* The Horn Book Magazine *(copyright © 1974 by the Horn Book, Inc., Boston), October, 1974.*

DONALD A. WOLLHEIM

In lists of leading science fiction writers such as might be compiled by academics or fan experts, it is probable that the name of Andre Norton would be missing, whereas such writers as Robert Heinlein, Poul Anderson, Arthur C. Clarke, John Brunner and others would be certainly present. Yet if these list compilers would take librarians and booksellers into investigation, they would discover that the name of Andre Norton would be right up there in any top ten list.

Why then would they have omitted her in their original off-the-top-of-the-head listings? It would be for a number of reasons. For one, Andre Norton has but rarely graced the pages of the standard science fiction magazines. Her novels are not serialized in the newsstand pulps. And she has

written but a handful of short stories and novelettes as compared with the others' output. . . .

[Her] novels do not push themselves to promote any sort of special pleading of the kind likely to attract controversy and debate.

Then also the greater part of her science fiction has been composed of novels written for hard-cover publishers as works for "young adults" and not promoted or even offered among the science fiction shelves of the adult fiction sections of book shops. Yet any bookseller could tell you that wherever her science fiction books are sold, however they may be labelled, they sell well, they sell steadily, they remain in print for years and years. (p. vii)

The world of science fiction and fantasy readers, the same people who devour Anderson and Simak and Farmer and Niven, also buy and read everything by Andre Norton they can get their hands on.

While they may spend a lot of time discussing the sociology and speculations of the other writers, Andre Norton they read for pleasure. This is not to say that her works lack the depth of the others, because they do not. But it is that these depths form part of the natural unobtrusive background of her novels whereas one's nose is, as it were, forceably shoved into the special pleading that the others so often project into their novels.

Andre Norton thought of herself as writing for young people; from the start she had an instinctive understanding of modern youth that many of her contemporaries and predecessors in juvenile fiction lacked. She knew that you did not have to write down to them; she knew that you did not have to explain the elementary details of futurology or infinity or other-worldly lore to them. She knew that the youth of today was already self-oriented to what came to their older contemporaries as "future shock."

So quite calmly she could speak of colonized planets and the problems of people living on them; she could write of alien beings, friendly and unfriendly; she could bring to the imagination the feel of what an alien mind could be, of what a wholly nonhuman intelligence might desire, or what unsolved mysteries the galaxy may very well hold for us.

She does this as part of a background in which flesh and blood humans develop—young people indeed, but not so young as not to be able to assume responsibilities for themselves, their causes, their loved ones. She could place a story in the grim setting of a ghetto for the dispossessed of a cosmic war—and her readers would understand. She could bring forth the thrill and commerce of space trade, of corporations and "free traders" and do it so that it all came alive, rang true. She could set a human being down alone on an alien landscape and make that alienness felt, make the reader live just what it had to be like.

She knows and loves animals and she utilizes her own feeling for the other living beasts of our Earth to place them or their like on other worlds and other futures—and she brings the magic of communication between man and his old allies of our terrestrial heritage into a reality desired by the legendry of mankind's rise, but possibly capable of achievement only through the knowledge of the ways of genetic structuring and mental revision. (pp. viii-ix)

Andre Norton is at home telling wonder stories.

She is telling us that people are marvelously complex and marvelously fascinating. She is telling us that all life is good and that the universe is vast and meant to enhance our life to infinity. She is weaving an endless tapestry of a cosmos no man will ever fully understand, but among whose threads we are meant to wander forever to our personal fulfillment. (p. x)

Basically this is what science fiction has always been about. And because she has always understood this, her audience will continue to be as ever-renewing and as nearly infinite as her subjects. (p. x)

> Donald A. Wollheim, in his introduction to The Many Worlds of Andre Norton by Andre Norton, edited by Roger Elwood (copyright © 1974 by Roger Elwood; reprinted with permission of the publisher), Chilton Book Company, 1974, pp. vii-x.

RICK BROOKS

The impression that a regular reader of Andre Norton's books might have is that of growing pessimism. From light hearted adventure stories like *Star Rangers* and *Sargasso of Space*, she has gone to books like *Dread Companion* and *Dark Piper* that give the feeling at the conclusion that it is best not to see or even guess what lies ahead.

While Miss Norton has never seemed too comfortable in the here-and-now, it seems that now the future that once beckoned has become another area for distrust. Even the latest Solar Queen story, *Postmarked the Stars*, is more subdued and grim in tone. The Patrol, a largely unsullied organization, comes in for its lumps in *The Zero Stone* and its sequel, *Uncharted Stars*. In *Ice Crown*, the Service makes no move to help those under a planetwide conditioning program. (p. 178)

Has Miss Norton lost faith in the future? . . . I see the answer as yes . . . and no. She has definitely lost some of her optimism—but haven't we all? In novels like *Dread Companion* and *Dark Piper*, she is trying for deeper characterization. This slows down the action and gives one more time to spot her usual lack of blind faith in the future. (pp. 178-79)

Star Man's Son takes place in a post-nuclear-war world. While the ending is upbeat with the hope of a rebirth of civilization, most of the story is rather bleak. This novel sees the birth of a theme that runs through all Norton's books—tolerance for other races.

[*Star Rangers*] extends this theme to non-humans and introduces the reptilian race of Zacan (the Zacathans) which have become almost a fixture in her later far future novels. The mighty stellar empire of Central Control seen at a much earlier stage is collapsing later in *Star Guard*, and a battered Patrol ship limps back to Terra, now long forgotten, to start anew. The upbeat ending again overshadows the brutal future pictured with a hardening of hereditary stratification in all groups, even the Patrol, and bloody power struggles in which entire worlds with all their people are burnt off with little apparent concern. The character's rather matter of fact acceptance of the latter is quite chilling.

The Stars Are Ours starts on another post-destruction Terra, this time by a satellite burn-off which triggers a program against Free Scientists. A few escape to Astra under cold sleep. The bleak repressive Terra miraculously gives way to the vividly drawn Astra. With this, Miss Norton comes into her major strength, the portrayal of other worlds. The switch between bleak winter on Terra and the verdant growing season on Astra also seems to mark a turning point in Norton's writing.

She now has a more optimistic tone as she explores the glory of other worlds. In *Sargasso of Space*, the planet Limbo has been partially burnt off, but in a long gone Forerunner war. *Star Guard* sees an attempt to set human mercenaries against each other, but no killings of non-combatants. *The Crossroads of Time* does show some brutal alternate presents. *Plague Ship* features a run-in with the Patrol and the danger of being shot on sight as plague carriers. *Sea Siege* is a downbeat near-future tale where radioactive mutated sea life and a nuclear war endanger humanity. *Star Born* features a clash with Those Others, the vicious native race of Astra. While there still is a lot of violence, the characters' attitude has changed from passive acceptance of it as a part of life to downright loathing.

Star Gate is a rather unique book as it concerns the alternate histories of another world. With the exception of Norton's later "Toys of Tamisan," this is the only science fiction that comes to mind covering both star travel and travel *sideways* in time. Creating an alien world is usually considered enough, without creating a history to go with it.

Andre Norton seems to have suffered a rough period in 1961-62. *Star Hunter* has the Patrol ignoring the mental conditioning of a young drifter so that a Veep can be nabbed. In *The Defiant Agents*, a group of Indians are mentally conditioned and sent off to occupy Topaz before the Reds can. The optimism of *Galactic Derelict*, where the universe and its wonders had been opened to man, have in its sequel turned to dread of the weapons of the earlier galactic empire in human hands. *Eye of the Monster* is Norton's most xenophobic story by far. The previous *Storm over Warlock* had a very nasty portrayal of the Throgs, but humans still try to make peace. Here there is no thought of peace. In all other stories, evil aliens are the result of forbidden researches. Here the crocs are vicious barbarians that suddenly start butchering all off-worlders. Several racial characteristics are adversely mentioned, especially odor. In all other Norton novels, aliens are evil for what they do, not what they are. Despite provocation, no other Norton hero has reacted by a hatred that could be classified as racial. This momentary failure underlines her usual tolerance for living beings.

Outside of these three novels, not much distinguished one Norton novel from another during the late fifties and most of the sixties except a little more polish in the writing of later ones. With *Dark Piper* (1968), a lessening of optimism is again visible. (pp. 179-80)

At least one fan has waged a titanic struggle in trying to sort out a consistent "future history" from Norton's books when she never has bothered with one. However, most of her stories do fall within a loose framework. It is almost like such terms as *Free Traders, Forerunners, First Ship, Patrol, Jack, Veep, First-in Scout,* and *Combine* fit so well that she doesn't bother to coin others. Races such as the Zacathans and planets such as Astra receive mention in many stories, as does the game of Stars and Comets. Whether this is a matter of sentiment, laziness, or practicality (it is work to create an entire world for just one story, let alone several worlds) is a point that can be argued.

Miss Norton, instead of being bound by a future history, has created a series of alternate universes that largely overlap. All her interplanetary stories, with the exception of *Star Gate* (though a planet Gorth is mentioned in *Moon of Three Rings*), *Secret of the Lost Race*, "Long Live Lord Kor!" and *Dark Piper* have interlocking references. The latter is probably to emphasize the isolation of the research planet of Beltane from the rest of the galaxy. I think that it is significant that the two novels date from 1958 and 1959, while the other is a novelette. Since Miss Norton's references to previous books have become more numerous in her last group of books, it would seem that certain races, planets, and things have become touchstones for her. (p. 181)

This is a good thing and gives depth to a story, but occasionally Miss Norton goofs in choosing a "spear-carrier" from an earlier story. The worst example is the Salarik who tended bar in *Star Hunter*. He could not have taken the odors of the place without protection.

Miss Norton's stories are born in many ways. *Star Rangers* started from the story of the Roman Emperor who ordered a legion eastward across Asia to the end of the world. Childe Roland and the Dark Tower became *Warlock of the Witch World*. *The Year of the Unicorn* owed its origin to the folk tale of "Beauty and the Beast." Even more obvious are the links between *Dark Piper* and the Pied Piper. However, few would realize that *Night of Masks* was sparked by the "powerful descriptions" of William Hope Hodgson's classic *The Night Land*. . . .

The stories are shaped by references to an "extensive personal library of natural history, archaeology, anthropology, native religions, folklore, and travel in off-beat sections of the world." The ". . . forests of Janus and *The Zero Stone* are both taken from the great forests of the Matto Grosso." And of course history plays an important part. (p. 182)

To create an alien culture, it is a big help to understand one. (p. 183)

So in the end, the chief value of Andre Norton's writing may not lie in entertainment or social commentary, but in her "re-enchanting" us with her creations that renew our linkages to all life. (pp. 184-85)

But Norton falls into a much more rigid pattern in her view of the complex technological future that largely ignores the individual. Her sympathies can be easily seen as the Norton hero or heroine never seems to fit into their society and often are outright misfits. In *Night of Masks*, Nik Kolkerne has a badly mutilated face and a personality to match. Diskan Fentress is a clumsy oaf crashing through the faerie world of Vaanchard in *The X Factor*. Ross Murdock is an alienated criminal when he becomes part of a time traveling team in *The Time Traders*. Roane Hume in *Ice Crown* finds the medieval life of Clio draws her from her relatives who treat her like an extra pair of hands.

Miss Norton seems to be fond of the medieval period. *Moon of Three Rings* was deliberately based on the culture of the European Middle Ages. . . . All six Witch World novels, *Key Out of Time*, *Star Gate*, *Star Guard*, "Toys of Tamisan," "Wizard's World," and to some extent *Plague Ship* feature a medieval-like culture. Some writers use such

a culture regularly because they are too lazy to work out another, but Miss Norton sees important values that we have bypassed in the medieval period.

Another major feature is the stressing of the bond between man and animal (and Iftin and tree in the Janus series). . . .

Star Rangers also introduces the theme of telepathy. In *The Beast Master* (1959) the two are fused together and we have Hosteen Storm, the Beast Master, and his team of African Black Eagle, Meerkats, and dune cat are telepathically linked. But like Diskan Fentress in *The X Factor*, his talent just covers animals. Kartr in *Star Rangers* as well as Zinga the Zacacathan can communicate telepathically with animals, but do not try for an emotional bond or work with them. (p. 185)

In places, Norton's consistency is disturbing as she insists on attacking the computer of ten or fifteen years ago. But Miss Norton is true to her daemon wherever it leads her. She sees a nuclear war as our probable future and it or the threat of it is a part of all her near future stories except *The Stars Are Ours*. The crosstime series, the time trader series, and *Operation Time Search* take place in the calm before the storm and this blights *The Defiant Agents*. Both *Star Guard* and *Plague Ship* note the changes wrought on Terra by such a war several hundred years past.

But her afterview is much too optimistic. Our civilization has delved deeply into the earth for the resources we now use. Let civilization collapse for very long and some of the resources needed to rebuild it will be out of reach. This is our main chance. Muff it, and most likely the stars will forever remain no more than points of light in the night sky.

However, Miss Norton's main thrust is not in the area of science and technology, but in that of human society. While all her stories are good entertainment, most contain more. (pp. 187-88)

Miss Norton's main problem seems to be that of the relationship between man and his machines. And her attitude is fairly obvious. I'd hardly expect a Norton story featuring a planet-bound misfit who finally realizes his dream of becoming a star ship mechanic. There have been sympathetic characters that have dealt with machines, but not recently. Since *Galactic Derelict* (1959) only Ali Kamil from the engine room of the Solar Queen in *Postmarked the Stars* comes to mind. And he had played a strong part in the first two books of the series.

Miss Norton is rather unacquainted with the "hard sciences" and her earlier books suffer a bit with her attempts to go into detail. This was especially true of astronomy. (p. 188)

By *The Stars Are Ours* and following books, Miss Norton avoids the trap most beginning sf writers fall into, and coins most of her planet names, mostly from mythology.

Even this early, Miss Norton showed a marked distrust of what Gene Marine in *America the Raped* termed the engineering mentality. (p. 189)

In the battle between technology and nature, Miss Norton took a stand long before the great majority of us had any doubts. Miss Norton has little knowledge of technology and rarely tries to explain the scientific wonders in her stories. . . . The less explanation, the less likely the science of the story is to date. But Andre Norton doesn't go into detail because she doesn't care. Technology is a necessary evil to get there for the adventure and to get some of the story to work. And the adventure is as much to mold her universe to her views as to entertain.

Two of the most extreme nature vs. technology novels are *Judgment on Janus* and its sequel, *Victory on Janus*. In this story the Iftin race have left "traps" that change humans sympathetic to nature into Iftin. Their lives are bound with nature and the massive trees. Technology becomes very distasteful. The chief villain turns out to be an alien computer.

The same type of villain turns up in *Star Hunter*, while a human built computer is the main evil in *Ice Crown*. In both *The Stars Are Ours* and *Dark Piper* where the computer performs a useful function, it isn't allowed any more scope than yesterday's model. In *Star Rangers*, a city computer directs a robot to destroy the heroes. (pp. 189-90)

Miss Norton sees no marriage of science and human powers. . . . So it should not be a surprise after traversing all the magical horrors the Witch World universe has to offer to find that the ultimate depth is a world from an environmentalist's nightmare where a degenerate humanity fights against men incorporated with machines both using weapons of advanced technology. (p. 190)

Norton consistently views the future as one where the complexity of science and technology have reduced the value of the individual. But the good of many is in the long run the good of the individual. As John Gardner points out in *Self-Renewal: The Individual and The Innovative Society,* our cultures become rigid and decay when they cease to allow a wide range of freedom to the individual.

So Miss Norton is actually wrestling with the prime problem, that of human worth and purpose. The question of human purpose has led to reams and reams of prose, most of it junk. Miss Norton is right in saying that it is not to be machine tenders, but she is vague on what human purpose should be. (p. 196)

We get glimpses of a Norton utopia in *Judgment on Janus* and *Victory On Janus* as well as scattered places throughout her books. The most appealing might well be the Valley of Green Silences which we see very little considering that parts of three Witch World novels take place there. While all her desirable places are those of nature, it is well to remember that man might not be man as we know him without his links to nature. (p. 197)

[No] matter how deeply Miss Norton's despair in the present and the future is germinating, she never councils quitting or even considering it. . . . Her heroes and heroines do not tamely bow their heads and accept their lot in a society that does not fit them. Some, like Diskan Fentress, may not seem to be concerned with others, but come through when the chips are down. Even if Norton's future societies do not value the individual, her sympathetic characters do.

Norton's future societies usually combine high ideals with a lack of concern for the people in it, an extrapolation of today's society that seems to be more comfortable treating men largely as interchangeable parts. And as our society worsens, so does her view of the future. *Catseye* (1961) marked the rise of organized crime. By *Night of Masks* (1964), crime syndicates had gone interstellar. *The Zero Stone* (1968) and *Uncharted Stars* show the Patrol reacting by trampling individual rights in their efforts to stamp out crime.

In *Sargasso of Space,* the Free Traders were recruited from the trainees that the Combines depended upon, too. By *Dread Companion* (1970) and *Exiles of the Stars,* the Free Traders are almost a separate race, rigidly controlling themselves on the planets, with their women and the declining feline race kept on their asteroid bases. It is almost as though the cats began to die out as their masters became less human, less linked to nature.

In the future, most of Miss Norton's work will probably be mainly the more aware and less hopeful novels such as *Dark Piper* and *Dread Companion*. But I shall miss seeing more light-hearted optimistic adventures. After all, anyone can be aware. But few can give us an Astra or a Witch World. (pp 199-200)

> *Rick Brooks, "Andre Norton: Loss of Faith," in* The Many Worlds of Andre Norton *by Andre Norton, edited by Roger Elwood (copyright © 1974 by Roger Elwood; reprinted with permission of the publisher), Chilton Book Company, 1974, pp. 178-200.*

One cannot but admire the fertility of Mrs. Norton's invention and the consistency of her imagined worlds. The logic of her technology is so beautifully developed, and her characters are just human enough to enable some identification on the part of the reader to take place. There is little room for romance but we are sustained by the old-fashioned virtues of courage, ingenuity and loyalty which were the mainstay of the stories in the old Boys' Own Paper.

The inhabitants of Vroom [in *Crosstime Agent*] are able to visit any planet at any time and have developed their own civilisation by sneaky trips of plunder. They are strictly controlled so that history is not disturbed. The multitude of worlds has enabled alternative cultures to prosper so that the Aztecs, not the Spaniards, inherited the world in which Marva and Marfy . . . come to grips with a plot to take over Vroom. Blake Walker is the linkman who holds together all those masterminding the opposition, and a very attractive hero he makes. On balance it is the human interest which dominates the story despite the ingenious scientific milieu. (p. 201)

> The Junior Bookshelf, *June, 1975.*

When Ramsey Kimball is time-zapped into the body of his other level twin Kaskar [in *Knave of Dreams*] he gets his bearings in no time at all. In a few days he's learned the language and customs of Ulad . . . and plunged into the intrigue over a successor to the crown. Maybe Ramsey is at home in Ulad because it's so familiar from reading other Norton books, though for better or worse, this world is less complicated than some. . . . Ramsey's motives are no more human than anyone else's and it's hard to figure out just what he's doing in this fancy dress game . . . and what you're doing playing with Norton's same old stacked deck one more time. (pp. 857-58)

> Kirkus Reviews *(copyright © 1975 The Kirkus Service, Inc.), August 1, 1975.*

MARGERY FISHER

The Jargoon Pard belongs to that section of André Norton's writing which she calls "sword and sorcery".... André Norton has always adopted a consciously archaic, literary style for this kind of story and in this one she has I think overdone it; inversions, archaisms, tortuous formality hold up even the highly dramatic opening scene and make the complex plot unnecessarily hard to follow. The chivalric note, the idea of personal honour is strong in the book but over and above this element there is something that seems still more important, the idea that man is distancing himself from the animal kingdom in which so much of his ancestry and aptitude rests. Kethan's changes from man to beast and back to man are far more than a device to hold the attention and further the plot. (pp. 2709-10)

> *Margery Fisher, in her* Growing Point, *October, 1975.*

The moral of this well written science fiction story [*The Iron Cage*] is strong; man must come to terms with himself and the animal world if he wishes to avoid the indignities and suffering he now inflicts on his own and other species.

This is a valid message but it is unfortunate that the author found it necessary to present such a disturbing picture of birth. A cat thrown out by thoughtlessly cruel humans gives an agonising birth to her kittens. A woman, experimented upon by a futuristic "higher species", forcibly impregnated by a "mind controlled" stud male and like the cat discarded, gives tortuous birth to her twins. The woman's name—it should have warned me—is Rutee! . . .

The monsters and advanced machinery of science fiction appeal to many children as fantasy—machine age fairy tale well outside the scope of reality. Birth is real life, and described cruelly as here may well cause distress, not perhaps at the reading but if related to birth within the family. (p. 413)

The Junior Bookshelf, *December, 1975.*

GERALD JONAS

Andre Norton's style is not to everyone's taste. She writes sentences like "Hunger was a discomfort within Sander" and "The creatures hopped rather than walked as might men, yet they were not slow." But she is a superb story-teller with a narrative pace all her own. [In "No Night Without Stars"] she tells the tale of Sander and Fanyi, a young man and woman in a post-nuclear-holocaust world who team up to seek the dangerous knowledge of the Before People.

Unlike some writers of S.F. juveniles, who pile sensation on sensation for fear of losing their audience, Norton slowly unfolds a succession of images that first intrigue and finally engulf the reader. To reach their destination, Sander and Fanyi must travel across a dry sea-bed where they discover not only those mutated hopping horrors but also the rusting hull of an ancient submarine and some even more ancient stone ruins—the remains of a great civilization that perished in an earlier eon, long before the Before People existed. With this evocative image of oceans periodically sweeping over the earth and then retreating, like a vast slow tide, the author places the quest of her hero and heroine against the grandest possible background. And even when that quest brings Sander and Fanyi into the conventionally sinister clutches of a mad computer and its mechanized minions, Norton never lets the reader lose sight of the larger framework she has so carefully created. (p. 12)

> *Gerald Jonas, in* The New York Times Book Review (ⓒ *1976 by The New York Times Company; reprinted by permission), January 25, 1976.*

MARGERY FISHER

As an adventure story *The Crossroads of Time* must rank with the best of André Norton's work, with its tremendous variety of landscape and atmosphere and its fast, forceful plot. She has given herself an almost limitless power of narrative as she describes Blake's sojourn on one alternative world after another, and has taken every opportunity to bring colour, action and thought to a multiplicity of scenes. Above all she has knit the practical and the philosophical brilliantly in describing how a courageous but untaught young agent adjusts himself to known and unknown worlds and peoples. (p. 2823)

> *Margery Fisher, in her* Growing Point, *March, 1976.*

NORMAN CULPAN

All André Norton's old skills are here [in *Iron Cage*], but they are here used to make explicit a theme, the important potential of animals, which has been implicit in many of her books from the beginning. Jony, of human origin, who has been nurtured on an alien planet by creatures of about stone-age intelligence who have developed from bears, throws in his lot with them and defeats the attempts of visiting men to colonise what has become to him his home planet. Some adult readers will share—and perhaps be surprised to share—my shock at a human being's choosing to bring disaster on an expedition of morally quite normal men; but few will deplore a plea for greater concern for and understanding of animals.

Young readers will need a certain amount of sophistication to link satisfactorily the Prologue and Epilogue in which a cat is dumped in a cardboard box to die and later rescued, with the imprisonment of the young Jony and his mother in cages by alien invaders, their escape, and their safe-keeping by the indigenous bear-like creatures. (p. 52)

> *Norman Culpan, in* The School Librarian, *March, 1976.*

Ashake, a Nubian princess of the blood, knows that she had a prior existence as black archaeologist Tallahassee Mitford before being pulled bodily through a time warp and into the ancient kingdom of Meroe as it is—or was—in some other continuum. . . . The combination of a with-it young scientist and evocative Egyptian talismans—and the omission of feline beings—get [*Wraiths of Time*] off to a promising start. However, the plot is opaque even by Andre Norton standards and Tallahassee's willingness to remain permanently in Ashake's body where she feels "real" and "welcomed" carries escapism farther than most will care to follow. (p. 740)

> Kirkus Reviews (copyright ⓒ *1976 The Kirkus Service, Inc.), July 1, 1976.*

S. WILLIAM ALDERSON

It is difficult to believe that *Outside* shares the same author as *Knave of Dreams,* for it is a very slight book, a mixture of *When the Machine Stops, Survivors* and many similar stories. It is loosely, but overtly based on the Pied Piper theme, though it is the children first, rather than the rats, that the Piper is taking, leading them to a new freedom outside the dying, machine-controlled city originally built to protect humans from the effects of pollution and radiation. That is all! No real plot, little excitement. It might entertain a few ten-year-olds, but it would be a sad disappointment for most SF readers. (p. 39)

> *S. William Alderson, in* Children's Book Review *(© 1976 Five Owls Press Ltd.; all rights reserved), October, 1976.*

NORMAN CULPAN

Kristie, [of *Outside*,] has lived all her life in a running-down city, completely domed and wholly shut off from the 'Outside', presumably long past devastated and rendered uninhabitable by nuclear war. She is obsessed with a desire to see the 'Outside', and when she gets there, with the aid of a mysterious Pied Piper, finds all is fresh and well again, with a small group of people planning a new and better world. . . .

Miss Norton has suitably simplified her vocabulary, sentence structure and plot for younger readers than she usually writes for, but in doing so loses some of her considerable power of imaginative evocation. (p. 324)

> *Norman Culpan, in* The School Librarian, *December, 1976.*

MARY M. BURNS

Recognizing the real meaning of courage and tentatively establishing the mutual understanding necessary for solid family relationships are the unifying elements of a skillfully constructed time-slip fantasy. [*Red Hart Magic*] recreates three troubled periods in English history from the seventeenth to the nineteenth centuries and allows the present-day Nan and Chris to observe their historical counterparts —who were as unassuming and as seemingly powerless as they—resolve great physical or moral dilemmas. The merging of past and present values is smoothly handled, the miniature model of an old English inn serves as an intriguing and effective device for transporting the two back in time, and the central characters solve their problems in a credible manner. (p. 160)

> *Mary M. Burns, in* The Horn Book Magazine *(copyright © 1977 by the Horn Book, Inc., Boston), April, 1977.*

Andre Norton is one of those writers who has the happy knack of writing for children and yet ensuring that her stories will be read just as eagerly by adults. There are no juvenile characters in [*Wraiths of Time*], and the story deals with difficult concepts like doorways through time, transferring a memory from a dead person to a live one, half-invisible wraiths who are lost in time, visitors from another planet and, of course, there is the usual fight of good against evil. The story combines all that is best in science fiction with all that is best in juvenile literature resulting in a book to be enjoyed by all ages. (p. 182)

> The Junior Bookshelf, *June, 1977.*

NORMAN CULPAN

Not being, in any sense of the word, science fiction, *Red Hart Magic* is not typical André Norton, though there are resemblances, both in theme and treatment, to a book she wrote in 1968 called *Octagon Magic*.

When teenagers Nan and Chris first meet they resent both each other and the recent marriage between their respective parents, both abroad. Through the agency of a model of the Red Hart Inn, near Rye, they move back in time to three separate adventures at the Inn, where they help one another, in the seventeenth, eighteenth and probably early nineteenth centuries. Interspersed are scenes at home and school, where they are severely tested by a dare to go shop lifting, bullying, and the attentions of a well meaning but rather insensitive aunt with whom they now live. The twentieth-century scenes are true to life but not fully alive; the three adventures in past time are excellent: they are fast-moving, fully involve the reader's imagination and sympathy, and are peopled with real adults, good and bad. (p. 60)

> *Norman Culpan, in* The School Librarian, *March, 1978.*

CHARLOTTE W. DRAPER

[Andre Norton] acknowledges that she has used the war game *Dungeons and Dragons* as the context for [*Quag Keep*]. Seven wayfarers, haunted by the memory of another world, are bound by a "geas"—an uncanny compulsion to seek out an alien force which menaces the precarious balance between Law and Chaos in their own world. The travelers wear bracelets of dice which warn them of new skirmishes with the agents of Chaos. When the companions arrive at Quag Keep, stronghold of the summoning power, they recognize the source of the spell: "[Y]ou aren't real, don't you understand that? I'm the game master." Chance is double-edged, however, and the Seven exert their own power over him. The landscape and its creatures—including some familiar inhabitants of Tolkien's Middle Earth—are cleverly devised and integrated. Skillful exposition in the first two chapters hints at previous incarnation for the Seven, but the reader remains as mystified as the actors in the drama, not understanding until the end why their behavior appears to be preordained. The characterizations derive from the magical or physical power of each player to oppose his or her adversary, and the plot structure is an analogue of the geometric pattern of a game board. The game seems deadly serious and involves a restructuring of the identity not only of the players—but ultimately of the game master himself. (pp. 285-86)

> *Charlotte W. Draper, in* The Horn Book Magazine *(copyright © 1978 by the Horn Book, Inc., Boston), June, 1978.*

FREDERICK PATTEN

[*Crossroads of Time*] is a well-written introduction to the concept of parallel worlds. It becomes slightly sidetracked when Blake is forced into his overlong ordeal through worlds not really connected with the plot, and Blake himself spends a lot of time being bewildered (though understandably so). However, the action and tension remain constant, and the settings are fascinatingly exotic. This 1956 novel displays its Cold War era origins in its gloomy succession of time-lines in which Earth has always been destroyed in a nuclear or similarly catastrophic war; but this supports Blake's resolution to keep the same fate from being brought by Pranj to our own world. There is an equally good sequel, *Quest Crosstime* . . . , in which Blake goes on his first mission as a full-fledged Wardsman into an alternate America dominated by a militaristic Aztec/Toltec society. (p. 8)

Frederick Patten, in Science Fiction & Fantasy
Book Review *(copyright © 1979 by The Borgo
Press), February, 1979.*

Jimmy Page

1944-

Robert Plant

1948-

British songwriters and filmmakers. Page and Plant are the two focal points of the premier heavy-metal rock band, Led Zeppelin, a group which for ten years has explored various musical forms and techniques while still adhering to their blues roots. By combining music both delicate and powerful with lyrics that reflect an interest in mystical and physical subjects, Led Zeppelin has developed a fanatical following and a reputation for always providing their audiences with the unexpected. They are the first band to have broken international concert attendance records set by the Beatles, and have spawned scores of imitators. Many critics and fans agree that they are the current embodiment of the quintessential rock band. Much of the credit for the group's success is given to Page, their leader and lead guitarist. Page was a member of the legendary blues-based group, the Yardbirds. When it folded in 1968, Page was left with the responsibility of completing a series of unfulfilled contractual obligations which prompted him to form Led Zeppelin with vocalist Plant, bassist John Paul Jones, and drummer John Bonham. Led Zeppelin expanded on the ground broken by the Yardbirds, Cream, and the Jeff Beck Group and redefined the genre these bands began with their spontaneous vocal improvisations, unusual chord progressions, and forceful instrumentation. Their song "Whole Lotta Love" is considered the classic representation of all these elements. Both Page and Plant collaborate on ideas for their music, but Plant is most often considered responsible for the band's lyrical stance. Often alluding to traditional English ballads, folklore, and works of fantasy such as J.R.R. Tolkien's *The Lord of the Rings*, Plant's lyrics create their own imaginative mythology with songs like "The Battle of Evermore" and "Stairway to Heaven," the latter being most consistently regarded as the band's best work. The lyrics often refer to sixties-based concerns such as universal love and world peace, causing Plant to be criticized as a naive, outdated flower child. Plant's darker side has also emerged in Led Zeppelin's lyrics, many of which are overtly sexual and often considered chauvinistic. The band has also been charged with lifting lyrics and music from uncredited blues sources and for creating music that is ponderous, boring, and excessive. Their film, *The Song Remains the Same*, has been criticized for similar reasons. However, Led Zeppelin is still looked to for music that is both physically exciting and spiritually uplifting, and despite sporadic album releases and tours, personal misfortune, and changing musical tastes, they remain among the favorite groups of many young people.

JOHN MENDELSOHN

[The] excesses of the [Jeff Beck Group's] *Truth* album (most notably its self-indulgence and restrictedness), are fully in evidence on Led Zeppelin's debut album [*Led Zeppelin*].

Jimmy Page, around whom the Zeppelin revolves, is, admittedly, an extraordinarily proficient blues guitarist and explorer of his instrument's electronic capabilities. Unfortunately, he is also a very limited producer and a writer of weak, unimaginative songs, and the Zeppelin album suffers from his having both produced it and written most of it (alone or in combination with his accomplices in the group). (pp. 6-7)

The album's most representative cut is "How Many More Times." Here a jazzy introduction gives way to a driving (albeit monotonous) guitar-dominated background for Plant's strained and unconvincing shouting (he may be as foppish as Rod Stewart, but he's nowhere near so exciting, especially in the higher registers). A fine Page solo then leads the band into what sounds like a backwards version of the Page-composed "Beck's Bolero," hence to a little snatch of Albert King's "The Hunter," and finally to an avalanche of drums and shouting.

In their willingness to waste their considerable talent on unworthy material the Zeppelin has produced an album which is sadly reminiscent of *Truth*. Like the Beck group they are also perfectly willing to make themselves a two- (or, more accurately, one-and-a-half) man show. It would seem that, if they're to help fill the void created by the demise of Cream, they will have to find a producer (and editor) and some material worthy of their collective attention. (p. 7)

> *John Mendelsohn, "'Led Zeppelin'" (originally published in* Rolling Stone, *March 15, 1969), in* Rolling Stone Record Review *by the editors of* Rolling Stone *(copyright © 1967, 1968, 1969, 1970, 1971, by Straight Arrow Publishers, Inc.; all rights reserved; reprinted by permission), Pocket Books, 1971, pp. 6-7.*

["Led Zeppelin II"] is an extension of "Communications Breakdown" from [the] first album. Loud, All-Out, Big-Fast, Steel-Grinding. . . .

Led Zeppelin *seem* to be a quartet of rough London kids who never had a guardian and who go running amok across stage and people's minds with no thought of Art, or Togetherness, or anything half-grossly aesthetic. They don't really need to, as their success shows—fans come to get their spines racked with illicitly obtained and consumed sexthrills, and they get it. (And leave feeling mighty inadequate.)

This album was probably made while having a good time around the studio. It certainly must be listened to in that manner, because if you are a purist, you'll eventually sling it out the window in a fit of genuine anger. "The Lemon Song," for instance, mixes in all the blues phrases stolen from other songs, mostly "Killing Floor," (a Howling Wolf song), and then the unforgettable & inimitable "you better squeeze my lemon, babe." line that they are famous for, (but which was actually stolen from Robert Johnson's "Terraplane Blues").

The inside painting pretty much shows the theme to this album: a huge, golden-plated king-phallic blimp mounted on a Grecian temple/pedestal. . . .

There are a total of nine songs here . . . , and only one, "Living Loving Maid," is a tightly arranged immediate piece, with the rest being between four and six minutes long. "Thank You" is actually a nice slow lovely-organy song but. . . .

THE REST all come on like exploding flashlights and hot twisted metal come erupting and shooting crooked sparks without a heavy rest and more more more bitumous blitzrock.

Some songs, like "Heartbreaker," make you shout in warbled pain, others sound borrowed, such an occasional riff that sounds familiar of Jeff Beck (though who actually did it first is beyond scoffed complaint), and another moment is borrowed from Steve Cropper. Nevertheless, working honest vinyl impressions of hot lust with sweated fervor into soapy orgasmic rock. . . this album will appeal to those who need it. (p. 10)

> *Go Magazine (copyright 1969 by GO Publishing Co., Inc.), November 7, 1969.*

JOHN MENDELSOHN

Hey, man, I take it all back! [*Led Zeppelin II*] is one fucking *heavyweight* of an album! OK—I'll concede that until you've listened to the album eight hundred times, as I have, it seems as if it's just one especially heavy song extended over the space of two whole sides. But, hey! you've got to admit that the Zeppelin has their distinctive and enchanting formula down stonecold, man. Like you get the impression they could do it in their sleep. . . .

"Whole Lotta Love," which opens the album, has to be the heaviest thing I've run across (or, more accurately, that's run across me) since "Parchmant Farm" on [Blue Cheer's] *Vincebus Eruptum*. . . .

Anyhow . . . Robert Plant, who is rumored to sing some notes on this record that only dogs can hear, demonstrates his heaviness on "The Lemon Song." When he yells "Shake me 'til the juice runs down my leg," you can't help but flash on the fact that the *lemon* is a cleverly-disguised phallic metaphor. Cunning Rob, sticking all this eroticism in between the lines just like his blues-beltin' ancestors!

John Mendelsohn, "'Led Zeppelin II'" (originally published in Rolling Stone, *December 13, 1969), in* The Rolling Stone Record Review *by the editors of* Rolling Stone *(copyright © 1967, 1968, 1969, 1970, 1971, by Straight Arrow Publishers, Inc.; all rights reserved; reprinted by permission), Pocket Books, 1971, p. 8.*

LESTER BANGS

I keep nursing this love-hate attitude toward Led Zeppelin. Partly from genuine interest and mostly indefensible hopes, in part from the conviction that nobody *that* crass could be all that bad, I turn to each fresh album expecting—what? Certainly not subtle echoes of the monolithic Yardbirds, or authentic blues experiments, or even much variety. Maybe it's just that they seem like the ultimate Seventies Calf of Gold.

The Zep, of all bands surviving, are *today*—their music is as ephemeral as Marvel comix, and as vivid as an old Technicolor cartoon. It doesn't challenge anybody's intelligence or sensibilities, relying instead on a pat visceral impact that will insure absolute stardom for many moons to come. Their albums refine the crude public tools of all dull white blues bands into something awesome in its very insensitive grossness, like a Cecil B. DeMille epic. If I rely so much on visual and filmic metaphors, it's because they apply so exactly. . . .

Their third album deviates little from the track laid by the first two, even though they go acoustic on several numbers. Most of the acoustic stuff sounds like standard Zep graded down decibelwise, and the heavy blitzes could've been outtakes from *Zeppelin II*. In fact, when I first heard the album my main impression was the consistent anonymity of most of the songs—no one could mistake the band, but no gimmicks stand out with any special outrageousness, as did the great, gleefully absurd Orangutang Plant-*cum*-wheezing guitar freakout that made "Whole Lotta Love" such a pulp classic. "Immigrant Song" comes closest, with its bulldozer rhythms and Bobby Plant's double-tracked wordless vocal croonings echoing behind the main vocal like some cannibal chorus wailing in the infernal light of a savage fertility rite. What's great about it, though, the Zep's special genius, is that the whole effect is so utterly two-dimensional and unreal. . . .

Unfortunately, precious little of *Z III*'s remaining hysteria is as useful or as effectively melodramatic. . . .

I must mention a song called "That's the Way," because it's the first song they've ever done that has truly moved me. Son of a gun, it's beautiful. Above a very simple and appropriately everyday acoustic riff, Plant sings a touching picture of two youngsters who can no longer be playmates because one's parents and peers disapprove of the other because of long hair and being generally from "the dark side of town." The vocal is restrained for once—in fact, Plant's intonations are as plaintively gentle as some of the Rascals' best ballad work—and a perfectly modulated electronic drone wails in the background like melancholy harbor scows as the words fall soft as sooty snow: "And yesterday I saw you standing by the river / I read those tears that filled your eyes / And all the fish that lay in dirty water dying / Had they got you hypnotized?" Beautiful, and strangely enough Zep. As sage [Chuck] Berry declared eons ago, it shore goes to show you never can tell. (p. 34)

Lester Bangs, in Rolling Stone *(by Straight Arrow Publishers, Inc. © 1970; all rights reserved; reprinted by permission), Issue 71, November 26, 1970.*

BRUCE HARRIS

There's something absurd about reviewing an album like [*Led Zeppelin III*]. It's like reviewing *Love Story*. No one is the least interested in what you say. Don't expect mass audiences to turn away from *Love Story* to go see an Italian western just because Bruce Harris said that the combined talent that went into making the movie wouldn't be enough to come up with an effective circular for the A & P.

Likewise, there isn't a reason in the world why Led Zeppelin should even bother to be good, having the charts sewn up the way they do, but the fact is, music lovers, that on this LP, if not on their previous two, the Zep have demonstrated that they are first-rate supermusicians, and that, with the current drought in Rock artistry, they aren't only good, they're one of the best. . . .

Immigrant Song, for instance, is one of the best things Led Zeppelin has ever done, and it's a pleasure to hear it on Top 40 Radio, not only because it drowns out the squeals of James Taylor and Elton John, but because *Immigrant Song* is not only louder, it's better: "How soft your fields so green / Can whisper tales of gore / Of how we calmed the tides of war, / We are your overlords. / On we sweep with threshing oar, / Our only goal will be, the western shore." That's poetry. No, it isn't great. Yes, it is sophomoric. But it is on Top 40 radio, and yes, yes, yes, it is a far cry from "Sugar, Sugar, Honey, Honey, You are my Candy Girl, and you got me wanting you." . . .

So ultimately, *Led Zeppelin III* is not only high-energy. It is also high-quality. There's an awful lot of good music included, the strongest cuts being the bizarre *Friends* which has a curious middle-period Yardbirds feeling, the lovely *Tangerine,* and the moving *That's The Way,* an unusual song about an unusual topic. However, besides the brilliant, booming *Immigrant Song,* the most wholly realized cut is the magnificent rendition of the traditional *Gallows Pole.* Here Plant's stirring vocal powers are given the perfect vehicle for their expression.

For a supergroup, Led Zeppelin has tried pretty hard here to gain critical validity. Don't mistake them for Grand Funk Railroad. And then again, don't mistake them for a trend. Perhaps Led Zeppelin, the last of the super-hard-rock bands, are not where music is going. But we can only hope, as rock music mellows and quiets down, that it does not mistake softness for profundity. If Led Zeppelin come on loud, maybe it's because they have something to say. (p. 50)

Bruce Harris, in Jazz & Pop *(© 1971 by Jazz Press Inc.; reprinted by permission of the author), March, 1971.*

JON LANDAU

Three or four years ago, rock reviewing was less problematic than it is today. For one thing, you knew what to write about. The Byrds, the Animals, the Dead, the Airplane, and the Beach Boys were fit subjects for comment; Gerry and the Pacemakers, Dave Clark and Freddie and the Dreamers were not. The Beatles, the Stones, and Dylan were the first inductees to rock's (as opposed to rock and roll's) pantheon; after that, everyone bowed in the direction of San Francisco and underground British groups until the appearance of Led Zeppelin.

Zeppelin forced a revival of the distinction between popularity and quality. As long as the bands most admired aesthetically were also the bands most successful commercially (Cream, for instance) the distinction was irrelevant. But Zeppelin's enormous commercial success, in spite of critical opposition, revealed the deep division in what was once thought to be a homogeneous audience.

That division has now evolved into a clearly defined mass taste and a clearly defined elitist taste. Critics may write pages and pages about elitist favorite Captain Beefheart, but it was sons of Grand Funk—namely Black Sabbath—who were the first new band in months to sell out the Fillmore East in advance. . . . Finally, let us never forget that the two best selling albums in the history of Atlantic Records are *In-A-Gadda-Da-Vida* and *Led Zeppelin II,* neither of them quite the subject of "critical acclaim."

If nothing else, it is obvious that people are able to decide what they like without the assistance of critics. (p. 48)

Jon Landau, in Rolling Stone *(by Straight Arrow Publishers, Inc. © 1971; all rights reserved; reprinted by permission), Issue 79, April 1, 1971.*

LENNY KAYE

It might seem a bit incongruous to say that Led Zeppelin—a band never particularly known for its tendency to understate matters—has produced an album [*#&@%*] which is remarkable for its low-keyed and tasteful subtlety, but that's just the case here. The march of the dinosaurs that broke the ground for their first epic release has apparently vanished, taking along with it the splattering electronics of their second effort and the leaden acoustic moves that seemed to weigh down their third. What's been saved is the pumping adrenaline drive that held the key to such classics as "Communication Breakdown" and "Whole Lotta Love," the incredibly sharp and precise vocal dynamism of Robert Plant, and some of the tightest arranging and producing Jimmy Page has yet seen his way toward doing. If this thing with the semimetaphysical title isn't quite their best to date, since the very chances that the others took meant they would visit some outrageous highs as well as some overbearing lows, it certainly comes off as their most consistently good.

One of the ways in which this is demonstrated is the sheer variety of the album: out of eight cuts, there isn't one that steps on another's toes, that tries to do too much all at once. There are Olde Englishe ballads ("The Battle of Evermore" . . .), a kind of pseudo-blues just to keep in touch ("Four Sticks"), a pair of authentic Zeppelinania ("Black Dog" and "Misty Mountain Hop"), some stuff that I might actually call shy and poetic if it didn't carry itself off so well ("Stairway to Heaven" and "Going to California"). . . .

. . . and a couple of songs that when all is said and done, will probably be right up there in the gold-starred hierarchy of put 'em on and play 'em agains. The first, coyly titled "Rock And Roll," is the Zeppelin's slightly-late attempt at tribute to the mother of us all, but here it's definitely a case of better late than never. (pp. 62-3)

The end of the album is saved for "When The Levee Breaks" . . . and it's a dazzler. Basing themselves around one honey of a chord progression, the group constructs an air of tunnel-long depth, full of stunning resolves and a majesty that sets up as a perfect climax. Led Zep have had a lot of imitators over the past few years, but it takes cuts like this to show that most of them have only picked up the style, lacking any real knowledge of the meat underneath.

Uh huh, they got it down all right. . . . Not bad for a pack of Limey lemon squeezers. (p. 63)

Lenny Kaye, in Rolling Stone *(by Straight Arrow Publishers, Inc. © 1971; all rights reserved; reprinted by permission), Issue 98, December 23, 1971.*

MIKE BOURNE

The point is this: even the most trivial art offers some virtue, even the most evanescent entertainment, even the most utter jive, even Led Zeppelin.

To hear a retrospective of their music is to recognize a variety, or simply a musiciality, that never before seemed evident. Not that their fourth LP [#&@%] proves all that exhilarating but in listening I realize a certain jadedness in myself; too often I've accepted their more egregious Top-40 like *The Lemon Song* (possibly the worst rock song ever) as their noisome hallmark—and this is not always so. . . .

[Despite] all the vile humors I've spewed upon the band, the music of Led Zeppelin is at least amusing. . . .

The album compares unfavorably to the more stylized and/or simply more creative recordings of Jack Bruce, Zappa, the Beach Boys and others. But Led Zeppelin nonetheless remains an original "heavy" band, far better than the horde of noisy nothings it spawned, especially the leprous Grand Funk—and in that there must be some value. (p. 28)

Mike Bourne, in down beat *(copyright 1972 by Maher Publications), March 16, 1972.*

LESTER BANGS

Robert Plant, the original hippie, has been responsible for all of Led Zeppelin's lyrics, and his peacelove doves and mushy stairways are all over *Houses of the Holy*. This is the first Zep set where they made the mistake of printing the lyrics; if they hadn't, we might have missed gems like "I got my flower, I got my power," or prime Rowan Brothers stuff like "Hare Hare" and "Singing in the Sunshine, laughing in the rain . . ."

That kind of stuff may bug you the first few playings if you bother to notice it, but that's not what pulls this album down from being a true masterpiece like their last one. Plant's just the easiest member to pick on, and *Houses* is as erratic as Zeppelin have been for most of their career. At its peaks it's amazing, but even though the peaks predominate, the valleys are so *unambitious* you get exasperated.

The perfect cuts are "Song," "Dancing Days," "No Quarter" and "Over the Hills and Far Away." "Days" is built on another one of those angular, dissonant, truly disorienting Page riffs like the one employed in "Misty Mountain Hop." It almost hurts, but you can't get enough of it, and even if some of Plant's lines are rather mawkish, the lyrics and the song's blinding strut make it a crazed '73 successor to "Dancing in the Streets"—a summer song!

"Over the Hills and Far Away" is simply fine, churning mainstay Zep expertise: a folky Page opening, a yearning vocal, a cinerama explosion. These boys breathe dynamics, and they've still got as fine and fierce a rhythm sense as any group on either side of the Atlantic. Just dig "The Crunge," which may put you off at first because it sounds like Plant and the band indulging themselves in a little James Brown wank with tighten-up guitar. But Plant's vocal has a genuine sense of humor, and when Page starts dragging those sproinging backwards riffs from underneath and counterposing them against all this mock-blackface (there is such a thing) it all gets a bit more, ah, intellectual, even if the blabbing at the end is a bunch of foolishness.

So is "D'yer Maker" (foolishness, that is). It sounds like a halfassed attempt at reggae mushed into another one of those cutesy 50s routines. . . . But it's so fucking goofy you end up liking it in spite of (because of?) its very asininity. Which certainly can't be said of "The Rain Song," a truly undistinguished ballad that drags on for far too long. (pp. 62-3)

So you can see why I'm tied up in knots and yodeling. *Houses of the Holy* is leagues from the perfect album Led Zeppelin are capable of making, and I hate to skip cuts. But fuck it! . . . You can see their songs even while you're hearing them in the best oldhat psychedelic sense. And since psychedelia is about due for a recycle anyway, even Plant's love-in lyrics are okay by me. I expected a little more than this after waiting over a year, but I know that at least "Song" and "Dancing Days" are gonna be with me long after they finally get around to releasing their next one, and that's enough. (p. 63)

Lester Bangs, "Getting By on Blood & Iron," in Creem *(© copyright 1973 by Creem Magazine, Inc.), June, 1973, pp. 62-3.*

STEVE SIMELS

The Zep is a band for which I have a sort of grudging respect; all their albums have had a few incandescent moments surrounded by great heaping gobs of overblown silliness, but those incandescent moments have been definitive rock-and-roll. The problem has always seemed to me that Jimmy Page (who *is* the group, for all intents) is either afflicted with a cynical contempt for his audience (justifiable, I'm afraid) or, less likely, blessed with extremely fitful good taste (there are too many moments when the only reaction to his music *has* to be "he must know better"). (p. 111)

Steve Simels, in Stereo Review *(copyright © 1973 Ziff-Davis Publishing Company), November, 1973.*

CHRIS WELCH

"Led Zeppelin" was and still is one of the finest rock albums devised, one that gave birth to a whole school of rock thought, and provided stimulus to countless other groups. . . .

This was the first "heavy" band. . . . The combination of feeling, technical ability and raw energy was quite overwhelming. . . .

Zeppelin were a revolution in 1969, but a lot has happened since then, and many imitators have passed under the bridge, let alone a whole breed of groups who have taken rock music to new frontiers.

There is no earthly reason Page should not take what he has already pioneered and polished, and simply go on producing vibrant and yet essentially humanist hard rock, with the freedom to side-step into intriguing side routes when the mood takes them. . . .

Whatever direction the next Zeppelin album takes us, one can be sure Jimmy will go on supplying excitement and continue his quest for artistic fulfilment.

There is certainly no sign of his withdrawing from the fray.

> Chris Welch, *"Jimmy Page: The Power and the Glory,"* in Melody Maker (© *IPC Business Press Ltd.), March 23, 1974, p. 27.*

MICHAEL OLDFIELD

["Physical Graffiti" is] a work of genius, a superbly performed mixture of styles and influences that encompasses not only all aspects of Led Zep's recording career so far but also much of rock as a whole.

This is not just a collection of great tracks, but a perfectly balanced selection of music that weighs heavy rock with acoustic, ballad with out-and-out rocker in such a way that you can play the album non-stop day and night without ever needing to pause for a bit of peace.

And for one of the world's heaviest bands, that's some achievement. . . .

[Led Zep] are, if you like, one of the few "progressive" bands left—you remember them, the groups who were always going to move forward and keep exploring new avenues.

Zeppelin have, and still are doing just that. They established their base with heavy blues/rock on "Led Zeppelin I", and have constantly sought to build on that, investigating new fields; from the folky "Battle Of Evermore" to the reggae influenced "The Crunge".

Now they've taken electronic space rock for "In The Light", one of the two most immediately striking cuts on "Physical Graffiti". . . .

What marks it as the work of true musical craftsmen . . . is the linking: those space sounds are not just a frill tagged on for the hell of it, but properly joined to the core of the song, first led in by Robert Plant's voice, then led out for a reprise in the middle by Jimmy Page's acoustic guitar.

"Kashmir" hits you just as immediately. It's in a completely different vein: heavily orchestrated, with a chopping string riff which builds up to a crescendo at the end of each verse. The nearest equivalent is the work of the classical composer Moondog, who uses the same richly descriptive style.

So effectively is it used though on "Kashmir" that it actually sounds like you're travelling on a caravanserai through the East. . . .

Certainly this is one of the most imaginative and outstanding numbers Led Zep have ever cut.

But the band's strength does not always rest on the new. They take that old, old theme of the blues on "In My Time Of Dying" and came up with a fresh approach, by constantly changing the pace, veering from the breakneck to the dead slow. . . .

And if it's heavy rock you want, Zeppelin can drive a number along like no other band on earth. Listen to them roar through "Custard Pie", "Night Flight" and "Sick Again", always giving that little bit extra that's the sign of class—a bubbling keyboard here, a nifty riff there, an intricate pattern elsewhere.

They can be wistful ("Down By The Seaside"), fun ("Boogie With Stu"), acoustic ("Bron-Yr-Aur"), melodic ("The Rover")—just about anything in fact. They can take as long as they like with the next album: "Physical Graffiti" will last 18 months or 18 years. And then some.

> Michael Oldfield, *"Led Zeppelin: Pure Genius,"* in Melody Maker (© *IPC Business Press Ltd.), March 1, 1975, p. 13.*

JIM MILLER

[With] the release of *Physical Graffiti*, Led Zeppelin's sixth album, the question [of what group is the world's best rock band] has actually become relevant. This two-record set, the product of almost two years' labor, is the band's *Tommy, Beggar's Banquet* and *Sgt. Pepper* rolled into one: *Physical Graffiti* is Led Zeppelin's bid for artistic respectability.

In a virtual recapitulation of the group's career, *Physical Graffiti* touches all the bases. There's a blues ("In My Time of Dying") and a cosmic-cum-heavy ballad ("In the Light"); there's an acoustic interlude ("Bron-Y-Aur") and lots of bludgeoning hard rock, still this band's forte ("Houses of the Holy," "The Wanton Song"); there are also hints of Bo Diddley ("Custard Pie"), Burt Bacharach ("Down by the Seaside") and Kool and the Gang ("Trampled under Foot"). If nothing else, *Physical Graffiti* is a tour de force.

The album's—and the band's—mainspring is Jimmy Page, guitarist extraordinaire. It was Page who formed Led Zeppelin in 1968. . . . And it is Page who continues to chart Zeppelin's contemporary course, not only as the group's lead guitarist, but also as the band's producer.

His primary concern, both as producer and guitarist, is *sound*. His playing lacks the lyricism of Eric Clapton, the funk of Jimi Hendrix, the rhythmic flair of Peter Townshend; but of all the virtuoso guitarists of the Sixties, Page, along with Hendrix, has most expanded the instrument's sonic vocabulary. . . .

Fronting the band onstage and sharing the spotlight with Page is vocalist Robert Plant. Like the Who's Roger Daltrey, he is a singer of limited range and feeling, but he projects himself with an irrepressible flair. Plant's acrobatics in fact complement Page's preoccupation with sound. Not only does Plant warble limply as well as scream, he also adds yet another gravelly component to the band. In his production of Plant, Page constantly plays on this grittiness, the vocal counterpart to the distorted sound of his own guitar. (p. 48)

The jerky meter and crude attack [that characterized "Communication Breakdown" on *Led Zeppelin*] remain favorite devices of Page, who, like Leiber and Stoller with the Coasters, understands the art of contriving a raucous sound (consider "Rock & Roll," Zeppelin's other masterpiece of distilled freneticism).

Thanks to Page's production, Led Zeppelin quickly outdistanced such predecessors as Cream and the Yardbirds. Not only was Plant a stronger singer than the Yardbirds' Keith Relf, but Page, in contrast to Clapton, Bruce and Baker, grasped the importance of crafting a coherent ensemble approach. Taking his cues from old Sun and Chess records, he used reverb and echo to mold the band into a unit, always accenting the bottom (bass and drums), always aiming at the biggest possible sound. As a result, Zeppelin's early records still sound powerful, while Cream tracks like "White Room" in retrospect sound pale and disjointed. On such classics as "Whole Lotta Love," Page's production set new standards for recording hard rock. . . .

[An] attention to detail and a sense of economy and nuance have become hallmarks of the Zeppelin style. "Four Sticks," from *Led Zeppelin IV,* to take a trifling example, sustains momentum by alternating a distorted electric riff with an acoustic progression doubled on keyboards. The percussion recalls Elvis's "Mystery Train" more than Cream's "Sunshine of Your Love," and it adds just the right touch of elegance to an otherwise elementary cut.

Physical Graffiti only confirms Led Zeppelin's preeminence among hard rockers. Although it contains no startling breakthroughs, it does afford an impressive overview of the band's skill. On "Houses of the Holy," Plant's lyrics mesh perfectly with Page's stuttering licks. Here again, the details are half the fun: Bonham kicks the cut along with a cowbell while the two final verses add what sounds like a squeaky chorus of "do-it"'s behind the vocal; Plant meanwhile is almost inaudibly overdubbed on the song's central chorus, underlining the phrase "let the music be your master."

Throughout the album, Page and the band tap a strange lot of sources, although the result is always pure Zeppelin. . . .

Naturally, *Graffiti* is not without faults—Zeppelin is too intuitive a band to cut a flawless album. Although Page and Bonham mount a bristling attack on "The Rover," this track, like several others, suffers from Plant's indefinite pitch. Other cuts, such as the ten-minute "Kashmir" and "In My Time of Dying," succumb to monotony. "In the Light," one of the album's most ambitious efforts, similarly fizzles down the home stretch, although the problem here is not tedium but a fragmentary composition that never quite jells: When Page on the final release plays an ascending run intended to sound majestic, the effect is more stilted than stately.

Despite such lapses, *Physical Graffiti* testifies to Page's taste and Led Zeppelin's versatility. Taken as a whole, it offers an astonishing variety of music, produced impeccably by Page. . . .

Physical Graffiti will likely . . . disappoint those who prefer their rock laced with lyrical significance: Led Zeppelin no more articulates a world view than Little Richard (or Cream) did. Yet while Zeppelin's stature as cultural spokesmen can be questioned, their standing as rock musicians cannot. True, Led Zeppelin misses the swagger of the Stones, the kinetics of the Who. But on *Physical Graffiti,* Led Zeppelin performs rock with creativity, wit and undeniable impact.

They have forged an original style, and they have grown within it; they have rooted their music in hard-core rock & roll, and yet have gone beyond it. They may not be the greatest rock band of the Seventies. But after seven years, five albums and now *Physical Graffiti,* they must be counted among them. (p. 51)

Jim Miller, "Anglo Graffitti: Hardest-Core Rock," in Rolling Stone (by Straight Arrow Publishers, Inc. © 1975; all rights reserved; reprinted by permission), Issue 183, March 27, 1975, pp. 48, 51.

JAAN UHELSKI

Physical Graffiti can stand on its own historically without the support of Zep's five other million sellers, but inevitably the cuts on this album will be scrutinized with Nancy Drew-like precision in search of a successor to "Stairway" or an equal to "Rock and Roll." *Graffiti* is, in fact, a better album than the other five offerings, the band being more confident, more arrogant in fact, and more consistent. The choice of material is varied, giving the audience a chance to see all sides of the band. Equal time is given to the cosmic and the terrestrial, the subtle and the passionate.

The exotic and musky "Kashmir" is intriguing in its otherworldliness. Jimmy Page's grinding, staccato guitar work sounds like a cosmic travelog to spiritual regeneration, swelling around the lyrics, which are heavily laden with mystical allusions and Hessean imagery. Although "Kashmir" is certainly the best cut on the album, it could be trimmed without losing any of its mesmeric effect, because at some point the incense grows a little murky, and the slow burning guitar degenerates into opulent cliches, causing the instrumental interludes to echo an *Exodus* soundtrack.

Not all of the cuts are exercises in advanced audial basketweaving, but trace a musical cycle running from Page's grandiose productions to basic drunken boogie. . . .

Led Zeppelin moves in strange ways. Sure they're gutsy, ballsy, and flamboyantly aggressive, always spiked with a lot of eroticism, but they're also cerebral . . . by way of the glands. They have this unique ability to wind you up and prime you for a full-throttled tilt. You rocked, you rolled, and oh mama those juices flowed—but you also listened to the words. (p. 64)

A Led Zeppelin album is like a select invitation to a key club of rock 'n' roll, where the kohl eyed gypsy Jimmy Page is finally accessible through his smoky guitar solos. Robert Plant preens and moans, lusts and longs for lost memories . . . and takes you along. Like a sonic vortex, Zeppelin draws you into their private caprice, spiraling, coaxing your willing psyche into a suprasensory haven where you can taste and savor this dream stuff that superstars thrive on. This is not pop music, but a harder stuff, more heady and potent, like a round of whiskeys and coke. Zeppelin are avatars in a cultural vacuum. (p. 65)

Jaan Uhelski, "Rock's Best Body English," in Creem (© copyright 1975 by Creem Magazine, Inc.), May, 1975, pp. 64-5.

CHRIS WELCH

Of all the great British groups that emerged towards the end of the sixties, [Led Zeppelin] represented the most raw and powerful approach to music, combining an intelligence and expertise, that made their appeal, to the vast bulk of fans, irresistible. . . .

For many fans "Led Zeppelin" is still the definitive album

by the group. There was a pace, an electrifying atmosphere about the pieces. And the way they blended into each other, especially the fade on "Your Time Is Gonna Come," leading into the unexpected Indian flavour of "Black Mountain Side," with Viram Jasani on tabla, gave the album a sense of performance that many a concept album has lacked.

The sizzling, spine-chilling effect of "Dazed And Confused," the grinding blues feeling engendered on Robert's tour de force on "I Can't Quit You Baby" and the sheer, exultant power of "Communication Breakdown," taken at racing tempo, was a remarkable piece of sustained creativity that makes it still one of the most enjoyable rock albums produced, and one of the most successful in capturing the ingredients of a British rock band in full flight. (p. 28)

Chris Welch, "The Led Zeppelin Story," in
Melody Maker (© *IPC Business Press Ltd.*),
May 10, 1975, pp. 28-9.

BUD SCOPPA

[Led Zeppelin plays] a basic, sinewy brand of music that depends for its impact more on simple relentlessness than on dramatic development. Not many bands could get away with working within such a simple framework, but Led Zeppelin takes a seemingly arrogant delight in flattening everything in its path through a perfect execution of fundamentals.

In the Sixties, it would have been hard to imagine a band like Zeppelin winning a mass following (it may now be the most popular single attraction in rock) with such hard, uncompromising music, but this outfit has certain other characteristics that have combined with its raw sound to make it appealing in a very broad way. One of the most important of these is Led Zeppelin's playing off its almost austere amplified blues and rock-and-roll against the flamboyant and exotic public personalities of Page and Plant. Both in the music itself and in the way it's perceived by the listener, this exotic suggestion has lent mood and mystery to the bulk of the group's recorded work.

If all this makes Led Zeppelin seem overwhelmingly ominous (and here comes characteristic number two), this great heaviness has always been balanced by a pervasive sense of humor; they're capable of making fun of their own identity: for example, Page and Plant originally called their publishing firm Superhype Music, and their second album's hit single, *Whole Lotta Love,* was at once a crushingly effective heavy-metal number and a winning heavy-metal *parody.*

A third aspect of Led Zep's character is the group's willingness to be adventurous within the stylistic parameters its members have set for themselves, and, as a consequence, each of their half-dozen albums has a distinctive identity. Of the six, the only ones not generally satisfying are "Led Zeppelin III" and the fifth album, "Houses of the Holy," the problem in each case being caused by the group's allowing itself to drift too far from its basic forms—that is, by their being *too* adventurous, *too* confident.

Led Zeppelin's most obvious success, the ubiquitous *Stairway to Heaven* (from their fourth album) was remarkable because it placed what may well be the band's most explosively passionate performance into a formal, sequential context, complete with appropriate imagery and a basic

metaphor that paralleled the relentlessly ascendant musical movement of the track. So, seemingly paradoxically, the group was best able to present its all-stops-out style by carefully measuring it to fit a precisely conceived structure. But that sort of adaptability is simply proof of the remarkable (if often masked) intelligence at the core of this band's work. What *Stairway to Heaven* makes clear is that the band is most successful when it innovates from *out* of its basic style, rather than by moving away from it.

Their new "Physical Graffiti" shows both that that intelligence is still very much present, and that, when it errs, Led Zeppelin still errs on the side of audacity. This is the band's first double album, and playing its four sides straight through is—as I've learned—*a whole lotta Led Zep.* But the wealth of ideas presented do justify the expanded format, even if some of those ideas don't quite come off.

This time out, Page has chosen to present the band in a context that is the antithesis of the sonically elaborate second and fourth albums—a stark, roomy, flatly realistic ambiance that serves to make the rockers roar like nothing they've done since their relatively crude (but still tremendously exciting) first album. And in the several quiet segments that are contained here, the roominess oddly lends a feeling of intimacy to Plant's heretofore cutting and two-dimensional singing; surprisingly enough, his restraint wears rather well.

What's wrong with the album is that it is programmed to showcase its three least successful tracks. . . . [*In My Time of Dying*] is an electric Delta blues in which the band attempts to transform—through endless repetition—a relatively standard progression into something tangibly, er, ghostly. Its Robert Johnson metaphysics notwithstanding, the track seems to me to be doubly irritating: it's interminable and it lacks Page's usual subtlety. *Kashmir* is a more ambitious failure. On this track, Page attempts to use the tone colors of Middle Eastern music to turn a medium-paced rocker into a dramatic, image-evoking piece. While its unorthodox textures produce a dusky and exotic effect, it never really gets beyond the point of sounding like the soundtrack to some Charlton Heston bigger-than-life epic about the Third Crusade.

In the Light provides a classic example of how a particularly dumb or ugly track can set up, by sheer contrast, the particularly pretty or tasteful track that immediately follows it. The first two-thirds of *In the Light* has the distinction of being both ugly *and* dumb. It begins with a collage of bleats and drones which combine to create a sort of sci-fi bagpipe, develops into the most unlistenable sort of heavy-metal dirge, only to open abruptly into a lovely guitar/electric-piano section. Then, after the progression is repeated and the track concludes, along comes *Bron-Yr-Aur,* a pastoral acoustic-guitar solo that introduces itself like a peppermint Cert into a tired mouth.

Much more successful (though less obviously ambitious) than the three aforementioned major clinkers are the companion pieces *Down by the Seaside* and *Ten Years Gone.* Although hampered somewhat by a plodding tempo in its primary section, *Seaside* makes good use of some unexpected devices, such as a Beatlesque "aahhh" chorus and segmented structure. The lyric is rather Beatleish, too, in its juxtaposition of hazy images and ambiguous lines, and it is inexplicably poignant, especially in the brief "twist again" middle segment. The track foreshadows *Ten Years*

Gone in both mood and theme, touching as it does on a half-recalled, half-dreamed scene. But *Ten Years Gone* goes directly into the past and comments overtly on change and the passage of time. . . . In a modulated, unflashy way (they seem almost meek at first by Led Zeppelin standards), these two tracks provide the album's most imaginative and dramatic moments. (pp. 84-5)

Because its big programmed moments don't work, and because its general tone is more serious than other Zeppelin albums . . . "Physical Graffiti" is not Led Zeppelin's most impressive work. But Plant's much more controlled and varied singing, the set's wealth of modest rockers, and its subtle innovations make it abundantly attractive nonetheless. As always, part of the fun stems from the fact that this band can do so much while working in such a severely limited idiom, from both the dramatic and textural viewpoints. Within the areas it has chosen, Led Zeppelin still has no peers. (p. 85)

> *Bud Scoppa, "Led Zeppelin: Erring on the Side of Audacity," in* Stereo Review *(reprinted by permission of the author), June, 1975, pp. 81-5.*

STEPHEN DAVIS

Led Zeppelin's seventh album confirms this quartet's status as heavy-metal champions of the known universe. *Presence* takes up where last season's monumentally molten *Physical Graffiti* left off—few melodies, a preoccupation with hard-rock rhythm, lengthy echoing moans gushing from Robert Plant and a general lyrical slant toward the cosmos. . . .

Physical Graffiti was a penultimate of sorts ("Trampled Under Foot" was the hardest rock ever played by humans, while "Kashmir" must be the most pompous) and the new record certainly tries to keep up. The opening track, "Achilles Last Stand," could be the Yardbirds, 12 years down the road. The format is familiar: John Bonham's furiously attacking drum is really the lead instrument, until Jimmy Page tires of chording under Plant and takes over.

Although Page and Plant are masters of the form, emotions often conflict and the results are mixed. A few bars from one piece convince the listener he's hearing the greatest of rock & roll, then the very next few place him in a nightmarish 1970 movie about deranged hippies.

Actually there is some fine rock on *Presence*. "Nobody's Fault but Mine" is strong, while "Candy Store Rock" perfectly evokes the Los Angeles milieu in which the Zep composed this album; it sounds like an unholy hybrid in which Buddy Holly is grafted onto the quivering stem of David Bowie

Zeppelin's main concern here is to establish a reliable riff and stick to it, without complicating things too much with melody or nuance. At their best, the riffs are clean and purifying. The two dreary examples of blooze ("Tea for One," "For Your Life") may stretch even the diehards' loyalty, but make no mistake: *Presence* is another monster in what by now is a continuing tradition of battles won by this band of survivors. (p. 64)

> *Stephen Davis, in* Rolling Stone *(by Straight Arrow Publishers, Inc. 1976; all rights reserved; reprinted by permission), Issue 213, May 20, 1976.*

JAMES WOLCOTT

No "Black Dog" [in *Presence*], no "Kashmir" either. Yet though *Presence* doesn't bombingly pockmark the landscape or scale snowy Himalayan heights—even if Jimmy Page's guitar is becoming a riff Osterizer and Robert Plant's voice is shredding at the edges and tearing in the middle—still, Zeppelin has such command of heavy-metal weaponry that even their modest efforts have scorched-earth capability. When Zeppelin doesn't launch search-and-destroy missions into your neocortex it's because they don't want to, not because they can't. This album, a quickie recorded in eighteen days, lacks the fleetness of *Houses of the Holy* and the architectural density of *Physical Graffiti,* but in its best moments still manages to rattle the windowpanes.

"Achilles' Last Stand" for example is lengthy, too lengthy, and drivingly singleminded (a detour or two would have been nice), but is rescued by Plant's parched-throat chanting which gives the track a raw thrilling lift. "For Your Life," however, features Plant at his most dreary: he boringly moans coital groans as if his vocal cords were located in his testicles; such singing should be vasectomized. "Royal Orleans" has teasing guitar licks; "Nobody's Fault but Mine" opens pretentiously but has a blasty harmonica break; "Candy Store Rock" is formula grindola, and "Tea for One" is the obligatory soul-dragging, slow-bluesy number, a recycle of "Since I've Been Loving You" from album three. The high on *Presence* is "Hots on for Nowhere" which is dynamically sporadic. . . .

Contrary to myth, critics have never really hated Led Zep the way they've hated units like Chicago, ELO, or Emerson Lake & Palmer; Zeppelin was just resented, and resented simply because despite their numero uno popularity, they're fundamentally so damned *uninteresting* to write about. Nearly all of the mavens . . . have written memorably about the Stones, but I've never read any analysis of Zeppelin which made them sound more provocative than the Doobie Brothers, BTO, Bad Company, or any of those other applause-machine bands that I assiduously avoid. Now I understand why: everything Led Zeppelin does is in the grooves, there's no spillover, no sauce for us young dogs to lap up, and the fans they don't care, they adore music which is so majestically self-contained. Though I enjoy Zeppelin, it's been a while since hermetic-studio music could have an equally enthralling effect. In fact, it's been a long time been a long time been a been a lonely-lonely-lonely-lonely-*time.*

> *James Wolcott, "Same Same Old Old (Do You Care?)," in* Creem *(© copyright 1977 by Creem Magazine, Inc.), July, 1976, p. 65.*

DAVE MARSH

The Song Remains the Same isn't the landmark in rock cinema Led Zeppelin would like it to be. In fact, it's barely a movie at all, just some concert footage interspersed with trick photography (in a fantasy sequence devoted to each member). This technique is meant to unify the best qualities of *A Hard Day's Night* and *Gimme Shelter,* but it doesn't work: there's none of the Beatles' wit, and the horror is phony. Still, in its misguided way, this blurry, pretentious monolith does offer some insights into what makes the most popular heavy-metal band tick. (p. 19)

Parsimony is one of the movie's themes, albeit accidentally. When a telegram arrives notifying Robert Plant of the impending tour, he stands and smiles at the waiting messenger. Finally, the kid shrugs and leaves: these rock stars don't even tip.

The other theme is sadism, principally expressed in the fantasy sequences, although there's an edge to the documentary footage, too. It hardly behooves a Sam Peckinpah fan such as myself to complain of gratuitous violence, but sadism is the only word for some of this. In Plant's fantasy, a hippie Camelot is transformed, without apparent reason, into a brief horror show of gore and rape; the effect is more sickening than shocking. This mood of semipsychopathic self-indulgence pervades *The Song Remains the Same.* Worse, the film lacks a single moment of catharsis—it's not only relentlessly vicious, but relentlessly antihuman and unthinking.

It is hard to imagine any other major rock act making a film so guileless and revealing. Far from a monument to Zeppelin's stardom, *The Song Remains the Same* is a tribute to their rapaciousness and inconsideration. While Led Zeppelin's music remains worthy of respect (even if their best songs are behind them), their sense of themselves merits only contempt. (p. 21)

> *Dave Marsh, "They Probably Think This Film Is about Them," in* Rolling Stone *(by Straight Arrow Publishers, Inc. © 1976; all rights reserved; reprinted by permission), Issue 227, December 2, 1976, pp. 19, 21.*

ROY HARPER

Robert Plant is one of the great "mediatricians" of the Sixties, and is likely to remain so into the Eighties and Nineties and beyond the year 2,000. . . .

In my estimation Robert's forte is twofold: one, I think, is his ability to be able to understand the forces at work in what we could loosely call the youth culture, and two, not only to understand them but to continue to assimilate them into the nucleus of his art, so that at no time in the last few years has his finger been anywhere other than on the pulse, the pulse of human youth on this planet.

To be that vital is no mean feat. . . .

In one sense, it is hard to talk about Robert's contribution to British art without a reference to Jimmy Page, his great co-pilot, because the vast majority of the musical forms and structures in which their work is contained can be traced, in my view, to solidly British foundations.

Although a great many of us are blues-influenced in this generation, our own original work manifests many of the great traditions of our own indigenous art. This is especially true of Robert, whose fantasies of the British past and future lend themselves admirably to Jimmy's flowing intricacy of design.

If you hold the great plate from Lindisfarne or Iona or the Book of Kells in your hand and you listen to "Battle Of Evermore," "Four Sticks" or even the global-village-influenced "Kashmir," the family resemblance is striking.

Robert's ability as a rock lyricist is second to none because of his awareness of the medium/people/world. In my view, he is at his best when he is not being portentous. "Stairway To Heaven" suffers in this way, perhaps, although it has brought many a tear to my eye, whereas lyrics like on "The Song Remains The Same," "The Rain Song," and "In The Light" are pure joy.

If Robert has a failing, it is his almost deification of all things Celtic, to the detriment of all things English, where, at one time, there was much Celtic basking to be had in mucho-reflected English glory. . . .

In a land where towers of strength are not a common phenomenon and great all-rounders are sadly a dying breed, if only temporaneously, I am proud to be contemporary with Robert, whose light and inspiration will shine, I am sure, for many long years. He will continue to produce, meanwhile, and I only hope that I'm around in another ten years because I've got a feeling that he's just coming into his own. The song, although remaining the same, is once-upon-an-age improved upon, and those of us around to see it do so are illuminated beyond time, by it.

> *Roy Harper, "Finger on the Pulse," in* Melody Maker *(© IPC Business Press Ltd.), March 19, 1977, p. 14.*

TONY PALMER

Stylistically, [the music of Led Zeppelin] is a tour de force, borrowing from Bo Diddley, the Stones, Cream, and Burt Bacharach, fusing jazz, rock, blues, flamenco. It is persuasive and snarling, whether acoustic or electric. It is deceptively facile, yet almost never overblown. It relies heavily on the blues for its emotional strength, yet has expanded the vocabulary of that ill-used idiom while remaining firmly locked within it. Some maintain that, like the best or the worst of rock, Page and his troupe have been schooled in the art of excess. They play too loud and too long. Yet the musical evidence dumbfounds such a view. A song like "Stairway to Heaven" is characteristic; it begins quietly with acoustic guitar playing an aching quasi-blues melody. The singer stutters out the simplest of themes. Gradually, but inevitably, the sound develops over ten minutes into a massive climax, the bass and drums providing an elemental roar from which the guitar (now electric) and singer tear a raging, hurting melody. Not all Zeppelin's songs are based on this pattern, but a sufficient number to recognize this as the group's signature. Again, it is the multiplicity of cross-references that makes the music arresting, as if the band were summing up rock and roll today and yet refashioning many of its conflicting elements into a new sound that has the possibility, thereby, of extended development. One hears snatches of the Beatles' chord progression, the miasmic, tortured blues line of Leadbelly, the rhythmic brutality of Pete Townshend. Yet the whole is different from the parts.

Of all those working in the rock milieu today, Page is the master craftsman. . . . Page recognized that rock contained within *itself* the possibility of development. (p. 296)

> *Tony Palmer, in his* All You Need Is Love: The Story of Popular Music *(copyright © Theatre Projects Film Productions Limited, EMI Television Productions Limited and Phongram Limited, 1976; all rights reserved; reprinted by permission of Viking Penguin Inc.), Viking Penguin, 1977.*

ROBERT SMITH

It's Plant's wailing, drifting, compelling voice and uninhibited stage presence, along with Page's electrifying musical direction (and guitar playing) that carry [Led Zeppelin]. The mystery of their success is partly in the surprising ways they take to the stage and *not let go,* as well as their ability—behind the scenes—to write and record with uncanny exactitude and excitement. They have mastered a unique sound: loud, spiritual and mesmerizing.

> *Robert Smith, "Robert Plant, Male Vocalist of the Year," in* Circus Magazine *(copyright © 1978 by Circus Enterprises Corporation), February 16, 1978, p. 24.*

JAMES SPINA

In every sense of the word this [article] is 'a ramble' on strictly intended to convey the incredible staying power, the historically heavy importance and the sometimes celtic prowisnish that is, in the christening words of Keith Moon, a LED ZEPPELIN. (p. 38)

[Despite] massive personal setbacks, constant critical abuse and a carefully controlled output of recorded music Led Zep are still the best at their business of heavy metal, rockironroll music. . . .

There isn't one bad cut on that first record. Some people are constantly griping about the fact that Page took all the ingredients of the first Jeff Beck Group and called it something new. That is totally unfair. Compare the two versions of "You Shook Me" and the distinctly different points of view become vary apparent.

Both guitarists shared similar roots and routes so of course they were shooting off from similar hips but whereas Beck never left much room for the group, Page was working towards a total sound that would survive while Beck's unit hit the kids. Zeppelin also had this folk fixation, even on the first album (check out "Black Mountain Side" and the soft interludes of "Babe I'm Gonna Leave You") that would eventually develop into the one side of Zeppelin no heavy band could grasp. (p. 39)

[The] most important (and popular) heavy rock record in the universe [is] *Led Zeppelin II*. Forget about Dylan being the first bootlegged rock star. There was this guy at Queens College selling truckloads of this record (with exactly duplicated cover and label) on campus at three bucks a clip. Nobody could get enough Led Zep. First FM then AM radio started playing "Whole Lotta Love" to death. To this day many people don't realize that this sonic sonnet opens up with an almost inaudible laugh-breath-cough-sigh of anticipation as Robert Plant clears his pipes before laying down one of the most aggressively spectacular rock vocals ever recorded.

The middle "meteor—metric—gnomed" break recalls early Yardbird rave ups right up until Page's chokeneck, breakneck solo. Many youngsters caught their first snatch of filth-infested blues licking on "The Lemon Song". . . .

Years later thirteen year old kids are still buying *II* as if it had been released yesterday. May these babes forever be the taste makers of time. Played today the record sounds totally undated and played side to side with The Stones "Some Girls" it makes that lusciously sexist slab of vinyl sound like outtakes from a recording session joining asexuals to cotton swabs. Though they would never lose that touch, never again would Page and Company sound so groin grown.

Now the story gets cerebrally disorienting. On the heels of massive monetary success Led Zeppelin withdrew and re-routed. Jimmy Page grew a beard and started sporting a massive old overcoat. *Led Zeppelin III* marked a drastic

shift in the group's material. On a more than equal footing with the band's on stage heavy-handedness, the new music (as recorded) shifted under the weight of cosmic acoustics and Anglo-folk, lyrical tapestries. Robert Plant emerged as a sometimes obvious but often engaging druid dabbler. One of the songs is in fact dedicated to an artist whose music bore similar celtic overtones, Roy Harper. Most of this charm can be closely tied to the band's (and especially Page's) spiritual ties to that 'place' clarioned in "Bron-Y-Aur Stomp".

It is here that Led Zeppelin transforms from some thick-steeled tank into a band of whimsical warriors armed to the teeth in an array of studio-sorcery, surreal screeching vocals and one part air/one part rock. By record number four they even discard the title, replacing it with four symbols. . . . [#&@%] carries on with the fairy battles ("Evermore") paced by pounding rock songs (like "Black Dog") that must have had countless garage bands spinning in amazement while trying to keep up with the tempo changes. . . .

"Evermore" remains as this record's mastergroove, a timeless slice of music on good footing in any sound idiom. . . .

Houses Of The Holy continues the secret ways of *IV*. . . . Page had become a master of the million and one strings approach to recording his guitar bits. Every song seems to hum along like some island of pleading sirens. Try that metaphor out on "Dancing Days" or "The Song Remains The Same" to hear what I mean. Even when he plays one guitar part it sounds like twelve. And live he began incorporating that civilization of alien sounds into his solos right up there with those trademark bent notes, slurs and bow-itific visions. Still chuckle over the campiness of "D'yer Maker" (the jamaica . . . get it . . . chuckle . . . but damn it if they don't do the best ever heavy metal reggae song ever recorded.) and 'where is that confounded bridge' on the James Brown take-off "The Crunge"?

Physical Graffiti Even the name sounds monsterously imposing. A double album of music that breaks with usual rock tradition by being wholly and unifyingly worth it. Don't ask me to pick out any clunker cuts. Also don't ask me to name all the cuts on the two records. This music is frightfully impressive. Musically as intricate as its cover, the whole project reeks of self satisfaction. This band knows its place in the universe and all pretenders will get "Trampled Under Foot". "Kashmir" has almost replaced "Stairway" as the most requested FM Zep cut and well it should. The bow technique previously resorted to as a gimmick takes on the guise of the song's very arrangement, propelling the piece into tense territories of Asian cultures and alienated relationships. Plant sounds like some sacrificial pig being electrocuted by a bolt of white noise. (pp. 40-1)

"Houses Of The Holy" (The song, not the lp) is nearly out of character with its title. Envisioning another "Evermore" the boy invites you to the movies but tricks you into his usual visions of angels and fancy figments. Or is it? Right smack in the center of this sound Plant starts screaming about sowing seeds and I think they have a bit to do with those lemons he wanted squeezed way back on *II*.

I can't say much about Zep's live soundtrack album for the film "The Song Remains The Same". It does work in the context of the film and it is better than the rash of countless live bootleg tapes of Led Zep shows but the real live lp is

yet to come. Page constantly promises to get to those endless reels of live material and work out a live testament to
the band's legendary performances. This disc remains as
my least favorite Zeppelin record. . . .

Presence is so complex, so ethereal, so Led Zeppelin that it
deserves an award all to itself. . . . I still haven't peeled my
way through the labyrinth of sounds on "Achilles Last
Stand" and just about every other track on the disc. Sure at
times the old Zep themes gets a bit overbearing and
boorish. But that is the point. This band earned the right to
be righteously heavy because they invented the place. . . .

Will the competition of the new wave affect them? Is there
a place in this rock arena for a group that seems more concerned with feudalism than anarchy? . . . I don't think a
tidal wave really has to worry about any fresh ripples in the
rock pond. (p. 41)

> *James Spina, "Good Times Bad Times: The Led
> Zeppelin Story," in* Hit Parader *(© copyright
> 1979 Charlton Publications, Inc.), January, 1979,
> pp. 38-41.*

Katherine Paterson

1932-

American young adult novelist. Paterson writes both historical and contemporary young adult fiction. She has also written several books for children, and has assembled a multi-media workshop on religious study which was distributed to Sunday Schools across the United States. Born and raised in China during the Japanese occupation, she later studied and served as a missionary in Japan. Her knowledge of Japanese culture and history has provided the background for three of her novels, which are set in feudal Japan. Paterson's most recent books have been set in present-day America; *Bridge to Terabithia* is based in part on the experience of her younger son. Whether set in East or West, her novels are characterized by their concern with moral decisions and the process of self-realization. In 1977 she won the National Book Award for *The Master Puppeteer* and the Newbery Medal for *Bridge to Terabithia*. (See also *Contemporary Authors*, Vols. 21-24, rev. ed., and *Something about the Author*, Vol. 13.)

Suspended in delicate imagery and among the many layered feuds between the Samurai clans of the Genji and Heike is the subdued quest of the nameless orphan Muna [in *The Sign of the Chrysanthemum*], who flees the burial of his peasant mother to search for a warrior father identifiable only by a small chrysanthemum tattoo. This introspective adventure, in which Muna learns to find his fortune within himself, will attract those readers who can be sustained by the carefully evoked setting and a realistic, stoical resolution which leaves some questions, philosophic and factual, open-ended. (pp. 1272-73)

Kirkus Reviews *(copyright © 1973 The Kirkus Service, Inc.), November 15, 1973.*

Twelfth-century Japan may seem a long way off but if you can accustom yourself to the fierce life of samurai you may enjoy [*The Sign of the Chrysanthemum*]. . . . The tale is simply told. There is plenty of action. It is a boy's book, and is at least a change from war stories of our own time. (pp. 335-36)

The Junior Bookshelf, *October, 1975.*

The deep bond between Jiro and the puppet-master's son Kinshi, both apparently unloved by their demanding fathers, forms [*The Master Puppeteer*'s] stable core, but Paterson's ability to exploit the tension between violence in the street and dreamlike confrontations of masked puppet operators is what makes this more lively and immediate than her other, equally exacting, historical fictions. (p. 71)

Kirkus Reviews *(copyright © 1976 The Kirkus Service, Inc.), January 15, 1976.*

DORA JEAN YOUNG

Making economical use of detail to set scene and atmosphere [in *The Master Puppeteer*], the author has chosen a period of lawlessness when Japan's old samurai tradition was dying and set against the teamwork and discipline of the puppeteers. Many of the themes in the *The Sign of the Chrysanthemum* . . . and *Of Nightingales That Weep* . . . reappear in this novel which should be very popular for its combination of excellent writing and irresistible intrigue. (p. 117)

Dora Jean Young, in School Library Journal *(reprinted from the March, 1976 issue of* School Library Journal, *published by R. R. Bowker Co. A Xerox Corporation; copyright © 1976), March, 1976.*

JEAN MERCIER

Osaka in the 1700s and the desperate plight of the impoverished Japanese are the chief elements in a brilliant novel by [Katherine Paterson]. . . . She offers not only a compelling drama but engrossing details on the art of puppetry. . . . ["The Master Puppeteer"] is swift and exciting. . . . (p. 85)

Jean Mercier, in Publishers Weekly *(reprinted from the April 19, 1976, issue of* Publishers Weekly *by permission of the critic, published by R. R. Bowker Company, a Xerox company; copyright © 1976 by Xerox Corporation), April 19, 1976.*

ZENA SUTHERLAND

Like intricate embroidery, [*The Master Puppeteer*] has deftly woven threads of several patterns that combine to make a cohesive and dramatic whole. The setting, as in other of [Paterson's] books, is feudal Japan; the milieu is the closed and intricate world of the puppet theater; the contrapuntal plot thread is the mysterious bandit who operates as an Osakan Robin Hood. . . . The plot is skilfully constructed, the characters are strong, and the historical background is as interesting as the details of the puppet theater. Good style, good story. (p. 181)

Zena Sutherland, in Bulletin of the Center for Children's Books *(© 1976 by the University of Chicago; all rights reserved), July-August, 1976.*

PATRICIA CRAIG

The exotic location and the distance in time make [the sentiments of *Of Nightingales That Weep*] palatable—just. It has something of the formality and simplicity of a retold folk tale. Its moral message is clear: that beauty is skin-deep.

The underlying theme is derived from the concept of loyalty and the ways in which it can be expressed. Takiko, daughter of a samurai, is lady-in-waiting to Princess Aoi when she becomes infatuated with a warrior from a rival clan. The subsequent story involved slaughter, mass suicide, death from plague and ultimate betrayal; but Takiko's own brand of courage enables her to face reality and come to terms with it. If there is an element of masochism in her final choice of husband, her decision is none the less fitting in terms of the plot. . . .

The elaborate, poetic and violent qualities of life in feudal Japan are sympathetically evoked. Occasionally the story seems to require a more oblique or individualistic touch—but on the whole the author's method works well. (p. 66)

Patricia Craig, in Books and Bookmen *(© copyright Patricia Craig 1977; reprinted with permission), March, 1977.*

MARGERY FISHER

[*Of Nightingales that weep*] could satisfy adolescents and adults alike with its exotic flavor and mature handling of character. . . . The unfamiliar pattern of events and the alien concepts of love, loyalty and ceremony which guide the characters are made clear in a story based on scholarship and on knowledge of the country whose contours and vegetation are skilfully used as background to a deliberate, convoluted narrative. (p. 3066)

Margery Fisher, in her Growing Point, *March, 1977.*

I must admit to a distinct reluctance to read [*Of Nightingales That Weep*]. The clan wars of twelfth century Japan are, to put it no more strongly, not a popular subject with English readers. The mindlessly brutal wars and the formality of court life make so sharp a contrast that it is difficult to bridge the gap between them. However, once started, *Of Nightingales That Weep* turns out to be a hypnotically dominating book. . . .

Mrs. Paterson tells the strong, action-filled narrative quietly, making its most powerful effects by understatement. (p. 239)

The Junior Bookshelf, *August, 1977.*

JACK FORMAN

Not only is [*Bridge to Terabithia*] . . . unusual because it portrays a believable relationship between a boy and a girl at an age when same-sex friendships are the norm but it also presents an unromantic, realistic, and moving reaction to personal tragedy. Jess and Leslie are so effectively developed as characters that young readers might well feel that they were their classmates. (p. 61)

Jack Forman, in School Library Journal *(re-*

printed from the November, 1977 issue of School Library Journal, *published by R. R. Bowker Co. A Xerox Corporation; copyright © 1978), November, 1977.*

RICHARD PECK

[Jesse and Leslie] create a wilderness hideaway kingdom, the "Terabithia" of the title . . . It lacks the elaboration of earlier childhood fantasy, perhaps to indicate they're already growing past the possibility of easy escape. The diction they adopt in their private principality may make some young readers uncomfortable. . . .

The author is at the top of her form in creating the uninspiring round of home and school. Jess contemplates, like most of his readers, that he may have been adopted—and abducted from a far more cultivated home. . . .

Like all the best books for the young, *Bridge to Terabithia* ends at a beginning. The young survivor offers love to a new and worthy recipient. And the reader of any age draws strength from the conclusion. (p. E3)

Richard Peck, "The Crime of Being Different," in Book World—The Washington Post *(© 1977, The Washington Post), November 13, 1977.*

BARBARA ELLEMAN

[*Bridge to Terabithia*] is not a message book, however, Paterson subtly handles [its] complex subject in an eloquent way that makes evident the expansion of her writing ability. The vivid and sensitive character portrayals and changing relationships . . . are superb. (p. 554)

Barbara Elleman, in Booklist *(reprinted by permission of the American Library Association; copyright 1977 by the American Library Association), November 15, 1977.*

PENELOPE CURTIS

What seems at first the main fault of [*Bridge to Terabithia*] —its light loosely woven structure—becomes its most important quality. The fabric of loosely woven thoughts is an integral part of the story. The short, sharp American dialogue is rather off-putting, as is the opening theme, but these are overcome by the developing charm and simplicity. This book grows on you, and you may not realise how much you have enjoyed it until the end. (pp. 23-4)

Penelope Curtis, in Book Window *(© 1978 S.C.B.A. and contributors), Winter, 1978.*

MRS. HILDAGARDE GRAY

Love stories, *good* love stories, are rare today. [*Bridge to Terabithia*] is a beautiful one, encompassing all the tones and nuances of deep feeling, all the entanglement lovers feel with each other's sensitivities and interpretations of life. . . .

This is not a love story of physical encounter but a fusion of souls and minds. To shy Jess, Leslie's philosophy opens new doors. Her sudden death threatens to crush him before he has learned to *live* her teachings. Her strength, however, continues to move within him, permitting him to move toward maturity and carry the land of Terabithia in his heart. There is a truth, a realism to the childlike expressions of fear, love, and friendship that should assure the author a permanent place among those whose books are sought by author, the kind whose names guarantees perfection of the writing craft. (p. 368)

Mrs. Hildagarde Gray, in Best Sellers *(copyright © 1978 Helen Dwight Reid Educational Foundation), February, 1978.*

ANN A. FLOWERS

Jess and his family are magnificently characterized; [*Bridge to Terabithia*] abounds in descriptive vignettes, humorous sidelights on the clash of cultures, and realistic depictions of rural school life. The symbolism of falling and of building bridges forms a theme throughout the story, which is one of remarkable richness and depth, beautifully written. (pp. 49-50)

Ann A. Flowers, in The Horn Book Magazine *(copyright © 1978 by the Horn Book, Inc., Boston), February, 1978.*

JEAN F. MERCIER

"God help the children of the flower children" is the theme of Paterson's ["The Great Gilly Hopkins"], a potentially rich story but disappointing in some ways. At 11, Gilly (who was abandoned by her hippie mother at birth) has been given up by a series of tired foster parents. In her new home, the guardian is obese, sloppy, semi-literate Maime Trotter whose other charge is a timid little boy.... Scheming to escape, Gilly gains the confidence of ... her new family by pretending to care for them. To her surprise she finds that she does and that "deliverance," when it comes unexpectedly, causes her wrenching sadness. [Katherine Paterson] writes expertly.... Still it's hard to accept the exaggeration of Trotter's virtues, the implication that ignorance plus slovenliness equals motherly love. (p. 127)

Jean F. Mercier, in Publishers Weekly *(reprinted from the February 13, 1978, issue of* Publishers Weekly *by permission of the critic, published by R. R. Bowker Company, a Xerox company; copyright © 1978 by Xerox Corporation), February 13, 1978.*

JACK FORMAN

Eleven-year-old Gilly Hopkins is a foster child seemingly modeled on the Tatum O'Neal character from *Paper Moon* and *Bad News Bears*. She is endowed with an above-average intelligence, a stubborn aggressiveness, and uncanny abilities to lie, steal, and see through hypocrisy.... Young readers might—as Gilly does—find Trotter's moralizing at the end a bit overdone, but they will appreciate the crisp, realistic dialogue, believable and humorous writing, and broad array of unorthodox characters. In Gilly and Mrs. Trotter, Paterson ... has created two of the most memorable and oddly appealing protagonists in contemporary juvenile novels. (p. 87)

Jack Forman, in School Library Journal *(reprinted from the April, 1978 issue of* School Library Journal, *published by R. R. Bowker Co. A Xerox Corporation; copyright © 1978), April, 1978.*

ZENA SUTHERLAND

Paterson's development of the change in Gilly is brilliant and touching, as she depicts a child whose tough protective shield dissolves as she learns to accept love and to give it

[in *The Great Gilly Hopkins*]. A well-structured story has vitality of writing style, natural dialogue, deep insight in characterization, and a keen sense of the fluid dynamics in human relationships. (p. 147)

Zena Sutherland, in Bulletin of the Center for Children's Books *(© 1978 by University of Chicago; all rights reserved), May, 1978.*

NATALIE BABBITT

[*The Great Gilly Hopkins*] is a book which, having a choice to make between a happy ending and a hard one—both being reasonable—chooses the latter, thereby finally declaring itself as something rather different from what it has led the readers to expect. For the story line has healthy antecedents in literature from *Oliver Twist* onward: an abandoned child, stranded in a bizarre place among bizarre people, learns how to value herself and others. (p. 1)

Katherine Paterson develops her characters thoroughly, avoiding the common pitfalls of stories of this type. While she eschews Dickensian sentimentality, she is strong on humor, and her writing is clear, inventive, and—except for a single line from the social worker, "God help the children of the flower children,"—entirely nonjudgmental. Gilly is a liar, a bully, a thief; and yet, because Paterson is interested in motivations rather than moralizing, the reader is free to grow very fond of her heroine—to sympathize, to understand, to identify with Gilly, and to laugh with her.

Still, the parallels to Dickens and others of his ilk are not unimportant. Familiarity with patterns in fiction directs the reader's expectations towards an ending to Gilly's story that is quite different from the one Paterson has chosen. For in spite of the hopelessness of the principal characters' situations, they are all full of hope—they are good-humored, steadfast, loving and even happy. They are, in other words, larger than life in a very particular way: they have a greatness of spirit which takes them a shade beyond reality. There is here, as with Dickens, an element of affectionate overdrawing, almost of caricature, and insofar as that element is present, the expectation is created for an ending which rewards these people's suffering.

Yet, when Gilly's mother appears in the closing chapter, she shows herself to be real in a flat, uncompromising way that her fellow characters are not. For her Paterson shows no affection, and she and the denouement she brings seem less than Gilly deserves. It is as if this book, as a movie, were filmed in the soft, warm, misty color that can find beauty even in a London alley, and then, at the end, turns suddenly to harsh black-and-white.

Paterson intended this to be the case—that seems clear. As Mrs. Trotter says to Gilly at the close of the story, 'You just fool yourself if you expect good things all the time. They ain't what's regular—don't nobody owe 'em to you." True enough, and therefore fair enough.... Perhaps, for Gilly, her days spent with Mrs. Trotter and William Ernest and Mr. Randolph can be compared, in a classic sense, to Dorothy's days in Oz: they are the true fantasy world of the hero from which he must at the end return, enriched but sobered, to reality.

In any case, *The Great Gilly Hopkins* is a finely written story. Its characters linger long in the reader's thoughts after it is finished. What Paterson has done is to combine a beautiful fairness with her affection for her creations, which makes them solidly three-dimensional. And that by itself, even if there were nothing else—and there is a great deal else—would be sufficient to make this a book worth reading. (pp. 1-2)

> *Natalie Babbitt, "A Home for Nobody's Child,"* in Book World—The Washington Post (© *1978*, The Washington Post), *May 14, 1978, pp. 1-2.*

ETHEL L. HEINS

Gilly—short for Tolkien's Galadriel—is not only a foster child but also, deliberately and blatantly, an *enfant terrible*. . . . In its similarity of theme and in its combination of poignancy and humor, [*The Great Gilly Hopkins*] may be compared with Betsy Byars's *The Pinballs*. . . . Yet despite the racy dialogue and the memorably eccentric characters, the author's second novel with a contemporary setting does not measure up to *Bridge to Terabithia* in subtlety, structural beauty, and emotional power. (p. 279)

> *Ethel L. Heins, in* The Horn Book Magazine *(copyright © 1978 by the Horn Book, Inc., Boston), June, 1978.*

VIRGINIA BUCKLEY

Katherine's knack for telling anecdotes is part of her gift as a writer. As you get to know her, you realize that the quick wit and strong loyalties with which she endows her characters are qualities that she herself possesses and extends to her family, friends, and the people she works with—even chance strangers. . . . (p. 368)

Every time I reread one of Katherine's novels, I find something new of value. Most recently I became aware of her abiding sympathy for the underdog, the lowly of this earth. Now that I think of it, that sympathy might be the ripening of this mature, engaged, and engaging women with the ready laugh, who can still recall that when she was a child in Shanghai, she and her friends dramatized over and over *The Wizard of Oz*—but that she was never allowed to play Dorothy and was always a Munchkin. (p. 371)

> *Virginia Buckley in* The Horn Book Magazine *(copyright © 1978 by the Horn Book, Inc., Boston), August, 1978.*

Richard Price

1949-

American novelist. Price's novels are realistic depictions of growing up male in New York City which explore both the specific and universal problems that arise from having to mature in an urban environment. The main question Price's characters ask themselves is whether they have the courage to break away from the security offered by a group: a gang, the traditions of a family, or even the heterosexual classification. Price's works have been written directly from experience, especially his first novel, *The Wanderers,* which deals with what he calls "my Bronx-housing project, pre-Beatle kidhood." Written at age 24, this novel received accolades from authors such as John Fowles, William Burroughs, and Hannah Green, and established Price's reputation as a literary boy wonder. Price's next novel, *Bloodbrothers,* continues his theme of adolescent searching, and relates it to a young man's questions about his family and his future. The success of these two books has caused Price to be considered, along with filmmaker Martin Scorcese and musician Bruce Springsteen, as part of the trio who are responsible for creating a contemporary mythology around East Coast street life. Price's latest novel, *Ladies' Man,* is a departure from his stories of the Italian-American experience, being a wry study of sexuality and the male mystique. Price's novels have been criticized for their excessive violence, explicit sex scenes, rawness of language, and similarity of characters and situations. Price has also been considered a pessimistic writer due to the hopelessness of his endings. However, he has been praised for his objective, sensitive portrayals and his respect for the dignity of his characters, as well as for his lively naturalistic writing style and accurate dialogue. As a chronicler of the wanderings of young people looking for meaning in life, Price brings the understanding that comes with recent personal experience to his works, and gives them relevance and a distinctive approach. Both *The Wanderers* and *Bloodbrothers* have been adapted for film. (See also *CLC*, Vol. 6, and *Contemporary Authors*, Vols. 49-52.)

CHRISTOPHER LEHMANN-HAUPT

At first it looks as if Richard Price is contriving extreme effects for their own sake in his first novel, "The Wanderers". . . . By the end of the second story we have been treated not only to a torrent of street language that can't be sampled here and a swamp of sexual byplay that can't be described, but also to one aborted race war, one gang skirmish complete with Molotov cocktails and a scene in which two preteen-agers are threatened with mutilation of their genitals. Mr. Price is never one to underplay his scenes. . . .

Still, it pays to keep reading "The Wanderers." For if Mr. Price's exaggerations seem troublesome at first, it is only because we haven't yet adjusted to the world in which they occur. We haven't yet appreciated the authenticity of his dialogue, which establishes itself only through its cumulative repetition of flat grammatical contortions ("Hey, this is Despie," says Buddy Borsalino, introducing to the Wanderers a girl whose "Juicy Fruit breath" has just begun to "intoxicate him." "Despie . . . this is the guys."). We haven't yet discovered that if Mr. Price's characters are pitched in a violent key—if they talk with their fists and dream of little else but treating their "seemingly incurable virginity"—their violence masks tenderness as well as brutality. . . .

And it hasn't yet dawned on us that if Mr. Price's exaggerations are occasionally contrived, then just as often they ascend to a surrealism that justifies them entirely—as for instance when that playground football game is broken up by a horde of Irish Catholic "midgets" called the Ducky Boys, and there follows a glorious melee so bloody and brutal, so flashing with tire chains, car aerials and straight razors, and yet so comparatively harmless in its physical consequences, that it can only be read as a sort of poem of violence.

And once we get used to Mr. Price's world, we believe it. . . .

Indeed, so accustomed do we become to the violence and obscenity of Mr. Price's world that any act short of outright murder assumes a quality of near-Chekhovian understatement. What had first seemed to be gratuitous brutality begins to impress us as a metaphor signifying the vitality of lower-class life. And so we find ourselves feeling gently nostalgic when the Wanderers take Buddy out for his final bachelor fling and present him with a going-away gift of "400 foil-wrapped Trojans." And when musclebound Emilio accepts the news of his son's departure from home without hitting him in the stomach or bloodying his nose, it seems nothing less than a scene of gentle blessing.

In the end the Wanderers take their separate paths out of innocent youth onto the treadmill of adulthood—some by way of marriage, others by way of the services. Eugene

Caputo, after standing helplessly by while his girl friend is raped by a black man wielding a razor, decides to join the Marines in order to absorb his mother's admonition "that the two greatest joys of being a man are beating the hell out of someone and getting the hell beaten out of you." The final measure of Richard Price's accomplishment in writing "The Wanderers" is that, after all we've been put through, we can read this warning to be meant ironically.

Christopher Lehmann-Haupt, "Brutality as a Sign of Life," in The New York Times *(© 1974 by The New York Times Company; reprinted by permission), March 20, 1974, p. 39.*

RICK KOGAN

Ah, to be 24 and have written "The Wanderers." To have captured the essence of the urban-American dream. To have taken a theme as old as the novel itself—the loss of innocence—and fashioned it as few have before. Ah, to be 24-year-old Richard Price and have written one of the few powerful and worthwhile novels of the year. . . .

The language of "The Wanderers" is tough, the gang's actions often crude and vulgar. But it is an important novel for just those reasons. It is real. It is a work that tells its tale in the best possible way—using real characters in a real world. There is no sermonizing, no agonizing wasted space.

Richard Price has gathered the pieces to the puzzle of his own youth and the puzzle of growing up in urban America. In "The Wanderers" he has put all the pieces together and they fit like a charm.

Rick Kogan, ". . . and a Gang of the 1960s," in The Chicago Sun-Times *(reprinted with permission of* The Chicago Sun-Times), *March 31, 1974.*

SUSAN HEATH

Richard Price, with a raunchy humor that smarts from the slap of reality, writes of growing up Italian in the Bronx during the early Sixties. He focuses on a teenage gang called the Wanderers as they skirmish through playgrounds, candy stores, and deserted lots during their last year together.

[*The Wanderers* is] a snappily paced novel that beats with the rhythm of street patter. And the sewer-mouthed boys who spit it out are characterized with deftness and economy. . . .

Though *The Wanderers* reeks of ghetto life, it is not just another first novel about the slums. It is, rather, a story about nothing less than the universal drama: growing up, getting laid, learning to cry "I am." (p. 52)

Susan Heath, in Saturday Review/World *(© 1974 by Saturday Review/World, Inc.; reprinted with permission), May 4, 1974.*

MICHAEL ROGERS

[*The Wanderers*] could be the flip side of *American Graffiti:* The time is the early Sixties, the kids are high-school age, the music is the Four Seasons, Dion, Smokey Robinson—but there the similarities end. These kids live in housing projects in the Bronx, run in gangs, rumble with car aerials and straight razors, and in general lead lives sufficiently grim to make the small-town pranks and repressed sexuality of the *American Graffiti* crew look like material for Hans Christian Andersen. Price's book chronicles the adventures and depredations of one gang, the Wanderers, during their last year of high school—an amalgam of sex, violence and humor, glued together with superb dialogue and unsentimental sensitivity. . . .

While the book is clearly episodic, and many of the chapters could easily stand on their own as short stories, Price nonetheless manages to blend his humor and horror to create a sense of wholeness. A novelist friend of mine contends no one in America really changes after high school, and that seems to be Price's conclusion as well. At the last full gathering of the Wanderers—at Buddy Borsalino's wedding—they "stood with arms around each other's shoulders, fingers pressing into flesh, trying to make a circle which nothing could penetrate—school, women, babies, weddings, mothers, fathers." But it is clear, as they drift away later, that the circle was never impermeable in the first place; that the words of the gang's theme song—"I roam from town to town / I go through life without a care" —are as aptly mocking of the kids from the Bronx as any they might have chosen. (p. 73)

Michael Rogers, in Rolling Stone *(by Straight Arrow Publishers, Inc. © 1974; all rights reserved; reprinted by permission), Issue 160, May 9, 1974.*

JOHN LAHR

There have been stunning books about black ghetto life, but Richard Price's *The Wanderers* finds its own place among the chronicles of urban turmoil by focusing on a white community, one step up from the black ghetto, in housing projects on the outskirts of the bourgeois dream. These are the children of blue-collar workers who with no stigma attached to their skin, no "heritage" of slavery, still find themselves excluded from America's abundant table.

The backbeat of rock'n roll pounds behind the cunning descriptions of family battles, the ferocious territorial feuds between gangs, and the make-out sessions. Rock'n roll promises action and joy in a world that offers little chance of change or happiness. The gang takes its name from the song "The Wanderer" by Dion and the Belmonts:

> I roam from town to town
> I go through life without a care. . . .

As the desperation in the gang's lives unfolds, the sounds which define their good times come to seem like their epitaphs. . . .

Mr Price's outrage at the violence of the city is matched by deep affection for its survivors. He captures the sweeter moments of city living—a love song dedicated over a request radio show; "elbow-titting" passers-by on the street; the strained patter when boy picks up girl. "I once went up in the elevator with Murray the K", says Despie, trying to impress her husband-to-be on their first encounter. "Jackie the K's a real piece", Buddy replies, one-upping her with the name of the disc jockey's wife and adding: "No offence." Every move Mr Price makes has this poise and sense of detail; and his novel represents a remarkable victory over his own past.

John Lahr, "School for Losers," in The Times Literary Supplement *(© Times Newspapers Ltd. (London) 1975; reproduced from* The Times Literary Supplement *by permission), May 30, 1975, p. 585.*

ELIOT FREMONT-SMITH

[*Bloodbrothers* is a] tough, dramatic novel about an Italian-American working-class family and a son's attempts to break out of a ruinously confining value system centered on mawkish or brutal (nothing in-between) images of masculinity.... The style is strictly "naturalistic," the momentum energetic, the mood at once gritty, funny, and quite horrendous. The novel's considerable force also derives from its authenticity: Price clearly knows what he is talking about, both the surface detail and the feelings roiling just beneath. He is sharply observant of these, understanding, not patronizing. (p. 46)

> *Eliot Fremont-Smith in* The Village Voice *(reprinted by permission of* The Village Voice; *copyright © The Village Voice, Inc., 1976), April 26, 1976.*

GREIL MARCUS

Price's first book, *The Wanderers* ... was not a great novel, but it was a stunning first novel (and not incidentally the first fiction to bring rock & roll into its characters' lives with the naturalness of Scorsese's *Mean Streets*). Unfortunately, *Bloodbrothers*, a sort of Italian working-class *Catcher in the Rye*, is not even a very good second novel. Eighteen-year-old Stony De Coco is trying to break free of his family and become his own man, but the reader may have to strain to care about the struggle, especially if the reader has already been through *The Wanderers*. Price has dressed up his earlier themes in new clothes, but that's all.... One would think the only story Price has to tell is that of Sisyphus. The one character who rises out of the book is a girl named Three-Finger Annette, who comes and goes in a few pages; she's who I wanted to read a novel about when I finished *Bloodbrothers*, but I wonder if Price isn't too locked into the romantic tragedies of adolescent males to write it. (p. 97)

> *Greil Marcus, in* Rolling Stone *(by Straight Arrow Publishers, Inc. © 1976; all rights reserved; reprinted by permission), Issue 213, May 20, 1976.*

RICHARD ELMAN

"Bloodbrothers" ... is a book with a thesis: family loyalty is the ultimate treason to oneself.

Like some proletarian fictions of a few decades back, this story of Stony De Coco, 18, and his clan grinds and blusters from point to point, undeterred by Price's feeling for life or his dramatic gifts. As Stony chooses between the family racket ... and realizing his own possibilities in the world of strangers beyond the confines of Co-op City, the Bronx, incidents from the psychopathic behavior of the De Cocos, their wives, friends and other wounded kinfolk, proliferate as illustrations of a subtext about the mutual destructiveness of those who still comply to the hoary doctrine that blood is thicker than water; however, the author never allows his substantial powers of observation and empathy to keep in focus, or perhaps animate this. When all else fails Price's rather distant and contemptuous estimation of what such unpleasant, chagrined, consuming, stupefied proles are about, he introduces a psychiatrist to sermonize to Stony. Or a best friend, who owns a hosiery shop, is made to deliver a summary that recalls what one might hear in Manhattan, perhaps, in therapy.

This sort of coercion of characters to do their author's dirty work is always a saddening, disappointing process. It's a sin against talent, and art, the eye, the ear, the emotions. In "Bloodbrothers" Price has closed his eyes and stopped up his ears and composed page after page of hostile, insult-laden dialogue interspersed with a hyped-up colloquial narrative through which the reader is bullied to sustain the illusion that the story has been composed by somebody with a background similar to that of the participants.

But, of course, this is just another literary device: within this work the author's total knowledge of what is happening to people is constantly pitted against the blindness of his characters, and the result is almost as brutalizing to us and Price, it would seem, as what we are told has been happening to Stony and his aunt and uncle, father, mother, kid brother and girlfriends. (pp. 42-3)

Most of the time Price isn't content to understate, to let things happen, or even take a chance that the situation of these people is even more ugly or desperate than he knows. If his characters won't cooperate in being utterly unredeemable, he twists their arms or stomps on them a bit. Stony sometimes sounds like a Lenny Bruce monologue and sometimes like an angry analysand; and I began to wonder if all the malice in the book could be attributed to the characters. Or was it not the work of imperfect patience and compassion of the part of the author?

Compassion doesn't mean liking; that was not a serious flaw in Price's much celebrated first novel, "The Wanderers," which depicted a similar milieu. But it's no help at all to a writer if he feels superior to his characters; [Maxim] Gorky knew that, as do our contemporaries, [Gilbert] Sorrentino and [Hubert] Selby. But this sort of stuff is more like a dirty-mouthed Italianate Hyman Kaplan: a few touches aspiring to art, and much of the rest simply kibitzing or commentary. (p. 43)

> *Richard Elman, in* The New York Times Book Review *(© 1976 by The New York Times Company; reprinted by permission), May 23, 1976.*

GERARD C. REEDY

Since the De Cocos, Price's main characters [in *Bloodbrothers*], and I live in the same borough, I am reluctant to admit that my fellow Bronxites realistically and constantly talk, think and act this dirtily. That aside, some of Price's episodes are achingly moving, especially when Stony, the hero, talks to the kids in the hospital and when Chubby, his uncle, reminisces. Will Stony become an electrician, like his dad and uncle? Or a worker with hospitalized children? Memorable minor characters make each option believable for him. Although Price's solution is ineptly premature, *Bloodbrothers* offers powerful writing on almost every page. The author, like his hero, has great story-telling gifts; he also has a good feel for loneliness in the high-rise buildings of New York, or anywhere. (p. 332)

> *Gerard C. Reedy, in* America *(© America Press, 1976; all rights reserved), November 13, 1976.*

JULIAN BARNES

[*Bloodbrothers*] is a smart, professional example of the post-Selby genre of lower-depths chic. Perhaps the continuing bankruptcy of New York is behind the flowering of this school, in which your archetypal American family beat and cheat one another, drive each other bananas, and then ensure that the vicious cycle continues into the next generation. . . . As one of the more detached characters puts it, 'the whole fuckin' Bronx is like a combination open-air loony bin an' Red Cross disaster tent, right?' If right, one ought to thank Price for his report from the battle-zone; instead, one worries about why he makes such a shapely, saleable artefact out of it, why the book-club classes will read the novel as they might go to the zoo to watch panthers, and whether the whole genre isn't the Gothic of our time, designed to be read in suburban ranch-houses, by affluent readers straight out of Charles Webb, as a nice change from the Sears Roebuck catalogue. (p. 681)

Julian Barnes, in New Statesman *(© 1977 The Statesman & Nation Publishing Co. Ltd.), May 20, 1977.*

STEPHEN FENDER

Bloodbrothers is an old American story with a new ending: an adolescent undergoes a *rite de passage*, then returns home instead of lighting out for the territories. Mr Price's technique mirrors this tension between freedom and captivity. On the surface the novel is liberated from decorum and cliché. The dialogue has the energetic authentic sound made familiar by [Hubert Selby's] *Last Exit to Brooklyn* and recent films like *Mean Streets* and *Dog Day Afternoon*. But underneath it is conventionally authoritarian: heavily plotted, not in the serio-comic manner of Thomas Pynchon, but in the more ordinary sense of seeming contrived. For instance, Stony has a friend who seems almost magically transformed from a moron to a sage dispenser of friendly counsel when he takes over the management of his uncle's lingerie store—a rather obvious foil for Stony. The events leading to Stony's final renunciation seem especially hard to credit; too much happens too quickly, without apparent cause or convincing effect.

This tension between surface and plot may, of course, be intended since there is a similar vacillation in point of view. The book seems anxious to break free from stereotypes about New York. Blacks and whites enjoy unselfconscious friendships. Policemen and nurses are not pigs and tyrants but wary, rather kindly people trying to help where they can. Even the "hard hats" get a voice. But along with this desire to accommodate, to see the other man's point of view, goes a nervousness about "point of view" in the narrative sense. No sooner does Stony finish telling his friend Butler about his wild night with Annette (a superb piece of writing) than the narrative bustles around to old Three Fingers's place to register her life-story, what *she* thought of their night together, how she imagines Stony talking about it later. No sooner do we witness the conversation between Dr Harris and Stony about Albert, than we go inside the doctor's head for his view of the case. Mr Price leaves very little white space. Like Tommy De Coco, he does not always trust his offspring.

Stephen Fender, "Electrical Storms," in The Times Literary Supplement *(© Times Newspapers Ltd. (London) 1977; reproduced from* The Times Literary Supplement *by permission), July 1, 1977, p. 812.*

Moving his Bronx characters downtown to Manhattan proves traumatic to Price (*The Wanderers, Bloodbrothers*); he picks up a bad case of *angst* [in *Ladies' Man*]. . . . What keeps this book afloat long past its torpedoing point is Price's Lenny Bruce-ish, shpritz-style riffery. The high

point is a first chapter in which Kenny accompanies La Donna to an audition at a nightclub that perversely caters to connoisseurs of no-talents; next best is Kenny listening to a late-night call-in show, with its requisite I'm-gonna-kill-myself caller. But the voice becomes tiring. Price's disdainful eye, really interested only in watching Kenny, often just winks nastily: a girl in a movie-theater lobby is one of those "minor dancers living in body stockings, hair in a bun, shy, always giving and getting something ceramic and Chinese for presents." Like one of the callers to those phone-in shows, Price is mostly talking to hear himself maintain a solo; the message—we all need someone—is small beer, and Kenny's concluding, scouring descent into S & M depravity comes off less like fiery purification than like a letter home to Mom from Camp Götterdamerung. Jazzy. Empty. (p. 773)

Kirkus Reviews *(copyright © 1978 The Kirkus Service, Inc.), July 15, 1978.*

JOHN FLUDAS

Kenny Becker [in *Ladies' Man*] narrates his own story of a week-long panic that breaks out when La Donna, the woman he lives with, leaves him and forces him to share his apartment with a person he knows to be part fraud, part dreamer, a college dropout going through some premature mid-life crisis: himself. Like the untalented comedians and singers who try out for a pitiful amateur showcase in the brilliant first chapter of *Ladies' Man*, Becker, too, wants his place in a spotlight, to be acceptable to others and to himself. . . .

In this book, Richard Price can do anything with words. He can shape a tightly structured novel, yet allow scenes to expand freely. Better than most writers who try to record street talk, he has a quick ear for the varieties of English spoken in New York. He gives Kenny a wit almost as sharp and jaundiced as Holden Caulfield's in *The Catcher in the Rye*. He captures the spurts of rage of Kenny's mind, gives him airborne fantasies, creates settings that reverberate with his emotional state—his isolation in a packed singles' bar, his frenzy in a porno booth as he peeps through glass at nude women shouting dirty talk into microphones, his terror and excitement in gay bars.

The novel ends on an upbeat that is neither forced nor sentimental. It grows naturally out of the fibers of Kenny's character. (p. 52)

John Fludas, in Saturday Review *(© 1978 by Saturday Review Magazine Corp.; reprinted with permission), September 30, 1978.*

LAURA MATHEWS

In two earlier books . . . Richard Price has documented the proud, cheerless world of New York City's white working-class youths, and the special bind of high school camaraderie. In *Ladies' Man* that mystique emerges, ambivalently, as the romantic anchor for Kenny's faltering confidence.

Price risks everything on the persuasiveness of his hero's voice, for the plot is static and the story has all the structure of a skin flick (which may be intentional). Kenny's speech verges on the solipsistic, yet is energized by urban patois ("did up some coffee," "whigged," "riffed"). It reflects both bravado and a panicky need to ward off the bad stuff he meets on the street ("I mean, I wasn't no depresso, was I?").

Though its gaminess will offend many readers, *Ladies' Man* is a remarkably sustained portrait of a present-day underground man. (p. 116)

> *Laura Mathews, in* The Atlantic Monthly *(copyright © 1978 by The Atlantic Monthly Company, Boston, Mass.; reprinted with permission), October, 1978.*

JEFFREY BURKE

Ladies' Man is an effective depiction of loneliness, and Richard Price is an expert on the fulsome and frenzied aspects of New York City. Kenny Becker is a perfectly conceived character; so perfect, in fact, that he is thoroughly unpleasant to listen to at book-length. The clichés, the hipness, the latest urban argot, the masculinity so overweening that it whines—in short, the unrelenting gracelessness, however true to the social type Kenny represents, demands a high degree of tolerance or a peculiar affection for dialect. But that is a native New Yorker's reaction: outside city limits Kenny may well be considered good company. (p. 97)

> *Jeffrey Burke, in* Harper's *(copyright © 1978 by* Harper's Magazine; *all rights reserved; reprinted from the October, 1978 issue by special permission), October, 1978.*

JEROME CHARYN

Richard Price has an amazing ear and eye for the street. He presents us [in "Ladies' Man"] with a cityscape that is filled with powerful spooks. . . .

Richard Price collects the dung and scrap heaps of our urban culture in a frightening, electrical style. But the book's main problem is Kenny himself; Kenny gets in the way of the narrative with his 50-cent truths. At times he sounds like a hip Benjamin Franklin in platform shoes, dreaming wise thoughts as he gobbles on a stale roll: "Why was it that everybody seemed to have more friends when they were kids than when they were adults?" (p. 32)

It's this sort of claptrap that harms the book, because it gives us Richard Price's silliness rather than Kenny Becker's infantile rage. But "Ladies' Man" still has its bite. It's a disturbing, freaky novel about sexual disgust and the pornography of our everyday lives. (pp. 32, 34)

> *Jerome Charyn, in* The New York Times Book Review *(© 1978 by The New York Times Company; reprinted by permission), November 12, 1978.*

Mary Rodgers

1931-

American novelist, columnist, playwright, screenwriter, composer, and lyricist. Rodgers's books are humorous and entertaining portraits of the Walter Mitty-esque fantasies of the modern young adult. Imagination is a primary quality of her books, from the wildly wicked reveries of Simon in *The Rotten Book* to the fantastic transformation that takes place in *Freaky Friday.* Her settings are contemporary but the lessons her characters are taught are traditional morals associated with cautionary tales and ugly duckling stories. This moral element is not overtly obtrusive and the entertainment value of the stories remains high. Critics note, however, that her stories are so rife with current phrases, events, and commercial slogans that they are already becoming dated and may in the future become mere artifacts of the early 1970s. Rodgers also wrote the screenplay for the film version of *Freaky Friday,* and, in collaboration with her mother, Dorothy, writes a monthly column for *McCall's* magazine entitled "Of Two Minds." (See also *Contemporary Authors,* Vols. 49-52, and *Something about the Author,* Vol. 8.)

The Rotten Book is really two books, a worldly satire and a simple, rather old-fashioned cautionary tale. The trouble starts—for Simon and the reader—at the breakfast table where Simon is dawdling with his egg and his father is holding forth on a "rotten" little boy who's ungrateful for what he has (which matches what Simon has) and who's "going to land up in jail one of these days." Whereupon Simon, wondering what the boy did, goes through a day of being absolutely rotten to everyone and everything. . . . [At the end of the day] Simon is taken away handcuffed while his family cheers. "He'd probably spend the rest of his life in jail (and) never even get an egg for breakfast." Cut to the breakfast table where Simon praises the egg and proceeds to behave like a model boy. The father's self-righteous condemnation of a *little* boy is odd to start with, and if he and Simon's mother are going through this elaborate charade on behalf of an egg, it's ludicrous. Either way, father's letter-perfect pompous and in today's context (and today's plots), the child is supposed to rebel, not capitulate. If he were to rebel, jail's not the timeliest deterrent; if it's meant simply as a warning, there are others more suitable. And suppose he didn't eat the **** egg—would he have to feel rotten? (p. 926)

> *Kirkus Reviews (copyright © 1969 The Kirkus Service, Inc.), September 1, 1969.*

Gregor Samsa's "Metamorphosis" to insect form is no more disconcerting than the opening of *Freaky Friday:* "When I woke up this morning, I found I'd turned into my mother. There I was in my mother's bed . . . with my father sleeping in the other bed. I had on my mother's nightgown and a ring on my left hand." But once past the alarming Oedipal implications, which Ms. Rodgers mercifully ignores, this becomes a conventional situation comedy in which 13-year-old Annabel, whose mother has switched "bods" to teach her a lesson, tries unsuccessfully to cope with cooking, laundry, budgeting, and all that. . . . At the height of a company crisis mother switches back (just how is never explained). . . . It all ends as a lesson in mother-knows-best, and the rest is like the silly TV show you hate yourself for laughing at . . . but can't stop. (p. 267)

> *Kirkus Reviews (copyright © 1972 The Kirkus Service, Inc.), March 1, 1972.*

JANE LANGTON

Mary Rodgers has the knack of catching the sound of a real child talking. When Annabel [in *Freaky Friday*] says, "Oh, wow," it is because writer, character, page of print, and reader have all been catapulted into an Oh, wow mood. Plenty of other writers try to hit young readers with "now" ideas and phrases—make love, not war; I mean; you know; Fascist pig. You wish they hadn't. Why didn't they try to be, like, universal and timeless? But in this book the pages rush by, . . . and it might all be happening in the apartment next door. *Freaky Friday* is unputdownable. It is a gem. (p. 5)

> *Jane Langton, in Book World—Chicago Tribune (© 1972 Postrib Corp.), May 4, 1972.*

ROBERT BERKVIST

God rest ye, Lewis Carroll. Alice, in one guise or another, is still tripping through the looking glass. Listen: "When I woke up this morning, I found I'd turned into my mother." How's that for a trip, eh, Lew? Oh, nothing serious, of course. Not that kind of trip, just one of those wish-fulfillment jobs.

The lass doing the wishing is Annabel Andrews, a feisty 13-year-old with crushing problems—a handsome, "fantastically cool" father, an attractive but annoyingly strict mother, a disgustingly neat 6-year-old brother named Ben

..., rampant orthodonture and, well you know, problems. There must be a way out. . . .

One Friday morning, Annabel wakes up in her mother's shoes. (She wakes up in her mother's bed, too, but that's someone else's trip, not Miss Rodgers's.) She sees her father—er, hubby—off to work, the kids off to school and then goes about her business. Her business turns out to be a matter of discovering what it's like to be Annabel's mother and, in other more complex ways, what it's like to be Annabel. There's lots of spiky, convincing dialogue and an ingenious wrap-up. (p. 8)

> *Robert Berkvist, in* The New York Times Book Review *(© 1972 by The New York Times Company; reprinted by permission), July 16, 1972.*

BERYL ROBINSON

[*Freaky Friday* is as] bright and breezy as the title, a truly funny story about a girl who awakens one morning in her mother's body, and who—during an incredible day of revelation and opportunity—sees herself as others see her and faces her mixed-up adolescent problems squarely. . . . She receives surprising insight into her mother's problems. . . . There is wisdom as well as humor in this fresh, original story, and the impact, despite the story's fantastic basis, is successful and convincing. (p. 378)

> *Beryl Robinson, in* The Horn Book Magazine *(copyright © 1972 by The Horn Book, Inc., Boston), August, 1972.*

[*Freaky Friday* takes place in New York and deals with adolescent growing pains. The characters are smart but the problems and preoccupations are not very far out]; middle-class television comedy is about the mark. It has a marvellous theme—bright but bolshie teenage Annabel wakes up one morning as her mother, and finds in the proper tradition of magical wish-fulfilment that life is not quite as cushy as she expects. Some of it is very well done, properly uncomfortable and again, very funny—for instance, the supposedly parental interview with her headmaster in which she starts by defending but ends up lambasting herself—but it is also a bit schmaltzy at times, and falters sadly at the revelation that mom herself has engineered the switch; she will not say how and Annabel cannot imagine—no doubt the author could not either. . . .

[The book is somewhat glossy and ends a little too neatly], with ugly duckling Annabel converted into a swan. (p. 1433)

> *The Times Literary Supplement (© Times Newspapers Ltd. (London) 1973; reproduced from* The Times Literary Supplement *by permission), November 23, 1973.*

VIRGINIA HAVILAND

[*A Billion for Boris* is a] deliciously original, engaging and consistently inventive story told by Annabel Andrews of *Freaky Friday*. Boris, who is Annabel's boyfriend, and Ben, her seven-year-old brother, complete a trio of brilliantly perspicacious and likeable characters, while a supporting cast of adults is equally well-drawn. Boris' defunct TV set, restored to working order by uncannily clever Ben, projects the next day's programs, thus providing remarkably valuable information. . . . Boris quickly perceives that the announcement of race-track results would be an open

sesame to untold amounts of money. The author adroitly resolves the ethical problem of Boris' success at the betting office, and she portrays with comedy and poignancy Boris' earnest endeavors to alter the life style of his mother. (p. 144)

> *Virginia Haviland, in* The Horn Book Magazine *(copyright © 1974 by The Horn Book, Inc., Boston), October, 1974.*

[When Boris] acquires a TV set that broadcasts tomorrow's programs [in *A Billion for Boris*], Annabel wants to use their foreknowledge for good deeds like helping the police entertain a lost child or providing a *Daily News* journalist with scoops, but Boris has bigger plans. It seems that Sascha, his mother, . . . is not after all evil but just a flighty writer, and the only way he sees to straighten her out and make his own life bearable is to win $12,000 on the races. . . . [When] he loses his sudden wealth in the end on a disqualified front runner, Sascha . . . comes up not only with a $50,000 check from Hollywood to pay the bills but also with the apparent revelation that she loves him. This leaves Boris, who has essentially learned his lesson without suffering for his mistakes, blubbering with joy—but it's poor reward for readers who have taken in all the cheap crises and social insensitivity of *Freaky Friday* without any of the compensating laughs. (p. 1104)

> *Kirkus Reviews (copyright © 1974 The Kirkus Service, Inc.), October 15, 1974.*

ALIX NELSON

It's too bad we don't reserve a special set of adjectives for books that really are commendable—witty, original, entertaining, well-plotted and well-wrought—as it is, copywriters . . . have so diluted those terms that when the genuine article [like "A Billion for Boris"] comes along it's like crying wolf. Wolf! . . .

While I'm not saying this is "Eloise" of the seventies, "A Billion for Boris" does assume an urban and sophisticated frame of reference on the part of the reader, and it evokes so much New York City local color . . . that it really is the perfect New York City book.

Ah, but its smart high-school repartee is so snappy (and so true!) it ought to delight the cognoscenti and their eccentric, rotten-housekeeper mothers from coast to coast. (p. 8)

> *Alix Nelson, in* The New York Times Book Review *(© 1974 by The New York Times Company; reprinted by permission), November 24, 1974.*

American children are apt to move through their fictional lives with great gusto, much wise-cracking and a columnist's wit. [In *A Billion for Boris*] Annabel Andrews and her young brother Ape Face join with Boris in the exploitation of a TV set which inexplicably shows tomorrow's programmes today. As in all the best folk tales the possession of wishes that come true or powers of foretelling the future never seem to work out. There is a lot of hilarious backchat and exchanges of verbal fireworks between children and parents. Why is that, to all American fictional children, adults are slightly soft in the head? As devoid of real emotion as a P. G. Wodehouse anti-hero, these superficial fun-loving urban descendants of Huck Finn will provide an amusing read. . . . (p. 336)

> *The Junior Bookshelf, October, 1975.*

JANET MASLIN

Freaky Friday is about a mother and daughter who magically exchange bodies for a day.... [This] production takes on a spooky, unexpected verisimilitude that ought to make it at least as interesting to adults as it is to children, perhaps even more so. Mary Rodgers's screenplay, based on her novel, supplies enough faintly Freudian undertones to pique a grownup's interest even further. Try to imagine how Annabel Andrews, a 13-year-old tomboy, must feel when she finds herself with a mature figure and a husband she suddenly starts calling "Daddy," and you begin to get the idea.

Rodgers's book concentrated mainly on Annabel and included a few soggy lessons in mutual understanding, but the movie is delightfully flip and evenhanded. . . .

Most of the day's mishaps involve stock situations . . . and none of it is likely to whiz over the heads of viewers who can still count their ages on their fingers.

> *Janet Maslin, "Switcheroo," in* Newsweek *(copyright 1977 by Newsweek, Inc.; all rights reserved; reprinted by permission), February 28, 1977, p. 72.*

J(erome) D(avid) Salinger

1919-

American novelist and short story writer. Salinger is recognized by critics and readers alike as one of the most popular and influential of contemporary writers. His only novel, *The Catcher in the Rye,* drew such great attention during the fifties and early sixties that those years have been called "the age of Holden Caulfield." The novel, in Ernest Jones's words, records "what every sensitive 16-year-old since Rousseau has felt." It has been banned even recently from a few libraries, schools, and bookstores for the starkness of its language and attitudes and the realism of some of its settings. Although Salinger has fallen out of critical favor of late because of his sentimentality, it is generally agreed that *Catcher* has yet to be surpassed in its portrayal of the pains and pleasures of a youth searching for love and direction. In all of his work Salinger draws upon the experience of his own life. For instance, his parents shared the same backgrounds as do those of his fictive Glass family. An undistinguished student, Salinger flunked out of private high school. His family sent him to Valley Forge Military Academy, the model for *Catcher*'s Pencey Prep. Later, in a short story class at Columbia University, Salinger made a poor first impression on his instructor, Whit Burnett; however, at the end of the first semester he turned in his first manuscript, which was so polished that Burnett published it without changes in his *Story* magazine. While Salinger was in the Army, Ernest Hemingway once visited his unit and looked at some of his written work. When asked about its quality, Hemingway replied, "He's got a hell of a talent." In 1946 *Collier's* magazine published "I'm Crazy," which marked the literary debut of Holden Caulfield. Salinger became one of the major contributors of short stories to *The New Yorker,* which has since premiered all of his later works. After *Catcher*'s popularity, Salinger withdrew from his audience. One reason given is that he has become a Zen Buddhist, since the precepts of that religion permeate so much of his fiction. Whatever the cause, his personal inscrutability has served to further popularize him among his admirers, creating a legendary aura around his name. To his series of young adult readers, Salinger's identification with and understanding of their situation has kept him relevant and appreciated for almost 30 years. (See also *CLC*, Vols. 1, 3, 8, and *Contemporary Authors*, Vols. 5-8, rev. ed.)

ARTHUR HEISERMAN and JAMES E. MILLER, JR.

It is clear that J. D. Salinger's *The Catcher in the Rye* belongs to an ancient and honorable narrative tradition, per-

haps the most profound in western fiction. The tradition is the central pattern of the epic and has been enriched by every tongue; for not only is it in itself exciting but also it provides the artist a framework upon which he may hang almost any fabric of events and characters.

It is, of course, the tradition of the Quest. (p. 129)

There are at least two sorts of quests, depending upon the object sought. [James Joyce's] Stephen Dedalus sought a reality uncontaminated by home, country, church; for . . . he knew that social institutions tend to force what is ingenious in a man into their own channels. He sought the opposite of security, for security was a cataract of the eye. Bloom [also in Joyce's *Ulysses*], on the other hand, was already an outcast and sought acceptance by an Ithaca and a Penelope which despised him. And, tragically enough, he also sought an Icarian son who had fled the very maze which he, Bloom, desired to enter. So the two kinds of quests, the one seeking acceptance and stability, the other precisely the opposite, differ significantly, and can cross only briefly to the drunken wonder of both heroes. (pp. 129-30)

American literature seems fascinated with the outcast, the person who defies traditions in order to arrive at some pristine knowledge, some personal integrity. (p. 130)

All the virtues of these American heroes are personal ones: They most often, as a matter of fact, are in conflict with home, family, church. The typical American hero must flee these institutions, become a tramp in the earth, cut himself off from Chicago, Winesburg, Hannibal, Cooperstown, New York, Asheville, Minneapolis. For only by flight can he find knowledge of what is real. And if he does not flee, he at least defies.

The protagonist of *The Catcher in the Rye,* Holden Caulfield, is one of these American heroes, but with a significant difference. He seems to be engaged in both sorts of quests at once; he needs to go home and he needs to leave it. Unlike the other American knight errants, Holden seeks Virtue second to Love. He wants to be good. When the little children are playing in the rye-field on the clifftop, Holden wants to be the one who catches them before they fall off the cliff. . . . But like these American heroes, Holden is a wanderer, for in order to be good he has to be more of a bad boy than the puritanical Huck could have imagined. Holden has had enough of both Hannibal, Missouri, *and* the Mississippi; and his tragedy is that when he starts back up the river, he has no place to go—save, of course, a California psychiatrist's couch.

So Salinger translates the old tradition into contemporary terms. The phoniness of society forces Holden Caulfield to leave it, but he is seeking nothing less than stability and love. He would like nothing better than a home, a life embosomed upon what is known and can be trusted; he is a very wise sheep forced into lone wolf's clothing; he is Stephen Dedalus and Leopold Bloom rolled into one crazy kid. And here is the point; for poor Holden, there is no Ithaca. Ithaca has not merely been defiled by a horde of suitors: it has sunk beneath waves of phoniness. He does, of course, have a Penelope who is still intact. She is his little sister Phoebe whom he must protect at all costs from the phantoms of lust, hypocrisy, conceit and fear—all of the attributes which Holden sees in society and which Huck Finn saw on the banks of the Mississippi and Dedalus saw in Dublin. So at the end, like the hero of [Aldous Huxley's] *Antic Hay,* Holden delights in circles—a comforting, bounded figure which yet connotes hopelessness. He breaks down as he watches his beloved little Phoebe going round and round on a carousel; she is so *damned* happy. From that lunatic delight in a circle, he is shipped off to the psychiatrist. For Holden loves the world more than the world can bear.

Holden's Quest takes him outside society; yet the grail he seeks is the world and the grail is full of love. To be a catcher in the rye in this world is possible only at the price of leaving it. To be good is to be a "case," a "bad boy" who confounds the society of men. So Holden seeks the one role which would allow him to be a catcher, and that role is the role of the child. As a child, he would be condoned, for a child is a sort of savage and a pariah because he is innocent and good. But it is Holden's tragedy that he is sixteen, and like Wordsworth he can never be less. In childhood he had what he is now seeking—non-phoniness, truth, innocence. He can find it now only in Phoebe and in his dead brother Allie's baseball mitt, in a red hunting cap and the tender little nuns. Still, unlike all of us, Holden refuses to compromise with adulthood and its necessary adulteries; and his heroism drives him berserk. Huck Finn had the Mississippi and at the end of the Mississippi he had the wild west beyond Arkansas. The hero of *The Waste Land* had Shantih, the peace which passes human understanding. Bloom had Molly and his own ignorance; Dedalus had Paris and Zurick. But for Holden, there is no place to go.

The central theme of Salinger's work is stated explicitly in one of his best short stories, "For Esme—with love and Squalor." Salinger quotes a passage from Dostoevski: "Fathers and teachers, I ponder 'What is Hell?' I maintain that it is the suffering of being unable to love." (pp. 130-32)

Salinger thus diagnoses the neurosis and fatigue of the world in one simple way: if we cannot love, we cannot live. (p. 132)

The flight out of the world, out of the ordinary, and into an Eden of innocence or childhood is a common flight indeed, and it is one which Salinger's heroes are constantly attempting. But Salinger's childism is consubstantial with his concern for love and neurosis. Adultism is precisely "the suffering of being unable to love," and it is that which pro-

duces neurosis. Everyone able to love in Salinger's stories is either a child or a man influenced by a child. All the adults not informed by love and innocence are by definition phonies and prostitutes. (p. 133)

[The] final note of irony in the book [is] that that frontier west which represented escape from "sivilization" for Huck Finn has ended by becoming the symbol for depravity and phoniness in our national shrine at Hollywood. (p. 134)

[Poignance] characterizes all of Salinger's humor, [a] catch in the throat that accompanies all of the laughs. Holden Caulfield is no clown nor is he a tragic hero; he is a sixteen-year-old lad whose vivid encounter with everyday life is tragically humorous—or humorously tragic. At the end of the novel, as we leave Holden in the psychiatric ward of the California hospital, we come to the realization that the abundant and richly varied humor of the novel has reenforced the serious intensity of Holden's frantic flight from Adultism and his frenzied search for the genuine in a terrifyingly phony world. (pp. 134-35)

Holden does not suffer from the inability to love, but he does despair of finding a place to bestow his love. The depth of Holden's capacity for love is revealed in his final words, as he sits in the psychiatric ward musing over his nightmarish adventures: "If you want to know the truth, I don't *know* what I think about it. I'm sorry I told so many people about it. About all I know is, I sort of miss everybody I told about. Even old Stradlater and Ackley, for instance. I think I even miss that goddam Maurice. It's funny. Don't ever tell anybody anything. If you do, you start missing everybody." We agree with Holden that it is funny, but it is funny in a pathetic kind of way. As we leave Holden alone in his room in the psychiatric ward, we are aware of the book's last ironic incongruity. It is not Holden who should be examined for a sickness of the mind, but the world in which he has sojourned and found himself an alien. To "cure" Holden, he must be given the contagious, almost universal disease of phony adultism; he must be pushed over that "crazy cliff." (p. 137)

> *Arthur Heiserman and James E. Miller, Jr., "J. D. Salinger: Some Crazy Cliff," in* Western Humanities Review *(copyright, 1956, University of Utah), Spring, 1956, pp. 129-37.*

FRANK KERMODE

What meaning, if any, can one attach to the expression 'a key book of the present decade'? It is used as a blurb in a . . . reprint of [*The Catcher in the Rye*]. . . . Whoever remembers the book will suppose that this is a serious claim, implying perhaps that *The Catcher,* as well as being extremely successful, is a work of art existing in some more or less profound relationship with the 'spirit of the age.' It is, anyway, quite different from saying that *No Orchids for Miss Blandish* is a key book. On the other hand, there is an equally clear distinction between this book and such key novels as *Ulysses* or *A Passage to India.* For it is elementary that, although these books have been read by very large numbers of people, one may reasonably distinguish between a smaller, 'true' audience and bigger audiences which read them quite differently, and were formerly a fortuitous addition to the "highbrow" public. But although Salinger is certainly a 'highbrow' novelist, it would be unreal to speak of his audience, large though it is, as divided in this way. What we now have is a new reader who is not only common but pretty sharp. This new reader is also a pampered consumer, so that the goods supplied him rapidly grow obsolete; which may explain why I found *The Catcher* somewhat less enchanting on a second reading.

It is, of course, a book of extraordinary accomplishment; I don't know how one reviewer came to call it 'untidy.' Nothing inept, nothing that does not look good and work well as long at it is needed, will satisfy this new public. Structural virtuosity is now taken for granted, particularly in American novels. This one is designed for readers who can see a wood, and paths in a wood, as well as sturdy, primitive trees—a large, roughly calculable audience: fit audience though many.

At the level of its untidy story, the book is about an adolescent crisis. . . . Repetitive, indecent, often very funny, it is wonderfully sustained by the author, who achieves all those ancient effects to be got from a hero who is in some ways inferior, and in others superior, to the reader. . . .

[The story] you get from listening to the boy, and it sounds untidy. What Mr. Salinger adds is design. Holden is betrayed at the outset by a schoolmaster (phoney-crumby) and at the end by another (phoney-perverted). The only time his parents come into the story, he has to remain motionless in the dark with his sister. The boy's slang is used to suggest patterns he cannot be aware of: whatever pleases him 'kills' him, sends him off to join his dead brother; almost everybody, even the disappointed whore, is 'old so-and-so,' and 'old' suggests the past and stability. More important, the book has its big, focal passages, wonderfully contrived. Holden hears a little neglected boy singing. 'If a body catch a body, etc.' This kills him. Then he helps a little girl in Central Park to fasten her skates. Next he walks to the Museum of Natural History, which he loved as a child; it seemed 'the only nice, dry cosy place in the world.' Nothing changed there among the stuffed Indians and Eskimos; except *you*. You changed every time you went in. The thought that his little sister must also feel that whenever she went in depresses him; so he tries to help some kids on a see-saw, but they don't want him around. When he reaches the museum he won't go in. This is a beautiful little parable, and part of my point is that nobody will miss it. . . .

Why, then, with all this to admire, do I find something phoney in the book itself? Not because there is 'faking,' as Mr. [E. M.] Forster calls it. In his sense, 'faking' doesn't lead one directly to some prefabricated attitude, and this does happen in *The Catcher*. The mixed-up kid totters on the brink of a society which is corrupt in a conventional way: its evils are fashionably known to be such, and don't have to be proved, made valid in the book. Similarly, the adult view of adolescence, insinuated by skilful faking, is agreeable to predictable public taste. Again, we like to look at the book and see the Libido having a bad time while the Death Wish does well, as in the museum scenes: but I don't feel that this situation occurs in the book as it were by natural growth, any more than sub-threshold advertising grows on film. *The Catcher* has a built-in death wish; it is what the consumer needs, just as he might ask that a toothpaste taste good *and* contain a smart prophylactic against pyorrhoea. The predictable consumer-reaction is a double one: how good! and how clever! The boy's attitudes to religion, authority, art, sex and so on are what smart people

would like other people to have, but cannot have themselves because of their superior understanding. They hold together in a single thought purity and mess, and feel good. The author's success springs from his having, with perfect understanding, supplied their demand for this kind of satisfaction. (p. 705)

Frank Kermode, "Fit Audience," in The Spectator *(© 1958 by* The Spectator; *reprinted by permission of* The Spectator), *May 30, 1958, pp. 705-06.*

PAUL LEVINE

No writer of recent years has captured the *New Yorker* market of Connecticut emigres the way J. D. Salinger has. From the defiant Holden Caulfield to the stoic Mrs. Glass all of his characters are strictly the contented-tormented people who inhabit New York City and its suburbs. But Salinger's importance in the school of younger writers comes from a moral awareness as well as a social perception. The hero in every Salinger story becomes a reflection of a moral code arising out of a cult of innocence, love, alienation, and finally redemption. These heroes form a particularly adolescent troupe of spiritual non-conformists, tough-minded and fragile, humorous and heartbreaking.

The basic predicament in Salinger's stories is that of a moral hero forced to compromise his integrity with a pragmatic society. What disaffiliates the hero is his peculiar off-center vision which sensitizes and distorts his sense of truth in a false world. As Salinger's talent develops, his hero's vision becomes his trademark, flowering in the extraordinary Glass family of Salinger's latest *New Yorker* stories. Moreover, the hero's misfitness in the modern world resolves as a moral problem rather than as the bitter fruit of a social injustice. If the significance of Salinger's emphasis on the moral right is kept in mind, then his recent embracing of Christian principles becomes less than surprising; if we are aware of them, there are indications all along the way.

In his second published story Salinger constructs the predicament that all his heroes will subsequently face: a young soldier marches out of step with the rest of his battalion in "Hang of It." . . . In "Varioni Brothers" Salinger, for the first time portrays his hero as an artist. The story stands as a transition between the hero who is a misfit and the misfit who is a hero. In the character of Joe Varioni, the writer-artist, Salinger crystallizes the character who will dominate his later fiction—the misfit hero. Unlike his predecessors, Joe is talented, kind, and sensitive; yet he stands apart from his society because he is docile as well as brilliant. Unequipped for the tough world around him, Joe's submissiveness leads to his downfall. (pp. 92-3)

Just as "Varioni Brothers" created the image of the misfit hero, so every succeeding story developed the hero's alienation from, and defeat by, society. All of Salinger's wartime stories accentuated the hero's isolation from the good past and the corrupt world. In "This Sandwich Has No Mayonaise" the hero, Vincent Caulfield, is separated from his family and removed from his brother, Holden, who is "missing in action." Cut off from love, alienated from the other soldiers by his thoughts, Vincent is "drenched to the bone, the bone of loneliness, the bone of silence." The soldier's initiation into the terrors of war parallels the child's initiation into the sordidness of the adult world. What is so horrifying is neither war's physical brutality nor society's overt prejudices but rather the subtle dehumanization, the insidious loneliness, and the paralyzing lovelessness. Thus each character becomes a war casualty just as the earlier characters were casualties of society. (p. 93)

Salinger's early vision—the vision of something so terrible that it cannot be communicated or forgotten which plagued the young soldier—is culminated in the post-war world of "The Inverted Forest" . . . in which an innocent and talented poet destroys himself. Raymond Ford, the talented poet, is Salinger's misfit hero, built from Joe Varioni's image, later to be developed into Seymour Glass. . . . What makes him a misfit in society—the fact that "his equipment differed from that of other men"—cannot be compromised.

The fate of Raymond's vision symbolizes the outcome of his life: real sight and metaphorical sight are one. In his adolescence he read poetry twenty hours a day, badly damaging his eyes. Finally, his impaired vision required him to wear two pair of glasses—one for reading and one for everyday use. In an attempt to reconcile these two worlds—the aesthetic and the real one—Ford ruined himself. . . . The point for Raymond—as for Holden and Seymour—is that he *is* a misfit and can never be accepted by, or accept, society. His vision—like his unimpaired sense of taste—renders his problem insoluble. With it he cannot live in society; without it he cannot live with himself. (pp. 93-4)

The off-center vision of "The Inverted Forest" is further developed in the first Salinger story to gain any attention, "A Perfect Day for Bananafish." . . . In it, the Glass family is born when Seymour Glass, the eldest son in the family, commits suicide at the age of twenty-five. Developing from the mold of Joe Varioni, Vincent Caulfield, and Raymond Ford, Seymour becomes the prototype for the whole Glass family: sensitive, intelligent, imaginative, loving, combining a whimsical sense of humor and an overbearing sense of his own misfitness in the modern world. Like Holden Caulfield, he is too full of love, with no worthy object on which to bestow it. Salinger juxtaposes the delightful conversation Seymour has with the little girl on the beach with his complete inability to communicate with any of the adults around him. Seymour's tragic obsession with his own inability to communicate with the outside world and live with it on its own terms is what kills him and plagues the rest of the Glass Family. (p. 94)

"Raise High the Roofbeam, Carpenters" . . . delves into the pre-suicidal days of Seymour Glass. That Salinger should resurrect Seymour is important not only because it sheds light on the earlier story, "A Perfect Day for Bananafish," but because it holds the key to the future evolution of the misfit hero. The problem becomes no longer one of merely co-existing with society but rather of living the good life. Indeed, this sprawling story—formless in contrast to earlier works like "A Perfect Day for Bananafish" or "Down at the Dinghy"—contains the element found in all of Salinger's stories. Present are the distraught misfit hero, unable to reconcile his Zen Buddhism with his society's Pragmatism; the mundane, misguided girl who cannot share her fiance's extraordinary world; the vulgar antagonist, insensitive and sophisticated enough to be harmful, insinuating that there is something homosexual about Seymour because he is too happy to show up for his own wedding; the narrator who tries to appear detached but obviously has a personal stake in Seymour's life; and the stifling environ-

ment in which love, communication and decent values have been lost.

Seymour says: "The human voice conspires to desecrate everything on earth." Indeed, all through Salinger's writing there is distrust of the spoken word. . . . At the same time, Salinger has made the written word the mode of communication for his hero. Joe Varioni is a writer; Raymond Ford a poet; and Teddy and Seymour keep diaries. . . . More lasting than speech, writing symbolizes both the honesty and the creativity of the artist. Like Stephen Dedalus and Tonio Kruger, but perhaps more like Kafka's Hunger Artist, Salinger's misfit hero is the artist, trying to reconcile his art to his soul.

If the artist communicates by writing, then the religious man communicates by silence: this is the paradox of Zen. Zen Buddhism places its prime burden on the relationship between man and nature, between the "I" of Martin Buber and any object outside the "I"—the "Thou." Without this essential relationship there can be no communication. Thus the "sound of two hands clapping" is the sound of the relationship. Without either partner—call them subject and object if you like—there can be no sound. The search for "the sound of one hand clapping" comes to an end in the spiritual life. Thus art is the way of the imagination and Zen is the way of the soul. Salinger is primarily interested in the souls of his characters.

However, it is one thing to espouse the way of the soul and quite another thing actually to follow it. In choosing the private world over the public the hero has compromised the basic Western principle of social responsibility. Salinger's heroes attempt not to compromise between the pure spiritual world and the corrupted mundane world but rather to disaffiliate themselves from the public world and flee to the private because they have confused the private world with the soul. . . . The way of the holy man is, truly, a difficult way, too difficult for either Holden or Seymour. In this sense, Salinger's misfit who is a hero is really a hero who is a misfit: a misfit in society because he refuses to adjust and a misfit in the private world because he cannot pass through its "dark night of the soul." Too much a product of his Western culture to follow Zen, the misfit hero makes the grave error of assuming that there are only these two alternatives and that one of them is unthinkable.

Salinger's choice for his hero is essentially a religious problem, that is, the problem of finding moral integrity, love, and redemption in an immoral world. We can illuminate the meaningfulness of this interpretation by comparing Salinger's last story, "Zooey" . . . , to T. S. Eliot's *The Cocktail Party* for the two works are much closer than one would suspect. In setting up their respective situations both Salinger and Eliot have used essentially the same pattern and relationships between their characters. In the play, Celia, a sensitive young woman concerned with the futility of the meaningless relationships she has established, is faced with the possibilities of her salvation. Similarly, in "Zooey," we pick up Franny where we last left her, still sick of her college environment, now at home, trying to decide whether to return to school or become a nun. (pp. 95-7)

Both Franny and Celia suffer from the same symptoms: frustration in love, loneliness and alienation, emptiness and failure. Celia says she feels she must "atone" for her failure while Franny actively does this by murmuring her prayer over and over in an attempt to regain what she feels she has lost. The two women are also presented with the same alternatives. (p. 97)

Like Eliot, Salinger finds that the path through the world reaches salvation as quickly as the way to the frontier. However, whereas Celia chooses the frontier, Franny chooses the world. In the respective choices lies the difference between the Anglican and American tempers. While William Wiegand points out in the *Chicago Review* . . . that Franny's embracing of "Christian love" is a reconciliation of the misfit hero, alias bananafish, to the world, it seems more likely that Franny's defection from the trail to the nunnery indicates a repudiation of the image of the misfit hero. Zooey tells her: "We're freaks, that's all. Those two bastards [Seymour and his twin brother, Buddy, the story's narrator] got us nice and early and made us into freaks with freakish standards, that's all. We're the Tattooed Lady, and we're never going to have a minute's peace, the rest of our lives, till everybody else is tattooed, too." The thing that counts in the religious life is "detachment" but the misfit hero has made the mistake of using his ego as the yardstick of holiness, replacing it with a holier-than-thou-ness. He has forgotten that "this is *God's* universe, buddy, not yours, and He has the final say about what's ego and what isn't." Like Job, the misfit hero is guilty of the deepest sin, spiritual pride: he has missed the distinction between being religious and being pious, between God's world and his personal world. Thus Franny is so busy searching her spiritual navel that she cannot recognize that her mother's bowl of chicken broth is "consecrated."

But a world of difference separates Franny from the earlier misfit heroes. Whereas Holden Caulfield runs away when he is in trouble, Franny goes home. . . . In a vast world full of misunderstanding and estrangement, the sensitive innocent must turn in towards the family to find the intimate love and communication that is so lacking in the outside world. It is through the family that he retains his equilibrium, balancing his moral integrity against the social pressures of the outside world. Thus the family becomes the place where self and society meet, where the moral and ethical realms are reconciled. The Glass family is a striking affirmation in an era dominated by the disintegrating families of O'Neill and Wolfe. The affirmation of the family and of the concept of social responsibility is traditionally moral in the sense that it is traditionally Judeo-Christian.

Not only are *The Cocktail Party* and "Zooey" essentially Christian, they are both concerned with the family unit. Arthur Miller has pointed out that the basic weakness of *The Cocktail Party* is that its poetic diction is unsuited to its familial subject matter. Likewise, the form of Salinger's latest stories may weaken their effectiveness. For while the stories retain the semblance of the realism of "Uncle Wiggily . . ." and "A Perfect Day for Bananafish," they blur the distance between the author and his subject matter. This lack of aesthetic distance creates a personal interplay between author and character rather than between character and character. The stories hold the reader's attention not through the revelation of character but through revelation of author, reducing Salinger's audience to his afficionados and troubled adolescents in general. His audience becomes cultish, his predicament personal, his characters begin "to give off a little stink of piousness," and the mean-

ingfulness of the problem and solution appears both too pat and even ludicrous in its juxtaposition to the facts that he gives. (pp. 98-9)

Paul Levine, "J. D. Salinger: The Development of the Misfit Hero," in Twentieth Century Literature *(copyright 1958, Hofstra University Press), October, 1958, pp. 92-9.*

DAN WAKEFIELD

It has only been in the past few years . . . that professional literary critics have taken Salinger under their microscopes for examination. Even this belated inspection has been not so much out of interest in his search as it has in him as a species held in high regard by "The Young Generation." Surely this is of interest, but to make it the most important thing in considering Salinger is to distort the meaning of his work.

Out of my own personal experience, which is that of a student of Columbia College in the early fifties who has spent the last several years in New York, I know that Salinger is indeed regarded highly by many young people. I have heard his work discussed among my friends and acquaintances more than any other contemporary author, and I have heard enough speculation about Salinger himself to feel that there is indeed a "Salinger Myth," as there was in the twenties, though in a different way, a "Fitzgerald Myth." Certainly any myth alive in our fact-smothered era is of interest, and this one perhaps especially since its nature is so extremely different from the twenties myth. The Fitzgerald myth had its hero in Gatsby-like parties and dunkings in the fountain at Union Square; the Salinger myth has its hero living in a cabin in the woods or going to Japan to study Zen. But in both cases the work of the man is of far more importance than the myth. Limiting Salinger's work to its interest as some kind of "document" that appeals only to people of a certain age and social background is as sensible and rewarding as considering *The Great Gatsby* as a sociological monograph once enjoyed by a now extinct species known as "Flaming Youth."

And yet it seems to follow in the eyes of some older observers that if Salinger is indeed a myth and mentor of many young people, interest in his work is restricted to young people and that this is symptomatic of the fact that it is really childish, sentimental, adolescent, and irrelevant. (pp. 78-9)

Moral senility can come at any age, or need not come at all, and we have recently borne painful witness through the Howls of the writers of the "Beat Generation" that moral senility can afflict quite young men and women. This group dismisses the search of Salinger on the grounds that he is "slick" (he writes for *The New Yorker,* and as any sensitive person can tell, it is printed on a slick type of paper). But now that the roar from the motorcycles of Jack Kerouac's imagination has begun to subside, we find that the highly advertised search of the Beat has ended, at least literarily, not with love but with heroin. (pp. 80-1)

Holden, through the course of his search, is repulsed and frightened, not by what people do to him . . . but rather by what people do to each other, and to themselves. (p. 81)

Dan Wakefield, "Salinger and the Search for Love," in New World Writing No. 14 *(copyright © 1958 by Dan Wakefield; reprinted by permission of the author and The Helen Brann Agency,*

Inc.), 1958 (and reprinted in Studies in J. D. Salinger: Reviews, Essays, and Critiques of 'The Catcher in the Rye' and Other Fiction, *edited by Marvin Laser and Norman Fruman, Odyssey Press, 1963, pp. 77-84.*

ARTHUR MIZENER

The essential reality for [Salinger] subsists in personal relations, when people, however agonizingly, love one another. "I say," remarks Buddy Glass as he begins to tell us the story "Zooey," "that my current offering isn't a mystical story, or a religiously mystifying story, at all. I say it is a compound, or multiple, love story, pure and complicated."

This is true of all Salinger's mature stories. Their subject is the power to love, pure and—in children and the childlike—simple, but in aware people, pure and complicated. Salinger's constant allusions to the Bhagavad Gita, Sri Ramakrishna, Chuang-tzu, and the rest are only efforts to find alternative ways of expressing what his stories are about. This power to love can be realized—and represented—most fully in complicated personal relations like those of the Glasses.

Salinger's conception of these relations is an impressive—and certainly unconscious—evidence of the way he fits into a major tradition of American literature, what might be called the effort to define The Good American. For this tradition, American experience creates a dilemma by encouraging the individual man to cultivate his perception to the limit according to his own lights and at the same time committing him to a society on which the majority has firmly imposed a well-meaning but imperceptive and uniform attitude. (p. 87)

The Glass children stand in this way at the center of our dilemma as, with less clarity of perception and less intensity of feeling, large numbers of Americans do. Like Thoreau and Henry Adams, Huck Finn and Ike McCaslin, Ishmael and Jay Gatsby, the Glass children are well aware of where they stand—committed, involved, torn.

"I'd enjoy [doing a movie in France], yes," says Zooey. "*God,* yes. But I'd hate like hell to leave New York. If you must know, I hate any kind of so-called creative type who gets on any kind of ship. I don't give a goddam what his reasons are. I was *born* here. I went to *school* here. I've been *run over* here—*twice,* and on the same damned *street.* I have no business acting in Europe, for God's sake."

This sounds like the speaker in Allen Tate's "Ode to the Confederate Dead," except that the voice is wholly Northern and urban and is—for all its desperateness—less despairing. (pp. 87-8)

It is the effort to convey their full sense of this situation that leads the Glass children to talk the way they do. For this extra dimension of understanding they use the everyday urban speech Salinger has been listening to all his life. The Glass children must speak the language of the place where they were born, went to school, were run over; it is their native language, the only one wholly theirs, just as the place itself is. But they need to express in this language an understanding of their experience which, if possessed to some degree by many Americans, is wholly clear to only a few of them.

An effort to resolve a similar conflict of feelings affects most of the writers of this tradition, with the result that they too develop odd, brilliant styles. Salinger's style most obviously resembles those of Mark Twain, Lardner, and Hemingway, who prided themselves on using homely American speech with great accuracy, but were saying things with it that few homely Americans are wholly conscious of.

Like Twain and Lardner, Salinger depends more than most prose writers on the fine shading of his style to convey his meaning. That is why he is at his best when one of his characters is speaking. When Buddy Glass writes his brother Zooey about Zooey's unprofitable love of Greek, he says, "Of course, you can go to Athens. Sunny *old* Athens." When Zooey wants to get out of the bathtub, he says to his mother, "I'm getting out of here in about three seconds, Bessie! I'm giving you fair warning. Let's not wear out our welcome, buddy." Each of these clichés is made absurd by the special quality of the Glass child's feeling, but it is at the same time what holds him, for all his special insight, in contact with the perception of ordinary people. (p. 88)

It is [a] delicately balanced perception that gives the Glass children their special quality.

But if it makes them remarkable, it is also a quite terrible burden. "Smart men," as Dick Diver said a long time ago about Abe North in *Tender Is the Night,* "play close to the line because they have to—some of them can't stand it, so they quit." Like Abe North, Seymour, the most gifted of the Glass children, kills himself. He knows that, in spite of—because of—the unusual depth and intensity of his perception of experience, he needs to be a part of the daily life of the ordinary world. He tries, by psychoanalysis and marriage, to become part of Muriel Fedder's world. This commitment is not merely an intellectual need; it is a desperate emotional necessity for him: "How I love and need her undiscriminating heart," he says of Muriel. But Seymour finds it impossible to live simultaneously the life of his own discriminating heart and Muriel's life, with its "primal urge to play house permanently—to go up to the desk clerk in some very posh hotel and ask if her Husband has picked up the mail yet, . . . to shop for maternity clothes, . . . [to have] her own Christmas-tree ornaments to unbox annually." He is torn apart by two incompatible worlds of feeling.

This, then, is the hard thing—not to find out "what it [is] all about," which the Glass children have known from very early, but "how to live it." Knowing what it is all about, in fact, is the burden.

"Those two bastards," says Zooey of Seymour and Buddy, who had taught Franny and him what wisdom is, "got us nice and early and made us into freaks with freakish standards, that's all. We're the Tattooed Lady, and we're never going to have a minute's peace, the rest of our lives, till everybody else is tattooed, too. . . . The minute I'm in a room with somebody who has the usual number of ears, I either turn into a goddam *seer* or a human hatpin. The Prince of Bores."

This, Zooey knows, is not a failure of love—he would not be concerned with his own freakishness if love failed—but a distortion of it. As his mother says to him:

> "If you [take to somebody] then you do all
> the talking and nobody can even get a word

in edgewise. If you *don't* like somebody—which is most of the time—then you just sit around like death *itself* and let the person talk themselves into a hole. I've seen you do it. . . . You do," she said, without accusation in her voice. "Neither you nor Buddy knows how to talk to people you don't like." She thought it over, "Don't love, really," she amended.

"Which is most of the time" because, apart from children and the occasionally simple adult, the world is made up of people who are innocently imperceptive and emotionally dead. (pp. 89-90)

Nevertheless the power to love can exist in unimaginative people, and when it does, as the Glass children know they ought to know, nothing else really counts. Bessie Glass "often seem[s] to be an impenetrable mass of prejudices, clichés, and bromides"; these are a continual irritation to her children: Franny is driven nearly frantic by Bessie's insistence on nice cups of chicken soup when Franny is suffering something like a crisis of the soul. But Zooey is right when he points out to her that she is "missing out on every single goddam religious action that's going on around this house. You don't have sense enough to *drink* when somebody brings you a cup of consecrated chicken soup—which is the only kind of chicken soup Bessie ever brings anybody around this madhouse."

Even if the acts of such people are not consecrated by love, they must not be hated. "What I don't like," Zooey says to Franny, ". . . is the way you talk about all these people. I mean you don't just despise what they represent—you despise them. It's too damned personal, Franny."

What Zooey knows he must learn to do in order to survive is to love even what he calls the "fishy" people—because they are all the Fat Lady for whom Seymour told him to shine his shoes before going on the air, even though the audience could not see his feet.

"This terribly clear, clear picture of the Fat Lady formed in my mind," he tells Franny. "I had her sitting on this porch all day, swatting flies, with her radio going full-blast from morning till night. I figured the heat was terrible, and she probably had cancer and—I don't know. Anyway, it seemed goddam clear why Seymour wanted me to shine my shoes when I went on the air. It made *sense*."

It makes sense because the highest standard of performance a man's own understanding can set for him must ultimately be embodied—however mystically—in the ordinary, suffering members of the community of his fellows. Otherwise there can be no solution to the dilemma the Glass children are caught in. Zooey puts this conviction in the highest possible terms:

> I'll tell you a terrible secret . . . [he says to Franny]. Are you listening to me? *There isn't anyone out there who isn't Seymour's Fat Lady. . . .* Don't you know that? Don't you know that goddam secret yet? And don't you know—*listen* to me, now—*don't you know who that Fat Lady really is?* . . . Ah, buddy. Ah, buddy. It's Christ Himself. Christ Himself, buddy.

What Salinger has seen in American life is the extraordi-

nary tension it sets up between our passion to understand and evaluate our experience for ourselves, and our need to belong to a community that is unusually energetic in imposing its understanding and values on its individual members. Whatever one may think of Salinger's answer to the problem, this view of American life is important; it has a long and distinguished history. But Salinger's achievement is not that he has grasped an abstract idea of American experience, important as that idea may be in itself; it is that he has seen this idea working in the actual life of our times, in our habitual activities, in the very turns of our speech, and has found a way to make us see it there, too. (p. 90)

Arthur Mizener, "The Love Song of J. D. Salinger," in Harper's *(copyright © 1959 by* Harper's *Magazine; all rights reserved; excerpted from the February, 1959 issue by special permission), February, 1959, pp. 83-90.*

GRANVILLE HICKS

Last spring I taught a course in contemporary fiction at New York University. When I was drawing up the reading list, a veteran teacher whom I consulted mildly questioned the inclusion of J. D. Salinger's "The Catcher in the Rye." "It's the one book," he said "that every undergraduate in America has read." I think he was pretty nearly right about that, but, for my own sake, I'm glad I decided to teach the book. To most of my students, I discovered, Holden Caulfield meant more than Jake Barnes or Jay Gatsby or Augie March or any other character we encountered in the course, and in the discussion of the novel there was a sense of direct involvement such as I felt on no other occasion.

For the college generations of the Fifties, Salinger has the kind of importance that Scott Fitzgerald and Ernest Hemingway had for the young people of the Twenties. He is not a public figure as they were; on the contrary, his zeal for privacy is phenomenal; but he is felt nevertheless as a presence, a significant and congenial presence. There are, I am convinced, millions of young Americans who feel closer to Salinger than to any other writer.

In the first place, he speaks their language. He not only speaks it; he shapes it, just as Hemingway influenced the speech of countless Americans in the Twenties. The talk of his characters is, so to speak, righter than right. The voice of Holden Caulfield is a voice we instantly recognize, and yet there is just that twist of stylistic intensification that always distinguishes good dialogue.

In the second place, he expresses their rebellion. Most of my undergraduates, so far as I could tell, were as nonpolitical as Holden Caulfield. . . . Yet they were far from complacency, and they delighted in Holden's attacks on meanness, stupidity, and especially phoniness. They admired his intransigence, too, which he often refers to as his craziness, and rejoiced in his gestures of defiance.

But Holden is not merely a rebel, and this also my students understood. What is strongest in him, as is indicated by the passage that gives the book its title, is compassion. . . .

I have been talking seriously about a book that on page after page is wildly funny, but it is fundamentally a serious book, as its younger readers know. Holden Caulfield is torn, and nearly destroyed, by the conflict between integrity and love. He is driven by the need not to be less than himself, not to accept what he knows to be base. On the other hand, he is capable of understanding and loving the persons to whom his integrity places him in opposition. The problem of values with which Salinger so persuasively confronts his sixteen-year-old is not exclusively a problem of adolescence. (p. 13)

There are many things to say about "Seymour," but I want to concentrate on two. The story is told in the first person by Buddy, the second oldest of the Glass children, and Salinger has chosen to identify himself completely with Buddy: for instance, Buddy describes three stories he has written, and they are three stories written and signed by J. D. Salinger. This does not entitle us to assume that Salinger had four brothers and two sisters or appeared on a quiz show or teaches in a women's college, but we cannot avoid the conclusion that when Buddy speaks on literary matters he speaks for Salinger. What we discover is that Salinger is acutely self-conscious, about his writing, about his philosophy, about his reputation. (Buddy alludes to "the bogus information that I spend six months of the year in a Buddhist monastery and the other six in a mental institution.") Indeed, self-consciousness gives the story its peculiar quality, and although the tone is beautifully sustained, as always in Salinger's later work, the self is exceedingly obtrusive. Buddy was prominent in "Raise High the Roof Beam, Carpenters," but he wasn't constantly talking about himself as a writer, and I think that was a better story than this. (So was "Zooey," if only by virtue of the wonderful bathroom conversation between Zooey and his mother, which "Seymour" has nothing to equal.)

On the other hand, as a piece of stylistic virtuosity, the story does make the reader's hair stand on end, and, what is more, the reader begins to see Seymour as Salinger wants us to see him. He was interesting and likeable in "A Perfect Day for Bananafish," but no more than that. In "Raise High the Room Beam, Carpenters" and "Zooey" we felt that he was a man of unusual powers, but we saw him only from a distance. Now, in brief glimpses, but in the most concrete way, Salinger makes us feel Seymour's brilliance, his high poetic gifts, and above all his capacity for love. "What was he, anyway?" Buddy asks. "A *saint*? Thankfully, it isn't my responsibility to answer that one." But that is exactly what Salinger is trying to create—a contemporary saint—and in the end he convinces me. (pp. 13, 30)

When we were discussing "The Catcher in the Rye" in class, there was one dissenting voice, one student who felt that Holden Caulfield's rebellion was too immature and ineffectual to be worth serious consideration. Most of the students loudly disagreed, and I went along with the majority. Holden is not rejecting maturity but is looking for a better model than his elders by and large present. Like the Glasses, though in a less ostentatious way, he is a seeker after wisdom. That Salinger can make the search for wisdom seem important to large numbers of young people is not exactly cause for alarm. (p. 30)

> *Granille Hicks, "J. D. Salinger: Search for Wisdom," in* The Saturday Review *(Entire issue copyright 1959 by Saturday Review Associates, Inc.; reprinted with permission), July 25, 1959, pp. 13, 30.*

MICHAEL WALZER

Young people today have no spokesmen. (p. 156)

Ideology, heroism, success: none of these seems suffi-ciently compelling. For the young today, the importance and excitement of the adult world have become somewhat problematic. On the one hand this can lead to that odd combination of indifference and professionalism which one sometimes encounters in college students. On the other hand, it produces an earnest confusion, less often critical than nostalgic, which contemplates without enthusiasm or alternatives its possible maturity.

Some sense of this confusion and of the painful sincerity that goes with it is necessary in order to understand the phenomenon of J. D. Salinger, the writer most admired and read by many young people today. In one sense, Salinger represents the indulgence of a mood; but he is also the confidant of those who indulge the mood. Affectionate and tender, he speaks to the adolescent soul with urgent but reassuring intimacy. Yet he is also full of advice. He understands the ways in which growing up is a misfortune, a process of compromise and surrender. Reconciliation, however, and not resistance is his eventual concern: he is whimsical, all right, but not absurd. His opening theme is childhood lost, his conclusion is a half-mystic, half-sentimental resignation—with an ultimate glimpse of childhood regained. Finally, he is successful, appealing and comforting because he suggests a kind of reconciliation with the adult world which is at the same time an evasion of worldliness.

It is in grateful recognition of this evasion that many young people have accepted Salinger's characters, Holden Caulfield as a brother and Seymour Glass as a private and sainted memory. Holden, it should be remembered, had his last fling at sixteen; Seymour committed suicide at thirty-one. The two events have the very moderate virtues of aimlessness and failure—we don't after all want moral lessons—but in their retelling, Salinger slips into sentimentality, contrived whimsy and a cagey, esoteric piety. So the academic critics, committed as they are to the surface seriousness of things, call Holden a pilgrim, and undoubtedly one of them will shortly grasp the somber truth that Seymour is a martyr and a saint.

This portentousness is Salinger's own fault—perhaps his intention—and it surely misrepresents the young; it even misrepresents Holden and Seymour. For precocious piety and innocent goodness are not yet wisdom, resourcefulness, or moral conduct; they cannot motivate martyrdom or, by themselves, make pilgrimage significant. They are qualities which remain to be tested, to be embodied and sharpened by worldly encounter. Salinger, however, turns them into the standardized equipment of a cautious, wistful rebel. When the earnest and uncertain young men identify with Holden Caulfield, they are expressing a deeply felt discontent. But it is a discontent devoid of all appetite for adult satisfaction. It seems on the one hand to lack purpose and on the other to be free from all anxiety about purposelessness. It lacks, above all, just that moral irascibility which was once thought the truest sign of youth. This vague rebelliousness is Salinger's material—what he both truly expresses and exploits. He cultivates a sense for its style, and he adds to its gentle ineptitude an engaging piety, at once sentimental and exotic. He does not, of course, suggest any actual confrontation between the discontented and the world of their discontent.

Salinger's characters are not heroic in part because they are members of the family. They are members, almost, of a

Victorian clan—the patriarch vague or missing, the clan more of a fraternal coterie—and it is familial feeling which provides the background for the affection, honesty, and love which he seeks to describe. (pp. 156-57)

Salinger's artfulness is best revealed in his ability to reconstruct the circumstances and sentiments of teenage revelation: sit down a minute, I want to tell you everything. He tirelessly reads us his family mail, prints fragments from the diaries of the dead Seymour, relates the unassorted jottings of his brothers and sisters. He gathers his stories through a presumably random (but he assures us, total) recall, and pays a public price for the remembering. He drags us into his living room for "home movies"—I think of Salinger as the only modern writer with a living room—and there we sit, silent members. He is insistently intimate, urgently garrulous, wordily familiar. For Salinger this familiarity has a moral (as well as a literary) motive, and that motive is affection. He seeks to draw us into the clan, to bind us by the somewhat tendentious (not to say, onesided) heatedness of his intimate, utterly candid communications. There is not a drop of cold blood in his veins. Outside the family "people never believe you," as Holden says. He means adults and he is right enough; adults are suspicious, and children, if they have a native honesty, have also a native gullibility.... [Today], Salinger seems to say, the only contrast to the innocence and fervor of the child is the affectation, the cruel conventionality, the phoniness of the adult world. The adult is not "real"; he lives amidst sham.

But not sham at all: that is what one would like, for it is at least the proper opposite of innocence and sincerity. If children are candid, then let adults be hypocrites and the war of generations rage. But neither Holden's complaint, nor that of Franny Glass, is about hypocrisy; they are not really concerned with the lie, nor with actual cruelty. It requires something like moral firmness to resent hypocrisy, and though Holden has, as do all of Salinger's children and, I would guess, many of his readers, a natural sense of the sweet and the good, Holden is no moralist. His true concern is with foible, affectation, minor pomposity, casual carelessness—all of which combine to make this a jungle of fallible (but ferocious) animals. The jungle itself, however, is no part of Holden's experience. Nor of Franny's; and when her brother tells her that every fat woman is Jesus Christ (and hence not to be resented), it is a counsel of imperfection which bears little relationship to the real imperfections of the world. Love, he tells her, can transcend foible and fatness alike: *it certainly had better*.

So the professor who goes into the men's room to muss up his hair before class is after all no villain. Nor is the Ivy Leaguer in the theater lobby who "said the play *itself* was no masterpiece, but the Lunts, of course, were absolute angels." With them, one can make emotional peace. But surely the hypocrite and the moralist have another difficulty, and a fairly simple one: they are permanently at odds, irreconcilable. This occurs to none of Salinger's characters, and for that reason I don't believe it is fair to say that they are simply unspoiled; I think they are untouched. At the same time as the child approaches the adult world, he escapes into fantasy. Holden's fantasies are relatively modest, though they bear a close relationship to the religious aspirations of Salinger's later characters: Holden dreams of being a "catcher in the rye," the defender of children at play, or a gas station attendant in the west, deaf,

dumb and solitary.... What is disturbing, however, is that his dreams do not lead him to any kind of adventure, not to anything at all but casual encounter and sensitive recoil. As Seymour's mother-in-law says, he doesn't relate. Salinger's characters can't like or even know anyone they don't love —*who isn't in the family, for chrissake.*

If this is really true, then why doesn't Holden set out for that gas station in the west? He might be a beat traveller. That, I suppose, is the real alternative and it is not especially interesting. Holden, instead, goes home to his ten year old sister; he doesn't want adventure, any more than do most of Salinger's readers; he wants affection. He will become an adult gently, carrying with him in the phony world only a single moral image, the image of childlike simplicity. (pp. 157-59)

Since Holden's last fling, Salinger has written almost entirely of the Glass family, a clan of seven precocious children, of Irish-Jewish stock and distinctly Buddhist tendencies. The main theme of these stories has been love. Love is the bond which holds the seven children together—and love, along with a touch of friendly condescension, is what binds them even to their parents. The family here is a mythical gang, truly fraternal, truly affectionate; it is as if, remembering Holden's loneliness, Salinger is determined never again to permit one of his characters to be alone.

The precocity of Salinger's children takes many forms.... But the most important form is an extraordinary religious and mystical insight. I think it fair to say that love for Salinger is either familial or Christlike; it is the love of brothers and sisters—or of brethren. The last of these is obviously the more difficult, and Salinger sensibly recommends but does not describe it. He writes of erotic love not at all, and it is worth at least entertaining the idea—though it contradicts many of the operative assumptions of our culture—that his young readers are really not interested in it, that they are entirely satisfied with the love of Holden and his sister or of Zooey and Franny. (pp. 159-60)

Love at a distance, whimsical appreciation ("the terrible Miss Zabel"), manages to combine commitment and withdrawal; I would guess that it makes both marriage and suicide unnecessary, But what does it do to the quality of love? In Salinger's stories love, familial and Christlike together, is primarily the habit and the wisdom of precocious children. It is almost inevitably, given Salinger's style and his subject matter, a bit precious. It is also indiscriminate and uninvolved. (p. 161)

Whimsy and religion are Salinger's ploys. He does not mean them to indicate willfulness, that is too harsh, nor mere childishness, that is too unimportant; nor morality, that is too difficult, and not pure contemplation, that would be farfetched. He means them to indicate *superiority*. Whimsy is the caprice of the precocious; religion, their secret insight. For such people does Salinger write: gentle, unconventional people, who find themselves behaving exactly like everyone else, but who know that they are different, if only because they remember that once they were young. But is that really such a precious or exclusive memory? Perhaps it is, and perhaps that moment of uncertainty before a young man surrenders himself to higher education and total organization is as important as Salinger's prose suggests. But I doubt that the moment is adequately represented by whimsy, or that it can survive in reminiscence, or be resurrected in esoteric piety.

The numerous silent members of the Glass family, Salinger's ardent readers, share a kind of emotional superiority, which, one must admit, has little that is worldly in it. They pursue their careers with a sense of grace, that is, with an assurance of style. They are reckless, but only in imagination; after all, they were rebels once. They are painfully sincere, which is to say, loquacious; and—their truest mark —they are whimsically discontented, that is, they complain only about unimportant things.

Membership in this fervent household, however, is for the good alone. And here I think Salinger and his admirers must be taken seriously. Goodness for many of us has always implied activity, vigor, commitment. Good men—let me put it strongly—are energizing centers of ethical action. This is simply not so for Salinger, and presumably it is not so for most of his readers. Goodness for them seems rather a matter of personal style and impulse; its quality is unpretentious, naive (indeed, willfully so), sincere, whimsical. It imitates the child because he presumably has these qualities naturally and indulges them freely; he represents the absence of convention and corruption. That is not, of course, because he is corruptible. But what is for him a merely temporary condition can easily become a permanent posture. The posture is not entirely incompatible with world activity, but questions of ambition, work and conflict evaded; the engaging precocity of the *wunderkind* makes them all seem irrelevant.

Salinger's idea of goodness is another version of disaffiliation, but it is the happiest version, and the easiest, because it makes disaffiliation a secret. Who, indeed, would guess that S. never moves his kings out of the back row? So far as society is concerned, the earnest, uncertain young man goes underground. But not to cultivate the resources of the rebel, not to test his capacity for silence or for patience. The underground is his irregular home, a unique realm of security and affection, sharply contrasted with the worlds of Hollywood, advertising, the organization. Up above, the young man may lie, it is a bit of whimsy; he may prove querulous, it is an indulgence; he may be a success, it doesn't matter; but he will not be active, involved, driving, lustful. He is the first among the disaffiliated to give up cult of experience, and therefore he is permanently untried. But for his readers, perhaps, that is Salinger's greatest appeal. I said above that he is seemingly incapable of cold-bloodedness; surely his readers understand this and appreciate it. Their lack of ambition is also an absence of taste for danger, even for the simple dangers of everyday human encounter. But what will their love come to, and what their goodness, if they do not calculate and take risks? (pp. 161-62)

> *Michael Walzer, "In Place of a Hero," in* Dissent *(reprinted by permission of* Dissent*), Spring, 1960, pp. 156-62.*

CARL F. STRAUCH

[In *The Catcher in the Rye*,] Salinger sharply accentuates the portrayal of Holden with a symbolic structure of language, motif, episode, and character; and when the complex patterns are discovered, the effect is to concentrate our scrutiny on a masterpiece that moves effortlessly on the colloquial surface and at the same time uncovers, with hypnotic compulsion, a psychological drama of unrelenting terror and final beauty. (p. 6)

Salinger has employed neurotic deterioration, symbolical death, spiritual awakening, and psychological self-cure as the inspiration and burden of an elaborate pattern—verbal, thematic, and episodic, that yields the meaning as the discursive examination of Holden's character and problem out of metaphoric context can never do. Structure *is* meaning.

As a start, the readiest way of understanding *The Catcher* lies in an awareness of the dualism or ambivalence of language, for Holden employs both the slob and the literate idiom. . . . Holden's slob speech is obviously justified as a realistic narrative device, since it is the idiom of the American male; yet from the psychological point of view, it becomes the boy's self-protective, verbalized acceptance of the slob values of his prep school contemporaries. He thus may justify himself in his overt being and may hope to secure immunity from attack and rationalize his "belonging"; slob language, therefore, hits off two important social themes—security and status. But the psychological intent becomes symbolical portent when we see that the mass idiom emphasizes a significant distinction between two worlds—the phony world of corrupt materialism and Holden's private world of innocence. . . . For his private world Holden uses a literate and expressive English, and so the profounder psychological and symbolical purposes of slob language may be detected only as that idiom functions in polarized relationship with the other. We need not labor the point that the full range of Salinger's portrayal would never be disclosed without an awareness of the ambivalence of language. (pp. 7-8)

Once we have recognized the ambivalence of language we are prepared to discover Salinger's elaborate use of several kinds of pattern that support and help to develop the narrative. The first verbal pattern to be examined stands in an ironic and mutually illuminating relationship with the image of the secret goldfish at the head of the narrative symbolizing Holden and his secret world. In D. B.'s short story "The Secret Goldfish" the boy would not let others see the goldfish "because he'd bought it with his own money." Holden likewise was to pay in far more than money for his secret world; and as a further parallel, nobody ever saw (or cared to see) this secret world, although Holden invites inspection in the confessional mode, "if you really want to hear about it." This mode is maintained throughout with frequent interpolations of "if you want to know the truth" or "if you really want to know." As the story uncovers more and more of Holden's dilemma, these phrasings, although employed in the most casual manner, transcend their merely conversational usage and become psychologically portentous. The inference is that society, including his own parents, has no desire to recognize the truth about Holden or its own obsessions. In the middle of the tale Holden learns from the psychoanalytical snob, Carl Luce, that his father had helped him to "adjust"; and the blunted resolution of the narrative on the Freudian couch represents society's final humiliating indifference to truth. Recognition of the truth would embrace the love and compassion that it has no time for but that Holden himself not only lavishes on his secret world but extends to the public world in episodes and reflections rounded off with a minor verbal pattern, "You felt sorry for her" or "I felt sorry as hell for him." The confessional mode embraces still another verbal pattern put variously, "People never notice anything," "He wasn't even listening," "People never believe you," and morons "never want to discuss anything." The failure in communication could not be more bleakly confirmed; and there is an immense irony in the contrast between Holden's telling the truth and the indifference surrounding him. Note, then, that the confessional mode, developed by several verbal patterns, provides a beautifully formulated enclosing structure for the tale—with the symbolic image of the secret goldfish at the start and at the end of the equally symbolic talking couch.

Two other patterns ironically reenforce the confessional mode. At Pencey Dr. Thurmer had talked to Holden "about Life being a game," and Mr. Spencer added for the truant's benefit, "Life *is* a game that one plays according to the rules." Toward the end Mr. Antolini sustained the cliché in his overblown rhetoric. Considering Holden's own honesty and the indifference of his seniors, "playing the game" becomes a grisly farce; and there is further irony in the fact that Holden is himself fervently devoted to the concept, first in his treasuring Allie's baseball mitt and then in his confiding in Phoebe that he would like to be a catcher in the rye to save children from falling off "some crazy cliff." And does he not wear his red hunting hat backwards like a catcher? Mr. Antolini, who speaks to Holden from a sophisticated height and warns him of a "terrible, terrible fall," a "special kind of fall," is capable, in these psychological terms, of no more than talk, for he arrived too late to catch young Castle, who jumped out the window to escape the persecution of his contemporaries. The second pattern furnishes an ironical grace note or two. At the beginning of the tale Holden thought that Mr. Spencer yelled "Good luck!" at him, and toward the close a teacher in Phoebe's school wished him "good luck." Unrelenting in its vision of the double-dealing of society, *The Catcher* portrays teachers as sentimentalists and guardians of an exploded ethic; and one of them, Antolini, is a linguistic phony. In these closing patterns, then, the reverberations of irony appear to be endless, and the structure of language and motif is all the more impressive because everything is presented in such an artless and colloquial fashion.

If the design thus far disclosed may be construed as the motif of unsportsmanlike sportsmanship and if the social corollary is that by playing the game (but what *are* the rules?) one may achieve security and status, it remains to be said that society reduces Holden to an ambivalence of acceptance and rejection, of boastful claims and humiliating admissions that are, in effect, destructive of the integrity of his personality. Holden seeks status with his contemporaries by talking slob language, but he shows the same impulse with his elders in more subtle fashion. (pp. 9-11)

If society were no worse than a somewhat difficult but rational enough arrangement for status-seeking and if a person had merely to pay a stiff psychological price in adjustment for the rewards, Holden's frequent charge of "phony" might be dismissed. But the matter goes far deeper than that: society, in the repulsive form of Stradlater, subjects Holden to humiliations that pass beyond the legitimacies of playing the game. Holden's career discloses intensified patterns of ambivalence—withdrawal and aggression, guilt feelings, fantasies of mutilation, the death-wish; and the reason lies almost as much in the social encounter as in the death of his brother Allie. A society that ignores or rejects his gesture for understanding, that preempts his possessions, body, and mind, that invades and violates his inner being—such a society is not only status-

seeking; it is actively and crudely anthropophagus and psychophagus. The vision of ugliness in *The Catcher* challenges anything else in the same genre. (p. 11)

The somewhat less than twenty pages of chapters four and six, the Stradlater episode, provide a brilliant instance of Salinger's technical virtuosity. Here we have convincing evidence that this completely selfish and indifferent young animal did push Holden, in his already neurotic state, down the nightmarish incline toward the psychoanalytical couch.... Since it is the despoiling and humiliation of Holden Caulfield, the cynically indifferent invasion and stripping bare of his person, property, and secret imaginative world that is the burden of this episode, we note with fascinated attention how Stradlater possesses himself of all things that are Holden's, one after another. He uses Holden's Vitalis on his "gorgeous locks," he borrows Holden's hounds-tooth jacket for his date, and yawning all the while, he expects Holden to write his theme for him. A sovereign indifference to all about him is Stradlater's salient characteristic. He could not be bothered to get Jane Gallagher's first name right; he called her Jean. When Holden, with his studious care for the other person, asked whether Jane had enjoyed the game, Stradlater didn't know. A bitter humiliation for Holden is that he must ask this gorgeous phony, who has made a theme-slave of him, not to tell Jane that he is being expelled from Pencey; most galling for the reader is Holden's admission that Stradlater probably won't tell "mostly . . . because he wasn't too interested."

It is, however, the imminently dangerous quality of sex that is frightening. In chapter four when Holden heard that Stradlater was to have a date with Jane Gallagher, he "nearly dropped *dead*" and "nearly went crazy," and in chapter six, through all the mounting ordeal, he "went right on smoking like a madman." The psychological significance of these verbalisms is unmistakable, for Stradlater has invaded Holden's secret world and violated a symbol of innocence and respect. Indeed, in the elaborate pattern of this episode, Stradlater, the "secret slob," matched Holden's secret world with his own, for when Holden was driven to ask the crude but important question, he announced with all the taunting impudence of his kind, "That's a professional secret, buddy."

When Holden recalls for this "sexy bastard" how he had met Jane and goes on to say that he used to play checkers with her, Stradlater's contemptuous comment is "*Checkers, for Chrissake!*" This girl, who had had a "lousy childhood" with a booze hound for a stepfather running "around the goddam house naked," always kept her kings in the back row. As Holden put it, "She just liked the way they looked when they were all in the back row." Half earnestly, half facetiously, he requests Stradlater to ask Jane whether she still keeps her kings in the back row; the symbolism of this imagery, portraying defense against sexual attack, is the central motif of the episode. Stradlater cannot, of course, know what a shocking and menacing figure he has become, for on the simple realistic level the request is merely casual reminiscence; but in the psychological context danger signals have begun fluttering in Holden's mind. If the request may be construed as Holden's desire to send Jane a secret warning against the slob who would himself be the bearer of the message, this defensive gesture, nevertheless, cannot issue in decisive action, and it remains no less symbolical than Holden's wearing his red hunting hat "with the peak around to the back and all." But these gestures indicate, so early in the narrative, that Holden is unconsciously preparing for his subsequent role as a catcher in the rye. In chapter six the futile best that he can do is to invite a beating at Stradlater's hands, and after the struggle he cannot, for a while, find the hat. All the protective gestures have dissolved in impotence, and with his nose "bleeding all over the place" Holden has had a thorough lesson in the game of life.

This lesson is all the more pathetic because in chapter five we have the first full glimpse of Holden's secret world and hence some indication of how, given a chance, Holden would play the game. The subject of his theme is his dead brother Allie's outfielder's mitt that has "poems written all over the fingers and pocket and everywhere." The mitt symbolically indicates that Holden would like to play the game with sensitivity and imagination, and Stradlater's crude rejection of the theme is itself a symbolic gesture, and a final one, shutting off all hope of communication. Holden tears the theme into pieces. But it should be added that, like Jane's kings in the back row, Holden's private world is impotent, and the effort at self-revelation in the theme is of a piece with this futility. His rapidly worsening neurotic condition has frozen him in this posture of feebleness, and indeed Holden must take Antolini's "special kind of fall" and disappear into the museum room where the mummies are and thus symbolically encounter death before he may be reborn to an active defense of his world. (pp. 12-14)

Holden's fantasy begins at the obvious and apparently extroverted level of "horsing around." With Ackley Holden pretends to be a "blind guy," saying, "Mother darling, give me your *hand*. Why won't you give me your *hand*?" Considering the view we get later of parental care *in absentia* or by remote control, and considering, furthermore, what has already been disclosed of the highly wrought design of *The Catcher,* we should not fail to note, so early in the novel, the motif of mutilation and the implied charge that a mother has not provided guidance and owes her son the hand that he has broken; with Holden the extroverted simply does not exist. Ackley's response is, "You're nuts, I swear to God." Ackley calls Holden's hat a "deer shooting hat," and Holden facetiously retorts, "I shoot people in this hat"; and once again, in the sequel, the facetious may be seen to envelop aggressive tendencies. The hat, indeed, is the central symbol of Holden's fantasy and so of the book —not only, as here, for aggression, but later for his humanitarian role, faintly foreshadowed, as we have already noted, in the Stradlater episode; and a third symbolic function of the hat is to hit off Holden's quest, which is in a large measure hysterical flight, as he rushes about New York before he comes home to Phoebe. Aggression and withdrawal follow each other rapidly in the opening scenes, the first with Stradlater when Holden leaps on him "like a goddam panther," and the second when he wakes up Ackley and asks about joining a monastery.

In his hotel room, after "old Sunny," the prostitute, has gone, he talks "sort of out loud" to Allie and expresses guilt feelings about his having refused to take Allie with him and a friend on a luncheon bike-trip because Allie was just a child. Since Allie's death, whenever Holden becomes depressed, he tries to make up for this past cruelty by saying that he may go along. Here, then, in his guilt feelings we have an explanation of why Holden broke his hand against the garage windows, and we may trace all the elements of his fantasying to this psychological cause. Mutilation is itself the physical symbol of a psychological state of self-accusation and self-laceration. Hence, when Holden, after discovering that he cannot pray, reflects that next to Jesus the character in the Bible that he likes best is the lunatic that lived in the tombs and cut himself with stones, we observe a consistent psychological development of the motif of mutilation and, linked to it, the death-wish; and . . . we note further Holden identifies himself with a madman. In *Mark,* V:1-20, we are told of the lunatic that broke all chains and fetters, for no man could tame him. Jesus drove the spirits that possessed him into the swine and told him to go home to his friends. If we are to comprehend what really happens in *The Catcher* we must attribute prime importance to this little scene of about two pages at the head of chapter fourteen; for Holden will subsequently break his morbid psychological fetters, he will go home to Phoebe, and, in a manner of speaking, he will be able to pray. (pp. 16-17)

The visit to Central Park and then home to Phoebe must be regarded as the two halves of a single, unfolding psychological experience; they provide the hinge on which *The Catcher* moves. Holden had started thinking about the ducks during his talk with "old" Spencer; and in New York he asked two cab drivers about what the ducks did in such wintry weather. Holden knew the park "like the back of [his] hand," for as a child he had roller-skated and ridden his bike there. But now, searching for the lagoon, he is lost, and, as he says, "it kept getting darker and darker and spookier and spookier." The park has become *terra incognita*. When at last he finds the lagoon there are no ducks. (pp. 18-19)

The psychological and thematic components of this little scene are profoundly rich and yet beautifully simple. Central Park represents Holden's Dark Tower, Dark Night of the Soul, and Wasteland; the paradise of his childhood is bleak, and the ducks that, in his fantasy, he has substituted for the human, have vanished. In effect, Holden is finished with childhood and is prepared for the burdens of maturity. But all the same he gathers up the pieces to be treasured, and in a final act of childhood profligacy—skipping coins over the lagoon—he symbolically rejects the materialism of the adult world that he is about to enter.

The apartment episode with Phoebe is so brilliant and so densely packed that we must examine it in two stages, here largely from Holden's point of view and later from Phoebe's. The meeting between brother and sister is presented as a conspiracy, for Holden enters the building under false pretenses and slips into his own apartment "quiet as hell." "I really should've been a crook." The anti-social bond is confirmed when Phoebe tells Holden that she has the part of Benedict Arnold in a Christmas play and when he gives her his symbolical hunting hat. They are rebels and seekers both.

Almost the first thing that Holden notices in D. B.'s room where Phoebe usually sleeps when D. B. is away is her fantasying with her middle name, which she changes frequently, the present one being "Weatherfield." The various kinds of fantasy have an important role in *The Catcher* and, in alliance with other motifs, hint at the philosophical question of the narrative: "What is the nature of reality?"

From this point onward the novel converges upon the answer. Meanwhile, Phoebe's fantasying "killed" Holden; and in this and later scenes with children his mood is good humored, indulgent, and parental. The word "kill" is used throughout the novel in colloquial fashion, as here; but presently it reflects a rising hysteria when Phoebe exclaims again and again about Holden's leaving school, "Daddy'll *kill* you." Paradoxically, the terror exists not for Holden but for Phoebe, and the boy who had been fleeing from one physical and psychological terror after another now finds himself in the role of the elder who must reassure his young sister that nobody is going to kill him.

The spotlight is, furthermore, powerfully focused upon Holden's problem when Phoebe acts out a killing. She had seen a movie about a mercy killing; a doctor compassionately put a crippled child (on his way to the apartment Holden, continuing his mutilation fantasy, had been "limping like a bastard") out of its misery by smothering it with a blanket. In symbolic mimicry Phoebe places her pillow over her head and resists Holden's plea to come out from under. Here, indeed, is killing—"mercy" killing, and assuredly one way of dealing with children. But it would be a "mercy" also to save children, to catch them as they are about to fall off "some crazy cliff," and this is the humanitarian solution that Holden expresses to Phoebe. The antisocial conspiracy has blossomed into a benevolent and protective order. Antolini's thesis, coming belatedly as it does, merely renders conceptually the courage and maturity that Holden, with his imaginative heart, had discovered in the stolen moments of domestic affection and security with Phoebe. Salinger is intimating that for the imaginatively endowed the living experience may become the source of precept and rule. The point is that Holden is way ahead of his elders. (pp. 18-20)

From the start Holden is convinced that by either standard —society's or his own, he is a coward. . . . The [museum episode], unmistakably illuminating the climax of the book, shows that he is not a coward and that, in effect, he essentially has business to transact only with himself, and he must therefore stop running. In the museum of art when Holden walks down "this very narrow sort of hall" leading to the room containing the mummies, one of the two boys with him bolts and runs, the other says, "He's got a yella streak a mile wide," and he also flees. Not Holden but society is yellow.

Since Holden's neurosis includes feelings of insecurity stemming from Allie's death and from Jan Gallagher's "lousy childhood" (like his own) and since both Allie and Jane have become inextricably bound together in his mind, Holden conquers the two-fold hysteria at one and the same moment. There is sexual imagery in "this very narrow sort of hall" and the room containing the mummies, especially since the obscene word is written "with a red crayon . . . right under the glass part of the wall." Once again as in Phoebe's school he reacts with weariness over the corruption of this world and solemnly reflects that if he ever dies and is buried, his tombstone will bear the ugly legend. Here, at last, the identity of the fear of death and the fear of sex is made clear, and these fears are to be seen, actually, as a pervasive fear of violence to body or spirit and the ensuing mutilation. If in the Stradlater episode and throughout the rest of the novel Holden is an innocent, he is so, not so much in terms of our popular literary tradition, but rather in a classical, Christian, or psychoanalytical schema. His very fears yield proof that his innocence represents a harmony of attributes and drives—intellectual, emotional, and physical, so that in the proper regulation of them harm will result neither for the person nor for others. Holden's obsession about faces indicates this fastidious care; the Egyptians tried to conquer the final violence of death by mummification so that, as Holden says, the face "would not rot." In Holden's encounter it is important that the spirit should not rot.

For insight into the psychologically symbolic meaning of the museum episode we turn once again to the structure of the novel. Allie's death has been such a traumatic experience that all Holden knows is death, for when "old" Spencer, who makes him "sound dead," confronts him with the unsatisfactory results of the history examination, it is clear that his historical knowledge is limited to the subject of mummification. It is to this knowledge, at the close of the book that he returns with a sense of how "nice and peaceful" it all is. The psychological journey from the fear of death to a calm acceptance of it is further highlighted at the beginning when we learn that Mr. Ossenburger, the mortician, has donated the dormitory wing named for him in which Holden has his room.

Holden's victorious encounter with death reveals psychological maturity, spiritual mastery, and the animal faith and resiliency of youth. The charmingly offhand and rather awesome conditional statement, "If I ever die" reminds the reader that in the last quarter of the book it is so difficult for Holden to think of Allie as dead that Phoebe must underscore the fact, "Allie's *dead*." Yet although Holden masters his neurosis he also falls victim to society, for in alternating stress the novel continuously presents two mingled actions—his own inner dealings with himself and society's brutal effect upon him. After his visit to the mummies Holden goes to the lavatory and proceeds to faint, i.e., symbolically dies; and his comment is that he was lucky in falling as he did because he "could've killed" himself. The parallelism with the earlier Stradlater episode leaps instantly to the mind, for then, as we recall, Holden "nearly dropped *dead*"; and that scene also took place in a lavatory —a fit symbol, in both instances, for a scatalogical society. Significantly, he feels better immediately after; and he is reborn into a new world of secure feelings and emotions, with himself fulfilling the office of catcher in his mature view of Phoebe. Thereafter the psychoanalytical couch can mean little to him, far less than Antolini's couch, to which it is thematically related.

The dense contrapuntal effect of the verbal patterns is, finally, enhanced by one that keeps a persistent drum beat in the background until the full thematic range of *The Catcher* is disclosed. If Holden symbolically and psychologically dies only to be reborn into the world of Phoebe's innocence and love, he has all through the novel been announcing the theme of regeneration in the "wake up" pattern. After the Stradlater episode Holden wakes up Ackley, then another schoolmate Woodruff (to sell him a typewriter), and as a derisive parting shot, "every bastard on the whole floor" with his yell, "*Sleep tight, ya morons!*" . . . [The] thematic implication of the pattern transcends both the episodes and the characters involved; in moral as well as psychological terms Salinger is suggesting that a brutalized society requires regeneration and must arouse itself from its mechanistic sloth.

In a development that parallels the "wake up" pattern Salinger shows that Holden, of course, must wake up in his own way; and it has been the thesis of this reading of *The Catcher* that he does effect his own psychological regeneration. . . . Holden's secret world fails the boy not only outwardly in the encounter with society, but also inwardly in his retreat from circumstance, for it is effectively sealed off, so that, as with the outside world, there is here likewise no communication. The pattern that discloses this aspect of Holden's isolation is "giving old Jane a buzz." Early in the novel Holden thinks of phoning Jane's mother; twice thereafter he thinks of phoning Jane, but instead phones Sally. On two separate occasions phoning Jane is part of his fantasy. Toward the close of the novel he thinks of phoning her before going out west, but this bit of fantasy does not reveal a need for her, since, as we have observed, Holden's mood has become rational and volitional. But in the violent Hollywood fantasy earlier in the middle of the book, Holden does phone Jane, and she does come to succor him; any comfort, however, that the boy might derive from Jane, who is one of the two nodal images in his private world (the other being Allie), is immediately destroyed by the *ersatz* sentimental form of the fantasy. Equally significant for Salinger's purpose in underscoring the psychological remoteness of the image of Jane is the one time when Holden does actually phone her: there is no answer. His own world fails to respond. Thereafter come the visit to Central Park, the return home to Phoebe, and a concomitant spiritual recovery. (pp. 21-5)

Although the humanitarian role of saviour that Holden assigns himself stands in the foreground, we must nevertheless not fail to see that Phoebe is the essential source; and if Holden, on the path up out of spiritual dilemma and crisis, must find the verbal and conceptual means of expressing his innermost needs, Phoebe, as easily as she wakes up, expresses an even more fundamental insight through symbolic gesture. The charm of the scene, when fully comprehended from this point of view, lies in the mingling of the naive and childlike with the spiritually occult; in the immense discrepancy between means (a child) and ends (spiritual insight); for adults it is a rather puzzling and even terrifying charm, when they acknowledge it, discoverable in fairy tales and some of the teachings of Jesus. (p. 26)

In Holden's maturing there is no repudiation of childhood or even of the secret world. In the organic processes of life the continuity between childhood and maturity, need not, must not, be severed. If the child is father of the man, as Wordsworth said, assuredly society at large and parents in particular have scarcely encouraged this teenaged boy, well over six feet, with a crippled right hand and the right side of his head full of "millions of gray hairs," to think of his days in Wordsworthian fashion as "bound each to each by natural piety." For that reason his secret world, when released from the death-like enchantment of neurosis, may well have been, ultimately, the real source of his salvation. Certainly in the daylight return to Central Park with Phoebe Holden experienced the natural piety that Wordsworth celebrated, being at once child and parent with her, both in the zoo (he need no longer search for the ducks) and at the carrousel, watching Phoebe go round and round, another symbol for the circular activity of life. Here the sense of continuity that Holden demands in his surroundings . . . receives a living affirmation when he comments with so much satisfaction that the carrousel "played that same song about fifty years ago when I was a little kid." When, to the adult reader's further amusement, Holden, like any apprehensive parent, says that Phoebe will have to take her chances with falling off the horse when reaching for the ring, the boy has added a cubit to his psychological stature.

The short concluding chapter, far from being the lame and defective appendage to a charming book that some think it, is like so much else in *The Catcher,* a triumph of technical virtuosity. In this reading of the novel the conclusion is blunted, and interestingly so, only because we cannot say what society will do to impose adjustment upon a boy who has effected his own secret cure; and we therefore close the narrative not with psychoanalytical questions, but ethical. In rejecting the formalism of psychoanalytical technique for the spontaneous personality Salinger follows D. H. Lawrence; and in boldly proposing that the resources of personality are sufficient for self-recovery and discovery, his book will stand comparison with Hermann Hesse's *Steppenwolf,* whose protagonist, Harry Haller, rises above his own neurosis in a discovery, based on Buddhistic thought, that the potentialities of the soul are limitless. Altogether, in this reading the answer to the question, "What is the nature of reality?" is both complex and simple, residing in the living, organic relation between childhood and maturity, continuity and change, the contemplative and the active, the external world and the inner spirit. This reality is not a philosophical abstraction, but an existentialist datum of physical and emotional experience. (pp. 26-8)

Once again there is an immense discrepancy between means (a child) and ends (spiritual insight). When the psychoanalyst (in the role of disciple) asks Holden (the master) whether he intends to apply himself at school, and Holden replies that he doesn't know because you don't know "what you're going to do till you do it," the surface impression is that of a typically unsatisfactory answer from a teenager. When D. B. asks him what he thinks about "all this stuff [he] just finished telling . . . about" and Holden replies that he does not know what to think, the surface impression is the same. Finally, Holden proposes a riddle. He says that he misses everybody, even Stradlater, Ackley, and "that goddam Maurice." "Don't ever tell anybody anything. If you do, you start missing everybody." Here is a shock to the conceptualizing, precept-laden intelligence, a puzzle or paradox that will not yield to logical analysis but that, on the contrary, sends the mind back over the experience recorded, even into the depths of the unconscious where both the malady and the cure lay. In the large, Whitmanesque acceptance of evil there is affirmation of the life-process as the personality "lets go"; and such Zen riddling is easily translatable into existentialist understanding.

In its emphasis on the conflict between the organic and the mechanistic, the secret and the public, reality and appearance, awakening and death, *The Catcher* hits off the strongest Romantic affirmations from Goethe and Wordsworth down to Lawrence, Joyce, and Hesse. Whether at Walden Pond, at Weissnichtwo, or in New York hot spots, the problem of personality remains; one surmises that, after a century and more, as *A Portrait of the Artist* and *Steppenwolf* likewise indicate, the struggle has become intensified. At the close of *The Catcher* the gap between society and the individual has widened perceptibly; and far from repudiating Holden's secret world, Salinger has added a secret of psychological depth. A mechanistic society, represented just as much by Antolini as by the psychoanalyst, may with the glib teacher continue to ignore the boy and talk of "what kind of thoughts your particular size mind should be wearing"; we may all comfort ourselves with the reflection that, after all, Holden is another bothersome case of arrested development, albeit rather charming in a pathetic and oafish manner.

No doubt Salinger has overdrawn the portrayal, but a work of literature is not a statistic, it is a special vision. In its pathetic and sentimental tone *The Catcher* faithfully reflects the surface of American life, and insofar, therefore, as it lacks intellectual substance and a valid universality based on a cultural heritage, it falls far below the Romantic masterpieces to which I have made passing reference. But as I have tried to make clear, *The Catcher* is strongest where these are strongest. Whatever the dreadful odds, the human spirit, though slain, refuses to stay dead; it is forever hearing the cock crow, forever responding to the Everlasting Yea. So in *The Catcher;* and the blunted, ambiguous ending mingles with this affirmation the doubt whether now at last, in the long travail of the spirit, the odds have not become too dreadful. If, as this reading interprets the book, the scales tip in favor of the affirmation, it is so because the history of youth is almost always hopeful. (pp. 28-9)

> Carl F. Strauch, "Kings in the Back Row: Meaning through Structure–A Reading of Salinger's 'The Catcher in the Rye'," in Wisconsin Studies in Contemporary Literature (© 1961, Wisconsin Studies in Contemporary Literature), Winter, 1961, pp. 5-30.

JOHN HERMANN

Salinger's story, "For Esmé—with Love and Squalor," has been anthologized, selected as his best story, and in general accorded the high point of his as yet beginning career. And the attention that has been given to Esmé is warranted, for it juxtaposes in one story two of Salinger's major theses, love and squalor, in one of his favorite subjects, children: Esmé, the distillation of squalor, of people who are, according to the choir director in the story, "silly-billy parrots" if they sing without knowing the meaning of the words; and Charles, Esmé's five year old brother, the epitome of love. Not all critics agree, but I should like to suggest, contrary to some recent interpretations, that it is Charles, rather than Esmé, who is the key to the story. It is his riddle of what one wall says to another: "Meetcha at the corner," which is the nexus between Sergeant X and the world, and it is Charles's final, spontaneous, and insistent Hello, Hello, Hello, Hello, Hello, affixed to the end of Esmé's letter, that brings Sergeant X's F-A-C-U-L-T-I-E-S back together.

The contrast between Charles and Esmé is the burden of the first half of the story. The second half, in which the *I* point-of-view is shifted to Sergeant X "so cunningly that even the cleverest reader will fail to recognize me," is the squalid or moving part of the story, and shows a projection of Esmé's squalor (lack of compassion, of affection) in Corporal Clay, his girl friend, Loretta in the States, her psychology professor, Sergeant X's older brother—the same squalor, magnified further, which war itself shows in the punishment of a German girl who has been a minor Nazi official. It is the extension of this squalor, that war engenders, that has driven Sergeant X to the brink of disin-

tegration, of faculties shattered. Esmé's letter, with Charles's P.S. at the end, brings the worlds of *I* and Sergeant X together at the conclusion of the story.

In the first half, the character of the narrator has been well established by the time he meets Esmé, Charles, and their governess, Miss Megley, in a tea-room in England during the war. (pp. 262-63)

Except for the two introductory paragraphs, the tone [of this half] has been wry, jocular—a man making fun not only of the army but of himself.

[Wandering] the streets in the rain, he hears children singing in church and enters. They are practicing. One of the singers is a young girl "whose eyes seemed to be counting the house." Even in a church. It is the first intimation we have of Esmé's character, and it is given by the narrator half in admiration, half in amazement.

After the practice, they meet by accident again at a nearby tea-room, where Esmé comes with Charles and their governess. Before the narrator quite realizes how, Esmé is standing with "enviable poise" beside his table. Invited, she sits down, a "truth lover or a statistics lover" of thirteen. He is the eleventh American she has met. She sits beautifully straight on her chair so that he too must come out of his army slouch. Her conversation with the narrator is that of a census taker—"Are you deeply in love with your wife?" "How were you employed before entering the army?"—or has the tone of an almanac dispensing facts— "To be quite candid Father really needed more of an intellectual companion than Mother was" (her parents become case histories in psychology); her wet hair, now straight, is when dry "not actually curly but quite wavy" (she is meticulously exact even in a situation in which a young girl might normally be tempted to alter truth a trifle, claiming curls rather than waves).

She finally asks the narrator, even though she is somewhat disappointed that he is not a published writer, to write her a story about squalor. "About what?" he says, incredulous, for he is confronted with a girl who believes everything can be learned by statistics, by so many notes taken, by so many Americans kept count of, by so many figures put together. "Silly-billy parrots" the choir director had said of those who mouth words without knowing their meanings. She is talking about Esmés.

In contrast is Charles, disdainful of appearances like wet hair, of the facts that his sister cherishes ("He certainly has green eyes. Haven't you, Charles?" the narrator asks him. "They're orange," Charles says); enjoying his game of riddles; arching his back across the chair in contrast to Esmé's perfectly achieved poise; covering up his face with his napkin; giving a Bronx cheer at one point of the conversation between his sister and the narrator; engulfed with laughter at his own jokes; and furiously disappointed when the Sergeant tells him the answer to the riddle when asked the second time. He is everything his sister is not (She takes his wet cap from his head when they enter the tea-room "by lifting it off his head with two fingers, as if it were a laboratory specimen"). The last image that we have of the two of them in this part of the story that remains: Charles, blushing but determined, comes back to kiss the Sergeant good-bye. Asked the answer to the riddle, his face lights up. He shrieks: "Meet you at the corner," (and he does at the end of the story, saying at the corner of sanity and insanity to the Sergeant, Hello, Hello, Hello) and races out of the room "possibly in hysterics." Esmé leaves too, "slowly, reflectively, testing the ends of her hair for dryness"; one risking embarrassment to show his friendship; the other, worried about her own appearance.

The second, or squalid part of the story, extends Esmé's attitude to other people, etching the dilettantism into callousness, into stupidity, into destruction. For what does it mean to know squalor without love? It means a Corporal Clay who uses Sergeant X to write letters home to impress his girl, Loretta. It means a Loretta who uses the war experiences of men overseas as case histories in her psychology class (Esmé's treatment of her father and mother's relationship).... It means finally the last protest of Sergeant X, scribbled almost illegibly underneath: "Fathers and teachers, I ponder 'What is hell?' I maintain it is the suffering of being unable to love," which are the words of Father Zossima in *The Brothers Karamazov*. (Esmé: "My Aunt says that I'm a terribly cold person." "I am training myself to be more compassionate.") And Sergeant X's faculties under these pressures begin to disintegrate.

On his desk is a pile of packages, letters, books, that he has left unopened for days. He pushes them aside to use his typewriter to write a letter connecting him to someone, somewhere. But he cannot. He collapses on the typewriter. When he opens his eyes again, he sees a green package ("He certainly has green eyes, haven't you, Charles?" "They're orange," Charles says). Unconsciously Sergeant X moves to open the package.

It is a present and a note from Esmé—her father's watch (broken), and the notation that it was an extremely pleasant afternoon that they had spent "in each other's company on April 30, 1944, between 3:45 and 4:15 P.M. in case it slipped your mind."

But appended to the note is a message from Charles, of one wall saying to another, without thought, without knowledge, without statistics, but with compassion and affection: Hello Hello Hello Hello Hello. And Sergeant X's F-A-C-U-L-T-I-E-S disintegrating under squalor gradually come back together again. Much as we like Esmé's intelligence, poise, and breath-taking levelheadedness, it is her brother Charles, with the orange eyes and the arching back and the smacking kiss, who knows without counting the house, without 3:45 and 4:15 P.M.'s, the riddles of the heart. (pp. 263-64)

John Hermann, "J. D. Salinger: Hello Hello Hello," in College English (copyright © 1961 by the National Council of Teachers of English), January, 1961, pp. 262-64.

ROBERT M. BROWNE

I'm for critical ingenuity and latitude of interpretation and all, but there is some stuff up with which I will not put. Like Mr. John Hermann's view of Salinger's Esmé [see excerpt above] as a symbol of squalor, of lack of compassion and affection. Mr. Hermann gets facts wrong, as when he says that Charles, "blushing but determined . . . risking embarrassment to show his friendship," comes back into the tearoom to kiss Sergeant X good-bye. In context it is obvious that Esmé has to "drag" and "push" Charles to get him to kiss the sergeant.

But more important, Mr. Hermann has committed two basic errors. One is to read the story in the light of a rather romantic preconception, the other is to neglect the role of the narrator. The romantic preconception is that love of truth, including statistics, makes one unable to love people. Since Esmé is a statistic-lover, she must be unable to love people.... But Esmé's love of truth is simply part of her admirable integrity. She is still child enough not to have lost wonder and curiosity; her intelligence has not been corrupted by wishful thinking (her cool appraisal of her mother, her refusal, which Mr. Hermann thinks abnormal, to pretend that her hair is curly when it's only wavy). True enough, her literalness is a trifle comic, but it is not morally disabling, as it might be in an adult.

In the tearoom Esmé approached X in part because her aunt had told her she was "terribly cold," and she was "training herself to be more compassionate." Despite Mr. Hermann, this passage does not put her in Dostoevsky's hell of being unable to love; on the contrary, her willingness to try is enough to save her. Esmé's fidelity to truth and her acute though unseasoned intelligence do not prevent her from loving people; on the contrary they cause her to bestow her love fully on adults who, she perceives, have somehow escaped the general corruption: her father and X, whose "extremely sensitive face" attracted her in church. Though Mr. Hermann found her inattention in church objectionable, she wasn't simply counting the house, she was making an acute judgment of X, and ultimately the right response to him. For aren't we too meant to like him, and to think him worthy of love? If Esmé doesn't love him, why in the world does she write him and send him her dearest possession, the watch?

Of course her love of people, like her love of truth, has its comic side. The nervous concern about her hair, the question about X's love for his wife, the fear of seeming either too childish or too forward, these all indicate a schoolgirl's crush on a soldier. But it seems unfortunately necessary to insist on the obvious: Esmé is comic as well as admirable. . . . Throughout the story there is nothing in X's tone, explicit or implicit, which modifies the admiration for Esmé he so frequently exhibits: for her forehead, voice, smile, dress, posture, feet and ankles.

And how authoritative a narrator is X? By Mr. Hermann's own account of the preliminary section, he is wry and jocular. This sophisticated, ironic person is the most intelligent and mature observer in the story. Without discussing X's views, Mr. Hermann accepts the position of the aunt and of the choir coach with the dissonant voice, who sees Esmé and her choirmates as "silly-billy parrots." (The choir coach gets the treatment she deserves from the children, "a steady, opaque look.") When Esmé asks X if he, like her aunt, finds her terribly cold, the reply of this ordinarily reserved man is "absolutely not—very much to the contrary, in fact." I will back him against the aunt, the choir coach, and Mr. Hermann. (pp. 584-85)

Robert M. Browne, "In Defense of Esmé," in College English (copyright © 1961 by the National Council of Teachers of English), May, 1961, pp. 584-85.

JOAN DIDION

Among the reasonably literate young and young in heart, [J. D. Salinger] is surely the most read and reread writer in America today, exerting a power over his readers which is in some ways extraliterary. Those readers expect him to teach them something, something that has nothing at all to do with fiction. Not only have his vague metaphysical hints been committed to rote by *New Yorker* readers from here to Dubuque, but his imaginary playmates, the Glass family, have achieved a kind of independent existence; I rather imagine that Salinger readers wish secretly that they could write letters to Franny and Zooey and their brother Buddy, and maybe even to Waker (who is a Jesuit and apparently less disturbed than his kin), much as people of less invincible urbanity write letters to the characters in *As the World Turns* and *The Brighter Day*.

What actually happens in *Franny and Zooey* . . . is really nothing much. (p. 233)

To anyone who has ever felt over-exposed to the world, to anyone who has ever harbored hatred in his or her heart toward droppers of names, writers of papers on Flaubert, toward eaters of frogs' legs, [*Franny and Zooey*] has a certain seductive lure; there is a kind of lulling charm in being assured in that dazzling Salinger prose, that one's raw nerves, one's urban hangover, one's very horridness, is really not horridness at all but instead a kind of dark night of the soul. . . .

However brilliantly rendered (and it is), however hauntingly right in the rhythm of its dialogue (and it is), *Franny and Zooey* is finally spurious, and what makes it spurious is Salinger's tendency to flatter the essential triviality within each of his readers, his predilection for giving instructions for living. What gives the book its extremely potent appeal is precisely that it is self-help copy: it emerges finally as *Positive Thinking* for the upper middle classes, as *Double Your Energy and Live Without Fatigue* for Sarah Lawrence girls. (p. 234)

> *Joan Didion, "Finally (Fashionably) Spurious," in* National Review *(© National Review, Inc., 1961; 150 East 35th St., New York, NY 10016), November 18, 1961 (and reprinted in* Studies in J. D. Salinger: Reviews, Essays, and Critiques of 'The Catcher in the Rye' and Other Fiction, *edited by Marvin Laser and Norman Fruman, Odyssey Press, 1963, pp. 232-34).*

LESLIE FIEDLER

I am not sure why I have liked so much less this time through a story which moved me so deeply when I first read it in *The New Yorker* four or five years ago. I mean, of course, "Zooey," to which "Franny" is finally an appendage, like the long explanatory footnote on pages 52 and 53, the author's apologetic statement on the jacket, the pretentiously modest dedication: all the gimmicks, in short, which conceal neither from him nor from us the fact that he has not yet made of essentially novelistic material the novel it wants to become.

It was, I guess, the novel which "Zooey," along with a handful of earlier stories, seemed to promise to which I responded with initial enthusiasm: the fat chronicle of the Glass family which might have caught once and for all the pathos and silliness of middle-class, middle-brow intellectual aspiration—the sad and foolish dream that certain families, largely Jewish, dreamed for their children listening to the Quiz Kids perform on the radio two long decades ago. For the sake of that novel, Salinger seemed at the point of making a new start. . . . Certainly in "Zooey" Salinger had

begun untypically to specify the times and circumstances of his characters; to furnish patiently the rooms through which they moved; to eschew slickness and sentimentality and easy jokes in favor of a style almost inept enough to guarantee honesty; to venture beyond an evocation of adolescent self-pity and adolescent concern with sex titillating chiefly to adolescents themselves.

But there is, as yet, no novel—only "Zooey," well-leaded and in hard-covers, flanked by apologies and new promises, but still unfulfilled: and it is this, I suppose, which has left me baffled and a little disappointed. In a magazine, Salinger's documentation seemed not quite so irrelevant, his furnishings not quite so disproportionate to the events they frame, the awkwardness of his writing not quite so much a tic of embarrassment or a posture of false modesty.

"Franny" itself, which I had not read before, seems to me an eminently satisfactory piece of reportage, turned in as evidence (at the demonstration trial of the generations, in which it is not clear who is the plaintiff, who the defendant) by a middle-aged eavesdropper on station-platforms and at restaurants where the Ivy League young ritually prepare for watching games and getting laid. It is, at least, scarcely ever cute, like much of "Zooey" and all of the mere apparatus which with it ekes out a book; and it ends ambiguously before its author, whose resolutions are often disasters, can manage to be either sentimental or sage. In "Franny" for once Salinger demonstrates that he can write of adolescence without disappearing into it; but "Franny," alas, is completed by "Zooey," which itself completes nothing. (pp. 235-36)

[Salinger] speaks for the cleanest, politest, best-dressed, best-fed and best-read among the disaffected (and who is not disaffected?) young; not junkies or faggots, not even upper-bohemians, his protagonists travel a road bounded on one end by school and on the other by home. They have families and teachers rather than lovers or friends; and their crises are likely to be defined in terms of whether or not to go back for the second semester to Vassar or Princeton, to Dana Hall or St. Mark's. Their *angst* is improbably cued by such questions as: "Does my date for the Harvard Weekend *really* understand what poetry is?" or "Is it possible that my English instructor hates literature after all?"

I do not mean by reduction to mock the concerns of Salinger's characters; they cannot, in any case, be reduced, and I should mock myself making fun of them. For better or for worse, a significant number of sensitive young Americans live in a world in which the classroom and the football game provide customary arenas for anguish and joy, love and death; and to that world, Salinger has been more faithful than it perhaps deserves. Which is why in the end he is a comic novelist or nothing. If the Temple Drake of Faulkner's *Sanctuary* stands as the classic portrait of a co-ed in the 'twenties, the Franny of Salinger's Glass stories bids to become her equivalent for the 'fifties, and the decline in terror and intensity from one to the other, the descent toward middlebrow bathos is the fault not of Salinger but of the times. Temple's revolt was against vestigial Puritanism and obsolescent chivalry and her weapons were booze and sex; Franny's is against literature and the New Criticism and her weapon is the "Jesus Prayer."

Certainly, this is fair enough; for, in the thirty years that separate the two refugees from college, the Culture Religion of Western Europe has replaced Christianity as the orthodox faith for middle-class urban Americans; and the Pastors to whom our hungry sheep look up in vain are Ph.D.'s in Literature and the "section men" who are their acolytes.

Before the present volume, Salinger had always presented madness as a special temptation of males; perhaps because, in the myth he was elaborating, it is a female image of innocence that, at the last moment, lures his almost-lost protagonists back from the brink of insanity: a little girl typically, pre-pubescent and therefore immune to the world's evil, which, in his work, fully nubile women tend to embody. (p. 238)

In "Zooey," where the brother saves, the sister is redeemed and neither is a child, the myth struggles back toward the tragic dimension; and it is for this, too, perhaps, that I responded so strongly at first to the story, to its implicit declaration of Salinger's resolve to escape what had become for him a trap. (p. 239)

But "Zooey" is, at last, a fable of reconciliation as well as of salvation; for the saved Franny, we are left to believe, will return perhaps to school, certainly to "acting," as her brothers recommend, not so much for her own sake as for the sake of what Seymour had been accustomed to call, in their Quiz Kid days, the Fat Lady, i.e., the audience out front. But the Fat Lady, Zooey announces as his story ends, is Christ; the mass audience is Christ. It is an appropriate enough theophany for a popular entertainer, for Salinger as well as Zooey, and the cue for a truce with all the world, with bad teachers, mad television producers, bad psychoanalysts, bad everyone.

Finally, like his characters, Salinger is reconciled with everything but sex. The single voice in his novella which advocates marriage is the voice of Bessie Glass, a stage-Irish comic mother married to an off-stage comic Jew; but she raises it in vain in a fictional world where apparently only women marry and where certainly no father appears on the scene. It is to Zooey she speaks, the one son of hers not already killed by marriage like Seymour, or safe in monastic retirement, secular like Buddy's or ecclesiastical like his Jesuit brother Waker's. Zooey, who fears his own body and his mother's touch on it, turns her aside with a quip; though he might well have repeated what he had cried earlier in deep contempt, "That's just sex talking, buddy . . . I know that voice." These words, too, he had addressed to her; since for him men and women alike are "buddy," as if unlike the actual Buddy, he needed no little girl to remind him of what Seymour had once tried to teach them all: that "all legitimate religious study *must* lead to unlearning . . . the illusory differences between boys and girls . . ."

To unlearn the illusory differences: this is what for Salinger it means *to be as a child.* And the Glasses, we remember, are in this sense children, holy innocents still at twenty or thirty or forty, Quiz Kids who never made the mistake of growing up, and whose most glorious hours were spent before the microphones on a nation-wide radio program called "It's a Wise Child." The notion of the Quiz Kids, with their forced precocity, their meaningless answers to pointless questions faked by station employes as heroes, sages, secret saints of our time is palpably absurd. But Salinger himself ironically qualifies what he seems naively to offer by the unfinished quotation he uses to give his only half-

mythical program its name. It is with his collaboration, we remind ourselves, that we are able to say of his hidden saints, when they become insufferably cute or clever or smug, "The little bastards!" Surely, this is Salinger's joke, not just one on him and on his world. (pp. 239-40)

Leslie Fiedler, "Up from Adolescence," in Partisan Review *(copyright © 1962 by Partisan Review, Inc.), Winter, 1962 (and reprinted in* Studies in J. D. Salinger: Reviews, Essays, and Critiques of 'The Catcher in the Rye' and Other Fiction, *edited by Marvin Laser and Norman Fruman, Odyssey Press, 1963, pp. 235-40).*

JOHN UPDIKE

Salinger's conviction that our inner lives greatly matter peculiarly qualifies him to sing of an America where, for most of us, there seems little to do but to feel. Introversion, perhaps, has been forced upon history; an age of nuance, of ambiguous gestures and psychological jockeying on a national and private scale, is upon us, and Salinger's intense attention to gesture and intonation help make him, among the contemporaries, a uniquely pertinent literary artist. As Hemingway sought the words for things in motion, Salinger seeks the words for things transmuted into human subjectivity. His fiction, in its rather grim bravado, its humor, its morbidity, its wry but persistent hopefulness, matches the shape and tint of present American life. It pays the price, however, of becoming dangerously convoluted and static. A sense of composition is not among Salinger's strengths. . . . (pp. 53-4)

The Franny of "Franny" and the Franny of "Zooey" are not the same person. The heroine of "Franny" is a pretty college girl passing though a plausible moment of disgust. . . .

The Franny of "Zooey," on the other hand, is Franny Glass, the youngest of the seven famous Glass children, all of whom have been in turn wondrously brilliant performers on a radio quiz program, "It's a Wise Child." (p. 54)

One wonders how a girl raised in a home where Buddhism and crisis theology were table talk could have postponed her own crisis so long and, when it came, be so disarmed by it. (pp. 54-5)

The more Salinger writes about them, the more the seven Glass children melt indistinguishably together in an impossible radiance of personal beauty and intelligence. . . .

In "Raise High the Roof Beam, Carpenters" (the best of the Glass pieces: a magic and hilarious prose-poem with an enchanting end effect of mysterious clarity), Seymour defines sentimentality as giving "to a thing more tenderness than God gives to it." This seems to me the nub of the trouble: Salinger loves the Glasses more than God loves them. He loves them too exclusively. Their invention has become a hermitage for him. He loves them to the detriment of artistic moderation. "Zooey" is just too long; there are too many cigarettes, too many goddams, too much verbal ado about not quite enough.

The author never rests from circling his creations, patting them fondly, slyly applauding. He robs the reader of the initiative upon which love must be given. Even in "Franny," which is, strictly, pre-Glass, the writer seems less an unimpassioned observer than a spying beau. . . . (p. 55)

"Franny," nevertheless, takes place in what is recognizably our world; in "Zooey" we move into a dream world whose zealously animated details only emphasize an essential unreality. . . . Not the least dismaying development of the Glass stories is the vehement editorializing on the obvious—television scripts are not generally good, not all section men are geniuses. Of course, the Glasses condemn the world only to condescend to it, to forgive it, in the end. Yet the pettishness of the condemnation diminishes the gallantry of the condescension.

Perhaps these are hard words; they are made hard to write by the extravagant self-consciousness of Salinger's later prose, wherein most of the objections one might raise are already raised. On the flap of this book jacket, he confesses, ". . . there is a real-enough danger, I suppose, that sooner or later I'll bog down, perhaps disappear entirely, in my own methods, locutions, and mannerisms. On the whole, though, I'm very hopeful." Let me say, I am glad he is hopeful. I am one of those—to do some confessing of my own—for whom Salinger's work dawned as something of a revelation. I expect that further revelations are to come.

The Glass saga, as he has sketched it out, potentially contains great fiction. When all reservations have been entered, in the correctly unctuous and apprehensive tone, about the direction he has taken, it remains to acknowledge that it *is* a direction, and that the refusal to rest content, the willingness to risk excess on behalf of one's obsessions, is what distinguishes artists from entertainers, and what makes some artists adventurers on behalf of us all. (pp. 55-6)

> *John Updike, " 'Franny and Zooey' " (originally published in* The New York Times Book Review, *September 17, 1961), in his* Assorted Prose *(copyright © 1961 by John Updike; reprinted by permission of Alfred A. Knopf, Inc.), Knopf, 1965, pp. 234-39.*

WARREN FRENCH

[Can] a decade be labeled with the name of one writer? During the 1950s, Jerome David Salinger published his single novel to date, *The Catcher in the Rye,* and eight rather long stories—all but one of them connected at least thematically with the saga of a family named Glass. . . . This small body of work enjoyed a popularity unparalleled during the decade. (p. 23)

Salinger's significant writing was almost entirely confined to the 50s. (p. 24)

Certainly no writer has won a remotely similar place in American affections during the 60s; nor did any single writer so largely monopolize readers during any earlier decade. Because of the singular relationship between Salinger and the years of the "silent generation," it would seem that we might learn something about the feelings of the inarticulate youth of the period by examining the assumptions underlying the fiction of the writer that most attracted them.

First, though, we must bear in mind that Salinger was not universally acclaimed during the 50s. His works have always polarized opinion. *The Catcher in the Rye* was widely denounced and rejected. Older critics dismissed it impatiently; school boards and self-appointed professional moralists objected to its colloquial style and obscene language. Although some older readers had the perceptiveness to admire Salinger, his novel appealed principally to high school and college students; and he is important—among other things—as one of the earliest chroniclers of the now formidable "generation gap."

The first and last of Salinger's stories to attract widespread attention concerned the same event—the suicide of Seymour Glass in a Miami Beach hotel. Indeed "The Age of Salinger" can be precisely designated as extending from January, 1948, when "A Perfect Day for Bananafish" introduced readers of the *New Yorker* to the extraordinary Glass family to June, 1959, when the far longer and more garrulous "Seymour: An Introduction" appeared in the same magazine and cleared up the most important chapter in this family chronicle. These dates are important in discussing the rage for Salinger, because not since the enthusiasm during the early Romantic period for Goethe's young Werther had fictional characters so completely dominated the imaginative fancies of a decade as Seymour Glass and Holden Caulfield dominated the dim, defensive 50s. When in the 60s John F. Kennedy helped inspire a new dynamic activism among American youth, interest in Salinger and his creations began to dwindle.

With a decade's perspective on the body of Salinger's major work, we can see that Holden and Seymour are actually polar opposites and that from the contrast between them we can achieve a sharply black-and-white outline of the hopes, fears, and convictions of the sensitive young people growing up during the 50s. Both Seymour and Holden are, paradoxically, triumphant and defeated figures, depending upon the code of values of the perceiver. For those who believe in the sacredness of the life force, who feel that survival even at the expense of repression is the highest value, Holden Caulfield is a hero of his time and Seymour Glass is anomic, the personification of neurotic self-righteousness. For those who believe that the maintenance of principle is worth any sacrifice ("Better dead than red," as some shouted during the 50s), who find their highest values in personal integrity even at the sacrifice of their lives, Seymour Glass is not just a hero, but a saint—a spiritual exemplar to less noble and dedicated men, and Holden Caulfield is a "cop-out," a man who demeans himself by compromising in the interest of self-preservation. (pp. 24-6)

If we can correctly assume that Salinger's values are representative of those of a sizeable and influential segment of the youth of the 50s (and this argument remains hypothetical because the 50s are still close enough to remain an exasperating puzzle), it is clear that a principal conviction of this witch-hunting era was that a man could not retain his integrity and stay alive. (p. 26)

"If you want to stay alive," Holden observes, "you have to say that stuff," like "Glad to've met you" to people you're not at all glad to meet.

Holden surely spoke for many of his contemporaries even if they didn't always recognize his message. The 50s were a period of supreme disillusionment. (pp. 27-8)

Most people of the 50s resembled Holden Caulfield. When he says, "If you want to stay alive, you have to say that stuff," he speaks for his readers. Extraordinarily for a book that has been so frequently and intensively read, *The*

Catcher in the Rye has often been completely misinterpreted. Both youthful partisans and older fault-finders have viewed the novel as an account of a callow rebellion against pompous propriety. On the contrary, the book preaches not rebellion, but resignation. More than that, it is not even romantic in its approach.... The clearest indication of the intention of *The Catcher in the Rye* is found in Holden's remark after spending a night in the waiting room at Grand Central Station, "It wasn't too nice. Don't ever try it. I mean it. It'll depress you." Even at the climax of the novel, though Holden realizes that kids can't be protected from falling over "some crazy cliff," he continues to tell *the reader* what to do, "The thing with kids is, if they want to grab for the gold ring, you have to let them do it, and not say anything." Holden is not a Romantic urging his readers —like the later Beatniks—to go "on the road" and discover life for themselves.... Far from encouraging rebellion and flight, Salinger attempts to make *The Catcher in the Rye* a surrogate for them, so that the reader by vicariously sharing Holden's depressing experiences need not himself undergo a parallel ordeal.

Although few young readers could probably have articulated their response to the book and although few of them probably even tried to analyze this response (as Holden said of Jesus, "He didn't have time to go around analyzing everybody"), many of them probably were provided by the novel with the vicarious experience that enabled them to compromise with their own private, impractical dreams— the aesthetic resolution of their frustrations. In the many battles that have raged over *The Catcher in the Rye*, few have noted that the novel is a virtually flawless fictional embodiment of the traumatic experience of accepting the destruction of one's illusions as the price for moving from childhood to manhood. (pp. 28-9)

Seymour Glass is the necessary complement to Holden Caulfield. We can, in fact, only fully grasp the significance of Holden by contemplating his polar alternative. Holden's old teacher Antolini urges upon Holden a quotation from Wilhelm Stekel, "'The mark of the immature man is that he wants to die nobly for a cause, while the mark of the mature man is that he wants to live humbly for one.'" Whether Antolini is good angel or devil's advocate (and I doubt that Salinger accepts the idea that to die nobly for a cause is a mark of immaturity), the statement that he treasures does express what Salinger conceives to be the only alternatives open to people. Either one lives humbly (as Holden will if he continues to accept suffering) for a cause or one dies nobly for it. Salinger seems to reject the Socratic possibility of leading the truly "examined life" (like Jesus, one doesn't have time to go around "analyzing everybody"), but so probably did most of his contemporaries, too caught up in the "rat race" to have the leisure or even the inclination to scrutinize their own and other's behavior.

Seymour Glass embodies the possibility of dying nobly (and the danger of viewing the talkative Antolini as Salinger's spokesman is shown by the tenderness with which the author presents a character for whom Holden's teacher would have to feel great distaste). The motive behind Seymour's suicide remains enigmatic in "A Perfect Day for Bananafish." The only clue to his behavior is found in his earlier explanation of the bananafish to a little girl Sybil (who calls him "Seemore Glass"):

"Well, they swim into a hole where there's a

lot of bananas. They're very ordinary-looking fish when they swim *in*. But once they get in, they behave like pigs.... Naturally, after that they're so fat they can't get out of the hole again. Can't fit through the door.... They die.... They get banana fever. It's a terrible disease."

A possible interpretation of this fable is that Seymour sees himself as a bananafish, doomed by his addiction to material things; but this explanation scarcely holds water because Seymour kills himself quite deliberately, whereas the bananafish enter blithely upon their doomed course without understanding the consequences. They behave just like the little kids in *The Catcher in the Rye* grabbing for the gold ring. It is more likely that the other characters are the bananafish. Seymour's wife Muriel and her mother, for example, are clearly obsessed with material things, so that their doom is certain. Seymour finds the only escape from their vulgar obsession with "things" (Salinger could scarcely have set the story in a more appropriate place than Miami Beach, which must be the most garishly vulgar place in the world) in the childlike innocence of Sybil; but when Sybil says that she sees the bananafish, Seymour recognizes that she is going to go the way that Muriel has gone—that he can't prevent her falling any more than Holden can prevent the kids in the field of rye from doing so and that, therefore, there is literally nothing that he can do to save this world while he remains alive. (pp. 30-2)

Salinger returned to the problem of Seymour's suicide at the end of his great decade.... In "Seymour: An Introduction," Buddy Glass is quite explicit about Seymour's reasons for taking his life: "I say that the true artist-seer, the heavenly fool who can and does produce beauty, is mainly dazzled to death by his own scruples, the blinding shapes and colors of his own sacred human conscience."

I don't think that it matters whether or not Salinger actually had this clearly articulated concept in mind when he wrote the first story about Seymour. The important thing is that although there are differences between the early and the late Seymour Glass, both manifestations of the character are incapable of "adjusting" to the "phony" world. That Seymour is not intimidated as Holden is by the knowledge that "If you want to stay alive, you have to say that stuff" is evident from his conversations about an imaginary tattoo and his remark to a woman whom he accuses of looking at his feet. In both stories, he will not compromise with squalor; and this refusal makes it impossible for him to continue to live in a squalid world.

Salinger's other major stories are principally reinforcements or elaborations of the principles laid down in his portraits of Holden and Seymour. (pp. 32-3)

The range of ideas in Salinger's work is extremely narrow. He is like a searchlight exploring a small area intensely rather than like a sun illuminating a landscape. (The simile is doubly appropriate because his vision is nocturnal. Most of the action in his stories takes place at night, and the characters tend to spend their days largely in dim apartments or darkened theatres.) He sees the material world as absolutely corrupt (once more he recalls Eliot, whose "Gerontion" observes "... what is kept must be adulterated"). One can save one's self only by limiting one's criticism to one's self and resisting the temptation for public acclaim. The man whose vision is too clear to enable him to close his eyes to this world cannot hope to communicate with it. He can hope to make a spectacular exit that may keep alive some glimmering memory of the "niceness" we can know only momentarily.

It is easy to see that these ideas had enormous appeal to young people of the 50s. The continued cold War, the venal leadership of the "industrial-military" complex, the "crew-cut" mentality that denounced any deviation as heresy made the world seem squalid indeed. One could enjoy his vision only—like the poet in "The Inverted Forest"—by throwing away his glasses so that he could not see the "phony" world and keeping quiet about the world inside his head. Survival demanded either a debasing acceptance of the acclaim of an "unskilled" public or else an undiscriminating acceptance of all men and things. (Significantly, Eisenhower, the most appropriate figurehead the age could have found, had a reputation based on his being undiscriminatingly "liked" by everyone on the basis of a vacuous smile that served to hide any ideas or visions he might have had.) The man who would not compromise his vision was either literally driven to his death (like French film director Max Ophuls or Czech leader Jan Masaryk) or into long seclusion (like Charles DeGaulle or Boris Pasternak). The direction of society was left in the grasping hands of insensitive egotists like Lane Coutell.

Since the end of the 50s Salinger's works—though still widely read and admired—have declined in popularity. Sensitive youth has turned activist in the 60s, and Salinger does not speak as clearly to a dynamic generation as he did to a passive one. The shortcoming of the quite justified attitude of withdrawal from the world held by sensitive people of the 50s is that it is self-indulgent. By assuming that any effort to improve conditions is going to be defeated and will probably simply get one into trouble, one can rationalize a failure even to make any effort. Celebrity is undoubtedly accompanied by formidable problems; but Salinger's characters—and Salinger himself—never tried to surmount these problems. (pp. 37-8)

"The Age of Salinger" provides compelling reasons for describing as sentimental and decadent an "either/or" vision which perceives defeat or death as the only alternatives in the struggle between the affectionate individual and squalid society. None of Salinger's characters ever expresses the attitude championed by Marlow in Conrad's *Heart of Darkness* that "for good or evil mine is the speech that cannot be silenced."

What a writer has his characters say is, of course, as much his own business as his attitude toward the world. What matters is not that a defeatist attitude underlies Salinger's work, but that works embodying such an attitude were extremely popular during the 50s. Salinger's writings have sometimes been called "decadent" for the wrong reasons by unthinking people reacting automatically to words or incidents in the stories. Perhaps in the long run the most important contribution made by *The Catcher in the Rye* to the development of American literature was the novel's providing the perennially necessary refurbishing of the colloquial idiom; and Salinger needed to "invent" very few of the things that happen to Holden. As the poet in "The Inverted Forest" insisted one should, the novelist "found" his material by observing the world around him. (pp. 38-9)

Warren French, "The Age of Salinger," in The

Fifties: Fiction, Poetry, Drama, *edited by Warren French (copyright © 1970 by Warren French), Everett/Edwards, Inc., 1970, pp. 1-39.*

CAROL and RICHARD OHMANN

Holden's sensitivity is the heart of [*The Catcher in the Rye*]; that which animates the story and makes it compelling. Events are laden with affect for Holden. He cannot speak of an experience for long in a neutral way, apart from judgment and feeling. And of course those judgments and feelings are largely negative. Not so entirely negative as Phoebe says—"You don't like *any*thing that's happening"—but this novel is first the story of a young man so displeased with himself and with much of the world around him that his strongest impulse is to leave, break loose, move on. From his pain follows rejection and retreat.

But what exactly is it that puts Holden out of sorts with his life? What does he reject? The critics answer [with] phrases that universalize: an immoral world, the inhumanity of the world, the adult world, the predicament of modern life, the human condition, the facts of life, evil. As we see it, the leap is too quick and too long. Holden lives in a time and place, and these provide the material against which his particular adolescent sensibility reacts.

Holden has many ways of condemning, and an ample lexicon to render his judgments. Some people are bastards, others jerks. The way they act makes you want to puke. What they do and say, can be—in Holden's favorite adjectives—depressing, corny, dopey, crumby, screwed-up, boring, phony. "Phony" is probably Holden's most frequent term of abuse, definitely his strongest and most ethically weighted. For that reason his application of the word is a good index to what he finds most intolerable in his life. And Holden is quite consistent in what he calls phony. (pp. 27-8)

[Twin] themes run through the book. When a situation or act seems phony to Holden, it evidences bad class relationships, or public ritual, or both. The first theme is foregrounded when Holden stigmatizes the word "grand," or the phrase "marvelous to see you"; the second when he notes the hollow formality of "glad to've met you." (pp. 29-30)

Holden rounds on mores and conventions that are a badge of class. He also revolts against convention itself. We would remark here that although these two feelings often blend, they have quite different origins. Society is imaginable without privilege, snobbery, unequal wealth. To banish *all* convention would be to end society itself. (p. 30)

Any society provides identities for its members to step into; Holden's is no exception. We can hardly consider his quest for identity apart, for instance, from the fact that his father is a corporation lawyer ("Those boys really haul it in") on the edge of the ruling class, who has tried, however fruitlessly, to open for Holden the way to a similar identity by apprenticing him in a series of private schools. For Holden, such an identity is imaginatively real, and coercive. . . . Holden understands well enough that such an identity is incompatible with the spontaneous feeling and relatedness he wishes for.

But what vision can he entertain of some alternate self? Here imagination darkens. Holden has no idea of changing society, and within the present one he can see forward only to the bourgeois identity that waits for him. So he fantasizes another identity which fulfills desire by escaping society almost entirely. (pp. 32-3)

Here is the main equivocation of the book, and it seems to be both Holden's and Salinger's.... [The] force of Holden's severest judgment is divided. "Phony" stigmatizes both the manners and culture of a dominant bourgeoisie—class society—and ceremonies and institutions themselves—any society. As long as we listen to the critical themes of the novel, the equivocation doesn't matter much: after all, the only society around *is* bourgeois society. But when we listen to those hints in the novel of something better, of alternative futures, of reconstruction, it makes a great deal of difference. Given Salinger's perception of what's wrong, there are three possible responses: do the best you can with this society; work for a better one; flee society altogether. Only the second answers to the critical feeling that dominates the book, but Salinger omits precisely that response when he shows Holden turning from that which his heart rejects to that which has value, commands allegiance, and invites living into the future without despair. So, when Holden imagines an adult self he can think only of the Madison Avenue executive or the deaf-mute, this society or no society.

And what does he like in the present? ... For Holden, images of the valuable are generally images of people withdrawn from convention—people who are private, whimsical, losers, saints, dead. Holden's imagination cannot join the social and the desirable. At the beginning and again at the end of the novel he has the illusion of diappearing, losing his identity altogether—both times when he is crossing that most social of artifacts, a street.

So long as the choice is between this society and no society, Holden's imagination has no place to go. He wants love and a relatedness among equals. These do not thrive in the institutions that surround him, but they cannot exist at all without institutions, which shape human feeling and give life social form. When Phoebe retrieves Holden from nothingness and despair she draws him, inevitably, toward institutions: the family, school, the Christmas play, the zoo in the park, the carrousel where "they always play the same songs." In short, toward the same society he has fled, and toward some of its innocent social forms, this time magically redeemed by love.

Holden returns to society, the only one available. It is unchanged; he has changed somewhat, in the direction of acceptance. To go the rest of the way back, he requires the help of another institution, and a psychoanalyst. Society has classified him as neurotic—a fitting response, apparently, to his having wanted from it a more hospitable human climate than it could offer. He will change more. Society will not. But that's all right, in the end: the very act of telling his story has overlaid it with nostalgia, and he misses everybody he has told about.... In a word, *Art* forms the needed bridge between the desirable and the actual, provides the mediation by which social experience, rendered through much of the story as oppressive, can be embraced.

The Catcher in the Rye is among other things a serious critical mimesis of bourgeois life in the Eastern United States, ca. 1950—of snobbery, privilege, class injury, culture as badge of superiority, sexual exploitation, education subor-

dinated to status, warped social feeling, competitiveness, stunted human possibility, the list could go on. Salinger is astute in imaging these hurtful things, though not in explaining them. Connections exist between Holden's ordeal and the events reported on the front page of the *Times*, and we think that those connections are necessary to complete Salinger's understanding of social reality. (pp. 33-5)

The novel draws readers into a powerful longing for what-could-be, and at the same time interposes what-is, as an unchanging and immovable reality. (p. 35)

In short, the esthetic force of the novel is quite precisely located in its rendering a contradiction of a particular society, as expressed through an adolescent sensibility that feels, though it cannot comprehend, this contradiction. Short of comprehension, both Holden and Salinger are driven to a false equation—to reject this society is to reject society itself—and a false choice—accept this society or defect from society altogether.

It is here that the novel most invites criticism, informed by history and politics. But the critics have instead, with few exceptions, followed Salinger's own lead and deepened the confusion of the novel with the help of mystifications like "the adult world," "the human condition," and so on. Pressing for such formulations, they have left history and the novel behind. They have failed both to understand its very large achievement—for we consider it a marvelous book—and to identify the shortcomings of its awareness and its art. And in this way they have certified it as a timeless classic. (pp. 35-6)

> *Carol and Richard Ohmann, "Reviewers, Critics, and 'The Catcher in the Rye'," in* Critical Inquiry *(copyright © 1976 by The University of Chicago), Vol. 3, No. 1, Autumn, 1976, pp. 15-37.*

GERALDINE De LUCA

[One] can say, in dubious celebration of Salinger, that *The Catcher in the Rye* is the one book that the adolescent novel comes from. It is a difficult, deceptive heritage: satirical and ostensibly designed to offer a clearer mode of life and thought than that which the heroes witness. But certainly in Salinger's case..., there really are no alternatives. One's only salvation is to remain a child.

Even in his works about the Glass Family, where he has turned to the adult world, Salinger is still celebrating childhood. While the Glass family can get quickly under one's skin, the books ultimately do not satisfy because the characters never quite get past what Zooey himself termed their "tenth-rate nervous breakdowns," never accepting or confronting the ills of the adult world that so oppress them. They remain Salinger's children, sanctified and damaged by their sensibilities.

In all of Salinger's work, children alone offer solace to his tormented characters: twelve-year-old Esme is the only one of the narrator/Sergeant X's correspondents who can help him; Seymour Glass, the oldest of the Glass family children, now unhappily married, has a sad tryst in the ocean at Miami Beach with a little girl named Sybil before he blows his brains out. The family reminisces about Franny sitting in the kitchen as a child, having a small glass of milk with Jesus. And of course there is Holden's younger sister Phoebe, dressed in her pajamas with the elephants on the collar, urging Holden to face his parents—if not his problems. These are the ideal characters in Salinger's world, and adults are appealing insofar as they share the qualities and voice of childhood. Franny and Zooey, for all their sophistication, are still pained children. Zooey's small, beautiful back—observed mostly by his mother who sits talking to him as he takes a bath—suggests a child's; Franny recovers from her depression by listening, open-mouthed, on the phone to her brother Zooey, who disguises his voice as their brother Buddy's and tells her the old adage of their brother Seymour that she should live for the fat lady, because the fat lady is Christ. Seized and calmed by the truth of that simple notion, Franny climbs into her father's empty bed and goes beatifically to sleep. How comfortably, innocently incestuous they all are. "It's a Wise Child," the radio program on which each of the Glass family in turn spouted their wisdom, might be the name of any of Salinger's works.

The casual reader might be beguiled into the belief that Salinger's nay-saying characters are simply confused and shortsighted and that the author is implying they can mature and change. Zooey's pep talks with his sister—self-mocking, ironic, good humored—sound optimistic. But Salinger's humor comes more from desperation than distance. The unhappiness Holden feels because of his intolerance for compromise and his discomfort with sexuality cannot easily be helped. There is no successful model for him. One either compromises or goes under. And none of the Glass family is doing much better. Their fat lady—in the prophetic Seymour's extended description—has cancer and sits on her porch listening to the radio. In the face of this dismal vision, the Glass family must simply bear up under their crown of thorns.

In terms of what he finds acceptable, Salinger is not, in fact, very far from Lewis Carroll. He has much more sympathy for the compromises of the common man, but no more hope. Yet, like Carroll, he is authentic. He may have descended from Twain, but he is not an imitator. Unfortunately, the same cannot be said of his descendants. The idiosyncracies—not to say excesses—of his style, along with his simplifications and his celebration of innocence have been adopted by a host of followers. The fat lady has been succeeded by M. E. Kerr's Miss Blue [of *Is That You, Miss Blue?*], who hangs pictures of Jesus in the dormitory bathroom, and Paul Zindel's invalid Irene [of *I Never Loved Your Mind*], who spits into a sputum cup all day, and writes doggerel verse which she sends to *The London Observer*. Almost all the adolescent novels use the familiar and by now too predictable first person narrator whose alienated-innocent voice confines, constricts, and dominates the work. They are all sanctified, all wise children. Salinger's gimmicks appear everywhere: in the lists, like the contents of Bessie Glass's medicine cabinet; the footnotes, that "aesthetic evil" for which Buddy Glass asks indulgence; the physical grotesques and caricatures, like Old Spencer, surreptitiously picking his nose, or Mr. Antolini, ambiguously stroking Holden's hair. (pp. 89-91)

> *Geraldine De Luca, in* The Lion and the Unicorn *(copyright © 1978 The Lion and the Unicorn), Fall, 1978.*

JAMES LUNDQUIST

This is 1979, and it has been twenty-eight years since Holden Caulfield dragged his deer-hunting cap and his prep-school heart through Manhattan. But J. D. Salinger's

ideas on the true and the false in American culture, his religious solutions to the crises of alienation and isolation, and his overriding sentimentality may have had more impact on the American brainscape than anyone yet has taken into account. Since the publication of a long story, "Hapworth 16, 1924," in *The New Yorker* in 1965, Salinger has maintained a silence that has turned him into the Howard Hughes of American literature. But Salinger's lasting significance has not declined. The startling thing for many of us to realize is that the confidential ravings of Holden Caulfield, the enigma of Seymour Glass's suicide, and the pathetic pragmatism of the Jesus Prayer embraced by Franny Glass, remain part of our consciousness—and it is not just simply nostalgia for that time in the 1950s and early 1960s when Salinger's characters provided just about the only voices that did not sound phony. As a whole new generation of readers indicates, the appeal of his work is enduring. His influence remains, and we cannot get around it, perhaps cannot get over it. (p. 1)

Looking back, one can now discern at least four phases in Salinger's career. His early stories generally portray characters who feel estranged and marooned because of World War II. His second phase is represented by *The Catcher in the Rye,* and Salinger's attempt in that book to deal with estrangement and isolation through a Zen-inspired awakening and lonely benevolence. The third phase, seen in *Nine Stories,* involves bringing together the principles of Zen art and the tradition of the short story. The fourth phase is one in which Salinger's work becomes more and more experimental, resulting in the philosophical mood of his last two books, *Franny and Zooey* and *Raise High the Roof Beam, Carpenters;* and *Seymour: An Introduction.* These four phases indicate that Salinger should be read as a writer who is seeking solutions, as a writer who is trying to give direction to his thought based on an initial disturbing event. And that event is World War II.

This is not to say that Salinger should be considered a war novelist in at all the same way that one has to think about Mailer or James Jones. Nor is Salinger's relationship to the war at all as direct as that of Kurt Vonnegut, whose life and thought, as Vonnegut has admitted himself many times, revolves around the firebombing of Dresden. Unlike Vonnegut, Salinger apparently did not go through a single, harrowing experience that stayed with him from that point on. Rather it was a mood that seemed to have influenced him, a mood of loneliness, isolation, ineffectuality, and a sense of being a misfit in an unfit society. (pp. 2-3)

Many of Salinger's early stories do not deal directly with the war . . . but a war atmosphere permeates them—and it is not one of patriotism, nor is it representative of the kind of thought found in so much writing to come out of the war . . . that suggests war might be hell, but at least it can make a man out of you. . . . Instead, there is a sense that whatever the ideological banner, the state inevitably becomes omnivorous and omnipotent and the individual is helpless against it. The question, unstated, but there nonetheless in Salinger's earliest work, is this: What can one think and do when all possible beliefs are gone? (pp. 3-4)

Salinger has been charged, because of his essential optimism, because of his refusal to be as grimly existential as Sartre or as bleak as Beckett (if Salinger had written *Waiting for Godot*, Godot—or at least a near relative—would have shown up to drink milk in the kitchen), of retreating into mysticism. Yet in reality, the movement of his stories suggests a kind of pilgrim's progress, a journey from the melancholia of the war stories, through the trauma of *The Catcher in the Rye* and *Nine Stories,* to the moments of revelation in the later dialogues. Again and again he writes on the relationship of man to God—or, to state it more subtly and accurately, man's relationship to the *lack* of God and how that sense of emptiness may be treated and perhaps alleviated. At the same time, Salinger's humor, often wry, often understated, but never bitter, is there. . . . [The] humor directs us away from the tragic and toward the comic; poignancy turns into hopefulness, and the objective is enlightenment, not despair. (pp. 4-5)

The Catcher in the Rye appeared in a sober and realistic time, a period when (by comparison with the 1960s, at any rate) there was a general disenchantment with ideologies, with schemes for the salvation of the world. Salinger's novel, like the decade for which it has become emblematic, begins with the words, "If you really want to hear about it," words that imply a full, sickening realization that something has happened that perhaps most readers would not want to know about. What we find out about directly in the novel is, of course, what has happened to Salinger's hero-narrator, Holden Caulfield; but we also find out what has happened generally to human ideas on some simple and ultimate questions in the years following World War II. Is it still possible to reconcile self and society? Is it any longer possible to separate the authentic from the phony? What beliefs are essential for survival? What is the role of language in understanding the nature of our reality? Is it possible to create value and endow the universe with meaning? That Salinger deals with these questions in one way or another points to a problem with *The Catcher in the Rye* that has often been ignored or simply not taken seriously—that the climate of ideas surrounding the novel is dense, and that the book is not just the extended and anguished cries of a wise-guy adolescent whose main trouble is that he does not want to grow up. (p. 37)

In describing Holden's predicament, one cannot avoid using existential platitudes, for Holden is, undoubtedly, in the midst of an existential crisis. Yet for all his despair, Holden is not a character who adequately illustrates the bitter pessimism and seriousness of a character out of the writings of Sartre, nor does he convey the simple message of popular existentialism as suggested by Camus—choose a path, commit yourself, be yourself, realize your own dignity. Salinger conceives of character much the same way Sartre and Camus do, but his use of language, his humor, and his ultimate willingness to look elsewhere for his answers make him a far different writer, even though he begins at the same point: The world with all its obscenities.

The way Holden Caulfield sees the world is stated in the novel's most famous line: "If you had a million years to do it in, you couldn't rub out even half the 'Fuck you' signs in the world." . . . It is ironic that this sentence is the one that is most responsible for the various bannings of the novel in the years following its appearance. . . . [The] controversial line, instead of being obscene itself, is directed, as almost all of Salinger's fiction is, *against* obscenity. Holden tries to explain to us not only what is offensive, disgusting, and repulsive to him in human behavior, but also what goes against prevailing notions of modesty and decency. "The things that Holden finds so deeply repulsive are things he

calls 'phony,'" writes Dan Wakefield, "and the 'phoniness' in every instance is the absence of love, and, often, the substitution of pretense for love" [see excerpt above]. Holden is a rebel, but he is hardly a rebel without a cause: He begins in a screaming rage against a society of convention, immorality, and the patently false, but he ends by establishing love and acceptance as a saving grace. (pp. 38-9)

The influence of Holden's example on an entire generation of readers is impossible to measure, but it is difficult to ignore in considering the development of the "counterculture" of white American youth in the 1960s. The conventional virtues they rejected—competitive masculinity, military supremacy, and the emphasis on self discipline in order to channel energy into economic achievement—are all virtues rejected by Holden. And the belief that non-Western thought could provide humanizing answers that centuries of Christianity and European philosophy had not is as much a part of Salinger and *The Catcher in the Rye* as it is of the Beat movement. Like Gary Snyder, Salinger suggests the use of Zen Buddhism as a means of discipline necessary to cleanse the mind of certain untruths promoted by mass culture in America. Holden Caulfield's long digression is a pilgrimage to find meaning, one he has doubtless encouraged others to follow on the path back to a revitalized sense of inner direction.

But however extensive the influence of Salinger's most notorious character, he is a major reason for Salinger's fame and popularity. In the real and relevant idiom of Holden, Salinger caught and dissected modern society through a symbolic structure of language, motif, and episode that is as masterful as anything in contemporary literature. *The Catcher in the Rye* is a novel that fights obscenity with an amazing and divine mixture of vulgarity and existential anguish, and it does this through a style that moves the narrative effortlessly along on a colloquial surface that suddenly parts to reveal the terror and beauty of the spiritual drama that Holden enacts. It may be Salinger's only novel, but it is still one of the best we have. (pp. 67-8)

The secret of balancing form with emptiness and in knowing when one has said enough is behind the art of the modern short story. This secret is also behind the art forms of Zen Buddhism with its emphasis on an idea that must be at the center of every good short story: One showing is worth a hundred sayings. The short-story writer and the Zen artist must work to convey the impression of unhesitating spontaneity, realizing that a single stroke is enough to give away character, and avoiding filling in the essential empty spaces with explanation, second thoughts, and intellectual commentary. These principles are brought together in Salinger's *Nine Stories,* a collection of his finest work and a startling blend of West and East in its aesthetic assumptions. (p. 69)

What happens in the short stories of Chekhov or Joyce also happens in the short stories of Salinger—character is revealed through a series of actions under stress, and the purpose of the story is reached at the moment of "epiphany," when the reader comes to know the true nature of a character or situation. Looked at from a distance and in light of the development of the short story, Salinger's stories are rather conventional. But when looked at from another way, the way suggested by the Zen *koan* that prefaces the collection, they become calligraphic paintings, reach their artistic high point in a tea ceremony, and have the arrangement of a Japanese garden.

Such a view of *Nine Stories* is not suggested as simply a critical metaphor or yet another way of getting at the problem of "pattern" that has bothered so many readers of the book. It is an acknowledgement that in these stories, Zen attitudes toward art and human experience are consciously being used by Salinger in dealing with and expressing such major themes as the survival of the despairing individual in a mass society, the redeeming possibilities in a lonely benevolent, intuitive kind of love, and the necessity of overcoming the pervasive obscenity of life by passing through the boundaries of personality to enlightenment, liberation, or *satori*. (p. 70)

It is in *Nine Stories* . . . that Zen is most pointedly being used as a conceptualizing force for Salinger's fiction, and the puzzle that we are presented with before we can even start reading the stories is this one:

> We know the sound of two hands clapping.
> But what is the sound of one hand clapping?

This, of course, is one of the most famous Zen *koan*, originated by Hakuin . . . , generally acknowledged as the greatest of the Zen masters. The word *Zen* means thinking, meditation, to see, to contemplate, and the *koan* is central to the Zen process. (p. 74)

[What] is the point of the "one-hand" *koan?* It leads us through a series of questions. Can you hear something that is not making any noise? Can you get any sound out of a hand that has nothing to hit against? Can you obtain any knowledge of your own real nature—can the mind hit against itself? It is this final question that Salinger comes down to in his stories as he presents characters who achieve or fail to achieve *satori*, who either do or do not achieve a sudden and intuitive way of seeing into themselves. And for those who do solve the *koan* that is crucial to their awakening, what happens is described by Dumoulin this way: "He who lifts one hand and while listening quietly can hear a sound which no ears hear, can surpass all conscious knowledge. He can leave the world of distinctions behind him; he may cross the ocean of the *karma* of rebirths, and he may break through the darkness of ignorance. In the enlightenment he attains to unlimited freedom."

To the western mind, this unlimited freedom is most easily symbolized in children, and this, of course, is why Salinger relies on the child as symbol so often in *Nine Stories*. (p. 78)

Because of the Zen emphasis on "indirectness," on signs and symbols in expressing the nature of reality, art forms, particularly painting and poetry, are especially important in Zen. Salinger's awareness of Zen art is apparent in his stories. Two examples that spring immediately to mind are M. Yoshoto's painting of the white goose in the pale blue sky and Teddy's recitation of two Japanese poems (the only kind of poetry he can stand): "Nothing in the voice of the cicada intimates how soon it will die" and "Along this road goes no one, this autumn eve." . . . And the impression left by each of his stories is similar to the feeling left by the calligraphic style of painting done with black ink on paper or silk that was practiced by Chinese artists as early as the eighth century, a form of painting in which the objective, as in a Salinger story, is unhesitating spontaneity, and where a single stroke is often enough to give away one's character, the picture itself designed to bring about *satori*. (pp. 110-11)

The most obvious relationship between Zen art and Salinger's writing is, of course, between the "wordless" poetry of the *haiku* and the careful use of language in the stories. The *haiku*, which reached its fullest form in the seventeenth century, consists of just seventeen syllables, and tries, through a single image, to convey the same effect as Zen painting does through its use of empty space. . . . The same effect is achieved by many of Salinger's stories. It is the silence we feel as much as anything at the end of "A Perfect Day for Bananafish," "The Laughing Man," and "Teddy," a silence that is the sound of one hand clapping.

Given the direct reference to Zen painting and poetry in *Nine Stories*, it is not surprising that the Zen practice that has evoked the most curiosity in the Western world, the tea ceremony, should figure in what most critics agree is the best-written story in the collection, "For Esmé—With Love and Squalor." In Buddhism, tea has nearly the same sacramental function as wine does in Christianity. Its slightly bitter yet clarifying taste is said to suggest the same taste as Buddhist awakening itself, and it has long been used by Zen monks as a stimulant for meditation. . . . Included in the ceremony, which is frankly accepted as an escape from the concerns of business and worldly competition, is non-argumentative discussion of philosophical matters. In Salinger's story there is no attempt at direct representation of the tea ceremony, but the Sergeant has entered the tearoom as an escape (both from the rain and the barracks), the experience does figure in his awakening, and he and Esmé do carry on a non-argumentative discussion that ultimately turns on the philosophical meaning of squalor—the very thing the tea ceremony enables one to escape.

If the tea ceremony is central to one of the most memorable stories of the book, perhaps it is not pushing the metaphor of Zen art and its influence on *Nine Stories* too far to point out that the overall arrangement is much like that found in a Japanese garden, where the attempt, as in the stories, is not to make a strictly realistic illusion of a miniature landscape, "but simply to suggest the general atmosphere of 'mountain and water' in a small space, so arranging the design of the garden that it seems to have been helped rather than governed by the hand of man" [from Alan W. Watts, *The Way of Zen*]. The arrangement of Salinger's stories in the literal sense of the order in which they appear in the book seems to follow this principle. They give the impression of pattern and structure to the collection, yet the order is simply the order of magazine publication. They are arranged but they are not arranged. Another similarity between the stories and Zen gardening is in *bonseki*, the art of "discovering" rocks along the seashore and mountains that have been shaped by wind and water into living contours and then positioning them in the garden so that they look as if they have "grown" there. Salinger does much the same thing in his use of otherwise insignificant objects (a chicken sandwich, a red piece of waste paper, a watch) as beatific signs. And just as the Zen gardeners, Salinger is always sparing and reserved in his use of color.

Zen art requires incredible care and by its very nature cannot be prolific—something that must be taken into consideration in any discussion of Salinger's relatively "slight" output. Once a writer accepts the Zen principles of art, as Salinger's *Nine Stories* indicates he has, he becomes like the Zen gardener who can never cease to weed, prune, and train his plants, and who must do so with the realization that he is part of the garden himself, not some sort of controlling agent standing outside. This is what Salinger accomplishes in *Nine Stories;* he is so much inside the stories that they become an interior monologue in which we can perceive the writer's own movement toward *satori* as he faces the essential Zen fact of all that side of life completely beyond the control of logic. And how has he done this? Perhaps through gaining the same insight as the Zen master teaches in Eugene Herrigel's *Zen in the Art of Archery:* "What is true of archery and swordsmanship also applies to all the other arts. Thus, mastery in ink-painting is only attained when the hand, exercising perfect control over technique, executes what hovers before the mind's eye at the same moment when the mind begins to form it, without there being a hair's breadth between. Painting then becomes spontaneous calligraphy. Here again the painter's instructions might be: spend ten years observing bamboos, become a bamboo yourself, then forget everything and—paint." (pp. 110-14)

[*Franny and Zooey*] actually consists of two long stories put together into what almost, but not quite, becomes a novel. An abrupt shift in narrative technique from omniscient point of view in the first story . . . to having Buddy serve as the narrator in the second . . . gives the book an awkward structure. But despite the narrative shift, the two stories are best considered as one unit, not only because the second story serves to resolve the first, but also because the two of them taken together mark an essential change in Salinger's fiction. Through his use of the Glass family as an organizing concept for his vision, and through his increased reliance on Buddy as the narrator in that portrayal, Salinger attempts to more firmly capture the paradoxical splendor and squalor of life, while concurrently presenting a vision of twentieth-century America that is ultimately positive. The source of that vision is something that comes as a relief after the occasional overemphasis on the efficacy of Oriental thought in *Nine Stories*, and Holden Caulfield's apparent attainment of Buddhahood at the end of *The Catcher in the Rye*. What we perceive through Salinger's ventriloquial act . . . is a deeper awareness engendered by the paradox itself—that there are no pat answers to the problems of existence—not even Zen—and that the paradox of splendor and squalor, or of the nice and the phony, can be resolved only through character and being. *Franny and Zooey* thus places emphasis on character rather than action, and clearly shows Salinger moving from the well-made structures of his early stories to the discursive narrative insights of Buddy Glass working from his position within the conceptual and focusing frame of the family. (pp. 120-21)

[The volume containing *Raise High the Roof Beam, Carpenters* and "Seymour: An Introduction"] is somewhat similar in structure to *Franny and Zooey*. The first section consists of a story . . . complete with plot and even something of a resolution, and the second section . . . is a dialogue of sorts between Buddy and Seymour (or rather, Seymour's ghost) that serves peripherally as a commentary on the first story, provides us, as the title indicates, with more information on Seymour, and finally comes down to a discussion of the nature of art, the crucial differences be-

tween poetry and prose, and the predicament of the artist. But even though both sections are this time narrated by Buddy, the two parts of the book do not fit together tightly, and "Seymour: An Introduction" comes about as close to being an essay as a piece of fiction can. However, the overall effect is one of intended delight. As in *Franny and Zooey*, Salinger is clearly writing about characters for whom he feels great affection because of the way they provide him with a means of centralizing his vision. (p. 136)

Salinger's later work should be seen . . . as part of a general development in American fiction that has been going on since World War II when the conservative stability of form that had long dominated American writing was challenged by a growing awareness of the work, not only of Joyce and Kafka (remember that Salinger uses a Kafka quotation as an epigraph at the start of "Seymour: An Introduction"), but also of more exotic talents such as Hesse, Robbe-Grillet, Cortazar, and Borges. It should also be seen as part of a different reaction that involved a certain public distrust of what fiction can do. . . . (p. 153)

Another important point is that Salinger's development is not unlike that of Kurt Vonnegut and other writers of his generation. He moves steadily away from old-fashioned stories of the sort that lead us to believe that life has leading characters and minor characters, important details and unimportant details, beginnings, middles, ends—"Fundamentally, my mind has always balked at any kind of ending," Buddy confesses at the conclusion of "Seymour: An Introduction." Like Vonnegut by the time he gets to *Breakfast of Champions*, Salinger seems to have resolved to avoid storytelling in favor of a kind of writing that, through its observations on the process by which it was created, and through the conceptualizing frame of the Glass family, shows us one way of combatting the obscenity of modern life and adapting to a chaotic, but ultimately benign, universe.

All phases of Salinger's career must be taken into account in assessing his importance, and few readers would argue with the view that *The Catcher in the Rye* and *Nine Stories* remain Salinger's most satisfying work. In his only novel, he lays claim to a few years that, without much exaggeration, could be called "The Age of Salinger" because of his (sometimes schoolroom-enforced) influence on a generation of readers. With *Nine Stories*, he establishes a reputation as a short-story writer that puts him in the class of [Ring] Lardner, Fitzgerald, and Hemingway (as well as that of [John] Cheever, [John] Updike, Flannery O'Connor, and James Purdy). And despite his long silence, Salinger's work shows a surprising growth and increasing sophistication of technique. It is a long way from "The Young Folks" to "Seymour: An Introduction." In the process of change, Salinger has become, at points in his performance, a stylist whose comic mastery of language approaches that of Mark Twain, and a writer of considerable religious vision whose books themselves remain in the mind as incarnations of spirit long after they are put down. (pp. 153-54)

James Lundquist, in his J. D. Salinger *(copyright © 1979 by Frederick Ungar Publishing Co., Inc.), Frederick Ungar, 1979.*

Charles M(onroe) Schulz

1922-

American cartoonist and illustrator. Schulz's comic strip, "Peanuts," is internationally popular for its humorous and sensitive portrayal of children and their reactions to life. Schulz grew up knowing he would someday be a cartoonist. Lacking confidence, however, he studied art via correspondence rather than facing the instructors in person. His strip entitled "Li'l Folks" first appeared in *The Saturday Evening Post* before it was bought and renamed "Peanuts" by the United Feature Syndicate in 1950. Many of the characters and their predicaments are personal observations and autobiographical elements in Schulz's life; he thinks of them as a second family. A compulsive worrier like his character Charlie Brown, he is concerned that his characters always reflect the sentiments of their creator. Schulz, therefore, is one of the few cartoonists who has no ghost writers. Throughout the cartoon's lifetime, the "Peanuts" gang has become more defined in character, appealing to children on a literal level, and to adults for their astute observations of human nature at its most precarious moments. Most of the strips carry a message of some sort, be it humorous or profound, which often reflects Schulz's religious background. Critics agree that it is the dialogue that supports the simply drawn figures. The daily strip has branched out to include other media, such as books and television, the most popular of these creations being Schulz's first TV special "A Charlie Brown Christmas." Schulz has been criticized for the commercialization of his strip, which has resulted in a barrage of "Peanuts" products, from greeting cards to Christmas ornaments. However, Charlie Brown and his friends show the wisdom of innocence, and have escaped the limits of the four paneled cartoon into the realm of the American cultural symbol. Schulz was twice presented with the Reuben Award, the cartoonist's equivalent of the Oscar, in 1955 and 1964. (See also *Contemporary Authors*, Vols. 9-12, rev. ed., and *Something about the Author*, Vol. 10.)

In a decade that has seen much of the fun leak out of the funnies, a Popsicle-set Punchinello named Good Ol' Charlie Brown has endeared himself to millions of newspaper readers with a quietly wistful brand of humor that is both fresh and worldly-wise. . . .

The appeal of *Peanuts* lies in its sophisticated melding of wry wisdom and sly one-upmanship. Unlike such funny-page small fry as Hank Ketcham's *Dennis the Menace* or Jimmy Hatlo's *Little Iodine*, its characters are disingenuous and uncute. Charlie, whose peanut-bald head is surmounted by a single dispirited curl, is a junior-grade Walter Mitty, whose highflying dreams of popularity crash in endless ignominies.

> *"Child's Garden of Reverses," in* Time *(reprinted by permission from* Time, The Weekly Newsmagazine; *copyright Time Inc. 1958), March 3, 1958, p. 58.*

NATHAN A. SCOTT, JR.

[The] art of the cartoon strip must not have been wholly corrupted if it can still afford a working medium for so scrupulous and lively an imagination as that of Charles Schulz. For, in and through the fabulous little world of Charlie Brown and Lucy and Linus and Snoopy and Shermy and Violet, Mr. Schulz has been turning a remarkably penetrating searchlight on the anxieties and evasions and duplicities that make up our common lot; and . . . the analysis of human existence that Mr. Schulz is giving us is essentially theological and, in its basic inspiration, deeply Christian. (pp. ix-x)

> *Nathan A. Scott, Jr., in his foreword to* The Gospel According to Peanuts *by Robert L. Short (© 1965 by M. E. Bratcher; used by permission of John Knox Press), John Knox, 1964 (and reprinted by Bantam Books, 1968), pp. ix-x.*

ROBERT L. SHORT

Peanuts, the famous cartoon strip, often assumes the form of a modern-day, Christian parable. To illustrate how closely the parables of *Peanuts* can parallel the parables of the New Testament—in lessons suggested, in ways of suggesting these lessons, and in indirect method—[the cartoon showing Linus' kingdom of sand washed away by rain] is coupled with Christ's parable of "The house on the rock and the house on the sand." (p. 19)

And so there *are* lessons to be found in *Peanuts;* but just as in the parables of Christ, we are not always sure what these lessons are. Or, as Lucy would put it, also in *Peanuts* we have trouble "reading between the lines." . . .

[Mr. Schulz] has confessed . . . to presenting something of a religious message in *Peanuts,* but evidently he has not gone much further in specifying exactly what this message is. Again, why should he? . . . [The] job of the interpreter (whether minister, priest, professional critic, or perceptive layman) and the job of the artist should usually be kept apart. ''How can you give a personal evaluation of a work of art?'' was Schulz's guarded reply when one reporter attempted to force him into becoming his own critic. Both the Church and the artist must constantly beware of cheapening what they have to say by making it *too* accessible. . . .

[Lessons] ''to be found,'' if they are to be seriously *appreciated* when found, will always first require a corresponding amount of serious *seeking*. And so then, like Charlie Brown, the job of Charles Schulz probably should not be the *interpretation* of ''prophetic literature'' as much as it is the *creation* of it. . . . (p. 20)

The doctrine of Original Sin is a theme constantly being dramatized in *Peanuts*. And as Lucy asks Charlie Brown, after demonstrating to him how his pebble-like virtues are no match for the boulder representing his ''countless faults,'' ''Don't you think you're lucky to have me around to point up these things in such a graphic manner?'' Indeed we are lucky! For as Hume maintained, one of the best ways of putting new flesh onto the bones of old and misunderstood creeds is precisely to point up these things in a graphic manner. (pp. 26-7)

The captivity of man's will is most often dramatized in *Peanuts* just as it is most often dramatized in men's lives— by *the significant change* that never takes place. In talking about the egotism and brutality of children, Schulz has said, ''We grown-ups don't change so much, except on the surface, because we get along better that way.'' (p. 31)

The inability of the *Peanuts* kids to produce any radical change for the better in themselves—or in each other—is a constant *Peanuts* theme. . . . The classic *Peanuts* commentary on this rather pessimistic view of human nature is the running gag every year when Charlie Brown's courageous views on man's freedom and goodness are invariably brought back to earth by Lucy [when she promises not to pull the football away as Charlie Brown kicks it]. . . . Lucy's ''bonded word'' . . . sounds more like what theologians have called ''the bondage of the will''; and Charlie Brown sounds very much like a follower of Pelagius, who also was ''accustomed . . . to call attention to the capacity and character of human nature and to show what it is able to accomplish.'' (pp. 32-3)

The ''children of men'' of the preceding psalm could be well represented by the children of *Peanuts,* for in both cases *all* seem to have ''gone astray.'' Even the lovable and long-suffering Charlie Brown, as Schultz has said of him, ''never does anything mean, but he is weak, vain and very vulnerable. . . . And aren't all kids egotists?'' Schulz asks. ''And brutal? Children are caricatures of adults.'' Indeed Mr. Schulz had originally planned to call his strip *Li'l Folks,* and evidently was quite disappointed with the ''terrible insignificance'' of the ''Peanuts'' title, when the strip was renamed by a cartoon syndicate. (pp. 40-1)

Children can be a good symbol for the original sinfulness of man since all men originate as children *and* as sinners. . . . For this reason the children of *Peanuts* can be seen as a sort of comic counterpart to the kind of children found in William Golding's terrifying tract of the times, *Lord of the Flies.* Golding's children, along with an increasing number of young people in modern literature, help us to see the

unaccommodated man—left completely free to be himself, to do what comes naturally, without gospel and in spite of law—is a savage. . . . Seeing the infant as a sinner, however, probably never has been nor will be a popular point of view. It may be, therefore, that the modern ''cult of the child,'' which holds to the child's ''original innocence,'' is partly a reaction against the doctrine of Original Sin. . . . Whenever they can, even the youngest *Peanuts* children are crafty enough to take advantage of this point of view. . . . This kind of ''original innocence'' of children, as Lucy says of it, ''doesn't solve anything, but it makes us all feel better.'' But the innocence of the *Peanuts* kids is never an innocence of shallow and sinless ''cuteness''; it is always an innocence with biblical or metaphysical overtones, an innocence of being ''innocent but not too well informed,'' as Schulz has said of Linus. (pp. 41-2, 45)

All the *Peanuts* kids are guilty . . . of serving a false god; and all receive their inevitable wages in [a] kind of emotional clobbering.

This theme is so constant in *Peanuts* that the strip truly can be seen as a kind of ''child's garden of reverses.'' Take Linus for instance. His blanket (this ''portable security,'' this source of ''mental therapy,'' this ''spiritual blotter'' soaking up ''fears and frustrations''!) is obviously intended to cover a multitude of sins for him, but it inevitably turns out to be only a drag, as it is surely the world's longest and most vulnerable Achilles' heel. One might wonder why he continues to suffer for it so; but, as he says, it is all he has: ''Only one yard of outing flannel stands between me and a nervous breakdown!'' . . . No one can part with one's *god* until one *has* to, until there is no part of it left to cling to. A *god,* by definition, is all we have ''to keep us going,'' as Linus has put it. (pp. 50-2)

But *Peanuts* manages to demonstrate the hazards of worshiping deities that are far more familiar than blankets, winning, Beethoven, or Schroeder. There is for instance the belief we can have in ourselves, or in our abilities—the well-known ''power of positive thinking.'' . . . Poor Charlie Brown! The psalmist surely must have had him in mind when he wrote, ''Insults have broken my heart, so that I am in despair. I looked for pity, but there were none and for comforters, but I found none.'' . . . Indeed the psalmist *could* have had ''Charlie Brown'' in mind. For Charlie Brown, with his globe-like head (Lucy has used it as a globe several times) and his T-shirt of thorns, can be seen as a sort of twentieth-century representation of Everyman. We love him just as misery loves company; for usually he is just as miserable as most of mankind is. (pp. 53, 55)

In *Peanuts* religious heresy seems to be represented by the ''Great Pumpkin,'' Linus' substitute for Santa Claus. . . . Futhermore, the ''Great Pumpkin'' will only appear in ''the pumpkin patch that he thinks is the most sincere.'' Over and over, Schulz seems to be saying that *sincerity* is no more a guarantee of truth than it is a guarantee of success. . . . Schulz seems to be in agreement with Kierkegaard, who said, ''Evil, mediocrity, is never so dangerous as when it is dressed up as 'sincerity'.'' The ''Great Pumpkin,'' then, may be symbolic of popular religious sentiment, which currently seems to have more ''faith in faith,'' or faith in ''sincerity,'' than faith in anything in particular. At any rate, the cult of the ''Great Pumpkin'' is surely ''religious,'' as also is its rival the Santa Claus sect. When Charlie Brown is asked if he believes there really *is* a Santa

Claus, he replies, ''I refuse to get involved in a theological discussion.'' (p. 59)

The ''child's garden of reverses,'' *Peanuts*, seems . . . at times to be an unweeded garden that grows to seed. For here the ''weeds of the heart'' often seem to be represented by weeds that can be seen, and yet weeds that are nonetheless a threat to the *Peanuts* patch. They are a threat because they are so easy to get ''lost'' in—just as were the weeds in Jesus' ''parable of the sower'' and ''parable of the weeds of the field.'' . . . Snoopy has a very peculiar malady Charlie Brown calls ''weed-claustrophobia.'' . . . For whether Snoopy represents a kind of cosmic catcher in the rye, or comic outfielder in the weeds, he is literally terrified of weeds. . . . ''What's the difference between 'claustrophobia' and '*weed*-claustrophobia'?'' Lucy asks Charlie Brown after seeing Snoopy's horror of the weeds. ''Regular claustrophobia is *nothing* compared to '*weed*-claustrophobia','' he explains. Even the very worst sufferings ''the natural man'' can endure are like a ''jest,'' Kierkegaard tells us, when compared to the dreadful ''sickness unto death.'' ''Thus may we gather honey from the weed, / And make a moral of the Devil himself,'' as Shakespeare put it; thus Schulz would not seem to be above the same strategem. (pp. 67-8)

Schulz gives all of us a lot of high-protein food for thought; but . . . , the job of unshelling *Peanuts* is largely up to us. (p. 81)

[We] . . . turn more directly to the element of redemption expressed in *Peanuts* by extremely subtle suggestion, we now turn to Jesus Christ.

Snoopy we would hesitate to call ''Christ.'' He comes closer, rather, to being ''a little Christ''—that is, a Christian. For as Schulz himself has pointed out, Snoopy is capable of being ''one of the meanest'' members of the entire *Peanuts* cast. Futhermore, Snoopy has other faults . . . : he is lazy, he is a ''chow hound'' without parallel, he is bitingly sarcastic, he is frequently a coward, and he often becomes quite weary of being what he is basically—a dog. He is, in other words, a fairly drawn caricature for what is probably the typical Christian. (pp. 87-8)

Snoopy, as a little Christ, quite obviously takes on Christ's ambivalent work of humbling the exalted and exalting the humble, ''that those who do not see may see, and that those who see may become blind,'' . . . as Jesus put it. ''The love that follows us sometimes is our trouble, / Which still we thank as love,'' quoth Shakespeare. And Snoopy is certainly a troubling love that follows. For as his name implies, Snoopy is given to constant prying and meddling. None of the popular false gods of the *Peanuts* patch are secure when he is around. He is a ''hound of heaven,'' fled from ''down the labyrinthine ways,'' who uses his snoopy nose to smell out faults not immediately discernible to the eye. (p. 89)

Snoopy seems to realize that his lowliness and lonely separation means beatitude, that he is ''rejected by men but in God's sight chosen and precious.'' . . . For to be a Christian is to be ''a little Christ''; and to be ''the Christ'' is to be the anointed one, the chosen one, the one who is specially called-out, set apart, or elected—it is to be ''the lucky one.''

Snoopy's being ''the lucky one'' may also help to explain why the happiness of the Li'l Folks seems dependent to an extent on their relationship to him. ''Happiness is a warm puppy!'' says Lucy in one strip, as she pats Snoopy on the head and gives him a big hug. (pp. 98-9)

We would not have the reader think that every *Peanuts* cartoon contains some profound theological meaning. If this were the case, Schulz probably could not keep his audience with him any more than a Shakespeare could if he had composed his plays of nothing but Hamlet-like soliloquys. But on the other hand, as Schulz has pointed out, ''if you do not say anything in a cartoon, you might as well not draw it at all!'' The Christian faith must learn to speak meaningfully to men where they are; and when it comes to ''serious'' reading, there are probably many people who never get far beyond the comics section of the daily newspaper, who read only the comics ''religiously.'' (p. 106)

Peanuts lends itself easily to this kind of Christian interpretation, whether these thoughts were always in the artist's mind or not. Thus *Peanuts*—and countless other efforts in the modern arts—can play a vital part in the life of the Church by providing meaning-full ''conversation pieces'' between the Church and culture, by being wonderfully imaginative parables of and for our times. . . . (p. 107)

> *Robert L. Short, in his* The Gospel According to Peanuts *(© 1965 by M. E. Bratcher; used by permission of John Knox Press), John Knox, 1964 (and reprinted by Bantam Books, 1968).*

''Peanuts'' it isn't. The eminent multi-millionaire creator of ''Peanuts'' is also a well-known and active worker for his church. . . . [He] turned out three little cartoon collections especially for church young people. They deal mostly with teen-agers' relationship with the church and are as wholesome as all-get-out. Bantam has selected [for ''Teenagers, Unite!''] the 100 least religious, most ''general'' cartoons from the three Warner Press paperbacks, but, as we said before, ''Peanuts'' it isn't. (p. 60)

> *Publishers Weekly (reprinted from the April 17, 1967, issue of* Publishers Weekly *by permission, published by R. R. Bowker Company, a Xerox company; copyright © 1967 by Xerox Corporation), April 17, 1967.*

WILLIAM H. McNEILL

''On a beautiful day like this it would be best to stay in bed so you wouldn't get up and spoil it,'' says Charlie Brown in Charles M. Schulz' latest triumph, *You're Something Else, Charlie Brown*. To review it is like getting out of bed—too risky to be undertaken seriously; safe only for the lighthearted. And if you're lighthearted you may read it and chuckle or smile, but chuckles and smiles have never made it in English orthography, even with the license accorded comic-strip artists. So let us merely say hurrah and pass on swiftly to some earnest thoughts about the Charlie Brown phenomenon in general, and another and far less successful Charlie Brown book in particular [*You're a Good Man, Charlie Brown*].

The celebrated Pooh perplex perploxed the Depression generation of privileged children and parents—those, that is, who could afford two bucks for a book of sentiment—and whumsy. But the present pullulation of Charlie Brownisms utterly dwarfs what went before. Who can pooh-pooh the eclipse of Pooh? By who? By you! But what did you do? Why, read Charlie Brown instead.

What does it signify? A coming of age of American culture? The apartments of New York instead of the purlieus of Kensington Gardens as exercise ground for childhood imagination—and parents, too, of course?

Or are we playing a freudulent trick upon the young by offering them not one but a whole company of anti-heroes to feel superior towards or learn from, as the case may be?

Or is it the new psychological perspective—the knee-high view—that recognizes big sister as a tyrant, and the ability to catch a baseball as the pinnacle of manly success?

All of these, no doubt, plus merchandising skills, the mass media boys in the back room will have, and the antic imagination that first generated Linus and Lucy, Schroeder, Snoopy and Charlie Brown within the straitened frame of a daily newspaper comic strip.

The peculiarities of that art form survive in large degree in the musical "Peanuts." . . . Deprived of music and spectacle, most musical comedies are poor things; the same, alas, is true here. There is no plot, no overall structure; no movement of pace or tone that runs through the whole in any pattern I could perceive. It is, in short, a comic strip in two acts.

> William H. McNeill, "The Peanuts Perplex," in Book World—Chicago Tribune (© 1968 Postrib Corp.), June 2, 1968, p. 17.

If there is anything being written, drawn or scored for tuba that's funnier or indeed wiser and more human than the daily doings of Charlie Brown, crabby Lucy, Linus-of-the-security-blanket, Schroeder and of course everybody's favorite beagle, Snoopy himself, we'll have to be shown. ["Peanuts Treasury"] contains the best of ten years of Peanuts cartoons, and in our library ranks with the First Folio of Shakespeare. (p. 65)

> Publishers Weekly (reprinted from the September 16, 1968, issue of Publishers Weekly by permission, published by R. R. Bowker Company, a Xerox company; copyright © 1968 by Xerox Corporation), September 16, 1968.

ROBERT L. SHORT

"Art-Parable is that creation of man with no practical use except to communicate meaning indirectly through forms that capture one's attention." This is the kind of definition that could easily help wear someone out, but it is also why all art is parable, and vice versa. . . . Charles Schulz's famous comic strip, *Peanuts*, certainly meets this definition of Art-Parable. But since this cannot be said of all comic strips, we need to distinguish between "art" and "entertainment." All art involves "entertainment" of sorts, but not all entertainment is art. Mere entertainment leads us away from reality; indeed it can even be considered an escape from reality. . . . Art, on the other hand, can also entertain us, but it goes further. It leads us through its dream back to a reality that perhaps we had not seen before or to a reality that we now see in a new light. It helps us to see our lives as they really are and frequently provides suggestions as to how those lives can better be faced and accepted without the constant need for escape. . . . Art-Parable . . . always has "something to say." . . . (pp. 14-15)

This extra dimension of Art-Parable no doubt accounts for much of the phenomenal popularity of *Peanuts*. For in ad-

dition to being consistently well drawn and funny and entertaining, it is easy to see that this important "plus factor" is also there. Not only can we see it, but we know that Schulz intends for it to be there. "In a sense, anyone can learn to draw, but having something to say makes the difference," he says in regard to the strip's success. (pp. 15-16)

It is to Schulz's credit then that he has taken such a popular entertainment medium and raised it to the level of art. For everything we have a right to expect from art is there. Therefore, in considering *Peanuts* as a significant body of *art*, we should not be put off by the fact it remains hilariously funny and is enjoyed by almost everyone. This is exactly the same audience that Jesus wanted to attract— "everyone." Hence we have his parables, or "word-pictures," as the New Testament word for "parables" can be translated. The parables, then, in a very valid way, can be thought of as the cartoons of the Bible. And *Peanuts,* more than any other strip we know of, is "the Bible" among cartoons. There is little doubt that someday in the future, when we are browsing among the literary classics that have had wide appeal for young and old, literary scholars and pure pleasure seekers—titles such as *Moby Dick, Gulliver's Travels, Huckleberry Finn*—we shall also find *The Collected Cartoons of Charles Schulz*. (p. 17)

Schulz could hardly avoid preaching even if he should want to, given the basic recipe he has chosen for *Peanuts*: take a few small children; render them honestly in the way that children really think and act; put into their midst one small, "peculiar" dog; and stir this mixture into the framework of spare simplicity and high comedy. It seems to me that with these ingredients (the strip "is full of ingredients," as Linus says about a box of cocoa-mix) one will necessarily concoct a strip that not only will speak eloquently about man and his problem, but also a strip that at least will be highly suggestive of the *answer* to that problem. The hallmarks of *Peanuts* are its simplicity and its honesty about life; and these are precisely the hallmarks of the parables of Jesus. (p. 18)

[Schulz] says, "It's much better to be a good cartoonist than a terrible minister," But . . . he still considers himself a minister even though a cartoonist. . . . [He] recognizes that in working "for the secular press through a newspaper syndicate I must exercise care in the way I go about expressing things. I have a message that I want to present, but I would rather bend a little to put over a point than to have the whole strip dropped because it is too obvious." This then is his answer—to "bend a little," a *parabolic* expression of his faith. For this is literally what a parable is —a *bending*, a curved or roundabout or less than obvious way of getting to "a point." And this bending can constantly be seen in *Peanuts*. Both the parables of Jesus and the parables of *Peanuts*, to use [Dietrich] Bonhoeffer's famous phrase, "speak in a 'secular' way about God." (p. 21)

[Both] the parables of Peanuts and the parables of the New Testament are best not seen as *allegories*—that form of Art-Parable that attributes special significance to every last detail. Just as New Testament scholars can tell us "that most of the parables have each of them one main point and only one," it has also been observed that in *Peanuts* "each strip is usually a lesson, complete in itself." Also, allegories use a quite *consistent* symbolism; and this certainly is not always true of *Peanuts*. Although there are symbols that can be seen in the strip, Schulz is no slave to any intricately devised symbolic scheme that will solve all of the world's problems in a single cartoon. . . . Schulz has said that he believes his characters "should be as inconsistent as most of us unfortunately are." His characters are best seen then, I think, as a small repertory company of actors, the same type of company that Shakespeare wrote and acted for, in which "one man in his time plays many parts." Schulz has even compared himself to a "playwright" with a small "cast of characters"—a cast of characters who must frequently change roles, if on this tiny stage it is really possible to see "all the world." (pp. 43-4)

Schulz tells us that at one time early in his career he attempted to illustrate the entire Old Testament book of Ecclesiastes with cartoon figures, but later scrapped the effort as he "didn't know what to do with it." Nevertheless, the major themes of Ecclesiastes still constantly reappear in *Peanuts*. For instance, Ecclesiastes begins by lamenting the family of man's ancient "charter," from which there seems to be no escape and in which man seems to be beaten before he begins. In this sense no generation is different from any other: the "vanity" or hollowness of man's life is inherited from generation to generation in the same sense that men beget men and not angels. ("That's always been the trouble with our family," says Linus. "We have too much heredity.") . . . We break off and limit ourselves to the first chapter of Ecclesiastes, as Schulz—very much like Dante—could easily furnish us with tour guides who could help us to see the entire book as a sort of divine comedy.

One of the purposes of Art-Parable is, as Shakespeare could put it, "to hold the mirror up to nature." Schulz is a master in this regard, especially in holding the mirror up to *human* nature. This job is made easier for him by the fact that he deals exclusively with small children—and deals with them honestly. If one man is a microcosm, "a little world," a child is—in several ways—an even more clearly defined and concentrated microcosm. One of these ways is the clearer view we can obtain from children of the primitive, unadulterated evil in man. Evil is literally "unadulterated" in children as children lack the adult's sophisticated ability to mask and disguise evil. By "evil" we mean "sin." . . . In Art-Parable, . . . as well as in "real life," sin is most often dramatized by "sins." This is why, as [*Time* magazine] could say of Schulz, "There is no doubt that Schulz, a fervent Bible reader, is aware of original sin. He owns up to making his Peanuts mean because he believes that kids are born mean. But by making his characters cruel on occasion, he has also made them believable." Cruelty, like crabgrass, runs rampant throughout the *Peanuts* patch, so much so that there is no need to cite particular examples. Rather, it should be sufficient to say that in the Christian's view of things, including Schulz's, the games people play as children do not essentially change by the time they are adults. . . . (pp. 57-8, 60)

To say that it is possible to see the devil in the figure of the dreaded "Red Baron" should be "no wonder, for even Satan disguises himself as an angel of light" . . . , and "the Prince of Darkness *is* a gentleman," as Shakespeare can tell us—a gentleman traditionally symbolized in red. Also, it is quite obvious that for Snoopy at least, the Red Baron *does* represent the forces of evil in the world. For instance, in one cartoon, after getting shot down for the umpteenth time, Snoopy grimly makes his way back to his outfit, mut-

tering to himself, "Curse the Red Baron and his kind! Curse the wickedness in this world? Curse the evil that causes all this unhappiness!" But not only is Snoopy's *real antagonist* very much like the Christian's, but Snoopy is engaged in exactly the same *kind* of struggle "the church militant" is *engaged* in. . . . Snoopy's encounters with the Red Baron are comical for the same reason that the Christian is involved in a divine comedy: regardless of how narrowly perilous and difficult the situation becomes for both of them, we know they will always *finally* escape; the war in which they are fighting has *already* been fought and won: the final outcome is assured long before the individual skirmishes ever begin. Both Snoopy and the Christian may get shot down time after time; but we know, as they do, that "Someday I'll get you, Red Baron!" We know this because we know that "the Red Baron" has, in actual fact, already been *got*. "For our fight," just as Snoopy's, this little peanut-sized "hound of heaven" who persistently dogs the Red Baron, "is not against human foes, but against cosmic powers, against the authorities and potentates of this dark world, against the superhuman forces of evil in the heavens." . . . (pp. 155-57)

Schulz has frequently been asked why *Peanuts* does not "seem to deal with controversial issues . . . like war, or sex, or something similar," as one student so aptly put it. The answer to this question, of course, as Schulz indicated in his reply, is that *Peanuts* is more concerned with gospel than with law. The strip refuses to give us little homilies or moral lessons or rules to live by, but goes straight to the heart of the matter where *the* question and *the* answer lie. For example, Schulz cites "Charlie Brown's adulation of the little red-haired girl [which] touches upon the fact that there are some people—maybe all of us—who never really get to meet the little red-haired girl." *Peanuts*, then, like all real art, is a *metaphor* for the universal; it is more interested in the larger implications than the specifics. As Thoreau could say, "There are a thousand hacking at the branches of evil to one who is striking at the root." And, we believe, such a one is Schulz. For it is rare when we see the moralizing game played in *Peanuts*, whether in the social or religious or political fields. This is one comic strip that is really playing a deeper, far more crucial game than "right and wrong": it is concerned with the "game" of good and evil. For this reason, it is very easy to apply to Schulz the statement T. S. Eliot made of Baudelaire: "In . . . an age of bustle, programmes, platforms, scientific progress, humanitarianism and revolutions which improved nothing, an age of progressive degradation, [he] perceived that what really matters is Sin and Redemption." (pp. 228-29)

Charlie Brown, whose globe-like head the other kids enjoy ridiculing, is a zero, a sort of walking cipher, "a no one" (as he says). He is also "everyone"—the very world itself. For in this suffering little child of the world, we can also see the rest of the world, made "the victim of frustration" by the Creator. But he is even something more than this; because a circle is also a symbol for eternity. Charlie Brown's perfectly round head is also a built-in halo with the face of all mankind on it. In Charlie Brown, Schulz has done in cartoon form exactly what van Gogh wanted to do in his paintings: "In a picture I want to say something comforting, as music is comforting. I want to paint men and women with that something of the eternal which the halo used to symbolize, and which we seek to convey by the actual radiance and vibration of our coloring.'' (p. 293)

Schulz has probably best summed up his approach to the Bible by saying, ''Let the Bible speak to you!'' By this, we are sure that he does not mean to minimize the importance of historical criticism and biblical research, but that he does feel ''that intelligent and fruitful discussion of the Bible begins when the judgment as to its human, its historical and psychological character has been made and *put behind* us'' (Barth). (p. 295)

The world of *Peanuts* is a world of *sighs*, ''sighs too deep for words''—which is another way of saying that *Peanuts* is a world of prayer. (p. 314)

> *Robert L. Short, in his* The Parables of Peanuts *(copyright © 1968 by Robert L. Short; reprinted by permission of Harper & Row, Publishers, Inc.), Harper, 1968.*

JOHNNY HART

Since the very beginning, each era or generation has had its satirical cartoonist; one who stands above the others, points to what we have really become, and teaches us to laugh.

Our time has given us the best yet. He is Charles M. Schulz. . . . Charlie is a dear man who has taken it upon himself to make children of us all. Let us be eternally grateful for his foresight. We are God's children after all, and are meant to be no more than that. As a jealous child who loves to laugh, I sometimes . . . resent the laughs that God must surely enjoy at the expense of his clumsy, faltering children. He shares, of course, an equal amount of sorrow, which I do not wish to get into. Charlie Schulz does get into this. He gives us our pathetic side, and we laugh with dewy eyes. (pp. v-vi)

There are times when Charlie Brown and the red-headed girl cause me more tears than laughter. Not knowing whether to cry or laugh is, at its best, an exhilarating feeling. We've all felt it. The invariable result is laughter, which feels good.

Charlie Schulz is a man who not only knows the intricate parts of the funny bone, but proves his knowledge day by day. All things to Schulz contain the element of fun. You and I and the world can rest assured that the day cannot come when a herd of angry, pumpkin-headed kids trample Charlie Schulz. . . . (p. vi)

> *Johnny Hart, in his foreword to* PEANUTS TREASURY *by Charles M. Schulz (copyright © 1968 by United Feature Syndicate, Inc.), Holt, Rinehart and Winston, 1968.*

[The] fine examples of neoprimitive art [in *You're In Love, Charlie Brown*] are marred by running commentary with mythic overtones, exploiting the motif of *eros* and *agape,* but lacking penetration into the depths of human emotions. (p. 267)

> *The Antioch Review (copyright © 1969 by the Antioch Press; reprinted by permission of the Editors), Vol. 29, No. 2, 1969.*

JOHN TEBBEL

One of the most remarkable facts about [*Peanuts*] is the way its popularity cuts across every kind of classification.

People from very young children to the very old admire it, for all kinds of special reasons. Schroeder, the Beethoven-loving character who is usually seen playing the piano when he isn't playing baseball, appeals to people who had never heard of Beethoven before. The little tyrant Lucy is seen by the small fry as a deliciously contrary girl, and by some adults as the typically abrasive female in American life. Linus, with his security blanket, seems to speak to everyone who would like to have a blanket of his own in troubled times. And Snoopy, the beagle who has Van Goghs hanging in his doghouse and a World War I aviator's helmet on his head, is the kind of fantasy dog everyone would like to own. (p. 72)

In the hierarchy of immortal comic strips—*Blondie, Little Orphan Annie, Andy Gump, L'il Abner, Krazy Kat,*—Schulz has created something unique, more successful than all the others, but paradoxically more fragile. Perhaps it is because the strip is so personal that it elicits an unprecedented identification and affection from its vast readership. People don't take it literally, like *Little Orphan Annie,* whose characters are real people to some readers. Neither is its appeal pure fantasy shaped into barbed, slightly acid social satire, like *L'il Abner.* Nor is it a vehicle for the creator's political philosophy, as *Little Orphan Annie* was for Harold Gray.

Everyone sees something different, and something of himself, in Charlie Brown and his friends. He's everybody's boy. (p. 91)

> *John Tebbel, ''The Not-So Peanuts World of Charles M. Schulz, Part I: Happiness Is a Comic Strip,'' in* Saturday Review *(© 1969 by Saturday Review, Inc.; reprinted with permission), April 12, 1969, pp. 72-3, 90-1.*

CHARLES M. SCHULZ

During these twenty years, I have had the opportunity to observe what makes a good comic strip. I am convinced that the ones that have survived and maintained a high degree of quality are those which have a format that allows the creator room to express every idea that comes to him. . . .

[What] is funny in a comic strip today will not necessarily be funny the following week. A good example of this is the character of Snoopy. The mere fact that we could read Snoopy's thoughts was funny in itself when *Peanuts* first began. Now, of course, it is the content of those thoughts that is important, and as he progresses in his imagination to new personalities, some of the things which he originally did as an ordinary dog would no longer be funny. Snoopy's personality in the strip has to be watched very carefully, for it can get away from me. (p. 73)

[Children] see more than we think they do, but at the same time almost never seem to know what is going on. This is an interesting paradox, and one with which adults should try to acquaint themselves. . . . (p. 74)

> *Charles M. Schulz, ''The Not-So Peanuts World of Charles M. Schulz, Part II: But a Comic Strip Has to Grow,'' in* Saturday Review *(© 1969 by Saturday Review, Inc.; reprinted with permission), April 12, 1969, pp.73-4.*

CLARENCE PETERSEN

[*Snoopy and the Red Baron*] was Schulz's first full-length

cartoon adventure and, as the publisher describes it, "In the tradition of the great war novels, it is an odyssey of love, guts, and tears." In case you don't read the comics, Snoopy is Charlie Brown's hound dog, and the life he leads would do credit to Walter Mitty. In his most persistent fantasy Snoopy is a World War I air ace, and his doghouse is the Sopwith Camel in which he ventures at dawn into the wild blue yonder to do battle with the butcher of the skies, Baron von Richtofen. Ridiculous? Don't be silly! Think of it—Snoopy under anti-aircraft fire over France; Snoopy smiling coldly in the shadow of the familiar Fokker Triplane; Snoopy piercing the skies with a defiant cry of "Nyahh, Nyaah, Nyaah, Red Baron!"; Snoopy plummeting to earth; Snoopy making his way across barbed wire through enemy lines to safety; Snoopy, secure at last back in headquarters and already dreaming of the next epic dogfight: "Someday I'll get you, Red Baron!" This is what war and heroism are all about, friends. This is what Dos Passos and Hemingway and Republic Pictures were trying to tell us all along. (p. 13)

Clarence Petersen, in Book World—Chicago Tribune *(© 1969 Postrib Corp.), August 10, 1969.*

MICHAEL RUBY

"Peanuts" [is] the evocative, touching and wise comic strip that has quietly become an American institution. As unpretentious as Schulz himself, the strip has restored to use idioms of a simpler day: "Good grief," "Rats!" and "You blockhead." It has invented the cult of the Great Pumpkin, and the concept of the Failure Face. It has given the world a dozen definitions of happiness and a store of homespun philosophical reflections. . . . It has expressed what may be the quintessential American lament: "How can we lose when we're so sincere?" . . .

The magic begins with the characters, an appealing lot whose foibles, anxieties and frustrations make a human comedy that hovers always on the lip of despair. (p. 40)

[Throughout the years] the strip itself has changed in subtle ways—the features are sharper now, the dialogue more sophisticated, the heads larger in relation to the bodies. . . . Schulz's dialogue has always carried his strips, and lately he has moved steadily away from straight gags and trick humor, the kind invariably revealed in the last panel. "I want to get the humor from the personalities of the characters, to get people to know them. . . . It's a mistake to try to please all the readers every day. It's unreasonable to think someone should be able to pick up the paper for the first time and enjoy Peanuts. We have to tease the reader along from day to day." (pp. 42-3)

Michael Ruby, "Good Grief, $150 Million!" in Newsweek *(copyright 1971 by Newsweek, Inc.; all rights reserved; reprinted by permission), December 27, 1971, pp. 40-4.*

REINHOLD REITBERGER and WOLFGANG FUCHS

That Charles M. Schulz, the creator of *Peanuts,* is a lay preacher in the 'Church of God', a conservative, biblically orientated Protestant sect, is today common knowledge; and books like *The Gospel According to Peanuts* and *The Parables of Peanuts,* both by Robert L. Short [see excerpts above] have made it clear that Peanuts has a metaphysical background. Short's biblical paraphrase of the human condition is illustrated by sequences from *Peanuts* and it is evident that Schulz, in his own way, gives a much clearer picture of humanity's malaise than Short's often cited favourite authors Kierkegaard, Barth and Tillich. (p. 54)

The Peanuts children have aged only about two or three years since 1950, but spiritually they have undergone much greater changes. Right at the beginning Charlie Brown and his friends acted like any other normal children. Sally liked Charlie better than Shermy and even quarrelled with Violet, who insisted she loved him even more.

Those were happy days for Charlie Brown; but soon his balloon-shaped head became a target for malicious personal remarks, and whilst the other kids developed more and more odd traits and even phobias, which they paraded quite openly, Charlie Brown remained normal and human and consequently became the outsider. The time of childish innocence had passed. Schulz is always at his best when he portrays the inability of the naïvely simple and humane Charlie Brown to integrate into the community, in contrast to all the other Peanuts characters who find no difficulty in doing so. He shows how society attaches a stigma to the lone wolf, the individualist who wishes to remain himself. . . . Lucy and the other Peanuts, integrated conformists, slaughter Charlie Brown emotionally and the latter's inability to defend himself stems from the fact that he is a vulnerable character, quite untypical for this day and age. . . . Charlie Brown is not as intellectual as his interpreters: he does not indulge in vast metaphysical questioning or deep theological suffering, for he simply wants to be a human being.

Charlie Brown elicits the admiration of the reader because he refuses to take refuge in neurosis. (pp. 54-5)

Charlie Brown does not want to be alone; his efforts at integration, doomed to failure because of his separateness, are mute demonstrations of John Donne's 'no man is an island' thesis. . . . When will Schulz, his creator, let a little sunshine into his life? When will Charlie's unrequited love for the little red-haired girl be returned—at least to the degree of allowing him to eat his sandwiches in her company during recreation time?

Schulz reflects the literary tendencies of the day most accurately in *Peanuts.* In the fifties it was psychoanalysis (Lucy); in the sixties Charlie Brown showed traits of Herzog, the title hero of a psychological-philosophical novel by Saul Bellow . . . , and the inclination towards pure fantasy which followed equally paralleled the literary scene.

Charlie Brown is another fall guy with whom everyone can identify. He is the son of a hairdresser (like Charles M. Schulz) and dreams, like all American children, of becoming a baseball hero, perhaps even President of the USA. The other Peanuts, adjusting and conforming to society, have an easier time ahead of them; they will not find it so difficult to accept their stereotyped roles in the adult world of American suburbia. They have already chosen their spiritual crutches. . . .

The beagle hound Snoopy . . . gradually pushed himself into the foreground until he became the centre of attraction and the main character of the strip. (p. 55)

In the beginning Snoopy's main interest was food and apart from a few minor attacks of claustrophobia whilst lost in high grass, he acted natural; but after a while he began to outgrow his dogginess. . . .

A Walter Mitty of the canine world, Snoopy dreamed himself into all sorts of situations. He imitated vultures, gorillas, dinosaurs and became a real menace as 'The Mad Punter'. (p. 56)

Snoopy's imagination soon ran amuck, dream and reality became indistinguishable. He developed a weakness for the air aces of the first World War. . . .

But the charm of *Peanuts* does not depend on the daydreams of Walter Mitty Snoopy, it lies in the metaphysical content: the whole point of Snoopy's activities as author, ice hockey player, or 'world-famous check-out man in a grocery store' lies in the fact that—in appearance at least—he is a dog, and this is neither funny nor ludicrous in the long run, but becomes a symbolic formula. Charles Schulz has shown however, that he wants to get back to his old formula, to the type of content which will make him immortal in the world of comics. (p. 57)

> *Reinhold Reitberger and Wolfgang Fuchs, in their* Comics: Anatomy of a Mass Medium, *translated by Nadia Fowler (translation copyright © 1972 by Studio Vista Publishers; reprinted by permission of Little, Brown and Co.), Little, Brown, 1972.*

ROBERT G. MINER, JR.

Without even venturing into the possibilities [the *"Snoopy Come Home" Movie Book*] suggests—among them the cliché that this is a post-literary generation—I can't help feeling that the "Movie Book" may herald a new trend. Instead of the book-to-movie progression of the past decades, TV, ironically enough, may have made the moving picture commonplace for today's children and the moving word intriguingly new. Schultz's book is graced with the laconic humor and pointed jabs of pure feeling that already have made Peanuts a staple for adults of all ages. The book also offers some startling double-page illustrations that share, in their unconventional focus and perspective, some of the unnerving aptness of perception about small people's relationship to the full-size world that marks the work of all great writers of children's literature. (pp. 219-20)

> *Robert G. Miner, Jr., in* Children's Literature: Annual of The Modern Language Association Seminar on Children's Literature and The Children's Literature Association, *Vol. 2, edited by Francelia Butler (© 1972 by Francelia Butler; all rights reserved), Temple University Press, 1973.*

ARTHUR ASA BERGER

Charles Schulz, the creator of *Peanuts*, is a rather shy person who personifies the American Dream. (p. 181)

Peanuts is now so ubiquitous that it is literally part of the fabric of modern American society, and Schulz is the spokesman for millions of mute Americans. (p. 182)

Because the comic strip does not have much status as an art form, and because the characters in *Peanuts* are little children and a dog, we tend to underestimate Schulz's achievement, even though almost everybody admires his work. *I believe that Schulz is one of the greatest humorists of the twentieth century.* . . . [He] has developed a distinctive style of art work, an incredible assortment of characters, and a positively amazing command of the techniques of humor.

His *ouvrage* is monumental. And though his earlier work was not particularly exceptional, he has developed his talent to an extraordinary level over the years. We find his work all about us. . . . The strip is also popular abroad—some hundred million people read it daily—though I believe it is essentially American in its spirit.

We enjoy *Peanuts* because it is extremely funny. Schulz mixes graphic, verbal, and ideational humor in a genuinely inventive manner. He is a master of representing expressions in his characters. His characters tend to be monomaniacs who pursue their destinies with all the zany abandon of divinely inspired zealots. We seldom see them this way, however, because we have been taught to regard children (and dogs) as innocent and mildly amusing.

Schulz does not accept this notion; he portrays children in all their Augustinian corruptness. The characters in *Peanuts* exist after the fall of man from the Garden of Eden. They are corrupted by original sin and therefore can be selfish egoists without any strain on our credulity.

There are no adults in the strip; there are no authority figures, though Lucy, by virtue of her domineering personality and ready resort to fisticuffs, is probably the locus of power for all practical purposes. The strip is a fascinating study in anarchy. Without any central organizing power to set limits and establish boundaries, we find a collection of self-important petty sovereigns—or perhaps petty tyrants. A peanut is an "insignificant or tiny person," and Schulz's characters are in reality peanuts in both senses of the word. As far as their self-image is concerned, however, they are giants.

They are also lovable. Guilt does not make people nasty or hateful. (pp. 182-83)

The love in *Peanuts* is based upon understanding, not illusion; Schulz is a supreme realist. One of the strip's charms is that it openly acknowledges pride and stupidity and gullibility and all the other evil qualities (or nasty ones) in man, and still is able to be accepting. Somehow we all feel that Schulz accepts man for what he is, not what he claims to be. Schulz relieves us of the awesome burden of innocence, and we are all grateful.

Schulz's characters are only innocent in the sense they are asexual and pregenital; they have all the vices of adults in every other aspect. They are subject to passions, susceptible to whims, motivated by greed or love, and they never learn. Lucy pursues Schroeder relentlessly, never understanding (or admitting to herself) that he does not particularly like her. Linus is insecure, and an emotional cripple without his blanket. Charlie Brown is continually suffering ignominious defeats on the baseball diamond and is victimized by people who take advantage of his trusting nature.

Since the characters are children (and animals), we are not offended by the light they throw on our vices. Naive commentators have long been used as a literary device by humorists to point out our shortcomings. Huck Finn is a case in point. But Twain's humor has a savage intensity, founded on a sense of moral outrage that we do not find in Schulz, whose satire is infinitely more gentle and genial. Schulz deals with a wider perspective and operates at a higher level of abstraction.

Peanuts is a commentary on the human condition, from the perspective of a person who understands human nature and man's invincible ignorance and propensity toward folly. The comic strip format does not easily lend itself to the more biting satire of Twain or Swift, but it does lend itself to satire and social commentary, and Schulz is probably the king of popular psychologists and lighthearted critics of man in America. (pp. 184-85)

An important element behind humor—an insight we get from Freud and psychoanalysis—is that it serves to mask aggression. The energy that we expend laughing at the ridiculous releases pent-up hostilities. Under the guise of wit, Schulz says things we would rather not hear. He does this by defining things in an amusing way. "Happiness," he tells us, "is a warm puppy"; or "happiness is feeling the wind and rain in your hair." These definitions, which have a folksy quality to them, are really like proverbs—and Schulz is following a long line of humorists in America from Benjamin Franklin on, who cloaked their moralizing in witty phrases and comic maxims. Humor is implicitly social, and we must expect a certain amount of moralizing from our humorists. Proverbs, really, are moral directives. Schulz disguises this ethical element in his work so beautifully that we seldom see it.

Snoopy, from atop his doghouse, is very much a commentator from a mock-pulpit, calling man to see his errors and return to the straight and narrow path. . . . There is something about being on doghouses, pulpits or even soapboxes that brings out the moralist in man—and dogs like Snoopy.

Schulz is a mirthful moralist; he continues to point out our frailties and calls upon us to lead the good life. His particular instrument is his comic genius and the remarkable collection of many characters he has created in his strip. He does not sentimentalize childhood, and perhaps goes a step or two in the opposite direction at times, but then childhood is a period with many bitter and painful experiences.

Peanuts does a number of things for us. It points out, by implication, the danger of a society full of egoists who pursue their particular passions; it offers us little homilies and morality plays to help us maintain our righteousness; it offers us insights into the many frailties of man and human nature; and it enables us to release our aggressions by having a remarkable assortment of comic characters and fools for us to laugh at. It is no wonder that the strip is so popular with adults, for it is very reassuring. (pp. 186-87)

Peanuts is full of inversions. We find children who act like adults, dogs who act like humans, and a comic strip which deals with many of the profundities of life and does not sentimentalize children. Inversion is also central to the pastoral, and I believe we must understand *Peanuts* as a kind of pastoral. When we think of the pastoral, we usually imagine shepherds and maidens frolicking on the grass. But in its modern manifestations we can interpret the pastoral as a device which uses inversion and puts the complex into the simple. Schulz's children act like adults in a society where adults often act like children.

There is a certain abstract quality to the strip. The characters do not seem to live in society, *per se*—though society is intimated in the form of schools and psychiatrists and holidays. Much of the action takes place beyond society in a state of nature, with modern shepherds and shepherdesses playing out their roles. (pp. 187, 190)

Schulz's genius . . . is in finding ways of manipulating his stock characters so that unexpected resolutions occur or that the resolutions that we anticipate do not occur. (p. 191)

By all odds the greatest of Schulz's characters, and the one he relies most upon, is Snoopy. Snoopy is . . . one of the greatest manifestations of the talking animal convention. Not only does he talk, but he has a brilliant personality—he carries on human relationships, he is a *bon vivant,* he participates in history, he has an incredible imagination, he is witty, he expresses himself with virtuosity in any number of ways (eye movements, ear movements, tail movements, wisecracks, facial expressions), and he is superb as mimic and dancer. He has energy and spirit and a heart overflowing with kindness, though he has been known to boot a bird or two, or snatch a blanket.

There is, in fact, an existential dimension to Snoopy. He is an existential hero in every sense of the term. He strives, with dogged persistence and unyielding courage, to overcome what seems to be his fate—that he is a dog; that he is *just* a dog. And somehow he does it! I think we see Snoopy as a "person" who happens to be a dog, rather than a dog who happens to become a person. . . . (p. 192)

What Snoopy demonstrates, to all his readers, is that ultimately we are all free to create ourselves as we wish, no matter what our status on the Great Chain of Being might be. We can all be authentic if only we will have the courage *to* be what we can be. And this applies even to dogs.

Snoopy is an animal who has transcended his limitations, though he still has some. How curious that in a society characterized . . . by a growing sense of alienation and apathy, a dog in a comic strip is just bursting with *joie de vivre,* vitality, and hope. Perhaps we have reached the stage in which we live vicariously through Snoopy. . . . (pp. 192-93)

This is somewhat farfetched, but there is little question in my mind that one of the reasons for the popularity of *Peanuts* is that it helps assuage our hunger for *personality* in a world that is full of dehumanizing forces and in which identity is so much under attack. Snoopy shows that man's spirit has resiliency and that there is hope yet.

Schulz has said that his greatest ambition is to create a comic strip as good as *Krazy Kat,* probably the greatest comic strip produced to date. There is little question, I think, that he has come close to this goal. Schulz has transformed a comic strip into part of the very essence of American life. Charlie Brown and Linus and Snoopy and their cohorts are not just comic strip characters; they have long since transcended their roles and now are part of the galaxy of great comic creations, in any form of popular art. His characters have become legends in their own comic strip lifetimes. (p. 193)

> Arthur Asa Berger, "Peanuts: The Americaniza-
> tion of Augustine," in his The Comic-Stripped
> American (copyright © 1973 by Arthur Asa Ber-
> ger), Walker and Company, 1973, pp. 181-90.

SHERWIN D. SMITH

["Peanuts" is the] General Motors of comic strips, it sometimes seems. The latest count was 44 in print, not all of them by any means proper reprints of newspaper strips. At their best, they're very, very good—a mixture of pop philosophy and fantasy. At other times, they go icky-commercial. (p. 27)

Sherwin D. Smith, in The New York Times Book
Review (© *1974 by The New York Times Company; reprinted by permission), June 9, 1974.*

PAUL ENGLE

It should have been expected that Peppermint Patty would
kick the national holiday around [in "A Charlie Brown
Thanksgiving"], and that Marcie and Franklin would find a
fresh way of celebrating the traditional event. Their faces
are precise, highly individual and their remarks full of wit
and irony. Imagine—the real Thanksgiving comes in out of
the comic page, which may say something very authentic
about the U.S.A. right now, when there is so much for
which the country really can't give thanks. (p. 27)

Paul Engle, in The New York Times Book Review (© *1974 by The New York Times Company;
reprinted by permission), November 3, 1974.*

JOHN SEELYE

That Snoopy! If recollection serves, Charlie Brown's dog
began where Dagwood's Daisy left off, a silent, even passive witness to human folly, occasionally giving off a
bubble of gassid comment. He was a generic descendant of
Buster Brown's Tige, that fabulous canine who smiled with
human teeth, and both were variations on a traditional
genre touch, the Boy and his Dawg. But, in time, as the
Peanuts gallery expanded to include more unlikely children, increasing our suspicion that they are actually midgets, Snoopy took on a larger and more complex role, until,
as [*The Snoopy Festival*] reveals, he has become a little
dogpersonality, walking, very nearly talking, even sitting at
table and enjoying an occasional root beer. Once a distinctly minor character, at times he now threatens to take
over the strip.

Such are the joys and dangers of serial literature, as
Shakespeare (Falstaff), Fenimore Cooper (Leather-
stocking) and Mark Twain (Huckleberry Finn) discovered.
But when anthropomorphics are the subject, then we are in
the world of Mickey Mouse, where some interesting analogies to *Peanuts* hold. . . . Starting out as a raffish, vulgar,
often violent manifestation of id, Mickey ended up as a
stolid, middle-class citizen, complete with hat, business suit
and pointed-toe shoes, becoming at last the equivalent of
Walt himself, a sort of middle-mouse, more a manager than
an actor in the company.

Snoopy provides the Dionysian element, the free-floating
shadow for a thoroughly Freudened Jung *Mensch*. Charlie
Brown is not a *Mittel*—but an *Untermensch;* though he
shares Mickey's mantle as a member of the managerial
class, he can't ever get his crazy team to play ball. A
mousey Durocher, he is the eternal victim of plots, jibes,
sneers, a *Schlemiel* Hamlet. . . . As Schulz grew rich and
famous among the apple-cheeked masses, Snoopy grew
rampant, his masquerade more varied, giving the collective
id of *Peanuts* a wider and wider range of identities to match
the aggregate ego of Charlie and his team, until he now
threatens to become *Überhund,* top if not super dog. (p. 27)

As family dog he has become top banana (nose), the Mister
Peanut of them all. From a *bona fide* cartoon Fido, li-
censed to give off occasional indigestive comments, Snoopy
has become a veritable repertory company of exchangeable
personae, from a World War I pilot of a Sopwith Camel to
Joe Cool, campus cutout. . . . More important he is given

loose leash, granted the freedom to go on those kinds of
quests traditionally associated with the *Bildungsroman*
qualities of the American novel: the return home again, the
search for a parent, the voyage into the great unknown,
etc., a *Steppenhund,* a *Wilhelm* in search of his *Meister.* As
if to emphasize his literaryness, Snoopy has recently become a would-be author, but as *auteur* he is still his own
best creation, and his favorite role remains that William
Faulknerian projection of wish fulfillment, the flying cava-
lier engaged in an endless, invisible dogfight with the Red
Baron, his humble doghouse the vehicle of perilous flights
of fancy.

Schulz has in effect miniaturized the cast of the Thurber
carnival in his *Snoopy Festival,* his battle of the sexes being
an infinite number of triste-go-rounds between his beleaguered little boys and a growing legion of threatening, sexless mini-Amazons. Lucy shares with the Thurber woman a
helmet of clotted hair and a swift punch to the polar sexes,
and more often than not gets her comeuppance, the agent of
same being not Charlie Brown but Snoopy, a dreamy
beagle clearly descended from those amorphous dogs of
Thurber's wild imagination. If Charlie Brown and the
Thurber male owe something to Webster's Milquetoast,
then Snoopy is a dogged derivation from that singular
Thurber male, Walter Mitty, even if his flying doghouse
does not make funny noises. He has increasingly become
the dog that walks on two feet, a comic strip equivalent, not
of Disney's animated pups, but a gentled-down re-creation
of the dogs of Jack London and James Oliver Curwood.
(pp. 27-8)

John Seelye, in The New Republic *(reprinted by
permission of* The New Republic; © *1974 by The
New Republic, Inc.), December 7, 1974.*

RICHARD R. LINGEMAN

[Everybody] likes Peanuts, and that is as much a tribute to
Mr. Schulz's Lilliputian genius as it is to his avoidance of
controversy. The Peanuts children precociously know that
life can be lousy and their popularity from the late fifties on
may be due to their reflecting a secret, self-doubting, self-
questioning mood abroad in the nation: Charlie Brown is
everybody's loser because everybody is a loser much of the
time. Peanuts offers a gentle philosophy of human relations, of stoically coping with existence, that is the underside of the preachments of those eupeptic middle-class yea-
sayers from Norman Vincent Peale to "How to Be Your
Own Best Friend." (p. 7)

Richard R. Lingeman, in The New York Times
Book Review (© *1975 by The New York Times
Company; reprinted by permission), December 7,
1975.*

JOHN JACOBUS

[For] the true *Peanuts* fan, accustomed to the more func-
tionally proportioned soft-cover collections, the giant *Peanuts Jubilee* is a bit much. However, its creator, Charles
Schulz, in his modestly phrased text, lets us know that,
one, he doesn't much care for the title "Peanuts," wished
upon his strip by syndicate biggies; and, two, he dislikes
the strip's small format—so, bigness may be important for
Schulz.

Peanuts graphics are in the classic American cartoon tradition, to which the Disney atelier contributed not only its

Parthenon frieze but its Arch of Constantine as well. This simple, laconic manner, a world removed from the late-'30s baroque of Alex Raymond and Milton Caniff . . . , was not drawn into the mainstream of American visual culture through the instrument of High Pop Art. *Peanuts,* like Disney, is too much the creation of our heartland; its fantasies are domestic, excluding the foreign or exotic and abjuring any ventures in space or time. . . .

Peanuts is something of a pastoral fantasy. Like Disney, it reaches back into early-20th-century small-town America where people walked or took the bus. There was no busing to school. They walked, and this established many of the situations. If Disney's strips are today admired in the backwash of '30s nostalgia . . . he is now more remembered for that little-understood genre known as the family film, and, above everything else, for Disneyland and Disneyworld. . . . Schulz, a neo-classic in his art, has not reached so far, has not sought to be so encyclopedic and seems (in spite of the size of *Peanuts Jubilee*) to have none of the classic Disney megalomania.

Smallness and conciseness are virtues in Schulz's work, and perhaps it is just as well that circumstances have forced him to create in restricted format. His best work is in the daily strip; typically four panels for which he early found the perfect episode structure. Apparently the working method is to find the climactic situation or epigram for the last panel and then construct backwards. . . . Schulz has been attracted recently to continuous, strip-to-strip narrative but only when he has been able to work it into his established style, so that each concise episode, as well as advancing the plot, also stands by itself as a discrete thing. The larger Sunday features, in color have been more of a challenge, as Schulz himself points out. Some esthetes, like myself, would argue that his daily black-and-white strips are the place to look for his greatest work, but I am sure that all children and most adults find much more pleasure in the Sunday color episodes. In either format the images gain an almost Egyptian rhythm through repetition and a sense of relatedness across the vertical bars dividing the panels. (p. 29)

Simplicity is a virtue in the eye of the critics, not of the public. Yet we can revel, one and all, in the familiar simplicity of the settings and props of *Peanuts:* a tree, the television set . . . , the old-fashioned school desk, even the bench and fence at the ballpark. . . .

Snoopy's home has become the preferred setting, and the guises and disguises of its occupant, this Woody Allenish beagle, have come to dominate the strip in recent years. . . . [It] is Snoopy's adventures that are the most innovative, forming the leading edge of the strip. . . . More recently, Snoopy has turned to literary dreams, providing Schulz a vehicle for punning and name-twisting. This adds another dimension to the otherwise conventional conceit of the strip, which is based upon the idea of little people, a modest and innocent device which has now grown to mythic proportions. . . .

[*Peanuts Jubilee*] is interesting and quite revealing. . . . But the trouble with the books is that it is simply not a sufficiently thorough anthology of *Peanuts* themes and episodes over the years. . . . It is of course useful to have the chronological survey, but this is a bit thin for the first decade and a half; indeed, much of the earliest work does not hold up

too well, either in subject or graphically. It took two or three years for Schulz to get the strip moving and to sharpen his line, to give it the right edge of gentle caricature. . . . The remarkable thing about *Peanuts* is its continual growth, the careful addition of characters and the stretching out of the themes that fans can respond to with recognition, as in the repetitions of pop music. Anticipation and surprise are used gingerly and with consummate understanding of the needs of this art form. (p. 31)

Basic and more encyclopedic—indeed, as comprehensive as could be wished for—is *The Snoopy Festival:* probably every Snoopy episode down to about a year ago. Given the ever-growing importance of this character in the *Peanuts* hierachy, this may be the most important volume yet published. (p. 33)

> *John Jacobus, in* Art in America *(copyright © 1976 by Art in America, Inc.), March-April, 1976.*

ALASTAIR FOWLER

[Charles Schulz's] autobiographical memoir *Peanuts Jubilee* reads almost like a story, a myth of middle America. However modestly told, it must be a great success story. . . .

The memoir gives the real-life origin of many Peanuts events and characters. But this is a little deceptive: Mr Schulz often divulges less than he seems to.

He would have us think of him as the real Charlie Brown, a loser, stimulated to creativity by failures or disappointments in love. But if Charlie Brown ever wrote a comic strip, it would not be successful like Peanuts: it would be an international flop. Mr Schulz, we feel, must have something in him of Schroeder and Lucy—to say nothing of that typewriter ace Snoopy. . . .

[The technical accounts of Mr Schulz's art] are not exactly secrets. About his own development away from gag cartooning, he is interesting but more reserved. . . . What is one to make of the cubist faces in Li'l Folks, or Snoopy's two right (seldom two left) eyes? Such matters are presented as technical problems. Thus, Mr Schulz abandoned the brush because his characters needed a tighter line; and he abandoned cats because he could not do them very well (a just appraisal, as a glance at *We're Right Behind You, Charlie Brown* will show).

Much—perhaps too much—of the Peanuts iconography is attributed to trivial causes. "It would be difficult to draw some of these characters from different angles." The front-view pose of Linus is obligatory because from the side his arm would be too short for thumbsucking. Schroeder, however, would be difficult from front. It is possible that Mr Schulz really sees it all in this reductive way: "Cartooning, after all, is simply good design." But he must know that while his own draughtsmanship is limited (at best unnoticeable, like the transparent literary style of some great novelist), his cartooning has more value than that of better draughtsmen. . . .

Two principles of Mr Schulz's art emerge. First, realism. He either treats familiar subjects (behind Schroeder's gratuitous information lies much reading of Beethoven biography); or else he gets subjects up to find out what is "authentic", that is, ordinary. . . . In one mood, Mr Schulz pursues statistical realism. Hence our characteristic response is one of recognition: Peanuts is just like the real thing. . . . People long to inhabit the humane, egalitarian Peanuts idyll.

The more subtle principle of variety . . . alternates probable and fantastic stories, and assigns them to a cast of diverse characters. When Snoopy threatens to take over the feature —he affects not to remember the name of "that round-headed kid"—the principle of compensating variations restores him to proportion. Mr Schulz's art is firmly classical. More abstractedly, the same principle governs the alternation of daily episodes and extended stories. The latter are too long for *Peanuts Jubilee;* which is a pity. . . .

The long stories are not planned ahead, but allowed to develop spontaneously. This daily encounter with the blank page could be construed as a form of self-interrogation, issuing in expressions of the various Peanuts archetypes. Such terms may seem disproportionate to a comic strip. But Mr Schulz himself more than once speaks of cartooning in connection with depressive phases, dreams, and curious mental states whose "examination" actually produces the past for self-analysis. Mythology, emblems, even witty epigraphs have provided interfaces with wisdom. And today, for some who lack a good ten-cent psychiatrist, the equivalent may well be Peanuts.

Theological allegorizing threatens to take over Peanuts criticism, and Mr Schulz tries . . . to put it in perspective. . . . This is not to deny that Peanuts introduces theological ideas . . . , or uses the Scriptures "in a gentle manner". But Mr Schulz prefers to leave discussion of such matters "for a time when you can look the other person directly in the eye". The dark glass of print distorts. This is almost too well judged for simplicity. . . . Mr Schulz claims not to have realized the subject he had touched on; and is careful to observe that people on both sides approved (and disapproved) of the strip. Before marvelling at his obliviousness: observe the real "point" of the strip: "that people all too frequently discuss things that they know little about." Charlie Brown's face, again, is round and ordinary because he represents Everyman.

Alastair Fowler, "The Round Face of Everyman," in The Times Literary Supplement (© *Times Newspapers Ltd. (London) 1976; reproduced from* The Times Literary Supplement *by permission), December 3, 1976, p. 1508.*

BENNY GREEN

For some time now I have been mystified by the sheer extent of the *Peanuts* trend. That the average casual reader is a schoolboy I have always realised. . . . But the discovery that he is not a schoolboy after all but a child comes as a bit of a smack on the face, especially as it seems to me that the Peanuts cartoons disappeared, aesthetically speaking, a long time ago down the chasm which separates adult sensibility from infant sentimentality. . . .

[The] draughtsmanship . . . is, of course, where Schulz scores. It appears that his line, his proportions, and his sense of colour convey something to small children which reminds them of the way they see the world. The captions, on the other hand, please those adults whose arch explorations into what they think they remember childhood ought to have been leads them into all manner of critical excesses. . . . The *Peanuts Jubilee* book is beautifully produced . . . , and is for children of all ages who can't read. (p. 25)

Benny Green, in The Spectator (© *1976 by* The Spectator; *reprinted by permission of* The Spectator), *December 11, 1976.*

JOYCE SWARTNEY

[*Charlie Brown's Second Super Book of Questions and Answers: About the Earth and Space . . . From Plants to Planets!*] will answer questions such as where do the stars go in the daytime and what is a tornado. The answers are written in a manner understandable to children and adults. Frequently the questions are interspersed with color-coded squares containing interesting facts. . . . Some of the illustrations appear to be copies of daily "Peanuts" comic strips, while others seem to have been prepared for this publication. They are chosen with care and often support the text as well as amuse the reader. The content is accurate and instructional, but the sections on Earth, weather and climate, and on the stars and planets are more interesting than those on plants and on space travel. This book is appropriate for a wide range of readers, including parents of inquisitive children. (p. 110)

Joyce Swartney, in Science Books & Films (*copyright 1978 by the American Association for the Advancement of Science), Vol. XIV, No. 2 (September, 1978).*

JEAN MARIE HIESBERGER and PAT McLAUGHLIN

A major problem with *What A Nightmare, Charlie Brown* by Charles M. Schulz is that the format and illustrations suggest it was written for young children. The familiar and popular Snoopy and Charlie Brown are presented in full color, comic strip style. The small quantity of text does not form a cohesive or credible story. Basically, the "plot" concerns Snoopy's nightmare encounter with frightening monsters and terrifying dogs in Alaska following his overindulgence of pizza. The monsters in this book are consistently vicious and realistic and Snoopy only manages to save himself from them by magically becoming more vicious than they are. The whole thing seems purposeless, confusing, and somewhat frightening for small children. (p. 92)

Jean Marie Hiesberger and Pat McLaughlin, in New Catholic World, *March/April, 1979.*

Patti Smith

1946-

American songwriter, poet, playwright, and journalist. Smith's works have synthesized the influences of French and American literary figures of the nineteenth and twentieth centuries and rock musicians of the sixties into reflections of her own unique fantasies and visions. Her mergings of passionate stream-of-consciousness lyrics with rock and reggae rhythms, coupled with an exciting delivery in concert, have helped to move the image of the contemporary poet away from an ivory-tower stereotype. She uses powerful imagery in her poetry and song lyrics to frame subjects of violence, anarchy, and eroticism. She can, however, be delicate and sensitive, and often colors her work with religious themes and allusions, as with "Easter," which is based on the first communion of her greatest influence, French Symbolist poet Arthur Rimbaud. It is this combination of rawness and tenderness that defines her art and seems to give Smith her greatest appeal. One of her major themes is that of artist as outcast, and she sees her own life as following that tradition. Smith moved to New York in 1967 after dropping out of teacher's college and working in a New Jersey toy factory, which served as the stimulus for her first song, "Piss Factory." She developed a legendary reputation as an unconventional journalist and started writing verses and plays in 1970. She coauthored the play "Cowboy Mouth" with Sam Shepard and began to give readings of her poetry in churches and small clubs, accompanied by rock critic Lenny Kaye on guitar. In 1974 she formed the Patti Smith Group and started setting her poems to music. One of the first performers to appear at New York club CBGB, a spawning-ground for New Wave talent, Smith achieved underground notoriety and cult status for her improvisatory lyrics, intense performances, and tough, cool style. Her work has been criticized for its shapelessness and lack of discipline, especially for the song "Radio Ethiopia," a torrent of words and feedback. She has also been considered pretentious and unoriginal for her conscious emulation of Rimbaud, Bob Dylan, William Burroughs, Mick Jagger, and others, and has been called sexually ambiguous for often writing her poetry from the male viewpoint. Smith has recently become commercially successful with "Because the Night," on which she collaborated with Bruce Springsteen. Her obvious pleasure in this achievement has been criticized, with both fans and critics expressing the fear that this success signals her movement away from her punk roots. However, Smith speaks directly to her young adult audience, and has said that she cares only about their agreement with what she says. She seems to understand their alienation from society and desire for freedom, and delivers her messages with sincerity.

TONY GLOVER

The four plays in [*Mad Dog Blues and Other Plays*] all tend to be basic (most with little scenery), and full of street talk and rock-and-roll images. . . .

[The] main reason I got the book is for the second play, "Cowboy Mouth" [which Sam Shepard] co-authored with Patti Smith, who is one of the greatest poets writing in English. (Probably other languages too, but English is all I got covered right now.) The play is heavily auto-biographical; the two characters, Slim the Coyote and Cavale the Crow were played onstage by Shepard and Smith. The premise is basic, and bizarre enough to be real; Cavale has kidnapped Slim from his wife and kid at gunpoint—she wants to make him a rock and roll star. Slim is torn between leaving and embracing her fantasy. The action takes place in Cavale's room. . . . In the room and their minds they run through all the changes of demon-doomed lovers; they tell each other stories, they play coyote and crow, they curse each other out, they howl at the moon, they collapse from exhaustion. Each author wrote their own character's speeches, and a rough and ragged poetry spurts out. . . .

Words in this play are more than words, they're vehicles for lots of emotion. The whole man-woman thing is dug into, overlaid and under-cut by all the sounds out the window that affect every bedroom, no matter how the air is conditioned. . . .

Try this one out—and keep an eye out for future works by Patti Smith. . . . (p. 57)

Tony Glover, in Creem *(© copyright 1972 by Creem Magazine, Inc.), June, 1972.*

TONY GLOVER

[There's] a new kind of poetry being made—a poetry that exists in equal partnership with the rhythm and sound of music, poetry that needs performing to make it real.

A few poets have realized this to some extent, and there are more and more readings—but Patti Smith, New Jersey swamp child and angel-envisioning rock-and-roll street punk, says that poets are killing poetry.

"The idea of reading to a bunch of people is really self-centered . . . it takes a lot to get somebody off when you're reading," she told me. . . . [I] "figure if you're gonna put yourself publicly, any performer better be able to stand behind his performance—especially a poet. I don't wanna be no simp reading boring intellectual shit to a YMCA . . ."

There isn't much to worry about that on any count . . . as [*Seventh Heaven*] will show. Patti is one of the first poets of rock&roll; she has a literary background, on top of that she's placed the pulse and beat of the stereo and street—to make a modern combination with something for everybody . . . brain and boogie freak alike. (p. 52)

All of Patti's work is heavily autobiographical, some true, some fantasy, but all very much a part of her world. . . .

The first poem, "seventh heaven" . . . talks about Eve and all the badmouthing she took after eating the apple:

> She bit. Must we blame her. abuse her.
> poor sweet bitch. Perhaps theres more to the story.
> think of Satan as some stud.
> maybe her knees were open . . .

I won't spoil it for you by quoting more, except like most of the poems here, it would help if you read this aloud—cocky, sly, and sweet. (And don't forget the beat.) In the second poem, Eve becomes "sally" who's been "ripping it up with someone. down in the briar patch":

> torn pants
> torn pants
> and juice all down your dress

This poem could be a song—and in fact, now it is. "jeanne d'arc" is a new look at a female martyr; Patti pictures her not with mysticism, but instead sees her as an itchy virgin who wants to come before her time does. And this is absolutely the *horniest* poem I've ever come across. . . .

"girl trouble," and "Judith" both deal with girl love, and have several word puns wandering thru them—they're also a release, as they lead into "fantasy", a brutal man-woman love poem with a real Mike Hammer *gun* in it.

Patti says she structured the order of poems the way you would a record—and this ends side one. "marilyn miller" (four interesting positions of a retired child star) is "like a commercial while you're turning the record over", according to Patti. Side Two begins with "mary jane", a Saturday night hustler laying down a hype, and "amelia earheart" is both word play and soaring: ing. . . . "Linda" is for Patti's sister, all air and light—"death by water" is a tribute to Brian Jones and Jim Morrison.

"dog dream" is many people's single favorite poem—it's in the form of a little chant, which came to Patti and friend Sam Shepard in a simultaneous dream—Patti says the poem was told to . . . her by a "Fellini-like communion child" who wouldn't go away till she wrote it down. . . .

"Female" is pure self-knowing and growing, a record of the way she grew to womanhood—and "Longing" is the fulfillment of all that being a woman is. The last words in the book are from the few lines that Anita Pallenberg had in "Barbarella":

> come to me my
> pretty pretty

So we fade out, and the needle's scratching as the book ends. What's Patti *up to* and *who* is she? This book will give you some clues—she stands more naked than most artists—but even in revealing, the secrets are like the mirror.

Patti is one of the best poets writing—but think of this book as just a sampler, damn good but only a part of her flow. A look inside the head and body of a fascinating, sensitive, complex and very creative person. . . . (p. 53)

> *Tony Glover, in* Creem *(© copyright 1972 by Creem Magazine, Inc.), October, 1972.*

STEPHEN HOLDEN

Over the past three years, Patti Smith . . . has developed into a New York legend. Onstage . . . , she exudes an inimitable aura of tough street punk and mystic waif, in whose skinny, sexy person the spirits of Rimbaud and William Burroughs miraculously intersect with the mystic qualities of Jim Morrison, Jimi Hendrix, the Stones, the Velvet Underground, the Marvelettes and Mary Wells, to name but a few. . . . Her improvised raps, often very humorous, combine graphic sexual fantasy with surreal, extraterrestrial visions of violence and supernatural redemption, delivered in ungrammatical streetwise diction whose rhythms she instinctively elevates into stream-of-consciousness poetry. . . .

I hesitate to say it, but I will: Patti Smith is the best new solo artist I've seen since Bruce Springsteen. She seems destined to be the queen of rock & roll for the Seventies. (p. 62)

> *Stephen Holden, in* Rolling Stone *(by Straight Arrow Publishers, Inc. © 1975; all rights reserved; reprinted by permission), Issue 193, August 14, 1975.*

GREIL MARCUS

The first question about "Horses," Patti Smith's debut album, might be called the Janis question—it comes up whenever a particularly exciting performer has fashioned a distinctive style, attracted a fierce public following, and then steps into a studio for the first time. Either the style informs the record, or the process of making a record causes the performer to alter the style, the result being, more often than not, a garish parody that is forced, hysterical, or both. In that case, the record can be counted on to provide a spurious, instant satisfaction; about a month later, it drops dead. Cheap thrills.

What has happened in Patti Smith's case is something else again. She had made an authentic *record* that is in no way merely a transcript once-removed of her live show. The record not only captures Smith whole, it offers shadows, perspectives, and shadings that few of her fans could have caught before. (p. 97)

But if the disc captures Smith, it also exposes her. Those new shadows and perspectives that come off the record add power to her music, but they also, after a few listenings, begin to undermine its incantatory momentum. The concepts that lie behind Smith's performance—her version of rock and roll fave raves, the New York avant-garde, surrealist imagery and aesthetic strategy, the beatnik hipster pose, the dark night of the street punk soul, and so on—emerge more clearly with each playing, until they turn into shtick.

Which is to say that after a time one hears points of reference more clearly than a point of view. The brutal, physical details of the self-mutilation in Smith's most ambitious number, "Horses," take one right back to the terminal violence best represented by Bunuel and Dali's [short film] "Un Chien Andalou"—you might even think that on some level the horses of the title are the same horses that were stuffed into Dali's piano. But the sheer surrealistic classicism of Smith's violence song—after a bit it seems like a matter of artistic formality—finally makes one doubt that Smith has really thought about why Bunuel centered his film around a shot of himself holding a razor over a woman's eye and an immediately following shot of the eye sliced open; if that was a tradition Smith is trying to understand or a posture she wants to imitate.

For Smith's posture ultimately seems an end in itself. The success of the album in putting Smith across isolates *what* she is putting across—raising, and begging, questions of depth, substance, and the like. If the concepts, sources, and references in her lyrics and in her singing overwhelm the music, and the singing *as* singing, then, if her record shrinks over the next month or so, it will not be because the music has diminished in power, as one kept playing the record, as happens when a style is forced; it will be because her concepts wore out. If you're going to mess around with the kind of stuff Bunuel, Dali, and Rimbaud were putting out, you have to come up with a lot more than an *homage*.

That said, there is much on "Horses" that gets home free. "Gloria" takes the listener past its hopelessly tough-chick spoken intro into a realm that shows Patti Smith at her best, all fury and desire. The double-tracked chants and vocals on "Horses," where Smith sounds with no self-consciousness like two very different people telling very different stories, are hypnotic. The strongest piece on "Horses," though, is "Free Money," a nice, straightforward rock and roll song about someone with nothing who wants everything. Here, it all comes together: Smith as a writer, singer, poetry reader; and the musicians playing for their lives. . . . Smith soars, as she does nowhere else on the album, till the momentum is unbreakable, and then pulls out like a pilot buzzing the house of her ex-lover.

I love "Free Money," and I have no doubt I always will. The rest of the album is attractive, but it breaks too easily into its parts under the attention it demands. It seems, in the end, an "art statement," which is to say, more a comment on an aesthetic than an aesthetic in action. That, of course, may come. (pp. 97-8)

> Greil Marcus, *"Patti Smith Exposes Herself,"* in The Village Voice *(reprinted by permission of* The Village Voice; *copyright © The Village Voice, Inc., 1975), November 24, 1975, pp. 97-8.*

STEVE LAKE

You'll find Patti Smith, poetess, in the Gotham Book Mart, New York's hippest bookstore, where her slim volumes of manic poetry nestle snugly between volumes of Burroughs, Ginsberg, Goray and Rimbaud. Patti Smith enjoys a literary reputation. Jerzy Kosinki is one of her fans.

I don't feel particularly qualified to assess her poetry. I've browsed through it and wasn't conscious of being in the presence of greatness, but I'm no Harvard poetry professor, that's for sure.

Better, perhaps, that we leave posterity to hassle over Patti's prosody. But Patti Smith, rock singer, is a subject closer to home. . . .

Her interviews liberally compare her to Jim Morrison, William Burroughs, Iggy Stooge, Verlaine (not the Television guitarist, the other one) and Rimbaud who, she has claimed in moments of monumental banality, "woulda made a great lead guitarist." Of course, the New York press laps all this up and proclaims her the "biggest thing since Bruce Springsteen" (which, by my watch, is only five minutes ago). . . .

I can't believe that there's any honest listeners left on earth who aren't up to here with calculated decadence and incompetence. And does anybody really need to hear Patti Smith's band [on "Horses"] play appallingly sloppy reggae on "Redondo Beach," or screw up Van Morrison's "Gloria" with the rantings of a Charlie Manson? Or cross-breed "Land Of A Thousand Dances" with "Sister Ray" and hurl in yet more references to Rimbaud for cultural appeal?

The drag is, of course, that half-assed critics with no musical sensibilities whatever will drag their volumes of Freud from dusty top shelves and begin to chunder about Oedipal tendencies and bore us all over again like they once did with Jim Morrison and the Doors. I wouldn't mind at all if Patti Smith was a bona fide nut. But she doesn't even have that distinction.

There's no way that the completely contrived and affected "amateurism" of "Horses" constitutes good rock and roll. That old "so bad it's good" aesthetic has been played to death. "Horses" is just bad. Period.

> Steve Lake, *"Poet and a No-Man Band . . . ,"* in Melody Maker *(© IPC Business Press Ltd.), December 13, 1975, p. 52.*

TONY HISS and DAVID McCLELLAND

Patti's music [is] a unique combination of fairy tales, gleeful excitement, melodic singing, spitting, unshed tears of childhood, hypnotic reiteration, teasing, dancing, masturbatory fantasies, sheet-metal schooldays and chunks of real 50's and 60's hard-rock songs. . . . (p. 24)

Patti Smith knows she's got it. On stage, she burns like a white filament dressed in black, spitting, crooning, screaming a volcano of lyrics about sex, U.F.O.'s, horses, internal voyages, Jimi Hendrix, Jim Morrison, loneliness, adolescence, beaches, possibilities, Arthur Rimbaud. You have to listen hard to Patti Smith, and that's part of her appeal. She's the first legit, published . . . poet to move her poetry completely into rock 'n' roll, and because rock is now 20 years old, she can play on a wealth of associations that any audience will be bringing to her performances. So she splices phrases like "Do the Watusi!" and "She's so fine" into her intricate and often highly intellectual songs. (p. 26)

Patti's a smart performer. Using techniques similar to those recommended by Antonin Artaud, who created the "Theater of Cruelty," she sets up a powerful dramatic tension by alternately scaring and eliciting protective feelings from an audience. She aims for the groin and the spine, and as soon as people realize she wants them to like her, they usually do, and things start to cook. Energy flows up the spine. The words, Patti's own, are generally very important and occasionally just there to set up a texture of good old straight id material. Patti explains that she tries to work herself into a certain state where she won't know what she's going to say next, but can speak directly from a certain myth-generating part of her mind. She is really an expert at that and can obviously do it under any circumstances. . . .

It's certainly the most literate magic in rock 'n' roll. "Birdland," the song set at Wilhelm Reich's funeral, was written after Patti read Peter Reich's "A Book of Dreams." It is her visionary interpretation of young Reich's experience as a little boy, his experience imagining his father returning for him in a fleet of black flying saucers that looked somewhat like the black limousines in the cortege. Patti's "Birdland" lyrics phosphoresce with a dark glow never before found in any kind of rock. . . .

Patti, who is writing rock songs about saucers and death and sex and gritty street violence, can look at all these potentially scary subjects with a sense of humor and thereby demonstrate that they do not have real power over her. Patti's songs, in a sense, are counterspells, attempts to release herself and the audience from all the dark forces of late 20th-century delusions. To accomplish this feat, she will sometimes play off deeply disturbing lyrics against comfortable, upbeat, finger-poppin' rock tunes. "Redondo Beach" is a stark lyric about a girl friend's suicide at a Lesbian beach. . . .

Patti makes the song bearable by throwing it away as a light Jamaican reggae tune and singing it almost as a parody with stylized 50's tear-drying mime. (p. 29)

> *Tony Hiss and David McClelland, "'Gonna Be So Big, Gonna Be a Star, Watch Me Now!'" in* The New York Times Magazine (© *1975 by The New York Times Company; reprinted by permission), December 21, 1975, pp. 24-31.*

STEVE SIMELS

[If] ever there was an *adult* record, ["Horses"] is it. It's a fiendishly difficult piece of work, and I suspect that as a result it's going to polarize people like crazy, which is too bad, because for all its overreaching, I can't remember a first album that exhibited such overwhelming potential.

What it boils down to is whether or not we are willing to admit that rock means anything more than "it's got a good beat and you can dance to it." . . .

And so, either you'll be simply knocked out by what Patti is attempting with "Horses"—the mating of "traditional" poetic diction (in her case the Symbolists and the Beats) with the diction of rock and creating an appropriate musical style to go with it—or you'll hear only a mannered, technically limited chick singer waxing obscure in front of a monochromatic rock band, the whole sounding like an only slightly less pretentious version of the Velvet Underground. I am myself convinced up front, despite the album's limp production job, because there's real passion here—you can tell what a labor of love this was for Patti, on all levels. (p. 42)

> *Steve Simels, in* Stereo Review *(reprinted by permission of the author), February, 1976.*

JOHN ROCKWELL

Patti Smith is the hottest rock poet to emerge from the fecund wastes of New Jersey since Bruce Springsteen. But Smith is not like Springsteen or anybody else at all.

Springsteen is a rocker; Smith is a chanting rock & roll poet. . . .

For Smith, the words generate everything else. Her "singing" voice has an eerie allure and her "tunes" conform dimly to the primitive patterns of Fifties rock. But her music would be unthinkable without her words and her way of articulating them—and that remains true even if they are occasionally submerged in sound. Patti Smith is a rock & roll shaman and she needs music as shamans have always needed the cadence of their chanting.

Her first record, *Horses,* is wonderful in large measure because it recognizes the overwhelming importance of words in her work. (p. 85)

The range of concerns in *Horses* is huge, far beyond what most rock records even dream of. . . .

To say that any of these songs is "about" anything in particular is silly—it limits them in a way that hopelessly confines their evocativeness. Like all real poets, Smith offers visions that embrace a multiplicity of meanings, all of them valid if they touch an emotional chord. Her poems are full of UFOs and shining light that illuminates parallel worlds, mirrors you step through and cracks in our common realities. She leaps between meanings of words like an elf across dimensions, deliberately dizzying you with crisscrossings between comfortable perceptions: you see, the see becomes a sea, the sea a sea of possibilities.

But with all her Martian weirdness, Patti Smith doesn't drift hopelessly beyond comprehension, and her music isn't synthesized neo-British progressivism. Her visions repay consideration but don't lose their immediate impact. Partly that's because she couches them in the common words and experiences of everyday life. And partly it's because she anchors her imagination with the sturdy ballast of rock & roll. (pp. 85-6)

All eight songs [on *Horses*] betray a loving fascination with the oldies of rock. The *hommage* is always implicit—the music just *sounds* like something you might have heard before, at least in part—and sometimes explicit.

It is Smith's elaborations of rock standards that provide the most striking songs in her repertory. On her limited-edition, long out-of-print, privately released single of Hendrix's version of "Hey, Joe," she spun a Patty Hearst fantasy full of sex and revolutionary apocalypse. On *Horses* she subjects "Gloria" and "Land of a Thousand Dances" to a similar treatment. Each becomes something far more expansive than their original creators could have dreamed. And with all due respect to Van Morrison's "Gloria" and all those who recorded "Land of a Thousand Dances," Patti's versions are better. The other songs on *Horses* aren't so overt in their appropriations of the past, although, as in "Elegie," with its return to Hendrix and a direct quotation from him, they are permeated with a feeling for rock historicism.

Smith is a genuine original, as original an original as they come. But all these debts to rock's past may make some in the rock audience wonder about that originality. And indeed, if one looks beyond rock, there are all sorts of other antecedents for her, too, and the question is whether a perception of those antecedents undermines her newness or merely places it in its proper context. The Beat poets are the easiest to spot, and particularly the Romantic/surrealist,

Blake/Rimbaud sort of visionary mysticism that has always lurked behind the Beats. Such cosmic quests have rarely been prized by the establishment rationalists, leftist revolutionaries and rock & roll populists among us, but that hasn't fazed the poets much. One reason is that the whole lower Manhattan avant-garde community has for at least 20 years acted as a self-contained world, incubating art on its own. The art toddles blithely across traditional borders: poets sing, composers dance, dancers orate, painters act, rockers make art. These artists owe everything to one another and far less to the outside, even the outside practitioners within any given medium. Patti Smith cares a lot more about Lou Reed than Robert Lowell. . . .

Originality is always something tricky to prove. An artist's detractors rush to dredge up antecedents in order to deny the claimant's newness: the artist's fans stress what is unprecedented about their idol. In Smith's case, most of the response so far has focused on her debts to the Velvet Underground, the Stones, Jim Morrison and even Iggy Pop, while ignoring her nonrock roots. *Horses* is a great record not only because Patti Smith stands alone, but because her uniqueness is lent resonance by her past. (p. 86)

> *John Rockwell, "Patti Smith: Shaman in the Land of a Thousand Dances," in* Rolling Stone *(by Straight Arrow Publishers, Inc. © 1976; all rights reserved; reprinted by permission), Issue 206, February 12, 1976, pp. 85-6.*

PAUL NELSON

If critics are having nightmares these days, one of the worst of them will undoubtedly be about not liking "Horses," Patti Smith's ubiquitous debut album. Without missing a beat, the nation's linotypers seem to have shifted from Springsteen to Smith, and there is no escaping this strange New Jersey Nightingale. Sneakers are out, Rimbaud is in, and I feel so poeticized I could die. However, after listening to the record a dozen times, not only do I not *like* "Horses," I never want to hear it again—these days a difficult admission to make.

"Horses" is so clearly a classically idiosyncratic "first" album that perhaps the artist's subsequent records will illuminate its not inconsiderable virtues and make it seem much better in years to come than it seems now—even the mistakes of heroes can be heroic. I doubt it, but I hope so. Inwardly vulnerable and outspokenly naïve, Patti Smith is after all a heroine only half-baked, though she seems to have accepted her (possible) stardom as if it were a divine right. . . .

"Horses" plods far more than it prances.

Poet Patti Smith loved rock-and-roll long before she decided to become a rock-and-roll singer. And once the decision was made, I suspect, she accepted it as already accomplished fact, rushing through her first album as if some kind of transition or training period were unnecessary. She can talk all she wants to about Mick, Keith, and Brian, but "Horses" sounds less like a Rolling Stones record than a poetry reading at the local "Y." She may look, she may even *think,* rock-and-roll, but more often than not her carefully precise recitations lack the craziness of the real pandemonium she is striving for. Right now, it's all too serious, not enough fun.

Try as I might, I simply cannot warm to the music and po-

etry of "Horses." I respect the effort behind it, but how much can you respect a record you wouldn't dream of playing for pleasure? "Patti Smith is nothing if not new" is the line of defense her admirers offer to mockers, but the album sounds to me like a morbid, pretentious rehash of Jim Morrison and Lou Reed, Smith's two major late-Sixties influences. Even *Land,* the best song in it, said to be based on a vision of Jimi Hendrix's last hours, metamorphoses from the Velvet Underground into the Doors for one of its neatest tricks. *Free Money,* another of the better cuts, cleverly weds love to money, making all the double entendres triple, but musically it is again derivative of the late, lamented Underground. . . .

Poetry, I suppose, is the part which defies translation. Patti Smith is a good poet, but even the best of her work seems —I've struggled hard to characterize it—pointlessly pregnant. "Horses" is too pregnant to be taken seriously, yet it is surely not funny nor meant to be. It is pregnant past the point of aesthetic return, so heavy at times that it cannot make the simplest movement with grace. And when those huge coils of self-important surrealism unwind aggressively toward me, I find it urgent to look for a way out of this place. I've been here before, and it hasn't aged well. Razorblade Alley and Eyeball Lane still look the same, and over there on Arcane Avenue at the Dying Swan Motel and Piano Shop, where only the upper cases hang out, they still measure a man by the width of his donkey and the height of the A in his Art. And you never could get a good meal there anyway. In the early Sixties, I had a friend on Philosopher's Row; he used to play all his "serious" records in a dark room lighted only by black and purple light bulbs and iridescent art. Incense burned. Nonsense reigned. He would have loved "Horses." (p. 96)

> *Paul Nelson, in* Stereo Review *(reprinted by permission of the author), April, 1976.*

MARIANNE PARTRIDGE

Patti Smith certainly has one hell of a lot to answer for. Not only does she unashamedly use her band as a backcloth for her pretentious "poetic" ramblings, but she simultaneously comes on as the saviour of raw-power rock and roll as it struggles to survive the onslaught of esoteric rock. In other words, she's into the myth-making business. And in this, her second album, the myth is exposed . . . as cheap thrills. At least "Horses" had the dubious privilege of a rabble-rousing version of Them's "Gloria," but on "Radio Ethiopia" all the cuts are by Patti and Band. . . . An inarticulate mess. (p. 24)

> *Marianne Partridge, in* Melody Maker *(© IPC Business Press Ltd.), October 23, 1976.*

R. MELTZER

[There] really ain't no way I'm gonna be anything but thrilled to my shorthairs by a Patti LP and [*Radio Ethiopia* is] no exception. Altho the last one was a bit less *grave* cause y'know her live show (still—when it's *on*—the best by a cunny since Billie Holiday and best by either gonad group since James Morrison's prime) has its moments of excruciating gravity but it's also got her laffing it up and spitting on the stage. Like the title cut's great and tense and all that but it could've extracted a *wee* bit more from the lesson of the Fugs' "Virgin Forest" (y'know like even the *first* experiment in self-conscious homogeneous length hadda yield to the inevitability of self-parody and stuff like that) cause like you can't do "Goin' Home"—"Sister Ray"—"The End" forever cause after a while it just kinda bristles with more than a morsel of, uh, *datedness per se.* Less Velvets in evidence than last time tho but in its stead you got Patti paying abundant vocal homage to currently faddish punkdom (wake of the Velvets anyway) which is okay for the *band* to indulge in but why waste your pipes straining for functionless punk poses that make you force your notes thru all sortsa dumb strainers like George Foreman tryin to punch in a straight line? Like this sweety was already vocally past punk forever by '74 . . . and by the winter of '75 she was so far ahead of all other femmesingers in the orchestration-of-it-all that almost anything with an intense easy-croon feel for any kinda cosmos sounded like it could very well've been somethin Pat just *dashed off.* . . . Singin on side one of this one sounds like too much needless *struggle.*

But that's mostly just nitpickin cause "Ain't It Strange" is an improvement on [Jefferson Starship's] "Miracles" at its own game. . . . "Pumping" is as rewardingly hot & desperate as trash pulp sex circa '58 and "Distant Fingers" is "Third Stone from the Sun" as told by the stone (as well as a nifty play on Pearlman-Roeser's "ETI" [performed by Blue Oyster Cult] so it's really a bonafide certified *good'un,* y'know?

> R. Meltzer, "'A Certified "Good 'un," Y' Know?'" in Creem (© copyright 1977 by Creem Magazine, Inc.), January, 1977, p. 56.

DAVE MARSH

On [*Radio Ethiopia*] Patti Smith lays back, refusing to assert herself as she did on last year's *Horses.* The key is in the billing: on *Radio Ethiopia,* her group dominates. But while Smith can be an inventive, sometimes inspired writer and performer, her band is basically just another loud punk-rock gang of primitives, riff-based and redundant. The rhythm is disjointed, the guitar chording trite and elementary. Even at best ("Distant Fingers," for instance), the Patti Smith Group isn't much more than a distant evocation of psychedelic amateurs like Clear Light.

Smith seems to lack the direction necessary to live up to her own best ideas—the song-poem structure of the first album wasn't completely effective, but here there's no structure at all. Even her lyric writing, the most captivating and polished part of her work, seems depersonalized—there's nothing as moving as "Redondo Beach" or "Kimberly" on this album. (pp. 51-2)

Smith obviously would like to be just another rock singer, with a band that could reach a broad, tough teenage audience. Ceding control to a band that lacks her best qualities and encourages her worst ("Pissing in a River" is only vulgar, without the transcendent quality of the earlier "Piss Factory") is hardly the way to go about it.

But the most disturbing image on *Radio Ethiopia* is the picture on the liner notes of Smith gazing reverently at Harry Crosby's opium pipe: the false artist worshiped by the real. (p. 52)

> Dave Marsh, in Rolling Stone (by Straight Arrow Publishers, Inc. © 1975; all rights reserved; reprinted by permission), Issue 230, January 13, 1977.

ROBERT CHRISTGAU

Patti Smith is in trouble. She's caught in a classic double bind—accused of selling out by her former allies and of not selling by ner new ones. Maybe she's just too famous for her own good. Habitues of the poetry vanguard that provided her initial panache, many of whom mistake her proud press and modest sales for genuine stardom, are sometimes envious and often disdainful of her renown as a poet, since she is not devoted to the craft of poetry and they are. Music-biz pros both in and out of her record company, aware that her second album, *Radio Ethiopia,* is already bulleting down the charts, are reminded once again that print exposure is the least reliable of promotional tools in an aural medium, not least because the press can be fickle. Somewhere in between are the journalists and critics, who count as former allies and new allies simultaneously, and who can now be heard making either charge, or both. . . .

Although Patti was personally acquainted with more than a few critics, the nationwide journalistic excitement she initially aroused went far beyond cliquishness. Like Bruce Springsteen, she answered a felt need. . . . She recalled a time when rock and roll was so conducive to mythic fantasies that pretentiousness constituted a threat. Patti had her pretentious side, everybody knew that, but in her it seemed an endearing promise that she would actually attempt something new. Moreover, she had earned her pretensions: what other rock and roller had ever published even one book of poetry without benefit of best-selling LP? Nor was it only critics who felt this way. A rock audience that includes six million purchasers of *Frampton Comes Alive!* spins off dissidents by the hundreds of thousands, many of whom are known to read. People were turned on by Patti Smith before they'd seen or heard her. Even in New York, the faithful who had packed into CBGB's for her shows were only a small fraction of her would-be fans, and elsewhere she was the stuff of dreams.

The problem with this kind of support is that it is soft—it's not enthusiasm, merely a suspension of the disbelief with which any savvy rock fan must regard the unknown artist. In Patti's case this openness lasted even after her first album, *Horses,* came out in October 1975. Patti has always attracted a smattering of sensitive types who are so intrigued by the word "poet" that they pay no heed to its customary modifier, "street"; these poor souls will attend one show and leave early, wincing at the noise. But they don't count—it's the informed fence sitters Patti could use. There's no way to know how many of the almost 200,000 adventurous rock fans who purchased *Horses* feel equivocal about it, but I wouldn't be surprised if half of them balanced the unusual lyrics, audacious segues, and simple yet effective vocals and melodies against what is admittedly some very crude-sounding musicianship. These were people who wouldn't rule out the next LP—a genuine rock poet deserves patience, after all—but wouldn't rush out for it, either. For although Patti is a genuine rock poet, what she does—her art, let's call it—is not calculated to appeal to those attracted by such a notion. (p. 14)

[The music of avante-garde band The Velvet Underground] inspired a whole style of minimal American rock, a style that rejects sentimentality while embracing a rather thrilling visceral excitement. Patti Smith . . . performs directly and consciously in this tradition. . . .

[Though] the melodies be spare, the rhythms metronomic,

the chords repetitive, at its most severe this is still rock and roll. . . . One reason *Horses* . . . was so well received critically—and sold so much better than critics' albums like the first [New York Dolls] or Ramones LPs—was that it managed to meld the pop notes with both basic instrumentation (the back-up singing on "Redondo Beach") and poetic fancies (the revelatory transition from Johnny's horses to "Land of a Thousand Dances," or from the sweet young thing humping the parking meter to "Gloria"). But Patti's and Lenny Kaye's public pronouncements on rock and roll have always indicated that something rather different was also to be expected.

Sure Patti and Lenny love mid-'60s pop-rock. Patti's fondness for both Smokey Robinson and Keith Richard is well documented; Lenny's credits as a record producer include Boston's poppish Sidewinders and *Nuggets,* the recently reissued (on Sire) singles compendium that defines the original punk rock of a decade ago at its most anonymous and unabashed. But Lenny also christened heavy-metal music and has been known to say kind things about abstract shit all the way from Led Zeppelin to the Art Ensemble of Chicago, while Patti's rock writin' included paeans to Edgar Winter as well as the Stones. Moreover, both have always been enamored of unpunkishly hippie-sounding notions about rock culture and the rock hero. Patti sometimes seems to prefer Jim Morrison to Bob Dylan and obviously relates to Keith Richard more as someone to look at than someone to listen for—as does Lenny, which is doubly dangerous. It is out of all these buts that *Radio Ethiopia*—which by comparison to *Horses* is ponderous, postliterate, anarchically communal—proceeds.

Unlike almost all of my colleagues, . . . I am an active fan of Patti's second album. It's unfortunate that its one bad cut is its title cut and lasts 11 minutes, but I wouldn't be surprised if I reached a place where I even liked that one. I've already gotten there with "Poppies" and "Pissing in a River," two cuts I originally considered dubious, as I did long ago with some of the more pretentious stuff on *Horses.* . . .

When it works, *Radio Ethiopia* delivers the charge of heavy metal without the depressing predictability; its riff power—based on great ready-made riffs, too—has the human frailty of a band that is still learning to play. . . .

I'm a sucker for the idea I perceive in "Radio Ethiopia," a rock version of the communal amateur avant-gardism encouraged by the likes of jazzman Marion Brown. And it works acceptably on stage, where Lenny's sheer delight in his own presence gets him and the band through a lot of questionable music. But I've never found Marion Brown at all listenable, and I guess I'd rather see the "Radio Ethiopia" idea than play it on my stereo. The same does not go, however, for the other dubious artistic freedom on the LP, the swear words. (p. 15)

[Patti] is a utopian romantic whose socioeconomic understanding is so simplistic that she can tell a Hungerthon that rock-and-roll power will feed Ethiopia . . . ; she is an autonomous woman with such shameless male identifications that she can cast herself cheerfully as a rapist in one poem and begin another: "female, feel male. Ever since I felt the need to / choose I'd choose male." Clearly, her line is not calculated to appeal to the politicos and radical feminists who actually live up to her challenge; it can also be counted

on to turn off most intelligent, settled adults, by which I mean people pushing Patti's age—30. But Patti won't miss those uptights—she wants kids. Her sense of humanity's potential is expressed most often in the dreamscape images of heavy rock: sex-and-violence, drugs, apocalypse, space travel. She theorizes that rock and roll is "the highest and most universal form of expression since the lost tongue (time: pre-Babel)." She believes that the "neo-artist" is "the nigger of the universe." In short, she would appear to be full of shit.

Well, so did Rimbaud, who, while no longer dominating Patti's cosmology, continues to exemplify her artist hero, theoretical inadequacies and all. I say artist hero, not artist, to avoid the absurdity of comparing poetry, but Patti's poetry itself is a place to begin. Both rock critics and poets have been known to put it down. Observers of the world of poetry inform me that some of this censure can be attributed to envy, and I suspect the same of the rock critics. In any case, as a reader who reveres Whitman, Yeats, and Williams and whose tastes in contemporary poetry—at those rare times when he has wanted to read it—have run to Creeley, Wieners, Padgett, Denby, I've found most of Patti's published work likable and some of it remarkable; one poem—"judith," in *Seventh Heaven*—strikes me as, well, a great poem, and one great poem is a lot. Still, I'll go along with the poet who told me he liked her wit and quickness but found her work unfinished. Patti reports that she works hard, tediously hard, on most of what she writes. But if it didn't seem unfinished at the end, like her rock and roll, then it wouldn't do what she clearly wants it to do.

In her search for a "universal form of expression," Patti rejects the whole idea of the avant-garde. She will talk about the way Bobby Neuwirth and Eric Andersen encouraged her to write but never mention Frank O'Hara, who others cite as a major influence on her. Obviously, she doesn't want to be associated with the avant garde's limitations. But this in itself is a kind of vanguard position that places her firmly where she belongs—in the camp of anarchists like Jarry or Tzara, as opposed to the unofficial academy of formalists like Gide or Mondrian. Avant-garde anarchists have always been especially fascinated by popular imagery and energy, which they have attempted to harness to both satirical and insurrectionary ends. Patti simply runs as far as she can with the insurrectionary possibility: Her attempt to utilize the popular form authentically is her version of the formal adventurousness which animates all artistic change.

Can I possibly believe that this deliberately barbaric sometime poet and her glorified garage band are worthy of comparison with Rimbaud, Jarry, Tzara, Gide, Mondrian? The short version of my answer is yes. The long version must begin with a reminder that Jarry and Tzara are obviously more relevant than Gide and Mondrian before returning inexorably to Rimbaud. One poet I spoke to posited rather icily that Patti reads Rimbaud in translation. This is more or less the case—but it is also one appropriate way to get to the whole of what Rimbaud created, whether monists of the work of art like it or not. For although her verse may strive (with fair success) for a certain unrefined *alchimie du verbe,* it is Rimbaud the historical celebrity Patti Smith emulates—the hooligan *voyant,* the artist as troublemaker. Even the formal similarities—such as Patti's exploitation of the cruder usages of rock and roll, which disturb elitists much as Rimbaud's youthful vulgarisms did—are in this mold. For if Patti is clearly not the artist Rimbaud was, she can compete with him as an art hero, at least in contemporary terms. Rimbaud, after all, would appear to have quit poetry not to make up for his season in hell but simply because he couldn't find an audience in his own time. So far, that has not been a problem for Patti.

Of course, one understands that even the most attractive art-hero/celebrity must actually produce some art, lest she be mistaken for Zsa Zsa Gabor, and that it is appropriate to scrutinize this art critically. Well, here is one critic who values it highly. Settled, analytic adult that I am, I don't have much use for its ideational "message," for the specific shamanisms it espouses—astral projection, Rastafarianism, whatever. But I'm not so settled that I altogether disbelieve in magic—the magic power of words or the mysterious authority of an assembly of nominally unconnected human beings—and I find that at pivotal moments Patti quickens such magic for me.

The secret of her method is her unpredictability. To a degree this is assured by the very ordinary technical accomplishments of her musicians, but even her intermittent reliance on shtick and intermittently disastrous tendency to dip into onstage fallow periods help it along by rendering those moments of uncanny inspiration all the more vivid and unmistakable. Actually, her comedic gift is so metaphysical, so protean, that sometimes her musings and one-liners, or even her physical attitudes as she sings, will end up meaning more than whatever big-beat epiphanies she achieves. But when she's at her best, the jokes become part of the mix, adding an essential note of real-world irony to the otherworldly possibility. "In addition to all the astral stuff," she boasts, "I'd do anything for a laugh." Thus she is forever set apart from the foolish run of rock shaman-politicians, especially Jim Morrison.

Discount Morrison, assign Jimi Hendrix's musical magic to another category, and declare Patti Smith the first credible rock shaman, the one intelligent holdout/throwback in a music whose mystics all pretend to have IQs around 90. Because spontaneity is part of the way she conjures, she is essentially a live artist, but through the miracle of phonographic recording conveys a worthy facsimile of what she does in permanent, easy-to-distribute form. I don't equate these records with Rimbaud's poetry or Gide's fiction or Mondrian's paintings, although without benefit of historical perspective I certainly do value them as much as I do the *works* of Jarry or Tzara, both of whom survive more as outrageous artistic personages, historical celebrities, than as creators of works of art. Since popular outreach is Patti's formal adventure, I might value what she does even more if I thought she could be more than a cult figure—and retain her authenticity, which is of course a much more difficult problem. But in a world where cult members can number half a million and mass alliances must be five or 10 times that big, I don't. If you like, you can believe that her formal failure reflects her incompetence. I think it reflects her ambition, the hard-to-digest ugliness and self-contradition of what she tries to do. (p. 16)

Robert Christgau, "Save This Rock & Roll Hero," in The Village Voice *(reprinted by permission of* The Village Voice; *copyright © The Village Voice, Inc., 1977), January 17, 1977, pp. 14-16.*

ALBERT H. JOHNSTON

Rock star Patti Smith is one of the newer phenomena on the far-out youth scene, one of the most brilliantly gifted pop performers and poets since Dylan. Here [in "Babel"], in a single volume that includes her photos and line drawings, are her poems, prose sketches and other lyrical outpourings composed during the period of her rise to rock-stardom—a collector's item, most likely, and certainly a mind-boggling expression of the surrealist temper that will have some readers shouting bravo while others pull out the plug. This is post-Dylan discothèque writing steeped in the cocaine mystique, savage and invincibly poignant, a volcanic spewing of image and metaphor and immures the sacred in the obscene and profane. Smith is one of the "adrenal people," by turns Scheherazade or Nefertiti (there's an Oriental-exotic strain here) performing a literary gutspill right out of a "high" and veering to straight elegy or tribute, as in her poems on the short-lived Edie Sedgewick and "great lady painter" Georgia O'Keefe. Nothing-barred sex is celebrated with heat, and it is almost impossible to read Smith's dithyrambs at a single sitting—her imagination numbs with its corruscating images and kaleidoscopic turns. (pp. 44-5)

Publishers Weekly *(reprinted from the November 28, 1977, issue of* Publishers Weekly *by permission, published by R. R. Bowker Company, a Xerox company; copyright © 1977 by Xerox Corporation), November 28, 1977.*

[With *Babel*, Patti Smith] turns out an aptly titled mix of prose poems, pseudo-Oriental fables, and ditties, despite her fear that "i'll never squeeze enough graphite from my damaged cranium to inspire or asphyxiate any eyes grazing like hungry cows across the stage or page." Helping enormously with the squeezing are all those modern muses grass, hash, coke, morphine, and a chaser of Calvados. They inspire opaque, largely unreadable, sado-masochistic ruminations on sex and violence interspersed with curious tributes to Rimbaud ("the syphilis oozes") "jeanne darc" ("feel like fucking") and Georgia O'Keefe ("no bull shit"). People and things are laid out, strapped in, impaled, crucified, cut, raped, etc. unless of course they are the ones laying out, strapping in, impaling, and so forth. The whole book squishes with oil, grease, worms, mire, and a vast assortment of body fluids, and were it not for shitting and fucking, it would be a lot shorter. Smith, however, seems to agree with a character in one of her fables: "i can never rest and repetition makes me nauseous." Yes, indeed. (p. 1313)

Kirkus Reviews *(copyright © 1977 The Kirkus Service, Inc.), December 1, 1977.*

ROCHELLE RATNER

[*Babel* is composed of] fast-paced, visionary poems and prose poems, but the fact that the visions seem to be drug-induced makes them frequently difficult to follow. It's hard to separate Smith the writer from Smith the cult figure (a difficulty which she herself seems all too conscious of—when she succeeds, it's almost in spite of herself). The writing includes everything a cult figure needs: drugs, sex, the wrestling with religious concepts. Most of her best poems fall into this last category; even if she sets herself up as a martyr at times, there are other poems which convey a real sense of struggle in the search for meaning. . . . The emphasis on orgiastic rites makes it inappropriate for many, but the book is likely to have a large, enthusiastic young audience. (p. 463)

Rochelle Ratner, in Library Journal *(reprinted from* Library Journal, *February 15, 1978; published by R. R. Bowker Co. (a Xerox company); copyright © 1978 by Xerox Corporation), February 15, 1978.*

JONATHAN COTT

The writer Grace Paley once talked in an interview about the fact that many women missed the sense of boyhood when they were children, "the freedom and excitement of boyhood," and that girls would try "to invent some kind of risky, boyhood life for [their] girlhood—which creates imagination, which means imagination."

Patti Smith—poet and rock-and-roll star—accepted her boyhood life right from the beginning. "Female. feel male," she wrote in her little book "Seventh Heaven." "Ever since I felt the need to choose / I'd choose male.". . .

A kind of cross between Alice in Wonderland and Huck Finn—a working-class kid who took off from the New Jersey backwater to become a *poète maudit* in New York City—Patti Smith seems to have nurtured her contradictions not so much with "joy and terror"—as Baudelaire said he nurtured his hysteria—but with a tomboyish sense of comedy and curiosity. (p. 9)

Her sensibility is one that borrows and embraces Gnostic-tinged, heterodoxical ideas and feelings that have appeared in the cosmogony of William Blake, the ritualism and paranoia of Baudelaire, the illuminations of Rimbaud, the menacing sexual fantasies of Lautréamont, Bataille and Genet. And her esthetic program is one that owes an incalculable debt to Antonin Artaud, who, in the words of Roger Shattuck, "concocted a magic amalgam of theatrical style, occult and esoteric knowledge . . . antiliterary pronouncements, drug cultism and revolutionary rhetoric without politics."

Patti Smith has taken this magic amalgam and manifested it in what she calls "3 chord rock merged with the power of the word," claiming that rock-and-roll is "the highest and most universal form of expression since the lost tongue (time: pre-Babel)." Certainly, since the 1960's, rock-and-roll has been a perfect arena for sympathetic magic and convulsive theatrics, for ecstatic poetry and collective transcendence. As with Artaud, however, it is hard to separate Smith's poetry and recordings from her public persona, for she has been producing—as Susan Sontag has said of Artaud—not so much a literary and musical body of work as a "self." And it is a self that consciously draws on the mythological presence of rock stars such as Jim Morrison and Lou Reed (both of whom are also published poets), Mick Jagger, Bob Dylan and Jimi Hendrix.

As an intense, thin, almost etiolated figure . . . she imitates and mirrors the image of the androgynous male rock-and-roll hero, which allows her to avoid the stereotyped victim-or-vamp role-playing of most female performers. And by adopting a paradoxical theatrical stance—one that confuses male and female roles and that combines the acoustic magic of Rimbaud and the Ronettes—Patti Smith has been able to develop, explore and create a certain shamanistic presence

that has eluded many aspiring rock-and-roll seers and heroes. (pp. 9, 29)

And in the role of shaman she bridges this world, the underworld and the heavens, and brings back news from the shadows; she contacts ghosts, makes love with the dead and transforms herself into animals (a black-haired, blue-eyed skunk dog in one poem). As she said in an interview with Amy Gross in Mademoiselle: "I get into so many genders I couldn't even tell you. I've written from the mouth of a dog, a horse, dead people, anything. I don't limit myself. Some of the best sex I ever had was with Rimbaud or Jimi Hendrix. I call them my brainiac-amours. Nothing sick about it, ya know. I get a lot of good poetry out of it. Me and Rimbaud have made it a million times."

To many people, most or all of the above will sound demented if not pretentious. And to them, her new book "Babel"—about 60 lyrics, poems and prose poems (most of them previously unpublished) that are set in lower case typeface with expressive but intentionally crude punctuation and spelling—will prove to be the work of an overwrought poetaster suffering from dysphoria and delirium tremens. To me, it is an alternately dazzling, uneven, arousing, annoying, imitative, original work.

Of course Patti Smith sounds like everyone who has influenced her—especially Lautréamont, Rimbaud, Bataille, Burroughs and Paul Bowles—and even like those who probably haven't—Mina Loy and Else von Freytag-Loringhoven come to mind. Of course her obsession with "love / and sex drugs and death," with "the freedom to be intense," with her pantheon of heroines including Joan of Arc and Marianne Faithfull, and with the ideas that vision places one in a state of grace and that "the cross is just the true shape of a tortured woman" are hyperalgesic pubescent and adolescent concerns. As Baron von Hugel once wrote, true illumination results in a special sweetness of temper; and in "Babel" there is more violence than grace, more bravado, swagger, machine-like lovemaking, "cooked" lesbian encounters, embodiments of rapists, masturbatory fantasies of sexual vengeance, reveries of saints and studs, Ethiopians and lepers, "disintegration and bending notes."

But out of the "realm of dreams and of fever" and in the "forbidden cinema" of her naturally hallucinating mind, Patti Smith has also given us some wonderful passages. . . .

The 16th-century Venetian courtesan poet Gaspara Stampa used outworn Petrarchan forms and imagery to write powerful sonnets on the themes of "fever and love." Patti Smith employs such overused surrealistic ideas as "the omnipotence of dream" and "the disinterested play of thought" to give us a number of poems—and two wonderful records . . .—that have more energy and passion than many well-regarded works by American surrealists like Parker Tyler and Philip Lamantia. And if Patti Smith lacks the range of poets such as Diane di Prima, Anne Waldman and Carolyn Forché, she must still be praised for her insistence that one "never let go of the fiery sadness called desire," for her striving to attain the kind of vision Rimbaud nicknamed "voyance"—and this at a time when many writers settle simply for being voyeurs. (p. 29)

Jonathan Cott, "Rock and Rimbaud," in The New York Times Book Review *(© 1978 by* The New York Times Company; *reprinted by permission), February 19, 1978, pp. 9, 29.*

KEN TUCKER

Patti Smith's pretensions are as important to her as feedback—both give the music the kind of kick and quirk that makes falling off a stage a transcendent experience. Her unwarranted assertions are grandiose, self-serving, impossible but noble. They hold out cosmic solutions, received philosophy, and, especially on *Easter,* lavish hope. Frequently they don't even fuck up the music; their profusion of exhortation, drivel, hallucination, and poetry complements the verve and, increasingly, the wit of the loud music played by the Patti Smith Group.

However all-inclusive they may seem, Smith's pretensions have never extended to matters of technique, and thematic coherence is not something you look for from her. It's tempting, therefore, to make much of the Christian imagery that runs through *Easter.* "Till Victory," the album's opening clarion call, is a spacey "Onward Christian Soldiers," very gung-ho on astral holy wars. At the other end is the title tune, . . . [which] ends with Patti Smith ascribing to herself . . . well, *everything:* "I am the seed of mystery, the veil, the thorn . . . I am the Prince of Peace . . ."

Provoking stuff for word lovers, but those who also heed the music will quickly figure out that Smith uses the New Testament in the same way she used "Gloria" on *Horses*—as a hunk of raw myth for her and her boys to gnash and wail over. What Smith admires about Jesus is not His teachings (she is too much the earnest blasphemer to even feign piety) but His example, His ordeal and triumph—that He was a real little scrapper, just like Patti. Thus Christ gains admission to Smith's eccentric pantheon of "Rock 'n' Roll Niggers," besides Jackson Pollock, Jimi Hendrix, and, unless my ears deceive me, Smith's grandmother. But even though "Rock 'n' Roll Nigger" has pretty silly lyrics, it's also the album's best rocker, with . . . Smith's most concise, magnetic hook yet: the refrain "Outside of society." . . .

Other heathen pleasures include "Ghost Dance," an American Indian chant . . . that is every bit as haunting as it's meant to be. And vying for the Most Secular award are: a paean to shit, "25th Floor"; "Space Monkey," a jagged lament that closes with an act of bestiality or God knows what; and the song that may well pull Patti's gristle out of the commercial fire—"Because the Night," a ballad by Smith and Bruce Springsteen. The cavernousness of sound and sentiment is very Springsteeny, yet the song is gratifyingly Smithish, with its elliptical metaphors and refreshing s&m interpretation of Asbury Park puppy love. But *Easter* is not without tender moments, it just finds them in odd places. "Privilege" is a good song plucked from a garish movie that probably appeals to the group's garish romanticism. . . .

Smith's own triumph—and the climax of the album—occurs during the segue from "Babelogue," spoken in her poet's thin keen, into "Rock 'n' Roll Nigger," sung in her new deep-throated bark, when she abruptly avers, "I am an American artist and I have no guilt." This admission, delivered just as the guitars are spiraling up to the album's fiercest song, has the force of catharsis: Smith's lyrics usually make their effects by an accretion of detail and metaphor; she is not given to the self-important confessional, to say nothing of declarative sentences. But then Smith goes on to make the moment her own—denies her revelation even as she proffers it—by screwing up, inten-

tionally. First she stutters the sentence, and then confuses it with the red-herring assertion that precedes it, "I am Moslem." The listener is left inexplicably moved and immediately plunged into the guitar wash of "Rock 'n' Roll Nigger." Some may dismiss all of this as intellectual sloppiness, but if so it is sloppiness worthy of deKooning, Neil Young, or the Three Stooges—endearing and gloriously artless, making its points by piling everything on too thickly.

All of which splendid disparity suggests that Patti Smith has outgrown her mentors to become her own rock star. Previously, she has taken solace and inspiration from the suffering and nihilism of old Niggers like Rimbaud, Jim Morrison, Artaud. Their worst influence on her music was to make all of its passion seem born out of self-induced derangement; *Easter* sees through this notion. In place of *Horses'* livid dreamscapes and *Radio Ethiopia*'s frustrating visions of perpetual struggle against the world, the flesh, and radio programmers, *Easter* offers a radical, nutty optimism, banishing the unearned fatalism that mired crucial sections of the previous albums. Beneath the juggled imagery, the only "message" on *Easter* is that Patti Smith prevails, not with a grimace but a grin.

> *Ken Tucker, "Onward Heathen Soldiers," in* The Village Voice *(reprinted by permission of* The Village Voice; *copyright © The Village Voice, Inc., 1978), May 1, 1978, p. 51.*

CHARLES M. YOUNG

Patti Smith has set about creating a movement to free the world through rock & roll. Her personal charm, when she wants it to be, is enormous. Her followers are increasing every day, and they are among the most ardent anywhere. . . . She is a poet for the people. . . .

Patti Smith's detractors think Radio Ethiopia, a loosely defined organization of her supporters, amounts to a Kiss Army for intellectuals who like to be mystified by poetry without capital letters. They think she is a fool. Because she cultivates the look of a possessed poet, she can say things like "the word art must be redefined" and get away with it. Her fans, in fact, eat it off a stick. And she is happy to feed them, so long as they don't question the menu too closely.

With her goal of creating a Sixties-style social movement out of the music, she is reminiscent of a charismatic sect leader who has convinced her followers that she alone has the secret of life. The secret is so heavy, of course, that it can only be revealed through the leader's interpretation of *Das Kapital* / visions of the Scripture / mumbo jumbo about the creative process. And like the best of the sect leaders, Smith believes her own line and has constructed an imposing edifice of egomania to protect her mediocre ideas from doubt. (p. 52)

> *Charles M. Young, "Visions of Patti," in* Rolling Stone *(by Straight Arrow Publishers, Inc. © 1978; reprinted by permission), Issue 270, July 27, 1978, pp. 51-4.*

SIMON FRITH

"Wave" is a much better record than I expected, but to explain why I'll have to go back a bit.

Patti Smith's problem is that what was touching in a rock fan is obnoxious in a rock star. Her desperate faith in the cleansing spiritual power of rock 'n' roll was inspiring as long as she was on the outside. "Horses" was a gripping debut album that rekindled the rock faith of even the most jaded critics. What Patti the poet brought to her versions of "Gloria" and "Land Of A Thousand Dances" was less lyrical than emotional vision. She reminded us (in 1975, just prepunk) that rock 'n' roll was primarily a musical *feeling*.

Unfortunately, inevitably, once Patti had made it . . . she became, given her belief in rock stars as shamans, her own myth. Her music became self-indulgent, bombastic, arrogant. The declaiming poet became the haranguing priestess. Patti claimed a special access to god; she placed herself in the tradition of the oppressed vagabond (Rimbaud and all that); she wrote silly songs like "Rock 'n' Roll Nigger."

"Wave", thank the Lord (the Pope features here, rather than Haile Selassie), restores to the Patti Smith Group some sense of perspective. This is partly because Patti herself is in love and subordinates her spiritual and bohemian conceits to a new account of her muse: "for one human being to love another," she quotes Rilke, "that is perhaps the most difficult of our tasks." . . .

The most moving track on the album is a swirling version of the Byrds' "So You Want To Be (A Rock 'n' Roll Star)"— still a song of disillusion, but still optimistic: Patti accepts at last that that's all she is, a rock 'n' roll star.

As such, especially on side 1, she isn't bad at all. "Frederick" is a love lyric, with a melodic line reminiscent of "Be-cause The Night" but gentler, less forced, more authentically pop. "Hymn" is just that, a Sunday School lullaby . . . "Dancing Barefoot" is dedicated to Modigliani's mistress, to all women who sacrifice themselves to men, drawn as if addicted. "Citizen Ship" is a vagabond song, but Patti singing now like she wanted to get on board, "Revenge" is a giving-the-man-his-come-uppance song, a big blues. . . .

Side 2, after "So You Want To Be (A Rock 'n' Roll Star)", is less satisfactory. "Seven Ways Of Going" is the PSG at its most pretentious. Patti runs through an obscure list of "seven" images—seven seas of Galilee, seven hills of Rome, etc. . . . "Broken Flag" brings to the fore the hint of the hymnal that recurs throughout this record. It's a Victorian dirge that only makes sense as marching music—a song for a poppy day parade. But "Wave" is the worst track here: Patti as a self-abasing girl, fancying a man on the beach as the waves crash—the Shangri-Las did it better.

No doubt the song means something (it is the title track), just like the arty trappings . . . that are now a necessary part of Patti Smith as commodity. But I understand this record better as commerce than as art. The Patti Smith Group are making a hard (radio-aimed) bid to move from cult to middle of the road. . . . Who knows. they might just make it.

Simon Frith, "Patti: Love Conquers All," in Melody Maker (© IPC Business Press Ltd.), May 5, 1979, p. 31.

Mary Stolz

1920-

American novelist and short story writer. Stolz's works are recognized as among the first written for young people that accurately represented their concerns, feelings, and lifestyles, and did so with empathy and respect. Her plots and themes are realistic ones: family relationships, divorce, social problems, and the expectations and disappointments of growing up. Although many of her works include a standard boy/girl relationship as their basis, Stolz is mainly interested in the increased awareness and maturity of her characters, whom both readers and critics generally consider exceptionally well developed and true to life. After she completes writing a book, she has said, "I know the characters as if they were friends. They're still there—real." Stolz started her writing career by selling her first stories to periodicals such as *Ladies Home Journal* and *Seventeen*. In 1948 she was hospitalized for three months; to combat her depression her doctor (who later became her husband) suggested that she write something of greater length. The book that followed, *To Tell Your Love*, set the standard for Stolz's portrayals of adolescents and their families. Much of Stolz's fiction is based on fact, especially on things that have happened to her son and young relatives. In order to keep her situations, settings, and dialogue correct and relevant, she quizzes the members of her family to find out if all the details ring true. Her respect for young people is evident in the way she characterizes them: her protagonists, often young women, are intelligent and ambitious, and are interested in literature and the arts. They are aware of the larger world that surrounds them, and are often anxious to become involved in its betterment; Stolz herself has been a part of several movements for peace. She has been criticized for writing novels that are too issue-oriented, and for the similarities among some of her characters and dialogue. However, she has published over 40 books, many for younger children and a few for adults, which have been printed in nearly 30 languages. In 1954, her *In a Mirror* was given the Child Study Association Award, which is presented to a children's book which deals realistically with the problems of childhood. Her analyses of social relationships and human values in the often complicated world of the young adult have been written with sensitivity and perception for almost three decades. (See also *Contemporary Authors*, Vols. 5-8, rev. ed., and *Something about the Author*, Vol. 10.)

[*To Tell Your Love* is a] lively, better than average romance-family novel for teen-age girls. As in the 18th century novels of sensibility, the Armacost family leads tremulously emotional lives. The school teacher, bird-watching father, charming gentle mother, twenty-three year old poetry loving nurse, Theo, lovely and impetuous eighteen year old Anne, and self-conscious, sensitive, fourteen year old Johnny—all vibrate to each other's problems like overwrought canaries. Meditations, snatches of poetry and diaries reflect the Armacost problems. . . . There may be a surfeit of nobility here, but the family relationships are warm and happy, the dialogue witty, and the sobering picture of a moneyless teen-age marriage gives the book substance. Also the sympathetic glimpse of a kid brother may inspire the teen-age girl to take a second look at the traditional pest. (p. 424)

> Virginia Kirkus' Bookshop Service, *August 1, 1950.*

ELLEN LEWIS BUELL

["To Tell Your Love"] is a wise and sensitive story of first love. . . .

The essential poignancy of Anne's experience is balanced by an amusing family background. The Armacosts are attractive people, blessed with humor and imagination. Through them the author manages to say a number of perceptive things about the business of everyday living. (p. 34)

> Ellen Lewis Buell, in The New York Times Book Review (© 1950 by The New York Times Company; reprinted by permission), October 8, 1950.

[*The Organdy Cupcakes*] has the same freshness of touch, depth of characterization and charm in heroines [as *To Tell Your Love*]. The three girls who pace the action of this novel—which could double as a career story for prospective nurses—are refreshingly intelligent, ambitious and womanly at the same time, but hardly superwomen. . . . To be sure, the girls pair off with suitable men, but their affection and dedication to their work is enriched, not diverted, by masculine attention. A realistic inside view of the hospital, too, with basins as well as starched uniforms. (p. 66)

> Virginia Kirkus' Bookshop Service, *February 1, 1951.*

ELLEN LEWIS BUELL

Mrs. Stolz' "To Tell Your Love" introduced a talented new writer. Like that novel, "The Organdy Cupcakes" is witty, perceptive and mature. It hasn't quite the poignancy of that story of first love, but it has the same freshness of characterization and writing.

Although it is a story of three student nurses in a suburban hospital it is far removed from the stereotyped career novel. . . . The girls seem real, not made. So too, do the other characters—Nelle's bat-brained, charming mother; the patients, the doctors. It is this feeling for people which gives the story its vitality and richness. (p. 24)

> *Ellen Lewis Buell, in* The New York Times Book Review (© *1951 by The New York Times Company; reprinted by permission), April 8, 1951.*

The careers, home life and romances of three girls . . . at nursing school are woven deftly into ["The Organdy Cupcakes"]. It is by far the best "career book" of the spring; also it is much more mature in the approach of the older teen age girl audience than was "To Tell Your Love." . . .

The hospital background is very well done: the atmosphere, the different sorts of work, the relations of nurses, interns, doctors and the rest of the staff are very realistic, honest and interesting. In Gretchen Bemis we meet an unusual character, one we are at first uncertain about, whose love affair will be very satisfying to young readers. Rosemary's troubles with her stepmother, Nelle finding out how to keep a beau, add interesting subplots.

This is "older" than most "junior novels," and therefore most welcome for high school libraries and youth rooms. What separates it, in style and content, from a "regular" novel is a point we shall not press here. Girls over fourteen will be keen on it, whatever their dreamed-of careers. (p. 24)

> *The New York Times Book Review (©* 1951 by *The New York Times Company; reprinted by permission), May 13, 1951.*

ELLEN LEWIS BUELL

["The Sea Gulls Woke Me"] is simpler in construction and in theme than are Mrs. Stolz's earlier books, "To Tell Your Love" and "The Organdy Cupcakes," but for that reason it may be even more popular, especially among the younger teen-agers. It has, too, the humor, the sharp awareness of character and scene which have made her one of the best present-day novelists for older girls. (p. 28)

> *Ellen Lewis Buell, in* The New York Times Book Review (© *1951 by The New York Times Company; reprinted by permission), September 16, 1951.*

LOUISE S. BECHTEL

A book to delight teen-age girls, ["The Sea Gulls Woke Me"] is the best yet of the three junior novels, or first love stories, by this writer. The problem of her sixteen-year-old heroine is a vital one: to escape the domination of a fussy, smothering sort of mother, and find herself as an individual. . . . [Jean's mistaken "crush" and] her first real love affair, are very well handled. The philosophy offered, the underlying tone, and Jean's relation to all the adults concerned are fine. There is a bitter "older man" (of twenty-five, a writer) who causes her roommate trouble, and is a bit overdone. But he adds speed to a rather quiet plot.

Miss Stolz has a wide range of references to books, places, poetry, people, also a quick sense of humor. All this she pours out easily, but a bit too freely, with an over-use of carefully unusual adjectives and crowded metaphor that makes some pages lush. But she's able to interpret teen-age feelings so that they ring true. (p. 16)

> *Louise S. Bechtel, in* New York Herald Tribune Book Review (© *I.H.T. Corporation; reprinted by permission), October 28, 1951.*

MARGARET A. EDWARDS

The nearest rival in quality [to Maureen Daly] is probably Mary Stolz. In both *To Tell Your Love* and *The Sea Gulls Woke Me* she draws sharp characterizations, brings poignancy to the problems of youth, and has well-developed plots. And yet, while her stories are enjoyed, girls in Baltimore who read them do not send their friends to the library with the general understanding that their lives will not be worth living until they read these books. It may be that this author has limited her audience by writing a junior novel so mature in its concepts that it is best understood by college girls who choose their junior novels, however good they may be. In *The Sea Gulls Woke Me* Mrs. Stolz includes brief discussions of T. S. Eliot and Macaulay; she skilfully depicts the hopeless fascination that an "arty" author, an older man, has for a young college girl, thereby giving her story a very grown-up tone, which many girls read with pleasure and profit but not too often with a deep enough understanding, because they are unacquainted with some of her characters or have not come across some of her situations in their limited experiences. So while librarians and book reviewers compare Stolz with Maureen Daly, the young people themselves do not. (pp. 70-1)

> *Margaret A. Edwards, in* English Journal *(copyright* © *1952 by the National Council of Teachers of English), September, 1952 (and reprinted in* Readings about Adolescent Literature, *edited by Dennis Thomison, The Scarecrow Press, Inc., 1970).*

JENNIE D. LINDQUIST and VIRGINIA HAVILAND

When her mother died, Morgan Connor [in *Ready or Not*] had to take on the responsibility of caring for her younger brother and sister and keeping house for them and their father, whose job as a subway clerk barely supported the family. I question whether a young girl could possibly run a household as smoothly as she did and gone to school at the same time, but that is the only flaw I find in a far-above-average story remarkable for its perceptive character delineation. Not only the Connors but also Morgan's high school friends and their families, and Tom, the boy with whom she falls in love, are as real and as individual as living people. Mrs. Stolz seems to me our most outstanding writer of teen-age novels today. (p. 414)

> *Jennie D. Lindquist and Virginia Haviland, in* The Horn Book Magazine *(copyrighted, 1952, by The Horn Book, Inc., Boston), December 1952.*

The characters [in *Ready or Not*] are very real people, not completely good and not completely bad. Morgan, in particular, is unusual as a heroine in a teen-age novel, for she is neither very pretty nor very bright, but the reader is drawn to her with a feeling of real understanding and sympathy for her problems. The author writes with a maturity and a depth of perception that are as welcome as they are rare in books written for teen-age readers. (p. 54)

Bulletin of the Center for Children's Books (published by the University of Chicago), March, 1953.

ELLEN LEWIS BUELL

In her previous novels for older girls Mrs. Stolz has explored with wit, originality and a rare maturity the problems of growing up. ["Ready or Not"] is even more adult in tone and is, in one sense, more ambitious in its probing of family relationships. It is also new in setting, for here the author moves from the comfortable, suburban background of her earlier characters to the bare, hard-won respectability of a low-cost housing project in New York City. . . .

Each of [the] characters is sharply individualized and the interplay of family relationships is brilliantly stated. Pitched in a minor key, the story may disappoint those who are hot for certainties, but for thoughtful readers it will be an unusual experience. (p. 24)

Ellen Lewis Buell, in The New York Times book Review (© 1953 by The New York Times Company; reprinted by permission), March 22, 1953.

RICHARD SULLIVAN

A quiet, sensitive, close textured novel, "Truth and Consequence." It deals with the diverse events of a single day; its numerous characters are all sharply defined; its phrasing is precise and economical; and its parts come together to make a unified total effect that may be remember with satisfaction after the book is closed.

The central figure is 13-year-old Geraldine. . . .

But the narrative, while centering on Geraldine, switches quietly from character to character, and ranges up and down the street. The fussy housewife; the blind old man; the high school girl miserable in love with her math teacher; the anxious young mother protecting her precocious son; the young wife restless in her infidelity; the mad widow awaiting the return of her husband—these are some of the persons whose common day is here subtly, significantly revealed.

Into certain of their lives this day brings partial or tentative resolution. In the deep purpose of fiction is, as [Joseph] Conrad suggested, to make the reader "see," then "Truth and Consequence" very justly and rightly fulfills that difficult intention. (p. 4)

Richard Sullivan, in Chicago Sunday Tribune, Part 4, August 23, 1953.

JANE COBB

There are several good things to be said for Mary Stolz's "Truth and Consequence." The characters are believable and the situations in which they find themselves are convincing. The dialogue is excellent. The flaw in the book is its completely unrelieved glumness. In the entire narrative there is scarcely a shred of hope or humor.

Most of the action takes place in a suburban town where 13-year-old Gerry has been taken to stay with her Aunt Proud. . . .

[Some] pieces in the pattern of misery include a wife who doesn't like her husband and has a lover she can never

marry and, of course, Gerry's agonized parents. Miss Stolz has also included a mildly demented woman called Cassandra, who has been waiting for five years for her dead husband to come home, and an embittered colored woman whose little boy was born with no legs.

This all sounds too dismal to be true, and it is greatly to Miss Stolz's credit that she has made it as believable and interesting as she has. She has talent, and this reader hopes that in her next book she will cheer up a little.

Jane Cobb, "Catalogue of Despairs," in The New York Times Book Review (© 1953 by The New York Times Company; reprinted by permission), August 30, 1953, p. 15.

BERNICE FRANKEL

All of Mary Stolz's novels are notable for their eloquence, maturity, and insight. [In a Mirror] is rich in these qualities. The diary form adopted for the story is ideal for Miss Stolz's purpose, which is to disclose the inmost thoughts of a college junior who seeks to understand herself and those about her. (pp. 68, 70)

Bessie's relationships—with Til, the instructor, her parents—are sensitively drawn and serve to enlighten her. Girls who read her story will be enlightened, too, as well as deeply moved. (p. 70)

Bernice Frankel, in The Saturday Review (Entire issue copyright 1953 by Saturday Review Associates, Inc.; reprinted with permission), November 14, 1953.

MARGARET FORD KIERAN

[In a Mirror] is as penetrative and analytical as anything [Mary Stolz] has ever done. But is it a *teen-age* book? I confess I bogged down for a minute while I went through it because, as a stream-of-consciousness journal of a present-day college girl, it would surely have Henry James looking to his laurels.

It is extremely well done, once you accept the heroine as a product of the "majoring in psychology" group. Smoothly written and as fascinating as certain psychiatric case histories can be, I nevertheless would not recommend it except to those teenagers of your acquaintance whose emotional balance is well established. They could handle it and would thoroughly enjoy it, no doubt, but for the more immature I think it is too introspective and somehow disturbing. (p. 98)

Margaret Ford Kieran, in The Atlantic Monthly (copyright © 1953 by The Atlantic Monthly Company, Boston, Mass.; reprinted with permission), December, 1953.

MARGARET C. SCOGGIN

The tragedy of the fat girl is handled [in In a Mirror] with perception and some humor. Bessie Muller has brains and a certain objectivity in looking at herself and her easygoing family, but it takes time for her to realize that her overeating is a compensation for certain lacks she must overcome. Her journal reveals her discovery that just as the basilisk died when it saw its image in a mirror, so one can overcome faults when one sees them clearly and stops making excuses for them. Of course, there is more to the plot—college life, dates and parties, Bessie's determination to write, her roommate's devotion to dancing and hopeless love for a young married professor. But the special appeal lies in felicity of phrase and delightful people. This is a work of art. (pp. 469-70)

Margaret C. Scoggin, in The Horn Book Magazine (copyrighted, 1953 by The Horn Book, Inc., Boston), December, 1953.

ANNE BROOKS

So fragmentary as hardly to be called a work of fiction, Mary Stolz' ["Truth and Consequence"] is a series of sketches of people who are merely linked together by the circumstance of living in the same neighborhood. But these are singularly alive and acute sketches. Miss Stolz has an exceptional talent for understanding people. . . .

Miss Stolz' greatest merit is that she does not overheighten the characteristics of her people. They are real and reasonable. . . . Miss Stolz is quietly understanding of the Negro maid, Coral, . . . and the great pride which makes Coral classify white people into groups which are stereotypes, never intimates. There is the same understanding of Karen, the young woman married to a perfect but boring physical specimen, and of all the others who people this gifted little novel. Some day Miss Stolz will round out her unusual sympathy for people into a more concrete and meaningful form. But in the meantime here is a talent to be watched. (p. 14)

Anne Brooks, in New York Herald Tribune Book Review (© I.H.T. Corporation; reprinted by permission), December 13, 1953.

ANDREA PARKE

To explore, to interpret, to define the struggles of youth's raw, aching emotions has proved a pitfall for more than one writer. But Mary Stolz, who has written several novels about adolescents for adolescents, understands her young people thoroughly, and in ["Two by Two"] has written a first-rate novel. . . .

Harry . . . discovers he is in love with Nan Gunning, a childhood playmate. Before the summer is over, thanks to the inept blundering of both families, Harry has accidentally killed a man and has been hurt in a way it will take him years to overcome. Thanks to his own courage, one feels that his and Nan's love will survive. One has only to read the scenes between Harry and his father, between Harry and Nan, to listen to the talk of a group of teen-agers to know that the author hears and sees true.

Andrea Parke, "Midsummer Love Story," in The New York Times Book Review (© 1954 by The New York Times Company; reprinted by permission), September 26, 1954, p. 33.

ELLEN LEWIS BUELL

Never an adherent to the cozier conventions of teenage fiction, Mary Stolz has given us another of her provocative novels [with "Pray Love, Remember"]—this time about a girl who isn't sure what she wants but knows quite well what she doesn't want. . . . On first acquaintance, Dody is not an entirely agreeable person, but she is very real in her uncertainties, her paradoxes and in her fierce desire to escape the mediocrities of the Plattstown pattern. . . .

All Mrs. Stolz' novels have been distinguished by a mature approach to the problems of young people but this is the most challenging and the best of them all. (p. 50)

Ellen Lewis Buell, in The New York Times Book Review (© 1954 by The New York Times Company; reprinted by permission), November 7, 1954.

Miss Stolz remembers teen-age emotions well, and always chooses problems acutely important to that age. She has often touched on the theme of money as it affects youth and first love, and always shows her characters in a rounded social setting. Her well balanced sense of values has made a definite contribution; so have the poetic feeling and love of books which sometimes have led her to a rather lush style.

Now [in "Pray Love, Remember"] she traces the growing-up pains of Dody Jenks. . . .

Her love affair with a talented, poor young Jew from Brooklyn is well done. . . . His sudden death makes a tragic ending, but one that is also revealing and hopeful for Dody, drawing together her thinking about religion, work and people. It may not be the best of this writer's books for girls, and the rather trite theme could be better handled, but it has a lot to say to dreamy teen-agers who need to wake up as Dody did. (p. 22)

New York Herald Tribune Book Review (© I.H.T. Corporation; reprinted by permission), November 14, 1954.

How does a boy grow up? This is the question that lies at the center of Mary Stolz's new novel, "Two by Two." . . . During his seventeenth summer Harry Lynch faces many typical problems. How is he to emerge as an adult personality in the face of a father who does not understand him, who treats him like a two-year-old? How is he to cope with the dead weight of the past—represented by his mother, who has died six months earlier, whose memory he worships? Above all, how is he to handle his first experience of loving a girl?

Mary Stolz has painted her portrait of Harry with warmth, understanding and loving care. Other portraits in the book emerge solid and clear to stand beside the boy; Harry's older sister in particular, torn by neurotic conflicts, is a very moving study. And the picture of Harry's family as a whole, and of the way of life, is well realized.

Some readers will feel that the final resolution of "Two by Two" is unnecessarily violent and melodramatic. But a deep respect for human beings and a firm belief in the values of good human relations are implicit in the narrative. (p. 18)

New York Herald Tribune Book Review (© I.H.T. Corporation; reprinted by permission), November 28, 1954.

[Rosemary is a] merciless, understanding look at an average small town girl, the kind who had been popular in high school but is now beginning to feel the effects of a rather shopworn gaiety, [and it] also provides a close scrutiny of Rosemary's community—a college town where there are students as well as private citizens and a rather full blown town-gown complex. . . . A deep, well worked story, this probes many values and is healthy reading for all young people. (pp. 543-44)

Virginia Kirkus' Service, August 1, 1955.

RICHARD S. ALM

Mary Stolz, surely the most versatile and most skilled of

[the writers who followed Maureen Daly, but did not imitate her], writes not for the masses who worship Sue Barton Barry [married name of the heroine of *Sue Barton, Neighborhood Nurse* and the entire series written by Helen Boylston] but for the rarer adolescent who sees in Anne Armacost *(To Tell Your Love)* a girl of warmth and charm, in love unfortunately with a boy who is afraid to return her love. In a summer of endless days with a telephone which does not ring, Anne slowly understands what has driven Doug away. The poignancy of her losing this first, intense love is a bitter-sweet experience which makes her a little sadder, but a good deal more perceptive of the emotions and reactions of those around her.

The other characters, too, in *To Tell Your Love* are individuals, not types. In shifting her point of view from one to another and giving an intimate glimpse of the feelings and thoughts of each one, Stolz reveals a talent that few writers have.... Stolz' other novels—*In a Mirror, The Seagulls Woke Me, Pray Love, Remember,* and *Organdy Cupcakes* are significant contributions, too, to fiction for the adolescent. In all of them, she tells an engrossing story but, equally important, she presents characters who emerge as sensitively-drawn individuals. (pp. 358-59)

> *Richard S. Alm, in* English Journal *(copyright © 1955 by the National Council of Teachers of English), September, 1955 (and reprinted in* Readings about Children's Literature, *edited by Evelyn Rose Robinson, David McKay Company, Inc., 1966).*

LILLIAN MORRISON

Mary Stolz stands alone among the authors who now write fiction for the teen-age girl—alone and above. Her characters and situations have the reality and the depth one hopes for in a good adult novel and yet she truly speaks the language of her teenager readers. She seems to live and to be her girl characters, so well does she understand them. "Rosemary" is the story of two girls in a college town who know each other largely through a common interest in several boys. Helena, who comes of a well-to-do family, goes to the college. Rosemary works as a salesgirl and yearns for what the college stands for. It is a town-versus-gown story and it is written with the perception, sympathy, and also the warm understanding of family relationships that we have come to expect from this author. (p. 82)

> *Lillian Morrison, in* The Saturday Review *(Entire issue copyright 1955 by Saturday Review Associates, Inc.; reprinted with permission), November 12, 1955.*

MARGARET C. SCOGGIN

Mary Stolz is quite at the top of those writing for and about today's teen-agers. She gives them to us with all their faults and perplexities, as real as the next-door neighbors. She never provides a conventional happy ending for she knows that the best endings (or beginnings) come when her characters change what they can and accept what they must—when, in short, they grow up.

The setting [of "Rosemary"] is a college community where high school graduates split into two groups, those who do not go on to college and those who do.... Into a former group comes Sam Lyons, college senior.... It is Sam who

sets in motion conversations and events which give each of [the] young people a change of perspective.

The matter is serious but the touch is deft and light. "Rosemary" is an outstanding junior novel. (p. 10)

> *Margaret C. Scoggin, in* New York Herald Tribune Book Review *(© I.H.T. Corporation; reprinted by permission), November 13, 1955.*

Dody [in *Pray Love, Remember*] is in some ways a realistic character, and many of her problems will be recognized by teen-age girls as similar to their own. The character of Stephen Roth, the boy who dies, is less skillfully handled and the reader is left with the feeling that his death was brought in as much to give the author a solution to the religious problem which his and Dody's love affair would have raised as it was to give Dody a chance to exercise her new-found maturity. The other characters vary in quality of development from obvious stereotypes to well-rounded individuals. The plot development is quite weak. (p. 55)

> Bulletin of the Center for Children's Books *(published by the University of Chicago), December, 1955.*

ELLEN LEWIS BUELL

One of the most moving of Mary Stolz's earlier novels was "Ready or Not," a portrait of a New York family living precariously on the edge of poverty, held together by the love and instinctive wisdom of Morgan, the elder daughter. Now Mrs. Stolz continues the story of the Connors [with "The Day and the Way We Met"], taking it up four years later at a time of strain precipitated by Morgan's marriage.... Julie, at 17, feels painfully inadequate to take her sister's place. Impatient, thorny, remote, Julie has also her private problems: her secret, hopeless love for an older man, her boredom with her one steady beau, the uncertainties of her future.

As always, Mrs. Stolz is interested more in people's thoughts and feelings than in what they do. Except for Ned [the little brother] who takes one brief, reluctant step toward delinquency, nothing of great outward import happens. Yet, during those weeks of readjustment Ned and Julie have moved toward a closer understanding. Julie herself breaks free from her shell of dreamy isolation, is ready, at last, to meet the world—"to be hurt and made happy by reality." If, in her probing of moods and emotions, Mrs. Stolz occasionally allows her story to lag, she is always perceptive and convincing and the final affirmation, Julie's acceptance of life, should be both a challenge and an encouragement to her contemporaries in real life. (p. 32)

> *Ellen Lewis Buell, in* The New York Times Book Review *(© 1956 by The New York Times Company; reprinted by permission), April 22, 1956.*

Mary Stolz's stories are unfailingly good, the kind that show that writing for the teens can be both realistic and well received, in fact, better received than the ordinary run of comforting moral pointers. [In *Hospital Zone*] we meet a new girl in a new environment—Honey Kirkwood in her senior year of nurse's training in a Boston hospital. Actually her story is nothing more than a character sketch, or a collection of character sketches, but as such, and although all but plotless in form, they make memorable young reading as an examination of that all important question—what makes people tick? . . . [This is an] honest book, exciting in its dialogue and commentary and provocative understanding. (p. 578)

Virginia Kirkus' Service, *August 15, 1956.*

[*The Day and the Way We Met*] seems rather diffuse at times because of the lack of focus on one main character, and an occasional incident, such as Ned's brush with juvenile delinquency, is over-simplified both in the statement of the problem and its solution. The characterizations are well-rounded and perceptive and the story will have appeal for readers who want a novel that gives them more than just surface emotions and trivial problems. (p. 14)

Bulletin of the Center for Children's Books (*published by the University of Chicago), September, 1956.*

A junior novel by Mary Stolz with a nurse as heroine should gather in the fans in droves. Many young girls like the complicated agonizing and introspection of Mary Stolz's heroines, and those who do not are usually just the ones that read every nurse story they can lay their hands on. The hospital background [in "Hospital Zone"] is quite fully realized, especially the relation of the young nurse to her patients and the impact of their tragedies and troubles on her even while she is engrossed in her own young problems. Honey Kirkwood, the heroine, is outwardly a cool character. . . . She is pretty [and a flirt]. . . . One of her friends wisely says that she is "riding for a fall," and she was. Honey had not counted on Dr. Dragone. In the end, unable to forget the doctor and considering falling back on good old Joe, she muses in a Stolzian way about her experience, "It's life itself that has the rich meaning. To live, to learn, to know things, to suffer and recover. The thing is to live." No. The nurse-story fans, looking for wedding bells as well as starched uniforms, won't like that. This story like most of Mary Stolz' novels will be enjoyed most by girls of similar temperament to the heroine's. (p. 8)

New York Herald Tribune Book Review (© *I.H.T. Corporation; reprinted by permission), December 30, 1956.*

Miss Stolz has undertaken an exacting task in [*Because of Madeline*]—the tracing of the effect of a single personality on the lives of others. In this goal she has fallen somewhat short though her story is again reminiscent of her other books in the frankness and free expression and understanding of the teen-ager. . . . [Madeline] remains a shadowy figure. Only occasionally does her effect on Dot and some of the more sensitive girls come through. . . . There are many elements [here] too often sidetracked in school stories—the snobbery, uncertain standards and difficulties of adjustment. But the whole book does not measure up to Miss Stolz's best. (pp. 4-5)

Virginia Kirkus' Service, *January 1, 1957.*

VIRGINIA HAVILAND

At nineteen, from the university, Dorothy looks back [in *Because of Madeline*] to the year when she was a fourteen-year-old student at a co-educational private school near Central Park. Christmas holidays brought a change to her life, to her brother and "the rest of us" because of Madeline, the brilliant gum-chewing daughter of a cleaning woman who entered the school on scholarship. How, be-

cause Madeline was an *individual* and the first non-conformist the students had met, she affected their thinking and made them willing to be less alike is a significant theme, characteristic of this author. Dorothy, who wanted everyone to be happy; her quixotic boarding-school brother; his roommate; and Celia, a less different scholarship girl, are well revealed through changes wrought by the catalyst Madeline who had no wish to change herself "except by her own rules." Fresh and rewarding reading, with clear, intense, and natural views of young people's relationships. (p. 141)

Virginia Haviland, in The Horn Book Magazine (*copyrighted, 1957 by The Horn Book, Inc., Boston), April, 1957.*

ELLEN LEWIS BUELL

["Because of Madeline"] is a subtle story, complex in structure as the narrator shifts back and forth in time, remembering and analyzing those disturbing moments of self-evaluation—especially the realization of latent snobbery. It is one of Mrs. Stolz' most searching studies of motives and manners, of social and human values. And, for all its knowledgeable, witty picture of sub-deb life, it presents a situation that could happen in almost any school (p. 20)

Ellen Lewis Buell, in The New York Times Book Review (© *1957 by The New York Times Company; reprinted by permission), April 21, 1957.*

JENNIE D. LINDQUIST

Fifteen years old, with charming parents and two small brothers whom she loved, and a very happy home, Barbara Perry [in *Good-by My Shadow*] still had to go through the stage of adolescence when everything seemed black. She herself realized that she was unreasonable in being dissatisfied with everything but she could not seem to pull herself out of her self-centered sadness. This story of her gradual growth back to happiness is, I think, one of Mary Stolz' best books. Barbara's shyness with the group of boys and girls of which she wanted so much to be a part is perceptively pictured. These young people who seemed so gay and carefree to Barbara are convincing, too; and her completely delightful parents are so real in their puzzled approach to her problems that mothers and fathers, as well as their daughters, will appreciate the book. (pp. 406-07)

Jennie D. Lindquist, in The Horn Book Magazine (*copyrighted, 1957 by The Horn Book, Inc., Boston), October, 1957.*

MARGARET C. SCOGGIN

["Good-by My Shadow"] is an uncommonly subtle study of a girl emerging from adolescent self-concern to level-headed appreciation of herself, her family and her friends. Its appeal is for those past 15 who relish the author's flashes of humor, care with words, regard for family relationships—and who remember their own growing pains. This seems to me one of the more adult of Mary Stolz's books. (p. 34)

Margaret C. Scoggin, in The New York Times Book Review, Part II (© *1957 by The New York Times Company; reprinted by permission), November 17, 1957.*

PHYLLIS A. WHITNEY

One of the best of Mary Stolz's fine novels, ["Second Nature"] is a story about life and human beings and love. About different kinds of love because there are so many different kinds of human beings. . . .

The mature teen-ager will find more than a good story in these pages. "Second Nature" has the gift of helping readers to meet their own problems more honestly and clearly. (p. 8)

> *Phyllis A. Whitney, in* Chicago Sunday Tribune, *Part 4, May 11, 1958.*

ELLEN LEWIS BUELL

Once again [with "Second Nature"] Mary Stolz has taken a familiar teen-age situation and, eschewing the easy ending, has turned it into a wise commentary on life. The book is moving without being sombre, witty and knowing in its portrayal of teen-agers and grown-ups alike. And, like nearly all of Mrs. Stolz's books, it calls for more maturity than does the average novel for girls, provoking, at the same time, mature thinking. (p. 34)

> *Ellen Lewis Buell, in* The New York Times Book Review (© *1958 by The New York Times Company; reprinted by permission), May 18, 1958.*

ZENA SUTHERLAND

Mrs. Stolz is adept at writing in first person and has created, in [*Second Nature*'s] Anne, a sympathetic and real person. Anne's relationships to her family, her understanding of the need for tolerance and acceptance in maintaining friendships, and her painful adjustment to unrequited love are told with keen insight. The picture of a group of young people, their shifting intragroup relationships and the different ways in which each meets the common problems of courtship, love and adult status, is drawn with nuance and with strength. All the members of Anne's circle are described with candor and are quite realistic. The style is natural and the action consistent with the characters. (p. 114)

> *Zena Sutherland, in* Bulletin of the Center for Children's Books *(published by the University of Chicago), June, 1958.*

ELIZABETH C. MANN

Mary Stolz has done it again—this mature, beautifully written novel ["Some Merry-Go-Round Music"] is one of the season's few worthwhile books for girls. Again, the story's theme is determined by the personality of the main character, a heroine who exists everywhere but whose unheroic qualities have made her unrepresented in fiction.

Miranda Parrish is a young woman with plenty of potential but an unhappy life. Bickering parents, a dull job, and never enough money can happen to anyone, but Miranda's overwhelming desire is for peace at any price—and the price is high. . . . Only when circumstances force her does she take a stand and find that integrity and self-confidence make a better life than servility. The end of the book should be labeled "the beginning." (p. 38)

> *Elizabeth C. Mann, in* Chicago Sunday Tribune, *Part 2, November 1, 1959.*

LILLIAN MORRISON

"Some Merry-Go-Round Music" lacks the prolonged in-

trospection we sometimes get in [Mary Stolz's] books, but there are the unusually accurate perceptions we have come to expect, the wry wit, and a basic human kindness, an underlying compassion for families, for drab lives, and above all, for young loves and aspiration. (p. 34)

> *Lillian Morrison, in* The New York Times Book Review, *Part II* (© *1959 by The New York Times Company; reprinted by permission), November 1, 1959.*

ZENA SUTHERLAND

[*Some Merry-Go-Round Music* is one] of the most delightful books this dependable author has produced. Miranda is typical without being typed: an ordinary girl from an ordinary lower middle-class family. Living in a Washington Heights apartment and commuting to a dull job in an obscure office, Miranda dreams of romance . . . and she almost finds it, but the man isn't really interested. Realistically, the book ends on a happy note of optimism because Miranda realizes that her chance will come—a refreshing contrast to the usual patterned happy ending. The book is absorbing chiefly because it is peopled with amazingly vivid people. . . . Honest and perceptive writing. (p. 68)

> *Zena Sutherland, in* Bulletin of the Center for Children's Books *(published by the University of Chicago), December, 1959.*

Once again [with *The Beautiful Friend and Other Stories*] Mary Stolz proves that writing for teen-agers can be a serious and valuable literary enterprise. Here, in a collection of stories, she reveals her particular gift for insight and irony: a plain girl attains beauty through love; a possessive father drives his daughter into a sanctuary of lies; a bit of gossip disrupts a tentative romance; a dumb athlete teaches his flirtatious girl to appreciate him; a wife learns her place. These and other stories of a high literary quality will move, entertain, and enrich the readers into whose fortunate hands the collection will fall. (p. 686)

> Virginia Kirkus' Service, *August 15, 1960.*

ZENA SUTHERLAND

[In *The Beautiful Friend* each story gives] a vignette of some turning point in the life of a young person moving toward emotional maturity. . . . There is no variation in the excellence of the stories—they are beautifully written, perceptive, and sympathetic. Especially penetrating are the situations in which a young woman is struggling to free herself from the loving parents who do not realize they are clinging and overprotective. (p. 49)

> *Zena Sutherland, in* Bulletin of the Center for Children's Books *(published by the University of Chicago), November, 1960.*

MAUREEN DALY

Mary Stolz is a consistently modern writer for young people. But she should no more be classed as a "teenager's" writer than—say—Katharine Brush in her day. Miss Stolz' characters may be in the teen to 20 group, but her approaches and her techniques are mature, skillful, and poised. The nine short stories in this collection [*The Beautiful Friend and Other Stories*] are carefully polished little gems.

And Miss Stolz is modern because she knows that many

college students commute by airplane, some girls do marry in the teenage bracket and that it's no longer square to study in college and quote from semi-obscure poets. Yet the stories that are so up-to-date in framework might benefit from a little old-fashioned, raw emotion. All the heroines have problems which are solved in the end. Not happily, necessarily, but satisfactorily. And perhaps it is that very quality of predestination (Miss Stolz likes a tidy plot) that makes the total group of stories unsatisfactory. So pleasant to read, but without enough ache to remember. (p. 49)

> Maureen Daly, in Chicago Sunday Tribune, *Part 2, November 6, 1960.*

ELLEN LEWIS BUELL

Perhaps it is because we have come to expect so much from Mary Stolz—more than we get from almost any other writer for older girls—that her first collection of short stories ["The Beautiful Friend and Other Stories"] is a little disappointing. The compact form does not allow for the gradual unfolding of personality, the intricate development of situations, the colorful secondary characters and the detailed backgrounds which are the hallmarks of her novels. In comparison to those novels certain of the short stories seem a little slick, too quickly resolved, as in "The Robin" in which a young matron frees herself from a subtly domineering older sister.

This is not to say, however, that Mrs. Stolz cannot tell a good deal in a short space about situations in which many girls find themselves and of immediate interest to others. The title story, with its unexpected ending is an adroit reassurance to not-so-beautiful girls about beauty and the beholder.... Both "A Very Continental Weekend" and "The Turning Point" (the best of them all) deal with girls who are trying to wrench a little privacy and independence for themselves from over-protective, possessive parents. These are sharp, compassionate and sensible and ought to be required reading for all doting parents. (p. 28)

> Ellen Lewis Buell, in The New York Times Book Review (© 1960 by The New York Times Company; reprinted by permission), November 13, 1960.

MARY LOUISE HECTOR

"Wait for Me, Michael," is a beautifully constructed document that works out its psychological puzzle about emerging maturity with neatness. As a novel, it is flat. It has a final chapter of benevolent summary that will offend readers who know the author's usual subtlety and strong sense of reality. Perhaps the most glaring advertisement of the weakness of the narrative is the fact that the plot turns not once, but twice, on an episode of eavesdropping. (p. 30)

> Mary Louise Hector, in The New York Times Book Review (© 1961 by The New York Times Company; reprinted by permission), April 16, 1961.

MARGARET C. SCOGGIN

[*Wait for Me, Michael*] is well toward the top of my list of Stolz books, for it has unity as well as subtlety, and the presentation of adolescent feeling is unusually deft. Anny's moments may be sweet, bitter, or bittersweet, but they are always touched with a flash of humor or common sense or

intuition on the part of the heroine. Anny suffers but, underneath, she and her readers sense that this is a part of growing pains. For girls beyond girls' stories who ask for something true to life. (p. 285)

> Margaret C. Scoggin, in The Horn Book Magazine (copyright, 1961, by the Horn Book, Inc., Boston), June, 1961.

PAMELA MARSH

Mary Stolz's books are not the kind that can be described by a brief plot summary for she is one of the few who write for teen-age girls as sensitively as they would for adults. Her heroine's thoughts and actions spring naturally from a complete background with a sense of past and future, and so do the people who surround her. [*Who Wants Music on Monday?*] begins with a familiar conflict, glamorous sister versus plain, sensitivity versus obtuseness. But gradually, skillfully, the emphasis seesaws until empty-headedness is pitted despairingly against intellect.... As in her other books Mary Stolz shows especially an understanding of the unconforming thinker, too sensitive about her appearance, too proud of her intellect, but very appealing for all that. (p. 137)

> Pamela Marsh, in The Christian Science Monitor (reprinted by permission from The Christian Science Monitor; © 1963 The Christian Science Publishing Society; all rights reserved), November 14, 1963.

MADELEINE L'ENGLE

Mary Stolz stands high among the fine writers for young people. Although "Who Wants Music on Monday?" is not her best book, it stands head and shoulders above most teen-age novels in the quality of its writing.

The Dunne children are interesting young people, alive and intensely believable.... [Their] vital concerns are seen by the reader in a vacuum, rather than in action or conflict. At the end of the book Vincent is expected at home with his Negro roommate, but we are not shown the expected encounter. The reader is left with a sense of disappointment and incompleteness. We want very much to know the rest of the story. (p. 22)

> Madeleine L'Engle, in The New York Times Book Review (© 1964 by The New York Times Company; reprinted by permission), February 23, 1964.

VIVIAN J. MacQUOWN

The plots of teenage novels amount to the statement of a problem and its solution, which makes them puzzles or games, rather than genuine plots. E. M. Forster, in *Aspects of the Novel*, says that a plot is a narrative of events which arouses not only the curiosity of the reader but his intelligence and his memory. "Characters, to be real," he says, "ought to run smoothly, but a plot ought to cause surprise." But what could be more predictable than the plot of the ordinary teenage novel?

It is only fair to say at this point that some writers have a much better record than others in this matter. Mary Stolz, for instance, writes movingly in *To Tell Your Love* of the heartbreak of a 17-year-old girl whose first true love abandons her for no reason that she can discover; and by the end of the book he has not come back, nor will he. In *Be-*

cause of Madeleine this same author describes the career of an arrogant underprivileged girl who is awarded a scholarship to an exclusive, expensive private school. No, she is never accepted as a member of the gang nor does she want to be. But she is a brilliant student and gets what she wants from life, to the bewilderment of the "establishment."

These books are exceptions in the great sea of stories where girl loses but regains boy, where she is a misfit among her companions but is finally accepted, where she fails in the preliminary talent show but wins the big one. (p. 196)

> *Vivian J. MacQuown, in* School Library Journal *(reprinted from the April, 1964 issue of* School Library Journal, *published by R. R. Bowker Co. A Xerox Corporation; copyright © 1964), April, 1964 (and reprinted in* Readings about Adolescent Literature, *edited by Dennis Thomison, Scarecrow, 1970).*

The defect of *Goodbye my Shadow* is that the situation and the characters are abnormal, but they purport to be normal. One is therefore left unconvinced. Miss Stolz suggests that Barbara's teenage insecurity is normal, and continuous. It is possible to believe in it for a short period, which would be recognizably a crisis, but hardly as a long-term state. . . . [Barbara's insecurity] is well observed, and many teenagers will recognize something of themselves, but her father's indulgence in homely psychology and her mother's affectionate anxiety may well seem to them like a well-sugared pill, offered with the intention of persuading them to understand their parents' point of view. And in this they are unlikely to be very interested. Nor will they be fundamentally convinced that Barbara can come out of her self-imposed misery as a result of her chance invitation to participate in group social activity with the most desirable school "set", followed by a chance meeting with a fifteen-year-old boy who discusses Kafka and Hardy with her father, but at the same time takes an interest in her. Barbara does make considerable headway in self-knowledge during the course of the book, but not enough to justify the ending. However, *Goodbye my Shadow*, within these limitations, is well written and well observed and will be thoroughly enjoyed, in a slightly self-indulgent way, by many young teenagers. (p. 1074)

> The Times Literary Supplement *(© Times Newspapers Ltd. (London) 1964; reproduced from* The Times Literary Supplement *by permission), November 26, 1964.*

ZENA SUTHERLAND

Revised by the author, [*A Love, on a Season* is a novel first published in 1954 under the title *Two by Two*. . . . This is an] honest and a tender story, perceptive in analysis of human relationships and candid in approach to the problem of sex. Although the tension (and misunderstanding) between a father and son is particularly well-described, it does not overshadow the crucial problem of the book: what do two young people in love do to restrain the feelings they cannot deny? (pp. 63-4)

> *Zena Sutherland, in* Bulletin of the Center for Children's Books *(copyright 1964 by the University of Chicago; all rights reserved), December, 1964.*

RUTH HILL VIGUERS

Girls rejecting fantasy and period novels and eager for the reassurance in "real stories of girls today" can be deluded by the pseudo realism and false values predominating in many of their books. Mary Stolz's remarkable empathy with the characters in her books is particularly important in her stories about older boys and girls. At a time when many teen-age stories are misleading, she always plays fair. The people of her books are alive, their world is the contemporary world, and their stories are told with truth and dignity. (p. 107)

> *Ruth Hill Viguers, in her* Margin for Surprise: About Books, Children, and Librarians *(copyright © 1964 by Ruth Hill Viguers; reprinted by permission of Little, Brown and Co.), Little, Brown, 1964.*

MARY K. EAKIN

[*Who Wants Music on Monday?* is a] quite wonderful book. The individual characters are drawn with sharp perception; relationships between characters are described with the rarely found combination of deep and intelligent insight and that seemingly easy flow of prose that marks the craftsman. Cassie is a thorny, gawky fourteen; blazing with integrity, she resents the easy charm of her older sister, Lotta. Lotta is a case-history belle, a vain and pretty creature who blithely uses people. Their brother and his Negro roommate are concerned about their goals: about marriage, about race relations. Perhaps the most penetrating analysis is seen in the mother of the family, a woman of limited intellect, bewildered by her children, bored by her life, aimlessly unhappy. The changes in all their lives are realistic: Lotta falls in love with a man who finds her boring and rejects her; Cassie finds security in the friendship of the same man; Vincent and his roommate, often disturbed by the world in which they live, still have the optimism of youth and the sustenance of being in love. Mother doesn't change. (p. 319)

> *Mary K. Eakin, in her* Good Books for Children *(reprinted by permission of The University of Chicago Press; © 1959, 1962, and 1966 by The University of Chicago), third edition, University of Chicago Press, 1966.*

MAY HILL ARBUTHNOT

Mary Stolz, whether writing for six or sixteen, is first of all a competent writer. She has a sense of form, style, and outstanding story-telling appeal. Her approach to adolescent girls' problems in dealing with the opposite sex is sensitive and understanding. . . . [Her books] are free of didacticism, although they are built around some of the common problems that trouble adolescent girls and that need to be brought into the open. This Mary Stolz does admirably in the course of a good story. (pp. 215-16)

> *May Hill Arbuthnot, in her* Children's Reading in the Home *(copyright © 1969 by Scott, Foresman and Company; reprinted by permission), Scott, Foresman, 1969.*

JEAN FRITZ

When Mary Stolz first began writing teen-age fiction, she was hailed not only as a distinguished writer but as a ground breaker, a realist not afraid to introduce a fat heroine into a field dominated by pretty, slim girls, not afraid to let unrequited love go unrequited although traditionally romances were expected to produce happy endings. But now it is 20 years later; realism in teen-age books means drugs, ghettoes, knives, illegitimate babies, alcoholic fathers, and Mary Stolz, after a seven-year absence from the teen-age field returns with ["By the Highway Home,"] a story her publishers say is of a modern girl coping with "contemporary issues."

Thirteen-year-old Catty Reed's brother was killed in Vietnam some months before the story opens; her father loses his job as a chemical engineer and eventually decides he would rather work on the land than to continue a profession oriented toward war. Yet Catty's story has little to do with these issues. It is the story of a girl's grief over a lost brother, her difficulties in getting along with a beautiful, self-centered sister, and her adjustment to a new life in Vermont.... As far as we are concerned, Catty is protected from the problems of her contemporaries since, except for an ambiguous moment with a boy, she is only seen in relationship to her family and the old people.

This is not to criticize the story, only to place it. In spite of the surrounding circumstances, the story is not contemporary in feeling; with minor changes it might have been written 20 years ago—or seven years ago when Miss Stolz wrote "Who Wants Music on Monday?" about a similar girl.... But this is a stronger book and relevant to today's youth as perceptive stories of family relationships will always be relevant. Indeed, as grief is relevant, and certainly Miss Stolz has remarkable insight into that long, aching grief that settles down to live with a family. She has given us an appealing heroine—sensitive and articulate but so sturdy and level-headed that we can't really worry about her. We simply enjoy. (p. 8)

> *Jean Fritz, in* The New York Times Book Review *(© 1971 by The New York Times Company; reprinted by permission), October 24, 1971.*

MARILYN GARDNER

[*By the Highway Home*] is another in a growing body of teenage books that have had the spun sugar coating scraped off in order to be "relevant." Relevancy here is two-pronged, dealing with a family's grief after a beloved brother is killed in Vietnam, and with their despair when the economic recession puts their father out of a job. The story is told by Catty, a sensitive, likable, feet-on-the-ground 13-year-old, and it is Catty who both makes and saves the story. Not all the events are credible (readers who have ever moved may wonder if such a major change in lifestyle could be quite as instantly accepted and accomplished). But on balance the story is a realistic treatment of mostly realistic situations, and a pleasant bit of reading.... (p. B5)

> *Marilyn Gardner, in* The Christian Science Monitor *(reprinted by permission from* The Christian Science Monitor; *© 1971 The Christian Science Publishing Society; all rights reserved), November 11, 1971.*

[This] story of a girl's survival of her parent's separation and divorce [*Leap Before You Look*] is long, heavy, and humorless.... [Characterization] (even though some of the people "change" or are seen by Jimmie in a changing light) is too often either sledgehammer stereotype ... or static repetition of the same projection.... The continuity is frequently interrupted by gratuitous references and tiresome conversations about new lifestyles, fem lib, encounter groups and ecology, which instead of providing a convincing 1971 background just add to the strain. (p. 486)

> *Kirkus Reviews (copyright © 1972 The Kirkus Service, Inc.), April 15, 1972.*

ZENA SUTHERLAND

Fourteen-year-old Jimmie (Janine) sits alone amid the Christmas litter and looks back over the past unhappy year in which her parents have been divorced.... Much of [*Leap Before You Look*] is concerned with Jimmie's concern for issues, her relationship with her friends, her first love affair, and her love for her small brother, and the story is therefore balanced and realistic. The characterizations and relationships are excellent, the development perceptive, so that when Jimmie, alone on Christmas morning, decides to telephone her father (whose marriage she has resented) it is an adjustment arrived at gradually and convincingly. (p. 18)

> *Zena Sutherland, in* Bulletin of the Center for Children's Books *(© 1972 by the University of Chicago; all rights reserved), September, 1972.*

LAEL SCOTT

["*Leap Before You Look*"] is very bright and busy. Although divorce is the pivot, the author has added so many "with-it" subjects—Women's Lib, ecology, drop-outs, encounter groups—that at times her fiction resembles a new variety of the "Whole Earth Catalog." Her characters ring true, and so does her dialogue. Unfortunately her heroine, Jimmie (whom we pick up as a tomboy and leave a romantic teen-ager), falls disastrously out of character in the middle of the book. From the onset Jimmie seems to understand—better than they—her parents' constant dissension and her mother's peculiar withdrawal and hostility. But when her parents finally announce that they are actually going through with a divorce, Jimmie reacts with rage compounded by complete astonishment. How can this "perfectly happy marriage" break up? This kind of nonsequential thinking is inconsistent and—at the least—disconcerting. (p. 8)

> *Lael Scott, in* The New York Times Book Review *(© 1972 by The New York Times Company; reprinted by permission), September 3, 1972.*

[In *The Edge of Next Year*] Mary Stolz first gives fourteen-year-old Orin Woodward an idyllic family life: home is a rustic, unworked farm; Father a journalist who reads poetry aloud; brother Victor a delightfully grave youngster fascinated by snakes and bugs; his mother, Rose, a lover of plants and word play and given to watching the moon through binoculars. No sooner is all this established, than it is shattered by a freak auto accident that leaves Orin's mother dead—"thrown to the side of the road like a woodchuck, or a dog"—and plunges his father into alcoholism. The shock and numbness of sudden tragedy are sharply drawn. What follows is not so much an examination of the problem of alcoholism as of the burdens borne by the alcoholic's family. Indeed, Orin's father remains enigmatic, his recovery as well as his decline inadequately motivated, whereas Orin's moods are probed layer by layer, and are most revealing in the degree to which his bitterness, resentment, and fear of abandonment are seen as acceptable and even sympathetic. The rather judgmental treatment of

Orin's father is enriched somewhat by the presence of some complex minor characters.... A mixture of good to middling moments—probably better as a study of the aftermath of a parent's death than of the drinking problem—this strengthens the introspective vein established in 1973's *Land's End.* (pp. 111-12)

Kirkus Reviews *(copyright © 1974 The Kirkus Service, Inc.), October 15, 1974.*

ZENA SUTHERLAND

It demands the skill of a writer like Mary Stolz to write a story [like *The Edge of Next Year,*] so honest and perceptive that the nuances of shifting relationships and the conflicts between love and resentment are solid and believable enough to compensate for the lack of action—no lack is felt. (p. 123)

Zena Sutherland, in Bulletin of the Center for Children's Books *(© 1975 by the University of Chicago; all rights reserved), March, 1975.*

VIRGINIA HAVILAND

[*Cat in the Mirror* is a skillfully wrought,] engrossing fantasy about a child who lives in two societies, three thousand years apart. Highly individualistic Erin Gandy, who has been miserable at five schools in three countries, is again an outsider at school.... (p. 597)

When school reopens in the fall, a new student, Seti, the attractive son of a United Nations official from Egypt, takes a liking to Erin. He also becomes part of the in-group, whose overbearing leader decides that they will make a film —"switching back and forth between modern days and ancient Egypt ...". When their teacher insists that the filming be a class project, Seti secures a role for Erin, for she is the most Egyptian-looking—"like one of the daughters of Amenhotep III." At the Metropolitan Museum with Flora, Erin overhears Seti refusing to take part in the film because the others are ridiculing her. Sobbing, she crashes into a limestone corner and plunges "back in time to another mastaba, another place, another life she had lived and then lived part way through again."

In the second half of the story, the author has created a brilliantly clear piece of historical fiction set in ancient Egypt, in and around the active household of Ha'tpet, Keeper of the King's Vineyards. The characters ingeniously parallel those in Part One.... (pp. 597-98)

There is impressive realism in the tightly constructed story, in which the details complete the symmetry, speech anachronisms help to unite the two parts of the story, and analogies and transitions are apt and smooth. Erin-Irun is a lovable, eager, and interesting child; however, it is the human relationships so sharply drawn and continued across time that make the story unique. (p. 598)

Virginia Haviland, in The Horn Book Magazine *(copyright © 1975 by The Horn Book, Inc., Boston), December, 1975.*

From the notion that present and past are concurrent, Stolz fashions a time-travel fantasy [in *Cat in the Mirror*] centered around adolescent problem solving on the part of protagonist Erin Gandy. Erin is saddled with a dual existence, one in present-day New York, where she worries about growing up and privately battles to cope with both her mother's low opinion of her and her schoolmates' ostracism. Her other self exists as Irun, an Egyptian girl of 3,000 years ago whose chief adversary is once again a disinterested mother. The time transitions are triggered by psychological or physical traumas.... A stereotypically haut monde mother and some worn situations block the evocative, gutsy impact that characterizes some of Stolz' other fiction, but the plot mechanics work smoothly, and Erin's psychological profile is well drawn. (p. 628)

The Booklist *(reprinted by permission of the American Library Association; copyright 1976 by the American Library Association), January 1, 1976.*

Elizabeth Swados

1951-

American playwright, composer, director, and juvenile novelist. The underlying theme behind Swados's theatrical works and music is the potential of the human spirit to overcome the harsh realities of life. Focusing especially on the resiliency of contemporary youth, she has presented their reactions to the world in her musical collection, *Nightclub Cantata*, and in *Runaways*, a musical theater piece about young people both literally and figuratively homeless. Swados synthesizes various forms of contemporary sound, combining them with Latin and tribal rhythms to create music that is vibrant, eclectic, and unconventional. She spent a year in Africa as composer and musical director for English director Peter Brook. Swados traveled with Brook's troupe throughout various African villages; the sense of community and the importance of ritual she experienced there has underscored much of her work, notably *Runaways*. Another important association for Swados was her partnership with director Andrei Serban, with whom she created contemporary stylizations of plays by such authors as Aeschylus and Chekhov. She also served as composer-in-residence with La Mama Experimental Theatre Club in New York City, and has been a faculty member at several universities. Swados has worked with producer Joseph Papp in many of his New York Shakespeare Festival productions, and it was Papp who was responsible for bringing *Runaways* to Broadway. The play evolved organically from Swados's interviews with students and runaways. Many of these young people later performed in the production, which has generally been praised as an honest and compassionate portrayal of the anger, energy, and courage of youth under pressure. Although Swados's songs are sometimes criticized for being too obvious, sentimental, self-conscious, or hysterical, and for having melodies that are unmemorable, songs like "To the Dead of Family Wars" and "We Are Not Strangers" from *Runaways* touchingly evoke the pain and pleasure of adolescence. She has been the recipient of two Obie awards: in 1972 for her score for Serban's production of *Medea*, and in 1977 for her direction of *Runaways*. In 1976 she wrote and illustrated *The Girl with the Incredible Feeling*, a fable about the importance of individuality, and recently adapted it for an off-Broadway production. Her musical adaptation of *Dispatches*, Michael Herr's autobiographical report of the Vietnam experience, was also recently staged off-Broadway. Merging highly charged emotional appeals with innovative dramatic techniques, Swados is credited with expanding the range of musical theatre and strengthening its appeal for a young adult audience.

CLIVE BARNES

["Nightclub Cantata"] is the most original and perhaps the most pleasurable form of nightclub entertainment I have ever encountered. . . . It is more in the pattern of the "Jacques Brel" show, but its accent, its manner and its atmosphere is quite different.

Miss Swados comes off as a force of nature. . . .

What is fascinating about this "Nightclub Cantata" is simply its unique mixture of music, drama and pop entertainment. Miss Swados's own staging is a knockout—the actors are trained like human acrobats—and her choice of source material, much of it written by herself, runs from Sylvia Plath and Frank O'Hara to Carson McCullers. But in the event it is the music that does it.

I have always been interested by her music for other people's scenes. It sounded like Mr. [Peter] Brook and Mr. [Andrei] Serban, a little like Muzak for listeners, or background music for the thinking classes. Heard on its own its amazing perceptions become far more apparent.

From Mr. Brook she has learned the humble but radiant virtue of eclecticism. Miss Swados picks around the storehouse of contemporary music like a bright-eyed jackdaw. To listen to her music is like hearing a collage of contemporary sounds; she is a sort of Kurt Schwitters of music. Her musical tone is both strange and familiar. Here you can pick up a touch of Kurt Weill, there will be more than a trace of calypso. But all this eclecticism is merger, as with the work of Mr. Brook, into a new formal pattern, a fresh realization of life and art.

Anyone who has worked with Mr. Brook would learn what to take from Mr. Serban. Miss Swados has taken Mr. Serban's visualization of the actor as a physical image, where both voice and form take on a special imagistic, even metaphorical value. For Mr. Serban, or so it seems, actors and dancers are only people differentiated slightly by their training, and of course, by their methods. But not by their purpose or function.

As a result "Nightclub Cantata" is an all-singing, all-dancing, all-acting show that represents all Swados. . . . [She] is presenting a show that is clearly a life view—about people, animals, and the things we do to one another. . . .

For anyone wanting a show that is different, involved and

engaging, and yet, on its own special terms, quite clearly cabaret, this is the show for you. I adored it.

Clive Barnes, "Art Is a Cabaret at Top of the Gate in Fine, Unique 'Nightclub Cantata'," in The New York Times *(© 1977 by The New York Times Company; reprinted by permission), January 10, 1977, p. 29.*

MICHAEL FEINGOLD

Let's go cautiously. Anyone expecting to discover a theatre piece in Elizabeth Swados's *Nightclub Cantata* had better take a second look at the title. It is not an opera, not one of the Greek plays Miss Swados is famous for setting, not a revue, not a play. It is a cantata, that quirky form halfway between opera and oratorio, a setting of somewhat dramatic texts that is meant to be sung rather than acted. And it is a cantata meant for performance in a nightclub, where the audience can smoke, drink, and at least whisper during the show, can observe coolly rather than being mobilized in a body to participate vicariously. . . .

Not, of course, a cantata in the normal sense of the word, for Swados does not write "normal" music. Her methods are monodic or responsive chant, recitative, patter-singing, the percussive use of unpitched sounds, intoning in unison or parallel thirds, and the repertory of clicks, shrieks, growls, and wails that we associate with birds, animals, and the tribal languages of Africa and Latin America. Swados is, in short, a neo-primitive—though her "primitivism" has more sophistication than a hundred years of hack composing in the traditional Western musical theatre, a fact that is pointed up by her choice of texts. No primitives here: Delmore Schwartz and Pablo Neruda, Muriel Rukeyser and Sylvia Plath, Frank O'Hara and Carson McCullers. If not for the wildly different nature of the music, it might be a Ned Rorem concert. . . .

The discrepancy between the complex, intellectual texts and the simple, repetitive accents of the music is one source of the evening's power. Swados's directing style, like her composing style, is aggressive—not hostile, but hortatory—and it can make one reel as sentences containing a dozen delicate nuances are hurled at you, at top speed and peak fervor, by her impeccably drilled young automata. If I have a criticism of her method, it is that it is too tight, too breakneck-paced, too clipped; it wants the looseness that, in a cabaret, allows for warmth and the revelation of personality—author's as well as performer's. . . .

Combined with the forcefulness of Swados's music, [her aggressive directing style] makes for an evening that is always powerful in its angularity, as it passes from the deeply moving and the humorous to numbers that are misguided or those that, at best, mark time. Only twice, I think, does Swados's method let her down at all: Once, at the very end of a lovely articulation of Delmore Schwartz's "In Dreams Begin Responsibilities," where her recitative barrels past what is properly the dramatic climax of the anecdote. (On the other hand, cantatas aren't supposed to be dramatic, and Swados's choice not to emphasize this emotional moment redoubles the impact when she does emphasize what immediately follows.)

Second, in a harrowing account of concentration-camp language, by Isabella Leitner, the words simply go by too fast, and I have a feeling that less striving for high-speed intensity and effect (the choral shouts, the flashlights in the audience) would make the moment harrow that much more deeply. It would for me, anyway. . . .

Footnote: Just to show you that the evening is not one of bleak intellectual austerity, I should add that "Indecision" is a very funny parody '50s rock number.

Michael Feingold, "Her Chants Are Sophisticated," in The Village Voice *(reprinted by permission of* The Village Voice; *copyright © The Village Voice, Inc., 1977), January 17, 1977, p. 83.*

EDITH OLIVER

Miss Swados' idea [in "Nightclub Cantata"] is to take poems and passages of prose by various hands (including her own), set them to music for various instruments (including her own guitar), and turn them over to the four young men and four young women of the company (including herself) for performance. Several of the numbers are fierce and angry, and they are delivered with passion—Muriel Rukeyser's "Waking This Morning" . . . , for example . . . , and Sylvia Plath's "The Applicant." . . . Something quite different is "Bird Lament," which Miss Swados sings entirely in bird language. . . . The weakest numbers, to get them over with as quickly as possible, are a passage from "The Ballad of the Sad Café," in which Carson McCullers makes several obvious points on the subject of love with unwarranted emphasis, and "Are You with Me?," a love ballad by Miss Swados that . . . made me long for Rodgers and Hart or the Gershwins, who handled this sort of thing with more finesse and just as much conviction. Lest I make the show sound too earnest (it *is* quite earnest), let me say right away that there is some comedy as well—a bit about two ventriloquists' dummies (written by Miss Swados and Judith Fleisher), and another bit, of venerable antecedents, about a troupe of maladroit acrobats. The strengths of "Cantata" far outnumber its weaknesses. . . . The climax of the evening (for me, at any rate) is Isabella Leitner's "Isabella"—a woman's horrifying, numbing memories of a concentration camp. . . . It must also be said that there are moments in the show when the delivery and the movements seem too intense for the material—perhaps a matter of overdisciplined direction (Miss Swados again)—but the absolute clarity of everything more or less cancels that out. . . . Miss Swados' music is undeniably dramatic, original, and effective, though it does tend to evaporate rather quickly once it is finished. (pp. 64-5)

Edith Oliver, in The New Yorker *(© 1977 by The New Yorker Magazine, Inc.), January 24, 1977.*

HAROLD CLURMAN

To call a Greenwich Village "barroom" show *Nightclub Cantata* may sound a bit uppity but as a matter of fact the name conveys the exact nature of its content. . . . There are numbers like the spoof on an acrobatic stunt act which fits a nightclub performance. For the rest, with a few exceptions, the show has a seriousness which justifies the designation of "cantata." On this occasion, [the Greenwich Village "barroom"] has been turned into an existentialist café.

The show's overall tone, "Conceived, composed and directed" by Elizabeth Swados is gritty, brave, somber and exhilarating withal. It reflects the best part of a youth which has for some time now lived in a discouraging world, a youth of few illusions, a youth emotionally and physically tattered, but yet eager to continue its life without renouncing joy, despite an experience and foreknowledge of anxiety, deception and pain. One has only to scan the list of the writers whose poems or prose Elizabeth Swados has set to her music: there is Nazim Hikmet, a Turkish poet who died in prison; contributions by Pablo Neruda, Sylvia Plath, Frank O'Hara, David Avidan, an Israeli who writes in Hebrew; by Delmore Schwartz, Muriel Rukeyser, Isabella Leitner and Ms. Swados herself.

The collective import of the words spoken or sung, and for the most part, distinctly heard, is that one must endure life and even "dance" in it, though it be heavy and rough as a "fat rock." The Leitner piece called *Isabella*—the author's first name—strikes the keynote of the evening: it tells of the garbled language, distortions of German, invented in the shadow of the Nazi crematoriums. The sounds uttered are ugly, and what they bespeak are of cruelties and atrocities the very thought of which make one flinch and shudder. Yet even in the camp, songs emerged and this particular chant concludes with, "You don't die of anything but death. Suffering is nothing; it doesn't kill you—only death."

Hardly any of the songs with their overtones of muted tenderness articulate all their apprehension, all the half-understood but nonetheless indelibly memorable hurts which the youths have sustained. Yet we know them to be real because we share in all of them. Hence the underlay of brooding sentiment throughout the evening; happily, however, we are made to rejoice in the resilient fiber, the bounce of recovery, the hardihood, spiky humor and the basic generosity of spirit which keep these youngsters "dancing."

The Swados music . . . is for the most part bony rhythm, stark, strong, insistent, with here and there—. . . a faintly plaintive touch which nevertheless reaches toward hope. There is little sensuousness in the music: there is only the energy of assertion and straight-in-the-eye determination. (pp. 124-25)

> *Harold Clurman, in* The Nation *(copyright 1977 by the Nation Associates, Inc.), January 29, 1977.*

ALAN RICH

The first time I came across music by Elizabeth Swados was at La Mama a couple of years ago, during one of Andrei Serban's stagings of some Greek play or other. The room, as I remember it, was full of flying bodies: actresses being thrown off balconies, things like that. Although I spent most of the evening cowering in protected areas, I do remember every now and then picking up a snatch of something that sounded like bad Carl Orff (*very* bad, in other words) to texts that sounded something like gratch, grotch, pook. I left with the firm resolve that the mysteries of Ms. Swados's art—to say nothing of Mr. Serban's—might be safer in other hands in the future.

But now there is *Nightclub Cantata* . . . , and with it comes reason for an upward evaluation of Ms. Swados's musical qualities. . . .

There are a couple of clunks, as there would be in twenty of any composer's songs. Ms. Swados is not on very firm ground in simple love ballads, and the one or two in *Nightclub Cantata* are somewhat awash in sentimentality. There are also a couple of rather hysterically angry pieces that

tend to fly apart from a failure to control their inner tension, somewhat the way so many Jacques Brel songs do. But a good three quarters of the material is absolutely top-notch, and it covers a wide range of expression, from a throaty inner rage ("The Applicant," to a text by Sylvia Plath . . . , to a wild, antic hilarity ("Pastrami Brothers," a teeming spoof of all those vaudevillian acrobatic skits that could demolish the genre forever).

I liked virtually everything about the show: most of the songs, the easy way one piece runs into the next without a touch of the preciousness or plasticized charm that the "intimate revue" can so often generate, and the sense the singers generate of being genuinely happy with their material. (p. 68)

> *Alan Rich, in* New York Magazine *(copyright © 1977 by News Group Publications, Inc.; reprinted with the permission of* New York *Magazine), January 31, 1977.*

IRENE S. LEVIN

The relating of a fable is, at best, a difficult task. When it is attempted with a Y.A. audience in mind, it is even more difficult. Elizabeth Swados has accomplished the impossible. She has managed to instill in this fable [*The Girl With the Incredible Feeling*], the story of a girl who was different and found that when she listened to a drummer other than her own she lost her own individuality and sense of being. . . . It is meant to be a short read and a long discussion. Excellent for the beginning of a discussion on "being" and "to thine own self be true". Forget about the format of the children's book, which it is, teenagers will hear about this by word of mouth and read it anyway. (p. 32)

> *Irene S. Levin, in* AJL Bulletin, *Spring, 1977.*

MEL GUSSOW

["Runaways"] is an inspired musical collage about the hopes, dreams, fears, frustrations, loneliness, humor and perhaps most of all, the anger, of young people who are estranged from their families and searching for themselves. There are moments of joyfulness and youthful exuberance, but basically this is a serious contemplative musical with something important to say about society today. . . .

[In a mosaic of songs, monologues, scenes, poems, and dances, we are given] a complete portrait of urban children on the run. We see what prods youngsters to leave home and what disturbs—and nurtures—them in their escapes. The musical takes a harsh and uncompromising look at the world of runaways, but it is written . . . with great compassion. . . .

With "Runaways," [Swados] steps right into the front line of popular American theatrical composers. This is the first musical since "Hair" to unite, successfully, contemporary popular music and the legitimate theater. . . .

A pivotal song—an absolute show-stopper and one of a dozen or so exciting numbers—is "Where Are Those People Who Did 'Hair'," a lowdown travesty of punk rock. On one level, "Runaways" poses the question: What happened after the Age of Aquarius? With the death of Woodstock, the wilting of the flower children, America was faced with nuclear dropout. Confused and undirected, adolescents unmounted their "Easy Rider" motorcycles and looked for methods of survival. In the words of one of the more infectious songs in ''Runaways,'' in order to survive, you've got to ''enterprise.'' . . .

Actually, the [Joseph] Papp show that ''Runaways'' is closest to in spirit and in having a strong central theme is Ntozake Shange's ''For Colored Girls Who Have Considered Suicide/When the Rainbow is Enuf.'' In common with Miss Shange, Miss Swados creates art with her nerve ends. . . .

''Runaways'' is a concerned citizen of a musical, but it is also a buoyant entertainment, filled with the bright colors, language, and vivacity of the street. . . .

[In] all respects, ''Runaways'' is a triumph. It is an eloquent and mature vision, a musical that touches our hearts.

> *Mel Gussow, ''Stage: Inspired 'Runaways','' in The New York Times (© 1978 by The New York Times Company; reprinted by permission), March 10, 1978, p. C3.*

EDITH OLIVER

There is no story [to ''Runaways'']—one number just follows another—but underneath run the themes of abandonment, anger, and bewilderment, and (lest you think all is unrelieved gloom and reproach) of chipper opportunism in any number of situations, and of innocence and humor and bravery and bravado. Rarely have I seen so much energy and spirit on a stage. In a sense, ''Runaways'' could be considered a confessional musical, like ''A Chorus Line,'' in that the characters talk directly about themselves to the audience and act out their stories. . . . Although these characters are for the most part victims (and for the most part victims of parents), there is not a moment of sentimentality or commercial wistfulness. It is their remarkable toughness and their ability to improvise in one dangerous situation after another that set the tone of the performance. . . . [Although] the theme of ''Runaways'' is sad and often agonizing, the show raises the spirits. For some reason, however, it lacks the absolute authenticity, the firsthand quality, of ''A Chorus Line'' . . . —or, more aptly, of the original production of ''Hair'' . . . , which was also about street children. These characters seem to be composites—devised by the shrewd, intelligent, and gifted Miss Swados but composites all the same.

About Miss Swados' gifts there can be no question. Every word spoken on that stage, whether in lyrics or in lines or in recitations, is plausible, and so is every movement; the music, which comes in many varieties, is dynamic and theatrical and sounds like the music of no one else on earth. (p. 88)

> *Edith Oliver, in The New Yorker (© 1978 by The New Yorker Magazine, Inc.), March 20, 1978.*

JACK KROLL

Multitalented 27-year-old Elizabeth Swados has what D. H. Lawrence called an intelligent heart. It's this quality of highly charged feeling shaped by insight, empathy and compassion that makes her extraordinary urban pop cantata ''Runaways'' an immensely affecting show. To call it far and away the best musical of the season is to insult it. ''Runaways'' seizes your heart, plays with your pulse, dances exuberantly across the line that separates entertainment from involvement.

Swados's runaways are the deracinated, disconnected kids of the metropolis who have been cut off from the human continuity that families are supposed to provide. As writer, composer and director, Swados over a ten-month period assembled and worked with a cast ranging in age from 11 to 20, many of them actually runaways or ''problem'' children. In an astonishing feat of theatrical and social creativity, she organized these young people into an expressive community that electrifies the stage with power, poignance and pride.

Swados calls ''Runaways'' a ''collage about the profound effects of our deteriorating families.'' Like some lost tribe of children bivouacked in a secret playground . . . , the nineteen kids play out their emotions—their fear, hope, despair and defiance—in shifting deployments from solos to choruses. For Swados everything is music: ''Runaways'' vibrates with city rhythms from rock to jazz, from soul to salsa. Swados's songs are sonic shapes that trap and project emotion: sometimes the feeling is so urgent that there's no time for melody and the words pour out in a strafing monotone. (p. 74)

[''Runaways'' is an] original and enriching show. (p. 75)

> *Jack Kroll, ''Babes Up in Arms,'' in Newsweek (copyright 1978 by Newsweek, Inc.; all rights reserved; reprinted by permission), March 27, 1978, pp. 74-5.*

JOHN SIMON

Let's pretend that nobody has overused the word ''nice.'' It is, therefore, still fresh and available to describe a show that is decent, appealing, enjoyable without being extraordinary. Such a nice show is *Runaways*, by Elizabeth Swados. . . . [The] most authentic runaway is Liz Swados herself. . . . The true runaway quality about her is mental; her invention races freely between the near-classical and the quasi-popular styles of composition, much of it in a special, somewhat fey, faraway province of the imagination. Miss Swados . . . writes tunes and words about a wonderland often as bizarre and menacing as Lewis Carroll's and, unfortunately, real.

Here the subject is, of course, runaway children from eleven to their early twenties, and the sequence of unconnected but strategically ordered songs concerns, sometimes, the brighter moments of being young and streetwise or -foolish, and, more frequently, the pains of being alone, alienated, and in the process of becoming one of the metropolis's victims or victimizers. There are, however, glimpses of home life as well, so that the show (to a certain extent improvised by the cast) is really about growing up—absurdly, tragically, and sometimes, despite everything, even triumphantly.

The music, in all conceivable pop, folk, and ethnic modes, is fair to excellent. Swados, like most composers with genuine theatrical facility, is sometimes a bit too facile, and there are passages of merely serviceable *Gebrauchsmusik* here, verging on latter-day versions of the old oom-pah-pah. But, suddenly, the composer will pull herself up by her guitar strings . . . and out comes a sinuously cajoling melody like ''Where Do People Go?'' Still, in the area of melodic invention, Swados, as of now, has her intermittencies.

Her lyrics, not infrequently delivered in a parlando style, have their raw beauty. Not your customary, disciplined rhymes, they rove in both form and meaning. But they are apt to be moving in a quirkily defiant, unpoignant, harshly affecting way; they can also be funny with the untrammeled, irreverent fantasy of children (from whom age has not yet detached Miss Swados fully) who bring a prodigality of gifts to a world that, at best, accepts them ungraciously. Oddly enough, Miss Swados's words often sound as genuine as, but less sentimental than, the charming and deeply involving ones in *The Me Nobody Knows,* the fine show that was based almost entirely on children's writings. (p. 70)

John Simon, in New York *Magazine (copyright © 1978 by News Group Publications, Inc.; reprinted with the permission of* New York *Magazine), March 27, 1978.*

LAURA SHAPIRO

"*Runaways* is about anybody who's in transition, anybody who's separated," said Swados; but the songs and monologues are about one sort of distance more than any other, the distance between ourselves and our families. Parental fights, divorce, child abuse and general neglect are what the kids describe: their fantasies are about belonging. "Let me be young before I get old," is the climactic plea. "Let me be a kid." They sing about life on the street, about heroin and prostitution and violence; they also demonstrate skateboard technique, play basketball and dream. . . .

The music composed for *Runaways* is as straightforward as the rest of the production, mainly variations on a few hard-hitting themes, contrasting with the plaintive monologues. "This music is the folk music of the village, the *Runaways* village," Swados remarked. "The music tries to cover what is consciously agreeable to their age—I use salsa, rock, jazz —and the monologues to me are music, too." . . .

Although its theatrical and emotional heritage is in productions like *Hair, Tommy* and the Joffrey Ballet's groaningly hip *Trinity, Runaways* successfully avoids the gaseous self-indulgence of those Broadway efforts. . . . Most musicals can be tied up with a bow and delivered whole; *Runaways* is different. There is no happy ending, no glorious resolution; the stark question, "Where do people go?/When they run away?/Where do they stay?" is never answered. The kids themselves can be strong and exuberant but the theme of loneliness and bitterness is constant. Both off-Broadway and on, what is disconcerting about the show is the rows and rows of cheerful parents applauding the anguish of their children. (p. 56)

Laura Shapiro, "Runaway Kids Find Home in Broadway Theater," in Rolling Stone *(by Straight Arrow Publishers, Inc. © 1978; all rights reserved; reprinted by permission), Issue 267, June 15, 1978, pp. 54-6.*

ERIKA MUNK

Once upon a time, Elizabeth Swados wrote a children's book called *The Girl with the Incredible Feeling.* In 1977— when I was still interested in Swados's work, though beginning to be troubled by it—I bought the book for my daughter Maja, then four. The story was about a girl who had a feeling (drawn as a multicolored blob) which made her sing, dance, "laugh at things others fought over," and have visions. . . . One day a man came out of the shadows and said the world could use this terrific feeling, so it was

dressed up, therapized, explicated, plagiarized. The girl became "more popular," but the feeling grew weak and disappeared. After a while the girl felt empty inside and had horrible dreams. Every thing and person looked the same to her. So despite the blandishments of the shadow-man and offers of other people's feelings and "amazing facts," she hunted for her feeling and, by returning to the place she started from, reclaimed it. The Blue Bird of Art is found in the Self.

The cartoony drawings and kindergarten vocabulary were about right for Maja, but she didn't like the story much. So I put the book away. It is more about Swados than for children. And her idea that feeling, or insight, or imagination, or skill is a precious blob one mustn't let others touch seemed a deadly notion for a child.

It's not such a terrific notion for a theatre artist either. From Swados's experimental (or Brook/Serban) phase, through *Nightclub Cantata*'s effective though ethically dubious attacks on our emotions, on to *Runaway*'s slick wringing of easy-come easy-go tears, to the hodgepodge of the never-opened *Alice in Wonderland,* one senses that the Feeling has become more and more a Blob. A blob, however, which is less and less unsullied by the shadow-man: indeed it's dressed up, therapized, explicated, and plagiarized.

Now we have *The Incredible Feeling Show*—produced by the First All Children's Theatre. . . . Although Meridee Stein, the company's director, calls it "the magical journey of a young girl's self-discovery," the piece is still a fable about art and commerce. . . .

As for Maja, she still didn't understand the story and has no patience with explanations, but now she's nagging me for tap shoes of her own. Which is fine, but not to be confused with magical journeys of self-discovery. She'll need different shoes for that, and they're not in Swados's store. (p. 84)

Erika Munk, in The Village Voice *(reprinted by permission of* The Village Voice; *copyright © The Village Voice, Inc., 1979), March 12, 1979.*

STANLEY KAUFFMANN

It may sound pat . . . to praise a small inexpensive show. I risk it happily. . . . Swados made a musical from her book for children, *The Girl with the Incredible Feeling,* and called it *The Incredible Feeling Show.* It's the perfect title. . . . It's a long while since an hour and a quarter in the theater has passed in such sheer delight.

Swados's songs, a few of them reminiscent of her past works, are ingeniously based on pop forms. . . .

If you're in New York during the run, even without children, take a plunge into a pool of bubbles. (p. 25)

Stanley Kauffmann, "Slay It With Music" (copyright © 1979 by Stanley Kauffmann; reprinted by permission of Brandt & Brandt Literary Agents, Inc.), in The New Republic, *March 24, 1979, pp. 24-5.*

JOHN BEAUFORT

[What] went wrong with "Dispatches"?

Certainly, in addition to all her other creative talents, Miss Swados proved (in "Nightclub Cantata" and "Runaways") an abundant aptitude for original musical-theater entertainment. "Dispatches," Michael Herr's hard-hitting, graphically authentic reportage from Vietnam, offered a challenge which unfortunately has not been met. . . .

The magnitude of the subject [of Vietnam] looms over the inadequacy of Miss Swados' noisy gallimaufry.

Using passages from Mr. Herr's book as spoken links and lyric themes, Miss Swados embellishes the text with 21 musical numbers in a score that features rock-and-roll but which also includes blues, country, and western, and even a setting of the 91st Psalm in a black-gospel treatment. Since she is a gifted melodist and lyric writer, "Dispatches" offers some rewards to relieve the general monotony. . . .

On the whole, however, this musical amalgam . . . trivializes its source material, and more important, the enormous subject with which it strives to deal. Besides seeming dated, the attempt underscores the limits of the rock idiom. (p. 18)

> *John Beaufort, in* The Christian Science Monitor *(reprinted by permission from* The Christian Science Monitor; © *1979 The Christian Science Monitor Publishing Society; all rights reserved), April 25, 1979.*

ERIKA MUNK

This is not an apocryphal story: A Vietnam combat veteran went to see Elizabeth Swados's *Dispatches* in preview. After the show he introduced himself, saying that he had been in Vietnam when Michael Herr was there and would like to talk to her whenever she had a moment. "I'm sorry, I can't," said Swados, "I'm too vulnerable."

Swados has always worked with material that cuts to the emotional quick and, based as it is on things that happen to real people, should allow us no recourse. At the same time she apparently needs to make art pretty, to create easy affect through coarse effects. To be moved by one of her pieces is to be pushed around; this was true of the concentration camp and political material in *Nightclub Cantata* . . . , and the child abuse and desertion in *Runaways*. . . . But to be pushed around emotionally is not, of course, to be moved. Swados provides experiences of a measured, mollified harshness and her ideal spectator is confronted just enough to be absolved of further thought. She wants us to be vulnerable: but only to her work, and only for the moment of watching. . . .

Herr's book is apolitical, almost antipolitical, all about looking-at-him-looking-at-the-war. But at least he looks at himself (and his colleagues) with some irony and toughness, and the book is understood to be a report of what he—scared, skewed, stoned, there by choice, and having his happy childhood—picked to see. It is not a history of the war. Swados has almost liquidated the reporter as character, so that the images and incidents she picks become representative of what she wants us to consider a whole truth. Thus she must be held responsible for a few omissions: the government which ordered the war, the military which decided where and how Americans would fight and be killed, the Vietnamese whom they in turn killed, the anti-war movement which tried to stop all this. Swados *is* vulnerable, but not the way she meant.

> *Erika Munk, "Crimes of Omission," in* The Vil-

lage Voice *(reprinted by permission of* The Village Voice; *copyright* © *News Group Publications, Inc., 1979), April 30, 1979, p. 88.*

MICHAEL FEINGOLD

Dispatches doesn't have any dramatic continuity; it is another Swados nightclub cantata, a setting of disconnected passages from Michael Herr's book of war reportage. Herr's main interest is what Vietnam did to one's consciousness, his own as much as the soldiers'. At one point he equates the moral upheavals caused by the war with the social upheavals going on back home, and refers to a "rock-and-roll war." This dubious phrase is the one that has misled Ms. Swados. Her war is staged as a rock concert. . . . It is not the silliest damn thing I've ever seen in my life (close, though), but it is certainly the most frustrating waste of a major opportunity. . . .

[The net effect of *Swados's*] tinpan tunes and cute diddy-bop routines is to soften and mute the gritty realities on which Herr's speculations are based; the words go racing by semi-audibly, usually cheapened by the visual component. An interesting anecdote about a female Viet Cong sniper is turned into a Lady-in-Red honky-tonk number; a disturbing list of the superstitions G.I.s clung to is lightened with a cheery ragtime tune.

Imitations of famous rock acts, and tableaux copied from news photographs, add to the distraction. What does the story of a legless soldier and the priest who lied to him have to do with Jimi Hendrix's guitar-smashing act? . . .

A performance that dealt with the facts, causes, and effects of the Vietnam war in an authentic way would probably make half the audience walk out in anger, and the other half sick in the aisles. Even so, I would rather be offended that way than be cajoled into swallowing the tiny bitter pill Swados has so carefully sugared; she doesn't seem to realize that the sugar is the rancid part: When she picks up on Herr's dubious philosophizing, and tries to make the audience believe that we're all swell folks who don't *like* liking war, and that those who stayed home suffered just as much, that "we've all been" to Vietnam, she is doing something actively pernicious, insulting to those who *were* there and confirming those who were not in an equality they have no real right to feel.

None of this is to say Swados isn't creative, dedicated, and sincere; she is. But she is rapidly becoming New York's most unthinking young artist, snatching up anything that can be ground through her musical mill. She has no right to do it with a subject as demanding of moral responsibility as Vietnam; she ought to know better. Even in this dismal welter, several of her melodies—the nonrock ones—are listenable. . . . On the other hand, her directing sabotages the spoken texts with the same kind of stuntiness that disfigures the show as a whole. There is no excuse for her adulterating this spare, exacting prose with fake-naturalistic ums and ers, fake-stoned pauses, and fake-black street jive; she is as unfair to Herr as she is to Vietnam.

> *Michael Feingold, "Hawkish on Swados," Part 1,* The Village Voice *(reprinted by permission of* The Village Voice; *copyright* © *News Group Publications, Inc., 1979), April 30, 1979, p. 89.*

STEPHEN HOLDEN

Though billed as a "rock-war musical," there's hardly a

moment of rock in Elizabeth Swados's adaptation of Michael Herr's *Dispatches* and only a child's storybook sense of war. One of Herr's triumphs was the invention of an electric-mosaic prose style whose intense emotional crosscurrents and streetwise rhythms are the literary equivalent of hard-rock music. *Dispatches* is a sustained riff on the romance of fear, the pornography of war, and the limits of machismo. Like the greatest rock music, especially the voodoo psychedelic funk of Jimi Hendrix, its mixture of pain, humor, and superstition is as close to unbearable as it is compelling. The book takes off on the McLuhanist assumption that the same technology that produced rock, produced Vietnam when America grafted its electric-circuit consciousness to Asia. One of the many ways Herr dramatized this interface was by sprinkling rock lyrics throughout his chronicle. The language dissolves into funk into technojargon and back, explosion, feedback, and reverb: amplification and remote control, technical precision guided by insane superstition.

There's no evidence in her musical that Swados has ever seriously considered Herr's techno-military ironies or their relation to American machismo. Swados carved a modest niche in the musical world by ignoring just such issues to forge a sentimental/primitive salon theatrical style, antithetical to the very concept of rock power. *Dispatches* shows just *how* antithetical. The only way it could even have been staged would have been as a mixed-media event with high-amp rock at the center. Instead, Swados has given us a collection of old-fashioned Broadway set pieces (none especially tuneful) for soloists and chorus—*Hair* without hits. . . .

In setting Herr's prose, Swados simply lifted the book's most obvious vignettes and dramatized them for superficial comedy or pathos. By fragmenting the book into 21 self-contained, stylized "numbers" that often render the text unintelligible, she's succeeded in turning the most personal and primal American graffiti imaginable into shtick. . . . Women don't figure in Michael Herr's book, and they shouldn't have been introduced here. Swados's vision is so prim, so smugly sensitive, she even makes the mistake of playing routine street obscenity for shock value rather than color and style. By systematically stripping *Dispatches* of its terror, humor, poetry, and finally its music, Swados has reduced Vietnam to nostalgia based on the fatally trite flower-power notion that we're all just kids; she might just as well have called this travesty *Springtime for Thieu*.

Stephen Holden, "Hawkish on Swados," Part 2,
The Village Voice *(reprinted by permission of* The
Village Voice; *copyright © News Group Publications, Inc., 1979), April 30, 1979, p. 89.*

JOHN SIMON

[*Dispatches* is a] sordid, even sinister, business. I am willing to believe that Herr's book is all they claim for it; all the more reason to bemoan the self-indulgent, sophomoric, and tuneless mess Miss Swados has made of it. Indeed, the entire Vietnam experience is trivialized, vulgarized, and, worst of all, made boring. It is one thing to take runaway children and portray their dropping out through clever verbal-musical vignettes; such kids do develop a gutter cleverness, are drawn to and drugged by rock music, and can be choreographed into dances of protest, wistful self-expression, kinetic energy as a substitute for purposeful activity.

But the Vietnam war, the soldiers, dismemberment and dying, national shame and personal tragedy submerged in heat, mud, humiliation, and sometimes modes of perishing that are denied even the dignity of combat (such as being shot by one's own buddies)—these cannot be judged by words cut out of context and turned into lyrics by a dubious art of découpage, and accompanied with music that, this time round, is all monotonous non-melody. Almost every "tune" here could be done full justice to by a penny whistle, baby's rattle, and tin drum. . . . (p. 85)

John Simon, in New York Magazine *(copyright ©
1979 by News Group Publications, Inc.; reprinted
with the permission of* New York Magazine*), May
7, 1979.*

J(ohn) R(onald) R(euel) Tolkien

1892-1973

British novelist, poet, editor, critic, short story writer, and Anglo-Saxon scholar. Tolkien created a complete mythology with his works of fantasy, which narrate a timeless cosmic struggle between good and evil and have captured the imaginations of a generation. He is credited with making the fairy tale accessible to adults through his trilogy, *The Lord of the Rings*, and essay, "On Fairy Stories." His success made fantasy a popular and acceptable genre for adult writers, many of whom have imitated his example. Tolkien was born in South Africa, and moved to England at the age of four following the death of his father. Perhaps Tolkien's greatest influence was his mother, who introduced him to history, legends, and the fascination of language. At an early age he began composing his own languages and later wrote stories and poems as a framework for them. Tolkien studied linguistics at Oxford, and in 1925 became Rawlinson and Bosworth Professor of Anglo-Saxon. From 1945 until his retirement he was the Merton Professor of English Language and Literature and became an emeritus fellow of Oxford. His scholarly works on philology and literature are considered major contributions to both subjects. While at Oxford he made the acquaintance of novelist and critic C. S. Lewis, who was later to talk a reluctant Tolkien into submitting *The Hobbit* for publication. *The Hobbit*, based on Tolkien's private mythology and the bedtime stories he told his children during the 1930s, began the history of Middle-earth. *The Lord of the Rings* continues the saga, having as its theme the corruption of power. *The Silmarillion*, which was begun in 1916 but published posthumously, forms the prologue to *The Lord of the Rings*. During the 1960s Tolkien was catapulted to fame as young adults discovered his books. The cult spawned clubs, journals, buttons, and graffiti, as well as societies devoted to the serious study of Tolkien and his works. Tolkien's critical reception has been less wholeheartedly enthusiastic: he has been criticized for characters, especially women, who are one-dimensional and for prose which is flat and lacking in imagery. Although the initial craze surrounding his work has ebbed, young people still respond positively to Tolkien's characters, identifying with their quests towards maturity and self awareness. (See also *CLC*, Vols. 1, 2, 3, 8, and *Contemporary Authors*, Vols. 17-18; obituary, Vols. 45-48; *Contemporary Authors Permanent Series*, Vol. 2; *Something about the Author*, Vol. 2.)

The publishers claim that "The Hobbit," though very unlike "Alice," resembles it in being the work of a professor at play. A more important truth is that both belong to a very small class of books which have nothing in common save that each admits us to a world of its own—a world that seems to have been going on before we stumbled into it but which, once found by the right reader, becomes indispensable to him. Its place is with "Alice," "Flatland," "Phantastes," "The Wind in the Willows."

To define the world of "The Hobbit" is, of course, impossible, because it is new. You cannot anticipate it before you go there, as you cannot forget it once you have gone. . . .

[This] is a children's book only in the sense that the first of many readings can be undertaken in the nursery. "Alice" is read gravely by children and with laughter by grown-ups; "The Hobbit," on the other hand, will be funniest to its youngest readers, and only years later, at a tenth or twentieth reading, will they begin to realize what deft scholarship and profound reflection have gone to make everything in it so ripe, so friendly, and in its own way so true. Prediction is dangerous: but "The Hobbit" may well prove a classic.

> *"A World for Children," in* The Times Literary Supplement *(© Times Newspapers Ltd. (London) 1937; reproduced from* The Times Literary Supplement *by permission), October 2, 1937, p. 714.*

C. S. LEWIS

[*The Fellowship of the Ring*] is like lightning from a clear sky; as sharply different, as unpredictable in our age as [William Blake's] *Songs of Innocence* were in theirs. To say that in it heroic romance, gorgeous, eloquent, and unashamed, has suddenly returned at a period almost pathological in its anti-romanticism, is inadequate. To us, who live in that odd period, the return—and the sheer relief of it—is doubtless the important thing. But in the history of Romance itself—a history which stretches back to the *Odyssey* and beyond—it makes not a return but an advance or revolution: the conquest of new territory.

Nothing quite like it was ever done before. . . . The utterly new achievement of Professor Tolkien is that he carries a comparable sense of reality unaided. Probably no book yet written in the world is quite such a radical instance of what its author has elsewhere called 'sub-creation'. The direct debt (there are of course subtler kinds of debt) which every author must owe to the actual universe, is here deliberately reduced to the minimum. Not content to create his own story, he creates, with an almost insolent prodigality, the whole world in which it is to move, with its own theology, myths, geography, history, palaeography, languages, and orders of beings—a world 'full of strange creatures beyond count'. The names alone are a feast . . . [and are] best of all . . . when they embody that piercing, high, elvish beauty of which no other prose writer has captured so much.

Such a book has of course its predestined readers, even now more numerous and more critical than is always realized. To them a reviewer need say little, except that here are beauties which pierce like swords or burn like cold iron; here is a book that will break your heart. They will know that this is good news, good beyond hope. To complete their happiness one need only add that it promises to be gloriously long: this volume is only the first of three. But it is too great a book to rule only its natural subjects. Something must be said to 'those without', to the unconverted. At the very least, possible misunderstandings may be got out of the way.

First, we must clearly understand that though *The Fellowship* in one way continues its author's fairy-tale, *The Hobbit,* it is in no sense an overgrown 'juvenile'. The truth is the other way round. *The Hobbit* was merely a fragment torn from the author's huge myth and adapted for children; inevitably losing something by the adaptation. *The Fellowship* gives us at last the lineaments of that myth 'in their true dimensions like themselves'. (p. 1082)

[The Hobbits] are not an allegory of the English, but they are perhaps a myth that only an Englishman (or, should we add, a Dutchman?) could have created. Almost the central theme of the book is the contrast between the Hobbits (or 'the Shire') and the appalling destiny to which some of them recalled, the terrifying discovery that the humdrum happiness of the Shire, which they had taken for granted as something normal, is in reality a sort of local and temporary accident, that its existence depends on being protected by the powers which Hobbits forget against powers which Hobbits dare not imagine, that any Hobbit may find himself forced out of the Shire and caught up into that high conflict. More strangely still, the event of that conflict between the strongest things may come to depend on him, who is almost the weakest.

What shows that we are reading myth, not allegory, is that there are no pointers to a specifically theological, or political, or psychological application. A myth points, for each reader, to the realm he lives in most. It is a master key; use it on what door you like. And there are other themes in *The Fellowship* equally serious.

That is why no catchwords about 'escapism' or 'nostalgia' and no distrust of 'private worlds', are in court. This is no Angria, no dreaming; it is sane and vigilant invention, revealing at point after point the integration of the author's mind. What is the use of calling 'private' a world we can all walk into and test and in which we find such a balance? As for escapism, what we chiefly escape is the illusions of our ordinary life. We certainly do not escape anguish. Despite many a snug fireside and many an hour of good cheer to gratify the Hobbit in each of us, anguish is, for me, almost the prevailing note. But not, as in the literature most typical of our age, the anguish of abnormal or contorted souls; rather that anguish of those who were happy before a cer-

tain darkness came up and will be happy if they live to see it gone.

Nostalgia does indeed come in; not ours nor the author's, but that of the characters. It is closely connected with one of Professor Tolkien's greatest achievements. One would have supposed that diuturnity was the quality least likely to be found in an invented world. And one has, in fact, an uneasy feeling that the worlds of *Furioso* or *The Water of the Wondrous Isles* weren't there at all before the curtain rose. But in the Tolkinian world you can hardly put your foot down anywhere from Esgaroth to Forlindon or between Ered Mithrinnd Khand, without stirring the dust of history. Our own world, except at certain rare moments, hardly seems so heavy with its past. This is one element in the anguish which the characters bear. But with the anguish comes also a strange exaltation. They are at once stricken and upheld by the memory of vanished civilizations and lost splendour. They have outlived the second and third Ages; the wire of life was drawn long since. As we read we find ourselves sharing their burden; when we have finished, we return to our own life not relaxed but fortified.

But there is more in the book still. Every now and then, risen from sources we can only conjecture and almost alien (one would think) to the author's habitual imagination, figures meet us so brimming with life (not human life) that they make our sort of anguish and our sort of exaltation seem unimportant. Such is Tom Bombadil, such the unforgettable Ents. This is surely the utmost reach of invention, when an author produces what seems to be not even his own, much less anyone else's. Is mythopoeia, after all, not the most, but the least, subjective of activities?

Even now I have left out almost everything—the silvan leafiness, the passions, the high virtues, the remote horizons. Even if I had space I could hardly convey them. And after all the most obvious appeal of the book is perhaps also its deepest: 'there was sorrow then too, and gathering dark, but great valour, and great deeds that were not wholly vain'. *Not wholly vain*—it is the cool middle point between illusion and disillusionment. (p. 1083)

> *C. S. Lewis, "The Gods Return to Earth," in* Time and Tide, *August 14, 1954, pp. 1082-83.*

W. H. AUDEN

I suppose readers exist who do not enjoy Heroic Quests, but I have never met them. For many of us they are so much the most delicious form of literature that we can devour one even when our critical faculties tell us it is trash. Those who remember *The Hobbit* as the best children's story written in the last fifty years will open any new work by Professor Tolkien with high hopes, but *The Fellowship of the Ring* is better than their wildest dreams could have foreseen. . . . (p. 59)

For a contemporary writer who sets out to create a convincing imaginary world, the task is much more formidable than it was for the authors of the Courtly Romances, since he can neither write nor expect to be read as if the naturalistic novel and scientific historical research did not exist. It may give some indication of Mr. Tolkien's astonishing powers that I can only find two questions of probability to raise, just as the questions themselves may illustrate the difference between a mid-20th-century reader and a contemporary of Spenser. We are told that the Hobbits have lived for many generations immune from war, pestilence, and famine; and that, normally, they have large families and are long-lived. In that case, I do not quite understand why population pressure has not forced them to emigrate from the Shire. Secondly—a minor point—the drying up of the Sirannon river is explained by the fact that it has been dammed; but the lake so formed has been full for years—where is the water going to?

The first problem for the maker of an imaginary world is the same as Adam's in Eden; he has to invent names for everything and everyone, and these names must be both apt and consistent with each other. It is hard enough to find the "right" names in a comic world; in a serious one, success seems almost magical. I can only say that in the nominative gift Mr. Tolkien surpasses any writer known to me, living or dead. (pp. 59-60)

Again, what other creator of imaginary landscapes has possessed so acute a topographical eye? For a journey to seem real, the reader must be convinced that he is seeing the landscape through which it passes as, given his mode of locomotion and the circumstances of his errand, the traveller himself saw it. By the end of the volume Frodo Baggins has covered some thirteen hundred miles, much of it on foot, and with his senses kept perpetually sharp by fear, watching every inch of the way for signs of his pursuers, yet Mr. Tolkien succeeds in convincing us that there is nothing which his hero noticed which he has forgotten to describe; indeed, so exact is he that a reader who consults the beautiful map at the end of the book will observe immediately that the course of the road between Hoarwell Bridge and Bruinen Ford is erroneously drawn.

In a heroic romance where the situations are those of elemental crisis to which the possible reactions are few, to stand one's ground or to flee, to be faithful or to betray, subtleties of character drawing are neither possible nor relevant. The characters must be representative specimens of a few archetypes, the Wise man, the Strong man, the Cheerful man, the Cautious man, the Lady of Light, the Lord of Darkness, etc. Mr. Tolkien manages very cleverly to give his types an uncommon depth and solidity by providing each of them with a past which is more that of the group to which he belongs than a personal one; what Aragorn, for instance, talks about is the history of the Rangers, not of himself. Only one character, and this may be an idiosyncracy of my own, does not come off. Sam Gamgee, the faithful squire, is certainly a very estimable person and I think that we are meant to love him; but, in me, he arouses a strong desire to kick him all round the block.

Perhaps Mr. Tolkien's greatest achievement is to have written a heroic romance which seems wholly relevant to the realities of our concrete historical existence. When reading medieval examples of this genre, enjoyable as they are, one is sometimes tempted to ask the Knightly hero—"Is your trip necessary?" (p. 60)

In *The Fellowship of the Ring,* on the other hand, the fate of the Ring will affect the daily lives of thousands who have never heard of its existence. Further, as in the Bible and many fairy stories, the hero is not a Knight, endowed by birth and breeding with exceptional *arete,* but only a hobbit pretty much like all other hobbits. It is not the wise Gandalf or the mighty Aragorn but Frodo Baggins who is called to undertake this deadly dangerous mission which he would much rather avoid, and if one asks why he and not one of a hundred others like him, the only answer is that chance, or Providence, has chosen, and he must obey. (p. 62)

> W. H. Auden, "A World Imaginary, But Real," in Encounter (© 1954 by Encounter Ltd.), November, 1954, pp. 59-60, 62.

MAURICE RICHARDSON

The Two Towers is the second volume of [Tolkien's] mammoth fairy tale, or, as some call it, heroic romance, *The Lord of The Rings.* It will do quite nicely as an allegorical adventure story for very leisured boys, but as anything else I am convinced it has been wildly overpraised and it is all I can do to restrain myself from shouting: Conspiracy! and slouching through the streets with a sandwichman's board inscribed in jagged paranoid scrawl in violet ink: "Adults of all ages! Unite against the infantilist invasion."

It has been compared by Richard Hughes to Spenser's *Faerie Queen;* by Naomi Mitchison to Malory; by C. S. Lewis to Ariosto. I can see why these three should have soft spots for its Norse and Celtic and mystical trappings. Mr. Auden has also gone into raptures over it [see excerpt above]. This, too, is not unexpected, because he has always been captivated by the pubescent worlds of the saga and the classroom. There are passages in *The Orators* which are not unlike bits of Tolkien's hobbitry. (p. 835)

My first impression is that it is all far too long and blown up. What began as a charming children's book has proliferated into an endless worm. My second that, although a great deal of imagination has been at work, it is imagination of low potential. The various creatures, hobbits, elves, dwarfs, orcs, ents (tree-wardens who seem at times to be almost walking vegetables) are nicely differentiated. Their ecology is described with scholarly detail and consistency. But not one of them has any real individuality; not one is a character. And though their dialogue is carefully varied, from coloquial-historical for men and wizards to prep school slang for hobbits and orcs, they all speak with the same flat, castrated voice.

I also find the story-telling (true, this is particularly difficult to judge in an isolated volume, and I should warn new readers who are going to begin here that they will find the synopsis barely adequate) confusing. Interest is diffused between too many characters and groups. In this volume the hobbits, Pippin and Merry, steal too much of the picture from the chief hobbit, Frodo, the original possessor of the Ring which all the fuss is about.

Naturally there are points in favour. The battle scenes are well done; the atmosphere of doom and danger and perilous night-riding often effective. The traditional mystical confusion attaching to a quest, and a struggle between good and evil . . . is neatly worked into the plot. And the allegorical aspect rouses interesting speculations. How much relation is there between the world—ruined, note—of the story and our own past, present and future? To what extent, if any, does the Ring tie up with the atomic nucleus, as well the orcs at all equated with materialist scientists? Nevertheless, the fantasy remains in my opinion thin and pale. And the writing is not at all fresh. (p. 836)

> Maurice Richardson, in The New Statesman & Nation (© 1954 The Statesman & Nation Publishing Co. Ltd.), December 18, 1954.

LOREN EISELEY

Beginning with *The Hobbit,* a tale of the adventures of Bilbo Baggins, a small, intelligent representative of a people whose simple underground houses have sometimes led me to suspect that they are remote relatives of rabbits, we pass from a fascinating child's tale to the great orchestra of *The Lord of the Rings,* in which a whole Secondary World is created and successfully sustained through three large volumes.

These are sure to remain Tolkien's life work, and are certainly destined to outlast our time. They stand as a major creative act, and it is not without significance that Tolkien tells us in *Tree and Leaf* that his full taste for fairy stories, using the term in its highest sense, arose during the war. He knows better than most that the adult mind has, if anything, greater need of fantasy than that of the child, greater need of consolation, and that if Christianity be a myth of secondary Creation, then it has permeated and enlightened and in some sense influenced the Primary World: the beautiful enchantment has become real. (p. 365)

[*Tree and Leaf*] may seem slight by contrast [with *The Lord of the Rings*], consisting as it does of an essay on the fairy tale and the account [in "Leaf by Niggle"] of an artist named Niggle. Niggle procrastinated upon making a journey we all must make. Of his once great picture only a single painting of a leaf remains. To the student of *The Lord of the Rings,* however, it is plain that no one but the author could have so clarified his purpose or illuminated the underlying dignity of that enchantment in which the true artist "may actually assist in the effoliation and multiple enrichment of creation." . . .

Can it be that long familiarity with Bacon's Primary World has reduced our present universe, for all the vast range of our instruments, to [what Samuel Taylor Coleridge calls] a "mass of little things?" "Of all faces," says Tolkien wisely, "those of our *familiares* are the ones both most difficult to play fantastic tricks with, and most difficult really to see with fresh attention. . . . Creative fantasy . . . may open your hoard and let all the locked things fly away like cage-birds . . . you will be warned that all you had (or knew) was dangerous and potent, not really effectively chained . . . no more yours than they were you."

This is the essential message of *Tree and Leaf:* to approach with care the interpretation of a wayward universe that in spite, or because, of our learning threatens to slip away without genuine comprehension, or—and much worse—to assume unexpectedly the vanished shape of Sauron. (p. 367)

Loren Eiseley, "The Elvish Art of Enchantment," in Book Week *(© I.H.T. Corporation; reprinted by permission), May 9, 1965 (and reprinted in* The Horn Book Magazine, *August, 1965, pp. 364-67).*

HENRY RESNIK

In recent months, *The Lord of the Rings* has been at the top of college best-seller lists across the country, and although the Tolkien people wince at the word "fad" as if it were sheer blasphemy, even they will admit that their enthusiasm has gone—perhaps inevitably—beyond all reason. The Tolkien people may be less noisy than the LSD-heads, but there are more of them, and they give the lie to most of the melodramatic scandal that has emanated from the

American campus within the past year. Look into the mirror of their emotion—the world of Tolkien—and you will probably find a clue to what today's students are really about; look into that mirror and you may even find the link that ties you to them. . . .

The books are essentially an adventure story, and this certainly accounts for part of the enthusiasm they generate. The adventure is founded on the well-known medieval convention of the quest, complete with hero (occasionally in armor), dragons of various sorts, treasure (or reward) at the end, and, although less important (the books are not very sexy), a smattering of fair ladies. (p. 91)

The easy answer to why *The Lord of the Rings* appeals so strongly to high-school and college students is that to them the ring represents the power of destruction which threatens and haunts them—the bomb. This sort of easy thinking raises problems, however. First, apparently all the Tolkien people have rejected the allegorical interpretation as pointless and uninteresting (some admittedly prompted by Tolkien's own distaste for allegory). Second, high-school and college students seem rarely to think about the bomb these days, much less construct allegorical connections concerning it. . . . The younger Tolkien fans, in fact, claim they read the books for the sheer "fun" of it. A Columbia freshman speaks eloquently for his fellow fanatics: "I'd be downcast if there were a social meaning." Yet here there is a certain division among the Tolkien people. The older ones readily grant that the books are a powerful and hopeful affirmation about man, filled with philosophical import, but even they do not think this is a good reason for reading the books.

To all readers, however, the world of Tolkien seems to offer a delicious, vintage-wine sort of escape. (pp. 91-2)

The most sophisticated evaluation of the fad inevitably turns, however, to the imaginative scope of Tolkien's world. . . . Tolkien's power of imagination seems to be, at any rate, the single element which all the Tolkien people praise, whatever their terminology.

But none of the Tolkien people have observed an important quality in themselves which may explain the explosion better than any other single factor. The majority of them are unified not by a need to find ethics in a hopeless modern world or a desire for escape or a passion for myths and languages (although these may explain their initial attraction to the books); rather, they share the hobbit spirit—the pluck, the taste for adventure, the *joie de vivre,* and, above all, the total commitment to their goals (once they decide to have goals) that unite them all. (p. 92)

Henry Resnik, "The Hobbit-Forming World of J.R.R. Tolkien," in The Saturday Evening Post *(© 1966 The Curtis Publishing Company), July 2, 1966, pp. 90-4.*

JOSEPH MATHEWSON

[At] college bookstores all across the country, students who formerly pounced on *The Catcher in the Rye* and *Lord of the Flies* are passing them up in favor of a new Lord, *The Lord of the Rings,* by J.R.R. Tolkien. The king of the campus novels is dead. Long live the king. (p. 130)

The Hobbits and their buddies are almost wholly good and, with one exception, light of skin. And no one has much more psychological depth than Rebecca of Sunnybrook

Farm. There seems to be no allegorical meaning to the trilogy. At least the author denies there is, and he also denies that World War II impinged on his plans for the cycle. If *The Lord of the Rings* has any message at all, it may be that good can win in conflict with evil, but that good is irreparably changed by the conflict. But even reading that much into the books may be reading too much, since they are in essence nothing more than fairy tales, grown up and grown exceedingly lengthy, escapist and nonintellectual.

How, then, did *The Hobbit* and the trilogy come to take the place of Salinger's appeal to the gut reactions of so many adolescents and Golding's fashionable pessimism? . . .

There was, at the outset, something cliquish about the reading of Tolkien, a hint of the secret society. It was as though the consumption of his works were a sort of ritual which, once fulfilled, admitted the reader to an inner circle of *cognoscenti*. But it was also a passport to Middle-earth, and those who have been there are generally as eager to talk about what they've seen as the tourist back from a ten-day jaunt through Europe. The true fan's need to rehash his discoveries endlessly with as many people as possible has tended to overbalance the pleasure he feels from being among the elite, and Tolkien's remarkable gossip value may be one of the major reasons why his books have ceased to be the province of cliques—or rather, why they have become the province of cliques so widely spread as to form a cult. (p. 131)

The non-fan might . . . think that an admiration for Tolkien was one of the higher forms of camp, and he might point for proof to the curious status of women in the trilogy. They are largely in the background, to say the very least. . . . And the symbolism involved in taking a ring to be destroyed is too obvious to require examination.

But the fans have little interest in the Freudian deeps of their totem. They are, for the most part, content to explore its sizable surface, studying lines of descent and gazing with inexhaustible wonder at the maps of Mordor and Gondor, Rohan and Eriador which decorate the books. (pp. 131, 221)

During the past few years, American college students have changed immensely from silent, or introspective, types to vocal, active members of the world outside their cloister. The foremost decloistering agent has been the civil-rights movement, a complex of issues that students tend to see in unequivocal terms: The little old Negro woman who wants to vote is good, and the redneck sheriff who keeps her from it is bad. Working for the good, students come in touch with a large number of adults who share their zeal, as a result of which they may be inclined to reject Holden Caulfield's blanket condemnation of all adults as phony. To carry on their work, they must be more or less convinced that they can remake the world and make it better, so they may also be inclined to reject the thesis of *Lord of the Flies* that if people were given a chance to start life anew, they would mess up just as badly as they did in the beginning.

But the world the students have entered is at times almost too real. Its inhabitants are often put in jail, often beaten and vilified, sometimes even murdered. They well may want to escape from it occasionally. The best escape is not just as way out, though, but a means of assurance, too: It's better to go down a ladder than to jump from a sixth-floor window. And the great appeal of the Tolkien books may be

that they offer both, not only page after page of faraway Middle-earth but also the victory of good over evil in a struggle where the lines are as clearly drawn as they ever were in Selma, Alabama. Having found such a febrifuge, the students have naturally done what they could to make it a lasting one, absorbing its every detail and coming in effect to believe in Middle-earth as an alternate reality.

A thoughtful student once compared destroying the ring to pasting the apple back on the tree of knowledge. "After it's gone, there's innocence again," she said, the seraphic look of the saved in her eyes. This generation of college students has lost its innocence early, in however good a cause. Perhaps they would rally to any books that tell them they can get it back by pushing their cause to success. But Tolkien got to them firstest with the mostest. (pp. 221-22)

> *Joseph Mathewson, "The Hobbit Habit" (first published in* Esquire *Magazine; copyright © 1966 by Esquire, Inc.), in* Esquire, *September, 1966, pp. 130-31, 221-22.*

PETER S. BEAGLE

The real surge of interest in Tolkien's writing has been among high school and college students. Students make strange and varied works their own, and if there is any significance to their adoption of *The Lord of the Rings*—beyond the fact that it's a good book—the hell with it; one or another of our explainers of the young will take note of it pretty soon. But there is one possible reason for Tolkien's popularity that I would like to put forward, because it concerns the real strength of *The Lord of the Rings*. Young people in general sense the difference between the real and the phony. They don't know it—when they begin to know that difference, and to try to articulate it, then they are adults and subject to all the pains and fallibilities of that state. They can be misled by fools or madmen, but they sense the preacher who doesn't feel a word of his sermon, the mountebank who is putting them on, the society that does not believe in itself. They rarely take a phony of any sort to their hearts.

Tolkien believes in his world, and in all those who inhabit it. This is, of course, no guarantee of greatness—if Tolkien weren't a fine writer, it could not make him one—but it is something without which there is no greatness, in art or in anything else, and I find very little of it in the fiction that purports to tell me about this world we all live in. This failure of belief on the authors' part is, I think, what turns so many books that mean to deal with the real things that really happen to the real souls and bodies of real people in the real world into the cramped little stages where varyingly fashionable marionettes jiggle and sing. But I believe that Tolkien has wandered in Middle-earth, which exists nowhere but in himself, and I understand the sadness of the Elves, and I have seen Mordor.

And this is the source of the book's unity, this deep sureness of Tolkien's that makes his world more than the sum of all its parts, more than an ingenious contrivance, more than an easy parable of power. Beyond the skill and invention of the man, beyond his knowledge of philology, mythology and poetry, *The Lord of the Rings* is made with love and pride and a little madness. There never has been much fiction of any sort made in this manner, but on some midnights it does seem to me that my time is cheating itself of even this little. So I have read the tale of the Ring and some other books many times, and I envy my children, who have not yet read any of them, and I envy you if you have not, and wish you joy. (pp. xv-xvi)

Peter S. Beagle, "Tolkien's Magic Ring," published by Travel Magazine, Inc., in Holiday Magazine, *1966 (and reprinted in* The Tolkien Reader, *by J.R.R. Tolkien, Ballantine Books, Inc., 1966, pp. ix-xvi).*

MATTHEW HODGART

Although I like reading epics, medieval romances, and folktales, for many years I could not get beyond the barrier of that first all-too-Hobbit sentence: "When Mr. Bilbo Baggins of Bag End announced that he would shortly be celebrating his eleventy-first birthday with a party of special magnificence, there was much talk and excitement in Hobbiton." When I forced myself inside I began to read with growing speed and excitement; then went back to *The Hobbit* (which is a very good children's book); then read most of the *Rings* for a second time, at first enjoying Tolkien's learning and craftsmanship, but ending up disenchanted. . . .

The war episodes and the spy episodes [in *The Lord of the Rings*] are beautifully synchronized, with a very precise chronology and no loose ends in the narrative. But although the war is presented in a pastiche of Anglo-Saxon and medieval epic and the spy part is a romantic Quest, the basic form is that of a John Buchan thriller. (p. 10)

Everything [in *The Lord of the Rings*] resolves itself into a simple conflict between Good and Evil. Drawing with immense skill on the *Iliad*, the *Edda*, *Beowulf*, the Irish epics of Cuchullin and the Tuatha Dé, the *Mabinogion*, Chrétien de Troyes, and Malory, Tolkien completely changes the spirit of heroic and romantic literature; there recognizable human beings suffer from some of the confusions and ambiguities of real life, but he brings everything down to the black-and-white of the fairy tales. But he goes even further than the fairy tales, where the opposition is usually not between moral good and evil but between the familiar world of men and the uncanny world of nature and the supernatural. That contrast he expresses perfectly in *The Hobbit* and in the forest episodes of the *Rings,* but throughout most of the latter he presents a much more radical opposition, which is in fact a theological one, between God and the Devil. For a parallel in medieval literature we must look to works written under the inspiration of Christian doctrine: to the *Chanson de Roland*, with its straight conflict between good Christians and bad Saracens, or to the oddest and least secular part of Arthurian romance, the *Queste del Saint Graal*. Somewhere in the background of the war between Gondor and Mordor is the war in heaven as described in *Revelations*.

This is not to say that the book is an allegory in the strict sense, like [John] Bunyan's *Holy War*. (pp. 10-11)

We can take [Tolkien's] word for it that the characters and actions do not stand for historical people or topical events: Sauron is not Hitler, the Scouring of the Shire is not about present-day England. But isn't the book really a parable, consciously aimed at putting across the general Christian view that the universe is a battlefield between the forces of good and evil? That Frodo is a Christ-like figure does not seem doubtful to me: his journey about Easter-time across the plain of Gorgoroth (cf. Golgotha) is a Calvary; he is

stripped of his garments, flogged by the soldiery, scratched by thorns: he saves the Shire and "dies" for it, finally going west over sea to the Elfish Tir-nan-Og or land of eternal youth. The Hobbits have apparently no formal religion; the men of Gondor only a silent grace before meals and a place called the Hallows. But it is hinted that Aragorn is really a monotheist and that the Quest takes place under divine providence. The *Rings* has a family likeness to the science fiction of C. S. Lewis and to the detective stories of Charles Williams, who were his friends and eloquent fellow-Christians at Oxford. Lewis and Williams deliberately chose forms of popular fiction to convey a general message about religion, at the least to predispose their readers to accept a supernaturalist view of the universe. Tolkien is a much better writer than either, but he seems, whether wholly consciously or not, to have attempted much the same thing. . . .

[The] extreme polarization of good and evil, which is so striking in the works of all three, is not only reminiscent of rigid medieval Christianity but is also, surely, rather infantile. The Hobbits are several times described as children, and that is quite acceptable, since the genres of fairy tale and romance rely on the childlike powers of the imagination. But the Hobbit view of life remorselessly divides the world up into Good Fathers (like Gandalf and Aragorn) and Bad, castrating Fathers (like Sauron, Saruman, and the Nazgul on their pterodactyls), while the terrors of the journey and the war read too often like infantile phobias. Carried into adulthood, such a view has been the basis of religious and political intolerance and persecution. One senses behind the author's tact and modesty a strongly authoritarian personality—as more obviously in C. S. Lewis —which insists on treating us all as children. If this is true, it may explain the astonishing success of the book among the young, who after a permissive upbringing may secretly want to be treated with authority like old-fashioned children. Tolkien appeals to the residual Christianity of our culture (which is probably stronger in America than in Britain) and by posing the problems of life in terms of absolute good and evil, he gives a pseudo-explanation more satisfactory to the imagination than the rational explanations of liberal humanism can ever be. (p. 11)

Matthew Hodgart, "Kicking the Hobbit," in The New York Review of Books *(reprinted with permission from* The New York Review of Books; *copyright © 1967 Nyrev, Inc.), May 4, 1967, pp. 10-11.*

ROBERT SKLAR

Tolkien's trilogy . . . resembles the Anglo-Saxon chronicles he studied as a scholar. *The Lord of the Rings* is a work of art but it is also history—even if invented history—and it bears comparison to works of Gibbon or Parkman more readily than it does to other novels. The great historians are equally artists and builders of worlds. Gibbon's Rome and Parkman's French America are worlds as strange and distant from our own as Tolkien's Middle Earth. On the level of great historical narrative it matters little whether the events described can be absolutely verified; what matters far more is the historian's attitude toward his world and his treatment of it.

As a work of history *The Lord of the Rings* is distinctly Spenglerian in tone. Tolkien has created a historical world with a comprehensive erudition and a philosophical audacity few historians since Spengler have been able to match—and with a sense of tragic destiny nearly equal to Spengler's.

For at its core *The Lord of the Rings* is the story of civilization's decline. Good may finally triumph over evil, but good is never unalloyed—in men or in hobbits or in cultures. The Third Age of Middle Earth, which the trilogy brings to a close, was founded on the powers of lesser rings, rings for dwarfs, elves and men. But the One Ring rules them all. Were Sauron to recover the ring he could only subjugate Middle Earth; when Frodo succeeds in destroying it the other rings must lose their power, too. Frodo and his company know from the start, whether they should succeed or fail, that a 3,000-year era is doomed to end.

In many ways the Third Age had been a time of peace and beauty. Yet Tolkien's historical panorama is too vast to allow mourning over the passing of an age. The elves had "attempted nothing new, living in memory of the past." The dwarfs selfishly hoarded their treasures. Their time now was passed, and they were fated to depart, leaving Middle Earth to men.

For the hobbits, too, time in Middle Earth is drawing to an end. But these little people, with their provincial narrowness, their agelong inconsequence, their simple love of beer and pipe smoking, provide the moral center and the humor of Tolkien's trilogy, and the deep recognition young people feel when they read it. Ignored and underrated by others; hedonistic and isolationist by choice—suddenly a handful of them, Frodo and Samwise, Pippin and Merry, are chosen; or choose themselves. Their moment on the great stage of history has come: to act, to dare, to be brave, to endure hardship, risk their lives, and lose forever their comfort and anonymity. This challenge, and their response, is the true moral drama in *The Lord of the Rings*.

If young people identify more with the hobbits than with the warriors and kings of men in Tolkien's tale, surely one reason—though of course Tolkien could not have envisioned such a remarkable coincidence—lies in the resemblance of the hobbits' situation to their own. Many in the present generation of American youth see themselves as just such a chosen band, called upon to leave behind a way of life equally as self-serving and as oblivious to social truths.

This represents in part a vast metaphor for coming of age— *The Lord of the Rings* provides a most dramatic and mythic analogy for the rite of passage to maturity. But it also suggests a distinctive attitude toward the present. Young people are not so saddened by the Third Age's passing, perhaps because they envision the present as a time when another outmoded era is being left behind—an era when humans are as selfish as dwarfs and as self-satisfied as elves. Like the hobbit band, they can rise above the limitations of their own society and thus prepare themselves to inherit the future. (pp. 599-600)

The fantasy and imagination and other-worldliness of Tolkien's work are all important, but what is most important is not that it serves as an escape, or leads to contemplation, or makes for livelier dreams but that it provides a paradigm for action. It asks not who you are, or your pedigree, or your past associations but simply states: this is the task; are you willing to carry it through? . . .

The most unusual aspect of Tolkien's popularity is his complete unconcern with the traditional and conventional issues of adolescence, particularly that ontological stumper, "who am I?" In the trilogy, characters may change their names and identities several times over, but they are the last ones to stew over it. They know who they are and what they must do, and if they use disguises or pseudonyms it is simply part of the job. Young people do not miss the usual questions in Tolkien because the immediacy of action cancels out all Hamlet-like musings on the self. (p. 600)

Robert Sklar, in The Nation *(copyright 1967 by the Nation Associates, Inc.), May 8, 1967.*

WILLIAM L. TAYLOR

The Lord of the Rings is an extremely valuable pedagogical instrument for heightening students' awareness of concepts and values which are difficult to grasp in the modern environment, but which are essential for full response to literary works we must teach them. (p. 819)

The central values of the book are thoroughly traditional, and the direct, immediate style and tone reinforce the fact that, however applicable they may be to our own age, these are the things that have always been true. It is curious that in an age so bound to "realism" and "verisimilitude" we should find the great truths of human nature so fully embodied in a fantasy. No student who has read it is likely to deride products of creative imagination as insignificant because they are "unscientific." The relevance of this story to real life is inescapable, and it will win a far more respectful and attentive reading of "fantasy," whether it be *A Midsummer Night's Dream* or *The Rime of the Ancient Mariner*.

Even the nature of actual sociological and international conflict is presented with vivid clarity, as Tolkien amplifies social, national, and racial differences into differences of species. Trolls are opposed to Ents, Orcs to Elves and Dwarves. Suspicions and hostilities between Elves and Dwarves, Orcs and Trolls, even Men and Hobbits, are laid aside in the face of the common enemy or for the achievement of common aspirations. Alliances, intermarriage, defections, all reflect the real world on which the fantasy is based. It is this aspect of the book which has tumbled so many critics into allegorical interpretations—the Crack of Doom itself for anyone trying to understand the work.

All who have tried to teach such books as *The Scarlet Letter* or *Moby Dick* are well aware that the present generation of high school students has a very weak concept of evil. It is extremely difficult to communicate to them the substance of these works, because they simply lack the emotional apparatus to respond to the forces of evil and corruption. I do not think there is another book available to us that will develop this sensitivity as fully as *The Lord of the Rings*. . . . One of Tolkien's greatest strengths as a novelist is his incredible sense of evil, and no reader can escape being affected by it.

Equally powerful is his presentation of the changes that occur in the human personality through contact with evil, even when that evil is not victorious. In *The Hobbit*, Bilbo Baggins does not slay the dragon—that is accomplished by a minor character—but he does confront the dragon, and he is not the same person after the experience. On an epic scale, and with vastly amplified ramifications, *The Lord of the Rings* treats the same phenomenon. (pp. 819-20)

The arena in which the immense conflict between virtue and the corruptive forces of evil is fought, the lands of Gondor and Mordor and even all of Middle-earth, is somehow progressively condensed into the remarkably durable soul of little Frodo, the Hobbit, and at the moment of greatest violence, the entire drama is enacted in a little cave in the side of Mount Doom. These parallels between internal violence, character conflict, and cosmic turmoil can render a student far more likely to grasp the relationship between the personal drives of the characters and the primal forces of the universe in such works as *Wuthering Heights* or *Moby Dick*. Evil seems to be far more powerful than Good in *The Lord of the Rings,* and yet, somehow, Good triumphs, apparently because, as Gandalf says, it was meant to be. A strong sense of Fate colors the entire story, and though it seems to be a benevolent force, at least for the time being, it can give the student a far better grasp of Destiny as it functions in Greek drama or the novels of Thomas Hardy. And since its origin is the *Wyrd* of Germanic mythology, it bears directly upon *Beowulf,* a story which almost all high school students read and almost none appreciate. . . .

The key to *Beowulf* and all heroic literature lies in this modern fantasy. (p. 820)

The characters in *The Lord of the Rings* are strongly drawn with simple, bold strokes, and are fine exemplars of the value as well as the limitations of character interpretation. Gandalf may well represent Hope, perhaps Conscience, but no one is in danger of forgetting that he is first of all that highly individual and vivid personality, Gandalf the Grey. His resurrection is an excellent instance of how a writer may use symbolism in a partial and restrictive way; the parallel to the resurrection of Christ is not maintained, and does not function at all at the conclusion of the story. Whatever Gandalf is, he is not a Christ-figure.

Many of the characters are valuably prototypic. For example, young readers often find Uriah Heep in *David Copperfield* too incredible to accept, but they may well look again when they realize his striking similarities to the possessed, maddened villain who won their complete belief, the astonishing creature, Gollum. Or again, no one has ever counted the protagonists in fiction who are supported by a loyal friend, but of them all, few are more winning than the lovable, plain-spoken Sam Gamgee, and few illustrate the structural function of the role so clearly.

Finally, there is the tiny heart of the entire massive creation, Frodo Baggins, the Hobbit. We rarely find characters in fiction who demonstrate so thoroughly the ability of a fine writer to force his audience into identification with his protagonist. We face Frodo's trials; we suffer Frodo's agonies; his life is ours. We identify unquestioningly—with a Hobbit. Tolkien has provided us an excellent demonstration of the powers of our own imagination caught up in creative fiction.

The book has its weaknesses, it is true. Tolkien's sense of the ugly and the evil far surpasses his sense of the beautiful and the good. His description of the lovely forest of Lothlórien falls short of the magical quality he aims at, while the desert surrounding Mount Doom veritably exhales the vapors of evil from every crevice in the devastated land. In details as well, there are flaws, such as the inadequate explanation given for the dark power known as the Balrog.

But the virtues of the work overwhelm its deficiencies, and beyond the various pedagogical uses which I have pointed out, the book is a valuable literary experience in itself, of a sort we rarely see well executed. (p. 821)

William L. Taylor, "Frodo Lives," in *English Journal (copyright © 1967 by the National Council of Teachers of English), September, 1967, pp. 818-21.*

MICHAEL WOOD

Tolkien is a Catholic and an Anglo-Saxon scholar, and the theology of his work is an extraordinary synthesis of heroic northern myth and Christian promise. Tolkien believes in Providence, both in and out of his fiction. He never mentions chance without a pious parenthesis—"if such it be"—yet he also believes, as he suggests the author of *Beowulf* believed, that within Time the monsters win. "We have fought the long defeat," Tolkien's Elf-Queen says, and the elves effectively leave the earth. God, in other words, is pulling his punches, to see how we make out against Sauron and his ilk. The treats come later, in the islands of the blessed.

This view accounts, I think, for two things in Tolkien's work. First, the fascination with the journey—not only in *The Hobbit* and *The Lord of the Rings* passim, but also in the rather thin stories, *Leaf by Niggle* and *Smith of Wootton Major*; the journey becomes a figure or type of death, the happy release, the blessed departure. And secondly, the elegiac tone of the trilogy, which seems strangely at odds with its heroic theme. (p. 168)

Tolkien's "old times" are only half-mythical. They are a magical Arthurian past, certainly; a lost age where lords and ladies dally sweetly on the greensward and talk like Tennyson, where elves and dwarves and hobbits and wizards and other, older creatures are available for chats with mortal men. It is a haunted world where trees move and mountains threaten and the weather is always a metaphor— a world where at least one of what Tolkien calls "primordial human desires" is satisfied: the desire to "hold communion with other living things." It is an elvish Eden, a world seen in the morning, when "al was this land fulfild of fayerye," as the Wife of Bath put it. But Tolkien's old times are also simply historical, a picture of pre-industrial England, a place of unspoiled greenery, fields and forests. Forests especially.

Tolkien writes beautifully about trees—largely, I suspect, because he prefers them to people. At the end of the trilogy, when the quest is over, the heroic hobbits return to the Shire to find that Sauron's agents have been busy there too. There are chimneys belching out black smoke, and mean houses have replaced the picturesque burrows. There is arbitrary imprisonment, and there are distinct unfairnesses in the distribution of beer and tobacco. It's a tame picture of the great darkness: a mingling of a dim view of socialism and a wishful view of Hitler's Germany.

What is there, then, in this Tory daydream to prevent it from being the mishmash that Edmund Wilson thought it was? Why would people like Richard Hughes, Naomi Mitchison and C. S. Lewis want to compare Tolkien with Spenser, Malory and Ariosto (respectively)? The answer lies less, I think, in the quality or texture of Tolkien's work than in the extent and variety of it, and in the power of the complex moral fable which he manages to sustain.

Tolkien's borrowings are considerable: lines from heroic lays, a horn from Roland, an interesting case of resurrection from *The Golden Bough*, and a swan from an expensive staging of *Lohengrin*. Some of his ''sources'' are less dignified. (pp. 168-69)

But I don't intend these remarks as a criticism of Tolkien—well, only partly. They also give an idea of his range, which is wider than it looks. So that although he is capable of all kinds of archaic awfulness . . . , he is also capable of this characterisation of Sauron's evil eye, seen in an elf-mirror: ''The Eye was rimmed with fire, but was itself glazed, yellow as a cat's, watchful and intent, and the black slit of its pupil opened on a pit, a window into nothing.'' Roughly, Tolkien is good when the action is moving, and embarrassing when it stops. He is a born storyteller and a bad writer. The battle between Gandalf and the Balrog, for example, an ancient evil awakened from its long sleep under the mountain, is as exciting as anything since *Moby Dick*, but the halt in Lorien, the land of the elves, is more like Maurice Hewlett or Anthony Hope.

Tolkien was born in 1892 (Nabokov and Borges were both born in 1899), but he belongs to an older generation: that of Yeats and the friends of Madame Blavatsky. The enemy is science, or rather the complacency of science, the self-satisfaction of people who think they can explain everything, who have no time for myths, for forms of truth which will not fit within a narrow rationalism. Hence Tolkien's fantasy, his insistence on the *possibility* of ''fayerye''; hence Yeats's flirtations with the occult. Frodo the hobbit ''looked at maps, and wondered what lay beyond their edges.''

This is the striking thing about Tolkien's imagined world: the precision of its geography, the colour of the map beyond the map's edges. Tolkien is not good at creating individuals, but his types, his races, are fascinating. There are dwarves, orcs, elves, hobbits, ents, men, dragons, wizards, trolls, goblins, ghosts, all sharply differentiated, all speaking their own dialects. (pp. 170-71)

But all this still sounds closer to *The Wizard of Oz* than to Ariosto. What else is there? First, there is Tolkien's unrelenting psychologism. There are heroic adventures here, but they are all carefully internalised. The authentic acts of courage—a hobbit deciding to face a dragon, a handful of men deciding to fight against all odds—always take place in the mind. And the authentic conflicts of the trilogy are always telepathic—clashes of wills, combats of concentration. Good and evil are thus not abstractions, they are a confrontation. They are congregations of like-minded creatures lined up in opposition. The recruiting and the battles and the weather are simply metaphors for this.

And then the conflict in any case is not a simple one. The ring which Frodo has to destroy is a ring of power. If Sauron gets it back, nothing will be safe from him. But why shouldn't an enemy of Sauron use it against him, for the good of the world? This is the argument and the temptation offered to several important characters. The answer is that the ring simply is evil. Anyone who tried to use it would either become a servant of Sauron, or if he were very strong, become Sauron himself, a new dark lord. There is no good in the ring, no way of using it well.

Tolkien has said that his work is not an allegory, and it isn't, in any narrow sense. But it certainly isn't just a jolly

tale either, and the rings represents something, whether Tolkien knows what it is or not. Ultimately, the ring represents the lure of the modern world itself, which must stain all those who try to change it or use it. ''The blood-dimmed tide is loosed,'' as Yeats wrote, and the only answer is high conservatism: war without compromise, and without resort to the engines of the enemy. This is the long defeat the Elf-Queen spoke of, because a modern war on those terms cannot be won. But Tolkien would say, I think, that the war cannot be won anyway, and that the alternatives are death with clean or with dirty hands. The model is a desperate, noble wager which works in romance and inevitably fails in real life.

I don't find this an attractive or a realistic position, but I think it is a powerful and a coherent one—it is the position of Swift and Pope faced with what they saw as the rising darkness—and I think it has a lot to do with Tolkien's success, whether with poets or writers or students or teachers or hippies. ''The world withers,'' Tolkien writes in an alliterating poem based on *The Battle of Maldon*, ''and the wind rises; / the candles are quenched. Cold falls the night.'' *Beowulf*, anyone? (pp. 171-72)

Michael Wood, ''Tolkien's Fictions,'' in New Society, *March 27, 1969 (and reprinted in* Suitable for Children? *edited by Nicholas Tucker, University of California Press, 1976, pp. 165-72).*

MARY ELLMANN

Eglerio! Praise them! I want to type fast and congratulate American Youth on the (J.R.R.) Tolkien Cult before it is over. Perhaps it ends today and thousands of people, shutting Volume I or II or III of *The Lord of the Rings*, are now never to know if Gollum came back or Frodo came to. Still, I would hope that no one, even on the West Coast where the time lags, missed the Door Scene in which two necromancers exert two separate spells, one to open a door and the other to shut it. The molecules of the door, flustered by these opposing influences, lose their grip on each other and go off every which way. The door achieves absolute Doorlessness.

The addiction of young people to scenes like that is unrivaled in its purity. In late and jaded adolescence, they have demanded their right to live innocuously. . . . [All] sorts of Tolkien readers grow innocent by association. Most of them, sick of being analyzed, are sick of analysis in fiction too. They could of course find book Be-Ins like *Alice in Wonderland* or *Finnegans Wake* in which there is no comprehensible motivation. But they prefer Tolkien in whom motivation is so comprehensible as to be less than none; at ones so limpid and yet so emphatic as to establish the only ambiguity that still pleases. Even the East Coast enthusiasts aren't quite sure whether their enthusiasm is epic or parodic, inspired by Tolkien real or Tolkien camp. The swollen smallness of the Rings, the swarming details of its self-evident circumstances, its colossal freedom from embarrassment create in the end a breathtaking puerility. It is a book like climbing to the top of Mount Everest to keep an appointment with one's sixth-grade teacher.

But (without precedent!) the teacher likes the same book the pupils like. The catholic charm of the *Rings* is its leaving out almost every complexity we know now: the young find this simplicity exotic, the middle-aged find it significant. The young enjoy transparency, the middle-aged take it for a moral *solution* of some previous or mutually premised opacity. It is as though at the bottom of a custard that the child swills down, the parent finds a single almond inscribed TRUTH. By good or bad luck (he himself seems undecided), the gap in Tolkien's writing between an intended sublimity and an actual absurdity doubles the audience. The simpler this writing becomes, the more it pleases the vestigial Matthew Arnolds who respond to clarity as to grandeur, *and* the hippies who want to float free of intricacies.

Tolkien nourishes the deprived impulse of them both given two dots on a piece of paper, to draw a line between them. In three volumes, he traces just such a narrative between a starting point, Bag End, Hobbiton, the Shire, in the west corner of the vast nursery called Middle-earth, to a final destination, the Cracks of Doom, Mount Doom, Mordor. The horizontal purpose is relentless, converts say irresistible: Frodo must get through to Mordor, Tolkien must get Frodo through, the reader must get through Tolkien. But even all this determination detaches itself from customary effort by its odd immateriality. It is true that Frodo Baggins is often said to have a Quest, an energetic concept of behavior, but his is not accumulative, he is not to come back with something he went after. He already has it: the First Ring of the Nine Rings of Power belongs to Frodo. But its use can only corrupt its user: Power Loves Evil. Still, it is not enough for Frodo to keep it hidden in his pocket or around his neck on a scapular string. For aligned against Frodo and all the cozy kitchen values of the hobbit culture are the eastern hordes headed by Sauron who is eager to frisk Frodo, find the Ring, and wear it himself: Evil Loves Power. It is, therefore, necessary for the Ring to go back where it came from, and for Frodo to take it there. (pp. 217-19)

[The] obsession of the hobbits with dark and light . . . determines the structure of their story. Their expedition is, in skeleton, a progress through a series of tunnels, like that of a well-accoutered toy train. In almost every chapter, hobbits are caught in a dark tight spot, they panic, they crawl or climb or fight, they emerge once again into light and space. And yet really, their enemies do to them only what they do to themselves. When they aren't forcibly inserted into little blind places, like dimes into a jukebox, they look for their own slots. That is, their system of values has, as they say in English class, a central ambivalence. While they don't want to be extinguished by others (put out like lights), they don't want to be brilliant either. Their ideal, and this is at once strange, ingenious, and alluring to Americans, is to be dim. So their temptation is to go too far, into total invisibility. The Ring offers Frodo this seductive chance, and in not keeping it on his finger, he proves he has the courage to be *seen*.

It would be painful to list the reasons American youth may have for wishing to disappear too. Fortunately, while Tolkien raises the possibility, he also argues strenuously against it. But in view of his influence here, one might wish he showed as much energy in urging a prompt maturity as well as a low but certain visibility. (pp. 221-22)

After so much labor, so much loss. The insolence of slimy things, and the unhealthy questions to be asked of them. Do words, then, have no certain commitment to dogma, are the two at cross-purposes here again? Tolkien himself is guiltless, oblivious of his own sudden insinuation—he endorses its opposite. His book is based on the assumption that all words, like the pigments of all skins, are indicative of either good or evil. Moreover, it is again the supposedly pretty that is good, and the supposedly ugly that is bad, in languages as in legs. (pp. 226-27)

[Both] the Elven and Coarse styles are only little lay-bys on the great highway, the M-1, of the Middle style. It is this blandness from which young people might have benefited the most, were it not for the linguistic distractions provided by that capricious Gollum. For the Middle style bears the intellectual brunt of Middle-earth. A sense of the unexceptional is omnipresent, the security of an unbroken line of commonplaces by means of which good dull creatures have regulated their thoughts and feelings for Generations Without Count. (pp. 227-28)

[Tolkien unites with a] settled syntax, never tense or impatient or dissatisfied, as predictable in form and as resonant in spirit as a bag of communion wafers. (p. 228)

But Gollum is a genuine subversion, not by evil so much as by idiosyncrasy. The almost whole fabric of predictability is broken by his speech defects, his *gollum* and his *ss*-sounds. He is a thing for a thing's sake, and so a coffee break from the business of the *Rings*, a reminder of surprise, singularity, and the new. It is perhaps with that first swerving motion of Gollum from the dead center that Tolkien, in a sense, gained and lost the Tolkien Society. For the present indications are that the young members tend to read their master in a spirit of impropriety. They express no enthusiasm for the Middle style and give no evidence as yet of having perfected it themselves. Their attention seems instead almost entirely directed toward those further eccentricities of background out of which Tolkien drew his Everyhobbit; and the long sleepy lessons of the book, like those of a late spring afternoon seminar, are passed over in an indecent hurry to play with elven penmanship or the Baggins family tree. An opportunity, rare in its pedagogical calm, is submitted to hectic and frivolous abuses. Even our estranged youth show our old incapacity to turn aside from any conceivable source of invention. (pp. 228-29)

> *Mary Ellmann, "Growing Up Hobbitic," in* New American Review *(copyright © 1968 by The New American Library, Inc.), No. 2, 1968, pp. 217-29.*

DONALD DAVIE

The Lord of the Rings is one of the most surprising products of British literature since 1945, and one of the most serious. Edmund Wilson's attack on the book [see *CLC,* Vol. 1], though it hearteningly insisted on the obvious—for instance, that Tolkien's prose is as undistinguished as his verse (someone ought to point out, for example, how much mileage he gets out of the one word "great")—quite fails to account for the seriousness of the undertaking, for the pressure that drove the author through these thousand or more pages, as it has driven many readers (this reader among them) to follow through the same pages eagerly. The avidity with which *The Lord of the Rings* is read, the appeal of it and the loyalty it evokes among admirers—these are self-evident facts which can't be explained convincingly by talk of frivolity and escapism. The fantasy which the narrative promotes and exploits and nourishes has to be something which answers to a specific need. And as to this, Edmund Wilson has nothing to say.

At first sight there seems an obvious solution: the book

answers to a hunger for the heroic. And to some degree this must be true; *The Lord of the Rings* is a grown-up's *Superman*. But the driving force of the book is unheroic, even anti-heroic. The logic of the plot (which is very logical and tidy, not at all like medieval romance) is quite unequivocal; heroes are not to be trusted, only anti-heroes.... Indeed the point of leverage for the whole of Tolkien's creation is an assumption the sourness of which is surprisingly little noticed, still less resented—the assumption that the hobbits, who are less than human, are the only beings in Tolkien's world that a human reader can, as we say, "identify with." We are forced to go along with this assumption because of the language that is put in the mouths of the hobbits, as contrasted with the more elevated and literary language that is spoken by everyone else. Though the language that the hobbits speak is not convincingly the language which the common Englishman does use ..., it is plainly meant to be so, and we register it as at least nearer to live spoken English than the archaic and rhetorical language given to all others.

What the narrative says is that neither Gandalf nor Aragorn can be trusted with the power of the magical Ring—a power which on the contrary can be entrusted safely only to the hobbit, Frodo. The idealistic and devotedly heroic capacities of men cannot be trusted with power; power can safely be invested (and even so not with complete safety, for even Frodo is tempted and falls right at the end) only in those "halfling" men who, lost in a sleep of modestly sensual gratification, can rise to idealism only reluctantly and mistrustfully under the pressure of outrageous events, who behave heroically as it were in spite of themselves and to their own surprise, without premeditation. Thus the whole vast work tends to one end—to the elevation of the common man, of the private soldier over his officers and the schoolboy over his schoolmasters, of the sensual man over the intellectual, and of the spiritually lazy man over the spiritually exacting and ambitious. This is "the Dunkirk spirit," or "Theirs not to reason why." ... (pp. 90-1)

Tolkien is concerned with [what makes behavior authoritative], but he's also concerned with power. Gandalf and Aragorn have authority without power; and this, it seems, is all right. Frodo the hobbit has power without authority; and this is all right too. What is not all right, in Tolkien's scheme of things, is to be like Saruman the wicked wizard who wants power *and* authority, both at the same time, the one to back the other. Creon and even Ismene would find this hard to understand. And so do I. Power without authority is unauthorised power is the power of the gangster. Authority without power is impotent authority, the authority of the figurehead, the merely nominal head of state. But that is not the worst of it. If, as ... does Tolkien by implication, you identify authority with *style* ("They only are secure who seem secure"), then power without authority means power where we least expect it, power that is exerted upon us without manifesting itself: the power, for instance, of the advertiser and the media-manipulator—power which is all the more dangerous for not having any of the external marks by which we might recognise it, a power which operates under wraps or under the mask of the entertainer and the discreet or fawning servant. And authority without power, when authority is identified with style, becomes the magnetic or hypnotic authority of the great performer and the charismatic leader, the authority of a Hitler,

whose authority *is* his power, and a very great power indeed. (pp. 91-2)

Tolkien, it is well known, is far more popular with American youth than with British; and among radicals and dissidents as much as with the squares.... And although American campus rebels are very different from the British rebels, it's reasonable to think that when they cry *"Pigs!"* at the representatives of authority on and off campus they, like their British counterparts, are conceiving of a society from which authority shall seem to have vanished, where at any given moment overt authority shall be vested in no one at all. *The Lord of the Rings* endorses such hopes, and feeds them. (p. 92)

> *Donald Davie, in* Encounter (© *1969 by Encounter Ltd.), October, 1969.*

HUGH CRAGO

When Bilbo Baggins chooses to rush out of his hobbit-hole without his handkerchief and accompany some disreputable dwarfs on a dangerous and seemingly impossible venture, Tolkien makes it quite clear that he is choosing rightly. By opting for hardship instead of comfort and (more important still) Romance instead of everyday life, he is, we know, choosing the life of imaginative experience. Wizards, elves, dragons and treasure are, as well as being superbly real in themselves, symbols for various aspects of this life. Bilbo returns a better person for having lived it, and is promptly classed by his fellow-hobbits as "queer." Imagination, then, says Tolkien, is a good thing, but most men do not want it. It involves a conscious decision to brave not only the unknown, but also the scoffs and sneers of those "sensible" people who live right next door. Through the metaphor of the journey, and its universal associations of strangeness, discomfort and homesickness, Tolkien is able to convey with simple power a good deal of the quality of the experience, to make his readers shiver too. Really, the source of the Tolkien magic is as simple as that: few people have not felt snug at home by the fireside when the wind howls outside, and it's not hard to envisage the reverse situation vicariously.

Those who have read that curious story, "Leaf by Niggle" ... will recall that in a simple allegory (and a remarkably successful one it is too) Tolkien develops these ideas a stage further. While the main point of the tale is an illustration of the theories expounded in the essay "On Fairy Stories", and contains the message that the imaginative man, the creative artist, has a responsibility towards his neighbour as well as towards his own work, there is also an explicit equation made between imaginative and spiritual experience. This time the journey is the ultimate one—Death, and the Mountains towards which the purged and perfected Niggle eventually sets off are clearly meant to correspond to Heaven.

In the magnum opus itself, the Ring trilogy, there is a great deal of emphasis on the central problem of power, but the theme of the imaginative/spiritual experience is still important. In fact I would contend that its presence is absolutely vital, and directly responsible for the magnificent minor-key ending—a conclusion the artistry and taste of which have been too little noticed by those who enthuse over the mere narrative excitement of the work. Frodo must leave Middle-Earth because he can no longer be happy there. His titanic spiritual test has left him wearied and transformed, so that he begins to resemble the Elves, whose doom-laden beauty and poignancy are so memorable. (pp. 125-26)

I have given only an outline of the development of this vital strand in Tolkien's work, but there is no real need to go into further details. By now it should be becoming clear what *Smith of Wootton Major* is: a restatement, a summary, a drawing-together of the ideas we have been following.

In this sense, then, there is little new in *Smith*. Its hero is a man who is granted the power to walk in Faery—to participate in the imaginative or spiritual experience, in other words. In token of this he wears a star on his forehead. Eventually, he has to give it up, and is saddened, but makes the right decision as to whom the grace shall go to next. His spiritual guardian (who later turns out to be the King of Faery) is Prentice, a figure markedly similar to Gandalf. Nokes, the villain of the piece, is the stock Tolkien materialist, who steadfastly refuses to believe in the existence of the spiritual—but he lacks the appeal that even the most unimaginative hobbits possess, and is rather an ugly figure.

In fact many people may feel that the replacing of the Shire with a village of men, complete with its slightly unsatisfactory Town Hall, Master Cook and ritual Great Cake, is a step in the wrong direction. While it is true that the writing lacks the assurance it has when Tolkien is talking about hobbits, and the characters that glorious individuality that hobbits have, it is obviously up to him to decide what suits his themes best. In this respect *Smith* falls into the same category as *Farmer Giles of Ham,* of which the setting is also generalised—Medieval. But on the whole, I think *Smith* is closest in tone and general character to "Leaf by Niggle." The very explicitness of its religious symbolism supports this, as well as the restricted scope, lack of humour (an important constituent in *Giles*) and lack of pace. *Smith* is not meant to be read primarily as a story, and as I have hinted, this fact in itself will disappoint many of its readers.

Though it is not particularly fast-moving, there is nevertheless considerable *compression* of events in *Smith,* and there is no doubt that the feeling of slight bewilderment one experiences during a first reading is at least partly due to the fact that there is a rapid succession of Master Cooks in the course of the story, and also two Smith Smithsons (since surnames in the village follow the standard Medieval practice.) Nor, one might add, does it help that Prentice is variously referred to as ''Prentice'', ''Alf'' and ''The King of Faery''.

The abruptness of the narrative due to the compression-factor is paralleled by a similar jerkiness in the style. The dialogue, for example, is a curious mixture of colloquial contractions and long-winded formalisms. Some of what Smith's children say simply doesn't come off at all:

> ''Daddy'.'' she cried, ''where have you been? Your star is shining bright'.'' . . .
>
> (pp. 126-27)

Prentice's habit of asking questions and then hurrying on to exclamations and commands without waiting for a reply tends to make his speech too undignified for his status as a spiritual being. Faults like these, small as they are, bulk larger in this book than they do in the longer works (where the attentive reader can easily notice them also), because

one is not reading so fast—another result of the smallness and lack of pace of *Smith*. Many of these defects could, however, be overcome by sympathetic and skilful reading aloud.

On the whole, though, *Smith of Wooton Major* must stand or fall on the portrayal of the ''Faery'' experience. In spite of Tolkien's careful distinction between this spiritual conception and Noke's idea of ''Fairyland'', there is more of the traditional fairyland in this Faery than one might expect with Tolkien. . . . There are, for example, a Fairy Queen, and a circle of dancing fairies—none of these is very memorable.

Some features of Faery are more successful, though. One thinks of the sudden advent of the Elven mariners, suggesting the awe and fear of the Faery experience, or of the clarity of the air in the Vale of Evermorn. . . . This is good stuff, and captures effortlessly the matter-of-fact flavour of the style of certain folktales.

Then there is the fiery lake, a splendid vignette, even if it does owe something to Lewis' picture of the land of Bism in *The Silver Chair*. . . . (p. 127)

These short-lived, vivid pictures, hurrying always onward like a speeded-up succession of stills, are highly successful in transmitting to the reader the quality of the experiences Smith undergoes. But unfortunately, Tolkien abandons image for quasi-philosophical statement at the climactic point, and nearly ruins the whole thing:

> . . . and a great stillness came upon him; and he seemed to be both in the world and in Faery, and also outside them and surveying them, so that he was at once in bereavement, and in ownership, and in peace.

Not only has Tolkien never previously attempted to describe this particular mystical condition—he has never tried to evoke ''Faery'' *as a place* before, except possibly in the chapter on Lothlórien in *The Lord of the Rings*. It is not surprising that the endeavour is in some ways unsuccessful. Such regions are better hinted at than charted in more detail. But at least we can see that some new ground has, after all, been broken in *Smith of Wootton Major*. We have guessed that it is perhaps because it is so full of basic Tolkien ideas that other aspects of the book suffer, but luckily it is not a summary only. There are some flashes of genuine fire, and if Faery is not as successful a symbol as the journey out of the warmth into the cold, that is no reason for not trying it. Tolkien, like Bilbo and Frodo, is not yet content with treading the well-worn path, and this is to his credit. (pp. 127-28)

> *Hugh Crago, ''Tolkien in Miniature,'' in* Tolkien: Cult or Culture? *by J. S. Ryan (© J. S. Ryan, 1969), University of New England, Armidale, 1969, pp. 125-28.*

ALEXIS LEVITIN

The Lord of the Rings focuses upon a particular episode in the eternal struggle between Good and Evil. Special emphasis is placed on the central role that Power plays in this conflict. Tolkien demonstrates that Power is the true weapon only of Evil, and that even in the hands of Good it eventually must result in corruption and suffering. . . .

[Louis J. Halle, in a review comparing Tolkien's work to

actual historical studies, says] "The two prime facts of Middle-earth.... are *power* and its *consequence,* suffering.... In the historian's view, power is not a neutral element that can be used for good or evil. It is always evil, for it enables the wicked to dominate the world or, in the hands of the good, is inescapably corrupting."

It is apparent that Tolkien considers the influence of Power to be ultimately pernicious. He associates Power, and all its concomitants, with his wicked characters, but, for the most part, he denies them to his heroes. (p. 11)

Tolkien unfortunately interchanges words such as Power and Force without distinction, although he does seem to distinguish between the two concepts....

It is clear that good people may be powerful without destroying their goodness. Gandalf, Elrond, Glorfindel, Galadriel, and Aragorn are all quite powerful, yet manage to avoid falling to evil ways. The mere possession of power, although potentially dangerous, need not lead to wickedness. It is the exertion of one's strength through Force that is corrupting. Galadriel possesses one of the three rings of power forged by the Elves themselves, ages before, under the deceitful advice of Sauron, and has the Ruling Ring come within her grasp. But she resists the temptation to use Force, recognizing that the Ruling Ring is an Evil Power that must dominate, compel, subjugate, and destroy....

The varying possibilities inherent in power are illustrated by the Rings.... [Power] for good does exist, but it is necessarily limited in scope. The power to heal and build, understand and create, is a good and marvelous power, but as such has no control over war, nor can it procure dominion over others.

When Tolkien uses the word Power he is almost always referring to the evil Force represented either by Sauron or his Ring. Force is based on fear rather than love. It is compulsive, demanding of its victims actions which they abhor, and forcing things upon them which they are too weak to resist. (It should be recalled that the powerful Wizards are sent to unite those who are *willing* to fight Sauron, but may not compel them to do so.) Power such as Gandalf's is personal, and vaguely spiritual. He recognizes the existence and importance of other beings. He sympathizes with them, and wants to help them in their plight. Force, such as Sauron's, is impersonal and materialistic. Sauron considers himself the living center of all existence, and the other beings with whom he must deal are only objects to him. He feels himself the real and true living Being surrounded by things. These things he desires to rule, command, distort, destroy, in effect, treat exactly as he likes.

Sauron's Power is the greatest of its kind in Middle-earth, but it has several inherent weaknesses, one of which in particular leads to his downfall. Sauron, so mighty and so evil, cannot conceive of other beings who think differently from himself, whose attitudes toward power could be different. This lack of imagination on his part proves fatal....

This weakness can be exploited because those fighting Sauron are able to guess how he looks at things. The Good can imagine what it is like to be bad, but Evil cannot imagine how it is to be good. Evil cannot imagine anyone else being different, basically, from itself. This proves its doom. (p. 12)

There are other elements intrinsic to Sauron's evil nature which prove of great detriment to his cause. He is filled with a lust for domination which drives him to extremes of cruelty far beyond the point of usefulness....

Sauron's craving to hurt others drives him to illogical actions....

A third weakness of Evil is its inability to command solidarity in its forces. An evil being only loves himself, and will not willingly help another for his own sake. The orcs, converted by Sauron into a thoroughly wicked race, always bicker and struggle amongst themselves. They serve Sauron, but only out of fear. In fact, they would never serve for any other reason, unless it were the enticement of great reward. Saruman, the renegade wizard, is an independent evil power who, although under Sauron's dominion, tries treacherously to gain the Ring for himself. He is first of all a traitor to the good cause which he originally served, and secondly a traitor to the Evil One who partially has enslaved him. He wants Power, incarnate in the Ring, for himself alone. The good, on the other hand, are able to unite, for they only want the end of the Ring of Power, so that all can be at peace....

The Ring plainly is a symbol of Power. It can provide unlimited Power to its possessor, but he is forced to lose his freedom and become a slave to that Power. Even the best intentions in the world will eventually be smothered by the Ring's insidious influence upon its user. Gandalf and Galadriel both refuse to wield the Ring, knowing that their good beginnings would be followed by evil results. (p. 13)

I think it important to stress the fact that the Ring attacks its victim through Pride, the primary sin of Christian theology. Boromir and his father Denethor, both noble men, fall prey to the lure of Power, entrapped by thoughts of the grandeur of their nation and of themselves.... Saruman the White, at one time a good wizard, also falls to evil through desiring the Ring, which he has never even seen [, corrupted by the desire for power]. (p. 14)

> Alexis Levitin, "Power in 'The Lord of the Rings'," in *Orcrist, No. 4, 1969-1970, pp. 11-14.*

C. STUART HANNABUSS

I believe that Tolkien was working out a quasi-Christian morality in pagan terms, using a former culture and literary tradition to furnish the scenario to a quest which incorporated the major issues of Life. His landscape is one of utter contrasts, images of good and evil.... The denizens of Tolkien's world fall into two camps, broadly good and bad; and, with a simplicity due to this moral viewpoint, as well as due to the simple characterization in epic, so we find Gandalf ranged against Sauron, Fangorn against Saruman, Sam against Gollum, and Bard against Smaug.... It is thus a dualistic scheme we see, with the ultimate victory to good (the "eucatastrophe"), and in this sense Christian.

Perhaps the most effective of the images representing this Good (or, in Christian terms, Love) is Sam's rehabilitation of the Shire.... [Sam] uses his "magic" creatively, for the good of others, as an attempt to transform the "primary world" into a "secondary world" with the "inner consistency of reality". (pp. 87-8)

Yet the victory good has over bad is almost Pyrrhic: so clearly do the heroes anticipate and acknowledge defeat that we are in the world of Beowulf and the Norse sagas.

And this is the culture which Tolkien so lavishly resurrects.... Tolkien's world is an arena, no paradisal garden or utopian golden age but a world shot through with archetypal threats and phobias.... (p. 88)

This "dream world" is not escapist.... Withdrawal into a secondary world, and the communication of that in the primary world, are coinherent in the scheme of life, and religio-fantasy creates a bridge between the two worlds: for they have parallel and cross-fertilizing eschatologies. (p. 89)

The Lord of the Rings is a story, a saga, stories within stories, a "what then?" story. It is a quest or odyssey undertaken by an Everyman figure, the Hobbit, who likes regular meals and the peace of his Shire. We believe in Hobbits, with their Hobbit-holes and genealogies, and we travel across mountains and plains, feeling the weight of the Ring. Man in a landscape of moral ambivalences and on a quest with metaphysical and mystical overtones. Parts of the route are purgatorial, as when Aragorn leads them through the Paths of the Dead like Aeneas with his golden bough; as when Frodo crawls up Mount Doom to wrestle for his life and soul against the power of the Ring. The fate of the participants moves from physical to metaphysical planes continually in the archetypally patterned symbolism, which subconsciously alludes at all times to Christian iconography.... But subsuming the overtly Biblical is the story which can in poetry mirror man's dilemmas and look Life in the eye. Whether we are refreshed depends on our faith, that bridge of the two worlds. (pp. 93-4)

However many uses Tolkien's text is put to, it has vindicated the fantasy tradition from the criticism that the genre is a mere "contamination of reality by dream". To have read it is to have come nearer, if not to Veritas, at least to verities, and one *has* joined an elite—not self-appointed but arising naturally—an elite of those with a clear view. (p. 94)

> C. Stuart Hannabuss, "Deep Down," in Signal (copyright © 1971 C. Stuart Hannabuss; reprinted by permission of the author and The Thimble Press, Lockwood Station Road, South Woodchester, Glos. GL5 5EQ, England), September, 1971, pp. 87-95.

GERALD O'CONNOR

There are [many] explanations for the popularity of [*The Lord of the Rings*] as anyone who has taught it knows. It's a great story. It has wildly original and interesting characters. It takes place in a delightful world of fantasy. And, finally, it communicates an extraordinary reverence for natural life. Long before ecology became fashionable, the trilogy celebrated the natural wonders of our world: the earth, the water, the trees, the flowers, the other living things that Tolkien lets us commune with.... To me, all of these are good reasons why any young person could enjoy *The Lord of the Rings*. In fact, so anesthetizing are they that a great many young people have not only willingly suspended their disbelief when reading the trilogy but their critical judgment as well. For, as I intend to show, read critically, *The Lord of the Rings* is really an Establishment book.

The first of the six crimes against the counter-culture state that the trilogy makes is genocide: it glorifies age and it disparages youth. Not only are the great figures in the book aged, their age is their greatness. (pp. 48-9)

[There are six superior creatures who] represent the greatness of extremely old age [and] Frodo and Aragorn who might be said to represent the virtues of middle-age.... Frodo is not the Marlowe of Conrad's *Youth* nor Harry Haller, the Steppenwolf. He is a shrewd, practical, cautious, solid citizen of the Shire who achieves a measure of heroism in spite of himself.

That Frodo is not to be seen as a representative of youth is made emphatically clear by Tolkien's treatment of Pippin who is. At twenty-nine the youngest of the Fellowship, Pippin is characterized in volume one as a thoughtless, disrespectful, irresponsible, foolish child.... In short, Tolkien does not seem to trust anyone under thirty, but almost everyone over three hundred.

Now as ignominious as it is to be young like Pippin, at least he is included in the Fellowship. No woman is. For if to be young is to be disestablished, to be female is to be disenfranchised. Accordingly, a second reason why the *Lord of the Rings* should turn off the young today is its institutional male chauvinism. In the trilogy this chauvinism takes two forms, the virtually total exclusion of women from the main action of the story, including membership in the Fellowship, and secondly the subordinate role that the few women do play, Galadriel excepted.

The Fellowship itself, like the *comitatus* of the Heroic Age, consists exclusively of males and affirms traditional male values: bravery, strength, loyalty, and above all the love of fellowship. (pp. 49-50)

[Another of the book's basic ideas is blood supremacy. The whole of *The Lord of the Rings* makes it clear that] your blood is your destiny. This idea, it seems to me, is a third reason why young people today should critically reject the book....

In the trilogy the theme of blood runs strong, deep, and blue. As a result a rigorous caste system exists, a Great Chain of Being for those who prefer euphemism.

The most important example of a caste relationship is, of course, that between Sam and Frodo. Sam treats his Mr. Frodo with unwavering devotion, loyalty, kindness, self-sacrifice, worship, love, and servility. In turn, Frodo treats his servant Sam with unwavering benevolence, paternalism, tolerance, pity, understanding, love, and patronage. In another context their relationship could easily be construed as a parable defending the institution of slavery. (p. 51)

The retainer to lord relationship is a microcosm of the whole social structure of *The Lord of the Rings*. From the wealthy Bagginses of Bag End to the galloping Rohirrim of Rohan, from the Mirkwood Forest to the Gulf of Lune waters, this land was not made for you and me but for them and theirs.

Implicit in this hierarchic structure is a value that, as all commentators agree, the young today uniformly and overwhelmingly reject—authoritarianism.... Yet somehow *The Lord of the Rings* has escaped this tidal wave of youthful rebellion.

This authoritarianism, the fourth reason why the trilogy should alienate and not attract its young readers, so completely informs the work that any documentation of it is necessarily arbitrary and selective. (p. 52)

As well as illustrating the great respect for authority which pervades the trilogy, the fall of Boromir . . . illustrates the two qualities of the book, the fifth and sixth reasons I will discuss, which are most completely and directly in contradiction to the ideals of the young today. I am referring to moral and political absolutism. Because these two are identified, or confused if you will, in the trilogy, as they have been in our lives, I will not attempt to distinguish between them but rather treat them as one overall world view.

The most explicit statement of the moral and political absolutism that informs the work is Aragorn's answer to Eomer's "How shall a man judge what to do in such times?" To convince Eomer that the war with Sauron is indeed a Holy War, that political neutrality is tantamount to moral depravity, Aragorn answers: "As he ever has judged. Good and ill have not changed since yesteryear; nor are they one thing among Elves and Dwarves and another among Men." In *The Lord of the Rings* good and ill do not change—shape or sides. (p. 53)

I am saying that in moral and political terms the *Lord of the Rings* is a monument to all the pious cliches, . . . all the self-righteous rhetoric, propaganda, and bullshit of the past. The War of the Rings is another war with God-on-our-side. As Tolkien's history tells it, and tells it so well, the cavalry charged and the orcs they fell. And you never ask questions when God's on your side. . . .

Young people are saying everywhere that they have had enough killing in the name of God and Country; that they are sick of body counts of orcs, slopes, Indians, blacks, trolls, or gooks. Young people today should be aghast at, not entranced by, Tolkien's heroes from Rohan who "sang as they slew, for the joy of battle was on them" and whose "hoofs of wrath rode over" the dead they had slain. Young people today, as Melanie tells us, bleed inside each other's wounds. Young people today sing songs of peace. (p. 54)

> Gerald O'Connor, "Why Tolkien's 'The Lord of the Rings' Should Not Be Popular Culture," in Extrapolation (copyright 1971 by Thomas D. and Alice S. Clareson), December, 1971, pp. 48-55.

RICHARD PURTILL

One criticism made of Tolkien is that his language is general, unspecific, not evocative of particular images unlike that of D. H. Lawrence, for example. But Tolkien writes in this way on theory and of set purpose. As some scattered remarks make clear, Tolkien distrusts overspecific description in fantasy for the same reason he is wary of pictures in such books: both have the effect of dragooning the imagination, forcing us to see the scene in a certain way. (pp. 40-1)

[Another] accusation is that the language in, for example, the *Rings* is "derivative," full of echoes of other literature. . . . Of course, this is a highly relative matter. If you have not read the other literature you will miss the echoes, and if you read *The Hobbit* before *Beowulf*, the dragon in *Beowulf* is likely to remind you of Smaug rather than vice versa. But again there is a principle behind the accusation, the principle that originality is valuable in itself and lack of originality vitiates any other merits a work may have. Yet, prevalent as this assumption is, it seems also to be false. Originality in itself does not make a work good, for a work can be a failure in an entirely new way. Complete originality is impossible; any work has a great deal in common with works that have gone before. Furthermore, originality is a matter of degree; a completely unoriginal work would

have to be an exact copy of another work. Traditional material traditionally treated occurs in many admittedly great works of literature. The idea that interesting work can no longer be done in some traditional form is always open to refutation by counter-example.

But there is also a confusion here between two kinds of unoriginality. Tolkien is unoriginal in his images in one way, original in another. He is unoriginal in that he uses familiar associations—light with goodness, darkness with evil, for example. (pp. 45-6)

However, the use Tolkien makes of these familiar images is far from unoriginal. (p. 46)

Archaisms, richness, and variety of proper names and imagery taken from sense experiences are all highly characteristic of Tolkien's works. (p. 47)

The use which Tolkien and Lewis make of language in their fiction grows out of their professional concern with language, in interesting ways. Tolkien's field of specialization is Anglo-Saxon. . . . The study of Anglo-Saxon itself would, I think, have some tendency to influence any imaginative person to think of roots and origins, the means by which language molds and is molded by history. The way in which modern English is built on an Anglo-Saxon foundation with Latin, French, and other borrowings, the way in which an Anglo-Saxon word (*cwik,* for example) can change and evolve over a period of time, has a tendency to remind us of how the present is based on the past and of the great gulf of history which lies behind us. Tolkien's chronologies, histories, and legends in the *Ring* trilogy surely owe something to this habit of mind. (pp. 61-2)

Tolkien has not merely borrowed from the early English epics which he dealt with as a scholar. He has created in our own time a work with something of the same fascination and the same mythical quality. In the making of this story, Tolkien's own experience of language and its history has played its part. (p. 66)

Both Lewis and Tolkien . . . are Christians, and their morality is essentially Christian morality. This is so clear in Lewis that we have found critics accusing him of propaganda. It is much less clear in Tolkien, and this has tempted some critics to say that Tolkien's view of the world is "really" the modern view and not the traditional Christian view. This is [a] major . . . misunderstanding of Tolkien. . . . (p. 95)

Tolkien's vision is profoundly his own and deeply Christian, and if we misunderstand this we seriously misunderstand him. (p. 101)

[The] real moral focus of Tolkien's story is on the two races, hobbits and men. They can sink to complete damnation, as the Ringwraiths have done, and as Bilbo or Frodo might have. But they can rise to something like sanctity, as Frodo does. We have detailed pictures of moral struggle in men (Boromir, Théoden, Denethor), in most of the hobbit characters (especially Frodo, Sam, and Bilbo, but also Merry and Pippin), and in the wizard Saruman who is at least ostensibly a man or elf-man.

The constant temptation of all the characters is to give in, give up the struggle and cooperate with the Dark Lord. Against this the virtues characteristic of the heroes of the story are courage, will and endurance, and loyalty and love. (p. 104)

The responsibility of each person to do God's work, the danger of using evil means—this is Tolkien's message. (p. 112)

[Tolkien] is telling us a story, which can be enjoyed purely in its own right. Like all good stories, it has echoes of others, including that greatest of all stories—which Tolkien believes is a true story—the life of Christ.

Gandalf and Frodo are not allegorical masks for Christ, as in a strict allegory, nor symbols for some aspect of human condition, as in a loose allegory. They are people in their own right. But because they are almost real people they can, as real people can, express Christ in their own way. (p. 127)

Tolkien's view is a world of purpose, a world where there is a real struggle between good and evil, a hope and danger which go beyond the personal. (p. 154)

> *Richard Purtill, in his* Lord of the Elves and Eldils: Fantasy and Philosophy in C. S. Lewis and J.R.R. Tolkien *(copyright © 1974 by The Zondervan Corporation; used by permission), Zondervan, 1974.*

RANDEL HELMS

[We] have in *The Hobbit* and its sequel what is in fact the same story, told first very simply, and then again, very intricately. Both works have the same theme, a quest on which a most unheroic hobbit achieves heroic stature; they have the same structure, the "there and back again" of the quest romance, and both extend the quest through the cycle of one year, *The Hobbit* from spring to spring, the *Rings* from fall to fall.

The episodic structures of the two books are so closely parallel one says without exaggeration that *The Lord of the Rings* is *The Hobbit* writ large. (p. 21)

But if *The Hobbit* and *The Lord of the Rings* are in essence the "same book," why did Tolkien feel obliged to write again what he had already done once? The answer is, of course, that far from being the same book, they have merely the same narrative husk; between them is a host of subtle and profound differences. (p. 23)

[Despite] the similarities between them, the first is in all respects *smaller* than its sequel, in direct proportion as the readers of the one are smaller than the readers of the other. In the earlier work, Tolkien is addressing children and dealing with a closely limited theme—growing up—telling about Bilbo's "birth" out of Bag End and his gradual initiation into full "manhood." Tolkien's moral is little more than "Be brave, enter life's dark secret places; there may be golden treasure hid within." *The Hobbit* is, at its narrative heart, a book about entering and grasping, and taking forth symbols of manhood. . . . [The] moral elements of *The Hobbit* are relatively simple, something evident to any adult reader, and really no damning criticism of a children's book; what is striking is the contrast to its sequel—a story grown vastly greater in import and application, heavy with the fate of civilizations and the weight of long history. (pp. 24-5)

In the earlier work, composed for his children, [Tolkien] adopts an "angle of address" of approximately forty-five degrees, talking down to his little listeners; this stance controls the tone, as in the opening paragraph: "In a hole in

the ground there lived a hobbit. Not a nasty, dirty, wet hole, filled with the ends of worms and an oozy smell." This first page, and indeed much of the book, is marred for the adult reader by a set of tonal quirks, perhaps the worst being the excessive number of modifiers—"perfectly," "very," "lots and lots," "on and on," "many," "little" (all from the first page)—and the frequent authorial intrusiveness, clearly taken over in imitation of oral storytelling style in which a narrator (Daddy at bedtime) breaks in to share private jokes with his diminutive listeners: "Yes, I am afraid trolls do behave like that, even those with only one head each." . . . (pp. 26-7)

Corollary to the tone of the early parts of *The Hobbit* is an obvious lack of moral inclusiveness, a narrowing of the range of good and evil permissible to its characters. There is a clear difference in moral depth, for example, between the initial adventures of Bilbo and Frodo on the road to Rivendell. Bilbo's adventures begin on the night of June 1. Inexplicably separated from Gandalf, the dwarves and the hobbit find themselves cold and supperless on a wet night, grimly preparing to sleep on the ground, when they spy a light ahead. Bilbo the burglar, sent forward to reconnoiter, discovers trolls, fierce, man-eating creatures, on a raiding expedition. But such trolls! "Mutton yesterday, mutton today, and blimey, if it don't look like mutton again tomorrer . . . Yer can't expect folk to stop here for ever just to be et by you and Bert. You've et a village and a half between yer, since we come down from the mountains." . . . Tolkien deliberately undercuts the force of our response to the trolls' wickedness by giving them a Cockney dialect, and a rather crudely presented one at that. We are asked to laugh as well as shudder, and caught between the two reactions, we finally have neither. But this is, of course, the adult response; what Tolkien has done with his trolls is altogether suitable for children, and there is no use in faulting him for undercutting the evil. The tone is at one with the substance of the scene and with the minds of the audience. All we can say here is that Tolkien has not yet purged himself of the notion of a natural connection between fairy stories and the minds of children. . . . (p. 27)

Compare, now, Bilbo's trolls with the account of Frodo's first adventure on the way to Elrond's. Again separated inexplicably from Gandalf, and again on the road at night, the hobbit and his companions trudge toward Rivendell. Suddenly hearing hoofbeats, they hide beside the road:

> As Frodo watched he saw something dark pass across the lighter space between two trees, and then halt. It looked like the black shade of a horse led by a smaller black shadow. The black shadow . . . swayed from side to side. Frodo thought he heard the sound of snuffling. The shadow bent to the ground, and then began to crawl towards him. . . .

The jocular authorial intrusiveness has disappeared, and the evil is distilled to its mythic and elemental basis— shadow—lacking not only a comic dialect, but even the humanizing force of speech itself. The hero faces not comic villains, but something wholly inexplicable, against which he has no defense at all—the stuff of bad dreams, perhaps, but essential fantasy. (pp. 27-8)

The Hobbit . . . lacks a certain intellectual weight, lacks the commitment, fully expressed in *The Lord of the Rings,* to exploring and revealing the enriching, ennobling functions of fantasy. (p. 30)

What, then, is the deepening impulse, where the magic moment, when Tolkien's vision begins to probe and plumb, touching at last richness and complexity? As we should expect, it begins when Tolkien's hero encounters Middle-earth's most compelling symbol, the Ring, and its most complex and engaging creature, that strange hobbit called Gollum. Almost, one could say, as soon as Gollum and the Ring appear, *The Lord of the Rings* is inevitable, for the two stimulate and deepen Tolkien's imagination, in the direction of a complex Secondary World, more than any other of the inventions in *The Hobbit.* With Gollum and the Ring is the beginning of Tolkien's exploration of the puzzlement and fascination of evil; with Gollum especially, Tolkien has hit upon his most complex representative figure of the satanic in Middle-earth, and one that will grow very quickly in his imagination into the never-seen title figure of *The Lord of the Rings,* Sauron the Great. Sauron, like Gollum, is a figure of immense age, once not evil to behold, who has lost something of incalculable importance to him and whose life's object is to get it back again. Clearly the distant but still recognizable model for Sauron (and even Gollum) is Milton's Satan, likewise a creature of immense age and former beauty, who has lost heaven and must forever seek to regain it, but just as clearly the imaginative transformation of the model has been very great. . . . With immense modesty and perspicuity, Tolkien has recognized the limits of his rich but narrow genius and keeps Sauron in the background, a hovering and unimaginable symbol of irredeemable evil, and gives us in the foreground only a worm's-eye view of wickedness, Sauron's wretched servant Gollum, who also has lost the precious Ring, and must again find it or be forever gnawed by its desire. (pp. 32-3)

It is hardly too much to say that Gollum and the Ring are the central figures in the history of the unraveling of *The Lord of the Rings* in Tolkien's imagination, the roots that fed the imaginative growth of Middle-earth from leaf to cosmos. (p. 33)

[Tolkien] changes on discovering his central symbol, his imagination grows and deepens, and even *The Hobbit,* in its later parts, feels the effects of the discovery of the Ring; it remains a children's book, narrow in moral range, but the tone shifts, and a greater sense of the possibilities of good and evil seems to erupt from the underside of Tolkien's imagination. First of all, the frequent authorial intrusions that mar the early part of the book change to direct comments with a much flattened angle of address—the audience seems taller now. . . . (p. 35)

One explanation for the tonal shift in *The Hobbit,* though far too simplistic to suffice, tells part of the truth. As in all books, form is, after all, content, style *is* substance, and a hobbit of the Shire, even one with Tookish blood, is, literally, the same height as the young audience of his story (three feet, sometimes approaching four), and until he grows in metaphoric stature (and his growth is the theme of the story), puzzled disorientation *must* be called "flummoxed," and an angry curse *will* be mouthed as "confusticate and bebother." As Bilbo grows, so do Tolkien's style and imagination.

But even if we reject as fanciful the notion that the matura-

tion of Tolkien's style is the objective correlative of Bilbo's growth to heroic stature, and even as we grant that a tonal shift is the sign of something more important than a developing technique, we must accept the obvious, that Tolkien did, somewhere about midpoint in the story, begin adjusting his tone with more skill. The first half of *The Hobbit* has only one tone—jocular down-talk—but the second becomes increasingly complex tonally. (pp. 35-6)

Tolkien's development as a prose stylist, Bilbo's growth toward heroic stature, Thorin's deepening character—here are the main, interrelated signs of the beginning of the depth and complexity of *The Lord of the Rings,* and the beginning as well of the one theme in *The Hobbit* with adult moral interest: the nature and meaning of power. (It is, of course, no accident that this is also a central theme in *The Hobbit*'s sequel.) It is, perhaps, a theme one would expect to find in any account of a fictional world, but it is one Tolkien only slowly grew toward. He had first to learn that a serious and important theme could be dealt with in a mythological narrative—in this case the theme was maturation. Next he learned, and again rather slowly, that serious themes could be dealt with in such a narrative *seriously* rather than whimsically or patronizingly. Then, at the end of *The Hobbit,* he learned one more lesson as he imaginatively explored the final growth and greatness of Thorin and Bilbo. He had to grasp the significance of the one great theme that differentiates the otherwise identical plot shells of the narratives of Bilbo and Frodo: the courageous renunciation of power. It is this theme that ennobles *The Lord of the Rings,* animating and supporting its far greater dignity and seriousness. For while both books are built upon the ancient structure of the quest, both concerned with the central plot of the maturation of an untried and apparently weak hero, they are differentiated in one great way: *The Hobbit* is a quest to *get* something, *The Lord of the Rings* a quest to *renounce* something. Tolkien is in the process of discovering that theme of renunciation in the final pages of his children's book. The minor expression of the theme in *The Hobbit* is Thorin's renunciation of his kingly pride and greed just before his death; the major expression is Bilbo's giving up the Arkenstone, an act directly foreshadowing Frodo's greatness in renouncing the Ring. (pp. 37-8)

[Tolkien's] real discovery is, of course, not the theme of the hero—that is ancient indeed—his real discovery is the thrilling potential of the mythic imagination, that it can tell us things about ourselves and our world we may not know in another way, things we need deeply. (p. 52)

[We] cannot take *The Hobbit* by itself, for it stands at the threshold of one of the most immense and satisfying imaginative creations of our time, *The Lord of the Rings.* The real importance of *The Hobbit* is what its creator learned in the writing. As Bilbo Baggins grew up, so did Tolkien's imagination. The childlike evocations of shivery evil in Bilbo's adventures awoke in Tolkien a sudden and disturbing perception of genuine evil and of the heroism it must elicit. So we have to begin again with *The Hobbit,* seeing it in the perspective it deserves, as an initiation (both Tolkien's and Bilbo's) into the perilous world of Faërie, a world Tolkien only slowly discovered and only with much labor gave, in turn, to us. (pp. 52-3)

The children's book began as a symmetrical quest-tale ("There and Back Again," its subtitle) about entering, grasping, and returning, but it grew into a story not about grasping but about renouncing, and thus in its own context turned out to be an asymmetrical plot. When, however, we place the end of *The Hobbit* up against the beginning of *The Lord of the Rings,* we indeed find a structural symmetry: a symmetry of renunciation. (p. 54)

Having discovered his pattern and his theme in *The Hobbit,* and their great potentials, Tolkien set about telling the same story again in *The Lord of the Rings,* yet with a difference.... *The Lord of the Rings* is not exclusively in the initiatory mode of *The Hobbit,* is not, that is, merely a book addressed to children, symbolically expressing their fears and wishes about growing up. *The Hobbit* is pure myth of maturation, with no other overlay of "meaning." *The Lord of the Rings,* however, despite Tolkien's demurrer that it has no "inner meaning or 'message',"... has a definite mythic argument and a positive moral and aesthetic, even a "political" program. In his children's story, Tolkien does little more than bore down to the artesian archetype and let it flow. But the more it flowed, the more he recognized the potential greatness of his theme and that the mythic devices he had rediscovered could, rightly used, be a searching and a healing tool. So in a generation that had forgotten the power and value of myth, he set about creating a group of myths of central concern to our age. (pp. 54-5)

Tolkien ... [reasserts] the supreme importance of the myth-making imagination and [provides] in the process, a set of myths that express, more fully than the works of any other contemporary writer I know, a complex of otherwise inexpressible emotions riving the breasts of a whole generation of readers. (p. 55)

In *The Lord of the Rings,* Tolkien has symbolically expressed our situation in a strikingly profound and useful set of myths that can evoke and pattern a healing emotional response to literary situations deeply symbolic of our own. We must carefully note that the *Rings* patterns a response to its *own* situation, not directly to ours. Literature gives no direct moral answers, it only exercises and enriches the wisdom of spirit that must ponder and respond to its own dilemmas. Tolkien himself has seen the possibilities for finding simple-minded allegory in his work and has repeatedly insisted that the Ring is not the atom bomb and the War of the Rings is not World War II. We need not doubt his sincerity; a powerful symbol is not the allegorical equivalent of a single technological item. The Ring does not equal the Bomb, but is rather a symbol for the entire complex fact that twentieth-century man has, like Frodo, suddenly found himself, without wanting it, without even guessing it would find a way into his pocket, in possession of a power over nature so immense even the desire to use it will inevitably corrupt his soul. And again, like Frodo, he would really rather throw the whole thing into the sea and forget it, but knows he cannot. Here we arrive at a perception of one of Tolkien's supremely valuable contributions to the imaginative health of us all—what I have called the anti-Faustian myth. (pp. 59-60)

Tolkien is indeed a keen analyst of the modern psyche and its need for realignment with the natural world; he was one of the first to grasp that everything depends on whether we can adjust our ego-ideals away from the Faustian and toward whatever it is Frodo represents—Frodo anti-Faust but by no means Frodo anti-hero. Frodo is hero, but surely that word must undergo some radical changes in meaning to

be applicable to a three-foot-high bundle of timidity with furry feet. This indeed is another of Tolkien's gifts to us in *The Lord of the Rings*—a profound criticism and revaluation of the meaning of heroic behavior. (p. 61)

[Part] of the reason Tolkien's vision is so necessary to so many is that it provides a richly satisfying experience of a fully worked out mythological perception of radical evil. Tolkien's particular myth parallels his Christianity, positing a malevolent and corrupting outside influence, spiritual and probably eternal, against which man is doomed to fight, but which he has no hope of conquering on his own—Sauron the Great, Lord of the Rings. (p. 67)

Randel Helms, in his Tolkien's World *(copyright © 1974 by Randel Helms; reprinted by permission of Houghton Mifflin Company), Houghton, 1974.*

C. N. MANLOVE

[*The Lord of the Rings*] came just when disillusion among the American young at the Vietnam war and the state of their own country was at a peak. Tolkien's fantasy offered an image of the kind of rural conservationist ideal or escape for which they were looking (it also could be seen as describing, through the overthrow of Sauron, the destruction of the U.S.). In this way *The Lord of the Rings* could be enlisted in support of passive resistance and idealism on the one hand and of draft-dodging and drugs on the other. A second factor may have been the perennial American longing for roots, a long-tradition and a mythology: these things are the fibre of Tolkien's book, where every place and character is lodged at the tip of an enormous, growing stem of time. (p. 157)

Tolkien's intention in his book was to create a species of heroic epic. (By the word 'intention' here is meant evidence from within the text.) The trilogy has epic scale: we journey over what W. H. Auden tells us is 1,300 miles from the Shire to Mordor, taking in a variety of races and regions on the way.... The sense of extension in space is complemented by one in time: we are made continually aware of thousands of years of the past lying behind the story of the Ring, indeed that the history of its evil maker stretches back into the First Age of Middle-earth. In Frodo's journey, the long ages come to a point, and all Middle-earth is involved in the crisis and the outcome.

Tolkien is trying to write what C. S. Lewis termed 'secondary' epic: that is, one which records a temporal crux, and rests on the assumption that history is not merely cyclic, but directional. Though other evils may come, Sauron is finally destroyed. The historical sense is thus similar to that of the *Aeneid* in that something permanent is achieved. Unlike the *Aeneid,* however, Tolkien's work is not so much concerned with beginnings as with endings. It is the close of the Third Age that he chronicles, the final defeat of an ancient antagonist and the subsequent departure of the Elves to the Far West.... *The Lord of the Rings* is permeated with the sense of an ending.

In keeping with this, Tolkien has set out to give his epic an elegiac character. The story is made heavy with awareness of the past. There is scarcely a mortal character whose descent is not chronicled or a racial history which is not mapped out either in the text or the appendices. The entire journey of the Fellowship lies amidst the relics of long-gone ages and events.... Remembrance of times past is pervasive. Not ten pages can pass without some figure or event from the backward abyss being recalled. . . . (pp. 171-72)

Part of the aim is to evoke a sense of mortality and the wearing action of time. To heighten this, Tolkien has given varying degrees of longevity to the different races. . . . The Ring, which can lengthen the life of its wearer (and in the cases of Bilbo and Gollum does so), is the only time-defier in the book, and it is destroyed. Time is indeed in the grain of Tolkien's work, down to our continued sense of the hours of the day, the date and the changing seasons during the quest. (pp. 172-73)

Since the subject of Tolkien's book is meant to be a mortal estate, it is not surprising that he allows no more than a small and rather veiled place to divine agency. (p. 173)

The fewness and the brevity of [the] references to providence are an index to Tolkien's purpose: if he had wanted us to have a sense of some destinal or divine agency at the forefront of our minds in reading his story, he would have stressed it much more than he has. (p. 174)

At the centre of his epic, Tolkien has set out to place an ethic of heroic endeavour: the Ring-bearer against the whole might of Sauron. Yet he has chosen no conventional hero, no Beowulf nor Aeneas nor Roland of almost un-thinking honour or courage, but a little man, a four-foot halfling of a race happiest just to eat and sleep. The idea is to give us in Frodo a protagonist who grows into being a hero as his journey proceeds. It is here that Tolkien's problems begin. (pp. 174-75)

Any conception of a hero demands that the hero's actions be substantially based on free choice and human will; and Tolkien certainly seems to have meant this to be a major spring in the action of his fantasy. Frodo's decisions in the Shire and at Rivendell to set out with the Ring are arranged to appear acts of independent resolution: in each case he is presented with the facts and we are to believe that he has a choice between the comforts of staying and the rigours of going which he alone must decide. (pp. 174-75)

Free choice is not meant to be the sole key to the action of Tolkien's book. Frodo, after all, is chosen to carry the Ring; and on one occasion Gandalf says that '"only a small part is played in great deeds by any hero."' . . . Nevertheless, whether by heroic or any other standards, free will must have a substantial part to play if the story is not to make mortals into puppets.

In fact, however, we find that this last is just what has happened. (p. 176)

The simple fact is that Tolkien was trying to write a novel as well as an epic, a story of ordinary lives faced with extraordinary demands, and he did not know how to start from cold. . . .

The same problems are present in the body of the work, the account of Frodo's journey. Even allowing, for Tolkien's benefit, that Frodo is a free agent capable of real choices, there are several factors in the narrative which restrict our sense of this. No one will deny that from Frodo's point of view there are difficulties—the long hike, the constant dangers, the burden of the Ring; but from the reader's vantage point these obstacles are less real than they should be.

For one thing, Frodo always chooses correctly; and if he is in doubt, as he is at Parth Galen whether to go to Minas

Tirith or Mordor, he is pushed into making the right decision (there by the attempt on the Ring by Boromir). The result of a string of correct choices is that the reader gets a sense of inevitability: the possibility of making a wrong choice recedes to vanishing point, and with it the very idea of choice. Nor is turning back ever temptation enough to force a real dilemma: it occasionally lures, but is readily forgotten, and attention settles back in its groove. (p. 177)

Not once does Frodo doubt that all that Gandalf has said about the evil nature of the Ring is right. He is not tempted for an instant by Boromir's suggestion that it is all surmise. In fact he is scarcely tempted at all: there is no such thing as a good and a bad side of his nature that he must choose between; and this is nowhere more evident than in the contradictory account of the power of the Ring. The Ring, we are told, corrupts: it excites in all who have it or come near it a sense of power; and though this urge may at first be good, it swiftly degenerates into pride and rapacity. . . . Yet Frodo, its bearer, is never tempted by this aspect of the Ring save at the very last moment, when his heavily-emphasized past mercies to Gollum immediately save him from the consequences. Nor does the fact that he is a simple hobbit make him immune: Sam is tempted on the walls of Mordor—and Tolkien is hard put to find good reason for his not falling. . . . (p. 178)

The Ring also tries to force its owner to use it, but here the assault is portrayed as more magical than spiritual. (pp. 178-79)

Tolkien is unhappy with the whole idea of inner conflict. (p. 179)

What has happened in the *Lord of the Rings* is that Tolkien has turned from the scheme of inner conflict—which both his conception of a protagonist unequal to the task and the whole idea of the Ring of Power demand—to a ready-made heroic psychology where struggle is with external forces—the Ring and Sauron's powers. There are several possible explanations of this. His reluctance to show Frodo or any of the other good characters as truly tempted may be accounted for by his normally absolute distinctions between good and evil (to show the good tempted would be to show them morally mixed); and this distinction may in turn stem from his concept of 'Recovery' [from his essay "On Fairy Stories" in *Tree and Leaf*], which requires the portrayal of things in their pure and unalloyed states. Explanation might also be found in another aspect of 'Recovery': the demonstration that things really are separate from us, 'no more yours than they [are] you' . . . , in this sense Tolkien's fantasy celebrates the objective, not the subjective world—or, as he says, he is 'primarily interested in Faërie, not tortured mortals.' . . . This last point is part of a belief that the nature of fantasy is opposed to the sort of character-delineation and 'internal' narrative that has its place in the novel or drama. Equally, of course, so does the nature of heroic epic as Tolkien knows it: there the hero rarely doubts his purpose or is seen to struggle with himself, and conflict is with something external to him—be it the purposes of a deity, a monster or simply human enemies. (p. 180)

If then struggle with the self is to be abandoned as the basis of Frodo's heroism, let us consider how far the idea of an *externalized* conflict, as in heroic epic, between a fully resolved soul and vicissitude can be taken seriously as the ethical basis of *The Lord of the Rings*.

There is a glaring feature of Tolkien's fantasy which critics have tended to play down or ignore, and which removes almost all possibility of regarding Frodo or anyone else in the book with any seriousness as a hero: the continued presence of a biased fortune. (pp. 180-81)

It may be true that from the point of view of the characters themselves, the constant assistance is not expected, and that to themselves, their fear and courage are real; but for the reader, who sees that it is not mortal will but luck which is the architect of success, the struggles with the evil forces become unreal, mere posturings in a rigged bout. And even if one were to argue that destiny or the Valar were the cause (which as we have seen there seems little justification for doing), this would only give a metaphysical base to what would remain a desertion of the heroic ethic. (p. 183)

The problem is not only one of Tolkien's having failed with the heroism and mortal will he set out to put at the centre of his fantasy: it is a problem too of the truth of his work to the fundamental character of reality. W. H. Auden said of the imaginary world,

> Its history may be unusual but it must not contradict our notion of what history is, an interplay of Fate, Choice, and Chance. Lastly, it must not violate our moral experience . . . The triumph of Good over Evil which the successful achievement of the Quest implies must appear historically possible, not a daydream. Physical and, to a considerable extent, intellectual power must be shown as what we know them to be, morally neutral and effectively real: battles are won by the stronger side, be it good or evil.

It is precisely these features which *The Lord of the Rings* lacks. Auden's concluding assertion that no Quest Tale does 'more justice to our experience of social-historical realities than *The Lord of the Rings*' [see *CLC*, Vol. 1] simply does not stand up to the facts. . . . A sense of inevitability comes over the reader: nothing is at risk, nothing can be lost; Frodo is home and dry under the umbrella of authorial fortune. (pp. 183-84)

Tolkien could have given us some significant instances of bad luck in his fantasy to convince us that fate is impartial. His refusal to do this is part of a more general weakness in *The Lord of the Rings*. He is simply not prepared to allow any really telling loss or vicissitude into the book. (p. 185)

[Though] he has set out to put free will and heroism at the centre of his fantasy, Tolkien has ended by cancelling them with luck; though he intends a picture of evil as continuous and no victory final, he gives us an absolute happy ending; though meant as a true elegy *The Lord of the Rings* gives only portable woes.

The weakness in Tolkien's fantasy is however not simply a matter of the author having slid away from the demands of his vision: it is also the result of an attraction towards something. At the centre of the book are Mordor and Sauron: not only in that they are the goal towards which the Ring-bearer is moving (though this arrangement of the plot is in its own way significant), but in that Tolkien has realized them far more vividly than anything he gives us to oppose to them. What we have is, unknown to the author, an imaginative imbalance: good is supposed to overcome

evil, but since it is less real to us, its victory does not convince. (p. 191)

Tolkien has done what Milton is sometimes accused of having done: he has unconsciously let the weight of his imagination fall on the wrong side. There is nothing to balance the Dark Lord, no opponent, whether Gandalf or the scarce-mentioned Valar, to whom he has given any corresponding mystical presence. Once in Mordor the thought comes to Sam the hobbit that 'in the end the Shadow was only a small and passing thing: there was light and high beauty for ever beyond its reach' (III, 199); but it remains only a single fleeting thought, of which nothing is made.

It is worth noticing that Tolkien's book sets out to be about Sauron: it calls itself *The Lord of the Rings*. No one else but the Dark Lord can be described by this title. Others cannot master the One Ring, but can only struggle against becoming slaves to it. The book is therefore entitled 'Sauron', and this suggests that somehow Tolkien felt the darker side of the story more meaningful to him personally. (pp. 192-93)

The weakness of the characterization in Tolkien's fantasy frustrates one of his primary aims. For he set out to recover for us in his book a freshness of vision which we are without; and if there is no vision, there can be no freshness. The way the characters tend to run together into a nondescript soup is also precisely counter to the moral polarity he has set up within his fantasy. His picture of the alliance of the peoples of Middle-earth against Sauron is one of a co-operative effort by different races, each with a separate identity, in which the author at least goes through the motions of taking a delight. It is precisely that they retain their generic individualities in coming together that should define the good; and under Sauron and the power of the Ring that identity should fade. . . . (pp. 200-01)

After [Tolkien's] failure with style, we are left only with what one might call the fantasist's 'long-stop': the mythic base, if any, of the book. Here, however, one must be wary of C. S. Lewis' insistence . . . that where a myth or some archetypal posture is present in a work, that work necessarily merits our reverence. There does seem to be a glimmer in Tolkien's book of a myth which is more definitely at the back of *Paradise Lost*: the idea of the minute yet enormously powerful Ring with its frail bearer, the long and difficult journey to enclosed Mordor and the casting of the Ring into the mountain suggests a process of fertilization. Of course there are inconsistencies: throwing the Ring into Orodruin results in destruction, not creation, and unless we are to grant an incest motif, a spermatozoon does not return to its ultimate point of origin. Nevertheless the basic pattern of the story does hint at this image.

There are further drawbacks to *The Lord of the Rings*, not the least of which, given the flabbiness of material, and allowing for the sense of scale demanded by epic, is its length. The epithet 'endless worm' coined by one critic seems only too apt. Doubtless there is such a thing as the sheer number of pages the reader has had to turn that can add poignancy to the story—one almost feels this is the case as we come to the great close of Malory's epic. But not with Tolkien's book, for we have never been very much involved anyway. Perhaps also the length of the story and the time he took to write it go some way towards explaining his failure of detachment: his involvement in Middle-earth may well have increased in direct proportion to the time and space at his disposal. Certainly he manages to avoid this fault in his short stories.

What then are we to make of Tolkien's book? From the evidence now assembled it can be concluded that none of 'Consolation', 'Fantasy' and 'Secondary Belief', nor 'Recovery' (and by further implication 'Escape') can properly emerge from this work: the first because nothing is at risk; the second two because in many basic features the book does not keep to its own terms, and thus is without the 'inner consistency of reality' on which they depend; and the others because for the most part the style is weak and bloodless.

It would be easy to conclude that all this results from Tolkien's having been sentimental, evasive and morally uncertain as a man and inadequate as an artist. Yet the weakness of *The Lord of the Rings* may equally come from the fact that he did not express himself fully. The book was largely born out of a reaction against the modern world in which he lived: nostalgia and wish-fulfilment, which were only one part of Tolkien the man, are its essence. That there was more to the author than the work shows can be argued from its very poverty of realization: Tolkien may have found that the good, the beautiful and the age-old did not excite him so much or so plainly as he liked to believe. It is possible that his work becomes facile and weak because of an oversimple judgement on the modern world which is its source and end. *The Lord of the Rings* would thus be a picture rather of Tolkien's uncertainty than of Tolkien himself. (pp. 205-06)

> C. N. Manlove, "J.R.R. Tolkien (1892-1973) and 'The Lord of the Rings'," in his Modern Fantasy: Five Studies (© Cambridge University Press 1975), Cambridge University Press, 1975, pp. 152-206.

DOROTHY MATTHEWS

J.R.R. Tolkien's *The Hobbit* has received very little serious critical attention other than as the precursor of *The Lord of the Rings*. It has usually been praised as a good introduction to the trilogy, and as a children's book, but anyone familiar with psychoanalysis cannot avoid being tantalized by recurrent themes and motifs in the three stories. Bilbo's story has surprising depths that can be plumbed by the reader who is receptive to psychoanalytic interpretations.

The central pattern of *The Hobbit* is, quite obviously, a quest. Like so many heroes before him, Bilbo sets out on a perilous journey, encounters and overcomes many obstacles (including a confrontation with a dragon) and returns victorious after he has restored a kingdom and righted ancient wrongs. However, this pattern is so commonplace in literature that it is not a very helpful signpost. But it may help in other ways.

Let us first look briefly at *The Hobbit* for its folk ingredients, that is, the common motifs or story elements which it shares with folk narratives. There are, of course, the creatures themselves: dwarves, elves, trolls, animal servants, helpful birds and, the most frequently recurring of all folk adversaries, the treasure-guarding dragon. There are magic objects in abundance: a ring of invisibility, secret entrances into the underworld, magic swords, and doors into mountains. Dreams foretell and taboos admonish, the violation of which could bring dire results.

There are tasks to be performed, riddles to solve, and foes to be outwitted or outfought. Folk motifs form the very warp and woof in the texture of this tale, which is not surprising since Tolkien, as a medievalist, is immersed in folk tradition, a tradition that gives substance not only to the best known epics but to most medieval narratives and to "fairy tales."

In fact, it is probably its resemblance to what today's readers see as the nursery tale that has resulted in *The Hobbit* being relegated to elementary school shelves. (pp. 29-30)

But even if *The Hobbit* is only a children's story, it should be analyzed more closely for deeper levels of meaning, for it is the kind of story that has provided the most profound insights into the human psyche. (p. 31)

Bilbo Baggins' journey [is] a metaphor for the individuation process, his quest . . . a search for maturity and wholeness, and his adventures . . . symbolically detailed rites of maturation. . . .

[At] the beginning of the tale, Bilbo's personality is out of balance and far from integrated. His masculinity, or one may say his Tookish aggressiveness, is being repressed so that he is clinging rather immaturely to a childish way of life. He has not even begun to realize his full potential. The womblike peace and security of his home is disturbed with the arrival of Gandalf, who may be seen as a projection of the Jungian archetype of the "wise old man" since he resembles the magic helper of countless stories. . . . (p. 33)

At the outset of their adventure, Bilbo, like a typical young adolescent, is uncertain of his role, or "persona," to use a Jungian term. (p. 34)

One of the most crucial incidents of the story takes place when Bilbo finds himself unconscious and separated from the dwarves within the mountain domain of the goblins. In this underground scene he must face an important trial; he must make a decision whose outcome will be a measure of his maturity. . . . With unprecedented courage he decides to face life rather than to withdraw from it. This decision marks an important step in his psychological journey.

The danger he decides to face at this time, of course, is Gollum, the vaguely sensed but monstrous inhabitant of the underground lake. The association of this adversary with water and the attention given to his long grasping fingers and voracious appetite suggest a similarity to Jung's Devouring-Mother archetype, that predatory monster which must be faced and slain by every individual in the depths of his unconscious if he is to develop as a self-reliant individual. The fact that the talisman is a ring is even more suggestive of Jungian symbology since the circle is a Jungian archetype of the *self*—the indicator of possible psychic wholeness. The psychological importance of this confrontation is further supported by the imagery of the womb and of rebirth which marks the details of Bilbo's escape. (pp. 34-5)

Whether the spider with whom Bilbo battles is interpreted as a Jungian shadow figure, embodying evil, or as the Devouring-Mother facet of the anima is immaterial. The symbolism is clear without specific terms: a lone protagonist must free himself from a menacing opponent that has the power to cripple him forever. With the aid of a miraculously acquired sword and a magic talisman, he is able to face the danger and overcome it. (p. 37)

From this point on, Bilbo has the self-esteem needed to fulfill his responsibilities as a mature and trustworthy leader. It is through his ingenuity that they escape from the dungeon prisons in the subterranean halls of the wood-elves. This last episode also reveals telling symbolic details in that the imprisonment is underground and the escape through a narrow outlet into the water is yet another birth image.

The climactic adventures of Bilbo are of course the episodes with Smaug, who, like the traditional dragon of folklore, has laid waste the land and is guarding a treasure. If viewed in the light of Jungian symbology, the contested treasure can be seen as the archetype of the self, of psychic wholeness. Thus this last series of events marks the final stages of Bilbo's quest of maturation. (pp. 38-9)

A truly critical question arises in considering [the incident where Bilbo acquires the Arkenstone] and the remainder of the story. I have taught this work many times and am constantly hearing complaints of dissatisfaction from students who feel that the last part of the book is both puzzling and anticlimactic. Many report that they felt a real loss of interest while reading the final chapters. Why does Bilbo keep the Arkenstone without telling the dwarves and then use it as a pawn in dealing with their enemies? Why, they ask, did Tolkien have a rather uninteresting character, rather than Bilbo, kill Smaug? Why is Bilbo, the previous center of interest, knocked unconscious so that he is useless during the last Battle of Five Armies? Isn't it a fault in artistic structure to allow the protagonist to fade from the picture during episodes when the normal expectation would be to have him demonstrate even more impressive heroism?

Answers to these questions are clear if the story is interpreted as the psychological journey of Bilbo Baggins. It stands to reason that Tolkien does not have Bilbo kill the dragon because that would be more the deed of a savior or culture hero, such as St. George, or the Red Cross Knight, or Beowulf. The significance of this tale lies in fact in the very obviously anti-heroic manner in which Tolkien chooses to bring Bilbo's adventures to a conclusion. As a result, Bilbo emerges as a symbol of a very average individual, not as a figure of epic proportion. Bilbo has not found eternal glory, but, rather, the self-knowledge that a willingness to meet challenge is not necessarily incompatible with a love of home. . . . [At] the conclusion of his adventures Bilbo finds the greatest prize of all: a knowledge of his own identity. In maturing psychologically, he has learned to think for himself and to have the courage to follow a course he knows to be right—in spite of possible repercussions. (pp. 40-1)

Dorothy Matthews, "The Psychological Journey of Bilbo Baggins," in A Tolkien Compass, *edited by Jared Lobdell (reprinted from* A Tolkien Compass *edited by Jared Lobdell by permission of The Open Court Publishing Company, LaSalle, Illinois; copyright © 1975 by The Open Court Publishing Company), Open Court, 1975, pp. 29-42.*

DEBORAH C. ROGERS

[The] hobbits are the *race* par excellence in *The Hobbit* and *The Lord of the Rings.* One can tell this in part because Tolkien uses their point of view, but even more because he obviously likes them very much indeed, and without evading their shortcomings in his portrayal. *I* can also tell from a letter which Tolkien sent me in 1958, in which he said, "I am in fact a hobbit."

So what are hobbits like, these original and most important creatures of Tolkien's? Their main qualities are apparent: they are small, provincial, and comfort-loving. (p. 71)

[Hobbits] are the aspect of humanity which I have dubbed, for the purposes of this paper, Everyclod—unjustly, of course. For as we all know, "there is more to them than meets the eye."

Tolkien has done his portraiture finely. We are all in some way small, provincial, and comfort-loving—and we see ourselves as such. At first we like to imagine ourselves as heroes, but experience makes us sceptical; we become convinced that, in fairness, we are not heroes. . . . One of the notable features of twentieth century literature is the antihero; Northrop Frye's ironic literary mode has taken over our everyday lives. Everyclod is at the center of our vision, which has become cloddish.

But this is not Tolkien's mode. One of the reasons he is likable and unusual among contemporary authors is that he does not focus on the cloddish, though he does focus on hobbits. Bilbo, Frodo, Sam, Merry, and Pippin are all to a greater or lesser extent billed as Everyclod at the beginnings of their stories, but as we know, each of them becomes a hero. . . . With the hobbits, what Tolkien shows us is that, and how, Everyclod really is Everyhero, and can develop his heroic nature when the need arises.

Hobbits, then, are Tolkien's primary picture of Man. But then, what of the characters he portrays as men, members of the human race? (pp. 71-3)

Tolkien's human race, in the specimens we encounter, has much more variety than any of the other races. . . . The first thing to be said of the human race, in Tolkien's portrait, is that it is capable of any act: treachery, warcraft, gentleness, domesticity, adventurousness, or poetry. And this leaves us where we were before: hobbits are Tolkien's basic kind of people, and the human race is too various to abstract a composite picture from its members and say, This is Tolkien's man.

In that case, look again. What if, instead of seeking a composite picture, we look for a representative? Can we say that in all this variety of men, there is one *man* par excellence? Of course we can. Obviously, Tolkien's man par excellence is Aragorn. So let us consider him and see what he adds to Tolkien's picture of humanity. So far, we have the image of Everyclod with Everyhero sleeping inside him. Aragorn is a hero already, and what sleeps in him is kingship. (p. 73)

Tolkien's man par excellence is very different from his race par excellence. Aragorn must, so to speak, "refer" to a different aspect of humanity from the hobbits, who (as we have seen) refer to Everyclod, the individual who has heroic potential. (p. 74)

But, what is Aragorn about? What other aspect of man is so important? There is his bad side, but Strider does not represent that, despite the mixed impressions created by his first appearance. Evils are amply covered by orcs, Saruman, Ted Sandyman, and so on. Nor does Aragorn represent our Everyclod aspect, even with its latent heroism, for his heroism is not latent. He is a heroic hero, the sort we feel shy of identifying ourselves with. He is a hero, and more than that, the king: the epitome of his race, and in that sense its representative.

But look at the condition this king is in throughout most of the story: he is not in his rightful place, and he is surrounded by symbols of a realm not in its rightful order. The throne is vacant. A steward governs in the city of Gondor, whose name is no longer the Tower of the Setting Sun but the Tower of Guard. In the city houses stand empty. The White Tree is withered. The sword Narsil is broken. Aragorn is the king's heir, but he is in exile from his realm. He is engaged to Arwen, but they are not married. In fact, the first time we see her, at a feast, he is closeted in council elsewhere.

By the conclusion of the story, these conditions are all set right: Narsil is reforged as Anduril; a seedling of the Tree is found; the city is on its way to being rebuilt and repopulated; Aragorn and Arwen are married and reigning. This is Tolkien's fortunate resolution, or if you will, happy ending.

Do we know anyone else who is out of his rightful position, whose restoration would be a fortunate event? Yes, we do. It is not you or me or him or her (Farmer Maggot, or Rosie Cotton); it is *us*.

Now I shall refer to Christian doctrine, which we have inherited in the form of Judeo-Christian myth. Tolkien is a Christian himself, and a look at this body of beliefs throws light on his story at this point. The rightful position of man is to be the ruling creature on this planet, to administer it in the best interests of all the local creatures, and God's viceroy. As you know, man now occupies only a parody of this position: he is the ruling creature here, but he kills his own kind and other creatures and damages and exploits the planet.

In the history of mankind, there are two men par excellence whom it behooves us to consider while talking of Aragorn: Adam, and Christ, who is called the new Adam.

Adam was set at his creation into the kingly position I have described. And he failed. And all his descendants after him have been dislocated from our place on earth. Adam (and in him all mankind) is parallel to Aragorn in that both are exiles. But Aragorn does not fail. He bides his time, works, follows his opportunities, resists temptations, and brings all the realm to good. Notice that he can only do this in cooperation with Everyclod—in fact, with all good creatures.

Tom Bombadil, by the way, has been called [by Alexis Levitin] "the unfallen Adam." This is a perceptive appellation. I don't mean Tolkien said to himself, "Now I will put in a prelapsarian"; but surely Adam in Eden must have been similar in many ways to Tom as described: the master of all natural things, but not their owner.... But Adam fell, and his race's predicament follows from that. Tom is a survivor from another age, and peripheral to the War of the Ring, while the king in exile is central to it. (pp. 74-5)

Aragorn's kingdom *is* of this world. He is born to reign in Middle-earth. Aragorn is parallel to Christ only in that each of them is the man of good events in his story, not in the kind of fortunate conclusion they bring. True, they have some manifestations in common: most noticeably, each can heal the sick and each is crowded upon by the sick in consequence. I do not think one need make much to-do about a Biblical parallel, on the crowding: it is only a piece of realism. If there is a healer, he will be pestered; think of the proverbial doctor at the cocktail party.

Aragorn's good work, then, is that of the restoration of the king on earth. And this is a type, a figure, a symbol, of the happy turnabout of the restoration of man as a race. Individually, we are hobbits; collectively, we are Aragorn. (p. 76)

> *Deborah C. Rogers, "Everyclod and Everyhero: The Image of Man in Tolkien," in* A Tolkien Compass, *edited by Jared Lobdell (reprinted from* A Tolkien Compass *edited by Jared Lobdell by permission of The Open Court Publishing Company, La Salle, Illinois; copyright © 1975 by The Open Court Publishing Company), Open Court, 1975, pp. 69-76.*

JOHN GARDNER

If "The Hobbit" is a lesser work than the Ring trilogy because it lacks the trilogy's high seriousness, the collection that makes up "The Silmarillion" stands below the trilogy because much of it contains *only* high seriousness; that is, here Tolkien cares more about the meaning and coherence of his myth than he does about these glories of the trilogy: rich characterization, imagistic brilliance, powerfully imagined and detailed sense of place, and thrilling adventure. Not that those qualities are entirely lacking here. The central tale, "The Silmarillion"—though not the others—has a wealth of vivid and interesting characters, and all the tales are lifted above the ordinary by Tolkien's devil figures, Melkor, later called Morgoth, his great dragon Glaurung, and Morgoth's successor Sauron. Numerous characters here have interest, almost always because they work under some dark fate, struggling against destiny and trapping themselves; but none of them smokes a pipe, none wears a vest, and though each important character has his fascinating quirks, the compression of the narrative and the fierce thematic focus give Tolkien no room to develop and explore those quirks as he does in the trilogy.

Character is at the heart of the Ring trilogy: the individual's voluntary service of good or evil within an unfated universe. The subject of "The Silmarillion" is older, more heroic: the effect on individuals of the struggle of two great forces, the divine order and rebellious individualism that flows through Morgoth. (p. 1)

Music is the central symbol and the total myth of "The Silmarillion," a symbol that becomes interchangeable with light (music's projection). The double symbol is introduced at once in the creation of myth, "Ainulindale." ...

Tolkien's vision in this book is a curious blend of things modern and things medieval. What is modern is for the most part the tawdriest of the modern—not that one cares, since Tolkien's vision transforms and redeems it. Walt Disney is everywhere, though his work may have had less influence on Tolkien than did that of equally childlike artists, such as Aubrey Beardsley. Tolkien's language is the same phony Prince Valiant language of the worst Everyman translations and modernizations—things like: "Death you have earned with these words; and death you should find suddenly, had I not sworn an oath in haste; of which I repent, baseborn mortal, who in the realm of Morgoth has learnt to creep in secret as his spies and thralls." But one pushes aside all such objections, because the fact is that Tolkien's vision is philosophically and morally powerful, and if some of the fabric in which he clothes the vision is bargain-basement, he has greatly elevated it by his art.

What is medieval in Tolkien's vision is his set of organizing principles, his symbolism and his pattern of legends and events. (p. 39)

As he borrows the organizing principles and symbols of medieval poets and philosophers, Tolkien borrows the standard legends of characters tricked by fate, characters damned by their own best (or worst) intentions, characters who found proper atonement. His characters are of course new, but their problems are standard, archetypal. . . . In all these stories there are splendid moments, luminous descriptions of the kind that enrich the Ring trilogy, moments of tenderness, though rarely moments of humor.

But in "The Silmarillion" what is finally most moving is not the individual legends but the total vision, the eccentric heroism of Tolkien's attempt. What Tolkien lacks that his medieval model possessed is serene Christian confidence. Despite the affirmation of his creation legend, Tolkien's universe is never safe like Chaucer's. The Providential plan seems again and again to hang by a thread above bottomless pits of disaster. Tolkien, in other words, has taken on the incredible task of seeking to rejuvenate the medieval Christian way of seeing and feeling, although—as all his legends reiterate—we can no longer see clearly (the songs of the elves are now all but forgotten, as was the First Age in the Ring trilogy) and our main feeling is now tragic dread.

Strange man! Strange mind! Why would anyone do it, we keep asking as we read. Why create a whole Christianlike religion, a whole new creation myth to set beside those of the Greeks, the Jews, the Northmen and the rest? Why write a mythic history, a Bible? Nevertheless, he has tried to do just that. . . . (pp. 39-40)

Art, of course, is a way of thinking, a way of mining reality. In the Ring trilogy, Tolkien went after reality through philosophy-laden adventure. In "The Silmarillion," for better or worse, he has sought to mine deeper. (p. 40)

> *John Gardner, "The World of Tolkien," in* The New York Times Book Review *(© 1977 by The New York Times Company; reprinted by permission), October 23, 1977, pp. 1, 39-40.*

ROBERT M. ADAMS

The Silmarillion, despite the cuts that have evidently been made in the original materials, the selection and arrangement that have been imposed on them, remains an empty and pompous bore. There are epic elements in it, but they have been smothered by an overgrowth of genealogy.

The narrative is not in itself very sturdy. Oaths, feuds, sword fights, lost cities, doomed lovers, and ill-starred friendships abound; but there is a dearth of characters and an oversupply of stereotypes. The familiar Tolkien divison prevails between level-eyed, steely-but-gentle good guys, and snarling, black-minded bad guys; but the action remains exterior and mechanical. Above all, Tolkien has a fascination with names for their own sake that will probably seem excessive to anyone whose favorite light reading is not the first book of Chronicles. . . .

Such a barricade of grotesque and semi-pronounceable names is no small obstacle to a venturesome reader; but in fact the names are also a good part of the book's reward. Like the portmanteau words of "Jabberwocky" or the deeper and more violent conglomerates of *Finnegans Wake,* many of them sink into the mind, disintegrating the

smooth and accepted conventions of everyday English to memorable effect. The dragon Smaug, the wicked and menacing Nazgûl, the Ents of Fangorn—such rich and mouthy names keep the mind busy tangling and untangling their phonemes. But when one has to keep Elendë (which is a name of Eldamar) distinct from Elendil the son of Amandil, and both distinct from Elendur the son of Isildur, while Elrond, Elros, Eluréd, and Elurín hover in the neighborhood, the effect is an irritating blur. (p. 22)

There's no need to dwell longer on the deficiencies of this latest volume, for which hardly anybody has had a good word to say. . . . *The Silmarillion* is a commercial and perhaps a social phenomenon of some interest, but not a literary event of any magnitude. The books which draw it along in their wake are another matter entirely. The appeal they exercise is deep as well as wide, and is based on their real literary qualities, not simply the quirks and fads of the popular mind. Still, they are very uneven books, both when compared to one another, and in their different parts as well. (p. 23)

[The] success of Tolkien's books may need no more explanation than this, that they contain a number of extremely good stories which many readers seem to be encountering for the first time. The books are a pastiche of stories and scenes in which the reader encounters motifs from Genesis and Revelation, bits of *Beowulf,* snatches of Wagner, pieces of Malory and of Macpherson's *Ossian,* fragments of the sagas, Gaelic legends, Breton lays, elements of the *Poema del Cid,* the *Chanson de Roland, Orlando Furioso, The Faerie Queene, Paradise Lost,* and more, much, much more. This rich gallimaufry of narrative is softened here and melodramatized there for the modern taste, and exempt by being a fairy tale from merely rational criticism. People who have enjoyed it would be well advised not to try prolonging the pleasure by studying *The Silmarillion.* Instead, if the thought isn't too solemn, they might try some of the books that Tolkien himself used to construct his Disney-ized cycle. (p. 24)

> *Robert M. Adams, "'The Hobbit' Habit," in* The New York Review of Books *(reprinted with permission from* The New York Review of Books; *copyright © 1977 Nyrev, Inc.), November 24, 1977, pp. 22-4.*

MARGERY FISHER

I feel that Tolkién did not revise and add to [*The Silmarillion*] over the years as an escape, though it does seem in one way to belong to a deep, almost childlike need to fix and possess for ever a part of the English countryside (and in this sense it could be said to bear the same relation to his practical life as "The Wind in the Willows" bore to Kenneth Grahame's.) The clue to reading it can be found, perhaps, in *Leaf by Niggle. The Silmarillion* is the creation of what Tolkien called a Secondary World, just as much as *Lord of the Rings* though in a different style. It is a piece of literary invention which depends on semantics rather than on social morality. It is true that the whole work reflects the rise of aggression in gods, elves and men, the effects of greed and the lust for power on races created as generous and civilised beings. Tolkien's experience of the world from the '20's onwards cannot but have affected the book in some measure. But ultimately the struggle for the Silmarils and the Rings of Power exists without moral comment, as the necessary impulse for a story, a work of continuous craftsmanship by which Tolkien earned a place in a long line of story-tellers.

The Silmarillion is a bardic work. Whatever it supplies of background to his other tales, it is narrated as if to a receptive and practised audience. The manner is not unlike that of *Beowulf:* the tone is one of celebrating, even of reminding, rather than of explaining. (pp. 3257-58)

Ancient taboos are touched upon in the tale of Beren and Luthien and their fraternal, forbidden love; Germanic folk-tale is recalled in the account of the origin and habitations of Dwarves and in the glimpses of Dragons, Orcs, Balrogs and other monstrous shapes; the ritual words and acts of medieval chivalry add dignity to many scenes of conquest and alliance. The sense of epic immensity is achieved not by mere length in the narrative but in the reiteration of measurements of time, by the way the names of people and places change with certain significant events, and by oratorical passages like the end of the first section:

> Here ends the SILMARILLION. If it has passed from the high and the beautiful to darkness and ruin, that was of old the fate of Arda Marred; and if any change shall come and the Marring be amended, Manwe and Varda may know; but they have not revealed it, and it is not declared in the dooms of Mandos.

In keeping with the epic nature of *The Silmarillion,* the style is concentrated, with the musical rhythms often giving place to the dry, measured words of a chronicler. Elsewhere, though, there is a plangency and emotional force that belong to high fantasy—for example, in the magnificent description of the engulfing of Numenor or the account of Mirkwood and the coming of the Wizards. This posthumous work of Tolkien's is bound to suffer the attentions of cryptographers, thesis-writers and fanatics in the years to come but with patience and good will the ordinary reader (including many in the 'teens) may obtain from it more true pleasure than they ever will. (pp. 3258-59)

Margery Fisher, in her Growing Point, *March, 1978.*

Garry Trudeau

1948-

American cartoonist, essayist, and screenwriter. "Doonesbury" evolved from a series of cartoons entitled "Bull Tales" written for the *Yale Daily News* while Trudeau was an undergraduate. The strip, which poked fun at campus celebrities, interested a newspaper syndicate and was launched nationally in 1970. Along the way the scope was broadened and the comic became a satire of contemporary politics and culture instead of campus hijinks. "Doonesbury" is one of a few politically oriented comic strips with a continuous story line. It was recognized as revolutionary in the medium because it satirized public officials without the mask of fictional locales such as Al Capp used in "L'il Abner." Real life characters appear as themselves and Trudeau allows them to damn themselves with their own words. All political persuasions come under attack from Trudeau's pen, and he is as unsparing with left-wing characters as he is with right-wing. An intelligent follower of the news and a meticulous researcher, Trudeau sometimes creates strips that are obscure to those without his knowledge of current political events and cultural trends. He does not write his strips far in advance of publication, which makes their appearance in the papers almost concurrent with the events he is satirizing. Because of this topicality and his cutting irony he is sometimes censored in newspapers when his satire strikes too close to home. A strip on Nixon's visit to Watts, for instance, was dropped from the *Los Angeles Times*. On occasion Trudeau has defended his work from editorial criticism, but such public statements of intention are rare. A reclusive man, he rarely interviews or makes public appearances, preferring to speak through his comic strip or in the essays that appear in various magazines. In addition to a 1975 Pulitzer Prize for editorial cartooning, Trudeau has received an Academy Award nomination for the short subject *A Doonesbury Special* and several honorary doctorates. (See also *Contemporary Authors*, Vols. 81-84.)

ROBERT C. MAYNARD

On [May 29, 1973], The Washington Post and about a dozen other American newspapers incurred the wrath of hundreds of their readers by making the decision to omit, on grounds of fairness, a popular comic strip, "Doonesbury" by Garry Trudeau. . . .

Doonesbury's well-earned popularity is based on the pithy way in which its characters sink their teeth into contemporary subjects. The strip is created with a sure-handed sophistication that is pointed even when it isn't funny.

The reason the Tuesday strip was dropped is that it was, in the opinion of the editors of The Washington Post, entirely too pointed and overstepped the bounds of decency, fairness and good judgment.

What Trudeau did was have his "WBBY" commentator give a little Watergate rundown which concluded with the judgment about a principal in the case as being "GUILTY! GUILTY, GUILTY, GUILTY!!"

Howard Simons, managing editor of The Washington Post, explained his decision to drop the strip by saying:

"If anyone is going to find any defendant guilty, it's going to be the due process of justice, not a comic strip artist. We cannot have one standard for the news pages and another for the comics." . . .

It has long been recognized that cartoons are very much the creation of their authors and the points of view they express are granted a special license. . . . Any number of strips have expressed a variety of political viewpoints, many of them quite contrary to the editorial stand of the newspapers in which they appear. . . .

What gives the current Doonesbury controversy special status is that it is a stark case of the conflict of rights. Garry Trudeau clearly has a right to his opinion about Watergate. It can even be argued that the way he portrays his commentator, Mark, declaring a Watergate defendant "Guilty, Guilty, Guilty!!" suggests something of the extreme view that many take of the Watergate case.

For all that, other rights have their place. These are the rights of a defendant to be considered innocent until proven guilty. It is that aspect of the matter which is so disturbing. . . .

Responsible journalists have taken pains to make a distinction between finding that there is a probable cause to believe wrongdoing has occurred and a flat conclusion of guilt.

To many, it has seemed at times a distinction without any substantive difference. And, to be sure, there have been times when major news organizations have made assertions in the Watergate case which would have been far better left for the determination of a judicial body.

I am very much of the belief that in a free society, it is always dangerous to suppress expression. I am equally sure that in a nation of laws, it is profoundly dangerous for comic strip artists to ignore the fundamental right of defendants to be presumed innocent.

If I had to weigh those rights in the Doonesbury case, I'd say that Mark and his creator, Trudeau, must yield. It is even more profoundly so for the reason that it is a cartoon appearing in the comic section. I'd like it never to be said that young readers received their first notions about fundamental rights from the comics and concluded that folk-hero characters are allowed to declare people guilty in advance of their trials. . . .

[There] is in my mind a line across which responsible expression cannot step without running the risk of excision. Trudeau, in my opinion, stepped across that line in having Mark speak as he did.

> *Robert C. Maynard, "The Comic Strip Isn't a Court," in* The Washington Post *(© 1973, The Washington Post), May 31, 1973, p. A 18.*

ALLAN PARACHINI

To Trudeau, [*Doonesbury*] is simply his public voice, his vehicle to inveigh against social and political wrongdoing, and to cuff wrongdoers. (p. 4)

What is it that has made *Doonesbury* such a runaway success? One simple reason is that it has attracted . . . support from young readers. . . . They find the strip believable and identify with its characters. . . . [Don Wright, Pulitzer Prize-winning editorial cartoonist,] has high praise for Trudeau's dialogue. "He's a damn good writer. His style is clean and uncluttered. . . ."

Nicholas Von Hoffman . . . catalogues another Trudeau strength. "He has a golden ear. He pays attention to words and the way they're said, and captures the essence of what's there that most people don't hear." The power of the dialogue and Trudeau's use of a device perfected by Jules Feiffer—keeping the art in each panel reasonably static—increases the impact of the message.

Some critics, including gun-shy editors, find the message all too strong, the humor too harsh and brittle. They also question Trudeau's ability to sustain the strip's momentum in the less turbulent post-Watergate milieu. The growing number of *Doonesbury* advocates among newspaper readers tends to refute the criticism about excessive harshness. In fact, on subjects other than Watergate, Trudeau displays a droll, subtle sense of humor that works because it underwhelms rather than overpowers. (p. 7)

> *Allan Parachini, "Social Protest Hits the Comic Pages," in* Columbia Journalism Review *(© 1974 Graduate School of Journalism, Columbia University), November-December, 1974, pp. 4-7.*

NORA EPHRON

I am not one of those who believe that there is nothing to laugh at about the women's movement; in fact, there is plenty to laugh about without in any way putting down the movement, and I become downright irritable when I read lengthy feminist tracts justifying the women's movement's lack of a sense of humor. "How can we laugh when we're so oppressed?" That kind of thing. It seems to be that the exact opposite is true: how can we *not* laugh when we're so oppressed. (p. 93)

In any case, the women's movement has spawned very little humor—much less any humor that amuses me. And Joanie Caucus hardly seemed a likely candidate; she was, after all, the creation of a man. Then I started reading "Doonesbury," and there was Joanie, the runaway wife, the day-care center supervisor, the law school applicant, the newly-single woman coping with passes from a hip priest with hot tickets to a Jeb Magruder concert, and I began to roar.

There is nothing more hopeless than attempting to explain why something is funny. . . . I have no idea why she is funny. I just know she kills me. . . . It's not just that I know women like her and that I'm a little like her myself. It's not just that my friends constantly tell me stories about trying to bring the movement to their children, stories that are remarkably like the episodes in this book. It's also that there is something about what she looks like and the way she behaves—so downtrodden and yet plucky, so saggy and yet upright, so droopy-eyed and yet wide awake, so pessimistic and yet deepdown slyly sure that she's on the right track. I don't want to take this too seriously, but she seems such a perfect, sympathetic mirror-image of all of us who are trying to make sense out of the contradictions, trying to assimilate all the new information and ideas and theories into our messy lives and minds. It's not easy, folks—and I love that Joanie makes it look so hard. It's occasionally absurd and ridiculous—and I love that she makes it look so funny. It seems to me that this book provides a perfect, absolutely painless way for parents to introduce some of these ideas to their children. (pp. 94-5)

> *Nora Ephron, in her afterword to* Joanie *by Garry Trudeau (copyright © 1974 by G. B. Trudeau; reprinted with permission from Andrews and McMeel, Inc.), Sheed and Ward, Inc., 1974, pp. 93-5.*

DOMINIQUE PAUL NOTH

[Trudeau is funny, pertinent and incisive and] daringly hard to categorize. At the same time [his work is] nothing new—at least in terms of bringing political statement to the comic pages. Trudeau, however, may be the best, the most plugged in to society of a long line of cartoonists with messages to drop. And instead of disguising his points within a whimsical swamp, Dogpatch or adventure, Trudeau uses today's locales. . . .

[Trudeau] has an uncanny radar that sweeps up material across the American scene. While many readers presume a leftist bent to his views, Trudeau has taken on the sacred cows and semantic bull of all sides. He has poked at both Nixon and the press, activists and reactionaries. He has looked with a strange mixture of sadness, love and humor at his own generation. . . .

[Trudeau rejects] the idea that his work ought to be isolated in some safe, adult compartment of a newspaper. He once wrote:

> I am often infuriated by the editor who responds to the cry that comics should remain irrelevant and sanitized to encourage moral rectitude on the part of the adolescent comic reader. Why the double standard? The same adolescent comic reader can watch "Mod Squad" in the evening, a kid shooting up in the playground and can even, God forbid,

browse through the rest of the newspaper, where topics forbidden on the comic page abound in great numbers.

Dominique Paul Noth, in Milwaukee Journal *(© 1975, by* The Milwaukee Journal*), May 20, 1975.*

RICHARD R. LINGEMAN

Beginning with B. D., the hard-helmet Jock, and on through Joanie Caucus, the feminist; Zonker Harris, the hippie; Mark Slackmeyer, campus radical—not to mention Michael Doonesbury himself, who is Charlie Brown's older brother kicked out into the world—Mr. Trudeau steadily evolved into a first-rate political satirist of contemporary immorals and unmanners. This progress is admirably charted in "The Doonesbury Chronicles," a collection of 572 of what Mr. Trudeau considers his best strips. They culminate in Watergate, and these are the most slashing, but reading the whole of Mr. Trudeau's work one comes to see him as a satirist who gentles his barbs with a laugh or a "what-can-you-do?" shrug, and who is always held back by a sense of the humanity of even his targets. (p. 7)

Richard R. Lingeman, in The New York Times Book Review *(© 1975 by The New York Times Company; reprinted by permission), December 7, 1975.*

CHUCK STONE

We'll Take It from Here, Sarge is a ba-a-ad book.

Not white folks' conventional notion of bad—invidious, malevolent, and naughty. But black people's revision of bad—hip, together, and super-good.

In this brief but brilliant burlesque on busing (apologies to Spiro Agnew), Garry Trudeau has captured a quality which eluded thousands of newspaper articles, editorials, and television reels on Boston. He has reduced America's cancer of race hate to the essential sadness of its humanity.

Little innocent white Bobby Matthews and his streetwise black friend, Rufus, A. B. (after busing) are juvenile pawns caught up in an adult savagery that is as vibrant today as it was 113 years ago when Lincoln signed that piece of paper.

Bobby's other friend is National Guardsman Sgt. DeRosa, who sits next to him in class, not to help him learn, but to help him survive. (p. 91)

After 113 years of this combative nonsense, an exhausted Sgt. DeRosa must be bewildered by its futility. After only one semester, Bobby Matthews is certainly fed up. From his hospital bed, a victim of racial violence in the school cafeteria, Bobby capsules an American absurdity:

"I mean, I understand busing has brought a lot of ugly passions to the surface. I understand white resentment and I even think I'm beginning to understand black resentment. But what I DON'T understand is all this emphasis on HITTING!" . . .

We'll Take It from Here, Sarge only touches with merciful brevity on the black self-hatred which frequently explodes into irrational aggression. An older black dude rips off Bobby's coke, a way of life in ghetto schools.

Well, you're not bringing it into my life, Bobby decides. He challenges the bigger black dude . . . , precipitates a spaghetti-slinging mini-riot and ends up in the hospital.

Yet, he still doesn't hate. Even though his parents do with their yellow plastic hardhats, their pink plastic hair curlers and their minds in Baggies.

Years ago, kings had court jesters. Today, America is blessed with cartoonists who wield satirical crayons with Lady Montagu's admonition that "satire should, like a polished razor keen, wound with a touch that's scarcely seen." America's number one political satirist, Trudeau, daily does exquisite surgery on our foibles in his "Doonesbury" cartoons. (p. 92)

If sanity somehow manages to prevail, it will be due in part to the Garry Trudeaus who will have ridiculed us into reason and the Bobby Matthews and Rufuses, upspoiled by parents, who will have embarrassed us into love. (p. 93)

Chuck Stone, in his afterword to We'll Take It From Here, Sarge *by Garry Trudeau (copyright © 1975 by G. B. Trudeau; reprinted with permission from Andrews and McMeel, Inc.),* Sheed and Ward, Inc., *1975, pp. 91-3.*

[In *The World of Doonesbury* the] lives of Mike, Zonker, Ms. Joanie Caucus and the rest of the Doonesbury gang whimsically and satirically become a commentary on the political and general cultural scene of the Vietnam and Nixon years and especially of Watergate. Trudeau shows that humor can often reveal more about America's values, attitudes and history than any number of learned tomes gathering dust on the shelves. (p. H 10)

Book World—The Washington Post *(© 1976, The Washington Post), December 5, 1976.*

RALPH SCHOENSTEIN

"An Especially Tricky People" is a nicely satirical look at certain parts of the current scene, from the inscrutable East to the inscrutable West. Unfortunately, the current scene changes too fast for political satire in a book: To talk about Mao Tse-tung and Gerald Ford today is to talk about the husband of a traitor and a golfer at N.B.C.; but Trudeau is so sharp that even his dated panels trigger laughs. For example, the questioning of an ambassador by a United States Senator:

"Did the President say anything about your accelerating obsession with drugs?"

"Of course not. Jerry and I have an understanding. I don't make any comments about his lack of motor skills and he doesn't hassle me about my interest in stimulants. Besides, his son's a pot head."

"Oh, c'mon—I heard he doesn't inhale."

Trudeau drawings are as static as Jules Feiffer's: Characters are frozen into poses, and then they just talk for a dozen frames; but the talk is intelligently funny, so the lack of animation doesn't diminish the pleasure you feel. (p. 28)

Ralph Schoenstein, in The New York Times Book Review *(© 1977 by The New York Times Company; reprinted by permission), May 15, 1977.*

WILLIAM F. BUCKLEY, JR.

What is there to say about *Doonesbury*, or even about the comic-strip mode? . . . There is, for instance, the nagging mechanical—and therefore artistic—problem of reintroducing the reader to the synoptic point at which he was dropped the day before. In a collection this is more aggravating than if twenty-four hours have gone by since arriving at the point where the artist left you, and you need a little nudge. Trudeau handles this very deftly, usually by introducing into the panel a tilt of some sort that takes the reader slightly beyond where he was left yesterday, so that he is relieved of that awful sensation of turning wheels without moving forward.

The other problem is the presumptive requirement of the climax—the gag—at the end of every strip. This cadence no artist can hope to satisfy, although they must all make the effort. A collection runs the risk of maximizing the disharmonies. Imagine reading a collection of the last paragraphs of Art Buchwald's columns. Or, as Zonker would put it, Imagine! Which digression beings me to note the awful overuse of the intensifier in Mr. Trudeau's captions. Nothing appears so workaday as to be merely remarkable. Everything is *arresting!* Now this is in sharp stylistic contrast with the very nearly expressionless faces Mr. Trudeau tends to draw. Nobody ever smiles, or hardly ever; and the effect is wonderful, insofar as it reminds the reader that no experience, no absurdity, no observation, is truly new. But nearly everything spoken must be punctuated with exclamation points and served up in boldface type. I am as unconvinced that this is necessary as I am persuaded that Trudeau scores remarkably well in wrenching a climax of sorts out of almost every one of his strips. There are the anticlimaxes; but the reader forgives them indulgently; he is well enough nourished, all the more so since there is all that wonderful assonant humor and derision in mid-panel: indeed, not infrequently the true climaxes come in the penultimate panel, and the rest is lagniappe.

And then—there is a sense of rhetorical leisure in Trudeau. *Whatever* is the *hurry?* It is very pleasurable, the more so when one realizes how compressive the form is by nature, like smoking a cigar on a parachute jump. After reading three years' worth of *Doonesbury* I am certain I have read as many words as are in *War and Peace*. The artist gives off a great air of authority by this device, rather like those notices in *The New Yorker* magazine in which even the most conventional abbreviations are spurned ("Closed on Sundays and holidays, except for Thanksgiving").

Consider the treatment of an essentially banal exchange. If it were honed less finely, it would not work. One of the characters is watching a television screen, whence the words sound out:

"At the very root of the Big Apple's problems seems to be the endless exodus of the middle class. 'Good Night, New York' is fortunate to have with us tonight Mr. Jamie Dodd, one such fugitive.

"Jamie, I take it you and your wife have always been anxious to leave New York? . . ."

"Oh no, not at all, Geraldo—in fact, at first the city seemed a marvelous place for an upwardly mobile couple like us! [Note the exclamation point.] But then one day last fall I was promoted to a $45,000 job. That same day my wife was assaulted in the park. The power went off, and the garbage people went on strike . . . And suddenly! Right! Suddenly Darien made *loads* of sense!"

It requires a hypnotic self-assurance to bring off (as Trudeau does) that sequence. As so often, he relies heavily on his meiotic pen to do it.

The longueurs are sometimes almost teasingly didactic. Who else in the funny-paper business would attempt the following?

[Again, the action is coming out of the television set.]

"Mr. Finkles, as one of New York's past comptrollers, how were you able to build up such a whopping deficit?"

"Well Geraldo, we had *many* great tricks. The most common one was selling city bonds on the strength of inflated estimates of anticipated federal funding. This device was very popular among top city money wizards. But let me show you my personal favorite. See Column B here? This is where we charged the final wage period of one fiscal year to the budget of the next! In so doing, we built up a hidden deficit of *two billion dollars!*"

"Wow!"

"Now I must caution the folks at home from trying this . . ."

Note the touch of the anticlimax in the last line, inserted in the way that Oliphant permits the kitten or the mouse to pronounce the moral coda. But the unapologetically literate account of the exact character of the financial hanky-panky gives a rollicking sense of reality to the episode. (pp. ix, xi)

William F. Buckley, Jr., "Overture" (copyright © 1978 by William F. Buckley, Jr.; reprinted by permission of Wallace & Sheil Agency, Inc.), in Doonesbury's Greatest Hits *by G. B. Trudeau, Holt, Rinehart and Winston, 1978, pp. vii, ix, xi, xiii.*

John R. Tunis

1889-1975

American novelist, nonfiction writer, and journalist. Tunis is considered by many critics and readers to be the dean of the American juvenile sports novel, and several of his books, such as *The Kid from Tomkinsville* and *Schoolboy Johnson*, are classics in that field. His sports books are characterized by their authentic athletic background, attributable to his experience as a newspaper sportswriter and radio commentator. This intimate knowledge of sports provides realistic settings, but his novels are more than simple sports chronicles. His well-plotted adventures are examinations of character as well as action, with sports being used to test both individual ethics and broader social values. Using complex characters who face a variety of ethical dilemmas, he invests his work with moral concerns that range from the growth of personal integrity to the effects of racism on the young. His success is attributed by many critics to the fact that he regards his readers as adults and does not talk down to them. However, it has also been noted that his work at times takes a too strongly didactic tone, as in *A City for Lincoln*, where one high school student's forthright statement of belief changes the attitude of an entire town. Tunis has incorporated his sports themes in several novels which treat the brutality of war in a realistic manner, particularly *His Enemy, His Friend*. Besides his sports novels, Tunis has written several analyses of the contemporary sports world, both professional and amateur. Like his novels, these nonfiction accounts are concerned with the social implications of sport. In all cases, his work is concerned with the dilemmas and decisions that are the constants in any situation in which pressure is placed on an individual. (See also *Contemporary Authors*, Vols. 61-64.)

"Sports"—we need not repeat the typesetter's wretched pun [changing the first and last letters of the title to dollar signs]—is a highly-amusing, highly-instructive paroxism of feeling. . . . Its aim is to lay bare what goes on in the locker-rooms at Olympic Games and Tennis Tournaments. . . .

The book has faults, but the faults certainly are not lack of sincerity, or lack of vigor, or pusillanimity, or lack of information; the outstanding trouble with it is that at times Mr. Tunis talks his information so rapidly and shouts so vigorously that neither he nor the reader is able to hear himself think. The horrors of the situation are flung out in a merciless bombardment; and the resulting effect, although di-

verting always, is frequently confusing. In the maelstrom the reader is tempted to take shelter by saying: "Oh, Olympic Games can't really be as bad as this!" . . .

In spite of the confusion, however, the book carries conviction. It is, of course, not a book for those who look for literature in their reading. It is rather for the reader who reads sports or plays sports or who has children who do those things. For such people Mr. Tunis's cruel and amusing outburst against the present equivocal state of amateur sport could not possibly be a waste of time. If you want to know the worst about your heroes, says Tunis, here it is. (p. 256)

The Saturday Review of Literature (copyright, 1928, by The Saturday Review Co., Inc.; reprinted with permission), October 13, 1928.

S. L. THOMAS

The title "American Girl" is rather unfortunate. It is too diffuse, covers too much territory, whereas the heroine, Florence Farley, with whom the book deals as child and young woman, is an individualized human being with a special life and a special soul of her own, and not just any American girl. The picture of her childhood is most vivid. An attractive, interesting, delicate little girl, she happens to show a particular aptitude for tennis playing. This determines her career. She becomes a tennis champion.

Mr. Tunis has done well to choose the background of sport. He is most at home in the world of sport, as we know from his various writings. But it is essential, in order to do justice to the book, to bear in mind that the author has used the knowledge of his specialty merely for the purpose of providing authentic and convincing settings. In all else he is purely the novelist with the artist's eye to the portrayal of his men and women and the unfolding of the life story of his heroine. He shows that he knows his men and women as well as he knows the technique of their profession. . . .

"American Girl" is [primarily] a tragedy, with Florence Farley as its pathetic heroine. Naturally, after she has grown to womanhood, her soul reactions, the direction of her emotions, the whole ensemble, in fact, which we call a person's character, is to a large extent determined by her career and the environment into which she is cast as a consequence. Insofar, what is true of Florence Farley would be equally true of anyone who is caught in the sports racket. But beyond that she is Florence Farley, not just a tennis champion. In her line she is a prima donna. . . . Mr. Tunis here displays a subtle art and an intuitive fidelity to realistic truth. The large effect is the same as with any temperamental, capricious diva, spoiled by success and the applause of crowded houses. She assumes dominance herself, but she does it without violence, with perfect dignity, and with the saving of all appearances. (p. 38)

Frankly, "American Girl" is muck-raking. We sometimes wonder whether the people who do the muck-raking are not in danger of covering themselves with the slime they are stirring up. Whatever may be true of others it is certainly not true of Mr. Tunis. (p. 39)

> *S. L. Thomas, "A Diva of the Courts," in* The Saturday Review of Literature *(copyright, 1930, by The Saturday Review Co., Inc.; reprinted with permission), August 9, 1930, pp. 38-9.*

BRUCE RAE

Tunis, doughty campaigner for the revival of the late-lamented Amateur Spirit, has, in "American Girl," attempted the "Uncle Tom's Cabin" of American amateur tennis. . . .

As a novel, "American Girl" is far from first-rate. Mr. Tunis rides his hobby too hard. Every single thing in the book is written in terms of tennis. That would be all right if Mr. Tunis had shown dramatically just how the business of being tennis champion inevitably tended to crowd all other things from Miss Farley's life. But he lets certain scenes—for example, the one in which Miss Farley renounces love to remain champion—pass with more than cinematographic speed.

> *Bruce Rae, "The Tennis Racket," in* The New York Times Book Review *(© 1930 by The New York Times Company; reprinted by permission), August 24, 1930, p. 7.*

ANNE T. EATON

[Tunis has succeeded in "The Iron Duke"] as few writers do succeed, in writing a college story for boys which is not a mere chronicle of . . . athletic triumphs of one kind or another and which . . . avoids the attempt at a critical summing up of college education and its effects that characterizes most college-fiction written for adults.

The story is modern and up-to-date, the situations unforced, the characters alive. One is not only interested in what Jim and his room-mates do . . . but in what they think and feel and in Jim's development as an individual. Tunis writes well, in a vivid, direct style. . . .

> *Anne T. Eaton, "Harvard Days," in* The New York Times Book Review *(© 1938 by The New York Times Company; reprinted by permission), March 27, 1938, p. 10.*

ELLEN LEWIS BUELL

The Kid from Tomkinsville [protagonist of the book of the same name] was a sand-lot rookie . . . who pitched and batted his way to fame, but this is more than the story of one man's success, for it turns inside out the making of a winning baseball team. Here, in prose which has the good hard smack of ash against leather and the quick impressions and scope of a candid camera, are portrayed the problems, the disappointments and the sheer nerve of a team. . . .

[Even] a reader who does not know a hit from an error will respond to the tense excitement of play-by-play accounts of games. It is, however, the finer values of sportsmanship interpreted in very human and masculine terms which make this more than just a tale of sport.

> *Ellen Lewis Buell, "A Baseball Story," in* The New York Times Book Review *(© 1940 by the New York Times Company; reprinted by permission), June 9, 1940, p. 9.*

ELLEN LEWIS BUELL

Mr. Tunis's champion [Janet Johnson in "Champion's Choice"] is his first heroine, a tennis star who scaled the heights of Wimbledon, and stayed there, not by technique and strength only but, as a champion must, by knowing how to call on the last ounce of fighting spirit. . . .

Her first victory at Wimbledon, where she perceived that tennis was a contest of character as well as skill, came early. . . . From then on Janet . . . became almost more champion than she was human being. . . . She was a sportsmanlike fighter and a smart one, but she was also a hard-boiled one, until . . . she realized there were other things in life more desirable than tennis honors.

It is not an entirely glamorous picture that Mr. Tunis has drawn of the tennis world, and therefore all the more worth considering. He does not get as close to the workings of Janet's mind as he did with "The Kid from Tomkinsville," but he does let us see clearly the development of her ambition as well as her game, and young tennis enthusiasts will find in his swiftly detailed descriptions of hard-fought contests much of the technique and the very heart of the game's spirit at its best.

> *Ellen Lewis Buell, "The Young Tennis Champion," in* The New York Times Book Review *(© 1941 by The New York Times Company; reprinted by permission), February 2, 1941, p. 10.*

ELLEN LEWIS BUELL

["World Series" is] the story of a team in its most important series, and especially of Dave Leonard, the game veteran manager for whom his men would give their last spurt of strength and skill. It is Dave . . . who rallies the team when . . . it falls into one of those inexplicable and costly slumps. . . .

There is less emphasis upon characters here, and a little less upon the qualities of mind and heart which make champions of individual players than in ["The Kid from Tomkinsville"], but there is even more of baseball . . . described with . . . tempo and force. . . .

> *Ellen Lewis Buell, "With the Dodgers," in* The New York Times Book Review *(© 1941 by the New York Times Company; reprinted by permission), October 19, 1941, p. 10.*

ALICE M. JORDAN

[All-American, a] fine football story, is soundly set against the background of life in a large city high school. Faced with the problems of race and social standing, as well as of real values compared with popularity, Ronald Perry has a chance to see what is meant by democracy. Mr. Tunis's name is guarantee both for the vigor and accuracy of the sport sections and for the high note of character and citizenship. Boys and girls will find it an exciting story and a timely one, firmly grounded in a liberal conception of the meaning of democracy. (p. 425)

> *Alice M. Jordan, in* The Horn Book Magazine *(copyrighted, 1942, by The Horn Book, Inc., Boston), November, 1942.*

ELLEN LEWIS BUELL

No one writing for boys today can describe a touchdown or a home run with more photographic clarity than John Tunis, but [he] always has a good deal more to say than just sports talk. ["All-American" is] his most penetrating book on sport in American life. . . .

As star halfback for the Academy team Ronald had his world in his hand until the day of the big game against the High School. Rivalry between the Academy and the High School went deeper than sport, . . . for there was real animus and scorn on both sides. When Ronald nearly killed a High School player in that game he was . . . deeply shocked at the callousness with which his friends (imbued with a snobbery which seems a little more obtuse than is entirely credible) dismissed the accident as of no importance since the victim was only a High School "tough" and a Jew.

Fumbling for a sense of values only dimly perceived, Ronald left the Academy and entered the High School. . . . [He] began to understand, bit by bit, a system which demanded self-discipline and self-reliance from the individual. . . . [Finally, he] started off on a crusade, the kind which can, and nearly did, tear a town and school in two—a youthful, gloriously quixotic crusade for justice which precipitated a climax in the best high-school tradition.

As a football story this has speed and tension. As a realistic story of the issues and values which underlie life in any American high school it offers meaty food for thought. . . . (p. 9)

> *Ellen Lewis Buell, in* The New York Times Book Review *(© 1942 by The New York Times Company; reprinted by permission), November 1, 1942.*

MARGARET C. SCOGGIN

John Tunis has long had a monopoly on sport stories because of his taut, vigorous style, his sure knowledge of games and lingo, and his understanding of players. Add to that a definite belief about the place of democracy in sport. His *All-American* . . . is not only a fast-paced football story but also an account of how a young athlete and his fellow high school students reacted when a neighboring school refused to play their team unless the star end, a Negro, was left behind. No punches are pulled in the handling of race prejudice and commercialism in sport; here are some specific problems of democracy in terms young people can understand.

Mr. Tunis has done much to kill the curse of namby-pamby, milk-and-water writing for boys. (p. 149)

> *Margaret C. Scoggin, in* The Atlantic Monthly *(copyright © 1942 by The Atlantic Monthly Company, Boston, Mass.; reprinted with permission), December, 1942.*

MAY LAMBERTON BECKER

A good baseball story can leave you in a lather of excitement—over baseball. But when it keeps you stirred up over baseball from first to last and leaves you excited over a vital issue in American life, it is something special in sports literature. "All-American" gave notice. . . what we might expect from Tunis. "Keystone Kids" is another exercise of the same special gift. (p. 6)

> *May Lamberton Becker, in* New York Herald Tribune Book Review *(© I.H.T. Corporation; reprinted by permission), September 5, 1943.*

ELLEN LEWIS BUELL

When those hypothetical historians of the next century begin to investigate the sports world of our day they will do well to turn to the works of John Tunis. . . . [They] will find in them an accurate picture of both the tempo and temper of American sports. Futhermore, they throw an interesting sidelight on certain contemporary issues of our times, for Mr. Tunis is much interested in the place of sports in the democratic way of life and vice versa.

[In "Keystone Kids"] he deals, as in "All-American," frankly and realistically with racial intolerance. . . .

At first, casually, carelessly, then with conscious animus, the players rag the [Jewish] newcomer, ruining his nerve and also the chances of the team. . . . It is [manager Spike Russell] . . . who gropes behind the immediate problem to its implications, who lays down the law to the team, and who shows Klein how to fight back.

Although there is less body to this story than to most of its predecessors, and not quite so much of the swift-paced action of the diamond, its theme of sportsmanship in the fuller sense rings clearly through its racing prose. . . .

> *Ellen Lewis Buell, "With the Dodgers," in* The New York Times Book Review *(© 1943 by The New York Times Company; reprinted by permission), September 5, 1943, p. 9.*

ARTHUR HEPNER

[Tunis is waging a successful campaign] to pose fundamental issues in young readers' minds. Twice before—in "Duke Decides" and "All American"—he told sports stories that put down the hard, tough facts of getting along in a democracy. Now he does it again, dramatically and trenchantly.

"Keystone Kids" is a baseball story, the tale of two inseparable orphaned brothers who are a sensation on the field because of their mastery of the game. The story is harsh and disillusioning, for it strips the glamor from big-league baseball. It shows how utterly ruthless, selfish and heartless professional athletes can be, how they have no interest in the game *qua* game and how they resent anyone who does. Yet, it is more than the mere narrative of what two open-eyed youngsters face when they reach the top on sincerity and merits of ability. For as success comes, there arises a circumstance which not only threatens the renascence they have effected on a disgruntled baseball team, but also the deep relationship between the brothers.

Just as Spike, the older of the two, is about to be made manager of the Brooklyn Dodgers, a lad names Klein joins the team. Immediately begin the cries, "Hey there Bugle-nose, throw us that ball. . . . Watch out, Jew-boy or you'll get yerself kilt up there. . . ."

The inseparable brothers veer toward a split over Klein's

presence. Bob, the younger, leads the anti-Semitic outbursts; Spike, as manager, defends the Jewish teammate. On the issue of whether a Jew shall remain on the team, morale is shattered. . . .

Spike finally decides to talk with Klein to see what can be done to reëstablish unity among the team. And slowly, at first hesitantly, flow the words from the strapping Jewish boy. Suddenly it is all out; the tragedy of the Jew, the 2,000 years of relentless hounding, the things which set Klein apart from the others.

Tunis could have left it there. But his understanding of the entire question of anti-Semitism is far too acute. "Now see," Spike tells Klein, "you say like this: I'll never be any good on account I'm Jewish. They realize you feel that way. They know it." Therefore, the ride. "Once they see you're a scrapper, they'll be for you all the way. You wait and see." . . .

Tunis believes two things. First, the writer need not write down for his audience, not even a young audience. Second, if a writer has something to say, he must say it in a medium his audience will understand. Anti-Semitism and its solution is a knotty, uncomfortable problem. But if it can be presented in terms of teamwork, the young mind can see how patently unjust discrimination is.

He is indeed bold to tempt young people with such provocative ideas. . . .

Time was when writers of juvenile fiction could duck from truth down an alley of appearance. Fantasy is one thing; distortion is another.

> *Arthur Hepner, "A New Kind of Juvenile," in* The New Republic *(reprinted by permission of* The New Republic; *© 1943 by The New Republic, Inc.), September 13, 1943, p. 370.*

MAY LAMBERTON BECKER

One who reads ["Rookie of the Year"], man or boy, sees baseball not from the stands but from the inside, sharing viewpoint and sensations with Spike Russell, young manager of the Dodgers. . . . Because he has been thinking of only one game at a time, the story's suspense begins over with each game, tightening from one surprise to another. This is no school story with climax in one game: professional baseball climaxes continually, and each chapter closes with the impact of spectators trooping out of the ball park.

There is no special social problem in this Tunisian, which gets its complications from baseball and human nature. . . .

Full of life, around the [central] story surges the special excitement that surrounds the Dodgers. (p. 5)

> *May Lamberton Becker, in New York Herald Tribune Book Review (© I.H.T. Corporation; reprinted by permission), April 2, 1944.*

MARY GOULD DAVIS

["Rookie of the Year"] is not as good a book as "Keystone Kids." It is as though Mr. Tunis has written it not out of an overwhelming urge but out of a mild desire to carry Spike and his team a bit farther on in their history. . . . The real value of the book lies in the games, especially toward the end when the Dodgers play the Cardinals for the pennant. Here is the good, honest thrill of a sport that has its devo-

tees in far-flung camps and outposts all over the face of the earth.

> *Mary Gould Davis, "Good Old Dodgers," in The Saturday Review of Literature (copyright, 1944, by The Saturday Review Co., Inc.; reprinted with permission), April 15, 1944, p. 74.*

ELLEN LEWIS BUELL

["A City for Lincoln"] represents something of a departure from [Tunis's] sports stories—there is only one basketball game, heard off-stage—but it is really a part of the main pattern which he has been depicting, the pattern of democracy in everyday American life. . . .

Though the story seems a little slick, a little too managed in spots, Mr. Tunis makes politics as exciting as sports and of immediate significance. . . . [He] gives youth something to think about and something to believe in. (p. 34)

> *Ellen Lewis Buell, in The New York Times Book Review (© 1945 by The New York Times Company; reprinted by permission), October 28, 1945.*

MAY LAMBERTON BECKER

You enter ["A City for Lincoln"] through a typical Tunis game, guaranteed to stir the blood even of one unfamiliar with finer points of basketball. . . . These opening chapters announce a purpose . . . : "Give kids responsibility and they'll come through for you, every time." . . .

[A Juvenile Aid Division and Junior Court is put in basketball coach Don Henderson's hands.] The procedure of this court, the students' gradual recognition that law-breaking is no joke, forms the body of the story which . . . is told in cases, with earnestness and power. . . . [The treatment of a case of teenage shoplifting] is the most sincere, sensible consideration a book for teens has given a problem not unknown to adolescence. . . .

[Though] a typical Tunis sport story is in its own way as much a morality as an Alger or a Frank Merriwell, we respect it more, not only because he writes ten times as well, but because . . . a Tunis story invigorates a formula by being savagely in earnest about it. (p. 11)

> *May Lamberton Becker, in New York Herald Tribune Book Review (© I.H.T. Corporation; reprinted by permission), November 11, 1945.*

RALPH ADAMS BROWN

Boys have long been used to good sport stories from the pen of John R. Tunis. [*The Kid Comes Back*] is, however, more than a good baseball story and so merits special attention. There is much baseball in it, with a smashing finale. . . . The story opens with the Kid's bomber making a forced landing in occupied France. . . .

[After various adventures the] Kid, badly injured, is shipped back to the United States.

All this adds up to a thrilling story. What makes it more significant is the struggle of the Kid to overcome the fear— a new word to him—which his injury has left in him. . . . The Kid's triumph over his fear, his final realization that "all we have to fear is fear itself," is what lifts this book above other action stories. (pp. 54, 56)

> *Ralph Adams Brown, in The Saturday Review of Literature (copyright, 1946, by The Saturday Re-*

view Co., Inc.; reprinted with permission), November 9, 1946.

ELLEN LEWIS BUELL

[In "Highpockets" Tunis explores the problems of Cecil (Highpockets) McDade.] He was a brilliant right fielder . . . , but it was very evident he was more interested in his batting average and a good contract than in the team. No one knew that behind his stinginess and his crass ambition lay a determination to reclaim a run-down North Carolina farm and to educate five brothers and sisters. . . . [He] went his stubborn, lonely way until he accidentally injured a boy. . . . [As] young Dean fought for his life Highpockets forgot his importance and his future security to discover the meaning of teamwork in personal relationships and on the diamond.

Perhaps because of the very tempo of Mr. Tunis' slashing, telegraphic style Highpockets doesn't emerge as a deeply realized personality; nevertheless this outwardly unsympathetic character wins one's sympathy and understanding, and the baseball sequences are, as one expects, as good as a lower grandstand seat right back of home plate. (p. 29)

> *Ellen Lewis Buell, in* The New York Times Book Review *(© 1948 by The New York Times Company; reprinted by permission), February 15, 1948.*

MARY GOULD DAVIS

["Highpockets"] is a character study that sets it apart from Mr. Tunis's earlier books. We find here a more mellowed and sensitive writer. [Cecil McDade] is projected into the spotlight of the baseball world too soon for his own good. He is a curious mixture of personal ambition, almost total ignorance of the ways of the world, and an insensitiveness that makes him extremely unpopular with the Dodger fans. He is so well drawn that the reader becomes exasperated with him, and curiously sorry for him. The change in Cecil, or Highpockets as he is known to his jeering public, comes through his concern for a [little boy] whom he injures through careless driving. Slowly the surface hardness, the selfishness of this awkward lad yield to the natural kindliness and decency that are innate in him. But it is a slow process. . . . This is an exciting tale and one that will be long remembered for its analysis of a sportsman who learns through adversity to adjust himself to his team and to his world. (p. 36)

> *Mary Gould Davis, in* The Saturday Review of Literature *(copyright, 1948, by The Saturday Review Co., Inc.; reprinted by permission), March 13, 1948.*

LOUISE S. BECHTEL

The studies of character and of citizenship in [Tunis's] popular books lead inevitably to new fields, [and in "Son of the Valley" it is the building of the T.V.A.] Mr. Tunis has made the relation of one antagonistic family and one hard-working boy to the whole great effort . . . so real that his readers in far different places will be absorbed.

The lead-up to the day when the Heiskells [and Johnny] must leave their farm, which must be flooded, and the relation of the government to their departure is moving and dramatic. . . .

As real as Johnny is his young sister. . . . [Her reactions] to selling her [pet calf] are splendidly told. (p. 6)

> *Louise S. Bechtel, in* New York Herald Tribune Book Review *(© I.H.T. Corporation; reprinted by permission), March 20, 1949.*

ELLEN LEWIS BUELL

[Mr. Tunis] has ever been concerned with the working-out of democratic ideals in American life. . . . [In "Son of the Valley" he explores] the significance of a great democratic experiment: that of the Tennessee Valley Authority.

The experiences of the Heiskell family . . . typify those of many a farming family of that region. Here is seen that deep love of the land, the fierce resentment of government authority, the rock-ribbed opposition to innovation. . . . It was a back-breaking struggle, but in the end the most stubborn old-timer acknowledged the benefits of TVA.

All of this is so true in essence, so far-reaching in its implications that one wishes this were a better story. Unfortunately, Mr. Tunis has so much to tell that he has skimped characterization. His book frequently reads more like a thesis on agriculture than work of fiction. Nevertheless serious-minded readers will find here much that is stimulating.

> *Ellen Lewis Buell, "Tennessee Farmer," in* The New York Times Book Review *(© 1949 by The New York Times Company; reprinted by permission), March 20, 1949, p. 26.*

HOWARD PEASE

One secret of Mr. Tunis' popularity is his ability to write a sports story that is more than a sports story. He discards the old formula to write about people who happen to move in the world of sports. The drama in ["Young Razzle"] arises from a conflict between . . . a father and son, both professional ball players.

Young Joe Nugent, the product of a split home, hates his father, who is a stranger to him. . . . How the relationship between these two slowly changes makes a warm-hearted story, written with intensity and understanding. The background is filled with fascinating sidelights on big time baseball. . . .

> *Howard Pease, "Drama on the Diamond," in* The New York Times Book Review *(© 1949 by The New York Times Company; reprinted by permission), September 18, 1949, p. 34.*

HENRY B. LENT

["The Other Side of the Fence" is the story of Robin Longe's trip across the country.] Some of his experiences as a hitchhiker have a slightly nightmarish quality. Others are wonderful and exciting. . . . John R. Tunis, with his usual skill and deep understanding of what makes a teenager tick, has given us another story that youngsters will enjoy immensely and that many a parent will find instructive.

> *Henry B. Lent, "Hitchhiker," in* The New York Times Book Review, Part II *(© 1953 by The New York Times Company; reprinted by permission), November 15, 1953, p. 12.*

RAYMOND SWING

[Tunis is] the only outstanding writer in the [sports] field who can make fair play compete for interest with winning a game. . . . Mr. Tunis is not overtly a missionary for democracy and refuses to preach. But his best books take up such issues as racial discrimination and individual integrity, and no boy can read them without sharpened perceptions about his own values and without realizing that Americanism is something that begins inside himself in his relations with his comrades.

Though his "Son of the Valley" is about the TVA, most of the Tunis books are about a single sport. They follow a pattern used in most sport books for boys. They are written crisply, the story has to move, there is not much contemplation and there is a great deal of action. In the end comes the crucial game or contest. Mr. Tunis is no illusionist, his hero does not always win. But he usually wins the test between the better and the worse in himself and on the field and in the community. . . .

"Go Team, Go!" is a basketball story. . . . If there is a better story about basketball, that gives more insight into the skills and refinements of the game, I do not know it. In all his books Mr. Tunis brings to bear an amazing amount of expert knowledge of the sport he is writing about. He has made basketball almost as thrilling to the armchair reader as it is to the delirious townsmen [in his book]. . . .

[The book] deals with a test of strength between a coach and some of his star high-school players, who go on a strike because one of their number is disciplined for promoting gambling in the school. . . . The excitement is about the ultimate victory of the coach and the part which the hero, one of the striking players has in the triumph of right values. Mr. Tunis has written with an economy of words and a drive of action that makes the book shake with excitement. Any boy loves a book like that. But he may cherish this one, as he has its predecessors, for leaving with him something beyond excitement. . . .

[Mr. Tunis] is as far from a "do-gooder" as one well can be, but one must look far to find someone who has contributed more usefully to the perpetation of good values.

> Raymond Swing, "The Boys' Mr. Tunis," in The Saturday Review (*Entire issue copyright 1954 by Saturday Review Associates, Inc.; reprinted with permission*), June 19, 1954, p. 40.

ANNE IZARD

Buddy, the captain and short stop of his elementary school team, has to learn the hard way that winning is not all important and bad sportsmanship is infectious [in "Buddy and the Old Pro"]. . . .

There is good baseball and a sound philosophy integral to the storytelling. As always, Tunis keeps his book full of action and excitement building toward a climax that never loses touch with reality.

> Anne Izard, "For the Boys," in New York Herald Tribune Book Review (© *I.H.T. Corporation; reprinted by permission*), May 22, 1955, p. 6.

John Tunis has a vital thesis [in *The American Way in Sport*], and uses his historical facts about American sports to buttress his point. He loves sports and has watched sporting events of all kinds for half a century. Now he is deeply concerned about the direction the growth of sports has taken and the attitude of the public towards it. He doesn't like the professionalism and the dollar mark. . . .

For those who seek an overall survey of American sports in a half century, that too is here. (p. 651)

> Virginia Kirkus' Service, *August 15, 1958.*

ROBERT DALEY

[Tunis] has always been a man of strong convictions. But few would have supposed convictions as strong, fearless and iconoclastic as those propounded in ["The American Way in Sport"].

This is not a book for boys, although they might profitably read it. It is for those adults willing to think deeply and seriously about the mighty force which sports exert in the life of the nation, a force which, according to Mr. Tunis, is destroying us physically and morally as a people. Thus he asks if Little League baseball . . . [does] not stimulate "the ego of the youngster (and Daddy), besides increasing the acquisitive traits of a boy in an acquisitive society." . . .

Mr. Tunis suggests abolishing all competition among youngsters under 13—they are simply too young. . . .

This is strong stuff, and few will be indifferent to Mr. Tunis' book. Agree with him, or not, it's something that needed to be said. His book is readable, even compelling, throughout. . . .

> Robert Daley, "*But Is It a Game?*" in The New York Times Book Review (© *1958 by the New York Times Company; reprinted by permission*), October 26, 1958, p. 38.

DAN WAKEFIELD

When the verdict was read on the famous Chicago Black Sox scandal, a tearful, unknown urchin broke through the crowd to "Shoeless Joe" Jackson, one of the players accused of throwing the World Series, and, the story goes, made an appeal that has since become a classic line in American history: "Say it ain't so, Joe; say it ain't so."

John R. Tunis, a writer who has followed sports in our time since the turn of the century and kept his faith in its virtues intact through the Black Sox scandal, has [in "The American Way in Sport"] set down a verdict of his own so deep in its condemnation and sincerity that any young sports-loving lad might approach him with a tearful request to "say it ain't so, John; say it ain't so." . . .

[Tunis' books] always found virtue as well as excitement in organized athletics. . . . Even in those novels Tunis was aware of the growing commercialization of sport, but his heroes always escaped its dangers and emerged on the side of right and sportsmanship. . . .

[But] Tunis feels that in its overorganization, its emphasis on victory at any cost, and its tremendous financial importance . . . big-time sport is threatening the moral values as well as the education of American youth. He reaches the drastic conclusion that we should "give up our amateur athletics, so-called" and recommends "the divorce of education and recreation."

Tunis does not want the abolishment of sport, but the revival of sport as it existed in the days before it became more business than fun. . . .

This book, in essence, is a stirring appeal to return to the values of a world that was more concerned with faces than numbers.

Dan Wakefield, "Big Business in the Ball Park," in The Saturday Review (Entire issue copyright 1959 by Saturday Review Associates, Inc.; reprinted with permission), January 17, 1959, p. 68.

[*Silence Over Dunkerque,* the] fictitious saga of Sergeant Williams, Second Battalion, Wiltshire Regiment, might easily have been the true story of any British soldier at Dunkerque. . . . [His] encounter with divergent elements of French opinion about the evacuation, [his] close shaves with the enemy build an adventure with a solid foundation in recent history. The swift pace holds the reader until the Sergeant's final and climactic escape to freedom. (p. 525)

Virginia Kirkus' Service, *June 15, 1962.*

WILLIAM JAY JACOBS

Whether wars really are lost or won on the playing field is of course debatable. Still, few persons would deny that important lessons sometimes may be learned there. John R. Tunis, now in his seventies, has written about sport as it relates to the larger questions of life in some two thousand articles and a score of books perennially popular with young people. . . . The qualities Tunis prizes—courage, persistence, teamwork, the evaluation of people according to merit instead of race or religion or social class—underlie his books. . . .

Tunis' appeal is to those who want simply to read exciting sports stories. Whatever "message" he imparts comes through vivid incidents and realistic characterizations. (p. 48)

The descriptions in Tunis' books have a remarkable vividness—the product of careful attention to detail, along with an almost intuitive talent for capturing the fleeting instant or the elusive mood. . . . The indelible quality of his descriptions is not an accident but the result of painstaking research on the scene. . . .

Yet Tunis is scrupulous in his use of action scenes, never employing them as a substitute for character development. Consequently, he avoids the stereotyped, wooden sports-story character who deals only in black-and-white issues. His personalities are complex and credible. (p. 49)

Many young readers have never suffered discrimination. . . . Others experience prejudice early. Picturing circumstances almost identical to those encountered by Lionel in J. D. Salinger's short story "Down at the Dinghy," Tunis captures in *Keystone Kids* the frustration and disbelief of a young ballplayer upon his first glimpse of the river [of racial prejudice] separating him from other men. (p. 50)

The issue of prejudice in sport strikes close at the values Tunis considers important, since the toleration of inequities in our leisure-time activities inevitably calls into question other premises operative in American society. Why, for example, is being a winner so important in the United States? . . .

Especially in *Yea! Wildcats* . . . and *A City for Lincoln* . . . , stories about high-school basketball in Indiana, Tunis tries to show how the doctrine of "victory at any cost" can make interscholastic sport nothing less than "a training ground for a jungle society." (p. 51)

What then are some of the finer qualities presumably encouraged by sport [in Tunis' books]? Two of the most important are persistence and courage. (pp. 51-2)

Courage is . . . a hallmark of Tunis' heroes [and not just physical courage]. . . . In *Son of the Valley* . . . , young Johnny Heiskell demonstrates to neighbors and his tradition-bound father that modern farming methods and cooperation with the Tennessee Valley Authority will help, not hurt, their prospects. In the course of his struggle against obstinacy Johnny becomes a man.

Tunis suggests other dimensions of courageous behavior: courage in battle, as in *Silence over Dunkerque* . . . ; courage to stand for a social principle in the face of one's friends and teammates, as in *All-American;* courage to keep trying, even after chance has delivered an apparently unjust blow, as in *The Kid from Tomkinsville.* . . .

With courage often comes growth and transformation: the realization that sometimes the team does not win on the last page, even if it deserves to, and that in life, as Tunis declares,

> you cannot always or even often have your own way, that the manner in which we face up to defeat and disappointment is a test of growth and part of the development of character.

The reader of the Tunis books learns that one really can be a success—possibly more of a success—after failing to make The Circle at Harvard or being cut from the freshman football squad. He learns that there is a world of bigger things than victory in the high-school basketball game; that a substantial outlay of honest, sometimes unpleasant self-examination may be required before one develops a proper sense of proportion; that becoming a man is not an easy process.

Persistence, courage, a sense of proportion. These are values to which Tunis subscribes. . . . The analogy [of democracy] to sport is scarcely novel, yet somehow Tunis presents it in fresh perspective. (pp. 52-3)

Tunis is perhaps alone in the attention he gives to the unsung workers of the democratic team, like the clubhouse attendant *Keystone Kids,* Old Chiselbeak. . . . (p. 53)

Superbly realistic and well-written stories, [Tunis' books] are above all the imaginative testimony of a man who stands for something, a man with a commitment to values. (p. 54)

William Jay Jacobs, "John R. Tunis: A Commitment to Values," in The Horn Book Magazine (copyright © 1967, by The Horn Book, Inc., Boston), February, 1967, pp. 48-54.

GILBERT MILLSTEIN

It is a little unusual for an author of boys' books to engage himself in the argument of a moral proposition any stronger than, say, one concerned with sportsmanship as exemplified in the homilies of the late Grantland Rice, or the salutory effects of telling the truth. But John R. Tunis, who is obviously a highly moral man and one equally troubled by the rising tide of brutality in the world, has attempted something more [in "His Enemy, His Friend"]: an examination of conscience arising out of an incident in World War II.

On the whole, he has brought it off, even though he has had to depend here and there on the conjunction of a couple of outrageous coincidences. Young people are not so apt to question outrageous coincidences as they are doubtful moral propositions, and so "His Enemy, His Friend," a frankly hortatory novel, is apt to do some good. (p. 44)

[The] moral imperatives are satisfied; judgments are made; punishment (possibly divine) is meted out, and the consciences of all men of good will ultimately are satisfied—not without small dollops of irony and pity. (p. 46)

> *Gilbert Millstein, in* The New York Times Book Review *(© 1967 by The New York Times Company; reprinted by permission), October 29, 1967.*

GERALD GOTTLIEB

[*His Enemy, His Friend* is concerned with] a severe crisis of conscience. . . . [The] crisis literally involves human life; the young protagonist, a German soldier in Occupied France during World War II, is ordered to kill six innocent hostages as reprisal for an unknown Resistance sniper's act. What happens then—and what happens 20 years later when the German faces the son of one of the hostages in an international soccer match—provides a sharp, sardonic view of war's sad effect on the ethics of decent folk. Mr. Tunis has written many fine sports stories for young people, and his tense account of a World Cup soccer match is knowledgeable and exciting. He unfortunately flaws his book with some excessive melodrama and a couple of absurdly long arms of coincidence, but the jarring effect of all this is largely offset by his superb depiction of the inhabitants of a Normandy fishing village reacting in an entirely real and human way to four years of German occupation. The passages about soccer are effective, but those about war are often magnificent. (p. 24)

> *Gerald Gottlieb, in* Book World—Chicago Tribune *(© 1967 Postrib Corp.), November 19, 1967.*

ALLEEN PACE NILSEN

His Enemy, His Friend is a fitting capstone to John Tunis's long years of doing first-rate sports stories for teenage readers. While there is a magnificent account of a soccer game in the book, it is basically not a sports story. The author says it is the story of a man and his conscience. It raises the eternal dilemma of the individual faced with a conflict between what the inner self thinks is right as opposed to what society demands. . . .

This story not only has a high interest level, but also considers fundamental moral issues. . . . (p. 91)

> *Alleen Pace Nilsen, in* English Journal *(copyright © 1974 by the National Council of Teachers of English), February, 1974.*

ZENA SUTHERLAND

[The plot of *Grand National*] is predictable—despite obstacles, [the hero's horse] wins the race, and the heavy hints of romance between Jack [the hero] and an Englishwoman who works with sick or injured horses ends with a last-page proposal. The story plods, the writing is mediocre in style, and it seems improbable that any reader but the steeplechase buff will find it appealing. (pp. 151-52)

> *Zena Sutherland, in* Bulletin of the Center for Children's Books *(© 1974 by the University of Chicago; all rights reserved), May, 1974.*

Kurt Vonnegut, Jr.

1922-

American novelist, short story writer, playwright, and essayist. Vonnegut is often considered a cultural spokesman for the present age, an heir to Jonathan Swift and George Orwell. He is a moralist who uses satire and iconoclastic humor to vividly portray the depravity of contemporary society. His novels combine fact and fantasy to raise many basic existential and epistemological questions. Although Vonnegut's plots are often bleak and pessimistic, his novels always contain some affirmation of man's essential decency, and a contention that our ability to love one another can save us from destruction and helplessness. Vonnegut's works seem to speak especially to young adults, who have identified with his humanistic concerns since the beginning of his career. It was the support of his student audience that first helped to bring him to prominence during the mid-1960s. World war and nuclear holocaust are central to an understanding of Vonnegut, as their influence on him permeates his fiction. He uses the novel as fable to exorcise the demons of his personal experience, and often appears as both character and author in his works. Vonnegut was captured by the Germans at the Battle of the Bulge and interned as a prisoner of war in Dresden, Germany, as was his character Billy Pilgrim in *Slaughterhouse-Five*. During the fire-bombing of Dresden, Vonnegut was sheltered in a meat storage cellar below a slaughterhouse; when the raid ended he was among those soldiers used by the Germans to recover the bodies of their dead from the ruins of the city, an experience which repeatedly recurs in his early work. Upon his return home, Vonnegut went to work as a public relations writer for the General Electric Research Lab in Schenectady, New York, an experience which figures in his first novel, *Player Piano*, and from which came several permanent themes: the impact of technological innovations on the ordinary person, the individual versus the institution, and the makeup (and satirization) of the writer. Vonnegut's first works were published as cheap sci-fi novels, and during his early career he remained virtually unknown. In *God Bless You, Mr. Rosewater* he satirizes this period of his life and introduces his most famous character, Kilgore Trout. An unsuccessful science fiction writer, Trout is Vonnegut's symbol for what he thought he might become; in a later novel, *Breakfast of Champions*, Vonnegut portrays Trout's rise to phenomenal literary success, again indulging in self-parody. Most critics feel that his finest synthesis of theme and technique occurs in *Slaughterhouse-Five*, a cathartic novel in which Pilgrim, a kind of Everyman, survives the horrors of Dresden and tries to make sense of the world which allowed it to happen. Von-

negut is sometimes criticized for his sentimentality, superficial characterizations, and formulaic prose style; his philosophy, also, has been criticized for not being deep enough to warrant the seriousness with which readers take his books. However, Vonnegut's reputation has always been solid among the young. He, in turn, seems to have great respect for this section of his audience and wants, he says, to catch them at school, "before they become generals and senators and Presidents, and poison their minds with humanity." (See also *CLC*, Vols. 1, 2, 3, 4, 5, 8, and *Contemporary Authors*, Vols. 1-4, rev. ed.)

[*Player Piano* is a] rather witty story of the future, with machines doing the work of men. The trouble with this book, as with many similar stories, is that the author gets his human beings so close to the machines that they are dehumanized, which means that although the nightmare remains, there is no sense of tragedy, and none of pity, and we are left with a feeling of disgust and weariness. (pp. 88-9)

> The New Yorker, (© 1952 by The New Yorker Magazine, Inc.), August 16, 1952.

DAVID GOLDKNOPF

Player Piano is a preview of American life after the third World War. . . . It is a country in which a man's station and future are totally controlled by a configuration of punched holes in a personnel card and men's minds have been ground down to a conformity as fine as our dust. That dust is occasionally stirred by ancient dreams and inchoate resentments, and such a stirring is taking place as the novel begins. But mostly America is a country in which life is intolerably dull.

That seems to be a quality shared by most versions of the future and it poses a very difficult problem for their creators: namely, how to write interestingly about a dull subject. *Player Piano*'s stereotyped or amorphous characters, inept construction, blunderbuss satire, and pedestrian prose help matters not at all.

And yet these defects, however serious, might be pardoned in a novel of ideas if the ideas themselves were profound or at least provocative. Mr. Vonnegut's are not; they are, in fact, demonstrably erroneous. . . . Of course the author is talking about the future; but the future in his eyes is obviously an extrapolation of the present—that's what makes the novel "significant"—and there is, in the history of technological development, no support whatsoever for the situation which Mr. Vonnegut envisions.

More disappointing than the author's misconceptions, however, is his evasiveness. Having created a false issue, he lacks the courage to face up to it. The scientist-hero of *Player Piano*, after an abortive return-to-nature, lends himself to a Saturnalian uprising against the machine. As the novel ends he is seen sardonically yielding himself up to his executioners while the machine like the phoenix rises from the reeking ashes of its predecessor. Well now what does the author recommend? It may be objected that it is for the novel to propose problems not to answer them, but a work as doctrinaire and ill-natured as this one may reasonably be expected to offer some alternative to the evils it so grimly prophesies. Shall we return to brutalizing drudgery, to caste, to superstition? Shall we surrender our ease of movement, the spaciousness of our lives, in general—half our life-span for that matter. I'm sure the author would not seriously suggest that. Nor need he. Mechanization, blind and irresistible, can be directed if not resisted. . . .

This novel, it seems to me, stems not so much from an intelligent apprehension as from the intellectual's sense of inferiority in the presence of the garage mechanic. . . .

> *David Goldknopf, "The Mechanistic Blues," in* The New Republic *(reprinted by permission of* The New Republic; © *1952 The New Republic, Inc.), August 18, 1952, p. 19.*

TERRY SOUTHERN

The narrator of "Cat's Cradle" purports to be engaged in compiling a responsibly factual account of what certain interested Americans were doing at the precise moment the atomic bomb was dropped on Hiroshima. Through correspondence with the three children of the late Felix Hoenikker, Nobel Prize winner and so-called "father of the atomic bomb," he evolves a portrait of the man in relation to his family and the community. . . .

"Cat's Cradle" is an irreverent and often highly entertaining fantasy concerning the playful irresponsibility of nuclear scientists. Like the best of contemporary satire, it is work of a far more engaging and meaningful order than the melodramatic tripe which most critics seem to consider "serious."

> *Terry Southern, "After the Bomb, Dad Came Up with Ice," in* The New York Times Book Review (© *1963 by The New York Times Company; reprinted by permission), June 2, 1963, p. 20.*

WILLIAM JAMES SMITH

The trouble with the Black Humorists is that they are not, as a rule, very humorous. They are, in fact, generally very depressing. . . . It is not necessarily the genre that is at fault but the execution. We have our classics of Black Humor which are very funny indeed. And if the young are said to admire them more than their elders it is because, as always, much of the cynicism goes over their pretty little heads. And even that is assuming—contrary to my observation—that the young read anything at all.

Kurt Vonnegut has risen, if that is the word, to Black Humor from an even more dubious genre, humorous sci-

ence fiction, having put out a couple of volumes of it before he eased over into the main stream with his first "serious" novel, *Cat's Cradle*. This is a tale of the end of the world as brought about through human stupidity, a theme always good for a few chuckles in terms of Black Humor. This novel, as his subsequent ones, carries some of the stigmata of Mr. Vonnegut's pulp fiction origins—the one-line paragraph, and the feeling that, at three cents a word, no word ever got x-ed out and no joke was ever deemed too feeble or tasteless for inclusion.

Nevertheless Mr. Vonnegut came through with real promise on his second serious novel, *God Bless You, Mr. Rosewater*. . . . [The] book is good because Mr. Vonnegut occasionally forgets about being Black and concentrates on being Humorous to real effect. These passages are oddly tangential, even irrelevant, to the main story line. They deal with the denizens of a New England fishing village and it is not difficult to say why these bizarre folk are funny in their madness while Mr. Vonnegut's Mad Millionaire is not. It is simply that they are believable. Even Pisquontuit's thirteen-year-old Lila Buntline, the town's leading dealer in smut, is real compared to the ingenious but heavy tendentiousness of Mr. Rosewater.

It all goes back to one of the eternal verities of fiction—create believable characters and you don't have to do a single blessed other thing right. The characters don't have to be literal—they can be just as grotesque as Mr. Vonnegut's wonderful minor characters, and just as Black in their Humors. It all comes down to the fact that there is good Black Humor and bad Black Humor—a critical perception slow to make headway.

In [*Mother Night*] Mr. Vonnegut tackles what should be a dilly for a Black Humorist—an American Counter-Intelligence agent who worked for the Nazis during World War II as an anti-Semitic propagandist. . . . There ought to be lots of good belly-laughs in this one, of course, but somehow they don't emerge.

But if there is anything that the Black Humorists have taught us it is that the venture was not necessarily foredoomed by its implausibility. We can thank them for showing us once again (it has happened often before in literary history without the tag of Black Humor) that no material is ultimately resistant to the alchemy of humor. . . . Mr. Vonnegut's attempts . . . to make us laugh, however bitterly, in areas presumed intractable to laughter may do something toward opening those areas out to a renewed consideration—a sort of shaking up in the kaleidoscope of laughter that enables us to see things in a new pattern.

Unfortunately, *Mother Night* does not completely succeed in its permutating bath of laughter. Only a few years ago we would have said that this was because his subject matter was unsuitable. Too many marvelous satiric feats, however, have been performed in recent years (not least by Mr. Vonnegut) for us to doubt that the trick can be done. It is the unsettling but healthy lesson the Black Humorists have taught us—that no disease is immune to laughter. And if the laughter frightens or angers us it only means that we must look once more at ourselves to see what is truly serious within us, and what is the mere facade of conviction without reason and without true belief. Perhaps this is another way of stating what Mr. Vonnegut says is the moral of his novel: We are what we pretend to be, so we must be careful what we pretend to be. (pp. 592-94)

William James Smith, in Commonweal *(copyright © 1966 Commonweal Publishing Co., Inc.; reprinted by permission of Commonweal Publishing Co., Inc.), September 16, 1966.*

CHARLES NICOL

We are best cheered by untruths, so the bigger the whopper, the better—says Vonnegut. In his masterpiece, *Cat's Cradle*, the founder of a new religion insisted at every step that his own doctrines were lies. Solace, apparently, came immediately.

In the preface to [*Welcome to the Monkey House*] he announces that one of the themes of his novels is "No pain." Kurt Vonnegut, Jr., probably our finest Black Humorist, is offering us comfort.

He is the little Dutch boy stopping the hole in the dike: while he conscientiously aids us, he reminds us that we live in the shadow of deep waters. Or, to use the idea that appears frequently in his work as a main character, a minor figure, part of the background, or the tail of a metaphor, he is the volunteer fireman, unselfishly and innocently rushing to put out the random blazes of civilization. His comforts frighten us with their inadequacy, and we laugh in self-defense.

Vonnegut's special enemies are science, morality, free enterprise, socialism, fascism, Communism, all government— any force in our lives which regards human beings as ciphers. His villains are simple egotists, indifferent to other people, his protagonists men who adapt events to their own discontent with the system, rolling with the times to create change, which is rarely, in Vonnegut's world, an improvement. His third group of characters, his saints, his volunteer firemen, are content to aid others in their own small world, unaware of the larger actions that swirl around them. Failing to participate in events, they nevertheless become the focus of all activity, their relevance being the undeniable fact that they exist.

Vonnegut is a pessimist. But he is also an idealist; his irony is not cynicism. His writing has a disarming directness, and his few statements about style reinforce this simplicity, yet the apparent slickness of his short, tight paragraphs—almost a paradigm of the popular magazine—fails to conceal the size of his concepts. And what appears at first to be gratuitous satire is always integral to the tale. (p. 123)

The style may bring to mind another Black Humorist, Terry Southern.... Both authors use the cliché for effect, but where the sardonic Mr. Southern uses the commonplace to reinforce our own complacency, Vonnegut uses it to throw new light on those thoughts which we hoped were *not* ordinary. A cliché is dead language, as when an author deliberately inserts one into the unresisting mouth of a character, he is registering contempt for that character, labeling him dead....

Roughly half of Vonnegut's published short stories are included in this collection. It is a good selection, although an unimpressive review of the big Random House dictionary has unaccountably crept in....

The reader should not expect full-fledged apocalypse from these pleasant tales, only brush fires of varying intensity that a good fireman can handle. (p. 124)

Charles Nicol, "The Volunteer Fireman," in The

Atlantic Monthly *(copyright © 1968 by the Atlantic Monthly Company, Boston, Mass.; reprinted with permission), September, 1968, pp. 123-24.*

LARRY L. KING

["Welcome to the Monkey House"] says much against "collections."... Most collections are little more than old soup warmed over. Possibly a few bridging pages or paragraphs will be added in an effort to spark new flame under the kettle. The literary gourmet will not be fooled, however. Old soup is old soup no matter how you ladle it.

"Welcome to the Monkey House" fails to enhance Kurt Vonnegut's reputation. There are only brief glimpses of the hilarious, uproarious Vonnegut whose black-logic extentions of today's absurdities into an imagined society of tomorrow at once gives us something to laugh at and much to fear. At his wildest best (as in his earlier "God Bless You, Mr. Rosewater" or in "Cat's Cradle") Kurt Vonnegut is a laughing prophet of doom. Too much of this book ... is slick, slapdash prose lifted from the pages of magazines of limited distinction. (pp. 4-5)

[In "Welcome to the Monkey House," Vonnegut is] content to write a three-page preface and then, apparently willy-nilly, toss together whatever materials appeared handiest....

Some few of the selections are worthwhile. There's a pleasant little essay on the Cape Cod village where the author lives, a funny review of The Random House Dictionary ... and some three or four stories dealing competently and wildly with improbable tomorrows. (p. 5)

Unhappily, such touches are rare. The rather pitiful state of magazine fiction is what one most remembers about this book. (p. 19)

Larry L. King, "Old Soup," in The New York Times Book Review *(© 1968 by The New York Times Company; reprinted by permission), September 1, 1968, pp. 4-5, 19.*

GRANVILLE HICKS

[Vonnegut] is a sardonic humorist and satirist in the vein of Mark Twain and Jonathan Swift. In earlier works, such as *Player Piano*, *Cat's Cradle*, and *God Bless You, Mr. Rosewater,* he has made fun of the worship of science and technology. Now we can see that his quarrel with contemporary society began with his experiences in World War II, about which he has at last managed to write a book [*Slaughterhouse-Five*]....

Vonnegut never does get around to describing the raid on Dresden, and that shows the wisdom of the strategy he was finally led to adopt. When the planes came over, Billy and a few other prisoners, together with four of their guards, took refuge in a meat locker.... In trying to tell what he and his fellow-survivors saw the next morning when they emerged from the locker, about all Billy can say is, "It was like the moon." It is by this and other kinds of indirection that Vonnegut makes his impression.

Vonnegut's satire sweeps widely, touching on education, religion, advertising, and many other subjects....

But the central target is the institution of war.... The terrible destruction of Dresden is, as Vonnegut sees it, an example of the way the military mind operates. (He quotes a military historian to the effect that the raid served no essential purpose.) He shows that in great matters as in small war is brutal and stupid. . . .

Like Mark Twain, Vonnegut feels sadness as well as indignation when he looks at the damned human race. Billy Pilgrim is a compassionate man, and meditates a good deal on the life and teachings of Jesus and on institutionalized Christianity. . . . Partly as a result of what he has learned on Tralfamadore, Billy is to some extent reconciled to life as it is lived on Earth. But Vonnegut is not, and in this book he has expressed his terrible outrage. . . .

As I read it, I could hear Vonnegut's mild voice, see his dead pan as he told a ludicrous story, and gasp as I grasped the terrifying implications of some calm remark. Even though he is not to be identified with Billy Pilgrim, he lives and breathes in the book, and that is one reason why it is the best he has written. (p. 25)

> *Granville Hicks, in* Saturday Review *(© 1969 by Saturday Review, Inc.; reprinted with permission), March 29, 1969.*

JOYCE CAROL OATES

Slaughterhouse-Five or *The Children's Crusade* is a book that hasn't yet been written. Vonnegut is so obsessed, so horrified by his subject that he quite literally cannot approach it, can only hint at it, surrounding it with semi-comic *non sequiturs*, a kind of toned-down *Catch-22*. The subject is the firebombing of Dresden. But this subject is not the content of this novel. The novel is about any number of other things, and it is also about Vonnegut's failure to write the novel, his sense of despair, his conviction that it is a lousy novel, and so forth. Rarely has the failure of a piece of fiction been so obviously tied up with the author's intense desire to write about it. Vonnegut says in his introductory chapter that he has been writing or trying to write the story of the firebombing of Dresden for years, this is his "famous" unwritten novel, and yet what he has finally turned out is a highly artificial, glib, picaresque tale of someone named "Billy Pilgrim." Billy is captured by a flying saucer from the planet Tralfamadore on his daughter's wedding night and, gifted with a peculiar talent for timelessness, he can see past, present, and future, and relive or live these various times, but without the power to alter anything. This gives Vonnegut the chance to jump maniacally back and forth and ahead in time, creating a jumble of events and non-events, since he is anxious not to write about his alleged subject, which is apparently the firebombing of Dresden. Of course, a writer writes about what he wants to write about, and it is quite possible that Vonnegut has been deluding himself for decades—what he really wants to write about is the nonsense of Billy Pilgrim, and not the seriousness of Dresden. It would have been kind of someone to tell him that he couldn't write about it anyway, since fiction is not written about events but about people: Vonnegut has not created any people here, only bizarre cut-outs mouthing lines that are sometimes funny and sometimes not. His grotesque scenes are unfelt because they are unimagined. (pp. 535-36)

> *Joyce Carol Oates, in* The Hudson Review *(copyright © 1969 by The Hudson Review, Inc.; reprinted by permission), Vol. XXII, No. 3, Autumn, 1969.*

LESLIE A. FIEDLER

[The] novel must cease taking itself seriously or perish. . . . Vonnegut has had what we now realize to be an advantage in this regard, since he *began* as a Pop writer, the author of "slick" fiction, written to earn money, which is to say, to fit formulas which are often genuine myths, frozen and waiting to be released. Fortunately, though he has sometimes written to suit the tastes of the middle-aged ladies who constitute the readership of the *Ladies' Home Journal*, he has tended more to exploit the mythology of the future. But he has, in any case—as writers of, rather than *about*, mythology must—written books that are thin and wide, rather than deep and narrow, books which open out into fantasy and magic by means of linear narration rather than deep analysis; and so happen on wisdom, fall into it through grace, rather than pursue it doggedly or seek to earn it by hard work. Moreover, like all literature which tries to close the gap between the elite and the popular audiences rather than to confirm it, Vonnegut's books tend to temper irony with sentimentality and to dissolve both in wonder. . . .

Vonnegut *does* belong to what we know again to be the mainstream of fiction; it is not the mainstream of High Art, however, but of myth and entertainment: a stream which was forced to flow underground over the past several decades, but has now surfaced once more. (p. 196)

[*Player Piano,*] despite its projection into the future and its science-fiction gimmicks, . . . represented quite obviously the kind of earnest social criticism which suggests comparisons with quite respectable writers like Aldous Huxley and George Orwell. In its earlier pages especially, it seems now, in fact, *too* bent on suggesting such comparisons, more committed to morality than play, more concerned with editorial than invention; grimly intent on proving (once more!) that machines deball and dehumanize men—and that the huge corporation, called the Ilium Works . . . corrupts those it nominates as an elite even as it strips of all dignity those it finds unworthy to program its computers. But before *Player Piano* is through, Vonnegut's sense of humor has mitigated his indignation, and he is pursuing . . . any possibility of a joke, no matter how poor or in the midst of no matter what horror: anticipating, in fact, the mode later called, ineptly enough, "Black Humor." . . .

Vonnegut is at his best in the book when he himself indulges in Pop fantasy—anticipating what he can do best as he invents the Ghost Shirt Society. . . . (p. 199)

[In *The Sirens of Titan* and *Cat's Cradle*] he seems at ease —in a way he was not earlier and would not be later—with science fiction; finding in its conventions not a kind of restriction, but a way of releasing his own sentimental-ironic view of a meaningless universe redeemed by love; his own unrecognized need to write a New Gospel or at least to rewrite the Old; his distrusted longing to indulge his fantasy without providing the unimaginative one more occasion for idle masturbation; his unconfessed desire to escape both the stifling inwardness of the traditional art-novel and the empty virtuosity of avant-garde experiment. . . .

[Reading] them, we are not tempted to believe ourselves set apart by the rareness of our pleasure or the subtlety of our understanding. Like all Pop art, they confirm our solidarity with everyone who can read at all, or merely dream over pages devoted to evoking the mystery of space and time, or to prophesying the end of man.

[*Mother Night*] temporarily interrupts Vonnegut's continuing exploration of the potentialities of science fiction—representing perhaps a desire to be more immediately topical, more directly political, more "serious" in short. It is not unsuccessful in its own terms, but finally irrelevant to Vonnegut's special vocation, though deeply concerned with Germany and World War II, which is Vonnegut's other obsessive subject matter: the past he remembers, rather than the future he extrapolates or invents. *Mother Night* does not quite manage to deal with the American fire-bombing of Dresden.... [He came] closer in *Slaughterhouse-Five;* but even that novel is less about Dresden than about Vonnegut's failure to come to terms with it—one of those beautifully frustrating works about their own impossibility. . . .

Eschewing science fiction in *Mother Night,* however, Vonnegut turns to another, more established Pop form, the spy novel. . . . The story itself is, however, serious enough; the tale of a double agent, unable to prove for a long time that he was really in the pay of the U.S. Government and unwilling, finally, to save himself from hanging when that proof is unexpectedly offered. Self-condemned and self-executed, Howard W. Campbell leaves behind a book intended to testify that one is always—hopelessly, irrecoverably—what he pretends to be, pretends to himself he is *only* pretending to be.

Campbell is, in fact, the first major author-protagonist in Vonnegut; and, like his own author, a Pop artist before history makes him an autobiographer. He has become for the large German public a successful playwright; and for the smaller public of two, constituted by himself and his wife, a private pornographer. . . .

[Vonnegut] is especially hung up on the subject of porn, the sole Pop form which, in fact, evades him—despite a theoretical dedication to freeing men to lead full sexual lives. Vonnegut cannot ever quite manage to talk dirty enough to be explicit about sex; though (because?) he is haunted throughout his work by a vision of his own books ending up in the display windows of pornographic bookshops, confused by owners and customers alike with hard-core pornography. He is aware really that the confusion is, on the deepest level, somehow valid; that the best of science fiction has in common with the shabbiest sort of erotica, not sex but "fantasies of an impossibly hospitable world."

But he is not really at ease with the fact; and throughout his work, especially as it grows more and more unguardedly confessional, there appears over and over the image of that first of all pornographic photos, in which a girl is vainly trying to screw a Shetland pony. . . .

Yet what bugs Vonnegut even more is the awareness that in his own time pornography is practiced, and accepted, as revolutionary art itself, a special way of telling the truth about the society we live in; and he parodies mercilessly, in *God Bless You, Mr. Rosewater,* a novelist presumably dedicated to absolute candor. . . . (p. 200)

In the end, however, the spy novel proved for Vonnegut almost as unsympathetic as pornography itself—more unsympathetic, in fact, since the story of espionage posits a world of total alienation rather than one of impossible hospitality. He could not find room in it, moreover, for magic and wonder, the religious dimension so necessary to his view of man. (pp. 200, 202)

The Sirens of Titan is his best book, I think—most totally achieved, most nearly dreamed rather than contrived. In it, he evokes all the themes, along with their sustaining images, for which we remember him with special affection and amusement: the unreality of time and the consequent possibility of traveling therein, the illusory nature of free will and the consequent possibility of heroism and sacrifice, the impossibility of really choosing one's mate and the consequent necessity to love whomever, whatever happens to come to hand. It is, moreover, his most *chutzpahdik,* his most outrageously and attractively arrogant book, for in it he dares not only to ask the ultimate question about the meaning of human life, but to answer it.

But what sets *The Sirens of Titan* apart is that, inventing it, Vonnegut has escaped from the limitations of an imagination narrower and more provincial than it is ever possible quite to remember. Despite his dedication to a form predicated on space-travel, Vonnegut is oddly earth-bound, American-bound. . . . In *The Sirens of Titan,* however, he imagined for the first time Tralfamadore, the transgalactic world he is to evoke again and again, but to which none of his space-travelers even actually go; until, perhaps, Billy Pilgrim . . . , and which we are free, therefore, to understand for the absolute Elsewhere, more easily reached by art or madness than by mere technology. (p. 202)

This is not, however, the work's final word, Vonnegut's final position: for that very messenger, it turns out, though an intricate machine, has learned somehow to love in the aeons he has spent as a castaway; and he provides—like a kindly Pop artist—a vision of Paradise to sustain Malachi's dying moments; a false vision sustained by posthypnotic suggesting, but sufficient to make dying more palatable than living. It is as much of a Happy Ending as Kurt Vonnegut could imagine at this point in his career. (pp. 202-03)

[*Cat's Cradle*] does not even offer us [a] token Happy Ending, for that book begins and ends with a vision of the total destruction of mankind, to which only an eternal gesture of contempt is an adequate response. It is a book which has nothing to do with Heaven except insofar as it is not there ("No cat! No cradle!"), though it takes place largely on an island paradise in the Caribbean, which stirs in us once more memories of that Master of Illusion, Prospero. . . .

Indeed, the not-quite nihilism of the book's close is a product of the tension between the religion of Bokononism, which advocates formulating and believing sacred lies, and the vision granted to the dwarfed son of the Father of the Bomb of the emptiness behind all lies, however sacred. The voice of the White Dwarf and the Black Prophet are both Vonnegut's, and they answer each other inconclusively throughout; creating an ambiguity quite like that produced by the opposite claims of High Art (the Dwarf, an avant-garde painter, renders his view in monochrome abstraction) and Pop Art (Bokonon, an entertainer, sings his creed in calypso form).

But, as ever in Vonnegut, something more is presented than the unresolvable conflict of mutually exclusive theories: namely, the possibility of actual joy. John, at any rate, is revealed as having experienced two great joys before his tale is told: one slow and long-continued, as he learns who are the other members of his *karass,* the handful of others in the world with whom, willy-nilly, he must work out the pattern of his destiny: one intense and momentary, as he plays footsie with the blonde Negress, Mona, whom he, and everyone else, loves. . . .

God Bless You, Mr. Rosewater . . . and *Slaughterhouse-Five* (1969) . . . constitute, in fact, a single work, with common characters, common themes, common obsessions and a common whimsy—and which together rifle his earlier books for other characters, themes, obsessions and whimsical asides; as if he is being driven to make his total work seem in retrospect a latter-day Human Comedy or Yoknapatawpha series. But [these] last novels are quite different in their tone and effect, being essentially autobiographical rather than mythic: quasi-novels really, in which the author returns to his early material reflectively rather than obsessively—and so ends writing *about* it, rather than simply writing it. . . . (p. 203)

God Bless You, Mr. Rosewater is not science fiction at all . . . but a work of "mainstream literature," in which Vonnegut has transposed from the Future and Elsewhere to the Present and Right Here the themes which he once mythologized in popular, fantastic modes: the compelling need to love the unlovable, whose ranks industrialization has disconcertingly swelled; the magical power of money and the holy folly of renouncing it; the uses and abuses of fantasy itself. But the profoundest and most central concern of *Rosewater* is new for Vonnegut. . . . We remember the novel chiefly as a book about madness, or more particularly, as one about the relationship between madness and holiness; since Eliot Rosewater . . . is the first of Vonnegut's gurus who lives *in* madness rather than *by* lies. He does not, that is to say, choose deliberately to deceive for the sake of the salvation of mankind, but is hopelessly self-deceived: insane enough to accept as truth what Rumfoord was forced to justify as useful fictions, or Bokonon to preach as *foma,* "harmless untruths."

But if *God Bless You, Mr. Rosewater* is not science fiction, it is compulsively *about* science fiction; and this time the writer nearest to its center . . . is Kilgore Trout, the author of scores of neglected and despised science fiction novels. . . .

[It] is given to Trout to play an equivocal St. Paul to Eliot Rosewater's absurd Christ: to rationalize Eliot's madness in terms acceptable even to his tycoon father. . . .

[In] *Slaughterhouse-Five,* Trout returns to play a similar role for a similar sub-messiah, this time an optometrist called Billy Pilgrim, who had, as a matter of fact, been introduced to the work of Trout by Eliot himself in the psycho-ward of a military hospital during World War II.

But Billy, unlike Eliot, travels in space and time, actually reaching Tralfamadore itself. . . . Oddly enough, however —as Vonnegut pointedly informs us—Trout had already imagined the zoo episode in fiction, and Billy had read it before living it, or dreaming it, or falling through time and space into it. Vonnegut will not, to be sure, let us side with the cynics and realists who would, by psychiatric means, cure Billy of his belief that he has been and is forever on Tralfamadore; but he leaves suspended, not quite asked, much less answered, the question of whether he travels there through Outer Space or Inner, via madness or flying saucer—or merely by means of Pop fiction, in which each of these is revealed as the metaphor of the other. . . .

And if at last Vonnegut does not understand, all the better

for him and for us. What he does not understand is precisely what saves him for readers like me who are disconcerted and dismayed as he grows more and more conscious of more and more in himself, turns more and more from fantasy to analysis. (p. 204)

> Leslie A. Fiedler, *"The Divine Stupidity of Kurt Vonnegut,"* in Esquire *(first published in* Esquire Magazine; *copyright © 1970 by* Esquire, Inc.*), in* Esquire, *September, 1970, pp. 195-204.*

EDITH OLIVER

["Happy Birthday, Wanda June"] is an attempt at a satire on the return of Odysseus. Mr. Vonnegut's Odysseus is a paunchy, bearded fellow named Ryan who has been missing for eight years, held captive by Indians in South America. He is a bully and a braggart who calls his young wife "Daughter," boasts of his heroism during the Spanish Civil War and the Second World War, and at the end goes offstage with a loaded rifle to shoot himself. In short, he is a caricature of Hemingway, drawn in pure venom. A dreadful, cheap idea, and certainly unworthy of the clever Mr. Vonnegut's considerable talent—talent for comedy, that is, which, while slighter than Hemingway's, for example, often pays off. No talent for abstract though is discernible. . . . Although I'd just as soon simply laugh at anyone as funny as Mr. Vonnegut and let it go at that, he demands to be taken seriously, and when he starts moralizing he becomes obvious and silly, almost sinking his play. (p. 143)

> *Edith Oliver, in* The New Yorker *(© 1970 by* The New Yorker Magazine, Inc.*), October 17, 1970.*

WALTER KERR

"Happy Birthday, Wanda June" is a Punch and Judy show acted out by pretended people, in case you've forgotten the real content of any Punch and Judy show. It adds up, simply, to this: Punch kills everybody, one by one, until the Devil gets him. (p. 1)

There are at least three things wrong with the play and one —much more important—that is right. The play is structurally ambivalent about death. A number of quite jolly interludes take place in a heaven that is conveniently composed of a driving rain of spotlights. There Wanda June, who has nothing to do with the play except that she has been killed by an ice-cream truck, sings girlish songs in her pretty white frock, playing shuffleboard with the Beast of Yugoslavia, a Nazi with a curled lip who deeply admires the way our hero made a mess of him during the war.

In heaven, everyone is content, happy really to be dead; even the hero's third wife has enough to drink to keep her drunk. But with death, so omnipresent, so inevitable, and so enjoyable, the main line is undercut. Does it matter so much that the victim is a killer if his victims are cheerful enough to be out of it and if we are all going to be killed anyway by ice cream trucks? The hero's killing comes to seem a bit redundant; we can't become much exercised about him, or even interested in him, if he's only expediting what's bound to come willy-nilly.

The thrust of the hero is further dulled, made to seem not terribly dangerous, by the fact that the role is [not as well written as the others]. . . . (pp. 1, 18)

The last thing wrong: Mr. Vonnegut has done what I thought he would never do, he has not only let himself preach, but he has also let us catch him doing it. A doctor gets out a skeletal chart of two men, asks us which of the two men can be identified as an "enemy." A wife gets too smug. "Education's my vice," she says, comparing herself to boozehounds. The doctor looks at the antiered walls and muses, "All this unending death." We don't need nudging like that—not from Vonnegut, who's burned whole cities without batting an eyelash.

But if the play has to cope with these burdens, it also brings to the theater something the theater desperately needs. An imaginative mind. An imaginative voice is not the same thing as an inventive one. An inventive mind makes things up—anything, everything. An imaginative mind doesn't. It looks around at the insane world we inhabit and reports it as it is, tells us what we knew; but it tells it in unmournful numbers that none of the rest of us would have ever used. We saw it before, we believe it now, but we'd never have said it that way. An imaginative mind makes the same contacts we do but it never recites them in our terms.

From the beginning of the evening . . . we hear a person, not a playwrighting computer, not a news bulletin on television, not a report to the President that the President will or won't like, but a man whose neurons and dendrites click together differently from our own. The same-plus-different is what enchants us in life, perhaps it is the only thing that ever does. And here is this man, this half-wild man, this voice, this wind-from-the-planets voice, unexpectedly and impudently and familiarly and backslappingly and despairingly speaking to us out of a one-of-a-kind head.

It's exhilarating at first, and then, when we see how much is wrong with the play, insistent. We can't turn away from it just because it makes mistakes. . . .

Vonnegut's noises, Vonnegut's colors *are* Punch and Judy noises and colors, abrupt, primary, murderous, childlike, funny in the sense of funny-I-thought-I'd-die. The play falters; I find the thwack and the quack irresistible. (p. 18)

> *Walter Kerr, "At Last, An Imaginative Mind," in* The New York Times, *Section 2 (© 1970 by The New York Times Company; reprinted by permission), October 18, 1970, pp. 1, 18.*

TONY TANNER

It is a growing awareness of the seriousness of Vonnegut's inquiries which has made people realize that he is not only the science fiction writer he first appeared to be.

His first novel, *Player Piano* (1952), was, to be sure, a fairly orthodox futuristic satire on the dire effects on human individuality of the fully mechanised society which technology could make possible. A piano player is a man consciously using a machine to produce aesthetically pleasing patterns of his own making. A player-piano is a machine which has been programmed to produce music on its own, thus making the human presence redundant. This undesirable inversion of the relationship between man and machine, suggested by the title, is at the heart of the novel. In this society of the future there is one part for the machines and the managers, and another part ('the Homestead') into which have been herded all the unnecessary people. Paul Proteus (whose initials suggest his relation to the theme of the title, and whose second name suggests a predisposition to change), is a top manager who believes in the system. But he starts to feel a 'nameless, aching need' which indi-

cates a nascent dissatisfaction with the very social structures he has helped to erect. He realises that he is trapped in the system he serves. (pp. 181-82)

[*Player Piano* presents] a basic dilemma in Vonnegut's work. Both sides want to *use* the hero; both sides want to impose a particular role on him and make him into a special sort of messenger or conveyor of information; and as Paul discovers, between the two sides, 'there was no middle ground for him'. Paul is a typical American hero in wanting to find a place beyond all plots and systems, some private space, or 'border area'—a house by the side of the road of history and society. He would like not to be used, not to be part of someone else's plan. But the book shows this to be an impossible dream.

The Sirens of Titan (1959), Vonnegut's next novel, is also about people being used, this time on the sort of inter-galactic scale permissible in science fiction. . . . [Rumfoord] is a man who now exists as 'wave phenomena' as a result of having run his space ship into an 'uncharted chrono-synclastic infundibulum'. He is *'scattered far and wide, not just through space, but through time, too'*, and with his new-found power to arrange things to suit his patterns, free to handle time and space as he pleases and put people where he wants them, he is a suitably fantastic analogue of Vonnegut himself, who is doing just that in his book. But if Rumfoord is the user, he is also the used. (pp. 182-83)

It is man's status as agent-victim which preoccupies Vonnegut; once one of his characters comes to see this double aspect of human life and action he usually, like Malachi, becomes 'hopelessly engrossed in the intricate tactics of causing less rather than more pain'. (p. 183)

[A] possible attitude to the discovery of [the human] fate is implied in Beatrice Rumfoord's conclusion that '"The worst thing that could possibly happen to anybody would be not to be used for anything by anybody."' A corollary of this is Malachi's late decision that one purpose of human life " 'no matter who is controlling it, is to love whoever is around to be loved.'" This formulation, albeit very sympathetic, points to a detectable strain of sentimental sententiousness which recurs in Vonnegut's work. (p. 184)

With *Mother Night* (1961) we are back into the bleakest years of contemporary history. In this book . . . one may discern a shift in Vonnegut's style. There is less attempt at narrative fulness, and a greater use of short chapters which give the sense of the intermittencies and incompletenesses inevitable in any written version. The impression is of compressed selections suspended in an encompassing silence. . . . Howard Campbell is a quintessential Vonnegut hero: *the* agent-victim, the most uncertain and perhaps the most hapless of all Vonnegut's bemused messengers. (p. 185)

Campbell is a special 'agent'; but in Vonnegut's vision we are all agents, and the perception that we can never be sure of the full content and effect of what we communicate to the world, by word or deed, is at the moral centre of this novel. It also carries the implicit warning that our lies may be more influential than our truths, a consideration which writers in particular must ponder. (p. 186)

The book presents, almost in shorthand, a whole spectrum of fiction-making, from the vilest propaganda to the most idealistic art. There is no cynical attempt to identify these two extreme ends of the spectrum, but it is part of Vonnegut's meaning to suggest that the artist cannot rest in confidence as to the harmlessness of his inventions. . . . In one way it comes down to that suspicion of all communication which seems to go so deep in contemporary American fiction. As no one can be fully aware of the 'information' that goes out through him (just as you cannot control the information that is fed into you), the artist as a professional inventor and sender of messages must be very careful about what he puts out. He may think that, in [Sir Philip] Sidney's terms, he is delivering a golden world from our brazen one. But he might, all unawares, be contributing to the restoration of the ancient reign of Mother Night. (p. 188)

[Vonnegut] has seldom been more comically inventive [than he is in *Cat's Cradle*,] but then the whole novel is an exploration of the ambiguities of man's disposition to play and invent, and the various forms it may take. . . .

[Each character on the island of San Lorenzo] is following his dream, creating his fiction. And it is from this island that the process which will end the world is unwittingly launched. This may be Vonnegut's mordant way of predicting the possible final outcome of the human instinct to play. When this island of invention contains both [ice-nine], *and* representatives of the artistic and Utopian dreams which console and dignify the race, one can see that Vonnegut is pushing quite hard for a recognition of the deeply ambiguous creative/destructive aspects of the innate human instinct to play. (p. 189)

The title is explained in the book. Newt recalls that the one game his father played with him on the day the first atom bomb was exploded, was to make a cat's cradle and push it jeeringly into his face. On the island Newt makes a painting of the ancient game of cat's cradle, and adds "'For maybe a hundred thousand years or more, grown-ups have been waving tangles of string in their children's faces.'" In Newt's view it is no wonder that children should grow up crazy, because when they look at the cross-crossed string, what do they see? *'No damn cat, and no damn cradle'*. A chapter in *Mother Night* is entitled 'No Dove, No Covenant'. It alludes to the same discovery which any child is likely to make; namely, that the religions or legends taught to him by adults are just fictions. There is no cat there; nor does God make a sign. On the other hand it is an axiom of Bokonism that man has to tell himself that he understands life even when he knows he doesn't. This is the justification for constructing fictions, for the necessity of art. It does, after all, take skill to weave the string, and something more again to imagine the cat. On the other hand one must confront the fact that the string *is* only string. The matter is summed up in what the narrator calls 'the cruel paradox of Bokonist thought, the heartbreaking necessity of lying about reality, and the heartbreaking impossibility of lying about it'. That, certainly, is what Vonnegut contrives to suggest in his own brilliant little fiction.

The distinctive tone of Vonnegut's work is very likeable and sympathetic; it obviously bespeaks a compassionate humane spirit. The economy and laconic wit prevent this from issuing in much overt sentimentality, though the tendency is there. However, at times it does seem as though he is using his fiction to issue short sermons on the state of contemporary America, or the world, and this can at times endanger the poise of his work. I think that some of the weaker aspects of his writing show up in *God Bless You, Mr. Rosewater* (1965), despite the wit and moral feeling with which the book is conceived and executed. (pp. 191-92)

[*Slaughterhouse-Five*] is a moving meditation on the relationship between history and dreaming cast in an appropriately factual/fictional mode. . . .

[Vonnegut] himself enters his own novel from time to time . . . and it becomes very difficult to hold the various fictional planes in perspective. . . . But the overall impression is that of a man who has brought the most graphic facts of his life to exist in the same medium with his more important fictions to see what each implies about the other. (p. 195)

[Although] one necessarily reads in sequence the many compressed fragments or messages which make up his novels, one nevertheless gets the impression of arrested moments suspended in time. In reading Billy Pilgrim's adventures we too become unstuck in time. As a result one is left with something approaching the impression of seeing all the marvellous and horrific moments, all at the same time. Vonnegut, the telephoner, has condensed and arranged his telegrams to good effect. He starts his account of the adventures of Pilgrim with the single word—'Listen'. This is to alert us. We are being messaged. (p. 197)

A motto which Billy brings from his life into his fantasy, or vice-versa, reads: 'God grant me the serenity to accept the things I cannot change, courage to change the things I can, and wisdom always to tell the difference'. In itself this is an open-ended programme. But immediately afterwards we read: 'Among the things Billy Pilgrim could not change were the past, the present, and the future'. Billy becomes completely quiescent, calmly accepting everything that happens as happening exactly as it ought to (including his own death). He abandons the worried ethical, tragical point of view of western man and adopts a serene conscienceless passivity. If anything, he views the world aesthetically: every moment is a marvellous moment, at times he beams at scenes in the war. Yet he does have breakdowns and is prone to fits of irrational weeping.

Here I think is the crucial moral issue in the book. Billy Pilgrim is a professional optometrist. He spends his life on earth prescribing corrective lenses for people suffering from defects of vision. It is entirely in keeping with his calling, then, when he has learned to see time in an entirely new Tralfamadorian way, that he should try to correct the whole erroneous Western view of time, and explain to everyone the meaninglessness of individual death. . . . The point for us to ponder is how are *we* to regard his new vision. According to the Tralfamadorians, ordinary human vision is something so narrow and restricted that, to convey to themselves what it must be like they have to imagine a creature with a metal sphere round his head who looks down a long thin pipe seeing only a tiny speck at the end. He cannot turn his head around and he is strapped to a flatcar on rails which goes in one direction. Billy Pilgrim's attempt to free people from that metal sphere, and his own widened and liberated vision, may thus seem entirely desirable. But is the cost in conscience and concern for the individual life equally desirable? (p. 198)

Perhaps the fact of the matter is that conscience simply cannot cope with events like the concentration camps and the Dresden air-raid, and the more general demonstration by the war of the utter valuelessness of human life. Even to try to begin to care adequately would lead to an instant and irrevocable collapse of consciousness. Billy Pilgrim, Everyman, needs his fantasies to offset such facts. (p. 199)

Billy's Tralfamadorian perspective is not unlike that described in Yeats's 'Lapis Lazuli'—'gaiety transfiguring all that dread'—and it has obvious aesthetic appeal and consolation. At the same time, his sense of the futility of trying to change anything, of regarding history as a great lump of intractable amber from which one can only escape into the fourth dimension of dream and fantasy, was the attitude held by Howard Campbell during the rise of Nazi Germany. Vonnegut has, I think, total sympathy with such quietistic impulses. At the same time his whole work suggests that if man doesn't do something about the conditions and quality of human life on Earth, no one and nothing else will. Fantasies of complete determinism, of being held helplessly in the amber of some eternally unexplained plot, justify complete passivity and a supine acceptance of the futility of all action. Given the overall impact of Vonnegut's work I think we are bound to feel that there is at least something equivocal about Billy's habit of fantasy, even if his attitude is the most sympathetic one in the book. At one point Vonnegut announces: 'There are almost no characters in this story, and almost no dramatic confrontations, because most of the people in it are so sick and so much the listless playthings of enormous forces'. It is certainly hard to celebrate the value of the individual self against the background of war, in which the nightmare of being the victim of uncontrollable forces comes compellingly true. In such conditions it is difficult to be much of a constructive 'agent', and Billy Pilgrim doubtless has to dream to survive.

At the end of the novel, spring has come to the ruins of Dresden, and when Billy is released from prison the trees are in leaf. He finds himself in a street which is deserted except for one wagon. 'The wagon was green and coffin-shaped'. That composite image of generation and death summarises all there is actually to see in the external world, as far as Vonnegut is concerned. The rest is fantasy, cat's cradles, lies. In this masterly novel, Vonnegut has put together both his war novel and reminders of the fantasies which made up his previous novels. The facts which defy explanation are brought into the same frame with fictions beyond verification. The point at which fact and fiction intersect is Vonnegut himself, the experiencing dreaming man who wrote the book. He is a lying messenger of course, but he acts on the assumption that the telegrams must continue to be sent. Eliot Rosewater's cry to his psychiatrist, overheard by Billy Pilgrim, applies more particularly to the artist. 'I think you guys are going to have to come up with a lot of wonderful *new* lies, or people just aren't going to want to go on living.' Of course, they must also tell the truth, whatever that may be. Kafka's couriers could hardly be more confused. What Vonnegut has done, particularly in *Slaughterhouse-Five*, is to define with clarity and economy —and compassion—the nature and composition of that confusion. (pp. 200-01)

Tony Tanner, "The Uncertain Messenger: A Study of the Novels of Kurt Vonnegut, Jr." (originally published in a slightly different version in Critical Quarterly, *Winter, 1969), in his* City of Words: American Fiction 1950-1970 *(copyright © 1971 by Tony Tanner; reprinted by permission of*

Harper & Row, Publishers, Inc.; in Canada by Jonathan Cape Ltd.), Harper, *1971, pp. 181-201.*

J. D. O'HARA

[*Breakfast of Champions*] is almost a deliberate curiosity, an earnest attempt to play after getting Dresden out of the way. It's filled with Vonnegut's cartoon drawings of items mentioned in the text; it plays the whimsical game of pretending that we know nothing about life on earth . . . and it delivers many straight-faced criticisms of Life. . . . He indulges in some obligatory no-no's: he talks about Niggers, he draws a vagina, he gives penis measurements of most of the male characters (but fudges about his own). (p. 26)

Well, all this—and the funny names and the slapstick events—is less amusing than it ought to be. The characters are still stick figures, still listless playthings; but the "enormous forces" are now reduced to Vonnegut himself, who wanders through his novel like Ed Sullivan through reruns of his Sunday nights—creating characters, endowing them with nonce pasts and qualities, hurting or sparing them, and then dismissing them indifferently. We tend to share that indifference. We soon learn to read *Breakfast* by the line, or by the one-liner, hoping for a joke here and there and keeping an eye out for the novel's chief blessings, its summaries of Kilgore Trout's science fiction. The Vonnegut who appears is less charming than his earlier avatars: here he is represented as on the verge of a nervous breakdown, troubled by schizophrenia and his mother, and not much involved in the novel: "'This is a very bad book you're writing,' I said to myself. . . ." It's not *that* bad; it's diverting . . . but it's pop, no snap or crackle. . . . Even simple communication requires the right kind of simple. At the University of Iowa [where he taught a writing workshop], one of Vonnegut's main themes was the "sense of wonder" needed by writers; here he describes—and draws —a rattlesnake with rattles and poison-filled fangs; then after a momentous pause he announces:

> Sometimes I wonder about the Creator of the Universe.

Even a sophomore will wince at *that* kind of simplicity. (pp. 26-7)

J. D. O'Hara, "Instantly Digestible," in The New Republic *(reprinted by permission of* The New Republic; © *1973 The New Republic, Inc.), May 12, 1973, pp. 26-8.*

MARTIN BURNS

In *Breakfast of Champions,* Vonnegut intends to release his characters from his control. In doing so, he shows their unreadiness to cope with freedom, or to measure up to its responsibilities. In a sense, he is telling us that we are all living in our own private novels, but our actions do not, in reality, follow a coherent plot. Our lives collide and interfere with each other. We inevitably become what we do. . . .

Vonnegut's people were once machines that one could wind up and set loose. He wants to change that, because they are also part of his own machinery. Even after his decision to free them, they continue to behave as if they were acting out a drama beyond their own control, with major roles and minor roles to play, and a Providence to grant them some means of atonement for their mechanical failures.

In *Breakfast of Champions* human machines are broken down into their chemical and physical components more thoroughly than ever before in a work by Vonnegut. The story is told in a sense of short, narrative bursts which describe the histories and actions of people in and around Midland City. . . .

Kilgore Trout is especially groomed to be Vonnegut's liason with the rest of creation. He is the only "machine" around possessing more than just the faintest glimmer of cosmic consciousness.

Existing as a character in the book, the author is, understandably, the most crucial being in the book. He presents himself candidly, by inserting personal asides and encouraging the reader to jump often from fiction to reality and back again. The resulting style is sometimes annoying. Vonnegut, though, is at his best when detailing the relations between the biographies of his characters, who can hardly begin to imagine the influences they exert on each other. He has so much sympathy, in fact, for their lack of imagination that occasional annoyance can be easily overlooked.

At any rate, the difficulties of emancipation are hopefully more evident to us, (having read the book) than to those with less imagination. Emancipation, we learn, is not equivalent to freedom. Wayne Hoobler has been "freed" from the security of prison and turned loose in a hostile world which offers him no purpose. Dwayne Hoover's mind is "freed" from the restrictions of reality by his madness, yet his body must remain a straight-jacketed machine, unable to follow where his fantasies lead. Kilgore Trout, who is freed (by Vonnegut's intervention) from any uncertainty as to the purpose of his existence, suffers, ironically, from the logical projection of Vonnegut's own plight. Having met his maker, Trout finds him omnisciently infallible, but unfortunately lacking the power to rejuvenate his elderly creation. (p. 75)

We can only guess that Vonnegut is not at all comfortable in the atmosphere he has bestowed upon those made in his likeness and image. Their world is too much like his own for complete comfort. There is little enough love, of any kind, except his own. The pathos of his beings' common plight serves, at times, to amuse and distract him from the awful burden of absolute and final authority. (pp. 75-6)

[Those] who have enjoyed Vonnegut's previous books can hardly begrudge the author his time in such a harsh spotlight as the one he turns on himself. (p. 76)

> *Martin Burns, in* The Critic (© *The Critic 1973; reprinted with the permission of the Thomas More Association, Chicago, Illinois), September-October, 1973.*

REBECCA M. PAULY

With a certain facile agility, [Vonnegut] has gone genre jumping, assuming the colors, alternately, of short story writer, novelist, playwright, and sometime poet. Critics have attempted to trace an evolutionary pattern through various categories, techniques, styles, and points of view. Yet, however much the form varies, Vonnegut's very personal, readily identifiable products persist in their family resemblance. . . .

Vonnegut entered literature through the door of science fiction, what some would unhesitatingly label the back door. . . . His works often project the consequences of the modern scientific world in nightmarish sequences of a shocking future, to wit, *Player Piano, Sirens of Titan,* and *Cat's Cradle.* The demon-scientist figure is especially well portrayed in the character of Dr. Felix Hoenikker, who fulfills the biblical prophesy that tasting of the tree of knowledge will bring destruction on the race. Man is undone by his presumption to tinker with the universe.

The notoriously schizophrenic quality of science fiction pervades Vonnegut's work, even to the center of his authorial identity: by writing *Player Piano,* he was able to escape G. E., and he has never stopped using fiction to project himself beyond the constraints of physical reality. In his terse telegraphic style, one finds impatience with even the confining nature of printed language. Often his characters' doubling of identity is accomplished by the juxtaposition of spatially and temporally irreconcilable sequences, as in *Sirens of Titan* and *Slaughterhouse Five,* where traditional boundaries burst before the power of imagination. And almost all Vonnegut's characters (foremost Howard Campbell of *Mother Night*) are torn by their dual quality, the inevitable incompatibility between the official, public identity and the real, private self. They search for shelter from the emptiness of institutionalized being. The world man has created is incapable of satisfying him; he is alienated by, and sacrificed to, the real villains, the monstrous machines of industry, in peace and war. (pp. 66-7)

For all its attractions, though, science fiction falls short in serving to express Vonnegut's views of man's fate; it loses him to fantasy, satire, black humor. The man-made, mechanized universe of science fiction is too presumptuous. Its technical realism, always on the side of the plausible, is founded on the basic tenet of progress and change, not necessarily positive, but involving a linear, cause-and-effect concept of human existence. Vonnegut rejects both the idea of verifiable reality and man's control of his destiny. In a universe governed by the absurd, empirical problems of human existence become irrelevant. There can be no qualitative distinction between reality and illusion, only the question of spiritual survival in a world gone mad. Thus ultimately Vonnegut, the anthropologist, rejects Vonnegut, the chemist. (pp. 67-8)

Vonnegut's mordant attacks on the absurdities of the human condition and the follies, inequities, and brutalities of man's making place him in a *karass* including such notables as [Jonathan] Swift, Voltaire, [Denis] Diderot, [Mark] Twain, [Henry] Mencken, [Sinclair] Lewis, and [John] Barth. With his own special brand of irreverence, he gives us private glimpses of the great and powerful, undermining their aura of importance. Often the ridiculous is allowed to speak for itself, the author believing that man's stupidity will reveal itself unaided. Vonnegut laughs at cruelty and injustice, at life, like Beaumarchais' Figaro, in order not to cry. He is too vigilant to cry; crying helps us to forget and lets us indulge in the luxury of self-pity.

In Voltaire's *Candide,* the Manichean philosopher Martin muses that the world has been created in order to enrage man. Like Martin, Vonnegut feels rage, as well as frustration and depression. But unlike those who rail, he exploits the power of the unsaid. Wielding classic understatement, he is a cool medium, eliciting intense reader participation. (p. 68)

[It] can be said that Vonnegut has indeed a strong moral response to man's fate—that of basic humanism. From *Player Piano* to *Slaughterhouse-Five*, the message is clear: love your fellow man, with compassion, with *caritas* not *eros*. Responsibility to one's neighbor becomes responsibility to oneself. Truth and falsehood are redefined irrespective of any point of reference in perceptually ascertainable reality. "We are what we pretend to be, so we must be careful about what we pretend to be," the stated moral of *Mother Night,* touches on existential questions of moral identity, echoing the Sartrian dialectic, "Nous sommes la somme do nos actes": we *are* what we *do*. Campbell commits suicide, like Salo, to punish himself for crimes against himself. In the existential sense, he is a microcosm of humanity; the acts of each man contribute to the identity of Man. When actions become institutionalized, official, the sense of responsibility is diluted: hence, the danger of a morally intolerable schizophrenia.

Vonnegut's loss of faith in an ordered universe leads him again and again to the question of religion. The Christian religion is rejected, because man learned the wrong lesson from the crucifixion: *"Before you kill somebody, make absolutely sure he isn't well connected."* . . . Any religion aspiring to authenticity must protect the unwanted, the unloved. In the rewritten Gospel Vonnegut offers us, Jesus is a nobody, whom God adopts as his son when he is tortured unjustly. "God said this: *From this moment on, He will punish horribly anybody who torments a bum who has no connections!"* . . . It must be a human religion, catering to man's spiritual needs here and now. . . . Central to Vonnegut's moral reality is the certainty of man's mortality: "When you're dead, you're dead." . . . And the basic element in his humanism is his acceptance of the human condition. "So be it" and "so it goes" echo through his works. In these amens, bitterness and resignation are mixed with a sense of nostalgic joy. (pp. 69-70)

In Vonnegut's world there are no saviors. The only hero is an everyman, at once the lowest and the highest common denominator. Like [Albert] Camus' stranger and [Bernard] Malamud's fixer, his central truth is, "I am a man." He faces a grim prospect: the impossibility of utopia is obviated by *Cat's Cradle;* there is no apparent reason, purpose, or justification for the mess man is in and no apparent way out. In a world of madness where [Samuel Beckett's] Godot will never come, where man is abandoned to his fate, he must survive without hope. Like Sisyphus pushing his boulder, Vonnegut's hero must strive for something with no anticipation of success, renewing his effort daily. Billy Pilgrim sees on his office wall and on the pendant Montana wears the ancient Sanskrit prayer for wisdom to distinguish the limits of man's control of his destiny. In *Happy Birthday, Wanda June,* Vonnegut conclusively rejects the image of the conquering hero as murderous, placing in its stead the shy healer. Humility is essential to Vonnegut's morality. Man is imperfect, frail, inefficient, alternately brilliant and stupid. . . . Man is mud. . . . Given these limitations, there is only one viable course of action: "God damn it, you've got to be kind." . . . Vonnegut asks us how long it will take us "to realize that a purpose of human life, no matter who is controlling it, is to love whoever is around to be loved." . . . The act of loving, accepting, tolerating one's fellow man becomes everyman's chance to be an artist, to create beauty in an ugly world. (p. 70)

Rebecca M. Pauly, "The Moral Stance of Kurt Vonnegut," in Extrapolation *(copyright 1973 by Thomas D. and Alice S. Clareson), December, 1973, pp. 66-71.*

IHAB HASSAN

Part satirist and part visionary, Kurt Vonnegut . . . enjoys a sudden vogue since the late Sixties, particularly among youths disaffected with militarism, greed, and excessive rationality, with various ecological and technological disasters. A dark comedian even more than a satirist, Vonnegut expresses his rage, guilt, and compassion, his sense of being alive in a world of death, in frightening dystopias. But as sly prophet, he presents alternatives to the human condition in science fictions, disporting the virtues of his favorite Tralfamadorians. His urgency carries itself lightly in fantasy or whimsy, though his gruff sentimentality also tends to weaken his hold on complex realities. (p. 45)

A fatalist and dreamer, he conceals his discomforts within strange levity. His harshest critics find him lacking in mind. Yet Vonnegut offers, more than levity, an honest perception of his moment; and creates a style both lax and gnomic, "telegraphic schizophrenic," which attempts to carry his sense of discontinuity toward some visionary end. (p. 47)

Ihab Hassan, "Kurt Vonnegut," in his Contemporary American Literature: 1942-1972 *(copyright © 1973 by Frederick Ungar Publishing Co., Inc.), Frederick Ungar, 1973, pp. 45-7.*

KATHLEEN CUSHMAN

[*Wampeters, Foma & Granfalloons* is a collection of Vonnegut's essays, reviews, and speeches.] His technique, properly applied, is unsurpassed. In a piece of speculative reporting such as "There's a Maniac Loose Out There," the account of a grisly crime on Cape Cod, . . . Vonnegut approaches his own opinion with a jigsawlike gallery of observations that leaves one meditating on one's own responses. And in "Excelsior! We're Going to the Moon! Excelsior!" he frequently follows his own paragraphs by repeating a word or phrase from within them, letting it reverberate as if to re-examine his own sentence from another, more interesting viewpoint. . . . Occasionally these techniques fall flat, leaving a sense of facility and emptiness. But more often their seemingly random perceptions provide a surprisingly acute moral juxtaposition.

Still, it is this very tone of moral insight which has gained Vonnegut his reputation as a humanist and a conveyor of wisdom that weakens his impact in the latter half of the collection. As his popularity grows and magazines begin to ask him to point his pithy pencil at politics and the like, Vonnegut loses strength as a writer. His message, after all, is the same in most of his works—a condemnation of the inhuman uses of technology, a bitter pessimism about the future, mixed with a romantic identification with the young and his own sunny little dream, the comforts of a folk society. He relates political events as well as the trivia of everyday life to such staggering absolutes as the end of the world, happiness to death, ambition to futility.

The essays and speeches here are dry, wry, self-deprecating. They brim over with humor. . . . Read all at once they may cloy, but sampled sparingly they provide as accurate a look at Vonnegut the man as can be found. But the only work of fiction in the collection, "Fortitude," reminds one of the double-edged satirical strength he achieves when he forgets about himself and recreates that enthusiastic intimacy with his own imagination that is not possible at the podium.

> Kathleen Cushman, "Vonnegut's Pithy Pencil Writes On. Pencil.," in The National Observer, June 29, 1974, p. 19.

JEAN E. KENNARD

[Almost] all the commentators on Vonnegut betray a certain uneasiness in talking about him as a satirist; he does not quite fit the mold. (p. 101)

Vonnegut's basic world view is Post-existential. He [rejects] all ethical absolutes. Vonnegut stresses the futility of man's search for meaning in a world where everything is "a nightmare of meaninglessness without end," where we are all the victims of a series of accidents, "trapped in the amber of this moment.... Because this moment simply is." In *Cat's Cradle* he shows how man's "nostalgia for unity," to use Camus' phrase, forces him to interpret mere chance as purposeful, leads him to create the meaning he wants to find and makes him believe in his own insubstantial structure, his own cat's cradle. Each of Vonnegut's novels shows us that there is no relation between human actions and the events that take place in human lives. All success—and, one supposes, failure—is the result of luck.... Man, like Billy Pilgrim in *Slaughterhouse-Five*, finds that among the things he cannot change are past, present and future. His actions serve no purpose he can hope to comprehend. Vonnegut also has his own version of [Jean-Paul] Sartre's theory of human identity. He talks about the desire of Being-For-Itself to become Being-In-Itself as the Universal Will to Become and claims that the moral of *Mother Night* is "We are what we pretend to be."

If Vonnegut denies the possibility of absolute values, then how can he be a satirist [since satire implies the existence of absolute values]? The answer is that he is not. He has the look of the satirist, but has no answer to give us. (pp. 102-03)

[He] employs the methods of satire as an attack upon satire itself, or rather upon the idea of a world in which the definite answers satire implies are possible. Vonnegut deliberately uses the expectations that satire arouses to tempt the reader into easy moral answers he subsequently undermines either by later attacking the acquired moral answer or by setting it in a Post-existential philosophic framework where no value is absolute....

Vonnegut frustrates the reader's expectations in order to bring about in him an experience of the absurd. He allows the reader the temporary illusion that he has the answer and then disillusions him. This is not just a question, as perhaps it is in the case of such other pessimistic satirists as Swift or [Samuel] Johnson, of not believing man likely to adopt the alternative to the vices under attack. Vonnegut does not merely disbelieve that man will become benevolent, ... but attacks the very idea of the workability of benevolence.

In his earlier novels, Vonnegut works chiefly against the expectations aroused by satire but more recently, particularly in his sixth novel, *Slaughterhouse-Five*, he has been making increasing use of those techniques of action, language, and characterization that work against the expectations of realism. (p. 103)

Vonnegut uses the form of the fable against the objectives of the fable. By suggesting, through obvious patterning of characters and contrasts between our own world and those of other planets, that he is arguing to a conclusion, he arouses our expectation for revelation. The pattern will work out; the final piece of the jigsaw puzzle will make the picture clear; the fable will reveal its moral. But Vonnegut's fables do not have morals, at least none which can stand as solutions to the Post-existential dilemma, just as his apparently satirical methods do not operate from any consistent ethical scheme. Again he is deliberately working to disillusion the reader.... [He] parodies himself; his novels gradually unmake themselves....

[The central figure of *Player Piano*, Paul Proteus] feels "love—particularly for the little people, the common people, God bless them. All his life they had been hidden from him by the walls of his ivory tower.... This was *real*, this side of the river, and Paul loved these common people, and wanted to help, and let them know they were loved and understood, and he wanted to them to love him too"....

If we accept, as most critics have, that this novel is a satire directed against technology, then the values expressed by Paul here are those Vonnegut expects us to accept also. But ... a careful reader would surely have to be suspicious of the tone of this passage. Vonnegut is too conscious of language to use such phrases as "the common people," "the little people," "ivory tower" "this was real," without recognizing them as clichés. He is giving us an easy answer —charity, fellow feeling, remorse—to the problems of mechanization and inhumanity, and is indicating that the answer is simplistic by his use of clichés.

Nevertheless, it is easy to miss these early clues, and the novel does for a long time seem to be a satire. Vonnegut's targets are standard ones: daytime soap operas designed to keep everyone satisfied with the status quo; the big business aspects of college football now no longer related to academic life at all; ambitious wives who feign affection. Each of these targets is attacked through the usual satirical method of slightly exaggerating a situation already present to a lesser extent in our society. Each of these targets also is an aspect of the apparently chief target of Vonnegut's novel, the mechanization of human lives. The great example of its opposite, human feeling and eccentricity, is Ed Finnerty, and Vonnegut sees to it that our sympathies lie with Finnerty and his friend Lasher throughout the novel. Who can resist the temptation to support man and human feeling against machines?

So far the novel is conventional. The methods are basically realistic, except for the use of a future world. Even the visitor from another country, the Shah of Bratpuhr, functions ... as a naive observer, not as he would in later Vonnegut novels as a creature with more knowledge from a totally different world. (p. 104)

But *Player Piano* does not end conventionally. The values established by the satirical methods at the beginning of the novel are finally completely undercut. This is not to deny, of course, that Vonnegut prefers human warmth to mechanization; but he does not, in his novel, appear to see it as a viable situation. Those representatives of human feeling against mechanization, Finnerty and Lasher, treat Paul as an object. "'You don't matter,' said Finnerty. 'You belong to History now'".... They are prepared to kill him if it is necessary. (p. 106)

In *Player Piano* the easy answers of [Vonnegut's] initial satirical attacks are not refuted by placing them in a Post-existential framework and there are only the earliest hints of absurd techniques. But nevertheless Vonnegut does use here the basic method of all his novels; he tempts the reader into easy answers through satirical methods and later disillusions him.

The subject of man as machine is fare more imaginatively treated in Vonnegut's second novel, his first attempt at science fiction, *The Sirens of Titan*. In this novel Vonnegut takes the old sophomoric debate about first cause—if God created the world, then who created God—and gives it some new turns. He is concerned with the absurdity of man's "appetite for the absolute," with his inescapable tendency to attribute meaning to his existence on earth. (pp. 106-07)

Religious belief, says Vonnegut, is based on no evidence at all. Rumfoord believes he knows the meaning of certain earthlings' lives, since they are part of his plan to establish the Church of God the Utterly Indifferent on earth by leading an attack from Mars. Malachi Constant, later Unk, is used by Rumfoord. What Rumfoord doesn't know is that he is part of a more complicated plan, the ultimate aim of which is to transport a replacement part for a space ship stranded on Titan. So the meaning of human life is reduced to an absurdity. (p. 107)

If human life has a pattern, a scheme, it is not a merciful one. . . . If the plan of the universe is not merciful, suggests Vonnegut, it might just as well not have one. Our religious fantasies of all truth being revealed to us in another world might well turn out to be the truth revealed to us through the other worlds of Vonnegut's novel. At all events there is no possible way of our finding the truth. Each man is doomed to his own subjective version of it. . . .

All events come about through luck, though like Malachi Constant we choose to believe that "somebody up there" likes us. (p. 108)

The Sirens of Titan invites us to read it as a satire just as *Player Piano* does. The many early targets of the book—posted bulletins about someone's health that reveal nothing; man's need to feel superior to his fellows by remembering his own achievements—suggest a satire operating from some base of consistent values. A favorite target is one that epitomizes the theme of the book: man's belief in image without substance. . . .

The major satirical method is a traditional one, to be found in [Swift's] *Gulliver's Travels,* for example; Vonnegut ridicules the target by making the abstract concrete. Thus the support religion has historically given to big business in the U.S.A. becomes in the novel the literal making of money by using initials from the first sentence of the Bible; the handicaps of life become actual weights carried around by some people to make the race of life fair. (p. 109)

There are some positive images of human experience in this novel. . . . Beatrice, Malachi, and their son, Chrono, together on Titan towards the end of the novel, can be seen as an illustration of the truth that Constant believes he has found; that one of the purposes of human life is to love "whoever is around to be loved." In this novel Vonnegut, . . . does appear to see human emotion as a value, even if a relative one. . . . [But] Vonnegut's picture of Constant is of

an old, lonely man accepting a comforting myth as the truth. Vonnegut, then, as in *Player Piano,* tempts the reader into accepting easy answers and then invalidates them. He also sets the assumed values in a Post-existential framework which makes them all relative. . . .

[In] Vonnegut's novels people are forced into new roles by others. The fact that people treat others as objects is illustrated by having the characters literally turn into machines —Malachi Constant becomes mechanized as Unk—much in the way Beckett's characters often do. In this way, of course, Vonnegut is working against the expectations of the reader for "human," rounded characters. He, then, undercuts his own method deliberately: Salo, a machine, is more humane than the earthlings. (p. 110)

The Sirens of Titan is the first Vonnegut novel to display an interest in the techniques of self-conscious art—in Vonnegut self-parody—that are so important in the later novels. His concern with the whole subject of the nature of fictional reality is revealed in the dedication: "All persons, places, and events in the book are real," reminding us of [Eugene] Ionesco's comment that fantasy is more real than realism. Throughout the novel Vonnegut draws our attention from what we are reading to the process of reading, by introducing other novels and stories which comment on the themes of his novel. (p. 112)

Superficially, at least, Vonnegut's third novel, *Mother Night,* is concerned with . . . the ways men use and destroy each other in the name of purpose. Given Vonnegut's concern with atrocities and his basic method of working against the expectations of the reader, it is not surprising that he should take as his subject the Nazis' treatment of the Jews. . . . [But in *Mother Night* an American is] about to be tried by Israel for broadcasting anti-Semitic speeches for Germany in World War II. As Campbell describes his postwar escape to New York and subsequent capture, the moral certainties become less clear. (pp. 112-13)

In *Mother Night* Vonnegut is primarily interested in two concepts. The first is the impossibility of absolute truth. We can only have absolute answers by blocking our minds to some obvious facts: "The dismaying thing about the classic totalitarian mind is that any given gear, though mutilated, will have at its circumference unbroken sequences of teeth that are immaculately maintained. . . . The missing teeth, of course, are simple, obvious truths". . . . All absolutes lead inevitably to tyranny. . . . There are no absolute reasons for action as Campbell discovers when he finds himself paralyzed, . . . because he has "absolutely no reason to move in any direction". (p. 113)

The second concept is Sartre's theory of human identity: "We are what we pretend to be." We cannot pretend to be evil, as Campbell does, and remain good secretly. We can choose our roles, but we are what we choose. Man, Vonnegut shows, has an infinite capacity for living in bad faith. Campbell can sustain a lovenest—a "nation of two"—while he helps destroy thousands. Stalin can love a romantic play about the Holy Grail and yet be Stalin. This play, one of Campbell's, functions as a comment on the novel itself for, in spite of its romantic treatment, its subject is the tyranny of Christianity, which, like the absolutes in *Mother Night,* has destroyed human lives.

The basic technique of *Mother Night* is that of *Player Piano:* to play against our preconceived attitudes and the expectations which the initial satirical attacks have aroused in us.... All absolutes, all preconceived notions, are undercut in this novel. The reader is left, as Campbell is, without any values to cling to....

Cat's Cradle is perhaps Vonnegut's most successful novel. The use of the methods of satire to attack satire is at its sharpest; the techniques of science fiction are turned upon science itself. But the novel works primarily because of the quality of the two central images, ice-nine and cat's cradle, and because of a fundamental irony underlying Vonnegut's conception of the narrator. (p. 114)

[The] using of clichés in new ways, which Vonnegut has occasionally employed before, becomes a major technique in the novel. He takes this cliché, reverses the traditionally benign associations of it, and shows how our inheritance from the past is not necessarily benign at all. Evil, cold like ice, spreads like water and is inevitably passed, like the ice-nine, from one generation to the next. (pp. 114-15)

Throughout the early scenes of the novel there is much ironic juxtaposing of Christianity with inhuman technology. Christmas Eve is the night Angela Hoenikker divides up the ice-nine among the children. We are tempted into believing Vonnegut offers Christian compassion as the answer. Yet Christianity is associated with destruction too.... Perhaps, then, if capitalistic Christianity is no answer, communism is? Vonnegut undercuts that solution also. (p. 115)

There can be no absolute solution, of course, because there is no meaning to human existence. The second important image of the novel is the image of the child's game cat's cradle.... Cat's cradle is a structure without substance or the meaning ascribed to it. Cat's cradle is a concrete example of the religious and philosophic structures man seems driven to build to explain his existence.

The Post-existentialist world view of *Cat's Cradle* is that of *The Sirens of Titan*. Vonnegut has invented a religion called Bokononism, which most critics have described as Existentialism and take as Vonnegut's own philosophy. Certainly Bokononism recognizes that life has no purpose.... It is equally true that "Man got to tell himself he understand" ... Bokonon recognizes that even his own cosmogony is a "pack of foma," all lies. Here, surely, is the point.... The narrator ... calls himself a Bokononist, just as he used to call himself a Christian, and thus is in the ironic position of believing in lies as his truth. Of course, Vonnegut claims, so are we all. (p. 116)

The action is full of [such] absurd coincidences as Jonah's chance meeting with Marvin Breed just after leaving his brother Asa, and the discovery of a pedestal on which his own name is engraved. There is little causal relation between the scenes; each is a short anecdote, often complete in itself. In many of these anecdotes action is exaggerated to the point of absurdity, ... (p. 117)

[*Slaughterhouse-Five*] comes to terms with the question that has in one way or another been central to all his novels: What is the significance of human suffering? Is it possible for human beings to be other than cruel to one another in an Existentialist world.... For Vonnegut the firebombing of Dresden ... is the ultimate symbol of purposeless human cruelty.... How, asks Vonnegut, can the knowledge of such suffering, the memory of it, be made bearable? Can anything make sense of it? (p. 122)

Vonnegut dramatizes for the reader that whatever scheme one may devise to handle the idea of death, nothing can minimize the fact of it. "So it goes" comes at us with increasing momentum....

One of the effects of the "so it goes" on the reader is the effect produced by the disjunction of tone and subject. We expect death to be treated with more apparent concern. (p. 123)

Vonnegut constantly moves the reader between real life and fiction, mentioning the Kennedys, Martin Luther King, Harry Truman.... [There] are numerous references also to characters from his own earlier novels.... In this way he reminds us of the fictional nature of all experience. (p. 124)

More or less everything, he announces at the beginning of the novel, is true, not just metaphorically true, but actually true. Billy Pilgrim's attempt to come to terms with the horrors of Dresden is Vonnegut's own attempt. Billy Pilgrim creates an imaginary world, Tralfamadore; Vonnegut creates an imaginary world, *Slaughterhouse-Five*. In fiction, of course, as on Tralfamadore, all time is eternal, the past can be recaptured, the dead returned to life. Art is apparently a way of dealing with death, but the novelist of number is not Zeus and must ultimately fail. (pp. 124-25)

[For] all its Post-existential world view, [*Breakfast of Champions*] appears to argue that there are ways of living with the absurd dilemma: "It is hard to adapt to chaos, but it can be done".... [We] may be able to improve the human situation. (p. 125)

[This] is a world of interdependent people; we have the power to be each other's saviour rather than his slavemaster, but we are unaware of that fact, Vonnegut seems to be arguing.

The solution, apparently, is to set each other free. What is valuable ... is the core of awareness in each one of us, an awareness which appears to be identical with Sartre's concept of Being-for-itself.... It is not enough to adopt the Kilgore Trout view, perhaps intended to represent Vonnegut's in his earlier novels, that everyone is a machine except oneself. (p. 126)

It seems to me, though, that Vonnegut, here as in all the other novels, undercuts this proposed solution which may remain an ideal but is seen in the novel as unworkable. Vonnegut decides to give Trout and all his other characters their freedom.... But Trout becomes once again Vonnegut's father, the man upon whom the character was modelled, and what he wants is not freedom but further control from his creator; "Here was what Kilgore Trout cried out to me in my father's voice: 'Make me young, make me young, make me young!'"....

Has Vonnegut become an optimist? Hardly. Even if one does not read the ending of *Breakfast of Champions* as ironic, recognition of each other's value is not a solution to the Post-existential dilemma; it is at best ... a way of making bearable the absurdity of the human condition. Vonnegut is ultimately a pessimist. (pp. 126-27)

Jean E. Kennard, "Kurt Vonnegut, Jr.: The Sirens of Satire," in her Number and Nightmare: Forms of Fantasy in Contemporary Fiction *(© 1975 by Jean E. Kennard), Archon Books, Hamden, Connecticut, 1975, pp. 101-28.*

STANLEY SCHATT

The thrust of Vonnegut's fiction has moved from detached, ironic observation to impassioned participation. His early works, *Player Piano* and *The Sirens of Titan*, were concerned with the external environment—the dangers of technology and the glorification of the machine. He also evinced a marked concern with the relationship between destiny and fate, but the detached tone of his novels made it difficult to penetrate the layers of ambivalence. In *Mother Night*, Vonnegut began to concern himself more with the internal state of consciousness and with the problem of schizophrenia, as well as with the epistomological question of what can be perceived as real and what is simply illusory. *Cat's Cradle* and *God Bless You, Mr. Rosewater* express Vonnegut's feelings about institutionalized religion, about the destructive nature of a social system that values money much more highly than love, and about the loneliness of the thousands of unloved that Eliot Rosewater wants to help but cannot without destroying himself. In *Slaughterhouse-Five* and in *Breakfast of Champions*, Vonnegut began to speak much more confidently with his own voice about himself and his views of society; and he culminated *Breakfast of Champions* by cutting his ties to Kilgore Trout, his erstwhile spokesman. Perhaps Vonnegut had outgrown his idealistic and very naïve *alter ego*.

Explicit in both *Breakfast of Champions* and *Slapstick* is Vonnegut's search for a philosophy of life that would explain its cruelties and injustices—for some code that would make life meaningful and understandable.... With the possible exception of Kilgore Trout, none of Vonnegut's characters are successful; in fact, the effort to create a harmonious world destroys Paul Proteus (*Player Piano*) and Howard W. Campbell, Jr. (*Mother Night*); and the attempt drives Bokonon (*Cat's Cradle*) and Eliot Rosewater (*God Bless You, Mr. Rosewater*) insane.

While Vonnegut's protagonists strive to create an harmonious world filled with love, the price they pay is their loss of any personal happiness and their abrogation of any love relationship with their spouses.... [The] choice of Vonnegut's fictional characters is always the greater good for all humanity rather than personal happiness.

Inevitably, despite the best efforts of Vonnegut protagonists who "bargain in good faith with their destinies," the world is destroyed or is so unpleasant that destruction would be a relief. Usually lurking behind the destruction is Vonnegut's favorite target—unbridled technology that is divorced from any concern for Humanistic values. (p. 114-16)

The strong eschatological thread that runs through all of Vonnegut's fiction seems to be linked closely to his continued preoccupation over the question of man's ability to control his own destiny. Skeptical of institutionalized religion, Vonnegut has long pondered whether life has any intrinsic meaning or is simply haphazard. This question is the more fundamental one behind Vonnegut's consideration of the fire-bombing of Dresden in *Slaughterhouse-Five*, of the lack of American culture in *Breakfast of Champions*, and of the loss of his sister in *Slapstick*. The autobiography he writes in *Slapstick* is simply his acceptance of the impossibility of ever discovering life's inherent meaning and his realization that the key to humanity's survival and happiness is its embrace of life with the good natured ear-

nestness and sincerity of Laurel and Hardy. In cinematic terms such as those Vonnegut uses in *Slapstick*, man is part of a Laurel and Hardy comedy and is not detached enough to see the entire film; he can only play one scene at a time, bargain good naturedly with his destiny, and be aware that he is not good at life and will often fail. (pp. 116-17)

Stanley Schatt, in his Kurt Vonnegut, Jr. *(copyright © 1976 by G. K. Hall & Co.; reprinted with the permission of Twayne Publishers, A Division of G. K. Hall & Co., Boston), Twayne, 1976.*

JOHN W. TILTON

Vonnegut has taken great care to date precisely various incidents and stages in the life of Billy Pilgrim [in *Slaughterhouse-Five*] and just as much care to date the appearances and intrusions of the narrator, who insists on at least a partial identification with Billy and becomes himself a character in the novel. Ultimately this observation leads to the realization that imbedded in the telegraphic, schizophrenic manner of the tale is a considerably detailed biography of Billy Pilgrim and that time-travel, together with the other science-fiction components of the novel, is a brilliant psychological technique devised by Vonnegut to interpret the life and philosophy of his created character. (p. 71)

Perhaps I attach too much importance to Vonnegut's biographical accuracy, but I have reason to believe that one's comprehension of the meaning and the aesthetic form of the novel may depend to a great extent on the isolation of Billy's biography.

The biographical path will lead, for example, to three corresponding points of time in the lives of Billy and the narrator that must be characterized as deliberate juxtapositions of salient events, functioning as elements of a conscious structural pattern of the novel, designed to signal the distance between the created character Billy and his creator Vonnegut and to alert readers to Vonnegut's critical but—as shall be seen—sympathetic and compassionate evaluation of Billy's response to the cruelty of life.

The first point of time is 1964. In that year Billy was *forced* to remember Dresden; he was not even aware of his inability to remember, so deeply in his subconscious had he buried a memory of Dresden. Vonnegut, too, was unable to remember, but he was aware of that inability and actively sought to overcome it. In 1964, Kurt Vonnegut visited his war buddy Bernard V. O'Hare for the *express purpose of recalling* Dresden. (pp. 71-2)

In 1967, the second point of time, Vonnegut's attempt to remember Dresden actually took him back to that city, whereas in 1967 Billy was kidnapped by a flying saucer and taken to Tralfamadore, "he says." More precisely, he escaped to a "planet" created in his own imagination in order to avoid his human responsibilities as surely as Vonnegut, together with O'Hare, in 1967 traveled on his real planet Earth to Dresden in an act of human responsibility. (p. 72)

The year 1968 is the climactic year: it brings the biography of Billy to its last moment in the narrative present (beyond 1968 there is only Billy's vision of his death in 1976), and it brings Vonnegut to the present moment of writing *Slaughterhouse-Five*.... The import of the juxtaposition of the creative acts engaged in by Vonnegut and Billy Pilgrim in 1968 seems clear: Vonnegut is writing a novel that rejects the Tralfamadorian philosophy while Billy is actively disseminating that philosophy, first preaching it orally on the all-night radio program and then by writing letters to the Ilium *News Leader*. The chronological correspondence works out with highly suggestive accuracy. (p. 73)

Billy's total incapacity to understand the significance of the death of human beings clearly distances him from Vonnegut. In effect, Vonnegut says in answer to Barbara's question—"Father, Father, Father—what *are* we going to *do* with you?" . . . that nothing *can* be done with Billy. (p. 74)

The reasons why Billy Pilgrim withdraws from humanity are clearly implicit in his isolable biography. In it, one can trace his indoctrination to the cruelty of the world and discover that his withdrawal from humanity was virtually complete well *before* Billy witnessed the firebombing of Dresden. As emotionally wounding as the Dresden holocaust may have been to Billy, it served largely to confirm a conception of life and death already a part of his being. . . . He had been "alarmed by the outside world" nearly since birth. . . . (pp. 74-5)

Though in the narrative sequence Billy's—and the doctors'—belief that he is going crazy does not surface until 1948, even at the age of twelve, in 1934, Billy had undergone the real crises of his life, had found life meaningless even if he could not then articulate that concept, and was in desperate need of reinventing himself and his universe. Vonnegut's biographical exposition of Billy's formative years implies that Billy was at twelve already well on his way to Tralfamadore. Here is the true time-travel of the novel: a linear, chronological development clearly based on a cause-and-effect relationship. The child is indeed the father of the man who searches for a prelapsarian Eden. And readers are in the presence, not of science fiction, but of profound satirical fiction probing the condition of modern man.

A brief examination of the implications of Billy's formative years shows that although Vonnegut is intensely concerned about World War II and the Vietnamese War, the novel transcends any specific events of our time. Vonnegut's ultimate concern is to question the origin and the viability of the myths man lives by and finally to reject any new lie that deprives man of his dignity and his life of significance. In this sense, *Slaughterhouse-Five* is a profoundly religious novel. (p. 76)

> *John W. Tilton, "'Slaughterhouse-Five': Life against Death-in-Life," in his* Cosmic Satire in the Contemporary Novel *(© 1977 by Associated University Presses, Inc.), Bucknell University Press, 1977, pp. 69-103.*

JAMES LUNDQUIST

There is a mystical, perhaps unnerving appeal in the way Vonnegut artistically maintains the clement aloofness that strangely accounts for much of his contemporaneity; but behind it all, behind the fantasy and the anti-establishmentarianism, is a deceptive fondness for the uncomplicated that enchants some readers, repels others, and seems downright anti-intellectual or, worse, silly to his least sympathetic critics. Which of the three reactions is most valid is a matter of taste or tastelessness (depending on how you look at it); but how Vonnegut, a distinctly bourgeois writer who has more in common with Sinclair Lewis than with

Hermann Hesse, came to achieve his present reputation and whether his artistry will sustain it is another matter. (p. 1)

Vonnegut's emphasis on the need for self-respect and his belief in the necessity of pacifism point to traits of character that are, one may argue, very much midwestern. Vonnegut's work can be read almost as if it is designed to illustrate attitudes that John T. Flanagan . . . sees as particularly midwestern: "individualism, self-reliance, a practical materialism, skepticism of custom and tradition unless rooted in common sense, political intransigence, and isolationism explained and heretofore justified by the geographical barriers and almost antagonistic apathy of the Old World."

Even Vonnegut's obsession with science-fiction techniques can be understood in terms of his regional background. "Vonnegut's fondness for vistors from other worlds is the drollest expression yet of the midwestern feeling that the Midwest *is* the Earth and that all other people are different," Alfred Kazin writes. "All that has changed since the West was the country of innocence is Vonnegut's feeling that innocence is dangerous." Vonnegut shares this feeling with Mark Twain, Sherwood Anderson, Sinclair Lewis, and other midwestern writers; but given Vonnegut's sense of imminent apocalypse, the feeling is expressed with much more urgency and is more to the point than ever.

Vonnegut returns to the midwest again and again for characters and settings. The novelist Dan Wakefield (*Going All Way*), who also hails from Vonnegut country, points out that in each of Vonnegut's books there is at least one character from Indianapolis and compares this to Alfred Hitchcock's practice of making a walk-on appearance in each of his movies. Vonnegut can even be seen as a literary embodiment of the midwesterner in the updated tradition of the vernacular storyteller. . . . (pp. 3-4)

This is an appealing approach and it may be a good reason for the success Vonnegut has had with a contemporary reading audience that uneasily accepts alienation as a fact of life. Even though the stability, the security, and the optimism associated with middle-class, midwestern attitudes are no longer to be found in Indianapolis or anywhere else, Vonnegut remains something of a homesick writer. In all of his attacks on pornography, pollution, war, and whatever other evils he chooses to name, there is an inescapable longing for an earlier, simpler time, for the midwest of his boyhood. . . . (p. 4)

[Vonnegut is] a transitional figure in a time when the antiegalitarian values of such earlier figures as T. S. Eliot, who believed that culture is the property of the tiny remnant that can appreciate highly abstruse and allusive symbolic forms of art, are being left behind. Pop, which has been seen as a vice of the populace, is now regarded as a fantastic and fantastically valuable storehouse of dreams, longings, and ancient myths retooled. What Vonnegut as a pop novelist does, in part, is what he himself attributes to Hunter S. Thompson: "He makes exciting, moving collages of carefully selected junk. They must be experienced. They can't be paraphrased." . . .

In just about every conceivable way Vonnegut's novels are what only can be termed "naïve" literature because he makes so much use of expected associations and conventions for the purpose of rapid communication with its readers. And what sets other writers apart from popular audiences is the very thing that Vonnegut seems to lack—sophistication. His manner suggests to his readers that he is not looking down on them, that he may even be right there, where they are and where it's at. (p. 10)

Vonnegut's revelations are often accomplished through the use of fables, another of the naïve forms he likes to work in. His stories always have morals, and they work to expose sins and folly.

Vonnegut uses another, perhaps more complex, association or convention—the structural discontinuity that appeals to the imagination of an audience accustomed to the montage of television. This is part of Vonnegut's fragmented idiom, which in itself suggests contemporary experience. The way Vonnegut times the talk of his characters, along with his short chapters, his sharp images, and his quick scenes—all of this makes reading his fiction a formal approximation of the experience of watching television.

But Vonnegut's popularity should not be interpreted only as a consequence of the modish appeal of his fiction or because his books make use of so many of the devices employed by the electronic media. Vonnegut's willingness to speak directly to his audience must have something to do with it. . . . (p. 11)

In a sense, all of Vonnegut's novels are *Welcome* books, full of attitudes and instructions on handling those attitudes that are useful if one is to avoid falling off the planet, or if one wishes to keep the planet here, wherever it is.

It is a mistake, however, to conceive of Vonnegut's significance entirely in terms of his popular success. Not only does he deal with concerns that are important to all of us, but he develops many ideas in startlingly refreshing ways. One surprising consideration is that Vonnegut a thoroughly middle-class writer who is, in some of his work at least, an apologist for the very kind of life he seems to be attacking. Vonnegut writes from a vantage point that is consistently middle class, and in his novels there is the suggestion, repeated many times, that the most unhappy people are those who do not have the blessings of middle-class life—a point that Vonnegut often expresses with considerable sentimentality. (p. 12)

Vonnegut's sentimentality is, of course, behind most of his social pronouncements and his remedy for the American experience, an experience he interprets as generally an unhappy one. One reason he sees for the unhappiness is that Americans suffer from living without a culture. In his view, American society is a lonesome one. He senses a longing for community, a longing that is frustrated by the shifting from house to house and from town to town that the economic system requires of so many Americans. . . . Vonnegut would also prefer that people live in "primitive" communities, folk societies, which he seems to think of in terms of small towns or of neighborhoods within cities (again the middle-class, midwestern vision of tree-shaded streets and old, comfortable homes).

Consideration of such economic and social pronouncements might have no place in a study of Vonnegut's achievement as a writer if it were not for his often stated opinion (which he wryly says is in agreement with that of Stalin, Hitler, and Mussolini) that a writer should serve society and that his own motives, at least, are political.

"Writers are a means of introducing new ideas into society," Vonnegut emphasizes, "and also a means of responding symbolically to life." His notion of what a writer should do is in conflict, however, with his assumption (perhaps another middle-class suspicion) that writers of fiction are simply not important and most certainly are not listened to by the government. (pp. 13-14)

The purpose of writing and of all the arts is to provide . . . myths of "frauds," as Vonnegut terms them, which make man seem wonderful and important even if we all know that in the long run he is not. . . . So, even though each of Vonnegut's novels shows that man in general is contemptible, Vonnegut always has a hero who denies that contemptibility through his ability to come up with or live through a myth that is usually redemptive, somehow.

There is, however, another way Vonnegut views the usefulness of the arts. In his address to the American Physical Society in 1969, he said that in teaching writing, he has come up with what he calls the "canary-in-the-coal-mine theory of the arts." His explanation is "that artists are useful to society because they are so sensitive. . . . They keel over like canaries in coal mines filled with poison gas, long before more robust types realize that any danger is there." His application of this theory is evident in all of his novels, each of which is a cry of danger, from *Player Piano* with its warning about computerization, to *Breakfast of Champions* with its warning about the consequences of failing to understand the chemical causes of schizophrenia. (pp. 14-15)

Time travel, visits by creatures from other planets, flying saucers, glimpses into a nightmare future—these and other science-fiction motifs are employed by Vonnegut to make the reader more aware of the absurdity of man's place in the universe. Vonnegut uses science fiction as a means of transmitting his vision, a vision that, because of its cosmically ironic implications, demands the intergalactic scope that science fiction affords. Given Vonnegut's attitudes toward his characters, if there were no such form as science fiction, he would be forced to invent it. . . .

[Science fiction] also serves as a mitigating element in Vonnegut's fiction as well as a means of carrying off many of the jokes that run through and structure his novels. . . .

[Vonnegut] uses science fiction not only as a way of carrying his ideas but as a way of making those ideas more palatable. If it were not for the science-fiction elements, Vonnegut would often be very unfunny indeed. (p. 86)

But, as even his first novel demonstrates, Vonnegut refuses to be limited by either the form of science fiction or its conventions. He shows from the start in *Player Piano* that he differs from most science-fiction writers in his characterization. Even though Vonnegut tends toward cartoonlike characters in his novels, purposely avoiding full development on principle, he nonetheless begins with a character, Paul Proteus, rather than an idea. Science may provide the conflict, but the resolution comes through character.

Most of Vonnegut's fiction concerns itself with technological problems but only insofar as those problems relate to and explicate character, with the point usually being that no matter what technology surrounds them, men and women remain essentially the same. *Player Piano* despite its EPICAC XIV computer and its checker-playing machine, comes down in the end to an ironic story about a disappointed middle-class revolutionist. . . . (p. 94)

The Trout novels retold in *Breakfast of Champions* are remarkably similar to Vonnegut's own in their resolutions and in their tendency to avoid any actual technical explanation of the strange futuristic technologies they rely upon. A good example is the story of Delmore Skag, who, as a way of protesting against the wastefulness and absurdity of large families, invents a means of reproducing replicas of himself by shaving living cells from the palm of his right hand and culturing them in chicken soup. He then invites his neighbors, all of whom have large families, to mass baptisms—sometimes as many as a hundred of his "babies" at once. But instead of passing a law outlawing families of more than one or two children, the government enacts legislation prohibiting the possession of chicken soup by an unmarried person. And the cosmically ironic joke is on Delmore Skag, a joke that goes along with one of Vonnegut's main themes—the destruction of the planet through the insane response human beings seem to make to any idea. (p. 97)

In one novel, *Cat's Cradle*, however, Vonnegut plays things straighter, especially with the substance that engenders the final catastrophe—*ice-nine*. Vonnegut generally makes no attempt to explain or make plausible the scientific wonders that occur in his futuristic worlds, and there admittedly is not much "science" in his fiction. But with *ice-nine*, at any rate, Vonnegut provides a technical lecture that makes *Cat's Cradle* read at times more like hard-core science fiction than any of Vonnegut's other novels. . . . The result is a suggestion of authentic science that makes the apocalyptic ending of the novel horrifying, despite Vonnegut's comic implications. (p. 98)

What Vonnegut is doing as he moves half mystically, half laughingly, in and out of science fiction is to try to come up with a definition of himself and others that will "stand in the terrifying light of twentieth-century knowledge." When he is writing simply as a science-fiction writer in the stories he published in *Galaxy* ("Unready to Wear" and "The Big Trip Up Yonder") or in the *Magazine of Fantasy and Science Fiction* ("Harrison Bergeron"), he does not move very far toward that definition. But when he combines the special effects of science fiction with extended cosmic irony in his novels, he transforms one of the most important forms of pop culture into his own distinctive form of astral jokebook. (p. 100)

> *James Lundquist, in his* Kurt Vonnegut *(copyright © 1977 by Frederick Ungar Publishing Co., Inc.), Frederick Ungar, 1977.*

CLARK MAYO

[Kurt Vonnegut, Jr.] is a Cosmic Fool, a clown who laughs at the world's failings and sorrows (and tries to tease, cajole and seduce us into laughing at them, too), rather than be overwhelmed by them (though sometimes it is touch and go). His satirical commentaries on business, war, politics, machine technology, organized religion, and organizations in general expose the foibles and inhumanities of a society of which he is always highly critical. Yet his satire and cosmic pessimism are paradoxically countered by his humor, gentleness and kindness, as well as his comic energy and individual optimism. (p. 3)

Faced with a world defined by Emersonian or Jungian polarities (what he calls in *Cat's Cradle* "Dynamic Tension,"

or Bokonon's "sense of a priceless equilibrium between good and evil" [one could add to his list nature and history, freedom and determinism, love and indifference, individuality and conformity, reality and illusion, and literature and life], Vonnegut consciously chooses a stance of naivety and wonder—the "child-like"—as well as sentiment and self-pity—the "childish." In many ways, he is sensitive and profound; in others, he remains a blurb-writer, still doing public relations work, but now for himself.

Vonnegut establishes throughout his writings a point of view intended to be outside our own moment in time and space. . . . This point of view—usually "a visitor from another planet"—is concerned fundamentally with problems of value: self-awareness, self-realization, self-fulfillment; the nature and destiny of man. On a primary level, Vonnegut's search for the sacred in human experience involves the attempt, as the narrator says in *Slaughterhouse-Five*, "to reinvent himself and his universe in his novel." Or, as Billy Pilgrim hears Eliot Rosewater say to a psychiatrist: "I think you guys are going to have to come up with a lot of wonderful *new* lies, or people just aren't going to want to go on living." These "new lies" (or Bokononist *foma*) and the reinvented selves are the moral centers of Vonnegut's fiction. (p. 4)

[What] makes a worthwhile life in a meaningless, arbitrary, contingent universe? Each of Vonnegut's works embodies in its characters a response to this predicament. . . . (pp. 4-5)

Vonnegut's other major themes, the nature of truth, the paradoxical contrast between illusion and reality, and the nature of man, all come together in his sense of the need for the creation of a reinvented universe (a "secondary universe" in fantasy terms), a perspective from which we may examine our primary universes and perhaps change them. His tactics include irony, paradox, and satirical humor, sometimes coupled with a didactic and sentimental tone, to delineate his own created universes. At one level, Vonnegut is a failed Romanticist who sees "no hope" in a world which does not care either for or about man. . . . (p. 5)

[*Player Piano*] is a satire of modern society, relationships, religion, and politics. . . . Some critics have argued that it is Vonnegut's finest novel, and even that it is the best work of modern science fiction. Others have argued that it is his poorest, and not science fiction at all. One of the reasons for this wide variance in opinion is Vonnegut's characterization: the characters who people this novel (and indeed all his novels) seem to many critics flat and stereotypic, to lack depth in their feeling and thinking, to fail to meet a prime criterion for fiction: making us *care* deeply about them. But this misses the point, for Vonnegut's characters are closer relatives to the figures in G. B. Trudeau's "Doonesbury" than they are to most of the characters in modern American fiction. They embody and reflect the ideas and values which come under close scrutiny in Vonnegut's work; they do not come into any "full life" of their own. (p. 9)

Vonnegut's satire . . . focuses on one of his consistent themes: the failure of love to provide a secure center for human relationships in the modern world. Paul makes a "dark muffled womb" of his bed every night, and his "barren" wife Anita (who would fit in rather easily with the Stepford wives) has social rather than sexual orgasms.

Their ritual love-refrain ("I love you, Paul." "I love *you*, Anita.") is repeated in one form or another eleven times in the novel, and along with Paul's "Hi ho," is the first of the refrains which become consistent thematic punctuations in Vonnegut's work. Yet Paul, in a pathetic yet poignant scene typical of Vonnegut (and reminiscent of Isaac Mc-Caslin's thoughts about his own wife in Faulkner's *The Bear*), thinks that Anita "was what fate had given him to love, and he did his best to love her." This problem with love, and its failure as a redeeming force in life, is reflected in much of Vonnegut's work, and becomes the center of [*Slapstick*]. . . . (p.11)

[*Player Piano's*] cast of characters is varied and impressive, and although they tend to be brittle, fallible, fragile, and weak, "losers" more than "winners," they inspire both irony and pity, Vonnegut's as well as the reader's. (pp. 11-12)

The Shah provides for us a point of view and perspective from outside the limited world and experience of the novel's cultural framework (and our own, Vonnegut suggests). (p. 13)

What the Shah never sees is Paul's personal world, and this lack of interaction or confrontation is one of the novel's weaknesses. For Paul is finally insubstantial, a "wraith" who is "little more than his station in life. . . ." [He] remains a figurative as well as literal prisoner at the novel's end. Like Malachi Constant in *The Sirens of Titan*, Paul is a manipulated messiah figure who inadvertently satirizes not only the Protestant work-ethic, but also the forms of old religions and the failures of new religions (like the Ghost Shirt Society) to replace them. (p. 14)

The central question of the novel concerns the nature and destiny of man. . . . Paul, on trial for sabotage (the greatest sin against a technocracy, states that "The main business of humanity is to do a good job of being human beings . . . not to serve as appendages to machines, institutions, and systems." Yet it is not always clear in the novel just what "doing a good job of being human beings" means. Indeed, Vonnegut struggles with this question throughout his work. (pp. 14-15)

Of all the characters in [*The Sirens of Titan*], it is Rumfoord who is the most intriguing. On one hand, he is described by the narrator in terms which would do justice to a Hemingway "code character": he has "un-neurotic courage," "style" . . . , and "gallantry." Yet he loves fraud, endlessly manipulating the other characters. . . . (p. 19)

The image of man in this novel is thus close to what e. e. cummings has called 'mostpeople." People are described as "whores for money, alcoholics, cynics, and scummy idiots who dream of greener pastures without being willing to work for them." Yet, in Rumfoord's eyes, man remains laughingly optimistic, expecting the species to last for millions of years. It is this laughter, along with memory, which is one of the few measures of man's freedom. (p. 20)

In many ways the characters in *The Sirens of Titan* have their parallels with the characters in *Player Piano*. There are: the central character who somewhat simple-mindedly struggles to make sense of his world, and in the process becomes more aware and more human, though still manipulated and used (Malachi and Paul); the observer from "outer space" who sees the action more clearly and hon-

estly than those who are involved in it (Salo and the Shah); the perceptive participant who tries to create a new religion to solve man's problems (Rumfoord and Lasher); and the plastic-hostess female figure who only at brief moments shows any humanity (Bee and Anita).

Both novels focus on the question of the meaning of life. (p. 22)

Love and kindness may be illusion and not reality, as are the Sirens of Titan (Malachi learns on Titan that they are not real women, but only statues made by Salo of Titanic peat); yet that may be all there is. As Woody Allen says to the psychiatrist who tells him to hospitalize his brother who thinks he is a chicken: "I can't; I need the eggs." The same is true, he says, of human relationships: we don't give them up, because we need the eggs. Perhaps the moral of *The Sirens of Titan* finally is: abandon expectations, live fully in the present moment, and love whoever is around to be loved. (pp. 22-3)

[At several levels *Mother Night*] is about pretending, duplicity, illusion, and multiple roles. . . . Campbell is in several ironic ways as much Nazi as pseudo-Nazi. He says that like Mata Hari—to whom he dedicated his book—he "whored in the interest of espionage"; but Wirtanen points out that historians would consider him *really* a Nazi, and asks what would have happened if Germany had won the war. Campbell's response is that he probably would have become a "Nazi Edgar Guest." Vonnegut extends the moral in his editor's note by quoting from a chapter Campbell later rejected, in which he dedicated the novel to "one familiar person, male or female, widely known to have done evil while saying to himself, 'a very good me, the real me, a me made in Heaven, is hidden deep inside,'" and rededicates the novel to himself, as a "man who served evil too openly and good too secretly, the crime of his times." Clearly, the moral is meant to apply to the reader as well as to Campbell. (pp. 24-5)

Mother Night might be subtitled "A Portrait of the Artist as Liar." It is a novel of escapes from reality, in which (like *Player Piano*) history overcomes art, love, and politics. Campbell, as playwright-artist, hides from reality in a world of the imagination, and sees the world—rather than himself—as diseased. (p. 26)

Though *Cat's Cradle* is in many ways an antidote to *Mother Night*, countering its view of lies as corrupting and destructive with a vision of lies as nurturing and sustaining, its fundamental focus is literature as game. In this novel Vonnegut is closer to [Vladimir] Nabokov, [Jorge Luis] Borges, [John] Fowles, and [John] Barth than he has been in his earlier works. The reader is more aware of being *played with* than he is of being instructed or amused, though Vonnegut continues to satirize science, religion, politics, sex, man's understanding, nationalism, and love. (p. 28)

Once again, man in Vonnegut's cosmos is obsessed with the search for meaning and purpose. . . . And once again, understanding is the booby-prize; man must accept what is, and not separate himself from his experience by constantly trying to analyze its meaning. (p. 31)

God Bless You, Mr. Rosewater deals with the confusions of money, power and love in a "Free Enterprise System." (p. 37)

But *God Bless You, Mr. Rosewater* is as much about love and integrity as it is about money and power. The only character with real integrity in the novel besides Kilgore Trout (the others either lack it or are searching for it) is the Hemingway-type caricature of Mr. Natural, Harry Pena. . . . (p. 40)

Eliot and his father argue periodically throughout the novel about the nature of love. . . . [The] point to Eliot, and to Kilgore Trout, is that "people can use all the uncritical love they can get." As Trout says, what Eliot wants is "treasuring human beings because they are *human beings*." This contrast in views on love is similar to that of John and Mona in *Cat's Cradle*. And what Eliot has learned is similar to what Howard Campbell learns in *Mother Night*, that people need uncritical love, love without judgment, love which accepts people just the way they are, and just the way they are not. (p. 41)

[*Happy Birthday, Wanda Jane*] deals fundamentally with death, the acceptance of death as a part of the natural order, and the place of women in the modern world. . . . However, the central conflict in the play is between those who enjoy killing, and those who don't, a conflict which is never clearly resolved, at least in part because once again Vonnegut has no real villains. The play is also about the need for rituals in society . . . male chauvinism . . . , and the human need for dignity and patience. . . . [His] plays are certainly less successful than the novels, due fundamentally to a lack of depth of motivation in the characters, and no clearly defined points of view. . . .

[*Slaughterhouse-Five*] focuses particularly on the horror and absurdity of war, man's helplessness in an absurd universe, the fact that life (and death) simply is what it is, and how man can deal with these realities: by inventing "wonderful new lies." It presents these ideas, however, in a style which is continuing to develop, and which is moving significantly closer to the form which might be called the Gestalt Novel, the form of *Breakfast of Champions* and *Slapstick*. (p. 45)

Beginning with *Slaughterhouse-Five*, Vonnegut is not only a character in his novels, but also, in dramatic terms, the producer and director as well. His authorial intrusions provide the framework for the entire novel (as the beginning and end of the actual novel, rather than as introduction and afterword), and also punctuate the work throughout, reminding us that Vonnegut as "author" and Vonnegut as "narrator" are not necessarily the same. (pp. 45-6)

There is no beginning, middle or end to the novel—not in terms of chronological time-scheme nor of plot development. There is also no suspense (we as readers, as well as Billy Pilgrim, learn quite early how and when he will "die"), and none of the cause and effect relationships of realistic fiction; the book simply reinforces the Tralfamadorian and Bokononist views that what is, is. In fact, the Tralfamadorians frequently tell Billy that men are "machines" and "bugs in amber," and that Earthlings are the universe's "great explainers," who keep needing to create artificial answers to the question "why?" rather than accept the irrelevance of the question. The disjointed time-scheme and short chapter form also create a clump of images, if not symbols, which come together in the mind of the reader as a montage which *does* often "produce an image of life that is beautiful and surprising and deep." It is

this technique of "Gestalt fiction" which Vonnegut extends in *Breakfast of Champions* and *Slapstick* as a vehicle for his naive vision. (pp. 49-50)

When Billy asks the Tralfamadorians that question which must be asked in all Vonnegut novels, "Why me?," they reply: . . . "Because this moment simply *is*. . . ." [Billy discovers] that this view totally eliminates guilt, and frees man to use his memory selectively. By concentrating only "on the happy moments" of life one is able to adopt the epitaph which Vonnegut says will serve for himself as well as Billy Pilgrim: "Everything was beautiful, and nothing hurt" (or, as he phrased it in *Monkey House*: "No Pain"). . . . What this *foma* (or "wonderful new lie") provides is a perspective beyond anxiety and alienation, a perspective which accepts the meaninglessness of the world (and says "so what?"), and then goes on to create a world in which man is paradoxically free because he has been released from the burden of irresponsible responsibility. It is a world in which what a man does is simply what he does; a world governed by a naive vision out of which, as Kilgore Trout says, one can open the window and make love to the world.

Breakfast of Champions is a further development in Vonnegut's naive vision, and in the techniques of "Gestalt fiction." (pp. 51-2)

It is [the] seemingly radical separation of art and reality, and of literature and life, which becomes the center of Vonnegut's naive vision. It is an attempt to break down the stereotypes of continuity, order and ordinary meaning which inform mainstream fiction, a fiction in which "people get what is coming to them in the end," a fiction which convinces readers that in this "fair and just" world, they too will be rewarded (and their enemies punished). (p. 53)

The central theme in *Breakfast of Champions* remains the same as it is in Vonnegut's other work. If human beings are "non-sacred machines" living on a "wrecked planet," if the real "breakfast of champions" is alcohol (which destroys the body) rather than any cereal which nourishes it, and if there is no Creator to cry "Olly-olly-ox-in-free" to us (as Dwayne does so ironically in this novel, and as Howard Campbell wishes it in *Mother Night*), what shall give us the will to live? How can we say goodbye to all the "Blue Mondays"? (p. 56)

[Commenting on the novel, Vonnegut] says that "the American experience has been an unhappy experience, generally, and part of it, as I say, is living without a culture" . . . , "all my books are my effort to . . . make myself like life better than I do."

Yet there is a gap (and in our contemporary culture, perhaps a chasm) between acknowledging a problem and solving it, and with each novel, the gap for Vonnegut seems to become wider. (p. 57)

In *Slapstick*, Vonnegut again reveals his disenchantment with the lack of supportive culture in America, particularly the disenfranchisement brought about by the breaking down of regionalism. . . .

Vonnegut, still the intrusive author, begins the novel with the sentence: "This is the closest I will ever come to writing an autobiography. . . ." And the novel does seem to be autobiographical, with Wilbur's relationship with his sister Eliza paralleling Vonnegut's own relationship with

his sister Alice; it is also grotesque, situational poetry—
"real life," as Vonnegut called it in *Breakfast of Champions;* and it is filled with a poignant longing for a recapitulation of the past . . . , the other side of Kilgore Trout's last cry at the end of *Breakfast of Champions: "Make me young, make me young, make me young!"* (p. 58)

The irony in [the novel] is that Wilbur is unable to have real intimacy, just as he is unable to share love. . . . [Love] "can often be poisonous" (Vonnegut wants it replaced by "common decency"), and when Wilbur and Eliza attempt a reconciliation the result is an incredibly intense, traumatic, and pathetic orgy which lasts for "five whole nights and days," and which terrifies them both. Eliza, the intuition, has spent her time in the institution singing the same song, over and over again: "Some Day My Prince Will Come;" Wilbur, the intellect, has spent his time justifying their separation. Neither the romanticist nor the rationalist alone is "really very good at life." Yet when Wilbur twice tells Eliza that he loves her, she tells him that she doesn't like it because its "just a way of getting somebody to say something they probably don't mean. What else can I say, or *anybody* say, but, 'I love you, too?'" (reminiscent of the ironic refrain Paul and Anita repeat in *Player Piano*). . . . Despite Vonnegut's admonition in the preface that this novel is "what life *feels* like to me," and the epigraph of Romeo's "Call me but love, and I'll be new baptiz'd," intuition bows and defers to intellect, and feeling to thinking, and love fails. (pp. 61-2)

Where will Vonnegut go from here? In *Breakfast of Champions* and *Slapstick,* the Gospel from Outer Space (the detached observer) has been replaced by the Gospel from Inner Space (the involved participant). Vonnegut remarked in the preface to *Wampeters, Foma, and Granfalloons* that "I keep losing and gaining equilibrium, which is the basic plot of all popular fiction." Though there are still no Nirvanas, Vonnegut may continue, if he overcomes his own fears (particularly embodied in Howard Campbell's desire for suicide in *Mother Night,* and Kilgore Trout's cry against growing old in *Breakfast of Champions*) and maintains his "equilibrium," to develop and refine his techniques of Gestalt fiction. Look also for an extension of his naive vision, for a literature which helps us laugh (as well as cry) at life's ironies, and helps us become our own folk heroes. Look for a book like Unk's letter, as it was described in *The Sirens of Titan*: "literature in the finest sense, since it made Unk courageous, watchful, and secretly free. It made him his own hero in very trying times." (p. 63)

> *Clark Mayo, in his* Kurt Vonnegut: The Gospel from Outer Space (or, Yes We Have No Nirvanas), *(copyright © 1977 by Clark Mayo), The Borgo Press, 1977.*

RICHARD GIANNONE

[*Player Piano*] intends to startle us with something sinister. Aspiring toward moral autonomy violates the order of creation. In grabbing for the complete freedom of God, the technological mind abuses the freedom God has given the human creature to share in life within limitations. The consequence of this overreaching is the degradation and oppression felt by all the figures in the story.

In *Player Piano* humanity lives under the curse brought about by its own arrogance. The novels that follow take the

reader to many remote, exotic places as they recount the adventures of many wonderfully strange persons; and yet they come back to this old—Old Testament, really—predicament of the fundamental break in the relationship among persons and between them and their universe. (p. 24)

The narrative line of Vonnegut's first two novels traces the way the hero makes his path through worlds that check his decent impulses, finally to be cleansed by a restoration of the human values that had been sacrificed. Both books show the need for a new human beginning. In *Player Piano,* Paul Proteus rebels against the technological violation of humanity, and in *The Sirens of Titan,* Malachi Constant reacts against his own debauchery; but what is constant for Paul and protean for Malachi is the final commitment to compassion and to life in all its unpredictability.

There are, however, between Vonnegut's first two books, telling differences in mode and in moral penetration of their common theme. By and large, *Player Piano* is a traditionally composed novel. Though Vonnegut uses nonsense, creates a nonlanguage, tries his hand at word catalogues, his techniques is not in the end experimental. The anthropological material is not esoteric, and the novel's futurism and anti-utopian satire leave our imagination unchallenged. The setting of Paul Proteus' renunciation of the political system is on recognizable Earth. Now these energies are also in *The Sirens of Titan,* but they swing out more widely and plumb deeper. The second novel sweeps cosmically through the solar system and depicts those outer worlds not satirically, but with visionary celebration. Moreover, the moral compass takes in spiritual principles of retribution that lay deeper than the political effects brought about by Proteus' rebellion. (pp. 25-6)

Though only his second novel, [*The Sirens of Titan*] signals a clear advance over the first. It has reached the large popular audience for which Vonnegut wrote it, and yet subtly works through patterns that we associate with his more recent and acclaimed books.

The novel's *cri-de-coeur*—"'Live!'"—expresses our most primal human need and implies that the universe is set against our fulfilling such a need. Where the struggle to make the most of life is the theme of *Player Piano,* in *The Sirens of Titan* it becomes the form. With all its cosmic range, the story is told with a pointed simplicity. The choice of a popular manner underscores the universality of Constant's desire to be free and to be decent. The simplest message is given in the simplest way. Naive literature is one name for this treatment; parable is another, and in this case is more apt because it conveys the moral tone underlying the tale. The nature of the parable is such that meaning can readily be extracted from it. This is the effect Vonnegut seeks. He even tells brief stories within the novel as a whole. But paradoxes, bewilderments, and reversals in the total story make any single extrapolation seem inadequate. That the story is not reducible to a statement of its meaning is its distinctiveness. What we have is a sophisticated treatment of the naive genre. *The Sirens of Titan* is *almost* a parable. (pp. 26-7)

The plain syntax suggests values of simplicity and community, which the action will affirm. Just as the parable is the simplest form in which to express the simplest lesson, so the loose declarative sentence is the simplest grammatical structure. It so dominates the novel that it becomes formulaic, achieving at times the quality of a chant. The style speaks for artlessness and commonplace. The narrative voice provides signals to the audience for the stance it should take, and here Vonnegut expects nothing more of the reader than would the modes of communication in the popular culture. The voice is the kind, knowing, legendary one of, say, fairy tales. (p. 27)

If the voice Vonnegut develops in *The Sirens of Titan* is folksy, it is also complex. The rhetorical gestures express a double mood. Set against the plain manner, but serving the same purpose—to communicate directly to a common reader—is a superlative idiom. Here we find Vonnegut the pop writer trying to give another kind of art a break by giving dignity to the petty experience of contemporary life. (p. 28)

[Exaggeration] allows Vonnegut gently to satirize the material he uses. What is especially noteworthy is how Vonnegut gives meaning to what in other hands would be mere bravura devices. Conventional science fiction presents the spectacle of enormity and of the outer world to dazzle us by honoring technology. Its verisimilitude requires that we suspend our disbelief. Not so with Vonnegut. His exaggerations make us stay aware of this tale as fiction, as imagined. For him, space exploration ventures into possibilities, not facts; and the possibilities are those of inner spiritual zones, not of a fake mechanism or fixed cosmography. . . .

The marvel that is the subject of *The Sirens of Titan* is the humanization of Malachi Constant of Hollywood, California, who has three billion dollars but is a spiritual pauper. He nevertheless evolves into a good man because his dissoluteness contains the seed of his virtue. In the beginning of the parable he lives in corruption. By passing through the *terra incognita* of his soul he comes out into magnificence. (p. 29)

In keeping with his desire to reach a large popular readership, Vonnegut vivifies Constant's trip into the inner *terra incognita* of love through the great contemporary mythic voyage, the space odyssey. (A Joyce or a Proust would use the less accessible metaphor of mental association to chart the route into the psyche's unknown areas.) . . . Winston Niles Rumfoord, who knows a great deal about space and time, says to his wife that " 'life for a punctual person is like a roller coaster.' " The contour of Constant's voyage proves his point: the ups, the dips, the turns are all there; and the time-caught person rides it out. The path of the roller coaster pictures times spatially, and one can see the whole life-course at once. Blocked out this way, events appear accidental, pointless, beyond our control. The roller coaster, then, is fate. (p. 30)

As for Constant, this weary traveler made it through the thick and thin of planet-hopping but dies waiting in the snow for a bus, the commuter's nightmare come true. Nevertheless, his life "would end well," the parabolist promises us; and it does. . . . Constant fulfills his destiny as an Earthling with the restoration of friendship. The blatant hallucinosis of Constant's reverie bids farewell to the actual world and reminds us of the fictiveness of this fiction. (p. 37)

The requirements of the sentimental adventure story are more than amply fulfilled in *The Sirens of Titan*. When the novel concludes, the world is brought into precise focus as things come into a harmonious whole. It is no longer the junkyard it once was. That debris-ridden world is gone. In the end our perception of the world is corrected because Constant's preceptions have been made new through his space pilgrimage. The perfect white world at the conclusion depicts the world as though seen through Constant's moral freshness. He has come to see—we have come to see in the act of reading his parable—that our humanity is forever present, not something to be pursued or awaited, but only to be perceived and realized by loving whoever is around to be loved, as we sail together on this planet through the cold blue. (pp. 37-8)

Mother Night takes place in jail, opening with Campbell behind bars in Jerusalem and concluding with him locked up in the same place, about to commit suicide. The bare facts of time and place, along with the polarities of its dramatic movement, say a great deal about the growth of Vonnegut's work, and we may pause briefly to note his development. Strife, brutality, spiritual loss—these and other themes from the first two books recur in *Mother Night;* but now the treatment of such issues is more personal, more psychological. It takes place in the present, not in the future. The setting shifts accordingly from the outer space of *The Sirens of Titan* to inner space. The story unfolds not by flinging out through celestial bodies but by burrowing down into psychic places within a single person. Having ventured into the cosmos, Vonnegut for this adventure confines himself to the microcosm of the self. The exploration of this inner galaxy is best made through introspection rather than the mock-utopian or parable treatments of the earlier novels. Such a book might very well have been expected, though its story could not have been predicted. Near the beginning of *The Sirens of Titan,* the narrator declares that "Only inwardness remained to be explored." Campbell's confession gives shape to that remaining exploration. Finally, we can say this about the thematic contours of Vonnegut's first three novels: if *Player Piano* affirms the growth of the individual through revolt, and if *The Sirens of Titan* goes on to show a positive, miraculous conversion of the self, *Mother Night* redirects the moral energy by dramatizing a negative artistic conversion. (pp. 40-1)

A particularly apt way into the complexity of *Mother Night* is through form. This confessional story requires of the reader a certain literary sophistication, for the book is, after all, told by a literary artist revealing his abuses of literary forms. . . . [His] display of various kinds of inventions is one aspect of Vonnegut's making form the subject of his novel. Another aspect comes through Campbell's direct comments on language, which ironically yield his best insights into his behavior. Art can do this. In Campbell's case it must because his absorption into this self-created Nazi monster equates the crisis of his life with the task of his art. (p. 42)

Campbell's personal history should have taught him that there are *forms* and that a work has *a* form, but *the* form does not exist except as an ideal or textbook exercise. A pattern based on clarity and causality could not accommodate his own life, which is a series of disconnections. But Campbell's fate is not to know all that he is communicating. While he states a preference for ideal form, his achieved form in his confessions is highly individual. The novel itself renders the shape of his experience. (p. 43)

The beginning establishes the fictive world of *Mother Night* as that of Campbell's mind. The rhetoric reveals a crisis. The litany of facts and repetitious syntax are part of Campbell's bafflement. Emotionally, he is stuck; the string of loose sentences cannot go forward. He is blocked in a cell of words; hence the physical jail. Setting and mind become interchangeable. The terms of his imprisonment further alter our sense of the beginning of the novel. He is awaiting trial and, as things stand certain execution by the Israeli government. The beginning of his memoir is really a crisis. The man who commends stories with a definite beginning starts his own memoir well past the middle of his life, very near the end. Vonnegut's formal irony here tells us more about Campbell than does his aesthetic manifesto. (p. 44)

Mother Night is not only a book about life, which is the classical business of the novel, but also is a book that has living going on in its pages. Put another way, it shows life in form while using form to represent life. This of course is Campbell's problem stated anew. (p. 45)

Though he proclaims his impending self-destruction, the novel leaves the reader with the sense that Campbell does not follow through with his announcement. We are left with the split response that is at the center of his personality. With characteristic dramatic flourish he bids, "Goodbye, cruel world!" Then, with an equally typical about-face, he speaks from another of his selves (now his dark, comic self) and follows his adieu with a histrionic gesture that raises the possibility that we will meet again—"*Auf wiedersehen?*" These words close the novel with the gallows humor that surrounds Vonnegut's stories. Moreover, by concluding the memoir with a question mark, Vonnegut suspends Campbell's self-examination in an unfinished state. Like Dante's damned, Campbell is doomed emotionally to relive his crime without ever coming to a releasing understanding. So it does seem likely, as he says that we will meet his many selves again and again. . . .

Vonnegut is making a moral point through the ambiguous ending of *Mother Night*. The scripts Campbell tries to live by are inadequate to the contingencies of life. The pain caused by remorse is awful, but worse pain comes from the recognition that there is no resolution. Early in the novel Campbell speaks of "'something worse than Hell'" to his Israeli prison guard. Hell is decisive next to the purgatorial rotation of pretenses that leads nowhere. We have a hung ending to parallel the hung beginning. Rhetorical gesture serves as moral retribution. Campbell's imminent suicide is a comment on the world he lives in as well as on his personal despair; only in a nihilistic world could the gratuitous taking of one's life be a way of affirming oneself, as it is for Campbell. Mother Night is in the throes of giving birth to another dark child of despondence.

The ironies of the ending remind the reader to view the maze wholly from the outside and invite us to exercise our moral imagination to piece together the confusion that destroys the protagonist. This is the responsibility ironic art such as Vonnegut's places on the reader. From the outside a pattern does suggest itself. In trying to comprehend his heartsickness and penitence, Campbell moves from an egocentric view of his personal importance (he will dazzle the world with his brilliant speeches) to a recognition of his personal insignificance. "'Nobody even knows I'm alive anymore.'" Doomed and with his fantasy defenses down, Campbell confronts the idea of his personal extinction. His

ego, which was once so grandiose that it hatched many make-believe selves to secure endurance, now is presented with the fact of its noncontinuance. The mind encounters no greater difficulty than realizing its nonexistence. Campbell deals with this intolerable dilemma with the same subterfuge he used to handle other dangers. Now he thinks of himself as dead, but his idea of suicide wrests only illusory power over impending doom. *Mother Night* lays bare for us the mechanism of the self-deceiving mind as it desperately tries to keep up with the uncontrollable distresses of life, which, for Vonnegut, are epitomized in the encompassing threat of war with its senseless violence. (pp. 50-1)

[*Cat's Cradle*] is a digression about the Hoenikker family, and this displacement of the narrator's proclaimed topic by a subsidiary one alerts us to Vonnegut's intention in his fourth novel. His meaning lies precisely in the book's narrative detour; for swerving reflects Dr. Hoenikker's deviation from responsibility in his scientific research, a deviation which brought about the Hiroshima disaster in the first place and then yielded *ice-nine,* which finally destroys the entire world.

John survives to tell about the later calamity and changes his name to one more in keeping with trial he has endured. "Call me Jonah," are his first words. His phraseology pointedly aligns Vonnegut's narrator with Melville's storyteller Ishmael in *Moby Dick,* and by extension with the classical American artists who are, as William Carlos Williams terms them in *Paterson,* "Ishmaels of the spirit." Having narrowly escaped in their pursuit of the great white whale of knowledge, such people survive to tell us of the world's incomprehensibility. The spirit of Ishmael is that of prophecy born of affliction. Vonnegut makes of his spiritual Ishamel a darker figure who shadows forth the dire warning that we must change our ways if we are to avoid universal annihilation. The bearer of cosmic news is as familiar a figure in Vonnegut's books as is the conflict between "know-how" and "know-what." The threat of technological advancement without regard for ethical purpose necessitates the omens issued by the messenger. By placing the pursuit of knowledge in the atomic age under the sign of Jonah, Vonnegut in *Cat's Cradle* has extended the responsibility of the envoy and, therefore, the character of his news. (pp. 53-4)

Vonnegut's first-person narration makes *Cat's Cradle* a personal testimony to the warning of *Mother Night*, namely, that pretense and lies can overtake truth; for in *Cat's Cradle,* as Jonah tells his tale, lies systematically overtake actuality. (p. 59)

Jonah is not a character in the customary sense so much as he is a mock author. He is not a narrator with a personality developed from inherent qualities, for his several names tell us that he is a reduction to narrative expedient. Whether he is John, as he once was, or "had been a Sam, I would have been a Jonah still" because the name evokes the disaster that determined his being. . . . For all his unique experience teaches him, Jonah's life remains "meaningless." He tries to believe that love will make sense amid vast disorder and resigns himself to a loveless universe. "And no love waiting for me anywhere. . . ." Passive resignation allows Jonah to live in the fallen world but it also allows him to be absorbed by the cynicism that destroyed the world. (p. 61)

Cat's Cradle concludes with [an] encounter between Jonah

and a swami leading to a promised infernal text about life. Like Blake, Jonah at the End sees a visionary, Bokonon, who was something of a prophet and now, by calculated inversion, becomes an outlawed devil. He is not consumed in flames but is dying slowly of *ice-nine.* Jonah and Bokonon talk of their text, *The Books of Bokonon,* which shares in the diabolical irreverence of [William] Blake's "The Bible of Hell." Dazed, Bokonon proffers Jonah the final sentence of *The Books of Bokonon,* which is an urging that Jonah write "a history of human stupidity." This is to be written in untruth because in a world of radical instability and deception, inverted language is all that is left for communication. Accordingly, the epigraph to the complete novel runs: "Nothing in this book is true." We are left in *Cat's Cradle* not only with the negation of vision but also with the negation of communication. Solipsism, the final divorce of relations, among persons, is the ruling condition in the novel. (p. 67)

[Vonnegut's view in *Cat's Cradle*] is personalist and immanent. "'Think of what paradise this world would be if men were kind and wise.'" Unfortunately what the novel dramatizes does not share this cheerfulness but rather encourages a judgment that a scientific and utopian belief in the limitless power and perfectibility of human nature is one of those evil illusions by which humankind tries to make life easy and wonderful while actually causing great pain. The proclamation of Vonnegut's Jonah points toward but does not reveal deliverance. He directs us to laugh at the disasters brought about by our scientific and political egotism in order that we may turn away from a prideful death-wish to appreciate what is good in the world and dear in other persons. (p. 68)

[*God Bless You, Mr. Rosewater*] is a companion book to *Cat's Cradle.* . . . Both novels show men of good will struggling to make sense of a bewildering, fallen universe by answering the naked needs of others. . . . Having discarded in *Cat's Cradle* the efforts of organized religion and science to improve life, and having questioned in *Mother Night* the capacity of art to penetrate the abiding deterioration, Vonnegut moves on to consider the power of money to humanize life through the kind offices of Eliot Rosewater. . . . (p. 69)

Eliot Rosewater's character is a résumé of the qualities Vonnegut developed in the principal figures of the preceding four novels. Eliot is born to privilege and, with Paul Proteus in *Player Piano,* turns against the system, which respects him for extrinsic reasons, in order that he can present himself as a person. Malachi Constant travels all around the solar system in *The Sirens of Titan* for the simple perspective of which his great material wealth deprived him, and the humility Malachi learns becomes the way of life that his fellow millionaire Eliot takes up in his backwater hometown. But noble intentions can boomerang. Howard J. Campbell goes crazy in *Mother Night* by trying to remain patriotic while serving the Nazi enemy. Or the high cause can overwhelm the endeavor to do what is right. Eliot openly works for the good of other, yet his mind gives way under the massive need he serves. . . .

The pervasive poverty in the Vonnegut world is that of love. Warm feeling between persons marks a special moment in his narratives, and there are few such moments. Intimacy is avoided rather than desired, and friendship is a passing bond. Trust of one person by another is so excep-

tional that we are likely to accept Jonah's isolation as the given condition. Mere awareness of emotional contact indicates a sympathetic figure who invariably comes across as vulnerable and not infrequently as a bit crazed. Where ignorance of emotion is the norm, sensitivity will inevitably seem to be a mental disorder. The masses of automatons crowding Vonnegut's fictions indicate that lovelessness has reached a crisis stage where indiscriminate affection is called for as a cure. (p. 70)

If we come to think of Eliot as living out Jesus' commandment to his disciples to answer the curse with a blessing, as Vonnegut seems to invite us to do, then we can sense the seriousness in the bitter comic ending. In the Bible the Father communicates life to his Son. Passing on life is the essential blessing. In the end Eliot does just this to his fifty-seven new, stray children: "'And tell them . . . to be fruitful and multiply.'"

These are the last words of the novel. They suspend the action in a mandate for regeneration. If only for this closing moment, love harmonizes the social disorder with which the story began. Eliot's presence assures us that there is one entirely good man in the world. The gesture magically shows that cruelty and confusion are merely at the service of order and goodness. The miracle Eliot performs does not wipe away the world's havoc. Chaos abides; it is the law of nature. His miracle amounts to correcting our vision; for his life teaches us that we have only to alter the way we look at the world to accept its unpredictability and to recognize the humanness in people through their need for affectionate contact. Eliot's potentiality has been intimated all along in the name Rosewater, which hints of gentleness, fairness, and transformation. The final wonder that Vonnegut observes is the transformation in Eliot's spirit. At the end he is not the lunatic philanthropist casting pearls before swine, to borrow from the novel's sardonic subtitle; nor is he the helpless madman cast in the prison of his mind or behind the bars of psychic conventionality. Rather, he is the good man casting life onto the world. (p. 81)

What I believe is most important for an understanding of *Slaughterhouse-Five* and for a study of Vonnegut's artistry is how his change of heart in directly confronting his subject brings about a change in the form of his fiction. In fact, the question of novelistic form is equated in the book with the task of writing about Dresden. The reader is forced to consider the very nature of the book that he is involved in through reading, just as Vonnegut forces himself to look squarely at his hellish knowledge. . . . Survival is what *Slaughterhouse-Five* is all about, and so to take up the question of the novel's survival links form to action: the problem of living through the fire-bombing of Dresden is rivaled by the problem of writing about it. The two acts are analogues, and from the tone of the passage on the viability of fiction we can pick up Vonnegut's meaning. He is not quite prediciting a future for the novel but he is negating its death notice. He is not quite prescribing a function for the novel, but he is deriding the cheap purposes it has been made to serve. We are at least made aware that the life of form relates to the form of our lives. Vonnegut comments on the reality of Dresden by treating the problems of fiction.

This indirect formulation of the novel's function expresses Vonnegut's approach to art. He questions the mold he uses. He begins *before* the first sentence of the story. The title page undermines our expectation about design with three titles. The proper one refers to a pig slaughterhouse in Dresden, which housed American prisoners in World War II. The second shows how language falsifies war: "The Children's Crusade" transforms brutality into sentimental heroism, calculation into innocence. The third title, "A Duty-Dance with Death," borrows from [Louis-Ferdinand] Céline to state that art must confront death frankly. The use of three titles effectively denies the adequacy of any one title for the book. Instead of a label we are given a deepening attitude toward the violence of war. (pp. 82-3)

The strategies that entangle *Slaughterhouse-Five* . . . offer clues to how its disparateness comes together. The shift, from the narrator's own predicament to Billy Pilgrim's, alters the perspective from introspection to observation, thereby making Vonnegut the narrator into a confessing witness. . . . Detached at the same time that he is sympathetic to Billy's experience, the narrator can suggest a way of seeing, through compassionate wisdom, the otherwise baffling war in the context of other catastrophes. The hurt and wonder of Billy's life become the hurt and wonder of every time. (p. 84)

Vonnegut's testimony puts a moral light on war to reveal alliances not shown by treaties. The essential battle here is waged by man against the violent bent in himself. Vonnegut plumbs the dark forces in the human spirit. Sentimentality, egotism, blind patriotism, materialism, these are the enemy; and for Vonnegut they are the signal qualities of American life. Against them stand conscience and feeling. Vonnegut, the witness, acts as a moral scout, smuggling himself across battle lines to reach the front of consciousness where he hopes to find final resistance to killing. His moral awareness accounts for the uncommon affection for a cherished city of the declared enemy and for the German people themselves. They are presented as fellow human beings struggling against their own propensity for violence. And to the degree that Americans yielded to their destructive urge (the violent style of postwar American life suggests a *high* degree), they—we—fell victims. Both political sides lost in the struggle for human decency. (p. 87)

Vonnegut, the witness to Dresden, whose survival from disaster is also his fate, draws strength from seeing how a gesture of helpless love redefines its fatal expression. (p. 88)

There is . . . a tension among three shaping forces in *Slaughterhouse-Five:* the ancient Christian news of victory over death; the Tralfamadorian message of no death; and the message implied in the reader's unfolding consciousness about the respective choices of each message. This deepening consciousness is Vonnegut's gospel. I would put their respective views of self in this way: whereas the Christian self exists between vanity and fulfillment, the science-fiction self is eternally in isolation. Vonnegut, working against both views, seeks to measure the self's relatedness in mutuality through its capacity to grow in consciousness and compassion. Vonnegut's new covenant stipulates the obligation of spiritual nurturance among persons. (p. 93)

[Vonnegut's strategy in *Slaughterhouse-Five*] is to register the mind in the act of confronting annihilation. In finding a form to tell of [the disaster of Dresden], Vonnegut is able to respond to the smoldering demand that this holocaust, which killed more people than did the atomic bombing of

Hiroshima in 1945, not pass silently into human history, as its planners had hoped it would. Faced boldly, narrated and thereby worked through, the trauma of Dresden is exorcised of its dark spell on Vonnegut's imagination. (pp. 96-7)

[*Breakfast of Champions*] fictionalizes the searching pronouncements Vonnegut was making on the potentialities of his fiction. With Prospero's affection, Vonnegut near the end of his tempestuous *Breakfast of Champions* proclaims the release of "all the literary characters who have served me so loyally" from the confines of his pages. He casts off, also, any vestige of the realistic novel with its meaningless accumulation of details and facts. Liberation and dispersal are possible because Vonnegut created those things; and his creation and what it imitates or represents are the subject of *Breakfast of Champions.* (p. 102)

In a book that dismisses detail as pointless, we can assume that facts of time and place create their own verisimilitude. The narrative present generates a mental excursion backward to action in 1492 and completed events in 1979 and 1981, all of which blend with the Ford Galaxies and Burger Chefs of our current moment that constitutes one indefinite past. Moreover, where the author hovers godlike over the events, his presence is likely to overtake the story. And it does. What I term the tale of *Breakfast of Champions* is its subtext. "'The Big show is inside my head,'" Vonnegut says to a character for both her benefit and the reader's. Vonnegut's mind is the arts festival for which the Midland City shindig is a metaphorical expedient. (p. 103)

In a universe where every substance is defined by its function in some experiment—"loving machines, hating machines . . . truthful machines, lying machines"—creatures do not encounter one another. Persons *meet;* robots and forces collide. The form of the tale of Trout's impact on Dwayne is that of collision. Collision in *Breakfast of Champions* is the unifying principle derived from a natural law of Vonnegut's cosmos. Continents, we are told, ride a slab that drifts precariously "on molten glurp"; and "when one slab crashed into another one, mountains were made." A violent crashing is continually "going on" in the universe, leading scientists to predict "that ice ages would continue to occur." Like world, like people, Nations grind against one another; creatures strike one another. We are "doomed to collide and collide and collide." Collision is the secret knowledge behind the revelations in [Trout's book] *Now It Can Be Told,* which implies that God moves not only in mysterious ways but also in disastrous ways. (pp. 106-07)

The destructive impact of Trout on Dwayne poses the novel's theme in structural terms: How do we respond to the inevitable collisions that make up our lives? The possible responses are obviously limited. Any attempt in the book to check disaster ends up hastening it. The agonized lives of the characters warn against such action, pursuit of money or science yield illusions of control over our lives. Passivity would seem less perilous. One can withdraw and hope, as Trout does, to spend one's days without touching another human again; but even Trout is lured out of his solitude to spread the very insight (that we are machines) that drove him there, and then he is caught in the pile-up. Again, our attempts to master the mysterious activity of the world finally implicate us further in its turmoil. . . . Vonnegut takes his cue from the Creator, the eternal black humorist. "For want of anything better to do, we became fans of collisions." The spectator's stance produces the peculiarly humorous wisdom documents recurring in the novels: Jonah in *Cat's Cradle* gives us his record of human stupidity; Eliot Rosewater's *Domesday Book* presents in apple-pie order a ledger of his philanthropic operations during the apocalypse; Trout tells it as it is in *Now It Can Be Told;* and to this imaginary library of visionary documents, Vonnegut makes a personal contribution of a notebook of a cosmic fan. The superstructure of *Breakfast of Champions* is that of an archeological scrapbook composed of wise precepts for life on a planet that was, Earth. (pp. 108-09)

Vonnegut wants to toss out junk in order to retain only "sacred things." His reason for going to Midland City is "to be born again." He is not reborn but he relearns that forces in our souls prevent transformation. Again collision images the spiritual turmoil that awaits us. "One force had a sudden advantage over another, and spiritual continents began to shrug and heave." The sacred, then, resides neither in himself nor in any individual human being. Robo Karabekian, a trashy minimalist painter who has been invited to the Festival, brings Vonnegut to his fullest understanding of the sacred: "'Our awareness is all that is alive and maybe sacred in any of us.'" Karabekian calls our awareness a band of light, which describes his kind of painting. The bogus painter-philosopher defines for Vonnegut, the doodler-novelist, what is sacred. Awareness is all that the fan of collision can hope to attain and awareness depends on collective, interpenetration of mind. Vonnegut writes from that band of unwavering light in himself, addressing the band at the core "of each person who reads this book," and thereby he furthers the collectivity of the sacred. (pp. 110-11)

Vonnegut in the book expresses a keen interest about what God would have to say about all the collisions going on. Vonnegut even plays God in the oldest of artistic guises, the omniscient Creator of his fictions, just to see if the giving and the taking of fictional life provides an insight into God's knowledge. How can he, as a second Creator of the world, transform reality back into its potentialities and so escape its chaos? Vonnegut's intrusion into the text, scaffolding an overstructure of reflection, is not a gimmick but an act of love. The final silence evoked by his self-portrait resonates with the recognition of the Creator's failure to comprehend and to save his world. (pp. 111-12)

Without essentially altering his established material or practiced style, Vonnegut advances his art in *Slapstick* through tone. Doom is handled quietly, philosophically, in the way that Laurel and Hardy throw pies with thoughtful poise. The novel's dramatic action revolves around cruelty and turmoil, yet it reaches across a long emotional distance that removes any trace of bitterness or sentimentality. And like Stan and Ollie, Vonnegut plays himself in *Slapstick*. He becomes the character in this work that he said in his Preface to *Between Time and Timbuktu* he wanted to be—and was encouraged to be, I believe by *A Time To Die,* Tom Wicker's moving account of how the Attica uprising of 1971 caused him to redirect the entire course of his life. Vonnegut now uses fiction to achieve just such a personal transformation of his writing. All the Alicelike trips through wonderland that comprise the new novel are falls down the rabbit holes of his mind, wending through the remote passages of his childhood to emerge in the channel of his crea-

tive achievement. *Slapstick* is deliberately a spiritual autobiography, an act of Vonnegut's mind, logging his responses to the disquieting origins of his creativeness. The fictionalized memoir is not nearly as melancholy an account as Vonnegut found Wicker's to be. Vonnegut looks back from the long perspective of very old age, which can see the human comedy in the trappings of utter defeat. (p. 114)

Vonnegut's talent comes through most effectively when he lifts a simple story with an explicit moral (which he often states for us) from a known genre and then satirizes his use of it. The result is a parody narrative in which Vonnegut does not imitate human action but imitates another imitation.

Vonnegut understands well that screen low-comedy presents the audience with a poem through a series of gestures. Continuity of action counts for much less in slapstick film than does gesture. Such comedy coheres through spare ritual conduct—stupidity creating catastrophe, dumb, ill-judged violence bringing about destruction in images that we can all grasp immediately. (p. 118)

[Stan and Ollie] personify human dignity born of its own ineptitude. *Slapstick* is peopled by the blundering idots and scurvy knaves of that zany world, and their perpetual blundering explains that our humanity is bound up with imperfection. This sympathy for human shortcomings leads Vonnegut to plead for simple kindness. Gentle decency, far more than idealistic theories, is needed for us to live with our salutary imperfections. (p. 119)

Laurel and Hardy and Chaplin also provide Vonnegut with a way to unify his introspective folktale. They are masters of inflection. Their comedy develops as they carefully shade their physical stance and emotional attitude toward the gag. In *Slapstick* Vonnegut proceeds by modulating his numerous attitudes toward the jungle of extinction. *Slapstick* is a sequence of mental positions without a climax. A minimal story line is ornamented with dialogue and situation. The effect is that of improvisation supporting an unobtrusive plan. Wilbur's chronological recollection of his life is the story's binding thread, which Vonnegut fastens to his personal prologue and epilogue. Vonnegut as usual delights in acknowledging "all the loose ends of the yarn" while composing in strip-cartoon layout a series of gallows gags that blend, in a carefully paced tempo, outlandish behavior with a feeling of inevitability. (pp. 119-20)

In the moral background of the novel are the atomic bomb and the killing of 100 million people in this century's wars and death camps. These events shape *Slapstick* as well as modern history. *Slapstick* is Vonnegut's meditative documentary—his sorrow and pity in low-comedy form—about how we live now in the aftermath of the holocaust. During such a crisis, human beings require a sense of continuity and relatedness to what comes before and after life. We find that struggle to achieve a new relationship with the world expressed in *Slapstick* through the image of the survivor as creator. Creativeness, like Wilbur's happy childhood, takes two forms. The external formulation of the struggle for meaning is the novel itself. The inner, spiritual mode generating the story is rendered through Melody. Simply to go on, as Melody does, taking things as they come, is to know how to live with suffering; and when everything falls apart, to pick up and begin again with clownish joyousness from the act of doing so is all there is to do. We learn by feeling. Such purity of heart is the beginning of unity within one's spirit. (pp. 120-21)

For Vonnegut, fiction serves the great moral purpose of breathing life back into life. Books are restorative, especially if they train readers to be cosmic fans. So in dark times he uses the therapy of laughter to evoke the brightness that is concealed by fear. Because the times are deceitful, he satirizes their false claims. Because we are caught in spiritual tyranny, he celebrates the liberating power of the imagination. Vonnegut wants to reveal what Blake called "the infinite which was hid" so that we can with new energy transform the nowhere of all the mental San Lorenzos we have made for ourselves into the now-here of love.

In such a place of the heart, love and power would unite to allow the compassionate real self to emerge from the secrecy it adopts for survival. Feeling and action could then be one . . . Vonnegut attempts through his novels to sensitize his readers to the need for reversing the way the politics of power have infiltrated the intimacies of experience. . . . His novels bear witness to the rareness and the danger of recognizing others in open affection. Paul Proteus can no longer fit into his society; Howard Campbell prefers to kill himself rather than live with the newly aroused idea that he is a feeling person responsible to others; Billy Pilgrim and Eliot Rosewater go mad; Kilgore Trout secludes himself; and Wilbur Daffodil-11 Swain resorts to drugs. If their collective discovery of the human is imperiling, it is also necessary. It provides the basis for a covenant relation between person and person for mutual validation at a time when conditions have made untenable any other recognition of our human purpose.

The image of the human mind strained by ideological oppression, within a body racked by pain, dominates Vonnegut's novels form the first, without any implication that life ever was or will be less burdened by suffering or exempt from death. But there is a change in Vonnegut's attitude toward his persistently apocalyptic stories, and it comes about through the same psychological introspection which attends his technical development. As the novels penetrate humanity's betrayed trusts in utopian perfectability, economic progress, scientific inquiry, social prerogative, military power, and the innate illusion of personal immortality, Vonnegut gradually affirms a true source of life: consciousness. Consciousness brings him to reject any false foundation for being, or "junk," as he calls it. Trusting in a transcendent source of being frees the human mind from laying its unlived life on institutions, which cannot fulfill the heart's yearning to live. It is significant that where Vonnegut's memory is most highly charged with social injustice and political tragedy, namely, in *Slaughterhouse-Five, Breakfast of Champions,* and *Slapstick,* consciousness holds in check the immense force of doom. Consciousness formulates hope, which is why Vonnegut calls it "sacred." Hope defies explanation, in Vonnegut's reflection, because it lies in the sovereignty of the Creator of the Universe, however unpredictably his will presents itself, and in the sovereignty of human love, however rare its presence. From the dramatic action of the novels, however, we see that Vonnegut addresses that hope to the disenfranchised, who do not nourish the illusion that they are masters of their present or future. This, the message of self-giving love, is the proclamation of Vonnegut's novels. It is the best of all possible news. (pp. 124-25)

Richard Giannone, in his Vonnegut: A Preface to His Novels *(copyright © 1977 by Kennikat Press Corp.; reprinted by permission of Kennikat Press Corp.), Kennikat, 1977.*

PETER J. REED

Slaughterhouse-Five from the start suggested the possibility that Vonnegut had written the crucial personal experiences out of his system, and I think that this is one reason we have all tended to wait with particular interest, and perhaps a little uncertainty, for what would subsequently come from him. In prefacing [*Happy Birthday, Wanda June*], Vonnegut declared that he was through with novels and with characters who were "spooks". . . . The end appeared at hand, if one dared take the author seriously. In *Breakfast of Champions* he announced the discarding of old characters and themes, while also bringing certain other lines of development in his fiction to their seeming logical ends. With Vonnegut's observation that *Breakfast of Champions* spun off from *Slaughterhouse-Five,* one could imagine that it represented a final housecleaning. But then came *Slapstick,* a continuation which seems to promise more of the same. (pp. 151-52)

[Vonnegut's self consciousness] appears to have grown. That is suggested by his talk of abandoning the novel in his preface to *Happy Birthday, Wanda June,* and by his decrying the qualities of his books . . . in the introduction to *Breakfast of Champions.* The preface to *Between Time and Timbuktu* reveals more of the same: Vonnegut talking about the inadequacy of film since the author cannot place himself in the work. . . . And in prefacing *Wampeters, Foma & Granfalloons* he speaks of the problems of being a "guru" addressing college audiences, about critics writing of him as if he were already dead, and about "British critics" who find him sometimes too sentimental. More important than these prefatory musings, however, are the signs of such preoccupations in the content and style of the works.

In this respect, the projection of self into the novel changes markedly in nature between *Slaughterhouse-Five* and *Breakfast of Champions.* Vonnegut has been "present" in many of the earlier novels, in the sense that they have directly or obliquely autobiographical content. The change at this point is in the manner of the intrusion of the autobiographical "I." In *Slaughterhouse-Five,* the appearance of Vonnegut himself in an intermittent minor role in the action —"that was me"—is framed by the first and last chapters, in which Vonnegut speaks from the present of the writing of the novel. The technique seems entirely appropriate in a novel with a subject matter which is at one level intensely personal and which is viewed reflectively. It enables Vonnegut to combine his retrospective perspective as author rationalizing and ordering past experience and his contemporaneous reactions as participant in the events shown. It is also appropriate (and an effective structural device) in a novel which emphasizes time, the interrelationships of time periods, and the effects of time on perception or "truth." In the later novel, the introduction of self as character seems a little less comfortable or natural. The difference in context *almost* provides a satisfactory answer: *Slaughterhouse-Five* is probably Vonnegut's most serious novel, while *Breakfast of Champions* may be his most whimsical. *Breakfast of Champions* is also intensely personal, as its preface explains. But even when an author writes a book as a birthday present to himself, if he publishes it, it will be read by others, who, even if disposed to wish him Many Happy Returns, are still likely to approach it much as they would any other work of fiction. The test then becomes one of how well the introduction of author as character is supported not by exterior, prefatory assertion but by thematic, structural, and generic context. This does not mean an expectation of a traditional concept of the fictional world as "real," not to be violated by authorial admissions of artifice to shatter our willing suspension of disbelief. . . . [What] Vonnegut does here is rather different. An author's admission that a fictional world *is* a fiction, *is* artifice, frequently works in the direction of emphasizing the involvement of the reader in the creative process. In *Breakfast of Champions* the direction is almost opposite. The author is present in the fictional world as character and creator simultaneously, telling us how he chooses to have other characters perform. This tends to put the reader in the position of observer, even if an observer who is "let in" on why actions occur or what will happen next. Vonnegut's projection of self into this novel is such that the reader finds it hard to escape the sense that *Breakfast of Champions* at least in the later chapters, is personal in a rather exclusive way. This particular kind of personal quality has a certain awkwardness, one which may be resolved in either first-person fiction (by a consistent character-narrator relationship) or autobiography, but which in *Breakfast of Champions* remains unsettled. The effect results in the reader's feeling partially estranged in the fictional world into which he has apparently been invited.

Vonnegut's increased self-consciousness also reveals itself stylistically. Here *Wampeters, Foma & Granfalloons* makes interesting reading. Some of the earlier pieces (for example, "Brief Encounters on the Inland Waterway") seem strikingly fluent and almost languid in comparison with the later prose. In *Breakfast of Champions* the statements are terse, the rhythms brusque, the sentences short and staccato in the manner of the later abrupt style. The novel also abounds with the repetitions which distinguish the later work. Where *Slaughterhouse-Five* uses the "So it goes" refrain effectively, this novel has the repeated injunction "Listen," the reiterated fade-out "And so on," and the inconclusive "Etc." There are other forms of repetition, such as the echoing of the last word of a paragraph as a solitary declaration proceding the next paragraph and the restatement of the thematic motto, "Goodbye Blue Monday." While this device has its purpose in the context of the novel, repetition succeeds rather less well here than in *Slaughterhouse-Five.* As with the curt phrasing, the resurrection of familiar characters and scenes, and even the characteristic, bitingly understated asides on current social events, it gives the impression of being self-consciously employed—as indeed Vonnegut's prefatory statement that he is saying "good-bye to all that" implies it is.

This impression becomes disturbing for several reasons. The most obvious one is that it might suggest a decline of powers, or efforts, on Vonnegut's part, since the phenomenon of the American novelist's succumbing to self-parody in later years is not an unfamiliar one. The personal, prefatory remarks in *Breakfast of Champions,* revealing ambivalence and weariness, might contribute to this impression. So might the relative lack of originality, of scope, power, of sheer size, in the content of the novel itself. The tendency to self-imitation might naturally invite the judgment that Vonnegut is playing to the known responses of an estab-

lished following. Doubtless the perennial Vonnegut detractors would say that. Some have always accused him of playing "guru" to one generation, although his publishing history and the content of his fiction make the charge ludicrous. What seems apparent is that in the wake of the success of *Slaughterhouse-Five,* as book and film, Vonnegut has felt the pressures of fame and of those who would cast him in the guru role, as he discloses in the preface to *Wampeters, Foma & Granfalloons.* This, and other personal circumstances, doubtless contributed to making the years following the publication of *Slaughterhouse-Five* distracting ones for Vonnegut. The precise relationship between personal trauma and the form of *Breakfast of Champions* would be difficult, if not impossible, to define. But Vonnegut's preface alone suggests that there is a relationship, and the plot almost certainly confirms it. (pp. 153-56)

[*Breakfast of Champions*] has more strengths than it has generally been credited with. . . . Perhaps inevitably, the novel's strengths are closely related to some of its relative weaknesses. One of these comes in the area of characterization. Vonnegut has often been apologetic about this part of his work, perhaps more than he need be. True, many of his characters appear two-dimensional or stereotyped. But that is also true of characters in some major "serious" American novels. Furthermore, Vonnegut has shown the ability, on the one hand, to create some major characters of considerable interest and depth and, on the other, to make a number of the two-dimensional lesser characters sharp and memorable. In *Breakfast of Champions* none of the characters amounts to what would normally be considered a really well-developed characterization. The two major figures, Dwayne Hoover and Kilgore Trout, though clearly defined, immensely amusing, and quite memorable, remain essentially enlarged, two-dimensional secondary characters. Yet that is appropriate. Kurt Vonnegut is the central character of this novel, and Hoover and Trout have supporting roles both in the sense of being secondary to the author-protagonist and in the way they effectively enlarge and complete the central character. (pp. 157-58)

The interjection of self directly as character is much expanded in *Breakfast of Champions,* yet that figure remains far from a complete autobiographical portrait. Vonnegut's own presence in the novel is filled out by Hoover and Trout, each of whom embodies aspects of the author, and even by lesser figures such as Rabo Karabekian, the painter. . . . Rather like the older Billy Pilgrim . . . , Hoover can be seen as a modern Everyman figure, a version of the standard middle-class norm of success. He thus provides a vehicle for one of Vonnegut's favorite themes— the man who attains the stereotyped American goals but is left asking "What is the meaning of life?" or "What are people for?" In Vonnegut, such characters are seldom merely conveniences for social satire: they are treated with sympathy and understanding, embodying much of the Ordinary Man from whom the author never distances himself very far. (p. 158)

Perhaps the most important interrelating theme is that presented in Trout's *Now It Can Be Told*—the perception of people as robots. . . . Obviously, the idea of humans as robots connects with the Dwayne Hoover side of the story, with its theme of human behavior biochemically controlled. The two themes merge when the two characters meet in the bar in Midland City, where Trout gives Hoover a copy of the novel. The general concept and its implications are not new in Vonnegut. People behaving "as it was meant to happen," questions of free will, characters being treated as neither virtuous nor evil because they were simply doing all that was possible to them, have had prominence in Vonnegut's novels at least since *The Sirens of Titan*. But here the twin themes emerge with peculiar force and particular personal relevance. (pp. 161-62)

[Again], Trout becomes a vehicle for the expression of the author's own misgivings. Yet ultimately the personal significance of the bad-chemicals-and-robots theme finds expression through the unlikely character of Rabo Karabekian. (p. 162)

The danger comically present in Trout's *Now It Can Be Told* is its "solipsistic whimsy." The story, like many of Trout's, is written solipsistically; Trout develops an idea into a personal fantasy which he then imposes on a vision of the world. That danger becomes explicit when the book falls into the hands of the already solipsistic [Dwayne Hoover]. . . . (p. 163)

But behind the irony [of Vonnegut's presentation of Karabekian] resides a serious truth which could effectively counter many of the nightmares of robots, bad chemicals, and solipsism. Recognizing that within each individual being, within the physical "meat machine," lives an immaterial core of awareness entails a recognition of the peculiar individuality, the uniqueness, the "sacredness" of that being. . . . Such an awareness counters the solipsism which reduces others to robots, by recognizing . . . their uniqueness, their individual worth as beings endowed with their own perceptions and feelings. This recognition thus becomes a key to behaving toward others with humaneness. Similarly—and the outward and inward directions of this recognition are coalescent—self-respect also comes from affirming . . . and respecting one's own humanity. Thus, this characteristically simple perception makes possible the reversal of character-Vonnegut's earlier pessimistic conclusion, by arguing that there *is* something "sacred about myself or about any human being" and that we are *not* all merely "machines, doomed to collide and collide and collide." That discovery is Vonnegut's cocktail-lounge epiphany, the cause of his subsequent "rebirth" and "serenity." (pp. 165-66)

Above all, the tone must always be kept in mind when discussing Vonnegut. In *Breakfast of Champions* there is plenty of "yin and yang," of taking away what has been offered and undercutting what has been affirmed. There is spoofing; despite the use made of Karabekian's speech, his own personality and his painting of "an unwavering band of light" are surely mocked. The irreverent and the poignant stand side by side—Vonnegut's pathetically psychotic mother is "crazy as a bedbug." And there is the everpresent mix of the joyful and the pessimistic. While Vonnegut says that he finds serenity, and the general tone of the novel is upbeat, gloom remains. After all, the sacred awareness which he discovers continues to be ignored in the world around him. Even Vonnegut's freeing of his slaves, his characters, is ambivalent. Freed from their creator, they cease to have existence. Of course, the freeing of characters is a comic conception, as the ironic reference to Jefferson's freeing of his slaves emphasizes. And there is a sense in which, ultimately, Vonnegut can be no more freed from these children than he can be from the parents he so

constantly recalls. Trout embodies much of the father—even his shins, his feet, and his voice—but he is also father to Vonnegut, in part the obscure writer he once was, in part the man he might have become, and in part the often bemused but patiently cheerful person he remains. So, while *Breakfast of Champions* celebrates a birthday, discarding old trappings and offering new beginnings, the happy anniversary is not wholly joyous. It is, after all, his fiftieth. Vonnegut's last words might echo Trout's—"Make me young, make me young, make me young"—and the final portrait shows him with a tear in his eye. (pp. 168-69)

[*Slapstick*] is a view of life as being as his dying sister described it: "Slapstick." Given the conditions he [describes] of isolation, of inevitable death, of bargaining in good faith with a meaningless universe—one might choose another word: "Absurd." Except that Vonnegut's word typically emphasizes the comic (or comical) potentialities so often overlooked by the existentialists. . . . Yet just as the prologue, which reflects on many such occurences in Vonnegut's own life, does not seem depressed, so the novel's tone transcends the gloom inherent in much of its content. And, for the same reason. Vonnegut himself seems steadier, more composed, more at terms with life in this prologue than in those which immediately precede it. Likewise, his narrator in *Slapstick,* though wearied and in some senses disillusioned, seems calm and resigned.

In casting himself as Wilbur Swain and his sister as Eliza Swain, Vonnegut has made both "monsters." This may seem perverse or whimsical, yet remains characteristic of Vonnegut. He is consistently self-denigrating in his fiction and the prefaces. Some of the characters with whom he might be most nearly identified and some of the "heroes" of his fiction are abnormal physically or psychologically, and when he approaches self in portraying artists and writers he typically undercuts. One senses a degree of embarrassment here in a writer who nevertheless feels compelled to be direct and personal. It is as if he needs the protection of irony and whimsy after having come so close to the nerve. Usually the protection serves well, saving him in tricky spots from what might otherwise become sentimental self-pity, didacticism, or plain morbidity. In *Slapstick* the character of Wilbur Swain works effectively as such a mask, but more importantly helps to advance thematic content. Most notably, casting the young Swains as seven-foot freaks gives comically dramatic emphasis to the notions of "common decency" in human relations and "bargaining in good faith with destiny." (pp. 172-73)

Where the autobiography lies in all of this (and one should not take the novel as some kind of psychological *roman à clef*) perhaps only Vonnegut can answer. His sister, Alice, was tall, embarrassed by her height, and developed bad posture—all hyperbolically reproduced in Eliza. Vonnegut felt especially close to her [and] claims that she was the only person he had written for. . . . (p. 174)

[The] need for "family" becomes the major theme of the novel, expressed personally as part of what life feels like to Vonnegut, and more broadly as a universal human requirement. (p. 175)

[The] novel ends with affirmation in terms of its major theme. Caring relatives behave with decency, and the bargaining in good faith with destiny goes on. And this affirmation arises out of a view of life bleak enough to contradict any suggestions of bland optimism. The last words—"Das Ende"—also nod toward relatives: those Vonneguts who "were all cultivated and gentle and prosperous, and spoke German and English gracefully". . . .

This, then, is the slapstick of life as Vonnegut feels it. Much of that experience seems painful. Wilbur's pill-popping, his birthdays, his father-son relationships, his loss of a sister, all echo phases in the author's life. Often the comical coexists with the painful, as agility and intelligence are sorely tested. Like a Laurel and Hardy film, Vonnegut's fictional world is "funny and adorable" but also poignant. . . . [Vonnegut has said in an interview that] "People are too good for this world". . . . For a moment this almost startles us, because although Vonnegut claims not to create villains or heroes, he portrays some rather nasty people and shows plenty of suffering caused by human action. Yet his prevailing attitude remains one of sympathy for the human lot. The destiny with which humans gamble does not always keep good faith; if gravity is not unpredictable, the weather certainly is. The best that humans can do is often not good enough, and Vonnegut breathes another "Hi ho," bespeaking a weary resignation but not, ultimately, rejection. He sees humans generally as limited in the same ways as himself, and that gives rise to one of the major strengths of *Slapstick* and of his other fiction: the ability to interconnect the intensely personal with the universally human. (pp. 183-84)

> *Peter J. Reed, "The Later Vonnegut," in* Vonnegut in America: An Introduction to the Life and Work of Kurt Vonnegut, *edited by Jerome Klinkowitz and Donald L. Lawler (copyright © 1977 by Jerome Klinkowitz and Donald L. Lawler; reprinted by permission of Delacorte Press/Seymour Lawrence), Delacorte Press, 1977, pp. 150-84.*

RICHARD LUPOFF

Vonnegut's novels are science fiction, will he or nil he. Listen, *Slapstick* is about a pair of telepathic twins whose intelligences synergize into super-genius when they're in close proximity but deteriorate to bright-normal when they're farther apart. They pretend to be idiots, however, as a form of protective coloration. Nice old science fiction device, first used by Olaf Stapledon around 1935, I believe. It also involves a scheme to relieve population pressures by breeding miniature humans—Bob Bloch did this in the 1960s. And there's a future plague which reduces most of the world to a state of neo-barbarism-in-the-ruins. Cf. Jack London, 1915. (pp. 52-3)

[*Slapstick* is] a science fiction novel if ever there was one. . . .

As for whether *Slapstick* is a good science fiction novel or not, that's another matter. It has all of the trademarks of Vonnegut's novels, since the first few: a bitter zaniness, a deceptively simple style relying on commonplace vocabulary, short sentences, scenes and chapters, and a many-times-repeated key phrase. (Back in *Slaughterhouse Five* it was "So it goes"; in *Slapstick* it's "Hi ho." It's stupid and irritating.)

Unfortunately, since writing *Slaughterhouse-Five* . . . , Vonnegut has obviously lost heart. He's done only two novels since then. *Breakfast of Champions* . . . was announced as Vonnegut's last novel. It was a pitiful wail of despair at the human condition. *Slapstick* is a bit better, but

once again, Vonnegut lacks the courage, energy and dedication to carry his scheme through to completion. The book starts promisingly, wanders off on a variety of tangents, and finally fizzles into nothingness at the end. It isn't Vonnegut's worst performance, but it's a poor one. . . .

I resonate with this guy. But I can't forgive him for putting out these defeated, sloppy, unsatisfactory and unsatisfying books. If he was written out after *Slaughterhouse-Five*, by damn he should have quit writing. . . .

Slapstick? A better title might have been *Slapdash*. (p. 53)

> *Richard Lupoff, in* Algol *(copyright © 1979 by Algol Magazine), Winter, 1978-79.*

DAVID BOSWORTH

Vonnegut expresses a relentlessly pessimistic vision of man, a pessimism far surpassing the cynic's belief in the eventual victory of evil or the fundamentalist's version of a fall from grace. For there can be no victory without a battle and no fall if one from the start is inescapably mired at the bottom of the pit. The moral drama between right and wrong loses all meaning if men are not free to choose and competent to act, and Vonnegut sees man as neither competent nor free. In his fictional world, there are no villains and, as well, no heroes to oppose them; both good and evil are beyond man's grasp. When he writes in the introduction to *Slaughterhouse-Five* that he learned in college "there was absolutely no difference between anybody," the ironic tone does not belie the accuracy of the words. Vonnegut does believe that all men are the same, and to read his fiction is to meet a cast of characters who are uniformly pathetic, helpless victims of a random, incoherent, meaningless existence, and whose suffering, unmitigated by any true higher purpose, is distinguished only by the self-delusions embraced to relieve it.

It is precisely this unrelievedly debased view of man that cripples Vonnegut's fiction and undermines his effectiveness as a moral critic. Caught in a conflict between what he wishes and what he believes, between what he wants for mankind and what he thinks mankind is fated to have, his fiction constantly exposes folly only to submit to inevitability. In Vonnegut's books, anger—which is, after all, a kind of hope—is always defeated by resignation, his criticism of society always emasculated by his final belief that man can do no better. (pp. 14-15)

Vonnegut's problem, you see, is that although he abhors our mechanized culture, he believes the world view upon which it is based; his vision on mankind—so many like individuals pushed by forces beyond their control—is really the same, nothing more than that same mechanistic metaphor misapplied again. And the result of that misapplication is always the same: pessimism, cynicism, resignation, despair. (p. 16)

But Vonnegut is, above all else, a compassionate man; he may not respect his characters, but he does care about them, is driven by an urge to ease their suffering. Given the pessimism of his outlook, however, all he can offer is the very solution he so often mocks: illusion, fantasy, the "harmless untruths" of Bokonism, of Tralfamadorian metaphysics, the soothing escapism of Billy Pilgrim's time-travel. As his recurring character, Eliot Rosewater, says to a psychiatrist in *Slaughterhouse-Five*, "I think you guys are going to have to come up with a lot of wonderful *new* lies, or people just aren't going to want to go on living.'' And there it is again, the same basic conflict resurfacing—between thought and feeling, between the artist and the humanitarian. Vonnegut wants to tell us the truth and at the same time spare us from it; he wants to ease our pain and at the same time show us that only ''lies'' can achieve that end. To comfort, he must lie; to tell the truth, he must hurt; for in the world as Kurt Vonnegut, Jr., sees it, happiness is utterly incompatible with truth. (pp. 16-17)

> *David Bosworth, in* The Antioch Review *(copyright © 1979 by the Antioch Press; reprinted by permission of the Editors), Vol. 37, No. 1, 1979.*

Lenora Mattingly Weber

1895-1971

American young adult novelist and adult short story writer and journalist. Weber, author of the popular Beany Malone series, was for years one of the most widely read authors of books for teenage girls. She published her first book, *Wind on the Prairie*, in 1929. In her more than forty years as an author Weber wrote over thirty books, most of which are romances stressing old-fashioned values, the age-old boy/girl crises of adolescence, and the importance of family relationships. Many of her novels, particularly her earlier efforts, are set on a ranch, reflecting the fact that Weber spent most of her life in Colorado. Although Weber's fiction is frequently criticized today for its sentimentality, its restricted vision of a woman's role, and its failure to confront contemporary issues, it has without question been an important literary influence on several generations of American girls. (See also *Contemporary Authors*, Vols. 19-20; obituary, Vols. 29-32, rev. ed.; *Contemporary Authors Permanent Series*, Vol. 1, and *Something about the Author*, Vol. 2.)

EDWIN L. SABIN

As with Mrs. Weber's preceding books, "Wish in the Dark" revolves around ranch life in Colorado. With its cast of striking characters bent upon making good or destined to be made good, and its element of mystery, it is again a tale capitally told. . . . In a rickety car Hope and the twelve-year-old twins, Becky and Baird, come from Iowa to Colorado, consigned, as orphans, to their Aunt Sarah who is assumed to be living in the town of Trail's End. . . . Their dramatic arrival in Trail's End, their rapidly growing list of new acquaintances, with lively ensuing adventures, brim a story that can be recommended to any family endowed with the spirit of the 'teens. (p. 356)

> *Edwin L. Sabin, in* The Saturday Review of Literature *(copyright, 1931, by The Saturday Review Co., Inc.; reprinted with permission), December 5, 1931.*

The scene of this mystery story for girls ["Wish in the Dark"] is laid on a ranch in a Colorado valley. . . . The plot has plenty of thrills from the stolen telegram and the disappearance of the green shirt to cattle rustling on a large scale. In the end the threads are all tied up neatly—a heart of gold is found under each forbidding exterior in true Western style. In spite of the author's tendency to sentimentalize and to use stock character types "Wish in the Dark" is lively and amusing and much less stereotyped than the average mystery story for girls. (p. 8)

> *New York Herald Tribune Book Review (© I.H.T. Corporation; reprinted by permission), March 6, 1932.*

ELLEN LEWIS BUELL

The Malones [in "Meet the Malones"] are certainly worth meeting. They are individuals in their own right, but you will see in them something of the family next door or down the street, for these four motherless youngsters and their companionable father are very much alive and of this day. And of our time and our country is their unspoken knowledge that democracy really begins at home, around the family council table. . . .

When Martie Malone [the father] went off to Hawaii he left his household running fairly smoothly. . . .

Nonna [the glamorous, efficient step-grandmother] fixed everything beautifully—at first—and the Malones reveled in ease and comfort. But somehow the old, generous, helpful way of life was managed out of existence, the debts and plans were half forgotten, until the arrival of three small refugees made them realize painfully that you can't have things for nothing, that independence and integrity are dearly bought but worth the price.

As the Malones sift their values of living, older girls will find their family crises full of humor and revealing bits of characterization; and if the story occasionally verges on the sentimental, this is more than offset by the tonic tone of the whole.

> *Ellen Lewis Buell, "Family Crises," in* The New York Times Book Review *(© 1943 by The New York Times Company; reprinted by permission), October 17, 1943, p. 8.*

MAY LAMBERTON BECKER

"Meet the Malones" is a story in which the world of an American high school appears as it does in many an American city today. . . .

[The Malone children are settling their family problems] very well in their own way when their step-grandmother, a high-pressure career woman, comes for a visit. She settles everything for them; all they need pay, for what they don't want, is self-respect. Nonna goes, but meanwhile there has been a series of demonstrations that Emerson was right when he said the highest price you could pay for anything was to get it for nothing. This is not a second "Little Women": we don't need one, having the first. But we do need good contemporary high school stories, and this is one. (p. 40)

> *May Lamberton Becker, in* New York Herald Tribune Book Review *(© I.H.T. Corporation; reprinted by permission), November 14, 1943.*

MAY LAMBERTON BECKER

Ever since I read "Sing for Your Supper" I have kept an eye out for anything by its author . . . because she writes about the West, old or contemporary, with a juicy vitality needed in stories about it. For "Westerns" tend to become stereotyped: her stories, for young people growing up, stay within the frame of this fiction, but make it seem as if it really happened.

Thus the bookful of short stories ["Riding High" has] basic elements one expects from ranches in fiction [a sweet young girl, a devoted foster-parent, a bow-legged cowboy confidant, and a young hero].

There is, incidentally, a good deal about habits and education of ranch horses. . . . If grown-up Westerns had as much in them, I might be able to read the things. (p. 7)

> *May Lamberton Becker, in* New York Herald Tribune Book Review *(© I.H.T. Corporation; reprinted by permission), July 21, 1946.*

RUTH HILL VIGUERS

In spite of her name, Beany Malone is a character one is likely to remember. The most reliable, although the youngest of her delightful but not always accountable family, Beany takes over the responsibility of the welfare of her brothers and sisters when their father, the overworked editor of the local paper, goes to Arizona to recuperate.

There is a story and a problem behind each member of the family [in "Beany Malone"]. . . .

There is warmth, quiet humor, and excellent suspense in this story of a young girl's growing up. The Malones are charming, loveable people with a strong sense of values and a fine social outlook, whose problems are real enough to become the problems of the reader.

This is a fine novel, well written, convincing and alive. (p. 36)

> *Ruth Hill Viguers, in* The Saturday Review of Literature *(copyright, 1948, by The Saturday Review Co., Inc.; reprinted with permission), August 14, 1948.*

[*Leave It to Beany!*] is another story of the charming Malones. Sixteen-year-old Beany, in the midst of a high school romance and diverse energetic family projects, finds that her desire to help people in unorthodox ways leads her into several ridiculous and difficult situations. . . . The cousin Sheila episodes, concerning the attempts of the Malones to stuff the lonely, glum girl into a pattern of the American Girl, present an amusing and often perceptive study of the iron defense mechanism which may be built up by a girl outside the magic circle of a high school clique. A warmhearted, very human story. (p. 63)

Virginia Kirkus' Bookshop Service, *February 1, 1950.*

LOUISE S. BECHTEL

["*Leave It to Beany!*" the fifth] book about the Malones will please all their fans in Junior High. Beany, the youngest, now sixteen, is shown in a humorous portrait, overdoing her role of helping every one and managing everything. . . . It is all fairly improbable, even for the high air of Denver, but it is at the same time warm-hearted and a good family portrait. It is rather a relief to find, in a children's book, a family going to mass together.

Motherless Beany rings true, so does the cooking by young and old, and the newspaper background. John's struggles with his history of Denver make a clever sub-plot, and the glimpses of several teachers are well done. The romance is played down, in a refreshingly humorous way. On the whole, better than most series books. (p. 10)

> *Louise S. Bechtel, in* New York Herald Tribune Book Review *(© I.H.T. Corporation; reprinted by permission), April 23, 1950.*

This time [*Beany and the Beckoning Road*] takes the already beloved Beany Malone of Miss Weber's series [on] a trip to California to bring about the further flowering of her romance with the *Morning Call*'s young red haired reporter, Norbett. . . . In the welter of events that includes scoops, caring for a friend's horse, finding out more about people and their feelings, this latest Malone story is a good bit of human interest, a good bit of newsworld background. Excellent for hours at the apple-supplied window-seat. (p. 78)

Virginia Kirkus' Bookshop Service, *February 1, 1952.*

LOUISE S. BECHTEL

["*Beany and the Beckoning Road*"] begins with Beany having a sad tiff with her beau Norbett. It sends her from Denver to San Diego to cure her troubled heart. On this wild jaunt by auto Beany and her absent-minded older brother take turns at the wheel. Their adventures are told with the mixture of humor, sentiment, and realism that have given the Malone books their wide appeal to junior-high-age girls. The horse in the trailer, the mysterious old lady, the trunk full of gold, all are utterly preposterous, yet cleverly related to Beany's love affair. That the lovable three-year-old could live through such a trip is the most miraculous touch of all. Those who already like the sensible, warm-hearted, direct Beany will have to read it. To listmakers who worry about such matters, it may be said that few teen-agers would wish to follow Beany on such a journey. (p. 10)

> *Louise S. Bechtel, in* New York Herald Tribune Book Review *(I.H.T. Corporation; reprinted by permission), March 16, 1952.*

[In *My True Love Waits* the] author of the loved *Beany Malone* series turns to the post Civil War South and Southwest in [a] sympathetically touching if over-long novel of a young girl's marriage to an actor and the trials of poverty and social disapproval that it entailed. . . . Prolonged overtones of sentimentality may bore some but character and atmosphere are sketched to give a fine picture of the times. (p. 73)

Virginia Kirkus' Bookshop Service, *February 1, 1953*.

JENNIE D. LINDQUIST

Already well known for her lively Beany Malone stories, Mrs. Weber has here written [*My True Love Waits,*] a book no less lively but of more permanent value.... The larger part of the book—and the best of it—is devoted to the hardships and adventures that Mary and the five people who go with her meet on their covered-wagon journey to Denver City. It is a realistic story that does not soft-pedal the grim side of such an undertaking, though the book has a happy and satisfactory ending. (pp. 128-29)

Jennie D. Lindquist, in The Horn Book Magazine *(copyrighted, 1953, by The Horn Book, Inc., Boston), April, 1953.*

[*Beany Has a Secret Life*] takes our heroine, now a junior at Harkness High in Denver, over some rough 16 year old bumps. There's a new stepmother in newsman Martie Malone's large family, and a discouraging if temporary rebuff from the school's clubs throws Beany into the arms of an executive secret club of six members, started by glamorous, unhappy Maurine. Adair, Martie's new wife, is young and artistic and Beany is determined to like her until a set of circumstances that includes the theft of Adair's car, seems to prove irrevocably that Adair is out for blood. Beany takes increased refuge with Maurine and the small gang, but with her brother taking a hand, she realizes at last why such groups are against school jurisdiction. Maurine too confesses both to the damage done Adair's car *and* to a serious if reparable step*father* problem. Warm, humorous and adult handling of these thorny issues. (p. 3)

Virginia Kirkus' Service, *January 1, 1955*.

ALBERTA EISEMAN

At 16, Beany, youngest of the Malones—a family well known to teen-age girls—was happy with the status quo. Then suddenly everything began to change [in "Beany Has a Secret Life"].... For over 200 pages the author puts every possible obstacle in the way of a reconciliation between Beany and her stepmother, but finally our freckle-faced heroine sees the light.

The Malones are a nice family and, as always, fun to read about. One wishes, however, that the author had not thrown so many contrived misunderstandings their way and had not tied everything up quite so neatly at the end. (p. 24)

Alberta Eiseman, in The New York Times Book Review *(© 1955 by The New York Times Company; reprinted by permission), March 6, 1955.*

BARBARA JOYCE DUREE

While more hackneyed and contrived than some of its author's earlier books, [*The More the Merrier*] will be welcomed by Beany's many fans. Left with her brother Johnny while their parents are in Mexico, Beany decides to turn the big Malone home into a boardinghouse, thereby earning enough to make a rumpus room in the basement. Although her boarders ... bring the kindhearted Beany more problems than profits, the summer ends happily for everyone concerned. (p. 160)

Barbara Joyce Duree, in The Booklist and Subscription Books Bulletin *(reprinted by permission*

of the American Library Association; copyright 1958 by the American Library Association), November 15, 1958.

BARBARA JOYCE DUREE

[*A Bright Star Falls*] finds its popular heroine [Beany Malone] now a senior at Harkness High and editor of the school paper.... The seriousness of ... new situations and problems makes the book seem somewhat more significant than many of the earlier titles in a growing series. (p. 124)

Barbara Joyce Duree, in The Booklist and Subscription Books Bulletin *(reprinted by permission of the American Library Association; copyright 1959 by the American Library Association), October 15, 1959.*

HELEN OAKLEY

In [*The Winds of March,* a] sequel to *Don't Call Me Katie Rose*, the heroine, a sophomore at Adams High, has the smugness blown out of her by "the winds of March." In this month she has two chastening experiences. First, she must learn to stand by while the irresistible Bruce Seerie overlooks her intellect in favor of her sister's exuberance. The other crisis, a horrifying kidnapping, well handled by both Katie Rose and the author, helps her revise some of her lofty attitudes. Mrs. Weber's teenage dialogue and school setting are authentic, and there is enough action to satisfy girls who can easily identify with this "delightsome" heroine. (p. 2039)

Helen Oakley, in Library Journal *(reprinted from* Library Journal, *April 15, 1965; published by R. R. Bowker Co. (a Xerox company), copyright © 1965 by Xerox Corporation), April 15, 1965.*

[*A New and Different Summer,* the third Katie Rose story,] consists of menu plans and grocery lists. Bringing the Katie Rose gossip up to date—Mrs. Belford has had to go to Ireland to look after a sick relative, leaving K.R. in charge of supervising all household arrangements for the other five children. Katie Rose sees this as her opportunity to change her mother's do-the-cooking from scratch policies.... Nothing very startling happens beyond the domestic routine, and there are enough shopping items to fill two or three more Katie Rose books. The characters are easy to like, though, and are nicely refreshing. And the Irish-American, financially struggling but not impoverished family help to balance out the extremes of the well-to-do and the poor which overpopulate teen books. (pp. 190-91)

Virginia Kirkus' Service *(copyright © 1966 Virginia Kirkus' Service, Inc.), February 15, 1966.*

EMMA KIRBY

Despite the predictable plot and characters and the story's pat resolution, [*A New and Different Summer*] is highly readable and has great appeal in its evocation of a happy, loving family. Not challenging fiction, but lighthearted and fun to read. One unnecessary scene gives the story an ugly flaw. At a baby shower, Katie asks a Negro girl if she is married.

"'I was' came the casual answer. 'I got me two little kids, but right now I ain't got no man'." ... The scene and comment are extraneous to the plot and needlessly perpetuate the stereotype of the shiftless Negro. (p. 174)

Emma Kirby, in School Library Journal *(reprinted from the May, 1966 issue of* School Library Journal, *published by R. R. Bowker Co. A Xerox Corporation; copyright © 1966), May, 1966.*

ZENA SUTHERLAND

The writing [of *A New and Different Summer*] has an easy flow, but the story moves slowly; it has the appeals of familiar characters, a modest home setting, and realistic events, but the main theme (Katie Rose's menus and shopping extravaganzas) is somewhat belabored. (p. 172)

Zena Sutherland, in Bulletin of the Center for Children's Books *(copyright 1966 by the University of Chicago; all rights reserved), June, 1966.*

Katie Rose Belford, who seemed, in earlier installments, to have some sense and spirit as well as brains . . . submits to the appeal of Gil(martin) Ames [in *I Met a Boy I Used to Know*]. . . . Gil is clearly a Lost Cause . . . but Katie Rose clings to her faith that "his showoff was only a cover for inner insecurity and unhappiness." . . . [She] finally realizes that her ill-starred hero is just plain unpleasant and unreliable, and moves "out from under his dark star." The Belford clan . . . is strictly in the background: instead of *One Girl's Family* it's *A Woman's Folly*. But Miguel—zany, dependable Miguel—is expected in thirty-eight and-a-half days; readers might well skip this inauspicious interlude and, with Katie Rose, await his return. (p. 1145)

Virginia Kirkus' Service (copyright © 1966 Virginia Kirkus' Service, Inc.), November 1, 1966.

Mostly Katie Rose is in the wings [in *Angel in Heavy Shoes*], waiting for the Muse; it's Stacy's and Ben's show. . . . Katie Rose is hung up over the subject of a play for a contest everyone expects her to win. . . . In his obtrusive institution shoes, [Irv, just back from reform school, has] been an angel unawares and just what Katie Rose needed to start her play, *Angel in Heavy Shoes*. The blarney is laid on without a brogue and the Good Samaritanship isn't all goody-goody; if you can stomach the series at all, you'll find this easier to take than some. (p. 126)

Kirkus Service (copyright © 1968 Virginia Kirkus' Service, Inc.), February 1, 1968.

The focus of [*Come Back, Wherever You Are*] is Beany's concern for Jodey [the four-year-old son of Kay, a hospitalized friend,] and what it does to her family life, expecially to her relationship with husband Carl—a shift of interest for teenage fiction but not for girls who watch afternoon TV. Before Kay's death and the final wrap-up, assorted relatives and classmates pose their own problems, and the solution for one of the latter is also the answer for Jodey and Joe. All very tidy, but Mrs. Weber's audience will still call it neat. (p. 58)

Kirkus Reviews (copyright © 1969 The Kirkus Service, Inc.), January 15, 1969.

ZENA SUTHERLAND

As in all the Beany Malone stories, [*Come Back, Wherever You Are*] is a smooth pastiche of family life and the problems of Beany's circle of friends and acquaintances. Here the crucial situation is that of a small, disturbed child whose mother, Beany's old friend, dies of leukemia. Beany's efforts to make little Jodey feel secure are partially suc-

cessful. . . . Although the story has a burden of subplots and minor characters, it is realistic, warm, and capably written. (p. 135)

Zena Sutherland, in Bulletin of the Center for Children's Books *(© 1969 by the University of Chicago; all rights reserved), April, 1969.*

PILAR SCHMIDT

[*Angel in Heavy Shoes*] is above the level of the ordinary because it attempts to treat relations among people from various socio-economic levels of society. In spite of some weaknesses, *Angel in Heavy Shoes* generally warrants consideration because it deals with the struggles of a middle-class teen-ager who tries to overcome distaste for a family of a lower socio-economic class and because it touches on the seamier side of life: alcoholism, juvenile delinquency, and crime. Even though the background details of the unfortunate Flood family are revealed rather awkwardly through Rita and Lennie Flood's mouths, the gradual change that occurs in Katie Rose Belford's attitude towards the Floods is well done and believable.

One of the major drawbacks of this novel is its structure. Dealing with one day or even one afternoon at a time, the author treats each one of the main characters and their adventures in turn before moving on to the next period of time. I found this technique monotonous, but students with reading problems might find it an asset rather than a liability. (pp. 779-80)

Pilar Schmidt, in English Journal *(copyright © 1969 by the National Council of Teachers of English), May, 1969.*

[*Separation*] from the Belford manse and menage impoverishes the proceedings and throws all the weight on [the] lightweight plot [of *How Long is Always?*]. Series-ly speaking, it's expendable. (p. 113)

Kirkus Reviews (copyright © 1970 The Kirkus Service, Inc.), February 1, 1970.

ZENA SUTHERLAND

A protagonist familiar to Katie Rose fans, younger sister Stacy Belford takes a summer job as driver-helper to an elderly man [in *How Long Is Always?*]. . . . Stacy has the usual problems of adapting to a new situation, falling in love with an older man, trying to thaw her employer's wife. The events are natural and realistic, although the book lacks the warmth of the Belford family stories; the characterization and story line are adequate, the writing marred by a trick that is overdone: Stacy has trouble with long words . . . and this becomes a bit cute. Stacy also exhibits occasional gaps in knowledge or intelligence that don't quite ring true. (p. 186)

Zena Sutherland, in Bulletin of the Center for Children's Books *(© 1970 by the University of Chicago; all rights reserved), July-August, 1970.*

Sure an' you'll be longin' for the sound of Granda O'Byrnes' brogue, the latest of the Belford chronicles [*Hello, My Love, Goodbye*] being low in lovable schmaltz, high in TV trauma. Optimistic extrovert Stacy, now seventeen, is manhandled by a boozy has-been and "this shameful and degrading experience" is aggravated by the failure of her assorted boy friends to assure her she couldn't be taken for "that kind of girl." . . . This one's not so easy to laugh off. (p. 181)

Kirkus Reviews *(copyright © 1971 The Kirkus Service, Inc.), February 15, 1971.*

REBECCA RICKY FRIESEM

Lenora Mattingly Weber's latest teen romance [*Sometimes a Stranger*] again pits stereotyped wholesomeness against stereotyped evil. Spirited Stacy Belford breaks off her romance with Bruce Seerie because he has not yet asserted his independence from his meddling, snobbish mother. While Stacy plunges into a whirl of activity to forget him, Bruce belatedly cuts the umbilical cord and consequently plunges into a deep depression. . . . Will these two finally get together? Of course, with the help of some new types for a Weber novel—hippies with hearts of gold. A further nod in the direction of the new age is Stacy's plan to embark on a career with no mention of marriage and "working 'til the baby comes." . . . Nevertheless, the characters here . . . are one dimensional, and the plot holds few surprises. (p. 141)

Rebecca Ricky Friesem, in School Library Journal *(reprinted from the April, 1972 issue of* School Library Journal, *published by R. R. Bowker Co. A Xerox Corporation; copyright © 1972), April, 1972.*

JOHN W. CONNER

Sometimes a Stranger is a fitting finale for the talents of Lenora Weber. She had an ever-present finger on the reading pulse of younger adolescent girls.

In *Sometimes a Stranger,* Stacy Belford's on-again-off-again-then-on-again love affair with wealthy Bruce Seerie is traced through Stacy's senior year at St. Jude High School and into the summer following her graduation. (pp. 1385-86)

Hours of heartache and moments of happiness alternate in *Sometimes a Stranger,* much as they do in an adolescent reader's own life. This element, of course, is what makes Lenora Weber's stories meaningful for her many readers. Stacy and Bruce both begin to face the future more realistically at the close of this novel. Each has learned that personal values are something one has to develop within oneself, not accept from parents or friends. Both young people are wiser and closer together at the close of *Sometimes a Stranger.* I predict that younger adolescent girls will enjoy this last Lenora Weber book for many years to come! (p. 1386)

John W. Conner, in English Journal *(copyright © 1972 by the National Council of Teachers of English), December, 1972.*

REBECCA RADNER

[The Beany Malone series is mentioned in Rebecca Radner's essay discussing the limiting effect on girls of some of the teenage literature written during the nineteen-forties and fifties.]

Recently I became curious about just what in these books exerted such a strong pull on our young imaginations. (p. 789)

The basic elements of this sort of story are simple. The sixteen or seventeen year old heroine meets the right boy and the wrong boy. We can tell them apart instantly, but she

can't until the end of the book. While her mother is cooking and cleaning for the family, our heroine goes through an identity crisis, usually brought on by a desire to impress the wrong boy. This leads to a temporary misunderstanding with the right boy. By the end of the story, she has made up with the right boy, been invited to the big dance after all, has become solidly popular with the crowd, and decided to be herself. As we shall see, this decision is less impressive than it sounds; the typical heroine of the period knows she is a girl who wants to be both nice and popular, and end up with a house and kids just like Mom. Her quest for identity usually ends with this comfortingly vague realization. (pp. 789-90)

Unpopularity is the greatest menace for all the girls. Even Beany Malone, one of the most independent heroines, surveys the unpopular girls at a dance with the resolve never to be one of them. . . .

One might think that . . . our heroine will challenge [the] system, but she never does. Her way of dealing with it is to exchange the wrong boy for the right boy, but she will end up secure in the knowledge of her popularity. (p. 790)

The main function these nice boys serve is to assure their girl friends' popularity, and bolster up their egos. All the girls want to feel they are special, that their lives are special, that their love affairs are special. . . .

Perhaps because there is so little inherent drama in this sort of relationship, every story has a misunderstanding part way through which threatens the heroine in her most vulnerable spot, the senior prom or its equivalent. . . .

The girl and the boy are reconciled, and the girl vows never again to try to act like anyone else. This rings all the more hollow as these passages have a similar tone of having your cake and eating it. In a little epiphany near the end of *Beany Has A Secret Life,* Beany decides, "Yes, it was nice to *be on her own* without her heart's happiness depending on any one boy." In the last scene, however, Beany welcomes Andy's claims on her. "Andy held out the apron for her, and wrapped the ties around her twice. He tied them snugly. 'There! Now you might say I've got strings on Beany Malone,'" he exclaims, in a classic demonstration of Male Chauvinism. (p. 792)

The game the girls seem to enjoy the most might be called little weak feminine me and big strong masculine you. Mary Fred Malone, Beany's big sister, assures her boy friend, "I'd like you to boss me, Ander." (p. 793)

It's true they don't seem to have many choices other than marriage. Very few of the girls seem to have any interests beyond boys, clothes, and an occasional round of housekeeping. Mary Fred Malone lives for horses, but that has always been an acceptable side-line for a teen-age girl, and that's how she gets her husband. Older sister Elizabeth goes from beauty queen to wife and mother, and Beany is decidedly the hausfrau type. (pp. 793-94)

Perhaps one reason the girls' choices seem so limited is that they don't know anyone who doesn't conform. (p. 794)

There are no non-conformists in [much of the literature of this period], with the possible exception of the Beany Malone series. Beany knows the only career woman mentioned (a lonely hearts columnist), an old homeless newspaperman, the only cripple (who is, luckily, beautiful, sweet and uncomplaining, and the younger sister of Beany's boy friend), and the only fat girl (who reduces, with Beany's help, in time to get her own boy friend by the last page). There are no minorities and no seriously poverty-stricken families; no one, in fact, who isn't automatically eligible for small town popularity, if they'll just make a slight effort to be pleasant. At least the Malone series does suggest that other people count too. . . .

The adults in these books are not much help at suggesting another way of life. They are contented with their own, which presents a range of choices even more limited than that of the girls. Beany Malone's father Marty is one of the exceptions. He is a crusading newspaperman who encourages the motherless Malone children to be self-reliant. The standard father figure is much more like the right boy grown older. He is solid, dependable, unimaginative, and convinced that woman's place is in the kitchen. He rewards his daughter for the use of feminine wiles. (p. 795)

Beany's Secret Life presents an interesting picture of a new stepmother who is an artist instead of a housekeeper. Beany is resentful at first, because "a stepmother ought to be more at home in a kitchen." Mary Fred tries to excuse Adair: "I think she wants to do for us, but she doesn't know how." Adair herself apologizes constantly for her ineptness and her preference for painting over housework, even suggesting that she go to cooking school. The problem is solved when motherly Miss Opal offers to stay with the Malones and do the work. Adair is delighted by the sugges-

tion but still feels guilty, telling Miss Opal she'd rather worry about her salary "than about what a wash-out I am as a housekeeper." Despite her long-time career, now that she is married, Adair's first duty is to the housework, and only the lucky presence of Miss Opal, who needs a place to stay, and Beany's hausfrau nature will allow her to escape it. (p. 796)

Why did we love these stories so much if they made us feel so bad? I think it was because they were the only literature we had that talked about girls a little older than we were in a contemporary setting. Most of us weren't supposed to read adult best sellers at eleven or twelve, and these books were the only ones that claimed to give us an idea of what it was like to be in high school, how we should behave, what would really happen to us. . . .

Many of these books are no longer generally available. They've been reevaluated by younger librarians and teachers as badly written, full of social stereotypes, and misleading. My friend the children's librarian says, "I'm really glad to see them go."

Before they went, though, they affected a whole generation of women. How much, it's impossible to tell. These books were part of a larger phenomenon, of course, and it's silly to blame them for all of our confusion. But I think they augmented it. (p. 798)

Rebecca Radner, in Journal of Popular Culture *(copyright © 1978 by Ray B. Browne), Spring, 1978.*

Rosemary Wells

American young adult novelist and children's book author/illustrator. Creating novels for young adult readers and picture books for children, and winning awards for both, Wells is a popular and versatile juvenile author. She writes and illustrates her picture books, which are generally lighthearted treatments of a child's growing experiences. Wells has written three young adult novels to date, *The Fog Comes on Little Pig Feet*, *None of the Above*, and a mystery novel, *Leave Well Enough Alone*. All the novels deal with ethical dilemmas of adolescence, presenting difficult moral solutions with honesty and humor.

ALICE MILLER

[*The Fog Comes on Little Pig Feet* is] fast-paced, adequately written entertainment.... Although the characters ... are stereotyped and one minor character never develops as expected, Wells does successfully portray the beginnings of puberty and an adolescent's need for privacy. Rachel's obsession about getting her period, counting her pubic hairs ... and examining her chest for signs of developing breasts are related with humor and understanding. (p. 89)

> Alice Miller, in School Library Journal (*reprinted from the May, 1972 issue of* School Library Journal, *published by R. R. Bowker Co. A Xerox Corporation; copyright © 1972*), May 1972.

JANE LANGTON

[*The Fog Comes on Little Pig Feet*] is the secret journal of Rachel Sasakian, scribbled after lights out while she crouches in a bathtub at boarding school....

Driven into a corner by the dumb rules of the school, she becomes crafty. Her father, she brags, is Norman Mailer. To escape compulsory chapel she declares herself a convert to Judaism. But the totalitarian pressure of the school mounts until Rachel's resistance is an act of heroism. The book says something true about life: Evil is not diabolical and nasty, but bland and blind. (p. 5)

> Jane Langton, in Book World—Chicago Tribune (© *1972 Postrib Corp.*), May 7, 1972.

To start with, Rachel's snobbish working-class mother, who saves and borrows to send Rachel to a $4,000-a-year high school with "nice girls from nice families," is just un-real. She's a type rather than an individual but she isn't true to any type, and Ms. Wells' unsympathetic treatment of her [in *The Fog Comes on Little Pig Feet*] indicates a little snobbery on her own part.... The initial picture of the rigid, repressive school gives a similar impression of garbled sociology, even to the expensive, out-of-season asparagus served at dinner. Once we're into the story, though, certain recognizable absurdities are given properly incidental notice..., and the quirky humor that has always been evident in Ms. Wells' pictures assumes some happy verbal manifestations here. And Rachel herself, a reluctant nonconformist who hates the school because it allows her no time to practice piano or just be alone, is quietly convincing all along. When she accidentally becomes involved with a disturbed older girl who runs away to the Village, the plot focuses on a real dilemma: should Rachel tell where Carlisle has gone, as authorities tell her the girl is self-destructive and needs help, or keep her vow of silence because Carlisle has a right to lead her own life and neither the school nor her parents are likely to do her any good if they do find her? In the end Rachel is not sure she has made the right choice but fortunately the trouble has brought her parents to their senses and they withdraw her from the school. The story too grows up as it goes along. (p. 581)

> Kirkus Reviews (*copyright © 1972 The Kirkus Service, Inc.*), May 15, 1972.

JEAN F. MERCIER

Ms. Wells writes with uncompromising honesty; the feelings of all characters [in "None of the Above"] are believably expressed and the plot concerns a vital area—the pitiful state of education in our public schools. The trouble with the story is that all its people are so unsavory. That goes double for the "heroine," a dolt who is more irritating than sympathetic. Her stepmother, a snob and a pseudointellectual, wants Marcia out of the dullard class in high school and into the college-prep group with her bright daughter, Chrissie. Marcia, though she's more interested in gaudy sweaters and french fries and in daydreams of sexual exploits, finds she can fake it and make it in the advanced courses until the day when she's required to think instead of cram her head with facts. At the story's end, she has opted for a sordid future instead of college, but who cares? (p. 58)

637

Jean F. Mercier, in Publishers Weekly (*reprinted from the August 5, 1974, issue of* Publishers Weekly *by permission of the critic, published by R. R. Bowker Company, a Xerox company; copyright © 1974 by Xerox Corporation*), August 5, 1974.

JONI BODART

When her father remarries, doltish Marcia . . . finds herself out of place with her sophisticated stepmother and her whiz-kid stepsister Chris. In the five years that [*None of the Above*] spans, Marcia becomes more acceptable to her new family . . . but in so doing seems to lose herself. . . . Wells refuses to provide any "happily ever after" solution to Marcia's problems. An unusual and oddly affecting heroine, Marcia seems, at times, to be sleepwalking through the events of her life. The author skillfully captures the girl's confusion in this timely, realistic and moving novel. . . . (p. 69)

Joni Bodart, in School Library Journal (*reprinted from the November, 1974 issue of* School Library Journal, *published by R. R. Bowker Co. A Xerox Corporation; copyright © 1974*), November, 1974.

DALE CARLSON

"None of the Above" is a sensitive novel of teen-age problems, the search for identity in a confusing world, the alien feeling within the context of an alien family, the discovery of answers to essentially unanswerable problems.

"None of the Above" is well-written and the characters well-conceived. I'm not sure about the ending—sentimentally, but I don't think realistically, conceived. (p. 8)

Dale Carlson, in The New York Times Book Review (© *1974 by The New York Times Company; reprinted by permission*), November 24, 1974.

SISTER MARY COLUMBA, P.B.V.M.

Marcia Mill discovers new pressures, new adjustments, new problems in her life after her father remarries. Her brilliant stepsister brings competition, so she tries to attain a higher academic standing. Her sister, Sharon, whose husband has been in Vietnam for over a year, becomes pregnant, but doesn't want her husband to know. Her father arranges for an abortion. . . .

The first part of [*None of the Above*] is an interesting story of family situations and events with a stepmother and her daughter trying to become part of this family. The stepmother counsels Marcia about getting "caught" as her sister did. Marcia promises to be virtuous.

The latter half is disgusting as it vividly depicts sexual relations. Raymond [Marcia's boyfriend] is a Catholic. He belittles prayer and confession. Sex seems to be the only thing in his life. Marcia's goal is now marriage—not a college education. She gets "sick" and later slips on Raymond's ring because she love him.

The book is definitely not for ages thirteen and up. Adults would find parts of it lacking in morality. (pp. 519-20)

Sister Mary Columba, P.B.V.M., in Best Sellers (*copyright 1975, by the University of Scranton*), February 15, 1975.

MARGERY FISHER

The boarding-school world depicted in *The fog comes on little pig feet*, though not quite St. Trinian's, would probably be taken as a satirical picture if the story were set in England; as it is, I cannot be sure whether the author has exaggerated the oppression and emotional aridity of North Place and, if so, whether this is because of her own experience of school or to give bite to her story. At any rate it has acquired enough bite through first person narration. The naïve, emotional words of the narrator, Rachel, whose battle against the school is also a battle against her parents, make Carlisle Daggett's misguided neurotic fight against authority seem all the more tragic because the author herself does not comment on it. She merely shows how the sight of an older girl's misery, and the conflicting claim on Rachel's loyalties, make the child set aside her own troubles for a time. This short, uncluttered tale, a good deal of it consisting of dialogue, implies a good deal about the difficulties of communication, between individuals and between the generations. (pp. 2891-92)

Margery Fisher, in her Growing Point, May, 1976.

ROSAMOND FAITH

The theme [of *The Fog Comes On Little Pig Feet*] inevitably recalls Salinger; the disastrous first week at a posh boarding school of Rachel, fierce, funny and working-class, sent there by her sad and anxious parents to meet "nice girls from nice families". . . . There isn't much of a plot; loyalty to a run-away delinquent friend, to her own scale of values, to those worried parents; these provide conflict enough.

The book is tougher and more sophisticated than any English equivalent I know, and certainly more literate: a friendship is sealed by a Carl Sandburg misquotation and the tone throughout is urbane. There are quite a few Americanisms (public school, Kotex, etc), which could well have been edited out. None of this, I hope, should prevent the book being enjoyed by literate young English readers. It's well written, it's funny, and it feels so right that it comes as no surprise to learn from the blurb that it is based on the author's own experience.

Rosamond Faith, "Lack of Promise," in The Times Literary Supplement (© *Times Newspapers Ltd. (London) 1976; reproduced from* The Times Literary Supplement *by permission*), October 1, 1976, p. 1243.

JANE ABRAMSON

[In *Leave Well Enough Alone*] Dorothy is . . . left on her own to decide the most moral course of action. Although the mystery is contrived and confusing at times with too many false or oblique clues, the characterizations are superb, especially Dorothy's "martyred" older sister who, at 20, is saddled with a baby and bunions; and, of course, Dorothy, herself, caught squarely between her Catholic conscience and ambitious nature. Wells' finest novel yet, this raises thorny ethical questions and discusses them compellingly and with great humor. (p. 73)

Jane Abramson, in School Library Journal (*reprinted from the May, 1977 issue of* School Library Journal, *published by R. R. Bowker Co. A Xerox Corporation; copyright © 1977*), May, 1977.

KATHERINE PATERSON

I began [*Leave Well Enough Alone*] laughing with delight at Rosemary Wells's marvelous re-creation of fourteenness —the fervid rejoicing over a mistake not made, the strain of drinking a Coke noiselessly in the presence of an adult one is struggling to impress, furtively removing and disposing of one's ruined stockings, only to have them returned by a smiling porter. And for those of us who grew up pious in the '40s and '50s there is that ever losing battle for goodness—the feverish yielding to the very temptation one has seconds before praised God for the power to overcome.

I began the book laughing. I ended it in goosebumps. In between I had gobbled up red herrings like gum drops.

To say that Wells deceived me right up until the next to the last page is to acknowledge her ability as a writer of suspense, but it is the shimmering threads of humor and human insight with which she has spun her tale that completely entrap the reader.

> *Katherine Paterson, "The Case of the Curious Babysitter," in* Book World—The Washington Post *(© 1977, The Washington Post), May 1, 1977, p. E4.*

SUSAN TERRIS

Not since Dorothy was whisked off to Oz have I encountered a Dorothy as impressionable and thoroughly sympathetic as the heroine of Rosemary Wells's "Leave Well Enough Alone." In this novel, set in 1956, Dorothy, almost 15, a policeman's daughter and student at the Sacred Heart School in Newburgh, N.Y., finds herself transported to Llewellyn, Pa. where, for the magnificent sum of $400, she is to spend the summer taking care of two beastly little girls.

At first blink, Maria and John Hoade's Llewellyn estate with its pastoral beauty and fabulous parties seems like an Emerald City to Dorothy Coughlin; but as the green glasses begin to slip down her nose she realizes that the place reeks of menace, mystery and lies. (p. 20)

As Dorothy pursues clue after clue in her search for truth and in a desire to gain personal recognition, she also begins to discover that the world is a very complex place with a gray area between right and wrong where even a person of conscience cannot easily cope. Despite the aura this serious issue gives to the novel, Mrs. Wells has not lost her touch for writing funny dialogue or her ability to develop believable characters. In fact, the Hoade girls' mother, Maria, is so pathetically real and zany—she wears her homemade sweater inside-out because she knitted the initials from the manual into it instead of her own—she sometimes threatens to steal the whole show from Dorothy.

All in all, this is a well-written book full of humor and suspense. It does, however, have the added plus of leaving the reader to wrestle with the question of whether "leaving well enough alone" *is* the right solution to a complicated moral dilemma. (p. 21)

> *Susan Terris, in* The New York Times Book Review *(© 1977 by The New York Times Company; reprinted by permission), July 10, 1977.*

ZENA SUTHERLAND

The characterization [in *Leave Well Enough Alone*] is strong and the dialogue natural; the story is overcrowded however, with the mystery and suspense of the adult coffin, with Dorothy's adjustment to a job and a situation for which she is equally ill-prepared, and with the dominating theme of her struggles with her conscience and her reiterated but abortive promises to herself and to God that she will stop lying and meddling. (p. 40)

> *Zena Sutherland, in* Bulletin of the Center for Children's Books *(© 1977 by the University of Chicago; all rights reserved), October, 1977.*

Brian Wilson

1942-

American songwriter, musician, musical arranger, and producer. Wilson's music is noted for authentically capturing the American teenage experience and for helping to create the international image of Southern California as a youthful utopia. The Beach Boys, which he formed as a teenager with his two brothers, Carl and Dennis, a cousin, Mike Love, and a friend, Al Jardine, gained fame in the early sixties with songs that depicted a mythic world of long-haired girls and golden boys who live for surfing, cars, and long summer nights. Wilson's descriptions of this free lifestyle did not come from experience; he wrote as an outsider looking in, and built his career out of his displacement. His music, which started as confident and joyous in the surf genre he created, gradually became more introspective with songs like "In My Room" and "When I Grow Up." Filled with inner turmoil, pain, and longing, these songs were wrapped in lush arrangements and were characterized by their distinctive chord progressions and unique harmonies. Influenced by the close-harmony vocals of the Four Freshmen, the jaunty rockers of Chuck Berry, and, especially, the mini-operas of producer Phil Spector, Wilson concentrated on creating and overall sound that would be both musically innovative and commercially successful, much as the Beatles were doing. The Beach Boys became phenomenally successful, and demands were made on Wilson to churn out hit singles in the fun-and-sun mold despite his own desire to concentrate solely on improving his composing and production talents. This pressure on his creativity caused him to retreat further into himself, and he stopped performing with the group and suffered a series of breakdowns. After the commercial failure of *Pet Sounds,* an album which some critics consider both Wilson's definitive work and a milestone in pop music, he retreated from the music scene, and the group floundered without his leadership. Musically, he released fragmented but exciting works such as *Smiley Smile,* but seemed to lose interest in his work and entered a period of creative inertia. During the late sixties and early seventies The Beach Boys became considered a reactionary, clean-cut anachronism that had no relation to a period of social change and revolution. Wilson's lyrics were criticized as being sophomoric, weak, and unworthy of the maturity of the music, and he became more well known for his eccentric behavior than for the quality of his work. However, the band returned to public favor in 1974, after dogged touring and the success of a greatest-hits compilation. Wilson returned to the group in 1976, but their recent albums have achieved only minimal success. It has been argued that no songwriter has been better at depicting the joy and sorrows of adolescents than Wilson, in a language that was specifically their own. Certainly many young people have related to his innocent, lyrical yearnings and have appreciated his undeniable musical gifts.

BARRY FANTONI

I think "Pet Sounds" is probably one of the best produced albums out, but it suffers because of it. I managed to listen to one side of it, and I heard just about a bellyfull. At times it was beautiful but the words were hazy which may have been unintentional—or that may have been the idea. It was rather a lazy record. Sometimes boring—not because of the way it was done—but the slight monotony. I've got "Beach Boys Today!" which is rougher but more exciting. Actually "Pet Sounds" reminded me of two classical composers—who I prefer—and shouldn't really compare, but it has similarities to Palestrini, and, also what happened to Mozart and Turner the painter in mid-career. Their techniques became immaculate and their production fantastic and you thought "who the hell managed to produce this?" That's how I feel about the Beach Boys. I preferred them when they were young and more loose and rough, as I did Turner and Mozart when they got older and loosened up. I agree it's probably revolutionary but I'm not sure that everything that's revolutionary is necessarily good. I'm not being anti-progressive—but I'm not convinced they're always good. (p. 8)

Barry Fantoni, in Melody Maker (© *IPC Business Press Ltd.), July 30, 1966.*

ANDREW OLDHAM

I think that "Pet Sounds" is the most progressive album of the year in as much as Rimsky-Korsakov's "Scheherezade" was. It is the pop equivalent of that. A complete exercise in pop technique. Personally I consider it to be a fantastic album. The lyrics are tremendous. The way Wilson has suited them to the songs is outstanding. I see pop music as a form of escapism, and "Pet Sounds" is a great example of escapism. (p. 8)

Andrew Oldham, in Melody Maker *(© IPC Business Press Ltd.), July 30, 1966.*

ARTHUR SCHMIDT

The Beach Boys have tried faithfully to render who and what they are. That what they are is in some ways a simply (existential but) foolish denial of reality, that Hawthorne is not the world that Watts is, is nothing other than the fact that art, like human action, when it impersonally duplicates reality, is more schizophrenia.

The group takes risks, however. After *Pet Sounds,* the only flaw of which was its indulgence in a sometimes over-lush sound, they cleaned up and came out with *Smiley Smile,* so controlled, precise and tight that it risked (and at times lost to) sterility. "Wild Honey" bet on keeping tight and somehow simultaneously releasing everything they had in a sustained emotional burst. The bet paid off. *Friends* is a transition. . . . Occasionally lapsing into the style of *Pet Sounds* (as on "Diamond Head," which is not as good as anything on that earlier LP), they more often mix the dry, silly-but-witty (like a fatigue high) style of *Smiley Smile* with the harder-driving, less still, more emotional feel of *Wild Honey.*

The best cuts are "Meant For You," the dedication; "Friends," a more mature (in that it lacks their usual immediacy) evocation of the surfer "pack" or "club" vision —why go out with a girl when you can go cruising with the guys on Saturday nights? It's really warm, simple, touching, saying in not so many words that friendship isn't about words. Other groups say what is happening, they talk about what has happened and what should have, and, by implication, why what has has and why what should have hasn't.

Everything on the first side is great. These cuts, "Wake the World," "Be Here in the Morning," and "When a Man Needs a Woman," all evoke the elation of "Wild Honey." (The lyrics on the last are a weird synthesis of R&B raunchiness and the group's own wholesome naivete.) (p. 323)

"Little Bird" and "Be Still," are tight, emotional and beautifully done, with fine lyrics that do not exploit the California-nature-youth idiom that is, as vision, as artistic as the music itself. "Transcendental Meditation" is unfortunate, because India Imports Gibranism is unfortunate, and because it experiments questionably with jazz. But for pop mysticism, it's not as pretentious as it might be.

"Busy Doing Nothing" words and music by Brian, is a great lyric, a matter-of-fact, vernacular exposition that well evokes a quiet mood with its small beauties. A good melody tapers off into embarrassingly sloppy jazz at its very end.

Like any entity that creates its own idiom, musically as well as culturally, the Beach Boys take getting into. Listen once and you might think this album is nowhere. But it's really just at a very special place, and after a half-dozen listenings, you can be there. (pp. 323-24)

Arthur Schmidt, "'Friends'" (originally published in Rolling Stone, *August 24, 1968), in* The Rolling Stone Record Review *by the editors of* Rolling Stone *(copyright © 1967, 1968, 1969, 1970, 1971, by Straight Arrow Publishers, Inc.; all rights reserved; reprinted by permission), Pocket Books, 1971, pp. 323-24.*

PAUL WILLIAMS

[The Beach Boys] are moving forward all the time.

Each Beach Boys album since *Pet Sounds* has been (or seemed) a little less sophisticated. Retrogression? Not at all, but to prove that, we'd better decide what "forward" is.

Forward is the direction in which time moves. It's kind of like "out," which is the direction in which cosmic matter moves. There is no possibility of reversal inherent in this movement, nor even of angular shift. Those concepts have no meaning. Can a line stretching from zero towards infinity turn around? I mean, try to visualize it. At best, it would no longer be a line; and the basic assumption we make in calling something a line is that it is, at least, a line. So forward is a description of how time moves, just as outward might describe how space moves, if we think of "space" the concept rather than the objects that move about *within* space.

Now, "forward" as applied to the Beach Boys must have to do with their relationship to time. Do they move forward in time (or rather, with it)? Yes, of course, everybody does. Do they make progress? To answer that, we must consider their work as existing in time, and ask: is there a real movement (if there is, it couldn't be anything but forward) from the Beach Boys' earlier creations to their more recent ones? Not, do they get better?—that would require a highly subjective judgment (I, personally, do not think they get better; I feel they are as great now, or conversely, were as great then—I don't favor any particular period). Rather, do they incorporate the past in the present, do they seem to learn, do they operate out of some kind of awareness of past accomplishment and failure, or are they striking out anew from the beginning, the origin, every time? The question is, is there some kind of real expansion evident in the achievements of the Beach Boys as time goes on, something that would justify our considering one album as a step forward from a previous one?

This is very difficult to answer; it breaks down into a matter of subjective judgment no matter how we try to avoid that. I would say that, taking the various albums the Beach Boys have done and shuffling them, it is not necessarily evident that there are "more advanced" and "less advanced" albums. They have reached different audiences at various times sophisticated. Retrogression? Not at all, but to prove that, we'd better [say] that they were only good up to this point, or since that point ("Good Vibrations" is one popular dividing line). However, I would argue that, from the point of view of the longtime listener who has taken them pretty much for what they are, the Beach Boys have covered more distance than almost any other group in rock.

Can I explain that statement? I hope so. It must be remembered that the consistent listener himself moves forward with time; he heard *Pet Sounds* in 1966 and *Smiley Smile* in 1967 and *Friends* in 1968. So each new record the group releases may well seem to him not merely another piece of plastic to be measured against past pieces, but rather the most recent advance of a continually expanding body of work. . . . (pp. 9-10)

In terms of the listener, he feels himself *moved further* (at least I do) by each new album the Beach Boys produce. This is not true with most groups, even very good ones. . . . The Beach Boys, in their work since *Pet Sounds* and I believe throughout their careers, have been pressing constantly on, relentless in dissatisfaction, in the need to express more and more of themselves (as opposed to the need for expressing the same thing more and more effectively).

So what happens to the listener is this: he is familiar with the Beach Boys, he likes them, meaning he enjoys most of what they've put out and rather expects that they will continue to create worthwhile (to him) music. He sees a new Beach Boys album in the shop window, purchases it, takes it home and plays it and lo and behold *he cannot relate!* Is this the same Beach Boys I know and love? he wonders, knowing full well it is, the voices certainly sound familiar, but somehow this is not what he expected. It is not more of the same. It is something entirely new as though the group had just appeared on the scene and expected to be listened to with no preconceptions whatsoever.

Not more of the same. And as a result, it is extremely difficult for the listener to say whether or not he likes the record. On first listening, it appears to have no relevance, either to him or to his idea of who the Beach Boys are.

But (I hope) he continues to play the record. And slowly but surely he finds one song and then another quite stuck inside his mind, he hears the music in his head as though his mind were a portable radio and the song were being picked up by him directly as waves in the air. He finds himself more and more deeply involved in the album, until he hears each separate song with great pleasure and feels an affection for the album itself. Quite unconsciously, he has come to like the record, and now he may say, after the fact, that it's good, I like it, the Beach Boys have done it again.

Do you know what has happened? His head has been opened. A whole new thing, which he responded to not at all at first, has been added to his consciousness, he now responds to this strange music warmly and with sensitivity, and he is not at all the same listener he was before he bought the album. He has, *bien sur*, made progress. Progress not just within a context but beyond the contexts he as a listener was familiar with.

I have seen this happen, with *Pet Sounds, Wild Honey, Friends.* I've had it happen to me and I've spoken to many people who seem to have had the same experience. And I know very many people who've turned off the Beach Boys because they never got beyond that first baffling exposure to the album. It seems to me essential, if we are to stay as children, if we are to remain open to the world and what's in it, that we not take defensive postures, that we never hold on tighter to what we have when faced with something strange and new. Our only chance at escaping stagnation is to continue to grow almost in spite of every urge towards security and safety that we feel. True security can only be found in the ability to respond fully to any situation.

So let us praise the Beach Boys for their progress. *Friends* is not the least like *Wild Honey,* though it retains *Wild Honey*'s achievement of the casual and the everyday and the immediate (and explores these things somewhat further). It is not at all *Smiley Smile,* although its explorations of organ sound as it relates to melody and to the human voice continue. *Friends* is, furthermore, no return to *Pet Sounds,* though it might please those who have been seeking in the Beach Boys the calm, the softness of *Pet Sounds (Friends* lacks *Pet Sounds'* passion—which you can find even more in *Wild Honey,* but it is in many ways both

more comforting and more adventurous). *Friends* is merely a new Beach Boys album and as such both the successful expression of their current interests and feelings and a real step forward on the part of the Beach Boys music in general —not because this is a better album than any before, but because Beach Boys music and Beach Boys' listeners' perception of music are now that much further developed— *more* sophisticated, through being deeply sensitive to apparently simpler stuff—than they ever were before. An important product indeed. (p. 10)

> *Paul Williams, in* Crawdaddy *(copyright © 1968 by Crawdaddy Publishing Co., Inc.; reprinted by permission of the author), September, 1968.*

GENE SCULATTI

Brian Wilson and company are currently at the center of an intense contemporary rock controversy, involving the academic "rock as art" critic-intellectuals, the AM-tuned teenies, and all the rest of us in between.

As the California sextet is simultaneously hailed as genius incarnate and derided as the archetypical pop music cop-outs, one clear-cut and legitimate query is seen at the base of all the turmoil: how seriously can the 1968 rock audience consider the work of a group of artists who, just four years earlier, represented the epitome of the whole commercial-plastic "teenage music industry?" . . .

The answer is a simple one. The Beach Boys' approach to their music is as valid now as it was in 1962 and *vice versa.* Brian Wilson owes no one any apologies for his music, present or past.

The most popular charge leveled at the Beach Boys is their apparently excessive immersion in and identification with mass culture and "commercialism". . . . [An] association with mass culture was indeed a characteristic of the Beach Boys' music up until 1966. Moreover, it was an "honest" association. . . . Wilson's world circa 1962 was seriously involved with all the then dead serious/now ludicrous manifestations of adolescence: hot rods, surfing and making-out in the school parking lot really do exist. A fascination with popular culture has proven to be a significant part of the twentieth century artist's personality. It has served [Andy] Warhol and Chuck Berry (the Beach Boys' earliest influence) equally well. Southern California teenage culture provided Brian Wilson with material for his art in *Surfin' Safari* and *Little Deuce Coupe,* as did the drug experience in *Good Vibrations,* as does whatever in *Wild Honey.*

The aforementioned charges would, however, have been valid (as certainly they are when applied to performers like Jan & Dean) if the Beach Boys' music had proven to be of no artistic merit, but such is not the case. Despite the oversaturation of the public with surf and drag argot, despite the fact that their recordings became somewhat anachronistic for a while, the Beach Boys have maintained a consistent impressive musical output. . . .

In retrospect, the first Beach Boys music was a relatively crude product. In their initial LP effort, *Surfin' Safari,* the only talent evidenced is Brian Wilson's empathy, his ability to assimilate his environment and structure it into lyrical form. . . .

In their third LP, *Surfer Girl,* the Beach Boys emerged as the first authentic "rock 'n' roll group," in the modern sense; they were at once composers, singers and musicians, arrangers and producers, the first major self-sufficient rock band. . . . In *Surfer Girl* Brian Wilson supervises the whole recording operation; still working with the formula, he is able to create a work of variety and subtlety. . . . By *Little Deuce Coupe* the formula has been polished to high gloss, directly working from Chuck Berry and Four Freshmen stylings. Brian's proficiency at composing intriguing melodies is displayed in *Car Crazy Cutie* and *Spirit of America.* The formula works perfectly, for the last time. (p. 38)

[What] ensued after *Little Deuce Coupe* was a period of artistic transition which lasted roughly from 1964 to 1966. From *Shut Down Volume 2* through *Beach Boys Party Album* formula is necessarily discarded and the LPs become uneven collections, replete with boring bull session fillers, displaying commendable experimentation and sophistication, moments of beauty amid dullness.

[The] most ambitious of the group's transition efforts [was] *The Beach Boys Today!* While it avoids contextual unity *Today!* is remarkable in its embodiment of Brian's oft-quoted "voices-as-instruments" philosophy. The perfect vocal intracacies of *She Knows Me Too Well* and *Please Let Me Wonder* originally elicited Jack Good's famous quote that "Beach Boys' records sound as if they were sung by eunuchs in the Sistine Choir." A precursor of *Pet Sounds* orchestration is found in the elaborate treatment given Spector's Ronettes' *I'm So Young.* Perhaps more than any previous work, *Today!,* substantiated Brian's stature as one of the all-time great composers of melody in rock (along with Lennon-McCartney, John Phillips and Smokey Robinson).

Two important singles mark the Beach Boys' final transition phase. *Sloop John B.* early in 1966 was a partially effective attempt at erasing youth cult leaders image by adapting folk-rock to traditional Beach Boys' style. *God Only Knows,* a truly distinctive 45 . . . was the lead-off cut on the most fascinating and creative Beach Boys album to date, *Pet Sounds. Pet Sounds* was by no means a revolutionary work in that it inspired or influenced the rock scene in a big way. It was revolutionary only within the confines of the Beach Boys' music. The concept behind the album was part of a tradition established by [the Beatles'] *Rubber Soul; Rubber Soul* was the definitive "rock as art" album, revolutionary in that it was a completely successful creative endeavor integrating with precision all aspects of the creative (rock) process—composition of individual tracks done with extreme care, each track arranged appropriately to fit beside each other track, the symmetrical rock 'n' roll album. *Rubber Soul* established itself as the necessary prototype that no major rock group has been able to ignore; *Rubber Soul,* [the Rolling Stones'] *Aftermath* and *Pet Sounds* are of the same classic mold. Brian's omniscience is surely felt in *Pet Sounds,* the master hand collecting and selecting, shaping his musical expression to exhibit all of the parts of the whole; the Freshmen harmonizing, [Phil] Spector's cavernous hollows of sound, lush 1940's movie music, adolescent romanticism. Like the prototype, *Pet Sounds* was a final statement of an era and a prophecy that sweeping changes lay ahead.

Good Vibrations may yet prove to be the most significantly revolutionary piece of the current rock renaissance; executed as it is in conventional Beach Boys manner, it is one of the few organically complete rock works; every audible note and every silence contributes to the whole three min-utes, 35 seconds, of the song. It is the ultimate in-studio production trip . . . , very much rock 'n' roll in the emotional sense and yet un-rocklike in its spacial, dimensional conceptions. In no minor way, *Good Vibrations* is a primary influential piece for all producing rock artists; everyone has felt its import to some degree, in such disparate things as [the Yellow Balloon's] *Yellow Balloon* and [the Beatles'] *A Day in the Life,* in groups as far apart as (recent) Grateful Dead and the Association, as Van Dyke Parks and the Who. . . .

[*Smiley Smile*] was an abrupt collection of comic vocal exercises. The most promising cuts, *Vegetables, Gettin' Hungry* and *She's Goin' Bald,* act as illustrations of the voice-as-instrument thing (they're mainly freaky-hip vocal diversions, not even songs), but *Smiley Smile* was predominantly a downer.

As if enough fuel hadn't been added to the fire, shortly after the radical (it is nothing if not experimental) *Smiley Smile,* an astonishingly conventional album, *Wild Honey,* made its appearance; the Beach Boys come on really schizoid now. In *Wild Honey* they have the audacity to fool around with r&b, a territory indeed alien to them. Surprisingly, *Wild Honey* works well. It isn't the least bit pretentious, it's honest, and convincing. A whole lot of soul is used up on *Wild Honey* and *Darlin',* as well as the re-make of Stevie Wonder's *I Was Made To Love Her. Aren't You Glad* achieves a Miracles style smoothness via a Bobby Goldsboro-type song, and Brian's weird ear . . . for melody is again evidenced in *Let the Wind Blow* and *Country Air. Wild Honey* is ambitious but not obnoxious. It's where the Beach Boys presently are at, in many ways it is where they have been all along (a kind of lyrical romance rock); and it is precisely where they belong, doing their thing uniquely like no one else can.

The Beach Boys' most recent work, *Friends,* may actually be their best. This album represents the culmination of the efforts and the results of their last three LPs. Demonstrating their highly distinctive approach and their own sense of organicism, *Friends* derives primarily from *Pet Sounds, Smiley-Smile, Wild Honey,* and little else. The characteristic innocence and somewhat childlike visions imparted to their music are applied directly to the theme of the album: friendships. As usual, the lyrics tend to be basic, yet as expressive as they need to be; words, like individual voices or instruments, are all part of the larger whole of *music;* the sole qualifications for Beach Boys' lyrics is that they partake of, and don't visibly harm, melody. *Friends* is certainly less "complex," as regards harmonic intricacies, than much recent Beach Boys work. Compared to *Pet Sounds* and *Smiley Smile, Friends* seems to be vocally thin. The emphasis is on very strong melodies and it is here that Brian Wilson scores again. . . . In *When A Man Needs A Woman* Wilson again treats sex as he did in *Gettin' Hungry (Smiley Smile),* with a stunning directness and surprisingly effective simplicity. . . . *Friends* differs little in effect from most other Beach Boys albums. It is another showcase for what is the most original and perhaps the most consistently satisfying rock music being created today. (p. 40)

Gene Sculatti, "Villains and Heroes: In Defense of the Beach Boys," in Jazz & Pop *(© 1968 by Jazz Press Inc.; reprinted by permission of the author), September, 1968, pp. 38, 40.*

JIM MILLER

After a long period of recovery, mediocrity, and general disaster, the Beach Boys have finally produced an album [*Sunflower*] that can stand with *Pet Sounds:* the old vocal and instrumental complexity has returned and the result largely justifies the absurd faith some of us have had that the Beach Boys were actually still capable of producing a superb rock album—or, more precisely, a superb rock muzak album. "Add Some Music to Your Day"; hip supermarkets might program this album for contented browsing among the frozen vegetables and canned fruit.

As a reassuring note, most of the lyric impotence of the group remains, though not so prominently displayed as on colorful recent outings as *Friends*. . . . [The] tracks are executed with a certain aplomb that often was lacking in post-"Good Vibrations" Beach Boy music, as if the self-consciousness of such homogenizing enterprise as making a new Beach Boy record has been again overcome. As a result, the naivete of the group is more astounding than ever —I mean, good Christ, it's 1970 and here we have a new, excellent Beach Boy's epic, and isn't that irrelevant?

In any case, Brian's new stuff is great, especially "This Whole World" and "All I Wanna Do." (pp. 325-26)

The inevitable saccharine ballads are present in abundance. "Deirdre" and particularly Brian's "Our Sweet Love" rejoin the ongoing tradition of "Surfer Girl," although "Our Sweet Love" is almost reminiscent of the mood of *Pet Sounds*. Of course there is some lesser stuff here, like "At My Window." No matter: as a whole, *Sunflower* is without doubt the best Beach Boys album in recent memory, a stylistically coherent tour de force. It makes one wonder though whether anyone still listens to their music, or could give a shit about it. This album will probably have the fate of being taken as a decadent piece of fluff at a time when we could use more Liberation Music Orchestras. It *is* decadent fluff—but *brilliant* fluff. The Beach Boys are plastic madmen, rock geniuses. The plastic should not hide from use the geniuses who molded it. (p. 326)

> *Jim Miller, " 'Sunflower' " (originally published in* Rolling Stone, *October 1, 1970), in* The Rolling Stone Review *by the editors of* Rolling Stone *(copyright © 1967, 1968, 1969, 1970, 1971, by Straight Arrow Publishers, Inc.; all rights reserved; reprinted by permission), Pocket Books, 1971, pp. 325-26.*

RICHARD WILLIAMS

Just as it's tied to emotional memories, so most pop music evokes specific times of year. Most of the best pop picks on summer, simply because that (idealistically speaking) is when the nights are longer, the girls are prettier, and you can take the hood off your sportycar and bomb off into the glorious sunset.

There's never been any better summer music than that created by Brian Wilson for the Beach Boys, between '62 and '67. More so even than Chuck Berry, Wilson's compositions sum up what pop was always about, and what we're the poorer for having lost.

The very early Sixties, the years just before the Beatles, were the most unproductive that white pop has known, until Wilson came along with "Surfin'," a weird mixture of goofy acappella-style vocal and Chuck Berry riffs recorded

in the Wilson's garage—wouldn't you know? Their first album, titled "Surfin' Safari" . . . , was incredibly naive, a combination of Berry-derived songs and "Pipeline" style instrumental work. In "409," though, you could hear the beginnings of a choral style, those stripped-down harmonies charging behind the light lead voice. . . .

"Surfin' Safari" . . . , the second album, contained intimations of genius. The title song was a straight rewrite of Berry's "Sweet Little Sixteen," but "Farmer's Daughter" and "Lonely Sea" were something else again. They both used falsetto leads; Mike Love took "Daughter" at a fast clip while the other voices echoed him, and Brian himself sang "Lonely Sea," an ambivalent hymn to the surfer's home made all the more poignant by the realisation that Brian himself was only a mediocre surfer.

This was the first in his magnificent sequence of love-ballads, all of which became marked by sumptuously rich harmonies, and usually by the aching falsetto. "Surfer Girl," from the album of the same name . . . was the next, and very possibly the best: from the first notes you could feel the sun, sense the texture of tanned skin.

"In My Room," from the same record, developed the theme of Brian's personal claustrophobia: "In my room I lock out all my worries and my fears." The wonderful interweaving harmonies at the end of the middle eight ("Laugh at yesterday") also hinted at complexities to come, and the whole record was a tight, compact statement of almost stifling intensity.

"Shut Down Vol. 2" . . . contained perhaps his most acclaimed ballad, the classic "Don't Worry Baby," in which production began to play a part: the voices seemed to melt into the softly pounding backing track, so that bass voice and bass guitar became almost indistinguishable. . . .

["Girls on the Beach"] still makes my toes curl, particularly those sudden modulations between major and minor keys (the kind of trick which brought Lennon and McCartney to intellectual respectability, but which, in Brian's hands, went unnoticed—maybe it worked too well).

"Wendy," though, was perhaps the most striking track, developing the spatial relationships intimated in "Don't Worry Baby." This in turn led to a series of superb up-tempo hit records: "Dance Dance Dance," "When I Grow Up," and "Help Me, Rhonda" . . . and "California Girls" and "Let Him Run Wild". . . .

Of these, "California Girls" was easily the most outstanding, a kind of ultimate anthem to the Wilsons' home state.

It begins with an out-of-tempo instrumental section, then moves into a loping beat over which the vocal strides. Fairground organ leads into a circular vocal fade which had its antecedents in "Kiss Me, Baby." . . . The voice lines interweave and overlap, wind round each other, producing a seamless whole in which not one note takes precedence over another.

This innovation seems to me to put Wilson on the same scale as any vocal music in the world, and I don't expect to be contradicted when I say that Brian Wilson is a genius.

But he was a genius who never received his just acclaim, and it's possible that he never will. The main reason for this is absurdly simply: during 1966, he released an album called "Pet Sounds" . . . which simply dwarfed all the rest of pop music put together. His entirely romantic songs were cloaked in shrouds of orchestra, massive arrangements sliding in and out with a subtlety and rightness which defied criticism.

Just as it was settling nicely into its position as the world's number one popular music record, the far more fashionable Beatles released "Sgt. Pepper," and "Pet Sounds" was forgotten, just like that.

The trouble was that the Beatles were eclectics, very clever at picking up on all kinds of influences, and Wilson was different. He'd only ever borrowed his beat from Berry and his harmonies from the Four Freshmen; everything else, all the development, came from within.

His last real throw was the "Smiley Smile" album . . . which contained the epic "Good Vibrations" (the second-best single ever?) and the much-underrated "Heroes And Villains". . . .

"Smiley Smile" was either ignored or dismissed by the reviewers, and has since become The Great Undiscovered Pop Album. It contains fragments—mostly vocal with minimal instrumental accompaniment—which have all the epigrammatic, enigmatic power of Japanese *haiku*. More: "Wonderful" and "Little Pad" contain passages written in the conditional tense (i.e. the songs move easily between reality and fantasy), a technique evolved by [Jean-Luc] Godard in the cinema and which only Wilson, as far as I know, has picked up in pop.

Since then, he seems to have lost heart. There have been some nice cuts, like "Darlin'" from "Wild Honey" . . . , and "I Can Hear Music" and "Cottonfields" from "20/20" . . . , but the focus, once so tight and sharp, has been lost.

The analogy with the cinema is quite a good one. Wilson always was a director, moving his camera around to find angles on a rather narrow subject, and his movie-songs comprise a body of work which few can match.

The fact that such a talent can possibly become "unfashionable" frankly sickens me.

> Richard Williams, "The Endless Summer: A Reappraisal of the Beach Boys," in Melody Maker (IPC Business Press Ltd.), May 22, 1971, p. 17.

MICHELE HUSH

Most people seem to love [*Surf's Up*]. They say the harmonies, production and instrumentation are perfect; they like the way it flows, its smoothness and sweetness. *Surf's Up* does possess all of these characteristics—it is made of ball-bearings, silicone and glycerine, with the friction kept down to a minimum. In essence, it is spun sugar, and that is precisely why I don't like it.

Consider the following hypothetical situation: the Vienna Boys' Choir, under the direction of Henry Mancini, records arrangements lifted from the California "cool jazz" school; the libretto is topical—lots of ecology, revolution, nostalgia and romanticism. Given a couple of years to play around in a well-equipped studio, and there is reason to believe they'd sound a lot like the Beach Boys.

This album is the safest thing I've heard in years, almost calculatedly inoffensive—something your mother could love. Consequently, its gut content is zero. People insist

upon associating the word "genius" with Brian Wilson—perhaps an aftershock of "Good Vibrations"—but so far I can't see why. Genius leads a person to take chances, to experiment; craftsmanship, on the other hand, leads one to perfect a given trade—vocal arrangement, for example. And, while Brian Wilson may well be a master craftsman, thus far a genius he is not.

The Beach Boys are basically a contemporary version of a barber shop quartet. They are outstanding because they are extraordinarily concordant—their voices sound custom-made for each other's company. On *Surf's Up*, they manage to tune their instruments to their vocal chords, and the result is one big super-harmony. If that's what you're into *Surf's Up* may be just what you've always wanted. But be forewarned—like cotton candy, it is pretty and very sweet, but it lacks substance. (p. 27)

> Michele Hush, in Rock (reprinted by permission of Countrywide Publications, Inc. and Rock Magazine), October 11, 1971.

ARTHUR SCHMIDT

I've been waiting impatiently for [*Surf's Up*] since *Sunflower*, and the small letdown I feel could be the other side of that impatience, the wish that they could have kept it a little longer to make it perfect. In this case that would not be a matter of production . . . but rather of waiting for the material to even out in quality. . . .

Still, I recall my own first reaction to *Sunflower*, some cuts at first seemed too thin, *too* light.

But the important thing about the Beach Boys is just this aspect of their music. The production is usually flawless and the melodies so frequently exquisite that one tends to hear, then listen for—and finally dismiss it as—surface. Yet the surface is manipulated so carefully and so brilliantly that (and here I am forced by a certain poverty of analogy to shift senses) it becomes hologrammatic. Cotton candy: bite into it and the pink fluff becomes sugar on your tongue—then, *poof!*—mere aftertaste. Yet wait, there's more pink fluff inside the cone, and more, and more . . . (Not to mention the best aftertaste in the business.) . . .

This is a good album, probably as good as *Sunflower*, which is terrific, and which I've had six months more to listen to. It is certainly the most original in that it has contributed something purely its own. Perhaps because of the ecology theme, it is not as joyous. But it will do to keep the turntable warm until their next. . . . They remain unique, and though they still promise more than they deliver, this group has delivered plenty throughout its history. For that reason, they are perhaps still the most important—and certainly the most "accomplished"—of all American groups.

You can come home, guys, all is forgiven. (p. 49)

> Arthur Schmidt, in Rolling Stone Magazine (by Straight Arrow Publishers, Inc. © 1971; all rights reserved; reprinted by permission), Issue 93, October 14, 1971.

STEPHEN DAVIS

Pet Sounds, aside from its importance as Brian Wilson's evolutionary compositional masterpiece, was the first rock record that can be considered a "concept album"; from first cut to last we were treated to an intense, linear personal vision of the vagaries of a love affair and the painful, introverted anxieties that are the wrenching precipitates of the unstable chemistry of any love relationship. This trenchant cycle of love songs has the emotional impact of a shatteringly evocative novel, and by God if this little record didn't change only the course of popular music, but the course of a few lives in the bargain. It sure as hell changed its creator, Brian, who by 1966 had been cruising along at the forefront of American popular music for four years, doling out a constant river of hit songs and producing that tough yet mellifluous sound that was the only intelligent innovation in pop music between Chuck Berry and the Beatles.

Previous Beach Boy albums were also based on strong conceptual images—the dream world of Surf, wired-up rods with metal flake paint, and curvaceous cuties lounging around the (implicitly suburban and affluent) high school. It was music for white kids; they could identify with the veneration of the leisure status which in 1963 was the ripest fruit of the American dream. It wasn't bullshit, you could dance your silly brains away to "Get Around" or "Fun Fun Fun" if you felt like it.

But *Pet Sounds*. . . . nobody was prepared for anything so soulful, so lovely, something one had to think about so much. It is by far the best album Brian has yet delivered, and it paradoxically began the decline in mass popularity that still plagues this band. It also reflected Brian's preoccupation with pure sound. . . .

The love songs of *Pet Sounds* begin with the gorgeous theme of frustrated mid-Sixties blueballed adolescence, "wouldn't it be nice to stay together, hold each other close the whole night through? . . ." That question lays the entire premise of the album immediately in front of us. "You Still Believe In Me" . . . carries the affair a little farther, through and past indiscretion into the reconciliation of "Don't Talk (Put Your Head on My Shoulder)." . . . There are also the perceptive songs of anxiety, malaise and self-doubt. . . .

The *Pet Sounds* story ends unhappily, or at least stoically. "Here Today" is an angry blaster, and portrays a pessimism and disaffection that jars with the previous optimism. It is the end of the affair, and our persona is clearly pissed. "I Just Wasn't Made For These Times" is an expression of general disenchantment with just about everything, rendered politely of course, in a low-key manner. These two tunes, like the rest of the record are great not only because of the lush, dramatic arrangements, but because the strangest of the brothers Wilson has his psyche on the pulse of universal subjectivity. Being extremely aware of fantasy himself, Brian knows how most people think. . . .

The final episode of *Pet Sounds* is "Caroline, No," three minutes of heartbreaking pathos, a haunting ballad that is the guts of hapless melancholy, the hollow and incredulous feeling at the loss of a lover.

Ah, *Pet Sounds*. Ah, the wonderful 20 second trailer right out of Thomas Hart Benton with the barking dogs, the signal bells and at the railroad crossing as a fast diesel roars by towards where you are not, the barking in the distance again and then silence. Ah, Brian.

So Tough is the first and maybe last album by Carl and the Passions, the aptly-named once and future Beach Boys. The mysterious, reclusive Brian (having endured another

aesthetic triumph with the last album, *Surf's Up*) seems to have abdicated the leadership of the organization into the capable hands of brother Carl. . . .

So Tough's insurmountable problem is that only four of the eight cuts fall into the subtly specialized class of "acceptable" Beach Boy material. It was, at least honest, to call the band Carl and the Passions. Because the difference is Brian, and the difference hurts. (p. 56)

> *Stephen Davis, in* Rolling Stone *(by Straight Arrow Publishers, Inc. © 1972; all rights reserved; reprinted by permission), Issue 111, June 22, 1972.*

PETER FORNATALE

There are vast differences between the 1966 and 1972 Beach Boys. This fact becomes painfully apparent with the release of their new double set *Carl and the Passions—So Tough* coupled with the re-release of their classic *Pet Sounds*. Spin for spin, *Pet Sounds* is the superior album. It soars. *So Tough* doesn't soar. It taxis all around the runway looking for a place to take off, but never quite finds it.

Of course, the biggest difference is one of leadership. In 1966, the Beach Boys were Brian Wilson's group. Their main function was to serve as the vehicle for Brian's unique and personal vision of life and reality. Nowadays, the musical chores are divided up pretty equally among all the group members resulting in a kind of conceptual schizophrenia.

There are just eight songs on *So Tough;* all would do better in the context of other Beach Boys albums. . . . There are occasional glimpses of familiar Beach Boys genius, but not enough to justify a new album.

Pet Sounds saves the day. It is every bit the masterpiece it was six years ago—still vital, still full of wonder, imagination and discovery. It is interesting to remember that *Pet Sounds* preceded *Sgt. Pepper* by a full year. It is a total album. In this major undertaking, Brian Wilson subtly, but masterfully, explored the thin line between adolescence and adulthood with tenderness, compassion and total empathy. It was, to say the least, ahead of its time . . . but maybe its time is now. I hope so. (p. 75)

> *Peter Fornatale, in* Words & Music *(© 1972 by Poppy Press Inc.; reprinted by permission of the author), September, 1972.*

RICHARD WILLIAMS

["Holland"] contains more fun and beauty than any dozen efforts by more fashionable bands.

The overwhelming quality of "Holland" (so called because they recorded it in a town outside Amsterdam) is consistency, in two respects: first, it fits right in with the sequence of Beach Boys music from '62 on; secondly, the consistency of writing and performance is on a higher level than anything since, perhaps, "Pet Sounds". . . .

First question: what is B. Wilson's contribution this time out? Answer: less than I'd expected, but as it happens that doesn't hurt at all. With four collaborators . . . he composed the opening cut, "Sail On, Sailor", which is also the upcoming single, and although it lacks instant 45 rpm magic it's as crisp and cooling as fresh orange-juice. . . . [The] chorus sticks in your head like . . . well, like a Brian Wilson chorus should. . . . Lastly, Brian contributed a 12-minute fairy tale called ''Mt. Vernon & Fairway,'' which comes on a separate 7-inch 33 rpm disc. Narrated by [Jack] Rieley in the approved Sparky's Magic Piano style, it's about a prince and a magic transistor radio, has lashings of amusing background noises from the amazing Wilson brain, and is performed in exactly the right tone for [children's program] Junior Choice—on which it deserves to make regular appearances for years to come. . . .

I expect more from the Beach Boys than from anyone else, and ''Holland'' has the goods.

Richard Williams, ''Beach Boys Go Dutch,'' in
Melody Maker (© *IPC Business Press Ltd.),*
January 27, 1973, p. 23.

GREG SHAW

[Except] for Dick Dale's, no surf music came out on major labels before the Beach Boys proved it could be more commercial than anyone had dreamed. They did it by blending together—probably not too consciously—elements of all the disparate styles they'd heard in records they liked, and they had the good taste to prefer the kind of records that approached a sort of summation of teenage consciousness. By distilling the essence from these, the Beach Boys emerged as perhaps the ultimate in teenage rock-and-roll groups.

Influenced by various Fours (Freshmen, Preps, Seasons), they added to the standard surf instrumentation a thick vocal sound laden with harmonies, falsetto singing, and constant background vocals. And their voices, rather than aping Little Richard and James Brown (as singers in white bands were wont to do in those days) or the New York doo-woppers, preserved a wholesome, clean-cut, high-school-cocky tone that identified them even more closely with their audience. The final touch was provided by Brian Wilson, whose obsession with the records of Phil Spector led him to place greater emphasis on production and pure *sound* than just about anybody else who was recording in 1963.

In retrospect, the records that started it all don't sound all that hot. *Surfin'*, *Luau*, and even *Surfin Safari* are primitive and amateurish. But to ears accustomed to endless guitar reworkings of 1952 Joe Houston riffs, they must have seemed fantastic. *Surfin'*, the Beach Boys' first release, was obviously based on such records as Jan & Dean's 1959 *Baby Talk*. But the remarkable thing about *Surfin*, as opposed to anything that had come before, was what it implied about its audience. Instead of trying to suggest the sensation of riding a wave, as all previous surf music had done, the Beach Boys were singing about how ''Surfin' is the only life, the only way for me. . . .'' Waking up, checking the surf reports, getting into a car to pick up a girl and drive to the beach—this is what the Beach Boys sang about, and this is what life *was* for the young people of southern California. They saw a reflection of their own lives they'd never seen before. It was *their* music, the one missing element in the whole developing teen culture, and it was also the source of that incredibly self-confident and eventually arrogant self-image that California teens disseminated and fashioned into the sand castles of folk-rock and flower-power—before it all came crashing down of its own not very heavy weight in 1969. The implications of surf music were far-reaching indeed.

By their third release [*Surfin' USA*], the Beach Boys had refined the basics of their sound. (pp. 80-1)

Surf music Beach-Boys-style was loved all over the world because, as has been said of Chuck Berry's storytelling songs and all the other enduring classics of popular music, its message and appeal were universal, not tied to any particular provincial scene. The surf and the beach were just convenient images—myths if you will—around which an attitude toward life on the part of California youth crystallized. The affluence and the restlessness that produced the attitude were spreading east, and, because (with certain regional exceptions) there were no other youth-culture myths that could match it, surf music was quickly adopted by American youth as a whole.

Although they were themselves surfing enthusiasts, the Beach Boys were smart enough to know their music didn't depend on the sport. The B side of *Surfin' Safari* was *409*, their first car song. There had been hot-rod songs before, of course, and teenage boys just naturally have a strong interest in cars—in the age we live in, the psychological needs behind an adolescent boy's obsession with cars can't be denied. The Beach Boys knew that, and they pulled cars into the larger mythology they were constructing by applying car themes to music already established as ''surf'' and writing songs about racing, winning, having the best car around, attracting girls as a result—and need I go on? The opportunities for reinforcing the adolescent ego were multiplied, and hot-rod music (since highways were more common than beaches between the coasts) had far greater potential for nationwide relevance. (p. 81)

[By] the peak years of 1965-1966 they were down to the basics—simply being young, alive, and free. Songs like *Dance, Dance, Dance, Girl Don't Tell Me, Help Me, Rhonda, California Girls, Barbara Ann,* and *Wouldn't It Be Nice,* classics all, probably represent the zenith of the teenage spirit in music. (p. 82)

[A] new sound, folk-rock, . . . was busily developing the generational consciousness set loose by surf music and getting set to become the next big trend.

What happened after that was perhaps inevitable. A youth culture conditioned to think of itself as such by hearing surf records began taking itself seriously—too seriously, in fact, demanding ponderously portentous statements from its music to the point where the whole thing fell apart. The Beach Boys, though not immune to the allures of health food, transcendental meditation, and the vapid intellectualism of, say, a Van Dyke Parks, managed to retain through it all their feeling for nature, and, though their late-Sixties records were as lacking in youth consciousness as youth itself was, their music was always about the most *real* to be found. (pp. 82-3)

But things slowly began to snowball, resulting in a refreshing trend that, while still quite minor in mass terms, speaks strongly for the continued relevance of mid-Sixties surf-inspired pop music. The world, it seems, is beginning to feel the way it did when the Beach Boys were making their mark—summer once again means fun, and not, as the Stooges said for so many in 1969, ''another year with nothing to do.'' What the Beach Boys unleashed was not merely a product of its time, but an inescapable byproduct of any world in which teenagers are growing up aware of themselves as teenagers, and it has taken the arrival of the first fresh teenage generation since the Sixties demoralization to prove it. (p. 83)

Greg Shaw, "Surf Music," in Stereo Review *(reprinted by permission of the author), October, 1973, pp. 79-83.*

GEOFF BROWN

No group has as consistently made music celebratory of sun, fresh air and youth as the Beach Boys and it is particularly appropriate that they should have two albums out during the present endless summer.

Hardly a June, July or August has passed since 1962 without a Beach Boys tune implanting itself in mind and heart, and 1976, what with bicentennial and all, will be no exception.

For me, this year's memory will be "It's O.K.", a Brian Wilson/Mike Love song from "15 Big Ones", which is vintage, euphoric, hot weather music. . . .

"15 Big Ones" is not an "advanced" Beach Boys album. After a decade and a half of serious and immeasurably enjoyable progression they are putatively looking back to their earliest days in an attempt, perhaps, to rekindle the flame of youth, which is odd, for they have always had the touch of Peter Pan about them.

Their voices and music never grow old. Nevertheless, recreation is at the core of "15 Big Ones," with rearrangements (all by Brian) of oldies. . . .

Of the new Beach Boys songs, two good Brian Wilson/Mike Love numbers eclipse the opening "Rock And Roll Music". They are "It's O.K." . . . and "Had To Phone Ya". . . . It's a pretty song of love long distance. . . .

The group is clearly building its energies before moving forward once more. As a new work "15 Big Ones" is no "Pet Sounds" or "Surf's Up", but it will most assuredly suffice for the present. Meanwhile, the album is important as a confident step in the rehabilitation of Brian Wilson, to whom—Welcome Back.

Geoff Brown, "Welcome Back to Vintage B.B.," in Melody Maker *(© IPC Business Press Ltd.), July 10, 1976, p. 21.*

BILL GUBBINS

Does Brian make that *big* a difference [in *15 Big Ones*]? Not really.

There is no question that Brian Wilson is a genuine talent in American music (mind you, we're talking about a category somewhat beyond rock 'n' roll) and the controversy about whether he did or did not destroy/burn the famous *Smile* tapes just might be the valid rock equivalent to the search/confusion over the missing portions of [Erich] Von Stroheim's alleged film masterpiece *Greed*. Nevertheless, *Smile* was ten years ago and one can wait only so long for the vanquished hero to return. Unfortunately, on *15 Big Ones* at least, he hasn't.

The overriding concept . . . behind *15* is not dissimilar to the recent work by another well-known concept artist, Todd Rundgren, on *Faithful:* re-recorded oldies mixed with new material.

The originals sound even more forced than the oldies.

Whatever happened to Brian Wilson the *composer*, the guy who was someday supposed to write these *symphonies* and be like Beethoven or somebody? Here he's reduced to merely a glorified producer, an arranger no less. In his heralded comeback, Brian Wilson remains an invisible man and the state of his talent in the Seventies an unanswered question. (p. 64)

Bill Gubbins, in Creem *(© copyright 1976 by Creem Magazine, Inc.), September, 1976.*

JIM MILLER

Gone are the white Levis, tennies and striped shirts. Gone too are the odes to affluent hedonism, replaced by a host of ecologic, mystic and poetic preoccupations. Yet despite the beards, beads and plugs for TM, the Beach Boys, after 15 years in the business, remain identifiably the Beach Boys. Alone among white American rock groups, their ingenuity has sustained them over a decade, at times shaping, at times ignoring the whims of passing fancy.

The elements of their style are by now legend: the vocals, densely clustered or moving in counterpoint, simultaneously frail and precise; the compositions, some complex, others elementary, some anthemlike, others confessional, some a catalog of clichés, others a revision of rock orthodoxy.

In the Sixties, when they were at the height of their original popularity, the Beach Boys propagated their own variant on the American dream, painting a dazzling picture of beaches, parties and endless summers, a paradise of escape into private as often as shared pleasures. Yet by the late Sixties, the band was articulating, with less success, a disenchantment with that suburban ethos, and a search for transcendence. It has been a curious trek from hot rods and high times to religion and conservation; yet through it all, the Beach Boys have remained wed to the California that Chuck Berry once called the "promised land"—and their resurgent popularity says as much about the potency of that chimera as it does about the Beach Boys. . . .

In surfing, the Beach Boys had hit upon a potent image. Leisure, mobility and privacy—it was the suburban myth transported to the Pacific Ocean, but rendered heroic. There had been "surf bands" . . . in California before the Beach Boys, but these bands played a homogeneous brand of instrumental rock, crossed with rhythm and blues; the Beach Boys, with their neatly trimmed harmonies, were projecting a world view. . . .

[For "Surfin' U.S.A."] Brian and Mike [Love] contrived a set of lyrics that revealed no small flair for constructing teen utopias ("If everybody had an ocean . . ."); and the music itself was no less striking. While the blanched vocals harked back to the Four Preps, the guitars had the crude drive of a high school band; coming in the midst of teen idols, Brill Building pop and seductive "girl groups," the first Beach Boys hits managed to sound raunchy and vital, yet clean, somehow safe—for here was a rock and roll band aspiring to the instrumental sleekness of the Ventures, the lyric sophistication of Chuck Berry, and the vocal expertise of some weird cross between the Lettermen and Frankie Lymon and the Teenagers. . . .

The first LP [Brian] produced for the Beach Boys, *Surfer Girl,* hinted at things to come. For the first time, Brian used his falsetto extensively, sharing lead vocals with Mike

Love, whose nasal drone propelled all of the group's early uptempo hits. The group's harmonies veered toward the modern voicings of the Four Freshmen, and the success of "Surfer Girl," a cool ballad, enabled Brian to fill the album with similarly romantic fare, tied to surfing in name only. More importantly, Brian let a little of himself be expressed; on "In My Room," his pure falsetto, soaring over violins (another innovation), carried a message of suburban-bred agoraphobia at variance with (although not unrelated to) the Beach Boys' official posture of nonstop kicks: "There's a world where I can go / And tell my secrets to / In my room. . . ." (p. 158)

[During this period], the group's pursuit of Fun, whether on a surfboard or in a car, set them apart and assured them of an audience, no matter how restrictive the specific motifs —although surfing, cars and the California locale all became emblematic, of course.

California—in 1963, it was the one place west of the Mississippi where everyone wanted to be. Rich and fast, cars, women, one suburban plot for everyone: a sea of happy humanity sandwiched between frosty mountains and toasty beaches, all an easy drive down the freeway. But was it that simple and bright? Behind the pursuit of fun, you might hear a hint of tedium, or a realization that each day blemished the pristine Youth this culture coveted. Brian Wilson understood this perfectly, and, characteristically, made it attractive and not a little heroic, as in "I Get Around," in which he expresses sheer frustration: "I'm gettin' bugged drivin' up and down the same old strip. . . ." His business was the revitalization of myths he wished were true and knew were false. The hollowness, properly dressed up as adolescent yearning, could itself be marketed in "teen feel" pop songs.

Brian Wilson in any case was after something more than simple celebrations of suburbia. Throughout 1963, Phil Spector's Crystals and Ronettes recordings poured epic crescendos of sound into three-minute singles. The resonance and self-conscious imagery of Spector's records caught Brian's ear. From 1964 to *Pet Sounds* (May 1966), he dedicated himself to duplicating that oceanic sound. He would wed the Beach Boys' own harmonic expertise to Spector's use of layered percussion and orchestration. But Brian was not after mere imitation; the same impacted density would amplify his own lyrical themes. Suburban values wouldn't be abandoned—they'd be rendered profound, their ambiguities expressed.

"Fun, Fun, Fun" and "Don't Worry Baby" marked the break. "Don't Worry," ostensibly about a drag race, represented an earnest confession of insecurity: "Well, it's been buildin' up inside of me for, oh, I don't know how long / I don't know why, but I keep thinkin' something's bound to go wrong." The vocal arrangement underlined this vulnerability at every turn, casting the lyric's anxiety against a soothing expanse of overdubbed harmony parts. The Beach Boys were beginning to push pop conventions to their limits.

Meanwhile, hit followed hit, each marking some small advance over its predecessor. After "I Get Around," a brilliant teen anthem mounted with unorthodox chord changes, the singles toyed with an ever broader palette of colors. . . . But "When I Grow Up (to Be a Man)" stands as Brian's most touching work of the period. Its sad queries ("Will I

dig the same things that turned me on as a kid?") formed an admission of the ephemerality of youth, the passage of time underlined by the tolling of years on the refrain ("16, 17").

By 1965, "California Girls" and *Summer Days (and Summer Nights)*, Brian's style had fully developed. The group's last unadulterated fling at summer in the suburbs, *Summer Days* included such highlights as "Let Him Run Wild," a cyclical construct that recalled Holland-Dozier-Holland at Motown as much as it evoked Phil Spector. Brian had tamed the studio. . . . (pp. 158, 160)

Yet Brian increasingly played the recluse, dropping all concert dates with the band to concentrate on composing and producing. . . .

Not without regret, the Beach Boys, presumably at Brian's behest, abandoned their search for the perpetual followup. Perhaps, as some have claimed, Brian Wilson was consumed by a desire to better the Beatles; or perhaps, more simply, he was intent on working out the music already in his mind. Whatever the reasons, Wilson now focused all of his energy on creating an album that would fully reflect the Beach Boys' capabilities, by elaborating a new intricacy and a new seriousness of intent. . . .

Pet Sounds ushered in a turbulent period for the group. While "Wouldn't It Be Nice," the opening cut, presented Brian's fantasy of marital bliss, the rest of the record vented Wilson's obsession with isolation, cataloging a forlorn quest for security. The whole enterprise, which smacked slightly of song cycle pretensions, was streaked with regret and romantic languor. "I had to prove that I could make it alone now / But that's not me." But it worked; sweetening each cut with everything from chamber strings to a lonesome koto, Wilson distilled a potent brew, both confessional and maudlin, in the melodramatic fashion of Paul Anka. The Beach Boys have never quite recaptured the sustained brilliance of Brian's settings for these songs: and it was his music that carried the lyrics and made them evocative rather than trite.

The record's conclusion was pessimistic, charting the inevitability of change. By closing the cycle on a note of resignation ("Where did your long hair go? / Where is the little girl I used to know?"), "Caroline, No" revealed the emptiness of Brian's daydream on "Wouldn't It Be Nice." Unfortunately, such expressions of adolescent angst were not everybody's cup of tea: compared to previous Beach Boy albums, *Pet Sounds* sold poorly. (p. 160)

[*Smiley Smile*] and its successor, *Wild Honey,* marked a turning point for the Beach Boys. In its heyday, the band had dominated the charts thanks to Brian's skill at cutting hit singles; since the early songs were composed by a performing member of a performing group, they could be successfully re-created onstage. But starting with *Pet Sounds,* the music's complexity virtually precluded live performance; even worse, many of the new lyrics hardly hinted at the sunny fare Beach Boy fans expected. Perhaps sensing defeat in his effort to broaden the group's scope, Brian retreated. . . .

On albums like *Friends,* it almost seemed as if they were attempting, defiantly, to be uncommercial. A return to *Smiley's* dryness, minus the weirdness, *Friends* cast the Beach Boys as auteurs: coming from anybody else, the album would have been embarrassing; coming from them, it had the ring of autobiographical truth.

Brian, in the songs he contributed to the venture, returned to the suburban themes that have always preoccupied him; only now, the good life appeared as an exercise in ennui: "I get a lot of thoughts in the mornin'," sang Brian in "Busy Doin' Nothin'," "I write 'em all down / If it wasn't for that, I'd forget 'em in a while." At their best, the Beach Boys have never flinched before their own banality. "Busy Doin' Nothin'," for example, featured an entire verse devoted to dialing a telephone and not getting an answer. It is one of Brian's most subtle lyrical conquests.

Friends, when set against the success of "Do It Again," a summer-fun rehash, illustrated the band's dilemma. On the one hand, by milking familiar formulas, they could still command an audience; on the other hand, whenever they released a personal statement, or experimental material, the group found themselves performing in a vacuum. . . .

[The] Beach Boys thus faced several questions. Should they disband in the face of sporadic sales and indifferent response? Should they change their name, a liability in "hip" circles, and aim exclusively at the burgeoning market for "progressive rock"? Or should they continue as before, retain their original name and identity, and record whatever material they felt appropriate?

The answers came in 1970. The Beach Boys signed with Reprise Records, reactivated their own Brother Records logo (which had appeared on *Smiley Smile's* label), played the Big Sur Folk Festival, and issued *Sunflower,* their strongest album since *Pet Sounds.* In name, style and sound, they remained the Beach Boys.

In the five years since, the group has reestablished a loyal following among a new generation, and emerged as one of the biggest live acts in the U.S. In addition, they have continued to record new original material, with fitful public response.

Surf's Up, released in 1971, epitomized the post-*Pet Sounds* Beach Boys. On such tracks as "Long Promised Road," Carl Wilson emerged as Brian's heir apparent, a composer with an intuitive grasp of the Beach Boys' style. But *Surf's Up* also contained large doses of puffery, pretentiousness and ecological nonsense. Truth to tell, the Beach Boys had evolved into an accomplished, idiosyncratic but sometimes sterile ensemble, at least in the studio. . . .

[In their successful concert appearances] it was the surfing and car songs that brought audiences to their feet. At first the group persisted in largely performing recent material, but as the crowds grew, the pressure to concentrate on the oldies became irresistible. (p. 161)

To Brian, the problem must have seemed particularly acute. On the one hand, he now composed moody, introspective miniature operas, like "Til I Die" on *Surf's Up* —although he was reportedly reluctant to release the song, because it wasn't "fun." On the other hand, he was still capable of writing happy-go-lucky songs like those behind the Beach Boys' initial popularity, as "Marcella" on *Carl and the Passions* showed. Unfortunately, almost all of his writing had become baroque, condensed, difficult to execute forcefully, and, apparently, difficult for an audience to hear. They wanted the cheerful values of the early Sixties reaffirmed, resoundingly, in the compelling and straightforward fashion of the early hits. What Brian for his part wanted was considerably less clear, perhaps just to trundle

around the house and run the Radiant Radish, his organic-foods shop in Hollywood.

Buried by a tidal wave of nostalgia, and more or less abandoned by Brian, their greatest creative asset, the Beach Boys had little choice but to embrace their past. . . .

Ironically, Brian Wilson remains the group's guiding light. It is Brian's old songs that the band plays night after night; and it is Brian's new songs that stand out on the later Beach Boy albums. Indeed, the Beach Boys remain beholden to a style bequeathed them by Brian. From the nasal raunch of "Surfin' Safari" to the convoluted elegance of "Surf's Up," that style has become a nearly autonomous fund of favored themes, production tricks and chord progressions. . . .

[The] future remains uncertain. For one thing, Brian by the end of 1975 had yet to resume an active role within the group despite persistent rumors to the contrary; for another, the group is almost exclusively identified in the public's mind with its hits from the early Sixties. Like Chuck Berry, the Beach Boys lyrically and musically reflect an era; yet like the Beatles, the band has matured and progressed within the confines of a unique style. In many respects, they are the most innovative white rock and roll band the United States has ever seen. But whether they will ever be able to lead their audience beyond the uncomplicated suburban utopia their early hits so brilliantly depicted is another question entirely. (p. 162)

> *Jim Miller, "The Beach Boys," in* The Rolling Stone Illustrated History of Rock and Roll, *edited by Jim Miller (copyright © 1976 by Rolling Stone Press; reprinted by permission of Random House, Inc.), Rolling Stone Press, Random House, 1976, pp. 158-62.*

RICHARD WILLIAMS

The dilemma facing the Beach Boys today is created simply by their audience's expectations. Those who throng to their concerts do so in anticipation of swooning to "Surfer Girl" and bopping to "Fun, Fun, Fun", and would be mightily put out were these demands denied.

On the other hand, critics and old-time aficionados approach each new album with an equally understandable lust for the exploratory daring enshrined in the likes of "Wendy", "Caroline No", "Wind Chimes" and "Surf's Up".

"15 Big Ones", the 1976 album which featured Brian Wilson's first wholehearted studio participation in several years, suffered a cruel backlash from the latter camp, whose members refuse to acknowledge that although former heights may one day be scaled and even surpassed, now is not the time.

"Pet Sounds" and "Smile" were conceived in an era (immediately after Kennedy) conducive to experimentation; by contrast, the post-Nixon age encourages the flippant, the nostalgic, and the easy, empty gesture. Most critics carelessly misread the intentions and function of "15 Big Ones", an album perfectly wedded to its time: perhaps no pop album in a decade has been so easy to put on at a party, or while doing chores, in the way that one used pop albums in the days before "Rubber Soul"; in the way, of course, that one used "The Beach Boys Today" and "Summer Days (And Summer Nights)". It's not too fanciful to suggest that the American fans who made "The

Beach Boys Party'' a million-seller and then ignored ''Pet Sounds'' perhaps felt that ''15 Big Ones'' was the first real Beach Boys album in a decade.

''The Beach Boys Love You'' finds Brian Wilson further entrenched in his personal struggle, his tactics more obviously conditioned by those outside expectations....
....There are no oldies, and very little fluff: the whole endeavour bears the stamp of effort, symbolised in the urgent straining lead vocals of the half-dozen numbers which feature Brian in that capacity....

Some of the songs are very good indeed: ''Roller Skating Child'' is, I would say, an obvious single, somewhat after the manner of ''Darlin''', with Spectorish cliff-hanging snare-drum and handclaps beneath a throughly infectious chorus. ''Mona'' is another Spector tribute, made explicit in its lyric as well as the bedrock saxes and tubular bells. ''The Night Was Young'' is a yearning love song, harking back to the featherweight romanticism of ''She Knows Me Too Well'' and ''We'll Run Away'', with a classically unexpected, perfectly judged fadeout. ''I'll Bet He's Nice''; all jangling harpsichords and tambourines, is constructed with the old imaginative care and delicacy....

The finest achievement, however, is a song called ''Johnny Carson'', which some commentators have already misunderstood. In fact, the lyric and the vocal arrangement are filled with deepest irony, very far from the blandness of which the group is often accused. The voices are used in blocks, alternating syllables to recreate Carson's mechanical bonhomie, and anyone who can't see the satire in these lines is beyond redemption: ''Who's the guy that we admire? Johnny Carson—he's a real live wire!'' ...

''The Beach Boys Love You'' can appear insubstantial on early acquaintance, but further attention yields many riches. Perhaps Brian does need the lyrics of a Van Dyke Parks or a Jack Rieley for full creative stimulus; and perhaps the oppressive nature of the group's weighty tradition means that the best music of all will appear on the eventual solo albums from Dennis, Carl and Brian. But, for 1977, what they present here is better than we have any right to expect.

> Richard Williams, ''More Wilson Riches,'' in Melody Maker (© IPC Business Press Ltd.), March 19, 1977, p. 27.

STEVE SIMELS

[There] is one group—and one group only—for whom [a] preoccupation with the aging process seems to have no relevance whatsoever. (p. 67)

[Despite] the attrition of years, the virtual disappearance of the surf and car culture from which they sprang, and the inevitable distancing from their audience their growth from boys to men must bring, the Beach Boys are *still* fueling the fantasies of adolescents *and* of those of us long beyond them. This is a most remarkable achievement; other musicians who, like them, began their careers at the same age as their first fans have for the most part hung on to these *same* fans as the greater part of their audience. Paul McCartney, Dylan, the Stones, and the Who (to say nothing of Elvis, who is in many ways outside time entirely) have, to be sure, attracted new devotees. But only the Beach Boys' audience, among those of the classic rockers', seems to remain forever young, forever fifteen.

The answer, I think, has something to do with Innocence, which, like most things in life, is a much more complicated proposition than it at first appears. Certainly, the Beach Boys *were* innocents when they began; how could they, a bunch of teenagers growing up in an unremarkable suburb like Hawthorne, California, as a tight little family unit and interested in nothing more sophisticated than cars and girls, have been otherwise? You can see it on their earliest album covers—those incredibly young faces smiling on the back of ''Surfing U.S.A.'' seem like extras from the cast of *Leave It to Beaver* or some weird, surreal foreshadowing of *Happy Days*. But there is pain in the passing of innocence, and Brian Wilson, who captained the group from its inception and who blossomed as an enormous talent almost overnight, felt it most strongly. (pp. 67-8)

But Brian was not merely an overly sensitive teenager; he was a remarkably gifted musician, and the fantasies that obsessed him turned into a series of records that sounded like nothing anyone had ever heard before.... Some rocked like mad (*Little Deuce Coupe, Dance Dance Dance, I Get Around*); some were ballads of aching melodic beauty (*Surfer Girl, The Warmth of the Sun, In My Room*). Either way, these evocations of youthful joys and sorrows were on a level approaching the very finest folk art, and few could resist them.

For the first few years of their career, the Beach Boys clung to their innocence as they traveled the world in triumph, enormous international stars....

As the world rapidly changed, their innocence began to weigh heavily against them. They had represented good times, hedonism, materialism, even an Andy Hardy-ish school spirit, and by the middle of the decade the teenagers who had once adored the Boys were rejecting those values with a vengeance....

The amazing thing is that, throughout [the] whole chaotic period [of the late sixties], the beset Beach Boys turned out a series of albums that are perhaps their best and certainly among the least dated relics of their era. There was ''Pet Sounds,'' Brian's pre-''Sgt. Pepper'' concept record, both a triumph of studio technology and a heart-rending chronicle of lost love. There was ''Smiley Smile,'' a curious but entertaining piecing together of fragments of a project Brian had been working on with Van Dyke Parks. And, finally, there was ''Wild Honey.'' Cut totally in Brian's basement studio, it anticipated the return to pre-psychedelic simplicity of Dylan's ''John Wesley Harding'' by several months, but, for all its primitive sound and back-to-the-roots naïveté, it was as perfect a piece of music as they had ever come up with—ten gorgeous originals and perhaps the first cover version of a Stevie Wonder tune [''I Was Made to Love Her''] ever attempted by any white rock band. Despite the success of the title track as a single, ''Wild Honey'' sold hardly at all, and it is only now beginning to get its critical due. It has been reissued, though, and if you don't own a Beach Boys record, it is certainly the one you should buy first....

[Through] it all, incredibly, ... original innocence has somehow endured, a slightly battered assurance of survival. If their obsession with the California dream of the early Sixties—cars, surfing, the good life—has a contemporary parallel, what is it if not their involvement with conservation and ecological matters, their continued dalliance with transcendental meditation? These are fitting backgrounds for dreams of more Endless Summers and other Promised Lands, and they now include the knowledge, derived from experience, of the price of those dreams, the understanding that good times have to be earned if they are to be worth having. How wonderful that you can get all of that along with some of the most beautiful songs and performances in American music. (p. 68)

> Steve Simels, "The Beach Boys: Eleven Years On," in Stereo Review *(reprinted by permission of the author), May, 1977, pp. 66-9.*

BILLY ALTMAN

The Beach Boys Love You is a truly wonderful album, and it is Brian's show from beginning to end. He wrote 11 of the 14 songs and coauthored the others. In light of last year's events—*15 Big Ones* is easily the worst album in the Beach Boys' long history—its success is even more amazing. The bad songs here are really embarrassing—"Let's Put Our Hearts Together," a duet between Brian and wife Marilyn, and "Love Is a Woman," with Brian's achingly strained vocal, should never have been released—but mostly this album presents a Brian Wilson who is again comfortable in the recording studio, functioning at a level not too far removed from his better days.

As usual, the strengths are musical, the weaknesses lyrical. Wilson's lyrics have always reached clumsily for rhymes and images, and the content has often been silly and child-like. But the fact that he's not trying to be either profound or cute redeems him—you wince, but you also smile. As often as not, it is the very simplicity and warmth of spirit in the words teamed with the very complex and well thought out arrangements that win you over. (pp. 63-4)

The Beach Boys Love You is reminiscent of many other Beach Boys albums. Like the best of them, it's flawed but enjoyable. Brian Wilson still isn't singing as well as he used to, but his playing and composing talents have certainly returned from wherever they've been the past few years. Considering what he's been through, it's some accomplishment. (p. 64)

> Billy Altman, "Brother Brian's Resurgin' Safari," in Rolling Stone *(by Straight Arrow Publishers, Inc. © 1977; all rights reserved; reprinted by permission), Issue 238, May 5, 1977, pp. 63-4.*

MITCH COHEN

There is no TM song, no music-is-swell song, or "unfolding enveloping missiles of soul," or political/ecological commentary [in *The Beach Boys Love You*]. Instead, what we have here is a collection of 14 Brian Wilson compositions (three are collaborations) and a return to the Beach Boys' musical-thematic values of the late 1960's. If the group had been traders in the slobbery hogwash endemic to the era, that would hardly be news worth celebrating; but who would be grumpy enough to complain when faced with a distillation of *Pet Sounds* atmospheric cohesiveness, *Wild Honey* plains peak domesticity and stripped-body instrumentation, *Smiley Smile* jokiness and *Friends* unadorned sentimentality. It would serve people who cavil about Wilson's lyrics right if Jack Rieley were to make a return as wordsmith.

All talk about Brian's "comeback" aside, *The Beach Boys Love You* does show clearly how much his guiding vision

was missed; his musicianship is continually surprising, subtle and tricky. This LP achieves through the use of synthesizer a unity of tone that has been absent from Beach Boys albums since his role was usurped by participatory democracy. He really does give them direction, deepening the sound without being heavy-handed. . . . [There's] complexity in the arrangements that makes them endlessly listenable.

And then there are those lyrics. While one may be totally disarmed by couplets like "If Mars had life on it/I might find my wife on it" ("Solar System") or "When guests are boring he takes up the slack / The network makes him break his back" ("Johnny Carson"), it's easy to see how others might find them and similar AABB rhyme schemes embarrassing. The Beach Boys have always been Champions of Silly, but here the words are so unaffected, so "one equals one" that they've reached new heights. Coming from anyone else the lyrics of "I Wanna Pick You Up" (the title is all it has in common with Ramones diction) would be taken as fetishistically infantile. . . . But Wilson's words say what they say. "Well oh my oh gosh oh gee" ("Roller Skating Child") seems like a reasonable critical response.

One thing that is missing is a sense of physical and emotional geography. Wilson's songs are no longer situated in a tangible place; he's been indoors a lot, but even if he were more social, the L.A. of the Eagles would probably be unrecognizable to him. T-shirts, cut-offs and a pair of thongs aren't standard Southern California haberdashery anymore. He's an isolated adult now, at a distance from the boy-girl encounters he's creating more out of memory and imagination than current experience. It's quite a jump from eulogizing James Dean ("A Young Man Is Gone") to praising Johnny Carson, from sneaking into drive-ins to exploring the solar system. Wilson never was much of a participant, but at least he was in touch. The high school mentality and humor on some of these songs—"falsies" really is a locker-room anachronism—suggests his disassociation from 1977 teenage.

So many songs on the album, "The Night Was So Young," "I'll Bet He's Nice," "Mona," "Let Us Go On This Way," are captivating enough, and as texturally sophisticated as they are lyrically naive, to quell any resistance. . . . Some of the lead vocals are a bit ragged (but not as bad as on *15 Big Ones*), and Wilson frequently tests the dividing line between child-like directness and stunning banality. If you love the Beach Boys, though, you can't help but feel immense affection for *The Beach Boys Love You.*

> Mitch Cohen, "This Ain't the Summer of Love, But the Beach Boys Love You Just the Same," in Creem *(© copyright 1977 by Creem Magazine, Inc.), July, 1977, p. 70.*

DAVID LEAF

Brian Wilson's special magic in the early and mid-1960s was that he was at one with his audience. There was no "writing down" to the listeners. Brian had a teenage heart, until it was broken. Before that happened, Brian used the Beach Boys music to "invent" California.

California has always occupied an exalted position in popular American culture, whether it was the Gold Rush days or the heyday of Hollywood. Brian Wilson's particular California Myth is a product of the 1960s, and it is important to remember that to teenagers in 1961, California was just a state, not yet a state of mind. . . .

For kids whose oceans and beaches were made by intersecting asphalt and fire hydrants, whose winters were filled with long, cold, snowy nights, California had to be the end of the rainbow. (p. 7)

The California clichés really haven't been changed or challenged since Brian Wilson created them fifteen years ago. For teenagers, they remain incredibly powerful fantasies, so powerful that in 1978 they have become institutionalized clichés. . . .

The myth was at its most potent in the early sixties before my generation came of age and decided that what Los Angeles had to offer wasn't worthwhile. When Southern California did epitomize the ideal youth, when the drive-in movie screens were showing films like "Girls on the Beach" or "Beach Blanket Bingo," the Beach Boys represented that way of life to the world. (p. 8)

California was once looked on by America as its final frontier. Today, it's more like a last chance on its last legs. The Beach Boys are in a similar position, but nobody wants to accept that fact. Even though they are balding and paunchy, they are all we have left to remind us of our own golden summers. The Beach Boys, like Southern California, are a fading jewel.

The 1970s are one long, nostalgic look at a better time. That means movies like *American Graffiti*, TV programs like "Happy Days," and rock groups like the Beach Boys. While the first two are idealized and cleansed versions of what it was like in the late fifties and early sixties, the Beach Boys are still the original. They may be in their thirties, with divorce, drugs, and personal disaster behind them, but they are still the same guys churning out a music that struck a basic chord in white middle-class American society. The Beach Boys' music created a myth that didn't work, for them or anyone else, and when nothing else worked, a disillusioned America returned to that myth.

The music, however, has transcended their personalities and the ravages of time. Brian Wilson's music is for the ages. . . . (p. 9)

> David Leaf, in his The Beach Boys and the California Myth *(copyright © 1978 by Delilah Communications, Ltd.), Grosset & Dunlap, 1978.*

TOM CARSON

You go to a rock and roll show in the hope of being moved by the unexpected; you go to see an institution, like the Lincoln Memorial, or the Grand Canyon, or the Beach Boys, to be moved by the expected—to trigger a response you already know is there. That they continue to be a working band, nominally in the present tense, hardly matters. The albums of new material that they release from time to time simply aren't part of the legend; they're appendages, and they feel incomplete, because the audience, the community of belief that made the Beach Boys' fantasies come to life, doesn't exist in the present tense to sustain them. Only as evokers of the past, passive agents of their fans' desire, does the band become whole again. The critical difference between the Beach Boys myth of 1965 and today is that the community of belief has turned into a community of suspended disbelief which makes the band's job slightly easier.

The point came clear during the second half of the Beach Boys' concert at Radio City Music Hall, the first show of a four-night stand there last week. After an abbreviated version of their current single, the discofied reworking of *Wild Honey*'s "Here Comes the Night," Mike Love announced —rather nervously—that they were going to play four more songs off their new LP, *L.A. (Light Album)*, which will be in the stores next week. The audience was receptive enough, but you could feel them counting; when Love introduced "Help Me Rhonda" by saying "Now we're going to go into a familiar one," they let out a huge cheer.

Me, I was a little disappointed. I like the new album—it's nothing spectacular, and I wish they'd pick up the pace a bit, but I still think it's the freshest, most accessible work they've done in some time—and I like the fact that they were doing untried material on stage even better. But the audience knew instinctively what I only came to understand after the concert: that, good or bad, this music was simply irrelevant. It had nothing to do with their conception of the Beach Boys, and their conception of the Beach Boys was all-important: it had far more life than the band itself. The *L.A.* material, well-performed though it was, interrupted the ritual—the serene contemplation of the recaptured, ageless past. . . . (pp. 57-8)

[When] the band launched into "Sloop John B," letting loose on the harmonies and hitting the changes hard, . . . the audience howled its first real enthusiasm of the night. The time machine had functioned after all—the evening settled into a timeless groove. "I Get Around" and "Fun, Fun, Fun" are historical songs now, recreated fragments of collective memory, like "The Night They Drove Old Dixie Down." It hardly makes any difference that they were never intended that way. To complain that most of the material was hardly less than 15 years old would be to miss the point of the ritual entirely: the reason people go to see the Beach Boys now is to erase those 15 years. . . .

Afterward, I went back to listen to *L.A.* again, and was struck by a wistful, melancholy undertone—an almost subliminal sense of futility—that I hadn't noticed before. The album starts off, or tries to, on a hopeful note, with a song called "Good Timin'"; but that mood soon gives way to a slightly mawkish, altogether more appropriate regret. Even the new "Here Comes the Night," with its synthesized rhythms and spacey mix, the most innovative thing they've done in years, echoes the past more than it anticipates the future: it seems like a one-shot bid for a hit single rather than the authentic new beginning it might have been. The pointless cover of "Shortnin' Bread" that closes the album is such a throwaway finish—a retreat into Brianesque eccentricity—that it's almost as if the band is saying, Here's another record that won't make any difference. (p. 58)

> Tom Carson, "Those Wonderful Pre-Disco Beach Boys," in The Village Voice *(reprinted by permission of* The Village Voice; *copyright © The Village Voice, Inc., 1979), March 12, 1979, pp. 57-8.*

DAVITT SIGERSON

The finest wit, the most affecting, and the most difficult to achieve, is the wit of tolerance. The Beach Boys have become masters of this medium in recent years. Although their output has been worrisomely uneven, they have not, as some argue, "gone soft." The Beach Boys have never worked with the facile arts of cynicism: so, in the Sixties, simple minds believed their surfing records to be naive, because they were uncontemptuous . . . so, in the Seventies, simple minds believe the Beach Boys are dead, because they are unrepentant.

The Beach Boys are not dead, as this fine album ["L.A. (Light Album)"] proves. Their gentle wit begins in the title, a double pun. For not only does LA stand for "Light Album" (at which unperceptive listeners may dismiss it)—the "Light," we are told, refers to "the awareness . . . and presence . . . of God." . . .

"Here Comes The Night" does for the dance-floor what "I Get Around" did for the wood-panelled station wagon. It's a disco record, a Beach Boys record and a great record, in no particular order.

The rest of "L.A." is comprised of short, melancholy, exquisite ballads. "Angel Come Home" is a great pop record on an old theme. "Good Timin'" and "Full Sail" are songs with positive messages that make you feel sad; its clear how imperfect we are, how pathologically misunderstanding and misunderstood, how seeing the light and employing it are not the same thing. That they communicate irony without bitterness, sadness without hoplessness, is the mark of their art.

Davitt Sigerson, "The Beach Boys' Divine Light," in Melody Maker *(© IPC Business Press Ltd.), March 31, 1979, p. 23.*

DAVE MARSH

The Beach Boys are easily the most overrated group in rock & roll history—which presents the reviewer with a problem: simply stating the facts invites an overreaction from the band's maundering cult who exaggerate the surf bums' importance. But the truth is that Brian Wilson was never a musical genius, though he executed some of the most crafty reworkings of Phil Spector's production style ever done and, for a few years, tapped into the heart line of teenage lifestyle; that the Beach Boys have not made great rock music since *Wild Honey;* that the Beach Boys have not made competent pop music since *Holland.*

Like the LPs that preceded it, *L.A. (Light Album),* the Beach Boys' CBS-distribution debut, offers hope to the faithful with a mix of the barely listenable and distant echoes of the good old days. Even the vaunted disco track, "Here Comes the Night," is not so much a sellout as it is simple padding. . . .

Don't get me wrong. It would be easy to attack *L.A. (Light Album)* as an awful record, if only out of spite for being bored to death by the jabbering of the Beach Boys' champions. But this LP is worse than awful. It is irrelevant. (p. 57)

Dave Marsh, in Rolling Stone *(by Straight Arrow Publishers, Inc. © 1979; all rights reserved; reprinted by permission), Issue 292, May 31, 1979.*

Stevie Wonder
1950-

(Born Steveland Judkins Morris) Black American songwriter, arranger, musician. Wonder is often considered responsible for expanding the range of rhythm and blues music through his use of diverse musical elements; reggae, jazz, blues, and rock are all part of his repertoire. Wonder's audience reflects this diversity; he was one of the first black artists to achieve the mass popularity and initial acclaim previously attributed to white performers. His keen sense of sound, perhaps enhanced by his blindness, steered him towards developing his musical interests as a young child. At the age of nine, he was under contract with Motown records, and was referred to as "the little boy wonder" around the studio, thus creating his recording name. A talented harmonica player, he soon mastered all the other instruments used as backup for his music, an accomplishment allowing for varied musical expression. As he matured both physically and stylistically, Wonder transcended the limiting image often set for Motown performers and their contract restrictions to develop a distinctive, personal approach. The year 1971 was pivotal for Wonder: he gained artistic control over his music, becoming one of the few artists who continues to govern his own creativity in this manner, and independently released *Music of My Mind*, an innovative album which set a precedent for all of his following recordings. Wonder's life was greatly affected by a near fatal auto accident in 1973. This brush with death led to a spiritual rebirth which is often expressed in his music, such as "Have a Talk with God" and "Higher Ground." Critics concede that his music sustains his lyrics, which have been called belabored and repetitious. His songs, however, reflect his genuinely optimistic and enthusiastic attitude towards life, often dealing with the many forms of love. The recipient of numerous Grammy awards, Wonder continues to be an inspiring songwriter and performer and one who, despite a sporadic recording career, consistently meets the expectations and maintains the respect of his audience.

JON LANDAU

[The range of material on *I Was Made to Love Her*] is very limited, making it difficult to listen to the album as a whole.

Stevie's . . . style is essentially a variation on the kind of thing he did on "Uptight," a fine record. On that cut he added to the standard components of a Motown single a very personal lyric, and then sang the whole thing in a driving style from beginning to end. Stevie doesn't go in for dynamics, rhythm changes, or crescendoes, but prefers to sing frenetically for the duration of a piece.

The "Uptight" style continues to be the basis for all of Stevie's recordings, and the title song of his new album, *I Was Made to Love Her,* is a beautiful example of what Stevie can do using this approach. By far the best cut on the album, it contains a personal, down home lyric, some of Stevie's wild harmonica, and the basic overdrive that characterizes all of his records. (p. 179)

[The] album has all the worst characteristics of the Motown sound with only a very few of the saving graces. The whole thing has a blatantly manufactured quality to it typical of Motown's capacity to crank out albums without giving any thought to experimentation or expanding the range of its artists' capacities. The result is an album of second-rate single material. (p. 180)

> *Jon Landau, "'I Was Made to Love Her'" (originally published in* Rolling Stone, *December 14, 1968), in* The Rolling Stone Record Review *by the editors of* Rolling Stone *(copyright © 1967, 1968, 1969, 1970, 1971, by Straight Arrow Publishers, Inc.; all rights reserved; reprinted by permission), Pocket Books, 1971, pp. 179-82.*

S. K. OBERBECK

"My Cherie Amour" and "Yester-Me, Yester-You, Yesterday," are more haunting ballads than soul tunes. The funky, grinding backgrounds of [Stevie Wonder's] early records have been replaced by a silky, sophisticated bank of swelling strings and brass. . . .

Hearing the old cuts of Stevie Wonder's high-jiving and scatting days, like "Uptight Everything's Alright" and "Be Cool, Be Calm and Keep Yourself Together," makes the changes in his current style apparent. You can turn on the radio today and hear white rock singers doing the same things, less gracefully, that Stevie was doing eight years ago. Now he is moving out, beyond blackness and beyond soul, ranging wider for what he likes and wants to sing.

> *S. K. Oberbeck, "Big Stevie," in* Newsweek *(copyright 1970 by Newsweek, Inc.; all rights reserved; reprinted by permission), January 12, 1970, p. 65.*

ARNOLD BRODSKY

[Stevie Wonder] specializes in sentimental novelty songs

which are very good when they work, very bad when they don't. "Never Had a Dream Come True" [from his album *Signed, Sealed, Delivered*] works. The best is reminiscent of "A Place in the Sun," one of Stevie's best early songs, but there is less of a dominant regularity here, and the added looseness enables his vocal straining to fit in better here than on the more stiffly structured "Yester You, Yester Me, Yesterday." (p. 199)

> *Arnold Brodsky, "'Never Had a Dream Come True'" (originally published in* Rolling Stone, *April 16, 1970), in* The Rolling Stone Record Review *by the editors of* Rolling Stone *(copyright © 1967, 1968, 1969, 1970, 1971, by Straight Arrow Publishers, Inc.; all rights reserved; reprinted by permission), Pocket Books, 1971, pp. 198-200.*

VINCE ALETTI

Any of the 12 songs on Stevie Wonder's [*Signed, Sealed & Delivered*] holds more creative singing than you're likely to find in another performer's entire body of work. And while everything may not reach the energy level of the title song, "Signed, Sealed, Delivered," there's not a bad cut on the LP. One of the best is a version of Lennon-McCartney's "We Can Work It Out," which had a startling, brand-new vitality even on an early unmixed tape. In its finished state, it's extraordinary.

The rest of the album is original material, most of it written in part by Stevie.... Nearly every number has single potential, but a few rise above the rest: "I Can't Let My Heaven Walk Away" is a beautifully-written Lost Love song ("I accused my angel of being a liar / I said the flesh is weak and guys keep tryin'") that Stevie delivers in fine style—the way he slashes at the work "flesh" in the quoted line is worth the whole cut....

Stevie Wonder shines throughout, yes he does, and joy (takes over me). (p. 48)

> *Vince Aletti, in* Rolling Stone *(by Straight Arrow Publishers, Inc. © 1971; all rights reserved; reprinted by permission), Issue 74, January 21, 1971.*

["Where I'm Coming From" represents Stevie Wonder's] final emergence from being just another cog in the Motown hit machine to become a fully-fledged songwriter/musician with something personal and worthwhile to say.

Not that Stevie really ever was just another cog; he has always stood slightly apart, remaining a resolute and instantly recognisable voice through all the successive "sounds" dictated by Motown producers. This album confirms his identity and reveals new depths. It really is impressive with something of a "Sgt Pepper" feel in its conscious use of widely-differing moods and styles and its touches of wry humour.... [This album is] a solid delight.

> *"Stevie Works Wonders," in* Melody Maker *(© IPC Business Press Ltd.), June 19, 1971, p. 40.*

VINCE ALETTI

It's only when I stop dancing and singing all around the room that it occurs to me Stevie Wonder's *Music of My Mind* may not be the great album of the year. It's certainly the best thing to come out of Motown since Marvin Gaye's *What's Goin' On* and perhaps even more impressive as a personal achievement, considering Wonder not only wrote,

arranged and produced the entire album but played every instrument.... Everything seems to fall quite comfortably within Steve's grasp and the effect is both satisfying and exciting. It's satisfying if you're willing to overlook a few flaws, some of which have cropped up in his other recent work. Most would fall under the heading Self-Indulgence: a tendency towards gimmickry that often eludes his fine sense of control.

[Wonder] seems to have come into his own as a songwriter. His lyrics are generally simple, playful, unpretentious; even some of the more self-conscious lines in "Girl Blue" work nicely. Yet the words have little inspiration when compared with the music, which is constantly inventive within a rather simple structure. Wonder never overloads his songs musically; instead, his weakness seems to be with the vocal tracks. (p. 48)

> *Vince Aletti, in* Rolling Stone *(by Straight Arrow Publishers, Inc. © 1972; all rights reserved; reprinted by permission), Issue 107, April 27, 1972.*

Stevie can no longer be considered as simply a Motown artist or a soul man but must be recognised for what he is: one of the most inventive and complete musicians around.

People are already talking about ["Music of My Mind"] as Motown's "Sgt. Pepper." I'm not sure that labels like that really help, but I know what they mean. Like "Pepper," there is a wholeness about this album which is completely satisfying: each track is a real song, beautifully constructed, instantly memorable and self-contained. Yet the tracks hang together and complement each other perfectly. They are linked not by any laborious theme or concept but by the underlying mood and the homogeneity of the playing....

If you can stand to have the "Sgt Pepper" comparison pushed a bit further, then I would say that Stevie's album, too, is remarkable because it owes very little, directly, to anything that has gone before—yet at the same time it is a beautiful synthesis of everything that has gone before. Several tracks, for example, have a subtle Latin flavour which reflects Stevie's recent interest in South American music, while "Sweet Little Girl" with its gruff vocals and harmonica is as funky as anything the "old" Stevie would have done. He's aware of the New Music, but he hasn't forgotten his roots.

Stevie warned us what to expect with his last album, "Where I'm Coming From" ..., but everything here is so much more sharply-focussed, particularly the lyrics ... which make their point without the kind of preaching which makes the Marvin Gaye "What's Going On" album less than perfect.

From the opening "Love Having You Around" ..., to the closing, climactic and very moving "Evil" this is a very "up" album. And the final touch which sets this apart from many other fine albums is Stevie's lightness of touch, his sense of fun and flashes of ad-lib, self-mocking humour on songs like "Sweet Little Girl." Throughout the impression is of a real musician in a natural groove, playing his ass off and having fun. And the wonder of it is that the best is probably yet to come.

> *"Stevie's Sgt. Pepper," in* Melody Maker *(© IPC Business Press Ltd.), May 13, 1972, p. 24.*

LENNY KAYE

Stevie Wonder has become the brightest light of all

[Motown's prodigies], his work since *Music of My Mind* consistently innovative and lustily creative, propelled by a confidence and artistic maturity that only comes through the dogged patience and understanding of day-to-day experience.

Innervisions is Wonder's 14th album, his third since fully becoming his own man, and it shows off his talents to luminous advantage.... Indeed, *Innervisions* may be as close to a concept album as Stevie will ever produce. Its tracks are coupled by a hovering mist of subdued faith, of a belief in the essential *rightness* of things; and if he seeks to offer no real solutions (should he?), neither does he allow for any easy outs, any quick glossings of the surface.

The themes are simple. Life is tough but life is beautiful; find your own way, but make sure you're not simply playing the fool and kidding yourself. He gently chides the escapism of drugs ("Too High"), as well as the "Misstra Know-It-All"'s who wear their ignorance like a shield. He saves his blessings for those who maintain a reverie of the world as it should be, as it inevitably is, the "Higher Ground" which must never be lost sight of or denied. It's interesting to note here that in the song Wonder directs at the "Jesus Children of America" (adding transcendental meditators and junkies into the spiritual mix), he merely asks them not to "tell lies." Later, in "Don't You Worry 'Bout a Thing": "Everybody needs a change / A chance to check out the new / But you're the only one to see/The changes you take yourself through."

In this sense—and it's to his credit that Wonder's preoccupations with such siddharthic messages never slide into the blandly predictable—Stevie functions a bit like Curtis Mayfield, aware of his role as a musical and spiritual leader, in that order, but hardly to the point of shrillness. His concern with the real world is all-encompassing, a fact which his blindness has apparently complemented rather than denied. "I'm not one who makes believe," he sings in "Visions"; "I know that leaves are green." Even when his characters run into crippling obstacles—the young Mississippi boy who's spent his life "Living for the City," only to arrive at Port Authority and be unjustly thrown in the slammer—he never loses that basic optimism, the ability to once again rise and return to the fray....

An eye for an eye. On *Innervisions*, Stevie Wonder proves again that he is one of the vital forces in contemporary music.

> Lenny Kaye, "Wonder's Own Third: Luminous Talent," in Rolling Stone *(by Straight Arrow Publishers, Inc. © 1973; all rights reserved; reprinted by permission), Issue 144, September 27, 1973, p. 98.*

JON LANDAU

Stevie Wonder has replaced Sly Stone as the most significant individual black innovator in the twin fields of R&B and rock. He has also replaced him as the most popular black music personality: Wonder's appeal now crosses every boundary. His music always sounds free and, at his best, he does things no one else can.... And though [the audio montage of "Living for the City" on *Innervisions*] would crumble in the hands of a lesser artist, he makes it work through the force of his personality. There is something complete about Stevie Wonder, and one senses that

he is not only exceptionally important today, but will continue to be for as long as he chooses. (p. 67)

> Jon Landau, in Rolling Stone *(by Straight Arrow Publishers, Inc. © 1974; all rights reserved; reprinted by permission), Issue 162, June 6, 1974.*

KEN EMERSON

[The cover of *Fulfillingness' First Finale* is] remarkably apt, for the careers of few performers in popular music have been such uninterrupted ascents. Nothing, not even a brush with death, has interrupted Wonder's progress toward ever higher ground, and *FFF* is a new plateau. As its title declares, the album is a culmination of what has come before, but it is by no means a final destination.

Since he assumed complete control of his musical direction in 1972 ..., Wonder's albums have been about vision. About the false visions that delude and undo people (ambition in "Superwoman," superstition in the hit of the same name, shady demagogy in "Big Brother" and "He's Misstra Know-It-All," and dope in "Too High"); about Wonder's idealistic "innervision," which is religious, romantic, and political at the same time; and about things as they are....

If *Talking Book* deals primarily with love of woman and *Innervisions* with love of humanity, *FFF* concerns the love of God. Wonder's faith has become more inner-directed and otherworldly, less easily threatened by the here-and-now.... A self-assured serenity pervades *FFF,* and it opposes the tension and urgency which made *Talking Book* and *Innervisions* more exciting albums. *FFF*'s tunes and tempi are for the most part easygoing, more like "Sunshine of My Life" than "Living for the City" or "Superstition." The album aims at relaxed enjoyment; it's not something to get hot and bothered about.

FFF is less funky, less specifically black than its predecessors. For Wonder's onward and upward development has consistently been away from strict soul music and racial categories or limitations. Because of this, his appeal—greater than that of almost any other performer today—cuts across social and ethnic barriers.... [Unlike] so many Detroit acts, whose wooing of white listeners leaves them pallid and gutless, Wonder's music expands and its integrity is strengthened, not diminished....

It's also the least representative, for Wonder realizes that such seriousness can be less entertaining to a pop music audience. More typically, he weds an earnest lyric to a lighthearted melody, as he did on *Talking Book*'s "Big Brother." Thus a mellow, easy-rolling tune sweetens the zeal of "Heaven Is 10 Zillion Light Years Away," and it also conveys the calm confidence of Wonder's devotion. Even when it touches upon lost love or abandonment, *FFF* is a cool album, for Wonder has reached the point where little can shake his convictions or composure....

FFF succeeds in making Stevie Wonder's dreams seem attractive and real.

> Ken Emerson, "In Excelsis Wonder," in Rolling Stone *(by Straight Arrow Publishers, Inc. © 1974; all rights reserved; reprinted by permission), Issue 170, September 26, 1974, p. 98.*

MAUREEN ORTH

Emotion—direct and straightforward—is the key to all of

Stevie's music. His only real weakness is an occasional lapse into sentimentality that comes precisely from his total emotional sincerity—there's no chic toughness à la Mick Jagger, no metaphysical melancholy à la James Taylor. Stevie writes and sings exactly what he feels—a very rare gift. (p. 65)

Maureen Orth, "Stevie, The Wonder Man," in Newsweek *(copyright 1974 by Newsweek, Inc.; all rights reserved; reprinted by permission), October 28, 1974, pp. 59-65.*

ROBERT CHRISTGAU

Stevie Wonder is a fool. I state it that way—baldly, without qualification—because the qualifications are so obvious that they tempt us away from the truth. I'm not saying he's a complete fool; in fact, I'm not saying he isn't a genius. But you can't deny that if you were to turn on a phone-in station and hear Stevie rapping about divine vibrations and universal brotherhood, especially with that inevitable dash of astrology, you would not be impressed with his intellectual discernment. . . .

Stevie's blather has more dimensions—about six in all—than that of the average Leon Lewis fan or rock and roll pundit. Foolishness is an annoyance; cosmic foolishness is an offense. Elton John and John Denver may be no smarter than the guy who tried to sell you Earth Shoes last week, but like most salesmen they do maintain a certain feel for the concrete. . . .

EJ and JD, together with SW, are the pop music heroes of the year, and perhaps the decade, and all three are united by simple-mindedness of a sort that seemed to have disappeared from rock and roll atavars a decade ago. . . .

Stevie's early precursors—blind genius Ray Charles, love-crowd soul fave Otis Redding, Grammy perennial Aretha Franklin—never indulged in the sort of wary self-knowledge that makes for contrasts as intense as Beatles/John and Taylor/Denver. Stevie might have seemed callow against their down-to-earth maturity, but callowness is natural in a child prodigy. His real model, however, was Sly Stone, who like so many rock (not soul) stars resolved the paradox of personal power within a supposedly communal music by pretending to inscrutability. Sly's public pronouncements are incoherent to the point of put-on, which opens that incoherence to further analysis, while Stevie's nonsense is accentuated by the earnest context in which it occurs. (p. 128)

I've often wondered about the visual imagery running through the songs of our blind genius. Maybe the eye bias of our thought and language forced him to go *lookin'* for another pure love, but it seems fair to surmise that only his deplorable penchant for cliches—metaphors so hackneyed they become abstract—turns that love into the apple of his *eye*. Even in "Visions" a title that refers explicitly to the phrase "vision in my mind," he goes on: "I'm not the one who make-believes / I know that leaves are green / They only turn to brown when autumn comes around." If he's blind, how does the fool know the leaves are green? . . .

I found myself moved by the "visions in my mind" idea, for obviously the man could enjoy no other, and suddenly I understood how he knew the color of the leaves—he had been told it was so, and he had no choice but to believe.

That was the definitive condition of his life. Much more than you or me, he was in contact with the unconscious acts of faith that get every one of us through each day.

I began by calling Stevie Wonder a fool because that is the kind of judgment we shy away from—after all, the man is blind, he is black, and we love him. But if he is a fool, he is a sainted fool. His simplicity will not save us—what will?—but it will do us more good than the simplicity of John Denver or Elton John. We may enjoy their simplicity, we may find it useful . . . but we do not need it. It just may be that we need Stevie Wonder.

The persistence of hope which we call faith has always energized black music, and in Stevie this energy is intensified—because of his blindness, and because of his fortune as a survivor. Stevie may sometimes be sanctimonious as well as sanctified; his musical expansiveness may puff him up; his dream of brotherhood for our grandchildren may cloud over the ironies of our condition more than he can ever understand. But he really isn't one who make-believes. Instead, he creates an aural universe—or maybe I should call it an aural condition—so rich that it makes us believe. His multiplicity of voices, his heavenly tunes, his wild ear humor, and even his integration of the synthesizer all speak of a free future not dreamt of in our philosophy. And it is not foolish to believe that the transcendence of philosophy is the reason we want music in our lives. (p. 129)

Robert Christgau, "Stevie Wonder Is a Fool," in The Village Voice *(reprinted by permission of* The Village Voice; *copyright © The Village Voice, Inc., 1974), December 16, 1974, pp. 128-29.*

ELLEN WILLIS

Wonder not only has attracted a huge interracial audience and made the cover of *Newsweek* at a time when there is little communication between black and white musical cultures but has engaged our imaginations, made connections, become more than a performer. . . . At his best, he has the power to make optimism and racial reconciliation marvellously credible. Without denying "the nightmare that's becomin' real life"—pain, anger, bitterness toward oppressors, even the petty spite that can arise out of disappointment in love are all present in his lyrics, in the strange, often tormented sounds he coaxes out of the synthesizer—he can suggest that the joy of being human ultimately prevails. And because the anarchic, exploratory textural busyness of his music enlarges our sense of possibility the way Dylan's words once did, because his pleasure in the exchange between performer and audience both communicates and inspires something like love—perhaps also because we know he hasn't exactly had it easy—we are ready to believe him. But there is a delicate balance involved here, and too often it tips in the direction of romantic and religious sentimentality. Wonder's lapses are disturbing, because they call into question his successes. Does his transcendent joy reflect some sort of reality we can grasp and build on, or is it, after all, just a pleasant distraction? Is there a possibility of racial détente based on hard times ahead, on the common disillusion and defiance expressed in a song like "You Haven't Done Nothin'"? Or will the more fatuous aspects of Wonder's message of universal love simply provide the growing horde of religious escapists with still another focus for their complacency? (pp. 56-7)

Ellen Willis, "Rock, Etc.: The Importance of

Stevie Wonder," in The New Yorker (© 1974 by
The New Yorker Magazine, Inc.), December 30,
1974, pp. 56-7.

[It] will come as little surprise to anyone that ["Songs In
The Key Of Life"] is as accomplished as its five predecessors. The songs, with a very few exceptions, are excellent,
and Wonder's arrangements and production realise them
perfectly....

Thematically, Wonder's writing continues to explore social
issues: the touch, taste and scent of ghetto life, and, centrally, love of every sort, from that of a father for his child
to man for woman to the spiritual love of man for his fellow, which remains the very essence of Wonder's work—
brotherly love, nation shall speak unto nation, and so on.

His lyrics are exceptionally exact on his two strongest
commentary songs. Their extremely terse words are flung
into sharp contrast by using a lush mood and delicate violin
arrangement. It's true of both the futuristic "Pastime Paradise," and "Village Ghetto Land," a blunt yet caring description of ghetto life covering fear, robbery, starvation,
police corruption, murder, disease, politicians' insensitivity, greed and vice—all in four verses of the six-verse song.

"Songs In The Key Of Life" is not, however, a dark or
brooding album. Wonder, by his very nature, couldn't produce one. Even his songs of lost love are presented in so
luxuriant a setting that the shade of blue is distinctly royal....

The whole of the first side indeed, is utterly successful.
There is the opening cut, "Love's In Need Of Love Today," which sums up the basic philosophy of the album....

If side three is less convincing, it's because it's more personal to Wonder. "Isn't She Lovely" is a gay, swinging
hymn to his daughter, Aisha, spoiled by an over-lengthy
fade....

There are many sides (no pun intended) to "Songs In The
Key Of Life," and not all will emerge to this listener, I
suspect, in the first week or two. All I can say is that it is
the sort of album which will make you replay all your other
Stevie Wonder albums. And that's the best sort of album.

"Stevie—A Key Set," in Melody Maker (© IPC
Business Press Ltd.), October 9, 1976, p. 33.

ROBERT CHRISTGAU

The first notes of Songs in the Key of Life waft up from a
choir of humming colored folks who might be refugees from
Vincente Minnelli's Cabin in the Sky. Their music is mellifluous, placid, and elevated; it seems to epitomize (as black
critic Donald Bogle wrote of Cabin in the Sky) "ersatz
Negro folk culture . . . passed off as the real thing." The
catch is that this ersatz culture may be the real thing. . . .

Fallacious or not, questions of intention arise immediately,
as they so often do in popular culture. In order to understand what is actually going on here we are well-advised to
try to determine what is supposed to be going on. So if
we've forgotten for a moment who this artist is, with his
"serious news for everybody," we are now obliged to remember. This is Stevie Wonder. He is black and considers
that an advantage; he is blind and given to mystic visions.
His music is both meticulous and wildly expressionistic; his

words combine a preacher's eloquence with an autodidact's
clumsiness. And a small detail: In one of his best and favorite jokes, he impersonates a disc jockey, everybody's
friendly announcer.

Who can gauge what intentions these credentials imply?
Perhaps Stevie Wonder hopes to reclaim an unfairly discredited manifestation of black culture—the genteel Hollywood gospel chorus—with his blessing. Or perhaps the
chorus . . . merely reifies the man's idealist notion of black
spirituality. Perhaps the musical ambiguity is deliberate, the
stilted language a gentle gibe at the "announcer," at Stevie
himself. Or perhaps it's all just sloppiness. Only two things
are clear. First, this man is too secure in his own artistic
power to concern himself with such quibbles; he doesn't
worry whether we think he's wise or foolish, careless or
precise. Second, this music is so audacious and so gorgeous
that it seems pointless for us to worry about it either.

That is to say, among other things, that this album has
presence—it's really out there—and that its presence
counts for something. (p. 50)

The irresistible beauty of this record calls for inept superlatives. . . . [Songs in the Key of Life] is a flawed [master-
piece] not in the manner of Dylan and the Stones, who cultivated a rough tone that made flaws inevitable, even
welcome . . . , but by identifiable mistakes, failures of taste
and concept. In this it reminds me a lot of Carole King's
Tapestry. Especially since Tapestry was King's breakthrough, whereas Songs in the Key of Life is Stevie Wonder's fulfillingness, the parallel is far from exact, and it may
bring sarcastic moans from the skeptical. But those who
remember how fresh Tapestry sounded before it was transmogrified into an aural totem—the delight of finding that
when a promising artist surpasses her potential, there's no
way a few banal passages can diminish the general affection
and admiration that results—will know what I mean.

There are errors of commission on Stevie Wonder's new
masterpiece. A lot of this music (the final refrain of "Isn't
She Lovely," for instance, or the homiletic "Black Man")
goes on for too long; there are many awkward phrases
("founder of blood plasma"), forced rhymes ("red, blue,
and white"), and uncolloquial constructions ("for
Christmas what would be my toy"); several of the songs (I
would name "Summer Soft" and "If It's Magic") are,
hopefully, quite forgettable. Talking Book is closer to a perfect album. . . . A more complex and satisfying delight—a
delight that combines the freewheeling energy of Dylan and
the Stones with the softer accessibility of a Carole King—is
provided by an artist with the ambition to ride his own considerable momentum and the talent to do more than just
hang on while doing so.

My reasoning, if that's what it is, is entirely appropriate to
this album. . . . To put it in the jargon of a time gone by,
I've overcome my own negative vibrations. Such a discipline is the key to Stevie Wonder's prescription for life,
what he means literally to denote when he says "love's in
need of love" or warns against living in a "pastime [that is,
"past time"] paradise," or, God knows, opines that "God
knew exactly where he wanted you to be placed." Sometimes he almost seems to mean that bad thoughts are the
source of all evil, and I should point out to those sympathetic to this interpretation that its practicality is questionable, because it supplies no surefire method of eliminating

the bad thoughts. I should also point out that Stevie acknowledges just this problem in "Village Ghetto Land," which serves as an empiricist postscript to the idealist "Love's in Need of Love Today" and "Have a Talk with God" by implying quite pointedly that poverty and happiness are often mutually exclusive. The man is obviously no giant ideologically, but he does have a reasonably accurate idea of what's going down.

Ideology can hardly be his specialty in any case, because the locus of ideology is written language, whereas for Stevie books must talk. In fact, no verbal analysis can do him justice. What makes the contradictory platitudes of his lyrics worth following through is the rhetorical impetus of his music. Even in the accompanying 24-page booklet the words aren't as stiff and preachy as his worst moments might have made you fear; sung or declaimed over a music much less vague and ballady than his worst moments might have made you fear, they take on a convincing vivacity. (pp. 50-1)

There is wit, pace, variety, and dimension to this music. In themselves, the words—especially as brought to life by Stevie's high-spirited multivoice—have it all over the musings of Maurice White, or Eddie Levert reciting the verse of Kenneth Gamble; they're funnier and trickier. But as validated by the music they come close to redeeming the whole genre; they make clear that no matter how annoying the sociospiritual bullshit of Earth, Wind & Fire or the O'-Jays may get, it still surpasses the escapist mythopoeia and greeting-card sentimentality that passes for poetry among too many white rock-ettes these days.

If Bob Dylan, say, scores an artistic punch with the rough tone, then Stevie Wonder is familiar with the artistic benefits of the genteel tone. He wants something like that gospel chorus in the sky—a chorus which has echoed through much of the most ambitious black music—just because of what it can say to masses of people. Sometimes he takes his advantage in a straightforward and seemly way—with synthesized strings, for instance, or with the beauty of that chorus itself—but sometimes he makes it work ass-backwards. His literary gaffes and ideological inadequacies can be blamed on confused cultural aspirations only after we're sure blame is called for; it may well be that it is only through such indiscretions that the earth-shattering, or/‑mending, presumption of his music can be conveyed. A blind man who can envision a time "when the rainbow burns the stars out of the sky" or write a song called "Ebony Eyes" is like a black man who can stick Glenn Miller in between Count Basie and Louis Armstrong in a litany of music heroes. He doesn't even acknowledge limitations that some would hope were beneath him. As in most rock and roll masterpieces, the flaws are a part of the challenge, and of the fun. (p. 51)

> Robert Christgau, "Stevie Wonder Is a Masterpiece," in The Village Voice (reprinted by permission of The Village Voice; copyright © The Village Voice, Inc., 1976), November 8, 1976, pp. 50-1.

MIKAL GILMORE

[How] does one approach the prodigy who technically deserves the highest of accolades, yet allows the grandeur of his work to obfuscate his perspective? . . . Stevie Wonder's *Songs In The Key Of Life* is the first album which has stirred such ambivalent—nearly dichotomous—reactions within me in a long, long time. . . .

[Since] when has it become incumbent upon Stevie Wonder to project himself as a spokesperson—spiritual, political, or otherwise? *Have A Talk With God*? Thanks, but my editor's heavy enough. *Black Man*? I'm not trying to slight Stevie's intentions, but I think we have more effective and less pedantic means at our disposal to impart historical lessons without catering to boring, endless recitations. I'm afraid many of us (myself included) have been screaming "genius" at Stevie Wonder for so long that it has impaired his judgment. "For I do believe it is that Stevie Wonder . . . must be carried on his mission to spread love mentalism," he declares in his opening liner notes. I'm sorry, but the man simply fails to qualify as a prophet or messiah. I'm not moved by Stevie the "leader," but rather Stevie the music maker. . . .

[So] *much* music on this record blows me away that I often end up thinking: So what if Stevie is preachy and extravagant? So what if he's lost the intuitive thread that made *Talking Book* a landmark? "Just because a record has a groove / Don't make it in the groove," cites Stevie in his Ellington tribute, *Sir Duke*, and though his art may be more notable for its artifice at this point, when he strikes those first few chords, I can't help but capitulate.

The entirety of sides one and two and the first three tracks from the EP are the real meat of this sacred cow. *Love's In Need Of Love Today*, *Have A Talk With God*, and *Saturn* are gorgeous pieces, brimming with full, rotund harmonies and seamless, multilayered instrumental weavings. *Knocks Me Off My Feet* and *Summer Soft* are the kind of guilessly sensitive songs so many of us have come to love Stevie for in the past, as close to offering personal feelings as this album gets. And while Stevie's head is definitely lost somewhere in the cosmic cloud of unknowing, his instincts are still terrestrial enough to reel off infectious rockers like *I Wish* (this album's *Superstition*), *Ordinary Pain* . . . , *Ebony Eyes*, and *All Day Sucker*.

But too many "endless endings" (which translates as filler) and not enough willingness to challenge the medium dilute *Key Of Life*'s impact. *Contusion* may show Stevie can hold his own with Corea and the rest, and *Sir Duke* convincingly and enchantingly demonstrates his affinity for swing; but the closest Wonder comes here to breaking new ground is *Village Ghetto Land*, with its chilling, bloody imagery set against a deceptive, alluring string section. Maybe too close for comfort. More incisive insight of that order and less didactic, gratuitous . . . moral and religious advice, and Stevie Wonder may still become the musical icon he so obviously longs to be. But I don't think music needs a "born again" Jimmy Carter. Nor even a soulful John Denver. (p. 24)

> Mikal Gilmore, in down beat (copyright 1976 by Maher Publications), December 16, 1976.

VINCE ALETTI

Wonder confronts us virtually single-handedly, grasps our expectations and wrestles them to the ground [in *Songs in the Key of Life*]. I give him four out of five falls gratefully, happily; were it not for his lyrics he might have won them all.

My immediate impression of *Songs in the Key of Life* is

that the album has none of the pinched, overwrought, over-refined quality one might expect from material that's been coddled and polished over a period of two years. If there are scattered traces of icy, brittle perfection, the overall feeling is expansive, spontaneous and startlingly immediate. Wonder's particular genius is that his carefully crafted perfection sounds so convincingly offhand. . . .

The album offers something fresh at each listening, something right for every mood. But it's also one of the record's annoyances—it has no focus or coherence. The eclecticism is rich and welcome, but the overall effect is haphazard, turning what might have been a stunning, exotic feast into a hastily organized potluck supper.

Part of the problem is the bulk of the material. The inclusion of four straggling cuts on a bonus EP comes across finally as a self-indulgent rather than generous gesture. Are we being given this heap of songs as a dog-biscuit reward for our patience or because Stevie had such a staggering amount of fine material that he wanted to release as much as possible? Though the first impulse is to begin editing it down, the more you listen, the less you want to cut. With some rather appalling exceptions, the quality does overwhelm the unwieldy format.

The best songs in the collection are love songs, which are classic in their directness and simplicity. . . . (p. 77)

Wonder's message songs have always been a bit heavy-handed, but "Black Man" . . . is one of his most effective. Set to a percolating, popping rhythm, the song is essentially didactic, a Bicentennial history lesson drawing together key figures in America's melting pot with a forceful chorus that preaches (and sometimes demands), "It's time we learned / This world was made for all men." It ends with a shrill, aggressive question-and-answer session that might work as a teaching tool but is too brutal for a piece of music. Elsewhere, Wonder sings of "Village Ghetto Land," describing an almost Brechtian scene of despair and corruption over a deliberately ironic piece of elegant, mock-classical music. Two other songs—"Love's in Need of Love Today," whose point is neatly summed up in the title, and "Ngiculela / Es Una Historia / I Am Singing," sung in Zulu, Spanish and English—are more predictable about Love, as in Peace and Love, but in Wonder's hands they take on a warmth that transcends the shallowness of the lyrics.

Wonder's lyrics aren't clever or particularly intelligent but, at their best, they're instinctive, straightforward and touchingly sincere. Unfortunately, at their worst they're convoluted, awkward, atrociously rhymed and so tangled up in their pretensions to "poetic" style that they become almost comical. *Songs in the Key of Life* has more than its share of Wonder at his worst. . . . "Pastime Paradise" sounds like a parody of a well-meaning protest song with its meaningless shuffle of words ("Consolation/Integration/Verification/of Revelations"). Even the best songs are marred by uncomfortably twisted phrasing ("To me came this melody"; "But listen did I not though understanding / I fell in love with one / Who would break my heart in two") and sunk with leaden platitudes. Stevie underlines this dismal writing with his rambling liner notes. (pp. 77-8)

If the lyrics are flawed and uneven, the productions are, without exception, excellent. What he can't say in words he can say more fluidly, subtly and powerfully in his music. So it's Wonder's music, his spirit, that dominates here and seems to fill up the room. It's his voice—also beyond mere words, into pure expression—that snatches you up. And won't let go. (p. 78)

Vince Aletti, in Rolling Stone *(by Straight Arrow Publishers, Inc. © 1976; all right reserved; reprinted by permission), Issue 228, December 16, 1976.*

JOHN ROCKWELL

[Stevie Wonder] isn't consistent; he has a distressing predilection for cosmic meanderings and soupy sentimentality. But listening to his albums in sequence is an instructive experience; it indicates that Wonder is perhaps most comfortable as a live performer and that his gifts are more constrained by the confines of the studio than those of some artists, and it suggests that the supposedly sharp break in his career around 1971—when he reached legal maturity and renegotiated his Motown contract to obtain a far-reaching artistic freedom—needs to be partially reevaluated. Certainly the post-1971 Wonder records are more innovative than those that preceded them. But the same polarities in his art can be observed from the beginning. . . .

The records of this period are highly variable, ranging from curious emulations of the then popular "surf sound" . . . to an inevitable homage to Ray Charles and a Christmas album. The hit singles of his adolescence include punchy R&B—"Uptight (Everything's Alright)," "I Was Made to Love Her"—to brassy pop ("For Once in My Life"), sentimental ballads ("My Cherie Amour"), even a Dylan tune ("Blowin' in the Wind") long before Motown discovered social consciousness. (p. 338)

[Some of Wonder's later characteristics were already in evidence.] There was the childlike ebullience of his fast tunes and the unabashed sentimentality of his slow numbers (no matter that at first he confined himself to the stock banalities of teen-dream love, only later to lap over into universal brotherhood). There was his carnivorous ability to devour diverse influences and put his own stylistic stamp on the results—from the basics of gospel, blues, rhythm and blues and soul to Dylan, the surf sound, jazz, adult white pop, and finally to rock, electronic music and African ethnicity. . . .

[With] *Music of My Mind* . . . , Stevie Wonder could be counted as a matured artist.

The maturity expressed itself in several ways. The records weren't "concept albums," but they were conceived as entities, the songs flowing together organically. The lyrics now embraced social, political and mystical concerns, and even his stock love-and-sex themes were deepened to include domesticity and religiousness. . . . Most crucially, both the shape and the color of his music had matured. Its shape, no longer bound to the rigid confines of the three-minute hit single, increasingly reflected the expansive spontaneity of his live performances. . . .

Although Wonder's big hits remained lively R&B material like "Higher Ground," "Boogie on Reggae Woman," and "You Haven't Done Nothin'," his albums have been largely devoted to balladic ramblings. Some white critics complain about his self-indulgence and bleary universal-love sentimentality. These are unquestionably parts of his nature, but his early records prove they're nothing new.

What is ultimately exciting about Wonder's music—and what makes his potential for growth so much more promising than that of more settled artists—is his unpredictable openness to new sounds and new styles. One imagines that he will keep plugging away, striking the chord of mass popular success every few years and proceeding on his own way in between. Isolated from the "real" world by race and blindness even as he is linked to it by his own extraordinary acuteness, Wonder is probably too original for guaranteed, comfortable mass acceptance. Which, of course, constitutes his ultimate strength. (p. 339)

> *John Rockwell, "Stevie Wonder," in* The Rolling Stone Illustrated History of Rock and Roll, *edited by Jim Miller (copyright © 1976 by Rolling Stone Press; reprinted by permission of Random House, Inc.), Rolling Stone Press, Random House, 1976, pp. 338-39.*

CHRIS ALBERTSON

[The multitude of songs on "Songs in the Key of Life"] is a generous portion by anybody's standards, but one that is praiseworthy only if the material presented on all that vinyl warrants so much of one's time. In this case it doesn't.

Let me point out right away that I am a Stevie Wonder *fan*. In fact, I went out and *bought* [the] album as soon as it became available, and *buying* albums is something people on my end of the record business rarely do. Though I confess to being disappointed, I must add that I don't feel the expenditure was a total waste—the album, besides representing the latest work of an important artist, does contain material of musical value, and, had I been given the opportunity to hear it beforehand, I would still have bought it.

Starting at the top of the program, side one provided me with my first disappointments. *Village Ghetto Land* attempts, in semi-baroque Beatles fashion, a social comment, but it is on an embarrassing high-school level; an instrumental aptly named *Contusion* sounds like a bad Weather Report out-take; *Sir Duke* seems to have something to do with Ellington, Basie, (Glenn?) Miller, and someone the printed lyrics call Sachimo (*sic*); and there are two other songs of Love and God that are best forgotten. *I Wish*, a highly rhythmic, catchy recollection of childhood, starts off the second side in a more promising vein, but, with the exception of that and *Past Paradise*—featuring the twenty-four voices of a Hare Krishna chorus and the West Los Angeles Church of God Choir—this side, too, is dispensable.

The Wonder of the Sixties opens side three with *Isn't She Lovely*—and she would be, if she didn't go on so interminably. There follows a mildly interesting six and a half minutes called *Joy Inside My Tears*, but *it* is followed by a wretched eight and a half minutes of *Black Man*. This pits no less than forty-three vocal participants against one of those "we-all-must-live-together" message songs; the theme is tiresomely common, and this example is among the worst examples. Much has been said and written lately about pop lyrics as "poetry," but reading Wonder's lyrics in the accompanying booklet I was struck by their puerility—and they do seem to be a little worse this time around. However, Stevie Wonder usually manages to rise above even the most inane lyrics, so their inadequacy is less noticeable in the listening.

The song *As* here must be considered Wonder's *pièce de résistance,* for it is a marvelously infectious, exciting song that will surely be remembered long after most of the others are forgotten. It leads right into *Another Star,* a spirited song of love—and Stevie Wonder's new album finally comes alive. But look, we've reached the end of side four, and, though there is something arresting about the tango rhythm of *Ebony Eyes* (one of the four selections on the seven-inch "bonus record"), the party is, I'm afraid, over.

In the final analysis, "Songs in the Key of Life" is a disappointment, but bear in mind that we have come to expect the extraordinary from Stevie Wonder. If this album does not live up to expectations, much of it is still noteworthy when measured against most of the other pop offerings of the day. The ingredients for an exceptional single album are here, but . . . this latest Stevie Wonder offering is marred by excess.

> *Chris Albertson, "The Extraordinary Stevie Wonder," in* Stereo Review *(reprinted by permission of the author), January, 1977, p. 94.*

JACK SLATER

[Stevie Wonder] has begun writing and producing music exploring several layers of experience—music that addresses itself not only to one's romantic needs but to racial grief, urban defeat, transcendental perception and, more recently, to religious experience.

Because of his music's transformation and also because of its variety, Stevie Wonder . . . has become all things to all who hear him: the child prodigy who made the transition to adulthood as a productive musician, the blind seer apocalyptically exposing America's injustices, the sightless man-child who still manages to smile, the musician who refused to accept the tyranny and paternalism of corporate recording interests, the black flower-child ruled by visions and astrological signs, the blind nature-boy telling us that the only thing which matters is to love and be loved in return, the black brother who has "made it," who is still "for real" and still funky and, finally—and perhaps most burdensome of all—the young man who has become, as some whites tell him, an example and an inspiration for his people. (pp. 30-1)

Since *Where I'm Coming From,* Stevie's albums have become increasingly mental, increasingly social and more spiritual in tone, a tone which is particularly evident in *Songs in the Key of Life.* And he succeeds in achieving that tone without ever becoming pious or academic or stilted; for much of his music is firmly rooted in a joyous gospel-like beat that often embraces lyrics of incredible beauty. If Stevie Wonder is a musician of considerable power, he is also a poet of considerable passion. (p. 34)

Since Stevie is, despite his various images, a rather self-contained and intensely self-absorbed person, his blindness may . . . accentuate, may feed the particular quality of that self-absorption, which in turn might feed his clearly spiritual bent. His self-absorption, however, is exactly what makes him such a remarkable entertainer, because an audience very naturally provides him with a release, a respite from self.

Since he is young and gifted—and open—his music will probably continue to grow, to expand in new directions. One can easily imagine a Stevie Wonder, at 50 or 60, becoming what would then be a kind of latter-day Duke Ellington.

For the moment, however, the extraordinary thing about the Wonder man is that he, a sightless child out of a Detroit slum ghetto, has managed through music to reach a world outside of himself, a world beyond the darkness surrounding him. The music in turn has helped countless others toward enough sight to see beyond themselves. (p. 36)

> Jack Slater, "Stevie Wonder: The Genius of the Man and His Music," in Ebony (© copyright, 1977, by Johnson Publishing Co., Inc.), January, 1977, pp. 29-36.

C. DRAGONWAGON

Stevie's songs of [his earliest songwriting] period undoubtedly have the Motown stamp on them, some of them also clearly have his special touch. With few exceptions, even the most canned lyrics and monotonous bass line and percussion can soar when the song is performed by that swelling, feeling voice. Of this genre, I particularly like *Signed, Sealed, And Delivered*. . . . It is one of the all-time great dancing tunes, and Stevie manages to imbue the ordinary lyrics with immense feeling and life. The frisky brass that is so often a part of Steve's early work is there; it's been toned down a little so it's less overbearing, yet none of its excitement has been lost. The melody line is far less predictable, much more compelling than most early Motown hits. *"Like a fool I went and stayed too long / Now I'm wondering if your love's still strong"*: because of the voice, there's anguish there, the mediocre lyric notwithstanding. And when the chorus comes in behind him, wailing strong and soulful, *"Ooooooh, baby, here I am, signed, sealed, and delivered, / I'm yours,"* how can you not sing along? (p. 22)

Music Of My Mind emanates the real personality of Stevie Wonder, the loose Stevie. . . . [He] listens to other people, really listens, without any of this waiting for the other guy to finish so he can jump in with *his* opinion. And when he talks about himself, there's always this gentle, funny self-mockery—no bitterness, no superstar tripping, just . . . folks. Somehow *Music Of My Mind* has something of that feeling. It has riffs the way Stevie does, floating effortlessly in and out. (p. 28)

Without exception, every single song on *Music Of My Mind* allows you to feel the pulse in Stevie's wings as he spreads them and soars. This exhilarating freedom is evident musically and lyrically, and in many ways the songs all seem like indications of things to come. The album contains, for example, *I Love Every Little Thing About You*, the first public reference in song to the spiritual, a side of Steve that had always been there but had never before found overt expression musically. . . . Basically a love song, it praises not only his beloved but also the transforming power of love itself. (p. 31)

Unlike many people drawn to a spiritual outlook, Steve's search for and expression of the truth within him did not lead him away from trying to call attention to the problems of the world. His commitment to social change is seen clearly in later songs like *Big Brother, Superstition, Black Man, Village Ghetto Land*, and *Living For The City*; the sadly questioning *Evil* on *Music Of My Mind* foreshadows this development. Its slow, solemn start leads to a fast emotional build-up and unusual, unpredictable musical transitions.

It is Stevie's unique talent that even in such a song no feeling of bitterness or cynicism comes across—just sadness and compassion for those who are afflicted by evil. (p. 32)

[There's] an underlying philosophy here of self-reliance that's not unlike what self-realization movements brought into prominence in the seventies: the idea that one has complete responsibility for one's own life, and one's happiness or unhappiness. (p. 35)

Stevie Wonder Presents Syreeta . . . is an autobiographical, sad, and, for the most part, beautiful portrayal of the beginning, middle, and end of an affair, and the struggle to trust and love again. It is the story of Steve and Syreeta's relationship, and even where it is weak musically or lyrically, one cannot help but respect the unusual honesty that went into the album as a whole. . . .

I like [*Spinnin' and Spinnin'*], but it's strangely uncharacteristic, both musically and lyrically, of the pair's writing. The string arrangements and the light xylophone instrumentation create a Broadway show tune effect. The lyrics add to this impression.

Stevie comes in on this one at the end, and, unfortunately, his incomparable voice—rich, smooth, effortlessly brimming with feeling and ease—completely overshadows Syreeta. She still lacks confidence and that special quality of relaxation and expertise that only comes with experience.

I can't understand why . . . *Your Kiss Is Sweet* was ever recorded. It's not only the worst song on this record, it's also the worst song Steve has had a hand in since the original Motown days. Repetitive, musically and lyrically simplistic, it is whiny and boring to listen to. (p. 43)

Talking Book is a far more finished album than *Music of My Mind*. It manages to maintain the high vitality of that record while cutting back on the jiving around. The sum total is a tight, hard-hitting, solidly professional product which went platinum. It was as if with the first flush of freedom over, Stevie could now relax into full artistic control. The spontaneity had always been there; what he had found now was a little more self-discipline.

The album begins with the lovely *You Are The Sunshine Of My Life*, probably the best known of Steve's later songs, and one of the most widely recorded. . . . Yet, pretty as it is, it seems just a little too predictable, and the crying lyrics are without Steve's usual solid emotional punch. (p. 49)

[In *Maybe Your Baby*, between] verses of gray, questioning feeling is the sneaking suspicion, *"Maybe your baby done made some other plans."* Stevie successfully evokes the obsessive wondering and depression one has about a lover who disappears, and the music backs this up effectively. Its repetitive, compelling beat is suggestive of going over and over the same facts in one's head. He knows the facts but just won't let them add up.

Then we're back to *"Maybe your baby done made some other plans / Not includin' future plans."* That "maybe" is a stroke of brilliance lyrically: it is the "maybe" that keeps anyone who's in an unhappy love affair unable to let go, and unable to feel good holding tighter.

Another technique the lyric uses effectively is one from Syreeta's *Heavy Day*—the switching of pronouns at the crucial moment. Thus *"maybe your baby"* changes to *"maybe my baby."* (pp. 49-50)

So much intensity hard-packed into [*Superstition*] could not help but make it a winner. *Superstition* richly deserved every scrap of attention it got. . . .

While *Superstition* deals with inner oppression, the kind of chains ignorant, poor, or ill-educated people are capable of throwing off by themselves, *Big Brother,* the next cut, deals with outer oppression. We meet a nightmarish mix of *1984*ish surveillance, ghetto poverty, hypocritical, do-nothing politicians.

At first one is strangely struck by the fact that although its lyrics are much more horrific than those of *Superstition,* musically *Big Brother* is far more low key, less riveting. (p. 51)

[*Songs in the Key of Life* deals] with the usual three-pronged range of subject material: the societal, the romantic, and the spiritual. The album opens with two spiritually oriented songs, *Love's in Need Of Love Today* and *Have A Talk With God.* Despite its title, *Have A Talk With God* (cowritten by Calvin Hardaway) is bubbly and irresistible. The arrangement, based on a jazz-rock syncopation, is infectiously good-natured and lightens up the preachy lyric. The song's message is optimistic and full of faith. . . .

Village Ghetto Land fails because it is too moralistic. Arranged for orchestrated strings, it lacks rhythm and force. The aim of the song is to contrast the life of the ghetto with that of the privileged upper class. Unfortunately, the song is monotonous, and over-romanticizes the very real problems of ghetto life. (p. 89)

Knocks Me Off My Feet, on Side Two, is a great romantic ballad. Stevie played all the instruments for this one and did the vocals. It somehow manages to capture the feeling of the wonder of love, the sense of communication that goes beyond words.

An equally beautiful but more "cosmic" love song is the stirring *As.* Repetition works effectively here, as the lyrics climb and soar against towering keyboard work.

A spoken part successfully avoids the fatal pitfall of mawkishness and is well-integrated into the music. Actually, it is half-chanted, the effect of which is inspiring instead of condescending. (p. 90)

There are lots of surprise guests on *Songs In The Key Of Life.* . . . It is almost as if Steve saw *Songs In The Key Of Life* as a huge ark on which he wanted to get as many friends, relatives, and acquaintances as possible before the flood. And if this diversity weakens the album, making it uneven and choppy in places, it also gives it strength and freshness. (pp. 90-1)

C. Dragonwagon, in her Stevie Wonder *(copyright © Flash Books, 1977), Flash Books, 1977.*

Appendix

THE EXCERPTS IN CLC, VOLUME 12, WERE REPRINTED FROM THE FOLLOWING PERIODICALS:

Africa Report
AJL Bulletin
Algol
The Alien Critic
America
American Anthropologist
American Libraries
American Literature
American Quarterly
The American Record Guide
The American West
The Antioch Review
Appraisal
The Armchair Detective
Art in America
The Atlantic Monthly
Best Sellers
The Black Scholar
Black World
Book Week
Book Week—The Sunday Herald Tribune
Book Window
Book World—Chicago Tribune
Book World—The Washington Post
Booklist
Books and Bookmen
Books for Your Children
Canadian Children's Literature
The Canadian Forum
Catholic Library World
Catholic World
Cheetah
Chicago Daily News
Chicago Review
The Chicago Sun-Times
Chicago Sunday Tribune
Children's Book News
Children's Book Review
Children's literature in education
Choice
The Christian Century
The Christian Science Monitor
Circus Magazine
College English
Columbia Journalism Review
Commentary
Commonweal
Contemporary Review
Crawdaddy
Creem
The Crisis
The Critic
Critical Inquiry
Critical Quarterly
Criticism
Critique: Studies in Modern Fiction
Delap's Fantasy and Science Fiction
  Review
The Dial
Dissent
down beat
Drama
Ebony
The Economist
Encounter

English Journal
Esquire Magazine
Extrapolation
Film Comment
Films and Filming
Freedomways
The Georgia Review
Go Magazine
Growing Point
Harper's
Harvard Educational Review
High Fidelity
Hit Parader
Holiday Magazine
Horizon
The Horn Book Magazine
Hound & Horn
The Hudson Review
In Review
The International Fiction Review
Interracial Books for Children Bulletin
Jahrbuch Für Amerikastudien
Jazz & Pop
The Journal of Negro Education
Journal of Popular Culture
Journal of Reading
The Junior Bookshelf
Junior Libraries
The Kenyon Review
Kirkus Reviews
Language Arts
Library Journal
Life
The Lion and the Unicorn
The Listener
London Magazine
Luna Monthly
Maclean's Magazine
McCartney: Beatle on Wings
Melody Maker
The Milwaukee Journal
The Minnesota Review
Modern Occasions
Monthly Film Bulletin
Ms.
Museum News
Music Educators Journal
The Nation
The National Observer
National Review
Natural History
New American Review
New Catholic World
The New England Quarterly
The New Leader
New Literary History
New Musical Express
The New Republic
New Society
New Statesman
New World Writing
New York Herald Tribune Books
New York Magazine
The New York Review of Books
The New York Times
The New York Times Book Review

The New York Times Film Review
The New York Times Magazine
The New Yorker
Newsweek
Nyctalops
The Ontario Library Review
Orcrist
Partisan Review
PHYLON
Poetry
Popular Music & Society
The Progressive
Psychology Today
Publishers Weekly
Punch
Ramparts
Renascence
The Reporter
Riverside Quarterly
Rock
Rolling Stone
The Saturday Evening Post
Saturday Review
The School Librarian
School Library Journal
Science Books
Science Books & Films
Science Fiction & Fantasy Book Review
Scientific American
Senior Scholastic
Sewanee Review
Sight and Sound
Signal
Sing Out!
The Social Sciences
South Atlantic Bulletin
The Southern Humanities Review
The Southern Review
Southwest Review
The Spectator
Stereo Review
The Sunday Times Magazine
The Texas Quarterly
Thoreau Journal Quarterly
Time
Time and Tide
The Times Educational Supplement
The Times Literary Supplement
TriQuarterly
TV Guide
Twentieth Century Literature
The Use of English
The Village Voice
Virginia Quarterly Review
The Washington Post
Western American Literature
Western Humanities Review
Wilson Library Bulletin
Wisconsin Studies in Contemporary
  Literature
Words & Music
The Yale Literary Magazine
The Yale Review
Young Adult Cooperative Book Review
  Group of Massachusetts

THE EXCERPTS IN CLC, VOLUME 12, WERE REPRINTED FROM THE FOLLOWING BOOKS:

Abramson, Doris E., Negro Playwrights in the American Theatre: 1925-1959, *Columbia University Press, 1969.*

Aldiss, Brian W., Billion Year Spree: The True History of Science Fiction, *Doubleday, 1973.*

Arbuthnot, May Hill, Children's Reading in the Home, *Scott, Foresman, 1969.*

Arbuthnot, May Hill, and Sutherland, Zena, Children and Books, *Scott, Foresman, 1972.*

Berger, Arthur Asa, The Comic-Stripped American, *Walker, 1973.*

Berger, Harold L., Science Fiction and the New Dark Age, *Popular Press, 1976.*

Blackmur, Richard P., The Double Agent: Essays in Craft and Elucidation, *Arrow Editions, 1935.*

Blishen, Edward, ed., The Thorny Paradise: Writers on Writing for Children, *Kestrel Books, 1975.*

Bluestein, Gene, The Voice of the Folk: Folklore and American Literary Theory, *University of Massachusetts Press, 1972.*

Broderick, Dorothy M., Image of the Black in Children's Fiction, *Bowker, 1973.*

Butler, Francelia, ed., Children's Literature: Annual of The Modern Language Association Seminar on Children's Literature and The Children's Literature Association, Vol. 5, *Temple University Press, 1976.*

Butts, Dennis, ed., Good Writers for Young Readers, *Hart-Davis Educational, 1977.*

Cadogan, Mary, and Craig, Patricia, You're a Brick, Angela! A New Look at Girls' Fiction from 1839 to 1975, *Victor Gollancz, 1976.*

Cameron, Eleanor, The Green and Burning Tree: On the Writing and Enjoyment of Children's Books, *Atlantic-Little, Brown, 1969.*

Carr, Roy, and Tyler, Tony, The Beatles: An Illustrated Record, *Harmony Books, 1975.*

Christgau, Robert, Any Old Way You Choose It: Rock and Other Pop Music, 1967-1973, *Penguin, 1973.*

Cook, Richard M., Carson McCullers, *Frederick Ungar, 1975.*

Council on Interracial Books for Children, Racism and Sexism Resource Center for Educators, Human (and Anti-Human) Values in Children's Books: A Content Rating Instrument for Educators and Concerned Parents, *The Council on Interracial Books for Children, 1976.*

Crouch, Marcus, The Nesbit Tradition: The Children's Novel in England 1945-1970, *Ernest Benn, 1972.*

de Mille, Richard, ed., The Don Juan Papers: Further Castaneda Controversies, *Ross-Erikson Publishers, 1980.*

Dragonwagon, C., Stevie Wonder, *Flash Books, 1977.*

Dumas, Bethany K., E. E. Cummings: A Rememberance of Miracles, *Barnes & Noble, 1974.*

Eakin, Mary K., Good Books for Children, *University of Chicago Press, 1966.*

Editors of Rolling Stone, The Rolling Stone Record Review, *Pocket Books, 1971.*

Egoff, Sheila, The Republic of Childhood: A Critical Guide to Canadian Children's Literature in English, *second edition, Oxford University Press, Canadian Branch, 1975.*

Egoff, Sheila, Stubbs, G. T., and Ashley, L. F., eds., Only Connect: Readings on Children's Literature, *Oxford University Press, Canadian Branch, 1969.*

Eisen, Jonathan, ed., The Age of Rock: Sounds of the American Cultural Revolution, *Random House, 1969.*

Elwood, Roger, ed., The Many Worlds of Andre Norton, _Chilton Book Company, 1974._

Evans, Oliver, The Ballad of Carson McCullers: A Biography, _Coward-McCann, Inc., 1966._

Eyre, Frank, British Children's Books in the Twentieth Century, _Longman Books, 1971._

Field, Elinor Whitney, ed., Horn Book Reflections: On Children's Books and Reading, _Horn Book, 1969._

Fisher, Margery, Intent upon Reading: A Critical Appraisal of Modern Fiction for Children, _Franklin Watts, Inc., 1962._

Fishwick, Marshall, and Browne, Ray B., eds., Icons of Popular Culture, _Bowling Green University Press, 1970._

Fox, Geoff, Hammond, Graham, Jones, Terry, Smith, Frederic, and Sterck, Kenneth, eds., Writers, Critics and Children, _Agathon Press, Inc., 1976._

French, Warren, ed., The Fifties: Fiction, Poetry, Drama, _Everett/Edwards, Inc., 1970._

Friedman, Norman, E. E. Cummings: The Art of His Poetry, _Johns Hopkins University Press, 1960._

Giannone, Richard, Vonnegut: A Preface to His Novels, _Kennikat, 1977._

Gillespie, John T., More Juniorplots: A Guide for Teachers and Librarians, _Bowker, 1977._

Goldman, Albert, Freakshow, _Atheneum, 1971._

Gray, Richard, The Literature of Memory: Modern Writers of the American South, _Johns Hopkins University Press, 1977._

Grossvogel, David I., Mystery and Its Fictions: From Oedipus to Agatha Christie, _Johns Hopkins University Press, 1979._

Hassan, Ihab, Contemporary American Literature: 1942-1972, _Frederick Ungar, 1973._

Hatch, James V., Black Theater, U.S.A.: Forty-five Plays by Black Americans, _Free Press, 1974._

Haycraft, Howard, Murder for Pleasure: The Life and Times of the Detective Story, _revised edition, Biblo and Tannen, 1972._

Heins, Paul, ed., Crosscurrents of Criticism: Horn Book Essays 1968-1977, _Horn Book, 1977._

Helms, Randel, Tolkien's World, _Houghton, 1974._

Huck, Charlotte S., and Kuhn, Doris Young, Children's Literature in the Elementary School, _second edition, Holt, 1968._

Kael, Pauline, Reeling, _Atlantic-Little, Brown, 1974._

Keating, H.R.F., ed., Agatha Christie: First Lady of Crime, _Holt, Rinehart and Winston, 1977._

Kennard, Jean E., Number and Nightmare: Forms of Fantasy in Contemporary Fiction, _Archon Books, 1975._

Kingman, Lee, ed., Newbery and Caldecott Medal Books: 1956-1965, _Horn Book, 1966._

Kingston, Carolyn T., The Tragic Mode in Children's Literature, _Teachers College Press, 1974._

Klinkowitz, Jerome, and Lawler, Donald L., eds., Vonnegut in America: An Introduction to the Life and Work of Kurt Vonnegut, _Delacorte Press, 1977._

Kostelanetz, Richard, ed., The Young American Writers, _Funk & Wagnalls, 1970._

Laser, Marvin, and Fruman, Norman, eds., Studies in J. D. Salinger: Reviews, Essays, and Critiques of 'The Catcher in the Rye' and Other Fiction, _Odyssey Press, 1963._

Leaf, David, The Beach Boys and the California Myth, _Grosset & Dunlap, Inc., 1978._

Lobdell, Jared, ed., A Tolkien Compass, _Open Court, 1975._

Lukens, Rebecca J., A Critical Handbook of Children's Literature, *Scott, Foresman, 1976.*

Lundquist, James, J. D. Salinger, *Ungar, 1979.*

Lundquist, James, Kurt Vonnegut, *Ungar, 1977.*

Manlove, C. N., Modern Fantasy: Five Studies, *Cambridge University Press, 1975.*

Mayo, Clark, Kurt Vonnegut: The Gospel from Outer Space (or, Yes We Have No Nirvanas), *Borgo Press, 1977.*

McCullers, Carson, The Mortgaged Heart, *Houghton, 1971.*

McCullers, Carson, Reflections in a Golden Eye, *New Directions, 1950.*

McGregor, Craig, ed., Bob Dylan: A Retrospective, *William Morrow, 1972.*

Meek, Margaret, Warlow, Aidan, and Barton, Griselda, eds., The Cool Web, *Bodley Head, 1977.*

Meigs, Cornelia, ed., A Critical History of Children's Literature, *revised edition, Macmillan, 1969.*

Mellers, Wilfrid, Twilight of the Gods: The Music of the Beatles, *Schirmer Books, 1973.*

Miller, Jim, ed., The Rolling Stone Illustrated History of Rock and Roll, *Random House, 1976.*

Noel, Daniel C., ed., Seeing Castaneda: Reactions to the "Don Juan" Writings of Carlos Castaneda, *G. P. Putnam's Sons, 1976.*

Nye, Russel, The Unembarrassed Muse: The Popular Arts in America, *Dial, 1970.*

Palmer, Tony, All You Need Is Love: The Story of Popular Music, *Viking Penguin, 1977.*

Pichaske, David R., Beowulf to Beatles: Approaches to Poetry, *Free Press, 1972.*

Poirier, Richard, The Performing Self, *Oxford University Press, 1971.*

Purtill, Richard, Lord of the Elves and Eldils: Fantasy and Philosophy in C. S. Lewis and J.R.R. Tolkien, *Zondervan, 1974.*

Reitberger, Reinhold, and Fuchs, Wolfgang, Comics: Anatomy of a Mass Medium, *Little, Brown, 1972.*

Riley, Dick, ed., Critical Encounters: Writers and Themes in Science Fiction, *Ungar, 1978.*

Rinzler, Alan, Bob Dylan: The Illustrated Record, *Harmony Books, 1978.*

Robinson, Evelyn Rose, ed., Readings about Children's Literature, *David McKay, 1966.*

Ryan, J. S., Tolkien: Cult or Culture?, *University of New England, Armidale, 1969.*

Schaffner, Nicholas, The Beatles Forever, *McGraw-Hill, 1977.*

Schatt, Stanley, Kurt Vonnegut, Jr., *Twayne, 1976.*

Scholes, Robert, Structural Fabulation: An Essay on Fiction of the Future, *University of Notre Dame Press, 1975.*

Short, Robert L., The Gospel According to Peanuts, *John Knox, 1964.*

Short, Robert L., The Parables of Peanuts, *Harper, 1968.*

Tanner, Tony, City of Words: American Fiction 1950-1970, *Harper, 1971.*

Thomison, Dennis, ed., Readings about Adolescent Literature, *Scarecrow Press, 1970.*

Thorburn, David, and Hartman, Geoffrey, eds., Romanticism: Vistas, Instances, Continuities, *Cornell University Press, 1973.*

Tilton, John W., Cosmic Satire in the Contemporary Novel, *Bucknell University Press, 1977.*

Tolkien, J.R.R., The Tolkien Reader, *Ballantine Books, Inc., 1966.*

Townsend, John Rowe, A Sense of Story: Essays on Contemporary Writers for Children, *Lippincott, 1971.*

Townsend, John Rowe, Written for Children: An Outline of English-Language Children's Literature, *revised edition, Lippincott, 1974.*

Tucker, Nicholas, ed., Suitable for Children?, *University of California Press, 1976.*

Updike, John, Assorted Prose, *Knopf, 1965.*

Vidal, Gore, Rocking the Boat, *Little, Brown, 1963.*

Viguers, Ruth Hill, Margin for Surprise: About Books, Children, and Librarians, *Little, Brown, 1964.*

Waggoner, Diana, The Hills of Faraway: A Guide to Fantasy, *Atheneum, 1978.*

Wegner, Robert E., The Poetry and Prose of E. E. Cummings, *Harcourt, 1965.*

Wilson, Edmund, Classics and Commercials: A Literary Chronicle of the Forties, *Noonday Press, 1950.*

Wolfe, Tom, The Electric Kool-Aid Acid Test, *Bantam Books, 1968.*

Cumulative Index to Critics

CRITIC INDEX

CRITIC INDEX

CRITIC INDEX

CRITIC INDEX

CRITIC INDEX

CRITIC INDEX

CRITIC INDEX

CRITIC INDEX

CRITIC INDEX

CRITIC INDEX

CRITIC INDEX

CRITIC INDEX

CRITIC INDEX

CRITIC INDEX

CRITIC INDEX

CRITIC INDEX

CRITIC INDEX

CRITIC INDEX

CRITIC INDEX

CRITIC INDEX

CRITIC INDEX

CRITIC INDEX

CRITIC INDEX

CRITIC INDEX

CRITIC INDEX

CRITIC INDEX

CRITIC INDEX

CRITIC INDEX

CRITIC INDEX

CRITIC INDEX

CRITIC INDEX

CRITIC INDEX

CRITIC INDEX

Cumulative Index to Authors

AUTHOR INDEX

AUTHOR INDEX